BANKS ON SENTENCE

VOLUME 2

11th edition

BANKS ON SENTENCE

VOLUME 2

11th edition

ROBERT BANKS
Barrister of the Inner Temple

www.banksr.com   book@banksr.com
Twitter @BanksonSentence

Banks on Sentence

First published January 2003 by Butterworths LexisNexis™

Second edition September 2005 published by Robert Banks

Third edition March 2008 published by Robert Banks

Fourth edition June 2009 published by Robert Banks

Fifth edition May 2010 published by Robert Banks

Sixth edition May 2011 published by Robert Banks

Seventh edition 9 May 2012 published by Robert Banks

Eighth edition 30 April 2013 published by Robert Banks

Ninth edition 29 April 2014 published by Robert Banks

Tenth edition 28 April 2015 published by Robert Banks

Eleventh edition 28 April 2016 published by Robert Banks

Production

www.banksr.com

enquiries@banksr.com

Banks on Sentence, PO Box 35, Etchingham, East Sussex TN19 7WS

Twitter: @BanksonSentence

Sentencing Alert: subscribe at www.banksr.com

Printed in the UK by CPI William Clowes, Copland Way, Ellough, Beccles, Suffolk NR34 7TL

Typeset by Letterpart Ltd, 3 Cricket View, Guards Avenue, Caterham on the Hill, Surrey, CR3 5XL

This book is printed on acid-free paper. The paper is responsibly manufactured and obtained from sustainable forests where at least two trees are planted for each one used in the production of paper.

Photographic credits

Volume 1 Royal Courts of Justice, with thanks to Magdanatka (Shutterstock).

Volume 2 HMP Dartmoor, with thanks to Roy Riley

ISBNs:

Volumes 1 and 2: 978-0-9932022-3-0

Volume 1: 978-0-9932022-1-6

Volume 2: 978-0-9932022-2-3

CONTENTS

Volume 1

Volume 2

Contents

200   ABDUCTION OF A CHILD

200.1

This chapter includes kidnapping when the victim is a child.

s 1 (by parent)

s 2 (by other person)

Mode of trial Triable either way

Maximum sentence On indictment 7 years. Summary 6 months and/or a £5,000 fine for offences committed before 12 March 2015 and an unlimited fine thereafter.[1] There are maximum fines for those aged under 18, see **14.38**.

This chapter is divided into three sections: a) Parent or stepparent, By, b) Relative, friend, employer etc. of the victim, By, and c) Stranger, By.

Children and vulnerable adults: barred lists Where the defendant is convicted of section 1 or 2 and is aged 18 or over he or she is automatically barred from engaging in regulated activity with vulnerable adults and with children.[2] The judge must tell the defendant that the Disclosure and Barring Service will include him or her in the barred lists.[3] The defendant may ask the Service to remove him or her from the lists.

Sexual Harm Prevention Orders For section 1 and 2 offences there is a discretionary power to make this order when it is necessary to protect the public from sexual harm.[4]

Law Commission report In a report published in November 2014, the Law Commission recommended that the maximum penalty should be increased from 7 to 14 years' imprisonment and that the ambit of section 1 should be extended.

200.2   *Crown Court statistics   England and Wales*

Child abduction Aged 21+

Year	Plea	Total sentenced	Type of sentencing %						Average length of custody in months
			Discharge	Fine	Community sentence	Suspended sentence	Custody	Other	
2013	G	43	2.3	–	14	20.9	60.5	2.3	15.1
	NG	11	–	–	–	9.1	63.6	27.3	48
2014	G	60	2	–	10	32	55	2	17.6
	NG	12	–	–	–	8	83	8	38.4

For explanations about the statistics, see page 1-xii. For statistics for male and female defendants etc., see www.banksr.com Other Matters Statistics tab

200.3   *Judicial guidance/Human rights*

R v A 2001 EWCA Crim 1777, 2002 1 Cr App R (S) 87 (p 473) It is the interests of the child which are paramount, not the interests or aspirations of the parent. Save in quite exceptional circumstances a person who commits a section 2 offence commits a serious offence, especially if it is done to thwart orders of the court. Orders must be respected by parents who have access to the courts and to legal advice. Real punishment is called for to punish and to deter others.

R v Kayani 2011 EWCA Crim 2871, 2012 2 Cr App R (S) 38 (p 214) LCJ At its most serious the offence of child abduction is akin to kidnapping. The maximum sentence for kidnapping is life. For child abduction the maximum sentence is 7 years. This wide discrepancy seems illogical. The offence, even if committed by a loving parent, is a serious offence and there should be a significant element of deterrence in the sentence.

---

[1] Legal Aid, Sentencing and Punishment of Offenders Act 2012 s 85(1) and (4) and Legal Aid, Sentencing and Punishment of Offenders Act 2012 (Commencement No 11) Order 2015 2015/504

[2] Safeguarding Vulnerable Groups Act 2006 s 2 and Sch 3 and Safeguarding Vulnerable Groups Act 2006 (Prescribed Criteria and Miscellaneous Provisions) Regulations 2009 2009/37 paras 3 and 6 and Sch paras 2 and 4

[3] Safeguarding Vulnerable Groups Act 2006 s 2 and Sch 3 para 25

[4] Sexual Offences Act 2003 s 103A as inserted by Anti-social Behaviour, Crime and Policing Act 2014 Sch 5 para 2 and Sexual Offences Act 2003 Sch 5

The abduction of children from a loving parent is an offence of unspeakable cruelty to the loving parent and to the child or children, whatever they may later think of the parent from whom they have been estranged as a result of the abduction. It is a cruel offence even if the criminal responsible for it is the other parent. Any reference in mitigation to the right to family life, whether at common law, or in accordance with European Convention on Human Rights art 8, is misconceived. In effect the submission involves praying in aid and seeking to rely on the very principle which the defendant has deliberately violated, depriving the other parent of the joy of his or her children and depriving the children from contact with a loving parent with whom they no longer wish to communicate. There is a distinct consideration to which full weight must be given. It has long been recognised that the plight of children, particularly very young children, and the impact on them if the person best able to care for them (and in particular if that person is the only person able to do so) is a major feature for consideration in any sentencing decision. These are offences of great seriousness, with the additional complexity arising just because the abducting parent is the person best able to provide the children with a home.

Dealing with it generally, where the only person available to care for children commits serious offences, even allowing fully for the interests of the children, it does not follow that a custodial sentence, of appropriate length to reflect the culpability of the offender and the harm consequent on the offence, is inappropriate. We can see no reason why the offence of child abduction should be placed in a special category of its own when the interests of the children of the criminal fall to be considered. Indeed in one sense, if the consequence is that the children wish to have nothing to do with the parent from whom they have been abducted, and have nowhere else to go, a further consequence of the abduction itself is the hardship then endured by the children.

Parent or stepparent, By

200.4   *Care, Child in*

R v RC and RC 2014 EWCA Crim 1169 D and R, a married couple, pleaded to abduction. They had been assessed as unfit to parent their two sons, aged four and three, who were then taken into care. D and R were allowed periodic access while the High Court dealt with the local authority applications. When the children's foster parents were at a wedding, D and R abducted them, taking them to Thailand, a country not signed up to the Hague Convention. No proceedings to return them could be instituted. Seven months later, D and R voluntarily returned to the UK and the children were again taken into care. The defence accepted that 9 months could not be faulted. Held. There had been a number of changes in circumstances post-sentence. A hearing was due to take place the following week to decide on a placement order for the youngest child, and a request for a residential assessment order from the parents. We do not want to restrict the options available to the High Court Judge dealing with the case. The parents would be unavailable if the existing sentences stood and the best interests of the children required their attendance. **5 months** enabling immediate release, not 9.

Note: If the welfare of the children is the dominant consideration here, why not substitute a suspended sentence to act as a deterrent for any future defiance of court orders? The Court said immediate imprisonment could not be faulted. However, if immediate release could be justified, so could a suspended sentence. Ed.

200.5   *Court order, In breach of a*

R v Kayani 2011 EWCA Crim 2871, 2012 2 Cr App R (S) 38 (p 214) LCJ D pleaded (20% credit) to two abductions. In 1996 his marriage deteriorated and his wife asked him to leave their home. He refused so she left the home with their two children. He said if they split up he would take the children to Pakistan. In 1998 an interim *interdict* prohibited D from taking the children away from their mother's care. Contact began and on each occasion he had custody of the children, he had to give his passport to his wife. D then falsely reported that his passport had been stolen and was issued with a replacement. He also obtained Pakistani passports for his children. In 2000, the mother handed her boys, then aged four and five, to D, and was given his passport. She has never seen the children since. D flew to Pakistan on the newly obtained passports and he rang her asking for the boys' UK passports. She refused. She flew twice to Pakistan to try to find the children. She began court proceedings there and hired investigators and lawyers. She also held a press conference. In 2009, D returned to the UK with the children, now aged 13 and 15. He attended the police station and the sons, on orders, refused to answer questions. They refused to have contact with their mother. D was aged 49 with no convictions. The pre-sentence report said he was manipulative, self-centred and deceitful. He said he should not be sent to prison because he was the boys' sole carer. Held. That was because of his offence. D was willing to use his sons to shield himself. She has lost her boys for ever. She has suffered extreme emotional hardship. **5 years** was not manifestly excessive.

R v SB 2012 EWCA Crim 240, 2 Cr App R (S) 71 (p 408) D pleaded at the first opportunity to kidnapping his five-year-old son. D had an arranged marriage and he and his wife separated in 2006. D and his family opposed this. D and his wife each found a new partner and had a new child. The family courts made a residence order directing that the child should live with his mother. Contact was initially supervised. D's contact with his son was not easy. The mother obtained a non-molestation order. Each side made complaints to the social workers that the boy had marks or bruises. There was nothing in these allegations. In 2010, the mother brought contact to an end unilaterally complaining that the boy didn't want to go. The social work report showed that the boy was torn by the antagonisms of his parents. In 2011, D recruited a taxi-driver friend who drove D from Portsmouth to Middlesbrough with a child car seat to bring the child back in, and a wig and sunglasses to serve as a disguise. Reconnaissance was carried out to find a suitable place to snatch the boy. The next day the boy was snatched and the car's number plate was covered up with a bin liner. A member of the public pulled part of it away which enabled the police to stop the car on the A1 three or four hours later. D was of positive good character and his family was very well respected and well established. D lied to the probation officer. The Court rejected part of D's counsel's mitigation as being incapable of being true. Held. Although these cases are sometimes dealt with in the family courts it was entirely right for this to be prosecuted. D will have felt frustrated and his frustration was not allayed by the disappointing social worker's recommendation that there should be no contact. Custody was absolutely inevitable. There was nothing wrong in **16 months**.

Older cases: Best ignored as sentences have increased. Ed.

Relative, friend, employer etc. of the victim, By

200.6   *General cases*

R v Galeas 2011 EWCA Crim 1548 D pleaded to abducting a child and affray. D had had a relationship with M. M had a son, V, who was not related to D. D had become fond of V. M had indicated that she wanted some time away from D. D drank alcohol and used cannabis and cocaine. He let himself into the house with his key. V was asleep under the care of his aunt. He took a knife from the kitchen and used it to prevent the aunt from getting close. He took V and threatened to kill the aunt if she did not let him go. D put V into his car. The aunt and two neighbours tried to prevent D from taking V. The aunt suffered bruising and superficial cuts. The neighbour took V from the car but D grabbed him back and returned him to the car, and pointed the knife at V. A second neighbour took V from the car and ran away. D gave chase and the neighbour and V fell over. D once again returned V to the car. V was screaming. The aunt threw the car keys away to further delay D. The police attended and had to use CS gas in order to arrest him. The motive was to attract the mother's attention. D, aged 29, was of previous good character.

Held. The determination and persistence shown by D, the use of the weapon towards the boy, the threat to kill and the effect on V are aggravating factors. **3 years 9 months** was severe but justified.

R v Wicks 2012 EWCA Crim 330 D pleaded to sexual activity with a child (×6) and abducting a child. D was a chef in a pub. V, aged 15 and from a troubled background, began to work in the kitchen. V was under the supervision of social services, at least partly because she was known to be sexually active with older men. D and V became friendly. V made it clear to D that she was attracted to him and their relationship became sexual. In January/February 2011 they started to have sexual intercourse and did so frequently over the following months. D told the police it was about 20 times. D knew from the start that: a) V was under 16, b) that she turned 16 in August 2011, and c) that it was an offence for him to have sexual relations with her. The police became involved at an early stage and D was given an informal warning by a police officer to 'stay away from V'. D ignored the warning and took care that their sexual encounters should be conducted surreptitiously thereafter. The police concern continued and in May 2011, D had a formal meeting with an officer from the Protection of Vulnerable Children unit. D was then served with a notice under Child Abduction Act 1984 s 2, prohibiting D from allowing V to enter D's flat or travel in D's car, or meeting or contacting V. D signed to say he understood the notice and that it had been explained to him by an officer. D ignored the notice and the relationship continued. It was a somewhat volatile relationship and when V suggested she might bring the relationship to an end, D suggested that he would kill himself. In June 2011, D and V drove in D's father's car to nearby woodland. They pitched a tent and consumed a 'fair amount' of alcohol. They had vaginal and anal intercourse. V left the tent wearing only pants and a T-shirt. She felt ill because of the heat and what she had drunk the previous night. She was found by a neighbour, clearly unwell and in a distressed state. D had left the tent and did not go to find her. D, aged 32 at appeal, was of good character. It was said that having regard to D's personality and the nature of his offence, he was finding life particularly difficult in prison. The Judge imposed 3 years 8 months on each count concurrently. Held. Aggravating features were the number of offences committed over a lengthy period of time during which D was given two warnings. The warnings should have left D in no doubt that V was a vulnerable person. It is also relevant that D put pressure on V to continue the relationship. Starting at **4½ years**, with the plea, **3 years**.

R v Sivillica 2013 EWCA Crim 1591 D pleaded to three abduction of a child counts. He formed a friendship with V, aged 14. After a time, V's parents became concerned about the relationship, in particular because of apparent cannabis use and a deterioration in V's behaviour. They raised their concerns with the police and made it clear they did not wish V to see D. The police served a 'harbouring notice' on D which informed him in stark terms that V's parents had 'absolutely banned outright with no exceptions' V from visiting any address which D was at or associating with D at any place. The notice warned D that if he allowed V to be at an address at which he resided or was at, or associated with V, he would be arrested for child abduction. A police officer checked that D had understood. Within days, officers found V at D's home. He was arrested and mobile phones were confiscated from V and D. D was bailed with a condition not to contact V. Text messages referred to D providing V with money in relation to a motorcycle and to sexual activity having occurred between the two some days earlier, after the notice had been served on D. D was charged and again bailed. The condition not to contact V was surprisingly removed. Days later, D was stopped whilst driving his car. The car contained D, M (who was then aged 15) and S, a girl aged 15. D claimed as the bail condition was removed he understood the harbouring notice no longer applied. D was aged 20 at the time of the offences. He had no convictions but had a caution when aged 17 for making indecent photographs of children. Held. These were serious and deliberate offences. The first was committed only days after the notice was served and explained to him and the second only days after he had been charged with the first offence and bailed. They offences were aggravated by the sexual aspect. An immediate custodial sentence was required. There was an element of genuine friendship between D and V, notwithstanding the sexual aspect and financial encouragement offered to V. There was no force or coercion present. D also had an unhappy childhood. **12 months' detention** not 18.

R v A 2014 EWCA Crim 566 D pleaded to two counts of abduction. D came to the UK from Ghana in 2001. He married V in Ghana and she then came to the UK to live with him. In 2004, he was out of work and was offered a job in Ghana. V did not want to leave the UK. (What happened to the job is not revealed. Ed.) In 2013 D gave up his tenancy and told his wife he was taking his two children to a zoo. In fact he flew with them to Ghana so they could join his extended family. Later when V asked about the children, he said they were in Ghana and let her have contact with them. V's solicitors wrote to D saying he had been ordered by a court to return the children. D came back to the UK but he had not obtained visas for the children in time. D assisted the police and the court with the return of the children. D paid for their tickets. It was not suggested the children were not looked after properly. D was aged 44 and had no convictions. The pre-sentence report said D did not know the abduction was against the law. Held. The tenancy termination meant it was planned. D lied to V. He did not bring the children back until there was a court order. However, the period of the abduction was relatively short, V knew where the children were and V could contact them. Starting at 12 months, with the plea, **8 months** not 21.

See also: *R v Cash* 2014 EWCA Crim 500, 2 Cr App R (S) 48 (p 382) (10% credit. V was aged 15 with a troubled background, and D was aged 24. V's grandmother was told about D's past and his true age but V defied her and saw D. V left with D, despite D trying to persuade her not to. V returned the next day, but had spent the night with a girlfriend, not D. D had many antecedents with a 2010 voyeurism conviction and was on the Sex Offender Register. Abduction short and no coercion. **8 months**, not 2 years.)
Old cases: Best ignored as sentences have increased. Ed.

Stranger, By

200.7   *General cases*

R v Mansatti 2010 EWCA Crim 2765 D pleaded to abducting a child. He was in a park with another drinking alcohol. The victim, V, was aged 15 and wearing her school uniform, but playing truant from school. D approached V and offered her a cigarette. D and V chatted, before D encouraged V to follow him out of the park. They boarded a bus and D, having led V upstairs, proceeded to kiss her cheek and rub her thigh and hand. They alighted and D purchased alcohol from an off-licence. A member of the public had alerted the police and D was arrested. A pre-sentence report recommended a community order. D was of good character with no friends or family in this country and unable to speak English. Held. No sentence other than an immediate custodial sentence of imprisonment was appropriate. The Judge was entitled to find that (this was) abduction with a sexual motive and to distinguish this case from mere abduction and the cases of sexual activity alone. **12 months**, not 18.

R v Wilson 2014 EWCA Crim 1848, 2015 1 Cr App R (S) 8 (p 64) D pleaded to abducting a child and common assault. M, who was unknown to D, was with her 11-month-old child, V, in the street. D seized V and walked a few metres. She held V above her head and waved her around. A bottle of alcohol fell from D's pocket. A security guard, S, intervened and challenged D. D handed him V, who was returned to M. The abduction lasted 6 seconds. D then seized S's neck and scratched it (the common assault, 2 months consecutive, no appeal). When arrested, D smelt of alcohol and lied. D was aged 40 and had 31 court appearances for 45 offences including dishonesty, drug supply, disorderly behaviour, assault PC, common assault and failure to comply with a community order. She had entrenched alcohol misuse issues. D had never been in paid employment and lived a chaotic and reckless lifestyle. She also had psychiatric issues including a persistent mood disorder and a history of ADHD. It was accepted that D did not wish to remove V from M permanently and D did not wish to harm V. Held. When in drink D had a history of violence. We start at 9 months, so with plea **6 months**, not 12, and with the common assault **8 months**, not 14.

R v Hawes 2015 EWCA Crim 702 D pleaded to child abduction. Police found D in bed with K, a 15-year-old girl. She was a troubled and vulnerable girl. He was tried for sexual activity with her and his defence was that he believed she was over 16. He was acquitted and was served with a child abduction warning notice, which prohibited him from allowing K to stay at a property where he was present. Days later, K left her foster home placement and contacted D. D took K to his aunt and said to her that K was aged 17 and gave a false surname for her. The two stayed there two nights. D was aged 19 and had four offences of sexual activity with a different girl aged between 13 and 15. D was then aged 14 and received a Referral Order. In the same year, he had a conviction for sexual assault, where he shouted at a woman in the street and seized her breasts. In 2010, D was convicted of false imprisonment when he seized another woman and tried to drag her down an alleyway. He received an 18-month DTO. D breached the training part of his order five times and was recalled. There were also low-level violence and dishonesty convictions. For the abduction offence he was in breach of a community order. The pre-sentence report assessed there was a high risk of serious sexual harm to children and young women. Held. The only mitigation was D's troubled youth and that K was not coerced. We start at 3 years so with plea, **2 years** not 30 months.

Older cases: Best ignored as the sentences have increased. Ed.

200.8   *Blackmail, With*

All these cases are listed in the **BLACKMAIL** chapter whether there is a count of blackmail or not.

Sex cases Cases where there is a sexual motive are listed in the relevant sex offences chapter.

201   ABH ASSAULT OCCASIONING ACTUAL BODILY HARM

201.1

Offences Against the Person Act 1861 s 47

Mode of trial Triable either way

Maximum sentence On indictment 5 years. Summary 6 months and/or a £5,000 fine for offences committed before 12 March 2015 and an unlimited fine thereafter.[5] There are maximum fines for those aged under 18, see **14.38**.

Sexual offences There is an offence of committing an offence with intent to commit a sexual offence, see Sexual Offences Act 2003 s 62. That offence can be ABH.

Approach Usually, the most important factor is the injury inflicted or the potential injuries. Ed.

Extended sentences This offence is listed in Criminal Justice Act 2003 Sch 15. The court may pass a 2012 extended sentence (EDS) if there is a significant risk of serious harm from future specified offences and either: a) the defendant has a Criminal Justice Act 2003 Sch 15B conviction (applicable only to defendants aged 18+), or b) the offence would justify a determinate sentence of at least 4 years.[6]

Criminal Behaviour Orders Where a defendant has engaged in behaviour that caused or was likely to cause harassment, alarm or distress to any persons and a Criminal Behaviour Order will help in preventing the offender from engaging in such behaviour, the court may make this order.[7]

---

[5] Legal Aid, Sentencing and Punishment of Offenders Act 2012 s 85(1) and (4) and Legal Aid, Sentencing and Punishment of Offenders Act 2012 (Commencement No 11) Order 2015 2015/504

[6] Criminal Justice Act 2003 s 226A-226B as inserted by Legal Aid, Sentencing and Punishment of Offenders Act 2012 s 124

[7] Anti-social Behaviour, Crime and Policing Act 2014 s 22(1)-(4)

Football Banning Orders Where the offence was committed relevant to a football match and where there are reasonable grounds to believe that making a banning order would help to prevent violence or disorder at or in connection with any regulated football match, the court <u>must</u> make a Football Banning Order under Football Spectators Act 1989 s 14A and Sch 1 para 1.

Licensed premises Where an offence is committed on licensed premises, the court may prohibit defendants from entering those premises or any other specified premises without the express consent of the licensee etc.[8] The minimum period is 3 months and the maximum period is 2 years.[9] Violent Crime Reduction Act 2006 s 65 and Sch 5 repeals these powers. The repeal and the commencement of the new powers are not expected soon.

Sexual Harm Prevention Orders There is a discretionary power to make this order when it is necessary to protect the public from sexual harm.[10]

201.2   *Sentencing Council guideline 2011*
Assault Guideline 2011, see www.banksr.com Other Matters Guidelines tab This guideline applies to all offenders aged 18+. In force 13 June 2011.

STEP ONE Determining the offence category
page 12 The court should determine the offence category using the table below.

Category 1	Greater harm (serious injury must normally be present) and higher culpability
Category 2	Greater harm (serious injury must normally be present) and lower culpability or lesser harm and higher culpability
Category 3	Lesser harm and lower culpability

The court should determine the offender's culpability and the harm caused, or intended, by reference only to the factors identified in the table below (as demonstrated by the presence of one or more). These factors comprise the principal factual elements of the offence and should determine the category.

Factors indicating greater harm
Injury (which includes disease transmission and/or psychological harm) which is serious in the context of the offence (must normally be present) Victim is particularly vulnerable because of personal circumstances Sustained or repeated assault on the same victim
Factors indicating lesser harm
Injury which is less serious in the context of the offence
Factors indicating lower culpability
Subordinate role in group or gang A greater degree of provocation than normally expected Lack of premeditation Mental disorder or learning disability, where linked to commission of the offence Excessive self-defence

---

[8] Licensed Premises (Exclusion of Certain Persons) Act 1980 s 1(1)
[9] Licensed Premises (Exclusion of Certain Persons) Act 1980 s 1(3)
[10] Sexual Offences Act 2003 s 103A as inserted by Anti-social Behaviour, Crime and Policing Act 2014 Sch 5 para 2 and Sexual Offences Act 2003 Sch 5

Factors indicating higher culpability
Statutory aggravating factors: Offence motivated by, or demonstrating, hostility to the victim based on his or her sexual orientation (or presumed sexual orientation) Offence motivated by, or demonstrating, hostility to the victim based on the victim's disability (or presumed disability) ***Other aggravating factors:*** A significant degree of premeditation Use of weapon or weapon equivalent (for example, shod foot, head-butting, use of acid, use of animal) Intention to commit more serious harm than actually resulted from the offence Deliberately causes more harm than is necessary for commission of offence Deliberate targeting of vulnerable victim Leading role in group or gang Offender motivated by, or demonstrating, hostility based on the victim's age, sex, gender identity (or presumed gender identity)

201.3

STEP TWO Starting point and category range

page 12 Having determined the category, the court should use the corresponding starting points to reach a sentence within the category range below. The starting point applies to all offenders irrespective of plea or previous convictions. A case of particular gravity, reflected by multiple features of culpability in step one, could merit upward adjustment from the starting point before further adjustment for aggravating or mitigating features, set out below.

	Category	Starting point	Category range
1	Greater harm (serious injury must normally be present) and higher culpability	1 year 6 months' custody	1 to 3 years' custody
2	Greater harm (serious injury must normally be present) and lower culpability, or lesser harm and higher culpability	26 weeks' custody	Low-level community order to 51 weeks' custody
3	Lesser harm and lower culpability	Medium-level community order	Band A fine to high-level community order

Note: A Band A fine is 50% of net weekly income. Bands B and C are 100% and 150%. For more detail, see **60.27**. Ed.

For the meaning of a high-level, a medium-level and a low-level community order see **16.12-16.14**.

The table below contains a non-exhaustive list of additional factual elements providing the context of the offence and factors relating to the offender. When sentencing Category 2 offences, the court should also consider the custody threshold as follows:

Has the custody threshold been passed?

If so, is it unavoidable that a custodial sentence be imposed?

If so, can that sentence be suspended?

When sentencing Category 3 offences, the court should also consider the community order threshold as follows:

Has the community order threshold been passed?

201.4   [Aggravating and mitigating factors]

Factors increasing seriousness

Statutory aggravating factors:
Previous convictions, having regard to a) the nature of the offence to which the conviction relates and its relevance to the current offence; and b) the time that has elapsed since the conviction Offence committed whilst on bail

Other aggravating factors include:
Location of the offence Timing of the offence Ongoing effect upon the victim Offence committed against those working in the public sector or providing a service to the public Presence of others including relatives, especially children or partner of the victim Gratuitous degradation of victim In domestic violence cases, victim forced to leave their home Failure to comply with current court orders Offence committed whilst on licence An attempt to conceal or dispose of evidence Failure to respond to warnings or concerns expressed by others about the offender's behaviour Commission of offence whilst under the influence of alcohol or drugs Abuse of power and/or position of trust Exploiting contact arrangements with a child to commit an offence Established evidence of community impact Any steps taken to prevent the victim reporting an incident, or obtaining assistance and/or from assisting or supporting the prosecution Offences taken into consideration (TICs)

Factors reducing seriousness or reflecting personal mitigation
No previous convictions or no relevant/recent convictions Single blow Remorse Good character and/or exemplary conduct Determination, and/or demonstration of steps taken to address addiction or offending behaviour Serious medical conditions requiring urgent, intensive or long-term treatment Isolated incident Age and/or lack of maturity where it affects the responsibility of the offender Lapse of time since the offence where this is not the fault of the offender Mental disorder or learning disability, where not linked to the commission of the offence Sole or primary carer for dependent relatives

Racially/religiously aggravated offences: the court should determine the appropriate sentence for the offence without taking account of the element of aggravation and then make an addition to the sentence, considering the level of aggravation involved. It may be appropriate to move outside the identified category range, taking into account the increased statutory maximum.

The court should then consider the following: a) other factors indicating a reduction, such as assistance to the prosecution, b) reduction for a guilty plea, c) dangerousness, d) totality, if sentencing for more than one offence, and e) compensation and ancillary orders.

201.5   *Judicial guidance about the guideline*

R v Thomas 2014 EWCA Crim 1715, 2015 1 Cr App R (S) 3 (p 16) D pleaded to ABH. Held. The expression 'serious injury' must be interpreted within the context of ABH and not a more serious offence, such as GBH. 'Serious injury' differentiates between an injury on the margin of being an actual injury and injury which is more substantial, and in the context of ABH, is serious. Chipped teeth and facial damage are not trivial matters to a young woman. In this case, V's injuries were serious and the Judge was entitled to place this in Category 1.

For more detail about the case see **201.16**.

201.6   *Magistrates' Court Sentencing Guidelines 2011 Update*

Magistrates' Court Sentencing Guidelines 2011 Update, see www.banksr.com Other Matters Guidelines tab The update repeats the main guideline. In the table indicating ranges and starting points, sentences exceeding the powers of the Magistrates' Court are replaced with 'Crown Court'.

For details about applying guidelines, see the **GUIDELINES** chapter in Volume 1.

Children, Against, see the **CRUELTY TO CHILDREN** chapter.

Child victims are listed in the **CRUELTY TO CHILDREN** chapter at **231.19**.

201.7   *Defendant under 18*

R v BW 2012 EWCA Crim 3178 D was convicted of ABH. V, a 'young man', was knocked to the ground and kicked by a group of three people which included D. There was evidence that D's mother was nearby and was encouraging the attack. D was committed to the Crown Court because he had adult co-defendants. The Judge gave him an 8-month DTO. D was aged 14 years 4 months at the time of the offence. Held. In other circumstances D would have been dealt with in the Youth Court where a custodial sentence would not have been available. Considering *R v Ghafoor* 2002 EWCA Crim 1857, 2003 1 Cr App R (S) 84 (p 428) and the principle that custody should be a last resort for a 14-year-old offender, the correct sentence was a Youth Rehabilitation Order. Taking account of the time spent in custody, a **2-year Youth Rehabilitation Order**, not an 8-month DTO.

Note: The *Assault Guideline 2011* does not apply to those aged under 18, see **201.2**. I expect most judges would determine the appropriate sentence for an adult and then make a reduction. Ed.

201.8   *Defendant aged 16-17*

R v Myers 2013 EWCA Crim 622 D pleaded to ABH. V, aged 17, was in the garden of D's home drinking alcohol with a number of others. D, unprovoked, punched V to the face. V staggered and P, D's friend, punched him to the face. V went to the floor and was "out of it". D stamped on V's face and head at least three times. P kicked him in the stomach and was egging D on, saying, "Go on Dan, fucking hurt him". D's mother then appeared and kicked V to the backside. She went through his pockets and stole money and a tobacco pouch. Witnesses described V as having passed out at this stage. D returned to 'have another go' but was prevented from doing so by a witness. V suffered bruising, grazes and cuts to his mouth which required two stitches. D was aged 16 and had no previous convictions. He had a reprimand and a warning in 2010 for criminal damage. The family was known to social services and the children were on the child protection register. D was described as bright and capable of attaining good GCSEs but his attendance at education was poor. He used alcohol and cannabis on a regular basis. Held. D had started the violence. The offence fell within Category 1; the higher culpability arose from the use of a shod foot. This was an extremely serious case of violence involving a group attack on an individual. The use of the shod foot to the head can lead to the most devastating of consequences. After a trial of an adult, we would not have been surprised at a sentence of **around 3 years**, even for a first offence. A **12-month DTO** was neither wrong in principle nor manifestly excessive.

201.9   *Extended sentences*

These cases are not summarised as the decision often turns on the characteristics of the defendant rather than the offence. Examples are: *R v Fazli* 2009 EWCA Crim 939 (No) *R v A* 2010 EWCA Crim 159 (Yes).

For principles about **medical staff** as victims, see the VICTIMS *Medical staff Judicial guidance* para at **121.7**.

201.10   *Parties having argument etc.*

R v Briggs 2012 EWCA Crim 2112 D pleaded to ABH. His basis of plea was contested and the Judge held a *Newton* hearing. The victim did not attend and so the basis of plea was accepted by default. V, D's girlfriend, held a party at her house. She was very drunk and an argument broke out between D and V. V attempted to leave the house through the first-floor window. D, being concerned for her safety, pulled her back and put her on the bed. They continued to argue and V grabbed D's throat. D punched her to get her off, but accepted that that went further than self-defence. V suffered a black and swollen left eye, swelling to the left side of her head and reddening to the forehead. D and V had two young children together. D, aged 21 at appeal, had a number of convictions, though none for violence. He was subject to a community order imposed some 18 months earlier. Subsequently, D was in breach of a Suspended Sentence Order imposed for his failure to attend appointments with the probation service and the suspended sentence imposed by the Judge was activated in full. Held. Taking a pragmatic view, the appropriate sentence is **6 weeks suspended** for 12 months, not **6 months suspended**.

R v Islam 2014 EWCA Crim 2484 D, S and F pleaded to ABH (10% credit). V suffered from schizophrenia and had trouble with noise outside his property. His neighbour was D and his three sons were S, F and J (who did not appeal). In the afternoon, V went out to remonstrate with J who was joined by D, S and F. V was then punched and kicked by the four. V was held down and unable to defend himself. A neighbour told the four to stop. D gave V five stamps over his back, arms and head. D's wife also pleaded for them to stop. Eventually the four stopped and V was unable to get up for some time. V had a 4 cm wound in his buttock, two 2 cm wounds to his thigh and a graze to his elbow and his calf. The wounds indicated a weapon had been used. D had no previous. S had nine convictions which included robbery, ABH, and affray. [Their ages and F's character are not recorded.] The Judge considered that D played a leading role. Held. This was an appalling attack on a defenceless, vulnerable victim with a weapon. The Judge must have been looking at the wrong guideline. For D, **2½ years** not 40 months. For S, **26 months** not 32, consecutive to a 3-month suspended sentence. For F, **21 months** not 27.

201.11   *Persistent offender*

R v Turay 2014 EWCA Crim 166 D pleaded (full credit) to ABH. D went to an address expecting to find his girlfriend, G, there. Her car was parked outside. The front door was unlocked and D went inside and upstairs. He saw a woman in bed with a man and thought it was his girlfriend, G. In fact, it was V, G's sister, who looked very similar. D dragged V out of the bed by the hair. He dragged her to the stairs whereupon they both fell down the stairs and D landed on top of V. D believed his knee may have collided with V's head at that point. D then realised that the person was G's sister, V. He immediately began to apologise. He got something from the kitchen for her to put on her knee. He offered to take her to the hospital but she told him to go home, which he did. V suffered a large bump and swelling to the right side of her head, four scratches to her cheek, swelling to her thumb, a chipped tooth and tissue damage to her right eye. D was aged 35 at the time of the offence. He had 12 convictions for 37 offences. Nine related to assault, ABH or GBH. In 2003, he received 6½ years for section 18 and ABH. The ABH was when he assaulted a female taxi driver. Later he had argued with his then partner and pushed her down the stairs. She suffered fractures to her head requiring reconstructive surgery. This was the GBH. In 2008, while on licence from the last sentence, he received a 5-year extended sentence for ABH against another partner during an argument. She suffered injuries to her face, teeth and nails. Held. The facts do not comfortably fit into any of the categories in the guideline. Being faithful to the basis of plea, D wrongly entered another person's home, trespassed into the occupier's bedroom, reached an incorrect conclusion as to what he saw and acted violently by dragging a wholly innocent and unsuspecting victim out of bed whereupon both of them fell down the stairs. The offence was gravely aggravated by the previous convictions. The culpability and harm in conjunction with the previous convictions elevate the case to the top of the category range for Category 1. Therefore the starting point was 3 years. With full credit, **2 years** not 3.

R v Elkington 2015 EWCA Crim 659 D pleaded (25% credit) to ABH and assault by beating (4 months concurrent). D, aged 42, was in an on/off seven-year relationship with V, aged 26. They both lived in a Salvation Army hostel. They argued and D told V she was a prostitute and she should go and sell herself. She laughed and D pushed her into a wall and she slumped to the ground. Feeling dizzy, she went upstairs to her room. D followed her and shouted abuse at her. She ran out of the room so she could be in the street. D followed her outside and punched her in the eye. She fell down and D kicked her and punched her. The following day, D knocked at her door and D pushed his way in and knocked her over. This was the beating charge. V had bruising and swelling around her eye and bruising to her arms. She was in pain from the kick in the ribs. D had 37 court appearances for 121 offences between 1983 and 2012. They included: 1997, manslaughter (8 years); 2003, common assault (3 months); 2005, ABH (extended sentence 17 months) and 2012, section 20 (extended sentence 56 months) for which he had been recalled. There were assaults on police in 1993, 1995, 1996 and 2004. D did appear to show remorse. The pre-sentence report said he presented a high risk of re-offending and high risk of harm to V and members of the public. Held. The starting point was one month short of the maximum. The sentence could not be justified by fear of future violence. 5-year extended sentence was correct but the custodial term should be **36 months** not 44.

201.12   Police officer, Against a

R v McNicoll 2012 EWCA Crim 568 D pleaded to ABH. V, an off-duty police officer, was in a pub with his brother. D was also in the pub and was drunk, shouting, and dancing around. Initially V ignored D. However, D became more aggressive and was threatening people encouraging them to fight him, saying that he would knock them all out. He was flexing his arms saying, "Who dares mess with this?" He ran into a group of men in the pub and began punching indiscriminately. V went to speak with D and believed that he had succeeded in trying to calm him down. Since it was almost closing time, V put his arm around D's shoulder and suggested that he leave. D grabbed V's wrist, which was weak as it had previously been broken, and began to twist it. D pulled and twisted V's arm such that V was lifted off the ground. Both men fell to the floor and D punched V below the left eye. V managed to pin D to the floor and D punched V several times in the back of the head. V told D to calm down and that he was a police officer. D responded, "Fucking copper, I'm going to kill you." V was holding D's arms above his head, and consequently his chest was level with D's face. D bit V's left nipple extremely hard and maintained the bite. The bite caused V to bleed. V got to his feet and as he did so, D bit V in the crotch area, biting only his jeans. He left a bite mark and blood on V's jeans. He then tried to bite V again on the leg, again only biting his jeans. He then tried again, and bit V on the right thigh causing excruciating pain. Eventually D let go but then tried biting V on his fingers. As V pulled his fingers away, D punched him in the right eye and tried to put his hands around his neck, causing more pain. Someone shouted that the police had arrived and D desisted and walked out of the pub. V suffered a hairline fracture of the wrist, there were bite marks which remained sore and there were two scars, one around his nipple and another on his leg. He subsequently had to undergo an operation to remove scar tissue from his leg. V remained on light duties at work nine weeks after the incident. In 2006, D, who was aged 24 at appeal, had a caution for common assault. He was married with a young son. Held. This was a sustained and vicious attack on a man who had intervened only to try to calm D down. The attack only stopped once the police arrived. It is an aggravating feature that when V told D he was a police officer, the attack persisted and D deliberately inflicted significant injury upon him. The offence was properly placed in Category 1. Starting at 18 months, **12 months** not 2 years.

R v Murray 2013 EWCA Crim 247 D pleaded (full credit) to ABH. He was also sentenced for escape from lawful custody (×2). He was one of three men drinking in a garden at night. Two of the men began a drunken argument with punches thrown. A police officer intervened. D, the third man, approached the police officer aggressively, banging his fists on his chest. The officer feared he was about to be attacked and pushed D back. D became more aggressive and used offensive language towards the officer who warned D that he would be arrested. He then arrested D, who struggled violently causing both men to fall to the floor. The officer felt his foot 'snap' and was unable to get up. He sustained three fractures and D made good his escape, shouting abuse in the process. When he came to be arrested at a later date, he pushed past officers and escaped again. D, aged 23, had a terrible record for offences of violence. Held. D was drunk, the offence was committed at night and in a public place. The first escape was treated as an aggravating factor of the ABH. This was Category 2 (greater harm but not higher culpability). **18 months** not 2 years. 2 months consecutive for the escape not challenged.

201.13   *Prison officers etc., Against*

R v Lusher 2010 EWCA Crim 384 D pleaded at the Magistrates' Court to breach of an ASBO and ABH. Police found him lying comatose on the pavement with two open cans of lager next to him. He was arrested for breach of the alcohol condition in his ASBO. In the Court cells he threw a cup of coffee into the face of a prison detention officer, who suffered reddening of the skin. The ASBO had been imposed for racially aggravated assault, disorderly behaviour and being drunk and disorderly. D was aged 45, with 60 convictions between 2002 and 2009 largely for drunk and disorderly and threatening etc. behaviour. There were also convictions for a common assault and a battery. The pre-sentence report said that: a) D was very remorseful and apologetic to the victim, b) he had attempted suicide on a number of occasions, c) he was unsuitable for unpaid work or a curfew, and d) he was unable to comply with a community-based sentence until he stopped drinking. The Judge said that: a) while he remained addicted to alcohol he was not merely a nuisance but a menace, b) he had assaulted a man who was helping him, and c) he had taken no notice of the ASBO which he had flagrantly breached on several occasions. The prison report said that his behaviour was erratic and unpredictable. Held. In the ordinary way these offences perhaps would not attract custody of any kind. However, D was a prolific offender who had paid scant respect for the Order, and his behaviour invited a robust response to bring him to his senses. Therefore, 9 months not 12 for the ASBO and **6 months** not 12 for the ABH consecutive, making **15 months** not 2 years.

Old cases: *R v Hills* and Others 2008 EWCA Crim 1871, 2009 1 Cr App R (S) 75 (p 441) (**3 years**) *R v Ravenhill* 2008 EWCA Crim 2984 (**2 years**) For a summary of the case see the 10th edition of this book.

201.14   *Pub fights/attacks*

R v McNicoll 2012 EWCA Crim 568 D pleaded to ABH. V, an off-duty police officer, was in a pub with his brother. D was also in the pub and was drunk, shouting, and dancing around. Initially V ignored D. However, D became more aggressive and was threatening people encouraging them to fight him, saying that he would knock them all out. He was flexing his arms saying, "Who dares mess with this?" He ran into a group of men in the pub and began punching indiscriminately. V went to speak with D and believed that he had succeeded in trying to calm him down. Since it was almost closing time, V put his arm around D's shoulder and suggested that he leave. D grabbed V's wrist, which was weak as it had previously been broken, and began to twist it. D pulled and twisted V's arm such that V was lifted off the ground. Both men fell to the floor and D punched V below the left eye. V managed to pin D to the floor and D punched V several times in the back of the head. V told D to calm down and that he was a police officer. D responded, "Fucking copper, I'm going to kill you." V was holding D's arms above his head, and consequently his chest was level with D's face. D bit V's left nipple extremely hard and maintained the bite. The bite caused V to bleed. V got to his feet and as he did so, D bit V in the crotch area, biting only his jeans. He left a bite mark and blood on V's jeans. He then tried to bite V again on the leg, again only biting his jeans. He then tried again, and bit V on the right thigh causing excruciating pain. Eventually D let go but then tried biting V on his fingers. As V pulled his fingers away, D punched him in the right eye and tried to put his hands around his neck, causing more pain. Someone shouted that the police had arrived and D desisted and walked out of the pub. V suffered a hairline fracture of the wrist, there were bite marks which remained sore and there were two scars, one around his nipple and another on his leg. He subsequently had to undergo an operation to remove scar tissue from his leg. V remained on light duties at work nine weeks after the incident. In 2006, D, who was aged 24 at appeal, had a caution for common assault. He was married with a young son. Held. This was a sustained and vicious attack on a man who had intervened only to try to calm D down. The attack only stopped once the police arrived. It is an aggravating feature that when V told D he was a police officer, the attack persisted and D deliberately inflicted significant injury upon him. The offence was properly placed in Category 1. Starting at 18 months, **12 months** not 2 years.

See also: *R v Gavin* 2011 EWCA Crim 2709 (Pleaded to three counts of assault. Full credit. Aged 22. After drinking, swung a hammer at bar staff, hitting one twice, and an unintended victim once. Caused swelling and bleeding. **2 years 6 months** not 3 years, making a total of **2 years 10 months** not 3 years 4 months for all three assaults.)

201.15   *Punish, Motive is to*

R v Thomas 2011 EWCA Crim 249 D was convicted of ABH. He telephoned V, with whom he was friends, and asked whether he could attend the house where V was celebrating another friend's birthday. D arrived at the party and was more intoxicated than the other guests. Some guests decided to go to bed and D thought he could stay. He was asked to leave at which he was horribly abusive to V. He called her a "slut". V pushed D on the shoulder and told him to go home. D responded by striking her a heavy blow on the side of her face. She suffered a perforated ear drum but no lasting hearing loss. D, aged 23 at appeal, had six offences in three years, none of which were for violence. The Judge noted that V was a young woman and therefore relatively vulnerable. The Judge dealt with D on the basis that this was a premeditated assault. Held. This was not a premeditated assault. This case plainly did not involve a minor injury, even though there was no evidence of any long-lasting effect. **6 months** not 12.

R v Pinchion 2013 EWCA Crim 242 D pleaded (full credit) to ABH. V, a 63-year-old man, was walking down an alley after an evening in a pub. D and his co-accused wrongly believed V to be a paedophile. V's legs were taken from beneath him and he was punched and kicked. D sat astride V and punched him several times in the face, taunting him. V sustained cuts to his nose, which was bloodied and bruised, his left eye was swollen and bruised and there was bruising to other parts of the face, head and arms. D, aged 21, had 21 offences including two ABHs, five battery offences and three public order offences. D failed to surrender during the proceedings on three occasions. Held. V was vulnerable. The assault was sustained and of a bullying nature. There was clearly a degree of premeditation. It was wrong to treat presumed paedophilia as coming within the Guideline's aggravating factor of an offence motivated by hostility based on sexual orientation. The kicking with a shod foot was an aggravating factor. The offence was therefore clearly a Category 1. D had previous convictions for bail offences. They were deliberate offences and there is nothing wrong with 2 months consecutive for each. 18 months plus 6 months for the bail offences making 2 years was not manifestly excessive.

R v Heffer 2013 EWCA Crim 253 D was convicted of ABH. V1 and V2 had been for a night out. They ended up at a pub and met D, M and S. S accused V1 of bullying a girl with whom they had been at college. S was aggressive and there was some pushing. V1 and V2 left the pub. There was more pushing outside, designed to initiate a reaction from V2, but V1 and V2 made their way towards V2's house. As they walked, they heard voices calling V1's name. They felt anxious but could not see anyone. The group stopped V1 and V2 outside a shop and S continued a discussion about V1 having 'bullied' a girl at college. S had four other males with him, including D. D pressed his head against V1's head and waved a lighter in front of his face. V1 and V2 were intimidated. M then came over and began to punch V1. V2 was also punched. Other males from the group joined in the punching. There was no evidence that S punched either victim. The punching stopped and V1 and V2 again made their way home. V2 was then attacked again. It was unclear whether V1 was hit by D at this stage. V1 suffered bruising to both eyes and swelling to his left cheekbone, and was examined in hospital for a suspected fracture. There was no fracture. D was aged 20 and of positive good character. His mother had been very ill and had died two weeks prior to the appeal hearing. That had had a great effect on him. Held. This was a Category 2 case, as higher culpability was present. There were significant aggravating factors. D struck V1 in the face more than once, in a premeditated attack. He was under the influence of alcohol and the attack happened late at night. Despite the mitigation there were no exceptional circumstances to suspend the sentence. 12 months' detention, not 2 years.

R v I 2014 EWCA Crim 314 D was convicted of assault. In a park at about 8.30 pm, V, aged 16, with his friends, were with some girls by a lake. D had with him some cans of alcohol and walked past V and his friends and said something whilst looking at one of the young girls. He then walked off and sat on a bench near the lake drinking the alcohol. He began to call the young girls over to him. One of the young girls said that D had 'dirty talked' to her and had been bothering her earlier in the day. As this was not the first time that this had happened, V and his friends decided to approach D. They said to keep clear of the girls who were only aged 14 or 15, that D had been 'perving' on them and that he should leave them alone. D dropped his bag, stood up and said "What did you say?" He then punched V in the side of the face. A scuffle took place and in the mêlée one of V's friends punched D in the face. D managed to drag V into the lake about 3 metres out. V tried to get out but D was holding him under the water. One of V's friends threw a rock at D, hitting him on the side of the head. D let go of V and he swam to the side and got out. D got out of the lake, smashed a glass bottle and chased the group. The police were called and D was found hiding in a bush. V suffered bruising to his ribs and to the right side of his face, a swelling to his right cheek, pain to his fingers, a laceration inside his mouth and bruises around his right eye socket. V said he believed he was going to die and there were obvious psychological effects of the assault. D was aged 28 at appeal and had five convictions for seven offences including ABH, common assault, possession of a bladed article, being drunk and disorderly and battery. D was sentenced for the initial assault and not the subsequent activity in the lake, of which he was acquitted. Held. Plainly the psychological effect did not all result from the first ABH of which, alone, D was convicted. Taking into account the plea and the previous convictions, 18 months was too long. But there must be a significant measure of contribution to the psychological effect from the first ABH which must be recognised in the sentence, which therefore should be at the very top of Category 1. **12 months** not 18.

R v Osman 2015 EWCA Crim 167, 2 Cr App R (S) 5 (p 36) D pleaded (full credit) to ABH. V had been punched and knocked down by a takeaway worker, J, following an altercation over the price of a kebab. As V was on the ground, D stamped on V's head two or three times. D was wearing boots and acted in revenge for an earlier slight. V sustained a fractured tooth and cheekbone, swelling, a black eye and bleeding in the eye. V had to undergo surgery for his cheekbone and could not chew food properly on one side of his mouth for six months. The Crown could not state who caused which injury. J pleaded to common assault only but V felt that his cheekbone had been fractured by J's punch. D was aged 20 on appeal with only two cautions for shoplifting. She lived with her four siblings and her mother, who also cared for D's daughter, aged 17 months. A report showed that D was immature and open to sexual exploitation. Held. The Judge was not entitled to conclude that D alone was responsible for V's injuries. The offence properly belonged at the cusp between Categories 1 and 2. **8 months' detention**, not 16. See also: *R v Halane* 2014 EWCA Crim 1842, 2 Cr App R (S) 46 (p 375) (Plea to ABH. D and V heavily intoxicated. V punched D first. D and a friend pushed V into the gutter. D then kicked V repeatedly and stamped on V's head twice. The friend tried to hold D back but V punched again. D, aged 27, no violent or custodial antecedents with caring responsibilities. V was vulnerable as intoxicated, therefore Judge entitled to place this sustained assault into Category 1. 16 months stiff, but not excessive.)

R v Merritt 2015 EWCA Crim 610 (Convicted. D complained to the police about boys knocking on his door and running away. Told to produce one of the miscreants. Four boys involved again. V, aged 11, had not knocked on the door. Pursued him and punched him. D took him back to his house and demanded the names of those involved. Aged 55. Previous for violence but none in last five years. Category 1, aggravated by age of V and previous. Because of mitigation **18 months** not 30.)

Old cases: *R v Scrimshaw* 2010 EWCA Crim 142 (**4 months**) *R v Conn* 2010 EWCA Crim 933 (**15 months**) *R v Rodham* 2010 EWCA Crim 1471 (**3 years**) For a summary of these cases see the 10th edition of this book.

Racially motivated, see the **RACIALLY OR RELIGIOUSLY AGGRAVATED OFFENCES** chapter.

For when there is no count specifying the racially aggravating matter, see **315.7**.

201.16   *Relationship offences*

Domestic Violence Guideline 2006, see www.banksr.com Other Matters Guidelines tab and the **DOMESTIC VIOLENCE** chapter.

R v James 2011 EWCA Crim 2630 D pleaded (late) to ABH. D had had an on and off relationship with V for about two years. She was five months' pregnant. He reported her to the authorities over her Housing benefit. They had an argument in a car. D drove to V's home and the argument continued. D called V "fat, worthless, a cunt and a whore". The argument continued in the front garden, after D left the house. He threw a sizeable stone at V, which missed. He got into his car and reversed, hitting some railings and a tree. V went into the road to call for her dog. D then drove recklessly in her direction, The car collided with her at between 11 and 13 mph. V fell to the ground underneath the car. D immediately reversed the car away from V and went to her assistance, although he told her not to go to the police. V suffered abrasions on both elbows, her knee, her chin, her chest and her abdomen. D pleaded on the basis that he did not intend to hit her, but that his driving was reckless. D, aged 35 at appeal, had a long record for violence in a domestic context, including unlawful wounding and common assault (×5). He had begun to drink heavily, and was in receipt of Incapacity benefit. The Judge particularly noted the offences against partners and former partners. Held. This was on any view a serious offence. Although there was no premeditation, the fact that V was pregnant, the use of a car as a weapon and D's record were significant aggravating factors. Starting at **4 years**, with ⅙ credit for the plea, **3 years 4 months** upheld.

R v Moore and Brown 2012 EWCA Crim 262 LCJ M and B pleaded (full credit) to ABH. V, aged 17, had had a brief relationship with M's daughter. When the relationship terminated, M's daughter suggested that M would be looking for V, as he had made threats to damage M's van. M approached V and a friend, and they ran away. They came across B, whom they knew to be M's friend. B told V to stop messing with M's family and pushed him to the ground. V was punched and kicked. M arrived and dragged V into the back of his van. M drove the van whilst B attacked V in the van by punching and kicking his head and body. B suggested that had M not been present, B would have slit V's throat. V was subsequently allowed to go. V suffered a cut to his lip, a bloodied nose, grazes, swelling to his head and a bruise under his eye. M, aged 36, had 15 convictions for 46 offences, mostly for driving offences. There were no convictions for violence, but he had been sent to custody in 1995, 1998, 2000, 2001, 2003 and 2004. B, aged 29, had convictions for 19 offences, including assault in 1998 and 2002. Held. Had it not been for the abduction and detention, this would have been a Category 2 offence. The injuries were not serious. However, in addition to the abduction, this was a sustained and unprovoked attack committed by two men partially in a public place. It must have been a terrifying experience for V. Starting at 18 months, **12 months** cannot be criticised.

R v Gunning 2013 EWCA Crim 179 D pleaded to two ABHs and criminal damage. He spent much of an evening arguing with his girlfriend, V. D engaged in boorish and provocative behaviour. He deliberately smashed some framed photographs of hers which were of sentimental value to her (the criminal damage). V did not rise to the bait and D made an attempt to cut himself. V told him he was sick and twisted. D then grabbed her tightly by the throat, brought his face repeatedly into contact with hers and then head-butted her. He held her down on the floor and hid her mobile so she could not contact anyone. V managed to hit him with a saucepan. Two days later, there was a further argument and D told V to leave his flat. She began to pack. D pushed her and again head-butted her. He tried to convince her he would kill himself. V did leave. A neighbour described V as in pain, extremely upset and fearful of what D might do to her. V had bruising to the face and arms, and a black eye. D was aged 36 and had numerous convictions involving dishonesty and drugs. He had a conviction for harassment of a different former partner. D put forward a basis of plea which was rejected. The Judge said the assaults were Category 1 and gave 25% credit for the plea, because D had tried to minimise his criminality. He started at 16 months for each assault. That made 12 months for each consecutive. Held. The first offence cannot be described as involving greater harm. He was entitled to full credit. We start at 12 months for the first assault. With totality we start at 15 months for the second. That makes 8 and 10 months consecutive so **18 months,** not 2 years.

R v Lee 2013 EWCA Crim 948 D pleaded (at the PCMH) to ABH and breach of a Restraining Order. V and D started a relationship in 2006 and thereafter there was a history of domestic abuse. D saw V in a shop, pulled her to the ground by her hair, hit her with a beer can and said, "The police have dropped the assault charge, you need to pull back on yours."[11] In early 2012, D, after convictions for intimidation and assault by beating, a 4-year Restraining Order was made. He received 30 months and was released in May 2012. The Restraining Order was varied at V's request, as she had contacted D in relation to their children and they were contemplating resuming their relationship. All but one condition was lifted, namely that D was prohibited from threatening violence against V. The relationship resumed and once again it deteriorated, with V feeling that D was controlling. V and the children spent one evening with her friends and at about 1 am D phoned her and asked her who she was with and where she was. They made arrangements for D to see the children the following day, but minutes later, D arrived at the address with a friend, G. V told D that the children were asleep and he could not just turn up unannounced. D became angry and V's next recollection was of being on the floor with D kicking her in the head. She placed her hands around her head to protect herself and could hear G shouting "That's enough". She lost consciousness and woke up in a pool of blood. She had a superficial laceration under her eye and a deep circular wound on her forehead. D, aged 31, had extensive convictions. There were 24 convictions for 52 offences including robbery, theft, arson, possession of cannabis and burglary. There were also convictions for criminal damage and battery. He had been to custody twice before for violent offences against V. Held. The Judge unlawfully imposed an extended sentence. That was quashed. This was a Category 1 offence and a bad case of domestic violence aggravated by D's previous convictions. Further, there was the breach of the Restraining Order. There is nothing wrong in principle with a consecutive

---

[11] The judgment contains no detail of the assault charge, or what 'yours' refers to. Ed.

sentence for that breach. There was similarly nothing wrong with 6 months, reflecting a sentence of 9 months before the plea. The custodial term of 3 years 9 months (before plea) imposed by the Judge was significantly outside the guidelines. That was not appropriate. The appropriate starting point was 3 years. With the plea, **2 years**. With 6 months consecutive for the breach, **2½ years**.

R v Zakacura 2013 EWCA Crim 2595 D pleaded to ABH. D was a Latvian national who came to the UK in 2011. He had had a relationship with V, and a more recent relationship with TL. TL had a stepdaughter, ND. It was alleged that he had assaulted TL and ND and a police officer and was to be tried for those offences subsequently. He had been drinking heavily and went to TL's address. ND and V were there. An argument arose and D took hold of V's hair and struck her in the area of her left eye. V began to bleed from the blow. It had caused two lacerations, one above and one below the eye, with attendant bruising and impaired vision. The wounds were treated with paper stitches. D, aged 35, had a history of violence and had received 9 months in Latvia after smashing windows of the home he shared with his former partner. In 2012, he received 8 months for making threats to kill and 4 months concurrent for threatening to destroy property. Following his release he received a caution for battery. He had a 'major problem' with alcohol abuse and had convictions for driving with excess alcohol. He had 'generally been in work' since arriving in the UK. Held. It can be inferred that the Judge took a starting point of about 15 months, allowing for full credit for the guilty plea. That was beyond the upper point of the Category 2 range. The Judge was entirely right to do so. The injuries to V, a young female victim, were very serious in the context of the offence. The aggravating factors were legion. He had recently been sentenced for making a threat to kill and had a caution for battery. The offence was committed on bail and at an address at which the conditions of bail expressly forbade him to be. The offence was committed in the home of the alleged victim of the first assault and in the presence of her child. He was under the influence of alcohol at the time and there was a clear pattern of serious alcohol abuse associated with crime. The Judge could properly have placed this offence in Category 1 with a starting point of 18 months. With full credit, **12 months** would have been in excess of what the Judge imposed. It follows that 10 months was not manifestly excessive.

R v Bullough 2014 EWCA Crim 1170 D pleaded to ABH. V, D's father, who was small and frail, left the house to go for a walk. He received a call from D's girlfriend and took the call in the street. D had been in a bad mood all day after arguing with his girlfriend and had been drinking. D ran outside accusing V of laughing at him and bundled him into the house, threatening to kill him. D began attacking V, punching him repeatedly about the head causing a laceration. When V fell, D kicked him, ignoring pleas to stop. Then he stopped and hugged V and asked to be forgiven. D, aged 27 and with 19 convictions for 28 offences, was subject to a community order with an alcohol treatment requirement at the time of the offence. The pre-sentence report highlighted D's mental health problems. Held. The attack was very nasty. However, D's mental health problems indicated lower culpability. With full credit, **12 months** not 20.

R v Thomas 2014 EWCA Crim 1715, 2015 1 Cr App R (S) 3 (p 16) D pleaded to ABH. He pleaded guilty at a mention just before his trial. D had lost his temper and dragged V, his partner, by the hair a short distance across a road with a significant degree of force. He then kicked her twice in the back as she lay on the floor. V suffered chipped teeth, bruising to her chin and back and cuts and grazes, but she made no complaint. The incident was captured on CCTV and her injuries were seen by her sister and the police. D was aged 29 and had 18 convictions (five as a juvenile) for violence. His last was in 2011 for affray and possessing a firearm with intent (12 months) but he had been out of trouble for 18 months since his release. D's longest custodial sentence was a 2-year DTO and he had received six immediate custodial sentences in all. Despite having regular arguments and threatening V, D indicated remorse and a need to change his outlook. The Judge placed this in Category 1 as V was vulnerable, since she knew D was capable of anger and violence, therefore greater harm. It was higher culpability as D had used his shod foot as a weapon and the offence occurred in a public place, leading to V's humiliation. Held. The expression 'serious injury' must be interpreted within the context of ABH and not a more serious offence, such as GBH. 'Serious injury' differentiates between an injury on the margin of being an actual injury and injury which is more substantial, and in the context of ABH, is serious. Chipped teeth and facial damage are not trivial matters to a young woman. In this case, V's injuries were serious and the Judge was entitled to place this in Category 1. He was also entitled to rely on D's antecedents and go outside the range. That said, regard was to be had to: a) the full extent of V's injuries, b) D's genuine remorse, c) D's pre-trial plea and d) D's previous attacks not warranting a term of over 12 months. **3 years**, not 5 years' extended sentence (4 years' custody 1 year extended licence).

R v Gulas 2015 EWCA Crim 1200 D pleaded to ABH (full credit). D had had a relationship with V for over a year. They had a 6-month-old child and V had two older children with another father. D and V argued for most of a day, mostly about money. The older children went to bed and the baby was downstairs with D and V. The arguments escalated and D punched V in the eye three times, causing it to bleed. V tried to protect herself with her arms and he punched them and [pushed] them out the way. D went to the kitchen and came back with a rolling pin. He hit V with it around her hip. She again tried to protect herself with her arms and he used a cigarette to burn her so she would move her arms. The noise woke the children up and the eldest took the baby upstairs. D wanted a drink so he went to a shop. He came back, threatened V and punched her in the eye again. Police arrived. V's temple was swollen and bleeding. There were cuts and bruising to V's arms and an injury to her hip. There was a burn and other marks. In interview D lied. He was aged 35 with no convictions in this country. D told the pre-sentence report writer that he had lost control and that V deserved it. The Judge said it was a most dreadful and sustained attack on a most vulnerable victim. Held. The injuries were significant. The Judge was able to go to the top of the range of Category 1. A fist, a rolling pin and a cigarette were used. We start at 3 years 4 months, so with plea, **27 months** not 32.

See also: *R v Corbett* 2011 EWCA Crim 2417 (Plea to ABH. Whilst in his ex-partner's home and after consuming alcohol, the defendant punched her in the head a number of times causing loss of a tooth. Threatened to smash a wine bottle on her. Aged 47. Drug user. 29 appearances for over 70 offences including manslaughter and a firearms offence. **2½ years** was not manifestly excessive.)

R v Mann 2013 EWCA Crim 1110 (Plea (no discount) to ABH on his girlfriend. Repeated allegations of infidelity. Slaps and punches. She escaped and he dragged her back into the flat. Black eye, bruising and swelling. Previous for ABH on same victim and ABH on person who defendant thought his girlfriend was sleeping with. Attempts to force victim not to attend. **2½ years** not 5 years' extended sentence (4 years' custody 1 year extended licence).)

R v Somerset 2014 EWCA Crim 1516 (Plea to four counts (very little credit). D, the son of a duke, subjected V, his wife, to repeated domestic violence for over 22 years. D and V both drank excessively. Hair pulling and V sustaining bruises and scratches. On two occasions D kicked V. Once was V's ankle with "an incredibly hard blow", the other was to V's body, leaving her with bruising, swelling and soreness. D was aged 56. Held. Persistent, deliberate violence treated extremely seriously. Overall sentence of **24 months** not excessive.)

R v Whitelock 2014 EWCA Crim 204 (Convicted of two ABHs. Repeated punches to the face of a female neighbour and her male partner. Both victims on the floor. Defendant delivered kicks to the face and ribs. Extensive bruising and cuts. Substantial and serious attack. Aged 53. No material convictions. 9 months consecutive for the assaults, making **18 months** not 24 and 2 months consecutive for a breach of bail.)

R v Maloney 2015 EWCA Crim 798, 2 Cr App R (S) 32 (p 276) (Plea to ABH and dangerous driving. Forced his partner, who was pregnant, into a car. Drove off, insulted her and punched her three times in the face and three times on the leg. Now aged 21. No convictions. **8 months** not 18, consecutive to and not concurrent with the 6 months for the driving offence.)
Old cases: *R v Parker* 2009 EWCA Crim 1226, 2010 1 Cr App R (S) 32 (p 199) (**2 years**) *R v A* 2010 EWCA Crim 159 (5 years' extended sentence (**4 years' custody** 1 year licence) *R v Bevan* 2010 EWCA Crim 255 (**3 years**) *R v Poules* 2010 EWCA Crim 399 (**18 months**) *R v Wilson* 2010 EWCA Crim 2138 (**50 weeks' suspended**) *R v Jenkins* 2010 EWCA Crim 2229 (**8 months**) For a summary of the last case see the 10th edition of this book.
Road rage, see the **ROAD RAGE** chapter.

201.17 Sporting offences
R v Noble 2015 EWCA Crim 1454 D was convicted of ABH. Five minutes after coming onto a football pitch as a substitute, D was closely marked by [another] during a goal kick. Both men, D and V, stood their ground and suddenly D struck V in the face with considerable force. V suffered mouth injuries. One of his teeth broke in half and another was loosened and hanging. In interview D said V was pushing and hitting him and would not stop. Out of frustration he used his arm to send V a message. D, aged 25, was a hard-working man with no convictions. The Judge held the assault was deliberate and V was knocked out for a few seconds. Held. The defendant had no history of violence except for a caution for common assault in 2009. This was a serious assault which comfortably passes the custody threshold. If the offence was Category 1 then it was at the lower end of the scale. **9 months** not 2 years.
Stalking, see the **STALKING** chapter.

201.18 Street fighting
R v Pullen 2012 EWCA Crim 1026 D pleaded to ABH. He was in a town centre with friends. They had been drinking heavily during the day. His friends had told him that V had been saying 'bad stuff' about D and his girlfriend. D approached V and punched him in the back of the head. V attempted to walk away, but D followed him and punched him a further two times. V suffered a fractured jaw, both to the right mandibular angle and the left mandibular body. He also lost a tooth. D made full and frank admissions and recognised the attack was unprovoked. The pre-sentence report noted D showed genuine remorse, victim empathy and understanding of the wider impact of his actions. D was aged 17, just short of his 18th birthday, was of good character and was attending college. Held. The Judge placed this into Category 2. It was a serious case of repeated assault. There was no provocation. Taking account of his good character, the plea and the personal mitigation, **4 months' detention**, not 10.
R v Pepper 2013 EWCA Crim 814 LCJ D pleaded to ABH. There was a *Newton* hearing at the Crown Court. The Judge found in his favour and D fell to be sentenced on the basis that he had fallen out with his girlfriend, went to a city centre, had too much to drink and got into another argument. Then V had thrown a jumper at him and D had punched him as an immediate reaction. V fell to the floor and D punched V twice while he lay on the ground. V lost three teeth, which required operative treatment. D, aged 22 at appeal, had no previous convictions. Held. It was conceded that this was properly categorised as a Category 2 case. There was an aggravating feature of drunken violence on city streets late at night. In considering the seriousness of the offending, there are two elements of greater harm: the loss of three teeth requiring operative treatment and the fact that D continued to assault V after he had fallen to the ground. An immediate custodial sentence in excess of the starting point of 26 weeks was justified. The Judge reduced the starting point to 24 weeks after the *Newton*. With full credit, **16 weeks** was not manifestly excessive.

R v Wright 2013 EWCA Crim 2672 D pleaded to ABH and affray. Whilst waiting for a taxi, D was approached by V1, who wrongly accused him of using racist words. D struck V1 causing bleeding and a fractured nose. Five days later, D and a friend had an altercation with V2 and V3 who were pushed and punched. V2 sustained bruising and swelling to the eye sockets with some concussion. V3 required no medical treatment. D was aged 20 and had no relevant convictions. Held. V1's injury was in part provoked by V1, was caused by a single blow and was not a particularly serious injury. V2's injuries, while more serious, if dealt with as ABH [were] likely [to] have been Category 3. The Judge was incorrect in passing deterrent sentences owing to a local problem with violence. There was no evidence that the problem was greater locally than nationally. 1 month not 5 for the ABH. 4 months, not 10 for the affray. Total concurrent sentence of **4 months**.

201.19   *Unprovoked/No reason   No weapon, no kicks*

R v Cooper 2011 EWCA Crim 1910 D pleaded on the day of trial to ABH. After drinking, he went to get a taxi. He attempted to get into a taxi which V had already started to get into. The taxi driver asked D to get out. There was a lengthy conversation. D got out but was abusive. He punched V in the face, knocking him to the ground. V had a glaucoma score of 15, a wound to his head, swelling over his zygoma (cheekbone), swelling to both lips and an abrasion to one lip. D had a previous conviction for section 20, threatening words or behaviour and excess alcohol. Held. It was clear that alcohol had played a significant part in his offending. The appropriate starting point was 16 months, so, with 10% for the plea, **14 months** not 21 months.

R v Pullen 2012 EWCA Crim 1026 D pleaded to ABH. He was in a town centre with friends. They had been drinking heavily during the day. His friends had told him that V had been saying 'bad stuff' about D and his girlfriend. D approached V and punched him in the back of the head. V attempted to walk away, but D followed him and punched him a further two times. V suffered a fractured jaw, both to the right mandibular angle and the left mandibular body. He also lost a tooth. D made full and frank admissions and recognised the attack was unprovoked. The pre-sentence report noted D showed genuine remorse, victim empathy and understanding of the wider impact of his actions. D was aged 17, just short of his 18th birthday, was of good character and was attending college. Held. The Judge placed this into Category 2. It was a serious case of repeated assault. There was no provocation. Taking account of his good character, the plea and the personal mitigation, **4 months' detention**, not 10.

R v Burgess and Torr 2012 EWCA Crim 1043 B and T pleaded to ABH. V was a taxi driver. B, T and two others got into V's taxi. After making two stops, all four men got out of the taxi. T said "Don't pay", but at the insistence of another of the group, they paid the fare. As V returned to his taxi, B and T began to attack him. V was punched on the nose and elsewhere by both men. A third also became involved. V's nose was broken and he suffered bruising, abrasions and a scratched cornea. He was unable to work for 10 days and suffered around £1,000 of lost income. The blood in the taxi needed extensive professional cleaning. V did not want to drive at night, and was concerned about the stress caused to his pregnant wife. B, aged 22 at appeal, had three appearances, for section 20 (2006) and battery (×2 2011). He also had five cautions and was subject to a community order, which he had breached. One of the battery offences was committed six days prior to this attack, and B was on bail pending sentence. T (age not revealed) had 25 appearances for 49 offences, including attempted ABH (April 2004), battery (November 2004), ABH (2005) and section 18 (2007). Held. There is no doubt that this was a Category 1 case. The offence bristles with aggravating features. For T, with his appalling history, a departure from the guideline is fully justified. For B, the fact that the offence was committed on bail was a serious aggravating factor. The Judge was not wrong to treat both men in the same way, despite the disparity in age and antecedents. **3 years** for both might be regarded as severe but it was not manifestly excessive.

R v Venables 2013 EWCA Crim 231 D pleaded (full credit) to ABH. He had spent the day at Chester Races and was drunk. V was cycling home at about 1 am after work. D ran across the road to V and pushed him off his bike. V fell into the middle of the road and a car narrowly missed him. He was wearing a helmet. D then rode V's bike along the road until he was stopped by a woman who returned the bike to V. D boarded a bus and was later arrested. V suffered grazes to his ankle and head. V took two weeks off work and was frightened to go into the town centre. D, aged 27 at sentence, had nine offences on five occasions. None involved violence and all were dealt with by fines or discharges. D demonstrated genuine remorse. Held. The fact that D was drunk and would not have committed this offence sober is an aggravating, rather than a mitigating, factor. Imprisonment was justified, but due to D's limited record, a suspended sentence would have been appropriate. Because D has been in custody for 2 months, we replace the 8-month sentence with 4 months, allowing immediate release.

R v Stevenson 2015 EWCA Crim 1140 D pleaded to ABH at the Magistrates' Court. D, who had been drinking, talked to V in a petrol station kiosk amicably. V then thought D had been rude to the cashier and D took exception to this and head-butted and punched V. D then left. V lost one of his teeth and had a small cut to his eyebrow. D was 27, with seven sentencing hearings for 21 offences. Between 2005 and 2007, there was a violent behaviour and an assault. There were other violent offences but there was no offending since he was released from prison in 2009. He had been using cocaine and was drinking up to a bottle of spirits a day. The pre-sentence report assessed he posed a high risk of harm to the public. The Judge said it was a Category 1 case, because D had hit V twice, making the offence one of higher culpability. She thought the head-butt was, in effect, the use of a weapon. Held. The Judge made no mention of the mitigation which was: a) D had been in full-time employment since two months after his release, b) he was now a team leader at his local factory, c) D was the sole breadwinner, d) his children were aged 3 years and 8 months, e) his wife was very ill with a perforated ulcer with complications and f) D had to support her and look after the children. The offence was Category 1. The aggravating factors did not warrant an extra year's imprisonment. We start at 2 years, not 30 months, so with plea, 16 months not 20 months.

R v Daines 2015 EWCA Crim 1475 D pleaded to ABH. At 2.30 am on New Year's Day, D, with another, walked past V, who was waiting for a taxi. All were under the influence of alcohol. After about 10 metres, D walked back and punched V hard in the face. V fell and was unconscious for about five minutes. V's friends intervened and D turned his attention to them. D's actions became out of view of the CCTV. In interview, D said he thought V had said, "What are you looking at?" which V had not said. D was aged 23. He had a good work record and was a valuable asset to his employer. In 2010, when aged 19, he received 4 months suspended for GBH. In a night club, D had fractured a man's jaw. The suspended sentence was extended when D committed a public order offence. In 2012, when drunk, he committed criminal damage. Held. The case was at the very top of Category 2. It was a single punch. [We start at 12 months] not 15, so with full credit, **8 months** not 10.

See also: *R v Bignell* 2012 EWCA Crim 346 (Late plea to ABH. Friction between defendant and his girlfriend's ex-partner, V, with whom she had a child. Defendant head-butted V, grappled him to the floor and punched him a number of times. Caused split lip, red mark on cheek, bleeding mouth and painful tooth. No stitches. Aged 24 with bad record for violence including three ABHs. Category 2 not 1. 10% credit for plea. **16 months** not 28.)

R v Myers 2013 EWCA Crim 622 (3 years for an adult. See **201.8**.)

Old cases: *R v Abbas* 2009 EWCA Crim 1386, 2010 1 Cr App R (S) 47 (p 292) (**15 months**) *R v Lloyd* 2010 EWCA Crim 2319 (**2 years**) *R v Melbourne* 2010 EWCA Crim 2230 (**12 months**) *R v O'Halloran* 2010 EWCA Crim 2332 (**14 months**) *R v Milhailsens* 2010 EWCA Crim 2545 (**16 weeks**) *R v Fleck* 2010 EWCA Crim 2811 (**12 months**)

For a summary of the first case see the 9th edition of this book and for the last four cases see the 10th edition of this book.

201.20   *Unprovoked/No reason   Kicks or weapon used*

R v Morris 2012 EWCA Crim 1965 D pleaded to ABH on rearraignment. A group of youths were acting in an unruly manner in the street. CCTV camera operators were monitoring their behaviour. V found himself surrounded by the group, and was attacked. He was pushed to the ground and punched and kicked whilst he was there. He managed to run off but was pursued by around six or seven youths who tried to trip him. He was again pushed to the ground and was repeatedly punched and kicked. The group left in various vehicles, although D did not go with them. V suffered a fractured foot and grazing and bruising to his elbows. D was identified by the CCTV images. D, aged 19 at appeal, but 18 at the time of the incident, had seven convictions for 12 offences in 2011 and 2012. The convictions were for threatening behaviour and obstructing the police, among other things. Held. The Judge was correct not to distinguish between the defendants. They were jointly responsible for the violence. A fractured foot is serious in the context of an ABH offence. The nature of the offence is made more serious by the combination of individuals, acting together, kicking a defenceless individual whilst he is on the ground. The Judge was correct that this was a Category 1 case. **13 months** was untouched.

R v Port 2013 EWCA Crim 2668, 2014 2 Cr App R (S) 26 (p 203) D pleaded (at his PCMH) to ABH and possession of an offensive weapon. V was a licensed mini-cab driver. He collected D from his home. D had been drinking alcohol and taking drugs, in particular cocaine. D offered payment for the journey at the outset but no payment was made. D asked V to stop en route so he could buy some cigarettes. V asked for some payment before he got out and D refused, saying he would pay for the journey at the end. He told V to "fuck off" and got out of the car. V followed him and told him that he could not just walk off without providing some form of payment. D said "If you don't fuck off I am going to punch you in the face." V said "Are you really going to punch me in the face?" Thereupon D punched V in the face causing swelling and bruising. A fight ensued and V got the upper hand, delivering a number of punches to D's face. They both ended up on the ground. D took out an extendable baton from his bag. He struck V once on the arm in order to free himself. V grabbed the baton and D let go and ran away. Four of V's teeth became loose and he suffered a cut lip. D pleaded on the basis that he punched V once, and used the baton (which was not his) to protect himself. D was aged 25 at appeal. He had seven previous court appearances between 2006 and 2013. Held. This offence was above Category 3 in the guidelines because of the particular position of taxi-drivers who provide a public service and who are frequently assaulted by passengers not wishing to pay their fare, or robbed. D punched V hard in the face after a reasonable request for some of the monies owed to V, causing four teeth to be loose. It was not a Category 2 case, however, as greater harm or higher culpability were not present. Immediate custody was required but a starting point of 12 months was not merited. Starting at 8 months was consistent with the offending. The appropriate credit for the plea was 25%. **6 months** not 9.

See also: *R v Candy* 2013 EWCA Crim 1158 (Plea. Street fight between defendant's boyfriend, P, and V. She became involved and threw punches and aimed numerous kicks at V's body. The kicks were not forceful. Aged 21. Previous for violence but none for 3 years. Showed remorse. She was a responsible mother. Category 2 offence. 7 weeks in custody. **14 weeks** not 8 months, to enable immediate release.)

Old cases: *R v Lawson* 2010 EWCA Crim 150 (**30 months**) *R v McCall* 2010 EWCA Crim 1452 (**2 years**) *R v Tierney* 2010 EWCA Crim 1465 (**3 years**) *R v Jones* 2010 EWCA Crim 2425 (**12 months suspended**)

For a summary of the first three cases see the 10th edition of this book.

202   ABH: RACIALLY OR RELIGIOUSLY AGGRAVATED
202.1
Crime and Disorder Act 1998 s 29
Mode of trial Triable either way
Maximum sentence On indictment 7 years. Summary 6 months and/or a £5,000 fine for offences committed before 12 March 2015 and an unlimited fine thereafter.[12] There are maximum fines for those aged under 18, see **14.38**.
For the ancillary orders, see **201.1**.

202.2   Sentencing Council guideline
For the guideline, see the **ABH** chapter at **201.2**.
Basic principles see the RACIALLY OR RELIGIOUSLY AGGRAVATED OFFENCES *Basic principles* para at **315.4**.

202.3   Cases
R v Jones 2013 EWCA Crim 397 D pleaded (full credit) to racially aggravated ABH. V, aged 19, was working as a taxi rank marshal. D, under the influence of alcohol, without any warning or provocation of any kind, approached V, a Sikh, from behind and 'tugged' at his turban. D pushed and punched him while shouting at him saying "Paki bastard" and "twat". When V retreated into the road, D head-butted V causing swollen lips and a bruised tooth. Throughout the attack, V did not retaliate but merely tried to restrain D. D, aged 29, had one conviction for criminal damage when aged 17. He had three references. One from a colleague from a minority ethnic background stated that he had never experienced or witnessed racist behaviour from D. The Judge started at 26 weeks, doubled it to take account of the aggravation and then reduced it by a third for the plea. Held. The Judge rightly noted that this was aggravated (above the statutory aggravation) by the fact that it occurred in a public place. This Category 2 offence clearly crossed the custody threshold. Although V was not a public employee, he was performing a public service. The inevitable custodial sentence had to be immediate. There was an element of double counting in relation to the racial aggravation, having brought the offence into the category, and then effectively doubled within the category. **26 weeks** not 34 weeks.

R v Eyles 2014 EWCA Crim 322 D pleaded to racially aggravated ABH, racially aggravated common assault and affray. At about 5 pm, V was out shopping. She was wearing a hijab and carrying her 16-month old son. She became aware of D running towards her. D was shouting and swearing, causing V to fear for her safety. Witnesses heard him shout at her, "I don't want to fucking scare you, but I will. It's all your fault. Don't think I won't smash your baby's head in because I will." D punched V several times and at one point took hold of her baby and 'knocked' his head against a wall. V stopped D but was assaulted again and knocked to the ground. V sustained cuts and grazes to her arms and legs. As she fell, her son fell too and hit his head on the ground. Bystanders saw what was going on and tried to intervene. D was described as being in a world of his own. D put his hand in his pocket and made out that he was armed with a weapon. Fortunately the baby sustained no injury and so the charge in respect of him was common assault. A supermarket security guard tried to help and D said "I've got a knife and I'll fucking kill you." D was told to calm down and responded by saying he wanted to shake the security guard's hand. In fact D ran off. He went up to another man, grabbed his hand and said he had a 9 mm firearm. That man froze with fear. The police arrived and D ran into a supermarket. D shouted "I've got a fucking gun. Get down or I'll shoot." The police followed him and fired at him with a Taser. He continued to run around the shop until he was stopped by a security guard. It turned out he was not armed with a weapon. D said he had taken a legal high and some cannabis and heard voices. D said he targeted V because she was a Muslim and Asian. He had been told that there

---

[12] Legal Aid, Sentencing and Punishment of Offenders Act 2012 s 85(1) and (4) and Legal Aid, Sentencing and Punishment of Offenders Act 2012 (Commencement No 11) Order 2015 2015/504

would be a terrorist attack. He said he had mental health issues. D was aged 30 at appeal and had been employed at a scrapyard. He had a conditional discharge in 2007 for assaulting a PC and a suspended sentence in 2011 for animal cruelty. The pre-sentence report said D had said he was having a nervous breakdown on the day of the offences brought on by anxiety about not having contact with his daughter. A decision from the Family Court was pending. Held. The Judge was right to categorise the ABH as a Category 1 offence. This was a serious and sustained assault in a public place on a woman carrying a small child. A total sentence of 3 years would have been appropriate, following a trial. With full credit, the appropriate sentences were as follows. For the ABH, 18 months for the basic offence and a 6-month uplift for the racial aggravation, making 2 years. For the common assault, 9 months. For the affray, 18 months. So **2 years** not 2 years 8 months.

See also: *R v Cawley* 2011 EWCA Crim 2817 (Convicted of racially aggravated ABH. Racial abuse of Afghan neighbour, followed by kicks with shod foot. She had convictions for assault and affray. Previous mental health issues. **23 months** was not manifestly excessive.)

R v Letchford 2014 EWCA Crim 1474 (D realised that he was being followed by a group of teenagers. He confronted them and ran up to and punched a man five or six times, saying, "I hate black people." Victim chased round town centre. Threats to kill made. Incident lasted 30 minutes. Abusive language to police. Previous convictions for violence against a police officer. With full credit **3 years** not 42 months. Sentence remains consecutive to burglary sentence.)

Old cases: *R v Comfort* 2007 EWCA Crim 104 (**2½ years'** detention) *Att-Gen's Ref No 75 of 2008* 2009 EWCA Crim 667 (LCJ Aged under 18. In a group attacking foreign students at a university. **18 months'** detention.)

For a summary of the first case, see the 7th edition of this book.

ABSTRACTING ELECTRICITY, see the THEFT *Electricity or gas* para at **346.17**.

ACCOUNTING, FALSE, see the FALSE ACCOUNTING chapter.

203   AFFRAY/VIOLENT DISORDER

203.1

1 Affray

   Public Order Act 1986 s 3

   Mode of trial Triable either way

   Maximum sentence On indictment 3 years. Summary 6 months and/or a £5,000 fine for offences committed before 12 March 2015 and an unlimited fine thereafter.[13]

   There are maximum fines for those aged under 18, see **14.38** in Volume 1.

2 Violent disorder

   Public Order Act 1986 s 2 (using/threatening violence such as to cause a person to fear for his personal safety etc.)

   Mode of trial Triable either way

   Maximum sentence On indictment 5 years. Summary 6 months and/or a £5,000 fine for offences committed before 12 March 2015 and an unlimited fine thereafter.[14]

   There are maximum fines for those aged under 18, see **14.38** in Volume 1.

Criminal Behaviour Orders For both offences, where a defendant has engaged in behaviour that caused or was likely to cause harassment, alarm or distress to any persons and a Criminal Behaviour Order will help in preventing the offender from engaging in such behaviour, the court may make this order.[15]

---

[13] Legal Aid, Sentencing and Punishment of Offenders Act 2012 s 85(1) and (4) and Legal Aid, Sentencing and Punishment of Offenders Act 2012 (Commencement No 11) Order 2015 2015/504

[14] Legal Aid, Sentencing and Punishment of Offenders Act 2012 s 85(1) and (4) and Legal Aid, Sentencing and Punishment of Offenders Act 2012 (Commencement No 11) Order 2015 2015/504

[15] Anti-social Behaviour, Crime and Policing Act 2014 s 22(1)-(4)

Extended sentences Both offences are listed in Criminal Justice Act 2003 Sch 15. The court may pass an extended sentence if there is a significant risk of serious harm from future specified offences and either: a) the defendant has a Criminal Justice Act 2003 Sch 15A[16] conviction (applicable only to defendants aged 18+), or b) the offence would justify a determinate sentence of at least 4 years.[17]

Depriving defendant of vehicle used These orders can be imposed for both offences, see *Depriving defendant of vehicle used* para at **203.10**.

Disqualification from driving There are occasions when it is appropriate to make this order for both offences.[18]

Football Banning Orders For both offences, where the offence was committed relevant to a football match and where there are reasonable grounds to believe that making a banning order would help to prevent violence or disorder at or in connection with any regulated football match, the court <u>must</u> make a Football Banning Order under Football Spectators Act 1989 s 14A and Sch 1 para 1.

Licensed premises For both offences where an offence is committed on licensed premises, the court may prohibit defendants from entering those premises or any other specified premises without the express consent of the licensee etc.[19] The minimum period is 3 months and the maximum period is 2 years.[20] Violent Crime Reduction Act 2006 s 65 and Sch 5 repeals these powers. Evaluation of the new powers continues. The repeal and the commencement of the new powers is not expected soon.

Sexual Harm Prevention Orders For both offences where is a discretionary power to make this order when it is necessary to protect the public from sexual harm.[21]

203.2   Crown Court statistics   England and Wales
Violent disorder

Year	Age	Plea	Total sen- tenced	Type of sentencing %						Average length of custody in months
				Dis- charge	Fine	Community sentence	Sus- pended sentence	Custody	Oth- er	
2013	18-20	G	86	2.3	0.0	4.7	12.8	79.1	1.2	16.2
		NG	14	–	–	–	7.1	85.7	7.1	27.8
	21+	G	243	–	–	3.7	39.9	56.4	–	19.4
		NG	52	–	–	9.6	17.3	73.1	–	28.3
2014	18-20	G	80	–	1	4	40	55	–	12.6
		NG	12	–	–	–	17	83	–	19.9
	21+	G	208	–	–	4	25	70	1	18.7
		NG	38	–	–	–	21	79	–	23.7

For explanations about the statistics see page 1-xii. For more statistics and for statistics for male and female defendants etc. see www.banksr.com Other Matters Statistics tab

203.3   Magistrates' Court Sentencing guidelines   Affray
Magistrates' Court Sentencing Guidelines 2008, see www.banksr.com Other Matters Guidelines tab The guidelines apply to the Magistrates' Court and to the Crown Court hearing appeals or sentencing for summary only offences.[22]

---

[16] Repealed by Legal Aid, Sentencing and Punishment of Offenders Act 2012 Sch 21 para 31 (as of 3/12/12)

[17] Criminal Justice Act 2003 s 225-229 as amended by Criminal Justice and Immigration Act 2008 s 13-20 and commenced by Criminal Justice and Immigration Act 2008 (Commencement No 2 and Transitional and Saving Provisions) Order 2008 2008/1586 para 2

[18] Powers of Criminal Courts (Sentencing) Act 2000 s 146, *R v Cliff* 2004 EWCA Crim 3139, 2005 2 Cr App R (S) 22 (p 118) and *R v Bye* 2005 EWCA Crim 1230, 2006 1 Cr App R (S) 27 (p 157)

[19] Licensed Premises (Exclusion of Certain Persons) Act 1980 s 1(1)

[20] Licensed Premises (Exclusion of Certain Persons) Act 1980 s 1(3)

[21] Sexual Offences Act 2003 s 103A as inserted by Anti-social Behaviour, Crime and Policing Act 2014 Sch 5 para 2 and Sexual Offences Act 2003 Sch 5

[22] See page 15 of the guidelines.

For details about applying the guidelines, see the GUIDELINES chapter in Volume 1. page 85 Starting points are based on a first-time offender pleading not guilty.

Examples of nature of activity	Starting point	Range
Brief offence involving low-level violence, no substantial fear created	Low-level community order	Band C fine to medium-level community order
Degree of fighting or violence that causes substantial fear	High-level community order	Medium-level community order to 12 weeks' custody
Fight involving a weapon/throwing objects, or conduct causing risk of serious injury	18 weeks' custody	12 weeks' custody to Crown Court

The following aggravating and mitigating factors may be particularly relevant:
Factors indicating higher culpability: 1 Group action 2 Threats 3 Lengthy incident. Factors indicating lower culpability: 1 Did not start the trouble 2 Provocation 3 Stopped as soon as police arrived. Factors indicating greater degree of harm: 1 Vulnerable person(s) present 2 Injuries caused 3 Damage to property.
Consider ancillary orders, including compensation and Football Banning Order.
A Band C fine is 150% of net weekly income. For more detail, see **60.27** in Volume 1. For the meaning of a high-level, a medium-level and a low-level community order see **16.12-16.14** in Volume 1.

203.4   *Magistrates' Court Sentencing guidelines   Violent disorder*

Magistrates' Court Sentencing Guidelines 2008, see www.banksr.com Other Matters Guidelines tab page 84 These offences should normally be dealt with in the Crown Court. However, there may be rare cases involving minor violence or threats of violence leading to no or minor injury, with few people involved and no weapon or missiles, in which a custodial sentence by the Magistrates' Court may be appropriate.
For details about applying the guidelines see the GUIDELINES chapter in Volume 1.

203.5   *Judicial guidance   Serious affrays*

R v Keys 1987 84 Cr App R 204 LCJ In cases of very serious affray where it is plain that there was some measure of preparation, central organisation and direction, those who are organisers and ringleaders can expect heavy sentences in the range of 7 years and upwards. At the other end of the scale, acts of individual participants on the edges of the affray cannot be taken in isolation. Even though a particular defendant never hit an opponent, never threw a missile, never physically threatened anyone, nevertheless, even if he participated simply by encouraging others and shouting insults and threats, he thereby helps to promote the totality of the affray. He must accordingly take some share of the blame for the overall picture. The more he is shown to have promoted the affray, the greater must be his punishment. Where there has been not only a concerted major affray, but also a prolonged and vicious attack on the police, any participant, however slight his involvement may have been, can expect a sentence of at least 18 months to 2 years. The carrying of weapons, the throwing of missiles and so on ought properly to be reflected in an increase in that minimum.
Note: The sentences were passed before Public Order Act 1986 came into force and the case is very old. Consequently I would ignore the suggested penalties. However, the guidance about participation appears to be applied now as then. Ed.
R v Fox and Hicks 2005 EWCA Crim 1122, 2006 1 Cr App R (S) 17 (p 97) In cases of public disorder it is important to look at the whole picture and what an individual may have done by himself is of relevance. [The defendant's actions are] simply part of the whole to which he is contributing in his way and the larger picture must be taken account of.

203.6   Judicial guidance   Violent disorder
R v Hebron and Spencer 1989 11 Cr App R (S) 226 The two defendants were involved in a serious New Year's Eve disturbance. Held. In cases of violent crowd disorder, it is not only the precise individual acts that matter. It is the fact that the defendant is taking part in violent disorder, threatening violence against other people, and is part and parcel of the whole threatening and alarming activity.
R v Tyler 1993 96 Cr App R (S) 332 Two defendants were convicted of riot and two offences of violent disorder. After a poll tax demonstration, buildings were damaged and police attacked. Held. It is not the individual act that is the essence of the offence here. It is the using of violence in circumstances where so many people are present as to cause or inspire fear in the general public. One must look at the individual act in the context of that fear. When it occurs in a busy street the dangers are obvious.
R v Chapman 2002 EWCA Crim 2346 The defendant pleaded to violent disorder. There was a full-scale riot which lasted 12 hours. The presiding Judge issued a policy for those being sentenced for the riot. Judges must regard the total picture and the individual's specific acts. The specific acts cannot be regarded in isolation. The Court must regard the level and nature of the violence used, the scale of the riot, the extent to which it is premeditated, and the number of persons in the context of the overall picture of the specific acts. I hope that this message will deter others from engaging in this type of behaviour. Held. These observations equally apply to violent disorder.
R v Fox and Hicks 2005 EWCA Crim 1122, 2006 1 Cr App R (S) 17 (p 97) The defendants pleaded to affray. In cases of public disorder it is important to look at the whole picture and what an individual may have done by himself is of relevance. [However], that is simply part of the whole [event] to which he is contributing in his way and the larger picture must be taken account of.

Cases
Note: The two offences are listed in the same chapter because the offences are very similar. However, it is important to remember that the two offences have different maximum penalties and different Magistrates' Court guidelines. Ed.

203.7   Defendant aged under 18
R v Cox 2012 EWCA Crim 476 D pleaded (20-25%) to **violent disorder** after a section 18 count was dropped. At about 10 pm, D was in a house with others when one of the group, X, received a telephone call from Y, who made threats. X was angry and challenged Y to a fight. It was agreed it should be in a car park. X took along a crate of milk bottles. Other weapons were taken by others. Fifteen people were present in two groups. X knocked Z out and Z was stabbed three times. Z also had two skull fractures. In a basis of plea, D said he became involved in the ensuing violence. He kicked out at Z once or twice but did not recall the kick connecting. He was not present when Z was stabbed. D was aged 17 and of good character. Held. With the late plea, good character and early disengagement, **14 months** not 20.
Old cases: *R v H* 2009 EWCA Crim 1453 (Violent disorder. **Custody** was appropriate but because of his education **Supervision Order**)
For a summary of the case see the 10th edition of this book.

203.8   Demonstrations, During   Judicial guidance
R v Gilmour 2011 EWCA Crim 2458 D pleaded to **violent disorder** during a demonstration. Held. It is an unavoidable feature of mass disorder that each individual act, whatever might be its character taken on its own, inflames and encourages others to behave similarly, and that the harm done to the public stems from the combined effect of what is done *en masse*.

203.9   Demonstrations, During
R v Lahouidek 2010 EWCA Crim 738 LCJ D pleaded to **violent disorder**. In 2009 she was part of a large crowd demonstrating outside the Israeli Embassy in West London. D was filmed throwing a stick into the crowd. She joined a smaller group who broke away

from the demonstration and attacked the front windows of a café. D and several of the demonstrators went inside the café. Another kicked over a counter. H picked up a chair, kicked a table, and helped D push the counter against another counter. Some of the windows were broken and frightened staff and customers inside who ran away or sought refuge inside. D, aged 19, had no convictions but had a caution for minor criminal damage. D made no comment in interview. The pre-sentence report said there was a low risk that D would reoffend or cause harm to the public, that she did not appear to fully understand the reasons for her behaviour and that she expressed remorse. H had no convictions and was sentenced to 51 weeks suspended. Held. **15 months'** detention was not manifestly excessive but because of disparity **51 weeks suspended**.

R v Al-Dahi 2013 EWCA Crim 1267 D pleaded (on rearraignment) to **violent disorder**. 150-200 protesters gathered outside the Syrian embassy in London. They were demonstrating against the Assad regime in Syria, based on reports overnight of 200 killings. There were barriers erected but at some point the protesters had breached them. D could be seen on CCTV challenging some of the police officers, at one point brandishing a traffic cone, which an officer subsequently removed from him. At another point, D attempted to climb over the barriers surrounding the embassy. He armed himself with a missile and threw it towards the embassy. D kicked out at police officers, but this was not recorded on the CCTV footage. As a result of one of D's kicks, a superintendent pivoted in such a way that he suffered a knee injury. The superintendent continued in his duties despite the injury. The prosecution was not able to say whether D had in fact connected with the superintendent. D was aged 30 and of previous good character. He was employed as a painter and decorator. Held. Unfortunately, the Judge was not taken to *R v Gilmour* 2011 EWCA Crim 2458. The context of this violent disorder was quite different from that of the London riots and the actions in *R v Gilmour* 2011. We are troubled that there may have been disparity in the way D was treated in comparison to other protestors as (prosecution counsel conceded) the police focused on D because of the superintendent's leg injury. That does not diminish the significance of that injury as D was performing his public duties, especially as he continued to perform them after sustaining the injury. **36 weeks suspended** for 18 months was appropriate, not 18 months' custody.

See also: *R v Alhaddad and Others* 2010 EWCA Crim 1760, 2011 1 Cr App R (S) 86 (p 517) (Pleas. **Violent disorder**. Demonstrations against invasion of Gaza by Israeli troops. Protesters threw objects at the police. Barrier clips weighing 2.5 lb were thrown. One officer was seriously injured. Starting point **2 years 3 months** not 3 years. Sentences should be **20 months, 21 months, 18 months** (×3), **12 months, 10 months** and **community order**.)

203.10   *Depriving defendant of vehicle used*

R v Bye 2005 EWCA Crim 1230, 2006 1 Cr App R (S) 27 (p 157) D was convicted of **affray**. He was driving his Aston Martin and after V had passed a parked car first, he overtook him and forced him to stop. D went to V's window and shouted at him, saying he had cut him up, threatened him and stamped or kicked him. D was aged 46 with 29 previous convictions including a similar one for road rage and 3 years for supplying class A drugs. He received 8 months (no appeal), a 12-month disqualification and a Deprivation Order for the car which instructed the solicitors to sell the car and pay £15,000 to the Crown. The car was worth about £75,000. Held. He presents a danger on the road. Although there will be a serious impact on D's ability to earn a living there can be no criticism of the disqualification. However, the prison and disqualification [are] enough. The financial penalty of £15,000 is manifestly excessive.

203.11   *Domestic premises, On*

R v Deere 2011 EWCA Crim 236 D pleaded (late) to **affray**. He turned up at his partner's home when she was with their 13-month old daughter and her 12-year-old sister. He appeared to be angry and 'in drink'. He said that he wanted a knife and was going to stab someone. His partner tried to calm him down. He ignored her and went into the kitchen. His partner continued to try to calm him down. D took a knife from the drawer. He made stabbing motions in mid-air and said, "I'm going to fucking stab you", although this was not directed at anyone in the house. He left the house and went to a nearby access road, still shouting. The police arrived and when requested by them to calm down, D responded, "Fuck off, you cunt". He did not have the knife with him at this stage. Following his arrest, he said "You watch, I'm gonna cut his fucking brake pipes. I'm gonna get a knife and stab the ginger cunt." When reminded of the reasons for his arrest, he said, "He's gonna take my little girl from me". D said in interview that he thought his drink had been spiked with drugs. D, aged 21 at appeal, had 18 convictions for 34 offences. They include a number for assault and a number of custodial sentences. The pre-sentence report noted D's remorse but assessed him as at high risk of reoffending. Held. D's behaviour was frightening to those who saw it. His entitlement to credit for his plea was limited. He had a poor record and was in breach of a community order specifically designed to address his intake of alcohol. However, the incident lasted a short time, the violence was not directed to those who observed it, no injury was caused, no damage to property occurred, and what happened took place largely on private property, where D was at least not unwelcome in normal circumstances. **10 months** not 15.

R v Pritchard 2013 EWCA Crim 2008 D pleaded to **affray**. He had a son who suffered from Asperger's syndrome with whom he had lost contact. In 2011 he met V and they became friends. Over time, he considered himself her boyfriend and became increasingly possessive of her. They fell out and subsequently bumped into each other, whereupon D told V he was back in contact with his son and wanted her help in looking after him. From then on, she would occasionally help him do so. D and his son went to V's address and asked to stay the night. V agreed that they could sleep on the sofa. D began drinking and became argumentative and antagonistic. V asked him to leave but agreed that his son could stay. V then went to bed. She was awoken by D who was leaning over her, punching her in the face and ribs and calling her a slut. She began to scream and D's son entered the room and tried to pulled D away from V. V told him to leave. D and his son went downstairs and D got a knife from the kitchen and waved it in front of V. When she tried to grab it, she suffered a cut to her finger which required three stitches. D was arrested. He had no relevant convictions. Held. The Judge wrote to the Court of Appeal acknowledging that he had taken too high a starting point. Starting at 2 years, not 3, was appropriate. With 25% credit, **18 months** not 27.

R v Crowsley 2014 EWCA Crim 1930 D pleaded (full credit) to **affray** and possessing an offensive weapon. V had a relationship with D's partner and there was a history of trouble. D sought revenge. D had harassed V on Facebook, receiving a police warning only the day before. V was at home with his partner and brother who, seeing the offenders, forewarned V of trouble. D and his co-accused kicked in V's door and, brandishing a snooker cue and baseball bat respectively, threatened to kill V. V escaped and hid and the offenders ran off. D made no comment in interview and expressed little remorse. He was also on bail. V was left concerned and anxious and considered moving. D was aged 24 on appeal and had significant antecedents, including section 18 from 2009, ABH, threatening behaviour and possession of an offensive weapon. Held. D took a leading role. It was planned. Weapons were taken. Two people were in the house at the time. D had been warned about his behaviour to V. D was on bail with a condition not to contact V. He had just been released from prison. The Judge overstated the case in saying that this was as bad an affray as could be imagined and in taking the maximum as a starting point. There was no violence, no vulnerable victim, it was not racially or religiously aggravated, it was relatively short-lived and, apart from the door, no damage was done. **18 months** in all, not 2 years.

R v Gilbert 2014 EWCA Crim 1533 D pleaded (full credit) to common assault and **affray** which arose from the same occasion. The police were called to a domestic incident at D's flat. V saw that D's partner's car was damaged and went and told her. D then appeared and remonstrated with V at the door saying that it wasn't any of his business. D then grabbed V's jacket and head-butted him in the forehead (the common assault). D went back into the flat and produced a meat cleaver. V, frightened, ran back to his flat with D following him for a short distance. A *Newton* hearing was due to be held, but D's partner didn't turn up. D had a poor record, having already served custody for violence which included witness or juror intimidation. Held. **15 months**, not 21 for affray. **3 months concurrent** for assault unaltered.

R v Hull 2010 EWCA Crim 1437 D pleaded to **affray**. D arrived home drunk and demanded sex from his wife, V, but she refused and told D to go to bed. D said he had a right to have sex with her because she was his wife. V went to her bedroom and went to bed with their 2-year-old daughter. Their 4-year-old son and stepchildren aged 11 and 17 were also in the house. D threatened to rape V if she would not have sex with him. V told him to go away and went to telephone a friend but D threatened to smash up the phone. D threatened to strangle V unless she had sex with him and threatened to urinate on her. V began to cry and D took off his trousers and said "I'm going to get my cock out". D had an 8-inch bladed knife. V was petrified and asked him to put it down but he did not. V said she would call the police. D continued to demand sex, said he would look at pornography on the computer and he would rape V if he did not get the computer to work. D put the knife down. V went to dial 999 in one of the children's rooms and D stuck the knife into a wall. The stepdaughter shouted at D to go away and D passed out. V tried to withdraw her statement and sought reconciliation with D. D, aged 42, had been before the courts once in 2005 for driving with excess alcohol. The pre-sentence report said D posed a low risk of reconviction but with a medium risk in the domestic context and posed a medium risk of harm to V or the children. Six character references spoke highly of D. Held. This was a serious case of threats of violence. Because of D's good character and mitigation **8 months** not 16.

R v Harrop and Others 2010 EWCA Crim 2915 (Violent disorder. **24 months' YOI** for D, **43 months** for H and **16 months** for W.)
For a summary of the case see the 10th edition of this book.

203.12   *Fists used*

R v Duffy and Burton 2012 EWCA Crim 63, 2 Cr App R (S) 50 (p 286) LCJ D pleaded on rearraignment to **affray**. B pleaded to affray. D and B were members of, or associated with, a group called the English Defence League (EDL). With others associated with the EDL, they met outside an Irish Centre in Newcastle, which was the proposed meeting place for the Socialist Workers' Party. The meeting was cancelled as the organisers had received warnings that the EDL were planning to attend. D, B and others were reluctant to accept that no meeting was taking place. The doormen at the Irish Centre decided to let D into the centre so he could see for himself that there was no meeting. A doorman put his hand on D's shoulder, and D turned round waving his fists in the doorman's face. D was pushed out of the door of the club. About 20 of the EDL group surged into the lobby of the Irish Centre. The doormen tried to keep the group out, but retreated into another room. The group were inside the Irish Centre for less than a minute. There were no weapons and no physical injury was caused. There were punches thrown and a fire extinguisher was sprayed around the hall. The group then left. D, aged 44, had 14 convictions for 36 offences including theft, drugs, public disorder and offensive weapons. Between the offence and sentence, D suffered two episodes of serious ill-health requiring a reconstructive operation. B, aged 28, had no convictions and only one caution for possession of an offensive weapon. Held. It is necessary to focus on the overall totality of what was involved. It was quite clear there was an element of pre-planning and the speed at which the group surged in indicated that there was little forethought. They were prepared for some form of trouble. This remains a bad piece of offending and there was the potential for considerable harm and personal injury. For D, **10 months** was not manifestly excessive. For B, **7 months** was not manifestly excessive.

R v Wright 2013 EWCA Crim 2672 D pleaded to ABH and affray. Whilst waiting for a taxi, D was approached by V1, who wrongly accused him of using racist words. D struck V1 causing bleeding and a fractured nose. Five days later, D and a friend had an altercation with V2 and V3, who were pushed and punched. V2 sustained bruising and swelling to the eye sockets with some concussion. V3 required no medical treatment. D was aged 20 and had no relevant convictions. Held. V1's injury was in part provoked by V1, was caused by a single blow, and was not a particularly serious injury. V2's injuries, while more serious, if dealt with as ABH [were] likely [to] have been Category 3. The Judge was incorrect in passing deterrent sentences owing to a local problem with violence. There was no evidence that the problem was greater locally than nationally. 1 month not 5 for the ABH. 4 months not 10 for the affray. Total concurrent sentence of **4 months**.

See also: *R v Cutter* 2011 EWCA Crim 240 (Plea to **affray** with 25% credit. 'Play-fighting' in a pub. Landlord asked the men to stop. Violence ensued. Punches thrown. Injuries including swelling to the brain. **9 months** not 15.)

Old case: *R v Kendrick* 2010 EWCA Crim 2301, 2011 1 Cr App R (S) 100 (p 592) (Affray **8 months**)
For a summary of the case see the 10th edition of this book.

203.13   *Football offences*
R v Asli 2012 EWCA Crim 1896 D pleaded (full credit) to **violent disorder**. There were 11 other defendants, aged 19 to 47, who pleaded to the same. Brighton were playing Aberdeen in a pre-season friendly. Aberdeen had support from some Tottenham supporters. A number, who were known to police to have Football Banning Orders, were seen drinking in public houses before going to the match. They left the match early and became involved in a large disturbance in a residential area of Brighton. On several occasions, two groups were seen to be violently charging at each other, armed with snooker cues, extendable batons, homemade bats and bottles. A number were injured. A bottle was smashed over one person's head. Frightened pedestrians tried to hide and a group with baby buggies stood frozen in fear. D could be seen on footage recorded by frightened homeowners at the front of the Tottenham group, leading the charge. He was also seen exchanging punches with more than one person and hitting out with a baton. Seized mobile phones showed that the disturbance had been subject to planning. D, aged 47, had six convictions, all for public disorder including threatening behaviour (×3). Between 1994 and 2008 he had received 2 years and 2½ years for football-related violent disorder. Held. The offence was of medium gravity. The offence was aggravated by the previous convictions. 3½ **years** was severe but not manifestly excessive.

R v Wiggins and Others 2014 EWCA Crim 1433, 2 Cr App R (S) 72 (p 560) D and nine others pleaded to violent disorder. Prior to a football match in Lincoln between Lincoln City and Luton Town, Luton supporters were drinking in a Wetherspoons pub. Many people were ordering and eating meals and there were young children about. Lincoln supporters entered the pub and some goaded the Luton fans and very quickly glasses were thrown. Customers left quickly. The Lincoln supporters left and regrouped on the street. They then ran back to the pub and attacked the Luton fans who were outside. It was one of the busiest commercial streets in Lincoln. Chairs and punches were thrown. Kicks were delivered. The whole incident was over in about 4 minutes. There had been 12 violent incidents involving Lincoln City matches. The Judge said there was extreme danger to the public and it was a miracle that nobody got seriously hurt. He divided the defendants into three groups. There was a 7½-month delay between all but one of their pleas and sentence. Four were in Group 1. They were aged 27, 34, 23 and 27. They all had relevant violent and/or public order previous convictions. One was only outside, one threw one glass, one threw glasses and led the charge and one was in the area glasses were thrown. One had had a Football Banning Order before. One had had three. G alone was in Group 2. He was aged 23 and threw a chair and kicked someone. D, W, Att, Wi and S were in Group 3. D was aged 20 with no previous convictions and only threw a punch. W was aged 21 and also punched a man outside. Att was aged 17 and now was aged 19 with no convictions. He was on the fringe, but hit a man with a chair. Wi pleaded on his 18th birthday. He punched someone. S was aged 26 and was a goader. He had twice breached a Football Banning Order. Held. It was an extremely nasty incident, but it was short-lived and there were no serious injuries. For Group 1 we start at 3 years and not 4½ years, which was very close to the maximum sentence. With plea **2 years**. For G, **18 months** not 2 years 8 months. D and W, **12 months'** YOI not 2 years 4 months. Att's **12-month** Detention and Training Order was correct. Wi, **12 months'** YOI not 2 years 1 month. S, **15 months** not 2 years 4 months.

See also: *R v P and Others* 2010 EWCA Crim 2081 (**Violent disorder**. Mob rampage. One of the most senior members. **30 months**. Others **18-month and 12-month DTOs**.) *R v Gornall and Others* 2011 EWCA Crim 1402, 2012 1 Cr App R (S) 36 (p 213) (Convictions for conspiracy. Early evening when it was expected police would have stood down. 20 men set off in taxis and a minibus to two pubs where 50 hooligans were waiting for a pre-arranged fight after an important local match. Police with horses waiting. Prime mover with seven threatening behaviour, four assault on police, three assault and other similar convictions. For one, **5-year** maximum appropriate. For others, **4 years, 3½ years, 3 years** and **21 months** upheld. Reductions in sentence for those less involved.)

Old cases: *R v Rees and Others* 2006 2 Cr App R (S) 20 (p 143) (**34 months, 30 months' detention, 27 months' detention** and **3 years 9 months**) *R v N and Others* 2010 EWCA Crim 1515 (Violent disorder **4 months' DTO**, **6 months**, and **6 months' YOI**)

For a summary of the first case see the 8th edition of this book and for the last case see the 10th edition.

203.14   *Kicking others*

R v Boyle and Others 2010 EWCA Crim 1056 LCJ B, C and D pleaded to **affray**. C walked towards a group of three men and was punched by P. C punched back and the two fought. B intervened and swung a bottle at P. C continued to tussle with P and fell to the ground. B went to P and D grappled with him. D punched another male and C got up and twice kicked P. B kicked out at P when he was on the ground. D punched another. B ran up to a male and hit him on the head, knocking him to the ground. Females intervened to protect P. As the police arrived, B, C and D ran off. The defendants claimed the other group was aggressive, and had started the incident. B was aged 26 with 61 convictions including four for ABH, three for threatening behaviour, two for battery, one for assault with intent to resist arrest and an affray. Most of the convictions were over 10 years old. He was serving a sentence for a breach of a community order and battery. C was aged 29 with 25 convictions including five for common assault or battery. D was aged 22 with 25 convictions including robbery, GBH, ABH, affray and battery. The Judge said the incident was drink-fuelled. Held. It was spontaneous. There was no serious injury or damage. There may have been some provocation. With the maximum 3 years, **18 months** not 2 years for B and C and **12 months** not 18 for D.

R v McKenzie 2010 EWCA Crim 2311 W pleaded to **affray** and J pleaded to wounding with intent. Early in the morning, V was part of a group of around 30 people including W and J outside a nightclub, which was closing. V did not know J or W. J approached a woman and tried to 'chat her up'. There was some degree of unpleasantness between the two of them resulting in J exposing himself to her. V approached J and reproved him, asking him to treat the woman with respect. There was an argument. J turned his back on V and was struck by what he believed to be a bottle. Believing that V was responsible, J punched and kicked V, who fought back. Bystanders and friends became involved. V ran across the road and was hit by a car. J and W caught up with V, and J accepted in his basis of plea that he kicked V in the head twice before passing out and being taken to the hospital. W accepted in his basis of plea that he used threatening words and behaviour including pushing and shoving and that he became involved in the fight towards the end.

The sentencing Judge's comments indicated a significant long-term traumatic effect. J had no previous convictions for violence, but a number for robbery and possession of class A drugs with intent to supply. W had convictions for violence and drug offences. A pre-sentence report noted that W suffered from Asperger's syndrome. The Judge remarked that the incident was a "deliberate, sustained and vicious attack". Held. The case merited a significant, even if not maximum reduction for the plea by W. This, though a bad case of its kind, cannot be described as one of the very worst. For W, **15 months** not 2 years. For J, **4 years** not 6.

R v Casey 2011 EWCA Crim 2254 D pleaded (full credit) to **violent disorder**. V, D's friend, was drunk and causing a nuisance. He was pushed to the ground by a group which included D. V was then assaulted, including kicks. No appreciable injury was caused. Held. Considering the maximum sentence of 5 years and with perhaps a generous discount for the plea, **2 years 4 months**.

See also: *R v Garforth and Hird* 2011 EWCA Crim 136 (Pleas to **affray**. Fight between two groups at taxi rank lasting 5 minutes. Punches and kicks. H had 13 and G had 15 previous convictions. For H, **2 years 10 weeks**, for G, **12 months' YOI**.)

R v Marks 2011 EWCA Crim 1416, 2012 1 Cr App R (S) 38 (p 229) (Plea to **affray**. At 2 am, D, who had been drinking, was involved in a fight outside a bar. There were numerous men involved. At one stage he was pulled away from V, but he renewed the attack. He kicked V whilst V was on the ground. V suffered no serious injury. D, aged 28, had no convictions but one caution for battery (2006). Held. Considering *R v Blazys* 2008 EWCA Crim 904, 2 Cr App R (S) 106 (p 615), **12 months** not 17.)

R v Mears and Flynn 2011 EWCA Crim 1706 (Pleas to **violent disorder**. Mob attack. Six youths attacked two at a petrol station. Repeated kicking and punching to the head. Unprovoked. Aged nearly 18 and 18. **12 months**.)

Old case: *R v Blazys* 2008 EWCA Crim 904, 2 Cr App R (S) 106 (p 615) (**Affray 8 months**). For a summary of the case see the 9th edition of this book.

203.15   Police officers, Actions against

R v Decker-Heath 2015 EWCA Crim 406 D pleaded early to violent disorder. D answered an advertisement on Facebook for an illegal rave. After drinking, D was one of up to 1,000 people who attended the venue and police tried unsuccessfully to contain the crowd. The crowd were pushing forward and gaining access to the venue for the rave. The prosecution considered it was a large-scale disturbance and the crowd was very hostile. D was behind some railings and he was attacking the police lines and fighting with the police. He struck out at them using both hands and his arms. D pulled a police shield off an officer and he tried to pull an officer's helmet off. D also ignored police instructions to get back. In interview D made full and frank admissions. D was aged 20 with no convictions. He was unemployed. The pre-sentence report said he expressed shame and remorse. Held. D had no weapon and he had not tried to injure anyone. We start at 9 months not 18, so with plea, **6 months** not 12. D is warned that if this happens again, he will be treated a lot more severely than this.

203.16   Public transport, Offence connected with

R v Jones 2015 EWCA Crim 2070 D pleaded to affray. V, who was driving a bus carrying about 30 passengers, had to stop when his path in a one-way street was blocked by an Audi. V flashed his lights and sounded his horn. The driver's door of the Audi opened and F leaned out of the door and shouted aggressively. The door closed and 5-10 seconds later F stepped out of the car. F approached V's window in a very aggressive way. D and his brother left the car went to the bus too. F tried to force the driver's window open and D joined him acting aggressively. D spat at the windscreen and the three tried to enter the bus by pressing the emergency door release. Luckily V was able to override this action. V was so worried about his passengers' safety he reversed the bus around a corner and then called the police. While the bus was reversed, the three gesticulated and shouted abuse. D then went to a pub while the others involved themselves in a much more serious incident. D was incapacitated through drink. D was aged 23 and had 14 previous convictions, including possession of a firearm with intent to cause fear of violence, two for threatening behaviour, an affray in 2009 (24 weeks) and being drunk and disorderly. D's pre-sentence report said D's lifestyle had involved binge drinking since he was aged 18. The likelihood of reconviction was high. Held. This drunken rampage was a frightening episode of public disorder with three men acting as a group. It was very distressing. We take into account the previous convictions. However, there was no actual violence. We start at 2 years, not 34 months, so with plea **16 months** not 22.

Old cases: *R v H* 2009 EWCA Crim 1453 (Violent disorder. Aged 16. **Supervision Order**) *R v Wasden and Others* 2010 EWCA Crim 2423 (Twelve defendants. Sentences between **12 months** and **2 years 8 months**)

For a summary of the first case see the 10th edition of this book.

Racially motivated, see the RACIALLY OR RELIGIOUSLY AGGRAVATED OFFENCES chapter.

203.17   *Weapon(s) used*

Magistrates' Court Sentencing Guidelines 2008, see www.banksr.com Other Matters Guidelines tab The guidelines apply to the Magistrates' Court and to the Crown Court hearing appeals or sentencing for summary only offences.[23]

page 85 **Affray**

Examples of nature of activity	Starting point	Range
Fight involving a weapon/throwing objects, or conduct causing risk of serious injury	18 weeks' custody	12 weeks' custody to Crown Court

For the rest of the guideline see **203.3**.

R v Deere 2011 EWCA Crim 236 D pleaded (late) to **affray**. He turned up at his partner's home when she was with their 13-month-old daughter and her 12-year-old sister. He appeared to be angry and 'in drink'. He said that he wanted a knife and was going to stab someone. His partner tried to calm him down. He ignored her and went into the kitchen. His partner continued to try to calm him down. D took a knife from the drawer. He made stabbing motions in mid-air and said "I'm going to fucking stab you", although this was not directed at anyone in the house. He left the house and went to a nearby access road, still shouting. The police arrived and when requested by them to calm down, D responded, "Fuck off, you cunt". He did not have the knife with him at this stage. Following his arrest, he said "You watch, I'm gonna cut his fucking brake pipes. I'm gonna get a knife and stab the ginger cunt." When reminded of the reasons for his arrest, he said "He's gonna take my little girl from me". D said in interview that he thought his drink had been spiked with drugs. D, aged 21 at appeal, had 18 convictions for 34 offences. They included a number for assault and a number of custodial sentences. The pre-sentence report noted D's remorse but assessed him as a high risk of reoffending. Held. D's behaviour was frightening to those who saw it. His entitlement to credit for his plea was limited. He had a poor record and was in breach of a community order specifically designed to address his intake of alcohol. However, the incident lasted a short time, the violence was not directed to those who observed it, no injury was caused, no damage to property occurred, and what happened took place largely on private property, where D was at least not unwelcome in normal circumstances. **10 months** not 15.

R v Bostan 2012 EWCA Crim 562 D pleaded to **affray**. D's family were part owners of a take-away restaurant called Aladdin's in a town centre. At night, D, S, M, B and N, who were brothers, were working at the restaurant or were nearby. A group of people went to the restaurant at about 1.30 am. An argument developed between a man and a

---

[23] See page 15 of the guidelines.

woman who were a part of that group. Various people tried to quieten down the argument, including one of D's brothers. There was no violence at this stage and one of the brothers asked them to take their argument outside the shop. There was a 'tussle'. Members of staff then intervened. An unidentified member of staff then stood on the counter and started to threaten those who were still in the shop. A number of other members of staff jumped onto the counter and some were armed with baseball bats and kebab skewers and were threatening to stab and shoot people. At that stage, none of D's brothers were involved, although some were present. The incident calmed down after the police attended, and the group moved away from the restaurant. A short time later, and a little distance from the restaurant, there was a chance meeting between V1 and V2, two members of the group from the take-away restaurant, and N. Offensive remarks were exchanged. N summoned others to come from the restaurant to their location. Two cars arrived within moments. One car was driven by B, the other was driven by D. A number of men armed with golf clubs, metal bars and baseball bats got out of the cars. M and B were making threats. Some members of the group from the take-away restaurant had returned to see what was happening. S followed V1 and V2 as they tried to escape. V1 pushed B, who was holding a golf club. B attacked V1 with the golf club until V1 and V2 left. That was the end of the incident. S was knocked over by the car driven by D. He later died. D did not take part in the violence but his role was to drive the others to the scene and encourage others by his presence. D, aged 19, had no convictions. He was married with two very young children and had a regular job. He simply helped at the restaurant at the weekends. Held. It was not wrong for the Judge not to suspend D's sentence of 12 months on the basis of the material presented to her. Since that time, things had moved on somewhat. D had spent 3 months in custody. He had been a model prisoner. **12 months suspended**, not 12 months.

R v Jabarkhall 2012 EWCA Crim 2133 D was convicted of **violent disorder**. When leaving a club in Barking at 3.40 am, B had a verbal argument with D. B struck D in the face and a fight ensued. A friend of D's ran over, armed with two or three half snooker cues. One of them was handed to D during the course of the fight. B retreated to the club and things appeared to calm down. B and his girlfriend were offered a lift home by a friend, and got into the car. D ran towards the rear of the car and smashed the rear window with the snooker cue. There was a fight involving a number of men in the street. The fight lasted several minutes. B and his girlfriend got into the car and drove off. They drove around 700 m then returned to confront D again. The fight once again broke out in the street. D was left injured at the scene, suffering a fractured spine causing paralysis, a punctured lung and a small stab wound in the lumbar region. He will remain in a wheelchair for the rest of his life. Held. It was mindless but significant violence. All were equally involved. There was no distinction to be drawn. But for his terrible injuries, D could have expected a sentence of 3 years like the other defendants. We might well not have given D an immediate custodial sentence, but as one was imposed and D has now served the equivalent of 12 months, we replace the 18-month sentence with **12 months** to effect his immediate release.

R v Brown 2013 EWCA Crim 20, 2 Cr App R (S) 53 (p 356) D pleaded to **affray**. D and others drank. In the early hours there were two groups in a High Street. The groups were shouting and behaving aggressively. D was in the larger group and someone gave him a crowbar. D's group pushed the other group up the street. D was attempting to hit people with the crowbar. The fact the bar did not connect was mere chance. Two women tried to wrestle the bar off him. D continued to brandish it. Eventually one of the women took the bar from D. The whole incident lasted only a fairly short time. D was aged 27 and had no employment history. He had been sentenced on 15 occasions. D had three convictions for disorder, one for a bladed article and one for possessing a butterfly knife. D's pre-sentence report said he had a disposition to violence. Held. There were three aggravating factors: a) the serious weapon which was used. The bar could cause life-threatening injuries, b) it was group violence in a high street in the early hours. It was drink-fuelled feral behaviour, c) D's striking record. The Judge's sentence of 20 months could not be faulted.

R v Bligh 2014 EWCA Crim 547 D pleaded to affray. V and another neighbour subjected D to a tirade of homophobic abuse. There had been a history of trouble and ill-feeling and D thought he was at the end of his tether. He had made complaints about his neighbours. In a fit of anger, D left the house and confronted V, holding a kitchen knife. D said the abuse against him continued. D held it handle-first toward V and invited V to stab him. M seized it and threw the knife away. A basis of plea indicated that at no time did D lunge at V with the knife. D, aged 39, had convictions for criminal damage and assault but was remorseful. A pre-sentence report recommended a community order or suspended sentence and concluded there were issues that D needed to address. A psychiatric report diagnosed depression. Held. Significant provocation, depression and an early plea were powerful mitigation and the Court could see the case for a suspended sentence. Nevertheless, the sentence passed was one open to the Judge and could not be criticised. **8 months** upheld.

Note: I would imagine few judges would pass this sentence on a victim of intimidation. I would also imagine most prosecutors would have sought to do a deal if there had been no plea to affray. Ed.

R v Crowsley 2014 EWCA Crim 1930 D pleaded (full credit) to affray and possessing an offensive weapon. V had a relationship with D's partner and there was a history of trouble. D sought revenge. D had harassed V on Facebook, receiving a police warning only the day before. V was at home with his partner and brother who, seeing the offenders, forewarned V of trouble. D and his co-accused kicked in V's door and, brandishing a snooker cue and baseball bat respectively, threatened to kill V. V escaped and hid and the offenders ran off. D made no comment in interview and expressed little remorse. He was also on bail. V was left concerned and anxious and considered moving. D was aged 24 on appeal and had significant antecedents, including section 18 from 2009, ABH, threatening behaviour and possession of an offensive weapon. Held. D took a leading role. It was planned. Weapons were taken. Two people were in the house at the time. D had been warned about his behaviour to V. D was on bail with a condition not to contact V. He had just been released from prison. The Judge overstated the case in saying that this was as bad an affray as could be imagined and in taking the maximum as a starting point. There was no violence, no vulnerable victim, it was not racially or religiously aggravated, it was relatively short-lived and, apart from the door, no damage was done. **18 months** in all, not 2 years.

R v Ozberkcan 2014 EWCA Crim 2377 D was convicted of affray. In the early hours, D, who had been drinking heavily, and another were prevented from entering a take-away by V, a doorman. A brief scuffle ensued between D and V. Shortly after, D and the other male re-entered the take-away and the male punched V repeatedly and grabbed his arms. Meanwhile D hit V on the back with a metal chair, forcing staff to intervene. All this was captured on CCTV. D, aged 38, had a young family and was of good character. The Judge did not order a pre-sentence report and additional medical mitigation was not available to him. Held. **6 months**, not 9.

See also: *R v Wood* 2011 EWCA Crim 935 (Plea to **affray**. Drunk. Ex-Army. Approached 15-year-old victim, who had laughed at him, and drew a large knife across his throat without cutting the skin. He said "Do you want to die tonight?" Continued to make stabbing motions at the windows of a building into which V had sought refuge. **18 months** not 2 years.)

Old cases: *R v Bowker* 2007 EWCA Crim 1608, 2008 1 Cr App R (S) 72 (p 412) (**2 years'** detention.) *R v Boyle* and *Others* 2010 EWCA Crim 1056 (Affray **18 months** and **12 months**) *R v Goodhead* 2010 EWCA Crim 1812 (Affray **27 months**) *R v Tebbeck* 2010 EWCA Crim 1993 (affray **10-month DTO**)

For a summary of the first case see the 7th edition of this book and for the rest see the 10th edition.

204   AGGRAVATED VEHICLE-TAKING

204.1

Theft Act 1968 s 12A

Theft Act 1968 s 12A(1) and (4) (Death caused)

Aggravated vehicle-taking is the taking of a mechanically propelled vehicle and either: a) the vehicle was driven dangerously, b) an accident occurred when either i) injury was caused to a person or ii) damage was caused to property other than vehicles or iii) a person was killed, or c) damage was caused to the vehicle taken. There are defences.

Mode of trial Triable either way unless the vehicle was only damaged and the value of the damage was less than £5,000, when it is summary only.

Maximum sentence On indictment where death is caused 14 years.[24] Otherwise 2 years. Summary 6 months and/or a £5,000 fine for offences committed before 12 March 2015 and an unlimited fine thereafter.[25] There are maximum fines for those aged under 18, see **14.38**.

Criminal Behaviour Orders Where a defendant has engaged in behaviour that caused or was likely to cause harassment, alarm or distress to any persons and a Criminal Behaviour Order will help in preventing the offender from engaging in such behaviour, the court may make this order.[26]

Endorsement and special reasons If special reasons found, 3 to 11 points. The fact that the defendant was not the driver of the car shall not be regarded as a special reason, Road Traffic Offenders Act 1988 s 34(1A).

Mandatory disqualification Mandatory disqualification of 1 year.[27]

Extended sentences This offence is listed in Criminal Justice Act 2003 Sch 15. The court may pass a 2012 extended sentence (EDS) if there is a significant risk of serious harm from future specified offences and either: a) the defendant has a Criminal Justice Act 2003 Sch 15B conviction (applicable only to defendants aged 18+), or b) the offence would justify a determinate sentence of at least 4 years.[28]

Sexual Harm Prevention Orders There is a discretionary power to make this order when it is necessary to protect the public from sexual harm.[29]

204.2   Crown Court statistics   England and Wales

Aggravated vehicle-taking

Year	Age	Plea	Total sen-tenced	Type of sentencing %						Average length of custody in months
				Dis-charge	Fine	Community sentence	Sus-pended sentence	Custody	Oth-er	
2013	18-20	G	101	1.0	–	27.7	14.9	55.4	1.0	9.0
		NG	2	–	–	50.0	–	50.0	–	12.0
	21+	G	302	–	–	7.3	22.8	69.9	–	10.6
		NG	10	–	–	10.0	30.0	60.0	–	12.2

[24] Criminal Justice Act 2003 s 285(1)

[25] Legal Aid, Sentencing and Punishment of Offenders Act 2012 s 85(1) and (4) and Legal Aid, Sentencing and Punishment of Offenders Act 2012 (Commencement No 11) Order 2015 2015/504

[26] Anti-social Behaviour, Crime and Policing Act 2014 s 22(1)-(4)

[27] Road Traffic Offenders Act 1988 s 34(1) and Sch 2 Part I

[28] Criminal Justice Act 2003 s 226A-226B as inserted by Legal Aid, Sentencing and Punishment of Offenders Act 2012 s 124

[29] Sexual Offences Act 2003 s 103A as inserted by Anti-social Behaviour, Crime and Policing Act 2014 Sch 5 para 2 and Sexual Offences Act 2003 Sch 5

Year	Age	Plea	Total sen-tenced	Type of sentencing %						Average length of custody in months
				Dis-charge	Fine	Community sentence	Sus-pended sentence	Custody	Oth-er	
2014	18-20	G	77	1	–	19	40	38	1	10.4
		NG	4	–	–	50	25	25	–	*
	21+	G	286	–	–	8	28	64	–	11.0
		NG	4	–	–	–	–	100	–	*

*: Not shown as based on too few cases to be meaningful

For the statistics for cases when death is caused, see **204.10**. For explanations about the statistics, see page 1-xii. For statistics for female and male defendants etc., see www.banksr.com Other Matters Statistics tab

204.3   *Magistrates' Court Sentencing Guidelines*

Magistrates' Court Sentencing Guidelines 2008, see www.banksr.com Other Matters Guidelines tab

The guidelines apply to the Magistrates' Court and to the Crown Court hearing appeals or sentencing for summary only offences.[30]

Starting points are based on a first-time offender pleading not guilty.

page 111 Damage caused to property other than the vehicle in an accident or damage caused to the vehicle

Examples of nature of activity	Starting point	Range
Exceeding authorised use of e.g. employers' or relative's vehicle, retention of hire car beyond return date, minor damage to taken vehicle	Medium-level community order	Low-level community order to high-level community order
Greater damage to taken vehicle and/or moderate damage to another vehicle and/or property	High-level community order	Medium-level community order to 12 weeks' custody
Vehicle taken as part of burglary or from private premises, severe damage	18 weeks' custody	12 to 26 weeks' custody (Crown Court if damage over £5,000)

The following aggravating and mitigating factors may be particularly relevant: Factors indicating higher culpability: 1 Vehicle deliberately damaged/destroyed 2 Offender under influence of alcohol/drugs. Factors indicating greater degree of harm: 1 Passenger(s) carried 2 Vehicle belonging to elderly or disabled person 3 Emergency services vehicle 4 Medium to large goods vehicle 5 Damage caused in moving traffic accident. Factors indicating lower culpability: 1 Misunderstanding with owner 2 Damage resulting from actions of another (where this does not provide a defence).

Consider ancillary orders, including compensation.

For the meaning of a high-level, a medium-level and a low-level community order see **16.12-16.14** in Volume 1.

204.4   **Dangerous driving or accident causing injury**

Examples of nature of activity	Starting point	Range
Taken vehicle involved in single incident of bad driving where little or no damage or risk of personal injury	High-level community order	Medium-level community order to 12 weeks' custody

---

[30] See page 15 of the guidelines.

Examples of nature of activity	Starting point	Range
Taken vehicle involved in incident(s) involving excessive speed or showing off, especially on busy roads or in built-up area	18 weeks' custody	12 to 26 weeks' custody
Taken vehicle involved in prolonged bad driving involving deliberate disregard for safety of others	Crown Court	Crown Court

The following aggravating and mitigating factors may be particularly relevant: Factors indicating higher culpability: 1 Disregarding warnings of others 2 Evidence of alcohol or drugs 3 Carrying out other tasks while driving 4 Carrying passengers or heavy load 5 Tiredness 6 Trying to avoid arrest 7 Aggressive driving, such as driving much too close to vehicle in front, inappropriate attempts to overtake, or cutting in after overtaking. Factors indicating greater degree of harm 1 Injury to others 2 Damage to other vehicles or property.

Consider ordering disqualification until appropriate driving test passed.

For details about applying the guidelines, see the GUIDELINES chapter in Volume 1.

204.5 *Judicial guidance*

R v Bird 1993 14 Cr App R (S) 343 at 346 In judging the gravity of the case, the most important of the statutory elements a) to d) of the offence of aggravated vehicle-taking is paragraph a), that the vehicle was driven dangerously on a road or other public place, for that concerns the culpability of the driver, whereas the incidence and severity of any injury or damage under paragraphs b), c) and d) are to some extent a matter of chance. The aggravating features of this offence will be primarily the overall culpability of the driving: how bad it was and for how long and, to a lesser extent, how much injury or damage or both was caused. Where drink has played a part, no doubt this will affect the dangerousness of the driving.

204.6 *Accident, Vehicle was involved in an*

R v Beard 2013 EWCA Crim 1284 D pleaded to aggravated vehicle-taking and theft. He was released from the Magistrates' Court and went to a pub to call a taxi but didn't get one. He took a jacket and found the keys to a car and a mobile which he stole. He then used the keys to take a car and within a few metres crashed into a Mercedes belonging to C, the Deputy Chief Constable, causing £5,000 damage to it. C went downstairs to detain D, but he was head-butted by D and suffered a cut lip. D threatened C by saying, "Today's the day you die". He was taken to the police station where he said he was full of Valium but refused to provide a specimen. D had effectively annual offending from 1994 to 2008. There were 'lots of dishonesty, lots of motoring offences including aggravated vehicle-taking'. The Judge started at the maximum, 2 years for the vehicle-taking and with 20% for the plea (because the case was overwhelming) gave him 20 months, with 1 month for the mobile and 3 months for assaulting a PC. All these were consecutive to each other. D also received 3 months concurrent for a specimen offence. Held. The driving was disgraceful but it only lasted a few metres. D may not have reached the carriageway. The distance was an important feature. The offence was aggravated by the driving when heavily under the influence of drugs. The starting point should have been **18 months**. With the plea, that was 14 months so with the consecutive sentences (for the mobile and assaulting a PC) **18 months** in all.

R v Navarro 2014 EWCA Crim 2146 D pleaded (full credit) to aggravated vehicle-taking. D took a car then drove it, having consumed cocaine, and proceeded to speed off when seen by the police. D drove dangerously pursued by police, passing vehicles around bends, forcing one vehicle to brake to avoid a collision. He also crossed a solid white line and drove 10 mph over the speed limit in 50 mph and 30 mph areas,

eventually crashing into a hedge when speeding in a village. The cocaine did not show up on a test. D was aged 23 on appeal and on licence for supplying cocaine. He was convicted in 2011 of various vehicle offences. Held. **12 months**, not 16.
See also: *R v Candir* 2011 EWCA Crim 1694, 2012 1 Cr App R (S) 44 (p 263) (Plea. Used brother's car to make deliveries at work. Speeding motorcyclist who was to blame for accident killed. 76 mph in 30 mph area. Good character. **10 months** not 18.)
Old cases: *R v Jones* 2010 EWCA Crim 675 D (**26 months**) *R v Duvivier* 2010 EWCA Crim 696 (**22 months**)
For a summary of the two cases see the 10th edition of this book.

204.7   *Alcohol, Defendant had excessive*
R v Duvivier 2010 EWCA Crim 696 D pleaded to aggravated vehicle-taking, using a motor vehicle with no insurance, driving it with excess alcohol, and driving whilst disqualified. D stole his brother's car and crashed it with such force the car rolled onto its side and caused damage to several parked cars. D punched his way out of the car window and hid. D was seen by the police trying to leave the scene in a taxi and was stopped. D refused to give his details so was taken to the police station. There it was discovered that D was disqualified from driving and had no insurance. He gave a reading of 111 µg of alcohol to 100 ml of breath, over three times the legal limit. D, now aged 27, had convictions for four ABHs, four affrays, wounding and a number of road traffic offences. Held. Insufficient credit was given for plea and other mitigation. Each offence was an aggravating feature of the others. **22 months** in all, not 28.

204.8   *Death is caused   Judicial guidance*
Note: The obvious starting point would be to consider the guidelines in the DEATH BY DRIVING: GENERAL PRINCIPLES and DEATH BY DRIVING, DISQUALIFIED, NO LICENCE, UNINSURED chapters and adjust them. Ed.
R v Woolley 2005 EWCA Crim 2853, 2006 1 Cr App R (S) 123 (p 723) D pleaded to aggravated vehicle-taking when death was caused. Held. The argument that the 14-year maximum is to allow for cases involving dangerous driving is misconceived. Causing death by dangerous driving reflects that offence. Parliament no doubt intended to increase the level of sentence when death was caused whether or not the driver's driving was at fault.
R v Clifford 2007 EWCA Crim 2442, 2008 1 Cr App R (S) 100 (p 593) The most significant feature is likely to be the culpability of the driving of the offender.
R v Roberts 2013 EWCA Crim 785 LCJ D pleaded to aggravated vehicle-taking. After drinking he was a passenger in a car which, after being driven at speed, crashed and overturned. Counsel for the prosecution enquired why the driver of the car had not been charged with causing death by dangerous driving. The charging officer at the CPS considered that there was insufficient evidence to sustain that charge and in any event, aggravating vehicle-taking carried the same maximum sentence (14 years). Consequently it was deemed appropriate to charge aggravated vehicle-taking. Held. That should not be the approach. Causing death by dangerous driving is, in sentencing terms, generally regarded as the more serious offence and it should be the norm for that to be charged where there is evidence to support it.

204.9   *Death is caused   Statistics*
Causing death by aggravated vehicle-taking

Year	Plea	Details
2008	Both guilty	One aged 21+, suspended; one aged 18-20 received 4 years.
2009	0	
2010	All guilty	Two aged 21+ Average custody 61.5 months. Two aged 18-20. Average custody 48 months.

2011	0	
2012	Both guilty	One aged 21+. Average custody 78 months. One aged 18-20. Average custody 12 months
2013	Three pleaded, one convicted.	Two aged 21+, one community sentence, one custody 40 months. Two aged 18-20, one community sentence, one, who was convicted, custody 48 months.
2014	Two guilty, one not.	One aged 21+, discharged. Two aged 18-20, One community sentence, one custody.

204.10   *Death is caused   Cases*

R v Gregory 2010 EWCA Crim 5, 2 Cr App R (S) 52 (p 365) D pleaded (full credit) to aggravated vehicle-taking and perverting the course of justice. He was arrested for common assault, gave a false name and was bailed. Two months later he was arrested for cruelty to a dog, gave a false name and was bailed. About four months later, D was drinking with two friends, V and K. When D came out of a kebab shop he found the two associates stealing a motorbike. He assisted and pushed the bike away. They went to V's home when they continued drinking and K left. V drove the bike at excessive speed with D on the back. Three minutes later V lost control and hit a traffic light. V died and D suffered minor injuries. D was abusive to medical staff. On his arrest D said, "I bet he's dead isn't he? He was the one riding the fucking bike not me." D lied in interview. Before he was 14, D had convictions for aggravated vehicle-taking and two TDAs. Between the ages of 14 and 21 he had 34 court appearances for 63 offences largely of damage, theft and breach of court orders. He had experimented with drugs and had binge-drinking offences. The Judge took into account that D was on bail for two offences, neither D nor V was insured, no helmets were worn, the headlights were not illuminated, the excessive speed of the bike in wet conditions in a residential area, the arrest remark which showed a lack of concern and D, although not driving, was complicit from an early stage. In prison D had acquired three adjudications. D received 3 months consecutive for the perverting (no appeal). Held. We accept the culpability of the passenger is unlikely to be as high as that of the driver unless there is active encouragement. D's willing participation in the drink-fuelled taking and joyriding showed a high degree of complicity. The starting point should not have exceeded **4 years**, so with plea **2 years 8 months**.

R v Roberts 2013 EWCA Crim 785 LCJ D pleaded to aggravated vehicle-taking. There was a house party for a youth and the next day, some friends of his went to the house to continue the celebrations. Later, D and a friend arrived. The owner of the house, M, owned an MG car which was parked outside. In the early hours of the following morning, D went with four other men, two of which were M's sons, in M's car without her permission. D was in the front passenger seat. The car was travelling at considerable speed snaking around the roads until it crashed into a parked vehicle and overturned. M's 13-year-old son was badly injured and later died. D remained at the scene, as did the other passengers. D later said that he had been asked by M to move the car, despite the fact he had no licence and was not insured. He moved the car a short distance and left the keys inside it. He told the police he was quite drunk. D knew the driver did not have permission to drive the car. D, aged 21, had two reprimands for theft. He was treated as being of good character. The pre-sentence report indicated D was remorseful. Held. This was a very bad case of its kind. D was the oldest of the group and he should have had the maturity to prevent it. **12 months' YOI** was justified, even without the aggravating factors. 3-year disqualification not 5.

See also: *R v Candir* 2011 EWCA Crim 1694, 2012 1 Cr App R (S) 44 (p 263) (Pleaded early to aggravated vehicle-taking. Aged 32. Good character. Provisional licence. Drove

to deliver food from restaurant at which he worked. Gave false details. His driving was
not at fault. A motorcyclist, who was three times over the drink-drive limit on the wrong
side of the road, died. **10 months** not 18.)
Old case: *R v Clifford* 2007 EWCA Crim 2442, 2008 1 Cr App R (S) 100 (p 593) (**6
months**) For a summary of this case see the 9th edition of this book.

204.11   *Defendant aged under 18 years*
R v F and Hansford 2010 EWCA Crim 144 (LCJ Aged 16, see **204.15**.)

204.12   *Disqualification for how long?*
R v F and Hansford 2010 EWCA Crim 144 (LCJ **1 year**, see **204.15**.)
R v Roberts 2013 EWCA Crim 785 (LCJ **3 years**, see **204.10**.)

204.13   *Police chase*
R v Roberts 2012 EWCA Crim 662 D pleaded to aggravated vehicle-taking, dangerous
driving, no insurance and no licence. A JCB was stolen and was used to ram the gates of
commercial premises to steal an expensive piece of machinery. A short while later the
JCB was spotted by police. D was driving it at about 10 mph. When D saw the police he
stopped and reversed into the front of a police van. Two officers were jerked forward,
severely shaken but not injured. The van was damaged. D drove off, drove over a grass
verge and turned the vehicle round so it was facing the police van. D jumped off and the
JCB crashed into a parked car and a tree. D was on licence and heavily convicted. He
had previous convictions for vehicle-taking and dangerous driving. In 2007, he received
4 years for burglary and other matters. In a *Newton* hearing the Judge rejected the
suggestion that the collision was accidental. Held. Because of the way the particulars
were drafted, the vehicle-taking was the same incident as the dangerous driving.
Consecutive sentences were wrong. There were serious aggravating factors. The only
mitigating factor was that the dangerous driving was short-lived. 18 months not 12
months for the vehicle-taking, concurrent not consecutive to the 10 months for the
dangerous driving making **18 months** not 22.
Note: There is no mention that D was charged with conspiracy to burgle or steal. If D
had been charged and convicted of that, the Court could have considered his previous
convictions and given him a significant sentence made consecutive to the driving
matters. Ed.
Old case: *R v Kirby* 2007 EWCA Crim 3410, 2008 2 Cr App R (S) 46 (p 264) (**22
months**) For a summary of this case see the 9th edition of this book.

204.14   *Speeding, Defendant was*
R v Harrison 2010 EWCA Crim 1794 D pleaded to aggravated vehicle-taking, bladed
article (4 months consecutive) and affray (8 months consecutive). Shortly before
5.30 am, officers saw D's grandfather's car being driven along a street. They heard a
scraping sound and indicated that the car should pull over. It failed to do so. It was
initially being driven at 35 mph but was swaying from side to side. It accelerated
through a red traffic light at about 50 mph. The car's speed increased to 70 mph and the
driver temporarily lost control. It went through another red traffic light and again the
driver lost control, colliding with a number of cones in the road. Its speed increased to
110 mph for about 1 mile until it approached a roundabout where the driver lost all
control of the car, turned 180° and ploughed into a ditch. Officers arrested D, who was
the passenger. The Judge noted that the chase had continued for a long time and the level
of driving was completely unacceptable and completely reckless. D, aged 18, was of
previous good character. Held. The seriousness of the offence required an immediate
custodial sentence. We do not regard the fact that the car belonged to the appellant's
grandfather as an aggravating feature which would merit an increase in sentence on that
ground. 12 months was excessive, bearing in mind the mitigation and the maximum
sentence of 2 years. **7 months' YOI**, so 19 months not 30 in total.
R v Morley 2013 EWCA Crim 609 D pleaded (20% credit) to aggravated vehicle-taking
and driving whilst disqualified. At about 6 pm, police saw D doing 'wheelies' on a stolen

motorcycle. As they approached, he sped up and drove away at around 50 mph. The area was one in which the speed limit was 30 mph. The road conditions were good, but there were parents with children around. As he turned a corner, the bike skidded and three pedestrians who were crossing the road had to step back onto the pavement. He stalled the bike and was unable to restart it, and so he fled on foot. He had driven about a mile. When arrested, he said "Who was it who chased me? I fucking smoked you." He was already disqualified from driving at the time of the offence. D, aged 24, had 13 convictions for 31 offences. His offending was mostly vehicle crime, often including dishonesty. There were convictions for disqualified driving, aggravated vehicle-taking and dangerous driving. The pre-sentence report noted a high risk of reoffending. The Judge imposed 16 months for the vehicle-taking and 4 months consecutive for the disqualified driving. Held. The sentences for each offence, with regard to plea and D's bad record, may not be seen as manifestly excessive. However, with totality, they should be concurrent, not consecutive. **16 months** not 20. **2-year disqualification**, not 5.

204.15   *Victim injured*
R v F and Hansford 2010 EWCA Crim 144 LCJ F and H pleaded (full credit) to aggravated vehicle-taking and perverting the course of justice. F took a car from the forecourt of his father's garage. F with H as a passenger lost control of the car at a roundabout through speed. The car went round the roundabout sideways then skidded, hit a livestock wagon and then hit a motorcycle. The motorcyclist suffered pain in his groin, wrist and pelvis. F gave his brother's details and both told police that H was driving. This lie was repeated. F, aged 16, was of good character and had substantial character references. The pre-sentence report said there was a low risk of reoffending and he was deeply remorseful. F had now passed his driving test. H was aged 19 with no particularly relevant convictions. His risk of reoffending was also assessed as low. The Judge sentenced them to 6 months and 4 months consecutive for the perverting. H only appealed the disqualification. F said the disqualification would have a substantial impact on his ability to work in his father's garage. Held. This was a serious incident which could easily have had much more serious consequences. However, there were indications the two had learnt their lesson. We are not impressed with the fact [that] H was the passenger because he was older and a willing party. **6 months** and **4 months** for F concurrent not consecutive because of the constraints on periods of detention and training and the total was too long and not because consecutive sentences are inappropriate. Because of their need to drive, **1 year** not 4 years' disqualification.

AIDS For where the victim fears he or she might have contracted AIDS although there was no evidence he or she had done so, see the VICTIMS *Victim fears that he or she has contracted AIDS from sex attack* para at **121.2** in Volume 1.
For where defendant has AIDS, see the DEFENDANT *AIDS, Defendant has* para at **240.1.**
For infecting someone else, see the OFFENCES AGAINST THE PERSON ACT 1861 S 18 *Sexual/HIV* para at **292.34** and the OFFENCES AGAINST THE PERSON ACT 1861 S 20 *Sexual/HIV infection* para at **293.19.**

205   ALCOHOL SALE OFFENCES
205.1
Licensing Act 2003
  s 141 (sale of alcohol to a person who is drunk)
  s 146 (sale of alcohol to persons under 18)
  s 147 (allowing the sale of alcohol to persons under 18)
  s 147A[31] (persistently selling alcohol to persons under 18)
Modes of trial Summary only

---

[31] As inserted by Violent Crime Reduction Act 2006 s 23

Maximum sentences Level 3 fine (£1,000) or for sections 147 and 147A a £5,000 and £10,000 fine respectively for offences committed before 12 March 2015 and an unlimited fine thereafter.[32]

Fixed penalties There is a £90 fixed penalty[33] for: a) sale of alcohol to a person who is drunk, b) sale of alcohol to persons aged under 18, c) purchase of alcohol on behalf of persons aged under 18, and d) delivery of alcohol to persons aged under 18 or allowing such delivery[34] with half the relevant victim surcharge. For more detail, see **61.1** in Volume 1.

Forfeiture and Suspension of liquor licence There is power to make these orders.[35]

Drug/driving Under the new list of prescribed drugs for drug/driving the prescribed limit for methylamphetamine, also known as amphetamine, is 10µg.[36] For more detail see **245.2**.

205.2 *Magistrates' Court Sentencing Guidelines*

Magistrates' Court Sentencing Guidelines 2008, see www.banksr.com Other Matters Guidelines tab

The guidelines apply to the Magistrates' Court and to the Crown Court hearing appeals or sentencing for summary only offences.[37]

page 19 Starting points are based on a first-time offender pleading not guilty.

Examples of nature of activity	Starting point	Range
Sale to a child (i.e. person under 18)/to a drunk person	Band B fine	Band A fine to band C fine

Where these offences are 'commercially motivated', see **60.10** in Volume 1.

The following aggravating and mitigating factors may be particularly relevant:

Factors indicating higher culpability: 1 No attempt made to establish age 2 Spirits/high alcohol level of drink 3 Drunk person highly intoxicated 4 Large quantity of alcohol supplied 5 Sale intended for consumption by group of children/drunk people 6 Offender in senior or management position.

Factors indicating greater degree of harm: 1 Younger child/children. 2 Drunk person causing distress to others 3 Drunk person aggressive.

Consider ancillary orders, including forfeiture or suspension of personal liquor licence.

Consultation It is expected that the Sentencing Council will issue a consultation document about updating this guideline in May 2016.

A Band A fine is 50% of net weekly income. Bands B and C are 100% and 150%. For more detail, see **60.27** in Volume 1.

See also the **DRUNK** chapter.

206 AMPHETAMINE

206.1 *General properties*

R v Wijs 1999 1 Cr App R (S) 181 LCJ Amphetamine is a synthetic stimulant which, in powder or tablet form, is a class B drug. There are two very obvious differences between cannabis and amphetamine: a) while market prices tend to fluctuate depending on the interplay of supply and demand, and there has been a sharp decline in the street value of amphetamine in the last two years or so, amphetamine has always, weight for weight, been vastly more valuable than cannabis, b) it has always been the practice to retail amphetamine to consumers in a highly adulterated form. Based on seizures in the last

---

[32] Legal Aid, Sentencing and Punishment of Offenders Act 2012 s 85(1) and (4), Legal Aid, Sentencing and Punishment of Offenders Act 2012 (Commencement No 11) Order 2015 2015/504 and Legal Aid, Sentencing and Punishment of Offenders Act 2012 (Fines on Summary Conviction) Regulations 2015 2015/664 para 4 and Sch 4 para 33(4)

[33] Penalties for Disorderly Behaviour (Amount of Penalty) Order 2002 2002/1837 Sch as amended

[34] Licensing Act 2003 s 141, 146(1) and (3), 149(3)-(4) and 151 respectively

[35] Licensing Act 2003 s 129

[36] Drug Driving (Specified Limits) (England and Wales) Regulations 2014 2014/2868 para 2

[37] See page 15 of the guidelines.

year or two, amphetamine now has a higher concentration of the drug than was once generally the case. While goods seized at the points of importation may contain a high percentage of amphetamine, at a retail level the purity may well be no more than [say] 10% to 12% or even less. It follows that a trafficker in possession of amphetamine stands to earn very much larger sums than a trafficker in possession of the same weight of cannabis, that a relatively small weight of amphetamine of maximum purity will, when adulterated, convert into a very large number of individual doses, and that the weight of amphetamine which a user may hold for his own personal consumption is likely, in many cases, to be much smaller than the weight of cannabis held for personal consumption. For reasons clearly given in *R v Aranguren* 1994 99 Cr App R 347 at 351 sentences in relation to amphetamine should depend not on market value but on the quantity of the amphetamine calculated on the basis of 100% pure amphetamine base (i.e. the maximum theoretical purity of 73% amphetamine base in amphetamine sulphate, the remaining 27% being the sulphate). As was held in relation to class A drugs we should not attempt to distinguish between different drugs in class B on the basis that one such drug is more or less pernicious than another.

See also the **DEFENDANT** *Drug users* paras at **240.21** and the **IMPORTATION OF DRUGS, PRODUCTION OF DRUGS** and **SUPPLY OF DRUGS** chapters.

206.2   *Assessing the weight of drugs*
R v Kerley 2015 EWCA Crim 1193, 2 Cr App R (S) 69 (p 475) LCJ D pleaded to conspiracy to supply amphetamine. The drugs were 9.95 kilos of wet amphetamine. When dried, the drugs weighed 5.42 kilos. An issue arose as to what the proper weight should be. Held. People should be dealt with for the actual drugs they have with them. Note: A more sensible approach would be to assume the amphetamine weights in the guideline are for dry amphetamine, as that is how it is usually found. Consequently the dry weight should be used and as a result there should be no anomalies with people dealing with the same amphetamine being dealt with differently depending on whether they handled the drug when it was wet or dry. Ed.

207   ANIMAL CRUELTY
207.1
Animal Welfare Act 2006
> s 4 (causing unnecessary suffering)
> s 8 (causing an animal to fight etc.)

Mode of trial Summary only

Maximum sentence 6 months and/or a £20,000 fine for offences committed before 12 March 2015 and an unlimited fine thereafter.[38] There are maximum fines for those aged under 18, see **14.38** in Volume 1.

Destruction Orders etc. There is power to destroy the animal and deprive ownership of the animal.[39]

Disqualification There is power to disqualify persons from owning, keeping, etc. animals.[40]

Forfeiture and seizure There is power to seize animals and forfeit qualifying items.[41]

Law Commission On 10 November 2015, the Law Commission issued its report and draft bill to reform and codify wildlife law. The report does not deal with domestic or farm animals. The proposed penalties for unlawfully killing or injuring certain wildlife is made a triable either way offence with a 2-year maximum sentence.

---

[38] Legal Aid, Sentencing and Punishment of Offenders Act 2012 s 85(1) and (4) and Legal Aid, Sentencing and Punishment of Offenders Act 2012 (Commencement No 11) Order 2015 2015/504
[39] Protection of Animals Act 1911 s 2
[40] Protection of Animals Act 1911 s 2
[41] Animal Welfare Act 2006 s 35 and 40

207.2   *Magistrates' Court Sentencing guidelines*

Magistrates' Court Sentencing guidelines 2008, see www.banksr.com Other Matters Guidelines tab The guidelines apply to the Magistrates' Court and to the Crown Court hearing appeals or sentencing for summary only offences.[42]
page 22 Starting points are based on a first-time offender pleading not guilty.

Examples of nature of activity	Starting point	Range
One impulsive act causing little or no injury, short-term neglect	Band C fine	Band B fine to medium-level community order
Several incidents of deliberate ill-treatment/frightening animal(s), medium-term neglect	High-level community order	Medium-level community order to 12 weeks' custody
Attempt to kill/torture, animal baiting, conducting or permitting cock-fighting etc., prolonged neglect	18 weeks' custody	12 to 26 weeks' custody

The following aggravating and mitigating factors may be particularly relevant: Factors indicating higher culpability: 1 Offender in position of special responsibility 2 Adult involves children in offending 3 Animal(s) kept for livelihood 4 Use of weapon 5 Offender ignored advice/warnings 6 Offence committed for commercial gain.
Factors indicating lower culpability: 1 Offender induced by others 2 Ignorance of appropriate care 3 Offender with limited capacity.
Factors indicating greater degree of harm: 1 Serious injury or death 2 Several animals affected.
Consider ancillary orders, including compensation. Also consider disqualification from ownership of animal.
A Band B fine is 100% of net weekly income and a Band C fine is 150% of net weekly income. For more detail, see **60.27** in Volume 1.
Consultation It is expected that the Sentencing Council will issue a consultation document about updating this guideline in May 2016.
For the meaning of a high-level and a medium-level community order see **16.13-16.14** in Volume 1.
For details about applying the guidelines, see the **GUIDELINES** chapter in Volume 1.

208   ANIMAL RIGHTS ACTIVISTS

208.1

Various offences and penalties including:
Serious Organised Crime and Police Act 2005 s 145-146 (section 145 interfering with the contractual relationships so as to harm animal research organisations and section 146 intimidating persons connected with animal research organisations)
Mode of trial Both offences are triable either way.
Maximum sentence On indictment 5 years. Summary 6 months and/or a £5,000 fine for offences committed before 12 March 2015 and an unlimited fine thereafter.[43] There are maximum fines for those aged under 18, see **14.38** in Volume 1.

208.2   *Judicial guidance*

R v Martin 1999 1 Cr App R (S) 477 Generally the sentences imposed for acts of violence relating to animal rights activism are in almost every case lower than for

---

[42] See page 15 of the guidelines.
[43] Legal Aid, Sentencing and Punishment of Offenders Act 2012 s 85(1) and (4) and Legal Aid, Sentencing and Punishment of Offenders Act 2012 (Commencement No 11) Order 2015 2015/504

terrorist offences fuelled by political extremism. There are obvious reasons why this should be so. The political threat presented by such offences is much less potent, and the general level of sophistication is a very great deal lower.

R v Gisbourne 2005 EWCA Crim 2491, 2006 1 Cr App R (S) 108 (p 636) D pleaded to conspiracy to damage property connected with Huntingdon Life Sciences. £40,000 worth of property was damaged. Held. Everyone can freely hold any personal opinion, however unusual, on any subject. But no one can seek to impose on others his or her opinion by intimidation or by violence or threats of violence to persons or property. All those who by such conduct disrupt the ability of others lawfully to live their lives challenge the essential peaceful fabric of our society and must expect to be severely punished. D's beliefs are of no consequence. What is of consequence is the misery which, with premeditation and planning, she chose deliberately and repeatedly to inflict on several particularly vulnerable law-abiding victims. (The length of her 6½-year sentence was challenged because of the lack of full discount for the plea. It was reduced on that ground alone to **5½ years.**)

208.3   *Attacking laboratories or their suppliers etc.*

R v Ablewhite and Others 2007 EWCA Crim 832, 2 Cr App R (S) 93 (p 604) The three defendants pleaded to conspiracy to blackmail. There was a six-year campaign against a farming business run by H's family which bred guinea pigs for medical research. In the course of that campaign the grave of Mrs H's mother was desecrated and her body removed. There were threats made against H's children's riding instructor. There was also a burglary in which 600 guinea pigs were taken. Threatening letters were sent to members of H's family. An improvised explosive device was left at the home of one of H's family. A cousin of the family was targeted and three cars outside his home were damaged with paint stripper. H's golf club had three greens dug up. Their employees were targeted. An employee was sent a threatening letter saying her husband's body would be taken. Graffiti appeared in her village and that went on for three years until she gave up her job. In the course of that harassment paint was thrown at her home, and windows were smashed. Her son and daughter were also targeted and their vehicles damaged. Another employee also gave up his job after he had threats in letters to blow up his house. Devices which had the potential to injure were left in his garden and his car was damaged. Another employee received threatening letters including threats of bombing. Two of his cars were damaged, and devices were left in his garden. His partner was targeted and her parents were threatened. Businesses that dealt with H were targeted. A firm of solicitors that had worked for them was affected by threats, and refused to take further instructions from them. Calor Gas ceased to deliver to the farm. There were 38 victim impact statements from the victims. Ultimately the body of Mrs H's mother was recovered as a result of information given by one of the defendants. The defendants each had previous convictions including convictions for similar activities. Held. The maximum sentence was 14 years. It was right to say that the defendants sought to enforce their view by a campaign of terror, and a severe sentence was necessary. Previous terms of imprisonment for similar offences had not deterred them. In view of the length of the campaign and the previous convictions **12 years** for each was fully merited.

Att-Gen's Ref No 113 of 2007 2008 EWCA Crim 22, 2008 2 Cr App R (S) 51 (p 319) D pleaded early to six counts of blackmail, one count of attempted blackmail and five counts of interference with contractual relations so as to harm animal research organisations, contrary to Serious Organised Crime and Police Act 2005 s 145. The offences were committed between August 2001 and June 2006. On the blackmail counts, she sent threatening letters to people who were in some way linked with animal research companies, threatening them that if they did not sever links with the animal research companies there would be adverse consequences. Two were sent to employees of a bank which provided financial services to Huntingdon Life Sciences (HLS). One said, 'Stop investing in HLS or you will die', which was taken to be a threat of murder, the other,

'Stop investing in the animal killers at the HLS. If not we will visit you'. This one was signed 'ALF' (the Animal Liberation Front). Two other threatening letters were directed at a vet who provided services to the Hall family, who bred guinea pigs for research. They said, 'Cut all ties to them (the Halls) or our campaign will focus on you next. ALF' and 'Stop doing business with Animal Killers the Halls. You have been warned'. The second of these contained a white powder, which it was thought might be anthrax. His staff were panicked and some of them considered leaving their jobs out of terror. The powder was in fact harmless. Two other letters were sent to companies that worked for Sequani, an animal research organisation. They said, 'Stop trading with Sequani or you're next'. Both contained white powder. In the first one, the recipient felt panicky and nervous and believed he was being poisoned. In the second, the powder fell onto the woman who opened the envelope and she was shocked and frightened. She was taken to the sterile area of a hospital and instructed to shower and change into paper clothing. She was there for 6-8 hours before being told there was no danger. She said the events had permanently affected her life and left a mental scar. In both cases the white powder was harmless. The attempted blackmail was when D sent a threatening letter in similar terms to a family she believed, incorrectly, were involved with the export of livestock. The four counts of interference with contractual relationships involved sending letters warning the recipients that unless they stopped all trade with 'animal abusers' they would be targeted. In interview D made no comment. A basis of plea was that she had never attended any animal rights meetings or demonstrations or been in contact with any individual animal rights campaigner and was not associated with any other campaign. She had acted entirely alone. D was aged 35. A psychiatric report said she had a number of problems including a personality disorder, alcohol dependency, anxiety and depression. She had had inpatient treatment for depression. A pre-sentence report said she was influenced by others with extreme views and her regret was genuine. Held. The starting point should have been **6 years**. The aggravating features were that she was engaged in a sustained campaign of intimidation for over 5 years. She deliberately gave the impression she was acting on behalf of dangerous extremists. The means she had employed, particularly the sending of powder, were calculated to cause fear of death and widespread alarm. She had targeted 11 victims but many more were affected. The early plea and personal mitigation meant the Judge should have sentenced her to **3 years**. As she is being sentenced twice, and is at this time nearly due for release, **2 years** concurrent on the counts involving white powder not 8 months concurrent, and **18 months concurrent** not 4 months concurrent on all other charges.

Note: This case is old so should be treated with care. Ed

Old case: *R v Harris* 2006 EWCA Crim 3303, 2007 2 Cr App R (S) 37 (p 238) **(2 years)** For a summary of this case see the 10th edition of this book.

208.4   *Rescuing animals from laboratories*

Att-Gen's Ref No 54 of 2005 2005 EWCA Crim 1896, 2006 1 Cr App R (S) 71 (p 378) D was convicted of conspiracy to burgle. He had been an animal rights activist for many years and he entered laboratory premises at night with two others. He said his intention was to obtain documentary evidence of alleged illegal experimentation on animals. He took laboratory records and 700 mice and their cages. He was arrested two days later and virtually all the mice were recovered. If they had not been recovered there would have been a loss to the company of £25,000, which included £3,000 damage to the building. After he had been sentenced and was leaving Court, D passed the technical director of the company who was in the public gallery and said, "Your troubles have only just started", which he admitted, and "You better start looking under your bed", which he denied. The Judge heard evidence and decided he had made both remarks and sentenced him to 6 months' imprisonment for contempt of court. The aggravating features were identified as: that the offence was carefully planned and sophisticated and was committed in furtherance of D's moral beliefs, that the deliberate removal of the mice exceeded the claimed purpose for committing the offence of exposing alleged illegal activity to the media, that he inflicted significant financial damage to a legitimate business and important scientific experimentation, that he was the prime mover and recruited others to carry out his plan and that he had previous convictions for similar offences. D was aged 39 and had been sentenced in 1996 to 14 years' imprisonment for offences committed in the course of animal rights activism: attempted arson, criminal damage, attempted incitement to commit arson, attempted incitement to steal, escape from lawful custody and having explosive substances. The Court of Appeal reduced that sentence to 11 years and a significant factor in this decision was that he told both courts that he no longer intended to pursue his belief in animal rights by illegal means. He had not been convicted of any offence since his release in 1999. A pre-sentence report in this case set out that he was the sole carer for his partner, who suffered from significant handicaps. She had had a brain haemorrhage and suffered from fybromyalgia[44] and had consequent physical and mental disabilities. She needed constant care. Held. The burglary and the contempt of court cast significant doubt on the genuineness of the intent to give up illegal means that he expressed at the time of the previous case. This was a carefully planned and sophisticated offence and had the benefit of inside information. The moral justification for the action does not make it any less illegal. In an appropriate case there may be room for some disposal other than a custodial sentence but not in this particular case. The contempt of court and the fact that this was repeat offending means that he should have forfeited any claim to leniency. The appropriate sentence would have been **18 months to 2 years**. As it was a reference and because of the circumstances of his partner, **12 months** to be served consecutively for the contempt of court, not 230 hours' Community Punishment Order.

ARMED FORCES, MEMBERS OF see the **COURT MARTIAL** chapter in Volume 1.

209   ARSON

209.1

Criminal Damage Act 1971 s 1

Mode of trial Simple arson is triable either way. Arson being reckless whether the life of another would be endangered and arson with intent are triable only on indictment.

Maximum sentence Simple arson: On indictment 5 years. Summary maximum 6 months and/or a £5,000 fine for offences committed before 12 March 2015 and an unlimited fine thereafter.[45] There are maximum fines for those aged under 18, see **14.38** in Volume 1. Reckless arson and arson with intent: Life

Criminal Behaviour Orders Where a defendant has engaged in behaviour that caused or was likely to cause harassment, alarm or distress to any person and a Criminal Behaviour Order will help in preventing the offender from engaging in such behaviour, the court may make this order.[46]

Extended sentences This offence is listed in Criminal Justice Act 2003 Sch 15. The court may pass a 2012 extended sentence (EDS) if there is a significant risk of serious harm from future specified offences and either: a) the defendant has a Criminal Justice Act 2003 Sch 15B conviction (applicable only to defendants aged 18+), or b) the offence would justify a determinate sentence of at least 4 years.[47]

Sexual Harm Prevention Orders There is a discretionary power to make this order when it is necessary to protect the public from sexual harm.[48]

---

[44] A long-term condition which causes pain all over the body.

[45] Legal Aid, Sentencing and Punishment of Offenders Act 2012 s 85(1) and (4) and Legal Aid, Sentencing and Punishment of Offenders Act 2012 (Commencement No 11) Order 2015 2015/504

[46] Anti-social Behaviour, Crime and Policing Act 2014 s 22(1)-(4)

[47] Criminal Justice Act 2003 s 226A-226B as inserted by Legal Aid, Sentencing and Punishment of Offenders Act 2012 s 124

[48] Sexual Offences Act 2003 s 103A as inserted by Anti-social Behaviour, Crime and Policing Act 2014 Sch 5 para 2 and Sexual Offences Act 2003 Sch 5

This chapter is divided into the following sections: a) General, b) Arson Simple, c) Arson Reckless whether life would be endangered and d) Arson Intending life would be endangered.

General
209.2   *Crown Court statistics   England and Wales*
Arson (Simple)

Year	Age	Plea	Total sen-tenced	Type of sentencing %						Average length of custody in months
				Dis-charge	Fine	Community sentence	Sus-pended sentence	Custody	Oth-er	
2014	18-20	G	26	–	–	12	15	65	8	19.7
		NG	1	–	–	–	–	100	–	not listed[49]
	21+	G	188	2	1	14	24	49	10	21.3
		NG	10	–	–	10	10	70	10	47.0

*: not shown as based on too few cases to be meaningful
For explanations about the statistics, see page 1-xii. For statistics for female and male defendants etc., see www.banksr.com Other Matters Statistics tab

209.3   *Psychiatric report, Need for*
R v Calladine 1975 The Times 3/12/75 It is unwise to pass sentence without a psychiatric report.

Arson Simple
209.4   *Criminal Damage Act 1971 s 1(1) and (3)*
Mode of trial Triable either way
Maximum sentence On indictment life. Summary 6 months and/or a £5,000 fine for offences committed before 12 March 2015 and an unlimited fine thereafter.[50] There are maximum fines for those aged under 18, see **14.38** in Volume 1.

209.5   *Magistrates' Court Sentencing Guidelines*
Magistrates' Court Sentencing Guidelines 2008, see www.banksr.com Other Matters Guidelines tab The guidelines apply to the Magistrates' Court and to the Crown Court hearing appeals or sentencing for summary only offences.[51]
page 23 Starting points are based on a first-time offender pleading not guilty.

Examples of nature of activity	Starting point	Range
Minor damage by fire	High-level community order	Medium-level community order to 12 weeks' custody
Moderate damage by fire	12 weeks' custody	6 to 26 weeks' custody
Significant damage by fire	Crown Court	Crown Court

The following aggravating and mitigating factors may be particularly relevant: Factor indicating higher culpability: 1 Revenge attack. Factor indicating lower culpability: 1 Damage caused recklessly.
Factors indicating greater degree of harm: 1 Damage to emergency equipment 2 Damage to public amenity 3 Significant public or private fear caused e.g. in domestic context.
Consider ancillary orders, including compensation.

---

[49] Not shown as based on too few cases to be meaningful
[50] Legal Aid, Sentencing and Punishment of Offenders Act 2012 s 85(1) and (4) and Legal Aid, Sentencing and Punishment of Offenders Act 2012 (Commencement No 11) Order 2015 2015/504
[51] See page 15 of the guidelines.

For the meaning of a high-level and medium-level community order see **16.13-16.14** in Volume 1.

209.6   Simple arson   Judicial guidance

R v Elsobky 2014 EWCA Crim 2035 It has always been recognised that the inherent dangerousness of setting fire to a building makes even simple arson a very serious offence. In *R v Hartley and Blevins* 1994 14 Cr App R (S) 198, this Court said, "Arson cases are difficult. Sentences passed must reflect the grave consequences which can flow, and in this case did flow, from the fire. It has to be remembered that firemen called to large fires are always in danger and that commercial companies whose premises are damaged by fire can also face serious consequences. Sentences passed on arsonists must contain an element of deterrence to dissuade others from behaving in an irresponsible and reckless manner."

209.7   Simple arson   Domestic premises

R v Roberts 2009 EWCA Crim 701, 2 Cr App R (S) 100 (p 657) D pleaded promptly to attempted arson. He was living by himself on the ground floor in the middle of a block of flats. D was drinking too much and became depressed. He turned two heaters on and draped blankets and towels over them. D went out and called the police from a nearby call box saying he was a mental patient and had set fire to his flat. Nothing caught fire and there was no damage. He was arrested in the call box and said to police he had had enough and wanted to go to prison. At the police station he said he wanted to burn down his place and the flats and made full admissions in interview saying it was a cry for help and he did not intend to kill anyone. The defendant had one previous conviction in 2004 for reckless arson. He had started a fire in the property he was living in. He had suffered from mental health problems and alcohol-related problems since 1994. A psychiatric report said the nature and severity of his problems varied over time. He suffered depressive symptoms, had some paranoid ideas, heard the voices of his dead parents and had been treated with anti-depressant and anti-psychotic medicine. He had resumed drinking because he was depressed and had impulsively tried to cause a fire. A pre-sentence report said there was a medium risk of reoffending and a high risk of harm to members of the public who live near him. He had said he would resume drinking when released from prison. Held. There was a case to charge reckless arson but we are careful to sentence only for arson. It was right to find that there was a significant risk to the public of serious harm. The harm which he might have caused was grave and he knew what he was doing. The appropriate determinate sentence after a trial would have been 4 years and given his early plea less, so IPP was not possible. **32 months** not IPP with a minimum term of 2 years.

R v Evans 2010 EWCA Crim 668 D pleaded to arson, battery, and breach of a Non-molestation Order. D and his wife of 7 years, V, began divorce proceedings but continued to live together. The house was jointly owned. Whilst watching television, D grabbed V round the throat, put his thumb into her windpipe and shouted, "Die". D told V he would torch the house, kill the cat and she would have nothing. V had bruising to the chin, chest and shoulders and a scratched face. V went to live with her daughter and obtained a Non-molestation Order which forbade D from contacting V, attending the address where she was living and damaging any jointly owned property. A neighbour saw D's car parked outside the property formerly shared by V and D and smoke was coming from the house. D contacted his son-in-law, told him the fire had been started and suggested he call the police. D also left a message on V's mobile telephone which said, "Morning bitch, I've torched the house. You'll have nothing." The house was ablaze for 10 minutes before the fire brigade arrived. An 89-year-old lady in the adjoining house had to be assisted from her home. The conservatory and all the internal fixtures and fittings were destroyed and some steel joists were structurally damaged. D, aged 65, said in interview that he had bought petrol and made sure the property was empty. The pre-sentence report said D had minimised his behaviour. Held. This was a very serious case of simple arson. The aggravating features were premeditation, spite, and it was committed in breach of the Non-molestation Order. **4 years** for the arson and 1 year consecutive for the breach was not manifestly excessive.

R v Loader 2012 EWCA Crim 1838 D pleaded (full credit) to simple arson and common assault. He had been in an on/off relationship with K. They had a 3-week old child together and K had a 3-year-old daughter from a previous relationship. D had been taking drugs and remained downstairs. K was upstairs with the children. D woke her at 2 am asking where his CDs were. He was swearing and gritting his teeth. He went downstairs and returned, upon which he started throwing items around the room. He pinched K's cheeks and was shouting at her. He lit a cigarette and said, "I don't give a shit anymore. Watch this, I'm going to burn the house down and you and the kids in it." He then set fire to K's dressing gown. The prosecution opening stated that D extinguished the fire with his own hands, upon which he returned downstairs. K was petrified for her safety and the safety of her children. When arrested, D said he had had "a wobble with the missus". D had 17 appearances for 57 offences, largely for dishonesty and motoring. Held. His behaviour that night must have been very frightening, notwithstanding that the fire was extinguished quickly. Looking at the events as a whole, **9 months** not 30.

See also: *R v Saleem* 2010 EWCA Crim 2801 (D convicted of arson and pleaded late to damaging property. Damage limited to bathroom, unoccupied house of husband of D's partner with no accelerant. **27 months** not manifestly excessive.)

Old cases: *R v Hales* 2009 EWCA Crim 98 (**IPP** (minimum term of 2 years 3 months)) *R v Saleem* 2010 EWCA Crim 2801 (**27 months**) For a summary of the second case see the 10th edition of this book.

209.8   *Simple arson   Evidence, To destroy*

R v Kramer 2013 EWCA Crim 1087 D pleaded to arson and TDA. D and T had been to a party. At about 2 am T carried out a burglary and took the keys to a BMW. D and T took the vehicle in order to drive home. They got lost and abandoned the vehicle where they set fire to it in an attempt to destroy any evidence that might identify them. The vehicle sustained substantial damage. D, aged 21, had 29 appearances for 59 offences, largely for dishonesty. He was on licence from a 16-month sentence for two burglaries and three TDAs. The pre-sentence report noted a high risk of reoffending. Held. These offences are not to be equated with aggravated vehicle-taking. 2½ years for the arson was undoubtedly severe but with an appalling record [and 3 months consecutive for the TDA]. 2 years 9 months was not manifestly excessive.

209.9   *Simple arson   Other fires*

R v H 2011 EWCA Crim 1913 D pleaded (full credit) to arson. In the early hours, a business dealing in vehicles suffered arson. Later that day, D, after encouragement from others, visited the business, and the group set fire to a vehicle, using an accelerant. D unsuccessfully attempted to set fire to a van. Damage estimated at between £500,000 and £750,000 was caused to 22 vehicles. An exclusion zone of several hundred metres was set up owing to the risk of gas cylinders present on the site. D, aged 13, had gone there out of curiosity but had been a willing participant. He admitted his involvement almost immediately. He had one reprimand for theft. Held. The fire threatened the business with bankruptcy. Bearing in mind D's family difficulties (his parents had separated and his uncle had recently died), his age (pertaining to his vulnerability in custody) and his frankness, **18 months' detention** under section 91, not 2 years.

R v Blackford 2011 EWCA Crim 2523, 2012 1 Cr App R (S) 111 (p 663) D pleaded (full credit) on rearraignment to simple arson. D set light to the inside of a church hall. It was an impulsive act which was influenced by alcohol without D appreciating the consequences. The cost of replacement was between £500,000 and £600,000, of which only a few hundred thousand would be covered by insurance. D, aged 18, demonstrated genuine remorse and had no convictions. There was one reprimand for ABH. Held. This was a serious offence with adverse consequences for the wider community. Starting at 4 years, not 5, with full credit **32 months' YOI** not 40.

R v Erdogan 2012 EWCA Crim 3104, 2013 2 Cr App R (S) 50 (p 343) D pleaded to simple arson and damaging a TV. He was in the Health Care Unit of prison. Staff asked him not to mingle or integrate with other prisoners. When he was abusive to them, he was encouraged back to his cell. The cells were monitored by CCTV. D threw his TV at his door. The TV broke. Next, D gathered bedding and papers etc., placed them by the door and set them alight. It created a very large amount of smoke. The other 15 prisoners had to be returned to their cells and the fire brigade had to be called. The cell was out of action for four days and the costs of putting the cell right were £400. In interview, D said he had tried to harm himself and he had started the fire to get out of the wing. D was aged 33. He had convictions for common assault, ABH, possession of an offensive weapon (×2, one of them 18 months) and wounding (27 months). Held. The aggravating factor was that the offence was in a prison. With full credit for the plea, **2 years** not 32 months.

R v Bradley 2014 EWCA Crim 488 D pleaded to arson. She lived alone and was no longer on good terms with her neighbour, K, with whom she had been in a relationship some eight years previously. There had been a history of disputes about a fence which divided their gardens. The fence belonged to D and she thought it was being damaged by K. D spent part of the day breaking pieces off the damaged fence and burning them in an incinerator. Abuse was exchanged between D and K about the fence. The next day, D continued to burn pieces of the fence in the incinerator. She had hitherto used her hands to break off the wood, but then began to use a lighter to set fire to some material which could be used to loosen a particular piece of fence which had proved obdurate. The piece of fence caught fire and spread from three fence panels to a wicker screen, erected by M. It damaged his fence, decking and a hot tub, in addition to the guttering and the doors on his house. His windows and brickwork were charred and scorched. The damage was about £12,000. Both D and K called the fire brigade and D attempted to extinguish the fire. When the fire brigade arrived, D was observed to be laughing and referring to K's lack of insurance. D appeared to be in drink. She accepted setting the fire but said the way it spread was an accident. She accepted that she didn't like K and did like burning things. D had three convictions for a public order offence in 2009 and a subsequent offence of excess alcohol and assaulting a constable. A psychiatric report noted a relatively mild history of mental illness. It suggested that alcohol might have played more of a part in the offence than D had admitted. A pre-sentence report noted that D said she found the burning 'therapeutic' after becoming stressed at her failure to get her daughter back from the father who had taunted her. Held. The harm was significant and K was uninsured, but it was not at the most serious level where this type of offence is committed. This was not deliberate setting of a fire.[52] The culpability was the reckless setting fire to part of the fence. The recklessness is in what she did when setting the fire. Her reaction afterwards, although to be deplored, did not add significantly to the culpability, and set against [that] was her apparent shock at what had happened as a result of her crime. There was considerable mitigation including the removal of her child and the stress of standing trial for arson with intent to endanger life. The correct starting point should have been in the order of 21 months. With credit for the plea, **14 months** not 21.

Note: Although there was some damage to a house, the start of the fire and the major damage was outside the house so the case is not listed as a dwelling fire. Ed.

See also: *R v Elsobky* 2014 EWCA Crim 2035 (Convicted. Simple arson and fraud. Business in financial difficulty. D recruited others to burn building for bogus £290,000+

---

[52] Presumably the Court meant that the setting of the fire was deliberate, but causing the damage was not deliberate. Ed.

insurance claim. Warehouse worth before fire about £330,000. Considerable planning, false invoices used and insurance increased before fire. Fire was severe. Aged 28, no convictions. **8 years** in all upheld.)

Old cases: *R v Grounds* 2009 EWCA Crim 2016 (**IPP** with a **2-year** minimum term) *R v Multi-Hungwe* 2009 EWCA Crim 2386, 2010, 2 Cr App R (S) 15 (p 88) (**5 years**) *R v Pay* 2010 EWCA Crim 1164 (**2 years**)

For a summary of the first two cases, see the 9th edition of this book and for the last case see the 10th edition.

Arson Reckless whether life would be endangered

209.10
Criminal Damage Act 1971 s 1(2)-(3)
Mode of trial Indictable only
Maximum sentence Life

209.11   *Crown Court statistics   England and Wales*
Arson endangering life

Year	Age	Plea	Total sen-tenced	Type of sentencing %						Average length of custody in months
				Dis-charge	Fine	Community sentence	Sus-pended sentence	Custody	Oth-er	
2014	18-20	G	37	–	–	5	19	59	16	38.0
		NG	1	–	–	–	–	100	–	not listed[53]
	21+	G	323	–	–	4	19	63	13	37.9
		NG	32	–	–	3	–	91	6	65.7

For explanations about the statistics, see page 1-xii. For statistics for female and male defendants etc., see www.banksr.com Other Matters Statistics tab

209.12   *Reckless arson   Judicial guidance*
Att-Gen's Ref No 1 of 1997 1998 1 Cr App R (S) 54 D pleaded to arson being reckless whether life would be endangered. Held. An offence of arson endangering life recklessly is one which, save in the most exceptional circumstances and/or in the case of mental trouble, must attract an immediate prison sentence. Further it is a case where the prison sentence will have to be severe, partly to protect the public, partly to deter the man himself and to deter anyone else from doing this sort of thing again.
Note: This case is old, but the policy seems to continue. Ed.

209.13   *Reckless arson   Defendant aged under 18*
R v Walsh 2010 EWCA Crim 1580 D and T pleaded (full credit) to reckless arson and theft. H received a telephone call from a neighbour stating that two individuals, D and T, were in his car. H looked out of the window and D and T ran off. The police were called and discovered that amongst other things the manual had been stolen. A policeman saw T and D and then D throwing a burning object to the ground which turned out to be the manual from the car. Just before D and T were detained, V, a disabled 81-year-old in sheltered housing, was awoken by a noise from an open window. V saw his net curtains alight. When D saw the flames were taking hold, he put them out with his hands. The two were then arrested. The damage was £10. D, aged 20, had 16 convictions, one of which was for criminal damage (no custodial sentences). T, aged 17, had two convictions for three offences, two of which were criminal damage (absolute discharges). D and T admitted the offences and D cited the fact that he was drunk as the explanation. The psychiatric report said D was emotionally immature. D and T showed remorse. The Judge said that the fact that D had put the flames out made "little difference". Held. We

---

[53] Not shown as based on too few cases to be meaningful.

start at 3 years not 5. Having regard to the fact that the flames were extinguished almost as soon as they were lit, 5 years was manifestly excessive. For D, with the plea, **2 years**, not 3 years 4 months, and for T, **18-month DTO**, not 3 years 4 months' detention.

Old cases: *R v G* 2006 EWCA Crim 3277, 2007 2 Cr App R (S) 32 (p 185) (**2 years** and an extension period of 5 years) *R v Goodfellow and Jevons* 2007 EWCA Crim 1733, 2008 1 Cr App R (S) 29 (p 147) (3 **years'** detention for both) *Att-Gen's Ref No 58 of 2007* 2007 EWCA Crim 2057, 2008 1 Cr App R (S) 71 (p 408) (**4 years'** detention) For a summary of the first case, see the 8th edition of this book, for the second case see the 9th edition and for the last case see the 10th edition.

209.14   *Reckless arson   Domestic premises etc. with no occupants (other than defendant)*

R v Humphries 2013 EWCA Crim 1748 D pleaded to attempted reckless arson. D and J were close friends, though their friendship had deteriorated. They had fallen out after J accused D of drink/driving whilst J was a passenger. Thereafter, D attempted to disrupt J's wedding. On the day of the wedding, she tried to spread false rumours about J, using Facebook. She also attended the reception uninvited. Other false allegations continued. J's stepson went back to J's home to collect some clothing. He found some papers just inside the door, some of which were slightly burnt with matches on top of them. D had pushed the papers through the door. By then, D was in custody having been arrested for driving her car, whilst intoxicated, into a brick wall. In two interviews she lied. D was aged 40 and of previous good character. The pre-sentence report indicated she was remorseful but failed to see the potential devastating consequences of her actions. A report stated that she suffered from a chronic adjustment disorder. The Judge sentenced her to 2 years, resulting in her children going to live with her former husband. Her family was ostracised within their community as a result of the offence. D attended a number of courses whilst in custody. Held. Though D's actions were highly dangerous, they were a crude attempt at lighting a fire. No accelerant was used and she remained at the property to ensure that it did not take hold. She undoubtedly had mental health issues and although this offence was driven by alcohol and anger, she had long-standing problems. **12 months** not 2 years. The sentence would not be suspended because of the overall seriousness and the dangerous nature of the offence.

R v Newman 2014 EWCA Crim 1116 D was convicted of reckless arson. A housing association sent her 27 letters regarding antisocial behaviour, the state of the property and her failure to allow access to the premises. Proceedings to evict her started. About 10 minutes after D took her children to school, a neighbour, N, saw smoke coming from D's letter box. D returned to the property with her children. N let them into D's home and D's son opened the back door to let the dog out. D rang the fire brigade, who came and extinguished the fire. D's son said D usually left him in bed while she took the other children to school, but on this occasion she had woken him up. D had taken her laptop, the only item of any real value in the property, on the school run. The seat of the fire was a chair in the living room and the fire service found the most likely cause was a deliberate ignition of a mixture of paper and textiles with a naked flame. D had no relevant convictions. She suffered from substance abuse and drug dependency. The Judge said the fire was lit out of frustration. He accepted that D was not dangerous or a pyromaniac and had to an extent turned her life around from someone who took drugs on a daily basis to someone who appreciated that if she continued that way she would lose her children forever. Held. It was a terraced house which was empty at the time. It cost £17,000 to repair. Taking account of the personal mitigation, notably that the property was D's own home, it was borne out of frustration not revenge, that the inevitable custodial sentence would have a serious effect on her children, the delay and that she had 'turned her life around', 4½ years was manifestly excessive. **3½ years** substituted.

Att-Gen's Ref No 35 of 2014 2014 EWCA Crim 2921 D pleaded to reckless arson which was indicated shortly after her plea of not guilty when the case was set down for trial. V1 and his wife, V2, lived in a mid-terraced house with their son, V3, aged 24 and another son. V3 became friends with D and her boyfriend, W. While D's parents were away looking after V1's father, the sons lived in the home and on a visit D and W stole V1's house keys. Using the keys they entered his house and started a fire. A pedestrian saw smoke and firemen attended. The house and the two neighbouring houses were empty. A cigarette had been used to start a fire in V3's bedroom, which was very badly damaged. The rest of the floor was smoke damaged. Two curtains separating the sitting room and the dining room had burn marks suggesting a flame had been applied to the hems and had taken hold but burnt out. No accelerant was used on either floor. V was arrested and made no comment when interviewed. On the same day, she sent a text saying, 'No one is dead tho so its kl and its not stupid I don't care about the money he can keep it but don't try to take me for a dickhead!' (sic). The prosecution said D was owed money. V2 suffered nightmares and their youngest son (who was probably V3) felt guilt and anger. D was aged 18. In 2011 she had an attempted theft conviction (Referral Order) and a supply cannabis conviction (Community Order with a supervision requirement). In 2013 she was conditionally discharged for handling. D was brought up in care. It was agreed she fell under the influence of W, who was older than her. The pre-sentence report considered there was a medium risk of further offending. She had personality disorders and had disengaged from mental health and psychological services. She had also stopped taking her medicine. The post-sentence report was positive. She was co-operative, pregnant and in regular contact with her psychiatric nurse and her probation officer. She was a very different woman from when she was sentenced. Held. The Judge did not identify any exceptional circumstances and he must have been merciful. He wanted her to make progress and all the indicators suggest the decision to suspend the sentence was well made. The appropriate sentence was **4-4½ years**, but we do not disturb the sentence with its activity and educational and training requirements.

Old cases: *R v Bal* 2008 EWCA Crim 1434, 2009 1 Cr App R (S) 52 (p 283) **(3 years)** *R v Moody* 2010 EWCA Crim 1370 **(9 months' suspended)** *R v Gibson* 2010 EWCA Crim 2126 **(2 years)**

For a summary of the first case, see the 9th edition of this book and for the second case see the 10th edition.

209.15 *Reckless arson   Domestic premises with occupants   Danger to occupants*
R v Hill 2011 EWCA Crim 35 D pleaded (full credit) to reckless arson. He had been drinking beer since 4 pm on the day of his mother's 50th birthday party at a local golf club. Whilst engaged in some 'horseplay', he found a flag and set it alight with a cigarette lighter. The flag, which was used to mark a golf hole, was waved about and then thrown to the ground. D thought nothing more about it. Unfortunately the flag set fire to a golf buggy which was outside the clubhouse. That in turn set other articles alight which then set the clubhouse alight. Above the clubhouse was an occupied domestic flat. £600,000 damage was caused. Initially declining to comment, upon seeing CCTV tapes he identified himself as one of the males present. There were two stewards clearing up after the party still present. The stewards called the fire brigade and the occupant. D's basis of plea was that he was drunk, careless, lacking intention, anticipated that the fire would have died out once thrown to the ground and was horrified at the result. D was of good character and had references. Held. As the Judge made clear, it was not a deliberate act. What D must be sentenced for was setting fire to the flag. 30 months was inconsistent with D's real culpability. A custodial sentence was inevitable. **18 months** was appropriate.

Att-Gen's Ref No 39 of 2011 2011 EWCA Crim 2617 During his trial, D pleaded (10% credit) to intentionally assisting etc. an offender to reckless commit arson. When D lost his job, he pursued a course of threats directed toward his employer, V. D was charged under Public Order Act 1986. (There were also pleas to drugs offences.) When V intended to give evidence, D offered £2,000 to an associate (whom he knew to have a history of non-fatal violence) as payment for setting light to the employer's home. D was unconcerned whether the employer or his family would be at home. He instructed his associate that he wanted petrol poured through the main entry of the property. D persisted in his requests and his associate reported the matter to the police. D had 13 convictions for 18 offences including violence and criminal damage. Held. The offence was motivated by revenge, was premeditated and involved planning. It was also committed on bail. V's family could have been seriously injured if not killed. Having already had an extended sentence imposed upon him, there is no doubt that the proper sentence is IPP. It is inappropriate to pass a consecutive term for the other offences. We start at somewhere in the region of 7 years. With plea discount that gives 6½ years. We raise that to 8 years for the drugs offences which he pleaded to. With double jeopardy, we arrive at 7 years, so **3½ years' IPP**, not 2 years 2 months determinate.

R v Hartley 2012 EWCA Crim 1722 D pleaded to reckless arson. She had spent a short time in a psychiatric unit before spending some time with her mother. She returned to her flat. A passer-by drove past D's house and saw that it was on fire. She stopped and approached D, who was standing outside holding a suitcase in one hand and her son in the other. When the passer-by said that her house was on fire, D replied, "Oh, is it?" The emergency services attended and all occupants were evacuated. D had remarked that a couple who lived above D may be in. In fact D had informed the wife of the couple that the building was on fire. When questioned by police, D said she had £15,000 worth of debts and had started the fire to enable her to claim on her insurance. She later told doctors that she had taken the drug MCAT on the day of the offence. The fire caused around £39,000 of damage. D, aged 24, had 25 convictions for 36 offences including supply, various offences of dishonesty and burglary with intent to commit GBH. D had a variable psychiatric history, ranging from normal to paranoid and delusional. She had been prescribed anti-psychotic medication, and a doctor's report stated that she had been suffering from a mental disorder at the time she committed the offence. She expressed remorse. Held. There were reports which indicated that D had made significant positive progress. To give D the support and guidance she would need over the next 12 months, enabling immediate release, **24-month community order** with supervision, not 3 years.

R v Maitland-Thomas 2013 EWCA Crim 1063, 2014 1 Cr App R (S) 22 (p 125) D pleaded (on the day of trial) to reckless arson. Police officers were alerted to a block of flats where D lived as someone had noticed there was smoke and a burning smell. The police could hear crying and a distressed voice coming from inside D's flat. Inside, D appeared to be dishevelled and distressed. The net curtain had been set fire to. As the officers spoke to D, she tried to set fire to other curtains in the room. D admitted acting in that way and the prosecution decided not to proceed with a separate count. Eight days later, D called 999 to report a fire at her home. The fire had taken hold and the flames could be seen coming from within the flat. There was £13,000 of damage caused. D had deliberately set fire to the sofa in her flat. D pleaded on the basis that she was depressed and heavily intoxicated at the time. A doctor's report stated she had recurrent depression and alcoholism. Another doctor's report expressed concerns that D had said she wanted to burn herself to death and that there was a pattern of suicidal ideation. It considered there was a risk of further fires. D did not accept responsibility for the fire, despite her plea. She was aged 55 and had no convictions. Held. The custody threshold was passed. The fire service was able to contain the fire but the risk to other occupants in the block was very real. The reason for the offence was not one of malice but due to D's depression aggravated by her alcoholism. The Judge was entitled to accept the view that there was a risk of D setting further fires. The risk to the lives of others was obviously considerable. The Judge's starting point of 5 years after a trial could not be criticised. That would have been higher if the offence [had been] motivated by malice, in the region of 8-9 years. With the late plea, **4½ years** was not manifestly excessive. The court recommended a 'strong supervision package' upon release to help D's release into the community.

See also: *R v Gask* 2011 EWCA Crim 1382 (Convicted of reckless arson (×3). On three occasions, set fire to the flat of an elderly man who had allowed D to stay with him, when he was homeless and addicted to drugs and alcohol. Nine elderly residents at risk. Committed whilst on bail. **8 years** was severe but not manifestly excessive.)

R v Thompson 2013 EWCA Crim 740 (Reckless arson. Tenant in block of flats. Knocked over his TV and smashed it. Then put newspaper on top of it and set it alight. It was smouldering as he walked away. Very little smoke damage. Mental health issues. Aged 35. Convictions for 45 offences since 1990 including criminal damage. Gravamen of the offence was the risk to others' lives, not the damage caused. Appropriate to start at 4 years. With full credit for the plea, 32 months was appropriate. There could be no complaint about **30 months**.)

R v Smith 2014 EWCA Crim 846 (Plea (full credit) to reckless arson. Mother and defendant argued. Repeatedly clicking a cigarette lighter. Set her curtain on fire to frighten her mother after their argument. Mother and young brother fled the property. Extensive fire and smoke damage. Three previous convictions but none for arson. Emotionally unstable personality disorder. Had engaged with mental health services. Exceptional case. **20 months suspended**, not 20 months.)

Att-Gen's Ref No 56 of 2015 2015 EWCA Crim 1442, 2016 1 Cr App R (S) 9 (p 57) (Reckless arson. At night in the middle of a terrace. Under influence of heroin and alcohol. After row with partner, made fire in wheelie bin outside house with wood etc. Window burnt and smoke damage in house. Previous convictions but none similar. Correct starting point 4½ years, so with plea **3 years** not 2.)

See also: *R v Wojcik* 2010 EWCA Crim 265 (**18 months**) *R v Sanders* 2010 EWCA Crim 1511 (**4 years**) *R v Walsh and Another* 2010 EWCA Crim 1580 (**18-month DTO** for D and **18 months** for T)

For a summary of the first case see the 10th edition of this book. If more old cases are required, see the 9th edition.

209.16   Reckless arson   Non-domestic premises

R v Bailey 2010 EWCA Crim 655 D pleaded (full credit) to reckless arson. D and his brother, X, pushed the door of an office block in the early hours. A security guard shouted at X and he moved away. The guard saw D open the lid of a wheelie bin and went back to the office to watch D and X on the CCTV. X used a lighter to set fire to the contents of a bin attached to the wall. D did the same to another bin. Both D and X then lit the contents of another bin each. After moving away, they returned to check if the fires were still lit and if not they reignited them. The fires were extinguished by the fire brigade. D was drunk. In interview D made admissions. D, aged 22, had convictions for ABH and one conviction for simple arson. The pre-sentence report said D showed little insight into his behaviour or the potential harm he could have caused. He posed a medium risk of reoffending and posed a high risk of harm to a named adult and to the general public. The psychiatric report said D was not suffering from any form of mental disorder, had suffered a difficult childhood and had learning difficulties. The offending appeared to be a repeating pattern of behaviour and D's risk of reoffending was medium-high. A further report said D was not a 'typical' arsonist and did not present a high risk of danger of reoffending. **3 years**, not 2 years' IPP.

R v Whale 2014 EWCA Crim 789 D pleaded (at the PCMH) to reckless arson. D had a very serious alcohol addiction. At about 2.50 am, he set fire to a wooden veranda in a restaurant. The restaurant was closed at the time but was immediately adjacent to a bar and nightclub containing between 100 and 150 people. There was a smoke machine in the club and it was hard to persuade people there was a genuine fire. The fire was spotted by a passing HGV driver who stopped and immediately alerted the manager of the bar. The fire had by then taken hold. D was seen by a taxi driver soon after the fire was set behaving in a strange manner. The taxi driver saw the fire and asked D if he had set it. D replied "I'm English and it is very, very cold." There were a number of compressed gas cylinders nearby which were beginning to activate as the fire heated. The premises needed to be completely rebuilt at an estimated cost of £436,000. CCTV showed that after setting the fire, D remained for some time to see that it was still burning. An hour or so before the fire, D attended a local police station and used a phone to report that he had been assaulted. He requested the help of the police and ambulance service. He suggested he should be put in prison and threatened to blow up the hospital. D was aged 54 and had a long list of previous convictions (antisocial offending of one kind or another), but none as serious as the instant offence. They were mostly for dishonesty and public order offences. There was a psychiatric report which noted that D had been drinking for 30 years, would spend £30 per day on alcohol and £10 per day on heroin or cocaine. The alcohol caused confabulation and problems with his memory. It was not clear whether D had any memory of setting the fire. A doctor considered that unless D addressed his alcoholism, there remained a risk of further arson and it was impossible to say when it would be safe for him to return to the community. Held. D deliberately targeted these premises and must have been aware of the risk to the building next door. Very many lives were endangered and extensive damage was caused. Despite D's troubled mental state…it did not reduce his culpability to any substantial degree, not least because it was his continued and voluntary consumption of alcohol that was causing his problems. There was no suggestion from the reports that D's mental responsibility was impaired by his alcoholism in a way that would justify any significant reduction in the sentence. **7½ years** after trial would have been perfectly justified, albeit at the top of the range. 10 years extended sentence (**5 years'** custody 5 years extended licence) upheld.

See also: *R v Thomson* 2011 EWCA Crim 3269 (Plea to reckless arson. Drunk. Set fire to lavatory paper in a bar's lavatories. Out of character. £100 damage. No evacuation of premises. Aged 23. Remorse. **6 months** not 18.)

209.17   *Reckless arson   Previous convictions for arson*

R v Bailey 2010 EWCA Crim 655 D pleaded (full credit) to arson being reckless as to whether life was endangered. D and his brother, X, pushed the door of an office block in the early hours. A security guard shouted at X and he moved away. The guard saw D open the lid of a wheelie bin and went back to the office to watch D and X on the CCTV. X used a lighter to set fire to the contents of a bin attached to the wall. D did the same to another bin. Both D and X then lit the contents of another bin each. After moving away, they returned to check if the fires were still lit and, if not, they reignited them. The fires were extinguished by the fire brigade. D was drunk. In interview D made admissions. D, aged 22, had convictions for ABH and one conviction for simple arson. The pre-sentence report said D showed little insight into his behaviour or the potential harm he could have caused. He posed a medium risk of reoffending and posed a high risk of harm to a named adult and to the general public. The psychiatric report said D was not suffering from any form of mental disorder, had suffered a difficult childhood and had learning difficulties. The offending appeared to be a repeating pattern of behaviour and D's risk of reoffending was medium-high. A further report said D was not a 'typical' arsonist and did not present a high risk of danger of reoffending. **3 years**, not 2 years' IPP.

See also: *R v Kettle* 2011 EWCA Crim 3108, 2012 2 Cr App R (S) 34 (p 191) (LCJ Plea to reckless arson. Set fire to pillow in his housing association flat. Crack cocaine addict. Drug-induced psychoses. £18-20,000 worth of damage. Previous convictions for reckless arson in 2004 (×2). Similar circumstances. Dangerous offender but life was wrong. Notional sentence of 12 years was too long. 10 years appropriate, less the plea, so **3 years 4 months' IPP**, not life with minimum term of 4 years.)

209.18   *Reckless arson   Relationship offences*

R v Black 2010 EWCA Crim 381, 2 Cr App R (S) 91 (p 583) D pleaded to reckless arson. He had a volatile marriage for 24 years and D and his wife, W, started sleeping apart. D reacted badly to this. W blamed alcohol and drugs. She went to friends nearby, and police were called to the house, where they found D drunk and throwing W's things about. Next day, W received a series of phone calls from D saying that he was going to set fire to the house and he was going to go up with it. W phoned 999, and a paramedic, P, found D sitting in a chair in the conservatory. D said that he had started a fire, and D was told to leave straight away. He refused to move. P found the fire in the living room, with flames 3-4 feet high. The sofa was well alight. D still refused to move, and was dragged out. D was aggressive. By now the living room was a mass of flames. The fire brigade arrived, and D claimed that he wanted to go back in to use a fire extinguisher. He smelt of alcohol and was again restrained. The damage to the living room was extensive and put at £3,000. D went to hospital and was thoroughly unco-operative. In interview he blamed the fire brigade but admitted that he had a serious alcohol problem. D was aged 62 and had 13 previous convictions, mostly for drugs and shoplifting. The risk of reoffending was assessed as high. The Judge described D: a) as aggressive, manipulative, deeply antisocial and acting in a controlling way, and b) as someone who well knew that the house was a semi-detached property. **5 years** was not manifestly excessive.

See also: *R v Ford* 2010 EWCA Crim 383 (Plea to reckless arson. Committed on Christmas Day when the woman he was seeing was with her mother. Mid-terrace house gutted. All her personal possessions destroyed. Previous conviction for murder. High risk of reoffending. After trial **12 years**. With plea 8 years, so **4 years' IPP** not 6.)

209.19   *Reckless arson   Series of fires started*
Example: *R v Brown* 2014 EWCA Crim 2015 (Convicted of reckless arson (×6) and simple arson (×10). Over 22 months 16 fires started, at domestic and commercial premises, increasing in seriousness and frequency. Two out of revenge. Five houses occupied, several with vulnerable people. Serious injury/death narrowly avoided. Shop targeted three times. Odd and disturbing features e.g. pretending to be a hero and taking photos. Very serious case so life with a **9-year** minimum term upheld.)

Arson Intending life would be endangered
209.20
Criminal Damage Act 1971 s 1(2)-(3)
Mode of trial Indictable only
Maximum sentence Life
Note: Cases of Offences Against the Person Act 1861 s 18 involving fire are listed in this section. Ed.

209.21   *Arson with intent   Judicial guidance*
Att-Gen's Ref No 68 of 2008 2008 EWCA Crim 3188, 2009 2 Cr App R (S) 48 (p 338) D pleaded to reckless arson. Following *R v Frankham* 2007 EWCA Crim 1320, 2008 1 Cr App R (S) 27 (p 132) in particular, the starting point for arson with intent is in the range of **8-10 years** after a trial.

209.22   *Arson with intent   Domestic premises with occupants*
R v Jan 2007 EWCA Crim 3223 J was convicted of causing a public nuisance and two counts of arson with intent to endanger life. In 1996 after his mother had expressed concerns about his mental health the victim, B, organised a Mental Health Act assessment for J. J became upset and agitated and began to make threats against those present, B, her colleague, Dr K and two police officers. The conclusion was that he was suffering from a psychopathic personality disorder for which it was not appropriate to order his detention, but he was arrested to prevent a breach of the peace. He was released without charge the following day. Shortly afterwards D wrote to B threatening that she would not 'get away with it'. He made an official complaint to her superior saying he would not forgive or forget as long as he lived. He then embarked on a series of official complaints against members of the assessing team and those who associated with them or supported them. This included a wide circle of people. Over the next few years D wrote over 6,000 pages of documents of complaint to the local Social Services. Mental health resource centres were flooded with calls from him. A very large number of different individuals were repeatedly harassed and subject to acts of vandalism. They received silent and threatening phone calls to their homes and places of work, and

threatening letters. Some were followed to their home addresses. Their property was damaged. Car tyres were slashed. Unwanted documents and services purported to have been ordered by them were delivered to their homes. Tradesmen and taxi drivers were sent to a number of different homes. D covered his tracks. He changed his identity, pretended to be people he was not, travelled in cars with false plates and changed addresses so that he was impossible to find. A social worker victim associated with B had his car set on fire twice. B was assaulted and required hospital treatment. On her discharge her car, parked outside her home, was set on fire. A petrol bomb was thrown outside the drive of the sector manager of a Healthcare Trust. Innumerable phone calls were made to other officials and councillors. One of these, a doctor, became the victim of a serious arson attack on her home when petrol was poured through or onto her front door and ignited. It caused serious damage to the property although she and her family escaped from the house. The house was uninhabitable for six months. The council leader received threatening angry calls in the middle of the night at his home address. D said to him, "I will fucking put an end to you. You need 24-hour protection." Following the fire at the home of the doctor D made a call to the council leader's wife saying that he had got back his arson bag and he asked for £75, saying, "If I go to hell you are coming with me". The threats continued. On arrest documents were seized which categorised into three orders of culpability lists of those described as forming 'The Grand Coalition' against him. He continued to threaten people including his own counsel during the trial. D had one previous conviction for assault in 1999. A psychiatric report recommended an Interim Hospital Order saying he would benefit from assessment in hospital. He said it was possible that D had a long-standing bipolar disorder. It referred to his persecutory ideation about various parties and said he was endeavouring to have D referred to a high-security unit. There were reports from two further psychiatrists before the Court of Appeal. One concluded that at the time of the offences D was suffering from an acute mental illness but he was at the time of the report free of symptoms of acute mental disorder. He recommended further psychological and pharmacological treatment. He described the risk of repetition of similar offences as low, as long as D stayed free of acute mental illness, which would be the case if he continued treatment. D refused to see the other psychiatrist or allow him to see his medical records. Based on paperwork, this second psychiatrist concluded that D suffered from a paranoid personality disorder. He said that the suggestion in the other report that D's condition had resolved through taking antidepressants of the same kind he was taking throughout the harassment campaign would only be credible if supported by firm and detailed evidence, which it was not. The evidence did not suggest that there had been any underlying change in his beliefs or self-justification for his actions. His campaigns were channelled into his appeal as his circumstances dictated. They have not ceased. The degree of dangerousness indicated by his previous actions speaks for itself. The psychiatrist could find no evidence that any effective intervention had occurred to lower his dangerousness. He recommended continuing treatment which could be carried out in prison. Held. The nature and gravity of the offences show that at the time he represented a serious danger to the public. The length of his campaign and the seriousness of his conduct lead to the conclusion that the danger to the public will remain for a period of time which it is impossible for us to assess. The offences were very serious. He has expressed no remorse. **Life** was right, with a **7½-year** minimum term.

Att-Gen's Ref No 24 of 2009 2009 EWCA Crim 1511, 2010 1 Cr App R (S) 23 (p 126) D pleaded to arson with intent to endanger life. She lived next door to V and his wife. They suffered an obsessive campaign of harassment by D's family and another family. D knew that V and his wife had had their front door set alight or petrol poured on it on a previous occasion and D knew it had upset them. D was charged with harassment and released on bail. She breached her bail conditions repeatedly. V and his wife considered they had no option but to move. They moved away and the police gave them a panic button. D was arrested for breach of bail and released. A week later D decided to exact revenge on V's wife for her being charged. She, under the influence of alcohol and a high dose of diazepam, filled a plastic washing-up bottle with petrol. D drove to V's secret address arriving at 9.50 pm. V saw D approach the house and activated the alarm. He opened the door to confront her and she started spraying his body with petrol. V seized her in a bear hug and she held a cigarette lighter in her hand trying to strike it, shouting, "I've got a fucking lighter. You're going up." Neighbours intervened and she continued to struggle fiercely, kicking and attempting to bite V. She continued to try to ignite the lighter and the petrol, shouting, "I'm going to fucking kill you". D was arrested and at the police station she said, "I wanted to kill him". A note was found in her pocket which read, "I'll be back". She admitted taking steps to disguise her features. D claimed V sprayed the petrol on himself, and her neighbours were conspiring against her. D was aged 35 with no convictions. She had a depressive illness with alcohol dependence. D had self-harmed on a large number of occasions. She had been a nurse and foster mother and had glowing references. Held. She planned her revenge with considerable care. She knew there were at least two people in the house and that people lived on either side. D did everything she could to set light to the property and to light V. The Judge placed too much weight on D's problems and not enough on the serious nature of the offence. For a not guilty plea 6-7 years, so **5 years** not 2.

R v Clark 2015 EWCA Crim 633 D was convicted of arson with intent. He pleaded to failing to provide a specimen. D left a public house in his car and collided with a wall which was part of an archway at the rear of some dwellings. V1 and her partner V2 were in their bedroom just above the car. D told them the car had broken down and said he would move it later. V1 accepted this. D returned half an hour later and set the car on fire. The flames appeared to be threatening their home. V2 received an injury to his eye. V1 and V2 had 9 months of anguish with insurers, builders and cleaners. V1 also needed counselling. Held. With the exceptional personal mitigation (not listed) 4 **years** not 5.

See also: *R v Pithiya* 2010 EWCA Crim 1766 (Convicted. Partner wanted to end relationship. Burnt carpet and damaged bed frame and covers. Assaultive behaviour to his partner and other women. **4 years' IPP** not 5.)

Old case: *R v Frankham* 2007 EWCA Crim 1320, 2008 1 Cr App R (S) 27 (p 132) (**7 years**) For a summary of the case, see the 9th edition of this book.

Note: All but one of these cases are old and should be approached with care. Ed.

209.23   *Arson with intent   Petrol/inflammable liquid used*

R v Clark-Webber 2009 EWCA Crim 514, 2 Cr App R (S) 95 (p 635) D pleaded (full credit) to GBH with intent. There was animosity between D and V, who was aged 15, relating to D's 1-year-old daughter. D approached V, who was with two friends, and pulled out a Lucozade bottle filled with white spirit. She threw the spirit over V and accused V of being intimate with her boyfriend. After a brief altercation D used a cigarette lighter to set fire to V's head saying, "You won't be pretty no more". V was now on the ground trying to extinguish the flames. V took off her top but that also caught fire. A man ran out of a house to help and took his shirt off to extinguish the flames, but extinguishing them proved difficult. V's bra melted into her skin and she lost consciousness. She came round screaming, "I'm going to die". V had severe burns to her face, neck, head and hands. She was treated for 11% burns, some partial, and some deep. V would bear the physical and emotional scars for the rest of her life as well as undergoing painful operations. D was aged 19, a single mother and of good character. Her partner was in custody for abusing her. D was pregnant, suffering from a mild reactive depression, and had tried to commit suicide. The Judge said the attack was determined and planned over several days to disfigure V because of jealousy. Held. V was clearly in immense pain. However, 13 years would have been appropriate if D had pleaded not guilty, so **9 years** instead.

Att-Gen's Ref No 24 of 2009 2009 EWCA Crim 1511, 2010 1 Cr App R (S) 23 (p 126) D pleaded to arson with intent to endanger life. She lived next door to V and his wife, the victims. The victims suffered an obsessive campaign of harassment by D's family and another family. D knew that V and his wife had had their front door set alight or petrol poured on it on a previous occasion, and D knew it had upset them. D was charged with harassment and released on bail. She breached her bail conditions repeatedly. V and his wife considered they had no option but to move. They moved away and the police gave them a panic button. D was arrested for breach of bail and released. A week later D decided to exact revenge on V's wife for her being charged. She, under the influence of alcohol and a high dose of diazepam, filled a plastic washing-up bottle with petrol. D drove to V's secret address arriving at 9.50 pm. V saw D approach the house and activated the alarm. He opened the door to confront her and she started spraying his body with petrol. V seized her in a bear hug and she held a cigarette lighter in her hand trying to strike it, shouting, "I've got a fucking lighter. You're going up." Neighbours intervened and she continued to struggle fiercely, kicking and attempting to bite V. She continued to try to ignite the lighter and the petrol, shouting, "I'm going to fucking kill you". D was arrested and at the police station she said, "I wanted to kill him". A note was found in her pocket which read, "I'll be back". She admitted taking steps to disguise her features. D claimed V sprayed the petrol on himself, and her neighbours were conspiring against her. D was aged 35 with no convictions. She had a depressive illness with alcohol dependence. D had self-harmed on a large number of occasions. She had been a nurse and foster mother and had glowing references. Held. She planned her revenge with considerable care. She knew there were at least two people in the house and that people lived on either side. D did everything she could to set light to the property and to light V. The Judge placed too much weight on D's problems and not enough on the serious nature of the offence. For a not guilty plea 6-7 years, so **5 years** not 2.

R v Ajmal 2010 EWCA Crim 536, 2 Cr App R (S) 92 (p 587) A week before his trial, D pleaded to arson and attempted arson intending to endanger life. At night the occupiers of a house heard a loud bang at their front door. They found outside a makeshift petrol bomb made of a bottle with a tissue in the neck. It had been lit but had failed to light the petrol. Two young children were in bed. Five minutes later D with an identical bomb attempted to set fire to a van belonging to F, the best friend of one of the occupiers targeted earlier. The fire, which caused £550 worth of damage, was put out. F was known to the police. D made denials. The Judge said that if the taper had stayed alight a few more seconds the whole house would have gone up. Held. That observation shows how wafer thin the distinction is between murder or manslaughter, the full offence of arson with intent where no one dies, and an attempted arson. These were targeted attacks. What lay behind this remains a mystery. Consecutive sentences were not appropriate, so 8 years not 9 for the house and 2 years concurrent, making **8 years** not 11.

Old case: *Att-Gen's Ref No 69 of 2005* 2005 EWCA Crim 3050, 2006 1 Cr App R (S) 130 (p 756) (**2 years**) For a summary of the case, see the 8th edition of this book.

Note: All these cases are old and should be approached with care. Ed.

210   ASSAULT ON A POLICE OFFICER

210.1

Police Act 1996 s 89(1)

Mode of trial Summary only

Maximum sentence 6 months and/or a £5,000 fine for offences committed before 12 March 2015 and an unlimited fine thereafter.[54] There are maximum fines for those aged under 18, see **14.38** in Volume 1.

Licensed premises Where an offence is committed on licensed premises, the court may prohibit defendants from entering those premises or any other specified premises

---

[54] Legal Aid, Sentencing and Punishment of Offenders Act 2012 s 85(1) and (4) and Legal Aid, Sentencing and Punishment of Offenders Act 2012 (Commencement No 11) Order 2015 2015/504

without the express consent of the licensee etc.[55] The minimum period is 3 months and the maximum period is 2 years.[56] Violent Crime Reduction Act 2006 s 65 and Sch 5 repeals these powers. The repeal and commencement are not expected soon.

210.2   Sentencing Council guideline

Assault Guideline 2011, see www.banksr.com Other Matters Guidelines tab This guideline applies to all offenders aged 18 and older. In force 13 June 2011.

STEP ONE Determining the offence category

page 19 The court should determine the offence category using the table below.

Category 1	Greater harm and higher culpability
Category 2	Greater harm and lower culpability, or lesser harm and higher culpability
Category 3	Lesser harm and lower culpability

The court should determine the offender's culpability and the harm caused, or intended by reference only to the factors identified in the table below (as demonstrated by the presence of one or more [factors]). These factors comprise the principal factual elements of the offence and should determine the category.

Factors indicating greater harm
Sustained or repeated assault on the same victim

Factors indicating lesser harm
Injury which is less serious in the context of the offence

Factors indicating lower culpability
Subordinate role in group or gang A greater degree of provocation than normally expected Lack of premeditation Mental disorder or learning disability, where linked to commission of the offence Excessive self-defence

Factors indicating higher culpability
Statutory aggravating factors: Offence racially or religiously aggravated Offence motivated by, or demonstrating, hostility to the victim based on his or her sexual orientation (or presumed sexual orientation) Offence motivated by, or demonstrating, hostility to the victim based on the victim's disability (or presumed disability) *Other aggravating factors:* A significant degree of premeditation Use of weapon or weapon equivalent (for example, shod foot, head-butting, use of acid, use of animal) Deliberately causes more harm than is necessary for commission of offence Leading role in group or gang Offender motivated by, or demonstrating, hostility based on the victim's age, sex, gender identity (or presumed gender identity)

210.3

STEP TWO Starting points and category ranges

Having determined the category, the court should use the corresponding starting points to reach a sentence within the category range below. The starting point applies to all offenders irrespective of plea or previous convictions. A case of particular gravity,

---

[55] Licensed Premises (Exclusion of Certain Persons) Act 1980 s 1(1)
[56] Licensed Premises (Exclusion of Certain Persons) Act 1980 s 1(3)

reflected by multiple features of culpability in step one, could merit upward adjustment from the starting point before further adjustment for aggravating or mitigating features.

Category		Starting point	Category range
1	Greater harm (serious injury must normally be present) and higher culpability	12 weeks' custody	Low-level community order to 26 weeks' custody
2	Greater harm (serious injury must normally be present) and lower culpability; or lesser harm and higher culpability	Medium-level community order	Low-level community order to high-level community order
3	Lesser harm and lower culpability	Band B fine	Band A fine to Band C fine

The table below contains a non-exhaustive list of additional factual elements providing the context of the offence and factors relating to the offender. Identify whether any combination of these, or other relevant factors, should result in an upward or downward adjustment from the starting point. In some cases, having considered these factors, it may be appropriate to move outside the identified range.

When sentencing Category 1 offences, the court should also consider the custody threshold as follows:

- Has the custody threshold been passed?
- If so, is it unavoidable that a custodial sentence be imposed?
- If so, can that sentence be suspended?

For the meaning of a medium-level and a low-level community order see **16.12-16.13** in Volume 1.

210.4   [Aggravating and mitigating factors]

Factors increasing seriousness
Statutory aggravating factors: Previous convictions, having regard to a) the nature of the offence to which the conviction relates and its relevance to the current offence; and b) the time that has elapsed since the conviction Offence committed whilst on bail *Other aggravating factors include:* Location of the offence Timing of the offence Ongoing effect upon the victim Gratuitous degradation of victim Failure to comply with current court orders Offence committed whilst on licence An attempt to conceal or dispose of evidence Failure to respond to warnings or concerns expressed by others about the offender's behaviour Commission of offence whilst under the influence of alcohol or drugs Established evidence of community impact Any steps taken to prevent the victim reporting an incident, or obtaining assistance and/or from assisting or supporting the prosecution Offences taken into consideration (TICs)

Factors reducing seriousness or reflecting personal mitigation
No previous convictions or no relevant/recent convictions Single blow Remorse Good character and/or exemplary conduct Determination, and/or demonstration of steps taken to address addiction or offending behaviour Serious medical conditions requiring urgent, intensive or long-term treatment Isolated incident Age and/or lack of maturity where it affects the responsibility of the offender Lapse of time since the offence where this is not the fault of the offender Mental disorder or learning disability, where not linked to the commission of the offence Sole or primary carer for dependent relatives

The court should then consider the following:
   a) other factors indicating a reduction, such as assistance to the prosecution
   b) reduction for a guilty plea
   c) totality, if sentencing for more than one offence
   d) compensation and ancillary orders

210.5   *Magistrates' Court Sentencing Guidelines*
Magistrates' Court Sentencing Guidelines 2011 Update page 209, see www.banksr.com Other Matters Guidelines tab The update repeats the main guideline. In the table indicating ranges and starting points, sentences exceeding the powers of the Magistrates' Court are replaced with 'Crown Court'.
For details about applying the guidelines, see the GUIDELINES chapter in Volume 1.

211   ASSAULT WITH INTENT TO RESIST ARREST
211.1
Offences Against the Person Act 1861 s 38
Mode of trial Triable either way
Maximum sentence On indictment 2 years. Summary 6 months and/or a £5,000 fine for offences committed before 12 March 2015 and an unlimited fine thereafter.[57] There are maximum fines for those aged under 18, see **14.38** in Volume 1.
Criminal Behaviour Orders Where a defendant has engaged in behaviour that caused or was likely to cause harassment, alarm or distress to any persons and a Criminal Behaviour Order will help in preventing the offender from engaging in such behaviour, the court may make this order.[58]
Football Banning Orders Where the offence was committed relevant to a football match and where there are reasonable grounds to believe that making a banning order would help to prevent violence or disorder at or in connection with any regulated football match, the court <u>must</u> make a Football Banning Order, Football Spectators Act 1989 s 14A and Sch 1 para 1.
Licensed premises Where an offence is committed on licensed premises, the court may prohibit defendants from entering those premises or any other specified premises without the express consent of the licensee etc.[59] The minimum period is 3 months and the maximum period is 2 years.[60] Violent Crime Reduction Act 2006 s 65 and Sch 5 repeals these powers. The repeal and the commencement of the new powers is not expected soon.

---

[57] Legal Aid, Sentencing and Punishment of Offenders Act 2012 s 85(1) and (4) and Legal Aid, Sentencing and Punishment of Offenders Act 2012 (Commencement No 11) Order 2015 2015/504
[58] Anti-social Behaviour, Crime and Policing Act 2014 s 22(1)-(4)
[59] Licensed Premises (Exclusion of Certain Persons) Act 1980 s 1(1)
[60] Licensed Premises (Exclusion of Certain Persons) Act 1980 s 1(3)

Sexual Harm Prevention Orders There is a discretionary power to make this order when it is necessary to protect the public from sexual harm.[61]

See also the OFFENCES AGAINST THE PERSON ACT 1861 s 18 *Police officers on duty as victims, Intent to resist arrest* para at **292.25**.

211.2 Sentencing Council guideline

Assault Guideline 2011, see www.banksr.com Other Matters Guidelines tab This guideline applies to all offenders aged 18 and older. In force 13 June 2011.

STEP ONE Determining the offence category

page 15 The court should determine the offence category using the table below.

Category 1	Greater harm and higher culpability
Category 2	Greater harm and lower culpability, or lesser harm and higher culpability
Category 3	Lesser harm and lower culpability

The court should determine the offender's culpability and the harm caused, or intended by reference only to the factors identified in the table below (as demonstrated by the presence of one or more [factors]). These factors comprise the principal factual elements of the offence and should determine the category.

Factors indicating greater harm
Sustained or repeated assault on the same victim
Factors indicating lesser harm
Injury which is less serious in the context of the offence
Factors indicating lower culpability
Subordinate role in group or gang A greater degree of provocation than normally expected Lack of premeditation Mental disorder or learning disability, where linked to commission of the offence Excessive self-defence
Factors indicating higher culpability
Statutory aggravating factors: Offence racially or religiously aggravated Offence motivated by, or demonstrating, hostility to the victim based on his or her sexual orientation (or presumed sexual orientation) Offence motivated by, or demonstrating, hostility to the victim based on the victim's disability (or presumed disability) *Other aggravating factors:* A significant degree of premeditation Use of weapon or weapon equivalent (for example, shod foot, head-butting, use of acid, use of animal) Intention to commit more serious harm than actually resulted from the offence Deliberately causes more harm than is necessary for commission of offence Deliberate targeting of vulnerable victim Leading role in group or gang Offender motivated by, or demonstrating, hostility based on the victim's age, sex, gender identity (or presumed gender identity)

---

[61] Sexual Offences Act 2003 s 103A as inserted by Anti-social Behaviour, Crime and Policing Act 2014 Sch 5 para 2

211.3

STEP TWO Starting points and category ranges

Having determined the category, the court should use the corresponding starting points to reach a sentence within the category range below. The starting point applies to all offenders irrespective of plea or previous convictions. A case of particular gravity, reflected by multiple features of culpability in step one, could merit upward adjustment from the starting point before further adjustment for aggravating or mitigating features, set out below.

Category		Starting point	Category range
1	Greater harm (serious injury must normally be present) and higher culpability	26 weeks' custody	12 weeks' to 51 weeks' custody
2	Greater harm (serious injury must normally be present) and lower culpability; or lesser harm and higher culpability	Medium-level community order	Low-level community order to high-level community order
3	Lesser harm and lower culpability	Band B fine	Band A fine to Band C fine

The table below contains a non-exhaustive list of additional factual elements providing the context of the offence and factors relating to the offender.

When sentencing Category 1 offences, the court should consider whether the sentence can be suspended.

For the meaning of a medium-level and a low-level community order see **16.12-16.13** in Volume 1.

211.4   [Aggravating and mitigating factors]

Factors increasing seriousness
Statutory aggravating factors: Previous convictions, having regard to a) the nature of the offence to which the conviction relates and its relevance to the current offence; and b) the time that has elapsed since the conviction Offence committed whilst on bail *Other aggravating factors include:* Location of the offence Timing of the offence Ongoing effect upon the victim Gratuitous degradation of victim Failure to comply with current court orders Offence committed whilst on licence An attempt to conceal or dispose of evidence Failure to respond to warnings or concerns expressed by others about the offender's behaviour Commission of offence whilst under the influence of alcohol or drugs Established evidence of community impact Any steps taken to prevent the victim reporting an incident, or obtaining assistance and/or from assisting or supporting the prosecution Offences taken into consideration (TICs)

Factors reducing seriousness or reflecting personal mitigation
No previous convictions or no relevant/recent convictions
Single blow
Remorse
Good character and/or exemplary conduct
Determination, and/or demonstration of steps taken to address addiction or offending behaviour
Serious medical conditions requiring urgent, intensive or long-term treatment
Isolated incident
Age and/or lack of maturity where it affects the responsibility of the offender
Lapse of time since the offence where this is not the fault of the offender
Mental disorder or learning disability, where not linked to the commission of the offence
Sole or primary carer for dependent relatives

The court should then consider the following:

a) other factors indicating a reduction, such as assistance to the prosecution,
b) reduction for a guilty plea,
c) dangerousness,
d) totality, if sentencing for more than one offence, and
e) compensation and ancillary orders.

211.5   *Magistrates' Court Sentencing Guidelines*
Magistrates' Court Sentencing Guidelines 2011 Update page 29, see www.banksr.com Other Matters Guidelines tab The update repeats the main guideline. In the table indicated ranges and starting points, sentences exceeding the powers of the Magistrates' Court are replaced with 'Crown Court'.

212   ASSISTING OFFENDERS/ENCOURAGING OFFENCES ETC.
212.1
1) Criminal Law Act 1967 s 4 (assisting offenders)
   Mode of trial On indictment
   Maximum sentence The maximum sentence depends on what the maximum sentence is for the offence that the defendant was assisting in.

When the maximum sentence for person being assisted:	The maximum sentence for the instant offence is:
Fixed by law (i.e. mandatory life in murder cases)	10 years
14 years	7 years
10 years	5 years
Other cases	3 years

Summary 6 months and/or a £5,000 fine for offences committed before 12 March 2015 and an unlimited fine thereafter.[62] There are maximum fines for those aged under 18, see **14.38** in Volume 1.

To determine whether the 14-year or 10-year level of sentence applies, it is necessary to exclude any uplift for the penalty for an offence which is dependent on the defendant having previous convictions.[63]

2) Serious Crime Act 2007 s 44-46
   s 44 (encouraging or assisting an offence)
   s 45 (encouraging or assisting an offence believing it will be committed)

---

[62] Legal Aid, Sentencing and Punishment of Offenders Act 2012 s 85(1) and (4) and Legal Aid, Sentencing and Punishment of Offenders Act 2012 (Commencement No 11) Order 2015 2015/504
[63] Criminal Law Act 1967 s 4(3)(b) and (c)

s 46 (encouraging or assisting offences believing one or more will be committed)
Mode of trial Sections 44 and 45 are triable in the same manner as the assisted offence. Section 46 is triable only on indictment.[64]
Maximum sentence Where the offence anticipated is murder, the maximum is discretionary life imprisonment. For all other offences anticipated the maximum is the same as the offence anticipated.[65]
See also the **PERVERTING THE COURSE OF JUSTICE/CONTEMPT OF COURT/PERJURY ETC.** chapter and for terrorist offences, see **TERRORISM** *Failure to disclose information/Assisting offenders* at **345.8**.

212.2   Judicial guidance
Att-Gen's Ref No 16 of 2009 2009 EWCA Crim 2439, 2010 2 Cr App R (S) 11 (p 64) LCJ D was convicted of assisting an offender. Held. Consider: a) the nature and extent of the criminality of the offender assisted, b) the nature and extent of the assistance provided, and c) the extent the interests of justice were damaged.
For more details about the case, see **212.5**.

212.3   Internet encouragement
R v Blackshaw and Others 2011 EWCA Crim 2312 LCJ In unconnected appeals, B pleaded to encouraging etc. offences believing one or more would be committed, contrary to Serious Crime Act 2007 s 46. S pleaded to encouraging etc. the commission of an offence, contrary to Serious Crime Act 2007 s 44. B and S used Facebook to post messages and create 'events' inciting local residents to engage in the rioting which had recently taken hold of their communities. In both cases, members of the public contacted the police and no one attended at the proposed meeting points, despite 47 people agreeing to attend S's event. S cancelled the event immediately before the police arrested him, with the suggestion that his motivation was that the police were searching for him. B was aged 21 and S aged 22. Held. We are conscious that no harm actually occurred. However, it is not accurate to state that neither had any adverse consequences. Some citizens were appalled at what they had read and some were put in fear. Deterrent sentences were entirely appropriate. Modern technology enables the incitement of many people in one step. Both were caught red-handed. **4 years** for both was appropriate.

212.4   Murder cases
R v Roberts and Mould 2008 EWCA Crim 59, 2 Cr App R (S) 59 (p 350) R pleaded to murder, and M, his father, pleaded to assisting an offender, both at the earliest opportunity. R's girlfriend phoned him from a party saying V was making advances towards her. R got a knife from his kitchen and went to the party. He spoke to his girlfriend, then went into the house, and after a very brief exchange of words stabbed V to the heart. The knife penetrated through to the backbone. There was no suggestion that V had threatened any violence against R. R went home and then to a friend's house. His father went to see him there the next morning and told him V had died. He took the clothes R had been wearing at the time of the stabbing and the knife and dropped them in a wheelie bin some distance away. R went to another area four days later but after discussions with his family including his father it was decided he should give himself up. His father drove him back and R surrendered to the police. M had advised him to make a full confession and he did. He made it plain from the start he intended to plead guilty whatever the state of the evidence. He said there had been no fault on the part of V. M tried to help the police by telling them what he had done and took the police to the wheelie bin but the items were not retrieved. R, aged 17, had some convictions, M had quite an extensive record but neither record was of real significance for sentencing purposes. They both felt sincere remorse. There were supportive letters and character references. Held. R was entitled to a significant and substantial discount from the starting point over and above that attributable to his plea. There were numerous

---

[64] Serious Crime Act 2007 s 55
[65] Serious Crime Act 2007 s 58

mitigating features, in particular the exceptional degree to which he acknowledged his guilt at an early stage. The correct minimum term for R was 9 years not 11. For M, he attempted to make amends for what he had done, encouraged his son to give himself up and make a full confession, and but for his admission the police would not have thought he had any hand in disposing of that evidence. His conduct is more understandable though no less wrong because it was the unplanned response to a traumatic situation involving his son. **12 months** not 18.

R v Khatab 2008 EWCA Crim 541, 2 Cr App R (S) 94 (p 530) D was convicted of assisting an offender, M, who had committed murder, by disposing of the murder weapon. D, who was a drug dealer, quarrelled with the murder victim, V. V demanded a payment of £10,000 from D with threats of violence. He bullied and slapped him. They parted near D's home. He arrived home in tears and told his two brothers, M and N, what had happened. N armed himself with a screwdriver, M with a stone pestle. All three left the house and the two brothers attacked V with their weapons. He sustained a serious injury to his head and died on the way to hospital from head injuries. D took the pestle off M and disposed of it. Two days later he went to the police and told them he was a drug dealer and had disposed of the pestle because it had blood on it. His trial was conducted on the basis that he had done these actions but that the prosecution had to prove M was guilty of murder or manslaughter, and that he had been aware of this at the time of disposing of the pestle, before they could prove his guilt. D, aged 23, had a number of previous convictions mainly for road traffic offences. He had been convicted in 2006 of perverting the course of justice and possession of a bladed article. He also had a conviction for obstructing the police. There were four character references. Held. Having regard to the way in which D conducted his defence he was entitled to a significant discount from the sentence which would have been appropriate had he maintained a steadfast plea of not guilty all along. Nevertheless he assisted an offender who was convicted of murder. **3 years** not 4.

R v Antonia 2012 EWCA Crim 1389 D was convicted of assisting an offender having claimed duress. Her co-accused and partner, S, was convicted of murder. D and S had been staying at V's flat. V had severe disabilities and would befriend street drinkers. S and D had an argument in the flat, and S punched D in the face. V intervened and S took a rounders bat from him and attacked him with it, causing skull and brain injuries in an extremely violent and sustained attack. S and D fled the area and changed their clothing. D instructed S to dispose of the murder weapon in a bin. D, aged 33, had 14 appearances for 28 offences including assault and possession of class A drugs. Held. S and D's relationship clearly centred [on] heroin and alcohol dependency. D deliberately and instinctively stood by her man. To D's credit, she helped the police considerably. **2 years** not 5.

See also: *R v Ramsey and Others* 2011 EWCA Crim 872 (Two counts. Late plea. Twice helped gang killers. Single mother. *Newton* hearing. Assisted police. 4½ years in all was tough but not too long.)

Old case: *R v Elfes* 2006 EWCA Crim 2799, 2007 1 Cr App R (S) 118 (p 727) (**5 years**) For a summary of the case see the 7th edition of this book.

212.5   *Robbery, firearms and drug supply cases*

R v Worthington-Hale 2010 EWCA Crim 1664, 2011 1 Cr App R (S) 64 (p 401) D pleaded on rearraignment to assisting an offender. There was a series of robberies carried out by S which involved the use of a firearm and a meat cleaver. There was press reporting and armed police attended D's address four days after a robbery in which the store owner was pistol-whipped. D initially told the police that there was no one in the house, but upon the police stating they wished to search the house, D alerted them to S's presence in the attic. He said: "He's in there. He'll kill me." The firearm used to assault the store owner had been purchased by D some months previously. The Crown sought to use this evidence against D. D, aged 36 at appeal, had convictions, but none relevant to the offence. Held. In view of the fact that [there was] no separate charge in relation to the gun, we must leave it to one side in approaching the question of the correct sentence. The correct approach was laid out in *Att-Gen's Ref No 16 of 2009* 2009 EWCA Crim 2439, 2010 2 Cr App R (S) 11 (p 64). Giving credit for the plea and considering the extent to which D actually assisted S, **2½ years** not 3½.

R v Lanphier 2012 EWCA Crim 731 D pleaded (on the day of trial) to encouraging an offence. B was interviewed by police in relation to an ongoing inquiry. B had apparently given the police information about what D had said when they shared a cell in prison. S apparently also provided information relating to the same inquiry. In another prison, he became friends with W. D wrote to W stating that he had been arrested on suspicion of witness intimidation in relation to S and B, and that W should 'do summat' about 'those grassing cunts'. W took it to mean that D wanted him to intimidate S and B, who were both serving prisoners at the same prison as W. He had no intention to carry out the request, and saw that the letter was passed to the authorities. D was arrested and gave a fanciful explanation of the purpose of the letter. D had a bad record, with convictions for significant violence, including section 47 and 20 (1999), section 18 and attempted robbery (2001), possessing a knife and ammunition (2006), battery (2009), possessing a knife (2010) and section 20 (2010). The Judge noted that D was "a very violent man" and that as W had a significant record for violence also, the step of asking for his help was not a hollow one. Held. The sentence imposed by the Judge was too high, given all the circumstances. **2½ years** not 3½.

R v Wickenden 2013 EWCA Crim 2505 D was convicted of assisting an offender. Three people came to his flat where he lived with his partner, P. They threatened to kill him and his family. D telephoned C, a friend, and was allowed to go and stay in his home.[66] C had a number of shotguns in a locked cabinet. A few days later, D and P returned to their home. By then, D had found the keys to the shotgun cabinet and taken one of the shotguns. It was an automatic weapon capable of firing three shots in quick succession. About one month later a number of people arrived at D's house. One of them banged on the door and demanded to speak to D. D and P did not answer the door and left through a side door. There was an altercation following which P shot and fatally wounded one of the men, V. D removed the shotgun from the scene and took it back to C's house. He did nothing to assist V, who lay dying in the street. C contacted the police and told them that D had confessed to taking the gun and had returned it to C. D and P were arrested and gave contradictory accounts of the shooting. D claimed that when the men arrived at his house, V forced him outside and beat him up. D had a large number of convictions, none of which were relevant, save for the fact that he had been convicted of possession of an offensive weapon. The Judge said that D had grossly exaggerated the threat posed by V, he had stolen the gun and loaded it, and although being assaulted by V, the assault was over by the time V was shot. Additionally, the Judge said the offence was aggravated by the fact that D did nothing to assist V and instead acted to assist P and to evade detection himself. Held. There was a letter from the prison commending D's behaviour whilst on remand. D was not peripheral to the offence but very central to it. How the weapon came to be at D's house was very relevant indeed. 5 years was a severe sentence but not manifestly excessive.

Old cases: *R v Robinson* 2007 EWCA Crim 3120, 2008 2 Cr App R (S) 35 (p 201) (**4 years**) *Att-Gen's Ref No 16 of 2009* 2009 EWCA Crim 2439, 2010 2 Cr App R (S) 11 (p 64) (**6 years'** detention was appropriate for the assisting offender counts, and **12 years** in all). For a summary of the first case see the 8th edition of this book and for the second case see the 9th edition.

212.6   *Corruption etc.*
R v McCarthy 2015 EWCA Crim 1117, 2 Cr App R (S) 47 (p 355) D pleaded at her PCMH to assisting an offender and misconduct in a public office. She had obtained a master's degree in criminal justice and in 2010 she qualified as a probation officer. D

---

[66] Although it does not explicitly say so in the judgment, the inference is that P also went to stay at C's address. Ed.

managed a cohort of high-risk offenders and had achieved some very encouraging results. One of her placements was S. He was addicted to crack and had spent 14 out of the last 20 years in prison. D worked tirelessly to assist S but became emotionally dependent on him. On a home visit, D provided S with a mobile phone. Shortly afterwards, S was locked out of his accommodation and D took him back to her flat for the night. She took S back to his accommodation in the morning. D then committed a burglary. Police investigated it and told D that S was wanted for it. D correctly started the process for the revocation of S's licence. When police asked D about the number of the phone she had given S, she said it was her phone and she had let S use it to phone his mother. This was a lie. The result of this was that the police did not seek to find S through his use of the phone. D's basis of plea was that the reason for this was not to help S but to avoid disciplinary proceedings. When D was away on holiday, she permitted S to live at her flat knowing he was still wanted by the police. A sexual relationship developed between them. During this time D committed four dwelling burglaries. When D appeared at the Crown Court D talked her way into the cells to speak to S. D was now aged 31. She lost her job and the relationship with S continued. Held. The seriousness lay in the period of time the offending persisted. S was a prolific offender and D harboured him when employed in a position of trust. Starting at 16-18 months was not inappropriate. **12 months** concurrent on each was not manifestly excessive.

Terrorism see the TERRORISM *Encouraging or assisting others to commit terrorism/ Soliciting to murder*

ATTEMPTS

Attempts are listed with the full offence except for murder, which is listed in the MURDER, ATTEMPTED, MURDER, CONSPIRACY TO ETC. chapter.

213   AVIATION OFFENCES
213.1
Various offences and penalties

213.2   *General principles*
R v Matlach 2005 EWCA Crim 2911, 2006 2 Cr App R (S) 1 (p 1) D pleaded to being drunk on an aircraft and common assault. The Judge said, "Travelling on an aeroplane places a special duty on passengers to behave. You are all confined in a tube in the sky and the safety of other passengers may well be put in jeopardy because a relatively small incident may have catastrophic consequences which may not always be foreseen." Held. This is the appropriate approach. Offences of being drunk on an aircraft, or similar offending, will always require condign punishment, especially for the reason that others must be deterred. Quite apart from the element of danger to the aircraft and the people on it, it is important to stress the effect on those immediately surrounding a drunken passenger in the confined space. Behaviour must be prevented by deterrent sentences.

213.3   *Drunk, Being*
R v Matlach 2005 EWCA Crim 2911, 2006 2 Cr App R (S) 1 (p 1) D pleaded at the Magistrates' Court to being drunk on an aircraft and common assault. He flew from Warsaw to London on a Boeing 757 the day after the 2005 London bombings took place. He started drinking before he boarded the flight. When on board he drank from a whisky bottle and spoke in Polish to the woman next to him. At times he was pleasant and at times aggressive. She was quite scared and he tried to kiss her face. When the food was served he took her drink without asking her but did ask her if she wanted him to do something to stop the plane from landing. She became very concerned. Speaking no English she had difficulty in asking for assistance. He asked her to buy further drink for him. She told him she was meeting her boyfriend and he said he would arrange for a gang to meet him and chop him to pieces. As the aircraft landed he said he would wait for her and get her. Before passengers were permitted to leave their seats he got up, took

his rucksack from the overhead locker and threw it at V while shouting at her. When she went to get her bag from the locker he pushed her forcibly in the chest causing her to fall back in her seat. He spat at her four times in the face and hair. He was unsteady on his feet and unruly with the ground staff. He was also abusive to the police. When sober enough to be interviewed he admitted consuming a bottle of whisky. He expressed remorse. The pre-sentence report said his fear of flying had been exacerbated by the London bombs and he used drink to escape his problems. He was attending Alcoholics Anonymous and his risk of reoffending was assessed as low. Aged 40, this was his first offence. The psychiatrist considered he suffered from a lifelong fear of flying which amounted to a phobia. He claimed he had no recollection of the flight. He received 6 months on each count consecutively. Held. A phobia cannot be an excuse. Because of the personal mitigation **6 months** concurrent instead.

See also: *R v Ator* 2011 EWCA Crim 769 (Pleas to being drunk in an aircraft, common assault (×2) and interfering with the duties of a crew member. During a flight, he was verbally abusive to staff and passengers. He bit a passenger who assisted the crew in restraining him. Aged 61. **6 months**, costs and compensation.)

See also the **Drunk** chapter.

213.4   *Endangering an aircraft or any person*
1) Civil Aviation Act 1982 s 61(1)(a) and Air Navigation Order 2009 2009/3015 Reg 137, 241(8) and Sch 13 Part D
(endangering the safety of an aircraft)
   Mode of trial Triable either way
   Maximum sentence On indictment a fine and/or 5 years. Summary a £5,000 fine for offences committed before 12 March 2015 and an unlimited fine thereafter.[67] There are maximum fines for those aged under 18, see **14.38** in Volume 1.
2) Civil Aviation Act 1982 s 61(1)(a) and Air Navigation Order 2009 2009/3015 Reg 138, 241(7) and Sch 13 Part C (endangering safety of any person or property)
   Mode of trial Triable either way
   Maximum sentence On indictment a fine and/or 2 years. Summary a £5,000 fine for offences committed before 12 March 2015 and an unlimited fine thereafter.[68] There are maximum fines for those aged under 18, see **14.38** in Volume 1.

R v Hussain and Miah 2008 EWCA Crim 1559, 2009 1 Cr App R (S) 65 (p 373) H and M pleaded to recklessly acting in manner likely to endanger aircraft. They had shone a laser pen at the cockpit of a police helicopter at night. The laser was so bright it meant that the pilot could not read his instruments or see out of the aircraft to navigate. He was forced to take emergency action. He turned the helicopter away from the laser beam but the defendants continued to shine the pen at the helicopter for several more minutes as the pilot manoeuvred. They ran away, discarding the pen. There was evidence of the great danger involved when night vision is lost, especially in the case of police helicopters, which often work at low altitudes. The use of this kind of laser caused the most trouble and distraction for pilots, and incidents of this sort have increased rapidly over the last three years. The defendants accepted that they had passed the laser pen between them. H, aged 21, had convictions for TDA, burglary, resisting arrest, attempting to obtain property by deception and two offences of criminal damage. M, aged 19, had convictions for assault with intent to resist arrest, burglary, theft, and criminal damage. Held. This case can be distinguished from *R v Voice* 2008 because in that case there was a legitimate reason for possession of the bright torch and the light fell on the aircraft through negligence. In this case the beam followed the aircraft even when the pilot tried to manoeuvre away. It was not a transitory moment but lasted for several

---

[67] Legal Aid, Sentencing and Punishment of Offenders Act 2012 s 85(1) and (4) and Legal Aid, Sentencing and Punishment of Offenders Act 2012 (Commencement No 11) Order 2015 2015/504
[68] Legal Aid, Sentencing and Punishment of Offenders Act 2012 s 85(1) and (4) and Legal Aid, Sentencing and Punishment of Offenders Act 2012 (Commencement No 11) Order 2015 2015/504

minutes. The two defendants are not law-abiding, hard-working citizens. Personal circumstances and mitigation would carry less weight in this case than it would in some others. **6 months'** imprisonment was the least that could be imposed.

R v Jafari 2010 EWCA Crim 2965 D was convicted of endangering the safety of an aircraft. When a helicopter landed unannounced on his property, he was said to have approached the helicopter aggressively and subsequently threw a rubbish bag at it whilst the rotor blades were in motion and took hold of the skid bar as the helicopter was lifting off. The pilot and passengers were alarmed and frightened. D, aged 58, was of effective good character and had glowing character references. Held. 12 months was manifestly excessive. **6 months** was appropriate.

R v Pitchers 2014 EWCA Crim 1350 D pleaded at the Magistrates' Court to entering an aircraft when drunk, criminal damage and being drunk on an aircraft. He boarded a plane at Heathrow bound for Australia. There were 477 passengers. The staff noticed D was drunk and he said he was suffering from depression and had left his medication in the hold. Because he was apologetic, the Captain agreed that the plane should take off. Three-quarters of the bottle of vodka he had was poured away by staff. Twenty minutes into the flight, D was aggressive with a passenger who wanted to remove a bag from the overhead locker. There was a tussle and D became aggressive and swore. The air stewardess was very frightened. A passenger came to her aid and D was restrained but continued to be aggressive. The passenger and the stewardess thought they would be assaulted. Five male crew members took over and took D to the business lounge where he became even more aggressive. He ripped a piece of wood from a cup holder and used it as a weapon. D shouted, swore and threatened to kill the crew. A doctor was found who advised D needed to be sedated. When the doctor mentioned D had a carpet burn, D said, "You're a condescending cunt". D was sedated and the aggression ended. The flight, which by then was near Germany, was diverted back to Heathrow. The cost of that diversion was £32,000. D was arrested and made frank admissions. D was aged 40 and had no convictions. For 10 years he had been his partner's sole carer and D was very badly affected when the relationship broke up. The Judge referred to the severe inconvenience to other passengers. Held. There was no significant violence. We start at 15 months, so with plea **10 months** not 13 in all.

Note: The lack of significant violence was irrelevant as he was charged with being drunk and criminal damage. Bearing in mind these incidents are every passenger's and crew member's nightmare, D seems to have been very fortunate. Ed.

Old cases: *R v Voice* 2008 EWCA Crim 953, 2009 1 Cr App R (S) 11 (p 54) (**conditional discharge**) *R v May* 2009 EWCA Crim 2204, 2010 1 Cr App R (S) 91 (p 589) (**6 months**) For a summary of the first case, see the 9th edition of this book.

213.5   *Endangering safety at aerodromes*
Aviation and Maritime Security Act 1990 s 1
Mode of trial Indictable only
Maximum sentence Life
Extended sentences This offence is listed in Criminal Justice Act 2003 Sch 15 and is not listed in Criminal Justice Act 2003 Sch 15B. The court may pass a 2012 extended sentence (EDS) if there is a significant risk of serious harm from future specified offences and either: a) the defendant has a Criminal Justice Act 2003 Sch 15B conviction (applicable only to defendants aged 18+), or b) the offence would justify a determinate sentence of at least 4 years.[69]
Sexual Harm Prevention Orders There is a discretionary power to make this order when it is necessary to protect the public from sexual harm.[70]
R v Lees 2003 EWCA Crim 243, 2 Cr App R (S) 47 (p 306) D pleaded to disrupting services at an aerodrome with intent contrary to Aviation and Maritime Security

---

[69] Criminal Justice Act 2003 s 226A-226B as inserted by Legal Aid, Sentencing and Punishment of Offenders Act 2012 s 124
[70] Sexual Offences Act 2003 s 103A as inserted by Anti-social Behaviour, Crime and Policing Act 2014 Sch 5 para 2

Act 1990 s 1(2)(b) and criminal damage. He was a helicopter pilot who used Coventry airport for leisure purposes. A dispute arose between him and the airport director after the director had mistaken D for someone with a criminal record, wanted by the police. The director appreciated that he had made a mistake, but then he found that D's medical certificate had expired. D said that that was an oversight. However, the director excluded D from the airport. Five weeks later D used the airport to refuel. The director walked over and asked him to leave the airport forthwith or be escorted off. D took off in his helicopter, but instead of leaving he went and hovered at the intersection of the two operational runways. He radioed the control tower and said that he had a problem with the airport director and that the airport was closed. By hovering at the intersection of the runways he had indeed effectively closed the airport. Two jets waiting to take off had to taxi to a position just off the runway. He then positioned his helicopter to face one in an intimidating fashion. He caused another helicopter which was coming in to land to pull up short so as to avoid a collision. Advised that the director was in the control tower, D said, "I am coming to talk to him". He then flew the helicopter at speed towards the control tower, only pulling to a hover directly outside the fourth-floor window. He then flew in a loop around the control tower, over-flew the fire station and then circled the control tower again before coming back to hover by the fourth-floor window. People tried to calm him. However, he finally said, "I've had enough", before dipping the nose of the helicopter and powering it up. It came straight for the control tower, only pulling away at the last minute. The control tower was evacuated. This happened only a month after 11 September 2001. He flew off, but as he did so he clipped a glide path monitor which had to be recalibrated at considerable cost. After landing he was arrested. He was aged 42 and of exemplary character. He lived for flying. He had glowing references. The pre-sentence report said that D was struggling to come to terms with his loss of good character, and reoffending risk appeared low. A psychiatric report said he suffered with a moderate to severe post-traumatic stress disorder and depression. He was extremely remorseful. Held. Custody was justified. The seriousness was reflected in the fact that the maximum sentence for the offence is life. Accepting that any custodial sentence would lead to loss of his livelihood, coupled with remorse and the mitigation, **2 years** not 3.

213.6   *Security   Assisting others to defeat security at airports*

R v Gale 2008 EWCA Crim 1344 D pleaded to a count of fraud by abusing a position of trust for gain. He worked as office manager for DHL based at Heathrow airport. He said he was rung up by a man he had never met who asked him to accept goods in a public house car park between 5 am and 6 am and take them to the despatching agents for the airline at Heathrow. D said to him "That's more likely not to be honest" and accepted £100 for his services. The crate was to be sent to New York. He had prepared all the paperwork for the consignment showing the crate as containing 'empty plastic pots' with an address which he knew was false. He prepared a consignment security certificate saying that the consignment had been made secure in compliance with the requirements of the Department of Transport security criteria and may be carried on any aircraft. He delivered the goods as known cargo to the airline agents early in the morning. He must have provided HMRC with the necessary certificate to enable them to endorse the goods' acceptance with an authority for export. The crate was intercepted in New York and found to contain 500 kilos of khat, a drug, then legal in the UK but illegal in the USA. In the USA the street value was about $170,000. He initially lied to police, but then made frank admissions in interview. He said he knew the crate would be neither hand-searched nor X-rayed. He said he anticipated the crate would have had to go through explosives screening. D was aged 25 and had no previous convictions. He lost his job with DHL but had got another as a driver. There was no reason to suppose that he presented any particular risk of further offending. Held. D took an enormous risk that the crate might contain if not explosives contents with a real security risk. People who work in airports are peculiarly valuable to serious criminals who want to get contraband through security procedures. It is important that it should be known that those who take a bribe to allow illicit unchecked substances into the airport must expect to receive a short sentence of imprisonment. **8 months'** imprisonment upheld.

When the goods are prohibited or restricted goods, see the **IMPORTATION OF DRUGS** and the **IMPORTATION/ EXPORTATION OF PROHIBITED/RESTRICTED GOODS** chapters.

214   BAIL OFFENCES

214.1

Bail Act 1976 s 6 (absconding when released on bail)

The offence is tried at the court where the offence took place.

It is possible for the offence to be prosecuted as a contempt of court.[71]

Maximum sentence At the Crown Court (including a committal for sentence and where prosecuted as a contempt of court[72]) 12 months. Summary maximum 3 months and/or a £5,000 fine for offences committed before 12 March 2015 and an unlimited fine thereafter.[73] There are maximum fines for those aged under 18, see **14.38** in Volume 1.

Contempt of court The sentencing powers are listed at **305.1**. Appeals for contempt of court orders are at **305.1**.

Appeals Although a Bail Act 1976 offence is not a contempt, the Court of Appeal uses the contempt of court procedures for any appeal. Where there is an appeal for a Bail Act 1976 offence (with or without other appeals) the papers are sent to the full court. For the contempt of court appeals see **305.1**.

Consultation paper A consultation paper about 'breach of order including bail' is expected in the autumn of 2016.

214.2   *Crown Court statistics   England and Wales*

Failing to surrender to bail

Year	Age	Plea	Total sen-tenced	Type of sentencing %						Average length of custody in months
				Dis-charge	Fine	Community sentence	Sus-pended sentence	Custody	Oth-er	
2013	18-20	G	65	4.6	10.8	3.1	1.5	49.2	30.8	0.7
		NG	1	100	–	–	–	–	–	–
	21+	G	581	3.6	4.8	3.8	7.7	50.9	29.1	1.1
		NG	2	50	–	–	–	50	–	0.1
2014	18-20	G	61	2	3	2	7	57	30	0.8
		NG	–	–	–	–	–	–	–	–
	21+	G	544	3	6	3	5	52	32	1.0
		NG	4	.	25	.	.	50	25	not listed[74]

For explanations about the statistics, see page 1-xii. For statistics for male and female defendants etc., see www.banksr.com Other Matters Statistics tab

Procedure

214.3   *Committals for sentence*

Bail Act 1976 s 6(1) If a person who has been released on bail in criminal proceedings fails without reasonable cause to surrender to custody he shall be guilty of an offence.

(2) If a person who:

---

[71] Criminal Practice Directions 2015 EWCA Crim 1567 para III 14C.7

[72] *R v White and McKinnon* 2002 EWCA Crim 2952, 2003 2 Cr App R (S) 29 (p 133)

[73] Legal Aid, Sentencing and Punishment of Offenders Act 2012 s 85(1) and (4) and Legal Aid, Sentencing and Punishment of Offenders Act 2012 (Commencement No 11) Order 2015 2015/504

[74] Not shown as based on too few cases to be meaningful

a) has been released on bail in criminal proceedings, and

b) having reasonable cause therefore,[75] has failed to surrender to custody,

fails to surrender to custody at the appointed place as soon after the appointed time as is reasonably practicable he shall be guilty of an offence.

Bail Act 1976 s 6(6) Where a Magistrates' Court convicts a person of an offence under subsection (1) or (2) above the court may, if it thinks:

a) that the circumstances of the offence are such that greater punishment should be inflicted for that offence than the court has power to inflict, or

b) in a case where it [sends] that person for trial to the Crown Court for another offence, that it would be appropriate for him to be dealt with for the offence under subsection (1) or (2) above by the court before which he is tried for the other offence,

commit him in custody or on bail to the Crown Court for sentence.

214.4   *Court procedure*

Bail Act 1976 s 6(5) An offence under [Bail Act 1976 s 6(1) or (2)] shall be punishable either on summary conviction or as if it were a criminal contempt of court.

Note: The first alternative way of proceeding is the procedure in the Magistrates' Court and the second is the procedure in the Crown Court. The effect of this is that at the Magistrates' Court, the matter is dealt with like an ordinary offence with the magistrates being the finders of fact. At the Crown Court there is no need for a jury as the judge finds the facts and either finds the offence made out or not. Ed.

Bail granted by a court

Criminal Practice Directions 2015 EWCA Crim 1567 para III 14C.3 Where a person has been granted bail by a court and subsequently fails to surrender to custody, on arrest that person should normally be brought as soon as appropriate before the court at which the proceedings in respect of which bail was granted are to be heard. (There is no requirement to lay an information within the time limit for a Bail Act offence where bail was granted by the court.)

14C.4 Given that bail was granted by a court, it is more appropriate that the court itself should initiate the proceedings by its own motion although the prosecutor may invite the court to take proceedings, if the prosecutor considers proceedings are appropriate.

14C.5 [see **214.6**]

14C.6 If the Bail Act offence is adjourned alongside the substantive proceedings, then it is still necessary to consider imposing a separate penalty at the trial. In addition, bail should usually be revoked in the meantime. Trial in the absence of the defendant is not a penalty for the Bail Act offence and a separate penalty may be imposed for the Bail Act offence.

Conduct of proceedings

14C.7 Proceedings under Bail Act 1976 s 6 may be conducted either as a summary offence or as a criminal contempt of court. Where proceedings are commenced by the police or prosecutor, the prosecutor will conduct the proceedings and, if the matter is contested, call the evidence. Where the court initiates proceedings, with or without an invitation from the prosecutor, the court may expect the assistance of the prosecutor, such as in cross-examining the defendant, if required.

14C.8 The burden of proof is on the defendant to prove that he had reasonable cause for his failure to surrender to custody (Bail Act 1976 s 6(3)).

Schiavo v Anderton 1986 83 Cr App R 228 An offence under Bail Act 1976 s 6 is not a contempt of court, although it may bear some relation to it in the sense that a person who commits it has acted in defiance of an essential condition of his bail, namely that he surrender so as to appear before the court at a place and at a time appointed.

---

[75] Parliament presumably meant 'therefor'.

214.5   Contempt of court, Dealing with offence as if it were a

Criminal Practice Directions 2015 EWCA Crim 1567 para III 14C.7 Proceedings under Bail Act 1976 s 6 may be conducted either as a summary offence or as a criminal contempt of court, see **214.4**.

Note: This direction can be reconciled with *R v Reader* 1987 below by inserting 'as if it were' just before 'a criminal contempt of court'. This would then be in line with Bail Act 1976 s 6(1), see **214.2b**. Ed.

R v Reader 1987 84 Cr App R 294 LCJ D was on bail and attended court. He left the building saying he was going to park his car. He did not return and went to Spain. The Judge said he was in contempt of court and D admitted that. He was sentenced to 2 years' imprisonment. The prosecution told the Judge that the maximum penalty was 1 year. The Judge said he was dealing with the matter as a contempt because it was an escape and not simply a breach of bail. The defence appealed saying it was not a contempt of court. Held. Because the defendant was not in lawful custody when he failed to return it was not an escape. The offence of absconding whilst on bail has never constituted a contempt. That is because of the wording of Bail Act 1976 s 6(5). 12 months, the maximum, not 2 years.

R v Lubega 1999 163 JP 221 D attended his trial and was late. The Judge said if he was late the next day he would regard it as a contempt. The next day D was 20 minutes late. D was given 28 days' imprisonment. Held. The Judge was not entitled to treat the conduct as a contempt, because the offence was contrary to Bail Act 1976 s 6. The effect of section 6(5) is not to convert an offence under Bail Act 1976 into a contempt but to provide a speedy and effective alternative method of dealing with such an offence. Therefore the Judge was not entitled to deal with the matter as a contempt.

Note: I interpret this as the court using the same procedure as a contempt when the offence isn't a contempt. The most important consequence of this is that a judge can make the finding and no jury is required.

214.6   When to sentence

Fail to Surrender to Bail Guideline 2007, see www.banksr.com Other Matters Guidelines tab para 24 The key principle is as soon as is practicable, even if the trial or other hearing for the offence is adjourned. The following factors are relevant: 1) when the proceedings are expected to conclude, 2) the seriousness of the original offence, 3) the type of penalty that might be imposed for both the bail and the original offence, and 4) any other relevant circumstances.

Whether or not the defendant is guilty of a bail offence should be determined as soon as possible. It will be central to the issue of whether bail should now be granted or refused. Even where the offence is denied, a trial is normally short. It should be held on the first appearance after arrest or surrender, unless an adjournment is necessary (for example, for the defence to obtain medical evidence). When there is a plea or finding of guilt, sentence should be imposed as soon as practicable. A key relevant circumstance is whether the substantive offence is to be adjourned, either for a pre-sentence report or for trial, and whether the remand is to be on bail or in custody. Where the defendant is remanded in custody, the sentencing options for the bail offence are limited. There will be occasions when it is more appropriate that all outstanding matters should be dealt with on one sentencing occasion. This may be where the totality of offending may affect the sentence.

Timing of disposal

Criminal Practice Directions 2015 EWCA Crim 1567 para III 14C.5 Courts should not, without good reason, adjourn the disposal of a Bail Act 1976 s 6(1) or 6(2) offence (failure to surrender) until the conclusion of the proceedings in respect of which bail was granted but should deal with defendants as soon as is practicable. In deciding what is practicable, the court must take into account when the proceedings in respect of which bail was granted are expected to conclude, the seriousness of the offence for which the defendant is already being prosecuted, the type of penalty that might be imposed for the Bail Act offence and the original offence, as well as any other relevant circumstances.

General matters

214.7   *How the breach undermines the administration of justice*

Criminal Practice Directions 2015 EWCA Crim 1567 para III 14B.1 The failure of defendants to comply with the terms of their bail by not surrendering, or not doing so at the appointed time, undermines the administration of justice and disrupts proceedings. The resulting delays impact on victims, witnesses and other court users and also waste costs. A defendant's failure to surrender affects not only the case with which he or she is concerned, but also the court's ability to administer justice more generally, by damaging the confidence of victims, witnesses and the public in the effectiveness of the court system and the judiciary. It is, therefore, most important that defendants who are granted bail appreciate the significance of the obligation to surrender to custody in accordance with the terms of their bail and that courts take appropriate action, if they fail to do so.

214.8   *Breach of conditions*

Note: This is not an offence, see Bail Act 1976 s 6(1)-(2) and 7(5). It is, however, an opportunity to reconsider bail, which, if it is refused, can mean the defendant stays longer in custody than if he was sentenced for a bail offence. Ed.

214.9   *Claims of being medically unable to attend*

Criminal Practice Directions 2015 EWCA Crim 1567 para III 14B.2 A defendant who will be unable for medical reasons to attend court in accordance with his or her bail must obtain a certificate from his or her general practitioner or another appropriate medical practitioner such as the doctor with care of the defendant at a hospital. This should be obtained in advance of the hearing and conveyed to the court through the defendant's legal representative. In order to minimise the disruption to the court and to others, particularly witnesses if the case is listed for trial, the defendant should notify the court through his legal representative as soon as his inability to attend court becomes known. 14B.3 Guidance has been produced by the British Medical Association and the Crown Prosecution Service on the roles and responsibilities of medical practitioners when issuing medical certificates in criminal proceedings. Judges and magistrates should seek to ensure that this guidance is followed. However, it is a matter for each individual court to decide whether, in any particular case, the issued certificate should be accepted. Without a medical certificate or if an unsatisfactory certificate is provided, the court is likely to consider that the defendant has failed to surrender to bail.

214.10   *Police station bail*

Bail granted by a police officer

Criminal Practice Directions 2015 EWCA Crim 1569 para III 14C.1 When a person has been granted bail by a police officer to attend court and subsequently fails to surrender to custody, the decision whether to initiate proceedings for a section 6(1) or section 6(2) offence will be for the police/prosecutor and proceedings are commenced in the usual way.

14C.2 The offence in this form is a summary offence although Bail Act 1976 s 6(10)-(14), inserted by Criminal Justice Act 2003 s 15(3), disapplies Magistrates' Courts Act 1980 s 127 and provides for alternative time limits for the commencement of proceedings. The offence should be dealt with on the first appearance after arrest, unless an adjournment is necessary, as it will be relevant in considering whether to grant bail again.

Fail to Surrender to Bail Guideline 2007, see www.banksr.com Other Matters Guidelines tab para 9 In general terms, the same approach to sentencing should be adopted whether the offence involves a failure to surrender to a court or to a police station since the legal obligation is the same. However, the harm that results from failure to surrender to a court will usually be greater than that resulting from failure to surrender to a police station and this will affect the assessment of the seriousness of an individual offence. A failure to attend results in police time being wasted and the course of justice being impeded. Potentially, it can also result in victims and witnesses being distressed and concerned about their safety and the ability of the system to protect the public and deliver justice. However, the circumstances in which such bail is granted are less formal than the grant of court bail and the history of the individual case should be examined. There may be less culpability where bail has been enlarged on a number of occasions and less harm if court proceedings are not significantly delayed.

214.11   Relationship with original offence

Fail to Surrender to Bail Guideline 2007, see www.banksr.com Other Matters Guidelines tab para 11 Failure to surrender to custody and the sentence imposed should be proportionate to the seriousness of the offending behaviour itself. The specific nature of the original offence may significantly affect the harm or likelihood of harm caused by the failure to surrender. Particular types of offence (such as violent or sexual offences) may have implications for public protection and safety, and the offender's failure to surrender might cause fear and distress to witnesses. Seriousness is not reduced automatically by subsequent acquittal of the original offence. Whilst it may seem harsh that a defendant before the court for an offence of which he is not guilty should be punished for the ancillary offence of failure to surrender during the course of the prosecution of that offence, both the culpability and the likely harm – delay, distress and inconvenience to witnesses, and additional costs – are the same. Moreover, one of the most serious effects of a Bail Act offence can be that a trial cannot take place because of the failure to surrender and it will often be invidious to expect a court to identify genuinely innocent defendants.

Sentencing for a Bail Act offence

Criminal Practice Directions 2015 EWCA Crim 1567 para III 14C.9 A defendant who commits an offence under Bail Act 1976 s 6(1) or s 6(2) commits an offence that stands apart from the proceedings in respect of which bail was granted. The seriousness of the offence can be reflected by an appropriate and generally separate penalty being imposed for the Bail Act offence.

For details about applying the guidelines, see the **GUIDELINES** chapter.

Guidelines case examples

214.12   Sentencing Guidelines Council guidelines

Fail to Surrender to Bail Guideline 2007, see www.banksr.com Other Matters Guidelines tab page 1 A prime objective of courts is to bring criminal proceedings to a conclusion as soon as practicable, and a rigorous and consistent response when offenders fail to answer bail is needed to help achieve this. When assessing the seriousness of an offence, the court must consider the offender's culpability and any harm which the offence caused, was intended to cause or might foreseeably have caused.[76] In assessing **culpability**, a court will need to consider whether the failure to surrender was intended to cause harm and, if so, what level of harm. In assessing **harm**, a court will need to consider to what extent the failure to surrender impeded the course of justice. 'Harm' includes not only the harm caused to individual victims and witnesses but the consequential drain on police and court resources and the wider negative impact on public confidence in the criminal justice system. The same approach to sentencing should be adopted whether the offence is committed contrary to section 6(1) or 6(2). However, section 6(2) offences require that there had been a reasonable excuse not to attend on the original date and so the degree of harm arising from the failure to attend as soon as reasonably practicable after that date is likely to be less. Accordingly, the seriousness of the offence is likely to be less also.

---

[76] Criminal Justice Act 2003 s 143(1)

para 6 Consider the immediate reason why the defendant failed to appear. This can range from forgetfulness or fear of the outcome of the hearing through to a deliberate act. Where the failure was deliberate, it will be relevant whether it was designed to disrupt the system to the defendant's advantage or whether the defendant simply gave no thought at all to the consequences. Some degree of harm, even if only a minor delay or inconvenience to the authorities, will always be caused when a defendant fails to surrender. The harm that the offence might foreseeably have caused[77] must also be taken into account. Where the defendant is to regain his or her liberty, there is the possibility of a non-custodial sentence. A community order, including an electronically monitored curfew requirement and, perhaps, a supervision requirement or an activity requirement, may be helpful in ensuring attendance at future court hearings.

Aggravating and mitigating factors

page 6 para 14 Aggravating factors: 1 The period of time for which a defendant absconds is also likely to influence the court when considering sentence. Whilst being absent for a long period of time will aggravate an offence, the fact that a defendant arrives at court only a few days, or even only a few hours, late, is not a factor that will necessarily mitigate sentence. In many cases, the harm will already have been done (e.g. the trial may have been put back, witnesses may have been inconvenienced and there may be an increased likelihood that witnesses will fail to attend at a future hearing). 2 Leaving the jurisdiction. 3 Actions designed to avoid the jurisdiction of the court such as changing identity and appearance. 4 Repeat offending. 5 Determined attempt to avoid the jurisdiction of the court/undermine the course of justice. 6 Previous relevant convictions and/or repeated breach of court orders or police bail.

para 18 Mitigating factors: 1 Prompt voluntary surrender might mitigate sentence where it saves police time. It may also be an indication of remorse. 2 Surrender initiated by the offender is. Surrender in response to follow-up action is not. 3 A misunderstanding (which does not amount to a defence) may be a mitigating factor but must be differentiated from a mistake on the part of the defendant, where the error must be regarded as his or her own responsibility.[78] 4 Being the sole or primary carer of dependent relatives may be personal mitigation when it is the reason why the offender has failed to surrender to custody. 5 Misunderstanding (when not a defence). 6 Failure to comprehend the requirements or significance of bail (when not a defence).

page 13 For a first-time offender convicted of absconding aged 18+ who pleaded not guilty. The type and degree of harm will affect where in the range the case falls.

Nature of failure and harm	Starting point	Sentencing range	
		Crown Court	Magistrates' Court
Deliberate failure to attend and/or interference with the administration of justice	14 days' custody	Community order (medium) to 40 weeks' custody	Community order (low) to 10 weeks' custody
Negligent or non-deliberate failure causing delay and/or interference with the administration of justice	Fine	Fine	Fine to community order (medium)
Surrenders late on day but case proceeds as planned	Fine	Fine	Fine

Additional aggravating factors: 1 Lengthy absence 2 Serious attempt to evade justice 3 Determined attempt seriously to undermine the course of justice 4 Previous relevant

---

[77] Criminal Justice Act 2003 s 143(1)
[78] *Laidlaw v Atkinson* 1986 The Times 2/8/86 QBD

convictions and/or breach of court orders or police bail. Additional mitigating factors: 1 Prompt voluntary surrender. Where not amounting to a defence: 1 Misunderstanding 2 Failure to comprehend bail significance or requirements 3 Caring responsibilities

For the meaning of a medium-level and a low-level community order see **16.12-16.13** in Volume 1.

214.13   *Magistrates' Court Sentencing Guidelines*
Magistrates' Court Sentencing Guidelines 2008, see www.banksr.com Other Matters Guidelines tab It is the same as the main guideline save the fines are defined.

page 31 The guidelines apply to the Magistrates' Court and to the Crown Court hearing appeals or sentencing for summary only offences.[79]

Nature of failure and harm	Starting point	Sentencing range
Surrenders late on day but case proceeds as planned	Band A fine	Band A to band B fine
Negligent or non-deliberate failure causing delay and/or interference with the administration of justice	Band C fine	Band B fine to medium-level community order
Deliberate failure to attend and/or interference with the administration of justice	14 days' custody	Low-level community order to 10 weeks' custody

For the meaning of a medium-level and a low-level community order see **16.12-16.13** in Volume 1.

214.14   *Defendant has a chaotic lifestyle*
Fail to Surrender to Bail Guideline 2007, see www.banksr.com Other Matters Guidelines tab para 19 The fact that an offender has a disorganised or chaotic lifestyle, which may be due to a dependency on drugs or alcohol, does not of itself reduce the seriousness of the offence. Depending on the particular facts, it may be regarded as personal mitigation.

R v Chowdhury 2013 EWCA Crim 943, 2014 1 Cr App R (S) 27 (p 168) D was found to have failed to surrender to bail without a reasonable excuse after a hearing. He was charged with harassment and making a threat to kill (×2). The complainant was his wife. He was bailed and failed to attend his trial. A warrant was issued for his arrest and he was at large for almost 13 years. He relocated from the south coast to the Leeds area and came to the attention of the police by virtue of his application for leave to remain. His wife's health had deteriorated and she was unable to give coherent evidence. The Crown offered no evidence but proceeded with the bail offence. Held. Where the failure is deliberate, it will be relevant whether it was designed to disrupt the system to the defendant's advantage. That was most certainly the case here. The offence was aggravated by the length of the delay and disruption to the administration of justice and the fact that this was a determined and successful attempt to avoid the jurisdiction of the court and undermine the course of justice. This was an extreme case of its kind, justifying a sentence beyond the guidelines. No fair trial was possible. **12 months** was not manifestly excessive, notwithstanding that it was the maximum sentence.

R v Spring 2013 EWCA Crim 1246 D pleaded (full credit) to theft and failing to surrender. He was arrested and bailed. D failed to answer his bail and was visited by police officers. He agreed to surrender the following day and did so. Held. For the bail offence, the likely explanation is that D gave no thought to the consequences. The delay caused was no more than one day. The guideline suggests a starting point of 14 days

---

[79] See page 15 of the guidelines.

where the failure to surrender was deliberate. 2 months was manifestly excessive. The degree of harm was truly minimal and there was moderate culpability. **7 days** for the bail offence **consecutive** to 12 months for the theft.

214.15   *Defendant has literacy or language difficulties*
Fail to Surrender to Bail Guideline 2007, see www.banksr.com Other Matters Guidelines tab para 21 Where an offender has literacy or language difficulties, steps should normally be taken by the police or the court to address this when bail is granted. Such difficulties may be mitigation (where they do not amount to a defence but contribute to the offender failing to surrender to bail) where potential problems were not identified and/or appropriate steps were not taken to mitigate the risk in the circumstances as known at the time that bail is granted.

214.16   *Defendant is late for hearing*
R v Archak 2011 EWCA Crim 2014 D was required to surrender to bail. He arrived at court about 30 minutes late. He had nine previous bail offences. The Judge commented that D had inconvenienced the court and interrupted a trial. He was given 2 months. Held. The Judge could have remanded D in custody on the substantive charges, which would then have counted against the resulting sentence. The Court understood the Judge's indignation, but **immediate release** not 2 months.

214.17   *Genuine mistake*
R v Davis 2011 EWCA Crim 2285 D pleaded (full credit) to theft, TDA, driving whilst disqualified and 10 counts of fraud. D had a long record. D failed to attend a hearing and a bench warrant was issued. He turned up the next day and said it was a mistake. Held. The fact he had requested the second day off from work supports his explanation of mistake. 7 days consecutive for the breach was not appropriate.
R v Randall 2014 EWCA Crim 71 D pleaded to failing to surrender. He appeared at the Magistrates' Court for a robbery charge. Conditional bail was renewed and a preliminary hearing was ordered to take place at the Crown Court some two weeks later. D failed to attend and the Judge issued a warrant. He was arrested at his mother's house the following afternoon. On arrest he told the officer that he thought he was in court the following day. When aged 18, D had two convictions for failing to comply with community orders. Held. D made a mistake, albeit as a result of negligence on his part. This type of offence is not dealt with by the guidelines. Even if the Judge had rejected D's account and found that he deliberately failed to attend, the starting point would only have been 14 days before discount for the plea. On the basis that this was a negligent failure to attend, the entire sentencing range in the guidelines fell below custody. The single day that D spent in custody from arrest to court appearance would have been sufficient. **1 day** not 30.

214.18   *Long absence*
R v Ball 2009 EWCA Crim 1265 D pleaded to dangerous driving and a bail offence. D was then aged 17. D then failed to answer his bail and was arrested over 3 years later. He had no convictions and four character references. His risk of reoffending was assessed as low. Held. His 18-month sentence failed to reflect the plea and his personal mitigation, particularly as he was only 17 at the time. The plea was worth 20-25% so with a maximum of 2 years, **12 months** consecutive to 6 months for failing to attend.
R v Baker 2011 EWCA Crim 150 D was convicted of two counts of obtaining property by deception[80] and failure to surrender to bail (**one year consecutive**). He absconded during his trial and 'laid low' for 18 months. D, aged 47, had significant previous convictions including robbery (7 years) and obtaining money by deception (similar to instant offence. 87-year-old victim. 4 years.) Held. This was a bad case. 6 years was appropriate for the deception. There was no problem with the total. The consecutive sentence for failing to surrender remains.

---

[80] This would appear to be a typo. Perhaps the offence was one of the Fraud Act 2006 offences. Ed.

R v Cinar 2011 EWCA Crim 524 D pleaded to failing to surrender to bail. D was charged with rape and absconded. Two years later he was arrested upon returning to the UK. D, aged 35, had no previous convictions. Held. This was a deliberate and serious offence and showed complete disregard to the criminal justice system and to the court. However, the justice of the case can be met by a sentence of **6 months**, not 9.

R v Stokes 2014 EWCA Crim 2772 D accepted a breach of bail. He had absconded before his trial in 2003. In 2014 he voluntarily surrendered. He had no previous convictions. The Judge gave him 10% for his plea because 'he had no option' but to plead. Held. There was nothing wrong with taking the maximum as the starting point. However, there should have been an allowance for voluntarily surrendering, so **8 months** not 10.

Old case: *R v Cockburn-Smith* 2008 EWCA Crim 3159, 2009 2 Cr App R (S) 20 (p 123) **(12 weeks)**

214.19   *Short absence*

Example: *R v Whitelock* 2014 EWCA Crim 204 (Convicted in absence of two ABHs. Didn't attend because he was offered employment and risked losing work if he did take the job. Arrested a few days later. Judge said offence had become all too prevalent. Aged 53. No material convictions. 18 months for the assaults and **2 months** not 3 months consecutive for the breach of bail.)

214.20   *Trial abandoned*

R v Howlett 2012 EWCA Crim 1031 D pleaded to failure to surrender to bail. He faced an indictment alleging sexual offences against a child. He travelled from his home in South Croydon to the court in Sheffield for the first day of his trial when the child gave evidence. He was granted conditional bail, requiring him to attend the following morning. He failed to attend. The trial was abandoned. A subsequent trial proceeded in his absence and he was acquitted. D continued to reside with his partner and their two children. When the police contacted his mother, D rang the police and as a result was arrested. The Court was told that the fear of being labelled a sex offender had driven him to become depressed and have suicidal thoughts. D, aged 26, had two previous convictions for criminal damage, but no custodial sentences and had never failed to surrender to bail before. Held. This was a Level 1 case. It was a serious offence. The potential for undermining the administration of justice is significant but **17 weeks** not 8 months.

214.21   *Voluntary surrender*

R v Stokes 2014 EWCA Crim 2772 D accepted a breach of bail. He had absconded before his trial in 2003. In 2014 he voluntarily surrendered. He had no previous convictions. The Judge gave him 10% for his plea because 'he had no option' but to plead. Held. There was nothing wrong with taking the maximum as the starting point. However, there should have been an allowance for voluntarily surrendering, so **8 months** not 10.

215   BENEFIT FRAUD

215.1

1) Social Security Administration Act 1992 s 111A and 114 (dishonest representation to obtain benefit/fraudulent evasions)
2) Tax Credits Act 2002 s 35 (fraudulently obtaining tax credit)
   Modes of trial All three offences are triable either way.
   Maximum sentences On indictment 7 years. Summary 6 months (for section 111A and 35 offences only) and/or a £5,000 fine for offences committed before 12 March 2015 and an unlimited fine thereafter.[81] For offenders aged under 18, see **14.38** in Volume 1.

---

[81] Legal Aid, Sentencing and Punishment of Offenders Act 2012 s 85(1) and (4) and Legal Aid, Sentencing and Punishment of Offenders Act 2012 (Commencement No 11) Order 2015 2015/504

3) Social Security Administration Act 1992 s 112 (false representations for obtaining benefit etc.)

Mode of trial Summary only

Maximum sentence 3 months and/or an unlimited fine.[82] For offenders aged under 18, see **14.38** in Volume 1.

Offences are also charged under Fraud Act 2006, or as false instruments and forgery. See also the **FRAUD AND FINANCIAL SERVICES OFFENCES** and the **TAX FRAUD AND DUTY EVASION OFFENCES** chapters.

Confiscation Where a defendant has a criminal lifestyle the court, once the confiscation proceedings are triggered (see **22.11** in Volume 1), <u>must</u> follow the Proceeds of Crime Act 2002 procedure. The list of 'criminal lifestyle' offences does not include the offences listed above or fraud offences.[83] For establishing a criminal lifestyle by another route see **22.48** in Volume 1.

Where social security benefits are obtained, the benefit figure is the whole amount obtained and that is not set off by what could have lawfully have been obtained, *R v Richards* 2005 EWCA Crim 491, 2 Cr App R (S) 97 (p 583), see **22.89** in Volume 1.

Fixed penalty There is a £50 fixed penalty for: a) incorrect statements (Social Security Administration Act 1992 s 115C(2)), b) failure to provide information (Social Security Administration Act 1992 s 115D(1)), and c) failure to notify (Social Security Administration Act 1992 s 115D(2)).[84]

215.2   Sentencing Guidelines Council guideline

Fraud, Bribery and Money Laundering Offences Guideline 2014, see www.banksr.com Other matters Guideline tab This guideline applies to Social Security Administration Act 1992 s 111A, Tax Credits Act 2002 s 35, Theft Act 1968 s 17, Social Security Administration Act 1992 s 112, Fraud Act 2006 s 1 and conspiracy to defraud. In force 1 October 2014.

STEP ONE: Determining the offence category

page 28 The court should determine the offence category with reference to the tables below. In order to determine the category the court should assess culpability and harm.

Culpability

The level of culpability is determined by weighing up all the factors of the case to determine the offender's role and the extent to which the offending was planned and the sophistication with which it was carried out.

Where there are characteristics present which fall under different levels of culpability, the court should balance these characteristics to reach a fair assessment of the offender's culpability.

Culpability
Culpability A – High Culpability
A leading role where offending is part of a group activity Involvement of others through pressure/influence Abuse of position of power or trust or responsibility Sophisticated nature of offence/significant planning
Culpability B – Medium Culpability
Other cases where characteristics for categories A or C are not present Claim not fraudulent from the outset A significant role where offending is part of a group activity

---

[82] Legal Aid, Sentencing and Punishment of Offenders Act 2012 s 85(1) and (4) and Legal Aid, Sentencing and Punishment of Offenders Act 2012 (Commencement No 11) Order 2015 2015/504

[83] Proceeds of Crime Act 2002 s 6 and 75 and Sch 2

[84] Social Security (Civil Penalties) Regulations 2012 2012/1990 paras 2-4

Culpability C – Lesser Culpability
Performed limited function under direction Involved through coercion, intimidation or exploitation

Harm – amount obtained or intended to be obtained

Category 1	£500,000–£2 million Starting point based on £1 million
Category 2	£100,000–£500,000 Starting point based on £300,000
Category 3	£50,000–£100,000 Starting point based on £75,000
Category 4	£10,000–£50,000 Starting point based on £30,000
Category 5	£2,500–£10,000 Starting point based on £5,000
Category 6	Less than £2,500 Starting point based on £1,000

215.3

STEP TWO: Starting point and category range

page 29 Having determined the category at step one, the court should use the appropriate starting point to reach a sentence within the category range in the table below. The starting point applies to all offenders irrespective of plea or previous convictions.

Where the value is larger or smaller than the amount on which the starting point is based, this should lead to upward or downward adjustment as appropriate.

Where the value greatly exceeds the amount of the starting point in Category 1, it may be appropriate to move outside the identified range.

Table 1

Social Security Administration Act 1992 s 111A, Tax Credits Act 2002 s 35 and Theft Act 1968 s 17

Harm	Culpability		
	A	**B**	**C**
Category 1 £500,000 or more	**Starting point** 5 years 6 months' custody	**Starting point** 4 years' custody	**Starting point** 2 years 6 months' custody
Starting point based on £1 million	**Category range** 4 years' to 6 years 6 months' custody	**Category range** 2 years 6 months' to 5 years' custody	**Category range** 15 months' to 3 years 6 months' custody
Category 2 £100,000 to £500,000	**Starting point** 4 years' custody	**Starting point** 2 years 6 months' custody	**Starting point** 1 year's custody
Starting point based on £300,000	**Category range** 2 years 6 months' to 5 years' custody	**Category range** 15 months' to 3 years 6 months' custody	**Category range** 26 weeks' to 2 years 6 months' custody
Category 3 £50,000–£100,000	**Starting point** 2 years 6 months' custody	**Starting point** 1 year's custody	**Starting point** 26 weeks' custody

Starting point based on £75,000	**Category range** 2 years' to 3 years 6 months' custody	**Category range** 26 weeks' to 2 years 6 months' custody	**Category range** High-level community order to 36 weeks' custody
Category 4 £10,000–£50,000	**Starting point** 18 months' custody	**Starting point** 36 weeks' custody	**Starting point** Medium-level community order
Starting point based on £30,000	**Category range** 36 weeks' to 2 years 6 months' custody	**Category range** Medium-level community order to 21 months' custody	**Category range** Low-level community order to 26 weeks' custody
Category 5 £2,500–£10,000	**Starting point** 36 weeks' custody	**Starting point** Medium-level community order	**Starting point** Low-level community order
Starting point based on £5,000	**Category range** Medium-level community order to 18 months' custody	**Category range** Low-level community order to 26 weeks' custody	**Category range** Band B fine to medium-level community order
Category 6 Less than £2,500	**Starting point** Medium-level community order	**Starting point** Low-level community order	**Starting point** Band A fine
Starting point based on £1,000	**Category range** Low-level community order to 26 weeks' custody	**Category range** Band A fine to medium-level community order	**Category range** Discharge to Band B fine

For the meaning of a high-level, a medium-level and a low-level community order see **16.12-16.14** in Volume 1.

215.4   Table 2
Social Security Administration Act 1992 s 112

	Culpability		
Harm	**A**	**B**	**C**
Category 5 Above £2,500	**Starting point** High-level community order	**Starting point** Medium-level community order	**Starting point** Low-level community order
Starting point based on £5,000	**Category range** Medium-level community order to 12 weeks' custody	**Category range** Band B fine to high-level community order	**Category range** Band A fine to medium-level community order
Category 6 Less than £2,500	**Starting point** Medium-level community order	**Starting point** Band B fine	**Starting point** Band A fine
Starting point based on £1,000	**Category range** Low-level community order to high-level community order	**Category range** Band A fine to Band C fine	**Category range** Discharge to Band B fine

For the meaning of a high-level, a medium-level and a low-level community order see **16.12-16.14** in Volume 1.

215.5   Table 3
Fraud Act 2006 s 1 and conspiracy to defraud

Harm	Culpability		
	A	**B**	**C**
Category 1 £500,000 or more	**Starting point** 7 years' custody	**Starting point** 5 years' custody	**Starting point** 3 years' custody
Starting point based on £1 million	**Category range** 5 to 8 years' custody	**Category range** 3 to 6 years' custody	**Category range** 18 months' to 4 years' custody
Category 2 £100,000– £500,000	**Starting point** 5 years' custody	**Starting point** 3 years' custody	**Starting point** 15 months' custody
Starting point based on £300,000	**Category range** 3 to 6 years' custody	**Category range** 18 months' to 4 years' custody	**Category range** 26 weeks' to 3 years' custody
Category 3 £50,000– £100,000	**Starting point** 3 years' custody	**Starting point** 15 months' custody	**Starting point** 36 weeks' custody
Starting point based on £75,000	**Category range** 2 years 6 months' to 4 years' custody	**Category range** 36 weeks' to 3 years' custody	**Category range** 26 weeks' to 1 year's custody
Category 4 £10,000– £50,000	**Starting point** 21 months' custody	**Starting point** 1 year's custody	**Starting point** High-level community order
Starting point based on £30,000	**Category range** 1 year's to 3 years' custody	**Category range** High-level community order to 2 years' custody	**Category range** Low-level community order to 26 weeks' custody
Category 5 £2,500– £10,000	**Starting point** 1 year's custody	**Starting point** High-level community order	**Starting point** Medium-level community order
Starting point based on £5,000	**Category range** High-level community order to 2 years' custody	**Category range** Low-level community order to 26 weeks' custody	**Category range** Band C fine-high level community order
Category 6 Less than £2,500	**Starting point** High-level community order	**Starting point** Low-level community order	**Starting point** Band B fine
Starting point based on £1,000	**Category range** Low-level community order to 26 weeks' custody	**Category range** Band B fine to medium-level community order	**Category range** Discharge to Band C fine

For the meaning of a high-level, a medium-level and a low-level community order see **16.12-16.14** in Volume 1.

215.6   *Aggravating and mitigating factors*
page 32 The table below contains a non-exhaustive list of additional factual elements providing the context of the offence and factors relating to the offender.
Identify whether any combination of these or other relevant factors should result in an upward or downward adjustment from the sentence arrived at so far.

Consecutive sentences for multiple offences may be appropriate where large sums are involved.

Factors increasing seriousness
Statutory aggravating factors Previous convictions, having regard to a) the nature of the offence to which the conviction relates and its relevance to the current offence; and b) the time that has elapsed since the conviction Offence committed whilst on bail ***Other aggravating factors*** Claim fraudulent from the outset Proceeds of fraud funded lavish lifestyle Length of time over which the offending was committed Number of false declarations Attempts to conceal/dispose of evidence Failure to comply with current court orders Offence committed on licence Offences taken into consideration Failure to respond to warnings about behaviour Blame wrongly placed on others Damage to third party (for example as a result of identity theft)
Factors reducing seriousness or reflecting personal mitigation
No previous convictions or no relevant/recent convictions Remorse Good character and/or exemplary conduct Serious medical condition requiring urgent, intensive or long-term treatment Legitimate entitlement to benefits not claimed Little or no prospect of success Age and/or lack of maturity where it affects the responsibility of the offender Lapse of time since apprehension where this does not arise from the conduct of the offender Mental disorder or learning disability Sole or primary carer for dependent relatives Offender co-operated with investigation, made early admissions and/or voluntarily reported offending Determination and/or demonstration of steps having been taken to address addiction or offending behaviour Offender experiencing significant financial hardship or pressure at time fraud was committed due to exceptional circumstances

215.7   *Suggested approach to the new guideline*
Note: There is nothing in the guideline to suggest it is intended that there should be a radical departure from the existing sentencing principles. I would suggest sentencers should: a) start with the guideline, b) consider the recent cases from the Court of Appeal to see if they are helpful, and then c) return to the guideline before deciding the appropriate sentence. Ed.

215.8   *Magistrates' Court Sentencing Guideline*
Magistrates' Court Sentencing Guideline 2008 (as amended), see www.banksr.com page 349 The section on benefit fraud of the *Fraud, Bribery and Money Laundering Offences Guideline 2014*, see www.banksr.com Other matters Guideline tab has been inserted.

215.9   *Compensation   Judicial guidance*
R v Stewart 1987 85 Cr App R 66 LCJ It may well be advisable as a first precaution for the court to enquire what steps the department proposes to take to recover its loss from the offender. Counsel for the Crown should be equipped to assist the court on this aspect of the matter.

215.10   *Cases   Less than £20,000 loss   Pre-guideline cases*
R v Gardiner 2012 EWCA Crim 1318 D pleaded to benefit fraud (×2). In 2005, he claimed Working Tax Credit and was working 16 hours per week. In April 2008, he stopped working, but continued to claim Working Tax Credit until August 2011. He received £14,820.94 to which he was not entitled. From April 2008, he was also in receipt of Council tax benefit and from September 2008, Housing benefit. He failed to declare his Working Tax Credit and received £5,508.18 and £1,800.59 respectively. The total fraudulently claimed was £22,129.71. D, aged 45 at appeal, had a number of convictions but only one for dishonesty, which was 13 years old. He had a production of drugs offence which was committed after these offences (suspended sentence). Held. This was not fraudulent from the outset, but was carried on over a very long time. A significant sum of money was received, [but] the amount of money was right at the bottom of the particular category in the guidelines. Immediate imprisonment was justified. 4 months concurrent on each, not 6.
R v Fiaz 2012 EWCA Crim 1823 D pleaded to benefit and Council tax fraud. He accepted voluntary redundancy with a package of over £40,000 and a pension paid monthly. In December 2008, he made a Jobseeker's Allowance application, claiming that neither he nor his wife were working and that their household had no other income nor savings over £16,000. That was fraudulent because he had over £40,000 in his bank account and was in receipt of £850 each month from his pension. Between then and February 2011, he received over £14,000 to which he was not entitled. At the same time, he continued to claim Council tax benefit, which was initially paid legitimately. D failed to notify the authority about his change in financial circumstances (namely the redundancy payment) and further received more than £1,900 to which he was not entitled. D, aged 59 at appeal, was of previous good character. Held. The Judge took too high a starting point. The correct starting point was 4 months. D was now responsible for caring for his ailing wife. **3 months**, not 6 months.
See also: *R v Chester* 2010 EWCA Crim 2147 (Total benefit fraud loss £850. Offences committed with assistance of his partner, a DHSS employee. Convictions for violence. **4 weeks** not 21 resulting in immediate release.)
R v Power 2012 EWCA Crim 2374 (Plea to failure to notify change of circumstances. Initial claim legitimate. Overpaid by £27,436. Aged 52. Previous good character. Considerable remorse. On medication for bipolar disorder. Family dependent on her. Had served 14 days. 28 days suspended, not 2 months.)

215.11   *Cases   £20,000 to £40,000 loss*
R v Begum 2011 EWCA Crim 2485 D pleaded (full credit) to dishonestly making a false statement (×2). D submitted dishonest benefit claims over a period of four years. £25,723 was claimed in Housing and Council tax benefit. The claims were fraudulent from the outset. The Judge imposed 6 months. It was argued that a sentence ought to have been suspended. D, aged 31, had no previous convictions. She had three children aged 11, 8 and 1. Held. This was not a case where D's imprisonment would force her children into local authority care. **6 months** cannot be said to be manifestly excessive.
R v Kireche 2012 EWCA Crim 1787, 2013 1 Cr App R (S) 91 (p 488) LCJ D was convicted of furnishing false information and failing to notify a change of circumstance, in relation to Housing and Council tax benefit. He had initially claimed Housing and Council tax benefit honestly, in 2002. In 2003, he declared a Lloyds Bank account and a Nationwide Building Society account. A claim form in 2005 referred to two accounts but only Nationwide by name. In 2005, 2006 and 2007, D completed a Housing and Council tax review form, each of which purported to show that he had no bank account, no savings or capital investments (other than the Nationwide account) and that he had no income. In fact, D had accounts with Lloyds, HSBC, HBOS and the Emirates Islamic Bank. He also had five credit cards and was involved in the purchase of property in Dubai. He had been on holidays and had made several trips to Dubai. He had also failed to disclose his property investments in Dubai. D had obtained at least £30,000 of benefit

to which he was not entitled between 2005 and 2010. D, aged 38 at appeal, had no convictions. Held. D's claims were not dishonest from the outset but as the Judge noted, he had shown a quite remarkable disregard for the criminality of what he had been doing. D's motive was plainly greed and not need. The fraud took place over a very long period of time and resulted in the obtaining of a very substantial amount of money. This was an extremely productive multiple fraud. 11 months was not manifestly excessive.

See also: *R v Baker* 2013 EWCA Crim 276 (Plea. Failed to notify a change of circumstances. Over a period of five years she was overpaid £12,900 Housing benefit and £30,200 Council tax benefit. Not fraudulent from the outset. Made another claim to switch benefit to Jobseeker's Allowance. Overpaid £6,250. Fraudulent from the outset. Total of nearly £50,000 falsely claimed. Aged 35. Good character. Three daughters aged 18, 15 and 13. Persistent dishonesty. Nothing wrong with starting at 36 weeks. Full credit. **24 weeks**.)

R v Blakeburn 2013 EWCA Crim 460, 2 Cr App R (S) 75 (p 500) (Made legitimate claims between 1995 and 2003. Failed to declare a change in circumstances. £23,310 in Housing and Council tax benefits and £51,706 in Income Support. Committed over an eight-year period. Repaying at a rate of £60 per month. Previous good character. Full credit. With the plea and long delay, **10 months** not 2 years 4 months.)

Old cases: *R v Lambert* 2010 EWCA Crim 234 (**22 weeks**) *R v Turner* 2010 EWCA Crim 2897, 2011 2 Cr App R (S) 18 (p 102) (**14 months**) Best ignored. Ed.

Post-guideline case

R v Siracusa 2015 EWCA Crim 268 D pleaded (full credit) to benefit offences. D started claiming Income Support in 1995 and Council tax benefit in 2002, both legitimately. She then inherited substantial sums of money in 2009 and 2010, totalling £155,000. D did not declare this and instead used it to buy properties. D's excuse was that the money did not stay in her account for very long. The total overpayment to D was £33,500 over a four-year period. The Judge described D's level of dishonesty as 'extraordinary' as there was no excuse for continuing to claim benefits. D, aged 58 on appeal, was the main carer for her 21-year-old daughter, who required help with almost all daily functions. D presented a 'remarkably low risk of reoffending'. Held. Immediate custody was appropriate. This fell into Category 4 with Category B culpability. **6 months** concurrent, not 18.

215.12   *Cases   £40,000+ loss   Pre-guideline cases*

R v McCormack 2011 EWCA Crim 1601 D pleaded (full credit) to seven counts of dishonesty relating to benefit fraud. In 1997 D legitimately claimed Income Support and Housing and Council tax benefits. From 2001, she lived with H as husband and wife. There were two children. He provided an average income of £34,406, and in 2003 she received just over £88,000 as a beneficiary from a will. Each year she completed fresh claims for Housing and Council tax benefits. She failed to declare that she lived with H as husband and wife and that their capital exceeded the prescribed limit. Over nine years, she dishonestly obtained £100,104. D pleaded on the basis that she was not living with H before March 2001 or after September 2008. She used the money primarily to pay off debts. D was aged 38 at appeal and of good character. Held. A claim for Income Support did not require the submission of fresh forms, whereas the Housing benefit and Council tax [benefit] did. For that reason the fraud fell between the two categories of: a) fraudulent from the outset and b) not fraudulent from the outset and [their subdivisions]. There were no aggravating features. Taking into account the sum, the plea and the powerful mitigation, **12 months suspended** with 60 hours' unpaid work, not 2 years.

R v Butler 2012 EWCA Crim 2184 D pleaded (full credit) to social security fraud (×3). Prior to 2004, she had been entitled to claim Income Support, Jobseeker's Allowance, Housing benefit and Council tax benefit. At the time, her partner, K, who was in full-time employment, began to live with her. D knew she was no longer entitled to claim the benefits. She continued to claim them all and was subject to one investigation but denied living with K. No charges were brought. There was a second referral in 2009 and surveillance evidence revealed that they were living together. She was interviewed in 2010 and was shown the surveillance evidence. Thereafter she declined to co-operate. The overpayments stopped in January 2011. The fraud was therefore carried on for 7 years and the 'total involved' was about £56,300. D was aged 44. Held. This was a multiple fraud over a significant period of time. D also lied to the authorities when she was first investigated. In mitigation, there was the plea and D's mental health. The Judge was right to suspend the sentence but 9 months was too long. 6 months suspended, not 9 months suspended.

R v Ekajeh and Others 2012 EWCA Crim 3125, 2013 2 Cr App R (S) 44 (p 291) E, K and F were convicted of conspiracy to defraud. All three were employed as fortnightly job review clerks at different job centres. E and K had been employed for about 10 years, F was employed for a much shorter period. Each was responsible for signing on customers who were claiming Jobseeker's Allowance and for carrying out job searches and reviews on their behalf. Each therefore had access to the DWP databases which stored vast amounts of personal data including names and addresses, dates of birth and NI numbers. K, E and F, and five others, were involved in a lengthy and sophisticated fraud in which large numbers of false benefits claims were submitted using the identities and details which K, E and F illegally accessed from the DWP database for that purpose. Over a period of almost two years, 1,562 false claims were made, claiming about £720,000. Of that sum, £107,000 worth of claims were successful and were paid to the conspirators. The sums claimed under the SSMG scheme for parents with newborn babies were paid into accounts set up by the conspirators, a number of which had been set up in the names of the stolen identities from the DWP database. E and F were also convicted of another count involving falsely claiming tax credits. This occurred over a period of 4½ years during which 205 claims were made for sums totalling just under £900,000. £170,000 was paid out. This was known as the tax credit fraud. E was also convicted of a different fraud. He accessed the DWP database and amended customers' genuine bank details so that payments would be made into the accounts controlled by the conspirators. This was known as the JSA fraud. E, aged 49 at appeal, was married with four young children and had no convictions. F was aged 35 at appeal and had seven convictions, the last of which was committed whilst on bail for these offences. One of his convictions involved fraudulent representation for gain. K was aged 48 at appeal. He had no convictions other than for driving matters in 2006. Held. The aggravating factors include: a) the gross breach of trust, E's breach of trust was more serious as he was sometimes entrusted with carrying out more senior roles as a deputy manager, b) the gross breach of trust occurred on a large number of occasions over a prolonged period of time, c) there were multiple frauds and high-value sums were targeted, d) the targeted money was public money intended for the neediest in society, e) the victims were not only HMRC and the DWP but also those who had had their identities stolen, f) their actions undermine public confidence in the protection of personal data and the public bodies to which such data is entrusted. For E, 5 years on the SSMG fraud, 5 years on the tax credit fraud, consecutive, and 12 months concurrent on the JSA fraud. The total sentence of **10 years** for E was not in error. E played a leading role and the aggravating features were plain. There was nothing wrong with consecutive sentences and the Judge could have made the sentence for the JSA fraud consecutive also. For F, there needed to be a reduction to reflect: i) the short period for which F was involved (6 months) and ii) the difference in scale of accessing information between E and F. Because of totality and parity with E, 3½ years for the SSMG fraud would be untouched, but 3 years not 4 for the tax fraud, consecutive. Total sentence for F, **6½ years**, not 7½. K's involvement was limited and the vast majority of his illegal access of the DWP database occurred on three days, giving rise to 27 claims totalling £13,500. He was only involved in the SSMG fraud. K stopped committing the fraud, not because he was caught but of his own volition. **4½ years** not 5½.

R v Hill 2013 EWCA Crim 121 D pleaded to three failing to notify offences at the Magistrates' Court. In 1999, as a single mother, she made a legitimate claim for benefits. Over 11½ years she obtained Income Support, Housing benefit, Council tax benefit and Jobseeker's Allowance. From March 2004, she had a partner living with her, and from April 2004 (so over 6 years 9 months) £55,000 was obtained unlawfully. The Judge considered the length of time and the amount obtained and started at the top of Category 3 in the guideline making 18 months. With plea he gave 12 months. Held. Considering *R v Rusher* 2012 EWCA Crim 2161, the proper starting point was 12 months making **8 months** with the plea.

R v Stone 2013 EWCA Crim 723 D pleaded (20% credit) to benefit fraud. He and his partner, P, claimed a number of benefits totalling £21,800+ on the basis that P was a single mother. In fact the two lived together. Forged documents and a considerable amount of deception were used, which was described as 'almost breathtaking'. D had no convictions. The Judge took 15 months as the starting point from the £20,000 to £100,000 category box. He reduced it to **12 months** for the plea. The defence argued the guideline should be applied proportionately so 15 months should equate with £60,000, the half-way figure between the two amounts. Held. We agree the table should be applied proportionately. However, because of the deceptions and the length of time the fraud was carried on for, 15 months as a starting point was not manifestly excessive.

R v Thomas 2013 EWCA Crim 1044 D pleaded (full credit) to conspiracy to defraud (×2) and money laundering. The names and addresses of 1,400 genuine people were used without their knowledge to make fraudulent claims for financial assistance by way of social fund or tax credits. Using these stolen identities, D made nearly 2,500 handwritten applications for grants and loans from the DWP social fund (count 1) and tax credits from HMRC (count 2). D controlled the accounts, which had been opened under the false names, into which the monies were requested to be paid. He then went to cash machines and withdrew the money. The offences were committed from January 2007 to October 2011. The value of the claims was £3.8m but the rate of return was low. The actual loss was close to £90,000. When arrested, he had over 20 post office account cards with PIN numbers written on the back. He also had further handwritten applications on him. Records showed that D sent money to Lagos. D, aged 38 at appeal, had no convictions in the UK or his native Nigeria. He was an illegal entrant and had never worked lawfully in the UK. Held. This was a benefit fraud. The enterprise was fraudulent from the outset. It was professionally planned and represented multiple frauds carried out over a significant period. There were very large sums claimed and identities stolen but this was not serious professional crime, it was more in the nature of a cottage industry. The guidelines do not apply but they plainly inform the sentencing process. The offences do not fit neatly into the guidelines. A substantial sentence was called for but a 10-year starting point was far too high. Starting at 6 years would fully represent the aggravating features. With full credit, **4 years** not 7.

R v Brindley 2014 EWCA Crim 1104 D pleaded to benefit fraud (×2). In 1999, she made a legitimate claim for benefits following separation from her partner. In 2003, she moved to her present address where she made declarations that she remained the single parent of two small children and that her circumstances had not changed. However, her partner had once again begun to reside with her at about that time. Between 2003 and 2012, she failed to declare that change in circumstances. As a result, she had claimed Housing benefit, Council tax benefit, Jobseekers Allowance and Income Support. She was not entitled to any benefits. The total sum obtained was just over £100,000. An investigation was conducted after it came to light that she lived with her partner, they had use of motor vehicles and that D kept a number of horses. It was common ground that the claims were not fraudulent from the outset but were carried out over a significant period of time. It was also common ground that the case fell within the second or third levels described in the guideline. Held. Due to the sum involved and the length of time over which the fraud was carried out, an immediate custodial sentence was fully justified and inevitable. The notes in the guidelines point out that the figure of £100,000 was taken as a starting point for the second category because the [Sentencing Guidelines Council] considered it unlikely that more than that could be obtained in a benefit fraud unless the offence was professionally planned. There was no suggestion of professional planning in this case. Given the mitigation, starting at 18 months was manifestly excessive. Starting at 12 months was appropriate. With the plea, **8 months**, not 12.

See also: *R v Blakeburn* 2013 EWCA Crim 460, 2 Cr App R (S) 75 (p 500) (Made legitimate claims between 1995 and 2003. Failed to declare a change in circumstances. £23,310 in Housing and Council tax benefits and £51,706 in Income Support. Committed over an eight-year period. Repaying at a rate of £60 per month. Previous good character. Full credit. With the plea and long delay, **10 months** not 2 years 4 months.) Old cases: Best ignored. Ed.

216   BIGAMY/MARRIAGE OFFENCES

216.1

1) Offences Against the Person Act 1861 s 57 (bigamy)
2) Perjury Act 1911 s 3 (false statements etc. with reference to marriage)
3) Civil Partnership Act 2004 s 80 (making, signing etc. false notices, declarations or certificates etc.)
4) Anti-social Behaviour, Crime and Policing Act 2014 s 121 (forced marriage).[85]

Modes of trial All the offences are triable either way.

Maximum sentences All the offences. On indictment 7 years.[86] Summary 6 months (except for section 80 offences which are non-imprisonable) and/or £5,000 fine for offences committed before 12 March 2015 and an unlimited fine thereafter.[87] There are maximum fines for those aged under 18, see **14.38** in Volume 1.

See also the **IMMIGRATION OFFENCES** and **PASSPORT OFFENCES** chapters.

216.2   *Crown Court statistics   England and Wales*
Bigamy Aged 21+

Year	Plea	Total sentenced	Type of sentencing %			Average length of custody in months
			Community sentence	Suspended sentence	Custody	
2012	G	2	50	50	–	–
	NG	0	–	–	–	–
2013 (Fem)	G	2	–	50	50	7.0
	NG	0	–	–	–	–
2013 (Male)	G	7	–	57	43	5.7
	NG	0	–	–	–	–
2014 (Fem)	G	3	–	–	100	–
	NG	0	–	–	–	–
2014 (Male)	G	5	–	80	20	–
	NG	0	–	–	–	–

[85] In force 16/6/14, Anti-social Behaviour, Crime and Policing Act 2014 (Commencement No 2, Transitional and Transitory Provisions) Order 2014 2014/949 para 5(b)

[86] Offences against the Person Act 1861 s 57 states the maximum penalty for that offence is 7 years' penal servitude. Perjury Act 1911 s 3 states that the maximum penalty for that offence is 7 years' penal servitude or 2 years' imprisonment. Criminal Justice Act 1948 s 1(1) provides that maximum sentences of penal servitude shall be construed as maximum terms of imprisonment.

[87] Legal Aid, Sentencing and Punishment of Offenders Act 2012 s 85(1) and (4) and Legal Aid, Sentencing and Punishment of Offenders Act 2012 (Commencement No 11) Order 2015 2015/504

For explanations about the statistics, see page 1-xii. For statistics for defendants aged under 21 and male and female defendants, see www.banksr.com Other Matters Statistics tab

216.3   Immigration controls, To evade   Judicial guidance

R v Lacko 2012 EWCA Crim 730, 2 Cr App R (S) 102 (p 600) D pleaded to conspiracy to facilitate breaches of immigration law. Held. It must be clearly understood that participating in sham marriages with a view to evasion of immigration control is a very serious matter. First, it is an abuse of the marriage ceremony itself and indeed a devaluation of the marriage state. Second, it is an abuse of immigration control. The maximum available sentence, it may be recalled, is one of 14 years' imprisonment. Those involved in offending of this kind can ordinarily expect an immediate custodial sentence.

216.4   Immigration controls, To evade   Cases

R v Olivieira and Others 2012 EWCA Crim 2279, 2013 2 Cr App R (S) 4 (p 18) D and N were convicted of conspiracy to facilitate the breach of immigration law. D was Dutch and so she benefited from free movement within the EU. N was Nigerian and was in the UK illegally, having, he claimed, arrived on a (now-expired) six-month visa of which there was no record. The marriage took place two days after D arrived in the UK. Over the next two years, N sent payments to D totalling £3,600. After the wedding, D applied to UKBA for leave to remain as the spouse of an EU national. Police attended N's address and found that D did not live there, but there were a number of documents, including a marriage certificate and wedding photographs, kept in a bag which could be used to substantiate a marriage if the need arose. Held. This was a single transaction and a ceremony in which each was a party. There was no sign of any organisation and no sign of facilitation of ceremonies for others. There was no exploitation. However, it was done for money. For both, **2½ years** not 3½.

R v Olivieira and Others Re C 2012 EWCA Crim 2279, 2013 2 Cr App R (S) 4 (p 18) C was convicted of facilitating a breach of immigration law. He was a Czech national living in Bradford. Over a period of 15 months he recruited five different Czech women and arranged for sham marriages to take place between them and Nigerian men who wanted to evade immigration controls. He was paid £4,000-£4,500 per time. He promised the women around £2,000, although he paid some of them as little as £500 and £900. Held. A sentence of 7½ years after a trial, amounting to 5 years after full credit, was deliberately severe. It recognised the element of exploitation and the sophisticated organisation and was clearly intended to send out a deterrent message to unscrupulous and callous commercial operators such as C. 5 years was very severe but the Judge was entitled to impose it.

See also: *R v Unuane and Uchuno* 2010 EWCA Crim 1167 (Pleas to bigamy etc. **5½ years** not 7)[88]

R v Olusanya and Sabina 2012 EWCA Crim 900, 2013 1 Cr App R (S) 32 (p 170) (Pleas (full credit) to facilitating a breach of immigration law. O and his partner entered the UK illegally. They had four young children. S, a Dutch national, flew to the UK twice in furtherance of the conspiracy. She obtained a National Insurance number. O married S. O's partner then took on the role of S, and took possession of her identity documents. S was paid £3,000. O and his wife claimed £8,200 in benefits. No forged documents. Assuming a false identity was just as serious as using false documents to effect an overstay or illegal stay. **2 years 8 months** for O, **16 months** for S upheld.)

Old cases: Best ignored.

216.5   Bigamy

R v Ballard 2007 EWCA Crim 751, 2 Cr App R (S) 94 (p 608) D was convicted of bigamy. After that verdict he admitted at the first opportunity being in contempt of court.

---

[88] This is not a simple case. Ed.

He married his first wife in 1999 and they separated after 6 months. In 2003, he went through a ceremony of marriage with a second woman. The bigamy was only discovered after he had separated from the second wife in 2005. In interview he said that he had heard through friends that his first wife had instituted divorce proceedings and made an assumption after three years that he had been divorced, but he made no attempt to contact her or her lawyers to confirm this. He had not signed any divorce paperwork. He accepted he had lied to the Registrar in 2003. The contempt was altering two doctor's sick notes provided to the Court. The doctor stated that he was unfit to attend work after a traffic accident but D altered them adding 'unfit to travel' so that he did not have to attend court. He said he did this because he was traumatised from the accident and could not face travelling in motor vehicles. D had some convictions but had never been to prison before. **Held.** The Judge was entitled to conclude that V had suffered distress as a result of the bigamy and that therefore the custody threshold had been crossed. However, it was only discovered after she had separated from him, which must have lessened her distress. The contempt of court richly deserved an immediate custodial sentence. It was deliberate forgery. The totality of the sentences was too long given that he had never been to prison before. **6 months** made up of **3 months** on each count to run consecutively, not 9 in all.

Old cases: *R v Mitchell* 2004 EWCA Crim 1516, 2005 1 Cr App R (S) 41 (p 193) **(9 months)** *R v Seed and Stark* 2007 EWCA Crim 254 LCJ (Immediate release.)

217   BLACKMAIL
217.1
Theft Act 1968 s 21 (blackmail)
Mode of trial Indictable only
Maximum sentence 14 years
Extended sentences Through no doubt an oversight, the draftsmen left this offence out of Criminal Justice Act 2003 Sch 15, so an extended sentence is not available.
Confiscation Where a defendant has a criminal lifestyle the court, once the confiscation proceedings are triggered (see **22.11** in Volume 1), _must_ follow the Proceeds of Crime Act 2002 procedure. Blackmail is a 'criminal lifestyle' offence.[89]
Restitution Orders There is power to make an order that the stolen goods etc. in the possession of the defendant or a third party be restored to the owner etc.[90]
Serious Crime Prevention Orders For Theft Act 1968 s 21 offences there is a discretionary power to make this order, when it would protect the public etc.[91]

217.2   *Crown Court statistics   England and Wales*
Blackmail Aged 21+

Year	Plea	Total sentenced	Type of sentencing %						Average length of custody in months
			Dis-charge	Fine	Commu-nity sentence	Sus-pended sentence	Custody	Other	
2013	G	99	–	–	3.0	22.2	72.7	2.0	30.6
	NG	26	–	–	–	23.1	76.9	–	56.8
2014	G	136	–	–	1	18	80	1	32.9
	NG	44	–	–	–	5	95	–	53.3

For explanations about the statistics, see page 1-xii. For statistics for defendants aged under 21 and male and female defendants, see www.banksr.com Other Matters Statistics tab

---

[89] Proceeds of Crime Act 2002 s 6 and 75 and Sch 2 para 9
[90] Powers of Criminal Courts (Sentencing) Act 2000 s 148(2) and Theft Act 1968 s 24(4)
[91] Serious Crime Act 2007 s 1 and Sch 1 para 11

217.3   Judicial guidance

R v Levison 2002 EWCA Crim 2580 LCJ D pleaded to blackmail. He extorted money from a publican by threats of violence to the publican and his staff. Held. We apply *R v Hoey and Sherwood* 1992 13 Cr App R (S) 177, which said, 'The crime of blackmail has two distinct components. There are the unlawful demand and the measures which accompany it. It follows therefore that any sentence passed for blackmail must take account of the means by which that blackmail is effected; in other words, the nature of the menaces. We would like to make it quite plain that blackmail in the form of a protection racket has got to be stamped out at once. This is blatant, arrogant lawlessness and the sooner it is realised that such conduct will always be severely punished by immediate terms of imprisonment the better for all concerned, not least those who might be tempted to indulge in it.'

R v Davies 2003 EWCA Crim 1868, 2004 1 Cr App R (S) 32 (p 209) Blackmail is a very nasty offence. A serious view will always be taken but its true gravity does of course vary considerably.

R v Arshad 2014 EWCA Crim 2485 This Court has emphasised the seriousness and nastiness of the offence of blackmail on a number of occasions, see *R v Hadjou* 1989 11 Cr App R (S) 29 [where the LCJ said blackmail is one of the ugliest and most vicious crimes in the calendar of criminal offences and it is perhaps due to the fact that the courts always impose severe sentences that one seldom, if ever, finds a person convicted for a second time for blackmail], *R v Christie* 1991 12 Cr App R (S) 540 [where it was said the offence of blackmail is regarded by the public, and rightly regarded, with loathing and contempt. The typical case of blackmail falls somewhere between robbery and simple theft in seriousness. It is clearly more serious than theft because of the mental anguish which is so often caused] and *R v Davies* 2003.

217.4   Bills, To enforce unreasonable

R v Williams and Stagg 2012 EWCA Crim 1483 LCJ W pleaded to conspiracy to blackmail, obtaining property by deception, engaging in an aggressive commercial practice and other offences. S pleaded to conspiracy to blackmail and obtaining property by deception (×3). With others, they were involved in a wheel clamping business which entered into contracts with local businesses and services. Vehicles were clamped and cash was demanded. However, motorists were never given the opportunity to pay the release fee before the fee escalated. A spotter vehicle was used which would inform the removal vehicle of the location of a parked car. The removal vehicle was dispatched before the owner of the car was aware their vehicle had been clamped. Signs detailing charges were usually partially or fully obscured from view. There was evidence to suggest that young women, particularly those with children, were targeted. The total sum extracted was £3,775. In one incident, a car was lifted by the removal truck with a young woman still inside. The clampers' van was then driven at the owner of the car as he attempted to prevent the van from leaving. The Judge noted that the men had taken steps to give an impression of propriety, for example the wearing of uniforms and badges. Held. The blackmail was arrogant, bullying and aggressive and involved the deliberate intimidation of victims by up to four men. S played a lesser role and had assisted the police. There was therefore a lesser degree of culpability. For the conspiracy, taking account of totality, for S, **2 years** not 3 and W, **3 years** not 4. Other sentences to run concurrently.

R v Swift 2014 EWCA Crim 2065 D pleaded (25% credit) to blackmail. D made numerous persistent demands of his parents for money, despite the fact that they were unable to support him. They handed D £6,820 over two years, typically giving him money three times a week. D had repaid only £75. D sent his mother, V, a text message purporting to be from a stepbrother of his partner. The message stated that D's friends had stolen £100 from D's partner and that, if it was not found, D would be in trouble. This message was re-sent twice and D then alleged that his partner's brother would not leave D's house until he was given the £100. Further messages were sent, including that

D was going to be sectioned and needed £1,000 a week for his rehabilitation. The message implied that D was in danger and had been kidnapped over a £125 debt. This same message was sent throughout the evening and into the next day with V and D's father being utterly terrified and reporting the matter to the police. Following a large police investigation, D was found safe and well and arrested. He denied sending the text messages in interview. D was aged 38 on appeal with good character. He said the £125 would have covered utility bills and rent due and that he would no longer ask for money. Held. Blackmail is a very nasty offence and a serious view will always be taken. Starting at 1 year not 2, **9 months**, not 18.

R v Cunningham and Others 2015 EWCA Crim 1884 C and his brother-in-law D pleaded on the fourth day of their trial to conspiracy to blackmail and J, C's son, was convicted of same offence. C and D were the prime movers in a tarmac fraud. There were 13 incidents. £168,000 was demanded and £61,850 paid. The group targeted small companies and provided sub-standard tarmac work. The work was often different from what had been agreed and the work often had to be done again by another contractor. The fees demanded were significantly inflated from the original quote. To enforce payment there were threats of serious violence and damage to property. The proceeds were laundered through a sophisticated arrangement of fake and legitimate companies using false identities. Police dismissed complaints as just civil debt issues. One victim, V, ran a company and he received a call from D who said he had heard there were pot holes in his car park. V said he would discuss it the next day. However on the same day, a 16 foot trench was dug across his car park and two men were there with tar laying equipment. D arrived with another man and claimed V had ordered the tarmac. V asked for the trench to be repaired and D became abusive and threatened to off-load tarmac in front of the entrance to the property. V refused to pay and men began tipping the tarmac. V then agreed they could finish the work. £2,740.50 was demanded. Numerous threats were made including that 20 gypsy families would park in the car park and they would cause £20,000 worth of damage. V was also told they knew where his properties were and V could not guard them all. There were also threats of violence and mutilation. Further, to avoid injury and damage, D was told that he would have to pay £10,000. The other incidents were similar and included particularly vile abuse to women. Before plea, the Judge indicated in the region of 15% plea discount might be made. C, aged 50, was treated as of good character. D, aged 46, and J, aged 27, had a joint conviction for fraud and conspiracy in Canada in 2010, involving a bogus paving company defrauding a church of over $5,000 (Canadian). The first incident was only weeks after they had arrived in the UK after their deportation. J also had a conviction for affray. C and D had character witnesses and medical issues. Held. The victims felt utterly helpless and beyond the protection of the law. The evidence was overwhelming. We start at between 8 and 9 years for C and D not 10. For C, with the health issue we move to 7 years and with plea **6 years** not 8 ½. For D, with the Canadian conviction and the health issue we move to 8 years. With plea, **6 years 9 months** not 8 ½. J was limited to the first incident and had done well in prison, so **4 ½ years** not 6.

Old case: *R v Havell and Miller* 2006 EWCA Crim 735, 2 Cr App R (S) 97 (p 633) (**3 years** and **2 years**) For a summary of the case see the 9th edition of this book.

217.5 *Debt collecting*

R v Norris 2010 EWCA Crim 689 D was convicted of aggravated burglary and blackmail. V was at home with a friend in his caravan. He saw D and U approach the caravan. D was carrying a bucket of petrol and some metal implements. V opened the door and D threw the contents of the bucket over him. It covered V from head to toe. V asked what this was about and was told that he owed the men £12,000. D lit a blowtorch and waved it at V, who handed the men £2,700 in cash which was all he had. V's friend was threatened by U with a butter knife and asked to leave. D told V if he did not receive the rest of the money soon he would gouge his eyes out, cut off his fingers and set light to him. D and U demanded V's mobile phone number, took an air rifle from the caravan and left. After reporting the incident to the police, V received phone calls from D who threatened to torture V and burn him and his caravan if he did not pay up. D also told V not to "fuck him about" as this was what D did for a living. Arrangements were made for V to leave the money under the steps of his caravan for a female to collect. D drove a female to the caravan. She walked towards the caravan and was stopped by police, who found she had a CS gas spray. D drove off but was stopped by police. He had a piece of paper with V's mobile phone number, and the butter knife and blowtorch were found at his home. D, aged 37, had one conviction for using threatening behaviour. The pre-sentence report said D posed a low risk of reoffending but as he did not appear to understand the effects of his behaviour he posed a high risk of harm to the public and V. D had references and a medical report in relation to his partner's autistic son. The prison report said D was an enhanced offender who posed no concerns or issues. The Judge said D's involvement was aggravated by his persistence and determination to threaten. Held. This was never a case for an indeterminate sentence. **10 years** not 6 years' IPP in all.

R v Currie 2011 EWCA Crim 600 D, with others, pleaded on rearraignment to false imprisonment. There was a dispute over a significant sum of money with V. V met D and the others at a pub. They travelled to a house. It is unclear whether this was with V's consent. There were discussions about money. A text message was sent to D by one of the co-defendants. It read 'shall I cover (V's) face'. The detention period was 6¼ hours. Whether V was able to leave during the period was unclear. The police were eventually alerted to his detention. D, aged 50, had two previous offences including theft. Held. The detention lasted some 20 hours and was not impulsive. The starting point was 42 months. So with full credit, **28 months**, not 40.

R v Fontan 2013 EWCA Crim 1904 D was convicted of blackmail (×3). D told AR that he was selling oil from a confiscated oil tanker, priced significantly under the market value, which would therefore generate a huge profit. AR assembled a group of buyers. D subsequently told AR that the deal had fallen through, that D had paid out £30,000 and that AR's share was £7,500. They later spoke on the phone and D threatened AR, saying that he would come round to his flat and 'knee-cap' him if he did not pay. D said that he and his minder would then take AR to a piece of land in Essex and bury him. AR believed these threats and was terrified. He borrowed the money and paid D. That was count 1. Counts 2 and 3 concerned a sum of money which had been loaned by DA, a businessman, to CT, his business partner, 10 years earlier. D told CT that the debt was now owed to him and that CT didn't want to owe him because he was "a nasty aggressive man". D then met CT and said that the debt had increased to £25,000 by compound interest. CT said he did not have the money. D replied that he would break CT's legs and bury him somewhere in Essex. CT borrowed £2,000 from his brother to make a down payment. Threats to rape his children and to insert barbed wire into his anus were made. CT then reported the matter to the police and D was arrested. D was aged 35 at appeal and had 12 convictions for 21 offences including threatening and abusive behaviour and criminal damage, but not blackmail. Held. The Judge was correct to say that the case possessed many features akin to robbery. This was an egregious case of its type and so a sentence above the reported authorities was justified. The threats were premeditated and vicious. The single Judge referred to the barbaric nature and extent of the threats made, the lack of remorse, the effect upon the victims and the need for a substantial punishment when refusing the application for leave. He also said that there could be no objection to consecutive sentences and a totality argument would not succeed. We agree. **11½ years** (7 years on count 1 and 4½ years on count 2) was not manifestly excessive.

R v Ford 2015 EWCA Crim 561, 2 Cr App R (S) 17 (p 177) D was convicted of blackmail. V was a drug user who purchased cocaine from D. D was a large well-built 33-year-old. V was a timid, submissive man. V would pay £1,000 in cash a month. By 2011, V ran into financial difficulties. On V's pay day, D would meet him and withdraw V's money from a cash machine. By mid-2012, D made V set up a standing order for

£1,000 a month. In November 2012, V lost his job. He paid the December payment and was then out of funds. Over seven months, D applied pressure on V, his father, F, and his sister. A series of highly threatening texts and phone calls followed. D threatened to smash or fire bomb their homes. He also threatened to break V's arms and legs. V was terrified. £12,000 was obtained. V and F had been significantly affected by D. D had about 40 convictions between 1996 and 2011. Eight were for harassment and threatening behaviour. During the trial he procured witnesses to lie. D put forward a wholly false 10-year service in army war zones when in fact he had been discharged after 75 days for stealing from his colleagues. The Judge said V was bled dry. Held. It is plain the Judge did not add to the sentence for his court room lies, [but it destroyed much of his mitigation]. D was also a significant drug dealer. The threats were over a long period. A severe sentence was required although no violence was used, so **7 years** not 8.

Note: Why D was not prosecuted for drug supply is not explained. Ed.

Old cases: *R v Temple* 2008 EWCA Crim 2511 (**3 years** not 4½) *R v Asare and Others* 2008 EWCA Crim 2516, 2009 1 Cr App R (S) 115 (p 644) (**3 years 2 months'** detention) *R v Razzaq* 2009 EWCA Crim 376, 2 Cr App R (S) 553 (A total of **11½ years**) *R v Mitchell and Kendrick* 2010 EWCA Crim 261 (**2 years 3 months**)

For a summary of the first case see the 7th edition of this book, for the next two cases see the 9th edition and for the last case see the 10th edition.

See also ***Kidnapping individuals for ransom/Debt collecting*** at **217.9**.

217.6 *Embarrassing material/behaviour*

R v Ayub 2011 EWCA Crim 423 D pleaded to blackmail. He and V, who had a sexual relationship, attended their employers' Christmas party. V had sexual intercourse with another man, and later returned to D's house, where they also had sexual intercourse. D subsequently learnt of V's encounter with the other man and sent threatening text messages. V had lent D £750. D stated he would not repay the money and that he wanted an additional £250. V was very fearful. Further text messages threatened V, stating it would be worse for her if she did not pay. D, aged 31, had one appearance for common assault. The instant offence was committed during the Suspended Sentence Order imposed for that offence. Held. **2½ years** not 3 years 4 months.

R v Iason 2014 EWCA Crim 1936 D pleaded (during his trial) to blackmail. D's father and V were friends and he had known D since he was young. V cared for his mother, who had cancer. She had been targeted by local youths. D, having been thrown out by his father and with no benefits, begged and harassed V for money over 12 months or so. D received £10-30 a time and over £1,000 in total. He was encouraged by his sister, with whom he now lived, to beg for both of them. On one occasion V threatened to call the police and D replied that he would, "tell them what you done when I was 16 then, when I come into your room." D referred to when V told D that he, V, had put a sexual video of himself on the Internet. D was aged 18 on appeal and with only a caution for theft. He had committed the offence out of desperation for money. D had an unhappy childhood, was allegedly sexually abused and had sought counselling for his mental health issues. He self-harmed to relieve his depression and was palpably anxious about custody. Held. This is the kind of offence that often called for a deterrent sentence, irrespective of the strength of any personal mitigation and the need for the offender to receive some kind of help and support in the community. However, D was sentenced on a somewhat wider basis than the agreed basis and insufficient weight was given to the fact that this was a first offence committed by someone of immaturity and emotional vulnerability. **6 months' YOI detention**, not 12.

R v C 2015 EWCA Crim 1519 D pleaded (full credit) to blackmail. D was aged 33 and married with three children. J, his wife's 14-year-old half-sister, was staying with D and they were together when J was sending messages to V, a 16-year-old boy from school. V sent J a photo of his erect penis, which D saw. D sent V a picture of himself saying he was J's brother and he would beat the shit out of him. D said he would report V, and V was apologetic. D referred to J being underage and told V he could go to prison for this.

V asked to make it up. D said that was not good enough and money might help to prevent the matter going to the police. V said he was skint and D said, "Police it is then". V pleaded for another chance. D said apologising was not enough and that V would go down for one picture. Various exchanges followed ending with '£75 in four weeks.' The exchanges lasted about 30 minutes. D was on bail for nearly a year and was barred from his own home and barred from unsupervised contact with anyone under the age of 16. (This is likely to have been because of a charge he was acquitted of. Ed.) Held. There was no sophistication or premeditation. With D's good character, we start at 12 months, so with plea, **8 months**.

Old cases: *R v A* 2007 EWCA Crim 245, 2 Cr App R (S) 62 (p 383) (**3½ years**) *Att-Gen's Ref No 67 of 2007* 2007 EWCA Crim 2878, 2008 1 Cr App R (S) 92 (p 549) (**4 years**) *R v M* 2008 EWCA Crim 1915, 2009 1 Cr App R (S) 88 (p 527) (**2 years 8 months**) *R v Clair and Clair* 2010 EWCA Crim 306 (**2 years 8 months**) For a summary of the first case see the 7th edition of this book, for the next two see the 9th edition and for the last case see the 10th edition.

217.7 Kidnap, Threats to
R v Singh 2014 EWCA Crim 1233 D pleaded to blackmail. He made calls to V, a lady in India, in which he demanded £5,000 from her brother, L, who lived in the UK. Threats were made that L's 3-year-old son would be kidnapped. Further calls were made to L using a different phone that was traced to D. D, aged 46, had no convictions and had been in the UK illegally for nine years. Held. Blackmail is an offence that strikes terror into the hearts of its victims, aggravated in this case by the nature of the threat against a child. Starting at 5 years not 6, with 20% credit, **4 years** not 5.

See also: *R v Taberer* 2011 EWCA Crim 1186 (Pleas to blackmail. Telephoned businessman threatening him and his family. Demanded £1m. Used false names. **4 years** not 8.)

217.8 Kidnapping individuals for ransom/Debt collecting   Judicial guidance
Att-Gen's Ref Nos 92-93 of 2014 2014 EWCA Crim 2713, 2015 1 Cr App R (S) 44 (p 323) D pleaded to and G was convicted of conspiracy to kidnap, false imprisonment and conspiracy to blackmail (×3). D threatened to kill V or slash V's face but D became more aggressive, demanding £2,600 that V owed him in drug debts. D and G also called V's family demanding payment and making further threats against V which they took extremely seriously, phoning the police. Later that day, V's family arranged to pay over a sum of money. Held. Clearly the correct approach in this case will be, first of all, to have regard to the kidnapping and false imprisonment…and then to make allowance for the considerable aggravation represented by the blackmailing demands. Relevant factors in accessing the gravity of cases of this type will include: the length of detention, the circumstances of detention, including location and any method of restraint, the extent of any violence used, the involvement of weapons, whether demands were made of others; whether threats were made to others, the effect on the victim and others, the extent of planning, the number of offenders involved, the use of torture or humiliation, whether what was done arose from or was in furtherance of previous criminal behaviour, and any particular vulnerability of the victim whether by reason of age or otherwise.

217.9 Kidnapping individuals for ransom/Debt-collecting   Cases
R v Hussain and Others 2012 EWCA Crim 2093 Ha, G, Ko and Ku pleaded to conspiracy to kidnap, conspiracy to commit false imprisonment, conspiracy to commit blackmail and section 18. Hu and F were convicted of kidnap, false imprisonment and blackmail. Plans were made to intercept V, the owner of a garage. They failed at their first attempt as V left the garage in a different car than was expected. R was with V and was in telephone contact with Ha. R asked V if they could test drive a vehicle. When they went outside, they were approached by Ku, G and Ha. He was shown what appeared to be a police warrant card and told to go with them. He refused and the men started to treat him roughly, restrained him and forced him into the car. V was told they

wanted £350,000 from his safe. V said he had no money and was driven to an address. He was slapped, threatened and tied up. He maintained he had no money and so a blanket was put over his head and boiling water was poured over his legs on more than one occasion. He screamed in pain and was jumped on. He was kept overnight and was in great pain. V's wife was telephoned and asked for £50,000. She telephoned the police and a kidnap unit was deployed. A girlfriend of V was also contacted and asked for money. D was burned with boiling water again, once on his arm and once on his back. She raised £7,000 and was told by the men she would be notified of a suitable location. Hu was an organiser but not present for the torture. He was in regular telephone contact with the others. V suffered burns over 5% of his body and will have scarring for the rest of his life. All of the defendants were aged between 20 and 24. None had convictions of any relevance except Ha, who had recently been released from a 4½-year sentence for robbery. Held. For Ha, starting at 18 years was appropriate, not 20. So with ⅓ for the plea, **12 years** not 13 years 4 months. For G and Ku, starting at 16 years was correct to reflect their good character. So **10 years 8 months**, not 12 years. For Ko, starting at 16 years, with 25% for the late plea, **12 years** not 13½. For Hu, **13 years** was appropriate, not 15. F did not carry out the kidnap and was only involved with the aborted attempted kidnap. **8 years** not 10.

R v Phillips and Baptiste 2013 EWCA Crim 841 P was convicted of false imprisonment. B was convicted of false imprisonment, ABH, possessing a firearm at the time of committing an offence and possession of a prohibited firearm. V was held against his will and demands for money were made. He was physically assaulted and threatened with a sawn-off shotgun. V received a phone call from P, arranging to meet. V said it was to buy an iPhone. P and B said it was all about drugs. The Judge thought that was almost certainly the case. P and B met V and got into a car. K, a co-defendant, was in the driver's seat. J, a co-defendant, got into the seat next to V and asked for money. K drove the car and when it arrived at its destination, V got out with the others. He tried to run off, notwithstanding that he had been threatened that he would be shot if he did so. V was tripped and fell to the ground. J and B punched and kicked V and at some point B hit V in the face with the gun. He was picked up and carried to a ground floor flat. He was threatened with a gun and told to make phone calls to get some money. He was further assaulted and was bleeding from facial injuries. At one point the gun was pointed at his foot. The safety catch on the gun was on. P had at various points played a more calming role. He sought to restrain the other when they were assaulting V. P had a conviction for common assault (2007) and two possession of drugs offences. B was aged 19 at the time of the offences and had no convictions. He had made a university application on the back of some credible examination results. Held. For P, who was acquitted of all counts in relation to the gun, 9 years was too long. With his leading role **7 years** was appropriate. For B, with his age and good character, **10½ years' YOI** was appropriate, not 12 years.

Att-Gen's Ref Nos 54-55 of 2013 2013 EWCA Crim 2067 R, S, L, W and K pleaded to false imprisonment and blackmail. V, aged 18, was telephoned and asked, and agreed, to meet W nearby. He walked there with a friend. W was there and they were asked to get into the rear of a car, which they did. R, who was sitting in the front passenger seat, rammed his seat backwards, trapping V. V was told that they wanted money from V's brother and that he would be held until they received it. S got into the rear of the car and V tried to escape. R punched V in the face. V contacted his brother and V told R and another that his brother was trying to obtain the money. Shortly afterwards, V's brother contacted the police. The car was driven to an address and W obtained two knives. They told V that if his brother tried anything, they would 'be ready for him'. V was taken from the car and placed in the boot. The friend was released. The car was driven to another location and V was taken from the boot to the rear of the car. The child locks on the doors were activated. The group spoke to V's brother again, threatening to cut off one of V's fingers. By that time, the phone calls were being recorded by the police. The group demanded £20,000 for V's return. V was taken by W to a flat belonging to L. S guarded

V. R did not enter the flat but remained in telephone contact. He later apologised to the group for not coming into the flat. V was detained for 7 hours in the car and 14 hours in the house. In the early hours, V's brother was told that V's body would be dumped in the river. S called V's brother and L was instructed to fetch a hot iron to torture V. V's brother was told that he was about to hear V scream whilst a hot iron was placed on him. L returned with pliers, an iron and curling tongs. W, L, K and S were present. The iron and tongs were connected to the electricity. V was then tortured with the iron and tongs, suffering 17 burns and abrasions to the ear, face, chest and arms. S and L told V he would be burned again and have some fingers cut off. V's brother could hear the screaming and threats that V would be stabbed were made. The burns were inflicted by W and S over half an hour. A neighbour complained to her landlord about the noise after which point the demand calls to V's brother stopped. V was dropped near a tube station and he walked home. Neither V nor his brother wanted to make a statement out of fear. V said he had lost his friends due to his fear of public contact. If he went outside, he would now conceal his appearance. S was aged 17 and had a conviction for possession of a bladed article and robbery. He had not served a custodial sentence. He had admitted his involvement at a comparatively early stage and claimed he was acting under direction. R was aged 21 and had convictions for robbery, conspiracy to commit robbery, section 20, four threatening behaviours, violent disorder and affray. He had not, however, served a custodial sentence. He was in breach of suspended sentences for the conspiracy to rob and section 20 offences. R was sentenced on the basis that he was involved in the early stages of the detention but not the torture. The Attorney-General appealed R and S's sentences and L and W appealed. Held. R did not enter the flat where V was held but had said sorry to the others for not doing so. R was fully involved with the demands made to V's brother. R had led the criminal enterprise with another and had personally made threats to V's brother. He was not to be sentenced for responsibility for the torture. For R, starting at 9 years, so with plea **6 years 9 months** not 4½ years with half of the suspended sentence activated making 7 years 3 months. S was involved at an early stage and was personally involved in the torture. Had he been an adult, the starting point would have been 12 years. Because of his age, the appropriate starting point was three-quarters of that, namely 8 years. With plea, **7 years' detention** not 3½. W's **15 years** and L's **9 years** were upheld.

Att-Gen's Ref Nos 92-93 of 2014 2014 EWCA Crim 2713, 2015 1 Cr App R (S) 44 (p 323) D pleaded to and G was convicted of conspiracy to kidnap, false imprisonment and conspiracy to blackmail (×3). D also pleaded to ABH. V had been selling drugs on D's behalf and owed him money. D sent V messages over several days chasing the debt, but V had avoided him. When D finally caught up with V, he was told to get into D's van, which he did. In the van, D shouted and struck V on the shoulder and to the head with a hammer, cutting V's forehead. V handed over £700 and then fled and hid in a shop. Later, V was in a fast food restaurant with a 'friend' who alerted D to V's presence. D and G escorted V away and kept him under their control. Initially, D threatened to kill V or slash his face but D became more aggressive, demanding £2,600 that V owed him. G's role was that of an 'enforcer' and, pretending to act as a restraint on D, he threatened to leave V alone with D unless the money was paid that day. Owing to continuing threats, V felt under duress to stay with D and G for the next ten hours or so, a lot of which time was spent at various pubs. V was extremely concerned for his safety throughout. D and G also called V's family demanding payment and making further threats against V which they took extremely seriously, phoning the police. Later that day, V's family arranged to pay over a sum of money but, suspicious of police involvement, V was abandoned in a car park. D was aged 31 and was on licence for two offences of possession of class A drugs with intent to supply (2005, 6½ years and 2012, 30 months). He was the organiser. G, aged 41, was heavily convicted with over 125 offences, mostly for violence or public disorder, the last being in 2013. He was also convicted of false imprisonment in 2004 where a victim was ransomed (7 years). The Judge asserted that the kidnap and false imprisonment were "made much worse by the blackmail demands of [V's] brother and father". Held. Clearly the correct approach in this case will be, first of all, to have regard to the kidnapping and false imprisonment...and then to make allowance for the considerable aggravation represented by the blackmailing demands. Relevant factors in accessing the gravity of cases of this type will include: the length of detention, the circumstances of detention, including location and any method of restraint, the extent of any violence used, the involvement of weapons, whether demands were made of others, whether threats were made to others, the effect on the victim and others, the extent of planning, the number of offenders involved, the use of torture or humiliation, whether what was done arose from or was in furtherance of previous criminal behaviour, and any particular vulnerability of the victim whether by reason of age or otherwise. The starting point was 10 years. For D, receiving 10% credit for the offences save for two blackmails, **9 years 9 months** overall, not 3 years 9 months (7½ years concurrent for the two blackmails, 9 months consecutive for the ABH and 9 years concurrent for the other offences). For G, **10 years concurrent**, not 5.

R v James 2015 EWCA Crim 339 D pleaded (at different times) to blackmail, false imprisonment and Class A drug supply. V owed C a £2,000 drug debt. V agreed to pay it off by selling drugs but instead consumed the drugs himself. The debt was then said to be £7,000. M and C visited V's address. They were angry and held V responsible for a burglary at C's house. V was told to get into a taxi and V was taken to C's house. As V walked in, D struck him with his hand on his face causing his nose to bleed. V was questioned about the burglary. D struck him again causing V to crouch on the floor. D punched him five to six times on the back of the head. D also placed his hand around V's throat and applied pressure. V was now told the debt was £14,000. V agreed to pay. After two hours, V was told to telephone his mother and meet her. The meet took place and C told the mother, M, that she should re-mortgage her house to repay the debt. An oblique threat was made about M's other son. M was told V would stay with C until the debt was paid. Further, if D was arrested, V would be killed. V was taken back to C's address. The next day, V managed to return home and learned that M had contacted the police. At D's address, police found 35.1 grams of cocaine (28% purity) and a dealers' list. D was aged 24 and had convictions for common assault and an offensive weapon and was on bail. The Judge found there were no weapons used and no serious injury. Held. Such violent, abusive and threatening behaviour will not be tolerated. A life was threatened. D was the lead player in the assault which was prolonged. The 8½-year starting point for the blackmail was not too high. **7 years** on the blackmail upheld. Because of totality we reduce the drug sentence making **9 years** not 11 in all.

See also: *R v Hang and Others* 2011 EWCA Crim 2089, 2012 1 Cr App R (S) 91 (p 550) (Pleas to conspiracy to blackmail and conspiracy to kidnap. Full credit. 18-year-old kidnapped. $2m ransom demanded. Tied up and detained for six days. Threatened, beaten, including with a screwdriver, and burned with cigarette butts. Carefully planned. Sophisticated. With plea, **12 years** not 13 years 3 months.)

R v Smickele and Others 2012 EWCA Crim 1470, 2013 1 Cr App R (S) 64 (p 354) (Late pleas (20% credit) to blackmail and false imprisonment. Gang of seven took a 14-year-old boy hostage and threatened his mother. Aged 15-18. Demanded £20,000. Held for 36 hours, during which he was beaten, suffered 16 deliberate cuts and forced against a hot pipe. Police intervention rescued the boy. Family decided to move abroad. For those of good character, **7 years** not 8. For the rest, **8 years** was not manifestly excessive.)

Old cases: *R v Serrant* 2007 EWCA Crim 717, 2 Cr App R (S) 80 (p 500) (**4 years**) *R v Shergill* 2008 EWCA Crim 451, 2 Cr App R (S) 81 (p 469) (**3 years**) *Att-Gen's Ref Nos 36-41 of 2009* 2009 EWCA Crim 2343, 2010 2 Cr App R (S) 9 (p 48) (8 years for B, **6½ years** for D-K, 6 years for N, **5½ years** for P, **4 years' detention** for K **and 4 years' YOI** for BB) *R v Yan and Lin* 2009 EWCA Crim 2686, 2010 2 Cr App R (S) 25 (p 157) (**11½ years** for Y and **11 years** for L) *R v Gisanrin* 2010 EWCA Crim 504 (IPP Yes) *R v*

Stephens 2010 EWCA Crim 911, 2011 1 Cr App R (S) 5 (p 27) (18-year starting point, **12 years, 10 years** and **8 years**) *R v Ahmed and Others* 2010 EWCA Crim 3133, 2011 2 Cr App R (S) 35 (p 217) (**9 years 9 months, 10½ years** and **8½ years**)
For a summary of the first case, see the 7th edition of this book, for the second case see the 8th edition, for the fourth case see the 9th edition and for the last case see the 10th edition.

217.10   *Supermarkets and retail stores*
R v Pearce 2000 2 Cr App R (S) p 32 D pleaded to nine counts of blackmail, three of ABH, causing an explosion likely to endanger life, doing an act with intent to cause an explosion likely to endanger life, unlawful wounding, two counts of possessing firearms with intent to commit an indictable offence, possessing explosives and possessing a prohibited weapon. He was the 'Mardi Gras bomber' who over 3½ years waged a campaign against Barclays Bank and Sainsbury's. In the Barclays Bank campaign he deployed 25 devices of six different types intending to produce explosions. Some were boxes designed to fire shotgun cartridges, others were modified gas cylinders filled with diesel fuel and a detonating charge and some were designed to fire pellets from a twin-barrel shotgun with a timer. One victim received minor injuries, one narrowly avoided injury to the eye, and a passing car was engulfed with flames with the driver managing to escape. The devices could cause serious injury and death. In the campaign against Sainsbury's he used a similar extremely ingenious mechanism involving shotgun cartridges. A man was injured. Another device went off in someone's car and one struck a man causing multiple puncture wounds. That victim had to end his athletic career. Others exploded in the street without causing injuries. He wanted very substantial sums of money from the bank and £500,000 from Sainsbury's. For each there was an ingenious method of payment to avoid the risk of being caught. He was aged 62 and needed psychiatric treatment. His life expectancy was 4-5 years. Held. A Hospital Order was not appropriate. **21 years** in all was entirely appropriate.
R v Dyer 2002 EWCA Crim 567, 2 Cr App R (S) 105 (p 490) D pleaded at the first opportunity to nine counts of blackmail and common assault. Not guilty verdicts were accepted for sending an explosive substance and causing an explosion. Both were with intent to cause GBH. D was short of money and repeatedly demanded £200,000 from Tesco. The money was to be withdrawn from ATMs by way of specially prepared loyalty cards. There were also messages posted in a local paper for communication with the store. After the first letter a post box was set alight. Later, two married pensioners in their seventies received a padded envelope in the post. It exploded creating a large flash and bang in the face of the wife. Smoke got into her eyes and she was in some discomfort for a time. Both were shaken. The device was made of shotgun cartridge powder and match heads. That was the common assault. Seven identical letters were delivered to Tesco customers in the area. The letter said anyone seen shopping in Tesco would be a potential target for bombs. The letters referred to bombs that had been sent to four addresses including the pensioners'. Three packages were found at the depot but hadn't been delivered because there was insufficient postage on them. Those packages contained a similar device to the one that went off. Next month a letter said the next generation was ready. Map references were given as to where a bomb was. It covered an area of a square kilometre. A hundred police officers, army personnel and bomb disposal officers tried to find it. A month later a further letter was received saying there was no bomb but there was no time to waste. The campaign lasted about six months but he never received any money. The Judge concluded that it was an evil campaign of extortion and intimidation. The planning was done with devious cunning and meticulous care. Many customers had been put in fear and there had been enormous public anxiety. Tesco had incurred great expense and there had been a very extensive police operation. He was aged 51 and of good character. Held. 14 years in total gave insufficient discount for the plea, so **12 years**.
Note: Both the above cases are old. Treat them with care. Ed.

R v Moncrieffe 2014 EWCA Crim 1237 D pleaded to blackmail. D targeted M, the manager of a Sainsbury's supermarket. Separate letters were sent to M and his wife using a phrase that M used regularly. D contacted M by telephone revealing knowledge of his family's daily lives. D also issued threats suggesting M should open the safe if he valued his family's safety. M stated he did not have access to the safe. D asked about the amount of money in the tills and numerous questions about security. D then told M he would tell his people to back off. M's family believed they were under surveillance. D, aged 39, was of effective good character and was genuinely remorseful. Held. The offence had a serious impact on the lives of M and his family and caused distress, severe anxiety and considerable upheaval. However, the blackmail was ultimately unsuccessful and was ended by D himself, who used his own mobile phone which enabled him to be traced. Starting at 7 years, with credit for the early plea, **4 years 8 months** not 6 years.

217.11   *Unsophisticated blackmail*

R v Wilson 2010 EWCA Crim 3076 D pleaded at the PCMH to blackmail. After approaching a landlord of a pub to enquire about job vacancies, he posted a threatening letter demanding £200 be placed in the envelope provided and deposited at a bus stop, or the pub would be burnt down. D was arrested some 18 months later on a separate charge and his fingerprints matched those taken from the letter and envelope. D, aged 20 at the time of the offence, stated that he was taking drink and drugs at the time and had no intention of carrying it out. He had previous convictions in 2003 for a dwelling house burglary (4-month DTO), in 2006 for criminal damage (community order), and 2007 for a Public Order Act offence (community order). In 2008, following the commission of this offence, he was given a custodial sentence of 8 weeks for a non-dwelling house burglary and in 2009 was subject to a 12-month community order for racially aggravated common assault. Held. This was a standard case of blackmail falling towards the bottom end of the range of seriousness. It was not repeated and there was no prospect of it being carried out. However, it was undoubtedly most alarming to V and his family. A starting point of 6 years was manifestly excessive. 4 years was appropriate, so with the plea and making a discount for delay, **2 years**.

R v Duffy 2011 EWCA Crim 231 D was convicted of blackmail and other counts. Whilst on bail for drug offences, he impersonated a member of security staff at a nightclub. He accused V of taking drugs in the lavatory, took his mobile phone and £40. D told V he could have his mobile phone back if he paid another £40. D took V to an ATM where £200 was withdrawn. D threatened V as they walked. D discovered V's PIN and withdrew a further £100. D, aged 27, had previous convictions for drugs and drunkenness. The Judge noted that he had picked on a vulnerable victim, duping him into believing that D was a member of security staff. The Judge remarked that the offence came very close to robbery and that he had taken into account the guideline for that offence. Held. The acquisition of the security jacket indicated a degree of premeditation. The Judge was undoubtedly correct to state that the offence was serious. It was clear that D's offending called for immediate imprisonment. **3 years** not 4 with the other sentences consecutive.

R v Ceesay 2012 EWCA Crim 2075, 2013 1 Cr App R (S) 101 (p 529) D pleaded (full credit) to blackmail. He met V, aged 20, through a website and they began dating. He gave V a false name. Their relationship continued for about 9 months until V found that she could not contact D. He subsequently contacted her and said he had been in hospital as he had been beaten up by an ex-girlfriend's boyfriend. V told D that she was pregnant and they arranged to meet. D did not show up and did not respond to text messages. About a week later, V received text messages stating that her 'so-called boyfriend' had been kidnapped and £10,000 was being asked for his release. D had provided £9,500 but was unable to raise the final £500. The messages asked for V to pay the £500 or D would be killed. V eventually alerted the police and D was found and arrested. He was seen moving freely around an area of London. D, aged 23, was of good character. Held. There were repeated demands made over a comparatively short period of time. The amount demanded was quite modest and there was no threat to reveal any wrongdoing on V's part, as is often so common. V was subject to real anxiety over a period of some hours, and 20 police officers were involved in the investigation. Starting at 12 months was appropriate. **8 months** not 2 years.

217.12 *Violence occurs*

R v Walker 2010 EWCA Crim 2184 D, aged 18, pleaded on the day of his trial to blackmail, causing unnecessary suffering to an animal and obstructing a constable in the execution of his duty (2 months' detention consecutive). D contacted C, and asked whether C owned a dog. C in fact did. D in fact had C's dog which had C's telephone number on the collar. D offered to return it. C offered D £10, but D asked for £20. C agreed. They agreed to meet. C received a phone call from D stating that the price was now £120. C was unhappy and began to contact the police. D appeared and asked for £150. During this discussion, D's partner appeared with the dog, dragging it roughly by a belt attached to its neck. D said, "Give me the £150 or you'll have a dead dog." C said that he'd already contacted the police. D said, "Pay me quick or you'll have a dead dog before the police come." D applied the belt like a tourniquet around the dog's neck and tightened it. C shouted for help and pleaded with D not to kill the dog. The dog collapsed and died of a heart attack. D left the scene. Officers gained entry to his flat and after a violent struggle in which D tried to punch, kick and bite the officers, D was arrested. It was accepted that D had come into possession of the dog by finding it as opposed to stealing it. D had 14 convictions including eight robberies and two threatening behaviour. The Judge disqualified D from owning a dog for 5 years. Held. This was an extraordinarily callous and cruel offence. A prison report details five adjudications for fighting whilst in custody. D had links to a local gang and appeared to have made money by selling drugs and other illegal activity. The Court was unimpressed by a letter from D asserting that he had seen the error of his ways, but essentially denying the offence. The obstructing a PC sentence was unlawful so 1 month consecutive instead. The **3 years'** detention was deserved.

Att-Gen's Ref Nos 54-55 of 2013 2013 EWCA Crim 2067 (**7 years'** detention, **15 years** and **9 years**, see **217.9**)

Att-Gen's Ref Nos 39-42 of 2014 2014 EWCA Crim 1557 Three defendants were convicted of false imprisonment. D pleaded guilty (20% credit) to the same charge. V bought cannabis from D. V was driven to D's flat. After a "horrendous" humiliating and brutal attack to V's face, with D wielding a hammer and others helping, V's family was told to pay a £1,500 debt. V was tied up, placed on top of a body bag and hit again. D hit V on the head with the hammer. He fell and was punched. D then repeatedly hit V in the face, particularly in the eye and mouth. V's teeth were deliberately broken. The attack was recorded. Threats were made to kill and rape V. V's belongings were taken and D hit V's legs with the hammer making walking difficult. Two defendants visited P, V's partner. A phone call was made to V. During the call, D held the hammer to V's head, demands were made for £1,500, and threats made that one of them would rape P. P had no money. V was driven to an isolated wood whilst the defendants discussed killing V there. V took the threats as genuine. Further demands for money were made. V was untied, driven back, his property returned and he was given some cannabis resin. D offered V money not to give evidence. D was aged 21 and had an extensive record, including violence. He was dependent on drugs. The others were aged 17 (with an ABH and drug conviction), 22 and 19 (neither with convictions). Held. For D, 14 years' extended sentence (**10 years'** custody 4 years' extended licence) with a 3-year consecutive sentence for two unrelated supply counts (as before). For the others **7 years'** YOI, not 4, **4 years**, not 2 and, **8 years'** YOI, not 5.

Old case: *R v Nissar* 2008 EWCA Crim 3016 (**15 years**) For a summary of the case see the 9th edition of this book.

BLADED ARTICLE see the **OFFENSIVE WEAPONS/BLADED ARTICLE, POSSESSION OF/THREATENING WITH** chapter.

218   BOMB HOAX, PLACING OR DISPATCHING ARTICLES OR SENDING FALSE MESSAGES

218.1

Criminal Law Act 1977

   s 51(1) (placing…or dispatching an article…with the intention of inducing in some other person a belief…that it will explode or ignite)

   s 51(2) (communicating any information which he knows or believes to be false to another person with the intention of inducing in him…a false belief that a bomb or other thing…liable to explode or ignite is present etc.)

Modes of trial Triable either way

Maximum sentences On indictment 7 years. Summary 6 months and/or a £5,000 fine for offences committed before 12 March 2015 and an unlimited fine thereafter.[92] There are maximum fines for those aged under 18, see **14.38** in Volume 1.

218.2   *Cases*

R v Altahan 2010 EWCA Crim 985 D pleaded to sending a malicious communication containing false information and an offence involving a bomb hoax. D sent emails to two schools claiming to be a suicide bomber named Qacim Haddad. The second email said, 'Warning, I am going to blow up Broomfield school, I'm a suicide bomber in Leeds'. Qacim Haddad, an asylum seeker from Iraq, was arrested and said he had met D online but had ceased communicating with her. In interview D said the messages were meant as revenge against Qacim for splitting up with her and she hoped he would be deported. D, aged 37, had a caution for harassment after she developed an obsessive attraction to her GP. The pre-sentence report said D struggled to accept responsibility, there was a low risk of re-conviction and D posed a medium risk of harm to staff or anybody with whom she formed, or wished to form, a relationship. The psychiatric report said D suffered from Asperger's syndrome, the risk of violence was 'absolutely minimal', and there was a substantial risk of further inappropriate or unrequited fantasy attachments to men. People such as doctors, police officers and those in positions of authority and status were most at risk. The Judge said she led a sad and lonely existence and appeared to be unable to function socially in an ordinary way. Held. It is in the public interest that she receives appropriate treatment. **Community order** with supervision and mental health treatment requirement, not 16 months.

R v Pinder 2014 EWCA Crim 1710 D pleaded to communicating false information (full credit). Four days after the Boston terrorist attack, D phoned police four times and texted them once in just over 1½ hours. She said bombs would be detonated at named police stations killing all police officers inside etc. D claimed to be a friend of hers in one call and used her own name in two later calls. She used her own mobile. Police played the message to the friend, who recognised D's voice. She was aged 33 at sentence with very many previous convictions, including numerous public order offences, criminal damage and persistently using telecommunication systems to cause annoyance offences. D was now aged 33 and had a personality disorder. Held. D was well known to police, who would have realised she was incapable of carrying out the threats. They would have known this from an early stage. The terrorist attack was not relevant. D made no reference to it. We start at 2 years, with plea, **16 months** not 4 years.

R v Perera 2015 EWCA Crim 1303 D pleaded to communicating false information with intent. He called Norwich airport and said a bomb would go off at 6. The airport was searched and nothing was found. By coincidence no flights were due to leave that day. The call was traced to a phone box and D was identified by CCTV. About a year after making the call, he pleaded guilty. D was aged 47, with a very low IQ of 60. He had a very limited understanding of what he had done and had mental difficulties. The

---

[92] Legal Aid, Sentencing and Punishment of Offenders Act 2012 s 85(1) and (4) and Legal Aid, Sentencing and Punishment of Offenders Act 2012 (Commencement No 11) Order 2015 2015/504

pre-sentence report said he was now showing an insight into what he had done. A prison report said D was well-behaved and had good discipline, but there was little they could do for him. The **6-month** sentence should be **suspended** with a supervision requirement. Old cases: *R v Philipson* 2008 EWCA Crim 1019, 2 Cr App R (S) 110 (p 631) (**6 months**) *R v McMenemy* 2009 EWCA Crim 42, 2 Cr App R (S) 396 (**2 years**) *R v McMenemy* 2009 EWCA Crim 42, 2 Cr App R (S) 396 (**2 years**) For a summary of the first two cases see the 9th edition of this book and for the last case see the 10th edition. **BREACH** see the back index.

219   BURGLARY

219.1

Theft Act 1968 s 9

Mode of trial Triable either way unless:
  a) the defendant could be sentenced to a minimum sentence of 3 years,[93] or
  b) the burglary comprises the commission of, or an intention to commit, an offence which is triable only on indictment (GBH only. Ed.),[94] or
  c) the burglary is in a dwelling and a person in the dwelling was subjected to violence or the threat of violence.[95]

In these cases the offence is triable only on indictment.

Maximum sentences On indictment, 14 years when the building is a dwelling, 10 years otherwise. Summary 6 months and/or a £5,000 fine for offences committed before 12 March 2015 and an unlimited fine thereafter.[96] There are maximum fines for those aged under 18, see **14.38** in Volume 1.

Minimum sentences Domestic burglary is a specified offence for a 3-year minimum sentence when the offence is a third domestic burglary,[97] see the *Minimum 3 years' custody* paras at **219.28**.

Extended sentences Burglary 'with intent to a) inflict GBH on a person, or b) do unlawful damage to a building or anything in it' is listed in Criminal Justice Act 2003 Sch 15. The court may pass a 2012 extended sentence (EDS) if there is a significant risk of serious harm from future specified offences and either: a) the defendant has a Criminal Justice Act 2003 Sch 15B conviction (applicable only to defendants aged 18+), or b) the offence would justify a determinate sentence of at least 4 years.[98]

Restitution Orders There is power to make an order that the stolen goods etc. in the possession of the defendant or a third party be restored to the owner etc.[99]

Sexual Harm Prevention Orders There is a discretionary power to make this order when it is necessary to protect the public from sexual harm.[100]

GENERAL

219.2   *Crown Court statistics*   ***England and Wales***
Burglary   Dwelling

---

[93] Powers of Criminal Courts (Sentencing) Act 2000 s 111(2)
[94] Magistrates' Courts Act 1980 s 17(1) and Sch 1, para 28b
[95] Magistrates' Courts Act 1980 s 17(1) and Sch 1, para 28c. In *R v McGrath* 2004 1 Cr App R 15 (p 173), violence was inflicted in response to the occupant's force when restraining the burglar. Held. para 28(c) was not to be taken to mean that the violence must have been part of the effecting of the burglary. It was sufficiently wide to cover cases such as this.
[96] Legal Aid, Sentencing and Punishment of Offenders Act 2012 s 85(1) and (4) and Legal Aid, Sentencing and Punishment of Offenders Act 2012 (Commencement No 11) Order 2015 2015/504
[97] Powers of Criminal Courts (Sentencing) Act 2000 s 111
[98] Criminal Justice Act 2003 s 226A-226B as inserted by Legal Aid, Sentencing and Punishment of Offenders Act 2012 s 124
[99] Powers of Criminal Courts (Sentencing) Act 2000 s 148(2)
[100] Sexual Offences Act 2003 s 103A as inserted by Anti-social Behaviour, Crime and Policing Act 2014 Sch 5 para 2 and Sexual Offences Act 2003 Sch 5

Year	Age	Plea	Total sen-tenced	Type of sentencing %						Average length of custody in months
				Dis-charge	Fine	Community sentence	Sus-pended sentence	Custody	Oth-er	
2013	18-20	G	1,292	0.3	0.1	13.1	15.0	71.0	0.5	20.5
		NG	50	2.0	–	10.0	8.0	80.0	–	28.8
	21+	G	6,369	0.1	0.1	5.7	15.7	78.1	0.3	25.8
		NG	472	–	0.6	4.2	14.4	79.9	0.8	34.8
2014	18-20	G	1,086	–	–	9	23	67	–	20.5
		NG	43	–	–	7	19	74	–	29.0
	21+	G	5,705			5	16	78		26.3
		NG	410	.	.	6	12	80	2	35.7

Burglary in a building other than a dwelling

Year	Age	Plea	Total sen-tenced	Type of sentencing %						Average length of custody in months
				Dis-charge	Fine	Community sentence	Sus-pended sentence	Custody	Oth-er	
2013	18-20	G	191	1.0	–	22.0	18.3	57.6	1.0	19.9
		NG	11	–	–	27.3	36.4	36.4	–	18.5
	21+	G	1,742	0.3	0.1	9.5	22.7	66.9	0.5	15.4
		NG	99	–	1.0	9.1	24.2	61.6	4.0	24.4
2014	18-20	G	174	–	–	20	30	49	1	11.8
		NG	4		25	–	25	50	–	not listed[101]
	21+	G	1,838	–	–	8	23	68	1	15.3
		NG	63	2	2	8	17	68	3	24.9

For explanations about the statistics, see page 1-xii. For statistics for male and female defendants etc., see www.banksr.com Other matters Statistics tab

DWELLING BURGLARY

Guidelines and drafting the indictment

219.3   Dwelling   Sentencing Council guideline
Burglary Offences Guideline 2012, see www.banksr.com Guidelines tab The guideline applies to all offenders aged 18+. In force 16 January 2012.

STEP ONE Determining the offence category

page 8 The court should determine the offence category using the table below.

Category 1	Greater harm and higher culpability
Category 2	Greater harm and lower culpability or lesser harm and higher culpability
Category 3	Lesser harm and lower culpability

The court should determine culpability and harm caused or intended, by reference only to the factors below, which comprise the principal factual elements of the offence. Where an offence does not fall squarely into a category, individual factors may require a degree of weighting before making an overall assessment and determining the appropriate offence category.

---

[101] Not shown as based on too few cases to be meaningful

Factors indicating greater harm
Theft of/damage to property causing a significant degree of loss to the victim (whether economic, sentimental or personal value), Soiling, ransacking or vandalism of property, Occupier at home (or returns) while offender present, Trauma to the victim, beyond the normal inevitable consequence of intrusion and theft, Violence used or threatened against victim, Context of general public disorder.

Factors indicating lesser harm
Nothing stolen or only property of very low value to the victim (whether economic, sentimental or personal), Limited damage or disturbance to property.

Factors indicating higher culpability
Victim or premises deliberately targeted (e.g. due to vulnerability or hostility based on disability, race, sexual orientation), A significant degree of planning or organisation, Knife or other weapon carried (where not charged separately), Equipped for burglary (e.g. implements carried and/or use of vehicle), Member of a group or gang.

Factors indicating lower culpability
Offence committed on impulse, with limited intrusion into property, Offender exploited by others, Mental disorder or learning disability, where linked to the commission of the offence.

219.4

STEP TWO Starting point and category range

page 8 Having determined the category, the court should use the corresponding starting points to reach a sentence within the category range below. The starting point applies to all offenders irrespective of plea or previous convictions.

Where the defendant is dependent on or has a propensity to misuse drugs and there is sufficient prospect of success, a community order with a drug rehabilitation requirement under Criminal Justice Act 2003 s 209 may be a proper alternative to a short or moderate custodial sentence.

A case of particular gravity, reflected by multiple features of culpability or harm [as set out above], could merit upward adjustment from the starting point before further adjustment for aggravating or mitigating features, set out [later].

The starting point applies to all offenders irrespective of plea or previous convictions.

Offence category	Starting point (applicable to all offenders)	Category range (applicable to all offenders)
Category 1	3 years' custody	2-6 years' custody
Category 2	1 year's custody	High-level Community Order to 2 years' custody
Category 3	High-level Community Order	Low-level Community Order to 26 weeks' custody

For the meaning of a high-level, a medium-level and a low-level community order see **16.12-16.14** in Volume 1.

219.5   [Aggravating and mitigating factors]

page 9 The table below contains a **non-exhaustive** list of additional factual elements providing the context of the offence and factors relating to the offender. Identify whether any combination of these, or other relevant factors, should result in an upward or downward adjustment from the starting point. **In particular, relevant recent convictions are likely to result in an upward adjustment**. In some cases, having considered these factors, it may be appropriate to move outside the identified category range.

When sentencing Category 2 or 3 offences, the court should also consider the custody threshold as follows:

Has the custody threshold been passed?
If so, is it unavoidable that a custodial sentence be imposed?
If so, can that sentence be suspended?

Factors increasing seriousness

Statutory aggravating factors
Previous convictions, having regard to: a) the nature of the offence to which the conviction relates and its relevance to the current offence; and b) the time that has elapsed since the conviction,
Offence committed whilst on bail.
Other aggravating factors
Child at home (or returns home) when offence committed,
Offence committed at night,
Gratuitous degradation of victim,
Any steps taken to prevent the victim reporting the incident or obtaining assistance and/or from assisting or supporting the prosecution,
Victim compelled to leave their home (in particular victims of domestic violence),
Established evidence of community impact,
Commission of offence whilst under the influence of alcohol or drugs,
Failure to comply with current court orders,
Offence committed whilst on licence,
Offences Taken Into Consideration (TICs)

Factors reducing seriousness or reflecting personal mitigation

Offender has made voluntary reparation to the victim,
Subordinate role in a group or gang,
No previous convictions **or** no relevant/recent convictions,
Remorse,
Good character and/or exemplary conduct,
Determination and/or demonstration of steps taken to address addiction or offending behaviour,
Serious medical conditions requiring urgent, intensive or long-term treatment,
Age and/or lack of maturity where it affects the responsibility of the offender,
Lapse of time since the offence where this is not the fault of the offender,
Mental disorder or learning disability, where not linked to the commission of the offence,
Sole or primary carer for dependent relatives.

219.6   Dwelling   Magistrates' Court Sentencing Guidelines
Note: The guidelines reproduce at page 217 the main guideline with a few amendments to reflect the lesser sentencing powers of the Magistrates' Court. Ed.

219.7   Dwelling   Judicial guidance
R v Franks 2012 EWCA Crim 1491, 2013 1 Cr App R (S) 65 (p 363) D and others pleaded to dwelling burglaries. £3,400 worth of goods were stolen. The police stopped the car used and most of the property was recovered. The Judge held for the guidelines there was significant loss. The defendants appealed saying there was not significant loss. Held. There was a significant loss at the time of the burglary so the Judge was right.
R v Sticklen 2013 EWCA Crim 615 D pleaded to a dwelling burglary. Held. The justification for treating a dwelling as being different from other properties (and the Judge mentioned a shed or a factory) is the very fact that it is someone's home,

occupied, with personal and sentimental property within it. It is for that reason that higher sentences are required, and for that reason that statutory minimum sentences have been deemed appropriate.

R v Steadman and Others 2013 EWCA Crim 742 D was convicted of conspiracy to burgle. They stole £1.2m worth of high-value cars after stealing the keys by entering houses. It was argued that *R v Johnson* 2009 EWCA Crim 649 set a maximum sentence of 11 years where there was an absence of violence in a burglary. Alternatively, the absence of violence was a mitigating feature. Held. There is no sentence rule or practice that where no violence is used in the course of a burglary the maximum is 11 years and the absence of violence is not a mitigating feature.

R v Blaydes 2014 EWCA Crim 798, 2 Cr App R (S) 54 (p 437) If two people take part in a dwelling-house burglary, that is a clear and substantial aggravating feature.

219.8   *Dwelling   Old guideline case and old judicial guidance*

Note: The guidelines take precedence over these cases. The cases are included as the new guideline is not always easy to apply and the old law has in some respects not been replaced. Ed.

Att-Gen's Ref Nos 19-21 of 2001 2001 EWCA Crim 1432, 2002 1 Cr App R (S) 33 (p 136) There can be little doubt that the two forms of criminal conduct which cause the public most concern are domestic burglary and street robberies. The effect of such offences goes way beyond the dreadful trauma suffered by the immediate victim and causes large sections of the public to alter their lifestyle to seek to avoid the danger. People are afraid to go out of their homes.

R v Saw 2009 EWCA Crim 1, 2 Cr App R (S) 54 (p 367) LCJ

The seriousness of burglary The starting point must always, we emphasise, always, be that burglary of a home is a serious criminal offence. The principle which must be grasped is that when we speak of dwelling house burglary, we are considering not only an offence against property, which it is, but also, and often more alarmingly and distressingly, an offence against the person. There is a long-standing, almost intuitive, belief that our homes should be our castles. The concept suggests impregnability and defiance against intrusion. In the phrase coined by Sir Edward Coke in 1628, when compiling his *Third Institute of the Laws of England*, our homes should be our 'safest refuge', where above all we should enjoy secure tranquillity and untroubled peace. Something precious is violated by burglary of a home, and those who perpetrate this crime should be sentenced and punished accordingly. We repeat the observations in *R v Brewster and Others* 1998 1 Cr App R (S) 181, and adopt them: 'Domestic burglary is, and always has been, regarded as a very serious offence.'

The loss of property Some of these homes may not include property or objects of any great financial worth, but for those whose material possessions are limited in number and value, the disappearance of what in a prosperous home would be treated as relatively small items will be correspondingly more significant. In any event the sense of disturbance and distress suffered by the home owner is not quantifiable in bare economic terms. Therefore in the sentencing decision particular focus is required on the impact of the offence on those living in the burgled house. Where goods of slight economic but significant sentimental value are taken or damaged the impact on the victim is likely to be high, not least because these objects are irreplaceable. A photograph is worth nothing, except to the person who owns it, but it may be the only image left of grandparents, or now-deceased parents. The loss or destruction of letters written in the early days of courtship may distress the widow or widower who has lost them far more than the disappearance of valuable electrical equipment.

Unintended consequences Whether or not the dwelling house burglar has any specific intention to cause harm, he runs the risk that the victim or victims may suffer serious adverse consequences. Where this happens, sentences should be reflective even of unintended consequences. We repeat the observations in *R v Brewster and Others* 1998 1 Cr App R (S) 181, and adopt them: 'Domestic burglary may involve considerable loss to the victim. Even when it does not, the victim may lose possessions of particular value to him or her. To those who are insured, the receipt of financial compensation does not replace what is lost. But many victims are uninsured: because they may have fewer possessions, they are the more seriously injured by the loss of those they do have. The loss of material possessions is, however, only part (and often a minor part) of the reason why domestic burglary is a serious offence.'

The effect on the victims 'Most people, perfectly legitimately, attach importance to the privacy and security of their own homes. That an intruder should break in or enter, for his own dishonest purposes, leaves the victim with a sense of violation and insecurity. Even where the victim is unaware, at the time, that the burglar is in the house, it can be a frightening experience to know that a burglary has taken place, and it is all the more frightening if the victim confronts or hears the burglar. Generally speaking it is more frightening if the victim is in the house when the burglary takes place, and if the intrusion takes place at night, but that does not mean that the offence is not serious if the victim returns to an empty house during the daytime to find that it has been burgled.' The intrinsic seriousness of each burglary offence may vary hugely. The presence of the victim at home in bed at night while the burglary occurs may well occasion especial trauma certainly if woken by the burglar, and even more so if he or she sees, or, worse, is confronted by the burglar. In these circumstances it would be unrealistic to regard the victim's presence at home during a night-time burglary as merely a medium-level aggravating feature. The same may apply when the householder is at home during the daytime when a forced entry takes place, particularly if the homeowner is someone on his or her own, or someone who by himself or herself is caring for children or the elderly. Such a burglary is likely to cause considerable alarm and distress, and, often perhaps overlooked, while it is taking place, uncertainty about what to do and great fear about what may lie ahead. To all this we would of course add the particular effect on the elderly and infirm, whose last years can be overshadowed by what sometimes becomes an ever-present, pervading fear and constant nervousness. Many warm and happy memories of bygone years can be destroyed as a direct consequence of burglary, and for some indeed, their home becomes something of a prison, as they barricade themselves behind the security arrangements they believe they need.

Minor examples [Where] the offence is committed by a man of good character who, passing an open window on a summer's day, puts his hand inside the window and steals a bottle of water. Without trivialising the offence, that smacks more of petty theft than burglary. Such exceptional cases should obviously be treated exceptionally. Thus although burglary has always been regarded as a serious offence, it has also been recognised that while some burglaries are higher-level offences of their kind, some remain lower-level offences.

Planning The inference of careful planning can usually be drawn where property of high economic value is taken, particularly if it is not recovered, and if the facts lead to the inference that whoever may have burgled the premises knew precisely which receiver or receivers would be willing and able to accept and pay for the stolen property. However, a degree of planning, not necessarily profound or detailed planning, may be demonstrated when burglars work in a group. The carrying and use of house-breaking implements will ordinarily dispose of any suggestion that the offence was simply impulsive. Obviously the carrying of any weapon speaks for itself and will often result in a charge of aggravated burglary, which is outside the scope of these guidelines.

The judge's task The task is properly to assess the true seriousness of the individual offence. The sentencer must focus on the realities. Different cases throw up different features, and sometimes the different features are unusual. Their absence from the list of aggravating features does not mean that they should be disregarded. At the same time, many cases involve more than one of these aggravating features, some at the particularly serious end of what may otherwise be regarded as a single individual feature, on its own indicative of the need for a severe sentence, some not so. In essence, all the various aggravating features require the court to address two specific features which may be present in every dwelling house burglary: first, the overall criminality of the defendant, in the light of his previous convictions, and second, the true impact of the offence on the victims.

Aggravating features They include: 1 Force used on, or threatened against, the victim, and especially if physical injury is caused, such cases will often be charged as robbery or as offences against the person. They fall outside the scope of these present guidelines, 2 Trauma to the victim beyond the normal inevitable consequence of intrusion and theft, 3 Premeditation and professional planning/organisation in the execution, this may be indicated by burglars working in a group or when housebreaking implements are carried, 4 Vandalism of the premises, 5 Deliberate targeting of any vulnerable victim (including cases of 'deception' or 'distraction' of the elderly), 6 Deliberate targeting of any victim, for example out of spite or upon racial grounds, 7 The particular vulnerability of the victim, whether targeted as such or not, 8 The presence of the occupier at home, whether the burglary is by day or by night, 9 Theft of or damage to property of high economic or sentimental value, 10 Offence committed on bail or shortly after the imposition of a non-custodial sentence, 11 Two or more burglaries of homes rather than for a single offence, and 12 The offender's previous record.

Mitigation We attempt no exhaustive list. Good character is substantial mitigation. If nothing, or only property of very low economic or sentimental value, is taken, that obviously reduces the gravity of the offence. The defendant may have played only a minor part in the burglary, and been treated by the other burglars as if he were on the fringes. He may indeed have been exploited by others. He may have committed it on impulse. Evidence of genuine regret and remorse, ready co-operation with the police, positive response to previous sentences and the age and state of health (mental and physical) of the defendant are all likely to be relevant factors. We emphasise that we are not seeking to limit the matters in mitigation, merely highlighting some of the more obvious and common factors.

The appropriate sentence There will therefore be some cases where, depending on the circumstances and the impact on the victim, the right sentence will be non-custodial. For example, the sentencing of a first offender, particularly a youthful offender, requires careful attention to the question whether the public interest would be best served by attempting his or her rehabilitation. Another example is a defendant who has reached a critical stage in his life with a real prospect of turning his back on crime, or breaking away from addiction to the drugs which led him into crime. If he is indeed making a genuine attempt to break the cycle, or to address its causes, then that is plainly a factor to be taken into account in his favour, and put into the balance against the aggravating features of the specific case. Successful and early rehabilitation often represents the best long-term advantage to the public, and a sentence which has a reasonable prospect of achieving that the offender will be deterred, or discouraged, or taught to avoid crime may well be appropriate where the burglary lacks significant attendant aggravating features.

Repeat offenders Once an offender has been caught and sentenced, and in particular if made subject to a non-custodial penalty on the basis that his rehabilitation may be achieved, he must understand that for dwelling house burglars such a chance rarely comes more than once, and then only if the subsequent court is satisfied that the offender has been making genuine efforts to break out of the cycle of offending and reoffending, and that the current lapse is temporary.

219.9   *Dwelling   How to draft the indictment*

R v Miller 2010 EWCA Crim 809, 2011 1 Cr App R (S) 2 (p 7) D pleaded to burglary of a care home. Held. The particulars in the count should include 'dwelling' if that is suggested because then there is a higher penalty, applying *R v Courtie* 1984 78 Cr App R (S) 292. Here where 'dwelling' was not in the particulars it could not be said D had admitted that it was a 'domestic' burglary for the purposes of the 3-year minimum sentence. D was sentenced on a wrong basis and we have to sentence on the basis that the burglary was not committed in respect of a dwelling.

Note: In *R v Courtie* 1984, C pleaded to buggery without there being an averment in the particulars stating there was no consent. The prosecution alleged there was no consent and the defence denied this. Consensual buggery carried a maximum of 5 years whereas non-consensual buggery carried a maximum of 10 years. The Judge refused to allow a fresh count alleging there was no consent to be added to the indictment and he and two Magistrates then found there had been no consent. The House of Lords held that where there were two different penalties for the same offence, Parliament had in fact created two offences. Therefore it was for the jury to determine whether the ingredients of the more serious offence had been made out and the Judge and Magistrates had usurped the function of a jury. Consequently C fell to be sentenced for non-consensual buggery. In future where non-consensual buggery is alleged the lack of consent should be specifically pleaded enabling a plea or a verdict of the jury to be returned dealing with that element. Ed.

R v Flack 2013 EWCA Crim 115, 2 Cr App R (S) 56 (p 366) D pleaded to burglary when the particulars averred it was a dwelling. D faced a minimum sentence. D contested that it was a dwelling and the Judge held a *Newton* hearing where the Judge concluded the property was a dwelling. Held. That was wrong. If the defendant did not accept it was a dwelling then a) he or she should plead not guilty, b) a count without the dwelling averment should have been added, c) [the defendant should plead to that] and d) a jury should be sworn to try the issue. Here D had pleaded to the offence including the averment.

Types of dwelling burglary

219.10   Dwelling, Types of
Note: It is important to remember that the guidelines take precedence over all the pre-guideline comparable cases. Ed.
Animal rights activists, see the **ANIMAL RIGHTS ACTIVISTS** chapter.

219.11   Dwelling   Attempted burglary
R v McGuire 2002 EWCA Crim 2689, 2003 2 Cr App R (S) 10 (p 40) Attempted burglary is not a qualifying offence for the purposes of Powers of Criminal Courts (Sentencing) Act 2000 s 111 [minimum sentences]. Sentence quashed.

R v Delaney 2010 EWCA Crim 2346 D pleaded on the day of his trial to attempted burglary. He was arrested after being spotted by police walking out of a garden at the rear of a house at around 3.50 am. There were footprints in the snow matching D's and an unknown other's. The handle of the door had been bent. The pre-sentence report stated that D claimed he was under the influence of drink and had foolishly allowed himself to go along with another whom he had met that evening. It also suggested a Suspended Sentence Order. D was aged 19 and had one previous conviction for ABH and a caution for another assault. Held. In view of D's age and the fact that he was lightly convicted, **3 months** not 9.

Post-guideline case
R v Smith 2013 EWCA Crim 996 D pleaded (25% credit) to attempted burglary. V, her daughter and her daughter's friend were in V's home. V was in bed when she was disturbed by a 'knock at the door followed by a louder knocking at the front door'. She looked out of the window and saw two men standing behind some bushes at the end of her driveway. They moved towards the rear of the property and tried both the patio doors and the kitchen door. V then called the police. When the police called back, D and his accomplice ran away. D was arrested shortly after and gave a false name. D, aged 24 at appeal, had convictions for dwelling and non-dwelling burglaries. In 2007 he received 3 years' YOI and in 2009 he received 3½ years. He was on licence when he committed the instant offence. Held. The Judge was justified in concluding that this was a Category 1

offence. This was an attempt and no entry was effected. Consequently, an adjustment needs to be made to reflect that. Starting at 4 years not 5, **3 years** not 3 years 9 months was appropriate.

R v Lothan 2015 EWCA Crim 1316 D pleaded at his PCMH to attempted burglary. Police noticed a ground floor window of a flat had been broken. A blood stain enabled D to be linked to it. D had 64 offences on 29 occasions. He had burglary convictions in 1997 (twice), 2001 and 2004 (21 months). There was regular and serious offending up to this offence. The Judge referred to his addiction to drink and drugs. Held. This was a Category 2 case with lower culpability. While the victim was at home there was limited damage to the property. The harm was neutral. As it was an attempt, **18 months**.

See also: *R v Abdi* 2015 EWCA Crim 1413 (At night one attempt and a burglary of a shed (damage £300). Smashed glass in occupied dwelling. No entry. Claimed he was drunk. No previous convictions. Doing an apprenticeship and caring for sister with Downs' syndrome, mother and uncle. We start at 15 months, making with plea **10 months** not 18.)

219.12 *Dwelling   Damage, Burglary with intent to cause   Post-guideline case*
Theft Act 1968 s 9(1)-(2)

Entering any building as a trespasser with intent to do unlawful damage to the building or anything therein.

R v Shepherd 2014 EWCA Crim 1800 D pleaded (full credit) to burglary with intent to do unlawful damage. D persisted in maintaining contact with V, with whom he had had a relationship. He called V up to 20 times a day and V described D as harassing her. On the day in question, D left V 11 voice messages which were increasingly rude, abusive and irate. Minutes following the final message, D broke into V's house and went through the property and damaged or disturbed all but two rooms. The damage was less than £500 but made V feel physically sick. She became extremely anxious and scared, leaving her unable to return to work, but D surrendered himself to police the next day. D was aged 49 and had over 100 convictions. His last was in 2008, and he had three for burglary (non-dwelling), but he had impressive references. He was remorseful but said he had initially no intention of breaking in, only later becoming angry and doing so. The defence argued there was limited damage as opposed to disruption and disturbance of the items in the property. Held. D's submission is inconsistent with admitting to burglary with intent to cause damage and the Judge was entitled to put the offence within Category 1. Such offences require a significant immediate custodial sentence, however, D's previous convictions are balanced out by his mitigation. We start at 3 years. With plea, **2 years**, not 30 months.

219.13 *Dwelling   Damage to the property, Very significant   Post-guideline cases*
R v Bibby 2013 EWCA Crim 1938 D pleaded (full credit) to burglary. He went to a wedding and got drunk. Then he argued with his partner and left. Next he broke into a 15th-century listed property. The occupiers were away. They had spent two years restoring the house. D broke down historic doors, threw a TV on the floor, ripped out and ruined a wine fridge, causing damage to the wiring, and urinated on an antique rug, which stained it beyond repair. D also smashed several mirrors including one in an antique cupboard, defecated in the bath, damaged a designer chair, ripped out a bath from its mounts which caused a flood, smashed interior windows and broke roof tiles. D was found in a nearby garden behaving bizarrely. He was wearing a dinner jacket stolen from the house. The repair costs were just under £20,000. The owners no longer felt safe in their home. D had a history of drug and alcohol abuse. The defence argued the Judge had placed the offence in the wrong category. Held. The offence does not fit easily in the guideline. There were very significant and numerous aggravating features. **3 years** could not be described as excessive.

See also: *R v J and J* 2013 EWCA Crim 117 (Pleas to attempted burglary. Aged 17. Twins. Because of guideline, **6 months'** DTO not 10.)

Death is caused, see the MANSLAUGHTER *Burglars/robbers/thieves, By* para at **284.13**.

219.14   Dwelling   Distraction burglaries (entering by a trick and stealing)
R v Thirkwell 2011 EWCA Crim 2759 LCJ D pleaded (full credit) to burglary. He
entered a ground-floor flat occupied by V, a 58-year-old woman who lived alone. She
suffered from multiple sclerosis and had carers visit her four times each day. She was
unable to move without assistance. D rang the doorbell and V let him in. He claimed to
be from the Blind Institution and had items to sell. He persuaded her to buy a lamp for
£10. He took one of her purses, ostensibly to take £10 from it, in payment for the lamp.
In fact, he took the entire contents totalling £170. The effect on V was considerable. She
would no longer answer the door and preferred to keep a knife by her side to protect her.
D, aged 26 at appeal, had convictions for a non-dwelling burglary aged 18 (community
punishment order), robbery and failure to surrender aged 21 (15 months), and possession
of class A drugs with intent (18 months). Held. This offence was committed whilst D
was on licence and he had a significant criminal record. V was clearly vulnerable but
does not appear to have been targeted. A substantial prison sentence was called for. **3
years** not 4.
Post-guideline cases
R v Dance 2013 EWCA Crim 1412, 2014 1 Cr App R (S) 51 (p 304) D was convicted of
dwelling burglary. His son and co-accused, S, pleaded guilty (4 years). V, aged 77 with a
severe hearing impairment, lived alone. She was tricked into allowing D and S into her
flat under the guise that they were selling household items. While one of them distracted
her, the other stole money from her bedroom and handbag. The loss amounted to £170.
The Judge noted that V was very vulnerable, there was a degree of planning, they acted
as a team once inside the flat and the effect on V was severe. She now wanted to move
out of her flat. D, aged 49 at appeal, had nine convictions for 27 offences including
convictions involving deception under Theft Act 1968. Held. This was a mean and
despicable offence. This was a Category 1 burglary. Distraction burglaries targeted at
vulnerable victims are a very serious crime. D had no convictions for burglary or theft
from a dwelling. The guidelines apply but the aggravating factors [lifted the sentence
above the guidelines]. **5 years** not 6.
R v King 2014 EWCA Crim 971, 2 Cr App R (S) 61 (p 478) D pleaded (25% credit) to
burglary. V was aged 88 and lived on her own. She walked with a stick and was reliant
on Meals on Wheels. She took a taxi to go and collect her pension, which was £600 in
cash. She took a taxi home and gave her address to the driver. D and an unidentified
accomplice tricked the driver into disclosing the address. The accomplice spoke to
another taxi driver in the queue, pretending to be V's granddaughter's boyfriend, and
said he wanted to check that V had given the driver the correct address. They obtained
V's address and made their way to her home. D knocked on the door and said that he had
come to cut her hedges. He then distracted her by engaging her in conversation in the
back garden, discussing the supposed hedge trimming. Meanwhile the accomplice
sneaked into the house through the open front door. He stole £720 in cash, a cheque
book and a pension folder. Once it was clear the burglary was complete, D said he must
have confused which house needed gardening work and they left. V discovered she had
been burgled and called the police. She was extremely distressed to the extent that she
could not bring herself to make a victim impact statement. D was identified by V in an
identification procedure. D had a bad record consisting of 29 convictions for 55
offences. There were a large number of dishonesty offences including burglary (1986),
deception and handling (1990), theft (1991), burglary and handling (1997), handling
(2000), domestic burglary (2005), assault, criminal damage, theft and breach of the
peace (2011) and shop theft (2012). Held. This case was certainly serious enough to
justify a starting point above 6 years. D had already received a 4-year sentence for a
similar offence. This was a particularly well-planned and executed burglary which in
reality had not begun in V's home but in the town at the taxi rank. V was targeted. A

substantial sum of cash was stolen. The impact of the offence on V was considerable. **5 years** was undoubtedly severe and at the top of the range but it was properly severe and cannot be said to be manifestly excessive.

See also: *R v Cassidy and Others* 2010 EWCA Crim 388 (Plea. 69 burglaries. Victims were mostly elderly. Defendants said they were police, Water Board officials etc. Some victims attacked. Sometimes phone wires cut. Considerable planning. Aged 30, **10 years**. Aged 17, **8 years**. Aged 19, **9 years**.)

R v Spooner 2010 EWCA Crim 2586, 2011 1 Cr App R (S) 125 (p 728) (Plea to distraction burglary. 78-year-old victim. 22 previous convictions including dwelling burglaries in 1996, 1998, 2005, 2006 and 2007. Targeted elderly victims. Despite strong mitigation, **8 years** was severe but upheld.)

Old cases: *R v Curtis* 2007 EWCA Crim 136, 2 Cr App R (S) 52 (p 322) (**5 years**) *R v Cawley and Cawley* 2007 EWCA Crim 2030, 2008 1 Cr App R (S) 59 (p 341) (**7 years** for J and **8 years** for M) *R v Casey and Maloney* 2007 EWCA Crim 2568, 2008 2 Cr App R (S) 2 (p 5) (M, **12 years** and C, **7 years**) *R v Myers* 2009 EWCA Crim 119, 2 Cr App R (S) 70 (p 495) (**6½ years**) *R v O'Driscoll* 2009 EWCA Crim 796 (**6 years**) *R v Casey* 2010 EWCA Crim 890 (**6 years**) *R v Johnson and Spence* 2010 EWCA Crim 1831, 2011 1 Cr App R (S) 82 (p 493) (**7½ years** and **3½ years**)

For a summary of the first three cases see the 8th edition of this book, for the next two see the 9th edition and the last two cases see the 10th edition.

219.15   *Dwelling   To steal keys for cars*

R v Baldacchino 2012 EWCA Crim 1394 D was convicted of conspiracy to burgle. D was part of a gang who burgled homes to steal the keys to cars. D's role was to drive the thieves to the addresses to be burgled. Over 19 days, 18 houses were burgled and car keys and cars stolen. D would sometimes drive in convoy with the stolen vehicle. D, aged 42 at appeal, had 19 convictions for 44 offences, mostly for dishonesty but not at a high level. In 2004 he received 18 months for theft, handling and obtaining by deception. Held. This case does not comfortably fit within the guidelines. It was organised and on a large scale but over a short period of time. D was neither an organiser nor a significant beneficiary of these offences. **8 years** not 10, taking account of his role and bad record.

See also: *R v Mount* 2011 EWCA Crim 164 (Pleaded to burglary. Broke into house at night to steal keys in an attempt to steal a car. Aged 26. Significant previous convictions. **12 months** not 18.)

Post-guideline cases

R v Bham 2013 EWCA Crim 10 D pleaded to conspiracy to burgle at the first opportunity. A team committed eight burglaries. D was involved in three of them. Each was at night when the occupant was asleep. Car keys were taken and then a car. Two Audis worth £30,000 and £70,000 and a Mercedes worth £70,000 were taken. The Judge said the conspiracy was well planned and the burglars were able to remove the tracking devices. D had no convictions and was the primary carer of his former partner who had limited mobility. Held. With the plea and the personal mitigation, **4 years** not 4½.

R v Steadman and Others 2013 EWCA Crim 742 S, P and M were convicted of conspiracy to burgle and conspiracy to steal. The conspiracies ran from May to December 2010. The conspirators conducted reconnaissance trips around a large area of the West Midlands, Staffordshire and Shropshire to identify houses with high-value cars. The houses were later broken into with the intention of taking car keys, but the burglars also took the opportunity to steal other valuable property which they came across. The burglaries usually took place at night when the occupants were asleep. The value of the vehicles targeted was £1.2m although the conspirators were not successful in all cases. The value of the cars they were successful in taking was about £0.5m. The cars were stored at remote locations to ensure they were not tracked and then moved on to other places. They were then exported abroad or broken up for parts. The conspirators could be connected to some 46 substantive offences, although not every conspirator could be connected to each offence. Held. The evidence placed S and P at the heart of the conspiracy. They were to be sentenced outside of the guidelines, which were not designed to deal with offending on this scale. Sentences of **11 years** for S and P, and **9 years** for M were not in any way manifestly excessive.

219.16   Dwelling, Occupied   One offence   Post guideline cases

R v Mansell and O'Gorman 2013 EWCA Crim 284 M and D pleaded to burglary. Just after midnight, they entered V1 and V2's house, with two others. It was in a rural and isolated location. They were wearing balaclavas. V1 and V2 heard noises and went downstairs. V2 handed V1 their lawfully held shotgun. V1 fired it at the men as one of them, believed to be D, reached into a kitchen drawer which V1 and V2 knew contained knives. V1 fired the shotgun, hitting D in the face and injuring him, and hitting M in the hand and injuring him. They fled and M and D were arrested in hospital. M believed, wrongly, that the house contained £170,000 in cash and drugs. M, aged 33, had four convictions for dwelling burglary, robbery and section 18. He was on licence at the time of the offence. D, aged 28, had been before the court 16 times but not for dwelling burglary. He had convictions for section 18 and was on licence for dangerous driving. Held. The appeals were wholly without merit. This was a deliberately targeted isolated house in the country, burgled at night. A significant degree of planning was involved. A group was involved. Face coverings were worn. Both were on licence and both had significant previous convictions. Remorse was expressed but it was not so far as to name the others involved. The Judge was entirely justified in taking 6 years as a starting point. With full credit for the pleas, **4 years**.

R v Kirmse 2014 EWCA Crim 79 D pleaded to burglary and (late) to damaging property. At about 5 am, he forced his way into a residential flat above a pub. The 22-year-old householder was disturbed by the noise and awoke. She went to the kitchen and was confronted by D. He was intoxicated. She asked him to leave and he began to do so. The police arrived and arrested him. The Judge held that D was equipped with an implement as a result of the damage caused to the kitchen window. The suggestion was that he picked up an implement nearby. It was said that it was not a Category 1 burglary. Held. It was clear that D used an implement in order to force open the kitchen window. It may well be that he became equipped to carry out the burglary at a very late stage, but equipped he was. There was also the high culpability that followed from the devastating effect on the victim. The case just came within Category 1. Bearing in mind that D equipped himself for the burglary at a late stage, it was not appropriate to move up from the starting point of 3 years. With 10% credit for the late plea, **2 years 8 months** not 3 years.

R v Shaban 2014 EWCA Crim 133 D pleaded to dwelling burglary. The house was occupied with a family of five who were asleep at the time. D gained entry through an insecure patio door. He stole property including a rucksack, wallet and credit cards, as well as keys to the house and vehicles. D was arrested the next day and some of the property was recovered. D was aged 38 at appeal and had 51 convictions for 109 offences. This was not a 'third strike' burglary, however. There was a history of failing to comply with community orders and he also fell to be sentenced for a bail offence. Held. There was little mitigation save for the guilty plea. The Judge placed this into Category 2, and was entitled to sentence above that, because of D's record. **Starting at 3 years** would not have been excessive. With full credit, **2 years** not 3 was appropriate. 2 months consecutive for the bail offence was not excessive.

Old cases: They add little.

219.17   Dwelling, Occupied   More than one offence

R v Bodman 2010 EWCA Crim 3284, 2011 2 Cr App R (S) 42 (p 249) D pleaded to five non-dwelling burglaries in 2009. Over £10,000 worth of goods were stolen, and damage caused. He received community sentences. D was then convicted of a dwelling burglary with six TICs, one of which was committed prior to the 2009 offences. No property was taken. He was in breach of his community order. D, aged 33, had 28 appearances for 70 offences, including dwelling and non-dwelling burglaries, attempt burglary and robbery. Held. The previous record was a significant aggravating factor. However, having regard to totality, **18 months** not 30 for the 2009 offences, and 18 months consecutive for the dwelling burglary.

R v Capel 2013 EWCA Crim 2805 D pleaded (full credit) to two burglaries. During the early hours D entered a house in which the owners slept. He disturbed their dogs and the occupiers went downstairs to find entry had been gained via an open window. The wife saw D leaving with an expensive laptop. That same morning a nearby property was ransacked, with three laptops, several phones, £50 in cash and an Armani watch taken. D had a quite appalling record, particularly for domestic burglary, and had received custodial sentences. Held. It was not possible to identify a factual element indicating higher culpability. The Judge was entitled to go outside both the starting point and range for a Category 2 burglary so as to give effect to section 111. We start at 5 years not 6, so with plea, **3 years 4 months** not 4½.

Post-guideline case

R v Parsonage 2014 EWCA Crim 306 D pleaded to three burglary (counts 1 and 3 early, count 2 late). V1 and his family returned home to find their property had been broken into. A dog flap had been removed in order to gain entry. Property to the value of £4,400 had been stolen, a small amount of which had been recovered. (This was count 3, Category 1.) V1 recalled that some 9 months earlier some items of jewellery had gone missing whilst they had employed D as an 'odd-job' man. Those items were worth £4,500 including items of sentimental value. D had not been permitted to go into the upstairs room where the jewellery was kept. (This was count 2, Category 2.) At the same time, D had been doing work at a property around the corner, owned by V2. The burglary of those victims came to light after D was arrested in respect of V1's property. (This was count 1, Category 2.) D was aged 26 when sentenced and had seven convictions for eight offences. A previous pre-sentence report (theft of a motor vehicle) did not speak well of him. There was a history of poor compliance with community orders and the commission of offences on bail. Held. This is a man of relatively young years. But it is plainly clear that the Judge was entitled to take the view that the sentences should be and properly were consecutive. Although counts 2 and 3 were burglaries of the same victims, D treated them as distinct by originally pleading not guilty to count 2, and they occurred on different occasions, each netting D a substantial haul. The 5 years given by the Judge does not take account of totality. **4 years** was appropriate, so 12 months on count 1, 6 months (not 18) on count 2 and 30 months on count 3, all consecutive.

R v Oracka 2015 EWCA Crim 1471 D pleaded to seven burglaries and two attempted burglaries. They were all daytime residential burglaries. Only in one were occupiers present. D stole cash or other items of low value. He absconded when released on police bail (14 days' imprisonment at the Magistrates' Court). D was a Slovakian national and aged 42. He was of good character prior to his arrest. D claimed the proceeds were for his sick sister in Slovakia. Held. The Judge did not structure the sentence properly. We start at 3 years not 4½ years because of the defendant's good character and other personal mitigation, so with plea **2 years**.

R v Mendoza 2015 EWCA Crim 1834 D pleaded to three domestic burglaries. In the first, at 8.45 pm, D entered by smashing patio doors. Property worth £840 was stolen and there was £1,600 worth of damage. About four weeks later, at about 5 pm, D smashed a rear door and fled when the alarm went off. The damage was £250. Five days later, while the occupiers were out, D smashed a window of a house with a brick. He stole property from all over the house including a large amount of jewellery, some of which was of enormous sentimental value. A laptop computer was also stolen. The total stolen was worth £18,361. D was aged 38, an illegal over-stayer with no convictions. The Judge found D had targeted particular areas where he thought there would be rich pickings.

Held. The Judge was right to make it a Category 1 offence because of the very significant loss and the ransacking. D had gone equipped for burglary and used a vehicle. D spoke no English and was separated from his wife and children, who were sent back to Colombia. Consecutive sentences were justified to reflect the distinct criminality. Looking at the total we start at 4½ years, not 6, so with plea, **3 years** not 4.
See also: *R v McKinley* 2011 EWCA Crim 1522 (Pleas to two night-time burglaries. Electronic equipment, other items, a car key and wallet stolen. Now aged 20. Convictions for 50 previous offences, many for dishonesty but including burglary. Global sentence. Starting at 5 years, **40 months' YOI** not 4 years.)
R v Blaydes 2014 EWCA Crim 798, 2 Cr App R (S) 54 (p 437) (Full credit. Two opportunistic dwelling burglaries in quick succession, one with another man. Given suspended sentence. Six weeks after, at night in occupied house of retired couple (but undisturbed). Electronics stolen. D, aged 21, of good character and cured M-KAT addiction on remand. Border between Categories 1 and 2. We give full credit for the last one, so 18 months for final burglary, 8 months activated consecutive, making 26 months.)
Old pre-guideline case: *R v Lumsden* 2010 EWCA Crim 1522 (Plea with four TICs.[102] Dwelling burglary at night of elderly couple whilst on licence for robbery. Kettle, foot warmer, two tins and a steering lock taken. 30 appearances for 73 offences. Full credit. **2 years**, not 3.)

219.18   *Dwelling, Unoccupied   Pre-guideline cases*
R v Gledhill 2011 EWCA Crim 645 LCJ D pleaded, with another, to burglary. D and J, equipped with mole grips and wearing hoods, acted as lookouts for a burglary of an unoccupied house. A large television, a computer console and a Freeview box worth around £670 were stolen. A CCTV console had been removed, causing damage. D and J had activated the alarm when they entered and no other items were taken. D, aged 18, had previous convictions for TDA (Referral Order), theft, being drunk and intimidation of a witness (DTO). He was in breach of a Suspended Sentence Order for dangerous driving. Held. This was a serious offence of burglary and D has a bad record. Considering the mitigation, his age and the plea, the sentence of an **18-month DTO** with 6-month DTO consecutive for breach of SSO was severe but not manifestly excessive.
R v Aspin 2011 EWCA Crim 2044 D pleaded on the day of his trial to burglary. D borrowed money from his uncle and regularly failed to pay it back. Knowing that £5,000 was hidden in his uncle's house, he sent a text asking if he was at work. Then he broke in and stole the money. Nothing else was taken. He had earlier been refused a loan for a smaller amount. D, aged 30 at appeal, had one conviction for affray in 1999. It was thought that he was suffering from post-traumatic stress disorder after distinguished service in Iraq and Afghanistan. Held. This was a planned offence involving a significant sum of money. V was a family member. **9 months** was not excessive.
R v Steele 2012 EWCA Crim 179 K and P pleaded to burglary. In the early hours they entered an untenanted flat and pulled the radiator off the wall. A quantity of copper pipe was ripped out and water damage was caused. The cost of the damage was just over £300. K and P were brothers who had lost their mother when they were aged 13 and 10, and their father five years later. They rapidly became dependent on drugs and had been engaged in persistent crime since then. K had 58 convictions involving non-dwelling burglaries, drugs, theft, and breaches of court orders. P had 127 convictions at 41 appearances involving one dwelling burglary in 1993, three non-dwelling burglaries in 2007, drug offences, theft, breaches of court orders and assaults. Held. This was technically a dwelling burglary. This was a case of lesser harm and lower culpability making it Category 3. Because of the convictions it was outside the guidelines and starts at 12 months. With plea, **8 months** each, not 16 and 15 months.

---

[102] The report does not give details of what these related to.

See also: *R v Buckingham and Catterall* 2011 EWCA Crim 171 (Pleas to burglary. Property worth £3,000 stolen. Unoccupied house targeted at night. B, minor previous convictions. C, previous convictions for non-domestic burglary. Both were aged 21. B, **13 months**, not 18, C, **12 months** not 16, which reflected the different discounts for their pleas.)

R v Aksu 2012 EWCA Crim 1498 (Late plea. Broke into an unoccupied house and stole £600 worth of property including a TV, a computer and an Xbox. He had ransacked nearly every room. Aged 21 at appeal. Convictions for robbery aged 16. Category 2. Starting at 21 months, **18 months** not 2 years.)

R v Le Butt Seal 2013 EWCA Crim 1210 (Plea to attempted burglary. Substantial dwelling-house. Thwarted by burglar alarm. Reconnaissance carried out under guise of legitimate enquiry of homeowner's business. Significant damage to the porch. Aged 23. 70 offences including an old conviction for dwelling and non-dwelling burglary. Category 2. Starting at 2 years was appropriate. **16 months** not 2 years.)

Old pre-guideline cases: *R v Saw Re K* 2009 EWCA Crim 1, 2 Cr App R (S) 54 (p 367) at para 48 (**18 months**) *R v Etiele* 2010 EWCA Crim 1022 (**20 months**) *R v Hammon and Whitmill* 2010 EWCA Crim 1410 (**2 years' detention**) *R v Mendy* 2010 EWCA Crim 2067 (**3 years**)

For a summary of the first case see the 9th edition of this book and for the second and third cases see the 10th edition.

219.19   Dwelling   Expensive properties with antiques etc.   Pre-guideline cases

R v Johnson and Others 2009 EWCA Crim 649 O, C, N, J and R were convicted of conspiracy to burgle. O and C pleaded to handling. Over about a year there were 16 burglaries at large, isolated country houses and commercial premises. Antiques, silver, porcelain and jewellery were stolen. There was careful planning. Balaclavas and other headgear were used. Stolen 4×4 vehicles were also used which were burnt out soon afterwards. In one case well over £10m of property was stolen. Very little property was recovered. In many instances the loss was in the hundreds of thousands of pounds. The defendants were aged 32, 33, 30, 24 and 55 respectively. All defendants had been sentenced many times and had committed offences involving prison sentences. O had 17 burglary offences. In 2007, he and C pleaded to a conspiracy to burgle. C had 35 offences including burglary. R had 57 offences including an old burglary. N had 28 offences including burglary. J had 10 offences including burglary. The Judge did not start at the maximum because there had been no violence. Held. **11 years** for O and C, **10 years** for N, **9 years** for J and **8 years** for R were not manifestly excessive.

Note: The total loss or any finding about how many burglaries each defendant was connected to, or the suggested roles of the defendants, are not in the judgment (save J's role was limited to reconnaissance). Ed.

Att-Gen's Ref Nos 50-53 of 2012 EWCA Crim 2558 LCJ L, E and F pleaded to conspiracy to commit burglary and conspiracy to steal. J pleaded to conspiracy to commit burglary. 2½ month period over which the four men and others targeted and burgled high-value targets in well-organised and well-planned domestic burglaries committed after dark. Not all members of the gang were present at each burglary and each played a different role. Cash, jewellery and electronics were taken along with sentimental items. In one burglary, a safe was stolen containing £200,000 worth of jewellery and £30,000 cash. Extreme violence was used in two of the burglaries including hitting one of the occupiers with a crowbar. Some of the gang wore crash helmets to conceal their identities. The cars stolen during the burglaries were often offered for sale. At appeal, L was aged 23, J and E were aged 22, and F aged 21. L had convictions for violence and dishonesty in 2004, 2005, 2006, 2007, 2010 and 2011. J had significant convictions including dwelling burglaries in 2005 and 2007 (×2). E had a number of convictions including seven dwelling burglaries from 2004 to 2009. F had no dwelling burglary convictions and only one non-dwelling burglary conviction aged 16. Held. Two of the offences could have been charged as robbery and section 18. L was recruited to take part in the burglaries and was not an organiser. F and J initially pleaded on a false basis. E was only involved on one day. E would receive full credit, the others, 20%. For L, **8 years** not 5. For J, **5½ years** not 3 years 3 months. For E **4½ years** not 3 years 4 months. For F, **5½ years** not 3 years 2 months.

219.20   Dwellings/Hotel rooms
R v Massey 2001 2 Cr App R (S) 80 (p 371) The defendant, aged 34, pleaded to two burglaries at the Magistrates' Court. He broke into a guest's room at a hotel through a window. From the room and the guest's car he stole property worth £1,500. He also stole the car. The second burglary was also a guest's room at another hotel with access also gained through a window. The property stolen was worth £3,078. He admitted the offences in interview. He had many previous convictions including 36 for burglary and three for attempted burglary. The risk of reoffending was assessed as high. Held. The burglary of a guest's bedroom was much more akin to burglary of domestic premises rather than of a small business. It is close to the burglary of a bedroom. 2 and 2 years consecutive not 2 and 3 years so **4 years** not 5 in all.

219.21   Dwelling   Providing access to others in breach of trust   Pre-guideline case
R v Hallcup 2013 EWCA Crim 1036 D was convicted of conspiracy to burgle. She was employed as a nanny for a family who lived in a substantial house. D lived in an annexe to the house with her son. She was trusted and treated as a family friend. The family went on holiday and left D with keys so she could tend to the property. D's boyfriend, B, had an extensive criminal record. He took advantage of their relationship and D gave him the keys. D entered the house and took property worth £30,000 including some sentimental items. Very little was recovered. A window was left ajar to support the fiction that there had been a burglary in the ordinary sense of the word. The annexe in which D lived was also made to look as if it had been burgled. The Judge accepted that B had pressured D. D was aged 28 with a very young child who had significant medical problems. She was of good character. Held. The burglary was well planned. The Judge correctly applied the Burglary guideline. This was a Category 1 domestic burglary, aggravated by the feeling of betrayal resulting from D's breach of trust. That was a very significant aggravating factor. There was loss, both economic and sentimental. It was accepted that **2 years** was correct. D's child was being cared for by her family members. There was nothing…to conclude that the Judge reached the wrong judgement [in not suspending the sentence]. The Judge was in a much better position to reach the appropriate conclusion. Appeal dismissed.

219.22   Dwelling   Pubs etc. with living quarters   Pre-guideline cases
Note: In these cases it is important to consider whether the dwelling part of a pub was entered. Ed.
R v Robinson 2011 EWCA Crim 205 D pleaded to burglary (×2) and possession of crack cocaine. There were nine burglaries TIC'd. D broke into a pub and smashed the locks on the pool table and quiz machine and pulled the payphone from the wall. He also smashed the alarm. He was disturbed and ran away, leaving behind a hammer and a key. D's DNA was found at the scene. D broke into another pub, stealing the cash hoppers from the fruit machine. The landlord was disturbed and he called the police. D was arrested at his home address and found to be in possession of a wrap of crack cocaine. The other offences TIC'd related to burglaries of public houses in the same area. D had a disrupted upbringing and was the child of a heroin addict. He was involved in offending from the age of 11 and had convictions for 150 offences. The Judge considered the burglaries more akin to dwelling burglaries as the landlords lived on the premises. Held. The non-dwelling authorities had the missing element of the resident landlords. However, only the public parts were entered and no personal items were taken. Taking into account

the progress since incarceration, and recognising the truly dreadful record, there seems to be at last some prospect of this man beginning to shake off his drug addiction. **3 years** for the burglaries, not 5. One month for the crack cocaine remained.

R v Stonnell 2011 EWCA Crim 221 D pleaded (late) to burglary. She was staying at a bed and breakfast. CCTV showed that during the night she allowed a co-defendant into the property. Later, D entered the laundry room by kicking the door until the lock broke. The police attended and left, having spoken to D. Later, D was seen taking two large laundry bags from the laundry room to her bedroom. The proprietor of the hotel subsequently found that clean bed linen and towels had been taken, totalling around £400. D, aged 40, had convictions for 71 offences between 1987 and 2010 including two burglary convictions, one dwelling in 2001 and one non-dwelling in 2009. She had a bad drug habit. D was on bail when the instant offence was committed. The Judge said that D had clearly targeted the room with a view to acquiring property to sell. Held. This was an unusual burglary. It was not a commercial burglary. However, the usual sentence for a dwelling house burglary would not have reflected the offending. There was little to choose between D and her co-defendant in terms of criminality, despite the co-defendant being charged with theft and not burglary. **10 months** not 15.

For non-dwelling pub burglaries, see the *Non-dwelling pubs* para at **219.46**.

219.23   Dwelling   Repeatedly burgling the same place
An example: *R v Fiurasek* 2012 EWCA Crim 1705, 2013 1 Cr App R (S) 57 (p 321) (D pleaded to conspiracy to burgle. With two others he burgled a 77-year-old's home three times. Victim was in poor health and traumatised. Aged 21. Previous for dwelling burglary. The Judge started at 9 years and with plea **6 years**. Appeal dismissed.)

219.24   Dwelling   Sexual element, With a
Note: Where a burglary has a sexual element, the prosecution charge a sexual offence and the case is listed in the relevant sex chapter of this book. This practice enables notification to occur. There are some old burglary cases with a sexual element but they are too old and were before the guideline came into force. Ed.

219.25   Dwelling   Victim badly affected
R v Mikolajczak 2012 EWCA Crim 1232, 2013 1 Cr App R (S) 47 (p 265) D pleaded (10% credit) to burglary and TDA. He entered a house via an insecure window in the early hours of the morning. V, the occupier, awoke and heard the crunching of the gears as D made off in his car. The vehicle was found a few streets away. D was seen walking away from the car, taking off a hat and gloves and entering a house. V's keys and purse were found in the house. Her TV was found in the car. All the property was returned, save for the patio door key. The impact on V was serious. She was prescribed sleeping tablets for 2 weeks and was very anxious and nervous. She had to move out of the house as she did not feel safe. D had 42 offences between 2008 and 2011. These included three non-dwelling burglaries and one dwelling burglary. He was subject to a community order imposed the day prior to the instant burglary. The Judge accepted it was a Category 2 offence, but the aggravation allowed him to sentence outside of the guidelines. With D's criminal background, the Judge was not prepared to give the factor that his age was 19 much weight. Held. Where there are especially serious consequences the sentence can be above the guideline figure. D had a very bad record, the offence was committed at night and there was a significant effect upon the victim. Further, the offence was committed just one day after a community order was imposed for a non-dwelling burglary. **2 years 3 months** was not manifestly excessive.

219.26   Dwelling   Victim over 65
See also *Distraction burglaries* at **219.14** (where the victim is invariably elderly).
R v Fowler 2010 EWCA Crim 2242 D pleaded to burglary on the day of her trial. V was aged 67 and lived alone. V had medical and other problems affecting her mobility. Her condition would have been obvious to anyone who entered her home from the way the premises were equipped. D went to V's property, making out that she had been sent by

someone in authority to do some cleaning. She remained for around two hours, asking various personal and financial questions, then left saying that she would return a week later. The next day, D and her co-defendant returned stating that they were cleaners from community services. They explained that they were there to check up on the flat as their boss was coming to inspect what work had been done. Both women went upstairs and V went to check on them a couple of times but was told to sit down and rest her leg. The next day V noticed that a number of items were missing including a mobile phone, a post office pension card, jewellery, her diary, two model buses, a piece of paper with her PIN on it and an appointment card for physiotherapy. D and her co-defendant were arrested, both denying the offence and blaming each other. A victim impact statement detailed how V was nervous about opening the door to people and that the incident had destroyed her trust in people. D had 40 convictions for 96 offences including burglary of dwellings, theft, fraud and handling. The instant offence constituted a breach of a community order. The Judge noted the 'very unpleasant aspects of the offence' and indicated a 5-year starting point. Held. It can be said that there was seriously raised culpability which justified a starting point at or near the top end of the range indicated in *R v Saw* 2009 but it is in our judgement not arguable that this offence is at such an extreme level of culpability or impact as to justify a starting point above the range indicated in that authority. With a starting point of 4 years, with 1/6 credit for the plea, the appropriate sentence is **3 years and 4 months** not 4 years and 2 months.

R v Fitzjohn 2013 EWCA Crim 148 D pleaded to two burglaries. She was acquainted with V1, a man aged 87, who lived in sheltered accommodation. She was aware that the building consisted of a number of flats for the elderly. She went to V1's flat. He suffered from Parkinson's and had poor mobility. She asked him for a cup of coffee and whilst he was distracted, she stole his wallet and left. The wallet contained £40, a bank card, a social club card and a photograph of V1's late wife. None of the items were recovered. The following day, she went to V2's flat. He too suffered from Parkinson's and had poor mobility. She pretended to be the manager at the sheltered accommodation. She gently but firmly took hold of him and placed him in a chair. She asked whether he had won any money at bingo and that question, plus the fact that she was barefoot, made him suspicious. He checked the box where he kept his money and discovered it was empty. He stood up and approached D. There was a physical confrontation and D left. She had taken £400. D, aged 28, had a bad record and was addicted to heroin. There were 31 offences on 14 occasions including one for domestic burglary and one for robbery (3 years). V2 blamed himself for being tricked, suffered a loss of confidence and was depressed. It was accepted that these were Category 1 offences. Held. There were no threats of violence and the physical confrontation was not violent. The appropriate starting point is between 5 and 6 years. The Judge was right to give 25% credit for the plea at the PCMH. Starting at 5½ years, with credit for the plea, 4 years 3 months not 5 years 3 months.

Att-Gen's Ref Nos 44-45 of 2013 2013 EWCA Crim 1640 M and C pleaded (early) to conspiracy to burgle. C also pleaded possession of criminal property and converting criminal property. Both were involved in a number of dwelling burglaries across the country in which cash and jewellery were stolen. The victims were usually elderly and some were particularly vulnerable, with 19 being aged between 70 and 90 years. There were 42 burglaries identified as being part of the wider conspiracy. M accepted he was present and a participant in 17 of them. C admitted participating in 24 of them. The Judge sentenced them for their part in the wider conspiracy and their direct involvement with the burglaries that they had admitted. C opened a savings account through which some of the proceeds were laundered. M, aged 33 at appeal, had 22 convictions for 60 offences including 27 of burglary (at least six were dwellings). C, aged 20 at appeal, had a caution for dwelling burglary in 2010 and a caution for sexual activity with a child under 13. He also had a conviction for failing to provide a specimen and failing to comply with notification requirements. Held. The Judge identified the relevant features:

planning by a group of burglars, targeting of the aged and vulnerable, the geographical breadth of the conspiracy, the number of burglaries and the fact that numerous victims were confronted in their homes. There was also the targeting of items which held sentimental value, such as wedding rings, and M's previous convictions. The one redeeming feature was the lack of violence, but the physical dominance of those involved undoubtedly resulted in the victims being cowed and frightened. These offences were so serious that personal mitigation in the case of either M or C was of very modest significance. The starting point for M should have been in the region of **13-14 years**. With full credit, **9 years** not 7. There was a justifiable distinction between M, an older man with experience, and C, his assistant. For C, **6 years' detention** was correct, not 5.

Post-guideline case

R v Summerfields 2014 EWCA Crim 1114 D pleaded to dwelling burglary (×2). V, aged 83, lived alone at an isolated address. D and three others forced their way into the house and demanded money, jewellery and gold. Three of the men were wearing balaclavas. They took V around the house and she was forced to hand over £80 in cash. Antiques and other items worth £10,000 were taken. All items were subsequently recovered. The police arrived and the men fled. D's DNA was found on a white glove near the property and cell site data showed he was in the vicinity of the property at the time of the offence. One month later, whilst under police surveillance, D and C were seen travelling in a two-car convoy to an unoccupied house which they entered. The car had false plates. The property was not occupied because the owner was receiving treatment in a hospice. One of the vehicles had been seen in the vicinity of the property on a number of earlier occasions. The vehicles drove away from the address and the police stopped one. D was found in the boot, and property stolen during the burglary together with gloves, a hat and a trolley jack were also found in the car. The other car was found burnt out the next day. The estimated total loss was a safe and contents worth £150,000 and other items worth £12,000 which were not recovered. D, aged 58 at appeal, had 34 convictions for 75 offences between 1969 and 2013. Twelve of the 13 burglary convictions were of dwellings. In a 34-year period, D had been sent to prison 18 times. The minimum sentence applied. Held. In relation to the first offence, there were a significant number of aggravating features which, taken together, would justify a finding that the starting point fell outside the normal sentencing range in the guidelines. However, starting at 12 years was too high. Starting at 9 years was appropriate. With full credit, 6 years not 8. The second burglary clearly also fell into Category 1. The starting point should have been 5 years. With full credit, 3½ years. It was not wrong in principle to impose consecutive sentences. For totality, the 3½ years would be reduced to 2½. In total, **8½ years**, not 9½ years.

R v Fawcett and Another 2014 EWCA Crim 1174 D1 and D2 pleaded to burglary. They had targeted the rural home of a couple in their 70s from which they ran a catering business. The couple were known to D1 as their son had visited him in prison. D1 and D2 entered the property while no one was in. They stole a laptop and a safe containing cash from the Christmas period and other items totalling between £7,000 and £10,000. Some of the items were of sentimental value. D1 aged 32 had a long history of offending, including repeated shoplifting for which he had only recently been released from custody. D2 was aged 35 and had convictions for dishonesty. Held. This was a very mean offence committed at the home of the parents of a man who had only ever been kind to D1. While this was undoubtedly a Category 1 offence, there was insufficient evidence of the offence being professional owing to D1 and D2 leaving by taxi, which was booked in D2's first name and destined for their own address. With full credit, **3 years 4 months** not 4.

R v Glover 2015 EWCA Crim 1333 D pleaded to 11 burglaries, theft and four charges of fraud at the Magistrates' Court. The offending was subject to two committals. She was a carer for frail and elderly individuals. She was given keys to some of their homes and the burglar alarm codes in others. D stole a ring given to V1, aged 79, by her husband 60 years earlier. The ring was pawned. Three burglaries related to V2, aged 76, where jewellery and crystal items were stolen. Another three related to V3, aged 85, who was bedbound and lost jewellery. Access was gained by deactivating the alarm when V3 was asleep. Two related to V4, aged 86, who was in a wheelchair and lost a handbag with £200 in it, a bank book and some jewellery. Another two related to V5, aged 92, who believed rightly that someone was entering her house at night. She was not believed and so refused to go to bed to try to catch the culprit. This adversely affected her health. She lost money and jewellery. One burglary and another offence related to V6, who was receiving end of life care. He lost a chain and gold bangles. D was arrested and made admissions. She said she used the money for amphetamine and gambling addictions. She was aged 43 with only a motoring conviction. She cared for two young children. The Judge started at 3½ years, gave full credit and then made the two groups of offences consecutive making **56 months**. Held. With the good character and remorse, starting at the equivalent of about 7 years was clearly a stern sentence, but it was justified.

See also: *R v Fiurasek* 2012 EWCA Crim 1705, 2013 1 Cr App R (S) 57 (p 321) (D pleaded to conspiracy to burgle. With two others he burgled a 77-year-old's home three times. Victim was in poor health and traumatised. Aged 21. Previous for dwelling burglary. The Judge started at 9 years and with plea **6 years**. Appeal dismissed.)

Old pre-guideline cases: *R v Saw Re T* 2009 EWCA Crim 1, 2 Cr App R (S) 54 (p 367) (**2 years**) *R v Saw Re S* 2009 EWCA Crim 1, 2 Cr App R (S) 54 (p 367) at para 44 (**18 months**) *R v Passoni* 2009 EWCA Crim 1217, 2010 1 Cr App R (S) 37 (p 222) (**5 years**) *R v Dahl* 2010 EWCA Crim 2121 (**4 years**) *R v Jones* 2010 EWCA Crim 2242 (**6 months' detention**)

For a summary of the first two cases see the 9th edition of this book and for the last two see the 10th edition.

219.27 Dwelling Victim over 65 Previous convictions for similar offending   Pre-guideline cases

R v Beggs 2012 EWCA Crim 2226 D pleaded on rearraignment to burglary. He rang the communal bell of a residential property for the elderly. He said he wanted to see "Barbara at flat 18", which was indeed where she lived. He was granted entry by an 82-year-old resident. D went to flat 18 but was denied entry. The occupant rang Careline, a company who monitored the residential home. A while later, D opened to door to flat 4. A 94-year-old woman lived there. He asked if he could leave a message for 'Babs' and told the resident to write down his name and address. He gave false details. While she was distracted, he looked in her handbag but did not take anything. D asked to use the bathroom and then left. The woman pulled the Careline cord in her flat. The police responded and found D outside the residential property knocking on doors and windows. He had overdosed on medication and could not recall what he had done. He did not believe he had gone inside the property. The woman at flat 4 said she was 'a bit shaken up'. D, aged 41, had 69 offences on 21 occasions between 1986 and 2009, including 30 dwelling burglaries. The Judge considered he was a career distraction burglar. He was on licence at the time of the instant offence. D suffered from either epilepsy or a seizure disorder. However, the diagnosis was not understood or controlled. A doctor concluded that D was 'a person in deep distress' and that his actions 'can be considered a cry for help'. Held. This case had great harm, as the occupier was at home, elderly and vulnerable. There was higher culpability as D targeted his victim. The starting point was 3 years with a range of 2-6 years. There was a statutory aggravating factor of his previous convictions for very similar offences. D is a hardened distraction burglar and was on licence. The Judge was entitled to go outside the guideline and start at 7½ years. With 20% credit for the plea, 6 years was not manifestly excessive.

See also: *R v Brooker* 2011 EWCA Crim 1836, 2012 1 Cr App R (S) 70 (p 398) (Pleaded to burglary (×3) and possession of heroin. Targeted elderly homeowners and asked for donations to a fake charity. 13 burglary TICs. Stole wallets, mobile phones and money. Used bank cards from one burglary. 31 convictions for 68 offences, largely drug-related. Aged 27. 6 years was near the top of the range but not manifestly excessive.)

Old cases: *R v Cawley and Cawley* 2007 EWCA Crim 2030, 2008 1 Cr App R (S) 59 (p 341) (**7 years** for J and **8 years** for M) *R v Saw Re M* 2009 EWCA Crim 1, 2 Cr App R (S) 54 (p 367) at para 56 For a summary of the first case see the 8th edition of this book.

Dwelling   Minimum sentences

219.28   *Dwelling   Minimum 3 years' custody   Statutes*

Powers of Criminal Courts (Sentencing) Act 2000 s 111(1) This section applies where:

a) a person is convicted of a domestic burglary committed after 30 November 1999,

b) at the time when that burglary was committed, he was 18 or over and had two relevant domestic burglary convictions,[103] and

c) one of those other burglaries was committed after he had been convicted of the other, and both of them were committed after the relevant date.[104]

(2) The court shall impose an appropriate custodial sentence for a term of at least three years except where the court is of the opinion that there are particular circumstances which:

a) relate to any of the offences or to the offender, and

b) would make it unjust to do so in all the circumstances.

Powers of Criminal Courts (Sentencing) Act 2000 s 111(6) In this section 'an appropriate custodial sentence' means b) in relation to a person who is under 21 at that time, a sentence of detention in a Young Offender Institution.

Powers of Criminal Courts (Sentencing) Act 2000 s 115 Where an offence is found to have been committed over a period of two or more days, or at some time during a period of two or more days, it shall be taken for the purposes of s 111 (third domestic burglary) to have been committed on the last of those days.

Serious Organised Crime and Police Act 2005 s 73(5) Nothing in any requirement which requires that a minimum sentence is passed, affects the power of the court to act under s 73(2) (power to take into account assistance given by the defendant where there is a written agreement). (Section summarised.)

Mental Health Act 1983 s 37(1A)(b) Nothing in section 111 shall prevent the court from making a [Hospital Order or a Guardianship Order].

219.29   *Dwelling   Minimum 3 years' custody   Servicemen/women*

Powers of Criminal Courts (Sentencing) Act 2000 s 111(1) Where a) a person has at any time been convicted of an offence under Armed Forces Act 2006 s 42 (criminal conduct), and b) the corresponding offence under the law of England and Wales (within the meaning given by that section) was a domestic burglary, the relevant section of this chapter shall have effect as if he had at that time been convicted in England and Wales of that corresponding offence.

(1A) Where a) a person has at any time been found guilty of a member State service offence committed after the relevant date, and b) the corresponding UK offence was a class A drug trafficking offence or a domestic burglary, the relevant section of this chapter and subsection (1) above shall have effect as if the person had at that time been convicted in England and Wales of that corresponding UK offence.

---

[103] Powers of Criminal Courts (Sentencing) Act 2000 s 110(2A) For the purposes of subsection (1): a 'relevant domestic burglary conviction' means: a) a conviction in England and Wales of a domestic burglary, or b) a conviction in any other part of the United Kingdom or any other member State of an offence which would, if done in England and Wales at the time of the conviction, have constituted domestic burglary.

[104] Powers of Criminal Courts (Sentencing) Act 2000 s 110(2A) b) 'the relevant date', in relation to a relevant domestic burglary conviction, means i) in respect of a conviction in England and Wales, 30 November 1999.

219.30   *Dwelling   Minimum 3 years' custody   Crown Court Statistics   England and Wales*

Minimum 3-year sentence for third domestic burglary Aged 18+

Year	2002	2003	2004	2005	2006	2007	2008	2009	2010	2011	2012
Orders	36	84	157	185	197	242	298	358	392	473	523

Statistics for 2013-14 were unavailable before going to press.
Sentences for third-time domestic burglars Aged 18+

	2007		2008		2009		2010		2011	
	Male	Female	Male	Female	Male	Female	Male	Female	Male	Female
Absolute discharge	1	0	0	0	0	0	0	0	0	0
Conditional discharge	2	0	6	0	4	0	5	0	2	0
Fine	2	0	1	0	0	0	0	0	0	0
Community sentence	37	1	36	2	32	2	50	1	44	4
Fully suspended	35	1	49	2	37	1	35	1	32	4
Immediate custody	484	16	602	18	670	22	757	20	859	26
Other	14	0	22	0	21	0	29	0	20	2
Total	575	18	716	22	764	25	876	22	957	36

The figures for 2012-14 were not available before printing. For explanations about the statistics, see page 1-xxii. For more detailed statistics, see www.banksr.com Other Matters Statistics tab

219.31   *Dwelling   Minimum 3 years' custody   How to determine whether rule applies?*

R v Hoare 2004 EWCA Crim 191, 2 Cr App R (S) 50 (p 261) D pleaded to three burglaries and other counts. In 2000 he was sentenced for a dwelling house burglary and three TICs. In 2003 he committed the instant offence. The total dwelling house burglaries on his record was seven. In the Crown Court the Judge was wrongly informed by both counsel that D qualified for a 3-year sentence. Held. In fact D had only been convicted of one dwelling burglary at the commission of the third burglary. Powers of Criminal Courts (Sentencing) Act 2000 s 111 requires that in order for the automatic sentence to be triggered, the sequence required is: a) commission of first offence, b) conviction for first offence c) commission of second offence, d) conviction for second burglary, e) commission of third burglary, f) conviction for third burglary. This was not so in D's case. The sentence is therefore unlawful.

R v McInerney 2002 EWCA Crim 3003, 2003 2 Cr App R (S) 39 (p 240) LCJ The purpose of the section is, in the absence of specific or particular circumstances which would render it unjust to do so, to oblige the court to impose the prescribed custodial sentence. This means that Parliament has chosen a term as the standard penalty. The object of the section quite plainly is to require the courts to impose at least the minimum sentence. However, that does not preclude situations arising where it would be unjust to impose a sentence of 3 years, even where the offender qualifies. It may be helpful to give examples of the type of situation where a 3-year sentence may be unjust. The sentence could be unjust if two of the offences were committed many years earlier than the third offence, or if the offender has made real efforts to reform or conquer his drug or alcohol addiction, but some personal tragedy triggers the third offence or if the first two offences were committed when the offender was not yet aged 16. Section 111 gives the sentencer a fairly substantial degree of discretion as to the categories of situations where the presumption can be rebutted. This approach is supported by the decision of this Court in the case of *R v Offen and Others* 2001 2 Cr App R (S) 10 (p 44). Understood in this way section 111 can be regarded as reflecting the current sentencing practice of the courts in relation to those who are convicted of burglary on three separate occasions even where the statutory requirements do not apply.

219.32   *Dwelling   Minimum 3 years' custody   Caravans, canal boats etc.*
R v Coleman 2013 EWCA Crim 544, 2 Cr App R (S) 79 (p 514) D pleaded to an amended indictment for burglary which specifically stated the place of the burglary, which was a narrowboat, was an inhabited vessel which was a dwelling rather than a building. The Judge ruled the offence triggered the minimum sentence provisions. On appeal it was argued that because Powers of Criminal Courts (Sentencing) Act 2000 s 111(5) defines domestic burglary as 'burglary in respect of a building or part of a building which is a dwelling' the provisions did not apply. Held. Theft Act 1968 s 9(4) extends the venue of a burglary to include 'an inhabited vehicle or vessel when a person having habitation in it is not there as well as at times he is'. The two sections should be read together so the minimum sentence provisions did apply.

219.33   *Dwelling   Minimum 3 years' custody   Judicial guidance*
R v Saw 2009 EWCA Crim 1, 2 Cr App R (S) 54 (p 367) LCJ [The three-year minimum term] is not a guideline starting point of 3 years' imprisonment: it is a minimum sentence and where the offence is characterised by significant or seriously raised culpability or impact, longer sentences will be appropriate. The record of the offender is of more significance in the case of domestic burglary than in the case of some other crime.
R v Miller 2010 EWCA Crim 809, 2011 1 Cr App R (S) 2 (p 7) D pleaded to burglary of a care home. The particulars in the indictment did not allege that the building was a dwelling as it should have done if that was suggested. The Judge felt that D was liable to be sentenced under Powers of Criminal Courts (Sentencing) Act 2000 s 111, which provided for a minimum term of 3 years for a third domestic burglary (a building which is a dwelling). Held. By pleading guilty, D did not admit that the offence concerned a dwelling, therefore there is no basis for saying that it was 'domestic' for the purposes of section 111.
Att-Gen's Ref No 39 of 2013 2013 EWCA Crim 1756 D pleaded to burglary and two counts of breach of a Restraining Order. He had extensive convictions and was liable to the minimum sentence provisions. The Judge found exceptional circumstances based on his hopes for D's family and the general public if D became drug-free. Held. Courts should be careful not to fall into traps set by apparently powerful but unfocused mitigation. There was no justification for not imposing the minimum sentence. However, we decline to interfere with the Judge's brave decision.
R v Silvera 2013 EWCA Crim 1764 D pleaded to burglary. He had 58 previous convictions and was liable for a minimum sentence. The Judge considered because he was on licence at the time and the number of previous convictions the starting point should be increased to 4½ years. Held. The 3-year minimum term was not the starting point. The correct approach is to have regard to the guidelines and ensure the final sentence is not less than the minimum required. (Note: This is 3 years if there is no plea or 3 years with up to 20% credit if there is a plea. Ed.) This was a Category 2 case with a starting point of 1 year. Treating the convictions as an aggravating factor was not double-accounting as they included a variety of offences including robbery and theft. The previous convictions and the fact that D was on licence were aggravating features. There should have been a 3-year starting point so with the plea, 30 months.
The record of the offender is of more significance in the case of domestic burglary than in the case of some other crimes. There are some professional burglars whose records show that from an early age they have behaved as predators preying on their fellow

citizens, returning to their trade almost as soon as each prison sentence has been served. Such defendants must continue to receive substantial terms of imprisonment. There are, however, other domestic burglars whose activities are of a different character, and whose careers may lack any element of persistence or deliberation. They are entitled to more lenient treatment. It is of importance that the efforts which an offender has or has not made to rehabilitate himself are taken into account.

There are some first-time burglaries which on their facts are so serious that a sentence of **3 years or more** might be appropriate but, conversely, some third-, fourth- or fifth-time burglaries where a sentence of lower than 3 years could properly be justified. (Note: The lower sentence being achieved by reliance on the exception to section 111. Ed.) An offender convicted of a single domestic burglary will accrue a qualifying conviction. Equally an offender convicted on one occasion of three burglaries who asked for another three burglaries to be taken into consideration will also only accrue one qualifying offence. The totality of the actual criminal behaviour is important.

See also: *R v McKay* 2012 EWCA Crim 1900 (D was convicted of domestic burglary. The minimum sentence applied. It was a Category 1 offence. The Judge thought that he had to add the 3-year minimum to the 3-year starting point in the guidelines, and imposed 6 years. Held. That was wrong in principle. The Judge should not have added them together.)

See also the *Persistent burglar* paras at **219.57**.

219.34   Dwelling   Minimum 3 years' custody   Is it unjust?
Powers of Criminal Courts (Sentencing) Act 2000 s 111(2) The court shall impose an appropriate custodial sentence for a term of at least 3 years except where the court is of the opinion that there are particular circumstances which: a) relate to any of the offences or to the offender, and b) would make it unjust to do so in all the circumstances.

R v Gibson 2004 EWCA Crim 593, 2 Cr App R (S) 84 (p 451) The Judge indicated at one of the case adjournments that if residential accommodation could be found for the defendant she would make a Drug Treatment and Testing Order (DTTO). It was found and she sent him to prison. Held. Because of the rules when judges send defendants to prison after the judge indicates a non-custodial sentence it was wrong. His expectation was a 'particular circumstance' which made the minimum sentence unjust. DTTO substituted.

R v Sparkes 2011 EWCA Crim 880 D pleaded to two burglaries and other charges. He was on bail for other burglaries and when he received 5 years for those offences he pleaded not guilty to the instant offences. After forensic evidence was served, the Judge passed 3 years consecutive for the second set of offences. Held. The overall sentences should have totalled 6½ years. But unquestionably, the sentences for the instant offences had to be consecutive. If the minimum term were applied consecutively, the totality principle would be breached. Therefore it would be unjust to impose consecutive sentences of 3 years for the instant offences. 18 months concurrent but consecutive to his existing 5-year sentence.

R v Stone 2011 EWCA Crim 2823, 2012 2 Cr App R (S) 12 (p 50) D pleaded (20% credit) to burglary on rearraignment. He was seen trying to open a gate in an alleyway next to a house. Being unable to do so, and upon noticing that a window was open, he reached through the window and removed a box containing items worth £60. D, aged 28, had convictions for dishonesty, mostly of a minor nature. He had served a 12-month custodial sentence (2005) for attempted robbery, dwelling burglary and obtaining by deception. There was another dwelling burglary in 2000 (community service). The Judge found no exceptional circumstances. Held. Section 111 gives the judge a fair degree of discretion. With the age of the previous offending and the characteristics of the instant offence, namely that it was opportunistic in nature and without any breaking or entry, the imposition of so long a sentence was not required. **8 months** not 2 years 5 months, enabling immediate release.

R v Flack 2013 EWCA Crim 115, 2 Cr App R (S) 56 (p 366) D pleaded to burglary. He entered a house which was being renovated to let. As he entered the property he saw a builder's mobile in a porch and ran off with it. He had two qualifying burglaries on his record. He was given a minimum sentence. The defence said that was unjust because a) D was only aged 16 for his first qualifying burglary, b) the offence was the opportunist taking of a phone, c) access may well have been easier because the house was being renovated, d) the harmful features of a normal domestic burglary were absent, e) there was no evidence the owner had left property in the premises, f) there was no invasion of the home, g) on the other two qualifying burglaries no property was taken, h) there was no evidence anyone lived there and i) one of the other qualifying dwellings was undergoing repair. Held. That combination of factors made it unjust. 18 months not 29 months. (D's age is not specified. Ed.)

R v Fletcher 2015 EWCA Crim 1709, 2016 1 Cr App R (S) 28 (p 173) D pleaded to domestic burglary. He lived in supported accommodation with V, aged 19. Both had a small bedsit. V went to stay with friends and his bedsit was left unlocked as V had lost his key. D entered and stole V's X-box and controller. On arrest D said he had taken the X-box to stop it being stolen. There were two attempts to sell the X-box, but when they failed D's partner returned the X-box to V. D was aged 44, and had 42 court appearances for 93 offences. 21 of those offences were for breaches of court orders. 55 of the offences were for theft and similar offences. Two were for domestic burglaries (2004, 15 months and 2006, 27 months). Held. D did have a poor record, but the two previous domestic burglaries were respectively 11 and nine years prior to the latest offence and the nature of the offence itself was not the most severe of this sort. The minimum sentence was unjust. We start at 27 months, so with the plea, 18 months.

See also: *R v Taylor* 2014 EWCA Crim 1611, 2 Cr App R (S) 85 (p 658) (Plea (20% credit) to a third dwelling burglary. D handed himself in. He was aged 19, and had a substantial record including two burglaries (2007 and 2010). Held. 3-year minimum was unjust. D was aged 13 when first burglary was committed over six years ago and received a supervision order. **2 years' detention**, not 876 days.)

219.35 Dwelling   Minimum 3 years' custody   Attempted burglary

R v McGuire 2002 EWCA Crim 2689, 2003 2 Cr App R (S) 10 (p 40) Attempted burglary is not a qualifying offence for the purposes of the Act. Sentence quashed.

219.36 Dwelling   Minimum 3 years' custody   Defendant under 18   Judicial guidance

R v McInerney 2002 EWCA Crim 3003, 2003 2 Cr App R (S) 39 (p 240) LCJ Where an offender who is now aged 18 or over has two qualifying previous convictions for domestic burglary as a juvenile, a third alleged domestic burglary must be tried in the Crown Court, and the presumptive minimum sentence is a custodial sentence of 3 years. Although section 111 does not apply until the offender has attained the age of 18, it would seem to follow that for an offender who is aged under 18 but is charged with a third domestic burglary, a custodial sentence **in excess of 24 months** (the maximum term available for a Detention and Training Order) will be the likely sentence and so the Youth Court should generally commit the case to Crown Court for trial with a view to sentence under section 91.

219.37 Dwelling   Minimum 3 years' custody   Plea of guilty

Criminal Justice Act 2003 s 144(2) Where a sentence is to be imposed under Powers of Criminal Courts (Sentencing) Act 2000 s 111 nothing in that section shall prevent the court from imposing a sentence of 80% or more of the minimum period.

Note: This section is summarised. The section means if the defendant pleads guilty the court can impose a sentence which is 80% or more of the minimum term. Ed.

R v Smith 2002 EWCA Crim 2531, 2003 1 Cr App R (S) 120 (p 630) D pleaded to two counts of burglary and asked for one offence of theft to be taken into consideration. The victim of all the offences was D's mother, who owned a public house. D broke into the bar area at night and smashed open a pay telephone, two gaming machines and stock cupboards, and stole cash and food to the value of £850. He caused £600 of damage. At the time of that offence he was on bail pending sentence for a dwelling house burglary, for which he received a 9-month sentence. Following his release D's mother found him in his bedroom with some drugs and told him he had to leave. She had left her handbag on the landing from which she discovered £40 was missing after he had gone. That was the theft. At about 9 pm that evening, D broke into the residential part of the premises, kicked in the bedroom door and stole £750. He was arrested within a few days and made full admissions in interview. D was aged 20 with a substantial record of previous convictions including a number of non-dwelling house burglaries. He also had two convictions for dwelling house burglaries and triggered PCC(S)A 2000 s 111, requiring the Judge to impose an appropriate custodial sentence of at least 3 years unless it would be unjust so to do. A psychiatric report concluded that D had a history of depressive disorder, had dyslexia and some symptoms of post-traumatic stress disorder following abuse as a child. D was severely addicted to heroin. A letter from D's mother was also considered. Held. It was not unjust to impose the statutory minimum. However, the sentencing Judge made no mention of the fact that D had pleaded guilty, giving the clear impression that he had overlooked PCC(S)A 2000 s 152,[105] which provides that where a court imposes a sentence under section 111 it is entitled to reduce the statutory minimum to a sentence not less than 80% of the maximum sentence where an offender has pleaded guilty. **2½ years** (about 82% of the statutory minimum term) not 3 years.

R v Gray 2007 EWCA Crim 979, 2 Cr App R (S) 78 (p 494) D pleaded to a burglary and an attempted burglary. The Judge considered 5 years was the starting figure with a 30% discount for the plea. He then gave a 20% discount to the first 3 years (because of the Act) and 30% to the other 2 years. Held. The Judge should have applied 30% to the whole figure as all the Act does is to say the judge may not impose less than a certain figure.

R v McCarthy 2011 EWCA Crim 3107 LCJ The sentencing Judge wanted to give the defendant a full one-third discount, but felt restrained by the statute. Held. He was not so restricted. He could give the full discount as long as the sentence did not fall below the 20% maximum discount from the minimum sentence of 3 years, which is 2 years 4.8 months.

R v Kemp 2014 EWCA Crim 200 D pleaded to possession with intent to supply class A drugs at his adjourned PCMH. He qualified for a 7-year minimum sentence and the Judge gave him 6 years 3 months, which was just over 10% plea credit. Held. D had pleaded reasonably early and before the trial date was fixed. Had there been no minimum sentence he would have been entitled to 25%. He was entitled to just under the statutory maximum 20%, which makes 5 years 9 months.

Note: Although the case relates to a different minimum term, the principle would also apply to the burglary minimum term. Ed.

See also the **GUILTY PLEA, DISCOUNT FOR** chapter in Volume 1.

NON-DWELLING BURGLARY

219.38   Non-dwelling   Sentencing Council guidelines 2011
Burglary Offences Guideline 2012,[106] see www.banksr.com Guidelines tab The guideline applies to all offenders aged 18+. In force 16 January 2012.

STEP ONE Determine the offence category
page 12 The court should determine the offence category using the table below.

Category 1	Greater harm and higher culpability
Category 2	Greater harm and lower culpability or lesser harm and higher culpability
Category 3	Lesser harm and lower culpability

---

[105] Repealed by Criminal Justice Act 2003 Sch 37(7) para 1 and Sch 1 para 44(r) on 4/4/05 by SI 2005/950
[106] In force 16/1/12 regardless of the date of the offence, see page 3 of the guideline.

The court should determine culpability and harm caused or intended, by reference only to the factors below, which comprise the principal factual elements of the offence. Where an offence does not fall squarely into a category, individual factors may require a degree of weighting before making an overall assessment and determining the appropriate offence category.

Factors indicating greater harm
Theft of/damage to property causing a significant degree of loss to the victim (whether economic, commercial, or personal value), Soiling, ransacking or vandalism of property, Victim on the premises (or returns) while offender present, Trauma to the victim, beyond the normal inevitable consequences of intrusion and theft, Violence used or threatened against victim, Context of general public disorder.

Factors indicating lesser harm
Nothing stolen or only property of very low value to the victim (whether economic, commercial or personal), Limited damage or disturbance to property.

Factors indicating higher culpability
Premises or victim deliberately targeted (to include pharmacy or doctor's surgery and targeting due to vulnerability of victim or hostility based on disability, race, sexual orientation and so forth), A significant degree of planning or organisation, Knife or other weapon carried (where not charged separately), Equipped for burglary (e.g. implements carried and/or use of vehicle), Member of a group or gang.

Factors indicating lower culpability
Offence committed on impulse, with limited intrusion into property, Offender exploited by others, Mental disorder or learning disability, where linked to the commission of the offence

219.39

STEP TWO Starting point and category range

Having determined the category, the court should use the corresponding starting points to reach a sentence within the category range below. The starting point applies to all offenders irrespective of plea or previous convictions.

Where the defendant is dependent on or has a propensity to misuse drugs and there is sufficient prospect of success, a community order with a drug rehabilitation requirement under Criminal Justice Act 2003 s 209 may be a proper alternative to a short or moderate custodial sentence.

A case of particular gravity, reflected by multiple features of culpability or harm in para **219.38**, could merit upward adjustment from the starting point before further adjustment for aggravating or mitigating features, set out [below].

The starting point applies to all offenders irrespective of plea or previous convictions.

Offence category	Starting point (applicable to all offenders)	Range (applicable to all offenders)
Category 1	2 years	1 to 5 years' custody
Category 2	18 weeks' custody	Low-level community order to 51 weeks' custody
Category 3	Medium-level community order	Band B fine to 18 weeks' custody

For the meaning of a medium-level and a low-level community order see **16.12-16.13** in Volume 1.

219.40   [Aggravating and mitigating factors]
page 13 The table below contains a **non-exhaustive** list of additional factual elements providing the context of the offence and factors relating to the offender. Identify whether any combination of these, or other relevant factors, should result in an upward or downward adjustment from the starting point. **In particular, relevant recent convictions are likely to result in an upward adjustment**. In some cases, having considered these factors, it may be appropriate to move outside the identified category range.

When sentencing Category 2 or 3 offences, the court should also consider the custody threshold as follows:

Has the custody threshold been passed?

If so, is it unavoidable that a custodial sentence be imposed?

If so, can that sentence be suspended?

When sentencing Category 3 offences, the court should also consider the community order threshold as follows:

Has the community order threshold been passed?

Factors increasing seriousness
Statutory aggravating factors: Previous convictions, having regard to: a) the nature of the offence to which the conviction relates and its relevance to the current offence; and b) the time that has elapsed since the conviction   Offence committed whilst on bail.   *Other aggravating factors include:*   Offence committed at night,   Abuse of power and/or position of trust,   Gratuitous degradation of victim,   Any steps taken to prevent the victim reporting the incident or obtaining assistance and/or from assisting or supporting the prosecution,   Established evidence of community impact,   Commission of offence whilst under the influence of alcohol or drugs,   Failure to comply with current court orders,   Offence committed whilst on licence,   Offences Taken Into Consideration (TICs).
Factors reducing seriousness or reflecting personal mitigation
Offender has made voluntary reparation to the victim,   Subordinate role in a group or gang,   No previous convictions or no relevant/recent convictions,   Remorse,   Good character and/or exemplary conduct,   Determination and/or demonstration of steps taken to address addiction or offending behaviour,   Serious medical conditions requiring urgent, intensive or long-term treatment,   Age and/or lack of maturity where it affects the responsibility of the offender,   Lapse of time since the offence where this is not the fault of the offender,   Mental disorder or learning disability, where not linked to the commission of the offence,   Sole or primary carer for dependent relatives.

219.41   *Non-dwelling   Commercial premises*
R v Liddle 2011 EWCA Crim 1700 D pleaded (full credit) to burglary with intent to do damage. He entered a warehouse, smashed a number of internal windows, forced open

locked drawers and smashed furniture. The repairs were estimated at £5,000-£6,000. That offence was committed only weeks after the imposition of three suspended sentences for racially aggravated offences (×2) and a firearms offence relating to a CS-gas canister. Aged 36 at appeal, D had 37 appearances for 51 offences, including nine non-dwelling burglaries. Held. It was significant that D pleaded to burglary with intent to do unlawful damage, i.e. simply to cause damage inside the building. This offence is a serious example of its kind. 2 years not 3. The activation of the suspended sentences in full (**40 weeks**) was not unjust.

219.42   Non-dwelling   *Former dwellings that are being renovated*
See also: *R v Sticklen* 2013 EWCA Crim 615 (Plea to burglary. Also sentenced for breach of community order imposed for burglary. Initially pleaded to dwelling burglary, but the charge was reduced as the property was empty and awaiting letting by the agents. Intended to steal copper piping to fund drug habit. £500 worth of damage. Aged 25 with 27 offences between 2006 and 2011. Judge regarded the unoccupied property as akin to a dwelling and sentenced outside of the guidelines. That was wrong. **9 months** for the burglary and **3 months** for the community order making **12 months**, not 15 months and 4 months.)
Note: The Judge's approach seems faultless. The Court of Appeal's decision seems flawed, because it doesn't appear to recognise that it is more serious to burgle a house being renovated than commercial premises. In any event, even with a plea, 15 months for a defendant with previous convictions for burglary could not be regarded as manifestly excessive. Further, 19 months for a burglary and a breach of community order imposed for a burglary also cannot be regarded as manifestly excessive. Further still, as the loss was 'significant', there was planning and it is assumed he was equipped in order to dislodge the pipework and the boiler, that would make it a Category 1 burglary with a 2-year starting point. With the breach for a burglary offence, 30 months in all (which is slightly more than the starting point taken by the Judge) cannot be inappropriate. Ed.

219.43   Non-dwelling   *Hospitals*
R v Gould 2010 EWCA Crim 2051 D pleaded at the Magistrates' Court to burglary and racially aggravated harassment. He entered a hospital from which he was banned excluding a real medical emergency. He was discovered by a security guard in an area off-limits to the public with a bag and a pillow case. The bag contained a defibrillator worth around £5,000 and the pillow case contained drugs, syringes and tubing worth around £100. Whilst detained by security staff he called one member of staff, who was a Muslim, "a fucking terrorist" and said, "You're bombing everywhere". D had 21 previous convictions for 35 offences, mainly dishonesty and drug-related offending, having received a 3-year custodial sentence for a dwelling burglary with 7 TICs. It was submitted that a) the starting point of 4 years was too high and beyond the guidelines, and b) a 25% reduction for the plea was insufficient. Held. a) The aggravating features were his previous convictions, the fact that he knew he was banned from the hospital and that he had targeted a vulnerable institution in the public sector. This justified a departure from the guidelines. b) This is a case of the most red-handed capture of a burglar one could imagine. 25% (discount) was generous. **3 years** was certainly in no way excessive let alone manifestly so.

219.44   Non-dwelling   *Metal thefts*
R v Ganescu 2012 EWCA Crim 1984 D pleaded (full credit) to burglary. At 4.30 am police were called to an address. They found a Transit van parked in the street, with D and P in the rear of the van, pretending to be asleep. They were lying on sacks containing copper wire. The wire was the proceeds of the burglary of a scrap yard committed earlier that morning. It was worth around £800. The scrap yard had been the victim of a number of burglaries in the previous 6 months. D, aged 36, was a Romanian national with convictions beginning in 2010 for six offences of shoplifting and failure to appear at

court. He had no legal right to work in the UK. Held. The scrap yard was targeted and therefore it was a planned, commercial burglary. There was a reasonable inference to be made that D knew this was a repeat offence of a series committed by others. It was appropriate to start at the top of Category 2, namely 12 months. With the plea, **8 months** not 12.

See also: *R v Rye* 2012 EWCA Crim 2797, 2013 2 Cr App R (S) 11 (p 50) (Plea. Full credit. Two burglaries committed at night on electricity substations. Left out of action and in a dangerous state. £8,000 worth of damage. Copper stolen. No disruption to railway service. D aged 37. 21 convictions. He had not previously received a custodial sentence. J aged 33. One short custodial sentence and 14 convictions. Category 1. For D 20 months not 28. For J, 28 months not 36.)

See also the **THEFT** *Metal thefts* para at **346.23**.

219.45   Non-dwelling Museums
R v Stanton 2013 EWCA Crim 1456, 2014 1 Cr App R (S) 56 (p 351) D and W pleaded to conspiracy to burgle. They visited the Oriental Museum at Durham University and their screwdriver was confiscated. They were seen on CCTV going straight to a display cabinet containing Chinese artefacts valued between £1m and over £2m. Six days later they returned at night in two cars and removed bricks from the wall. They entered the museum and smashed a cabinet. A figurine and jade bowl were removed and hidden on wasteland near the museum. They then left in one of the cars. Two days later, D and two others picked up the other car. The following day, W was seen in the area looking agitated and was unable to locate the pieces. The items were retrieved undamaged several days later. D was aged 33 and had 19 previous court appearances including five non-dwelling burglaries as a juvenile. W had convictions for four non-dwelling burglaries as a juvenile. In 2011 they burgled an amusement arcade and stole £10,500 in cash. They were given suspended sentences which were current when the instant offence was committed. D had recently breached the terms of the suspended sentence (activated in full). The Judge said that he sentenced at the top end of the bracket because of a) the immense consternation of the dedicated museum staff, b) the concerns that benefactors might be worried about donating in the future, c) the planning, d) the tenacious and audacious execution, e) the items' huge cultural importance in China, f) both their previous convictions and g) both were on suspended sentences. He also said the recovery of the items was no thanks to them. Held. The recovery of the stolen property was a relevant factor in reduction of sentence. We start at 8 years not 9, so with 10% plea credit, **7 years** not 8 with W's suspended sentence activated in full, making 9 years.

Note: If you factor in the Judge's reasons and a) the danger of the items being lost or damaged because of the reckless methods used, b) the items were irreplaceable, c) the inevitable danger to the items when the cabinet was smashed and d) the high value of the items, the Judge's approach does not seem open to criticism. Because of the outrage felt when national treasures are threatened and the bond between museums and their staff and the community, museums should perhaps be treated in Theft Act 1968 s 9(3)(a) and in the guidelines as being in the dwelling burglary category rather than the other/non-commercial category. Ed.

219.46   Non-dwelling   Pubs etc.
Note: In these cases it is important to consider whether the dwelling part of a pub was entered. Ed.
R v Robinson 2011 EWCA Crim 205 D pleaded to burglary (×2) and possession of crack cocaine. There were nine burglaries TIC'd. D broke into a pub, smashed the locks on the pool table and quiz machine and pulled the payphone from the wall. He also smashed the alarm. He was disturbed and ran away, leaving behind a hammer and a key. D's DNA was found at the scene. D broke into another pub, stealing the cash hoppers from the fruit machine. The landlord was disturbed and called the police. D was arrested at his home address and found to be in possession of a wrap of crack cocaine. The other

offences TIC'd related to burglaries of public houses in the same area. D had a disrupted upbringing and was the child of a heroin addict. He was involved in offending from the age of 11 and had convictions for 150 offences. The Judge considered the burglaries more akin to dwelling burglaries as the landlords lived on the premises. Held. The non-dwelling authorities had the missing element of the resident landlords. However, only the public parts were entered and no personal items were taken. Taking into account the progress since incarceration, and recognising the truly dreadful record, there seems to be at last some prospect of this man beginning to shake off his drug addiction. **3 years** for the burglaries, not 5. One month for the crack cocaine remained.

R v Stonnell 2011 EWCA Crim 221 D pleaded (late) to burglary. She was staying at a bed and breakfast. CCTV showed that during the night she allowed a co-defendant into the property. Later, D entered the laundry room by kicking the door until the lock broke. The police attended and left, having spoken to D. Later, D was seen taking two large laundry bags from the laundry room to her bedroom. The proprietor of the hotel subsequently found that clean bed linen and towels had been taken, totalling around £400. D, aged 40, had convictions for 71 offences between 1987 and 2010 including two burglary convictions, one dwelling in 2001 and one non-dwelling in 2009. She had a bad drug habit. D was on bail when the instant offence was committed. The Judge said that D had clearly targeted the room with a view to acquiring property to sell. Held. This was an unusual burglary. It was not a commercial burglary, but the usual sentence for a dwelling house burglary would not have reflected the offending. There was little to choose between D and her co-defendant in terms of criminality, despite the co-defendant being charged with theft and not burglary. **10 months** not 15.

R v Green 2012 EWCA Crim 112 D was convicted of burglary of a public house which was under renovation. The owner returned to discover D inside the property, having forced a window. D tried to flee and was restrained. He was found to have a screwdriver and a torch on him, and another was found nearby. D, aged 30, had a number of convictions, significantly four for commercial burglary and two for going equipped. Held. This was not a completed burglary. The pre-sentence report noted a high risk of reoffending. Though severe, 2 years was not manifestly excessive.

Post-guideline cases

R v Kadiri 2014 EWCA Crim 1106 D pleaded (at the first opportunity) to commercial burglary. D was seen in an office building by a cleaner who became suspicious and called the police. D had left by the time the police arrived. Two iPads and a laptop computer worth £2,500 had been stolen. D was identified by CCTV. D was aged 36 at appeal with a 'truly appalling' record. Since the age of 16, he had been convicted on 54 occasions of 109 offences. Those included drug offences and one rape (7 years, 2003). Non-dwelling burglaries greatly predominated over the previous 20 years. In June 2011 he received 33 months for five non-dwelling burglaries. He was on licence when the instant offence was committed. The Judge considered that the offence was pre-planned. He gave 20% credit as he considered the case overwhelming. Held. The Judge properly remarked that D was a career commercial burglar. The starting point [of just short of 50 months] could not be said to be arguably wrong, but case not overwhelming so with full credit **2 years 8 months**, not 3 years 3 months.

R v Murphy 2015 EWCA Crim 1523 D pleaded (full credit) to two burglaries. Both were at a social club where his girlfriend once worked and were just over a month apart. In both he forced a fire door. In the first he smashed gaming machines, doors, snooker tables and stole £300 cash. In the second, with two other people, he stole a TV worth £300, several bottles of spirits and a monitor for a computer. The goods were worth just over £1,000 and the damaged caused was £400. The club was not insured. D was aged 24 and had convictions but none for burglary. He lived with his mother and was unemployed. He said he was short of money. Held. Together the two merited 3 years, so with plea, **2 years**.

For dwelling pub burglaries see the *Pubs* para at **219.22**.

219.47   *Non-dwelling   Ram-raiding   Judicial guidance*
R v Percy 1993 14 Cr App R (S) 10 LCJ Inevitably cars are stolen and damaged. An offence of this kind is an affront to the people who are present. Furthermore there are risks that people will be injured. It was a heavy crime, much closer to armed robbery than ordinary theft.
R v Byrne 1995 16 Cr App R (S) 140 LCJ The defendants pleaded or were convicted of theft. It is almost always a composite offence. It involves the theft of other vehicles before the main theft is attempted. It involves targeting a particular prize and planning the offence with deliberation. There will almost always be serious damage to property. The offence is aimed at defeating even the best security. It is a kind of military operation against whatever security precautions may be in place. There is the element of breach of the peace. Here in the middle of the night there was an operation which roused people and put some of them in fear. It is an affront to civilised society. It is an outrageous offence.
R v Richardson and Brown 1998 2 Cr App R (S) 87 A real differential should be maintained between even domestic burglaries of some gravity and determined commercial burglary of this sort on a bank with vehicles and equipment used.
R v Lawlor 2012 EWCA Crim 1870 S pleaded and L was convicted of a conspiracy to rob a bank. Held. The nature of ram-raiding can differ. Whichever form it takes, and whether charged as theft, burglary or robbery, it is not easy to pigeon-hole ram-raiding within any particular guideline.

219.48   *Non-dwelling   Ram-raiding*
Att-Gen's Ref Nos 45-49 of 2007 2007 EWCA Crim 3383, 2008 1 Cr App R (S) 88 (p 525) C, Br, Bo, Bu and S pleaded to conspiracy to steal and conspiracy to burgle. They were involved in a campaign of ram-raiding over a four-month period. The conspiracy to steal was the obtaining of vehicles to use in their campaign. A health centre, a House of Fraser store (twice), a van with computer equipment, a Currys electrical store (twice), two garages, a Staples store, a Jessops store, a restaurant, a business centre and three other stores were attacked. Balaclavas and masks were worn. The damage caused was more than £116,000 and the property taken was worth more than £170,000. Each limited his plea to specific burglaries and stolen vehicles. C admitted four burglaries (two were ram-raiding) and six thefts. Br admitted four ram-raid burglaries and a theft. Bo and Bu admitted three ram-raid burglaries and five and four thefts respectively. S admitted two burglaries (one was ram-raiding) and four thefts. One theft he had already been sentenced for. The defendants were aged 20-23. All had substantial previous convictions. S had 10 court appearances for 21 offences including TDAs and commercial burglaries (one of which was ram-raiding). Br had 13 offences on eight court appearances, the majority of which were aggravated vehicle-taking or commercial burglaries. Bo had nine offences on six occasions, almost all of which were TDA or commercial burglaries, including one ram-raid. Bu had 23 offences on 11 occasions including TDA and commercial burglaries, one of which was a ram-raid. S had 39 offences on 19 occasions including TDA and two commercial burglaries. All were on licence. All continued to offend on bail. Br had been released from prison. Held. *R v Perry* 1993 14 Cr App R (S) 10 (plea, one ram-raid **5 years** upheld), *R v Byrne* 1995 16 Cr App R (S) 140 (plea to theft, one ram-raid against cash machine at building society, **5 years** upheld) and *R v Richardson and Brown* 1998 2 Cr App R (S) 87 (eight-man team against a bank's cash machine, £75,000 taken. **5 years** not 7 for the plea) suggest that in the context of a single ram-raid the starting point after a trial is a sentence of **approaching 7 years**. C **6½ years** not 3½. Br **5 years'** detention not 2½ with an extra allowance because of his release. Bo and Bu **5½ years'** detention not 2½. S **4 years** not 2.
R v Delaney 2010 EWCA Crim 988, 2011 1 Cr App R (S) 16 (p 117) D was convicted of two offences of burglary and four of TDA. In each case ATMs were ripped from buildings and taken away. A JCB and a Transit van were stolen. The front entrance doors

of a Co-op had been completely smashed and an ATM with £10,000 was stolen. A milkman had to move his float to avoid it being hit. The burglars were heavily disguised. For the second offence, a JCB and a Toyota car were stolen. In the early hours the JCB was seen being driven backwards and forwards ramming the front of a bank. The JCB reversed out dragging the ATM into the street. The JCB was abandoned and the Toyota was driven off with the ATM on the back. It contained £87,000. The total damage on this occasion was estimated at £40,000 or more. D told his wife that each of the burglars had received £27,000. D had a number previous convictions including one for burglary, theft, handling and taking vehicles without authority. Held. **10 years** not 12.

R v Lawlor 2012 EWCA Crim 1870 S pleaded to <u>conspiracy to rob</u> on rearraignment (25% credit), and L was convicted of the same offence. Car keys to a VW and a BMW were stolen in a burglary. The cars were then driven to a bank. L was driving the VW, with two masked men inside. L waited until the bank had closed and reversed the VW into the bank, twice, smashing the glass. The two masked men jumped out, shouted at the bank manager and two cashiers and grabbed cash boxes containing £108,000. The three staff were hit by flying glass. The two cars were then driven off in convoy at speed. The BMW and the money were never recovered. The Judge accepted that no weapons were used. The raid lasted 29 seconds. S's record was worse than L's, but the instant offence represented a significant increase in their offending. Held. There was sophistication and careful planning, a number of robbers were involved and masks/disguises were worn. We reject that no weapons were used, the VW was used as a weapon in order to gain entry. *R v Hibbert* 2008 EWCA Crim 1854 and *R v McCaffery and McCaffery* 2009 EWCA Crim 54, 2 Cr App R (S) 56 (p 392) suggest sentences of 10-15 years after a trial for a single offence of robbery. Moreover, the case falls to be considered in light of the higher sentences contemplated in *R v Thomas and Others* 2011 EWCA Crim 1497, 2012 1 Cr App R (S) 43 (p 252). For L, **12 years** and for S, **9 years** might be considered severe, but were not manifestly excessive.

Note: It is important to remember that this was a conspiracy to rob plea. The problem with this is that the three cases relied on involve firearms. If the distinction between robberies with and without firearms is blurred, sentencing will become more complex and unfair. The Court in its summary of the other cases never referred to the fact that the cases involved firearms. The Court also in its judgment did not refer to the guideline about using a weapon in a robbery. Ed.

Post-guideline case

Att-Gen's Ref Nos 74-78 of 2014 2014 EWCA Crim 2535, 2015 1 Cr App R (S) 30 (p 233) L, G, C, D, and J pleaded guilty to conspiracy to burgle and attempting to cause or, in the cases of L and G, actually causing an explosion. CCTV footage showed a car pulling up at a Barclays ATM in the early hours. Two masked and gloved men in dark clothing got out whilst a third remained in the driver's seat. One male carried a sledgehammer and crowbar from the car's boot to the bank's front door. The other male removed two gas canisters, one acetylene and one compressed oxygen, from the car and hid them at the side of the bank. The men then left in the car, returning nine minutes later. The two males got out again and, having forced the ATM's front, placed the gas canisters close to it. They then attached wires and hoses and detonated the canisters. The front door of the bank was smashed and the two men repeatedly went inside, retrieving £19,170 in cash. Replacing the ATM and repairing the damage cost almost £39,000 in total. The telephone data indicated the three individuals were L, C and D. Additionally, L's DNA was on the sledgehammer and both he and D contacted several gas canister suppliers. Three weeks later the trio, using the same *modus operandi*, tried to burgle another Barclays ATM but were unsuccessful. Two vehicles were spotted nearby and, shortly after the failed attempt, they drove off. Another week later, two very similar vehicles, one stolen and with false number plates, drove to the same Barclays and attempted the same burglary. G and C attempted to blow the ATM apart, but the police arrested them as they tried to hide. C said, "I suppose I'm bang to rights then. I suppose it's too late to say sorry." D was also arrested, after a struggle, as he attempted to drive off. S was arrested a short distance away in the second vehicle. Phone evidence was consistent with both D and J also being involved in the second and third attempts. Since March 2013, there had been an increasing vogue for gas attacks on ATMs. The method had been used on more than 70 occasions. Over £1m had been lost. L, aged 28, received full credit and had 13 convictions, mostly for dishonesty and violence. His last offences were ABH and GBH committed in 2013 and 2014 but he had had a very difficult upbringing. G, aged 39 on appeal, received full credit and had 17 convictions, mostly for dishonesty, drugs and violence. C, aged 29 on appeal, received full credit and had eight convictions, mostly for dishonesty. He received a 6-year extended sentence for his last offence, GBH with intent. D, aged 30 on appeal, received full credit and had 19 convictions, mostly for dishonesty. J, aged 29 on appeal, received full credit for the burglary conspiracy but only 25% credit for attempting to cause explosions (×2). He had 24 convictions, mostly for dishonesty and some violence. He had received custody as a youth. Held. Offences such as these, which include the use of gas cylinders, and which are increasing across the UK, require deterrent sentences. We would hesitatingly have imposed consecutive terms, not least to emphasise the gravity of the explosion count, and so that any court in future considering previous convictions would find the Court's approach obvious on the face of [the offenders'] antecedent history. We are not persuaded that the Judge adequately marked the element of deterrence. We have found it less straightforward than it might at first have appeared. Although all members of this Court would have passed consecutive sentences so as to mark the explosion offences, we intend to remain loyal to the Judge's concurrent sentencing. For L, J and G we start at 10 years. For the rest we start at 12 years. For L **6 years 9 months**, not 5 years 4 months. For G, C and D, **8 years**, not 6. For J, **7½ years** for the explosion offences, not 6.

219.49   Non-dwelling   Schools   Pre-guideline case
R v Adams 2010 EWCA Crim 974 D pleaded early to six counts of burglary with six other burglaries TIC'd. The burglaries were of schools. In the first burglary three computer screens and a hard drive were stolen. In the next three nothing was taken. In the last two a projector was stolen each time. The total value of equipment stolen was £3,000 and £300 damage was caused to premises. D had 23 convictions for burglary and had received custodial sentences including one of 6 years. **4 years** not 6.

219.50   Non-dwelling   Shops etc.   Pre-guideline cases
R v Derham 2012 EWCA Crim 342 D pleaded to burglary of shop premises (×5) and theft. He had previously worked at a Guess clothing store at a shopping centre. After ceasing to work at the store, he still had his key to the stockroom. On five occasions, he entered the stockroom and stole a quantity of clothing. They were the burglaries. The theft was committed in another shop in the same centre where D was working at the time. Again he entered the stockroom and stole a quantity of clothing. The total was in the region of £6,500. D, aged 27, had no previous convictions. There was one caution which was treated as being irrelevant. There was a report from prison which was distinctly unfavourable. His wife was expecting their second child. Held. The offences were committed to some extent in breach of trust. D is not a professional burglar. A proper starting point was 12 months. With the pleas, **8 months** not 16.
R v Scott 2013 EWCA Crim 2651 D pleaded to burglary. D and others wearing helmets used a hammer to smash the glass door of a John Lewis store in Oxford Street. They smashed display cases containing high-value watches. Property valued at £78,000 was taken, with damage estimated to be between £8,000 and £10,000. D was aged 29 and had ten convictions for 14 offences, including three for burglary or attempted burglary. A medical report indicated he had moderate learning difficulties and was more suggestible than average. Held. This was a very serious professional burglary justifying a substantial sentence. The Judge was entitled to go above the range suggested in the guidelines due to the aggravating factors. **4½ years** upheld.

R v Grieves and Others 2014 EWCA Crim 540 G, R and F pleaded to burglary (25% credit). At about 12.30 am, G and F disabled the alarm and security camera at a bookmaker's. The shutters in front of the premises were disabled so that they could not be opened. One and a half hours later, G and F returned to the premises with R. Two of them gained entry by forcing open the rear fire door. R acted as a lookout. They had cutting tools and gloves. They sprayed two bottles of bleach at the windows in an attempt to conceal scientific evidence. An attempt was made to break into the gaming machines and the safe was pulled from its mounting. The premises were 'wrecked'. The police attended and all three ran from the premises but were arrested. G had five burglary convictions but none since 2002. He suffered from panic attacks and had been looking after three children. F, aged 27 at the time, had two court appearances but nothing of this type. R had a very long record with 49 convictions for 137 offences including numerous convictions for burglary. There were none between 2006 and 2011. Held. This was a highly professional, determined, criminal venture with all the hallmarks of expertise gained from previous ventures. There was a significant degree of planning. The premises were targeted by a gang. There was major disturbance of the property and it was a burglary for high stakes. A starting point of 4 years was correct. Marking the fact that F had never previously been convicted of burglary or been to custody, **2 years** not 3. For R and G, **3 years** was not manifestly excessive.

Old case: *R v Whelan* 2010 EWCA Crim 2075 (**2 years**) For a summary of the case see the 10th edition of this book.

See also the **Commercial premises** para at **219.41** and the **Ram-raiding** paras at **219.47**.

219.51   Non-dwelling   Shops   Looting during public disturbance   Judicial guidance

R v Blackshaw and Others 2011 EWCA Crim 2312 LCJ The Court considered the appeals against the sentences imposed for burglary committed during, and as a part of, widespread public disorder. Held. Those who deliberately participate in disturbances of this magnitude, causing injury and damage and fear to even the most stout-hearted of citizens, and who individually commit further crimes during the course of the riots, are committing aggravated crimes. 'It is a wholly wrong approach to take the acts of any individual participator in isolation' (*R v Caird* 1970 54 Cr App R 499). The imposition of severe sentences, intended to provide both punishment and deterrence, must follow.

See also the **RIOT** chapter and the **ROBBERY** *Looting* para at **322.19**.

219.52   Non-dwelling   Shops   Looting during public disturbance   Internet encouragement/organisation

R v Blackshaw and Others 2011 EWCA Crim 2312 LCJ In unconnected appeals, B pleaded to encouraging etc. offences believing one or more would be committed, contrary to Serious Crime Act 2007 s 46. S pleaded to encouraging etc. the commission of an offence, contrary to Serious Crime Act 2007 s 44. B and S used Facebook to post messages and create 'events' inciting local residents to engage in the rioting which had recently taken hold of their communities. In both cases, members of the public contacted the police and no one attended at the proposed meeting points, despite 47 people agreeing to attend S's event. S cancelled the event immediately before the police arrested him, with the suggestion that his motivation was that the police were searching for him. B was aged 21 and S aged 22. Held. We are conscious that no harm actually occurred. However, it is not accurate to state that neither had any adverse consequences. Some citizens were appalled at what they had read and some were put in fear. Deterrent sentences were entirely appropriate. Modern technology enables the incitement of many people in one step. Both were caught red-handed. **4 years** for both was appropriate.

219.53   Non-dwelling   Shops   Looting during public disturbance

Examples: *R v Blackshaw and Others* 2011 EWCA Crim 2312 *Re H* (LCJ Plea to burglary (×5) and violent disorder. Orchestrated the group. Threw bricks at police and police dog. Stole £280 worth of alcohol and cigarettes. **4 years 8 months** upheld.) *Re V*

(Plea to burglary. Stole a camera worth £300 from a shop which had suffered £15-20,000 worth of damage. Aged 25, no relevant convictions. **20 months** was in the appropriate range.) *Re GD* (Pleaded. Aged 19. Previous convictions including robbery. Caught taking alcohol and cigarettes from a Sainsbury's store. **2 years' detention in YOI** was in the appropriate range.) *Re K* (Pleaded to burglary. Aged 18. Stole speakers, media centre and a camera from Comet. £855,000 stolen in total. With 25% credit, as he was caught red-handed, **12 months' detention in YOI** was within the appropriate range.) *Re M* (Plea to burglary. Stole a television from Argos. £40,000 damage caused and a total of £80,000 stolen. Her father received an eviction notice. Aged 19. Good character. **13 months' detention** in YOI was appropriate.)

Types of burglar (Dwelling and non-dwelling)

219.54   *Types of burglar   Defendant aged under 18   Guideline cases*
R v Saw 2009 EWCA Crim 1, 2 Cr App R (S) 54 (p 367) LCJ In the context of a young life which is at present being wasted away, a constructive, rehabilitative sentence, which includes a punitive element, may provide a better long-term solution for the public generally, and particularly for other householders, than an unconstructive custodial sentence. The Judge is not the prisoner of the sentencing tariff, but rather has the difficult task of arriving at the right sentence in the individual case. Whether an individual case is one for which such a course may be appropriate requires careful judgement. The age of the defendant is likely to be a relevant factor.
Note: The *Burglary Offences Guideline 2012* does not apply to those aged under 18, see **292.3**. I would expect most judges would determine the appropriate sentence for an adult and then make a reduction. Ed.

219.55   *Types of burglar   Defendant aged under 18   Cases*
R v G 2010 EWCA Crim 469 D was convicted of burglary. He had earlier pleaded to another burglary. On 11 July 2009, he went to a house made into bedsits for asylum seekers. D smashed the window above the door of two of them. Some of the property was found by the police in a third bedsit where he was with the resident. £1,300 worth of property was missing, including two laptops, an iPod and jewellery. D was two days short of his 16th birthday. In the three months before the offence, he had court appearances on 2 March for two robberies (a Referral Order), 31 March for theft, 27 April for theft, 18 May for shoplifting, 22 June for two witness intimidations and a robbery, and 7 July when he was sentenced to a Supervision Order for the previous four matters. From 22 July to 17 August he had been in custody. Then he was tagged with a curfew. D had an IQ of 61 with difficulties of verbal comprehension, which would put him last in a group of 1,000 children. Experts disagreed about his condition but some found autism and Asperger's syndrome. One said that he was extremely vulnerable and easily influenced. The risk of reoffending was assessed as high. Held. The case raises the difficulty of sentencing a young person with learning difficulties who is out of control. In many instances a custodial sentence becomes inevitable. The four-day gap between the Supervision Order and the burglaries is a grave aggravating factor. **6 months'** detention not 10.
R v F 2012 EWCA Crim 1142 F pleaded on the day of trial to a dwelling burglary. He acted as a lookout while an older man committed the burglary. The victim was a 17-year-old girl who was alone in the house. She was confronted by the man during the burglary. There was no violence. F, aged 14, had previous convictions for dwelling burglary and robbery. F had already served a custodial sentence. He was given a Youth Rehabilitation Order and told that he was being given a chance. He failed to comply with the order in almost every respect. F was brought back before the same Judge. Held. A custodial sentence was inevitable. Given his record and the offence, 12 months was excessive. Having regard to his very young age, an **8-month DTO** was appropriate.

Note: The defendant was then released almost immediately. Some may wonder why the defendant, who was so determined not to engage with society, was not given a longer sentence to deter him from further crime. Ed.

R v L and D 2015 EWCA Crim 59 L and D (a girl) pleaded (full credit) to a dwelling burglary. V lived in a room in a shared house. The front door was key operated and each room had its own PIN code. V knew both L and D. V went to F's house where D and others were. F was V's friend. V mentioned that she had £1,130 in cash in her room for buying a car. F asked V if she could borrow her Hoover. V returned to her own house with D in a taxi to get it. Both V and D then returned to F's house. Later that evening, V returned home, finding that she had been burgled. There was no damage to the front door, but she had lost her keys a few days earlier, and her room's door was damaged and hanging off the frame. The room was left intact and only the cash had been stolen. Text messages between L and D implicated L and another person breaking in. The messages also highlighted a complete and utter lack of remorse. D and L also continued to pretend to be V's friend whilst spending her money on hotels and alcohol. No money was ever recovered. V was affected badly, she had to move away, lost her room and had to pay for the damage. She took anti-depressants and felt frightened and vulnerable with D having betrayed her trust. It was accepted that the burglary fell into Category 1. L was aged 17 with only a reprimand and a caution for cannabis possession. Having left college at 16, he had no regular employment. He used the stolen money to fund his cannabis habit and to purchase luxury items. D was aged 16 and of good character. She was in full-time education with an interview for an apprenticeship. Held. L had no relevant previous convictions, a mitigating factor identified in the guideline and was still aged only 17. 2 years' detention in a YOI was too harsh, so **12-month community order with supervision** substituted. For D, Having regard to the *Overarching Principles: Seriousness Guideline 2004* and the welfare of D, **12-month youth rehabilitation order with supervision** not 1-year Detention and Training Order.

Old cases: Best ignored.

219.56   *Types of burglar   Drug addicts   Guideline and pre-guideline judicial guidance*

Burglary Offences Guideline 2012, see www.banksr.com Guidelines tab page 8 Where the defendant is dependent on or has a propensity to misuse drugs and there is sufficient prospect of success, a community order with a drug rehabilitation requirement under Criminal Justice Act 2003 s 209 may be a proper alternative to a short or moderate custodial sentence.

R v McInerney 2002 EWCA Crim 3003, 2003 2 Cr App R (S) 39 (p 240) It is common knowledge that many domestic burglars are drug addicts who burgle and steal in order to raise money to satisfy their craving for drugs. This is often an expensive craving, and it is not uncommon to learn that addicts commit a burglary, or even several burglaries, each day, often preying on houses in less affluent areas of the country. But to the victim of burglary the motivation of the burglar may well be of secondary interest. Self-induced addiction cannot be relied on as mitigation. The courts will not be easily persuaded that an addicted offender is genuinely determined and able to conquer his addiction.

In the case of offences committed because the offender is an alcoholic or a drug addict, while the taking of drink or drugs is no mitigation, the sentencing process must recognise the fact of the addiction and the importance of breaking the drug or drink problem. This is not only in the interests of the offender but also in the public interest since so commonly the addiction results in a vicious circle of imprisonment followed by reoffending. When an offender is making or prepared to make a real effort to break his addiction, it is important for the sentencing court to make allowances if the process of rehabilitation proves to be irregular. What may be important is the overall progress that the offender is making. This is part of the thinking behind drug and treatment orders.

R v Saw 2009 EWCA Crim 1, 2 Cr App R (S) 54 (p 367) LCJ Another example [of where the right sentence is non-custodial] is the defendant who has reached a critical stage in his life with a real prospect of turning his back on crime, or breaking away from addiction to the drugs which led him into crime. If he is indeed making a genuine attempt to break the cycle, or to address its causes, then that is plainly a factor to be taken into account in his favour, and put into the balance against the aggravating features of the specific case. Successful and early rehabilitation often represents the best long-term advantage to the public, and a sentence which has a reasonable prospect of achieving that the offender will be deterred, or discouraged, or taught to avoid crime may well be appropriate where the burglary lacks significant attendant aggravating features. In the context of a young life which is presently being wasted away, a constructive, rehabilitative sentence, which includes a punitive element, may provide a better long-term solution for the public generally, and particularly for other household-ers, than an unconstructive custodial sentence. The Judge is not the prisoner of the sentencing tariff, but rather has the difficult task of arriving at the right sentence in the individual case. Whether an individual case is one for which such a course may be appropriate requires careful judgement.

219.57   *Types of burglar   Persistent burglars (dwellings) Pre-guideline Judicial guidance*
R v Saw 2009 EWCA Crim 1, 2 Cr App R (S) 54 (p 367) LCJ Once an offender has been caught and sentenced, and in particular if made subject to a non-custodial penalty on the basis that his rehabilitation may be achieved, he must understand that for dwelling house burglars such a chance rarely comes more than once, and then only if the subsequent court is satisfied that the offender has been making genuine efforts to break out of the cycle of offending and reoffending, and that the current lapse is temporary.
R v Marcantonio 2012 EWCA Crim 1279 D had been a career burglar since 1980. Held. There will be cases where the record of the offender combined with his inability or unwillingness to rehabilitate himself and respond to non-custodial options are factors which will entitle a sentencing judge not just to depart from the relevant sentencing guidelines, but to depart radically from those guidelines so that there can be no doubt that the protection of the public is being considered first and foremost. Burglary worth 18 months but with record etc. we start at 7½ years.
R v Brooke 2012 EWCA Crim 1642 The [Sentencing] Council did not intend to reserve sentences above 6 years for burglaries committed only where they were accompanied by violence. The guideline provides specifically for the offender with a record. Where appropriate an offender's record may be a significantly aggravating feature.
See also the **Minimum sentences** section at **219.28** and the *Drug addicts* paras at **219.56**.

219.58   *Types of burglar   Persistent burglars (dwellings) One offence*
R v Brooke 2012 EWCA Crim 1642 D pleaded (full credit) to burglary. He was a career burglar who preyed on elderly and vulnerable victims. D went to V's bungalow. V, aged 77, had suffered two strokes and walked with the aid of a Zimmer frame. V answered the door and D told him he was from the council and had come to deal with asbestos. He walked past V, uninvited, into the bungalow. He looked around the property, opening drawers with a tea towel. When he moved a sideboard, V asked him what he was doing, to which he replied something about moving it for asbestos. He then took a chair and entered the loft. After some time, V became concerned and shouted up to him. D had left the property. No items were taken. He had been there for some 30 minutes. D, aged 44, had 17 appearances for 46 offences since 1979, 28 of which were for burglary and theft. In 2007, he received 10 years for burglary, reduced to 7 on appeal in 2011. Within a matter of weeks of being released, D had committed this offence. Held. This is an unusual case for two reasons. First, D is a recidivist of a relatively rare kind. It seems there is nothing the courts can do to deter him from preying on the elderly and the vulnerable and causing great harm. Second, D heard the Court of Appeal in 2011 set a benchmark of at least 7 years for his offending. The offence on the last occasion was

almost identical to the present. The judgment was admittedly pre the Definitive Guideline, however, the Definitive Guideline was not intended to reduce the level of sentences for burglaries overall. Thus, D must have known that if he offended again in a similar way, he would receive a sentence of 7 years or more. We are satisfied that the Judge was entitled to move significantly beyond the range identified. To reduce the sentence in this case, in the light of what happened on the last occasion before this court, would, in our judgment, amount to a mockery of justice. This was indeed a very severe sentence but given the unique features of this case, we are satisfied that a very severe sentence was justified. Starting at **12 years**, **8 years** upheld.

R v Petre 2013 EWCA Crim 422 D pleaded (25% credit) to dwelling burglary and theft. At about 1 am V was woken by a loud noise. He went into the living room of his home and saw that D and another were trying to gain entry with a jemmy. V walked to the local police station. He returned with police officers to discover that a jacket, a mobile phone, four fishing rods, a fishing reel and a penknife had been stolen. D and his accomplice also broke into a car the same evening and stole a jacket and £5 in cash, causing £50 worth of damage in the process. The two stolen jackets and four fishing rods were found at the property in which D was staying. V felt depressed as a result of the offence and no longer felt safe and secure in his home. He could not sleep at night and had requested a move to a top-floor flat, where he felt he would be less vulnerable to further such offences despite suffering from angina. He said he had lost all his happy memories, any security and his family home. He said that his world had been turned upside down by the offence. D, aged 37, had convictions for 88 offences between 1992 and 2012, largely for theft and similar matters. There were two dwelling burglaries, in 1998 (12 months) and 2004 (15 months). He was on bail for an offence of theft at the time of the instant offences. Held. The Judge was correct to place the burglary offence into Category 1. The appropriate starting point was 5 years. With the plea, **3 years 9 months**, not 4½ years.

R v Bancroft 2014 EWCA Crim 157 D pleaded to a dwelling burglary. He entered a house in the middle of the day by kicking the door in. A 13-year-old boy was alone in the premises at the time. He heard the smashing noise downstairs, saw D and hid under the bed. D stole property to the value of £3,500, which was recovered when D was arrested. D was aged 54 at appeal and had 29 convictions for 83 offences including 30 burglaries or attempts. Held. This was the third time D had been liable to the mandatory minimum sentence. The Judge made a fair assessment of the case by placing it into Category 1. A starting point of 7½ years taken by the Judge was significantly too high. The range was 2-6 years and the aggravating factors equivocal. The Judge was entitled to increase the starting point from 3 to 6 years but not any higher. With full credit, **4 years** not 5½.

R v O'Neill 2015 EWCA Crim 1181, 2 Cr App R (S) 71 D pleaded to burglary (25% credit). At 10.30 pm, D entered a house through an unlocked patio door. He stole car keys, an iPhone, and another mobile. D went to a shop to try and unlock the iPhone. Staff were suspicious and called the police. D left, leaving his wallet with his details behind. D was now aged 34 with over 20 burglary and attempted burglary convictions between 1996 and 2012. He received 3 years' detention in 2002, 3 years in 2004, 1 year in 2007, 32 months in 2008, 30 months in 2010 and 34 months in 2012, all for burglaries. He was a drug addict. Held. We start at 5 years not 6 so **3 years 9 months** not 4.

R v Jones 2015 EWCA Crim 1258 D pleaded to burglary early. When on licence he broke into a home by breaking the glass in a rear door. He took a laptop, a notebook computer and about £105. D had 53 convictions on 18 occasions of which 25 were burglaries or attempted burglaries. There were many burglary TICs. For burglaries he received 4 years in 2009 and 57 months in 2012. The defence said an 8-year starting point was wrong. Held. When offenders persist in such offending, then ever-increasing sentences are to be expected. But an invariable exponential increase on each succeeding occasion cannot be allowed to give rise to an end result which ultimately bears no true relationship to the actual offence. We start at 6 years, so with plea, **4 years**.

See also: *R v Flanders* 2011 EWCA Crim 2121 (Plea. Dwelling burglary. Stole £750 worth of belongings while family were asleep upstairs. No damage to property. Bad record including three dwelling burglaries. Aged 44. With 20% credit for plea, **4 years** not 5.)

R v Marcantonio 2012 EWCA Crim 1279 (Early plea. Over £12,000 of items stolen, some of great sentimental value. A career burglar starting at 1970. Third-time third-strike burglary. No response to non-custodial sentences. Over the years had received 12, 9 and 6 years for burglaries. Burglary worth 18 months but with record etc. we start at 7½ years, with the plea, **5 years** upheld.)

R v Ferries 2012 EWCA Crim 1307 (Plea. Entered dwelling. Owner returned and apprehended him. Defendant struck out causing owner slight injury. 63 previous offences. Mostly acquisitive. Heroin addict. Committed on licence. Third-strike case. 20% credit. **4 years 9 months** not 7 years.)

R v Andrews 2012 EWCA Crim 2332, 2013 2 Cr App R (S) 5 (p 26) (Convicted of burglary. Unoccupied flat. Broke window and stole two bracelets and some foreign currency. 53 convictions for burglary or attempted burglary. Aged 52. Care order for five dwelling burglaries when aged 10. Life of crime. Class A drug user for 20 years on and off. Poor mental health. Minimum sentence not unjust. His record meant a sentence outside the guideline range was permissible if not inevitable. Element of double counting. **3 years** was correct, not 5.)

219.59   *Types of burglar   Persistent burglar (dwellings) More than one offence*

R v John 2011 EWCA Crim 135 D pleaded to burglary with 12 dwelling house burglary TICs. D entered a dwelling by smashing a window and forcing the door open. He stole jewellery including items of sentimental value. Two days later, D gained entry to another dwelling. He stole electrical equipment, a camera, Nintendo games and jewellery. Twelve days later, D started to force entry into a third dwelling. The occupant was upstairs. The occupant heard the smashing of glass and confronted D. He remained in the vicinity and was arrested. D had 24 offences of burglary or theft previous. His last sentence for burglary was 5½ years. Community sentences had not worked and D had not complied with drug rehabilitation requirements. Held. The Judge correctly characterised D as a professional burglar. It was necessary to reflect the sheer number of burglaries and the appalling previous criminal record. However, in light of the plea, 7 years should have been a starting point. So, **6½ years**. 6 months consecutive for breaches of community orders untouched.

R v Whyte 2011 EWCA Crim 229 D pleaded to burglary and attempted burglary. He also pleaded to two further counts of burglary on a second indictment. D disturbed occupants in three of the four burglaries. Each was of a dwelling or a garage at a dwelling at night. When one occupant challenged him, he said, "Let go of me, I don't want to hurt you". D was in possession of a screwdriver during that offence. D, aged 48 at appeal, had 35 convictions for 88 offences of theft and kindred offences. He was a persistent dwelling house burglar and had committed all of these offences while on bail. In 2005 he received 4 years for dwelling burglaries. D had been given the opportunity to reform when released from a custodial sentence and had been given employment. He had to resign due to disciplinary proceedings after a vehicle was damaged. The pre-sentence report noted that his offending was governed by an addiction to alcohol and drugs. The Judge said he had an eye to totality and D's plea in mind. Held. The starting point which can be inferred from a sentence of 5 years is too high, despite D's awful record of offending. There also should have been some clear indication of what credit was given for the pleas, due to the complex nature of the timing of the pleas. The starting point was 5½ years before credit. We think 20-25% was appropriate. So **4 years**, not 5.

R v Johnson 2011 EWCA Crim 595 D pleaded to burglary with three other burglary TICs. He entered an unoccupied house at 9.50 am via a rear bathroom window. He stole a computer games system, a watch and a bank card with a total value of £886. The bank card had the PIN with it and he subsequently twice withdrew money from the account. D was a heroin addict and said that it was to fund his habit. D, aged 34, had 23 convictions for burglary and references speaking of his attempts to get off heroin. D was liable for a minimum sentence. Held. The previous convictions were aggravating factors. However, 5 years after an immediate plea suggests 7½ years following a trial. That would be too long. **4 years**.

R v Johnston 2011 EWCA Crim 2976, 2 Cr App R (S) 32 (p 182) D pleaded to three dwelling burglaries and one ABH. V1 was a 77-year-old lady who lived alone. She left the house for a short while and upon her return found that the patio door had been smashed. Seventeen rare and sentimental items of jewellery had been stolen, including gifts from her late husband. V2 was aged 63 and lived in a garden flat. D and another burst into her front room at lunchtime and she was restrained. Threats were made. They took the keys to the main house, mentioning the occupant, V3, by name. They then burgled the main house. V3, a 68-year-old woman, was returning to her house when she saw a man coming out of her house. The second man grabbed her wrist and pushed her outside. She screamed and the man bit her finger and pushed his finger into her eye. There was a graze to her cheek and her finger was swollen and bruised. There was reddening where she had been poked in the eye. V1 was unable to sleep properly after the burglary, and died a few weeks later. V2 and V3 had to have bars fitted to their windows. D, aged 50, was a professional criminal who had received prison sentences totalling 30 years. Convictions included numerous burglaries and an aggravated burglary (9 years). The Judge said V1 died broken-hearted. Held. The Judge was entitled to find that the offence on V2 fell little short of robbery. The Court reminded itself of the Robbery Guideline. The Judge was entitled to consider that the public required protection from D. Because of totality, **13 years** not 15.

See also: *R v Stevenson* 2011 EWCA Crim 1679, 2012 1 Cr App R (S) 55 (p 313) (Two burglaries a few hours apart. Early hours. One owner now too scared to leave home. 40 previous convictions for dwelling burglaries. Expect severe sentences. Starting at **8 years**, with plea 6 years not excessive.)

R v Gibson 2011 EWCA Crim 2160 (Plea. Two burglaries, attempted burglary and two theft. Stole from his sister and a friend among others. Appalling record. Dwelling burglaries in double figures. Had received minimum sentence for dwelling burglary on four occasions. **8 years** was severe but not excessive.)

Post-guideline case

R v Appiah 2014 EWCA Crim 472 D pleaded to four burglaries. Two were committed on a day in October 2011. Shortly after his release from prison, he smashed his way into two flats within the same building. He made untidy searches and took foreign currency to the value of £200 and a pair of cufflinks worth £100 with sentimental value from one flat. From the other flat he took an engagement ring worth £34,000, other jewellery and a games console together worth about £3,000. The engagement ring was recovered. D left his fingerprints at the scene. In March 2012, he received 28 days' imprisonment for fraud. In May 2012, he received 51 weeks for going equipped for theft. He was not arrested until March 2013 for those offences and pleaded on the day of trial. On a day in July 2013 with another, he broke into two flats in a building and made untidy searches. D or his accomplice had placed a kitchen knife near the front door. The occupier returned and challenged D and his accomplice. They ran, discarding the stolen property. D pleaded earlier in relation to the 2013 offences. D, aged 37 at appeal, had a bad record for dishonesty offences and dwelling burglary in particular. He had eight burglary/attempted burglary convictions. He committed the offences largely to fund a drug habit. He had spent a considerable proportion of his life in prison. The Judge passed 7½ years (so starting at around 9 years). Held. The first two offences (which without reference to D's previous convictions were Category 2 offences) were to be placed into Category 1. The 2013 offences were also to be placed into Category 1 as greater harm (the victim returned to the property) and higher culpability (D and his accomplice formed a group) were present. Individually, a starting point of 3 years with a range of 2-6 years was appropriate. The minimum sentence applied to each offence. It was understandable why the Judge felt such a substantial term was needed but even for a repeat offender with as bad a record as D, the sentence was too high. The appropriate starting point for the first two offences was 4 years, and for the second two offences, 4½ years. Giving credit of 10% and 25% respectively, the result would be about 7 years. From that, a reduction for totality was appropriate. That reduction could not be substantial and justice would be done by a sentence of **6½ years**.

219.60   *Types of burglar   Persistent offenders (non-dwelling)*
R v Langley 2011 EWCA Crim 2471 D pleaded to commercial burglary with one burglary TIC'd. At night, he broke into a hair salon through a window which had previously been broken and blocked by breeze blocks. He stole £1,300 in cash and £6,600 in stock, and caused £500 worth of damage. He also removed the keys. The owner lived in the flat above the premises but was unaware of the burglary. D had 26 convictions, nearly all for burglary. Early offences were domestic burglaries but D had then concentrated on commercial burglaries. Held. The guidelines are inapplicable to this defendant. His almost identical previous convictions undoubtedly aggravate the offence. A previous sentence for burglary had been postponed to establish whether D had 'turned a corner'. A community order was imposed and that was subsequently breached six weeks later. **3 years** (or a little longer) after a trial would have been merited by the need to protect the public. **30 months** was not manifestly excessive.

Post-guideline cases
R v Kadiri 2014 EWCA Crim 1106 D pleaded (at the first opportunity) to commercial burglary. D was seen in an office building by a cleaner who became suspicious and called the police. D had left by the time the police arrived. Two iPads and a laptop computer worth £2,500 had been stolen. D was identified by CCTV. D was aged 36 at appeal with a 'truly appalling' record. Since the age of 16, he had been convicted on 54 occasions of 109 offences. Those included drug offences and one rape (7 years, 2003). Non-dwelling burglaries greatly predominated over the previous 20 years. In June 2011 he received 33 months for five non-dwelling burglaries. He was on licence when the instant offence was committed. The Judge considered that the offence was planned. He gave 20% credit as he considered the case overwhelming. Held. The Judge properly remarked that D was a career commercial burglar. The starting point [of just short of 50 months] could not be said to be arguably wrong, but as the case was not overwhelming, with full credit **2 years 8 months**, not 3 years 3 months.
R v Wingfield 2015 EWCA Crim 18 D pleaded to commercial burglary at the Magistrates' Court. He was a registered drug addict and was unlawfully at large, having failed to appear for sentence at the Crown Court. D hoped to obtain the drugs he craved. Knowing that he would be arrested upon trying to collect his drugs at a chemist's, D forced a locked window at a vet's surgery and stole some drugs. D had an appalling record of almost 150 offences, many of which were for commercial burglary, and had received 4 years for another burglary of a vet's. Held. The proper starting point was 3 years, so **2 years**, not 3.
R v Bown 2015 EWCA Crim 2057 D was convicted of burglary. D stayed at a campsite in Dorset with his girlfriend. They used false names. At a nearby holiday park, a small shop was locked up for the night. In the morning, the manager found the front door of the shop had been damaged, the glass in the door had been smashed and the cigarette cabinet had been broken into. Cigarettes, cigars and tobacco worth £3,600 had been stolen. CCTV showed two individuals fumbling around outside the shop just after midnight and an hour later the same two breaking in. When arrested, D had tools including a cordless drill. Glass samples found on his jacket matched the smashed glass. In his interview D lied. D was aged 52, with 38 court appearances for 80 offences, 50 of which were burglaries (both domestic and commercial). They started in 1974, when D was aged 11, and the last prison term was in April 2007 when D received 30 months for a domestic burglary. D was in breach of a community order. Held. This was a Category

1 burglary. The harm was borderline. There was a significant economic loss. There was targeting and a substantial degree of planning and two people were involved. Culpability was particularly high. The offence was committed at night. D's convictions may have reduced over the last decade but D was a professional burglar who, in the 1980s and 1990s, was making between £50,000 and £100,000 a year. He had spurned attempts to help him reform. However, where a defendant has a significant criminal record, it is important that the sentence bears an appropriate relationship to the crime committed. **3 years** not 4.

220 BURGLARY, AGGRAVATED
220.1
Theft Act 1968 s 10
Mode of trial Indictable only
Maximum sentence Life
Minimum sentences Domestic burglary is a specified offence for a 3-year minimum sentence when the offence is a third domestic burglary.[107] The definition of a 'domestic burglary' is unhelpful as to whether the Act applies to aggravated burglary. There is no reason why an 'aggravated domestic burglary' should not be a 'domestic burglary'. If a non-aggravated burglary is subject to the rule, there is a powerful reason to consider an aggravated burglary should be subject to the provisions. For details of these provision, see **219.28**.
Extended sentences This offence is listed in Criminal Justice Act 2003 Sch 15. The court may pass a 2012 extended sentence (EDS) if there is a significant risk of serious harm from future specified offences and either: a) the defendant has a Criminal Justice Act 2003 Sch 15B conviction (applicable only to defendants aged 18+), or b) the offence would justify a determinate sentence of at least 4 years.[108]
Restitution Orders There is power to make an order that the stolen goods etc. in the possession of the defendant or a third party be restored to the owner etc.[109]
Sexual Harm Prevention Orders There is a discretionary power to make this order when it is necessary to protect the public from sexual harm.[110]

220.2 *Crown Court statistics   England and Wales*
Aggravated burglary in a dwelling

Year	Age	Plea	Total sen-tenced	Type of sentencing %						Average length of custody in months
				Dis-charge	Fine	Commu-nity sentence	Sus-pended sentence	Custody	Oth-er	
2013	18-20	G	41	–	–	–	–	97.6	2.4	59.8
		NG	13	–	–	–	–	100.	–	91.8
	21+	G	142	–	–	–	2.1	97.2	0.7	74.2
		NG	54	–	–	–	–	100.	–	110.9
2014	18-20	G	35	–	–	6	–	94	–	62.7
		NG	5	–	–	–	–	80	20	not listed[111]
	21+	G	146	–	–	1	1	97	1	75.5
		NG	29	–	–	–	–	97	3	103.9

Aggravated burglary in a building not a dwelling

---

[107] Powers of Criminal Courts (Sentencing) Act 2000 s 111
[108] Criminal Justice Act 2003 s 226A-226B as inserted by Legal Aid, Sentencing and Punishment of Offenders Act 2012 s 124
[109] Powers of Criminal Courts (Sentencing) Act 2000 s 148(2)
[110] Sexual Offences Act 2003 s 103A as inserted by Anti-social Behaviour, Crime and Policing Act 2014 Sch 5 para 2 and Sexual Offences Act 2003 Sch 5
[111] Not shown as based on too few cases to be meaningful

Year	Plea	Total sentenced	Type of sentencing %						Average length of custody in months
			Discharge	Fine	Commu-nity sentence	Sus-pended sentence	Custody	Other	
2013	G	5	–	–	–	20	80	–	48.5
	NG	1	–	–	–	–	100	–	54.0
2014	G	8	–	–	–	–	88	13	77.1
	NG	2	–	–	–	–	100	–	not listed[112]

For explanations about the statistics, see page 1-xii. For statistics for male and female defendants etc., see www.banksr.com Other Matters Statistics tab

220.3   *Sentencing Council guideline*

Burglary, Aggravated

Burglary Offences Guideline 2012, see www.banksr.com Guidelines tab The guideline applies to all offenders aged 18+. In force 16 January 2012.

Note: This guideline does not distinguish between: a) dwelling and non-dwelling aggravated burglary and b) a premises where persons are not expected to be present and premises where persons are present or likely to be present. Looking at the structure and the penalties, it can be inferred that the authors had in mind dwelling offences only. Ed.

STEP ONE Determine the offence category

page 4 The court should determine the offence category using the table below.

Category 1	Greater harm and higher culpability
Category 2	Greater harm and lower culpability or lesser harm and higher culpability
Category 3	Lesser harm and lower culpability

The court should determine culpability and harm caused or intended, by reference only to the factors below, which comprise the principal factual elements of the offence. Where an offence does not fall squarely into a category, individual factors may require a degree of weighting before making an overall assessment and determining the appropriate offence category.

Factors indicating greater harm
Theft of/damage to property causing a significant degree of loss to the victim (whether economic, commercial, sentimental or personal value), Soiling, ransacking or vandalism of property, Victim at home or on the premises (or returns) while offender present, Significant physical or psychological injury or other significant trauma to the victim, Violence used or threatened against victim, particularly involving a weapon, Context of general public disorder.

Factors indicating lesser harm
No physical or psychological injury or other significant trauma to the victim, No violence used or threatened and a weapon is not produced.

Factors indicating higher culpability
Victim or premises deliberately targeted (e.g. due to vulnerability or hostility based on disability, race, sexual orientation), A significant degree of planning or organisation, Equipped for burglary (e.g. implements carried and/or use of vehicle), Weapon present on entry, Member of a group or gang.

---

[112] Not shown as based on too few cases to be meaningful

Factors indicating lower culpability
Offender exploited by others, Mental disorder or learning disability, where linked to the commission of the offence.

220.4

STEP TWO Starting point and category range

page 4 Having determined the category, the court should use the corresponding starting points to reach a sentence within the category range below. The starting point applies to all offenders irrespective of plea or previous convictions. A case of particular gravity, reflected by multiple features of culpability or harm in step one, could merit upward adjustment from the starting point before further adjustment for aggravating or mitigating features, set out [below].

The starting point applies to all offenders irrespective of plea or previous convictions.

Offence category	Starting point (applicable to all offenders)	Range (applicable to all offenders)
Category 1	10 years' custody	9 to 13 years' custody
Category 2	6 years' custody	4 to 9 years' custody
Category 3	2 years' custody	1 to 4 years' custody

220.5   [Aggravating and mitigating factors]

The table below contains a **non-exhaustive** list of additional factual elements providing the context of the offence and factors relating to the offender. Identify whether any combination of these, or other relevant factors, should result in an upward or downward adjustment from the starting point. **In particular, relevant recent convictions are likely to result in an upward adjustment**. In some cases, having considered these factors, it may be appropriate to move outside the identified category range.

Factors increasing seriousness
Statutory aggravating factors: Previous convictions, having regard to: a) the nature of the offence to which the conviction relates and its relevance to the current offence; and b) the time that has elapsed since the conviction, Offence committed whilst on bail. *Other aggravating factors:* Child at home (or returns home) when offence committed, Offence committed at night, Abuse of power and/or position of trust, Gratuitous degradation of victim, Any steps taken to prevent the victim reporting the incident or obtaining assistance and/or from assisting or supporting the prosecution, Victim compelled to leave their home (in particular victims of domestic violence), Established evidence of community impact, Commission of offence whilst under the influence of alcohol or drugs, Failure to comply with current court orders, Offence committed whilst on licence, Offences Taken Into Consideration (TICs).

Factors reducing seriousness or reflecting personal mitigation
Subordinate role in a group or gang, Injuries caused recklessly, Nothing stolen or only property of very low value to the victim (whether economic, commercial, sentimental or personal), Offender has made voluntary reparation to the victim, No previous convictions or no relevant/recent convictions, Remorse, Good character and/or exemplary conduct, Determination and/or demonstration of steps taken to address addiction or offending behaviour, Serious medical conditions requiring urgent, intensive or long-term treatment, Age and/or lack of maturity where it affects the responsibility of the offender, Lapse of time since the offence where this is not the fault of the offender, Mental disorder or learning disability, where not linked to the commission of the offence, Sole or primary carer for dependent relatives.

220.6 Other guidance

For some additional guidance, see the **ROBBERY** *Guidelines* paras at **322.4**, **322.9** and **322.23**.

For an example of the Court of Appeal using the robbery guidelines in a case where the occupants were threatened, see *R v Ellis* 2009 EWCA Crim 173, 2 Cr App R (S) 73 (p 506).

220.7 Dwellings

Example: *R v M* 2012 EWCA Crim 374 (Entered flat posing as gasman with another and picked up knives in kitchen. Demands made. Aged 26 with one previous burglary. Acted as 'back-up' to the other. Because of early plea and role, 3½ years not 4½.

Post-guideline case

R v Wilcock 2014 EWCA Crim 1890 D pleaded (25% credit) to aggravated burglary, burglary and to handling stolen goods (×4). C pleaded to burglary and one handling offence, receiving 3 years. D and C smashed their way into a house opposite their own, knowing the occupier was absent. Following an untidy search of the house, C was seen by police carrying a large TV which was dropped. She wore dark clothing and gloves. D was caught after a short chase and denied any involvement. A month later, whilst on bail, D entered another house, with the door having been left on the latch. The occupants returned after 10 minutes to see D in their living room. V1 confronted D at the threshold. He was carrying a handbag filled with belongings, including a laptop and camera. D had also been carrying a 10 inch knife, found in the house. V1 told D to drop the goods and get out and then tried to grab the handbag. After a struggle, D ran off past V2 dropping most of the goods but still wielding the knife. The knife and a purse were later recovered. The four handling offences related to local burglaries where items were stolen and then pawned or sold soon after. D was aged 32 on appeal with convictions for 11 burglaries and nine for handling stolen goods. He was also on licence following his last handling conviction when he committed the aggravated burglary. D's complaint regarded totality. Held. These were serious offences committed by a serial burglar and handler. Aggravated burglary is always a serious offence and D went equipped for the first burglary. D found the knife in the second burglary at the property but made no overt threats with it. **5 years** for the aggravated one and a total of **9 years**, not 10½ years.

220.8 Dwellings Defendant has relevant previous convictions Post-guideline case

Att-Gen's Ref No 30 of 2014 2014 EWCA Crim 1248 D1 and D2 pleaded to aggravated burglary. On 8 May 2012, they entered a public house at about 2.30 am, above which the licensees V1 and V2 lived. D1 was armed with a claw hammer and D2 with a knife or screwdriver. They entered the victims' separate bedrooms, woke V1 and V2 and

demanded access to the safe. While holding the claw hammer, D threatened V2, saying, "Get a fucking move on or I'll smash your skull in". The safe was opened and more than £6,300 was taken. They sped away on a motorbike. D1 had 18 previous appearances for 32 offences (including four dwelling burglaries) and D2 had 21 appearances for 58 offences (including four burglaries, two of which were dwellings). In 2004, D2 pleaded to GBH with intent and having a firearm with intent. He and four others broke into a home with a firearm and other weapons in the early hours and used violence. D2 received 7 years. They had both been released from prison in March 2012 and were both in breach of their licence before the offence. Held. These were grievous offences committed as a pair and while armed, intruding upon the sense of safety of two licensees. Practically every statutory aggravating feature was present. We start at 11 years for both, so for D1, with full credit, **7 years 4 months** not 4 years. For D2, with 10% credit, **9 years 9 months** not 5 years.
Old pre-guideline case: *R v Ellis* 2009 EWCA Crim 173, 2 Cr App R (S) 73 (p 506) (**6 years**)

220.9   *Dwellings   Sexual attack, Involving a*
Note: Where a burglary has a sexual element, the prosecution now charge a sexual offence to mark the gravity of it and to enable notification to occur. There are some old burglary cases with a sexual element but they don't reflect current practice and were before the guideline came into force. Ed.

220.10   *Dwellings   Victim injured*
Att-Gen's Ref No 13 of 2010 2010 EWCA Crim 1067, 2011 1 Cr App R (S) 27 (p 181) LCJ D pleaded (full credit) to aggravated burglary and ABH. He entered a house in which V and her two sons, R and L, were asleep. V confronted D and shouted at him. D was holding a screwdriver and walked towards V. V grabbed at D's hand and lunged at V twice. There was a struggle and D grabbed V around the throat. D went upstairs and V followed. R came onto the landing and D moved towards him, waving the screwdriver. R struck D with a dog lead and barricaded himself into a room. D proceeded up the second flight of stairs, where L was asleep. V followed and D pushed her down the stairs, causing her injury. D tried to climb out of a window, and V said that he would fall and be hurt. D jumped from the window and injured himself on the pavement. V went to D's aid and called an ambulance. The Judge determined that D was not 'dangerous' for the purposes of Criminal Justice Act 2003. D, aged 34, had many convictions for residential burglary and one for aggravated burglary. D had a history of drug abuse. He was subject to the minimum 3-year sentence provisions. The Judge gave D a community order with residential rehabilitation and has engaged in 'very intensive' work. He also ordered D to attend court every month to show he was drug free. Since the order D had shown at his attendances that he was drug free. Held. The Judge's assessment was that the public interest in securing the full rehabilitation of the offender, and therefore the end of his criminal offending, was more likely to be served by a non-custodial sentence which would build on the positive progress the offender had already made. We understand that thinking, but the difficulty with the approach is that such a sentence would significantly underestimate the seriousness of the offence. **4 years**, not 24-month community order.
Note: The 4-year sentence was understandable but it raises the questions, 'Would the sentencing judge's approach be more likely to end the offending?' and 'Which is more important, punishment or rehabilitation?' The Court of Appeal sometimes solves this problem by saying that '4 years was the appropriate sentence but because the order was working so well we exercise our discretion not to disturb the success. However, if there is a breach, four years consecutive is inevitable'. Ed.
R v Gregory 2010 EWCA Crim 3095, 2011 2 Cr App R (S) 38 (p 232) D was convicted of conspiracy to burgle and aggravated burglary. Three men, one of whom was D, were seen at the back of V's house. Two were wearing balaclavas and D was wearing a ski mask. He also wore gloves, carried a torch and had a pocket knife. The men entered the

house by force and a struggle ensued. V picked up a kitchen knife to defend himself. Mrs V may have done the same. The man ran off. Mrs V suffered bruising. D sustained wounds to his stomach and arms. The wound penetrated his kidney. D, aged 25, had been sentenced on 11 previous occasions including burglary of a dwelling house (×4) and aggravated vehicle-taking. Held. The aggravating features in addition to the possession of the knife were: a) three men were equipped to burgle, b) they planned to burgle a house they knew was occupied (the lights were on), c) they entered by force, d) Mrs V suffered injuries, and e) D had a bad record. The Judge was not referred to the authorities. For the conspiracy, 6 years, the aggravated burglary, 9 years, and the theft remains at 6 months. In total, **9 years** is appropriate, not 12.

R v Garrod 2013 EWCA Crim 109 D was convicted of aggravated burglary and two ABHs. After drinking he met S, whom he knew vaguely, and they spoke for a few moments. The next day S received three threatening text messages from D. D seemed to believe S had assaulted a friend or relative of D. The last message indicated D was coming round to assault S. S lived in a flat below the house of his grandfather, V, and V's brother-in-law, V2. V was aged 70 and recovering from cancer. V2 was aged 65. The two were watching television. D and another arrived and broke the glass in their front door with a shovel which had been near the door. V went to investigate and was confronted by D with the shovel. D hit V in the jaw with it. V cried out to alert V2. V tried to disarm D. V2, who was ex-military, arrived and D and he grappled with each other. D tripped and fell, enabling V2 to restrain him. D then bit V2 with considerable force causing a nasty wound. D maintained the grip with the bite. D was still restrained and started to talk. Both men started to reduce their grip on D and D broke free and punched V in the face with a clenched fist causing V to fall backwards. D escaped. V and V2 were shocked and required medical treatment. There was £600 worth of damage caused, including a broken glass cabinet. In interview D lied and at the trial he ran self-defence. D was aged 22. In 2009 he received 30 months for robbery. In drink, he caused puncture wounds with a knife on the victim before taking his wallet. While serving that sentence he had an altercation with a prisoner and a prison officer intervened. D punched the officer on the head and kneed him several times before pursuing him down the corridor, still throwing punches at him. Held. We agree with the Judge [that] the case fell into Category 1 of the guideline. We start at 10 years, so 13 years' extended sentence (10 years' custody 3 years' licence) not 6 years' IPP.

See also: *Att-Gen's Ref No 53 of 2010* 2010 EWCA Crim 3245, 2011 2 Cr App R (S) 22 (p 118) (Plea to aggravated burglary. Attacked victims aged 84 and 87 with baseball bat, striking them several times around the head. Stole £7. Alcoholic. **10 years** not 3½.)

R v Armstrong 2012 EWCA Crim 320 (Late plea to aggravated burglary. With another, broke into neighbour's house. Armed with an iron bar and wearing hoods and scarves to cover their faces. Destroyed property and assaulted V, aged 50. Stole wallet and purse. One-year delay between offence and charge. Two-year delay between offence and plea. Aged 17. No convictions. ADHD. **5½ years' YOI** not 6½.)

Old cases: *Att-Gen's Ref No 12 of 2009* 2009 EWCA Crim 1438, 2010 1 Cr App R (S) 54 (p 339) (**4 years**) *Att-Gen's Ref No 29 of 2009* 2009 EWCA Crim 2169, 2010 1 Cr App R (S) 90 (p 583)[113] (The appropriate starting point was **6 years**) *R v Douglas* 2010 EWCA Crim 2760 (**24-month DTO**) *Att-Gen's Ref No 40 of 2010* 2010 EWCA Crim 2695, 2011 2 Cr App R (S) 6 (p 22) (**9 years**)

For a summary of the first two cases see the 9th edition of this book and for the next two see the 10th edition.

See also **OFFENCES AGAINST THE PERSON ACT 1861 S 18** *Robbery/Burglary/ Aggravated burglary, And* at **292.32**.

---

[113] Although the wounding was not to the householder who was burgled, the case is in this paragraph because there was an intent to cause GBH.

220.11   *Dwellings   Victim seized or tied up   Post-guideline cases*

R v Walsh and Brown 2014 EWCA Crim 1155 W and B pleaded (at the first opportunity) to aggravated burglary. W was at college with V, whom he disliked. W learned that V had told others that his father had received a cash payment of $10,000 for some work he had performed. W decided he wanted to steal the cash and told B and two others about it. All four went to V's house shortly before midnight. They wore masks or face coverings, dark clothes and gloves. B was armed with what appeared to be a metal crutch. They knocked on the door and when V's father answered, they immediately overpowered him. He was told to get on the floor, face down, and his hands and mouth were secured with tape. A bag was placed over his head. W and B stayed downstairs with V's father, repeatedly 'jabbing' him in the stomach or groin, whilst demanding $10,000. The other two went upstairs and tied up V and V's mother. One pretended that he had a gun and made frightening threats as to what would happen if the money was not handed over. In fact, V's father's $10,000 had already been stolen in a burglary some days earlier. V's mother had managed to make a 999 call before being tied up. The police arrived and the four men fled, taking with them several items from the house. V's family were left feeling unsafe in their home and were contemplating moving house and moving abroad, despite increasing their security provision. W was aged 17, just 12 days short of his 18th birthday at the time of the offence, and had two minor convictions which were treated as being irrelevant. B was aged 17 years and 9 months at the time of the offence and was of good character. One co-accused was aged 17 years and 11 months and another was approaching his 20th birthday. Held. There were a number of aggravating features. This was a premeditated and planned offence, targeted against a family who were believed to have a substantial sum of money in their house. It was committed at night by a group of four men who were masked and armed. It was common ground that this offence fell into Category 1. This was a very serious offence and it was necessary to mark that. The principles in the *Youths Sentencing Guideline 2009* were to be applied. The Judge should have given greater weight to the ages of W and B. The planning and execution of this crime involved features of criminal sophistication which one would not expect from youths of previous good character. On the other hand, it does seem clear that…they had failed to give any mature thought to the consequences to their unfortunate victims. Both B and W were remorseful. The Judge should have drawn a somewhat greater distinction than he did between W and B and the elder co-defendant on the grounds of [their] comparative youth. For B, we well understand why the Judge started at 10 years [reduced to 9 for his age], but he should have reduced that by more than 1 year to reflect his youth. W initiated the offence and that cannot be overlooked. Thereafter, his involvement was no greater than the others. The same starting point [of 10 years before the reduction for his youth] should have been adopted because the aggravating features in W's case were counter-balanced by his stronger personal mitigation. Reducing the sentences for their youth, the starting point was 8 years for both, not 9 years for B and 10 years for W. With full credit, for B, **5 years 4 months' detention**, not 6 years, and for W, **5 years' 4 months' YOI** not 6 years 8 months.

R v Grimshaw 2014 EWCA Crim 1348 (Plea to aggravated burglary and carrying a firearm with criminal intent (a taser pen). Under pressure from criminal associate. Entered jeweller's house by a trick and used taser on victim's neck. Victim screams in pain. Fled when man arrived with a knife. Over in 25 seconds. It was Category 1 but **6 years** not 8.)

220.12   *Dwellings   Victim over 65   Pre-guideline Judicial guidance*

Att-Gen's Ref Nos 32-33 of 1995 1996 2 Cr App R (S) 346 LCJ Both defendants pleaded to aggravated burglary. One also pleaded to attempted robbery. The general effect of the (reported) cases is that where an elderly victim, living alone, is attacked by intruders and is injured the likely sentence will be in double figures. We wish to stress that attacks on elderly people in their homes are particularly despicable and will be regarded by the court as deserving severe punishment. Elderly victims living alone are vulnerable, not only because of their lack of assistance but also because of their own weakness and isolation. Any attack on such a person is cowardly and can only be expected to be visited with a very severe punishment indeed.

220.13   *Dwellings   Victim over 65   Pre-guideline cases*

R v Keenan 2010 EWCA Crim 2484 D was convicted of aggravated burglary. V was an 86-year-old woman who lived alone. He smashed a window and entered her property in the early hours whilst she was asleep. He took credit cards and, wearing a pair of V's gloves, took a knife from the kitchen up to her bedroom. She was woken, and D, speaking in a false Polish accent, instructed V to give him more money and the PINs for the cards. He threatened to smash her with a hammer if she did not comply. He asked for car keys and left, returning to ask how to start the car. He then tied V up by the hands and feet, and gave her a cushion and her glasses. He also stole her handbag and jewellery. V lost her confidence and became very nervous. D, aged 31, had 20 appearances for 55 offences including dwelling burglaries in 1994, 1995, 1996, 1999, 2001 (2 years), 2003 (4 years), 2007 (3½ years) and 2009 (2½ years). There was also an attempted burglary in 2001. Held. The aggravating features were clear. A vulnerable and elderly woman, woken in the early hours, threatened with a hammer, and tied up. This case is at the top of the range of offences immediately below those involving both actual violence and injury. **12 years** not 14.

R v M and E 2012 EWCA Crim 2941 M and E pleaded to aggravated burglary. E befriended V, an 80-year-old widowed man who lived alone. E obtained some keys to the house. Some weeks later at about 10 pm, M and E went to the house and broke in. They took weapons to the scene and injured V, who suffered a cut thumb. M picked up a knife whilst in the house and brandished it at V. They took £800-£1,000 and V's deceased wife's wedding ring. The wedding ring was melted down and so was lost forever. M and E thereafter pawned the jewellery. M and E blamed each other for instigating the offence. V said that M was 'really vicious' and that both 'were vile and horrible to me'. He thought he would be killed and thereafter wore an alarm around his neck. V now considered it unsafe to be in his own bed. In interview, M said, "Fuck the victim" when charged. Both M and E were aged between 15 and 17. (No mention is made about whether they had convictions.) E was a couple of months younger than M and had Asperger's. Held. This was a Category 1 offence: E took a walking stick as a weapon and M brandished a knife in V's face. E's Asperger's syndrome in a young man does blunt victim empathy. M and E took no notice of V's frailty and used it to injure him. After a trial for an adult, the sentence would have been **12 years**. The appropriate discount was 25%, making 9 years. M was more culpable. A sentence of **5 years** gives him a discount of almost half for his youth and personal circumstances. For E, **4 years** takes into account his Asperger's syndrome, his plea and his youth. Both sentences upheld.

220.14   *Non-dwelling cases   Pre-guideline case*

R v Opara 2011 EWCA Crim 655 D pleaded (full credit) to aggravated burglary. A security guard at a Louis Vuitton store was seized and bundled into a store room. V was bound and gagged. D and others tried to enter the store with a key that they had brought with them, but it did not work. They took V's key and removed goods with a trade figure of £55,000 and a retail value of £144,000. V's jaw was fractured and it required a metal plate. D, whose role was to affix tape over the security cameras, was a former employee of Louis Vuitton and had provided information to the other participants. He had been sacked after his probationary period. He was approached by individuals from his neighbourhood and eventually succumbed to the pressure and agreed to participate in the offence. D, aged 29 at appeal, was of good character and showed remorse. Held. This was a serious offence involving a grave breach of trust. There were high-value goods and grave physical injury was caused to the security guard. **3 years** not 4.

221 CANNABIS

221.1

Drug/driving Under the new list of drugs for drug/driving the prescribed limit for delta-9-tetrahydrocannabinol, also known as THC, the main psychoactive ingredient in cannabis, is 5 µg.[114] For more detail see **245.2**.

See also the IMPORTATION OF DRUGS, POSSESSION OF DRUGS, and SUPPLY OF DRUGS chapters.

General

221.2 *How to assess the different types*

R v Ronchetti 1998 2 Cr App R (S) 100 Lord Lane's distinction in *R v Aramah* 1982 between cannabis, cannabis resin and cannabis oil should be read as cannabis and cannabis resin being equivalent and cannabis oil being 10 times that, as 10 kilos of cannabis or cannabis resin are required to produce 1 kilo of cannabis oil.

221.3 *The properties of the drug*

R v Auton 2011 EWCA Crim 76 The principal psycho-active ingredient of cannabis is THC (tetrahydrocannabinol). Recent research commissioned by the Home Office for the Advisory Council on the Misuse of Drugs reported that the mean THC concentration in sinsemilla seized was (albeit with a wide range) approximately double that of imported herbal cannabis and about three times that of cannabis resin. Correspondingly, the level of cannabidiol (CBD), which it is thought possible may moderate the effect of THC, is very low in herbal cannabis, including sinsemilla, by comparison with cannabis resin. The Advisory Council reported in 2008 that sinsemilla now accounts for a large majority of cannabis seizures (about 80%, compared with about 15% resin and about 2% imported herbal cannabis). As the Council observed, the potential overall effects of the drug depend not simply on potency but on a combination of potency and quantity taken. Users may need much less sinsemilla than less potent forms, or the extra potency may mean greater effects. Natural market forces mean that sinsemilla attracts a significantly higher price than less potent forms of cannabis.

Cultivation etc. of cannabis

221.4

Misuse of Drugs Act 1971
  s 6(2) (cultivation)
  s 4(2)(a)-(c) (production)
  s 8(a) (being concerned in the management of premises and knowingly permitting the production of cannabis)

Mode of trial All offences are triable either way.

Maximum sentences For all offences on indictment 14 years. Summary 6 months and/or £5,000 fine for offences committed before 12 March 2015 and an unlimited fine thereafter.[115] There are maximum fines for those aged under 18, see **14.38** in Volume 1.

Confiscation Where a defendant has a criminal lifestyle the court, once the confiscation proceedings are triggered (see **22.11** in Volume 1), <u>must</u> follow the Proceeds of Crime Act 2002 procedure. 'Criminal lifestyle' offences include Misuse of Drugs Act 1971 s 4(2)-(3) and Misuse of Drugs Act 1971 s 8 offences.[116] For what constitutes a criminal lifestyle, see **22.43** in Volume 1.

Serious Crime Prevention Orders For Misuse of Drugs Act 1971 s 4(2) and 6[117] offences there is a discretionary power to make this order, when it would protect the public etc.[118]

---

[114] Drug Driving (Specified Limits) (England and Wales) Regulations 2014 2014/2868 para 2
[115] Legal Aid, Sentencing and Punishment of Offenders Act 2012 s 85(1) and (4) and Legal Aid, Sentencing and Punishment of Offenders Act 2012 (Commencement No 11) Order 2015 2015/504
[116] Proceeds of Crime Act 2002 s 6 and 75 and Sch 2 para 1
[117] Misuse of Drugs Act 1971 s 6 was inserted by Serious Crime Act 2015 s 47(2). In force 3/5/15
[118] Serious Crime Act 2007 s 1 and Sch 1 para 1(1)(a)

221.5   Sentencing Council guideline
The guideline applies to class A, B and C production and can be found in the
PRODUCTION *Sentencing Council guideline* para at **310.2**.
Note: I consider the best approach to the guideline is to follow it and to ignore all the
pre-guideline tariff cultivation cases. Ed.

221.6   Calculating the factual background/Determining the category   Judicial
guidance
R v Healey and Others 2012 EWCA Crim 1005, 2013 1 Cr App R (S) 33 (p 176) In
production of drug cases, the quantities in the guideline are indicators of output or
potential output as the preamble says. The guidelines (page 18) have an assumption that
many cases seem to involve an output of about 28 to 40 grams for each plant. In the
cases here and perhaps more generally, productivity has increased markedly and was
sometimes 100 grams for a plant, sometimes 200 and sometimes apparently even more.
That kind of yield is a step change. It demonstrates that the number of plants is, as the
note to the guidelines makes clear, to be considered only as a route to the more
fundamental question of output or potential output. One of these defendants, M, obtained
no less than 1.47 kilos from only seven plants. para 17 If a defendant has half a dozen
plants or so in a grow-bag alongside his tomatoes outside the back window, he is no
doubt contemplated as engaged in what the guidelines would call a domestic operation
(see Category 4 of the harm). Assuming he is growing only for his own use, he would
clearly have what they envisage as the lowest level of culpability. However, those who
create a purpose-built room in a loft etc., having invested substantially in professional
equipment for watering, for lighting and/or for electronically controlled timing of those
operations and others, cannot be described as having a lesser role. Those people do so
because they are contemplating repeated cropping under professional or semi-
professional conditions with dedicated apparatus which has been bought for the purpose,
usually at a cost of some hundreds of pounds. Those people should be described as
[playing a] 'significant role'. Also in this 'significant role' will be those who have the
apparatus and the dedicated space for, but in whose case there is a real likelihood of,
additional wider circulation, in other words, supply, whether for money or not. There is
an essential and important distinction between cases where there is likely to be
circulation or supply and cases where there is not. The prospect of future supply does not
generally call for the inclusion of additional counts for possession with intent to supply.
The prospect of future supply very often has to be evaluated by the judge. Circulation in
this context is not confined to sale. The defendant who invests substantial sums in the
creation of a production line for the cultivation of cannabis, usually in a separate room
dedicated for the purpose, is properly to be located on the sliding scale of culpability at
the bottom end of the significant role category. Those who do the same where there is a
prospect of supply are higher up in the significant role category and those who do it
where it is frankly clear that there will be supply for money are a little further up again.
When the operation becomes commercial, in the ordinary sense, then one is talking
about the uppermost category of culpability. If the quantities are such as to put the case
into Category 3, then for those where there is no prospect of supply the appropriate level
for sentencing will very often be in the general region of **6-12 months** after trial. There
may of course be cases where it is entirely proper for there to be a **non-custodial**
penalty.
R v Bamford 2012 EWCA Crim 820, 2013 1 Cr App R (S) 4 (p 26) D pleaded to
producing cannabis. He grew 20 cannabis plants in his front bedroom. Someone
bypassed the electricity meter for him. There was a ducting system. The curtains came
adrift and someone mistook an orange glow for a fire and the fire brigade were called.
They told the police. The estimated yield was 40 grams per plant. D said he grew the
plants from seed, learnt the technique from the Internet and the equipment cost £100. D
was aged 27 and a cannabis user. He said since his arrest he had given up cannabis. His
employer spoke highly of him and said he had overcome considerable difficulties to

obtain and keep the job. If custody continued he would lose it. Held. For the guidelines, 20 plants was Category 3 and 'lesser role' because it was agreed the cannabis was for his own use. The bypassing of the electricity and the exposure of his six-year-old child were serious. Set against that [were] his genuine remorse, his positive good character and his giving up cannabis, which were strong mitigating features. The professional operation and the ability to have crop after crop meant the custody threshold was passed but a **suspended sentence** was justified. As he had served the equivalent of **9 weeks** we substitute that, quashing the 6 months.

R v Soloman 2015 EWCA Crim 64, 1 Cr App R (S) 57 (p 401) D pleaded to cultivating cannabis. The indictment said there were 18 plants. The Judge said the guideline assumed a yield of 40 grams per plant, which meant the 28 plants in the guideline for Category 3 would have a yield of 1,120 grams. In D's case there was expected to be a yield of between 680 and 1,077 grams, which was closer to a Category 3 case than a Category 4 case. He also said the category was between 3 and 4 and the operation was more akin to a commercial operation than a domestic one. D received 9 months' imprisonment. Held. The Judge was entitled to reach these findings. 9 months was at the top end but not manifestly excessive.

221.7   Cases   Post-guideline   Leading role
Note: Pre-guideline cases are best ignored. Ed.

R v Wiseman 2013 EWCA Crim 2492, 2014 2 Cr App R (S) 23 (p 162) D pleaded (on rearraignment) to producing a class B drug, cannabis. D operated a sophisticated and professional cannabis factory, growing over 1,000 cannabis plants. These could produce three crops per year of 120 kilos each. Each crop could retail at £300,000 at street value. D was found at the factory and stalled for time when the police arrived to enable the successful escape of his accomplice. The offence was committed partly when D was on bail for fraud. He gave no comment in interview. D's first trial was halted but D was found to have told a series of deliberate lies. His second trial began whilst he was serving a lengthy sentence for the fraud. There was then a *Newton* hearing at which the Judge disbelieved almost all of D's evidence. D had antecedents including serious dishonesty, but not drugs offences. Held. The Judge was right to place this in Category 1. D had played a leading role and had lied twice on oath. A comparison in relation to the guidelines for the supply and importation of controlled drugs is not apt because offences of producing drugs do not relate to a specific quantity seized or intercepted, unlike supplying and importing drugs. The guidelines use the phrase 'capable of producing', not an operation which produced a specific quantity. **6½ years** unaltered.

See also: *R v Descombre and Thomas* 2013 EWCA Crim 72, 2 Cr App R (S) 51 (p 345) (T pleaded to production and other offences. Commercial, well-organised and sophisticated system. Insulation, lighting and ventilation had been installed. 60 mature flowering plants. Yield £50,000. Electricity by-passed. Third crop. Made about £15,000 from the first two crops. Mid-40s and of good character. T had 'enormous financial problems' and was depressed. Husband and wife team. Leading role. Full credit. **3 years 4** months was not manifestly excessive.)

221.8   Cases   Post-guideline   Significant role
R v Greenhow 2013 EWCA Crim 886 D pleaded (full credit) to producing a class B drug and possession with intent to supply the same. Police searched D's address and found extensive hydroponic equipment for growing cannabis in two of the rooms. In one room, they found 14 young cannabis plants growing in a wardrobe, and the root balls or remains of about another 20 plants. There was also a quantity of cannabis leaves which had been left to dry. The accepted basis of plea was that the cannabis was for himself and three or four friends to whom he sold it. D said he made about £400 per month from those sales from which he funded his rent. It was an ongoing operation. The value of the cannabis seized was around £7,000, with a potential further £4,000 from the plants that were growing. D had numerous convictions, mainly for dishonesty and breaches of

orders. There was one possession of cannabis offence in 2007 (community order). D used to be a plasterer but due to an injury arising from a car accident he was unable to continue that work. Held. Although there was substantial financial gain, there were no other factors present to indicate a leading role. Therefore D probably had a significant, not a leading, role. This was ongoing, low-level commercial production involving between 30 and 40 plants. It is in the upper range of Category 3 [which specifies 28 plants] as it cannot be said that D was producing 'significant quantities of cannabis' as specified in Category 2. The appropriate starting point was **18 months**. With the plea, **1 year** not 2.

Att-Gen's Ref No 3 of 2014 2014 EWCA Crim 456 D pleaded (25% credit) to cultivation of cannabis. D telephoned the police to report he had been threatened by a friend with an air pistol. Police went to D's home and smelled cannabis. D said he had a few plants downstairs. In a 4 m × 4 m cellar, police found 46 female cannabis plants, four large lamps, a heater, two fans and four voltage regulators. The walls were lined with reflective material and the heat was removed by ducting. D said he had spent £1,500-£2,000 on setting the cellar up. Three plants were analysed and each had an average yield of two ounces of skunk cannabis. The estimated street value was £22,000-£33,000. D was in his late 30s and only had a fare evasion conviction. He had had particular difficulties in coping with the loss of his mother, which was followed by the loss of his grandmother. He was sentenced on the basis the cannabis was for himself, for his friends and for a commercial element. D was given an **18-month suspended sentence**, with supervision and 300 hours' unpaid work. D had made excellent progress with the order. The prosecution complained that the Judge did not ascribe a leading role. Held. The Judge was entitled to place D in the significant category. The case was between the top of Category 3 and the bottom of Category 2. We would have started at a little higher than 2 years. There was considerable personal mitigation, not all of it in the judgment. We do not interfere with the sentence.

R v Bergin 2014 EWCA Crim 1228, 2 Cr App R (S) 71 (p 555) D pleaded (around 25% credit) to producing cannabis and possession with intent to supply cannabis. D had cultivated 90 plants at his home, with a potential yield of 378 kilos of skunk cannabis valued at £30,000. This was not D's first crop. He also had bags, scales and two phones which contained messages regarding drug dealing. D was aged 55 on appeal with no significant criminal convictions. He suffered with heart disease and depression following his parents' deaths. Held. The Judge was entitled to treat D's role as significant. Starting at 4 years, **3 years** upheld.

R v McGrath 2015 EWCA Crim 1108 D was pleaded early to production of cannabis and possession of cannabis with intent to supply. D was stopped in his van and police found a small amount of cannabis and a cannabis grinder. He gave his mother's address but police were able to search his real address. Police found 44 cannabis plants about 32 inches high. There were also 10 large bags of prepared dried cannabis and a set of digital scales. Three further bags of cannabis were found in the freezer. An expert said each plant was worth between £280 and £840, making between £11,200 and £33,600. The bags in the freezer (2.40 kilos) were valued at £24,000 and the 10 bags (2.45 kilos) at £24,500. The overall total was between £59,760 and £82,160. D was aged 28 and had 27 sentencing hearings for 77 offences. In 2003 and 2005, he had convictions for possession of cannabis. In 2006 he had cocaine supply and other supply and possession counts (4 years' YOI). The pre-sentence report said the risk of re-offending was very high. There was a *Newton* hearing where the defence account was rejected. The Judge said the production offence was Category 2, because the operation was capable of significant production. Held. The Judge was entitled to consider that the operation was capable of significant production. However, **30 months** not 3 years.

Note: The court did not say what the role was. However, the range it took was for a significant role. Ed.

221.9   Cases   Post-guideline   Lesser role
R v Vu 2014 EWCA Crim 561 D pleaded to producing cannabis. Police received a complaint of a strong smell of cannabis in a residential street. They forced entry to the premises and found that several rooms had been converted into a cannabis farm. It was a very professional operation. There had been unlawful access to the electricity supply and there were 231 plants and 140 pots with soil and the roots of cannabis plants still in them. He was acting under pressure from others and his only gain was food and accommodation. D, aged 39, was of previous good character. The Judge assessed his role as lesser. Held. Although D was not to share in the profit, he must have known the scale of the operation. We start at 2 years, reducing that with personal mitigation to 18 months and with plea discount, **16 months** not 2 years.
Note: The Court said there was no criticism of the plea discount being one sixth and then gave him 16 months instead of 15. Ed.
R v Sobarasua 2015 EWCA Crim 1137 D pleaded to producing cannabis, abstracting electricity and possessing cannabis with intent. On 26 February 2013, police officers noticed a strong smell of cannabis coming from a van in convoy with a BMW driven by D. They stopped the vehicles and found in the van 15 potted cannabis plants in bags. The two men were arrested. At V's address, police found 137 cannabis plants in two stages of growth. The electricity meter had been bypassed. D made no comment in interview and was bailed. D was then told no action would be taken against him. In the middle of 2014, D was summoned to appear in court in October 2014. His basis of plea said he was in debt to his dealer and had allowed the dealer's plants to be grown in his house to cancel the debt. D was of good character and had a positive pre-sentence report. The Judge started at 5 years, gave 20% credit for D's plea at the PCMH, and a year off because of the delay. Held. The Judge could pass a global sentence on the production count. There was no reason why the credit should not be 25%. 24 months for the production and 3 months consecutive for the abstraction count making **27 months** not 3 years.

221.10   Assisting others to produce
Example: R v Dang and Others 2014 EWCA Crim 348, 2 Cr App R (S) 49 (p 391) (D pleaded to being concerned in the production of cannabis and other charges. 22 others were convicted of D's conspiracy. Some were convicted of that conspiracy and other similar separate conspiracies. They supplied hydroponic and other equipment to assist others to grow cannabis. The turnover of pots supplied was suitable for growing over 1 million cannabis plants. The potential yield was 40,000 kilos worth about £100m. There were 56 production farms. Not all appealed. Sentences of **14 years, 10 years, 9 years, 9 years 323 days, 7 years, 6 years** (×2), **5 years, 4 years** (×2), **2½ years** (×3), **42 months and 2 years suspended** upheld.)

221.11   Production information
R v Auton 2011 EWCA Crim 76 The object is a crop of flowering tops of the female plants, usually of the kind known as sinsemilla, which is to say without seeds, achieved by having an all-female population. This herbal, not resinous, material is to be contrasted with imported herbal cannabis, because it is significantly stronger. The non-scientific expression 'skunk' is often applied to it, particularly where it is a variety with high odour. Cannabis is an annual plant, so that its life cycle ends with flowering and the production of new seeds. When grown intensively indoors one, or sometimes two, crops can be obtained from a plant before it passes to senescence and dies, and a crop takes (generally speaking) something of the order of four months from the planting of the seed to harvest, or about three months from the seedling stage. Plants in the flowering stage have different lighting needs from those at the germination or growing stage, so either the lighting regime in a single space is altered or, if more continuous production is desired, different lighting regimes may be provided in different rooms or areas. This may well be indicated by the presence of plants at different stages of development in separate areas. Yield may vary according to the type and size of plant, how long they are left

before harvest, and the cultivation methods (for example spacing), but from the evidence in the cases before us seems likely to be in the general region of about one to one-and-a-half ounces (about 28-40g) per fully matured plant. We recommend that such estimates be provided in these cases.

The proper inference as to what the cultivation entailed and what would be likely to happen to the product depends on the facts of each case. In most cases, and not only where the plants have not as yet been harvested, it will not be possible to frame a count of possession of identified material with intent to supply. The issue must be dealt with by the judge. As with many other offences, care needs to be taken with assertions advanced by way of basis of plea. It hardly needs to be said that the Crown should accept (i.e. endorse) such a basis only when satisfied that it is proper to do so. To say that there is no evidence to 'gainsay' it is rarely discharging the Crown's responsibility. The evidence of the scale of the operation and the implausibility of the explanation may justify the inference that the basis advanced is false whether or not there is independent evidence of actual supply.

222   CARELESS DRIVING/DRIVING WITHOUT DUE CARE AND ATTENTION

222.1

Road Traffic Act 1988 s 3

Mode of trial Summary only

Maximum sentence A £5,000 fine for offences committed before 12 March 2015 and an unlimited fine thereafter.[119] There are maximum fines for those aged under 18, see **14.38** in Volume 1.

Disqualification Discretionary disqualification

Fixed penalty There is a fixed penalty (and financial penalty deposit) of £100 for this offence[120] with half the relevant victim surcharge. For more detail see **61.1** in Volume 1.

Penalty points 3 to 9. When certain conditions are met the court may order reduced penalty points for attendance on courses.[121] On 24 June 2013, Road Safety Act 2006 changes came into force.

Reduced periods of disqualification When certain conditions are met the court may order a reduced period of disqualification (not less than 3 months, not more than a quarter of the unreduced period) for Road Traffic Act 1988 s 3 offences for attendance on courses.

Court Martial The suggested penalty for careless driving is a fine of five days' pay with a recommendation that the military driving permit be withdrawn, *Guidance on Sentencing in the Court Martial 2013* para 5.11.4.

HGVs etc. For Passenger Carrying Vehicles (PCV) and Large Goods Vehicles (LGV) drivers, see **341.1**.

222.2   *Magistrates' Court Sentencing Guidelines*

Magistrates' Court Sentencing Guidelines 2008, see www.banksr.com Other Matters Guidelines tab The guidelines apply to the Magistrates' Court and to the Crown Court hearing appeals or sentencing for summary only offences.[122]

For details about applying the guidelines, see the **GUIDELINES** chapter in Volume 1. page 117 Starting points are based on a first-time offender pleading not guilty.

---

[119] Legal Aid, Sentencing and Punishment of Offenders Act 2012 s 85(1) and (4) and Legal Aid, Sentencing and Punishment of Offenders Act 2012 (Commencement No 11) Order 2015 2015/504
[120] Road Safety (Financial Penalty Deposit) (Appropriate Amount) Order 2009 2009/492 as amended.
[121] Road Traffic Act 1988 s 30A substituted by Road Safety Act 2006 s 34
[122] See page 15 of the guidelines.

Examples of nature of activity	Starting point	Range
Momentary lapse of concentration or misjudgement at low speed	Band A fine	Band A fine 3 to 4 points
Loss of control due to speed, mishandling or insufficient attention to road conditions, or carelessly turning right across oncoming traffic	Band B fine	Band B fine 5 to 6 points
Overtaking manoeuvre at speed resulting in collision of vehicles, or driving bordering on the dangerous	Band C fine	Band C fine Consider disqualification or 7 to 9 points

The following aggravating and mitigating factors may be particularly relevant: Factors indicating higher culpability: 1 Excessive speed 2 Carrying out other tasks while driving 3 Carrying passengers or heavy load 4 Tiredness. Factors indicating lower culpability: 1 Minor risk 2 Inexperience of driver 3 Sudden change in road or weather conditions 4 Tiredness. Factors indicating greater degree of harm: 1 Injury to others 2 Damage to other vehicles or property 3 High level of traffic or pedestrians in vicinity 4 Location e.g. near school.
Consider compensation.
A Band A fine is 50% of net weekly income. Band B and C are 100% and 150%. For more detail, see **60.27** in Volume 1.
Consultation It is expected that the Sentencing Council will issue a consultation document about updating this guideline in May 2016.
For details about the guidelines, see the **GUIDELINES** chapter in Volume 1.

222.3 *Judicial guidance*
R v Krawec 1984 6 Cr App R (S) 367 LCJ The primary considerations are the quality of the driving, the extent D fell below the standard of the reasonably competent driver, in other words the degree of carelessness and culpability. The unforeseen consequences may sometimes be relevant to those considerations. Here the fact that D failed to see the pedestrian until it was too late and therefore collided with him was plainly a relevant factor.
Note: This is an old case and it would be helpful if the Court of Appeal gave some fresh guidance. Ed.

222.4 *Cases*
R v Tomasso 2010 EWCA Crim 322 D pleaded early to driving without due care and attention. D was driving on an A-road, overtook a lorry and collided with an oncoming motorbike driven by V. V sustained serious injuries to his arm, leg, foot and side of his body. Operations to remove pins from his leg and to insert a long metal pin inside his thigh bone were required and further operations to his broken foot may be required. It was anticipated that V would suffer from arthritis as he got older and he would be off work for up to 12 months following the collision. D lived in a rural area. He had two fixed penalty notices for speeding and three active points on his licence. The Judge said this was a bad case of careless driving. Held. After a trial a fine of £1,200 would have been justified so there was nothing wrong with **£750**. D was at risk of losing his job so **6-month disqualification** not 2½ years.
R v Christie 2012 EWCA Crim 35, 2 Cr App R (S) 46 (p 273) D pleaded to careless driving. He was acquitted of dangerous driving. He pulled out of a garage forecourt and failed to see another motorist. That motorist had to take evasive action. D pulled onto the wrong side of the road and drove for around 185 metres (13 seconds). Then there was a head-on collision with a taxi. The driver suffered a fractured elbow, a fractured wrist, two broken legs and a broken ankle. There were serious economic consequences for his

business. One passenger suffered three or four broken ribs and a punctured lung. Another passenger suffered a broken leg, a broken hip and multiple facial fractures requiring significant surgical intervention. A third passenger suffered a knee injury. For two of the passengers, the accident occurred on their wedding day. D remained at the scene and called the emergency services. D, aged 51, was of good character and had not had any previous driving convictions. Held. This was a bad case of careless driving, bordering on dangerous. The injuries were due to pure inattention or lack of concentration, not merely for an instant but for a relatively significant period and distance. There were extremely serious injuries. Whilst this was a bad case, it does not fall into the very worst category. The appropriate fine was **£3,000** not £5,000, which was the maximum. The disqualification of 15 months would remain.

R v Sullivan 2013 EWCA Crim 97 D pleaded guilty as an alternative to dangerous driving. Aged 20, she lost control of her car due to speed and inexperience. The car hit a tree. Her passenger sustained very serious injuries. D was of good character with a clean licence. Held. **£3,000 fine** was reasonable.

R v Patterson 2015 EWCA Crim 1797 D pleaded in the Magistrates' Court[123] to careless driving and excess alcohol. D stopped at a red light and then over-accelerated away and lost control of his car. The car hit another car causing the other driver minor injury. D's alcohol reading was 91 μg (permitted max 35 μg). D was of good character and an oil trader with a good income. Held. For the due care, this was between the middle and highest level in the *Magistrates' Court Sentencing Guidelines 2008*. It is important not to double account. With full credit for the plea, **£4,000** global fine on the excess alcohol charge not £1,000 and £5,000 as separate fines.

Note: D's £5,000 fine was the maximum sentence available because the offence was committed before the maximum was increased. The fine clearly did not reflect the early plea but this point was not mentioned in the judgment. Ed.

See also: *R v Perkins and Salveson* 2012 EWCA Crim 218 (Pleas. S and P in separate cars travelling at 90 mph on M1. S's car hit V's car, which was then hit by P's. V's children, who were not wearing seatbelts, were thrown from the car and one broke an arm and another an ankle. V was straddling two lanes. S and P were on-duty police officers. P would not have avoided a collision if driving at 70 mph. Disqualification quashed. **5 penalty points**)

R v Drobac 2012 EWCA Crim 1733, 2013 1 Cr App R (S) 73 (p 409) (Plea. Fell asleep at wheel due to accumulated lack of sleep. Had happened on previous occasion. Driving at 45 mph. Veered into oncoming car. Multiple fractures, soft tissue injuries, severed artery and serious ligament damage. Six or seven hours of emergency surgery. Very bad case of careless driving. **£1,250 fine** was correct and **12-month disqualification** not 18 because of the need for driving at work and 8 months after he had handed in his licence to the DVLA.)

222.5   Death results
The law changed with the introduction of the new offence of causing death by careless driving, see the **DEATH BY DRIVING: CARELESS (SIMPLE)** chapter.

222.6   Disqualification
R v Kruger 2012 EWCA Crim 2166, 2013 1 Cr App R (S) 117 (p 608) (Plea. Drove into the back of another car and caused it to swerve and end up on the wrong side of the road. He was driving over the speed limit and had been drinking. His basis of plea stated he was not drunk. Victims suffered soreness and whiplash. Aged 25. Previous for dangerous driving in 2007. If the driving matter was on its own, a 2-year disqualification would have been excessive. In the context of committing this offence about one year after regaining his licence, a **2-year disqualification** was not excessive.)

---

[123] At the beginning of the judgment it says the pleas were made in the Crown Court. Later in the judgment it says it was in the Magistrates' Court, which must be correct.

222.7 HGV drivers
R v Morling 1998 1 Cr App R (S) 420 The fact that the defendant is an HGV driver is two-edged. The disqualification will hit the defendant hard, but being an HGV driver heightens the culpability of taking the risks he did.

223 COMMON ASSAULT
223.1
Criminal Justice Act 1988 s 39 (common assault and battery (usually particularised where there is contact as 'assault by beating' and sometimes known as assault by battery))
Mode of trial Summary only
Maximum sentence 6 months and/or a £5,000 fine for offences committed before 12 March 2015 and an unlimited fine thereafter.[124] There are maximum fines for those aged under 18, see **14.38** in Volume 1.
However, under Criminal Justice Act 1988 s 40 the offence is triable on indictment. According to the Divisional Court[125] it is then contrary to section 39 although certain academics and another set of judges at the Divisional Court[126] consider that the offence is then contrary to common law.
Where a defendant pleads to common assault as an alternative to another count and the other counts that the defendant is to be sentenced for are summary only, the maximum consecutive sentence is 6 months.[127]
Criminal Behaviour Orders Where a defendant has engaged in behaviour that caused or was likely to cause harassment, alarm or distress to any persons and a Criminal Behaviour Order will help in preventing the offender from engaging in such behaviour, the court may make this order.[128]
Licensed premises Where an offence is committed on licensed premises, the court may prohibit defendants from entering those premises or any other specified premises without the express consent of the licensee etc.[129] The minimum period is 3 months and the maximum period is 2 years.[130] Violent Crime Reduction Act 2006 s 65 and Sch 5 repeals these powers and includes powers to make Drinking Banning Orders. Evaluation of the new powers continues. The repeal and the commencement of the new powers are not expected soon.

223.2 Sentencing Council guideline
Assault Guideline 2011, see www.banksr.com Other Matters Guidelines tab This guideline applies to all offenders aged 18 and older, regardless of the date of the offence.

STEP ONE Determining the offence category
page 24 The court should determine the offence category using the table below.

Category 1	Greater harm (injury or fear of injury must normally be present) and higher culpability
Category 2	Greater harm (injury or fear of injury must normally be present) and lower culpability, or lesser harm and higher culpability
Category 3	Lesser harm and lower culpability

---

[124] Legal Aid, Sentencing and Punishment of Offenders Act 2012 s 85(1) and (4) and Legal Aid, Sentencing and Punishment of Offenders Act 2012 (Commencement No 11) Order 2015 2015/504
[125] *DPP v Little* 1992 95 Cr App R (S) 28
[126] *Haystead v DPP* 2000 The Times 2/6/00 164 JP 396
[127] Criminal Law Act 1967 s 6(3A) and 6(3B) and *R v James* 2007 EWCA Crim 1906, 2008 1 Cr App R (S) 44 (p 238)
[128] Anti-social Behaviour, Crime and Policing Act 2014 s 22(1)-(4)
[129] Licensed Premises (Exclusion of Certain Persons) Act 1980 s 1(1)
[130] Licensed Premises (Exclusion of Certain Persons) Act 1980 s 1(3)

The court should determine the offender's culpability and the harm caused, or intended, by reference **only** to the factors below (as demonstrated by the presence of one or more). These factors comprise the principal factual elements of the offence and should determine the category.

Factors indicating greater harm
Injury or fear of injury which is serious in the context of the offence (must normally be present)
Victim is particularly vulnerable because of personal circumstances
Sustained or repeated assault on the same victim
Factors indicating lesser harm
Injury which is less serious in the context of the offence

Factors indicating lower culpability
Subordinate role in group or gang
A greater degree of provocation than normally expected
Lack of premeditation
Mental disorder or learning disability, where linked to commission of the offence
Excessive self-defence

Factors indicating higher culpability
Statutory aggravating factors:
Offence motivated by, or demonstrating, hostility to the victim based on his or her sexual orientation (or presumed sexual orientation)
Offence motivated by, or demonstrating, hostility to the victim based on the victim's disability (or presumed disability)
Other aggravating factors:
A significant degree of premeditation
Threatened or actual use of weapon or weapon equivalent (for example, shod foot, head-butting, use of acid, use of animal)
Intention to commit more serious harm than actually resulted from the offence
Deliberately causes more harm than is necessary for commission of offence
Deliberate targeting of vulnerable victim
Leading role in group or gang
Offender motivated by, or demonstrating, hostility based on the victim's age, sex, gender identity (or presumed gender identity)

223.3

STEP TWO Starting point and category range

page 24 Having determined the category, the court should use the corresponding starting points to reach a sentence within the category range below. The table is applicable to all offenders.

Category	Starting point	Category range
1	High-level community order	Low-level community order to 26 weeks' custody
2	Medium-level community order	Band A fine to high-level community order
3	Band A fine	Band C fine

For the meaning of a high-level, a medium-level and a low-level community order see **16.12-16.14** in Volume 1.

223.4   [Aggravating and mitigating factors]

The table below contains a non-exhaustive list of additional factual elements providing the context of the offence and factors relating to the offender. When sentencing Category 1 offences, the court should also consider the custody threshold as follows:

Has the custody threshold been passed?
If so, is it unavoidable that a custodial sentence be imposed?
If so, can that sentence be suspended?

Factors increasing seriousness
Statutory aggravating factors:
Previous convictions, having regard to a) the nature of the offence to which the conviction relates and its relevance to the current offence; and b) the time that has elapsed since the conviction
Offence committed whilst on bail
Other aggravating factors include:
Location of the offence
Timing of the offence
Ongoing effect upon the victim
Offence committed against those working in the public sector or providing a service to the public
Presence of others including relatives, especially children or partner of the victim
Gratuitous degradation of victim
In domestic violence cases, victim forced to leave their home
Failure to comply with current court orders
Offence committed whilst on licence
An attempt to conceal or dispose of evidence
Failure to respond to warnings or concerns expressed by others about the offender's behaviour
Commission of offence whilst under the influence of alcohol or drugs
Abuse of power and/or position of trust
Exploiting contact arrangements with a child to commit an offence
Established evidence of community impact
Any steps taken to prevent the victim reporting an incident, or obtaining assistance and/or from assisting or supporting the prosecution
Offences taken into consideration (TICs)
Factors reducing seriousness or reflecting personal mitigation
No previous convictions or no relevant/recent convictions
Single blow
Remorse
Good character and/or exemplary conduct
Determination, and/or demonstration of steps taken to address addiction or offending behaviour
Serious medical conditions requiring urgent, intensive or long-term treatment
Isolated incident
Age and/or lack of maturity where it affects the responsibility of the offender
Lapse of time since the offence where this is not the fault of the offender
Mental disorder or learning disability, where not linked to the commission of the offence
Sole or primary carer for dependent relatives

Racially/religiously aggravated offences: the court should determine the appropriate sentence for the offence without taking account of the element of aggravation and then make an addition to the sentence, considering the level of aggravation involved. It may be appropriate to move outside the identified category range, taking into account the increased statutory maximum.

The court should then consider the following:
  a) other factors indicating a reduction, such as assistance to the prosecution,
  b) reduction for a guilty plea,
  c) dangerousness,
  d) totality, if sentencing for more than one offence, and
  e) compensation and ancillary orders.

223.5   *Magistrates' Court Sentencing Guidelines*

Magistrates' Court Sentencing Guidelines 2011 Update, see www.banksr.com Other Matters Guidelines tab page 213 The update repeats the main guideline.

223.6   *Cases*

R v Hichens 2011 EWCA Crim 1626 D was convicted of common assault, and acquitted of ABH. He moved into V's flat after O had introduced them. O and V had had a relationship. O attended the address and was abusive and threatening towards D. The police attended and O was given a warning under Protection from Harassment Act 1997. He returned. V wanted to let him in, but D prevented her from doing so. It was alleged that he put his hand around her throat and exerted pressure so that she lost consciousness. D admitted slapping V in order to prevent O from entering, thereby preventing the commission of an offence: an assault. It was also alleged that D threatened to break V's jaw. D, aged 40 at appeal, had repeated convictions for violence and he thought that he had a right to control women with whom he had an association. Held. Whilst on one view it seems a little startling that the maximum sentence was passed for a single slap, when considered in regard to D's bad record for violence and the fact he sought to control V in her own home, in light of his attitudes to women, **6 months** was not manifestly excessive.

R v Barnett 2011 EWCA Crim 2433 D pleaded to common assault at the Magistrates' Court. After an argument with V, his girlfriend, she left their house. She got into a car with her friend. The car stopped at some traffic lights and D happened to be walking past. He asked V to get out of the car several times and, when she continued to refuse, he reached into the car, grabbed her scarf and attempted to pull her out of the car. D, aged 20 at appeal, had 10 convictions for breach of community orders, five for threatening behaviour, three for common assault, one for harassment and one for attempted robbery. D was in breach of a suspended sentence for the robbery and was committed for sentence. Held. Notwithstanding that the plea was on the basis of recklessness, this was a serious matter. The Judge was entitled to impose a sentence of **3 months**. This was consecutive to the activated but reduced in length (due to work performed etc.) suspended sentence.

R v Fitzpatrick 2013 EWCA Crim 730 D was convicted of battery,[131] having been acquitted of ill-treatment of a person who lacks capacity. She was employed as a care assistant who visited clients and assisted in all aspects of their care. V, an 88-year-old woman, found it very difficult to swallow and was bedridden. She needed visits from two carers four times a day to administer her medication and feed and bathe her. She lacked capacity to run her own affairs and had a very poor short-term memory. She would therefore have been unable to complain about any incident of mistreatment. When D was trying to give V her medication, she shouted at V in an aggressive tone.[132] V spat the medication out and it went down D's front. V shouted "you're trying to kill me" at which point D swung her arm and struck V with a backhand across the face. D became aware that her co-worker was watching and said "Oh I've upset you, I'm sorry darling". The co-worker reported the incident. There was no evidence of injury arising out of the assault. D, aged 46 at appeal, had no convictions. She had been a carer for 10 years and had obtained qualifications for that occupation. She had a lost a son aged 7 and suffered depression and anxiety. Held. Anyone with these responsibilities, in great trust, and who strikes a patient clearly carries the burden of higher culpability. There was greater harm present. The Judge was correct to conclude that this offence passed the custody threshold because of the level of trust involved. The degree of trust and reliance in circumstances

---

[131] The report says assault by beating and Criminal Justice Act 1988 s 39. Battery is the offence, and the particulars should read 'assault by beating'.

[132] The report states 'D shouted at Mr Cole' but as there is no other mention of Mr Cole in the judgment it is assumed it is a typo for Mrs Cole, V. Ed.

like this and the consequent important breach of trust mean that it will be a rare case where a suspension of sentence, for a real blow, will be justified. **3 months** not 6 (which was the maximum).

R v Fuller 2013 EWCA Crim 2625 D pleaded (full credit) to three charges of assault by beating. D and his two brothers, B1 and B2, were involved in an altercation with two soldiers outside a nightclub. B1 later pleaded to GBH and B2 to ABH. D's offending consisted of a single blow to one of the soldiers and a later scuffle with the club doorman. The Judge highlighted alcohol as an aggravating feature of the offence but gave full credit. D was aged 19 and had no convictions. Held. The Judge was incorrect in putting the offences in Category 1 of the guidelines. D became tainted with the much more serious offences committed by B1 and B2. **2 months** concurrent not 4, enabling him to be released immediately.

Note: When the Court said the case was not a Category 1 case, the clear implication is that the case should have been dealt with by a non-custodial sentence. Ed.

R v Ukueku 2015 EWCA Crim 184 D was convicted of common assault. She was acquitted of racially aggravated assault. V and her son boarded a bus in London and V began talking on her phone in a foreign language. V and D sat next to each other and their arms touched. D then placed clothing over her arm which was closest to V. V took umbrage at this and interpreted the gesture as D thinking that V was 'garbage'. V then, finishing her phone conversation, said, "This is a public bus, if you don't want people to touch you, take a taxi or drive your own car." D replied, "Shut up! This is my country…Why don't you go back to your country? You have met your match." D then stood up and slapped V about the head and on her chest. She also scratched V and pulled her hair. Despite V's eight-year-old son shouting for D to stop, she continued to try to slap V whilst V attempted to push her away. V suffered scratches to her hands and her chest. D asserted in interview that she had acted in self-defence and V was the aggressor. D also falsely claimed to have suffered scratches during the attack. D was aged 38 with only two cautions, the second of which was in 2012 for a similar assault on a bus. D sought to minimise her offending to the author of the pre-sentence report, who thought the offence occurred due to D's inability to manage her emotions. D had experienced domestic violence as a child but was in employment with positive support. D's risk of reoffending was low, perhaps due to her distress during her experience of court. However, D posed a medium risk of serious harm to the public and the report recommended a medium-level community order. The Judge, however, placed the offence into Category 1 due to D's use of her nails, her persistence in the attack and the causing of more harm than necessary. Also, children were present. Held. The Judge was entitled to place this into Category 1 but it lacked some aggravating futures which would otherwise have justified a sentence at the top of the range. **3 months suspended** for 12 months, not 20 weeks' immediate custody. No unpaid work requirement because of the period in custody. £150 compensation not £1,000.

See also: *R v Bayley* 2015 EWCA Crim 940 (Two cases. D pleaded on day of trial. Other plea earlier. One offence, D hit another's face with his fist with some force. In other offence, D hit his friend's face (not hard, the late plea). Seven previous convictions for battery or common assault. Serious one worth as a Category 1 offence 4 months, not 6. With other one **5 months** in all upheld.)

Old case: *R v Walton and Parker* 2010 EWCA Crim 411 (**Community orders** with 150 hours' unpaid work and a curfew.) For a summary of the case see the 10th edition of this book.

224 COMMON ASSAULT: RACIALLY OR RELIGIOUSLY AGGRAVATED
224.1
Crime and Disorder Act 1998 s 29
Mode of trial Triable either way

Maximum sentence On indictment 2 years. Summary 6 months and/or a £5,000 fine for offences committed before 12 March 2015 and an unlimited fine thereafter.[133] There are maximum fines for those aged under 18, see **14.38** in Volume 1.

Criminal Behaviour Orders and **Licensed premises** For details, see the COMMON ASSAULT chapter.

Sexual Harm Prevention Orders There is a discretionary power to make this order when it is necessary to protect the public from sexual harm.[134]

For the basic principles, see the RACIALLY OR RELIGIOUSLY AGGRAVATED OFFENCES chapter.

224.2   *Sentencing Guidelines Council Guidelines*

The guideline is in the COMMON ASSAULT chapter. The Magistrates' Court Guideline is the same as the main guideline.

224.3   *Cases*

R v Johnson 2010 EWCA Crim 3077, 2011 2 Cr App R (S) 29 (p 164) D pleaded on rearraignment to racially aggravated common assault, having pleaded not guilty to racially aggravated ABH. V, aged 19, was attempting to park her car when she sounded her horn to get the attention of D, who was double parked. D, a black male, approached V's car and said, "What the fuck do you want? What the fuck are you doing you stupid white girl?" V explained she did not want to damage D's car. D shouted abuse at her so V drove away. She noticed that D had written down her registration number. Stopping at temporary traffic lights, V saw D approach her once more, proceeding to shout: "Who do you think you are? What the fuck do you think you are doing you stupid white bitch?" V explained that she was six months pregnant. D then punched V through the car window, hitting her six or seven times to the upper arm. She sustained bruising to her upper arm and to her left eye. D told V, "You're not going to get away with this you stupid white bitch." Two boys then pushed D away from the car and D drove off. D lied in interview. D, aged 47, had an 'extremely unpleasant' record, although he had fewer appearances in recent years. Held. The offence had aggravating factors: committed against a lone woman who was pregnant and stuck in traffic, in a car so unable to drive off and escape. It was premeditated in that V drove off and D followed. The maximum sentence for the assault was 6 months, with the maximum uplift for the racial element being 18 months. 4½ months was appropriate for the assault and 4½ for the racial element. Therefore, **9 months**, not 18.

R v Isitt 2013 EWCA Crim 265 D pleaded (full credit) to racially aggravated common assault. D went to a doctor's surgery. D was swearing as V came in with his five-year-old daughter. V sat down in front of D, who began to kick V's daughter's chair. V turned around and asked him what he was doing. D replied, "You fucking cunt. What are you going to do, you fucking Paki? I'm going to slice you up. I'll go to prison for you, you bastard. I'll make sure I damage you first. If I see you in the street, I'll fight you." D then spoke into his mobile phone, saying, "I've got some Paki here, I'm in the surgery. Are you guys coming? I'm going to slice him up." It was not known whether D was actually speaking to anyone or just pretending. V said he would call the police. D replied that that would give him even more reason to 'do' him. V called the police. D stood up and tried to grab V. V moved away and someone else in the surgery intervened. D was taken outside and when an officer arrived, D raised his fist as if to punch him. He was arrested. D, aged 36, had over 130 convictions on 71 appearances. He had received both custodial and non-custodial sentences with drug and alcohol courses. Most of his offences were for acquisitive offences, but included four assaults, six ABHs, two affrays, five batteries and seven threatening words and behaviour offences (two of which were

---

[133] Legal Aid, Sentencing and Punishment of Offenders Act 2012 s 85(1) and (4) and Legal Aid, Sentencing and Punishment of Offenders Act 2012 (Commencement No 11) Order 2015 2015/504

[134] Sexual Offences Act 2003 s 103A as inserted by Anti-social Behaviour, Crime and Policing Act 2014 Sch 5 para 2 and Sexual Offences Act 2003 Sch 5

racially aggravated). D also fell to be sentenced for successive breaches of community orders and suspended sentences. A pre-sentence report noted his deep-rooted drug and alcohol misuse. D was in breach of a 12-week Suspended Sentence Order. Held. There was a deliberate attempt to scare V by using his mobile phone to suggest D was recruiting others to attack V. The offence was very significantly aggravated by the fact it was committed in front of V's young daughter and it was in a doctor's surgery. The offence significantly crossed the custody threshold even without D's previous convictions. Taking account of the suspended sentences which were imposed concurrently, it can be assumed the Judge started at 18 months. With the plea and an uplift for D's previous convictions and the breach of the orders, **14 months** was not too long.

R v Niewulis 2013 EWCA Crim 556, 2 D was convicted of racially aggravated common assault. He was a customer in a supermarket. One of the security guards on duty was black. Whilst shopping, D constantly looked towards the guard and repeated the words "nigger" and "gay" interspersed with bad language. D passed through the tills and went into the lavatories in the store. The alarms went off and the security guard suspected (wrongly) that D had an item in his bag which he had not paid for. As he was searching through it, D brought his hand down onto the guard's arm with enough force to knock it to his side. This was the assault. The force was minimal and no injury resulted. D was taken to the manager's office and a tussle ensued. D was intimidating and aggressive throughout. He repeatedly shouted "fuck off" and further words of abuse including "gay" and "nigger". D, aged 32, had three convictions for racially aggravated threatening words or behaviour or harassment and distress. Held. We have no doubt that the custody threshold was passed. The appropriate sentence was **3 months** for the assault and an uplift of **3 months** for the racial aggravation. So **6 months** not 12.

Old cases: *R v Raybone* 2010 EWCA Crim 78, 2 Cr App R (S) 58 (p 390) (**10 months**) *R v Pullinger* 2010 EWCA Crim 756 (**3 months**) For a summary of these cases see the 10th edition of this book.

COMMUNITY ORDER, BREACH OF, see Volume 1

225   COMPANIES AND PUBLIC BODIES AS DEFENDANTS

225.1
Deferred Prosecution Agreements Crime and Courts Act 2013 s 45 and Sch 17 introduces this procedure. The procedure is that a bill of indictment is preferred and proceedings are automatically suspended. The powers include financial penalties, compensation, disgorgement of profits, donation of money to charity and implementation of compliance programmes. Commencement was on 24 February 2014.

For fraud, see the **FRAUD AND FINANCIAL SERVICES OFFENCES** chapter.

See also the **INSOLVENCY OFFENCES** chapter.

Procedure

225.2   *Corporations   Committals*
Powers of Criminal Courts (Sentencing) Act 2000 s 3(5) The preceding provisions of this section (see **99.4** in Volume 1) shall apply in relation to a corporation as if:
   a) the corporation were an individual aged 18 or over, and
   b) in subsection (2) above, the words 'in custody or on bail' were omitted.
Note: This provision means corporations can be committed for sentence. Ed.

R v F Howe and Son (Engineers) Ltd 1999 2 Cr App R (S) 37 In the case of a company, magistrates can properly commit for sentence on the basis that their powers to fine are insufficient.

225.3   *Basis for sentence, There must be a proper*
Corporate Manslaughter and H and S Offences Causing Death Guideline 2010, see www.banksr.com Other Matters Guidelines tab para 11 It will generally be appropriate to require the prosecution to set out in writing the facts of the case relied upon and any

aggravating or mitigating features which it identifies.[135] The defence may conveniently be required similarly to set out in writing any points on which it differs. If sentence is to proceed upon agreed facts, they should be set out in writing.[136]

Note: This guidance applies to corporate manslaughter and Health and Safety cases and the guideline has been replaced. In similar factual or legally complex cases the court would no doubt expect or order similar assistance. Ed.

Friskies Petcare (UK) Ltd 2000 EWCA Crim 95, 2 Cr App R (S) 401 Problems can arise when there is a dispute about whether the court sentenced the defendant on the basis on which the case was presented. This case illustrates the problem. The Health and Safety Executive should list in writing not merely the facts of the case but the aggravating features as set out in *R v F Howe and Son (Engineers)* Ltd 1999 2 Cr App R (S) 37. It should be served and the defence should set out in writing the mitigating features. If there is an agreed basis, it should be in writing.

225.4   Need for senior person to explain the offending and their response to it

R v Sellafield and Network Rail 2014 EWCA Crim 49 LCJ The two appeals were heard together. Network Rail pleaded to a section 3 Health and Safety failing. V1 drove onto a user-worked crossing on a railway line. He saw a train coming and braked. The car slipped on loose gravel and was hit by a train. V1's grandson, V2, was thrown out of the car and hit his head on the track. V1 was badly bruised and V2 suffered a brain stem bleed which had a devastating effect on him and his future. Held. It was important for Network Rail to ensure the fullest information was provided to the sentencing court. That is highly material when the court assesses the response of the board of the company to the statutory purposes of sentencing, when a fine inflicts no direct punishment on any one [individual].

R v Southern Water Services Ltd 2014 EWCA Crim 120, 2 Cr App R (S) 29 (p 235) LCJ the defendant pleaded to contravening its licence conditions. The company polluted the sea with untreated sewage. The Environment Agency was not notified for ten days and the problem was not remedied quickly enough. This was a breach of its licence. There were further discharges later in the year as the repairs were not permanent. The company's turnover was £0.75bn and its post-tax profit in 2013 was £156.9m. The company had 160 previous offences. Held. In offences of this seriousness it is incumbent on the Chief Executive and the main board of the company, particularly one with a serious record of minor criminality as here, to explain to the court the cause of the offending behaviour, the current offence and its proposals for protecting the public from further such offending, as set out in *R v Sellafield and Network Rail* 2014 EWCA Crim 49. £200,000 fine upheld.

Factors

225.5   Offence committed for 'commercial' purposes

Magistrates' Court Sentencing Guidelines 2008, see www.banksr.com Other Matters Guidelines tab page 150 para 26 Some offences are committed with the intention of gaining a significant commercial benefit. These often occur where, in order to carry out an activity lawfully, a person has to comply with certain processes which may be expensive. They include, for example, 'taxi-touting' (where unauthorised persons seek to operate as taxi drivers) and 'fly-tipping' (where the cost of lawful disposal is considerable).

27 In some of these cases, a fine based on the standard approach set out above may not reflect the level of financial gain achieved or sought through the offending. Accordingly: a) where the offender has generated income or avoided expenditure to a level that can be calculated or estimated, the court may wish to consider that amount when determining the financial penalty, b) where it is not possible to calculate or estimate that amount, the court may wish to draw on information from the enforcing authorities about the general costs of operating within the law.

---

[135] *Attorney-General's Guidelines on the Acceptance of Pleas and the Prosecutor's Role in the Sentencing Exercise 2009,* see www.banksr.com Other Matters Other Documents tab
[136] See *Friskies Petcare (UK) Ltd* 2000 EWCA Crim 95, 2 Cr App R (S) 401

225.6   *Directors and small companies both prosecuted   Avoid double punishment*
R v Rollco Screw and Rivet Co Ltd 1999 2 Cr App R (S) 436 LCJ The defendant
company and two of its directors, who were father and son, pleaded to failing to ensure
the health and safety of employees and persons other than their employees. The
defendants were prosecuted for stripping out asbestos in breach of the regulations and
exposing employees and others to risks. The father was in charge of the contractual
arrangements. The son was considered to be the father's lieutenant and did not fully
appreciate the risks. The Court imposed for the company a £40,000 fine and £30,000
costs in total. The father was fined £6,000 and £2,000 costs. The son was fined £4,000
and £2,000 costs. Held. In a small company the directors are likely to be the
shareholders and therefore the main losers if a severe sanction is imposed on the
company. One must avoid a risk of overlap and must not impose double punishment. On
the other hand it is important that fines should be imposed which make it clear that there
is a personal responsibility on directors and they cannot simply palm off their responsibilities to the corporation of which they are directors. The proper approach is to answer
two questions. First, what financial penalty does the offence merit? Second, what
financial penalty can a defendant, whether corporate or personal, reasonably be ordered
to meet? Addressing the first question, the total fine for the company and the directors
was £50,000. In considering that question we have to bear in mind the glaring public
need for effective sanctions where the health and safety of the public are so obviously at
risk. The situation is the more important when, as here, the ill-effects of exposure to
brown asbestos may take many years to appear. In the interim, of course, no individual
can know whether he will ultimately suffer or not. The division of **£40,000** and **£10,000**
was an appropriate split. The total sum divided between the two was an appropriate
recognition of the gravity of this offending. The directors' appeal was dismissed. The
fine on the company was reduced on other grounds.

225.7   *Employees etc. partly/fully to blame*
R v Patchett Engineering Ltd 2001 1 Cr App R (S) 40 (p 138) The company pleaded
guilty to Health and Safety at Work etc. Act 1974 s 2(1). The company supplied an
egg-collecting machine to a farm. A young worker who was collecting eggs caught his
jacket in the machine and was found suspended from a drive shaft. The clothing had
tightened round his neck and he was strangled. The worker must have climbed up the
frame of the cage to reach the position where his clothing was caught. The likely
explanation was that he noticed that the top-tier tray was not in place, and he climbed up
to let it down without turning the machine off. The defence argued that there was no
need for the worker to act in the unorthodox way he did and it was not foreseeable. The
Judge rejected this. Held. The Judge was right. Workers will take short cuts and not
follow proper practices. The need to guard the shaft should have been apparent. When it
was designed, someone should have considered that operatives do occasionally take
short cuts. The statutory duty has, as one of its objects, the protection of workers who
may be neglectful of their own safety in a way which should be anticipated.
Piercing the corporate veil see **22.46** in Volume 1

225.8   *Approach to different sized companies*
Corporate Manslaughter and H and S Offences Causing Death Guideline 2010, see
www.banksr.com Other Matters Guidelines tab
Note: Although the guideline only applies to two offences and the guideline has been
replaced, judges are likely to consider that the principles are helpful when dealing with
corporate defendants on other charges. Ed.
para 12 The law must expect the same standard of behaviour from large and small
organisations. Smallness does not by itself mitigate, and largeness does not by itself
aggravate, these offences. Size may affect the approach to safety, whether because a small

organisation is careless or because a large one is bureaucratic, but these considerations affect the seriousness of the offence via the assessment set out in paragraphs 6-8 above (see **284.23**), rather than demonstrating a direct correlation between size and culpability.

para 13 A large organisation may be more at risk of committing an offence than a small one simply because it conducts very many more operations. Some large corporate groups operate as a single company whereas others are structured as separate companies for separate operations. A large organisation may be operating upon a budget as tight (or tighter) than a small one because of the demands placed upon it, large local authorities, hospital trusts or police forces may be examples, but so might commercial companies with large turnover but small profit margins. However, in some instances, a large organisation may have less excuse for not dealing properly with matters affecting Health and Safety, since it may have greater access to expertise, advice and training resources, whether in-house or otherwise.

Fraud, bribery and money laundering

225.9   *Sentencing Council guideline*

Fraud, Bribery and Money Laundering: Corporate Offenders Guideline 2014, see www.banksr.com Other Matters Guidelines tab In force 1 October 2014

At page 47 of the *Fraud, Bribery and Money Laundering Offences Guideline 2014*, see www.banksr.com Other matters Guideline tab, there is an identical guideline.

page 3 [The guideline applies to:]

Fraud Conspiracy to defraud, [cheating] the public revenue, Fraud Act 2006 s 1, 6 and 7, Theft Act 1968 s 17 [false accounting] and Customs and Excise Management Act 1979 s 170 [fraudulent evasion of duty etc.]

Bribery Bribery Act 2010 s 1, 2, 6 and 7

Money laundering Proceeds of Crime Act 2002 s 327-329

225.10

STEP ONE Compensation

page 48 The court must consider making a compensation order requiring the offender to pay compensation for any personal injury, loss or damage resulting from the offence in such an amount as the court considers appropriate, having regard to the evidence and to the means of the offender.

Where the means of the offender are limited, priority should be given to the payment of compensation over payment of any other financial penalty.

Reasons should be given if a compensation order is not made. (See Powers of Criminal Courts (Sentencing) Act 2000 s 130.)

STEP TWO Confiscation

page 48 Confiscation must be considered if either the Crown asks for it or the court thinks that it may be appropriate.

Confiscation must be dealt with before, and taken into account when assessing, any other fine or financial order (except compensation). (See Proceeds of Crime Act 2002 s 6 and 13.)

225.11

STEP THREE Determining the offence category

page 49 The court should determine the offence category with reference to **culpability** and **harm**.

The sentencer should weigh up all the factors of the case to determine **culpability**. **Where there are characteristics present which fall under different categories, the court should balance these characteristics to reach a fair assessment of the offender's culpability.**

Culpability is demonstrated by the offending corporation's role and motivation. It may be demonstrated by one or more of the following **non-exhaustive** characteristics.

A High culpability
Corporation plays a leading role in organised, planned unlawful activity (whether acting alone or with others)
Wilful obstruction of detection (for example destruction of evidence, misleading investigators, suborning employees)
Involving others through pressure or coercion (for example employees or suppliers)
Targeting of vulnerable victims or a large number of victims
Corruption of local or national government officials or ministers
Corruption of officials performing a law enforcement role
Abuse of dominant market position or position of trust or responsibility
Offending committed over a sustained period of time
Culture of wilful disregard of commission of offences by employees or agents with no effort to put effective systems in place (Bribery Act 2010 s 7 only)

B Medium culpability
Corporation plays a significant role in unlawful activity organised by others
Activity not unlawful from the outset
Corporation reckless in making false statement (Value Added Tax Act 1994 s 72)
All other cases where characteristics for Categories A or C are not present

C Lesser culpability
Corporation plays a minor, peripheral role in unlawful activity organised by others
Some effort made to put bribery prevention measures in place but insufficient to amount to a defence (Bribery Act 2010 s 7 only)
Involvement through coercion, intimidation or exploitation

Harm

page 49 Harm is represented by a financial sum calculated by reference to the table below.

Amount obtained or intended to be obtained (or loss avoided or intended to be avoided)

	Harm
Fraud	For offences of fraud, conspiracy to defraud, cheating the Revenue and fraudulent evasion of duty or VAT, harm will normally be the actual or intended gross gain to the offender.
Bribery	For offences under Bribery Act 2010 the appropriate figure will normally be the gross profit from the contract obtained, retained or sought as a result of the offending. An alternative measure for offences under section 7 may be the likely cost avoided by failing to put in place appropriate measures to prevent bribery.
Money laundering	For offences of money laundering the appropriate figure will normally be the amount laundered or, alternatively, the likely cost avoided by failing to put in place an effective anti-money laundering programme if this is higher.
General	Where the actual or intended gain cannot be established, the appropriate measure will be the amount that the court considers was likely to be achieved in all the circumstances. In the absence of sufficient evidence of the amount that was likely to be obtained, 10-20 per cent of the relevant revenue (for instance between 10 and 20 per cent of the worldwide revenue derived from the product or business area to which the offence relates for the period of the offending) may be an appropriate measure. There may be large cases of fraud or bribery in which the true harm is to commerce or markets generally. That may justify adopting a harm figure beyond the normal measures here set out.

225.12

STEP FOUR Starting point and category range

page 50 Having determined the culpability level at step three, the court should use the table below to determine the starting point within the category range below. The starting point applies to all offenders irrespective of plea or previous convictions.

The harm figure at step three is multiplied by the relevant percentage figure representing culpability.

Culpability level	A	B	C
Harm figure multiplier	**Starting point** 300%	**Starting point** 200%	**Starting point** 100%
	Category range 200% to 400%	**Category range** 100% to 300%	**Category range** 20% to 150%

Having determined the appropriate starting point, the court should then consider adjustment within the category range for aggravating or mitigating features. In some cases, having considered these factors, it may be appropriate to move outside the identified category range. (See below for a non-exhaustive list of aggravating and mitigating factors.)

Factors increasing seriousness
Previous relevant convictions or subject to previous relevant civil or regulatory enforcement action
Corporation or subsidiary set up to commit fraudulent activity
Fraudulent activity endemic within corporation
Attempts made to conceal misconduct
Substantial harm (whether financial or otherwise) suffered by victims of offending or by third parties affected by offending
Risk of harm greater than actual or intended harm (for example in banking/credit fraud)
Substantial harm caused to integrity or confidence of markets
Substantial harm caused to integrity of local or national governments
Serious nature of underlying criminal activity (money laundering offences)
Offence committed across borders or jurisdictions

Factors reducing seriousness or reflecting mitigation
No previous relevant convictions or previous relevant civil or regulatory enforcement action
Victims voluntarily reimbursed/compensated
No actual loss to victims
Corporation co-operated with investigation, made early admissions and/or voluntarily reported offending
Offending committed under previous director(s)/ manager(s)
Little or no actual gain to corporation from offending

Note: An exact copy of this guideline has been placed in the Magistrates' Court Guidelines at page 273.

225.13 General principles to follow in setting a fine

page 51 The court should determine the appropriate level of fine in accordance with Criminal Justice Act 2003 s 164, which requires that the fine must reflect the seriousness of the offence and requires the court to take into account the financial circumstances of the offender.

225.14 Obtaining financial information

page 51 Companies and bodies delivering public or charitable services

Where the offender is a company or a body which delivers a public or charitable service, it is expected to provide comprehensive accounts for the last three years, to enable the court to make an accurate assessment of its financial status. In the absence of such disclosure, or where the court is not satisfied that it has been given sufficient reliable information, the court will be entitled to draw reasonable inferences as to the offender's means from evidence it has heard and from all the circumstances of the case.

1 For companies: annual accounts. Particular attention should be paid to turnover; profit before tax; directors' remuneration, loan accounts and pension provision; and assets as disclosed by the balance sheet. Most companies are required to file audited accounts at Companies House. Failure to produce relevant recent accounts on request may properly lead to the conclusion that the company can pay any appropriate fine.

2 For partnerships: annual accounts. Particular attention should be paid to turnover; profit before tax; partners' drawings, loan accounts and pension provision; assets as above. Limited liability partnerships (LLPs) may be required to file audited accounts with Companies House. If adequate accounts are not produced on request, see paragraph 1.

3 For local authorities, fire authorities and similar public bodies: the Annual Revenue Budget (ARB) is the equivalent of turnover and the best indication of the size of the defendant organisation. It is unlikely to be necessary to analyse specific expenditure or reserves unless inappropriate expenditure is suggested.

4 For health trusts: the independent regulator of NHS Foundation Trusts is Monitor. It publishes quarterly reports and annual figures for the financial strength and stability of trusts from which the annual income can be seen, available via www.monitor-nhsft.gov. uk. Detailed analysis of expenditure or reserves is unlikely to be called for.

5 For charities: it will be appropriate to inspect annual audited accounts. Detailed analysis of expenditure or reserves is unlikely to be called for unless there is a suggestion of unusual or unnecessary expenditure.

225.15

STEP FIVE Adjustment of fine

page 52 Having arrived at a fine level, the court should consider whether there are any further factors which indicate an adjustment in the level of the fine. The court should 'step back' and consider the overall effect of its orders. The combination of orders made, compensation, confiscation and fine ought to achieve:

    the removal of all gain,

    appropriate additional punishment, and

    deterrence.

The fine may be adjusted to ensure that these objectives are met in a fair way. The court should consider any further factors relevant to the setting of the level of the fine to ensure that the fine is proportionate, having regard to the size and financial position of the offending organisation and the seriousness of the offence.

The fine must be substantial enough to have a real economic impact which will bring home to both management and shareholders the need to operate within the law. Whether the fine will have the effect of putting the offender out of business will be relevant; in some bad cases this may be an acceptable consequence.

In considering the ability of the offending organisation to pay any financial penalty the court can take into account the power to allow time for payment or to order that the amount be paid in instalments.

The court should consider whether the level of fine would otherwise cause unacceptable harm to third parties. In doing so the court should bear in mind that the payment of any compensation determined at step one should take priority over the payment of any fine.

The table below contains a **non-exhaustive** list of additional factual elements for the court to consider. The Court should identify whether any combination of these, or other relevant factors, should result in a proportionate increase or reduction in the level of fine.

Factors to consider in adjusting the level of fine
Fine fulfils the objectives of punishment, deterrence and removal of gain
The value, worth or available means of the offender
Fine impairs offender's ability to make restitution to victims
Impact of fine on offender's ability to implement effective compliance programmes
Impact of fine on employment of staff, service users, customers and local economy (but not shareholders)
Impact of fine on performance of public or charitable function

For a note about the *Environmental Offences Guideline 2014*, see **249.3**.
Health and Safety offences see the HEALTH AND SAFETY OFFENCES chapter.
Railway accidents see the MANSLAUGHTER *Railway accidents* para at **284.54**.

225.16   *Magistrates' Court Sentencing Guideline*
Magistrates' Court Sentencing Guideline 2008 (as amended), see www.banksr.com
Other matters Guideline tab page 369 This guideline contains the corporate section of
the *Fraud, Bribery and Money Laundering Offences Guideline 2014*, see www.banksr.
com Other matters Guideline tab

225.17   *Judicial guidance*
R v Sellafield and Network Rail 2014 EWCA Crim 49 LCJ para 3 It is important to
[apply] the provisions laid down by Parliament. [These include] the purposes of
sentencing set out in Criminal Justice Act 2003 s 142, see **87.15** in Volume 1. The courts
must regard the culpability of the offender and the harm caused etc. when considering
the seriousness of the offence, Criminal Justice Act 2003 s 143, see **87.38** in Volume 1. If
the court is considering a fine it must take into account the criteria in Criminal Justice
Act 2003 s 164, see **60.16** and **60.19** in Volume 1. The objective when sentencing for
Health and Safety offences was set out in *R v F Howe and Son (Engineers) Ltd* 1999
2 Cr App R (S) 37 [at para 44], 'The objective is to achieve a safe environment for those
who work there and for other members of the public who may be affected. A fine needs
to be large enough to bring that message home where the defendant is a company not
only to those who manage it but also to its shareholders.' The fact a company has a £1
billion turnover makes no difference to the basic approach. para 6 The fine must be with
the objective of ensuring that the message is brought home to the directors and members
of the company/shareholders. For companies with a turnover in excess of £1 billion it
will be necessary to examine with great care and in some detail the structure of the
company, its turnover and profitability as well as the remuneration of the directors.

Specific defendants
225.18   *Public bodies/Hospitals*
Corporate Manslaughter and H and S Offences Causing Death Guideline 2010, see
www.banksr.com Other Matters Guidelines tab para 19 When considering the financial
consequences of a fine, the court should consider the effect upon the provision of
services to the public [to] be relevant, although a public organisation such as a local
authority, hospital trust or police force must be treated the same as a commercial
company, where the standards of behaviour to be expected are concerned (sic), and must
suffer a punitive fine for breach of them, a different approach to determining the level of
fine may well be justified. 'The Judge has to consider how any financial penalty will be
paid. If a very substantial financial penalty will inhibit the proper performance by a
statutory body of the public function that it has been set up to perform, that is not
something to be disregarded.'[137]
The same considerations will be likely to apply to non-statutory bodies or charities if
providing public services.
For [what means information is] required, see **225.24**.

---

[137] *R v Milford Haven Port Authority* 2000 2 Cr App R (S) p 423 at 433-434

Note: This guideline only applies to two offences and has been replaced, but the principle may be helpful for corporate cases. Ed.

Health and Safety Offences, Corporate Manslaughter and Food Safety and Hygiene Offences Guideline 2016, see www.banksr.com Other Matters Guidelines tab page 6 The offender is expected to provide comprehensive accounts for the last three years, to enable the court to make an accurate assessment of its financial status. In the absence of such disclosure, or where the court is not satisfied that it has been given sufficient reliable information, the court will be entitled to draw reasonable inferences as to the offender's means from evidence it has heard and from all the circumstances of the case, **which may include the inference that the offender can pay any fine.**

[Assessing the financial information Organisations]
page 6 Normally, only information relating to the organisation before the court will be relevant, unless exceptionally it is demonstrated to the court that the resources of a linked organisation are available and can properly be taken into account.
1. to 2. [see para **225.14**]
3. *For local authorities, fire authorities and similar public bodies*: the Annual Revenue Budget (ARB) is the equivalent of turnover and the best indication of the size of the organisation. It is unlikely to be necessary to analyse specific expenditure or reserves (where relevant) unless inappropriate expenditure is suggested.
4. *For health trusts*: the independent regulator of NHS Foundation Trusts is Monitor. It publishes quarterly reports and annual figures for the financial strength and stability of trusts from which the annual income can be seen, available via www.monitor-nhsft.gov.uk. Detailed analysis of expenditure or reserves is unlikely to be called for.

Magistrates' Court Sentencing Guidelines 2008, see www.banksr.com Other Matters Guidelines tab page 183 When sentencing public authorities, the court may have regard to the fact that a very substantial financial penalty may inhibit the performance of the public function that the body was set up to fulfil. This is not to suggest that public bodies are subject to a lesser standard of duty of care in safety and environmental matters, but it is proper for the court to take into account all the facts of the case, including how any financial penalty will be paid.

R v British Railways Board 1991 Unreported extract at 2000 2 Cr App R (S) 430 High Court Judge at CCC. The company was sentenced for Health and Safety offences following the Clapham rail crash. Held. In the case of a public authority that is funded by the taxpayer or, as here, by a combination of the taxpayer and the fare-paying public, the question of penalty raises an acute problem. A swingeing fine of the magnitude that some might consider appropriate could only be met by the board either by increasing the burden on the fare-paying passengers, which is hardly logical having regard to the fact that it is for the benefit of the fare-paying passengers that this legislation exists, or by reducing the funds available for improvements in the railway system in general. That can hardly be regarded as a desirable state of affairs. On the other hand, I must bear in mind the necessity of marking the disapproval of society at the failures demonstrated by those charged with British Rail management leading up to and causing this accident. An insignificant fine would rightly bring down on myself and upon the whole system of justice universal condemnation. I therefore have to steer a narrow course between those two alternative hazards. **£250,000** fine imposed.

R v Milford Haven Port Authority 2000 2 Cr App R (S) p 423 The company pleaded to causing oil to enter controlled waters. A pilot committed a serious navigational error, and a tanker grounded on rocks causing a crude-oil spill which was among the largest ever recorded. The authority was a public trust port. Held. Public bodies are not immune from appropriate penalties because they have no shareholders and the directors are not in receipt of handsome annual bonuses. However, it is proper for the Judge to take that factor into account. If a substantial financial penalty will inhibit the proper performance by a statutory body of the public function it has been set up to perform, that factor should not be disregarded.

R v Southampton University Hospital NHS Trust 2006 EWCA Crim 2971, 2007 2 Cr App R (S) 9 (p 37) The defendant pleaded to failing to discharge its duty to persons not in its employment (Health and Safety at Work etc. Act 1974 s 33(1)). On 27 June 2000, P died at the hospital of toxic shock syndrome following a minor operation and an infection. Two senior house officers (SHOs) were subsequently convicted of his manslaughter on the basis of gross negligence in their treatment of P. Each had failed to regularly observe P's pulse, temperature and blood pressure, which were abnormal, and to seek help. Concerns had been raised by others in the hospital about poor performance by these and other SHOs in this department and about a lack of supervision. There was no formal supervision, training or appraisal system in place. It was accepted that these were failures of implementation and maintenance, not a structural flaw. It was accepted that there were none of the aggravating factors listed in *R v F Howe and Son (Engineers) Ltd* 1999 2 Cr App R (S) 37. The basis of the plea was that the failure of supervision was not causative of P's death and that once the failing had been identified, rapid steps were taken by the defendant to correct it. Held. These failures were serious and had been in existence for a period of at least weeks and probably the whole of June. There were powerful mitigating factors: the prompt admission of responsibility, timely guilty plea, steps taken to remedy failings, otherwise good safety record, enormous contribution made by the defendant to the welfare of the public, its financial position and its complete co-operation with the prosecution. The failures related to one department only. They were corrected long before the prosecution. Following *R v Milford Haven Port Authority* 2000, the Court has to consider how a financial penalty will be paid and if it will inhibit proper performance of a statutory body that must be regarded. **£40,000** fine not £100,000.

R v Guy's and St Thomas' NHS Trust 2008 EWCA Crim 2187, 2009 1 Cr App R (S) 104 (p 585) The defendant pleaded to supplying a medical product not of the nature specified. There was human error in mixing a medical solution followed by an error by a supervisor. As a result a baby died following a massive glucose overdose. Held. Where a not-for-profit organisation exists for the public benefit and a failure occurs without actual fault on the part of that body, but through an act or default of an employee to whom the task has been properly delegated and who has been properly trained, the Court ought not to punish such a body by a financial penalty which would materially impact on its ability to discharge its public duty. The reason is that the public interest would not be served by doing so. Because of no management failures and the need not to impact on the work of the Trust, **£15,000** fine not £75,000.

Compensation and costs
225.19   *Compensation orders*
Corporate Manslaughter and H and S Offences Causing Death Guideline 2010, see www.banksr.com Other Matters Guidelines tab para 19 vi) The liability to pay civil compensation will ordinarily not be relevant, normally this will be provided by insurance or the resources of the defendant will be large enough to meet it from its own resources. The assessment of compensation in cases of death will usually be complex, will involve payment of sums well beyond the powers of a criminal court, and will ordinarily be covered by insurance. In the great majority of cases the court should conclude that compensation should be dealt with in a civil court, and should say that no order is made for that reason.[138] There may be occasional cases, for example if the

---

[138] Powers of Criminal Courts (Sentencing) Act 2000 s 130(3)

defendant is uninsured and payment may not otherwise be made, when consideration should be given to a compensation order in respect of bereavement and/or funeral expenses.[139]

Note: This guideline only applies to two offences and has been replaced, but the principle may be helpful for corporate cases. Ed.

See also: *R v Pola* 2009 EWCA Crim 655, 2010 1 Cr App R (S) 6 (p 32) at **18.32** in Volume 1.

225.20   Costs orders

Magistrates' Court Sentencing Guidelines, January 2004, see www.banksr.com Other Matters Guidelines tab page 97 The prosecution will normally claim the costs of investigation and presentation. These may be substantial, and can incorporate time and activity expended on containing and making the area safe. Remediation costs for pollution offences may also be significant. For water pollution offences enforcing authorities are able to recover them through the criminal courts (Water Resources Act 1991, as amended). In other cases there are powers for the courts to order offenders to remedy the cause of the offence, or for the Environment Agency to require them to undertake clean-up at their own expense, or for the agency to carry out remedial work and seek to recover its costs through the civil courts.

The enforcing authorities' costs should be fully recouped from the offender. The order for costs should not be disproportionate to the level of the fine imposed. The court should fix the level of the fine first, then consider awarding compensation, and then determine the costs. If the total sum exceeds the defendant's means, the order for costs should be reduced rather than the fine. Compensation should take priority over both the fine and costs. As always, magistrates should seek the advice of the legal adviser on sentencing options and guidelines in all cases. Note: The 2004 guideline has been suspended by the 2008 guideline but the guidance may be useful. For more detail, see the **COSTS** chapter.

R v F Howe and Son (Engineers) Ltd 1999 2 Cr App R (S) 37 The power to award costs is contained in Prosecution of Offences Act 1985 s 18(1) and permits an order that the defendant pay to the prosecutor such costs as are just and reasonable. This includes the cost of the prosecuting authority carrying out investigations with a view to prosecution, see *R v Associated Octel Ltd* 1996 EWCA Crim 1327, 1997 1 Cr App R (S) 435. Sometimes costs awarded have been scaled down so as not to exceed the fine. Neither the fines nor the costs are deductible against tax and therefore the full burden falls upon the company.

R v B&Q 2005 EWCA Crim 2297 The defendant company was convicted of three counts and acquitted of five counts. Two trials were halted because of problems with playback equipment. The company was fined £550,000 with £250,000 costs. Held. Because of the differing nature of the statutory provisions relating to costs and the way in which costs are borne by different departments of the Executive in this type of prosecution, the Judge should have adopted a global approach, as set out in the *Guide to the Award of Costs 1991*. The prosecution costs of the two aborted trials should not have been considered, because it was the prosecution that was required to make the equipment available. Leading counsel was a proper expense, see *R v Dudley Magistrates' Court ex parte Power City Stores* 1990 154 JP 654. An allowance should have been made for the acquittals on the direction of the trial Judge.

225.21   Costs out of central funds

Practice Direction (Costs in Criminal Proceedings) 2015 EWCA Crim 1568 para 2.1.2 (for the Magistrates' Court) and Practice Direction (Costs in Criminal Proceedings) 2015 EWCA Crim 1568 para 2.2.4 (for the Crown Court) In respect of proceedings in a

---

[139] Made under Powers of Criminal Courts (Sentencing) Act 2000 s 130(9)-(10)

Magistrates' Court/Crown Court commenced on or after 1 October 2012 legal costs (sums paid for advocacy, litigation services or experts' fees) may only be allowed to a defendant who is an individual.

225.22   Costs   Apportioning costs
R v Harrison 1993 14 Cr App R (S) 419 The defendants pleaded to trade description offences. The Judge considered the first defendant was the principal defendant, who stood to gain financially from the offence and had the means to pay, whereas the second defendant, who was his son, had little to do with running the business. He therefore made the principal defendant pay all the costs. Held. Where there are several defendants it will usually be appropriate when making a costs order to look to see what would be a reasonable estimate of the costs if each defendant were tried alone. However, the Judge's approach was proper.
R v Fresha Bakeries Ltd 2002 EWCA Crim 1451, 2003 1 Cr App R (S) 44 (p 202) The defendant company, FB Ltd, its sister company, H Ltd, the Chief Executive of the group (CE), the chief engineer at the plant (E), and the production director (PD), pleaded to offences under Health and Safety at Work etc. Act 1974 s 2-3. The companies and E pleaded at the first appearance. CE and PD pleaded the day before the trial was fixed. Two workmen were burnt to death trying to repair a bread oven when major breaches of Health and Safety procedures took place. It was agreed by the prosecution, the defence and the Judge that the Judge should fix the overall financial penalty as if it were a single company and apportion the fine and costs elements between the companies. The companies were able to pay a significant fine. The pre-tax profits of FB Ltd were £250,000, and H Ltd's profits were £400,000. The Judge distinguished *R v Ronson and Parnes* 1992 13 Cr App R (S) 153 (where costs were adjusted so that they were what they would have been if the defendant had been tried alone) and calculated the costs to include the work up until sentence, notwithstanding their early plea. FB Ltd was fined £250,000 with costs of £175,000, H Ltd was fined £100,000 with £75,000 costs, CE was fined £10,000 with £5,000 costs, PD was fined £1,000 and E was fined £2,000 (neither with a costs order). The revised figure for the costs when the companies pleaded was £108,451. The revised figure when the other defendants pleaded was £283,307. The companies appealed. Held. It was a very bad case. There was no basis for holding that the fines totalling £350,000 were manifestly excessive. It may be appropriate to order the defendant who is more responsible to pay a greater share of the costs than he would pay if he were tried alone. The Judge was entitled to conclude that the corporate defendants bore a greater responsibility than the individual defendants. However, the Judge took too little account of the fact that the companies had no control over the proceedings against CE and PD. If they had pleaded when the companies did, the costs would have been significantly less. Taking into account the costs incurred for the proposed trial after the corporate defendants had pleaded and the reduced costs figure now available, FB Ltd's costs should be £105,000 and H Ltd's costs should be £45,000.

Fines

225.23   Fines   Means   Guidelines
Corporate Manslaughter and H and S Offences Causing Death Guideline 2010, see www.banksr.com Other Matters Guidelines tab
para 12 The law must expect the same standard of behaviour from a large and a small organisation. Smallness does not by itself mitigate, and largeness does not by itself aggravate, these offences. Size may affect the approach to safety, whether because a small organisation is careless or because a large one is bureaucratic, but these considerations affect the seriousness of the offence via the assessment set out in paragraphs 6-8 above, rather than demonstrating a direct correlation between size and culpability.
13 A large organisation may be more at risk of committing an offence than a small one simply because it conducts very many more operations. Some large corporate groups operate as a single company whereas others are structured as separate companies for

separate operations. A large organisation may be operating upon a budget as tight (or tighter) than a small one because of the demands placed upon it: large local authorities, hospital trusts or police forces may be examples, but so might commercial companies with large turnover but small profit margins. However, in some instances, a large organisation may have less excuse for not dealing properly with matters affecting Health and Safety, since it may have greater access to expertise, advice and training resources, whether in-house or otherwise.

14 The means of any defendant are relevant to a fine, which is the principal available penalty for organisations. The court should require information about the financial circumstances of the defendant before it. The best practice will usually be to call for the relevant information for a three-year period including the year of the offence, so as to avoid any risk of atypical figures in a single year.

15 A fixed correlation between the fine and either turnover or profit is not appropriate. The circumstances of defendant organisations and the financial consequences of the fine will vary too much [for that]. Similar offences committed by companies structured in differing ways ought not to attract fines which are vastly different. A fixed correlation [between the fine and the profits] might provide a perverse incentive to manipulation of corporate structure.

Note: The language has been significantly tidied up. Ed.

16 The court should, however, look carefully at both turnover and profit, and also at assets, in order to gauge the resources of the defendant. When taking account of financial circumstances, statute[140] provides for that to either increase or decrease the amount of the fine and it is just that a wealthy defendant should pay a larger fine than a poor one. Whilst a fine is intended to inflict painful punishment, it should be one which the defendant is capable of paying, if appropriate over a period which may be up to a number of years (sic).

Note: Although the guideline only applies to two offences and has been replaced, judges are likely to consider that the principles are helpful when dealing with corporate defendants on other charges. Ed.

225.24   *Financial information a court should expect to be provided about a defendant*

Corporate Manslaughter and H and S Offences Causing Death Guideline 2010, see www.banksr.com Other Matters Guidelines tab para 17 Annex A sets out the kind of financial information with which, in the ordinary way, a court should expect to be provided in relation to a defendant. The primary obligation to provide it lies on the defendant. As a matter of practice it would be helpful if the prosecution takes the preliminary step of calling upon the defendant to provide it to the court and prosecution and, if the defendant does not do so, of assembling what can be obtained from public record and furnishing that to the court. If a defendant fails to provide relevant information, the court is justified in making adverse assumptions as to its means, and may be obliged to do so.

18 It will not ordinarily be necessary for the prosecution to analyse the figures. In a few complex cases of relevant dispute the prosecution can, if genuinely necessary, undertake such analysis either in-house or by the instruction of an accountant and if it can justify the expense as part of its necessary costs those costs will ordinarily be recoverable from the defendant.[141]

19 In assessing the financial consequences of a fine the court should consider (*inter alia*) the following factors: i) the effect on the employment of the innocent may be relevant, ii) any effect upon shareholders will, however, not normally be relevant, those who invest in and finance a company take the risk that its management will result in financial loss, iii) the effect on directors will not, likewise, normally be relevant, iv) nor would it

---

[140] Criminal Justice Act 2003 s 164(1) and (4)
[141] Criminal Justice Act 2003 s 164(5)(b)(iii)

ordinarily be relevant that the prices charged by the defendant might in consequence be raised, at least unless the defendant is a monopoly supplier of public services, v) the effect upon the provision of services to the public will be relevant, although a public organisation such as a local authority, hospital trust or police force must be treated the same as a commercial company, where the standards of behaviour to be expected are concerned (sic), and must suffer a punitive fine for breach of them, a different approach to determining the level of fine may well be justified. 'The judge has to consider how any financial penalty will be paid. If a very substantial financial penalty will inhibit the proper performance by a statutory body of the public function that it has been set up to perform, that is not something to be disregarded.'[142] The same considerations will be likely to apply to non-statutory bodies or charities if providing public services. (vi) The liability to pay civil compensation will ordinarily not be relevant; normally this will be provided by insurance or the resources of the defendant will be large enough to meet it from its own resources, vii) the cost of meeting any remedial order will not ordinarily be relevant, except to the overall financial position of the defendant, such an order requires no more than should already have been done, viii) whether the fine will have the effect of putting the defendant out of business will be relevant, in some bad cases this may be an acceptable consequence.

20 [see para **225.29**]

21 In some cases it may be apparent that a broadly quantifiable saving has been made by the defendant by committing the offence. In such cases it will normally be the proper approach to ensure that the fine removes the profit and imposes an appropriate additional penalty.

Note: This guideline only applies to two offences and has been replaced, but the principle may be helpful for corporate cases. For what financial information should be obtained for corporate offenders being sentenced for fraud, bribery and money laundering see the *Fraud, Bribery and Money Laundering: Corporate Offenders Guideline 2014* **Obtaining financial information** section at page 51 and **225.14**. Ed.

Health and Safety Offences, Corporate Manslaughter and Food Safety and Hygiene Offences Guideline 2016, see www.banksr.com Other Matters Guidelines tab

page 6 The offender is expected to provide comprehensive accounts for the last three years, to enable the court to make an accurate assessment of its financial status. In the absence of such disclosure, or where the court is not satisfied that it has been given sufficient reliable information, the court will be entitled to draw reasonable inferences as to the offender's means from evidence it has heard and from all the circumstances of the case, **which may include the inference that the offender can pay any fine.**

225.25   *Information required for different corporate entities*

Health and Safety Offences, Corporate Manslaughter and Food Safety and Hygiene Offences Guideline 2016, see www.banksr.com Other Matters Guidelines tab

[Assessing the financial information Organisations]

page 6 Normally, only information relating to the organisation before the court will be relevant, unless exceptionally it is demonstrated to the court that the resources of a linked organisation are available and can properly be taken into account.

1. *For companies*: annual accounts. Particular attention should be paid to turnover; profit before tax; directors' remuneration, loan accounts and pension provision; and assets as disclosed by the balance sheet. Most companies are required to file audited accounts at Companies House. **Failure to produce relevant recent accounts on request may properly lead to the conclusion that the company can pay any appropriate fine.**

2. *For partnerships*: annual accounts. Particular attention should be paid to turnover; profit before tax; partners' drawings, loan accounts and pension provision; assets

---

[142] *R v Milford Haven Port Authority* 2000 2 Cr App R (S) p 423 per Lord Bingham CJ at 433-434.

as above. Limited liability partnerships (LLPs) may be required to file audited accounts with Companies House. **If adequate accounts are not produced on request, see paragraph 1.**

3. *For local authorities, fire authorities and similar public bodies*: the Annual Revenue Budget (ARB) is the equivalent of turnover and the best indication of the size of the organisation. It is unlikely to be necessary to analyse specific expenditure or reserves (where relevant) unless inappropriate expenditure is suggested.

4. *For health trusts*: the independent regulator of NHS Foundation Trusts is Monitor. It publishes quarterly reports and annual figures for the financial strength and stability of trusts from which the annual income can be seen, available via www.monitor-nhsft.gov.uk. Detailed analysis of expenditure or reserves is unlikely to be called for.

5. *For charities*: it will be appropriate to inspect annual audited accounts. Detailed analysis of expenditure or reserves is unlikely to be called for unless there is a suggestion of unusual or unnecessary expenditure.

225.26   Fines   Means   Basic principles

R v F Howe and Son (Engineers) Ltd 1999 2 Cr App R (S) 37 Any fine should reflect not only the gravity of the offence but also the means of the offender, and this applies just as much to corporate defendants as to any other, see Criminal Justice Act 2003 s 164(3). Difficulty is sometimes found in obtaining timely and accurate information about a corporate defendant's means. The starting point is its annual accounts. If a defendant company wishes to make any submission to the court about its ability to pay a fine, it should supply copies of its accounts and any other financial information on which it intends to rely, in good time before the hearing, both to the court and to the prosecution. This will give the prosecution the opportunity to assist the court should the court wish it. Usually accounts need to be considered with some care to avoid reaching a superficial and perhaps erroneous conclusion. Where accounts or other financial information are deliberately not supplied, the court will be entitled to conclude that the company is in a position to pay any financial penalty it is minded to impose. Where the relevant information is provided late, it may be desirable for sentence to be adjourned, if necessary, at the defendant's expense, so as to avoid the risk of the court taking what it is told at face value and imposing an inadequate penalty. Where a defendant is in a position to pay the whole of the prosecution's costs in addition to the fine, there is no reason in principle for the court not to make an order accordingly. The court must look at the whole sum (fine and costs) and consider the impact upon the defendant.

R v Yorkshire Water Services Ltd 2001 EWCA Crim 2635, 2002 2 Cr App R (S) 13 (p 37) The defendant company pleaded to supplying water unfit for human consumption. A balance may have to be struck between a fitting expression of censure, designed not only to punish but to stimulate improved performance on the one hand, and the counter-productive effect of imposing too great a financial penalty on an already under-funded organisation on the other.

R v ESB Hotels Ltd 2005 EWCA Crim 132, 2 Cr App R (S) 56 (p 332) The defendant company pleaded at the Magistrates' Court to two counts of contravening the requirements of a fire certificate. The defendant was the occupier of a modern seven-storey hotel. The company's annual turnover was £4m. Its expected profits for the next year were just below £1m. Held. It is important that in determining the level of fine the court should have regard to the pre-tax profits rather than gross turnover.

R v New Look Retailers Ltd 2010 EWCA Crim 1268, 2011 1 Cr App R (S) 57 (p 359) It was suggested the fine was disproportionate to the breaches of duty admitted. Held. We disagree. There were three considerations when finding the appropriate balance. They were: a) the seriousness of the breach, b) the capacity of the company to meet the fine, and c) the need of the fine to make an impact upon the shareholders and senior managers.

225.27   Fines   Means   Wealthy companies
R v Transco Plc 2006 EWCA Crim 838, 2 Cr App R (S) 111 (p 740) LCJ The defendant company pleaded to an offence under Health and Safety legislation. It was fined £1m. Held. Where a court is considering the level of financial penalty to impose upon a corporate defendant, there is no principle which requires them to have details of the defendant company's financial position where its representations indicate that the means of the defendant company are substantial.
R v Sumal & Sons (Properties) Ltd 2012 EWCA Crim 1840 S was convicted in his absence for being the owner of a rented property without a licence. It was a summary only offence. S had a turnover of £600,000+. S was committed for sentence and was fined £2,000 with costs and a confiscation order. Held. Ordinarily a fine in this context can convey a degree of 'sting' geared to a particular landlord's financial situation. Appeal dismissed.

225.28   Fines   Company would be forced into liquidation
R v Cotswold Geotechnical Holdings Ltd 2011 EWCA Crim 1337, 2012 1 Cr App R (S) 26 (p 153) LCJ The defendant company was convicted of corporate manslaughter. It was involved with soil investigation. V, an employee, entered an unsupported pit, 3.5 m in depth. The pit collapsed and V was crushed. He died from traumatic asphyxia. The company was a small company employing only eight employees and was only just breaking even. The Judge recognised that the fine would mean liquidation and the employees losing their jobs. Held. It was plainly foreseeable that the way in which the company conducted its operations could produce not only serious injury but death. The standard by which it fell short of its duty of care was found by the jury to have been gross. In addition, there was an earlier incident in which the company had failed to heed advice from the Health and Safety Executive following a complaint from a young employee who had been required to go into deep, unsupported pits. The purpose of the fine is to inflict punishment, but it should be one that the defendant is capable of paying. The guideline states that when assessing the fine, regard should be had to whether the defendant would be forced into liquidation. In this case, that consequence was unavoidable. **£385,000** fine (250% of turnover) was upheld.

225.29   Fines   Time to pay single payment
Corporate Manslaughter and H and S Offences Causing Death Guideline 2010, see www.banksr.com Other Matters Guidelines tab para 20 In the case of a large organisation the fine should be payable within twenty eight days. In the case of a smaller or financially stretched organisation, it is permissible to require payment to be spread over a much longer period. There is no limitation to payment within twelve months, but the first payment should be required within a short time of sentencing. An extended period for the payment of further instalments may be particularly appropriate for an organisation of limited means which has committed a serious offence, and where it is undesirable that the fine should cause it to be put out of business.
Note: This guideline only applies to two offences and has been replaced, but the principle may still be helpful. Ed.
R v B&Q 2005 EWCA Crim 2297 The defendant company was fined £550,000 plus £250,000 costs. The Judge gave 28 days to pay. Held. That time to pay was an indulgence. Where a fine (which can only be viewed as modest when set against the defendant's overall turnover and profitability) is imposed on a company of anything approaching the size of the defendant's, the seriousness of the offending and the impact of the penalty can be brought home to it by its being required to pay the fine within a much shorter period of time than 28 days. An undertaking of the size of the defendant does not need 28 days to pay. Such fines ought as a matter of course to be paid either immediately or in a period to be measured in single-figure days, unless very cogent evidence is provided that more time is needed. In contradistinction, the principles applicable to very small companies are set out in *R v Rollco Screw and Rivet Co Ltd*

1999 2 Cr App R (S) 436 (see **225.6** and **225.30**). But even on very cogent evidence, the first instalment should be made payable at a very early date so that the effects of the criminality are brought home.

R v Deeside Metals Ltd 2011 EWCA Crim 3020, 2012 2 Cr App R (S) 29 (p 167) Deeside Metals, D, pleaded to failing to ensure the Health and Safety of employees. An employee died. D had a turnover of £975,000 ranging from a £31,000 loss to a £68,000 profit. Held. There were multiple failures. What matters here is funds to pay the fine. D provided three years of accounts. It barely breaks even. Over five years, its average profit after tax was £26,500. There is no sign on the horizon of significant improvement in profitability. The company exists, essentially, to pay its employees' wages. We propose a radical restructuring of the Judge's sentence, to allow the company to keep trading. £50,000 fine not £100,000, payable over 5 years not 4. £10,000 costs quashed.

225.30   *Fines   Instalments, Paying fines etc. by*

Corporate Manslaughter and H and S Offences Causing Death Guideline 2010, see www.banksr.com Other Matters Guidelines tab para 20 In the case of a large organisation the fine should be payable within 28 days. In the case of a smaller or financially stretched organisation, it is permissible to require payment to be spread over a much longer period. There is no limitation to payment within 12 months, but the first payment should be required within a short time of sentencing. An extended period for the payment of further instalments may be particularly appropriate for an organisation of limited means which has committed a serious offence, and where it is undesirable that the fine should cause it to be put out of business.

Note: This guideline only applies to two offences and has been replaced, but the principle may be helpful. Ed.

R v Olliver and Olliver 1989 11 Cr App R (S) 10 LCJ There is nothing wrong in principle with the period of payment (for a fine) being longer than a year, provided that it is not an undue burden, and so too severe a punishment, having regard to the offence and the nature of the offender. A two-year period will seldom be too long, and in an appropriate case three years will be unassailable. Every effort is required to find alternatives to custodial sentences.

Note: Although this is an old case it is line with the current practice. Ed.

R v Rollco Screw and Rivet Co Ltd 1999 2 Cr App R (S) 436 LCJ The defendant company and two of its directors, who were father and son, pleaded guilty to failing to ensure the Health and Safety of employees and persons other than their employees (section 2(1) and 3(1)). The defendants were prosecuted for stripping out asbestos in breach of the regulations and exposing employees and others to risks. The father was in charge of the contractual arrangements. The son was considered to be the father's lieutenant and did not fully appreciate the risks. The company was fined £40,000 with £30,000 costs in total (£5,000 within a year and the rest at £1,000 a month). The father was fined £6,000 and £2,000 costs (£1,000 a month). The son was fined £4,000 and £2,000 costs. Held. Reminding ourselves of *R v Olliver and Olliver* 1989 11 Cr App R (S) 10 the Court was at pains to avoid stipulating any period which should not be exceeded. With a personal defendant there are arguments for keeping the period within bounds. Those arguments are much weaker, if indeed they apply at all, when one is considering a corporate defendant. There is not the same anxiety as is liable to afflict an individual, and it is acceptable for a fine to be payable by a company over a substantially longer period than might be appropriate for an individual. It is not necessarily a more severe course to order a larger sum over a longer period than a smaller sum over a shorter period, since the former course may give the company a greater opportunity to control its cash flow and survive difficult trading conditions. If it wants to, the company can pay the sums sooner than is ordered. This period of payment over 6 years 5 months was excessive. Because of that the fine is reduced to £20,000, so the payment period is 5 years 7 months, which is an appropriate payment period.

R v Aceblade Ltd 2001 1 Cr App R (S) 105 (p 366) The company pleaded to failing to ensure the Health and Safety of an employee. It was fined £20,000 with £15,000 costs. The fine was payable over 42 months. Held. The payment period was not too long. See also the **INSTALMENTS, PAYMENT BY** chapter.

226   COMPUTER AND COMMUNICATIONS NETWORK OFFENCES
226.1
Serious Crime Prevention Order Serious Crime Act 2015 s 47(4) adds Computer Misuse Act 1990 s 1, 2, 3, 3ZA and 3A to Serious Crime Act 2007 Sch 1, thus enabling this discretionary order to be made for these offences, when it would protect the public etc.[143] In force 3 May 2015.[144]

This chapter is divided into three sections: a) Sending messages, b) Hacking, and c) Modification of electronic material and sending viruses.

Sending messages
226.2
1) Communications Act 2003 s 127 (improper use of public electronic communications network)

    Mode of trial Summary only

    Maximum sentence 6 months and/or a £5,000 fine for offences committed before 12 March 2015 and an unlimited fine thereafter.[145] There are maximum fines for those aged under 18, see **14.38** in Volume 1.

    Sexual Harm Prevention Orders There is a discretionary power to make this order when it is necessary to protect the public from sexual harm.[146]

    Fixed penalty There is a fixed penalty of £90 for this offence[147] with half the relevant victim surcharge. For more detail see **61.1** in Volume 1.

2) Wireless Telegraphy Act 2006 s 47 (sending or attempting to send misleading or false messages in relation to a safety of life service or to endanger the safety of a person, ship, aircraft or vehicle)

    Mode of trial Triable either way

    Maximum sentence On indictment 2 years. Summary 6 months and/or a £5,000 fine for offences committed before 12 March 2015 and an unlimited fine thereafter.[148] There are maximum fines for those aged under 18, see **14.38** in Volume 1.

3) Fire and Rescue Services Act 2004 s 49 (false alarms of fire)

    Mode of trial Summary only

    Maximum sentence 3 months and/or a Level 4 fine[149]

    Fixed penalty There is a fixed penalty of £90 for this offence[150] with half the relevant victim surcharge. For more detail, see **61.1** in Volume 1.

    Serious Crime Prevention Order

    Serious Crime Act 2015 s 47(2) adds Misuse of Drugs Act 1971 s 6 to Serious Crime Act 2007 Sch 1, thus enabling this discretionary order to be made for section 6 offences as well. Commencement is awaited.

See also the **HARASSMENT SECTION 2 AND 4** chapters and the **DATA PROTECTION ACT 1998 OFFENCES** chapter.

---

[143] Serious Crime Act 2007 s 1 and Sch 1 para 3
[144] Serious Crime Act 2015 (Commencement No 1) Regulations 2015 2015/820 para 2
[145] Legal Aid, Sentencing and Punishment of Offenders Act 2012 s 85(1) and (4) and Legal Aid, Sentencing and Punishment of Offenders Act 2012 (Commencement No 11) Order 2015 2015/504
[146] Sexual Offences Act 2003 s 103A as inserted by Anti-social Behaviour, Crime and Policing Act 2014 Sch 5 para 2 and Sexual Offences Act 2003 Sch 5
[147] Penalties for Disorderly Behaviour (Amount of Penalty) Order 2002 2002/1837 Schedule as amended
[148] Legal Aid, Sentencing and Punishment of Offenders Act 2012 s 85(1) and (4) and Legal Aid, Sentencing and Punishment of Offenders Act 2012 (Commencement No 11) Order 2015 2015/504
[149] Fire and Rescue Services Act 2004 s 49(2) and (3)
[150] Penalties for Disorderly Behaviour (Amount of Penalty) Order 2002 2002/1837 Schedule as amended

226.3   *Magistrates' Court Sentencing Guidelines   Communications Act 2003 s 127*
Magistrates' Court Sentencing Guidelines 2008, see www.banksr.com Other Matters
Guidelines tab The guidelines apply to the Magistrates' Court and to the Crown Court
hearing appeals or sentencing for summary only offences.[151]
page 42 Sending grossly offensive, indecent, obscene or menacing messages, s 127(1)

Examples of nature of activity	Starting point	Range
Single offensive, indecent, obscene or menacing call of short duration, having no significant impact on receiver	Band B fine	Band A fine to band C fine
Single call where extreme language used, having only moderate impact on receiver	Medium-level community order	Low-level community order to high-level community order
Single call where extreme language used and substantial distress or fear caused to receiver, or One of a series of similar calls as described in the box above	6 weeks' custody	High-level community order to 12 weeks' custody

Sending false message/persistent use of communications network for purpose of causing
annoyance, inconvenience or needless anxiety (section 127(2))

Examples of nature of activity	Starting point	Range
Persistent silent calls over short period to private individual, causing inconvenience or annoyance	Band B fine	Band A fine to band C fine
Single hoax call to public or private organisation resulting in moderate disruption or anxiety	Medium-level community order	Low-level community order to high-level community order
Single hoax call resulting in major disruption or substantial public fear or distress, or One of a series of similar calls as described in box above	12 weeks' custody	High-level community order to 18 weeks' custody

Consultation It is expected that the Sentencing Council will issue a consultation
document about updating this guideline in May 2016.
For how to apply the guidelines, see the **GUIDELINES** chapter in Volume 1.
For the meaning of a high-level, a medium-level and a low-level community order see
16.12-16.14 in Volume 1.

226.4   *Misleading messages, Sending*
R v Judge 2008 EWCA Crim 1820, 2009 1 Cr App R (S) 74 (p 439) D pleaded at the
Magistrates' Court to Wireless Telegraphy Act 2006 s 47. When drunk he used a marine
radio for which he had no licence and made a Pan call [a type of emergency call] on the
international distress and safety channel. It was far from coherent but claimed there was
a boat aground containing 40-45 illegal immigrants. He made another call saying there
was a body in the water. When found by police he was drunk and asleep. His previous
offences were old and had an alcohol theme. Held. The offence was not likely or
intended to endanger the safety of people, ships etc. It was the result of drunken folly
rather than malice. **8 months** not 12.

---

[151] See page 15 of the guidelines.

Sexual messages, Sending see the SEX OFFENCES: CHILDREN, WITH Grooming and seeking or asking for sexual activity section at **328.38**.
Social media offences see the PERVERTING THE COURSE OF JUSTICE/CONTEMPT OF COURT/PERJURY ETC. *Social media offences* para at **305.17**.

Hacking

226.5   *Hacking*

1) Computer Misuse Act 1990
s 1 (unauthorised access to computer material)
s 2 (unauthorised access with intent to commit or facilitate the commission of further offences)
s 3 (unauthorised modification of computer material respectively)
s 3ZA (unauthorised acts causing, or creating risk of, serious damage)
Mode of trial and maximum sentences Section 1 is summary only. 6 months and/or a £5,000 fine for offences committed before 12 March 2015 and an unlimited fine thereafter.[152] There are maximum fines for those aged under 18, see **14.38** in Volume 1.
Sections 2-3 are triable either way. On indictment 5 years. Summary 6 months and/or a £5,000 fine for offences committed before 12 March 2015 and an unlimited fine thereafter.[153] There are maximum fines for those aged under 18, see **14.38** in Volume 1.
Section 3ZA is indictable only. There is a maximum of 14 years, except where there is a 'significant risk of damage to human welfare of the kind mentioned in subsection (3)(a) or (3)(b) or serious damage to national security' when the maximum is life imprisonment.
2) Regulation of Investigatory Powers Act 2000 s 1 (interception of public postal systems or public telecommunication systems)
Mode of trial Triable either way
Maximum sentence On indictment 2 years. Summary, a £5,000 fine for offences committed before 12 March 2015 and an unlimited fine thereafter.[154] There are maximum fines for those aged under 18, see **14.38** in Volume 1.
For police officers accessing the police computer, see the CORRUPTION/MISFEASANCE IN PUBLIC OFFICE/BRIBERY *Police officers misusing the police computer* para at **228.8**.

226.6   *Hacking   Judicial guidance*

R v Mangham 2012 EWCA Crim 973, 2013 1 Cr App R (S) 11 (p 62) para 19 Aggravating factors are a) whether the offence is planned and persistent, b) the nature of the damage caused to the system itself and to the wider public interest such as national security, individual privacy, public confidence and commercial confidentiality. Revenge is a serious aggravating factor. The following are relevant: a) the cost of remediation, b) the motive, c) the benefit, and d) the value of the intellectual property involved. Courts are likely to take a very dim view where a hacker attempts to reap financial benefit by the sale of information which has been accessed. Whether or not the information is passed onto others is another factor. Among the mitigating factors the psychological profile of an offender will deserve close attention.

226.7 *Hacking and selling material*

R v Crosskey 2012 EWCA Crim 1645, 2013 1 Cr App R (S) 76 (p 420) LCJ D pleaded (full credit) to two Computer Misuse Act 1990 offences. D created an e-mail account similar to that of the father and manager (F) of the singer, Selena Gomez (SG). It was

---

[152] Legal Aid, Sentencing and Punishment of Offenders Act 2012 s 85(1) and (4) and Legal Aid, Sentencing and Punishment of Offenders Act 2012 (Commencement No 11) Order 2015 2015/504
[153] Legal Aid, Sentencing and Punishment of Offenders Act 2012 s 85(1) and (4) and Legal Aid, Sentencing and Punishment of Offenders Act 2012 (Commencement No 11) Order 2015 2015/504
[154] Legal Aid, Sentencing and Punishment of Offenders Act 2012 s 85(1) and (4) and Legal Aid, Sentencing and Punishment of Offenders Act 2012 (Commencement No 11) Order 2015 2015/504

rumoured that SG was in a relationship with Justin Bieber (JB). By representing himself to be F, D gained access to a Facebook account in SG's name, with millions of followers. D changed the password so as to have control over the site. F was therefore precluded from accessing the site and had to spend three days rectifying the situation with Facebook. Following D's access to the account, a post 'Justin Bieber sucks' was added to the publicly viewable page, prompting hostile responses from JB's fans. There was no proof that this was posted by D. D subsequently contacted *OK!* and *Hollywood Life* magazines, stating that he had accessed SG's Facebook account. He stated he could prove that SG and JB were in a relationship by reference to their personal e-mails. He stated he was motivated by a desire to expose Facebook's poor security measures. D then contacted F directly, stating that he had hacked SG's Facebook account, allowing him to 'do whatever [he] wanted'. He also claimed to have accessed four of SG's e-mail accounts, allowing him to read her personal emails, which 'her fans might want to see'. He further stated that he made a copy of every e-mail between SG and JB, and that the paparazzi would 'have a field day with these IF/when [he were to] release them onto the web [sic]'. D posted a video on YouTube boasting how he had accessed SG's account. He also posted a question on 'hackforums.net', deliberating whether to publicly release the information or to sell it. A police/FBI investigation took place. It took the UK police 180 days and cost £50,000. D, aged 21 at appeal, was of effective good character and a 'bright young man'. He had since begun a university course concerned with testing computer games. The pre-sentence report averred that the offences appeared to be youthful bravado and a desire to prove himself to his peers. Held. D had clearly given active consideration as to whether the information could be sold. The offending took place over a short period of time and D has expressed what appears to be genuine remorse. Starting at 12 months, **8 months** was appropriate.

226.8   *Hacking   Gaining access to material*

R v Mangham 2012 EWCA Crim 973, 2013 1 Cr App R (S) 11 (p 62) D pleaded to three counts of unauthorised access to computer material with intent, Computer Misuse Act 1990 s 1 and one count of unauthorised modification of computer material, Computer Misuse Act 1990 s 3. D hacked into Facebook's computers and infiltrated Facebook employees' e-mail accounts and e-mail archives. He then gained access to their Phabricator server and therefore their source code. This was their unique software which gives Facebook its functionality. Facebook estimated its costs as $200,000 which included their time investigating, accessing and remedying the damage done. The FBI and the US Dept. of Justice had three special agents working full time for about three weeks. The FBI sent two agents to the UK. D was aged 26 and of good character. He probably suffered from Asperger's syndrome, a personality disorder, social phobia and possibly major depression. He had exposed vulnerabilities at Yahoo. He was paid for this assistance. The Judge considered a) D was possibly emotionally younger than 26, b) D had never intended to pass any of the information on or make any financial gain, c) the conduct was not harmless experimentation, d) Facebook's entire operation was potentially at risk, and e) the behaviour was persistent and sophisticated. The information had not been passed to anyone and there was no financial gain. 6 months, reduced to **4 months** with the plea was more appropriate than 8 months.

See also: *R v Khan* 2012 EWCA Crim 2032, 2013 1 Cr App R (S) 113 (p 585) (Plea to six counts of unauthorised access to computer material with intent. 24 similar TICs. Worked for the council in a clerical role. Had access to records for very limited purpose. In a relationship with a man who was being investigated for exploiting young girls. She accessed the records to try to assist her partner over a 2-month period. No adverse effect on the preparations for his trial. Aged 21. Good character. Two young children with her partner. No arguable error in the approach taken by the Judge. **8 months**)

R v Martin 2013 EWCA Crim 1420, 2014 1 Cr App R (S) 63 (p 414) (Attacked the websites of Oxford and Cambridge Universities and Kent Police (each twice). The universities' IP addresses became unresponsive. In the first attack, the police computer had to shut down, after which normal services resumed. In the other attack, the server ran slowly. Interfering with two individuals' access to computer's financial information. Aged 21 and with police warning for computer access. 14 previous convictions. Motive not profit. With plea, **2 years** amply justified.)

226.9   Interception of e-mails etc.
R v Stanford 2006 EWCA Crim 258 LCJ The defendant pleaded after a ruling by the Judge to the unlawful and unauthorised interception of e-mails to a public company, Regulation of Investigatory Powers Act 2000 s 1(2). Held. The material factors for a section 1 offence are the nature of the material obtained and the object of obtaining it.
Old case: *R v Stanford* 2006 EWCA Crim 258 (LCJ) (**6 months suspended**)

226.10   Intercepting phone calls/messages
R v Goodman 2007 Times News 27/1/07 and Internet sites CCC G and M pleaded to conspiracy to intercept telephone communications. G was a royal reporter with the *News of the World*. M was a private investigator hired by the paper. 609 messages on royal aides' phones were intercepted over nine months. The aides worked for Princes William and Harry and their father and stepmother. Eight stories were printed from the material. The motive was profit. M hacked into the phones of Max Clifford, the publicist, Simon Hughes MP, two leading football figures and a supermodel. G, **4 months** and M, **6 months.** (Treat news reports with care. Ed.)

226.11   Electronic fraud
Phishing (false financial e-mails), pharming (cloned false websites for fraud) and Trojan installation (viruses) are treated as Fraud Act 2006 offences.
For the guidelines, see **FRAUD AND FINANCIAL SERVICES OFFENCES** *Articles, possessing, making etc. for fraud* at **265.15**.

Modification of electronic material and sending viruses
226.12
For the offences and penalties, see **226.5**.

226.13   Interference with computer data
Example: *R v Martin* 2013 EWCA Crim 1420, 2014 1 Cr App R (S) 63 (p 414) (Attacked the websites of Oxford and Cambridge Universities and Kent Police (each twice). The universities' IP addresses became unresponsive. In the first attack, the police computer had to shut down, after which normal services resumed. In the other attack the server ran slowly. Interfering with two individuals' access to computer's financial information. Aged 21 and with police warning for computer access. 14 previous convictions. Motive not profit. With plea, **2 years** amply justified.)

226.14   Unauthorised modification of material
R v Mangham 2012 EWCA Crim 973, 2013 1 Cr App R (S) 11 (p 62) see **226.8**.
Old case: *R v W* 2007 EWCA Crim 222 (**4 months** and **£6,500 costs**)

227   CONSPIRACY
227.1
Confiscation Where a defendant has a criminal lifestyle the court, once the confiscation proceedings are triggered (see **22.8**), <u>must</u> follow the Proceeds of Crime Act 2002 procedure. 'Criminal lifestyle' offences include conspiracy[155] to commit offences listed in Proceeds of Crime Act 2002 Sch 2, see **22.43**.
There are two different types of conspiracy. There are statutory conspiracies under Criminal Law Act 1977 s 1, which form the bulk of conspiracies charged. There are also three common law conspiracies, namely: a) conspiracy to defraud, b) conspiracy to

---

[155] Proceeds of Crime Act 2002 s 6 and 75 and Sch 2 para 10(1)

corrupt public morals, and c) conspiracy to outrage public decency. For those conspiracies, see the **FRAUD AND FINANCIAL SERVICES OFFENCES** and the **PUBLIC DECENCY, OUTRAGING** chapters.

Criminal Law Act 1977 s 3 provides for the following maximum penalties for statutory conspiracies: a) life, where the offence in question is murder, or is an offence which carries a maximum of life and where the offence has no maximum sentence provided, b) the same maximum term of imprisonment to be available as the offence in question carries, and c) in all other cases a fine. Conspiracy cases are listed under the offence which the defendant agreed to commit.

227.2 Conspiracy not carried out

R v Davies 1990 The Times 3/10/90 D was convicted of conspiracy to rob. Held. The fact that conspirators had desisted from the planned crime before carrying it out must be reflected in the sentence. If the conspirators desisted because they were overcome with better feelings then great credit must be given. If they desisted because they lost their nerve, nonetheless they should not be sentenced as if they had gone ahead with their design.

R v Hardy 2004 EWCA Crim 2906 H and S were convicted of a conspiracy to import up to 100 kilos of cocaine. The evidence was almost entirely from undercover officers. H was the introducer and attended three meetings after that. Nothing was imported. After his son died, S said he didn't want anything more to do with any plan. H had previously dealt in class A drugs. S was aged 60 with a conviction in 1991 for dealing in class B drugs for which he received 6 years. Just before the Court of Appeal hearing, S had had a successful liver transplant. Held. The reason why a conspiracy to import drugs comes to an end is material to sentence. If the conspiracy is frustrated because the authorities seize the drugs, the mitigation is slight. If the conspirators decide of their own free will that they will not continue with the importation, the mitigation may be substantial. For this amount where the conspiracy did not come to fruition the starting point is in the order of **14 years**. H **7 years** not 14. Because of S's age and health and his ceasing to be involved, **10 years** not 20.

Note: These cases are old, but they are in line with current sentencing practice. Ed.

See also the **DEFENDANT** *Withdrawing from criminal agreement It should be encouraged* para at **240.68**.

227.3 Conspiracy to commit a crime abroad

Criminal Law Act 1977 s 1A (power to prosecute when certain conditions are satisfied)

R v Patel 2009 EWCA Crim 67, 2 Cr App R (S) 67 (p 475) The US maximum was 10 years. The English maximum was 14 years. The maximum penalty is the English maximum. However, nothing prevents a judge from moderating the sentence because he or she thinks it would be unfair to impose a sentence which would involve a significantly greater real punishment than individual defendants would have imposed upon them if they had been prosecuted in the country in which the agreement was to be carried out.

227.4 Penalty for the offence alters during the conspiracy

R v Hobbs 2002 EWCA Crim 387, 2 Cr App R (S) 93 (p 425) The defendants were convicted of conspiracy to facilitate the illegal entry into the UK of illegal immigrants. During the dates particularised the maximum sentence was raised from 7 to 10 years. The Judge sentenced two of them to 9 and 7½ years. Held. The better course is to prefer distinct counts for the period before and after the date the maximum changed. Defendants should not be affected adversely, with respect to powers of sentence, by changes in the law occurring during the currency of a conspiracy entered into before the changes. A strict, narrow and certain view as to when the offence is complete should be applied and not a more extensive and flexible construction. Conspiracy is complete when the agreement is made. The Judge was restricted to the old maximum.

227.5 *Sentence to reflect participation in the conspiracy as well as the individual acts*

Att-Gen's Ref Nos 52-53 of 2006 2006 EWCA Crim 2571 T and R pleaded to conspiracy to rob. They participated in a wide-ranging and determined conspiracy to rob in which 54 individual offences were committed. These included a number of violent robberies of people in their cars or in the street. Valuable watches, cars and motor-cycles were forcibly taken. On a number of occasions completely gratuitous violence was used. Commercial premises were also robbed and there was a smash-and-grab burglary. T was caught preparing a robbery on a security van. Held. We shall, of course, look at the individual offences admitted by each of these offenders in the basis of plea, but we must emphasise at the outset that this was a wide-ranging conspiracy, in which there were a number of young men who came together to terrorise victims who happened to be chosen. For some time this group of young men was completely out of control, on the rampage, committing violent crime, and no doubt as each crime was committed, it encouraged them to commit the next one. The sentences on the individuals should reflect not only their participation in specific offences, but their involvement in the conspiracy in the broadest sense. In brief, therefore, for as long as he was party to the conspiracy each conspirator sustained and supported the other conspirators in the crimes in which they did not personally participate. It was, truly, a conspiracy in the broadest sense.

Att-Gen's Ref Nos 66-71 of 2006 2006 EWCA Crim 2777 The defendants pleaded to conspiracy to supply involving the wholesaling of cocaine. Except for two defendants, the defendants pleaded guilty to a single count of conspiracy to supply. There were 14 to be sentenced. Held. The prosecution submitted that conspiracy makes the offence more serious than it would have been with substantive charges. That may be the case in some instances, indeed very often it will. In other cases, however, the nature of the charge makes very little difference by the time one comes to the sentencing exercise. If an offence is committed on an organised basis, that is necessarily usually more serious than an isolated individual offence. That is particularly so where there is a team operating and where individual participants, although they act personally in a limited number of transactions, are plainly responsible for the wider range of dealings which are carried out by others as part of the overall operation. *R v Allsopp and Others* 2005 EWCA Crim 703 is a good example of just such a case. On the other hand, virtually every joint offence is also potentially capable of being charged as a conspiracy and it does not necessarily follow that a count of conspiracy automatically creates a case where a defendant is fixed with responsibility for actions beyond his own. That may be the position, but it may not always be true. In this case it did not make any difference at all whether a defendant fell to be sentenced for conspiracy on the basis of X transactions, or fell to be sentenced for X specific substantive counts.

R v Austin and Others 2009 EWCA Crim 394, 2 Cr App R (S) 74 (p 510) Where the conspirator knows that the conspiracy is wider than his own individual participation, he must when sentenced bear a responsibility for the results of the whole of that conspiracy.

R v Harding and Others 2014 EWCA Crim 538 LCJ Nine defendants were sentenced for conspiracy to steal BT cabling. The conspiracy was extremely professional and meticulously executed. Held. The sentence for each conspirator should reflect not only that conspirator's participation in specific acts done in furtherance of the conspiracy, but his involvement in the conspiracy in its broadest sense. Thus, for as long as they were parties to the conspiracy, they could be said to have sustained and supported the other conspirators in those acts in furtherance of the conspiracy in which they had not personally participated. However, the roles that individual conspirators played should not be ignored.

CONTEMPT OF COURT see the PERVERTING THE COURSE OF JUSTICE/CONTEMPT OF COURT/PERJURY ETC. chapter.

COPYRIGHT OFFENCES see the RETAIL OFFENCES chapter

228   CORRUPTION/MISFEASANCE IN PUBLIC OFFICE/BRIBERY

228.1

1) Bribery Act 2010

   s 1 (bribing another person)

   s 2 (requesting, agreeing to receive and accepting bribes etc.)

   s 6 (bribing foreign public officials)

   s 7 (commercial organisations failing to prevent bribery)

Modes of trial and maximum sentences Section 1, 2 and 6 offences are triable either way. On indictment, for an individual maximum is 10 years. Summary maximum 6 months and/or a £5,000 fine for offences committed before 12 March 2015 and an unlimited fine thereafter.[156] There are maximum fines for those aged under 18, see **14.38** in Volume 1.

For non-individuals, section 1, 2 and 6 offences and section 7 offences are indictable only. Maximum sentence a fine[157]

The four offences came into force on 1 July 2011.

Confiscation Where a defendant has a criminal lifestyle the court, once the confiscation proceedings are triggered (see **22.11** in Volume 1), must follow the Proceeds of Crime Act 2002 procedure. The list of 'criminal lifestyle' offences does not include Bribery Act 2010 offences.[158] For establishing a criminal lifestyle by another route see **22.43** in Volume 1.

Serious Crime Prevention Orders For Bribery Act 2010 s 1, 2 and 6 offences there is a discretionary power to make this order, when it would protect the public etc.[159]

Deferred Prosecution Agreements A designated prosecutor may apply to the court under Crime and Courts Act 2013 Sch 17 para 7 for this procedure to be applied to Bribery Act 2010 s 1, 2, 6 and 7 offences. The procedure is laid down in Crime and Courts Act 2013 Sch 17. In force 24 February 2014

2) Misfeasance in Public Office

   Common law offence

   Mode of trial Indictable only

   Maximum sentence Life

3) Criminal Justice and Courts Act 2015 s 26 (corrupt or other improper exercise of police powers and privileges)

   Mode of trial Indictable only

   Maximum sentence 14 years.

   In force 13 April 2015[160]

For **corporate offenders** see the *Fraud, Bribery and Money Laundering: Corporate Offenders Guideline 2014* at **225.9**.

228.2   *Sentencing Guidelines Council guideline   Bribery*

Fraud, Bribery and Money Laundering Offences Guideline 2014, see www.banksr.com Other matters Guideline tab page 41 This guideline applies to Bribery Act 2010 s 1, 2 and 6. In force 1 October 2014. Owing to the length of the guideline and the rarity of prosecutions for this offence it is not listed.

STEP ONE: Determining the offence category

Page 42 The court should determine the offence category with reference to the tables below. In order to determine the category the court should assess culpability and harm.

---

[156] Legal Aid, Sentencing and Punishment of Offenders Act 2012 s 85(1) and (4) and Legal Aid, Sentencing and Punishment of Offenders Act 2012 (Commencement No 11) Order 2015 2015/504

[157] Bribery Act 2010 s 11

[158] Proceeds of Crime Act 2002 s 6 and 75 and Sch 2

[159] Serious Crime Act 2007 s 1 and Sch 1 para 9

[160] Criminal Justice and Courts Act 2015 (Commencement No 1, Saving and Transitional Provisions) Order 2015 2015/778 para 3 and Sch 1 para 22

Culpability
The level of culpability is determined by weighing up all the factors of the case to determine the offender's role and the extent to which the offending was planned and the sophistication with which it was carried out. Where there are characteristics present which fall under different levels of culpability, the court should balance these characteristics to reach a fair assessment of the offender's culpability.

Culpability
Culpability A – High Culpability
A leading role where offending is part of a group activity Involvement of others through pressure/influence Abuse of position of significant power or trust or responsibility Intended corruption (directly or indirectly) of a senior official performing a public function Intended corruption (directly or indirectly) of a law enforcement officer Sophisticated nature of offence/significant planning Offending conducted over sustained period of time Motivated by expectation of substantial financial, commercial or political gain
Culpability B – Medium Culpability
Other cases where characteristics for categories A or C are not present A significant role where offending is part of a group activity
Culpability C – Lesser Culpability
Involved through coercion, intimidation or exploitation Not motivated by personal gain Peripheral role in organised activity Opportunistic 'one-off' offence; very little or no planning Limited awareness or understanding of extent of corrupt activity

Harm
Harm is assessed in relation to any impact caused by the offending (whether to identifiable victims or in a wider context) and the actual or intended gain to the offender. Risk of harm involves consideration of both the likelihood of harm occurring and the extent of it if it does. Risk of harm is less serious than the same actual harm. Where the offence has caused risk of harm but no (or much less) actual harm, the normal approach is to move to the next category of harm down. This may not be appropriate if either the likelihood or extent of potential harm is particularly high.

Category 1	Serious detrimental effect on individuals (for example by provision of substandard goods or services resulting from the corrupt behaviour) Serious environmental impact Serious undermining of the proper function of local or national government, business or public services Substantial actual or intended financial gain to offender or another or loss caused to others
Category 2	Significant detrimental effect on individuals Significant environmental impact Significant undermining of the proper function of local or national government, business or public services Significant actual or intended financial gain to offender or another or loss caused to others Risk of Category 1 harm

228.3   *Judicial guidance*

R v Innospec Ltd 2010 Lloyd's Rep FC 462 www.banksr.com Other Matters Other Documents Southwark Crown Court Thomas LJ Corruption is an insidious plague that has a wide range of corrosive effects on societies. It undermines democracy and the rule of law, leads to violations of human rights, distorts markets, erodes the quality of life and allows organised crime, terrorism and other threats to human security to flourish. This evil phenomenon is found in all countries, big and small, rich and poor, but it is in the developing world that its effects are most destructive. Corruption hurts the poor disproportionately by diverting funds intended for development, undermining a govern-ment's ability to provide basic services, feeding inequality and injustice and discourag-ing foreign aid and investment. Corruption is a key element in economic underperformance and a major obstacle to poverty alleviation and development.

R v Dougall 2010 EWCA Crim 1048, 2011 1 Cr App R (S) 37 (p 227) LCJ We illustrate the seriousness of corruption by quoting the Secretary General of the UN. (Note: This is the quote in *R v Innospec Ltd* 2010 above. Ed.) It is not a victimless crime. Sometimes entire communities are victims. Often the process of investigation and trial requires huge resources and protracted analysis.

R v Brealy 2010 EWCA Crim 1860, 2011 1 Cr App R (S) 89 (p 535) D was convicted of corruption. He was the managing director of a company which owned properties, let through managing agents. D allowed M, a councillor who sat on various committees relating to planning and development, to live in a property owned by the company. The unpaid rent totalled £34,000 spanning five years. Held. There are no guideline cases for sentencing in this area. However, it is possible to distil principles from the authorities. First, sentences contain substantial elements of punishment and deterrence. That is because the court regards corruption as a cancer in commercial and public life and makes clear that those who engage in it should expect little in the way of mercy, see *R v Harwood* 1985 7 Cr App R (S) 402. Second, since corruption is so damaging to commercial and public life, and public confidence in these, those who indulge in it should expect immediate imprisonment, despite previous good character, *R v Wilson* 1982 4 Cr App R (S) 33. We adopt '…for any who may be tempted to be less than absolutely scrupulous, the expectation of a custodial sentence should act as a deterrent', *R v Bennett and Wilson* 1986 1 Cr App R (S) 162. Third, the reach and character of the corruption has an important bearing on the nature of the custodial period.

R v Messent 2011 EWCA Crim 644 LCJ We adopt Thomas LJ's statement in *R v Innospec Ltd* 2010 without hesitation. Corruption of foreign government officials or foreign government ministers is at the top end of serious corporate offending both in terms of culpability and harm.

228.4   *Accepting bribes   Sportsmen and betting frauds*

R v Amir and Butt 2011 EWCA Crim 2914, 2012 2 Cr App R (S) 17 (p 68) LCJ D pleaded (full credit) to conspiracy to accept corrupt payments and conspiracy to cheat. B was convicted of the same offence. D and B had contracts with the Cricket Board of Pakistan. B was the captain of the team and D was a player. D and B played in a test cricket match against England. 'No balls' were bowled at predetermined points which benefited some in organised gambling. A third cricketer and D's agent were also involved. The men were very well rewarded for their part. The International Cricket Board conducted an investigation and banned D for 5 years (2 suspended) and B for 10 years (5 suspended). The Judge found that B was the orchestrator of the corrupt activity by three players and regarded him as having had an influence over D. At appeal, D was aged 19 and B 27. Held. The corruption was carefully prepared. The players had betrayed their team, their country and their sport which had given them their distinction. The discount for the serious ban from the ICB was adequate. B was undoubtedly the most involved and a malign influence on D and the other player. The Judge was entitled to find that B was the orchestrator. In the long term, cricket would be utterly impoverished if the court failed to make it clear that conduct like this is criminal conduct of a very serious kind which must be marked with a criminal sanction. For D, **6 months' YOI**. For B, **2 years 6 months**.

228.5   *Commercial organisations*

R v Thomas 2013 EWCA Crim 1447 D pleaded (25% credit) to conspiracy to corrupt. JM also pleaded while other defendants were acquitted. D was the managing director of OilExec, a company contracted by BP to recruit experienced divers to support its worldwide drilling operation. OilExec was a subsidiary of C-Mar Holdings, which owned a 51% controlling share. JM was the commercial director of C-Mar. Two of the acquitted defendants (directors of C-Mar) became concerned at OilExec's lack of profitability and put pressure on D to improve the performance. D did so by entering into a corrupt agreement with TH, an employee of BP responsible for engaging with the recruitment agencies who provided divers. D, with JM's knowledge and connivance, made payments to TH over a long period, totalling £250,000, in return for which TH engaged OilExec to provide divers to BP. In this way, over five years OilExec's business with BP amounted to about $17m. The corrupt payments were made directly to TH's wife's account and were concealed by bogus invoices for so-called marketing or consultancy services. D benefited as OilExec's business with BP increased considerably and D had access to generous expense accounts. D's actions removed competition and distorted the market. D initially denied knowledge of anything untoward. Held. A proper starting point would have been **3 years** not 4. With the plea, **2 years 3 months** not 3 years.

See also: *R v Ford* 2011 EWCA Crim 473 (D pleaded to five offences of corruption. He paid K £190,735 in order to obtain £920,145 worth of contracts for his business. D assisted the prosecution under Serious Crime Act 2007 s 73. D was aged 58 and of good character. With credit for the pleas, his assistance and reflecting his criminality, **18 months**, not 2 years.)

Old case: *R v Welcher and Others* 2007 EWCA Crim 480, 2 Cr App R (S) 83 (p 519) (**6½ years**) For a summary of the case see the 9th edition of this book.

228.6   *International corruption*

R v Tumukunde 2009 EWCA Crim 327 D pleaded late to corruption. He was a senior civil servant in Uganda. The Government wanted security assistance for the Commonwealth Heads of Government meeting in Kampala. A UK company was awarded contracts for training etc. They were signed. D travelled unexpectedly to the UK and asked the company directors to pay him £80,000 in total. It was a corrupt payment claimed to 'maintain good relations' with a senior official in Uganda. The payment was made and D may have received £20,000. The defence said the payment did not induce a contract and the Uganda Government was cheated. Held. Corruption is so corrosive of the commercial integrity of the UK in the international arena and is so corrosive of the ability of African countries to overcome the problem of corruption where sadly it has been endemic in the past, that it requires condign punishment and deterrent. **1 year** upheld.

R v Messent 2011 EWCA Crim 644 LCJ D pleaded (full credit) to two counts of corruption. 39 corruption offences were taken into consideration. He was head of property at a London-based reinsurance brokers. Between 1999 and 2002 he oversaw 41 corrupt payments to two state-owned institutions in Costa Rica, totalling £1,260,000. The contract cost the state companies $2m more than it should have done. The individuals receiving the money were able to influence whether D's company had its contract renewed with the Costa Rican institutions. D resigned in 2006 following an internal investigation. D's bonus was increased and he received £428,000 (£265,000 net). The corrupt payments were clawed back by the company in the form of disguised insurance premiums. The unexplained payments were uncovered after a presidential election in Costa Rica. At the outset of the investigation, D did not co-operate and offered untruthful explanations. D, aged 50, was of good character. The case had had a devastating impact on him and his family. The Judge gave D full credit. Held. We question whether that was appropriate but it does not affect our view of the sentence. The starting point of **4-5 years** was not too high. With plea and a discount for the delay, **21 months** was not outside the appropriate range. 5-year disqualification from being a director and £100,000 compensation also remain.

228.7   *Local government*

R v Davies 2010 EWCA Crim 1804 D pleaded on rearraignment to conspiracy to commit false accounting. R was a senior surveyor for a council. He oversaw the maintenance of their buildings. His role required him to order necessary parts and he used a company where D was employed. R abused his position and obtained almost £90,000 worth of goods spanning four years. D assisted R over that period and two methods were employed to avoid detection. An investigation was eventually undertaken and D admitted his involvement after initially denying all knowledge. D admitted to arranging work to be completed on R's property to the value of £14,834 exclusive of VAT. The pre-sentence report noted that D was ashamed of his actions. The Judge noted that D was entitled to substantial credit for his plea. Mitigating factors included pleading to a substantially lower sum than R, he was not a public employee, his remorse and an impressive set of letters and testimonials. Held. D did not receive any monetary benefit and there was no breach of trust. D lost his job as a result. D had a job offer but his home detention curfew would make employment very difficult, so **6 months** not 12.

R v Brealy 2010 EWCA Crim 1860, 2011 1 Cr App R (S) 89 (p 535) D was convicted of corruption. He was the managing director of a company which owned properties let through managing agents. D allowed M, a councillor who sat on various committees relating to planning and development, to live in a property owned by the company. The unpaid rent totalled £34,000 spanning five years. The managing agents wrote letters to M each year and D was kept appraised of the debt. The company's accountants were instructed to write off the debt, stating 'M smoothes things through planning at the council'. There was a note written by D on a meeting agenda which read: 'Getting good councillor backing. Remind the board this is linked to rent arrears.' He claimed that neither he nor the company had received a benefit and that his actions were to avoid making an enemy which was misguided rather than corrupt. The Judge noted that this was a very serious offence of corruption but accepted that D's actions were not overt in that he did not explicitly invite M to act in his or the company's favour. D was of good character. Held. An offence such as this is always liable to jeopardise public trust and confidence in public offices. In this case there was very strong mitigation and 15 months was harsh but not manifestly excessive.

228.8   *Police officers as defendants misusing the police computer*

Att-Gen's Ref No 68 of 2009 2009 EWCA Crim 2219 LCJ D pleaded when his case was listed for trial to two counts of misconduct and conspiracy to defraud. Police searched a co-defendant's address and found police documents. One had D's fingerprints on it. D was a serving police officer. It was discovered that over 18 months on a 'large number' of occasions he had accessed police computer records and passed them on to friends who were criminals. One of the criminals was a class A drug supply suspect. He used other police officers' details to conceal his computer activity. Some of the details obtained were used by others to commit fraud. On one day he viewed 421 documents relating to T, and some of these documents were found on T. Police paperwork was found in criminals' homes. D also provided false personal details of a criminal contact to a bank. A bank account was then provided. D had access to a debit card and made six £200 withdrawals in cash. The basis of plea accepted that the accessing was done for bravado and nosiness. Also there was no evidence that the evidence was intended to be used in furtherance of any criminal activity, nor was any police operation compromised. D was now aged 25 and of good character. There were commendable aspects to his police service. Held. The misuse of police records for any purpose is always very serious. Deterrent sentences are appropriate. Actual damage caused was relatively minor. **18 months** would have been appropriate. Because of the unpaid work done and it would be a return to custody, **12 months** not 12 months suspended.

R v Razaq 2011 EWCA Crim 1518 LCJ D, a serving police officer at the time of the offences, pleaded late to criminal property offences (×2), perverting the course of justice and conspiracy to pervert (×2), possession of prohibited firearms (×3), possession of ammunition, misconduct in public office and money laundering. His plea triggered his co-accused, including D's brother, H, to plead to offences including kidnap. D used the police computer system to access information about his acquaintances etc. H instructed D to deliver a bag containing money and other items to an associate. D received £500. H instructed D to prevent a witness in a forthcoming kidnap trial from giving evidence. D agreed. A search of D's home found £70,000 in cash in a bag, along with two sub-machine guns, a Sten gun and 228 live rounds of ammunition. D indicated to the authorities that a further 70-80 rounds of ammunition could be found at his address. His basis of plea was that the money belonged to H, and fearing for H's safety he agreed to mind it. Further, fearing for his safety, he agreed to mind the weapons etc. when approached by another. Held. These were a very serious series of offences, prolonged and repeated and in the gravest breach of trust. Focusing on totality, **11½ years** was well within the range.

See also: *R v Wilkie* 2012 EWCA Crim 247, 2 Cr App R (S) 68 (p 393) (Plea to misconduct in public office (×12) and theft. Police officer who used Police National Computer to obtain details of vulnerable girls and women, and subsequently sexually harassed them. 20 women over 18 months. The women had mostly been victims of crime and were aged 15 upwards. Gross breach of trust. Aged 51. **3 years 4 months** upheld.)

R v Nichols 2012 EWCA Crim 2650, 2013 2 Cr App R (S) 10 (Late plea to securing unauthorised access to computer material. Now aged 49. Detective Inspector in police with 30 years' service. Used police intelligence system to perform checks on his own family. Breach of trust. Information not used corruptly or disseminated to criminals. Now unemployed. 100 hours' unpaid work affirmed, attached to a **community order**, not a suspended sentence.)

Old cases: *R v Kassim* 2005 EWCA Crim 1020, 2006 1 Cr App R (S) 4 (p 12) (**2½ years**) *Att-Gen's Ref No 1 of 2007* 2007 EWCA Crim 760, 2 Cr App R (S) 86 (p 544) (**18 months**) For a summary of the first case see the 8th edition of this book and for the last case see the 9th edition.

228.9   *Police officers as defendants   Non-computer offences*

R v Stone 2011 EWCA Crim 1602 D was convicted of misconduct in a public office. D, a policeman, came to know M as a result of her son becoming known to the police. D and a colleague gave M a lift home whilst on duty. Later, D returned to M's address and they had consensual sexual intercourse. When on duty D subsequently harassed her. Whilst on duty, D followed M home in his police car and when he arrived he demanded to know who had bought her the flowers that she was holding. D went into M's house and they had consensual sexual intercourse. D was of positive good character. Held. An offence of misconduct by a police officer is a gross breach of the trust placed in every constable. However, the court is not a court of morals. **5 months** not 12, so immediate release.

R v Bunyan 2013 EWCA Crim 1885, 2014 1 Cr App R (S) 65 (p 428) D was convicted of eight counts of misconduct in public office. He was a Police Community Support Officer (PCSO) and between 2007 and 2011 he met vulnerable women in his work and engaged in sexual relationships with them. He accessed their computerised police records to further the relationships. He had relationships with four women, three of whom he had intercourse with whilst he was on duty. He had intercourse with one woman in a police office. He told one woman about confidential police activity in her area. One of the women had mental health difficulties, though D was sentenced on the basis that he had not taken advantage of the women and that there was no evidence that they were vulnerable in the conventional sentencing sense. He revealed police data to one woman about a friend's partner. D was aged 40 and of good character. Held. There was no element of breach of trust. This case was to be distinguished from those where police officers have taken blatant advantage of vulnerable women in the course of their duties, provided information to criminals and accessed police computers for the purposes of having sexual relationships with them. The use of the personal information was, however, intended to impress the women. There was a clear breach of his duties. **3 years** not 7.

R v Arthurs 2013 EWCA Crim 2407 D was convicted of misconduct in public office (×5). She was a constable in the Kent police. She separated from her husband in 2004 and the family home was put up for sale. LM made an offer to buy the property, which was accepted. The sale was delayed until 2005 so that D could find somewhere to live. After renting an address elsewhere, she purchased a similar property in the same street as the former family home. On four occasions between July 2004 and June 2005, D misused the police computer system to view the records relating to LM and on one occasion during that period accessed the records of LM's former partner. In February 2006, she accessed the records of IT. On the same day D became aware that LM was a suspect in the Tonbridge Securitas robbery. A colleague, aware she used to live at LM's address, asked her for a suitable position from which to observe the address. D was subsequently found to have accessed the PNC in relation to LM. Allegations relating to IT were not substantiated. Disciplinary proceedings were commenced and she was given a warning. In 2011, D completed a vetting renewal form and failed to disclose her association with LM, knowing that he had criminal convictions and associations. In March 2012, LM attended a police station and claimed someone was trying to have him killed. He believed than an Audi car was connected to the threat and supplied a registration number. D used the computer system to access and print records relating to an Audi car and its registered keeper. This followed her claim that she had seen an Audi driving suspiciously and wanted to carry out a PNC check. D was not permitted to use the PNC. A colleague said that there was no interest in the vehicle and he did not propose to carry out a PNC check. D told a more senior colleague, who advised her to make an intelligence report and carry out certain checks. She then asked another officer to carry out a PNC check on the vehicle, telling him that it was a suspected stolen vehicle. Her colleague printed out the result which contained the name and address of the registered keeper and the fact that there were no reports in respect of the vehicle. When D was arrested, the PNC print-out was discovered in her car. Her mobile phone revealed frequent telephone contact between her and LM. Her home was searched and photographs of D with LM and IT were found. D was aged 52 when sentenced and had no convictions. She had been prescribed medication for depression prior to her arrest. A prison report was wholly favourable. Held. Her actions related to a personal friendship with a criminal and involved deliberate and improper use of police computer files for a number of individuals. The police print-out contained highly confidential information and intelligence which D had obtained with the sole purpose of giving it to LM. D's motive for the first three offences was consistent with curiosity about a friend and his acquaintances, although she knew she should have disclosed their friendship. The motive for the final offence was clearly to help a criminal. She had concealed her friendship with LM and then taken active steps to assist him. The behaviour took place over a period of eight years. Her culpability was high and the potentially serious harm was only averted by her arrest. **2 years** concurrent was not manifestly excessive.

See also: *R v Lewis* 2010 EWCA Crim 579, 2 Cr App R (S) 104 (p 666) (LCJ Acquittal of the rapes. Plea to eight counts of misfeasance. Police officer demanded sexual activity with a witness, a victim and two defendants. Misuse of the police computer. **3 years** not 4.)

Att-Gen's Ref No 30 of 2010 2010 EWCA Crim 2261, 2011 1 Cr App R (S) 106 (p 624) (**6 years**)

R v Fletcher 2011 EWCA Crim 1802, 2012 1 Cr App R (S) 62 (p 356) (Pleas ×2. Police officer on patrol. Attended home of vulnerable woman. Engaged in oral sex. They agreed to meet that evening. They had intercourse. The officer left and she self-harmed. No previous convictions. **32 months** was not manifestly excessive.)

Old cases: *R v O'Leary* 2007 EWCA Crim 186, 2007 2 Cr App R (S) 51 (p 317) (**3½ years** upheld) *R v Ranson and Kerr* 2007 EWCA Crim 153, 2007 2 Cr App R (S) 55 (p 342) (**3 years** and **18 months**) *Att-Gen's Ref No 1 of 2007* 2007 EWCA Crim 760, 2 Cr App R (S) 86 (p 544) (The minimum appropriate sentence was **18 months.**) For a summary of the cases, see the 7th edition of this book.

See also the **DEFENDANT** *Police officers as defendant* para at **240.52**.

Prison officers, see the **PRISON OFFENCES** *Prison officers as defendants* para at **309.12**.

228.10   Public officials

R v Ozakpinar 2008 EWCA Crim 875, 2009 1 Cr App R (S) 8 (p 35) D was convicted of false accounting and three counts of corruption. He was Chief Procurement Officer for the CPS. He procured self-employed contractors for the CPS. In the first case he ensured that his friend, P, received a contract to supply a computerised shopping system for stationery by selecting P as the sole candidate to be interviewed. There had been no involvement of the usual system for the CPS to find service providers. The work was carried out. 'Milestone payments' had been agreed which meant that when a milestone was reached P would receive payments of £20,000. Two of these payments were made to P, and he in turn paid D a total of £12,000. In the second case he engaged N to complete a contract. Her application did not go through the normal process either and he ensured that she was on the short list of candidates to be interviewed. He then sat on the interviewing panel and there was evidence that he was instrumental in her obtaining the contract. Again, when N received a milestone payment she paid D £6,000 of it. The false accounting was when he appointed W to write guides on procurement. She was effectively freelance. He asked her for a blank draft invoice which he then completed purporting to show that all the work had been done. In fact it had not. W was paid £12,440 which she queried, believing that she was only due £5,000. D told her that the extra £7,440 was for additional future consultancy work and asked her to pay it over to him for safe keeping, which she did. He paid it into his bank account. After his arrest it was repaid. D, aged 45, had no relevant previous convictions. Held. Even if the false accounting did not in itself pass the custody threshold this is no reason for not taking it into account in fixing the overall prison sentence because it would have attracted significant punishment which in the present circumstances is not being imposed. The theft breach of trust sentencing cases do not apply. This defendant was a senior civil servant who had charge of substantial public funds. He bypassed proper procedures and was blatantly rewarded. **2½ years** was not manifestly excessive.

R v Patel 2012 EWCA Crim 3075, 2013 1 Cr App R (S) 48 (p 269) LCJ D pleaded (full credit) to bribery and misconduct in public office. He was employed as a court clerk and solicited and took bribes from those accused of motoring offences. He telephoned S, who was before the court for a speeding offence. He told S that unless D sorted the matter out for him, S would "get fucked" as the magistrates "don't like Asian bros". D also said that S was likely to get a £350 fine and his car insurance would "go through the roof". S contacted *The Sun* and arranged to meet with D. D identified himself with his ID card and explained to S how the fraud would operate. This was covertly recorded. The police were alerted and subsequently found court documents at his home address and summonses for various people in his work desk drawers. Text messages were found where D had offered advice on how to deal with reissued summonses. The investigation revealed no less than 53 cases where D had assisted offenders to avoid prosecution. All related to motoring offences. There were cash deposits totalling £54,000 and transfers totalling £42,000 which were unexplained. The Judge found that D's financial reward was at least £20,000. D, aged 22, was of previous good character. Held. This was a systematic and prolonged breach of trust in which D courted bribes for his own enrichment. He acted alone and enjoyed all the profits. The public are entitled to rely on the integrity of everyone who is involved in the administration of justice, whether as a judge, a magistrate, or a court official. All are expected to be incorruptible. That confident expectation was tarnished by D's criminal activities. Some drivers who should have been disqualified avoided disqualification and others avoided fines and penalty points which they would justly have incurred. Each incident represented a deliberate and successful perversion of the course of justice by an official of the court system. **4 years** not 6.

Note: The details of how the fraud worked were deliberately left out of the judgment. Ed.

R v McCarthy 2015 EWCA Crim 1117, 2 Cr App R (S) 47 (p 355) D pleaded at her PCMH to assisting an offender and misconduct in a public office. She had obtained a master's degree in criminal justice and in 2010 she qualified as a probation officer. D managed a cohort of high-risk offenders and had achieved some very encouraging results. One of her placements was S. He was addicted to crack and had spent 14 out of the last 20 years in prison. D worked tirelessly to assist S but became emotionally dependent on him. On a home visit, D provided S with a mobile phone. Shortly afterwards, S was locked out of his accommodation and D took him back to her flat for the night. She took S back to his accommodation in the morning. D then committed a burglary. Police investigated it and told D that S was wanted for it. D correctly started the process for the revocation of S's licence. When police asked D about the number of the phone she had given S, she said it was her phone and she had let S use it to phone his mother. This was a lie. The result of this was that the police did not seek to find S through his use of the phone. D's basis of plea was that the reason for this was not to help S but to avoid disciplinary proceedings. When D was away on holiday, she permitted S to live at her flat knowing he was still wanted by the police. A sexual relationship developed between them. During this time D committed four dwelling burglaries. When D appeared at the Crown Court D talked her way into the cells to speak to S. D was now aged 31. She lost her job and the relationship with S continued. Held. The seriousness lay in the period of time the offending persisted. S was a prolific offender and D harboured him when employed in a position of trust. Starting at 16-18 months was not inappropriate. **12 months** concurrent on each was not manifestly excessive.

See also: *R v John-Ayo* 2008 EWCA Crim 1651, 2009 1 Cr App R (S) 71 (p 416) (Civil servant convicted of 14 counts of misconduct. Issued travel documents known as 'refugee passports' to 64 people. She also granted 180 fraudulent applications for those documents. Done for gain over 15 months. **9 years** beyond criticism.)

R v Shoyeju 2014 EWCA Crim 486 (LCJ Home Office immigration officer. Corruption in an area such as immigration control, upon which public confidence and the system of controls is of paramount importance, must seriously aggravate the gross breach of trust involved in such corrupt activities. Factors to consider listed. Appeal wholly without merit.)

229   COUNTERFEIT CURRENCY OFFENCES

229.1

1) Forgery and Counterfeiting Act 1981
   s 14(1) (making)
   s 15(1) (passing etc.)
   s 16(1) (having custody or control of counterfeit notes or coin intending the notes or coins to be passed)

s 17(1) (making etc. counterfeiting materials etc. intending the notes or coins to be passed respectively)

Modes of trial All offences are triable either way.

Maximum sentences On indictment 10 years. Summary 6 months and/or a £5,000 fine for offences committed before 12 March 2015 and an unlimited fine thereafter.[161] There are maximum fines for those aged under 18, see **14.38** in Volume 1.

2) Forgery and Counterfeiting Act 1981

s 14(2) (making counterfeit notes or coin without lawful excuse etc.)

s 15(2) (delivering counterfeit notes or coin without lawful excuse etc.)

s 16(2) (having custody and control of counterfeit notes or coin without lawful excuse etc.)

s 17(2) (making etc. counterfeiting materials without lawful excuse etc.)

Modes of trial All offences are triable either way.

Maximum sentences On indictment 2 years. Summary 6 months and/or a £5,000 fine for offences committed before 12 March 2015 and an unlimited fine thereafter.[162] There are maximum fines for those aged under 18, see **14.38** in Volume 1.

Confiscation Where a defendant has a criminal lifestyle the court, once the confiscation proceedings are triggered (see **22.11** in Volume 1), must follow the Proceeds of Crime Act 2002 procedure. 'Criminal lifestyle' offences include those under Forgery and Counterfeiting Act 1981 s 14-17.[163] For what constitutes a criminal lifestyle see **22.43** in Volume 1.

Serious Crime Prevention Orders For section 14-17 offences there is a discretionary power to make this order, when it would protect the public etc.[164]

229.2   *Judicial guidance*

R v Fisher 2013 EWCA Crim 2055 D was convicted of conspiracy to pass counterfeit coins and conspiracy to have custody of items for the purpose of making counterfeit coins. The Judge accepted that D was not to be sentenced as a counterfeiter or manufacturer of the coins. Held. We do not accept the implied submission that the maximum should be reserved for those who mint or manufacture protected coins or notes. The maximum sentence was the same in each case. The seriousness of the individual offence with which the judge is concerned will be assessed according to its own facts and in particular the role played by the offender in its commission. We recognise that if an offender is to be sentenced as both a counterfeiter and a distributor, he will be in a more serious position than an offender who is either one or the other. Nonetheless, we consider that the culpability of a person in D's position, identified as an organiser of the distribution of massive quantities of counterfeit coins, will be the greater when he is also close to the source of manufacture.

R v Edirin-Etarreri 2014 EWCA Crim 1536, 2 Cr App R (S) 82 (p 641) D pleaded to having custody of counterfeit currency. Held. Cases that are 20 years old offer no real assistance. The court should have in mind the quantity involved and Lord Lane's words in *R v Howard* 1985 7 Cr App R (S) 320, "It is a trite observation made in these cases, but nevertheless correct, that the issue of counterfeit notes undermines the whole economy of the country and is likely to result in great loss being sustained by innocent people who find themselves in possession of these notes only to discover that they are worthless." For this type of offending immediate imprisonment is almost inevitable.

Old case: *R v Crick* 1981 3 Cr App R (S) 275 (About 150 fake 50p pieces which could not be put into general circulation. Used in vending machines. Held. Coining is a serious offence and calls for immediate imprisonment. However, not all offences are of the same

---

[161] Legal Aid, Sentencing and Punishment of Offenders Act 2012 s 85(1) and (4) and Legal Aid, Sentencing and Punishment of Offenders Act 2012 (Commencement No 11) Order 2015 2015/504

[162] Legal Aid, Sentencing and Punishment of Offenders Act 2012 s 85(1) and (4) and Legal Aid, Sentencing and Punishment of Offenders Act 2012 (Commencement No 11) Order 2015 2015/504

[163] Proceeds of Crime Act 2002 s 6 and 75 and Sch 2 para 6

[164] Serious Crime Act 2007 s 1 and Sch 1 para 10

gravity. At one extreme is the professional forger, with carefully prepared plates, and elaborate machinery, who manufactures large quantities of banknotes and puts them into circulation. A long sentence of imprisonment is appropriate in such a case. At the other end is this case.)

229.3   Large-scale production

R v Hartley and Others 2011 EWCA Crim 1957, 2012 1 Cr App R (S) 76 (p 429) On indictment 1, M pleaded to making counterfeit currency and conspiracy to tender counterfeit notes. B pleaded to a fresh count of possession etc. of counterfeiting materials. On indictment 2, M, B and H pleaded to conspiracy to tender counterfeit notes. M and B purchased printing equipment worth £4,000. They converted a room in a rented house into a factory to produce counterfeit currency. Their activities alerted police, who subsequently raided the house. They were found to be printing counterfeit £20 notes. Some 9 months later, 15,995 of the notes had been recovered. They were worth £318,100.[165] Those were the offences charged in indictment 1. M and B were charged and bailed. Both failed to appear. Both continued with their counterfeiting activities on a large scale. H drove to meet M, where he collected a holdall. He was stopped by police and admitted that he was carrying counterfeit notes. The value was £381,180. A farm garage had been adapted with a false wall, behind which was a significant quantity of printing and computer equipment. That was the offence charged in indictment 2. At sentence, £472,180 of the notes produced in the second offences had been recovered. M, aged 40 at appeal, had 11 convictions for 39 offences, mostly for dishonesty. B, aged 30 at appeal, had an attempted burglary conviction 10 years earlier. H, aged 62 at appeal, had a poor criminal record, mainly for dishonesty, including counterfeiting in 2003. Held. This was a very serious conspiracy to pass or tender large sums of counterfeit currency. M was a key player and the second offences were committed whilst on bail. This is a serious matter. For indictment 1, **4½ years** not 5, **2 months** for failure to surrender, and for indictment 2, **6 years** not 7, making **10 years 8 months**. B acted as an assistant to M and had pleaded to a single count over a shortened period. For indictment 1, **3½ years** not 5, **2 months** for failure to surrender, and for indictment 2, **8 years 8 months**, all concurrent. For H, **5½ years** was not manifestly excessive for this very serious conspiracy involving large sums of counterfeit currency. See also: *R v Allen* 2010 EWCA Crim 846, 2011 1 Cr App R (S) 10 (p 92) (Plea Conspiracy to counterfeit currency. Overall amount £500,000+. Defendant said he was involved with £200,000 to £250,000. High degree of sophistication. There could be no quarrel with **6 years**.)

229.4   Passing, tendering or having control of counterfeit currency

R v Miller 2010 EWCA Crim 257, 2 Cr App R (S) 62 (p 413) D pleaded to three counts of passing counterfeit currency and having control of counterfeit currency. He tendered three forged £20 notes in a bar. Police searched his home and found three more forged £20 notes. D was aged 27 with a large number of convictions. He had served custody for some of them. D had character references and was sole carer for his virtually bed-bound mother. Held. Custody was inevitable. Despite his record, the low value of notes, his early plea and personal mitigation means **15 months** not 2 years.

R v Hughes and Edwards 2010 EWCA Crim 453 H and E were convicted of custody of counterfeit currency. E drove to a truck stop and met H and another. E handed over £11,000 in counterfeit currency. Police seized the money and found £1,550 in genuine cash on E. H had £300 in genuine cash on him. Both had long histories of criminal offending. E was aged 50 and had a previous conviction for a counterfeit note. Held. Both were fully involved in the enterprise. **5 years** for E was not too long. (The Court reduced H's sentence because of his recall to prison.)

---

[165] The report states that 15,995 £20 notes are worth £318,100, when it would appear they are actually worth £319,900.

R v Forde 2013 EWCA Crim 2548 D pleaded (full credit) to tendering a counterfeit currency note and possessing cannabis (4 months concurrent and no appeal). He sought to purchase a top-up for his mobile phone using what appeared to be a genuine £20 note. However, the sales assistant looked more closely and it was discovered that it was a forgery. The police attended and arrested D. He was found to be carrying a small quantity of cannabis, for his own consumption. D admitted that he had purchased five counterfeit notes and had successfully used the others. He had previous convictions, albeit the last one involving dishonesty was a shoplifting in 2002. The last conviction involving drugs was for cultivation of cannabis in 2011 (community order). D was aged 44 at appeal. Held. With the potential harm to the UK economy, a custodial sentence would almost invariably be required in a case such as this. 20 months was manifestly excessive. With the plea, **15 months**.

See also: *R v Edirin-Etarreri* 2014 EWCA Crim 1536, 2 Cr App R (S) 82 (p 641) (Tried to use two £20 notes and had five £20 notes in his wallet. Starting at **18 months**, with plea, good character and aged 21, 10 months was proper.)

230   CRIMINAL DAMAGE

230.1

Criminal Damage Act 1971 s 1(1)

Mode of trial The offence is triable either way, except where the value of damage is believed to be £5,000 or less.

Maximum sentences There are the following maximum sentences at the Crown Court:
  a) Where the defendant is indicted following a voluntary bill, the maximum is presumably the Crown Court maximum, 10 years. This is because the count has not been before magistrates.
  b) Where the count is added to the indictment, the maximum is 10 years, *R v Alden* 2002 EWCA Crim 421, 2 Cr App R (S) 74 (p 326), *R v Saleem* 2010 EWCA Crim 2801. This is irrespective of the value.
  c) Where a charge has been dealt with summarily because the value has been found to be £5,000 or less and committed for sentence with another offence, the maximum is the summary maximum (both in relation to the individual maximum and the total for summary offences).
  d) If the defendant is sent for trial, under Crime and Disorder Act 1998 s 51 the Crown Court is obliged to perform the task the magistrates perform. If the estimated value of damage in a count or aggregate of damage is clearly over £5,000, the maximum is the Crown Court maximum. If subsequently this is found to be in error the maximum is still the Crown Court maximum. If the value is not estimated to be over £5,000 the maximum is the summary maximum.

The authorities for paras c) and d) are *R v Alden* 2002 EWCA Crim 421, 2 Cr App R (S) 74 (p 326), *R v Gwynn* 2002 EWCA Crim 2951, 2003 2 Cr App R (S) 41 (p 267) and *R v Tuplin* 2009 EWCA Crim 1572.

Summary maximum, when the value is £5,000 or more, 6 months and/or a £5,000 fine for offences committed before 12 March 2015 and an unlimited fine thereafter.[166] There are maximum fines for those aged under 18, see **14.38** in Volume 1. Otherwise 3 months and/or £2,500.

Criminal Behaviour Orders Where a defendant has engaged in behaviour that caused or was likely to cause harassment, alarm or distress to any persons and a Criminal Behaviour Order will help in preventing the offender from engaging in such behaviour, the court may make this order.[167]

---

[166] Legal Aid, Sentencing and Punishment of Offenders Act 2012 s 85(1) and (4) and Legal Aid, Sentencing and Punishment of Offenders Act 2012 (Commencement No 11) Order 2015 2015/504
[167] Anti-social Behaviour, Crime and Policing Act 2014 s 22(1)-(4)

Fixed penalty There is a £90 fixed penalty,[168] with half the relevant victim surcharge. For more detail see **61.1** in Volume 1.

Sexual Harm Prevention Orders There is a discretionary power to make this order when it is necessary to protect the public from sexual harm.[169]

Arson is listed separately in the ARSON chapter.

230.2   *Crown Court statistics   England and Wales*
Criminal damage endangering life (other than arson)

Year	Age	Plea	Total sen-tenced	Type of sentencing %						Average length of custody in months
				Dis-charge	Fine	Community sentence	Sus-pended sentence	Custody	Oth-er	
2013	18-20	G	2	100	–	–	–	–	–	–
		NG	0							
	21+	G	41	2.4	2.4	9.8	12.2	68.3	4.9	31
		NG	8	–	–	–	12.5	87.5	–	132.9
2014	18-20	G	5	–	–	20	20	60	–	not listed[170]
		NG	0							
	21+	G	27	–	–	11	15	70	4	33.4
		NG	4	–	–	–	25	50	25	not listed

Other criminal damage

Year	Age	Plea	Total sen-tenced	Type of sentencing %						Average length of custody in months
				Dis-charge	Fine	Community sentence	Sus-pended sentence	Custody	Oth-er	
2013	18-20	G	24	–	–	54.2	20.8	20.8	4.2	7.4
		NG	0							
	21+	G	171	10.5	5.3	29.2	29.8	24.6	0.6	7.2
		NG	12	–	16.7	–	25.0	58.3	–	14.6
2014	18-20	G	20	10	5	35	35	15	–	not listed[171]
		NG	1	100	–	–	–	–	–	–
	21+	G	149	11	4	31	20	28	6	8.7
		NG	11	18	18	–	18	27	18	not listed

For explanations about the statistics, see page 1-xii. For more statistics, statistics for 'threat etc. to commit criminal damage' and statistics for male and female defendants etc., see www.banksr.com Other Matters Statistics tab

230.3   *Magistrates' Court Sentencing Guidelines*
Magistrates' Court Sentencing Guidelines 2008, see www.banksr.com Other Matters Guidelines tab The guidelines apply to the Magistrates' Court and to the Crown Court hearing appeals or sentencing for summary only offences.[172]

page 44 Starting points are based on a first-time offender pleading not guilty.

---

[168] Penalties for Disorderly Behaviour (Amount of Penalty) Order 2002 2002/1837 Sch as amended
[169] Sexual Offences Act 2003 s 103A as inserted by Anti-social Behaviour, Crime and Policing Act 2014 Sch 5 para 2 and Sexual Offences Act 2003 Sch 5
[170] Based on too few cases to be meaningful
[171] Based on too few cases to be meaningful
[172] See page 15 of the guidelines.

Examples of nature of activity	Starting point	Range
Minor damage e.g. breaking small window, small amount of graffiti	Band B fine	Conditional discharge to band C fine
Moderate damage e.g. breaking large plate-glass or shop window, widespread graffiti	Low-level community order	Band C fine to medium-level community order
Significant damage up to £5,000 e.g. damage caused as part of a spree	High-level community order	Medium-level community order to 12 weeks' custody
Damage between £5,000 and £10,000	12 weeks' custody	6 to 26 weeks' custody
Damage over £10,000	Crown Court	Crown Court

The following aggravating and mitigating factors may be particularly relevant:

Factors indicating higher culpability: 1 Revenge attack 2 Targeting vulnerable victim. Factors indicating lower culpability: 1 Damage caused recklessly 2 Provocation. Factors indicating greater degree of harm: 1 Damage to emergency equipment 2 Damage to public amenity 3 Significant public or private fear caused e.g. in domestic context. Consider compensation.

A Band B fine is 100% of net weekly income. Band C is 150%. For more detail, see **60.27** in Volume 1.

For the meaning of a high-level, a medium-level and a low-level community order see **16.12-16.14** in Volume 1.

The guidelines are also for racially or religiously aggravated criminal damage offences where the sentence should be increased to reflect that element.

For how to apply the guidelines, see the GUIDELINES chapter in Volume 1.

230.4   *Cases*

R v Paxon 2013 EWCA Crim 2260 D pleaded (early) to theft and destroying property. In the early hours of the morning, D gained access to the secure compound at a Tesco store and removed copper piping. During the theft he cut himself and left blood on one of the units, which led the police to arrest him. D had 27 convictions for 64 offences spanning 2000 to 2013. There were 41 offences of theft from shops, buildings and from the person. There were 20 for failure to comply with court orders. Held. D can properly be described as a prolific offender. The copper piping cost the store a substantial sum of money, including, but not limited to, £7,500 worth of stock. The Judge generously accepted D's mitigation that he did not realise it would cause significant financial loss to Tesco. D sold the piping to fund his class A drug habit. He had a long history of acquisitive crime and the pre-sentence report noted a high risk of reoffending (95% within 24 months). The correct starting point was 18 months. There would be full credit for the plea. For the destroying property count, **12 months** not 16 months. 4 months consecutive for theft would be untouched. **20 months** not 24.

Note: The case is listed here as the significant point for sentencing was the amount of damage caused. Ed.

R v Reader 2014 EWCA Crim 2145 D pleaded (full credit) to threatening to damage property (×2). D's two young children were removed following allegations of child cruelty and were placed with D's sister, V. D's 16-year-old son, S, lived with V. D drunkenly sent S text messages. In them, D threatened to fire-bomb V's house so she would feel the pain of losing children. D told S to pass the messages on to V. Shortly after, D phoned V's husband, making the same threats. D admitted that problems with his young children had upset him and he had made the threats due to his drinking. He was arrested but later had no recollection of his actions, blaming alcohol. D was aged 40 on appeal with over a record of over 70 offences, including section 18 and other violence. They were linked to alcohol. The pre-sentence report noted that D posed a high risk of re-offending and a medium risk of harming the public if his drinking continued. Held. Immediate custody was warranted but the offences should properly be considered as one episode of offending with a starting point of 3 years. **2 years concurrent**, not consecutive.

R v Moses 2015 EWCA Crim 1010 D pleaded early to criminal damage and squatting (no penalty). The criminal damage value was limited to £20,000. Neighbours heard noise coming from a flat and saw floorboards, radiators and kitchen units being thrown out of the windows. Police attended and were abused by D. He said he was the owner and issued more threats. At the police station he said he was squatting and was renovating the property. D was bailed and continued squatting in the property. He breached his bail twice and was re-interviewed when it was clear he was convinced the property was his. D was now aged 47. He had been before the courts on 36 occasions for 126 offences in 20 years. Most of the offences were burglary, theft and other dishonesty offences. He was on licence for an attempted burglary offence for which he had received 12 months. The pre-sentence report said the offending was linked to extensive alcohol and amphetamine use. Further D did not intend to address those problems. Held. We start at 2 years. With plea, **16 months**.

230.5   Graffiti   Judicial guidance

R v Austin and Others 2009 EWCA Crim 394, 2 Cr App R (S) 74 (p 510) The defendant pleaded to a train graffiti conspiracy. The Judge said, "This type of offending sickens members of the public who have their travelling lives blighted by this sort of criminal damage and vandalism by graffiti on a massive scale. Sentences of course must be deterrent sentences to send a message out to those who may be tempted to do this for their own gratification." Held. We agree.

230.6   Graffiti   Cases

R v Moore 2011 EWCA Crim 1100, 2012 1 Cr App R (S) 5 (p 19) D pleaded (early) to 25 counts of destroying or damaging property. He trespassed on railway property and left his graffiti tag on various structures. The prosecution said the cost of removing D's graffiti was at least £40,000. The total cost of removing the graffiti in the various counts was more than £113,000. D, aged 24, had an extreme form of diabetes that left him especially vulnerable in custody. D had previous convictions for criminal damage between September 2007 and August 2009, when he was given a 2-month suspended sentence. This was activated in full and made consecutive. The Judge said the repair work would cost between £40,000 and £100,000. He started at 3 years and gave 2 years with the plea and mitigation. Held. The Judge took all relevant considerations into account. We start at **2 years**, so **18 months** with the plea, plus 2 months making 20 months in all.

Note: Why the Court of Appeal only gave 25% credit whereas the Judge had given 33% is not explained. Ed.

R v Whitehead 2011 EWCA Crim 1619 D pleaded to 10 counts of criminal damage. He was a part of an organised graffiti group which vandalised trains and infrastructure belonging to London Underground and Network Rail. D caused just over £20,000 worth of damage between November 2007 and February 2010. The motive was to show off. It was submitted that an immediate custodial sentence was not necessary as D was only 15 years old when most of the offending occurred. Held. This is not a victimless crime. These are serious offences. 12 months' YOI not 15.

See also: *R v Brzezinski* 2012 EWCA Crim 198, 2 Cr App R (S) 62 (p 314) (Pleas to eight criminal damage counts. In breach of community order for handling (value around £400) and on bail. Wrote in marker pen on inside of tube train. Incidents spanned 2007-2010. Heavily convicted. Aged 22. Immediate custody called for. Re-sentenced for the handling offence to 3 months not 9. **21 months** not 27. **ASBO** upheld.)

Old cases: *R v Dolan and Whittaker* 2007 EWCA Crim 2791, 2008 2 Cr App R (S) 11 (p 67) (**conditional discharges**) *R v Pease and Others* 2008 EWCA Crim 2515 (**2 years**,

1½ **years** and **15 months** for each defendant). *R v Austin and Others* 2009 EWCA Crim 394, 2 Cr App R (S) 74 (p 510) (**18 months, 20 months, 15 months'** YOI, **12 months'** YOI) For a summary of the first two cases see the 9th edition of this book.
For offences on the railway network, see the **RAILWAY OFFENCES** chapter.

230.7   *Racially or religiously aggravated*
Crime and Disorder Act 1998 s 30
Mode of trial Triable either way
Maximum sentence On indictment 14 years. Summary 6 months and/or a £5,000 fine for offences committed before 12 March 2015 and an unlimited fine thereafter.[173] There are maximum fines for those aged under 18, see **14.38** in Volume 1.
Basic principles, see the **RACIALLY OR RELIGIOUSLY AGGRAVATED OFFENCES** *Basic principles* para at **315.4**.

230.8   *Case*
Old case: *R v Johnston* 2005 EWCA Crim 2737, 2006 1 Cr App R (S) 115 (p 665) (**6 years**) For a summary of the case, see the 9th edition of this book.

230.9   *Reckless whether life would be endangered*
Criminal Damage Act 1971 s 1(2)
Mode of trial Indictable only
Maximum sentence Life
Sexual Harm Prevention Orders There is a discretionary power to make this order when it is necessary to protect the public from sexual harm.[174]
Extended sentences This offence is listed in Criminal Justice Act 2003 Sch 15. The court may pass a 2012 extended sentence (EDS) if there is a significant risk of serious harm from future specified offences and either: a) the defendant has a Criminal Justice Act 2003 Sch 15B conviction (applicable only to defendants aged 18+), or b) the offence would justify a determinate sentence of at least 4 years.[175]

230.10   *Reckless whether life would be endangered   Cases*
R v Cotter and Others 2009 EWCA Crim 1441, 2010 1 Cr App R (S) 55 (p 347)[176] C, T and R pleaded to damaging motor cars reckless whether P's life was endangered. The count was a specimen count. They were aged 16, 15 and 13. They, with others, threw stones etc. at vehicles on an A-road with two lanes running one way and one lane the other way. It was a very busy and dangerous stretch of road. Three of the youths were wearing hoods. Eleven vehicles were damaged by having their windscreens smashed or bodywork dented. The vehicles included HGVs, a commercial van and family cars carrying children. One driver stopped his car in panic, and this caused P in his car to overtake the stationary car and lose control of his car. It collided with an oncoming car and P was killed. The other motorist broke her arm. The defendants were seen laughing at the chaos. An HGV swerved when its windscreen was smashed. In interview, C said he had thrown 15 stones. T said he was having a laugh. R admitted presence only. C had seven convictions including ABH (female kicked and punched), making false 999 calls, harassment involving stone throwing and since the incident aggravated vehicle-taking. T, with his half-brother, committed after this offence a Public Order Act 1986 s 5 offence against his father (Referral Order). R was of good character. C was threatening and aggressive at his secure centre. His family could not control him. He had a low IQ and an attention deficit hyperactivity disorder. T had a low IQ and low self-esteem. R had a disturbed background and was abusing alcohol and paracetamol. He was a victim of bullying and self-harmed. They were sentenced on the basis that T was a follower and R

---

[173] Legal Aid, Sentencing and Punishment of Offenders Act 2012 s 85(1) and (4) and Legal Aid, Sentencing and Punishment of Offenders Act 2012 (Commencement No 11) Order 2015 2015/504
[174] Sexual Offences Act 2003 s 103A as inserted by Anti-social Behaviour, Crime and Policing Act 2014 Sch 5 para 2 and Sexual Offences Act 2003 Sch 5
[175] Criminal Justice Act 2003 s 226A-226B as inserted by Legal Aid, Sentencing and Punishment of Offenders Act 2012 s 124
[176] Also known as *R v T 2009* EWCA Crim 347

only gathered stones for the others. Held. It was a frightening and shocking experience for motorists. The sentences had to act as a deterrent. The offence was extremely serious. It required severe punishment. **4 years** for C, **3 years** for T and **2 years** for R upheld. See also the ARSON **Arson, Reckless whether life would be endangered** section at **209.10**.

230.11   *Revenge, Motive was*

R v Thompson 2012 EWCA Crim 2275 D was convicted of criminal damage. W was the manager of a bus company. For a short period, W employed D. When D left the company, he believed that W owed him wages of £60-70. The company disputed that. D returned to the company and asked for the money owed to him. He acted aggressively and there was a confrontation in which W was apparently struck. No action was taken. D later assaulted a member of staff, from whom he took money claiming it was in lieu of wages. Subsequently, a robbery charge was dropped and D pleaded to common assault. Whilst on bail, however, he filled a bottle full of corrosive liquid and proceeded to spray it on almost every panel of W's Bentley Continental, which was parked on his drive. W chased D but did not catch him. D denied he was the perpetrator. The damage amounted to about £23,000, plus £3,000 loss to his no claims bonus and an £8,000 loss for vehicle hire over a period of months, and the costs of added home security because of the fear felt by his family. D had a number of convictions, including a post office robbery (7 years). There were no convictions since 1993. Held. The offence was committed whilst D was on bail for an assault on one of W's employees. It was calculated and planned. There were earlier incidents of aggressive confrontation. W was to be a witness in the proceedings to come, albeit only to give only formal evidence. D's culpability was high. **2 years** was not manifestly excessive.

230.12   *Threatening to destroy or damage property*

Criminal Damage Act 1971 s 2
Mode of trial Triable either way
Maximum sentence On indictment 10 years. Summary 6 months and/or a £5,000 fine for offences committed before 12 March 2015 and an unlimited fine thereafter.[177] There are maximum fines for those aged under 18, see **14.38** in Volume 1.
CRUELTY TO ANIMALS, see the ANIMAL CRUELTY chapter.

231   CRUELTY TO CHILDREN

231.1

Guidelines see also the DOMESTIC VIOLENCE chapter.
Historical abuse The maximum sentence for Children and Young Persons Act 1933 s 1 was increased from 2 years to 10 years on 29 September 1988, Criminal Justice Act 1988 s 45(1).
Sexual Harm Prevention Orders There is a discretionary power to make this order when it is necessary to protect the public from sexual harm.[178]
The approach The important matters for sentence appear to be the defendant's intent, the injuries if any, the length of time over which the offences took place and most crucially of all the trauma of the victim(s). Judges stress their duty to protect the vulnerable and those who cannot protect themselves. Readers are invited to bear in mind the different intents required for each section and consider all the sections when considering a case.
See also the MANSLAUGHTER *Child victims* paras at **284.15**.

---

[177] Legal Aid, Sentencing and Punishment of Offenders Act 2012 s 85(1) and (4) and Legal Aid, Sentencing and Punishment of Offenders Act 2012 (Commencement No 11) Order 2015 2015/504
[178] Sexual Offences Act 2003 s 103A as inserted by Anti-social Behaviour, Crime and Policing Act 2014 Sch 5 para 2 and Sexual Offences Act 2003 Sch 5

Guidelines and judicial guidance

231.2 *Sentencing Guidelines Council guideline*

Assaults on Children and Cruelty to a Child Guideline 2008 page 5 para 7, see www.banksr.com Other Matters Guidelines tab This guideline applies to offenders aged 18 or over. The Court of Appeal has given a consistent message that an assault against a child will normally merit a custodial sentence. The Council's view is that such a presumption will not always be appropriate.

page 7 para 20 The gender of an offender is irrelevant for sentencing purposes.

page 9 para 33 A court must strike a balance between the need to reflect the serious view which society takes of the ill-treatment of very young children and the need to protect those children, and also the pressures upon immature and inadequate parents attempting to cope with the problems of infancy.

Aggravation

page 5 para 8 [In addition to the factors] listed in the *Overarching Principles: Seriousness Guideline 2004* (see **66.23** in Volume 1) many of those are most likely to be present where the defendant has caring responsibilities for the child: victim is particularly vulnerable, abuse of power, abuse of position of trust, an especially serious physical or psychological effect on the victim, even if unintended, presence of others e.g. relatives, especially other children, additional degradation of the victim. Additional aggravating factors are: sadistic behaviour, threats to prevent the victim reporting the offence, deliberate concealment of the victim from the authorities, and failure to seek medical help. The following additional factors will aggravate offences of child cruelty: targeting one particular child from the family, sadistic behaviour, threats to prevent the victim from reporting the offence, deliberate concealment of the victim from the authorities and failure to seek medical help.

Mitigation

page 6 para 12 [Where] an offender [seeks] to argue that any harm caused to the child amounted to lawful chastisement a court might form the view that the offender held a genuine belief that his or her actions amounted to no more than a legitimate form of physical punishment. The defence of lawful chastisement is available only in relation to a charge of common assault. Where that defence is not available, or, in relation to a charge of common assault, such a defence has failed, sentence for the offence would normally be approached in the same way as any other assault.

para 13 There will be circumstances where the defendant has been charged with an ABH and the court finds the defendant only intended to administer lawful chastisement to the child and the injury that was inflicted was neither intended nor foreseen by the defendant.

para 14 [This] finding of fact should result in a substantial reduction in sentence and should not normally result in a custodial sentence. Where not only was the injury neither intended nor foreseen, but was not even reasonably foreseeable, then a discharge might be appropriate.

page 11 para 43 Seeking medical help or bringing the situation to the notice of the authorities will mitigate offences.

The adverse effect of the sentence(s) on the victim

page 7 para 16 Where imprisonment of the offender deprives a child victim of his or her sole or main carer (and may result in the child being taken into care), it may punish and revictimise the child.

para 17 In view of the seriousness of the offence committed and the risk of further harm to the victim or other children, even though a child may be distressed by separation from a parent or carer, imposing a custodial sentence on the offender may be the only option. However, where sentencing options remain more open, the court should take into account the impact that a custodial sentence for the offender might have on the victim.

para 18 There will be cases where the child victim is the subject of concurrent care proceedings and, indeed, the child's future care arrangements may well have been determined by the time the offender is sentenced. Both the sentencing court and the Family Court need to be aware of the progress of any concurrent proceedings.

Offenders who have primary care responsibilities

page 7 para 21 In cases where an immediate custodial sentence of less than 12 months is justified, it is possible that a Suspended Sentence Order (where available) might be the most appropriate sentence. This could enable the offender, subject to the necessary risk assessment being made, to resume care for, or at least have regular contact with, the child and could also open up opportunities for imposing requirements to rehabilitate and support an offender in need.

Personal mitigation

page 13 para 59 The most relevant areas of personal mitigation are likely to be: mental illness/depression, inability to cope with the pressures of parenthood, lack of support, sleep deprivation, offender dominated by an abusive or stronger partner, extreme behavioural difficulties in the child, often coupled with a lack of support and inability to secure assistance or support services in spite of every effort having been made by the offender.

para 60 However, some of these factors, in particular sleep deprivation, lack of support and an inability to cope could be regarded as an inherent part of caring for children, especially when a child is very young. Thus, such factors could be put forward in mitigation by most carers charged with an offence of child cruelty. It follows that, before being accepted in mitigation, there must be evidence that these factors were present to a high degree and had an identifiable and significant impact on the offender's behaviour.

231.3   *Judicial guidance*

R v Andrew 1995 16 Cr App R (S) 899 A court must strike a balance between the need to reflect the serious view which society takes of the ill-treatment of very young children and the need to protect those children and also the pressure upon immature and inadequate parents attempting to cope with the problems of infancy.

R v Ali 2002 EWCA Crim 884, 2 Cr App R (S) 120 (p 542) D pleaded to ABH on a child. Held. The Lord Chief Justice gave some guidance in *R v Durkin* 1989 11 Cr App R (S) 313 where the defendant pleaded to a section 20 offence on a boy aged 19½ months. He said, "These cases are among the most difficult a judge has to deal with. First, it is necessary to punish. Second, it is necessary to provide some form of expiation[179] of the offence for the defendant. Third, it is necessary to satisfy the public conscience. Fourth, it is necessary to deter others by making it clear this behaviour will result in condign punishment."

R v Ahmed 2002 EWCA Crim 1398, 2003 1 Cr App R (S) 40 (p 187) The defendant pleaded to ABH. Held. Infants are entitled to care at the hands of those who, despite stresses and strains, nevertheless can contain their temper and control unwelcome impulses. For an attack upon a child, custody will almost always be inevitable. But here a community penalty would have been suitable.

R v F 2012 EWCA Crim 1928 Parenthood brings heavy responsibilities.

Children and Young Persons Act 1933 s 1, ABH and Offences Against the Person Act 1861 s 20

231.4

1) Children and Young Persons Act 1933 s 1
   Mode of trial Triable either way

---

[179] This means atonement.

Maximum sentence On indictment 10 years. Summary 6 months and/or a £5,000 fine for offences committed before 12 March 2015 and an unlimited fine thereafter.[180] There are maximum fines for those aged under 18, see **14.38** in Volume 1.

Extended sentences This offence is listed in Criminal Justice Act 2003 Sch 15. The court may pass a 2012 extended sentence (EDS) if there is a significant risk of serious harm from future specified offences and either: a) the defendant has a Criminal Justice Act 2003 Sch 15B conviction (applicable only to defendants aged 18+), or b) the offence would justify a determinate sentence of at least 4 years.[181]

Licensed premises Where an offence is committed on licensed premises, the court may prohibit defendants from entering those premises or any other specified premises without the express consent of the licensee etc.[182] The minimum period is 3 months and the maximum period is 2 years.[183] Violent Crime Reduction Act 2006 s 65 and Sch 5 repeals these powers and includes powers to make Drinking Banning Orders. Evaluation of the new powers continues. The repeal and the commencement of the new powers are not expected soon.

Sexual Harm Prevention Orders There is a discretionary power to make this order when it is necessary to protect the public from sexual harm.[184]

Children and vulnerable adults: barred lists Where the defendant is aged 18 or over he or she is automatically barred from engaging in regulated activity with vulnerable adults and with children.[185] The judge must tell the defendant that the Disclosure and Barring Service will include him or her in the barred lists.[186] The defendant may ask the Service to remove him or her from the lists.

2) ABH and Offences Against the Person Act 1861 s 20

Modes of trial Both offences triable either way

Maximum sentences On indictment 5 years. Summary 6 months and/or a £5,000 fine for offences committed before 12 March 2015 and an unlimited fine thereafter.[187] There are maximum fines for those aged under 18, see **14.38** in Volume 1.

For the ancillary powers, see the **ABH** and **OFFENCES AGAINST THE PERSON ACT 1861 s 20** chapters.

Guidelines and judicial guidance, see the *Sentencing Guidelines Council guideline* para at **231.2**.

231.5   *Crown Court statistics England and Wales   Section 1 cruelty*
Cruelty to children or neglect of children[188]

Year	Age	Plea	Total sen-tenced	Type of sentencing %						Average length of custody in months
				Dis-charge	Fine	Community sentence	Sus-pended sen-tence	Cus-tody	Oth-er	
2013 female	18-20	G	9	–	–	55.6	44.4	–	–	–
		NG	2	–	–	–	100.0	–	–	–
	21+	G	143	4.2	–	34.3	43.4	18.2	–	19.3
		NG	35	–	–	14.3	25.7	60	–	30.9

[180] Legal Aid, Sentencing and Punishment of Offenders Act 2012 s 85(1) and (4) and Legal Aid, Sentencing and Punishment of Offenders Act 2012 (Commencement No 11) Order 2015 2015/504

[181] Criminal Justice Act 2003 s 226A-226B as inserted by Legal Aid, Sentencing and Punishment of Offenders Act 2012 s 124

[182] Licensed Premises (Exclusion of Certain Persons) Act 1980 s 1(1)

[183] Licensed Premises (Exclusion of Certain Persons) Act 1980 s 1(3)

[184] Sexual Offences Act 2003 s 103A as inserted by Anti-social Behaviour, Crime and Policing Act 2014 Sch 5 para 2 and Sexual Offences Act 2003 Sch 5

[185] Safeguarding Vulnerable Groups Act 2006 s 2 and Sch 3 and Safeguarding Vulnerable Groups Act 2006 (Prescribed Criteria and Miscellaneous Provisions) Regulations 2009 2009/37 paras 4 and 6 and Sch paras 2 and 4

[186] Safeguarding Vulnerable Groups Act 2006 s 2 and Sch 3 para 25

[187] Legal Aid, Sentencing and Punishment of Offenders Act 2012 s 85(1) and (4) and Legal Aid, Sentencing and Punishment of Offenders Act 2012 (Commencement No 11) Order 2015 2015/504

[188] Although these figures do not add up to 100%, they are the figures provided by the Ministry of Justice. Ed.

Year	Age	Plea	Total sentenced	Type of sentencing %						Average length of custody in months
				Dis-charge	Fine	Community sentence	Sus-pended sen-tence	Cus-tody	Oth-er	
2013 male	18-20	G	4	–	–	25	50	25	–	8.0
		NG	0							
	21+	G	130	3.1	–	16.9	39.2	40.8	–	20
		NG	27	–	3.7	11.1	22.2	63	–	28.9
2014 female	18-20	G	9	–	–	44	44	11	–	not listed[189]
		NG	0							
	21+	G	198	2	–	25	53	21	–	15.8
		NG	28	–	–	11	43	39	7	30.8
2014 male	18-20	G	2	–	–	–	100	–	–	–
		NG	0							
	21+	G	153	3	–	10	44	42	–	17.9
		NG	25	–	–	20	16	64	–	26.2

For explanations about the statistics, see page 1-xii. For statistics for male and female defendants etc., see www.banksr.com Other Matters Statistics tab

231.6   *Sentencing Guidelines Council Guideline   Section 1 cruelty*

Assaults on Children and Cruelty to a Child Guideline 2008, see www.banksr.com Other Matters Guidelines tab Starting points and sentencing ranges

Note: The table below is clearly relevant where a defendant is convicted of ABH or Offences Against the Person Act 1861 s 20. Ed.

page 17 These starting points will apply to a first-time offender who has been convicted after a trial and has not been assessed as dangerous.

Nature of failure and harm	Starting point	Sentencing range
i) Serious cruelty over a period of time. ii) Serious long-term neglect. iii) Failure to protect a child from either of the above.	6 years' custody	5 to 9 years' custody
i) Series of assaults (the more serious the individual assaults and the longer the period over which they are perpetrated, the more serious the offence). ii) Protracted neglect or ill-treatment (the longer the period of ill-treatment or neglect and the longer the period over which it takes place, the more serious the offence). iii) Failure to protect a child from either of the above.	3 years' custody	2 to 5 years' custody
i) Assault(s) resulting in injuries consistent with ABH. ii) More than one incident of neglect or ill-treatment (but not amounting to long-term behaviour). iii) Single incident of long-term abandonment OR regular incidents of short-term abandonment (the longer the period of long-term abandonment or the greater the number of incidents of short-term abandonment, the more serious the offence). iv) Failure to protect a child from any of the above.	36 weeks' custody	26 weeks' to 2 years' custody

---
[189] Based on too few cases to be meaningful

Nature of failure and harm	Starting point	Sentencing range
i) Short-term neglect or ill-treatment. ii) Single incident of short-term abandonment. iii) Failure to protect a child from any of the above.	12 weeks' custody	Community Order (low) to 26 weeks' custody

Additional aggravating factors: 1 Targeting one particular child from the family 2 Sadistic behaviour 3 Threats to prevent the victim from reporting the offence 4 Deliberate concealment of the victim from the authorities 5 Failure to seek medical help. Additional mitigating factor: Seeking medical help or bringing the situation to the notice of the authorities.

231.7 *Magistrates' Court Sentencing Guidelines Section 1 cruelty*
Magistrates' Court Sentencing Guidelines 2008, see www.banksr.com Other Matters Guidelines tab page 47 The guideline mirrors the main guideline except '36 weeks' custody' and '26 weeks' to 2 years' custody' become 'Crown Court'.

231.8 *How to apply the guideline*
R v Mason 2013 EWCA Crim 1666, 2014 1 Cr App R (S) 78 (p 482) The circumstances in which a child might be wilfully neglected, and the consequences of that neglect in terms of potential and actual harm for the child, are infinitely variable and the descriptions in the guidelines necessarily blunt. In cases of wilful neglect, the particular circumstances of the case are of especial importance. They may well take a case, one way or the other, outside the category in the guidelines that might otherwise best describe it.

For more details of the case see **231.11**.

For more detail on how to apply the guidelines, see the **GUIDELINES** chapter in Volume 1.

231.9 *Cultural/Religious events*
R v Z 2008 EWCA Crim 2847 LCJ D was convicted of two counts of cruelty to a person under 16. Shia Muslim men are accustomed to mark the festival of Ashura by flagellating themselves with a zanjeer, an instrument which has light-weight curved blades attached to it. D was a devout Shia Muslim attending a local mosque. The centre management of that mosque ruled 48 hours before the festival that boys below the age of 16 would not be allowed to use the zanjeer. At the festival, D used the zanjeer on himself and allowed his two sons aged 15 and 13 to use it on themselves. The boys used it briefly and sustained cuts to their backs. When D thought they were about to do too much damage to themselves he intervened and stopped them. They did not need medical intervention. They later said that they had used it before on more than one occasion and were both keen to use it this time. The boys' mother was estranged from D. When she found out what had happened she contacted the police. On arrest D denied that he had forced his sons to take part in the ritual but accepted that he had allowed them to at their request. D, aged 44, was hard-working and of exemplary good character. He was living apart from his wife and their sons. There was monthly contact with the boys but there was considerable difficulty about it. A pre-sentence report said his motivation was his fervent religious belief but suggested that allowing the boys to participate in the ritual was his method of asserting familial control. He minimised his responsibility. Risk of reconviction was low. He had positive community links and was suitable for a community order. Held. He is of exemplary character and has personal difficulties, but he was on notice that the mosque elders advised that they deprecated what he allowed impressionable youths to do. Given their advice it is inevitable that this passed the custody threshold. **26 weeks suspended for 12 months** upheld.

231.10   *Danger, Exposing child to*

R v MG 2012 EWCA Crim 2150 D pleaded to cruelty. He was a heroin addict who was prescribed methadone. V's mother left V, aged 21 months, in D's care. V was on the bed in the bedroom next to D's bottle of methadone which was open. D left the bedroom and it is not clear for how long. V ingested some methadone. On D's return there was some liquid on the bed and round the child's mouth. D said he licked round V's mouth. D took no medical steps. V's mother returned home about 45 minutes later and all three of them went to a party. Initially V appeared to be fine. He later became unresponsive and lifeless. Only at this stage deal did D tell V's mother that the child might have taken some methadone. V was rushed to hospital some two hours after the incident. There was evidence that had there been 15 minutes' more delay V might well have died. Luckily he made a full recovery. The Judge sentenced D on the basis of initial carelessness followed by reckless disregard for the safety of the child and reckless placing V's life in danger by not summoning medical assistance. Held. The correct starting point was **18 months** so **12 months** with the plea not 2 years.

See also: *R v RR* 2012 EWCA Crim 250 (Plea to neglect. Anal and vaginal rape by partner on 15-year-old daughter. Allowed partner to stay overnight after social services removed him from the home. Good character. **1 year** not 2)

231.11   *Medical help, Delay in seeking/Not telling doctors the truth*

R v Haskey 2011 EWCA Crim 2208, 2012 1 Cr App R (S) 102 (p 616) D pleaded (full credit) to cruelty to a child. The case against her was that she did not seek prompt medical attention for her child, V, who was just short of her 2nd birthday. D and V lived with D's boyfriend, X, who was not V's father. X was abusive to D. D left V in his care and V suffered a burn on her foot, caused by her foot being held against a hot kettle for several seconds. D did not immediately telephone an ambulance when she discovered the injury. A medical examination found numerous bruises under the left eye, on the right cheek, behind the right ear lobe, on the left forearm, left buttock and left thigh. D said she did not know how the bruises had been caused. A report said that D suffered from a personality disorder, was immature and needed to address her alcohol use and anger management. D, aged 23 at appeal, had various convictions for violence and dishonesty, and three cautions for violence, as recent as three months prior to this incident. Held. This was correctly categorised as a Level 2 case. The injuries went well beyond ABH into GBH. D must have known that V was being physically abused but did nothing about it. D's age, immaturity, social background and abusive relationship were mitigation. **18 months** not 2 years.

R v MG 2012 EWCA Crim 2150, see **231.10**.

R v H 2013 EWCA Crim 453 D pleaded (full credit) to cruelty. She was the mother of V, who was four months old. She also had two sons from previous relationships, aged 6 years and 2 years. They lived with D's then boyfriend and co-accused, W, who was aged 20 at appeal. In April 2011,V had serious scalding to her face. A consultant plastic surgeon considered that it had been caused by the submersion of her face into hot liquid, probably hot water. The area around her mouth had escaped injury, probably because she had a dummy in her mouth. W eventually admitted that he had held V's face down in a hot bath thereby causing the injury. D was sentenced on the basis that she was asleep in bed at the time the injury was inflicted but was informed of the cause of the injury when she awoke. W's initial account (adopted by D to hospital staff and police) was that W had spilled hot tea over V. W was reluctant for D to take V to hospital as he did not want to get into trouble. The delay lasted about five hours. V was X-rayed and fractures of the bones of her lower legs were found dating from a maximum of 18 days before the scalding injury. They were typical of non-accidental injuries. V made an excellent recovery. W pleaded to ABH (biting V), section 18 (the scalding) and cruelty. GBH (fracturing V's legs) was left to lie on the file. He received 8½ years. D had two convictions in 2010 for battery and obstructing a police officer. She received a community order and a Restraining Order. The pre-sentence report noted that D appeared unaware and even disinterested in the pain that V must have suffered. D and W's lives were chaotic and drugs and alcohol played a major part. D had offered to be a prosecution witness against W. Held. Immediate custody was inevitable. D fell to be sentenced for a relatively short period of neglect. It was in Category 4 of the guideline. But the severity of V's injuries and V's very young age increased the starting point significantly in excess of the range. However, starting at 32 months, as the Judge did, was not justified. That would have been appropriate for a protracted period of neglect. Starting at 18 months, **12 months** not 21.

R v Mason 2013 EWCA Crim 1666, 2014 1 Cr App R (S) 78 (p 482) D pleaded to cruelty to a child by wilful neglect. D lived with his wife, W, and their son, V. D worked during the day and W worked during the evenings. V was born in January 2009. In September 2009, Social Services conducted an investigation as a result of bruising to his face and a cut to his lip. W explained that the injuries were caused by V rolling into the bars of his cot. In November 2010, W went to work leaving D at home with the two children in his charge. When she returned, V was sick and drowsy, but W did not think that he was particularly unwell. Just after 3 am V was unwell. W thought he was fitting. An ambulance arrived at about 4 am and the medics found V on the bed, with a dark bruise over the top of his right eye and bruising to one of his ears. He was flushed and whimpering and had a decreased level of consciousness. He was described as being 'a little floppy' and was shaking. D said nothing about what had caused the bruises. V was urgently admitted to hospital, arriving at 4.30 am. A specialist paediatric team was called in. W told the medical staff that nothing untoward had happened to V that evening. D said V had cried on one occasion whilst W was out but had quickly settled and there had been no cause for concern. A consultant paediatrician noticed the bruising on V's head and also some older bruising on his abdomen, back and leg. He then asked for a CT scan, which subsequently showed swelling of the brain and damage to the skull which was thought to be a fracture. At 9 am V was intubated and ventilated and transferred to a specialist intensive care unit. The consultant told D and W that he thought their account was insufficient to account for the degree of bruising or V's evolving neurological picture. He said the most likely cause was trauma to the head. D still said nothing about anything occurring the previous evening. The police were alerted to the possibility of a non-accidental injury to a child and attended the hospital. They spoke to D, who repeated the account he had given to the medical staff. He was subsequently arrested and interviewed, again repeating that nothing untoward had occurred. V remained in a critical state with his cranial pressure increasing and his condition worsening. Two days later, a nurse pressed D and W to tell her if anything had happened to V that evening. D subsequently told his mother that he had sat V on a kitchen work surface and turned away. When he turned back, V was on the floor, whimpering, with a red mark on his head. D said he put a cold flannel on V's head, given him a drink and thereafter he appeared to be all right. He said he felt stupid about his inattention and frightened because he did not know whether V's injury was related to the fall. He was frightened for himself following the Social Services investigation into what they suspected was non-accidental bruising. His mother told D he had to tell someone about the fall, but he did not. Three days later, V was certified as dead. He was 22 months old. D subsequently contacted the police and told them about the fall. The post mortem revealed damage to the skull but not a fracture. Expert evidence stated that the fall could have caused the damage to the skull. The delayed reaction (suffering a collapse some nine hours later) was improbable but possible. The medical evidence could not form the basis of a charge relating to the death. D was charged with cruelty based only on his failure to tell anyone that V had suffered a recent impact to the head, however that impact had occurred. A paediatric neurosurgeon said D's failure to tell the medical staff about the fall had delayed optimal treatment by about five hours. He said it was possible, but not certain, that earlier ventilation would have prevented V's death, but had V survived, it was likely that he would have been permanently and severely disabled. D was aged 33 and had no relevant convictions. D and W had another child subsequent to V's death. The child was subject to care proceedings in Ireland and it was argued that any custodial sentence should be suspended as D wished to be with his partner to help in her attempts to obtain residence of the child. Held. The guideline suggested a starting point of 12 weeks for a Category 4 offence characterised by short-term neglect or ill-treatment. However, the circumstances in which a child might be wilfully neglected…are infinitely variable and the descriptions in the guidelines necessarily blunt. In cases of wilful neglect, the particular circumstances of the case are of especial importance. D's criminal failure lay in failing to tell the medics straightaway that V had fallen from the work surface onto the floor. He withheld that information solely out of fear for himself. He told no one, apart from his mother, until after the child had died. His culpability was high. To an unquantifiable extent, D's failing gave a higher risk of serious injury or death, but it was very likely that V would have died in any event. The fact that death ensued was not of any substantial weight for the purposes of sentencing. D's remorse was deep and genuine. 15 months not **10 months** and notwithstanding the issue of care proceedings, it was not appropriate to suspend the sentence.

See also: *R v Flatley* 2013 EWCA Crim 1808 (Plea to cruelty. Husband caused injury to their six-week-old baby, including spinal fracture (receiving 30 months). Baby in very considerable pain for a week. Defendant claimed she only realised just before the end of the week when the baby was taken to hospital. No convictions. Both her children put into care. Aged 21. **6 months** not 9.)

R v Barley 2014 EWCA Crim 1609, 2 Cr App R (S) 86 (p 663) (Plea. D's partner, P, shook and threw V hard into his cot. V was D's son, aged 10 months. Baby taken to hospital. No outward signs of V's injuries. D lied to have V successfully discharged from hospital. Carried on lying each time medical help sought. V died of vertebrae fractures about four weeks later. Prior to assault, P's behaviour towards V and his own children entirely proper. P received 8 years for manslaughter. D, aged 23 and of good character, a loving mother, but had limited intellect and past mental health issues. **6 months**, not 15. Some judges might not have given immediate custody.)

R v F 2014 EWCA Crim 2742, 2015 1 Cr App R (S) 46 (p 337) (Pleas (10% credit) to cruelty to a child (section 1). Iron applied deliberately to arm twice. Superficial injuries but painful. Mother, aged 30, and stepfather, aged 27, could give no explanation. 30 hours' wait for treatment and after prompt from social services. Not knowing who did act, both have to be sentenced on basis of failing to obtain treatment. 8 months for each upheld.)

Old case: *R v KB* 2010 EWCA Crim 2339 (**15 months**)

For a summary of this case see the 10th edition of this book.

231.12   *Inappropriate medical treatment*

R v MB 2013 EWCA Crim 910, 2014 1 Cr App R (S) 29 (p 173) D was convicted of cruelty to a person under 16. She was a Nigerian national who arrived in the UK in 2012 when heavily pregnant. After the birth, she wanted to have the child circumcised according to her Muslim faith and Nigerian custom. She had two appointments to have the child circumcised but failed to make them. She was given a phone number of a woman who performed circumcisions at her home with scissors. Later, the child's nappy was full of blood. This was noticed by shop staff when she was stopped on suspicion of shoplifting. She had been instructed to keep the child at home for 5-7 days. She had in fact taken him shopping the same day as the circumcision. He required surgical repair to stem the bleeding and fluid resuscitation because of the blood loss. It was potentially life threatening. She had no convictions and was generally a good mother to her children. Held. It was difficult to fit this into any of the relevant guidelines. The Judge was entitled to consider that there had been real neglect of the child. A custodial sentence was appropriate in principle. This was a case of neglect and not intentional harm. She was cavalier about the interests of her child. **4 months,** not 10, would properly reflect the gravity of the offending and would enable immediate release.

231.13   *Leaving a child or children unsupervised*
R v Ryan 2011 EWCA Crim 1434, 2012 1 Cr App R (S) 40 (p 235) D pleaded (full
credit) to cruelty to a child under 16. She was caring for her son, V, aged 5 months. She
went to the supermarket twice, with V, and purchased two bottles of wine. She drank
them. She returned a third time, leaving V alone at home, and purchased a third bottle.
She drank it and was very drunk. She later became aware she could not find V. She
enlisted the help of neighbours, and they searched for V. Neighbours noticed excrement
on V's cot, and on D's arms and hands. V's father returned to help search. He found V
between a bed and a wall, face down in plastic bags, covered in excrement. He died. The
cause of death was not established, but it was accepted that D was responsible. D had
been diagnosed with post-natal depression two months previously. She was dependent
on alcohol and had been drunk when caring for V on previous occasions. She concealed
her problem from her partner. D was aged 39 at appeal and had no convictions. Held.
The guideline really does not cover the facts of this case. This was an incident waiting to
happen, as D was dependent on alcohol and sought to cover it up. That put V at risk. **16
months** not 2 years.
R v NT 2012 EWCA Crim 759 D pleaded to cruelty to a child. In 2000, aged 17, she
formed a relationship with F. In 2003, they had a child, S. In 2009, the relationship had
allegedly become violent and D was forced to flee, with S, to a refuge. D found a job but
struggled with child care. She would leave S on her own for a period of hours after
collecting her from school. From Wednesday morning until Sunday night, D effectively
abandoned S, who was aged 6 at the time. D returned on Friday evening and provided
one meal. S had otherwise been eating Monster Munch crisps and yoghurt and drinking
chocolate milkshake. When D didn't return, she knocked on her neighbour's door. She
was cold and distressed. D claimed she had left S for only a matter of hours. The
pre-sentence report noted an inversion of the normal relationship where S felt responsible for D. D had a cannabis caution and bail offence conviction in 2011. She had served
on remand the equivalent of an 8-month prison sentence. S was settled with her
grandmother and D was thereafter no longer the sole carer of S. Held. The gravamen of
the offending was the single incident of long-term abandonment. There is an interest in
alleviating any sense of guilt felt by S and in restoring her relations with D. The
background is stable, enabling D to fulfil her obligations to S. **10 months suspended** not
18 months.
R v EMSG 2014 EWCA Crim 225 D was convicted of one count of neglect and pleaded
to one count of neglect. The police attended D's address to report the arrest of her
husband for drink/driving. V, aged 2½, opened the front door wearing an unfastened
babygro. D was asleep in the chair, drunk. A breathalyser revealed she had 138 µg per
100 ml of breath (approximately four times the drink/drive limit). There were signs of
drinking all around and the room smelt heavily of cigarette smoke. D was interviewed
and bailed, on condition that she seek assistance. She was permitted to keep custody of
V. Two months later, she burst into a neighbour's flat with V in a pram. It was 2 degrees
but V had no hat or gloves. Her hands were 'frozen' and her nappy heavily soiled. The
neighbour called the police and a Police Protection Order was put into effect. The
following day, officers arrived at D's address. D arrived 20 minutes later smelling
strongly of drink, not knowing where V was. She was arrested. In the intervening hours,
she had abandoned the pram with V in it and made no attempt to contact anybody to
report her absence. V had been abandoned for almost 11 hours, from 11.15 pm until
10 am. D had convictions for shoplifting in 2011 and 2012 and a caution for 'being
drunk while in charge of a child'. The pre-sentence report noted that she did not accept
responsibility for her actions. She posed a medium risk to V but not to others. Held.
When in drink, D lost sight of the need to care for her child and on the second of the two
occasions, abandoned her on a cold winter's night in circumstances where her child
could well have come to significant harm. There was no evidence, however, that V had
come to harm. The local authority subsequently made arrangements for V to be adopted.

D opposed that process and proceedings were pending. This case should have been dealt with as falling within the third most serious category for which the range is 26 weeks to 2 years. 15 months consecutive to 3 months **making 18 months**, not 27 months.

Note: Taking into account the length of time V was in danger, the fact that the child could have died (when the charge would have been manslaughter), the number of incidents and the previous conviction, it appears the sentencing Judge correctly focused on the danger to the child whereas the Court of Appeal focused on the interests of the mother. Ed.

See also: *R v S* 2013 EWCA Crim 1491 (Late pleas to cruelty (×2). Children aged 4 and 5 living in utter squalor. Dirty, smelling of urine and excrement and obese but they appeared friendly and happy. Social worker described conditions as the worst she had ever seen. Child protection plan put in place. Continued to neglect the children. Aged 46. No convictions. **12 months** was appropriate, not 2 years.)

Old cases: Best ignored as there is now less emphasis on the parents' situation and more emphasis on the protection of the victims. Ed.

231.14   Neglect

R v R 2011 EWCA Crim 1969 D pleaded to cruelty to a person under 16. Police raided D's house. D and her partner, who were both drug users, had five children aged between 3 and 10. The children were dirty and smelly but not malnourished. The youngest child was considered to be suffering considerable neglect. Three children had bad burn marks although it was accepted these were not inflicted deliberately. Rotten food was discarded around the property and mice and mouse droppings were also discovered. A crack pipe and other drug paraphernalia were found in the middle of the room. In custody, D had remained drug-free. Held. There is a distinction to be drawn between wilful ill-treatment and neglect. This was a case of neglect and the headline term 'cruelty' is misleading. 6 months suspended with curfew and other requirements, not 2 years' imprisonment.

R v O 2013 EWCA Crim 232 D pleaded to child cruelty (×3). D lived with V1, V2 and V3, aged 6, 5 and 4 respectively. Police were called to D's address for an unrelated matter. The officer saw V1, V2 and V3 lying on a double bed with no pillows. The room smelled strongly of vomit, there were three or four piles of vomit on the bed and more vomit on the floor. The mattress was heavily stained. The officer asked why there was vomit, to which D said to the children, "Why didn't you tell me?" The officer began to look around and D came up behind him. There was a struggle and the children screamed in distress. D was restrained. The living conditions in the house were described by police as squalid and disgusting. There were piles of rubbish and rotting food, discarded bottles and cans. The only sign of heating was a single bar electric fire downstairs. Two other bedrooms were unusable. There was a quantity of rubbish in one and the smell of excrement in the other. Downstairs was serviceable but very dirty. The children told the police that they got their food from the fridge. The fridge smelled horrible and contained rotting and out-of-date food. The children warned the officers not to open the freezer. When the officer did so, the smell was quite dreadful. It caused him to gag and he thought he was going to be sick. One of the children told him, "I am usually sick after eating out of there and I have already been sick once today." The children had been placed on the child protection register for neglect in 2010. They were examined by a paediatrician in August 2011, who noticed they were grubby and had missed their vaccine and dental appointments. They had rotten teeth and severe dental decay. Social services instituted a voluntary child protection plan but subsequently D did not allow social services officers into her address. V1 and V2 were re-examined after the police attended the address. They were still dirty despite having been bathed. V3 was too distressed to be seen at that stage. One of the children had gaps in her teeth where just brown pegs were left. They had still not received their vaccinations. The Crown's case was that the cruelty was due to indifference or apathy resulting from D's drug or alcohol dependence. D had six previous offences, two of which were for shoplifting. They had been dealt with by community penalties or conditional discharges. D made an effort to overcome her drug addiction, but her alcohol problems continued. Held. This was a serious example of child neglect. There was, however, no deliberate infliction of harm or sadistic cruelty. D did not have the requisite parenting skills. The appropriate starting point was **3 years**. With 25% credit for the plea, **2 years 3 months** not 3 years.

R v EMSG 2014 EWCA Crim 225 D was convicted of one count of neglect and pleaded to one count of neglect. The police attended D's address to report the arrest of her husband for drink/driving. V, aged 2½, opened the front door wearing an unfastened babygro. D was asleep in the chair, drunk. A breathalyser revealed she had 138 µg per 100 ml of breath (approximately four times the drink/drive limit). There were signs of drinking all around and the room smelt heavily of cigarette smoke. D was interviewed and bailed, on condition that she seek assistance. She was permitted to keep custody of V. Two months later, she burst into a neighbour's flat with V in a pram. It was 2 degrees but V had no hat or gloves. Her hands were 'frozen' and her nappy heavily soiled. The neighbour called the police and a Police Protection Order was put into effect. The following day, officers arrived at D's address. D arrived 20 minutes later smelling strongly of drink, not knowing where V was. She was arrested. In the intervening hours, she had abandoned the pram with V in it and made no attempt to contact anybody to report her absence. V had been abandoned for almost 11 hours, from 11.15 pm until 10 am. D had convictions for shoplifting in 2011 and 2012 and a caution for 'being drunk while in charge of a child'. The pre-sentence report noted that she did not accept responsibility for her actions. She posed a medium risk to V but not to others. Held. When in drink, D lost sight of the need to care for her child and on the second of the two occasions, abandoned her on a cold winter's night in circumstances where her child could well have come to significant harm. There was no evidence, however, that V had come to harm. The local authority subsequently made arrangements for V to be adopted. D opposed that process and proceedings were pending. This case should have been dealt with as falling within the third most serious category for which the range is 26 weeks to 2 years. 15 months consecutive to 3 months **making 18 months**, not 27 months.

Note: Taking into account the length of time V was in danger, the fact that the child could have died (when the charge would have been manslaughter), the number of incidents and the previous conviction, it appears the sentencing Judge correctly focused on the danger to the child whereas the Court of Appeal focused on the interests of the mother. Ed.

See also: *R v S* 2013 EWCA Crim 1491 (Late pleas to cruelty (×2). Children aged 4 and 5 living in utter squalor. Dirty, smelling of urine and excrement and obese but they appeared friendly and happy. Social worker described conditions as the worst she had ever seen. Child protection plan put in place. Continued to neglect the children. Aged 46. No convictions. **12 months** was appropriate, not 2 years.)

Att-Gen's Ref Nos 53 and 62 of 2014 2014 EWCA Crim 2262[190] (Both defendants neglected their five young children over many years. Inadequate diet, children underweight and malnourished. Very poor care, with a refusal to engage with healthcare workers. D1, aged 42 and D2, aged 36, both with no relevant convictions. Held. This was neglect of the worst possible kind. We start at at least 7 years. With plea, **6 years** for both as global sentences.)

Old cases: Best ignored as there is now less emphasis on the parents' situation and more emphasis on the protection of the victims. Ed.

231.15   *Punishments etc. to children, Unlawful*

Assaults on Children and Cruelty to a Child Guideline 2008, see www.banksr.com Other Matters Guidelines tab page 6 para 12 This guideline applies to offenders aged 18 or over. [Where] an offender [seeks] to argue that any harm caused to the child amounted to lawful chastisement a court might form the view that the offender held a genuine belief that his or her actions amounted to no more than a legitimate form of physical

---

[190] There are two Att-Gen's Ref No 53 of 2014. They are in fact different cases. The other is 2014 EWCA Crim 1929.

punishment. The defence of lawful chastisement is available only in relation to a charge of common assault. Where that defence is not available, or, in relation to a charge of common assault, such a defence has failed, sentence for the offence would normally be approached in the same way as any other assault. para 13 There will be circumstances where the defendant has been charged with an ABH and the court finds the defendant only intended to administer lawful chastisement to the child and the injury that was inflicted was neither intended nor foreseen by the defendant. para 14 [This] finding of fact should result in a substantial reduction in sentence and should not normally result in a custodial sentence. Where not only was the injury neither intended nor foreseen, but was not even reasonably foreseeable, then a discharge might be appropriate. page 11 para 43 The following additional factor will mitigate offences of child cruelty: seeking medical help or bringing the situation to the notice of the authorities.

R v LA 2010 EWCA Crim 1314 D and her partner pleaded to ill-treatment of a child. They had a boy, aged 4, and a girl, aged 2. The girl had been annoying her father and he placed her on the 'naughty step' as a punishment. The child's misbehaviour continued. The father then took a reel of duct tape, sat the girl on the sofa, passed the tape across her legs, abdomen and chest and put a piece across her mouth, apparently loosely. One of her parents took a photograph. This photograph was then uploaded onto Facebook, with the caption 'The naughty step did not work'. This photo was seen and reported to the police. The children were removed by Social Services and an intensive investigation was conducted. The outcome was positive and the children were in due course returned. The parents were genuinely sorry for what they had done. The Judge was referred to the *Assaults on Children and Cruelty to a Child Guideline 2008*, judging the incident to fall into Category 3 of 4, the second-least serious. He said that the photo was a "shocking image" and that in other circumstances it might have been put there by the sadistic, or as an indication of rotten parenting. This was not the case. Held. This was a single act of ill-treatment and not on any view analogous with assaults resulting in actual harm, repeated neglect or ill-treatment or long-term abandonment (Category 3 requirements). The appropriate range was a low-level community order to 6 months' custody. With the plea, a **community order** requiring 12 months' supervision, not 28 weeks' imprisonment, suspended.

R v J 2014 EWCA Crim 1442 D was convicted of 23 child cruelty offences against his three children and one stepchild. The counts were sample counts pleaded from the children's date of birth to their 16th birthday. This made the dates from 1982 to 2000. He hit the children with a belt and with implements, sometimes every day. He traced the mother and the children when they were in refuges and carried on the violence. The children's upbringing had been dominated by domestic violence meted out for D's own gratification. D was effectively of good character and was now aged 49. The Judge sentenced the defendant to 30 months for each child and made the sentences consecutive. Held. Our summary can convey little about the appalling nature of these crimes. We apply the *Assaults on Children and Cruelty to a Child Guideline 2008* and *R v H* 2011 EWCA Crim 2753, 2012 2 Cr App R (S) 21 (p 88). These offences would merit **10 years**. However, because of the change in maximum sentence from 2 years to 10 years, we reduce it to 8½ years.

Old cases: *R v Hobbs* 2006 EWCA Crim 1597 (**4 months suspended**) *R v G* 2006 EWCA Crim 3097, 2007 2 Cr App R (S) 14 (p 63) (**2 years 9 months**) *R v Reynolds and Others Re L* 2007 EWCA Crim 538, 2 Cr App R (S) 87 (p 553) (**2 years**) *R v S* 2008 EWCA Crim 1662, 2009 1 Cr App R (S) 40 (p 220) (**community order**) For a summary of the first case see the 7th edition of this book, for the second case see the 8th edition and for the last case see the 9th edition.

231.16   *Selling children*

R v P 2011 EWCA Crim 2825, 2012 2 Cr App R (S) 13 (p 53) D and MJ were convicted of conspiring to commit cruelty to a person under 16 and holding a person in slavery. Their daughter, Y, was aged 11 months. D planned to sell Y. MJ was married to DP. MJ told an acquaintance that he had a baby for sale. A newspaper sting operation was set up. Meetings between MJ, D and the prospective buyers took place. Y was present. The price was agreed at £35,000. After their arrest, D alleged that MJ had raped her. He was 20 years her senior and known to D and DP as 'Uncle'. D lied to police upon arrest. D, aged 29, was of good character. Held. This case does not sit easily with the guideline as it is concerned with actions that have been taken, not with the risk of harm if intended actions had been carried out. It is of some relevance that the couple posing as prospective buyers were presented as a happy and successful married couple who would bring up the child well. D was an active participant, but in some ways a victim also. There is much room for mercy in this case. **4 years** not 7.

231.17   Sexual attacks, Assisting

R v Sawdon 2012 EWCA Crim 1660 D was convicted of cruelty to a child (×2) and arranging etc. a child sex offence (×2) and causing a child under 13 to engage in sexual intercourse. D appealed only against one of the child cruelty counts. She met and began a relationship with H. H was convicted of rape (×4), sexual assault (×4), assault on a female (×6), making indecent photographs and possessing an extreme pornographic image. He received 21 years. D had two daughters, G and C, aged 6 and 17 months. G informed D that H had been having sex with her. D then told her aunt that she had 'found child porn on [H's] laptop'. G and C were taken into care. G thereafter described how H had anally raped her while D was present and how D had said, "…If [H] wants to have sex with you, let him have sex with you". D had smacked G when she wet the bed, made her sleep in the wet bed, threw a hairbrush at her and cut her with a knife. The count against D was that D knew G was being sexually abused and failed to stop it or respond to the complaints. There was a further incident when D woke G and carried her to H's bed, upon which H put his penis in G's mouth. The Judge said this was one of the worst cases of breach of trust he had seen in 30 years and placed the cruelty count in the highest category. D had betrayed her child in an utterly appalling and deliberately cruel way. D had no previous convictions. Held. D's wilful cruelty to G extended over a substantial period when H was carrying out numerous and utterly horrific sexual offences on her daughter. Notwithstanding the horrific nature of the offences and the gross breach of trust, there was no element of real physical violence and no sadistic element. 9 years, so close to the maximum permissible, was manifestly excessive. **7 years** substituted. Overall sentence of **10 years** unaltered.

Note: It is unlikely that Parliament would have envisaged this type of conduct when they fixed the maximum sentence. Many would consider that the wrong offence was charged and that the original sentence made sense. Ed.

See also: *R v RR* 2012 EWCA Crim 250 (Plea to neglect. Anal and vaginal rape by partner on 15-year-old daughter. Allowed partner to stay overnight after social services had removed him from the home. Good character. **1 year** not 2)

231.18   Victim dies

Examples: *R v Sutherland* 2010 EWCA Crim 1855, 2011 1 Cr App R (S) 90 (p 541) (Plea. Mother of baby, aged 13 months, who had been dead for two or three days. Baby covered in faeces with numerous injuries. Baby otherwise well cared for. 'Gross neglect'. Cause of death unknown. D had a depressive disorder and suffered abuse as a child and an adult. **2 years 3 months**)

R v Mason 2013 EWCA Crim 1666, 2014 1 Cr App R (S) 78 (p 482) (D failed to tell hospital of fall. Victim may have died in any event. Factor not of any substantial weight, see **231.11**)

See also the **MANSLAUGHTER** *Child victims* paras at **284.15**.

231.19   Violence to child aged less than 2 years

Note: ABH offences are listed in these violence paragraphs. Ed.

R v W 2011 EWCA Crim 340 D pleaded to section 20. She had got angry with her eight-month-old child, shaken him and dropped him on the carpet. He then became unresponsive and was struggling to breathe. She persisted with the story that she had returned to the bedroom, after leaving him for a short while, to find him in that state. He was left with permanent and significant brain injury and total blindness. He would also need 24-hour care and care for the rest of his life. For two months her husband had been under suspicion, which caused him great distress. There was no evidence of previous abuse. D, aged 38, had no convictions. Held. The injuries caused were truly catastrophic. That should be marked by a significant sentence of imprisonment. **2 years** was not in the least excessive.

R v S 2011 EWCA Crim 2410 D pleaded to ABH. She was in a relationship with P and had two children by him: R, the eight-year-old complainant, and S, a six-year-old son. D and P never cohabited and the children lived with D. A previous allegation of assault had led to an agreement that P would collect the children from school. P asked D to collect the children and she did so. She was witnessed as being drunk. At home, with D, there was an argument about the playing of a computer game. D threw her stiletto at R, striking her in the face around the right eye. R fell to the ground. D then stamped on her leg and twisted her arm. The person who had seen D drunk had contacted the police and they attended to make a welfare check. They noted R's injuries and called an ambulance. R was taken to hospital and kept overnight. D was drunk when arrested and made reference to hitting R with her shoe harder than she intended. She made no reference to the stamping. R suffered 14 injuries including a blackened eye, a bruise above the eye, and scratches to the left arm, the side of her body and her ear. S did not witness the causing of the injuries but was present in the home at the time. He was distressed. D had convictions for theft, breach of a Reparation Order and threatening behaviour. She had cautions for battery and child cruelty in respect of R, when she threw a glass at R which cut her arm. Held. This offence was not just a momentary loss of temper instantly regretted. D went on to stamp on R's leg and twist her arm. In addition, she was drunk at a time when she was the child's primary carer, and did not seek any assistance for R. The earlier caution puts an additional dimension on the seriousness of this case. **2 years** was high but not manifestly excessive.

R v M 2011 EWCA Crim 2673 D pleaded (full credit) to ABH (×2) against his sons who were aged 9 and 10 at appeal. The elder child told his teacher at school that his leg hurt. He showed the teacher very severe bruising at the top of his left leg, which he said had been caused by D striking him with a lead from a PlayStation. He also had scratches on his neck, caused by D. The younger child confirmed that D had struck him and his brother with an electrical flex and plug because they had forgotten to replace the lid on a carton of juice. The younger brother had a large bruise on his shin, injuries on his buttocks, bruising on his arm, the back of his legs, his back and his hands. D was quick to admit the offences to the police. D did not have a history of violent offending. Held. The offence was aggravated by the breach of trust involved, and the fact that similar offences were committed against two children in the presence of each other. Starting at **18 months**, with the plea and prompt admissions **12 months** not 20.

R v T 2013 EWCA Crim 2015 D was convicted at a retrial of section 20 (×2) and wilful neglect. V was D's son. He was aged 7½ weeks. At some point during the day, V was under the sole care of D. D claimed that V had slipped from his grasp and fallen head first onto the floor, striking his head on the bed frame as he fell. V was examined at the hospital and no injury was found. Subsequently, when V was aged 11½ weeks, V was again injured whilst under the sole care of D. D claimed V had fallen head first from the sofa where D had placed him in order to change his nappy. D called 999 and a paramedic arrived and took V to hospital. By the time he arrived at hospital V had suffered seizures. A CT scan of V's brain revealed the injuries V had suffered. There were chronic bilateral subdural haematomas caused during the first incident and separate bilateral haemorrhages caused during the second incident. He was transferred to a specialist neurosurgical intensive care unit where he remained for some time until he was discharged into the care of foster parents. D had shaken V when holding him by the chest region. The neglect charge related to D's behaviour when he took V to the hospital after the first incident. He failed to give a proper account of V's symptoms, in particular those consistent with him having had a fit. D was aged 34 at the time of the offences. He had no previous convictions. D lived with V's mother and her two children from a separate relationship. They separated after the commencement of proceedings. Medical reports suggested that V would be unaffected by the incidents in the long term. Held. The two assaults taken together would fall into the second category of the guideline. These were very significant and serious offences. They were four weeks apart and perpetrated against a very young baby. They could have resulted in terrible injury or death. A sentence at the upper end of the appropriate range was called for. With totality in mind, 5½ years was manifestly excessive. A sentence beyond the guideline was not justified. **4½ years** was proper. The 2-year sentence for the first assault would remain. Reducing the consecutive 3-year sentence to 2½ years for the second assault and making the 6-month consecutive sentence for cruelty concurrent was appropriate.

R v MM 2014 EWCA Crim 1622 D pleaded to child cruelty (25% credit). D's seven-month-old girl, V, fell asleep and after 40 minutes D's partner returned home to find V's ear was very red. V was examined at a hospital and the redness lasted for over nine hours. V's ear had swelling, three bruises and discolouration which it was agreed amounted to ABH. D said V fell asleep on her rattle but medical opinion disagreed. In interview D accepted pulling V's ear when trying to feed her in frustration. D worked night shifts and his partner had been ill. D was aged 23 at sentence and of positive good character. Social services had no concerns and D was having regular unsupervised access to V. Held. The Judge was entitled to pass immediate custody but suspension should have been seriously considered. **5 months** not 9.

Note: Whether the access was required because the child had been taken into care (which seems unlikely) or because his relationship had broken up is not revealed. Ed.

Old case: *R v KB* 2010 EWCA Crim 2339 (**15 months**) For a summary of the case see the 10th edition of this book.

231.20   *Violence to child aged 2-5 years*
Att-Gen's Ref No 59 of 2014 2014 EWCA Crim 1926 D was convicted of cruelty to her children (×3). V1 was aged 12 years, V2 10 years and V3 18 months old. V1, although terrified of the possible consequences flowing from her allegations, disclosed that D had hit her twice on the head with a bottle, causing swelling and bleeding. D had assaulted V1 from the age of 2 years including rubbing chillies in her eyes and vagina, pulling her hair and biting her hands, leaving her unable to write. Punishments were meted out for minor misbehaviour. It was also disclosed that D had assaulted V2 and V3 over a sustained period. When the victims were examined at hospital, V1 then lied about the multiple scars on her forearms as D was listening. A doctor concluded the scars were consistent with V1 and V2 being burnt with hair straighteners. V2 had several small scars on her upper body, which were compatible with being stabbed with a pen, and hair straightener burns. V2 was slapped across the face, her hair was pulled and she was locked in the bathroom. D told V2 to give false explanations to cover up the injuries. V3 was found uninjured but, when she was a baby, had previously been repeatedly slapped on the face, back and legs and was thrown across the bed. At the hospital D made a phone call in Bengali and when police later called, the bottle used against V1 was missing. The children were then placed in foster care, but during a supervised visit D told V1 not to say anything. D's violence left her children 'really scared'. D was aged 35 at sentence and of good character, but posed a serious risk to children. She provided supposedly innocent explanations for the injuries and showed no remorse. Held. This was a deeply troubling breach of D's duty towards her own offspring and her violence was sometimes administered after a period of reflection. There were aggravating factors. The psychological scars will probably be profound and the physical scars will be borne throughout the older children's lives. This case is, at the least, towards the top end of the second bracket. **5 years**, not 2½ in all.

Att-Gen's Ref No 73 of 2014 2014 EWCA Crim 1932 D was convicted of cruelty to a child (×2). The offences were carried out over a period of five years or so, beginning in 1997, when V, her daughter, was aged 5. V is now in her twenties. The abuse included hitting V to the stomach and other areas where bruising was not visible, pinching, kicking and slapping V. D also threw objects at V, forced her to take cold baths, walked V to and from school using a dog lead and pulled V's hair. D had also blamed V for her problems and described her as "a cancer". D said that she should have aborted V and wished that V was dead. D threatened to kill V if she told anyone. It seemed to V that D took pleasure in hurting her. The abuse ended only when D left the family home. V told her father and stepmother after D repeatedly tried to contact her when she had turned 18. V was left with psychological scars which V continued to endure. V suffered from low self-esteem, feelings of isolation and depression. D was in her late forties and of good character. However, she continued to deny the offences and portrayed herself as the victim. D had a low level of intellectual functioning and a psychiatrist noted that immediate imprisonment was likely to severely exacerbate D's anxiety, possibly making her suicidal. Held. This case is very serious [and] called for a significant custodial sentence. The impacts remain serious. The case falls into the second category. [As it was an old offence] there needed to be exceptional circumstances. [There weren't any.] Even taking her mental state into account, **2 years** was the least sentence available, not 2 years suspended.

R v MA 2015 EWCA Crim 1209 D pleaded (15% credit) to cruelty. He was looking after his three-year-old son, V, who was eating an ice lolly. Some of the lolly and the wrapper fell on the floor and D got angry. He slapped V three to four times on his legs, arms and buttocks. The smacks were not hard. This caused reddening and bruising to the buttock area. D had references. Held. It was an isolated incident. Held. There were three aggravating factors. First, when V's mother attended, D showed no contrition. He placed his face 30 cm from V and said, "Yes, I did hit you and you know why. It is because you do not listen." Second, the assault had taken place in front of other children. Third, the incident happened only days after a 15-month Child Protection Plan had expired. **12 months** was severe but not manifestly excessive.

See also: *R v L and O* 2013 EWCA Crim 526 (Pleas to neglect. L and O were the parents of Fa and F, twins aged 15 months. Da, aged 5 years, was L's son and O's stepson. Neglect over 10 days to Da included bruising caused by beating. Neglect in respect of Fa and F over 11 weeks included malnourishment and multiple fractures. Level 2 offence. Previous good character. Provided contradictory and inconsistent accounts. With the pleas, **3 years 4 months** not 4 years.)

R v Giwa and Giwa 2013 EWCA Crim 1424 (Husband convicted of cruelty by wilful assault and neglect. Wife convicted of cruelty by wilful neglect. Both in the UK illegally. Not registered childminders. Child aged just over 2 years placed in their care. Displaced fracture to the skull. Severe and life-threatening injuries causing significant residual disability. Likely impact with a table or wall. Head swollen to twice usual size. Delay in taking victim to hospital. Both of good character. Husband aged 46. **7 years** was richly deserved. Wife aged 34. Lied about the proximity of the hospital. **3 years** well justified.)

Old cases: *R v Reynolds and Others Re L* 2007 EWCA Crim 538, 2 Cr App R (S) 87 (p 553) **(2 years)** *R v Dickinson* 2009 EWCA Crim 2119, 2010 1 Cr App R (S) 93 (p 596) **(2½ years)** *R v MG* 2010 EWCA Crim 304 **(21 months)**

For a summary of the first two cases, see the 9th edition of this book and for the last case see the 10th edition.

231.21   *Violence to a child aged over 5 years*

R v M 2013 EWCA Crim 2078 D pleaded to ABH and common assault. His son, V, who was aged 9, had been playing football after school in his school shoes rather than in trainers. His shoes became muddy. The family finances were tight. D lost his temper, instructed V to strip to his underwear and lie on the floor and beat him with a belt. V suffered a large number of bruises to the face, arms, chest and buttocks. Some had been caused by an open hand but most were by the belt. D held the buckle end of the belt. In interview D made full admissions. The common assault was in the previous month. D, aged 35, was very remorseful after the incident and the pre-sentence report identified him as having a very low risk of re-offending. Held. The gravity of the offence was such that it had to be marked by an immediate prison sentence. The courts must be astute to protect children against violence of this nature. D was the main breadwinner and incarceration would cause much suffering and hardship for the other family members. D was also a primary carer and the case had had a very adverse effect on V. These mitigating factors were afforded insufficient weight. We start at 1 year not 2, so with full credit, **8 months** not 16.

See also the **ABH** and the OFFENCES AGAINST THE PERSON ACT 1861 S 20 chapters.

Causing serious injury (Offences Against the Person Act 1861 s 18 and Domestic Violence, Crime and Victims Act 2004 s 5)

231.22   *Offences Against the Person Act 1861 s 18   GBH with intent*

Mode of trial Indictable only

Maximum sentence Life

Ancillary orders For the ancillary powers, see the OFFENCES AGAINST THE PERSON ACT 1861 S 18 chapter.

R v G 2012 EWCA Crim 2359 D was convicted of section 18. The victim was his four-week-old baby boy, V. V was found to have multiple rib fractures and metaphyseal fractures of his lower limbs. The medical evidence suggested that the rib injury had been caused by a squeezing motion involving grossly excessive force on more than one occasion and the fractures to the legs were caused by V's ankles being jerked upwards with considerable force. The injuries would have caused obvious distress to V. V's injuries were resolved without treatment so there was no permanent disability. It was accepted that the injuries were caused on three separate occasions, as a result of a sudden loss of temper. D was aged 43 at his appeal. Held. This was not a case which easily fitted into Category 1 or 2. The aggravating factors include the vulnerability of V, the extent of his injuries, the injuries required substantial force to inflict, the gross breach of trust, the fact that the injuries were deliberate, and there was a lack of remorse. This case is considerably more significant than what one might call the normal or even an aggravated Category 2 case. This case was between categories and so the sentence ought to have been **11 years** not 13.

R v C 2015 EWCA Crim 1866 D was indicted for three incidents. For each there was a section 18 and a section 20 count. He was convicted of one section 18 count (count 5) and two section 20 counts (counts 2 and 4). D lived apart from his partner, P, and son, V, aged 2. He would stay at their address and on occasions he would be left in charge of V. In July 2013, D was left in charge of V for 15 minutes. On her return P found V crying and screaming. He had a bruise and a spot of blood on his lip. There was also a graze to V's elbow. D said he did not know how the injuries had been caused. D knew that P was going to her GP that afternoon with V but said nothing. That afternoon V was taken to her grandmother for the night. The following morning, V was holding his right leg tightly to his chest and was uncomfortable if his leg was not in that position. V was also unsettled and cried when his nappy was changed. Two days later, V was in pain and if anyone tried to move him he shrieked. V's leg caused the most distress. V was taken to the GP, who found it difficult to examine V because he was in pain if his leg was moved. V was agitated and screamed. The GP noticed a crusted lesion on V's arm. In hospital it was discovered that V had serious injuries on four separate sites. In interview, D was upset but lied. The Judge found the following facts: a) the injury to the leg (count 2) was caused by a twisting and pulling action by D, b) the injury to the ribs (count 4) was caused by D squeezing V's torso when he was violently shaking V, c) this caused haemorrhaging to the brain (count 5). D was aged 22. In July 2014, D received 14 weeks for two offences of causing unnecessary suffering to an animal over Christmas. A psychiatric report said D thought V hated him. D told probation that he felt frustrated and D expressed regret and shame. Both the psychiatric report and the probation report said D posed a risk of causing serious harm to children in his care and he was unable to control his temper. Further he had a tendency to be violent and cruel when frustrated. The Judge relied on D's flagrant abuse of power and trust, his attempts to blame P and the grandmother, the extent and severity of the injuries and the delay in seeking medical help. She placed the offence in Category 1. Held. These cases are always difficult and sensitive. D's intent to cause serious harm was formed in an instant. D was comparatively young and immature. The case was either a lower end Category 1 or an upper end Category 2. **9 years** not 11 with the other concurrent sentences not altered.

See also: *R v T* 2011 EWCA Crim 1954 (Plea to section 18 after trial started (20%). He was only allowed supervised contact with his daughters. When unsupervised, he held his daughter's hand in hot water for at least 5 seconds as a punishment. Caused third-degree burns. Needed skin graft. Permanent scarring. Aged 41. Starting at 12-13 years, so **10 years** not 12.)

Att-Gen's Ref Nos 58-59 of 2012 2012 EWCA Crim 2547 (LCJ Convicted. F was the father, W his wife. Years of violent abuse of a child. Child was F's son and W's stepson. W inflicted the many instances of violence and abuse over 5 years. F's negligence allowed the abuse to continue. Included holding the boy's feet against a hot radiator and jumping onto his abdomen. Caused burns, fractured ribs and bowel herniation. In surgery hard work done to save life. F had one caution for common assault. **10 years** not 7 for W, and **18 months** not 6 months for F.)

See also the OFFENCES AGAINST THE PERSON ACT 1861 S 18 chapter.

231.23   *Causing etc. serious injuries to child or vulnerable adult*

Domestic Violence, Crime and Victims Act 2004 s 5 (causing or allowing a child or vulnerable adult to suffer serious physical harm)[191]

Commencement Offences must be committed on or after 2 July 2012.[192]

Mode of trial Indictable only

Maximum sentence 14 years

The maximum sentence is subject to the automatic life provisions.

Automatic life This section is listed in Criminal Justice Act 2003 Sch 15B Part 1.[193] The Lord Chief Justice said in *Att-Gen's Ref No 27 of 2013* 2014 EWCA Crim 334[194] para 8 iii) (*obiter*) that in rare cases the provisions could lead to the imposition of a life sentence where the offence does not carry life imprisonment.

The court must (unless the particular circumstances make it unjust[195]) pass automatic life if: a) the defendant is aged 18+ at the date of the conviction, b) the offence was committed on or after 3 December 2012, c) the court considers a determinate sentence of at least 10 years is appropriate, d) at the time the offender was convicted he had a conviction for a Criminal Justice Act 2003 Sch 15B offence, and e) the defendant at the time of his or her conviction had previously been sentenced to either: i) a life sentence where he or she was not eligible for release during the first five years of the sentence, or ii) a determinate sentence or extended sentence where the custodial part was 10 years or

---

[191] The amendments to the section were made by Domestic Violence, Crime and Victims (Amendment) Act 2012, which extended section 5 to include victims who 'suffer serious physical harm'.

[192] Domestic Violence, Crime and Victims (Amendment) Act 2012 (Commencement) Order 2012 2012/1432

[193] Although Domestic Violence, Crime and Victims Act 2004 s 5 is listed, the description of the offence does not include the serious injury alternative. It is assumed the section is what determines whether automatic life is available.

[194] This case is also known as *R v Burinskas* 2014 EWCA Crim 334.

[195] Criminal Justice Act 2003 s 224A(2)

more.[196] For a pre-2012 extended sentence, when determining whether the custodial term was 10+ years, the period deducted for time on remand or on a curfew and tag is included.[197]

Children and vulnerable adults: barred lists The section is a scheduled offence, see the VULNERABLE GROUPS: BARRING chapter in Volume 1.

Extended sentences This offence is listed in Criminal Justice Act 2003 Sch 15. The court may pass a 2012 extended sentence (EDS) if there is a significant risk of serious harm from future specified offences and either: a) the defendant has a Criminal Justice Act 2003 Sch 15B conviction (applicable only to defendants aged 18+), or b) the offence would justify a determinate sentence of at least 4 years.[198]

232   DANGEROUS DRIVING (SIMPLE)

232.1

Road Traffic Act 1988 s 2 (dangerous driving)

Mode of trial Triable either way

Maximum sentence On indictment 2 years. Summary maximum 6 months or a £5,000 fine for offences committed before 12 March 2015 and an unlimited fine thereafter.[199] There are maximum fines for those aged under 18, see **14.38** in Volume 1.

Disqualification Minimum disqualification 1 year[200]

Disqualification until test is passed Where the defendant is disqualified under Road Traffic Offenders Act 1988 s 34, the defendant must be disqualified until an appropriate driving test is passed.[201] In force 13 April 2015

Penalty points 3-11 penalty points when special reasons found[202]

Depriving defendant of vehicle used There is power to deprive the defendant of the vehicle used[203] for the purposes of committing the offence.

Passenger Carrying Vehicles (PCV) and Large Goods Vehicles (LGV) drivers, see **341.1**.

232.2   *Crown Court statistics   England and Wales*

Dangerous driving

Year	Age	Plea	Total sentenced	Type of sentencing %						Average length of custody in months
				Discharge	Fine	Community sentence	Suspended sentence	Custody	Other	
2013	18-20	G	215	–	0.5	25.1	25.1	49.3	–	8.6
		NG	13	–	23.1	7.7	30.8	38.5	–	11.8
	21+	G	1,596	0.3	1.1	10.0	37.5	50.3	0.8	10.1
		NG	128	–	5.5	10.2	30.5	52.3	1.6	11.5
2014	18-20	G	265	–	2	18	43	36	–	9.2
		NG	8	–	–	13	50	38	–	not listed[204]
	21+	G	1,592	–	1	9	37	52	1	10.1
		NG	121	2	7	13	38	40	–	11.4

---

[196] Criminal Justice Act 2003 s 224A as inserted by Legal Aid, Sentencing and Punishment of Offenders Act 2012 s 122. The requirement in a) is at section 224A(1)(a), the requirement in b) is at section 224A(1)(b), the requirement in c) is at section 224A(1)(c) and the requirement in d) is at section 224A(4)-(9). For details see para **76.2** in Volume 1.
[197] Criminal Justice Act 2003 s 224A(9)-(10)
[198] Criminal Justice Act 2003 s 226A-226B as inserted by Legal Aid, Sentencing and Punishment of Offenders Act 2012 s 124
[199] Legal Aid, Sentencing and Punishment of Offenders Act 2012 s 85(1) and (4) and Legal Aid, Sentencing and Punishment of Offenders Act 2012 (Commencement No 11) Order 2015 2015/504
[200] Road Traffic Offenders Act 1988 s 34(1) and Sch 2 Part I
[201] Road Traffic Offenders Act 1988 s 36(2)(d)
[202] Road Traffic Offenders Act 1988 s 28, 34 and Sch 2 Part I
[203] Powers of Criminal Courts (Sentencing) Act 2000 s 143(6)-(7)
[204] Based on too few cases to be meaningful

For explanations about the statistics, see page 1-xii. For statistics for male and female defendants etc., see www.banksr.com Other Matters Statistics tab

232.3   Guideline cases

Some assistance can be found in the DEATH BY DRIVING: DANGEROUS DRIVING *Guidelines* para at **238.3**. Ed.

232.4   Magistrates' Court Sentencing Guidelines

Magistrates' Court Sentencing Guidelines 2008, see www.banksr.com Other Matters Guidelines tab The guidelines apply to the Magistrates' Court and to the Crown Court hearing appeals or sentencing for summary only offences.[205]

page 120 Starting points are based on a first-time offender pleading not guilty.

Examples of nature of activity	Starting point	Range
Single incident where little or no damage or risk of personal injury	Medium-level community order	Low-level community order to high-level community order. Disqualify 12-15 months
Incident(s) involving excessive speed or showing off, especially on busy roads or in built-up area	12 weeks' custody	High-level community order to 26 weeks' custody. Disqualify 15-24 months
Prolonged bad driving involving deliberate disregard for safety of others	Crown Court. Consider interim disqualification after conviction	Crown Court

Disqualify for at least 2 years if offender has had more than one disqualification for a period of 56 days or more in preceding 3 years.

The following aggravating and mitigating factors may be particularly relevant: Factors indicating higher culpability: 1 Disregarding warnings of others 2 Evidence of alcohol or drugs 3 Carrying out other tasks while driving 4 Carrying passengers or heavy load 5 Tiredness 6 Aggressive driving, such as driving much too close to vehicle in front, inappropriate attempts to overtake, or cutting in after overtaking 7 Driving when knowingly suffering from a medical condition which significantly impairs the offender's driving skills 8 Driving a poorly maintained or dangerously loaded vehicle, especially where motivated by commercial concerns. Factors indicating lower culpability: 1 Genuine emergency 2 Speed not excessive 3 Offence due to inexperience rather than irresponsibility of driver. Factors indicating greater degree of harm: 1 Injury to others 2 Damage to other vehicles or property.

Consider ancillary orders, including compensation.

For details about applying the guidelines, see the GUIDELINES chapter in Volume 1.

For the meaning of a high-level, a medium-level and a low-level community order see **16.12-16.14** in Volume 1.

For how to apply the guidelines, see the GUIDELINES chapter in Volume 1.

232.5   Court Martial

Guidance on Sentencing in the Court Martial 2013 para 5.11.1 There is no power to impose penalty points or order disqualification from driving.

para 5.11.3 The sentences for dangerous driving…and similar very serious matters should be based on those in the Sentencing Council guidelines.

232.6   Alcohol, Driving under the influence of

R v Sheill 2010 EWCA Crim 22, 2 Cr App R (S) 53 (p 368) D, a doctor, pleaded to dangerous driving. D attended a dinner and drove home with his mobile switched off.

---

[205] See page 15 of the guidelines.

His host rang his mobile saying his wife had had a heart attack. The ambulance took 25 minutes to arrive and the wife died. D received the message when it was too late. A year later, there was an anniversary lunch and D drank too much. He drove his Bentley Continental home. He hit kerbs on several occasions and drove on the wrong side of the road. D collided with another vehicle on the brow of the hill. £5,000 damage was caused. D failed to stop, crossed a junction without stopping and hit another car. He did stop. The other driver was taken to hospital with bruising to her chest and abdomen. She also had a 'bang' to her leg. D's alcohol reading was 126 mg (limit 80 mg). It was accepted that D had no recollection about the first collision because of drink. He said he felt obliged to go to the lunch. D was aged 50, of good character and suffered from depression. The Judge said he was an asset to the community. Held. The **12-month** sentence was not manifestly excessive and there were no grounds to suspend it.

R v Francis 2011 EWCA Crim 1660 LCJ D was convicted of dangerous driving, failing to stop and obstructing an officer. Having consumed alcohol, he drove a Range Rover over 2½ miles erratically and dangerously. The car veered from side to side, narrowly avoiding collisions and striking the kerb. He negotiated three roundabouts in a dangerous manner. When crossing the fourth, he entered the wrong side of the carriageway and hit a small car head-on. The driver of the small car suffered a broken nose and had to be cut from the wreckage. D immediately fled, with no concern for the other driver's safety. D, aged 37, had committed driving offences some 20 years previously. Held. The aggravating factors are: a) D drove dangerously for 2½ miles, b) the manner in which he drove made it 'a matter of time before an accident happened', c) there was evidence he had consumed alcohol, and d) he fled the scene. The maximum sentence is 2 years, and there are worse cases than this. **12 months** not 16.

R v Ward 2013 EWCA Crim 2667, 2014 1 Cr App R (S) 74 (p 466) D pleaded to dangerous driving and other matters (short consecutive sentences). After drinking on Saturday night, D drove to a shop the following morning with V1, aged 15 and V2, his partner. D was staggering and obviously drunk in the shop at around 9.20 am. On the drive home, D drove very fast. V1 and V2 repeatedly asked him to slow down. D lost control of the vehicle on a bend and mounted a pavement, rolling over onto a grass verge. A bus driver estimated the speed at 60 mph. V1 suffered a broken collarbone and D suffered a punctured lung. A back calculation concluded that D's blood alcohol level would have been approximately 206 mg at the time of the accident. D had two convictions for five offences, none of which were driving offences. Held. This was a very serious case of dangerous driving. D and V1 were injured, V2 quite seriously. It was fortunate that they did not suffer more serious injury. The Judge was correct to take a starting point of the maximum sentence. **21 months** upheld.

Concurrent or consecutive? Should the sentences be see the Concurrent and Consecutive Sentences *Driving and other offences* para in Volume 1.

232.7   *Disqualification for how long?   Judicial guidance*
R v Bell 2013 EWCA Crim 2549 Police chase. The purpose of disqualification was not to punish but to protect. **3 years** was appropriate, see **232.8**.

R v Shipley 2014 EWCA Crim 1572 D pleaded to dangerous driving and appealed against the length of disqualification. Held. Save in exceptionally severe cases, the period of disqualification should not be so long as to impair the prospects of rehabilitation.

232.8   *Disqualification for how long? 3 years or less appropriate*
R v Ziad 2011 EWCA Crim 209 D pleaded early to dangerous driving and failing to stop. D drove behind V's car. He then passed V on her near side, pulled in front of her car and braked, causing her to perform an emergency stop. V pulled into the slow lane. D's car slowed down so that it was level with V. He pulled over and collided with V's car. He also forced her into a kerb at a roundabout. He then drove off at speed. The incident was witnessed by an off-duty police officer. D contended that the damage caused was

unintentional. D had previous convictions, but none for driving offences. Held. 5 years' disqualification bears too heavily upon D. He has a family to support. We can see that the period of 5 years does have the potential effect in that it appears to result in, say, some 3 years during which this man is unable to utilise his driving skills in any way pending the termination of the period of disqualification, once he is released from custody for other offences. **3-year disqualification**, not 5.

R v Jawid 2013 EWCA Crim 1081 D pleaded to dangerous driving and no insurance. An unmarked police car drove in the opposite direction to D's car, which was in a left-turn filter lane. D was accelerating too fast to turn the corner and swerved back into the main line of traffic. The officer in the unmarked car activated his lights and D pulled into a layby. The officer pulled in front of D's car and got out. D then revved the engine and drove off at speed. The officer gave chase and D drove on the wrong side of the road, then immediately turned right causing traffic to brake hard. He drove on the wrong side of the road at 70 mph in a 30 mph zone. After returning to the correct side of the road, he encountered a queue of traffic and overtook them on the wrong side of the road. The officer abandoned the chase. D was later arrested and said, "Sorry I drove off. I've got no insurance. It's my granddad's car." The prosecution were unable to say the time or distance during which D's dangerous driving continued. D was aged 20 at appeal and was of good character. He had completed a Level 2 NVQ in motor vehicles and was about to begin a Level 3. He would be able to begin that upon his release. Held. 3 months' detention would not be reduced. There was force in the argument that, given his educational opportunities, his rehabilitation should not be inhibited by disqualification for such a long period. **15-month disqualification**, not 3 years, was appropriate.

R v Rasul 2013 EWCA Crim 1458 D was convicted of dangerous driving. He drove at a police officer. At 15 mph the officer was hit. D had a clean driving licence but was on prison licence. He received 3 months' imprisonment. Held. In the absence of injury and considering the speed, **15-month disqualification**, not 3 years.

R v Bell 2013 EWCA Crim 2549 D pleaded (full credit) to dangerous driving. In the early hours of the morning, a police patrol vehicle discovered that D was driving his Vauxhall Astra without insurance and without an MOT certificate. The officer illuminated his car's blue lights in an attempt to stop D's car. D drove off at speed. He drove at grossly excessive speeds over a distance of about five miles. This included driving at 70 mph in a 40 mph restricted area and driving the wrong way around a roundabout. D eventually brought his vehicle to a stop at a red traffic light and allowed the police vehicle to pull alongside him. When one of the officers began to get out of the car, D drove off at speed, colliding with the open door and forcing the officer to take evasive action. D then drove through eight red lights, one of them at 80 mph. D had a number of convictions including making off without payment (×4 in 2012) and driving whilst disqualified, without insurance and having defective tyres (2013). There were also three breaches of a community order imposed for the 2012 offences. Held. This was a prolonged piece of very bad driving involving a high risk of potential injury to police and other road users. The evidence was overwhelming but this was a case in which the full discount should be given. 12 months' imprisonment. **3-year disqualification** was appropriate.

R v Ditta and Ditta 2013 EWCA Crim 2765 D was convicted of dangerous driving. D and his brother, T, were in a car when they were racially abused by a pedestrian after an altercation at a crossing. D and T got out of the car and armed themselves with an iron bar and a car jack. They pleaded to affray. A car driven by D mounted the pavement on two separate occasions causing pedestrians, including someone with a child in a pushchair, to jump out of the way. A bystander suffered a bruised hand after it was hit by the car's wing mirror. D was aged 21 and T was aged 25. Held. It was fortunate that serious injury to pedestrians was avoided. The use of the car was deliberate. However, D, as a car mechanic, would be significantly affected by such a period of disqualification. **18-month disqualification**, not 3 years.

R v Atkinson 2014 EWCA Crim 1079 D pleaded to dangerous driving. He tried to perform a three-point turn in an area where V had parked her car. He verbally abused her and deliberately reversed into her car at slow speed causing £400 worth of damage. He verbally abused her again and then drove away. Held. It was characterised as a road rage incident. Having regard to the limited degree that the driving was bad and D's occupation as a taxi driver, **12- month disqualification**, not 18.

R v Shipley 2014 EWCA Crim 1572 D pleaded to dangerous driving and appealed against the length of disqualification. D was driving along an A road at 90 mph in drizzly conditions overtaking and undertaking at speed and dangerously. He was far too close to cars in front and was attempting to undertake when he lost control and collided with another vehicle, which then hit a third. Four vehicles were seriously damaged but no one was injured significantly. D was aged 26 and of exemplary character with no driving offences. He was ordered to take a re-test and he was going to lose his job due to his disqualification. Held. D was wise not to challenge the suspended sentence with 250 hours' unpaid work. Death could have occurred. But the case was not exceptional in its severity so **30-month disqualification**, not 5 years.

See also: *R v Normoyle* 2011 EWCA Crim 824 (Pleas to wounding, dangerous driving and excess alcohol. 60 mph in 40 mph zone. Passengers egging him on. Drove towards pedestrian intending to scare him. Hit pedestrian, causing broken ankle and abrasions. **3-year disqualification**, not 7)

R v Jenkinson 2011 EWCA Crim 2330 (Lorry driver ran into stationary traffic when vision obscured. **3-year disqualification** not 5, see **232.11**.)

R v Murray 2014 EWCA Crim 886 (**2-year disqualification** not 5 for speeding, see **232.13**.)

Old cases: These provide very little assistance so they are not listed.

232.9   *Disqualification for how long? More than 3 years appropriate*
Examples: *R v Smith* 2010 EWCA Crim 2228 (D was convicted. Street race. High-performance cars. Speed possibly in excess of 100 mph on an A-road. D lost control and was thrown through the rear window. Partner and child in the car. Good character. **3-year disqualification**, not 4)

R v Gray 2012 EWCA Crim 475 (D pleaded to dangerous driving, failing to provide a specimen and failing to stop. He crashed into another vehicle and drove off the wrong way along a motorway slip road. Previous conviction for excess alcohol. **4-year disqualification**, not 10)

R v O'Connor 2012 EWCA Crim 785 (Plea to dangerous driving, failing to stop and cannabis possession. Asked to stop by police officers in marked vehicle. 1½ times the speed limit. Mounted the pavement. Drove on wrong side of road. Caused other vehicles to take swift action to avoid a collision. 2 minutes of driving. Aged 30. Conviction for a public order offence. Given 12 weeks' custody. **18-month disqualification**, not 3 years)

232.10   *Driving at people*
R v Bowen 2013 EWCA Crim 376 D pleaded on rearraignment to dangerous driving. D's brother, DB, had damaged a car belonging to CF, who DB believed had been having an affair with his former partner. CF was informed of the damage and arranged to meet DB. DB armed himself with a large knife and recruited D to drive him to the scene. At the meeting, CF charged at DB, unaware that he had a knife. DB stabbed CF, who pleaded to section 18 and received 12 years. A fourth man, V, saw the violence and ran towards DB with a hockey stick. He hit DB with the stick. D was still in the car and drove towards V, hitting him and knocking him into the air. He did not suffer any serious injuries. DB and D drove away. D's basis of plea was that his intention was to protect his brother and not to injure V. D was aged 28 and had three convictions for four offences, but none since 2003. Held. It was appropriate to suspend the sentence, thereby not risking D's

employment, home and family. D's employers deferred their decision on D's employment until the result of the appeal. **16 months suspended** with 120 hours of unpaid
work, not 6 months.

232.11   HGV drivers
R v Jenkinson 2011 EWCA Crim 2330 D, a professional lorry driver of 16 years, pleaded
late to dangerous driving. He was driving at 56 mph on the A1. Traffic had slowed and
brake lights were illuminated. Some motorists had activated their hazard lights. D failed
to brake and drove straight into the cars in front of him. Some were stationary and some
were moving slowly. Six victims suffered serious injuries including a spinal fracture,
neck and shoulder injuries. D claimed that he was blinded by the sun and an
investigation report said this could have hindered D's view. The angle of the sun could
have been 18°. D only applied the brakes after his vehicle collided with the first vehicle.
D was aged 49 at appeal and had convictions for careless driving and two failures to
stop. Held. D was carrying a heavy load, which gave him a greater responsibility. Others
had managed to stop and photographs showed how fortuitous it was that no one was
killed. Immediate imprisonment was inevitable and correct. With the late plea, the
correct sentence was **9 months** not 12. Disqualification should have been for 3 years not
5 as this was not a case of a driver disregarding the rules of the road.

232.12   Overtaking
R v Ball 2009 EWCA Crim 1265 D pleaded to dangerous driving. He was driving a van
with six vehicles in front of him. The van in front of him overtook the group on a hill in
what was considered to be an obviously dangerous manoeuvre. D followed and on the
brow of the hill crashed into a car going the other way. The driver, V, had to be cut out by
the fire brigade and suffered extremely serious injuries. V had a broken arm, leg and
nose and injuries to the face with permanent scarring. There was severe damage to one
eye. She had a head injury and memory impairment. V was a swimming instructor who
could no longer swim. D was then aged 17 and was aged 18 when he pleaded not guilty
at the Magistrates' Court. D then failed to answer his bail and was arrested over three
years later. He had no convictions and four character references. His risk of reoffending
was assessed as low. Held. There was no evidence of prolonged bad driving, nor
influence of drink or drugs. His 18-month sentence failed to reflect the plea and his
personal mitigation (particularly as he was only aged 17 at the time). The plea was worth
20-25% so with a maximum of 2 years, **12 months** consecutive to 6 months for failing to
attend.
R v Baublys 2015 EWCA Crim 1411 D pleaded to dangerous driving. He was working as
a delivery driver. He drove on a notoriously twisting and dangerous stretch of road. The
speed limit was 50 mph and he was in a queue of traffic travelling at about 40 mph. On
a blind bend and when there were central double white lines he tried to overtake two
vehicles in the queue. A witness described it as a total gamble. As D was almost past the
second vehicle, his van hit an oncoming car. The force of the van pushed that car
backwards and it was hit from behind by another car. In the first car was a driver, who
suffered whiplash injuries, an adult, who suffered severe bruising, and a child. In the
second car, the driver sustained injuries to the neck and abdomen, trauma to her breast
and a suspected broken rib. The injured persons suffered significant mental trauma and
one could not work, which affected her finances. D remained behind the wheel until
arrested. He lost his job. D had no convictions and a clean licence. The Judge said it was
an astonishing piece of driving with a high likelihood of a head-on collision. Held. It was
a short aberration, but the danger was plain. The court should impose only the minimum
term so we start at 9 months making **6 months** with the plea.

232.13   Police chases
R v Kilara 2012 EWCA Crim 2110 D pleaded (full credit) to dangerous driving. He was
driving an Audi, carrying one passenger, when the police decided to stop him. He pulled
over but just as the police stopped their car behind the Audi, he sped off. D stated he did

not realise that it was the police who were attempting to stop him. In built-up areas he drove at over 50 mph in 30 mph limited zones. He drove on the wrong side of the road causing other drivers to take evasive action. One pedestrian had to jump out of the way. There were no injuries and no damage caused. D, aged 29 at appeal, had acquired an extensive criminal record between the ages of 16 and 22, including an 8-year sentence for serious firearms offences in 2005. Held. After a trial, the appropriate starting point would be towards the top of the 3-12 month range for this kind of offence. **8 months** not 15.

R v Gaskin 2013 EWCA Crim 244 D pleaded to dangerous driving. A VW Golf, driven by D, was seen by a police officer, who followed and saw it accelerate to in excess of the 60 mph limit on an A-road. The officer illuminated his blue lights, indicating that the Golf should stop. It did not. For 7 minutes and 8 miles, D engaged in a prolonged period of dangerous driving. He continued along A-roads at speeds of more than 90 mph. D drove through a village where the limit was 30, then 40 mph at more than 80 mph. He then reached speeds of more than 100 mph where the limit was 60 mph. He performed dangerous overtaking manoeuvres, forcing oncoming traffic to take evasive action. He overtook cars on a left-hand bend, straight into the path of an oncoming motorbike. The rider had to 'stand the bike up and slide down the offside' between the Golf and the nearside verge over the mud on the road. Had the rider not done so, there would have been a fatal collision. D drove into a private drive and decamped from the car. He was caught hiding in bushes after a police helicopter located him. D's 12-year-old cousin was in the rear of the Golf, shaking and crying. He was so distressed he found it difficult to talk. D's one-year-old child was in the front of the car in a child seat. D, aged 31, had eight convictions for 39 offences. Most of the offences were driving offences including failing to stop and dangerous driving whilst a juvenile. There were also eight drugs offences. He was on licence. Held. This was a very bad case with many aggravating features. D drove over a considerable distance in a manner showing total disregard for his own safety, the safety of the public and of the children in his car. D was on licence for another offence. The absence of serious injury was relevant, notwithstanding the new offence of dangerous driving causing serious injury. This was not at the top of the category. **16 months** not 18 months.

R v Murray 2014 EWCA Crim 886 D pleaded to dangerous driving. At 1 pm, he was driving a Vauxhall Corsa in excess of the speed limit. He was caught on a camera and a police unit was dispatched to apprehend him. He failed to stop when requested to do so. In order to evade the police and for some 15 minutes covering 10 miles, he drove through four red traffic lights at speeds of up to 50 mph in a 30 mph zone, up to 77 mph in a 50 mph zone, up to 52 mph in another 30 mph zone and up to 60 mph in a 20 mph zone. The incident only came to a conclusion when he drove into a cul-de-sac. One elderly man had to take evasive action. D had a full UK driving licence and was driving a rental car which was fully insured. D, aged 30 at appeal, was on licence at the time of the offence, being under a 9-year sentence imposed for assault, burglary, theft, ABH, aggravated burglary and threats to kill. D had two character references. Held. Motorists and pedestrians were placed in obvious danger. The fact that the police were involved and that D was on licence were seriously aggravating factors. There was a very high risk of harm to innocent members of the public and it was fortunate that no one was hurt. Starting at 20 months was too high. There was excessive speed but no intention to cause harm or fear. There was no injury or involvement of alcohol or drugs and significantly an absence of any additional relevant offences. D was a model of compliance with his licence, has stable accommodation and had obtained qualifications and a good job as a painter and decorator. However, this was still a very serious offence and the absence of injury was a matter of chance. Starting at 15 months was appropriate. With the plea, **10 months** not 14. The sentence had to be immediate, given the aggravating features. 5 years' disqualification was manifestly excessive, 2 years was appropriate.

See also: *R v O'Connor* 2012 EWCA Crim 785 (Plea to dangerous driving, failing to stop and cannabis possession. Asked to stop by police officers in marked vehicle. 1½ times the speed limit. Mounted the pavement. Drove on wrong side of road. Caused other vehicles to take swift action to avoid a collision. 2 minutes of driving. Aged 30. Conviction for a public order offence. Starting at 18 weeks, **12 weeks** not 6 months. 18-month ban not 3 years)
See also **DEATH BY DRIVING: DANGEROUS DRIVING** *Police chases* at **238.17**.

232.14   *Police officers or traffic wardens, Driving at*
R v Lee 2010 EWCA Crim 69 D pleaded (full credit) to dangerous driving, driving whilst disqualified and two common assault offences. Police officers were investigating a burglary and approached D's car, which was stuck in traffic. One officer went to each side of the car. They attempted to open the doors but D tried to drive off. The police tried to break the windows but D reversed, causing a minor injury to one officer's leg. D then drove forward, causing a minor injury to the other officer's knee. D then mounted the pavement and drove down it for about 150 metres and then drove off on the road. D was aged 39 with a large number of dishonesty and driving offences, including reckless driving and driving whilst disqualified. He also had convictions for common assault, ABH, assault PC and robbery. The Judge said that he would reflect the common assault in the driving sentence but consecutive to 6 months for the driving whilst disqualified. Held. Because of the plea, **15 months** not 2 years, making 21 months.
Old case: *R v Watson* 2007 EWCA Crim 1595, 2008 1 Cr App R (S) 55 (p 315) (**12 months**) For a summary of the case see the 9th edition of this book.
Road rage, see the **ROAD RAGE** chapter

232.15   *Revenge*
R v Mohammed 2010 EWCA Crim 1061 D pleaded to dangerous driving and battery. V stopped his car at some traffic lights and was hit from behind by D's car. D then drove in front of V and boxed him in. D got out, went to V's car, opened the door and punched V several times in the face and kicked him once. D was pulled off by a bystander and D drove away. V had swelling to both sides of his face. There was £600 damage to V's car. In interview D admitted the offence and claimed that V, a university student, had threatened D's girlfriend with a razor blade and had slightly cut her lip. D accepted that the collision was deliberate. He was aged 20, a first-year university student and of good character. Held. This was a serious and disturbing offence. The incident was frightening and alarming. **8 months** overall was entirely justified.
R v Wilson 2013 EWCA Crim 1745, 1 Cr App R (S) 79 (p 490) D pleaded (25% credit) to dangerous driving. V and her brother, L, visited someone's home and a fight broke out between L and D. V tried to stop it and she was hit on the head. All three left and D got in his car and drove towards V, L, and others who had joined them. Most of them jumped out of the way but V was hit. She was thrown onto the bonnet, hit the windscreen and then fell on the ground. She was unconscious. D stopped and fled. V had a glass bottle in her pocket, which broke. Her thigh was cut, requiring stitches. V also suffered bruising and grazes. D went to the police and pretended his car had been stolen. V and another picked D out from an ID parade. D claimed they were mistaken. D was now aged 21. He had numerous convictions for theft, and some assaults and breaches of public order. The Judge accepted that D drove the car to scare L, V was intoxicated and D did not intend to cause any injury. He considered D's driving to be reckless and it was fortunate that V was not more severely injured. He started at 20 months and reduced it to 16. Held. The offence was aggravated by the injury and the potential harm that could have been caused to others. However, only a short distance was driven, there were no relevant previous convictions and the offence was totally out of character. An immediate custodial sentence, absent exceptional features, was inevitable. Although it was a highly dangerous incident, this court has seen many worse cases. With his youth and relatively minor record, 12 months, and with the plea, **9 months**.

232.16   Speeding

R v Hudson 2011 EWCA Crim 2693 D pleaded (full credit) to dangerous driving, driving without insurance, no licence, failing to stop and failing to report an accident. D took his aunt's car after going to visit her. It was unclear whether he had taken the vehicle without her consent. Travelling at 50-60 mph in a 30 mph limited zone, he did not slow down before a crossroads where he was required to give way. He continued over the crossroads and collided with another vehicle, which in turn collided with another. D drove off before the police attended the scene. D then abandoned the car. D, aged 33, had never held more than a provisional licence. He had 84 offences including domestic violence, public disorder, drug and dishonesty offences. With full credit the Judge must have started at 24 months for the driving and 6 months for the reporting. Held. This was an appalling piece of bad driving. D's bad record was an aggravating feature. Considering totality and the maximums, starting at 18 months, **12 months** for the dangerous driving, and 4 months consecutive for the failing to stop and the failing to report, making **16 months** not 22 months in total.

R v Joel 2013 EWCA Crim 634 D pleaded to failing to stop and failing to report an accident. He was convicted of dangerous driving. At 1 am, he was driving in a town centre. He drove into a series of police cones designed to prevent access to a particular street. He then turned his car around and drove back down the street, in contravention of the one-way designation. D then sought to turn left and was prevented doing so by a further police barrier. He therefore reversed at speed before getting out of his vehicle. Two police officers witnessed part of this incident and indicated to D that he should stay. D gesticulated to the officers, got back into his car and drove off at speed without illuminating the lights on the vehicle. In doing so, he narrowly missed one of the officers who had to step out of the way as D's vehicle approached. D then drove back through the original set of police cones and onto a roundabout. He lost control of his car on a dual carriageway, causing him to crash through the brick wall central reservation and onto the other carriageway. D escaped on foot. When interviewed he told police he had little or no recollection of the incident but admitted driving too fast and losing control of his car. He told police he was taking medication for anxiety at the time and he left the scene because he was in shock. D, aged 29 at appeal, had a conviction for driving with excess alcohol and whilst uninsured (2006, a fine). D suffered from depression and anxiety. In the period leading up to the offences, he was unable to sit his final examinations at university. He expressed remorse. Held. We accept that D did not drive at the officers intending them injury. However, D had driven in contravention of various road restrictions and was fully aware that the officers wished to speak to him about those matters. He displayed contempt by gesturing at them and drove past them in circumstances which were clearly dangerous. It involved a significant risk that they may be seriously injured. It was good fortune rather than judgement that no other vehicles or individuals were directly involved. D's driving was aggressive and involved inappropriate speed. Taking account of the fact that the driving was of relatively short duration, **6 months** not 12.

R v Ward 2013 EWCA Crim 2667, 2014 1 Cr App R (S) 74 (p 466) D pleaded to dangerous driving and other matters (short consecutive sentences). After drinking on Saturday night, D drove to a shop the following morning with V1, aged 15 and V2, his partner. D was staggering and obviously drunk in the shop at around 9.20 am. On the drive home, D drove very fast. V1 and V2 repeatedly asked him to slow down. D lost control of the vehicle on a bend and mounted a pavement, rolling over onto a grass verge. A bus driver estimated the speed at 60 mph. V1 suffered a broken collarbone and D suffered a punctured lung. A back calculation concluded that D's blood alcohol level would have been approximately 206 mg at the time of the accident. D had two convictions for five offences, none of which were driving offences. Held. This was a very serious case of dangerous driving. D and V1 were injured, V2 quite seriously. It was fortunate that they did not suffer more serious injury. The Judge was correct to take a starting point of the maximum sentence. **21 months** upheld.

R v Nazeer 2014 EWCA Crim 2236 D pleaded on rearraignment to dangerous driving following a *Goodyear* indication. D drove past a marked police car travelling at an estimated 60 mph, double the limit. He then jumped red traffic lights and continued at speed, overtaking at least one vehicle on the wrong side of the road. When stopped by the police, D admitted he was at fault and apologised, but said that he needed to pick his mother up from the airport. D was aged in his mid-30s and a schoolteacher. He had convictions for failing to stop and report an accident from 2004 but was of essentially good character. Held. This offending was nowhere near the top end of the scale. **Community order with unpaid work**, not 12 months suspended for 2 years.

See also the SPEEDING chapter.

Victim seriously injured The cases are not listed because of the new offence below.

233   DANGEROUS DRIVING CAUSING SERIOUS INJURY

233.1

Road Traffic Act 1988 s 1A[206] (Causing serious injury by dangerous driving)

Mode of trial Triable either way

Maximum penalty On indictment 5 years. Summary maximum 6 months and/or a £5,000 fine for offences committed before 12 March 2015 and an unlimited fine thereafter.[207] There are maximum fines for those aged under 18, see **14.38** in Volume 1.

Disqualification Obligatory disqualification for 2+ years[208]

Disqualification until test is passed Where the defendant is disqualified under Road Traffic Offenders Act 1988 s 34, the defendant must be disqualified until an appropriate driving test is passed.[209] In force 13 April 2015.

Penalty points 3-11 points, when special reasons found

Commencement The offence only applies when committed on or after 3 December 2012.[210]

Guidelines I would expect sentencers to refer, where appropriate, to the aggravating and mitigating factors in both the dangerous driving (simple) and the death by dangerous driving guidelines.

233.2   *Disqualification   How long?*

R v Ellis 2014 EWCA Crim 593 D pleaded to causing serious injury by dangerous driving (2 years' imprisonment). At night and with two passengers, D attempted to race and overtake another car. He drove at consistently fast speeds, accelerating and braking suddenly. V, a care home owner, exited a roundabout to be confronted by two cars coming towards her. The other car braked and D collided with it, skidding left and hitting V head on. V was seriously injured with fractures to the skull and ankle. Her sight was affected, she could no longer drive nor work and her permission to run the care home was withdrawn. D, aged 24, had no convictions and a clean licence. He was in full time work on a farm. The pre-sentence report concluded that he was prone to impulsive and risk-taking behaviour, but assessed him as low risk. He expressed remorse. D appealed the disqualification. Held. Guidance can be obtained from the *Causing Death by Driving Guideline 2008* paras 30-31 (see **235.20**). Disqualification operates to both

---

[206] As inserted by Legal Aid, Sentencing and Punishment of Offenders Act 2012 s 143. In force 3/12/12 by Legal Aid, Sentencing and Punishment of Offenders Act 2012 (Commencement No 3 and Saving Provision) Order 2012 2012/2770 para 2
[207] Legal Aid, Sentencing and Punishment of Offenders Act 2012 s 85(1) and (4) and Legal Aid, Sentencing and Punishment of Offenders Act 2012 (Commencement No 11) Order 2015 2015/504
[208] Road Traffic Offenders Act 1988 s 34(4)(iia) as inserted by Legal Aid, Sentencing and Punishment of Offenders Act 2012 Sch 27 para 5. In force 3/12/12 by Legal Aid, Sentencing and Punishment of Offenders Act 2012 (Commencement No 3 and Saving Provision) Order 2012 2012/2770 para 2
[209] Road Traffic Offenders Act 1988 s 36(2)(c)
[210] Legal Aid, Sentencing and Punishment of Offenders Act 2012 s 143(4). In force 3/12/12 by Legal Aid, Sentencing and Punishment of Offenders Act 2012 (Commencement No 3 and Saving Provision) Order 2012 2012/2770 para 2

protect the public and punish offenders. This was an extremely bad case of dangerous driving which was prolonged, persistent and deliberate. A lengthy disqualification was inevitable, although it would make it harder for D to get employment. **5-year disquali-fication** not 8. This would mean he had 4 years of disqualification on release.

See also: *R v Hussain* 2015 EWCA Crim 1016, 2 Cr App R (S) 52 (p 379) (Plea. D, a taxi driver, at work but without a passenger, sped at about 50 mph in a 30 mph area. Jumped pedestrian lights and hit an 18-year-old woman with a glancing blow. She had her leg amputated and sustained other horrific and life-changing injuries. D had three speeding offences. Age 33. Given 2 years' imprisonment. **4-year** disqualification not 7.)

R v Sandulache 2015 EWCA Crim 1502 (Plea. Overtaking when it was prohibited. **5 years** not 10. For more detail see **233.3**.)

233.3   Cases

R v Sandulache 2015 EWCA Crim 1502 D pleaded at the Magistrates' Court to dangerous driving causing serious injury. D drove on a twisty road with white lines prohibiting overtaking. He overtook at least two cars and whilst overtaking a third he hit a motorcyclist. The driver, V, was thrown off his bike and suffered a bleed to his brain, haematoma to his vertebrae, bruising to his lungs, 'some loss of dentition' and extensive injuries to both knees. V was an inpatient in hospital for six weeks. Afterwards he continued to suffer pain and loss of sleep. He had only been married for two months and the accident had changed him from being active and independent to largely inactive and dependent on his wife for many of his physical needs. He suffered from depression and frustration about his inability to look after himself. In interview, D said he was collecting members of his family from an airport and had started his journey later than he had expected. Further he knew that overtaking was prohibited and he 'regretted it terribly'. D was aged 22 and had lived most of his life in Romania. He had no convictions and worked as a lorry driver. Held. The collision had the most appalling consequences for V and his wife. In considering whether the maximum sentence was merited we consider the harm and the culpability. There was the highest level of harm. This was a very bad piece of driving, which created an obvious danger to other road users. If V had been killed, the case would have been Level 1. There were no other road traffic offences committed at the same time. He did not flee the scene and he was not under the influence of drink and drugs. We start at 4½ years, so with plea, **3 years** not 4.

233.4   Cases   Alcohol taken

R v Vincer 2014 EWCA Crim 2743, 2015 1 Cr App R (S) 51 (p 353) D pleaded guilty to causing serious injury by dangerous driving. He was also sentenced for excess alcohol (4 months concurrent). D was at home and had consumed a considerable quantity of alcohol. He was not intending to drive. His sister-in-law, S, phoned asking for help, saying his brother had assaulted her. D knew his brother was very drunk. D said he phoned members of his family but failed to get help for S. Then D drove to S, who was less than a mile away. When speeding, he clipped a kerb and lost control of his car. The car went onto the wrong side of the road and failed to turn left at a roundabout. The car was out of control for about 15 metres and hit V's car. V and her husband, who was in the car, were in their seventies. V suffered a heart attack, fractured ribs, bruising and lacerations. Her husband suffered a rib injury and bruising. V also suffered the financial cost of the accident. D stayed at the scene. He suffered a head injury and had psychological problems. D's alcohol reading was 153 µg (nearly twice the limit). He was aged 24 and of good character. He was in work and was the sole breadwinner. Held. D could have walked to S or called a cab. *R v Dewdney* 2014 EWCA Crim 1722, 2015 1 Cr App R (S) 5 (p 36) was a worse case than this. D's motive provided some mitigation. We start at **3 years**, so with plea 2 years not 3.

See also: *R v Buckle* 2015 EWCA Crim 229, 1 Cr App R (S) 68 (p 477) (Plea. 2¼ times over drink/drive limit. Left pub with two children. Drove whilst disqualified. Children sustained fractures and internal bleeding. One now has difficulty in walking. Aged 34.

81 previous convictions including burglary, robbery, 10 TDAs and motoring offences. Drink/drive convictions in 1994, 2004, 2006 and 2013. Judge started at maximum of 5 years, making **42 months** with plea. Upheld.)

233.5   *Overtaking*

R v Smart 2015 EWCA Crim 1756 D pleaded early to dangerous driving causing serious injury. At dusk, D was overtaking slow-moving vehicles and then sought to overtake two at once. He was slightly exceeding the speed limit. D had repeatedly claimed he did not see the oncoming motorbike which he hit. The rider, V, aged 54, suffered life-changing injuries (which the Court chose not to list). They included a below-the-knee amputation and left him with very serious disadvantages. D was aged 71 with a clean driving record for over 50 years. His wife had health issues. A police officer said V bears D no ill-will. Held. D has been a safe and conscientious driver. It was a momentary albeit serious misjudgement. The accident has impacted on D very significantly. He has genuine remorse and finds it impossible not to relive the accident. This would be a Level 3 offence in the *Causing Death by Driving Guideline 2008* (Dangerous driving section). 3 years was the starting point. The fact that V did not die and the very compelling mitigation means we start at 2 years not 3, making with plea **16 months** not 2 years.

233.6   *Cases   Speeding*

R v Jenkins 2015 EWCA Crim 105, 1 Cr App R (S) 70 (p 491) D pleaded to two counts of causing serious injury by dangerous driving. No penalty was given for offences of no licence and no insurance. D was travelling at 73 mph in a 30 mph area. It was raining heavily. D's car collided with Mr and Mrs V's car in a head-on collision on their side of the road. The closing speed was estimated to be 90-100 mph. Mr and Mrs V were trapped in their vehicle for about an hour. All three had to be cut free. Mr V had a broken arm and an open fracture to his leg, a fractured ankle, two fractured ribs and a fractured hip. Part of his calf muscle had to be removed from his leg. He was confined to a wheelchair for some time and at the sentence hearing he had to walk with a stick. Mrs V had a broken arm, seven broken ribs, a punctured lung, internal bleeding and other injuries. D had fractures too. Mr and Mrs V's recovery was slow and painful. They had to postpone their daughter's wedding for a year. D had been in a similar accident not long before this one. D was aged 27 and had 23 convictions. In November 2013, he was convicted of driving without due care. D was in breach of two community orders. The Judge found D was showing off and thrill seeking. Held. This was a very serious case of bad driving. The driving was deliberate, sustained and prolonged. The case was aggravated by D's motoring record, the fact that two people were injured, the lack of insurance and that he only had a provisional licence. However, the Judge should not have passed consecutive sentences. *R v Noble* 2002 EWCA Crim 1713, 2003 2 Cr App R (S) 65 (p 312) applied. We agree with the Judge's starting point of 4½ years to reflect the aggravating features. We consider the case was evidentially overwhelming. D was trapped in his car so there was no issue as to identity. There could be no issue about causation or that the driving was dangerous. We consider 20% credit not full credit was appropriate. That makes **3 years 7 months** not 4 years 6 months in all.

See also: *R v Dewdney* 2014 EWCA Crim 1722, 2015 1 Cr App R (S) 5 (p 36) (Plea. At 8.00 am after ignoring warnings, D drove well in excess of 50 mph over humpback bridge. Lost control of car. Ecstasy in blood. Three passengers injured. One had a brain haemorrhage and several fractures. One had fractured vertebrae and spine. One lost part of scalp. D had a fractured skull. Convicted of dangerous driving when aged 14. Other relevant previous convictions. Starting at **4½ years** was severe but upheld.)

R v Chrzaszcz 2014 EWCA Crim 2185 (30% credit. D reversed, stopped, and then continued at speed, with five-year-old son in back of vehicle. Vehicles were hit, property damaged, and V struck. V had a fractured pelvis, knee and lower back and a ruptured bladder. D, drunk, was almost five times over the limit (2½ hours after). Aged 28, remorseful with references and good character. This case was one of the worst of its kind. Starting at about 4½ years, making **3 years**, was severe but upheld.)

R v Iqbal 2014 EWCA Crim 2353 (Pleas to three counts and aggravated vehicle-taking. Took mother's car, driving at over 100 mph in a 30 mph limit. Passengers feared for their lives. D lost control of the car, crashed into a tree and his passengers were seriously injured. D fled the scene. Aged 21, very bad record and on licence. As it was a very bad case, the Judge was able to start at 5 years, the maximum. **40 months** after plea upheld.)

R v Hussain 2015 EWCA Crim 1016, 2 Cr App R (S) 52 (p 379) (Plea (10% credit). D, a taxi driver, at work but without a passenger, sped at about 50 mph in 30 mph area. Jumped pedestrian lights and hit an 18-year-old woman with a glancing blow. She had her leg amputated and sustained other horrific and life-changing injuries. D had three speeding offences. Aged 33. **2 years** was severe not manifestly excessive.)

234   DATA PROTECTION ACT 1998 OFFENCES

234.1

Data Protection Act 1998 s 55 (obtaining or disclosing personal data without consent)
Mode of trial Triable either way
Maximum sentence On indictment a fine. Summary a £5,000 fine for offences committed before 12 March 2015 and an unlimited fine thereafter.[211] There are maximum fines for those aged under 18, see **14.38** in Volume 1.
Financial penalties The Information Commissioner has power to impose monetary penalties for serious contraventions of Data Protection Act 1998 s 4(4).[212]
Consultation paper In 2006, the Department of Constitutional Affairs (DCA)[213] published a consultation paper (CP/6) proposing custody for this offence. On 7 February 2007 the DCA said[214] it would make the offence punishable with 2 years on indictment and 6 months (rising to 12 months when CJA 2003 s 154 is in force) on summary conviction. No further intentions are known.
See also the **COMPUTER AND COMMUNICATION NETWORK OFFENCES** chapter.

235   DEATH BY DRIVING: GENERAL PRINCIPLES

There are five chapters dealing with death by driving. They are:
DEATH BY DRIVING: GENERAL PRINCIPLES,
DEATH BY DRIVING: CARELESS DRIVING (DRINK/DRUG-RELATED),
DEATH BY DRIVING: CARELESS DRIVING (SIMPLE),
DEATH BY DRIVING: DANGEROUS DRIVING and
DEATH BY DRIVING: DISQUALIFIED/NO LICENCE/UNINSURED, WHEN

235.1   *Sentencing Guidelines Council guideline*
Causing Death by Driving Guideline 2008, see www.banksr.com Other Matters Guidelines tab The guidelines apply to sentences for offenders aged 18+.
Introduction
page 2 para 1 This guideline applies to the four offences of causing death by dangerous driving, causing death by [careless][215] driving under the influence of alcohol or drugs, causing death by careless driving and causing death by driving: unlicensed, disqualified or uninsured drivers.
para 2 [About the CPS policy and the offence definitions, which are not listed]

---

[211] Legal Aid, Sentencing and Punishment of Offenders Act 2012 s 85(1) and (4) and Legal Aid, Sentencing and Punishment of Offenders Act 2012 (Commencement No 11) Order 2015 2015/504
[212] Data Protection Act 1998 s 55A-55E as inserted by Criminal Justice and Immigration Act 2008 s 144(1). In force 1 October 2009, Criminal Justice and Immigration Act 2008 (Commencement No 11) Order 2009 2009/2606. See also the Data Protection (Monetary Penalties) Order 2010 2010/910, in force 6/4/10.
[213] This was renamed the Ministry of Justice in 2007. Ed.
[214] News and press document no. AR0038906.
[215] There is a typo in the guideline. The word 'careless' was omitted.

para 3   Because the principal harm done by these offences [the death of a person] is an element of the offence, the factor that primarily determines the starting point for sentence is the culpability of the offender. Accordingly, for all offences other than causing death by driving: unlicensed, disqualified or uninsured drivers, the central feature should be an evaluation of the quality of the driving involved and the degree of danger that it foreseeably created. These guidelines draw a distinction between those factors of an offence that are intrinsic to the quality of driving (referred to as 'determinants of seriousness') and those which, while they aggravate the offence, are not.

para 4   The levels of seriousness in the guidelines for those offences based on dangerous or careless driving alone have been determined by reference only to determinants of seriousness. Aggravating factors will have the effect of either increasing the starting point within the sentencing range provided or, in certain circumstances, of moving the offence up to the next sentencing range. The outcome will depend on both the number of aggravating factors present and the potency of those factors. Thus, the same outcome could follow from the presence of one particularly bad aggravating factor or two or more less serious factors.

para 5 [About Death by careless driving (drink-related), see **236.3**]

para 6 [About Death by driving: disqualified/no licence/uninsured, when, see **239.3**]

para 7   The degree to which an aggravating factor is present (and its interaction with any other aggravating and mitigating factors) will be immensely variable and the court is best placed to judge the appropriate impact on sentence. Clear identification of those factors relating to the standard of driving as the initial determinants of offence seriousness is intended to assist the adoption of a common approach.

page 3 **Assessing seriousness Determinants of seriousness**

para 8 There are five factors that may be regarded as determinants of offence seriousness which can be demonstrated in a number of ways. Common examples of each of the determinants are set out below and key issues are discussed in the text that follows in paragraphs 10-18 [which deal with alcohol/drugs, see **235.2**, avoidable distractions, see **235.6**, and vulnerable road users, see below].

Examples of the determinants are:

Awareness of risk
   a) a prolonged, persistent and deliberate course of very bad driving,

Effect of alcohol or drugs (see **235.2**)
   b) consumption of alcohol above the legal limit,
   c) consumption of alcohol at or below the legal limit where this impaired the offender's ability to drive,
   d) failure to supply a specimen for analysis,
   e) consumption of illegal drugs, where this impaired the offender's ability to drive,
   f) consumption of legal drugs or medication where this impaired the offender's ability to drive (including legal medication known to cause drowsiness) where the driver knew, or should have known, about the likelihood of impairment,

Inappropriate speed of vehicle (see **238.20**)
   g) greatly excessive speed, racing, competitive driving against another vehicle,
   h) driving above the speed limit,
   i) driving at a speed that is inappropriate for the prevailing road or weather conditions,
   j) driving a PSV, HGV or other goods vehicle at a speed that is inappropriate either because of the nature of the vehicle or its load, especially when carrying passengers,

Seriously culpable behaviour of offender
   k) aggressive driving (such as driving much too close to the vehicle in front, persistent inappropriate attempts to overtake, or cutting in after overtaking),
   l) driving while using a hand-held mobile phone,

m) driving whilst the driver's attention is avoidably distracted, for example by reading or adjusting the controls of electronic equipment such as a radio, hands-free mobile phone or satellite navigation equipment,

n) driving when knowingly suffering from a medical or physical condition that significantly impairs the offender's driving skills, including failure to take pre-scribed medication,

o) driving when knowingly deprived of adequate sleep or rest, especially where commercial concerns had a bearing on the commission of the offence,

p) driving a poorly maintained or dangerously loaded vehicle, especially where commercial concerns had a bearing on the commission of the offence,

Victim

q) failing to have proper regard to vulnerable road users.

page 4 para 9 Issues relating to the determinants of seriousness are considered below.

Vulnerable road users

page 4 para 17 Cyclists, motorbike riders, horse riders, pedestrians and those working in the road are vulnerable road users and a driver is expected to take extra care when driving near them. Driving too close to a bike or horse, allowing a vehicle to mount the pavement, driving into a cycle lane, and driving without the care needed in the vicinity of a pedestrian crossing, hospital, school or residential home, are all examples of factors that should be taken into account when determining the seriousness of an offence.

para 18 The fact that the victim of a causing death by driving offence was a particularly vulnerable road user is a factor that should be taken into account when determining the seriousness of an offence.

Aggravating and mitigating factors

a) paras 19-21 More than one person killed (see **235.10**)

b) paras 22-23 Effect on the offender (see **235.9**)

c) Actions of others

page 5 para 24 Where the actions of the victim or a third party contributed to the commission of an offence, this should be acknowledged and taken into account as a mitigating factor.

d) para 25 Offender's age/lack of driving experience (see **235.14**)

Personal mitigation

a) para 26 Good driving record (see **235.13**)

b) Conduct after the offence

para 27 Giving assistance at the scene (see **235.3**)

Remorse

page 6 para 28 Whilst it can be expected that anyone who has caused death by driving would be expected to feel remorseful, this cannot undermine its importance for sentencing purposes. Remorse is identified as personal mitigation in the Council guideline[216] and the Council can see no reason for it to be treated differently for this group of offences. It is for the court to determine whether an expression of remorse is genuine, [and] where it is, this should be taken into account as personal mitigation.

para 29 **Summary** (see **235.13**)

235.2   *Alcohol/drugs, Driving under the influence of*

Causing Death by Driving Guideline 2008, see www.banksr.com Other Matters Guide-lines tab The guidelines apply to sentences for offenders aged 18+.

Introduction

page 3 paras para 8 **Determinants of seriousness** There are five factors (1-5 below) that may be regarded as determinants of offence seriousness each of which can be demon-strated in a number of ways. Common examples of each of the determinants are: (For the other four factors see **235.1**)

---

[216] *Overarching Principles: Seriousness Guideline 2004* para 1.25

2 Effect of alcohol or drugs
  b) consumption of alcohol above the legal limit,
  c) consumption of alcohol at or below the legal limit where this impaired the offender's ability to drive,
  d) failure to supply a specimen for analysis,
  e) consumption of illegal drugs, where this impaired the offender's ability to drive,
  f) consumption of legal drugs or medication where this impaired the offender's ability to drive (including legal medication known to cause drowsiness) where the driver knew, or should have known, about the likelihood of impairment,

page 4 para 10 The guidelines apply to sentences of offenders aged 18+. For those offences where the presence of alcohol or drugs is not an element of the offence, where there is sufficient evidence of driving impairment attributable to alcohol or drugs, the consumption of alcohol or drugs prior to driving will make an offence more serious. Where the drugs were legally purchased or prescribed, the offence will only be regarded as more serious if the offender knew or should have known that the drugs were likely to impair driving ability.

para 11 Unless inherent in the offence or charged separately, failure to provide a specimen for analysis (or to allow a blood specimen taken without consent to be analysed) should be regarded as a determinant of offence seriousness.

para 12 Where it is established to the satisfaction of the court that an offender had consumed alcohol or drugs unwittingly before driving, that may be regarded as a mitigating factor. However, consideration should be given to the circumstances in which the offender decided to drive or continue to drive when driving ability was impaired.

For more detail see careless driving (drink/drug related) chapter and the alcohol paragraphs for death by dangerous driving at **238.6**.

Note: The Death by Driving: Careless driving offence has now been widened to include drug-related offences, see the **Drug-related offences** note at **236.1**. Ed.

235.3   *Assisting at the scene   Defendant takes positive action*
Causing Death by Driving Guideline 2008, see www.banksr.com Other Matters Guidelines tab page 6 para 27 **Giving assistance at the scene** There may be many reasons why an offender does not offer help to the victims at the scene – the offender may be injured, traumatised by shock, afraid of causing further injury or simply have no idea what action to take and it would be inappropriate to assess the offence as more serious on this ground (and so increase the level of sentence). However, where an offender gave direct, positive assistance to victim(s) at the scene of a collision, this should be regarded as personal mitigation.

R v Richardson 2006 EWCA Crim 3186, 2007 2 Cr App R (S) 36 (p 211) It is a specific mitigating feature that the defendant behaved responsibly and took positive action to assist at the scene. It is not a mitigating feature that he merely waited or remained at the scene. We have in mind direct action to assist the victim(s).

235.4   *Defendant distraught etc./What purpose does a prison sentence serve?*
Att-Gen's Ref No 36 of 1994 1995 16 Cr App R (S) 723 at 726 LCJ The sentencing Judge said that human life could not be brought back and he did not think any useful purpose would be served by sending the defendant to prison. Held. We cannot agree with that. There are many cases, unhappily, where offences of this kind are committed by persons of otherwise good character, who will be distraught by what has happened and who will have the fact that they have killed someone with them for the rest of their lives. But to say that no useful purpose is served by sending offenders to prison is to ignore the deterrent factor and the need to establish, to the knowledge of the public (and the driving public in particular), that where one drives with a substantial amount of drink, and one drives in such a way as to kill someone, then a sentence of imprisonment will almost always be required.

235.5 Defendant not the driver of the vehicle that killed the victim
R v Bowyer 2009 EWCA Crim 1112, 2010 1 Cr App R (S) 22 (p 121) D was convicted of death by dangerous driving. He and H were racing each other and overtaking each other at speeds of 80 mph+ over 4-7 miles on two A-roads with two roundabouts. The driving was aggressive and competitive. The cars were seen almost bumper to bumper. A van was nearly driven off the road. H overtook a lorry and collided with an oncoming car. H and the other driver died. Three other cars were involved in the incident. D was aged 23. In 2003, he cut across the front of his girlfriend's car at a traffic light. She drove off and when she stopped he kicked her car door. Criminal damage was charged. In 2004, D failed to give way to an oncoming motor-cyclist at a roundabout. The motor-cyclist fell and was injured. Due care and failing to stop were charged. **6½ years** upheld. 5-year disqualification not 7. (The judgment makes no point on the fact the accident was caused by H's car. Ed.)
Att-Gen's Ref No 61 of 2009 2009 EWCA Crim 2561, 2010 2 Cr App R (S) 4 (p 21) D was racing with V at 80 mph for over 1.84 km. V was killed and the other road user was severely injured. Held. The deceased did contribute to his own death but it was little mitigation as he had plainly been egged on by this offender and the very vice of racing or competitive driving is to incite another to join in that activity.

235.6 Distractions   Mobile phones etc., Defendant using   Guidelines and Judicial guidance
Causing Death by Driving Guideline 2008, see www.banksr.com Other Matters Guidelines tab
page 4 para 13 **Avoidable distractions** A distinction has been drawn between ordinary avoidable distractions and those that are more significant because they divert the attention of the driver for longer periods or to a greater extent. In this guideline these are referred to as a gross avoidable distraction. The guideline for causing death by dangerous driving provides for a gross avoidable distraction to place the offence in a higher level of seriousness.
para 14 Any avoidable distraction will make an offence more serious but the degree to which an offender's driving will be impaired will vary. Where the reaction to the distraction is significant, it may be the factor that determines whether the offence is based on dangerous driving or on careless driving. In those circumstances, care must be taken to avoid 'double counting'.
para 15 Using a hand-held mobile phone when driving is, in itself, an unlawful act. The fact that an offender was avoidably distracted by using a hand-held mobile phone when a causing death by driving offence was committed will always make an offence more serious. Reading or composing text messages over a period of time will be a gross avoidable distraction and is likely to result in an offence of causing death by dangerous driving being in a higher level of seriousness.
para 16 Where it is proved that an offender was briefly distracted by reading a text message or adjusting a hands-free set or its controls at the time of the collision, this would be on a par with consulting a map or adjusting a radio or satellite navigation equipment: activities that would be considered an avoidable distraction.
Page 10 para 3 For death by dangerous driving cases, Level 2 is likely to be characterised by 'gross avoidable distraction such as reading or composing text messages over a period of time' with an **8-year** starting point. Level 3 is likely to be characterised by 'driving whilst avoidably distracted' with a **3-year** starting point, see **238.3**.
Att-Gen's Ref No 17 of 2009 2009 EWCA Crim 1003, 2010 1 Cr App R (S) 12 (p 62) LCJ Inevitably drivers using mobile phones are distracted to some degree. Their driving does not have the full attention it needs. Drivers may continue to be distracted after they have just been using the phone or texting. This reduced attention is the consequence of a deliberate choice by drivers. The message still has not been heeded that it is always dangerous to be texting or using a hand-held mobile phone while driving

and that there is never any excuse for doing so. If and when something urgent needs attention so badly that it requires the use of the phone or the sending of a text, it is then urgent enough to stop the vehicle. A custodial sentence is inevitable. The only question is its length. That, as ever, is fact-specific. Perhaps the most significant fact is whether the phoning or texting happened at the moment of, or in the immediate few seconds before, impact, or whether the earlier phoning or texting may have played some part in the driver's lack of proper attention to the road ahead.

235.7   *Distractions   Mobile phone etc., Defendant using   Cases*
R v Knox 2009 EWCA Crim 1880, 2010 1 Cr App R (S) 52 (p 331) D was convicted of causing death by dangerous driving. He had been a taxi driver for some years. In the early hours, he was returning to base after dropping off a fare. He was travelling on the A1, a dual carriageway, at about 88 mph in a 70 mph area. D overtook a Clio which was travelling at about 70 mph. He pulled into the nearside lane and hit a motor-cycle travelling at 35-40 mph. The Clio ran over the motor-cyclist, who was wearing a high-visibility jacket, and the motor-cyclist died. D had been using a hand-held open phone line to his partner for 18 minutes before the collision. His Bluetooth device was not charged up. When interviewed he lied about the phone. D was aged 32 with no previous driving convictions. The Judge placed the offence at Level 3. Held. **4 years** not 5 and **4 years' disqualification** not 7, because of his impressive previous driving record.
R v Arora 2014 EWCA Crim 104 D pleaded to causing death by careless driving and was convicted of causing death by dangerous driving. V, a wife and mother, drove a Vauxhall Corsa and it broke down. The weather was fine and visibility was excellent. M came to assist V. M towed V's car at a very slow speed. There was no 'Towing' warning sign and whilst M's van had its hazard lights illuminated, V's Corsa did not. Three other vehicles overtook M and V without incident. M was aware of D's 44-tonne lorry in the inside lane, about 50 metres behind. There were no other vehicles between them. A fraction of a second later, M felt a thud and saw the lorry scraping down the side of his van, taking the wing mirror with it. In that time the lorry hit the Corsa, causing 'massive' damage, and V was killed. V was not wearing her seatbelt at the time, but it was not possible to say whether her so doing would have prevented the fatal injuries. It was discovered that D made two voice calls and received and sent one text message from his hands-free phone. This activity was timed when D was travelling at the maximum limited speed of 56 mph. D was travelling at that maximum speed when he hit the Corsa, and had slowed to 53 mph when he hit the van towing the Corsa. The accident examiner concluded that M's and V's vehicles were travelling at a speed which would have been hazardous to other road users. D had a clear, unobstructed view of the road ahead of him for about 8 seconds prior to the collision. The only plausible explanation for his failure to act appropriately was the distraction caused by the use of his telephone. D was aged 45 at appeal and had one conviction for 79 offences of making false records or entries on his tachograph. The Judge placed the case in Category 3. Held. As to the contribution of the victims, their actions were of no real consequence. It was lawful for slow-moving vehicles to use the A-road, visibility was good and D had an unobstructed view. There was no basis to suggest that had the Corsa had its hazard lights illuminated, D would have seen the vehicles. The same applies to the conclusion that V was not wearing a seatbelt. Although not using his phone at the time, D had been doing so immediately beforehand. The potential but avoidable consequences of his reduced attention were so much more serious given that the vehicle he was driving was a 44-tonne lorry. The fact that D was on bail for a tachograph offence was plainly relevant. 3½ years was severe, but not manifestly excessive.
Old cases: *R v Payne* 2007 EWCA Crim 157, 2 Cr App R (S) 45 (p 287) (**4 years**) *R v Hopkins* 2008 EWCA Crim 2971 (**6½ years**) *Att-Gen's Ref No 17 of 2009* 2009 EWCA Crim 1003, 2010 1 Cr App R (S) 12 (p 62) (**21 months** was a lenient sentence) *R v Taylor* 2009 EWCA Crim 38, 2 Cr App R (S) 55 (p 388) (**6 years**)

For a summary of the first case, see the 6th edition of this book, for the second case see the 8th edition and for the third case see the 9th edition.

235.8   *Fleeing the scene of the crime/Failing to stop*
Causing Death by Driving Guideline 2008, see www.banksr.com Other Matters Guidelines tab The guidelines apply to sentences of offenders aged 18+.
page 11 **Additional aggravating factors** 7 'Driving off in an attempt to avoid detection or apprehension' is now an 'additional aggravating factor', see also **239.3**.
Note: Strangely the factor is only listed in the 'Death by dangerous driving' guideline. However, judges treat this factor as relevant to all death by driving offences. Ed.
R v Rosevere 2008 EWCA Crim 2142 D was convicted of causing death by dangerous driving. The Judge did not hold the failure to stop after the event as an aggravating factor as this was a 'difficult area' of Bolton and D gave evidence that he feared for his personal safety. Held. Even if this was a difficult area this would not have prevented D from calling the police when he got home. The failure to report aggravated the offence.
R v Williams 2014 EWCA Crim 147 D pleaded to death by careless driving when over the prescribed limit. His car with three passengers overturned and came to rest on the passenger side. V died. D went down on his hands and knees crying, but was unhurt. One of the other passengers lived nearby and his father came to the scene. The father was urged to take D out of sight of the car because D was in such shock and it was freezing. D was ushered away. Held. This was not a case where D ran away to avoid the police and there was evidence not before the Judge that D was shepherded away from the scene out of compassion. The Judge should not have considered that as aggravation.

235.9   *Injuries, The defendant's own*
Causing Death by Driving Guideline 2008, see www.banksr.com Other Matters Guidelines tab page 5 para 22 **Effect on the offender** Injury to the offender may be a mitigating factor when the offender has suffered very serious injuries. In most circumstances, the weighting it is given will be dictated by the circumstances of the offence and the effect should bear a direct relationship to the extent to which the offender's driving was at fault – the greater the fault, the less the effect on mitigation. This distinction will be of particular relevance where an offence did not involve any fault in the offender's standard of driving.
R v Cooksley 2003 EWCA Crim 996, 2004 1 Cr App R (S) 1 (p 1) LCJ The offender's own injuries are a relevant consideration. The injuries can make the sentence of imprisonment a greater punishment than usual. His injuries are also in themselves a punishment and should bring home to the offender, in the most direct possible way, what can be the consequences of dangerous driving. The fact that the offender has been injured should not automatically be treated as a mitigating factor and that only 'very serious, or life-changing, injury' should have a <u>significant</u> effect on the sentence. Some indication of the scale of the effect is provided by the facts of *R v Maloney* 1996 1 Cr App R (S) 221. The offender had a very severe head injury, severe facial injuries, he lost the sight of his right eye and he lost his right little finger, and there was continuing loss of use of his right arm and leg. This Court reduced the sentence from 5 to **4 years** but in doing so were taking into account not only the injuries, but the fact that the trial Judge had erroneously sentenced the appellant on the basis that he had consumed an excessive amount of alcohol.
Note: This is an old guideline case and the *Causing Death by Driving Guideline 2008* takes precedence over it. Ed.
See also *R v Stanko* 2010 EWCA Crim 1883 at **238.7**.
See also the **DEFENDANT** *Injured during offence, Defendant* para at **240.38**.
See also the **MOTHERS** chapter.

235.10   *More than one person killed   Guidelines and judicial guidance*
Causing Death by Driving Guideline 2008, see www.banksr.com Other Matters Guidelines tab page 5 para 19 **More than one person killed** The seriousness of any offence

included in these guidelines will generally be greater where more than one person is killed since it is inevitable that the degree of harm will be greater. In relation to the assessment of culpability, whilst there will be circumstances in which a driver could reasonably anticipate the possible death of more than one person (for example, the driver of a vehicle with passengers (whether that is a bus, taxi or private car) or a person driving badly in an area where there are many people), there will be many circumstances where the driver could not anticipate the number of people who would be killed.

para 20 The greater obligation on those responsible for driving other people is not an element essential to the quality of the driving and so has not been included amongst the determinants of seriousness that affect the choice of sentencing range. Although concurrent sentences are likely to be imposed (in recognition of the fact that the charges relate to one episode of offending behaviour), each individual sentence is likely to be higher because the offence is aggravated by the fact that more than one death has been caused.

para 21 Where more than one person is killed, that will aggravate the seriousness of the offence because of the increase in harm. Where the number of people killed is high and that was reasonably foreseeable, the number of deaths is likely to provide sufficient justification for moving an offence into the next highest sentencing band.

R v Kallaway 1998 2 Cr App R (S) 220 The defendant pleaded to three counts of causing death by dangerous driving. Three people died. Held. The Judge had perhaps been overly affected by the fact there were three deaths. That was clearly relevant but the number of deaths is sometimes a matter of chance and does not necessarily reflect the seriousness of the driving which caused the deaths. (For further details of the case, see the 2nd edition of this book.)

R v Cooksley 2003 EWCA Crim 996, 2004 1 Cr App R (S) 1 (p 1) LCJ Even where there is no reason to suggest that the defendant is knowingly putting more than one person at risk, the fact that the consequences of dangerous driving are particularly serious, for example involving multiple deaths, is a relevant factor as to the length of sentence. That is the view that will be taken by the public. However, we are certainly not suggesting that the sentence should be multiplied according to the number of persons who sadly lose their life. It is still necessary to regard the offender's culpability in relation to the driving as the dominant component in the sentencing exercise. While the sentence is increased to reflect more than one death the sentence must remain proportionate to the nature of an offence which does not involve any intent to injure.

Note: The guidelines must take precedence over these two cases. Ed.

235.11   *More than one person killed*   *Cases*

R v Kibble 2009 EWCA Crim 592, 2 Cr App R (S) 93 (p 616) D was convicted of three offences of causing death by dangerous driving. In the early hours, 10 days after he passed his driving test, D took three 15-year-old boys to obtain some take-away food. He had bought the car a few days before. Two of the boys asked O, the assistant at the food outlet, to deliver the food to a car park. This was done and the food was taken without payment. One of the boys called O "a Turkish cunt". D drove away with one of the boys saying, "Go, go, go". At an early stage D must have known he was being pursued by O. The road became an unlit rural A-road with a number of bends. Both drivers drove with a complete disregard for the rules of the road. At one point O's car made contact with D's car. D drove without any thought for the safety of his passengers. The road was dry and in good condition. Some 1.7 miles from the car park O attempted to overtake. D tried to negotiate a bend and crossed to the other side of the road, hitting O's car and then a tree. All the passengers were killed. An expert said D's car had been orientated towards the nearside of the carriageway and mounted the grass verge. D attempted to correct that and over-steered, hitting O's car, which was overtaking dangerously. D, aged 17, had no convictions but was someone who liked to show off. O was also convicted of the same counts and sentenced to 8 years. Held. The road had a 60 mph speed limit but bearing in mind D's inexperience and that he was being closely and dangerously pursued

D's speed (not specified. Ed.) was wholly excessive. Were it not for the three deaths this would have been a Level 2 case. Because of the chase it would lie at the upper end. The three deaths justified a move to Level 1. The mitigation was his youth, his remorse, his lack of driving experience and his lack of convictions. **6 years'** detention not 8.

R v Stanko 2010 EWCA Crim 1883 D pleaded to causing death by dangerous driving, driving with excess alcohol and failing to stop. He attended a barbecue and drank about one-third of a bottle of whisky[217] mixed with Coca-Cola over four to five hours along with some other alcoholic drinks. His hostess, M, offered him a bed for the night, taking the view that he was too drunk to drive. M took D's keys. D searched for the keys for a couple of hours, then drove away after finding them. He returned to the house and asked P if he would like to accompany him. P attempted to persuade D not to drive. An independent witness then saw D drive away at 45-50 mph. Six pedestrians, one of whom was 12 years old, were walking along the pavement when D drove around the corner. It was not possible to establish how fast D was driving. However, he lost control, mounted the pavement and collided with a wall and the pedestrians. Five out of six pedestrians were hit. One died at the scene. Another was pronounced dead some three hours later. Another suffered serious injuries including fractures. The fourth suffered injuries including possible nerve damage. The fifth, the 12-year-old, suffered severe traumatic brain injuries and when D was sentenced, was confined to a wheelchair and had to be fed through a tube. It was likely that she would remain significantly disabled. D drove away from the collision but was found by police standing by his car. He claimed his car had been stolen but changed his story several times. Two hours after the collision a breathalyser showed 69 μg (almost twice the legal limit). D claimed he could not remember whether he was driving or not. The Judge said that this was a tragic and extremely serious case and took for his starting point 12½ years. Held. We have no doubt that the sentence of **10 years** was neither wrong in principle nor manifestly excessive. This was a Level 1 offence. The expert evidence was that D was travelling in excess of the speed limit. There were other aggravating factors. In our view D had no choice but to plead guilty therefore the Judge was entitled to withhold some credit for the guilty plea.

R v Etherington 2014 EWCA Crim 1867, 2015 1 Cr App R (S) 7 (p 59) D pleaded at the first opportunity to causing death by dangerous driving. V1 and V2, aged 14 and 16, were close friends. D drove past in his significantly modified car. As D did so, he revved the engine making a significant noise due to the modified exhaust. V1 and V2 then shouted abuse at D. He returned shortly afterwards, driving over a bridge and accelerating from 61 to 71 mph. V1 and V2 were in the road, their arms over each other's shoulder and, being 30 m from the bridge, were in plain sight of D. D drove through them and failed to stop, despite his car being very badly damaged. D stopped at a petrol station and phoned the police. V1 died instantly and V2, rendered unconscious and with her leg amputated, died six hours later, holding her mother's hand. D failed a drugs test, having taken mephedrone and ketamine. He claimed initially that the victims had jumped out in front of him and in interview claimed V2 was 'playing chicken' and, "it was as if V2 wanted to be hit". He also said he had slowed down, only leaving the scene for his own safety. His car was fitted with a black box recorder, revealing his true speed. D was aged 20 and had convictions for speeding (×2 and one was for racing) and failing to stop. D pleaded under the Early Guilty Plea Scheme. He told probation that he wished that he was the one who had died and was prescribed medication for nightmares he suffered in prison. Whilst there, he had also saved the life of a cellmate. The Judge started at near 14 years and reduced it to 12 years to reflect his age and the mitigation. Then he gave D only a 25% discount due to the overwhelming prosecution evidence.[218]

---

[217] It is not known how large the bottle of whisky was. Ed.

[218] At paragraph 9, when dealing with the discount, the principles have been mixed up. This summary is based on what it is assumed the Judge meant to say.

Held. D was driving under the influence of drugs, whether or not it affected his driving. D knew the girls were in the road and deliberately increased his speed. He failed to brake when it must have been obvious a tragedy was imminent. He lied to the police and sought to blame the girls. The Judge's approach cannot be faulted. The sentence was fully merited. **9 years' imprisonment**[219] upheld.

See also: *R v Girdler* 2010 EWCA Crim 2775 (Convicted on two counts. Erratic speeding driving killing two drivers, one in parked car. Estimated at 100 mph. Failure to provide a specimen on four occasions. **11 years** was not manifestly excessive.)

Old case: *R v Smith* 2007 EWCA Crim 2539, 2008 2 Cr App R (S) 1 (p 1) **(9 years)** For a summary of the case see the 8th edition of this book.

See also the *Consecutive or concurrent? Should the sentences be* para at **235.18**.

235.12   *Mothers of young children*
R v Petherick 2012 EWCA Crim 2214, 2013 1 Cr App R (S) 116 (p 598) (Speeding, persistent and inappropriate overtaking and twice over the limit. Principles considered), see **238.7**.)

235.13   *Personal mitigation, Defendant's   Guideline and judicial guidance*
Causing Death by Driving Guideline 2008, see www.banksr.com Other Matters Guidelines tab page 6 para 26 **Good driving record** This is not a factor that automatically should be treated as a mitigating factor, especially now that the presence of previous convictions is a statutory aggravating factor. However, any evidence to show that an offender has previously been an exemplary driver, for example having driven an ambulance, police vehicle, bus, taxi or similar vehicle conscientiously and without incident for many years, is a fact that the courts may well wish to take into account by way of personal mitigation. This is likely to have even greater effect where the driver is driving on public duty (for example, on ambulance, fire service or police duties) and was responding to an emergency.

para 29 Evidence that an offender is normally a careful and conscientious driver, giving direct, positive assistance to a victim and genuine remorse may be taken into account as personal mitigation and may justify a reduction in sentence.

R v Braid 2002 EWCA Crim 737, 2 Cr App R (S) 110 (p 509) The Judge said that personal circumstances do not weigh heavily in the balance in cases of causing death by dangerous driving. Held. We agree with the Judge about the weight of personal circumstances. Those falling to be sentenced not infrequently have the highest personal credentials and so generate very real sympathy. The courts have to reflect the loss of a precious life and to demonstrate to all that dangerous driving is a very serious social evil, which if it causes death will almost inevitably lead to a substantial custodial sentence.

Note: This case was cited with approval in *R v Cooksley* 2003 EWCA Crim 996, 2004 1 Cr App R (S) 1 (p 1), the old guideline case, but both cases are old and both should be treated carefully. Ed.

See also the **DEFENDANT** *Personal mitigation* para at **240.51**.

235.14   *Unqualified driver/Lack of driving experience*
Causing Death by Driving Guideline 2008, see www.banksr.com Other Matters Guidelines tab The guidelines apply to sentences of offenders aged 18+.

page 6 para 25 **Offender's age/lack of driving experience** The *Overarching Principles: Seriousness Guideline 2004* [see www.banksr.com Other Matters Guidelines tab] includes a generic mitigating factor 'youth or age, where it affects the responsibility of the individual defendant'. There is a great deal of difference between recklessness or irresponsibility, which may be due to youth, and inexperience in dealing with prevailing conditions or an unexpected or unusual situation that presents itself, which may be

---

[219] The sentence was unlawful as D should have received detention in a YOI, not imprisonment.

present regardless of the age of the offender. The fact that an offender's lack of driving experience contributed to the commission of an offence should be treated as a mitigating factor. In this regard, the age of the offender is not relevant.

Note: The offences are dealt with by the causing death by driving when disqualified offences, see the **DEATH BY DRIVING\: DISQUALIFIED/NO LICENCE/UNINSURED, WHEN** chapter. Ed.

235.15   *Victims   Judicial guidance*

Criminal Practice Directions 2015 EWCA Crim 1567 para VII F.3 e) The court must pass what it judges to be the appropriate sentence having regard to the circumstances of the offence and of the offender, taking into account, so far as the court considers it appropriate, the impact on the victim. The opinions of the victim or the victim's close relatives as to what the sentence should be are therefore not relevant, unlike the consequences of the offence on them. Victims should be advised of this. If, despite the advice, opinions as to sentence are included in the statement, the court should pay no attention to them.

R v Cooksley 2003 EWCA Crim 996, 2004 1 Cr App R (S) 1 (p 1) LCJ Where death does result often the effects of the offence will cause grave distress to the family of the deceased. The impact on the family is a matter that the courts can and should take into account. However, as was pointed out by Lord Taylor CJ in *Att-Gen's Ref Nos 14 and 24 of 1993* 1994 15 Cr App R (S) 640 at 644, 'We wish to stress that human life cannot be restored, nor can its loss be measured by the length of a prison sentence. We recognise that no term of months or years imposed on the offender can reconcile the family of a deceased victim to their loss, nor will it cure their anguish.' We refer to [what is now Criminal Practice Directions 2015 EWCA Crim 1567 para VII F] and to *R v Roach* 1999 2 Cr App R (S) 105 where the Court accepted that they could, as an act of mercy, reduce a sentence if relatives of a victim indicated that the punishment imposed on the offender was aggravating their distress. Lord Bingham LCJ said, "The court is not swayed by demands for vengeance and has to be very cautious in paying attention to pleas for mercy".

Att-Gen's Ref Nos 24 and 45 of 1994 1995 16 Cr App R (S) 583 at 586 LCJ No court can bring back to life those who have been killed. We understand the feelings of those relatives and friends of the deceased who believe that there ought to be a correlation between the loss of life and the length of sentence. We also understand that no length of sentence will ever satisfy those who lose loved ones that a proper correlation has been made. We must emphasise that this Court cannot be persuaded by campaigns or by clamour to pass extremely long sentences where the criminality of the offender does not justify it. This Court is concerned primarily with the criminality of the person who has caused the death. The fact of the death is, of itself, a factor in contributing to the length of sentence which should be passed. But essentially we have to look at the cases in the light of the offender's criminality.

Att-Gen's Ref No 66 of 1996 1998 1 Cr App R (S) 16 LCJ The families of the victims feel bitter and vindictive towards the defendant, whom they see as the author of their irreparable loss. This case contains such a feature. The family members of one of the victims have succeeded in reconciling themselves towards the consequences of this tragedy. The family of the other victim has not. Their feelings are understandable. No one who has not suffered such a loss is in a position to understand how they feel, and it would be entirely inappropriate to disparage or belittle the emotions of those who suffer in this way. It is nonetheless the duty of the trial judge and of this Court to judge cases dispassionately. The court must of course take account of the understandable outrage felt against any defendant who has caused consequences such as these. That is a sense of outrage shared by the wider public, which feels acute anxiety about the cruel, avoidable loss of life which is a feature of cases such as this. On the other hand, the court must take account of the interests of a defendant who has often, as here, not intended these consequences and is often, as here, devastated by them. The court cannot overlook the fact that no punishment it can impose will begin to match the deep sense of responsibility which defendants often feel. It is important that courts should do their best to approach their task objectively and dispassionately. They should not be overborne or intimidated into imposing sentences which they consider are unjust.

R v Porter (No 2) 2002 EWCA Crim 1121, 2 Cr App R (S) 50 (p 222) All judges are careful not to be over-influenced by the devastation that is caused.

Att-Gen's Ref No 77 of 2002 2002 EWCA Crim 2312, 2003 1 Cr App R (S) 111 (p 564) D pleaded to causing death by driving without due care having consumed alcohol above the prescribed limit. D and his passenger were said to be like brothers. They were in fact cousins. The cousin was killed. D was aged 20, of previous good character and genuinely remorseful. He was deeply depressed, had expressed suicidal thoughts and was spending a great deal of time at his cousin's grave. He had the support of all of his family (including the support of the sisters of the deceased). Since his sentence, a further report said that his attendance and standard of work had been very good. A sister of the deceased wrote movingly: 'Should (D) be taken away from us now [it] would be devastating.' Held. Both the impact of the crime on the victims and impact of the crime on D have to be approached with great care. Just as the impact of the death affects the level of sentence, the impact of death on D may do so too. A husband who is responsible for the death of a beloved wife, or a mother who kills her own child, will be carrying his or her own punishment to the grave and that is the sort of feature which may be relevant and weighed in the sentencing decision. It has always been recognised that in an exceptional case a non-custodial sentence is sometimes possible. The ability to exercise mercy and to identify the appropriate case in which mercy should be exercised has long been acknowledged as a judicial attribute. (For further details, see next section.)

R v Ritchie 2014 EWCA Crim 2114 D pleaded to causing death by careless driving. Held. There is no correlation between the length of the sentence and the loss of life. Nobody pretends that any sentence given to the offender can properly compensate for what had happened.

See also the **Victims** chapter.

235.16   *Victim dies after defendant dealt with for dangerous driving*

R v Munro 2001 1 Cr App R (S) 14 (p 45) D pleaded to dangerous driving and was sentenced to 15 months' imprisonment. A week later the case was re-listed and the Judge suspended the sentence because of D's family circumstances. At that stage, which was 7 months after the accident, the victim was still in hospital and was a quadriplegic. Thirteen months after the accident the victim left hospital but still required 24-hour care. A month later she died. D was then charged with causing death by dangerous driving. She pleaded and nearly two years after her first sentence was given **12 months'** imprisonment. D had driven in a highly dangerous way to and from her children's school. She drove at high speed on a road with bends. She lost control of the car both before and after collecting her children. She finally mounted the pavement and knocked over an elderly lady. Since her first sentence she had been stricken with guilt and had difficulty living with what she had done. The sentence of imprisonment had had a very considerable effect on her children which was likely to increase. A recent report showed she had suffered from post-traumatic stress disorder and had attempted to take her life. Held. The Judge was faced with a most difficult sentencing problem. The intrinsic culpability of D's conduct had not significantly changed. The victim's quality of life had been destroyed when she had been knocked down. If D had been dealt with for causing death by dangerous driving to start with the Judge would have been obliged to pass a sentence of **at least 3 years** which he could not have suspended. Sentences should reflect the gravity of the offences. The Judge had balanced all the competing interests and it was hard to criticise his decision. Notwithstanding the new information the appeal was dismissed.

See also the **Manslaughter** *Victim dies after defendant sentenced for the violence* para at **284.9**.

235.17   *Victims   The views of the relatives of the defendant who was related to/was friendly with deceased   Cases*

Causing Death by Driving Guideline 2008, see www.banksr.com Other Matters Guidelines tab page 5 **Effect on the offender** para 23 Where one or more of the victims was in a close personal or family relationship with the offender, this may be a mitigating factor. In line with the approach where the offender is seriously injured, the degree to which the relationship influences the sentence should be linked to offender culpability in relation to the commission of the offence. Mitigation for this reason is likely to have less effect where the culpability of the driver is particularly high.

R v Nunn 1996 2 Cr App R (S) 136 The opinions of the victim or the surviving members of the family about the sentence do not provide any sound basis for reassessing a sentence. If the victim feels utterly remorseful towards the criminal, and some do, the crime has still been committed and must be punished as it deserves. If the victim is obsessed with vengeance, which can in reality only be assuaged by a very long prison sentence, as also happens, the punishment cannot be made longer by the court than would otherwise be appropriate. Otherwise cases with identical features would be dealt with in widely different ways leading to improper and unfair disparity.

R v O'Brien 2001 1 Cr App R (S) 22 (p 79) D pleaded to causing death by dangerous driving. D showed remorse from the very beginning. The relatives said no useful purpose could be served by a custodial sentence. Held. The views of the family are to be greatly respected. Applying *R v Nunn* 1996 2 Cr App R (S) 136 and *R v Roche* 1999 2 Cr App R (S) 105 the views of the victims are not a relevant consideration whether they seek leniency or severity save in exceptional circumstances.

R v Matthews 2002 EWCA Crim 1484, 2003 1 Cr App R (S) 26 (p 120) D pleaded to the manslaughter of his brother. The family wrote letters about their support for D and their double loss. Held. Applying *R v Nunn* 1996 2 Cr App R (S) 136, we balance the public duty to indicate the gravity of the offence and on the other hand not adding to the punishment and anguish of the family by a sentence which causes them distress.

Att-Gen's Ref No 77 of 2002 2002 EWCA Crim 2312, 2003 1 Cr App R (S) 111 (p 564) On the day of his trial, D pleaded to causing death by driving without due care having consumed alcohol above the prescribed limit, having no insurance and no driving licence. Although D had had a number of driving lessons and a provisional licence he had never taken a test. D and his passenger were said to be like brothers. They were in fact cousins. D had been driven to a public house by his father, having had one or two drinks at home. He did not intend to drive that evening and so had had a further four or five pints of lager. At the end of the evening D's cousin, a long-distance lorry driver, asked D to drive him home in his (the cousin's) car. D, although feeling the worse for drink, agreed. D's girlfriend was also given a lift. At about 12.40 am D was driving along a single-carriageway road, subject to a 60 mph speed limit. There were no road markings or street lighting. The car suddenly veered to the right. This may have been due to the actions of his girlfriend who admitted that she might have grabbed the wheel because she was 'messing about, having a laugh'. A car travelling in the opposite direction collided with the nearside of the car driven by D. The cousin was pronounced dead at the scene, the girlfriend suffered cuts to her forehead and the driver of the other car was unhurt physically, but deeply shocked. A back calculation provided a likely figure of 120 mg of alcohol in 100 ml of blood at the time of the accident (equal to 52 µg in breath) (i.e. one-and-a-half times the legal limit). No defects were found to have contributed to the accident and there was no evidence that excessive speed had been a contributory factor. D was aged 20, of previous good character and genuinely remorseful. He was deeply depressed, had expressed suicidal thoughts and was spending a great deal of time at his cousin's grave. He had the support of all of his family (including the support of the sisters of the deceased). Since his sentence, a further report said that his attendance and standard of work had been very good. A sister of the deceased wrote movingly: 'Should [D] be taken away from us now [it] would be devastating.' Held.

Both the impact of the crime on the victims and impact of the crime on D have to be approached with great care. Just as the impact of the death affects the level of sentence, the impact of death on D may do so too. A husband who is responsible for the death of a beloved wife, or a mother who kills her own child, will be carrying his or her own punishment to the grave and that is the sort of feature which may be relevant and weighed in the sentencing decision. It has always been recognised that in an exceptional case a non-custodial sentence is sometimes possible. The ability to exercise mercy and to identify the appropriate case in which mercy should be exercised has long been acknowledged as a judicial attribute. This was a lenient sentence and a merciful sentence. **6-month Curfew Order and a Community Punishment Order** of 180 hours upheld.

R v Barker 2002 EWCA Crim 3070, 2003 2 Cr App R (S) 22 (p 110) D killed the three children of his partner. Held. The attitude of the mother is something that the Court should take into account. (For a summary of the case, see the 4th edition of this book.) Note: All these cases are old but they reflect the law that is applied today. Ed.

Passing the sentence

235.18   *Concurrent or consecutive? Should the sentences be*

R v James 2001 2 Cr App R (S) 32 (p 153) D was convicted of causing death by dangerous driving and driving while disqualified. D was disqualified from driving. Held. As the Judge had considered the fact he was disqualified in considering the aggravating factors it was wrong to make the disqualified driving sentence consecutive. The sentences were made concurrent. (For further details, see the 2nd edition of this book.)

R v Noble 2002 EWCA Crim 1713, 2003 1 Cr App R (S) 65 (p 312) It would be wrong in principle to impose consecutive sentences in respect of each death arising from a single piece of dangerous driving. For case details, see the 4th edition of this book.

See also the CONCURRENT AND CONSECUTIVE SENTENCES chapter in Volume 1 and the *More than one person killed* para at **235.10**.

235.19   *Deprivation Order   Guideline*

Causing Death by Driving Guideline 2008, see www.banksr.com Other Matters Guidelines tab page 7 para 32 **Deprivation order** A general sentencing power exists which enables courts to deprive an offender of property used for the purposes of committing an offence. A vehicle used to commit an offence included in this guideline can be regarded as being used for the purposes of committing the offence.

235.20   *Disqualification   Guideline*

Note: Disqualification is obligatory unless there are special reasons. The details are in the first paragraph of the relevant offence chapter and in the DISQUALIFICATION FROM DRIVING: OBLIGATORY chapter in Volume 1. Ed.

Causing Death by Driving Guideline 2008, see www.banksr.com Other Matters Guidelines tab. page 7 para 30 **Disqualification** For each offence, disqualification is a mandatory part of the sentence (subject to the usual (very limited) exceptions), and therefore an important element of the overall punishment for the offence. In addition, an order that the disqualification continues until the offender passes an extended driving test order is compulsory for those convicted of causing death by dangerous driving or by careless driving when under the influence, and discretionary in relation to the two other offences.

para 31 Any disqualification is effective from the date on which it is imposed. When ordering disqualification from driving, the duration of the order should allow for the length of any custodial period in order to ensure that the disqualification has the desired impact. In principle, the minimum period of disqualification should either equate to the length of the custodial sentence imposed (in the knowledge that the offender is likely to be released having served half of that term), or the relevant statutory minimum disqualification period, whichever results in the longer period of disqualification.

235.21   *Disqualification for how long?   Guideline case and judicial guidance*
Note: The new guideline replaces the old guideline case. However, the new guideline provides no assistance about the appropriate length of the disqualification. Consequently the pre-guideline law continues to be applied. Ed.
R v Cooksley 2003 EWCA Crim 996, 2004 1 Cr App R (S) 1 (p 1) LCJ Disqualifying the offender is a real punishment. The risk represented by the offender is reflected in the level of culpability which attaches to his driving so that matters relevant to fixing the length of the driving disqualification for the offence of causing death by dangerous driving will be much the same as those factors we have listed already. We have adopted four categories.
While those convicted of causing death by dangerous driving are likely to regard disqualification as an onerous part of the punishment for the offence, the main purpose of disqualification is forward-looking and preventative, rather than backward-looking and punitive. A driving ban is designed to protect road users in the future from an offender who, through his conduct on this occasion, and perhaps other occasions, has shown himself to be a real risk on the roads. In general, the risk represented by the offender is reflected in the level of culpability which attaches to his driving, so that matters relevant to fixing the length of the driving disqualification for the offence of causing death by dangerous driving will be much the same as those appearing in the list of aggravating factors for the offence itself. Shorter bans of **2 years** or so will be appropriate where the offender had a good driving record before the offence and where the offence resulted from a momentary error of judgment. Longer bans, between **3 and 5 years**, will be appropriate where, having regard to the circumstances of the offence and the offender's record, it is clear that the offender tends to disregard the rules of the road, or to drive carelessly or inappropriately. Bans between **5 and 10 years** may be used where the offence itself, and the offender's record, show that he represents a real and continuing danger to other road users. Disqualification for **life** is a highly exceptional course, but may be appropriate in a case where the danger represented by the offender is an extreme and indefinite one. *R v Noble* 2002 EWCA Crim 1713, 2003 1 Cr App R (S) 65 (p 312) was described by the Court of Appeal as 'one of those rare cases' where disqualification for life was necessary in order to protect the public.
The length of the ban should [not] be tailored to take into account the anticipated date of early release of the offender. On the other hand we accept that to extend the ban for a substantial period after release can be counter-productive particularly if it is imposed on an offender who is obsessed with cars or who requires a driving licence to earn his or her living, because it may tempt the offender to drive while disqualified. The balancing of these conflicting considerations is very much the responsibility of the sentencer. In doing so the balancing exercise will require the sentencer to take into account the requirement which now exists that an order must be made that the offender is required to pass an extended driving test.
R v France 2002 EWCA Crim 1419, 2003 1 Cr App R (S) 25 (p 108) Periods of disqualification vary substantially. The bracket appears to be that of **3-6 years**, but likely to be near the top of that bracket where more than one death has been caused but a bad previous driving record is absent.
R v Mair 2005 EWCA Crim 2532, 2006 1 Cr App R (S) 110 (p 643) D pleaded to death by dangerous driving. Held. 5 years' disqualification is appropriate where it is clear that the offender tends to disregard the rules of the road or to drive carelessly or inappropriately.
R v Woolston 2009 EWCA Crim 1295 The Court of Appeal considered the principles for disqualification in a death by dangerous driving case. Held. We have full regard to what was said in *R v Cooksley* 2003 EWCA Crim 996.

235.22   *Disqualification for how long? Less than 5 years*
R v Knox 2009 EWCA Crim 1880, 2010 1 Cr App R (S) 52 (p 331) (Taxi driver with impressive previous record. **4 years**) see **235.7**.

R v Smith 2011 EWCA Crim 241 D pleaded to causing death by dangerous driving. He had held a licence for 4 months. D was driving at around 50 mph, 20 mph in excess of the limit. He collided with two women, aged 60 and 84, as they crossed a road. They died as a result. His basis of plea was that he was not racing or showing off, and that his inexperience had led him to miss the brake pedal. D, aged 18, was of good character with references. The Judge accepted D's remorse as being genuine and deep. Held. But for the speed, the accident would not have happened. There was one major aggravating factor and that was the death of two innocent people. That of course does not affect the culpability of the offender. It is the same driving whether two people die, or one, or none. But the outcome matters to the sentence of the court, and in particular to the public sense of justice. There were a number of important mitigating factors, including the fact that this was a case of misjudgement, not reckless or deliberate action. 3 years' detention not 5 years' YOI and **4 years'** disqualification, not 7.

R v Coe 2015 EWCA Crim 169 D pleaded to causing death by careless driving and other related driving matters. D was riding a motorcycle along a three-lane road just before dawn at around 40 mph in a 30 mph zone. The road was wet and both light and visibility were poor. V, wearing dark clothes but with a white dog, began to cross the road. Two-thirds of the way across, V turned back. She waited for two vehicles to pass and then crossed the eastbound lane. She waited in the westbound lane momentarily for what has been calculated as being a quarter of a second. D drove into V. D left V, seriously injured, by the side of the road and stopped in a nearby pub's car park. Other motorists called an ambulance. D did not, despite having a mobile phone. D ran back to the scene to ask after V and to see if an ambulance had been called. D was uninsured and, after the accident, made a fraudulent application for insurance. V suffered serious injuries but deteriorated and died due to complications. D was sentenced to 12 months. Held. Each case depends on its own facts and circumstances and what is set out at para 31 of the *Causing Death by Driving Guideline 2008* cannot cater for every type of bad driving. This was a bad case of causing death by careless driving, but the period of disqualification was excessive. **2 years' disqualification**, not 3. Extended driving test upheld.

See also: *R v Smith* 2011 EWCA Crim 2844 (Plea to death by careless driving whilst over the limit and dangerous driving. Under speed limit but too fast for conditions. 45 µg. Failed to stop. Genuine remorse. Aged 39. **3-year** disqualification not 4.)

R v Dixon 2012 EWCA Crim 3149, 2013 2 Cr App R (S) 39 (p 270) (Plea. Dangerous driving case. 2 years' custody. Aged 23. After his stag weekend abroad. Driving home from delivery work which he had done all day. Tired. Hit three cars after veering into oncoming traffic. One died. Three injured. New driver. **3 years** not 5.)

235.23   *Disqualification for how long? 5+ years*

R v Woolston 2009 EWCA Crim 1295 D was convicted of death by dangerous driving. He drove a Hummer H2 on the M25. He hit queuing traffic where repairs were being carried out. A two-year-old passenger in the first car died and his five-year-old brother suffered a broken jaw and knee. The mother of the boys and her brother suffered whiplash injuries and bruising. The Hummer collided with four other cars whose occupants were all injured but not seriously. Two other cars were damaged. D was aged 41, of good character and had deep remorse. He was a bus driver who also drove limousines. The bus company sacked him for moonlighting. The pre-sentence report considered a repetition was highly unlikely. The Judge found that D had failed to notice warning signs about the repairs, was tired and deliberately took a risk to continue to drive. He found the case was at Level 2 in the guidelines. He was sentenced to 6 years and appealed the 10-year disqualification. Held. There was nothing to show that D would represent so great a risk to justify longer than 5 years, which is 2 years after halfway through his sentence. Despite the horror, death and injuries, as he was 41 with an unblemished driving record it was not right to impose more than a **5-year disqualification**.

R v Petit 2015 EWCA Crim 958 D pleaded to <u>manslaughter</u> and robbery. D drove with F from Bedford to Peterborough to supply V with some cannabis. V handed over the cash and F snatched it. Within seconds, D accelerated hard away. V was unable to disentangle himself from the car. The speed of the car reached up to 30 mph and V was dragged 138 metres and was thrown off, falling to the ground. He received massive head injuries and died. D carried on driving, initially the wrong way on a one way street. When seen by police he lied. He received 8½ years (no appeal) and a 10-year disqualification. The defence said the dangerous driving was over a short distance and relied on the guideline for disqualification where the offence is death by driving (see **235.20**). That says the period of disqualification should equate with the length of the custodial term, knowing that the defendant is likely to be released halfway through the term. The prosecution said the driving was deliberate and sustained and there was a very high degree of danger to V which was obvious. Held. This is only a rule of thumb. The pre-plea starting point was about 10 years. The actual term (10 years) was only 1½ years longer than the custodial term imposed (8½ years). Because of the high degree of danger and the nature of the driving, **10-year disqualification** was not manifestly excessive.
See also: *R v Maddison* 2010 EWCA Crim 1099 (Mistook distances in cone reducing area on M1. Two passengers killed. Said he would never drive again. **5-year disqualification** not 8) For more detail, see **238.16**.
R v Hopkins 2008 EWCA Crim 2971 (**10-year disqualification**).
R v Anderson 2014 EWCA Crim 180 (Plea to death by careless driving (drink/drug-related). Drank three pints of beer and 10 whiskey miniatures whilst waiting for, and during, a delayed domestic flight. Collected rental car after the flight and drove on a motorway substantially in excess of 70 mph limit. Drove into the rear of another vehicle, killing driver instantly. Attempted to flee the scene then hid in bushes for 2 hours. Severe financial impact on family. Two and two-thirds over the limit at the time of the crash. Not far short of dangerous driving. Positive good character. Full credit. 7 years' imprisonment not challenged. D was not a driver by profession but his employment would be assisted by a shorter period of disqualification. **7-year disqualification**, not 10.)
R v Rosoman 2015 EWCA Crim 986 (Convicted. Death by careless driving (based on alcohol). Joy ride at speed. At bend hit V's car. Aged 51. Following the guideline we substitute **6 years** for 8 making it the same length as the prison term.)

236   DEATH BY DRIVING: CARELESS DRIVING (DRINK/DRUG-RELATED)

236.1
Road Traffic Act 1988 s 3A (causing death when driving without due care and under the influence of drink or drugs or after failing to provide an alcohol or drug specimen)
Mode of trial Indictable only
Maximum sentence 14 years[220]
Drug-related offences Crime and Courts Act 2013 Sch 22 inserted in the description of the offence as another alternative a person who 'has in his body a specified controlled drug above the specified limit'. In force 2 March 2015[221]
Extended sentences This offence is listed in Criminal Justice Act 2003 Sch 15. The court may pass a 2012 extended sentence (EDS) if there is a significant risk of serious harm from future specified offences and either: a) the defendant has a Criminal Justice Act 2003 Sch 15B conviction (applicable only to defendants aged 18+), or b) the offence would justify a determinate sentence of at least 4 years.[222]

---

[220] Criminal Justice Act 2003 s 285(4)
[221] Crime and Courts Act 2013 (Commencement No 1) (England and Wales) Order 2014 2014/3268
[222] Criminal Justice Act 2003 s 226A-226B as inserted by Legal Aid, Sentencing and Punishment of Offenders Act 2012 s 124

Disqualification There is a minimum disqualification period of 2 years.[223] Where a defendant has a conviction for driving while unfit, causing death under the influence of drink or drugs, driving with excess alcohol or drugs and failing to provide a specimen in the previous 10 years, the minimum disqualification is 3 years.[224] For guidelines and cases, see the **DEATH BY DRIVING: GENERAL PRINCIPLES** *Disqualification* paras at **235.20**.

Disqualification until test is passed The defendant must be disqualified until an extended driving test is passed.[225]

Penalty points 3 to 11 penalty points when the court finds special reasons.[226]

Courses There is power to order reduced disqualification for attendance on courses.[227] On 24 June 2013, Road Safety Act 2006 changes came into force. For details see the **DISQUALIFICATION FROM DRIVING: OBLIGATORY** *Reduced periods of disqualification for attendance on courses* para at **44.8** in Volume 1.

Depriving defendant of vehicle used There is power to deprive the defendant of the vehicle used[228] for the purposes of committing the offence.

Funeral expenses There is no power to make a compensation order for funeral expenses where death is due to an accident arising out of the presence of a motor vehicle on the road.[229]

Sexual Harm Prevention Orders There is a discretionary power to make this order when it is necessary to protect the public from sexual harm.[230]

236.2   *Crown Court statistics England and Wales*
Death by careless driving when under the influence of drink or drugs

Year	Age	Plea	Total sentenced	Type of sentencing %						Average length of custody in months
				Discharge	Fine	Community sentence	Suspended sentence	Custody	Other	
2013	18-20	G	4	–	–	–	–	100	–	31
		NG	0							
	21+	G	23	–	–	4.3	4.3	91.3	–	66.1
		NG	0							
2014	18-20	G	2	–	–	–	–	100	–	not listed
		NG	0							
	21+	G	19	–	–	5	–	95	–	50.8
		NG	4	–	–	–	–	100	–	not listed[231]

For explanations about the statistics, see page 1-xii. For statistics for male and female defendants etc., see www.banksr.com Other Matters Statistics tab

Guidelines
236.3   *Sentencing Guidelines Council guideline*
For the basic guidelines for causing death when driving carelessly, see the **DEATH BY DRIVING: GENERAL PRINCIPLES** chapter.

---

[223] Road Traffic Offenders Act 1988 s 34(1) and (4) and Sch 2
[224] Road Traffic Offenders Act 1988 s 34(3)
[225] Road Traffic Offenders Act 1988 s 36(1) as amended by Driving Licences (Disqualification until Test Passed) (Prescribed Offence) Order 2001 2001/4051
[226] Road Traffic Offenders Act 1988 s 28, 34 and Sch 2 Part I
[227] Road Traffic Offenders Act 1988 s 34A
[228] Powers of Criminal Courts (Sentencing) Act 2000 s 143(6)-(7)
[229] Powers of Criminal Courts (Sentencing) Act 2000 s 130(1)(b)
[230] Sexual Offences Act 2003 s 103A as inserted by Anti-social Behaviour, Crime and Policing Act 2014 Sch 5 para 2 and Sexual Offences Act 2003 Sch 5
[231] Based on too few cases to be meaningful

Causing Death by Driving Guideline 2008, see www.banksr.com Other Matters Guidelines tab The guideline applies to those aged 18 or over who were convicted after a trial and were not assessed as a dangerous offender.

page 2 para 5 The determinants of seriousness likely to be relevant in relation to causing death by careless driving under the influence are both the degree of carelessness and the level of intoxication. The guideline sets out an approach to assessing both those aspects but giving greater weight to the degree of intoxication since Parliament has provided for a maximum of 14 years' imprisonment rather than the maximum of 5 years where the death is caused by careless driving only.

page 12 para 2 When assessing the seriousness of any offence, the court must always refer to the full list of aggravating and mitigating factors in the Council guideline *Overarching Principles: Seriousness Guideline 2004*, see **66.23** in Volume 1, as well as those set out on the facing page as being particularly relevant to this type of offending behaviour.

para 3 [the definition of the offence, now out of date]

para 4 In comparison with causing death by dangerous driving, the level of culpability in the actual manner of driving is lower but that culpability is increased in all cases by the fact that the offender has driven after consuming drugs or an excessive amount of alcohol. Accordingly, there is considerable parity in the levels of seriousness with the deliberate decision to drive after consuming alcohol or drugs aggravating the careless standard of driving onto a par with dangerous driving.

para 5 The fact that the offender was under the influence of drink or drugs is an inherent element of this offence. For discussion on the significance of driving after having consumed drink or drugs, see paragraphs 10-12 and **235.2**.

para 6 The guideline is based both on the level of alcohol or drug consumption and on the degree of carelessness.

para 7 The increase in sentence is more marked where there is an increase in the level of intoxication than where there is an increase in the degree of carelessness reflecting the 14-year imprisonment maximum for this offence compared with a 5-year maximum for causing death by careless or inconsiderate driving alone.

para 8 [Failure to supply a specimen, see **236.9**]

para 9 Sentencers should take into account relevant matters of personal mitigation; see in particular guidance on good driving record at **235.13**, giving assistance at the scene at **235.3**, and remorse in paragraphs 26-29 above at **236.15**.

Causing death by careless driving (drink/drug related) or having failed to provide a specimen

The legal limit of alcohol is 35 µg breath (80 mg in blood and 107 mg in urine)	Careless/ inconsiderate driving arising from momentary inattention with no aggravating factors	Other cases of careless/ inconsiderate driving	Careless/ inconsiderate driving falling not far short of dangerousness
71 µg or above of alcohol/high quantity of drugs or deliberate non-provision of specimen where evidence of serious impairment	Starting point: 6 years' custody Sentencing range: 5-10 years' custody	Starting point: 7 years' custody Sentencing range: 6-12 years' custody	Starting point: 8 years' custody Sentencing range: 7-14 years' custody

The legal limit of alcohol is 35 µg breath (80 mg in blood and 107 mg in urine)	Careless/ inconsiderate driving arising from momentary inattention with no aggravating factors	Other cases of careless/ inconsiderate driving	Careless/ inconsiderate driving falling not far short of dangerousness
51-70 µg of alcohol/moderate quantity of drugs or deliberate non-provision of specimen	Starting point: 4 years' custody Sentencing range 3-7 years' custody	Starting point: 5 years' custody Sentencing range: 4-8 years' custody	Starting point: 6 years' custody Sentencing range: 5-9 years' custody
35-50 µg of alcohol/minimum quantity of drugs or test refused because of honestly held but unreasonable belief	Starting point: 18 months' custody Sentencing range: 26 weeks to 4 years' custody	Starting point: 3 years' custody Sentencing range: 2-5 years' custody	Starting point: 4 years' custody Sentencing range: 3-6 years' custody

Additional aggravating factors
1 Other offences committed at the same time, such as driving other than in accordance with the terms of a valid licence, driving while disqualified, driving without insurance, taking a vehicle without consent, driving a stolen vehicle 2 Previous convictions for motoring offences, particularly offences that involve bad driving or the consumption of excessive alcohol before driving 3 More than one person was killed as a result of the offence 4 Serious injury to one or more persons in addition to the death(s) 5 Irresponsible behaviour such as failing to stop or falsely claiming that one of the victims was responsible for the collision.

Additional mitigating factors
1 Alcohol or drugs consumed unwittingly 2 Offender was seriously injured in the collision 3 The victim was a close friend or relative 4 The actions of the victim or a third party contributed significantly to the likelihood of a collision occurring and/or death resulting 5 The driving was in response to a proven and genuine emergency falling short of a defence.

236.4   *Judicial guidance*
R v Holburt 2012 EWCA Crim 1199 LCJ The seriousness of these offences is principally gauged by the extent to which the defendant's ability to drive is impaired through drink.

236.5   *Court Martial*
Guidance on Sentencing in the Court Martial 2013 para 5.11.1 There is no power to impose penalty points or order a disqualification from driving.
para 5.11.3 The sentences for…causing death…and similar very serious matters should be based on those in the Sentencing Council guidelines.
para 5.11.4 [The suggested penalty for] causing death by dangerous or careless driving is imprisonment in accordance with Sentencing Council guidelines and dismissal from HM Services.

Matters relating to the offence
Alcohol For the basic position, see DEATH BY DRIVING: GENERAL PRINCIPLES *Alcohol, Driving under the influence* at **235.2**.

236.6   *Alcohol   Less than twice over the limit*
R v Smith 2011 EWCA Crim 2844 D pleaded to death by careless driving whilst over the limit and dangerous driving. At 11 pm, he was driving a Porsche with dipped headlights at 55 mph on a 60 mph road. There was no street lighting or other ambient light. D collided with V, a 74-year-old man with mild Alzheimer's disease. He was wearing a black jacket and dark trousers and was walking in the road, 1.1 m out from the kerb.

Police investigators calculated that D would have had only 1.5 seconds to identify and react to V. D did not stop and drove 5 miles to a friend's house. He told his friend, who was a vehicle body repairer, that he had collided with a deer, causing the damage to his car. Police traced D's car and attended his home in the early hours of the morning. He gave a breath sample of 28 μg per 100 ml of breath. The back calculation indicated that at the time of the accident, the reading would have been between 45 and 100 μg. D's basis of plea was that he was just over the prescribed limit, with no more than 45 μg at the time of the incident. The dangerous driving was the driving of a damaged car after the collision. D, aged 39 at appeal, was of good character and had glowing references. Held. D should either have been driving with his full beam headlights on, or driving around 15 mph slower. The serious aggravating factor was that D did not stop. D had shown genuine and profound remorse. **30 months** not 4 years was appropriate.

R v Williams 2014 EWCA Crim 147 D pleaded to death by careless driving when over the prescribed limit. After drinking in a pub with some friends, at about 1.45 am he drove home. The journey was about 2 miles. There were four passengers in his car, one of whom died as a result of the crash. They were driving on a narrow country road and, having left the 30 mph restricted zone, D increased his speed. He approached a right-hand bend and failed to manoeuvre the car correctly as he went around the bend. He tried to correct the manoeuvre but lost control of the car and it mounted the verge. The car overturned and came to rest on the passenger side. V, who was sitting in the rear of the car behind the front passenger seat, died as a result of his head becoming trapped between the vehicle and the road. D went down on his hands and knees crying, but was unhurt. He then left the scene. The other three passengers were treated for minor injuries. D had been driving at 35-39 mph around the bend. An expert concluded that the maximum speed at which the bend could be safely negotiated was 39 mph. At 4.50 am, he blew 57μg, which was just over 1.5 times the legal limit. A family impact statement told of the devastation the death of V had caused. D was of good character. Held. It was common ground that D's driving came within the lowest level of carelessness. The driving amounted to an error of judgement as he travelled around a bend at speed. It was a bad error but it was not combined with any bad driving beforehand, nor was the speed so excessive so as to elevate it into the next category. This was not a case where D ran away to avoid the police and there was evidence that D was shepherded away from the scene out of compassion. The Judge should not have considered that as aggravation. This should not have been elevated to the middle category of the guidelines. Additionally, there was mitigation in the form of his good character, the remorse, the good references and the fact that the person who died was a good friend of his. Starting at 4 years, with the plea, **2 years 8 months** not 3 years 4 months.

R v Samuel 2015 EWCA Crim 487 D pleaded to drink-related causing death by careless driving. D spent the evening celebrating V's 22nd birthday. V was D's cousin and friend. V had set up his own successful business and was due to be married. At about 5 am, they tried to book a taxi but were told it would take 50 minutes. V asked D to drive them to his home in V's car and V gave D the keys. On the way, D managed to negotiate a series of bends and then failed to identify a bend or miscalculated a bend due to intoxication. The car hit a tree and V died. Neither was wearing a seat belt. D received a head wound requiring 20 stitches. D walked away from the scene. D lied about his involvement to a paramedic who saw him over half a mile away. D made no comment to the police. A backtracked blood test had an alcohol reading of 159 ml. The legal limit is 80 ml. D was aged 21 with no convictions and [an irrelevant] caution. He had a partner and character references. The defence said D could not read or write and the references said he tried to please others. The Judge considered there was momentary inattention with no aggravating factors when setting the starting point. When setting the sentence he found the following aggravating factors: a) did not ensure V was wearing a seat belt, b) the distance travelled before the collision, c) D fleeing the scene, and d) D denying he was the driver, although this might have been attributable to intoxication. With these the

Judge started at the top of the range, namely 7 years. The Judge reduced this to 6 years with the mitigation, and 4 years with the plea. He accepted D had remorse. Held. The impact statements make heart-rending reading. There was no evidence of excessive speed. Because of the alcohol reading, we place this offence at the very top of the range. In truth it was on the cusp between the two categories. There were considerable aggravating factors. However, with the mitigation we start at 5 years, so with plea, **3 years 4 months**.

236.7   *Alcohol reading over twice the legal limit*

R v Jenkins 2011 EWCA Crim 2436 D pleaded (full credit) to causing death by careless driving, driving whilst disqualified, uninsured, under the influence of drink or drugs and excess alcohol. D and his girlfriend, V, were at a party. Both had been drinking. D then drove them both to a house, where there was more drinking, and D took cocaine. D then drove them from the address. The car was travelling at between 58 and 65 mph in a 30 mph zone. V applied the handbrake but the accelerator was still applied. The car rotated to the right, crossed onto the other side of the carriageway and collided with parked vehicles and a garden wall. V died. D gave a blood sample indicating 172 mg of alcohol per 100 ml of blood. Back calculation showed that D had between 200 and 240 mg of alcohol per 100 ml of blood at the time of driving (2½ to 3 times the legal limit). D expressed his profound regret. However, the pre-sentence report noted that D sought to minimise his offending, stating that V had applied the parking brake after asking D to stop the car. V had a very young daughter. D, aged 23 at appeal, had two previous convictions for excess alcohol. Held. This offence had devastating consequences. A young woman lost her life and her death has left her family bereft, including her very young daughter. D continued to drive after V had implored him to stop. **9 years** was harsh, but not manifestly excessive. 10 years' disqualification, not 20, would reflect both punishment and the need to protect the public.

See also: *R v Holburt* 2012 EWCA Crim 1199 (LCJ Plea. Failed to see a boy on a bike. 48 mph in 40 mph area. 68 µg 2 hours later. Save for two speeding tickets D, aged 53, was of exemplary character. 4 years not manifestly excessive.) Note: This case is listed in this paragraph as, at the time of the offence, the defendant would have been over twice the legal limit. Ed.

R v Creathorne 2014 EWCA Crim 500, 2 Cr App R (S) 48 (p 382) (D pleaded. Ejected from pub with friend. Drove him in poorly maintained car at speed in built-up area when road wet. Hit tree after a bend. Friend killed. D seriously injured. Over twice the limit. 9 years 4 months starting point not in error.)

236.8   *Drugs, Driving under the influence of*

R v Martin 2010 EWCA Crim 1802 D pleaded to causing death by careless driving when unfit through drugs. He was driving his partner's car on a road with a 50 mph restriction. His partner, V, who was 8 months pregnant, was in the front passenger seat. Approaching a double bend with 'Slow' painted on the road, D lost control of the car and collided with a vehicle travelling in the opposite direction. The road surface was wet. V was partially thrown from the vehicle. D positioned himself between the passenger and driver seats and informed police that he had not been driving. A blood test showed that he was under the effect of diazepam, as he was a heroin addict. The prescription stated D should take one tablet three times a day. In fact D had not eaten and had taken five or six tablets. He was patently unfit to drive. V suffered serious neck injuries. An emergency caesarean was unsuccessful. V later died. The driver of the other vehicle suffered injuries which would result in life-long restricted elbow use and the development of osteoarthritis. D suffered fractures to the right arm, leg and shoulder. D had an appalling driving record (ignoring earlier convictions), in 1997 for driving without a licence or insurance and failing to provide a specimen, in 2003 for excess alcohol and no insurance and in 2008 for no insurance and no licence. He was disqualified for 12 months. This incident occurred around 3 weeks later. The Judge made a finding of dangerousness. Held. The

Judge was correct in making a finding of dangerousness. The Judge's reference to a propensity to flout the law and orders of the court was demonstrated by the fact that this offence occurred only a matter of a few weeks after he had been disqualified from driving and by his persistent pattern of driving without a licence for many years. A 10-year extended sentence (**7 years'** custody 3 years' licence) was not excessive.
Old cases: Best ignored.

236.9   *Offence based on failing to provide a specimen   General principles*
Causing Death by Driving Guideline 2008, see www.banksr.com Other Matters Guidelines tab page 12 para 8 A refusal to supply a specimen for analysis may be a calculated step by an offender to avoid prosecution for driving when having consumed in excess of the prescribed amount of alcohol, with a view to seeking to persuade the court that the amount consumed was relatively small. A court is entitled to draw adverse inferences from a refusal to supply a specimen without reasonable excuse and should treat with caution any attempt to persuade the court that only a limited amount of alcohol had been consumed.[232]
Att-Gen's Ref No 21 of 2000 2001 1 Cr App R (S) 50 (p 173) D pleaded to causing death by careless driving and failing to provide a specimen. Held. Where D has refused to provide a specimen the gravity lies in part in the fact that D has avoided the appropriate sentence for driving with excess alcohol. If D asks to be sentenced on the basis that he has drunk only limited alcohol the court should treat that with caution and circumspection. The onus of establishing that lies on D. The court is likely to require him to give evidence. In the absence of evidence, a court is able to draw adverse inferences about the amount of alcohol consumed. The ordinary inference will be that he has refused because he knows he has consumed alcohol well in excess of the limit. Normally a substantial custodial sentence will be required.
R v Pinchess 2001 EWCA Crim 323, 2 Cr App R (S) 86 (p 391) Courts should not examine whether the defendant was below the limit or unaffected by the drinking. They should approach the case as if there had been proven excess alcohol.
Note: The Court does not appear to have been referred to *Att-Gen's Ref No 21 of 2000* 2001 1 Cr App R (S) 50 (p 173). Ed.
Multiple deaths, see the **DEATH BY DRIVING: GENERAL PRINCIPLES** *More than one person killed* paras at **235.10**.
Victim dies after defendant dealt with for careless driving, see the **DEATH BY DRIVING: GENERAL PRINCIPLES** *Victim dies after defendant dealt with for dangerous driving* para at **235.16**.
Victims, The views of, see the **DEATH BY DRIVING: GENERAL PRINCIPLES** *Victims, The views of the relatives of the defendant who was related to/friendly with deceased* para at **235.17**.

Matters relating to the defendant

236.10   *Defendant aged 16-18*
R v Thorogood 2010 EWCA Crim 2123 D pleaded to death by careless driving whilst over the prescribed limit. D, aged 17, had recently passed his driving test. When his parents were away, he had some friends at his house. At about 5 pm, they drank alcohol and smoked a cannabis cigarette. At 1.30 am, D decided to drive his car, which he had had for two weeks, to a petrol station a short distance away. In an unlit, rural area, on a 60 mph limited road, D lost control of the car and hit a number of trees. The road was wet. The car rotated and overturned. One of his passengers was thrown from the vehicle. Another motorist collided with D's car. Two other passengers were trapped. When asked by police, D stated there were three people in the car. It was not until another passenger asked about the fourth that the other casualty was discovered. He was found dead at the base of a tree. Blood samples were taken at the hospital and with back calculation, the

---

[232] *Att-Gen's Ref No 21 of 2000* 2001 1 Cr App R (S) 50 (p 173)

alcohol concentration was found to be between 90 and 125 mg/100 ml blood. D had no previous convictions. Held. There is some force in the submission that the Judge did not have full regard to the credit due for the plea and other mitigation, in particular D's age. **33 months** not 42. Disqualification for 5 years.

Note: The guideline does not apply to those aged under 18. However, most judges consider what the appropriate sentence would be if the defendant was an adult and then they make a reduction. Ed.

Injuries, The defendant's own, see the **DEATH BY DRIVING: GENERAL PRINCIPLES** *Injuries, The defendant's own* para at **235.9**.

237 DEATH BY DRIVING: CARELESS DRIVING (SIMPLE)

237.1

Road Traffic Act 1988 s 2B

Mode of trial Triable either way

Maximum sentence On indictment 5 years. Summary 6 months and/or a £5,000 fine for offences committed before 12 March 2015 and an unlimited fine thereafter.[233] There are maximum fines for those aged under 18, see **14.38** in Volume 1.

Disqualification Obligatory 12 months' disqualification unless special reasons[234]

Penalty points 3-11 penalty points, if special reasons found[235]

237.2 *Crown Court Statistics   England and Wales*

Causing death by careless or inconsiderate driving Aged 21+

Year	Plea	Total sentenced	Type of sentencing %						Average length of custody in months
			Discharge	Fine	Commu-nity sentence	Sus-pended sentence	Custody	Other	
2013	G	123	0.8	–	35.8	34.1	29.3	–	13.6
	NG	25	–	4.0	20	36	40	–	13.8
2014	G	95	–	–	25	35	39	1	10.0
	NG	24	–	–	38	29	33	–	13.8

For explanations about the statistics, see page 1-xii. For statistics for male and female defendants etc., see www.banksr.com Other Matters Statistics tab

Guidelines

237.3 *Guidelines*

Causing Death by Driving Guideline 2008, see www.banksr.com Other Matters Guidelines tab The guideline applies to those aged 18 or over who were convicted after a trial and were not assessed as a dangerous offender.

page 14 paras 1-4 [These describe the guideline and the offence]

para 5 Since the maximum sentence has been set at 5 years' imprisonment, the sentence ranges are generally lower for this offence than for the offences of causing death by dangerous driving or causing death by careless driving under the influence, for which the maximum sentence is 14 years' imprisonment. However, it is unavoidable that some cases will be on the borderline between dangerous and careless driving, or may involve a number of factors that significantly increase the seriousness of an offence. As a result, the guideline for this offence identifies three levels of seriousness, the range for the highest of which overlaps with ranges for the lowest level of seriousness for causing death by dangerous driving.

---

[233] Legal Aid, Sentencing and Punishment of Offenders Act 2012 s 85(1) and (4) and Legal Aid, Sentencing and Punishment of Offenders Act 2012 (Commencement No 11) Order 2015 2015/504
[234] Road Traffic Offenders Act 1988 s 34(1) and Sch 2 Part I
[235] Road Traffic Offenders Act 1988 s 28, 34 and Sch 2 Part I

para 6 The three levels of seriousness are defined by the degree of carelessness involved in the standard of driving. The most serious level for this offence is where the offender's driving fell not that far short of dangerous. The least serious group of offences relates to those cases where the level of culpability is low – for example in a case involving an offender who misjudges the speed of another vehicle, or turns without seeing an oncoming vehicle because of restricted visibility. Other cases will fall into the intermediate level.

para 7 [Describes the ranges]

page 15 para 8 Where the level of carelessness is low and there are no aggravating factors, even the fact that death was caused is not sufficient to justify a prison sentence.

para 9 A fine is unlikely to be an appropriate sentence for this offence. Where a non-custodial sentence is considered appropriate, this should be a community order. The nature of the requirements EWCS will be determined by the purpose identified by the court as of primary importance. Requirements most likely to be relevant include unpaid work requirement, activity requirement, programme requirement and curfew requirement.

para 10 Sentencers should take into account relevant matters of personal mitigation; see in particular guidance on good driving record at **235.13**, giving assistance at the scene at **235.3**, and remorse in paragraphs 26-29 above at **235.13**.

Nature of offence	Starting point	Sentencing range
Careless or inconsiderate driving falling not far short of dangerous driving	15 months' custody	36 weeks' to 3 years' custody
Other cases of careless or inconsiderate driving	36 weeks' custody	Community order (high) to 2 years' custody
Careless or inconsiderate driving arising from momentary inattention with no aggravating factors	Community order (medium)	Community order (low) to Community order (high)

Additional aggravating factors
1 Other offences committed at the same time, such as driving other than in accordance with the terms of a valid licence, driving while disqualified, driving without insurance, taking a vehicle without consent, driving a stolen vehicle 2 Previous convictions for motoring offences, particularly offences that involve bad driving 3 More than one person was killed as a result of the offence 4 Serious injury to one or more persons in addition to the death(s) 5 Irresponsible behaviour, such as failing to stop or falsely claiming that one of the victims was responsible for the collision.

Additional mitigating factors
1 Offender was seriously injured in the collision 2 The victim was a close friend or relative 3 The actions of the victim or a third party contributed to the commission of the offence 4 The offender's lack of driving experience contributed significantly to the likelihood of a collision occurring and/or death resulting 5 The driving was in response to a proven and genuine emergency falling short of a defence.

For the meaning of a high-level, a medium-level and a low-level community order see **16.12-16.14** in Volume 1.

237.4   Magistrates' Court Sentencing Guidelines
Magistrates' Court Sentencing Guidelines 2008, see www.banksr.com Other Matters Guidelines tab page 118A The guideline restates the main guideline.

237.5   Judicial guidance
R v Odedara 2009 EWCA Crim 2828, 2010 2 Cr App R (S) 51 (p 359) D pleaded to causing death by careless driving. Held. This offence does not inevitably or necessarily carry imprisonment. Cases where it is likely to call for imprisonment may be where the

driver drives deliberately when his attention is elsewhere, e.g. when trying to use a phone, or when the driver has consumed alcohol or drugs or there is the theft of the car.

237.6   Court Martial
Guidance on Sentencing in the Court Martial 2013 para 5.11.1 There is no power to impose penalty points or order a disqualification from driving.
para 5.11.3 The sentences for…causing death…and similar very serious matters should be based on those in the Sentencing Council guidelines.
para 5.11.4 [The suggested penalty for] causing death by dangerous or careless driving is imprisonment in accordance with Sentencing Council guidelines and dismissal from HM Services.

Matters relating to the offence/defendant's conduct
Alcohol For the basic position, see **DEATH BY DRIVING: GENERAL PRINCIPLES** *Alcohol, Driving under the influence* at **235.2**.

237.7   Asleep, Defendant fell
R v Crew 2009 EWCA Crim 2851, 2010 2 Cr App R (S) 23 (p 149) D pleaded to causing death by careless driving. D arrived at Heathrow airport following a flight. In the preceding 24 hours D had 4½ to 5 hours' sleep. D hired a car and began driving with his two young children in the car to Lincolnshire. V, aged 21, was travelling in the opposite direction. D momentarily fell asleep, veered across the road and collided head-on with V's vehicle, forcing it off the road and into a tree. V died soon afterwards. D had no convictions, a long unblemished driving record and was full of remorse and shame. Held. The carelessness was of a high order bordering on dangerous driving. There were no aggravating features but D's culpability was very high. **14 months** and 2 years' disqualification not 5.
See also the **DEATH BY DRIVING: DANGEROUS DRIVING** *Asleep, Defendant fell* para at **238.9**.

237.8   Deceased more culpable than defendant
Example: *R v Arshad* 2011 EWCA Crim 2092 (Convicted of causing death by careless driving. Plea to death by driving whilst disqualified. When driving a taxi, and whilst performing a three point-turn, he collided with motor-cyclist who was speeding at twice the limit. Culpability reduced due to the motor-cyclist being largely responsible for the accident.)

237.9   Driving too close to car in front
R v Cox 2010 EWCA Crim 1285, 2011 1 Cr App R (S) 43 (p 292) D was convicted of causing death by driving without due care. D was driving on a B road. The vehicle in front braked sharply, D swerved into the opposite carriageway on a bend and collided head-on with a Mitsubishi Shogun travelling in the opposite direction. Neither D nor the driver of the Shogun had time to avoid a collision. The rear seat passenger of the Shogun, V, died. She was in her seventies and she sustained severe chest and spinal injuries. The driver of the Shogun was V's son. He suffered a fractured sternum and ankle and cuts and bruises. The front seat passenger of the Shogun was his partner. She suffered fractures to both arms, a fractured kneecap and had enduring physical and psychological problems. D was of excellent character, was described as a normally good, careful driver and had testimonials. He was in his second year at university. D was deeply remorseful. The Judge said the verdict meant that he was too close to the car which braked. The Judge also said it was the actions of a third party that contributed towards the commission of this offence. This case was at the bottom of the middle category of seriousness for the purpose of the guidelines. Held. The accident was obviously dreadful. The serious aggravating factor in relation to the consequences, although not the culpability, of this offence was the serious injury to the driver and second passenger of the other car. **Community order** with 200 hours' unpaid work affirmed. 16 weeks' detention suspended quashed.

237.10   Failing to see other road users

R v Odedara 2009 EWCA Crim 2828, 2010 2 Cr App R (S) 51 (p 359) D pleaded to causing death by careless driving. He was delivering for a pizza parlour in a company car. It was dark or nearly dark with adequate street lighting. He turned into a side road and failed to see a motor-cyclist who had no way of avoiding the collision. D's car was travelling at 5 to 10 mph. The motor-cyclist died. D was aged 29 and had come from India in 2008. He was married with two young children. D was in regular work and was of good character here and in India. He had no intention to drive again. Held. This was a momentary failure of attention. D did not keep a proper lookout. There were no aggravating features. This case did not pass the custody threshold, so a **community order** with 100 hours' unpaid work.

R v Jones 2012 EWCA Crim 972, 2013 1 Cr App R (S) 20 (p 109) D was convicted of causing death by careless driving. At 9.45 pm, he was driving on a dual carriageway. The speed limit was 70 mph and he was driving his car at 70 mph using cruise control. V, a 16-year-old boy, was riding a moped travelling in the same direction. Both D and V were in the inside lane. D drove into the back of V's moped, knocking him off. V sustained head injuries and subsequently died. Witnesses described D as being visibly upset and saying "I didn't see him". The rear light of the moped was displayed and the brake light had been illuminated for about three seconds prior to impact. The road conditions were good and the road was well lit at the time. The moped would have been visible for around 16 seconds. D had an old and now irrelevant speeding conviction and was 'well into middle age'. Held. There was no credit for the plea. D failed to see V for 16 seconds, which equates to around 500 m. The conclusion is that, in absence of any obstruction, poor lighting or any other explanation, D was not paying attention to what he was doing whilst travelling at considerable (but legal) speed. The Judge was entitled to conclude that lack of adequate sleep or rest provided an explanation for what happened. That is an aggravating factor. So was trying to blame V at times by saying he was on the wrong side of the road and that the moped didn't have rear lights. This was driving falling not far short of dangerous. This neutralised D's good character. **3 years** was not manifestly excessive.

R v Dhuck 2014 EWCA Crim 2865 D pleaded to causing death by careless driving. On his way to work, D stopped at a junction with a main road. He initially intended to turn right but because of the traffic, moved into the left-hand lane to go straight on. He waited for four seconds and then moved to cross the junction. For part of the four seconds, D's view was obscured by traffic. D failed to see a motor-cyclist, V, who hit D's car. V, who was driving at an appropriate speed, died at the scene. D remained at the scene and co-operated with the police. D was aged 45 with no convictions. He had an unblemished driving record. The Judge put the case at the upper end of Category 2. The pre-sentence report noted D's remorse and deep regret. Held. It was more serious than momentary inattention. The case was at the top of Category 3 or the bottom of Category 2. The appropriate sentence was a high-level **community order**. As D had served six weeks, we substitute 3 months.

See also: *R v Palmer* 2010 EWCA Crim 1863 (Plea. Failed to see motor-cyclist when defendant turned right. Victim married with three-year-old son and pregnant wife. No aggravating factors. Good character with unblemished driving record. Following the guideline 300 unpaid work hours reduced to 200.)

R v Sims 2010 EWCA Crim 2721 (Plea. Collision with motor-cycle he didn't see. Previous for careless driving where victim died. Full credit. **16 months** was not manifestly excessive.)

R v Hampton 2014 EWCA Crim 450 (Plea (25% credit). Also two driving whilst disqualified counts and no insurance charges. Struck a 16-year-old girl on her moped. Did not stop. **2 years** was appropriate. For more details, see **305.29**.)

Old cases: *R v Larke* 2009 EWCA Crim 870, 2010 1 Cr App R (S) 5 (p 28) (**39 weeks suspended**) *R v Campbell* 2009 EWCA Crim 2459, 2010 2 Cr App R (S) 28 (p 175) (**Community order** and 100 hours' unpaid work)
For a summary of these cases, see the 10th edition of this book.

237.11   *Foreign drivers on wrong side of road*
Example: *R v Fleury* 2013 EWCA Crim 2273, 2014 2 Cr App R (S) 14 (p 109) (Convicted. Frenchman living in France. Drove to UK to visit girlfriend. Awake for 16 hours, travelling for 6 or 6½ hours. Short period of sleep whilst crossing the channel. Head-on collision with another car after driving on the wrong side of the road for 200-400 metres. Both cars travelling at 40 mph. 60 mph limit. Held. Terribly serious careless driving. Culpability markedly lower than if he was a British driver. Top category, but insufficient allowance for the fact that he was French driving in UK. Starting at 12 months, not 2 years. 25% for the mitigation. **9 months** not 18.)
See also **DEATH BY DRIVING: DANGEROUS DRIVING** *Foreign drivers on wrong side of road* at **238.12**.

237.12   *HGV/coach drivers*
R v Gordon 2012 EWCA Crim 772, 2013 1 Cr App R (S) 9 (p 52) D pleaded (full credit) to causing death by careless driving. At about 6.30 pm he drove his flatbed lorry across the central reservation of a dual carriageway to turn right into the southbound carriageway. It was in January and the road was unlit. There was no signage at the entries to the central reservation. He waited there but the back of the lorry protruded into the northbound carriageway by 1.8 metres. D knew it was so protruding. A number of motorists saw the hazard and avoided it. V in his car did not, and hit the lorry. V sustained very serious head injuries and died. V's family spoke of their dreadful sorrow. It was accepted that D did not know the junction. D was aged 49 with no relevant convictions. He had an unblemished motoring record. D and his partner had two very young children. D had to cancel his wedding and suffered financial loss and he lost his job. More than 13 months passed between the accident and the sentence. The Judge placed the case at the upper end of the intermediate level. Held. That was wrong. We start at **36 weeks**. As is very often the case D was of positive good character and that, if there are no aggravating factors, must be given its proper weight. That brings the sentence down to 24 weeks and with plea **16 weeks**, not six months.
R v Coveney 2012 EWCA Crim 843, 2013 1 Cr App R (S) 10 (p 58) D pleaded (full credit) to causing death by careless driving. He drove his 34-ton lorry on the M20 with the cruise control on. He left the M20 at a proper speed at an uphill slip road which led to a roundabout. D disengaged the cruise control at a suitable time. He meant to dab the brake pedal but in fact he dabbed the accelerator at 100, 70 and 40 metres from the junction and again virtually at the point of impact. D thought his brakes had failed. He waved and sounded his horn but hit a car driven by a 71-year-old nurse. The lorry 'toppled over' and hit another car. The nurse died and was grievously missed by her family. D was aged 63 and had been a driver for over 40 years and had been an HGV driver for 34 years. He had lived a responsible life and had just one speeding conviction when driving his car. D provided considerable support for his adult disabled stepson who was deaf and blind. Held. This case was at the upper part of the middle category or in the lower/middle of the upper category. There were no aggravating factors. We start at 2 years so **16 months** with plea.
See also: *R v Marjoram* 2010 EWCA Crim 1600, 2011 1 Cr App R (S) 55 (p 351) (Plea. Coach driver collided with car at junction turning across carriageway. Good character. Between Categories 2 and 3. **Community sentence** with 300 hours of unpaid work, not 24 months suspended with 300 hours.)
R v Geale 2012 EWCA Crim 2663, 2013 2 Cr App R (S) 17 (p 74) (Plea. Coach driver. Momentary inattention caused by another driver. Incorrectly positioned when turning into a side road. Hit 10 year old boy at 10 mph. He was run over by the rear wheels

causing him catastrophic injury. Genuine remorse. 2 years suspended with unpaid work not challenged. Aged 53. One speeding conviction. Good references. Chronic blood disorder requiring treatment. No exceptional circumstances. Low culpability. **2-year** disqualification, not 3.)

237.13   *Inappropriate manoeuvres*
R v Hassan 2012 EWCA Crim 2786, 2013 2 Cr App R (S) 25 (p 170) D pleaded to causing death by careless driving. She approached a traffic light controlled junction with three lanes. The lights changed to green just as V1 and V2 began to cross the road not using the traffic lights. The right-hand lane was empty of traffic and was for traffic turning right. Traffic in the two other lanes slowed to let them cross. [V1 and V2's view of the right-hand lane was obscured by a van in the middle lane.] D drove at not less than 33 mph in the right-hand lane. She braked and skidded for just over 11 metres before she hit V1 and V2. She continued to skid for almost 14 metres afterwards. V1 was badly injured. V2 died 9 days later. D said she was turning right but in a *Newton* hearing she was disbelieved. D was of exemplary character and was the mother of six young children and the breadwinner. She expressed remorse. Held. The effect on the sentence on D's family was of limited assistance as the effect on V2's family was even more serious. However, V1 and V2 should not have been in the right-hand lane at all. We start at 10 months and with plea, **8 months** not 12.

See also: *R v Arshad* 2011 EWCA Crim 2092 (Convicted of causing death by careless driving. Plea to death by driving whilst disqualified. When driving a taxi, and whilst performing a three-point turn, he collided with a motor-cyclist who was speeding at twice the limit. Disqualified in 1996, but never took an extended retest. Did not realise he remained disqualified. Previous driving offences including dangerous driving and driving whilst disqualified. Level 2. **36 weeks** not 15 months.)

R v Ritchie 2014 EWCA Crim 2114 (Plea (25% credit). D, in a car, swerved entirely inexplicably, lost control and spun. D hit V, on a motorbike, travelling in the opposite direction. Seemingly perfect conditions. Both within speed limit. D, aged 23, of positive good character, had minor injuries. Lower end of Category 2. Start at 24 weeks, so **18 weeks**, not 10 months.)

237.14   *Medical problem, Accident caused by*
R v Rigby 2013 EWCA Crim 34 D pleaded to causing death by careless driving. Another motorist saw his car drifting from lane to lane along the A62. D's car stopped at some red lights and the motorist left her car and remonstrated with D about his driving. D's car then rolled back into the car behind him. The driver of that car found D unresponsive. D was described as messing about with the gear stick looking straight ahead. The police were called. D continued to drive. It was dark but the streets were illuminated. The pavements were covered with ice and pedestrians were walking in the road. V was walking in the road, which was straight and subject to a 30 mph limit. There was no problem with visibility. D drove into V. A witness spoke to D, who was shaking non-stop. D was very pale, mumbling and 'drifting out of conversation'.[236] The basis of plea was that D suffered a hypoglycaemic episode without warning. That day he had an unusually high blood-sugar level, one he had never had before. D was unaware of it and was unable to correct it. The day before the accident, D's wife had had surgery for breast cancer which would have related to the high stress levels. D did not check his blood-sugar level before leaving hospital after visiting his wife. His doctor said he was controlling his type 1 diabetes excellently. D had no previous convictions and had an exemplary character. The prosecution expert found D to be unaware of the steps recommended by the DVLA for diabetics, along with many other diabetes sufferers. The Judge sentenced D on the basis that he had failed to manage his condition, which was akin to someone drinking alcohol. Held. That was in error. D's culpability was less than

---

[236] It may be that this is a typo for 'consciousness'.

a driver who drinks. This type of case poses acute sentencing difficulties. The guidelines are not applicable here where the culpability lies in the failure to take precautions rather than the driving itself. D had chosen to drive knowing there was some risk of a hypoglycaemic attack. The single error was the failure to check before he left hospital. A short custodial sentence was appropriate. Given the exceptional circumstances and as D had served the equivalent of 4 months, immediate release.

See also the **DEATH BY DRIVING: DANGEROUS DRIVING** *Medical problem, Accident caused by* para at **238.15**.

237.15   *Overtaking*

R v Elliot 2012 EWCA Crim 243, 2 Cr App R (S) 70 (p 404) D, a former police officer, pleaded to causing death by careless driving. He was driving on an A-road, in a 40 mph zone, behind four other vehicles. The vehicles entered a derestricted zone, at which point the vehicle in front of D decided to overtake all the cars in front. D decided to do the same. As he did so he collided with a motor-cycle. The rider fell underneath the following car. D was punched by a witness and did not respond. In his second interview D stated that he did not see the motor-cycle, but the accident investigator described a line of sight of 850 metres. D said he had attempted to avoid the motor-cycle when he saw it, but he could not explain why he didn't pull into the gap left by the other overtaking vehicle. D, aged 41 at appeal, was of outstanding character with 38 references. He had shown remorse and accepted responsibility. The Judge accepted that the accident was partly caused by the other overtaker. Held. This offence was at the top end of the intermediate category of the guidelines. **12 months** upheld. **2-year disqualification** not 3.

Old case: *R v Rice* 2009 EWCA Crim 1967, 2010 1 Cr App R (S) 92 (p 591) (Plea. Cyclist killed by motorist overtaking. Exemplary character. Deep remorse. After accident took responsible action. Because of character, chance of offending in the future etc., the **20 weeks** should be **suspended** with 100 hours' unpaid work (reduced because of time served).)

237.16   *Parking, Dangerous*

R v Jenkins 2012 EWCA Crim 2909, 2013 RTR 21 (p 288) D was convicted of causing death by careless driving. He was working as a delivery driver for a builder's merchant. He was making a delivery to a property on a single carriageway two-lane A-road. The driveway was inaccessible partly because vehicles were already parked there and partly because snow had collected on the sides of the carriageway. The sky was clear but the sun was very low. Several witnesses who had driven towards D had stated that visibility was seriously impaired. D parked his lorry on the road adjacent to the address and in doing so blocked the majority of that side of the road. The lorry was parked at or just before a right-hand bend in the road. D had left the engine running, his headlights and hazard lights on and was away from the vehicle for about 10 minutes. V was driving a van in the same direction as D had been driving and collided with his vehicle. It was impossible to be precise about the speed but it was estimated at 50-60 mph. V suffered catastrophic injuries and died. Another vehicle had earlier had to execute an emergency stop to avoid hitting D's vehicle. Other drivers had given statements to the effect that they had taken to driving unusually slowly because of the conditions. D was aged 62 at appeal and of good character. He had held an HGV licence since 1974 and had an excellent work record. He had only one conviction for speeding some years ago. The pre-sentence report stated that D was remorseful and still shaken by the event. Held. We cannot fault the Judge's placing of the case in the highest category. It was little short of dangerous driving to park on that bend in those conditions. Equally, the Judge cannot be faulted for the conclusion that the offence fell towards the upper end of the range of seriousness. To take proper account of D's age, his virtually unblemished record and personal mitigation, 15 months not 2 years.

237.17   No insurance/No licence etc.
R v Middlebrook 2011 EWCA Crim 502 see **237.18**.
See also the DEATH BY DRIVING: DISQUALIFIED/NO LICENCE/UNINSURED, WHEN chapter.

237.18   Single misjudgement/Momentary inattention
R v Middlebrook 2011 EWCA Crim 502 D pleaded (full credit) to causing death by careless driving, causing death when not having insurance and causing death by driving otherwise than in accordance with a licence. He was driving his Audi A3 car which he had recently purchased and there were no 'L' plates displayed. His passenger was not a qualified driver. The road was a 60-mph-limit single carriageway which was wet. D was driving at 50 mph and on a slight right-hand bend he lost control, crossing into the oncoming lane. He collided with a car driven by the victim, a man known to D, and the Audi went into a violent spin. The victim died from his injuries. D's passenger was thrown from the vehicle and suffered two broken legs. D suffered a fractured neck, leg and arm with internal injuries. D's car had suffered a slow puncture from a screw in the tyre, which would have affected the steering ability and stability of the car. However, the screw could not have been in the car very long and D could not have known about it. D, aged 20, had no previous convictions and would be offered a job with an electrical firm once business improved. D was devastated by the death and was described as kind and trustworthy. The Judge placed the case in Category 1, but "only just", and passed a global sentence. Held. With the plea and full acceptance of responsibility, **2 years** not 3. It may be that the Judge gave insufficient weight to the under-inflated tyre.
R v Jones 2012 EWCA Crim 972, 2013 1 Cr App R (S) 20 (p 109) D was convicted of causing death by careless driving. At 9.45 pm, he was driving on a dual carriageway. The speed limit was 70 mph and he was driving his car at 70 mph using cruise control. V, a 16-year-old boy, was riding a moped travelling in the same direction. Both D and V were in the inside lane. D drove into the back of V's moped, knocking him off. V sustained head injuries and subsequently died. Witnesses described D as being visibly upset and saying "I didn't see him". The rear light of the moped was displayed and the brake light had been illuminated for about 3 seconds prior to impact. The road conditions were good and the road was well lit at the time. The moped would have been visible for around 16 seconds. D had an old and now irrelevant speeding conviction and was 'well into middle age'. Held. There was no credit for the plea. D failed to see V for 16 seconds, which equates to around 500 m. The conclusion is that, in the absence of any obstruction, poor lighting or any other explanation, D was not paying attention to what he was doing whilst travelling at considerable (but legal) speed. The Judge was entitled to conclude that lack of adequate sleep or rest provided an explanation for what happened. That is an aggravating factor. So was trying to blame V at times by saying he was on the wrong side of the road and that the moped didn't have rear lights. This neutralised D's good character. This was driving falling not far short of dangerous. **3 years** was not manifestly excessive.
R v Farwell 2013 EWCA Crim 2194 D pleaded (full credit) to death by careless driving. D was the owner of a motor repair workshop and was in possession of an Ariel Atom sports car which required servicing. The car has been described as having similar acceleration to a 1,000 cc motorcycle. D contacted B, a motor sport enthusiast and the boyfriend of D's niece, exchanging text messages containing photographs of the vehicle. It was arranged that B would accompany D on the test drive following the service. During the drive, D changed down a gear in order to accelerate but reapplied the power too quickly, which caused the wheels to lose traction. The vehicle hit a kerb, travelled across the carriageway and into trees and bushes, with the nearside striking a tree. Both men were seriously injured but B did not recover and died six days later. A basis of plea was agreed whereby the crash was attributed to unduly harsh acceleration. D was aged 46 and a man of positively good character, a fact highlighted in the pre-sentence report and in many testimonials provided to the court. Held. The Judge was not entitled to form

the view that the crash was caused by D's wish to "show off" to B as this formed no part of the agreed basis of plea. In light of the significant mitigating factors (presumably his own injuries, his good character and that the victim was soon to join his family) present in the case, **3 months** not 8. 12-month disqualification not 24.

R v Zhao 2013 EWCA Crim 1060, 2014 1 Cr App R (S) 17 (p 97) D pleaded to causing death by careless driving. At about 7.15 pm, V was riding a motorcycle on an A-road. D was ahead of him waiting to cross the A-road. D was stationary. A car ahead of V had turned at the junction at which D was waiting. Another motorcyclist had then passed ahead of D. D then pulled out into the A-road, into the path of V. V was travelling at a proper speed and was unable to avoid the collision. D did not see V. The line of sight from D's position to his right, from which V approached, was 138 metres. It would have been possible to see V from 44-48 metres away from the junction from which D emerged. The Judge accepted that this was a case of momentary inattention. Held. D's line of sight was somewhat impeded by the manoeuvre of the vehicle ahead of V. There were no aggravating features which took this case beyond the lowest category. A **medium-level community order** would have been appropriate. However, as D had spent the equivalent of a 4-month sentence in custody, a community order with 50 hours of unpaid work was appropriate, not 9 months.

R v Smart 2014 EWCA Crim 1119 D pleaded to causing death by careless driving. At about 1.30 pm, D was driving along a road. She was not speeding, nor was she distracted by a mobile phone or other distraction. V, aged 80, was crossing the road. A witness stated that V seemed unaware of D's vehicle approaching but also saw that D made no attempt to avoid V or to brake or stop. It seemed that D simply did not see V. She drove into V, who suffered a spinal injury and subsequently died. D brought her car to a stop and remained at the scene. When interviewed, she admitted that she had not seen V but could not explain why. D would have had a clear view of V for 6 seconds before impact. D was aged 59 and had no previous convictions. She was of 'positively excellent character'. Held. This was not a Category 1 case, as found by the Judge. In this case, D was driving in a perfectly lawful fashion without any aggravating features and her fault was an unexplained failure to stop or steer her vehicle during the 6 seconds that V was in her sight. This fell into the middle category, probably somewhere in the middle of that. Consideration should have been given as to whether an immediate custodial sentence was necessary. A custodial sentence would not be said to be wrong in principle given the guidelines, but...a sentence which would equate with the period of the custodial sentence which D had already served, namely the equivalent of 4 months' imprisonment, would have been sufficient. Furthermore, that should have been **suspended**. She had served approximately 2 months. To achieve that end, **4 months** immediate not 9, making immediate release.

Note: In motoring terms, failing to look for 6 seconds is a long time. The irresistible inference is that D was doing something in those 6 seconds and did not want to say what it was. If you take that into account and the harm D caused, 9 months appears correct. Ed.

See also: *R v Delduca* 2011 EWCA Crim 2454 (Plea to death by careless driving. Motor-cyclist slowed down, but driver following behind failed to do so. Collision between car and motor-cycle, pushing motor-cyclist into the vehicle in front. Momentary inattention. No aggravating features. **Community order** with 200 hours' unpaid work, not suspended sentence.)

R v Daniel 2012 EWCA Crim 2530 (Late plea with 20-25% discount. Missed correct turning on roundabout. Performed a U-turn to travel back to the roundabout. Did not indicate. U-turn was permitted. Collided with motorbike. Rider thrown over the car, which then ran over him. Victim trapped under car. Aged 51. Momentary but significant carelessness. **9 months** not 12.)

R v East 2014 EWCA Crim 1651 (Plea (10%). D, driving a coach full of students, failed to see V, riding a motorbike, and to give way. V hit D as D pulled out from a junction.

V's driving was not at fault and he had no time to avoid D. D may have had a restricted view because of another vehicle. D, aged 67, had a good driving record. Held. All surrounding circumstances must be considered, including D's inattention. Passengers and busy traffic are not significant aggravation. The appropriate sentence would have been a **community order**, not 10 months.)

Old case: *R v Marjoram* 2010 EWCA Crim 1600, 2011 1 Cr App R (S) 55 (p 351) (**Community sentence** with 300 hours of unpaid work.)

237.19   *Speeding*

R v Smith 2011 EWCA Crim 241 D pleaded to causing death by dangerous driving. He had held a licence for four months. D was driving at around 50 mph, 20 mph in excess of the limit. He collided with two women, aged 60 and 84, as they crossed a road. They died as a result. His basis of plea was that he was not racing or showing off, and that his inexperience had led him to miss the brake pedal. D, aged 18, was of good character with references. The Judge accepted D's remorse as being genuine and deep. Held. But for the speed, the accident would not have happened. There was one major aggravating factor and that was the death of two innocent people. That of course does not affect the culpability of the offender. It is the same driving whether two people die, or one, or none. But the outcome matters to the sentence of the court, and in particular to the public sense of justice. There were a number of important mitigating factors, including the fact that this was a case of misjudgement, not reckless or deliberate action. **3 years' detention** not 5 years' YOI and 4-year disqualification, not 7.

R v Singh 2013 EWCA Crim 62, 2 Cr App R (S) 52 (p 352) D pleaded to causing death by careless driving the day before his trial. D was driving his car at about 50 mph towards a cross-roads with traffic lights, which were green. The speed limit was 30 mph. V, who was riding his motor-cycle from the opposite direction, stopped. Then V turned right across D's path. There was some stationary traffic in the junction which restricted the view of both D and V. V collided with D's car, hit the bonnet and went into the windscreen. He landed 30 metres away. V, aged 18, died. V's blood alcohol level was investigated and it was discovered that it was 48 μg per 100 ml. The legal limit was 80 μg. D was aged 28 at his sentence and had convictions for using a mobile phone and failing to comply with traffic lights (the latter offence occurring after the instant offence occurred). Held. The Judge was entirely correct that this offence fell within Level 1. D was driving very substantially above the speed limit. Although the speed limit was 30 mph, it would not have been appropriate to enter the junction at that speed. D ought to have been driving at less than 30 mph. 2 years was a perfectly proper starting point. With 25% credit, **18 months** was not manifestly excessive.

R v Pattison 2014 EWCA Crim 544 D was convicted of causing death by careless driving (×2). At about 1.30 pm, he was driving his lorry. The weather and visibility were good. A lorry driven by P broke down. Extremely thick smoke drifted from it. For ¼ mile D could see it. Behind that smoke was an Army ambulance ahead of D which went into the smoke and did not slow down to any appreciable extent, if at all. It collided with the rear of P's lorry. D's lorry collided with the ambulance, pushing it further into P's lorry. V1, aged 24 and V2, aged 40, in the ambulance were killed. D had been driving at 48 mph but had reduced his speed to 39 mph some 20-30 m before the impact. His speed was estimated at 30 mph at the impact. It was estimated that he had commenced braking 1.5 seconds before the impact. D had been driving lorries for 30 years. D was aged 53 at appeal and 'of impeccable previous character' with a totally clean driving licence. The pre-sentence report detailed D's complete remorse. The Judge placed the driving into the highest category in the guidelines, falling not far short of dangerous driving. Held. D was driving a very heavy vehicle capable of doing immense damage. D must take his share of responsibility. He saw the smoke but elected to drive on without slowing down to any appreciable effect. The fact that others, including V1, had driven too fast and had not slowed down did not justify the conclusion that D was not driving too fast.[237] The Judge found that anyone driving into the thick smoke was taking a risk as to what might be within it. She was very well placed to make that assessment. It was incumbent on drivers to slow down accordingly. As a result of those findings, there could be no criticism of the categorisation of the offence. Consequently, **18 months** was not excessive. A 6-year disqualification order was excessive. 2 years would have sufficed.

R v Shadbolt 2014 EWCA Crim 1131 D pleaded (20% credit) to causing death by careless driving. D was driving his Corsa with his fiancée, F, in the front passenger seat. He had only been driving for a few months. It was sunny and dry. D was driving on an A-road and nearly missed his intended exit. He overtook a vehicle, returned to the inside lane and made a very late exit onto the slip road. He lost control on a severe bend, crossed a grassy area and drove onto another slip road with cars travelling in the opposite direction. D crashed head-on into a car driven by R. In R's car were G in the front passenger seat and V in the rear. R and G were badly injured and V died. In his basis of plea D accepted that a) he was driving too quickly for the severe bend that was ahead of him, and b) he was not familiar with the bend. D was aged 30 and had no convictions. He was very badly shocked by what happened and he had expressed strong remorse. R and G expressed a degree of forgiveness and asked for mercy. Held. It was a Category 1 case. There was serious injury to two people in addition to V's death, which constituted a seriously aggravating feature. The fact that D's fiancée was seriously injured was a mitigating factor, as was the fact that D had only been driving for a few months. It is also important to bear in mind that whilst this was [not over in an instant], it was a brief episode. With 20% credit, **15 months**, not 2 years.

R v Waseem 2014 EWCA Crim 247 D pleaded to death by careless driving. One evening V, aged 9½ years, was sitting on the handlebars of his brother's mountain bike. The two, neither helmeted, had travelled the wrong way along a residential road. D drove his car along a road to a T-junction with the road V was on. The speed limit was 20 mph. Nearby, there was a well-used park and there was a good deal of pedestrian traffic. V and his brother travelled into D's road. D braked and tried to steer clear but struck the front wheel of the bike. V hit the windscreen and was thrown into the air before landing on the ground. D lost control of the car and drove into a parked vehicle. D and his passenger decamped. A group of youths attacked him but he got away. V died from catastrophic head injuries. An expert placed D's speed at between 33 and 39 mph, not only in excess of the limit, but too fast for the prevailing conditions. Once aware that the police wanted to speak to him, D attended the police station with his solicitor. He wept throughout. He offered a prepared statement estimating his speed at 20-25 mph. He explained a serious congenital heart condition and his state of anxiety. He claimed he fled the scene fearing the angry youths. D was not insured. He was aged 23 at appeal. He had a 2008 conviction for driving without insurance. The pre-sentence report suggested a community order. The Judge accepted that he was extremely remorseful. Held. This was a difficult sentencing exercise. The time of the incident, near a park, in the summer, in a 20 mph restricted area, might be expected to concentrate the mind of a driver. Additionally, there was no obstruction to either party's view of the other and the collision was with the front of D's car. The Single Judge noted that with full credit, a sentence of 21 months must have started at (rounded up) 32 months, more than twice the starting point for Category 1 in the guidelines, which was 15 months. Driving in that category should fall not far short of dangerous. The primary aggravating factor was that this was the second time D had driven without insurance, coupled with his speed so far in excess of the 20 mph limit, in this type of area with which he was familiar. Starting at 32 months was manifestly excessive. Remaining loyal to the Judge's decision to give full credit for the plea, the sentence should have been **12 months**.

---

[237] The defence suggested that V1's failure to slow down as a result of the smoke created a false sense of security for D in relation to his speed. Ed.

See also: *R v Lawes* 2009 EWCA Crim 2767, 2010 2 Cr App R (S) 43 (p 276) (Plea. Lost control of his car on bend on wet road and hit an oncoming car because he was driving too fast for road conditions. Other driver and unborn child killed. **6 months** should have been **suspended**.)

R v Shepherd 2010 EWCA Crim 46, 2 Cr App R (S) 54 (p 370) (Plea. Aged 18. Excessive speed and showing off with faulty braking system six days after passing test. Three days before offence warned about speed and tyres. Going round bend, wheels locked. Head-on crash. No previous convictions. **4 years** after trial so **3 years'** detention.)

R v Tyro 2010 EWCA Crim 2597 (Plea. Lost control of car at difficult corner. Going too fast although not above speed limit. Lost control of car, which hit tree. Two deaths. Third victim seriously injured and life ruined. Aged 22 and treated as of good character and with a clean licence. **2 years** not 2½.)

R v Brassington 2010 EWCA Crim 2726, 2011 2 Cr App R (S) 7 (p 29) (Plea. Wet road surface. Approximately 60 mph in 40 mph zone. Car skidded sideways on a bend. Lost control and collided with another vehicle. A passenger died. Injuries sustained by other passengers. **18 months**.)

R v Landon 2011 EWCA Crim 1755 (Early plea. Defendant had held licence for one month. Drove at 64-71 mph in a 40 mph area. Wet road, poorly lit. Killed two passengers. Good character. Aged 17. Remorseful. **20 months' YOI** upheld.)

Old cases: *R v Tyson* 2010 EWCA Crim 601, 2 Cr App R (S) 96 (p 632) (**2 years**) *R v Brassington* 2010 EWCA Crim 2726, 2011 2 Cr App R (S) 7 (p 29) (**18 months**) *R v Powell* 2010 EWCA Crim 3265, 2011 2 Cr App R (S) 41 (p 244) (**15 months' YOI**) For a summary of these cases, see the 10th edition of this book.

Matters relating to the defendant
237.20   Defendant aged 16-20
Note: The *Causing Death by Driving Guideline 2008* does not apply to those aged under 18. I would expect most judges would determine the appropriate sentence for an adult and then make a reduction. Ed.

Examples: *R v Shepherd* 2010 EWCA Crim 46, 2 Cr App R (S) 54 (p 370) (Plea. Aged 18. Excessive speed and showing off with faulty braking system six days after passing test. Three days before offence warned about speed and tyres. Going round bend, wheels locked. Head-on crash. No previous convictions. **4 years** after trial so **3 years'** detention.)

R v Landon 2011 EWCA Crim 1755 (Early plea. Defendant had held licence for 1 month. Drove at 64-71 mph in a 40 mph area. Wet road, poorly lit. Killed two passengers. Aged 17. Good character. Remorseful. **20 months' YOI** upheld.)

237.21   Previous conviction for causing death when driving
Example: *R v Sims* 2010 EWCA Crim 2721 (Plea. Collision with motor-cycle. Previous conviction for careless driving where victim died. Full credit. **16 months** was not manifestly excessive.)

The sentence
237.22   Disqualification For how long?
R v Ebrahimi 2014 EWCA Crim 841 D pleaded to causing death by careless driving. He approached a junction and failed to give way as required. D drove into the path of V's vehicle and a collision occurred. V's car had to veer into the other carriageway and collided with an articulated lorry. V suffered a severe brain injury and died. D was not insured to drive at the time of the offence. It was unclear whether D was aware that he was uninsured. D was aged 38 and had a conviction in 2005 for a number of motoring offences including driving without due care, driving whilst uninsured and failing to stop after an accident. D had lost his job as a forklift truck driver as a result of the accident. He found a job as a carpet fitter and had a wife and three children to support. 6 months suspended for 2 years was not challenged. Held. For disqualification, public protection

was important. D's previous convictions justified a conclusion that D represented a continuing danger to road users in light of his conviction for this offence. The lack of a driving licence may inhibit D's ability to find and retain work, which was a relevant consideration. The appropriate range for disqualification in this case was 3 to 5 years. **4 years' disqualification**, not 7.

See also: *R v Henry* 2011 EWCA Crim 630 (Conviction of causing death by careless driving. Momentary inattention. Previous convictions for speeding and using a mobile phone. Employed as a salesman. Aged 53. **12 months** not 3 years.)

R v Sarginson 2012 EWCA Crim 1555 (Plea (first opportunity). Driver of a vehicle collecting waste for the council. V was workmate and friend. V guided vehicle as it reversed. Driver drove 1 mph over the 5 mph limit. Lost sight of victim in his mirror and hadn't turned the rear camera on. Trained to stop when losing sight of persons behind the vehicle but did not do so. Level 2. No previous driving convictions. **18-month disqualification** not 3 years.)

R v Daniel 2012 EWCA Crim 2530 (Late plea. Missed correct turning on roundabout. Performed a U-turn to travel back to the roundabout. Did not indicate. U-turn was permitted. Collided with motorbike. Rider thrown over the car, which then ran over him. Because of imprisonment and rehabilitation, **2 years** not 3.)

R v Geale 2012 EWCA Crim 2663, 2013 2 Cr App R (S) 17 (p 74) (Plea. Coach driver. Momentary inattention caused by another driver. Incorrectly positioned when turning into a side road. Hit 10-year-old boy at 10 mph. He was run over by the rear wheels causing him catastrophic injury. Genuine remorse. 2 years suspended with unpaid work not challenged. Aged 53. One speeding conviction. Good references. Chronic blood disorder requiring treatment. No exceptional circumstances. Low culpability. **2-year** disqualification, not 3.)

R v Bagshawe 2013 EWCA Crim 127, 2 Cr App R (S) 62 (p 393) (Pleaded. Pulled out at a junction causing motor-cyclist to hit him. Middle category case. Aged 86. **3 years** was not wrong.)

R v Farwell 2013 EWCA Crim 2194 (Acceleration causes loss of traction. **12 months** not 24, see **237.18**.)

R v Pattison 2014 EWCA Crim 544 (Speeding into some smoke. Lorry hit ambulance which had hit another lorry. Two died. Impeccable character. **2 years** not 6, see **237.19**.)

R v Ritchie 2014 EWCA Crim 2114 (Plea. D, in a car, swerved entirely inexplicably, lost control and spun. D hit V, on a motorbike, travelling in the opposite direction. Seemingly perfect conditions. Both within speed limit. D, aged 23, of positive good character, had minor injuries. Lower end of Category 2. No reason to be more than the minimum term.)

Old cases: These are not listed as these disqualification cases provide so little assistance. Ed.

237.23   *Custody threshold*
Causing Death by Driving Guideline 2008, see www.banksr.com Other Matters Guidelines tab The guidelines apply to sentences for offenders aged 18+.

page 15 para 8 Where the level of carelessness is low and there are no aggravating factors, even the fact that death was caused is not sufficient to justify a prison sentence.

R v Odedara 2009 EWCA Crim 2828, 2010 2 Cr App R (S) 51 (p 359) D pleaded to causing death by careless driving. Held. This offence does not inevitably or necessarily carry imprisonment. Cases where it is likely to call for imprisonment may be where the driver drives deliberately when his attention is elsewhere, e.g. when trying to use a phone, or when the driver has consumed alcohol or drugs or there is the theft of the car.

An example: *R v Marjoram* 2010 EWCA Crim 1600, 2011 1 Cr App R (S) 55 (p 351) (Plea. Coach driver collided with car at junction turning across carriageway. Good character. Between Categories 2 and 3. **Community sentence** with 300 hours of unpaid work, not 24 months' suspended with 300 hours.)

See also the **DEFENDANT** *Custody threshold, Passing the* para at **240.13**.

238   DEATH BY DRIVING: DANGEROUS DRIVING
238.1
Road Traffic Act 1988 s 1

Mode of trial Indictable only

Maximum sentence 14 years[238]

Penalty points 3-11 penalty points,[239] if special reasons found.

Disqualification Minimum disqualification 2 years[240]

Disqualification until test is passed The defendant must be disqualified until an extended driving test is passed.[241]

Extended sentences This offence is listed in Criminal Justice Act 2003 Sch 15. The court may pass a 2012 extended sentence (EDS) if there is a significant risk of serious harm from future specified offences and either: a) the defendant has a Criminal Justice Act 2003 Sch 15B conviction (applicable only to defendants aged 18+), or b) the offence would justify a determinate sentence of at least 4 years.[242] For two examples of an extended sentence being quashed, see *R v Peart* 2012 EWCA Crim 3240.

Depriving defendant of vehicle used There is power to deprive the defendant of the vehicle used[243] for the purposes of committing the offence.

Funeral expenses There is no power to make a compensation order for funeral expenses where death is due to an accident arising out of the presence of a motor vehicle on the road.[244]

Sexual Harm Prevention Orders There is a discretionary power to make this order when it is necessary to protect the public from sexual harm.[245]

See also **MANSLAUGHTER** *Vehicle, Death caused by a* at **284.62**.

238.2   *Crown Court statistics England and Wales*
Causing death by dangerous driving

Year	Age	Plea	Total sen-tenced	Type of sentencing %						Average length of custody in months
				Dis-charge	Fine	Community sentence	Sus-pended sentence	Custody	Oth-er	
2013	18-20	G	16	–	–	–	–	87.5	12.5	84.4
		NG	0							
	21+	G	68	–	–	1.5	4.4	94.1	–	54.2
		NG	22	–	–	–	4.5	95.5	–	51.5
2014	18-20	G	11	–	–	–	–	100	–	65.1
		NG	1	–	–	–	–	100	–	not listed
	21+	G	92	–	–	–	5	95	–	61.0
		NG	18	–	–	–	11	89	–	61.9

For explanations about the statistics, see page 1-xii. For more statistics about defendants aged 10-20 and female defendants, see www.banksr.com Other Matters Statistics tab

---

[238] Criminal Justice Act 2003 s 285(3)
[239] Road Traffic Offenders Act 1988 s 28, 34 and Sch 2 Part I
[240] Road Traffic Offenders Act 1988 s 34(1) and (4) and Sch 2
[241] Road Traffic Offenders Act 1988 s 36(2)(b)
[242] Criminal Justice Act 2003 s 226A-226B as inserted by Legal Aid, Sentencing and Punishment of Offenders Act 2012 s 124
[243] Powers of Criminal Courts (Sentencing) Act 2000 s 143(6)-(7)
[244] Powers of Criminal Courts (Sentencing) Act 2000 s 130(1)(b)
[245] Sexual Offences Act 2003 s 103A as inserted by Anti-social Behaviour, Crime and Policing Act 2014 Sch 5 para 2 and Sexual Offences Act 2003 Sch 5

Guidelines
238.3   *Sentencing Guidelines Council guideline*
Causing Death by Driving Guideline 2008, see www.banksr.com Other Matters Guidelines tab The guidelines apply to a first-time offender aged 18 or over convicted after trial who has not been assessed as a dangerous offender.

page 10 para 2 When assessing the seriousness of any offence, the court must always refer to the full list of aggravating and mitigating factors in the Council guideline *Overarching Principles: Seriousness Guideline 2004*, see **66.23** in Volume 1, as well as those set out on the facing page as being particularly relevant to this type of offending behaviour.

para 3 **Levels of seriousness**
The three levels are distinguished by factors related predominantly to the standard of driving. The general description of the degree of risk is complemented by examples of the type of bad driving arising. The presence of aggravating factors or combinations of a small number of determinants of seriousness will increase the starting point within the range. Where there is a larger group of determinants of seriousness and/or aggravating factors, this may justify moving the starting point to the next level.

Level 1 The most serious offences encompass driving that involved a deliberate decision to ignore (or a flagrant disregard for) the rules of the road and an apparent disregard for the great danger being caused to others. Such offences are likely to be characterised by:
   a prolonged, persistent and deliberate course of very bad driving and/or
   consumption of substantial amounts of alcohol or drugs leading to gross impairment and/or
   a group of determinants of seriousness which in isolation or smaller number would place the offence in Level 2.

Level 1 is that for which the increase in maximum penalty was aimed primarily. Where an offence involves both of the determinants of seriousness identified, particularly if accompanied by aggravating factors such as multiple deaths or injuries, or a very bad driving record, this may move an offence towards the top of the sentencing range.

Level 2 This is driving that created a substantial risk of danger and is likely to be characterised by:
   greatly excessive speed, racing or competitive driving against another driver, or
   gross avoidable distraction, such as reading or composing text messages over a period of time, or
   driving whilst ability to drive is impaired as a result of consumption of alcohol or drugs, failing to take prescribed medication or as a result of a known medical condition,
   or a group of determinants of seriousness which in isolation or smaller number would place the offence in Level 3.

Level 3 This is driving that created a significant risk of danger and is likely to be characterised by:
   driving above the speed limit/at a speed that is inappropriate for the prevailing conditions, or
   driving when knowingly deprived of adequate sleep or rest, knowing that the vehicle has a dangerous defect or is poorly maintained or is dangerously loaded, or
   a brief but obvious danger arising from a seriously dangerous manoeuvre, or
   driving whilst avoidably distracted or failing to have proper regard to vulnerable road users.

The starting point and range overlap with Level 2 is to allow the breadth of discretion necessary to accommodate circumstances where there are significant aggravating factors.

para 4 Sentencers should take into account relevant matters of personal mitigation; see in particular guidance on good driving record at **235.13**, giving assistance at the scene at **235.3**, and remorse in paragraphs 26-29 above at **235.13**.

Nature of offence	Starting point	Sentencing range
Level 1 The most serious offences encompassing driving that involved a deliberate decision to ignore (or a flagrant disregard for) the rules of the road and an apparent disregard for the great danger being caused to others	8 years' custody	7-14 years' custody
Level 2 Driving that created a substantial risk of danger	5 years' custody	4-7 years' custody
Level 3 Driving that created a significant risk of danger (where the driving is markedly less culpable than for this level, reference should be made to the starting point and range for the most serious level of causing death by careless driving)	3 years' custody	2-5 years' custody

Additional aggravating factors
1 Previous convictions for motoring offences, particularly offences that involve bad driving or the consumption of excessive alcohol or drugs before driving 2 More than one person killed as a result of the offence 3 Serious injury to one or more victims, in addition to the death(s) 4 Disregard of warnings 5 Other offences committed at the same time, such as driving other than in accordance with the terms of a valid licence, driving while disqualified, driving without insurance, taking a vehicle without consent, driving a stolen vehicle 6 The offender's irresponsible behaviour such as failing to stop, falsely claiming that one of the victims was responsible for the collision, or trying to throw the victim off the car by swerving in order to escape 7 Driving off in an attempt to avoid detection or apprehension.

Additional mitigating factors
1 Alcohol or drugs consumed unwittingly 2 Offender was seriously injured in the collision 3 The victim was a close friend or relative 4 Actions of the victim or a third party contributed significantly to the likelihood of a collision occurring and/or death resulting 5 The offender's lack of driving experience contributed to the commission of the offence 6 The driving was in response to a proven and genuine emergency falling short of a defence.

238.4   *Court Martial*
Guidance on Sentencing in the Court Martial 2013 para 5.11.1 There is no power to impose penalty points or order a disqualification from driving.
para 5.11.3 The sentences for dangerous driving, causing death...and similar very serious matters should be based on those in the Sentencing Council guidelines.
para 5.11.4 [The suggested penalty for] causing death by dangerous or careless driving is imprisonment in accordance with Sentencing Council guidelines and dismissal from HM Services.

Matters relating to the offence
238.5   *Aggravated vehicle-taking, and*
R v Roberts 2013 EWCA Crim 785 LCJ D pleaded to aggravated vehicle-taking. After drinking, he was a passenger in a car which, after being driven at speed, crashed and overturned. Counsel for the prosecution enquired why the driver of the car had not been charged with causing death by dangerous driving. The charging officer at the CPS considered that there was insufficient evidence to sustain that charge and, in any event, aggravating vehicle-taking carried the same maximum sentence (14 years). Consequently it was deemed appropriate to charge aggravated vehicle-taking. Held. That

should not be the approach. Causing death by dangerous driving is, in sentencing terms, generally regarded as the more serious offence and it should be the norm for that to be charged where there is evidence to support it.

Aggressive driving see *Racing, competitive or aggressive driving* at **238.18**

238.6   *Alcohol, Driving under the influence of   Guideline case*
See **Death by Driving: General Principles** *Alcohol, Driving under the influence of* para at **235.2**.

Note: Normally one would expect these offences to be prosecuted as careless driving (drink-related) offences. If they are not, one would expect the judge to consider the careless driving (drink/drug-related) guidelines, which are quite specific about the sentences for the different amounts of alcohol found, see **236.3**.

Causing Death by Driving Guideline 2008, see www.banksr.com Other Matters Guidelines tab page 10 para 3 [For] death by dangerous driving cases, 'consumption of substantial amounts of alcohol or drugs leading to gross impairment' is Level 1 with a starting point of 8 years. 'Driving whilst ability to drive is impaired as a result of consumption of alcohol or drugs' is Level 2 with a 5-year starting point, see **236.3**.

238.7   *Alcohol, Driving under the influence of   Cases*
R v Pell 2010 EWCA Crim 704, 2 Cr App R (S) (p 663) D pleaded to death by dangerous driving when under the influence of drink. V, aged 88, was crossing a B road which had a 30 mph speed limit. The road was wet but the sun was shining. D was driving towards V, did not slow down or take any evasive action and struck V, who was knocked onto the bonnet. V died. When D was tested at the police station the lower of two readings was 76 µg of alcohol in 100 ml of breath. It was calculated that D had been travelling at 44 mph. D had a bad history of driving offences. D showed remorse. **10 years** was severe but not excessive.

R v Stanko 2010 EWCA Crim 1883 D pleaded to causing death by dangerous driving, driving with excess alcohol and failing to stop. He attended a barbecue and drank about one-third of a bottle of whisky[246] mixed with Coca-Cola over four to five hours along with some other alcoholic drinks. His hostess, M, offered him a bed for the night, taking the view that he was too drunk to drive. M took D's keys. D searched for the keys for a couple of hours, then drove away after finding them. He returned to the house and asked P if he would like to accompany him. P attempted to persuade D not to drive. An independent witness then saw D drive away at 45-50 mph. Six pedestrians, one of whom was 12 years old, were walking along the pavement when D drove around the corner. It was not possible to establish how fast D was driving. However, he lost control, mounted the pavement and collided with a wall and the pedestrians. Five out of six pedestrians were hit. One died at the scene. Another was pronounced dead some three hours later. Another suffered serious injuries including fractures. The fourth suffered injuries including possible nerve damage. The fifth, the 12-year-old, suffered severe traumatic brain injuries and when D was sentenced, was confined to a wheelchair and had to be fed through a tube. It was likely that she would remain significantly disabled. D drove away from the collision but was found by police standing by his car. He claimed his car had been stolen but changed his story several times. Two hours after the collision a breathalyser showed 69 µg (almost twice the legal limit). D claimed he could not remember whether he was driving or not. The Judge said that this was a tragic and extremely serious case and took for his starting point 12½ years. Held. We have no doubt that the sentence of **10 years** was neither wrong in principle nor manifestly excessive. This was a Level 1 offence. The expert evidence was that D was travelling in excess of the speed limit. There were other aggravating factors. In our view D had no choice but to plead guilty therefore the Judge was entitled to withhold some credit for the guilty plea.

---

[246] It is unknown how large the bottle of whisky was. Ed.

R v Petherick 2012 EWCA Crim 2214, 2013 1 Cr App R (S) 116 (p 598) D pleaded to causing death by dangerous driving and excess alcohol. She was the single mother of a boy who was aged 16 months. One evening, D was drinking steadily with some friends, two men and two women. They finished a large and a small bottle of brandy. D decided to drive to the shops with the whole group to buy some more, although the shops were close enough for them to walk. On returning from the shop, D was driving along an urban high street, which had many fast food outlets and plenty of traffic and pedestrians. She was driving too fast and the two men in the rear of the car were encouraging D to drive faster and more recklessly. The woman in the front passenger seat, who was the only one sober, warned D that it was dangerous. D began to drive faster. She overtook two cars. As she attempted to overtake a third, she was unable to pull back onto the correct side of the road, and struck a double-decker bus travelling in the opposite direction. The offside of the car was ripped away and V1, one of the rear passengers, was ejected from the car by the impact and suffered fatal injuries as a result. The other male passenger suffered two collapsed lungs and fractured ribs. D's speed was put at not less than 60 mph in a 30 mph restricted area. D's breath sample was 77 µg, putting her more than twice the legal limit. D initially lied to the police, claiming that one of the passengers had been driving. She also lied about the amount of alcohol that she had consumed. The car had been refused an MOT certificate, but the condition of the car had nothing to do with the collision. D, aged 22, was of good character. She had made arrangements with her son's father's family for them to look after him to avoid the child going into care. Held. A substantial sentence of imprisonment was plainly unavoidable. D demonstrated genuine remorse and had undergone counselling and sought to address her drinking. There was also her youth and the effect that the sentence would have on her relationship with her son, and more importantly, his relationship with her. Aggravating features included the grossly excessive speed, driving whilst intoxicated and the persistent, inappropriate overtaking. We start at 8 years, like the Judge, so with plea credit 5 years 4 months and with 18 months discount for the mitigation **3 years 10 months** not 4 years 9 months.

R v Howson 2013 EWCA Crim 1863 D pleaded to death by dangerous driving. D, V, and B had been drinking to celebrate a birthday. D only held a provisional driving licence, a fact known to V. D was chosen to be the driver, having consumed less alcohol than the other two. The vehicle was being driven erratically and at an excessive speed. B said D ignored several requests from V to slow down. D lost control of the vehicle, which crossed the central reservation and rolled over onto a grass verge. At the scene D reportedly said "I am the driver, I was driving like an idiot". D had no convictions. The pre-sentence report said the risk of reoffending was low. The Judge said the aggravating factors were: a) being twice over the limit, b) D was speeding to show off and wind up V, c) D had no licence and no insurance, and d) he had ignored warnings. Held. The 8-year starting point was correct. D was entitled to full credit so **5 years 4 months** not 6 years. See also: *R v Taylor* 2009 EWCA Crim 38, 2 Cr App R (S) 55 (p 388) (Plea. Using a mobile phone when speeding and over twice the alcohol limit. **6 years** struck the balance.)

Old cases: *R v Robinson* 2009 EWCA Crim 450, 2 Cr App R (S) 79 (p 532) (**8 years**) *R v Gutierrez-Perez* 2009 EWCA Crim 2713, 2010 2 Cr App R (S) 36 (p 236) (**7 years**) For a summary of these cases, see the 10th edition of this book.

238.8   Alcohol, Driving under the influence of   Defendant avoids test
Att-Gen's Ref No 58 of 2000 2001 2 Cr App R (S) 19 (p 102) D pleaded guilty to causing death by dangerous driving after having pleaded not guilty. D left a pub and drove to his girlfriend's house, where they had an argument. He left and was seen by two pedestrians to be driving at about 50 mph in a 30 mph area. The car moved from the kerb to the centre of the road so that oncoming vehicles had to move towards their kerb. The engine was heard revving and after going over a bridge it collided head-on with a motor-cyclist. The accident was only a short distance from the house. The rider died. D left the scene

but surrendered to the police 18 hours later. Held. D had prevented the police from determining his alcohol level. Applying *Att-Gen's Ref No 21 of 2000* 2001 1 Cr App R (S) 50 (p 173) the Court is able to draw an adverse inference about the amount of alcohol consumed.

R v May 2005 EWCA Crim 1217, 2006 1 Cr App R (S) 29 (p 167) D pleaded to causing death by dangerous driving and driving while disqualified. In the early hours, he was driving a car borrowed from a friend. He had been drinking. He was attempting to negotiate a bend when he lost control and collided with a cyclist, V, who was killed instantly. His car continued across the road, smashed through a fence, crashed through the patio doors of a house and became embedded in the living room. His speed was later estimated at between 45 mph and 51 mph in a 30 mph area. He was seen to leave the car and run away appearing to be dazed and disorientated. He attended the police station late that morning. In interview he said he had drunk three pints of Stella Artois the night before. He expressed remorse for the death and said he was not a good driver. D, aged 18, had some minor previous convictions. Six weeks before this accident he had been fined and disqualified for two years for driving with excess alcohol. He had never held a driving licence or had driving lessons. A pre-sentence report recorded his regret and remorse. It said he was aware of the deep grief he had caused to V's family. There was a letter from his mother and a testimonial from his employer. There was also a statement of V's fiancée, who was the mother of his young daughter. Held. Some proportionality must be maintained between these cases and the sort of offences of violence where serious injury is positively intended, and between this case and other similar cases which come before other courts around the country. This case falls into the most serious level of culpability set out in *R v Cooksley* 2003 EWCA Crim 996, 2004 1 Cr App R (S) 1 (p 1). The three serious aggravating features were the previous conviction for drink/driving, the fact he was so recently disqualified, and although there was only one death there was very serious damage which caused great alarm to the residents of the house. He also ran away and did not go to the police until the following morning. The notional starting point of 12 years was too high. **6½ years'** detention not 8.

See also the **DEATH BY DRIVING: CARELESS DRIVING (DRINK/DRUG RELATED)** *Offence based on failing to provide a specimen* para at **236.9**.

238.9   *Asleep, Defendant fell*

Causing Death by Driving Guideline 2008, see www.banksr.com Other Matters Guidelines tab page 3 para 8 There are five factors that may be regarded as determinants of offence seriousness, each of which can be demonstrated in a number of ways. Common examples of each of the determinants are set out below. [One of the five determinants is] **Seriously culpable behaviour of the offender**. [One of the six examples of that behaviour is] para o) driving when knowingly deprived of adequate sleep or rest, especially where commercial concerns had a bearing on the commission of the offence. page 10 para 3, see www.banksr.com Other Matters Guidelines tab For death by dangerous driving cases, **Level 3** is likely to be characterised by 'driving when knowingly deprived of adequate sleep or rest' with a 3-year starting point, see **239.3**.

Att-Gen's Ref No 1 of 2009 2009 EWCA Crim 657, 2 Cr App R (S) 114 (p 742) LCJ D was convicted of two counts of causing death by dangerous driving. He was a van driver and started work at 7 am. He made deliveries with his passenger. On his way back to the depot his passenger fell asleep. At about 3 pm D fell asleep on a major A-road. At a bend the van went into oncoming traffic and narrowly missed a car containing a young family. The van collided head-on with another van and killed its driver and passenger. Another collision was caused and that driver sustained a fractured sternum and bruising. D's passenger sustained a fractured spine. The road conditions were good and D's van was faultless. D was discharged from hospital the same day. No one proved positive for drink or drugs. The prosecution said that D must have ignored his steadily declining ability to drive. D was aged 33 and of good character. He had a good driving record and showed genuine remorse. The jury said that in their number were people with experience of commercial vehicles and D's schedule was extremely demanding. **3½ years** not 28 months.

R v Wilson 2010 EWCA Crim 991, 2011 1 Cr App R (S) 3 (p 11) D pleaded (full credit) to two counts of causing death by dangerous driving and dangerous driving. D had 9-9½ hours' sleep over two nights and had been awake for 19½ hours. D began a 45-minute journey driving a minibus containing 15 people. D fell asleep at the wheel and the minibus mounted a pavement, carried on for about 60 metres and hit five pedestrians before coming to rest against a wall. None of the passengers was injured. Two women, aged 35 and 22, died. One other sustained serious injuries to her leg, injuries to her face and had to use a prosthesis to walk as one leg was 1 cm shorter than the other. The bus also struck two men. The first man suffered minor injuries and the other was dragged under the bus and suffered a minor skull fracture. An expert said D must have known she was losing consciousness but fought against it. D, aged 33, had an eight-year old son and a new baby, no convictions, an unblemished driving record, and references that described her as somebody who helps others and is looked up to. Held. This was a Level 2 case because of the two deaths and the three injured. **3 years** not 5.

R v Vinayagasivampilla 2015 EWCA Crim 1769 D pleaded early to causing death by dangerous driving. D worked a 12-hour night shift at Sainsbury's, seven days in a row. After the last shift, at 7 am he went home and had a shower. His uncle, U, asked D to drive him to a cash and carry in a van. D did that and dropped U back at U's home. At about 11 am, D drove in the van to U's shop to drop off the goods that had been purchased. D drove at an appropriate speed but fell asleep and the van hit V, who was jogging on the verge. D continued to drive for about 100 metres when he stopped and returned to V. Police arrived and noticed D was falling asleep. This was repeated at the police station. V died the next day. V was married with a 21-month-old daughter. Her husband continues to suffer from depression and a stress disorder. It was discovered that D was not insured to drive the van. D had convictions for excess alcohol and two for driving whilst disqualified and when uninsured. He came from a very poor background in Sri Lanka. D was now suffering from depression and said he never wanted to drive again. Held. It was a Level 3 case with a range of 2-5 years. We take into account the earlier convictions, his references and D's genuine remorse and assiduously hard-working character. We start at close to the top of the range, 4½ years, not 6, making with plea **3 years** not 4.

See also the **DEATH BY DRIVING: CARELESS DRIVING (SIMPLE)** *Asleep, Defendant fell* para at **237.7**

238.10   *Drugs, Driving under the influence of*

R v Cockroft 2012 EWCA Crim 2675, 2013 1 Cr App R (S) 29 (p 199) D pleaded (25%) to causing death by careless driving whilst unfit through drugs, causing death by driving whilst uninsured, possessing a class A drug and breach of a community order. V, aged 77, was crossing a road. It was dark and the street lights were on. There was a lot of traffic and a number of parked cars. D approached in his car. V crossed from right to left and was struck by D's car, suffering serious injuries from which he died. There was a 30 mph limit on the road and D was driving at between 26 and 31 mph. He would have had a clear view of V and the evidence showed that a driver with the normal one-second reaction time would have come to a stop 25 m before the point of impact. A driver with a two-second reaction time would still have avoided the impact. When arrested D was unsteady on his feet and had difficulty walking in a straight line. A blood sample taken showed the presence of heroin and cocaine. He was in possession of three wraps of heroin and one of cocaine. He later admitted that he was delivering drugs for others. D had previous convictions for drugs, including supply of heroin and crack cocaine in 2011. That was the breach of the community order. D told probation that he had been delivering drugs on a systematic basis for about 6 years and had had a 16-year drug habit. Held. The aggravating features were that D was uninsured, he was in possession of

more drugs than those responsible for his condition, he was in breach of a community order and on bail at the time. In mitigation, there was D's plea, his genuine remorse and that he had never served a custodial sentence before. This is a very serious example of this class of offence. A severe sentence was called for. A **10-year starting point** was the highest the Judge could have reasonably chosen. With 25% credit, **7½ years** not 9 years. *R v Etherington* 2014 EWCA Crim 1867, 2015 1 Cr App R (S) 7 (p 59) D pleaded at the first opportunity to causing death by dangerous driving. V1 and V2, aged 14 and 16, were close friends. D drove past in his significantly modified car. As D did so, he revved the engine making a significant noise due to the modified exhaust. V1 and V2 then shouted abuse at D. He returned shortly afterwards, driving over a bridge and accelerating from 61 to 71 mph. V1 and V2 were in the road, their arms over each other's shoulder and, being 30 m from the bridge, were in plain sight of D. D drove through them and failed to stop, despite his car being very badly damaged. D stopped at a petrol station and phoned the police. V1 died instantly and V2, rendered unconscious and with her leg amputated, died six hours later, holding her mother's hand. D failed a drugs test, having taken mephedrone and ketamine. He claimed initially that the victims had jumped out in front of him and in interview claimed V2 was 'playing chicken' and, "it was as if V2 wanted to be hit". He also said he had slowed down, only leaving the scene for his own safety. His car was fitted with a black box recorder, revealing his true speed. D was aged 20 and had convictions for speeding (×2 and one was for racing) and failing to stop. D pleaded under the Early Guilty Plea Scheme. He told probation that he wished that he was the one who had died and was prescribed medication for nightmares he suffered in prison. Whilst there, he had also saved the life of a cellmate. The Judge started at near 14 years and reduced it to 12 years to reflect his age and the mitigation. Then he gave D only a 25% discount due to the overwhelming prosecution evidence.[247] Held. D was driving under the influence of drugs, whether or not it affected his driving. D knew the girls were in the road and deliberately increased his speed. He failed to brake when it must have been obvious a tragedy was imminent. He lied to the police and sought to blame the girls. The Judge's approach cannot be faulted. The sentence was fully merited. **9 years' imprisonment**[248] upheld.
Note: On 2 March 2015, causing death by careless driving when over the prescribed drug limit became a specific offence, see **236.1**. Ed.

238.11   *Failing to see other vehicles, obstacles etc. within time*
Example: *R v Oakley* 2011 EWCA Crim 712 (Early plea to causing death by dangerous driving. Queuing traffic on motorway at road works. The defendant's van collided with rear of small car. The brakes were not applied. Was distracted. Three penalty points for speeding. **18 months** not 2½ years.)
Old cases: Best ignored. Ed.
For *Fleeing the scene* see **DEATH BY DRIVING: GENERAL PRINCIPLES** *Fleeing the scene* at **236.10**.

238.12   *Foreign drivers on wrong side of road*
R v Pulido-Sanchez 2010 EWCA Crim 2375 D, a Spanish national, pleaded to causing death by dangerous driving. He regularly drove his vehicle and had 11 years' experience driving in Spain. The road conditions on the night were dry and fine. He was driving his Volvo HGV from Portsmouth to Burnley. He had had 11 hours' rest whilst waiting for the ferry and during the crossing. Arriving at Portsmouth, he drove for 4 hours 20 minutes before looking for a place to stop. It appears that he lost his way. Officers in a police car thought he was lost. D pulled into a lay-by. After a few minutes he pulled out of the lay-by but drove on the wrong side of the road and continued to do so for 1½ miles. A taxi driver also driving northbound but on the correct side of the carriageway

[247] At paragraph 9, when dealing with the discount, the principles have been mixed up. This summary is based on what it is assumed the Judge meant to say.
[248] The sentence was unlawful as D should have received detention in a YOI, not imprisonment.

tried to alert D by flashing his lights and sounding his horn. Another road user driving behind D also tried to alert him. The taxi driver passed D on the correct side of the road. He then saw a motor-cyclist, V, and tried to alert V by flashing his lights. D was seen to suddenly pull towards the centre of the carriageway, immediately followed by the sound of a head-on collision. V died. The location was such that V would have only appreciated that D was on the wrong side of the road at the very last minute. D, aged 43, was well respected within his family and the community. The Judge sentenced D on the basis that he created a substantial risk of danger to other road users. That placed the driving at Level 2 in the guidelines with a suggested starting point of 5 years. Held. There was no question of alcohol or drugs or of excessive speed. His original error is one made by many if not most. The gravamen of the offence, as the Judge noted, lay in his failure to appreciate his error, continuing to drive for 1½ miles on the wrong side of the road. The degree of culpability does not easily fit within Level 2 of the guidelines, and on any view must be placed at the lower end of the bracket. There can be no doubt that D feels the most profound remorse. We consider that the Judge was in error taking a starting point at the upper end of the Level 2 bracket. Taking account of the plea and mitigation, **2½ years** not 4.

See also **DEATH BY DRIVING: CARELESS DRIVING SIMPLE** *Foreign drivers on wrong side of road* at **237.11**.

Health, Accident caused by defendant's poor state of health, see the **Medical problem, accident caused by** para at **238.15**.

238.13   HGV drivers   Judicial guidance
R v Caucheteux 2001 EWCA Crim 2960, 2002 2 Cr App R (S) 41 (p 169) Those who drove HGV vehicles owed a particular responsibility because of the nature of the vehicles they drove and because the results of errors could be, as in this case, catastrophic.

238.14   HGV/Coach drivers   Cases
R v Marjoram 2010 EWCA Crim 1600, 2011 1 Cr App R (S) 55 (p 351) D pleaded to causing death by careless driving. D was driving a coach along a B-road. On preparing to turn right he slowed down at give-way lines but did not make a complete stop. The coach drove across the opposite carriageway and collided with a vehicle travelling in the opposite direction. The female driver of the vehicle, V, died. After checking his 18 mostly elderly passengers he went to assist V. In interview he said he knew the road well and had assumed V's car had turned off. D had no convictions. The Judge said this was a tragedy involving two people, both of whom had led blameless lives. **Community sentence** 300 hours' unpaid work, not 24 weeks' suspended.

R v Oughton 2010 EWCA Crim 1540, 2011 1 Cr App R (S) 62 (p 390) D pleaded to manslaughter through gross neglect and causing death by dangerous driving. D was a partner with P in a coach firm. He was driving one of the firm's coaches with adults and a significant number of children. Passengers noticed an intense smell of burning when the coach went down a hill. Later the brakes failed and D lost control of the coach. After attempting to slow the vehicle down, it continued through a set of traffic lights which were on red, narrowly missed a vehicle pulling a horsebox and collided with another car, before coming to rest in a nearby garden. A married couple in the car died, making their son an orphan. Four on the coach received minor injuries and D suffered significant injuries. It was discovered that D and the other partner were responsible for failing to properly maintain the vehicle and in fact the Court heard that there were flagrant breaches of the licence, namely that the vehicle should be inspected every six weeks. This was not done. An expert: a) found the coach was poorly maintained and all four brakes were severely out of alignment, and b) said that had a competent mechanic inspected the vehicle, the defects in the braking system would have been identified. D was of good character with exemplary references. A prison report noted his excellent behaviour. The Judge: a) judged the neglect as joint with P, b) said they were equally responsible for the manslaughter, c) found the motive was commercial concerns, d) D had ignored the queries about the smell, e) found there were health issues for D, f) recognised D's deep and genuine remorse and g) gave D 25% discount for his plea. P received 3 years for the manslaughter. Held. The family loss was terrible. The Judge sought to strike the balance by applying the guidelines in a fair and impartial way. We think that he did that, and he took properly into account all the aspects of the criminal conduct and the mitigating features. 13 months for the manslaughter and **5 years** for the driving concurrent.

See also: *R v Pulido-Sanchez* 2010 EWCA Crim 2375 (HGV driver on wrong side of road, see **238.12**)

R v Arora 2014 EWCA Crim 104 (HGV driver using a mobile prior to fatality. **3½ years**, see **235.7**)

Old cases: *R v Payne* 2007 EWCA Crim 157, 2 Cr App R (S) 45 (p 287) (HGV driver crashed into queue of traffic, **4 years**) *Att-Gen's Ref No 137 of 2006* 2007 EWCA Crim 310 (Coach driver. **2½ years** would be expected) *Att-Gen's Ref No 146 of 2006* 2007 EWCA Crim 570, 2 Cr App R (S) 74 (p 470) (HGV driver. The appropriate starting point should have been **5 years**) *Att-Gen's Ref No 142 of 2006* 2007 EWCA Crim 662, 2 Cr App R (S) 84 (p 524) (HGV driver. **5½ years**) *R v Parry* 2007 EWCA Crim 1528, 2008 1 Cr App R (S) 49 (p 276) (HGV driver. **30 months**) *R v Stow* 2007 EWCA Crim 2354, 2008 1 Cr App R (S) 102 (p 603) (HGV driver. **3 years**)

For a summary of the first, third and fourth cases, see the 7th edition of this book and for the last two cases, see the 9th edition.

Inattention see the *Single misjudgement/Momentary inattention* para at **238.19**.

238.15   Medical problem, Accident caused by

R v Sims 2009 EWCA Crim 1454, 2010 1 Cr App R (S) 62 (p 415)[249] D was convicted of causing death by dangerous driving, having knocked down a traffic-sign pole which hit a 20-year-old woman who died. D said he must have blacked out. He was being treated for blackouts which were indicative of epilepsy. He was a train driver. In 2005 and 2006, in January, February and March 2007, and on 22 March and 5 April 2007 he was told not to drive by consultant doctors. On 13 April 2007, his work medical advisor passed D fit to drive a train although ignorant of two seizures. Held. There was consistent medical advice for D not to drive a car or a train. The Judge was able to put this case in Level 1, so **8 years** was not manifestly excessive.

Note: This case highlights the failure of the authorities to have a system in place to ensure that doctors have to inform the DVLA and train operators etc. that someone is unfit to drive a car, train etc. If D's licence had been suspended, this death would probably have been avoided. I, and no doubt others, sent this judgment to the Department for Transport. No doubt we will have to wait until scores of people die in a train crash for something to happen. Ed.

R v Seviour 2010 EWCA Crim 699 D was convicted of two counts of causing death by dangerous driving. D suffered a blackout in 2007 but did not seek medical advice. In 2008 D was driving on an A-road, suffered a sharp abdominal pain and veered across to the opposite side of the road. D's car collided head-on with a car travelling in the opposite direction, killing an engaged couple in their twenties. D, aged 67, had no convictions. In interview D said when he felt the pain he recognised it from his previous blackout and thought, 'Oh crikey, it's coming on', but had no recollection himself of what happened. D had an exemplary driving record and a settled home life. The pre-sentence report said D felt profound remorse. D was sentenced on the basis that he had enough time when the pain came on to avoid the accident. Held. It was a Level 3 case. The seriousness of an offence requires consideration of the harm that is caused as well as culpability. The aggravating feature was that the dangerous driving cost two lives. **12 months** not 2 years.

---

[249] The neutral citation in the Cr App R report is incorrect.

Old cases: *R v Rosevere* 2008 EWCA Crim 2142 (**2½ years**) *R v Clarke* 2009 EWCA Crim 921, 2010 1 Cr App R (S) 26 (p 158) (**12 months**)
For a summary of the cases, see the 9th edition of this book.
See also the DEATH BY DRIVING: CARELESS DRIVING (SIMPLE) *Medical problem, Accident caused by* para at **238.15**.
Mobile phone etc., Defendant using, see DEATH BY DRIVING: GENERAL PRINCIPLES *Distractions, Mobile phones etc., Defendant using* at **235.6**.
Multiple deaths see the DEATH BY DRIVING: GENERAL PRINCIPLES *More than one person killed* paras at **235.10**.

238.16   *Overtaking or starting to overtake, Driver*
Causing Death by Driving Guideline 2008, see www.banksr.com Other Matters Guidelines tab page 3 para 8(k) 'aggressive driving such as…persistent inappropriate attempts to overtake or cutting in after overtaking' are 'factors determinate of offence seriousness', see **235.1**.
R v Maddison 2010 EWCA Crim 1099 D pleaded to causing death by dangerous driving. He drove on the M1 where cones reduced the lanes from three to one. D misjudged the distances when trying to overtake a lorry. His car hit the lorry cab and scraped down the tractor and trailer unit and then struck a stationary truck. The car became sandwiched between the two lorries. D's car was forced down and forward and the trailer's wheel ran over it leaving it a mangled wreck. The weather was dry and the visibility was good. His two passengers, a father and his 14-year-old son, died. D was seriously injured and spent five weeks in hospital. D was aged 69 and had now lost both legs (not through the accident[250]). He also suffered from hypertension, diabetes and underlying ischaemic heart disease. In 2007, he had a cardiac arrest. D had two speeding convictions in 2006 and 2008. D accepted he would never drive again. Held. It was a single misjudgement. The Judge was right to put the case in Level 3. The aggravating factors were two people died, D had disregarded warnings and his record. The mitigating factors were he was seriously injured, he had lost a close friend, his age and his health. These factors cancelled each other out so starting at 3 years made it **2 years**.
Old cases: Best ignored.

238.17   *Police chases*
R v Casey 2012 EWCA Crim 623, 2 Cr App R (S) 94 (p 562) D pleaded to causing death by dangerous driving. In 2005, 2006 and 2011, D had been sentenced for driving whilst uninsured and without a licence. Barely two weeks after the last court appearance, D was driving a car which had had its registration plate changed. The car had been purchased by a woman who had paid cash and given a false name and address. Police officers approached the car. Despite the officers' requests, the occupants did not intend to remain. One of the officers smashed the windscreen using his baton and the car was driven off at speed. D was driving aggressively, with a police helicopter monitoring its movements. The car drove on the wrong side of road. The car approached some road works, where there was a 40 mph restriction. D approached at speed, overtook the first car, braked fiercely and then shot out to overtake the second car, in the face of an HGV travelling in the opposite direction. D managed to pull back in, onto the correct side of the road, but collided at 70 mph with the third vehicle, which was travelling in the same direction as he was. That vehicle was shunted into oncoming traffic, causing a head-on collision with a second HGV. The driver, a 50-year-old father of two, was killed instantly. The occupants of the car, including D, attempted to run from the scene. D had never held a full driving licence. Held. This was a Level 1 offence. D was driving to deliberately evade justice, in a car that was intended for a criminal purpose, in a manner

---

[250] It appears that that is the case, but it isn't clear. Ed.

which was deliberately extremely dangerous. He had previous convictions for relevant driving offences. The evidence was overwhelming. Consequently, starting at **10 years**, with 15% credit for the plea makes **8½ years** which was not manifestly excessive.

See also: *R v Britton* 2010 EWCA Crim 331 (Plea. 60 mph in 30 mph area. Went through at least one set of red lights. Killed motor-cyclist. Aged 21 and already served periods of detention. **5 years 4 months** was not manifestly excessive.)

Old case: *R v Buckland* 2006 EWCA Crim 2516 (**9 years**)

See also the **DANGEROUS DRIVING (SIMPLE)** *Police chases* para at **232.13**.

238.18   *Racing, competitive or aggressive driving*

Causing Death by Driving Guideline 2008, see www.banksr.com Other Matters Guidelines tab page 3 para 8(g) 'Racing and competitive driving against another driver' are 'factors determinate of offence seriousness'.

page 10 para 3 The guideline lists 'racing or competitive driving against another driver' when creating a substantial risk of danger as a **Level 2** offence so the starting point is **5 years**. Where there is a 'flagrant disregard for the rules of the road and an apparent disregard for the great danger being caused to others' it would be a **Level 1** case. For the guidelines, see **238.3**.

Att-Gen's Ref No 34 of 2013 2013 EWCA Crim 2135 D was convicted of causing death by dangerous driving. He was seen driving his white BMW 1 Series immediately behind a Ford Fiesta driven by V. They appeared almost to be touching. In front was a car driven by R, which was stationary at a pedestrian crossing with lights. D drove towards the crossing at a fast speed and appeared to be gesticulating and shouting at V, who was now stationary at the crossing. When the lights changed, V undertook R and drove away fast. R moved into the nearside lane and D overtook her and also drove away fast. D appeared to be pursuing V. The two cars approached a speed camera and both braked hard and then accelerated away. V was in the nearside lane and D in the outside lane. D then suddenly went in front of V. V braked sharply, went into the outside lane and hit a kerb on the central reservation. V lost control of his car, spun and went sideways along the road into the nearside lane and into a tree. The car was nearly cut in two. D drove off. V and his passenger died. In interview D admitted the driving and that he was angry at V but denied driving dangerously. He was aged 53 at appeal and was the owner of a successful building company. He had a drink/drive conviction in 1990 and a speeding conviction in 2010. He was essentially of good character. The Judge treated D and V as being as bad as each other. Held. This was a Level 2 offence involving prolonged aggressive and competitive driving culminating in a dangerous manoeuvre aimed at V. Had we been satisfied D intended V to take emergency avoiding action, we may well have concluded that this was a Level 1 offence. D's first and second thoughts were to evade responsibility. Two people died. **5 years** not 30 months. 5 years' disqualification not 3.

R v Paul 2013 EWCA Crim 2034, 2014 2 Cr App R (S) 7 (p 38) D pleaded (on the second day of trial) to causing death by dangerous driving and driving whilst disqualified. He owned an Audi R8 supercar. He was previously disqualified from driving after an excess alcohol conviction. He re-registered the car in his sister's name and continued to drive it. D was part of a group of friends who also owned high-powered, high-value cars. A number of them, D and V included, met in a pub. At about 11.45 pm, they got into their respective vehicles, and left the pub. V was driving an Audi TT, with passengers. D also had a passenger. Initially, they drove 'conservatively'. However, at a set of traffic lights, D pulled alongside V and they agreed to drive at speed or race. Over a distance of about two miles, in 30 and 40 mph limited areas, they drove at speeds in excess of 80 mph. D reached 100 mph at one point. D drove on the wrong side of a single carriageway causing oncoming drivers to take evasive action. V then decided not to continue to race. D fell behind V's car and drove very close to his rear bumper. He was flashing his lights indicating that he wanted the race to continue. D overtook V at speed and shortly after V, who was not racing at this stage, lost control.[251] His car hit a wall and then a lamp post. His passengers were unscathed but V died at the scene. D continued his journey for a short distance and then turned around to return to the scene of the crash. A witness attempted to open D's car door but it was locked. D drove off. The average speed over the two-mile distance was 45 mph. D and V had been good friends for a considerable period of time. D failed to report the accident. He lay low for a while, and had the car cleaned and replaced its tyres in an attempt to avoid detection. D, aged 27 at appeal, had a previous conviction for excess alcohol (2011). At the Crown Court, the defence accepted that it was a Category 1 case. Held. The driving fell on the boundary between Levels 1 and 2. It is clear that D was showing off. At the time of the accident, D was trying to provoke V into continuing to race. It was a continuation of earlier dangerous driving characterised by high-speed racing and dangerous overtaking manoeuvres. The excessive speed was not causative of V's death. The appropriate starting point was 7 years. The previous conviction and driving whilst disqualified and uninsured were aggravating features, as was the lamentable failure to stop after the accident. The mitigation of the loss of a close friend did not carry much weight, neither did the belated remorse and late plea. A sentence of 9 years before the plea was appropriate. 10% credit for the plea as granted by the Judge was more than generous but would remain. **8 years** not 9. There was nothing wrong with the 10-year disqualification.

See also: *Att-Gen's Ref No 40 of 2012* 2012 EWCA Crim 2531, 2013 2 Cr App R (S) 7 (p 34) (Convicted. Woman, D, speeding up and slowing down with boyfriend, B, each trying to get home from pub first. Expert said D's speed was 69 mph and B's speed 81 mph. B lost control of the vehicle and it overturned, mounted the pavement and struck two cyclists, V1, aged 23, and V2, aged 13. V2 died. V1 injured. D, aged 19, no convictions and pregnant. Category 2. **3½ years** not 18 months.)

R v Etherington 2014 EWCA Crim 1867, 2015 1 Cr App R (S) 7 (p 59) (Plea (25% credit). Accelerated from 61 to 71 mph at two girls on a bridge who had earlier shouted abuse. It appears this was because of the noise of his car's exhaust which was modified to make extra noise. [Appears to be a 30 mph area.] Both died. Defendant on drugs at time. Aged 20 with previous speeding convictions. Starting at close to 14 years, with mitigation 12 years, with reduced discount because case overwhelming, making **9 years** cannot be faulted. For more detail, see **235.8**.)

Old cases add little. If they are required, they are listed in the 9th edition of this book.

238.19   *Single misjudgement/Momentary inattention*

R v Maddison 2010 EWCA Crim 1099 D pleaded to causing death by dangerous driving. He drove on the M1 where cones reduced the lanes from three to one. D misjudged the distances when trying to overtake a lorry. His car hit the lorry cab and scraped down the tractor and trailer unit and then struck a stationary truck. The car became sandwiched between the two lorries. D's car was forced down and forward and the trailer's wheel ran over it leaving it a mangled wreck. The weather was dry and the visibility was good. His two passengers, a father and his 14-year-old son, died. D was seriously injured and spent five weeks in hospital. D was aged 69 and had now lost both legs (not through the accident[252]). He also suffered from hypertension, diabetes and underlying ischaemic heart disease. In 2007, he had a cardiac arrest. D had two speeding convictions in 2006 and 2008. D accepted he would never drive again. Held. It was a single misjudgement. The Judge was right to put the case in Level 3. The aggravating factors were two people died, D had disregarded warnings and his record. The mitigating factors were he was seriously injured, he had lost a close friend, his age and his health. These factors cancelled each other out so starting at 3 years made it **2 years**.

---

[251] Why V lost control is not stated. Ed.
[252] It appears that that is the case, but it isn't clear. Ed.

See also: *R v Oakley* 2011 EWCA Crim 712 (Early plea to causing death by dangerous driving. Queuing traffic on motorway at roadworks. The defendant's van collided with rear of small car. The brakes were not applied. Was distracted. Three penalty points for speeding. **18 months** not 2½ years.)

Old cases: *R v Evans* 2006 EWCA Crim 2040, 2007 1 Cr App R (S) 89 (p 555) (**2 years**) *R v Akujee* 2007 EWCA Crim 2981, 2008 2 Cr App R (S) 32 (p 188) (**18 months**) *R v Maltby* 2009 EWCA Crim 10, 2 Cr App R (S) 352 (**16 months**) *Att-Gen's Ref No 18 of 2009* 2009 EWCA Crim 1004, 2010 1 Cr App R (S) 13 (p 69) (**12 months' detention**) *R v Foster* 2009 EWCA Crim 1184, 2010 1 Cr App R (S) 36 (p 219) (**12 months suspended**)

For a summary of the first case, see the 6th edition of this book, for the third case, see the 8th edition and for the last case, see the 9th edition.

Sleeping, Defendant see the DEATH BY DRIVING: DANGEROUS DRIVING *Asleep, Defendant fell* paras at **238.9**.

238.20   Speeding   Guidelines

Causing Death by Driving Guideline 2008, see www.banksr.com Other Matters Guidelines tab page 3 para 8 g) 'Greatly excessive speed…, h) driving above the speed limit, i) driving at a speed that is inappropriate for the prevailing road or weather conditions and j) driving a PSV, HGV or other goods vehicle at a speed that is inappropriate either because of the nature of the vehicle or its load, especially when carrying passengers' are 'factors determinate of offence seriousness', see **235.1**.

page 10 para 3 [Where there has been] a deliberate decision to ignore (or a flagrant disregard for) the rules of the road with greater danger etc. it will be a Level 1 case, with an 8-year starting point. Level 2 is likely to be characterised by 'greatly excessive speed', with a **5-year** starting point. Level 3 is likely to be characterised by 'driving above the speed limit/at a speed that is inappropriate' with a **3-year** starting point, see **238.3**.

238.21   Speeding   Cases

Att-Gen's Ref No 76 of 2012 2013 EWCA Crim 458 D pleaded (full credit) to causing death by dangerous driving. V, aged 67, drove a white campervan along a dual carriageway with a 70 mph speed limit. The vehicle was adequately lit and travelling at 51-54 mph. D was driving a BMW sport coupé at speed with a friend. Neither vehicle had mechanical defects. The vehicles were in the same lane and D drove into the campervan pushing it up a grassy verge and into a traffic stanchion. V died of multiple injuries and trauma. D's average speed until 9 km before the impact was 117 mph and was 96 mph over the final 5.3 km. Over the final 1.6 km the speed was 91 mph. At the collision, his speed was in the low nineties. At a closing speed of 48 mph, V's van would have been in view for 25 seconds and for 16 seconds there would have been a direct line of sight. D was breathalysed and the test was negative. D said he had not seen any tail lights on the van and claimed he was travelling at "roughly 60". Later he admitted he had reached a speed of 128 mph and that he was showing off to his passenger. D, aged 22 at appeal, had offences of speeding in 2009 (speed awareness course) and 2011 and for using his mobile phone whilst driving in 2010. Held. There had been excessive speed for a prolonged period of about 11 km. His previous convictions demonstrate propensity and a failure to respond positively both to help offered and penalties imposed. In mitigation, there was the plea and D's previous exemplary behaviour. This was a level 2 case. Starting at 5 years, the appropriate sentence was **3 years 4 months.** Because it was a reference, **3 years** not 2.

Att-Gen's Ref No 33 of 2013 2013 EWCA Crim 1398[253] D pleaded (full credit) to causing death by dangerous driving and causing death by driving whilst unlicensed, disqualified or uninsured. D was driving a vehicle lent to him by a friend. There was no

---

[253] This was an Attorney-General's reference. However, the official transcript bears the name *R v Palmer* in error. Ed.

street lighting and the road was dry and subject to a 50 mph limit. The road was undulating, which meant oncoming cars could be obscured from view. D was travelling northbound and 'tailgating' another vehicle. He eventually moved to overtake. A witness said he was wholly or partly on the wrong side of the road and his view of any oncoming vehicles was obscured by the undulation in the road. D was driving 'fast'. After overtaking, D approached a sharp double bend with signs indicating that the road narrowed ahead and that drivers should slow down. D collided with a car driven by V, who was travelling south. The collision happened in the southbound lane on the apex of the double bend. D's speed was unknown but the maximum speed at which the bend could be negotiated was between 61 and 66 mph. V's car rotated through 180° and came to rest in a wooded embankment. V was trapped in the car and suffered head injuries, respiratory failure and leg injuries. D's vehicle was badly damaged but he managed to exit the car and he left the scene. V died in hospital days later. D, aged 28 at the appeal, had a bad driving record. He was convicted as a juvenile of TDA (×2), aggravated vehicle-taking and driving without insurance and a licence. There were also convictions for excess alcohol (2002), driving whilst disqualified (×2) (2003) and, as an adult, TDA, aggravated vehicle-taking and driving whilst uninsured and disqualified. In 2009, he pleaded to dangerous driving (12 months). Held. This was a Category 1 offence. D made a deliberate decision to ignore the rules of the road. The appropriate starting point could not have properly been lower than **12 years**, when considering D's record. With the plea, **8 years** not 5½.

R v Howson 2013 EWCA Crim 1863 D pleaded to death by dangerous driving. D, V, and B had been drinking to celebrate a birthday. D only held a provisional driving licence, a fact known to V. D was chosen to be the driver, having consumed less alcohol than the other two. The vehicle was being driven erratically and at an excessive speed. B said D ignored several requests from V to slow down. D lost control of the vehicle, which crossed the central reservation and rolled over onto a grass verge. At the scene D reportedly said "I am the driver, I was driving like an idiot". D had no convictions. The pre-sentence report said the risk of reoffending was low. The Judge said the aggravating factors were: a) being twice over the limit, b) D was speeding to show off and wind up V, c) D had no licence and no insurance and d) he had ignored warnings. Held. The 8-year starting point was correct. D was entitled to full credit so 5 years 4 months not 6.

See also: *R v Banasik* 2011 EWCA Crim 140 (Plea. Level 3 offence. Drove at speed killing student crossing road. Never passed a driving test. Then aged 24. In the region of 7 years would have been appropriate after trial. **5 years** was not manifestly excessive.) *R v Etherington* 2014 EWCA Crim 1867, 2015 1 Cr App R (S) 7 (p 59) (Plea (25% credit). Accelerated from 61 to 71 mph at two girls on a bridge who had earlier shouted abuse. It appears this was because of the noise of his car's exhaust which was modified to make extra noise. [Appears to be a 30 mph area.] Both died. Defendant on drugs at time. Age 20 with previous speeding convictions. Starting at close to 14 years, with mitigation 12 years, with reduced discount because case overwhelming, making **9 years** cannot be faulted. For more detail, see **235.11**.)

Old cases: *R v Hooker* 2010 EWCA Crim 461 (**3 years**) *R v Murphy* 2010 EWCA Crim 713 (**3 years 8 months**) *R v Kingsley* 2010 EWCA Crim 1717 (**15 months'** detention) *R v Searles* 2010 EWCA Crim 2279 (**6½ years**) *R v Hardy* 2010 EWCA Crim 2704 (**8 years**) *R v Girdler* 2010 EWCA Crim 2775 (**11 years**)

For a summary of the first, second and fourth cases, see the 10th edition of this book. If more old cases are required, see the 9th edition of this book.

See also the **Police chases** para at **238.17**.

Victim dies after defendant dealt with for dangerous driving, see **235.16**.

Matters relating to the defendant

238.22   *Defendant aged 14-17*

Note: The *Causing Death by Driving Guideline 2008* does not apply to those aged under 18. I would expect most judges to determine the appropriate sentence for an adult and then make a reduction. Ed.

R v Z 2008 EWCA Crim 753, 2 Cr App R (S) 108 (p 623) D changed his plea to guilty on counts of causing death by dangerous driving and aggravated vehicle-taking. He had no proper driving experience. He took a Jeep and drove it erratically, swerving and accelerating and driving too fast. He was showing off to a co-accused. He lost control, rounded a corner on two wheels and mounted a pavement. He hit a tree which fell on a buggy carrying two babies. V, aged 19 months, died from multiple injuries. He had been knocked out of the buggy and into a wall. His 10-week-old brother, although pinned to the wall in the buggy, was uninjured, as were their mother and another brother. D and his co-accused fled. V's family had suffered appallingly. They had to move out of the area, some had panic attacks and difficulty sleeping and some needed counselling. In interview he denied being in the collision. He later made admissions to a security officer guarding him but when re-interviewed made no comment. He was remanded to foster parents and absconded. He was found and spent six months in custody before pleading guilty. D, aged 14 at the time, had a conviction for common assault. Social services had become involved because his mother said she found him difficult to cope with. After the common assault conviction he had been remanded to a referral unit. He absconded from that. He had been excluded from school on several occasions. Social services had a high level of concern about his inappropriate sexualised and aggressive behaviour. D said he smoked cannabis daily. A pre-sentence report said that he had failed to comprehend the risks he was taking because of his lack of maturity and insight. He was assessed as posing a high risk of harm to others, but that he had made real efforts to address his offending behaviour. Recent reports from custody showed that he had caused a number of problems although on occasion he could respond well to being controlled, supervised and helped, but only when it suited him. Held. D knew full well that he had no business behind the wheel of a car. He was underage, he had no licence, no relevant experience and no insurance. He drove in a residential area where it must have been obvious that people might get hurt. He ran away and made no attempt to help those he had injured. **3½ years' detention** was thoroughly deserved.

R v Bennett 2009 EWCA Crim 591, 2 Cr App R (S) 651 D pleaded to causing death by dangerous driving. He and his best friend, V, drank through the night and when both drunk they left a club at about 2.30 am. D drove V towards V's father's house. The car hit a mini island and knocked down a bollard. The rear tyre was damaged but D continued driving. Within 75 metres the car became difficult to steer because the tyre became deflated, and 370 metres from the bollard the car swerved onto the wrong side of the road and at about 22 mph hit a tree. V died of his injuries. D was uninjured. His alcohol reading was 99 µg (permitted maximum 35 µg). He had driven about 1½ miles. The pre-sentence report assessed his risk of reoffending as low. There were 12 character references and very real remorse. D was aged 17 and had passed his driving test three months before the crash. The Judge considered that the starting point was 8 years aggravated by a fixed penalty for being drunk two weeks before, the high reading and the two warnings that something was wrong (the bollard crash and the tyre being deflated). Held. V's family suffered a devastating loss but they supported the appeal. The Judge was entitled to take the near treble reading and the penalty notice as aggravating factors. However, his age was the most significant factor. There was also his (good) character, the remorse, the loss of his intended army career, a good prison report, lack of driving experience and loss of his best friend. He had been frank and honest. The starting point was **6 years'** detention making with the plea **4 years**.

R v Kibble 2009 EWCA Crim 592, 2 Cr App R (S) 93 (p 616), see **235.11**.

R v Theaker 2009 EWCA Crim 620, 2 Cr App R (S) 683 D pleaded to causing death by dangerous driving. After drinking in the evening she, V and others went to a flat. Two of them said that D pestered V to let her drive his car. D and V left the flat in V's car, a BMW 316 Compact. Two miles later the car driven by D crashed into a wall after a sharp bend causing some injury to users of a restaurant. The examiner thought that the car's speed was no more than 30 mph. V died two weeks later. D was abusive in an ambulance and gave false details. Police said she smelt strongly of drink. With backtracking she had somewhere between 75 and 178 mg in her blood. The mean reading was 123 mg. D had only recently passed her test either 3 or 17 days before. She had been in trouble with the police three times and was on a Referral Order. Held. The car was quite powerful. There were strong indications that she was well over the limit but it could not be proved she was over the limit. There were no aggravating features and momentary inattention. Taking her inexperience, youth etc. the starting point should have been **18 months** so with the plea, **12 months'** detention not 2 years.

Old cases: *R v P* 2007 EWCA Crim 1003, 2008 1 Cr App R (S) 9 (p 38) (**3½ years**) *R v Herbert* 2007 EWCA Crim 3034, 2008 2 Cr App R (S) 28 (p 161) (**extended sentence of 8 years'** detention with an extension period of 4 years)

For a summary of the first case, see the 8th edition of this book and for the last case, see the 9th edition.

Note: I suspect the lack of recent cases is because judges adopt the rounded approach to sentencing youths, which means appealable sentences are rare. Ed.

Defendant takes positive action to assist at the scene see the DEATH BY DRIVING: GENERAL PRINCIPLES *Assisting at the scene Defendant takes positive action* para at **235.3**.

Injuries, the defendant's own Guideline case see the DEATH BY DRIVING: GENERAL PRINCIPLES *Injuries, the defendant's own* para at **235.9**.

Unqualified driver see the DEATH BY DRIVING: GENERAL PRINCIPLES *Unqualified driver/Lack of driving experience* para at **235.14**.

The sentence

238.23   *Custody threshold, Crossing the*

Att-Gen's Ref No 76 of 2002 2002 EWCA Crim 2344, 2003 1 Cr App R (S) 100 (p 519) The public demand that the seriousness of causing death by dangerous driving should be acknowledged. However, dangerous driving varies in its seriousness. We do not accept that in virtually every case of dangerous driving where death results a prison sentence must follow. In every case there are competing considerations.

Note: This view appears consistent with the principle that the court can depart from the guidelines where justice demands it. However, a non-custodial sentence must be rare. Ed.

Att-Gen's Ref No 56 of 2007 2007 EWCA Crim 1605, 2008 1 Cr App R (S) 66 (p 383) D was convicted of causing death by dangerous driving. A little after lighting-up time, he attempted to overtake two vehicles travelling at 20 mph. One was a pick-up truck and the other a tractor with a trailer. They were about 160 metres before a long bend. He would not have then been able to see an oncoming motor-cyclist who was driving within the speed limit. He saw the light of a motor-cyclist and tried to move to the left and hit the tractor, which caused it to go into the hedge. D's vehicle moved to the right, hit the motor-cycle and hit the tractor again. The motor-cyclist was thrown into the air and killed. There was no street lighting. Occupants of cars behind D were able to appreciate the length of the convoy. One described the overtaking as impatient. D was aged 59 and an ambulance driver. He recalled little of the collision and had glass in his head, a laceration and a fracture to his arm. He was suffering from post-traumatic stress disorder. The prosecution appeal made him very exhausted, very frightened and low. His remorse was genuine. Four hundred people attended the funeral of the motor-cyclist, whose father said their lives were shattered beyond repair. The prosecution said that there were no aggravating features. The Judge said that it was a momentary and unprecedented error. Held. The error was to underestimate the time it would take to overtake the convoy. There was nothing to suggest that D appreciated it was dangerous. The death may well have been caused in part by the tractor and trailer being unlit. Because of D's amnesia there should not necessarily be the normal disparity between the sentences for a conviction and a plea. The appropriate sentence was **1 year**. A suspended sentence (with 200 hours of unpaid work) was not, however, unduly lenient.

R v Foster 2009 EWCA Crim 1184, 2010 1 Cr App R (S) 36 (p 219) D was convicted of causing death by dangerous driving. Since 2005, he had cared for his wife, who suffered from motor neurone disease. She was unable to speak. The hospital told him that her treatment would not be continued as she was not going to survive. While driving her home, D's car crossed to the other side of the road and collided with a motor-cyclist head-on. The motor-cyclist died. The effects of the death on his family and others were devastating. D was aged 64 and a retired accountant. He had a distinguished career. He was of good character with no driving convictions. He showed deep remorse. The Judge found it was inattention as a result of a distraction for a matter of seconds at the most. Held. It is difficult to imagine a case in which the dangerous nature of the driving was less culpable than here. The emotions from the hospital visit must have made D susceptible to distraction. None of the aggravating factors was present. The starting point was **15 months** which we reduce to **12 months** because of his good character and personal mitigation. D had spent nearly 3 months in custody and it was a proper case with mercy to **suspend it**.

Note: The guidelines do not deal with this situation but the sentencing statistics show that judges continue to pass non-custodial sentences for exceptional cases. Ed.

See also the **DEFENDANT** *Custody threshold, Passing the* para at **240.13**.

Disqualification see the **DEATH BY DRIVING: GENERAL PRINCIPLES** *Disqualification* para at **235.20**.

239   DEATH BY DRIVING: DISQUALIFIED/NO LICENCE/UNINSURED, WHEN

239.1

Road Traffic Act 1988 s 3ZB[254] Causing death when at the time driving: a) without a licence authorising the vehicle to be driven, or b) while uninsured etc.

Mode of trial Triable either way

Maximum sentence On indictment 2 years. Summary maximum 6 months and/or a £5,000 fine for offences committed before 12 March 2015 and an unlimited fine thereafter.[255] There are maximum fines for those aged under 18, see **14.38** in Volume 1.

Disqualification Obligatory disqualification of 1 year,[256] unless there are special reasons.

Road Traffic Act 1988 s 3ZC[257] Causing death when at the time driving while disqualified. In force 13 April 2015

Mode of trial Indictable only

Maximum sentence 10 years

Disqualification Obligatory disqualification of 2 years,[258] unless there are special reasons.

---

[254] As inserted by Road Safety Act 2006 s 21(1) and amended by Criminal Justice and Courts Act 2015 Sch 6
[255] Legal Aid, Sentencing and Punishment of Offenders Act 2012 s 85(1) and (4) and Legal Aid, Sentencing and Punishment of Offenders Act 2012 (Commencement No 11) Order 2015 2015/504
[256] Road Traffic Offenders Act 1988 s 34(1) and Sch 2 Part I
[257] As inserted by Criminal Justice and Courts Act 2015 s 29(1)
[258] Road Traffic Offenders Act 1988 s 34(4) as amended by Criminal Justice and Courts Act 2015 Sch 6 para 4

Disqualification until test is passed Where the defendant is disqualified under Road Traffic Offenders Act 1988 s 34, the defendant must be disqualified until an appropriate driving test is passed.[259] In force 13 April 2015

Extended sentences This offence was added to Criminal Justice Act 2003 Sch 15.[260] The court may pass a 2012 extended sentence (EDS) if there is a significant risk of serious harm from future specified offences and either: a) the defendant has a Criminal Justice Act 2003 Sch 15B conviction (applicable only to defendants aged 18+), or b) the offence would justify a determinate sentence of at least 4 years.[261] In force 13 April 2015.[262]

Commencement Offences of causing death when disqualified committed before 13 April 2015 are contrary to section 3ZB, which then dealt with all three offences. The new section 3ZC only applies to offences committed after the new provisions are in force, Criminal Justice and Courts Act 2015 s 29(5).

Penalty points 3-11 penalty points for both offences when special reasons apply[263]

Depriving defendant of vehicle used For both offences there is power to deprive the defendant of the vehicle used[264] for the purposes of committing the offence.

239.2 Crown Court Statistics

Causing death by driving unlicensed, disqualified or uninsured Aged 21+

Year	Plea	Total sentenced	Type of sentencing %						Average length of custody in months
			Discharge	Fine	Commu-nity sentence	Suspended sentence	Cus-tody	Other	
2013	G	9	–	11.1	22.2	22.2	33.3	11.1	16
	NG	0							
2014	G	0							
	NG	1	–	–	–	–	100	–	not listed[265]

For explanations about the statistics, see page 1-xii. For more statistics about defendants aged 10-20 and female defendants, see www.banksr.com Other Matters Statistics tab

239.3 Sentencing Guidelines Council guideline

Causing Death by Driving Guideline 2008, see www.banksr.com Other Matters Guidelines tab The guidelines apply to sentences of offenders aged 18+. For the bulk of the guidelines, see the **DEATH BY DRIVING: GENERAL PRINCIPLES** chapter.

Factors to take into consideration

page 2 para 6 Since there will be no allegation of bad driving, the guideline for causing death by driving, unlicensed, disqualified or uninsured drivers links the assessment of offender culpability to the nature of the prohibition on the offender's driving and includes a list of factors that may aggravate an offence.

page 16 para 1 The following guideline applies to a "first-time offender" aged 18 or over convicted after trial (see page 8 above [not listed]). An offender convicted of causing death by driving whilst disqualified will always have at least one relevant previous conviction for the offence that resulted in the disqualification. The starting point and range take this into account; any other previous convictions should be considered in the usual way.

---

[259] Road Traffic Offenders Act 1988 s 36(2)(e)
[260] Inserted by Criminal Justice and Courts Act 2015 Sch 7 para 11. In force 13/4/15
[261] Criminal Justice Act 2003 s 226A-226B as inserted by Legal Aid, Sentencing and Punishment of Offenders Act 2012 s 124.
[262] Criminal Justice and Courts Act 2015 (Commencement No 1, Saving and Transitional Provisions) Order 2015 2015/778 para 3 and Sch 1 para 81
[263] Road Traffic Offenders Act 1988 s 28, 34 and Sch 2 Part I as amended
[264] Powers of Criminal Courts (Sentencing) Act 2000 s 143(6)-(7)
[265] Based on too few cases to be meaningful

para 2 When assessing the seriousness of any offence, the court must always refer to the full list of aggravating and mitigating factors in the Council guideline *Overarching Principles: Seriousness Guideline 2004*, see **66.23** in Volume 1, as well as those set out on the facing page as being particularly relevant to this type of offending behaviour.

paras 3 to 5 [These paragraphs describe the offence and the court's powers including disqualification.]

para 6 Because of the significantly lower maximum penalty, the sentencing ranges are considerably lower than for the other three offences covered in this guideline; many cases may be sentenced in a Magistrates' Court, particularly where there is an early guilty plea.

para 7 A fine is unlikely to be an appropriate sentence for this offence; where a non-custodial sentence is considered appropriate, this should be a community order.

para 8 Since driving whilst disqualified is more culpable than driving whilst unlicensed or uninsured, a higher starting point is proposed when the offender was disqualified from driving at the time of the offence.

para 9 Being uninsured, unlicensed or disqualified are the only determinants of seriousness for this offence, as there are no factors relating to the standard of driving. The list of aggravating factors identified is slightly different as the emphasis is on the decision to drive by an offender who is not permitted by law to do so.

para 10 In some cases, the extreme circumstances that led an offender to drive whilst unlicensed, disqualified or uninsured may result in a successful defence of 'duress of circumstances'.[266] In less extreme circumstances, where the decision to drive was brought about by a genuine and proven emergency, that may mitigate offence seriousness and so it is included as an additional mitigating factor.

para 11 A driver may hold a reasonable belief in relation to the validity of insurance (for example having just missed a renewal date or relied on a third party to make an application) and also the validity of a licence (for example incorrectly believing that a licence covered a particular category of vehicle). In light of this, an additional mitigating factor covers those situations where an offender genuinely believed that there was valid insurance or a valid licence.

para 12 Sentencers should take into account relevant matters of personal mitigation; see in particular guidance on good driving record at **235.13**, giving assistance at the scene at **235.3**, and remorse in paragraphs 26-29 above at **235.13**.

Nature of offence	Starting point	Sentencing range
The offender was disqualified from driving or the offender was unlicensed or uninsured plus two or more aggravating factors from the list below	12 months' custody	36 weeks' to 2 years' custody
The offender was unlicensed or uninsured plus at least one aggravating factor from the list below	26 weeks' custody	Community order (high) to 36 weeks' custody
The offender was unlicensed or uninsured – no aggravating factors	Community order (medium)	Community order (low) to community order (high)

Additional aggravating factors: 1 Previous convictions for motoring offences, whether involving bad driving or involving an offence of the same kind that forms part of the present conviction (i.e. unlicensed, disqualified or uninsured driving) 2 More than one

---

[266] In *DPP v Mullally* 2006 EWHC 3448 (Admin) the Divisional Court held that the defence of necessity must be strictly controlled and that it must be proved that the actions of the defendant were reasonable in the given circumstances. See also *R v Hasan* 2005 UKHL 22.

person was killed as a result of the offence 3 Serious injury to one or more persons in addition to the death(s) 4 Irresponsible behaviour such as failing to stop or falsely claiming that someone else was driving.

Additional mitigating factors: 1 The decision to drive was brought about by a proven and genuine emergency falling short of a defence 2 The offender genuinely believed that he or she was insured or licensed to drive 3 The offender was seriously injured as a result of the collision 4 The victim was a close friend or relative.

For the meaning of a high-level, a medium-level and a low-level community order see **16.12-16.14** in Volume 1.

239.4   *Magistrates' Court Sentencing Guidelines*

Magistrates' Court Sentencing Guidelines 2008, see www.banksr.com Other Matters Guidelines tab The guideline restates the main guideline, in the last paragraph.

239.5   *Cases*

Note: The Supreme Court in *R v Hughes* 2013 UKSC 56 decided that, where the defendant driver is not at fault, the offence is not made out. Consequently, *R v Hussain* below should be read with that in mind. Ed.

R v Hussain 2011 EWCA Crim 1893, 2012 1 Cr App R (S) 66 (p 378) D pleaded (full credit) to causing death by driving whilst uninsured, aggravated vehicle-taking and doing an act intending to pervert the course of justice. (The last two matters, 6 months concurrent each.) D was driving his uncle's car, without consent, and whilst uninsured to do so. V, who lived in a care home because of her mental problems, was walking back from the shops. V walked from a central reservation towards the pavement. Very shortly after, D's car hit her. A collision was inevitable. D remained at the scene but gave his brother's name (who was insured) when first asked (the perverting). He admitted the offences at the police station the next day. D, aged 21 at sentence, had no convictions and was studying for a degree in IT. Held. There was no criticism of his driving. The combination of circumstances requires an immediate custodial sentence. Starting at 12, not 16, **8 months** not 12 was appropriate.

R v Headley 2012 EWCA Crim 1212, 2013 2 Cr App R (S) 40 (p 224) D1 pleaded to: a) aiding and abetting the causing of death by driving whilst unlicensed and uninsured and b) permitting another, D2, to drive without a licence and without insurance. V, a 13-year-old boy, was riding his bike in a car park on a housing estate. D2 was also there driving a Toyota in first gear very slowly. D1 was in the passenger seat. Neither of them had insurance and D2 did not have a licence to drive. V drove into the path of the car and the car neither braked nor changed direction. V was crushed under the car, which hit a parked car. V died. D told police he was giving D2 driving lessons. He said he knew she did not have insurance or a licence. He also said D2 had panicked when she saw V and he told her to brake but she did not. D1 thought she might have hit the accelerator by mistake. He claimed he had pulled the handbrake. It was discovered that D2 had virtually no driving experience. D1 was of good character save for a conviction for no insurance (£350). D2, aged 21 at appeal, pleaded to the same unlicensed/uninsured offence and was sentenced to 12 months. Held. **8 months** was not manifestly excessive. 2-year disqualification not 3. The disqualification until driving test is passed was not necessary.

240   DEFENDANT

For *Absconding defendants* and *Absent defendants* see the back index.

240.1   *AIDS/HIV, Defendant has*

R v Stark 1992 Crim LR 384 D was sentenced to 4 years for drug trafficking. Because of AIDS his life expectancy was estimated by one doctor as not more than a year and another 12-18 months. The offences had originally been allowed to lie on the file because of his condition but five weeks later he was arrested for a similar offence. Held. It was not for the Court of Appeal to manipulate a sentence to achieve a social end. That matter was for the royal prerogative of mercy. Adjustments could be made as an act of mercy but it would not be right to change radically a perfectly proper sentence. His arrest showed there was a grave risk he would continue to traffic in drugs as long as he was able to do so. The medical reports should be forwarded to the prison authorities.

R v Bernard 1997 1 Cr App R (S) 135 The fact that an offender is HIV positive or has a reduced life expectancy should not generally affect the sentence. A serious medical condition, even when it is difficult to treat in prison, will not automatically entitle an offender to a lesser sentence. An offender's serious medical condition may enable a court to impose a lesser sentence as an act of mercy in the exceptional circumstances of a particular case rather than by virtue of any general principle.

R v Cahill 2009 EWCA Crim 420 D pleaded at the Magistrates' Court to possessing ketamine (class C, as it then was) and amphetamine with intent to supply. Police found 15.5 grams of ketamine with a street value of £566 and 46.9 grams of amphetamine with a street value of £467 at his home. A book with names and sums of money was also found. In interview he said he had been supplying drugs to 80-100[267] people and did so because of debts. He was aged 54 with a conviction in 1989 for stealing from old people at their home where he worked (community sentence). In 1986 he was diagnosed as HIV positive and in 1996 with AIDS. His consultant said, 'D has advanced HIV infection with multiple drug resistance maintained on a salvage antiretroviral regime. His Kaposi sarcoma is still active. He has recurrent nausea, vomiting, night sweats and diarrhoea. D is underweight. His health is very vulnerable and the control of his HIV is only possible with two new drugs. It is critically important that his drug supply is maintained and his adherence is full. He requires regular visits to hospital.' His partner of 21 years suffered from angina and a heart attack and needed D's care. The Judge took into account his health, his co-operation with the police and that he was a persistent class B and C drug dealer. Held. He has a very serious condition needing hospital supervision. It was exceptional so **9 months' suspended** not immediate.

See also the *Health of the defendant, Poor* paras at **240.29**, the *Disabled defendants* paras at **240.17** and the **RAPE AND ASSAULT BY PENETRATION** *Sexually transmitted disease, Defendant has* para at **317.94**.

240.2   Alcohol, Defendant under the influence of/Binge drinking etc.
Overarching Principles: Seriousness Guideline 2004, see www.banksr.com Other Matters Guidelines tab para 1.22 Commission of an offence while under the influence of alcohol or drugs is an aggravating factor/factor indicating higher culpability. For the other factors see the **GUIDELINES** *Factors indicating higher culpability Guidelines* para at **66.23** in Volume 1.

R v Rees and Others 2006 2 Cr App R (S) 20 (p 143) LCJ The Court dealt with a football-related violent disorder case. Held. When it is the habit of young men [and young women] to drink excessively and then behave out of character, it is important that the courts send a message that there are very real dangers in embarking on that sort of binge drinking.

Assisting the prosecution see the **INFORMANTS/GIVING EVIDENCE FOR THE PROS-ECUTION** chapter in Volume 1 and the **IMPORTATION OF DRUGS** *Assisting the prosecution* para at **273.38**.

Anonymity see the **CHILDREN AND YOUNG OFFENDERS GENERAL PRINCIPLES Reporting Restrictions** section at **14.20** in Volume 1.

For *Bad character* see the back index.

240.3   Bail   Offence(s) committed when on bail
Criminal Justice Act 2003 s 143(3) In considering the seriousness of any offence committed while the offender was on bail, the court must treat the fact that it was committed in those circumstances as an aggravating factor.

---

[267] Assuming I have amended a typo correctly. Ed.

Note: Where a civilian court deals with a service offence, the words 'or charged with a service offence and released from service custody' are inserted after the words 'on bail', Armed Forces (Civilian Courts Dealing with Service Offences) (Modification of the Criminal Justice Act 2003) Regulations 2009 2009/2042 regs 3-4.
Criminal Practice Directions 2015 EWCA Crim 1569 para III 14C.10 Where the appropriate penalty is a custodial sentence, consecutive sentences should be imposed unless there are circumstances that make this inappropriate.
Overarching Principles: Seriousness Guideline 2004, see www.banksr.com other Matters Guidelines tab para 1.21 The lists below bring together the most important aggravating features with potential application to more than one offence or class of offences...
para 1.22 **Factors indicating higher culpability** [One of the factors is] Offence committed whilst on bail for other offences, see **66.23** in Volume 1.
Example: *R v Megia-Grande* 2015 EWCA Crim 1205 (D shoplifted and was bailed, then shoplifted again and was bailed. D pleaded to both matters and was bailed. Two days later he shoplifted again and was given a community sentence. The third matter could not aggravate the earlier conduct, but the Judge could have it in mind. For more detail see **346.41**.)
See also the **BAIL OFFENCES** chapter.

240.4   Bail   Consecutive or concurrent sentences for the on bail offence and the original offence?

Fail to Surrender to Bail Guideline 2007 para 33, see www.banksr.com Other Matters Guidelines tab A court should normally impose a consecutive sentence. However, a concurrent sentence will be appropriate where otherwise the overall sentence would be disproportionate to the combined seriousness of the offences.
Criminal Practice Directions 2015 EWCA Crim 1567 para III 14C.9 A defendant who commits an offence under Bail Act 1976 s 6(1) or 6(2) commits an offence that stands apart from the proceedings in respect of which bail was granted. The seriousness of the offence can be reflected by an appropriate and generally separate penalty being imposed for the Bail Act offence.
C.10 As noted above, there is a sentencing guideline on sentencing offenders for Bail Act offences and this must be followed unless it would be contrary to the interests of justice to do so. Where the appropriate penalty is a custodial sentence, consecutive sentences should be imposed unless there are circumstances that make this inappropriate.
R v Thackwray 2003 EWCA Crim 3362 The Judge was entitled to take the commission of the offence when on bail as an aggravating factor even when the defendant was later acquitted of the other offence.

240.5   Bail   Offence(s) committed when released from service custody/ Bail   Court Martial

Armed Forces Act 2006 s 238(1) A court or officer dealing with an offender for a service offence ('the current offence') must, in considering the seriousness of the offence:
  c) if the offender committed the current offence while:
    i) charged with another service offence and released from service custody, or
    ii) on bail,
treat the fact that it was committed in those circumstances as an aggravating factor.

240.6   *Change of lifestyle*

R v Wilkinson 2005 EWCA Crim 811 D (presumably) pleaded to three counts of possession of drugs with intent to supply and one breach of bail. These offences had been committed in 1995 when D was aged 25. He was arrested in a nightclub after being observed supplying a white tablet. He had 16½ ecstasy tablets, nine wraps of amphetamine sulphate and a quantity of herbal cannabis estimated at £230 worth on him. He also had £44 in cash and £125 at home. In interview he said he had bought £300 worth of drugs some days earlier and that he intended to supply some of these at cost to his friends and keep the rest for his own consumption. He gave details of the person from whom he had bought the drugs. The case was committed to the Crown Court and it was anticipated he would plead guilty: a pre-sentence report had been prepared. He failed to answer to bail and a bench warrant was issued. Police did nothing about executing that warrant until a 'clear-up' operation in January 2005. In the intervening period he had done nothing to hide from the authorities and had lived openly under his own name. When arrested he admitted the offence. In 1995 D's life was 'at a low ebb'. He had dropped out of university. His parents had both died and he had squandered the money they left him on drink and drugs. However, he had no previous convictions and he had been frank when caught with the drugs. By 2005 he was a changed man. He had gone back to university and got a first-class honours degree. He then took an MA and was working for an MPhil/PhD while employed as a lecturer at university. He had gained certificates in mountain leadership and rock-climbing instruction and introduced scores of undergraduates to the sport. He had got married and had two daughters and was an excellent father. There were six testimonials about the transformation in his life, speaking of him as being a dedicated family man and a loving husband, a thoughtful student and a reliable trustworthy academic. Held. The circumstances of the case were exceptional. D has completely altered his way of life and is now making a very positive contribution. However, we cannot fault the decision that an immediate custodial sentence was necessary. We have information that was not before the Judge about university commitments which involve others which make it desirable he should be available and not in prison. As an act of mercy, **6 weeks** concurrent on all charges not 4 months, so immediate release.

R v Dalby and Berry 2005 EWCA Crim 1292, 2006 1 Cr App R (S) 38 (p 216) Four years was appropriate on a plea for this section 20 wounding. The Judge described it as the worst possible case of section 20. However, we are particularly impressed by the remarkable change in this young man. The prison report shows a remarkable improvement on the gloomy pre-sentence report. He has passed exams and has great promise. He appears to have made genuine progress. For this reason alone we reduce the sentence to **3½ years**.

Child defendant see the CHILDREN AND YOUNG OFFENDERS chapters in Volume 1 and the *Vulnerable defendants, Treatment of* para at **240.67** (because that is how children are classified).

240.7 Co-defendant's personal mitigation

Att-Gen's Ref No 73 of 1999 2000 2 Cr App R (S) 209 LCJ A co-defendant's sentence was reduced because of his personal mitigation. The Judge then reduced the defendant's sentence to prevent him having a burning sense of injustice. Held. It is not a reason to reduce the sentence. **18 months** substituted for CSO.

R v JF and NE 2015 EWCA Crim 351 LCJ J, a boy aged 14½ and D, a girl aged 16 were convicted of manslaughter. The Judge chose not to differentiate between them. Held. Because of the reports (no details given) and the seriousness of the offence, **3 years' detention** was not manifestly excessive. Because of the progress D had made and because she will be moved to a different type of establishment when she becomes 18, we reduce her sentence to 2 years. Because the defendants were treated the same by the Judge we do the same for J.

240.8 Conduct of the defence during a trial

R v Khatab 2008 EWCA Crim 541, 2 Cr App R (S) 94 (p 530) D was convicted of assisting an offender, M, who had committed murder, by disposing of the murder weapon. The victim sustained a serious injury to his head and died on the way to hospital. D took the murder weapon from M and disposed of it. Two days later he went to the police and told them he was a drug dealer and had disposed of it because it had blood on it. D's trial was conducted on the basis that he had done these actions but that the prosecution had to prove M was guilty of murder or manslaughter, and that D had been aware of this at the time of disposing of the weapon, before they could prove his guilt. His counsel asked virtually no questions. He put the prosecution to proof that M was the killer. Held. Having regard to the way in which D conducted his defence he was entitled to a significant discount from the sentence which would have been appropriate had he maintained a steadfast plea of not guilty all along.

R v Lowndes 2013 EWCA Crim 1747 The Judge took into account the fact the defendant sought to blame a co-defendant. Held. para 12 This was an impermissible approach. In *R v Scott* 1983 5 Cr App R (S) 90, the Judge took into account the immense amount of lying that has taken place. It was held in no circumstances should a sentence of imprisonment be passed simply because of the way in which the defence was presented. This would only be relevant when considering the value of a mitigation.

See also: *R v Hercules* 1987 9 Cr App R (S) 291 (Sentence reduced because the Judge implied the defendant received more because he lied.)

R v Fyad 2011 EWCA Crim 2039 (The fact that D lied to both the police and the jury was not an aggravating factor.)

240.9   *Confession evidence, Case based only on*

R v Thompson 2012 EWCA Crim 1764 D pleaded to burglary and theft. He received 32 months in part because of his bad record. He was visited in prison by police and invited to help them 'clear the books'. Held. We doubt that this case called for any significant downward adjustment on the grounds that D's admissions helped the victims. What it did call for was a significant downward adjustment in recognition of the fact that D had provided the evidence against himself. Sentence reduced from 32 months to 2 years.

R v Keeley 2013 EWCA Crim 1014 D pleaded to sexual assault of a child under the age of 13 (×6). D met his wife, W, over the Internet. She lived in the Philippines. He went to visit her on three occasions in 2009 and 2010. Her daughter, V, was aged 6 or 7 at that time. The six counts were sample counts reflecting some 20 incidents of sexual abuse during the visits. D touched V's vagina with his hand (×3) and rubbed his penis against her back, to the point of ejaculation (×3). D and V were clothed on all occasions. D married W and they returned to England. V remained in the Philippines with relatives but planned to come to England at some point, to live with D. D's offending weighed on his conscience and he wondered whether, when W and V came to England, he would be tempted to commit similar offences. D told W and social services, who informed the police. When V was interviewed, she made no reference to D's offending, stating simply that he was affectionate towards her. A pre-sentence report stated that D was unable to fully understand why he had committed the offences and that D misinterpreted normal child behaviour and sexualised them. D was aged 67 at appeal. Held. This was a wholly exceptional case in which D took the initiative of reporting himself to the authorities out of concern for his future offending. That there was no evidence from V is of significance. D appears to be highly motivated to address his offending. The Judge failed to reflect the wholly exceptional nature of the case. **3-year community order** not 2 years' imprisonment. A SOPO was quashed.

R v Graham 2015 EWCA Crim 503 Plea to robbery. 15 years was the correct starting point. The fact his confession was the reason why he was charged merits more than a third off for the plea and so, with that and other factors, **6 years** not 8.

R v Green 2015 EWCA Crim 1218 D pleaded (full credit) to two burglaries (one dwelling, one not). He accepted ten dwelling-burglary TICs. Police saw a bicycle leaning against a car and D coming out of a driveway. D ran off. Police caught him. A handbag he had discarded was found. It was discovered that the bicycle had been stolen from a shed and the handbag from a house. D took part in a police 'clean-slate' operation, in which he pointed out burglaries he had committed where there was no other evidence. Police considered that D's motivation was remorse and spoke well of D's realistic assessment of himself. D was aged 28 with an extensive criminal record. There were three appearances for more than one dwelling burglary with TICs. In 2006, D was sentenced to 18 months' YOI. In 2009, D was sentenced to 3 years. In 2010, he was sentenced to 47 months. There were problems with the health of his young son. Held. D was a prolific burglar who steals to feed his cocaine addiction. Considering the police assessment of him we can be more lenient [than usual]. We start at 5 years not 7½, so with plea, **3 years 4 months** not 5. For the shed burglary, we substitute 2 years concurrent for 3.

See also: *R v A* 2014 EWCA Crim 2143 (Plea. Sexually assaulted two girls but prosecution due to be dropped. D went to police voluntarily, confessed to those assaults and told them about two further victims. Given extended sentence with 4-year extended licence. Held. The Judge was right to start at about 10 years. With full credit and the confessions, **5½ years'** custody not 7.)

Corporate defendants see the COMPANIES AND PUBLIC BODIES AS DEFENDANTS chapter.

For *Corrosive effect of custody*, see CHILDREN AND YOUNG OFFENDERS: GENERAL PRINCIPLES *Corrosive effect of prison on young offenders* at **14.36** in Volume 1.

240.10   Confession evidence   Early and repeated admissions of guilt
Att-Gen's Ref No 21 of 2015 2015 EWCA Crim 953 D, now aged 77, made an early plea to 10 counts of indecent assault. Held. para 30 Rarely will an offender admit what he has done when confronted by his victim, then admit it to his wife, then the police and then the court. Even more rarely will an offender admit he has abused another victim when that person had made no complaint. These matters entitled the defendant to receive very considerable credit.

240.11   Custodial sentence, First
R v Howells 1999 1 Cr App R (S) 335 at 338 LCJ While the court will never impose a custodial sentence unless satisfied that it is necessary to do so, there will be even greater reluctance to impose a custodial sentence on an offender who has never before served such a sentence.

240.12   Cultural background
Att-Gen's Ref No 1 of 2011 2011 EWCA Crim 930 LCJ D was convicted of 16 rapes on his wife. It had been an arranged marriage. She was subject to domination, aggression and significant violence. They were both Pakistani. Held. The cultural background was not a feature which justified or could be said to begin to justify any reduction in sentence.
R v MA 2012 EWCA Crim 1646 D was convicted of five rapes and an ABH on his wife. He and his wife had an arranged marriage in Pakistan. D's counsel said, "The Judge could have treated [him] slightly differently from a man who had been brought up in the United Kingdom." That, she submitted, would be to reflect that his offending was based on his belief that he had a right to rape his wife, and so his offending was not aggravated by a deliberate disregard of what is culturally acceptable or by the norms in this country. Held. We reject that submission out of hand.

240.13   Custody threshold, Passing the
Criminal Justice Act 2003 s 152(2) The court must not pass a custodial sentence unless the offence, or combination of the offence and one or more offences associated with it, was so serious that neither a fine alone nor a community sentence can be justified for the offence.
Overarching Principles: Seriousness Guideline 2004, see www.banksr.com Other Matters Guidelines tab para 1.32 In applying the threshold test, sentencers should note that the clear intention of the threshold test is to reserve prison as a punishment for the most serious offences, it is impossible to determine definitively which features of a particular offence make it serious enough to merit a custodial sentence, passing the custody threshold does not mean that a custodial sentence should be deemed inevitable, and custody can still be avoided in the light of personal mitigation or where there is a suitable intervention in the community which provides sufficient restriction (by way of

punishment) while addressing the rehabilitation of the offender to prevent future crime. For example, a prolific offender who currently could expect a short custodial sentence (which, in advance of custody plus, would have no provision for supervision on release) might more appropriately receive a suitable community sentence.

para 1.33 The approach to the imposition of a custodial sentence should be as follows:
   a) Has the custody threshold been passed?
   b) If so, is it unavoidable that a custodial sentence be imposed?
   c) If so, can that sentence be suspended (sentencers should be clear that they would have imposed a custodial sentence if the power to suspend had not been available)?
   d) If not, can the sentence be served intermittently?
   e) If not, impose a sentence which takes immediate effect for the term commensurate with the seriousness of the offence.

For other custody threshold paragraphs see the back index.
Dangerous Offenders see the EXTENDED SENTENCES (EDS) chapter in Volume 1.

240.14   Debt   Defendant claims he or she is in debt
R v Mullany 2012 EWCA Crim 687 D pleaded to conspiracy to rob. A householder suffered a violent robbery. D claimed he was put under pressure because he was in drug debts. Held. Increasingly the court sees that those who have allowed themselves through drug addiction to acquire a debt to criminals who should supply class A drugs in particular are brought under pressure to commit offences. Those who are in that position must realise that that kind of excuse cannot radically affect the sentence to be passed on them if they offend, particularly if they offend in such a way as this. Offences causing intrusion into homes, offences of robbery with violence to the individual, offences which are bound to affect in an important way other people, cannot be excused to any significant extent by the fact that the offender has permitted himself to fall into debt and chooses to pass on the pain in this kind of way.
Deeming defendant is aged 21 see para **14.10** in Volume 1.

240.15   Delay in being sentenced etc. (after arrest)
European Convention on Human Rights art 6(1) Everyone is entitled to a fair and public hearing within a reasonable time.
Boolell v State of Mauritius 2006 UKPC 46 Privy Council D was interviewed about a dishonoured cheque in February 1991. At the first hearing in March 1993 he pleaded not guilty. After that he mounted a series of applications, many without notice to the prosecution. Many of his counsel withdrew. D pleaded guilty then withdrew his plea. There were over 50 hearings for the first trial and 90 hearings for the second trial. In March 2003, he was convicted and was sentenced to six months and a fine. He appealed his conviction and in May 2004, his appeal was dismissed. His appeal to the Privy Council was heard in June 2006. The cases were reviewed. Held. The delay was caused to a considerable extent by the defendant. The delay from February 1991 to March 2003 gives grounds for real concern and is *prima facie* unreasonable. It is incumbent on the court to take such steps as it could to expedite matters. There should have been an injection of an element of urgency after the [second] trial had started. However reprehensible the conduct of the defendant, the trial was not completed within a reasonable time. That was a breach of the constitution, which requires trials to be completed within a reasonable time. It would be wrong to send the defendant to prison 15 years after the offence, so we raise the fine from 500 Rs to 10,000 Rs instead.
R v Ali and Hussain 2008 EWCA Crim 146 The offences took place between 1997 and 2001. The first convictions were quashed in June 2005, *R v Ali and Others* 2005 EWCA Crim 87, 2006 1 Cr App R 8 (p 143). The next appeal was heard in July 2008. Held. The delay was not the defendants' fault, save that they contested the charges. There is ample

authority for a reduction for the delay, *Mills v HM Advocate* 2002 3 WLR 1597 and *R v Farquhar* 2003 EWCA Crim 2668, 2004 1 Cr App R 22 (p 270).[268] 2 years deducted to reflect the substantial delay, so **10 years** not 12.

R v Evans 2010 EWCA Crim 1090 D was convicted of possessing cocaine with intent to supply. The offence was in September 2008, the PCMH was in June 2009 and the trial was in January 2010. During the delay D kept drug-free and he worked well. D had also engaged well with the Drug Intervention Programme. Held. **4 years** was within the appropriate range. Because of the delay and the good use he had made of the delay **3 years**. For more details of the case, see the SUPPLY OF DRUGS chapter.

Att-Gen's Ref No 79 of 2009 2010 EWCA Crim 338 D pleaded to five sample counts of historical rape in the early 1980s. Now aged 67, he had assumed the role of the victim's father. The victim, aged 11-13, was interviewed in November 2005. D was interviewed in November 2007 and nine months later summonses were issued. Abuse proceedings were started and only in August 2009 was the trial started. The Judge reduced the sentence by the equivalent of 2 years for the inactivity. Held. There is no measure for the reduction in delay cases. Each case was far too variable for that. The breach of article 6 rights calls for some remedy. The delay should be reflected in the sentence, but not as much as this case.

R v Shaw and Others Re W and K 2011 EWCA Crim 98 D, with others, pleaded to offences relating to the importation and supply of cocaine. £100,000 was spent preparing to import quantities of cocaine. In the event, no drugs were ever imported. The quantities discussed were 200 and 260 kilos, and later, 75 kilos. There was a 2-year delay between each pleading to conspiracy and their eventual sentence. It was argued that the rights enshrined in article 6(1) to a fair and public hearing within a reasonable time were infringed. The Judge declined to reduce the sentences for the delay stating that it was inappropriate to reduce the sentence for the anxiety of awaiting sentence. Held. In this case, the three principal offenders had all pleaded guilty, those awaiting trial were lesser players and it may be that, in order to protect the article 6 rights of offenders waiting to be sentenced, once it became apparent that a lapse of time of this order was likely to occur, the court should have proceeded to sentence irrespective of the preferable approach that points to the sentencing exercise being undertaken once in order that all the facts can be considered at the same time. Although each case falls to be considered on its own merits, a delay of two years so that the trials of those not alleged to be principal offenders could take place means the Judge should have reduced the sentence (albeit slightly). We reduce the sentence by 6 months.

R v Burgin 2015 EWCA Crim 49 D pleaded to a section 20 assault. D was on licence at the time for a sentence of 3 years' detention. That was for three robberies. The recall lasted 9 months, which would not count towards the sentence. The co-defendant caused a nine-month delay to D's sentencing. Held. In *R v Kerrigan and Another* 2014 EWCA Crim 2348, 2015 1 Cr App R (S) 29 (p 221) this Court considered that a person…subject to the discretion on particular facts, such as excessive delay…is not entitled to…credit for time in custody awaiting sentencing, which coincides with time spent in custody having been recalled on licence.

Old cases: *R v Ashton* 2002 EWCA Crim 2782 (4½-year delay from sentence to appeal. Because of the article 6(1) breach **17 years** not 18.)

R v McCartney 2003 EWCA Crim 1372 (*R v Ashton* 2002 applied. Sentences of 22 years, 19 years, 11 years consecutive to 8 years not excessive. However, all reduced by 12 months because of the delay. Unclear what the delay in all was. One defendant was arrested in October 1998, convicted in April 2000 and appealed in May 2003.)

See also the *Historical cases* paras at **240.32**.

---

[268] Also known as *R v Petkar*.

240.16   *Defendants conducting their own cases*

Equal Treatment Bench Book 2013 www.banksr.com Other matters Other documents tab para Guilty pleas

Chapter 4 page 25 **Key points** Most litigants in person are stressed and worried, operating in an alien environment in what for them is a foreign language. They are trying to grasp concepts of law and procedure about which they may be totally ignorant.

They may well be experiencing feelings of fear, ignorance, frustration, bewilderment and disadvantage, especially if appearing against a represented party. The outcome of the case may have a profound effect and long-term consequences upon their life.

Role of the judge

Judges must be aware of the feelings and difficulties experienced by litigants in person and be ready and able to help them, especially if a represented party is being oppressive or aggressive.

Maintaining patience and an even-handed approach [are] also important where the litigant in person is being oppressive or aggressive towards another party or its representative or towards the court or tribunal. The judge should, however, remain understanding so far as possible as to what might lie behind their behaviour.

Maintaining a balance between assisting and understanding what the litigant in person requires, while protecting their represented opponent against the problems that can be caused by the litigant in person's lack of legal and procedural knowledge, is the key.

Particular areas of difficulty

page 28 para 21 Litigants in person may face a daunting range of problems of both knowledge and understanding.

The judge's role

page 32 para 48 It can be hard to strike a balance in assisting a litigant in person in an adversarial system. A litigant in person may easily get the impression that the judge does not pay sufficient attention to them or their case, especially if the other side is represented and the judge asks the advocate on the other side to summarise the issues between the parties.

a) Explain the judge's role during the hearing.

b) If you are doing something which might be perceived to be unfair or controversial in the mind of the litigant in person, explain precisely what you are doing and why.

c) Adopt to the extent necessary an inquisitorial role to enable the litigant in person fully to present their case (but not in such a way as to appear to give the litigant in person an undue advantage).

Criminal cases

55 Under European Convention on Human Rights art 6(3) (Sch 1, Human Rights Act 1998), everyone charged with a criminal offence has the right to defend him or herself in person or through legal assistance of his or her own choosing or, if he or she has not sufficient means to pay for legal assistance, to be given it free where the interests of justice so require.

56 Those who dispense with legal assistance do so usually because they decline to accept the advice which they have been given, whether as to plea or the conduct of the trial. This, a defendant is entitled to do. However, guidance as to the value of representation may persuade such defendants that they are better advised to retain their representatives. If a defendant decides, notwithstanding advice and guidance, to represent [him] or herself, then the judge must explain the process and ensure proper control over the proceedings is maintained.

Note: This is a very edited selection from a fairly long section of the Bench Book. Ed.

240.17   *Disabled/blind defendants   General principles*

European Convention on Human Rights art 3 No one shall be subject to torture or to inhuman or degrading treatment or punishment.

Equal Treatment Bench Book 2013 www.banksr.com Other matters Other documents tab para 24 Special provisions govern the different forms of disability discrimination.

Equality Act 2010 recognises that more than formal equality is required to enable disabled people to participate as fully as possible in society. As acknowledged in the *UN Convention on the Rights of Persons with Disabilities*, it can be the interaction with various barriers in society that hinder the full and effective participation of disabled people on an equal basis with others.[269] In addition to protection from direct and indirect discrimination, reasonable adjustments may be required to assist a disabled person who, because of his or her disability, is placed at a substantial disadvantage in comparison to others without that disability (section 20). These may be, for example, by adaptations or modifications to premises, physical features or different arrangements, such as sitting times or provision of a sign language interpreter, or provision of an auxiliary aid or service.

para 25 The gist of the duty is that it is to take reasonable steps, at no cost to the disabled person, to avoid the disadvantage or provide the aid or service.

Price v UK 2001 No 33394/96, see www.banksr.com Other Matters Other Documents tab ECtHR Third Section In civil proceedings the appellant refused to answer questions about her financial position and the Judge committed her for 7 days for contempt. At court she said that the battery charger for her wheelchair was taken away because it was a luxury item. She was a thalidomide victim and was detained in a police station overnight. She had numerous deformities, with bladder and bowel problems. Held. To detain a severely disabled person in conditions where she is dangerously cold, risks developing sores because her bed is too hard or unreachable, and is unable to go to the toilet or keep clean without the greatest of difficulty, constitutes degrading treatment contrary to article 3 of the Convention. There was a violation of article 3 in the present case. I can see no justification for the decision to commit the applicant to an immediate term of imprisonment without at the very least ensuring in advance that there existed both adequate facilities for detaining her and conditions of detention in which her special needs could be met. £4,500 awarded.

Gelfman v France 2004 No 25875/03 see www.banksr.com Other Matters Other Documents tab ECtHR Second Section D was suffering from AIDS. Held. Article 3 requires the State to ensure that prisoners are detained in conditions which are compatible with respect for human dignity, that the manner and method of the execution of the measure do not subject them to distress or hardship of an intensity exceeding the unavoidable level of suffering inherent in detention and that, given the practical demands of imprisonment, their health and well-being are adequately secured by, among other things, providing them with the requisite medical assistance.

240.18   *Disabled/blind defendants   Cases*

R v Draper, Easterbrook and Frost 2008 EWCA Crim 3206 F, aged 53, had long-standing and serious rheumatoid arthritis. A medical report said he was wholly dependent on medication, that he was significantly handicapped, and was vulnerable to infection. He had had both knees, both hips and a shoulder replaced. He had trouble dressing and needed aids or help. He was unable to do most of the activities available to other prisoners. Within a short time of being in prison he had lost three stone. Held. The medical condition of a defendant may not be relevant to sentence at all. But it may be if imprisonment is a significantly greater punishment than it would be for other people. 4½ **years** not 5½ in recognition of the additional punishment prison is for him.

R v Hetherington 2009 EWCA Crim 1186 D was sentenced to 18 months for possession of indecent child photos. D had spina bifida and hydrocephalus. He could walk only very short distances. He had a wheelchair and had a shunt to drain water from his brain. D was doubly incontinent and occasionally needed an enema. The defence questioned whether a prison sentence was in breach of article 3. The Judge made a reduction from the normal sentence. The Court of Appeal heard that: a) due to a broken lift he was unable to go outside, b) there were difficulties in using the toilet and washing facilities,

---

[269] Article 1

c) a doctor was concerned about cell cleanliness but his needs were mostly addressed, and d) he was confined to his cell overnight when he needed to catheterise himself. The prison provided cold water through a hatch for this. Held. The prison authorities have a continuing obligation to ensure that his needs and rights are respected. A failure to achieve optimum standards or an ideal level of support is very different from subjecting a person to inhuman or degrading treatment. It would be preferable if he had access to a washbasin. The catheter arrangements are far from ideal but do not lead to a breach of D's Convention rights. His needs can be met.

R v Arshad 2015 EWCA Crim 1111, 2 Cr App R (S) 54 (p 391) (D was registered blind with impaired hearing. Involved at a high level in the distribution of heroin and cocaine. Arrested, bailed and carried on. Judge refused to reduce sentence because his blindness hadn't stopped him offending. In prison, D found custody difficult as he was left exposed and vulnerable. He had to be assisted by other prisoners. Held. His blindness did not prevent him from playing a leading role in the conspiracy. The Judge was right. Only because of totality, sentence reduced to 19 years.)

Note: This judgment seems out of line. Discounts are given for those who are elderly, young, speak no English, have their family abroad, have young children, are disabled and have serious health problems. To be blind seems a greater hardship than any of these because it severely limits what you are able to do in prison and it would make it very difficult to live in a hostile environment. The argument that the difficulty did not stop the defendant from committing the offence would apply to all the other defendants with the characteristics listed above, where a discount is given. Let's hope the blind are not singled out for special unfair treatment to add to the difficulties they would experience in prison. Ed.

See also: *R v Jabarkhall* 2012 EWCA Crim 2133 (We might well not have given D an immediate custodial sentence, see **240.38**.)

Old case: *R v Griffiths* 2004 EWCA Crim 2656, 2005 1 Cr App R (S) 108 (p 600) (**15 years** reflected the defendant's disability.)

For a summary of the case, see the 9th edition of this book.

See also the *Health of the defendant, Poor* paras at **240.29**.

240.19   *Doctors abusing patients*
R v Bradbury 2015 EWCA Crim 1176, 2 Cr App R (S) 72 (p 485) Doctor sexually abusing boys aged 10-16. 22 years' extended sentence (**16 years'** custody 6 years' extended licence), see **328.26**.

240.20   *Domestic violence, Defendant is the victim of*
R v Smith 2010 EWCA Crim 6 D pleaded to section 20 on the day of her trial, which was listed for section 18. The plea was accepted. D, aged 15, started a relationship with V, aged 16. They had two children. For some of the time they lived apart. V was a heroin and cocaine user with convictions for violence against D. He hit and bit her and made threats. Police were called on five occasions. V on his mobile demanded to know what D was doing. In the afternoon both were drinking. V turned up at D's flat. Her friends returned and found D crying. She said V had threatened her with a knife and he had threatened to kill her and the baby if she went with another man. V had a small kitchen knife in his waistband and was the worse for drink. V said he was going to take the baby home. He was told to get rid of the knife and he threw it on a mattress in the living room. D seized the knife and flew at V aiming ten blows at V while he was holding the baby. Two penetrated his chest and four went into his legs. V required open-heart surgery and was in hospital for nine days. He will require regular medication for life. D first claimed she was acting in self-defence and then said V had stabbed himself. D was aged 19. She was described as quiet and timid. She had a conviction for shoplifting and carrying a bladed article. She was assessed with a high risk of serious harm particularly to future partners. The psychiatrist said she showed features of a woman subjected to domestic violence including emotional detachment, low self-esteem and inability to remove

herself from the violent relationship. Further, it was not the classic battered woman syndrome, and alcohol was likely to be a significant disinhibiting factor. Held. This case did not fall into either the top or second tier of the guidelines. The injury was particularly grave. There could be no criticism of the **3½-year** starting point. There was no fault with **2 years' detention**.

See also the **DOMESTIC VIOLENCE** chapter.

240.21 *Drug users   Judicial guidance*

R v McInerney 2002 EWCA Crim 3003, 2003 2 Cr App R (S) 39 (p 240) It is common knowledge that many domestic burglars are drug addicts who burgle and steal in order to raise money to satisfy their craving for drugs. This is often an expensive craving, and it is not uncommon to learn that addicts commit a burglary, or even several burglaries, each day, often preying on houses in less affluent areas of the country. But to the victim of burglary the motivation of the burglar may well be of secondary interest. Self-induced addiction cannot be relied on as mitigation. The courts will not be easily persuaded that an addicted offender is genuinely determined and able to conquer his addiction.

In the case of offences committed because the offender is an alcoholic or a drug addict, while the taking of drink or drugs is no mitigation, the sentencing process must recognise the fact of the addiction and the importance of breaking the drug or drink problem. This is not only in the interests of the offender but also in the public interest since so commonly the addiction results in a vicious circle of imprisonment followed by reoffending. When an offender is making or prepared to make a real effort to break his addiction, it is important for the sentencing court to make allowances if the process of rehabilitation proves to be irregular. What may be important is the overall progress that the offender is making. This is part of the thinking behind drug and treatment orders.

R v Saw 2009 EWCA Crim 1, 2 Cr App R (S) 54 (p 367) LCJ Cases require careful attention where a defendant has reached a critical stage in his life with a real prospect of turning his back on crime, or breaking away from addiction to the drugs which led him into crime. If he is indeed making a genuine attempt to break the cycle, or to address its causes, then that is plainly a factor to be taken into account in his favour, and put into the balance against the aggravating features of the specific case. Successful and early rehabilitation often represents the best long-term advantage to the public, and a sentence which has a reasonable prospect of achieving that the offender will be deterred, or discouraged, or taught to avoid crime may well be appropriate where the burglary lacks significant attendant aggravating features. In the context of a young life which is presently being wasted away, a constructive, rehabilitative sentence, which includes a punitive element, may provide a better long-term solution for the public, and particularly for other householders, generally than an unconstructive custodial sentence. The Judge is not the prisoner of the sentencing tariff, but rather has the difficult task of arriving at the right sentence in the individual case. Whether an individual case is one for which such a course may be appropriate requires careful judgement.

R v Mullany 2012 EWCA Crim 687 D pleaded to conspiracy to rob. A householder suffered a violent robbery. D claimed he was put under pressure because he was in drug debts. Held. Increasingly the court sees that those who have allowed themselves through drug addiction to acquire a debt to criminals who should supply class A drugs in particular are brought under pressure to commit offences. Those who are in that position must realise that that kind of excuse cannot radically affect the sentence to be passed on them if they offend, particularly if they offend in such a way as this. Offences causing intrusion into homes, offences of robbery with violence to the individual, offences which are bound to affect in an important way other people, cannot be excused to any significant extent by the fact that the offender has permitted himself to fall into debt and chooses to pass on the pain in this kind of way.

Old case: *Att-Gen's Ref No 105 of 2002* 2003 EWCA Crim 182, 2 Cr App R (S) 50 (p 319) (Those who commit criminal offences in order to feed their drug habit should, if possible, be weaned from that habit, because, if they are, the public may, in the future, suffer less from the depredations than they have in the past. On the other hand, the imposition of a community penalty for offences of robbery,…would usually be wholly inappropriate, having regard to the public interest and the interests of the victims.)

240.22   Drug users   Determined efforts to break addiction

R v Howells 1999 1 Cr App R (S) 335 at 337 LCJ Where offending has been fuelled by addiction to drink or drugs, the court will be inclined to look more favourably on an offender who has already demonstrated (by taking practical steps to that end) a genuine, self-motivated determination to address his addiction.

Att-Gen's Ref No 21 of 2005 2005 EWCA Crim 1675, 2006 1 Cr App R (S) 51 (p 279) D pleaded about a month after the PDH to two counts: possession of 489 grams of heroin at 54% purity with intent to supply and simple possession of 5.27 grams of heroin. He was stopped by police getting off a train in London and threw a carrier bag under the train. That bag contained the larger amount of heroin. His home was searched and the smaller amount found in 11 wraps. Also at his home there were a set of electronic scales, four rolls of cling film and two envelopes with writing on, apparently about drugs transactions. The larger amount was worth between £19,560 and £34,230, the smaller between £210 and £368. His plea was accepted on the basis that he was simply the courier of the larger amount. The aggravating features were said to be the type of drugs seized and their quality and that he was subject to a CPRO at the time of the offence. D, aged 22, had a number of previous convictions including ABH and handling stolen goods. He had one previous drugs conviction for possession of a small quantity of cannabis. He had been a drug addict until at least September 2004. He was granted bail before trial to attend a Prince's Trust course to see whether he had become drug-free and turned a corner in his life. A pre-sentence report presented him in a very positive light, noting he was drug-free and had moved back with his family. There was a glowing reference from the centre where D had attended part of the Prince's Trust course saying he was head and shoulders above the rest of the group and stood out as a gifted person. There was similar evidence from the person running the residential section of the course. A further report said that he was testing negative for heroin and cocaine and that his progress on the CPRO was entirely satisfactory. The assessment of risk of harm to the public was low. It strongly recommended that he should not be returned to prison and said that the programme of intervention had been effective in tackling his offending behaviour and managing the risk of reoffending. The restriction on his liberty through the Curfew Order and the demand of unpaid work was punishment and the work enabled him to make reparation to the community. The Appeal Court was also shown an extremely positive letter from a nursery at which he had been carrying out voluntary work. Held. The Judge was not bound as a matter of law to pass a sentence of immediate imprisonment providing that he was properly satisfied that the circumstances were so exceptional that it would be appropriate to pass a different sentence. He was also entitled to conclude that the circumstances were exceptional. The success of the order to date points to the conclusion that the constructive work done so far should be allowed to continue. This is not intended to suggest that a course of this kind could be taken save in very exceptional circumstances indeed. In this case a **Community Punishment Order** for 100 hours, a Community Rehabilitation Order for 3 years with a condition to attend a Think First programme and a curfew for 6 months between 9 pm and 7 am not altered.

R v Kituba 2014 EWCA Crim 2127 D pleaded (full credit) to conspiracy to supply Class A drugs. A courier was seen going into D's bedsit in the hostel. Following a search, D and the courier were found in D's bedsit, surrounded by drugs paraphernalia. D played a significant role in the conspiracy. He was aged 24 on appeal with references, but had previous convictions for possessing class A drugs and a robbery conviction from 2010, receiving 3½ years, so he was on licence. Held. In the ordinary way this Court would not criticise a sentence of 4 years. The personal mitigation demonstrates that all hope is not yet lost for this young man. Further reports demonstrate the significant progress D has made whilst in prison, and his determined efforts to change his offending behaviour and steer clear of drugs in the future. **3½ years**, not 4.

240.23 *Education would be interrupted*

Example: *R v Trace* 2010 EWCA Crim 879 (Drunken attack on delivery driver. Sentence suspended because of damage sentence would do to defendant's university studies and the unlikelihood of repetition. Defendant's age not revealed.)

For those aged under 18, see the **CHILDREN AND YOUNG OFFENDERS: GENERAL PRINCIPLES** *Education, training and welfare* para at **14.34** in Volume 1.

240.24 *Elderly defendants*

R v Evans 2007 EWCA Crim 1158 D was convicted of harassment and six breaches of her ASBO. She was involved in a dispute with a neighbour and found it impossible to be law-abiding or civilised. In 1999 she was convicted of three harassment offences (section 2). She was fined and given a Restraining Order. In 2001 she was given 6 months suspended for seven breaches of the order. The breaches were offensive, abusive and threatening behaviour. In 2004, there was a further breach. She was fined. Following further incidents she was fined and given an ASBO in 2005. In 2006, she shouted abuse at the neighbours and made derogatory remarks about their Italian origin (the current offences). She was aged 82 and had some typical ailments for her age. The victims spoke of the huge pressure and strain they were under. After her conviction she breached her bail so that no pre-sentence report could be written. In 2004 her pre-sentence report said she refused to accept any blame or responsibility for her actions. Held. She has persistently flouted the orders of the court. Even now there is no contrition. The court will only send individuals in their eighties to prison as a last resort and with great reluctance. Old age is not a licence to disregard the law. The Judge had no alternative but to imprison, but because of her age, **4 months** not 6.

R v Whincup 2010 EWCA Crim 73 D, now aged 74, was convicted of three counts of indecent assault. Between 1985 and 1989,[270] he abused his wife's great-niece. Held. **3 years** was merited but reduced to **2 years** because of his age, not 7.

R v Beaver 2015 EWCA Crim 653 D pleaded to manslaughter based on diminished responsibility. D killed V using a large kitchen knife. He was now aged 82 with early dementia and depressive symptoms. Held. He had just snapped, which was attributed to his mental and other problems. We are wholly unable to say **3 years** was wrong in principle or manifestly excessive. Mercy nonetheless remains. We substitute a **Suspended Sentence Order** of **2 years** [with mental health and other conditions]. For more details, see **240.24**.

See also: *Att-Gen's Ref No 65 of 2011* 2011 EWCA Crim 2277 (Prison bites differently, harder and deeper on persons either of advanced age or significant infirmity or both. With that principle there can be no quarrel.)

R v Marcussen 2015 EWCA Crim 1302 (Convicted. 25 indecent assault counts from 1947 to 1983. Some sample counts. PE teacher abusing boys aged 11-16. Two instances of anal digital penetration. Now aged 92. For younger man 13-14 years suitable. 9 years had a substantial discount.)

Old case: *R v Fontes* 2005 EWCA Crim 2103, 2006 1 Cr App R (S) 76 (p 401) (The risk of D becoming ill in prison, or so ill he is unable to return home, or even of his dying in prison is one which must be taken into account by the court. It is right to reflect the age and health in a substantially greater discount than the Court has given.)

For a summary of this case, see the 9th edition of this book.

See also the **SEX OFFENCES: HISTORICAL** chapter and the **MURDER** *Defendant over 65 or very old on release* para at **288.85**.

---

[270] These dates are inconsistent with the other dates in the report. Ed.

240.25   *Employment, Others will lose their***

R v D Roche Ltd 2013 EWCA Crim 993 The company, D, pleaded to two Health and Safety offences. The Judge ordered fines of £50,000 on each count, plus costs. D appealed on the basis that a £100,000 fine would result in D being unable to continue trading and the consequential loss of 75 jobs. Held. The guideline indicates that a fine is intended to inflict painful punishment. It should also have the effect of operating as a deterrent to others as well as the individual defendant in the future. The court is enjoined to consider the effect of the fine on the employment of innocent employees and on the business as a whole. The guideline [at para 25] relates to the position after trial and before credit for a guilty plea and is subject to the financial condition of the company being taken into account. [On examining the accounts the Court noted that D had continued profitably and appeared capable of 'withstanding the blow' from the £100,000 fine. The 12-month period for payment was insufficient, and extended to 3 years in the light of D's financial position.]

Old case: *R v Nichols* 1998 2 Cr App R (S) 296 (With a great deal of hesitation the company mitigation means that the sentence should be **6 months** not 9.)

For a summary of the case, see the 9th edition of this book.

240.26   *English, Defendant does not speak***

R v Rainho 2002 EWCA Crim 1981, 2003 1 Cr App R (S) 77 (p 389) D was convicted of importing 10 kilos of cocaine. She was aged 53 and with a good character after checks were made in Brazil. She spoke no English and the defence said prison would bear more harshly on her. Held. That is not something to which much weight can be given. Otherwise those are simple circumstances which would lead to the selection of particular types of courier by drug dealers, in order to encourage couriers to believe that sentences would be mitigated on account of those personal circumstances. It is to be noted that prisoners can be repatriated to their own country to serve part of their sentences.

240.27   *Female defendants***

Att-Gen's Ref No 67 of 2008 2009 EWCA Crim 132, 2 Cr App R (S) 60 (p 428) LCJ D pleaded to four offences of sexual activity with a child and offering to supply a class A drug. The victim, V, was the 14-year-old male friend of D's teenage son. D's 23-year marriage with her husband was experiencing difficulties. D and V had begun a relationship in which they had sexual intercourse twice, and V penetrated D's mouth with his penis twice. She later offered to supply him with cocaine. Held. We have been asked to note that guidelines proposed in these cases are put forward on the basis that they should apply irrespective of the gender of the victim or of the offender, except in specified circumstances where a distinction is justified by the nature of the offence. We agree that young boys, as well as young girls, are vulnerable. Parliament has not sought to distinguish between them in the legislation. Neither should we.

R v Townsend-Oldfield 2010 EWCA Crim 2451 D pleaded to causing or inciting a child to engage in sexual activity, aiding and abetting buggery and aiding and abetting unlawful intercourse with a child under 13. Her common-law husband, F, pleaded to rape, buggery and unlawful sexual intercourse with a child under 13 (×2). F told D that he wished to have intercourse with KA, their 14-year old neighbour. IP, aged 12, visited D's home and agreed to have sex for money. F put his fingers and penis into IP's anus and D put her fingers into IP's vagina and touched her breasts. There was a plain element of breach of trust as D and F had befriended the victims. D had been abused as a child and forced to sleep with certain men by her mother. It was asserted that D was controlled by F. Held. There is no reason to think that D will commit further offences. This was echoed in the pre-sentence report and the Judge must also have taken this view, not imposing a Sexual Offences Prevention Order. **4 years**, not 5.

See also the **MOTHERS** chapter.

Foreign penalties are irrelevant see the **IMPORTATION OF DRUGS** *Foreign penalties are irrelevant, Future* para at **273.43**.

240.28   *Good character*

R v Howells 1999 1 Cr App R (S) 335 LCJ p 337-8 Some measure of leniency will ordinarily be extended to offenders of previous good character, the more so if there is evidence of good character (such as a solid employment record or faithful discharge of family duties) as opposed to a mere absence of previous convictions. It will sometimes be appropriate to take account of family responsibilities, or physical or mental disability. *R v CO and Others* 2008 EWCA Crim 2790 para 73 LCJ The defendant was sentenced for sex offences against his family over 40 years. Held. There is no realistic basis for treating him as of good character because of his 40 years of offending.

Note: It must be remembered that the starting points and ranges in the guidelines are for first-time offenders, see para **66.1** in Volume 1. Many of the guidelines have 'no previous convictions or no relevant or recent convictions' as a factor reducing seriousness. This means that for offences with a guideline, a discount for being of good character will be appropriate.

However, for offences where there is no guideline, it is not possible to apply mathematical principles about the discount that is applicable. It will all depend on the circumstances. Where there is serious professional criminal behaviour, for example an offence of conspiracy to commit armed robbery, good character will be of little significance.[271] At the other end of the scale, good character can tip the balance in deciding whether it is necessary to give a defendant a custodial sentence. Good character is more important the older the defendant is. However, it can be very significant for defendants aged under 21. Courts try to avoid sending young people of good character into custody because it can be counter-productive. If the defendant is in employment, custody will normally destroy this and harm his or her chances of finding another position. Further, custody will introduce him or her to corrupting influences, which can be hard to undo. Courts will prefer a lenient sentence, which may stop defendants reoffending, rather than a custodial sentence, which may affirm his or her criminal behaviour. Ed.

R v Clifford 2014 EWCA Crim 2245, 2015 1 Cr App R (S) 32 (p 242) D was convicted of eight indecent assaults. Held. It is a well-established principle of sentencing that the mitigation of good character weighs less in the scales where the offending is serious.

See also **IMPORTATION OF DRUGS** *Good character* at **273.44**.

240.29   *Health of the defendant, Poor   General principles*

R v Qazi 2010 EWCA Crim 2579, 2011 2 Cr App R (S) 8 (p 32) D pleaded to fraud involving making false insurance claims. One of the means used was to deliberately engineer accidents. He suffered virtually his whole life from a genetic disorder known as Beta Thalassaemia Major, which requires him to undergo blood transfusions every three to four weeks. There were complications from an unsuccessful bone marrow transplant. He received 5 years' 6 months' imprisonment. He was transferred to a Category B prison where it became apparent that there were difficulties in providing the level of treatment required. There was a delay in attempting to secure a transfer to a Category D prison, and medical evidence suggested further imprisonment would result in a deterioration of his mental health. D had a high risk of developing life-threatening infections which had been increased by his imprisonment. He needed to be near his specialist hospital but that prison had turned down a transfer because they were unable to provide D with any medical support. After some time the transfer was accepted. He appealed relying on his article 3 rights. The Court considered extensive and detailed reports from both inside and outside prison and from the Ministry of Justice. Held. The first Governor was doing as much as he could. After the transfer D's care was so disappointing his imprisonment was in breach of article 3. There were regrettable and unexplained failures of central direction at NOMS. Later reports indicated D's article 3 rights were no longer breached. The ECHR obligation is consistent with common law obligations.

---

[271] *R v Turner* 1975 61 Cr App R 67 The defendants appealed their sentences for armed robbery. The Court in a guideline case said, "The fact that a man has not much of a criminal record is not a powerful factor in cases of this gravity."

We have had the benefit of considering at much greater length the correct approach a sentencing court should adopt. We have reached the following conclusions:

   i) The court is entitled to take into account the fact that there are the arrangements...to ensure that prisoners with severe medical conditions in public sector prisons are treated in accordance with their Convention rights, and there are the duties of the Secretary of State...to release the prisoner if that is the only way a breach of article 3 can be remedied.

  ii) On the basis of those arrangements and their continued operation in practice, a sentencing court need not be concerned in the allocation of a prisoner to a specific prison in the discharge of its duties under article 3. Furthermore, provided that the arrangements that we have set out for the provision of health care under the overall responsibility of the Secretaries of State are maintained and work in practice, a sentencing court does not need to enquire into the facilities in prison for the treatment of a medical condition.

  iii) It is only in circumstances where the very fact of imprisonment itself might expose the individual to a real risk of an article 3 breach that the court will be called upon to enquire into whether sentencing a person to custody will mean a breach of article 3. That is a quite different circumstance from the kind of enquiry carried out in *R v Hetherington* 2009 EWCA Crim 1186 as to whether facilities in a particular prison were adequate. It is an enquiry that can only arise where there is proper medical evidence before a court that any sentence of imprisonment *ipso facto* would cause a breach of article 3. If this arose it would be exceptionally rare.

  iv) If any such circumstances should ever arise, then the sentencing court must be provided with detailed medical evidence with an attached statement of truth by a properly qualified medical expert setting out the ground why imprisonment *ipso facto* will cause a breach of article 3. Such a statement must be served on the court and on the CPS well in advance of the hearing so that the CPS can, in conjunction with the Secretary of State for Justice, make the appropriate enquiries and produce medical evidence to the court.

  v) Once a sentence of imprisonment has been imposed, unless it is to be contended on appeal that the Judge should not have imposed a sentence of imprisonment because imprisonment anywhere would *ipso facto* cause a breach of article 3, the relevance of an appellant's medical condition relates solely to the assessment of the overall length of the sentence in accordance with the principles established in *R v Bernard* 1997 1 Cr App R (S) 135.

  vi) Any issues as to breach of the duties of the Secretary of State in relation to medical treatment and conditions in prison are matters for civil remedies and not for this division of the Court of Appeal.

Note: The judgment helpfully lists the arrangements for treating prisoners with serious health problems. Ed.

Att-Gen's Ref No 14 of 2015 2015 EWCA Crim 949 D was convicted of historical abuse on two male relatives. The first group was in the 1950s and 1960s. The second group was 40 years later. D, now aged 90, had a number of health problems including diabetes, having a catheter, heart problems and early dementia. His wife gave a very stark assessment of his health problems but a doctor said his physical and mental health were not so severe as to preclude imprisonment. Held. The principles are clear. A judge is entitled to make some allowance for an offender's mental condition and that the offences date back many years. However, such allowance is limited. The court cannot lose sight of the overall and principal purposes of sentencing, particularly in cases as serious as this.

For more detail see **240.30**.

See also: *R v Hall* 2013 EWCA Crim 82, 2 Cr App R (S) 68 (p 434) (Needing 24-hour care. 'Quite dreadful' multiple medical conditions. No breach of articles 2 or 3. However, it was appropriate to exercise exceptional mercy. Imported 2.8 kilos of cocaine. Starting at 7 years, 18 months not 3 years.)

240.30   *Health of the defendant, Poor   Cases*
R v Hepworth 2010 EWCA Crim 2338 D pleaded to causing death by dangerous driving. V was in the front passenger seat, F in the rear, behind D. D drove at excessive speed, somewhere in the low seventies, in a 30 mph area. As the car approached a mini-roundabout it skipped out to the right and left the road. The car hit a tree, flipped onto its side, collided with a lamp post and went onto its roof. It caught fire as soon as it stopped moving. D and F were able to crawl out of the vehicle. V died. D suffered 80% burns and F suffered 23% burns. V was D's best friend. D now needed to use a wheelchair and had limited mobility in his hands. His voice box was also damaged by the fire. F's victim impact statement stated that she thought D had suffered enough as a result of his injuries. She said putting him in prison would only cause her further heartache. V's family remained supportive of him and he remained friends with F. A different estimate said that D had suffered 75% total body surface burns which required a significant amount of surgery and grafting of the burns. There had also been partial distortion of both ears and he had lost a substantial amount of hair on his scalp. He would need future surgery and had a permanently altered voice. Survival after such burns was relatively unusual. He had also developed a chronic pain disorder with adjustment depressive disorder and had commenced anti-depressant medication. He suffered from post-traumatic stress disorder. He had significant facial and body scarring…this undermined his confidence and self-esteem. He required further surgery to his hands and had limited day-to-day functioning with them. A doctor felt a custodial sentence would compromise his ongoing care and specialist treatment and planned surgery would be a logistical challenge in custody. The Judge had enquired into prison capabilities of coping with his condition and was satisfied it was manageable. D, aged 25, had no previous convictions. A subsequent prison report stated that contractions (shortening of the skin) had led to D being unable to open his hands fully and his grip was poor. Held. The Judge was correct to categorise the incident at Level 2 in the guidelines. The risk here was substantial. The Judge took the starting point to be 5 years and we consider that that was an appropriate starting point. We are able to show a measure of further mercy, so **15 months** not 21.
R v Qazi 2010 EWCA Crim 2579, 2011 2 Cr App R (S) 8 (p 32) D pleaded to fraud involving making false insurance claims. One of the means used was to deliberately engineer accidents. Claims were made for accidents which never happened. Other claims were exaggerated. £280,000 had been paid by the insurance companies. £305,000 had been claimed for damage and £50,000 for personal injury. If the fraud had been successful £1.6m would have been realised. D had played a central role. D and another had also been involved with dishonestly obtaining mortgages. He suffered virtually his whole life from a genetic disorder known as Beta Thalassaemia Major, which requires him to undergo blood transfusions every three to four weeks. There were complications from an unsuccessful bone marrow transplant. He received 4 years for the insurance fraud and 18 months for the mortgage fraud. He was transferred to a Category B prison where it became apparent that there were difficulties in providing the level of treatment required. There was a delay in attempting to secure a transfer to a Category D prison, and medical evidence suggested further imprisonment would result in a deterioration of his mental health. D had a high risk of developing life-threatening infections which had been increased by his imprisonment. He needed to be near his specialist hospital but that prison had turned down a transfer because they were unable to provide D with any medical support. After some time the transfer was accepted. The Court considered extensive and detailed reports from both inside and outside prison and from the Ministry

of Justice. Held. There was no fault in the sentence. However, in light of the new information we make a further discount because of his health problems, so **5 years** in total not 5½.

R v James 2011 EWCA Crim 2441 D pleaded to handling. On the third night of heavy rioting in London, he was seen by police carrying a 50-inch television outside a shopping centre. It had been taken from a Currys store which had been extensively looted. He was sentenced on the basis that he had been cycling past the shop while it was being looted and the television was on the ground. D, aged 32, had convictions but none for dishonesty. Held. Relying on *R v Blackshaw and Others* 2011 EWCA Crim 2312, 9 months is unarguable. However, D was suffering from a cancer lymphoma and the day before the offence had begun a treatment of radiotherapy. It was in everybody's interests that the course of treatment should continue. D missed a hospital appointment, no doubt due to entirely understandable pressures on the Prison Service. The unavoidable interruption to his hospital treatment is an illustration of the inevitable consequence of his state of health on the administration of his sentence. 9 months was right in principle. However, we will adjust the sentence so that D can receive the hospital treatment. **6 months** not 9, which will enable the treatment to continue.

R v W 2012 EWCA Crim 355 D was convicted of buggery (×3), rape, indecent assault on a male (×5) and indecency with a child (×2) in a historical sexual abuse case. There was medical evidence that D had respiratory difficulties, epilepsy, Parkinson's disease and was a type 1 diabetic. He had a history of self-harm and depression and posed a moderately high to high risk of serious or fatal cardiovascular incident. D was aged 78 at appeal. Held. 22 years would have been appropriate. Solely because of the age and very poor health of D, a further reduction was appropriate, *R v Hall and Others* 2011 EWCA Crim 2753 applied. **12 years** not 18.

Att-Gen's Ref No 10 of 2013 2013 EWCA Crim 724 D was convicted of numerous historical sexual offences against his partner's daughter. Two rapes, multiple indecent assaults including forced oral sex, masturbation and digital penetration. Threats to kill victim's mother if she told anyone. D was aged 55 at appeal and suffered from a 'catalogue of medical conditions' requiring treatment. He was only able to walk short distances with the aid of a frame. The Attorney-General contended that either the starting point was too low, or the discount for D's health problems was too great. Held. D's conditions restricted his movement, caused him pain and required him to use a machine to ease his breathing at night. Those were conditions which would affect his life outside a prison establishment. Within a prison establishment, if he should require further medical treatment, it would be provided. The appropriate starting point was 15 years, as was conceded by D's counsel. The discount given by the Judge was manifestly too high. Taking account that this is the second time D is being sentenced, the maximum discount was 3 years, so **12 years** not 9.

Att-Gen's Ref No 14 of 2015 2015 EWCA Crim 949 D was convicted of a number of indecent assault and indecency with a child offences. In the 1950s and 1960s, when he was in his thirties, he abused V1, a male relative, when V1 was aged 9-16. D touched V1's penis, performed oral sex on him and got V1 to masturbate him. Forty years later, when D was in his seventies, D did similar acts with V1's son V2, when he was aged 8-14. He also encouraged V2 to perform oral sex on him. When aged 19, V2 felt anger, shame and depression. C2 told his mother in 2003 and the police in 2013. D, now 90 years old, had a number of health problems including diabetes, having a catheter and early dementia. He had a heart attack in his forties, a heart bypass in 2001 and a stroke in 2004. His wife gave a very stark assessment of his health problems saying he was unable to put on shoes and socks and that she could not leave him for fear of him having a panic attack. She said he couldn't use stairs and his memory was fading. A doctor said he would be highly vulnerable if custody was given but his physical and mental health were not so severe as to preclude imprisonment. The prosecution said D owed a duty of care to V1 and V2, there was grooming, the activity was over a very long period and the effect on V2 had been devastating. They also said the starting point for the penile penetration was 8 years. Held. We have doubts that the overall sentence starting point was 8 years as the Judge said. The lowest figure is **5 years**, not 2 years suspended.

Old cases: *R v Bernard* 1997 1 Cr App R (S) 135 (An offender's serious medical condition may enable a court to impose a lesser sentence as an act of mercy in the exceptional circumstances of a particular case rather than by virtue of any general principle.)

For a summary of the case, see the 9th edition of this book.

240.31 *Health of defendant, Poor Circumstances change after sentence*

R v Nall-Cain 1998 2 Cr App R (S) 145 *Obiter* Where, for example, there is a deterioration in D's health, or it is impossible, by reason of a prisoner's physical disabilities, for the prison to cope with him, the Court of Appeal may exercise mercy.

R v Shaw 2010 EWCA Crim 982 D was sentenced to 3 years for drug supply, handling and dangerous driving. When on remand he went blind and was weak on one side. He was taken to hospital in a wheelchair. Two days after sentence, he had a stroke in prison and was in an extremely serious condition. The prison report said there hadn't been any difficulty in managing the defendant in prison. Held. Those sentences might be regarded as generous. The general rule is the Court does not interfere unless the sentence is wrong in principle or manifestly excessive. The Secretary of State has power to release prisoners on compassionate grounds under Criminal Justice Act 2003 s 248(1). That power can be exercised by the prison governor in certain circumstances. In cases like this it will normally be appropriate to leave it to the Secretary of State to decide. He will be able to obtain full and up-to-date reports. Appeal refused.

240.32 *Historical cases Sentencing regime at time of sentence applies/Human rights/No heavier penalty to be imposed*

European Convention on Human Rights art 7(1) Nor shall a heavier penalty be imposed than the one that was applicable at the time the criminal offence was committed.

R v Secretary of State for the Home Dept ex parte Uttley 2004 UKHL 38 Lords The appellant challenged his parole provisions and relied on his article 7(1) right. Held. 'The penalty…that was applicable at the time' under article 7(1) referred to the maximum penalty the court could prescribe at the time an offence was committed and not the sentence that would probably have been imposed had the offender been convicted at that time.

Note: So the maximum is what matters, rather than the actual penalty. Ed.

R v H 2011 EWCA Crim 2753, 2012 2 Cr App R (S) 21 (p 88) LCJ para 14 Consistently with the statutory provisions, the starting point for the sentencing decision should normally be assessed by reference to the guidance in force on the sentencing date.

para 16 In principle, the defendant must be sentenced in accordance with the sentencing regime applicable at the date of sentence. Nevertheless [where a defendant committed an offence] years earlier which contravened the criminal law in force at the date when it was committed, he is liable to be convicted of that offence and no other, therefore the sentence is limited to the maximum sentence then available for the offence of which he has been convicted. Changes in the law which create new offences, or increase the maximum penalties for existing offences, do not apply retrospectively to crimes committed before the change in the law. In short, the offence of which the defendant is convicted and the sentencing parameters (in particular, the maximum available sentence) applicable to that offence are governed not by the law at the date of sentence, but by the law in force at the time when the criminal conduct occurred.

R (Massey) v Secretary of State for Justice 2013 EWHC 1950 (Admin) High Court In 2008, D was sentenced to IPP with a term of 2½ years. He was still in prison. Held. D cannot complain because IPP has been abolished. The United Kingdom is not obliged under the Convention to reopen historical sentences and re-sentence merely because it has introduced a new sentencing regime.

240.33   *Historical cases   Basic approach*

R v Millberry 2002 EWCA Crim 2891, 2003 2 Cr App R (S) 31 (p 142) LCJ Where the offence is reported many years after it occurred and where the offender at the time of sentencing is old, even in his eighties, the same starting points should apply. The fact that the offences are stale can be taken into account but only to a limited extent. It is after all always open to an offender to admit the offences and the fact that they are not reported earlier is often explained because of the relationship between the offender and the victim, which is an aggravating factor of the offence. A different factor that could cause the court to take a more lenient view than it would otherwise is the consequence which results from the age of the offender. In these cases the experience is that the offender may be only a danger to members of the family with whom he has a relationship. So this is a dimension that can be taken into account if there is a reduced risk of reoffending. In addition, the court is always entitled to show a limited degree of mercy to an offender who is of advanced years, because of the impact that a sentence of imprisonment can have on an offender of that age.

R v H 2011 EWCA Crim 2753, 2012 2 Cr App R (S) 21 (p 88) LCJ para 28 When passing sentence, the court should reflect on all the facts, including events since the offence was committed, with, according to *R v Bird* 1987 Cr App R (S) 77, account to be taken of the defendant's subsequent positive good character. para 46 The following considerations should be treated as guidance.

para 47 a) Sentence will be imposed at the date of the sentencing hearing, on the basis of the legislative provisions then current, and by measured reference to any definitive sentencing guidelines relevant to the situation revealed by the established facts.

b) Although sentence must be limited to the maximum sentence at the date when the offence was committed, it is wholly unrealistic to attempt an assessment of sentence by seeking to identify [at the date of sentence] what the sentence for the individual offence was likely to have been if the offence had come to light at or shortly after the date when it was committed. Similarly, if maximum sentences have been reduced, as in some instances, e.g. theft, they have, the more severe attitude to the offence in earlier years, even if it could be established, should not apply.

c) As always, the particular circumstances in which the offence was committed and its seriousness must be the main focus. Due allowance for the passage of time may be appropriate. The date may have a considerable bearing on the offender's culpability. If, for example, the offender was very young and immature at the time when the case was committed, that remains a continuing feature of the sentencing decision. Similarly if the allegations had come to light many years earlier, and when confronted with them, the defendant had admitted them, but for whatever reason, the complaint had not been drawn to the attention of, or investigated by, the police, or had been investigated and not then pursued to trial, these too would be relevant features.

d) In some cases it may be safe to assume that the fact that, notwithstanding the passage of years, the victim has chosen spontaneously to report what happened to him or her in his or her childhood or younger years would be an indication of continuing inner turmoil. However, the circumstances in which the facts come to light vary, and careful judgement of the harm done to the victim is always a critical feature of the sentencing decision. Simultaneously, equal care needs to be taken to assess the true extent of the defendant's criminality by reference to what he actually did and the circumstances in which he did it.

e) The passing of the years may demonstrate aggravating features if, for example, the defendant has continued to commit sexual crime or he represents a continuing risk to the public. On the other hand, mitigation may be found in an unblemished life over the years since the offences were committed, particularly if accompanied by evidence of positive good character.

f)[272] Early admissions and a guilty plea are of particular importance in historical cases. Just because they relate to facts which are long passed, the defendant will inevitably be tempted to lie his way out of the allegations. It is greatly to his credit if he makes early admissions. Even more powerful mitigation is available to the offender who, out of a sense of guilt and remorse, reports himself to the authorities. Considerations like these provide the victim with vindication, often a feature of great importance to them.

Note: In *R v H* 2011 EWCA Crim 2753, 2012 2 Cr App R (S) 21 (p 88) the Lord Chief Justice said at para 46, "[Only] *R v Millberry* 2003, the definitive sentencing guideline, used in the measured way we suggest, and this guidance [should be used]. Reference to earlier decisions is unlikely to be helpful, and, dealing with it generally, to be discouraged. Subsequent decisions of this court which do not expressly state that they are intended to amend or amplify this guidance should be treated as fact-specific decisions, and therefore unlikely to be of assistance to court." Ed.

See also the *Change of lifestyle* para at **240.6**.

240.34   *Historical cases   Case examples*

R v Bird 1987 9 Cr App R (S) 77 There may be exceptional cases where the sentencing court ought not to shut its eyes to subsequent events. It is the duty of the court to sentence for the offence. The offence had not changed but the man had.

R v MS 2013 EWCA Crim 1960 (Two-judge court) D pleaded to eight counts of indecent assault (maximum 10 years). D was then a teenager. He was aged 28 at appeal. Held. The passage of time between the offence and the sentence cannot have the result of increasing the penalty he now faces. The maximum then was a 2-year DTO. 18 months not 3 years. For more detail about the case see **330.15**.

R v Wright 2014 EWCA Crim 1328 Whereas the passage of time *per se* since the commission of sexual offences cannot amount to a mitigating factor, the absence of any convictions or criminal conduct thereafter can do. The extent to which it should be reflected in any sentence will vary from case to case, but in our judgement the Judge was, on the facts of this case, wrong in principle to exclude it from the reckoning.

Att-Gen's Ref No 14 of 2015 2015 EWCA Crim 949 D was convicted of historical abuse. Held. A judge is entitled to make some allowance for the [fact that] offences date back many years. However, such allowance is limited. The court cannot lose sight of the overall and principal purposes of sentencing, particularly in cases as serious as this. For more detail see **240.30**.

See also: *Att-Gen's Ref No 33 of 2012* 2012 EWCA Crim 2391 (Plea to section 18. In 2003, caused 7 cm wound with bread knife after confrontation outside pub. Bailed and absconded to native Ireland. Sentenced in 2012. Principles in *R v H* 2011 EWCA Crim 2753 apply to sentencing historical cases. The change in his circumstances could not be ignored. **3 years** not 2.)

For an example of a case where being aged 17 at the time of the offending, exemplary behaviour since and an interval of 38 years reduced a 15-year starting point to 6½ years, see *R v S* 2014 EWCA Crim 272 at **330.6**.

See also the **SEX OFFENCES: HISTORICAL** chapter and the *Historical abuse Judicial guidance* para at **330.3**.

240.35   *Historical cases   Offences which have been repealed*

R v BM 2010 EWCA Crim 1454, 2011 1 Cr App R (S) 34 (p 214) D pleaded to unlawful sexual intercourse, Sexual Offences Act 1956 s 5. Six rape offences were left on the file. D was aged 40 and a music teacher at V's school. D took V, a 12-year-old girl, on a shopping trip and then to his house. D had full sexual intercourse with V but she made no complaint. Twenty years later in 2007, D pleaded to sexual assault upon a child and a number of counts of making and possessing indecent photographs of children. V saw a report in the newspaper when D was sentenced and she made her complaint. V said D's

---

[272] This paragraph is listed as g) in the judgment, which is assumed to be a typo. Ed.

conduct had passed a shadow over her adult life and she had tried to bury the memory. She had taken an overdose and had sought counselling. D, now aged 65, was wheelchair bound, had suffered three strokes, had osteoarthritis in his spine and joints and was incontinent. The Judge observed that under current legislation, the offence would have been charged as rape of a child under 13 years and the appropriate starting point for sentence after a trial would have been 13 years. Held. The Judge considered what the offence would be today and what the sentence would be today. That approach was wrong. Unlawful sexual intercourse in the 1956 Act was a different offence from the offence of rape of a child under 13 within the current Act. The same offence had different parameters. The correct approach is to look at the sentencing guidelines at the time when the offence was committed and prior to the introduction of the new Act. We have read the authorities for unlawful sexual intercourse. If D had been sentenced at the time on a plea of guilty to unlawful sexual intercourse with a girl under 13 the likely sentence, subject to one caveat, would have been in the order of 4 years. The caveat is that 4 years was said to be appropriate where there was what we have called a course of conduct. The sentencing climate has changed, but the authorities require us to sentence in accordance with the principles of the day. This was a wicked offence, an offence which robbed the complainant of a significant part of her childhood and cast a shadow over her young life. However, with the mitigation and the sentencing rules **3 years** not 6.

240.36   *Historical cases/Old cases   Penalties change*
R v R (B) 2003 EWCA Crim 2199 The defendant pleaded guilty to indecent assault. The Judge passed an extended sentence which was not available at the time the offences were committed. Held. The licence is to protect the public on the defendant's release. 'Penalty' in European Convention on Human Rights art 7 applies to the whole penalty rather than its constituent elements. The licence is preventive not punitive. It is not a heavier penalty.

R v Gorman 2008 EWCA Crim 2907, 2009 2 Cr App R (S) 36 (p 259) D was convicted of manslaughter and sentenced to IPP. The victim was attacked before IPP came into force and he died after the provisions came into force. The defence sought to quash the sentence applying article 7. Held. The offence of manslaughter was not committed until the victim died. We do not resolve the issue whether article 7 relates to the act or the death. However, as the maximum sentence for manslaughter when the victim was attacked was life and IPP was no greater than that, the sentence was lawful.

R v RGB 2009 EWCA Crim 906 *R v R (B)* 2003 EWCA Crim 2199 was correctly decided even when other cases are considered.

See also the **CHANGE IN SENTENCING LAW** chapter and the **PROCEDURE, SENTENCING** *Explain the sentence, Sentencer must Explanation wrong* para at **87.49** in Volume 1.

240.37   *Historical cases   The release provisions change*
R v Bright 2008 EWCA Crim 462, 2 Cr App R (S) 102 (p 578) The Judge passed a 7-year sentence telling the defendant that he would only serve half of the sentence. In fact the defendant was entitled to release after one-third of the sentence. The defence submitted that the sentence should be reduced accordingly. Held. That submission was based on a fallacy. The actual sentence was 7 years. The release provisions did not and should not have affected the Judge's sentencing decision.

R v Rhule 2010 EWCA Crim 2177 In 1999, D raped a girl and pleaded not guilty. He then absconded. In 2010 D pleaded guilty and was sentenced to 5 years, which was agreed was the appropriate penalty. Between the offence and the sentence the release provisions changed from two-thirds off to half off. It was submitted the sentence should be reduced to take that into account. Held. The Judge had well in mind the release provisions. Applying *R v Bright* 2008 the appeal is dismissed.

See also: *R v Giga* 2008 EWCA Crim 703, 2008 2 Cr App R (S) 112 (p 638) (*R v Bright* 2008 EWCA Crim 462, 2 Cr App R (S) 102 (p 578) followed.)

R v Round and Dunn 2009 EWCA Crim 2667, 2010 2 Cr App R (S) 45 (p 292) (*R v Bright* 2008 EWCA Crim 462, 2 Cr App R (S) 102 (p 578) approved.)

Ill-health of the defendant see the *Health of the defendant, Poor* paras at **240.29**.

240.38   *Injured during offence, Defendant*

R v Jabarkhall 2012 EWCA Crim 2133 D was convicted of violent disorder. When leaving a club in Barking at 3.40 am, B had a verbal argument with D. B struck D in the face and a fight ensued. A friend of D's ran over, armed with two or three half snooker cues. One of them was handed to D during the course of the fight. B retreated to the club and things appeared to calm down. B and his girlfriend were offered a lift home by a friend and got into the car. D ran towards the rear of the car and smashed the rear window with the snooker cue. There was a fight involving a number of men in the street. The fight lasted several minutes. B and his girlfriend got into the car and drove off. They drove around 700 m, then returned to confront D again. The fight once again broke out in the street. D was left injured at the scene, suffering a fractured spine causing paralysis, a punctured lung and a small stab wound in the lumbar region. He will remain in a wheelchair for the rest of his life. Held. It was mindless but significant violence. All were equally involved. There was no distinction to be drawn. But for his terrible injuries, D could have expected a sentence of 3 years like the other defendants. We might well not have given D an immediate custodial sentence, but as one was imposed and D has now served the equivalent of 12 months, we replace the 18-month sentence with **12 months** to effect his immediate release.

See also the **DEATH BY DRIVING**: *General principles Injuries, The defendant's own* para at **235.9**.

240.39   *Inside man*

R v Graham 2015 EWCA Crim 503 D pleaded (full credit) to robbery. He worked for a small high-value electronics firm. He and V were engaged in loading five pallets of iPhones, worth £1.4m to £1.6m, onto a van. The two were attacked and V was punched repeatedly and struck in the face with what appeared to be a hard object. Next V was dragged into an office. D was seized by a hooded man and also taken to the office. They were tied up with cable ties. Their mobiles were taken and the goods were stolen. While freeing himself, V injured his leg. V suffered injuries to his eye, bruising, swelling, cuts to the face and wrist, torn ligaments and a broken finger. Because of the robbery the firm lost contracts. The owner of the business was suspicious about whether D was involved but D was not charged with the robbery. D was dismissed and went to live in Spain. Sixteen months later, D returned and went to the police and said he was the inside man. He said he had informed the gang about the cargo and the time to strike. D also said he had positioned the van to assist the gang and disabled various security locks. D was now aged 67 with 21 court appearances for 72 offences. They included 18 months for two burglaries and 9 years for a robbery. D's last conviction was in 2003. He said he had wanted a pension and believed he would receive £200,000. D said he only received about £35,000. He had lung and liver problems. D also said he was missing his family, worried about health care and feeling remorse. The Judge found there was a) gross breach of trust, b) violence, c) use of a weapon and, because of the high value, started at 15 years. He took into account the fact that the confession was borne out of remorse and D's medical problems. Held. The movement of the goods was a vulnerable process. D played a vital role in the robbery. The company had given him a chance of honest employment after years of crime and that was an additional breach of trust. The motive was greed. 15 years was the correct starting point. His confession was the reason why he was charged and merits more than a third off for the plea. With that and his relatively short life expectancy, **6 years** not 8.

240.40   *Joint enterprise*

R v D and S 2006 EWCA Crim 1694, 2007 1 Cr App R (S) 67 (p 391) The defendants were convicted of murder. They were some of about a dozen people who killed C. Held.

It needs to be remembered that this was a joint attack where the vice lies not only in what individuals do, but in the combined effect of what they all do. The combined effect of such an attack is often, if not usually, greater than the sum of identifiable individual actions, and all are responsible for all.

R v Jabarkhall 2012 EWCA Crim 2133 D was convicted of violent disorder. When leaving a club in Barking at 3.40 am, B had a verbal argument with D. B struck D in the face and a fight ensued. A friend of D's ran over, armed with two or three half snooker cues. One of them was handed to D during the course of the fight. B retreated to the club and things appeared to calm down. B and his girlfriend were offered a lift home by a friend and got into the car. D ran towards the rear of the car and smashed the rear window with the snooker cue. There was a fight involving a number of men in the street. The fight lasted several minutes. B and his girlfriend got into the car and drove off. They drove around 700 m, then returned to confront D again. The fight once again broke out in the street. D was left injured at the scene, suffering a fractured spine causing paralysis, a punctured lung and a small stab wound in the lumbar region. He will remain in a wheelchair for the rest of his life. Held. It was mindless but significant violence. All were equally involved. There was no distinction to be drawn. But for his terrible injuries, D could have expected a sentence of 3 years like the other defendants. We might well not have given D an immediate custodial sentence, but as one was imposed and D has now served the equivalent of 12 months, we replace the 18-month sentence with **12 months** to effect his immediate release.

240.41 *Licence revoked, Defendant has his or her*

R v Tahid 2009 EWCA Crim 221 D served his custodial sentence for murder and was released on licence. He committed a drug offence and his licence was revoked. D pleaded to supplying heroin and was given **3½ years**. The defence asked for the time he had spent in prison before sentence to be taken into account. Held. We reject this suggestion out of hand.

R v Kerrigan and Another 2014 EWCA Crim 2348, 2015 1 Cr App R (S) 29 (p 221) K pleaded to robbing a man, V, in the street. D punched V repeatedly and stole V's phone, keys and wallet. In a separate case, W pleaded to attempted robbery. He provided a large hunting knife and transport for the main assailant. Both had been on licence and appealed against orders preventing time spent in custody on recall counting towards sentence. For K this was 7 months and for W it was 11 months. K was aged 26 and W aged 22 on appeal and both had multiple previous convictions, including recent ones. Held. K and W did not qualify for any automatic reduction in their sentences. They breached their licence. They were recalled to serve the balance, or part of the balance, of an existing sentence and they were, therefore, detained pursuant to a custodial sentence. Unless K and W can bring themselves within the Judge's general discretion to do justice, the periods they spent on remand which coincided with time spent in custody on recall should not be counted twice. They didn't, so appeal dismissed.

For the bar on making a new sentence consecutive to a licence recall, see CONCURRENT AND CONSECUTIVE SENTENCES *Licence Defendant serving a sentence for a revoked licence* at **19.19** in Volume 1.

240.42 *Mentally disordered defendants*

Criminal Justice Act 2003 s 157(1)-(2) Where a defendant is or appears to be mentally disordered, the court must obtain and consider a medical report before passing sentence other than one fixed by law, unless the court considers that it is unnecessary to obtain one.

Note: This is a summary of the section. For the full section, see para **78.7** in Volume 1. Criminal Justice Act 2003 s 166 enables the court to mitigate the penalties on mentally disordered defendants without many of the restrictions imposed by statute on other defendants. Ed.

Overarching Principles: Seriousness Guideline 2004 www.banksr.com Other Matters Guidelines tab para 1.25 Mental illness or disability is a factor indicating significantly lower culpability. For the other factors see the GUIDELINES *Factors indicating lower culpability Guidelines* para at **66.25** in Volume 1.

R v Meenan 2009 EWCA Crim 140 D pleaded to section 18 wounding and other offences. The psychiatric reports indicated that he was suffering from schizophrenia and acute psychotic symptoms. An addendum report said that he still had significant symptoms of mental illness but that his condition had improved with medication. However, he had declined to engage in other treatment and had expressed a determination to return to prison from the hospital where he was being treated. His illness was said to be treatable but his resistance to psychiatric intervention meant that treatment was impracticable. He posed a high risk of serious harm to the public. Held. The element of public protection is achieved by the imposition of an indeterminate sentence. The minimum term is just that and does not mean he will be released after that time. It is fixed on the artificial hypothesis that the offender is not dangerous. On that hypothesis the fact that he was suffering from mental illness would have been some mitigation. Sentence reduced.

R v Barrett 2014 EWCA Crim 1222 D pleaded to robbery. V, aged 56, was totally blind. V had taken his guide dog to the vet and was standing, with the dog, at a bus stop. Suddenly he felt someone hit him in the face and the gold chain around his neck was snatched from him. He suffered reddening of the skin around his neck and the blow knocked his head against the bus shelter. A witness subsequently identified D. The gold chain, which was never recovered, had recently been valued at £3,500. D claimed he saw V and heard voices in his head telling him to attack him. He expressed remorse and said he did not realise V was blind. D was aged 22 and had no convictions. He had one caution for affray in 2010. It was common ground that D was suffering schizophrenia which involved associated external auditory experiences, which had been diagnosed in 2012. He was discharged from hospital on the basis that he agreed to take oral anti-psychotic medication. He failed to do so and avoided visits from and appointments with those who were there to help him. A report stated that D's condition was as a result of his cannabis use since the age of 15. The writer described it as a severe and enduring illness which significantly contributed to D's behaviour on the date of the offence. A subsequent report stated D's risk of re-offending would be significantly reduced with sustained successful treatment. Held. This was an unusual case. It is clear that the treatment in prison is not effective. Very often a robbery committed by a 22-year-old man is preceded by a number of earlier offences and interventions. This attack did not meet that characterisation. The offence fell squarely within the second category of the guidelines, 'force used which results in injury to the victim' (with a starting point of 4 years). On the other hand, the force was not that great. The starting point fell at the upper range between the lowest category of seriousness (starting point 12 months) and the intermediate level (starting point 4 years). There was no reason to disagree with the Judge's assessment that the particular aggravation of V's vulnerability and the particular mitigation of D's mental condition were of equivalent forensic weight. In which case, with full credit for the plea, the sentence should have been 2 years. On that basis, the sentence should have been suspended. This was a very nasty attack on an entirely innocent and vulnerable victim. But the public interest is better served by the management of D's condition so that such an offence never happens again. A Hospital Order was not required. **2 years suspended** with a mental health treatment requirement, not 2 years 8 months.

Old cases: *Att-Gen's Ref No 83 of 2001* 2001 EWCA Crim 2443, 2002 1 Cr App R (S) 139 (p 588) (It is fundamental to the responsibilities of sentencing judges that while they must always pay proper regard to the sentencing guidance given, they are required also to reflect on all the circumstances of the individual case. Where sentencing judges are satisfied that the occasion requires it, they have to balance the demands of justice with what is sometimes described as the calls of mercy. There were occasions where it was right to take a constructive course and seek to achieve the rehabilitation of the offender.) *R v Lomey* 2004 EWCA Crim 3014 (Despite sympathy with D, a **life sentence** for the section 18 wounding was unchanged.) *R v Nafei* 2004 EWCA Crim 3238, 2005 2 Cr App R (S) 24 (p 127) (We do not say that in circumstances like these a Hospital Order for drug importation can never be justified, but we would find it difficult to envisage such a case.) *R v Bryan* 2006 EWCA Crim 379, 2 Cr App R (S) 66 (p 436) at 447 (LCJ The greater the mental disability and the more it contributes to the behaviour, the greater its effect in mitigating culpability. For more details, see **284.71**.) For a summary of the first three cases, see the 9th edition of this book. See also the *Vulnerable defendants, Treatment of* para at **240.67**. See also the **CHILDREN AND YOUNG OFFENDERS: GENERAL PRINCIPLES Welfare** section at **14.33** in Volume 1 and the **IMPORTATION OF DRUGS** *Mentally disordered defendants* para at **273.45**.

240.43   *Defendant found insane or unfit to plead   Statute etc.*
Criminal Procedure (Insanity) Act 1964 s 5
Supervision Order This order is only available in the Crown Court, after a person has been found unfit to plead or not guilty by reason of insanity.
Powers to deal with persons not guilty by reason of insanity or unfit to plead etc.
Criminal Procedure (Insanity) Act 1964 s 5 (1) This section applies where:
  a) a special verdict is returned that the accused is not guilty by reason of insanity, or
  b) findings have been made that the accused is under a disability and that he did the act or made the omission charged against him.
(2) The court shall make in respect of the accused:
  a) a Hospital Order (with or without a restriction order),
  b) a Supervision Order, or
  c) an order for his absolute discharge.
(3) Where:
  a) the offence to which the special verdict or the findings relate is an offence the sentence for which is fixed by law, and
  b) the court have power to make a Hospital Order,
the court shall make a Hospital Order with a Restriction Order (whether or not they would have power to make a Restriction Order apart from this subsection).
(4) In this section:
'Hospital Order' has the meaning given in Mental Health Act 1983 s 37,
'Restriction Order' has the meaning given to it by Mental Health Act 1983 s 41,
'Supervision Order' has the meaning given in Criminal Procedure (Insanity) Act 1964 Sch 1A Part 1.
Criminal Procedure (Insanity) Act 1964 s 5A(1)-(3) makes consequential changes to Mental Health Act 1983 so Hospital Orders can be made for those unfit to plead and those found to be insane. Criminal Procedure (Insanity) Act 1964 s 5(4) deals with the opportunity to try those found with either disability when their health improves.
Criminal Procedure (Insanity) Act 1964 s 5A(5) Schedule 1A to this Act (Supervision Orders) has effect with respect to the making of Supervision Orders under subsection (2)(b) of section 5 above, and with respect to the revocation and amendment of such orders.
(6) In relation to the making of an order under subsection (2)(c) of section 5 above, Powers of Criminal Courts (Sentencing) Act 2000 s 12(1) (absolute and conditional discharge) shall have effect as if:
  a) the reference to a person being convicted by or before a court of such an offence as is there mentioned included a reference to the case where section 5 above applies, and

b) the reference to the court being of opinion that it is inexpedient to inflict punishment included a reference to it thinking that an order for absolute discharge would be most suitable in all the circumstances of the case.

Criminal Procedure (Insanity) Act 1964 Sch 1A(1) In this schedule 'Supervision Order' means an order which requires the person in respect of whom it is made ('the supervised person') to be under the supervision of a social worker, an officer of a local probation board or an officer of a provider of probation services ('the supervising officer') for a period specified in the order of not more than two years.

(2) A supervision order may, in accordance with paragraph 4 or 5 below, require the supervised person to submit, during the whole of that period or such part of it as may be specified in the order, to treatment by or under the direction of a registered medical practitioner.

(3) The Secretary of State may by order direct that sub-paragraph (1) above shall be amended by substituting, for the period for the time being specified there, such period as may be specified in the order.

(4) An order under sub-paragraph (3) above may make in paragraph 11(2) (not listed) below any amendment which the Secretary of State thinks necessary in consequence of any substitution made by the order.

(5) [Deals with regulatory powers. The rest of the Schedule is not listed.]

240.44   *Mentally disordered defendants   Defendant found insane or unfit to plead-Case*

R v Chinegwundoh 2015 EWCA Crim 109, 1 Cr App R (S) 61 (p 429) D was unfit to plead but found to have committed fraud and used a false instrument. D was a practising barrister but was disbarred for forging court documents. The Judge sentenced D to a Supervision Order requiring him to 'attend as an out-patient South London Maudsley Hospital under the supervision of [named doctor] or her appointed colleagues'. D appealed, signing the document, 'Prince Harold Chinegwundoh, King's Counsel'. The Registrar instructed counsel. Held. The Supervision Order did not comply with Criminal Procedure (Insanity) Act 1964 s 5 and Sch 1A. The point of general principle to be learnt is that particular care needs to be taken with the precise form of these orders. We amend the order for him to be under the supervision of [the relevant] social services.

240.45   *Mentally disordered defendants   Court Martial*

Armed Forces Act 2006 s 258(1) Subject to subsection (2), before passing a custodial sentence for a service offence on an offender who is or appears to be mentally disordered, a court must obtain and consider a medical report.

(2) Subsection (1) does not apply if, in the circumstances of the case, the court is of the opinion that it is unnecessary to obtain a medical report.

(3) Before passing a custodial sentence for a service offence on an offender who is or appears to be mentally disordered, a court must consider:

a) any information before it which relates to his mental condition (whether given in a medical report, a pre-sentence report or otherwise); and

b) the likely effect of such a sentence on that condition and on any treatment which may be available for it.

(4) No custodial sentence which is passed in a case to which subsection (1) applies is invalidated by a failure of a court to comply with that subsection, but any court on an appeal against such a sentence:

a) must obtain a medical report if none was obtained by the court below; and

b) must consider any such report obtained by it or by that court.

(5) In this section:

'medical report' means a report as to an offender's mental condition made or submitted orally or in writing by a registered medical practitioner who is approved for the purposes of Mental Health Act 1983 s 12 by the Secretary of State as having special experience in the diagnosis or treatment of mental disorder.

For hostility to a mentally disordered victim, see the VICTIMS *Hostility towards disabled, gay and transgender victims* paras at **121.4**.

240.46   *Mentally disordered defendants   Defendant fails to take his medication*
R v Nurthen 2014 EWCA Crim 83 D pleaded to wounding with intent and false imprisonment. For some weeks he failed to take his medication. On Christmas Day D drank a bottle of champagne and became highly delusional and psychotic. He seized V, a stranger, in the street and held a knife to his throat, saying at first he wanted it all and later that he was fed up with his life and was going to kill V. Police arrived and asked a question whereupon D cut V. V was absolutely terrified. D suffered from a delusional disorder. He self-harmed when he was under high levels of distress and anxiety. A psychiatrist said D would be dangerous in the future if he failed to take his medication and/or took alcohol. Held. Where an individual commits acts of violence whilst suffering a mental condition, that condition may provide mitigation, on occasion, very strong mitigation, even if it does not provide a defence. However, where an individual is aware that he or she has a mental condition that is well controlled by medication and exacerbated by alcohol or other drugs, and knows that without that medication or with those drugs he or she becomes delusional and distressed, but nevertheless chooses to omit the medication or take the drugs with the result that he or she commits offences whilst in that state, then that mitigation may be greatly reduced or entirely eliminated. Extended sentence upheld.

240.47   *Mentally disordered defendants   Asperger's syndrome*
R v Jackley 2013 EWCA Crim 774, 2 Cr App R (S) 80 (p 521) D pleaded to five robberies, three attempted robberies, seven related imitation firearm charges and other less serious offences. The robbery offences were at four banks, three betting shops and a building society. They were committed just before, and during, his time at university. After the offences, D travelled to the US and sought to buy real handguns. D was prosecuted and served 10 months in prison. He served 2 months awaiting deportation. Prior to that he was of good character. He was a loner. While offending he was completely isolated. The Judge was not told that D had Asperger's syndrome and said the only mitigation was his pleas and that the firearms were imitations. The Judge started at 20 years. A report prepared for the appeal dealt with his Asperger's syndrome and said D would find it more difficult to serve his sentence, was vulnerable, prone to be bullied and that his desire to collect money was an obsession. Held. D well knew the difference between right and wrong. He would have appreciated the terror he was causing. D's excessive consumption of alcohol and cannabis was relevant. His condition made it more likely he would become obsessed and continue to offend. With this extra information **12 years** not 13.
See also: *R v Palmer* 2011 EWCA Crim 1286 (One cannot ignore the link in appropriate circumstances between [Asperger's syndrome] and the offence which has occurred.)

240.48   *Mentally disordered defendant   Post-natal disorders*
R v Abdulrahman 2013 EWCA Crim 1983 D was convicted of section 20. She was acquitted of attempted murder and section 18. Six days after giving birth she put her baby, V, in a bin bag and put that in a rubbish chute. The baby, which was in a Moses basket, fell five floors into a bin below. She rang her husband saying strangers had taken the baby. V suffered catastrophic skull fractures and will be dependent on others for the rest of her life. A midwife who visited D the day before said D and her husband were loving parents, confident and competent in handling V. D was an Iraqi Kurd who spoke little English. She was aged 25 and had no convictions. The psychiatric reports came to different conclusions. One said D had a severe mental and behavioural disorder following the birth. The Judge held the condition was missed. D had now served nearly 12 months. Held. The only explanation was that V suffered acute puerperal psychosis. Her culpability was extremely limited. Considering *R v Sainsbury* 1989 11 Cr App R (S) 533, the best course is to substitute **12 months** for 30 months enabling her release.

240.49   *Mercy should season justice*
Att-Gen's Ref No 4 of 1989 1989 11 Cr App R (S) 517 LCJ It must always be remembered that sentencing is an art rather than a science, that the trial judge is particularly well placed to assess the weight to be given to various competing considerations, that leniency is not in itself a vice. That mercy should season justice is a proposition as soundly based in law as it is in literature.

Att-Gen's Ref No 83 of 2001 2001 EWCA Crim 2443, 2002 1 Cr App R (S) 139 (p 588) What the authorities do not show are the cases where the individual circumstances of the defendant and the mitigation available to him have led to a justified departure from the guidance provided by the reported decisions. It is fundamental to the responsibilities of sentencing judges that while they must always pay proper regard to the sentencing guidance given, they are required also to reflect on all the circumstances of the individual case. Where sentencing judges are satisfied that occasion requires it, they have to balance the demands of justice with what is sometimes described as the calls of mercy. There were occasions where it was right to take a constructive course and seek to achieve the rehabilitation of the offender. The Judge was satisfied it provided the best possible long-term solution for the community and the defendant. It was right to take a constructive course. So far he has been proved right. The prospects of reoffending are now lower than if he had had a custodial sentence. The sentence was lenient on paper but sentencing is not and never can be an exercise on paper. Each case, ultimately, is individual. It would be wrong to interfere.

R v Wilkinson 2005 EWCA Crim 811 (Supply and change of lifestyle case, see **240.6.**)

R v Adeojo and Mugambwa 2008 EWCA Crim 1552, 2009 1 Cr App R (S) 66 (p 376) The defendants pleaded to robbery. A guard delivering cash was attacked by a four-man gang. Two defendants alleged disparity because one of them, a 16-year-old, received a non-custodial sentence. Held. The Court had to regard the welfare of the child or young person. He was on the facts less culpable. From time to time the court is not only encouraged but entitled to show mercy to a young offender.

Att-Gen's Ref Nos 64-65 of 2009 2009 EWCA Crim 2322, 2010 2 Cr App R (S) 8 (p 43) LCJ T and G were convicted of manslaughter and acquitted of murder. Held. The act was very dangerous, best described as an instant unjustified retaliation rather than revenge. It was reckless and aggravated by the fact that no one went to V's aid. T and G had not started the altercation. One defendant was very seriously injured and the other had seen his friend injured. The offence was miles out of character committed by persons who are otherwise wholly to be recommended. The year's wait for their murder trial cannot be ignored. The offence might call for a sentence significantly beyond the **3 years** given. On paper it was worth something like **4-5 years**. In some circumstances it was permissible to pass a merciful sentence. The Judge was deliberately lenient and merciful and the sentence was not varied.

R v Hussain 2010 EWCA Crim 94, 2 Cr App R (S) 60 (p 399) LCJ T and his brother M were convicted of GBH with intent against a robber who entered the home of one of them and attacked his family. The robber's skull was fractured causing brain injury so that he was unfit to plead when he was charged. There were other fractures. Held. Where a gang produces injuries as serious as these, very lengthy prison sentences are required. The attack was revenge. It did not follow careful or even momentary reflection. M acted under extreme provocation. It was a response to the dreadful and terrifying ordeal and the emotional anguish he had undergone. His relief that he and his family were safe and his understandable fury combined to make a decent, peaceful man act entirely out of character. He might have reacted out of an overwhelming sense of relief and fatigue. Guidelines do not cover this case. The call for mercy is intense so we pass such a sentence. For T, **2 years** not 3 years 3 months, and for M, **suspended sentence** substituted.

R v Beaver 2015 EWCA Crim 653 D pleaded to manslaughter based on diminished responsibility. D killed V using a large kitchen knife. He was now aged 82 with early dementia and depressive symptoms. Held. He had just snapped, which was attributed to his mental and other problems. We are wholly unable to say **3 years** was wrong in principle or manifestly excessive. Mercy nonetheless remains. We substitute a **Suspended Sentence Order** of **2 years** [with mental health and other conditions]. For more details, see **240.24**.

240.50   *Meritorious conduct (unrelated to the offence), Defendant's*
R v Wenman 2004 EWCA Crim 2995, 2005 2 Cr App R (S) 3 (p 13) D pleaded to causing death by careless driving. Shortly before D was sentenced, a motorist swerved to avoid a deer and skidded on ice. His car slid down a bank and into a stream. The motorist lost consciousness and was choking on his blood and saliva. D, who was driving by, saw the red tail lights of the car. He stopped his car and gave assistance. The motorist's car was in a perilous position and was at risk of toppling further into the stream. D telephoned for help, opened the car door and held the victim's head for 30 minutes until assistance arrived. To do so he had to stand in knee-deep water. The fire brigade arrived and were not prepared to do anything until they had secured the car. They cut the car around D to free the motorist. Two policemen and the Chief Fire Officer wrote in praise of D. The motorist believed that D had saved his life. Held. The behaviour was highly commendable. D was entitled to substantial credit for his selfless and courageous conduct. **3 years** not 4.

240.51   *Personal mitigation*
Criminal Justice Act 2003 s 166(1) makes provision for a sentencer to take account of any matters that 'in the opinion of the court are relevant in mitigating the sentence'. Ed.
Att-Gen's Ref No 84 of 2001 2002 EWCA Crim 7, 2 Cr App R (S) 51 (p 226) The defendant pleaded to attempted robbery and having a firearm with intent to resist arrest. He tried to rob a Securicor guard delivering cash to a cash dispenser. Held. Personal factors in relation to offences of this gravity can have only a very small effect in determining what the appropriate sentence is.
R v Brown 2010 EWCA Crim 845 D pleaded to robbery. He attacked a companion with a pole and punched him. Personal possessions and £17 were taken. D had convictions including affray and ABH. He was deeply ashamed and had been drinking heavily at the time. D was sentenced to 2 years 3 months after the robbery. Subsequently he had obtained work as a fisherman, then the merchant navy and then worked for an emergency response and rescue vehicle. D had a good prison report. Held. The guidelines indicate 4 years for a first-time offender, which he wasn't, but he was entitled to very considerable credit for the way he had turned his life round. There could be no criticism for **3 years** if it had been imposed shortly after the robbery. It was an exceptional case so **2 years**.
Note: Most sentences are determined primarily by the offence. Personal mitigation can make little or no difference to the sentence. Occasionally, where the defendant has some terrible illness or has taken valiant steps to overcome his or her drug addiction and changed his or her whole lifestyle, courts can exercise mercy and impose a constructive sentence.[273] When three defendants of equal culpability are sentenced for the same offence, the one with good personal mitigation will usually receive the same sentence as the others. Each case will be decided critically on its own specific facts. However, deductions can be made. Character witnesses may show that an onerous community penalty is appropriate as well as custody. Ed.
See also the **DEATH BY DRIVING: GENERAL PRINCIPLES** *Personal mitigation* para at **235.13** and the **IMPORTATION OF DRUGS** *Personal mitigation* para at **273.47**.

---

[273] *Att-Gen's Ref No 83 of 2001* 2001 EWCA Crim 2443, 2002 1 Cr App R (S) 139 (p 588)

240.52   *Police officers as defendants*
R v Keyte 1998 2 Cr App R (S) 165 Police officers are given considerable powers and privileges. If they dishonestly abuse their position and do so for profit, then not only must a prison sentence follow, but it must of necessity be a severe sentence.
R v Nazir 2003 EWCA Crim 901, 2 Cr App R (S) 114 (p 671) The Judge said that the public should have absolute faith and trust in their police officers who, by the nature of their job, have extensive powers and responsibilities. Those who do exploit that trust must inevitably serve a prison sentence. Held. We agree.
Note: These are old cases, but the principles seem in line with current sentencing practice. Ed.

240.53   *Police officers as defendants   Community support officers etc.*
R v Scott 2015 EWCA Crim 411 D was convicted of six thefts and one count of misfeasance in a public office. She was a police community support officer. When on duty, in uniform and working at Gatwick airport, D would approach passengers very shortly before their plane was due to leave. She would take them to an area where they could not be overheard and ask them if they were taking any cash out of the country. She told them they were only able to take out £1,000, which was a lie. She told them any surplus had to be left with her and collected when they returned. She appeared to be writing down details in her notebook. In all she had obtained £13,500 with this trick. If a receipt was asked for she refused to give one and in panic they handed over the money. Impact statements revealed the profound effects the thefts had had. Some victims were not treated seriously and one or two were thought of as being involved in a scam. D had two children aged 16 years and 4 months. The Judge emphasised the loss of morale of officers when they discovered they had disbelieved victims and in some cases treated them quite severely. Held. We bear in mind the vulnerability of the victims, the persistence of the behaviour and that the offence will erode confidence in the police. The money, whilst objectively small, was of great value to the victims. There must be a deterrent sentence. In light of her good character, positive references and other factors, **5 years** not 6½ years in all.
See also the:
> CORRUPTION/MISFEASANCE IN PUBLIC OFFICE *Police officers misusing computer data* para at **228.8** and the *Police officers Defendants, As* para at **228.9**, and the PERVERTING THE COURSE OF JUSTICE *Police officers Defendants, As* para at **305.27**.

240.54   *Political protests*
R v Jones and Others 2006 EWCA Crim 2942 The defendants pleaded to obstructing railway engines etc. They made a political protest at an arms fair. They had excellent character, good records of voluntary work and/or academic distinction. Held. If the offence was committed in the course of a political protest that was a relevant factor. **Conditional discharges** not community orders.
R v Alhaddad and Others 2010 EWCA Crim 1760, 2011 1 Cr App R (S) 86 (p 517) The right to peaceful protest, to demonstrate and to march in favour of or against particular causes, or in favour of or against the policies of foreign states such as Israel, is a hallmark of our democratic society governed by the rule of law. That right the courts have always safeguarded and will always safeguard. Yet the rule of law requires that those engaged in protest do not engage in violence against anyone, particularly the police who were simply seeking to protect others from violence and to discharge the important duty of this state to, in this case, foreign embassies.

240.55   *Poor defendants*
Criminal Justice Act 2003 s 164(3) In fixing the amount of any fine to be imposed…a court shall take into account…the financial circumstances of the defendant so far as they are known, or appear, to the court.

(4) Subsection (3) applies whether taking into account the financial circumstances has the effect of increasing or reducing the amount of the fine.

For more detail, see the FINES *Poor defendants* paras at **60.33** in Volume 1.

Present, Right to be the see PROCEDURE, SENTENCING *Defendant's right to be present and represented* para at **87.20** in Volume 1.

Previous convictions see back index.

Prison conditions, Harsh see PRISONERS: SENTENCING PRINCIPLES *Harsh prison conditions* at **308.2**.

240.56   *Professional defendants*

R v Richards 1980 2 Cr App R (S) 119 LCJ A doctor was convicted of obtaining money dishonestly from his Health Authority. He was aged 57. Held. It is obvious he will have to face the Disciplinary Committee of the GMC. One must bear in mind that for a person such as this, a prison sentence, be it a week or be it 30 months, is a disaster. It is the end of his career. It is the end of his life as a doctor. The disgrace will remain with him for evermore. That must be borne in mind. Also one must not lose sight of the disciplinary proceedings which are inevitable, which in themselves mean a very large financial penalty, albeit indirectly, likewise the loss or probable loss of his pension rights. The sentence was reduced.

Note: This does not mean that professional defendants will always be treated less severely than non-professional defendants. Each case will depend critically on its own facts. Where there is a breach of trust to clients, other considerations will be present. Ed. See also the SOLICITORS chapter.

240.57   *Race of the defendant, Judge referring to the*

R v Odewale and Others 2004 EWCA Crim 145, 2 Cr App R (S) 47 (p 240) The defendants were convicted of conspiracy to defraud financial institutions by means of identity theft. The Judge said, 'A disproportionate number of participants in these sorts of crimes, are either Nigerians or people who have connections to other Nigerians, the Court has a responsibility…to seek to deter others'. Held. The Judge should not have made those remarks and it is regrettable that he did so. The language used may well have given the impression that their Nigerian background added to the defendants' sentences. We take this specific failing into account when adjusting the sentence.

Old case: *R v George* 1994 Unreported 3/11/94 (In the normal case the colour, race and religion of the victims and defendants are wholly irrelevant. There may be exceptional cases such as public order offences inspired by racial or colour prejudice or religious beliefs, where reference to those motives and to the race, religion or colour of those involved as victims, or as offenders, will be necessary for a proper explanation to be made of the circumstances of the offence. This was not such a case. For a judge to refer to the fact that the defendants were black can only leave in the minds of the defendants and their relatives and friends the suspicion that the defendants' colour was a factor in the Judge's mind when he passed sentence. We make a specific reduction so there is no lingering sense of injustice.)

240.58   *Release   Don't take release into account when sentencing*

R v Kenway and Cunningham 1986 7 Cr App R (S) 457 The defendants pleaded to three burglaries and other charges. The Judge said, 'It is difficult to see what will stop his offending. The Home Office let them out as soon as they dare. If this man gets a tariff sentence he will be out within a very short time and he would burgle again. A man who gets 18 months can be sure of being out after 6. 2 years and he will only serve 8 months. That would not be long enough'. Held. It is well established that to take account of parole is improper. **3 years** in all and 15 months' not 5 years' extended.

R v Round and Dunn 2009 EWCA Crim 2667, 2010 2 Cr App R (S) 45 (p 292) The Court considered the various anomalies of the curfew scheme, HDC, which depended on how the sentence was constructed, in particular whether the shorter of two consecutive sentences is served first or second. Held. The general principle that early release, licence and their various ramifications should be left out of account is of some importance. The HDC rules might change between sentence and when available. It is not incumbent on sentencers to alter the ordinary manner of expressing their sentences to maximise the uncertain possibilities of HDC. It is not wrong in principle for a judge to refuse to consider early release possibilities when calculating his sentence or framing the manner or order in which they are expressed to be imposed. It is neither necessary nor practicable to undertake such examinations, although there may be particular cases in which an unusual course is justified.

R v Dunn 2012 EWCA Crim 419 D was sentenced to 15 years each for 12 offences of rape. The Judge said D would be released after 7½ years. In prison he learnt that for the earlier offences he would not be entitled to be released until 10 years. For the rest the release date would be 7½ years. The case was re-listed but the time limit for variation had expired. The Judge wanted to reduce the sentences for the earlier offences so D would be released after 7½ years. It was agreed that D should appeal with an indication from the Judge that he wished the Court of Appeal to reduce the sentence for the earlier offences. The Judge told D that he did not want him to be disadvantaged and it was a procedural anomaly which was going to be resolved. Held. Early release provisions should not be considered. The Parole Board may release him after 7½ years. There was no injustice.

R v R 2012 EWCA Crim 709 D pleaded to various sex offences. All parties overlooked the fact that some of the older offences were under the pre-CJA 2003 regime. The case was brought back to Court after the time limit for amending the sentence had expired. The Judge encouraged D to appeal. Held. If the Judge states the wrong release date that is most unfortunate, but the principle in *R v Dunn* 2012 EWCA Crim 419 must stand.

R v Hardy 2013 EWCA Crim 36 D was sentenced to 6 years and the Judge said he would serve half the sentence. In fact, as the offences were historical, D had to serve two-thirds. The defence said the sentence should reflect what the Judge had in mind as the correct period of custody. Held. There may be rare and exceptional circumstances where the Judge selects a length of sentence after which the defendant should be released. Here, the Judge expressed no such intention. The sentence was not wrong.

See also the **HOME DETENTION CURFEW SCHEME** chapter in Volume 1 for an example of a similar principle.

240.59   *Release   Offences have different release dates*
R v Dunn 2012 EWCA Crim 419 see the previous paragraph.

For judge stating the wrong release date, see the **PROCEDURE, SENTENCING** *Explain the sentence, Sentencer must Explanation wrong* para at **87.49** in Volume 1.

Representation, Right to see the **PROCEDURE, SENTENCING** *Defendant's right to be present and represented* para at **87.20** in Volume 1.

240.60   *Re-sentenced, Discount for being*
R v Broomfield 2004 EWCA Crim 363, 2 Cr App R (S) 70 (p 381) D was in breach of a Community Punishment and Rehabilitation Order. When given the order he was in breach of his prison licence. He was sentenced to 9 months with the Judge taking into account the 6 months he had served on remand which he considered didn't count towards his sentence. The prison authorities released D after one day because they thought it did. The Judge re-listed the case and sentenced him again to 9 months saying that the period on remand didn't count. The prison adhered to its view and the Court re-listed it. The Court was told that if it wanted D to serve 9 months it must sentence D to 18 months. The Judge did so. Held. The prison was wrong. 9 months should be reinstated with **1 month** discount to reflect the history of the case.

Note: This discount seems less generous than the discount given when a defendant is re-sentenced after the prosecution appeal a sentence to the Court of Appeal. Ed.

240.61   Sentence served for which the conviction was later quashed
R v Exley and Day 2000 2 Cr App R (S) p 189 The defendant is not entitled to any discount for time in custody for a conviction that was later quashed.

240.62   Socially challenged, Defendant
R v Gilchrist 2009 EWCA Crim 1015 A co-defendant, W, pleaded to robbery. He had severe problems arising from a development disorder. W had an IQ of 61 which was in the bottom 1%. A psychologist said it was unlikely he would ever lead a fully independent life or manage his own affairs. He would need support throughout his life. W also had learning difficulties and dyslexia. Primarily because of his medical condition the Judge reduced his sentence from 7 years to **5 years**. Held. The Judge was perfectly entitled to do that.
R v Altahan 2010 EWCA Crim 985 D pleaded to sending a malicious communication containing false information and an offence involving a bomb hoax. D sent e-mails to two schools claiming to be a suicide bomber named Qacim Haddad. The second e-mail said 'Warning, I am going to blow up Broomfield school, I'm a suicide bomber in Leeds'. Qacim Haddad, an asylum seeker from Iraq, was arrested and said he had met D online but had ceased communicating with her. In interview D said the messages were meant as revenge against Qacim for splitting up with her and she hoped he would be deported. D, aged 37, had a caution for harassment after she developed an obsessive attraction to her GP. The pre-sentence report said D struggled to accept responsibility, there was a low risk of re-conviction and D posed a medium risk of harm to staff or anybody with whom she formed, or wished to form, a relationship. The psychiatric report said D suffered from Asperger's syndrome, the risk of violence was 'absolutely minimal', and there was a substantial risk of further inappropriate or unrequited fantasy attachments to men. People such as doctors, police officers and those in positions of authority and status were most at risk. The Judge said she led a sad and lonely existence and appeared to be unable to function socially in an ordinary way. Held. It is in the public interest that she receives appropriate treatment. **Community order** with supervision and mental health treatment requirement, not 16 months.
See also: R v Holland 2014 EWCA Crim 855 (Convicted of sex abuse with two nieces when one was aged between three and six years old and the other from when she was aged five. Over a six-year period. Defendant had learning difficulties and had the emotional maturity of an eight-year-old. Very low IQ in a dysfunctional family. Vulnerable and of good character. Unusual risk of being bullied. 3 years would have been merciful. Factors take it well outside the sentencing range so **2 years**.)
See also the **Vulnerable defendants, Treatment of** para at **240.67**.

240.63   Taking the law into your own hands
R v Hussain 2010 EWCA Crim 94, 2 Cr App R (S) 60 (p 399) LCJ T and his brother M were convicted of GBH with intent. M lived with his wife, two sons, S1 and S2, and a daughter, Ar. V, a professional criminal with a long record for serious offences, went to M's house with two others disguised with masks or balaclavas. They carried knives and cable ties and disabled the security lighting. M and his sons returned home just before 11 pm. They were ambushed by V's gang. M and his sons were threatened with a knife and bundled into their house. M, his wife and S1 were pushed to the floor and threatened that if they moved they would be killed. S2 dashed upstairs. Ar went downstairs and was also told to lie on the floor. M and Ar started crying. M was desperate that his family would be raped and then killed. S2 climbed out of an upstairs window and went to T's house nearby. The robbers went looking for S2, leaving only V guarding M etc. M threw a table at V and escaped. S1 punched V and pulled off V's balaclava. The robbers fled. Believing their relations were still being held, T, S2 and others went to M's house. They were armed with cricket bats etc. V was brought down and attacked with the cricket bat etc. M and T and others were involved. V's skull was fractured causing brain injury, so that he was unfit to plead when he was charged. He also had fractures to his ribs, jaw,

elbow and finger. T was aged 35 and M aged 53. They were both of impeccable, positive good character. M had made a positive contribution to the community. He was thought to have suffered post-traumatic stress disorder. The police thought he might be at risk of harm (from criminals). Held. Where a gang produces injuries as serious as these, very lengthy prison sentences are required. The burglary was over. The burglars had left. No one was in any danger from them. The attack was revenge. It was not vigilante activity. It did not follow careful or even momentary reflection. M acted under extreme provocation. It was a response to the dreadful and terrifying ordeal and the emotional anguish he had undergone. His relief that he and his family were safe and his understandable fury combined to make a decent, peaceful man act entirely out of character. He might have reacted out of an overwhelming sense of relief and fatigue. Guidelines do not cover this case. The call for mercy is intense. The principle that no one can take the law into his own hands and administer punishment has been vindicated. T **2 years** not 3 years 3 months. M **12 months** suspended with supervision not 2½ years. Old case: *R v McHale* 2001 2 Cr App R (S) 92 (p 417) (These were serious assaults. People cannot be permitted to take the law into their own hands. Severe prison sentences are virtually inevitable for this sort of conduct by people of good character.)

240.64   *Totality Basic rule*
TICs and Totality Guideline 2012 Crown Court, see www.banksr.com Other Matters Guidelines tab (*Magistrates' Court Sentencing Guidelines Update March 2012* page 18g) page 5 The principle of totality comprises two elements:
1 All courts, when sentencing for more than a single offence, should pass a total sentence which reflects all the offending behaviour before it and is just and proportionate. This is so whether the sentences are structured as concurrent or consecutive. Therefore, concurrent sentences will ordinarily be longer than a single sentence for a single offence.
2 It is usually impossible to arrive at a just and proportionate sentence for multiple offending simply by adding together notional single sentences. It is necessary to address the offending behaviour, together with the factors personal to the offender as a whole.
R v Sparkes 2011 EWCA Crim 880 Although it may be proper to make a sentence consecutive to one passed on an earlier occasion, particularly where the second offence was committed on bail for the first offence, the court must nevertheless have regard to the total sentence to be served.
See also the CONCURRENT AND CONSECUTIVE SENTENCES chapter.

240.65   *Totality   Defendant sentenced on separate occasions*
R v May 2013 EWCA Crim 850, 2014 1 Cr App R (S) 13 (p 58) D was sentenced on different occasions for two robberies committed three days apart. Held. para 3 The explanations given for this were not satisfactory. However, the principles of totality require us to approach the sentence, as the second Judge did, as if we were dealing with both offences at the same time and to ensure the totality of the sentence imposed is just and proportionate.

240.66   *Trafficked victim, Defendant was a*
R v O 2008 EWCA Crim 2835 D pleaded to an offence of possessing a false identity card with intent. She attempted to leave France by using a Spanish identity card and was arrested at Dover. She finally admitted the card was not hers and explained that she had lost her passport and wanted to visit her uncle in France. She gave her date of birth as 10 December 1985. Over the following months, she informed her advisors that her correct date of birth was 10 December 1991, making her aged 16, although she claimed she was aged 17. She stated that she had fled Nigeria due to threats to her life as a result of her refusal to enter an arranged marriage to a 63-year-old man. Her travel to the UK was to be repaid through work involving prostitution. She had no family in the UK. Held. No steps were taken by the defence to investigate the history. No consideration was given by the defence as to whether she might have a defence of duress. The possibility that she might have been trafficked was ignored. There is nothing in the transcript to suggest that

any thought had been given to the State's duty to protect her as a young victim, under the Council of Europe's Convention on Action against Trafficking in Human Beings 197/2005. Nobody considered that if she was aged 17 or less, she should not have been in the Crown Court at all. Counsel for the defence thought it right to refer to 'an inevitable prison sentence'. The Judge passed what she described as an 'inevitable prison sentence' of 8 months and for good measure had no report. If the appellant was aged 17 or less, a sentence of imprisonment as such was unlawful. The Crown did not oppose the appeal. This appeal against conviction must obviously be allowed.

240.67   *Vulnerable defendants, Treatment of*

Criminal Practice Directions 2015 EWCA Crim 1567 para I 3D.1…'Vulnerable' includes those under 18 years of age and people with a mental disorder or learning disability, a physical disorder or disability, or who are likely to suffer fear or distress in giving evidence because of their own circumstances or those relating to the case.

para 3D.2…This includes enabling a witness or defendant to give their best evidence, and enabling a defendant to comprehend the proceedings and engage fully with his or her defence. The pre-trial and trial process should, so far as necessary, be adapted to meet those ends. Regard should be had to the welfare of a young defendant as required by Children and Young Persons Act 1933 s 44 and generally to Criminal Procedure Rules 2015 2015/1490 Parts 1 and 3 (the overriding objective and the court's powers of case management).

Criminal Practice Directions 2015 EWCA Crim 1567 para I 3G.2 It may be appropriate to arrange that a vulnerable defendant should visit, out of court hours and before the trial, sentencing or appeal hearing, the courtroom in which that hearing is to take place so that he or she can familiarise him or herself with it.

3G.3 Where an intermediary is being used to help the defendant to communicate at court, the intermediary should accompany the defendant on his or her pre-trial visit. The visit will enable the defendant to familiarise him or herself with the layout of the court, and may include matters such as where the defendant will sit, either in the dock or otherwise, court officials (what their roles are and where they sit), who else might be in the court, for example those in the public gallery and press box, the location of the witness box, basic court procedure, and the facilities available in the court.

3G.4 If the defendant's use of the live link is being considered, he or she should have an opportunity to have a practice session.

3G.5 If any case against a vulnerable defendant has attracted or may attract widespread public or media interest, the assistance of the police should be enlisted to try and ensure that the defendant is not, when attending the court, exposed to intimidation, vilification or abuse. Criminal Justice Act 1925 s 41 prohibits the taking of photographs of defendants and witnesses (among others) in the court building or in its precincts, or when entering or leaving those precincts. A direction reminding media representatives of the prohibition may be appropriate. The court should also be ready at this stage, if it has not already done so, where relevant to make a reporting restriction under Children and Young Persons Act 1933 s 39 or, on an appeal to the Crown Court from a Youth Court, to remind media representatives of the application of section 49 of that Act.

Criminal Practice Directions 2015 EWCA Crim 1567 para I 3G.8 Subject again to the need for appropriate security arrangements, a vulnerable defendant, especially if he is young, should normally, if he wishes, be free to sit with members of his family or others in a like relationship, and with some other suitable supporting adult such as a social worker, and in a place which permits easy, informal communication with his legal representatives. The court should ensure that a suitable supporting adult is available throughout the course of the proceedings.

3G.9 It is essential that at the beginning of the proceedings, the court should ensure that what is to take place has been explained to a vulnerable defendant in terms he or she can understand and, at trial in the Crown Court, it should ensure in particular that the role of the jury has been explained. It should remind those representing the vulnerable defendant and the supporting adult of their responsibility to explain each step as it takes place and, at trial, explain the possible consequences of a guilty verdict and credit for a guilty plea. The court should also remind any intermediary of the responsibility to ensure that the vulnerable defendant has understood the explanations given to him/her. Throughout the trial the court should continue to ensure, by any appropriate means, that the defendant understands what is happening and what has been said by those on the bench, the advocates and witnesses.

Note: This section of the directions deals primarily with trials and the giving of evidence. However, the above edited parts may also assist sentencing hearings although the pressures then are not so protracted or acute. Ed.

For *Wealthy defendants* see the FINES *Wealthy defendants* paras at **60.31** in Volume 1.

240.68   *Withdrawing from criminal agreement   It should be encouraged*
Att-Gen's Ref Nos 65-66 of 2001 2001 EWCA Crim 2406 D pleaded to robbery of a guard of a security van. He sat beside the getaway driver wearing a balaclava helmet throughout the robbery. His basis of plea was that when the two assailants who attacked the guard got out of the car he was unaware that weapons were to be used. When he saw the weapons he decided not to go with the other two and he remained in the car. Held. The basis of the plea was supported by the fact he just remained in the car. Courts ought to encourage people who at the last minute decide not to go through with a criminal enterprise and who withdraw their own involvement even if they remain a party to what is going on.

Note: This is an old case. I am unaware of any more recent cases. As the case seems sensible I have kept it. Ed.

See also the CONSPIRACY *Conspiracy not carried out* para at **227.2**.

DELAY, for general principles, see the DEFENDANT *Historical case* paras at **240.32**.

241   DISQUALIFIED DRIVING (SIMPLE)
241.1
Road Traffic Act 1988 s 103
Mode of trial Summary only. Under Criminal Justice Act 1988 s 40(3)(c) it may be included in an indictment.
Maximum sentence 6 months and/or a £5,000 fine for offences committed before 12 March 2015 and an unlimited fine thereafter.[274] There are maximum fines for those aged under 18, see **14.38** in Volume 1.
Endorsement Obligatory, unless there are special reasons not to disqualify
Penalty points 6 points
Disqualification Discretionary
Depriving defendant of vehicle used There is power to deprive the defendant of the vehicle used[275] for the purposes of committing the offence.
When death is caused, see the DEATH BY DRIVING: DISQUALIFIED, NO LICENCE, UNINSURED chapter.

241.2   *Magistrates' Court Sentencing Guidelines*
Magistrates' Court Sentencing Guidelines 2008, see www.banksr.com Other Matters Guidelines tab
The guidelines apply to the Magistrates' Court and to the Crown Court hearing appeals or sentencing for summary only offences.[276]
For details about applying the guidelines, see the GUIDELINES chapter in Volume 1.
page 122 Starting points are based on a first-time offender pleading not guilty.

---

[274] Legal Aid, Sentencing and Punishment of Offenders Act 2012 s 85(1) and (4) and Legal Aid, Sentencing and Punishment of Offenders Act 2012 (Commencement No 11) Order 2015 2015/504
[275] Powers of Criminal Courts (Sentencing) Act 2000 s 143(6)-(7)
[276] See page 15 of the guidelines.

Examples of nature of activity	Starting point	Range
Full period expired but retest not taken	Low-level community order	Band C fine to medium-level community order 6 points or disqualify for 3-6 months
Lengthy period of ban already served	High-level community order	Medium-level community order to 12 weeks' custody Lengthen disqualification for 6-12 months beyond expiry of current ban
Recently imposed ban	12 weeks' custody	High-level community order to 6 weeks' custody Lengthen disqualification for 12-18 months beyond expiry of current ban

The following aggravating and mitigating factors may be particularly relevant: Factors indicating higher culpability: 1 Never passed test 2 Planned long-term evasion 3 Vehicle obtained during ban 4 Driving for remuneration. Factors indicating lower culpability: 1 Defendant not present when disqualification imposed and genuine reason why unaware of ban 2 Genuine emergency established. Factors indicating greater degree of harm: 1 Distance driven 2 Evidence of associated bad driving 3 Offender caused accident.

Consultation It is expected that the Sentencing Council will issue a consultation document about updating this guideline in May 2016.

For the meaning of a high-level and a medium-level community order see **16.13-16.14** in Volume 1.

For *Imposing preventive orders to inflate the maximum sentence*, see **85.11** in Volume 1.

241.3   Cases

R v Taylor 2014 EWCA Crim 2411 D pleaded (full credit) to driving whilst disqualified. D's lights were not on after sunset when there was rain and poor visibility. He was stopped by police. D was disqualified in 2013 under the totting regime. D was aged 38 and, since the incident, had led an industrious life. He had no relevant recent previous convictions. The prosecution dropped the main but unrelated count which caused the matter to be heard at the Crown Court. The Judge described him as "a menace to others whilst on the road". Held. **2 months**, not 3, and **disqualification of 12 months**, not 24. See also: *R v Ledgard* 2010 EWCA Crim 1605 (Plea to three offences of driving whilst disqualified and associated no insurance offences. D suffered from bipolar affective disorder and during manic episodes his driving was adversely affected. A **2-year community order** not 12 months suspended.)

242   DISQUALIFIED DRIVING (CAUSING SERIOUS INJURY)

242.1

Road Traffic Act 1988 s 3ZD[277]

Mode of trial Triable either way

Maximum sentence On indictment 4 years. Summary maximum 6 months and/or an unlimited fine.[278] There are maximum fines for those aged under 18, see **14.38** in Volume 1.

Commencement Section 3ZD only applies to offences committed after 13 April 2015, Criminal Justice and Courts Act 2015 s 29(5).

Endorsement Obligatory, unless there are special reasons not to disqualify

Disqualification Obligatory, 2 years[279]

Penalty points 3-11 points when special reasons found[280]

---

[277] As inserted by Criminal Justice and Courts Act 2015 s 29(1)
[278] Road Traffic Offenders Act 1988 Sch 2 Part 1
[279] Road Traffic Offenders Act 1988 s 34(4)
[280] Road Traffic Offenders Act 1988 Sch 2 Part 1

Disqualification until test is passed Where the defendant is disqualified under Road Traffic Offenders Act 1988 s 34, the defendant must be disqualified until an appropriate driving test is passed.[281] In force 13 April 2015.

Depriving defendant of vehicle used There is power to deprive the defendant of the vehicle used[282] for the purposes of committing the offence.

243 DOGS, DANGEROUS

243.1

1) Dangerous Dogs Act 1991 s 1(2) and (7) (breeding, selling, exchanging, giving away or advertising etc. a prohibited dog)

Dangerous Dogs Act 1991 s 1(3) and (7) (possession of a prohibited dog)

Dangerous Dogs Act 1991 s 3(1) (dogs dangerously out of control in any place in England and Wales)

The Dangerous Dogs Act 1991 s 3(3)(b) offence (dog in a private place where he/she is not permitted to be, which makes a person fear injury) was repealed on 13 May 2014.

Modes of trial Summary only

Maximum sentences 6 months and/or £5,000 fine for offences committed before 12 March 2015 and an unlimited fine thereafter.[283] There are maximum fines for those aged under 18, see **14.38** in Volume 1.

These offences were created by Anti-social Behaviour, Crime and Policing Act 2014 s 106. In force 13 May 2014[284]

2) Dangerous Dogs Act 1991 s 3(1) (dogs injuring a person or assistance dog in any place)

Mode of trial Triable either way

Maximum sentence On indictment: a) 14 years when a person dies as a result of being injured, b) 5 years in any other case where a person is injured, and c) 3 years in any case where an assistance dog is injured (whether or not it dies). Summary sentence 6 months and/or a £5,000 fine for offences committed before 12 March 2015 and an unlimited fine thereafter.[285] There are maximum fines for those aged under 18, see **14.38** in Volume 1.

The Dangerous Dogs Act 1991 s 3(3)(b) offence (dog in a place where he/she is not permitted who injures a person) was repealed on 13 May 2014.

Old offences For offences committed before 13 May 2014, there are the following differences: a) the offence had to be in a public place, b) injuring an assistance dog was not an offence, and c) the maximum sentence for a section 3(1) and (3) offence was 2 years on indictment.

Criminal Behaviour Orders The post-conviction ASBO was replaced by the Criminal Behaviour Order on 20 October 2014,[286] see **26.1** in Volume 1.

Destruction Orders For both offences there is power to order the destruction of the dog. For the section 3(1) and (3) offence there is a requirement to order destruction of the dog, unless the court is satisfied that the dog would not constitute a danger to public safety.[287] For more detail, see the **DESTRUCTION ORDERS: DOGS** chapter.

Disqualification from having custody of a dog For both offences there is a discretionary power to order the destruction of the dog and the disqualification of the defendant from having custody of a dog.[288] For more detail see that chapter.

---

[281] Road Traffic Offenders Act 1988 s 36(2)(f)

[282] Powers of Criminal Courts (Sentencing) Act 2000 s 143(6)-(7)

[283] Legal Aid, Sentencing and Punishment of Offenders Act 2012 s 85(1) and (4) and Legal Aid, Sentencing and Punishment of Offenders Act 2012 (Commencement No 11) Order 2015 2015/504

[284] Anti-social Behaviour, Crime and Policing Act 2014 (Commencement No 2, Transitional and Transitory Provisions) Order 2014 2014/949 Sch para 6

[285] Legal Aid, Sentencing and Punishment of Offenders Act 2012 s 85(1) and (4) and Legal Aid, Sentencing and Punishment of Offenders Act 2012 (Commencement No 11) Order 2015 2015/504

[286] Anti-social Behaviour, Crime and Policing Act 2014 (Commencement No 7, Saving and Transitional Provisions) Order 2014 2014/2590

[287] Dangerous Dogs Act 1991 s 4(1)-(1A)

[288] Dangerous Dogs Act 1991 s 4(1)

Statistics The Sentencing Council's consultation paper 2015 at page 6 says that in the last 10 years at least eight adults and 13 children have died from attacks by dogs. In 2013, 6,740 people required hospital treatment resulting from dog attacks. This was an increase of 6% from the previous year.

243.2   Dogs [dangerously] out of control causing injury   Sentencing Council Guidelines
Dangerous Dog Offences Guideline 2012, see www.banksr.com Other Matters Guidelines tab
page 3 Owner or person in charge of a dog dangerously out of control in a public place, injuring any person, Dangerous Dogs Act 1991 s 3(1)
The guideline refers to 'Owner or person in charge allowing a dog to be in a private place where the dog is not permitted to be, injuring any person, Dangerous Dogs Act 1991 s 3(3)(a)'. This offence was repealed on 13 May 2014.

Not in force from 1 July 2016

STEP ONE Determining the offence category
page 4 The court should determine the offence category using the table below.

Category 1	Greater harm and higher culpability
Category 2	Greater harm and lower culpability; or lesser harm and higher culpability
Category 3	Lesser harm and lower culpability

page 4 The court should determine culpability and harm caused or intended, by reference **only** to the factors below, which comprise the principal factual elements of the offence. Where an offence does not fall squarely into a category, individual factors may require a degree of weighting before making an overall assessment and determining the appropriate offence category.

Factors indicating greater harm
Serious injury (which includes disease transmission and/or psychological harm) Sustained or repeated attack Victim is a child or otherwise vulnerable because of personal circumstances

Factor indicating lesser harm
Minor injury

Factors indicating higher culpability
Statutory aggravating factors: Offence racially or religiously aggravated Offence motivated by, or demonstrating, hostility to the victim based on his or her sexual orientation (or presumed sexual orientation) Offence motivated by, or demonstrating, hostility to the victim based on the victim's disability (or presumed disability) *Other aggravating factors:* Failure to respond to warnings or concerns expressed by others about the dog's behaviour Goading, or allowing goading, of dog Dog used as weapon or to intimidate victim Offence motivated by, or demonstrating, hostility based on the victim's age, sex, gender identity (or presumed gender identity)

Factors indicating lower culpability
Attempts made to regain control of dog and/or intervene Provocation of dog without fault of the offender Evidence of safety or control measures having been taken Mental disorder or learning disability, where linked to the commission of the offence

Not in force from 1 July 2016

Not in force from 1 July 2016

243.3

STEP TWO Starting point and category range

page 4 Having determined the category, the court should use the corresponding starting points to reach a sentence within the category range below. The starting point applies to all offenders irrespective of plea or previous convictions. A case of particular gravity, reflected by multiple features of culpability or harm in Step 1, could merit upward adjustment from the starting point before further adjustment for aggravating or mitigating features, set out on the next page.

Offence category	Starting point (applicable to all offenders)	Category range (applicable to all offenders)
Category 1	6 months' custody	Medium-level community order to 18 months' custody
Category 2	Medium-level community order	Band B fine to 6 months' custody
Category 3	Band B fine	Discharge to Band C fine

For the meaning of a medium-level community order see **16.13** in Volume 1.

243.4   [Aggravating and mitigating factors]

page 5 The table below contains a **non-exhaustive** list of additional factual elements providing the context of the offence and factors relating to the offender. Identify whether any combination of these, or other relevant factors, should result in an upward or downward adjustment from the starting point. In some cases, having considered these factors, it may be appropriate to move outside the identified category range.

When sentencing **Category 1 or 2** offences, the court should also consider the custody threshold as follows:
Has the custody threshold been passed?
If so, is it unavoidable that a custodial sentence be imposed?
If so, can that sentence be suspended?

When sentencing **Category 2** offences, the court should also consider the community order threshold as follows: Has the community order threshold been passed?

Factors increasing seriousness
Statutory aggravating factors: Previous convictions, having regard to a) the nature of the offence to which the conviction relates and its relevance to the current offence; and b) the time that has elapsed since the conviction Offence committed whilst on bail *Other aggravating factors include:* Injury to another animal(s) Location of the offence Ongoing effect upon the victim and/or others Failure to take adequate precautions to prevent dog escaping Allowing person insufficiently experienced or trained to be in charge of dog Ill-treatment or failure to ensure welfare needs of dog, where not charged separately Dog known to be prohibited Lack or loss of control of dog due to influence of alcohol or drugs Offence committed against those working in the public sector or providing a service to the public Established evidence of community impact Failure to comply with current court orders Offence committed whilst on licence

Factors reducing seriousness or reflecting personal mitigation
No previous convictions **or** no relevant/recent convictions Isolated incident No previous complaints against, or incidents involving, the dog Remorse Good character and/or exemplary conduct Evidence of responsible ownership Determination and/or demonstration of steps taken to address addiction or offending behaviour Serious medical conditions requiring urgent, intensive or long-term treatment Age and/or lack of maturity where it affects the responsibility of the offender Mental disorder or learning disability, where not linked to the commission of the offence Sole or primary carer for dependent relatives

Compensation and ancillary orders

page 6 In all cases, the court should consider whether to make a compensation order and/or other ancillary orders.

Compensation order

The court should consider compensation orders in all cases where personal injury, loss or damage has resulted from the offence.[289] The court must give reasons if it decides not to award compensation in such cases.

Other ancillary orders available include:

Disqualification from having custody of a dog

The court **may** disqualify the offender from having custody of a dog.[290] The test the court should consider is whether the offender is a fit and proper person to have custody of a dog.

Destruction order/contingent destruction order

In any case where the offender is not the owner of the dog, the owner must be given an opportunity to be present and make representations to the court.

The court **shall** make a destruction order unless the court is satisfied that the dog would not constitute a danger to public safety.[291]

In reaching a decision, the court should consider the relevant circumstances, which include:

the incident – what degree of harm was caused by the dog's behaviour?

past behaviour of the dog – is this an isolated incident or have there been previous warnings or incidents? and

owner's character – is the owner a fit and proper person to own this particular dog?

If the court is satisfied that the dog would not constitute a danger to public safety, it **shall** make a contingent destruction order imposing certain available conditions.[292] A contingent destruction order should specify the measures to be taken by the owner for keeping the dog under proper control, which include:

muzzling; keeping on a lead; neutering in appropriate cases; and excluding it from a specified place.[293]

Where the court makes a destruction order, it **may** order the offender to pay what it determines to be the reasonable expenses of destroying the dog and of keeping it pending its destruction.[294]

243.5   *Dogs out of control   Sentencing Council guideline*

Dangerous Dog Offences Guideline 2012, see www.banksr.com Other Matters Guidelines tab

---

[289] Powers of Criminal Courts (Sentencing) Act 2000 s 130
[290] Dangerous Dogs Act 1991 s 4(1)(b)
[291] Dangerous Dogs Act 1991 s 4(1)(a)
[292] Dangerous Dogs Act 1991 s 4A(4)
[293] Dangerous Dogs Act 1991 s 4A(5)
[294] Dangerous Dogs Act 1991 s 4(4)(b)

page 9 1 Owner or person in charge of a dog dangerously out of control in a public place, Dangerous Dogs Act 1991 s 3(1)

The guideline refers to the 'Owner or person in charge allowing a dog to be in a private place where the dog is not permitted to be, which makes a person fear injury, Dangerous Dogs Act 1991 s 3(3)(b)' offence. This was repealed on 13 May 2014.

STEP ONE Determining the offence category
page 10 The court should determine the offence category using the table below.

Category 1	Greater harm and higher culpability
Category 2	Greater harm and lower culpability or lesser harm and higher culpability
Category 3	Lesser harm and lower culpability

page 10 The court should determine culpability and harm caused or intended, by reference **only** to the factors below, which comprise the principal factual elements of the offence. Where an offence does not fall squarely into a category, individual factors may require a degree of weighting before making an overall assessment and determining the appropriate offence category.

| **Factors indicating greater harm** |
| Presence of children or others who are vulnerable because of personal circumstances
Injury to another animal(s) |
| **Factor indicating lesser harm** |
| Low risk to the public |
| **Factors indicating higher culpability** |
| *Statutory aggravating factors:*
Offence racially or religiously aggravated
Offence motivated by, or demonstrating, hostility to the victim based on his or her sexual orientation (or presumed sexual orientation)
Offence motivated by, or demonstrating, hostility to the victim based on the victim's disability (or presumed disability)
Other aggravating factors:
Failure to respond to warnings or concerns expressed by others about the dog's behaviour
Goading, or allowing goading, of dog
Dog used as weapon or to intimidate victim
Offence motivated by, or demonstrating, hostility based on the victim's age, sex, gender identity (or presumed gender identity) |
| **Factors indicating lower culpability** |
| Attempts made to regain control of dog and/or intervene
Provocation of dog without fault of the offender
Evidence of safety or control measures having been taken
Mental disorder or learning disability, where linked to the commission of the offence |

243.6

STEP TWO Starting point and category range
page 10 Having determined the category, the court should use the corresponding starting points to reach a sentence within the category range below. The starting point applies to all offenders irrespective of plea or previous convictions. A case of particular gravity, reflected by multiple features of culpability or harm in step one, could merit upward adjustment from the starting point before further adjustment for aggravating or mitigating features, set out on the next page.

Not in force from 1 July 2016

Offence category	Starting point (applicable to all offenders)	Category range (applicable to all offenders)
Category 1	Medium-level community order	Band C fine to 6 months' custody
Category 2	Band B fine	Band A fine to low-level community order
Category 3	Band A fine	Discharge to band B fine

For the meaning of a medium-level and a low-level community order see **16.12-16.13** in Volume 1.

243.7   [Aggravating and mitigating factors]

page 11 The table below contains a **non-exhaustive** list of additional factual elements providing the context of the offence and factors relating to the offender. Identify whether any combination of these, or other relevant factors, should result in an upward or downward adjustment from the starting point. In some cases, having considered these factors, it may be appropriate to move outside the identified category range.

When sentencing **Category 1** offences, the court should also consider the custody threshold as follows:

Has the custody threshold been passed?

If so, is it unavoidable that a custodial sentence be imposed?

If so, can that sentence be suspended?

When sentencing **Category 1 and 2** offences, the court should also consider the community order threshold as follows:

Has the community order threshold been passed?

Factors increasing seriousness
Statutory aggravating factors:
Previous convictions, having regard to a) the nature of the offence to which the conviction relates and its relevance to the current offence; and b) the time that has elapsed since the conviction
Offence committed whilst on bail
Other aggravating factors include:
Location of the offence
Ongoing effect upon the victim and/or others
Failure to take adequate precautions to prevent dog escaping
Allowing person insufficiently experienced or trained to be in charge of dog
Ill-treatment or failure to ensure welfare needs of dog, where not charged separately
Dog known to be prohibited
Lack or loss of control of dog due to the influence of alcohol or drugs
Offence committed against those working in the public sector or providing a service to the public
Established evidence of community impact
Failure to comply with current court orders
Offence committed whilst on licence

Factors reducing seriousness or reflecting personal mitigation
No previous convictions or no relevant/recent convictions
Isolated incident
No previous complaints against, or incidents involving, the dog
Remorse
Good character and/or exemplary conduct
Evidence of responsible ownership
Determination and/or demonstration of steps taken to address addiction or offending behaviour
Serious medical conditions requiring urgent, intensive or long-term treatment
Age and/or lack of maturity where it affects the responsibility of the offender
Mental disorder or learning disability, where not linked to the commission of the offence
Sole or primary carer for dependent relatives

Not in force from 1 July 2016

Not in force from 1 July 2016

Compensation and ancillary orders
page 12 In all cases, the court should consider whether to make a compensation order and/or other ancillary orders.
Compensation order
The court should consider compensation orders in all cases where personal injury, loss or damage has resulted from the offence.[295] The court must give reasons if it decides not to award compensation in such cases.
Other ancillary orders available include:
Disqualification from having custody of a dog
The court may disqualify the offender from having custody of a dog.[296] The test the court should consider is whether the offender is a fit and proper person to have custody of a dog.
Destruction order/contingent destruction order
In any case where the offender is not the owner of the dog, the owner must be given an opportunity to be present and make representations to the court.
The court may make a destruction order.[297] Alternatively, it may make a contingent destruction order imposing certain available conditions.[298] A contingent destruction order should specify the measures to be taken by the owner for keeping the dog under proper control, which include:
Muzzling, keeping on a lead, neutering in appropriate cases; and excluding it from a specified place.[299]
In reaching a decision, the court should consider the relevant circumstances which include:
the incident – what degree of harm was caused by the dog's behaviour?
past behaviour of the dog – is this an isolated incident or have there been previous warnings or incidents? and
owner's character – is the owner a fit and proper person to own this particular dog?
Where the court makes a destruction order, it may order the offender to pay what it determines to be the reasonable expenses of destroying the dog and of keeping it pending its destruction.[300]

243.8   *Possession [of dangerous dogs]   Sentencing Council guideline*
Dangerous Dog Offences Guideline 2012, see www.banksr.com Other Matters Guidelines tab
page 15 1 Possession of a prohibited dog, Dangerous Dogs Act 1991 s 1(3)
2 Breeding, selling, exchanging or advertising a prohibited dog, Dangerous Dogs Act 1991 s 1(2)

STEP ONE Determining the offence category
page 16 The court should determine the offence category using the table below.

Category 1	Greater harm and higher culpability
Category 2	Greater harm and lower culpability or lesser harm and higher culpability
Category 3	Lesser harm and lower culpability

page 16 The court should determine culpability and harm caused or intended, by reference **only** to the factors below, which comprise the principal factual elements of the offence. Where an offence does not fall squarely into a category, individual factors may require a degree of weighting before making an overall assessment and determining the appropriate offence category.

---

[295] Powers of Criminal Courts (Sentencing) Act 2000 s 130
[296] Dangerous Dogs Act 1991 s 4(1)(b)
[297] Dangerous Dogs Act 1991 s 4(1)(a)
[298] Dangerous Dogs Act 1991 s 4A(4)
[299] Dangerous Dogs Act 1991 s 4A(5)
[300] Dangerous Dogs Act 1991 s 4(4)(b)

Not in force from 1 July 2016

Factors indicating greater harm
Injury to person
Injury to another animal(s)

Factors indicating higher culpability
Possessing a dog known to be prohibited
Breeding from a dog known to be prohibited
Selling, exchanging or advertising a dog known to be prohibited
Offence committed for gain
Dog used to threaten or intimidate
Permitting fighting
Training and/or possession of paraphernalia for dog fighting

243.9

STEP TWO Starting point and category range

page 16 Having determined the category, the court should use the corresponding starting points to reach a sentence within the category range below. The starting point applies to all offenders irrespective of plea or previous convictions. A case of particular gravity, reflected by multiple features of culpability or harm in step one, could merit upward adjustment from the starting point before further adjustment for aggravating or mitigating features, set out on the next page.

Offence Category	Starting point (applicable to all offenders)	Category range (applicable to all offenders)
Category 1	Medium-level community order	Band C fine to 6 months' custody[301]
Category 2	Band C fine	Band A fine to medium-level community order
Category 3	Band A fine	Discharge to band B fine

For the meaning of a medium-level community order see **16.13** in Volume 1.

243.10   [Aggravating and mitigating factors]

page 17 The table below contains a **non-exhaustive** list of additional factual elements providing the context of the offence and factors relating to the offender. Identify whether any combination of these, or other relevant factors, should result in an upward or downward adjustment from the starting point. In some cases, having considered these factors, it may be appropriate to move outside the identified category range.

When sentencing **Category 1** offences, the court should also consider the custody threshold as follows:

   Has the custody threshold been passed?

   If so, is it unavoidable that a custodial sentence be imposed?

   If so, can that sentence be suspended?

When sentencing **Category 1 or 2** offences, the court should also consider the community order threshold as follows:

   Has the community order threshold been passed?

Factors increasing seriousness
Statutory aggravating factors:
Previous convictions, having regard to a) the nature of the offence to which the conviction relates and its relevance to the current offence; and b) the time that has elapsed since the conviction
Offence committed whilst on bail

Not in force from 1 July 2016

---

[301] Imprisonment is not available if the provisions of Dangerous Dogs Act 1991 s 1(7) apply.

> ***Other aggravating factors include:***
> Presence of children or others who are vulnerable because of personal circumstances
> Ill-treatment or failure to ensure welfare needs of dog, where not charged separately
> Established evidence of community impact
> Failure to comply with current court orders
> Offence committed whilst on licence

> **Factors reducing seriousness or reflecting personal mitigation**

> No previous convictions or no relevant/recent convictions
> Unaware that dog was prohibited type despite reasonable efforts to identify type
> Evidence of safety or control measures having been taken by owner
> Prosecution results from owner notification
> Remorse
> Good character and/or exemplary conduct
> Evidence of responsible ownership
> Determination and/or demonstration of steps taken to address addiction or offending behaviour
> Serious medical conditions requiring urgent, intensive or long-term treatment
> Age and/or lack of maturity where it affects the responsibility of the offender
> Lapse of time since the offence where this is not the fault of the offender
> Mental disorder or learning disability
> Sole or primary carer for dependent relatives

Ancillary orders

page 18 In all cases, the court should consider whether to make any ancillary orders.

Ancillary orders available include:

Disqualification from having custody of a dog

The court may disqualify the offender from having custody of a dog.[302] The test the court should consider is whether the offender is a fit and proper person to have custody of a dog.

Destruction order/contingent destruction order

The court shall make a destruction order unless the court is satisfied that the dog would not constitute a danger to public safety.[303]

In reaching a decision, the court should consider the relevant circumstances which include:

> danger to the public – what is the potential risk of harm posed by the dog?
> behaviour of the dog – have there been any warnings or incidents involving the dog? and
> owner's character – is the owner a fit and proper person to own this particular dog?

If the court does not make a destruction order, the court shall make a contingent destruction order providing that unless the dog is exempted from the prohibition within two months it shall be destroyed.[304] Statutory procedures and conditions automatically apply to exempted dogs and no other conditions can be imposed.[305] Where the offender is the owner of the dog, it would not normally be appropriate to make a contingent destruction order in conjunction with a disqualification order.

Furthermore, the court must not transfer ownership of the dog to another.[306]

Where the court makes a destruction order, it may order the offender to pay what it determines to be the reasonable expenses of destroying the dog and of keeping it pending its destruction.[307]

---

[302] Dangerous Dogs Act 1991 s 4(1)(b)
[303] Dangerous Dogs Act 1991 s 4(1)(a)
[304] Dangerous Dogs Act 1991 s 4A(1)
[305] Dangerous Dogs Compensation and Exemption Schemes Order 1991 1991/1744 (as amended by Dangerous Dogs Compensation and Exemption Schemes (Amendment) Order 1991 1991/2297)
[306] Dangerous Dogs Act 1991 s 1(2)(b)
[307] Dangerous Dogs Act 1991 s 4(4)(b)

243.11 Sentencing Council guideline (in force 1 July 2016)
As the book was being sent to print, this guideline was published. The details are on www.banksr.com Other matters Guidelines.

243.12   Aggravated offences (Person(s) injured) Statute and judicial guidance
Dangerous Dogs Act 1991 s 3(1) and (3)
R v Cox 2004 EWCA Crim 282, 2 Cr App R (S) 54 (p 287) LCJ Parliament has demonstrated by the penalties the clearest intention that the courts should in no small measure look at the consequences of the offence when determining the penalty. An analogy can be seen with dangerous driving.

243.13   Aggravated offences (Person(s) injured) Cases
R v Richards 2008 EWCA Crim 1427, 2009 1 Cr App R (S) 48 (p 264) D pleaded at the Magistrates' Court to two counts of being the owner of a dog which was dangerously out of control, in the aggravated form because of injuries to a member of the public, Dangerous Dogs Act 1991 s 3(1)(d). D had two pit-bull type dogs, male and female, which he kept in a yard at the back of his house. The male was the more aggressive. The local postman, V, spoke to D about the dogs, which were trying to jump the fence to get at him. D promised to chain them. V's supervisors also wrote to D about the dogs. The neighbours had also complained to the Housing Association about the dogs and a letter had been sent to D's partner about them. The female dog pushed her way through a gap in the fence in the yard and followed V. The male dog joined her and they went straight for V, barking and growling and lunging at him. He jumped into a garden where they couldn't get at him and he went through other gardens until he thought it was safe to continue his deliveries. The dogs again appeared and attacked him, one on each leg, gripping him and shaking him. They pulled him to the ground and dragged him. He was in great pain and screaming. Other people tried to make the dogs desist, including by attacking them with a hammer and metal bar, but they continued to tear at V's leg. The attack lasted about 15 minutes. Eventually the dogs released him. The female dog was never found. V had open wounds on his leg and arm. He spent six days in hospital and had two operations, one involving skin grafts. He had deep lacerations to both legs, his right knee and right forearm, and puncture wounds to his chest. He needed physiotherapy and was told it would be at least six weeks before he could walk properly. He would be permanently scarred. D was aroused from his bed at about 11.15 am that day and confirmed that the dogs were his and should have been in the yard. In interview he admitted the dogs were his and said that they had not attacked anyone before but they had had fights with other dogs in the park. He said he could not chain them all the time because the RSPCA would object. He had put bins in front of the gap in the fence. He had never knowingly let the dogs out onto the public road. He consented to them both being destroyed. D, aged 19, had no relevant previous convictions. A pre-sentence report spoke of his genuine and deep remorse. Held. An important factor in sentencing for the aggravated form of this offence is the nature of the consequences to the person injured. In this case those were serious. Given D's mitigation and pleas, **4 months' detention** not 9.
R v Lee 2009 EWCA Crim 2046, 2010 1 Cr App R (S) 94 (p 600) D pleaded to two counts of allowing a dog to enter a place and injure. In April, D acquired two pit-bull terriers which lived in his rear garden. In October one of them entered V's garden and killed one of V's cats. V became scared of the dogs and stayed out of her garden. On Boxing Day, at about 2.30 am, V heard noises from her garden and saw one of V's dogs with her cat in his mouth. She went into the garden with a broom and one of the dogs bit her and dragged her to the ground. V thought she would be killed. Eventually the dog backed off. A police officer heard the screams and found V bleeding heavily. Her upper arm flesh had been torn exposing her biceps muscle. She needed a skin graft and was in hospital for four days. D was aged 21. The Judge said: a) V had been almost a prisoner

in her house because of the vicious dogs, b) there was a gross failure to ensure the dogs were restrained and c) the October incident had been a warning in the clearest possible terms. **6 months** not 10.

R v Shallow 2011 EWCA Crim 1443, 2012 1 Cr App R (S) 33 (p 197) D pleaded to owning a dog which caused injury whilst dangerously out of control in a public place. A nine-year-old girl, V, and her friend were cycling near some shops when they saw D's dog, a Staffordshire bull terrier. The dog was loosely muzzled, allowing it to open its jaw. The dog ran in front of her, causing her to swerve. V may have collided with the dog. She fell off her bike and the dog bit her on the thigh. It held on to her for about 30 seconds, causing a nasty gash. Someone grabbed the dog and took it away. V suffered scarring around her knee. The wounds were treated by bandages and sterile strips. The dog later caught a virus and died. D had previously had concerns about the dog's temperament and suspected it might be a Staffordshire pit-bull cross-breed. D showed contrition. D, aged 40, was of good character. Held. Because of the previous concerns regarding the dog's temperament, the custody threshold was passed. A Suspended Sentence Order was appropriate, but the custodial element did not have to be 12 weeks. **6 weeks** suspended with 150 hours' unpaid work was appropriate.

See also: *R v Murphy* 2013 EWCA Crim 433, 2 Cr App R (S) 70 (p 448) (Plea. Drunk owner in charge of very dangerous dog which killed another dog and bit its 83-year-old owner. A custodial sentence was appropriate, so **6 months suspended** with 6-month curfew requirement upheld.)

244   DOMESTIC VIOLENCE

244.1

This can be charged under a wide variety of offences.

For paragraphs in this book about domestic violence, see **Domestic violence** and **Relationship offences/attacks** entry in the back index.

Domestic violence protection order A police officer with a rank not below a superintendent may apply to the Magistrates' Court for a Domestic violence protection notice against an adult aged 18+ when certain conditions are met, Crime and Security Act 2010 s 24. The procedure is laid down in Crime and Security Act 2010 s 24-32.

244.2   *Sentencing Guidelines Council guideline*

Domestic Violence Guideline 2006, see www.banksr.com Other Matters Guidelines tab

A   Definition of domestic violence

page 3 para 1.1   There is no specific offence of domestic violence and conduct amounting to domestic violence is covered by a number of statutory provisions. For the purposes of this guideline, wherever such offending occurs, domestic violence is: 'Any incident of threatening behaviour, violence or abuse (psychological, physical, sexual, financial or emotional) between adults who are or have been intimate partners or family members, regardless of gender or sexuality'.[308]

para 1.2   Most incidents of domestic violence can be charged as one of a wide range of offences including physical assault (with or without a weapon), harassment, threats to cause injury or to kill, destroying or damaging property, false imprisonment (locking the victim in a room or preventing that person from leaving the house), and sexual offences.

para 1.3   Under the above definition, the domestic context includes relationships involving intimate partners who are living together, intimate partners who do not live together and former intimate partners. It is also wide enough to include relationships between family members, for example between a father and a daughter, or a mother and a daughter, perhaps where the daughter is the mother's carer.

---

[308] This is the Government's definition of domestic violence agreed in 2004. It is taken from *Policy on Prosecuting Cases of Domestic Violence*, CPS, 2005.

B Assessing seriousness

para 2.1   As a starting point for sentence, offences committed in a domestic context should be regarded as being no less serious than offences committed in a non-domestic context.

C Aggravating and mitigating factors

para 3.1   The history of the relationship will often be relevant in assessing the gravity of the offence. Therefore, a court is entitled to take into account anything occurring within the relationship as a whole, which may reveal relevant aggravating or mitigating factors.

para 3.2   The following aggravating and mitigating factors (which are not intended to be exhaustive) are of particular relevance to offences committed in a domestic context, and should be read alongside the general factors set out in the *Overarching Principles: Seriousness Guideline 2004*.

Aggravating factors

   i) *Abuse of trust and abuse of power*

para 3.3   The *Overarching Principles: Seriousness Guideline 2004* identifies abuse of a position of trust and abuse of power as factors that indicate higher culpability. Within the nature of relationship required to meet the definition of domestic violence set out above, trust implies a mutual expectation of conduct that shows consideration, honesty, care and responsibility. In some such relationships, one of the parties will have the power to exert considerable control over the other.

para 3.4   In the context of domestic violence: a) an abuse of trust, whether through direct violence or emotional abuse, represents a violation of this understanding, b) an abuse of power in a relationship involves restricting another individual's autonomy which is sometimes a specific characteristic of domestic violence. This involves the exercise of control over an individual by means which may be psychological, physical, sexual, financial or emotional.

para 3.5   Where an abuse of trust or abuse of power is present, it will aggravate the seriousness of an offence. These factors are likely to exist in many offences of violence within a domestic context.

para 3.6   However, the breadth of the definition of domestic violence (set out in 1.1 above) encompasses offences committed by a former spouse or partner. Accordingly, there will be circumstances where the abuse of trust or abuse of power may be a very minor feature of an offence or may be deemed no longer to exist – for example, where the offender and victim have been separated for a long period of time.

   ii) *Victim is particularly vulnerable*

para 3.7   For cultural, religious, language, financial or any other reasons, some victims of domestic violence may be more vulnerable than others, not least because these issues may make it almost impossible for the victim to leave a violent relationship.

para 3.8   Where a perpetrator has exploited a victim's vulnerability (for instance, when the circumstances have been used by the perpetrator to prevent the victim from seeking and obtaining help), an offence will warrant a higher penalty.

para 3.9   Age, disability or the fact that the victim was pregnant or had recently given birth at the time of the offence may make a victim particularly vulnerable.

para 3.10 Any steps taken to prevent the victim reporting an incident or obtaining assistance will usually aggravate the offence.

   iii) *Impact on children*

page 5 para 3.11   Exposure of children to an offence (either directly or indirectly) is an aggravating factor.

para 3.12   Children are likely to be adversely affected by directly witnessing violence or other abuse and by being aware of it taking place while they are elsewhere in the home.[309]

---

[309] The definition of 'harm' in Children Act 1989 s 31(9) as amended by Adoption and Children Act 2002 s 120 includes 'impairment suffered from seeing or hearing the ill-treatment of another'.

iv) *Using contact arrangements with a child to instigate an offence*

para 3.13   An offence will be aggravated where an offender exploits contact arrangements with a child in order to commit an offence.

v) *A proven history of violence or threats by the offender in a domestic setting*

para 3.14   It is important that an assessment of the seriousness of an offence recognises
the cumulative effect of a series of violent incidents or threats over a prolonged period,
where such conduct has been proved or accepted.

para 3.15   Where an offender has previously been convicted of an offence involving
domestic violence either against the same or a different partner, this is likely to be a
statutory aggravating factor.[310]

vi) *A history of disobedience to court orders*

para 3.16   A breach of an order that has been imposed for the purpose of protecting a
victim can cause significant harm or anxiety. Where an offender's history of disobedience has had this effect, it will be an aggravating factor.

para 3.17   Commission of the offence in breach of a Non-molestation Order imposed in
civil proceedings, in breach of a sentence (such as a conditional discharge) imposed for
similar offending, or while subject to an ancillary order, such as a Restraining Order, will
aggravate the seriousness of the offence.

para 3.18   The appropriate response to breach of a civil order is dealt with in the *Breach
of a Protective Order Guideline 2006.*

vii) *Victim forced to leave home*

para 3.19   An offence will be aggravated if, as a consequence, the victim is forced to
leave home.

244.3   *Mitigating factors*

i) *Positive good character*

para 3.20   As a general principle of sentencing, a court will take account of an
offender's positive good character. However, it is recognised that one of the factors that
can allow domestic violence to continue unnoticed for lengthy periods is the ability of
the perpetrator to have two personae. In respect of an offence of violence in a domestic
context, an offender's good character in relation to conduct outside the home should
generally be of no relevance where there is a proven pattern of behaviour.

para 3.21   Positive good character is of greater relevance in the rare case where the
court is satisfied that the offence was an isolated incident.

ii) *Provocation*

para 3.22   It may be asserted that the offence, at least in part, has been provoked by the
conduct of the victim. Such assertions need to be treated with great care, both in
determining whether they have a factual basis and in considering whether in the
circumstances the alleged conduct amounts to provocation sufficient to mitigate the
seriousness of the offence.

para 3.23   For provocation to be a mitigating factor, it will usually involve actual or
anticipated violence including psychological bullying. Provocation is likely to have
more of an effect as mitigation if it has taken place over a significant period of time.

D Other factors influencing sentence

Wishes of the victim and effect of the sentence

para 4.1   As a matter of general principle, a sentence imposed for an offence of
violence should be determined by the seriousness of the offence, not by the expressed
wishes of the victim.

para 4.2   There are a number of reasons why it may be particularly important that this
principle is observed in a case of domestic violence: a) it is undesirable that a victim
should feel a responsibility for the sentence imposed, b) there is a risk that a plea for

---

[310] Criminal Justice Act 2003 s 143(2)

mercy made by a victim will be induced by threats made by, or by a fear of, the offender, c) the risk of such threats will be increased if it is generally believed that the severity of the sentence may be affected by the wishes of the victim.

para 4.3   Nonetheless, there may be circumstances in which the court can properly mitigate a sentence to give effect to the expressed wish of the victim that the relationship be permitted to continue. The court must, however, be confident that such a wish is genuine, and that giving effect to it will not expose the victim to a real risk of further violence. Critical conditions are likely to be the seriousness of the offence and the history of the relationship. It is vitally important that the court has up-to-date information in a pre-sentence report and victim personal statement.

para 4.4   Either the offender or the victim (or both) may ask the court to take into consideration the interests of any children and to impose a less severe sentence. The court will wish to have regard not only to the effect on the children if the relationship is disrupted but also to the likely effect on the children of any further incidents of domestic violence.

E Factors to take into consideration
page 7 The following points of principle should be considered by a court when imposing sentence for any offence of violence committed in a domestic context.

1   Offences committed in a domestic context should be regarded as being no less serious than offences committed in a non-domestic context.

2   Many offences of violence in a domestic context are dealt with in a Magistrates' Court as an offence of common assault or assault occasioning actual bodily harm because the injuries sustained are relatively minor. Offences involving serious violence will warrant a custodial sentence in the majority of cases.

3   Some offences will be specified offences for the purposes of the dangerous offender provisions.[311] In such circumstances, consideration will need to be given to whether there is a significant risk of serious harm to members of the public, which include, of course, family members. If so, the court will be required to impose a life sentence or an extended sentence.[312]

4   Where the custody threshold is only just crossed, so that if a custodial sentence is imposed it will be a short sentence, the court will wish to consider whether the better option is a suspended sentence order or a community order, including in either case a requirement to attend an accredited domestic violence programme. Such an option will only be appropriate where the court is satisfied that the offender genuinely intends to reform his or her behaviour and that there is a real prospect of rehabilitation being successful. Such a situation is unlikely to arise where there has been a pattern of abuse. See also the **Relationship offences/attacks** entry in the back index.

245   DRINK/DRUG DRIVING
(including alcohol etc. offences when performing a prescribed duty)
245.1
Road Traffic Act 1988 s 4-5A
For the modes of trial and the maximum sentences, see **245.4** and **245.7**.
Driving/being in charge under the influence of drugs Crime and Courts Act 2013 s 56 created new offences by inserting Road Traffic Act 1988 s 5A. The offences are to drive or attempt to drive or be in charge of a motor vehicle when there is in [the driver's] body a specified controlled drug exceeding the specified limit. The offences are triable summarily only and have the same penalties as drink/driving. In force 2 March 2015.[313]
Courses for drink/drive offences For defendants convicted of Road Traffic Act 1988 s 4 or 5 offences, there is power to order reduced disqualification for attendance on

---

[311] Criminal Justice Act 2003 Part 12
[312] 'Imprisonment for Public Protection' has been removed as the order has been repealed. Ed.
[313] Crime and Courts Act 2013 (Commencement No 1) (England and Wales) Order 2014 2014/3268

courses.[314] On 24 June 2013, Road Safety Act 2006 changes came into force. For details see the **Disqualification from Driving: Obligatory** *Reduced periods of disqualification for attendance on courses* para at **44.8** in Volume 1.

Depriving defendant of vehicle used For both drink/driving and drug/driving offences, there is a power.[315]

Reduced periods of disqualification for attendance on courses There is a power to order reduced periods of disqualification where the offender completes a course, see the **Disqualification from Driving: Obligatory** *Reduced periods of disqualification for attendance on courses* para at **44.8** in Volume 1.

Football Banning Orders Road Traffic Act 1988 s 4-5A are relevant offences under Football Spectators Act 1989 s 14A and Sch 1 para 1. Where: a) the offence was committed during a journey, b) the court makes a declaration that the offence related to football matches, and c) there are reasonable grounds to believe that making a banning order would help to prevent violence or disorder at or in connection with any regulated football match, the court must make a Football Banning Order (except where the defendant is given an absolute discharge).

High-risk offenders Where a defendant has been disqualified for being 2½ or more times over the alcohol limit, or has two or more disqualifications for drink/driving within 10 years or has a disqualification for failure to provide a specimen[316] he or she will be classified by the DVLA as a high-risk offender. Offenders will be treated as persons potentially suffering from a disability requiring medical investigation.[317] Road Safety Act 2006 s 13 provides that high-risk offenders be denied 'cover to drive' under Road Traffic Act 1988 s 88. Licences will only be returned when they have completed the medical review procedure. Road Safety Act 2006 s 15 also introduced a new power to make an alcohol ignition interlock programme order.[318] This is unlikely to ever be in force.

For Passenger Carrying Vehicles (PCV) and Large Goods Vehicles (LGV) drivers, see **341.1**.

Report In June 2010, Sir Peter North issued his report to the Department of Transport about drink/driving and drug/driving, see www.banksr.com The report made 51 recommendations including that a) the drink/driving limits should be reduced, b) there should not be lower limits for HGV, PSV, taxi drivers or young or novice drivers, c) there should be an unrestricted power to demand a preliminary breath test, d) there should be no requirement for a preliminary breath test before an evidential breath test, e) there should be specified limits for a list of prohibited drugs, and f) the laboratory allowance for blood and urine tests should be reduced to 3%. Except for the driving when under the influence of drugs, there appear to be no other changes made as a result of the report. (I consider that is a pity as the recommendations would have been likely to reduce accidents. Ed.)

The chapter is divided into four subsections: a) General matters, b) Excess alcohol or drugs/Driving etc. when unfit, c) In charge and d) Servicemen and women.

See also the **Failing to Provide a Specimen** chapter.

General matters

245.2   *Drink/drive and drug/drive prescribed limits*

Drink/driving: Prescribed limits

---

[314]

[315] (6)-(7). See paras **64.4-64.11** in Volume 1.

[316] Motor Vehicles (Driving Licences) Regulations 1999 1999/2864 reg 74(1)

[317] Motor Vehicles (Driving Licences) Regulations 1999 1999/2864 reg 74(1)

[318] inserted by Road Safety Act 2006 s 15

	Breath µg (micrograms)	Blood mg (milligrams)	Urine mg (milligrams)
Magistrates' Court England and Wales	35	80	107
Scotland from 5/12/14	22	50	67
Service personnel performing a regulated duty, see **245.9** — Reg 4 duty	35	80	107
Service personnel performing a regulated duty, see **245.9** — Reg 5 duty	9	20	27

Drug/driving: Prescribed limits

Drug Driving (Specified Limits) (England and Wales) Regulations 2014 2014/2868 para 2

	Blood µg (micrograms)
Amphetamine[319]	250
Benzoylecgonine [the human body converts cocaine into this]	50
Clonazepam	50
Cocaine	10
Delta-9-tetrahydrocannabinol [the main active ingredient in cannabis]	2
Diazepam	550
Flunitrazepam [commonly known as Rohypnol]	300
Ketamine	20
Lorazepam	100
Lysergic acid diethylamide [commonly known as LSD]	1
Methadone	500
Methylamphetamine [commonly known as amphetamine]	10
Methylenedioxymethamphetamine [commonly known as ecstasy]	10
6-Monoacetylmorphine [the human body converts heroin into this and morphine]	5
Morphine	80
Oxazepam	300
Temazepam	1,000

245.3   *Test avoided   Is disqualification appropriate?*
R v Waring 2005 EWCA Crim 1080, 2006 1 Cr App R (S) 9 (p 56) D pleaded to escaping from lawful custody. He was stopped by a police officer for speeding and took a roadside breath test, which was positive. He was then arrested. His passenger became abusive and was also arrested. In the car on the way to the police station the passenger behaved badly and the arresting officer stopped the car to handcuff him. While she did this D ran off. D was arrested at home the following day and so had avoided taking an intoximeter test at the police station. He had a bad driving record and had previously been disqualified for

---

[319] Added by Drug Driving (Specified Limits) (England and Wales) (Amendment) Regulations 2015 2015/911. In force 14/04/15

3 years for driving with excess alcohol. Held. The Judge was right to ensure that D got no possible benefit from escaping and avoiding a breath test. **18 months'** disqualification upheld (4 months' imprisonment not appealed).

Note: The report does not reveal whether D would have been liable to a 3-year ban for a second drink/driving conviction in 10 years, if there had been a positive breath test. Ed.

Excess alcohol or drugs, Driving when unfit

245.4   *Excess alcohol or drugs, Driving when unfit*

Road Traffic Act 1988 s 4(1) and 5(1)(a) (drink/driving)

Road Traffic Act 1988 s 5A(1)(a) and 5A(2) (drug/driving)

Modes of trial Summary only

Maximum sentences 6 months[320] and/or a Level 5 fine (a £5,000 fine for offences committed before 12 March 2015 and an unlimited fine thereafter.[321] There are maximum fines for those aged under 18, see **14.38** in Volume 1.)

Disqualification and penalty points Minimum disqualification 1 year, or 3-11 penalty points, if special reasons not to disqualify are found. Where a defendant has a conviction for driving while unfit, causing death under the influence of drink, driving with excess alcohol and failing to provide a specimen 10 years prior to the date of the new offence, the minimum disqualification is 3 years.[322]

Driving under the influence of drugs Crime and Courts Act 2013 s 56 created a new offence by inserting Road Traffic Act 1988 s 5A. The offence is to drive or attempt to drive a motor vehicle when there is in [the driver's] body a specified controlled drug exceeding the specified limit. The offence is triable summarily only and has the same penalties as drink/driving offences. In force 2 March 2015

The Drug Driving (Specified Limits) (England and Wales) Regulations 2014 2014/2868 lay down the number of micrograms per litre of blood to be over the limit, see **245.2**.

For drink/driving offences, there is power to order reduced disqualification for attendance on courses, Road Traffic Offenders Act 1988 s 34A. For details see the DISQUALIFICATION FROM DRIVING: OBLIGATORY *Reduced periods of disqualification for attendance on courses* para at **44.8** in Volume 1.

245.5   *Magistrates' Court Sentencing Guidelines*

Magistrates' Court Sentencing Guidelines 2008, see www.banksr.com Other Matters Guidelines tab and page 124 (the Excess Alcohol guideline) and page 132 (the Unfit to Drive guideline). Ed.

The guidelines apply to the Magistrates' Court and to the Crown Court hearing appeals or sentencing for summary only offences.[323]

page 124 [Explanatory] note re final column below: the period to be imposed in any individual case will depend on an assessment of all the relevant circumstances, including the length of time since the earlier ban and the gravity of the current offence.

Note: The first three columns are taken from the Excess Alcohol guideline and the fourth column is taken from the Unfit to Drive guideline and the last four columns are common to both guidelines. Ed.

---

[320] Although '51 weeks' is listed as the penalty for the drug/driving offence in Road Traffic Offenders Act 1988 Sch 2, that should be read with Crime and Courts Act 2013 s 56(5), which says that until Criminal Justice Act 2003 s 281(5) is in force, the penalty is 6 months.

[321] Legal Aid, Sentencing and Punishment of Offenders Act 2012 s 85(1) and (4) and Legal Aid, Sentencing and Punishment of Offenders Act 2012 (Commencement No 11) Order 2015 2015/504

[322] Road Traffic Offenders Act 1988 s 34(3)

[323] See page 15 of the guidelines.

Level of alcohol			Examples of nature of activity (unfit cases)	Start-ing point	Range	Disqualifica-tion	Disqualification Second offence in 10 years, see note above
Breath µg	Blood mg	Urine mg					
36-59	81-137	108-183	Evidence of moderate level of impairment and no aggravating factors	Band C fine	Band C fine	12-16 months	36-40 months
60-89	138-206	184-274	Evidence of moderate level of impairment and presence of one or more aggravating factors listed below	Band C fine	Band C fine	17-22 months	36-46 months
90-119	207-275	275-366	Evidence of high level of impairment and no aggravating factors	Medium-level commu-nity order	Low-level to high-level commu-nity order	23-28 months	36-52 months
120-150 and above	276-345 and above	367-459 and above	Evidence of high level of impairment and presence of one or more aggravating factors	12 weeks' custody	High-level commu-nity order to 26 weeks' custody	29-36 months	36-60 months

Factors indicating higher culpability: 1 LGV, HGV, PSV etc. 2 Poor road or weather conditions 3 Carrying passengers 4 Driving for hire or reward 5 Evidence of unacceptable standard of driving. Factors indicating greater degree of harm: 1 Involved in accident 2 Location e.g. near school 3 High level of traffic or pedestrians in the vicinity. Factors indicating lower culpability:[324] 1 Genuine emergency established 2 Spiked drinks 3 Very short distance driven.

Consider offering drink/driving rehabilitation course and ancillary orders.

R v St Albans Crown Court ex parte O'Donovan 2000 1 Cr App R (S) 344. The defendant was convicted of driving with excess alcohol. The guidelines only apply where there are no special reasons. For more details, see below.

Consultation It is expected that the Sentencing Council will issue a consultation document about updating this guideline in May 2016.

245.6   *Disqualification for how long?*

R v St Albans Crown Court ex parte O'Donovan 2000 1 Cr App R (S) 344 D was convicted of driving with excess alcohol. D's car was partially blocking a service gate in a pub car park. D was moving his car to assist. He bumped another car and had 103 mg of alcohol in his blood. The prosecution accepted that he lived 5 minutes' walk away and he was not going to drive out of the car park, but was simply moving his car to attempt to clear the access to the rear of the pub. D was aged 39 with no relevant convictions. He was a forklift driver on building sites and his loss of job affected his ex-wife and two daughters whom he supported. He was sentenced to **£750 fine** and 20 months' disqualification with a 5-month reduction for going on a course. He appealed to the Crown Court, who dismissed his appeal. Each court found special reasons. The Crown Court relied on the *Magistrates' Court Sentencing Guidelines 2008*. Held. It would be

---

[324] Even where not amounting to special reasons.

hard to justify disqualification of more than 12 months. The guidelines only apply where there are no special reasons. The disqualification was reduced to **12 months** with a 3-month reduction for going on a course.

In charge

245.7   *In charge*
Road Traffic Act 1988 s 4(2), 5(1)(b) and 7(6) (drink/driving)
Road Traffic Act 1988 s 4(2), 5A(1)(b) and 5A(2) (drug/driving)
   Modes of trial Summary only
   Maximum sentences 3 months and/or Level 4 fine (£2,500)[325]
   Disqualification Discretionary
   Endorsement Mandatory, unless there are special reasons
   Penalty points 10
Being in charge under the influence of drugs Crime and Courts Act 2013 s 56 created the new offence by inserting Road Traffic Act 1988 s 5A. The offence is being in charge of a motor vehicle when there is in [the driver's] body a specified controlled drug exceeding the specified limit. In force 2 March 2015
For the prescribed limits, see **245.2**.
For drink/driving offences, there is a power to order reduced disqualification for attendance on courses, Road Traffic Offenders Act 1988 s 34A. For details see the **DISQUALIFICATION FROM DRIVING: OBLIGATORY** *Reduced periods of disqualification for attendance on courses* para at **44.8** in Volume 1.

245.8   *Magistrates' Court Sentencing Guidelines*
Magistrates' Court Sentencing Guidelines 2008, see www.banksr.com Other Matters Guidelines tab page 126
page 126 Excess alcohol (in charge)

Level of alcohol			Starting point	Range
Breath **µg**	**Blood** **mg**	**Urine** **mg**[326]		
36-59	81-137	108-183	Band B fine	Band B fine [and] 10 points
60-89	138-206	184-274	Band B fine	Band B fine [and] 10 points or consider disqualification
90-119	207-275	275-366	Band C fine	Band C fine to medium-level community order Consider disqualification or 10 points
120-150 and above	276-345 and above	367-459 and above	Medium-level community order	Low-level community order to 6 weeks' custody 6-12 month disqualification

Unfit through drink or drugs

Examples of nature of activity	Starting point	Range
Evidence of moderate level of impairment and no aggravating factors	Band B fine	Band B fine [and] 10 points

---

[325] Although '51 weeks' is listed as the penalty for this offence in Road Traffic Offenders Act 1988 Sch 2, that should be read with Crime and Courts Act 2013 s 56(6), which says that until Criminal Justice Act 2003 s 280(2) is in force, the penalty is 3 months.
[326] The guideline says 'ml'. It should read 'mg' as printed.

Examples of nature of activity	Starting point	Range
Evidence of moderate level of impairment and presence of one or more aggravating factors listed below	Band B fine	Band B fine [and] 10 points or consider disqualification
Evidence of high level of impairment and no aggravating factors	Band C fine	Band C fine to medium-level community order [or] 10 points Consider disqualification
Evidence of high level of impairment and presence of one or more aggravating factors	High-level community order	Medium-level community order to 12 weeks' custody Consider disqualification or 10 points

The factors are the same for both tables.
Factors indicating higher culpability: 1 LGV, HGV, PSV etc. 2 High likelihood of driving 3 Driving for hire or reward. Factor indicating lower culpability: Low likelihood of driving.
Consider ancillary orders.
Bands B and C are 100% and 150% of net weekly income. For more detail, see **60.27** in Volume 1.
Consultation It is expected that the Sentencing Council will issue a consultation document about updating this guideline in May 2016.
For the meaning of a high-level, a medium-level and a low-level community order see **16.12-16.14** in Volume 1.

Servicemen and women
245.9   *Performing a prescribed duty etc. when proportion of alcohol above prescribed limit*
Armed Forces Act 2006 s 20A
(as inserted by Armed Forces Act 2011 s 10)
Performing a prescribed duty etc. when proportion of alcohol above prescribed limit
Maximum sentence Any punishment in the table in Armed Forces Act 2006 s 164 but not more than 2 years' imprisonment.
Prescribed limits There are two limits, set out in Armed Forces (Alcohol Limits for Prescribed Safety Critical Duties) Regulations 2013 2013/2787 Reg 4 and 5. For the limits, see **288.2**. An example of a Reg 4 duty is an officer afloat on one of HM's ships and an example of a Reg 5 duty is a pilot during a flight.
Disqualification and endorsement There is no power to do either.
Note: There is no corresponding offence relating to drugs rather than alcohol yet. Ed.

245.10   *Guidance*
Guidance on Sentencing in the Court Martial 2013 para 5.11.1 There is no power to impose penalty points or order a disqualification from driving.
para 5.11.3 The sentences for…alcohol over twice the limit…should be based on those in the Sentencing Council guidelines.
para 5.11.4 The suggested penalty is: a) when the level is under twice the limit, a fine of 28 days' pay and b) when the level is over twice the limit, 90 days' detention.

246   DRUNK
246.1
1) Criminal Justice Act 1967 s 91 (drunk and disorderly)
   Mode of trial Summary only
   Maximum sentence Level 3 fine (£1,000)[327]

---

[327] *R v Boughtwood* 2002 EWCA Crim 1948 A sentence of 1 day's imprisonment is unlawful.

2) Sporting Events (Control of Alcohol etc.) Act 1985 s 2(2) (being drunk at a designated sports ground)

Mode of trial Summary only

Maximum sentence Level 2 fine (£500)

Fixed penalties There is a £90 fixed penalty[328] for a) disorderly behaviour while drunk in a public place,[329] b) sale of alcohol to a person who is drunk,[330] c) sale of alcohol to persons under 18,[331] d) delivery of alcohol to persons under 18 or allowing such delivery,[332] and e) purchase of alcohol on behalf of persons under 18.[333]

There is a £60 fixed penalty[334] for a) being drunk in a highway, other public place or licensed premises,[335] b) purchase of alcohol by persons under 18 on relevant premises,[336] and c) consumption of alcohol by persons under 18 on relevant premises or allowing such consumption.[337] For more detail see **61.1** in Volume 1.

Football Banning Orders For both offences when they were committed relevant to a football match the court must make a Football Banning Order where there are reasonable grounds to believe that making a banning order would help to prevent violence or disorder at or in connection with any regulated football match under Football Spectators Act 1989 s 14A and Sch 1 para 1.

See also the **ALCOHOL SALE OFFENCES** and the **DRINK/DRUG DRIVING** chapters and the **AVIATION OFFENCES** *Drunk, Being* para at **213.3**.

246.2   *Magistrates' Court Sentencing Guidelines*

Magistrates' Court Sentencing Guidelines 2008, see www.banksr.com Other Matters Guidelines tab The guidelines apply to the Magistrates' Court and to the Crown Court hearing appeals or sentencing for summary only offences.[338]

page 55 Starting points are based on a first-time offender pleading not guilty.

Examples of nature of activity	Starting point	Range
Shouting, causing disturbance for some minutes	Band A fine	Conditional discharge to band B fine
Substantial disturbance caused	Band B fine	Band A fine to band C fine

The following aggravating and mitigating factors may be particularly relevant: Factors indicating higher culpability: 1 Offensive words or behaviour involved 2 Lengthy incident 3 Group action. Factors indicating lower culpability: 1 Minor and non-threatening 2 Stopped as soon as police arrived.

Factors indicating greater degree of harm: 1 Offence committed at school, hospital or other place where vulnerable persons may be present 2 Offence committed on public transport 3 Victim providing public service.

Consider ancillary orders, including compensation and Football Banning Order.

A Band A fine is 50% of net weekly income. Bands B and C are 100% and 150%. For more detail, see **60.27**.

Consultation It is expected that the Sentencing Council will issue a consultation document about updating this guideline in May 2016.

For details about the guidelines, see the **GUIDELINES** chapter in Volume 1.

---

[328] Penalties for Disorderly Behaviour (Amount of Penalty) Order 2002 2002/1837 as amended.
[329] Criminal Justice Act 1967 s 91
[330] Licensing Act 2003 s 141
[331] Licensing Act 2003 s 146(1) and (3)
[332] Licensing Act 2003 s 151
[333] Licensing Act 2003 s 149(3)-(4)
[334] Penalties for Disorderly Behaviour (Amount of Penalty) Order 2002 2002/1837 as amended
[335] Licensing Act 1872 s 12
[336] Licensing Act 2003 s 149(1)
[337] Licensing Act 2003 s 150
[338] See page 15 of the guidelines.

247 ELECTION OFFENCES

247.1

Representation of the People Act 1983 (various sections and penalties)

Law Commission On 4 February 2016, the Law Commission issued an extensive interim report on electoral law. It proposed a comprehensive overhaul of the law.

247.2 *Judicial guidance*

R v Hussain 2005 EWCA Crim 1866, 2006 1 Cr App R (S) 62 (p 336) LCJ D pleaded to conspiracy to defraud. Held. Among the most important features of the way of life is, first, the fact that this country is a democracy. It has a form of government based, subject to limited exceptions, on each individual member of the public being entitled to a single vote to elect the Government of the day, whether national or local. Every vote should be of equal value. The second feature is that, although we have no reason for complacency, the Government in this country (both national and local) is usually free from any form of corruption. The third feature is that the two principles are every bit as important in local government. If the electoral system is contaminated by corruption or fraud, it will be rendered worthless. It is the responsibility of the courts to protect the country's electoral system, to which the courts must attach the greatest of importance. The Government and the legislature have recognised the dangers that the reduced proportion of the population who vote has for our democratic form of government. Particularly in the case of local elections, the percentage of those who vote is worryingly small. The Government as a result extended greatly the availability of postal voting. The advantage is that there has been an increase in the percentage of those who vote. The disadvantage is that it is easier for the system to be corrupted and more difficult to bring to justice those responsible for activities that undermine the voting system. It is important that the punishment that was passed was one which would deter others from committing offences of that sort.

R v Khan and Others 2009 EWCA Crim 2483 LCJ The defendants pleaded or were convicted of conspiracy to defraud and other charges. They created ghost voters by using false addresses, false documents etc. such that the ghost voters enabled their candidate to become a councillor when without the ghost voters the candidate would have lost. Held. The vote is at the very heart of the democratic process. At the moment when each citizen places his vote into the ballot box or casts his vote by post, that is a moment when the right of each and every citizen is absolutely equal. A single falsified vote distorts our democratic process. When the voting system is corrupted, as it was here, to suggest that one man was chosen by the community to represent it, when he was not, and when the community chose a different person to represent it, that is a very serious matter indeed. If this fraud had not been discovered, power would have invested in an individual who was not elected. Such crimes deserve severe punishment.

247.3 *Cases*

R v Hussain 2005 EWCA Crim 1866, 2006 1 Cr App R (S) 62 (p 336) LCJ D pleaded on rearraignment to conspiracy to defraud which involved the widespread abuse of the postal voting system for a local election in which he stood as the Labour Party candidate. In 1999 he was defeated by 92 votes. In the election in 2002, he and others systematically collected from households postal votes before they were completed and completed them to indicate a vote in the applicant's favour at the election. He won by 685 votes. After the election, the police spoke to a number of householders and discovered that there were numerous instances of householders being visited by people who said that they had come to collect the postal votes. Incomplete voting documents were handed over. In one ward 233 postal votes had been submitted with falsified documents. A substantial percentage of the constituents in the ward were from the Indian sub-continent and had limited, if any, English. He was now aged 62 and suffers from angina. He had been a community leader. The Judge said that he was imposing a deterrent sentence. Held. He took advantage of members of his own community who were less educated and less able to protect themselves than the majority of the electorate.

A fraud on this scale has even more dangerous consequences than an offence undermining the administration of justice. **3 years 7 months** (reduced from **4 years** because he pleaded at the first opportunity) was the appropriate sentence. We hope that the sentence will send the message to anyone else minded to indulge in action of this sort. The message is that that sort of conduct which undermines our system of democracy will not be tolerated.

R v Fadaka 2015 EWCA Crim 1017 D pleaded, on the day fixed for his trial, to making a false statement as to his qualification for being elected, Representation of the People Act 1983 s 65A(1A)(b). He applied to stand as a conservative councillor in a London Borough. He was seen by a party official and completed a form saying he had never been convicted of a criminal offence and sentenced to 3 months or more in the last five years. The party had found out before the election about a fraud conviction he had but could not substitute another candidate. The party found the publicity damaging. In the election he received 7% of the votes and his party spent £2,000 promoting him. D was now aged 34. He had a conviction for dishonesty in 2005. In 2011, he had pleaded to 11 counts of making a false claim for benefit. D received a 12-month suspended sentence. D had mental health problems. Held. Immediate imprisonment was called for as he had lied to gain public office. **6 months upheld**.

See also: *R v Khan and Others* 2009 EWCA Crim 2483 (LCJ D pleaded and M was convicted of conspiracy to defraud and other charges. They created ghost voters by using false addresses, false documents etc. such that the ghost voters enabled D to become a councillor when without them he would have lost. Held. D (**3½ years**) and M (**4½ years**) were wise not to appeal their sentences.)

248   ENTRAPMENT/*AGENTS PROVOCATEURS* AND SIMILAR SITUATIONS

248.1

Where police conduct amounts to state-generated crime, the court may stay that part of the indictment.[339] However, the police are permitted to make test purchases of drugs etc. (either where a statute authorises it or when it has been authorised by a senior officer) and take part in similar activity.

248.2   *Journalists*

R v Tonnessen 1998 2 Cr App R (S) 328 D pleaded to supplying heroin. She was approached by a man who claimed to know her. He was accompanied by two others who turned out to be from the *News of the World*. They said that they worked for a Sheikh and they were instructed to buy drugs. She was a heroin addict and a cannabis user and said that these drugs were widely available. They said that they wanted to buy heroin and asked her whether she was prepared to get it for them. They gave her £50 and she bought four wraps of heroin. She and a friend spent the rest of the evening with them. Immediately after, her name and photograph appeared in the paper. The police felt obliged to arrest her and she admitted the offence. After the publicity she was assaulted and received a threat to her life. She was aged 31 and had already served a prison sentence for an unrelated offence. She had no supply convictions. She suffered from a serious pre-cancerous condition. The Judge did not refer to the involvement of *agents provocateurs* and appeared not to have taken it into account. The defence said that there can be considerable mitigation where it can be shown that the offence would not otherwise have been committed. The defence submitted that it was legitimate for policemen to entrap criminals. When the entrapment is by a journalist even more consideration and more weight should be given. Held. We consider that there is substance in those submissions. However, it merited immediate custody. We cannot ignore the fact that she was set up. If these men had been police officers, that would provide mitigation. Different considerations must apply to investigatory journalists.

---

[339] *R v Looseley* 2001 UKHL 53, 2002 1 Cr App R (S) 29 (p 360) This case is also known as *Att-Gen's Ref No 3 of 2000* 2000 UKHL 53, 2002 1 Cr App R (S) 29 (p 360).

Their purpose was perfectly honourable. But we feel the public would be left with a sense of unease by the identification in the paper. The consequences were most unfortunate. It is appropriate to reflect the entrapment in the sentence. It should have been expressly mentioned in the remarks. In the exceptional circumstances we reduce the sentence from 12 months to **6 months**.

R v Barnett 2007 EWCA Crim 1625, 2008 1 Cr App R (S) 61 (p 354) D pleaded at the first opportunity to sexual grooming. He used his home computer to access an Internet chat room for teenagers. He struck up a conversation with someone who said that she was called Katie, aged 12. In fact she was a journalist assisting in a *Sunday People* investigation into teenage chat rooms and predatory older men. Over two days they had lengthy conversations in which D was clearly grooming 'Katie' for sexual purposes. He asked her, 'How naughty are you?' When she said that she had not tried anything sexual, he said, 'Would you like help? I don't mind if you're inexperienced. I can show you.' He was persistent in organising a meeting, and eventually one was arranged at a tube station. 'Katie' was a young-looking journalist and posed as a 12-year-old. She pretended to be nervous at the meeting. The resulting conversation was recorded by 'Katie'. She initially said tearfully she wanted to go home but he calmed her down. During the meeting he hugged her with both arms, touched her on the legs, squeezed her left calf and touched her hair. He told her not to tell anyone about their meeting and they arranged a further meeting the following week. In the week that followed there was further Internet contact of an overtly sexual nature. D sent 'Katie' nude pictures of his genitals and bottom. He went to the next arranged meeting but 'Katie' was not there. A journalist from the paper approached him and introduced himself, and D ran off. The newspaper then published the story and informed the police. D made no comment in interview. D, aged 46, was of previous good character. A pre-sentence report said that 'there was a low to medium risk of reoffending generally but a high risk of reoffending in a similar manner, and a high risk of harm to children until he addressed his sexual offending against children. He was ashamed of his actions but showed very limited insight into his motivation for committing such an offence.' Held. Any sexual grooming of a child is a very serious matter. There is some force in the cumulative effect of the submissions that he pleaded guilty at the first opportunity, that he was of previous good character, that he had expressed remorse, that he had been exposed in the national press and humiliated, no child was actually approached, there was no victim, the offence arose out of a newspaper sting operation, and he had been treated for depression and anxiety after his arrest. In the present case he is a man of good character caught in a sting operation with no actual victim, and he had been subjected to very considerable humiliation as a result of exposure in the national press. **18 months** not 30 months.
See also: *R v Pennant* 2009 EWCA Crim 845 (The entrapment contributed to a reduction.)

248.3   *Police collect evidence of continuing activity, e.g. drug dealing*

R v Springer 1999 1 Cr App R (S) 217 D pleaded at the Magistrates' Court to three charges of supplying heroin and was committed to the Crown Court. D was a suspected drug dealer. The police tested their suspicions by making three telephone calls. He was asked, 'Have you got anything'. He replied, 'Yeah', and arrangements were made to meet him. In response to each call a meeting was arranged, and about 1.5 grams of heroin were supplied. The calls were recorded and the meetings were videoed. The defence argued that he was entitled to a discount because of entrapment. Held. There was a need for the police to adopt this method of detection. There was need for there to be more than one supply to provide evidence that he was a dealer. This was not a case of entrapping a suspect into supplying drugs who would otherwise never have engaged in that activity. *R v Underhill* 1979 1 Cr App R (S) 270 at 272 applied. Here there was legitimate police activity and not activity that could provide mitigation or any reduction at all.

R v Mayeri 1999 1 Cr App R (S) 304 D pleaded at the earliest opportunity to four counts of supplying ecstasy. One tablet was involved in each case. Four undercover police officers approached him in a nightclub and he agreed to sell them a tablet for £10. He claimed there was an element of entrapment. D relied on *R v Tonnessen* 1998 2 Cr App R (S) 328. Held. The entrapment argument is not a good one. Where undercover officers discover that a man is prepared to sell drugs by approaching him it is not a matter that the courts need normally take into account as amounting to entrapment. It might be said, 'Seller beware'. These premises are frequently used to sell drugs.

248.4   *Refer to the agents provocateurs etc. in the sentencing remarks, Must*
R v Tonnessen 1998 2 Cr App R (S) 328 The Judge did not refer to the involvement of *agents provocateurs* and appeared not to have taken it into account. Held. Applying *R v Mackey* 1993 14 Cr App R (S) 53, it should have been expressly mentioned in the remarks.
See also the **SUPPLY OF DRUGS** *Test purchases/Entrapment* para at **340.40**.

249   ENVIRONMENTAL OFFENCES
249.1
Various offences and penalties
Agency penalties The Environment Agency and Natural England have power to impose civil sanctions for a range of environmental offences.[340] Since 6 April 2010, the fixed penalty for an individual is £100 and for a body corporate is £300.[341] There is also power to impose variable monetary penalties which must not exceed £250,000.[342] For more detail see **61.1** in Volume 1.
Serious Crime Prevention Orders For Environmental Protection Act 1990 s 33 offences there is a discretionary power to make this order, when it would protect the public etc.[343]
The principles for dealing with corporate defendants are listed in the **HEALTH AND SAFETY OFFENCES** chapter and the **COMPANIES AND PUBLIC BODIES AS DEFENDANTS** chapter in Volume 1.

249.2   *Crown Court statistics   England and Wales*
Public Health Aged 21+

Year	Plea	Total sentenced	Type of sentencing %						Average length of custody in months
			Discharge	Fine	Community sentence	Suspended sentence	Custody	Other	
2014	G	49	8.2	38.8	16.3	18.4	18.4	–	7.4
	NG	7	14.3	28.6	–	42.9	14.3	–	6.0
2015	G	20	–	35	15	40	10	–	not listed[344]
	NG	3	–	100	–	–	–	–	–

For explanations about the statistics see page 1-xii. For statistics for male and female defendants etc. see www.banksr.com Other Matters Statistics tab

249.3   *Environmental Offences Guideline*
Environmental Offences Guideline 2014, see www.banksr.com Other Matters Guidelines tab
The guideline came into force on 1 July 2014 and applies regardless of the date of the offence.

---

[340] Regulatory Enforcement and Sanctions Act 2008 s 36-40
[341] Environmental Civil Sanctions (England) Order 2010 2010/1157 para 3 and Sch 1 para 1(3)
[342] Environmental Civil Sanctions (England) Order 2010 2010/1157 para 3 and Sch 2 para 1(5)
[343] Serious Crime Act 2007 s 1 and Sch 1 para 13(3)
[344] Based on too few cases to be meaningful

Note: The guideline covers 'Unlawful or harmful deposit, treatment or disposal of waste' and 'Illegal discharges to air, land and water' offences, Environmental Protection Act 1990 s 33 and Environmental Permitting (England and Wales) Regulations 2010 2010/675 reg 12 and 38(1)-(3). The guideline also applies to Control of Pollution (Amendment) Act 1989 s 1, Environmental Protection Act 1990 s 34 and 80, Water Industry Act 1991 s 111 and Transfrontier Shipment of Waste Regulations 2007 2007/1711. The guideline is divided into two sections, Organisations and Individuals. The guideline is 24 pages long and for reasons of space and how seldom these offences are prosecuted, the details are not reproduced. Ed.

249.4   *Magistrates' Court Sentencing Guidelines*
Magistrates' Court Sentencing Guidelines 2008 (as amended), see www.banksr.com page 305 The *Environmental Offences Guideline 2014* has been inserted, see www. banksr.com Other Matters Guidelines tab

249.5   *Judicial guidance*
R v Anglian Water Services Ltd 2003 EWCA Crim 2243, 2004 1 Cr App R (S) 62 (p 374) The environment in which we live is a precious heritage and it is incumbent on the present generation to preserve it for the future. Rivers and watercourses are an important part of that environment and there is an increasing awareness of the necessity to preserve them from pollution. There is a heavy burden on [water companies] to do everything possible to ensure that they do not cause pollution.
Post-guideline case
R v Thames Water 2015 EWCA Crim 960, 2 Cr App R (S) 63 (p 439) LCJ D, the defendant company, pleaded to polluting a water course with raw sewage. Held. In Category 1 cases, the objectives of punishment, deterrence and the removal of gain must be achieved by the level of penalty imposed. This may result in a fine equal to a substantial percentage, up to 100%, of the companies' pre-tax net profit, even if it results in fines in excess of £100m. That is necessary because of the importance that is attached to environmental protection.

249.6   *Magistrates' Guidance   Pre-guideline*
Costing the Earth Magistrates' Guidance 2009 www.banksr.com Other Matters Other Documents tab Note: The Magistrates' Association has reissued its guidance, which contains a series of case examples on the following offences: Air Pollution, Animal Health, Environmental Permitting Regulations 2007,[345] fishing, genetic modification, Health and Safety, dog fouling, breaches of tree preservation orders, planning, pesticide, radiation, statutory nuisance and noise, waste, water, wildlife and nature conservation. As the guidance provides no suggested penalties, the case studies are not listed. Ed.

249.7   *Litter, Dropping*
Fixed penalty For depositing and leaving litter,[346] and where there is a notice under Environmental Protection Act 1990 s 88, the amount is £75 (where no amount is specified).[347] In all other cases, the amount is £60.[348] All penalties have had added to them half the relevant victim surcharge. For more detail see **61.1** in Volume 1.

249.8   *Radioactive waste   Pre-guideline case*
R v Sellafield and Network Rail 2014 EWCA Crim 49 LCJ S pleaded (full credit) to six breaches of regulatory requirements and carrying radioactive waste unlawfully. That waste must be passed through a measuring device twice. One of the monitors at the second stage was not calibrated correctly. As a result, five out of 5,000 bags left the company's site outside the permitted level of radioactivity. The error was detected by chance. The authorities were alerted immediately. After that S did all it could to ensure no one was harmed. Exposure to four bags of waste was no greater exposure to

---

[345] Now replaced by Environmental Permitting (England and Wales) Regulations 2010 2010/675 (as amended)
[346] Environmental Protection Act 1990 s 87(1)
[347] Environmental Protection Act 1990 s 88(6A)
[348] Penalties for Disorderly Behaviour (Amount of Penalty) Order 2002 2002/1837 as amended

radioactivity than a passenger would experience on a flight to Paris. An investigation revealed that S's staff had numerous opportunities to avoid the error. Not only were the specifications wrong but there were other breaches such as the recalibration was not carried out by a staff member, and the tests and checks were not properly carried out. S had a previous conviction for emissions of radioactive material, leading to fines of £500,000 and £75,000. S had a turnover of £1.6 billion. The Judge found basic management failures and the problem was undetected for four months. Further, the failure was not confined to specific individuals but the customs within the company were too lax and to a degree complacent. The Judge accepted no harm had been done. Held. The processing and storage of nuclear waste carries with it potentially grave risks. To mitigate those risks the most stringent standards have been adopted at national and international levels. The public rightly expects strict compliance with [the licence provisions]. There was the clearest negligence. The fine was little more than a week's profit. The **£700,000** fine could not be criticised.

249.9   *Tree preservation orders, Breach of/Sites of special scientific interest offences*
R v Davey 2013 EWCA Crim 1662, 2014 1 Cr App R (S) 34 (p 205) D was convicted of causing the destruction of a tree. D wanted a better view of Poole harbour. While he was in France he arranged for a tree surgeon to cut down a maritime pine in his neighbours' garden which was subject to a preservation order. In interview he lied about the tree. D was of some wealth. He was given a £75,000 confiscation order based on an unchallenged assessment of the increase to the value of the house of the removal of the tree. The Judge said D was remarkably arrogant and had complete contempt for the property rights of his neighbours and put their lives at risk. They were upset and distressed. Held. It was a notable tree. D not only had the increased value of his house, but he had the amenity value of the improved view. This was one of the most serious cases of its type. A **£50,000** fine was not manifestly excessive.
See also: *R v Day* 2014 EWCA Crim 2683, 2015 1 Cr App R (S) 53 (LCJ Plea after court ruling to carrying out an operation to an SSSI without giving notice to Natural England, Wildlife and Countryside Act 1981 s 28E. Felled 43 trees, constructed a track to take vehicles, constructed banks and stripped flora to assist a pheasant shoot. Threats made to those who complained. *Newton* hearing lost. One of the richest men in England. Held. SSSIs are a common heritage. Protection of the environment and SSSIs is of great importance. A fine **significantly greater** than **£450,000** was amply justified and costs of just over £457,000 remain.)
See also the **PLANNING OFFENCES** chapter.

249.10   *Waste: Unauthorised keeping, treating, depositing or disposal   Pre-guideline cases*
Offences include Environmental Protection Act 1990 s 33
Mode of trial Triable either way
Maximum sentence On indictment 5 years. Summary 6 months and/or a £5,000 fine for offences committed before 12 March 2015 and an unlimited fine thereafter.[349] There are maximum fines for those aged under 18, see **14.38** in Volume 1.
Note: The Court of Appeal in *R v Bairstow* 2011 EWCA Crim 2423, 2012 1 Cr App R (S) 98 (p 602) (see below) indicated that the cases before the maximum was increased (in 2005) do not 'give assistance'. Ed.
See also the **WATER OFFENCES** chapter and for the law about sentencing companies see the **COMPANIES AND PUBLIC BODIES** chapter in Volume 1.

249.11   *Waste: Unauthorised keeping, treating, depositing or disposal   Cases*
R v Bairstow 2011 EWCA Crim 2423, 2012 1 Cr App R (S) 98 (p 602) D pleaded (full credit) to unlicensed depositing of controlled waste (×6). There were a number of TICs which were committed whilst on bail. He was already serving a 48-week sentence for

---

[349] Legal Aid, Sentencing and Punishment of Offenders Act 2012 s 85(1) and (4) and Legal Aid, Sentencing and Punishment of Offenders Act 2012 (Commencement No 11) Order 2015 2015/504

theft and kindred offences. D committed commercial fly tipping over a period of 12 months in public places or open spaces. The waste was domestic and commercial and included asbestos. D, aged 36 at appeal, had 27 convictions for 133 offences between 1993 and 2011. D had health problems and suffered a stroke in 2010. Held. The offences were serious, blatant, persistent and over an extended period of time. The tipping was aggravated by the asbestos, organised, and his disregard for the law was for financial motives. There was a high level of culpability. There was no evidence that custody was aggravating his condition. **2 years** consecutive to D's other sentence was not manifestly excessive.

R v Hinchcliffe and Hinchcliffe 2012 EWCA Crim 1691, 2013 1 Cr App R (S) 79 (p 434) (Pleas (full credit) to four environmental regulations offences. Ran a company with a permit for waste disposal on one site, but not for two others. Site with permit was breaching its limit and waste was not contained. Ignored improvement notices for months. More than 3,000 tonnes over the 700 tonne limit. A fire at the site burned for one month costing the fire brigade £850,000. Showed a prolonged and cynical disregard for the regulations. Net income £661,649. Purpose was financial gain. Son cleaned up the site. Aged 71. Good character. **2 years** was fair.)

R v Williams 2013 EWCA Crim 1708 D was convicted of: a) depositing waste without a permit (section 33(1)(a)), and b) failing to complete a duty of care transfer notice. D was asked by a builder to deposit 750 kilos of plasterboard and he put it in a field. Environmental officers saw it and traced the builder. The next day, an officer saw burning roofing felt on top of the plasterboard. D was interviewed and said that he had deposited the plasterboard and that he was a tenant of the field. He agreed he had no permit or an exemption for the site in question. D removed the waste. In 2005 D was fined £3,000 for waste deposit offences, two offences of burning waste and two offences of failing to comply with a notice (£1,000 costs). In 2008, D had been fined for making false representations about benefit. Held. A **6-month suspended sentence** and a **£1,500 fine** with a £7,000 costs order was not manifestly excessive.

R v Rory J Holbrook Ltd 2015 EWCA Crim 1908 D pleaded early to operating a waste operation and depositing waste without permits. D agreed to construct and landscape a golf course. No permits were obtained notwithstanding D had a conviction in 2008 for operating without a waste management licence. The basis of plea was that: a) D did not deliberately flout the permit regime as it believed it was exempt, b) the employee responsible was not sufficiently experienced or competent, and d) no mixed or contaminated waste was deposited. D's turnover was about £5m. The Judge found D was significantly reckless and the notification was financial. The Judge considered it was a Category 3 case to reflect the significant adverse effect from the offending. Further the company was a small company so a starting point of £10,000 would be appropriate. A confiscation order for £247,278 was made. Held. A £30,000 fine cannot be faulted. For the confiscation appeal see **22.99**.

See also: *R v Brightmore* 2010 EWCA Crim 2119 (Plea. Commercial dumping over 10 months. **16 months** concurrent to other matters.)

249.12   *Waterways/sea pollution*

Offences include Water Resources Act 1991 s 85 (polluting controlled waters)
Mode of trial Triable either way
Maximum sentence On indictment 2 years. Summary 3 months and/or a £20,000 fine for offences committed before 12 March 2015 and an unlimited fine thereafter.[350]
Example: *R v Southern Water Services Ltd* 2014 EWCA Crim 120, 2 Cr App R (S) 29 (p 235) (LCJ Plea. Discovered sewage station was faulty and pumping effluent into the sea. Up to 50% of the sewage discharged was untreated. Environment Agency not notified for ten days and problem not remedied quickly enough. It was a breach of their

---

[350] Legal Aid, Sentencing and Punishment of Offenders Act 2012 s 85(1) and (4) and Legal Aid, Sentencing and Punishment of Offenders Act 2012 (Commencement No 11) Order 2015 2015/504

licence. Further discharges later in the year as the repairs were not permanent. No evidence of actual harm. The Judge was entitled to conclude that there was potential for serious harm. Turnover of £0.75bn and post-tax profit in 2013 of £156.9m. 160 previous offences, representing persistent offending. No explanation of how the company had reformed itself. **£200,000** fine upheld.)

Post-guideline case

R v Thames Water 2015 EWCA Crim 960, 2 Cr App R (S) 63 (p 439) LCJ D, the defendant company, pleaded early to an offence under Environmental Permitting (England and Wales) Regulations 2010 2010/675 Reg 38 and 39. Over five days D discharged untreated sewage into a brook which flowed through a 143 acre National Trust nature reserve in an area of outstanding natural beauty. The discharge was caused by a failure of two pumps which had been clogged by material inappropriately put in the sewage system. Alarms had been triggered 24 hours and four hours before. In the five months before the incident, there had been 16 instances of failure of one or both pumps. Since 1991, D had been convicted of 162 environmental offences. In 2014, D's turnover was £1.9 billion and its profit was £346m. D was categorised as a very large company. The Judge found that D was negligent in replacing the pumps. She found it was a Category 3 case and multiplied the starting point by five. This Court has not interfered with very significant fines for environmental offences, *R v Southern Water Services* 2014 EWCA Crim 129 para 21 and *R v Day* 2014 EWCA Crim 2683, 2015 1 Cr App R (S) 53 para 46. We estimate D had a conviction for a serious offence about once a year. That leaves substantial room for improvement. The fine should have been significantly into seven figures. We would have in mind a figure **very substantially over £250,000** as that was lenient.

Old cases: Best ignored. Sentences have increased significantly.

250   ESCAPE FROM CUSTODY ETC.

250.1

1) Escape from prison or police detention or when in transit (common law)

2) Breach of prison (common law)

   Modes of trial Both offences are indictable only.

   Maximum sentences Neither offence has a specified maximum, so the maximum is life.

3) Prison Act 1952 s 39 (aiding prisoner to escape[351] etc.)

   Mode of trial Indictable only

   Maximum sentence 10 years

4) Prisoners (Return to Custody) Act 1995 s 1 (remaining at large after temporary release)

   Mode of trial Triable either way[352]

   Maximum sentence On indictment 2 years. Summary maximum 6 months and/or a £5,000 fine for offences committed before 12 March 2015 and an unlimited fine thereafter.[353] There are maximum fines for those aged under 18, see **14.38** in Volume 1.

For offences committed before 13 April 2015, the offence is triable only summarily.

5) Crime (Sentences) Act 1997 s 32ZA, Criminal Justice Act 2003 s 255ZA (both remaining unlawfully at large after recall)

   Modes of trial Both offences are triable either way.

---

[351] This section was replaced with a new section by Offender Management Act 2007 s 21.

[352] The offence was made triable either way by Criminal Justice and Courts Act 2015 s 13. In force 13/4/15

[353] Legal Aid, Sentencing and Punishment of Offenders Act 2012 s 85(1) and (4) and Legal Aid, Sentencing and Punishment of Offenders Act 2012 (Commencement No 11) Order 2015 2015/504

Maximum sentences On indictment, both offences have a maximum of 2 years and a summary maximum of 6 months and/or an unlimited fine[354] for those aged 18+. For those under 18, see **17.25** in Volume 1.
These two offences were inserted by Crime Justice and Courts Act 2015 s 12(1)-(2). In force 13 April 2015.[355]

250.2   *Crown Court statistics   England and Wales*
Absconding from lawful custody

Year	Age	Plea	Total sentence	Type of sentencing %						Average length of custody in months
				Discharge	Fine	Community sentence	Suspended sentence	Custody	Other	
2013	18-20	G	25	–	–	–	20	80	–	6.9
		NG	0							
	21+	G	244	0.8	2.9	5.3	7.4	83.2	0.4	7.4
		NG	5	–	20	–	20	40	20	58
2014	18-20	G	21	–	5	19	5	67	5	7.1
		NG	4	–	–	–	–	25	75	not listed[356]
	21+	G	259	1	–	2	5	92	1	6.6
		NG	16	–	–	–	6	44	50	14.7

For explanations about the statistics see page 1-xii. For statistics for male and female defendants etc. see www.banksr.com Other Matters Statistics tab

250.3   *Judicial guidance*
R v Coughtrey 1997 2 Cr App R (S) 269 For prison escape, factors include: i) the nature and the circumstances of the crime for which he was in prison, ii) his conduct while in prison, iii) the methods employed in effecting escape and in particular whether any violence was involved and whether there was extensive planning and outside assistance, iv) whether he surrendered himself and how soon after, and v) a plea of guilty. It is a very serious offence for which a substantial sentence of imprisonment is expected because of the fear and apprehension it generates, the disruption to prison life, the violence and disorder that it may lead to and the need to deter the culprit and others. A consecutive sentence should almost always be imposed.
R v Jarvis 2002 EWCA Crim 885, 2 Cr App R (S) 123 (p 558) D pleaded to escaping and appealed. The defence posed a series of questions: 1) Was it pre-planned? 2) What level of violence was used and what level of injury, if any, was suffered? 3) Was the attempt successful and if so how long was D at large? Held. We bear in mind the criteria which have been helpfully summarised. Those who seek to escape violently must expect a custodial sentence.
R v Rumble 2003 EWCA Crim 770 D was convicted of escape from lawful custody. Held. Guidance is given in *R v Sutcliffe* 1992 13 Cr App R (S) 538 at page 540, "Escape from lawful custody is always a serious offence. It is quite essential for the courts to mark out the seriousness of escapes from custody of this kind, whether in the Magistrates' Court or in the Crown Court, by immediate sentences of imprisonment. It is not only intended as a punishment. It is also intended to be a clear deterrent to others contemplating escapes from custody."
R v Purchase 2007 EWCA Crim 1740, 2008 1 Cr App R (S) 58 (p 338) D pleaded to escape. The level of sentence divides roughly into two: 1) where a prisoner on his or her own has some kind of personal pressure which persuades him or her to escape, 2) where

---
[354] Legal Aid, Sentencing and Punishment of Offenders Act 2012 s 85(1) and (4)
[355] Criminal Justice and Courts Act 2015 (Commencement No 1, Saving and Transitional Provisions) Order 2015 2015/778 para 3 and Sch 1 para 8
[356] Based on too few cases to be meaningful

professional criminals are assisted to escape by confederates outside or inside prison. The sentences for the first group are in months and sentences for the second group are in years. Factors include the following: Was there planning or was it an impulse? Was there violence or damage caused? What was the reason for the escape? Did the offender surrender or make arrangements to surrender? For how long was he at large? What else did he do while he was at large?

250.4   *Police detention, Escape from*
R v Tiwary 2011 EWCA Crim 836 D pleaded to attempting to escape from custody and common assault. Having been arrested for aggravated vehicle-taking he complained of feeling ill as a result of ingesting numerous wraps of heroin and cocaine. He was taken to hospital in police custody. The officers escorted him to the lavatory whereupon he ran in the direction of the exit. He ran at three nurses, barging a female nurse and causing her injury (the common assault). He attempted to escape via an open door, which turned out to be a cupboard. Held. D was pretending to be ill. The injury was an obvious and important aggravating factor. The assault was a part of the escape. **16 months** and **4 months concurrent,** not 21 months and 4 months consecutive.
R v Baverstock 2013 EWCA Crim 1502, 2014 1 Cr App R (S) 64 (p 425) D pleaded to escape and theft of police handcuffs. D broke into a car and stole items valued at around £200. He was subsequently arrested at his flat and handcuffed. Whilst a search of his flat was being conducted he jumped out of the open first-floor window and disappeared. Eight weeks later, the police arrested him. He was in breach of an earlier conditional discharge. Held. The relevant considerations were set out in *R v Jarvis* 2002 EWCA Crim 885, 2 Cr App R (S) 123 (p 558). D had a bad record but the authorities suggest that is not a major factor in cases of escape. No violence was used and the escape was neither from a prison nor a court. **6 months** not 12, consecutive to other sentences.

250.5   *Prison, Walking out of/Failing to return to prison*
R v Patmore 2010 EWCA Crim 2887, 2011 2 Cr App R (S) 21 (p 115) D pleaded to escape. He was serving 16 years' YOI for conspiracy to rob and escape. Whilst in prison he had been compliant and had been moved to a Category D open prison. One day he simply walked out of the prison. Three months later police received information regarding his potential whereabouts. When he saw police officers outside the house he was in, he went upstairs and smashed a bathroom window. He jumped out and down into neighbouring gardens. He climbed onto the roof of another property and refused to come down for 30-45 minutes. He subsequently did so, on the understanding that a particular officer would arrest him. The Judge accepted that D had escaped for what appeared to be personal reasons. Whilst at large he committed no further offences. Held. D will now be held in a maximum security facility for which he only has himself to blame. This was D's second attempt to escape, no attempt was made to surrender and being an open prison, a greater degree of trust was placed in D. The effect is that D will serve approximately an extra 3 years, not attracting parole where he otherwise might have. There is a deterrent element. **15 months concurrent,** not 21.
R v Powter 2014 EWCA Crim 2360, 2015 1 Cr App R (S) 31 (p 240) D pleaded (full credit) to escape following his absconding from an open prison. He was serving IPP with a 2-year term. While serving he received a 40-month determinate sentence. In 2011 and 2013, he was released on licence and each time he was recalled for breaching his licence. After absconding, D remained at large for two weeks, then handed himself in. D escaped due to his anxiety at the prospect of a possible imminent release. D also suffered from depression and had a brain cyst causing him to have seizures and lose consciousness. Held. Starting at 9 months, **6 months**, not 18.
See also: *R v Fitchett* 2012 EWCA Crim 1375 (Plea to escaping from custody. Serving 3½ years for domestic burglary. Booked a taxi from an open prison. At large for 48 hours. Committed no offences. Voluntarily surrendered to police. **28 days** not 8 months.)

R v Perry 2013 EWCA Crim 1598 (Plea to escape. Serving 50 months for third-strike dwelling burglary. Failed to return after leave. Handed himself in to a police station three days later. No offences whilst at large. Went to visit family members. Large number of previous convictions including burglary. Enhanced prisoner status prior to escape. Three months after a trial. **2 months** not 8.)

R v McDonagh 2014 EWCA Crim 2977 (Plea with full credit. Serving 30 months' DPP. Minimum term well served. Walked out of open prison. Felt under duress from other prisoners. Surrendered four days later. No offences committed. Sentence should be the same whether the sentence is fixed or indeterminate. **6 months** not 12.

Old cases: *R v Golding* 2007 EWCA Crim 118, 2 Cr App R (S) 49 (p 309) (**10 months consecutive**) *R v Purchase* 2007 EWCA Crim 1740, 2008 1 Cr App R (S) 58 (p 338) (**9 months consecutive**) *R v Brockway* 2007 EWCA Crim 2997, 2008 2 Cr App R (S) 4 (p 13) (**1 year**)

For a summary of the first case, see the 8th edition of this book, for the second case, see the 9th edition and for the last case, see the 10th edition.

250.6   *Running from the dock   Opportunist*

R v Jarvis 2002 EWCA Crim 885, 2 Cr App R (S) 123 (p 558) D pleaded to escaping. D was charged with aggravated burglary and remanded in custody. D appeared in the Crown Court and the case was adjourned. He leapt over the dock and was tackled by two security officers and an off-duty police officer before he could get through the court doors. There was a struggle lasting 4-5 minutes. The police officer sustained a slight cut to his knuckle. Later the prosecution dropped the burglary charge because a witness had died. The Judge refused to give him credit for the time that he was in custody for the other matter. Held. The Judge was right not to give him credit. Bearing in mind the criteria (see *Judicial guidance*), **6 months** not 12.

251   EXCISE LICENCE, FRAUDULENT USE ETC. OF AN

251.1

Vehicle Excise and Registration Act 1994 s 44

Mode of trial Triable either way

Maximum sentence On indictment 2 years. Summary maximum a £5,000 fine for offences committed before 12 March 2015 and an unlimited fine thereafter.[357] There are maximum fines for those aged under 18, see **14.38** in Volume 1.

251.2   *Magistrates' Court Sentencing Guidelines*

Magistrates' Court Sentencing Guideline 2008, see www.banksr.com Other Matters Guidelines tab The guideline applies to the Magistrates' Court and to the Crown Court hearing appeals or sentencing for summary only offences.[358]

page 109 Starting points are based on a first-time offender pleading not guilty.

Examples of nature of activity	Starting point	Range
Use of unaltered licence from another vehicle	Band B fine	Band B fine
Forged licence bought for own use, or forged/altered for own use	Band C fine	Band C fine

---

[357] Legal Aid, Sentencing and Punishment of Offenders Act 2012 s 85(1) and (4) and Legal Aid, Sentencing and Punishment of Offenders Act 2012 (Commencement No 11) Order 2015 2015/504
[358] See page 15 of the guidelines.

Examples of nature of activity	Starting point	Range
Use of number plates from another vehicle, or licence/number plates forged or altered for sale to another	High-level community order (in Crown Court)	Medium-level community order to Crown Court Note: Community order and custody only available in Crown Court

The following aggravating and mitigating factors may be particularly relevant: Factors indicating higher culpability: 1 LGV/PSV/LGV/taxi etc. 2 Long-term fraudulent use. Factors indicating lower culpability: 1 Licence/registration mark from another vehicle owned by defendant 2 Short-term use. Factors indicating greater degree of harm: 1 High financial gain 2 Innocent victim deceived 3 Legitimate owner inconvenienced.

For the meaning of a high-level and a medium-level community order see **16.13-16.14** in Volume 1.

Consider disqualification from driving and deprivation of property (including vehicle).

A Band B fine is 100% of net weekly income. Band C is 150%. For more detail see **60.27** in Volume 1.

252 EXCISE LICENCE, NO

252.1

Vehicle Excise and Registration Act 1994 s 29 (using or keeping an unlicensed vehicle)
Mode of trial Summary only
Maximum sentence Level 3 fine (£1,000) or five times the amount of duty chargeable, whichever is greater[359]
Back duty The court must, upon conviction of a section 29 offence, order the defendant to pay 'back duty'.[360] Back duty is an amount equal to one-twelfth of the annual rate of vehicle excise duty appropriate to the vehicle for each month, or part of a month, in the relevant period.[361]

On 1 October 2014, the Finance Act 2014 Sch 19 paras 13 and 22 repealed Vehicle Excise and Registration Act 1994 s 33 (the offence of not exhibiting an excise licence). The enforcement of excise duty will now be through digital cameras and databases.

252.2 *Magistrates' Court Sentencing Guidelines   No excise licence*
Magistrates' Court Sentencing Guideline 2008, see www.banksr.com Other Matters Guidelines tab The guideline applies to the Magistrates' Court and to the Crown Court hearing appeals or sentencing for summary only offences.[362]

page 135 **No excise licence** Starting points are based on a first-time offender pleading not guilty. Starting point a) 1-3 months' unpaid duty: Level A fine, b) 4-6 months' unpaid duty: Level B fine, c) 7-12 months' unpaid duty: Level C fine.

In each case add the duty lost. For owner-drivers the starting point is the same as for drivers but consider an uplift of at least 25%. Fine bands A, B and C are 50%, 100% and 150% of relevant weekly income, respectively.

For how to apply the guidelines see the **GUIDELINES** chapter in Volume 1.

253 EXPLOSIVE OFFENCES

253.1

Explosive Substances Act 1883
    s 2 (causing explosion likely to endanger life or property)

---

[359] Vehicle Excise and Registration Act 1994 s 29(3)
[360] Vehicle Excise and Registration Act 1994 s 30(1)
[361] Vehicle Excise and Registration Act 1994 s 30(2). The relevant period is defined by Vehicle Excise and Registration Act 1994 s 31.
[362] See page 15 of the guidelines.

s 3 (attempt to cause explosion, or making or keeping explosive with intent to endanger life or property)
s 4 (punishment for making or possession of explosive under suspicious circumstances)
Modes of trial Indictable only
Maximum sentences Sections 2 and 3, Life. Section 4, 14 years
Extended sentences Both section 2 and section 3 offences are listed in Criminal Justice Act 2003 Sch 15. For these offences, the court may pass a 2012 extended sentence (EDS) if there is a significant risk of serious harm from future specified offences and either: a) the defendant has a Criminal Justice Act 2003 Sch 15B conviction (applicable only to defendants aged 18+), or b) the offence would justify a determinate sentence of at least 4 years.[363]
Sexual Harm Prevention Orders There is a discretionary power to make this order when it is necessary to protect the public from sexual harm.[364]
See also the **FIREWORKS, OFFENCES AGAINST THE PERSON ACT 1861 s 29** (sending any explosive substance etc.) and the **TERRORISM** chapters.

Causing an explosion with intent to endanger life etc.

253.2
Explosive Substances Act 1883 s 2-3
Modes of trial Indictable only
Maximum sentences Life
Extended sentences These offences are listed in Criminal Justice Act 2003 Sch 15. The court may pass a 2012 extended sentence (EDS) if there is a significant risk of serious harm from future specified offences and either: a) the defendant has a Criminal Justice Act 2003 Sch 15B conviction (applicable only to defendants aged 18+), or b) the offence would justify a determinate sentence of at least 4 years.[365]

253.3 *Cases*
R v Griffiths 2004 EWCA Crim 2656, 2005 1 Cr App R (S) 108 (p 600) D was convicted of having an explosive substance with intent (count 1) and doing an act with intent to cause an explosion (count 2). He had previously pleaded to one count of having an explosive substance (count 3). D went to a co-accused's house and there set about making letter bombs using PE4 (British military high explosive) and detonators. The explosives detonated and caused him serious injuries. £7,000 worth of damage was done to the house. When his own house was searched police found 349 grams of PE4 (count 3). His motives remained obscure. In the course of the trial he 'belatedly' said that he was going to deliver the devices to two people who owed him £5,000 to frighten them into paying the debt, after initially claiming at trial that the explosives had been forced on him by people he had picked up in his minicab earlier in the year. D was aged 42 with some old previous convictions but nothing approaching this one in seriousness. The longest sentence he had received was 6 months in a detention centre for possession of an offensive weapon. Both his hands had been amputated and he suffered injuries to his thighs, genitalia, anterior trunk, neck and face as well as perforated eardrums. A psychiatric report said that there were no suicidal or psychotic issues and he was coming to terms with his injuries. A medical report expressed concern that while in custody he was not receiving the medical care he required. Held. The only substantial point was whether the disability suffered merited further discount beyond making the sentence for count 3 (3 years) concurrent with counts 1 and 2 (**15 years**). It did not.
R v Larsen 2014 EWCA Crim 1514, 2 Cr App R (S) 81 (p 635) D was convicted of causing an explosion likely to endanger life or cause serious injury to property,

---

[363] Criminal Justice Act 2003 s 226A-226B as inserted by Legal Aid, Sentencing and Punishment of Offenders Act 2012 s 124.
[364] Sexual Offences Act 2003 s 103A as inserted by Anti-social Behaviour, Crime and Policing Act 2014 Sch 5 para 2 and Sexual Offences Act 2003 Sch 5.
[365] Criminal Justice Act 2003 s 226A-226B as inserted by Legal Aid, Sentencing and Punishment of Offenders Act 2012 s 124

possessing an explosive substance with intent to endanger life or cause serious injury to property and three arson offences. D set off a series of homemade explosions and fires in part of his home town over a 2½-month period. He was a local councillor and a former mayor of the town. He enjoyed the media attention it gave him. He talked about the fears he had for himself and his family. In one attack, D exploded a bomb containing 13 ball bearings just after midnight. Four ball bearings smashed windows and caused damage to a neighbouring house. One hit an upstairs bed. The owner was so frightened she sold her house. A mental health residential home was also hit and had broken windows. Three cars were damaged by fire. D was aged 46 and of good character with references. He was diagnosed with a serious illness. The Judge made a reduction for this and thought D had an inflated sense of his own importance and enjoyed being at the centre of attention. He applied the terrorist guideline case of *R v Martin* 1999 1 Cr App R (S) 477, see **345.3**. The defence said that was inappropriate. Held. This was a sustained campaign of deliberate terror. The motive for the attacks was unclear. D was not engaged in terror for political aims nor had [he] any connection with terrorist groups. [However, using the explosive cases (see the last two cases in this para) which were less serious than this, we consider] **18 years** concurrent was severe but not excessive.

R v Hines-Randle 2014 EWCA Crim 2364 D pleaded (20% credit) to having an explosive substance with intent, having an explosive substance and making a threat to kill. D, unable to cope with his son's autism, became depressed and started drinking to excess. His wife then left him, taking their children. After Family Court proceedings, D had no contact with the children. D became gradually more mentally unstable and spoke to a friend of 'doing away' with his wife, mother and two professionals involved in the family proceedings. He had allegedly followed those two. D also sought 200 cool packs from first aid kits to make explosive devices and said he would use them to create a diversion. D then showed the friend one of the clocks he proposed to use as a detonator in conjunction with mobile phones and claimed to have tested one explosive device. He also referred to using a shotgun. D was found homeless, sleeping in his car. In the car, explosive components and gunpowder were found which formed the basis of a viable device. D was aged 55 and of good character but had paranoia and was considered to present a high risk of violence to others. His personality traits were described as ingrained and unlikely to alter significantly in the future. Further, there may be re-emergence of violent fantasies. His wife, his mother and a friend all thought their lives were in danger. The Judge considered D to be dangerous. Held. D was perhaps lucky to have avoided a life sentence. Referring to *R v Larsen* 2014 EWCA Crim 1514, 15 years' extended sentence (**10 years' custody** 5 years' extension), not 17 years' extended sentence. Indefinite Restraining Order upheld.

Making or possessing explosives
253.4   *Explosive Substances Act 1883 s 4*
Mode of trial Indictable only
Maximum sentence 14 years
Criminal Justice and Courts Act 2015 s 1 raises the maximum to life. In force 13 April 2015.[366]

Extended sentences Section 4 is listed in Criminal Justice Act 2003 Sch 15. For these offences, the court may pass a 2012 extended sentence (EDS) if there is a significant risk of serious harm from future specified offences and either: a) the defendant has a Criminal Justice Act 2003 Sch 15B conviction (applicable only to defendants aged 18+),

---

[366] Criminal Justice and Courts Act 2015 (Commencement No 1, Saving and Transitional Provisions) Order 2015 2015/778 para 3 and Sch 1 para 1

or b) the offence would justify a determinate sentence of at least 4 years.[367] Criminal Justice and Courts Act 2015 s 2(1)-(2) adds section 4 to the Schedule 15 list. In force 13 April 2015.[368]

253.5   Cases

R v Riding 2009 EWCA Crim 892, 2010 1 Cr App R (S) 7 (p 37) D was convicted of making an explosive substance. When he was aged 18 he created a pipe bomb which was six inches long and made of copper wire. D said that he followed a recipe from the Internet. It was found in a safe. The explosive was from fireworks. There was a cord fuse at one end. An expert said that it had the potential to generate substantial shrapnel and it might just function as a firework. There was no attempt to detonate it. Also found were two replica firearms, three substantial knives and a knuckleduster he had made. The reports did not disclose any particularly concerning obsession. D was aged 21 when sentenced. He had no convictions and had been an assistant manager at a store. D had lost his next sales job due to the publicity about his pipe bomb. Held. D's motivation is only part of the story. The potential for harm is the other important aspect of the offence and that was not inconsiderable. The Judge's reference to lethal firearms seems appropriate. Here the fact of imprisonment was the principal punishment. He had served 4 months, which was enough, so **8 months** not 12.

See also: *R v Kasprazak* 2013 EWCA Crim 1531, 2014 1 Cr App R (S) 20 (p 115) (Late pleas to having an explosive substance. Eight counts. Large quantities of various chemicals which could be used to make explosives found. Large amount of research material into explosives also found on his computer. Large quantity of pyrotechnic fuses and other chemical equipment. Very dangerous chemicals capable of causing serious injury. Limited experimentation arising out of curiosity. 10% credit. **4 years** was appropriate. Sentence concurrent to 20 years for attempted murder and kidnapping.)

254   EXPOSURE

254.1

Sexual Offences Act 2003 s 66 (exposure)

Mode of trial Triable either way

Maximum sentence On indictment 2 years. Summary 6 months and/or a £5,000 fine for offences committed before 12 March 2015 and an unlimited fine thereafter.[369] There are maximum fines for those aged under 18, see **14.38** in Volume 1.

Extended sentences This offence is listed in Criminal Justice Act 2003 Sch 15. The court may pass a 2012 extended sentence (EDS) if there is a significant risk of serious harm from future specified offences and the defendant has a Criminal Justice Act 2003 Sch 15B conviction (applicable only to defendants aged 18+).[370] Because of the need for proof of 'serious harm' an extended sentence is unlikely ever to be imposed.

Sexual Harm Prevention Orders There is a discretionary power to make this order when it is necessary to protect the public from sexual harm.[371]

Notification For offences where the defendant was:
 a) aged under 18 and sentenced to imprisonment of at least 12 months, or
 b) aged 18+ and: i) the victim was aged under 18, or ii) the defendant was sentenced to imprisonment or detained in a hospital or given community service for at least 12 months,

---

[367] Criminal Justice Act 2003 s 226A-226B as inserted by Legal Aid, Sentencing and Punishment of Offenders Act 2012 s 124
[368] Criminal Justice and Courts Act 2015 (Commencement No 1, Saving and Transitional Provisions) Order 2015 2015/778 para 3 and Sch 1 para 2
[369] Legal Aid, Sentencing and Punishment of Offenders Act 2012 s 85(1) and (4) and Legal Aid, Sentencing and Punishment of Offenders Act 2012 (Commencement No 11) Order 2015 2015/504
[370] Criminal Justice Act 2003 s 226A-226B as inserted by Legal Aid, Sentencing and Punishment of Offenders Act 2012 s 124
[371] Sexual Offences Act 2003 s 103A as inserted by Anti-social Behaviour, Crime and Policing Act 2014 Sch 5 para 2 and Sexual Offences Act 2003 Sch 3

the defendant must notify the police within three days (or three days from his or her release from imprisonment, hospital etc.) with his or her name, home address, national insurance number etc. and any change and addresses where he or she resides for seven days[372] (in one or more periods) or more in any 12-month period.[373]

Children and vulnerable adults: barred lists Where the offence is committed against a child under the age of 16 and the defendant is aged 18 or over, he or she is automatically barred from engaging in regulated activity[374] with children and with vulnerable adults.[375] The judge must tell the defendant that the Disclosure and Barring Service will include him or her in the barred lists.[376] The defendant may ask the Service to remove him or her from the lists.

254.2   *Sentencing Council guideline   Sexual Offences Act 2003 s 66*
Sexual Offences Guideline 2014 www.banksr.com Other Matters Guidelines tab. In force 1 April 2014. The guideline only applies to offenders aged 18+, see page 7 of the guideline. For the usual practice, see **66.21** in Volume 1.

STEP ONE: Determining the offence category
page 129 The court should determine the offence category using the table below.

Category 1	Raised harm **and** raised culpability
Category 2	Raised harm **or** raised culpability
Category 3	Exposure **without** raised harm or culpability factors present

page 129 The court should determine culpability and harm caused or intended, by reference only to the factors below, which comprise the principal factual elements of the offence. Where an offence does not fall squarely into a category, individual factors may require a degree of weighting before making an overall assessment and determining the appropriate offence category.

Factors indicating raised harm
Victim followed/pursued
Offender masturbated

Factors indicating raised culpability
Specific or previous targeting of a particularly vulnerable victim
Abuse of trust
Use of threats (including blackmail)
Offence racially or religiously aggravated
Offence motivated by, or demonstrating, hostility to the victim based on his or her sexual orientation (or presumed sexual orientation) or transgender identity (or presumed transgender identity)
Offence motivated by, or demonstrating, hostility to the victim based on his or her disability (or presumed disability)

254.3

STEP TWO: Starting point and category range
page 130 Having determined the category, the court should use the corresponding starting points to reach a sentence within the category range on the next page. The

---

[372] Sexual Offences Act 2003 s 84(1)(c) and (6)
[373] Sexual Offences Act 2003 s 83 and Sch 3 para 18
[374] As amended by Safeguarding Vulnerable Groups Act 2006 (Controlled Activity and Miscellaneous Provisions) Regulations 2010 2010/1146 para 9(4)
[375] Safeguarding Vulnerable Groups Act 2006 s 2 and Sch 3 and Safeguarding Vulnerable Groups Act 2006 (Prescribed Criteria and Miscellaneous Provisions) Regulations 2009 2009/37 para 4 and 6 and Sch para 2 and 4
[376] Safeguarding Vulnerable Groups Act 2006 s 2 and Sch 3 para 25

starting point applies to all offenders irrespective of plea or previous convictions. Having determined the starting point, step two allows further adjustment for aggravating or mitigating features, set out on the next page.

A case of particular gravity, reflected by multiple features of culpability or harm in step one, could merit upward adjustment from the starting point before further adjustment for aggravating or mitigating features, set out on the next page.

Where there is a sufficient prospect of rehabilitation, a community order with a sex offender treatment programme requirement under Criminal Justice Act 2003 s 202 can be a proper alternative to a short or moderate-length custodial sentence.

Category	Starting point	Category range
1	26 weeks' custody	12 weeks' to 1 year's custody
2	High-level community order	Medium-level community order to 26 weeks' custody
3	Medium-level community order	Band A fine to high-level community order

For the meaning of a high-level and a medium-level community order see **16.13-16.14** in Volume 1.

254.4   [Aggravating and mitigating factors]
page 131 The table below contains a **non-exhaustive** list of additional factual elements providing the context of the offence and factors relating to the offender. Identify whether any combination of these, or other relevant factors, should result in an upward or downward adjustment from the starting point. **In particular, relevant recent convictions are likely to result in an upward adjustment.** In some cases, having considered these factors, it may be appropriate to move outside the identified category range.

When sentencing **Category 2 offences**, the court should also consider the custody threshold as follows:
   Has the custody threshold been passed?
   If so, is it unavoidable that a custodial sentence be imposed?
   If so, can that sentence be suspended?

When sentencing **Category 3 offences**, the court should also consider the community order threshold as follows:
   Has the community order threshold been passed?

Aggravating factors
Statutory aggravating factors: Previous convictions, having regard to a) the nature of the offence to which the conviction relates and its relevance to the current offence; and b) the time that has elapsed since the conviction Offence committed whilst on bail *Other aggravating factors:* Location of offence Timing of offence Any steps taken to prevent the victim reporting an incident, obtaining assistance and/or from assisting or supporting the prosecution Failure to comply with current court orders Offence committed whilst on licence Commission of offence whilst under the influence of alcohol or drugs Presence of others, especially children

Mitigating factors
No previous convictions **or** no relevant/recent convictions
Remorse
Previous good character and/or exemplary conduct*
Age and/or lack of maturity where it affects the responsibility of the offender
Mental disorder or learning disability, particularly where linked to the commission of the offence
Demonstration
No previous convictions or no relevant/recent convictions
Remorse
Previous good character and/or exemplary conduct*
Age and/or lack of maturity where it affects the responsibility of the offender
Mental disorder or learning disability, particularly where linked to the commission of the offence
* Previous good character/exemplary conduct is different from having no previous convictions. The more serious the offence, the less the weight which should normally be attributed to this factor. Where previous good character/exemplary conduct has been used to facilitate the offence, this mitigation should not normally be allowed and such conduct may constitute an aggravating factor.

Note: An exact copy of this guideline has been inserted into the *Magistrates' Court Sentencing Guidelines 2008* at page 295. Ed.

254.5   *Cases   No similar previous convictions   Pre-guideline cases*

R v Lam-Callinan 2009 EWCA Crim 1316, 2010 1 Cr App R (S) 49 (p 316)[377] D was convicted of seven counts of exposure. He was a learning monitor at a school. D approached seven women fellow employees at the school and made inappropriate sexual comments like, "I have a 10-inch cock". D either took out his penis or it was visible. He asked one woman to measure his penis. He exposed himself to another woman on four or five occasions. He pressed his penis against a third. At trial he suggested consent or fabrication. The Judge said that the offences were planned and D tried to gain the trust of the women. D had impressive testimonials. Held. We don't consider that there has to be a previous conviction for the defendant to be a repeat offender. **9 months** not 15 months. (His age and character are not revealed.)

R v U 2011 EWCA Crim 2094 D was convicted of exposure. He was a heating engineer who was servicing a 76-year old woman's heating. When in the shower room, he started talking to the woman. She thought he wanted something and said she couldn't hear him. D opened the door and stood with his erect penis in his hand. The woman was shocked and went downstairs. The woman called her friend and discovered that D had acted similarly in two other houses a few weeks earlier. D, aged 33, had previous offences but none for sex. Held. The Judge was wrong to take into account the other incidents when sentencing. The aggravating features included the targeting of an elderly woman in her own home, and the fact that D gained entry to the house by reason of his job as an engineer. It is not a breach of trust case but this should be taken into account. **Community order with 180 hours' unpaid work**, not 9 months' suspended with 180 hours' unpaid work.

See also: *R v Abdulliah* 2010 EWCA Crim 2170 (Convicted of exposure. Exposed his penis and masturbated near a woman. Followed her twice and continued his behaviour. Lasted 15 minutes. Previous convictions, none for sex. **9 months**)

Old case: *R v Bell* 2008 EWCA Crim 55, 2002 Cr App R (S) 55 (p 337) (**Community order**)

For a summary of this case, see the 8th edition of this book.

---

[377] The neutral citation in the Cr App R (S) report is wrong.

254.6   Cases   Similar previous convictions

R v Pennant 2010 EWCA Crim 2117 D pleaded to two offences of exposure. V, a 16-year-old girl, was on a train. D made regular eye-contact with V throughout the journey. V felt uncomfortable and alighted. D also alighted. He waited for passengers to disperse. He then stood 20 feet away from V with his trousers around his knees with his penis exposed. He masturbated for around two minutes. He briefly went away but returned, exposed himself for a second time and continued to masturbate for several more minutes. Three days later, a woman saw D with his penis exposed through the flies of his trousers. He was masturbating near two girls aged about 10 and 13. D was arrested and interviewed and made full and frank admissions. D had appeared before the court on six previous occasions relating to seven offences of exposure. In November 2007 he was given a community order for two such offences. In April 2008 he was given a suspended sentence for possessing an offensive weapon, with no action taken for breach of the order. In June 2008 he was sentenced to 8 months' detention for four offences of exposure and the community and suspended sentences were revoked. In November 2009 he was sentenced to 122 days' detention for another offence of exposure. D had had a troubled childhood and suffered from attention deficit hyperactivity disorder. A pre-sentence report stated: a) D recognised his need for help but was reluctant to discuss his sexual motivations and feelings, b) he had attended supervision appointments but did not engage well, c) he displayed immaturity and aggression, d) until he could be honest about his thoughts and behaviour, the risk of further sexual offending, specifically exposure, would remain high, and e) he posed a high risk of harm to women whom he found sexually attractive. Held. 9 months and 9 months consecutive were appropriate, with the plea, **6 months** and **6 months consecutive** not 12 months and 12 months.

R v Ashford 2013 EWCA Crim 720 D pleaded to two exposures and possession of a CS gas canister. He was on his way to north Wales to celebrate his son's birthday. He diverted into Warrington. At about 6 pm, he was wearing skimpy and loose fitting running shorts. He approached V1, aged 31, as she was leaving a doctor's surgery. D deliberately exposed his penis and testicles to her. He laughed before leaving her company. About 30 minutes later, he encountered his second victim, V2, aged 17, at a bus stop. D pulled down his shorts, exposed his erect or partially erect penis towards her, manipulating it as he did so. V2 turned in shock and D moved to stand directly in front of her, then to sit next to her on a seat at the bus stop. D was wearing a peaked hat which concealed the top part of his face and something which looked like a mask. He was wearing a backpack. V2 ran away. She spotted D making his way towards a camper van parked nearby. The police were contacted and arrested D in the camper van. The vehicle was searched and a woman's stocking, a backpack containing a second stocking, a CS gas canister, a pot of Vaseline and a number of metal and rubber rings were discovered. A second backpack contained pornographic magazines, condoms, a machete, rope and various items of clothing. D, aged 49, had been married for 21 years and was a senior lecturer at Manchester Metropolitan University. He was highly regarded by his colleagues but he had convictions for indecent assault on a female and indecent exposure (×3) when aged 25 (3 years' probation). The pre-sentence report revealed that the offences were committed in furtherance of D's sexual fantasies. The Judge considered the circumstances in which the offences were committed, including the possession of the CS gas canister which was a serious aggravating factor, and imposed a sentence outside the guidelines. Held. The starting point for a repeat offender committing exposure offences is 12 weeks' custody with a range of 4-26 weeks. The canister would be used to deter anyone who challenged him. These were aggressive exposure offences. **8 months** concurrent for the exposure, consecutive to **8 months** for the CS gas canister, making **16 months**, was not manifestly excessive.

R v Nicholson 2014 EWCA Crim 2710 D pleaded to six counts of exposure. In prison, he would press his emergency bell. Staff could not ignore it as he was on suicide watch. When a female officer attended, he would expose his erect penis, masturbate and make sexual comments. He targeted one particular officer but a number of officers were subjected to this abuse. Once, when he was masturbating in the exercise yard, he told other inmates to push the button for the officer. He made comments like, "If she comes to the cage I'm going to rape her and you can watch." His privileges were withdrawn but his behaviour did not change. Between the plea of guilty and the date of sentence there were two further incidents. D was aged 22 and had convictions in each year between 2009 and 2012 for exposure or breach of his SOPO. In 2009, he exposed himself to a schoolgirl telling her to suck it and threatened her with rape if she didn't. When on bail, he followed two 17-year-old girls down the street saying he would "ram it up your fucking arse." In 2010, there was a further threatening exposure. In the same year, he touched a woman sexually and when she resisted, he punched her, breaking her jaw. In 2011, he received 3 years for a SOPO breach. In the same year, he exposed himself to two 14-year-old girls. In 2012, he was transferred to a medium secure hospital where he was disruptive and lacked any motivation. In one-to-one sessions he refused to stop masturbating. In another hospital he repeated similar conduct. Since November 2010, he had only been at liberty for four days. D had an IQ in the bottom 1%. He had a grossly abnormal personality and described rape fantasies. He told one psychiatrist he would do serious harm if he could get hold of females. He was assessed as posing a very high risk of harm and his offending was likely to lead to rape. He was also assessed as being incapable of engaging in treatment. The Judge said he had a poor understanding of his SOPO. Held. D was clearly dangerous. D possesses a continuing threat of a very serious nature and will do so unless and until he can receive treatment which currently he won't engage with. Protection of the public was a relevant consideration, Criminal Justice Act 2003 s 142(1). The Judge was entitled to take into consideration the dangers D posed. We start at **6 years**, so with plea 4 years not 4½ years in total.

See also: *R v Jones* 2013 EWCA Crim 145, 2 Cr App R (S) 66 (p 419) (Pleaded. On 1 October 2012, pushed down tracksuit bottoms exposing non-erect penis for a few seconds. Woman angry and shaken. Aged 37. In breach of community order for exposure, imposed in August 2012. In 1990s, he had four exposure convictions. Then five appearances for sexual assault and exposure. He had already been given 30 months and 15 months' custody. Judge entitled to depart from the guideline and impose **1 year** and 1 year making **2 years**.)

R v Hardy 2013 EWCA Crim 2125, 2014 1 Cr App R (S) 70 (p 452) (Convicted. Showing his semi-erect penis in a car park. At 4.45 pm, near a takeaway where children were likely to congregate. **4 months** not 12)

Old cases: *R v Hawkins* 2007 EWCA Crim 2221 (**community order**) *R v McMahon* 2008 EWCA Crim 3104, 2009 2 Cr App R (S) 31 (p 226) (**6 months**) *R v Audoire* 2008 EWCA Crim 822, 2009 1 Cr App R (S) 5 (p 20) (**2 years**) *R v Ferguson* 2008 EWCA Crim 2940, 2009 2 Cr App R (S) 8 (p 39) (**21 months**)

For a summary of the first two cases, see the 8th edition of this book.

Post-guideline case

R v Ketteridge 2014 EWCA Crim 1962, 2015 1 Cr App R (S) 11 (p 89) (Two offences, one three days after being given bail for the other. D exposed his penis, masturbating and staring at: a) schoolgirls aged 17/18, and b) girls aged 13-16, whilst driving slowly or stationary. D was aged 45, had a caution for exposure shortly before the first incident, had no convictions and had supportive statements. Counsellor diagnosed 'disassociation', a symptom of PTSD. Obviously not a case for a community order. **9 months** in all and **1-year driving ban** upheld.)

255   FAILING TO PROVIDE A SPECIMEN

255.1

Road Traffic Act 1988 s 7(6) (failure to provide a laboratory specimen)
   Mode of trial Summary only

Maximum sentence 6 months and/or a £5,000 fine for offences committed before 12 March 2015 and an unlimited fine thereafter.[378] There are maximum fines for those aged under 18, see **14.38** in Volume 1.

Disqualification Driving or attempting to drive, obligatory disqualification of minimum 1 year. When defendant in charge, discretionary disqualification. Where certain conditions are met the court may order a reduced period of disqualification. See the **Reduced disqualification for attendance on courses** note below for details.

Penalty points: Driving or attempting to drive: 3-11 points. In charge: 10 points if special reasons not to disqualify are found

Driving/being in charge under the influence of drugs There are offences of 'to drive or attempt to drive or be in charge of a motor vehicle when there is in [the driver's] body a specified controlled drug exceeding the specified limit', Road Traffic Act 1988 s 5A inserted by Crime and Courts Act 2013 s 56. The offences are triable summarily only and have the same penalties as drink/driving. In force 2 March 2015.[379]

For roadside drink/drugs tests, see **255.3**.

Reduced disqualification for attendance on courses There is power to order reduced disqualification for attendance on courses.[380] On 24 June 2013, Road Safety Act 2006 changes came into force. For details see the DISQUALIFICATION FROM DRIVING: OBLIGATORY *Reduced periods of disqualification for attendance on courses* para at **44.8** in Volume 1.

Depriving defendant of vehicle used There is power to deprive the defendant of the vehicle used[381] for the purposes of committing the offence.

Report In June 2010, Sir Peter North issued his report to the Department of Transport about drink/driving and drug/driving, see www.banksr.com The report made 51 recommendations including that: a) the drink/driving limits should be reduced, b) there should not be lower limits for HGV, PSV, taxi drivers or young or novice drivers, c) there should be an unrestricted power to demand a preliminary breath test, d) there should be no requirement for a preliminary breath test before an evidential breath test, e) there should be specified limits for a list of prohibited drugs, and f) the laboratory allowance for blood and urine tests should be reduced to 3%. Except for the driving when under the influence of drugs, there appear to have been no other changes made as a result of the report.

For Passenger Carrying Vehicle (PCV) and Large Goods Vehicle (LGV) drivers see the note at **341.1**.

Failure to provide a laboratory specimen

255.2   *Magistrates' Court Sentencing Guidelines*

Magistrates' Court Sentencing Guidelines 2008, see www.banksr.com Other Matters Guidelines tab The guideline applies to the Magistrates' Court and to the Crown Court hearing appeals or sentencing for summary only offences.[382]

page 128 Starting points are based on a first-time offender pleading not guilty. [Explanatory] note re final column: the period to be imposed in any individual case will depend on an assessment of all the relevant circumstances, including the length of time since the earlier ban and the gravity of the current offence.

Drive/attempt to drive

---

[378] Legal Aid, Sentencing and Punishment of Offenders Act 2012 s 85(1) and (4) and Legal Aid, Sentencing and Punishment of Offenders Act 2012 (Commencement No 11) Order 2015 2015/504
[379] Crime and Courts Act 2013 (Commencement No 1) (England and Wales) Order 2014 2014/3268
[380] Road Traffic Offenders Act 1988 s 34A
[381] Powers of Criminal Courts (Sentencing) Act 2000 s 143(6)-(7)
[382] See page 15 of the guidelines.

Examples of nature of activity	Starting point	Range	Disqualification	
			Normal	Second offence in 10 years
Defendant refused test when had honestly held but unreasonable excuse	Band C fine	Band C fine	12 to 16 months	36 to 40 months
Deliberate refusal or deliberate failure	Low-level community order	Band C fine to high-level community order	17 to 28 months	36 to 52 months
Deliberate refusal or deliberate failure where evidence of serious impairment	12 weeks' custody	High-level community order to 26 weeks' custody	29 to 36 months	36 to 60 months

page 129 **In charge**

Examples of nature of activity	Starting point	Range
Defendant refused test when had honestly held but unreasonable excuse	Band B fine	Band B fine [and] 10 points
Deliberate refusal or deliberate failure	Band C fine	Band C fine to medium-level community order Consider disqualification or 10 points
Deliberate refusal or deliberate failure where evidence of serious impairment	Medium-level community order	Low-level community order to 6 weeks' custody 6-12 month disqualification

The following aggravating and mitigating factors may be particularly relevant: Factors indicating higher culpability: 1 Evidence of unacceptable nature of driving[383] 2 LGV, HGV, PSV etc. 3 Obvious state of intoxication 4 High likelihood of driving (in charge cases only) 5 Driving for hire or reward. Factors indicating lower culpability: 1 Genuine but unsuccessful attempt to provide specimen 2 Low likelihood of driving (in charge cases only). Factor indicating greater degree of harm: Involved in accident.

For the meaning of a high-level, a medium-level and a low-level community order see **16.12-16.14** in Volume 1.

Consider offering drink/driving rehabilitation course.

A Band B fine is 100% of net weekly income. Band C is 150%. For more detail see **60.27** in Volume 1.

Consultation It is expected that the Sentencing Council will issue a consultation document about updating this guideline in May 2016.

For how to apply the guidelines see the GUIDELINES chapter in Volume 1.

Failure to provide roadside breath, saliva or sweat sample or co-operate with an impairment test

255.3

Road Traffic Act 1988 s 6(6)

   Mode of trial Summary only

---

[383] Not for in charge cases

Maximum sentence Level 3 fine (£1,000)
Disqualification Discretionary
Penalty points 4 points

255.4   *Magistrates' Court Sentencing Guidelines*

Magistrates' Court Sentencing Guideline 2008, see www.banksr.com Other Matters
Guidelines tab page 135 The starting point for a first-time offender pleading not guilty is
a band B fine (100% of net weekly income).
For more detail about fine bands see **60.27** in Volume 1.

256   FAILING TO STOP/FAILING TO REPORT

256.1

Road Traffic Act 1988 s 170 (failure to stop, report an accident and give information or
documents)
Mode of trial Summary only
Maximum sentence 6 months and/or a £5,000 fine for offences committed before 12
March 2015 and an unlimited fine thereafter.[384] There are maximum fines for those aged
under 18, see **14.38** in Volume 1.
Penalty points 5-10 points[385]
Depriving defendant of vehicle used There is power to deprive the defendant of the
vehicle used[386] for the purposes of committing the offence.
For failing to stop when required to by a constable (Road Traffic Act 1988 s 163) see the
Magistrates' Court Sentencing Guidelines 2008 Part 3, page 136, at **321.4**.

256.2   *Magistrates' Court Sentencing Guidelines*

Magistrates' Court Sentencing Guidelines 2008, see www.banksr.com Other Matters
Guidelines tab The guideline applies to the Magistrates' Court and to the Crown Court
hearing appeals or sentencing for summary only offences.[387]
page 127 Starting points are based on a first-time offender pleading not guilty.

Examples of nature of activity	Starting point	Range
Minor damage or stopped at scene but failed to exchange particulars or report	Band B fine	Band B fine [and] 5 to 6 points
Moderate damage or failed to stop and failed to report	Band C fine	Band C fine [and] 7 to 8 points Consider disqualification
Serious damage and/or evidence of bad driving	High-level community order	Band C fine to 26 weeks' custody 6-12 month disqualification or 9-10 points

The following aggravating and mitigating factors may be particularly relevant: Factors
indicating higher culpability: 1 Evidence of drink or drugs or evasion of test 2
Knowledge or suspicion that personal injury caused (where not an element of the
offence) 3 Leaving injured party at scene 4 Giving false details. Factors indicating lower
culpability: 1 Believed identity known 2 Genuine fear of retribution 3 Subsequently
reported.
For the meaning of a high-level community order see **16.14** in Volume 1.
Consider ancillary orders, including compensation.

---

[384] Legal Aid, Sentencing and Punishment of Offenders Act 2012 s 85(1) and (4) and Legal Aid, Sentencing and Punishment of
Offenders Act 2012 (Commencement No 11) Order 2015 2015/504
[385] Endorsement code AC10
[386] Powers of Criminal Courts (Sentencing) Act 2000 s 143(6)-(7)
[387] See page 15 of the guidelines.

A Band B fine is 100% of net weekly income. Band C is 150%. For more detail see **60.27** in Volume 1.

Consultation It is expected that the Sentencing Council will issue a consultation document about updating this guideline in May 2016.

257   FALSE ACCOUNTING

257.1

Theft Act 1968 s 17

Mode of trial Triable either way

Maximum sentence On indictment 7 years. Summary 6 months and/or a £5,000 fine for offences committed before 12 March 2015 and an unlimited fine thereafter.[388] There are maximum fines for those aged under 18, see **14.38** in Volume 1.

Serious Crime Prevention Order For Theft Act 1968 s 17 offences there is a discretionary power to make this order, when it would protect the public etc.[389]

Deferred Prosecution Agreements A designated prosecutor may apply to the court under Courts and Crime Act 2013 Sch 17 para 7, for this procedure to be apply. The procedure is laid down in Crime and Courts Act 2013 Sch 17. In force 24 February 2014.

257.2   *Crown Court statistics   England and Wales*

False accounting Aged 21+

Year	Plea	Total sentenced	Type of sentencing %						Average length of custody in months
			Discharge	Fine	Commu- nity sentence	Sus- pended sentence	Custody	Other	
2013	G	62	3.2	1.6	16.1	53.2	25.8	–	22.1
	NG	8	–	–	50	37.5	12.5	–	68
2014	G	47	4	–	13	53	30	–	16.9
	NG	5	–	–	20	20	60	–	not listed[390]

For explanations about the statistics see page 1-xii. For statistics for male and female defendants etc. see www.banksr.com Other Matters Statistics tab

257.3   *Sentencing Guidelines Council guideline*

Fraud, Bribery and Money Laundering Offences Guideline 2014, see www.banksr.com Other Matters Guidelines tab.

Which guideline to use depends on what offence the false accounting supported. If it was: a) benefit fraud (page 27), see **215.2**, b) fraud (page 8), see **265.3**, or c) tax fraud and duty evasion (page 19), see **343.3**. If the defendant is a company or public body (page 47), see **225.9**.

There are no recent reported cases, but similar cases are listed in the FRAUD AND FINANCIAL SERVICES OFFENCES and THEFT ETC. chapters.

Where the essence of the fraud is tax evasion, see the TAX FRAUD AND DUTY EVASION chapter.

258   FALSE IMPRISONMENT/KIDNAPPING

258.1

Both offences are common law offences.

Modes of trial Both offences are indictable only.

Maximum sentence Life[391]

---

[388] Legal Aid, Sentencing and Punishment of Offenders Act 2012 s 85(1) and (4) and Legal Aid, Sentencing and Punishment of Offenders Act 2012 (Commencement No 11) Order 2015 2015/504
[389] Serious Crime Act 2007 s 1 and Sch 1 para 7
[390] Based on too few cases to be meaningful
[391] *R v Szczerba* 2002 EWCA Crim 440, 2 Cr App R (S) 86 (p 387) at 392

Extended sentences This offence is listed in Criminal Justice Act 2003 Sch 15. The court may pass a 2012 extended sentence (EDS) if there is a significant risk of serious harm from future specified offences and either: a) the defendant has a Criminal Justice Act 2003 Sch 15B conviction (applicable only to defendants aged 18+), or b) the offence would justify a determinate sentence of at least 4 years.[392]

Sexual Harm Prevention Orders There is a discretionary power to make this order when it is necessary to protect the public from sexual harm.[393]

Children and vulnerable adults: barred lists Where the defendant is convicted of kidnapping and is aged 18 or over, he or she is automatically barred from engaging in regulated activity with children and with vulnerable adults.[394] The judge must tell the defendant that the Disclosure and Barring Service will include him or her in the barred lists.[395] The defendant may ask the Authority to remove him or her from the lists.

Law Commission On 20 November 2014, the Law Commission published its final report on kidnapping, false imprisonment and related offences. Two new statutory offences are recommended to replace the common law offences. Kidnapping would be a slightly narrower offence and more defined. False imprisonment would be replaced with an offence of 'unlawful detention'. One of the objectives is to update the law for offences involving children.

When linked to prostitution see the PROSTITUTION OFFENCES **Trafficking of prostitutes** section at **311.18**.

Taking the law into your own hands see DEFENDANT *Taking the law into your own hands* at **240.63**.

258.2 Crown Court statistics England and Wales
Kidnapping etc. Aged 21+

Year	Plea	Total sentenced	Type of sentencing %						Average length of custody in months
			Discharge	Fine	Community sentence	Suspended sentence	Custody	Other	
2013	G	168	–	–	3.6	10.7	84.5	1.2	37.5
	NG	58	1.7	–	5.2	5.2	86.2	1.7	56.8
2014	G	167	–	–	2	15	82	1	46.0
	NG	74	1	–	4	7	88	–	79.0

For explanations about the statistics see page 1-xii. For statistics for male and female defendants etc. see www.banksr.com Other Matters Statistics tab

258.3 Judicial guidance
Att-Gen's Ref Nos 92-93 of 2014 2014 EWCA Crim 2713, 2015 1 Cr App R (S) 44 (p 323) D pleaded to and G was convicted of conspiracy to kidnap, false imprisonment and conspiracy to blackmail (×3). D threatened to kill V or slash V's face but D became more aggressive, demanding £2,600 that V owed him in drug debts. D and G also called V's family demanding payment and making further threats against V which they took extremely seriously, phoning the police. Later that day, V's family arranged to pay over a sum of money. Held. Clearly the correct approach in this case will be, first of all, to have regard to the kidnapping and false imprisonment…and then to make allowance for the considerable aggravation represented by the blackmailing demands. The case of *R v Spence and Thomas* 1983 5 Cr App R (S) 413 was long regarded as providing guidance for levels of sentencing. It is clear, however, that in more recent times levels of

---

[392] Criminal Justice Act 2003 s 226A-226B as inserted by Legal Aid, Sentencing and Punishment of Offenders Act 2012 s 124
[393] Sexual Offences Act 2003 s 103A as inserted by Anti-social Behaviour, Crime and Policing Act 2014 Sch 5 para 2 and Sexual Offences Act 2003 Sch 5
[394] Safeguarding Vulnerable Groups Act 2006 s 2 and Sch 3 and Safeguarding Vulnerable Groups Act 2006 (Prescribed Criteria and Miscellaneous Provisions) Regulations 2009 2009/37 para 4 and 6 and Sch para 2 and 4
[395] Safeguarding Vulnerable Groups Act 2006 s 2 and Sch 3 para 25

sentencing in cases of this type, where the victim has been detained, subjected to violence and made the subject of monetary demands are better reflected by more recent decisions. Those decisions include *R v Ahmed* 2010 EWCA Crim 3133, 2011 2 Cr App R (S) 35 (p 217), see **217.9**, *R v Smickele and Others* 2012 EWCA Crim 1470, 2013 1 Cr App R (S) 64 (p 354)[396], see **217.9**, *Att-Gen's Ref No 57 of 2013* 2013 EWCA Crim 2144, see **258.5**, and *Att-Gen's Ref Nos 39-42 of 2014* 2014 EWCA Crim 1557, see **292.19**. In *R v Spence and Thomas* 1983 Lord Lane CJ commented on the wide possible variation of seriousness in kidnapping and similar cases. It seems to us that relevant factors in accessing the gravity of cases of this type will include the length of detention; the circumstances of detention, including location and any method of restraint; the extent of any violence used; the involvement of weapons; whether demands were made of others; whether threats were made to others; the effect on the victim and others; the extent of planning; the number of offenders involved; the use of torture or humiliation; whether what was done arose from or was in furtherance of previous criminal behaviour, and any particular vulnerability of the victim whether by reason of age or otherwise.

Att-Gen's Ref Nos 102-103 of 2014 2014 EWCA Crim 2922, 2015 Cr App R (S) 55 (p 389) para 29 Generally speaking, cases involving hostage taking and demands for ransom will attract figures close to the 16-year starting point. Others, where such behaviour [was] absent, will still attract double figures, regardless of the degree of violence meted out.

Relevant factors in accessing the gravity of cases of this type will include: the length of detention, the circumstances of detention, including location and any method of restraint, the extent of any violence used, the involvement of weapons, whether demands were made of others, whether threats were made to others, the effect on the victim and others, the extent of planning, the number of offenders involved, the use of torture or humiliation, whether what was done arose from or was in furtherance of previous criminal behaviour, and any particular vulnerability of the victim whether by reason of age or otherwise.

R v Mahmood and Others 2015 EWCA Crim 441, 2 Cr App R (S) 18 (p 182) D made a late plea to conspiracy to kidnap, false imprisonment, section 18 and section 20. He and another put V in a shipping container where he was tortured with hammers etc. Other violence inflicted. We do not consider *R v Ahmed and Others* 2010 EWCA Crim 3133, 2011 2 Cr App R (S) 35 (p 217) sets the upper limit for kidnapping. Nothing wrong with starting at 18 years here.

Blackmail, with see the **BLACKMAIL** chapter. Where the motive is blackmail, the case is listed under **BLACKMAIL** whether or not there was a conviction for blackmail.

Debt collecting see the **BLACKMAIL** *Debt collecting* paras at **217.5**.

258.4   Defendant aged 10-17

R v R and S 2012 EWCA Crim 1459, 2013 1 Cr App R (S) 58 (p 327) R pleaded to false imprisonment, criminal damage and theft. S pleaded to false imprisonment, threats to kill and criminal damage. V, a 42-year-old lady with learning difficulties, was at times particularly vulnerable to people taking advantage of her. She had been to a pub and was going to bed in the early hours when she heard a knocking at the door of her upper flat, in which she lived alone. V heard a girl asking to be let in. She opened the door and R and S followed what was probably a group of three girls into the flat. They began to misbehave, the cooker was switched on and a frying pan put on the heat by R. The fire alarm was triggered and subsequently broken by S. Body cream was spread on the walls and S cut and damaged the chair and sofa in the living room. Clothing was flung out of drawers, tampons were spread about and washing-up liquid was placed in the kettle. V became increasingly distressed. S threatened her with a machete-style knife. He threatened to chop her fingers and toes off. She was told to kneel and beg for her life. She was dressed in her night clothes. She was continually threatened including being

---

[396] The reference to this case in the judgment is wrong.

told that reprisals would be carried out if she contacted the police. She was told she would have to pay a small sum to them and the suggestion made that V's son, who did not live with her, might be kidnapped. V's phone was taken and S broke her SIM card to prevent communication. V tried to get them to leave but they ignored her. One of the group said that they had in effect taken over her house and kidnapped her. Two of the girls left, leaving D, S and one girl. V was tied to a chair by her arms and legs. R acquired a knife from the kitchen and S and R threatened her, holding knives close to her neck and eyes. Part of that activity was recorded on S's mobile phone. The actions were meant to humiliate and demean V. S continued to threaten V and told her that he would kill her. He told her to beg for her life. The girls who had left returned and V was freed from the chair. This was at about 7 am. V had therefore been detained for approximately six hours. Threats were made that they would return and kill her if she told anyone about the incident. R showed the recorded footage to his mother, who thought it had been manufactured. S telephoned the police to admit the offences and answered questions in interview. R declined to answer questions. R pleaded on a basis stating that he did not have a knife when he went to V's address, he had gone to sleep in an adjacent room with his girlfriend and heard S's voice. He was told that S had held a knife to V's throat and had made her beg for her life. R passed the cables to S so that he could tie V up and then became involved in the recording. R was aged 17 and S aged 16 at the time of the offences. R had convictions for theft (×4) and burglary. He had a warning for threatening behaviour. S had convictions for arson, assault, disorderly behaviour and breaching ASBOs, together with offences of criminal damage and burglary. He had one previous custodial sentence (4-month DTO). The pre-sentence report stated that S showed no victim empathy. He had become a father aged 13 and presented a high risk of reoffending. He had to be segregated whilst on remand because of his negative behaviour. The pre-sentence report indicated that R minimised his culpability and blamed others. He presented a high risk of reoffending. Held. S had a worse record but did hand himself in to the police. R didn't. This was closely akin to a violent personal robbery within the home, even though no property was stolen. The recording of the incident and of the distress to V aggravates the offence. The appropriate starting point for an adult after a trial would be 12 years. Significant allowance had to be made for their youth and their pleas of guilty entered at the first opportunity. The Judge reduced the starting point by just under one half, which was a legitimate approach. The appropriate sentence was **6½ years'** detention under section 91, not 8.

Old case: *R v P* 2006 1 Cr App R (S) 113 (p 658) (**3 years**)

For a summary of the case, see the 9th edition of this book.

Firearms, With (real or imitation) see the **FIREARM OFFENCES** chapter.

258.5   *Domestic offences*

R v Ashworth 2009 EWCA Crim 1028, 2010 1 Cr App R (S) 15 (p 84) D pleaded (full credit) to false imprisonment and criminal damage. At his parents' home, D sought payment from his father, F, for some gardening work that D had done. An argument about that went on for several hours. Then there was an argument with F as to who should walk the dogs. F thought that D was trying to provoke an argument. He told D to leave him alone. D threw an orange at the wall, saying, "You fucking bastard". D also said with real venom, "You don't deserve to live". D threw a plate against the wall, saying, "It's your fault I'm in this position". Next, D poured the contents of a glass over F. F went upstairs and took his mobile. He said, "If you don't leave me alone I will call the police". D said, "You're not calling them, I have too much to lose". F said, "I've had enough, I'm phoning". F got up to go downstairs and D seized him by the wrist and wrenched the phone from him. F went upstairs. D stood at the top of the stairs, blocking F's way. F went to reach for the bedroom phone and dialled 999, but D punched the phone out of his hand. Police responded because it was a silent call. Meanwhile D pushed F onto the bed saying, "I'll stand here all night". D's mother was very anxious because of the similarity to an incident she suffered from D. The police arrived. When aged 17 D was convicted of an affray directed against his mother. When aged nearly 18, D was convicted of battery against his mother. When aged nearly 20, he was dealt with for false imprisonment (with a knife), battery, criminal damage and intimidation against his mother (21 months' detention). When aged 24, D took his mother's car and used it with others to commit a burglary in a church. Still aged 24 he was dealt with for aggravated vehicle-taking. When pursued by police D wrote the car off. Two months later, in the same month as the instant offence, he was dealt with for criminal damage to his sister's car. There were other offences involving the police and at least one involving paramedics. Also there was affray (with a knife) and racially aggravated assault against a police officer. At the time of the instant offences he was subjected to a community order, a suspended sentence, and was on bail for his sister's car offence. D was aged 24 with episodes of psychosis due to drug taking. The pre-sentence report said that there was a high risk of reoffending and a high risk of D's committing violent offences. He had manipulative and predatory behaviour associated with the targeting of his mother. He showed a great deal of antipathy towards the legal system and its agencies. D tended to turn to alcohol as a means of addressing any emotional or psychological disturbance. Held. This was a very serious incident. However, the detention was of short duration, the actual violence was modest, no weapon was used and it occurred spontaneously. **2 years** not 2 years' IPP.

R v Saker 2011 EWCA Crim 1196, 2012 1 Cr App R (S) 16 (p 87) D pleaded to false imprisonment. Her daughter, V, aged 18, had confessed to a drug addiction. Following a number of items going missing, including money, about £1,000, V said that she was obtaining drugs from an older man, who was pressuring her into performing sexual acts as payment. V later claimed this was untrue. V stated that the older man was outside and she wished to leave with him. V's former boyfriend, B, and D detained V in her bedroom. D co-operated with B in restraining V, and also lent support to the suggestion of violence against her. V was tied up with parcel tape and had a sock inserted into her mouth. D stated that B would inflict violence on V, before leaving the room. V was duly assaulted. D was of good character. The Judge noted that D's efforts were an extremely misguided attempt to scare V into halting her addiction. Held. Immediate imprisonment was justified given the degree of violence. **12 months** was not manifestly excessive.

258.5a *Relationship offences*

R v Higgins 2014 EWCA Crim 2776 D pleaded to kidnapping, ABH and breach of a Restraining Order (2 months). There was a long history of problems between D and V, his former long-standing partner. On 22 May 2014, D was given a suspended sentence and a Restraining Order. On 12 June 2014, neighbours heard screaming coming from V's house. One, N, went to the house and banged on the door and D answered it. He told N to go away. She didn't and saw V run from the house with her five-year-old daughter. The daughter was handed to a neighbour. D seized V and pushed her towards a waiting car with a male in the driver's seat. Then he pushed her face into the side of the vehicle and 'bundled' her into the back seat. The car drove away. It was not suggested that the other male was involved in the kidnap. V shouted to be let out. The car stopped and V managed to get out of the car and go home. She was crying and had a facial injury. She had pains in her head, eyes and chest with shortness of breath. D was aged 22 when sentenced and had a number of previous convictions including racially aggravated ABH, public order offences, criminal damage, possession of an offensive weapon and harassment. Held. Everything took place in the presence of the child. Consecutive sentences for the kidnapping and ABH were wrong. There should have been a [global] sentence. We start at 30 months not 2 years for the kidnapping. The ABH was Category 2 not 1. On its own, after a trial, it was worth 6 not 12 months but it is reflected in our [global] sentence. So with plea **20 months**. The 2-month sentence for the breach and 10 weeks for the breach of the suspended sentence to remain consecutive.

See also: *R v F* 2013 EWCA Crim 2698 (Plea. With W, tied friend of W's ex-girlfriend to a bed with belts. Imprisoned for short duration. Lack of violence toward W or his ex-girlfriend. Previous good character and just aged 18. With full credit, **16 months** not 24.)

258.6   *Victim tied up/Violence used*

R v R and S 2012 EWCA Crim 1459, 2013 1 Cr App R (S) 58 (p 327) R pleaded to false imprisonment, criminal damage and theft. S pleaded to false imprisonment, threats to kill and criminal damage. V, a 42-year-old lady with learning difficulties, was at times particularly vulnerable to people taking advantage of her. She had been to a pub and was going to bed in the early hours when she heard a knocking at the door of her upper flat, in which she lived alone. V heard a girl asking to be let in. She opened the door and R and S followed what was probably a group of three girls into the flat. They began to misbehave, the cooker was switched on and a frying pan put on the heat by R. The fire alarm was triggered and subsequently broken by S. Body cream was spread on the walls and S cut and damaged the chair and sofa in the living room. Clothing was flung out of drawers, tampons were spread about and washing-up liquid was placed in the kettle. V became increasingly distressed. S threatened her with a machete-style knife. He threatened to chop her fingers and toes off. She was told to kneel and beg for her life. She was dressed in her night clothes. She was continually threatened including being told that reprisals would be carried out if she contacted the police. She was told she would have to pay a small sum to them and the suggestion made that V's son, who did not live with her, might be kidnapped. V's phone was taken and S broke her SIM card to prevent communication. V tried to get them to leave but they ignored her. One of the group said that they had in effect taken over her house and kidnapped her. Two of the girls left, leaving D, S and one girl. V was tied to a chair by her arms and legs. R acquired a knife from the kitchen and S and R threatened her, holding knives close to her neck and eyes. Part of that activity was recorded on S's mobile phone. The actions were meant to humiliate and demean V. S continued to threaten V and told her that he would kill her. He told her to beg for her life. The girls who had left returned and V was freed from the chair. This was at about 7 am. V had therefore been detained for approximately six hours. Threats were made that they would return and kill her if she told anyone about the incident. R showed the recorded footage to his mother, who thought it had been manufactured. S telephoned the police to admit the offences and answered questions in interview. R declined to answer questions. R pleaded on a basis stating that he did not have a knife when he went to V's address, he had gone to sleep in an adjacent room with his girlfriend and heard S's voice. He was told that S had held a knife to V's throat and had made her beg for her life. R passed the cables to S so that he could tie V up and then became involved in the recording. R was aged 17 and S aged 16 at the time of the offences. R had convictions for theft (×4) and burglary. He had a warning for threatening behaviour. S had convictions for arson, assault, disorderly behaviour and breaching ASBOs, together with offences of criminal damage and burglary. He had one previous custodial sentence (4-month DTO). The pre-sentence report stated that S showed no victim empathy. He had become a father aged 13 and presented a high risk of reoffending. He had to be segregated whilst on remand because of his negative behaviour. The pre-sentence report indicated that R minimised his culpability and blamed others. He presented a high risk of reoffending. Held. S had a worse record but did hand himself in to the police. R didn't. This was closely akin to a violent personal robbery within the home, even though no property was stolen. The recording of the incident and of the distress to V aggravates the offence. The appropriate starting point for an adult after a trial would be 12 years. Significant allowance had to be made for their youth and their pleas of guilty entered at the first opportunity. The Judge reduced the starting point by just under one half, which was a legitimate approach. The appropriate sentence was **6½ years'** detention not 8.

R v Williams and Others 2012 EWCA Crim 2108, 2013 1 Cr App R (S) 105 (p 549) W was convicted of false imprisonment. W and B were convicted of false imprisonment and making an indecent image of a child. V, a vulnerable girl aged 16, lived in a hostel on her own. She was friends with some of the defendants. It was believed that V had stolen a watch belonging to Q and about £50 from SR. W and J, an acquaintance, were at another hostel with V. W and J started asking V about her suicide attempt a few days before. J grabbed V and tied her wrists with a dressing gown cord. He demanded her mobile phone. She was locked in a cupboard by W, who went to look for the phone. V hid it. W returned empty-handed and J became aggressive. He searched V and pulled her trousers down. He found the phone in the cupboard and demanded to know the PIN code to unlock it. V gave him the wrong number and he locked her in a cupboard for about an hour. She could not get out and was not permitted to go to the lavatory. J threatened her with a knife and when he allowed her out of the cupboard, he beat her with W's leather belt. He pushed her back into the cupboard and threatened her again. SR arrived about four hours after the incident began. V had been allowed out of the cupboard and had most of her property returned to her, excluding her phone and a silver chain. S was determined to get her money back from V. V wanted to settle the debt and asked her mother for £100 as she had 'got into trouble'. She told her mother that she had been tied up and the call was cut off. SR forcibly dragged V into a car. V was then free to leave but remained in the car because SR was her best friend. B was in the car with her young child. They drove around for several hours before picking up S, B's best friend. S got into the car and punched V in the face. They drove to a poorly lit car park and demanded that V get out of the car. She did so. She was given a choice between stripping naked and putting her hands in boiling water. B removed that choice and told her to strip. V did so, feeling that she could not leave. When V was naked, B and S took pictures using their mobile phones. They were sent to W and posted on the Internet, although it is not known by whom. W was aged 20 at appeal. S was aged 30 at appeal. She had convictions for assault, battery and theft. B was aged 28 at appeal. She had six convictions, mostly for driving offences and possession of cannabis. Held. This was a bad case of bullying and humiliation. V was vulnerable and in a fragile mental state. This was known by both W and J. W and J were equally responsible and no distinction was to be drawn between them on the sentences imposed. The behaviour in the car park amounted to the deliberate humiliation of V. No violence was actually used but the photograph was distributed on Facebook. For W **4 years** was severe but not manifestly excessive. For B and S, **3 years** not 4 was appropriate.

R v Hamaizia 2013 EWCA Crim 796 LCJ D was convicted of section 20, having earlier pleaded to false imprisonment. He was part of a group who wanted V to help 'set up' MH, for revenge. MH was later murdered. D was tried for that but was acquitted. The group kidnapped V and took him to a flat. V was hit by one of the group with a baseball bat. D hit him with a saucepan. His ankles and wrists were bound. A lit cigarette was placed on his leg and D hit V across the knees with the baseball bat. The group left, save for D and V. D went to the kitchen to fetch a knife. He returned, threatened to stab V and proceeded to cut him twice across the cheek. V freed himself and raised the alarm. He was unco-operative with the police. He suffered grazes and swelling to the face, lacerations to his back, swelling to his right knee and cuts to his cheek. The assaults lasted 10 or 11 minutes. D, aged 20 at appeal, suffered from Asperger's syndrome. Consequently he was detained in hospital. The pre-sentence report noted that: a) D struggled to appreciate the likely impact of his behaviour on V, b) D would have struggled to understand the complexities of the motivations of the group when they might have differed from his own, c) D was naïve and had a complete disregard for the nature of the activities he was involved with, and d) the reason for the level of violence D used was to impress and 'fit into' his new circle of friends. Held. This was a serious offence of its kind. It was planned and its purpose was to inflict violence and fear on V. D played a crucial role and joined in when members of the group inflicted serious injuries on V. It was significant that D continued with the acts of violence after the group had left. D had reduced culpability as a result of his Asperger's syndrome. The sentence was not excessive before the Asperger's condition was considered. That should be reflected in a somewhat lower sentence than the others. **5 years' detention in a YOI**, not 6 years.

R v Pierre 2014 EWCA Crim 733 D pleaded to false imprisonment and ABH. D was part of a gang. The gang believed that V had made detrimental comments about them. V was lured to a flat belonging to another member of the gang. When asleep, V was kicked in the face by D. Others who were present looked on as he was kicked, slapped, punched and bitten. He was unable to defend himself. The assault was filmed on a phone and forwarded to others using the BlackBerry Messaging service. After two hours, V nosedived through a window to escape. D, aged 26, had 11 convictions for 15 offences. The pre-sentence report highlighted his lack of empathy for V, saying D felt V had deserved what he got. Held. Gang behaviour could not be tolerated. The assaults were designed to be degrading. The Judge's starting point of 7 years could not be criticised. To give a distinction between H, the ringleader and D, his lieutenant and with full credit, **4 years 3 months** not 4 years 9 months.

R v Yousef 2015 EWCA Crim 1315 D was convicted of false imprisonment and ABH. V was invited to a party by D and she arrived at 11.30 pm. Another guest took V to a bedroom and raped her. V was punched by him during and after the rape. V told D and others she had been raped and she intended to call the police. D and another 'dragged her out', pulled her hair and forced her into another room. The two kicked V without shoes but caused bruises and other injuries. They took V's mobile and kept her for at least two hours. V was eventually able to escape. V had bruising to the face and loose teeth. D was aged 45 and had a conviction for child cruelty (Community Rehabilitation Order) which she breached (12 months' imprisonment). She did not co-operate with probation properly. The Judge said a) the assault was to humiliate and frighten V, b) it was very nasty and terrifying, c) it was designed to stop V calling the police, and d) and that it was to protect her tenancy. The defence relied on her depression from her experiences during the Somalian civil war. Held. It was traumatic, but the assault was relatively short. **4½ years** in all not 6.

See also: *R v Parkins and Others* 2011 EWCA Crim 968 (Pleas to false imprisonment (×2) and ABH (×2). Victim accused of setting up another for robbery. Victim was bound, gagged and beaten. Cut off victim's hair with scissors. Four defendants used a metal bar and plastic handcuffs, and had with them a knife and some wire. Took victim to another address. Incident lasted about an hour. For three defendants **4 years' YOI** and for the fourth, **42 months' YOI**.)

Att-Gen's Ref No 57 of 2013 2013 EWCA Crim 2144 (D pleaded to false imprisonment, ABH, perverting the course of justice and administering a noxious substance. Prolonged attack on V for claimed rumours when V was baby-sitting at night. Waved knife at V, punched and kicked him. Forced V to admit he had had gay oral sex and filmed confession. Denigrated V and poured salt in his wounds. Forced him to drink D's urine. Starting at 12 years not 8. The sentence could have been longer. With plea **9 years** not 6.)

Att-Gen's Ref No 9 of 2014 2014 EWCA Crim 952 (Plea on day of trial (10% credit) to false imprisonment and ABH (×5). Victim was next-door neighbour. He was vulnerable. Made to live in the garage. Treated like a slave, shouted at, fed one meal a day and made to defecate in a bucket. He was free to leave but pressure exerted on him to remain. Routinely subjected to violence with weapons. Suffered bruising, swelling and fractures. 2½ years for false imprisonment consecutive to 4 years for the ABH, making **6½ years** which was not unduly lenient.)

Att-Gen's Ref Nos 102-103 of 2014 2014 EWCA Crim 2922, 2015 Cr App R (S) 55 (p 389) (Convicted false imprisonment, ABH and two threats to kill. Two defendants suspected V had stolen a wallet. V was punched, kicked in head and stamped on. Later V was tied up and blindfolded. Iron used to burn arm. Later repeatedly plunged in water so he thought he was going to drown. Held over second-floor balcony. Eventually released and told if he complained he and his grandmother would be killed. V refused to go to hospital and only spoke to police when he was in breach of his bail conditions. Defendants had previous convictions for serious violence. 13 years' extended sentence (**10 years'** custody 3 years' extended licence))

Att-Gen's Ref Nos 109-111 of 2014 2014 EWCA Crim 2859 (Plea to false imprisonment and burglary. Hoods and gloves used. Victim of burglary aged 69, tied up. Engagement ring taken. Terrible effect on victim. We start at 7+ years so with full credit, **4½ years** each.

Old cases: There are plenty of recent cases. If old cases are required, they are listed in the 9th edition of this book.

Robbery, With see the **ROBBERY** chapter.

258.7 *Sexual activity, With or threats of*
Note: These cases are now prosecuted with a sex offence, no doubt to indicate the seriousness of sex offending and to enable notification to be triggered. The old cases under false imprisonment are best ignored. Ed.

259   FIREARM OFFENCES

259.1
1) Firearms Act 1968
   s 1, 2, 3(1)(a), 4(4), 5, 5(1)(b), 5(2A), 16, 16A, 17(1), 18(1), 19(1) and 21(4)
   For the modes of trial and the penalties, see the specific offences which start at **259.12**.
2) Firearms Act 1968 s 22(1) (purchase or hire any firearm or ammunition by a person under 18)[397]
   Mode of trial Summary only
   Maximum sentence 6 months in certain circumstances[398] and/or £5,000 fine for offences committed before 12 March 2015 and an unlimited fine thereafter.[399] There are maximum fines for those aged under 18, see **14.38**.
3) Firearms Act 1968 s 24ZA (failing to prevent minors from having air weapons)[400]
   Mode of trial Summary only
   Maximum sentence Level 3 fine (£1,000)
4) Customs and Excise Management Act 1979
   s 50 (improper importation of goods)
   s 68 (exportation of prohibited or restricted goods)
   s 170(1)-(2) (fraudulent evasion of duty etc.)
   For the penalties see **274.1** and **343.1**.

Extended sentences Sections 16, 16A, 17(1), 17(2) and 18 are listed in Criminal Justice Act 2003 Sch 15. The court may pass a 2012 extended sentence (EDS) if there is a significant risk of serious harm from future specified offences and either: a) the defendant has a Criminal Justice Act 2003 Sch 15B conviction (applicable only to defendants aged 18+), or b) the offence would justify a determinate sentence of at least 4 years.[401]

Minimum sentences Firearms Act 1968 s 5(1)(a), (ab), (aba), (ac), (ad), (ae), (af), (c), 5(1A)(a) and 5(2A)[402] and Firearms Act 1968 s 16, 16A, 17-20(1)[403] offences, in respect

---

[397] As inserted by Firearms (Amendment) Regulations 2010 2010/1759
[398] In force 28/7/10, Firearms (Amendment) Regulations 2010 2010/1759
[399] Legal Aid, Sentencing and Punishment of Offenders Act 2012 s 85(1) and (4) and Legal Aid, Sentencing and Punishment of Offenders Act 2012 (Commencement No 11) Order 2015 2015/504
[400] As inserted by Crime and Security Act 2010 s 46. In force 10/2/11
[401] Criminal Justice Act 2003 s 226A-226B as inserted by Legal Aid, Sentencing and Punishment of Offenders Act 2012 s 124
[402] Anti-social Behaviour, Crime and Policing Act 2014 s 108(6) inserts section 5(2A).
[403] Firearms Act 1968 s 51A(b)(iii) as inserted by Violent Crime Reduction Act 2006 s 30

of firearms or ammunition specified in Firearms Act 1968 s 5(1)(a), (ab), (aba), (ac), (ad), (ae), (af), or (c) or s 5(1A)(a) or 5(2A), carry a minimum sentence of 5 years for defendants aged 18+ years unless there are exceptional circumstances.[404] Where the offender is aged under 18, the minimum sentence is 3 years' detention.[405] The offence of using someone to mind a weapon under Violent Crime Reduction Act 2006 s 28 has its own minimum sentences created by that Act.[406] The minimum periods are the same. See the **Minimum sentences** section at **259.49**.

Confiscation Where a defendant has a criminal lifestyle the court, once the confiscation proceedings are triggered (see **22.11** in Volume 1), <u>must</u> follow the Proceeds of Crime Act 2002 procedure. 'Criminal lifestyle' offences include those under Firearms Act 1968 s 3(1).[407] For what constitutes a criminal lifestyle see **22.43** in Volume 1.

Forfeiture and cancellation of a firearm certificate There is power to make these orders, see **259.68**.

Serious Crime Prevention Orders For Customs and Excise Management Act 1979 s 68(2) and 170 where the offence is committed in connection with a firearm or ammunition and Firearms Act 1968 s 3(1) offences there is a discretionary power to make this order, when it would protect the public etc.[408]

Sexual Harm Prevention Orders For offences under Firearms Act 1968 s 16, 16A, 17(1)-(2) and 18 there is a discretionary power to make this order when it is necessary to protect the public from sexual harm.[409]

Serious Crime Act 2015 s 47(3) adds Firearms Act 1968 s 1(1), 2(1) and 5(1), (1A) and (2A) to Serious Crime Act 2007 Sch 1, thus enabling this discretionary order to be made for those offences as well. In force 3 May 2015.[410].

Law Commission On 16 December 2015, the Law Commission issued its report paper on reforming firearms law, Law Com No 563. The recommendations include new definitions and minor alterations. It is suggested that the law should be codified, but after the current recommendations have been enacted. The urgent need for an increase in certain penalties is not addressed.

259.2 *Crown Court statistics* *England and Wales*
Firearms Act offences

Year	Age	Plea	Total sentenced	Type of sentencing %						Average length of custody in months
				Dis-charge	Fine	Commu-nity sentence	Sus-pended sentence	Cus-tody	Other	
Possession of firearms [offences] indictable only										
2014	18-20	G	11	–	9	–	36	55	–	35.7
		NG	0							
	21+	G	88	2	–	1	23	73	1	45.7
		NG	13	–	–	–	8	92	–	77.0

---

[404] Firearms Act 1968 s 51A inserted by Criminal Justice Act 2003 s 287
[405] Firearms Act 1968 s 51A(4)-(5)
[406] See Violent Crime Reduction Act 2006 s 29(4) and (5).
[407] Proceeds of Crime Act 2002 s 6 and 75 and Sch 2 para 5(2)
[408] Serious Crime Act 2007 s 1 and Sch 1 para 3
[409] Sexual Offences Act 2003 s 103A as inserted by Anti-social Behaviour, Crime and Policing Act 2014 Sch 5 para 2 and Sexual Offences Act 2003 Sch 5
[410] Serious Crime Act 2015 (Commencement No 1) Regulations 2015 2015/820 para 2

Year	Age	Plea	Total sentenced	Type of sentencing %						Average length of custody in months
				Dis-charge	Fine	Commu-nity sentence	Sus-pended sentence	Cus-tody	Other	
Possession of firearms [offences] triable either way										
2014	18-20	G	53	–	2	11	13	74	–	31.1
		NG	3	–	–	–	–	100	–	not listed[411]
	21+	G	404	3	3	11	34	47	2	39.3
		NG	34	6	–	6	15	74	–	58.3
Possession of firearms with intent										
2014	18-20	G	38	–	–	5	21	68	5	32.3
		NG	6	–	–	–	17	83	–	31.2
	21+	G	190	2	–	5	29	60	4	25.3
		NG	24	–	–	–	–	92	8	48.1
Other firearm offences										
2014	18-20	G	2	–	50	–	–	50	–	not listed
		NG	1	–	–	–	–	100	–	not listed
	21+	G	34	3	–	–	18	71	9	55.7
		NG	11	–	–	–	–	100	–	57.8

For explanations about the statistics see page 1-xii. For statistics for male and female defendants etc. see www.banksr.com Other Matters Statistics tab

259.3   *Guideline cases and judicial guidance*

R v Avis 1998 2 Cr App R (S) 178 LCJ The number convicted of some firearms offences has very sharply increased. The unlawful possession and use of firearms is generally recognised as a grave source of danger to society. The reasons are obvious. Firearms may be used to take life or cause serious injury. They are used to further the commission of other serious crimes. Often the victims will be those charged with the enforcement of the law or the protection of persons or property. In the conflicts which occur between competing criminal gangs, often related to the supply of drugs, the use and possession of firearms provoke an escalating spiral of violence. The appropriate level of sentence for a firearms offence, as for any other offence, will depend on all the facts and circumstances relevant to the offence and the offender, and it would be wrong for this court to seek to prescribe unduly restrictive sentencing guidelines. It will, however, usually be appropriate for the sentencing court to ask itself a series of questions:

1) What sort of weapon is involved? Genuine firearms are more dangerous than imitation firearms. Loaded firearms are more dangerous than unloaded firearms. Unloaded firearms for which ammunition is available are more dangerous than firearms for which no ammunition is available. Possession of a firearm which has no lawful use (such as a sawn-off shotgun) will be viewed even more seriously than possession of a firearm which is capable of lawful use.

2) What (if any) use has been made of the firearm? It is necessary for the court, as with any other offence, to take account of all circumstances surrounding any use made of the firearm: the more prolonged and premeditated and violent the use, the more serious the offence is likely to be.

3) With what intention (if any) did the defendant possess or use the firearm? Generally speaking, the most serious offences under the Act are those which

---

[411] 'Not listed' means that it is considered that there are too few cases to make the data meaningful

require proof of a specific criminal intent (to endanger life, to cause fear of violence, to resist arrest, to commit an indictable offence). The more serious the act intended, the more serious the offence.

4) What is the defendant's record? The seriousness of any firearm offence is inevitably increased if the offender has an established record of committing firearms offences or crimes of violence.

Where there are breaches of Firearms Act 1968 s 4, 5, 16, 16A, 17(1) and (2), 18(1), 19 or 21 the custodial term is likely to be of considerable length, and where the four questions suggested above yield answers adverse to the offender, terms at or approaching the maximum may in a contested case be appropriate. An indeterminate sentence should, however, be imposed only where the established criteria for imposing such a sentence are met.

Att-Gen's Ref No 43 of 2009 2009 EWCA Crim 1925, 2010 1 Cr App R (S) 100 (p 628) LCJ The gravity of gun crime cannot be exaggerated. Guns kill and maim, terrorise and intimidate. That is why criminals want them: that is why they use them: and that is why they organise their importation and manufacture, supply and distribution. Sentencing courts must address the fact that too many lethal weapons are too readily available: too many are carried; too many are used, always with devastating effect on individual victims and with insidious corrosive impact on the well-being of the local community. Whenever a gun is made available for use as well as when a gun is used, public protection is the paramount consideration. Deterrent and punitive sentences are required and should be imposed. The value of the *R v Avis* 1998 series of questions for use by the judiciary in the Crown Court is undiminished. But, the broad guidance requires further amplification both in the light of subsequent legislation and because *R v Avis* 1998 did not address large-scale importation and/or manufacture, sale and distribution of guns. The possession of a firearm, without more, and without any aggravating features beyond the fact of such possession, is of itself a grave crime.

R v Sheen and Sheen 2011 EWCA Crim 2461, 2012 2 Cr App R (S) 3 (p 7) The defendants pleaded to possession with intent to endanger life. The court considered the four *R v Avis* 1998 questions and added two new ones. 5) Where was the firearm (or were the firearms) discharged, and who and how many were exposed to danger by its or their use? 6) Was any injury or damage caused by the discharge of a firearm or firearms, and if so how serious was it? para 12 The sentence may be longer than a sentence for attempted murder.

Note: I do not consider the Court intended to add these two questions so that the *R v Avis* 1998 test would be diluted. If six answers rather than four are considered, it would be easier to say the majority were not adverse to the defendant (which means that sentence would not have approached the maximum). It may be that these additional questions are factors to consider when the court is considering the more serious offending. Ed.

Specific offences

259.4 *Ammunition, Possession of*

R v Rudups 2011 EWCA Crim 61 D pleaded (full credit) to unlawful possession of ammunition. The prosecution offered no evidence on the count of unlawful possession of a prohibited weapon. He was a Latvian national who drove through Poland and Germany to Dover. There, D informed customs officers that he had a gun. He was arrested. In interview he informed officers that he had purchased the weapon for the purpose of defending himself as he drove from Latvia to the UK as he intended to sleep in his car. The weapon was a 9 mm calibre blank pistol, and he also had in his possession CN 'Mace cartridges' designed to discharge noxious substances. It was designed to fire CS gas cartridges. The weapon and cartridges were not prohibited items in Latvia, Germany or Poland. He had not considered whether it was legal to import them into the UK. A pre-sentence report assessed D as posing a low risk of reoffending. It voiced concern at how D would provide for his daughter should he be given a custodial sentence and

recommended a Suspended Sentence Order. D was of excellent previous character. Held. D was ignorant of the illegality of importing the weapon and its ammunition into the UK. Persons coming to this country should familiarise themselves with the law relating to guns and ammunition before they arrive. However, we underline the fact that he handed over the items as soon as he stepped onto British soil for the first time. The Judge was correct in identifying that he should depart from the statutory 5-year minimum sentence as required by Firearms Act 1968 s 51A on the existence of exceptional circumstances. **6 months** not 12.
Death results see the MANSLAUGHTER *Firearms, With* para at **284.34**.

259.5   *Imitation firearms   Judicial guidance*
R v Avis 1998 2 Cr App R (S) 178 LCJ Where imitation firearms are involved, the risk to life and limb is absent, but such weapons can be and often are used to frighten and intimidate victims in order to reinforce unlawful demands. Such imitation weapons are often very hard to distinguish from the real thing – for practical purposes, impossible in the circumstances in which they are used – and the victim is usually as much frightened and intimidated as if a genuine firearm had been used. Such victims are often isolated and vulnerable.

259.6   *Importation/exportation of firearms   Basic principles*
(Including other goods subject to sanctions)
Customs and Excise Management Act 1979 s 50, 68, 170(1)-(2) and Trade in Goods (Control) Order 2003 2003/2765 art 9(2).
Modes of trial Triable either way
Maximum sentence On indictment for offences involving a prohibited weapon or ammunition[412] restricted by Firearms Act 1968 s 5(1)(a), (ab), (aba), (ac), (ad), (ae), (af), (c), (1A)(a) and (2A)[413] the maximum sentence is life for offences committed on or after 14 July 2014 and 10 years for offences committed before 14 July 2014.[414] Otherwise 7 years. Summary maximum 6 months and/or a fine of £5,000 or three times the value of the goods, whichever is greater.[415]
Confiscation Where a defendant has a criminal lifestyle the court, once the confiscation proceedings are triggered (see **22.11** in Volume 1), underline{must} follow the Proceeds of Crime Act 2002 procedure. 'Criminal lifestyle' offences include those under Customs and Excise Management Act 1979 s 68(2) and 170 when committed in connection with a firearm or ammunition.[416] For what constitutes a criminal lifestyle see para **22.43** in Volume 1.
Note: These offences would now be prosecuted under Firearms Act 1968 s 5(2A), the supplying offence, which is easier to prove and has a maximum of life. Ed.
R v Knight 2008 EWCA Crim 478, 2 Cr App R (S) 76 (p 425) D pleaded to being knowingly concerned in the movement of controlled goods with intent to evade a prohibition etc. between third countries (Trade in Goods (Control) Order 2003 2003/2765 art 9(2)[417]). Held. The court should have regard to these factors: 1) an assessment of the goods involved e.g. military weapons. Also whether they are single use e.g. grenades or continuing use and their potential for multiple deaths, e.g. pistols as against machine guns. 2) The quantities and value of the weapons. 3) The intended customer. For example, supply direct to an insurgent group will be an aggravating factor. 4) The level of involvement of D. 5) The degree of planning by and length of involvement of D coupled with the degree of knowledge of D and his status, e.g. whether he is a generally licensed arms dealer. Also relevant would be persistence in effecting the transaction in

---

[412] Customs and Excise Management Act 1979 s 50(5A) 68(4A) and 170(4A) inserted by Criminal Justice Act 2003 s 293.
[413] Anti-social Behaviour, Crime and Policing Act 2014 s 108(6) inserts section 5(2A).
[414] Anti-social Behaviour, Crime and Policing Act 2014 s 111(2), (4)-(6) and Anti-social Behaviour, Crime and Policing Act 2014 (Commencement No 2, Transitional and Transitory Provisions) Order 2014 2014/949 para 6(d)
[415] When Legal Aid, Sentencing and Punishment of Offenders Act 2012 s 85 is in force, the fine will be unlimited.
[416] Proceeds of Crime Act 2002 s 6 and 75 and Sch 2 para 5(1)
[417] The maximum penalty is 10 years, article 9(4).

deliberate breach of export control laws. 6) The sophistication of the transaction and any attempts to evade responsibility or create a false impression. This list is not exhaustive. Consider also the potential consequences in terms of death, disorder and the effect on international relations. It is likely to be a rare case that a successful prosecution under article 9(2) will not result in a **significant immediate custodial** sentence.

Att-Gen's Ref No 43 of 2009 2009 EWCA Crim 1925, 2010 1 Cr App R (S) 100 (p 628) LCJ Where, however, statutory intent involving danger to life has been established, and it is clear that the firearms were subsequently used with homicidal intent by others to whom they were supplied or who obtained them in the criminal firearms market, the sentences on the importer or supplier should always reflect these dreadful consequences. In the context of Criminal Justice Act 2003 s 225, the fact that the importer or supplier is not an individual who pulled any trigger, or discharged any firearm, or caused serious injury himself, does not resolve the issue of future dangerousness in his favour. Criminals who are prepared to deal in such lethal weapons invariably represent a serious public danger, and it cannot be assumed that the danger they represent will have dissipated when the determinate element of their sentences has been completed. We therefore supplement the guidance in *R v Avis* 1998 by emphasising that for criminals involved in this level of gun crime along with very lengthy determinate sentences, indeterminate sentences, whether discretionary imprisonment for life or IPP, inevitably arise for consideration. Here he must be sentenced for the consequences of his actions, and the life sentence reflected that.

See also: *R v Hyde* 2014 EWCA Crim 713 (Convicted of two offences under 2003 control order. Partly lawful business. Brokered agreements with China to sell to Nigerian government. Never asked for a licence. Good character. 70,000 rifles, 10,000 pistols and 32 million rounds of ammunition. $400,000 commission paid into Liechtenstein bank. Delay. Business employing 20 people ended. **7 years** was severe but not manifestly excessive.)

259.7   *Importation/exportation of firearms   Cases*

R v Cardwell 2012 EWCA Crim 3030, 2013 2 Cr App R (S) 43 (p 284) D was convicted of conspiracy to possess firearms with intent to endanger life, conspiracy to import firearms and conspiracy to transfer prohibited firearms. The conspiracies ran from December 2009 to July 2010. They involved the purchase of 81 semi-automatic handguns from retail outlets in North Carolina, USA for importation into the UK by aeroplane in hold luggage for onward sale to criminals in Merseyside. G was the importer and made 10 trips to the USA to purchase the guns. D was the receiver in Merseyside who transferred the guns to a co-defendant. D also acted as a 'banker' for G. Three of the guns were sold to undercover officers and others were traced to a murder in Scotland, an attempted murder in Manchester and a robbery in Liverpool. D was of previous good character. It was submitted that the life sentence imposed by the Judge was inappropriate on the basis that the dangerousness provisions were not met. The Judge sentenced immediately after the conviction without the benefit of a report from the probation service as to the assessment of dangerousness. Held. The offending was grave and it merited a deterrent sentence. We agree with the Judge that **a notional 22-year determinate sentence** was appropriate. However, on the material before the Judge including the facts of the various offences, it cannot be concluded that D was dangerous within the meaning of the 2003 Act. **22 years**, not life with an 11-year term. Old cases: *R v Saltmarsh and Others* 2007 EWCA Crim 876, 2 Cr App R (S) 99 (p 643) (With endanger life conspiracy. For S **20 years** and V **14 years** cannot be faulted. S also received **6 years consecutive** for a supply of drugs matter.) *R v Knight* 2008 EWCA Crim 478, 2 Cr App R (S) 76 (p 425) (**4 years**) *R v Wright and Garrod* 2009 EWCA Crim 943 (With drug supply conspiracy. **7 years** for the firearms making **15 years**. For G **7 years**)

For a summary of these cases, see the 9th edition of this book.

259.8   *Manufacturing/Converting firearms   Judicial guidance*
Att-Gen's Ref Nos 48-49 of 2010 2010 EWCA Crim 2521 We find it very difficult to envisage a case of a deliberate attempt to create a working handgun (now a prohibited weapon) which will not require a sentence of at least 5 years after trial.

259.9   *Manufacturing/Converting firearms*
Att-Gen's Ref Nos 120-121 of 2004 2005 EWCA Crim 890 H and B pleaded on the first day of trial to three counts on which they were jointly charged: 1) conspiracy to manufacture prohibited weapons, 2) conspiracy to sell or transfer prohibited weapons, and 3) conspiracy to possess firearms with intent to enable others to cause fear of violence. Over a 10-month period they obtained from two suppliers in London a large quantity of blank-firing handguns and corresponding blank ammunition. They then converted the weapons into lethal prohibited weapons capable of firing the ammunition, and sold the weapons and ammunition direct to interested criminal parties or through one of their supplying shops. On a conservative basis they made and sold more than 150 weapons. The weapons were destined for the criminal fraternity. Their pleas followed an unsuccessful submission by their counsel to exclude evidence. After this H's counsel received a message from the Judge that if the defendants pleaded guilty they would receive full credit. Written bases of plea were submitted for both men. H's counsel said that he was not responsible for the manufacture of all guns (over 300 were referred to in the evidence). B's counsel said that although he had been a party to the conspiracy in count 1 he had played a minimal role in the manufacture, that the conduct charged in the other two counts was incidental to that charged in count 1, and that he had a lesser role than H. The Judge indicated to counsel in chambers that both men would receive full credit for their pleas and that his provisional view was that he would sentence concurrently on all counts as they were part and parcel of the same enterprise. The prosecutor indicated to the Judge that he could not agree the proposed bases of plea although there were some assertions of fact which he could not gainsay, in particular it was the prosecution's case that the defendants were involved over the course of the conspiracy with hundreds of guns. The aggravating features were identified as being the vast quantity of weapons involved, the 10-month length of the conspiracy and the defendants' intention to equip criminals with fully functioning firearms to put fear into others. H was aged 47, B aged 45. Held. This was a case where the prosecution evidence was strong and it was not a case for a full discount for pleas of guilty. Where the seriousness and range of the separate counts calls for a higher sentence than any of them on its own there should be consecutive sentences. Despite the Judge's early indication that he had concurrent sentences in mind he gave no commitment to that course, and the defendants cannot have had a legitimate expectation that he would impose concurrent sentences. These conspiracies required sentences of a very high order, not 6 years. The appropriate starting point for these offences was about **15 years** reduced to **9 years** after allowing for the full discount promised to the defendants by the Judge and taking into account that it was a reference.

Att-Gen's Ref No 43 of 2009 2009 EWCA Crim 1925, 2010 1 Cr App R (S) 100 (p 628) LCJ W was convicted of two counts of possession of a firearm with intent to enable another to endanger life, possession of ammunition with intent to endanger life, and other selling/transferring and converting a firearm counts. Police discovered a large arms factory where machine guns were created from replicas. W ordered 90 blank-firing replica submachine guns costing £55,201, together with 25 'shot magazines', saying that the guns were for a film. He also purchased a large number of precision tools including lathes and a centrifugal machine. A workshop was reinforced, alarmed and sound-proofed. There was a test firing room in a secure steel container. Three machine guns (one of which was converted), 2,695 discarded cartridges, 1,100 bullets and primers and packaging for 1,500 were found. W took police to another address where eight further machine guns, 9,000 bullets, 22,800 spent cartridges and other gun material were found. Fifty-one shootings had involved these converted machine guns, resulting in eight fatalities and 13 injuries. Fifty-three guns had been recovered. W was born in 1974 and had many convictions, some for dishonesty, some connected with drugs, and some for violence. In 1996 he was convicted of GBH with intent (4 years). In 2004 he was convicted of affray (community penalty). The Judge gave credit for the co-operation but described his activity as 'essential' to the operation. She started at 22 years and gave **life** (11-year minimum term) and **17 years** in total concurrent with the other offences. Held. W must be sentenced for the consequences of his actions and the life sentence reflected that.

See also: *Att-Gen's Ref Nos 48-49 of 2010* 2010 EWCA Crim 2521 (C and M purchased four starting pistols and sought to convert them to handguns. Effective good character. Operation was amateurish in the extreme. Motive was to pay off a drug debt. For C, **30 months** and for M, **25 months** was lenient but not increased.)

For penalties etc. for manufacturing firearms see the *Firearms Act 1968 s 3(1)(a)* para at **259.15** and for converting a shotgun see the *Firearms Act 1968 s 4* para at **259.16**.

259.10   Minding/Housing/Warehousing firearms   Guideline remarks

R v Dixon 2013 EWCA Crim 601 D pleaded to possession of a prohibited weapon, a Smith & Wesson revolver, and a bullet. She agreed to allow them to be stored at her house after someone had been shot at with the revolver. Held. The policy which Parliament has laid out is that [the minimum sentence] places the highest possible weight on deterring a gun culture and the use of guns. It is well known that those who live in communities where gun culture is prevalent suffer terribly from such a culture. It is part and parcel of such a culture that those that use guns to kill or maim or to inflict terror will need somewhere to place their weapons when they are not in use. The importance to those who engage in the use of guns in finding a place where it is thought that no one will suspect that a gun has been left is of the utmost importance. It is to deter anyone from being the repository of such guns that Parliament has decided such a severe sentence should be passed.

Robbery, With see the **ROBBERY** *Firearm, With* para at **322.13**.

259.11   Police officers as victims

R v Lewis 2013 EWCA Crim 48, 2014 2 Cr App R (S) 27 (p 207) L, F, G, J, T, C and R were convicted of possession of firearms with intent to endanger life, riot and other associated offences. Three days after the 2011 London riots started and late in the evening, 42 masked or hooded men assembled outside a pub in Birmingham. They then broke in and set the ground floor alight with petrol bombs. There were occupants on the first floor. Furniture from the pub was strewn in the road outside to entice police to the scene. The police arrived and at least 12 rounds from four firearms were discharged at the police. The police withdrew unharmed. The group moved off and at least two shots were fired at a police helicopter. Later, about 30 of them split into two to form a group on either side of a police car. The car was then attacked. The group then moved on and four firearms were discharged in the general direction of police vans. L was aged 29 and was one of the organisers. He [was] armed. He had a very bad record which included an armed robbery and possession of a loaded firearm (2004, 6½ years). (For L **35 years**, including 5 years consecutive for an unrelated firearms offence.) F was aged 27 and played a full part in the violence. In 2005 he had a conviction for robbery (5 years). He was a member of a gang and enjoyed using guns. (For F **30 years**.) G was aged 27 with a bad record. There were robberies in 2002 and 2004 (6 years). (For G **29 years**.) J was aged 27 with no significant record. He was an active member of a gang. He drove F to a scene so they could fire on police. (For J **23 years**.) T had a firearm and shot at the police helicopter. He was aged 19 and had limited previous convictions. (For T **23 years'** **detention**.) C went with F knowing he was armed. He was aged 25, in work and had a limited record. (For C **18 years**.) R was aged 16 and effectively of good character. He was close to a man reloading a handgun. He was still in the group for the police van incident. (For R **12 years' detention**.) Held. J's attitude to guns was highly relevant to F's sentence. All appeals rejected.

Firearms Act 1968 offences
259.12   *Firearms Act 1968 s 1*
Mode of trial Triable either way
Maximum sentence Indictment 5 years. Summary maximum 6 months and/or a £5,000 fine for offences committed before 12 March 2015 and an unlimited fine thereafter.[418] There are maximum fines for those aged under 18, see **14.38** in Volume 1.
Serious Crime Prevention Order Serious Crime Act 2015 s 47(2) adds Firearms Act 1968 s 1 to Serious Crime Act 2007 Sch 1, thus enabling this discretionary order to be made for this offence, when it would protect the public etc.[419] In force 3 May 2015.[420]
R v He 2011 EWCA Crim 2180 D pleaded to possession of a firearm without a certificate and possession of a stun gun (1 year concurrent). The car he was travelling in was stopped by police and searched. A stun gun was found in the glove box. His home address was searched and a silencer was found. D was aged 29 at appeal. Held. None of the aggravating features existed. **3 years** not 4.
R v Fraser 2013 EWCA Crim 799 D pleaded to possessing a firearm without a certificate. He was acquitted of attempted murder and section 18. D was in a relationship with L. That relationship was ended by D, but the two remained in contact. He subsequently appeared to have wanted to resume the friendship but L did not. L's house was damaged in an arson attack. D helped L clean up after the fire. Two months later, L was shot by someone using a 12-bore shotgun as she was leaving her house. L thought that it might be her former husband or D. D was a farmer and when the police were investigating, they found a single-barrelled shotgun and 40 cartridges hidden in some bales of hay. D denied ownership but later admitted it after his DNA was found on the gun. He said that the gun belonged to his father and had been used on the farm to kill vermin for as long as he could remember. He had never obtained a licence for it. D was aged 64 at the appeal, a hard-working man and of good character. Held. The Judge was right to treat this as a serious case of its kind. The gun was not stored securely but hidden in a barn with a large number of cartridges. It could have been found by anyone. **8 months** was not manifestly excessive. Suspension of the sentence was not appropriate. Old cases: Best ignored. Ed.

259.13   *Firearms Act 1968 s 1 and 4(4)*
Possession of a shortened shotgun or firearm which has been converted.
Mode of trial Triable either way
Maximum sentence Indictment 7 years. Summary maximum 6 months or a £5,000 fine for offences committed before 12 March 2015 and an unlimited fine thereafter.[421] There are maximum fines for those aged under 18, see **14.38** in Volume 1.
R v Flitter 2009 EWCA Crim 2152, 2010 1 Cr App R (S) 85 (p 563) D pleaded to possessing a shortened shotgun at the Magistrates' Court. The police searched his home and found behind a wardrobe in his bedroom a carrier bag containing a gun in three pieces wrapped in a towel. It was a 12-gauge single-barrelled smooth-bore shotgun shortened to 23 inches. The gun was in relatively poor condition but in working order. In a locked outbuilding was a box of shotgun ammunition which did not fit the shotgun. Also found were amphetamines (1 month concurrent). D said he had purchased the gun in the late 1980s when he had another gun and a firearm certificate. He was convicted of possession of cannabis and his certificate was revoked but he surrendered only one gun.

---

[418] Legal Aid, Sentencing and Punishment of Offenders Act 2012 s 85(1) and (4) and Legal Aid, Sentencing and Punishment of Offenders Act 2012 (Commencement No 11) Order 2015 2015/504
[419] Serious Crime Act 2007 s 1 and Sch 1 para 3
[420] Serious Crime Act 2015 (Commencement No 1) Regulations 2015 2015/820 para 2
[421] Legal Aid, Sentencing and Punishment of Offenders Act 2012 s 85(1) and (4) and Legal Aid, Sentencing and Punishment of Offenders Act 2012 (Commencement No 11) Order 2015 2015/504

D said he forgot about it and then was frightened to hand it in so he cut it up to make the gun inoperative. His account was accepted. D was 'some 50 years of age' with five previous convictions for relatively minor offences, none of which were similar. D was married with two children. His wife suffered from depression and he was the main carer for his elderly widowed mother who was in poor health. There was character evidence. Held. **2 years** was stern but not manifestly excessive.

R v Davies 2012 EWCA Crim 201, 2013 1 Cr App R (S) 121 (p 625) D pleaded to possessing a shortened shotgun (presumably section 4(4)). Police attended his address acting on information and asked D whether he had a shotgun. D immediately replied that it was upstairs and took an officer to it. The shotgun was in very poor condition and incapable of being fired. It was stored in a bag on top of a wardrobe. There was no ammunition. D claimed he found it in a field and intended to hand it in and he owed money to criminals. There was a *Newton* on the first issue and the Judge found that D was either holding it so he could use it for those he owed money to or holding the weapon for someone else. D, aged 31, had no recent convictions, but had committed offences including theft, affray and possession of a bladed article between 2005 and 2006. There were no firearms offences. Held. Considering *R v Avis* 1998, the weapon had no lawful use but there was no suggestion that the weapon had been used in criminal activity. D was holding the weapon for another and so he had no intent to commit a specific offence. D was entitled to some credit for his plea, despite the *Newton*. **3 years** was not manifestly excessive.

Old cases: *R v Jalloh* 2009 EWCA Crim 456, 2 Cr App R (S) 613 (**4 years** consecutive for the drugs matter.) For a summary of this case see the 9th edition of this book. Older cases are best ignored. Ed.

259.14   *Firearms Act 1968 s 2*
Possession of a shotgun
Mode of trial Triable either way
Maximum sentence Indictment 5 years. Summary maximum 6 months and/or a £5,000 fine for offences committed before 12 March 2015 and an unlimited fine thereafter.[422] There are maximum fines for those aged under 18, see **14.38** in Volume 1.
Serious Crime Prevention Order Serious Crime Act 2015 s 47(2) adds Firearms Act 1968 s 2 to Serious Crime Act 2007 Sch 1, thus enabling this discretionary order to be made for this offence, when it would protect the public etc.[423] In force 3 May 2015.[424]

259.15   *Firearms Act 1968 s 3(1)(a)*
Manufacturing a firearm
Mode of trial Triable either way
Maximum sentence Indictment 5 years. Summary maximum 6 months and/or a £5,000 fine for offences committed before 12 March 2015 and an unlimited fine thereafter.[425] There are maximum fines for those aged under 18, see **14.38** in Volume 1.
Note: With the low maximum sentence, prosecutors will normally charge another offence like supply. Ed.
Confiscation Where a defendant has a criminal lifestyle the court, once the confiscation proceedings are triggered (see **22.11** in Volume 1), <u>must</u> follow the Proceeds of Crime Act 2002 procedure. 'Criminal lifestyle' offences include those under Firearms Act 1968 s 3(1).[426] For what constitutes a criminal lifestyle see **22.43** in Volume 1.

---

[422] Legal Aid, Sentencing and Punishment of Offenders Act 2012 s 85(1) and (4) and Legal Aid, Sentencing and Punishment of Offenders Act 2012 (Commencement No 11) Order 2015 2015/504
[423] Serious Crime Act 2007 s 1 and Sch 1 para 3
[424] Serious Crime Act 2015 (Commencement No 1) Regulations 2015 2015/820 para 2
[425] Legal Aid, Sentencing and Punishment of Offenders Act 2012 s 85(1) and (4) and Legal Aid, Sentencing and Punishment of Offenders Act 2012 (Commencement No 11) Order 2015 2015/504
[426] Proceeds of Crime Act 2002 s 6 and 75 and Sch 2 para 5(2)

Serious Crime Prevention Order For Firearms Act 1968 s 3(1) offences there is a discretionary power to make this order, when it would protect the public etc.[427]
For cases see the *Manufacturing/Converting firearms* paras at **259.8**.

259.16   Firearms Act 1968 s 4
Converting weapons and shortening the barrel of a shotgun
Mode of trial Triable either way
Maximum sentence Indictment 7 years. Summary maximum 6 months and/or a £5,000 fine for offences committed before 12 March 2015 and an unlimited fine thereafter.[428]
There are maximum fines for those aged under 18, see **14.38** in Volume 1.
R v Avis 1998 2 Cr App R (S) 178 LCJ Where there are breaches of Firearms Act 1968 s 4 the custodial term is likely to be of considerable length, and where the four questions suggested above (see the *Guideline cases* para at **259.3**) yield answers adverse to the offender, terms at or approaching the maximum may in a contested case be appropriate.
See the *Manufacturing/converting firearms* paras at **259.8**.

259.17   Firearms Act 1968 s 5
Possession of a prohibited weapon/ammunition
For section 5(1)(b) and 5(1A)(a) offences see **259.21**. For section 5(2A) offences see **259.22**.
Mode of trial Offences under subsections 5(1)(a), (ab), (aba), (ac), (ad), (ae), (af), (c), and (1A)(a) are indictable only.[429] All other offences are triable either way.
Maximum sentence Indictment 10 years. Summary maximum 6 months and/or a £5,000 fine for offences committed before 12 March 2015 and an unlimited fine thereafter.[430]
There are maximum fines for those aged under 18, see **14.38** in Volume 1.
Minimum sentences Minimum sentence rules apply to ten of the offences under Firearms Act 1968 s 5. For details of which and other matters see the **Minimum sentences** section at **259.55**.
Detention Defendant aged 16-17 convicted of the indictable only offences can be detained under Powers of Criminal Courts (Sentencing) Act 2000 s 91,[431] when there are exceptional circumstances to justify not imposing the minimum term under Firearms Act 1968 s 51A.
Note: This offence only carries a maximum of 10 years so the 14-year requirement for section 91 orders would not be triggered. Hence there is a special statutory provision under Powers of Criminal Courts (Sentencing) Act 2000 s 94(1A). Ed.
Serious Crime Prevention Order Serious Crime Act 2015 s 47(2) adds Firearms Act 1968 s 5(1), (1A) and (2A) to Serious Crime Act 2007 Sch 1, thus enabling this discretionary order to be made for this offence, when it would protect the public etc.[432] In force 3 May 2015.[433]

259.18   Firearms Act 1968 s 5   Guideline case
R v Avis 1998 2 Cr App R (S) 178 LCJ Where there are breaches of Firearms Act 1968 s 5 the custodial term is likely to be of considerable length, and where the four questions suggested above (see the *Guideline cases* para at **259.3**) yield answers adverse to the offender, terms at or approaching the maximum may in a contested case be appropriate.

259.19   Firearms Act 1968 s 5   Cases   5 years or less
R v Rudups 2011 EWCA Crim 61 D pleaded (full credit) to unlawful possession of ammunition. The prosecution offered no evidence on the count of unlawful possession of

---

[427] Serious Crime Act 2007 s 1 and Sch 1 para 3(2)
[428] Legal Aid, Sentencing and Punishment of Offenders Act 2012 s 85(1) and (4) and Legal Aid, Sentencing and Punishment of Offenders Act 2012 (Commencement No 11) Order 2015 2015/504
[429] Criminal Justice Act 2003 s 28
[430] Legal Aid, Sentencing and Punishment of Offenders Act 2012 s 85(1) and (4) and Legal Aid, Sentencing and Punishment of Offenders Act 2012 (Commencement No 11) Order 2015 2015/504
[431] Powers of Criminal Courts (Sentencing) Act 2000 s 91(1A)
[432] Serious Crime Act 2007 s 1 and Sch 1 para 3
[433] Serious Crime Act 2015 (Commencement No 1) Regulations 2015 2015/820 para 2

a prohibited weapon. He was a Latvian national who drove through Poland and Germany to Dover. There, D informed customs officers that he had a gun. He was arrested. In interview he informed officers that he had purchased the weapon for the purpose of defending himself as he drove from Latvia to the UK as he intended to sleep in his car. The weapon was a 9 mm calibre blank pistol, and he also had in his possession CN 'Mace cartridges' designed to discharge noxious substances. It was designed to fire CS gas cartridges. The weapon and cartridges were not prohibited items in Latvia, Germany or Poland. He had not considered whether it was legal to import them into the UK. A pre-sentence report assessed D as posing a low risk of reoffending. It voiced concern at how D would provide for his daughter should he be given a custodial sentence and recommended a Suspended Sentence Order. D was of excellent previous character. Held. D was ignorant of the illegality of importing the weapon and its ammunition into the UK. Persons coming to this country should familiarise themselves with the law relating to guns and ammunition before they arrive. However, we underline the fact that he handed over the items as soon as he stepped onto British soil for the first time. The Judge was correct in identifying that he should depart from the statutory 5-year minimum sentence as required by Firearms Act 1968 s 51A on the existence of exceptional circumstances. **6 months** not 12.

R v Nightingale 2012 EWCA Crim 2734 Court Martial Appeal Court LCJ D was a Sergeant in the SAS. He pleaded at the last moment to possession of a prohibited firearm and possession of ammunition. In 2007, D was given a Glock automatic pistol as a present by the Iraqi Special Forces. During his tour of duty, he and two colleagues were overwhelmed by exhaustion. The two colleagues were later killed in action. Just before his tour ended, he was asked to accompany their bodies home because of his closeness to them and their families. His kit and the pistol were packed by others and sent to the UK. D intended to deactivate the pistol but never did so. He kept the pistol first of all in his room in the Sergeants' mess and then in January 2011, when he moved to civilian accommodation, in the bedroom where it was later found. In the meantime, he continued with his military duties, some of which were in the UK. In 2009, D took part in a jungle marathon in the Amazon Basin to raise funds for injured soldiers. The run was to last five days and was for 220 km. At the end of the race D collapsed and remained in a coma for three days. He suffered a significant brain injury and was seriously ill. He underwent a large number of seizures, which left him in a state of confusion. There were prolonged impairments to his brain function. D had difficulties with memory and word-finding. At the appeal there were some continuing residual cognitive abnormalities. An expert considered that these cognitive and emotional changes would have made a significant contribution to his continued failure to decommission his pistol and to return it and the ammunition to the amnesty box system. In October 2010, just over a year after he had sustained the brain injury, notwithstanding his continuing difficulties, D returned to active service in Afghanistan. In September 2011, police officers searched D's rented accommodation. D was serving in Afghanistan. The Glock pistol, in working order, was found in a hard plastic case in a wardrobe along with three magazines suitable for use. The following ammunition was also found: a) 122×9 mm live rounds, b) 40×7.62 mm live rounds, c) 50×90 mm frangible rounds, d) $50 \times .338$ armour piercing live rounds, e) $2 \times .308$ live rounds, and f) 74×5.56 mm live rounds. The remaining ammunition was found in a plastic box under the bed. The ammunition found was supplied to him when he was range training officer. He took it to his own quarters. D knew he was in breach of orders.

D was married with two young children. He had no previous convictions or cautions, although there was one military transgression recorded against him many years ago. His Commanding Officer regarded his disciplinary record as exemplary and D was described as an exemplary soldier. D had seen service in Northern Ireland, Bosnia, Lebanon, Turkey, Iraq, Afghanistan, Syria and Libya. His life had been at risk. When in Iraq, D had helped a group of medical consultants to design a new type of bandage which would seal chest wounds by the use of a revolutionary gel-like substance. The new bandage was named, and is known as, the 'Nightingale Dressing' in recognition of his contribution. It is used by military and paramedics throughout the UK. The Judge Advocate found the following exceptional circumstances to disapply the minimum sentence: a) his medical condition permits a more than usual credit for the plea at the court door, b) his exemplary character, c) his co-operation and genuine remorse, d) D was a highly valued soldier of great practical experience, e) the gun was not fired and f) but for his particular work, he would not come into contact with such weapons and ammunition. D was not reduced in rank or dismissed. The Judge Advocate hoped D would be of use to the Army in the future. Held. The Glock was a modern, highly dangerous revolver in full working order, with ammunition for use in it. The ammunition in the wrong hands was capable of wreaking havoc. There was not the slightest shred of evidence that it was D's intention to use [the gun and ammunition] for any criminal purpose. Nothing was further from his mind. We agree with the conclusion about the exceptional circumstances. D was held in high regard by his colleagues and those who commanded him. D and his colleagues were engaged in desperately serious operations against a ruthless enemy. The tour of duty [where the gun was given] was relentless, exhausting and dangerous. Throughout, Sergeant Nightingale was, and remained, a quiet, tough, calm, stalwart and stoical soldier. His continued possession of the firearms was not motivated by any wish to sell them for profit, nor to pass them on to anyone else who might misuse them. However, it was an offence of great folly. Firearms might well quickly have passed into the hands of serious criminals. **12 months suspended** not 18 months' detention.

Note: Some of the facts have been taken from the Judge Advocate's sentencing remarks, see www.banksr.com Other Matters Other Documents tab. Ed.

Att-Gen's Ref No 125 of 2014 2015 EWCA Crim 240 D pleaded to possession of a prohibited firearm (×3) (s 5(1)(aba)), possessing ammunition (×11), possessing a firearm and a smoothbore gun, both without certificate, and possession of a prohibited weapon (s 5(1)(b)). In D's house police found a deactivated and reactivated Tommy gun, belonging to D's father, and several other firearms in D's bedroom. These included two deactivated and reactivated pistols, a magazine, eight converted blank-firing pistols and a sawn-off pump-action shotgun. All bar one were immediately capable of causing lethal injury. Police also recovered 224 live cartridges along with paraphernalia for assembling new cartridges. A search of D's two caravans, where he spent most of his weekends, revealed further ammunition and firearm paraphernalia. D was silent in interview. He was aged 51 on appeal and of effective good character. D had suffered a nervous breakdown, received counselling, his mother had cancer and he had a new partner and a two-month-old baby. He was medicated for depression and his demeanour was impressive. Held. D's circumstances are not exceptional. Starting at 8 years, **5 years**, not 20 months.

See also: *Att-Gen's Ref No 64 of 2010* 2010 EWCA Crim 2956 LCJ (Early plea to possessing a prohibited weapon (×2). Young woman was arrested for large-scale shoplifting and a search of her home revealed two shortened shotguns stored on behalf of another for about a month. Both in working order. Because of the delay and the suspended sentence already served, **3 years** not 12 months' suspended with 200 hours' unpaid work.)

R v Danks 2011 EWCA Crim 72 (Pleas to possessing a shotgun, a prohibited firearm (a handgun) and three rounds of ammunition. Ignorant as to the need for a shotgun licence. Handgun had never been fired. Aged 68. Exceptional circumstances present. 5-year starting point was correct. One-third off for plea, not 20%, so **3 years 4 months**.)

R v Jones 2011 EWCA Crim 1448, 2012 1 Cr App R (S) 25 (p 149) (D was convicted of possessing a prohibited firearm, expanding ammunition, a firearm without a certificate and possession of cocaine. A .38 calibre revolver, 13 .22 long rifle cartridges, one 9 mm Parabellum cartridge, three .32 automatic cartridges and 0.77 grams of cocaine.

Threatened by unknown man who asked her to collect a bag. Frightened. Fell short of duress. Kept items for three weeks. Aged 22. Good character. Minimum sentence wholly arbitrary. **6 months** not 5 years.)

R v McQuaid 2014 EWCA Crim 2353, 2 Cr App R (S) 78 (p 622) (Plea. D suicidal. Dismantled pump-action shotgun found in his car along with cartridges and .22 ammunition. D was unfit for interview and voluntarily attended a psychiatric unit, where he was diagnosed with severe depression. Aged 56, homeless and still intended to commit suicide. Good character and a former Royal Marine, having served 12 years and been a reservist for seven more years. Judge found exceptional circumstances. The fact that D had held the gun illegally for a number of years required an immediate custodial sentence. **2 years**, not 4.)

Old cases: *R v Havill and Others* 2008 EWCA Crim 2952, 2 Cr App R (S) 254 (**5 years**) *R v Smith* 2009 EWCA Crim 472, 2 Cr App R (S) 578 (**2½ years**) For a summary of these cases see the 9th edition of this book.

For cases on the manufacture of prohibited weapons see the ***Manufacture/Converting*** paras at **259.8**.

259.20   *Firearms Act 1968 s 5   Cases   More than 5 years*

R v Razaq 2011 EWCA Crim 1518 LCJ D, a serving police officer at the time of the offences, pleaded late to criminal property offences (×2), perverting the course of justice and conspiracy to pervert (×2), possession of prohibited firearms (×3), possession of ammunition, misconduct in public office and money laundering. His plea triggered his co-accused, including D's brother, H, to plead to offences including kidnap. D used the police computer system to access information about his acquaintances etc. H instructed D to deliver a bag containing money and other items to an associate. D received £500. H instructed D to prevent a witness in a forthcoming kidnap trial from giving evidence. D agreed. A search of D's home found £70,000 in cash in a bag, along with two submachine guns, a sten gun and 228 live rounds of ammunition. D indicated to the authorities that a further 70-80 rounds of ammunition could be found at his address. His basis of plea was that the money belonged to H, and fearing for H's safety he agreed to mind it. Further, fearing for his safety, he agreed to mind the weapons etc. when approached by another. Held. These were a very serious series of offences, prolonged and repeated and in the gravest breach of trust. Focusing on totality, **11½ years** was well within the range.

R v Ajala 2012 EWCA Crim 21 D pleaded (15% credit) to possession of a prohibited firearm and possession of prohibited ammunition (×2). After an undercover operation, police arrested D and an associate. A search of D's house produced a .32 calibre revolver which was loaded with hollow point bullets. There were eight other .32 cartridges and two home-made bullets. Also found were a balaclava and some latex gloves, which had D's fingerprints on the inside and gunshot residue on the outside. D's basis of plea stated that: a) he was a custodian, b) he was keeping the gun after being put under pressure (which fell short of duress), c) he was stabbed some days earlier by associates of the man for whom he was holding the weapon and ammunition, and d) he was aware of what the items could be used for, but had no intention of using them himself. The Judge held that the minimum sentence provisions applied. D, aged 19 at the time of the offence, had 16 convictions for 24 offences, including violence, possession of offensive weapons and the supply of drugs. D had been involved in gangland activity from the age of 14, and was now displaying some maturity and insight into his criminal activity. He was in breach of a suspended sentence. Held. The possession of a formidable weapon and ammunition by someone involved in gang culture and the trade of drugs, even if he had no personal intention to use the gun, was a matter of considerable concern and aggravation. After a trial, a sentence of 7 to 7½ years was appropriate, so with the late plea, **6 years' YOI**, with 2 years concurrent for the ammunition, not consecutive.

R v Lewis 2014 EWCA Crim 2622, 2015 1 Cr App R (S) 38 Three counts with ammunition counts. Sentence reduced to **10 years** because sentences should not be consecutive, see **259.66**.

See also: *R v Robinson and Others* 2012 EWCA Crim 1525 (Two pleas, one conviction with possession of an offensive weapon and ammunition without a certificate. A MAC-10 sub-machine gun and ammunition used in a murder were transported and kept by various individuals before and after the murder. 5 years was too low a starting point. **9 years** (convicted) and **7 years** untouched. Both had similar previous convictions. 7½ **years** not 8 to reflect a lesser role and good character.)

R v Morrison 2012 EWCA Crim 1255, 2013 1 Cr App R (S) 35 (p 193) (Convicted of possession of a prohibited firearm and possessing ammunition without a certificate. Loaded Browning pistol found in wardrobe with 30 rounds of ammunition. Balaclava and gloves also found. Previous convictions for supply of heroin and cocaine, and possession of firearm/ammunition. Aged 27. Maximum sentences of **10 years** and 5 years concurrent were not manifestly excessive.)

R v Morgan 2013 EWCA Crim 1506 (Early plea. Submachine gun, 38 cartridges, a drum magazine and a silencer found in defendant's shed. Firearm of Eastern European origin. Capable of being fired. Minding the weapons. Previous for supply but none for firearms. Not a member of a gang. Could not complain about **6 years**. Concurrent, not consecutive, to a drugs offence (32 months.))

Old cases: *Att-Gen's Ref No 16 of 2009* 2009 EWCA Crim 2439, 2010 2 Cr App R (S) 11 (p 64) (**12 years** in all) *Att-Gen's Ref No 57 of 2009* 2009 EWCA Crim 2555, 2010 2 Cr App R (S) 30 (p 190) (**8 years**)

For a summary of these cases, see the 9th edition of this book.

For cases on the manufacture of prohibited weapons, see the ***Manufacture/Converting*** paras at **259.8**.

259.21   Firearms Act 1968 s 5(1)(b) and 5(1A)(a)   CS gas canisters/Stun guns, possession of

Note: Section 5(1A)(a) carries a minimum sentence unless exceptional circumstances are established. Section 5(1)(b) does not carry a minimum sentence. For more detail see **259.50**. Ed.

R v Ramzan 2012 EWCA Crim 2891, 2013 2 Cr App R (S) 33 (p 221) D pleaded to possession of a prohibited firearm disguised as another object (section 5(1A)(a)). Police searched his address and found a stun gun disguised as a mobile phone in his bedroom. There was also a charger for the device. He admitted that he had had the weapon for 3 years but was not prepared to say how he had come by it. He said that he had forgotten it was there. He also said that he knew it was illegal to 'walk around outside with it', but thought he was permitted to keep it in the house. He explained that he had had trouble with a boy who he believed tried to kill him and he had kept the weapon as protection. The boy was sectioned and D had kept the weapon for self-defence. He had never used it. In the pre-sentence report, he gave a different version. He had not realised the gravity of the situation when arrested and said that the story given to the police was just one that sounded plausible and that the weapon actually belonged to his uncle. His uncle had left some items at D's house including a jacket. One year prior to his arrest, D found the jacket under the bed and found it had the gun in it. He said he hadn't realised it was a gun and threw it back under the bed. D was aged 29 at appeal and of previous good character. Held. D had not sought out or purchased the gun. It had been left at the premises by his uncle. It had not been removed from D's home and D was not aware that it was an offence to have the item in his home. It had never been used, inside or outside the home. Notwithstanding that there was a charging device with the gun, D had never charged it. None of the four questions posed in *R v Avis* 1998 produced answers adverse to D. However, D did knowingly have possession of the stun gun, which had the capability to be charged and used. There was potential for anyone to take it and use it to cause significant injury. Exceptional circumstances were made out. However, those factors justified a significant custodial sentence. **2 years** not 5.

R v Stoker 2013 EWCA Crim 1431, 2014 1 Cr App R (S) 47 (p 286) D pleaded to possession of a disguised firearm (section 5(1A)(a)) and possessing a prohibited weapon (section 5(1)(b)) and possession of a pepper spray (×2) (section 5(1)(b)). Police officers executed a search warrant. The officers encountered D outside his address and informed him that they understood that he was in possession of a stun gun. D accepted that he was, showed the officers into his bedroom and indicated that the gun was in a jacket pocket in the wardrobe. The officers recovered the weapon, which was disguised as a mobile phone. They also found two 'pepper spray' canisters. When interviewed, D said he had ordered the items over the Internet a number of years ago and that he did not know they were illegal. He also said that he believed the police information about the weapons had come from a friend of his wife with whom he had had an employment dispute and who was carrying on a campaign of harassment against him. The pre-sentence report was positive. D, aged 47 at appeal, was very remorseful. Held. The minimum sentence applied to the stun gun. The illegal possession of firearms is a menace in society. Considering the *R v Avis* 1998 questions, the answers were: 1) a stun gun which was disguised and in the circumstances could not be used as it was not charged and was not capable of being so, 2) none, 3) to defend himself some years ago then put away and not thought about. D did not know the possession was illegal, 4) a man of good character. The two other questions were irrelevant. The Judge was wrong to say there were no exceptional circumstances. Stun guns can be very dangerous weapons in the wrong hands. We accept the point made in *R v Rehman and Wood* 2005 that a deterrent sentence is no deterrent if the offender does not know [that] what he has done is illegal. The appropriate sentence for the stun gun was **2 years**, not 5. For the other counts, the correct sentence was 1 year concurrent, not 2.

R v Zhekov 2013 EWCA Crim 1656, 2014 1 Cr App R (S) 69 (p 448) D pleaded to possessing a disguised firearm. D, a lorry driver from Bulgaria, entered the UK to make a delivery. He was routinely stopped by Border Agency staff who located the torch-style stun gun in a drawer in his cab. It looked like a torch and could be used as a torch. It was described as a non-lethal defence weapon. D, aged 50, was of exemplary character, genuinely remorseful and unaware that such items were illegal in the UK. Possession of such items was permitted in Bulgaria. Held. The factors were a) the purchase, possession and use were legal in Bulgaria, b) D was a foreign national who had lived his entire life in Bulgaria, c) he was in the UK for a lawful purpose, d) his stay was just the time it took to deliver his load and for most of that time he would be in his cab, e) D had no knowledge of the UK law, and f) there was no charging device and there was no evidence the stun gun had ever been used. His regret and remorse [were] genuine. The Judge was correct to find exceptional circumstances that justified departure from the mandatory provisions but wrong to find that immediate custody was required. A deterrent sentence was not necessary as any publicity would highlight that possession was illegal in the UK. **52 weeks suspended**, not 2 years' immediate custody.

R v Sayer 2014 EWCA Crim 2197 D was convicted of possessing a disguised firearm (s 5(1A)(a)), an offensive weapon and a prohibited weapon (s 5(1)(b)). D was stopped at the airport where stun guns disguised as mobile phones (×4), knuckle dusters (×5), extendible batons (×2) and a stun gun adapted to discharge a noxious liquid were discovered in his luggage. D had travelled from Thailand where such items were purportedly lawful. D was aged 50 on appeal with references, but had six convictions. In 2010, he received a suspended sentence for possessing a prohibited weapon, also a stun gun. It was accepted that the minimum sentence provisions applied. No exceptional circumstances were suggested. Held. Clearly the Judge was right to take a grave view of this case in light of the risk and nature of the weapons, which could easily be concealed. In the absence of any finding connecting the gun directly to further crime, **5 years**, not 6.

R v Withers 2015 EWCA Crim 132, 1 Cr App R (S) 64 (p 455) D pleaded to possession of a stun gun (section 5(1A)(a)). Police searched her flat and found a taser-type device that looked like a mobile phone in her bedside cabinet. There was no charger with it and the battery was flat. D said that it was given to her by a friend. She also said that in September 2013 her previous flat had been burgled. The next month, she had moved and there were continuing problems in the area. It was confirmed that she had made a call to the police about the problem before the search. A large man under the influence of drugs had knocked on her door at night. She had difficulty in getting him to leave and he had returned and kicked her front door in. Her door remained insecure and she remained concerned about anti-social behaviour in her area. D accepted she knew it was unlawful to possess a stun gun. The landlord refused to repair the door because D was in rent arrears. It was then she obtained the stun gun. D was aged 28 and had two minor convictions. A psychiatrist said D had an emotionally unstable personality disorder, which would mean she was likely to cope with imprisonment badly. Held. We cannot ignore the dangers of people possessing disguised stun guns. The answers to the *R v Avis* 1998 2 Cr App R (S) 178 questions were as follows: 1) the weapon did not shoot bullets, 2) no use was made of the weapon, 3) D's intention with the weapon was effectively none, save a defensive intention by which she hoped a 'buzz' would frighten away an intruder, and 4) D's previous convictions were not of any particular relevance. The minimum sentence was arbitrary and disproportionate. Her personal circumstances and her vulnerability had to be considered. **2 years** not 5.

See also: *R v Hudson* 2011 EWCA Crim 1812, 2012 1 Cr App R (S) 67 (p 382) (Late plea to possession of a prohibited weapon. CS gas canister. Attempted to conceal it from police. Bad record including possession of firearm with intent and robbery on a train (×2). Because of personal mitigation, **15 months' YOI** not 21.)

Old cases: *R v Kirby* 2009 EWCA Crim 14, 2 Cr App R (S) 49 (p 345) (**Community service**) *R v McDonnell* 2009 EWCA Crim 2922, 2010 2 Cr App R (S) 49 (p 341)[434] (Convicted. CS gas canister near defendant's home. No previous convictions. **6 months** not 9.)

For a summary of the first case, see the 9th edition of this book and for the second case, see the 10th edition.

259.22   *Firearms Act 1968 s 5(2A) Supplying a firearm*

Anti-social Behaviour, Crime and Policing Act 2014 s 108 amended Firearms Act 1968 s 5 by removing the references 'manufacture, sell and transfer' in section 5(1) and creating a new offence by inserting section 5(2A) of 'manufacturing, selling, transferring, having possession for sale or transfer and purchasing for sale or transfer prohibited weapons or prohibited ammunition'. The section came into force on 14 July 2014.[435]

Mode of trial Triable only on indictment

Maximum sentence Life

Minimum sentences Minimum sentence rules apply. For details see the **Minimum sentences** section at **259.55**.

Ancillary orders Due no doubt to drafting errors, the new offence does not enable the court to pass extended sentences, Financial Reporting Orders or Travel Restriction Orders. Neither is the offence listed in the schedule of offences for confiscation orders.

259.23   *Supplying or storing firearms for criminals   Guideline case and judicial guidance*

R v Ali and Mahmood 2007 EWCA Crim 1843, 2008 1 Cr App R (S) 69 (p 400) Gun crime in the cities has become all too prevalent. Anyone found facilitating the unlawful dissemination of [firearms] must expect to be punished severely.

---

[434] The neutral citation in the hard copy of Cr App R (S) is wrong.
[435] Anti-social Behaviour, Crime and Policing Act 2014 (Commencement No 2, Transitional and Transitory Provisions) Order 2014 2014/949 para 6(a)

Att-Gen's Ref No 43 of 2009 2009 EWCA Crim 1925, 2010 1 Cr App R (S) 100 (p 628) LCJ Where, however, the statutory intent involving danger to life has been established, and it is clear that the firearms were subsequently used with homicidal intent by others to whom they were supplied or who obtained them in the criminal firearms market, the sentences on the importer or supplier should always reflect these dreadful consequences. In the context of Criminal Justice Act 2003 s 225 the fact that the importer or supplier is not an individual who pulled any trigger, or discharged any firearm, or caused serious injury himself, does not resolve the issue of future dangerousness in his favour. Criminals who are prepared to deal in such lethal weapons invariably represent a serious public danger, and it cannot be assumed that the danger they represent will have dissipated when the determinate element of their sentences has been completed. We therefore supplement the guidance in *R v Avis* 1998 by emphasising that for criminals involved in this level of gun crime along with very lengthy determinate sentences, indeterminate sentences, whether discretionary imprisonment for life or IPP, inevitably arise for consideration. Here he must be sentenced for the consequences of his actions and the **life** sentence reflected that.

259.24 Supplying or storing firearms for criminals   Cases   Less than 15 years' imprisonment

R v Dixon 2013 EWCA Crim 601 D pleaded to possession of a prohibited weapon, a Smith & Wesson revolver (section 5(1)(aba)). At a party, P and W had a fight. P bit part of W's ear off. D, P and others who had been at the party left to go to D's house. P made a number of calls using D's phone and arranged to meet W. W arrived and was shot at by P. P returned to D's house and told D he wanted to put his bag in her cupboard. She agreed. She noticed that he left without it the following morning. Police searched the address. D was asked whether she had anything to say. She initially said no. Later, she drew their attention to the bag. In it was a Smith & Wesson double action .44 revolver with one bullet. She was arrested and given an *Osman* warning (a police warning to protect that person). She pleaded on the basis that she was drunk at the time the bag was placed in the cupboard and she had no knowledge of what was in the bag. D was aged 34 at appeal and had no convictions. She had two cautions for violence. She had children to support, aged 13, 14 and 16. The Judge said shootings in Birmingham were a very serious problem. Held. D was at the end of a period of binge drinking when the package was placed in the house. Despite initially refusing to say anything, she then took the police to where the package was. It has been said that all she failed to do was to enquire what the package was and look into it. We must ask ourselves whether the Judge went outside the independent judgement which a judge must give. We have regard to the *Osman* warning, her depression, drinking and drug-taking. The Judge was correct in his decision. **5 years**.
Note: The original appeal was *R v Dixon* 2011 EWCA Crim 924. The principles behind the decision can be found in **259.10**. Ed.

R v Gribbin 2014 EWCA Crim 115, 2 Cr App R (S) 28 (p 229) D pleaded to possession of a prohibited firearm counts and other related offences. Police executed a drugs warrant and discovered nine firearms including self-loading pistols, sawn-off shotguns, an Army-issue light support rifle and 446 live rounds of ammunition which could be fired from the weapons. There was a self-loading pistol in a lockable tool box which had had its serial numbers ground down. One of the weapons was linked to four shootings in Manchester between 2008 and 2010. D shared the house with his partner and children. The Judge imposed consecutive sentences on the basis that the weapons had been acquired at different times and storage had been at two addresses where he had lived. The defence appealed on the basis that the Judge imposed consecutive sentences in order to circumvent what he felt was an inadequate maximum sentence. The Judge found that D played a significant role in the preservation and storage of the weapons so they could be used by criminals. Held. The Judge was fully entitled to reach that conclusion. A deterrent sentence was fully justified. Credit was given for his pleas and **13 years** (6½ years × 2, consecutive) was not excessive or wrong in principle.

R v Valnuchinas 2014 EWCA Crim 652 D pleaded to selling or transferring a prohibited firearm (×3) and possessing ammunition without a certificate. Police officers on surveillance saw D drive onto a shop forecourt. Five seconds later S drove onto the forecourt and parked next to D. D got out of his car with a carrier bag. He went straight to the boot of S's car and placed the carrier bag inside. D then sat in the front passenger seat of S's car and D and S spoke for a short time. D returned to his car and S drove off. The officers followed S and stopped it shortly after. In the carrier bag was another carrier bag inside which was a black bin liner. The bin liner contained three handguns. There was another bin liner inside which were three magazines containing live ammunition. The firearms were Soviet 7.62 self-loading pistols, all in working order. They were originals as opposed to converted or reactivated weapons, thereby making them more desirable in the criminal market. The bullets were live bullets for those pistols. D was sentenced on the basis that he knew what was in the bags. There was an eight-month delay between plea and sentence. D was aged 38 at conviction and was treated as if he was of good character. Held. The Judge failed to identify any circumstance which required a departure from the normal practice, namely that consecutive sentences are not normally appropriate for offences arising out of the same incident. The 8 years for the firearms would remain, but the 3 years consecutive for the ammunition would be concurrent. So **8 years** not 11.

See also: *R v Bennett and Others Re S* 2014 EWCA Crim 2652 (Conspiracy to possess firearms with intent to endanger life and similar ammunition count. Garage converted into armoury. Supplier of firearms for spate of local firearm offences. Manufactured some firearms. Purchased some in Serbia. Age 33. No previous. We start at **20 years** not 24 so with plea **13 years 6 months** not 16. Extended sentence quashed.)

Old cases: *Att-Gen's Ref No 57 of 2009* 2009 EWCA Crim 2555, 2010 2 Cr App R (S) 30 (p 190) (**8 years**) *R v Alexander* 2010 EWCA Crim 1336 (**7 years' IPP**) For a summary of these cases see the 10th edition of this book.

259.25   *Supplying or storing firearms for criminals   Cases*

Att-Gen's Ref No 43 of 2009 Re A 2009 EWCA Crim 1925, 2010 1 Cr App R (S) 100 (p 628) para 42 LCJ D, W and S eventually pleaded to conspiracy to possess firearms and ammunition to enable another to endanger life. K was convicted of the offence. They obtained, converted and distributed self-loading Russian pistols to criminals. The guns were coated with an oil to hamper forensic tests. A high level of skill was involved in the modification process. They also were connected with distributing ammunition originally from South Africa and Brazil. Fifty-six weapons were seized with 8,000 bulleted cartridges. D was the co-ordinator. He was close to the top and was the Manchester manager. His role was pivotal. He gave instructions to K who in turn instructed S. D dealt with the man who brought the weapons from the South of England to Manchester. K and S co-ordinated their onward distribution. S repackaged them and was arrested with 13 pistols and silencers. The conspirators set about replacing them. W purchased some weapons from K and distributed them. D was aged 31 with no relevant previous convictions. His plea was based on his being the link between the South of England suppliers and Manchester. K was aged 31 and with no relevant convictions. W was aged 38 and had a substantial criminal record, including convictions for firearms and supplying heroin (10 years) for which he was on licence. S was aged 28 with no convictions. The Judge started at **25 years**. He said that D was not the main beneficiary but he was at the heart of the conspiracy. He started for him at **22 years** and reduced it to **18 years** because of the plea and the belated remorse. The Judge sentenced W on the basis that he recruited another to take a gun and ammunition to Scotland and liaised with other defendants for that man to collect and distribute weapons. The Judge started at **16 years** and gave **11½ years**. He started at **16 years** for S, and with the plea reduced it to

10 years 8 months. Held. The 56 weapons were only a proportion of the weapons involved. The guns were an assassin's armoury. The silencers justified that. Without a plea and with his prominent and important role, **20 years** for K was merited. S was a trusted employee playing a crucial role. W was steeped in very serious criminal conduct. No defendant could complain. Sentencers should consider whether to use their 'dangerousness' powers.

Att-Gen's Ref No 43 of 2009 Re O 2009 EWCA Crim 1925, 2010 1 Cr App R (S) 100 (p 628) LCJ para 64 O and F were convicted of possessing firearms and ammunition with intent to endanger life. D pleaded to those two charges. Two police officers approached G, who was next to a Porsche, and found on him just under £1,600 in cash. He was handcuffed. The police noticed a Mégane next to the Porsche with O, O-H and F in it. The occupants were told to stay in the car, and one of the policemen, C, kicked the driver's door shut. A rear passenger door opened and O pointed a gun at point-blank range at C, who kicked the door shut, causing O to drop the gun. It was a Browning 9 mm automatic pistol with 15 rounds in it. O struck one of the policemen, and O and F escaped. After a struggle D was arrested. There was a butt of a second firearm, a black BBM handgun, and four rounds of live ammunition in the Mégane. D had facilitated the meeting. He was not in possession of the weapons but had access to them. O-H was the purchaser of the weapons. F was the driver and participated in the transaction and helped arrange the meeting. He was considered to have been granted an enormous level of trust. D was a link between O-H and the others. O was born in 1984 and had convictions but none were this serious. F was born in 1981 and had many convictions including robbery (5 years). D was born in 1974 and had received custody for his previous convictions. The pre-sentence reports said that all posed a high risk to the public. The offence was too old for IPP. The Judge started at **14 years** for A. Held. 14 years was the right starting point for the purchasing and selling of two firearms with suitable ammunition. O's use of the gun justified his **18-year** sentence. F's sentence should be lower, so **14 years** not 18. **9 years** for D generously reflected his plea.

R v Hampson 2010 EWCA Crim 1254 D pleaded to conspiracy to sell or transfer prohibited firearms and other associated firearm offences. Undercover police officers, C, X and W, went to D's home. D was in the kitchen wearing surgical gloves. D showed C a variety of weapons and said he was "making a fortune". D had 5-6 Maglite torches which he said he was able to modify so that they were capable of firing. D said he had supplied a silencer to someone with another weapon, showed C a silencer and demonstrated how it fitted onto a pistol. D discussed the cost of weapons and C agreed to purchase weapons from him. A search of D's home revealed equipment for modification, conversion and re-activation of firearms. The computer showed in-depth research and an image of how to build a Beretta handgun. There was reloading equipment, ammunition components, mini Maglite torches in various states of modification, Maglite firearms, a 9 mm Browning semi-automatic, a 6.35 mm self-loading pistol, a 9 mm calibre pistol, a 9 mm revolver and 392 ammunition cartridges. D, aged 44, had 14 convictions for 26 offences including a conviction for conspiracy to convert an imitation firearm in 2002 (5½ years). The Judge said that the case concerned the supply of lethal weapons onto the streets where their use would have devastating consequences. Held. **20 years** was not manifestly excessive.

R v Sabir 2013 EWCA Crim 2261 D was convicted of 10 counts of possessing prohibited firearms and ammunition, including expanding ammunition. He claimed he was in debt to a drug gang who had been violent towards him and threatened to kill him. They wanted to store the guns at his address but he suggested another address, then empty, as a safer alternative. The items found included a self-loading Russian pistol and silencer, a 9 mm self-loading pistol and a pump-action smoothbore shotgun with a shortened barrel with the serial numbers removed. All were in working order. Duress was rejected by the jury. D volunteered the location of further weapons but this was in an attempt to create a false trail to be followed by police to 'curry favour' with them (6 years consecutive). D had a serious record although nothing for firearm offences. He had fled the country whilst on bail. He was eventually arrested in Canada. The Judge found that D was a well-trusted associate of the drug gang and a willing participant who was harbouring the firearms for a criminal organisation. She made the sentences consecutive because she believed a 15-year sentence was appropriate. Held. There [were] a significant number of weapons. There was a strong need for deterrent sentences. The offences were different. **15 years** (9 years and 6 years consecutive) was not manifestly excessive.

See also: *R v Cardwell* 2012 EWCA Crim 3030, 2013 2 Cr App R (S) 43 (p 284) (Convicted. 81 semi-automatic handguns bought in USA. Over 50 in unlawful circulation. Guns traced to a murder, an attempted murder and robbery. **22 years** was appropriate not life (11 year-minimum term). For more detail of the case see **259.7**.)

Old case: *Att-Gen's Ref No 43 of 2009* 2009 EWCA Crim 1925, 2010 1 Cr App R (S) 100 (p 628) (Judge started at **22 years** and gave **life (11-year** minimum term))

For a summary of the case, see the 9th edition of this book.

See also the ***Importation/Exportation of firearms*** paras at **259.6**.

259.26   *Firearms Act 1968 s 16*
Possession with intent to endanger life.
Mode of trial Indictable only
Maximum sentence Life
Minimum sentences Minimum sentence rules apply to ten of the offences under Firearms Act 1968 s 5. For details of which and other matters see the **Minimum sentences** section at **259.55**.
Automatic life This offence is listed in Criminal Justice Act 2003 Sch 15B Part 1. The court must (unless the particular circumstances make it unjust[436]) pass automatic life if: a) the defendant is aged 18+ at the date of the conviction, b) the offence was committed on or after 3 December 2012, c) the court considers a determinate sentence of at least 10 years is appropriate, d) at the time the offender was convicted he had a conviction for a Criminal Justice Act 2003 Sch 15B offence, and e) the defendant at the time of his or her conviction had previously been sentenced to either: i) a life sentence where he or she was not eligible for release during the first five years of the sentence or ii) a determinate sentence or extended sentence where the custodial part was 10 years or more.[437] For a pre-2012 extended sentence, when determining whether the custodial term was 10+ years the period deducted for time on remand or on a curfew and tag is included.[438]
Extended sentences This offence is listed in Criminal Justice Act 2003 Sch 15. The court may pass a 2012 extended sentence (EDS) if there is a significant risk of serious harm from future specified offences and either: a) the defendant has a Criminal Justice Act 2003 Sch 15B conviction (applicable only to defendants aged 18+), or b) the offence would justify a determinate sentence of at least 4 years.[439]
Sexual Harm Prevention Orders There is a discretionary power to make this order when it is necessary to protect the public from sexual harm.[440]

259.27   *Firearms Act 1968 s 16   Guideline case and judicial guidance*
R v Avis 1998 2 Cr App R (S) 178 LCJ Where there are breaches of Firearms Act 1968 s 16 the custodial term is likely to be of considerable length, and where the four

---

[436] Criminal Justice Act 2003 s 224A(2)
[437] Criminal Justice Act 2003 s 224A as inserted by Legal Aid, Sentencing and Punishment of Offenders Act 2012 s 122. The condition for a) is at section 224A(1)(a), for b) is at section 224A(1)(b), for c) is at section 224A(1)(c) and for d) is at section 224A(4)-(9).
[438] Criminal Justice Act 2003 s 224A(9)-(10)
[439] Criminal Justice Act 2003 s 226A-226B as inserted by Legal Aid, Sentencing and Punishment of Offenders Act 2012 s 124
[440] Sexual Offences Act 2003 s 103A as inserted by Anti-social Behaviour, Crime and Policing Act 2014 Sch 5 para 2 and Sexual Offences Act 2003 Sch 5

questions suggested above (see the *Guideline cases* para at **259.3**) yield answers adverse to the offender, terms at or approaching the maximum may in a contested case be appropriate.

Att-Gen's Ref Nos 4-8 of 2014 2014 EWCA Crim 651, 2 Cr App R (S) 51 (p 414) D and others were convicted of possession of a firearm with intent to endanger life. Held. para 21 Courts are taking an ever-increasing and stern view of firearms offences of this particular kind.

259.28 Firearms Act 1968 s 16 Cases

R v Mansende 2012 EWCA Crim 489, 2012 2 Cr App R (S) 52 (p 294) D was convicted of possessing a firearm with intent to endanger life, and possessing a prohibited firearm. He was hiding on the opposite side of the street to a social club. D fired a number of shots towards the club, hitting a parked car and the wall. No one was injured. D was chased by men from inside the club. He fired two shots at his assailants. No one was injured. He was apprehended and beaten up. The pre-sentence report stated that D talked of links to gang-related activity, but denied being directly linked to a gang. D, aged 23, had convictions for assault, robbery and possession of knives. He had served four custodial sentences. There was also possession of a pistol when aged 17. He committed the instant offence shortly after being released after 3 years' detention for possession of a knife. Held. All the aggravating features in *R v Avis* 1998 were present. This was a genuine firearm with live ammunition used to endanger life. Plainly a very substantial custodial sentence was called for. The appropriate notional term was 16 years, not 19, so **8 years' IPP**, not 9½.

Att-Gen's Ref No 7 of 2012 2012 EWCA Crim 1846 D was convicted of possessing a firearm with intent to cause fear of unlawful violence (×2) and putting a person in fear of violence by harassment. He had a history of abusive relationships, including offences of head-butting, battery, threatening words and behaviour, harassment and damaging property. From 2008, D had been in a relationship with V. V had a son. The relationship had been volatile. He had been drinking vodka and Coke and was smashing glasses on the floor. He took an air rifle, fired it into the air (unloaded) and then fired it 20 times (loaded) against a target containing a photograph of V and himself. V's son, aged 7, was present. D aimed the gun at the boy and fired near to him. D claimed the gun was not loaded. The boy was frightened and hid behind the chair V was sitting on. V called her daughter. In retaliation, D aimed the gun near her, upon which V held her handbag up to protect herself. D said, "You stupid cow, I can shoot through that." The boy cowered behind V's chair. D ordered V to take the phone away from her ear. He re-loaded the weapon and fired towards her, so the pellet flew past her head and lodged in the fence behind her. V ran into the house with her son. They moved out the following morning and did not return. D pursued V with text messages of a highly offensive and threatening nature. One said, 'I will find you and I will kill you'. When arrested, officers found a .22[441] air rifle and a large hunting knife. D was aged 48. Held. It is a gravely aggravating feature that D behaved as he did towards V and then aimed the gun towards the boy and pulled the trigger. All of the questions in *R v Avis* 1998 are to be answered adversely to D. He had no reason to have the weapon, he used the weapon to exercise power and violence towards two victims, he did so with the intent of causing them the fear he had caused in the past and he had a bad record of domestic violence. The Judge significantly underestimated the gravity of this offence. For the possession, **2 years** not 12 months for the offence against V, **3 years consecutive** not 18 months for the offence against V's son, and **12 months** not 9 for the harassment consecutive, making **6 years**, not 39 months in all.

R v Lewis 2013 EWCA Crim 48, 2014 2 Cr App R (S) 27 (p 207) L, F, G, J, T, C and R were convicted of possession of firearms with intent to endanger life, riot and other associated offences. Three days after the 2011 London riots started and late in the

---

[441] The judgment says 2.2 but it is assumed that is a typo.

evening, 42 masked or hooded men assembled outside a pub in Birmingham. They then broke in and set the ground floor alight with petrol bombs. There were occupants on the first floor. Furniture from the pub was strewn in the road outside to entice police to the scene. The police arrived and at least 12 rounds from four firearms were discharged at them. The police withdrew unharmed. The group moved off and at least two shots were fired at a police helicopter. Later about 30 of them split into two to form a group on either side of a police car. The car was then attacked. The group then moved on and four firearms were discharged in the general direction of police vans. L was aged 29 and was one of the organisers. He [was] armed. He had a very bad record which included an armed robbery and possession of a loaded firearm (2004, 6½ years). (For L **35 years**, including 5 years consecutive for an unrelated firearms offence.) F was aged 27 and played a full part in the violence. In 2005 he had a conviction for robbery (5 years). He was a member of a gang and enjoyed using guns. (For F **30 years**.) G was aged 27 with a bad record. There were robberies in 2002 and 2004 (6 years). (For G **29 years**.) J was aged 27 with no significant record. He was an active member of a gang. He drove F to a scene so they could fire on police. (For J **23 years**.) T had a firearm and shot at the police helicopter. He was aged 19 and had limited previous convictions. (For T **23 years' detention**.) C went with F knowing he was armed. He was aged 25, in work and had a limited record. (For C **18 years**.) R was aged 16 and effectively of good character. He was close to a man reloading a handgun. He was still in the group for the police van incident. (For R **12 years' detention**.) Held. J's attitude to guns was highly relevant to F's sentence. All appeals rejected.

R v Sugulle 2013 EWCA Crim 170, 2 Cr App R (S) 61 (p 389) D pleaded (full credit) to possession of a firearm and ammunition (both with intent to endanger life) and two bladed article offences. Police stopped a taxi in London and D, the passenger, was seen fiddling with a bag. D ran off but was detained. The bag contained a Smith & Wesson revolver and two kitchen knives. The gun was loaded with six bullets and the safety catch was off. The police said D was part of a well-known violent gang in Woolwich and the gun had been used in two shootings, one four days before the offence. D was aged 24 with no relevant previous convictions. The Judge identified four aggravating factors: the gun was loaded, it was ready to be fired, it was in a residential street and it was held in connection with gang-related activity. Held. The only mitigation was that the gun was not fired. The starting point was **15 years**, so **10 years** not 12.

R v Rukwira 2013 EWCA Crim 875 D was convicted of possessing a firearm with intent to endanger life, having pleaded to possessing ammunition with intent to endanger life, and simple possession of the same gun and ammunition. The police executed a warrant at the home of D's friend. They found nothing but when they returned later, they found a fully loaded .25 self-loading pistol with a spare magazine also loaded. D's friend was arrested and gave a prepared statement to the effect that she believed that 'Jordan' had left the items in her bedroom without her knowledge. Within a week, D informed the police that it was he who had placed the items in the bedroom without his friend's knowledge. Examination of their telephones revealed this to be a lie as they had been discussing the gun and ammunition in coded language. D was just short of his 18th birthday. He was treated as being of good character. Held. The fact that there was a loaded magazine was an aggravating feature. The public has to be protected from gun crime. **8 years** was severe, but rightly so.

Att-Gen's Ref Nos 4-8 of 2014 2014 EWCA Crim 651, 2 Cr App R (S) 51 (p 414) D and TD (who were brothers), K, W and T were convicted of conspiracy to possess firearms with intent to endanger life or to enable another to endanger life. Some were convicted of similar counts relating to ammunition. D and TD were the 'leading lights' in the conspiracy. With W and T, they were members of a south London gang with a very significant reputation for drugs and violence. D and TD were prominent members and W and T were 'juniors'. The gang members travelled in a hired car to avoid detection, and went to collect a gun from K in Bedford. K was a drug dealer who had regularly supplied the two brothers with drugs in the past. W and T travelled back by train and were stopped by police at Kings Cross. W had a rucksack with a .38 Ivor Johnson revolver and five rounds of ammunition in it. D and TD travelled back to London in the hired vehicle. D was aged 24 and TD was aged 26. Both had been arrested for murder before the offence. After the offence, D was convicted of murder and received a 30-year minimum term. He also had a robbery and drug offences on his record. TD was acquitted of murder but convicted of perverting the course of justice (8 years). He had a robbery with an imitation firearm conviction (54 months' detention). K was aged 22 and had convictions for robbery and other less serious offences. W was aged 19 and had no convictions. T was aged 18 and had a concealing property offence (community order). He was at university. The Judge sentenced W and T on the basis that they knew the other two would use the gun. K was sentenced on the basis that he had dealt with TD on a regular basis. Held. The entire gangland context must be reflected in the sentence. For D and TD the sentence had to be not less than 15 years, so **15 years** not 10. K was not a gang member but he knew the sort of man TD was. **11 years** not 8. W and T were younger. They were under the influence of the brothers. They were making real efforts educationally and otherwise to advance themselves. The Judge was right to have regard to the statutory minimum sentence even though it did not strictly apply. There were no exceptional circumstances so it was wrong to go below the minimum. For W and T **7 years**, not 4.

See also: *R v Sheen and Sheen* 2011 EWCA Crim 2461, 2012 2 Cr App R (S) 3 (p 7) (D1 and D2 pleaded (20% credit) to possession of firearms and ammunition with intent to endanger life. After a dispute between two travelling families, D1 and D2 discharged a shotgun at a car containing the victims. Pellets in face. Both occupants injured. **14 years** was entirely justified.)

Att-Gen's Ref No 6 of 2012 2012 EWCA Crim 86, 2 Cr App R (S) 67 (p 387) (Pleas to possession of a prohibited weapon and prohibited ammunition. They were alternative charges to possession of those items with intent to endanger life, to which the defendant later pleaded. 10% credit. Convictions for possession of class A and criminal damage. The gun was loaded but not discharged. Aged 23. Considering only the possession with intent count, 10 years not 5.)

R v Kumar 2012 EWCA Crim 503, 2 Cr App R (S) 84 (p 487) (Early plea to having a firearm and ammunition in a public place. Later plea to possession of a firearm with intent. Threatened by a gang. Informed an attack was imminent. Obtained a gun and ammunition. Shots fired at his house. He fired back. Hit one attacker in the groin. Previous convictions for threats to kill and battery. In breach of suspended sentence. Starting at 7 years was correct. 25% credit. **5 years 3 months**.)

R v Hagan 2012 EWCA Crim 1822, 2013 1 Cr App R (S) 90 (p 483) (LCJ Pleas to possession of a prohibited firearm and ammunition without a certificate. Convicted of possessing a firearm with intent. Beretta pistol and loaded magazine with six rounds. Gang association. Asked by local gang member to collect a package. Suspected it to be a gun. Used in 15 shootings between 2009 and 2011. Returned the weapon on request. Had also stored another gun, returned on request a matter of days prior to collecting the Beretta. One conviction for robbery and possession of an offensive weapon. Aged 16, living with parents. **9 years** was in no way manifestly excessive.)

R v Jones and Skyers 2014 EWCA Crim 632 (J convicted, S pleaded on rearraignment, to conspiracy to supply heroin, cocaine and cannabis and conspiracy to possess a firearm with intent (×3). Members of a south London gang involved. Violent dispute with a rival gang. Over 7 months, firearms used to protect drugs stored in a safe house. Weapons included a self-loading rifle with hollow point bullets. Weapons linked to two previous shootings. 200 g of heroin, 60 g of cocaine and half a kilo of skunk cannabis found. J aged 19 with previous convictions for firearms and robbery. He was on licence. S aged

20 with previous for robbery. S and J both leaders and organisers. 15% credit for S could not be faulted. For J **19 years' YOI**. For S **16 years' YOI**. The sentences were undoubtedly severe but not unduly long for what was extremely serious offending.)
Old cases: There are plenty of recent cases. If old cases are required, they are listed in the 9th edition of this book.
For when the firearm is supplied to criminals, see **259.22**.

259.29   *Firearms Act 1968 s 16A*
To have in his possession any firearm or imitation firearm with intent: a) by means thereof to cause, or b) to enable another person by means thereof to cause, any person to believe that unlawful violence will be used against him or another person.
Mode of trial Indictable only
Maximum sentence 10 years
Minimum sentences Minimum sentence rules apply to ten of the offences under Firearms Act 1968 s 5. For details of which and other matters see the **Minimum sentences** section at **259.55**.
Extended sentences This offence is listed in Criminal Justice Act 2003 Sch 15. The court may pass a 2012 extended sentence (EDS) if there is a significant risk of serious harm from future specified offences and either: a) the defendant has a Criminal Justice Act 2003 Sch 15B conviction (applicable only to defendants aged 18+), or b) the offence would justify a determinate sentence of at least 4 years.[442]
Sexual Harm Prevention Orders There is a discretionary power to make this order when it is necessary to protect the public from sexual harm.[443]

259.30   *Firearms Act 1968 s 16A   Guideline case*
R v Avis 1998 2 Cr App R (S) 178 LCJ Where there are breaches of Firearms Act 1968 s 16A, the custodial term is likely to be of considerable length, and where the four questions suggested above (see the ***Guideline cases*** para at **259.3**) yield answers adverse to the offender, terms at or approaching the maximum may in a contested case be appropriate.

259.31   *Firearms Act 1968 s 16A   Handguns*
R v Bent 2009 EWCA Crim 1847 D pleaded to possession of a firearm with intent to cause fear, and possession of cannabis. V was driving and came across D driving very slowly. V overtook him, and D shouted and pointed at him. V made an obscene gesture. V saw D behind him raising a handgun to the windscreen. They both accelerated. V phoned the police. Armed police stopped D and found an air pistol and some cannabis. The pistol did not require a licence and was not loaded. D was aged 20 and of good character. He had good reports from his work. Held. The gun had not been pointed at V. It was just shown to him. The incident was over in seconds. D did not follow V afterwards. Possession of a firearm coupled with an intent to cause fear in a public setting is a serious offence which merits custody but **4 months** not 12.
R v Wypych 2010 EWCA Crim 1166 D pleaded to possession of an imitation firearm with intent to cause fear of violence. Whilst driving her car, V stopped to pick up her partner, M. D and another approached the vehicle. D tapped on the driver's door window with a handgun. V was startled and frightened by the noise and turned to find a gun pointing in her face. D shouted "Get out of the car" three times. V drove off and had travelled a short distance before stopping at traffic lights. D chased on foot and tapped again on the window with the handgun. When the traffic lights changed V drove off at speed. The gun was never recovered. V was frightened and M thought she was going to be killed. D, aged 25, had no convictions. In interview D said it was a stupid joke. The pre-sentence report said D seemed to lack any awareness of the potential consequences

---

[442] Criminal Justice Act 2003 s 226A-226B as inserted by Legal Aid, Sentencing and Punishment of Offenders Act 2012 s 124
[443] Sexual Offences Act 2003 s 103A as inserted by Anti-social Behaviour, Crime and Policing Act 2014 Sch 5 para 2 and Sexual Offences Act 2003 Sch 5

of his actions and said he posed a medium risk of harm to the public. Held. This was a serious case of its kind. The aggravating factor was the degree of terror inflicted on the girls. **16 months**, not 2 years.

See also: *R v Charrington* 2010 EWCA Crim 2372 (Plea. Officers try to resolve domestic dispute. Threats to police officer. **4 years**.) For more detail see **259.33**.

Old case: *R v Oddy* 2009 EWCA Crim 245, 2 Cr App R (S) 528 (**6 years**)

For a summary of this case, see the 9th edition of this book. (Older cases are best ignored. Ed.)

259.32   Firearms Act 1968 s 16A   Imitation weapons, starting pistols etc.

R v Boyce 2011 EWCA Crim 2982, 2012 2 Cr App R (S) 28 (p 164) D pleaded (full credit) to possession of an imitation firearm with intent to cause fear of violence. He was swimming in a reservoir with a number of other people. Swimming in the reservoir was not permitted. Two park rangers approached the group in a boat to speak to them. When they were about 50 m away, they were met by jeering and abuse. Missiles were thrown including bricks and stones. D stood with both arms outstretched holding a firearm which was pointed at the boat. The rangers believed that it was real. Two shots were fired that coincided with something hitting the boat. In fact, it was not a bullet and must have been a stone or something similar. The rangers ducked and one of them took a photograph of D on his mobile phone. When D was arrested he said that he had been drinking. He said he found the gun by the river and thought it would be a joke to pick it up, point it and shoot with it. D, aged 29, had 9 convictions for 10 offences relating to theft, driving offences and breaches of court orders. He had not previously been to custody. D appeared to be remorseful. Held. The weapon was an imitation, recently found and not ordinarily carried. It was fired at two people who were performing a public service, who were isolated and vulnerable in a boat and were traumatised. There was no premeditation and the incident was an ill-judged joke by someone with no previous convictions for firearms or violent offences. The mitigation justified a reduction in what would otherwise be appropriate. **2 years** not 3.

R v Marsh 2012 EWCA Crim 1217, 2013 1 Cr App R (S) 18 (p 99) D pleaded to possession of a firearm with intent to cause fear. V and two other youths went to D's home complaining that D's son had burgled V's home and stolen a laptop. D's wife told them that her son was at home at the time. D then appeared and the discussion continued. V said what he would do if he sorted the son out. D responded by saying, "I'll blow your fucking brains out". D went back into the house and came back with an imitation Valtro 8 mm pistol which was a replica of a Beretta pistol. D made as if to prepare the gun for firing and pulled something on the top of the gun which made a clicking noise. D then pointed the gun at V's abdomen. D threatened to shoot V if he did not go away and said, "Get off my drive or I'll give you one". D's wife pushed D back inside and the gun was put down. V was shocked. The police were called and the pistol found. D was now aged 46 with a good record and no relevant convictions. Held. There were serious aggravating factors, the gun looked real, by moving the part D intended it to look real, there was an element of premeditation by going into the house to obtain the pistol and such use even with an imitation gun was fraught with danger. However, the threat was short-lived and there was no history of firearm use. **9 months** not 12.

R v Morris and Reader 2013 EWCA Crim 1248 M (at a preliminary hearing) and R (at the PCMH) pleaded to possession of an imitation firearm with intent to cause fear of violence. M, R and C were friends. C had been in a relationship with AS, who was aged 16 and pregnant by him. With C, they went to AS's house and knocked on the door. AS's mother answered the door and saw three men standing outside dressed in black and wearing balaclavas. C pointed a gun at her. AS's mother was very frightened and immediately shut the door. The three ran away. C's house was searched and a Beretta .177 air pistol was found under his bed. It was a very realistic imitation. M was aged 16 and aged 17 when sentenced and had seven previous offences, all of shoplifting save for one possession of a bladed article. R was aged 18. R and C were of previous good character. Held. The weapon was a realistic imitation, taken to a house in the hours of darkness with the clear intention of frightening one or more of those present. The weapon was in C's possession but M and R knew he had it, knew his intentions and willingly lent their support. For M, a 12-month DTO consecutive to a 4-month DTO for another bladed article making **16 months** was well justified. For R, there should have been a distinction between him and C (who received 3 years on conviction). Starting at **27 months**, with full credit for the plea, **18 months** not 2 years.

Att-Gen's Ref No 130 of 2014 EWCA Crim 378, 2015 2 Cr App R (S) 3 (p 24) D pleaded to section 16A. V and his partner, H, lived opposite D and were irritated and kept awake by a security light. D and H drove round in their night clothes to where they believed the light was coming from. V climbed over D's fence to check it was the right house. D challenged him but V did not respond. D and his partner, M, were very frightened. There had been problems in the area with anti-social behaviour. D said to M, "Get the gun." She did and handed it to him. It was a ball bearing gun which could fire pellets and was a lawful gun to keep. D pointed it at V. Abuse followed. Both sides called the police. D was arrested and police found the gun. D admitted V and H would have been absolutely terrified. H said she was still feeling the effects 3 months later. D was aged 49 and of previous excellent character. He was in a trusted position as a public servant which he would lose if he was sent to prison. D supported his disabled ex-wife. Held. This offence is usually serious. There should be an element of deterrence. However, this was an exceptional case. D reacted spontaneously believing there was a night-time intruder. D's culpability was low. The length of terror was exceedingly short. A **conditional discharge** was lenient but not unduly so.

Old cases: *R v Finch* 2010 EWCA Crim 688 (**12 months' detention**) *R v Webber* 2010 EWCA Crim 1102, 2011 1 Cr App R (S) 32 (p 204) (**30 months**) *R v Bentley* 2010 EWCA Crim 1169 (**18 months**)

For a summary of the first and last cases, see the 10th edition of this book.

259.33   *Firearms Act 1968 s 16A   Police, Offence directed at*

R v Charrington 2010 EWCA Crim 2372 D pleaded to possession of a firearm with intent to cause fear of violence. A police officer attended an address in relation to a domestic dispute. He was admitted to the house by W. D was sitting in the lounge and was unhappy that the officer was there. W stated she wanted D out of the house so the officer asked D to collect some belongings. D said, "I'm not leaving and if you fucking touch me I'll fucking kill you". Another officer arrived at that point. D also threatened to kill the second officer. W was upstairs and D, along with the officers, followed her. D was acting in an abusive and threatening manner towards the first officer. Referring to his body armour, he said: "That won't save you against me. What's that for?" The officer explained that it was designed to stop bullets and knives, and D laughed. W handed D a holdall from which D pulled out what looked like a black handgun and pointed it at the first officer's head. The officers fled, barricaded themselves in the lounge and called for armed back-up. D said: "It's a fucking BB gun you fucking idiots." Armed officers negotiated with D after he said he would shoot anyone who came through the door. The gun was a toy gun designed to fire ball bearings but had no magazine and no ball bearings in the firing chamber. Held. There were significant aggravating factors correctly identified by the Judge: the officer was unarmed and in an unfamiliar environment with D at a natural advantage, there were threats of violence and a considerable build-up to the production of the imitation gun, which was immediately preceded by a reference to the officer's body armour and its apparent inadequacies. Moreover, the gun was pointed at the officer's head from a very close range. There was, however, no planned premeditation but instead impulsivity. D took an opportunity which presented itself. **4 years** not 5.

R v Roberts 2011 EWCA Crim 2283 D pleaded to possession of a firearm with intent to cause fear of violence. He telephoned police and stated that he had a firearm and intended to shoot himself or police officers. A large number of officers attended, including two negotiators, and a helicopter was used. The street was also cordoned off. He appeared upset and pleaded with an armed officer to shoot him. He had a .22 rifle, which was loaded and with the safety catch 'off', and held it out with his left hand. He did not point it at the officers. He shouted, "I've killed men and I'll do it again." This was perhaps a reference to his time in the armed forces. There was a three-hour stand-off. He had drunk vodka and taken a large number of pain-killers. He eventually came out of the house and when arrested, stated that he had no intention of shooting the officers, that he wanted help with his mental health and that he was sorry. D, aged 47, had 10 previous convictions, including violence, but no firearm offences. Held. D did not suffer from a mental disorder of a degree which required care or treatment in hospital. There was a lengthy stand-off, in which D had a firearm which was loaded and capable of being fired. 12 pellets were found in D's house. In mitigation, no threats were issued to the police or public and D was deeply remorseful. **2 years 6 months** not 3 years 9 months.

259.34   *Firearms Act 1968 s 16A   Servicemen and women*
R v Moffat 2014 EWCA Crim 332, 2014 2 Cr App R (S) 37 (p 307) D pleaded to possession with intent to cause another to fear violence. He was a leading seaman and gunner who wanted to be present for his child's birth since he had missed his first child's birth, which had been a very difficult one. The Navy would not give him an absolute assurance he would be on leave but he thought it was his entitlement. While on his ship, he became overwrought and said to a Petty Officer, P, and a Lieutenant, L, that he had access to weapons and ammunition. P told him not to be stupid. L said he would take the matter up and D said if he didn't get home he was going to get a gun. L warned him that he could be on a charge. D raised the matter the next morning and it appeared he would get leave. D collected an SA80 assault rifle and bullets. He kept them separate and went to the second in command of the ship, a Lieutenant Commander, C. D stood in the doorway, clearly angry and intense, and said, "This is a loaded gun, you know what this means: I want to talk to you." C asked D if his junior officer could leave the room. D agreed and C asked D to hand over the weapon. D did so. D then broke down in tears. The incident was over in seconds. D was aged 45. The Board found the incident was a gross breach of naval discipline. They also found there were exceptional circumstances, namely: a) D immediately regretted his actions and was tearful, b) no magazine was attached to the gun, c) the weapon was not aimed at anyone, d) there was no evil intent and e) D was emotionally overwrought. D was found to have an adjustment disorder which had impaired his judgement. The offence was considered to be completely out of character as D was the very epitome of steady reliability, honesty and commitment. He had an unblemished record. The dismissal with its financial loss was not challenged. Held. This approach was unimpeachable. Taking the fleeting nature of the loss of judgement and the reduction of his mental responsibility which had overwhelmed him, **14 months** not 3 years, which meant immediate release.

259.35   *Firearms Act 1968 s 16A   Shotguns*
R v Dring 2010 EWCA Crim 2063 D pleaded, after the jury was empanelled, to possessing a firearm with intent to cause fear of violence. V was taking a balloon ride with his wife and others which was followed by a control vehicle. The balloon landed on a farm owned by D and her husband, whose principal business was the production of free-range eggs. D's brother-in-law was unhappy that the balloon had landed on the farm and remonstrated with the pilot. The pilot offered an apology and a bottle of whiskey and champagne were handed over. D, who was not present, was telephoned and informed of what had occurred. She was unhappy about the potential disturbance caused to the hens and returned immediately. Upon returning, she saw a number of cars parked on a private road. There were people in at least one of the cars, 'dressed up and drinking champagne'. Following a vicious verbal altercation with J, D allegedly threatened to "set the bloody dogs" on him. D then drove off to the farm. She returned with a double-barrelled

shotgun and shouted at V, "get off my land, get off my fucking land". She poked the broken gun in V's chest. She loaded the gun and closed it. Again she poked the gun in V's chest. V put his hands in the air and walked to his car. D drove behind him revving the engine. V did not think it was safe to ask if he could pick up his family members. D was arrested and denied the offence. D, aged 50, had no previous convictions and the Judge assessed that there was very little risk of her offending again. Held. The use of a firearm in this kind of threatening and intimidatory fashion cannot be tolerated. The Judge was correct to take the view that there was little benefit to come from sending D to prison, an educated woman posing very little risk of reoffending, however, also correctly, he noted that the offence was serious and that a loaded weapon pushed into V's chest created significant danger. With the plea and mitigation, **9 months'** imprisonment not 18.

Att-Gen's Ref Nos 20-21 of 2010 2010 EWCA Crim 2323 S and N were convicted of possession of a firearm with intent. On a motorbike, they drove to the address of V, whom S thought had been having a sexual relationship with his former girlfriend. A shortened shotgun-type weapon was placed against the letter box and discharged whilst the occupants were inside. The offenders were identified by CCTV. Due to evidence, the Judge felt unable to treat the weapon as a prohibited weapon and therefore the minimum term did not apply. S, aged 21, had two court appearances, resulting in community penalties. N, aged 21, had three appearances, two for arson, and was on bail at the time of the instant offence. Held. The firearm was real, loaded and discharged. It was in a public place and the prior acquisition suggested premeditation. There was also a suggested link to more sophisticated criminals. **5 years** not 3½.

See also: *R v Hulse* 2010 EWCA Crim 1914 (Plea. Discharged a shotgun into the air after he 'snapped'. Defendant under considerable strain and socially isolated. **18 months** not 2½ years.)

259.36   Firearms Act 1968 s 17(1)
Making use of a firearm with intent to resist arrest.
Mode of trial Indictable only
Maximum sentence Life
Automatic life This offence is listed in Criminal Justice Act 2003 Sch 15B Part 1. The court must (unless the particular circumstances make it unjust[444]) pass automatic life if: a) the defendant is aged 18+ at the date of the conviction, b) the offence was committed on or after 3 December 2012, c) the court considers a determinate sentence of at least 10 years is appropriate, d) at the time the offender was convicted he had a conviction for a Criminal Justice Act 2003 Sch 15B offence, and e) the defendant at the time of his or her conviction had previously been sentenced to either: i) a life sentence where he or she was not eligible for release during the first 5 years of the sentence or ii) a determinate sentence or extended sentence where the custodial part was 10 years or more.[445] For a pre-2012 extended sentence, when determining whether the custodial term was 10+ years the period deducted for time on remand or on a curfew and tag is included.[446]
Minimum sentences Minimum sentence rules apply to ten of the offences under Firearms Act 1968 s 5. For details of which and other matters see the **Minimum sentences** section at **259.55**.
Extended sentences This offence is listed in Criminal Justice Act 2003 Sch 15. The court may pass a 2012 extended sentence (EDS) if there is a significant risk of serious

---

[444] Criminal Justice Act 2003 s 224A(2)
[445] Criminal Justice Act 2003 s 224A as inserted by Legal Aid, Sentencing and Punishment of Offenders Act 2012 s 122 The condition for a) is at section 224A(1)(a), for b) is at section 224A(1)(b), for c) is at section 224A(1)(c) and for d) is at section 224A(4)-(9).
[446] Criminal Justice Act 2003 s 224A(9)-(10)

harm from future specified offences and either: a) the defendant has a Criminal Justice Act 2003 Sch 15B conviction (applicable only to defendants aged 18+), or b) the offence would justify a determinate sentence of at least 4 years.[447]

Sexual Harm Prevention Orders There is a discretionary power to make this order when it is necessary to protect the public from sexual harm.[448]

R v Avis 1998 2 Cr App R (S) 178 LCJ Where there are breaches of Firearms Act 1968 s 17(1) the custodial term is likely to be of considerable length, and where the four questions suggested above (see the *Guideline cases* para at **259.3**) yield answers adverse to the offender, terms at or approaching the maximum may in a contested case be appropriate.

Old cases: Best ignored. Ed.

259.37   *Firearms Act 1968 s 17(2)*

Committing or being arrested for a Schedule 1 offence and in possession of a firearm

Mode of trial Indictable only

Maximum sentence Life

Minimum sentences Minimum sentence rules apply to ten of the offences under Firearms Act 1968 s 5. For details of which and other matters see the **Minimum sentences** section at **259.55**.

Extended sentences This offence is listed in Criminal Justice Act 2003 Sch 15. The court may pass a 2012 extended sentence (EDS) if there is a significant risk of serious harm from future specified offences and either: a) the defendant has a Criminal Justice Act 2003 Sch 15B conviction (applicable only to defendants aged 18+), or b) the offence would justify a determinate sentence of at least 4 years.[449]

Sexual Harm Prevention Orders There is a discretionary power to make this order when it is necessary to protect the public from sexual harm.[450]

259.38   *Firearms Act 1968 s 17(2)   Cases*

R v Avis 1998 2 Cr App R (S) 178 LCJ Where there are breaches of Firearms Act 1968 s 17(2) the custodial term is likely to be of considerable length, and where the four questions suggested above (see the *Guideline cases* para at **259.3**) yield answers adverse to the offender, terms at or approaching the maximum may in a contested case be appropriate.

R v R 2010 EWCA Crim 2651 D pleaded to: a) possession of a firearm (9 mm machine pistol) whilst committing a specified offence (criminal damage), b) possession of a prohibited firearm (9 mm machine pistol), c) possession of a prohibited firearm (9 mm semi-automatic pistol), and d) possessing ammunition without a firearm certificate. In relation to a) and b), D and another fired at a man from a motorcycle. The man was unhurt. In relation to c) and d), a police officer witnessed D take something from inside a BT connection box and get in a taxi. Armed officers stopped the taxi to discover D, with others, in the footwell of the taxi in the foetal position. D pleaded to c) and d) on the basis that he was acting as a courier for the weapon. All offences were committed whilst on licence and c) and d) were committed whilst on bail for a) and b). D, aged 17, had 14 appearances for 27 offences, none of which related to firearms. Held. Offence a): The Judge was amply justified in concluding that D was dangerous for the purposes of CJA 2003 Part 12. Further, the Judge correctly identified that the notional minimum term would have been in excess of 2 years, therefore satisfying CJA 2003 s 226(3). DPP was correct. For a) **14 years** after trial was appropriate, not 16½. With full credit, **9 years**. Therefore, the minimum term is **4½ years**. Remainder concurrent.

Old cases: Best ignored. Ed.

---

[447] Criminal Justice Act 2003 s 226A-226B as inserted by Legal Aid, Sentencing and Punishment of Offenders Act 2012 s 124
[448] Sexual Offences Act 2003 s 103A as inserted by Anti-social Behaviour, Crime and Policing Act 2014 Sch 5 para 2 and Sexual Offences Act 2003 Sch 5
[449] Criminal Justice Act 2003 s 226A-226B as inserted by Legal Aid, Sentencing and Punishment of Offenders Act 2012 s 124
[450] Sexual Offences Act 2003 s 103A as inserted by Anti-social Behaviour, Crime and Policing Act 2014 Sch 5 para 2 and Sexual Offences Act 2003 Sch 5

259.39   *Firearms Act 1968 s 18(1)*
Having a firearm or imitation firearm with intent to commit an indictable offence
Mode of trial Indictable only
Maximum sentence Life
Minimum sentences Minimum sentence rules apply to ten of the offences under Firearms Act 1968 s 5. For details of which and other matters see the **Minimum sentences** section at **259.55**.
Automatic life This offence is listed in Criminal Justice Act 2003 Sch 15B Part 1. The court must (unless the particular circumstances make it unjust[451]) pass automatic life if: a) the defendant is aged 18+ at the date of the conviction, b) the offence was committed on or after 3 December 2012, c) the court considers a determinate sentence of at least 10 years is appropriate, d) at the time the offender was convicted he had a conviction for a Criminal Justice Act 2003 Sch 15B offence, and e) the defendant at the time of his or her conviction had previously been sentenced to either: i) a life sentence where he or she was not eligible for release during the first five years of the sentence or ii) a determinate sentence or extended sentence where the custodial part was 10 years or more.[452] For a pre-2012 extended sentence, when determining whether the custodial term was 10+ years the period deducted for time on remand or on a curfew and tag is included.[453]
Extended sentences This offence is listed in Criminal Justice Act 2003 Sch 15. The court may pass a 2012 extended sentence (EDS) if there is a significant risk of serious harm from future specified offences and either: a) the defendant has a Criminal Justice Act 2003 Sch 15B conviction (applicable only to defendants aged 18+), or b) the offence would justify a determinate sentence of at least 4 years.[454]
Sexual Harm Prevention Orders There is a discretionary power to make this order when it is necessary to protect the public from sexual harm.[455]

259.40   *Firearms Act 1968 s 18(1)   Guideline case and judicial guidance*
R v Avis 1998 2 Cr App R (S) 178 LCJ Where there are breaches of Firearms Act 1968 s 18(1) the custodial term is likely to be of considerable length, and where the four questions suggested above (see the *Guideline cases* para at **259.3**) yield answers adverse to the offender, terms at or approaching the maximum may in a contested case be appropriate.

259.41   *Firearms Act 1968 s 18(1)   Cases*
R v Scott 2010 EWCA Crim 2340 On the first day of trial D pleaded to having a firearm to commit an indictable offence, two counts of wounding with intent, wounding, possessing ammunition without a firearm certificate and possessing a firearm without a firearm certificate. D and his girlfriend, G, were at a bar when a member of the public made an accusation against D. The head of security and his colleague accompanied D down the fire escape to discuss the matter. D strongly denied the accusation and became abusive and threatening. When he was asked to leave, D punched the head of security causing him to buckle at the knees. D was pursued by the head of security and two other door staff. CCTV showed D lying on the ground and the three staff making their way back to the premises. D was helped up by G and another and drove off. D had fractured his leg. D later returned with a silver revolver and wearing a balaclava, and shot the head of security in the leg, the bar owner in the foot and a member of the public in the ankle. D fled but two door staff pursued him and managed to wrestle the firearm from his hand. The driver of the getaway vehicle drove at the three men as they wrestled, colliding with

---

[451] Criminal Justice Act 2003 s 224A(2)
[452] Criminal Justice Act 2003 s 224A as inserted by Legal Aid, Sentencing and Punishment of Offenders Act 2012 s 122. The condition for a) is at section 224A(1)(a), for b) is at section 224A(1)(b), for c) is at section 224A(1)(c) and for d) is at section 224A(4)-(9).
[453] Criminal Justice Act 2003 s 224A(9)-(10)
[454] Criminal Justice Act 2003 s 226A-226B as inserted by Legal Aid, Sentencing and Punishment of Offenders Act 2012 s 124
[455] Sexual Offences Act 2003 s 103A as inserted by Anti-social Behaviour, Crime and Policing Act 2014 Sch 5 para 2 and Sexual Offences Act 2003 Sch 5

one of the door staff. This allowed D to make his escape, but not before one of the door staff had managed to remove the balaclava. Police found six empty casings and three fired bullet heads on the pavement. D was arrested and his home address was searched along with another property to which he and G had keys. Forty-four 0.38 calibre cartridges were found along with six shotgun cartridges, two pairs of woollen gloves, a ball-bearing (BB) pistol, nine gas canisters and a box of premium grade BBs. A sawn-off shotgun was also found. D, aged 29, had convictions for ABH, possession of an offensive weapon, possession of cannabis and possession of cannabis with intent to supply. The pre-sentence report stated D claimed he was being paid £250 per month to look after the weapons. He did not seek to minimise his offending. Held. The starting point is 8 years, for a first-time offender after a trial. It appears to us that after a trial on those three offences a total sentence of some 13 or 14 years could not be regarded as manifestly excessive. It is necessary to look at the totality of offending relating to firearms. It is well-known sentencing policy that sentences for firearm offending should be ordered to run consecutively to other offending upon the indictment. Here there are two quite distinct elements to the offending of D. We look at the sentence in the round. It appears to us that a very lengthy sentence in this case was called for. Had there been a determinate sentence after a trial a sentence in excess of 20 years could not be complained against. With a little over 10% credit for the plea, **17 years** was not manifestly excessive.

Old cases: Best ignored.

259.42   *Firearms Act 1968 s 19*

Having in a public place a loaded shotgun, an air weapon or a firearm whether loaded or not or an imitation firearm.[456]

Mode of trial For offences where the firearm is one specified in Firearms Act 1968 s 5(1)(a), (ab), (aba), (ac), (ad), (ae) or (af) or s 5(1A)(a) the offence is triable only on indictment.[457] Otherwise triable either way unless the firearm is an air weapon, when it is a summary only offence. Offences with an imitation firearm are summary only.[458]

Maximum sentence On indictment 7 years. Summary maximum 6 months and/or a £5,000 fine for offences committed before 12 March 2015 and an unlimited fine thereafter.[459] There are maximum fines for those aged under 18, see **14.38** in Volume 1.

Minimum sentences Minimum sentence rules apply to ten of the offences under Firearms Act 1968 s 5. For details of which and other matters see the **Minimum sentences** section at **259.55**.

259.43   *Firearms Act 1968 s 19   Guideline case*

R v Avis 1998 2 Cr App R (S) 178 LCJ Where there are breaches of Firearms Act 1968 s 19 the custodial term is likely to be of considerable length, and where the four questions suggested above (see the *Guideline cases* para at **259.3**) yield answers adverse to the offender, terms at or approaching the maximum may in a contested case be appropriate.

259.44   *Firearms Act 1968 s 19   Magistrates' Court Sentencing Guidelines*

Magistrates' Court Sentencing Guidelines 2008, see www.banksr.com Other Matters Guidelines tab The guideline applies to the Magistrates' Court and to the Crown Court hearing appeals or sentencing for summary only offences.[460]

page 61 Starting points are based on a first-time offender pleading not guilty.

---

[456] This wider offence was inserted by Anti-social Behaviour Act 2003 s 37.
[457] As inserted by Violent Crime Reduction Act 2006 s 30(3)
[458] Violent Crime Reduction Act 2006 s 41 and Violent Crime Reduction Act 2006 (Commencement No 4) Order 2007 2007/2518
[459] Legal Aid, Sentencing and Punishment of Offenders Act 2012 s 85(1) and (4) and Legal Aid, Sentencing and Punishment of Offenders Act 2012 (Commencement No 11) Order 2015 2015/504
[460] See page 15 of the guidelines.

Examples of nature of activity	Starting point	Range
Carrying an unloaded air weapon	Low-level community order	Band B fine to medium-level community order
Carrying loaded air weapon/imitation firearm/unloaded shotgun without ammunition	High-level community order	Medium-level community order to 26 weeks' custody (air weapon) Medium-level community order to Crown Court (imitation firearm, unloaded shotgun)
Carrying loaded shotgun/carrying shotgun or any other firearm together with ammunition for it	Crown Court	Crown Court

The following aggravating and mitigating factors may be particularly relevant: Factors indicating higher culpability: 1 Brandishing the firearm 2 Carrying firearm in a busy place 3 Planned illegal use. Factors indicating lower culpability: 1 Firearm not in sight 2 No intention to use firearm 3 Firearm to be used for lawful purpose (not amounting to a defence). Factors indicating greater degree of harm: 1 Person or people put in fear 2 Offender participating in violent incident.

For the meaning of a high-level, a medium-level and a low-level community order see **16.12-16.14** in Volume 1.

Consider compensation, forfeiture or suspension of personal liquor licence and Football Banning Order.

A Band B fine is 100% of net weekly income. For more detail see **60.27** in Volume 1.

259.45   *Firearms Act 1968 s 21(2C)*

Possession of a firearm or ammunition or antique firearm[461] by persons previously convicted of crime (meaning a sentence of 3 months or more of immediate or suspended[462] custody.)

Often called 'possession of a firearm when prohibited'.

Mode of trial Triable either way

Maximum sentence Indictment 5 years. Summary maximum 6 months and/or a £5,000 fine for offences committed before 12 March 2015 and an unlimited fine thereafter.[463] There are maximum fines for those aged under 18, see **14.38** in Volume 1.

R v Avis 1998 2 Cr App R (S) 178 LCJ Where there are breaches of Firearms Act 1968 s 21, the custodial term is likely to be of considerable length, and where the four questions suggested above (see the ***Guideline cases*** para at **259.3**) yield answers adverse to the offender, terms at or approaching the maximum may in a contested case be appropriate.

R v Ellis 2010 EWCA Crim 1066 D pleaded to possession of a firearm when prohibited. Police searched his address and found an Anschutz .22 subloading rifle in a plastic bag and blanket in his wardrobe. D claimed it was a rifle, that he wanted it as an ornament and that he had bought it for £21 at a boot fair. He expressed remorse. The firearm was in poor condition but could fire, but only if the cartridges were fed into the chamber by hand as it had no magazine. D was aged 23 with convictions for criminal damage, affray,

---

[461] Firearms Act 1968 s 58(2) as substituted by Anti-social Behaviour, Crime and Policing Act 2014 s 110(2). Section 110(1)-(2) came into force on 14/7/14, Anti-social Behaviour, Crime and Policing Act 2014 (Commencement No 2, Transitional and Transitory Provisions) Order 2014 2014/949 para 6(c).
[462] Firearms Act 1968 s 21(2C) inserted by Anti-social Behaviour, Crime and Policing Act 2014 s 110(1)
[463] Legal Aid, Sentencing and Punishment of Offenders Act 2012 s 85(1) and (4) and Legal Aid, Sentencing and Punishment of Offenders Act 2012 (Commencement No 11) Order 2015 2015/504

false accounting and burglary (8 months in 2008). In 2007 he had been cautioned for possession of an imitation firearm in a public place. D said this was a joint possession of an air rifle at a fairground. Held. The risks of firearms are well known but **18 months** not 3 years.

R v Turley 2011 EWCA Crim 2163, 2012 1 Cr App R (S) 99 (p 606) D pleaded (full credit) to possessing a firearm when prohibited. He worked as a security guard and was patrolling a scrap yard, carrying with him a loaded .41 single-barrelled shotgun. He was aware of some intruders and shouted at them, "Come out of there you bastards". One escaped but the other two were shepherded into the office by D, who pointed the gun at them. One of the intruders had a panic attack. Once inside the office, D was concerned about the third intruder. He heard a noise outside and as a result there was an accidental discharge of the weapon. There was a ricochet and one of the intruders was injured. D had a substantial criminal record including three convictions for violence. Held. The injuries were not intentionally committed and D was misguidedly using the weapon in order to carry out his job more efficiently, not for an unlawful purpose. However, D was on licence at the time and should not have had the weapon. Starting at 3½ years, with the plea, **2 years 4 months,** not 3 years.

R v Coles 2013 EWCA Crim 1019 D pleaded (20% credit) to possessing a firearm without a certificate and possessing a firearm when prohibited. He had previously pleaded to possession of cannabis, going equipped and being in enclosed premises for an unlawful purpose. Armed police responded to a call from a member of the public reporting a man carrying a firearm in the street. Police attended and saw D leave his flat. He told the officers that they could find his air rifle in his bedroom. He appeared to be intoxicated. The rifle was on the bed alongside a tin of pellets and a separate sighting system. Further analysis confirmed that the muzzle velocity classified the weapon as one which required a fitness certificate for possession. The gun had been adapted, giving rise to the need for a certificate. D had a conviction for battery (2010) and by reason of that conviction he was prohibited from possessing a firearm. D, aged 39 at appeal, had numerous convictions for dishonesty but also for drugs and driving offences. Six days before the offence he received a suspended sentence for burglary and theft. It was argued that D did not adapt the air gun himself, was unaware of it and unaware of the need for a certificate. Held. The Judge was correct to activate the suspended sentence and the 10-month term would stand. For the firearms, **7 months** not 14, concurrent with 6 months, not 8. The 3 months consecutive (cannabis) would remain. In total, **20 months**, not 27.

Old cases: Best ignored. Ed.

Matters relating to the defendant

259.46   *Defendant aged under 18 years   Judicial guidance*
Att-Gen's Ref No 45 of 2008 2008 EWCA Crim 2019, 2009 1 Cr App R (S) 89 (p 529) The defendant pleaded to possession of a prohibited weapon. He was aged 16. Held. The prevalence of crimes involving firearms committed by young offenders in areas of our cities requires substantial sentences to be passed even in the case of young offenders.

259.47   *Defendant aged under 18 years   Cases*
R v F 2010 EWCA Crim 758 D pleaded (full credit) to possessing a prohibited firearm and possessing ammunition. Police saw D, aged 15, hand a carrier bag to a male. The male was arrested and there was a revolver in the bag. At her premises police found ammunition which D had had for a month. In interview she said she had been pressurised to commit the offence and was too frightened to say no. D had no convictions, remands or warnings. The pre-sentence report said there was a low risk of reoffending and D had displayed an appropriate level of remorse. The remand and tagging discount was 54 days (which did not count, so the court normally takes that into account when fixing the term. Ed.). The Judge said he had to send a clear message to those who might act as she had and gave her 30 months. Held. That sentence was

unlawful as she was aged only 15 when the offence was committed.[464] The maximum was therefore 18 months' DTO and the next lowest sentence was 12 months, so **12 months**.

R v Rukwira 2013 EWCA Crim 875 D was convicted of possessing a firearm with intent to endanger life, having pleaded to possessing ammunition with intent to endanger life and simple possession of the same gun and ammunition. The police executed a warrant at the home of D's friend. They found nothing but when they returned later, they found a fully loaded .25 self-loading pistol with a spare magazine also loaded. D's friend was arrested and gave a prepared statement to the effect that she believed that 'Jordan' had left the items in her bedroom without her knowledge. Within a week, D informed the police that it was he who had placed the items in the bedroom without his friend's knowledge. Examination of their telephones revealed this to be a lie as they had been discussing the gun and ammunition in coded language. D was just short of his 18th birthday. He was treated as being of good character. Held. The fact that there was a loaded magazine was an aggravating feature. The public has to be protected from gun crime. **8 years** was severe, but rightly so.

See also: *R v Morris and Reader* 2013 EWCA Crim 1248 (M aged 16. Possession with intent to cause fear. A **12-month DTO** was well justified. For details see **259.32**.)

R v Addy 2013 EWCA Crim 1276 (Plea to possession of pistol with intent to endanger life. Engaged in a shoot-out on a London estate. Bullet entered bedroom window. Gun (not recovered) used in seven other shootings. Aged 15 and proud member of a gang. Defence relied on age and immaturity. The Judge started at 18 years for an adult offender and reduced it to 12. He reduced it to **8 years** for the plea. This was gangland turf warfare using firearms. Appeal dismissed.)

Old cases: Best ignored.

259.48   *Servicemen and women*

Guidance on Sentencing in the Court Martial 2013 para 5.12.1 The Services are the nation's professional users of firearms and aspire to be exemplary in this matter. As such they are subject to the same laws as any other citizen outside their use on duty. It may be that soldiers can come to possess arms or ammunition negligently in a way that private citizens may not and that may be taken into account but the same rules should generally apply. A claim to be ignorant of the lethal effect of firearms would not be persuasive. There is a concern amongst the police that the Army is a source of illicit weapons. The rules for the safeguarding of service weapons including the decommissioning of trophy weapons are clear.[465] para 5.12.2 Entry points Presumption of dismissal unless there are truly exceptional circumstances.

Minimum sentences

259.49   *Minimum sentences   Crown Court Statistics   England and Wales*

Firearms: Minimum sentences

Year	Age	Total sentenced	Total sentenced to immediate custody	Received minimum sentence	% receiving minimum term	Average custodial term in months[466]
2013	16-17	3	1	1	33.3	
	18+	99	81	48	48.5	50.5
2014	16-17	2	0	0	0.0	
	18+	113	82	49	43.4	49.5

---

[464] Powers of Criminal Courts (Sentencing) Act 2000 s 91
[465] JSP [Joint Service Publication] 440 Part 7
[466] Excluding life and indeterminate sentences

For explanations about the statistics see page 1-xii. For more detailed statistics see www.banksr.com Other Matters Statistics tab

259.50   *Minimum sentences   Statutes*
Minimum sentence for certain offences under section 5
Firearms Act 1968 s 51A(1) This section applies where:
a) an individual is convicted of:
   i) an offence under section 5(1)(a), (ab), (aba), (ac), (ad), (ae), (af) or (c) of this Act,
   ii) an offence under section 5(1A)(a) of this Act, or
   iii) an offence under any of the provisions of this Act listed in subsection (1A) in respect of a firearm or ammunition specified in section 5(1)(a), (ab), (aba), (ac), (ad), (ae), (af) or (c) or section 5(1A)(a) of this Act, and
b) the offence was committed after the commencement of this section and at a time when he was aged 16 or over.
(1A) The provisions are:
za) section 5(2A) (manufacture, sale or transfer of firearm, or possession etc. for sale or transfer)[467]
a) section 16 (possession of firearm with intent to injure),
b) section 16A (possession of firearm with intent to cause fear of violence),
c) section 17 (use of firearm to resist arrest),
d) section 18 (carrying firearm with criminal intent),
e) section 19 (carrying a firearm in a public place),
f) section 20(1) (trespassing in a building with firearm).
(2) The court shall impose an appropriate custodial sentence (or order for detention) for a term of at least the required minimum term (with or without a fine) unless the court is of the opinion that there are exceptional circumstances relating to the offence or to the offender which justify its not doing so.
(3) Where an offence is found to have been committed over a period of two or more days, or at some time during a period of two or more days, it shall be taken for the purposes of this section to have been committed on the last of those days.
(4) In this section 'appropriate custodial sentence (or order for detention)' means:
a) in relation to England and Wales:
   i) in the case of an offender who is aged 18 or over when convicted, a sentence of imprisonment, and
   ii) in the case of an offender who is aged under 18 at that time, a sentence of detention under Powers of Criminal Courts (Sentencing) Act 2000 s 91,
b) in relation to Scotland (not listed).
(5) In this section 'the required minimum term' means:
a) in relation to England and Wales:
   i) in the case of an offender who was aged 18 or over when he committed the offence, 5 years, and
   ii) in the case of an offender who was under 18 at that time, 3 years, and
b) in relation to Scotland (not listed).
Note: So the listed offences above carry a minimum sentence of 5 years for defendants aged 21 years or over unless there are exceptional circumstances. The minimum sentence rules apply to 18- to 20-year-olds.[468] Where the offender is aged under 18, the minimum sentence is 3 years' detention.[469] Ed.
Mental Health Act 1983 s 37(1A)(a) Nothing in Firearms Act 1968 s 51A(2) or Violent Crime Reduction Act 2006 s 29(4) or (6) shall prevent the court from making a (Hospital Order or Guardianship Order).

---

[467] As inserted by Anti-social Behaviour, Crime and Policing Act 2014 s 108(6)
[468] *R v Campbell* 2006 2 Cr App R (S) 626
[469] Firearms Act 1968 s 51A(4)-(5)

Serious Organised Crime and Police Act 2005 s 73(5) 'Nothing in any requirement which requires that a minimum sentence is passed, affects the power of the court to act under section 73(2)' (power to take into account assistance given by the defendant where there is a written agreement). (Section summarised.)

The offence of using someone to mind a weapon introduced by Violent Crime Reduction Act 2006 s 28 has its own minimum sentence created by that Act.[470] The minimum periods are the same.

259.51   *Minimum sentences   Defendant under 18*

Firearms Act 1968 s 5

Offenders under 18 convicted of certain serious offences: power to detain for specified period

Powers of Criminal Courts (Sentencing) Act 2000 s 91(1) [Not listed. Deals with sex offences.]

(1A) Subsection (3) below applies where:
   a) a person aged under 18 is convicted on indictment of an offence:
      i) under Firearms Act 1968 s 5(1)(a), (ab), (aba), (ac), (ad), (ae), (af) or (c) (prohibited weapons), or
      ii) under subsection (1A)(a) of that section,
   b) the offence was committed after the commencement of Firearms Act 1968 s 51A at a time when he was aged 16 or over, and
   c) the court is of the opinion mentioned in Firearms Act 1968 s 51A(2) (exceptional circumstances which justify its not imposing required custodial sentence).

Powers of Criminal Courts (Sentencing) Act 2000 s 91(1B) Subsection (3) below applies where:
   a) a person aged under 18 is convicted on indictment of an offence under Firearms Act 1968 s 51A(1A)(b), (e) or (f) and which was committed in respect of a firearm or ammunition specified in Firearms Act 1968 s 5(1)(a), (ab), (aba), (ac), (ad), (ae), (af) or (c) or 5(1A)(a),
   b) the offence was committed after the commencement of Violent Crime Reduction Act 2006 s 30 and for the purposes of Firearms Act 1968 s 51A(3), at a time when he was aged 16 or over, and
   c) the court is of the opinion mentioned in Firearms Act 1968 s 51A(2).

(1C) Subsection (3) below also applies where:
   a) a person aged under 18 is convicted of an offence under Violent Crime Reduction Act 2006 s 28 (using someone to mind a weapon),
   b) section 29(3) of that Act applies (minimum sentences in certain cases), and
   c) the court is of the opinion mentioned in section 29(6) of that Act (exceptional circumstances which justify not imposing the minimum sentence).

(3) If the court is of the opinion that neither a Youth Rehabilitation Order nor a Detention and Training Order is suitable, the court may sentence the offender to be detained for such a period, not exceeding the maximum term of imprisonment with which the offence is punishable, as may be specified in the sentence.

(4) Subsection (3) above is subject to (in particular) Criminal Justice Act 2003 s 152 and 153.

(5) Where:
   a) subsection (2) of Firearms Act 1968 s 51A, or
   b) subsection (6) of Violent Crime Reduction Act 2006 s 29,

requires the imposition of a sentence of detention under this section for a term of at least the term provided for in that section, the court shall sentence the offender to be detained for such period, of at least the term so provided for but not exceeding the maximum term of imprisonment with which the offence is punishable in the case of a person aged 18 or over, as may be specified in the sentence.

---

[470] See Violent Crime Reduction Act 2006 s 29(4)-(5)

Violent Crime Reduction Act 2006 s 29(6)[471] Criminal Justice Act 2003 s 142A(3),[472] which provides that for offenders under 18 the purposes of sentencing are: the punishment of offenders, the reform and rehabilitation of offenders, the protection of offenders and the making of reparation by offenders to persons affected by their offences, does not apply to minimum sentences for firearm offences or for minimum sentences for certain cases of using someone to mind a weapon. (Section 29(6) is in force and section 142A(3) is not expected to be in force in the near future, if ever. Ed.) See also: *R v Jeffries* 2012 EWCA Crim 2339 (Plea to possessing a prohibited firearm. He was worried his brother planned to kill him and their parents with a sawn-off shotgun. He disposed of the gun by throwing it over a stream into a wood. He informed the police what he had done about a month later. Shotgun found on the bank of the stream, rusted, with one live cartridge inside. Full working order. Exceptional circumstances present. **12 months** not 5 years.)

259.52   *Minimum sentences   Basic principles*
R v Rehman and Wood 2005 EWCA Crim 2056, 2006 1 Cr App R (S) 77 (p 404) LCJ para 15 We have no doubt the fact that an offender is unfit to serve a 5-year sentence may be relevant, as is the fact that he or she is of very advanced years. This is necessarily to be read into the words used, otherwise a sentence may be inappropriately harsh and even fall within the language of European Convention on Human Rights art 3. Circumstances are exceptional for the purposes of Firearms Act 1968 s 51A(2) if it would mean that to impose 5 years' imprisonment would result in an arbitrary and disproportionate sentence.

R v Raza 2009 EWCA Crim 1413, 2010 1 Cr App R (S) 56 (p 354) D was convicted of possessing a prohibited weapon, possession of cocaine with intent to supply, and possession of ammunition. The Judge started at 10 years for the drugs and reduced it to 8 years for totality. She gave the minimum 5 years for the firearm and the 8 years consecutive. Held. The 5-year sentence was the same as he would have received if he had pleaded. The 10-year starting point was in no way excessive. There is a need to respect the express wish of Parliament so as not to dilute the impact of the minimum term by reducing the other sentence to take account of the mandatory sentence. The adjustment should not have been any greater.

Note: There is a clear inference that the imposition of concurrent sentences should not be used to defeat the will of Parliament. Ed.

Att-Gen's Ref No 23 of 2009 2009 EWCA Crim 1638, 2010 1 Cr App R (S) 70 (p 471) D pleaded at the PCMH to possession of four prohibited firearms. Held. It is always important to bear in mind what the Lord Chief Justice said in *R v Kelly* 1999 2 Cr App R (S) 176 about life sentences: "To relieve the duty of the court to impose a life sentence, the circumstances must be exceptional and in forming that opinion the court must have regard to the purposes of Parliament in enacting the legislation." For more details of the case see **259.62**.

Att-Gen's Ref Nos 48-49 of 2010 2010 EWCA Crim 2521 The defendants pleaded to conspiracy to possess and distribute prohibited firearms and ammunition. They purchased four starting pistols and sought to convert them to handguns. Held. The minimum sentences under section 51A do not apply, as it was not Parliament's intention for them to do so.

R v Shaw 2011 EWCA Crim 167 A guilty plea, whilst not in itself being in any way an exceptional circumstance, was capable of supporting a general finding of exceptional circumstances.

R v Dixon 2013 EWCA Crim 601 D pleaded to possession of a prohibited weapon, a Smith & Wesson revolver, and a bullet. She agreed to allow them to be stored at her house after someone had been shot at with the revolver. Held. The scourge of guns to

---

[471] Criminal Justice Act 2003 s 142A(4)
[472] As inserted by Criminal Justice and Immigration Act 2008 s 9

any society is too self-evident to need explanation. The importance to those who engage in the use of guns in finding a place where it is thought that no one will suspect that a gun has been left is of the utmost importance. It is very difficult to see how one can say that the circumstances where a person who knows that she has received a package from a man of violence (even though the violence might not have been associated with guns), without enquiring, who then finds that what she has is a gun, of a particularly dangerous kind, can be said on its own to amount to exceptional circumstances. It is so important that we uphold that solely for deterring those who use guns from depositing them with people and to deter anyone from taking a package from someone known to be violent without enquiring. The policy which Parliament has laid out is that [the minimum sentence] places the highest possible weight on deterring a gun culture and the use of guns. It is well known that those who live in communities where gun culture is prevalent suffer terribly from such a culture. It is part and parcel of such a culture that those that use guns to kill or maim or to inflict terror will need somewhere to place their weapons when they are not in use. It is to deter anyone from being the repository of such guns that Parliament has decided such a severe sentence should be the minimum passed. It may seem very harsh to this individual but [passing the sentence] follows a clear policy designed to deter the use of guns.

Att-Gen's Ref Nos 4-8 of 2014 2014 EWCA Crim 651, 2 Cr App R (S) 51 (p 414) D and others were convicted of conspiracy to possess firearms with intent to endanger life. They were members of a South London gang with a significant reputation for drugs and violence. Held. The Judge was right to have regard to the statutory minimum sentence even though it did not strictly apply. There were no exceptional circumstances, so it was wrong to go below the minimum.

259.53   *Court Martial*

Armed Forces Act 2006 s 227(1) This section applies if:

    a) a person is convicted by the Court Martial of an offence under section 42 (criminal conduct); and

    b) if his conviction had been by a civilian court in England and Wales of the corresponding offence under the law of England and Wales, Firearms Act 1968 s 51A (minimum sentences for certain firearms offences) would apply.

(2) The Court Martial must impose the sentence required by section 51A(2) of that Act (as that provision has effect in relation to England and Wales), unless it is of the opinion that there are exceptional circumstances relating to the offence or to the offender which justify its not doing so.

(3) In section 51A(4)(a)(ii) of that Act (interpretation of section 51A(2)), as applied by this section, the reference to a sentence of detention under Powers of Criminal Courts (Sentencing) Act 2000 s 91 is to be read as a reference to a sentence of detention under section 209 of this Act.

Minimum sentences   Exceptional circumstances

Note: The division of the cases into the following paragraphs is to stop the section being too long. It does not, however, create factors which amount or do not amount to exceptional circumstances. Many of the cases have more than one factor and so they cover more exceptional circumstances than the title of the paragraph suggests. Sometimes a factor will not be enough on its own, but when taken with other factors, exceptional circumstances will be made out. Each case will depend critically on its own facts. Ed.

259.54   *Minimum sentences   Are these exceptional circumstances?   Ammunition*

R v Beard 2007 EWCA Crim 3168, 2008 2 Cr App R (S) 41 (p 232) D pleaded early to possession of a firearm without authority, possessing prohibited ammunition and possessing a prohibited weapon. Police had searched the caravan where he lived for drugs. They found no drugs, but in the caravan was a Webley air rifle which looked like an ordinary air rifle but which had been subtly altered and had a muzzle velocity in excess of the specifications. That was count 1. They also found 78 cartridges of which 66 had a CS gas component (count 2) and a CS gas canister (count 3). It was accepted that he did not know that the air rifle had been modified and that he thought the ammunition was blank. He was functionally illiterate and the label on the box of ammunition was in German, although it did say in English that it contained CS gas. He said that a friend had left the ammunition in the caravan some years before. He did not possess a weapon capable of firing the ammunition and there was nothing to show that it had been used or would ever be used. D, aged 24, had one previous conviction and no convictions for violence. He expressed remorse. A pre-sentence report said that his risk of reoffending was minimal. He was married with two young children, the younger only two weeks old. He received the 5-year minimum for the prohibited ammunition. Held. It was entirely reasonable for him to think that it was blank. He has no criminal associates. These are truly exceptional circumstances, and the operation of the minimum term of 5 years in respect of the ammunition does operate here in an arbitrary manner entirely disproportionate to the circumstances of the case. There is, though, a clear obligation on those who possess such ammunition to ensure that they comply with the law. After a trial the proper sentence would have been 3 years. **2 years** not 5 for the ammunition, concurrent with other sentences as before.

259.55   *Minimum sentences   Are these exceptional circumstances?   Custodians*
R v Edwards 2006 EWCA Crim 2833, 2007 1 Cr App R (S) 111 (p 669) D pleaded to possession of a prohibited firearm. D was approached by police following information received. D immediately admitted that she was holding a gun on behalf of two men who had asked her to look after it. D led the police to where the semi-automatic gun was in her house. In interview D gave a complete account of how she became in possession of the gun, which she had kept for two months. She knew the men only as acquaintances and gave the police their names. She stated that she felt that she could not deny their request. The weapon was in a very poor state of repair. It was usable but scarcely so. It could be fired but only at risk to the firer. D was aged 29, a single woman with three children. She had a weak personality and was vulnerable to pressure. There were three convictions for benefit fraud in 2001. Held. The weapon was unlikely to be of significant use in the criminal context. Following the case of *R v Rehman and Wood* 2005 EWCA Crim 2056, 2006 1 Cr App R (S) 77 (p 404) we take a 'holistic approach' to 'exceptional circumstances'. The factors could collectively create 'exceptional circumstances' where individually they would fail. The Court found that seven factors constituted an exceptional circumstance: a) D's inability to resist the pressure of the criminal acquaintances, b) those who asked her to hide the gun were probably the source of her detection, c) she immediately admitted the offence and named those who had given her the gun, d) her plea of guilty, e) the gun was barely capable of any meaningful use, f) the low risk of her reoffending, and g) that she is a mother of three children. 2 years not 5.
R v Boateng 2011 EWCA Crim 861 D pleaded to possessing a prohibited firearm and possessing ammunition (×2). Police searched her address and discovered a .22 calibre pistol and 305 rounds of ammunition. 149 of those rounds would have fitted the pistol. Three had been modified to make them expanding ammunition. They were stored in a rucksack which D claimed had been left at her flat by a friend. She claimed she had been told not to touch the bag and that she thought the contents were 'dodgy'. After a *Newton* hearing, the Judge was satisfied D was unaware as to the contents of the bag. However, he found no exceptional circumstances, but said that if he could have imposed a lesser sentence, he would have done. D, aged 20 at appeal, was of impeccable character and was studying for a degree. Held. There were exceptional circumstances[473] that were not argued before the Judge. With full credit for the plea, 2 years not 5.
R v Nightingale 2012 EWCA Crim 2734 Court Martial Appeal Court LCJ D was a Sergeant in the SAS. He pleaded at the last moment to possession of a prohibited firearm

---

[473] Regrettably, the Court did not indicate what they were. Ed.

and possession of ammunition. D was given a Glock automatic pistol as a present by the Iraqi Special Forces. He kept ammunition that he had been given on range duties. The Judge Advocate found the following exceptional circumstances to disapply the minimum sentence: a) his medical condition permitted a more than usual credit for the plea at the court door, b) his exemplary character, c) his co-operation and genuine remorse, d) D was a highly valued soldier of great practical experience, e) the gun was not fired, and f) but for his particular work, he would not come into contact with such weapons and ammunition. Held. We agree with the conclusion about the exceptional circumstances. For more details of the case, see the *Firearms Act 1968 s 5 Cases 5 years or less* para at **259.19**.

Note: Some of the facts have been taken from the Judge Advocate's sentencing remarks, see www.banksr.com Other Matters Other Documents tab. Ed.

See also: *Att-Gen's Ref No 64 of 2010* 2010 EWCA Crim 2956 (LCJ Early plea to possessing a prohibited weapon (×2). Young woman was arrested for large-scale shoplifting and a search of her home revealed two shortened shotguns stored on behalf of another for about a month. Both in working order. Telling police about the firearms, good character, period only a month, naïve and impressionable 18-year-old who did not consider the consequences of doing a favour, and delay were exceptional circumstances.) *R v Dixon* 2013 EWCA Crim 601 (No, see para **259.52**.)

259.56   *Minimum sentences   Are these exceptional circumstances? Defendant's personal circumstances*

R v Blackall 2005 EWCA Crim 1128, 2006 1 Cr App R (S) 22 (p 131) D pleaded to possessing a prohibited firearm and possessing ammunition without a certificate. In 1995 he had been shot and rendered paraplegic by an unknown gunman who was never caught and no reason for the attack was ascertained. Since then D kept a revolver in his house to protect himself from future attack. It had always been unloaded until four months before this offence when he was subject to a further attack. A man knocked at his front door and put a gun to his head. He reported that to the police but no one was apprehended. After that he kept his gun loaded with six rounds of live ammunition. When police went to his house he told them where the gun was. This account was not disputed by the prosecution. The Judge took the view that there were no exceptional circumstances in relation to the offence that would justify a decrease from the minimum sentence. Held. We agree with the Judge about the circumstances of the offence. The fact that D was keeping the gun for his own defence cannot be an exceptional circumstance. But he also has to decide about the circumstances of the offender. A sentence of imprisonment represents a more severe sentence for him than it would for the average prisoner. In this case there were exceptional circumstances relating to the offender. 3 years not 5.

R v Rehman and Wood 2005 EWCA Crim 2056, 2006 1 Cr App R (S) 77 (p 404) (see para **259.62**)

Att-Gen's Ref No 23 of 2009 2009 EWCA Crim 1638, 2010 1 Cr App R (S) 70 (p 471) D pleaded at the PCMH to possession of four prohibited firearms. He was a tailor, and instead of payment had asked an American customer to send him a Ruger pistol from the USA concealed in other items and in two separate packages. One package was detected, and eventually the defendant's home was searched. Several firearms and a quantity of ammunition were discovered. D, aged 40, was of good character. He had served in the Army Cadet Force for some years. He had been married for 23 years and had five children. He had participated in many activities of benefit to the community. His tailoring business was successful and took him all over the world. A medical report before the Appeal Court said that one of his children was suffering from a very aggressive illness, that the child might not survive the illness, and that the child's treatment would be debilitating. Held. The Judge was in error in treating this case as amounting to exceptional circumstances because of his positive good character, his services to his country through charitable and army activities, his industrious life, and that he was not seeking to use the guns in a criminal way. These were all irrelevant considerations. D had deliberately tried to bring a weapon into this country. A minimum sentence of 5 years should have been imposed. However, the illness of his child could be characterised as exceptional circumstances because it goes to particular and unusual circumstances that affect this defendant, given the severe nature of the illness and the strain it imposes on the family. The correct sentence originally was 5 years not 3, but because of the exceptional circumstances we have identified, we reduce it back to 3 years. For details about the part that did not amount to exceptional circumstances see **259.63**.

R v Shaw 2011 EWCA Crim 167 D pleaded to possession of: a) a prohibited weapon, b) a smoothbore gun, and c) a shotgun without a certificate (×2). Officers executed a search warrant and discovered a 12-bore shotgun, a pump-action sawn-off shotgun, over 100 shotgun cartridges, a stun gun, a dismantled bolt-action shotgun and 12 CO_2 gas cartridges. D had purchased the weapons some eight to ten years earlier at a car boot sale. He claimed that he did not realise that the weapons were not lawful to possess as he believed that none of them were in working order. D was aged 76 at appeal. There was: a) a lack of significant previous convictions, b) a low risk of reoffending and c) no evidence that the weapons had been used in a crime. Held. That was not sufficient in itself of amounting to exceptional circumstances. However, D's very poor health did tip the balance in a finding of exceptional circumstances when taken with the other features identified. 3 years not 5.

See also: *R v K* 2007 EWCA Crim 744 (Scrap dealer who acquired Luger pistol. 'Kept it safe' with its ammunition under floorboards. Aged 63, no antecedents and sole carer of ill elderly mother, 83. No danger to society. This was not exceptional.)

R v Jones 2011 EWCA Crim 1448, 2012 1 Cr App R (S) 25 (p 149) (D was convicted of possessing a prohibited firearm, expanding ammunition, a firearm without a certificate and possession of cocaine. A .38 calibre revolver, 13 .22 long rifle cartridges, one 9 mm Parabellum cartridge, three .32 automatic cartridges and 0.77 g of cocaine. Threatened by unknown man who asked her to collect a bag. Frightened. Fell short of duress. Kept items for 3 weeks. Aged 22. Good character. Minimum sentence wholly arbitrary. 6 months not 5 years.)

R v Burton 2012 EWCA Crim 1781, 2013 1 Cr App R (S) 84 (p 458) (Plea to possession of a prohibited firearm. Tried to commit suicide by firing a single-barrelled shotgun into his face. Severely injured. Long history of offending. The firearm was the sort often used by criminals. It was loaded and he had it for at least 6 months. No exceptional circumstances. 12 months suspended for 18 months was untouched.)

Att-Gen's Ref No 125 of 2014 2015 EWCA Crim 240 (Good character, depressed, new partner, baby, mother with cancer, nervous breakdown were not exceptional circumstances. For more detail see **259.19**.)

See also the ***Minimum sentences Are these exceptional circumstances? Positive good character/Mother etc.*** para at **259.63**.

259.57   *Minimum sentences Are these exceptional circumstances? Defendant's personal circumstances Medical problems*

R v McEneaney 2005 EWCA Crim 431, 2 Cr App R (S) 86 (p 531) His mental illness did not amount to an 'exceptional circumstance'.

Att-Gen's Ref No 82 of 2012 2013 EWCA Crim 135, 2 Cr App R (S) 64 (p 406) D pleaded to possession of a prohibited weapon (×6). Police visited his home address and D directed an officer to a stun baton. They also found a stun gun in the shape of a knuckleduster. D said he sold such items. They also searched his car where they found three Taser devices disguised as mobile phones and a knuckle duster with a Taser. A minimum sentence applied to the stun guns disguised as mobile phones but not to the other three items. An expert said each was capable of discharging 8,000 volts. All were in working order. One was capable of discharging 800,000 volts. The Judge concluded there were exceptional circumstances because of his age, his depression, his lack of convictions and his tendency to self-harm. D's GP said a custodial sentence could produce a significant risk of self-harm. Held. These items were plainly items to which Parliament deemed it fit to apply the minimum term. They were not in a secure place. The exceptional factors relied on were in no way unusual. D had been able to maintain his employment. There were no exceptional circumstances. The sentence might be hard for the defendant but applying the law, 5 years, not 12 months suspended.

Att-Gen's Ref No 37 of 2013 2013 EWCA Crim 1466, 2014 1 Cr App R (S) 62 (p 411) D pleaded to possession of a prohibited weapon and ammunition. Police executed a search warrant at a house and D left through a window and ran. Police chased him and he threw away a Browning self-loading pistol loaded with five rounds of ammunition. In interview D made no comment. D had a conviction and caution for theft. In 2012 he received a conditional discharge for possession of class C drugs. At court he claimed he was addicted to ecstasy and had drug debts. He was threatened with harm to him and his partner if he did not allow his home to be used to grow cannabis and store the gun and ammunition. The prosecution said they could not controvert this and the Judge accepted the account. The Judge found exceptional circumstances because of D's depression and the plea and gave D 2 years. On appeal the prosecution said: a) D kept a loaded pistol so it could be available for criminal activity, b) he left the house with the loaded pistol, c) there was insufficient regard for the need to deter others, d) courts should expect people like D to seek help from the authorities and e) if these were exceptional circumstances the legislation would be blunted. Held. We agree and substitute the statutory minimum of 5 years.

Att-Gen's Ref No 51 of 2013 2013 EWCA Crim 1927, 2014 1 Cr App R (S) 83 (p 512) D pleaded to possessing a prohibited firearm and possessing ammunition without a firearm certificate (×2). Police officers attended D's home to execute a search warrant. Shortly after their arrival, D was seen retrieving a metal box from under a haystack. He walked towards a wooden area and attempted to dispose of the box. Officers followed him and asked him what was in the box. D replied that it was his father's gun and he was intending to hand it in to the police. The weapon was a Luger P08 pistol which held six 9 mm rounds. A further 9 mm round was located in the chamber. There were 15 rounds in the metal box. All rounds were of the right calibre to be fired by the pistol. D's basis of plea said, among other things, that: a) the firearm did not belong to him and he had never used it, b) he had found the weapon whilst digging and panicked, c) he wasn't sure it worked. He had held the pistol for two months. This was not accepted but the parties said it would not make a difference to the sentence. D, aged 58 at appeal, had six convictions for nine offences dating back to the 1970s including burglary and conspiracy to handle stolen goods. He was in breach of an 18-month suspended sentence imposed for making a false representation. A report suggested that D showed significant cognitive impairment. He also suffered from type 2 diabetes which affected his eyesight and hearing. The Judge found exceptional circumstances not to impose the minimum sentence. This was based on D's medical condition. Held. The agreement about the no difference to the basis of plea was surprising. The Judge was wrong to ignore the breach of the suspended sentence. D's health was undoubtedly poor and his family's concerns are understandable. However, it is far from the kind of ill-health which would, standing alone, amount to exceptional circumstances. Taking the factors relating to the offence and the offender individually or cumulatively, this case does not come close to amounting to exceptional circumstances. 5 years not 18 months.

See also: *R v Robinson* 2009 EWCA Crim 2600, 2010 2 Cr App R (S) 20 (p 127) (Stole gun from uncle to commit suicide. When he decided not to, the gun was stored in a reasonably secure place. Barrel shortened so it could fit in a bag more easily. Suffered from depressive episodes. Judge's finding of no exceptional circumstances not clearly wrong.)

R v Parke 2010 EWCA Crim 1220 (Depression and personal difficulties etc. No exceptional circumstances.)

R v Bate 2013 EWCA Crim 1327, 2014 1 Cr App R (S) 48 (p 292) (Threatened staff at McDonald's with a pistol. Pointed weapon at armed officers, wanted to be shot. Diagnosed with depressive disorder. Weapon incapable of firing live rounds, used by father for Wild West games. Exceptional circumstances present, so 2½ years not 5.)
See also: *R v McQuaid* 2014 EWCA Crim 2353, 2 Cr App R (S) 78 (p 622) (Plea. D suicidal. Dismantled pump-action shotgun found in his car along with cartridges and .22 ammunition. D unfit for interview and voluntarily attended a psychiatric unit, diagnosed with severe depression. D, aged 56, homeless and still intended to commit suicide. Good character and a former Royal Marine, having served 12 years and a reservist for seven more years. Judge found exceptional circumstances. Held. There were exceptional circumstances for both the offence and the offender. **2 years**, not 4.)

259.58   Minimum sentences   Are these exceptional circumstances?   Firearm originally held lawfully

R v Mehmet 2005 EWCA Crim 2074, 2006 1 Cr App R (S) 75 (p 397) D pleaded to possession of a prohibited weapon. The firearm was a self-contained gas-cartridge revolver in working order and capable of discharging airgun pellets. No ammunition was found in the course of a thorough drug search of his home. The weapon had been originally acquired by a friend of D in 1996 and he came into possession of it in 1999 or 2000. He intended that if he did use it, it would be for sporting purposes in a gun club or similar. On all these dates possession of it was lawful. The weapon became unlawful in January 2004 but at that time D was suffering from depression and knew nothing of the change in the law. There was a four-month period of grace to allow holders of these weapons to dispose of them or to apply for a licence for their continued possession. D was of previous good character. Held. The matters that could be identified as exceptional circumstances are: the weapon was lawfully in D's possession for a significant period of time, during the period of grace he was in a state of depression and was not aware of what had happened, and the nature of the weapon and the fact that it was originally a perfectly lawful weapon are both significant. None of those circumstances by itself is capable of constituting an exceptional circumstance. They present an unusual and cumulative picture. We recognise that the cases where exceptional circumstances can be found are rare. We find this is one of those cases. The material factors are: the early guilty plea, that no ammunition was found to exist, that there has never been any evidence of criminal intent in D, who is a man without previous convictions, and the nature of the weapon. Against that, part of the sentence is designed to reflect public policy that these weapons shall simply not be in existence, whatever the mitigation. 2½ years, not 5.

R v Barber 2005 EWCA Crim 2217, 2006 1 Cr App R (S) 90 (p 515) Failure to renew the authority inadvertently or a war trophy discovered among a deceased person's effects may be helpful examples to show purely technical offences which are not intended to be caught by the Act.

R v Rudups 2011 EWCA Crim 61 D pleaded to unlawful possession of ammunition. The prosecution offered no evidence on the count of unlawful possession of a prohibited weapon. He was a Latvian national who travelled in a vehicle through Poland and Germany to Dover. There D informed customs officers that he had a gun. He was arrested. In interview he informed officers that he had purchased the weapon for the purpose of defending himself as he drove from Latvia to the UK as he intended to sleep in his car. The weapon was a 9 mm calibre blank pistol, and he also had in his possession CN 'Mace cartridges' designed to discharge noxious substances. The weapon and cartridges were not prohibited items in Latvia, Germany or Poland. He had not considered whether it was legal to import them into the UK. Held. D was ignorant of the illegality of importing the weapon and its ammunition into the UK. Persons coming to this country should familiarise themselves with the law relating to guns and ammunition before they arrive. However, we underline the fact that he handed over the items as soon as he stepped onto British soil for the first time. The Judge was correct in identifying that he should depart from the statutory 5-year minimum sentence as required by Firearms Act 1968 s 51A on the existence of exceptional circumstances. (For more detail of the case, see **259.19**.)

R v Zhekov 2013 EWCA Crim 1656, 2014 1 Cr App R (S) 69 (p 448) D pleaded to possessing a disguised firearm. D, a lorry driver from Bulgaria, entered the UK to make a delivery. He was routinely stopped by Border Agency staff who located the torch-style stun gun in a drawer in his cab. It looked like a torch and could be used as a torch. It was described as a non-lethal defence weapon. D, aged 50, was of exemplary character, genuinely remorseful and unaware that such items were illegal in the UK. Possession of such items was permitted in Bulgaria. Held. The factors were: a) the purchase, possession and use were legal in Bulgaria, b) D was a foreign national who had lived his entire life in Bulgaria, c) he was in the UK for a lawful purpose, d) his stay was just the time it took to deliver his load and for most of that time he would be in his cab, e) D had no knowledge of the UK law, and f) there was no charging device and there was no evidence the stun gun had ever been used. His regret and remorse [were] genuine. The Judge was correct to find exceptional circumstances that justified departure from the mandatory provisions but wrong to find that immediate custody was required. A deterrent sentence was not necessary as any publicity would highlight that possession was illegal in the UK. 52 weeks suspended, not 2 years' immediate custody.

259.59   *Minimum sentences   Are these exceptional circumstances?   Intending to dispose of firearm*

R v Harrison 2006 EWCA Crim 345, 2 Cr App R (S) 56 (p 352) D pleaded to possessing a prohibited weapon, possessing ammunition, excess alcohol, no insurance and using a fraudulent licence. Police stopped his car and found a stolen tax disc. In his coat, which he was not wearing, they found an 8 mm Bruni handgun and a magazine containing live rounds. He was significantly over the alcohol limit. He was sentenced on the basis that he was on the way to dispose of the gun for C, who was his niece's boyfriend, and he had only received the gun that day. The gun was covered in wax but when the wax was removed it was in working order. He named C to the police. A fortnight later, C accused D of grassing him up and stabbed D in the shoulder. D's arm mechanism was damaged. D was aged 48 with a bad record for theft and burglary. There were 23 offences but only one for violence (ABH with an absolute discharge). There was nothing similar to firearms. Held. The Judge concentrated on only one factor, namely the nature of the weapon rather than the overall view, including the way he came into possession of it, how long he had had it, what he had done with it and what he intended to do with it. There were exceptional circumstances, so 2 years not 5.

R v Bowler 2007 EWCA Crim 2068 D pleaded to four counts of possessing a prohibited firearm and two counts of possessing ammunition without a certificate. Police came to his garage premises on an unconnected matter and asked to see inside his safe. He sent for the keys to be fetched from his house, and told the police that the items were inside, having been dumped at his premises three weeks earlier. He said that he had put them in the substantial commercial safe for safe keeping and intended to take them to the police if there were an amnesty. He had panicked, and that was why he did not call the police straight away. The items were a Colt revolver, two Colt self-loading pistols, a Smith & Wesson revolver, 372 cartridges and 2,330 rounds of .22 cartridges. He held a firearm certificate which authorised him to possess these cartridges but limited to 2,000 rounds. He pleaded on the written basis that the items were dumped three weeks before police came, that he placed them in his safe, that they were not used nor did he intend to use them, and that he did not intend to pass them to anyone except to the police if there were an amnesty. The prosecution said that it could not gainsay this basis. He had held a shotgun licence since he was aged 17 and a firearms licence since he was aged 25. D, aged 39, had no convictions. He had good references. He suffered from stress since his arrest. He showed deep and profound regret. His business might not survive with him in prison. Held. There are a number of unusual features: the guns were dumped on him, he

kept them locked in a secure safe, he eventually intended to hand them to the police, there was no suggestion that he had any intent to use them for a criminal purpose or hand them to anyone else for such a purpose, [and] the fact they were in a secure safe meant there was no real risk they might fall into wrong hands. There was a total absence of contact with criminals. To that should be added his good character, plea, low risk of reoffending and remorse. The cumulative effect of these points is that they amount to exceptional circumstances. The proper starting point after a trial would have been 3 years. Taking into account the plea, 2 years on all counts, not 5, all as before concurrent.
R v Munson 2008 EWCA Crim 1258, 2009 1 Cr App R (S) 39 (p 214) D pleaded to possession of a firearm,[474] a sawn-off shotgun. He found the gun and 13 cartridges in a plastic bag on waste ground near a scrap yard. He took the bag back to the house of a friend, W, who lived nearby. D, W and G, another friend, agreed that he would take G home in his car and then drop the gun off at a nearby police station. However, he took G home and then returned to W's house with the bag. By this time W had left to go on holiday. D went to W's garage and left the bag in a camper van there. A few days later, police officers found the gun in the van, lying on top of the plastic bag which still had the cartridges in. The gun was in poor condition but in working order. The 13 cartridges were capable of being fired. W was arrested on his return from holiday and denied all knowledge of the gun. He contacted D who then went to the police and gave his account of events. There was a *Newton* hearing and the Judge accepted that account. D, aged 26, had received a conditional discharge for possession of a bladed article in 2002 and the year before had served a short custodial sentence for driving while disqualified. He was in regular employment. A pre-sentence report said that he had poor problem-solving skills which had contributed to the offence. Held. At the heart of the Judge's remarks was the finding that the gun had no lawful purpose whatsoever. We cannot accept there were exceptional circumstances for two reasons: D left the items in a place and in circumstances which gave rise to a serious risk of them falling into the wrong hands, and the nature of the weapon adapted it to be particularly suitable for use in crime. If he had obtained this sort of weapon and ammunition in a more reprehensible way linking him more closely to criminal activity, a very significantly longer sentence than 5 years would have been justified. We recognise the harshness of this provision generally and in this case, but cannot find a reason for avoiding the statutory minimum of 5 years.
See also: *R v Manzoor* 2013 EWCA Crim 537 (Plea to possessing adapted starter pistol and ammunition. Found them in his father's garden. Intended to hand them to police or dispose of them. No criminal purpose. Never used. No convictions. 12 months not 5 years.)

259.60   Minimum sentences   Are these exceptional circumstances?   Momentary possession
R v Moffat 2014 EWCA Crim 332, 2014 2 Cr App R (S) 37 (p 307) D pleaded to possession with intent to cause another to fear violence. He was a leading seaman and gunner who wanted to be present for his child's birth since he had missed his first child's birth, which had been a very difficult one. The Navy would not give him an absolute assurance he would be on leave but he thought it was his entitlement. While on his ship, he became overwrought and said to a Petty Officer, P, and a Lieutenant, L, that he had access to weapons and ammunition. P told him not to be stupid. L said he would take the matter up and D said if he didn't get home he was going to get a gun. L warned him that he could be on a charge. D raised the matter the next morning and it appeared he would get leave. D collected an SA80 assault rifle and bullets. He kept them separate and went to the second in command of the ship, a Lieutenant Commander, C. D stood in the doorway, clearly angry and intense, and said, "This is a loaded gun, you know what this means: I want to talk to you." C asked D if his junior officer could leave the room. D agreed and C asked D to hand over the weapon. D did so. D then broke down in tears.

---

[474] For the minimum sentences to apply, it must have been a section 5 offence.

The incident was over in seconds. D was aged 45. The Board found the incident was a gross breach of naval discipline. They also found there were exceptional circumstances, namely: a) D immediately regretted his actions and was tearful, b) no magazine was attached to the gun, c) the weapon was not aimed at anyone, d) there was no evil intent and e) D was emotionally overwrought. D was found to have an adjustment disorder which had impaired his judgement. The offence was considered to be completely out of character as D was the very epitome of steady reliability, honesty and commitment. He had an unblemished record. The dismissal with its financial loss was not challenged. Held. This approach was unimpeachable. Taking the fleeting nature of the loss of judgement and the reduction of his mental responsibility which had overwhelmed him, 14 months not 3 years, which meant immediate release.

259.61   *Minimum sentences   Are these exceptional circumstances?   Nature of the prosecution*
Att-Gen's Ref No 7 of 2007 2007 EWCA Crim 902, 2007 2 Cr App R (S) 101 (p 1) A plea of guilty and the circumstances relating to the offence (full admissions, told a real likelihood he would not be charged, short duration) cannot amount to exceptional circumstances. However, because the offender has completed 65 hours of unpaid work to the very best of his ability and it was a reference etc., 3 years.
R v Ramzan 2012 EWCA Crim 2891, 2013 2 Cr App R (S) 33 (p 221) D pleaded to possession of a prohibited firearm disguised as another object (section 51(1A)). Police found a stun gun disguised as a mobile phone under his bed. The defence contended that the decision to charge D with section 5(1A)(a) (possession of a firearm disguised as another object) as opposed to section 5(1)(b) (possession of a weapon designed to discharge a noxious liquid, gas or other thing) was arbitrary and unfair in the particular circumstances of the case as the former attracted the minimum sentence and the latter did not. Held. CPS Guidance recommended that the section 5(1A)(a) offence should be charged for stun guns disguised as other objects. Throughout the proceedings, the decision to charge the section 5(1A)(a) offence was consistent, kept under review and was reviewed after the decision in *R v Brereton* 2012 EWCA Crim 85 (where the prosecution had repeatedly changed its mind as to which offence to charge). The decision to charge the section 5(1A)(a) offence was neither arbitrary nor unfair. Therefore the minimum sentence applied. The court found exceptional circumstances on other grounds and reduced the sentence to 2 years.
See also: *R v Antoine* 2014 EWCA Crim 1971 (The fact he had served 4 months for possession of the firearm and then was charged with a section 5 offence for the same incident was an exceptional circumstance.)

259.62   *Minimum sentences   Are these exceptional circumstances?   No knowledge it was unlawful*
R v Rehman and Wood 2005 EWCA Crim 2056, 2006 1 Cr App R (S) 77 (p 404) LCJ R pleaded to having a venting handgun less than 60 cm long and with a barrel less than 30 cm long (section 5(1)(aba)). It was a replica blank-firing handgun, but it was also a type of handgun which could easily be altered so as to be capable of firing blank ammunition. He bought it via a French Internet site in his own name using his own credit card and had it delivered to his own address which he shared with his parents. He put it in a box under his bed and left it there. Police easily traced him. He showed the police where the gun was and said that he did not think it was illegal to own it. He said that he did not know that the gun could be converted. D, aged 24, had a positively good character. He had a degree and was working for Customs and Excise. His training was continuing. The Judge heard from a senior executive officer in Customs and Excise who said that he was amazed that D was in this position. He had created a most favourable impression on those with whom he came into contact. Held. The Judge was wrong to conclude that there were no exceptional circumstances in this case. The background of D was particularly important and so was the fact that he had no knowledge of the

unlawfulness of the weapon. Matters set out in the skeleton argument viewed collectively make it possible to come to the conclusion that this was a case where the Court was not required to impose the minimum sentence. The Court was not required to pass a minimum sentence because: a) he had pleaded guilty at the first opportunity, b) he was a man aged 24 of good character, c) he and his family were entirely co-operative, d) he was a valued employee of Customs and Excise, e) the weapon was a blank-firing replica purchased from France, f) it had not been converted, g) no blank-firing ammunition was associated with it, h) it had not been fired, i) it was found in its original wrapping under D's bed where it had been since he received it, j) he had done nothing to disguise his identity as a purchaser, k) it was apparent from the contents of his room that he was a collector of memorabilia including other models, and l) he was not aware that the replica was capable of being converted until he was told so in the interview following the arrest. We would regard a custodial sentence as necessary in this case to achieve the deterrent message Parliament intended, but 12 months not 5 years.

R v Rudups 2011 EWCA Crim 61 D pleaded to unlawful possession of ammunition. The prosecution offered no evidence on the count of unlawful possession of a prohibited weapon. He was a Latvian national who travelled in a vehicle through Poland and Germany to Dover. There D informed customs officers that he had a gun. He was arrested. In interview he informed officers that he had purchased the weapon for the purpose of defending himself as he drove from Latvia to the UK as he intended to sleep in his car. The weapon was a 9 mm calibre blank pistol, and he also had in his possession CN 'Mace cartridges' designed to discharge noxious substances. The weapon and cartridges were not prohibited items in Latvia, Germany or Poland. He had not considered whether it was legal to import them into the UK. Held. D was ignorant of the illegality of importing the weapon and its ammunition into the UK. Persons coming to this country should familiarise themselves with the law relating to guns and ammunition before they arrive. However, we underline the fact that he handed over the items as soon as he stepped onto British soil for the first time. The Judge was correct in identifying that he should depart from the statutory 5-year minimum sentence as required by Firearms Act 1968 s 51A on the existence of exceptional circumstances. (For more detail of the case, see **259.19**.)

R v Zhekov 2013 EWCA Crim 1656, 2014 1 Cr App R (S) 69 (p 448) D pleaded to possessing a disguised firearm. D, a lorry driver from Bulgaria, entered the UK to make a delivery. He was routinely stopped by Border Agency staff who located the torch-style stun gun in a drawer in his cab. It looked like a torch and could be used as a torch. It was described as a non-lethal defence weapon. D, aged 50, was of exemplary character, genuinely remorseful and unaware that such items were illegal in the UK. Possession of such items was permitted in Bulgaria. Held. The factors were: a) the purchase, possession and use were legal in Bulgaria, b) D was a foreign national who had lived his entire life in Bulgaria, c) he was in the UK for a lawful purpose, d) his stay was just the time it took to deliver his load and for most of that time he would be in his cab, e) D had no knowledge of the UK law, and f) there was no charging device and there was no evidence the stun gun had ever been used. His regret and remorse [were] genuine. The Judge was correct to find exceptional circumstances that justified departure from the mandatory provisions but wrong to find that immediate custody was required. A deterrent sentence was not necessary as any publicity would highlight that possession was illegal in the UK. 52 weeks suspended, not 2 years' immediate custody.

See also: *R v Ramzan* 2012 EWCA Crim 2891, 2013 2 Cr App R (S) 33 (p 221) (Prohibited firearm disguised as another object (section 5(1A)(a)). Stun gun, disguised as a mobile phone. D had not sought out or purchased the gun. It had been left at the premises by his uncle. It had not been removed from D's home and D was not aware that it was an offence to have the item in his home. It had never been used, inside or outside the home. D had never charged it. None of the four questions posed in *R v Avis* 1998 produced answers adverse to D. Circumstances made out.)

For a stun gun that the defendant did not know was unlawful, see *R v Stoker* 2013 EWCA Crim 1431, 2014 1 Cr App R (S) 47 (p 286) (Stun gun. D didn't know it was unlawful, see **259.21.**)

259.63   *Minimum   sentences   Are   these   exceptional   circumstances?   Positive good character/ Mother etc.*

R v Rehman and Wood 2005 EWCA Crim 2056, 2006 1 Cr App R (S) 77 (p 404) W pleaded at the first opportunity to: a) two counts of possession of a prohibited weapon related to blank-firing pistols to which section 51 did not apply (although the sentencing Judge wrongly thought that it did), b) four counts of possession of a firearm without a certificate, c) one count of shortening of a shotgun contrary to Firearms Act 1968 s 4(1), d) possession of a single-barrelled hammerless shotgun with a barrel less than 30 cm long (section 5(1)(aba)) which carried the minimum-term provisions, and e) theft. The police went to D's home as a result of an investigation into a company selling weapons on the Internet. He was a collector of weapons. Most of the collection was in locked cabinets. In the loft was a shotgun with a shortened barrel. The weapon had been inherited from D's grandfather. The theft related to munitions taken at a time when he was acting as a cadet instructor. He said that he intended to return them but they became obsolete so he couldn't. It took two days to search D's house. He was co-operative and helpful with the police. D, aged 41, was of extremely good character. He was the manager of a surveillance company and had carried out important work with army cadets. He had provided help to the police. On one occasion he had confronted a violent criminal. Apart from these matters he was a most responsible and impressive man. He had glowing references. Held. He of all people should have understood that this was not the sort of weapon which should have been in his possession. He did not take the action he should have done to check whether it was lawful to possess it. The fact that he had committed the other offences demonstrates that he did not attach sufficient significance to the very strict statutory provisions. That showed a carelessness with regard to the possession of firearms which prevents us treating the circumstances as exceptional. We have reluctantly come to the conclusion that we would not be properly applying the statutory provision imposed by Parliament if we interfered with the sentence of 5 years). *R v Edwards* 2006 EWCA Crim 2833, 2007 1 Cr App R (S) 111 (p 669) (No, see para **259.55.**)

Att-Gen's Ref No 23 of 2009 2009 EWCA Crim 1638, 2010 1 Cr App R (S) 70 (p 471) D pleaded at the PCMH to possession of four prohibited firearms. He was a tailor, and instead of payment had asked an American customer to send him a Ruger pistol from the USA concealed in other items and in two separate packages. One package was detected, and eventually the defendant's home was searched. Several firearms and a quantity of ammunition were discovered. Some of the firearms were possessed lawfully. Three were not: a Brocock Orion-6 self-contained pistol, a Remington self-loading shotgun and a BSA sawn-off shotgun. In interview D made false excuses. It was accepted that he did not intend the guns for criminal purposes and had no connections with criminals. D, aged 40, was of good character. He had served in the Army Cadet Force for some years. He had been married for 23 years and had five children. He had participated in many activities of benefit to the community. His tailoring business was successful and took him all over the world. A medical report before the Appeal Court said that one of his children was suffering from a very aggressive illness, that the child might not survive the illness, and that the child's treatment would be debilitating. Held. The Judge was in error in treating this case as amounting to exceptional circumstances because of his positive good character, his services to his country through charitable and army activities, his industrious life, and that he was not seeking to use the guns in a criminal way. These were all irrelevant considerations. D had deliberately tried to bring a weapon into this country. A minimum sentence of 5 years should have been imposed. For the grounds for finding special reasons see **259.62.**

R v Ocran 2010 EWCA Crim 1209, 2011 1 Cr App R (S) 36 (p 223) D pleaded (early) to possessing a prohibited weapon (×2) and possession of a firearm (late). Police executed a warrant to search a flat of which D was the tenant of the acting housing trust. A police dog found underneath a free-standing wardrobe a Baikal semi-automatic pistol with a barrel of less than 30 cm and an overall length of less than 60 cm. Also found there was a Belgian-made shotgun which had a shortened barrel of less than 30 cm and a silencer for use with the firearms. These are what the Judge described as a "robber's kit". The 'indication' in the interview was that D was keeping the items in her flat for the convenience of the two people she identified. D, aged 24, was of previous good character and a single mother. It was argued that the Judge erred in not finding exceptional circumstances and erred in imposing the minimum sentence. First, that the firearms were only in D's possession for three weeks at most. Second, D had not taken possession of the firearms as their custodian, in a positive sense. Instead, the firearms were deposited in the property when D was living with her mother at another address, following her release from hospital. Third, that there was no question of D using the firearms for any criminal offence. She had found them in her flat and had failed to notify the police of that fact. Fourth, there was personal mitigation of a strong nature in this case. Held. After considering the authorities on 'exceptional circumstances' the Court cannot accept D's submissions. Personal mitigation is not sufficient to establish exceptional circumstances (see *R v Edwards* 2006 EWCA Crim 2833, 2007 1 Cr App R (S) 111 (p 669)) and considering the case as a whole, the appeal must be dismissed.

R v Welsh 2012 EWCA Crim 1331, 2013 1 Cr App R (S) 31 (p 164) D pleaded to various firearm offences, five of which attracted the minimum sentence. They were possession of a firearm with a barrel less than 30 cm (×3) and purchasing etc. prohibited ammunition (×2). Other counts alleged possession of firearms and ammunition without a certificate (×5). D asked for other firearm offences to be TIC'd, including 13 possession of a firearm with a barrel less than 30 cm offences and 21 possession of ammunition without a certificate offences. Some of the weapons were D's personal firearms collection worth about £44,000. D ordered a package from America containing a rifle stock. It was intercepted and investigation revealed that D had ordered numerous parcels from America containing antique gun parts. They were ordered in his own name, for delivery to his own address, paid for by his own account. A search warrant was executed and the search revealed a number of firearms and collections of ammunition. There were 42 firearms including a large number of rifles and handguns, many from the 1900s. D had converted a wardrobe into a display cabinet and there was a firing range in the property. He was also able to produce ammunition for the weapons. Twenty of the firearms were classified as antiques and 19 were prohibited. D confirmed that he had amassed the collection over a 20-year period. Following the introduction of the prohibition on possession of the weapons in D's collection in the 1990s, a scheme was introduced whereby individuals could hand in the weapons. D purchased replicas and re-tagged them with serial numbers to pass them off as the originals. He handed those in to the police. The ammunition in his possession worked in just about every weapon in his possession. He was aware that it was illegal to possess the firearms and ammunition and have the ability to fire them. D said that the weapons had a high sentimental value to him. There was no suggestion that he had intended to use the weapons for any harmful purpose. The defence submitted that the collection was maintained by a responsible enthusiast for purely artistic reasons. D, aged 48, lived with his mother, who was in poor health. He was the sole carer for her, on a 24-hour basis. He had driving convictions which were not relevant. Held. This was not a case where D was in ignorance of the law, nor had he been led into error by others whose pressures had been hard to withstand. This was a case of deliberate flouting of the law, and moreover, deception was employed to preserve his collection. The deceit, the creation and availability within the house of ammunition which would fit the weapons, the existence of what was essentially a firing range, the size of the collection and the continuing risk of the weapons falling into the wrong hands, militated against a finding of exceptional circumstances. This was a deliberate and prolonged breach of the law. D had shown an unhappy recklessness in the way he had handled the collection. The Judge was not wrong in concluding that there were no exceptional circumstances. 5 years upheld.

See also: *R v Bennett* 2010 EWCA Crim 902 (Elderly man. No criminal intent. Many items legitimately held. Genuine affection for weapons etc.)

For *Defendant's personal circumstances*, see para at **259.57**.

259.64   Minimum sentences   Are these exceptional circumstances?   Firearm previously belonged to another
R v Barber 2005 EWCA Crim 2217, 2006 1 Cr App R (S) 90 (p 515) Failure to renew the authority inadvertently or a war trophy discovered among a deceased person's effects may be helpful examples to show purely technical offences which are not intended to be caught by the Act.

259.65   Minimum sentences   Are these exceptional circumstances?   Stun guns
R v Zhekov 2013 EWCA Crim 1656, 2014 1 Cr App R (S) 69 (p 448) D pleaded to possessing a disguised firearm. D, a lorry driver from Bulgaria, entered the UK to make a delivery. He was routinely stopped by Border Agency staff who located the torch-style stun gun in a drawer in his cab. It looked like a torch and could be used as a torch. It was described as a non-lethal defence weapon. D, aged 50, was of exemplary character, genuinely remorseful and unaware that such items were illegal in the UK. Possession of such items was permitted in Bulgaria. Held. The factors were: a) the purchase, possession and use were legal in Bulgaria, b) D was a foreign national who had lived his entire life in Bulgaria, c) he was in the UK for a lawful purpose, d) his stay was just the time it took to deliver his load and for most of that time he would be in his cab, e) D had no knowledge of the UK law, and f) there was no charging device and there was no evidence the stun gun had ever been used. His regret and remorse [were] genuine. The Judge was correct to find exceptional circumstances that justified departure from the mandatory provisions but wrong to find that immediate custody was required. A deterrent sentence was not necessary as any publicity would highlight that possession was illegal in the UK. 52 weeks suspended, not 2 years' immediate custody.

R v Withers 2015 EWCA Crim 132, 1 Cr App R (S) 64 (p 455) D pleaded to possession of a stun gun (section 5(1A)(a)). Police searched her flat and found a taser-type device that looked like a mobile phone in her bedside cabinet. There was no charger with it and the battery was flat. D said that it was given to her by a friend. She also said that in September 2013 her previous flat had been burgled. The next month, she had moved and there were continuing problems in the area. It was confirmed that she had made a call to the police about the problem before the search. A large man under the influence of drugs had knocked on her door at night. She had difficulty in getting him to leave and he had returned and kicked her front door in. Her door remained insecure and she remained concerned about anti-social behaviour in her area. D accepted she knew it was unlawful to possess a stun gun. The landlord refused to repair the door because D was in rent arrears. It was then she obtained the stun gun. D was aged 28 and had two minor convictions. A psychiatrist said D had an emotionally unstable personality disorder, which would mean she was likely to cope with imprisonment badly. Held. We cannot ignore the dangers of people possessing disguised stun guns. The answers to the *R v Avis* 1998 2 Cr App R (S) 178 questions were as follows: 1) the weapon did not shoot bullets, 2) no use was made of the weapon, 3) D's intention with the weapon was effectively none, save a defensive intention by which she hoped a 'buzz' would frighten away an intruder, and 4) D's previous convictions were not of any particular relevance. The minimum sentence was arbitrary and disproportionate. Her personal circumstances and her vulnerability had to be considered. **2 years** not 5.

Concurrent or consecutive sentences
See also the **CONCURRENT AND CONSECUTIVE SENTENCES** chapter.

259.66   *Concurrent or consecutive sentences to other firearm offences*
Att-Gen's Ref No 57 of 2009 2009 EWCA Crim 2555, 2010 2 Cr App R (S) 30
(p 190) LCJ D pleaded to possession of two prohibited weapons, five counts of
possessing ammunition and possessing an accessory to a firearm. D was minding the
articles. The prosecution considered that the sentences should be consecutive to ensure
an adequate sentence. Held. That would disapply well-understood sentencing principles
and was a step too far.
R v Sabir 2013 EWCA Crim 2261 (It was appropriate, see **259.25**.)
R v Gribbin 2014 EWCA Crim 115, 2 Cr App R (S) 28 (p 229) D pleaded to possession
of a prohibited firearm counts and other related offences. Police discovered nine
firearms including self-loading pistols, sawn-off shotguns, an Army-issue light support
rifle and 446 live rounds of ammunition which could be fired from the weapons. The
Judge imposed consecutive sentences on the basis that the weapons had been acquired at
different times, storage had been at two addresses where he had lived, payments of
money were made and the offences were committed over a number of years. The
defence appealed on the basis that the Judge imposed consecutive sentences in order to
circumvent what he felt was an inadequate maximum sentence. Held. Consecutive
sentences are appropriate if offences are not all committed at the same time. **13 years**
(6½ years × 2, consecutive) was not excessive or wrong in principle.
R v Lewis 2014 EWCA Crim 2622, 2015 1 Cr App R (S) 38 D and F were convicted of
three prohibited firearm counts, three associated firearm counts and possession of crack.
Police searched D's bedroom and found a loaded Smith & Wesson gun and a loaded
pistol. In the same flat, in F's bedroom, police found a loaded pistol. In the kitchen they
found 2.19 grams of crack cocaine. The Judge thought the firearms were ready for use
by criminals. He thought the 10-year maximum was inadequate for all the offending
because of the danger to the public. He made the Smith & Wesson sentence consecutive
to one of the pistol counts making 11 years. The defence said the sentences should have
been concurrent. F received 12 years (no appeal then but one in 2015). Held. These were
terrible weapons capable of causing death and dreadful injury. Although the firearms
were found in separate rooms in a substantial property, we cannot uphold consecutive
sentences, following *Att-Gen's Ref No 57 of 2009* (see above). We have to reduce the
sentence to 10 years.
Note: It is not explained why there should not have been consecutive sentences for the
ammunition. This would be in line with the *TICs and Totality Guideline 2012: Crown
Court* page 6 and *R v Dillon* 1983 5 Cr App R (S) 439 and other cases. The ammunition
was a very significantly aggravating factor. Ed.
See also: *R v Robinson and Others* 2012 EWCA Crim 1525 (Possession of a prohibited
weapon (a sub-machine gun) and possession of ammunition. The Judge fell into error in
making the sentences for the ammunition consecutive on the basis that the intended
purpose of the weapon could not be doubted as it was loaded and accompanied by
ammunition. *Att-Gen's Ref No 57 of 2009* above applied.)
R v Valnuchinas 2014 EWCA Crim 652 (The Judge failed to identify any circumstance
which required a departure from the normal practice, namely that consecutive sentences
are not normally appropriate for offences arising out of the same incident. Sentences
made concurrent.) For more details, see para **259.24**.

259.67   *Concurrent or consecutive sentences to other offences*
See also the **ROBBERY** *Firearms, With concurrent or consecutive sentences* para at
322.14 and the **ROBBERY** *Firearm, With No firearm count* para at **322.15**.
Att-Gen's Ref No 311 of 2004 2005 EWCA Crim 1837, 2006 1 Cr App R (S) 57 (p 310)
(It is likely that the reference number is wrong but that number is in the judgment.) D
was convicted of conspiracy to blackmail and conspiracy to possess a firearm with intent

to endanger life. Held. The incident was part of a gang feud. Firearm offences are normally dealt with by way of consecutive sentences to any other matter. But bearing in mind the length of the appropriate sentence for the firearm offence and that it was a reference, the concurrent sentence on the conspiracy to blackmail of **4 years** was unchanged. For D it was wrong in principle not to have imposed consecutive sentences and his total sentence was lenient. Bearing in mind again that it was a reference, the individual sentences were not increased. **4 years** for conspiracy to possess a firearm, **6 months** for the offence of witness intimidation and **2 years** for possession with intent to supply all **consecutive** not concurrent, making a total of **6½ years** not 4.

R v Johnson 2005 EWCA Crim 2281, 2006 1 Cr App R (S) 99 (p 594) at 597 The defendant was convicted of GBH with intent and having a firearm with intent to commit that offence. Held. The Court cited *R v McGrath* 1986 8 Cr App R (S) 373 and said that was the general rule. However, where the firing of the firearm directly gives rise to another offence by way of serious injury to the person, the other offence is the primary offence and cannot be separated from the firearm offence. It would be artificial to pass consecutive sentences. It is quite different where the carrying of the gun is used to support a robbery.

Att-Gen's Ref No 16 of 2009 2009 EWCA Crim 2439, 2010 2 Cr App R (S) 11 (p 64) LCJ D was convicted of possessing a prohibited weapon and two offences of assisting an offender. D supplied a gun to a killer and then helped the killer to dispose of incriminating articles and washed him down to remove firearm residue. Held. The firearm sentence should have been consecutive not concurrent with the assisting offender counts.

Ancilary orders

259.68   *Forfeiture/Cancellation of a firearm certificate*

Firearms Act 1968 s 52(1) Where a person:

   a) is convicted of an offence under this Act (other than an offence under section 22(3) or an offence relating specifically to air weapons) or is convicted of a crime for which he is sentenced to imprisonment, or detention in a detention centre, or is subject to a detention and training order, or

   b) has been ordered to enter into a recognisance to keep the peace or to be of good behaviour, a condition of which is that he shall not possess, use or carry a firearm, or

   c) is subject to a community order containing a requirement that he shall not possess, use or carry a firearm, or

   d) [a Scottish provision],

the court by or before which he is convicted, or by which the order is made, may make such order as to the forfeiture or disposal of any firearm or ammunition found in his possession as the court thinks fit and may cancel any firearm certificate or shotgun certificate held by him.

Note: This provision is absurdly narrowly drawn. There should be a power under this section to forfeit firearms and air weapons when a defendant is convicted or acquitted of any offence. The test should be that the public interest in forfeiting the article outweighs the convicted or acquitted person's interest in having the article. Ed.

R v Hyde 2014 EWCA Crim 713 D was convicted of two offences under Trade in Goods (Control) Order 2003. He brokered agreements with China to sell 70,000 rifles, 10,000 pistols and 32 million rounds of ammunition to the Nigerian government (or so the documents said). D had over 14,200 firearms lawfully in a secure storage facility. Eleven months after the custodial sentence was imposed and five months after a confiscation order was made, the local Chief Constable applied to the trial Judge for an order that the firearms be forfeited and destroyed. The Judge held that possession was to be given a wide meaning. The application was granted. Held. All parties agreed D could appeal [to this Court]. The Judge was not entitled to hold that the property was in the possession of

D or that it was appropriate to pierce the corporate veil. We quash the order. The two companies involved will have to determine a mechanism whereby safe and lawful disposal of the firearms can be achieved.

260   FIREWORK OFFENCES
260.1
Various offences including:
1) Fireworks Act 2003 s 11 (Contravention of a prohibition or failure to comply with a requirement imposed by or under fireworks regulations or making false statements)
2) Explosives Act 1875 s 80 (Throwing fireworks in a thoroughfare)[475]

Fixed penalty There is a £90 fixed penalty for both offences[476] with half the relevant victim surcharge. For more detail see **61.1** in Volume 1.

261   FISHING OFFENCES
261.1
Various offences and penalties
Non-court penalties Where an authorised officer has reason to believe that a person has committed a penalty offence, the authorised officer may issue that person with a penalty notice for an amount not exceeding £10,000.[477]
Serious Crime Prevention Order For Salmon and Freshwater Fisheries Act 1975 s 1 offences there is a discretionary power to make this order, when it would protect the public etc.[478]

261.2   *Magistrates' Guidance*
Costing the Earth Magistrates' Guidance 2009 www.banksr.com Other Matters Other Documents tab The Magistrates' Association has reissued its guidance, which contains a series of case examples including fishing. As the guidance no longer contains suggested penalties, they are not listed. Ed.

261.3   *Over-fishing etc.*
Fisheries Act 1981 s 5, 12, 17 and 30(2)
There are many different orders made under this Act which create offences including some triable either way. There are various penalties.
R v Anglo-Spanish Fisheries Ltd 2001 1 Cr App R (S) 73 (p 252) The defendant company pleaded at the Magistrates' Court to an offence under Fisheries Act 1981 s 30(2) and the relevant EEC regulations. There were three charges of failing to record accurately the quantity of fish, one of landing a quantity of undersized fish and one of failing to keep a drawing of a fish storage room. The Spanish company owned a British-registered boat, which was boarded by officers from the Sea Fisheries Inspectorate. They weighed the fish on board and compared it with the entries in the logbook. There was significant under-recording of three fish. There was no recording of Megrim, a fish much sought after in Spain, in the book. 1,154 kilos of the fish was found on board. To conceal the Megrim an elaborate scheme of deception had been devised. The top layer of the boxes of fish was covered by Witch, a fish for which there was no quota, and the boxes were labelled Witch. The Witch fish was over-recorded. Of the other two fish in the charges of failing to record, the fish was hidden under nets and empty boxes. The total value of the under-declared fish was £12,400. In 1998 the company had four convictions dealt with at the same court as this offence for similar charges for over-quota fishing. The company was fined £80,000 with £6,371 prosecution costs. The company was fined in total **£115,000** and ordered to pay £3,869 prosecution costs. It appealed the

---

[475] Explosives Act 1875 s 80 repealed by Fireworks Act 2003. Commencement is awaited.
[476] Penalties for Disorderly Behaviour (Amount of Penalty) Order 2002 2002/1837 as amended
[477] Sea Fishing (Penalty Notices) (England) Order 2011 2011/758 art 3(1)
[478] Serious Crime Act 2007 s 1 and Sch 1 para 13(1)

fine in this case for failing to record the amount of Megrim fish for which it was fined £80,000. Held. Policing and enforcement of the quota system is exceptionally difficult for ships nominally registered in the UK but [which] operate out of ports of other countries. There was a paramount need to protect the fishing stocks. The offences were extremely serious and were motivated by greed. Penalties must strip the offenders of the profits and act as a very real deterrent. The penalties imposed were no more than adequate. The Judge would have been justified in imposing substantially larger fines on the other charges. We are surprised the Judge did not suspend the fishing licence.

R v Ramosa 2005 1 Cr App R (S) 77 (p 396) The defendant company pleaded to 11 counts of failing to comply with EU provisions relating to fisheries. The offences were strict liability and concerned failing to record quantities of fish and the alteration of log books, pursued with a commercial motive. The 11 counts spanned 16 months for approaching £500,000 worth of undeclared fish. The defendant company had no previous convictions. Held. The defendant company had pleaded to strict liability offences but that did not inhibit the Judge from sentencing on the basis that there were aggravating features of knowledge and a commercial motive. The company could have purchased additional quota entitlements for £50,000. **£250,000 fine** not £500,000.

261.4   *Unlicensed fishing*
Salmon and Freshwater Fisheries Act 1975 s 27
1) If the instrument is a rod and line:
  Mode of trial Summary only
  Maximum sentence Level 4 fine (£2,500)
2) In all other cases:
  Mode of trial Triable either way
Maximum sentence On indictment 2 years. Summary 3 months and/or £5,000 fine for offences committed before 12 March 2015 and an unlimited fine thereafter.[479] There are maximum fines for those aged under 18, see **14.38** in Volume 1.
Non-court penalties There is power to issue a variable monetary penalty[480] which must not exceed £250,000.[481]

262   FOOD OFFENCES
262.1
Food Safety Act 1990
  s 7 (rendering food injurious to health)
  s 8 (selling food not complying with food safety requirements)
  s 14 (selling food not of a nature or quality demanded)
  s 15 (falsely describing or presenting food etc.)
Modes of trial Triable either way
Maximum sentences On indictment 2 years. Summary maximum 6 months and/or £5,000 fine for offences committed before 12 March 2015 and an unlimited fine thereafter.[482] There are maximum fines for those aged under 18, see **14.38** in Volume 1.
Food Safety and Hygiene (England) Regs 2013 2013/2996 reg 19(1) (failing to comply with specified EU provisions)
Food Hygiene (Wales) Regs 2006 2006/31 reg 17(1) (failure to comply with the specified Community provisions)
General Food Regs 2004 2004/3279 reg 4 (failure to comply with EC requirements) This provision no longer applies to England but does apply to Wales.
Mode of trial Triable either way

---

[479] Legal Aid, Sentencing and Punishment of Offenders Act 2012 s 85(1) and (4) and Legal Aid, Sentencing and Punishment of Offenders Act 2012 (Commencement No 11) Order 2015 2015/504
[480] Salmon and Freshwater Fisheries Act 1975 s 37A
[481] Environmental Civil Sanctions (England) Order 2010 2010/1157 para 3 and Sch 2 para 1
[482] Legal Aid, Sentencing and Punishment of Offenders Act 2012 s 85(1) and (4) and Legal Aid, Sentencing and Punishment of Offenders Act 2012 (Commencement No 11) Order 2015 2015/504

Maximum sentences For these three offences on indictment and summarily an unlimited fine. For a regulation 4 offence there is on indictment a 2-year maximum with a 6-month summary maximum.

Hygiene Prohibition Order Where a food business operator is convicted of an offence under Food Safety and Hygiene (England) Regs 2013 2013/2996, the court shall make a Hygiene Prohibition Order when the conditions are met. This enables prohibitions to be made (reg 7(1)), including a prohibition of managing any food business (reg 7(4)). For more detail see **71.1** in Volume 1.

Licences If the defendant is licensed under Slaughterhouses Act 1974 s 1 or 6 there is power to cancel the licence.[483]

262.2   *Crown Court statistics   England and Wales*
Adulteration of Food Aged 21+

Year	Proceeded against	Found guilty	Sentenced
2012	54	44	45
2013	54	40	41
2014	83	56	55

Note: There is also a small set of statistics for 'Adulteration of Food, Drug etc.' The difference between the two sets of statistics is far from clear. Ed

For explanations about the statistics see page 1-xii. For more statistics see www.banksr. com Other Matters Statistics tab

262.3   *Sentencing Council Guideline 2010 and 2016*
Health and Safety Offences, Corporate Manslaughter and Food Safety and Hygiene Offences Guideline 2016, see www.banksr.com Other Matters Guidelines tab page 29 (for organisations) and page 39 (for individuals) In force 1 February 2016

As these offences are comparatively rare and the guideline is so long, the details are not reproduced here. The guideline contains sections on Determining the culpability and harm of the offence, the starting points and ranges, obtaining financial information, assessing whether the fine is proportionate and consideration of Hygiene Prohibition Orders and compensation.

One matter that survives from the old *Corporate Manslaughter and H and S Offences Causing Death Guideline 2010* page 3, see www.banksr.com Other Matters Guidelines tab is the basis of plea section.

Basis of plea

para 11 It will generally be appropriate to require the prosecution to set out in writing the facts of the case relied upon and any aggravating or mitigating features which it identifies.[484] The defence may conveniently be required similarly to set out in writing any points on which it differs. If sentence is to proceed upon agreed facts, they should be set out in writing.[485]

263   FOOTBALL OFFENCES
263.1
Various and penalties.

Football Banning Orders For: a) all Football (Offences) Act 1991 offences, b) Football Spectators Act 1989 s 2(1), 5(7), 14J(1) and 21C(2) offences, c) Sporting Events (Control of Alcohol etc.) Act 1985 s 2 or 2A offences, and d) offences committed relevant to a football match the court must make a Football Banning Order where there

---

[483] Food Safety Act 1990 s 35(4)
[484] Attorney-General's *Guidelines on the Acceptance of Pleas and the Prosecutor's Role in the Sentencing Exercise*, published November 2009, see www.banksr.com Other Matters Guidelines Attorney-General's guidelines section
[485] See *R v Friskies Petcare (UK) Ltd* 2000 EWCA Crim 95, 2 Cr App R (S) 401.

are reasonable grounds to believe that making a banning order would help to prevent violence or disorder at or in connection with any regulated football match, under Football Spectators Act 1989 s 14A and Sch 1 para 1.

See also the OFFENCES AGAINST THE PERSON ACT 1861 S 20 *Sporting* para at **293.20**, and the AFFRAY/VIOLENT DISORDER *Football offences* para at **203.13**.

For drunken football-related offences see the DRUNK chapter.

263.2   *Magistrates' Court Sentencing Guidelines*

Magistrates' Court Sentencing Guideline 2008, see www.banksr.com Other Matters Guidelines tab The guidelines apply to the Magistrates' Court and to the Crown Court hearing appeals or sentencing for summary only offences.[486]

page 62 Football-related offences. Starting points are based on a first-time offender pleading not guilty.

Examples of nature of activity	Starting point	Range
Being drunk in, or whilst trying to enter ground	Band A fine	Conditional discharge to band B fine
Going onto playing or other prohibited area Unauthorised sale or attempted sale of tickets	Band B fine	Band A fine to band C fine
Throwing missile, indecent or racist chanting	Band C fine	Band C fine
Possession of alcohol whilst entering or trying to enter ground	Band C fine	Band B fine to high-level community order

The following aggravating and mitigating factors may be particularly relevant: Factors indicating higher culpability: 1 Commercial ticket operation, potential high cash value, counterfeit tickets 2 Inciting others to misbehave 3 Possession of large quantity of alcohol 4 Offensive language or behaviour (where not an element of the offence). Factor indicating greater degree of harm: Missile likely to cause serious injury e.g. coin, glass, bottle, stone.

For the meaning of a high-level community order see **16.14** in Volume 1.

Consider ancillary orders, including compensation and Football Banning Order.

A Band A fine is 50% of net weekly income. Bands B and C are 100% and 150%. For more detail see **60.27** in Volume 1.

Consultation It is expected that the Sentencing Council will issue a consultation document about updating this guideline in May 2016.

263.3   *Football violence*   *Judicial guidance*

R v Doyle and Others 2012 EWCA Crim 995, 2013 1 Cr App R (S) 36 (p 197) The defendants were convicted of affray. They travelled home to Reading from a football match at West Ham. They were foul-mouthed, rowdy and drunk. A passenger asked them to stop their behaviour and they assaulted him. The defendants were of good character, with decent jobs and references. Held. The scourge of football violence has blighted the sport for years. It is well known that it has very seriously affected this country's reputation abroad and has greatly damaged the willingness of other countries to compete with British teams. It is also obvious that it carries with it the real likelihood that innocent people are either prevented from attending football matches, especially with their children, as they ought to be able to do, or are at risk of suffering disorder, harassment and serious violence if they do. Moreover such disorder and violence can do real injury to people who have nothing to do with football but happen to be present

---

[486] See page 15 of the guidelines.

where the offences are committed. It is a sad but well-established feature of the phenomenon that whilst sometimes the offenders are people with a history of violent behaviour unrelated to football, many others are often otherwise hard-working and unconvicted persons, who behave in the context of football matches in a way that they would not otherwise. One clear problem is the way in which violent behaviour is fuelled by numbers, and by a sense of tribal identity, which can lead people to think that violence and threats are acceptable. Often actions of a crowd are greater in their effect than the sum of the individual actions of its members.

264   FORGERY

264.1

Where the forgery is used to steal, see the THEFT ETC. chapter.

Deferred prosecution agreements A designated prosecutor may apply to the court under Courts and Crime Act 2013 Sch 17 para 7 for this procedure to be used for Forgery and Counterfeiting Act 1981 s 1-5 offences. The procedure is laid down in Crime and Courts Act 2013 Sch 17. In force 24 February 2014.

For other guidance see the COUNTERFEIT CURRENCY OFFENCES, ELECTION OFFENCES, FRAUD AND FINANCIAL SERVICES OFFENCES and PASSPORT/ID DOCUMENTS OFFENCES chapters.

264.2   *Crown Court statistics   England and Wales*

Forgery etc. of drug prescription Aged 21+

Year	Plea	Total sentenced	Type of sentencing %						Average length of custody in months
			Discharge	Fine	Commu-nity sentence	Sus-pended sentence	Custody	Other	
2013	G	11	–	–	27.3	45.5	27.3	–	6
	NG	1	–	–	–	–	100	–	15
2014	G	3	–	–	67	–	33	–	not listed[487]
	NG	0							

Vehicle insurance offences Aged 21+

Year	Plea	Total sentenced	Type of sentencing %						Average length of custody in months
			Discharge	Fine	Commu-nity sentence	Sus-pended sentence	Custody	Other	
Fraud, forgery, etc. associated with vehicle or driver records (MOT)									
2014	G	24	–	4	25	42	25	4	4.7
	NG	1	–	–	–	100	–	–	–
Vehicle insurance offences – triable either way (MOT)									
2014	G	7	14	43	14	14	–	14	–
	NG	0							

---

[487] Based on too few cases to be meaningful

Other forgery

Year	Age	Plea	Total sen- tenced	Type of sentencing %						Average length of custody in months
				Dis- charge	Fine	Community sentence	Sus- pended sentence	Custody	Oth- er	
2013	18-20	G	79	1.3	–	10.1	22.8	65.8	–	9.4
		NG	4	25.0	–	–	25.0	50.0	–	7.5
	21+	G	1,269	0.7	0.3	4.6	21.4	72.8	0.2	9.2
		NG	92	–	2.2	–	22.8	75.0	–	15.6
2014	18-20	G	35	–	–	17	37	46	–	7.0
		NG	6	–	–	–	33	67	–	8.5
	21+	G	201	1	1	6	35	56	–	13.3
		NG	34	–	–	6	26	68	–	29.3

For explanations about the statistics see page 1-xii. For statistics for male and female defendants etc. see www.banksr.com Other Matters Statistics tab

264.2a *Case*

R v Cano-Uribe and Others 2015 EWCA Crim 1824 F, C, L, D, H, W and K were sentenced for various forgery offences. The group worked for a company which was contracted by the Department of Work and Pensions (DWP) to provide courses to help people obtain work. The firm was paid for 588 claims and at least 345 had substantial irregularities. 167 files were forged by ten individuals and the loss was £288,595. An advisor received £50 for each person who found work. The Judge found it was not a victimless crime and the use of targets and bonuses had caused a high degree of pressure and stress, but this did not justify the wholesale fabrication of documents. It was agreed that the offences did not fit neatly into any of the guidelines. The Judge took a benchmark figure of 5 years from which she worked out the sentences. Held. [That was wrong] because there was no overarching allegation. There was an element of abuse of trust and public money was involved. F pleaded to nine specimen counts. The loss involved for her was £44,395 and her gain was only £1,150. She was aged 32, with only motoring previous convictions. We start at 18 months so with plea, **12 months** not 22. C was convicted of conspiracy to make a false instrument and forgery. She was involved in the overall control of the contract with staff. There was no financial motive for her offending. C was aged 39 with no convictions. She had two young children. We start at **9 months** and pass that sentence not 18 months. L pleaded to 13 counts. He was involved in 29 forged files which was 54% of the total. The loss to DWP was £51,503 and L made £1,450. He had no relevant convictions and gave evidence for the prosecution. The Judge started at 40 months. **12 months** not 15. D pleaded to seven counts of forgery. She was involved in 16 transactions and the loss to DWP was £6,216. Her gain was £350. We start at 15 months, so with the plea **10 months** not 15. H and W were charged with conspiracy to make a false instrument with C. H was a team leader and W was a whistle-blower. They made no money from the offence. The activity was to deceive the auditor. H was W's boss. H was aged 31 with no convictions. W was aged 27. K was convicted of forgery of one file. He was uneasy about taking part. **6 months suspended** not 12 suspended for H, W and K.

265   FRAUD AND FINANCIAL SERVICES OFFENCES

265.1

Where a forgery is made to steal, see the **THEFT ETC.** chapter.

Where the offence is identity fraud the cases are listed in this chapter. Where the offence is primarily the possession of the documents whether as simple possession, for use in obtaining work or misleading immigration officials etc. the cases are listed in the **PASSPORT/ID DOCUMENTS OFFENCES** chapter.

Various statutes and penalties including the following:

1) Fraud Act 2006

s 1 (fraud comprising: a) fraud by false representation, b) fraud by failing to disclose information and fraud by abuse of position)

s 6 (possession of articles for use in frauds)

s 7 (making or supplying articles for use in frauds)

s 9 (participating in fraudulent business carried out by a sole trader)

s 11 (obtaining services dishonestly)

Modes of trial Triable either way

Maximum sentences On indictment for sections 1, 2, 3, 4, 7, and 9 the maximum is 10 years and for sections 6 and 11 the maximum is 5 years. Summary maximum 6 months and/or a £5,000 fine for offences committed before 12 March 2015 and an unlimited fine thereafter.[488] There are maximum fines for those aged under 18, see **14.38** in Volume 1.

2) Conspiracy to defraud

Mode of trial Indictable only

Maximum sentence 10 years

3) Companies Act 2006 s 993 (fraudulent trading)

Mode of trial Triable either way

Maximum sentence On indictment 10 years.[489] Summary maximum 6 months and/or a £5,000 fine for offences committed before 12 March 2015 and an unlimited fine thereafter.[490] There are maximum fines for those aged under 18, see **14.38** in Volume 1.

4) Identity Documents Act 2010

s 4 (possession of false identity documents etc. with improper intention)

s 5 (possession etc. of apparatus designed etc. for making false identity documents)

s 6 (possession of false identity documents etc. without reasonable excuse)

Modes of trial and maximum sentences Sections 4 and 5 are indictable only. Maximum sentence 10 years. Section 6 is triable either way. On indictment maximum 2 years. Summary maximum 6 months and/or a £5,000 fine for offences committed before 12 March 2015 and an unlimited fine thereafter.[491] There are maximum fines for those aged under 18, see **14.38** in Volume 1.

Confiscation Where a defendant has a criminal lifestyle the court, once the confiscation proceedings are triggered (see **22.11** in Volume 1), <u>must</u> follow the Proceeds of Crime Act 2002 procedure. The list of 'criminal lifestyle' offences does not include any of the fraud offences listed above.[492] For what constitutes a criminal lifestyle see **22.43** in Volume 1.

Disqualification from being a company director A court may make a disqualification order against a defendant who is convicted of an indictable offence in connection with the management etc. of a company.[493]

---

[488] Legal Aid, Sentencing and Punishment of Offenders Act 2012 s 85(1) and (4) and Legal Aid, Sentencing and Punishment of Offenders Act 2012 (Commencement No 11) Order 2015 2015/504

[489] The maximum under the old Act was 7 years.

[490] Legal Aid, Sentencing and Punishment of Offenders Act 2012 s 85(1) and (4) and Legal Aid, Sentencing and Punishment of Offenders Act 2012 (Commencement No 11) Order 2015 2015/504

[491] Legal Aid, Sentencing and Punishment of Offenders Act 2012 s 85(1) and (4) and Legal Aid, Sentencing and Punishment of Offenders Act 2012 (Commencement No 11) Order 2015 2015/504

[492] Proceeds of Crime Act 2002 s 6 and 75 and Sch 2

[493] Company Directors Disqualification Act 1986 s 2

Serious Crime Prevention Order For Fraud Act 2006 s 1, 6, 7, 9 and 11 and conspiracy to defraud offences there is a discretionary power to make this order, when it would protect the public etc.[494]

Deferred prosecution agreements A designated prosecutor may apply to the court under Crime and Courts Act 2013 Sch 17 para 7 for this procedure to be applied for the following offences: a) Companies Act 1985 s 450, b) Companies Act 2006 s 658, 680 and 993, c) conspiracy to defraud, d) Financial Services and Markets Act 2000 s 23, 25, 85, 346, 397 and 398, e) Forgery and Counterfeiting Act 1981 s 1-5, f) Fraud Act 2006 s 1, 6, 7 and 11, g) Theft Act 1968 s 20 and 24A and h) certain other offences (see Crime and Courts Act 2013 Sch 17 para 15-30). The procedure is laid down in Crime and Courts Act 2013 Sch 17. In force 24 February 2014.

Corporate offenders See the *Fraud, Bribery and Money Laundering: Corporate Offenders Guideline 2014* at **225.9**.

See also the **RETAIL OFFENCES** chapter.

265.2   Crown Court statistics   England and Wales
Fraud by company director etc. Aged 21+

Year	Plea	Total sentenced	Type of sentencing %						Average length of custody in months
			Dis-charge	Fine	Commu-nity sentence	Sus-pended sentence	Custody	Other	
2013	G	18	–	–	11.1	33.3	55.6	–	21.9
	NG	7	–	–	–	14.3	71.4	14.3	63.6
2014	G	28	–	–	–	32	68	–	35.8
	NG	10	–	–	–	20	80	–	26.8

Other fraud

Year	Age	Plea	Total sen-tenced	Type of sentencing %						Average length of custody in months
				Dis-charge	Fine	Community sentence	Sus-pended sentence	Custody	Oth-er	
2013	18-20	G	116	1.7	3.4	30.2	26.7	37.9	–	10.6
		NG	8	12.5	–	50	12.5	25	–	3.0
	21+	G	3,686	1.5	0.9	13.1	42	42.1	0.3	16.6
		NG	503	1.4	1.4	14.3	26.4	55.5	1.0	31.5
2014	18-20	G	14	21	–	21	21	36	–	10.8
		NG	1	–	–	–	–	100	–	not listed[495]
	21+	G	251	1	1	11	24	62	1	12.6
		NG	41	–	2	12	20	66	–	23.5

For explanations about the statistics see page 1-xii. For statistics for male and female defendants etc. see www.banksr.com Other Matters Statistics tab

265.3   Sentencing Guidelines Council guideline
Fraud, Bribery and Money Laundering Offences Guideline 2014, see www.banksr.com Other Matters Guidelines tab

This guideline applies to Fraud Act 2006 s 1, conspiracy to defraud and Theft Act 1968 s 17. In force 1 October 2014.

---

[494] Serious Crime Act 2007 s 1 and Sch 1 para 7
[495] Based on too few cases to be meaningful

STEP ONE: Determining the offence category

page 6 The court should determine the offence category with reference to the tables below. In order to determine the category the court should assess culpability and harm.

Culpability

page 6 The level of culpability is determined by weighing up all the factors of the case to determine the offender's role and the extent to which the offending was planned and the sophistication with which it was carried out.

Where there are characteristics present which fall under different levels of culpability, the court should balance these characteristics to reach a fair assessment of the offender's culpability.

Culpability
Culpability A – High Culpability
A leading role where offending is part of a group activity Involvement of others through pressure/influence Abuse of position of power or trust or responsibility Sophisticated nature of offence/significant planning Fraudulent activity conducted over sustained period of time Large number of victims Deliberately targeting victim on basis of vulnerability
Culpability B – Medium Culpability
Other cases where characteristics for categories A or C are not present A significant role where offending is part of a group activity
Culpability C – Lesser Culpability
Involved through coercion, intimidation or exploitation Not motivated by personal gain Peripheral role in organised fraud Opportunistic 'one-off' offence; very little or no planning Limited awareness or understanding of the extent of fraudulent activity

265.4
Harm

page 7 Harm is initially assessed by the actual, intended or risked loss as may arise from the offence.

The values in the table below are to be used for actual or intended loss only.

Intended loss relates to offences where circumstances prevent the actual loss that is intended to be caused by the fraudulent activity.

Risk of loss (for instance in mortgage frauds) involves consideration of both the likelihood of harm occurring and the extent of it if it does. Risk of loss is less serious than actual or intended loss. Where the offence has caused risk of loss but no (or much less) actual loss the normal approach is to move down to the corresponding point in the next category. This may not be appropriate if either the likelihood or extent of risked loss is particularly high.

Harm A – Loss caused or intended	
Category 1	£500,000 or more	Starting point based on £1 million
Category 2	£100,000-£500,000 or Risk of Category 1 harm	Starting point based on £300,000
Category 3	£20,000-£100,000 or Risk of Category 2 harm	Starting point based on £50,000

Category 4	£5,000-£20,000 or Risk of Category 3 harm	Starting point based on £12,500
Category 5	Less than £5,000 or Risk of Category 4 harm	Starting point based on £2,500
	Risk of Category 5 harm, move down the range within the category	

page 7 The court should then take into account the level of harm caused to the victim(s) or others to determine whether it warrants the sentence being moved up to the corresponding point in the next category or further up the range of the initial category.

Harm B – Victim impact demonstrated by one or more of the following	
High impact move up a category; if in Category 1 move up the range	Serious detrimental effect on the victim whether financial or otherwise, for example substantial damage to credit rating Victim particularly vulnerable (due to factors including but not limited to their age, financial circumstances, mental capacity)
Medium impact move upwards within the category range	Considerable detrimental effect on the victim whether financial or otherwise
Lesser impact no adjustment	Some detrimental impact on victim, whether financial or otherwise

265.5

STEP TWO: Starting point and category range

page 8 Having determined the category at step one, the court should use the appropriate starting point (as adjusted in accordance with step one above) to reach a sentence within the category range in the table below. The starting point applies to all offenders irrespective of plea or previous convictions.

Where the value is larger or smaller than the amount on which the starting point is based, this should lead to upward or downward adjustment as appropriate.

Where the value greatly exceeds the amount of the starting point in Category 1, it may be appropriate to move outside the identified range.

Culpability and harm

page 8 **Table 1**

Fraud Act 2006 s 1 Conspiracy to defraud

	Culpability		
Harm	**A**	**B**	**C**
Category 1 £500,000 or more	**Starting point** 7 years' custody	**Starting point** 5 years' custody	**Starting point** 3 years' custody
Starting point based on £1 million	**Category range** 5 to 8 years' custody	**Category range** 3 to 6 years' custody	**Category range** 18 months' to 4 years' custody
Category 2 £100,000-£500,000	**Starting point** 5 years' custody	**Starting point** 3 years' custody	**Starting point** 18 months' custody
Starting point based on £300,000	**Category range** 3 to 6 years' custody	**Category range** 18 months' to 4 years' custody	**Category range** 26 weeks' to 3 years' custody
Category 3 £20,000-£100,000	**Starting point** 3 years' custody	**Starting point** 18 months' custody	**Starting point** 26 weeks' custody

Culpability			
Harm	**A**	**B**	**C**
Starting point based on £50,000	**Category range** 18 months' to 4 years' custody	**Category range** 26 weeks' to 3 years' custody	**Category range** Medium-level community order to 1 year's custody
Category 4 £5,000-£20,000	**Starting point** 18 months' custody	**Starting point** 26 weeks' custody	**Starting point** Medium-level community order
Starting point based on £12,500	**Category range** 26 weeks' to 3 years' custody	**Category range** Medium-level community order to 1 year's custody	**Category range** Band B fine to medium-level community order
Category 5 Less than £5,000	**Starting point** 36 weeks' custody	**Starting point** Medium-level community order	**Starting point** Band B fine
Starting point based on £2,500	**Category range** High-level community order to 1 year's custody	**Category range** Band B fine to 26 weeks' custody	**Category range** Discharge to medium-level community order

For the meaning of a high-level, a medium-level and a low-level community order see **16.12-16.14** in Volume 1.

265.6
page 9 **Table 2**
Theft Act 1968 s 17

Culpability			
Harm	**A**	**B**	**C**
Category 1 £500,000 or more	**Starting point** 5 years 6 months' custody	**Starting point** 4 years' custody	**Starting point** 2 years 6 months' custody
Starting point based on £1 million	**Category range** 4 years' to 6 years 6 months' custody	**Category range** 2 years 6 months' to 5 years' custody	**Category range** 15 months' to 3 years 6 months' custody
Category 2 £100,000-£500,000	**Starting point** 4 years' custody	**Starting point** 2 years 6 months' custody	**Starting point** 15 months' custody
Starting point based on £300,000	**Category range** 2 years 6 months' to 5 years' custody	**Category range** 15 months' to 3 years 6 months' custody	**Category range** 26 weeks' to 2 years 6 months' custody
Category 3 £20,000-£100,000	**Starting point** 2 years 6 months' custody	**Starting point** 15 months' custody	**Starting point** High-level community order
Starting point based on £50,000	**Category range** 15 months' to 3 years 6 months' custody	**Category range** High-level community order to 2 years 6 months' custody	**Category range** Low-level community order to 36 weeks' custody

	Culpability		
Harm	**A**	**B**	**C**
Category 4 £5,000-£20,000	**Starting point** 15 months' custody	**Starting point** High-level community order	**Starting point** Low-level community order
Starting point based on £12,500	**Category range** High-level community order to 2 years 6 months' custody	**Category range** Low-level community order to 36 weeks' custody	**Category range** Band B fine to medium-level community order
Category 5 Less than £5,000	**Starting point** 26 weeks' custody	**Starting point** Low-level community order	**Starting point** Band B fine
Starting point based on £2,500	**Category range** Medium-level community order to 36 weeks' custody	**Category range** Band B fine to medium-level community order	**Category range** Discharge to low-level community order

For the meaning of a high-level, a medium-level and a low-level community order see **16.12-16.14** in Volume 1.

R v Vaughan-Williams 2015 EWCA Crim 476 D pleaded early to fraud. He induced a friend, V, to invest in a company on the basis of lies. V lost about £25,000 which he had saved all his life for a house and that was now gone. V said he was financially crippled by the fraud. The Judge started with the offence in Category 3A with a leading role. Because of the effect on the victim, he moved it to Category 2 with a 5-year starting point. Because the loss was only £25,000 not the £50,000 midpoint, he moved it down to 4½ years, making 3 years with plea. Held. The Judge was entitled to move the case into Category 2 but in value terms it was near the bottom of the range in Category 3 [which should have been reflected in the sentence]. We start at 42 months, making 28 months with plea.

265.7   [Aggravating and mitigating factors]
Seriousness

page 10 The table below contains a non-exhaustive list of additional factual elements providing the context of the offence and factors relating to the offender.

Identify whether any combination of these or other relevant factors should result in an upward or downward adjustment from the sentence arrived at so far.

Consecutive sentences for multiple offences may be appropriate where large sums are involved.

Factors increasing seriousness
Statutory aggravating factors: Previous convictions, having regard to a) the nature of the offence to which the conviction relates and its relevance to the current offence; and b) the time that has elapsed since the conviction Offence committed whilst on bail ***Other aggravating factors:*** Steps taken to prevent the victim reporting or obtaining assistance and/or from assisting or supporting the prosecution Attempts to conceal/dispose of evidence Established evidence of community/wider impact Failure to comply with current court orders Offence committed on licence Offences taken into consideration Failure to respond to warnings about behaviour Offences committed across borders Blame wrongly placed on others

Factors reducing seriousness or reflecting personal mitigation
No previous convictions or no relevant/recent convictions
Remorse
Good character and/or exemplary conduct
Little or no prospect of success
Serious medical conditions requiring urgent, intensive or long-term treatment
Age and/or lack of maturity where it affects the responsibility of the offender
Lapse of time since apprehension where this does not arise from the conduct of the offender
Mental disorder or learning disability
Sole or primary carer for dependent relatives
Offender co-operated with investigation, made early admissions and/or voluntarily reported offending
Determination and/or demonstration of steps having been taken to address addiction or offending behaviour
Activity originally legitimate

265.8   Suggested approach to the new guideline
Note: There is nothing in the guideline to suggest it is intended that there should be a radical departure from the existing sentencing principles. I would suggest sentencers: a) start with the guideline, b) consider the recent cases from the Court of Appeal to see if they are helpful and then, c) return to the guideline before deciding the appropriate sentence. Ed.

265.9   Magistrates' Court Sentencing Guideline   Bribery
Magistrates' Court Sentencing Guideline 2008 (as amended), see www.banksr.com page 363 The section on bribery of the *Fraud, Bribery and Money Laundering Offences Guideline 2014* has been inserted, see www.banksr.com Other Matters Guidelines tab

265.10   Pre-2014 guideline judicial guidance   Fraud
R v Darwin and Darwin 2009 EWCA Crim 860, 2 Cr App R (S) 115 (p 746) LCJ D pleaded to eight counts of obtaining by deception. His wife, AD, was convicted of six counts of obtaining by deception and some money laundering offences. D faked his death in a canoeing accident and £250,000 was paid out in insurance. Their two adult sons believed that their father was dead, suffered grief and tried to comfort their mother. Held. The Judge was right to attach considerable importance to the impact on the sons. They suffered totally unnecessary emotional distress. This was the grossest form of betrayal. Consideration is not confined to those who have lost financially as a result of fraud, but may properly be extended to those who have suffered a devastating impact by it. A number of people became involved in the unpleasant and potentially dangerous task of trying to find D when he disappeared, which was an aggravating feature. The financial element of the fraud would suggest a shorter sentence, but the case cannot be limited to its financial element alone.
Note: This guidance was issued before the *Fraud Guideline 2009* and the *Fraud, Bribery and Money Laundering Offences Guideline 2014* were published. Ed.
For judicial guidance in *City frauds* see **265.25**.

Plea discussions in complex fraud cases, discount for guilty plea and delay
265.11   Complex fraud, Plea discussions in   Guidelines
Attorney-General's Guidelines on plea discussions in cases of serious or complex fraud 2004 www.banksr.com Other Matters Other Documents tab
para A1 These Guidelines set out a process by which a prosecutor may discuss an allegation of serious or complex fraud with a person who he or she is prosecuting or expects to prosecute, or with that person's legal representative. They come into force on the 5th day of May 2009 and apply to plea discussions initiated on or after that date.
A2 The Guidelines will be followed by all prosecutors in England and Wales when conducting plea discussions in cases of serious or complex fraud. For the purposes of the

Guidelines, fraud means any financial, fiscal or commercial misconduct or corruption which is contrary to the criminal law. Fraud may be serious or complex if at least two of the following factors are present:
a) The amount obtained or intended to be obtained is alleged to exceed £500,000.
b) There is a significant international dimension.
c) The case requires specialised knowledge of financial, commercial, fiscal or regulatory matters such as the operation of markets, banking systems, trusts or tax regimes.
d) The case involves allegations of fraudulent activity against numerous victims.
e) The case involves an allegation of substantial and significant fraud on a public body.
f) The case is likely to be of widespread public concern.
g) The alleged misconduct endangered the economic well-being of the United Kingdom, for example by undermining confidence in financial markets.
h) Taking account of these matters, it is for the prosecutor to decide whether or not a case is one of fraud, and whether or not it is serious or complex.

Discussion of sentence
D9 Where agreement is reached as to pleas, the parties should discuss the appropriate sentence with a view to presenting a joint written submission to the court. This document should list the aggravating and mitigating features arising from the agreed facts, set out any personal mitigation available to the defendant, and refer to any relevant sentencing guidelines or authorities. In the light of all of these factors, it should make submissions as to the applicable sentencing range in the relevant guideline. The prosecutor must ensure that the submissions are realistic, taking full account of all relevant material and considerations.
D10 The prosecutor should bear in mind all of the powers of the court, and seek to include in the joint submission any relevant ancillary orders. It is particularly desirable that measures should be included that achieve redress for victims (such as compensation orders) and protection for the public (such as directors' disqualification orders, Serious Crime Prevention Orders or Financial Reporting Orders).

Conducting plea discussions
D11 Due regard should be had to the court's asset recovery powers and the desirability of using these powers both as a deterrent to others and as a means of preventing the defendant from benefiting from the proceeds of crime or funding future offending. Proceeds of Crime Act 2002 requires the Crown Court to proceed to the making of a confiscation order against a convicted defendant who has benefited from his criminal conduct where the prosecutor asks the court to do so, or the court believes that it is appropriate to do so. Fraud is an acquisitive crime, and the expectation in a fraud case should be that a confiscation order will be sought by the prosecutor reflecting the full benefit to the defendant. However, in doing so it is open to the prosecutor to take a realistic view of the likely approach of the court to the determination of any points in dispute (such as the interest of a third party in any property).
D12 In the course of the plea discussions the prosecutor must make it clear to the defence that the joint submission as to sentence (including confiscation) is not binding on the court.
Note: This is a brief summary of a nine-page document. Ed.
See also: Criminal Practice Directions 2015 EWCA Crim 1567 para VII B.15-27 where the procedure etc. is set out.

265.12   *Complex fraud, Plea discussions in   Cases*
R v Innospec Ltd 2010 Lloyd's Rep FC 462 www.banksr.com Other Matters Other Documents tab Crown Court decisions Thomas LJ The defendant company pleaded to conspiracy to corrupt. Innospec had conspired with its directors and others to make corrupt payments to public officials of the Government of Indonesia to secure contracts for the supply of goods. The 'best estimate' of the amount of the bribes was $8m. There were concurrent criminal proceedings in the USA surrounding a corruption involving the

UN Oil for Food Programme in Iraq. A 'global settlement' was agreed along with the division of that agreement. The Director of the SFO, acting as prosecutor, also agreed with Innospec the nature of the penalty to be imposed for the offences it had pleaded to. Held. The SFO (or other prosecutor) cannot enter into an agreement under the laws of England and Wales with an offender as to the penalty in respect of the offence charged. This is particularly so in corruption cases. Further, as it is for the court to determine the sanction to be imposed upon an offender, an agreement between prosecutors as to the division of the sanction cannot be in accordance with basic constitutional principles. Any agreement as to penalty is to no effect.

R v Dougall 2010 EWCA Crim 1048, 2011 1 Cr App R (S) 37 (p 227) D pleaded to conspiracy to corrupt. The SFO, the prosecutor, entered into an agreement with the defence that D's sentence would be a suspended sentence. The prosecution then all but made submissions for the defence to that effect. Held. It was noted that the prosecution did not have the benefit of Thomas LJ's comments in *R v Innospec Ltd* 2010 and that in light of his judgment that situation would not recur.

Old case: *R v Whittle and Others* 2008 EWCA Crim 2560 at **265.46**

265.13 Delay, Discount for

R v Takkar 2008 EWCA Crim 646, 2 Cr App R (S) 92 (p 518) D was convicted of: 1) conspiracy to cheat, 2) cheating, and 3) fraudulent trading. There was a delay of three years between the last offence and the sentence. The defence asked for a 15% discount for the delay relying on *Att-Gen's Ref Nos 88-91 of 2006* 2006 EWCA Crim 3254, 2007 2 Cr App R (S) 28 (p 155). Held. The discount in that case was not met with approval or disapproval by the Court of Appeal. Investigation of such sophisticated frauds is a time-consuming process, involving international investigation and co-operation. Some of the delay was because D asked for the trial date to be moved. We do not want to give the impression that there is an entitlement to an additional discount, let alone one fixed at 15%. That would erode the plea of guilty discount. Absent an abuse of process or unreasonable delay by the prosecution the offenders should not benefit from delay resultant on a fraud covered by the perpetrators under complex layers. If delay is a feature it will depend on the facts of each case.

265.14 Guilty plea, Late

R v Buffrey 1993 14 Cr App R (S) 511 LCJ D pleaded to conspiracy to trade fraudulently and other connected counts after the case had been opened to the jury. The Court of Appeal considered to what extent, when someone pleads guilty at a late stage and so saves the holding of a very lengthy trial, ought the sentence which would otherwise have been imposed be discounted? Held. It must not be thought by those who are minded to commit fraud that after indulging in devious deception – which necessitates a long trial to unravel it – they can, by pleading guilty at a late stage, earn such praise from the court for their public-spirited acceptance of what they have done that they can have a great reduction of their sentence. But some reduction must be made, and because frauds of this kind are complex and do take a long time to unravel, they have become a burden on the criminal justice system. They are very costly, both in time and money. They cause stress to jurors, judges, those who conduct them and not least the witnesses and the defendants. These matters justify the court in applying a considerable discount where someone late in the day pleads guilty. There is no absolute rule as to what the discount should be. There will be considerable variance between one case and another. As a general guidance something of the order of one-third would very often be appropriate. Here the sentence could have been perhaps something of the order of 6 years (after a trial). With the plea **4 years** substituted.

R v Oprey and Pinchbeck 2002 1 Cr App R (S) 75 (p 317) The defendants O and P pleaded to conspiracy to defraud and other dishonesty etc. counts. O agreed to give evidence against P and then P made a late plea. Held. P's plea although late was a very strong piece of mitigation.

These cases must be considered with the new guidelines. However, they may show how a judge might exercise his or her discretion. Ed.
See also the **GUILTY PLEA, DISCOUNT FOR** chapter.

Particular frauds

265.15 *Articles   Possessing, making or supplying articles for use in fraud*
Fraud Act 2006
    s 1 (general fraud)
    s 6 (possession of articles for fraud)
    s 7 (making or supplying articles for fraud)
Modes of trial Triable either way
Maximum sentences On indictment 10, 5 and 10 years respectively. Summary maximum 6 months and/or a £5,000 fine for offences committed before 12 March 2015 and an unlimited fine thereafter.[496] There are maximum fines for those aged under 18, see **14.38** in Volume 1.

265.16 *Articles   Possessing, making or supplying articles for use in fraud-Guidelines*
Fraud Guideline 2009, see www.banksr.com Other Matters Guidelines tab For first-time offenders aged 18+ who were convicted after a trial.
Note: Although the *Fraud Guideline 2009* has been replaced, this information may be helpful. The information seems as relevant now as it was in 2009. Ed.
page 21 para 3 'Articles' will include any electronic programs or data stored electronically.[497] Examples of articles for use in frauds include false fronts for cash machines, computer programs for generating credit card numbers, lists of credit card or bank account details, 'sucker lists' and draft letters or e-mails for use in advance fee frauds. 4 As lists of credit card and bank account details constitute 'articles', the making of such lists through certain electronic programs, which contravenes section 1 of the Fraud Act 2006, is also criminalised by section 7 of the same Act.
Note: The entries about *Phishing*, *Vishing*, *Pharming* and *Use of a 'Trojan'* can be found at **265.24**. Ed.
5 Making, adapting, supplying or offering to supply computer programs, e-mails or websites for the above activities amounts to an offence under section 7 of the Fraud Act 2006.
6 Offenders who possess, make or supply articles for use in fraud intend their actions to lead to a fraud. Such offenders therefore have the highest level of culpability.[498] Whilst in many cases no financial harm will have been caused, in some cases, particularly where the 'article' is a list of credit card or bank account details, the victim(s) may have been inconvenienced despite not suffering any financial loss.[499]
7 There are three types of activity relating to articles for use in fraud: making or adapting, supplying or offering to supply and possession. The guideline does not distinguish between the first two categories, they carry the same maximum penalty and, depending on the sophistication and planning involved and the harm resulting from an offence, they may be equally serious.
8 The three offences in this group all involve an element of planning (whether by the offender or by another person). The planning of an offence has been identified by the Council as a factor indicating a higher level of culpability and the proposed starting points incorporate this aggravating factor.

---

[496] Legal Aid, Sentencing and Punishment of Offenders Act 2012 s 85(1) and (4) and Legal Aid, Sentencing and Punishment of Offenders Act 2012 (Commencement No 11) Order 2015 2015/504
[497] Fraud Act 2006 s 8
[498] See *Overarching Principles: Seriousness Guideline 2004*, www.banksr.com Guidelines tab para 1.7
[499] Where the article is a list of credit card or bank account details, the victims will need to cancel their cards and obtain new ones and/or change their bank accounts, *Overarching Principles: Seriousness Guideline 2004*, see www.banksr.com Guidelines tab

page 22 para 9 In relation to harm, the value of the fraud (either that intended by the offender where that can be ascertained, or that which was likely to be achieved) is not a determinant of seriousness for these offences in the way that it is for other offences of fraud. However, it is a factor that should be taken into account.

See also the COMPUTER AND COMMUNICATION NETWORK OFFENCES chapter.

265.17

Fraud, Bribery and Money Laundering Offences Guideline 2014, see www.banksr.com Other Matters Guidelines tab This section applies to Fraud Act 2006 s 6 and 7. In force 1 October 2014.

STEP ONE: Determining the offence category

page 14 The court should determine the offence category with reference to the tables below. In order to determine the category the court should assess culpability and harm.

Culpability

The level of culpability is determined by weighing up all the factors of the case to determine the offender's role and the extent to which the offending was planned and the sophistication with which it was carried out.

Culpability
Culpability A – High culpability
A leading role where offending is part of a group activity Involvement of others through pressure/influence Abuse of position of power or trust or responsibility Sophisticated nature of offence/significant planning Fraudulent activity conducted over sustained period of time Articles deliberately designed to target victims on basis of vulnerability
Culpability B – Medium culpability
Other cases where characteristics for Categories A or C are not present A significant role where offending is part of a group activity
Culpability C – Lesser culpability
Performed limited function under direction Involved through coercion, intimidation or exploitation Not motivated by personal gain Opportunistic 'one-off' offence; very little or no planning Limited awareness or understanding of the extent of fraudulent activity

Where there are characteristics present which fall under different levels of culpability, the court should balance these characteristics to reach a fair assessment of the offender's culpability.

Harm

page 14 This guideline refers to preparatory offences where no substantive fraud has been committed. The level of harm is determined by weighing up all the factors of the case to determine the harm that would be caused if the article(s) were used to commit a substantive offence.

Harm
Greater harm
Large number of articles created/supplied/in possession Article(s) have potential to facilitate fraudulent acts affecting large number of victims Article(s) have potential to facilitate fraudulent acts involving significant sums Use of third party identities Offender making considerable gain as result of the offence

Lesser harm
All other offences

265.18   *Magistrates' Court Sentencing Guideline*

Magistrates' Court Sentencing Guideline 2008 (as amended) p 335, see www.banksr. com Other Matters Guidelines tab The section on possession etc. of articles for fraud of the *Fraud, Bribery and Money Laundering Offences Guideline 2014* has been inserted, see www.banksr.com Other Matters Guidelines tab

265.19

STEP TWO: Starting point and category range

page 15 Having determined the category at step one, the court should use the appropriate starting point to reach a sentence within the category range in the table below. The starting point applies to all offenders irrespective of plea or previous convictions.
page 15 Fraud Act 2006 s 6

	Culpability		
Harm	**A**	**B**	**C**
Greater	**Starting point** 18 months' custody	**Starting point** 36 weeks' custody	**Starting point** High-level community order
	Category range 36 weeks' to 3 years' custody	**Category range** High-level community order to 2 years' custody	**Category range** Medium-level community order to 26 weeks' custody
Lesser	**Starting point** 26 weeks' custody	**Starting point** Medium-level community order	**Starting point** Band B fine
	Category range High-level community order to 18 months' custody	**Category range** Low-level community order to 26 weeks' custody	**Category range** Band A fine to medium-level community order

page 15 Fraud Act 2006 s 7

	Culpability		
Harm	**A**	**B**	**C**
Greater	**Starting point** 4 years 6 months' custody	**Starting point** 2 years 6 months' custody	**Starting point** 1 year's custody
	Category range 3 to 7 years' custody	**Category range** 18 months' to 5 years' custody	**Category range** High-level community order to 3 years' custody
Lesser	**Starting point** 2 years' custody	**Starting point** 36 weeks' custody	**Starting point** Medium-level community order
	Category range 26 weeks' to 4 years' custody	**Category range** Low-level community order to 2 years' custody	**Category range** Band C fine to 26 weeks' custody

For the meaning of a high-level, a medium-level and a low-level community order see **16.12-16.14** in Volume 1.

265.20   [Aggravating and mitigating factors]
page 16 The table below contains a non-exhaustive list of additional factual elements providing the context of the offence and factors relating to the offender.

Identify whether any combination of these or other relevant factors should result in an upward or downward adjustment from the sentence arrived at so far.

Consecutive sentences for multiple offences may be appropriate where large sums are involved.

Factors increasing seriousness
Statutory aggravating factors:
Previous convictions, having regard to a) the nature of the offence to which the conviction relates and its relevance to the current offence; and b) the time that has elapsed since the conviction
Offence committed whilst on bail
Other aggravating factors:
Steps taken to prevent the victim reporting or obtaining assistance and/or from assisting or supporting the prosecution
Attempts to conceal/dispose of evidence
Established evidence of community/wider impact
Failure to comply with current court orders
Offence committed on licence
Offences taken into consideration
Failure to respond to warnings about behaviour
Offences committed across borders
Blame wrongly placed on others
Factors reducing seriousness or reflecting personal mitigation
No previous convictions or no relevant/recent convictions
Remorse
Good character and/or exemplary conduct
Little or no prospect of success
Serious medical conditions requiring urgent, intensive or long-term treatment
Age and/or lack of maturity where it affects the responsibility of the offender
Lapse of time since apprehension where this does not arise from the conduct of the offender
Mental disorder or learning disability
Sole or primary carer for dependent relatives
Offender co-operated with investigation, made early admissions and/or voluntarily reported offending
Determination and/or demonstration of steps having been taken to address addiction or offending behaviour
Activity originally legitimate

For suggested approach to the guideline see **265.8**.

265.21   *Articles   Possessing, making or supplying articles for use in fraud   Pre-2014 guideline cases*
R v Burciu 2010 EWCA Crim 875 D pleaded early to theft (full credit). D and X placed a device on an ATM which retained three bank cards. D retrieved the cards and X used two of them to withdraw £530 in cash. £520 was recovered. D, aged 24, had no convictions. The pre-sentence report said D was unemployed, had expressed remorse and posed a low risk of reoffending. The basis of plea was that it was someone else's device and he would have given some of the money to the other man. X wasn't caught. The prison report said D was a good worker and a quiet and compliant prisoner. **4 months** not 8.

R v Graduiaru 2012 EWCA Crim 1312, 2013 1 Cr App R (S) 50 (p 282) D was convicted of possession of articles for use in fraud. He was arrested operating with a gang who had inserted a Lebanese loop device into an ATM machine. It was unclear whether D was a 'shoulder surfer', who would obtain PINs, or whether he had inserted the device. The device was basic in that it was designed to retain the cards as opposed to reading or photographing the PIN. The prosecution conceded that this case fell into the lower [category] of the guidelines. Held. There was no evidence that the gang was involved in more extensive fraud. However, this was a well-planned and executed operation. **8 months** not 12.

R v Strachinaru 2012 EWCA Crim 1612 D pleaded to fraud (×2) and possessing an article for use in fraud (6 months consecutive). Over a 4-4½ hour period, D and another carried out frauds at various ATMs. They made 11 attempts to withdraw money, with nine of those being successful. They obtained £2,750. They used 'transactional reversal fraud' where the machine is tampered with in order to obtain the money requested in the transaction, but the machine does not register the withdrawal and therefore the account is not debited. D had an MP3 player which contained a video demonstrating how to perform a transactional reversal fraud. The MP3 player had been partially modified in a manner associated with skimming frauds, although there was no evidence that it had been used on the night of these frauds. The MP3 player was seized from D's address, along with £9,000 in cash. The Judge described the outfit as a professional, skilful, criminal enterprise. D, aged 29, had been present in the UK since 2007 and had no convictions or cautions. Held. The nature and seriousness of the offences justify treating these offences as falling into a higher category than the amount stolen would indicate. The correct starting point was 12 months. With the plea, **8 months** making 14 months in all not 22.

R v Munteanu 2012 EWCA Crim 2221, 2013 1 Cr App R (S) 107 (p 555) D pleaded to possession of an article for use in fraud. V tried to use an ATM in High Holborn. She was unable to withdraw any cash and her card was retained by the machine. The machine displayed an 'Out of service' message. Two men had been intending to use the ATM after her. They observed two people approach the machine, remove items from it and then drive away. The police were called and the car was stopped nearby. A 'Lebanese loop' was found. D entered the UK from his native Romania in 2011. He had no regular employment since then and had previous convictions for theft and possession of an article for use in fraud (2011, arising out of the same incident). This was the same offence as the instant offence. D was aged 25. Held. The only aggravation was D's previous convictions. Our starting point is the guidance applicable to possession of 'articles intended for use in an extensive and skilfully planned fraud', which is indeed the appropriate guideline for cases of this character. Cases of this kind inherently fall to be sentenced at the top end of the recommended range, particularly where the item is used. Of its nature it is sophisticated and requires deliberate planning. The Judge was justified in starting far above the recommended range. This was deliberate reoffending with the same co-defendants as his previous convictions. **2 years** was severe but not manifestly excessive.

See also: *R v Curran* 2013 EWCA Crim 1477 (Plea to conspiracy to make an article for use in fraud. Created false identities and cloned others. False business offering non-existent jobs set up in order to acquire personal details. False documents created then used to open bank accounts. Accounts then used to enter credit agreements and electrical goods were obtained. Goods, including proceeds of burglaries, were advertised on eBay. Payments made into the false accounts and withdrawn from ATMs. £75-80,000 obtained. D played a supporting role, including using paperwork to open 14 false bank accounts. 84 previous offences including theft and fraud. Further offences since these offences. **3 years** not 3½.)

Old cases: *R v Kazi* 2010 EWCA Crim 2026 (**12 months**) *R v Pakiyanthur* 2010 EWCA Crim 2312 (**4 years**)

For a summary of the cases, see the 10th edition of this book.
Bank accounts, Letting others use your see the MONEY LAUNDERING ETC. chapter.

265.22   Banking and insurance fraud and obtaining credit through fraud   Pre-2014 guideline cases
R v Ndamba 2011 EWCA Crim 139 D pleaded to two counts of conspiracy to defraud. He was involved in a sophisticated conspiracy to steal and alter cheques from the Ministries. The cheques were altered to match bank cards which had also been stolen and taken from London to Birmingham. The cheques were then backed up by the bank cards in order to withdraw money, usually in the sum of £250-£350. There were five co-defendants who were categorised by the Judge as either 'droppers' (those who obtained the cash) or 'minders' (those who were handed the money after it was obtained). The fraud totalled £60,000. D was arrested with £1,600 in cash and a folder containing ten envelopes each with a name, address and an amount of money. There were also six bank cards each with a cheque matching the name borne on the card. D, aged 52 at appeal, had one recent conviction for a similar offence (conditional discharge). He had prostate cancer and his treatment would be delayed if he was sent to prison. The Judge said of D, "You were running back and forth between London…and Birmingham. You I regard as the most high up in the dock." It was argued that the Judge misconstrued the factual basis in relation to D's role. Held. The Judge may have overstated: a) D's role given that the prosecution accepted that his involvement was limited to one day, and b) the significance of the money and documentation found in his possession. In parity to M, **18 months** on each count concurrent, not 27 months.
R v Garcha 2012 EWCA Crim 177 D pleaded early to section 1 fraud. He ran a Post Office and grocer's. An audit showed a £95,000 shortfall in the PO accounts. D said the grocery side of the business had suffered. D offered to make up the shortfall but was unable to do so. D was aged 27 and of good character. It was suggested that the *Fraud Guideline 2009* recommended 12-18 months. The Judge thought the *Theft and Burglary in a Building other than a Dwelling Guideline 2008* was more appropriate but claimed to apply both guidelines. Held. The *Fraud Guideline* was the appropriate one. With the gross and repeated breaches of trust and the plea, **21 months** not 3 years.
R v Eason 2013 EWCA Crim 143 D pleaded (full credit) to transferring criminal property. He was employed by Halifax Bank of Scotland. He was promoted and eventually became temporary area business manager. As a result, he had full access to the banking system, including customers' accounts. Two of the bank's customers were his parents. He set up accounts in their names. The bank's rules prohibit staff from dealing with family members' accounts. He redirected their statements to his e-mail address. He increased the overdraft limit on the accounts and withdrew funds. He was interviewed after a colleague noticed suspicious activity on the accounts. He tendered his resignation that day but continued to have access to the accounts. For a further 12 months, he continued to withdraw funds. The total withdrawn was £93,300 in 471 transactions. His parents settled their claim against the bank for £72,801 and bore the remainder of the loss themselves. D explained that he was using a lot of cocaine at the time and spending money on clothes, social activities and a car. He was aged 25 at appeal and had no previous convictions. He accepted full responsibility. Held. The Judge applied the theft guidelines. The reality is that this offending neither fits neatly into the *Theft and Burglary in a Building other than a Dwelling Guideline 2008* nor the *Fraud Guideline 2009* Banking/insurance fraud section. There was abuse of a position of trust, both to his employers but also to his parents. His behaviour was persistent and the conduct persisted for 12 months after he resigned. Custody was inevitable. Starting at 3 years, **24 months** not 27 months.
Att-Gen's Ref Nos 7-8 of 2013 2013 EWCA Crim 709, 2014 1 Cr App R (S) 26 (p 140) K and W were convicted of two conspiracies to defraud. The first was against the Allied Irish Bank, AIB, and the second against the Bank of Scotland, BoS. K claimed he was a wealthy member of a Greek shipping family who wanted to diversify into property. The

AIB fraud was a property fraud relying on false documents. AIB advanced money for valuable properties in London with a 'reverse premium' which was in fact taken by the fraudsters. K was in overall control and W was the managing director of the controlling company. The loans for the properties included £18.8m, £47.5m, £12m and £152m. The total lent was £743m. The BoS fraud involved obtaining a money advance to convert a passenger ferry into a luxury yacht. False documents were produced and false representations made. The loss to BoS was €5.8m. Both were aged 44 at appeal. In 1995, K and W were convicted (in different names) of conspiracy to commit forgery and were given community service with unpaid work. The Judge considered the carelessness of the banks was no mitigation. In the AIB fraud the Judge declined to quantify the loss suffered or the gain to the fraudsters. He concluded that the AIB fraud was not the worst offence of its type. The Judge made the sentences concurrent because it was the same conduct. Held. We have no doubt that a consecutive sentence for the offence was required, subject to the principle of totality. For AIB, an 8-year starting point for K would properly reflect the probability no financial loss would be realised. For K, 7 and 4 years consecutive making **11 years**, not 7. For W, 5 and 3 years making **8 years**, not 5.

R v Iyer 2013 EWCA Crim 754 D pleaded (full credit) to false accounting and forgery (×2). He was a solicitor and later became a partner. Over a 12-year period, D submitted fictitious invoices from external suppliers to the accounts department in his firm. The invoices totalled about £2.8m. D was in possession of a blank invoice document in the name of a company which had gone into administration in the 1990s. The firm had done some work on that administration under D's direction. Most invoices had been expensed to, and paid by, clients of the firm, with about £200,000 paid for by the firm itself. The money had been spent on an extravagant lifestyle including a yacht, expensive cars and properties. D admitted the offences when challenged by the firm. D paid back about £2.15m as a result of a civil action by the firm. The forgery offences were unconnected and related to false documents created by D in support of an application that he be honoured with an OBE. The application claimed he had written a book and donated the proceeds to Cancer Research. D was aged 46. He had no convictions and showed remorse. He had written letters of apology to the affected clients. Held. The offending occurred over a lengthy period and the amount stolen was very considerable. There was a significant amount recovered but there remained a considerable loss outstanding. The offending was well planned, determined and was used to fund high living. There was an obvious profound breach of trust of the firm at which he was a partner, but also in relation to a number of the firm's clients. However, D made immediate admissions followed by early guilty pleas and he co-operated in the recovery of a very substantial amount of the money. D had been struck off as a solicitor and had become bankrupt, which led to the breakdown of his marriage. 6 years after a trial would adequately reflect the aggravation and mitigation. With the plea, **4 years 8 months** was correct.

R v Adetukasi 2013 EWCA Crim 851, 2014 1 Cr App R (S) 11 (p 52) D pleaded (20% credit) to acquiring criminal property. Over a three- or four-day period, persons purporting to be the owners of three different bank accounts telephoned the banks and answered the security questions correctly. They then asked for money to be transferred to a Co-op bank account belonging to D. D removed the bulk of that money within a short period of time and was said to have accounted for it to the principal fraudster. D's basis of plea accepted that £20,657 had come into his account. He suspected that the money was the benefit of criminal conduct of another. He did not carry out the transactions from others' accounts and did not assume anyone's identity. The single Judge regarded D's role as extremely important. D, aged 48, had a conviction from 1993 for importing class A drugs (7 years). Held. The Judge took too high a starting point. After a trial, **20 months** was appropriate, so with the plea, **16 months**, not 2 years.

Note: The two cases above were not indicted as a fraud but they could have been. Ed.

R v Malik 2013 EWCA Crim 2209 D pleaded at the PCMH to fraud. He was employed by Lloyds Bank as a part of the 'mass affluent team'. The team's responsibility concerned payment instruction requests from customers. Customers would send an e-mail to the team with an attached form which they had signed. D was responsible for administering the bulk of those transactions and in a three-week period he created a false payment instruction for £18,300 from a customer's account. D signed the authorisation form in the name of one of his colleagues. The transaction was queried and an investigation mounted. D's colleague was interviewed during the internal investigation and denied he was responsible. When D was interviewed, he admitted that he had forged his colleague's signature. The matter was reported to the police and D gave a no comment interview, stating that he was assisting with the internal investigation. D was aged 41 at appeal and of previous good character. He lost his job as a result of the offence. Held. The banking section of the *Fraud Guideline 2009* applied and this fell at the top of the bracket. The two aggravating features were the clear breach of trust and that the conduct caused an innocent colleague to fall under suspicion. The appropriate sentence would have been in excess of 6 months after a trial. With a reduction for the plea,[500] **18 weeks** not 9 months.

R v Brown 2014 EWCA Crim 695 D was convicted of possession of articles for use in fraud and securing unauthorised access to computer material with intent (×2). D possessed stolen bank and credit card details and accessed 83 accounts over a matter of days. He would change the details online and impersonate account holders in order to obtain a new card and PIN. Unsuccessful attempts in October 2011 involved £6,350. The loss sustained on the 83 accounts between August 2010 and October 2011 was almost £25,000. The potential loss was almost £500,000 (based on the maximum credit limits on the accounts) but the prosecution agreed that the potential loss was in fact just over £200,000. D's laptop contained software whereby he had access to a number of websites which conducted a trade in stolen credit cards. D was born in Zambia and had one conviction for a public order offence. The pre-sentence report noted that D committed the offences due to his financial situation. Held. The figure of £200,000 was the potential loss, not the established intended loss. The potential loss is not the determining means by which the fraud should be valued. The strongest evidence of intended loss was the figure of £6,350, although that must be aggravated by the value of the potential loss. There was no actual loss caused to Barclaycard customers as a result of D accessing the accounts (the computer counts) and the offending occurred over a relatively short period. The correct sentence was 18 months on the possession count, and 2 years and 18 months concurrent on the computer counts. **2 years** not 3.

See also:*R v Allmand* 2011 EWCA Crim 1530 (Early plea to nine counts of fraud. Over 18 months bank employee transferred £46,000 of interest from accounts he managed to family and friends' accounts then to his account. Breach of trust. Good character. **40 months concurrent**, not 4½ years.)

R v Shepherd 2012 EWCA Crim 1523 (Plea. Full credit. Conspiracy to use false instruments and conspiracy to commit fraud by false representation. Director of company. Made enquiries with a bank in Guernsey. Obtained letters and created false letters with letterheads purporting to be affirmations from the bank that the company had over £76m in deposits. Obtained £90,000 and €20m on that basis. Main organiser and beneficiary. Sophisticated fraud. Aged 51. Six previous convictions for dishonesty. Serious escalation in offending. Starting at 8 years. With the plea, **5 years 4 months**. Because of a non-qualifying curfew, **5 years** not 6 years 3 months.)

Old cases: *R v Siaw* 2010 EWCA Crim 395 (**2 years** and **2 years consecutive**) *R v Yates* 2010 EWCA Crim 1028, 2011 1 Cr App R (S) 15 (p 112) (**2½ years**) *R v Tommis* 2010 EWCA Crim 2262 (**9 months**)

For a summary of the first and the last cases, see the 10th edition of this book.

See also the *Identity fraud* para at **265.37** and the *Mortgage fraud* para at **265.44**.

---

[500] The judgment does not state the exact starting point nor the discount for the plea, but the figures indicate a plea discount of more than 25% and a starting point of between 6 and 7 months. Ed.

Benefit fraud see the **BENEFIT FRAUD** chapter.
Betting frauds see the **CORRUPTION/MISFEASANCE IN A PUBLIC OFFICE/BRIBERY** *Accepting bribes Sportsmen and betting frauds* para at **228.4**.

265.23   Breach of trust frauds
R v Chaytor 2011 EWCA Crim 929 LCJ D pleaded (25% credit) to three counts of false accounting. As an MP, on 13 occasions he dishonestly submitted false claims for expenses. The total was just short of £23,000, and D received just over £18,000. D had submitted falsified tenancy agreements to facilitate the claims. He had repaid a little more than was dishonestly claimed. D, aged 61 at appeal, was of good character and had a large number of references. Held. This sad fall from grace was entirely self-inflicted. It was surprising that D made dishonest claims as much of the money claimed could have been recovered by legitimate means, because it was no easier to make a dishonest claim than an honest one. The claims were bogus in their entirety. This was a grave breach of trust. **18 months** was not manifestly excessive.
R v Ekajeh and Others 2012 EWCA Crim 3125, 2013 2 Cr App R (S) 44 (p 291) E, K and F were convicted of conspiracy to defraud. All three were employed by the DWP as fortnightly job review clerks at different job centres. E and K had been employed for about ten years, F was employed for a much shorter period. Each was responsible for signing on customers who were claiming Jobseeker's Allowance and for carrying out job searches and reviews on their behalf. Each therefore had access to the DWP databases which stored vast amounts of personal data including names and addresses, dates of birth and NI numbers. K, E and F, and five others, were involved in a lengthy and sophisticated fraud in which large numbers of false benefits claims were submitted using the identities and details which K, E and F illegally accessed from the DWP database for that purpose. Over a period of almost two years, 1,562 false claims were made, claiming about £720,000. Of that sum, £107,000 worth of claims were successful and were paid to the conspirators. The sums claimed under the SSMG scheme for parents with newborn babies were paid into accounts set up by the conspirators, a number of which had been set up in the names of the stolen identities from the DWP database. E and F were also convicted of another count involving falsely claiming tax credits. This occurred over a period of 4½ years during which 205 claims were made for sums totalling just under £900,000. £170,000 was paid out. This was known as the tax credit fraud. E was also convicted of a different fraud. He accessed the DWP database and amended customers' genuine bank details so that payments would be made into the accounts controlled by the conspirators. This was known as the JSA fraud. E, aged 49 at appeal, was married with four young children and had no convictions. F was aged 35 at appeal and had seven convictions, the last of which was committed whilst on bail for these offences. One of his convictions involved fraudulent representation for gain. K was aged 48 at appeal. He had no convictions other than for driving matters in 2006. Held. The aggravating factors included: a) the gross breach of trust, E's breach of trust was more serious as he was sometimes entrusted with carrying out more senior roles as a deputy manager, b) the gross breach of trust occurred on a large number of occasions over a prolonged period of time, c) there were multiple frauds and high-value sums were targeted, d) the targeted money was public money intended for the neediest in society, e) the victims were not only HMRC and the DWP but also those who had had their identities stolen, f) their actions undermine public confidence in the protection of personal data and the public bodies to which such data is entrusted. For E, 5 years on the SSMG fraud, 5 years on the tax credit fraud, consecutive, and 12 months concurrent on the JSA fraud. The total sentence of **10 years** for E was not in error. E played a leading role and the aggravating features were plain. There was nothing wrong with consecutive sentences and the Judge could have made the sentence for the JSA fraud consecutive also. For F, there needed to be a reduction to reflect i) the short period for which F was involved (6 months) and ii) the difference in scale of accessing information between E and F. Because of totality and parity with E, 3½ years for the SSMG fraud would be untouched, but 3 years not 4 for

the tax fraud, consecutive. Total sentence for F, **6½** years, not 7½. K's involvement was limited and the vast majority of his illegal access of the DWP database occurred on three days, giving rise to 27 claims totalling £13,500. He was only involved in the SSMG fraud. K stopped committing the fraud, not because he was caught but of his own volition. **4½ years** not 5½.

R v Waqanika 2014 EWCA Crim 902 D pleaded to fraud by abuse of position. He was the manager of a company that was engaged to erect and move scenery at the Barbican theatre. D worked there with his four ultimate victims. D was responsible for obtaining payment for their services and for distributing it among them. Each worker received a daily rate that was paid on a monthly basis. When arranging payment for the services, D asked for the sums to be paid into the account of one worker. He'd then ask that worker to withdraw the money overpaid. For the first three months, D paid the workers in accordance with his obligations. There were no outstanding monies. Following a night out, D fell out badly with his co-workers. At the end of the next month, rather than distribute the cash, £6,815, he squandered it. He [at some time] went to the police and made full admissions in interview. The Judge noted that there was evidence that this had been committed between May and August and rejected that it was 'a spur of the moment thing'. D had previous convictions largely related to driving matters. Subsequent to the instant offence, he received a custodial sentence for breach of an earlier community order. Held. The Judge was wrong to sentence this as multiple transactions and/or as a fraud perpetrated over a period of months. The most relevant guidelines would appear to be a single fraudulent transaction confidence fraud involving the targeting of a vulnerable victim. The Judge correctly identified the aggravating features including the large sum of money and that D's actions amounted to an abuse of trust as he was their manager. Due to their reliance on D's integrity, they were to be regarded as vulnerable. Starting at 24 weeks was appropriate. With full credit for the plea, **16 weeks**, not 9 months.

Note: There is no mention in the judgment about breach of trust but the offence was committed in breach of trust. Ed.

R v Rouse 2014 EWCA Crim 1128 D pleaded to fraud (×4) and theft. He was employed as a deputy manager at a care home providing accommodation for vulnerable adults at two locations. All the residents suffered from learning difficulties. D had access to debit and credit cards belonging to the residents and also to other account information which allowed him to withdraw money from their accounts and to use their credit cards. D used three residents' cards to withdraw money from ATMs for his own purposes. He also used their credit cards to pay personal bills. The total loss was £8,278. A fourth resident had been given £600 to pay into his account. D took the money and kept it. D was dismissed after the matters came to light. He then obtained employment with a company responsible for re-stocking vending machines and collecting the money. D stole £4,863 there. Held. A breach of trust sentence was appropriate. This was a series of offences against a group of residents in the care of D's one employer. The fact that the form of the fraud was slightly different or that it took place in a different home does not...justify such separate treatment [so as to warrant a consecutive 12-month sentence]. The sentence imposed by the Judge was based on a starting point more than double that for an offence involving £10,000 and 50% more than the top of the range for offences of this sort. To reflect the aggravation of the multiple victims and the different ways of perpetrating the thefts, the starting point would be raised to 3 years. With full credit, 2 years was appropriate for the care home offences. In the context of the overall offending, 6 months could not be criticised, so with full credit **2½ years** not 3½.

R v Williams 2014 EWCA Crim 1356 D pleaded (20% credit) to fraud. He falsely told his family and friends that he had terminal cancer. He put that information up on Facebook and opened a 'giving page' to raise money. His purported progress was uploaded. When his family became suspicious, he produced a forged latter from a hospital to perpetuate the lies. £840 was raised and D kept £99.50. He was aged 28. A psychiatric report recorded a degree of instability in D's relationships and employment. The Judge said the offence was contemptible. The defence on appeal said that the sentence failed to take into account D's good character and the value was less than £100, so the sentence should have been suspended. Held. An immediate custodial sentence was inevitable. **6 months** was not manifestly excessive.

R v McClue 2010 EWCA Crim 311 D pleaded to fraud by misrepresentation. D was a deputy manager at a betting shop and was involved in a scheme where she put £285,470 worth of fraudulent transactions on the system. D stood to gain £28,000 but the transactions were discovered, so the betting shop suffered no loss. The money was going to support her child and her sister's child. D was a single mother who had always been in work. D, aged 28, made admissions in interview and had no convictions. The pre-sentence report said D was remorseful and that she accepted full responsibility. Held. We take into account the disastrous consequence for D's child. Because of mitigation, **8 months** not 18 months. Others should not assume they would receive the same leniency. See also: *R v Russell* 2011 EWCA Crim 2528 (Pleas to obtaining property (×2) and forgery (×2). Responsible for Y's financial affairs. Y received royalties, bequeathed to her in a will by X. Upon Y's death, the royalties were to pass to the trustee of X's estate. D did not notify anyone that Y had died. Between 1995 and 2006, she received £30,000 (£45,000 with inflation). Unpleasantly dishonest. Breach of trust. Aged 49 and of good character. **12 months** not 15.)

Old cases: *R v Chase* 2010 EWCA Crim 1630 (**2½ years**) *R v Sammons* 2010 EWCA Crim 2548 (**6 months**)

For a summary of these cases, see the 10th edition of this book.

Post-2014 guideline frauds

R v E 2015 EWCA Crim 445 D was convicted of a section 3 fraud. He was the father of V, aged 8, who suffered from a rare terminal illness that accelerates ageing. She was not expected to live beyond the age of 12 or 13. A motorcycle club devoted their annual fundraising efforts to her so she could go to America and swim with dolphins. £3,500 was raised and given to D. He spent the money on himself. When questioned, he lied. The motorcycle club said they no longer collected for individuals. D was aged 41 with 19 court appearances for 50 offences including dishonesty. In 1989, he was given 18 months detention for child cruelty. In 1988 and 1989, he was given community orders for theft from an employer. In 1989, he received 21 months for a dwelling burglary and concurrent sentences for obtaining by deception and another theft from an employer. In 2000, he was given a short prison sentence for various dishonesty offences. In 2005, a community order was given for a firearm offence and handling. A charity attested to his work for his daughter. The Judge said D had greatly abused the members of the motorcycle club. Further, D had blighted those who needed the club's charity and those who give or raise money for charity. The actual loss did not give significant assistance to him. Held. D had betrayed V, the givers and damaged the confidence of those involved in charity. **3 years** allowed for D's family mitigation.

R v Ousey 2015 EWCA Crim 984 D pleaded (full credit) to fraud at the Magistrates' Court. For 23 years he was employed by a group of companies and he became Financial Director and then Chief Financial Officer. Over four years, he submitted 11 bogus invoices worth about £227,000. He paid the money into a bank controlled by himself. He was able to buy two properties in Portugal. It was also discovered that he had paid himself substantial benefits to which he was not entitled. The group issued civil proceedings for that loss. He settled with them by paying about £1.4m to them, which included him giving up his pension rights and paying back the £227,000 as well. D helped in the investigation and paid money for that. D also paid the money before the criminal proceedings were started. D was aged 51 and of good character. He was remorseful and had a very favourable prison report. The Judge put it as Category 2A and started at 5 years as that was the guideline figure. Held. There was very substantial mitigation available. There were no aggravating factors. We start at 4 years, so with the plea **32 months**.

See also: *R v Choi* 2015 EWCA Crim 1089, 2 Cr App R (S) 55 (p 396) (Early plea to dishonestly making false representation. Former school finance officer able to access funds. Took £40,000 but never spent it. Good character. High culpability, but **18 months** not 2 years.)

265.24   *Charging for work that is not necessary or not done*
R v Baker 2011 EWCA Crim 150 D was convicted of two counts of obtaining property by deception[501] and failure to surrender to bail (1 year consecutive). S was the leader of a team of rogue builders who defrauded householders in the south-east of England by dishonestly charging for work which was not carried out, or carrying out incompetent or unnecessary work. Between January 2003 and September 2007 about 43 householders were defrauded and around £800,000 was obtained. Matters came to light when police were alerted after bank staff became suspicious when a victim, who police deemed was a vulnerable adult, sought to withdraw large sums of money on repeated occasions. D was present when extracting money from this particular victim. The prosecution proceeded on the basis that whilst D was only involved in February and March 2006, he was a trusted subordinate of S. S received 7½ years on a plea. D, aged 47, had significant previous convictions including robbery (7 years) and obtaining money by deception (similar offence, 87-year-old, 4 years). Held. This was on any view a bad case of its type. We ask ourselves whether a difference of only 18 months between S and D was too little. We think that it was. **6 years** not 8½. The consecutive sentence for failing to surrender remains.

Att-Gen's Ref Nos 21-23 of 2014 2014 EWCA Crim 1247 D and his two sons, M and B, pleaded to conspiracy to defraud, contempt of court and converting criminal property. The sentence for the contempt was concurrent and not challenged. D set up a company as a vehicle to defraud the elderly and vulnerable. Over 8 years, D defrauded five principal victims and others. V1, aged 62, had mobility and speech difficulties. The team did numerous pieces of work for her which was not fit for purpose. One piece of work was not required and made the roof worse. V1 was charged nearly £59,000. It should have cost £28,000. D also persuaded him to invest nearly £178,000 on land with false promises about planning. V1 lost the lot. In all, V1 lost over £244,000. V2, aged 92, suffered from dementia. She was confused and forgetful. Cheques were missing from her cheque book. The cheque stubs were blank or were without a final '0' which was on the cheque. Shoddy work was done and V2 lost over £18,500. V3, aged 93, and V4, aged 86, lived together. Both had health problems. Shoddy work was done on their two homes and they lost over £26,600. V5, aged 76, was regularly visited by nurses. He gave a large amount of cash and cheques worth at least £12,200 for poor work. Trading Standards had numerous complaints about the company overcharging mostly aged and vulnerable victims. V6 obtained a County Count judgment for shoddy work and nearly £4,000 was ordered to be paid. It never was. The three were arrested and given restraining orders which they breached by committing a similar fraud on a 73-year-old. She lost £2,300 and had to spend £1,050 to repair the damage to her house. This offence became a TIC. The total loss was over £338,000. D and M had no relevant convictions. B had no convictions. D and M were organisers. B was an assistant. M was sentenced on the basis of a £63,000 loss. He relied on 30 satisfied customers. B, aged 24, said he accepted directions from his father and his involvement was a £40,000 loss. Held. It was mean and carefully thought out. For D, we start at 9 years, with ⅙ credit **7½ years** not 5. For M, we start at 6 years, so with full credit, **4 years** not 2½. For B, we start generously at 5 years. His sentence of 12 months was unduly lenient but because of a GP's letter and a return to custody we do not alter it.

---

[501] This must be a typo. Perhaps he pleaded to some offence under Fraud Act 2006. Ed.

See also: *R v Field and Williams* 2011 EWCA Crim 1753, 2012 1 Cr App R (S) 69 (p 393) (Pleas to conspiracy to defraud. Targeted elderly and infirm individuals for home improvement. Total fraud £622,000. W involved for 2½ years concerning over £61,000, F, for a significantly shorter period, concerning £16,000 and 15 victims. Many victims repeatedly targeted. For W, full credit. **8 years** was severe but not manifestly excessive. For F, reduced credit, **4½ years** not 6.)

Att-Gen's Ref Nos 41-45 of 2011 2011 EWCA Crim 2174, 2012 1 Cr App R (S) 97 (p 587) (Pleas (25%) to conspiracy to defraud. Well-organised and nationwide confidence fraud, including threats. 29 victims. Related to building work not necessary or not done. Targeted and re-targeted elderly. £140,528 obtained and a further £45,090 sought. All defendants had previous convictions for dishonesty. **6 years** not 4 (13 victims) and **4 years 8 months** not 3 years 4 months (7 victims).)

R v Higgins and Others 2011 EWCA Crim 2246, 2012 1 Cr App R (S) 101 (p 613) (Convicted of conspiracy to defraud. Ran two companies who searched for building applications made to councils and made unsolicited offers to conduct building work. Not one of 50 projects was completed. False names were used. Threats to sue. Many customers paid more than the work completed was worth. Around £½m obtained. For the organiser, **8 years**, for two others, **7 years** and **6 years**.)

Old cases: *R v Frankham and Stevens* 2010 EWCA Crim 1861, 2011 1 Cr App R (S) 80 (p 487) (**2 years**) For more old cases, see the 9th edition of this book.

Post-2014 guideline cases

R v Hamilton 2015 EWCA Crim 278 D pleaded (full credit) to engaging in a commercial practice contravening the requirement of due diligence contrary to Consumer Protection from Unfair Trading Regulations 2008 2008/1277. V1 and V2, a couple aged 84 and 68 respectively, wanted a dividing wall in their house. D, describing himself as a builder and competent bricklayer, quoted them £800, a figure that was subsequently raised to £2,000. He asked for £500 on account and then a further £800, on top of the £2,000, and all was paid. A surveyor, asked by V2 to inspect D's work, concluded that two lintels were inadequate and badly inserted and that D's bricklaying was poor. The estimated cost of properly done work was £1,200 but it would cost £2,600 to put D's mistakes right. D was aged 28 on appeal with low-level public order convictions but he asserted he had done a good job. Held. Although a custodial sentence was justified, it would have been appropriate to suspend it. **12 weeks suspended for 1 year**, not immediate.

R v Reza 2015 EWCA Crim 2062 D changed his plea[502] to conspiracy to defraud and seven other offences (not revealed but fraud-related). He was deaf and assisted in training other deaf people on courses that were set up and paid for by the Department for Work and Pensions. To start with D submitted genuine invoices and then he submitted false invoices. Between 2008 and 2011, D established six sham companies with family members as directors. He recruited his wife and six other deaf people and pretended they were employed by him. They were given cover stories and they signed false invoices. Over four and a half years, he obtained about £800,000 of which more than £743,000 was overpayment. The money was laundered through accounts in Canada, the United Arab Emirates and the UK. The proceeds were spent on investment flats, jewellery, bonds and high-value insurance policies. D made dishonest claims for housing benefit (just under £87,000 overpaid) and council tax (nearly £12,000 overpaid) between 2002 and 2010. There were overpaid student loans to D's son and daughter (about £3,000 overpaid to each) and an overpaid National Health bursary of about £5,500 paid to D's son. These were procured by false statements about the family's income. D was aged 52 with only a battery conviction in 2012. Held. Consecutive sentences were justified, but **7½ years** in all not 9.

Charity offences see the **FRAUD AND FINANCIAL SERVICES OFFENCES** *Confidence frauds* paras at **265.28**.

---

[502] How late the plea was is not revealed.

Cheque frauds see the IDENTITY FRAUDS para at **265.37**
Complex fraud, Plea discussions in Guidelines see para **265.11**.

265.25   City frauds   Judicial guidance
R v Feld 1999 1 Cr App R (S) 1 LCJ As well as the guidelines in *R v Barrick* 1985 7 Cr
App R (S) 142 (now replaced by a Sentencing Guidelines Council Guideline for Breach
of Trust Theft) the following are relevant considerations: 1 The amount involved and the
manner in which the fraud is carried out. 2 The period over which the fraud is carried out
and the degree of persistence with which it is carried out. 3 The position of the accused
within the company and the measure of control over it. 4 Any abuse of trust which is
revealed. 5 The consequences of the fraud. 6 The effect on public confidence in the City
and the integrity of commercial life. 7 The loss to the small investors, which will
aggravate the fraud. 8 The personal benefit derived by the defendant. 9 The plea. 10 The
age and character of the defendant. It is vitally important if confidence in the City is to
be maintained [that] documents sent out in support of rights issues should be honest and
complete.
Note: This guidance must be read with the new fraud guideline taking precedence. Ed.
R v Hayes 2015 EWCA Crim 1944 LCJ D was convicted on eight counts of conspiracy
to defraud. He manipulated the London Interbank Offered Rate (LIBOR) in order to
advance his trading interests, the profits of the bank for which he worked and indirectly
his bonuses and his status, to the disadvantage of the counterparties to the trades. The
Judge considered that it was hard to overstate the seriousness of the appellant's conduct
and said: "High standards of probity are to be expected of those who operate in the
banking system. This case has shown the absence of that integrity that ought to
characterise banking. The reputation of LIBOR is important to this city and to the
banking industry. Probity and honesty are essential [in that area]." Held. The Judge
correctly identified all the relevant factors. Those who act dishonestly in these markets
must receive severe sentences to deter others from criminality that is often hard to detect
and has such a damaging effect not only on the markets, but more broadly on the general
prosperity of the state. However, conduct of this type will result in severe sentences
which, depending on the circumstances, may be significantly greater than the present
total sentence (11 years).
For more details see **265.26**.

265.26   City frauds   Post-guideline case
R v Hayes 2015 EWCA Crim 1944 LCJ D was convicted on eight counts of conspiracy
to defraud. Between 2006 and 2010 D, together with others, agreed to manipulate Yen
LIBOR in order to advance his trading interests, the profits of the bank for which he
worked and indirectly his bonuses and his status, to the disadvantage of the counterparties to the trades. The separate counts related to employment with different banks. He
conspired with employees of other banks and inter-dealer brokers in the fixing of the
rate. It was not possible to estimate the loss to the counterparties. D was aged about 27
when he started the fraud and was now aged 36. He was of good character and married
with a young child. He had been diagnosed with Asperger's syndrome which two
doctors assessed as mild (another said it was very mild). In 2006, his pay was £40,726
(including a bonus of £11,983). By 2009, his pay was £409,821 (including a bonus of
112,911). In December 2009, D was paid £1.96m when he joined Citibank, and his pay
in the next 9 months was £1.54m (including a bonus of £943,225). Held. The Judge
correctly set out D's high level of culpability, the serious harm and correctly identified
all the relevant factors. The conspiracy was over a very substantial period of time. D was
a trader and not a manager, whose conduct was condoned, if not encouraged, by his
immediate managers. Consecutive sentences were appropriate. A deterrent element was
plainly required. However, with his age, his non-managerial position in the two banks,
and his mild Asperger's condition, **11 years** not 14 years.
For the details of the judicial guidance in this case, see **265.25**.

265.27   *Computer fraud*

Fraud Guideline 2009, see www.banksr.com Other Matters Guidelines tab For first-time offenders aged 18+ who were convicted after a trial.

Note: Although the *Fraud Guideline 2009* has been replaced, this information may be helpful. The information seems as relevant now as it was in 2009. For the sentencing guideline that would normally apply, see **265.3**. Ed.

page 21 para 3 'Articles' will include any electronic programs or data stored electronically.[503] Examples of articles for use in frauds include false fronts for cash machines, computer programs for generating credit card numbers, lists of credit card or bank account details, 'sucker lists' and draft letters or e-mails for use in advance fee frauds.

para 4 As lists of credit card and bank account details constitute 'articles', the making of such lists through certain electronic programs, which contravenes Fraud Act 2006 s 1, is also criminalised by section 7 of the same Act. The [Sentencing Guidelines] Council considers that carrying out the following activities should be treated as making articles for use in fraud and sentenced using this guideline, regardless of whether the offence is charged under section 1 or section 7:

Phishing Where an offender sends an e-mail purporting to come from a financial institution, which asks victims to follow a hyperlink to a (false) website and induces them to enter their card or account details (which may include their PIN),

Vishing Where an offender uses an automated telephone system, purporting to be the telephone system of a financial institution, to induce victims to disclose their card or account details (which may include their PIN),

Pharming Where victims intend to visit a financial institution's website but are redirected to the offender's website (which purports to be the financial institution's website) and induced to enter their card or account details (which may include their PIN), and

Use of a 'Trojan' Where an offender installs a virus on victims' computers (often a 'keystroke logger', which captures all of the keystrokes entered into a computer keyboard) in order to gain access to their card or account details. Often the offender will send an e-mail inducing victims to visit a website, where the virus is automatically downloaded onto their computer.

5 Making, adapting, supplying or offering to supply computer programs, e-mails or websites for the above activities amounts to an offence under section 7 of the Fraud Act 2006.

6 Offenders who possess, make or supply articles for use in fraud intend their actions to lead to a fraud. Such offenders therefore have the highest level of culpability.[504] Whilst in many cases no financial harm will have been caused, in some cases, particularly where the 'article' is a list of credit card or bank account details, the victim(s) may have been inconvenienced despite not suffering any financial loss.[505]

7 There are three types of activity relating to articles for use in fraud: making or adapting, supplying or offering to supply and possession. The guideline does not distinguish between the first two categories, they carry the same maximum penalty and, depending on the sophistication and planning involved and the harm resulting from an offence, they may be equally serious.

8 The three offences in this group all involve an element of planning (whether by the offender or by another person). The planning of an offence has been identified by the Council as a factor indicating a higher level of culpability and the proposed starting points incorporate this aggravating factor.

---

[503] Fraud Act 2006 s 8

[504] See *Overarching Principles: Seriousness Guideline 2004*, at www.banksr.com Guidelines tab para 1.7

[505] Where the article is a list of credit card or bank account details, the victims will need to cancel their cards and obtain new ones and/or change their bank accounts, *Overarching Principles: Seriousness Guideline 2004*, see www.banksr.com Guidelines tab

page 22 para 9 In relation to harm, the value of the fraud (either that intended by the offender where that can be ascertained, or that which was likely to be achieved) is not a determinant of seriousness for these offences in the way that it is for other offences of fraud. However, it is a factor that should be taken into account.

See also the **COMPUTER AND COMMUNICATION NETWORK OFFENCES** chapter.

265.28   *Confidence frauds*   *Pre-2014 guideline cases*   *Loss less than £100,000*

R v Clugston 2012 EWCA Crim 98 D pleaded early to six frauds and asked for 25 similar offences to be TIC'd. He would enter business premises claiming to have champagne to sell, left over from a reception. Victims would hand him money, expecting him to return with the champagne. He left with the money and would not return. This occurred on 31 occasions, with £19,500 being obtained. The TICs were possible because of his help. D, aged 65 at appeal, was a professional conman with offences dating back 55 years. In 2008 he received 3 years for similar fraud offending. Held. D had an appalling record. With the plea, **4 years** not 5 was appropriate.

Note: For his 2005 case where his sentence for similar offences was reduced from 6 years to 4, see para **189.25** in the 6th edition of this book.

R v Moonesamy 2013 EWCA Crim 434 D pleaded to eight frauds. D was a professional ballet dancer. He contacted three local dance schools and explained that he had been authorised to organise a dance routine to form part of the closing ceremony for the 2012 Olympic Games. The dance school principals expressed an interest and D held auditions. He selected 25 students from each school aged between 8 and 18, 20 of whom were to be participants, with five reserves. He had the children measured for costumes and discussed travel arrangements with them. Those selected had to agree to a long list of conditions and each student or parents of each student had to pay a fee of £60 to the dance schools, and each school paid D £625. He received £1,875. Rehearsals were held over a period of four months. Halls were rented by the schools for those rehearsals, at some expense. Publicity took place, including an appearance on Blue Peter, on local radio and in newspapers. Significant sacrifices were made including one child, who suffered from a medical condition, who rescheduled her operation in order to participate in the dance performance. The result was that she had to defer her entry to sixth form for 12 months. Another child was a member of the English equestrian vaulting squad. An event clashed with one dance rehearsal and D told the child that she would lose her place in the team if she missed a rehearsal. The child withdrew from the equestrian team. D also contacted a number of people and organisations to obtain funding and free or discounted merchandise. He offered them free tickets to a champagne reception in a private box at the closing ceremony. A Birmingham clothing company agreed to provide £10-12,000 worth of clothing for a discounted price of £3,600. He also sought funding from the local council and they were in the process of authorising £2,000 for that purpose. Some companies suffered a financial loss but more significant was the time they wasted dealing with D. When arrested, D claimed he had hoped for authorisation from the Olympic Committee and that his contact in the Olympic organisation team had let him down. D was aged 36 at appeal and of good character. A report produced at the request of the single Judge revealed that D had failed to accept full responsibility for the offences. Three counts represented deception on the children and parents. Five counts concerned attempts to obtain funding and free or discounted merchandise. Held. This case is outside the normal run of confidence fraud cases. The effect on these children and their families is described as disappointment, but that is a serious understatement. **2 years** was a proper sentence.

R v Williams 2014 EWCA Crim 1356 D pleaded (20% credit) to fraud. He falsely told his family and friends that he had terminal cancer. He put that information up on Facebook and opened a 'giving page' to raise money. His purported progress was uploaded. When his family became suspicious, he produced a forged latter from a hospital to perpetuate the lies. £840 was raised and D kept £99.50. He was aged 28. A psychiatric report recorded a degree of instability in D's relationships and employment.

The Judge said the offence was contemptible. The defence on appeal said that failed to take into account D's good character and the value was less than £100, so the sentence should have been suspended. Held. An immediate custodial sentence was inevitable. **6 months** was not manifestly excessive.

See also: *R v Harris* 2011 EWCA Crim 3348 (Plea to four frauds. Obtained sums of money from elderly or disabled victims by concocting stories about needing urgent cash. These included needing the bus fare to visit his ill sister in hospital. Total obtained a little under £60.[506] Caused victims to feel scared and vulnerable. Very mean offending which took advantage of their generosity. Some degree of planning. Targeted the vulnerable. Heroin addiction reason for offending. Bad record including burglary and violence. Two TICs. **12 months** not manifestly excessive.)

R v Cooper 2012 EWCA Crim 162, 2 Cr App R (S) 57 (p 344) (Late plea to confidence fraud. With another, claimed 77-year-old victim's drains were damaged. Total claimed £29,200. Total loss £10,000. Fraud stopped before all cheques could be cashed. Deliberately targeted vulnerable man. No work was necessary on victim's property. Previous conviction for conspiracy to defraud in 2006 (total loss then was £300,000). Committed whilst on licence for previous fraud. **6 years after a trial**, so **5½ years** was not manifestly excessive.)

R v McCrae and Others 2012 EWCA Crim 976, 2013 1 Cr App R (S) 1 (p 1) (Plea to conspiracy to defraud. Plots of land sold to vulnerable investors. Lies told about planning hopes. 26 losers. £87,000 obtained. **2 years** for two defendants and 18 months for other defendant upheld.)

Old cases: *R v Clatworthy* 2010 EWCA Crim 1073 (**2½ years**) *R v Aquino and Mejia* 2010 EWCA Crim 3081 (**8 months**) For a summary of the last case, see the 10th edition of this book.

For rogue builders etc. see the ***Charging for work that is not necessary or not done*** para at **265.24**.

265.29   *Confidence frauds   Loss £100,000+*

R v Ahmad and Iqbal 2010 EWCA Crim 2882 D1 and D2 pleaded to a complex fraud relating to gift certificates issued by Apple Inc. over a five-month period. The counts were added on the day of trial. More than 7,000 certificates at £100 were bought using cloned or otherwise compromised credit or debit cards. D1 laundered certificates with a face value of £96,300 through eBay. D1 sold them to buyers for £27,946. D2 sold certificates to the value of £492,300 for £262,229. D2 pleaded on the basis that he did not benefit directly, financially or otherwise. The Judge found that the pleas were not entered at the earliest opportunity. The Judge made it clear that had there been a number of PCMHs leading up to trial, early compromise and pleas would attract more credit than otherwise. He fixed the discount at 20%. At the PCMH, the defendants had indicated a willingness to plead guilty to the offences they subsequently pleaded to, had they been included on the indictment at that stage. This was repeated when the case came for trial. The prosecution then indicated for the first time a willingness to accept those pleas. Held. The Judge's starting point was unimpeachable. The sense of the matter is that D1 pleaded guilty at the first opportunity and the Judge was wrong to suggest otherwise. They were entitled to ⅓ credit. For D1, **20 months**, not 2 years, and for D2 **2 years**, not 2 years 5 months.

R v Dosanjh 2011 EWCA Crim 1246, 2012 1 Cr App R (S) 17 (p 92) D pleaded to three frauds and failure to comply with notification requirements. Properties were rented by D under a false name. He then assumed the name of the legitimate owner and the property was sold to a 'quick purchase' company. This was repeated on two occasions. D set up numerous false bank accounts. The total value of the properties was £423,000. The total being paid into the bank accounts was about £297,000. The money was quickly withdrawn. When arrested, D admitted the offences, stating that he was the front man for

---

[506] The judgment later states 'the sum of about £16' and so the amount is unclear. Ed.

someone else, being paid £5,000 per transaction and a retainer of £30 per week. D, aged 39 at sentence, had a conviction for rape (in 2000) and a subsequent failure to comply with notification requirements. Held. The Judge carefully considered the guideline and reached a proper starting point of 5 years after a trial. There was no reason to consider a departure downwards. D was an essential figure in the fraud. He was a willing participant and was prepared to use false identities in connection with the transactions. This was a significant and sophisticated fraud. **3 years 4 months** for the frauds and **2 months** for the notification making **3½ years** was not manifestly excessive.

See also: *R v Field and Williams* 2011 EWCA Crim 1753, 2012 1 Cr App R (S) 69 (p 393) (Pleas to conspiracy to defraud. Targeted elderly and infirm individuals for home improvement. Total fraud £622,000. W involved for 2½ years concerning over £61,000, and F for a significantly shorter period, concerning £16,000 and 15 victims. Many victims repeatedly targeted. For W, full credit. **8 years** was severe but not manifestly excessive. For F, reduced credit, **4½ years** not 6.)

R v Higgins and Others 2011 EWCA Crim 2246, 2012 1 Cr App R (S) 101 (p 613) (Convicted of conspiracy to defraud. Ran two companies who searched for building applications made to councils and made unsolicited offers to conduct building work. Not one of 50 projects was completed. False names were used. Threats to sue. Many customers paid more than the work completed was worth. Around £½m obtained. For the organiser, **8 years**, for two others, **7 years** and **6 years**.)

R v Cash 2012 EWCA Crim 1583, 2013 1 Cr App R (S) 60 (p 341) (Late plea to fraud. Victims were an elderly couple aged 73 and 68 with learning difficulties. Defendant offered to clear their garden. Discussed selling their house and persuaded them to transfer it to him for no value. Worth £194,000. Instructed solicitors and convinced them to sign a solicitor's letter. Aged 25. Confidence trick of the worst kind. Category 2. Aggravated by targeting of vulnerable victims, planning, the potential gain and the effect on the victims. Not arguable that **4 years** was manifestly excessive.)

R v Ball 2013 EWCA Crim 2012 (Plea to fraud and conspiracy to commit fraud. D was a professional conman who preyed on vulnerable householders, inducing them to part with excessive sums of money for substandard or non-existent work. Cold calling over a 15-month period. One man was convinced to sell his house at almost half the market value (nearly £200,000) in order to invest in a business opportunity. He lost his house and all his savings and had to sleep rough. D had five convictions for 10 offences including conspiracy to defraud and blackmail (7 years), theft (×2) and making a false representation (×2). 25% credit. **8½ years** was entirely justified.)

Old cases: *R v Mokelu* 2010 EWCA Crim 288, 2 Cr App R (S) 87 (p 555) (**4 years**) *R v Asekomhe* 2010 EWCA Crim 740 (**4½ years**) For a summary of these cases, see the 10th edition of this book.

Post-guideline case
R v Moyse 2015 EWCA Crim 231 D pleaded (full credit) to fraud (×5), false accounting and fraudulent trading. As D's motor trade business grew, he adopted a high-risk strategy of offering guaranteed prices for cars, which ultimately failed, and D perpetrated a series of linked frauds. This caused losses to creditors, both individuals and businesses, totalling over £1.1m. D denied being dishonest and had intended to pay everyone. D was aged 39 on appeal and had a recent conviction for false accounting (conditional discharge) shortly before the frauds were committed. The Judge applied the confidence fraud guideline and, for one count, the obtaining credit guideline. Held. This was plainly a most unpleasant series of offences. The business wasn't fraudulent from the start, but it soon fell apart. In selecting an appropriate guideline…the Judge faced difficulties. Neither guideline was really appropriate. We adopt a pragmatic approach, so **7 years** in all, not 10.

265.30   *Confidence frauds   Commercial suppliers   Pre-2014 guideline case*
An example: *R v Kalian* 2012 EWCA Crim 652, 2 Cr App R (S) 86 (p 513) (Late plea (10% credit) to 22 counts of fraud. Owned a security business selling alarms. All were

faulty. Targeted the elderly. Customers were cold-called and misled that the alarms were tailor-made and had National Security Inspection approval. Alarms contacted monitoring stations unnecessarily causing telephone bills of £400-500. Extortionate prices charged. Pleaded to amount of just under £28,000. Repaid over £8,000. Treated as no previous convictions. Starting at 5 years, **4½ years**)

Conspiracy to defraud
The cases are distributed in the other paragraphs of this chapter.
For **corporate offenders** see the *Fraud, Bribery and Money Laundering: Corporate Offenders Guideline 2014* at **225.9**.

265.31   Employment frauds   Pre-2014 guideline cases
R v Sammons 2010 EWCA Crim 2548 D pleaded to four counts of fraud by false representation. He was employed by the NHS through a recruitment agency. After completing work, he continued to submit timesheets and was subsequently paid for the amounts submitted, about £88,000. This was discovered and D offered to repay the sums to the agency. D wrote a cheque but stated that, as he had no funds, it would probably bounce. D had been paid £14,339. He was arrested and bailed but failed to appear, having travelled to South Africa. D had a wife and young child to support. Held. This was a calculated, systematic and deliberate fraud in breach of trust which continued over a period of six months. The Judge made reference to a starting point of 18 months and in doing so had treated this offence as a confidence fraud, thus triggering a higher penalty. It is very doubtful whether the Sentencing Guidelines Council had in mind the kind of offence here in question when referring to confidence fraud. **6 months** not 12.
See also: *R v Akinpelu* 2010 EWCA Crim 2754 (Pleas to fraud for obtaining employment with false birth certificate and driving licence and possessing a false driving licence with intent. Used to obtain work. **6 months** not 12.)

265.32   False representation, Fraud by   Pre-2014 guideline cases
R v Chaytor 2011 EWCA Crim 929 LCJ D pleaded (25% credit) to three counts of false accounting. As an MP, on 13 occasions he dishonestly submitted false claims for expenses. The total was just short of £23,000, and D received just over £18,000. D had submitted falsified tenancy agreements to facilitate the claims. He had repaid a little more than was dishonestly claimed. D, aged 61 at appeal, was of good character and had a large number of references. Held. This sad fall from grace was entirely self-inflicted. It was surprising that D made dishonest claims as much of the money claimed could have been recovered by legitimate means, because it was no easier to make a dishonest claim than an honest one. The claims were bogus in their entirety. This was a grave breach of trust. **18 months** was not manifestly excessive.
R v Kelly 2011 EWCA Crim 2055 D pleaded to four counts of fraud. As a qualified nurse, she obtained a more senior position for which she was not sufficiently qualified. When challenged, she presented forged certificates created by her husband. She held the position for 2½ years. D, aged 45, had no previous convictions and had good character references. Held. She had gone to great lengths to deceive her employees. Because of the mitigation and the low risk of reoffending, **8 months** suspended, not 8 months.
R v Dittman and Anderson 2012 EWCA Crim 957, 2013 1 Cr App R (S) 21 (p 113) D and G pleaded (full credit) to fraud by representation. An unidentified woman, purporting to be D, attended a driving test centre for the theory test. She presented both parts of D's driving licence. The woman sat the test and passed. She was never traced. Subsequently, D was booked in for the practical driving test. G attended the test centre for the driving part of the test, purporting to be D. She was accompanied by C, who was recognised to be a driving instructor (in fact he was a trainee). G had both parts of D's driving licence and C said G was D. When challenged, G admitted that she was not D. She was arrested and admitted she had taken the test as a favour to D. D declined to comment in interview. D was aged 51 and had two children. One was aged 23 and the other was aged 13. His father lived in Germany. G was aged 39 and had two children,

aged 12 and four. G lived with her husband, who was not the father of her children. Neither had previous convictions and both were employed. C was given 6 months (no appeal). The Judge said M organised it and the offence potentially put the public at risk. Further the offence was prevalent and if D and G were concerned with the consequences of the loss of liberty they should have thought about that before they committed the offence. He drew a parallel with those who take other people's penalty points. Held. There was no commercial motive. It is clear from *R v Suleman* 2009 EWCA Crim 2205 that this crossed the custody threshold. The Judge passed sentences which were significantly lower than if those family circumstances were not present. **2 months** was not excessive.

Note: Perhaps the sentencing Judge could also have said the offence put D's passengers (including her children) at risk. Ed.

R v McGrath 2012 EWCA Crim 2018, 2013 1 Cr App R (S) 108 (p 560) D pleaded (full credit) to 14 counts of fraud by false representation. D met H and let him know that he needed somewhere to live. H allowed D to become his lodger. Within a month, D began to make credit card applications to various institutions pretending to be H. Cards were issued and he proceeded to use them to purchase goods and services and to pay off his gambling debts. One purchase was a car worth £3,908. He paid for the insurance with one of the fraudulent cards and named H as the driver of the vehicle. In order to conceal the fraud, he diverted correspondence intended for H, including those relating to genuine bills. H eventually found a bill from a credit card account in his name of which he was completely unaware. H contacted D, who told him that 'people were after him'. He claimed he had acquired debts of £40,000 which he owed to a drug dealer. D also purchased luxury goods and funded stays in hotels. H unknowingly fell into debt of around £1,000. Two finance houses failed to reinstate H's credit rating so he could not obtain credit. He was required to take a loan from members of his family. The total sum expended in D's fraud was almost £22,000. D committed the offences in breach of a suspended sentence imposed for fraud in 2010. He had cashed bogus cheques in a 'sophisticated fraud' involving producing complex documents. He was dealt with for the breach of the suspended sentence at the Magistrates' Court (6 weeks). Held. The aggravating features were the use of H's identity, his previous fraud offences, the breach of the suspended sentence and the loss caused to H. These were mean and utterly selfish offences. The Judge's starting point of 3 years 8 months was not manifestly excessive. **30 months** upheld.

R v Agunu 2013 EWCA Crim 1281 D pleaded (10% credit) to conspiracy to commit fraud by false representation. He used a dating agency to make contact with middle-aged and elderly ladies who had been widowed or divorced and who were therefore susceptible to a promise of a loving long-term relationship. The ladies were mostly located in the USA but some were in Canada and some in the Caribbean. He used false identities and bombarded the ladies with e-mails, telephone calls and text messages. They believed he was interested in a long-term relationship. Some believed that there was a prospect of marriage. He produced photographs and bogus documents to support his story that he was a successful businessman, including stating he had lucrative construction contracts. He subsequently asked for money from the ladies to support him, claiming he had encountered difficulties and needed money in order to release substantial sums. £365,000 was obtained. D admitted playing an integral part in the conspiracy but said that the concept was not his idea. He was not the ringleader but was acting on instructions from those higher up. D was aged 25 at appeal and had no convictions or cautions. He expressed remorse and a letter before the Judge asked for leniency so that he could complete an engineering course. Held. This was an offence with very serious aggravating features. It was a sustained fraud with a large number of victims. It was premeditated and the victims were vulnerable. The amount gained was very substantial. The mitigation was his late plea, his subordinate role and his character. Starting at **5½ years**, with the plea **5 years** not 6 years 4 months.

See also: *R v Shepherd* 2012 EWCA Crim 1523 (Plea. Full credit. Conspiracy to use false instruments and conspiracy to commit fraud by false representation. Director of company. Made enquiries with a bank in Guernsey. Obtained letters and created false letters with letterheads purporting to be affirmations from the bank that the company had over £76m in deposits. Obtained £90,000 and €20m on that basis. Main organiser and beneficiary. Sophisticated fraud. Aged 51. Six previous convictions for dishonesty. Serious escalation in offending. Starting at 8 years. With the plea, **5 years 4 months**. Because of a non-qualifying curfew, **5 years** not 6 years 3 months.)

R v Monsey 2014 EWCA Crim 723 (Convicted. Former employee of housing team at London borough used information acquired at work to defraud landlords of about £11,500. Gain significantly less. No evidence that the work was unnecessary. Remorse and previous good character. **18 months**, not 2½ years.)

Old case: See also: *R v Damji* 2010 EWCA Crim 648 (**15 months**)

For a summary of this case see the 10th edition of this book.

265.33 *False representations, Fraud by   Driving tests*

R v Mbangi and Silva 2013 EWCA Crim 1419 M (×2) and S (×1) pleaded (full credit) to conspiracy to commit fraud by false representation. The conspiracy was for S to take the theory part of the driving test in M's name. An attempt was made where an unidentified man tried to take the test. The test centre staff refused to allow him to do so because he did not resemble the picture on M's provisional licence. A second test was booked and S turned up to take the test. Staff spotted M's name and the police were called. S was arrested and admitted trying to sit the test for M, his friend. M, aged 49, had no convictions. He came to the UK from the Congo in 1995, where he held a full driving licence. He had indefinite leave to remain in the UK and had a partner and two children. He had worked continuously from 1998 as a porter. His job remained open to him after his sentence. He was extremely remorseful. S was aged 39 or 40 and had no convictions. He denied that there was any financial motivation. He had been in the UK since 1995 and had worked for the previous 10 years as a security officer. He had three children. Held. We endorse the decisions in *R v Dittman and Anderson* 2012 and *R v Suleman* 2009. The whole point of the licensing system is to ensure only those who are competent to drive on our roads are authorised to do so. Starting at **9 months** for M, who instigated the offence and was its potential beneficiary, was not excessive. The Judge doubled the 9 months to reflect the fact that he committed a second offence to reach 18 months. That failed to take account of the powerful mitigation. An additional 3 months would have been sufficient, making 12 months. With full credit, **8 months** not 12. For S, if 9 months is appropriate for someone in M's (and Suleman's) position, then it was appropriate to start at slightly lower than that for S. Starting at 6 months, with full credit, **4 months** not 6.

See also: *R v Suleman* 2009 EWCA Crim 2205 (Plea. Failed driving test twice. Arranged someone to impersonate him. **8 months** not 13.)

265.34 *Fraud by false representation, Fraud by   Servicemen and women*

Guidance on Sentencing in the Court Martial 2013 paras 5.8.4 to 5.8.10 set out the service policy, the way the money is recovered and the suggested penalties.

265.35 *Fraudulent trading   Judicial guidance*

R v Mackey 2012 EWCA Crim 2205, 2013 1 Cr App R (S) 100 (p 522) Although the guideline does not apply, it is appropriate to pay some regard to it. Offences of fraudulent trading cover a wide spectrum of offences. At one extreme there may have been deliberate reckless trading on a large scale, aimed at a rapid return with no genuine intention to discharge the company's debts. At the other end there may have been a properly funded business which ran into financial difficulties, out of which the directors attempted to trade themselves in order to save their own and their employees' jobs but reached a point where they became reckless as to the reality.

The factors that are relevant to sentence include the amount of the fraud, the manner in which it was carried out, the period over which it was carried out, the position of the defendant in the company and his or her measure of control over it, any abuse of trust involved, any effect on public confidence in the integrity of commercial life, any loss to small investors, the personal benefit to the defendant, the plea, and the age and character of the defendant.

265.36   *Fraudulent trading   Trading with intent to defraud   Long firm frauds Pre-2014 guideline cases*
R v Leaf 2007 EWCA Crim 802, 2008 1 Cr App R (S) 3 (p 14) D was convicted of 13 counts of fraudulent trading. In the early 1990s there was a tax avoidance scheme which was lawful until its subsequent abolition by legislation, known as a company purchase scheme. A purchaser would buy a dormant company which held a large amount of cash which had been set aside to meet outstanding corporation tax liability. The purchaser would then use various forms of tax relief which had not been available when the company was in its previous ownership to extinguish or greatly reduce the tax liability of the company and therefore make a profit out of the remaining cash held. The case against D was that he had purchased 13 companies of this type but that he had then unlawfully evaded liability for corporation tax. He used two fraudulent methods. The first involved false loan transactions in which a company, ABC, controlled by D, purported to lend the companies large sums of money. The companies then set about reducing their corporation tax liability by reference to the interest payments on the false loans. The second method involved bogus foreign exchange transactions through two entities, both controlled by D. They purported to carry out foreign exchange transactions on behalf of the purchased companies resulting in profits from which the purchased companies paid dividends. This enabled the companies to claim that their corporation tax liability had been extinguished in respect of the current year and also previous years by virtue of advance corporation tax, and facilitated claims to be made for repayment of tax in respect of sums previously paid in satisfaction of corporation tax liability. The aggregate corporation tax liability of the companies was about £55m. The prosecution case was that D had benefited by approximately £22m, the whereabouts of which was unknown. Normally, the charges would have been ones of defrauding the revenue. However, D had been in Switzerland, which does not extradite for fiscal offences. As a result of that the maximum for any one of these offences was 7 years. D was of previous good character. There were some public-spirited aspects to his life. He was responding to his sentence in very positive ways and by the time his case came to the Appeal Court there was some evidence of remorse. Held. This was fraud on a truly massive scale to satisfy his monumental greed. It was sustained, sophisticated and immensely serious. The offences were the product of premeditation, careful planning and intricate execution. The crimes were not victimless. He had denied the country substantial resources. Concurrent sentences would not begin to reflect the gravity of the case. We suspect that the loss to the Revenue is significantly lower than in excess of £50m. At the time of the offences there was a market in such companies for lawful schemes, and a significant amount of the tax which was due would have been lawfully avoided. However, D has benefited personally by some £22m which remains unaccounted for. He preferred the dishonest and criminal route to satisfy his monumental greed. A total of **10 years** not 12½.
See also: *R v Freeman* 2011 EWCA Crim 2534, 2012 1 Cr App R (S) 105 (p 629) (Pleaded to fraudulent trading. Full credit. Nine counts including two relating to being an undischarged bankrupt. 335 victims. Losses around £14m. Three phases. Misled investors and falsified documents. Appalling record of dishonesty including fraud. Committed when on bail. Because there was a 10-year maximum sentence with the plea, **6 years** not 7, consecutive to 1 year for a bankruptcy offence.)
R v Mackey 2012 EWCA Crim 2205, 2013 1 Cr App R (S) 100 (p 522) (Convicted. Formed a letting agency. Started as a genuine business. D took around £60,000 from

clients. Deposits were not protected as legally required. Landlords were not paid. Company folded and reformed. That folded soon after. Sought to blame her employees when arrested. Aged 38. Good character. Significant medical issues. Bottom end of the scale but not bottom of the range. Benefit of £60,000 was to keep the business going. **18 months** was within the appropriate range.)

Old cases: *R v Furr and Flint* 2007 EWCA Crim 19 (**4½ years** for one, **2½ years** for the other) *R v Philippou and Kemp* 2009 EWCA Crim 416 (**7 years** for one, **3 years** for the other) *R v Shulton* 2009 EWCA Crim 665 (**27 months**)

For a summary of the first case, see the 9th edition of this book.

265.37   *Identity frauds   Pre-2014 guideline cases*

R v Sivakumar 2011 EWCA Crim 1594 D was convicted of fraud (×3). He was the area manager of 10 KFC stores. Somehow he came into possession of a bank card belonging to a student. He used the card to purchase two cameras using a telephone at one of the stores. The value was £400. He then unsuccessfully attempted to purchase items worth about £1,000. On one of the occasions he was surrounded by his group managers. The student returned to the store in an attempt to retrieve the card. She was unsuccessful on two occasions. D was present on one of these occasions. D, aged 36, with a wife and child, had one theft conviction from 1994. Held. There were serious aggravating factors involved in this offence. There was good reason for the Judge to depart from the guidelines. However, 9 months was manifestly excessive. **6 months**.

R v Dias-Monteiro and Minchev 2013 EWCA Crim 1215 D and M pleaded to conspiracy to commit fraud. They were involved in a complicated conspiracy to obtain information about valid credit cards which occurred over a period of about 12 months. That information was used to produce cloned cards with which fraudulent transactions were carried out by purchasing high-value items and selling them for profit. Counterfeit cards would be used until it became apparent that the card or account had reached its credit limit. The cards used were frequently American cards where the chip and PIN system is not used. Instead, merely a signature was required to complete the transaction. A main target of the frauds were Apple stores. Estimates were that 250 cards were cloned and used to obtain goods to a total in excess of $1.5m. £30,000 was seized by police and bank accounts showed that monies were being sent abroad. There was evidence of a further 786 credit card accounts and account information stored on computers. D pleaded on the basis that she was not involved in obtaining the confidential information or making the cloned cards. She admitted that on approximately 15 occasions she used cloned cards, at the direction of others. After her arrest and bail, she continued with the fraud. D had been paid about £2,000 for her involvement. She was pregnant. M was aged 21 and had educated himself. He had no convictions. He had not continued to offend after his arrest and bail. Held. M was present on 13 occasions and was a willing participant. Others who had received a similar sentence had a greater level of seniority than M. **2 years 4 months** not 3 years. For D, this was serious criminality in which she played a significant role. We consider a starting point of 3 years was understandable. Giving prominence to the rights of the unborn child, **2 years' detention suspended** not 2 years.

R v Agrigoroaie and Another 2015 EWCA Crim 50 D pleaded with full credit to seven fraud-related offences. Compromised or stolen credit cards were used to pay for flights between Romania and the UK. The bookings were traced to S and D's flat and a search revealed a large amount of equipment including computers, USB items, encoding devices and items for cloning cards and identity documents, including blank and embossed cards. Also found were various documents with photos of S and D with false names and bank statements in different names. The computer contained a large number of emails, passwords and the details of around 150 bank accounts from around the world which were obtained by phishing. The fraud had been running for at least a month with 15-20 transactions totalling £15,410, and attempts were made to gain a further £10,000, although that was just 'the tip of the iceberg' as the computers were heavily encrypted. D made no comment in interview and had herself entered the UK using a booking made with a compromised credit card a year earlier. She was aged 23 on appeal, a Romanian national and of good character. Held. This was a highly professional fraud, which would generate a large return for those involved. The Court shares the single Judge's view that a starting point of 9 years was wrong. The fact that the offence was committed across borders and involved damage to third parties and card issuers, because of identity theft, are serious aggravating factors. Frauds such as these cause harm to others and the direct victim. They also…cause aggravation and stress to those who have to unravel the consequences. They lead to erosion of public confidence in payment mechanisms. For these reasons we consider that identity fraud, and frauds of this sort, are particularly serious. 4 years, not 6. For S (convicted of fraud in 2010), 5 years not 8.

See also: *R v Aleksic* 2011 EWCA Crim 92 (Plea to possession of false identity document counts with intent (×10) fraud (×15) and five theft TICs. Photo-card driving licences and passports. Accounts opened in false names. Stole banking documents from neighbours. A little under £40,000 obtained. **2 years** not 3.)

R v Webber 2011 EWCA Crim 3135, 2012 2 Cr App R (S) 41 (p 240) (Plea. Full credit. With others, operated sophisticated and sustained fraud via Internet. Set up website enabling credit card details to be obtained and used. Almost 8,000 members on the website. Reported loss was around £470,000. Cards used by him suffered loss of £40,000. Actual loss unknown as details passed on. Willing to sell the credit card details. Aged between 17½ and 18½. Breached bail and went to Majorca. **5 years** was not manifestly excessive.)

R v Curran 2013 EWCA Crim 1477 (Plea to conspiracy to make an article for use in fraud. Created false identities and cloned others. False business offering non-existent jobs set up in order to acquire personal details. False documents created then used to open bank accounts. Accounts then used to enter credit agreements and electrical goods were obtained. Goods, including proceeds of burglaries, were advertised on eBay. Payments made into the false accounts and withdrawn from ATMs. £75-80,000 obtained. D played a supporting role, including using paperwork to open 14 false bank accounts. 84 previous offences including theft and fraud. Further offences since these offences. **3 years** not 3½.)

Old cases: *R v Awoyemi* 2009 EWCA Crim 1725, 2010 1 Cr App R (S) 79 (p 515) (**6 years** for B and D, **5 years** for O.) *R v Mallu* 2010 EWCA Crim 1537 (**10 months' detention**)

For a summary of the last case, see the 10th edition of this book. For older cases, see the 9th edition.

See also **Banking frauds** at **265.22**.

See also the **PASSPORT/ID DOCUMENTS OFFENCES** chapter.

Immigration frauds see the **IMMIGRATION OFFENCES** chapter.

265.38   *Insider dealing   Pre-2014 guideline judicial guidance*

R v McQuoid 2009 EWCA Crim 1301 LCJ D pleaded to insider dealing. Held. It was not a victimless crime. Those involved are criminals and it is not just regulatory abuse. The principles of confidentiality and trust, which are essential to the operations of the commercial world, are betrayed and public confidence in the integrity of the system which is essential to its proper function is undermined. The message must be clear: when done deliberately it is a species of fraud. It is cheating. Those who expect to be subject to just regulatory proceedings can have no legitimate expectation of avoiding prosecution and sentence. The fact that the defendant was subject to the new policy (of prosecutions) is no reason to reduce the sentence. The relevant considerations are:

   a) the nature of the defendant's employment or retainer, or involvement in the arrangements which enabled him to participate in the insider dealing,

   b) the circumstances in which he came into possession of confidential information and the use he made of it,

c) whether he behaved recklessly or acted deliberately, and almost inevitably therefore, dishonestly,

d) the level of planning and sophistication involved in his activity, as well as the
period of trading and the number of individual trades,

e) whether he acted alone or with others and, if so, his relative culpability,

f) the amount of anticipated or intended financial benefit or (as sometimes happens)
loss avoided, as well as the actual benefit (or loss avoided),

g) although the absence of any identified victim is not normally a matter giving rise
to mitigation, the impact (if any), where proved, on any individual victim, and

h) the impact of the offence on overall public confidence in the integrity of the
market. Because of its impact on public confidence it is likely that an offence
committed jointly by more than one person trusted with confidential information
will be more damaging to public confidence than an offence committed in
isolation by one person acting on his own. Age and good character will always be
relevant.

However, it must be borne in mind that it will often be the case that it is the individual of
good character who has been trusted with information just because he or she is an
individual of good character. By misusing the information, the trust reposed as a result of
the good character has been breached.

265.39   *Insider dealing   Pre-2014 guideline cases*

R v McQuoid 2009 EWCA Crim 1301 LCJ The defendant was convicted of insider
dealing. As a solicitor working in a company he knew about a proposed takeover. He
with his father-in-law bought £20,310 worth of shares in his company and made nearly
£49,000 profit. He was aged 45, of good character, with young dependent children. He
was sentenced to **8 months**, £35,000 confiscation and £30,000 prosecution costs. Held.
The Judge gave full weight to the impact on him, his family and the destruction of his
professional reputation. The sentence was as merciful as it could have been. No
complaint could have been made of a **12-month** sentence.

See also: *R v Rollins* 2011 EWCA Crim 1825, 2012 1 Cr App R (S) 64 (p 366) (LCJ
Convicted of insider dealing (×5) and transferring criminal property (×4). Aged 47, good
character with dependants. Senior manager in a company. Sold shares when prohibited
including once after he was dismissed. Transferred proceeds to father whilst under
investigation by FSA. No distinction between those who trade for profit and those who
trade to avoid a loss. Concurrent sentences for insider dealing (**15 months**) but
consecutive to the money laundering (3 months), making 18 months.)

Old case: *R v Butt* 2006 EWCA Crim 47, 2 Cr App R (S) 59 (p 364) (**4 years**)
For a summary of this case, see the 9th edition of this book.

265.40   *Insurance frauds   Pre-2014 guideline cases*

R v Darwin and Darwin 2009 EWCA Crim 860, 2 Cr App R (S) 115 (p 746) LCJ JD
pleaded very early to eight counts of obtaining by deception. His wife, AD, was
convicted of six counts of obtaining by deception and some money-laundering offences.
(The differing charges did not give rise to a distinction in their involvement.) AD
pleaded not guilty on the basis of coercion by JD. They had planned JD's disappearance
because they were in financial difficulties. In December 2001 they took out a life
insurance policy on JD. In March 2002 he staged a drowning at sea in a canoe. The
Coast Watch, the Coast Guard, Air Sea Rescue, Northeast Air Support and the Royal
National Lifeboat Institution searched the coastline. A team of police officers continued
the search until the end of May 2002 when police divers found part of the canoe. A
coroner's inquest in 2003 concluded that he had died at sea. After that various claims
were made on insurance and pension policies. About £250,000 was paid out. Their two
adult sons believed that their father was dead, suffered grief and tried to comfort AD. To
launder part of the funds, sums were transferred into their accounts. Shortly after his
disappearance JD returned to his home area and lived there. He falsely used the identity

of someone who had died, and obtained false documents. AD sold properties and laundered money carefully. Eventually she told her sons she had set up a company in Panama, and in October 2006 emigrated there, taking with her over $1m. JD was also in Panama. In December 2007 JD went to police in the UK, saying he was suffering from amnesia. He was arrested a few days later. AD returned to the UK and was arrested. In interview they both initially told lies. Eventually they admitted that they had staged JD's death to clear their debts. They were of good character. A pre-sentence report on JD said that he was unlikely to reoffend. The pre-sentence report on AD said that she was a low risk of harm and reconviction although she minimised her behaviour. Held. The Judge's view that they operated as a team was amply justified. AD's involvement was whole-hearted. The conspiracy lasted 6½ years. JD returned to the UK not through guilt or remorse but probably to try to resume his relationship with his sons. The discount for JD's plea was adequate given the overwhelming nature of the evidence. The Judge was right to attach considerable importance to the impact on the sons. They suffered totally unnecessary emotional distress. This was the grossest form of betrayal. Consideration is not confined to those who have lost financially as a result of fraud, but may properly be extended to those who have suffered a devastating impact by it. The defendants got every penny available following JD's supposed death. A number of people became involved in the unpleasant and potentially dangerous task of trying to find him when he disappeared, which was an aggravating feature. The financial element of the fraud would suggest a shorter sentence, but the case cannot be limited to its financial element alone. For AD, **6½ years** in total, and for JD, **6 years 3 months** in total, though severe, were not manifestly excessive.

R v McLaren 2011 EWCA Crim 2701, 2012 2 Cr App R (S) 1 (p 1) D pleaded on rearraignment to fraud (×7). His wife pleaded to lesser offences. D was a dentist who had had made against him a number of complaints. As a result, he had changed his name and his area of practice a number of times. The General Dental Council were unaware the names referred to the same person. After his then employers learnt of his deficiencies as a dentist, they terminated his employment. He applied for passports in two different names and had 12 active credit cards with debts of £41,000. He owed £110,000 on a loan account. The prosecution totalled his indebtedness at £379,000. He notified his bank he was taking his mother to Jordan for medical treatment. In fact he took his family on holiday to Greece. The family returned but D did not. D's wife was telling people that D had been killed in a road accident, and D provided his wife with documents to support that claim. Thereafter, a number of claims were made against insurance companies. The first was for £1m. The second was for £96,000. The fourth was for three NatWest policies totalling £739,256. There was another relating to a credit card for £16,306. There were others. NatWest investigated and found D to be living in Scotland, practising as a dentist. In all, £1.8m was claimed, but only £51,000 was received. The prosecution did not suggest the policies were taken out for a fraud. Held. On the basis of the amount sought to be obtained, the offences fell within the first box in the guidelines, namely sums over £750,000. That provides for a range of 4-7 years. The guidelines state that the court should take into account the difference between the loss intended and resulting. The Judge should therefore have considered also the sum of £51,000. Whether that moved the offences out of the 4-7 year range was a matter of degree. However, a starting point of 6 years was too high. A sentence of **4 years** was appropriate after a trial. With 25% credit for the plea, **3 years** not 5.

R v Hillaman and Naqshbandi 2013 EWCA Crim 1022 H pleaded (20% credit) to conspiracy to defraud and N was convicted of the same. RAHL was registered as an accident management company assisting motorists who had been in road traffic collisions. Claims were made in respect of fictitious accidents, or where a real accident had occurred claims were made by fabricating the existence of phantom passengers or making charges for fictitious storage. This was a 'crash for cash' conspiracy. H and N were in the lower order of importance in the conspiracy. H had become company secretary and N became a company director. For N, the sum of money obtained during his involvement was £524,580 and the reserve figure (set aside but not paid out) was in excess of £4m. His bank account suggested that he personally benefited to the tune of £101,000. For H, during his involvement the total paid out was £70,692 with the reserve figure at £979,914. His bank account showed credits of almost £20,000 but the Judge considered that only represented a fraction of his true personal benefit. N was aged 32 with no convictions or cautions. He had references referring to his positive good character. H was aged 24 (19 at the time) and had a conviction for arson, violent disorder and damaging property arising from the riots in 2011 (3½ years). He also had references. Held. This was not a true breach of trust case. N had a full and active role in the fraud. He was a company director and was responsible for registering the company. When H joined, he knew it to be an ongoing conspiracy to defraud. For H, it was fraudulent from the outset. For N it was not. Given the prevalence, deterrent sentences were appropriate. For N, **6 years** not 7 years 3 months. For H, the appropriate starting point was 5 years. With the plea, **4 years** not 5. N would be disqualified from being a company director for 5 years not 7.

See also: *R v McKenzie* 2013 EWCA Crim 1544 (False accident claims. D was convicted. 25 claims. £483,000 paid out. £49,000 worth of claims rejected. Leading light given 7 years. D claimed to be a passenger when collision never occurred. Vehicles doctored. Examined by doctors three times. **15 months**, which was above the guideline, was not too long.)

R v Elsobky 2014 EWCA Crim 2035 (Convicted. Simple arson and fraud. Business in financial difficulty. D recruited others to burn building for bogus £290,000+ insurance claim. Very serious fire. Warehouse worth before fire about £330,000. Considerable planning, false invoices used and insurance increased before fire. Fire was severe. Aged 28, no convictions. **8 years** in all upheld.)

Old case: *R v Bright* 2008 EWCA Crim 462, 2 Cr App R (S) 102 (p 578) (**7 years**) For a summary of the case, see the 8th edition of this book.

265.41   *Investments, false promises/Bogus investment schemes etc.*   *Pre-2014 guideline judicial guidance*

R v Bailey and Rigby 2005 EWCA Crim 3487 The defendants had both been found guilty of recklessly making a statement, promise or forecast that was false and deceptive contrary to Financial Services and Markets Act 2000 s 397(c). Held. Amongst matters which need to be taken into account on sentence are: the degree of recklessness, the financial context in which the statement was made, the financial consequences of the falsity of the statement, whether the offender took any deliberately deceptive steps in the making of the statement, and the real personal responsibility that the offender had in the whole process involved in the making of the statement. The purpose behind the provision is to protect investors by reinforcing openness and integrity in financial markets. This was a serious offence.

For the pre-2014 fraud guideline see the *City frauds* paras at **265.25**.

265.42   *Investments, false promises/Bogus investment schemes etc.*   *Pre-2014 guideline cases*

R v Whitehead 2010 EWCA Crim 3252, 2011 2 Cr App R (S) 16 p (93) D pleaded (full credit) to an indictment containing 49 counts, including 15 of obtaining a money transfer by deception and fraud. D was an independent financial adviser. With contacts he had built through legitimate business, he began to run a pyramid fraud in 2004. D received £11.9m from the fraud, which lasted five years. Investors were repaid £4.7m. The losses amounted to £7.2m. D used Credit Suisse to prepare forged statements to allay suspicions. After a 'cease and desist' letter from Credit Suisse, D decided to use the Salvation Army's name. There were 25 victims for each fraud. After arrest, D did not seek to hide his crime. The Judge regarded the two sets of offences, 'the Credit Suisse offences' and 'the Salvation Army offences', as separate and imposed consecutive sentences. The defence proposition was that many if not most confidence frauds with multiple victims and transactions ought not to be regarded as multiple frauds. Held. It was wholly appropriate for the Judge to deal with these offences by way of consecutive sentences. D had the opportunity to end his offending behaviour after the Credit Suisse letter. With the plea and mitigation, **8 years** in total not 10 was appropriate.

Att-Gen's Ref Nos 7-8 of 2013 Re L 2013 EWCA Crim 709, 2014 1 Cr App R (S) 26 (p 140) L appealed his sentence and was joined with a prosecution appeal. D pleaded (20% discount) to two groups of offences. In group 1 were an offence under Theft Act 1968 s 15A, false accounting and two frauds. In group 2 were seven specimen fraud counts. D was a city trader who had worked there since 1984. From 2000, he traded honestly on his own account. Between 2005 and 2009, he operated a 'Ponzi' fraud in which £252m was given by clients on the understanding it would be invested whereas it was spent on paying interest to investors or used for D's benefit. Only £183m was returned. The overall loss was about £100m. D spent over £18m on lifestyle expenditure which included yachts, property and vehicles. Eventually, he faced extensive civil claims and was declared bankrupt. There were worldwide freezing orders in place which L ignored. The Judge considered there was 'the whole panoply'[507] of aggravating features: a) the fraud was well planned and professionally executed, b) it involved huge sums and huge profits, c) there were multiple victims whose trust was betrayed, d) it ran for a long period of time, and e) steps were taken to conceal the fraud and money was moved out of the reach of his creditors. The mitigation was he self-reported to the SFO (but only after the litigation had started and as the net was closing round him) and his good character. Held. The mitigation was modest. Starting at **15 years** not 17 makes **12 years** with the plea, based on 7 years for group 2 and 5 years for group 1, consecutive.

See also: *R v Maudsley* 2010 EWCA Crim 3315 (Pleas to false accounting, obtaining by deception and theft. Financial adviser deceived clients and investment companies. Massive and sophisticated scale. Preyed on elderly or retired victims. Abuse of trust. Also stole from victims. Net loss of £1m. Net gain £465,000. Starting at 12, **8 years** was not manifestly excessive.)

Old cases: *R v Hipwell* 2006 EWCA Crim 736, 2006 2 Cr App R (S) 98 (p 636) (**6 months**) *R v O'Hanlon* 2007 EWCA Crim 3074, 2008 2 Cr App R (S) 16 (p 96) (**18 months**) *R v Powell and Hinkson* 2008 EWCA Crim 1214, 2009 1 Cr App R (S) 30 (p 158) (**15 months**)

For a summary of the first case see the 7th edition of this book, for the second case see the 8th edition and for the last case see the 9th edition.

265.43   *Making false statements   Pre-2014 guideline judicial guidance*

R v Bailey and Rigby 2005 EWCA Crim 3487 The defendants had both been found guilty of recklessly making a statement, promise or forecast that was false and deceptive contrary to Financial Services and Markets Act 2000 s 397(c). Held. Amongst matters which need to be taken into account on sentence are: the degree of recklessness, the financial context in which the statement was made, the financial consequences of the falsity of the statement, whether the offender took any deliberately deceptive steps in the making of the statement, and the real personal responsibility that the offender had in the whole process involved in the making of the statement. The purpose behind the provision is to protect investors by reinforcing openness and integrity in financial markets. This was a serious offence. For more details see the 6th edition of this book.

265.44   *Mortgage fraud/Property fraud   Pre-2014 guideline   Judicial guidance*

R v Stevens 1993 14 Cr App R (S) 372 There are different sorts of mortgage fraud, some more sophisticated than others. In some instances false names and values are used. Properties, as well as borrowers, may even be invented for the purposes of defrauding financial institutions. One must take into account the fact that some loans are obtained

---

[507] Meaning 'a complete or impressive collection of things'. Ed.

for commercial purposes under the guise of being for domestic occupation and so at domestic rates. An important consideration is the part played by any given defendant in the fraud, that is to say his role may be anything from prime mover to nominee. It is an aggravating factor if he recruits others to participate in the fraud. Of relevance, also, is the length of the involvement in the fraud or frauds by any particular defendant, as well as the extent of any personal benefit that he may have derived. It is of consequence whether there was a genuine intention to repay loans advanced, thereby ultimately avoiding loss to the financial institutions concerned. It is common to pay regard to the amounts obtained by the lenders, as well as the losses incurred. It is important to bear in mind whether any particular defendant is a professional person or a quasi-professional person, for the special reason that if such a participant he must be guilty of breach of trust, and his role may be an important one in the deception of the lending institutions. Delay may be a relevant feature.

R v Yates 2010 EWCA Crim 1028, 2011 1 Cr App R (S) 15 (p 112) D was convicted of obtaining a money transfer by deception. D applied for a mortgage based on wholly false declarations of his and his partner's income. Forged payslips and at least one bank statement were provided in support of the application. Held. We would suggest that…in the case of a loan or loans obtained by fraud of this kind some of the potentially relevant features may be (in no particular order) as follows: a) whether one or several transactions are involved, b) whether the fraud is committed by a professional person or is otherwise committed in breach of trust, c) the nature of the fraud will need to be considered and the means by which it is carried through, d) whether the fraud was an isolated incident or involved ongoing deception, e) the amount of money sought and obtained, f) the amount of actual loss, so far as it can be identified, to the lender, g) whether the offender has involved others, or is involved with others, in the fraud, and h) whether at the time there was an intention to repay (and, if so, the anticipated means of repayment) or whether there was no intention to repay. There may well be other factors, and regard will of course need to be had in the usual way to matters such as a guilty plea, relevant previous convictions or lack of previous convictions, and so on. In particular, regard must, of course, always be had to the relevant Definitive Guidelines.

Att-Gen's Ref Nos 70 and 83 of 2014 2014 EWCA Crim 2267 D was convicted of conspiracy to defraud (×2) and H pleaded (very little credit) to conspiracy to defraud (×3) and to retaining a wrongful credit. H was struck off the Roll of Solicitors and in total, he attempted to obtain £6.1m from mortgage providers, actually gaining over £5.5m. D was a barrister without pupillage and a fellow of ILEX (now the Chartered Institute of Legal Executives). He set up a firm of solicitors and a bridging loan company. D was responsible for £3m of losses, none of which was recovered. Held. Financial arrangements of this kind which enable people to buy houses by way of a mortgage depend on trust and this type of criminality seriously undermines the confidence the public and the relevant financial institutions have in the solicitors and brokers involved.

265.45   *Mortgage fraud/Property fraud   Pre-2014 guideline cases*
R v Petkova 2011 EWCA Crim 109 K pleaded to conspiring to commit fraud by false representations (×5), obtaining services by deception (×4) and conspiring to obtain services by deception, with a similar offence TIC'd. P requested that K, an ACCA-registered accountant, create false accountant's certificates in relation to self-certified mortgage applications. K pleaded on a written basis that he acted under P's instruction and that he did not know nor had he come into contact with any person seeking to obtain a mortgage. K also pleaded to falsifying his own or his wife's income in applications for personal mortgages. The overall value of loans secured by K was just under £2m. The loans enabled K to purchase his matrimonial home and other properties, either for relatives to live in or as investments. P pleaded to making false representations when working as or for a mortgage broker, four for other persons and three for herself. The total value of loans secured by P was just over £1.8m. Many of the applications were falsified

on behalf of persons with low income or in receipt of benefit. K received only £1,200 for his assistance. Both P, aged 40, and K, aged 39, were of previous good character. The Judge noted that these frauds were on a significant scale. In mitigation, it was said that with one exception, there were no losses recorded as a result. He indicated that there was a difference between a fraudster who 'took the money and ran' and a fraudster who remained, intending to make a profit. The Judge found that P was the leading figure in the frauds. Held. Undoubtedly this was a difficult sentencing exercise. The abuse that had been given by his professional status could not be overlooked. With reference to *R v Yates* 2010 EWCA Crim 1028, there were many aggravating features present. For P, **4 years 4 months**, not 5 years 4 months. For K, **2 years**, not 4 years 4 months.

R v Hunter 2012 EWCA Crim 2869, 2013 2 Cr App R (S) 32 (p 219) D pleaded (at the PCMH) to fraud. On three occasions after 2000, he applied for planning permission to conduct work on his house. Inspectors visited the house in 2007 and highlighted areas of concern which needed to be addressed before consent could be granted. D was fully aware that consent could not be granted without a final inspection with the areas of concern addressed. Subsequently there was no contact between D and the local council and D went ahead and carried out the works. This included a loft conversion, a back extension and a conservatory. Three years later, he wished to sell his house. V1 and V2, who were in their 80s, wished to buy D's house. Before they did so, they needed to see the planning certificates for the work carried out by D. D forged the documents and handed them to her solicitors who passed them on to V1 and V2's solicitors. The sale was completed. In 2011, V1 and V2 wanted to sell their house. When their purchaser wanted to see the certificates, V1 and V2 asked the council for them and they were told that none existed. The sale collapsed and V1 and V2 had to pay £11,365 and to hire a skip in order to perform remedial works. They were unable to move out of the house as they had wished. D, aged 51, was of good character with good references. Held. This case is hard to categorise in the guidelines. It was a mean-spirited fraud. It affected vulnerable people who were caused distress by the discovery that they could not sell their house until they paid a considerable amount of money. That was very considerable aggravation. Whether this was, as the Judge determined, a Category 2 offence or not, it clearly called for a custodial sentence. **12 months** was appropriate and there was no hesitation in saying that it should not be suspended.

Att-Gen's Ref Nos 70 and 83 of 2014 2014 EWCA Crim 2267 D was convicted of conspiracy to defraud (×2) and H pleaded (very little credit) to conspiracy to defraud (×3) and to retaining a wrongful credit. H was struck off the Roll of Solicitors but later, using a solicitor's bank accounts and a false name, he played a central role in a scheme whereby mortgages were mainly obtained for properties not for sale. On other occasions, a title was not registered and a mortgage was obtained at a highly inflated value. H also 'cut and pasted' an authorising signature to permit the dissipation of funds, often abroad and via H's company. H then, working with D, cloned a solicitors' firm and perpetrated similar frauds, £1.2m of which was laundered through companies D and H owned. Finally, whilst on bail, H attempted to obtain a bridging loan fraudulently. In total, H attempted to obtain £6.1m from mortgage providers, actually gaining over £5.5m. D was a barrister without pupillage and a fellow of ILEX (now the Chartered Institute of Legal Executives). He set up a firm of solicitors and a bridging loan company. Using bogus property transactions involving H's company, D fraudulently obtained £385,000 on one occasion and was intimately involved in the firm laundering money from H's fraud. D was responsible for £3m of losses, none of which was recovered. There was a delay of five years from arrest to sentence, not the fault of the defendants. D was aged 30 on appeal and of good character with significant caring responsibilities. H was aged 51 with a dishonesty conviction from 2011 (unpaid work). Held. This was sophisticated offending by two men who had qualified as lawyers, which involved very significant sums of money. For D, **3 years** overall, not 18 months. For H, **6½ years** overall, not 4 years 9 months.

See also: *R v Stratford and Stirzaker* 2011 EWCA Crim 888 (Plea. 10 counts of mortgage fraud. He fraudulently charged valuations and forwarded details to proposed lenders. £2.3m worth of mortgages obtained. Starting point of 5 years appropriate. Because of plea and assistance to police, **2½ years**.)

R v Khan 2011 EWCA Crim 1234 (Plea to 10 counts of fraud. Sophisticated and large-scale mortgage fraud. £6.7m obtained, the defendant personally linked to £1.3m. False documents including passports used to open 68 bank accounts. **5 years** was not manifestly excessive.)

R v White 2011 EWCA Crim 2280, 2012 1 Cr App R (S) 100 (p 609) (Plea (25% credit), fraud (×2), obtaining a pecuniary advantage by deception (×2). Four fraudulent loan/mortgage applications. Each used to pay off the last. Amount obtained £265,000 over several years. **2 years** not just under 3½.)

R v McGarry 2012 EWCA Crim 255, 2 Cr App R (S) 60 (p 354) (Late pleas. Classic mortgage fraud. £50m defrauded. Starting at **11 years** was entirely appropriate. With discounts, 6½ years not 7.)

Att-Gen's Ref Nos 7-8 of 2013 2013 EWCA Crim 709, 2014 1 Cr App R (S) 26 (p 140) (Bank property loan fraud and a loan fraud. **15 years**, see **265.22** for details.)

R v Shah 2013 EWCA Crim 1279 (Convicted of section 1 fraud. Set up a business renting out high-performance vehicles. Insurance was high so he falsely represented to his broker that the business was a garage carrying out repairs and MOTs. Claimed he had never had a policy cancelled and that the business did not rent out vehicles. All assertions were false. Policy in force for about six weeks. Aged 28. Married with two-year-old child. Previous convictions for riot, handling a stolen vehicle and no insurance, among others (all 2002). No monies were lost. Risk to the public of renting vehicles without valid insurance was an aggravating feature. Relatively unsophisticated and short-lived fraud. **4 months** was appropriate, not 12.)

Old cases: *R v Yates* 2010 EWCA Crim 1028, 2011 1 Cr App R (S) 15 (p 112) (**2 years 6 months**) *R v Matthews* 2010 EWCA Crim 3115 (**6 years**)

For a summary of the first case, see the 10th edition of this book.

265.46   *Price fixing, illegal cartels and illegal anti-competitive measures*   *Pre-2014 guideline case*

R v Whittle and Others 2008 EWCA Crim 2560 All the defendants pleaded at the first opportunity to a cartel offence under Enterprise Act 2002 s 188. They had all been involved in fixing the price of marine hose, used for transporting oil and ancillary equipment. Each had a close association with a company that had been involved for many years before the Enterprise Act in an international cartel operating in the marine hose market. The cartel consisted of all the principal manufacturers worldwide. They were all party to a long-standing agreement to share the market, and this involved price fixing and bid rigging. The defendants were arrested in the USA during a meeting of the cartel in Houston at the annual Offshore Technology Conference. The cartel meeting was clandestine. The total value of the UK contracts affected between June 2003 and May 2007 (the dates on the indictment) was about £17.5m. The activities of the cartel caused an uplift of about 15% over what would otherwise have been the market price. An additional profit therefore of about £2.5m was made for the company during that period. On arrest in the USA they all made full and detailed admissions and indicated they would also plead guilty to a UK cartel offence. They entered into detailed plea bargain agreements which agreed sentences in the USA. They were allowed to return to the UK and the agreement provided that the US terms would be reduced by one day for each day of any sentence the UK court imposed. It also provided that they would not seek shorter prison terms in the UK than the ones agreed in the USA. The UK terms were to be calculated for this agreement as the original UK sentence terms, not the days actually to be served in the UK. The net effect of the agreement was that provided that each were sentenced in the UK to a term not less than the agreed US one, they would not be expected to return to the USA to serve any sentence there. Each defendant was of good character, each admitted his involvement readily and each offered to assist the authorities further. W had given evidence in the USA. Each lost his livelihood, and there would be significant financial consequences for each. Held. In general the following points should be considered: the gravity and nature of the offence, the duration of the offence, the degree of culpability of the defendant in implementing the cartel agreement, the degree of culpability of the defendant in enforcing the cartel agreement, whether the defendant's conduct was contrary to guidelines laid down in the company compliance manual, and mitigating factors, e.g. any co-operation the defendant has provided, whether or not he was compelled to participate under duress, whether it was the first offence, and any personal circumstance which the court may regard as a factor suggesting leniency. Whatever the starting point would have been, these mitigating matters would have led to significant discounts on sentence. Had we not been constrained by the agreement we may well have been persuaded to reduce the sentence further. In the light of the circumstances of the US agreement in this case this cannot be a guideline case. With considerable misgivings, but to avoid injustice, we substitute the sentences in the agreement. For W **2½ years** not 3, for D **2 years** not 3 and for B **20 months** not 30.

Property fraud see the ***Mortgage fraud/Property fraud*** para at **265.44**.

265.47   *Regulated activity when not authorised, Carrying out*

R v Epton 2009 EWCA Crim 515, 2 Cr App R (S) 96 (p 639) D pleaded to carrying out regulated activity when not authorised and transferring criminal property. B set up an Internet pyramid investment scam. Extremely high returns were promised but few if any investments were made. D was originally an investor but he became the UK manager of funds. A company and bank accounts were opened, and credit would be entered on the victim's Internet account. Returns would be paid if requested but many 'reinvested' them. Some investors were assured that everything was FSA compliant. D became concerned and took legal advice, and was told that it looked as though it involved regulated activity and the solicitor had concerns about money laundering. He raised those concerns with B but continued to accept investments. £423,658 was drained from an account. D had invested £50,000 and received a £75,000 return. He received about £65,000 in wages or commission. The FBI raided the US offices but D continued to invest. He took £10,000 from the UK bank account for himself. This was the basis for the second charge. In interview he said that he received instructions from B and said his concerns were swayed by him. D was aged 65, in poor health and of good character. The Judge said that he knew that there were no underlying investments and that he was greedy. Held. **15 months** and **9 months** were not excessive, neither was the **2 years** totally wrong.

R v Dixon 2012 EWCA Crim 815, 2 Cr App R (S) 100 (p 589) D pleaded to eight counts of engaging in a consumer credit business without a licence. Over a period of 7½ years, D engaged in lending substantial sums of money to individuals whom she knew. She had no licence. She had loaned out about £400,000, in amounts from £50 to £30,000. When police searched D's address, they found £9,000, short loan agreements and loan books containing the personal accounts of the borrowers. It was a well-organised and lucrative illegal money-lending operation. D did not inform the borrowers that the APR rates were between 1,300% and 1,700%. Large charges were levied against borrowers who missed repayments, in addition to threats made by D against those who did so. To ensure that regular payments were made, D took borrowers' bank cards and PINs. Although D pleaded, it was apparent in the pre-sentence report that her pleas were as a result of legal advice to that effect, as opposed to an acceptance of responsibility. D, aged 35 at appeal, was of positive good character. D was a single parent and sole carer for two young children, and D was receiving treatment for depression. Held. Although D's case was serious, it lacked many features of an aggressive loan shark. With the mitigation, 3 years was the starting point. With the plea, **2 years** not 3 years 9 months.

Stock market/share frauds see the *Insider dealing* paras at **265.38** and the *Investments, false promises/Bogus investment schemes etc.* paras at **265.41**.

For guidelines see the *City frauds* paras at **265.25**.

265.48   *Share fraud   Boiler room fraud   Pre-2014 guideline cases*

An example: *R v Wilmot* 2012 EWCA Crim 1424, 2013 1 Cr App R (S) 61 (p 344) (LCJ Convicted of conspiracy to defraud. Boiler room fraud. Based overseas. Losses of around £13.5m. Conducted over four years involving four companies. Aged 65 at appeal. Good character. Suffered from health problems. Masterminded the fraud. **9 years** not manifestly excessive.)

265.49   *Wills   Judicial guidance*

R v Kidd and Bianchy 2008 1 Cr App R (S) 82 (p 471) The two defendants, K and B, pleaded to attempting to obtain property by deception at the Magistrates' Court. Held. However exceptional the circumstances, forgery, particularly forgery of [wills], must in all but the most exceptional circumstances be visited [with] immediate custody.

Old cases: Best ignored.

266   GOING EQUIPPED TO STEAL

266.1

Theft Act 1968 s 25

Mode of trial Triable either way

Maximum sentence On indictment 3 years. Summary 6 months and/or a £5,000 fine for offences committed before 12 March 2015 and an unlimited fine thereafter.[508] There are maximum fines for those aged under 18, see **14.38** in Volume 1.

Disqualification from driving If the offence concerns the theft or taking of a motor vehicle, the offence carries discretionary disqualification.[509]

266.2   *Crown Court statistics   England and Wales*

Going equipped to steal Aged 21+

Year	Plea	Total sen- tenced	Type of sentencing %						Average length of custody in months
			Discharge	Fine	Commu- nity sentence	Sus- pended sentence	Custody	Other	
2013	G	131	0.8	1.5	16.8	20.6	58	2.3	8.4
	NG	12	–	–	16.7	50	33.3	–	7.5
2014	G	121	1	1	15	22	60	1	8.6
	NG	13	–	–	8	23	69	–	12.7

For explanations about the statistics see page 1-xii. For statistics for those aged under 21 and for male and female defendants etc. see www.banksr.com Other Matters Statistics tab

266.3   *Sentencing Council Guideline*

Theft Offences Guideline 2016, see www.banksr.com Other matters Guidelines tab In force 1 February 2016.

STEP ONE: Determining the offence category

page 22 The court should determine the offence category with reference only to the factors identified in the following tables. In order to determine the category the court should assess culpability and harm.

The level of culpability is determined by weighing up all the factors of the case to determine the offender's role and the extent to which the offending was planned and the sophistication with which it was carried out.

---

[508] Legal Aid, Sentencing and Punishment of Offenders Act 2012 s 85(1) and (4) and Legal Aid, Sentencing and Punishment of Offenders Act 2012 (Commencement No 11) Order 2015 2015/504

[509] Road Traffic Offenders Act 1988 s 9, 34, 97 and Sch 2 Part II

CULPABILITY demonstrated by one or more of the following:
A – High Culpability
A leading role where offending is part of a group activity Involvement of others through coercion, intimidation or exploitation Significant steps taken to conceal identity and/or avoid detection Sophisticated nature of offence/significant planning Offender equipped for robbery or domestic burglary
B – Medium Culpability
A significant role where offending is part of a group activity All other cases where characteristics for categories A or C are not present
C – Lesser Culpability
Involved through coercion, intimidation or exploitation Limited awareness or understanding of offence Little or no planning

Where there are characteristics present which fall under different levels of culpability, the court should balance these characteristics to reach a fair assessment of the offender's culpability.

Harm

This guideline refers to preparatory offences where no theft has been committed. The level of harm is determined by weighing up all the factors of the case to determine the harm that would be caused if the item(s) were used to commit a substantive offence.

Greater harm
Possession of item(s) which have the potential to facilitate an offence affecting a large number of victims Possession of item(s) which have the potential to facilitate an offence involving high value items
Lesser harm
All other cases

266.4

STEP TWO: Starting point and category range

page 23 Having determined the category at step one, the court should use the starting point to reach a sentence within the appropriate category range in the table below.

The starting point applies to all offenders irrespective of plea or previous convictions.

	Culpability		
Harm	**A**	**B**	**C**
Greater	**Starting point** 1 year's custody	**Starting point** 18 weeks' custody	**Starting point** Medium level community order
	Category range 26 weeks' to 1 year 6 months' custody	**Category range** High level community order to 36 weeks' custody	**Category range** Low level community order to High level community order

	Culpability		
Harm	**A**	**B**	**C**
Lesser	**Starting point** 26 weeks' custody	**Starting point** High level community order	**Starting point** Band C fine
	Category range 12 weeks' to 36 weeks' custody	**Category range** Medium level community order to 12 weeks' custody	**Category range** Discharge to Medium level community order

Consecutive sentences for multiple offences may be appropriate – please refer to the [*TICs and Totality Guideline 2012*].

The court should then consider further adjustment for any aggravating or mitigating factors. The following is a **non-exhaustive** list of additional factual elements providing the context of the offence and factors relating to the offender. Identify whether any combination of these, or other relevant factors, should result in an upward or downward adjustment from the starting point.

Factors increasing seriousness
Statutory aggravating factors: Previous convictions, having regard to a) the nature of the offence to which the conviction relates and its relevance to the current offence; and b) the time that has elapsed since the conviction Offence committed whilst on bail ***Other aggravating factors:*** Attempts to conceal/dispose of evidence Established evidence of community/wider impact Failure to comply with current court orders Offence committed on licence Offences taken into consideration

Factors reducing seriousness or reflecting personal mitigation
No previous convictions or no relevant/recent convictions Good character and/or exemplary conduct Serious medical condition requiring urgent, intensive or long-term treatment Age and/or lack of maturity where it affects the responsibility of the offender Mental disorder or learning disability Sole or primary carer for dependent relatives Determination and/or demonstration of steps having been taken to address addiction or offending behaviour

267 HANDLING STOLEN GOODS

267.1

Theft Act 1968 s 22

Mode of trial Triable either way

Maximum sentence On indictment 14 years. Summary 6 months and/or a £5,000 fine for offences committed before 12 March 2015 and an unlimited fine thereafter.[510] There are maximum fines for those aged under 18, see **14.38** in Volume 1.

Restitution Orders There is power to make an order that the stolen goods etc. in the possession of the defendant or a third party be restored to the owner etc.[511]

---

[510] Legal Aid, Sentencing and Punishment of Offenders Act 2012 s 85(1) and (4) and Legal Aid, Sentencing and Punishment of Offenders Act 2012 (Commencement No 11) Order 2015 2015/504

[511] Powers of Criminal Courts (Sentencing) Act 2000 s 148(2)

267.2   Crown Court statistics   England and Wales
Handling stolen goods

Year	Age	Plea	Total sen-tenced	Type of sentencing %						Average length of custody in months
				Dis-charge	Fine	Community sentence	Sus-pended sentence	Custody	Oth-er	
2013	18-20	G	212	5.2	2.8	34	17	41	–	8.1
		NG	17	–	5.9	47.1	23.5	23.5	–	9.5
	21+	G	1,291	1.9	1.4	19.8	27	49.5	0.4	11.4
		NG	157	1.9	3.8	24.2	28.7	40.8	0.6	19.5
2014	18-20	G	167	6	2	36	18	38	1	7.5
		NG	13	–	–	38	23	38	–	12.0
	21+	G	1,295	2	2	18	30	48	1	11.7
		NG	138	3	4	21	27	46	–	17.9

For explanations about the statistics see page 1-xii. For statistics for male and female defendants etc. see www.banksr.com Other Matters Statistics tab

267.3   Sentencing Council's guideline
Theft Offences Guideline 2016, www.banksr.com Other matters Guidelines tab In force 1 February 2016. The guideline only applies to offenders aged 18+, see page 2 of the guideline. For the usual practice, see **66.21**.

STEP ONE: Determining the offence category
page 16 The court should determine the offence category with reference only to the factors identified in the following tables. In order to determine the category the court should assess culpability and harm.
The level of culpability is determined by weighing up all the factors of the case to determine the offender's role and the extent to which the offending was planned and the sophistication with which it was carried out.

CULPABILITY demonstrated by one or more of the following
A – High Culpability
A leading role where offending is part of a group activity
Involvement of others through coercion, intimidation or exploitation
Abuse of position of power or trust or responsibility
Professional and sophisticated offence
Advance knowledge of the primary offence
Possession of very recently stolen goods from a domestic burglary or robbery
B – Medium Culpability
A significant role where offending is part of a group activity
Offender acquires goods for resale
All other cases where characteristics for categories A or C are not present
C – Lesser Culpability
Performed limited function under direction
Involved through coercion, intimidation or exploitation
Little or no planning
Limited awareness or understanding of offence
Goods acquired for offender's personal use

Where there are characteristics present which fall under different levels of culpability, the court should balance these characteristics to reach a fair assessment of the offender's culpability.

267.4   *Harm*

page 17 Harm is assessed by reference to the financial value (to the loser) of the handled goods and any significant additional harm associated with the underlying offence on the victim or others – examples of additional harm may include but are not limited to:

Property stolen from a domestic burglary or a robbery (unless this has already been taken into account in assessing culpability)

Items stolen were of substantial value to the loser, regardless of monetary worth

Metal theft causing disruption to infrastructure

Damage to heritage assets

Category 1	Very high value goods stolen (above £100,000) **or** High value with significant additional harm to the victim or others
Category 2	High value goods stolen (£10,000 to £100,000) **and** no significant additional harm **or** Medium value with significant additional harm to the victim or others
Category 3	Medium value goods stolen (£1,000 to £10,000) **and** no significant additional harm **or** Low value with significant additional harm to the victim or others
Category 4	Low value goods stolen (up to £1,000) **and** Little or no significant additional harm to the victim or others

267.5   *Suggested approach to the harm category*

Note: These financial categories are likely to be considered in the same way as the *Drug Offences Guideline 2012* categories are. This would mean that Category 2 has a midpoint of £45,000 and Category 3 has a midpoint of £4,500. Where the value of the goods stolen in a given category is more or less than the midpoint value an adjustment should be made. These categories are clearly not a series of steps but a graduated scale. Ed.

267.6

STEP TWO: Starting point and category range

page 18 Having determined the category at step one, the court should use the starting point to reach a sentence within the appropriate category range in the table below.

The starting point applies to all offenders irrespective of plea or previous convictions.

Culpability			
Harm	**A**	**B**	**C**
Category 1 Where the value greatly exceeds £100,000, it may be appropriate to move outside the identified range. Adjustment should be made for any significant additional harm where very high value stolen goods are handled	**Starting point** 5 years' custody	**Starting point** 3 years' custody	**Starting point** 1 year's custody
	Category range 3-8 years' custody	**Category range** 1 year 6 months' to 4 years' custody	**Category range** 26 weeks' to 1 year 6 months' custody

Culpability			
Harm	**A**	**B**	**C**
Category 2	**Starting point** 3 years' custody	**Starting point** 1 year's custody	**Starting point** High-level community order
	Category range 1 year 6 months' to 4 years' custody	**Category range** 26 weeks' to 1 year 6 months' custody	**Category range** Low-level community order to 26 weeks' custody
Category 3	**Starting point** 1 year's custody	**Starting point** High-level community order	**Starting point** Band C fine
	Category range 26 weeks' to 2 years' custody	**Category range** Low-level community order to 26 weeks' custody	**Category range** Band B fine to Low-level community order
Category 4	**Starting point** High-level community order	**Starting point** Low-level community order	**Starting point** Band B fine
	Category range Medium-level community order to 26 weeks' custody	**Category range** Band C fine to High-level community order	**Category range** Discharge to Band C fine

Consecutive sentences for multiple offences may be appropriate – please refer to the [*TICs and Totality Guideline 2012*].

267.7 [Aggravating and mitigating factors]
Seriousness

page 19 The court should then consider further adjustment for any aggravating or mitigating factors. The following is a non-exhaustive list of additional factual elements providing the context of the offence and factors relating to the offender. Identify whether any combination of these, or other relevant factors, should result in an upward or downward adjustment from the starting point.

Factors increasing seriousness
Statutory aggravating factors: Previous convictions, having regard to a) the nature of the offence to which the conviction relates and its relevance to the current offence; and b) the time that has elapsed since the conviction Offence committed whilst on bail *Other aggravating factors:* Seriousness of the underlying offence, for example, armed robbery Deliberate destruction, disposal or defacing of stolen property Damage to a third party Failure to comply with current court orders Offence committed on licence Offences taken into consideration Established evidence of community/wider impact

Factors reducing seriousness or reflecting personal mitigation
No previous convictions or no relevant/recent convictions
Good character and/or exemplary conduct
Serious medical condition requiring urgent, intensive or long-term treatment
Age and/or lack of maturity where it affects the responsibility of the offender
Mental disorder or learning disability
Sole or primary carer for dependent relatives
Determination and/or demonstration of steps having been taken to address addiction or offending behaviour

267.8   *Suggested approach to the guideline*

Note: The new guideline is a different approach to determining the sentence from the old guideline case of *R v Webb* 2001 EWCA Crim 1217, 2002 1 Cr App R (S) 22 (p 82). On the other hand, the Sentencing Council in its press release introducing the new guideline said, 'the Sentencing Council has not set out to change overall sentencing levels, but rather to provide comprehensive guidance and introduce a standard approach.' In balancing these factors I have included most of the old cases. If the old cases are used, it would be wise to begin and end the consideration with the guideline. Where the main factor in a pre-guideline case is the financial value I have not included it because the reader would be wise to simply apply the guideline, which is based on value. Ed.

267.9   *Pre-2016 judicial guideline*

R v Webbe 2001 EWCA Crim 1217, 2002 1 Cr App R (S) 22 (p 82) para 3 The offence can attract a penalty from a conditional discharge or modest fine at one end, up to 14 years' imprisonment at the other.

para 15 The relative seriousness of a case depends upon the interplay of different factors. One important issue is whether the handler has had advance knowledge of the original offence, or has directly or indirectly made known his willingness to receive the proceeds of the original offence, as compared with a handler who has had no connection with the original offence but who has dishonestly accepted the stolen goods at an undervalued [price]. Where the handler has had knowledge of the original offence, the seriousness of the handling is inevitably linked to the seriousness of that original offence. The link to the original offence explains the need for the high maximum penalty of 14 years' imprisonment, which might otherwise look anomalous. Sentences approaching the maximum should clearly be reserved for the most serious and unusual cases where the handler had previous knowledge of a very serious offence such as an armed robbery, which itself carries life imprisonment as its maximum.

para 17 There is an obvious difference, for example, between the gravity of receiving in a public house £100 worth of stolen television sets, and the gravity of receiving £100 in cash from the proceeds of a robbery which has taken place in the receiver's presence. Furthermore, accurate values in relation to the property received may very often be extremely difficult to ascertain.

para 18 The [Sentencing Advisory] Panel identified [that] other factors significantly affecting the relative seriousness of the handling offence are the level of sophistication of the handler, the ultimate designation of the goods, the criminal origin of the goods, the impact on the victim, the level of profit made or expected by the handler and, especially in cases of actual or intended disposal of goods, the precise role played by the handler. Those factors are correctly identified.

para 20 The Sentencing Advisory Panel identify nine factors which aggravate the offence. We agree with all nine:

1) The closeness of the handler to the primary offence (we add that closeness may be geographical, arising from presence at or near the primary offence when it was committed, or temporal, where the handler instigated or encouraged the primary offence beforehand, or, soon after, provided a safe haven or route for disposal),

2) Particular seriousness in the primary offence,

3) (This factor is about value, about which the sentencer should refer to the new guideline),
4) (This is about the proceeds of a domestic burglary, which is dealt with in the guideline),
5) Sophistication in relation to the handling,
6) A high level of profit made or expected by the handler,
7) The provision by the handler of a regular outlet for stolen goods,
8) Threats of violence or abuse of power by the handler over others, for example, an adult commissioning criminal activity by children, or a drug dealer pressurising addicts to steal in order to pay for their habit.

Note: *Theft Offences Guideline 2016* takes precedence over this old guideline case. However, some of the principles may still assist.

Types of handling

267.10   *Burglary (Dwelling)/robbery, Proceeds of*

Note: *Theft Offences Guideline 2016*, www.banksr.com Other matters Guidelines tab page 16 One of the Level A High culpability factors in the guideline is 'Possession of recently stolen goods from a domestic burglary or robbery', see **267.3**. page 17 One of the 'harm' factors in the guideline is 'Property stolen from a domestic burglary or robbery (unless that has already been taken into account in assessing culpability', see **267.4**. page 19 One of the aggravating factors is 'Seriousness of the underlying offence, for example armed robbery', **267.7**. In the press release when the guideline was issued, the Sentencing Council said, 'the guideline will bring a clear focus on the impact of thefts on victims beyond financial loss. These offences can cause emotional distress, loss of confidence and great disruption and inconvenience.' I consider that this applies as much to handling as it does to theft offences. As the Level A-C factors determine the starting points and ranges, I do not think the pre-2016 cases can assist for most types of handling. I think it is better for most offences just to apply the guideline. Where there is something special that is not included in the guideline, I have listed a few old cases. Ed.

267.11   *Looting, Proceeds of   Judicial guidance*

R v Blackshaw and Others 2011 EWCA Crim 2312 LCJ The Court considered the appeals against the sentences imposed for handling committed during, and as a result of, widespread public disorder. Held. In cases like these, a line needs to be drawn between the offences which arose from and were directly connected with the disorder (which is an aggravating feature in itself) and those which were intrinsic to the disorder (an even more aggravating feature).

267.12   *Looting, Proceeds of   Cases*

R v Blackshaw and Others 2011 EWCA Crim 2312 LCJ The Court considered the appeals against the sentences imposed for handling committed during, and as a result of, widespread public disorder. None of these cases of dishonest handling involves someone who handled stolen goods by way of encouragement of the commission of burglary and theft as part of the disorder. Rather each represents opportunistic involvement after the burglaries had occurred, and although in close proximity to the scenes of disorder, the appellants did not participate or contribute to them. Sentences of 12 months, 18 months and 16 months were reduced to **6 months**, **9 months** and **8 months** respectively, to reflect the distance between the instant offences and the widespread disorder of which they were a part.

267.7a   *Metal theft*

Note: *Theft Offences Guideline 2016*, www.banksr.com Other matters Guidelines tab page 17 One of the Harm factors in the guideline is 'Metal theft causing damage to infrastructure', see **346.4**. In the press release when the guideline was issued, the Sentencing Council said, 'Other factors making an offence more serious under the new guidelines include thefts that risk harm to people. This would include offences where electricity cables are stolen, which present an obvious danger of injury to the public.' Ed.

Matters relating to the defendant

267.13   *Persistent offenders*

R v Kiracoglu 2010 EWCA Crim 328 D pleaded to theft and handling. A resident chained her £2,700 bicycle to a staircase. D stole all of it except the frame. A nurse chained her £750 bike to another bicycle and D was seen struggling in the street with the two bikes chained together. The police were called. D was aged 28 with 23 convictions, mainly for dishonesty. There were a significant number for stealing bicycles. There were also convictions for possessing drugs. He had received a range of community punishments. D was the sole carer for his mother. He was in breach of a community order for theft of items from a car. He broke appointments on 20 occasions. The pre-sentence report said he was a long-standing heroin addict and there was a high risk of reoffending until he addressed his addiction to drugs. His case was adjourned to assess suitability for a drug rehabilitation programme. He failed to attend for his assessment. Held. D deliberately targeted valuable bicycles. Community service had not deterred him. 6 months, **8 months** and 2 months for the breach consecutive were not individually or collectively (**16 months**) excessive. (Interestingly, D pleaded to handling no doubt thinking it was less serious than theft. In fact he received 2 months less for stealing the more valuable bicycle than handling the others. Ed.)

R v Jack 2010 EWCA Crim 883 D was convicted of handling stolen goods. Following a search at a halfway house, computer games and a wristwatch which had been stolen from a house the day before were found in D's room. D, aged 32, had 70 previous convictions, including robbery (2 years), burglary, theft and two for handling, and was on licence at the time of these offences. Held. The aggravating factors were the goods had been stolen in a domestic burglary, the handling was close in time to the burglary, the offence was committed whilst D was on licence and D's bad record. **18 months** not 27.

R v Dixon 2010 EWCA Crim 2606 D pleaded to four counts of handling. The charges related to selling CDs and DVDs at an exchange store on four consecutive days. The property had come from four dwelling house burglaries which had been committed just before each of the sales. D also tried to sell a digital camera. D tried to escape when store staff attempted to detain him. The property was sold to the store for a total of £71.70. A large number of CDs and DVDs were recovered.[512] D was aged 44 at appeal. A pre-sentence report noted that D attempted to blame his brother, who had accompanied him to the exchange store. There was a medium risk of reconviction. D had 35 court appearances for 131 offences, mostly for offences of dishonesty including a high number of burglaries. Held. **4 years** not 5 years 3 months.

See also: *R v Stockton* 2014 EWCA Crim 321 (Plea to handling. Proceeds of a burglary. Value about £300. Arrested near the property soon after the burglary. Aged 37. Appalling record including 27 convictions for 99 offences from 1992 to 2013. Four handling offences and six dwelling burglaries. The proximity in time and distance to the burglary aggravated the offence. Starting at 3 years, with full credit for the plea, **2 years** was not manifestly excessive.)

R v Allgood and Allgood 2014 EWCA Crim 2581 (£7,500 worth of garden furniture. **30 months** not 3 years,)

267.14   *Professional handlers*

R v Webbe 2001 EWCA Crim 1217, 2002 1 Cr App R (S) 22 (p 82) In the more serious cases where the value of the goods is in excess of £100,000, or where the offence is highly organised and bears the hallmarks of a professional commercial operation, a sentence of **4 years and upwards** is likely to be appropriate, and it will be higher where the source of the handled property is known by the handler to be a serious violent offence such as armed robbery.

---

[512] Presumably from D's address. Ed.

Note: *Theft Offences Guideline 2016*, www.banksr.com Other matters Guidelines tab page 16 One of the Level A High culpability factors in the guideline is 'Professional and sophisticated offence', see **267.3**. Ed.

The sentence

267.15   *Compensation, confiscation and restitution*

R v Webbe 2001 EWCA Crim 1217, 2002 1 Cr App R (S) 22 (p 82) A court should always have in mind the power to make Restitution Orders under Powers of Criminal Courts (Sentencing) Act 2000 s 148-149, to make compensation orders under Powers of Criminal Courts (Sentencing) Act 2000 s 130, and to make confiscation orders in relation to profits under Criminal Justice Act 1988 and Proceeds of Crime Act 1995. (These two Acts have been replaced by Proceeds of Crime Act 2002. Ed.) A Magistrates' Court cannot, of course, make a confiscation order in a case of handling. But it is open to magistrates, in such a case, to commit to the Crown Court for sentence.

267.16   *Fines and compensation more appropriate than custody*

R v Webbe 2001 EWCA Crim 1217, 2002 1 Cr App R (S) 22 (p 82) LCJ *R v Khemlani* 1981 3 Cr App R (S) 208 shows the sentence that was appropriate for a man of good character, who pleaded to handling 350 stolen watches (wholesale value £7,350). K was imprisoned for **3 months**. The Court of Appeal took the view that this matter could be far better met by imposing a fine and making a compensation order in favour of the owners of the goods.

268   HARASSMENT SECTION 2

268.1

Protection from Harassment Act 1997 s 2 (pursuing a course of harassment)

Mode of trial Summary only

Maximum sentence 6 months and/or a Level 5 fine (£5,000 fine for offences committed before 12 March 2015 and an unlimited fine thereafter.[513] There are maximum fines for those aged under 18, see **14.38** in Volume 1).

Criminal Behaviour Orders Where a defendant has engaged in behaviour that caused or was likely to cause harassment, alarm or distress to any persons and a Criminal Behaviour Order will help in preventing the offender from engaging in such behaviour, the court may make this order.[514]

Restraining Order There is power to make a Restraining Order to protect the victim etc. from further conduct.[515] There is power to impose an order after an acquittal, Domestic Violence, Crime and Victims Act 2004 s 12 etc.[516]

Sexual Harm Prevention Orders There is a discretionary power to make this order when it is necessary to protect the public from sexual harm.[517]

See also the **PUBLIC ORDER ACT 1986 S 4**, **PUBLIC ORDER ACT 1986 S 5**, and **STALKING** chapters.

268.2   *Magistrates' Court Sentencing Guidelines*

Magistrates' Court Sentencing Guidelines 2008, see www.banksr.com Other Matters Guidelines tab The guideline applies to the Magistrates' Court and to the Crown Court hearing appeals or sentencing for summary only offences.[518] It also deals with racially or religiously aggravated offences where the sentence should be increased to reflect this element.

For how to apply the guidelines see the **GUIDELINES** chapter.

---

[513] Legal Aid, Sentencing and Punishment of Offenders Act 2012 s 85(1) and (4) and Legal Aid, Sentencing and Punishment of Offenders Act 2012 (Commencement No 11) Order 2015 2015/504
[514] Anti-social Behaviour, Crime and Policing Act 2014 s 22(1)-(4)
[515] Protection from Harassment Act 1997 s 5
[516] Domestic Violence, Crime and Victims Act 2004 (Commencement No 11) Order 2009 2009/2501
[517] Sexual Offences Act 2003 s 103A as inserted by Anti-social Behaviour, Crime and Policing Act 2014 Sch 5 para 2 and Sexual Offences Act 2003 Sch 5
[518] See page 15 of the guidelines.

page 70 Starting points are based on a first-time offender pleading not guilty.

Examples of nature of activity	Starting point	Range
Small number of incidents	Medium-level community order	Band C fine to high-level community order
Constant contact at night, trying to come into workplace or home, involving others	6 weeks' custody	Medium-level community order to 12 weeks' custody
Threatening violence, taking personal photographs, sending offensive material	18 weeks' custody	12 to 26 weeks' custody

The following aggravating and mitigating factors may be particularly relevant: Factors indicating higher culpability: 1 Planning 2 Offender ignores obvious distress 3 Offender involves others 4 Using contact arrangements with a child to instigate offence. Factors indicating lower culpability: 1 Limited understanding of effect on victim 2 Initial provocation. Factors indicating greater degree of harm: 1 Victim needs medical help or counselling 2 Action over long period 3 Children frightened 4 Use or distribution of photographs.

Consider a Restraining Order and ancillary orders, including compensation.

For the meaning of a high-level and a medium-level community order see **16.13** in Volume 1.

A Band C fine is 150% of net weekly income. For more detail see **60.27** in Volume 1.

268.3   *Guideline case*
R v Liddle and Hayes 2000 1 Cr App R (S) p 131 see **269.3**.

268.4   *Racially or Religiously aggravated*
Protection from Harassment Act 1997 s 2 and the Crime and Disorder Act 1998 s 32(1)(a) (pursuing a course of harassment which is racially aggravated)
Mode of trial Triable either way
Maximum sentence On indictment 2 years. Summary 6 months and/or a £5,000 fine for offences committed before 12 March 2015 and an unlimited fine thereafter.[519] There are maximum fines for those aged under 18, see **14.38** in Volume 1.
The guideline and ancillary orders are the same, see **268.1**.
For ***Basic principles*** *see* the RACIALLY AGGRAVATED OFFENCES ***Basic principles*** para at **315.4**.

269   HARASSMENT SECTION 4: PUBLIC NUISANCE ETC.
269.1
1) Protection from Harassment Act 1997 s 4 (putting people in fear of violence)
   Mode of trial Triable either way
   Maximum sentence On indictment 5 years.[520] Summary 6 months and/or a £5,000 fine for offences committed before 12 March 2015 and an unlimited fine thereafter.[521] There are maximum fines for those aged under 18, see **14.38** in Volume 1.
2) Public nuisance
   Mode of trial Common law, so indictable only
   Maximum sentence There is no maximum provided, so the maximum is life imprisonment.

---

[519] Legal Aid, Sentencing and Punishment of Offenders Act 2012 s 85(1) and (4) and Legal Aid, Sentencing and Punishment of Offenders Act 2012 (Commencement No 11) Order 2015 2015/504
[520] Where the jury convict of a section 4 offence as an alternative to the racially aggravated offence, the maximum sentence at the Crown Court is the Magistrates' Courts' maximum, *R v Alden* 2002 EWCA Crim 421, 2 Cr App R (S) 74 (p 326).
[521] Legal Aid, Sentencing and Punishment of Offenders Act 2012 s 85(1) and (4) and Legal Aid, Sentencing and Punishment of Offenders Act 2012 (Commencement No 11) Order 2015 2015/504

Criminal Behaviour Orders Where a defendant has engaged in behaviour that caused or was likely to cause harassment, alarm or distress to any persons and a Criminal Behaviour Order will help in preventing the offender from engaging in such behaviour, the court may make this order.[522]

Extended sentences This offence is listed in Criminal Justice Act 2003 Sch 15. The court may pass a 2012 extended sentence (EDS) if there is a significant risk of serious harm from future specified offences and either: a) the defendant has a Criminal Justice Act 2003 Sch 15B conviction (applicable only to defendants aged 18+), or b) the offence would justify a determinate sentence of at least 4 years.[523]

Restraining Orders There is power to make this order to protect the victim etc. from further conduct.[524] There is power to impose an order after an acquittal, Domestic Violence, Crime and Victims Act 2004 s 12 etc.[525]

Sexual Harm Prevention Orders There is a discretionary power to make this order when it is necessary to protect the public from sexual harm.[526]

Law Commission On 25 June 2015, the Law Commission issued a consultation paper suggesting the offence should be replaced with one which requires the defendant intended to cause, or was reckless about causing, a public nuisance.

269.2   Magistrates' Court Sentencing Guideline

Magistrates' Court Sentencing Guideline 2008, see www.banksr.com Other Matters Guidelines tab The guideline applies to the Magistrates' Court and to the Crown Court hearing appeals or sentencing for summary only offences.[527] The guideline also deals with racially or religiously aggravated offences where the sentence should be increased to reflect this element.

For how to apply the guidelines see the **GUIDELINES** chapter in Volume 1.

page 68 Starting points are based on a first-time offender pleading not guilty.

Examples of nature of activity	Starting point	Range
A pattern of two or more incidents of unwanted contact	6 weeks' custody	High-level community order to 18 weeks' custody
Deliberate threats, persistent action over a longer period, or intention to cause fear of violence	18 weeks' custody	12 weeks' custody to Crown Court
Sexual threats, vulnerable person targeted	Crown Court	Crown Court

The following aggravating and mitigating factors may be particularly relevant: Factors indicating higher culpability: 1 Planning 2 Offender ignores obvious distress 3 Visits in person to victim's home or workplace 4 Offender involves others 5 Using contact arrangements with a child to instigate offence. Factors indicating lower culpability: 1 Limited understanding of effect on victim 2 Initial provocation. Factors indicating greater degree of harm: 1 Victim needs medical help/counselling 2 Physical violence used 3 Victim aware that offender has history of using violence 4 Grossly violent or offensive material sent 5 Children frightened 6 Evidence that victim changed lifestyle to avoid contact.

Consider making a Restraining Order and ancillary orders, including compensation.

For the meaning of a high-level community order see **16.14** in Volume 1.

---

[522] Anti-social Behaviour, Crime and Policing Act 2014 s 22(1)-(4)
[523] Criminal Justice Act 2003 s 226A-226B as inserted by Legal Aid, Sentencing and Punishment of Offenders Act 2012 s 124
[524] Protection from Harassment Act 1997 s 5
[525] Domestic Violence, Crime and Victims Act 2004 (Commencement No 11) Order 2009 2009/2501
[526] Sexual Offences Act 2003 s 103A as inserted by Anti-social Behaviour, Crime and Policing Act 2014 Sch 5 para 2 and Sexual Offences Act 2003 Sch 5
[527] See page 15 of the guidelines.

For the *Domestic Violence Guideline 2006*, see www.banksr.com Other Matters Guidelines tab and see also the **DOMESTIC VIOLENCE** chapter.

269.3   Guideline case
R v Liddle and Hayes 2000 1 Cr App R (S) p 131 The court should consider:
a) Is the offence a section 2 or a section 4 offence?
b) Is there a history of disobedience to court orders in the past?
c) The seriousness of the defendant's conduct, which can of course range from actual violence through to threats, down to letters, which of course may even express affection rather than any wish to harm the victim.
d) Is there persistent misconduct by the defendant or a solitary instance of misbehaviour?
e) The effect upon the victim, whether physical or psychological. Does the victim require protection? What is the level of risk posed by the defendant?
f) The mental health of the offender. Is the defendant willing to undergo treatment or have the necessary help from the probation service, which is readily available under special schemes?
g) What is the defendant's reaction to the court proceedings? Is there a plea of guilty? Is there remorse? Is there recognition of the need for help?
For a first offence a short sharp sentence may be appropriate, though much will depend on the factors of repetition and breach of court orders and the nature of the misconduct. Obviously, the facts of each case vary and the facts of any particular case may require a longer sentence. For a second offence longer sentences of about **15 months** on a plea of guilty would be an appropriate starting point, and from then on it is possible to see from the maximum of 5 years where each case fits into the statutory framework working from the figure of 15 months, which may be appropriate.
Note: It would appear that the guidance is for both section 2 and 4 offences. Ed.
Animal rights activists see the **ANIMAL RIGHTS ACTIVISTS** *Attacking laboratories or their suppliers etc.* and *Rescuing animals from laboratories* paras at **208.3** and **208.4**.

269.4   General cases
R v Dallinger 2012 EWCA Crim 1284, 2013 1 Cr App R (S) 38 (p 212) LCJ D pleaded to public nuisance. The lease on his static caravan required him to vacate it for a proportion of the year. When he did so, he rented temporary accommodation. The accommodation was too small for his dogs and so at that time they would live with his daughter, who was arrested. Later the police visited her address as they learned that a young child had been left alone. They also found D's two dogs. The dogs were removed as it was thought they might be a prohibited breed. D became very disturbed at the seizure of his dogs and telephoned the police. He said he would "lean over the railings of a motorway bridge" if he could not find out what was happening to them. Three days later, D stood on the wrong side of the railings on a bridge over the M6 motorway. All patrols were sent out to the destination with lights flashing and sirens sounding. Road closures were implemented. Both northbound and southbound carriageways were closed. Police officers asked D why he was on the wrong side of the barriers and he said "because it is the only way I am going to get my dogs back. Get them here now." Officers persuaded him to return to the correct side of the barrier. That took about 15 minutes. He was arrested and said that if his dogs were not returned to him he would mount another demonstration. The cost of the disruption was estimated at nearly £1m. D was aged 51 at appeal and had convictions of a very different nature between 1980 and 1984. There was also a conviction in 2007 for obtaining benefit by deception (community penalty). A pre-sentence report proposed a community sentence. Held. This is a case where the impact on the public was notable and considerable. The Judge was correct to consider the prospective impact of any sentence which did not consist of an immediate custodial sentence. **6 months** upheld.

R v Harman 2015 EWCA Crim 2166 D pleaded (full credit) to harassment contrary to section 4(1). V, aged 84, lived in a block next to the flat of D's partner, P. V complained to her landlord about noise and nuisance from P's flat. On 10 June 2015, in a hallway, D called V a 'bitch'. On 11 June, D shouted through V's letter box, "You fucking slag." On 12 June, D took a picture of her in the hallway of the block and said, "That will do for court." On 13 June, V saw that D had written on a wall next to her front door, 'Stop your fucking shit or I will kill you, that is a promise, you fucking ugly slag.' D was arrested and in interview D denied harassing V and blamed her for harassing P. When asked about the harassment he had meted out to V, D said she deserved it. D was aged 46 with a poor record for dishonesty and begging. He had no conviction for harassment or anything similar. The Judge said it was a disgraceful campaign of harassment against V, who was vulnerable because of her age and that she lived alone. **9 months** not 18.
Old cases: *R v Jan* 2007 EWCA Crim 3223 (**Life** with a **7½-year** minimum term.) *R v Marchese* 2008 EWCA Crim 389 (**9 years**)
For a summary of these cases, see the 9th edition of this book.

269.5   *Racially or Religiously aggravated*
Protection from Harassment Act 1997 s 4 and Crime and Disorder Act 1998 s 32(1)(b) (putting people in fear of violence which is racially aggravated)
Mode of trial Triable either way
Maximum sentence On indictment 7 years. Summary 6 months and/or a £5,000 fine for offences committed before 12 March 2015 and an unlimited fine thereafter.[528] There are maximum fines for those aged under 18, see **14.38** in Volume 1.
The guideline and ancillary orders are the same as for a non-aggravated case, see **269.1**. *General approach* see the RACIALLY AGGRAVATED AND RELIGIOUSLY AGGRAVATED OFFENCES *Basic principles* para at **315.4**.

269.6   *Racially or Religiously aggravated   Cases*
R v Daniels 2010 EWCA Crim 2767 D pleaded to racially aggravated harassment causing intentional alarm or distress and to a breach of a community order which was imposed for an earlier offence of theft. D entered a branch of Sainsbury's with his dog. He was asked to leave as dogs were not permitted to be in the shop. A security guard came to assist and D said, "I know what you look like and I will get you outside. You're going to lose your licence, you black bastard." When arrested he continued to shout racist abuse. D, aged 18, had previous convictions for violence, harassment and racially aggravated threatening behaviour. He had a history of drug abuse which started at the age of 12. It was noted in the pre-sentence report that D insisted that he had been "stitched up". Held. There can be no doubt that the incident at the supermarket was very unpleasant. It is aggravated by D's previous offending. Furthermore, the imposition of a consecutive sentence for the offence for which the community order was imposed was clearly correct in principle. However, 18 months in total is manifestly excessive. So, **4 months** and **4 months consecutive**.
Old case: *R v McDermott and Melaney* 2008 EWCA Crim 2345, 2009 1 Cr App R (S) 110 (p 619) (**3 years**)
For a summary of the case, see the 9th edition of this book.

269.7   *Relationship offences*
R v Taylor 2010 EWCA Crim 1581 D pleaded to harassment. He had been in a ten-year on-and-off relationship with the victim, V. They did not live together but D regularly stayed at V's house and had possessions in the property. V told D she wished the relationship to end and that D had a few days to move out. D drank heavily and after consuming alcohol went into V's bedroom and began an argument. V called for her children and subsequently D pulled V's hair. V's adult daughter, L, attempted to intervene and D also pulled L's hair. V broke free and left the house with her children. D

---

[528] Legal Aid, Sentencing and Punishment of Offenders Act 2012 s 85(1) and (4) and Legal Aid, Sentencing and Punishment of Offenders Act 2012 (Commencement No 11) Order 2015 2015/504

caught up with them and banged V and L's heads together, once more grabbing them both by the hair. He was voluntarily interviewed and was not charged or put on bail. About a month later, D started a barrage of calls to V. The first was after 3 am, in a later one he said, "I ain't bothered about the police. I'm going to kick you to fuck" and "I am going to fucking strangle you". V saw D outside and the police were called. D kicked the front door and punched V. The police then arrived. No damage was caused. The Judge said that D, when drunk, was a "brutish and frightening bully". D, aged 41 at appeal, had a number of very serious convictions when a young man. Held. The Judge was not aware of the guidelines. The appropriate sentence was **28 weeks** not 12 months.

Att-Gen's Ref No 92 of 2011 2011 EWCA Crim 3284 D pleaded at the PCMH to robbery. He had known V for five or six years. She had two small children. He claimed they had had a close relationship, but V stated that their relationship was merely platonic. D had been harassing V by making telephone calls in the early hours. He was on bail for an offence of assault against V. So obsessive was his attitude, D ignored his bail conditions, and he broke into her house in the middle of the night. The door was forced. V phoned the police. D seized the phone and punched V to the back of the head a couple of times. No serious harm was caused. He took the phone and left. The following day, V went to the police station. D pursued her out of the driveway carrying a wheelie bin, which hit her car as she left. He then hung around outside the police station and as V left to go to her car, D ran up to her, shouted threats and seized her. D, aged 31 at appeal, had one conviction for possession of an offensive weapon, and other irrelevant offences. The Judge took into account the 6 months D had been on remand. After receiving a suspended sentence he continued to abuse her and broke his Restraining Order. Held. We do not take into account the later behaviour as that is for the breach hearing. The offence took place in V's home, where there were two small children, whilst D was on bail and prohibited from contacting V. However, the robbery was not the purpose of the exercise. D's purpose was harassment and intimidation. The Judge erred in not passing a sentence of imprisonment. He took the view that this was a Level 1 robbery. The correct approach is stated in *Att-Gen's Ref Nos 38-40 of 2007* 2007 EWCA Crim 1692. The court emphasised that the guideline is not relevant and the fact of a robbery taking place in the home was a seriously aggravating feature, making it more serious than a street robbery. **4½ years** was appropriate after a trial, so with the plea, **3 years**.

Note: The prosecution accepted a plea to robbery and did not pursue the harassment count. The item stolen is not referred to. The Court of Appeal treated this case as domestic abuse. Ed.

R v Iqbal 2012 EWCA Crim 267 D pleaded on the day of trial to section 4 harassment. D had harassed V, his estranged wife. He had left a threatening voicemail on her mobile phone, including a threat to chop her up into "countless little pieces". He also twice attended her place of work, making threats and physically restraining her. V felt frightened. D had no previous convictions and was the main carer for his sister. Held. D had been in custody for 3 months and that was sufficient. We reduce the sentence to **6 months** to allow for immediate release.

See also: *R v Smith* 2011 EWCA Crim 980 (Late plea to harassment. After separating from his wife, D followed her to work and later forced her into his car. He took her back to his address. Lasted 40 minutes. Good character. Two incidents only. **15 months** not 21.)

R v Brickwood 2013 EWCA Crim 2789 (Plea (full discount). Drunk, sent 200 abusive texts to daughter. Repeated previous breaches. Wanted daughter out of life to break connection with ex-wife. Daughter was sympathetic to him. Starting at 3 years, with full credit, **2 years** not 3.)

Old case: *R v Nagy* 2009 EWCA Crim 1623, 2010 1 Cr App R (S) 74 (p 41) (**12 months**) For a summary of this case, see the 9th edition of this book.

269.8   Sexual element

Note: These cases are now prosecuted with a sexual offence, no doubt to convey the seriousness of sexual offending and also to trigger notification. The cases which are just prosecuted as harassment are best ignored, as sentencing has changed since then. Ed.

269.9   Telephone calls

R v Taylor 2010 EWCA Crim 1581 (See para **269.7**.)

R v Hall 2010 EWCA Crim 1919 D pleaded (full credit) to breach of a Restraining Order and an offence under Malicious Communications Act 1988. In July 2008 D was subject to a community order imposed for offences of harassment. He had made telephone calls and sent text messages to an ex-partner. He threatened to smash windows. In November 2009, and in breach of the community order, he telephoned another ex-partner and threatened to "slit (her) throat". He pleaded to offences under Malicious Communications Act 1988 and Protection from Harassment Act 1997. He received 4 weeks suspended for 12 months and was made subject to a Restraining Order. The order prohibited him from contacting the ex-partner or her family. In February 2010, D left a gift at a venue where the ex-partner was due to sing. The gift was for her son. He then telephoned twice, leaving a lengthy message and subsequently a threatening message. D claimed that he had been told by V's parents that giving a gift would be acceptable. A victim impact statement detailed V's stress and inability to work due to fear. D had 27 convictions for 53 offences, including violence. Held. The original sentence of 15 months for the breach of the Restraining Order and 4 months for the Malicious Communications Act 1988 offence related to the same behaviour. To add a further period of imprisonment in respect of the same behaviour seems to us to have been wrong in principle. So, **15 months** for the breach of the Restraining Order and **4 months concurrent** for the Malicious Communications Act 1988 offence. The suspended sentence was activated in full and consecutively (**4 weeks**) making **16 months**.

R v Wood 2012 EWCA Crim 156, 2 Cr App R (S) 49 (p 283) D pleaded to public nuisance. He was also in breach of a 3-month suspended sentence (made concurrent). Over a five-month period, he made hundreds of calls to the charity Childline. Each time he called it cost the charity £4 because the caller is not charged. He had previously received a fixed penalty notice and signed an officer's notebook confirming he made the calls to Childline for sexual gratification. Next month he made more calls to Childline for which he received the suspended sentence. D would make calls to the charity and give graphic descriptions of how he was sexually abusing his nine-year-old daughter. In fact, he had no daughter. One of the calls lasted 55 minutes. The calls caused great distress to the volunteer staff and a number of them had been so distressed that they wanted to give up their voluntary work, even though it costs Childline £1,500 to train each volunteer. He was arrested and bailed. A condition of his bail was that he was not to make any further calls. He obtained a different phone and continued to make calls, using a facility on the phone to withhold his telephone number. There were 890 calls costing Childline some £3,500. D accepted that he made the calls for sexual gratification. D, aged 46, was a very isolated figure. He had convictions for sending an offensive letter (×3), wasting police time (×3), making hoax calls (×2), public nuisance and harassment by sending sexually explicit messages. The public nuisance conviction pertained to 3,000 calls made to the Samaritans charity in 2008. There was a long history of alcohol abuse. Held. This is plainly a more serious case than *R v Kavanagh* 2008 EWCA Crim 855. **4½ years** was the starting point. With full credit for the plea, **3 years** was not manifestly excessive.

See also: *R v Scott* 2010 EWCA Crim 2995, 2011 2 Cr App R (S) 37 (p 227) (Late plea to putting a person in fear of violence by harassment. Threatened a bank employee she would be sold to persons in the Middle East. Eight calls in three weeks. Previous conviction for threats to kill 18 years before, which was similar. **3 years** was severe but upheld.)

See also the **COMPUTER AND COMMUNICATION NETWORK OFFENCES** chapter.

See also the PUBLIC ORDER ACT 1986 S 4, PUBLIC ORDER ACT 1986 S 5 and STALKING chapters.

270   HEALTH AND SAFETY OFFENCES
270.1
Offences under various statutes and regulations can be prosecuted. The main statute is Health and Safety at Work etc. Act 1974 s 33(1) and Sch 3A[529] (failing to discharge the duty to ensure the health, safety and welfare of the employees and contravening regulations etc.). The offence can be committed in 15 different ways. The key ones are failing to discharge a duty or contravening a duty.
Mode of trial Triable either way except for three offences which are summary only.
Maximum sentence Section 33(1)(a) (failure to discharge a section 2 to 6 duty) On indictment 2 years. Summary maximum 6 months and/or a £20,000 fine for offences committed before 12 March 2015 and an unlimited fine thereafter.[530]
Compensation The Court of Appeal in *R v Pola* 2009 EWCA Crim 655, 2010 1 Cr App R (S) 6 (p 32) considered the principles of ordering compensation in Health and Safety cases and upheld £90,000 compensation to a victim who received severe brain injuries.
Funeral expenses Where a death results from an offence, other than death due to an accident arising out of the presence of a motor vehicle on a road, the court may make a compensation order for funeral expenses or bereavement. For more details, see **18.26** in Volume 1.
See also the COMPANIES AND PUBLIC BODIES AS DEFENDANTS chapter in Volume 1.

270.2   *Crown Court statistics   England and Wales*
Health and Safety at Work etc. Act 1974 Aged 21+

Year	Plea	Total sentenced	Type of sentencing %						Average length of custody in months
			Discharge	Fine	Community sentence	Suspended sentence	Custody	Other	
2013	G	48	–	35.4	18.8	37.5	4.2	4.2	9
	NG	12	–	75	16.7	8.3	–	–	–
2014	G	113	3	50	13	23	8	4	9.6
	NG	11	–	45	9	18	18	9	not listed[531]

For explanations about the statistics see page 1-xii. For more statistics see www.banksr. com Other Matters Statistics tab

Sentencing Council guideline Organisations
270.3   *Sentencing Council guideline   Organisations*
Health and Safety Offences, Corporate Manslaughter and Food Safety and Hygiene Offences Guideline 2016, see www.banksr.com Other Matters Guidelines tab. In force 1 February 2016.
page 3 [This guideline applies to] Health and Safety at Work etc. Act 1974 s 33(1)(a) for breaches of sections 2 and 3, and breaches of Health and Safety regulations, Health and Safety at Work etc. Act 1974 s 33(1)(c)
STEP ONE: Determining the offence category
page 4 The court should determine the offence category using only the culpability and harm factors in the tables below.

---

[529] As inserted by Health and Safety (Offences) Act 2008 s 1
[530] Health and Safety at Work etc. Act 1974 Sch 3A para 1 Legal Aid, Sentencing and Punishment of Offenders Act 2012 (Fines on Summary Conviction) Regulations 2015 2015/664 para 4(1) and Sch 4 para 7(a)-(b)
[531] Based on too few cases to be meaningful

Culpability

Where there are factors present in the case that fall in different categories of culpability, the court should balance these factors to reach a fair assessment of the offender's culpability.

CULPABILITY
Very high
Deliberate breach of or flagrant disregard for the law
High
Offender fell far short of the appropriate standard; for example, by: •failing to put in place measures that are recognised standards in the industry •ignoring concerns raised by employees or others •failing to make appropriate changes following prior incident(s) exposing risks to health and safety •allowing breaches to subsist over a long period of time Serious and/or systemic failure within the organisation to address risks to health and safety
Medium
Offender fell short of the appropriate standard in a manner that falls between descriptions in 'high' and 'low' culpability categories Systems were in place but these were not sufficiently adhered to or implemented
Low
Offender did not fall far short of the appropriate standard; for example, because: •significant efforts were made to address the risk although they were inadequate on this occasion •there was no warning/circumstance indicating a risk to health and safety Failings were minor and occurred as an isolated incident

270.4   Harm   [Organisations]

page 5 Health and safety offences are concerned with failures to manage risks to health and safety and do not require proof that the offence caused any actual harm. **The offence is in creating a risk of harm.**

1) Use the table below to identify an initial harm category based on the **risk of harm created by the offence**. The assessment of harm requires a consideration of **both**:

the seriousness of the harm risked (A, B or C) by the offender's breach, **and**

the likelihood of that harm arising (high, medium or low).

Seriousness of harm risked			
	Level A •Death •Physical or mental impairment resulting in lifelong dependency on third party care for basic needs •Significantly reduced life expectancy	**Level B** •Physical or mental impairment, not amounting to Level A, which has a substantial and long-term effect on the sufferer's ability to carry out normal day-to-day activities or on their ability to return to work •A progressive, permanent or irreversible condition	**Level C** •All other cases not falling within Level A or Level B
High likelihood of harm	Harm category 1	Harm category 2	Harm category 3

Seriousness of harm risked			
Medium likelihood of harm	Harm category 2	Harm category 3	Harm category 4
Low likelihood of harm	Harm category 3	Harm category 4	Harm category 4 (start towards bottom of range)

2) Next, the court must consider if the following factors apply. These two factors should be considered in the round in assigning the final harm category.

i) **Whether the offence exposed a number of workers or members of the public to the risk of harm.** The greater the number of people, the greater the risk of harm.

ii) **Whether the offence was a significant cause of actual harm.** Consider whether the offender's breach was a **significant cause*** of actual harm and the extent to which other factors contributed to the harm caused. Actions of victims are unlikely to be considered contributory events for sentencing purposes. Offenders are required to protect workers or others who may be neglectful of their own safety in a way which is reasonably foreseeable.

If one or both of these factors apply the court must consider either moving up a harm category or substantially moving up within the category range at step two overleaf. If already in harm category 1 and wishing to move higher, move up from the starting point at step two on the following pages. The court should not move up a harm category if actual harm was caused but to a lesser degree than the harm that was risked, as identified on the scale of seriousness above.

* A significant cause is one which more than minimally, negligibly or trivially contributed to the outcome. It does not have to be the sole or principal cause.

270.5

STEP TWO: Starting point and category range

page 6 Having determined the offence category, the court should identify the relevant table for the offender on the following pages. There are tables for different sized organisations.

At step two, the court is required to focus on the organisation's annual turnover or equivalent to reach a starting point for a fine. The court should then consider further adjustment within the category range for aggravating and mitigating features.

At step three, the court may be required to refer to other financial factors listed below to ensure that the proposed fine is proportionate.

270.6   Obtaining financial information

page 6 The offender is expected to provide comprehensive accounts for the last three years, to enable the court to make an accurate assessment of its financial status. In the absence of such disclosure, or where the court is not satisfied that it has been given sufficient reliable information, the court will be entitled to draw reasonable inferences as to the offender's means from evidence it has heard and from all the circumstances of the case, **which may include the inference that the offender can pay any fine.**

270.7   [Assessing the financial information Organisations]

page 6 Normally, only information relating to the organisation before the court will be relevant, unless exceptionally it is demonstrated to the court that the resources of a linked organisation are available and can properly be taken into account.

1. *For companies*: annual accounts. Particular attention should be paid to turnover; profit before tax; directors' remuneration, loan accounts and pension provision; and assets as disclosed by the balance sheet. Most companies are required to file

audited accounts at Companies House. **Failure to produce relevant recent accounts on request may properly lead to the conclusion that the company can pay any appropriate fine.**

2. *For partnerships*: annual accounts. Particular attention should be paid to turnover; profit before tax; partners' drawings, loan accounts and pension provision; assets as above. Limited liability partnerships (LLPs) may be required to file audited accounts with Companies House. **If adequate accounts are not produced on request, see paragraph 1.**

3. *For local authorities, fire authorities and similar public bodies*: the Annual Revenue Budget (ARB) is the equivalent of turnover and the best indication of the size of the organisation. It is unlikely to be necessary to analyse specific expenditure or reserves (where relevant) unless inappropriate expenditure is suggested.

4. *For health trusts*: the independent regulator of NHS Foundation Trusts is Monitor. It publishes quarterly reports and annual figures for the financial strength and stability of trusts from which the annual income can be seen, available via www.monitor-nhsft.gov.uk. Detailed analysis of expenditure or reserves is unlikely to be called for.

5. *For charities*: it will be appropriate to inspect annual audited accounts. Detailed analysis of expenditure or reserves is unlikely to be called for unless there is a suggestion of unusual or unnecessary expenditure.

For the pre-guideline law, which has more detail, see **270.29**.

Very large organisation

Where an offending organisation's turnover or equivalent very greatly exceeds the threshold for large organisations, it may be necessary to move outside the suggested range to achieve a proportionate sentence.

270.8   [Starting points and ranges: Organisations]

Note: It would be dangerous to regard these tables as compartments to fit a case into. To do so would mean a company with an £11m turnover would receive the same starting point as an equally culpable firm with a £49m turnover. It would also mean a company with a £10.5m turnover would receive a starting point more than three times that of a company with a £9.5m turnover. I would expect many judges to treat the suggested penalties as if they were for a company with a turnover between the two values and move the fine up or down from that figure depending on the turnover of the company they are dealing with. The profitability of the company is considered in step three, see **270.10**. Ed.

page 7

Large Turnover or equivalent: £50 million and over		
	Starting point	**Category range**
Very high culpability Harm category 1 Harm category 2 Harm category 3 Harm category 4	£4,000,000 £2,000,000 £1,000,000 £500,000	£2,600,000 to £10,000,000 £1,000,000 to £5,250,000 £500,000 to £2,700,000 £240,000 to £1,300,000
High culpability Harm category 1 Harm category 2 Harm category 3 Harm category 4	£2,400,000 £1,100,000 £540,000 £240,000	£1,500,000 to £6,000,000 £550,000 to £2,900,000 £250,000 to £1,450,000 £120,000 to £700,000

Large
Turnover or equivalent: £50 million and over

	Starting point	Category range
Medium culpability Harm category 1 Harm category 2 Harm category 3 Harm category 4	£1,300,000 £600,000 £300,000 £130,000	£800,000 to £3,250,000 £300,000 to £1,500,000 £130,000 to £750,000 £50,000 to £350,000
Low culpability Harm category 1 Harm category 2 Harm category 3 Harm category 4	£300,000 £100,000 £35,000 £10,000	£180,000 to £700,000 £35,000 to £250,000 £10,000 to £140,000 £3,000 to £60,000

Medium
Turnover or equivalent: between £10 million and £50 million

	Starting point	Category range
Very high culpability Harm category 1 Harm category 2 Harm category 3 Harm category 4	£1,600,000 £800,000 £400,000 £190,000	£1,000,000 to £4,000,000 £400,000 to £2,000,000 £180,000 to £1,000,000 £90,000 to £500,000
High culpability Harm category 1 Harm category 2 Harm category 3 Harm category 4	£950,000 £450,000 £210,000 £100,000	£600,000 to £2,500,000 £220,000 to £1,200,000 £100,000 to £550,000 £50,000 to £250,000
Medium culpability Harm category 1 Harm category 2 Harm category 3 Harm category 4	£540,000 £240,000 £100,000 £50,000	£300,000 to £1,300,000 £100,000 to £600,000 £50,000 to £300,000 £20,000 to £130,000
Low culpability Harm category 1 Harm category 2 Harm category 3 Harm category 4	£130,000 £40,000 £14,000 £3,000	£75,000 to £300,000 £14,000 to £100,000 £3,000 to £60,000 £1,000 to £10,000

Small
Turnover or equivalent: between £2 million and £10 million

	Starting point	Category range
Very high culpability Harm category 1 Harm category 2 Harm category 3 Harm category 4	£450,000 £200,000 £100,000 £50,000	£300,000 to £1,600,000 £100,000 to £800,000 £50,000 to £400,000 £20,000 to £190,000
High culpability Harm category 1 Harm category 2 Harm category 3 Harm category 4	£250,000 £100,000 £54,000 £24,000	£170,000 to £1,000,000 £50,000 to £450,000 £25,000 to £210,000 £12,000 to £100,000

Small Turnover or equivalent: between £2 million and £10 million		
	Starting point	**Category range**
Medium culpability Harm category 1 Harm category 2 Harm category 3 Harm category 4	£160,000 £54,000 £24,000 £12,000	£100,000 to £600,000 £25,000 to £230,000 £12,000 to £100,000 £4,000 to £50,000
Low culpability Harm category 1 Harm category 2 Harm category 3 Harm category 4	£45,000 £9,000 £3,000 £700	£25,000 to £130,000 £3,000 to £40,000 £700 to £14,000 £100 to £5,000

Micro Turnover or equivalent: not more than £2 million		
	Starting point	**Category range**
Very high culpability Harm category 1 Harm category 2 Harm category 3 Harm category 4	£250,000 £100,000 £50,000 £24,000	£150,000 to £450,000 £50,000 to £200,000 £25,000 to £100,000 £12,000 to £50,000
High culpability Harm category 1 Harm category 2 Harm category 3 Harm category 4	£160,000 £54,000 £30,000 £12,000	£100,000 to £250,000 £30,000 to £110,000 £12,000 to £54,000 £5,000 to £21,000
Medium culpability Harm category 1 Harm category 2 Harm category 3 Harm category 4	£100,000 £30,000 £14,000 £6,000	£60,000 to £160,000 £14,000 to £70,000 £6,000 to £25,000 £2,000 to £12,000
Low culpability Harm category 1 Harm category 2 Harm category 3 Harm category 4	£30,000 £5,000 £1,200 £200	£18,000 to £60,000 £1,000 to £20,000 £200 to £7,000 £50 to £2,000

270.9   [Aggravating and mitigating factors   Organisations]
The table below contains a **non-exhaustive** list of factual elements providing the context of the offence and factors relating to the offender. Identify whether any combination of these, or other relevant factors, should result in an upward or downward adjustment from the starting point. **In particular, relevant recent convictions are likely to result in a substantial upward adjustment.** In some cases, having considered these factors, it may be appropriate to move outside the identified category range.

Factors increasing seriousness
Statutory aggravating factors: Previous convictions, having regard to a) the nature of the offence to which the conviction relates and its relevance to the current offence, and b) the time that has elapsed since the conviction

| **Other aggravating factors:** |
| Cost-cutting at the expense of safety |
| Deliberate concealment of illegal nature of activity |
| Breach of any court order |
| Obstruction of justice |
| Poor health and safety record |
| Falsification of documentation or licences |
| Deliberate failure to obtain or comply with relevant licences in order to avoid scrutiny by authorities |
| Targeting vulnerable victims |

| **Factors reducing seriousness or reflecting personal mitigation** |
| No previous convictions or no relevant/recent convictions |
| Evidence of steps taken voluntarily to remedy problem |
| High level of co-operation with the investigation, beyond that which will always be expected |
| Good health and safety record |
| Effective health and safety procedures in place |
| Self-reporting, co-operation and acceptance of responsibility |

Steps three and four

The court should 'step back', review and, if necessary, adjust the initial fine based on turnover to ensure that it fulfils the objectives of sentencing for these offences. The court may adjust the fine upwards or downwards, including outside the range.

270.10 [Organisations]

STEP THREE

page 10 Check whether the proposed fine based on turnover is proportionate to the overall means of the offender

General principles to follow in setting a fine

The court should finalise the appropriate level of fine in accordance with Criminal Justice Act 2003 s 164, which requires that the fine must reflect the seriousness of the offence and that the court must take into account the financial circumstances of the offender.

The level of fine should reflect the extent to which the offender fell below the required standard. The fine should meet, in a fair and proportionate way, the objectives of punishment, deterrence and the removal of gain derived through the commission of the offence; it should not be cheaper to offend than to take the appropriate precautions.

The fine must be **sufficiently substantial to have a real economic impact which will bring home to both management and shareholders the need to comply with health and safety legislation**.

Review of the fine based on turnover

The court should 'step back', review and, if necessary, adjust the initial fine reached at step two to **ensure that it fulfils the general principles** set out above. The court may adjust the fine upwards or downwards including outside of the range.

The court should examine the financial circumstances of the offender in the round to assess the economic realities of the organisation and the most efficacious way of giving effect to the purposes of sentencing.

In finalising the sentence, the court should have regard to the following factors:

• The profitability of an organisation will be relevant. If an organisation has a small profit margin relative to its turnover, downward adjustment may be needed. If it has a large profit margin, upward adjustment may be needed.

• Any quantifiable economic benefit derived from the offence, including through avoided costs or operating savings, should normally be added to the fine arrived at in step two. Where this is not readily available, the court may draw on information available from enforcing authorities and others about the general costs of operating within the law.

• Whether the fine will have the effect of putting the offender out of business will be relevant; in some bad cases this may be an acceptable consequence.

In considering the ability of the offending organisation to pay any financial penalty, the court can take into account the **power to allow time for payment or to order that the amount be paid in instalments**, if necessary over a number of years.

270.11

STEP FOUR

Consider other factors that may warrant adjustment of the proposed fine

page 11 The court should consider any wider impacts of the fine within the organisation or on innocent third parties, such as (but not limited to):

• the fine impairs offender's ability to make restitution to victims,

• impact of the fine on offender's ability to improve conditions in the organisation to comply with the law,

• impact of the fine on employment of staff, service users, customers and local economy (but not shareholders or directors).

Where the fine will fall on public or charitable bodies, the fine should normally be substantially reduced if the offending organisation is able to demonstrate the proposed fine would have a significant impact on the provision of its services.

STEPS FIVE AND SIX

Note: Step five is factors which indicate a reduction, such as assistance to the prosecution. Step six is reduction for a guilty plea. The text provides no detail. Ed.

270.12   Compensation and ancillary orders   [Organisations]

STEP SEVEN

page 12 In all cases, the court must consider whether to make ancillary orders. These may include:

Remediation

Under Health and Safety at Work etc. Act 1974 s 42(1), the court may impose a remedial order in addition to or instead of imposing any punishment on the offender. An offender ought by the time of sentencing to have remedied any specific failings involved in the offence and if it has not, will be deprived of significant mitigation.

The cost of compliance with such an order should not ordinarily be taken into account in fixing the fine; the order requires only what should already have been done.

Forfeiture

Where the offence involves the acquisition or possession of an explosive article or substance, section 42(4) enables the court to order forfeiture of the explosive.

Compensation

Where the offence has resulted in loss or damage, the court must consider whether to make a compensation order. The assessment of compensation in cases involving death or serious injury will usually be complex and will ordinarily be covered by insurance. In the great majority of cases the court should conclude that compensation should be dealt with in the civil court, and should say that no order is made for that reason.

If compensation is awarded, priority should be given to the payment of compensation over payment of any other financial penalty where the means of the offender are limited.

Where the offender does not have sufficient means to pay the total financial penalty considered appropriate by the court, compensation and fine take priority over prosecution costs.

Sentencing Council guideline: Individuals

270.13   Sentencing Council guideline   Individuals

Health and Safety Offences, Corporate Manslaughter and Food Safety and Hygiene Offences Guideline 2016, see www.banksr.com Other Matters Guidelines tab page 13 [This guideline applies to] Health and Safety at Work etc. Act 1974 s 33(1)(a) for breaches of sections 2, 3 and 7, breaches of Health and Safety regulations, section 33(1)(c) and secondary liability, Health and Safety at Work etc. Act 1974 s 36 and 37(1) for breaches of sections 2, 3 and 33(1)(c)

STEP ONE: Determining the offence category

page 14 The court should determine the offence category using only the culpability and harm factors in the tables below.

Culpability

Where there are factors present in the case that fall in different categories of culpability, the court should balance these factors to reach a fair assessment of the offender's culpability.

CULPABILITY
Very high
Where the offender intentionally breached, or flagrantly disregarded, the law
High
Actual foresight of, or wilful blindness to, risk of offending but risk nevertheless taken
Medium
Offence committed through act or omission which a person exercising reasonable care would not commit
Low
Offence committed with little fault, for example, because: •significant efforts were made to address the risk although they were inadequate on this occasion   •there was no warning/circumstance indicating a risk to Health and Safety   •failings were minor and occurred as an isolated incident

270.14   Harm   [Individuals]

page 15 Health and safety offences are concerned with failures to manage risks to health and safety and do not require proof that the offence caused any actual harm. **The offence is in creating a risk of harm**.

1) Use the table below to identify an initial harm category based on the **risk of harm created by the offence**. The assessment of harm requires a consideration of **both**:

the seriousness of the harm risked (A, B or C) by the offender's breach, **and**

the likelihood of that harm arising (high, medium or low).

Seriousness of harm risked			
	Level A •Death •Physical or mental impairment resulting in lifelong dependency on third party care for basic needs •Significantly reduced life expectancy	**Level B** •Physical or mental impairment, not amounting to Level A, which has a substantial and long-term effect on the sufferer's ability to carry out normal day-to-day activities or on their ability to return to work •A progressive, permanent or irreversible condition	**Level C** •All other cases not falling within Level A or Level B
High likelihood of harm	Harm category 1	Harm category 2	Harm category 3

Seriousness of harm risked			
Medium likelihood of harm	Harm category 2	Harm category 3	Harm category 4
Low likelihood of harm	Harm category 3	Harm category 4	Harm category 4 (start towards bottom of range)

2) Next, the court must consider if the following factors apply. These two factors should be considered in the round in assigning the final harm category.

   i) Whether the offence exposed a number of workers or members of the public to the risk of harm. The greater the number of people, the greater the risk of harm.

   ii) Whether the offence was a significant cause of actual harm. Consider whether the offender's breach was a significant cause* of actual harm and the extent to which other factors contributed to the harm caused. Actions of victims are unlikely to be considered contributory events for sentencing purposes. Offenders are required to protect workers or others who may be neglectful of their own safety in a way that is reasonably foreseeable.

If one or both of these factors apply the court must consider either moving up a harm category or substantially moving up within the category range at step two overleaf. If already in harm category 1 and wishing to move higher, move up from the starting point at step two overleaf. The court should not move up a harm category if actual harm was caused but to a lesser degree than the harm that was risked, as identified on the scale of seriousness above.

* A significant cause is one which more than minimally, negligibly or trivially contributed to the outcome. It does not have to be the sole or principal cause.

270.15   [Individuals]

STEP TWO: Starting point and category range

page 16 Having determined the category, the court should refer to the starting points on the following page to reach a sentence within the category range. The court should then consider further adjustment within the category range for aggravating and mitigating features, set out on page 18.

Obtaining financial information

In setting a fine, the court may conclude that the offender is able to pay any fine imposed unless the offender has supplied any financial information to the contrary. It is for the offender to disclose to the court such data relevant to his financial position as will enable it to assess what he can reasonably afford to pay. If necessary, the court may compel the disclosure of an individual offender's financial circumstances pursuant to Criminal Justice Act 2003 s 162. In the absence of such disclosure, or where the court is not satisfied that it has been given sufficient reliable information, the court will be entitled to draw reasonable inferences as to the offender's means from evidence it has heard and from all the circumstances of the case **which may include the inference that the offender can pay any fine.**

Starting points and ranges

Where the range includes a potential sentence of custody, the court should consider the custody threshold as follows:

• Has the custody threshold been passed?

• If so, is it unavoidable that a custodial sentence be imposed?

• If so, can that sentence be suspended?

Where the range includes a potential sentence of a community order, the court should consider the community order threshold as follows:

• Has the community order threshold been passed?

Even where the community order threshold has been passed, a fine will normally be the most appropriate disposal where the offence was committed for economic benefit. Or, if wishing to remove economic benefit derived through the commission of the offence, consider combining a fine with a community order.

	Starting point	Category range
Very high culpability		
Harm category 1	18 months' custody	1 to 2 years' custody
Harm category 2	1 year's custody	26 weeks' to 18 months' custody
Harm category 3	26 weeks' custody	Band F fine or high-level community order to 1 year's custody
Harm category 4	Band F fine	Band E fine to 26 weeks' custody
High culpability		
Harm category 1	1 year's custody	26 weeks' to 18 months' custody
Harm category 2	26 weeks' custody	Band F fine or high-level community order to 1 year's custody
Harm category 3	Band F fine	Band E fine or medium-level community order to 26 weeks' custody
Harm category 4	Band E fine	Band D fine to Band E fine
Medium culpability		
Harm category 1	26 weeks' custody	Band F fine or high-level community order to 1 year's custody
Harm category 2	Band F fine	Band E fine or medium-level community order to 26 weeks' custody
Harm category 3	Band E fine	Band D fine or low-level community order to Band E fine
Harm category 4	Band D fine	Band C fine to Band D fine
Low culpability		
Harm category 1	Band F fine	Band E fine or medium-level community order to 26 weeks' custody
Harm category 2	Band D fine	Band C fine to Band D fine
Harm category 3	Band C fine	Band B fine to Band C fine
Harm category 4	Band A fine	Conditional discharge to Band A fine

page 18 The table below contains a **non-exhaustive** list of factual elements providing the context of the offence and factors relating to the offender. Identify whether any combination of these, or other relevant factors, should result in an upward or downward adjustment from the starting point. **In particular, relevant recent convictions are likely to result in a substantial upward adjustment.** In some cases, having considered these factors, it may be appropriate to move outside the identified category range.

270.16   [Aggravating and mitigating factors   Individuals]

Factors increasing seriousness
Statutory aggravating factors: Previous convictions, having regard to a) the nature of the offence to which the conviction relates and its relevance to the current offence, and b) the time that has elapsed since the conviction Offence committed whilst on bail ***Other aggravating factors:*** Cost-cutting at the expense of safety Deliberate concealment of illegal nature of activity Breach of any court order Obstruction of justice Poor health and safety record Falsification of documentation or licences Deliberate failure to obtain or comply with relevant licences in order to avoid scrutiny by authorities Targeting vulnerable victims
Factors reducing seriousness or reflecting personal mitigation
No previous convictions or no relevant/recent convictions Evidence of steps taken voluntarily to remedy problem High level of co-operation with the investigation, beyond that which will always be expected Good health and safety record Effective health and safety procedures in place Self-reporting, co-operation and acceptance of responsibility Good character and/or exemplary conduct Inappropriate degree of trust or responsibility Mental disorder or learning disability, where linked to the commission of the offence Serious medical conditions requiring urgent, intensive or long term treatment Age and/or lack of maturity where it affects the responsibility of the offender Sole or primary carer for dependent relatives

270.17

STEP THREE

Review any financial element of the sentence

page 19 Where the sentence is or includes a fine, the court should 'step back' and, using the factors set out below, review whether the sentence as a whole meets the objectives of sentencing for these offences. The court may increase or reduce the proposed fine reached at step two, if necessary moving outside of the range.

General principles to follow in setting a fine

The court should finalise the appropriate level of fine in accordance with Criminal Justice Act 2003 s 164, which requires that the fine must reflect the seriousness of the offence and that the court must take into account the financial circumstances of the offender.

The level of fine should reflect the extent to which the offender fell below the required standard. The fine should meet, in a fair and proportionate way, the objectives of punishment, deterrence and the removal of gain derived through the commission of the offence; it should not be cheaper to offend than to take the appropriate precautions.

Review of the fine

Where the court proposes to impose a fine it should 'step back', review and, if necessary, adjust the initial fine reached at step two to **ensure that it fulfils the general principles** set out above.

Any quantifiable economic benefit derived from the offence, including through avoided costs or operating savings, should normally be added to the fine arrived at in step two. Where this is not readily available, the court may draw on information available from enforcing authorities and others about the general costs of operating within the law.

In finalising the sentence, the court should have regard to the following factors relating to the wider impacts of the fine on innocent third parties, such as (but not limited to):

• impact of the fine on offender's ability to comply with the law,

• impact of the fine on employment of staff, service users, customers and local economy.

270.18   Compensation and ancillary orders

STEPS FOUR AND FIVE

Note: Step four is factors which indicate a reduction, such as assistance to the prosecution. Step five is reduction for a guilty plea. The text states matters well known to court users. Ed.

STEP SIX

page 20 **Compensation and ancillary orders**

In all cases, the court must consider whether to make ancillary orders. These may include:

Disqualification of director

An offender may be disqualified from being a director of a company in accordance with Company Directors Disqualification Act 1986 s 2. The maximum period of disqualification is 15 years (Crown Court) or 5 years (Magistrates' Court).

Remediation

Under Health and Safety at Work etc. Act 1974 s 42(1), the court may impose a remedial order in addition to or instead of imposing any punishment on the offender. An offender ought by the time of sentencing to have remedied any specific failings involved in the offence and if not, will be deprived of significant mitigation.

The cost of compliance with such an order should not ordinarily be taken into account in fixing the fine; the order requires only what should already have been done.

Forfeiture

Where the offence involves the acquisition or possession of an explosive article or substance, section 42(4) enables the court to order forfeiture of the explosive.

Compensation

Where the offence has resulted in loss or damage, the court must consider whether to make a compensation order. The assessment of compensation in cases involving death or serious injury will usually be complex and will ordinarily be covered by insurance. In the great majority of cases the court should conclude that compensation should be dealt with in the civil courts, and should say that no order is made for that reason.

If compensation is awarded, priority should be given to the payment of compensation over payment of any other financial penalty where the means of the offender are limited.

Where the offender does not have sufficient means to pay the total financial penalty considered appropriate by the court, compensation and fine take priority over prosecution costs.

270.19   *Suggested approach to the guideline*

Note: The new guideline is a radical departure from the old sentencing system. I would expect sentencers to carefully apply the guideline and ignore all the old tariff cases. Consequently I have not listed any. Ed.

270.20   *Judicial pre-guideline guidance*
R v F Howe and Son (Engineers) Ltd 1999 2 Cr App R (S) 37 The objective of
prosecutions is to achieve a safe environment for those who work there and for others
who may be affected. A fine needs to be large enough to bring that message home where
D is a company not only to those who manage it but also to its shareholders.
R v Graham 2010 EWCA Crim 2846, 2 Cr App R (S) 48 (p 335) The standards of Health
and Safety expected from smaller businesses must be the same as those expected of
larger ones.
Note: Most of the previous guidance has been incorporated into the guideline and is not
listed. The snippets above are consistent with the new guideline. Ed.

The procedure
270.21   *Basis for sentence, There must be a proper*
Corporate Manslaughter and H and S Offences Causing Death Guideline 2010, see
www.banksr.com para 11 It will generally be appropriate to require the prosecution to set
out in writing the facts of the case relied upon and any aggravating or mitigating features
which it identifies.[532] The defence may conveniently be required similarly to set out in
writing any points on which it differs. If sentence is to proceed upon agreed facts, they
should be set out in writing.[533]
Friskies Petcare (UK) Ltd 2000 EWCA Crim 95, 2 Cr App R (S) 401 Problems can arise
when there is a dispute about whether the court sentenced the defendant on the basis on
which the case was presented. This case illustrates the problem. The Health and Safety
Executive should list in writing not merely the facts of the case but the aggravating
features as set out in *R v F Howe and Son (Engineers) Ltd* 1999 2 Cr App R (S) 37. It
should be served and the defence should set out in writing the mitigating features. If
there is an agreed basis, it should be in writing.
Note: These principles will not be affected by the guideline. Ed.
For **District Judges accepting jurisdiction** see **60.7** in Volume 1. Where very large fines
are required, the decisions must be taken by District Judges, see the same paragraph.
Need for senior person to explain the offending and their response to it see **225.4**.

The offences
270.22   *Railway accidents*
The pre-guideline cases are listed in the 10th edition of this book but I think they are best
ignored. Ed.
See also the **MANSLAUGHTER** *Railway accidents* para at **284.54** and the **RAILWAYS**
chapter.

Special factors
270.23   *Directors and small companies both prosecuted   Avoid double punishment*
R v Rollco Screw and Rivet Co Ltd 1999 2 Cr App R (S) 436 LCJ The defendant
company and two of its directors, who were father and son, pleaded to failing to ensure
the Health and Safety of employees and persons other than their employees. The
defendants were prosecuted for stripping out asbestos in breach of the regulations and
exposing employees and others to risks. The father was in charge of the contractual
arrangements. The son was considered to be the father's lieutenant and did not fully
appreciate the risks. The total fines and costs for the company were £40,000 fine and
£30,000 costs. The father was fined £6,000 and £2,000 costs. The son was fined £4,000
and £2,000 costs. Held. In a small company the directors are likely to be the
shareholders and therefore the main losers if a severe sanction is imposed on the
company. One must avoid a risk of overlap and must not impose double punishment. On
the other hand, it is important that fines should be imposed which make it clear that there

---

[532] Attorney-General's guidelines on the *Acceptance of Pleas and the Prosecutor's Role in the Sentencing Exercise*, published
November 2009.
[533] See *Friskies Petcare (UK) Ltd* 2000 EWCA Crim 95, 2 Cr App R (S) 401.

is a personal responsibility on directors and they cannot simply palm off their responsibilities to the corporation of which they are directors. The proper approach is to answer two questions. First, what financial penalty does the offence merit? Second, what financial penalty can a defendant, whether corporate or personal, reasonably be ordered to meet?

Note: This is an old case, but the principle still seems valid. Ed.

270.24   *Employees etc. partly/fully to blame*
Old case: *R v Patchett Engineering Ltd* 2001 1 Cr App R (S) 40 (p 138) (Workers will take short cuts and will not follow proper practices. The statutory duty has, as one of its objects, the protection of workers who may be neglectful of their own safety in a way which should be anticipated.)
For a summary of this case, see the 9th edition of this book.

Matters relating to the defendant
270.25   *Public bodies/Hospitals*
Corporate Manslaughter and H and S Offences Causing Death Guideline 2010, see www.banksr.com Other Matters Guidelines tab para 19 In assessing the financial consequences of a fine, the court should consider: [para i-iv not listed] v) the effect upon the provision of services to the public will be relevant; although a public organisation such as a local authority, hospital trust or police force must be treated the same as a commercial company where the standards of behaviour to be expected are concerned, and must suffer a punitive fine for breach of them, a different approach to determining the level of fine may well be justified.
'The Judge has to consider how any financial penalty will be paid. If a very substantial financial penalty will inhibit the proper performance by a statutory body of the public function that it has been set up to perform, that is not something to be disregarded.'[534]
The same considerations will be likely to apply to non-statutory bodies or charities if providing public services.
page 5 para 17 and page 10 Annex A para 3 The courts should expect the following information.
For local authorities, police and fire authorities and similar public bodies: the Annual Revenue Budget (ARB) is the equivalent of turnover and the best indication of the size of the defendant organisation. It is published on www.local.communities.gov.uk/finance/bellwin.HTM. It is unlikely to be necessary to analyse specific expenditure or reserves unless inappropriate or grandiose expenditure is suggested. Such authorities also have attributed to them a 'Bellwin factor', which represents the level of exceptional and unforeseen expenditure that they are expected by central Government to meet themselves in any one year without any claim to recourse to central funds. But since that is arithmetically related to the ARB (currently 0.2%) it will ordinarily add little of significance beyond an indication of budgetary discipline.
para 4 *For health trusts*: the independent regulator of NHS Foundation Trusts is Monitor. It publishes quarterly reports and annual figures for the financial strength and stability of trusts from which the annual income can be seen, available via www.monitor-nhsft.gov.uk/home/our-publications. Detailed analysis of expenditure or reserves is unlikely to be called for. Note that Monitor has significant regulatory powers including over membership of the boards of directors or governors.
Magistrates' Court Sentencing Guidelines 2008, see www.banksr.com Other Matters Guidelines tab page 182 para 11[535] When sentencing public authorities, the court may have regard to the fact that a very substantial financial penalty may inhibit the performance of the public function that the body was set up to fulfil. This is not to

---

[534] *R v Milford Haven Port Authority* 2000 2 Cr App R (S) p 423 *per* Lord Bingham CJ at 433-434
[535] This section of the guideline was amended by Update 11 in February 2014.

suggest that public bodies are subject to a lesser standard of duty of care in safety and environmental matters, but it is proper for the court to take into account all the facts of the case, including how any financial penalty will be paid.[536]

Note: These guidelines may still assist. Ed.

R v Guy's and St Thomas' NHS Trust 2008 EWCA Crim 2187, 2009 1 Cr App R (S) 104 (p 585) The defendant pleaded to supplying a medical product not of the nature specified. There was human error in mixing the solution and an error by a supervisor. A baby died following a massive glucose overdose. Held. Where a not-for-profit organisation exists for the public benefit and a failure occurs without actual fault on the part of that body, but through an act or default of an employee to whom the task has been properly delegated and who has been properly trained, the court ought not to punish such a body by a financial penalty which would materially impact on its ability to discharge its public duty. The reason is that the public interest would not be served by doing so. Because of no management failures and the need not to impact on the work of the Trust, £15,000 not £75,000.

See also: *R v Sellafield and Network Rail* 2014 EWCA Crim 49 (LCJ Network Rail Health and Safety assessment failure. para 69 Profits invested into rail network. This factor is to be taken into account.)

Old cases: *R v British Railways Board* 1991 Unreported extract at 2000 2 Cr App R (S) 430 (A swingeing fine of the magnitude that some might consider appropriate could only be met by the board either by increasing the burden on the fare-paying passengers, which is hardly logical, having regard to the fact that it is for the benefit of the fare-paying passengers that this legislation exists, or by reducing the funds available for improvements in the railway system in general. That can hardly be regarded as a desirable state of affairs. On the other hand, I must bear in mind the necessity of marking the disapproval of society at the failures demonstrated by those charged with British Rail management leading up to and causing this accident.)

R v Milford Haven Port Authority 2000 2 Cr App R (S) p 423 (Public bodies are not immune from appropriate penalties because they have no shareholders and the directors are not in receipt of handsome annual bonuses. However, it is proper for the Judge to take the factor into account. If a substantial financial penalty will inhibit the proper performance by a statutory body of the public function it has been set up to perform, that factor should not be disregarded.)

For a fuller summary of these cases, see the 9th edition of this book.

Note: These principles would seem as relevant as ever. Ed.

The sentence

270.26   *Costs*

Magistrates' Court Sentencing Guidelines, January 2004 page 183 para 17 The prosecution will normally claim the costs of investigation and presentation. These may be substantial, and can incorporate time and activity expended on containing and making the area safe. Remediation costs for pollution offences may also be significant. For water pollution offences enforcing authorities are able to recover them through the criminal courts (Water Resources Act 1991, as amended). In other cases there are powers for the courts to order offenders to remedy the cause of the offence, or for the Environment Agency to require them to undertake clean-up at their own expense, or for the agency to carry out remedial work and seek to recover its costs through the civil courts.

The enforcing authorities' costs should be fully recouped from the offender. The order for costs should not be disproportionate to the level of the fine imposed. The court should fix the level of the fine first, then consider awarding compensation, and then determine the costs. If the total sum exceeds the defendant's means, the order for costs

---

[536] *R v Southampton University Hospital NHS Trust* 2006 EWCA Crim 2971, 2007 2 Cr App R (S) 9 (p 37) (see later in this paragraph)

should be reduced rather than the fine. Compensation should take priority over both the fine and costs. As always, magistrates should seek the advice of the legal advisor on sentencing options and guidelines in all cases.
Note: This material is from an old guideline. However, it would appear still to be valid. Ed.

R v F Howe and Son (Engineers) Ltd 1999 2 Cr App R (S) 37 The power to award costs is contained in Prosecution of Offences Act 1985 s 18(1) and permits an order that the defendant pay to the prosecutor such costs as are just and reasonable. This includes the cost of the prosecuting authority carrying out investigations with a view to prosecution, see *R v Associated Octel Ltd* 1996 EWCA Crim 1327, 1997 1 Cr App R (S) 435. Sometimes costs awarded have been scaled down so as not to exceed the fine. Neither the fines nor the costs are deductible against tax and therefore the full burden falls upon the company.

R v B&Q 2005 EWCA Crim 2297 The defendant company was convicted of three counts and acquitted of five counts. Two trials were halted because of problems with play-back equipment. The company was fined £550,000 with £250,000 costs. Held. Because of the differing nature of the statutory provisions relating to costs and the way in which costs are borne by different departments of the Executive in this type of prosecution, the Judge should have adopted a global approach, as set out in the *Guide to the Award of Costs* 1991. The prosecution costs of the two aborted trials should not have been considered, because it was the prosecution that was required to make the equipment available. Leading counsel was a proper expense, see *R v Dudley Magistrates' Court ex parte Power City Stores* 1990 154 JP 654. An allowance should have been made for the acquittals on the direction of the trial Judge.
See also the **Costs** chapter in Volume 1.

270.27   Costs, Apportioning

R v Harrison 1993 14 Cr App R (S) 419 D1 pleaded to trade description offences. The Judge considered D1 was the principal defendant and stood to gain financially from the offence and had the means to pay, whereas D2, who was his son, had little to do with running the business. He therefore made D1 pay all the costs. Held. Where there are several defendants it will usually be appropriate when making a costs order to look to see what would be a reasonable estimate of the costs if each defendant were tried alone. However, the Judge's approach was proper.

R v Fresha Bakeries Ltd 2002 EWCA Crim 1451, 2003 1 Cr App R (S) 44 (p 202) D, the defendant company, H Ltd, its sister company, B, the Chief Executive of the group, M, the chief engineer at the plant, and J, the production director, pleaded to offences under Health and Safety at Work etc. Act 1974 s 2 and 3. The companies and M pleaded at the first appearance. B and J pleaded the day before the trial was fixed. Two workmen were burnt to death trying to repair a bread oven when major breaches of Health and Safety procedures took place. It was agreed by the prosecution, the defence and the Judge that the Judge should fix the overall financial penalty as if it were a single company and apportion the fine and costs elements between the companies. D was able to pay a significant fine. D's pre-tax profits were £250,000, and H Ltd's profits were £400,000. The Judge distinguished *R v Ronson and Parnes* 1992 13 Cr App R (S) 153 (where costs were adjusted so that they were what they would have been if the defendant had been tried alone) and calculated the costs to include the work up until sentence, notwithstanding their early plea. D was fined **£250,000** with costs of £175,000, H Ltd was fined **£100,000** with £75,000 costs, B was fined **£10,000** with £5,000 costs, J was fined **£1,000** and M was fined **£2,000**. The revised figure for the costs when the companies pleaded was £108,451. The revised figure when the other defendants pleaded was £283,307. Held. It was a very bad case. There was no basis for holding that the fines totalling **£350,000** were manifestly excessive. It may be appropriate to order the defendant who is more responsible to pay a greater share of the costs than he would pay if he were tried alone. The Judge was entitled to conclude that the corporate defendants bore a greater responsibility than the individual defendants. However, the Judge took too little account of the fact that the companies had no control over the proceedings against B and J. If they had pleaded when the companies did, the costs would have been significantly less. Taking into account the costs incurred for the proposed trial after the corporate defendants had pleaded and the reduced costs figure now available, D's costs should be £105,000 and H Ltd's costs should be £45,000.

Note: Both these cases are old, but the principle seems valid today. Ed.

270.28   *Fines   Instalments, Paying fines etc.* by
R v Olliver and Olliver 1989 11 Cr App R (S) 10 LCJ There is nothing wrong in principle for the period of payment (for a fine) being longer than a year, provided that it is not an undue burden, and so too severe a punishment, having regard to the offence and the nature of the offender. A two-year period will seldom be too long, and in an appropriate case three years will be unassailable. Every effort is required to find alternatives to custodial sentences.

R v Rollco Screw and Rivet Co Ltd 1999 2 Cr App R (S) 436 LCJ The defendant company and two of its directors, who were father and son, pleaded to failing to ensure the Health and Safety of employees and persons other than their employees (Health and Safety at Work etc. Act 1974 s 2(1) and 3(1)). The defendants were prosecuted for stripping out asbestos in breach of the regulations and exposing employees and others to risks. The father was in charge of the contractual arrangements. The son was considered to be the father's lieutenant and did not fully appreciate the risks. The total fines and costs for the company were £40,000 fine and £30,000 costs (£5,000 within a year and the rest at £1,000 a month). The father was fined £6,000 and £2,000 costs (£1,000 a month). The son was fined £4,000 and £2,000 costs. Held. Reminding ourselves of *R v Olliver and Olliver* 1989 11 Cr App R (S) 10 the Court was at pains to avoid stipulating any period which should not be exceeded. With a personal defendant there are arguments for keeping the period within bounds. Those arguments are much weaker, if indeed they apply at all, when one is considering a corporate defendant. There is not the same anxiety as is liable to afflict an individual, and it is acceptable for a fine to be payable by a company over a substantially longer period than might be appropriate for an individual. It is not necessarily a more severe course to order a larger sum over a longer period than a smaller sum over a shorter period, since the former course may give the company a greater opportunity to control its cash flow and survive difficult trading conditions. If it wants to, the company can pay the sums sooner than it need. This period of payment over 6 years 5 months was excessive. Because of that the fine is reduced to £20,000, so the payment period is **5 years 7 months**, which is an appropriate payment period.

R v Aceblade Ltd 2001 1 Cr App R (S) 105 (p 366) The company pleaded to failing to ensure the Health and Safety of an employee. It was fined £20,000 with £15,000 costs. The fine was payable over **42 months**. Held. The payment period was not too long.

Note: This guidance was not incorporated into the new guideline but it seems very helpful. All these cases are old, but I expect the principles will be applied by the judges today. Ed.

270.29   *Fines, the means of the defendant and company   Guidelines*
Corporate Manslaughter and H and S Offences Causing Death Guideline 2010, see www.banksr.com Other Matters Guidelines tab
Although the guideline only applies to two offences, judges are likely to consider that the principles are helpful when dealing with corporate defendants on other charges. Ed.

Financial information, size and nature of organisation
para 12 The law must expect the same standard of behaviour from a large and a small organisation. Smallness does not by itself mitigate, and largeness does not by itself aggravate, these offences. Size may affect the approach to safety, whether because a

small organisation is careless or because a large one is bureaucratic, but these considerations affect the seriousness of the offence via the assessment set out in paras 6-8 above, rather than demonstrating a direct correlation between size and culpability.

13 A large organisation may be more at risk of committing an offence than a small one simply because it conducts very many more operations. Some large corporate groups operate as a single company whereas others are structured as separate companies for separate operations. A large organisation may be operating upon a budget as tight (or tighter) than a small one because of the demands placed upon it – large local authorities, hospital trusts or police forces may be examples, but so might commercial companies with large turnover but small profit margins. However, in some instances, a large organisation may have less excuse for not dealing properly with matters affecting Health and Safety, since it may have greater access to expertise, advice and training resources, whether in-house or otherwise.

14 The means of any defendant are relevant to a fine, which is the principal available penalty for organisations. The court should require information about the financial circumstances of the defendant before it. The best practice will usually be to call for the relevant information for a three-year period including the year of the offence, so as to avoid any risk of atypical figures in a single year.

15 A fixed correlation between the fine and either turnover or profit is not appropriate. The circumstances of defendant organisations and the financial consequences of the fine will vary too much, similar offences committed by companies structured in differing ways ought not to attract fines which are vastly different, a fixed correlation might provide a perverse incentive to manipulation of corporate structure.

16 The court should, however, look carefully at both turnover and profit, and also at assets, in order to gauge the resources of the defendant. When taking account of financial circumstances, statute[537] provides for that to either increase or decrease the amount of the fine and it is just that a wealthy defendant should pay a larger fine than a poor one. Whilst a fine is intended to inflict painful punishment, it should be one which the defendant is capable of paying, if appropriate over a period which may be up to a number of years.

Financial information a court should expect to be provided about a defendant

17 The primary obligation to provide such information lies on the defendant. It would be helpful if the prosecution takes the preliminary step of calling upon the defendant to provide the information. If the defendant does not do so, the prosecution can assemble what can be obtained from public records and furnish that to the court. If a defendant fails to provide relevant information, the court is justified in making adverse assumptions as to its means, and may be obliged to do so.

18 It will not ordinarily be necessary for the prosecution to analyse the figures. In a few complex cases of relevant dispute the prosecution can if genuinely necessary undertake such analysis either in-house or by the instruction of an accountant and if it can justify the expense as part of its necessary costs those costs will ordinarily be recoverable from the defendant.[538]

19 In assessing the financial consequences of a fine the court should consider (*inter alia*) the following factors:

i) the effect on the employment of the innocent may be relevant,

ii) any effect upon shareholders will, however, not normally be relevant, those who invest in and finance a company take the risk that its management will result in financial loss,

iii) the effect on directors will not, likewise, normally be relevant,

iv) nor would it ordinarily be relevant that the prices charged by the defendant might in consequence be raised, at least unless the defendant is a monopoly supplier of public services,

---

[537] Criminal Justice Act 2003 s 164(1) and (4)
[538] Criminal Justice Act 2003 s 164(5)(b)(iii)

v) the effect upon the provision of services to the public will be relevant. Although a public organisation such as a local authority, hospital trust or police force must be treated the same as a commercial company where the standards of behaviour to be expected are concerned, and must suffer a punitive fine for breach of them, a different approach to determining the level of fine may well be justified. [The Lord Chief Justice in *R v Milford Haven Port Authority* 2000 2 Cr App R (S) p 423 at para 433 said,] "The Judge has to consider how any financial penalty will be paid. If a very substantial financial penalty will inhibit the proper performance by a statutory body of the public function that it has been set up to perform, that is not something to be disregarded." The same considerations will be likely to apply to non-statutory bodies or charities if providing public services,[539]

vi) the liability to pay civil compensation will ordinarily not be relevant; normally this will be provided by insurance or the resources of the defendant will be large enough to meet it from its own resources,

vii) the cost of meeting any remedial order will not ordinarily be relevant, except to the overall financial position of the defendant; such an order requires no more than should already have been done,

viii) whether the fine will have the effect of putting the defendant out of business will be relevant; in some bad cases this may be an acceptable consequence.

para 21 In some cases it may be apparent that a broadly quantifiable saving has been made by the defendant by committing the offence. In such cases it will normally be the proper approach to ensure that the fine removes the profit and imposes an appropriate additional penalty.

Information required for different corporate entities

page 10 Annex A para 1 *For companies*: published audited accounts. Particular attention should be paid to a) turnover, b) profit before tax, c) directors' remuneration, loan accounts and pension provision, d) assets as disclosed by the balance sheet (note that they may be valued at cost of acquisition, which may not be the same as current value). Most companies are required to lodge accounts at Companies House. Failure to produce relevant recent accounts on request may properly lead to the conclusion that the company can pay any appropriate fine.

2 *For partnerships*: annual audited accounts. Particular attention should be paid to: a) turnover, b) profit before tax, c) partner's drawings, loan accounts and pension provision, d) assets as above. If accounts are not produced on request, see paragraph 1.

3 *For local authorities, police and fire authorities and similar public bodies*: the Annual Revenue Budget (ARB) is the equivalent of turnover and the best indication of the size of the defendant organisation. It is published on www.local.communities.gov.uk/finance/bellwin.HTM

It is unlikely to be necessary to analyse specific expenditure or reserves unless inappropriate or grandiose expenditure is suggested. Such authorities also have attributed to them a 'Bellwin factor', which represents the level of exceptional and unforeseen expenditure that they are expected by central Government to meet themselves in any one year without any claim to recourse to central funds. But since that is arithmetically related to the ARB (currently 0.2%) it will ordinarily add little of significance beyond an indication of budgetary discipline.

4 *For health trusts*: the independent regulator of NHS Foundation Trusts is Monitor. It publishes quarterly reports and annual figures for the financial strength and stability of trusts from which the annual income can be seen, available via www.monitor-nhsft.gov.uk/home/our-publications. Detailed analysis of expenditure or reserves is unlikely to be called for. Note that Monitor has significant regulatory powers including over membership of the boards of directors or governors.

---

[539] To enable this paragraph to be understood, the language had to be tidied up considerably. Ed.

5 *For 'third sector' organisations*: it will be appropriate to inspect annual audited accounts. Detailed analysis of expenditure or reserves is unlikely to be called for unless there is a suggestion of unusual or unnecessary expenditure.

page 7 **D. Level of fines**

para 22 There will inevitably be a broad range of fines because of the range of seriousness involved and the differences in the circumstances of the defendants. Fines must be punitive and sufficient to have an impact on the defendant.

23 Fines cannot and do not attempt to value a human life in money. Civil compensation will be payable separately. The fine is designed to punish the defendant and is therefore tailored not only to what it has done but also to its individual circumstances.

24 The offence of corporate manslaughter, because it requires gross breach at a senior level, will ordinarily involve a level of seriousness significantly greater than a Health and Safety offence. The appropriate fine will seldom be less than £500,000 and may be measured in millions of pounds.[540]

25 The range of seriousness involved in Health and Safety offences is greater than for corporate manslaughter. However, where the offence is shown to have caused death, the appropriate fine will seldom be less than £100,000 and may be measured in hundreds of thousands of pounds or more.

270.30   *Fines, Time to pay*

Corporate Manslaughter and H and S Offences Causing Death Guideline 2010, see www.banksr.com Other Matters Guidelines tab page 7 para 20 In the case of a large organisation the fine should be payable within 28 days. In the case of a smaller or financially stretched organisation, it is permissible to require payment to be spread over a much longer period. There is no limitation to payment within 12 months, but the first payment should be required within a short time of sentencing. An extended period for the payment of further instalments may be particularly appropriate for an organisation of limited means which has committed a serious offence, and where it is undesirable that the fine should cause it to be put out of business.

R v B&Q 2005 EWCA Crim 2297 The defendant company was fined **£550,000** plus £250,000 costs. The Judge gave 28 days to pay. Held. That time to pay was an indulgence. Where a fine (which can only be viewed as modest when set against the defendant's overall turnover and profitability) is imposed on a company of anything approaching the size of the defendant, the seriousness of the offending and the impact of the penalty can be brought home to it by its being required to pay the fine within a much shorter period of time than 28 days. An undertaking of the size of the defendant does not need 28 days to pay. Such fines ought as a matter of course to be paid either immediately or in a period to be measured in single-figure days, unless very cogent evidence is provided that more time is needed. In contradistinction, the principles applicable to very small companies are set out in *R v Rollco Screw and Rivet Co Ltd* 1999 2 Cr App R (S) 436 (see **270.23**). But even on very cogent evidence the first instalment should be made payable at a very early date so that the effects of the criminality are brought home.

Note: This guidance was not incorporated into the new guideline but it may assist. Ed.

271 HUNTING/HARE COURSING

271.1

Hunting Act 2004

    s 1 (hunting a wild mammal with a dog)

    s 5 (participating in a hare coursing event etc.)

Mode of trial Both offences are summary only.

---

[540] Observations in *R v Friskies Petcare (UK) Ltd* 2000 EWCA Crim 95, 2 Cr App R (S) 401 notwithstanding, it is no longer the case that fines of £500,000 are reserved for major public disasters.

Maximum sentence A £5,000 fine for offences committed before 12 March 2015 and an unlimited fine thereafter.[541] There are maximum fines for those aged under 18, see **14.38** in Volume 1.

Forfeiture There is power to forfeit dogs, hunting articles and vehicles.[542]

272   IMMIGRATION OFFENCES

272.1

1) Immigration Act 1971 s 24A (obtaining leave etc. by deception)
   Mode of trial Triable either way
   Maximum sentence On indictment 2 years. Summary 6 months and/or a £5,000 fine for offences committed before 12 March 2015 and an unlimited fine thereafter.[543] There are maximum fines for those aged under 18, see **14.38** in Volume 1.
2) Immigration Act 1971
   s 25 (assisting unlawful immigration)
   s 25A (helping asylum seeker to enter UK)
   s 25B (assisting entry to UK in breach of Deportation Order or Exclusion Order)
   Mode of trial Triable either way
   Maximum sentence On indictment 14 years. Summary 6 months and/or a £5,000 fine for offences committed before 12 March 2015 and an unlimited fine thereafter.[544] There are maximum fines for those aged under 18, see **14.38** in Volume 1.
3) Asylum and Immigration (Treatment of Claimants, etc.) Act 2004 s 4
   Mode of trial Triable either way
   Maximum sentence On indictment 14 years. Summary 6 months and/or a £5,000 fine for offences committed before 12 March 2015 and an unlimited fine thereafter.[545] There are maximum fines for those aged under 18, see **14.38** in Volume 1.

Confiscation Where a defendant has a criminal lifestyle the court, once the confiscation proceedings are triggered (see **22.11** in Volume 1), <u>must</u> follow the Proceeds of Crime Act 2002 procedure. 'Criminal lifestyle' offences include those under Immigration Act 1971 s 25, 25A and 25B and Asylum and Immigration (Treatment of Claimants, etc.) Act 2004 s 4.[546] For what constitutes a criminal lifestyle, see **22.48** in Volume 1.

Serious Crime Prevention Orders For Immigration Act 1971 s 25, 25A and 25B and Asylum and Immigration (Treatment of Claimants, etc.) Act 2004 s 4 offences there is a discretionary power to make this order, when it would protect the public etc.[547]

272.2   *Crown Court statistics   England and Wales*

Assist entry of illegal immigrant Aged 21+

Year	Plea	Total sentenced	Type of sentencing %						Average length of custody in months
			Discharge	Fine	Commu-nity sentence	Sus-pended sentence	Custody	Other	
2013	G	207	0.5	–	–	17.9	81.6	–	16.7
	NG	76	–	–	1.3	6.6	92.1	–	36.4
2014	G	237	–	–	1	28	70	–	18.8
	NG	54	–	–	–	11	89	–	28.0

---

[541] Legal Aid, Sentencing and Punishment of Offenders Act 2012 s 85(1) and (4) and Legal Aid, Sentencing and Punishment of Offenders Act 2012 (Commencement No 11) Order 2015 2015/504
[542] Hunting Act 2004 s 9
[543] Legal Aid, Sentencing and Punishment of Offenders Act 2012 s 85(1) and (4) and Legal Aid, Sentencing and Punishment of Offenders Act 2012 (Commencement No 11) Order 2015 2015/504
[544] Legal Aid, Sentencing and Punishment of Offenders Act 2012 s 85(1) and (4) and Legal Aid, Sentencing and Punishment of Offenders Act 2012 (Commencement No 11) Order 2015 2015/504
[545] Legal Aid, Sentencing and Punishment of Offenders Act 2012 s 85(1) and (4) and Legal Aid, Sentencing and Punishment of Offenders Act 2012 (Commencement No 11) Order 2015 2015/504
[546] Proceeds of Crime Act 2002 s 6 and 75 and Sch 2 para 4
[547] Serious Crime Act 2007 s 1 and Sch 1 para 2

For explanations about the statistics see page 1-xii. For more statistics and for statistics
for male and female defendants etc. see www.banksr.com Other Matters Statistics tab
See also the **BIGAMY/MARRIAGE OFFENCES** *Immigration controls, to evade* paras at
216.3 and the **PASSPORT/ID DOCUMENTS OFFENCES** chapter.

272.3   Judicial guidance

R v Le and Stark 1999 1 Cr App R (S) 422 LCJ The problem of illegal entry is on the
increase. The offence calls very often for deterrent sentences. The following are
aggravating features: a) where the offence has been repeated, b) where there is financial
gain, c) where it involves a stranger rather than a spouse or a close member of the
family, d) in a conspiracy where it has been committed over a period, e) high degree of
planning, organisation and sophistication, f) there are a large number of illegal immigrants as opposed to one or a very small number. Plainly the more prominent the role of
the defendant the greater the aggravation of the offence.
Note: Although this is an old case it may be helpful. Ed.
R v Ali 2001 EWCA Crim 2874, 2002 2 Cr App R (S) 32 (p 115) The defendant pleaded
to a section 24A offence. Held. Previous good character and personal circumstances are
of very limited value. Cases will be sentenced on a deterrent basis.
R v Ding 2010 EWCA Crim 1979, 2011 1 Cr App R (S) 91 (p 546) D pleaded at the first
opportunity to securing etc. the avoidance of an enforcement action (Immigration
Act 1971 s 24(1)(b)). When stopped at a service station and asked to provide his
documents, D handed over a photocard in a false name, which purported to be a
translation of a Chinese driving licence. Held. We are unpersuaded by the attempt to
draw a general difference of culpability between using deception to remain and using
deception to prevent the authorities discovering that he is unlawfully in the UK.

272.4   Adoption, Unlawful

R v Thomas 2013 EWCA Crim 1005 D pleaded to attempting to facilitate a breach of
immigration law. She arrived in the UK from the Philippines in 2001. In 2007, she
married M. She continued to live with him in the UK after the marriage. She obtained
British citizenship in 2010. D and M decided they wished to adopt a child. In May 2012,
D and M travelled to the Philippines. In June 2012, she submitted a UK settlement visa
application for N, a baby, at the British Embassy in Manila. She submitted a Philippines
birth certificate in support, which gave the date of birth as December 2011. She attended
the Embassy for interview and an immigration officer noticed that D may not have been
in the Philippines at the time of the birth. When cautioned and questioned, D admitted
that she was not the biological mother. She said the biological parents had sent the birth
certificate to her in the UK and she had signed it and returned it to the Philippines. The
child had not been registered by the biological parents and D had been contributing
financially to the child's maintenance. The application was refused, but D continued to
contribute to the child's maintenance, despite the child being cared for by her family in
the Philippines. In the UK she was arrested and claimed that she thought she had
adopted the child. She also said she had claimed to be the biological mother because of
the time it would have taken to complete the paperwork. Held. Offending of this nature
calls for general deterrence. However, it is important to note that this was not a case of
trafficking. It was not a sophisticated attempt. Immediate custody was inevitable and the
sentence must reflect the need for general deterrence. However, **4 months** not 6.

272.5   Assisting unlawful immigration (section 25)

R v Dhall 2011 EWCA Crim 2774 D pleaded (20% credit) to assisting unlawful
immigration. He acted as an immigration advisor and assisted applicants in completing
their forms and submitting them to the UK Border Agency. Ten applications were
presented with false supporting documentation in the names of companies with which D
was associated. D would produce, or collaborate in the production of, false payslips, and
subsequently transfer the appropriate sums to the applicants' bank accounts, to show that
they had been paid the sums that were stated on the forged payslips. D received £6,000

per application and the offending was repeated over the course of 12 months. Held. This case concerned illegal extension of stay, rather than illegal entry, and though there may be some force in the submission that those who facilitate illegal entry ought to be more severely dealt with than those falling into D's category, this offence was a serious one of its kind. **6 years** could not be criticised.

R v Miessan and Miessan 2013 EWCA Crim 733 D pleaded (early) to assisting unlawful immigration. RM, a French national, was contacted by her mother and told of a baby boy who had been found in the Ivory Coast. RM was childless, despite having fertility treatment. She discussed the matter with KM, her husband. RM went to the Ivory Coast in June 2011 and registered the birth of the baby as her own. She obtained a French birth certificate and passport for the baby using the false birth registration. She returned to the UK in April 2012 and she lived, with her husband and child, as a family in Kent. Following a civil court case in which KM gave evidence, it came to the attention of social services and the police that RM and KM had lied about the origin of the baby. They made full admissions upon arrest and a DNA test proved that the boy had no biological link to the couple. The Family Division had ordered the child to be removed from the parents and placed for adoption in the UK. There was no suggestion that the couple's care for the child was not satisfactory. Held. This was not a case of trafficking. Offending of this nature calls for general deterrence but the motivation was the desire to adopt a child. RM and KM had served 5 months in custody, having been sentenced to 12 months each by the Judge. The public interest did not require them to remain in custody any longer. **5 months,** not 12, to enable **immediate release**.

272.6   Consider the role of the agent, The court must

R (Q) v Secretary of State for Home Department 2003 EWCA Civ 364 It is clear that some asylum seekers are so much under the influence of the agents that they cannot be criticised for accepting implicitly what they are told by them. There is no valid comparison between agents of this kind, whose interests at the point of entry may well be in serious conflict with those of the asylum seekers, and professional advisors. To disregard the effect that they have on their charges would be both unrealistic and unjust.

R (K) v Crown Court at Croydon 2005 EWHC 478 (Admin), 2 Cr App R (S) 96 (p 578) High Court The defendant pleaded to seeking leave to enter by deception (Immigration Act 1971 s 24(a)). She made the application under the influence of the agent, and he persuaded her not to reveal her previous attempt to enter the UK. Held. Relying on *R (Q) v Secretary of State for Home Department* 2003 EWCA Civ 364, those seeking the aid of agents are powerfully under their influence. That fact and the defendant's age of 17 make it all the more important to take into account the influence that the agent must have had. Had the significance of the agent been brought home to the previous courts it would not have been possible to say that custody was the only appropriate method of dealing with this defendant. To ignore the influence of the agent amounted to an error of law. Sentence reduced.

R v Ai 2005 EWCA Crim 936, 2006 1 Cr App R (S) 5 (p 18) D pleaded at the Magistrates' Court to failing to produce at leave or asylum interview an immigration document contrary to Asylum and Immigration (Treatment of Claimants, etc.) Act 2004 s 2. He arrived at Stansted airport with no documents. He said that he had given the false passport back to his agent. His counsel gave a somewhat different version of events to the Appeal Court, saying that D had travelled from China to Russia on a genuine passport which he had then handed back to his agent. Held. There is a strong deterrent element needed in sentencing to send a clear message to agents or people traffickers that the requirements they are said to impose on their clients will not avail them and that their clients face a real risk of a custodial sentence. If significant weight is given to the instructions of an agent the effect of the Act would be significantly undermined. Whilst the instructions of an agent may in certain circumstances be a mitigating component, it cannot be so strong a component that it undermines the purpose of the legislation.

272.7   Disqualification from driving
R v Woop 2002 EWCA Crim 58, 2 Cr App R (S) 65 (p 281) D pleaded on rearraignment to facilitating the illegal entry of 35 people. He drove his lorry to the freight depot on the French side of the Channel Tunnel. A Customs officer asked him what he was towing and he said, 'Quartz sand'. A customs officer detected movement, and 35 people were found. D denied knowledge of them. He was a 38-year-old German man of good character with two young children. The trip was to fund treatment for his wife's chronic asthma. That treatment was not covered by their health insurance. Held. The gravity and prevalence of this offence requires no special emphasis. Sentences are heavy and intended to deter. 6 years was too long, so 5 years substituted. The offence had nothing to do with his driving. He earns his living from driving. The disqualification was reduced from 5 to **3 years**.

272.8   Failure to have immigration document at asylum interview
R v Jeyarasa 2014 EWCA Crim 2545, 2015 1 Cr App R (S) 39 (p 290) D pleaded to failing to have an immigration document at an asylum interview. He arrived at Manchester Airport from Paris and told passport control he had no passport or travel documents. An asylum screening interview took place. He said an agent had supplied false documents for him to leave Paris and had taken the documents off D before he arrived in the UK. D claimed he was tortured in Sri Lanka. His asylum application failed. The Single Judge said the Judge was entitled to take into account D's asylum application had failed but there was no evidence as to why. It could not be inferred D was disbelieved. It might have been because the application should have been made in France. Held. We agree. The fact he wished to claim asylum was relevant. The facts are similar to *R v Ai* 2005 EWCA Crim 936, 2006 1 Cr App R (S) 5 (p 18) where 5 months was substituted but we are bound to have regard to the changed climate about immigration since 2005. We start at 9 months not 18, so **6 months** not 12.

272.9   Driving illegal immigrants through ports etc.   Reward to be paid
R v Chocat and Chocat 2010 EWCA Crim 1468 D and his mother, C, pleaded to assisting unlawful immigration. They arrived at the ferry port in Portsmouth from Cherbourg in a Transit van. C was driving. A search of the van revealed 16 people of Vietnamese origin ranging in age from 15 to 35. D said he expected to receive €24,000 when he returned to France. D was aged 20 and C was aged 51. Neither had any convictions. C's basis of plea was: a) she had a limited knowledge of what was taking place, b) her motive was to help her son, c) she was not involved in the planning, and d) she did not expect a reward. She was resident in France with a daughter who was significantly dependent on her. Held. For D, **5 years** with a deterrent element. For C, 3 years after a trial and because of plea and mitigation, **2 years**, not 3.
R v Balta 2012 EWCA Crim 79, 2013 1 Cr App R (S) 8 (p 48) D, a Romanian lorry driver, pleaded at his PCMH to attempting to facilitate the commission of a breach of immigration laws. D's co-defendants brought 20 illegal immigrants, mostly of Asian origin, to his lorry in the East End of London. D drove the lorry to Dover to take the cargo to France. His lorry was searched at the port and the illegal immigrants were found in the back. £2,000, which was D's payment, was found in the lorry. The operation was sophisticated. D was of good character. Held. The aggravating factors were a) there were 20 and b) it was for a reward. The mitigating factors were it was a one-off and his character. Starting at **4½ years** makes **3 years** quashing the 5 years.
See also: *R v Naumann* 2010 EWCA Crim 2838, 2011 2 Cr App R (S) 12 (p 63) (Early plea in overwhelming case. He drove a van into the country containing 16 illegal immigrants from India for profit. Good character, aged 51. Isolated offence. With 25% discount, **4½ years**.)
Old cases: Earlier cases are best ignored.

272.10   *Driving illegal immigrants through ports etc./Assisting with travel   No reward*

R v Ballas 2013 EWCA Crim 2445 D pleaded (full credit) to attempting to facilitate the commission of a breach of immigration law. Police officers saw a van parked near a junction. There were three men standing by the van and a BMW car. The BMW drove off and the officers stopped and approached the van. D was present with two men and a 14-year-old boy. They refused to say what they were doing but D told the officers that it was his van and he had come to collect the others. A search of the van revealed Albanian passports, spare clothing, food and water. The officers asked D whether he knew the others. He said he did not. He claimed that he had come to help a friend whose car had broken down (the BMW) and that the three others had appeared from nowhere. The three were arrested. One had entered the country that day via a lorry from the Netherlands. The other man was his cousin. The boy had travelled via Italy to the Netherlands with his father and from the Netherlands to Dover by himself because his father did not have enough money for them both to travel. One of the men had a mobile phone and was in contact with another man who made all the arrangements. Both men were deported. D pleaded on the following basis: He knew nothing of the operation which brought the men to the UK. He received a phone call from an Albanian man with whom he had worked, asking him to collect his son who was stranded and lost. He went to help out of friendship with the man. He only expected one person. He was not offered any money, nor did he receive any. The van was his work van and the only vehicle he had. D had no convictions, had been in the UK since 2009 and had always worked. **Held.** Even with regard to the basis of plea, we note the importance attached to deterrence in this field, together with the public concern that relates to it. The correct starting point was 18 months. With full credit, **12 months** not 2 years.

272.11   *Employers, Offences by*

R v Rahman 2011 EWCA Crim 1985, 2012 1 Cr App R (S) 51 (p 295) D pleaded on the day of trial to seven counts of assisting unlawful immigration. He owned three restaurants in Cumbria. The UK Border Agency conducted an enforcement visit at two of his restaurants. At the first, they discovered nine people who had failed in their asylum applications or held only a visitor's visa. Eight people were found at the second premises. These findings resulted only in civil penalties totalling £55,000. Search warrants were subsequently executed and a total of seven illegal workers were found at two restaurants. Their living conditions were basic and cramped. The employees slept three or five persons per room on mattresses on the floor. One restaurant had no electricity in the employees' quarters. D's basis of plea was in effect that the employees received food and shelter in return for their work. D, aged 47 at appeal, had no relevant convictions. References spoke very highly of him. **Held.** To D, the illegal workers represented a financial gain. The numbers were not confined to just one or two and nor were they members of D's family. D was not, however, involved in facilitating entry to the UK. **2 years** was not manifestly excessive.

R v Wahiduzzama 2012 EWCA Crim 584, 2 Cr App R (S) 91 (p 549) D pleaded (after a jury had been sworn) to three counts of assisting unlawful immigration. UK Border Agency officials searched an Indian restaurant in Cumbria. D was the part owner and manager of the business. A chef who was working in the kitchen was illegally in the UK, having overstayed a short-term visa. He had been employed by the restaurant for over seven years. He had been identified as an illegal immigrant in 2010 on a Border Agency visit. He was permitted to remain in the flat above the restaurant, awaiting removal, provided he did not undertake any work. D had been fined £12,500 for the 2010 incident. A subsequent visit by police and the Border Agency discovered that two more men were working in the kitchen and were illegal immigrants. One was an absconder from the Border Agency control, and the other was subject to reporting restrictions at a Home Office centre in London. D claimed he was unaware that the chef was not permitted to undertake any work. He claimed that the other two men had only begun work recently and on the basis that they provided satisfactory permissions to be in the UK. D was of previous good character. Since these events, D was forced into bankruptcy with debts of £80,000 and had given up the business. His wife was expecting their second child and his first child had special educational needs. His wife spoke very little English and was entirely dependent on him. D accepted full responsibility. Held. This was a bad case of reoffending by D, who knew full well he was breaking the law. After the discovery of the chef, he offended again. This was done for financial gain, which would have been considerable. **23 months** was not manifestly excessive. The impact of the sentence on D's wife and daughter carried considerable weight so, as an act of mercy, we reduce the 23 months to **18 months**.

272.12   Enforcement action, Avoiding
R v Ding 2010 EWCA Crim 1979, 2011 1 Cr App R (S) 91 (p 546) D pleaded at the first opportunity to securing etc. the avoidance of an enforcement action (section 24(1)(b)). When stopped at a service station and asked to provide his documents, D handed over a photocard in a false name, which purported to be a translation of a Chinese driving licence by the International Automobile Association. In fact, that organisation did not exist. D's fingerprints were taken and his true identity was ascertained. He then admitted that he had purchased the photocard for £100. The defence sought to draw a distinction between the instant offence and the offence of obtaining etc. leave to enter/remain. Held. The statute makes no distinction between the two and we are unpersuaded by the attempt to draw a general difference of culpability between using deception to remain and using deception to prevent the authorities discovering that he is unlawfully in the UK. **12 months** was not manifestly excessive.

272.13   Entering the UK without a passport
Asylum and Immigration (Treatment of Claimants, etc.) Act 2004 s 2 (arranging etc. the arrival of an individual who he intends to exploit)
Mode of trial Triable either way
Maximum sentence On indictment 14 years. Summary 6 months and/or a £5,000 fine for offences committed before 12 March 2015 and an unlimited fine thereafter.[548] There are maximum fines for those aged under 18, see **14.38** in Volume 1.
Note: All the reported cases are old and are best ignored. Ed.

272.14   Exploiting immigrants through employment
Att-Gen's Ref No 28 of 2014 2014 EWCA Crim 1723 D was convicted of conspiracy to facilitate a breach of immigration law and of using unlicensed security operatives (2 years concurrent not altered). D ran a business providing security guards and employed 155 people during the conspiracy. Near the end of the scheme, D generated false paperwork or altered documents to hide the fact that employees were working illegally in the UK. D assured clients that his employees' credentials were genuine, even when challenged. The employees were exploited, some working for £3 per hour and for periods of 24 hours without rest. D denied knowledge of what was going on despite making annual profits of between £45,000 and £278,000 from employing around 75 illegal workers over the course of 5½ years. D was aged 44 at sentence with no previous convictions. He was not involved in the facilitation of entry into the UK. Held. There was a high degree of planning. D was the ringleader. There was substantial gain. The following non-exhaustive considerations apply: a) whether the offence is isolated or not, b) the duration of offending, c) [antecedents], d) motivation, whether commercial or humanitarian, e) the number of individuals involved in the breach of immigration law, f) whether they were strangers or family, g) the degree of organisation, h) whether the defendant recruited others, i) the defendant's role and j) whether D's conduct involved

---

[548] Legal Aid, Sentencing and Punishment of Offenders Act 2012 s 85(1) and (4) and Legal Aid, Sentencing and Punishment of Offenders Act 2012 (Commencement No 11) Order 2015 2015/504

exploitation of or pressuring others. D's company was designed to circumvent immigration controls and involved several people on a large scale over a considerable period. It
was aggravated by the false documents to government departments. Although some of
the business was legitimate, a significant part was not. **8 years**, not 4½.

272.15   *Large-scale organisations*
R v Naumann 2010 EWCA Crim 2838, 2011 2 Cr App R (S) 12 (p 63) D pleaded to
assisting unlawful immigration. He was a German national whose van was searched by
the UK Border Agency. The search uncovered 16 illegal immigrants. D advanced a
wholly false story in the first two interviews, subsequently admitting knowing that there
were persons concealed in the van, but not the number. He cited economic reasons for
committing the offence, namely that he had become unemployed after a lifetime of
employment. D was of good character. Held. This was an isolated offence. D's good
character is relevant. The number of immigrants is also relevant, as is the fact it was an
enterprise for profit. It was a sophisticated enterprise and D had been given money to
hire the van and had done so. The van was then handed over to those he was working for,
who adapted it to conceal the immigrants. Foreign nationals will not be dealt with more
leniently because they will be serving their sentence among those who speak a different
language and will be far from their families. They had only themselves to blame. 25%
discount for plea was proper. **4½ years** was stiff but well deserved.
R v Wolanski and Rakovskij 2013 EWCA Crim 1020 R pleaded (25% credit) to
conspiracy to facilitate a breach of immigration law and possession of criminal property.
W pleaded to conspiracy to [facilitate] a breach of immigration law. Illegal entrants to
the UK were provided with passports or identity cards, most of which were genuine
Polish or Lithuanian documents. The chosen entrant bore a strong resemblance to the
genuine document holder's photograph. Other supporting documents could also be
provided. The entrants were provided with transport into the UK, often crossing in
freight lorries from France. Once in the UK they were met and escorted to a
pre-arranged address. The prosecution was not able to say how many entries were
facilitated over the 15-month period but a large number of identity documents were
discovered. R was the organiser and W worked for him, carrying out errands. On one
occasion, a package containing identity documents was sent to Italy, demonstrating the
international nature of the conspiracy. R's address was searched and numerous identity
documents were found, along with false UK immigration stamps, a false Brussels Air
departure stamp and numerous tablets, phones, laptops and SIM cards. There was
extensive phone contact between R and others in Poland, Ukraine, France and Italy. W's
basis of plea was that he was a driver. He worked for R and his role was to collect
passengers from lorries that had brought them into the UK, and transport them to an
address. He was paid for his role and he knew the people he was collecting were illegal
immigrants but were not trafficked or exploited. He also carried out errands for R,
including collecting packages. R's basis of plea asserted that he had agreed with others
to facilitate entry of non-EU nationals to the UK for reward and that the entrants were
not trafficked or exploited. £10,000, which represented proceeds from the operation, and
148 passports and other ID documents were found in two safety deposit boxes belonging
to R. R had a degree in economics and had convictions in France for illegal entry and
assisting illegal entry (26 weeks, 6 of which were suspended). R said his motive was to
fund fertility treatment for his wife. W had no convictions. Held. This was a grave
conspiracy. The aggravating factors were: a) the conspiracy lasted for a number of
months, b) it involved strangers, not family members, c) the methods were highly
sophisticated including numerous false and forged documents, e) it was done for
financial gain. R's case contains virtually all the relevant aggravating factors one can
think of. He was the sole organiser. It was not possible to calculate the number of entries.
However, the number must have been very considerable. R's mitigation was his plea
and, to a very limited extent, the motivation to fund the fertility treatment. W's position
was different. His role was important and he assisted R. W may not have known the full

details of the operation but he knew the nature of the conspiracy. For R, **9 years** was severe but not manifestly excessive. For W, **4 years** was perhaps severe but not manifestly excessive.

R v Kytz 2013 EWCA Crim 1749 D pleaded (25% credit) to conspiracy to facilitate a breach of immigration law. He lived in Ukraine and from 2007 to 2012 he assisted 40 Ukrainians to enter and remain in the UK illegally. He exploited weaknesses in the system which allowed Ukrainians to gain admission to the UK without the visa they would normally require to enter. They were permitted to do this once they had satisfied the authorities that they would be leaving the UK within 24 hours. The usual way this was done was by presenting a valid aeroplane ticket for onward travel. D would buy the ticket for the individual to present to customs officials, then cancel it before the time came for the individual to board the plane. The individual would then disappear. D, or one of his associates, would travel to the UK with the client to ensure that everything went smoothly. D owned a number of boats and the reason for travel that was given by a number of the individuals was that they were learning to sail. The individuals were not vulnerable. Held. The conspiracy lasted for a considerable period. The conspiracy did not require forged documents but it was sophisticated because the system which D devised was so simple. It required very few procedures that could lead to discovery. This was a serious offence which called for the sentence the Judge imposed. He started at **12 years**, so with plea and other mitigation **8½ years**.

R v Hussain 2015 EWCA Crim 1352 K, D, N and G were convicted of conspiracy to defraud. D pleaded to two benefit fraud counts (3 months consecutive). D and G were K's sons. N was K's nephew. Two others were convicted of the conspiracy (K's wife (a suspended sentence) and the other (7 years). No appeal.) K was the originator and organiser of the conspiracy. He recruited the others. From January 2006 to September 2012, the team produced and sold false documents for 107 travel visas to the UK. Employment letters, wage slips and property particulars were forged. 81 had false solicitor's stamps. Some of the applicants were duped and deprived of making a legitimate application. The group obtained £175,000. K was now aged 62 and had a serious medical condition. In 1994 he had a conviction for dishonesty which increased the seriousness of the offence. He was the primary carer for his 82-year-old mother, who had medical problems. D was aged 31 with no relevant previous. N joined the conspiracy in 2010 when aged 20. He was of good character. G was now aged 26. The Judge said it was a highly sophisticated, wholesale assault on the immigration procedures and solicitors and estate agents had their reputations put at risk. Held. Financial harm is not at the heart nor the gravamen of a conspiracy to defraud. He found D, G and N played a significant and important part with full knowledge of what was occurring. Held. The guidelines are not an adequate way of dealing with this case. Deterrent sentences are called for. The time the conspiracy lasted and the sophistication were aggravating factors. **9 years** for K and **7 years** for the others were not manifestly excessive.

See also: *R v Shahi* 2010 EWCA Crim 2480, 2011 1 Cr App R (S) 115 (p 676) (Convicted of obtaining leave by deception, conspiracy to defraud and possessing criminal property. Set up a bogus immigration business. Forged documents for 574 applicants. £1m passed through the accounts. Top of conspiracy. Sophisticated conspiracy carried on for two years. **8 years** was justified.)

Att-Gen's Ref No 49 and 50 of 2015 2015 EWCA Crim 1402, 2016 1 Cr App R (S) 4 (p 14) (Convicted conspiracy to breach immigration law. One, a part-time lecturer who was the mastermind (aged 68) and the other, a director of a company recruiting overseas students who were in ill-health. 117 students with false documents. Value of fraud probably close to £300,000. No previous. Held. We consider the acute human misery to the students. **8 years** and **5 years** not 5 and 2½.)

Old cases: *R v Kvec* 2008 EWCA Crim 594, 2 Cr App R (S) 90 (p 510) (**8 years**) *R v Kashyap* 2008 EWCA Crim 775, 2 Cr App R (S) 109 (p 627) (**7 years**) *R v Kao and*

Others 2010 EWCA Crim 2617, 2011 2 Cr App R (S) 4 (p 13) (For K, X and M, **7 years**. For T, **3 years**) *R v Kugbeadzor* 2010 EWCA Crim 2685, 2011 2 Cr App R (S) 5 (p 19) (**3 years**)
For a summary of the first two cases, see the 8th edition of this book and for the last two see the 10th edition.

272.16   Obtaining leave etc. by deception
Examples: *R v Arinze* 2010 EWCA Crim 1638 (Pleas to having a false instrument, a passport, with intent and obtaining leave by deception. Nigerian national. Three children. Because of totality, **9 months** not 15.)
R v Kaur 2010 EWCA Crim 1989 (D, aged 19, pleaded to seeking to obtain leave by deception. She was an overstayer and an absconder. With agent completed false application form. Previous good character. 15-month starting point, so with the plea, **10 months** not 15.)
R v Kugbeadzor 2010 EWCA Crim 2685, 2011 2 Cr App R (S) 5 (p 19) (Pleas to possession of false identity documents with intent, seeking leave to remain by deception, and conspiracy to facilitate a breach of immigration control. Six sham marriages. Assisted the police. Previous good character. **3 years** not 4.)
R v Ilesanmi 2010 EWCA Crim 3083, 2011 2 Cr App R (S) 36 (p 222) (Pleas to fraud etc. Forged Nigerian passport, National Insurance card, and utility bill. Used to gain employment after overstaying visa. Sham marriage for right to remain in UK halted by police officers. **3 years**.)
Old cases: Best ignored.

272.17   Providing accommodation etc. for illegal immigrants
R v Anser 2011 EWCA Crim 55 D pleaded (full credit) to an offence under Immigration Act 1971 s 25(1), 'facilitating the commission of a breach of immigration law'. SA was a failed asylum seeker from Pakistan. After being removed from the UK, SA and his family returned 18 months later and entered a fresh application for asylum. At appeal it was still undecided. D provided SA, his younger brother, and SA's family with accommodation and basic subsistence. D's basis of plea stated that there was no loss, financial or otherwise, and that he genuinely believed that if SA was removed from the UK to Pakistan, he faced a real risk of a European Convention on Human Rights art 3 and 8 violation. D, aged 42 at appeal, was of previous good character. Held. We are satisfied an offence was committed. The Court considered the instant offence against the decision in *R v Ovieriakhi* 2009 EWCA Crim 452, 2 Cr App R (S) 91 (p 607). Unlike *Ovieriakhi*, here there was no deception. Perhaps understandably, D did not appreciate that he was committing an offence by assisting SA. It is to be noted that there was no profit to the defendant. This case is towards the lower end of the spectrum. **4 months**, not 12.
See also: *R v Ansari* 2011 EWCA Crim 1640, 2012 1 Cr App R (S) 37 (p 224) (Plea to unlawfully assisting immigration (×5). Full credit. Failed asylum seeker who then absconded. Provided accommodation, food and employment for illegal immigrants over a number of years. Did not assist entry. Aged 45. Good character. **12 months** was not manifestly excessive.)

272.18   Trafficked immigrants, Exploitation of
Asylum and Immigration (Treatment of Claimants, etc.) Act 2004 s 4
Protection of Freedoms Act 2012 s 110 amends and redefines Asylum and Immigration (Treatment of Claimants, etc.) Act 2004 s 4. The mode of trial, the maximum sentence and the ancillary orders remain the same. In force for offences committed on or after 6 April 2013.[549]
Mode of trial Triable either way

---

[549] Protection of Freedoms Act 2023 (Commencement No 5 and Savings and Transitional Provisions) Order 2013 2013/470 para 2

Maximum sentence On indictment 14 years. Summary 6 months and/or a £5,000 fine for offences committed before 12 March 2015 and an unlimited fine thereafter.[550] There are maximum fines for those aged under 18, see **14.38** in Volume 1.
Confiscation Once the confiscation proceedings are triggered (see **22.11** in Volume 1), the court <u>must</u> follow the Proceeds of Crime Act 2002 procedure.[551]
Serious Crime Prevention Orders For Asylum and Immigration (Treatment of Claimants, etc.) Act 2004 s 4 offences there is a discretionary power to make this order, when it would protect the public etc.[552]

272.19   *Trafficked immigrants, Exploitation of   Guideline remarks*
Att-Gen's Ref Nos 37, 38 and 65 of 2010 2010 EWCA Crim 2880, 2011 2 Cr App R (S) 31 (p 186) Under the Asylum and Immigration (Treatment of Claimants, etc.) Act 2004 s 4, assessing seriousness will include considering:

1) the nature and degree of deception or coercion exercised upon the incoming worker. Coercion will be an unusual aggravating feature in a case of economic exploitation. The gravamen of the offence committed against economic migrants is the deceitful promise of work on favourable terms,
2) the nature and degree of exploitation exercised upon the worker on arrival in the work place. This will involve a consideration both of the degree to which what is promised is in fact denied on arrival and the extent to which treatment in the work place offends common standards within the United Kingdom,
3) the level and methods of control exercised over the worker with a view to ensuring that he remains economically trapped,
4) the level of vulnerability of the incoming worker, usually economic but also physical and psychological,
5) the degree of harm suffered by the worker, physical, psychological and financial,
6) the level of organisation and planning behind the scheme, the gain sought or achieved, and the offender's status and role within the organisation,
7) the numbers of those exploited,
8) previous convictions for similar offences.

We think it probable that victims of these offences will routinely be strangers rather than family members. In cases of facilitating illegal entry to the United Kingdom, the fact the entrant is a family member and not a stranger may constitute some mitigation of the seriousness of the offence. The fact the victim of economic exploitation is a stranger is not, we consider, an aggravating feature of the basic offence.

272.20   *Trafficked immigrants, Exploitation of   Cases*
Att-Gen's Ref Nos 37, 38 and 65 of 2010 2010 EWCA Crim 2880, 2011 2 Cr App R (S) 31 (p 186) S, R and P were convicted of conspiracy to traffic persons for exploitation. P, the mother of K and R, ran a restaurant. S and R worked in the restaurant with responsibilities, but P oversaw activities. They enticed nine men from the Middle East and the Indian subcontinent to the UK with the promise of good wages and working conditions. In fact they were subjected to abuse, deprivation and economic exploitation. The men had their passports and personal documents confiscated. They were required to work more than 12 hours per day for six to seven days a week and were subject to threats and abuse. The men were not, as promised, registered with the NHS nor were they given National Insurance numbers or pay slips. The victims were allowed to leave the UK to visit family members. They returned having been promised that conditions and treatment would improve. After arrest, the defendants sought to persuade the victims to give false accounts of their treatment to the police. It was conceded that several workers were kept

---

[550] Legal Aid, Sentencing and Punishment of Offenders Act 2012 s 85(1) and (4) and Legal Aid, Sentencing and Punishment of Offenders Act 2012 (Commencement No 11) Order 2015 2015/504
[551] Proceeds of Crime Act 2002 s 6 and 75 and Sch 2 para 4 as substituted by Nationality, Immigration and Asylum Act 2002 s 114 and Sch 7 para 31
[552] Serious Crime Act 2007 s 1 and Sch 1

in conditions that were close to slavery. A comparison was drawn with Immigration Act 1971 s 25 (facilitating the arrival of an asylum seeker). S and R had previous convictions for affray. P was suffering from a depressive disorder. The Judge considered for P a Hospital Order after recommendations by experts. Held. This was a persistent campaign of exploitation involving nine vulnerable men over a prolonged period of time. The motivation was financial and there was a significant degree of organisation and planning. We consider that the Judge carried out the task of weighing the relevant factors with conspicuous care. He concluded that P exaggerated her symptoms. None of the offenders demonstrated any remorse. The starting point was **6 years**. For R and S, **4 years**, not 3 and for P 3 years untouched.

R v Bala 2011 EWCA Crim 534 D pleaded to conspiracy to traffic people within the UK for exploitation. A co-defendant pleaded to two similar offences. Advertisements were placed in newspapers in Poland offering jobs in construction in the UK. The individuals were required to pay £60 up front for rent and £200 for work permits etc. They were promised payment of £8 p/h. None were paid or properly registered. The accommodation provided was dirty and often cold. 25 workers were exploited. It was accepted that D was effectively a driver responsible for driving and collecting the workers. The organisation was run by a family in Poland. D eventually refused to do as asked and was instructed to leave, upon which he reported the matter to the police. The Judge noted that D had lost his own papers and therefore this was the only employment open to him. D, aged 41, was of good character. Held. D made no more than £10 per day from the activities. He took what he thought was a legitimate job and there was no way of extricating himself. A deterrent sentence was not appropriate. D also took positive steps to assist courts in Poland, which was unknown to the lower courts. **9 months**, not 2 years.

R v Suchy 2014 EWCA Crim 1245 D was convicted of two conspiracies to traffic for exploitation, and pleaded late to conspiracy to assist unlawful immigration. D was approached by U, a Pakistani national who had a student visa which was about to expire. D was asked to find a woman whom U could marry to remain in the UK. U was to be charged £1,380. Associates of D approached V, a Slovak national in Slovakia. D and his wife were also Slovakian. V was promised a better life if she came to the UK. She had been in prison for obtaining goods by fraud and was destitute. D bought her a ticket. She was repeatedly assaulted by D over three days. V wanted to go home but D took her ID card. V was taken to meet U. Then V was taken by D to his associates to try to sell her sexual services. They did not find any customers. V was made to do domestic work at D's house. U paid D £600 and U was given V's ID card. V was taken to U's flat where she was raped by U so violently she required hospital treatment. She bled heavily. D had no convictions. The Judge found D was in control of the operation at least in the UK. Held. Consecutive sentences were required owing to the distinction between the two offences. 6 years for the first two conspiracies and 4 years for the third was not wrong but because of totality, **8 years** not 10 in all.

Prostitution, Trafficking see the **PROSTITUTES, CONTROLLING ETC.** *Trafficking* paras at **311.19** and **311.22**.

273   IMPORTATION OF DRUGS (CLASS A, B AND C)

273.1
1 Customs and Excise Management Act 1979 s 170(2)(b) (knowingly concerned in the fraudulent evasion of a prohibition etc.)

> **Mode of trial** Triable either way unless the defendant could receive the minimum sentence of 7 years for a third drug trafficking offence, when the offence is triable only on indictment.

Maximum sentence On indictment class A life, class B and C 14 years.[553] On summary conviction 6 months (3 months for class C drugs) and/or a fine of £5,000 for offences committed before 12 March 2015 and a £20,000[554] fine thereafter, or three times the value of the goods, whichever is greater.

Why the maximum is £20,000 and not unlimited is far from clear. Large fines would only be appropriate for corporate offenders. It may be because the appropriate forum for such drug importations is considered to be the Crown Court.

For drugs on the high seas destined for other countries, the offences are prosecuted under Criminal Justice (International Co-operation) Act 1990 s 19, which has the same penalties (save the three times the value of the goods is omitted) and has the same 'triable either way' provisions.

Minimum sentences Importation and exportation (Customs and Excise Management Act 1979 s 50(2)-(3), 68(2) and 170) are specified offences for the 7-year minimum sentence for a third class A drug trafficking offence,[555] see the **Minimum sentences** section at **273.34**.

Travel Restriction Orders For importation and exporting offences, where 4 or more years' imprisonment is appropriate, the court is under a duty to consider whether it is appropriate to make a Travel Restriction Order.[556] Where there is a direction in the order, the Secretary of State may retain the defendant's passport.[557]

2 Psychoactive Substances Act 2016 s 8 (importing or exporting a psychoactive substance)
Mode of trial Triable either way
Maximum sentence On indictment 7 years. Summary maximum 6 months and/or an unlimited fine.
Commencement Commencement is awaited.
Meaning Psychoactive Substances Act 2016 s 2 provides that a psychoactive substance is one that is capable of producing a psychoactive effect subject to the exceptions listed in the Act. A substance produces a psychoactive effect in a person if, by stimulating or depressing the person's central nervous system, it affects the person's mental functioning or emotional state.
Prohibition order Where a person has been convicted of this offence, the court may make a prohibition order if the court considers it necessary and proportionate for the purpose of preventing the person from carrying on any prohibited activity.[558] The proceedings are civil and the standard of proof is the balance of probabilities.[559]

Confiscation For both offences where a defendant has a criminal lifestyle the court, once the confiscation proceedings are triggered (see **22.11** in Volume 1), must follow the Proceeds of Crime Act 2002 procedure. 'Criminal lifestyle' offences include those under Customs and Excise Management Act 1979 s 50(2)-(3), 68(2) and 170 when they are committed in connection with the prohibition or restriction on importation or exportation by virtue of Misuse of Drugs Act 1971 s 3.[560] For what constitutes a criminal lifestyle see **22.50** in Volume 1.

Serious Crime Prevention Orders For Customs and Excise Management Act 1979 s 50(2)-(3), 68(2) and 170 (when in connection with prohibited drugs), Psychoactive Substances Act 2016 s 8 and Criminal Justice (International Co-operation) Act 1990 s 19 offences, there is a discretionary power to make this order, when it would protect the public etc.[561]

---

[553] Criminal Justice Act 2003 s 284 and Sch 28 para 2.
[554] Legal Aid, Sentencing and Punishment of Offenders Act 2012 (Fines on Summary Conviction) Regulations 2015 2015/664 para 2 and Sch 1 para 23 and Sch 2 para 1(21)
[555] Powers of Criminal Courts (Sentencing) Act 2000 s 110
[556] Criminal Justice and Police Act 2001 s 33
[557] Criminal Justice and Police Act 2001 s 33(5)
[558] Psychoactive Substances Act 2016 s 19(1)
[559] Psychoactive Substances Act 2016 s 32(1) and (2)
[560] Proceeds of Crime Act 2002 s 6 and 75 and Sch 2 para 1(2) and 1A.
[561] Serious Crime Act 2007 s 1 and Sch 1 paras 1(2), 1A and 3(b)

Forfeiture The court may make a forfeiture order for the drugs and psychoactive substance.[562]
See also the **SUPPLY OF DRUGS** chapter.

273.2   *Crown Court statistics   England and Wales*
Unlawful importation class A

Year	Sex	Age	Plea	Total sentenced	Type of sentencing %						Average length of custody in months
					Discharge	Fine	Community sentence	Suspended sentence	Custody	Other	
2013	Male	18-20	G	2	–	–	–	–	100	–	42
			NG	2	–	–	–	–	100	–	42
		21+	G	185	–	1.1	–	2.7	96.2	–	67.9
			NG	54	1.9	–	–	–	98.1	–	170.8
	Female	18-20	G	4	–	–	–	–	100	–	47.5
			NG	0							
		21+	G	35	–	–	–	–	100	–	50.4
			NG	6	–	–	–	–	100	–	87
2014	Male	18-20	G	4	–	–	–	25	75	–	not listed
			NG	4	–	–	–	25	75	–	not listed
		21+	G	198	–	–	1	2	97	–	73.7
			NG	47	2	–	–	–	98	–	131.8
	Female	18-20	G	3	–	–	–	–	100	–	not listed
			NG	0							
		21+	G	22	–	–	–	5	95	–	52.7
			NG	7	–	–	–	14	86	–	100.0

Unlawful importation class B 21+

Year	Sex	Plea	Total sentenced	Type of sentencing %						Average length of custody in months
				Discharge	Fine	Community sentence	Suspended sentence	Custody	Other	
2013	Male	G	81	–	–	1.2	9.9	88.9	–	22.7
		NG	17	–	–	–	–	100	–	45.4
	Female	G	9	–	–	22.2	55.6	22.2	–	8.5
		NG	5	–	–	–	40	60	–	22.7
2014	Male	G	72	–	1	3	24	72	–	31.5
		NG	9	–	–	–	–	100	–	60.0
	Female	G	22	–	–	–	5	95	–	52.7
		NG	7	–	–	–	14	86	–	100.0

For explanations about the statistics see page 1-xii. For other importation and exportation statistics and for statistics for those aged under 21 see www.banksr.com Other Matters Statistics tab

---

[562] Misuse of Drugs Act 1971 s 27 and Psychoactive Substances Act 2016 s 54(1).

The guideline and the proper approach

273.3   *Sentencing Council guideline*
Drug Offences Guideline 2012, see www.banksr.com Other Matters Guidelines tab. In force 27 February 2012. The guideline only applies to offenders aged 18+, see page 2 of the guideline. For the usual practice, see **66.21**.

STEP ONE Determining the offence category
page 4 The court should determine the offender's culpability (role) and the harm caused (quantity/type of offender) with reference to the tables below.

In assessing culpability, the sentencer should weigh up all the factors of the case to determine role. Where there are characteristics present which fall under different role categories, the court should balance these characteristics to reach a fair assessment of the offender's culpability.

In assessing harm, quantity is determined by the weight of the product. Purity is not taken into account at step one but is dealt with at step two. Where the operation is on the most serious and commercial scale, involving a quantity of drugs significantly higher than Category 1, sentences of 20 years and above may be appropriate, depending on the role of the offender.

Culpability demonstrated by offender's role One or more of these characteristics may demonstrate the offender's role. These lists are not exhaustive.	Category of harm Indicative quantity of drug concerned (upon which the starting point is based):
LEADING role: directing or organising buying and selling on a commercial scale; substantial links to, and influence on, others in a chain; close links to original source; expectation of substantial financial gain; uses business as cover; abuses a position of trust or responsibility.	**Category 1** heroin, cocaine – 5 kilos; ecstasy – 10,000 tablets; LSD – 250,000 squares; amphetamine – 20 kilos; cannabis – 200 kilos; ketamine – 5 kilos.
SIGNIFICANT role: operational or management function within a chain; involves others in the operation whether by pressure, influence, intimidation or reward; motivated by financial or other advantage, whether or not operating alone; some awareness and understanding of scale of operation.	**Category 2** heroin, cocaine – 1 kilo; ecstasy – 2,000 tablets; LSD – 25,000 squares; amphetamine – 4 kilos; cannabis – 40 kilos; ketamine – 1 kilo.
LESSER role: performs a limited function under direction; engaged by pressure, coercion, intimidation; involvement through naivety/exploitation; no influence on those above in a chain; very little, if any, awareness or understanding of the scale of operation; if own operation, solely for own use (considering reasonableness of account in all the circumstances).	**Category 3** heroin, cocaine – 150 grams; ecstasy – 300 tablets; LSD – 2,500 squares; amphetamine – 750 grams; cannabis – 6 kilos; ketamine – 150 grams.
	Category 4 heroin, cocaine – 5 grams; ecstasy – 20 tablets; LSD – 170 squares; amphetamine – 20 grams; cannabis – 100 grams; ketamine – 5 grams.

Note: For assistance in how to determine the indicative output of drugs and into which category that weight should be placed, see the **SUPPLY OF DRUGS** paras in relation to indicative weight at **340.6** and **340.7**. Ed.

273.4

STEP TWO Starting point and category range

page 5 Having determined the category, the court should use the corresponding starting point to reach a sentence within the category range below. The starting point applies to all offenders irrespective of plea or previous convictions. The court should then consider further adjustment within the category range for aggravating or mitigating features, set out [at **273.5**]. In cases where the offender is regarded as being at the very top of the 'leading' role it may be justifiable for the court to depart from the guideline.

Where the defendant is dependent on or has a propensity to misuse drugs and there is sufficient prospect of success, a community order with a drug rehabilitation requirement under Criminal Justice Act 2003 s 209 can be a proper alternative to a short or moderate length custodial sentence.

Class A	Leading role	Significant role	Lesser role
Category 1	**Starting point** 14 years' custody	**Starting point** 10 years' custody	**Starting point** 8 years' custody
	Category range 12-16 years' custody	**Category range** 9-12 years' custody	**Category range** 6-9 years' custody
Category 2	**Starting point** 11 years' custody	**Starting point** 8 years' custody	**Starting point** 6 years' custody
	Category range 9-13 years' custody	**Category range** 6½-10 years' custody	**Category range** 5-7 years' custody
Category 3	**Starting point** 8½ years' custody	**Starting point** 6 years' custody	**Starting point** 4½ years' custody
	Category range 6½-10 years' custody	**Category range** 5-7 years' custody	**Category range** 3½-5 years' custody
Category 4	Where the quantity falls below the indicative amount set out for Category 4 in step one, first identify the role for the importation offence, then refer to the starting point and ranges for possession or supply offences, depending on intent. Where the quantity is significantly larger than the indicative amounts for Category 4 but below Category 3 amounts, refer to the Category 3 ranges above.		

Class B	Leading role	Significant role	Lesser role
Category 1	**Starting point** 8 years' custody	**Starting point** 5½ years' custody	**Starting point** 4 years' custody
	Category range 7-10 years' custody	**Category range** 5-7 years' custody	**Category range** 2½-5 years' custody
Category 2	**Starting point** 6 years' custody	**Starting point** 4 years' custody	**Starting point** 2 years' custody
	Category range 4½-8 years' custody	**Category range** 2½-5 years' custody	**Category range** 1½-3 years' custody
Category 3	**Starting point** 4 years' custody	**Starting point** 2 years' custody	**Starting point** 1 year's custody
	Category range 2½-5 years' custody	**Category range** 1½-3 years' custody	**Category range** 12 weeks' to 18 months' custody

Class B	Leading role	Significant role	Lesser role
Category 4	Where the quantity falls below the indicative amount set out for Category 4 in step one, first identify the role for the importation offence, then refer to the starting point and ranges for possession or supply offences, depending on intent. Where the quantity is significantly larger than the indicative amounts for Category 4 but below Category 3 amounts, refer to the Category 3 ranges above.		

Class C	Leading role	Significant role	Lesser role
Category 1	**Starting point** 5 years' custody	**Starting point** 3 years' custody	**Starting point** 18 months' custody
	Category range 4-8 years' custody	**Category range** 2-5 years' custody	**Category range** 1-3 years' custody
Category 2	**Starting point** 3½ years' custody	**Starting point** 18 months' custody	**Starting point** 26 weeks' custody
	Category range 2-5 years' custody	**Category range** 1-3 years' custody	**Category range** 12 weeks' to 18 months' custody
Category 3	**Starting point** 18 months' custody	**Starting point** 26 weeks' custody	**Starting point** High-level community order
	Category range 1-3 years' custody	**Category range** 12 weeks' to 18 months' custody	**Category range** Medium-level community order to 12 weeks' custody
Category 4	Where the quantity falls below the indicative amount set out for Category 4 in step one, first identify the role for the importation offence, then refer to the starting point and ranges for possession or supply offences, depending on intent. Where the quantity is significantly larger than the indicative amounts for Category 4 but below Category 3 amounts, refer to the Category 3 ranges above.		

For the meaning of a high-level and a medium-level community order see **16.13** in Volume 1.

273.5   [Aggravating and mitigating factors]
page 7 The table below contains a non-exhaustive list of additional factual elements providing the context of the offence and factors relating to the offender. Identify whether any combination of these, or other relevant factors, should result in an upward or downward adjustment from the starting point. In some cases, having considered these factors, it may be appropriate to move outside the identified category range.

For appropriate class C ranges, consider the custody threshold as follows:
Has the custody threshold been passed?
If so, is it unavoidable that a custodial sentence be imposed?
If so, can that sentence be suspended?

Factors increasing seriousness
Statutory aggravating factors: Previous convictions, having regard to a) nature of the offence to which conviction relates and relevance to current offence; and b) time elapsed since conviction Offender used or permitted a person under 18 to deliver a controlled drug to a third person Offence committed on bail

Other aggravating factors include:
Sophisticated nature of concealment and/or attempts to avoid detection
Attempts to conceal or dispose of evidence, where not charged separately
Exposure of others to more than usual danger, for example drugs cut with harmful substances
Presence of weapon, where not charged separately
High purity
Failure to comply with current court orders
Offence committed on licence

Factors reducing seriousness or reflecting personal mitigation[563]
Lack of sophistication as to nature of concealment
Involvement due to pressure, intimidation or coercion falling short of duress, except where already taken into account at step one
Mistaken belief of the offender regarding the type of drug, taking into account the reasonableness of such belief in all the circumstances
Isolated incident
Low purity
No previous convictions or no relevant or recent convictions
Offender's vulnerability was exploited
Remorse
Good character and/or exemplary conduct
Determination and/or demonstration of steps having been taken to address addiction or offending behaviour
Serious medical conditions requiring urgent, intensive or long-term treatment
Age and/or lack of maturity where it affects the responsibility of the offender
Mental disorder or learning disability
Sole or primary carer for dependent relatives

273.6   *Applying the guideline*

R v Boakye and Others 2012 EWCA Crim 838, 2013 1 Cr App R (S) 2 (p 6) In step one, the quantities of drug which are listed under the categories of harm in the new guideline are deliberately described as 'indicative quantity of drug upon which the starting point is based'. They are not thresholds at which the sentencing range changes. They could not be if the starting point, which by definition is a mid-range of sentence, is to be based upon it.

Note: I read this to mean that in fixing the starting point, sentencers take the given weight and the given starting point and adjust either up or down to reflect the actual assessment of weight in the case. Ed.

R v Healey and Others 2012 EWCA Crim 1005, 2013 1 Cr App R (S) 33 (p 176) The quantities that appear in the pictorial boxes as broad indicators of harm are neither fixed points nor are they thresholds. They are 'indicative', designed to enable the judge to put the case into the right context on the sliding scale.

Att-Gen's Ref Nos 15-17 of 2012 2012 EWCA Crim 1414, 2013 1 Cr App R (S) 52 (p 289) If the Sentencing Council had intended to lower the level of sentencing that was not reflected in their press release, 'Under the new guidelines there are likely to be increased sentence lengths for those guilty of large-scale production offences and reduced sentences for drug mules. There will be no change in sentencing for possession or drug supply offences.' The essential nature of a drugs hierarchy remains the same even if the terminology has changed. There was a time when some judges divided offenders according to military ranks: generals, lieutenants and foot soldiers. The Council has chosen the categories of 'leading', 'significant' and 'lesser' roles. This is not a change in substance. The categories do not provide some kind of straitjacket into which every case must be squeezed. The judge must do his or her best to reach a fair

---

[563] As amended in April 2012

assessment of the overall offending, namely culpability and harm, before proceeding to the next stage (step two). The judge should declare their conclusions on step one in their sentencing remarks, for the benefit of the offender, those advising the offender, and this Court.

R v Descombre and Thomas 2013 EWCA Crim 72, 2 Cr App R (S) 51 (p 345) TD pleaded to cultivating cannabis. Held. The proposition that the leading role should be reserved for cases where there is an operational hierarchy and a chain of employees and significant role should apply to where there is no chain is an incorrect analysis of the guideline.

273.7   *Suggested approach to the guideline*

Note: The guideline introduced a whole new system to determine the appropriate penalty. Some drug penalties increased some drug penalties decreased others. The court routinely ignores most of old tariff cases. As the guidelines do not suggest suitable penalties for exceptionally large conspiracies or very small imports, I list those cases which continue to be considered when sentencers work out sentences using the new guidelines. The Court of Appeal approach has been consistent with this. The non-tariff cases continue to be used and they are listed. There are some drugs which are not listed in the 'Category of harm' section. For these drugs sentencers look for a drug of the same category which is listed and then try to work out where in the table the amount of drugs involved in their case would be. Since the guidelines have been in force, the cases taken to the Court of Appeal have mostly turned on whether the judge selected the right offence category and the right role. None of them set a precedent and the majority are not helpful when considering the penalty for another case. These cases have been listed. Ed.

For determining the role see **340.9**.

273.8   *Cutting agents   Pre-guideline case*

Example: *R v Watling* 2012 EWCA Crim 2894, 2013 2 Cr App R (S) 37 (p 256) (Plea to assisting in supply of cocaine. He imported about 75 kilos of benzocaine in 15 shipments. Drove to Holland. His company was initially involved with legitimate importation of benzocaine. He then supplied it as a cutting agent. That would make 225 kilos of cocaine at 66% purity or 375 kilos of cocaine at 20% purity.[564] Value £9 to £13.5m. Used in six separate and substantial drug enterprises. Good prison reports while on remand. High culpability. Pivotal role. Commercial scale. Starting at 15 years was not manifestly excessive. The 2-year discount for the plea could not be impugned. **13 years** upheld.)

Note: Although the offence charged was supply, the activity was importation. Ed.

273.9   *Exporting drugs*

R v Powell 2000 The Times News 5/10/00 LCJ There was no difference in criminality between the importation and exportation of controlled drugs.

273.10   *Harbouring*

Note: Cases of harbouring etc. drugs with intent to evade the prohibition are normally sentenced as if the defendant was involved in the onward distribution of drugs in an importation case. Importation is a continuing offence.[565] This level of sentence will equate with a supply sentence, where sentences approaching those for importation can be imposed.[566] The nearer the defendant is to the importation, the greater the sentence will be. Ed.

Old cases: Best ignored. Ed.

---

[564] It looks as though the judgment contained a mathematical error. I have corrected the figures. Ed.
[565] *DPP v Doot* 1973 57 Cr App R 600
[566] *R v Aramah* 1982 76 Cr App R 190

273.11   Purity   Proper approach
Drug Offences Guideline 2012, see www.banksr.com Other Matters Guidelines tab page 4 Purity is not taken into account at step one but is dealt with at step two. For more detail see **273.4**.

273.12   Purity   What is required?
R v Morris 2001 1 Cr App R (S) 87 (p 297) Purity analysis is essential for sentencing purposes for cases of importation, or in other circumstances where 500 grams or more of cocaine, heroin or amphetamine are seized. It may be desirable in cases where quantities less than 500 grams of those substances are seized. But, bearing in mind the cost of purity analysis and that analysis may cause delay, purity analysis will not generally be required where a defendant is in possession of only a small amount consistent with either personal use or only limited supply to others. As purity can indicate proximity to the primary source of supply, if there is reason for the prosecution to believe that a defendant in possession of a small quantity of drugs is close to the source of supply and is wholesaling rather than retailing, it will be necessary for purity analysis to be undertaken before a court can be invited to sentence on this more serious basis. In the absence of purity analysis or expert evidence, it is not open to a court to find or assume levels of purity, except in the case of ecstasy and LSD [because sentencing for them is based on tablets and squares] and currently with an assumed average purity of 100 mg of ecstasy (*R v Warren and Beeley* 1996 1 Cr App R (S) 233) and 50 µg of LSD (*R v Hurley* 1998 1 Cr App R (S) 299 at 304) unless prosecution or defence, by expert evidence, show the contrary (*R v Warren and Beeley* 1996 1 Cr App R (S) 233 and *R v McPhail* 1997 1 Cr App R (S) 321 at 322).
R v Boakye and Others 2012 EWCA Crim 838, 2013 1 Cr App R (S) 2 (p 6) Whereas the previous case law proceeded upon the basis of quantity of drugs measured at 100% purity, the new guideline does not. The reason is that the Council was advised that in many cases, especially at the lower end of offending, scientific analysis of purity may not be available. For this reason, amongst others, the indicative quantities of weight, which the new guideline adopts as a broad measure of harm, are not the same as those spoken of in *R v Aramah* 1982 76 Cr App R 190, as subsequently modified. They are gross, not 100% purity weights. Of course, in dealing with a large consignment where there has been analysis and the weight at 100% purity is known, a court may well pay attention to the additional information which it has been given. It may determine to adjust up or down, either for very high or very low purity. However, the initial indicator of the category of offence is the weight as seized.
Note: The explanation for the change given in lines 2-6 does not deal with the problem of those who import or supply at cocaine at 1%. Consider two individuals who both have 1 kilo of cocaine at 88% and intend to cut it to make 5 kilos. If police arrest the first before he cuts it and the second just after he cuts it, why should they have different starting points? The ability to adjust the sentence for purity is little help as different judges would no doubt give different adjustments for similar cases. Ed.

Types of drug
273.13
Note: There is limited assistance from Court of Appeal cases involving drugs that are listed in the guideline, as the real question in each case is where in the guideline a particular case fits. Any decision about that rarely assists with another case, which will inevitably have different facts. For more details see **273.7**. Ed.

4-Mec
273.13a   4-Mec/NRG-2   class B   Case
Note: 4-Mec is Methylethylcathinone. It is sometimes known as NRG-2. The drug is a synthetically produced stimulant relating to the parent compound cathinone and is a

naturally occurring chemical available to purchase in bulk from China or the Ukraine, *Att-Gen's Ref Nos 15-17 of 2012* 2012 EWCA Crim 1414, 2013 1 Cr App R (S) 52 (p 289). Ed.
R v Hughes 2014 EWCA Crim 2338 4-Mec equates with cannabis and not amphetamine. Example: *Att-Gen's Ref Nos 15-17 of 2012* 2012 EWCA Crim 1414, 2013 1 Cr App R (S) 52 (p 289) at para 52 (Plea (25% credit). Lorry driver bringing in 240 kilos of 4-Mec. Wholesale value between £0.96-1.4m. We would expect 8 years before plea credit. **6 years** not 3½.)

Amphetamine class B

273.14   *Sentencing Council guideline*
Drug Offences Guideline 2012, see www.banksr.com Other Matters Guidelines tab and **273.4**.
Note: page 4 Amphetamine is a listed drug in the 'Category of harm' section in the guidelines. Category 1 is 20 kilos, Category 2 is 4 kilos, Category 3 is 750 grams and Category 4 is 20 grams. Ed.

Cannabis class B

273.15   *Sentencing Council guideline*
Drug Offences Guideline 2012, see www.banksr.com Other Matters Guidelines tab and **273.4**.
Note: page 4 Cannabis is a listed drug in the 'Category of harm' section in the guidelines. Category 1 is 200 kilos, Category 2 is 40 kilos, Category 3 is 6 kilos and Category 4 is 100 grams. Ed.

273.16   *Cannabis class B   Amount less than Category 4*
Drug Offences Guideline 2012, see www.banksr.com Other Matters Guidelines tab page 6 Where the quantity falls below the indicative amount set out for Category 4 (100 grams of cannabis), first identify the role for the importation offence, then refer to the starting point and ranges for possession or supply offences, depending on intent.

273.17   *Cannabis class B   Amount between Categories 3 and 4*
Drug Offences Guideline 2012, see www.banksr.com Other Matters Guidelines tab page 4 Where the quantity is significantly larger than the indicative amounts for Category 4 (100 grams of cannabis) but below Category 3 amounts (6 kilos of cannabis), refer to the Category 3 ranges (at **273.4**).

273.18   *Cannabis class B   'Most serious and commercial' offending*
Drug Offences Guideline 2012, see www.banksr.com Other Matters Guidelines tab page 4 Where the operation is on the most serious and commercial scale, involving a quantity of drugs significantly higher than Category 1 (200 kilos of cannabis), sentences of 20 years and above may be appropriate, depending on the role of the offender.
R v Greenwood 2010 EWCA Crim 1163 D changed his plea to guilty to conspiracy to import cannabis during his trial. Dutch customs officers discovered 326 kilos of cannabis hidden in a consignment bound for Harwich. After seizing the drugs the load was re-sealed and allowed to continue on its journey. The load was collected at Harwich and driven to Essex Freight at Clipper Park. Two people at Clipper Park had been arrested in relation to another consignment of cannabis. The manager at Essex Freight refused delivery and redirected the driver to another warehouse, Twin Wheels. The driver returned to Harwich. D attempted to divert the Dutch load to Twin Wheels. He sent a fax instructing Twin Wheels to take delivery of the load. D, aged 67, had no relevant convictions. On arrest he was found in possession of a large quantity of cash and his passport. He suffered from type 2 diabetes and suffered episodes of atrial fibrillation and other medical problems. Whilst on remand D had a permanent pace-maker fitted. The Judge said the sums were significant and huge profits were to be made. D's involvement was limited to one day. **3½ years** not 5.

Post-guideline case
R v Cox 2013 EWCA Crim 235 D pleaded (full credit) to attempting to import cannabis. His motor home was stopped and searched when it was disembarking the Roscoff to Plymouth ferry. 422 kilos of what was believed to be cannabis were found. It transpired that the material was not cannabis. D said his son was in trouble with drug dealers and those dealers had prevailed upon him to import drugs by threatening his son. He was paid €3,000 for expenses and would receive a further €25,000 on delivery. He admitted to previously smuggling tobacco using the same method of concealment. D, aged 63, had convictions but none for drugs. The most recent conviction was from 1997. D had a history of cancer and suffered a number of ischaemic attacks. Held. It required a fair amount of work to adapt the vehicle to take that quantity of cannabis. This offence was well within Category 1. Disregarding the adaptation of the vehicle, D is still appropriately described as playing a leading role as the fee he was due to receive was considerable. He was entrusted with a very large quantity of cannabis which was left in his charge for a considerable period of time. We reject any criticism of the Judge's attribution of a leading role to D. There was a substantial reduction to be made as the material imported turned out to be harmless. Starting at 10 years, 6 years after a trial was appropriate because of D's health problems and that the material was not in fact cannabis. With the plea, **4 years** not 5.

Cocaine/heroin class A
273.19   *Cocaine/heroin class A   Sentencing Council guideline*
Drug Offences Guideline 2012, see www.banksr.com Other Matters Guidelines tab and **273.4**.
Note: page 4 Cocaine and heroin are listed drugs in the 'Category of harm' section in the guidelines. Category 1 is 5 kilos, Category 2 is 1 kilo, Category 3 is 150 grams and Category 4 is 5 grams. Ed.

273.20   *Cocaine/heroin class A   Amount less than Category 4*
Drug Offences Guideline 2012, see www.banksr.com Other Matters Guidelines tab page 6 Where the quantity falls below the indicative amount set out for Category 4 (5 grams of cocaine or heroin), first identify the role for the importation offence, then refer to the starting point and ranges for possession or supply offences, depending on intent.

273.21   *Cocaine/heroin class A   Amount between Categories 3 and 4*
Drug Offences Guideline 2012, see www.banksr.com Other Matters Guidelines tab page 4 Where the quantity is significantly larger than the indicative amounts for Category 4 (5 grams of cocaine or heroin) but below Category 3 amounts (150 grams of cocaine or heroin), refer to the Category 3 ranges (at **273.4**).

273.22   *Quantities significantly higher than Category 1   Guideline and judicial guidance*
Drug Offences Guideline 2012, see www.banksr.com Other Matters Guidelines tab page 4 Where the operation is on the most serious and commercial scale, involving a quantity of drugs significantly higher than Category 1 (200 kilos of cannabis), sentences of 20 years and above may be appropriate, depending on the role of the offender.
R v Jaramillo and Others 2012 EWCA Crim 2101, 2013 1 Cr App R (S) 110 (p 569) para 16 In any case in which the importation falls significantly outside the range of Category 1, the judge will apply the same principles as those which apply within the categories. Accordingly, the role of the offender will be an important factor in determining the seriousness of the offence. Where (as here) quantities exceed Category 1, it is an exercise of judgment to scale up the corresponding sentences for those at the bottom rung of leading along with significant and lesser roles in such a way that fairly reflects not only the part played by the offender then being sentenced but also his comparative significance within the offending as a whole. Given the limit beyond which

a sentence for this type of offence does not normally extend, it is not surprising that at the highest levels, sentences on different offenders will be nearer to each other than might otherwise be the case.

273.23   *Quantities significantly higher than Category 1   Cases*
R v Zaman 2010 EWCA Crim 209 D pleaded to conspiracy to import cocaine, assisting an offender and conspiracy to import heroin. D and another agreed to import ½ kilo of cocaine (at 100% purity). He and another went to Amsterdam but the cocaine was intercepted. Afterwards D was involved in a flurry of calls about the interception. Z also gave shelter to a drug supplier of 11.5 kilos in his home (the assisting count). D was the liaiser for about 5 kilos of pure heroin. D travelled to Turkey. There was a dispute about the price, and the deal was called off. D was now aged 40 with a number of convictions including a firearm offence (12 months). D was much appreciated by the prison service for his work as a counsellor, and telling staff when matters had been left out or locked when they should not have been. He also talked an inmate out of a hunger strike and raised the alarm about an attempted suicide. Held. There are limits for exceptional personal mitigation but it is not without any value. **12 years** not 15.
Old cases: *Att-Gen's Ref No 61 of 2008* 2009 EWCA Crim 1123, 2 Cr App R (S) 517 (14.45 kilos. **14 years**) *R v Heron* 2009 EWCA Crim 94, 2 Cr App R (S) 362 (16 kilos at 100%. **10 years**) *R v Back and Others* 2009 EWCA Crim 754 (3.07 kilos of high purity, 8.5 kilos at 100%, 2 kilos of high purity would have been imported and 2.3 kilos of pure cocaine. After trial in the order of **25 years**) *R v Clough* 2009 EWCA Crim 1669, 2010 1 Cr App R (S) 53 (p 334) (337 kilos of cocaine. He played an important role. **26 years**) *R v Quinn and Others* 2009 EWCA Crim 1097, 2010 1 Cr App R (S) 34 (p 209) (**10½ years**)
For a summary of the first case, see the 9th edition of this book and for the last case, see the 10th edition. Ed.
Post-guideline case
R v M 2014 EWCA Crim 249 D was convicted of conspiracy to import heroin. He was sentenced on the basis that he was involved in the importation of at least 463 kilos of heroin (at about 60% purity). He received 25 years. Held. 25 years was in line with sentences imposed in other cases where there have been very large importations. Examples include *R v Black* 2009 EWCA Crim 754 (25-year starting point for 15 kilos of pure cocaine), *R v Clough* 2009 EWCA Crim 1669, 2010 1 Cr App R (S) 53 (p 334) (26-year starting point for the equivalent of 273 kilos of pure cocaine) and *R v Kahn* 2011 EWCA Crim 2049 (27-year starting point for the equivalent of 154 kilos of pure heroin).
Note: There are other factors to consider as well as the weight when the starting point (meaning the figure arrived at before any plea discount is considered) is determined. Ed.
Att-Gen's Ref Nos 82 and 90 of 2014 2014 EWCA Crim 2884, 2015 2 Cr App R (S) 1 D was convicted of conspiracy to import cocaine. W pleaded to the same count. Both were sentenced for cannabis matters which were not material. Customs officers stopped a lorry and trailer which had 52 kilos of high purity (67% to 91%) cocaine hidden in the load of redundant rubber. The driver was given a telephone number to ring on his arrival which belonged to D. This led to an investigation of a commercial unit on a remote farm. The load came from Malaga in Spain and customs discovered there were 31 similar importations of rubber with no commercial reason to import. D had paid about £20,000 rent in cash over about 18 months. Both had been to Malaga. D was aged 33 and had no convictions. He had a painful medical condition. W was aged 36 and had two cautions for drug possession. The Judge said he had a management function. He found W had substantial links to others in the chain of supply. Held. All the indications were that these two organised this enterprise. It was a generous finding to say D and W were at the top end of significant role, but we will respect that finding. We [note] the large number of trips, the planning and the sophistication of the enterprise. For D, with his mitigation,

nothing less than **20 years** will suffice, not the 15 years given. For W, the plea discount should be 15% not 20% and we keep his starting point 3 years longer than D. That makes **19 years** not 14.

See also: *Att-Gen's Ref No 8 of 2015* 2015 EWCA Crim 620 (Convicted of four counts of importation. Drove car with 52 kilos (78%) and 3 kilos (48%) of cocaine hidden in his car. Five previous stays at the hotel he had used with same car included in the indictment. Aged 68. Significant role not lesser. **16 years** not 8 in all.)

273.24   Cocaine/heroin class A   Couriers

R v Lopez-Sacido 2012 EWCA Crim 1732, 2013 1 Cr App R (S) 80 (p 440) D pleaded at the PCMH to importation of cocaine. He arrived from Barbados and was stopped at Gatwick airport after a narcotics dog took an interest in his bags. His suitcase contained two bin liners full of chocolate. The chocolate contained 2.77 kilos of cocaine, equating to 2.06 kilos of pure cocaine, with a street value of £547,000. D admitted in interview he had committed the offence because he was in financial difficulties. Others had organised the offence and he was to be paid €6,000 on his arrival in Belgium. The Judge placed the offence in Category 2 and noted that D was a courier. D had no convictions. Held. This is not a leading role case. This was a one-off offence driven by financial desperation and not for profit. There was no one under D's direction. The Judge was right to conclude that D had played a significant role. He was not unduly and oppressively taken advantage of. Starting at 8 years, **5 years 3 months** took adequate account of the plea and mitigation.

R v Jaramillo and Others 2012 EWCA Crim 2101, 2013 1 Cr App R (S) 110 (p 569) D, E, P and S pleaded (full credit) to importing cocaine. They were Spanish nationals and they flew from the Dominican Republic to Gatwick. They worked in pairs. D and E had 23.95 and 18.86 kilos of cocaine respectively in their luggage. P and E had 18.86 and 16.96 kilos respectively in their luggage. The purity was between 50 and 70%. The defendants were all of good character and to a greater or lesser extent were naïve and exploited because of their dire financial circumstances. D, E, P and S were aged 40, 27, 18 and 19 respectively. The Judge considered them couriers and ascribed them a lesser role. Held. They were different from 'mules' because they had exposed themselves to the risk of intimidation on their arrival. The Judge's starting point did not recognise, to a sufficient degree, the substantial gap in culpability between those who organise and manage and those towards the bottom of this pernicious hierarchy. Starting at **12 years** not 16, for D and E **8 years** not 11 and for P and S **7 years** not 10.

R v Klints and Others 2013 EWCA Crim 12 K, H and S pleaded to conspiracy to import heroin (all full credit). Couriers took a circuitous route to travel from London to Brazil and back. They were stopped and found to have swallowed cocaine. The conspiracy was based on 12 such journeys over two years. The Judge assessed the weight to be 9-12 kilos. K and H were important organisers and right-hand men to S, who was at the centre of the conspiracy. The Judge said the guidelines were not appropriate. K and H played a significant role. Held. The Judge was entitled to conclude that K and H were at the top end of 'significant role'. It was not appropriate to go beyond the guidelines. For S **10 years** not 12, for K and H **7½ years** not 9.

Post-guideline case

R v Nunez-Lopez 2015 EWCA Crim 1451 D pleaded to importation of cocaine. He was stopped in his Spanish-registered lorry at Dover and Customs officers found about 50 kilos of cocaine with an average purity of 70% under a false floor in his cab. In interview he said he had bought the vehicle himself. D was now aged 38 and treated as being of good character. The Judge considered D's role was between a leading role and a significant role. He also held that D was using his business as cover and there was an expectation of substantial financial reward. The defence contended that D was a courier who had no involvement higher up the chain. They relied on *R v Virgradaula* 2014 EWCA Crim 1200 where a 10-year sentence was given for a lorry driver with 63 kilos of cocaine and a full plea discount. Held. There was no evidence that D was acting in a leading role. The use of a legitimate business cover was limited to the concealment of the drugs amongst a legitimate cargo. There was no evidence of an expectation of substantial gain. In order for there to be a significant role there had to be evidence of an operational or management function within a chain, or that he involved others, or was motivated by financial or other advantage, or had some awareness of the scale of the operation. Whether or not he had an operational function or had involved others, clearly this appellant was motivated by financial reward and in our view he had some awareness of the scale of this operation. His role was therefore a significant one. However, there was no evidence that he personally had helped to load the cocaine into this lorry or knew precisely how extensive the operation was. We start at 15 years, so with plea, **10 years** not 14.

Ecstasy class A

273.25   *Ecstasy class A   Sentencing Council guideline*
Drug Offences Guideline 2012, see www.banksr.com Other Matters Guidelines tab and **273.4**.
Note: page 4 Ecstasy is a listed drug in the 'Category of harm' section in the guidelines. Category 1 is 100,000 tablets, Category 2 is 2,000 tablets, Category 3 is 300 tablets and Category 4 is 20 tablets. Ed.

273.26   *Ecstasy class A   Amount between Categories 3 and 4*
Drug Offences Guideline 2012, see www.banksr.com Other Matters Guidelines tab page 4 Where the quantity is significantly larger than the indicative amounts for Category 4 (20 tablets of ecstasy) but below Category 3 amounts (300 tablets of ecstasy), refer to the Category 3 ranges above.

273.27   *Ecstasy class A   'Most serious and commercial' offending   Pre-guideline case*
Drug Offences Guideline 2012, see www.banksr.com Other Matters Guidelines tab page 4 Where the operation is on the most serious and commercial scale, involving a quantity of drugs significantly higher than Category 1 (10,000 tablets of ecstasy), sentences of 20 years and above may be appropriate, depending on the role of the offender.
R v Paul 2010 EWCA Crim 2103 D was convicted of importing MDMA. He was a long-distance lorry driver and was stopped by Customs officers at Dover. A search of his lorry yielded 11 cardboard boxes containing white tablets. They proved to be 611,000 MDMA tablets, the active ingredient of which weighed 42 kilos with a wholesale value of between £200,000 and £600,000. The street value was £2.4m at £4 per tablet. D, aged 54, had no previous convictions, was married and had lived a hard-working, industrious life. Held. Making some allowance for personal mitigation, **16 years'** imprisonment was not manifestly excessive.
See also the ECSTASY chapter.

Ketamine class B

273.28   *Ketamine class B   Sentencing Council guideline*
Reclassification: Ketamine is a class B drug for offences committed on or after 10 June 2014, Misuse of Drugs Act 1971 (Ketamine etc.) (Amendment) Order 2014 2014/1106 para 4.
Drug Offences Guideline 2012, see www.banksr.com Other Matters Guidelines tab and **275.3**.
Note: page 4 Ketamine is a listed drug in the 'Category of harm' section in the guidelines. Category 1 is 5 kilos, Category 2 is 1 kilo, Category 3 is 150 grams and Category 4 is 5 grams. For offences committed before 10 June 2014, the class C guideline table should be used. Ed.
An example of a post-guideline case: *R v Bhatia* 2013 EWCA Crim 1121 (Convicted. Ketamine. Rented a self-storage unit. Purporting to import saris. Worked with his brother-in-law. 144.5 kilos worth £3.6m. Played a leading role in UK. Organiser for nine shipments. Good character and work record. **11 years** was perhaps severe but upheld.)

Khat

273.29   Khat   class C   Case
Note: Khat is a leafy green herb, *Catha edulis*, which is used mostly in North-East Africa, on the Arabian Peninsula and by people in the UK from those regions. It was previously a legal drug. It was made a class C drug on 24 June 2014,[567] Misuse of Drugs Act 1971 (Amendment) Order 2014 2014/1352 para 3. Ed.
Example: *R v Sidlauskas* 2014 EWCA Crim 2338 (Plea to importing khat. Full credit. Paid £250 to import 14.5 kilos of khat, valued at £680 on the street or £400 wholesale. D, aged 24, had minor previous, including recently failing to surrender to custody. The Judge considered he played a significant role. Held. We were told the drug is normally sold in 100 gram deals so this would be 140 deals. That means it can't be Category 4, so it is Category 3. **4 months** upheld.)

LSD class A

273.30   LSD class A   Sentencing Council guideline
Drug Offences Guideline 2012, see www.banksr.com Other Matters Guidelines tab and **273.4**.
Note: page 4 LSD is a listed drug in the 'Category of harm' section in the guidelines. Category 1 is 250,000 squares, Category 2 is 25,000 squares, Category 3 is 2,500 squares and Category 4 is 170 squares.

Opium class A

273.31   Opium   class A   Guidelines
R v Mashaollahi 2001 1 Cr App R (S) 96 (p 330) The court should proceed on the assumption that any given consignment of opium is unadulterated and of 100% purity. Should the defence wish to persuade a judge that the active ingredient was of a lesser percentage, it is open to them to call the evidence. Heroin is eight times more valuable than opium, so 40 kilos of opium at 100% would be equivalent to 5 kilos of heroin at 100%. There is at least the remote possibility that opium might be imported to convert it into morphine or heroin. Then base the sentence on the amount of heroin or morphine that could be produced from the opium seized. The ratio to apply would be 10:1 i.e. 10 kilos of opium would be needed to produce 1 kilo of morphine or heroin, assuming average levels of purity. The guideline for the importation of opium should be based on weight, and cross-checked with street value to ensure that at least an approximate equivalence with heroin and cocaine is maintained. For importation of opium, the appropriate guidelines would be **14 years** and upwards for 40 kilos or more of opium, **10 years** and upwards for 4 kilos or more of opium. To this rule of thumb we would make one exception, and that is in cases where it is established that the importation of opium was carried out for the purpose of conversion into morphine or heroin we consider that the appropriate sentence should be based on the equivalent value of those drugs.

273.32   Opium   Class A   Judicial guidance
R v Talebi 2012 EWCA Crim 3040, 2013 2 Cr App R (S) 49 (p 339) D pleaded to conspiracy to import opium. Held. For the purposes of the new guidelines, we should work on the assumption that 1 kilo of heroin is equivalent to 8 kilos of opium.

273.33   Opium class A   Pre-guideline case
R v Achmad 2013 EWCA Crim 871 D was convicted of conspiracy to import opium. The conspiracy related to 3½ kilos and 30 kilos of opium imported on two occasions. The Judge found that D had been involved in the importation of at least 100 kilos. The Judge referred to 21,000 telephone calls. Held. D was an organiser. The factors that influenced the court in their cases can have no bearing on D's case. **18 years** was a severe sentence but justifiably so.
See also the **OPIUM** chapter.

---

[567] The Court in *R v Sidlauskas* 2014 said the drug was made an illegal drug on 14 June 2014 but that must be a typo.

Minimum sentences

273.34   *Statutory provisions*

Powers of Criminal Courts (Sentencing) Act 2000 s 110(1) This section applies where:

a) a person is convicted of a class A drug trafficking offence committed after 30 September 1997,

b) at the time when that offence was committed, he was 18 or over and had two relevant drug convictions,[568] and

c) one of those other offences was committed after he had been convicted of the other.

2) The court shall impose an appropriate custodial sentence for a term of at least 7 years except where the court is of the opinion that there are particular circumstances which:

a) relate to any of the offences or to the offender, and

b) would make it unjust to do so in all the circumstances.

Powers of Criminal Courts (Sentencing) Act 2000 s 110(6) In this section 'an appropriate custodial sentence' means:...

b) in relation to a person who is under 21 at that time, a sentence of detention in a Young Offender Institution.

Powers of Criminal Courts (Sentencing) Act 2000 s 115 Where an offence is found to have been committed over a period of two or more days, or at some time during a period of two or more days, it shall be taken for the purposes of section 110 (third drug offence) to have been committed on the last of those days.

Mental Health Act 1983 s 37(1A)(b) Nothing in Powers of Criminal Courts (Sentencing) Act 2000 s 110(2) shall prevent the court from making a (Hospital Order or a Guardianship Order).

Coroners and Justice Act 2009 s 144 and Sch 17 para 10(2) widens the convictions that can be taken into account to include EU drug trafficking offences committed after 15 August 2010, the commencement date.[569]

See also the **FIREARM OFFENCES Minimum sentences** section at **259.49**.

Note: For firearm minimum sentences there is a need to find 'exceptional circumstances' to avoid a minimum sentence, which is a higher test than 'unjust'. Ed.

273.35   *Minimum sentences   Servicemen/women*

Powers of Criminal Courts (Sentencing) Act 2000 s 111(1) Where a) a person has at any time been convicted of an offence under Armed Forces Act 2006 s 42 (criminal conduct), and

b) the corresponding offence under the law of England and Wales (within the meaning given by that section) was a class A drug trafficking offence, the relevant section of this chapter shall have effect as if he had at that time been convicted in England and Wales of that corresponding offence.

(1A) Where:

a) a person has at any time been found guilty of a member State service offence committed after the relevant date, and

b) the corresponding UK offence was a class A drug trafficking offence,

the relevant section of this chapter and subsection (1) above shall have effect as if the person had at that time been convicted in England and Wales of that corresponding UK offence.

273.36   *Minimum sentences   How to determine whether Act applies*

R v Hoare 2004 EWCA Crim 191, 2 Cr App R (S) 50 (p 261) D pleaded to three burglaries and other counts. In 2000, he was sentenced for a dwelling house burglary and

---

[568] Powers of Criminal Courts (Sentencing) Act 2000 s 110(2A) For the purposes of subsection (1)(a) a 'relevant drug conviction' means: i) a conviction in any part of the United Kingdom of a class A drug trafficking offence, or ii) a conviction in another member State of an offence which was committed after the relevant date and would, if done in the United Kingdom at the time of the conviction, have constituted a class A drug trafficking offence.

[569] Coroners and Justice Act 2009 (Commencement No 5) Order 2010 2010/1858 para 3

three TICs. In 2003, he committed the instant offence. The total number of dwelling house burglaries on his record was seven. In the Crown Court the Judge was wrongly informed by both counsel that D qualified for a 3-year sentence. Held. In fact D had only been convicted of one dwelling burglary at the commission of the third burglary. Powers of Criminal Courts (Sentencing) Act 2000 s 111 requires that in order for the automatic sentence to be triggered, the sequence required is: a) commission of first offence, b) conviction for first offence, c) commission of second offence, d) conviction for second burglary, e) commission of third burglary, f) conviction for third burglary. This was not so in D's case. The sentence is therefore unlawful.

Note: Although the drug section of the Act is slightly different from the burglary section for minimum sentences, the structure is the same, so the two sections should be applied in the same way. Ed.

273.37   *Minimum sentences   Plea of guilty*

Criminal Justice Act 2003 s 144(2) Where a sentence is to be imposed under Powers of Criminal Courts (Sentencing) Act 2000 s 110, nothing in that section shall prevent the court from imposing a sentence of 80% or more of the minimum period.

Note: The section has been summarised. The section means if the defendant pleads guilty, the court can impose a sentence which is 80% or more of the minimum term. Ed.

Factors and matters relating to the defendant

273.38   *Assisting the prosecution*

R v Aramah 1982 76 Cr App R 190 LCJ It is particularly important that offenders should be encouraged to give information to the police, and a confession of guilt coupled with considerable assistance to the police can properly be marked by a substantial reduction. See also the INFORMANTS/GIVING EVIDENCE FOR THE PROSECUTION chapter.

273.39   *Believing goods to be a different drug*

R v Wolin 2005 EWCA Crim 3066, 2006 1 Cr App R (S) 133 (p 773) The defendant was convicted of attempted importation. She flew from Amsterdam to Heathrow and her holdall had an inner compartment with 3.85 kilos of lignocaine, which can be used to dilute cocaine. It is an anaesthetic and not a controlled substance. She gave no comment in interview. She had no convictions. Held. In essence she was a courier who tried to import cocaine and failed. Taking into account that it was an attempt and that the goods were not prohibited **5 years** not 8.

R v Cox 2013 EWCA Crim 235 D pleaded (full credit) to attempting to import cannabis. His motor home was stopped and searched when it was disembarking the Roscoff to Plymouth ferry. 422 kilos of what was believed to be cannabis was found. Held. We reject any criticism of the Judge's attribution of a leading role to D. There was a substantial reduction to be made as the material imported turned out to be harmless. Starting at 10 years, 6 years after a trial was appropriate because of D's health problems and that the material was not in fact cannabis. With the plea, **4 years** not 5.

R v Ward 2013 EWCA Crim 403 D pleaded to importation of 26 kilos of cocaine (15.4 kilos at 100%) with a street value of over £5.8m. The drugs arrived in the UK on a ship from Costa Rica. D was a courier in the conspiracy and his role was to collect drugs from the docks and deliver them to those further up the hierarchy. At the docks he was known as someone who had regularly been a courier collecting goods from the docks. D met B at the docks and B loaded holdalls into the van which D was driving. D drove out of the docks and was arrested. The drugs were found. D immediately said he thought they were cannabis. D had a long record of previous convictions, mostly for dishonesty. In 2001, he was convicted of importing[570] drugs (4 years). The guidelines were not yet in force. Held. The Judge treated D as though he thought the drug was cannabis and not

---

[570] At one stage of the judgment this is referred to as possession, but importation, which is also referred to, seems more likely.

cocaine. The 15-year starting point as selected by the Judge was appropriate before the cannabis allowance was considered. It should have been reduced by 2 years, making 13 years. With full credit for his plea, **8½ years** not 10.

See also the SUPPLY OF GOODS *Believing the goods to be a different drug* para at **340.20**.

Conspiracy not carried out see the CONSPIRACY *Conspiracy not carried out* para at **227.2**.

273.40   *Couriers*

R v Rimmer 1999 1 Cr App R (S) 234 The defendant pleaded to importing amphetamine. Held. A courier can be involved in a wide variety of ways. The critical fact is the degree and extent of his involvement and the nature of the enterprise.

R v Boakye and Others 2012 EWCA Crim 838, 2013 1 Cr App R (S) 2 (p 6) para 9 The Sentencing Council…anticipated that its approach would result in reductions in sentence for a certain sub-class of courier (commonly, if inaccurately, known as 'mules'). The sub-class in question is the group of disadvantaged defendants, particularly those from an under-developed country, who have been exploited by serious drugs criminals and persuaded to carry drugs often for very small reward. We agree that for such defendants the new guideline will often result in a shorter sentence, and on many occasions a significantly shorter sentence.

R v Terraza de Leon 2013 EWCA Crim 198 D pleaded to importing cocaine. She travelled from Guatemala to Zurich and then to London City airport. She had swallowed 82 packages containing cocaine. A man who had taken the same route was also stopped and had swallowed packages. D had HIV and was the primary carer for dependent relatives, at least one of whom was unwell. Her children were looked after by their grandmother, who was also unwell. The Judge concluded the two had been jointly responsible for nearly 3 kilos of cocaine with a purity between 30% and 40%. He placed the offence between Categories 1 and 2 and said the role was significant. He started at 8 years 9 months. Held. D was motivated by financial advantage. She swallowed the packages under direction. We think she played a lesser role. For a kilo the starting point is 6 years. We increase that for the extra weight and reduce it for the plea and other mitigation making **4 years** not 5.

R v Horton 2013 EWCA Crim 1801 D pleaded (20% credit) to importing heroin and cocaine. He picked up some frozen spinach in Belgium. At Dover 9.62 kilos of heroin (at 63% purity) and 11.39 kilos of cocaine (at purity between 72% and 88%) were found in the back of his lorry. When arrested he said, "It's £2,000 for two packages. I'm a family man." In interview he explained he had left the back of his lorry open during a rest period and the package was put in. D was aged about 43 with four handling and three making off without payment convictions. The Judge said the concealment lacked sophistication and couriers were a vital part of drug importation. D was ascribed a significant role with some awareness of the operation. The Judge started at 20 years because it was over three times the Category 1 weight and reduced the sentence to 18 years before the plea discount, because it was an isolated incident and the lack of sophistication. Held. It was plainly a significant role. The starting point was beyond the Category 1 level. The high purity and the aggravating and mitigating factors made it 15 years. With plea, **12 years** not 14.

273.41   *Drug addict, Defendant is*

Drug Offences Guideline 2012, see www.banksr.com Other Matters Guidelines tab page 5 Where the defendant is dependent on or has a propensity to misuse drugs and there is sufficient prospect of success, a community order with a drug rehabilitation requirement under Criminal Justice Act 2003 s 209 can be a proper alternative to a short or moderate-length custodial sentence.

273.42   Drugs not destined for the UK
R v Mouzulukwe 1996 2 Cr App R (S) 48 The defendant claimed that the drugs were
destined for the USA. Held. That made no difference whatsoever to the sentence.
R v Maguire 1997 1 Cr App R (S) 130 The defendant was convicted of being concerned
with cannabis in transit on the high seas, contrary to Criminal Justice (International
Co-operation) Act 1990 s 19(2)(b). The boat carrying the drugs was on the high seas in
international waters and not in UK waters. The boat was going to Holland where the
maximum would have been 4 years. The likely sentence would have been 18 months.
Held. That was irrelevant. Courts should use English cases.
R v Wagener and Pronk 1997 1 Cr App R (S) 178 The fact the drugs were targeted for a
country where the maximum penalties were lower was irrelevant. The fact that the drugs
never entered the UK did not affect the sentence.
Note: All these cases are old. However, they reflect the law as applied today.
See also the *Foreign penalties are irrelevant, Future* para at **273.43**.
English, Defendant does not speak see the DEFENDANT *English, Defendant does not
speak* para at **240.26**.

273.43   Foreign penalties are irrelevant, Future
R v Ogburu 1992 The Times News 14/10/92 Ignore foreign penalties in the future.
R v Nwoko 1995 16 Cr App R (S) 612 A Nigerian defendant faced a further term of
imprisonment on his return. Held. It was not a relevant consideration.
R v Ukoh 2005 2 Cr App R (S) 38 (p 231) D pleaded to importing 3.13 kilos of heroin at
100%. He was a Nigerian who feared further imprisonment on his return home because
the Government was, it was claimed, reactivating a 1990 decree. Held. We affirm
R v Ogburu 1992 and *R v Nwoko* 1995. No judge can anticipate what the law and
practice in a foreign state will be or how it will be applied when D is released. The Home
Secretary can decide in each case whether it will be unduly harsh to return D.
Note: All these cases are old. However, they reflect the law as applied today.
See also the *Drugs not destined for UK* para at **273.42**.

273.44   Good character
Note: Having previous convictions is a statutory aggravating factor, Criminal Justice
Act 2003 s 143(2), see **86.2** in Volume 1. In step two of the *Drug Offences Guideline
2012* page 7, 'No previous convictions or no relevant or recent convictions' and 'Good
character and/or exemplary conduct' are 'factors reducing seriousness or reflecting
personal mitigation' see **273.4**. In *R v Aramah* 1982 76 Cr App R 190, the Lord Chief
Justice said, "Good character of a courier of drugs was less important than good
character in other cases. The large-scale operator looks for couriers of good character
and for people of a sort who are likely to exercise the sympathy of the court if they are
arrested. Consequently, one will frequently find students, sick and elderly people used as
couriers for two reasons: first of all they are vulnerable to the offer of quick profit, and
second, it is felt that the courts will be moved to show misplaced sympathy in their
case." A similar observation was made in *R v Rainho* 2002 EWCA Crim 1981, 2003 1 Cr
App R (S) 77 (p 389). The guideline should be followed and it would appear that these
two cases may no longer reflect the law. However, reductions for good character will
vary and may be minimal. Ed.
See also the DEFENDANT *Good character* para at **240.28**.
Lawful substances, Material turns out to be see the SUPPLY OF DRUGS *Lawful
substances, Material turns out to be* para at **340.30**.

273.45   Mentally disordered/impaired defendants
R v Nafei 2004 EWCA Crim 3238, 2005 2 Cr App R (S) 24 (p 127) D pleaded to the
importation of 15.38 kilos of cocaine (at 100% purity). He was stopped at Dover driving
a Mercedes, and the drugs were found hidden in the car. The street value was estimated
at £1.8m. During the course of attempts to interview him it became apparent that he did
not understand the caution and that he might be suffering from some form of mental

illness. There were various psychiatric reports before the sentencing Judge. The reports said that D had a long history of mental illness and was suffering from schizophrenia. Several reports recommended a disposal under Mental Health Act 1983 s 37. D, aged 42, had a history of depressive illness. He had had a troubled and fractured life. He was at first assessed as having an acute psychotic illness and being unfit to plead. A later report diagnosed a major mental illness in the form of schizo-effective disorder, and said that D's condition was such as to require regular medication and hospital treatment. Another report confirmed this diagnosis and recommended in-patient treatment in a 24-hour nursing environment and that he be detained under section 37. It said that his illness required treatment for the foreseeable future, and that if he were given a custodial sentence and then transferred to hospital under Mental Health Act 1983 s 47 this would be detrimental to his mental health because there would be no statutory requirement on him to accept medication. He might also relapse into substance misuse with the attendant dangers to himself and others. Two further reports before the Judge both recommended a Hospital Order under section 37. They described his illness as severe and enduring, and said that because of his lack of insight he was unlikely to receive treatment voluntarily. Several psychiatric reports were obtained after sentence. They indicated a degree of relapse as a result of non-compliance with medical treatment and referred to the continuing risk to D and others in the absence of appropriate treatment and medication. They recommended again a disposal under section 37, with an alternative recommendation, if the custodial sentence were to stand, of transfer under section 47 to hospital. Held. It was of the greatest significance that there was no causal link between the mental illness and the offending. D knew that what he was doing was wrong and went into it with his eyes open. We do not say that in circumstances like these a Hospital Order for drug importation can never be justified, but we would find it difficult to envisage such a case. Nor do we wish to indicate that where there is a causal link a Hospital Order would normally be appropriate. It depends on the circumstances of the case. Any sentencing judge in those circumstances will need to bear very carefully in mind the important policy considerations which cause the courts to focus primarily on the offence in these cases, and the need to maintain effective deterrence. Treatment is or ought to be available to mentally affected offenders in prison, and powers are available for transfer to hospital. Given the huge quantities of drugs involved and given that D went into the offence with his eyes open, **12 years** was not excessive.
Note: This case is old. However, the principles are still applied today. Ed.
See also the **DEFENDANT**, *Mentally disordered defendants* para at **240.42**.

273.46   *Own use*
R v Aramah 1982 76 Cr App R 190 LCJ Importation of very small amounts of cannabis for personal use can be dealt with as if it were simple possession.
R v De Brito 2000 2 Cr App R (S) p 255 The defendant is entitled to a discount if the importation is solely for the their consumption, but the larger the amount the smaller the discount. This is because whatever the intention of the offender may be, the larger the amount the greater the danger that the drugs may pass into the hands of others.
Note: These cases are old. However, the principles are still applied today. Ed.

273.47   *Personal mitigation*
Note: In step two of the *Drug Offences Guideline 2012* page 7, some personal mitigation is set out which amounts to 'factors reducing seriousness or reflecting personal mitigation'. Often personal mitigation makes little difference, especially in drug trafficking cases. I have not listed the old cases on this topic because it is unclear how the guideline has affected them and they added little. Ed.
See also the **DEFENDANT** *Personal mitigation* para at **240.51**.

274 IMPORTATION/EXPORTATION OF PROHIBITED/RESTRICTED GOODS

274.1

Customs and Excise Management Act 1979 s 50(2), 68(2) and 170(2)

Modes of trial Triable either way

Maximum sentences On indictment: 7 years, except for:

Firearms, counterfeit currency, military goods and torture equipment Anti-social Behaviour, Crime and Policing Act 2014 s 111 raised the penalty for importing certain firearms to life imprisonment, see **259.6**. The section came into force on 14 July 2014.[571] Where the prohibition is in relation to military goods, military technology, torture equipment etc. and the offence is Customs and Excise Management Act 1979 s 68 or 170, the penalty is 10 years.[572] The statutory details are at **263.1** and the sentencing details are at **274.6**.

Iran For offences of importation and exportation of various goods contrary to Customs and Excise Management Act 1979 s 50(4)(b), 68(3)(b) and 170(3)(b) in connection with: a) Export Control (Iran Sanctions) Order 2012 2012/1243 arts 2(1), 3(1), 4, 8(1), 11(1)(a), 13(1)(a) and 15(1)(a), or b) Iran Sanctions Regulations EU 267/2012 art 15(1)(b) and 16 or c) Iran Human Rights Regulations EU 359/2011 art 1(b)(1), the maximum is 10 years, Export Control (Iran Sanctions) Order 2012 2012/1243 art 18(4) and (5).[573] Certain naval equipment and other articles were added to the list of goods which are subject to the 10-year penalty by Export Control (Iran Sanctions) (Amendment) Order 2013 2013/340.

North Korea and the Ivory Coast For: a) North Korean gold, precious metals, banknotes and certain North Korean technology and other goods, and b) equipment and other goods involving the Ivory Coast, the maximum penalty is 10 years, Export Control (North Korea and Ivory Coast Sanctions and Syria Amendment) Order 2013 2013/3182.

Seal skins For Import of Seal Skins Regulations 1996 1996/2686 reg 2, the maximum penalty is 2 years, Customs and Excise Management Act 1979 s 170(4B).

On summary conviction 6 months (except for seal skin offences where it is 3 months) and/or a fine of £5,000 for offences committed before 12 March 2015 and a £20,000[574] fine thereafter, or three times the value of the goods, whichever is greater.

Note: Why the maximum is £20,000 and not unlimited is far from clear. It may be because the appropriate forum for large-scale importations is considered to be the Crown Court. Ed.

Confiscation Where a defendant has a criminal lifestyle the court, once the confiscation proceedings are triggered (see **22.11** in Volume 1), <u>must</u> follow the Proceeds of Crime Act 2002 procedure. 'Criminal lifestyle' offences include those under Customs and Excise Management Act 1979 s 68(2) and 170 when committed in connection with a firearm or ammunition.[575] For what constitutes a criminal lifestyle and conducting confiscation proceedings under a different route, see **22.50** in Volume 1.

Serious Crime Prevention Orders For Customs and Excise Management Act 1979 s 68(2) and 170 where the offence is committed in connection with a firearm or ammunition and Criminal Justice (International Co-operation) Act 1990 s 19 offences there is a discretionary power to make this order, when it would protect the public etc.[576]

---

[571] Anti-social Behaviour, Crime and Policing Act 2014 (Commencement No 2, Transitional and Transitory Provisions) Order 2014 2014/949 para 6(d)

[572] Export Control Order 2008 2008/3231 Part 2 and para 42

[573] In force 1/6/12

[574] Legal Aid, Sentencing and Punishment of Offenders Act 2012 (Fines on Summary Conviction) Regulations 2015 2015/664 para 2 and Sch 1 para 2, 23 and 24 Sch 2 para 1(3), 1(11) and 1(21).

[575] Proceeds of Crime Act 2002 s 6 and 75 and Sch 2 para 5(1)

[576] Serious Crime Act 2007 s 1 and Sch 1 para 3 and 1(3)(b)

Sexual Harm Prevention Orders There is a discretionary power to make this order when it is necessary to protect the public from sexual harm.[577]

Notification For offences under Customs and Excise Management Act 1979 s 170 where:

a) the goods were prohibited by Customs Consolidation Act 1876 s 42 (indecent or obscene articles), and

b) the photograph showed a person under 16, and

c) i) the defendant is 18 or over, or ii) the defendant is sentenced to at least 12 months' imprisonment,

the defendant must notify the police within three days (or three days from his or her release from imprisonment, hospital etc.) with his or her name, home address, national insurance number etc. and any changes to those, and addresses where he or she resides for seven days[578] (in one or more periods) or more in any 12-month period.[579]

No doubt due to drafting errors, Customs and Excise Management Act 1979 s 50(2) and 68(2) do not trigger notification.

Children and vulnerable adults: barred lists For offences under Customs and Excise Management Act 1979 s 170 where: the goods were prohibited by Customs Consolidation Act 1876 s 42 (indecent or obscene articles), the defendant is automatically barred from engaging in regulated activity with children and vulnerable adults.[580] The judge must tell the defendant that the Disclosure and Barring Service will include him or her in the barred lists.[581] The defendant can ask the Service to remove him or her from the lists. No doubt due to more drafting errors, Customs and Excise Management Act 1979 s 50(2) and 68(2) do not trigger automatic barring for the same prohibited goods.

Deferred Prosecution Agreements A designated prosecutor may apply to the court under Courts and Crime Act 2013 Sch 17 para 7 for this procedure to be applied to Customs and Excise Management Act 1979 s 68 and 167 offences. The procedure is laid down in Crime and Courts Act 2013 Sch 17. In force 24 February 2014.

For movement of legal goods which are prohibited in another country etc. see the AVIATION *Security, Assisting others to defeat security at airports* para at **213.6**.

For **corporate offenders** see the *Fraud, Bribery and Money Laundering: Corporate Offenders* guideline at **225.4**.

274.2   *Birds and animals   Judicial guidance*

R v Noonan 2009 EWCA Crim 2917, 2010 2 Cr App R (S) 35 (p 229) D pleaded to evading the restrictions on the export of elephant tusks and sperm whale teeth. Held. These are serious crimes as the Court recognised in *R v Sisson* 2001 1 WLR 902. Without an illegal market there would be no need to catch these endangered species. It is the market that feeds the destruction of the species. Earlier cases fail to reflect the gravity of these cases. A serious deterrent sentence might stop this trade. Significant and serious sentences ought to be passed.

274.3   *Birds and animals   Cases*

R v Noonan 2009 EWCA Crim 2917, 2010 2 Cr App R (S) 35 (p 229) D pleaded late to evading the restrictions on the export of elephant tusks and sperm whale teeth and associated counts of altering or falsifying permits and certificates. The offences spanned a year. Count 1 involved an African elephant tusk. He offered the tusk to undercover agents on eBay in an e-mail and they bought it for just under $2,000. D described it as a 'faux' tusk. Count 2 was similar with a paid price of $2,200. In an e-mail he said he had held six auctions on eBay which included sales of tusks and whale teeth. Counts 3 and 5

---

[577] Sexual Offences Act 2003 s 103A as inserted by Anti-social Behaviour, Crime and Policing Act 2014 Sch 5 para 2 and Sexual Offences Act 2003 Sch 3

[578] Sexual Offences Act 2003 s 84(1)(c) and (6)

[579] Sexual Offences Act 2003 s 83 and Sch 3 para 14

[580] Safeguarding Vulnerable Groups Act 2006 s 2 and Sch 3 and Safeguarding Vulnerable Groups Act 2006 (Prescribed Criteria and Miscellaneous Provisions) Regulations 2009 2009/37 paras 4 and 6 and Sch paras 2 and 4

[581] Safeguarding Vulnerable Groups Act 2006 s 2 and Sch 3 para 25

involved a sperm whale tooth and an elephant tusk sold for something over $150 and $100. D also listed for sale another tusk. Count 7 was seven sperm whale teeth which were protected specimens. D was in his mid-forties and in poor health. His wife was suffering difficulties and he cared for his 93-year-old grandfather. **10 months** was fully justified.

R v Lendrum 2011 EWCA Crim 228 D pleaded to importation of prohibited goods. D was spotted at Birmingham airport acting suspiciously. A cleaner subsequently found two egg boxes in the shower facilities and the police were called. D was searched and was found to have 14 peregrine falcon eggs strapped to his chest. The police looked at his luggage and found a Leica viewing scope, a thermometer, binoculars, a GPS system, a walkie-talkie, a golf ball retriever, an insulated bag, £5,000, $3,500 and some South African rand. His car was searched. Various items were recovered, including an incubator, a cool bag, egg wrappings, a backpack containing other equipment and a satellite navigation unit. At a storage facility in Northampton belonging to him they recovered an incubator top, three syringes and another incubator. When questioned he made 'fatuous excuses'. Peregrine falcons were in the highest level of protection for endangered species. D had two convictions relating to wild bird's eggs in Canada and Zimbabwe. Had all 14 eggs hatched, the birds might have been sold for £70,000. The Judge sentenced D on the basis the profit was a commercial profit. Held. **18 months** not 30 aligns this case with the general pattern of sentencing for these cases.

Note: Many will think the sentencing Judge's sentence took into account the eggs' high level of protection for endangered species, the two previous convictions and the need for deterrence, whereas the Court of Appeal's sentence did not. Ed.

Cigarettes and tobacco see the TAX FRAUD AND DUTY EVASION *Duty evasion Cigarettes and tobacco* para at **343.15**.

274.4   False identity documents
Policing and Crime Act 2009 s 101 This section makes the importation or export of false identity documents prohibited, so that importers can be prosecuted under Customs and Excise Management Act 1979.[582]

Firearms see the FIREARM OFFENCES *Importation/Exportation of firearms* para at **259.6**.

274.5   Knives etc.
Policing and Crime Act 2009 s 102 This section amends Criminal Justice Act 1988 by adding s 141ZB, so making the importation of offensive weapons prohibited (subject to exceptions) so that importers can be prosecuted under Customs and Excise Management Act 1979.[583]

R v Price 2005 EWCA Crim 1757, 2006 1 Cr App R (S) 55 (p 302) D pleaded to two charges of importing flick knives. Held. In order to determine the sentence for importing prohibited weapons it is necessary to bear in mind the need to deter others and to take note of the nature of the weapons and the risk to the public if they are disseminated, the number of weapons, the offender's actual intention, which might not be the same as the offender's expressed intention, and the likely eventual use of weapons in this country. Old cases: Best ignored.

274.6   Sanctions, Contrary to
Example: *R v Summerskill* 2014 EWCA Crim 2173 (Plea. D's export licence to Iran was refused and he sent high-specification valves to Hong Kong to defeat the ban. D lied and persuaded a Hong Kong firm that no export licence was needed. He also sent goods that might be used for weapons/nuclear development twice, to Iran via Azerbaijan, by deceiving another company. D was of good character and had a previous military career.

---

[582] This section came into force on 25/1/10, Policing and Crime Act 2009 (Commencement No 2) Order 2010 2010/52.
[583] This section came into force on 25/1/10, Policing and Crime Act 2009 (Commencement No 2) Order 2010 2010/52.

D's company made annual profits of around £750,000. Held. The goods had potential use for weapons of mass destruction. **30 months** was merciful and a considerably greater sentence would have been justified. D's **company fine of £225,000** upheld.)

Note: The Court applied the principles for importing/exporting set out in the firearms chapter at **259.6**.

274.7   *Sexual images, Unlawful*

Children and vulnerable adults: barred lists For Customs and Excise Management Act 1979 s 170 offences, where the goods are 'indecent or obscene prints, paintings, photographs, books, cards, lithographic or other engravings, or any other indecent or obscene articles'[584] this scheme applies. A defendant who is aged 18+ will be automatically barred from engaging in regulated activity with children and with vulnerable adults.[585] The judge must tell the defendant that the Disclosure and Barring Service will include him or her in the barred lists.[586] The defendant may ask the Service to remove him or her from the lists.

Extended sentences This offence is listed in Criminal Justice Act 2003 Sch 15. The court may pass a 2012 extended sentence (EDS) if there is a significant risk of serious harm from future specified offences and either: a) the defendant has a Criminal Justice Act 2003 Sch 15B conviction (applicable only to defendants aged 18+), or b) the offence would justify a determinate sentence of at least 4 years.[587]

Note: These cases are now prosecuted with a sexual offence, no doubt to convey the seriousness of sexual offending and also to trigger notification. The cases which are just prosecuted as importation are best ignored as sentencing has changed since then. Ed.

275   INCEST

275.1

Sexual Offences Act 2003

    s 64 (sex with an adult relative where the defendant penetrates)

    s 65 (sex with an adult relative where the defendant is penetrated)

Modes of trial Both offences are triable either way.

Maximum sentences On indictment 2 years. Summary 6 months and/or a £5,000 fine for offences committed before 12 March 2015 and an unlimited fine thereafter.[588] There are maximum fines for those aged under 18, see **14.38** in Volume 1.

Historical offences Offences committed from 1 January 1957 to 30 April 2004 are charged under Sexual Offences Act 1956 s 10-11. The maximum penalty for men (section 10) was life if the victim was aged under 13 and otherwise 7 years. The maximum for women was 7 years.

For offences committed against a child under the new law, see the SEX OFFENCES: CHILD FAMILY MEMBER chapter.

See also the **Incest** section in the SEX OFFENCES: HISTORICAL CHAPTER at **330.8**.

Sexual Harm Prevention Orders There is a discretionary power to make this order when it is necessary to protect the public from sexual harm.[589]

Notification For offences under: 1) Sexual Offences Act 1956 s 10 (where the other party was aged under 18) and 2) Sexual Offences Act 2003 s 64-65 where: a) the defendant is aged less than 18 and is sentenced to imprisonment for 12 months or more or b) the defendant is aged 18 or over and is sentenced to imprisonment or detained in a

---

[584] As defined by Customs Consolidation Act 1876 s 42
[585] Safeguarding Vulnerable Groups Act 2006 s 2 and Sch 3 and Safeguarding Vulnerable Groups Act 2006 (Prescribed Criteria and Miscellaneous Provisions) Regulations 2009 2009/37 paras 4 and 6 and Sch paras 2 and 4
[586] Safeguarding Vulnerable Groups Act 2006 s 2 and Sch 3 para 25
[587] Criminal Justice Act 2003 s 226A-226B as inserted by Legal Aid, Sentencing and Punishment of Offenders Act 2012 s 124
[588] Legal Aid, Sentencing and Punishment of Offenders Act 2012 s 85(1) and (4) and Legal Aid, Sentencing and Punishment of Offenders Act 2012 (Commencement No 11) Order 2015 2015/504
[589] Sexual Offences Act 2003 s 103A as inserted by Anti-social Behaviour, Crime and Policing Act 2014 Sch 5 para 2 and Sexual Offences Act 2003 Sch 3

hospital, the defendant must notify[590] the police within three days (or three days from his or her release from imprisonment, hospital etc.) with his or her name, home address, national insurance number etc. and any changes to those, and addresses where he or she resides for seven days[591] (in one or more periods) or more in any 12-month period.[592] See also the NOTIFICATION: SEXUAL OFFENDERS chapter.

Children: barred lists For section 10 and 11 offences, where the other person was aged under 16 or did not consent to the act and the defendant is aged 18 or over, he or she is automatically barred from engaging in regulated activity with children.[593] For section 10-11 offences, where the other person was a child or did not consent to the act and the defendant is aged 18 or over, he or she is automatically barred from engaging in regulated activity with vulnerable adults.[594] The judge must tell the defendant that the Disclosure and Barring Service will include him or her in the barred lists.[595] The defendant can ask the Service to remove him or her from the lists.

275.2   *Crown Court statistics England and Wales*
Familial sexual offences with a relative aged 18 or over (Incest) Aged 21+

Year	Plea	Total sen- tenced	Type of sentencing %							Average length of custody in months
			Discharge	Fine	Community sentence	Sus- pended sentence	Custody	Oth- er		
2014	G	7	–	–	43	–	57	–		Not listed
	NG	0								

The previous years' statistics combined statistics for 'child family member' sex offences and incest. They are not listed here because the offences are so different.

For explanations about the statistics, see page 1-xii. For statistics for those aged under 21 and for male and female defendants etc. see www.banksr.com Other Matters Statistics tab

275.3   *Sentencing Council Guideline   Sexual Offences Act 2003 s 64-65*
Sexual Offences Guideline 2014 page 137 www.banksr.com Other Matters Guidelines tab
The guideline only applies to offenders aged 18+, see page 7 of the guideline. For the usual practice, see **66.21** in Volume 1.

STEP ONE: Determining the offence category
page 138 The court should determine the offence category using the table below.

Category 1	Raised harm **and** raised culpability
Category 2	Raised harm **or** raised culpability
Category 3	Sex with an adult relative **without** raised harm or culpability factors present

The court should determine culpability and harm caused or intended, by reference only to the factors below, which comprise the principal factual elements of the offence. Where an offence does not fall squarely into a category, individual factors may require a degree of weighting before making an overall assessment and determining the appropriate offence category.

---

[590] Sexual Offences Act 2003 s 80(1)(a) and Sch 3 para 4, 11 and 32
[591] Sexual Offences Act 2003 s 84(1)(c) and (6)
[592] Sexual Offences Act 2003 s 83
[593] Safeguarding Vulnerable Groups Act 2006 s 2 and Sch 3 and Safeguarding Vulnerable Groups Act 2006 (Prescribed Criteria and Miscellaneous Provisions) Regulations 2009 2009/37 para 4 and Sch para 2
[594] Safeguarding Vulnerable Groups Act 2006 s 2 and Sch 3 and Safeguarding Vulnerable Groups Act 2006 (Prescribed Criteria and Miscellaneous Provisions) Regulations 2009 2009/37 para 6 and Sch 1 para 4
[595] Safeguarding Vulnerable Groups Act 2006 s 2 and Sch 3 para 25

Factors indicating raised harm	Factors indicating raised culpability
Victim is particularly vulnerable due to personal circumstances Child conceived Victim is particularly vulnerable due to personal circumstances	Grooming behaviour used against victim Use of threats (including blackmail)

275.4

STEP TWO: Starting point and category range

page 138 Having determined the category, the court should use the corresponding starting points to reach a sentence within the category range on the next page. The starting point applies to all offenders irrespective of plea or previous convictions. Having determined the starting point, step two allows further adjustment for aggravating or mitigating features, set out on the next page.

A case of particular gravity, reflected by multiple features of culpability or harm in step one, could merit upward adjustment from the starting point before further adjustment for aggravating or mitigating features, set out on the next page.

Where there is a sufficient prospect of rehabilitation, a community order with a sex offender treatment programme requirement under Criminal Justice Act 2003 s 202 can be a proper alternative to a short or moderate-length custodial sentence.

Category	Starting point	Category range
1	1 year's custody	26 weeks' to 2 years' custody
2	High-level community order	Medium-level community order to 1 year's custody
3	Medium-level community order	Band A fine to high-level community order

275.5   [Aggravating and mitigating factors]

page 139 The table below contains a non-exhaustive list of additional factual elements providing the context of the offence and factors relating to the offender. Identify whether any combination of these, or other relevant factors, should result in an upward or downward adjustment from the starting point. In particular, relevant recent convictions are likely to result in an upward adjustment. In some cases, having considered these factors, it may be appropriate to move outside the identified category range.

When sentencing Category 2 offences, the court should also consider the custody threshold as follows:

   Has the custody threshold been passed?

   If so, is it unavoidable that a custodial sentence be imposed?

   If so, can that sentence be suspended?

When sentencing Category 3 offences, the court should also consider the community order threshold as follows:

Has the community order threshold been passed?

For the meaning of a high-level and a medium-level community order see **16.13** in Volume 1.

Aggravating factors
Statutory aggravating factors: Previous convictions, having regard to a) the nature of the offence to which the conviction relates and its relevance to the current offence; and b) the time that has elapsed since the conviction Offence committed whilst on bail

Other aggravating factors:
Failure to comply with current court orders
Offence committed whilst on licence
Failure of offender to respond to previous warnings
Any steps taken to prevent reporting an incident, obtaining assistance and/or from assisting or supporting the prosecution
Attempts to dispose of or conceal evidence

Mitigating factors
No previous convictions or no relevant/recent convictions
Remorse
Previous good character and/or exemplary conduct*
Age and/or lack of maturity where it affects the responsibility of the offender
Mental disorder or learning disability, particularly where linked to the commission of the offence
Demonstration of steps taken to address offending behaviour
* Previous good character/exemplary conduct is different from having no previous convictions. The more serious the offence, the less the weight which should normally be attributed to this factor. Where previous good character/exemplary conduct has been used to facilitate the offence, this mitigation should not normally be allowed and such conduct may constitute an aggravating factor.

275.6   *Post-2014 guideline case*

R v SD 2015 EWCA Crim 526 D pleaded to five specimen counts of sexual intercourse with an adult relative (section 64) and sexual assault. The five counts covered about 12-15 occasions of sexual intercourse. D had consensual sexual intercourse with V, a close family member, over about eight months. The assault was feeling V's bottom. V was emotionally vulnerable with matrimonial difficulties and mental health issues. V suffered a serious deterioration in her mental health and was admitted to hospital, where the activity was revealed. D was aged 54 and of good character. The pre-sentence report noted D's shame and regret. The pre-sentence report said there was a medium risk of serious harm to other adult family members. It was agreed it was a Category 2 case for the section 64 counts. Held. For the section 64 counts we start at 12 months, so with plea **8 months**, not 12. The Judge was wrong to consider there was an element of breach of trust for the assault. It was in Category 2A and not 3. 2 months, not 9 consecutive, making 10 months not 21 months.

Note: There are no other useful reported cases in the last 13 years. I suggest the reader simply applies the guideline. Ed.

INDECENT ASSAULT AND OTHER REPEALED SEX OFFENCES, see the SEX OFFENCES: HISTORICAL chapter.

276   INFANTICIDE

276.1

Infanticide Act 1938 s 1 (a woman causing the death of her child when her mind was disturbed)

Mode of trial Indictable only

Maximum sentence Life

Infanticide Act 1938 s 1[596]

Extended sentences This offence is listed in Criminal Justice Act 2003 Sch 15. The court may pass a 2012 extended sentence (EDS) if there is a significant risk of serious harm from future specified offences and either: a) the defendant has a Criminal Justice Act 2003 Sch 15B conviction (applicable only to defendants aged 18+), or b) the offence would justify a determinate sentence of at least 4 years.[597]

---

[596] The section was slightly amended by Coroners and Justice Act 2009 s 57.
[597] Criminal Justice Act 2003 s 226A-226B as inserted by Legal Aid, Sentencing and Punishment of Offenders Act 2012 s 124

Sexual Harm Prevention Orders There is a discretionary power to make this order when it is necessary to protect the public from sexual harm.[598]

Children and vulnerable adults: barred lists Where the defendant is aged 18 or over he or she is automatically barred from engaging in regulated activity with vulnerable adults and with children.[599] The judge must tell the defendant that the Disclosure and Barring Service will include him or her in the barred lists.[600] The defendant may ask the Service to remove him or her from the lists.

See also the **MOTHERS** chapter.

276.2   *Crown Court statistics   England and Wales*

Infanticide

Plea	Sentence	Year						
		2008	**2009**	**2010**	**2011**	**2012**	**2013**	**2014**
G	Community penalty	0	1	2	0	0	1	1
	Suspended sentence	0	0	0	0	0	0	0
	Other	0	0	0	0	1	0	2
NG	–	0	0	0	0	0	0	0

For explanations about the statistics see page 1-xii. For more statistics see www.banksr. com Other Matters Statistics tab

276.3   *Cases*

R v Sainsbury 1989 11 Cr App R (S) 533 D pleaded to infanticide. When aged 14 she was permitted to share the same bed as her boyfriend at her boyfriend's parents. She became pregnant but did not tell her parents. Earlier, her sister had become pregnant and had been turned out of her parents' house. She and the boyfriend moved to a bed-sit. When aged 15, she gave birth on a lavatory in squalid circumstances without any medical assistance. She and her boyfriend wrapped the baby in a blanket and took it across country to a river where it was discovered 3 months later. The psychiatrist said, 'she had the mental age of 12 and in an understandable state of fear, exhaustion and panic took part in the disposal of the baby whether alive or dead in the river'. The court proceedings were delayed. When she was aged 17, the Judge said: "You were a very immature 14-year-old and were quite unable to cope with the pregnancy or understand its implications. The effect of giving birth left the balance of your mind disturbed so as to prevent rational judgement and decisions. Your responsibility was greatly diminished. I accept you have now greatly matured under the care of your foster parents and your future would be best served if you were left in their care, but my duty is not just to your welfare but to the welfare of society." Held. In the last ten years there have been 59 cases of infanticide. No custodial sentences were passed. Fifty-two received probation or supervision and six received Hospital Orders. That is the pattern of sentences for this offence. Was there anything to take this case out of that pattern? Emphatically no. We profoundly disagree with the Judge that the welfare of society demanded a custodial sentence. The welfare of society is least at risk by the course adopted. The offence was serious but the mitigating features were so overwhelming we without any hesitation substitute **probation** for 1 year's YOI. That will serve the interests of her and society.

R v Lewis 1989 11 Cr App R (S) 577 D pleaded to manslaughter of her baby when she was severely depressed. The plea was based on diminished responsibility. She was aged

---

[598] Sexual Offences Act 2003 s 103A as inserted by Anti-social Behaviour, Crime and Policing Act 2014 Sch 5 para 2 and Sexual Offences Act 2003 Sch 5

[599] Safeguarding Vulnerable Groups Act 2006 s 2 and Sch 3 and Safeguarding Vulnerable Groups Act 2006 (Prescribed Criteria and Miscellaneous Provisions) Regulations 2009 2009/37 paras 4 and 6 and Sch 1 paras 2 and 4

[600] Safeguarding Vulnerable Groups Act 2006 s 2 and Sch 3 para 25

21 and gave birth in a bathroom. She sought no medical attention. She put the baby in two plastic bags and carried the baby into the garden in the belief that the baby was stillborn. Outside she detected movement and stabbed the baby with scissors through the bag several times. She hid the baby in a garden shed. A day or so later she became unwell and was taken to hospital where she told the staff what had happened. She was of good character and showed remorse. The psychiatrist said that the prison environment, far from alleviating the girl's problems, would have a deleterious effect upon them. Held. She was plainly deeply depressed. She had no one to turn to. Her reaction was not rational. However, the mental condition did not remove the responsibility altogether. Sometimes it has to be remembered that the interests of society must prevail over the interests of a defendant. Sometimes a sentence to mark public revulsion has to be passed. Her behaviour was of course wicked and a young life has been lost. That must never be forgotten. But prison was not the only option. **Probation** not 1 year.

Note: The Judge will normally be greatly influenced by the psychiatric reports. Usually the Judge will recognise the importance that a life has been taken, yet show understanding and give assistance rather than simply punish. There are no recent reported cases, maybe because no one has been given an immediate custodial sentence for at least 20 years. The recent statistics indicate that the sentencing principles in the above cases are still applied.

See also the **MANSLAUGHTER** *Child victims* para at **284.19**.

277   INSOLVENCY OFFENCES

277.1

Insolvency Act 1986

s 206-211 (Fraud, misconduct and falsification etc. when a company is to be or is wound up)

s 262A (False representations)

s 353-362 (Non-disclosure, concealment of property, falsification, making false statements and fraudulent disposal of property etc. by a bankrupt)

s 389 (Acting as an insolvency practitioner when not qualified to do so)

(and many other sections)

Modes of trial All the offences are triable either way.[601]

Maximum sentences On indictment 7 years (except for section 207, 354(3), 357-358, 360-362 and 389 where it is 2 years). Summary 6 months and/or a £5,000 fine for offences committed before 12 March 2015 and an unlimited fine thereafter.[602] There are maximum fines for those aged under 18, see **14.38** in Volume 1.

Disqualification Where the defendant is convicted in connection with the liquidation or receivership of a company etc. there is power to disqualify from being a director, receiver etc.[603]

See also the **FRAUDS AND FINANCIAL SERVICES OFFENCES** and the **THEFT ETC.** chapters.

277.2   Crown Court statistics England and Wales

Bankruptcy offences Aged 21+

---

[601] Insolvency Act 1986 s 431 and Sch 10
[602] Legal Aid, Sentencing and Punishment of Offenders Act 2012 s 85(1) and (4) and Legal Aid, Sentencing and Punishment of Offenders Act 2012 (Commencement No 11) Order 2015 2015/504
[603] Company Directors Disqualification Act 1986 s 2

Year	Plea	Total sentenced	Type of sentencing %						Average length of custody in months
			Discharge	Fine	Community sentence	Suspended sentence	Custody	Other	
2013	G	47	4.3	6.4	8.5	59.6	21.3	–	9.7
	NG	9	–	–	11.1	55.6	33.3	–	6.7
2014	G	60	3	2	3	75	17	–	10.5
	NG	4	25	–	25	50	–	–	–

For explanations about the statistics see page 1-xii. For more statistics and for statistics for male and female defendants etc. see www.banksr.com Other Matters Statistics tab

277.3   *Concealing/disposing of assets*

R v Ferguson 2013 EWCA Crim 1089 D pleaded to fraudulent disposal of property (section 357). He entered a contract to buy two properties. The property market had fallen by the date of completion. The mortgage that he had arranged was withdrawn and he was unable to complete the purchases. The developers began proceedings against him. The properties were eventually sold for £114,395 less than the contract price and the developers sought payment for that sum. Two judgments were given against him which he had not satisfied in full. Further, a former client of his made a £10,000 claim against him. D failed to enter a defence and judgment was obtained. D subsequently transferred £29,920 to his partner, which was used as part payment for a Range Rover. By this point he knew that he had a bankruptcy order against him. The deficiency was £185,120, most of which was the sum owed to the developer. The transfer to his partner was a removal of property with intent to defraud or conceal his affairs. The sum was transferred to the trustee in bankruptcy before the prosecution was commenced. D was aged 48 and had appeared before the court on five prior occasions. He had been sentenced to 15 months for blackmail. Held. The blackmail conviction was a seriously aggravating factor. The diversion of funds to purchase a luxury item represented a cynical disregard by D of his obligations to the creditors. D should have received 25% credit. **4 months** not 6.

R v Hussain 2013 EWCA Crim 2243, 2014 2 Cr App R (S) 15 (p 114) D pleaded (after the PCMH) to making a false statement and fraudulent concealment of property contrary to Insolvency Act 1986 s 356 and 357. D began trading in 2007. The business ran into financial difficulties and ceased trading in 2010. In 2007, D opened a gas account with British Gas. He was unable to maintain the payments and ended up owing £30,000. British Gas sought to obtain the sum and obtained judgment in default. D did not respond to any attempts to contact him. There were telephone conversations between British Gas and a man at D's home address during which the man claimed to be D's father and claimed that he did not live there any more. Shortly after the claim by British Gas, D transferred his interest in his property to his wife. There was no consideration for the transfer and she was registered as the new proprietor shortly afterwards (count 2). D subsequently petitioned for his own bankruptcy. Accompanying the petition was a statement of truth which contained false representations and admissions. In particular, D failed to disclose that he had gifted the property to his wife (count 1). He was interviewed after making the false statement and informed the Official Receiver's office of the transfer. D did not have any previous convictions. He had been under considerable financial strain. The pre-sentence report assessed the risk of reoffending as low. Held. It was accepted that the custody threshold was passed. The Judge was not wrong in deciding not to suspend the sentence. The short period of time for which the deception was practised leads to the conclusion that a starting point of 12 months was too long. 8 months was appropriate, so with 25% credit, **6 months** not 9.

Managing a company when bankrupt

See the DISQUALIFICATION FROM BEING A DIRECTOR OF A COMPANY ETC., BREACH OF chapter.

277.4   *Cases*

R v Hindley 2013 EWCA Crim 859 D pleaded to: a) being concerned in the management of a company while subject to a bankruptcy restriction order and b) fraud. In and before 2005, D traded as Choice Landscapes. In June 2005, he was adjudicated bankrupt on his own petition. There was an estimated deficiency of nearly £250,000. In July 2006, a bankruptcy restriction order was made against him, prohibiting him from acting as a director of a company etc. for a period of nine years. In 2007, D pleaded to concealment of financial transactions from the Receiver in his bankruptcy, making a false statement and obtaining credit without disclosing his bankruptcy. He received a 6-month suspended sentence with an unpaid work requirement. In 2008, Ripe Ventures was incorporated as a limited company which provided building services. It engaged in work for Mr and Mrs M, who needed their home extending and adapting to provide suitable accommodation for their disabled son. Mr and Mrs M paid £150,000 but there was a dispute as to the work's quality and part of the work had to be completed by another firm. Ripe Ventures repaid £15,000 in compensation. This was the fraud offence, namely obtaining a building contract for a house when D had told the householder in answer to a specific enquiry that he was entitled to be involved in management of a company and had never been made bankrupt. In 2008, Ripe Ventures was wound up on a creditor's petition. D was charged in 2010. D accepted that he carried out a management role in Ripe Ventures. There was a delay of four years of which only nine months was attributable to D due to his late plea of guilty. Held. The appropriate sentence for both offences was **18 months** not 26. So 9 months on each consecutive not 15 and 9. The Judge was correct to activate the suspended sentence but 3 months consecutive, not 6, was appropriate, because the unpaid work was completed. In all **21 months** not 30.

INSURANCE FRAUDS see the FRAUD AND FINANCIAL SERVICES OFFENCES *Insurance frauds* para at **265.40**.

278   INSURANCE, NO

278.1

1) Road Traffic Act 1988 s 143

Using a motor vehicle without insurance

Mode of trial Summary only

Maximum sentence A £5,000 fine for offences committed before 12 March 2015 and an unlimited fine thereafter.[604] There are maximum fines for those aged under 18, see **14.38** in Volume 1.

Disqualification Discretionary

Penalty points 6-8 points[605]

Fixed penalty There is a fixed penalty (and financial penalty deposit) of £300 for this offence[606] with half the relevant victim surcharge. For more detail see **61.1** in Volume 1.

2) Road Traffic Act 1988 s 144A (keeping a vehicle which does not meet insurance requirements)

Mode of trial Summary only[607]

Maximum sentence Level 3 fine (£1,000)[608]

---

[604] Legal Aid, Sentencing and Punishment of Offenders Act 2012 s 85(1) and (4) and Legal Aid, Sentencing and Punishment of Offenders Act 2012 (Commencement No 11) Order 2015 2015/504
[605] Endorsement code IN10
[606] Fixed Penalty Order 2000 2000/2792 Sch 1 as amended and Road Safety (Financial Penalty Deposit) (Appropriate Amount) Order 2009 2009/492 as amended
[607] para 1
[608] para 1

Disqualification Not applicable
Endorsement Not applicable
Fixed penalty £100[609]

For causing death by drivers unlicensed, disqualified or uninsured, see the DEATH BY DRIVING: DISQUALIFIED, NO LICENCE, UNINSURED chapter.

For fraudulent claims, see FRAUD AND FINANCIAL SERVICES OFFENCES *Insurance frauds* at **265.40**.

278.2   Statistics
Vehicle insurance offences Aged 21+

Year	Plea	Total sentenced	Type of sentencing %						Average length of custody in months
			Discharge	Fine	Community sentence	Suspended sentence	Custody	Other	
2013	G	5	20	–	40	20	20	–	5
	NG	0							
2014	G	7	14	43	14	14	–	14	
	NG	0							

For an explanation of the statistics see page 1-xii. For more statistics see www.banksr. com Other Matters Statistics tab

278.3   Magistrates' Court Sentencing Guidelines
Magistrates' Court Sentencing Guidelines 2008, see www.banksr.com Other Matters Guidelines tab The guideline applies to the Magistrates' Court and to the Crown Court hearing appeals or sentencing for summary only offences.[610]
page 130 Starting points are based on a first-time offender pleading not guilty.

Examples of nature of activity	Starting point	Range
Using a motor vehicle on a road or other public place without insurance	Band C fine	Band C fine 6 points to 12 months' disqualification

The following aggravating and mitigating factors may be particularly relevant:

Factors indicating higher culpability: 1 Never passed test 2 Gave false details 3 Driving LGV, HGV, PSV etc. 4 Driving for hire or reward 5 Evidence of sustained uninsured use.

Factors indicating lower culpability: 1 Responsibility for providing insurance rests with another 2 Genuine misunderstanding 3 Recent failure to renew or failure to transfer vehicle details 4 Vehicle not being driven. Factor indicating greater degree of harm: 1 Involved in accident 2 Accident resulting in injury.

Consider range from 7 points to 2 months' disqualification where vehicle was being driven and no evidence that the offender has held insurance.

Consider disqualification of 6-12 months if evidence of sustained uninsured use and/or involvement in accident.

For failure to produce insurance documents (Max fine Level 4) the guideline is starting point Band A fine and fine per offence not per document.

A Band A fine is 50% of net weekly income. Band B and C are 100% and 150%. For more detail see **60.27** in Volume 1.

Consultation It is expected that the Sentencing Council will issue a consultation document about updating this guideline in May 2016.

---

[609] Road Traffic Act 1988 s 144C(8) inserted by Road Safety Act 2006 s 22
[610] See page 15 of the guidelines.

279   KETAMINE

279.1

The drug is a class B drug.[611] It was reclassified from class C on 10 June 2014.[612]

279.2   *Drug properties etc.*

R v Johnson 2009 EWCA Crim 2745, 2010 2 Cr App R (S) 24 (p 154) D was convicted of possession of ketamine with intent to supply. Held. Ketamine is an anaesthetic drug which was originally used for veterinary and occasionally dental purposes. It is a dissociative anaesthetic which has the effect of blocking signals to the conscious mind from other parts of the brain. That can cause a state of reduced bodily sensation, and may prompt hallucinations. It is those psychedelic properties to which its present popularity on the clubbing scene can be attributed. It is a drug associated with drug-assisted sexual assault. It has dangers in that higher doses can render the taker paralysed. It can affect memory. One effect is to shrink the bladder and the urinary tract. This causes vastly increased frequency and discomfort of urination to the extent that D was required to relieve himself as much as twice an hour.

KIDNAPPING see the FALSE IMPRISONMENT/KIDNAPPING chapter. When for ransom, see BLACKMAIL *Kidnapping individuals for ransom/Debt collecting* at 217.9.

280   LANDLORDS, OFFENCES COMMITTED BY

280.1

Protection from Eviction Act 1977 s 1

Mode of trial Triable either way

Maximum sentence On indictment 2 years. Summary 6 months and/or a £5,000 fine for offences committed before 12 March 2015 and an unlimited fine thereafter.[613] There are maximum fines for those aged under 18, see **14.38** in Volume 1.

Criminal Behaviour Orders Where a defendant has engaged in behaviour that caused or was likely to cause harassment, alarm or distress to any persons and a Criminal Behaviour Order will help in preventing the offender from engaging in such behaviour, the court may make this order.[614]

Confiscation There was no power to make a confiscation order following a conviction for Housing Act 2004 s 95(1) (owner renting out property without a licence), *R v Sumal & Sons (Properties) Ltd* 2012 EWCA Crim 1840.

Restraining Orders There is power to make a restraining order to protect the victim by prohibiting the defendant from doing anything described in the order.[615] The order may be for a specified period or until further order.[616]

280.2   *Crown Court statistics   England and Wales   Crown Court*

Protection from Eviction Act Aged 21+

Year	Plea	Total sentenced	Type of sentencing %						Average length of custody in months
			Discharge	Fine	Commu-nity sentence	Sus-pended sentence	Custody	Other	
2013	G	1	–	100	–	–	–	–	–
	NG	1	–	–	–	100	–	–	–

---

[611] Misuse of Drugs Act 1971 Sch 2 Part III
[612] Misuse of Drugs Act 1971 (Ketamine etc.) (Amendment) Order 2014 2014/1106
[613] Legal Aid, Sentencing and Punishment of Offenders Act 2012 s 85(1) and (4) and Legal Aid, Sentencing and Punishment of Offenders Act 2012 (Commencement No 11) Order 2015 2015/504
[614] Anti-social Behaviour, Crime and Policing Act 2014 s 22(1)-(4)
[615] Protection from Harassment Act 1997 s 5(1)
[616] Protection from Harassment Act 1997 s 5(3)

Year	Plea	Total sentenced	Type of sentencing %						Average length of custody in months
			Discharge	Fine	Community sentence	Suspended sentence	Custody	Other	
2014	G	3	33	–	–	33	33	–	not listed[617]
	NG	2	–	50	–	50	–	–	–

For an explanation about the statistics see 1-xii. For more statistics see www.banksr.com Other Matters Statistics tab
The last reported case was in 2001 and is best ignored.

281   LAVATORY, SEX IN A
281.1
Sexual Offences Act 2003 s 71
Mode of trial Summary only
Maximum sentence 6 months and/or a £5,000 fine for offences committed before 12 March 2015 and an unlimited fine thereafter.[618] There are maximum fines for those aged under 18, see **14.38** in Volume 1.

281.2   *Sentencing Council guidelines*
Note: *The Sexual Offences Guideline 2014* does not have a section about this offence. It is understood that the old guideline remains in force. Ed.
Sexual Offences Act 2003 Guideline 2008, see www.banksr.com Other Matters Guidelines tab
The starting points and ranges apply to a first-time offender who was convicted after a trial.
page 95

Type/nature of activity	Starting points	Sentencing ranges
Repeat offending and/or aggravating factors	Community order	Community order or a fine
Basic offence as defined in SOA 2003, assuming no aggravating or mitigating factors	Fine	Community order or a fine

Additional aggravating factor: Intimidating behaviour/threats of violence to member(s) of the public.
For the meaning of a high-level, a medium-level and a low-level community order see **16.12** in Volume 1.
For general principles about sentencing in sex cases, see the **SEX OFFENCES: GENERAL PRINCIPLES** chapter.

281.3   *Magistrates' Court Sentencing Guidelines*
Magistrates' Court Sentencing Guidelines 2008, see www.banksr.com Other Matters Guidelines tab The guideline applies to the Magistrates' Court and to the Crown Court hearing appeals or sentencing for summary only offences.[619]
page 92 Key factors: a) This offence is committed where an offender intentionally engages in sexual activity in a public lavatory. It was introduced to give adults and children the freedom to use public lavatories for the purpose for which they are designed, without the fear of being an unwilling witness to overtly sexual behaviour of a kind that most people would not expect to be conducted in public. It is primarily a public

---

[617] Based on too few cases to be meaningful
[618] Legal Aid, Sentencing and Punishment of Offenders Act 2012 s 85(1) and (4) and Legal Aid, Sentencing and Punishment of Offenders Act 2012 (Commencement No 11) Order 2015 2015/504
[619] See page 15 of the guidelines.

order offence rather than a sexual offence. b) When dealing with a repeat offender, the starting point should be a low-level community order with a range of Band C fine to medium-level community order. The presence of aggravating factors may suggest that a sentence above the range is appropriate. c) This guideline may be relevant by way of analogy to conduct charged as the common law offence of outraging public decency. First-time offender pleading not guilty

Type/nature of activity	Starting points	Sentencing ranges
Basic offence as defined in the Act, assuming no aggravating or mitigating factors	Band C fine	Band C fine
Offence with aggravating factors	Low-level community order	Band C fine to medium-level community order

Factors indicating higher culpability: 1 Intimidating behaviour/threats of violence to member(s) of the public 2 Blatant behaviour.
Consider ancillary orders, including compensation.
Consultation It is expected that the Sentencing Council will issue a consultation document about updating this guideline in May 2016.
For the meaning of a medium-level and a low-level community order see **16.12** in Volume 1.

282 LSD

282.1
Drug/driving Under the new list of drugs for drug/driving the prescribed limit for LSD is 1 μg.[620] For more detail see **245.2**.
See also the **DEFENDANT *Drug users*** paras at **240.21** and the **IMPORTATION OF DRUGS (CLASS A, B AND C), POSSESSION OF DRUGS, PRODUCTION OF DRUGS** and **SUPPLY OF DRUGS** chapters.
282.2   *Don't treat the drug as less serious than other class A drugs*
R v Hurley 1998 1 Cr App R (S) 299 at 302 LCJ Principle stated
282.3   *How should the amount of drugs be presented to the court?*
R v Hurley 1998 1 Cr App R (S) 299 at 303 LCJ Don't use resale value, although it may be appropriate for the street value to be given to give an idea of the scale of the operation. The number of impregnated squares usually of approximately ¼ inch in size provides the best way. There is, however, evidence that it is now the fashion for dosage units to approximate to 50 μg and since any effect is unlikely to be detectable very much below 25 μg a dose of 50 μg is accepted as being a realistic dose. The practical evidence suggests that in the market place this is the average level of dose as judged by the seizures which are made. Of course, one would not expect the squares to be impregnated with exactly 50 μg. There must be a plus or minus. If, however, one takes the number of squares as the primary starting point, then allowance must be made appropriately upwards or downwards if there is convincing evidence that the squares are significantly more or less heavily impregnated. By 'significantly' we have in mind something in excess of 10 μg one way or the other. It is therefore possible, where weaker dosage units are intentionally produced, to adjust the scale accordingly, while bearing in mind that in such a situation those who produce these squares may well have done so quite deliberately in order to maximise their profits. Since the object of the legislation is to deter the use of unlawful drugs and strip dealers of their profits, it seems to us appropriate that the penalties should be related to the number of dosage units put, or to be put, on the market, subject to such adjustment as may be appropriate in the light of a

---

[620] Drug Driving (Specified Limits) (England and Wales) Regulations 2014 2014/2868 para 2

significant deviation from the standard dose. The sentence therefore should ordinarily be based on the number of squares to be marketed, assuming an LSD content of about 50 µg of pure LSD per square, plus or minus about 10 µg, but with discretion in the sentencer to vary the sentence upwards or downwards where there is any more significant variation.

Note: This is an old case, but it may be helpful. Ed.

282.4   *Scientific evidence*
R v Hurley 1998 1 Cr App R (S) 299 at 302 LCJ Dr Jansen and Professor Nichols told us that in the 1960s and 1970s LSD was regularly used in much larger quantities than is usual today. They testified that it was at about a dose of 50 µg that most people start to begin to experience hallucinatory effects.

283   MAKING OFF WITHOUT PAYMENT
283.1
Theft Act 1978 s 3
Mode of trial Triable either way
Maximum sentence On indictment 2 years. Summary 6 months and/or a £5,000 fine for offences committed before 12 March 2015 and an unlimited fine thereafter.[621] There are maximum fines for those aged under 18, see **14.38** in Volume 1.
Restitution Orders There is power to make a Restitution Order under Powers of Criminal Courts (Sentencing) Act 2000 s 148.
For guidance about general dishonesty offences, see the **THEFT ETC.** chapter.

283.2   *Sentencing Council Guideline*
Theft Offences Guideline 2016, www.banksr.com Other matters Guidelines tab. In force 1 February 2016. The guideline only applies to offenders aged 18+, see page 2 of the guideline. For the usual practice, see **66.21** in Volume 1.

STEP ONE: Determining the offence category
page 30 The court should determine the offence category with reference only to the factors identified in the following tables. In order to determine the category the court should assess culpability and harm.
The level of culpability is determined by weighing up all the factors of the case to determine the offender's role and the extent to which the offending was planned and the sophistication with which it was carried out.

CULPABILITY demonstrated by one or more of the following
A – High Culpability
A leading role where offending is part of a group activity Involvement of others through coercion, intimidation or exploitation Sophisticated nature of offence/significant planning Offence involving intimidation or the use or threat of force Deliberately targeting victim on basis of vulnerability
B – Medium Culpability
A significant role where offending is part of a group activity Some degree of planning involved All other cases where characteristics for categories A or C are not present

---

[621] Legal Aid, Sentencing and Punishment of Offenders Act 2012 s 85(1) and (4) and Legal Aid, Sentencing and Punishment of Offenders Act 2012 (Commencement No 11) Order 2015 2015/504

C – Lesser Culpability
Performed limited function under direction Involved through coercion, intimidation or exploitation Little or no planning Limited awareness or understanding of offence

Where there are characteristics present which fall under different levels of culpability, the court should balance these characteristics to reach a fair assessment of the offender's culpability.

283.3   Harm

page 31 Harm is assessed by reference to the actual loss that results from the offence and any significant additional harm suffered by the victim – examples of additional harm may include but are not limited to:

A high level of inconvenience caused to the victim
Emotional distress
Fear/loss of confidence caused by the crime
A greater impact on the victim due to the size or type of their business

Category 1	Goods or services obtained above £200 **or** Goods/services up to £200 with significant additional harm to the victim
Category 2	Goods or services obtained up to £200 **and** Little or no significant additional harm to the victim

283.4

STEP TWO: Starting point and category range

Having determined the category at step one, the court should use the starting point to reach a sentence within the appropriate category range in the table below.

The starting point applies to all offenders irrespective of plea or previous convictions.

	Culpability		
Harm	A	B	C
Category 1 Where the value greatly exceeds £200, it may be appropriate to move outside the identified range. Adjustment should be made for any significant additional harm for offences above £200.	**Starting point** 12 weeks' custody	**Starting point** Low-level community order	**Starting point** Band B fine
	Category range High-level community order to 36 weeks' custody	**Category range** Band C fine to High-level community order	**Category range** Band A fine to Low-level community order
Category 2	**Starting point** Medium-level community order	**Starting point** Band C fine	**Starting point** Band A fine
	Category range Low-level community order to 12 weeks' custody	**Category range** Band B fine to Low-level community order	**Category range** Discharge to Band B fine

Consecutive sentences for multiple offences may be appropriate – please refer to the [*TICs and Totality Guideline 2012: Crown Court*].

The court should then consider further adjustment for any aggravating or mitigating factors. The following list is a non-exhaustive list of additional factual elements providing the context of the offence and factors relating to the offender.

Identify whether any combination of these, or other relevant factors, should result in an upward or downward adjustment from the starting point.

Factors increasing seriousness
Statutory aggravating factors: Previous convictions, having regard to a) the nature of the offence to which the conviction relates and its relevance to the current offence; and b) the time that has elapsed since the conviction   Offence committed whilst on bail   Offence motivated by, or demonstrating hostility based on any of the following characteristics or presumed characteristics of the victim: religion, race, disability, sexual orientation or transgender identity   **Other aggravating factors:**   Steps taken to prevent the victim reporting or obtaining assistance and/or from assisting or supporting the prosecution   Attempts to conceal/dispose of evidence   Failure to comply with current court orders   Offence committed on licence   Offences taken into consideration   Established evidence of community/wider impact

Factors reducing seriousness or reflecting personal mitigation
No previous convictions or no relevant/recent convictions   Remorse, particularly where evidenced by voluntary reparation to the victim   Good character and/or exemplary conduct   Serious medical condition requiring urgent, intensive or long-term treatment   Age and/or lack of maturity where it affects the responsibility of the offender   Mental disorder or learning disability   Sole or primary carer for dependent relatives   Determination and/or demonstration of steps having been taken to address addiction or offending behaviour

284 MANSLAUGHTER

284.1

1) Common law
 Mode of trial Indictable only
 Maximum sentence Life[622]

2) Homicide Act 1957 s 2(3) (diminished responsibility)
 Mode of trial Indictable only
 Maximum sentence Life

2) Corporate Manslaughter and Corporate Homicide Act 2007 s 1
 Mode of trial Indictable only
 Maximum sentence A fine

Coroners and Justice Act 2009 s 54 introduced a partial defence to murder of loss of control, which replaced provocation.[623]

Automatic life Manslaughter is listed in Criminal Justice Act 2003 Sch 15B Part 1. The court must (unless the particular circumstances make it unjust)[624] pass automatic life if: a) the defendant is aged 18+ at the date of the conviction, b) the offence was committed on or after 3 December 2012, c) the court considers a determinate sentence of at least 10

---

[622] Offences Against the Person Act 1861 s 5
[623] In force 4/10/10, Coroners and Justice Act 2009 (Commencement No 4, Transitional and Saving Provisions) Order 2010 2010/816
[624] Criminal Justice Act 2003 s 224A(2)

years is appropriate, d) at the time the offender was convicted he had a conviction for a Criminal Justice Act 2003 Sch 15B offence, and e) the defendant at the time of his or her conviction had previously been sentenced to either: i) a life sentence where he or she was not eligible for release during the first 5 years of the sentence, or ii) a determinate sentence or extended sentence where the custodial part was 10 years or more.[625] For a pre-2012 extended sentence, when determining whether the custodial term was 10+ years, the period deducted for time on remand or on a curfew and tag is included.[626]

Extended sentences This offence is listed in Criminal Justice Act 2003 Sch 15. The court may pass a 2012 extended sentence (EDS) if there is a significant risk of serious harm from future specified offences and either: a) the defendant has a Criminal Justice Act 2003 Sch 15B conviction (applicable only to defendants aged 18+), or b) the offence would justify a determinate sentence of at least 4 years.[627]

Disqualification from driving When committed by a driver of a motor vehicle, there is obligatory disqualification for 2 years unless there are special reasons, and endorsement with 3-11 points.[628] The court must order him to be disqualified until he has passed the appropriate driving test unless there are special reasons. For the requirement to extend the period when custody is imposed, see **42.16** in Volume 1.

Depriving defendant of vehicle used There is power to deprive the defendant of the vehicle used[629] for the purposes of committing the offence.

Funeral expenses The court may make this compensation order,[630] see the *Funeral expenses of the deceased* para at **284.68**.

Sexual Harm Prevention Orders There is a discretionary power to make this order when it is necessary to protect the public from sexual harm.[631]

Children and vulnerable adults: barred lists Manslaughter is not a scheduled offence for automatic barring. Where the defendant commits a Domestic Violence, Crime and Victims Act 2004 s 5 offence and is aged 18 or over, he or she is automatically barred from engaging in regulated activity with children and vulnerable adults.[632] The judge must tell the defendant that the Disclosure and Barring Service will include him or her in the barred lists.[633] The defendant can ask the Authority to remove him or her from the lists.

Law Commission The Law Commission has published a Report on Murder, Manslaughter and Infanticide (No 304) 29 November 2006, www.lawcom.gov.uk. Its recommendations were ignored.

Cases The cases in this chapter are in part divided into sections for the weapon that was used, as that part of the case is usually clear. Often of more importance is the intent and the surrounding circumstances. One of the most critical factors is whether there was an intention to kill or cause GBH, which would be present when the offence is based on diminished responsibility or provocation. It is not possible to divide the cases by intent because many of the cases provide insufficient information to do that.

Consultation The Sentencing Guidelines Council is working on a guideline for manslaughter. The consultation paper is not expected until 2017 or 2018.

---

[625] Criminal Justice Act 2003 s 224A as inserted by Legal Aid, Sentencing and Punishment of Offenders Act 2012 s 122. The condition for a) is at section 224A(1)(a), for b) is at section 224A(1)(b), for c) is at section 224A(1)(c) and for d) is at section 224A(4)-(9).

[626] Criminal Justice Act 2003 s 224A(9)-(10)

[627] Criminal Justice Act 2003 s 226A-226B as inserted by Legal Aid, Sentencing and Punishment of Offenders Act 2012 s 124

[628] Road Traffic Offenders Act 1988 s 34(1), (4) and Sch 2 Part II

[629] Powers of Criminal Courts (Sentencing) Act 2000 s 143(6)-(7)

[630] Powers of Criminal Courts (Sentencing) Act 2000 s 130(1)(b)

[631] Sexual Offences Act 2003 s 103A as inserted by Anti-social Behaviour, Crime and Policing Act 2014 Sch 5 para 2 and Sexual Offences Act 2003 Sch 5

[632] Safeguarding Vulnerable Groups Act 2006 s 2 and Sch 3 and Safeguarding Vulnerable Groups Act 2006 (Prescribed Criteria and Miscellaneous Provisions) Regulations 2009 2009/37 regs 4 and 6 and Sch para 2 and 4

[633] Safeguarding Vulnerable Groups Act 2006 s 2 and Sch 3 para 25

Statistics and guidelines
284.2   *Crown Court statistics   England and Wales*
Manslaughter

Year	Sex	Age	Plea	Total sen-tenced	Type of sentencing %						Aver-age length of custody in months
					Dis-charge	Fine	Com-munity sen-tence	Sus-pended sen-tence	Cus-tody	Oth-er	
2013	Male	18-20	G	14	–	–	–	–	85.7	14.3	83.5
			NG	2	–	–	–	–	100	–	90
		21+	G	95	–	–	–	2.1	89.5	8.4	102.2
			NG	34	–	–	–	–	97.1	2.9	82.4
	Female	18-20	G	0							
			NG	0							
		21+	G	6	–	–	–	16.7	83.3	–	92
			NG	7	–	–	–	14.3	85.7	–	129
2014	Male	18-20	G	17	–	–	–	–	100	–	99.4
			NG	1	–	–	–	–	100	–	Not listed[634]
		21+	G	75	–	–	–	–	87	13	97.1
			NG	36	–	–	–	3	94	3	96.9
	Female	18-20	G	3	–	–	–	33	33	33	Not listed
			NG	1	–	–	–	.	100	–	Not listed
		21+	G	10	–	–	–	10	80	10	61.5
			NG	2	–	–	–	–	100	–	Not listed

Manslaughter due to diminished responsibility Aged 21+

Year	Plea	Total sentenced	Type of sentencing %						Average length of custody in months
			Dis-charge	Fine	Commu-nity sentence	Sus-pended sentence	Custody	Other	
2013	G	14	–	–	–	–	42.9	57.1	–
	NG	0							
2014	G	9	–	–	–	11	22	67	Not listed[635]
	NG	0							

For explanations about the statistics see page 1-xii. For more statistics and for statistics for male and female defendants and for causing or allowing the death of a child, see www.banksr.com Other Matters Statistics tab

284.3   *Judicial guidance*
R v Butler 1999 2 Cr App R (S) 339 Little use is gained in sentencing in manslaughter cases from an exhaustive view of the authorities since it is clear that this Court has repeatedly said that sentencing in manslaughter cases is: a) very difficult and b) turns on the particular facts of the case under consideration.
R v Barker 2002 EWCA Crim 3070, 2003 2 Cr App R (S) 22 (p 110) Manslaughter cases of this kind (gross negligence) are very difficult because the court is sentencing for

---

[634] 'Not listed' means the statistic was based on too few cases to be meaningful
[635] Based on too few cases to be meaningful

consequences the defendant did not intend. The public interest requires the imposition of a prison sentence where lives are taken in these circumstances. (For more details, see the 4th edition of this book.)

R v Clarke 2005 EWCA Crim 3047, 2006 1 Cr App R (S) 132 (p 768) The defendant pleaded to manslaughter. Held. The taking of innocent life is always very serious, especially when it is done in the course of committing crime, but the level of culpability for the act of causing death must be distinguished from the general level of culpability for the other underlying offence.

R v Briggs 2007 EWCA Crim 452, 2 Cr App R (S) 67 (p 425) The defendant was convicted of manslaughter. Held. One of the factors highly relevant in cases of involuntary manslaughter is the degree of risk of death or serious injury inherent in the defendant's conduct.

Att-Gen's Ref Nos 60, 62-63 of 2009 2009 EWCA Crim 2693, 2010 2 Cr App R (S) 46 (p 311)[636] LCJ (five-judge court) We reconsider the approach to sentencing in cases of manslaughter when, notwithstanding that the defendant intended neither to kill nor to cause the deceased grievous bodily harm, he is convicted of manslaughter on the basis that the death was consequent on an act of unlawful violence. They cannot be sentenced as if it was murder. If the defendant is convicted of manslaughter, the consequences must be treated as if they were unintentional, and unintended crimes which result in death should be treated more seriously, not so as to equate the sentencing in unlawful act manslaughter with the sentence levels suggested in Criminal Justice Act 2003 Sch 21, but so as to ensure that the increased focus on the fact that a victim has died in consequence of an unlawful act of violence, even where the conviction is for manslaughter, should, in accordance with the legislative intention, be given greater weight. For more detail see **284.50**.

Att-Gen's Ref No 125 of 2010 2011 EWCA Crim 640, 2 Cr App R (S) 97 (p 534) LCJ The *dicta* above apply equally to the manslaughter of babies and children as they do to disorder in the street.

R v Thompson 2014 EWCA Crim 2892 D pleaded to manslaughter on the basis of diminished responsibility. This Court in *R v Wood* 2009 EWCA Crim 651, 2010 1 Cr App R (S) 2 (p 6) and the subsequent authorities has made it plain that a large disproportion between sentences for murder and sentences for manslaughter which came close to murder would be inimical to the administration of justice.

Att-Gen's Ref Nos 107-108 of 2014 2015 EWCA Crim 405 Since *Att-Gen's Ref Nos 160, 62-3 of 2009* (see above), particular regard must be had to the dreadful consequences of manslaughter and as a result sentences have increased in recent years.

Att-Gen's Ref No 36 of 2015 2015 EWCA Crim 1174 D was convicted of manslaughter. Held. para 16 *Att-Gen's Ref Nos 60, 62 and 63 of 2009* (see above) signals a clear change to the approach to sentence in unlawful act manslaughter cases. There is to be an upward movement in sentences to reflect the new focus on harm under Criminal Justice Act 2003 s 143, the sentencing regime for offences of murder contained in Schedule 21, and the sterner approach in cases involving the carrying of knives and other weapons, see *R v Povey* 2008 EWCA Crim 1261, 2009 1 Cr App R (S) 42 (p 228). para 25 There is now a much greater focus on the fact a death has been caused. For more details see **284.40**.

For other guidelines, see the ***Diminished responsibility*** para at **284.24** and ***Loss of control*** para at **284.46**.

---

[636] The judgment refers to the case as *R v Appleby* 2009 EWCA Crim 2693.

Factors and the factual basis for sentencing

284.4   *Body, Dismembering and disposing of the*
Manslaughter by Reason of Provocation Guideline 2005, see www.banksr.com Other
Matters Guidelines tab page 1 Foreword This guideline is for use where the conviction
for manslaughter is clearly founded on provocation alone.
page 6 para 3.6 Concealment or attempts to dispose of evidence or dismemberment of
the body may aggravate the offence.
page 10 Additional aggravating factors: 1 Concealment or attempts to dispose of
evidence 2 Dismemberment or mutilation of the body.
R v Masefield 2012 EWCA Crim 1873, 2013 1 Cr App R (S) 77 (p 426) LCJ D pleaded
to manslaughter. In 1987, then aged 19, he struck a friend, V, over the head with a metal
pole after an argument. V died. D then wrapped V's body in bed sheets and pushed it
into a sewage pipe under a manhole cover in the garden. About three months later
council workers tried to clear the blockage and V's body was found. Unfortunately the
council workers had inadvertently used 'robust methods', which masked the fatal injury.
About a month later, D was interviewed and denied being involved. He did, however,
refer to the bickering between V and his brother, B. B was arrested for different reasons
and a number of his family thought B was responsible and turned completely against
him. In 2010, in a drunken conversation with H, D said he had killed V. B heard about it
and went to the police. D was interviewed and again denied involvement. Meanwhile H
died. In 2011, D approached the police and confessed. D, aged (presumably) 44 at
appeal, had previous convictions including in 1985 an assault with intent to rob when he
used a three-foot pole to demand money in a shop. There was also a battery in which D
kicked his son and a burglary in 2011. A basis of plea said D had not aimed at V's head
and there was a single blow. B said that D had wrecked 25 years of his life. The Judge
considered the most serious aggravating factor was the cover-up, which lasted many
years. Held. The following were serious aggravating factors: a) V was to an extent
vulnerable and killed in his own home, b) a weapon was used (although it was not taken
there), and c) D had disposed of the body in the most appalling way with a total lack of
respect for V, d) B and his sister spoke of how [the disposal] had affected them and
because of D's lies suspicion fell on B, and e) D must have known the anguish this had
caused. If D had been charged with obstructing the coroner or perverting the course of
justice he could have expected a very substantial sentence, see *R v Lang* 2001 EWCA
Crim 2690, 2002 2 Cr App R (S) 15 (p 44), where a sentence of 6 years was imposed.
The Judge was right to apply *R v H* 2011 EWCA Crim 2753, 2012 2 Cr App R (S) 21
(p 88). With late plea and modest mitigation **11½ years** was well merited.)
Note: In *R v Lang* 2001, the Court reduced an 8-year sentence to 6 years for perverting
the course of justice in a drug-related gang case. The victim was killed with a shotgun
and the defendant dug a grave and buried the victim. The grave was covered over with a
patio. The plea was late and the defendant was aged 33 with a previous conviction for
possession of a firearm for which he received 4½ years. The Judge found that D was
involved in professional organised crime. This was all very different from the facts in
R v Masefield 2012. For more details about *R v Lang* 2001, see the 7th edition of this
book. Ed.
See also the **MURDER** *Body, Disposal, moving, concealment, dismembering etc*. para at
288.21.

284.5   *Factual basis, dangerous offenders and the jury's verdict*
Manslaughter by Reason of Provocation Guideline 2005, see www.banksr.com Other
Matters Guidelines tab page 9 para 1 Sentences for public protection <u>must</u> be considered
in all cases of manslaughter.
R v Brook 2012 EWCA Crim 136, 2 Cr App R (S) 76 (p 433) D was convicted of
manslaughter on the basis of provocation. The attack was ferocious and relentless. D had
no convictions. The pre-sentence report concluded D was a 'dangerous' offender. Held.

para 14 The Judge was bound to make the assumption that the defendant's loss of control was reasonable in all the circumstances. It is therefore difficult to see how loss of control could provide the basis for a 'significant risk'. The analysis in the pre-sentence report was compelling but in critical respects it was wholly inconsistent with the jury's verdict. IPP quashed.

284.6   Multiple deaths

R v Hussain 2004 EWCA Crim 763, 2 Cr App R (S) 93 (p 497) D pleaded to conspiracy to commit arson and was convicted of conspiracy to commit arson with intent to endanger life and eight counts of manslaughter. D had four co-accused. He and others had made petrol bombs, and D had obtained the petrol. One of the co-accused wanted to attack one of the victims who had been telling tales about his relationship with a girlfriend. In the early hours of the morning D and others drove to the house where the victim was, and two of the co-accused threw the petrol bombs at the house. In the subsequent fire eight people died: a woman, her daughter, a student and girls aged between 6 months and 13 years. Four other people escaped the fire. The Judge said that the offences of manslaughter came very close to murder, and that no one who heard the evidence of family members who saw the fire would ever forget it. Further, it was a gross understatement to say that the surviving family members were devastated. Held. The Judge was bound to have regard to the number of persons unlawfully killed. This was manslaughter in horrific circumstances involving eight persons. It could not be argued that **18 years** for the manslaughter charges and a concurrent 14 years for the conspiracy to commit arson were manifestly excessive.

Note: This case is old. The sentence is, if anything, on the low side when compared with sentencing today. Ed.

Old case: *R v Ren and Others* 2006 Times News 29/3/06 and Internet sites (Crown Court. Cockler gangmaster convicted of 21 counts of manslaughter when 21 cockle pickers died in rising tides at Morecambe. **14 years** in total.)

See also the **MURDER** *Multiple murders* paras at **288.50**.

284.7   Racially or religiously aggravated

An example: *Att-Gen's Ref No 78 of 2006* 2006 EWCA Crim 2793, 2007 1 Cr App R (S) 114 (p 699) (Aged 20. Pleaded. Offence with racist remarks. Should have had a starting point of **2½ years** with a 9-month racist uplift making **3 years 3 months'** detention. As it was a reference, 3 years)

284.8   Uncertainty over jury's verdict

R v Cawthorne 1996 2 Cr App R (S) 445 There were three bases for this manslaughter conviction: insufficient intent, provocation or gross negligence. The foreman was asked if he wanted to indicate the basis and he declined. The Judge sentenced D on the basis of lack of sufficient intent. Held. It was quite proper for the foreman to decline. Having considered the authorities, we are quite clear that whether the judge asks is entirely a matter for the trial judge's discretion. In many cases the judge will not wish to do so, and doing so will throw an unnecessary additional burden on the jury. In a case like the present, and there are many other cases of this nature, there are grave dangers in asking juries. For example, they may not all have reached the verdict by the same route. The Judge was entitled to decide the basis of the sentence.

R v Bowen 2001 1 Cr App R (S) 82 (p 282) The jury was not asked which basis it was. The Judge did not indicate whether it was provocation or lack of sufficient intent. Held. It was for the Court of Appeal to decide.

R v Byrne 2002 EWCA Crim 1979, 2003 1 Cr App R (S) 68 (p 338) The defendant's case in his murder trial was there was a lack of intent. The Judge left the issue of provocation to the jury. The jury convicted of manslaughter, and the Judge decided it was not appropriate to ask them for the basis of their verdict. Held. The Judge was entitled not to ask, and decided that the basis of the verdict was provocation. The Judge has a duty to explain his decision, and it would have been better if he had gone into greater detail. The sentence was upheld.

R v Bertram 2003 EWCA Crim 2026, 2004 1 Cr App R (S) 27 (p 185) The judge is not bound to accept the most favourable version to the defence. The judge should carefully apply the criminal standard of proof and give the defendant the benefit of any doubt.

284.9   *Victim dies after defendant sentenced for the violence*

R v Owen 2009 EWCA Crim 702, 2 Cr App R (S) 738 In December 2008 D pleaded to manslaughter. In 2000, he caused serious injuries to a baby by shaking her. She was starved of oxygen, had four-limb spasticity, was unable to be fed and required constant attention. D pleaded to section 20 and was sentenced to 3 years. He was warned by the Judge that if the baby died he faced a return to prison. In 2007, the baby died. The Judge indicated that had it been manslaughter to start with, the sentence would have been 4 to 5 years. The defence argued that since then D had turned his life round, and there was no point in sending him back to prison. Held. The purpose was to mark the death of the baby and to punish him not only for destroying her quality of life, for causing her years of pain and misery, but also killing her. **1 year** upheld.

See also the **DEATH BY DRIVING: GENERAL PRINCIPLES** *Victim dies after defendant dealt with for dangerous driving* para at **235.16**.

284.10   *Victim's health precarious/Eggshell skull/Victim not expected to die*

R v Harrison 1996 2 Cr App R (S) 250 A blow sufficient to fracture an eggshell skull is very much less culpable than one which fractures a normal skull.

Note: This means that the sentencing factor is the force of the blow and not the victim's individual strengths or weaknesses. Ed.

R v Grad 2004 EWCA Crim 44, 2 Cr App R (S) 43 (p 218) D was convicted of manslaughter. He was with a group of friends at a nightclub on a balcony overlooking the club's beer garden. One of his group spat some beer over the balcony which landed on V, who was in a second group. There was verbal abuse between the two groups, and bottles and glasses were thrown by the second group towards the group on the balcony. Some witnesses said that glasses were thrown down from D's group. One of the glasses thrown up by the second group hit D and cut his head, which bled profusely. The security staff ushered D's group out of the club. One of the second group followed them because he wanted to continue with the confrontation. He shouted abuse outside but was then restrained by security staff. V had followed him out, not because he was looking for trouble but because he wanted to support his friend. D approached V and punched him once in the head (according to the witnesses) or the top of the neck (according to the scientific evidence). The punch was delivered with moderate force. V fell to the floor and was motionless. D did not play any part in any fighting save for that single punch. V died almost immediately. The medical evidence was that the cause of death was a very unusual combination of circumstances: a haemorrhage in the brain caused by the combination of the twisting of the neck by the blow, the angle of the blow and the dilation of the blood vessels caused by the victim's drinking. D and his friends had left the scene but when he heard of the death D surrendered voluntarily to the police. The prosecution said that the offence was as near to accident as a criminal offence could be. He was of previous good character. He had made a financial contribution to V's family, and there was a wide range of references showing that he had good business qualities and a bright future. There were letters showing that the companies he was involved with were suffering serious difficulties because of his imprisonment. He had shown genuine remorse. Held. The combination of factors which led to the death was very unusual. It was understandable that D did not plead guilty, having regard to the parties before the Court. This was a case where the seriousness of the offending must be marked by a custodial sentence. The appropriate sentence is at the very bottom of the bracket for this type of case. **9 months** substituted for 18 months.

R v Harvey 2010 EWCA Crim 1317, 2011 1 Cr App R (S) 42 (p 286) D pleaded early to manslaughter. The unlawful act was common assault. D, aged 47, was at home with his wife, V. They had been drinking and using a limited amount of cocaine. An argument flared up and D threw a television remote control which was not aimed at V. The remote control struck V just above her left ear. V died. Unknown to anyone, V had an unusual weakness of the vertebral artery and the blow had dissected the artery. The medical evidence said V could have died at any stage just from turning her head. D phoned for an ambulance immediately and did what he could to help. D had four convictions including for ABH in 1987, when he head-butted a police officer (1 month suspended), and for ABH in 2002 when he struck a guest at a party causing a fractured cheekbone. The Judge said this was an unintended death from unnecessary violence. Held. This was not a one-punch manslaughter but the intemperate throwing of a television remote control towards V. There was a streak of anger and violence within him. **21 months** not 3 years. See also the **MURDER** *Victim's health precarious/Eggshell skull/Victim not expected to die* para at **288.24**.

284.11   Victims, The views of the relatives of the
The law is most clearly stated in the cases about causing death by dangerous and careless driving.
See the **DEATH BY DRIVING: GENERAL PRINCIPLES** *Victims, The views of the relatives of the victim who was related to/was friendly with the deceased* para at **235.17** and the **VICTIMS** chapter in Volume 1.

Types of manslaughter
284.12   Bullying/Showing off etc.
Att-Gen's Ref Nos 64-65 of 2009 2009 EWCA Crim 2322, 2010 2 Cr App R (S) 8 (p 43) LCJ T and G were convicted of manslaughter and acquitted of murder. They and others were celebrating the Nepalese New Year on a boat moored on the Thames embankment. By 4 am everyone had had a great deal to drink. V was responsible for an argument and he swore and pushed a young woman who was a cousin of T. T verbally intervened. V's associate, B, struck T on the head with a bottle. The force was as hard as B could manage and T suffered a large cut on the head which bled copiously and required eight stitches. Friends of T, including G, pursued V thinking he had caused the wound. They chased him and V was brought down and punched and kicked. He was not badly hurt but was dazed. V was incapable of further retaliation. T then joined the group and suggested throwing V in the river. T, G and others bundled him over the waist-high embankment and V fell into the river and drowned. V's mother, a widow, was devastated by the loss of her only son. T was aged under 21 and G aged just 20. Their fathers were both Gurkha soldiers of the highest standards. They were both studying with a view to being accountants. Each was of good character. They accepted responsibility and showed profound remorse. Held. The act was very dangerous, best described as an instant unjustified retaliation rather than revenge. It was reckless and aggravated by the fact no one went to V's aid. T and G had not started the altercation. One was very seriously injured and the other had seen his friend injured. The offence was miles out of character, committed by persons who are otherwise wholly to be recommended. The year's wait for their murder trial cannot be ignored. The offence might call for a sentence significantly beyond the **3 years** given. On paper it was worth something like **4-5 years**. In some circumstances it was permissible to pass a merciful sentence. The Judge was deliberately lenient and merciful and the sentence was not varied.
R v Steanson 2010 EWCA Crim 1306 D pleaded to manslaughter. D was in a relationship with B, the father of her two-year-old son. B lived in a bail hostel and D spent the afternoon there with him and others. D challenged V, a resident of the hostel, as she was convinced that V had taken heroin in front of her son. D demanded that B challenge V. B went into V's room and gave V a severe beating. V had extensive bruising to his eyes, ears, jaw, neck and wrists. M came into the room followed by his girlfriend,

S, and then D. M joined B in the assault, kicking V. M's girlfriend tried to stop M without success and left the room. When she came back M and B were laughing and thought V was dead. They discussed hiding the body and moved V's body outside. B and M attacked V again, punching and kicking him. D joined them outside. All those involved then returned to the room, cleaned up the blood, tried to remove blood from their clothes or hid them. V's cause of death was significant head wounds. He had many blunt trauma injuries caused by kicking or stamping and stab wounds. In interview D lied. D, aged 25, was of good character and expressed regret. She had three children. B pleaded to murder. The Judge said D had lit the spark for this fatal violence. Held. The appropriate starting point was 8 years, not 12. **6 years** not 8.

Old case: *Att-Gen's Ref Nos 27-28 of 2008* 2008 EWCA Crim 2027, 2009 1 Cr App R (S) 87 (p 521) **(7½ years)**

For a summary of the case, see the 9th edition of this book.

See also the **MURDER** *Bullying/Showing off etc.* para at **288.29** and the **OFFENCES AGAINST THE PERSON ACT 1861 S 18** *Bullying/Showing off* para at **292.9**.

284.13   *Burglars/Robbers/Thieves, By*

R v Wingfield 2013 EWCA Crim 2274 D pleaded to manslaughter and robbery. V1 went to sleep in her house with her two-year-old son and a female friend. At almost 1 am, D and three others broke into the property by kicking in the door. D and one other walked into V1's bedroom and said "Give me your money or I'll cut your fingers off". He was opening and closing a lock knife as he made the threat. D also threatened to "tear the house apart". V1 shouted at the men and one of the others shouted back "Shut your fucking mouth, I'll cut your fingers off". The group took V1's car keys and a small amount of money. As they were leaving, D shouted "If you ring the police, there's not just me. There's other boys will come back for you. They'll kill you." He demanded and took the mobile phones from the women and drove away in V1's car. D altered the registration plates of the car.

V2 was aged 42. He used his house to sell crack cocaine for the two years prior to his death. D, W and R drove to V2's address in V1's car. W had a gun and a bayonet with him. All three had knives. They had previously spoken about 'taxing' drug dealers through extortion. D knocked on the door and V2 answered. W and R appeared and there was a struggle. W produced the gun and it was discharged. The bullet travelled through D's forearm and hit V2, passing through his throat and spinal canal. W went inside and returned with drugs and money. The three then escaped in V1's car. V2 was taken to hospital in a critical but stable condition. However, complications arose and he subsequently died. The three took steps to conceal their tracks and disposed of V1's car. D was arrested 'as a result of another episode' and admitted his involvement early on.

He indicated a willingness to enter into a formal agreement but in the meantime entered a defence case statement. The police declined to treat him as a formal informant but D decided to speak to them voluntarily. The case was listed for trial. The police were able to trace W as a result of D's information. D accepted the Crown's case regarding the robbery and entered a basis of plea regarding the manslaughter. The basis was that he was party to a joint enterprise to rob V2 of drugs and money. He foresaw the possibility that V2 would be caused some harm but did not foresee or agree to the infliction of grievous or fatal injury. That was accepted. V1 recognised D as a friend of a friend. She felt unable to identify him until after his arrest and was so frightened that she abandoned her house and moved to a new address. This was at a considerable cost. She also suffered greatly diminished trust and greatly raised anxiety. D was aged 23 at appeal and had previous convictions for much less serious matters. He had never been to custody. Held. The Judge's starting point was to be inferred as 23 years. Having reviewed the authorities, the appropriate starting point was 21-22 years. The 10% credit for the plea, as given by the Judge, was correct. There was also credit to be given for D's co-operation and it was appropriate to mark a distinction between D and R, who was older and had a far worse record. For D, starting at 21 to 22 years, the plea reduced the sentence to **19 years**. With credit for the co-operation, 17 years for the manslaughter, not 20. The consecutive sentence of 5 years for the robbery remained. **22 years** not 25.

R v Garner 2014 EWCA Crim 926 D pleaded to manslaughter and attempted robbery after her jury was sworn (10% credit). There were a series of robberies on a towpath where gay men met for casual sex. In the early hours, V1 was robbed of a packet of cigarettes by C and M. V2 and V3 came to V1's assistance. V2 was stamped on and V3 was thrown into the canal but managed to get out. B and S joined the group and pursued V4. The group then left but returned. The group followed V5 and tried to rob him. That was frustrated and V5 was pushed in the canal. B admitted that V5 shouted, "I can't swim." B fled, followed by D. The whole group ran off. V5 drowned and V3 suffered injuries. D was sentenced on the basis that she was present when B was pushed into the canal and encouraged others to intimidate V5. D was aged 21 and had 27 previous convictions including a number of robberies and attempted robberies. One was committed after the canal death. The Judge commented that: a) the men who visited the area were vulnerable because those who preyed on them did so knowing that they were unlikely to complain because of their situation, b) the robberies were in the dark, and the group created fear and were prepared to use violence, and c) D had been treated leniently before and she had not responded to that. C was given a 13-year extended sentence (10 years' custody 3 years' extended licence). M received 9 years' detention in a YOI. Held. There was evidence [that] robberies were unreported in this area. D lent support and added to the threat by her presence. The Judge drew the inference [that] D heard V5's cry as well as B. It was callous to abandon V5 in the canal. **10 years** upheld.

See also: *R v Delija* 2013 EWCA Crim 2735 (Convicted. Planned attack on elderly couple in bungalow by two men. Balaclava and ski mask worn and tied up victims. Husband repeatedly beaten to find out where keys to safe were. Keys found and safe opened. Substantial amount of cash taken. Threats to kill made. Imprisoned for best part of half an hour. Wife bound with tape. Husband suffered from significant heart disease and died. **20 years** at the top of the range but justified.)

Old cases: *Att-Gen's Ref Nos 38-40 of 2007* 2007 EWCA Crim 1692, 2008 1 Cr App R (S) 56 (p 319) (**5 years'** detention) *Att-Gen's Ref Nos 32-35 of 2010* 2010 EWCA Crim 2900, 2011 2 Cr App R (S) 32 (p 200)[637] (For J, **18 years** For M, **DPP** with a minimum term of **6 years** consecutive to the earlier mandatory life for murder. For O, **9 years'** detention)

For a summary of the first case, see the 9th edition of this book and for the last case see the 10th edition.

284.14   Cannibalism
R v Bryan 2006 EWCA Crim 379, 2 Cr App R (S) 66 (p 436) see **284.71**.
See also the **MURDER** *Cannibalism* para at **288.30**.

284.15   Child victims   Causing the death of a child
Domestic Violence, Crime and Victims Act 2004 s 5 (causing or allowing the death of a child or vulnerable adult)
Domestic Violence, Crime and Victims (Amendment) Act 2012 extended section 5 to include victims who 'suffer serious physical harm'. In force 2/7/12.[638]
Mode of trial Indictable only
Maximum sentence 14 years
Automatic life Section 5 is listed in Criminal Justice Act 2003 Sch 15B Part 1. The Lord Chief Justice said in *Att-Gen's Ref No 27 of 2013* 2014 EWCA Crim 334[639] para 8 iii) (*obiter*) that in rare cases the provisions could lead to the imposition of a life sentence where the offence does not carry life imprisonment.

---

[637] The transcript lists the case as *R v Jumah and Others* 2010, which is in error.
[638] Domestic Violence, Crime and Victims (Amendment) Act 2012 (Commencement) Order 2012 2012/1432
[639] This case is also known as *R v Burinskas* 2014 EWCA Crim 334.

The court must (unless the particular circumstances make it unjust)[640] pass automatic life if: a) the defendant is aged 18+ at the date of the conviction, b) the offence was committed on or after 3 December 2012, c) the court considers a determinate sentence of at least 10 years is appropriate, d) at the time the offender was convicted he had a conviction for a Criminal Justice Act 2003 Sch 15B offence, and e) the defendant at the time of his or her conviction had previously been sentenced to either: i) a life sentence where he or she was not eligible for release during the first five years of the sentence or ii) a determinate sentence or extended sentence where the custodial part was 10 years or more.[641] For a pre-2012 extended sentence, when determining whether the custodial term was 10+ years the period deducted for time on remand or on a curfew and tag is included.[642]

Extended sentences This offence is listed in Criminal Justice Act 2003 Sch 15 (as amended). The court may pass a 2012 extended sentence (EDS) if there is a significant risk of serious harm from future specified offences and either: a) the defendant has a Criminal Justice Act 2003 Sch 15B conviction (applicable only to defendants aged 18+), or b) the offence would justify a determinate sentence of at least 4 years.[643]

Sexual Harm Prevention Orders There is a discretionary power to make this order when it is necessary to protect the public from sexual harm.[644]

Children and vulnerable adults: barred lists see the VULNERABLE GROUPS: BARRING chapter in Volume 1.

284.16   *Causing death of a child etc.   Statistics*
Causing death of a child or vulnerable person

	2011		2012	2013		2014	
Plea	1 pleaded	1 convicted	Not available	1 pleaded	3 con- victed	2 pleaded	4 convicted
Sen- tence	Suspended Sentence Order	36 months		48 months	84 months (aver- age)	Not listed as based on too few cases to be meaningful	

284.17   *Causing the death of a child   Judicial guidance*
R v Ikram and Parveen 2008 EWCA Crim 586, 2 Cr App R (S) 114 (p 648) Both defendants were convicted of causing or allowing the death of a child (Domestic Violence, Crime and Victims Act 2004 s 5). Held. A conviction means it has been established that the defendant had failed to protect the victim and that he or she either appreciated or ought to have appreciated that there was significant risk that the victim would endure serious harm at the hands of the ultimate perpetrator in circumstances which that defendant foresaw or ought to have foreseen. Its link with manslaughter is clear and the general approach to sentencing in manslaughter cases provides useful assistance to the court in sentencing. Neither was to be sentenced as the perpetrator, both were to be sentenced for allowing the perpetrator to act as he or she did.
For more details of this case, see the next paragraph.

284.18   *Causing the death of a child   Cases*
R v Ikram and Parveen 2008 EWCA Crim 586, 2 Cr App R (S) 114 (p 648) Ik and P were convicted of causing or allowing the death of a child. V was Ik's 16-month-old son

---

[640] Criminal Justice Act 2003 s 224A(2)

[641] Criminal Justice Act 2003 s 224A as inserted by Legal Aid, Sentencing and Punishment of Offenders Act 2012 s 122. The condition for a) is at section 224A(1)(a), for b) is at section 224A(1)(b), for c) is at section 224A(1)(c), and for d) is at section 224A(4)-(9).

[642] Criminal Justice Act 2003 s 224A(9)-(10)

[643] Criminal Justice Act 2003 s 226A-226B as inserted by Legal Aid, Sentencing and Punishment of Offenders Act 2012 s 124

[644] Sexual Offences Act 2003 s 103A as inserted by Anti-social Behaviour, Crime and Policing Act 2014 Sch 5 para 2 and Sexual Offences Act 2003 Sch 5

by his former wife. V lived with Ik and P, who had one child from a previous relationship and one with Ik.[645] P had expressed some hostility to V. On 14 August he was taken to hospital with a fracture of the left tibia. He also had some bruising. His leg was put in plaster. He was taken to hospital a number of times thereafter with problems with the plaster. It was replaced four times, three times because it had come loose. On 2 September Ik took V to hospital because he had blood coming from behind the cast, and a further cast was fitted. On 4 September he attended the hospital for a follow-up appointment and he seemed comfortable. On 5 September he was found apparently lifeless in his cot. Ik called the emergency services. The cause of death was a pulmonary fat embolism resulting from a recent fracture to the left femur. In addition he had a deep hole in the back of his knee and 21 other injuries which were not more than 48 hours old, including abrasions and bruises to various parts of his face and body and an injury to his thumb. There were three recently fractured ribs. He had an indented blackened lesion about two days old consistent with a burn from a lighted cigarette. The fracture of the femur had probably been caused when the femur was grabbed around the knee joint and exposed to an extensive range of movement. It took considerable force to break it. The injuries and abrasions on the face and under the chin were consistent 'with grappling and fingernails from either impact or gripping'. The expert's opinion was that he had been subject to repetitive inflicted trauma. The original broken tibia had probably been broken some days before he was taken to hospital on 14 August, not on that day. The defendants were arrested and interviewed, and both maintained that V had been well when put to bed on 5 September. Subsequently they gave various accounts, including that V had fallen off a chair, and that P had fallen downstairs holding him. Ik had previously been cautioned for child neglect (leaving V alone asleep at home when he was 11 months old). **Held.** There was compelling evidence that V's multiple injuries were the result of deliberate and repeated violence. There was a brutal attack on V. The death occurred in circumstances which were close to murder or manslaughter of the most serious kind. Whichever defendant deliberately fractured V's femur, the other allowed it to occur without taking steps to protect him from awful foreseeable violence. The Judge was not able to discern any meaningful distinction between the defendants. This conclusion is critical to any sentencing decision in cases like these and must always be regarded as case-specific. **9 years' imprisonment** for both, though severe, upheld.

R v Vestuto 2010 EWCA Crim 721, 2 Cr App R (S) 108 (p 682) D pleaded early to causing or allowing the death of a child and cruelty to a child. D and her partner had two children. R was aged 18 months and Z was aged three years. D told a neighbour she had given R some medicine to help him sleep. R was sweating profusely, was in distress and relatives were worried about him. R cried for about an hour, then in the early hours R woke up distressed, went back to sleep then woke again screaming. D alerted her partner, who called an ambulance. D attempted to resuscitate R (whose condition presumably had deteriorated). Paramedics found R to be grey, silent and without a pulse. R was not breathing and did not respond to resuscitation attempts. He was pronounced dead in hospital. A post-mortem concluded R's cause of death was poisoning by Amitriptyline, an anti-depressant and sedative. The traces found were ten times the therapeutic dose for an adult. Further testing showed use of the drug over a period of time. Tests were carried out on Z and low traces of Amitriptyline were found in his hair samples. R had been exposed to a number of sedatives and painkillers in the weeks and possibly months leading to his death. In interview D lied. D, aged 28, had no convictions. The pre-sentence report said D was 'borderline intelligent', was an isolated individual, had limited support networks, had been placed on the child protection register as a child due to neglect and physical abuse, and struggled to accept responsibility for her actions. The prison report said D was a difficult prisoner, she bullied other prisoners and had another baby whilst in prison, which had been taken away. The Judge

---

[645] Assuming there is an error about the dates.

said this was a planned, ordered and controlled administration of the drug to the children. Held. This was a sustained, determined, persistent course of cruel conduct towards two helpless children. D was callous and controlling, her family expressed concerns and she did not ask for assistance. **6 years** upheld.

Old cases: *R v Khan* 2009 EWCA Crim 2 (**2 years**) *R v Brown* 2009 EWCA Crim 2133 (**6 years**)

284.19   *Child victims   Neglect, starvation etc.*

R v H 2009 EWCA Crim 397, 2 Cr App R (S) 90 LCJ D pleaded to manslaughter of her daughter T (based on gross neglect) and to cruelty to her child, E. D lived with her husband, H, and they ran a pub. T was born in September 2004, and D and H had a son, E, born in October 2006. Shortly after E's birth a midwife called, and H said that he did not have access to the living quarters. D returned, and the midwife found E dressed only in a nappy. He was cold, screaming and crying uncontrollably. D was given firm advice particularly about not leaving the children alone. T was not fed properly during a number of different periods. E was cared for a little better but was kept in conditions of squalor and deprivation. T and E were left unattended for long periods while D and H worked and went out. Throughout T's life there were periods when she was not fed at all. Visitors etc. recalled numerous occasions when the children were left alone. D and H made colourful excuses, and D told repeated lies. Two people heard a noise and went upstairs and found the children poorly dressed, fending for themselves, while D and H were out. They spoke to D and after that the door to the living quarters was kept securely locked when they went out. During T's last few days no one appeared to have looked after T at all. D was preoccupied with the pub and other business. She expressed concerns for the health of her dogs. CCTV picked up D talking to H, who said, "We've fucked it all up". They talked about being arrested and expressed concern just for themselves. H said, "Look at the state of her, she has obviously been dead for two days". A few hours later D called the emergency services saying that her daughter was dead. Ambulance men found T with clear signs of decomposition. The living quarters were filthy, squalid, unsafe and a serious health hazard in a number of ways. The rooms were full of highly dangerous electrical hazards. There were dog faeces and other excrement where the children were. T's growth and development were retarded. A post-mortem found T significantly underweight. In October 2005 she weighed 8.3 kilos. In September 2007 she weighed 9 kilos. Medical evidence suggested that T had neither food nor water for at least 20 hours before she died. It was considered that she had died two to three days before the phone call. D was an intelligent woman of good character. She had ample funds. Her pre-sentence report said that she was in denial. Held. The photographs indicate truly appalling, abject squalor. The children suffered from systemic neglect. It was a case of dreadful cruelty beyond comprehension. T was starved to a lonely, unloved death. D was neither inadequate nor disturbed. Her conduct was inexplicable. **12 years** was not manifestly excessive.

R v Reeves 2012 EWCA Crim 2613, 2013 2 Cr App R (S) 21 (p 129) D pleaded (25% credit) to gross negligence manslaughter. She was at home with her two children, one aged 2½ years, the other aged 12 months. She left them in the bath secured to a safety seat while she went outside to speak to some of her neighbours. She was tipsy but not drunk. She remained outside for a period of 45 minutes, occasionally looking back inside the flat but not into the bathroom. At one point the older child began to scream but D shouted at him to be quiet. There was evidence that D had told the boy to turn the tap on to entertain himself. Eventually, D returned to the bathroom and emerged moments later holding the younger child screaming that he had had a fit. Neighbours then realised that he had been in the bath. They tried to resuscitate him. The emergency services were summoned. D was hysterical and unhelpful. The child was taken to hospital but died on the same day. The causes of death were cerebral hypoxia (lack of oxygen to the brain), cardiac arrest and immersion. D's basis of plea stated that although the child was secured in his safety seat he was unsupervised for a period of 40-50 minutes and that during that period she was in the kitchen and from time to time outside speaking with neighbours. She asserted that she was not drunk but had been drinking. D was aged 24 at appeal and of effective good character. The surviving child was being cared for by his father by order of the Family Court. A pre-sentence report spoke of D's need to address her drug and alcohol misuse. It stated that D took full responsibility for the neglect and subsequent death of her child. Held. The child was left alone for around 45 minutes in a bath which had either been over-filled by D or had become over-filled by D's instructions to the older child. The facts by definition show great harm and the culpability is high. D's actions were counter-intuitive. There were clear warning signs on the baby's chair as to the appropriate water level. The older child's screams were ignored. The 25% credit given by the Judge was appropriate. **3 years 9 months** was a firm sentence, but was not manifestly excessive.

Old case: *R v Onley* 2004 EWCA Crim 1383, 2005 1 Cr App R (S) 26 (p 122) **(6 years' detention)**
For a summary of the case, see the 9th edition of this book.

284.20   Child victims   With violence
R v Abuhamza 2011 EWCA Crim 642 LCJ D and G pleaded to manslaughter of a child and five counts of cruelty to five more children (the dead child's brothers and sisters) during his second trial. G pleaded after D. After months of violent ill-treatment, six children aged between four and 12 suffered from malnutrition in a home which was full·of food. Until G became acquainted with A, there was evidence that she was a good mother. D moved in with G and immediately introduced into the household a strange routine. He took the children out of school despite them having special needs. D admitted to beating the children with a stick and sometimes sent them into a small garden shed. The children were also required to stand with their hands on their heads for up to an hour, or to stand in front of a coal fire. The surviving children alleged that punishments also included sitting in cold water or being sent out into the cold in the winter months. An ambulance was called when G discovered one of the children had died. She had severe malnutrition and 60 marks, many of which were the result of deliberate violence. D admitted to controlling the children's diet for disciplinary reasons. D suffered from schizophrenia and had suffered a psychotic episode leading up to the death. G had developed clinical depression exacerbated by D's psychotic episode. D was guilty by reason of diminished responsibility. G pleaded on the basis of unlawful conduct. The Judge dealt with the case as one of horrific cruelty, not being prepared to deal with it as a case of neglect. Further, the cruelty began before the mental impairment. Held. The ill-treatment of the children took two forms: one was deliberate starvation, the other was violent ill-treatment. The ill-treatment was of a most serious kind for five children in addition to the ill-treatment culminating in the death of a sixth. For D, **7½ years IPP** and for G **15 years**. There were concurrent sentences for the cruelty offence.

R v Thompson 2014 EWCA Crim 2892 D pleaded (full credit) to manslaughter on the basis of diminished responsibility. His marriage broke down but he continued to live with W, his wife. She bought out his share in the home and D paid W rent. V, their 11-year-old daughter, and D shared the same bedroom and he was exceptionally close to her. W started a new relationship with B and demanded D leave by 1 June 2013. He didn't and a new deadline of 1 July 2013 was given. In early June, W and B went on holiday together with V. On their return, tension in the house increased and D became distraught at the prospect of separation from V. On 21 June 2013, D told V's school she was ill. It was a lie and he took her to London Zoo for the day. They returned at 6 pm. Later that evening, he took a cord from her dressing gown and strangled her while she was asleep. He turned off the lights, secured the house and at 11.30 pm drove off in his car. About half an hour later, he drove his car into a tree at a speed of over 90 mph. He was badly injured and was taken to hospital. W phoned the hospital and D lied about the whereabouts of his daughter. When W visited D in hospital, he said V was at home. W, without warning, discovered V's body later. The three psychiatrists did not agree. One considered D suffered from Asperger's syndrome and was clinically depressed. Further he thought killing V was the only option to save her. Another said D had an abnormal personality with schizoid, avoidant and obsessive compulsive features. As a result, the applicant's emotional development was stunted and he had rigid, obsessional and inflexible thought. The third said D was in an extreme state of distress. Held. We start at 25 years, so with plea **17 years** not 20.

See also: *R v Burridge* 2011 EWCA Crim 2847 (D was convicted of murder and manslaughter was substituted on appeal. D's son, aged 8 weeks, stopped breathing and subsequently died. He suffered bleeding of the brain and broken ribs. Held. It was legitimate to infer that D inflicted the fatal injuries in temper and under stress. However, the offence was committed without premeditation or intent to kill. **10 years.**)

See also the **INFANTICIDE** chapter.

Control, Loss of see the *Loss of control* paras at **284.46**.

284.21   *Corporate manslaughter*

Corporate Manslaughter and Corporate Homicide Act 2007 s 1
Mode of trial Indictable only
Maximum sentence A fine

The Act enables the court to make a Remedial Order (Corporate Manslaughter and Corporate Homicide Act 2007 s 9) and a Publicity Order (Corporate Manslaughter and Corporate Homicide Act 2007 s 10), see the next paragraph.

284.22   *Corporate manslaughter   Guidelines*

Health and Safety Offences, Corporate Manslaughter and Food Safety and Hygiene Offences Guideline 2016, see www.banksr.com Other Matters Guidelines tab page 21 The guideline sets out the guidance over eight pages. Because of the length of the section and how rare these offences are prosecuted, the content is not listed.

284.23   *Corporate manslaughter guidelines*

Health and Safety Offences, Corporate Manslaughter and Food Safety and Hygiene Offences Guideline 2016, see www.banksr.com Other Matters Guidelines tab page 21 In force 1 February 2016

As these offences are so rare and the guideline so long, the details are not reproduced here. The guideline contains sections on determining the seriousness of the offence, the starting points and ranges, obtaining financial information, assessing whether the fine is proportionate and consideration of Publicity Orders, remediation and compensation.

One matter that survives from the old *Corporate Manslaughter and H and S Offences Causing Death Guideline 2010* page 3, see www.banksr.com Other Matters Guidelines tab is the basis of plea section.

Basis of plea

para 11 It will generally be appropriate to require the prosecution to set out in writing the facts of the case relied upon and any aggravating or mitigating features which it identifies.[646] The defence may conveniently be required similarly to set out in writing any points on which it differs. If sentence is to proceed upon agreed facts, they should be set out in writing.[647]

284.24   *Diminished responsibility*

Homicide Act 1957 s 2

Coroners and Justice Act 2009 s 52 substituted a new Homicide Act 1957 s 2(1).[648]

---

[646] Attorney-General's *Guidelines on the Acceptance of Pleas and the Prosecutor's Role in the Sentencing Exercise*, published November 2009, see www.banksr.com Other Matters Guidelines Attorney-General's guidelines section
[647] See *R v Friskies Petcare (UK) Ltd* 2000 EWCA Crim 95, 2 Cr App R (S) 401.
[648] In force 4/10/10, Coroners and Justice Act 2009 (Commencement No 4, Transitional and Saving Provisions) Order 2010 2010/816

284.25   *Diminished responsibility   Judicial guidance etc.*
Note: The diminished responsibility cases are distributed among the other paragraphs in this section. However, if there is a plea based on diminished responsibility, it means that D accepts that he or she intended to kill or cause GBH to the victim. Ed.
R v Limani 2013 EWCA Crim 1513 D pleaded to manslaughter by reason of diminished responsibility. The defence relied on the decision in *R v Wood* 2009 EWCA Crim 651, 2010 1 Cr App R (S) 2 (p 6) to argue the minimum term imposed was too long. Held. It is important to remember, however, that the offence in *R v Wood* 2009 occurred in 2005, the first trial in 2006 and the Court of Appeal hearing in April 2009. All predate the effect of Criminal Justice Act 2003 Sch 21 para 5A. From March 2010 onward, minimum terms for homicide were raised. It is difficult to conceive that the factual circumstances in *R v Wood* 2009 heard by a court today would have resulted in a similar term: first, it is overwhelmingly likely that the originally imposed term would have been very significantly higher, and second, the reduction would have been less.
Att-Gen's Ref No 34 of 2014 2014 EWCA Crim 1394, 2 Cr App R (S) 84 (p 649) D pleaded (full discount) to two counts of manslaughter (diminished responsibility). D said he would kill V1, his mother, and then attempt to commit suicide. [Presumably nothing happened.] D was hospitalised, having taken a cocktail of drugs and alcohol, but released after his mental state was assessed. Two days later he killed V1 with an axe in a premeditated attack. When V2 discovered what had happened, D killed her with the same axe. The killings were minutes apart. He also killed his dog with the same axe. D was later found in a very disturbed state. D was aged 24 at sentence and of good character. The Judge found that D had significant responsibility for the offences because they were based on the voluntary taking of LSD, which had triggered a vulnerability to psychosis. The Judge made a Hybrid Order with the sentence. Held. The aggravating factors were two victims, the significant degree of culpability, the clear intent to kill, a degree of premeditation and the use of the axe. A nuanced approach must be taken to Criminal Justice Act 2003 Sch 21 to reflect diminished responsibility. The same approach should also reflect the extent of the offender's residual culpability. The greater it is, the greater the impact of the Schedule 21 factors (which are used in murder cases) [will be]. Here, the serious aggravating factor of more than one intentional homicide should have its own impact on sentence. Starting with a 20-year minimum term, with plea, **13 years 4 months**, not 6 years.
Note: There is a problem here with using the murder guidelines for non-murder cases. If the Court thought a 20-year minimum term was appropriate, then the determinate term would have started at 40 years, which is significantly out of line with comparable cases. Ed.
R v Thompson 2014 EWCA Crim 2892 D pleaded to manslaughter on the basis of diminished responsibility. Held. In cases of diminished responsibility, a defendant's impairment may be so gross that his responsibility may be minimal; conversely, his impairment may be such that a substantial amount of mental responsibility remained. For details, see **284.20**.
See also: *R v Welsh* 2011 EWCA Crim 73 (Plea to manslaughter based on diminished responsibility. Took a knife to a party and for no reason stabbed victim in the neck. The issue was whether his responsibility for his actions was sufficient to justify a life sentence. Convictions for violence. Both prosecution and defence doctors recommended a Hospital Order. A Hospital Order with Restriction Order would not maintain public confidence. **Life imprisonment**.)
Old cases: Best ignored. Ed.
See also the ***Mentally disordered defendants As a mitigating factor*** para at **284.65**.

284.26   *Doctors killing patients Guideline remarks*
R v Kovvali 2013 EWCA Crim 1056, 2014 1 Cr App R (S) 33 (p 199) D pleaded to manslaughter. He failed to diagnose diabetes and the patient died. Held. *R v Holtom*

2010 EWCA Crim 934, 2011 1 Cr App R (S) 18 (p 128) indicated that there is now a greater emphasis on the fatal consequences of a criminal act for road death cases. Similar considerations would apply to cases of medical gross negligence.

284.27   Doctors killing patients   Cases

R v Garg 2012 EWCA Crim 2520, 2013 2 Cr App R (S) 30 (p 203) LCJ D pleaded (full credit) to gross negligence manslaughter. He was a highly qualified consultant urologist at a hospital. V, aged 37, was admitted to A&E on a Friday. She was healthy but complaining of abdominal pain and pain when passing urine. She was kept in over the weekend under D's care. D reviewed her condition over the weekend and it was decided that a procedure would be carried out on Monday morning. After the procedure, V suffered a cardiac arrest and died. After V's death, D changed the notes concerning V's care. He gave inaccurate information on the cremation certificate and as such the Coroner's Office was not alerted to the possibility that her death was as a result of neglect. No post mortem was carried out. D had disposed of a number of charts and notes and replaced documents which gave a different impression of V's care in order to conceal the true situation of V's condition. D, aged 44, was of positive good character. Held. There were the following failures: a) to ensure V's condition was properly identified, b) to identify or diagnose the possibility of closed renal infection/sepsis, c) to arrange urgent interventional treatment, d) to arrange a transfer to an appropriate hospital. So far as medical negligence is concerned, there will be more serious cases. The negligence was over a protracted period while V was in hospital. Had D not fallen significantly below the standards of accepted practice, the dangers would have been identified. The alteration of the records is an obvious aggravating feature. Starting at 3 years, as the Judge did, was appropriate. With full credit, **2 years** was not manifestly excessive.

See also: *R v Kovvali* 2013 EWCA Crim 1056, 2014 1 Cr App R (S) 33 (p 199) (Plea. Aged 65. Good character. Working as an out-of-hours locum doctor. Visited the victim after his condition worsened. Died from diabetic ketoacidosis. Didn't measure blood sugar. Failure to diagnose the condition was the main cause of death. Similar failure to check on another patient. Starting at **3 years** was not manifestly excessive. With 25% credit, **2½ years**.)

Old cases: Best ignored.

284.28   Drug abuse   Judicial guidance

R v Braybrooks 2002 EWCA Crim 2399, 2003 1 Cr App R (S) 114 (p 603) D was convicted of manslaughter. D injected the victim with heroin. Held. A clear pattern of sentences appears, with the court emphasising the need for stern, deterrent sentences where the supply of heroin is concerned, particularly in the circumstances which have led to death. The scope for mitigation may be limited. The authorities demonstrate that, after a trial, a sentence of **5 years** is appropriate in such cases.

R v Wilson 2007 EWCA Crim 1895, 2008 1 Cr App R (S) 75 (p 434) The authorities suggest a consistent approach of a sentence in the order of **5 years**, with a scaling down for plea and other mitigation.

284.29   Drug abuse   Cases

R v Finn 2010 EWCA Crim 1788, 2011 1 Cr App R (S) 70 (p 431) D pleaded to manslaughter and supplying heroin. J had been at D's home. She had been out drinking with D. D, who had an addiction to alcohol, was a recovering heroin addict and used prescribed methadone. D and J returned from drinking and D went alone to the bathroom in order to inject himself with heroin. J asked for some heroin to smoke, but there was none left in a smokable form. D initially refused to provide her with any. He subsequently acquiesced and agreed that she could have 20 ml of the remaining prepared solution. She asked if she could have the remaining 10 ml, making 30 ml. With some assistance from D, the heroin was injected into J and she immediately fell backwards onto the floor. D ran from the bathroom and instructed his wife to phone for an ambulance. When the police arrived he volunteered the comment, "I was the one who gave it to her". In interview he made the fullest admissions. J died in hospital. Before the Court there were statements declaring that J had broken free from her heroin addiction and had been drug-free for a considerable period of time. D maintained that he was unaware of this. D was truly remorseful. He had previous convictions for petty dishonesty but none for supplying drugs. Held. We accept that the Judge could not properly proceed on the basis that D knew that J was drug-free. He has always maintained that as far as he was concerned, she was still taking heroin. The Judge was in error in going above the conventional starting point of in the region of 5 years. It is only because of his full admissions in interview (and contrary to the legal advice that he received) that the full facts were known and indeed that a prosecution for manslaughter was able to be mounted. **3 years** not 4.

R v Phillips 2013 EWCA Crim 358, 2 Cr App R (S) 67 (p 423) D pleaded (full credit) to gross negligence manslaughter and possession of heroin. He was convicted of perverting the course of justice. He was an experienced user of heroin. He met V through his former partner, with a view to D helping V with his drug use. V was a recreational drug user. D had referred himself for assistance with his heroin dependency and had received overdose training. Others commented that V's drug use had spiralled since he met D. They jointly purchased some heroin and cooked it up. D drew 20 mm of the liquid heroin and gave it to V. V injected himself and began to snore. That was a normal response that D had observed when V had previously had taken heroin. D drew 70 mm of the liquid heroin and injected himself with ⅔ of it. He thought to himself that the mixture was strong. D came round approximately 30-45 minutes later. V's snoring had turned into a gurgle. D tried to wake V to no avail, although V did exhale and move his finger. D attempted mouth-to-mouth and then injected V with adrenaline. He did so again some 20 minutes later. Each time there was some sign of life. D saw blood running from V's nose about 1 hour later. At no time did D attempt to call for medical help. D later told J, who lived in the next room, that V had overdosed and was dead. D took a tarpaulin from a cot and wrapped V's body in it. D and J laid the body against the back wall of the house. D had previous convictions but they were not directly relevant. Held. There are no guidelines for this offence. V voluntarily took the heroin himself. D knew that V was not an habitual injector of heroin. Importantly, D knew the signs of overdose and knew what he should do. Yet he did nothing. **4 years** was severe but not wrong in principle or manifestly excessive. For perverting the course of justice, **8 months consecutive** was not wrong in principle, having regard to totality. **4 years 8 months** was not manifestly excessive.

Old cases: *R v Keen* 2007 EWCA Crim 1095, 2008 1 Cr App R (S) 8 (p 34) (**2 years**) *R v Wilson* 2007 EWCA Crim 1895, 2008 1 Cr App R (S) 75 (p 434) (**3½ years**)

For a summary of the first case, see the 8th edition of this book and for the second case, see the 9th edition.

See also the **Supply of Drugs** *Death occurs* para at **340.26**.

Drunken attack see the *No reason/Minor provocation/Drunken attack* paras at **284.50**.

284.30   *Death caused by the fall and not any blow   Judicial guidance*
Att-Gen's Ref Nos 60, 62-63 of 2009 2009 EWCA Crim 2693, 2010 2 Cr App R (S) 46 (p 311) LCJ The Court heard three cases together. B and R were convicted of manslaughter. After an incident in a club involving V1, R pointed V1 out to B saying, "That's him there". B struck V1 full force and V1 fell, hitting his head on the ground. This caused his skull to fracture, and he died. C and T pleaded to manslaughter. They punched V2 to death. The cause of death was the blows and not any fall. The other case was not a 'death by fall' case. Held. Defence advocates frequently refer to *R v Coleman* 1992 13 Cr App R (S) 508 where death resulted from a single blow followed by a fall which 'almost accidentally' fractured the deceased's skull, which caused the death. That principle should be 'strictly confined' to where the death was indeed almost accidental. We acknowledge the analysis made by Dr David Thomas, where an accidental death

resulted from a minor assault in *R v Mallett* 1972 Crim LR 260. He suggested that where death is the wholly accidental result of an unlawful act of a relatively trivial nature, the sentence is on the basis of the act he did and the consequences he intended. That approach continued for many years.

An additional feature of manslaughter cases which is a significant aggravating feature of any such case is the public impact of violence on the streets, whether in city centres or residential areas. Each of these three cases involved such public violence. Specific attention should be paid to the problem of gratuitous violence in city centres and the streets, *R v Miah* 2005 EWCA Crim 1798. para 13 The *R v Coleman* 1992 approach is no longer appropriate. What is now required, without of course diminishing the attention to be paid to the actions of the defendant and his intentions at the time, and the true level of his culpability, is that specific attention must also be paid to the consequences of his crime. para 21 Parliament's intention is clear. Crimes which result in death should be treated more seriously and dealt with more severely than before. para 22 Crimes which result in death should be treated more seriously to ensure that the increased focus on the fact that a victim has died in consequence of an unlawful act of violence, even where the conviction is for manslaughter, should, in accordance with the legislative intention, be given greater weight.

For some additional guidance in the case, see **284.3**.

Note: The problem with this case is that it was decided for a late night 'yobbery' case, where deterrent sentences are applied. It does not deal with the real 'death by fall' case. Suppose after lunch, outside a private house in a fit of temper, a young girl of impeccable character strikes her boyfriend causing little injury but he is killed by hitting a kerb stone when he falls. She is unlikely to be charged, as it would be called an accident. However, if it was the boyfriend hitting the girlfriend, it is likely that he would be charged, as it would be called domestic violence. Surely the death by fall factor is the dominant factor. There are no Court of Appeal cases on this type of fact pattern. It may be because those defendants are given Suspended Sentence Orders and do not appeal their sentences. Ed.

284.31 *Fall   Death caused by the fall and not any blow   Cases*

R v Rowell 2010 EWCA Crim 2736 D was convicted of manslaughter. After a pub football match there was a fight outside a pub between a member of the opposing team and D's team. V, aged 48, who was an organiser of one of the teams, went with D to assist the victim of that incident. After the incident was broken up by the door staff, D lost his temper and knocked V to the ground. V got up and walked to the pub doorman. D entered the pub. He subsequently exited 'like a bullet' and struck V in the face. V fell to the ground and struck his head on the pavement and suffered a fractured skull. He died from a subdural haemorrhage. D, aged 27 at appeal, had a number of previous convictions, including GBH, public order offences and possession of an offensive weapon. The Judge accepted that this was a single-punch manslaughter. However, he described it as a very heavy blow and 'a haymaker'. Held. The Judge was not entitled to sentence on excessive force and self-defence. There was ample evidence upon which the Judge could properly decide that this was a deliberate attack and this was not simply the use of excessive force in self-defence. The earlier episode takes this case out of the realms of a single-punch manslaughter because it was preceded by earlier violence. **6 years** not 7.

R v Bebbington 2011 EWCA Crim 1206, 2012 1 Cr App R (S) 19 (p 99) D was convicted of manslaughter. D was at his flat (with friends, including V). The group drank alcohol and also smoked cannabis for some time. D claimed that V touched D's brother's girlfriend inappropriately. V was asked to leave. D followed V outside onto the landing and was heard to shout at him. V tried to re-enter the flat and D pushed him away. V stumbled back a few feet because he was drunk and fell down the stairs. V was taken to hospital and it was discovered that he was brain dead as a result of the fall. D had no relevant convictions. Held. D's culpability was very low. He did not intend any harm and the death was a true accident. **2 years** not 3½.

R v Smylie 2015 EWCA Crim 133 LCJ D pleaded to manslaughter and theft on the day of his trial. V, aged 45, was a single man with a private drink problem. He met D to try to buy some cannabis. There was a disagreement between the two and V took out his wallet. D then pushed V and his forehead struck the ground causing an internal head injury. Whilst V was on the ground, D took £80 from V's wallet. V was next seen on some nearby stairs with D. D pushed V aggressively causing V to fall backwards but not onto the ground. V was then able to visit a local housing office and to go to the police station to report the events but V was not prepared to wait to be seen. Over the next few days V told others he was not well and three days after the incident his forehead looked swollen and haemorrhaged. Two further days later he died. The cause of death was subdural haemorrhage. D was aged 26 with 37 court appearances for 79 offences. He was assigned to a Prolific Priority police officer, which had little effect. In February 2012, D was given 6 weeks for theft. In April 2012, he was sent back to prison for 14 weeks for another theft. Very soon after his release, he committed this offence. The Judge identified two mitigating factors, a) no previous convictions for violence and a lifetime post-traumatic stress disorder. Held. It was a hard push, but it was only a push. V's heavy drinking may have made him more vulnerable. We start at 4½ years not 6.[649] With plea, 4 years. We make the theft sentence of three months concurrent not consecutive, making **4 years** not 5 years 3 months.

See also: *R v Hayes* 2015 EWCA Crim 199 (4½ years would have been unimpeachable for an adult, but because he was then aged 17, 45 months' YOI, see **284.63**.)

Old cases: *R v Chapman* 2007 EWCA Crim 2593, 2008 1 Cr App R (S) 103 (p 607) (**3 years** appropriate) *R v Hynds* 2009 EWCA Crim 1486, 2010 1 Cr App R (S) 64 (p 429) (**21 months' IPP**)

For a summary of the first case, see the 7th edition of this book and for the last case, see the 10th edition.

284.32   *Fighting (no knife)*

R v Stuart 2007 EWCA Crim 233 D pleaded to manslaughter (based on lack of intent), but not at the earliest opportunity. D and V were long-time close friends who often drank to excess together. On such an afternoon they started drinking in D's flat, and at about 6 pm a neighbour heard them shouting at each other and then a loud bang. At around midnight another neighbour opened the door of her flat and heard a low moan from D's flat. At 5.55 am D called the emergency services, saying that he had found his mate and he thought he was dead. The ambulance crew found V with a head injury. He had been dead for some time. The cause of death was lacerations caused by blunt trauma to the abdomen. This was consistent with blows, probably stamps or kicks or a combination of both. There were 25 recent marks of injury comprising three cuts to the head, bruises and abrasions over the body and a fractured nasal bone. In the fourth interview D said that they were arguing about money and trading insults. D had 11 appearances for 17 offences including five ABHs between 1982 and 1986. In 1997, he pleaded to manslaughter of his female partner to whom he had been violent on a number of occasions before. He punched her and she choked on her own vomit. D received 4½ years. He was a model prisoner. The Judge said that he was capable of great violence and was a very dangerous man, particularly when in drink. The Judge started at 18 years, reduced to 14 for the plea and gave life with a term of 7 years. Held. The **life** sentence could not be faulted. In view of the use of the shoe at least once, the other assaults, the indifference to the injuries, the failure to summon help and the initial prevarication when

---

[649] The Court said the starting point would have been 6 years before the plea and the plea credit was about 10%, which made 5 years. This is in fact a 17% reduction so it may be the Judge started at 5½ years with a 10% discount.

interviewed, this was at the top of the range. Added to this must be the other manslaughter. We start at **14 years** reducing it to 11 for the plea, giving a **5½-year** term. See also: *R v Gray* 2011 EWCA Crim 1878, 2012 1 Cr App R (S) 73 (p 410) (D pleaded to manslaughter. Full credit. Victim, V, involved in disturbance in a nightclub. D, acted as peacemaker. V pushed D. D punched V once. In street, powerful blow causing V to hit head on ground. V never regained consciousness. Previous convictions for violence in social context after drinking. **4 years 8 months** not manifestly excessive.)

See also the *Fall Death caused by fall and not any blow* para at **284.31** and the *One-punch manslaughter* para at **284.52**.

284.33   Fire, By

R v Daley 2010 EWCA Crim 602 D pleaded to reckless arson. The prosecution later added a count of manslaughter to which he pleaded. He was tried for murder and was acquitted. D was convicted of criminal damage against his then partner and stopped living with her. He moved in with his long-term friend, V, a 39-year-old male. D had taken drugs and drink for some time which made him angry, aggressive and unpredictable. On Christmas Eve D and V had been drinking and there was an argument. V called the police and said that D had hit him and had refused to leave his flat. The police operator spoke to D, who seemed drunk but calm. In a second call, at 11.14 pm, V said that D was banging on a communal door and refusing to leave. One minute later, a witness saw D outside the property shouting and swearing at someone inside. At 2 am D walked out and returned to the flat. He set light to the only door, knowing that V was inside. D said that he had lit a T-shirt. At 3.30 am the fire brigade found V's body. V died of smoke inhalation and had injuries. In a pub D said that he had started the fire. D was aged 34 and in breach of a 6-month suspended sentence for possession of an offensive weapon. In 2007 and 2008 he had a conviction for criminal damage. D had made several threats in the past to commit arson. The threats were not carried out. The Judge said he gave full credit for the plea and D had abused V's trust and friendship. Held. D set fire to the only means of exit, knowing that V was asleep or less than fully conscious. The Judge was entitled to start at **15 years**, so **6 years' IPP** upheld. The credit for the plea was entirely fair.

Att-Gen's Ref No 18 of 2013 2013 EWCA Crim 1161[650] D pleaded to manslaughter. V, aged 18, was vulnerable, suffering from Asperger's syndrome, a speech impairment, learning difficulties and epilepsy. He lived alone in a flat. S, who was V's friend, described V as easily influenced and suggestible. V held a party at his flat to celebrate his 18th birthday. D arrived with others. V said he had invited them, but seemed unsure. V was openly gay. During the course of the evening, JS and his friends persuaded V to take his clothes off. JS mocked him calling him a "gay cunt" and wrote on D's stomach 'I love dick'. 'Gay boy' was written on the bathroom door. Later, V was angry and was telling D and another to get out of his bedroom as they had been 'trashing' it. S saw D with a small hammer, told him off and took the hammer from him. D's plea was on the basis that he had seen two people in V's bedroom and had gone in to stop them, and had seen and removed the hammer. By 2 am, a number of people had left. V's trousers had been pulled down and his genitals were exposed. One of D's friends sprayed V's genitals with tanning oil. The label on the bottled displayed a warning that the contents were flammable. V did not object. JS held a lit cigarette lighter to V's groin. V immediately caught fire and ran into another room. He suffered 60% burns and died two days later. D's basis of plea included that: a) D had been invited to the party, b) he had been egged on to light the cigarette lighter and c) the references to D's sexuality were good-natured horseplay. The prosecution rejected b) and c) and agreed with the defence that a *Newton* hearing could be conducted on the papers. The Judge was surprised that no evidence was to be called but agreed to resolve the matter on the papers. The dispute related to the alleged cruel behaviour surrounding V's vulnerability and sexuality. The Judge found

---

[650] The judgment refers to the case as *R v Sheard* 2013 EWCA Crim 1161. Ed.

that the prosecution hadn't proved it and that D was to be sentenced according to his basis of plea. The Attorney-General argued that the aggravating factors merited a lengthier sentence than was imposed, and that the *Newton* hearing was decided without referring to evidence which might have affected the findings. He said that the Judge paid insufficient regard to the victim's vulnerability. Held. The Judge might have been prompted to review whether a *Newton* without evidence was the appropriate course. Hearing witnesses, potentially for both sides, could have affected the Judge's findings as to the appropriate loss of liberty. Though this Court might have directed the attendance of witnesses to better satisfy us of the true position, we must be careful now to avoid reaching a confident conclusion without that very advantage. D lost the chance to give evidence during the *Newton* and consequently it would not be fair or right to penalise him at this stage. The sentence of **3½ years** would not be increased.

Note: The Court said that had the Attorney-General's contentions been supported by oral evidence at the *Newton* hearing, it is likely that the sentence would have been increased. Ed.

R v Khatoon 2014 EWCA Crim 881 D pleaded to manslaughter and reckless arson. Her marriage to V1 had broken down some weeks previously. V1 was in a new relationship with V2. V2 lived with her mother, V3. D was furious and embarked on a campaign of relatively minor harassment. She telephoned V1 and made threats. D also resented V3, telephoned her calling her a whore and threatened to kill her. There were also physical attacks on the property including a smashed light and paint being poured over her car. V1 received a phone call stating that 15 Sikh males would 'get him' if he did not leave V2. One evening, V1 and V2 were staying at V3's address, along with V2's friend, V4. At 6.30 am the following morning, D and her co-accused travelled to V3's house, dressed in dark clothing. They set a fire which spread to the house and a passer-by heard screaming from inside. V1, V2 and V3 managed to escape the property by jumping from a window. V1 suffered fractured heel bones, V2 suffered a fractured femur and V3 suffered a broken back. V4 was unfamiliar with the layout and was unable to find her way out of the property. She died from thermal injuries. D had previously had contact with mental health services. She had no mental disorder although she claimed to be able to hear voices. An expert report considered that she had an emotionally unstable personality disorder. The Judge considered that the notional determinate term was 14 years. Held. Life with a minimum of 7 years was too high by a significant amount, considering the authorities. The **life sentence** was correct and the appropriate minimum term was **6 years**.

See also: *R v Mahmood* 2012 EWCA Crim 400, 2 Cr App R (S) 63 (p 373) (Convicted of manslaughter ×3. Brother was convicted of murder ×3. Disagreement with V over car bought for business venture. Threats made to V by the brother. The two men set fire to property of V's ex-wife using petrol. She was inside with her two children. Children died from smoke inhalation, mother died after suffering fractured spine from jumping from a first-floor window. Aged 18. **17 years' YOI** was not excessive. Brother received minimum term of 29 years.)

R v M and Others Re P 2013 EWCA Crim 673, 2014 1 Cr App R (S) 18 (p 501) (Convicted of gross negligence manslaughter. V was lured by a girl to her flat. V had previously sexually assaulted her. A number of men were waiting for him. They assaulted him and put him in the boot of a car. P did not participate in the violence. V was driven to a secluded location and petrol was poured over him. The car was set alight. V's hands had been tied together. P participated in setting fire to the car and knew that V was in the boot. He was paid £300 for his involvement. Effective good character. He failed to take any reasonable steps to check whether he was alive or dead. Death was a virtual certainty. **12 years** was fully justified.)

Old cases: *Att-Gen's Ref No 133 of 2006* 2007 EWCA Crim 809, 2 Cr App R (S) 91 (p 594)[651] (**11 years' detention**) *R v Gleadhill* 2009 EWCA Crim 493 (**12 years**) *R v Sheen* 2010 EWCA Crim 1862 ((**7 years' IPP**)

For a summary of the first case, see the 8th edition of this book and for the second case, see the 9th edition.

284.34 Firearm, With

R v Duffy and Others 2008 EWCA Crim 1436, 2009 1 Cr App R (S) 53 (p 286) T, F and L were convicted of murder. D was convicted of manslaughter. The victim, S, was a member of a gang in Liverpool habitually in dispute with the Croxteth Crew. S was visiting an inmate at a prison in Liverpool when he saw L in the visitors' area. L, a member of the Croxteth Crew, was on remand for firearms offences. There was some kind of argument between the two men. L returned to his cell and, using his mobile phone, set about arranging for S to be ambushed outside and killed. He called D, although he did not get through, then F and T. Within half an hour about 20 young men arrived outside the prison to attack S. The identity of the killer was never established. He had been hiding in some bushes, emerged and shot S in the head at point-blank range with a sawn-off shotgun. This took place in broad daylight in front of members of the public and prison officers. All involved escaped from the scene. Evidence which might link the offenders to the murder was destroyed. Cars were burned out and phones were disposed of. The police were obstructed by a mixture of lack of co-operation and fear. F and T were convicted on the basis that they joined the attack, formed part of the numbers which were a critical part of the plan, and did so knowing that the object was to attack S with at least the foreseeable possibility that he would be shot dead. T remained in one of the vehicles. F could have been one of those hiding in the bushes. L called on D for help, and D took an organising and leading role in the ambush. He made 35 calls in the relevant period. Some were before the attack to organise the participants, and some afterwards, presumably in part to organise the elimination of evidence. He was also at the scene at some stage. He was convicted on the basis that he knew that a firearm might well be used but that he did not have the intention or foresight that S would be killed or seriously injured, as distinct from frightened or threatened with the gun. L, aged 18, had relatively minor convictions with a history of being expelled from school for breaking someone's nose and reprimands for assaults. He was convicted of the firearms offences for which he was on remand at the time of these offences. It was suggested that he was immature. T, aged 17, had a previous conviction for possession of cannabis and had also been expelled from school for disruptive behaviour. He was awaiting trial for racially aggravated criminal damage which was still outstanding. At his home drawings were found showing a fascination for firearms. He admitted some involvement in a previous shooting. F, aged 15, had minor previous convictions and a record of disruptive behaviour at school. There was a psychological report which showed he had a very low IQ of 71. D, aged 25, had a number of convictions, mainly for the supply of drugs. He told the probation officer that he had supplied drugs since he had left school. Held. For D, there must be some sensible relationship between the statutory prescribed periods for murder and sentences for manslaughter. This does not mean there is an arithmetical relationship between the two offences. Sometimes a defendant convicted of manslaughter can plainly be seen to have played a minor role. This is not the case with D. He played a central part in arranging and organising the ambush. There can be no complaint against the sentence of **20 years.** The murder sentences were as follows. For L, the Judge took into account that his sentence of IPP, with a notional determinate term of 6 years for the firearms offences, would now be subsumed into this life sentence. Given the instigation by L of this murder, there is nothing wrong with a minimum period of **28 years**. Minimum terms for T of **20 years** and for F of **18 years**, while very long, are the correct sentences for this kind of blatant and chilling gang warfare.

---

[651] The case number in the report is wrong.

See also: *R v Wingfield* 2013 EWCA Crim 2274 (Manslaughter and robbery. **22 years**, see **284.13**.)
Old cases: Best ignored.
Gross neglect see the ***Neglect, Gross*** para at **284.49**.

284.35   Gross negligence   Judicial guidance

R v Johnson 2008 EWCA Crim 2976, 2009 2 Cr App R (S) 28 (p 210) For cases of gross negligence the offence is aggravated by: i) multiple deaths, ii) a prolonged and deliberate dangerous course of conduct, iii) an awareness of a significant risk of death or serious injury, iv) ignoring warnings that the course of conduct was dangerous or potentially dangerous, and v) pursuing[652] a course of conduct for financial gain.

R v Holtom 2010 EWCA Crim 934, 2011 1 Cr App R (S) 18 (p 128) LCJ D pleaded to manslaughter by gross negligence. D was a builder who killed a 15-year-old employee. Held. In the sentencing process for homicide cases, including deaths on the road, there is now a greater emphasis to be placed on the fatal consequences of a criminal act. The Lord Chief Justice explained the reason for this in *Att-Gen's Ref Nos 60, 62-63 of 2009* 2009 EWCA Crim 2693, 2010 2 Cr App R (S) 46 (p 311) (for details see **284.51**), see particularly para 13, and in relation to deaths on the road, para 20. It seems to us today that a similar consideration applies to cases of manslaughter by gross negligence in the workplace. (For more detail see the next paragraph.)

Note: Other gross negligence cases have been divided up between other paragraphs of this chapter. Ed.

284.36   Gross negligence   Cases

R v Brown 2010 EWCA Crim 2832, 2011 2 Cr App R (S) 11 (p 59) D pleaded (full credit) to manslaughter. She was at home with her sister, S, S's boyfriend, V, and a friend, F. They had all had a good deal to drink. An argument ensued during which D pushed V, and V pushed S onto the floor. S then took a kitchen knife and stabbed V in the thigh, before fleeing. V was bleeding heavily and had lapsed into unconsciousness. D did not want the emergency services called. Later, F called an ambulance but D terminated the call before the location could be disclosed. D consistently refused to call an ambulance. At least an hour after the stabbing, D called an ambulance and lied about how the incident had occurred. D, aged 25, had no convictions. She had two very young children and excellent references. Held. She let him bleed to death over a prolonged period of at least an hour. Not only did she not call an ambulance but she physically cut off her friend when she tried to do so. We acknowledge that she was driven by a misplaced sense of loyalty to her sister. **4 years** was not manifestly excessive.

R v Reeves 2012 EWCA Crim 2613, 2013 2 Cr App R (S) 21 (p 129) D pleaded (25% credit) to gross negligence manslaughter. She was at home with her two children, one aged 2½ years, the other aged 12 months. She left them in the bath secured to a safety seat while she went outside to speak to some of her neighbours. She was tipsy but not drunk. She remained outside for a period of 45 minutes, occasionally looking back inside the flat but not into the bathroom. At one point the older child began to scream but D shouted at him to be quiet. There was evidence that D had told the boy to turn the tap on to entertain himself. Eventually, D returned to the bathroom and emerged moments later holding the younger child screaming that he had had a fit. Neighbours then realised that he had been in the bath. They tried to resuscitate him. The emergency services were summoned. D was hysterical and unhelpful. The child was taken to hospital but died on the same day. The causes of death were cerebral hypoxia (lack of oxygen to the brain), cardiac arrest and immersion. D's basis of plea stated that although the child was secured in his safety seat he was unsupervised for a period of 40-50 minutes and that during that period she was in the kitchen and from time to time outside speaking with neighbours. She asserted that she was not drunk but had been drinking. D was aged 24 at appeal and

---

[652] Assuming there is a typo in the judgment.

of effective good character. The surviving child was being cared for by his father by order of the Family Court. A pre-sentence report spoke of D's need to address her drug and alcohol misuse. It stated that D took full responsibility for the neglect and subsequent death of her child. Held. The child was left alone for around 45 minutes in a bath which had either been over-filled by D or had become over-filled by D's instructions to the older child. The facts, by definition, show great harm and the culpability is high. D's actions were counter-intuitive. There were clear warning signs on the baby's chair as to the appropriate water level. The older child's screams were ignored. The 25% credit given by the Judge was appropriate. **3 years 9 months** was a firm sentence, but was not manifestly excessive.

R v Bowler 2015 EWCA Crim 849 D was convicted of manslaughter by gross negligence. D suffered from cerebral palsy and lived with his carer, C (who was acquitted). D had a history of physical and sexual abuse. He needed crutches and had a sexual dysfunction which meant he had difficulties in staying in a relationship. V was interested in extreme masochistic experiences and put his interest on a gay web site. He enjoyed submission and being wrapped in cellophane or PVC or both. V liked to be left after sex in a mummified state. In 2009, there was contact between D and V. V introduced D to his sexual practices and asked D to be his master. V said he had done it many times with other men. D agreed and he had sex with D using cellophane about 10-15 times. Holes were made in the cellophane to allow V to breathe. D said V asked to be additionally wrapped in PVC. In 2013, V e-mailed D late asking if he could come round. V arrived at 11.30 pm and D wrapped him in cellophane and taped it. There were holes around his nose and mouth and over his anus. At V's request, V was also wrapped in PVC. There were no air holes but it was wrapped loosely to allow the air in. C then spanked V and D had anal sex with V using a strapped-on penis. The sex tired D and he told V he was going downstairs to rest. V agreed to this. D went upstairs half an hour later and V was moving. Next time he came up V was lifeless. Both D and C panicked. Eventually, at 5.50 am, C went to a taxi office and told his mother he had killed someone. About three hours after, D contacted his brother and the emergency services were called. D accepted the advice from the ambulance service on the phone on how to revive V. The police arrived and V had been dead for some time. Tests showed that V had taken ketamine, norketamine and methamphetamine in normal recreational amounts. Death was caused not by suffocation but by a heart attack caused by overheating while under the influence of drugs. D was aged 35 with no convictions. The Judge assessed the period of time V was left wrapped up [after the sex] at between half an hour and three hours. On appeal the defence said, V positively encouraged the bondage, death was caused in a large measure by the victim's misjudgment and D was unaware of the dangers of overheating. The prosecution relied on the time V was left when he could not look after himself. Held. Unusual sexual practices are a matter for the individuals themselves. Here the practice of wrapping up was not an aggravating factor. The relevance of that was the creation of danger to V. The aggravating factor was the time V was left helpless and in danger. The culpability here was different from other cases because V [asked] for the actions to take place. **3 years** not 5.

See also: *R v M and Others Re P* 2013 EWCA Crim 673, 2014 1 Cr App R (S) 18 (p 501) (Convicted of gross negligence manslaughter. V was lured by a girl to her flat. V had previously sexually assaulted her. A number of men were waiting for him. They assaulted him and put him in the boot of a car. P did not participate in the violence. V was driven to a secluded location and petrol was poured over him. The car was set alight. V's hands had been tied together. P participated in setting fire to the car and knew that V was in the boot. He was paid £300 for his involvement. Effective good character. He failed to take any reasonable steps to check whether he was alive or dead. Death was a virtual certainty. **12 years** was fully justified.)

Old cases: *R v Johnson* 2008 EWCA Crim 2976, 2009 2 Cr App R (S) 28 (p 210) (**2½ years**) *R v Winter and Winter* 2010 EWCA Crim 1474, 2011 1 Cr App R (S) 78 (p 476) (For M, **7 years**. For N, **4 years**)
For a summary of the first case, see the 9th edition of this book and for the last case, see the 10th edition.
Health see the *Victim's health precarious/eggshell skull/Victim not expected to die* para at **284.10**.

284.37   Health and Safety failures
R v Holtom 2010 EWCA Crim 934, 2011 1 Cr App R (S) 18 (p 128) LCJ D pleaded (full credit) to manslaughter by gross negligence. D was subcontracted by F to carry out building works to a residential property. D employed three brothers, G, C and V, as casual labourers. V was aged 15 but told D he was 16. F told D a wall at the property was unstable and it would have to be taken down 'brick by brick or course by course'. D instructed G, aged 18, and V to demolish the wall and provided them with a sledgehammer and a pneumatic hammer. G and V were not wearing protective equipment. D returned to the front of the property leaving G and V unsupervised to demolish the wall. The wall began to lean and V went to tell D, who did not go to look at the wall himself. On V's return, the wall toppled towards him, pinning him between the wall and a shed. V died almost immediately from severe head injuries. D, aged 62, had no convictions and had testimonials. The GP report said D was remorseful and suffered from stress, depression and anxiety following the accident. The Judge said D had adopted a cavalier and thoroughly irresponsible attitude to others' safety. Held. There were substantial aggravating features: V should not have been working at all other than in strictly regulated circumstances because of his age, and D did not go to the scene when informed of the danger of the wall collapsing. **3 years** upheld.
Old cases: *R v Roys* 2008 EWCA Crim 2021, 2009 1 Cr App R (S) 91 (p 539) (**12 months**) *R v Johnson* 2008 EWCA Crim 2976, 2009 2 Cr App R (S) 28 (p 210) (**2½ years**)
For a summary of the first case, see the 9th edition of this book.

284.38   Historical manslaughter
R v Bell 2015 EWCA Crim 1426, 2016 1 Cr App R (S) 16 (p 113) D pleaded to manslaughter. The offence was in 2000. The defence sought to argue that European Convention on Human Rights art 7(1) and the principles in *R v Sullivan and Others* 2004 EWCA Crim 1762, 2005 1 Cr App R (S) 67 (p 308) applied so the Judge was bound to pass a sentence which was no more than what would have been imposed in 2000. Held. para 37, 47 and 54 *R v Sullivan* 2004 is plainly distinguishable as the case was manslaughter, which is determined by judicial discretion, and murder is determined by Criminal Justice Act 2003 Sch 21, laid down by Parliament. para 50 *R v Sullivan* 2004 does not apply to discretionary life cases. paras 42-44 We apply *R v Secretary of State for the Home Dept ex parte Uttley* 2004 UKHL 38 to say the heavier penalty provision of article 7(1) applies to the maximum penalty. The Court should apply *R v H* 2011 EWCA Crim 2753, 2012 2 Cr App R (S) 21 (p 88), see para **240.33**. para 63 In discretionary life cases, the minimum term should reflect current sentencing practice. Appeal dismissed.
See also: *R v Masefield* 2012 EWCA Crim 1873, 2013 1 Cr App R (S) 77 (p 426) (LCJ Plea to manslaughter. In 1987, after an argument, struck friend over the head with metal pole, killing him. In 2011, he approached the police and confessed. Aged 19 at the time of the offence. Judge right to apply *R v H* 2011 EWCA Crim 2753, 2012 2 Cr App R (S) 21 (p 88). **11½ years** was well merited. For a full report, see **284.4**.)

284.39   Knife, With   Judicial guidance
R v Thornley 2011 EWCA Crim 153 LCJ D pleaded to manslaughter by reason of provocation. The offence was committed before the introduction of the new minimum sentence for knife crime in murder and the new definition for provocation. Held. These

changes cannot be ignored by sentencing judges. It is clear to us…that the use of a knife, even in cases of manslaughter by provocation, shall now be regarded as a more significant feature of aggravation than it was when the provocation guideline was published (2005). In the end everything depends upon the individual circumstances of each case: why and how the knife came to be picked up and eventually used.

For more details of the case, see **284.47**.

R v Odegbune and Others 2013 EWCA Crim 711 para 29-30 From 2 March 2010 the starting point for murders where a knife or other weapon was taken to the scene where the intention was to commit an offence or have it available as a weapon became 25 years. In order to preserve consistency of approach to sentencing across the range of offences, that change for murder inevitably has an impact on lesser offences of violence committed with a knife or similar weapon.

Note: The sentences for manslaughter where the weapon is a knife have risen significantly. Ed.

284.40   Knife, With   Cases

R v Harris 2010 EWCA Crim 534 (**8 years**) See **284.57**.

R v Banaszek 2010 EWCA Crim 1076 D was convicted of manslaughter. D stabbed V and V bled to death. V sustained around 30 wounds to his face, scalp and legs. At trial D said he had been drinking heavily and had taken some crack cocaine. He said he believed he had been anally raped by V whilst drunk and some weeks later V, aged 42, touched D's bottom, saying, "It never happened rent boy", and laughed at him. D had convictions in Poland for violence, possession of drugs and dishonesty offences. The pre-sentence report said D's previous convictions showed a pattern of offending behaviour involving a predisposition to resort to violence in confrontational situations where he feels he may have been unfairly treated. The Judge said that because of the passage of time the provocation was low. Held. Despite the time elapsed between the alleged rape and the provocation, the provocation in such circumstances was substantial. The aggravating features were that D was armed with one or two knives, the ferocity of the attack and D's conduct after the attack. **4½ years' IPP** not 6 years' IPP.

R v Oakley 2010 EWCA Crim 2419, 2011 1 Cr App R (S) 112 (p 659) D pleaded to manslaughter by reason of diminished responsibility, having been charged with murder. He had been in a relationship with V, a sixth-form student, for around 10 months. V's mother was concerned about D's temper and how he monopolised V's time. D was controlling and had been aggressive. V decided to end the relationship. D did not accept this and had to be formally warned by police about his behaviour. He held a knife to V's throat, threatening to kill her and then himself. He continued to attempt to contact V via friends and neighbours. D's mother was concerned about his mental health and contacted the police. D was taken to hospital and was discharged, showing no signs of clinical mental illness. D confronted V in public and V was taken to stay with her friend. D visited the address, and asked to enter. Following a refusal, D entered and closed the door. V asked D to leave. V's friend's father went to telephone the police. As he did so, D quickly took a knife from the kitchen and stabbed V 34 times to the chest. V also suffered eight minor wounds to her arms, face and head. She died. The wounds were consistent with a frenzied dynamic assault with severe force. D fled, and was subsequently arrested. D, aged 24, had previous convictions for offences relating to former girlfriends. Held. The Judge was entitled to treat this as a particularly grave case warranting a life sentence. D has pursued V against her wishes and disregarded warnings from friends, family and the police. 18 years would have been appropriate for murder. Making a reduction for plea (⅙), and the substantial impairment of responsibility, **12-year minimum term**, not 15.

R v Bishop 2011 EWCA Crim 1225, 2012 1 Cr App R (S) 13 (p 60) D was convicted of manslaughter and acquitted of murder. J and V had a child. Later V's relationship with J broke down and there were allegations of domestic violence. D then began a relationship with J. There was a pronounced decline in V's behaviour and his mental health. V went out drinking and made abusive and harassing telephone calls to J. D, having heard this abuse, told J he was going to work. In fact he went looking for V armed with a knife, seeking a confrontation with V. He watched V in a bar but did not approach him. D left, shortly followed by V. D introduced himself as J's partner. V was stabbed seven times and died. The force of the stab wounds was described as 'moderate force', connoting the force of a 'firm punch'. D telephoned J and said, "I did it for you and Joe". He subsequently fled the country. An expert said the type of wound was consistent with a knife that was missing from a set of knives in J's kitchen. D had no previous convictions. The Judge said D had ruined the lives of many people. Held. **12 years** would not be reduced.

R v Lawton 2011 EWCA Crim 2106 (**8 years**) See **284.55**.

Att-Gen's Ref No 36 of 2015 2015 EWCA Crim 1174 D was convicted of manslaughter as an alternative to murder (based on lack of intent). D and V had known each other for some time and there was no animosity. They both went to a funeral and after the service they encountered each other. A fight broke out and D called V a grass, which was denied. There was evidence that D used this term for people he did not like. D punched V to the head and both men fell to the ground. D then kicked V and a knife with a 6-inch blade fell out of D's pocket. Both men reached for the knife but D picked it up and stabbed V in the neck. D drove off. D later called 999 but the information given was too little for the service to act on it. When found, V was taken to hospital but he was dead on arrival. V had a 4-inch-deep stab wound to the neck, which severed his jugular vein causing severe haemorrhaging. There were further knife injuries to V's chin and upper chest. D disposed of his blood-soaked clothing and tried to clean the blood from his shoes. D was aged 53. He had many previous convictions over a significant period. There was a section 18 in 1982 and possession of an offensive weapon in 1982, 1989, 1990 and 2013, just a year before this offence. In 1997 he received 9 years for conspiracy to rob, possession of a firearm with intent and two possessions of prohibited weapons. There was no remorse. Held. Sentences have moved upwards (see **284.3**). The principal aggravating feature was that D took a knife to the scene. D did not expect a confrontation but he chose to pick the knife up and he knew V was unarmed. The case was of high culpability. The offence was aggravated by D being the aggressor in the initial confrontation, the offence was witnessed in a public place, D made off and D disposed of the evidence. The least sentence is **14 years** not 9.

See also: *R v Balasubramaniam* 2010 EWCA Crim 168 (D was convicted of manslaughter and acquitted of murder. In a dispute over a £20 amount of cannabis he stabbed V in the stomach. D had a conviction for an offensive weapon. **7 years' IPP** not 8)

R v Dighton 2011 EWCA Crim 1372, 2012 1 Cr App R (S) 30 (p 178) (Convicted. Stabbed both of his parents, who had been generous to him. Two knives used. Mother stabbed 20 times. Diminished responsibility. Aged 35. Good character. **12 years'** IPP not 15 years' IPP.)

Old cases: Best ignored.

284.41 *Loss of control*
Coroners and Justice Act 2009 s 54, 56 and 178 and Sch 23 repealed Homicide Act 1957 s 3 and replaced the defence of provocation with the defence of loss of control.[653]
Note: The provocation guideline continues to be used. Ed.
Manslaughter by Reason of Provocation Guideline 2005, see www.banksr.com Other Matters Guidelines tab page 1 **Foreword** This guideline is for use where the conviction for manslaughter is clearly founded on provocation alone. There will be additional, different and more complicated matters to be taken into account where the other main partial defence, diminished responsibility, is a factor.

---

[653] In force 4/10/10, Coroners and Justice Act 2009 (Commencement No 4, Transitional and Saving Provisions) Order 2010 2010/816

page 3 para 2.1 The Court of Appeal in *Att-Gen's Ref Nos 74, 95 and 118 of 2002* 2002 EWCA Crim 2982, 2003 2 Cr App R (S) 42 (p 273) [set out the assumptions]. (They are at **284.46** and are not repeated here.)

Bearing in mind the loss of life, the starting point should be a **custodial sentence**. Only in a very small number of cases involving very exceptional mitigating factors should a judge consider a non-custodial sentence.

Factors influencing sentence

page 4 para 3.1 A number of elements must be considered and balanced by the sentencer. Some of these are common to all types of manslaughter by reason of provocation. Others have a particular relevance in cases of manslaughter in a domestic context.

para 3.2 The degree of provocation as shown by its nature and duration. An assessment of the degree of the provocation as shown by its nature and duration is the critical factor in the sentencing decision.

a) In assessing the degree of provocation, account should be taken of the following factors:

   i) if the provocation (which does not have to be a wrongful act) involves gross and extreme conduct on the part of the victim, it is a more significant mitigating factor than conduct which, although significant, is not as extreme,

   ii) the fact that the victim presented a threat not only to the offender, but also to children in his or her care,

   iii) the offender's previous experiences of abuse and/or domestic violence either by the victim or by other people,

   iv) any mental condition which may affect the offender's perception of what amounts to provocation,

   v) the nature of the conduct, the period of time over which it took place and its cumulative effect,

   vi) discovery or knowledge of the fact of infidelity on the part of a partner does not necessarily amount to high provocation.

b) Whether the provocation was suffered over a long or short period is important to the assessment of gravity. The following factors should be considered:

   i) the impact of provocative behaviour on an offender can build up over a period of time,

   ii) consideration should not be limited to acts of provocation that occurred immediately before the victim was killed. For example, in domestic violence cases, cumulative provocation may eventually become intolerable, the latest incident seeming all the worse because of what went before.

c) When looking at the nature of the provocation the court should consider both the type of provocation and whether, in the particular case, the actions of the victim would have had a particularly marked effect on the offender:

   i) actual (or anticipated) violence from the victim will generally be regarded as involving a higher degree of provocation than provocation arising from abuse, infidelity or offensive words unless that amounts to psychological bullying,

   ii) in cases involving actual or anticipated violence, the culpability of the offender will therefore generally be less than in cases involving verbal provocation,

   iii) where the offender's actions were motivated by fear or desperation, rather than by anger, frustration, resentment or a desire for revenge, the offender's culpability will generally be lower.

284.42   The extent and timing of the retaliation

page 5 para 3.3 It is implicit in the verdict of manslaughter by reason of provocation that the killing was the result of a loss of self-control because of things said and/or done. The intensity, extent and nature of that loss of control must be assessed in the context of the provocation that preceded it.

para 3.4 The circumstances of the killing itself will be relevant to the offender's culpability, and hence to the appropriate sentence:

i) in general, the offender's violent response to provocation is likely to be less culpable the shorter the time gap between the provocation (or the last provocation) and the killing – as evidenced, for example, by the use of a weapon that happened to be available rather than by one that was carried for that purpose or prepared for use in advance,

ii) conversely, it is not necessarily the case that greater culpability will be found where there has been a significant lapse of time between the provocation (or the last provocation) and the killing. Where the provocation is cumulative, and particularly in those circumstances where the offender is found to have suffered domestic violence from the victim over a significant period of time, the required loss of self-control may not be sudden as some experience a 'slow-burn' reaction and appear calm,

iii) choosing or taking advantage of favourable circumstances for carrying out the killing (so that the victim was unable to resist, such as where the victim was not on guard, or was asleep) may well be an aggravating factor – unless this is mitigated by the circumstances of the offender, resulting in the offender being the weaker or vulnerable party.

para 3.5 The context of the relationship between the offender and the victim must be borne in mind when assessing the nature and degree of the provocation offered by the victim before the crime and the length of time over which the provocation existed. In cases where the parties were still in a relationship at the time of the killing, it will be necessary to examine the balance of power between one party and the other and to consider other family members who may have been drawn into, or been victims of, the provocative behaviour. Although there will usually be less culpability when the retaliation to provocation is sudden, it is not always the case that greater culpability will be found where there has been a significant lapse of time between the provocation and the killing. It is for the sentencer to consider the impact on an offender of provocative behaviour that has built up over a period of time. An offence should be regarded as aggravated where it is committed in the presence of a child or children or other vulnerable family member, whether or not the offence takes place in a domestic setting.

Post-offence behaviour

para 3.6 The behaviour of the offender after the killing can be relevant to sentence:

i) immediate and genuine remorse may be demonstrated by the summoning of medical assistance, remaining at the scene, and co-operation with the authorities,

ii) concealment or attempts to dispose of evidence or dismemberment of the body may aggravate the offence. Post-offence behaviour is relevant to the sentence. It may be an aggravating or mitigating factor.

When sentencing, the judge should consider the motivation behind the offender's actions.

Use of a weapon

para 3.7

a) In relation to this offence, as in relation to many different types of offence, the carrying and use of a weapon is an aggravating factor. Courts must consider the type of weapon used and, importantly, whether it was to hand or carried to the scene and who introduced it to the incident.

b) The use or not of a weapon is a factor heavily influenced by the gender of the offender. Whereas men can and do kill using physical strength alone, women often cannot and thus resort to using a weapon. The issue of key importance is whether the weapon was to hand or carried deliberately to the scene, although the circumstances in which the weapon was brought to the scene will need to be considered carefully.

The use of a weapon should not necessarily move a case into another sentencing bracket. In cases of manslaughter by reason of provocation, use of a weapon may reflect the imbalance in strength between the offender and the victim and how that weapon came to hand is likely to be far more important than the use of the weapon itself. It will be an aggravating factor where the weapon is brought to the scene in contemplation of use before the loss of self-control (which may occur some time before the fatal incident).

284.43   *Sentence ranges and starting points*
Identifying sentence ranges
para 4.2 The key factor that will be relevant in every case is the nature and the duration of the provocation.

   a) The process to be followed by the court will be:
      i) identify the sentence range by reference to the degree of provocation,
      ii) adjust the starting point within the range by reference to the length of time over which the provocation took place,
      iii) take into consideration the circumstances of the killing (e.g. the length of time that had elapsed between the provocation and the retaliation and the circumstances in which any weapon was used).
   b) This guideline establishes that:
      i) there are three sentencing ranges defined by the degree of provocation: low, substantial and high,
      ii) within the three ranges, the starting point is based on provocation taking place over a short period of time,
      iii) the court will move from the starting point (based upon the degree of provocation) by considering the length of time over which the provocation has taken place, and by reference to any aggravating and mitigating factors.

Factors to take into consideration
page 9 para 1 The sentences for public protection must be considered in all cases of manslaughter.

2 The presence of any of the general aggravating factors identified in the *Overarching Principles: Seriousness Guideline 2004* [see www.banksr.com Other Matters Guidelines tab] or any of the additional factors identified in this Guideline will indicate a sentence above the normal starting point.

3 This offence will not be an initial charge but will arise following a charge of murder. The *Reduction in Sentence for a Guilty Plea Guideline 2007* (see www.banksr.com Other Matters Guidelines tab) will need to be applied with this in mind. In particular, consideration will need to be given to the time at which it was indicated that the defendant would plead guilty to manslaughter by reason of provocation.

4 An assessment of the degree of the provocation as shown by its nature and duration is the critical factor in the sentencing decision.

5 The intensity, extent and nature of the loss of control must be assessed in the context of the provocation that preceded it.

6 Although there will usually be less culpability when the retaliation to provocation is sudden, it is not always the case that greater culpability will be found where there has been a significant lapse of time between the provocation and the killing.

7 It is for the sentencer to consider the impact on an offender of provocative behaviour that has built up over a period of time.

8 The use of a weapon should not necessarily move a case into another sentencing bracket.

9 Use of a weapon may reflect the imbalance in strength between the offender and the victim, and how that weapon came to hand is likely to be far more important than the use of the weapon itself.

10 It will be an aggravating factor where the weapon is brought to the scene in contemplation of use before the loss of self-control (which may occur some time before the fatal incident).

11 Post-offence behaviour is relevant to the sentence. It may be an aggravating or mitigating factor. When sentencing, the judge should consider the motivation behind the offender's actions.

284.44   *Penalties*
Note: The guideline does not say to whom the guidelines apply. In 2005, the Sentencing Guidelines Council invariably constructed starting points and ranges for a first-time offender who was convicted after a trial. Ed.
page 10

Type/Nature of activity
Low degree of provocation A low degree of provocation occurring over a short period
Substantial degree of provocation A substantial degree of provocation occurring over a short period
High degree of provocation A high degree of provocation occurring over a short period
Sentence ranges and starting points
Sentence range: 10 years to life Starting point: 12 years' custody
Sentence range: 4 to 9 years Starting point: 8 years' custody
Sentence range: if custody is necessary, up to 4 years Starting point: 3 years' custody

Additional aggravating factors
1 Concealment or attempts to dispose of evidence (subject to para 3.6). 2 Dismemberment or mutilation of the body (subject to para 3.6). 3 Offence committed in the presence of a child/children or other vulnerable family member.
Additional mitigating factors
1 The offender was acting to protect another. 2 Spontaneity and lack of premeditation. 3 Previous experiences of abuse and/or domestic violence. 4 Evidence that the victim presented an ongoing danger to the offender or another. 5 Actual (or reasonably anticipated) violence from the victim.

284.45   New sentences: Criminal Justice Act 2003
The Council guideline recognised the potentially more demanding nature of custodial sentences of 12 months or longer imposed under the new framework introduced by Criminal Justice Act 2003. The sentencing ranges and starting points in the above guideline take account of this.
Note: Judges sensibly universally ignore these considerations. Ed.

284.46   *Loss of control   Judicial guidance*
Att-Gen's Ref Nos 74, 95 and 118 of 2002 2002 EWCA Crim 2982, 2003 2 Cr App R (S) 42 (p 273) The Judge must make certain assumptions in the defendant's favour. First, he must assume that the offender had, at the time of the killing, lost his self-control. Mere loss of temper or jealous rage is not sufficient. Second, he must assume that the offender was caused to lose his self-control by things said or done, normally by the person he has killed. Third, he must assume that the defendant's loss of control was reasonable in all the circumstances, even bearing in mind that people are expected to exercise reasonable control over their emotions, and that as society advances it ought to call for a higher measure of self-control. Fourth, he must assume that the circumstances were such as to make the loss of self-control sufficiently excusable to reduce the gravity of the defendant's offence from murder to manslaughter. Note: This remark must be read in conjunction with the new law and the guideline. Ed.
R v Ward 2012 EWCA Crim 3139, 2013 2 Cr App R (S) 35 (p 233) D pleaded to manslaughter on the basis of loss of control. Held. When determining a sentence for manslaughter by reason of loss of control, the [provocation] guidelines continue to

provide useful assistance. The Court must take account of the existence of a higher and different threshold for loss of control manslaughter than that which existed at common law for manslaughter (which results from the need for there to be a qualifying trigger); and of the greater significance given to the loss of life in manslaughter cases. There is scope within the ample brackets in the guidelines to make allowance for both. Sentencing is not, however, a mechanical exercise and depends upon the individual circumstances of the case.

284.47 *Loss of control   Cases*

R v Banaszek 2010 EWCA Crim 1076 D was convicted of manslaughter. D stabbed V. V bled to death. V sustained around 30 wounds to his face, scalp and legs. At trial D said he had been drinking heavily and had taken some crack cocaine. He said he believed he had been anally raped by V whilst drunk and some weeks later V, aged 42, touched D's bottom, saying, "It never happened rent boy", and laughed at him. D had convictions in Poland for violence, possession of drugs and dishonesty offences. The pre-sentence report said D's previous convictions showed a pattern of offending behaviour involving a predisposition to resort to violence in confrontational situations where he feels he may have been unfairly treated. The Judge said that because of the passage of time the provocation was low. Held. Despite the time elapsed between the alleged rape and the provocation, the provocation in such circumstances was substantial. The aggravating features were that D was armed with one or two knives, the ferocity of the attack and D's conduct after the attack. **4½ years' IPP** not 6 years' IPP.

R v Thornley 2011 EWCA Crim 153 LCJ D pleaded to manslaughter by reason of provocation. There was some friction over a practical joke between D and V, his neighbour. As a result D called the police. Because of that friction D and his wife hosted a barbecue at their house for V and some friends and neighbours. D and V drank alcohol. Something went wrong and they exchanged words. There was shouting and finger pointing. Some of the guests separated them and left the barbecue. He quarrelled with his partner before returning. D armed himself with a knife but was disarmed by his wife. V once again left. V returned and was angry. D had armed himself with a second knife. V, a strongly built man, took hold of D and a struggle ensued. D deliberately stabbed him once in the right side of the stomach and once in the left side of his back above the kidney. The blows were severe. They caused disastrous bleeding. V died after suffering a cardiac arrest. D returned to his house, washed the knife and made a complaint to the police that V had attacked him, initially not mentioning V's injuries. D, aged 44 at appeal, was of effective good character. The Judge accepted that D may have feared for his wife's safety, but he noted that D had taken a knife into a dangerous situation at a point when he had not lost control. Held. The aggravating features are plain. D armed himself deliberately with a knife on a second occasion. After the stabbing he behaved in an entirely selfish way in order to divert attention away from himself as the individual responsible for V's injuries and for his death. On the other hand, taking a measured, balanced look at how it came about that D armed himself with a knife for a second time, insufficient allowance was made for the fact that, at the time when D picked up the knife, his wife was engaged in an altercation with V, a powerful man, who was in an angry mood and spoiling for a fight with D, and who had then physically taken hold of him by the throat at the time when the stabbing occurred. D did not act in self-defence. The violence that he used was wildly excessive. Considering those circumstances, **12 years**, not 16.

R v Ward 2012 EWCA Crim 3139, 2013 2 Cr App R (S) 35 (p 233) D pleaded to manslaughter on the basis he was acting in self-defence and the defence of his brother, B, and it went too far. The prosecution accepted the plea on the basis of loss of control and offered no evidence against B. D, B and the victim, V, spent much of the day drinking and taking cocaine in two different houses. At 6 am a taxi was called and V went outside to wait for it. It was cold and V tried to come back into the house but B did not want him to do so. There was pushing and shoving which escalated to V

head-butting B. D went to B's aid and picked up a pick-axe handle spontaneously. D struck V and V suffered multiple heavy and sustained blows, mainly to his head. There were multiple skull fractures, fractures of the cheekbone, fractures to both eye sockets and the base of the skull. Severe force was required to cause a fracture of the spinal column. There were five areas of linear bruising to V's back and legs consistent with blows from a pick-axe handle. Some of the injuries could have been caused by punches and kicks or falls to the ground. The pathologist believed V was struck repeatedly to the head by a heavy blunt instrument and death would have been fairly immediate. There were no significant injuries on B. D and B made no attempt to assist V. D and B returned to the house possibly an hour later and called their solicitor, who called the police. D and B handed themselves in to the police. V had significant previous convictions for violence. D was aged 28. The Judge found there was a low degree of provocation over a short time. He started at 12 years and thought the aggravating and mitigating factors balanced each other out and with the plea gave **9 years**. Held. The aggravating features were the multiple heavy blows with a weapon and the sustained attack, which carried on when V was at least helpless and probably dead. The mitigation was [initially] D was protecting B fearing further acts of violence, it was spontaneous, the weapon [was not brought to the scene] and the violence D anticipated could have been extensive. The Judge did not err in imposing 9 years.
Old cases: *R v Gant* 2007 EWCA Crim 901, 2 Cr App R (S) 100 (p 652) (**6 years**) *R v K* 2008 EWCA Crim 2647 (**6 years' DPP**) *R v O'Reilly* 2008 EWCA Crim 209, 2 Cr App R (S) 67 (p 380) (**6 years' YOI**) *R v Celmins* 2009 EWCA Crim 1646, 2010 1 Cr App R (S) 77 (p 509) (**4 years**)
For a summary of the first case, see the 7th edition of this book, for the second case, see the 8th edition and for the last case, see the 9th edition.
For *Mentally disordered defendants* see **284.65** and for *Diminished responsibility* see **284.24**.

284.48   Mercy killing
An example: *R v Webb* 2011 EWCA Crim 152 (LCJ Convicted of manslaughter. Diminished responsibility. Offered to plead to manslaughter. Wife desperately anxious to end own life but had difficulty. Attempted an overdose. Began to wake up. Husband smothered her, at her own request. Akin to assisted suicide. Good character. Aged 73. Depression and adjustment disorder. Had served 6 months. Because of that, **12 months suspended** not 2 years.)
See also the MURDER *Mercy killing* para at **288.49**.

284.49   Neglect, Gross
Example: *R v Oughton* 2010 EWCA Crim 1540, 2011 1 Cr App R (S) 62 (p 390) see **284.62**.
See also the *Child victims, Neglect, starvation etc.* para at **284.19**.

284.50   No reason/Minor provocation/Drunken attack   Judicial guidance
Att-Gen's Ref Nos 60, 62-63 of 2009 2009 EWCA Crim 2693, 2010 2 Cr App R (S) 46 (p 311)[654] LCJ (five-judge court) An additional feature of manslaughter cases which has come to be seen as a significant aggravating feature of any such case is the public impact of violence on the streets, whether in city centres or residential areas. Specific attention should be paid to the problem of gratuitous violence in city centres and the streets. What is now required, without of course diminishing the attention to be paid to the actions of the defendant and his intentions at the time, and the true level of his culpability, is that specific attention must also be paid to the consequences of his crime. Crimes which result in death should be treated more seriously, not so as to equate the sentencing in unlawful act manslaughter with the sentence levels suggested in Criminal Justice

---

[654] The judgment refers to the case as *R v Appleby* 2009 EWCA Crim 2693.

Act 2003 Sch 21, but so as to ensure that the increased focus on the fact that a victim has died in consequence of an unlawful act of violence, even where the conviction is for manslaughter, should be given greater weight. For more detail of the case, see **284.51**. See also: *R v Barrass* 2011 EWCA Crim 2629 (*Att-Gen's Ref No 60 of 2009* 2009 EWCA Crim 2693 introduced a step change in the tariff of sentencing in such cases, each of which, of course, rests particularly on its own facts.)

284.51   No reason/Minor provocation/Drunken attack   Fists etc.

R v Harrison 1996 2 Cr App R (S) 250 An unlucky punch in the course of a spontaneous fight is very different from a wholly unprovoked blow to an innocent bystander.

Att-Gen's Ref Nos 60, 62-63 of 2009 Re B and T 2009 EWCA Crim 2693, 2010 2 Cr App R (S) 46 (p 311) para 66[655] LCJ (five-judge court) B and T pleaded to manslaughter (not full credit) and affray. B also pleaded to ABH. At about 3 am a group of friends, V1, V2, V3 and others, who had been out drinking, headed for the taxi rank. V4, his partner and his son were on their way to an all-night shop and were subjected to an aggressive verbal assault and confrontation by B's group including T and M. B forced V4 back into some fencing and attacked him with his fists and knees. V4 was defenceless. A witness spoke out and tried to stop the attack and was asked, "Do you want some?" V1's group saw this and went to stop the violence. They said, "That is out of order". The response was, "Fuck off or you would get the same". B ran towards V1 and, without warning, punched him heavily to the head. Then he punched V2 in the head and grabbed him by the eye. T grabbed V1 in a vicious headlock and punched him with his spare hand at least six times. M punched V3 in the head, knocking him over. V1 managed to get up, received another blow and fell again. T punched V2 powerfully, and B punched and knocked out V3. B then punched V2 again in the back of the head. B, T and their group fled, and V1 died. The cause of death was a rupture of the vertical artery at the base of the skull. It was likely that the tear occurred during the headlock. There were no fewer than 24 marks of injury to V1's head and body. There were abrasions, bruising, swellings to the face, bruises to the right arm, abrasions to the left arm and bruising and abrasions to both knees, as well as a swelling to the back of the head. There was also internal damage to the neck area with fracturing of the superior horn to the thyroidal cartilage and fractures of both the left and right horns. Fractures like these are frequently noted following forcible strangulation. V2 suffered a soft-tissue injury to his neck and his back, and bruising to his left eye. V3 had a cut to his lip which was stitched. V4's eye was blackened, and there was swelling and bruising above an eye, and swelling to the back of his head and left shoulder. In interview B and T relied on self-defence and blamed the victims. B was aged 20 and T 21. They were effectively of good character with good references. Held. V1's intervention was justified and courageous. It was likely that T's action with his headlock caused the fatal injuries. The injuries to the others underlined the extent of the violence. Heavy force was deliberately used. **7½ years** for B and **7 years** for T reflected their youth and character.

R v Duckworth 2012 EWCA Crim 1712, 2013 1 Cr App R (S) 83 (p 454) D was convicted of manslaughter. He was also convicted of assault by beating (no separate penalty). V and his friend were walking along a road when they passed D's girlfriend, who was standing alone. There was some 'light-hearted banter' between them, but D saw them talking and ran over. He said aggressively, "Oh yeah, you think you can chat up my fucking girlfriend" and punched V in the face with the full force of his fist. It was a powerful blow and D was a powerfully built man. V's friend described hearing V's head and jaw 'rattling'. V was knocked unconscious and hit his head on the road. V's friend described the shocking hollow sound of the impact. D then kicked out at V and swore at him. He swung a punch at V's friend (the assault), which connected with V's friend's ear. D was seen arguing with his girlfriend, assaulting her and then telling her to

---

[655] The judgment refers to the case as *R v Appleby* 2009 EWCA Crim 2693.

shut up or she would "get the same". V suffered skull fractures, an extensive life-threatening intracranial haemorrhage, a fracture to his jaw and a depressed fracture of the sinus, along with significant soft tissue damage as a result of the blunt force impact. V died. D, aged 36 at appeal, had 13 convictions for 26 offences including violence and public disorder. Held. This incident was of short duration, but it was not a spontaneous incident. D used gratuitous violence in the street, in an attack of considerable ferocity against a wholly innocent victim. The **extended sentence** was correct, but **6 years' custody** not 8. **5-year extension** period was wholly appropriate.
R v Jackson 2014 EWCA Crim 355 see **284.67**.
See also: *R v Robinson* 2010 EWCA Crim 2678, 2011 1 Cr App R (S) 127 (p 745) (One-punch manslaughter. After drinking, the defendant approached V in a hostile manner and punched him once from behind. V fell to the ground and hit his head. He suffered a serious brain injury. Sentenced to 2 years for GBH while V was still alive. Sentence served. Behaved well in prison and afterwards. Aged 25. Good character. **18 months** was not manifestly excessive.)
R v Green 2010 EWCA Crim 3069 (Three men drinking alcohol. One suffered head injuries and subsequently died. Bottle used as weapon. Previous for violence. **4 years' IPP**, not 5.)
R v Masefield 2012 EWCA Crim 1873, 2013 1 Cr App R (S) 77 (p 426) (LCJ Plea to manslaughter. In 1987, after an argument, he struck a friend over the head with a metal pole, killing him. Wrapped his body in bed sheets and pushed it into a sewage pipe under a manhole cover in the garden. The body was subsequently found. He was interviewed but denied all knowledge. In 2011, he approached the police and confessed. Aged 19 at the time of the offence. Previous convictions including violence and dishonesty offences. **11½ years** was well merited. For details of the case, see **284.4**.)
Old cases: *R v Chapman* 2007 EWCA Crim 2593, 2008 1 Cr App R (S) 103 (p 607) (**3 years' IPP**) *R v D and P* 2007 EWCA Crim 3200, 2008 2 Cr App R (S) 23 (p 127) (**DPP** with **3 and 3½ years** minimum terms) *R v Jones* 2008 EWCA Crim 1762, 2009 1 Cr App R (S) 73 (p 435) (**4 years**) *R v Wood (No 2)* 2009 EWCA Crim 651, 2010 1 Cr App R (S) 2 (p 6) (**Life, 13 years** minimum term) *R v Worsman* 2009 EWCA Crim 1588, 2010 1 Cr App R (S) 71 (p 476) (**5 years**) *R v Celmins* 2009 EWCA Crim 1646, 2010 1 Cr App R (S) 77 (p 509) (**4 years**) *Att-Gen's Ref No 83 of 2009* 2009 EWCA Crim 2611, 2010 Cr App R (S) 26 (p 161) (**IPP** with a **6-year** minimum term) *Att-Gen's Ref No 112 of 2009* 2010 EWCA Crim 351 (**3½ years'** detention)
For a summary of the first case, see the 7th edition of this book, for the fourth to seventh cases, see the 9th edition and for the last case, see the 10th edition.
Offer to plead rejected, convicted of that count see the GUILTY PLEA, DISCOUNT FOR *Offer to plead rejected, convicted of that count/Plea later accepted* para at **67.29** in Volume 1.

284.52   *One-punch manslaughter   Judicial guidance*
R v Edwards 2001 2 Cr App R (S) 125 (p 540) Where a single blow produced tragic consequences clearly unintended, the gravity of the consequences does have to be marked by a custodial sentence in most cases.
R v Furby 2005 EWCA Crim 3147, 2006 2 Cr App R (S) 8 (p 64) LCJ D pleaded to manslaughter. He struck a good friend one blow with a fist with moderate force. Held. The circumstances in which the punch was delivered will have a significant effect on the length of the sentence, but where the consequences of the punch were not reasonably foreseeable, care must be taken to see that the effect was not disproportionate. Where there is a guilty plea and no aggravating circumstances, the starting point is as in *R v Coleman* 1992 13 Cr App R (S) 508. With aggravating circumstances the sentence can rise to **4 years**. Getting drunk and resorting to violent behaviour will be a significant aggravating factor, particularly in a public place.
Att-Gen's Ref No 78 of 2006 2006 EWCA Crim 2793, 2007 1 Cr App R (S) 114 (p 699) The 4-year figure in *R v Furby* 2005 (see above) is after a plea.

Att-Gen's Ref Nos 60, 62-63 of 2009 2009 EWCA Crim 2693, 2010 2 Cr App R (S) 46
(p 311)[656] LCJ (five-judge court) *R v Coleman* 1992 13 Cr App R (S) 508 was clearly
intended to be strictly confined to cases where a single blow with a bare hand or fist was
followed by a fall where the death was 'almost accidental'. This description is apt to
mislead unless it is indeed 'strictly confined' to cases where death results from a single
blow with a bare hand or fist. Within that confined ambit a further distinction must be
drawn arising from the force used by the offender himself. This can vary from an almost
half-hearted blow, which would be unlikely to topple over many victims of such a blow,
or produce more than a minor bruise or small reddening of the skin, to a blow
administered with the offender's full force which, irrespective of any fall or secondary
impact, itself caused fatal injury. *R v Furby* 2006 2 Cr App R (S) 8 (p 64) continues to
provide valuable assistance about the approach of the Court to extreme cases where a
single punch, in circumstances where, although unlawful, the delivery of a punch is
understandable, a merciful course is appropriate. It is a true 'one-punch manslaughter'
case where, acting under provocation, in his own home, a defendant offered a single
punch which, but for the death, would have amounted to no more than a common assault
within the Crown Prosecution Service Charging Standard, or at the very worst an assault
occasioning very minor bodily harm, and in which the death was not only unintended,
but effectively a true accident arising from an unfortunate and unusual combination of
circumstances. An additional feature of manslaughter cases which has come to be seen
as a significant aggravating feature of any such case is the public impact of violence on
the streets, whether in city centres or residential areas. Specific attention should be paid
to the problem of gratuitous violence in city centres and the streets. What is now
required, without of course diminishing the attention to be paid to the actions of the
defendant and his intentions at the time and the true level of his culpability, is that
specific attention must also be paid to the consequences of his crime. Crimes which
result in death should be treated more seriously, not so as to equate the sentencing in
unlawful act manslaughter with the sentence levels suggested in Criminal Justice
Act 2003 Sch 21, but so as to ensure that the increased focus on the fact that a victim has
died in consequence of an unlawful act of violence, even where the conviction is for
manslaughter, should be given greater weight.
Att-Gen's Ref No 112 of 2009 2010 EWCA Crim 351 LCJ D pleaded to manslaughter.
The description 'one-punch manslaughter' fails to do justice to the many different
circumstances in which a single blow can cause death.
R v Waters 2013 EWCA Crim 936 D pleaded to manslaughter. Held. The decision in *R v
Coleman* 1992 13 Cr App R (S) 508 is over 20 years old [and at that time] sentencing in
cases where death had occurred was very different. In *R v Furby* 2005 EWCA Crim
3147, 2006 2 Cr App R (S) 8 (p 64) death was an unusual consequence of a blow of only
moderate severity. *R v Furby* 2006 provides guidance in extreme cases in which the
death was not only unintended but effectively a true accident arising from an unfortunate
and unusual combination of circumstances. In this case, the blow was a ferocious blow
with a closed fist, delivered without warning and delivered with the intention that at the
very least a significant amount of actual bodily harm would be caused. (5 years upheld.)
See also: *R v Jackson* 2014 EWCA Crim 355 at **284.67**.

284.53   One-punch manslaughter   Cases
R v Waters 2013 EWCA Crim 936 D pleaded (25-30% credit) to manslaughter as an
alternative to murder. He had been drinking all evening with L. He later described
himself, on a scale of 1-10 of drunkenness, as a nine. V, an Albanian national aged 27,
had had a drink but was not intoxicated. It was about 3 am and V and his friends walked
through a town centre, acting perfectly peaceably. K and M were walking in the same
area as V and his friends. D and L met K and M. D and L tried to start a fight with M and
were trying to goad him into striking them. He did not respond. D and L continued to

---

[656] The judgment refers to the case as *R v Appleby* 2009 EWCA Crim 2693.

pester the couple and D threw a bottle in their direction. It did not hit anyone. V and his friend went up to D to try to defuse the situation. He said, "Leave them alone" or words to that effect. Wholly unprovoked, D punched V to the side of the face. V fell to the floor with his head hitting the ground. A friend said he appeared to be unconscious as he fell. The injury caused to V's head was fatal and he died in hospital. V's family were devastated. When arrested, D said it was he who had been assaulted. He said he could not even remember the incident and demonstrated some genuine remorse. D was of good character but had one caution for assault. Held. Before the attack on V, there was a history of trouble-making and an attempt to cause violence. This was essentially an attack on a peacemaker. **5 years** was not manifestly excessive.

R v Lynch 2015 EWCA Crim 1130, 2 Cr App R (S) 73 (p 493) D pleaded to manslaughter. D, aged 41 and V, aged 62, had been close friends for a number of years. They lived in the same block of flats and had a father/son relationship. They socialised and drank together. D and his brother, B, went drinking after work and that led to an impromptu party at D's flat. As the night wore on, D and B began to argue, which became confrontational. D became extremely agitated and told everyone to leave. When they didn't, D lost his temper. He threw a coffee table into the air and put his foot through the TV screen. D, now worse for drink, attacked B, The confrontation spilled out onto the landing at the top of the stairs. V, acting as a peacemaker, tried to separate the two men. D swung a blow at B but hit V by mistake. V fell backwards and banged his head. There was some delay in calling an ambulance and when a call was made, the phone was handed to D who said, "We have all had a fight and I have hit my neighbour too hard. He is paralysed and I didn't mean to do it." V had a severe fracture to his neck. Corrective surgery was carried out and V had a stroke. This caused irreversible brain damage and V died. D was very remorseful. He only had a conviction for spitting at his girlfriend. The Judge accepted there was no animosity between D and V. Held. The blow was deliberate and aggressive. The culpability was high. The punch was thrown in the context of a fight. Before that there had been criminal damage. The level of sentencing was in the order of **6-8 years**. We agree with a 6-year starting point, the credit for the mitigation and the 20% plea credit, making **4 years 3 months**.

Note: The fact that V's death was caused by the fall rather than the severity of the blow was not taken as a factor by the defence or the Court. Ed.

See also: *R v Robinson* 2010 EWCA Crim 2678, 2011 1 Cr App R (S) 127 (p 745) (One-punch manslaughter. After drinking, the defendant approached V in a hostile manner and punched him once from behind. V fell to the ground and hit his head. He suffered a serious brain injury. Sentenced to 2 years for GBH while V was still alive. Sentence served. Behaved well in prison and afterwards. Aged 25. Good character. **18 months** was not manifestly excessive.)

R v Gray 2011 EWCA Crim 1878, 2012 1 Cr App R (S) 73 (p 410) (D pleaded to manslaughter. Full credit. Victim, V, involved in disturbance in a nightclub. D acted as peacemaker. V pushed D. D punched V once. In street, powerful blow causing V to hit head on ground. Never regained consciousness. Previous convictions for violence in social context after drinking. **4 years 8 months** not manifestly excessive.)

R v Duckworth 2012 EWCA Crim 1712, 2013 1 Cr App R (S) 83 (p 454) (11 years' extended sentence (**6 years'** custody 5 years' licence)). See **284.51**.)

R v Jackson 2014 EWCA Crim 355 see **284.67**.

R v Hayes 2015 EWCA Crim 199 (4½ years would have been unimpeachable for an adult, but because he was then aged 17, 45 months' YOI, see **284.63**.)

Old cases: *Att-Gen's Ref No 64 of 2008* 2009 EWCA Crim 88, 2 Cr App R (S) 424 LCJ (**3 years**) *R v Hynds* 2009 EWCA Crim 1486, 2010 1 Cr App R (S) 64 (p 429) (**IPP** with a minimum term of **21 months**) *Att-Gen's Ref No 112 of 2009* 2010 EWCA Crim 351 (**3½ years' detention**) *R v Rowell* 2010 EWCA Crim 2736 (**6 years**)

For a summary of the first two cases, see the 9th edition of this book and for the last two cases, see the 10th edition. For numerous other old cases, see the 8th edition of this book.

Passion, Crime of see the ***Relationship killings*** paras at **284.55**.

284.54   *Railway accidents*

R v Connolly and Kennett 2007 EWCA Crim 790, 2 Cr App R (S) 82 (p 509) C was convicted of four counts of manslaughter. C owned and operated a company called MAC. K was his employee. MAC had supplied a road rail vehicle (RRV) and two rail trailers to a company which was carrying out engineering works at night on the West Coast main line. They were removing redundant track. The two rail trailers loaded with track were standing waiting for unloading on a line which had a gradient of 1:75, quite significant for a railway line. One of the trailers started to move, gathering speed as it went downhill. It collided with and killed four workmen working on the track lower down, and injured others. The accident happened because the two trailers, and in particular the one that had run away, had no effective brakes. Important component parts of the brakes and hydraulic lines had been deliberately removed or dismantled so that the brakes were completely inoperative. The prosecution case was that C was responsible for disconnecting the braking system on both trailers and that K knew this. It was suggested that C had disabled the braking system to avoid the cost of repairing it. After the incident C and K tried to persuade another to forge assessment papers and a competency certificate for K. There was also evidence that C tried to persuade two of his employees to do or say things to cover up elements of what had happened. He did not give evidence. The defendants were of good character. Held. It was a very, very serious offence. It has been said that there was too great a disparity between C's and K's sentences, 2 years on the same counts. The main question is whether C's sentence was manifestly excessive, not whether K's was too lenient. Sentencing decisions on convictions for manslaughter based on gross negligence are troubling. Although we do not have a rationally explicable process which reaches a particular number, we think that 9 years was too great, and substitute **7 years'** imprisonment.

See also: *R v McGee* 2013 EWCA Crim 1012 (Convicted of gross negligence manslaughter. Employed by Merseyrail for 20 years. He was a train guard. Victim, aged 16, drank to excess at a party. She alighted at a station. She had her hands on a carriage, talking to someone in the train. The guard, who was a few feet away, indicated to the driver it was safe to depart. The moving train knocked her off balance and she fell between the platform and the train. Catastrophic injuries caused, from which she died. Treated as good character. Opportunity to stop the train not taken. Gross negligence of a very high order. **5 years** was within the appropriate range.)

See also the ***Corporate manslaughter*** paras at **284.21**.

Reckless manslaughter Cases on this type of manslaughter are distributed in the other paragraphs in this chapter.

284.55   *Relationship killings   Men killing wives, partners or former partners*

R v Lawton 2011 EWCA Crim 2106 D pleaded (25% credit) to manslaughter and was acquitted of murder. The conviction was based on 'an unlawful act'. He had a volatile relationship with V, his partner, which included violence on both sides. During an argument, in which V wanted to leave their house armed with a knife in order to attack another, D tried to restrain V. There was a struggle and V suffered a stab wound to the upper left chest which punctured her heart. D asked a neighbour for help and then fled the scene. He was arrested two days later. The Judge accepted that there was no intent to kill or do really serious injury. D had previous convictions including 14 offences of assault and a serious robbery. Held. Sentencing in this type of case was a balancing exercise between D's culpability and the fact that death resulted. **9 years** was not manifestly excessive.

R v Brown 2011 EWCA Crim 2796, 2012 2 Cr App R (S) 27 (p 156) LCJ D was convicted of manslaughter by reason of diminished responsibility, having been acquitted of murder, and convicted of obstructing the coroner. His marriage with V had broken down and divorce proceedings were in progress. D and V had two school-age children. D felt betrayed and was convinced that she was concealing her assets and running up costs in an attempt to manipulate the divorce proceedings, so that he would end up with as little as possible. The children had been staying with D for the weekend. Before D drove them to V's house, he put a hammer in his daughter's bag. When they arrived at V's, the children went into the house, with D's daughter carrying the bag containing the hammer into the house. D was talking to V in the hallway. The children were in a room two doors away. D violently and repeatedly struck V on the head with the hammer, 14 times. She sustained defensive wounds consistent with her covering her head. Once unconscious, D wrapped up V's body and put it into the boot of his car. His daughter saw him doing so. His son asked if he was taking V to the hospital. D drove his children back to his house, and left them with his girlfriend. He then drove to a park where he had previously dug a large hole and buried a garden box in a remote spot. He placed a bin liner over V's head to prevent blood leakage. He then put the body in the box and buried it in the hole. He disposed of his blood-stained clothing, the murder weapon, and the CCTV tape from V's house. D was of good character. Medical evidence diagnosed D as suffering from an adjustment disorder as a reaction to the severe stress of the divorce. The Judge gave D credit for offering a plea to manslaughter. He considered the disorder a mild one which rarely led to violence. Further, the sentence for murder would have been 28+ years. Held. D eventually handed himself in and had offered a plea to manslaughter. However, the aggravating features included the planning and premeditation, the proximity of the children to the attack, the fact that they heard what happened and were driven in the car with V's body in the boot, and the concealment of the body. The daughter knew that the body was in the boot. Finally, although D lost control, his culpability was high and his loss of control was in the context of his anger and resentment towards V arising out of their acrimonious divorce. D retained real culpability. Consecutive sentences were probably unnecessary and inappropriate but, considering the overall sentence, **24 years** for the manslaughter and **2 years consecutive** for the concealment, making **26 years**, was not excessive.

R v Bird 2012 EWCA Crim 1613, 2013 1 Cr App R (S) 69 (p 391) D pleaded (full credit) to manslaughter by reason of loss of control. He had been in a relationship with V for over 20 years. They had two daughters, aged 17 and 21. V had complained to her friends that D was jealous and controlling. V could be loud and aggressive when drunk. Police had been called to the house on many occasions as a result of domestic arguments after alcohol had been consumed. However, the allegations of domestic violence against D had almost invariably turned out to have no basis in fact. On the day in question, V had been drinking and D and V began to argue. The argument escalated and D stabbed V several times with a knife. He went out leaving V lying on the floor. He went to the pub and ordered a glass of wine. A barmaid noted that he was 'anxious and edgy'. He telephoned his daughters and told them that V was upset and he had gone out for a walk. He returned home half an hour later with a bottle of wine and some flowers, some of which he laid on V's body. The next morning, one of the daughters came to the house but no-one answered the door. The daughter was able to force her way in through the back door and found D covered in blood with a wound to his neck and a knife in his hand. D had inflicted knife wounds on himself, including a 6-inch horizontal cut across his neck, cuts to his forearms, wrists and stomach. He had drunk two bottles of wine and taken an overdose of painkillers. He said, "I wish you had let me die yesterday" and "Everyone has got their breaking point". V died from multiple stab wounds. Seven knives were discarded in the kitchen and bathroom, four of which had V's blood on them. D never sought to deny responsibility for the killing and was of good character. Held. The Judge was entitled to regard the degree of provocation as falling below 'a substantial degree' and marginally above 'a low degree'. The starting point was 10 years. With the plea and other matters of mitigation, **6 years 8 months** not 9 years.

R v Jones 2013 EWCA Crim 2839 D pleaded early to manslaughter. He was acquitted of murder. V, who came from Korea, was a student in Birmingham. In 2011, she began a relationship with D. On 23 March 2012,[657] D assaulted her and V reported it to the police. She considered moving away to somewhere he would not know. However, she went back to D. On 8 April 2012, they had an argument and D put his hand over her mouth and the other on her chest. D straddled her body by her waist. His hand moved up her chest to her neck and he held her by the throat. V changed colour and she stopped moving. The pressure on her windpipe was for 15-30 seconds during which time signs of asphyxia appeared. His other hand was over her mouth to stop her screaming. D took her body to the bedroom and had a bath. He covered the body with a duvet and left spending the next night at her student accommodation. Next day he went to Bristol to see his daughter and former partner to whom he admitted the strangulation. Her family called the police, who found V's body. The cause of death was extreme asphyxia. D was aged 28 with a caution. Because of a violent incident with a previous girlfriend (the caution) and the nature of the instant attack, D was assessed as 'dangerous' (no appeal). The Judge started at 15 years, and with plea made it a 15-year extended sentence (**10 years'** custody 5 years' extended licence). Held. There were serious aggravating factors. D committed an act of extreme dangerousness. It was an intentional assault, intended to frighten and terrify V to demonstrate control. It was not an isolated act of violence. D's behaviour after the killing was important. He did not call for help. He went to her accommodation and tried to 'wipe it' and remove his belongings from it. He tried to book a flight to New York. D had every expectation that an overseas student's absence would be unnoticed. The effect on V's family was appalling. Her parents had saved for her to study here. V's sister's grief still wracks her. This all justifies the 15-year starting point. Appeal dismissed.

Att-Gen's Ref No 29 of 2014 2014 EWCA Crim 1314 D pleaded to manslaughter (loss of control) on the first day of his trial for murder, of which he was acquitted. D had been with his partner, P, for about 18 months. V began a relationship with P. The next day, V told D about it on the phone. P was annoyed about that. Later, V happened to be driving past D and he threw a photo of P and him kissing at D. D went to P's flat and trampled on some flowers V had given P. (It seems P was not there.) D waited the rest of the day and the following night for V to arrive. In fact he stayed away as he had heard D was threatening to stab him. P took an overdose and was taken to hospital. Both D and V visited her. D later contacted P to say their daughter had gone missing. V collected P from hospital and they went to look for the daughter. The daughter was found and V and P went to the flat of a former partner of P, T. Shortly after D arrived, P went to lie down. D questioned V about his relationship and T left the room. V screamed and T returned and saw V curled up with D repeatedly punching V. Next he saw a knife fall to the floor. D then went to the kitchen and he picked up a large kitchen knife. P persuaded him to put it down and D left. V was found to have seven stab wounds which would have required severe force to inflict. One entered the lungs and the pericardial sac of the heart. D was aged 45 with no relevant convictions. The Judge sentenced D on the basis he had not brought the knife to the scene and the stabbing may have followed a humiliating remark by V about D. The Judge started at 10 years saying that was half-way between the 15-year and 25-year starting points. With 25% credit he gave 7½ years' custody. He later reduced this to 6 years because of D's low IQ. Held. The Judge gave insufficient weight to D's desire for a violent confrontation. He also gave too much weight to the low IQ. The guidelines should have led to a sentence of 11 years at least. With the 25% plea discount, **8 years'** custody with the **extended licence of 5 years** remaining.

---

[657] The judgment says it was 2013 but that would have been after D's trial.

See also: *R v Tyler* 2011 EWCA Crim 543 (Strangled his wife to death following low provocation over a short period of time. Allegations of prior domestic abuse. Previous convictions for violence including threats to kill. **6 years' IPP** not 8 years' IPP.)

Att-Gen's Ref No 8 of 2011 2011 EWCA Crim 1461, 2012 1 Cr App R (S) 53 (p 303) (Plea offered. Prolonged low-level provocation. Knife taken from another room. 22 stab wounds, some to full depth of the blade. Positive good character. Poor health. Starting point could not be less than 10 years. **7½ years** was the least sentence that could now be imposed.)

R v Pisano 2014 EWCA Crim 2519, 2015 1 Cr App R (S) 33 (p 258) (D was convicted based on an unlawful act. Plea to preventing burial (2½ years consecutive). Lived with gay victim, who was vulnerable and aged 62. D, aged 37, was financially dependent on V. As money ran out D became violent to V. After last attack, V left D injured in flat to 'rot' without obtaining any assistance. (How and when D died was not known.) **18½ years** in all not excessive.)

Old case: *R v Oakley* 2010 EWCA Crim 2419, 2011 1 Cr App R (S) 112 (p 659) **(12-year minimum term)**

For a summary of the case, see the 10th edition of this book.

For the *Domestic Violence Guideline 2006*, see www.banksr.com Guidelines tab or the **DOMESTIC VIOLENCE** chapter.

284.56   *Relationship killings   Men killing wives, partners or former partners   Elderly partner having difficulty in coping*

R v Beaver 2015 EWCA Crim 653 D pleaded to manslaughter based on diminished responsibility. D, now aged 81, had been married for over 60 years to V. For some time D had cared for V conscientiously. She had dementia and diabetes and had suffered mini strokes. She also had ulcerated legs from prolonged sitting. D did the housework and gave her injections. V called for D so often that he had to sleep on a chair in the downstairs room she lived in. A neighbour described how V would shout at D and noticed D did not complain. He was loving and caring. However, he became more forgetful and was not coping well. He suffered severe weight loss. She was also aggressive to her other carers, whom she hit. One day, D killed V using a large kitchen knife. D told a psychiatrist that he had had an argument about porridge or his lack of sleep and lost his self-control. D was of good character. A psychiatrist said D was in the range for dementia and suffered from depressive symptoms. Further D was normally a person of great commitment and tolerance. After the sentence, a prison supervisor said D's memory was deteriorating and his dementia was getting gradually worse. He was also becoming more and more forgetful and confused. Held. It was a tragic case but it was not a mercy killing. The attack was brutal. D had just snapped, which was attributed to his frontal lobe damage, his dementia, depression, urinary tract infection, sleep deprivation and exhaustion. We are wholly unable to say **3 years** was wrong in principle or manifestly excessive. Mercy nonetheless remains. We substitute a **Suspended Sentence Order** of **2 years** [with mental health and other conditions].

284.57   *Relationship killings   Women killing husbands or partners*

R v Harris 2010 EWCA Crim 534 D was acquitted of murder and convicted of manslaughter. Her relationship with V was over, or at least in serious trouble. The two had rows. D said that V had threatened to break her windows. At 4.46 pm D made a 999 call but the connection was broken. At 4.53 pm D phoned her sister and said that she was having problems with V. At 5 pm D called for an ambulance. After that D gave conflicting accounts. V had been stabbed through the stomach and the intestines. The knife then cut the aorta and struck a vertebra. An expert said that considerable force was used. D was aged 29 with two irrelevant convictions. She felt considerable remorse. The jury did not agree whether it was provocation or lack of intent. The Judge sentenced her on the basis that she went to the kitchen, took a knife from the drawer, lost her temper and stabbed V. Held. The separation from her son will be difficult for them both. **8 years** was not manifestly excessive.

Old case: *R v Lynch* 2007 EWCA Crim 300 (**18 months**)

For a summary of the case, see the 8th edition of this book.

284.58   *Revenge attack*

R v Thornley 2011 EWCA Crim 153 LCJ D pleaded to manslaughter by reason of provocation. There was some friction over a practical joke between D and V, his neighbour. As a result D called the police. Because of that friction D and his wife hosted a barbecue at their house for V and some friends and neighbours. D and V drank alcohol. Something went wrong and they exchanged words. There was shouting and finger pointing. Some of the guests separated them and left the barbecue. He quarrelled with his partner before returning. D armed himself with a knife but was disarmed by his wife. V once again left. V returned and was angry. D had armed himself with a second knife. V, a strongly built man, took hold of D and a struggle ensued. D deliberately stabbed him once in the right side of the stomach and once in the left side of his back above the kidney. The blows were severe. They caused disastrous bleeding. V died after suffering a cardiac arrest. D returned to his house, washed the knife and made a complaint to the police that V had attacked him, initially not mentioning V's injuries. D, aged 44 at appeal, was of effective good character. The Judge accepted that D may have feared for his wife's safety, but he noted that D had taken a knife into a dangerous situation at a point when he had not lost control. Held. The aggravating features are plain. D armed himself deliberately with a knife on a second occasion. After the stabbing he behaved in an entirely selfish way in order to divert attention away from himself as the individual responsible for V's injuries and for his death. On the other hand, taking a measured, balanced look at how it came about that D armed himself with a knife for a second time, insufficient allowance was made for the fact that, at the time when D picked up the knife, his wife was engaged in an altercation with V, a powerful man, who was in an angry mood and spoiling for a fight with D, and who had then physically taken hold of him by the throat at the time when the stabbing occurred. D did not act in self-defence. The violence that he used was wildly excessive. Considering those circumstances, **12 years**, not 16. Note: Although there is no mention of revenge in the judgment, revenge seems the likely motive. Ed.

R v Bishop 2011 EWCA Crim 1225, 2012 1 Cr App R (S) 13 (p 60) D was convicted of manslaughter and acquitted of murder. J and V had a child. Later V's relationship with J broke down and there were allegations of domestic violence. D then began a relationship with J. There was a pronounced decline in V's behaviour and his mental health. V went out drinking and made abusive and harassing telephone calls to J. D, having heard this abuse, told J he was going to work. In fact he went looking for V armed with a knife seeking a confrontation with V. He watched V in a bar but did not approach him. D left, shortly followed by V. D introduced himself as J's partner. V was stabbed seven times and died. The force of the stab wounds was described as 'moderate force', connoting the force of a 'firm punch'. D telephoned J and said "I did it for you and Joe". He subsequently fled the country. An expert said the type of wound was consistent with a knife that was missing from a set of knives in J's kitchen. D had no previous convictions. The Judge said D had ruined the lives of many people. Held. **12 years** would not be reduced.

R v Stonehouse 2011 EWCA Crim 2234 D was convicted, along with his father, F, of manslaughter. They had been drinking and were in a McDonald's restaurant. D spent a long time looking at T, who was 8 months pregnant. T called D a pervert and D approached T's table, closely followed by F. D and F launched a ferocious attack on T's partner, V, who did not fight back. V was punched, stamped on, kicked and attacked whilst helpless on the floor. The incident lasted 20 seconds and was stopped by a member of the public and staff. D and F left the restaurant. F returned. V died having suffered a tear in the right vertebral artery, arising from a blunt force impact in the region of the junction of the head and neck, consistent with a fist blow of moderate or greater force. D, aged 18½, was in breach of a conditional discharge, imposed for interfering with a vehicle. Held. This was a wholly unjustified vicious and ferocious attack in public, in front of V's heavily pregnant girlfriend. V at no time aimed any blow in retaliation and, in the latter stages of the attack, was utterly defenceless. In mitigation, there was D's youth, the lack of premeditation and the violence was short-lived, albeit sustained and violent. Even allowing for D's age, **9 years** on a contested trial was severe but not outside the range.

See also: *R v Mackevic* 2011 EWCA Crim 1688 (Convicted of manslaughter and section 20. Revenge attack following racial abuse. Punched and kicked a 17-year-old girl while accomplice repeatedly struck 17-year-old boy with a wooden post, causing his death (15-year minimum term). No previous convictions. Secondary party to fatal attack. **10 years** was not excessive.)

R v M and Others Re P 2013 EWCA Crim 673, 2014 1 Cr App R (S) 18 (p 501) (Convicted of gross negligence manslaughter. V was lured by a girl to her flat. V had previously sexually assaulted her. A number of men were waiting for him. They assaulted him and put him in the boot of a car. P did not participate in the violence. V was driven to a secluded location and petrol was poured over him. The car was set alight. V's hands had been tied together. P participated in setting fire to the car and knew that V was in the boot. He was paid £300 for his involvement. Effective good character. He failed to take any reasonable steps to check whether V was alive or dead. Death was a virtual certainty. **12 years** was fully justified.)

Old cases: *R v Fisher and Others* 2007 EWCA Crim 3303, 2008 2 Cr App R (S) 34 (p 196) (**9 years**) *R v Gosling* 2008 EWCA Crim 896, 2009 1 Cr App R (S) 10 (p 47) *Att-Gen's Ref Nos 60, 62-63 of 2009* 2009 EWCA Crim 2693, 2010 2 Cr App R (S) 46 (p 311)[658] at para 45 (For B, **5 years** and R, **3½ years**) *R v Kelly* 2010 EWCA Crim 197 (**11 years**) *R v Steanson* 2010 EWCA Crim 1306 (**6 years**) *R v Rowell* 2010 EWCA Crim 2736 (**6 years**)

For a summary of the first case, see the 7th edition of this book, for the second case, see the 8th edition, for the third case, see the 9th edition and for the last two cases, see the 10th edition.

Road traffic see the ***Vehicle, Death caused by*** para at **284.62**.

Robbers, By see the ***Burglars/robbers/thieves, By*** para at **284.13**.

284.59   *Sexual cases*

R v Doblys 2014 EWCA Crim 402 D was convicted of manslaughter and two rapes. V placed a lonely hearts entry in a Lithuanian newspaper. D answered it and they met in a hotel. A room was booked and paid for by D. During the night, D vaginally and anally raped V. V died during the night and certainly before 7.15 am. D checked out at 11.20 am and told the receptionist that he thought V was dead. D did not leave the hotel. Police and paramedics attended and found V face-down on the floor. During the examination by paramedics, D sat in a chair drinking vodka. He was calm. The numerous bruises to V's breasts, arms and thighs suggested there had been 'use of force by gripping'. The numerous injuries to her vaginal and anal area indicated there had been repetitive and deep penetration. V had died from postural asphyxia as a result of her position not allowing her sufficient air. Alcohol was considered a contributory factor. D, aged 49, had convictions for robbery, assault and carrying a knife. A psychiatric report concluded D was a "self-centred, grandiose man with limited empathy". Held. Recent authorities demonstrated there should be a correlation between sentences for murder (with a 30-year starting point) and sentences for manslaughter. The two rapes, the callous disregard for V, his lies and the painting a bogus picture of consent etc. were

---

[658] The judgment refers to the case as *R v Appleby* 2009 EWCA Crim 2693.

factors. The crimes committed were grotesque and appalling and deserved condign sentences. 20 years' extended sentence (**16 years'** custody 4 years' licence) was severe but wholly justified.

R v Bowler 2015 EWCA Crim 849 (3 years, see **284.36**.)

See also the **MURDER:** *Sexual* para at **289.18**.

Single-punch manslaughter see the **One-punch manslaughter** para at **284.52**.

284.60   Temper, Attack after loss of

R v Harvey 2010 EWCA Crim 1317, 2011 1 Cr App R (S) 42 (p 286) D pleaded early to manslaughter. The unlawful act was common assault. D, aged 47, was at home with his wife, V. They had been drinking and using a limited amount of cocaine. An argument flared up and D threw a television remote control not aimed towards V. The remote control struck V just above her left ear. V died. Unknown to anyone, V had an unusual weakness of the vertebral artery and the blow had dissected the artery. The medical evidence said V could have died at any stage just from turning her head. D phoned an ambulance immediately and did what he could to help. D had four convictions including for ABH in 1987, when he head-butted a police officer (1 month suspended), and for ABH in 2002 when he struck a guest at a party causing a fractured cheekbone. The Judge said this was an unintended death from unnecessary violence. Held. This was not a one-punch manslaughter but the intemperate throwing of a television remote control towards V. There was a streak of anger and violence within him. **21 months** not 3 years.

Unlawful act cases These cases are distributed in the other paragraphs in this chapter. For judicial guidance about violence, see the *Judicial guidance* para at **284.3**.

284.61   Vehicles   Offence committed by driver of a motor vehicle   Endorsement and disqualification

When the offence is committed by the driver of a motor vehicle the following provisions apply.[659]

Disqualification Obligatory disqualification 2 years[660] unless special reasons found.

Disqualification until test is passed The defendant must be disqualified until an extended driving test is passed.[661]

Endorsement Obligatory unless special reasons found.[662]

Penalty points 3-11 penalty points if there are special reasons.

R v Brown 2005 EWCA Crim 2868, 2006 1 Cr App R (S) 124 (p 727) The defendant pleaded guilty to manslaughter. Held. **8 years'** disqualification not 12 (see the transcript, as that part is not in the law report).

R v Petit 2015 EWCA Crim 958 D pleaded to manslaughter and robbery. D drove with F from Bedford to Peterborough to supply V with some cannabis. V handed over the cash and F snatched it. Within seconds, D accelerated hard away. V was unable to disentangle himself from the car. The speed of the car reached up to 30 mph and V was dragged 138 metres and thrown off, falling to the ground. He received massive head injuries and died. D carried on driving, initially the wrong way on a one-way street. When seen by police he lied. He received 8½ years (no appeal) and a 10-year disqualification. The defence said the dangerous driving was over a short distance and relied on the guideline for disqualification where the offence is death by driving (see **235.20**). That says the period of disqualification should equate with the length of the custodial term, knowing that the defendant is likely to be released half-way through the term. The prosecution said the driving was deliberate and sustained and there was a very high degree of danger to V which was obvious. Held. This is only a rule of thumb. The pre-plea starting point was

---

[659] Road Traffic Offenders Act 1988 s 9, 34, 97 and Sch 2 Part II
[660] Road Traffic Offenders Act 1988 s 34(1) and Sch 2 Part I
[661] Road Traffic Offenders Act 1988 s 36(2)(a)
[662] Road Traffic Offenders Act 1988 Sch 2 Part II

about 10 years. The actual term (10 years) was only 1½ years longer than the custodial term imposed (8½ years). Because of the high degree of danger and the nature of the driving **10 years** was not manifestly excessive.

Victim under 16 see the *Child victims* paras at **284.15**.

For the *Victim's health precarious/eggshell skull/Victim not expected to die* para, see the factual basis section at **284.10**.

284.62 *Vehicle, Offence committed by driving of a motor vehicle* **Cases**

R v Dwyer 2004 EWCA Crim 2982, 2005 2 Cr App R (S) 9 (p 43) The first thing to note is that the maximum for manslaughter is life and the maximum for the statutory offence is [different]. We refer to *R v Gault* 1995 16 Cr App R (S) 1013 where the Lord Chief Justice said, "Where a court has to punish an offender for manslaughter rather than for one of the statutory offences, a different approach is both justifiable and proper".

R v Dudley 2006 EWCA Crim 387 D pleaded to two counts of manslaughter. Held. Manslaughter involving the use of a vehicle is not to be equated with death by dangerous driving when it comes to sentence.

R v Oughton 2010 EWCA Crim 1540, 2011 1 Cr App R (S) 62 (p 390) D pleaded to manslaughter through gross neglect and causing death by dangerous driving. D was a partner with P in a coach firm. He was driving one of the firm's coaches with adults and a significant number of children. Passengers noticed an intense smell of burning when the coach went down a hill. Later the brakes failed and D lost control of the coach. After attempting to slow the vehicle down, it continued through a set of traffic lights which were on red, narrowly missed a vehicle pulling a horsebox, and collided with another car, before coming to rest in a nearby garden. A married couple in the car were killed, making their son an orphan. Four on the coach received minor injuries and D suffered significant injuries. It was discovered that D and the other partner were responsible for failing to properly maintain the vehicle and, in fact, the Court heard that there were flagrant breaches of the licence, namely that the vehicle should be inspected every six weeks. This was not done. An expert: a) found the coach was poorly maintained and all four brakes were severely out of alignment, and b) said that had a competent mechanic inspected the vehicle, the defects in the braking system would have been identified. D was of good character with exemplary references. A prison report noted his excellent behaviour. The Judge: a) judged the neglect as joint with P, b) said they were equally responsible for the manslaughter, c) found the motive was commercial concerns, d) found D had ignored the queries about the smell, e) found there were health issues for D, f) recognised D's deep and genuine remorse, and g) gave D 25% discount for his plea. P received 3 years for the manslaughter. Held. The family loss was terrible. The Judge sought to strike the balance by applying the guidelines in a fair and impartial way. We think that he did that, and he took properly into account all the aspects of the criminal conduct and the mitigating features. **13 months** for the manslaughter and **5 years** for the driving **concurrent**.

R v Hussain 2012 EWCA Crim 188, 2 Cr App R (S) 75 (p 427) D was convicted of manslaughter. V1, a two-year-old boy, was walking with two 13-year-old girls, V2 and V3, one of whom was his aunt. V1 ran between two parked cars and into the road. V2 ran after him. They were both struck by a car being driven by D. V2 suffered a broken ankle, cuts and bruises. V1 was hit on the head and thrown into the road. His head impacted with the road surface. D stopped the car for a second and then drove off. V1 had become caught underneath the car and D drove for some 350 m (around 30 seconds) with V1 underneath the car. When D turned right, V1 was thrown clear. D still drove on. V1 suffered multiple head injuries and subsequently died. D had been travelling within the 30 mph limit, and the prosecution's view was that D was entirely blameless in the primary incident. D abandoned the vehicle a short distance away. He denied being the driver. He was not the owner of the vehicle. The owner was arrested and interviewed. D was convicted on the basis that he knew V1 was underneath the car. D was aged 19 at the time of the offence and had an IQ of 58. He was of good character. He had not passed his test and had barely driven a car before. Held. This was reckless manslaughter. D could do nothing to prevent the accident. However, the medical evidence was clear: the initial impact did not kill V1, it was the brain damage sustained whilst being dragged along the road. Further, D lied on a number of important matters. There was a significant delay between the incident (2004), the conviction (2008) and the appeal hearing (2008) as he had had four trials. The submissions on delay had very little merit. Because of his age, the short distance driven, the low IQ and that his driving was less culpable than in *R v Hussain* 2006 EWCA Crim 3269, **6 years** not 8.

Att-Gen's Ref Nos 107-108 of 2014 2015 EWCA Crim 405[663] D1 and D2 pleaded (15% credit) to manslaughter and two conspiracies to steal. The two, who were established criminals, carried out a number of thefts from vehicles parked in cash and carry car parks over a weekend. Cloned vans were used. Four offences or preparation work were committed on the Saturday and three before the relevant one. During that one, a victim, V, jumped into van driven by D1 to prevent their escape. Inside there was a struggle between V and M, another conspirator. It ended with V being forcibly ejected through the sliding door. Through the force of M and D1's 'wiggling' of the van, V lost his grip and fell, with the back of his head hitting the ground with great force. M slid the door shut and shouted to D1, "Move it." D1 drove away dangerously and at speed. D2 was in a second vehicle about 300-400 metres away. V suffered a fractured skull and associated brain damage and died. V was aged 35, married with a child, hardworking and a central figure in his wider family. D2 accepted he foresaw the possibility that unlawful and dangerous violence might be deployed by people [intervening while they were stealing]. D1 was aged 34. In 2006, he drove dangerously whilst escaping from an attempted theft from a vehicle at a cash and carry. In 2011, he attempted to break into unattended vehicles at a cash and carry. In 2012, he was [convicted] of dangerous driving when he tried to escape from police who were interested in him at a shop car park. D1 was disqualified from driving. D2 was aged 46 and had dishonesty and driving convictions. His wife's health was poor. Held. There was a strong likelihood of members of the public seeking to intervene. Had the thefts stood alone 4 years [would have been appropriate]. The thefts were organised crime with a degree of sophistication by experienced criminals. At least 12 years would have been appropriate for D1, so **12 years** not 10½ years. We do not alter D2's **7½-year** sentence.

See also: *R v Willett* 2011 EWCA Crim 2710, 2012 2 Cr App R (S) 18 (p 76) (Convicted. Stealing from vehicles in a car park with brother who was convicted of murder. Drove away when disturbed by one owner, hitting victim in the process causing fatal injuries. Defendant was passenger. Aged 22. Bad record, mostly for dishonesty, motoring and breaches of court orders. Sentenced on basis that it was agreed the driver would drive dangerously to escape. Drug problem. **14 years** not 16.)

Old cases: *R v Bissell* 2007 EWCA Crim 2123, 2008 1 Cr App R (S) 79 (p 452) (**8 years**) *R v Lunn* 2010 EWCA Crim 166 (**5½ years DPP**)

For a summary of the first case, see the 7th edition of this book and for the second, see the 10th edition.

Matters relating to the defendant

284.63   *Defendant aged under 18*

R v E 2011 EWCA Crim 2744 D was convicted of manslaughter (unlawful act route). He was the victim of aggressive bullying by R, who was aged 16. D was aged 13 at the time of the offence. R took D's bicycle. V, aged 17, who was R's cousin, attempted to calm matters. R left with D's bicycle, but later telephoned V and arranged to meet D and V, so that D could collect the bicycle. At some stage, D anticipated some violence, and armed himself with a flick knife. R was older and bigger than D. R armed himself with a heavy stick and struck D a couple of times. D took out the flick knife and waved it around. V

---

[663] The judgment is wrongly entitled *R v O'Driscoll and O'Driscoll* 2015 EWCA Crim 405.

attempted to calm the situation and in doing so, D struck V with the knife whilst swinging it around. Held. There was no intention to injure V or anyone else, save for the intention of protecting himself against R. D showed remorse and reports about him in custody were favourable. **4 years' detention**, not 6.

R v Hayes 2015 EWCA Crim 199 D was convicted of manslaughter. D and V, both aged 17 at the time, knew each other and they attended a birthday party. They each consumed a moderate amount of alcohol. After the party and in the early hours, several attendees became involved in antisocial behaviour. D's friend was assaulted and D intervened angrily. Others had tried to calm him down. Another friend then told D that his hand was cut, which led D, by now 'pumped up', to angrily confront and shout at the person D thought had cut his hand. V then intervened by shouting at D and trying to push D away. D then shouted at V to get out of the way and punched V once to the face with moderate force. V fell to the ground and was knocked unconscious when his head hit the road. This also caused a skull fracture and arterial bleeding. D then ran off but V came round after a short while and went home to bed. V never woke up and a post-mortem revealed that he died from his brain being starved of oxygen due to the bleeding. D meanwhile had phoned V's friend, apologising and saying that he had not meant to punch V. At trial D's defence of self-defence was rejected. He was aged 18 on appeal and of exemplary character. V's family and friends suffered an immeasurable loss. Held. It was appropriate and necessary for the Judge to have proper regard to *Att-Gen's Ref Nos 60, 62-63 of 2009* 2009 EWCA Crim 2693, 2010 2 Cr App R (S) 46 (p 311), see **284.3**. Although the sentence would have been unimpeachable had D been older, the current sentence inadequately reflected the significance of D's age at the time. **3 years 9 months' custody** not 4 years 6 months' YOI.

R v JF and NE 2015 EWCA Crim 351 LCJ J, a boy aged 14½ and D, a girl aged 16, were convicted of manslaughter. They were acquitted of arson being reckless whether life was endangered and convicted of arson. They and two others, X and Y, visited a derelict building. Inside the basement, one needed torches to be able to see. J and D set fire to a discarded duvet which was on top of some tyres. On a table there was a tin of baked beans. X and Y asked what they were doing and said a man could have been inside. Within five minutes acrid smoke filled the basement rooms and shortly after they all ran off. A homeless man who was inside was killed. J admitted he knew people slept there. J had an IQ of 68-74. He was said to be child-like. The Judge chose not to differentiate between them. Held. Because of the reports (no details given) and the seriousness of the offence, **3 years' detention** was not manifestly excessive. Because of the progress D had made and because she will be moved to a different type of establishment when she becomes 18, we reduce her sentence to 2 years. Because the defendants were treated the same by the Judge we do the same for J.

See also: *R v Jackson* 2014 EWCA Crim 355 (For a summary, see **284.67**.)

R v S 2014 EWCA Crim 558, 2 Cr App (S) 29 (p 290) (Convicted. Age 15. Shot girlfriend aged 15. Pulled trigger to scare her. Previous convictions for two robberies. Worrying attitude to weapons. Remorseful. **9 years** but not extended.)

Old cases: There are a large number of old cases in the 9th edition of this book. They add little, as these cases are so fact-specific and manslaughter sentences have changed in the last five years.

284.64   *Defendant aged 18-20*

R v Mahmood 2012 EWCA Crim 400, 2 Cr App R (S) 63 (p 373) (Convicted of manslaughter (×3). Brother was convicted of murder (×3). Disagreement with V over car bought for business venture. Threats made to V by the brother. The two men set fire to property of V's ex-wife using petrol. She was inside with her two children. Children died from smoke inhalation, mother died after suffering fractured spine from jumping from a first-floor window. Aged 18. **17 years' YOI** was not excessive. Brother received minimum term of 29 years.)

Old cases: *R v O'Reilly* 2008 EWCA Crim 209, 2 Cr App R (S) 67 (p 380) (**6 years' YOI**) *R v Gosling* 2008 EWCA Crim 896, 2009 1 Cr App R (S) 10 (p 47) (**3 years' detention**)
For a summary of the second case, see the 8th edition of this book.

284.65   *Mental disorder   As a mitigating factor*
Note: There are a few old cases but sentencing in this area has changed significantly since they were reported. Mental disorientation remains a factor but cases do not assist in how great a discount should be given. Ed.

284.66   *Mentally disordered defendants   Grave cases*
R v Dighton 2011 EWCA Crim 1372, 2012 1 Cr App R (S) 30 (p 178) D was convicted of manslaughter on the grounds of diminished responsibility, having been acquitted of murder. After an argument with his mother, he took two knives, with 16 cm and 18 cm blades respectively, and stabbed both of his parents. His mother suffered 20 stab wounds, including two to the heart. His father suffered four stab wounds, one puncturing a lung. The wounds showed that the knives were buried to the hilt. He suffered from a low performance IQ, being equivalent to that of a ten-year-old. His underlying mental state consisted of cognitive deficits and schizoid traits. The Judge accepted that D's responsibility was 'substantially diminished'. D, aged 35, previously had a good relationship with his parents and was of good character. Held. Having regard to D's mental state, the substantially diminished responsibility, his real remorse, his character and the lack of premeditation, among other things, **12 years' IPP** not 15.
R v Brennan 2015 EWCA Crim 1449 and 2014 EWCA Crim 2387 D pleaded (full credit) to manslaughter based on diminished responsibility. He was tried for murder and his conviction was quashed by the Court of Appeal because it was not open to the jury to reject the unchallenged medical evidence. D was obsessed with videos featuring ritualistic and satanic killings. His sexual experiences had always been with men. He worked as a male escort and one of his clients was V. D said V required him to engage in particularly disgusting sexual acts which he particularly disliked. D was in a relationship with B and when B was away D used a set of keys he had had cut to enter and use B's flat. D texted V suggesting they meet at the flat. At that time he typed into his computer, 'Hide in bedroom stab heart cut throat bang head cut solar then groin at mo of death Krishna rhade jaya jaganatha place body in pentagram'. At about 9.15 pm, V went to the flat. Just after midnight V left the flat and rang 999 saying he had murdered someone. D later said to the police, "I have killed someone. I hate men. They just do what they want." Police went to the flat and found V naked in the bedroom and dead. He had been stabbed 22 times, primarily in the back but also in the chest. Three knives were used. Two hammers were also found. D said in an interview that the scratching and scorings on V's back were to release V's spirit. Police discovered that after the killing D had cleaned himself, put on new clothes, taken V's car keys and cash from the flat, thrown some of the cash in the street and left a note on the flat door with a pentagram symbol saying, "Do not enter, call 999 straight away." Forensic examination found no sign of sexual activity. At D's home were found pagan material corresponding with those found at the murder scene. D was aged 22 and had no convictions. He was small in stature. He had personality and mental health problems going back to when he was aged 13. D had suffered repeated abuse from another family member. At school he was bullied. There were incidents of self-inflicted violence including smashing his face with a rock. Around the time of the killing he was increasingly depressed and unwell. D told his appropriate adult that he had been having thoughts of killing people. D's mother said he was obsessed with witchcraft and Hare Krishna. A psychiatrist said D's behaviour was consistent with Schizotypal Disorder and Emotional Unstable Personality Disorder. She believed drink and drugs had inhibited him and made the killing easier. She did not think that sexual activity triggered the killing. Held. This was a shocking and savage murder on a defenceless man. D was a deeply troubled and damaged young man. However, he

retains significant responsibility for the killing. On the one hand there was a high level of culpability. On the other, D was in an almost total mental turmoil. Since his remand there had been a profound improvement. Two psychiatrists said because of the treatment his risk to others was low. D was not [now] dangerous whatever the position was in 2013. We start at 23 years, so with plea discount **15 years**.

See also: *R v Limani* 2013 EWCA Crim 1513 (Late plea. Diminished responsibility. Waiter at a restaurant where the victim was the manager. Decapitated the victim using a cheese knife taken from two floors above the scene. No obvious motive. Aged 33. Previous psychiatric treatment. One previous incident of violence, in Sweden. An attack with the gravest of features. Life with minimum term of **19 years** was unexceptional.)

Old case: *R v Oakley* 2010 EWCA Crim 2419, 2011 1 Cr App R (S) 112 (p 659) **(12-year minimum term)** The rest are best ignored.

For a summary of the case, see the 10th edition of this book.

See also the **Diminished responsibility** para at **284.24** and the **HOSPITAL AND GUARDIANSHIP ORDERS** *Serious offending, Public protection is paramount* para at **69.15** in Volume 1.

284.67   Secondary parties

R v Jackson 2014 EWCA Crim 355[664] D was convicted of manslaughter. V, aged 40, was out with his friends. They had been to several pubs and, at about 7.15 pm, D set off on his own to buy some food. He phoned his friends to say he was having some trouble with a group of youths. They set off to meet him. CCTV footage showed that D was part of a group of young people behaving in an antisocial way. Members of the group could be seen throwing road signs around, obstructing the pavement to get in the way of passers-by and being 'loutish'. D was not shown on the CCTV throwing anything, but was a part of the group. V approached the group and something was said to V. V stopped and remonstrated with them. While the exchange was going on, other people gathered. Two friends of V tried to defuse the situation. D sought to inflame matters and tried to provoke one of V's friends, saying that he was going to 'crack' him and knock him out. There was a further verbal confrontation with V. V did not try to provoke or try to hit anyone. He wanted to give the group a piece of his mind, which was, in the Judge's view, reasonable. Someone in the group shouted for assistance from D. He came running towards V from some 50 metres or so and delivered a single full-force punch to the side of V's head. V did not see him coming. The blow was so severe that it caused him to fall and strike his head on a pillar and then on the pavement. He suffered serious skull fractures and brain damage and died soon afterwards. D was sentenced on the basis that he was aggressive, looking for violence and trying to provoke one of the other men. D was aged 16. He had four court appearances predominantly for public disorder and criminal damage. The pre-sentence report noted that D had consumed a great deal of alcohol. Held. There was no intent to kill or to do really serious harm. The Judge knew every detail of the case and we do not seek to undermine his findings. He correctly identified 6 years as the starting point, [but] he fell into error in failing to reduce the sentence to take account of D's age. 6 years was manifestly excessive. **4 years** was appropriate.

R v Garner 2014 EWCA Crim 926 D pleaded to manslaughter and attempted robbery after her jury was sworn (10% credit). There were a series of robberies on a towpath where gay men met for casual sex. In the early hours, V1 was robbed of a packet of cigarettes by C and M. V2 and V3 came to V1's assistance. V2 was stamped on and V3 was thrown into the canal but managed to get out. B and S joined the group and pursued V4. The group then left but returned. The group followed V5 and tried to rob him. That was frustrated and V5 was pushed in the canal. B admitted V5 shouted, "I can't swim." B fled, followed by D. The whole group ran off. V5 drowned and V3 suffered injuries. D was sentenced on the basis that she was present when B was pushed into the canal and

---

[664] Reporting restrictions were lifted.

encouraged others to intimidate V5. D was aged 21 and had 27 previous convictions including a number of robberies and attempted robberies. One was committed after the canal death. The Judge commented that: a) the men who visited the area were vulnerable because those who preyed on them did so knowing that they were unlikely to complain because of their situation, b) the robberies were in the dark, and the group created fear and were prepared to use violence, and c) D had been treated leniently before and she had not responded to that. C was given a 13-year **extended** sentence (**10 years'** custody 3 years' extended licence). M received 9 years' detention in a YOI. Held. There was evidence [that] robberies were unreported in this area. D lent support and added to the threat by her presence. The Judge drew the inference [that] D heard V5's cry as well as B. It was callous to abandon V5 in the canal. 10 years upheld.

Old case: *Att-Gen's Ref Nos 60, 62-63 of 2009 Re B and R* 2009 EWCA Crim 2693, 2010 2 Cr App R (S) 46 (p 311)[665] (at para 45 LCJ (five-judge court) **5 years** and **3½ years**)

For a summary of the case, see the 9th edition of this book.

The sentence

284.68 *Funeral expenses of the deceased, Power to make an order for compensation for the*
Powers of Criminal Courts (Sentencing) Act 2000 s 130(1) The court may on application or otherwise make an order requiring him to make payments for funeral expenses or bereavement in respect of a death resulting from an offence other than death due to an accident arising out of the presence of a motor vehicle on a road.

Powers of Criminal Courts (Sentencing) Act 2000 s 130(3) A court shall give reasons if it does not make a compensation order in a case where this section empowers it to do so.
Note: The current specified amount is £12,980.[666] Ed.

R v Williams 1989 Unreported 10/3/89 It is important that sentencers bear in mind the words (which had just been added to the then statute) giving the court power to order compensation for funeral expenses. If the court decides not to order compensation, it must give its reasons.

284.69 *Concurrent or consecutive sentences   Should the sentence be concurrent or consecutive to the sentence for the illegal activity?*
R v Wacker 2002 EWCA Crim 1944, 2003 1 Cr App R (S) 92 (p 487) D was convicted of conspiracy to facilitate illegal entry and 58 counts of manslaughter. Sixty illegal immigrants travelled from China to Holland where they were loaded into an adapted container on D's lorry. The deaths were caused by lack of air. The basis for the manslaughter was gross negligence. D received 8 years for the conspiracy and 6 years consecutive for the manslaughter counts. The defence argued the total was too much and the Attorney-General argued the 6 years for the manslaughter counts was too lenient, although the total sentence was not challenged. Held. The causing of so many deaths to avoid detection puts this case in a category of its own. Concurrent sentences were the correct approach so there is no danger of punishing the underlying criminality twice. Therefore **14 years for the manslaughter** substituted, which would not have the appearance of devaluing the loss of life.
For more detail see *Multiple deaths* at **284.6**.

284.70 *Life sentences   Whole life orders*
Powers of Criminal Courts (Sentencing) Act 2000 s 82A(4) If the offender was aged 21 or over when he committed the offence and the court is of the opinion that, because of the seriousness of the offence or of the combination of the offence and one or more

---

[665] The judgment refers to the case as *R v Appleby* 2009 EWCA Crim 2693.
[666] See Fatal Accidents Act 1976 s 1A(3) and Damages for Bereavement (Variation of Sum) (England and Wales) Order 2013 2013/510 para 2. For deaths before 1/4/13 the figure is £11,800, Damages for Bereavement (Variation of Sum) (England and Wales) Order 2007 2007/3489 para 2.

offences associated with it, no order should be made under subsection (2) (the release provisions) above, the court shall order that the early release provisions shall not apply to the offender.

284.71 *Life sentences   Whole life orders   Cases*
R v Bryan 2006 EWCA Crim 379, 2 Cr App R (S) 66 (p 436) LCJ In 2005, D pleaded to two manslaughter counts on the grounds of diminished responsibility. In 1994 he was convicted of manslaughter on the grounds of diminished responsibility and wounding. Aged 23, he was working in a clothes shop. At 7 pm, armed with a claw hammer, he went to the shop and struck the owner's 20-year-old daughter with it, killing her, and struck her brother, aged 12. D was diagnosed as schizophrenic and received a Hospital Order. In 2002 he was released to a hostel. In 2003 there were concerns that he was relapsing. In February 2004 he was transferred to hospital so that he could be monitored. A week later he was allowed out for the day and went to the flat of C, someone he knew. A visitor found D holding a knife and C naked and dead. Police found C's brains in a frying pan in the kitchen. His arms and a leg had been severed. Strewn around the floor were blood-stained knives and a claw hammer. He said that he ate the brains with butter, and they were really nice. Further, he would have 'done' someone else if the police had not come along, and he wanted their souls. Examination showed he had broken the bones by stamping on them. He was taken to Belmarsh prison and assaulted staff. He was sent to Broadmoor and put in a medium-secure ward.
With him was L, a 60-year-old patient, awaiting trial for murder. Staff heard two bangs and found L on the floor. He had a ligature mark round his neck and head injuries. Eventually D admitted smashing his head on the floor and trying to strangle him. He said that he wanted to eat him but did not have time and that he was the weakest on the ward and the lowest in the food chain. He identified another patient who would have been next. He told doctors that he fantasised about killing L and wanted to cook him. He considered eating him raw but was sexually excited by the killing and attracted by necrophilia. He retained a desire to eat flesh and drink blood. He was a paranoid schizophrenic who was extremely dangerous. The Judge gave him **automatic life** and ordered that the release provisions should not apply. Held. The harm was immense and horrifying. It was important to disregard how long it would be before it was safe to release him because that was not part of the minimum term. D's mental abnormality diminished his culpability. It did so to the extent of reducing his crimes from murder to manslaughter. Thus, as a matter of law, it reduced his responsibility for the killings and his culpability. The Judge treated the bizarre sexual and sadistic overtones as increasing the gravity of the offences without reflecting the fact that these were symptomatic of D's illness. Assuming (unlikely though it is) that D is cured so he becomes a new man, how long does justice demand that he should be held to punish him for the crimes committed when he was ill? The appropriate term was **15 years** for each **consecutive**, making **30 years**. Therefore, the minimum term should be **15 years** with no reduction for the time in custody as we treat the time in hospital as if it were a licence from his previous offence. The reality is that it is hard to conceive that he will ever be released.
See also the **MURDER Whole life** section at **288.90**.
For whole life and article 3 ECHR, see **288.92**.
For whole life in cases other than murder and manslaughter, see **75.16** in Volume 1.

285   MEDICINE OFFENCES
285.1
Medicines Act 1968 s 7-8 and 45 (sell, supply etc. medicinal products, substances etc.)
Mode of trial Triable either way

Maximum sentence On indictment 2 years. Summary a £5,000 fine for offences committed before 12 March 2015 and an unlimited fine thereafter.[667] There are maximum fines for those aged under 18, see **14.38** in Volume 1.

There is no summary power of imprisonment.

See also the **DEFENDANT** *Drug users* paras at **240.21** and the **IMPORTATION OF DRUGS**, **POSSESSION OF DRUGS**, **PRODUCTION OF DRUGS** and **SUPPLY OF DRUGS** chapters.

285.2 Cases

R v Bacai 2013 EWCA Crim 1204 D pleaded (full credit) to conspiracy to supply: a) prescription-only medicines, b) medicines not on general sale, and c) class C drugs. He also pleaded to possession of false identity documents with intent and forgery. D was involved in a conspiracy to import and supply unlicensed medicines, prescription-only medicines and class C drugs to members of the public. D was at the hub of the British end of what was a significant shipping operation from abroad. He opened mailboxes in false names using false documents. The drugs were delivered to the mailboxes and D took them to his home, processed and distributed them. None involved were qualified to prescribe the medicines, which were potentially dangerous and could have significant side effects. D's address was searched and a large number of boxes and packages from China and India were found. There were mailing lists for people in the UK and throughout the world. The drugs seized were 220,000 benzodiazepine tablets (worth £1.5m) and various other medicinal products worth around £125,000. D, aged 38 at sentence, had no convictions or cautions. Held. The Judge was correct to note the attempt to bypass the regulatory authority whose objective was to protect public health. The offences were difficult to detect and D was involved in deliberate conduct designed to cause significant losses to legitimate companies. This was one large-scale business operation. D was also assisting, in albeit a remote and peripheral way, [at] the fringes of the importation. However, he was charged with conspiracy to supply. The correct starting point was **4½ years**. So 3 years not 3 years 8 months.

R v Tahir 2013 EWCA Crim 1866, 2014 2 Cr App R (S) 2 (p 8) D was convicted of using a false instrument with intent (×2). D was a doctor who, in 2002, joined a GP's partnership. In 2011 he was expelled from the partnership after a breakdown of relations. In 2012, his former practice was alerted by a pharmacist at Boots to a prescription which had been presented the day before. It was for 180 tablets which were a central nervous system stimulant. 30 tablets were dispensed, with the balance ordered in. It had been written on a pad belonging to one of D's former partners, Dr B, and purportedly signed in his name, and made out to a patient at the practice. The partners at the practice recognised D's handwriting. It was then discovered that a similar prescription had been presented on the previous day, again from Dr B's pad. The prescription was made out to a different patient at the practice. No tablets were dispensed as they needed to be ordered. The 30 tablets obtained were worth £200, but the full amount would have been worth £2,000. D's house was searched and Dr B's pad was found, along with a quantity of the tablets. His mobile phone contained details of two patients whose names were on the forged prescriptions. D was of previous good character with good character references. Held. There was a grave breach of trust. He stole the pad and forged the prescriptions. Deterrent sentences need to be imposed in this sort of context. There is no doubt that the Judge was right to impose an immediate custodial sentence. Due to the collateral punishment to D (the loss of his medical career), **10 months** not 15.

See also: *R v Guy's and St Thomas' NHS Trust* 2008 EWCA Crim 2187, 2009 1 Cr App R (S) 104 (p 585) (Plea to supplying medical product not of nature specified. Human error in mixing solution and error by supervisor. Baby died following massive glucose overdose. Because of no management failures and the need not to impact on the work of the trust **£15,000** not £75,000)

---

[667] Legal Aid, Sentencing and Punishment of Offenders Act 2012 s 85(1) and (4) and Legal Aid, Sentencing and Punishment of Offenders Act 2012 (Commencement No 11) Order 2015 2015/504

R v Gillespie 2011 EWCA Crim 3152, 2012 2 Cr App R (S) 24 (p 127) (Convicted of conspiracy to defraud, supplying a medicinal product without authorisation (×3), selling counterfeit goods (×3), and acting as a director when disqualified. Drugs manufactured in China were sold in the UK purporting to be French prescription drugs, previously on sale in France. High-value drugs. Aged 65. Deterrent sentence necessary. **8 years** was affirmed.)

Old cases: *R v French* 2007 EWCA Crim 2717, 2008 2 Cr App R (S) 13 (p 81) (**12 months concurrent**) *R v Haywood and Others* 2009 EWCA Crim 69, 2 Cr App R (S) 62 (p 443) (**6 years** for H. **4½ years** for D and **3 years** for P)

For a summary of the first case, see the 9th edition of this book and for the last case, see the 10th edition.

286   MONEY LAUNDERING ETC.

286.1

Proceeds of Crime Act 2002

　s 327 (concealing etc. criminal property)

　s 328 (entering into an arrangement etc. about criminal property)

　s 329 (acquiring, using and possessing criminal property)

Modes of trial Triable either way

Maximum sentences On indictment 14 years. Summary 6 months and/or a £5,000 fine for offences committed before 12 March 2015 and an unlimited fine thereafter.[668] There are maximum fines for those aged under 18, see **14.38** in Volume 1.

Cases which are charged under other offences but which are essentially money laundering are also listed in this chapter.

Confiscation Where a defendant has a criminal lifestyle the court, once the confiscation proceedings are triggered (see **22.11** in Volume 1), must follow the Proceeds of Crime Act 2002 procedure. 'Criminal lifestyle' offences include those under Proceeds of Crime Act 2002 s 327-328.[669] For what constitutes a criminal lifestyle see **22.48** in Volume 1.

Deferred Prosecution Agreements A designated prosecutor may apply to the court under Crime and Courts Act 2013 Sch 17 para 7 for these agreements to apply to offences under Proceeds of Crime Act 2002 s 327-330 and 333A and Money Laundering Regulations 2007 2007/2157. The procedure is laid down in Crime and Courts Act 2013 Sch 17. In force 24 February 2014.

Serious Crime Prevention Orders For section 327-329 offences, there is a discretionary power to make this order, when it would protect the public etc.[670]

For **corporate offenders** see the *Fraud, Bribery and Money Laundering: Corporate Offenders Guideline 2014* at **225.4**.

286.2   Crown Court statistics   England and Wales

Money laundering Aged 21+

Year	Plea	Total sentenced	Type of sentencing %						Average length of custody in months
			Dis-charge	Fine	Commu-nity sentence	Sus-pended sentence	Custody	Other	
2013	G	717	705	1.4	1.6	14.9	39.1	42.8	0.1
	NG	194	213	1.9	0.9	13.1	22.1	61.5	0.5
2014	G	639	2	1	16	41	39	–	19.2
	NG	194	2	1	7	34	57	1	30.6

---

[668] Legal Aid, Sentencing and Punishment of Offenders Act 2012 s 85(1) and (4) and Legal Aid, Sentencing and Punishment of Offenders Act 2012 (Commencement No 11) Order 2015 2015/504

[669] Proceeds of Crime Act 2002 s 6 and 75 and Sch 2 para 2

[670] Serious Crime Act 2007 s 1 and Sch 1 para 6

For explanations about the statistics see page 1-xii. For more statistics and for statistics for male and female defendants etc., see www.banksr.com Other Matters Statistics tab

286.3   *Sentencing Guidelines Council guideline*

Fraud, Bribery and Money Laundering Offences Guideline 2014, see www.banksr.com Other Matters Guidelines tab The guideline applies to Proceeds of Crime Act 2002 s 327, 328 and 329. In force 1 October 2014. The guideline only applies to offenders aged 18+, see page 4 of the guideline. For the usual practice, see **66.21** in Volume 1.

STEP ONE: Determining the offence category

page 28 The court should determine the offence category with reference to the tables below. In order to determine the category the court should assess culpability and harm.

Culpability

The level of culpability is determined by weighing up all the factors of the case to determine the offender's role and the extent to which the offending was planned and the sophistication with which it was carried out.

Where there are characteristics present which fall under different levels of culpability, the court should balance these characteristics to reach a fair assessment of the offender's culpability.

Culpability
Culpability A – High culpability
A leading role where offending is part of a group activity Involvement of others through pressure/influence Abuse of position of power or trust or responsibility Sophisticated nature of offence/significant planning Criminal activity conducted over sustained period of time
Culpability B – Medium culpability
Other cases where characteristics for Categories A or C are not present A significant role where offending is part of a group activity
Culpability C – Lesser culpability
Performed limited function under direction Involved through coercion, intimidation or exploitation Not motivated by personal gain Opportunistic 'one-off' offence; very little or no planning Limited awareness or understanding of extent of criminal activity

Harm A
This is initially assessed by the value of the money laundered.

Category 1	£10 million or more Starting point based on £30 million
Category 2	£2 million-£10 million Starting point based on £5 million
Category 3	£500,000-£2 million Starting point based on £1 million
Category 4	£100,000-£500,000 Starting point based on £300,000
Category 5	£10,000-£100,000 Starting point based on £50,000
Category 6	Less than £10,000 Starting point based on £5,000

Harm B
Money laundering is an integral component of much serious criminality. To complete the assessment of harm, the court should take into account the level of harm associated with the underlying offence to determine whether it warrants upward adjustment of the starting point within the range, or in appropriate cases, outside the range.
Where it is possible to identify the underlying offence, regard should be given to the relevant sentencing levels for that offence.

286.4

STEP TWO: Starting point and category range

page 37 Having determined the category at step one, the court should use the appropriate starting point to reach a sentence within the category range in the table below. The starting point applies to all offenders irrespective of plea or previous convictions.

Where the value is larger or smaller than the amount on which the starting point is based, this should lead to upward or downward adjustment as appropriate.

Where the value greatly exceeds the amount of the starting point in Category 1, it may be appropriate to move outside the identified range.

Proceeds of Crime Act 2002 s 327, 328 and 329

	Culpability		
Harm	**A**	**B**	**C**
Category 1 £10 million or more	**Starting point** 10 years' custody	**Starting point** 7 years' custody	**Starting point** 4 years' custody
Starting point based on £30 million	**Category range** 8 to 13 years' custody	**Category range** 5 to 10 years' custody	**Category range** 3 to 6 years' custody
Category 2 £2 million–£10 million	**Starting point** 8 years' custody	**Starting point** 5 years' custody	**Starting point** 3 years 6 months' custody
Starting point based on £5 million	**Category range** 6 to 9 years' custody	**Category range** 3 years 6 months' to 7 years' custody	**Category range** 2 to 5 years' custody
Category 3 £500,000–£2 million	**Starting point** 7 years' custody	**Starting point** 5 years' custody	**Starting point** 3 years' custody
Starting point based on £5 million	**Category range** 5 to 8 years' custody	**Category range** 3 to 6 years' custody	**Category range** 18 months' to 4 years' custody
Category 4 £100,000–£500,000	**Starting point** 5 years' custody	**Starting point** 3 years' custody	**Starting point** 18 months' custody
Starting point based on £300,000	**Category range** 3 to 6 years' custody	**Category range** 18 months' to 4 years' custody	**Category range** 26 weeks' to 3 years' custody
Category 5 £10,000–£100,000	**Starting point** 3 years' custody	**Starting point** 18 months' custody	**Starting point** 26 weeks' custody

Culpability			
Harm	A	B	C
Starting point based on £50,000	Category range 18 months' to 4 years' custody	Category range 26 weeks' to 3 years' custody	Category range Medium-level community order to 1 year's custody
Category 6 Less than £10,000	Starting point 1 year's custody	Starting point High-level community order	Starting point Low-level community order
Starting point based on £5,000	Category range 26 weeks' to 2 years' custody	Category range Low-level community order to 1 year's custody	Category range Band B fine to medium-level community order

For the meaning of a high-level, a medium-level and a low-level community order, see **16.12-16.14** in Volume 1.

286.5   [Aggravating and mitigating factors]
page 38 The table below contains a non-exhaustive list of additional factual elements providing the context of the offence and factors relating to the offender.
Identify whether any combination of these or other relevant factors should result in an upward or downward adjustment from the sentence arrived at so far.
Consecutive sentences for multiple offences may be appropriate where large sums are involved.

Factors increasing seriousness

Statutory aggravating factors:
Previous convictions, having regard to a) the nature of the offence to which the conviction relates and its relevance to the current offence; and b) the time that has elapsed since the conviction
Offence committed whilst on bail
Other aggravating factors
Attempts to conceal/dispose of evidence
Established evidence of community/wider impact
Failure to comply with current court orders
Offence committed on licence
Offences taken into consideration
Failure to respond to warnings about behaviour
Offences committed across borders
Blame wrongly placed on others
Damage to third party, for example loss of employment to legitimate employees

Factors reducing seriousness or reflecting personal mitigation

No previous convictions or no relevant/recent convictions
Remorse
Little or no prospect of success
Good character and/or exemplary conduct
Serious medical conditions requiring urgent, intensive or long-term treatment
Age and/or lack of maturity where it affects the responsibility of the offender
Lapse of time since apprehension where this does not arise from the conduct of the offender
Mental disorder or learning disability
Sole or primary carer for dependent relatives
Offender co-operated with investigation, made early admissions and/or voluntarily reported offending
Determination and/or demonstration of steps having been taken to address addiction or offending behaviour
Activity originally legitimate

286.6   Suggested approach to the new guideline
Note: There is nothing in the guideline to suggest it is intended that there should be a radical departure from the existing sentencing principles. I would suggest that sentencers: a) start with the guideline, b) consider the recent cases from the Court of Appeal to see if they are helpful, and then c) return to the guideline before deciding the appropriate sentence. Ed.

286.7   Magistrates' Court Sentencing Guideline
Magistrates' Court Sentencing Guideline 2008 (as amended), see www.banksr.com page 357 The section on money laundering of the *Fraud, Bribery and Money Laundering Offences Guideline 2014* has been inserted, see www.banksr.com Other Matters Guidelines tab

286.8   Pre-guideline judicial guidance
R v Greenwood 1995 16 Cr App R (S) 614 The defendant pleaded to assisting another to retain the proceeds of drug trafficking. Held. Launderers are nearly as bad but not quite as bad as those who do the actual dealing.

R v Basra 2002 EWCA Crim 541, 2 Cr App R (S) 100 (p 469) Money laundering is a stand-alone offence where the constituent elements may be many and varied. There may be circumstances where the launderer has no knowledge of the source of the money laundered and indeed may choose not to know. He may know that it represents the proceeds of criminal activity, but beyond that he is careful not to ask any questions. Many such offenders say they are ignorant of the origin of the proceeds in question and that this should isolate them from the original crime. In this case the maximum sentence for money laundering is 10 years (in fact, it is 14 years. Ed.), whereas the maximum sentence for the evasion of duty was 7 years. The former makes allowance for the many and varied antecedent offences to which it could relate. There is no necessary direct relationship between the sentence for the laundering offence and the original antecedent offence. The criminality in laundering arises from the encouragement and nourishment it gives to crime in general. Without it many crimes would be rendered much less fruitful and perhaps more difficult to perpetrate. Nonetheless, the sentence for laundering cannot be wholly disproportionate to the sentence for the original antecedent offence, where the offence is that of being involved in an arrangement whereby the retention or control of the proceeds of criminal conduct results.
Note: This case was applied in *R v Raza* 2013 EWCA Crim 1772. Ed.

R v El-Delbi 2003 EWCA Crim 1767 Those who launder large sums which are the proceeds of drug trafficking play an essential role in enabling the drug conspiracy to succeed, and as such they can expect severe sentences compared with others playing a significant role in the supply of drugs, although it has to be borne in mind that Parliament has provided different maximum sentences for dealing in class A drugs (life) and money laundering (14 years). There will be no direct arithmetical relationship between the sums recovered but nonetheless sentences very close to the maximum should be reserved for laundering on a very large scale.

R v Monfries 2003 EWCA Crim 3348, 2004 2 Cr App R (S) 3 (p 9) D was convicted of conspiracy to assist another to retain the proceeds of drug trafficking and/or criminal conduct money. Held. The relevant considerations that apply in cases of this type include the following: i) The circumstances of assisting another to retain the benefit of drug trafficking and/or criminal conduct vary so widely that this Court has not, to date, provided detailed guidelines, ii) There is not necessarily a direct relationship between the sentence for the laundering offence and the original antecedent offence. Where, however, the particular antecedent offence can be identified, some regard will be had to the appropriate sentence for that offence, when considering the appropriate sentence for the laundering offence, iii) The criminality in laundering is the assistance, support and encouragement it provides to criminal conduct, iv) Regard should be had to the extent of the launderer's knowledge of the antecedent offence, and v) The amount of money laundered is a relevant factor.

Att-Gen's Ref No 48 of 2006 2006 EWCA Crim 2396, 2007 1 Cr App R (S) 90 (p 558) The defendant pleaded to two counts of money laundering. Mathematical calculations are not appropriate because so much turns on the facts. In sentencing, deterrence must play a part.

R v Griffiths and Pattison 2006 EWCA Crim 2155, 2007 1 Cr App R (S) 95 (p 581) The defendant, P, an estate agent who provided financial services, was convicted of entering into a money laundering arrangement. Organising the cover-up or laundering the proceeds of crime is always particularly serious, especially if organised or set up as an operation. Custodial sentences are absolutely inevitable in almost every case, if not in every case [sic].

R v Yates 2010 EWCA Crim 1028, 2011 1 Cr App R (S) 15 (p 112) D was convicted of obtaining a money transfer by deception, among other offences. He obtained a loan of £807,500 in a mortgage fraud by false statements. Held. Clearly the relevant factors will vary from case to case. However, we would suggest that, and subject always to the Definitive Guidelines, in the case of a loan or loans obtained by fraud of this kind, some of the potentially relevant features may be (in no particular order) as follows: a) whether one or several transactions are involved, b) whether the fraud is committed by a professional person or is otherwise committed in breach of trust, c) the nature of the fraud will need to be considered and the means by which it is carried through, d) whether the fraud was an isolated incident or involved ongoing deception, e) the amount of money sought and obtained, f) the amount of actual loss, so far as it can be identified, to the lender, g) whether the offender has involved others, or is involved with others, in the fraud, and h) whether, at the time, there was an intention to repay (and, if so, the anticipated means of repayment) or whether there was no intention to repay. There may well be other factors and regard will, of course, need to be had in the usual way to matters such as a guilty plea, relevant previous convictions or lack of previous convictions, and so on. A starting point of four years for offending of this kind perhaps was a severe starting point, but it was not too high. For the fraud, **2½ years**.

R v Fay 2012 EWCA Crim 367 D pleaded to converting criminal property and possession of 1 kilo of cannabis and 400 Nimetazepam tablets (class C), both with intent to supply. His mobile phone records were examined and the prosecution inferred that text messages referred to class A, B and C drugs. D denied dealing in class A drugs. There was no *Newton* hearing. Held. The amount of money is obviously important but not determinate of any sentence. Just as important, if not more, is the criminal conduct from which the criminal proceeds have been obtained. A further factor is how close the defendant is to that conduct. The defendant should not be sentenced on the basis he was dealing in class A drugs. It is well known the sentences are significantly more severe for class A drugs.

Note: I was counsel in the case. The implication was that the Court should determine the class of drugs involved and that this was a significant factor when determining the sentence. Unfortunately class A drug money laundering was not listed as a Culpability A factor in the guidelines. Harm B includes a requirement, 'to take into account the level of harm associated with the underlying offence to determine whether it warrants upward adjustment of the starting point within the range, or in appropriate cases, outside the range,' see **284.3**. Ed.

R v Sowden 2014 EWCA Crim 1419 D pleaded to possession of criminal property. Held. Those who provide ready and willing assistance to those who perpetrate confidence frauds as here should expect an element of deterrence in the sentence.

286.9   *Concurrent or consecutive. Should the sentence be?*

R v Bell 2008 EWCA Crim 3211 D pleaded to producing cannabis and conspiracy to possess criminal property. He was sentenced to 4½ and 2½ years consecutive. It was argued that the sentences should have been concurrent. The prosecution said that the gravamen of the money laundering was different. Held. Each case depends on its own facts. Here the Judge was entitled to pass consecutive sentences because of D's ostentatious use of his wealth and a letter which showed how he glamorised the nature of his criminal activity.

R v Greaves and Others 2010 EWCA Crim 709, 2011 1 Cr App R (S) 8 (p 72) The defendants pleaded and were convicted of conspiracy to contravene Financial Services and Markets Act 2000 s 19 and 21 and money laundering under Proceeds of Crime Act 2002 s 328. The offence was a £2.4m share fraud. Money was transferred to Hong Kong. Held. If the conduct involved in the Proceeds of Crime Act offence in reality adds nothing to the culpability of the conduct involved in the primary offence, there should be no additional penalty. A person should not be punished twice for the same conduct. That can be achieved either by imposing 'no separate penalty' on the Proceeds of Crime Act offence or by a concurrent sentence where the primary sentence is imprisonment. Where conduct involved in a Proceeds of Crime Act offence does add to the culpability of the conduct involved in the primary offence an additional penalty is appropriate, see *R v Brown* 2006 EWCA Crim 1996, 2007 1 Cr App R (S) 77 (p 468) and *R v Linegar* 2009 EWCA Crim 648. Where the primary offence has a maximum sentence, that is the maximum which Parliament has thought appropriate for conduct constituting the offence. In a case where the Proceeds of Crime Act offence does not add to the culpability of the conduct involved in the primary offence, there should not be a consecutive sentence on the latter on the ground that the maximum permitted on the primary offence is too low. Any difficulty posed by a low maximum for the primary offence may possibly be avoided if it is foreseen by the prosecution. Thus, in the present case there might have been a number of specimen substantive counts rather than one count of conspiracy. Where the conduct involved in the Proceeds of Crime Act offence does add to the culpability of the conduct involved in the primary offence, the maximum sentence permitted on the primary offence may be relevant to the sentence on the Proceeds of Crime Act offence because the seriousness of the primary offence reflects on the seriousness of the laundering, see for instance *R v Greenwood* 1995 16 Cr App R (S) 614 and *R v Basra* 2002 EWCA Crim 541, 2 Cr App R (S) 100 (p 469). But it does not, as a matter of principle, provide a limit, see *R v Linegar* 2009. If the Proceeds of Crime Act offence merits it, the sentence for it may add to that for the primary offence bringing it above the maximum for the latter, and it may if appropriate itself exceed the maximum on the latter, see *R v Linegar* 2009. It is not necessary for the Proceeds of Crime Act offence to have a different gravamen from that of the primary offence. The conduct involved in the former must add to the culpability of the conduct involved in the latter. Put shortly, there must be 'something more'. The offender is not to be sentenced twice for the same conduct. Here, the money laundering counts did add something so the offences should attract consecutive sentences.

See also the CONCURRENT OR CONSECUTIVE SENTENCES chapter in Volume 1.

Criminal conduct money

286.10   *Category 1   Criminal conduct etc. money   More than £10m   Pre-guideline case*

Example: *R v Ibori* 2013 EWCA Crim 815, 2014 1 Cr App R (S) 15 (p 73) (Plea to money laundering and related fraud offences on two indictments. Massive frauds perpetrated in Nigeria. He was Governor of Delta State, Nigeria. Changed his date of birth to enable him to run for election. Sum involved was **£50m** at its lowest. Aged in his fifties. A sentence close to the maximum was appropriate for the money laundering. The Judge was fully entitled to start at **24 years** (the 14-year and 10-year maximums). With full credit, that was reduced to 16 years. Considering totality, **13 years** was wholly appropriate.)

286.11   *Category 3   Criminal conduct etc.   money   £500,001 to £2m   Pre-guideline case*

R v Bettie 2010 EWCA Crim 176 D was convicted of acquiring and using criminal property. He was acquitted of conspiracy to defraud. D ran a fraud in which over 300 investors lost all that they had invested in shares worth nearly £4m. Every penny was lost. Some victims lost their life savings. Between April and December 2005, D received over **£800,000** from the fraud. D's company was involved in selling the worthless shares using high-pressure sales techniques and lies about returns and who had invested in the shares. D was aged 34 and of good character. Held. D knew what was happening at his company. **4½ years** not reduced.

Example: *R v Khan* 2011 EWCA Crim 1234 (Plea to 10 counts of fraud. Sophisticated and large-scale mortgage fraud. £6.7m obtained, the defendant personally linked to **£1.3m**. False documents including passports used to open 68 bank accounts. **5 years** was not manifestly excessive.)

286.12   *Category 4   Criminal conduct etc.   money   £100,000 to £500,000   Pre-guideline cases*

R v Valentine 2011 EWCA Crim 1463, 2012 1 Cr App R (S) 42 (p 246) D pleaded (late) to money laundering. She was married to S, who headed a criminal gang. S was in custody for a series of robberies in which in excess of £1m was stolen. D lived a lavish lifestyle off the proceeds of S's criminal activity. S and D shared a house worth over £1m, sent their five children to private school, travelled extensively and purchased expensive jewellery. Those items, with cash deposits, amounted to **over £360,000**. However, the Crown asserted that this represented only a small portion of the total sums spent to fund D's lifestyle. D's basis of plea was that S was the dominant character in the relationship, that financial decisions were made by him and that she didn't realise at the outset of the relationship that he was involved in crime. She accepted that towards the end she deliberately closed her eyes to the origin of S's money. The Crown did not accept the basis of plea in its entirety. However, there was no *Newton* hearing. D was aged 38 at appeal and treated as if of good character. She had five children by S, three of whom were aged between 10 and 14. The Judge started at 2 years and reduced it for plea, her family and a period in custody for another matter. Held. The amount of money could not be precisely calculated, but clearly it ran into hundreds of thousands of pounds. There was no encouragement or assistance given to S by D. However, it is incorrect to state that because of S's dominating character, D had no option but to accept the benefits that were showered upon her. The Judge was correct to conclude that it would be an affront to both the victims of S's gang, and to the public, if the sentence were to be suspended. **12 months** was upheld.

See also: *R v Carmichael* 2013 EWCA Crim 1290 (Convicted. Eleven defendants defrauding account holders at Santander. Unauthorised changes were made to accounts and attempts were made to transfer money from those accounts. Some successful, some not. Total **£350,000+**. Some recovered, so net loss was £160,000+. Defendant, an employee of Santander, altered account details. Monies transferred into his account. Total benefit to him £32,000. Significant previous for dishonesty. Planned and sophisticated to a degree. **2½ years** not 3½.)

R v Akpan 2014 EWCA Crim 167 (Plea to transferring and possessing criminal property. Under police surveillance. Bag moved from a van to defendant's car. Contained £49,440. £74,905 found at her address. Had possessed another £52,460 on another occasion. Involved over 14-month period with **at least £250,000**. Convictions for dishonesty. She had young children. That was no reason to expect to escape a custodial sentence and there was no question of the sentence being suspended. Substantial custodial term merited. No merit in the appeal. **3 years** upheld.)

286.13   Category 5   Criminal conduct etc. money   £10,000 to £100,000

R v Coyle 2011 EWCA Crim 36 D pleaded to money laundering (×3), transferring criminal property (×1) and converting criminal property (×5). All counts related to D allowing his bank accounts to be used to launder money which had been defrauded by others. The scams related to building work in which elderly and vulnerable people were targeted and convinced to hand over large sums, in the region of £15,000, for building work which was either unnecessary or not carried out. In total, **£35,553** had been laundered through D's accounts. The Judge accepted that he was not 'the boss of the team' but considered that he did play an important role. He had targeted the elderly and vulnerable and had admitted his part in that. The Judge did not accept that D had not benefited. D, aged 21, had four previous appearances for 10 offences, including dishonesty offences. He was illiterate, and had no knowledge of numeracy or banking. He had never before served a custodial sentence. Held. D played no part in the active defrauding of these elderly and vulnerable victims. The accounts were set up by exploiters in his name. All D had to do was to sign his name when required. He got nothing [out of it] and in particular never saw any cash. The Judge fell into error when sentencing D on the basis that he played an active part in the defrauding of these very vulnerable victims. **2½ years** not 3½.

R v Ramdas 2011 EWCA Crim 244 D was convicted of possession of criminal property. He was a dealer in scrap metal. Police executed a search warrant at D's business premises. They were looking for stolen car parts. They found, hidden on the back of a truck in plastic barrels, Jamaican currency which had been stolen in 2000. The coins found represented 10% of the five million $20 coins stolen. The value was around £36,000, but at the time of the theft it would have been around **£77,000**. The circumstances in which D had come to be in possession of the coins were never properly established. D, aged 59, had no previous convictions. Held. Sentence of 21 months' imprisonment was indeed a significant term for an offence of this kind. There are no guidelines which could have assisted the sentencing Judge and there are no guidelines to assist this Court. Offences of this type, i.e. possessing criminal property, although comparatively frequent, are often of very differing circumstances and, in the experience of this Court, this is a somewhat unusual manifestation of this kind of offence. **12 months**, not 21, would have achieved the deterrent and punitive effect that this offence required.

R v Swan and Woolf 2011 EWCA Crim 2275, 2012 1 Cr App R (S) 90 (p 542) S pleaded (early) to seven charges of failing to disclose money laundering. She was a senior employee and a director (although she took little or no part in running the business) in a safe deposit company. She advised an undercover police officer how best to launder money without being reported. She oversaw the opening of boxes and the deposit of around **£54,000**. She suggested to another undercover officer a way in which business could be conducted anonymously. At sentence, searches had led to the recovery of more than £12m, which was being returned to the Treasury. A further £12.5m was being held pending investigations and £20m might further be recovered. The boxes contained criminal property in excess of £4.5m. S was of excellent character. Held. S played an important day-to-day role in the business and was amply placed to notice suspicious behaviour. She was a highly trusted employee whose failures to report the suspicious conduct were persistent and continued over a period of some considerable time. **9 months** not 12.

R v Aleksejevs 2013 EWCA Crim 94 D pleaded to seven counts of acquiring criminal property and a conspiracy to acquire the same. From 2007 to 2010, he received fraudulent funds and paid them into his and others' bank accounts. The funds were mostly fraudulent bank transfers and one was a stolen company cheque. The total was about **£45,000**. D, now aged 29, was a Latvian who had been resident since 2004. D had 20 convictions on nine occasions. He had been sent to prison twice. The Judge considered the offending widespread, organised, professional crime with an international dimension. He started at 4 years. Held. The offence did involve others. It was wide-ranging but we start at 3 years, making **27 months** with the plea.

R v Stubbs 2013 EWCA Crim 1077 D pleaded (full credit) to converting criminal property (×2). S, a solicitor, pleaded to 16 thefts. S did conveyancing work. D, who was a local estate agent, cashed 13 cheques to the value of **£12,580** from S's firm's client account. S used false invoices and other methods to cover the payments. D gave S cash in exchange for the cheques and D was paid about 5% for cashing the cheques. The basis of plea stated that D played a lesser role. The pre-sentence report was positive and D was ashamed of his behaviour. He was of good character. Held. Though there was powerful personal mitigation, an immediate custodial sentence was not wrong in principle. The Judge failed to properly reflect the powerful mitigation. There was also some disparity between D (very much a secondary party) and S (who received 16 months). 9 months was appropriate so with plea, **6 months** not 12.[671]

R v Cooper 2013 EWCA Crim 1152 D pleaded (15%) to transferring criminal property. His name was 'used for' a website, Cooper's Cars. Adverts were placed in motoring magazines and purported to offer motor cars for sale. Purchasers paid deposits into D's bank account. The total was **£20,300**. The vehicles did not exist and the prospective purchasers lost their money. D allowed his account to be used and although he had quickly realised that the transactions were part of a fraudulent scheme, he continued to do so. He accepted that he had withdrawn the money and paid it to a third party. D, aged 26 at appeal, had a young daughter who suffered from defects to both her kidneys. Held. The **21-month** starting point was not wrong. D's ill daughter was compelling mitigation. **15 months** not 18. It would not have been appropriate for this sentence to have been suspended.

R v Silevicius 2013 EWCA Crim 1527 D pleaded (full credit) to transferring criminal property. A sham website was set up, which offered cameras and other photographic equipment for sale. A number of orders were placed from around Europe. Payment for the equipment was sent to D's account. **Nearly £18,000** was credited to that account. A series of withdrawals were made effectively resulting in the removal of fraudulently obtained funds. D was not involved in setting up the website. He entered into an agreement that his account would be used, for which he would receive 25% of the value of the sums deposited. In the event, he received about 8%, amounting to nearly £1,700. D had personally made three withdrawals with the others being made by another, alone. D, aged 23, had no convictions but later pleaded to handling (×2). D had been addicted to heroin which may have provided a motive. At conviction he had been abstinent for 9 months. Held. It was appropriate to start at **30 months** not 3 years. With full credit, **20 months** not 2 years.

R v Imasuen 2014 EWCA Crim 1256 D pleaded to 14 counts of money laundering. He laundered the proceeds of two advance fee frauds. V1, an Australian retired civil servant, was told that a relative had died leaving him a large inheritance. He was persuaded to pay for lawyers and other fees. V1 lost just over **£64,000**. V2, an American, was a lured into a similar scam and lost about £31,000. The proceeds from both frauds passed through D's bank account. He was paid 10% of the funds making £9,500. D, aged 33 and originally from Nigeria, was a student with no convictions since his arrival in the UK in 2010. He claimed to know nothing of the details of the fraud. Held. This was a truly dreadful deceit on hapless victims. D was the facilitator of the fraud but not central to the conspiracy. Starting at 4 years, with full plea credit, **2 years 8 months** not 4 years.

See also: *R v Kerr* 2013 EWCA Crim 905 (Plea to money laundering. Used an innocent person's bank account. 'Cuckoo smurfing' case. Legitimate transactions bought and used as a vehicle to bank money without arousing suspicion. Controlled from Pakistan. £2m

---

[671] The report initially states that D received 12 months in the Crown Court but later states that the Court quashed the 18-month sentences. S received 16 months, which would suggest that it is more likely that D received 12 months. Ed.

over 6 months laundered. K's role was in a one-off transaction dropping off **£25,000** in cash. Acted under direction. No knowledge of the origin of the funds. There is a degree of trust given to a courier. Nothing wrong with **15 months**.)
Old cases: Best ignored.

286.14   Category 6   Criminal conduct etc. money   Less than £10,000
R v Sowden 2014 EWCA Crim 1419 D pleaded late to possession of criminal property. V was tricked into giving his bank account details to someone who phoned him. About **£4,000** was transferred to D's bank account in two amounts. D's basis of plea was he did not benefit from the bulk of the money and his reward was €200. D was aged 24 and of good character. He was assessed as suitable for doing unpaid work. The Judge found V had been caused considerable distress and found D's account to the probation officer was a calculated attempt to deceive. She started at 50 weeks and with plea made it 45 weeks, then with the mitigation **32 weeks**. Counsel said immediate imprisonment was wrong. Held. It is not inevitable that a 9-month sentence has to be immediate. But those who provide ready and willing assistance to [others] who perpetuate confidence frauds should expect an element of deterrence. Appeal dismissed.
Note: The maths is wrong here. 32 weeks is just over 7 months. In addition, the sentencing Judge should have deducted the plea discount after the mitigation discount. This meant the discount was larger than it should have been. Interestingly, the Court was surprised to learn D had been released after only 8 weeks. Ed.
R v Pereira 2010 EWCA Crim 347 D pleaded (25% credit) to transferring criminal property. The fraud concerned a Trojan Horse computer virus which requested, obtained and stored banking details of customers under the guise of a legitimate security check. The total unrecovered loss was almost £500,000. For the fraud to be effective, it was necessary for bank accounts to be available to receive the funds. D received two payments of **£2,850** and **£3,350**. The Judge said that it was necessary to look at D's (and his co-defendants') actions, and also the bigger picture. It was a determined and sophisticated international attack. Held. Taking into account the importance of deterrence, and the antecedent offending of the conspiracy as very serious, **21 months** was not manifestly excessive, nor was it wrong in principle.
Post-guideline case
R v Haygreen 2015 EWCA Crim 292 D pleaded very late to attempting to acquire criminal property. V, a vulnerable 68-year-old man, was defrauded out of around £100,000 over three months. D was to be paid £500 out of a sum of **£7,000** which was part of the overall defrauded sum. D had no idea that the money was from a fraud but admitted his role. He was aged 28 on appeal and of effective good character. The Judge gave a *Goodyear* indication of 9 months, suspended for 2 years, with 'any condition'. The pre-sentence report reflected D's remorse and concluded that unpaid work would be suitable. Held. Under the system before the guideline and under the guideline, given D's limited role in the circumstances, a **community order with unpaid work**, not 5 months suspended with unpaid work.

Drug money
286.15   Category 2   Class A drug money   £2m to £10m   Pre-guideline cases
R v Haidary and Others 2013 EWCA Crim 1584 H was convicted of money laundering. An organised crime group was responsible for laundering an estimated £120m over a two-year period, believed to have represented the profits from the sale of drugs. There were links to various countries world-wide. Cash handovers of amounts over £100,000 were co-ordinated by Dubai-based controllers. Money was paid into a business account in banks in Birmingham and Manchester. Once the account was credited, US dollars were bought and then sent to bank accounts in China, Pakistan and Dubai. Money bureaux were also used. They were used to create the impression that the money had come from genuine business. In reality, money did not go via any of the bureaux. False records of transactions were created to conceal their true provenance. H played a central

role. He was in regular contact via text messages and telephone calls with the controller in Dubai. He was involved in setting up a money bureau in Birmingham and records showed that £60,000 per day was going through the business. Between September 2008 and August 2009 that bureau transmitted **around £8m**. He acted as a guarantor for another bureau. H was involved in the collection of cash on around 11 occasions. He received instructions from the controller and made deposits into different accounts. The deposits accounted for around £212,000. This activity continued after his arrest and release on bail. He was surveilled and seen meeting other defendants and collecting holdalls of cash. He was arrested and £195,000 was found in the boot of his car. £5,000 and €100,000 were found at his address. H's role was significant and long-lived. He was a co-ordinator and organiser in the UK but to a lesser extent than another defendant. Held. The Judge was entitled to find that H knew that the money had come from drug trafficking. Given the scale of this money laundering, a **starting point of 12 years** could not be criticised. **11 years** would not be reduced.

R v Barnett and Keenan 2014 EWCA Crim 208 B and K pleaded to converting criminal property. K also pleaded to making an untrue statement to obtain a passport and possession of articles for use in fraud. In 2009, B was stopped near Marble Arch with a satchel containing €535,400 (in large denominations of €500 notes) and £1,500. The documentation found on him revealed he had just changed £488,000 into euros at a nearby exchange. B had been engaged to change money using an account that K set up in 2008. False documents were used by K to set up the account. Among those documents was a genuine passport of B. K had applied for an MSB (money service business) licence and with the trading account established in 2008, he was able to go to other MSB traders who were offering advantageous rates and change large sums of money that others had provided to him. The Judge concluded that overall **£19.5m** had passed through K's business in a 22-month period. K believed that the money he was laundering came from illegal gambling but soon after realised that it was from a source of really serious crime, namely class A drug dealing. B personally exchanged **£5m** but his role may not have been limited to that. He was aware of the larger scale activity and there was some reason to believe that later on he knew of the false documentation used by K. B's basis of plea averred that he became involved in early 2009. B was aged 49 at appeal with no convictions. K, aged 41 at appeal, had fraud and blackmail convictions in 2006 but had failed to disclose these when applying for an MSB licence. The appeal was heard in 2014 due to an application to stand the appeal out pending confiscation proceedings. K had subsequently suffered serious health issues. Held. K's previous conviction, the breach of licence, the fraudulent activity to set up the company using false documents, his realisation that the money had come from class A drug dealing and the vast sums of money were aggravating features. K's sentence of **11 years** (with 15% credit) was certainly at the top of the range but it was not wrong in principle nor manifestly excessive. B's role and culpability were materially different. B was an assistant and courier. At least 40 times he took cash to the exchange and on eight of those occasions he was carrying over £400,000. He was involved for a lesser period than K and was not a knowing party to the company. He was an assistant not the principal organiser. With something less than 25% credit (for pleading at the PCMH), **5 years** not 6.

286.16   *Category 5   Class A. money   £10,000 to £100,000*
Example: *R v Robinson* 2012 EWCA Crim 1898 (Convicted. Disguising criminal property (×9). Transferring criminal property (×3). Drug dealer. Lied in confiscation hearing. Concealed profits from drug dealing through his mother. Concealed money and transferred a house bought with drug profits to his girlfriend. Total appears to be **£37,715**. **3 years** not 4.)

286.17 Category 4 Class B drug money £100,000 to £500,000 Pre-guideline cases

R v Fay 2012 EWCA Crim 367 D pleaded (full credit) to four converting criminal property counts and possession of 1 kilo of cannabis and 400 Nimetazepam (class C) tablets, both with intent to supply. Police found the drugs in his house with £55,460 in cash. His wife's bank accounts were examined, as were his, and the Court of Appeal sentenced D on the basis of **£185,000** criminal conduct money on top of the cash. His mobile records were examined and the prosecution inferred that text messages referred to class A, B and C drugs. D was of positive good character and a hard-working family man with a referee who spoke extremely highly of him. D denied dealing in class A drugs. The Judge gave D 5 years for the criminal conduct money and 1 year consecutive for the drugs. Held. Here the source of the money was the sale of the drugs. The Judge could have made them concurrent. The cannabis was the stock-in-trade from which he was obtaining the money. We do not say the police were wrong in their interpretation of the texts, but there was no count on the indictment for class A drugs. There should have been clarity for that. **4½ years** for the money and 1 year concurrent for the drugs, not 6 in all.

286.18 Category 3 Drug money (class not determined) £500,001 to £2m Pre-guideline case

R v Gibson 2014 EWCA Crim 301 D was convicted of money laundering. He was seen to drive his van to a car park in Blackburn where he had a conversation with a man who was under police surveillance. The man got into the van and they drove around for about 8 minutes before the man left the vehicle. D then drove to a service station on the motorway. He went to the rear of the van, opened the back door and returned to the driver's door. He then returned to the back of the van wearing a pair of orange gloves. He closed the van door and went into the service station. He returned 20 minutes later and continued his journey. He was stopped on the motorway and police discovered two holdalls in the rear of the van. They contained **£621,285**. Over £570,000 were in vacuum wraps, with the remaining £50,000 in loose notes. D claimed he had been delivering goods in accordance with his legitimate business, a company involved in transporting goods from Spain to England for returning expatriates. D delivered four boxes to an address and received the two holdalls in return. The Judge found that he made that delivery knowing that he was moving the proceeds of drug crime. The Judge considered that because of D's legitimate business, he was the perfect conduit for the proceeds of crime. D was of good character and had a good prison report. Held. The Judge was perfectly entitled to come to that conclusion. One of the reasons that a person like D is chosen to launder money is that he is respectable. **4½ years** not 5½.

287 MOTHERS

287.1 Judicial guidance

JSB Equal Treatment Bench Book 2013, see www.banksr.com Other Matters Other Documents 'Social exclusion and poverty' section page 1 para 46 Lone parents are over-represented among those at risk of social exclusion. Custodial sentences for this group are likely to have significant adverse impacts on the children, whatever alternative arrangements are made for their care.

R v Khan 2011 EWCA Crim 2761 D pleaded to conspiracy to steal and was sentenced to 18 months. Held. Having children is not some form of licence which entitles a mother to commit whatever offences she likes, however serious, and avoid the normal consequences of such offending.

R v Boakye and Others 2012 EWCA Crim 838, 2013 1 Cr App R (S) 2 (p 6) para 32 The position of children in a defendant's family may indeed be relevant, but it will be rare that their interests can prevail against society's plain interest in the proper enforcement of the criminal law. The more serious the offence, generally the less likely it is that they can possibly do so.

R v Smak 2012 EWCA Crim 1280, 2013 1 Cr App R (S) 45 (p 258) LCJ Even where the offender is the mother and sole carer of a young child, there can be a place for deterrent sentences.

For more details of the case, see **309.6**.

R v Truby 2013 EWCA Crim 227 D pleaded to possessing firearms and ammunition. Held. We reiterate what *R v Petherick* 2012 EWCA Crim 2214, 2013 1 Cr App R (S) 116 (p 598) made clear, a defendant who is looking after children, even the sole carer of the children, is not thereby immune from a sentence of immediate custody. However, as *R v Petherick* 2012 also said, the impact of a sentence on young children in that situation always has to be considered and sentences must weigh up whether the disruption, which immediate custody [causes], is proportionate in the circumstances of the case.

See also: *R v Akpan* 2014 EWCA Crim 167 (Plea to money laundering. Involved over 14-month period with at least £250,000. Nobody can use the fact of young children needing to be cared for by other family members...as a licence to commit financial crimes on this scale and then to escape a custodial sentence.)

287.2   *Courts must obtain the fullest information*
R (P) v Secretary of State for the Home Dept 2001 EWCA Civ 1151, 1 WLR 2002 C of A (Civ Div) P gave birth to a baby shortly after starting her 8-year sentence. Q began her 5-year sentence with her nine-month old baby. Initially the babies were allowed to live with their mothers but they were notified that their babies would be taken from them. They applied to the High Court, relying on European Convention on Human Rights art 8. Held by the Master of the Rolls *obiter*. If the passing of a custodial sentence involves the separation of a mother from her very young child (or, indeed, from any of her children) the sentencing court is bound by Human Rights Act 1998 s 6(1) to carry out the balancing exercise identified by Hale LJ in *Re W and B (Children: Care Plan)* 2001 EWCA Civ 757 at para 54, especially at sub-para iii), before deciding that the seriousness of the offence justifies the separation of mother and child. (The case is about local authority care decisions. para 54 iii) deals with the interference with article 8 requiring a 'pressing social need' and the need for the interference to be proportionate. It was partly overruled in the House of Lords in *Re S (Minors)* 2002 UKHL 10. Ed.) If the court does not have sufficient information about the likely consequences of the compulsory separation, it must, in compliance with its obligations under section 6(1), ask for more. It will no longer be permissible, if it ever was, for a court to choose a custodial sentence merely because the mother's want of means and her commitments to her children appear to make a fine or community sentence inappropriate if the seriousness of the offence does not itself warrant a custodial sentence. In such circumstances it must ensure that the relevant statutory authorities and/or voluntary organisations provide a viable, properly packaged solution, designed to ensure that the mother can be punished adequately for her offence without the necessity of taking her into custody away from her children. The fathers also have rights. The Prison Service was not allowed to operate the removal policy rigidly. Q's baby will be aged 3 on Q's parole date. There was no contact with the father. The Social Services had difficulty in finding a placement. The harm done to the child if there was separation would be very great indeed. Q's appeal allowed. If we made an exception for P, it would be difficult to maintain the policy at all. P's appeal dismissed.

Note: Perhaps this case says little more than that judges should obtain the fullest information and they must reach a balanced decision. Ed.

287.3   *Human rights and separation of the child from the mother*
R v Petherick 2012 EWCA Crim 2214, 2013 1 Cr App R (S) 116 (p 598) D pleaded to causing death by dangerous driving. She drove at speed, persistently and inappropriately

overtaking when twice over the limit. The Judge gave her 4 years 9 months. The Court considered the effect of a sentence of imprisonment on an individual's article 8 rights to family life. Held.

1 The sentencing of a defendant inevitably engages not only her own article 8 family life but also that of her family and that includes (but is not limited to) any dependent child or children. The same will apply in some cases to an adult for whom a male or female defendant is a carer, and whether there is a marital or parental link or not.

2 The right approach in all article 8 cases is to ask these questions:
   a) Is there an interference with family life?
   b) Is it in accordance with law and in pursuit of a legitimate aim within article 8.2?
   c) Is the interference proportionate given the balance between the various factors?
   That is carefully set out by Lady Hale in her speech in *HH v Deputy Prosecutor of Genoa* 2012 UKSC 25.

3 Long before any question of article 8 or of Human Rights Act 1998 was thought of, sentencing practice in England and Wales recognised that where there are dependent children, that is a relevant factor to sentencing (see *HH v Deputy Prosecutor of Genoa* 2012 at paras 128-9)

4 It follows that a criminal court ought to be informed about the domestic circumstances of the defendant and where the family life of others, especially children, will be affected it will take it into consideration. It will ask whether the sentence contemplated is or is not a proportionate way of balancing such effect with the legitimate aims that sentencing must serve.

5 In a criminal sentencing exercise, the legitimate aims of sentencing, which have to be balanced against the effect that a sentence often inevitably has on the family life of others, include the need of society to punish serious crime, the interest of victims that punishment should constitute just deserts, the needs of society for appropriate deterrence (see Criminal Justice Act 2003 s 142) and the requirement that there ought not to be unjustified disparity between different defendants convicted of similar crimes.

6 It will be especially where the case stands on the cusp of custody that the balance is likely to be a fine one. In that kind of case the interference with the family life of one or more entirely innocent children can sometimes tip the scales and means that a custodial sentence otherwise proportionate may become disproportionate.

7 The likelihood, however, of the interference with family life which is inherent in a sentence of imprisonment being disproportionate is inevitably progressively reduced as the offence is the graver.[672]

8 In a case where custody cannot proportionately be avoided, the effect on children or other family members <u>might</u>, which we emphasise, afford grounds for mitigating the length of sentence, but it may not do so. If it does, it is quite clear that there can be no standard or normative adjustment or conventional reduction by way of percentage or otherwise. It is a factor which is infinitely variable in nature and must be trusted to the judgment of experienced judges.

9 Those briefly stated principles are, we think, sufficient to guide sentencing judges and do no more than reflect what has been the practice of the criminal courts since long before arguments were habitually couched in terms of article 8 or human rights generally.

R (P) v Secretary of State for the Home Dept 2001 EWCA Civ 1151, 1 WLR 2002 See **287.2**.

H (H) v Deputy Prosecutor of the Italian Republic 2012 UKSC 25 Supreme Court D and his wife, W, were convicted in their absence of drug trafficking offences in Italy. The authorities applied for their extradition. The wife suffered mental and physical collapse such that the husband had to become the primary carer of their three children. In a conjoined case, D2 and her husband settled in the UK in 2002. In two warrants dated

---

[672] This is what was said even if it is not very clear what it means.

2006 and 2007, the Polish authorities applied for her extradition for dishonest behaviour involving £6,000, dating back to 1997-2001. D, W and D2 resisted the warrants relying on their article 8 right to privacy and family life. The District Judges rejected their claims. The High Court Judges dismissed their appeals. Held. Although there might be a closer analogy between extradition and the domestic criminal process than between extradition and deportation, the court had still to examine the way in which extradition would interfere with family life. The question was always whether the interference with the private and family lives of the extraditee and members of his family was outweighed by the public interest in extradition. para 130 The principle therefore is well established, and habitually applied in practice. In the overwhelming majority of cases, when the criminal is convicted and sentenced for offences which merit a custodial sentence, the innocent members of his family suffer as a result of his crimes. Although custodial sentences are sometimes avoided altogether where the level of seriousness is relatively minor and are sometimes reduced by reference to the needs of dependent children, care must also be taken to ensure that considerations like these do not produce injustice or disparity as between co-defendants with different family commitments, or undermine the thrust towards desirable consistency of approach to sentencing decisions on a national basis. Accordingly, while for generations making allowances for the interests of dependent children, and what would now be described as their article 8 interests, the need to impose appropriate sentences in accordance with established, and now statutory provisions, is unchanged. para 131 The starting point in the sentencing decision involves an evaluation of the seriousness of the crime or crimes and the criminality of the offender who committed them or participated in their commission and a balanced assessment of the countless variety of aggravating and mitigating features which almost invariably arise in each case. In this context the interests of the children of the offender have for many years commanded principled attention, not for the sake of the offender, but for their own sakes, and the broader interests of society in their welfare, within the context of the overall objectives served by the domestic criminal justice system. Sadly the application of this principle cannot eradicate distressing cases where the interests even of very young children cannot prevail.

For D: a) the limited role which she had played in the children's lives, b) the seriousness of the offences which she had committed, and c) the breach of bail, the interference with the children's article 8 rights was justified by the public interest in her extradition. For D2, [we take into account] that a) the loss of the wife to her younger children would be exceptionally severe, b) her husband's ill-health would render him incapable of becoming the effective primary carer, c) the offences for which her extradition was sought were of no great gravity, d) the overall period of delay between the commission of the offences and the bringing of the Polish prosecutions was considerable, and e) during that lapse of time the wife and her family had led new and blameless lives and the younger children had been born, without there being any reason to believe that the Polish authorities were seeking her return. The public interest in returning D2 to Poland was not such as to justify the inevitable harm to the interests of the two younger children. Appeal allowed.

R v Mackey 2012 EWCA Crim 2205, 2013 1 Cr App R (S) 100 (p 522) D was involved in a £60,000 fraud. She relied on her daughter's special needs. Held. The principles to be applied were *H (H) v Deputy Prosecutor of the Italian Republic* 2012 UKSC 25 paras 126-131. It is clear that a sentencing court has a duty to consider the interests of the children of a criminal defendant. However, it is also clear that it will be rare that the children's interests can prevail against society's plain interest in the proper enforcement of the criminal law. Generally, the more serious the offence, the less likely it is that they can possibly do so.

287.4   *Child, The interests of the*

R v Whitehead 1996 1 Cr App R (S) 111 The courts are always reluctant to send the mother of young children to prison. Sometimes they have no alternative.

R v Attuh-Benson 2004 EWCA Crim 3032, 2005 2 Cr App R (S) 11 (p 52) This Court is acutely conscious of the effects of long sentences upon families of offenders, be they mothers or fathers. We need no reminding that it is very often the innocent who suffer from crime.

Att-Gen's Ref Nos 132-133 of 2004 2005 EWCA Crim 354 The defendants pleaded to conspiracy to supply heroin and crack cocaine. The **2½-year** and **2-year** sentences were unduly lenient. The supply was well organised and substantial. One defendant had been released and returned to her children. The other was about to give birth. Their father was abroad. We have to bear in mind the interests of the children. No order to increase the sentence made.

R v Greaves 2007 EWCA Crim 2693, 2008 2 Cr App R (S) 7 (p 42) D pleaded at the Magistrates' Court to possession of two tablets of ecstasy with intent to supply. She was visiting an inmate in prison and had the tablets secreted in her bra. She went to the canteen area to try to take them out, and was seen by prison staff to be extremely nervous. They asked what she was doing, and she dropped the tablets on the floor. She stopped and made immediate admissions. In interview she repeated those admissions. She said that she had been approached by a friend of the inmate and asked to take in the tablets. D, aged 35, was of positive good character. She was married and had a 10-year-old child. She was employed as a hairdresser and had been involved in charitable activities. She was assessed as being of no risk to the public. Held. Personal circumstances and personal mitigation do not always count for so much in cases of this kind. There is a need for a deterrent approach to be adopted. We are not persuaded that **18 months'** imprisonment was excessive.

R v Kayani 2011 EWCA Crim 2871, 2012 2 Cr App R (S) 38 (p 214) LCJ It has long been recognised that the plight of children, particularly very young children, and the impact on them if the person best able to care for them (and, in particular, if that person is the only person able to do so) is a major feature for consideration in any sentencing decision. Where the only person available to care for children commits serious offences, even allowing fully for the interests of the children, it does not follow that a custodial sentence, of appropriate length to reflect the culpability of the offender and the harm consequent on the offence, is inappropriate.

See also: *R v Spencer-Whalley* 2014 EWCA Crim 912, 2 Cr App R (S) 56 (p 461) (Plea to £1.63m fraud with husband, whose part was mortgage application forms worth £750,000. Not the principals. 2 years for each. Before sentence D's two daughters, aged 10 and 14, had been in France, where they were educated and integrated. Since then, they had had to return to the UK, where they needed to be re-integrated, with difficulty, into UK schooling, adversely affecting their education. Held. Impact upon family unsurprising and a direct result of D and her husband's criminality. Appeal dismissed.)

287.5   Cases

R v Dittman and Anderson 2012 EWCA Crim 957, 2013 1 Cr App R (S) 21 (p 113) D and G pleaded (full credit) to fraud by representation. An unidentified woman, purporting to be D, attended a driving test centre for the theory test. She presented both parts of D's driving licence. The woman sat the test and passed. She was never traced. Subsequently, D was booked in for the practical driving test. G attended the test centre for the driving part of the test, purporting to be D. She was accompanied by C, who was recognised to be a driving instructor (in fact he was a trainee). G had both parts of D's driving licence and C said G was D. When challenged, G admitted that she was not D. She was arrested and admitted she had taken the test as a favour to D. D declined to comment in interview. D was aged 51 and had two children. One was aged 23 and the other was aged 13. His father lived in Germany. G was aged 39 and had two children, aged 12 and 4. G lived with her husband, who was not the father of her children. Neither had previous convictions and both were employed. C was given 6 months (no appeal). The Judge said M organised it and the offence potentially put the public at risk. Further the offence was prevalent and if D and N were concerned with the consequences of the loss of liberty they should have thought about that before they committed the offence. He drew a parallel with those who take other people's penalty points. Held. There was no commercial motive. It is clear from *R v Suleman* 2009 EWCA Crim 2205 that this crossed the custody threshold. The Judge passed sentences which were significantly lower than if those family circumstances were not present. **2 months** was not excessive.

Note: Perhaps the sentencing Judge could also have said the offence put D's passengers (including her children) at risk. Ed.

Att-Gen's Ref No 26 of 2015 2015 EWCA Crim 1119, 2 Cr App R (S) 53 (p 384) D pleaded to section 18. D was dancing in a bar and at 1.25 am she accidently danced backwards into V. Words were exchanged and then D seized V's wine glass and pushed it into V's face. An artery was cut near V's ear causing profuse bleeding. Without the prompt action of door staff and a medical team, V's life could have been in serious danger. Staff thought D was drunk. V then suffered from anxiety and depression. D was of good character. She was the mother of five children aged 20, 19, 18, 13 and 12. She had been the victim of two violent and abusive relationships. She had lived in a series of refuges and temporary homes. D suffered from depression and Bell's palsy. She worked in a care home. After taking the children to school, she started work at a care home at 8 am. She worked until 8 pm and returned home at 8.30 pm. Her 74-year-old mother and her older children helped her. Following her mother's arrest, her 20-year-old daughter had to return home ending her relationship and her hopes to train as a nurse. The pre-sentence report said D was affected by anti-depressants and alcohol on the night. The probation officer considered arrangements could be made but was [worried about it]. The officer was concerned about the impact of imprisonment on D's two youngest children and whether the house would be lost because of the rent arrears. Although the plea was tendered at the PCMH, the Judge accepted that counsel's commitments had caused a problem and gave a 50% discount. He considered that it was a Category 2 case as the case was not of the most serious kind and assessed the risk of re-offending as low. The Judge was concerned about the family structure and imposed a 2-year Suspended Sentence Order with a supervision requirement. Held. D's deep remorse did mean the plea discount was not inappropriate. We reject the suggestion the Judge's categorisation was wrong. The offence was completely out of character. D had struggled with domestic and mental health problems for some time. The Judge was looking for a proportionate sentence. The sentence was not unduly lenient.

See also the **DEFENDANT** *Female defendants* para at **240.27**.

288   MURDER

288.1

Common law

Mode of trial Indictable only

Mandatory sentence Mandatory sentence of life imprisonment[673] (or detention at HM's Pleasure and custody for life for children and young offenders, see **288.80**)

Minimum terms/Whole life orders The court must either: a) order that the seriousness is so high that the early release provisions do not apply, or b) set a minimum term which must elapse before the defendant can be considered for release by the Parole Board.[674]

Children and young offenders Where a person convicted of murder appears to the court to have been aged under 18 at the time the offence was committed, the court shall sentence him to be detained at HM's Pleasure.[675] Where a person aged under 21 is

---

[673] Murder (Abolition of Death Penalty) Act 1965 s 1
[674] Criminal Justice Act 2003 s 269
[675] Powers of Criminal Courts (Sentencing) Act 2000 s 90

convicted of murder, the court shall sentence him to custody for life unless he is liable to be detained under Powers of Criminal Courts (Sentencing) Act 2000 s 90 (detention at HM's Pleasure)[676] (see **288.80**).

Automatic life and extended sentences Murder is a specified offence in Criminal Justice Act 2003 Sch 15B[677] If the defendant is reconvicted of certain offences, the conviction for murder may oblige the court to: a) impose automatic life, or b) enable the court to pass an extended sentence (EDS) for those aged 18+.

Transitional cases Offences committed before 18 December 2003 are dealt with under the transitional provisions, see the *Transitional arrangements* para of the **MURDER** chapter in the 3rd edition of this book. These transitional provisions ensure that offenders are not dealt with more severely than they would have been had they been sentenced under the old regime. Criminal Practice Directions 2015 EWCA Crim 1567 para VII N deals with this, see **288.10**.

Funeral expenses The court may make this compensation order, see the *Funeral expenses of the deceased* para at **288.95**.

Court Martial The requirement to pass mandatory life is governed by Armed Forces Act 2006 s 217. The requirement to pass detention at HM's Pleasure is set out in Armed Forces Act 2006 s 218. The Court may pass mandatory life imprisonment/Custody for life/Detention during HM's Pleasure for all ranks, ex-servicemen and women, and civilians, see *Guidance on Sentencing in the Court Martial 2013* Annex B and **288.28**.

Sexual Harm Prevention Orders There is a discretionary power to make this order when it is necessary to protect the public from sexual harm.[678] However, such orders would be very unusual.

Victim surcharge Where all the offences were committed after 1 October 2012, the court must impose a victim surcharge of £120[679] when the sentence is life or custody for life. When the sentence is detention during HM's Pleasure, there is a £20 surcharge when the defendant is aged under 18 and no surcharge for those aged over 18 at the time of sentence.

Children and vulnerable adults: barred lists Where the defendant is aged 18 or over, he or she is automatically barred from engaging in regulated activity with vulnerable adults and with children.[680] The judge must tell the defendant that the Disclosure and Barring Service will include him or her in the barred lists.[681] The defendant may ask the Service to remove him or her from the lists.

Release and supervision The release provisions for mandatory life (life imprisonment, custody for life and detention during HM's Pleasure) are the same. Except for those serving 'whole life' life sentences, release is via the Parole Board on expiry of the minimum term. The test is 'the prisoner's confinement is no longer necessary for the protection of the public', Crime (Sentences) Act 1997 s 28(6)(b). On release the prisoner is subject to supervision for life.

Removal from UK A prisoner who has served the minimum term of a life sentence and is liable for removal from the UK may be removed at any time. No direction from the Parole Board is required and a direction as to release does not prevent removal, Crime (Sentences) Act 1997 s 32A created and inserted by Legal Aid, Sentencing and Punishment of Offenders Act 2012 s 119. If, having been removed, he or she returns to the UK, he or she is to be treated as unlawfully at large and is liable to be detained

---

[676] Powers of Criminal Courts (Sentencing) Act 2000 s 93
[677] Inserted by Legal Aid, Sentencing and Punishment of Offenders Act 2012 s 122. In force for offences committed after 3/12/12
[678] Sexual Offences Act 2003 s 103A as inserted by Anti-social Behaviour, Crime and Policing Act 2014 Sch 5 para 2 and Sexual Offences Act 2003 Sch 5
[679] Criminal Justice Act 2003 (Surcharge) Order 2012 2012/1696
[680] Safeguarding Vulnerable Groups Act 2006 s 2 and Sch 3, and Safeguarding Vulnerable Groups Act 2006 (Prescribed Criteria and Miscellaneous Provisions) Regulations 2009 2009/37 para 4 and 6 and Sch 1 para 2 and 4
[681] Safeguarding Vulnerable Groups Act 2006 s 2 and Sch 3 para 25

pursuant to the sentence. If there has been a previous Parole Board direction as to release, he is to be treated as having been recalled, Crime (Sentences) Act 1997 s 32B.
Law Commission The Law Commission published a Report on Murder, Manslaughter and Infanticide (No 304) on 29 November 2006, www.lawcom.gov.uk. The report has been ignored.

288.2   *Crown Court statistics   England and Wales*
The number of convictions for murder were as follows:

Year	Age	Plea	Male	Female	Both sexes	Totals
	10-17		Not available			
2013	18-20	G	5	0	5	30
		NG	25	0	25	
	21+	G	41	2	43	272
		NG	204	25	229	
2014	10-17		Not available			
	18-20	G	6	0	6	39
		NG	32	1	33	
	21+	G	44	2	46	277
		NG	215	16	231	

For details and explanations about the statistics see 1-xii. For more statistics see www.banksr.com Other Documents Other Matters Statistics tab

Judicial approach to setting the minimum term

288.3   *Basic principles*
Criminal Justice Act 2003 s 269(3) The court takes into account:
   a) the seriousness of the offence, or the combination of the offence and any one or more offences associated with it, and
   b) the effect of any direction which it would have given under section 240 (crediting periods of remand in custody) if it had sentenced the offender to a term of imprisonment.
Criminal Practice Directions 2015 EWCA Crim 1567 para VII M.2 Under [Criminal Justice Act 2003] s 269, all courts passing a mandatory life sentence must either announce in open court the minimum term the prisoner must serve before the Parole Board can consider release on licence under the provisions of Crime (Sentences) Act 1997 s 28 (as amended), or announce that the seriousness of the offence is so exceptionally high that the early release provisions should not apply at all (a 'whole life order').
M.3 In setting the minimum term, the court must set the term it considers appropriate taking into account the seriousness of the offence. In considering the seriousness of the offence, the court must have regard to the general principles set out in Criminal Justice Act 2003 Sch 21 as amended and any guidelines relating to offences in general which are relevant to the case and not incompatible with the provisions of Schedule 21. Although it is necessary to have regard to such guidance, it is always permissible not to apply the guidance if a judge considers there are reasons for not following it. It is always necessary to have regard to the need to do justice in the particular case. However, if a court departs from any of the starting points given in Schedule 21, the court is under a duty to state its reasons for doing so ([Criminal Justice Act 2003] section 270(2)(b)).
R v Sullivan and Others 2004 EWCA Crim 1762, 2005 1 Cr App R (S) 67 (p 308) LCJ para 7 Minimum terms can range from **whole life** to even less than **8 years**. When comparing minimum terms with determinate sentences it is necessary to double[682]

---

[682] The Judge must have meant to say halve. Ed.

(approximately) the determinate term. para 9 When the judge is considering the minimum term, he or she is only considering seriousness, as the protection of the public is provided by the imposition of the life sentence. The principal task of the court is to consider what is appropriate (section 269(3)). para 11 Thus, notwithstanding statutory guidance, the decision remains one for the judge, who has to have regard to the principles in Criminal Justice Act 2003 Sch 21. para 12 The judge complies with the section if he has 'regard' to the principles set out in the Schedule. As long as he bears that in mind he or she is not bound to follow them.

R v Peters 2005 EWCA Crim 605, 2 Cr App R (S) 101 (p 627) The 'minimum term' prescribed by section 269(2), to reflect punishment and deterrence, requires the court to assess 'the seriousness of the offence, or of the combination of the offence and any one or more offences associated with it' (section 269(3)). In short, the legislative framework itself recognises that, even in murder cases, an identical level of seriousness cannot be attributed to each case. For the purpose of assessing seriousness, the court must have regard to what section 269(5) describes as the 'general principles' in Criminal Justice Act 2003 Sch 21, as well as any general guidelines relevant to the individual case, which are not incompatible with Schedule 21. This provides a series of criteria to be taken into account when the court is determining the appropriate minimum term to reflect the 'seriousness' of the individual offence. The process of determination begins with the identification of the starting point, which should normally, but we emphasise, not invariably or inevitably, be taken. None of these provisions enables the court to avoid its obligation to make a careful analysis of all the relevant facts, including the statutory criteria and guidelines. Under Schedule 21 they are required to identify the starting point they have taken, and if they depart from what is described as the 'normal' starting point, they are obliged to explain their reasons. Nevertheless, the reality, as the statute acknowledges, is that justice cannot be done by rote. This principle applies equally to cases where the judge considers that the seriousness of the offence calls for a longer sentence than the normal starting point, as it does to cases where the proper minimum term is lower. One problem arising from the legislative framework is that the sentencing court may approach the decision, or be invited to do so, as if the ultimate sentence represents a mathematical calculation. It does not. The true seriousness of the offence, which the minimum term is intended to reflect, inevitably represents a combination, and simultaneously a balancing, of all the relevant factors in the case.

288.4   *Discretion whether to apply the guidelines*
Criminal Practice Directions 2015 EWCA Crim 1567 para VII M.3…Although it is necessary to have regard to such guidance, it is always permissible not to apply the guidance if a judge considers there are reasons for not following it. It is always necessary to have regard to the need to do justice in the particular case. However, if a court departs from any of the starting points given in Schedule 21, the court is under a duty to state its reasons for doing so (section 270(2)(b) of the Act).

R v Last 2005 EWCA Crim 106, 2 Cr App R (S) 64 (p 381) LCJ The Sentencing Guidelines Council guideline was no more than a guideline. The guidelines are to assist. The court is only required to have regard to Schedule 21. As long as it gives reasons, the court is free to depart from Schedule 21. Guidelines and Schedule 21 do not remove the judge's discretion.

R v West 2007 EWCA Crim 701 D was convicted of murder. She shot her husband with a firearm. The trial Judge said that it was inevitable he should take the 30-year starting point. Held. It was not inevitable. The word in the Schedule is 'normally'. The determinative consideration is whether the seriousness of the offence was particularly high. Each case will depend on its own facts. The starting point should have been **15 years**.

For more detail about the case, see the 7th edition of this book.

288.5   *The stepped approach and dealing with previous convictions*
Criminal Practice Directions 2015 EWCA Crim 1567 para VII M.4 Schedule 21 states
that the first step is to choose one of five starting points: 'whole life', 30 years, 25 years,
15 years or 12 years. Where the 15-year starting point has been chosen, judges should
have in mind that this starting point encompasses a very broad range of murders. At
para 35 of *R v Sullivan and Others* 2004 EWCA Crim 1762, 2005 1 Cr App R (S) 67
(p 308), the court found it should not be assumed that Parliament intended to raise all
minimum terms that would previously have had a lower starting point to 15 years.
Criminal Practice Directions 2015 EWCA Crim 1567 para VII M.12 The second step
after choosing a starting point is to take account of any aggravating or mitigating factors
which would justify a departure from the starting point. Additional aggravating factors
(other than those specified in paragraphs 4(2), 5(2) and 5A) are listed at Schedule 21
paragraph 10. Examples of mitigating factors are listed at Schedule 21 paragraph 11.
Taking into account the aggravating and mitigating features, the court may add to or
subtract from the starting point to arrive at the appropriate punitive period.
M.13 The third step is that the court should consider the effect of Criminal Justice
Act 2003 s 143(2) in relation to previous convictions (see **86.2** in Volume 1), Criminal
Justice Act 2003 s 143(3) where the offence was committed whilst the offender was on
bail; and Criminal Justice Act 2003 s 144 where the offender has pleaded guilty
(Schedule 21 paragraph 12). The court should then take into account what credit the
offender would have received for a remand in custody under Criminal Justice Act 2003
s 240 or 240ZA and/or for a remand on bail subject to a qualifying curfew condition
under section 240A (see **288.94**), but for the fact that the mandatory sentence is one of
life imprisonment. Where the offender has been thus remanded in connection with the
offence or a related offence, the court should have in mind that no credit will otherwise
be given for this time when the prisoner is considered for early release. The appropriate
time to take it into account is when setting the minimum term. The court should make
any appropriate subtraction from the punitive period it would otherwise impose, in order
to reach the minimum term.
M.14 Following these calculations, the court should have arrived at the appropriate
minimum term to be announced in open court. As Criminal Justice Act 2003 Sch 21
para 9 makes clear, the judge retains ultimate discretion and the court may arrive at any
minimum term from any starting point.
Crown Court Bench Book 2013 www.banksr.com Other Matters Other Documents tab
page 8 To fix the minimum term the court must consider the seriousness of the
offence(s). In doing so the court must have regard to the general principles in
Schedule 21 and follow any relevant guidelines which are not incompatible with the
provisions of that schedule.
Having chosen a starting point, the court should take into account any aggravating and
mitigating factors, noting that (i) the lists of such factors set out in paragraphs 8-11 are
not exclusive and (ii) other aggravating factors may include previous convictions and the
offence(s) having been committed whilst on bail. This exercise may result in fixing a
minimum term of any length.
R v Ennis 2008 EWCA Crim 969 D was convicted of murder. There was a co-defendant.
Held. This sentencing exercise was a broad-brush exercise. It is particularly unfortunate
that the guidance prescribed by Schedule 21 was not followed so as to provide
fact-finding and an assessment of the sentence for this defendant.
R v Dillon 2015 EWCA Crim 3, 1 Cr App R (S) 62 (p 434) D was convicted of murder.
D stabbed V just outside his flat. D had many previous convictions for relatively minor
violence (all under 6 months, the last in 2009) and dishonesty, spanning 30 years. The
Judge considered that D's previous convictions were an aggravating factor. Held. D's
dishonesty convictions are almost entirely immaterial and his violence convictions are of
limited significance. For more details, see **288.44**.

288.6   *Judicial flexibility*
Criminal Justice Act 2003 (Mandatory Life Sentence: Determination of Minimum Term) Order 2010 2010/197 Explanatory Memorandum There is no limitation on the degree of adjustment that a court can make in consideration of aggravating and mitigating factors. Criminal Practice Directions 2015 EWCA Crim 1567 para VII M.14 Following these calculations, the court should have arrived at the appropriate minimum term to be announced in open court. As Criminal Justice Act 2003 Sch 21 para 9 makes clear, the judge retains ultimate discretion and the court may arrive at any minimum term from any starting point. The minimum term is subject to appeal by the offender under Criminal Justice Act 2003 s 271 and subject to review on a reference by the Attorney-General under Criminal Justice Act 2003 s 272.

R v Jones 2005 EWCA Crim 3115, 2006 2 Cr App R (S) 19 (p 121) at 130 The guidance in Schedule 21 is to assist judges. The judge must have regard to the guidance, but each case will depend critically on its particular facts. If the judge concludes it is appropriate to depart from the guidance, he should explain his reasons. Where aggravating factors have led the judge to adopt the higher of two starting points, or mitigating factors have led him to adopt a lower one, he or she must be careful not to apply those factors a second time. The starting points must not be used mechanically to produce in effect three categories of murder. Full regard must be had to the features of the individual case, so that the sentence truly reflects the seriousness of the particular offence. It is important to bear in mind that it is the task of the Parole Board to ensure that the offender is not released after serving the minimum term unless this presents no danger to the public. Schedule 21 paragraph 9 recognises that 'detailed consideration of aggravating and mitigating factors may result in a minimum term of any length'.

Att-Gen's Ref No 126 of 2006 2007 EWCA Crim 53, 2 Cr App R (S) 59 (p 362) D pleaded guilty. Held. It is clear that the appropriate sentence remains fact-specific. It is trite law that irrespective of the 'starting point', the end result may be a minimum term of 'any length', well below or well above the defined starting point. The court must take account of every aggravating and mitigating feature, with specific reference to those in Criminal Justice Act 2003 Sch 21 paras 10-11. These lists are not exhaustive.

R v Height and Anderson 2008 EWCA Crim 2500, 2009 1 Cr App R (S) 117 (p 656) LCJ D was sentenced for having killed his wife not for financial gain but because he wished to be rid of her, with a starting point of 15 years. H was sentenced as having committed the offence for 'not insubstantial' financial gain, with a starting point of 30 years. Held. The Judge must identify the starting point he has chosen, his reason for doing so and, where appropriate, his reasons for departing from the normal starting point. The sentencing provisions of section 269 are not intended to be applied inflexibly. Something must be wrong with the conclusion that the starting point for a man who wishes to have his wife murdered, and arranges and agrees to pay for it, should be different from the starting point for the man he employs to carry out the killing. It is difficult to conceive of many cases where one defendant acting for gain should be subject to a different starting point [from] the individual who paid or agreed to pay him. The potential absurdity is highlighted here because on the approach to the section adopted, different starting points were applied even when it was D and not his hired associate who actually carried out the killing. The Judge overlooked that there would be cases which, because of all the aggravating circumstances, would nevertheless make the seriousness 'particularly high' even if none of the express criteria applied to it. Although H's financial motivation made a 30-year starting point appropriate, D's culpability with all its aggravating features should also have been regarded as making his case one of particularly high seriousness and the same starting point should have applied.

288.7   *The exercise is a balancing exercise not a mathematical one*
R v Peters 2005 EWCA Crim 605, 2 Cr App R (S) 101 (p 627) The reality, as the statute acknowledges, is that justice cannot be done by rote. This principle applies equally to cases where the judge considers that the seriousness of the offence calls for a longer

sentence than the normal starting point, as it does to cases where the proper minimum term is lower. One problem arising from the legislative framework is that the sentencing court may approach the decision, or be invited to do so, as if the ultimate sentence represents a mathematical calculation. It does not. The true seriousness of the offence, which the minimum term is intended to reflect, inevitably represents a combination, and simultaneously a balancing, of all the relevant factors in the case.

R v Ennis 2008 EWCA Crim 969 D was convicted of murder. There was a co-defendant. Held. This sentencing exercise was a broad-brush exercise. It is particularly unfortunate that the guidance prescribed by Schedule 21 was not followed so as to provide fact-finding and an assessment of the sentence for this defendant.

R v Beckford 2014 EWCA Crim 1299, 2 Cr App R (S) 34 (p 285) This Court has said on many occasions that the setting of the minimum term is not achieved by slavishly and mechanically following Criminal Justice Act 2003 Sch 21. Courts must achieve a just result.

288.8   Standard of proof
R v Davies 2008 EWCA Crim 1055, 2009 1 Cr App R (S) 15 (p 79) LCJ The standard of proof for the judge when determining the aggravating features that establish the starting point is the criminal standard. For more detail of the case, see **288.71**.

Note: This is no more than affirming the standard of proof in sentencing cases which is the criminal standard, *R v Ahmed* 1984 6 Cr App R (S) 391. The accused is given the benefit of the doubt. Ed.

See also the FACTUAL BASIS FOR SENTENCING *Defendant should have the benefit of any doubt* para at **59.2** in Volume 1.

288.9   Don't add a period for public protection
R v Sullivan and Others 2004 EWCA Crim 1762, 2005 1 Cr App R (S) 67 (p 308) LCJ When the judge is considering the minimum term, he or she is only considering seriousness as the protection of the public is provided by the imposition of the life sentence. The principal task of the court is to consider what is appropriate (section 269(3)).

R v Peters 2005 EWCA Crim 605, 2 Cr App R (S) 101 (p 627) In murder cases, the protection of the public, rightly regarded as the prime consideration, is achieved by the mandatory life sentence itself.

R v Jones 2005 EWCA Crim 3115, 2006 2 Cr App R (S) 19 (p 121) at 130 The guidance in Schedule 21 is to assist judges. The judge must have regard to the guidance, but each case will depend critically on its particular facts. If the judge concludes it is appropriate to depart from the guidance, he should explain his reasons. Protection of the public is not a relevant factor as that is the task of the Parole Board when considering release.

288.10   Historical offences
Criminal Practice Directions 2015 EWCA Crim 1567 para VII N 1 This section deals with offences of murder committed before 18/12/03. It adds a fourth step to the stepped approach at para **288.5**.

The starting points

288.11   Judicial guidance
R v Challen 2011 EWCA Crim 2919, 2012 1 Cr App R (S) 20 (p 85) LCJ These starting points are not to be applied mechanistically. What is important is to determine where in the scale of seriousness a particular case comes.

For details of the judicial flexibility, see **288.6** and **288.7**.

288.12   The different starting points
Note: The normal starting points for setting the minimum term are as follows. The offender's age is his or her age at the time of the murder.[683] Ed.

---

[683] Criminal Justice Act 2003 Sch 21 para 4(1)(b), 5(1)(b), 6 and 7

Sch 21 para number	Offender aged under 18	Offender aged 18-20	Offender aged 21+
Cases within para 4, see **288.90**	12 years	30 years	Whole life
Cases within para 5, see **288.15**	12 years	30 years	30 years
Cases within para 5A, see **288.44**	12 years	25 years	25 years
All other cases, see **288.17**	12 years	15 years	15 years

288.13   *Determining the starting point*
Criminal Practice Directions 2015 EWCA Crim 1567 para VII M.4 Schedule 21 states that the first step is to choose one of five starting points: 'whole life', 30 years, 25 years, 15 years or 12 years. Where the 15-year starting point has been chosen, judges should have in mind that this starting point encompasses a very broad range of murders. At para 35 of *R v Sullivan and Others* 2004 EWCA Crim 1762, 2005 1 Cr App R (S) 67 (p 308), the court found it should not be assumed that Parliament intended to raise all minimum terms that would previously have had a lower starting point to 15 years.
R v West 2007 EWCA Crim 701 D was convicted of murder. She shot her husband with a firearm. The trial Judge said that it was inevitable that he should take the 30-year starting point. Held. It was not inevitable. The word in the Schedule is 'normally'. The determinative consideration is whether the seriousness of the offence was particularly high. Each case will depend on its own facts. The starting point should have been 15 years. For more details see the 7th edition of this book.
Att-Gen's Ref No 24 of 2008 2008 EWCA Crim 2936, 2009 2 Cr App R (S) 41 (p 289) The Judge said that he would not be taking a statutory starting point. Held. Criminal Justice Act 2003 s 270(2) requires the Judge to state the starting point and the reasons for doing so.
R v Morley 2009 EWCA Crim 1302, 2010 1 Cr App R (S) 44 (p 275) LCJ D was convicted of murder. He stabbed V many times and then cooked part of his flesh. A chewed piece of flesh was found in D's waste bin. The Judge said that when D was in drink he was highly dangerous. Further, because of the gruesome conduct after the death, the murder was a particularly serious one meriting a sentence of 30 years. Held. The Judge was right to find that this was not a murder 'involving sexual conduct' or 'aggravated by sexual orientation'. The attack was one of extreme ferocity following sexual activity. There is the dreadful element of the way in which he desecrated the body of his victim after death. Desecration and cannibalism are not expressly identified in Schedule 21 but are profoundly significant features of seriousness which would justify bringing the case into the 'particularly high level of seriousness'. The question is not what is in the schedule but whether this was a case of particularly high seriousness. It was, and the **30-year minimum term** was correct. For more detail see **288.15**.
R v Kelly and Others 2011 EWCA Crim 1462, 2012 1 Cr App R (S) 56 (p 316) LCJ Schedule 21 did not create a stepped sentencing regime with fixed dividing lines between specified categories. Schedule 21 paragraphs 4 and 5 do not create impenetrable compartments and every case will be subject to its own specific individual features of mitigation and aggravation. Cases which are expressly described in paragraphs 4 and 5 may be treated as cases of exceptional or particularly high seriousness, and cases which on their face appear to fall within one or other of the paragraphs may, on examination, be assessed at a lower level of seriousness than at first appearance.
R v Griffiths and Others 2012 EWCA Crim 2822, 2013 2 Cr App R (S) 48 (p 330) para 10 The prosecution contended the murder was for gain. The Judge determined the murder was not for gain. He said the cases itemised in paragraph 5(2)(c) are simply examples of what the court would normally hold to be murders of which the seriousness

was 'particularly high' and that the list is in no sense exhaustive. Further, a murder in the perceived protection and enforcement of the interests of a commercial drugs supply, even if not precisely a killing for gain, is very closely analogous to it. Held. para 15 We entirely agree with the Judge's self-direction that Schedule 21 cannot be applied mechanically and that paragraph 5(2) is in no sense an exhaustive list of the kinds of case which a court may determine to be of particularly high seriousness. The Judge was entitled to hold that this murder was comparable with the examples given in paragraph 5(2).

R v Blackman 2014 EWCA Crim 1029, 2 Cr App R 18 (p 244) Court Martial Appeal Court LCJ D was convicted of murder. He was a sergeant in the Royal Marines and calmly shot an unarmed, badly injured, Afghan insurgent. D had spent 15 years in the Royal Marines and character witnesses commented on his exceptional qualities as an outstanding commander. He had completed six tours of duty. A medical report produced two years after the incident noted that D suffered from accumulated frustration and could have suffered from combat stress disorder, though it was not possible to say with any certainty. Held. para 63 The Court Martial was correct to use Criminal Justice Act 2003 Sch 21 as providing [some] guidance for a murder occurring in circumstances which Parliament had not contemplated. It was correct to select the starting point as 15 years. para 73 The Court Martial was correct that a very substantial reduction from the starting point was required. **8 years**, not 10. For more detail see para **288.68**.

Note: This case would fall neatly into Schedule 21 para 5, 'a murder involving the use of a firearm', giving a starting point of 30 years. However, the Schedule says the listed examples which include the firearm entry 'normally fall' within this paragraph. Although the Court did not say so, this appears to be an example of where special and unusual factors determine that a lower starting point should be selected. Ed.

R v Patraucean 2015 EWCA Crim 957 D pleaded (full credit) to murder. Under the influence of cocaine, cannabis and alcohol, he picked up a prostitute, V. D went back to her flat in her car. He had a Stanley knife with him. About two hours later he drove away in her car. V was found with a number of knife wounds, some of which appeared to have been made after she died. The deepest wound was 9.6 cm long and gaped to 2.6 cm. Her neck was severed right through her cervical spine. Injuries indicated that D had manually strangled her. The pathologist determined that there had been a ferocious attack including blunt force trauma from a fist. There was no evidence of recent sexual activity. She was fully clothed. His blood-stained Stanley knife was found. D claimed that V had stolen £200 from him and an argument had broken out. D was aged 20 with no previous convictions. A *Newton* hearing was held [but it did not provide much help as to the required starting point]. The prosecution relied on *R v Jones* 2005 EWCA Crim 3115, 2006 2 Cr App R (S) 19 (p 121) to suggest that it mattered whether the seriousness of the case was particularly high and not whether one of the examples in Schedule 21 para 5 was made out. The Judge rejected a) that the murder involved sadistic conduct, b) that a 25-year knife starting point was not made out because D had not taken the knife back to the flat, c) that there were attempts to dismember the body and d) that there was a robbery motive. He gave D the benefit of the doubt that she had taken his money. However, because of the ferocity of the attack and the terrible injuries, this was a murder where the seriousness was particularly high. He started at 30 years and with the plea and mitigation, made the minimum term 25 years. Held. That was wrong. The starting point was 15 years. With the aggravating factors we increase that to 24 and with the plea make it 20 years.

Note: This case dramatically illustrates the problem of the courts trying to squeeze these cases into either a 15-year starting point or a 30-year starting point, which are so far apart. Schedule 21 para 5(2) lists examples of types of case where the offence would 'normally' be one of 'particularly high seriousness'. This case provides no help as to how the word 'normally' should be considered, nor does it mention any other case than *R v Jones* 2005. Hopefully next time there is a case which has a starting point not based on the examples, some more guidance can be given. Ed.

288.14   Whole life orders   Exceptionally high seriousness   Defendant aged 21+
Criminal Justice Act 2003 Sch 21 para 4 see **288.90**.

288.15   Starting points   Particularly high seriousness   30 years   Defendant aged 18+
Criminal Justice Act 2003 Sch 21 para 5(1) If:
a) the court considers that the seriousness of the offence (or combination of the offence and one or more offences associated with it) is particularly high, and
b) the offender was aged 18 or over when he committed the offence,
the appropriate starting point in determining the minimum term is **30 years**.
(2) Cases that would normally fall within para 5(1) include:
a) [para a) was repealed[684] on 13 April 2015 and placed in the whole life list of cases, see **288.90**.][685],
b) a murder involving the use of a firearm or explosive,
c) a murder done for gain (such as a murder done in the course or furtherance of robbery or burglary, done for payment or done in the expectation of gain as a result of the death),
d) a murder intended to obstruct or interfere with the course of justice,
e) a murder involving sexual or sadistic conduct,
f) the murder of two or more persons,
g) a murder that is racially or religiously aggravated or aggravated by sexual orientation, or
h) a murder falling within para 4(2) (see **288.90**) committed by an offender who was aged under 21[686] when he committed the offence.
R v Griffin 2010 EWCA Crim 149 LCJ A case may fall within para 5(1) even if none of the special features in sub-para (2) have been established. Here the features may have justified a 30-year starting point which with deductions would give a 22-year term. Had the starting point been 15 years, the aggravating factors would have produced the same term. For more detail see **288.75**.
For an example of a knife case satisfying the 25-year starting point criteria being raised to the 'particularly high seriousness' category see *R v Williams* 2013 EWCA Crim 933 at **288.61**.

288.16   Starting points   Knife or other weapon taken to the scene   25 years   Defendant aged 18+
Criminal Justice Act 2003 Sch 21 para 5A, see **288.44**.

288.17   Starting points   All other murders   15 years   Defendant aged 18+
Criminal Justice Act 2003 Sch 21 para 6 If the offender was aged 18 or over when he committed the offence and the case does not fall into paras 4(1) or 5(1) (see paras **288.90** and **288.15**), the appropriate starting point, in determining the minimum term, is **15 years**.

288.18   Starting points   12 years   Defendant aged under 18
Criminal Justice Act 2003 Sch 21 para 7 If the offender was aged under 18 when he committed the offence, the appropriate starting point, in determining the minimum term, is 12 years. See **288.79** for more details.

---

[684] Repealed by Criminal Justice and Courts Act 2015 s 27(1) and (3). The repeal only applies to offences committed after the section is in force, Criminal Justice and Courts Act 2015 s 27(4).
[685] For cases before 13/4/15, para a) read, 'the murder of a police officer or prison officer in the course of his duty'.
[686] When Criminal Justice Act 2003 Sch 21 para 7, which determines a 12-year starting point for those under 18, is considered, in this context 'aged under 21' means aged '18-20'. Ed.

Aggravating, mitigating and other factors

288.19   *Aggravating and mitigating factors   Statutory provisions*

Criminal Justice Act 2003 Sch 21 para 8 Having chosen a starting point, the court should take into account any aggravating or mitigating factors, to the extent that it has not allowed for them in its choice of starting point.

para 9 Detailed consideration of aggravating or mitigating factors may result in a minimum term of any length (whatever the starting point), or in the making of a whole life order.

Criminal Justice Act 2003 Sch 21 para 10 Aggravating factors (additional to those mentioned in paras 4(2) and 5(2) (see **288.90** and **288.15**) that may be relevant include:

a) a significant degree of planning or premeditation,

b) the fact that the victim was particularly vulnerable because of age or disability,

c) mental or physical suffering inflicted on the victim before death,

d) the abuse of a position of trust,

e) the use of duress or threats against another person to facilitate the commission of the offence,

f) the fact that the victim was providing a public service or performing a public duty, and

g) concealment, destruction or dismemberment of the body.

para 11 Mitigating factors that may be relevant include:

a) an intention to cause serious bodily harm rather than to kill,

b) lack of premeditation,

c) the fact that the offender suffered from any mental disorder or mental disability which (although not falling within Homicide Act 1957 s 2(1)), lowered his degree of culpability,

d) the fact that the offender was provoked (for example, by prolonged stress) in a way not amounting to a defence of provocation,

e) the fact that the offender acted to any extent in self-defence,

f) a belief by the offender that the murder was an act of mercy, and

g) the age of the offender.

288.20   *Judicial approach to aggravating and mitigating factors*

Criminal Justice Act 2003 (Mandatory Life Sentence: Determination of Minimum Term) Order 2010 2010/197 Explanatory memorandum There is no limitation on the degree of adjustment that a court can make in consideration of aggravating and mitigating factors.

R v Last 2005 EWCA Crim 106, 2 Cr App R (S) 64 (p 381) LCJ Schedule 21 does not seek to identify all the aggravating and mitigating factors. It merely provides relevant examples.

R v Peters 2005 EWCA Crim 605, 2 Cr App R (S) 101 (p 627) The judge is not rigidly bound by or limited to the specific features included in the list of aggravating or mitigating factors in paragraphs 10 and 11. The present cases provide two clear examples of unspecified features relevant to the determination of the minimum term. One of these deaths occurred as the result of a fight between rival groups of young men in broad daylight. Such a crime has a significant public element. It produces huge public dismay. It is therefore an aggravating feature of the case not included in the aggravating features in paragraph 10. Another of these cases involves a young woman, just 18 years 2 months old at the time of the murder, whose life until that date was rightly described by the Judge as 'wretched'. Her catastrophic start, with its link with the killing and the impact of the killing on her, provide mitigating features, properly to be taken into account, which, again, are not specified in paragraph 11. In short, the mitigating features identified in paragraph 11 of Schedule 21 do not all work in the same way, nor do they always have the same effect.

R v Jones 2005 EWCA Crim 3115, 2006 2 Cr App R (S) 19 (p 121) para 7 Where aggravating factors have led the Judge to adopt the higher of two potential starting points, or mitigating facts have led him to adopt the lower, he must be careful not to apply those factors a second time when making to that starting point any adjustment that may be appropriate to reflect the other material facts. The starting points give the Judge guidance as to the range within which the appropriate sentence is likely to fall having regard to the more salient features of the offence, but even then, as paragraph 9 recognises, 'detailed consideration of aggravating or mitigating factors may result in a minimum term of any length (whatever the starting point) (emphasis ours), or in the making of a whole life order'.

R v Waters 2006 EWHC 355 (QB) High Court Mere drunkenness leading to extreme violence cannot be a mitigating factor.

R v Simmons 2006 EWCA Crim 1259, 2007 1 Cr App R (S) 27 (p 140) The defendant was convicted of murder. Held. Parliament did not intend that the lists of aggravating and mitigating factors were exhaustive. Good character could be a factor.

Att-Gen's Ref No 73 of 2012 2012 EWCA Crim 2924, 2013 2 Cr App R (S) 38 (p 261)[687] D pleaded to murder. There was a sexual context and the Judge found that the starting point was 30 years. The Attorney-General submitted that the aggravating factors, viewed cumulatively, should have attracted a significant uplift in the starting point from the 30 years as provided by paragraph 5. The submission was based upon the assumption that once it is established that there is a sexual context in the murder, the lowest minimum term must be 30 years before aggravating and mitigating factors are taken into account. We do not accept that. Under paragraph 5, it is the judge's responsibility to make an assessment whether the seriousness of the offence is particularly high, and if so, what minimum term should reflect that seriousness. Schedule 21 is not a sentencing grid. Paragraph 5 does not set a non-reducible starting point. It is a guide which the sentencing judge should follow.

R v Odegbune and Others 2013 EWCA Crim 711 para 31 Schedule 21 might suggest that sentences upon those aged over 18 are stepped with minimum starting points at 15 years, [25 years], 30 years and whole life. In reality, however, these steps merely provide the architecture or framework within which the judge must exercise discretion moving upwards or downwards depending on his or her assessment of the seriousness of the offence then being considered along with the aggravating or mitigating features. The result could be described not as a series of steps but, rather, as fixed points on a continuum which allows for an approach which is consistent with the legislative intent, but which allows the sentencing judge an appropriate discretion to balance the various features of the case in order to achieve a just result.

288.21 *Body, Disposal, moving, concealment, dismembering etc.*
Criminal Justice Act 2003 Sch 21 para 9 Detailed consideration of aggravating or mitigating factors may result in a minimum term of any length (whatever the starting point), or in the making of a whole life order.

Para 10 Aggravating factors (additional to those mentioned in paras 4(2) and 5(2) (see **288.90** and **288.15**) that may be relevant include: g) concealment, destruction or dismemberment of the body.

R v Ibe 2009 EWCA Crim 1489, 2010 1 Cr App R (S) 72 (p 480) D was convicted of murder. For about two years before the murder he had a relationship with V, a 32-year-old mother of four who was separated from her husband. She went to D's house one evening, they had sex and spent some time together. For unknown reasons he strangled her, put her body in a laundry bag, and drove her body in the boot of his car to a car park some miles away. D then used his mobile phone to create false texts, suggesting that she was alive. The next day the children, aged between 8 and 13, could not find their mother and contacted their grandparents. Police interviewed D twice, and he said that he did not know where she was. Police found V's body in the boot of D's car. At about the same time he voluntarily went to the police station and told police that he

---

[687] This case is called *R v Halliwell* 2012 EWCA Crim 2924 in the judgment in error.

had killed her and where her body was, not knowing that the police had already found her body. There was no post-death ill-treatment of the victim. D's defence at trial was self-defence and/or diminished responsibility. D, aged 29, had no relevant previous convictions. Two psychiatrists gave evidence that he was suffering life-long disability as a result of a road accident, described as frontal lobe syndrome with organic bipolar affective disorder. They disagreed about whether that undoubted disability amounted to diminished responsibility. The Judge accepted that the murder was not planned or premeditated. Held. We cannot accept that D's culpability for the offence was lowered because of his disability. The Judge saw the psychiatrists give evidence, heard evidence from D, and expressed his firm view that it did not. The only aggravating factor was the concealment of the body. The correct starting point was **15 years**. The Judge added too long a period to reflect that one aggravating factor. It does not seem justifiable that D should have to spend a further 7 years in prison because he concealed the body for five days. The appropriate uplift was 2 years, so a minimum period of **17 years** not 22.

See also: *R v Ghafelipour* 2011 EWCA Crim 112 (Late plea. Defendant had begun short friendship with victim and then stole from her. 130 stab wounds to head and neck. Removed hair from her head by the roots, removed her right eye. Bite marks. **23 years**) *R v Dunkley* 2015 EWCA Crim 330 (Convicted of murder, theft and fraud. Pleaded to preventing burial. Killed paraplegic, V, for his savings when he was V's carer. Used Internet search engine to research about humans bleeding to death. Chopped up body into 10 pieces with chain saw and used freezer and incinerator in attempt to dispose of it. 30 years right starting point. We move it to 34 years not 36 for a) V's vulnerability, b) D was a trusted carer, c) significant degree of premeditation, and d) most significant, the gross dismemberment of V. Adopting the 2 years off for the mitigation, **32 years** not 34) See also the *Cannibalism* para at **288.30** and the OBSTRUCTING THE CORONER chapter and the MANSLAUGHTER *Body, Dismembering and disposing of the* para at **284.4**. For an example of how significant the uplift can be, see *R v Masefield* 2012 EWCA Crim 1873, 2013 1 Cr App R (S) 77 (p 426) at **291.4**.

Old cases: *R v McGrady* 2007 EWCA Crim 192, 2 Cr App R (S) 56 (p 347) (**whole life**) (see **288.93**) *Att-Gen's Ref Nos 25-26 of 2008* 2008 EWCA Crim 2665, 2009 1 Cr App R (S) 116 (p 648) (**24 years** and **18 years**) *R v Sykes* 2008 EWCA Crim 2990, 2009 2 Cr App R (S) 37 (p 263) (**24 years**) *R v Tailor* 2007 EWCA Crim 1564, 2008 1 Cr App R (S) 37 (p 199) (**25 years**)

288.22   *Intent to kill*
Criminal Justice Act 2003 Sch 21 para 11 Mitigating factors that may be relevant include: a) an intention to cause serious bodily harm rather than to kill, and b) lack of premeditation.
R v Peters 2005 EWCA Crim 605, 2 Cr App R (S) 101 (p 627) All other features of the case being equal, the seriousness of a murder committed with intent to kill is normally more grave and serious than one committed with intent to cause grievous bodily harm. para 11(a) gives effect to that common understanding. That said, no specific distinction based on the offender's intent is made in any of the starting points under paragraphs 4 or 5(1) and (2), 6 and 7, and there is no specific or special starting point for cases where the offender intended really serious harm rather than death. Moreover, paragraph 11(a) underlines that such an intention to cause grievous bodily harm, as opposed to an intention to kill, 'may' provide relevant mitigation, but not necessarily, and not always. Thus, murder committed with an intention to kill may attract yet greater mitigation than a killing to which paragraph 11(a) applies. For example, where the killing represents an act of mercy, motivated by love and devotion, as envisaged in paragraph 11(f), the intention is indeed to kill, to provide a merciful release. It is unlikely that the mitigation in such a case will be less than the mitigation allowed to an offender who involves himself in an unlawful violent incident and, intending to do really serious harm, causes death. Similarly, there are cases in which death, even if unintended, is a possible or likely consequence of the offender's premeditated conduct. For example, those who

abduct a child intending to blackmail the parents into providing a large ransom may deliberately make the parents aware that the child is being tortured, to encourage a positive response from the parents. In the course of torture the child may die. Just because the very objective of the criminal is a ransom, death may not be intended. If it is a consequence of the abduction or torture, we doubt whether much, if any, allowance would normally be made in mitigation for the fact that the death of the child was an unintended consequence of the deliberate infliction of bodily harm. It cannot be assumed that the absence of an intention to kill necessarily provides any or very much mitigation. It does not automatically do so. That said, in many cases, particularly in cases where the violence resulting in death has erupted suddenly and unexpectedly, it will probably do so, and it is more likely to do so, and the level of mitigation may be greater, if the injuries causing death were not inflicted with a weapon.

R v Jones 2005 EWCA Crim 3115, 2006 2 Cr App R (S) 19 (p 121) LCJ The victim was shot by a firearm. Held. Re J: The age of the defendant (19) and the lack of an intention to kill enable us to reduce the 30-year starting point to 20 years. Re D: Setting fire to a person's home with the intention of causing death or really serious personal injury is peculiarly horrifying. The Judge approached sentencing on the basis that the jury had found only an intention to cause really serious injury rather than an intention to kill. We do not think that in a case such as this the difference is very material. Deliberately to cause really serious injury by fire is likely to involve agony for the victim and the possibility of permanent injury or disfigurement. Furthermore, such conduct carries with it the obvious risk of causing death.

Note: This case primarily shows that perhaps it's the individual facts that matter. Ed.

R v Ainsworth 2006 EWCA Crim 2311 The Judge added 2 years because of an intent to kill. Held. An intention to kill was assumed in the 15-year starting point and it was not an aggravating factor.

R v Connor 2007 EWCA Crim 2591, 2008 1 Cr App R (S) 89 (p 537) D set fire to a house. A couple were trapped and died. Held. This is a clear example where no credit for the absence of an intention to kill was appropriate. (For more details see **288.37**.)

R v Walker 2010 EWCA Crim 109 D fired a gun into a crowd at a nightclub. The victim was shot in the head. He had some mitigation including being aged 21, some disability and a lack of premeditation and/or intent to kill. The term was reduced from 30 years to 27. D asked for a greater reduction. Held. The lack of a (proved) intent to kill and/or lack of premeditation was largely if not completely negated by D's possession of a loaded gun in a nightclub and willingness to produce it. (For more details, see **288.39**.)

R v Cameron 2010 EWCA Crim 1282, 2011 1 Cr App R (S) 24 (p 163) D was convicted of murder and conspiracy to rob. D was recruited with others to rob a man who it was thought had large quantities of drugs and money at his address. D, with others, went to V's home. V was tied up and tortured. There were 56 separate injuries. The facial skeleton had been shattered by blows that had also caused underlying brain damage, which it was concluded was the cause of death. It was argued that D had no intention to kill and had removed himself from the situation. The Judge accepted that D had suffered injuries but that they were the reason for D removing himself from the house, whereas D sought to argue that he had disengaged with the violence. Held. The lack of an intention to kill was but the other side of the coin to the specific intention of keeping the victim alive, if necessary through a period of torture and extreme violence, because only by so doing could he be expected to divulge the assumed presence of the money and the drugs. In those circumstances it is difficult to conceive of a situation in which the lack of an intention to kill counts for as little by way of mitigation.

R v Krezolek and Luczak 2014 EWCA Crim 2782, 2 Cr App R (S) 2 (p 12) A mother and stepfather beat and starved her child to death over weeks or months so his appearance was like the concentration camp victims who did not survive. The defence relied on a lack of intent to kill. Held. Here the lack of intent adds very little. **30 years** affirmed.

288.23   *Self-defence, Partial*
Criminal Justice Act 2003 Sch 21 para 11 Mitigating factors that may be relevant include: e) the fact that the offender acted to any extent in self-defence.
R v Peters 2005 EWCA Crim 605, 2 Cr App R (S) 101 (p 627) Precisely the same considerations for lack of an intention to kill (see **288.22**) apply to, for example, paragraph 11(e): 'the fact that the offender acted to any extent in self-defence'. Cases will vary from the offender faced with serious and direct violence who nevertheless went too far in self-defence, to the defendant faced with a very minor threat, whose response in killing his assailant was grotesquely disproportionate.

288.24   *Victim's health precarious/Eggshell skull/Victim not expected to die*
R v Master 2007 EWCA Crim 142 D was convicted of murder. During a quarrel he stabbed V 11 times with a kitchen knife and inflicted various other injuries. Before agreeing to call an ambulance, D spent some hours persuading her to agree to say that she had stabbed herself and had stabbed him. She had a history of self-harm. When she eventually agreed, he called an ambulance. She was taken to hospital and treated for stab wounds, bruising and a collapsed lung. There was a 5 cm stab wound between the shoulder blades which would have required little short of severe force to inflict. The wounds to the front of the chest included one or more requiring moderate force which penetrated the lung. She appeared to be recovering when, two days later, she collapsed and died. The immediate cause of death was an acute massive pulmonary embolism. Post-mortem evidence showed that she had an asymptomatic deep vein thrombosis in her right leg which pre-dated the stabbing incident. There was conflicting evidence about whether the stab wounds caused or contributed to her death but by their verdict the jury found that they did. D initially denied all responsibility for the offence. Many months later he accepted that he had done the stabbing, after the defence had obtained medical evidence that the wounds could not have been self-inflicted, but that there was a medical issue on causation. The trial issue was causation only. D was aged 26. Held. The key factors in assessing the degree of moral culpability are the nature and quality of D's conduct, his intent and the circumstances in which it occurred. It is a relevant factor that his intent was GBH, not to kill. But some of these stab wounds were more than superficial. If a person stabs another person in the chest or back with a knife with moderate force, it is frankly a matter of luck whether the result will be life-threatening. We do not think in such circumstances that it affects D's moral culpability, so long as his conduct made a significant contribution to her death. We regard as morally unacceptable the argument that, because there was an underlying risk of her life being cut short, it was somehow worth less to her and her friends and family. This Court should not place a lower value on the life of its weaker members than its stronger. The minimum period of **16 years** was quite proper.
Note: This is an old case, but it reflects current sentencing practice. Ed.
See also **MANSLAUGHTER** *Victim's health precarious/Eggshell skull/Victim not expected to die* at **284.10**.

Guilty pleas
288.25   *Guilty plea   Statute and guidelines*
Criminal Justice Act 2003 s 269(1) This section applies where after the commencement of this section a court passes a life sentence in circumstances where the sentence is fixed by law.
Criminal Justice Act 2003 s 269(3) The part of his sentence is to be such as the court considers appropriate taking into account:
a) the seriousness of the offence, or of the combination of the offence and any one or more offences associated with it, and
b) the effect of Criminal Justice Act 2003 s 240ZA (crediting periods of remand in

custody) or of any direction which it would have given under Criminal Justice Act 2003 s 240A (crediting periods of remand on certain types of bail) if it had sentenced him to a term of imprisonment.

(3A) The reference in subsection (3)(b) to section 240ZA includes Armed Forces Act 2006 s 246 (crediting periods in service custody).

Criminal Justice Act 2003 Sch 21 para 12(c) Nothing in this Schedule (of minimum terms) restricts the application of section 144 (the reduction for guilty pleas).

Reduction in Sentence for a Guilty Plea Guideline 2007, see www.banksr.com Other Matters Guidelines tab para 6.4 There are important differences between the usual fixed-term sentence and the minimum term set with a life sentence for murder. The most significant of these, from the sentencer's point of view, is that a reduction for a plea of guilty in the case of murder will have double the effect on time served in custody when compared with a determinate sentence. This is because a determinate sentence will provide (in most circumstances) for the release of the offender on licence halfway through the total sentence, whereas in the case of murder a minimum term is the period in custody before consideration is given by the Parole Board to whether release is appropriate.

6.5 Given this difference, the special characteristic of the offence of murder and the unique statutory provision of starting points, careful consideration will need to be given to the extent of any reduction and to the need to ensure that the minimum term properly reflects the seriousness of the offence. Whilst the general principles continue to apply (both that a guilty plea should be encouraged and that the extent of any reduction should reduce if the indication of plea is later than the first reasonable opportunity), the process of determining the level of reduction will be different.

288.26   *Guilty plea   Judicial approach*

Reduction in Sentence for a Guilty Plea Guideline 2007, see www.banksr.com Other Matters Guidelines tab para 6.6 1. Where a court determines that there should be a *whole life* minimum term, there will be no reduction for a guilty plea.

2. In other circumstances:

   a) the court will weigh carefully the overall length of the minimum term taking into account other reductions for which offenders may be eligible so as to avoid a combination leading to an inappropriately short sentence,

   b) where it is appropriate to reduce the minimum term having regard to a plea of guilty, the maximum reduction will be one sixth and will never exceed 5 years,

   c) the sliding scale will apply so that, where it is appropriate to reduce the minimum term on account of a guilty plea, the recommended reduction (one sixth or five years, whichever is the less) is only available where there has been an indication of willingness to plead guilty at the first reasonable opportunity, with a recommendation of 5% for a late guilty plea,

   d) the court should then review the sentence to ensure that the minimum term accurately reflects the seriousness of the offence taking account of the statutory starting point, all aggravating and mitigating factors and any guilty plea entered.

R v Peters 2005 EWCA Crim 605, 2 Cr App R (S) 101 (p 627) There are a number of cases where a defendant facing a charge of murder requires expert legal advice before he can sensibly decide on his plea, particularly in the case of a defendant who is young, or who suffers from mental problems or emotional inadequacy. The defendant may accept that he was responsible for the fatal injuries, or contributed to them, or was responsible for the injuries which the prosecution witnesses say caused death (even if his experts do not), but he will nevertheless often need expert legal advice whether the case should properly be contested on the basis of absence of intent, self-defence, provocation, or diminished responsibility. In relation to the allowance for pleas of guilty, even if there is a delay in obtaining the advice of leading counsel, the defendant should not normally expect to obtain the maximum discount unless a very early indication is given that, as a matter of fact, he accepts responsibility for the fatal injuries, or involvement in death.

Once he has seen his leading counsel and received advice, if he is then to benefit from the maximum discount, it is necessary for a plea to be indicated as soon as practicable thereafter. Subject to this consideration, we are not unsympathetic to the argument that, in some murder cases at any rate, the first reasonable opportunity firmly and finally to indicate an intention to plead guilty to murder may not arise until after the defendant has seen leading counsel. Equally, it is essential for leading counsel instructed in such cases to arrange a consultation with the defendant at the earliest practicable date.

R v Latham 2006 EWCA Crim 213, 2 Cr App R (S) 64 (p 427) D pleaded to murder. He killed his girlfriend. On 9 May 2005 he pleaded to manslaughter. The trial had been fixed for 18 July 2005. He indicated his plea to murder on 5 July 2005. By that stage the trial had been put back but the case was virtually prepared. The Judge started at 15 years, moved to 22 and reduced it to 20 for the plea. Held. We think 5% for the plea. 18 years not 20 was right.

R v R 2007 EWCA Crim 1874, 2008 1 Cr App R (S) 65 (p 379) The need to explore diminished responsibility was understandable. The sentence was adjusted to grant a full discount.

Note: The three cases are old. The first was a guideline case. All three reflect current sentencing practice. Ed.

Types of murder

Note: The cases in this section and other sections give the minimum period and ignore the time that was deducted for the defendant being remanded before sentence. Ed.

288.27   *Abduction and whole life orders*

Criminal Justice Act 2003 s 269(4) The statutory source of the power of the court to order that the early release provisions should not apply to the offender.

Criminal Justice Act 2003 Sch 21 para 4(1) If:

    a) the court considers that the seriousness of the offence (or combination of the offence and one or more offences associated with it) is exceptionally high, and

    b) the offender was aged 21 or over when he committed the offence,

the appropriate starting point is a whole life order.

(2) Cases that would normally fall within sub-paragraph (1)(a) include:

    a) the murder of two or more persons, where each[688] murder involves any of the following:...ii) the abduction of the victim,

    b) the murder of a child if involving the abduction of the child.

Accomplices, Aiding and abetting, and *Assisting offenders* see **288.67**.

288.28 *Armed forces, Murder by members of*

R v Blackman 2014 EWCA Crim 1029, 2 Cr App R 18 (p 244) Court Martial Appeal Court LCJ D was convicted of murder. He was a Royal Marines sergeant deployed to Afghanistan between March and September 2011. In 2012, a video recording taken from a helmet camera worn by a corporal under his command was discovered during an investigation into an unrelated matter. V, an Afghan insurgent, had been seriously wounded, having been lawfully engaged by an Apache helicopter. D found V, who was no longer a threat. D caused V to be moved to a place where he would be out of sight of the operational headquarters so that "[Persistent Ground Surveillance Systems] can't see what we're doing to him". V was handled by those under D's command in a rough manner, clearly causing him additional pain and D did nothing to stop them from treating him in that way. D failed to ensure V was given the appropriate medical treatment quickly, and then ordered those giving him some first aid to stop doing so. When D was sure the Apache helicopter was out of sight, he calmly discharged a 9 mm round into V's chest, killing him. V may have died of his wounds after the engagement by the Apache helicopter in any event. D then told his patrol that they were not to say anything about

---

[688] There is clearly a drafting error here. It would be absurd if two abduction murders trigger the whole life provisions but four abduction murders and one non-abduction murder do not. Ed.

what had just happened and he acknowledged that he had broken the Geneva Convention by his actions. D had spent 15 years in the Royal Marines and character witnesses commented on his exceptional qualities as an outstanding commander. He had completed six tours of duty abroad. A medical report produced two years after the incident noted that D suffered from accumulated frustration and could have suffered from combat stress disorder, though it was not possible to say with any certainty. Held. para 63 The Court Martial was correct to use Criminal Justice Act 2003 Sch 21 as providing a degree of guidance on sentencing for a murder occurring in circumstances which Parliament had not contemplated. It was correct to select the starting point as 15 years.

para 64 There were three aggravating factors. First was the circumstances of the shooting: a) the decision to stop first aid, b) the order to move V to a place where they would not be seen, c) the discharge of the weapon into V's chest, and d) the instruction to the patrol to say nothing about what happened. V's vulnerability did not add anything material to those acts. There was no threat from V, who had been seriously wounded and disarmed. para 66 The second aggravating feature was the deliberate involvement in a dishonest cover-up by soldiers who looked to him for leadership. para 67 Third, D's failure to follow (personally as a soldier and as a person in command of the patrol) the standards of conduct for HM Forces in Afghanistan.

para 68 In mitigation, D had an outstanding service record. para 69 Second, the effects on him of the nature of the conflict and the command he exercises. Most serious was the effect of stress. para 70 It is self-evident that forces sent to combat insurgents will be placed under much greater stress than forces sent to fight a regular army. para 72 D was under considerable stress dealing with insurgency and significant further stress because of the remote location of his command post. He had had little face-to-face contact with those commanding him and they could not assess the effect of the conditions upon him. para 73 The Court Martial was correct that a very substantial reduction from the starting point was required. para 75 D's mental welfare had not been assessed in the ordinary way. The combat stress should have been accorded greater weight.

para 76 The particular circumstances did not require an additional term by the way of deterrence to the sentence as the Court Martial found. The open and very public way in which the proceedings were conducted overall, the worldwide publicity given to D's conviction, the life sentence imposed on him and the significant minimum term he must in any event serve before any consideration of parole will be sufficient deterrence. **8 years**, not 10.

288.29 *Bullying/Showing off etc.*

Criminal Justice Act 2003 Sch 21 para 10 Aggravating factors (additional to those mentioned in paras 4(2) and 5(2) (see **288.90** and **288.15**) that may be relevant include:..c) mental or physical suffering inflicted on the victim before death.

R v Bonellie and Others 2008 EWCA Crim 1417, 2009 1 Cr App R (S) 55 (p 297) LCJ H and M pleaded to murder on rearraignment. B was convicted of murder. V was a 23-year-old man who had spent the previous nine years in psychiatric hospitals and who suffered from a learning disability and other psychiatric conditions. He was of a gentle disposition. He was with these defendants when they dared each other to hit him for money. M hit him first and knocked him to the ground. He got up. Then H hit and knocked him to the ground. The defendants bet with each other who could knock him out. M punched him, knocking him over, and hit him again. B said that he was going to knock him unconscious but H then hit him, knocking him over. The defendants laughed at him. He got up, was punched again and fell off a wall. He was crying and apologised to them. H punched him three more times so that he fell to the ground. The violence continued and became worse. As V lay on the ground they all jumped and stamped on him. H kicked him hard in the face. They dragged his unconscious body, pulled his underclothes down to his ankles and walked off. When found, he was deeply uncon-scious and he later died. A post-mortem report said that he had 22 recent injuries, with 18 separate blows delivered to his head and neck. The defendants surrendered to the police. B admitted presence but denied any violence. H said that he hit him a couple of times, and blamed the other two. M said in a prepared statement that he was there and had assaulted V, but that V was alive and conscious when he left. Both B and M had trained as amateur boxers. B, aged 17, had two convictions for threatening behaviour. A pre-sentence report assessed the risk of reoffending as medium to high. He was said to be ashamed of his actions and genuinely remorseful. M had a conviction for battery. A psychologist assessed his IQ as low at 79. A pre-sentence report assessed the risk of him reoffending and causing serious harm to the public as high. H had a conviction for ABH in 2003. They were sentenced on the basis that this was a sadistic murder of particularly high seriousness. The Judge found no intent to kill. Held. The behaviour of these defendants was appalling, they behaved like a pack of animals for amusement and to make themselves look big. It is often the case that those who attack others derive pleasure from it, including from kicking someone on the ground, baiting an individual or showing off to friends. That is not enough to conclude there was sadistic conduct as envisaged by subsection (e). That contemplates a greater degree of awareness of pleasure in the infliction of pain, suffering or humiliation. The starting point for H (the only adult) should have been **15 years** not 30. For H, **19-year** minimum term not 22. For B, not as involved and younger than H and with minor convictions, **15-year** minimum term not 18. For M, the youngest and who pleaded guilty, **13-year** minimum term not 15.

R v Herbert and Others 2008 EWCA Crim 2501 LCJ. H pleaded on the day of trial to the murder of V1 and section 18 wounding of V2. Ha was convicted of the murder and pleaded to the section 18 wounding. The two victims, V1, aged 20, and her boyfriend, V2, aged 21 were attacked without provocation by H, Ha and three others, who had been drinking. They first attacked V2, bringing him to the ground with kicks and punches. When on the ground they kicked him viciously to the head and body, and at least one of them stamped on his head. They goaded each other. V2 was rendered unconscious. V1 rushed to give him assistance and cradled his head in her lap, calling for help. H and Ha then attacked her, kicking and stamping until she was also unconscious. The motive for the attack was that the victims were dressed as 'Goths', known as 'moshers' in that area. Immediately afterwards H said to others, 'There's two moshers nearly dead up Bacup Park', and the group was seen to be behaving in a boastful, hyperactive way. The facial injuries of the two victims meant that it was impossible at first to tell what sex they were. V2 had blood around his brain tissue and was on a ventilator for two days. He was discharged from hospital 13 days after the attack. He had extensive facial injuries in the form of bruises, abrasions and swellings. As a consequence of the attack he suffered from short-term memory loss and poor balance. He became a recluse, would not leave home, and was undergoing psychiatric treatment. V1 died 13 days later. She had 17 injuries to her head and body, the principal target being her head. In interview, H admitted presence but denied any violence. In subsequent interviews he was silent. H said that he struck the first blow by hitting V2 when he was drunk and showing off. He said that he had no further involvement in the violence. H, aged 15, had a conviction for violence involving kicking. Ha, aged 15, had a conviction for violence involving kicking. Held. The Judge was fully justified in taking the view that this was an offence of particularly high seriousness. The attack on V2 made it close to double murder. The victims were singled out because of their appearance, analogous to race, religion or sexual orientation being the cause of the attack. The brutality of the attack on V1 while she cradled her boyfriend verged on cruel and sadistic behaviour. Had the defendants been adults, a 30-year starting point would have been appropriate. For H, the psychiatric report was not available until the day of trial. He was then advised to plead guilty and accepted that advice. Bearing in mind his age and the charge, it was right for this investigation to be carried out. He had admitted at least manslaughter in his defence case statement. It was to his credit that he accepted the advice. Allowance for his guilty plea should have been somewhat higher, so a minimum term of **15½ years** not 16¼. For Ha, a minimum term of **18 years** upheld.

For the co-defendants' appeal over their OAPA 1861 s 18 sentences, see the **OFFENCES AGAINST THE PERSON ACT 1861 S 18** *Bullying/Showing off* para in the 8th edition of this book.

R v Swellings and Sorton 2008 EWCA Crim 3249, 2009 2 Cr App R (S) 30 (p 220)[689] S1 and S2 were convicted of murder. At about 10.30 pm a gang of young men were causing damage to parked vehicles. V went to remonstrate with S1 and S2. They punched and kicked him to the ground, and kicked him while he lay on the ground. One of the kicks caused a tear in a major artery near the brain, and he died from a brain haemorrhage. His teenage daughters witnessed the attack. The prosecution case was that S1 was the person who had struck the first blow. He joined in the punching and kicking when V lay on the ground and inflicted the fatal kick. He had been involved in three violent incidents with others immediately before this incident. The Judge found S2 to be one of the leaders of the group. S1, aged 18 at the time, had a moderate record of convictions, including previous offences of violence. He was on bail at the time of the offence and was in breach of a bail condition by being in the town. S2, aged 16 at the time of the offence, had no previous convictions. Held. S1 was the leading figure and capable of exercising a degree of influence over the others. He must bear significantly the greater responsibility. The Judge took adequate account of his age and lack of full intent. **17 years** was not manifestly excessive. S2 was less culpable than S1, and his age and lack of full intent gave a starting point of 12 years. **13 years** not 15.

Note: All these cases are old. The sentences appear to be in the range that would be given today. Ed.

288.30   *Cannibalism*
Criminal Justice Act 2003 Sch 21 para 10 Aggravating factors (additional to those mentioned in paras 4(2) and 5(2) (see **288.90** and **288.15**) that may be relevant include:..g) concealment, destruction or dismemberment of the body.

R v Morley 2009 EWCA Crim 1302, 2010 1 Cr App R (S) 44 (p 275) LCJ D was convicted of murder. He had pleaded to manslaughter by reason of provocation and/or diminished responsibility. He and V knew each other as acquaintances. V was outwardly gay and proud of it. D was 'conflicted' about his sexuality. A month before the murder they met each other by chance in a gay bar and went back to V's home where they kissed and cuddled but there was no further sexual activity and they slept separately. They exchanged text messages of a flirtatious nature. In one of these D said that he wanted things to be taken slowly. They met by agreement one evening. D had been drinking and continued to drink with V. They went back to D's home where he cooked a meal and they drank two bottles of wine and some beer. There was kissing and cuddling. They went to bed to watch 'Brokeback Mountain'. D said that V had assured him there would be no sexual activity. He said that he woke up to find V performing oral sex on him. He felt betrayed and went downstairs to calm down and then went back upstairs. He said that he had no recollection of events after that. Scientific evidence was that he cut V's throat as he slept, and then stabbed him many times. After death, sections of V's flesh were removed and cooked. A chewed piece of flesh was found in D's waste bin. He then left the house in his dressing gown and slippers and went to a shop where he asked for the police to be called. When police arrived he told them he had killed the deceased because he had been raped, although he later explained he was referring to a much earlier rape, not by V. He said that he had asked V to take things slowly. He said that the rib cage is 'hard to get through especially from the back, harder than you think'. The Judge did not accept his version of events, which was that the sexual running had all been made by V. D, aged 36, had no relevant convictions. He had recently taken a meat cleaver to his former lover of five years, and only accident prevented him from injuring him seriously. When an ambulance arrived, he threatened the paramedics with an air rifle, so that police were called. He said that he had been raped as a 17-year-old by his

---

[689] The neutral citation in the Cr App R (S) report is wrong.

then-employer, although that employer gave evidence that their sexual relationship had been after D was 18 and was consensual. A psychiatric report noted that he had expressed an interest in a website showing photographs and news relating to violent fatalities, murder, suicide and other bizarre events. There was no evidence of personality disorder or that he had ever suffered from a mental illness. He was disturbed in his psychological functioning. There was no evidence to suggest any inherent cannibalistic interests. When sober he was a decent, caring man and could work hard. Held. The Judge was right to find this was not a murder 'involving sexual conduct' or 'aggravated by sexual orientation'. It was rightly accepted that there was a sexual background to this killing. The nature of the attack and the sexual element is a significant feature. The attack was one of extreme ferocity following sexual activity. D decided that he was going to punish V, who was at peace with his own sexuality. There was an element of clear deliberation. There is the dreadful element of the way in which he desecrated V's body after death. Desecration and cannibalism are not expressly identified in Schedule 21 but are profoundly significant features of seriousness which would justify bringing the case into the particularly high level of seriousness. The question is not what is in the schedule but whether this was a case of particularly high seriousness. It was, and the **30-year minimum term** was correct.
See also the **MANSLAUGHTER** *Cannibalism* para at **284.14**.

288.31   *Child murders and whole life orders*
Criminal Justice Act 2003 s 269(4) The statutory source of the power of the court to order that the early release provisions should not apply to the offender.
Criminal Justice Act 2003 Sch 21 para 4(1) If:
   a) the court considers that the seriousness of the offence (or combination of the offence and one or more offences associated with it) is exceptionally high, and
   b) the offender was aged 21 or over when he committed the offence,
the appropriate starting point is a whole life order.
para 4(2) Cases that would normally fall within sub-paragraph (1)(a) include:..b) the murder of a child if involving the abduction of the child or sexual or sadistic motivation.

288.32   *Child murders   Cases*
Criminal Justice Act 2003 Sch 21 para 10 Aggravating factors (additional to those mentioned in paras 4(2) and 5(2) (see **288.90** and **288.15**) that may be relevant include:..b) the fact that the victim was particularly vulnerable because of age or disability.
R v Donnison 2012 EWCA Crim 3073, 1 Cr App R (S) 39 (p 216) LCJ D was convicted of two murders. Her defence of diminished responsibility failed. D had two children. In 2001 she married F. In 2004, her daughter M died of cot death and D suffered from depression. Later she miscarried. In 2006 and 2008 the victims were born. In July 2009, D was made redundant. In September the children's father, F, discovered a note from D saying D was moving out with the children. F said this was totally unexpected. She took her four children and went to live in Surrey. In January 2001, in her old home town, she bought Nytol and Anadin tablets at 9.32 pm. Next day at 10.07 am, she bought 16 more tablets of Nytol. A few minutes later she bought 16 more Nytol. At 10.45, she walked into a police station and said she had killed her two children. She spoke in a monotone with no emotion. She appeared to have a fit. She was bleeding from both her wrists. D was unfit to be interviewed because of the Nytol. She did not say where the victims were but the police found them in a holdall in the boot of a car. They had been asphyxiated. It was likely they had been killed the previous evening. Neither death had been instantaneous. A note was found saying she had gone to be with the victims and M. D did not challenge her responsibility for the deaths but her counsel cross-examined F at length. F did say she was a good mother. D had no convictions. The experts did not agree about the mental situation. The Judge said the murders were deliberate and wicked acts which defied logical explanation. He thought the murders had something to do with her

feelings to F and her narcissistic personality traits. The Judge started at 30 years. He said there was the grossest breach of trust. He accepted there was some mental disorder, a lack of premeditation and the murders had not been long planned. Held. There was serious question about whether there was a serious suicide attempt. F underwent a significant ordeal and must have thought he was on trial. Set against the serious aggravating factors, **32 years** was within the appropriate range.

Att-Gen's Ref No 11 of 2014 2014 EWCA Crim 843 D was convicted of murder. She fell pregnant and concealed the pregnancy from her family and partner. D gave birth to the child but placed the child with foster parents as she did not wish to keep him. After seven months, she indicated that she wanted the child back and he was returned to her. Just over a year later, D gave birth to V, when she was aged 22. Again, the pregnancy was concealed. D took both children to weekly playgroup sessions. The staff and other mothers described V as being increasingly withdrawn with his general condition being described as blank, emotionless and listless. Witnesses observed a marked contrast between the attention given by D to the older child as compared with the way she treated V. D did not acknowledge that V was her child, instead claiming that he was a child of a cousin whom she was looking after. After V's death, the post mortem showed that he had suffered a number of serious injuries in the fortnight or so prior to his death. There were nine fractures to his ribs (five to the front), a fracture to his right wrist and a fracture of the upper part of his left tibia. Evidence showed that very significant force was required to fracture the front ribs of an 11-month-old child as at that age the ribcage is composed of compliant, bendable cartilage. The mechanism for causing the fractures was likely to have been severe gripping and squeezing, involving considerable force. The tibial fracture was likely to have been caused by a blow against a hard surface or from a snapping action. In the immediate aftermath of the time during which those injuries were caused, D kept V away from a parenting course and from the playgroup. The child was seen by a doctor and health worker, neither of which saw anything untoward. One evening, D's downstairs neighbours heard a series of very loud bangs and described the ceiling shaking with the force of the impact. Help was not sought for V until 8 am the following morning. Paramedics arrived and found V to be very pale, his breathing shallow and his pulse very weak. He had suffered a fatal brain injury and died two days later. Hospital staff observed that D was not in a distressed or concerned condition. V's brain had swollen so that the brain stem was compressed, caused by a direct impact to the head, or by V's head being struck forcibly against a surface. Rib fractures sustained earlier had been refractured and there were severe retinal haemorrhages and a detached retina. There were 26 areas of bruising. In interview, D claimed she had not inflicted the injuries and suggested that V's older brother must have been responsible. D had no mental illness or personality disorder. D was aged 23 and of previous good character. Held. The aggravating features are that V was particularly vulnerable, had been subjected to an attack or assaults prior to his death of a serious nature which would have caused physical suffering, and abuse of trust. Mitigating features included a lack of intention to kill, a lack of premeditation and D's age. The Judge found that D was a good mother to her older son. This was not a case of an otherwise loving parent who had become angry on an isolated occasion and then fatally assaulted their child, nor was it a case of an offender living in very difficult social circumstances or without the support from a wider family. There was no mental disorder and D had not exhibited deep remorse. The absence of those features does not aggravate the case but they provide nothing to set against the aggravating features. The shortest minimum term that could be imposed was **17 years**, so 17 years not 14.

See also: *R v Oyediran* 2010 EWCA Crim 2431 (D convicted of murder. Ten-week old baby shaken in sudden outbreak of anger. Two earlier incidents of violence. Baby suffered fractured arm, and brain injury (×2). **13 years** was right for the one event of violence that caused the death.)

R v Krezolek and Luczak 2014 EWCA Crim 2782, 2 Cr App R (S) 2 (p 12) (Both convicted. V, aged 4, suffered incomprehensible and unspeakable cruelty at hands of his mother, D2. Her partner, D1, beat V in a locked small room. V was forced to exercise, his arms broken, he was force-fed salt, held under water and starved over many months. Lived in poor conditions and stole food at school and lost weight, such that he was like one of the concentration camp fatalities. Became pale and withdrawn. V's sister, aged 6, coached to cover up abuse. Ambulance called as V unconscious for long period. Extensive lies to authorities. V died from deliberately inflicted head injury and had very high sodium level. D1, aged 35, with mainly driving convictions and D2, aged 29, of effective good character. No remorse. For both, **30-year** minimum severe but upheld.)
Old cases: *R v Randall* 2007 EWCA Crim 2257, 2008 1 Cr App R (S) 93 (p 556) (**30 years**) *R v Samuel* 2007 EWCA Crim 1954, 2008 1 Cr App R (S) 76 (p 439) (**30 years**) *R v Mullen* 2008 EWCA Crim 592, 2 Cr App R (S) 88 (p 501) (**35 years**) *R v Essilfie* 2008 EWCA Crim 2818, 2009 2 Cr App R (S) 11 (p 65) (**13 years**)
For a summary of the first case, see the 7th edition of this book, for the second, see the 8th edition and for the last two cases, see the 9th edition.

288.33   *Criminal gangs, Killings by/Drug disputes etc.*
R v Griffiths and Others 2012 EWCA Crim 2822, 2013 2 Cr App R (S) 48 (p 330) D, T, L and J were convicted of murder and perverting the course of justice. D was the mastermind and leader of a drug network selling mostly heroin. His son, T, was his trusted secondary participant. One of the 'minions' used as a driver and street seller was V, who was an addict and in very bad health. D became convinced that V was going to betray the gang either by informing, or stealing money, or doctoring the drugs. V went to hospital with air-gun pellets in his neck and chest. Later L put a knife to his neck. Next the four defendants arranged to seize, beat and interrogate V. T punched him and L kicked V hard. They tortured him over one to two weeks. He was freed from time to time. V was in such fear he lost control of his bowels. V died and had damage to his spleen and multiple broken ribs, probably attributable to being stamped on. V had been struck at least three times on the head by a weapon, such as an axe, a hatchet or a golf club. These blows caused his death. The defendants divided his body into six parts with a hacksaw. These parts were disposed of in separate watercourses. Some of the bones and clothing were burnt. This disposal was the perverting the course of justice element. D was aged 42 with 22 convictions, chiefly for dishonesty. There was no violence save a public order offence. T was aged 21 and had no convictions. He had been reprimanded for assault in 2005 and had signs of paranoid aggressive antisocial personality disorder. L, aged 19, was another son of D and had no convictions. J, D's stepson, was aged 26 and had convictions for disorder and violence. He had served 6 months for affray and 18 months (twice) for ABH. The Judge considered the aggravating factors were V's vulnerability, V's suffering and the disposal of the body. The mitigating factors were the younger defendant's age and for all a lack of intent to kill. The Judge considered D was irrationally dominant over the others. The Judge started at 30 years and moved it up to 35. He considered the perverting the course of justice was worth 8 years, so 4 years of a minimum sentence. D and T had a count of supply but did not add that to the sentences. Held. The Judge was entitled to hold that this murder was comparable with the examples given in paragraph 5(2). He could take into account the historical background of the ill-treatment of V. The lack of an intent to kill had less force here with its sustained violence than a spontaneous attack murder. For D, **30 years** not 35. The other defendants were under D's influence. L and J could say they had not been convicted of the drug supply matter. Taking an overall view, T **25 years** not 27, J **25 years** not 29 and L **23 years** not 26. Had we started at 15 years, the sentences would not have been very different.
R v Haigh 2013 EWCA Crim 2359 (**32 years**, see **288.39.**)
R v Bidace-Anthony 2014 EWCA Crim 359 (Convicted of murder, attempted murder and possession of a firearm with intent to endanger life. Murdered V1, a drug dealer, and

attempted to murder V2, V1's partner, who was disabled. He went to their flat under the guise of buying cocaine. V2 recognised him, which is why he tried to kill her. Shot V1 in back of head with handgun brought to the scene. Fired twice at V2, hitting her once. The third shot jammed and D fled. Committed in front of two others and a baby. Starting at 30 years. Life with minimum of **42 years** was very severe but entirely justified.)

R v Wilkinson and Ward 2014 EWCA Crim 678 (Plea by D. Conviction for J. Long-standing feud. D chased victim through home and shot him repeatedly. Grenade thrown which caused dreadful injuries. Heavy degree of planning. D on licence for serious armed robbery and drugs offences. Co-defendant given whole life for this and other murders. Notorious and particularly grave offence. Judge fully entitled to increase minimum term due to horrific aggravating features. For D, with limited plea credit and an uplift for possession of another loaded firearm at the time, **35 years**. For J, who did not fire the weapon and no relevant previous convictions, **33 years** upheld.

Old cases: *R v Coleman and Petch* 2007 EWCA Crim 2318 (**18 years** for P and **12 years** for C) *R v Henson and Magraw* 2007 EWCA Crim 1308, 2008 1 Cr App R (S) 19 (p 83) (For M, **35 years**. For H, **18 years**)

For a summary of the second case, see the 9th edition of this book.

See also the **MURDER, ATTEMPTED, CONSPIRACY TO MURDER, ETC.** *Criminal gangs, Attempted killings by/Drug disputes etc.* para at **289.6**.

288.34   *Disability, Aggravated by   Not whole life*

Criminal Justice Act 2003 Sch 21 para 3[690] For the purposes of this Schedule:..

   b) an offence is aggravated by disability if it is committed in circumstances mentioned in section 146(2)(a)(ii) or (b)(ii).

Criminal Justice Act 2003 s 146(2) Those circumstances are:

   a) that, at the time of committing the offence, or immediately before or after doing so, the offender demonstrated towards the victim of the offence hostility based on:..

     ii) a disability (or presumed disability) of the victim, or

   b) that the offence is motivated (wholly or partly):..

     ii) by hostility towards persons who have a disability or a particular disability.

Criminal Justice Act 2003 Sch 21 para 5(2) Cases that (if not [whole life]) would normally fall within [the **30-year term**]) include:…

   g) a murder that is…related to disability.

288.35   *Family etc. killings (Children over 13 etc.)*

Criminal Justice Act 2003 Sch 21 para 10 Aggravating factors (additional to those mentioned in paras 4(2) and 5(2) (see **288.91** and **288.15**) that may be relevant include:..d) the abuse of a position of trust.

Att-Gen's Ref No 73 of 2009 2009 EWCA Crim 2701, 2010 2 Cr App R (S) 42 (p 270) LCJ D was convicted of murder, wounding with intent (against Y) and attempted murder (against G). G married D in 2002. She had a daughter, Y, and a son, V, aged 15, from a previous relationship. The marriage produced seven sons. All the family lived together. D was a very jealous man who drank a lot and tried to control the family by bullying. D liked to dominate his family in extreme ways. D had tried to prevent V developing relationships with his natural father and their paternal grandparents,[691] and had developed a sexual relationship with Y. Y told D she was going to leave. D found his lack of control unacceptable. V had been to visit his dying grandfather. On returning home, V went to sleep in his sister's bedroom. Y, aged 18, went to sleep in her mother's bedroom whilst D stayed downstairs drinking. At 3 am, armed with a table leg and a 12-inch knife, D went to the room where V was sleeping and attacked him. V's cries woke G, Y and some of the other children. Part of the attack was witnessed by D's 9-year-old son and G. Y and G confronted D, who tried to stab G with the knife but

---

[690] As inserted by Legal Aid, Sentencing and Punishment of Offenders Act 2012 s 65(7)-(9)
[691] This may be a typo and maybe it should read 'his paternal grandparents'.

Y stepped in front and suffered injuries. D left the house. Emergency services attempted unsuccessfully to resuscitate V. V had sustained 18 separate stab wounds. His spine was severed, a lung collapsed and four ribs were damaged. D was aged 43. In the weeks prior to the attack, D told G that if she ever left him he would kill her and plead diminished responsibility. In interview D claimed that he could not remember what had happened. The psychiatric report said D was highly dangerous but did not suffer from any condition which could be treated. The Judge found an intention to kill. Held. The remorseless killing of a defenceless boy was a case of particularly high seriousness. The aggravating features were: the circumstances and facts of the associated offences, the victim died in circumstances of extreme vulnerability, and there was an attempt to kill the wife which failed, causing injury to her daughter instead. Life with a minimum term of **25 years** not 16.

Att-Gen's Ref No 100 of 2009 2010 EWCA Crim 935, 2011 1 Cr App R (S) 17 (p 122) LCJ D was convicted of murder. D lived with his pregnant girlfriend, L, her two children and V, who was L's mother, at V's house. V was a wealthy widow. D's relationship with V was occasionally strained. V asked D to leave the house and he went to live with his mother. D arranged to meet L, but was late. After eventually meeting D, L returned home and found V dead on the kitchen floor. V, aged 65, had been strangled with a ligature, had a number of bruises to her back and there was evidence of impacts to her head. D was jealous and possessive, cutting L off from other members of her family. D was upset by a holiday arrangement to which he was not invited. D, aged 46, lied in interview. He had no convictions. The prosecution said the motive was to make the relationship easier and to obtain V's inheritance. The Judge said this killing was an act of desperation but did not treat the case as a murder for gain. Held. There was no evidence of provocation. The aggravating features were: a) the killing was premeditated, b) D made sure he would not be disturbed, c) V knew and trusted D so allowed him access to her home, d) V was a vulnerable woman on her own, e) D disposed of the weapons and staged a show of innocence, and f) some suspicion initially fell wrongly on L. Life with a minimum term of **18 years** not 13.

R v Uddin 2010 EWCA Crim 2325 D was convicted of murder. The family of V, aged 40, were unable to contact her by telephone so visited her home. Upon seeing her body on the floor through the letterbox, they forced the door open and discovered that she had been brutally and repeatedly stabbed. There was no sign of a break-in and nothing had been stolen. Until a few days earlier V had shared the house with D, who was her youngest son, and his family. D had made repeated attempts to make members of his family let V live with them or take her to Bangladesh. These attempts failed and so D and his family moved out. D returned to the house in a final attempt to persuade V to leave and 'in all likelihood she refused and D took up a knife and killed her in anger and frustration'. D subsequently falsely claimed that he had been in a long conversation with a woman he knew at the time of the murder. V sustained several stab wounds to the body, some of which indicated that severe force had been used. Held. This was a terrible and abhorrent crime. It was accompanied by several features that made the crime far worse than the sort of murder for which Parliament had established a minimum term of 15 years. D betrayed his mother's trust and killed her in the home that she shared with him and his family. Once the murder was done, he set about establishing a bogus alibi. He was a man of previous good character, and in mitigation it can be said that the murder was not premeditated and that prior to the killing he had been a dutiful and loving son to his mother. **20 years** not 22.

See also: *R v Holmes* 2010 EWCA Crim 896, 2011 1 Cr App R (S) 19 (p 133) (Late plea to murder. Loss of temper. Defendant kicked and punched his father to death. Aged 20. Good character. **17 years** not 19.)

See also the *Child murders* para at **288.32** and the *Relationship killings* para at **288.60**.

288.36   *Fire, By.   Judicial guidance*
R v Jones 2005 EWCA Crim 3115, 2006 2 Cr App R (S) 19 (p 121) para 61 Setting fire
to a person's home with the intention of causing death or really serious personal injury is
peculiarly horrifying. The Judge approached sentencing on the basis that the jury had
found only an intention to cause really serious injury rather than an intention to kill. The
difference is not very material. Deliberately to cause really serious injury by fire is likely
to involve agony for the victim and the possibility of permanent injury or disfigurement.
Furthermore, such conduct carries with it the obvious risk of causing death. Although
causing death by arson does not feature in the list in Schedule 21 paragraph 5(2) of
examples of cases where the seriousness is likely to be particularly high, the Judge was
right to conclude that murder as a result of using petrol to set fire to a victim's home falls
within that category. Were there any doubt, we think that this fell to be resolved by the
fact that there was a second victim who was seriously injured as a result of jumping out
of an upstairs window to escape the fire. The Judge cannot be criticised for taking **30
years** as a starting point.

288.37   *Fire, By   Cases*
R v Clarke 2009 EWCA Crim 2484, 2010 2 Cr App R (S) 13 (p 78) LCJ D was
convicted of murder. He watched a spoof horror film depicting a gagged woman tied to
a tree. Liquid representing petrol was thrown over her. A masked man using matches
tried to set her alight without success. He then turned a flame-thrower on her, setting her
alight. D commented, "Wouldn't it be wicked to do this to someone in real life?" D and
V had differences over a girl and, about 15 months after watching the video, there was
an arranged meeting. D attacked V and then, armed with a baseball bat, pursued V later,
boasting that he had given him a good kicking. He was arrested and released on bail. The
following evening V was abducted, bundled into the boot of a car and driven to a
deserted spot in woods. V was tied to a tree and a mock trial was conducted involving
interrogation, answers and a confession from V to having had sexual intercourse with the
girl. D poured petrol into V's throat and over him and V was set alight. V's remains were
then moved to a swampy area where they were covered up. When found, the body was
badly decomposed. D later boasted to his friends about what had happened. D admitted
that he habitually carried two hunting knives. D gloried in his evidence during the
interrogation that, if he had been present, the killing would have been "a blood bath" and
V would have been "mutilated limb by limb". D was 'a few years younger than 22'. A
pre-sentence report assessed D as having a high risk of harm to the public. D suffered
from ADHD. His IQ was in the bottom 14% of the population. He had left home at the
age of 17 and lived independently since then. The Judge believed D had planned the
abduction, torture and murder, and that this was a sadistic killing, so started at 30 years.
Held. The reduction to **27 years** plainly reflected D's youth and no complaint could be
made.
Att-Gen's Ref No 50 of 2013 2013 EWCA Crim 2573 LCJ D was convicted of murder
(×3). He met V3 on the Internet when she was aged 15. He groomed her and she became
infatuated with him. She said that she loved him and let him dominate her life. She
truanted from school and on occasions lived rough with him. He separated her from her
friends and often came between her and her mother. A sexual relationship developed
between them. She became pregnant with twins. One twin was stillborn, the other, V1,
was premature and had severe physical disabilities. She had underdeveloped lungs and
needed assistance breathing. V1 remained in hospital for about six months. D was
envious of V3's love for V1. He was controlling and worried that his position in her life
would be threatened. He showed no interest in V1. This was demonstrated by the fact
that the care plan drawn up by social services did not include him. When V1 was due to
be discharged, D damaged the home of V3 and her mother, V2. He sent threating text
and Facebook messages and said that he hoped that V1 would die. He threatened to set
the house on fire and kill them all. V3 repeatedly cried at work as a result of the threats.
After that, the front door lock was changed and D slept in a tent in the garden. V1 was

taken home for the first time. D accused V3 of being unfaithful and questioned his paternity of the twins. He became abusive and threatening. At midnight he set fire to the tent. He sent threatening text messages to V3 saying that the house would 'look like the tent' and 'that oxygen will blow you up and [that's] what I want'. The reference to 'oxygen' was a reference to oxygen cylinders which had been provided for V1. At 3 am, when V1, V2, and V3 were asleep, D started a fire in the porch of the house. This was the night after the baby was discharged. The stairwell became impassable within minutes and the family were trapped. The flames burnt through the ceiling and V3 and V1 were heard screaming for help. Neighbours tried to get into the house but were unable to do so. V3 was urged to jump but she would not leave V1. V3, V1 and V2 died as a result of the fire. D denied having set the fire. He admitted to being drunk that night and to sending the text messages. He claimed that he had not meant what he said. Held. The starting point was 30 years. This was not a case involving a substantial degree of premeditation or planning. D had shown no remorse despite his actions condemning the family to a horrifying death. There was a serious degree of pain suffered by V2 and V3 before their deaths. There are three factors which showed that D's culpability was extremely high: first, the threats made, second, V1 was extremely disabled and was D's child, and third, he knew that the oxygen cylinders were in the house and the text messages showed he knew the effect they would have. Additionally, there was the way in which the family died. Those were very serious aggravating factors. This case warranted a sentence significantly above the 30-year starting point. Minimum term **35 years** not 30.

See also: *R v George-Davies* 2010 EWCA Crim 919, 2011 1 Cr App R (S) 13 (p 103) (Convicted. V remonstrates with D after D exposes himself. V punches D and D later spreads petrol round V's front door. Five escape and V dies badly burnt. **22 years**.)

R v Mahmud 2014 EWCA Crim 1008 (Convicted of two murders and three attempted murders. M bought 7 litres of petrol having told work colleagues he thought of harming his wife, V, who was divorcing him. He and D went to V's address and set it alight using the petrol. M's wife, her father and his wife's infant son died. His wife's mother and her brother suffered life-threatening injuries. He assisted in M's escape. D had no convictions and did not instigate the plan. M was to pay D £10,000 for his part. Aged 37 at conviction. Starting at 30 years. D's **34-year** minimum term upheld.)

Old cases: *R v Connor* 2007 EWCA Crim 2591, 2008 1 Cr App R (S) 89 (p 537) (**32 years**) *R v Taylor* 2007 EWCA Crim 2755, 2008 2 Cr App R (S) 9 (p 55) (**20 years**) For a summary of the cases, see the 9th edition of this book.

288.38   *Firearms, With   Basic principles*

Criminal Justice Act 2003 Sch 21 para 5(1)-(2) Cases for a defendant aged 21+ that would normally fall within the **30-year** starting point include murder involving the use of a firearm (unless it fulfils the criteria for a whole life term).

R v Jones 2005 EWCA Crim 3115, 2006 2 Cr App R (S) 19 (p 121) para 26 We have no doubt that the reason why the seriousness of such an offence (murder when firearm used) is normally considered to be particularly high is that it results from the unlawful carriage of a loaded firearm and that the usual purpose of carrying such a firearm is to be able to kill or to cause really serious injury. It is possible to envisage circumstances where this is not the case, but they will be very rare. Where a firearm is carried for the purpose of being used as an offensive weapon, we find it hard to envisage what reason there could be for not following the guidance in Schedule 21 and adopting **30 years** as a starting point.

R v West 2007 EWCA Crim 701 D was convicted of murder. She shot her husband with a firearm. The trial Judge said that it was inevitable he should take the 30-year starting point. Held. It was not inevitable. The word in the Schedule is 'normally'. The determinative consideration is whether the seriousness of the offence was particularly high. Each case will depend on its own facts. The starting point should have been **15 years**. (For more details, see the 7th edition of this book.)

288.39   *Firearms, With   Cases*

R v Ramsey and Others 2011 EWCA Crim 872 C, DR, NR and M were convicted of murder. C and NR were also convicted of attempted murder of the same victim. The defendants were members of a faction of the S3 gang in Sheffield. The gang engaged in robberies, drug dealing and extreme violence. V, aged 17, was also a member of the gang, and had a 'foot' in that faction and a rival faction. V was stabbed and, just days after being discharged from hospital, was shot with a sawn-off shotgun. It was thought V was murdered as revenge for aiding the murder of another gang member. NR ordered the killing whilst he was in custody (DPP for wounding). NR, aged 23 at sentence, had convictions for supplying hard drugs and wounding. M, aged 16, was not a member of the gang. He had a number of previous convictions (no custodial sentences) and was described as 'an enthusiastic hanger-on'. NR was the leader of the gang. The murder was planned and premeditated. NR's culpability was higher than that of those who carried out the murder. **35 years** was justified. For M, the appropriate starting point was 12 years because he was aged under 18. 20 years was too high. Taking into account the disparity between M and the other defendants, **17 years** was appropriate.

R v Hassan 2011 EWCA Crim 1229, 2012 1 Cr App R (S) 7 (p 30) D was convicted of murder, attempted murder and possessing a firearm with intent to endanger life. There was a minor argument in a pub between D and another, X. X was in the wrong. V1 and V2, two sons of the licensee, L, separated the two and ejected D. After about 7 minutes, D returned with a loaded automatic. L said it was not the time to discuss the incident. V1 and V2 approached him and D pointed the gun at V1. D fired at close range at V1's forehead and each arm. V1's skull was fractured and he died instantly. D fired four or five times at V2. One bullet grazed his head and lodged in the skull, two hit his shoulder and lodged in his jaw. Eight cartridges were found. Both incidents were in front of V1's father, mother and 13-year-old brother and pub customers. V2 was in hospital for six weeks. His brain damage affected his ability to walk and talk. Three bullets remained in his skull because it was thought too dangerous to remove them. D booked two tickets to New York. The incident devastated V1's family. His parents were unable to work and it was doubtful if they would ever work again. They were likely to lose their home. D was aged 31 and only had a drink/driving conviction with associated other charges. The Judge found: a) that V1 and V2 had tried to disarm D, b) that it was likely that D had the gun in his car or, if not, had visited a friend to secure it, and c) for the fatal shot there was an intent to kill. Held. The 37-year term was within the appropriate bracket.

R v Tucker 2011 EWCA Crim 3046, 2012 2 Cr App R (S) 30 (p 173) D was convicted of murder. He ran a public house with his partner, V. They lived on the premises together. V was having a bath and she talked with D. D later said that V taunted him, saying that she was seeing someone else and that she would not let D see his children, who lived in Ireland with D's ex-wife. D shot V in the back of the head with a .410 shot gun. She died instantly. He left the body in the bath for two days, before wrapping it in sheets and storing it in a large freezer outside. He continued to run the public house, making excuses for V's absence and bringing in extra help to manage the work. He became involved with a woman to the extent of having sexual intercourse with her in the living quarters of the public house, about a week after the murder. He then made his way to the Isle of Wight, taking his passport with him. He checked into a hotel in a false name and wrote a letter to the police confessing to the killing. He then sent text messages to the woman with whom he had had a brief relationship, telling her where the body could be found. She informed the police. The body was found some 12 days after the murder. D, aged 50, claimed that V's references to another man and his children amounted to provocation. He had tried to commit suicide twice prior to the murder. Held. D's position would have been stronger had he, as it is not uncommon in domestic offences to do, immediately notified the authorities. D in fact concealed the body for a time, misled people as to V's whereabouts and fled to the Isle of Wight. He did, however, eventually notify the police. V could not have been more vulnerable than lying in her bath. Breach of trust was not an aggravating factor as the concept of breach of trust does not cover the circumstances of this case. Life with **22-year** minimum term not 26.

R v Haigh 2013 EWCA Crim 2359 D was convicted of two murders. A co-accused, RS, was acquitted of both counts of murder. D, RS, V1 and V2 were involved in 'the underworld of drugs' in Liverpool and Cornwall. RS owed drug debts to those with whom V1 and V2 were associated. The drug creditors had threatened RS, his partner and their child. RS had constructed a sophisticated underground cannabis cultivation operation in St Austell to try to repay the debt. The operation was taken over by V1 and V2. D also owed drug money to V1. V1 had threatened D's ex-partner and child and had set fire to their house. The debt was considerable and to repay it D originally agreed to go to Brazil, ingest 1 kilo of heroin and bring it back to the UK. D's friend undertook a similar trip and was arrested and imprisoned. D then heard that he was going to be ordered to go to Brazil. D said he did not want to go. He stayed at a farm to keep watch over RS's cannabis production.

V1 and V2 travelled to Cornwall and had intended to meet someone in St Austell. That meeting did not take place. V1 and V2 were shot with a shotgun, V1 from behind and V2 in the face. Their bodies were dumped by RS in a trench and then dug up and transferred to a deep hole and set alight. Later their bodies were found by the police in two trenches at the farm. RS later admitted that he had dug the trenches with a JCB. RS stated that D had killed V1 and V2 and that he, RS, had disposed of the bodies. D was aged 27. (D's character was not referred to in the judgment.) Held. There was no doubt that the starting point had to be 30 years. The Judge regarded the concealment of the bodies as an aggravating feature but accepted that the murders were not premeditated. The Judge was correct to say that there were no real mitigating features. These were vicious murders at practically point blank range. A 5-year uplift was too much. The minimum term ought to have been **32 years**, not 35.

Old cases: *R v West* 2007 EWCA Crim 701 (**13 years**) *R v Henson and Magraw* 2007 EWCA Crim 1308, 2008 1 Cr App R (S) 19 (p 83) (**35 years**) *R v Tucker* 2007 EWCA Crim 3370, 2008 2 Cr App R (S) 27 (p 153) (**25 years**) *R v Kelly and Andrews* 2007 EWCA Crim 1715 (**32 years** and **29 years**) *R v Ennis* 2008 EWCA Crim 969 (**25 years**) *R v Walker* 2010 EWCA Crim 109 (**27 years**)

For a summary of the first case see the 6th edition, for the second and third cases, see the 7th edition, for the fifth case, see the 8th edition and for the last case, see the 10th edition.

288.40   *Gain, Defendant's motive was   Basic principles*

Criminal Justice Act 2003 Sch 21 para 5(1)-(2) Cases for a defendant aged 21+ that would normally fall within the **30-year** starting point include a murder done for gain (such as a murder done in the course or furtherance of robbery (unless it fulfils the criteria for a whole life term).

R v Bouhaddaou 2006 EWCA Crim 3190, 2007 2 Cr App R (S) 23 (p 122) D was convicted of murder and pleaded to burglary. He entered a home and was disturbed. He then stabbed the householder. The defence argued that the murder was not committed for gain but to facilitate an escape. Held. Escape is an integral part of burglary. The murder was in the 'for gain' category.

R v Tailor 2007 EWCA Crim 1564, 2008 1 Cr App R (S) 37 (p 199) D pleaded to murder. Held. Murder for gain in a domestic context is apt to include cases where the gain is not only financial but also involves other ends such as lust and selfishness. These cases are to be distinguished from those where professional criminals kill for gain or kill in the course of an offence such as robbery. The domestic cases will not ordinarily require such a long minimum term. Here the Judge should have discounted the starting point by reference to the mixed motives.

Att-Gen's Ref No 12 of 2008 2008 EWCA Crim 1060, 2009 1 Cr App R (S) 18 (p 97) LCJ D was convicted of murder. The Judge's starting point was 15 years rather than 30 as it was not clear that the murder was done for gain, rather it may have been done because of a failure to gain money. Held. We are concerned that at the sentencing hearing there seems to have been a mechanistic or arithmetical approach. Whether the court starts at 15 or 30 years, the exercise requires an assessment of seriousness having regard to the facts of the particular case, and that can result in a sentence that is some distance from the starting point. It does not seem to us that the seriousness of the offence is greatly affected by whether the violence was inflicted in the course of trying to obtain money from the victim or after such an attempt had failed.

R v Height and Anderson 2008 EWCA Crim 2500, 2009 1 Cr App R (S) 117 (p 656) LCJ D was sentenced as having killed his wife not for financial gain but because he wished to be rid of her, with a starting point of 15 years. H was sentenced as having committed the offence for 'not insubstantial' financial gain, with a starting point of 30 years. Held. The Judge must identify the starting point he has chosen, his reason for doing so and, where appropriate, his reasons for departing from the normal starting point. The sentencing provisions of section 269 are not intended to be applied inflexibly. Something must be wrong with the conclusion that the starting point for a man who wishes to have his wife murdered, and arranges and agrees to pay for it, should be different from the starting point for the man he employs to carry out the killing. It is difficult to conceive of many cases where one defendant acting for gain should be subject to a different starting point from the individual who paid or agreed to pay him. The potential absurdity is highlighted here because on the approach to the section adopted different starting points were applied even when it was A and not his hired associate who actually carried out the killing. The Judge overlooked that there would be cases which, because of all the aggravating circumstances, would nevertheless make the seriousness 'particularly high' even if none of the express criteria applied to it. Although H's financial motivation made a 30-year starting point appropriate, A's culpability with all its aggravating features should also have been regarded as making his case one of particularly high seriousness, and the same starting point should have applied.

R v Healy 2008 EWCA Crim 2583 D stole £10 and stabbed V. Held. There need be no conviction for robbery. The Judge was entitled to form his own view whether it was done for gain. He was not bound to take the view that because it was a murder for gain it was necessarily a murder of particular seriousness. This is a case where whatever starting point was correct, the eventual minimum term would lie between the two starting points.

R v Hood 2012 EWCA Crim 1260, 2013 1 Cr App R (S) 49 (p 273) D pleaded to murder. His girlfriend, G, was convicted of murder. The motive was that G didn't want her former partner, V, to see their six-month-old child. G lured V to a lake at night. D attacked V with a hammer and killed him. Held. para 18 This was not a murder for gain in the terms of paragraph 5(2)(c). The gain that is there contemplated is clearly principally a monetary one or one of equivalent kind. Having an ulterior motive for killing is not the same in every case as killing for gain. If it were, and an ulterior motive for killing meant that the murder was done for gain, that would apply to a very large number of killings, indeed most other than those spontaneously arising.

288.41   *Gain, Defendant's motive was   Cases*

R v King 2013 EWCA Crim 930 D was convicted of murder and robbery. He contacted V via a gay dating website. V was a slightly built, 5 foot 5 inch tall, quiet, gentle widower in his early sixties. D then spoke to a friend about a plan to target a victim to obtain goods or money. D asked the friend to wait outside a house while he stole keys to a vehicle. He spoke about stabbing the victim and showed the friend a knife. The friend did not want to be involved. D and V's conversation revealed that D was interested in whether V lived alone and whether he owned a vehicle. D and V arranged to meet two days later and their conversations on the Internet made it clear that the meeting was to be of a sexual nature. D went to V's home after they met at about 8 pm. At about 2.30 the following morning, neighbours smelled smoke coming from V's property. Firefighters discovered three seats of fire at V's address and the interior of the property was in considerable disarray. V's body was found naked with an ornamental wreath placed on his head. V's cat had been killed and placed on the body. V's body had multiple sharp and blunt force trauma injuries to the head, neck and chest, with dozens of incised wounds and multiple fractures to the skull and face. He had suffered 17 rib fractures and sub-arachnoid haemorrhage. There were 31 defensive wounds to the arms, indicating a sustained knife attack. D remained in the property for a period of about 3½ hours after the murder. During that time an audio recording was made on his phone, in which D can be heard to say "Fucking dead bastard". His phone also recorded a video clip showing V, either deeply unconscious or dead, with severe wounds to the head and face. A further video clip recorded 2 minutes later showed D repeatedly stamping on V's apparently dead body and face whilst saying things including "When you fuck with me, you fuck with the best". Two condoms recovered from the scene indicated that there had been sexual activity between D and V prior to the attack. D then left V's home, loaded up V's vehicle with his personal financial documents, a laptop, a hi-fi and a television, and drove away. He was stopped by the police for driving in an erratic fashion. They noticed that he was heavily bloodstained. He was still in possession of the knife. D, aged 18 at the time of the offences, had two convictions for shoplifting. He was obsessed with his physical stature. The Judge found D intended to kill before he met V and had enjoyed the murder. Held. This was a truly dreadful offence which falls into the 30-year starting point category because it was done for gain, and also because of the circumstances in which it was committed. There was significant premeditation. A knife was taken to the scene with violent intent. That alone would attract a starting point of 25 years. The vulnerable victim was attacked after the killing, and his body was subject to further gross violence. That violence was recorded on a mobile phone. This offence would have mandated a sentence of well in excess of 30 years for a mature adult. The Judge made a significant reduction for D's age. A **28-year** minimum term was not arguably excessive.

R v Senechko 2013 EWCA Crim 2308 D was convicted of murder. He lived in Ukraine but had come to the UK about eight months before the incident. He attended a New Year party at a restaurant part-owned by V's cousin. V was employed to provide music and entertainment in the restaurant. D was joined by K, L and M. At around 4 am, they went to L and M's flat where they continued to drink and then slept. In the morning, L remained in bed while the other three got up. K went to the shops and returned with more alcohol and the four continued to drink. D left the room and when he returned, he jumped on K and stabbed him in the neck with a kitchen knife. M witnessed this. K fell to the floor and there was a significant spray of blood across the room. The wound was 15 cm deep and had penetrated several major blood vessels. D walked into the kitchen, cleaned the knife and placed it back on the shelf. He said to M, "You can't prove anything." D told L and M that they should call the emergency services. The Judge found that although it was not a long-premeditated crime, D had formed the intention before he went to fetch the knife from the kitchen. D had no convictions in the previous ten years and was well regarded by his friends and colleagues. Held. D stabbed K with a six-inch knife up to the hilt and then calmly washed the weapon and boasted that the witness would not be able to prove anything. D did nothing to help K and instead he made off and disposed of his mobile phone in a further attempt to cover his tracks. The knife was not taken to the scene and so the starting point was 15 years. This was a horrific crime, carried out in cold blood for no good reason. D was fuelled by alcohol and his anger, if there was any, was utterly irrational. A 20-year minimum term was too high. Taking into account all the factors, a **minimum term of 18 years** was appropriate.

R v De Silva 2014 EWCA Crim 2616, 1 Cr App R (S) 52 (p 359) D was convicted of murder. He pleaded late to aggravated burglary (12 years consecutive). At about 6 am, he broke into V's home through a window. V, aged 73, heard the noise and went to investigate. Shortly after, V was subjected to an attack of horrifying savagery when D stabbed him 22 times. The wounds were mainly to the chest and abdomen but some were to V's back and sides. A few minutes later, V was found dead or dying by his family and friends. D was aged just 19. When aged 7, seven armed police entered his home and arrested his father, who was sentenced to a very substantial prison term. When aged 9, there were concerns about extreme violence in his home and he became a 'looked after' child. When aged 11, he was placed in a residential school. When aged 12, he started his [regular] appearances at the Youth Court for offences including ABH, burglary (five offences) and bladed article (four offences). Thereafter he was convicted of robbery. His longest sentence was 18 months' YOI. After his arrest he was transferred from a YOI to prison because of his aggressive and disruptive behaviour. A psychiatrist said there was 'no evidence of a psychotic mental disorder, but D suffered from a dissocial personality disorder. He was callously unconcerned for others, grossly irresponsible and had a low threshold for discharge of aggression including violence.' Judge concluded that a) the wounds were inflicted for D to make his escape, b) there was an intent to kill, c) it was a murder for gain (the burglary), d) D had the knife before he entered the house, e) V was elderly and vulnerable and f) D's mental condition did not lower the culpability 'discernibly'. Held. It was a dreadful crime. The Judge was entitled to conclude neither D's disorder nor the absence of a premeditated intent to kill were significant factors. Because of his age, **28 years** not 32.

R v Francis 2015 EWCA Crim 780 LCJ D was convicted of murder and robbery. In the early hours, he with another set out to rob. They entered a churchyard where they attacked V, who was eating a take-away. The two kicked him to death. (V's injuries are not listed.) £12 and an iPhone were stolen. D was aged 32. He had a robbery finding of guilt at 16 and less serious offences since. The Judge said it was a vicious, rapid and mindless attack. He started at 30 years and chose not to factor in D's record. Held. This was a robbery at the very bottom end of the scale. There was no intent to kill and no weapon. **24 years** not 26.

See also: *R v Orlowski* 2011 EWCA Crim 454 (Polish national aged 20. Homeless and dependent on alcohol. Convicted of murder having pleaded to manslaughter. Hit elderly victim with a vase at least 10 times about the head. Stole from victim's house and sought to return to Poland. Due to his immaturity and alcohol dependence, **20 years** not 23.)

R v Young 2011 EWCA Crim 2637, 2012 1 Cr App R (S) 103 (p 621) (Plea. Stole money from wallet of 89-year-old man living alone. Struck him with a hammer 6+ times causing significant head injuries. Murder for gain, therefore starting point of 30 years. Aggravating factors such as age and vulnerability of victim and brutality of the attack. Previous convictions for burglary and affray with knives and a hammer. With the plea, **28 years** was certainly not manifestly excessive.)

R v Bayliss 2012 EWCA Crim 269, 2 Cr App R (S) 61 (p 360) (Convicted of murder. Planned robbery. Stabbed taxi driver after driver taken to secluded spot. 14 blows including 6 times in the head. Fatal injury punctured the brain. Aged 29. Good character. 30-year starting point was correct. With character and aggravating features, **30-year** minimum term.)

R v Royle 2013 EWCA Crim 1461, 1 Cr App R (S) 49 (p 296) (Convicted. Robbed woman aged 79 who later died from a heart attack. Used considerable force. Aggravated by V's age and vulnerability. Sentenced for a separate robbery. Aged 37 with 111 previous convictions. Insufficient discount for absence of premeditation. **25-year minimum term** not 28.)

R v Dunkley 2015 EWCA Crim 330 (Convicted of murder, theft and fraud. Pleaded to preventing burial. Killed paraplegic, V, for his savings when he was V's carer. Used Internet search engine to research about humans bleeding to death. Chopped up body into 10 pieces with chain saw and used freezer and incinerator in attempt to dispose of it. 30 years right starting point. We move it to 34 years not 36 for a) V's vulnerability, b) D was a trusted carer, c) significant degree of premeditation, and d) most significant, the gross dismemberment of V. Adopting the 2 years off for the mitigation, **32 years** not 34.)

R v Hesse and Lewis 2015 EWCA Crim 884 (H and L convicted. Plan to steal contents of cannabis farm. Owner fatally stabbed. Judge able to start at 30 years. The fact that H and L initially only intended to carry out a burglary until there was a confrontation was mitigation. So 27 years not 30.)

Old cases: There are plenty of recent cases. If old cases are needed, five can be found in the 10th edition and many more in the 8th edition.

288.42   *Gay, lesbian and transgender murders   Not whole life*

The legislative provisions below were inserted by Legal Aid, Sentencing and Punishment of Offenders Act 2012 s 65(7)-(9). In force 3 December 2012.

Criminal Justice Act 2003 Sch 21 para 3 For the purposes of this schedule: a) an offence is aggravated by sexual orientation if it is committed in circumstances mentioned in section 146(2)(a)(i) or b)(i)...c) an offence is aggravated by transgender identity if it is committed in circumstances mentioned in section 146(2)(a)(iii) or (b)(iii).

Criminal Justice Act 2003 s 146(1) This section applies where the court is considering the seriousness of an offence committed in any of the circumstances mentioned in subsection (2).

(2) Those circumstances are:

a) that, at the time of committing the offence, or immediately before or after doing so, the offender demonstrated towards the victim of the offence hostility based on:
   i) the sexual orientation (or presumed sexual orientation) of the victim,..
   iii) the victim being (or presumed to be) transgender, or
b) that the offence is motivated (wholly or partly):
   i) by hostility towards persons who are of a particular sexual orientation,..or
   iii) by hostility towards persons who are transgender.

(3) The court:

a) must treat the fact that the offence was committed in any of those circumstances as an aggravating factor, and
b) must state in open court that the offence was committed in such circumstances.

(4) It is immaterial for the purposes of paragraph (a) or (b) of subsection (2) whether or not the offender's hostility is also based, to any extent, on any other factor not mentioned in that paragraph.

Criminal Justice Act 2003 s 146(6) In this section references to being transgender include references to being transsexual, or undergoing, proposing to undergo or having undergone a process or part of a process of gender reassignment.

Criminal Justice Act 2003 Sch 21 para 5(2) Cases that (if not [whole life]) would normally fall within [the 30-year term] include:...e) a murder involving sexual or sadistic conduct...g) a murder that is...aggravated by sexual orientation.

Note: Armed Forces Act 2006 s 241 contains an identical section save for a different description of the court. The amendment by Legal Aid, Sentencing and Punishment of Offenders Act 2012 is the same. Ed.

R v McDowell 2006 EWCA Crim 1836, 2007 1 Cr App R (S) 56 (p 320) D was convicted of murder. He met a 37-year-old student in a gay pub, took him to his flat and strangled him. He borrowed a saw, dismembered the body and put it in bin bags which he concealed in bins near his home. He boasted about his crime. He made no comment in interview and ran diminished responsibility at trial. He was aged 28 with no convictions. He had been very badly sexually abused as a child. Reports said that he had an untreatable psychopathic personality. Further, he presented a very great risk and continuing danger, in particular to homosexuals. The Judge agreed and said that the offence was planned and that he lured V back. It was a transitional case. Held. The means of disposal of the body and the psychosis did give rise to concern. His childhood abuse and his mental conditions mitigated the offence. The premeditation or planning and dismemberment were serious aggravating factors. The starting point was 15 years. **20-year** minimum term, not whole life.

Note: This was not considered a sexual orientation crime. The reason for this was not given. Ed.
For an example of the court saying that a murder after gay sex was not aggravated by sexual orientation, see *R v Morley* 2009 EWCA Crim 1302, 2010 1 Cr App R (S) 44 (p 275) at **288.30**.
Historical cases, see **288.5**.

288.43   Knives etc.   Judicial guidance
Note: Murders when a knife is used can have many different starting points. There is a starting point of 25 years, which only applies to certain knife crime and where the offence does not qualify for a 30-year or whole life starting point. There are also the offences involving a knife where the date of the offence is before the guideline came into force (2 April 2010). Finally, there are those knife murders outside the knife criteria. Ed.
R v M and Others 2009 EWCA Crim 2544, 2010 2 Cr App R (S) 19 (p 117) LCJ The use of a knife and the precise circumstances in which it was used aggravate the seriousness of the individual offence. Deaths in these circumstances outrage and horrify the collective conscience of the community as a whole. Anyone who goes into a public place armed with a knife and uses it to kill must expect condign punishment.
R v Odegbune and Others 2013 EWCA Crim 711 paras 29-30 From 2 March 2010 the starting point for murders where a knife or other weapon was taken to the scene where the intention was to commit an offence or have it available as a weapon became 25 years. This means the citation of reported decisions of sentences for similar offences committed prior to 2 March 2010 is unlikely to be helpful.
R v Beckford 2014 EWCA Crim 1299, 2 Cr App R (S) 34 (p 285) D drove a stolen car into V, ramming him off his bicycle with tremendous force. Held. The Judge was entitled to conclude that D took a weapon to the scene.

288.44   Knives etc.   25-year starting point   Statute and judicial guidance
Criminal Justice Act 2003 Sch 21 para 5A[692] For offences which do not fall within paragraph 4(1) (see **288.91**) or 5(1) (see **288.15**), if the offender:
   a) is aged 18+ at the time of the commission of the offence,
   b) took a knife or other weapon to the scene, intending to commit any offence or have it available to use as a weapon, and
   c) used that knife or other weapon in committing the murder,
the offence is normally to be regarded as sufficiently serious for the starting point to be 25 years.
The new provision does not apply to offences committed before 2 March 2010.
Criminal Justice Act 2003 (Mandatory Life Sentence: Determination of Minimum Term) Order 2010 2010/197 Explanatory memorandum The Government included both knives and other weapons (based on ordinary common English usage).
R v Kelly and Others 2011 EWCA Crim 1462, 2012 1 Cr App R (S) 56 (p 316) LCJ K, B and S in separate unrelated cases were convicted of murder. H and R were convicted of murder in the same trial. All the cases involved the use of knives. Held. It does not follow that a murder committed with a knife in the offender's home, or house, automatically falls outside the ambit of paragraph 5A. para 12 If X walks home intending to kill his wife, goes to the kitchen, picks up a knife and stabs his wife, his starting point is 15 years. If Y walks home, with exactly the same frame of mind, buys a knife from a shop and goes home and stabs his wife, he faces a 25-year starting point. That starting point can apply to murders in the home. No-one could believe that is justice, as the levels of culpability are the same. para 14 Problems arise with what is meant by 'the scene' in para 5A. If Z takes a knife from the kitchen which adjoins the living room without a partition, and stabs V in the living room, the knife is not 'taken to the scene'. Complications will arise where Z passes through doors which are open,

---

[692] As inserted by Criminal Justice Act 2003 (Mandatory Life Sentence: Determination of Minimum Term) Order 2010 2010/197

closed or locked on his way to murder. The situation will be additionally complicated if one of the doors in the premises through which the assailant went with the knife had been open, or closed, or locked. Given some of the difficulties that may arise with joint enterprise murders where a weapon is used by one, but only one, the difficulties are likely to multiply. There will continue to be convictions for multi-handed murders where one or more of the defendants was not aware that a knife or knives were being taken to the scene but who, once violence erupted, were participating in it well aware that the knife would be or was being used with murderous intent. Although guilty of murder, they were not party to the taking of the fatal weapon to the scene. For them, their offence is aggravated by the fact that they participated in a knife murder. Paragraph 5A would not provide the starting point in the sentencing decision. For those who did take part or were party to the taking of the knife to the scene, then it would, but care has to be taken not to double count the fact that they participated in a knife murder which has already been factored into the normal paragraph 5A starting point. The judge will therefore be required to make the necessary findings of fact to identify the appropriate starting point, and thereafter to reach the sentencing decision required by the justice of the case. On the basis of the single case [involving H and R involved in joint enterprise], we cannot give any broader guidance.

Looking at the individual cases, K took a knife from a kitchen drawer, went upstairs, broke down a locked bathroom door and stabbed the victim. A knife taken from the kitchen of a home, whether a flat, maisonette or house, to another room in the same home, even if a locked door is forced, is not 'taken to the scene'. The prosecution relied on the door being broken down. It is arguable either way whether the knife was 'taken to the scene'. If it was not, it is difficult to see how that could make any difference to the sentence.

V went to B's parents' home armed with a rounders bat, saying, "You're fucking dead mate". B, who was inside, armed himself with a knife and came out of the house onto the pavement. The two ran towards each other and V swung the bat. B stabbed V. The knife was 'taken to the scene'.

S lived in a bedsit above a factory. He heard an insult from V2. He took a knife from an upstairs kitchen in his own premises and went downstairs into the working area of the factory. He did not travel outside, he simply walked through an open door and a distance of some 50 metres before he killed V2. It is difficult to avoid the conclusion that the knife was 'taken to the scene'.

H took one knife to the scene and took a second knife from the kitchen drawer which was used in the stabbing. This means the first knife was not 'taken to the scene'. R bought a knife but would not have used it. He had taken it to pass on to H and H knew that the knife was taken to the scene. As it was a joint enterprise, [both were caught by paragraph 5A].

R v Fielding 2011 EWCA Crim 1942 D was convicted of murder. He stabbed V with a knife taken from the kitchen during a drunken argument. Held. When considering the knives taken to the murder scene provisions, in some circumstances it will be right to say that a knife has been picked up spontaneously as a weapon that happened to come to hand. In others it will be possible to discern a more considered decision. The distinction drawn by the defence between a spontaneous attack and 'the type of circumstance to which that provision was directed' was too rigid.

R v Folley 2013 EWCA Crim 396 D was convicted of murder. He had resented V being on the landing of his block of flats. D worked himself up into a fit of rage, armed himself with a kitchen knife from his flat and went outside. D then slit V's throat. V died. The defence contended the 25-year term did not apply. Held. That provision, as *R v Kelly and Others* 2011 explains, is not to be analysed by reference only to the distance the knife is carried. It is capable of being engaged if the offender leaves his home with the knife and the incident, for example, occurs in the street outside or in the same building as is his home. A murder with a knife in the home of the offender or the home of the victim may fall within the ambit of the paragraph. It is expressly not confined to murders committed by the use of a knife which has been taken out onto the streets. One of the cases in *R v Kelly and Others* 2011 was B, whose case was factually similar to this. A starting point of 25 years was upheld. We uphold this one.

R v Senechko 2013 EWCA Crim 2308 D was convicted of murder. He was drinking in a flat. D left the room and went to the kitchen and took a knife. He then returned to the living room, jumped on K and stabbed him in the neck with the knife. D walked back into the kitchen, and placed the knife back on the shelf. The Judge treated the kitchen and the living room as the same scene. Held. The 15-year starting point was correct. For more details, see **288.41**.

R v Dillon 2015 EWCA Crim 3, 1 Cr App R (S) 62 (p 434) D was convicted of murder. After repeated aggressive behaviour between D and V, V started banging on D's flat door. D came out of the door and stabbed V without saying a word. V died in a pool of blood. Held. The following emerges from the authorities: a) a knife taken from a kitchen to another part of the same flat or house, including a balcony, will not normally be regarded as having been taken to the scene, even if a door is forced open, b) conversely, if the knife is taken out of the house or flat into the street, or into another part of the premises, or onto a landing outside a flat, it will normally be regarded as having been taken to the scene, c) however, a starting point is not the same thing as a finishing point [in determining sentence]. For more details, see **288.45**.

288.45   Knives etc.   25-year starting point   Cases

R v Parr 2013 EWCA Crim 2007 D was convicted of murder and pleaded to having an offensive weapon, conspiracy to pervert the course of justice and threatening to take revenge.[693] V, aged 19, was walking home from a party. D and his 15-year-old cousin, J, were on the opposite side of the road. They knew each other. There had been a disagreement between V and J about a week previously. J was heard to say that he would stab V. D walked across the road and stabbed V three times in the thigh and once in the chest with a knife. He struck the blows with severe force. The wounds were 7, 9 and 14 cm deep in the thigh, and 10 cm to the chest. His heart was punctured and his sternum penetrated. D and J fled and went to C's house. C's friend described D as being 'in drink'. D told the friend how he had stabbed a man four times. C heard D on the phone say, "No one threatens my family. I did it for my family". He showed C the knife. It appeared to C that D was getting a 'buzz' from it. D handed himself in to the police the following day. D was overheard whilst on remand telling someone on the telephone that "someone should do the little rat's house tonight", meaning C's house. The windows were smashed in her house. In other calls, he issued threats and said he was certain if particular witnesses didn't attend the trial, he would be convicted of manslaughter, not murder. The threats affected C and she took a drug overdose and did not appear at the trial. D was aged 19 at the time of the offence. He had no previous convictions. The Judge treated him as though he did not have an intention to kill. Held. D's behaviour was cold-blooded and he boasted about it afterwards. D had plotted revenge against those who had the temerity to give evidence for the prosecution. One attempted suicide. D took the knife to the scene and the Judge was correct in starting at 25 years. The Judge was not wrong to add 1 year to the starting point for the other offending. There was, however, strong mitigation including the lack of an intention to kill, his youth and his good character. The minimum term should have been **20 years** not 23.

Att-Gen's Ref No 43 of 2014 2014 EWCA Crim 1289 D was convicted of murder. D and H, a co-defendant, had a verbal confrontation with V and J. This was initiated by V. After that, D and H walked on, and V and J drove to a gym where V armed himself with a 5-kilo dumbbell. A further confrontation ensued where V was backed by others also wielding dumbbells. At some stage this must have been dropped. D confronted V and H. V was fatally stabbed and D attempted to leave the country. V was a respected member

---

[693] 'Threatening to take revenge' is the term used by the Court. Ed.

of the community with no known gang affiliation and was of positive good character. D, aged 19, had recently been released from custody and had relocated to the area because of a civil 'gang injunction' imposed in London. He had convictions from 2011 for possession of a bladed article, burglary and violent disorder, all committed whilst on bail. The latter two offences occurred during the London riots. The Judge took as mitigation D's age, the element of provocation, the intent to kill was not proved and the lack of premeditation. Held. Insufficient weight was given to the antecedent history of D. The background of gang conflict, D's preparedness to use a knife and the fact that V was stabbed in the back were all aggravating features. **22 years** not 15.

R v Dillon 2015 EWCA Crim 3, 1 Cr App R (S) 62 (p 434) D was convicted of murder. He lived alone in a block of flats next to P, whose boyfriend, V, lived elsewhere. V regularly visited P. P argued with a close friend of D. P made complaints about D playing loud music day and night which affected P and V's baby. P and D's relationship was affected by untrue rumours that D was a paedophile. V stayed with P and in the morning they argued and after V had left, they exchanged angry text messages. P spent the afternoon drinking. Also during the afternoon, D was seen by P drinking on the balcony of his flat. Later that afternoon, P went out and returned in the evening and saw D in the car park behaving strangely. P followed D into the front door of the flats and in the communal area outside their flat doors, P thought D said "fat whore" or something similar. The words were repeated and P told D to "fuck off". D approached P angrily and P struggled to push her front door open. D tried forcibly to stop P entering her flat and shouted abuse. This led to P calling the police. D went out to buy beer and M, a mutual friend of V and P, phoned V. V then entered the flat landing and angrily banged on D's door, shouting, "Get the prick out here". P told him to stop, but V returned to D's door and continued banging on the door. D opened his door and, without saying a word, plunged a knife into V's chest to a depth of 23 cm with 80% of the 11-inch blade buried. The knife damaged V's lung and penetrated his heart. A second, forceful and substantial blow was dealt by D with the knife to the back of V's head. This caused a groove in V's skull. V also received a 4 cm wound to his cheek. D then pushed V out of sight and returned to his flat where he washed the blood from the knife and replaced it in a drawer. V died shortly after at the scene having lost a great deal of blood. D then calmly went to another flat, carrying a small knife. He then calmly called the police saying that his door had been attacked and that, "I was so scared…that I got a knife". He also admitted stabbing V. The police arrived. D was incredulous at his arrest and was found to have a small stab wound which he claimed V inflicted. It was unclear how it was caused, but V did not use a knife.

D had many previous convictions for relatively minor violence (all under 6 months, the last in 2009) and dishonesty, spanning 30 years. The Judge considered that the knife was taken to the scene and started at 25 years. He considered the previous convictions to be an aggravating factor. He reduced the term because of the lack of an intention to kill, a lack of premeditation and because D suffered from a fear that V was going to be violent to him. Held. This case falls within paragraph 5A. However, D's dishonesty convictions are almost entirely immaterial and his violence convictions are of limited significance. With the Judge's mitigating factors, **20-year minimum term**, not 22.

See also: *R v Beckford* 2014 EWCA Crim 1299, 2 Cr App R (S) 34 (p 285) (D convicted. V, aged 19, was a member of a rival gang. D drove a stolen car into V, ramming him off his bicycle with tremendous force. D aged 22 but no licence and poor record with three violent offences, including two robberies in 2009. Held. Judge entitled to conclude that D took a weapon to the scene. In setting minimum terms courts should achieve just results, not slavishly follow Criminal Justice Act 2003 Sch 21. **24-year** term upheld.)

Att-Gen's Ref No 19 of 2014 2014 EWCA Crim 1322 (Convicted. Sharing home pending separation. Tried to falsely blacken V's reputation. Talked about killing V. Killed her with commercial rolling pin (taken to the home as a weapon) causing severe brain injury. Motive was to obtain sole custody of child. 25-year starting point as weapon taken to scene so **23 years** not 18.)

288.46   Knives etc.   No 25-year starting point   Cases

R v Jogee 2013 EWCA Crim 1433 D was convicted of murder. D and his co-defendant, H, went to R's house at 2.23 am. They had both previously been at R's house that evening and had spent a large part of the evening together, becoming increasingly drunk and intoxicated by cocaine. Their behaviour was aggressive. After leaving the address earlier on in the evening, R sent a text to D instructing him not to bring H to the address again. They returned very shortly after. They knew that R and V (with whom R was in a sexual relationship) were at the address. H entered unasked and D remained at the door and was shouting about S, R's partner and the father of her children. Threats were made by H and D was egging H on to 'do something' to V. H confronted V, took a knife from the kitchen block and stabbed V in the chest. D had remained at the door. The knife was later disposed of. V, who was a paralegal, had previously represented both D and H. He had also represented S. There was evidence of earlier bad feeling between him and V. H, aged 25, was a friend of D. D, aged 22, used and dealt in drugs. He had convictions for common assault (2002 and 2003), possession of an offensive weapon (2003), possession of a prohibited weapon (2003, 2004 and 2006), battery (2009) and aggravated vehicle-taking (2010). Held. The single Judge refused leave, stating that D: a) was under the influence of alcohol, b) knew that H was drunk and dangerous, c) encouraged him to attack V, including when he had the knife, and d) had a substantial record including drug and violent offences. We consider the correct starting point to be 15 years. It should be reduced for the lack of an intention to kill. It has to be increased because of the aggravating features. There was, on the other hand, no planning and there was no great distinction between the sentences imposed for D (20 years) and H (22 years). The correct starting point was significantly above 15 years. Minimum term **18 years** not 20.

R v Senechko 2013 EWCA Crim 2308 D was convicted of murder. He lived in Ukraine but had come to the UK about eight months before the incident. He attended a New Year party at a restaurant part-owned by V's cousin. V was employed to provide music and entertainment in the restaurant. D was joined by K, L and M. At around 4 am, they went to L and M's flat where they continued to drink and then slept. In the morning, L remained in bed while the other three got up. K went to the shops and returned with more alcohol and the four continued to drink. D left the room and when he returned, he jumped on K and stabbed him in the neck with a kitchen knife. M witnessed this. K fell to the floor and there was a significant spray of blood across the room. The wound was 15 cm deep and had penetrated several major blood vessels. D walked into the kitchen, cleaned the knife and placed it back on the shelf. He said to M, "You can't prove anything." D told L and M that they should call the emergency services. The Judge found that although it was not a long-premeditated crime, D had formed the intention before he went to fetch the knife from the kitchen. D had no convictions in the previous ten years and was well regarded by his friends and colleagues. The Judge treated the kitchen and the living room as the same scene. Held. The 15-year starting point was correct. D had stabbed K with a six-inch knife up to the hilt and then calmly washed the weapon and boasted that the witness would not be able to prove anything. D did nothing to help K and instead he made off and disposed of his mobile phone in a further attempt to cover his tracks. This was a horrific crime, carried out in cold blood for no good reason. D was fuelled by alcohol and his anger, if there was any, was utterly irrational. A 20-year minimum term was too high. Taking into account all the factors, a **minimum term of 18 years** was appropriate.

R v Patraucean 2015 EWCA Crim 957 D pleaded (full credit) to murder. Under the influence of cocaine, cannabis and alcohol, he picked up a prostitute, V. D went back to her flat in her car. He had a Stanley knife with him. About two hours later he drove away in her car. V was found with a number of knife wounds, some of which appeared to have been made after she died. The deepest wound was 9.6 cm long and gaped to 2.6 cm. Her neck was severed right through to her cervical spine. Injuries indicated that D had manually strangled her. The pathologist determined that there had been a ferocious attack including blunt force trauma from a fist. There was no evidence of recent sexual activity. She was fully clothed. His blood-stained Stanley knife was found. D claimed V had stolen £200 from him and an argument had broken out. D was aged 20 with no previous convictions. A *Newton* hearing was held [but it did not provide much help as to the required starting point]. The prosecution relied on *R v Jones* 2005 EWCA Crim 3115, 2006 2 Cr App R (S) 19 (p 121) to suggest that what mattered was whether the seriousness of the case was particularly high and not whether one of the examples in Schedule 21 para 5 was made out. The Judge rejected: a) that the murder involved sadistic conduct, b) that a 25-year knife starting point was established, c) that there were attempts to dismember the body, and d) that there was a robbery motive. He gave D the benefit of the doubt that she had taken his money. However, because of the ferocity of the attack and the terrible injuries, he found this was a murder where the seriousness was particularly high. He started at 30 years and with the plea and mitigation, made the minimum term 25 years. Held. That was wrong. The starting point was 15 years. With the aggravating factors we increase that to 24 and with the plea make it **20 years**.

R v Jefferson 2015 EWCA Crim 1953 D was convicted of murder. He went to a party and was drunk and in a bad temper. He left the party and became involved in an argument with two youths in the street. D punched one of them, a girl, and knocked her out. People shouted abuse at D and he shouted back. D's co-accused,[694] N, was dancing in the street and waving a knife about which he had taken from the kitchen where the party was held. V had also been drinking and was in a foul mood. V came 'after N' and shouted, "Well come on then, you've got the knife". The two chased each other around. N dropped the knife and the confrontation appeared to have ended. Others told V to leave. D then approached V and started to usher him away. D had a concealed knife and as the two walked away, D thrust the knife into the back of V's thigh. The knife had originally come from kitchen drawer where the party was being held, but there was a conflict of evidence as to whether it had been taken by D or he had found it in the street. As V walked away, D kept thrusting the knife firmly into V's thigh. The wound had two tracks, one 7 cm long and one penetrating 18 cm though skin, muscle and tissue. That wound completely severed the femoral vein and partly severed the femoral artery. V collapsed. An ambulance attended but V died. D was aged 22 and had 33 previous convictions. When aged 15 he had been convicted of affray and possessing a bladed article, (Referral Order). His only custodial sentence was 12 weeks for driving offences in 2012. The Judge could not completely rule out the possibility that the knife was not taken to the scene. He also found a) the stabbing was not spontaneous and there was an element of guile, b) the previous convictions were insignificant, c) D had not started or provoked the disturbance, d) there was no intent to kill, e) his youth was a factor, and f) none of these factors carry great weight. The Judge started at 15 years. Held. The knife was used in the course of a serious incident of disorder. The Judge was entitled to take into account the use of the knife, the thrusting blows, the fact that the situation had calmed down and that he was walking away. The most important factor was the lack of an intent to kill. Taking that and D's youth into account, **18 years** not 20.

See also: *R v Braithwaite* 2010 EWCA Crim 1082 (Convicted. After a quarrel B returned with a knife and in a confrontation stabbed the victim in the neck. GBH intent. Premeditated revenge attack. Defendant in employment with family and previous convictions for carrying a knife. Nothing wrong with **19 years**.)

R v Matthews 2010 EWCA Crim 2023 (D, aged 17 at the time of the offence, pleaded to murder. During a burglary, D stabbed the victim four times, kicked, stamped and hit her with a saucepan. He was high on drugs. Full credit of one-sixth. **18 years** not 20.)

---

[694] News reports say he was convicted of affray and possession of offensive weapons.

R v Davies-Jones 2013 EWCA Crim 2809 (Attack on wife. **18 years** not 20, see **288.60**.) Old cases: Best ignored.

288.47   Knives etc.   30-year starting point   Case
R v Williams 2013 EWCA Crim 933 (**28 years**. See **288.61**.)
Mental disorder or mental disability, Defendant suffering from see **288.87**.

288.48   Mercy killing   Factor and judicial guidance
Criminal Justice Act 2003 Sch 21 para 11 Mitigating factors that may be relevant include:..f) a belief by the offender that the murder was an act of mercy.
R v Douglas 2014 EWCA Crim 2322, 2015 1 Cr App R (S) 28 (p 214) Defendant killed mother after drinking. Held. *R v Inglis* 2010 EWCA Crim 2637, 2011 2 Cr App R (S) 13 (p 66) (see below) decided that where there is a subjective genuine belief that an act of mercy is being performed, the potential aggravating factors of premeditation, vulnerability and abuse of trust may not be aggravating at all, or only to a moderate degree. For more details, see **288.77**.

288.49   Mercy killing   Cases
R v Inglis 2010 EWCA Crim 2637, 2011 2 Cr App R (S) 13 (p 66) LCJ D was convicted of murder and attempted murder of her son, V. He had suffered a head injury during a fight and against his wishes was taken to hospital by ambulance. During the journey the back doors opened three times and on the third occasion V fell out and suffered catastrophic head injuries. He was initially in a deep coma. Doctors were optimistic about his recovery. D felt she needed to relieve V's suffering. She injected V with heroin, causing a cardiac arrest. His condition deteriorated significantly. D initially denied the attempted murder. She subsequently indicated a willingness to plead guilty on the basis that it was an act of mercy. However, she did not accept that her actions were unjustified. A condition of D's bail was that she did not visit V in hospital. She subsequently did so under the guise of being his aunt. One afternoon when the hospital was understaffed, D visited V and injected him with a lethal dose of heroin. A nurse entered and D shouted at her to "get out" and threatened her that she had AIDS. When the nurse left the room D superglued the lock and barricaded the door with a chair and an oxygen tank. V died. D was diagnosed with post-traumatic stress disorder and suffered from a depressive disorder. After V's death, D's mental state improved. Held. The law of murder does not distinguish between murder committed for malevolent reasons and murder motivated by familial love. D's condition of depression and post-traumatic stress disorder diminished her ability to view V's condition, and all the events that surrounded it, in an objective way, and reduced her ability to cope with the awful stresses and strains likely to be imposed on any loving parent. However, her compulsive objective was indeed to kill V and there was no sense of remorse. The mitigation consequent on her grief should not be reduced by the absence of remorse for the killing. She was ill-equipped psychologically to cope with the disaster which befell V. Her culpability is reduced but not extinguished. She tried to kill V and did eventually kill him without a thought for the feelings of anyone else, including his father and his brothers, and indeed the members of the medical professions who were doing their very best to care for him. The minimum term should have been **5 years**, not 9.
Note: It would be easy to say it wasn't mercy killing because it was more like an execution based on one woman's view of what was best. In any event the sentencing Judge's decision reflected both incidents and the sanctity of life rather more than the Court of Appeal's decision. Ed.
R v Douglas 2014 EWCA Crim 2322, 2015 1 Cr App R (S) 28 (p 214) Defendant killed mother after drinking. Held. *R v Inglis* 2010 EWCA Crim 2637, 2011 2 Cr App R (S) 13 (p 66) (see below) decided that where there is a subjective genuine belief that an act of mercy is being performed, the potential aggravating factors of premeditation, vulnerability and abuse of trust may not be aggravating at all, or only to a moderate degree. For more details, see **288.77**.

For a case where the defendant cracked under pressure when caring for his elderly father, who had dementia, see *R v Zebedee* 2012 EWCA Crim 1428, 2013 1 Cr App R (S) 37 (p 207) at **288.74**.
See also the **MANSLAUGHTER** *Mercy killing* para at **284.48**.

288.50   *Multiple murders and whole life orders*
Criminal Justice Act 2003 Sch 21 para 4(1) If:
  a) the court considers that the seriousness of the offence (or combination of the offence and one or more offences associated with it) is exceptionally high, and
  b) the offender was aged 21 or over when he committed the offence,
the appropriate starting point is a whole life order.
(2) Cases that would normally fall within sub-paragraph (4)(1)(a) include:
  a) the murder of two or more persons, where each[695] murder involves any of the following:
      i) a substantial degree of premeditation or planning,
      ii) the abduction of the victim, or
      iii) sexual or sadistic conduct.

288.51   *Multiple murders and the 30-year starting point*
Criminal Justice Act 2003 Sch 21 para 5(1) If a) the court considers that the seriousness of the offence (or combination of the offence and one or more offences associated with it) is particularly high, and b) the offender was aged 21 or over when he committed the offence, the appropriate starting point in determining the minimum term is 30 years.
(2) Cases that would normally fall within para 5(1) include…f) the murder of two or more persons.

288.52   *Multiple murders Judicial guidance*
R v Malasi 2008 EWCA Crim 2505, 2009 1 Cr App R (S) 51 (p 276) D was convicted of murder, robbery and firearm offences. After the verdicts he pleaded to another murder. The Judge considered 24 years for the first and 12 years for the second appropriate, and reduced the total to **30 years**. He then passed concurrent sentences for the other offences. Held. The Act requires the fixing of a single overall term. The judge should take into account all the factors for each murder. The Judge had conducted a model approach.
R v Miah and Choudhury 2011 EWCA Crim 945, 2012 1 Cr App R (S) 11 (p 47) para 90 M and C were convicted of two murders and three attempted murders. Two people died and three were injured in a revenge arson attack. Held. When a defendant is convicted of two murders in one set of proceedings, then each murder is an associated offence of the other, Criminal Justice Act 2003 s 305 and Powers of Criminal Courts (Sentencing) Act 2000 s 161(1)(a). paras 101-102 The judge must set one overall minimum term in respect of each murder. The three attempted murders were also associated offences.

288.53   *Multiple murders   Cases*
R v Miah and Choudhury 2011 EWCA Crim 945, 2012 1 Cr App R (S) 11 (p 47) M and C were convicted of two murders and three attempted murders. M, aged 14 at the time of the offences, had been in a relationship with V1, aged 15. Their relationship had broken down. The Crown's case was that M wanted revenge. C, aged 20 at the time of the offences, who was M's cousin, was enlisted by M to help set fire to V1's home. C travelled to London with K to meet M. M and C set fire to V1's home. V1 and V2 died. Three other members of the family were injured. C played a secondary role. The Judge found an intent to kill. Held. The approach taken by the Judge, to consider the minimum terms for each murder, then consider one overall minimum term, as outlined in *R v Malasi* 2008, was correct. For M, the Judge took account of all the relevant factors, including his youth and the signs of problematic personality traits. **23 years'** detention at

---

[695] There is clearly a drafting error here. It would be absurd if two abduction murders trigger the whole life provisions but four abduction murders and one non-abduction murder do not. Ed.

HM's Pleasure was not manifestly excessive. For C, the starting point was 30 years. A very substantial reduction properly reflected his lesser role and mental difficulties. **Life with a 21-year minimum term** was not manifestly excessive.

See also: *R v Haigh* 2013 EWCA Crim 2359 (**32 years**, see **288.39**.)

Att-Gen's Ref No 50 of 2013 2013 EWCA Crim 2573 (LCJ **35 years**, see **288.37**.)

R v Mahmud 2014 EWCA Crim 1008 (Convicted of two murders and three attempted murders. M bought 7 litres of petrol having told work colleagues he thought of harming his wife, V, who was divorcing him. He and D went to V's address and set it alight using the petrol. M's wife, her father and his wife's infant son died. His wife's mother and her brother suffered life-threatening injuries. He assisted in M's escape. D had no convictions and did not instigate the plan. M was to pay D £10,000 for his part. Aged 37 at conviction. Starting at 30 years. D's **34-year** minimum term upheld.)

Old cases: *R v Henson and Magraw* 2007 EWCA Crim 1308, 2008 1 Cr App R (S) 19 (p 83) (**18 years** for H and **35 years** for M) *R v Connor* 2007 EWCA Crim 2591, 2008 1 Cr App R (S) 89 (p 537) (**32 years**)

For a summary of the first case, see the 9th edition of this book and for a summary of the second case, see the 8th edition.

288.54 *Passion, Crime of*

R v Heywood 2011 EWCA Crim 224 D was convicted of murder. D was a contented family man and a pillar of the local community. He nursed his wife through a long illness. After his wife died, D began another relationship. They bought a house with D's money and they married. His wife took two lovers, the first lasting five years causing D much distress. She announced she was leaving D for the second lover, V, to set up home with him. D was distraught, hurt, angry and even suicidal. D tracked V down and went to a hotel where he knew V would be. D took with him an iron bar and gloves. D hit V on the back of the head and neck with the iron bar about three or four times. V was seriously injured and died in hospital. The Judge noted that there were no aggravating features to the murder but noted that D had planned the offence and had worn dark clothing. The Judge took the view that D had not intended to kill V so the starting point should be 15 years. D, aged 69, was of good character. Held. We entirely accept that this is a difficult case and it involved for the Judge, as it does for us, a very difficult sentencing exercise. There are many mitigating features in D's favour. **9 years** not 11.

See also: *R v Singh* 2010 EWCA Crim 2951, 2011 2 Cr App R (S) 19 (p 107) (Convicted of murder and GBH with intent. Struggled to come to terms with ex-partner's new relationship. Poisoned him and his new partner with Indian aconite, bought in India. Partner died, his new partner suffered injuries. **23-year** minimum term.)

See also the *Relationship killing* paras at **288.59**.

288.55 *Police/prison officer(s)on duty*

Criminal Justice Act 2003 s 269(4) The statutory source of the power of the court to order that the early release provisions should not apply to the offender.

Criminal Justice Act 2003 Sch 21 para 4(1) If:

    a) the court considers that the seriousness of the offence (or combination of the offence and one or more offences associated with it) is exceptionally high, and

    b) the offender was aged 21 or over when he committed the offence,

the appropriate starting point is a whole life order.

4(2) Cases that would normally fall within sub-paragraph (1)(a) include:

(ba) the murder of a police officer or prison officer in the course of his duty.

Note: Criminal Justice and Courts Act 2015 s 27(1)-(2) moved these cases from the para 5(2) (30-year starting point) list to the para 4(2) (whole life) list. In force 13 April 2015.[696] The provision will only apply to offences committed after the section is in force, Criminal Justice and Courts Act 2015 s 27(4). Ed.

---

[696] Criminal Justice and Courts Act 2015 (Commencement No 1, Saving and Transitional Provisions) Order 2015 2015/778 para 3 and Sch 1 para 23

R v Bieber 2008 EWCA Crim 1601 D was convicted of one count of murder, two counts of attempted murder and two counts of possession of a firearm with intent to endanger life. He was in a badly parked stolen car, and two police officers on routine patrol approached because the car's tax disc was not genuine. He was put in their patrol car and, after a check had been made on the car, they told him that he was under arrest. A recovery vehicle arrived to remove the car, and a third officer arrived to take D to the police station. All three officers (B, R and A) went to the car door to handcuff him. He produced a handgun and fired five times. The first shot hit B in the chest. The second hit R, who had turned to run, in the lower back. The third hit both R and A, both now running. B was lying on the ground, and D stood over him and shot him in the head. D ran off with the gun. He approached a car and pointed the gun at the passenger. That car drove off. Holding the gun, D approached a second car, and the people in it ran off, leaving him to take the car. The Judge said that the aggravating feature leading him to impose a whole life tariff was the shot to the head of B, which made certain of his death. (D's age and character are not mentioned.) Held. The case fell within the 30-year starting point for two reasons: because the murder was of a police officer, and it involved the use of a firearm. The fact that two criteria were present is a possible reason for raising the term above the 30-year starting point. Added to this is the effect of the associated offences of attempting to murder two other police officers, which justified a substantial increment above the 30-year starting point. It must be remembered that the 30-year point already assumes an intention to kill. The criminal conduct was committed within a space of some eight seconds. Horrifying though this was, a minimum term of **37 years**, not a whole life tariff.

R v Ness 2011 EWCA Crim 3105, 2012 2 Cr App R (S) 39 (p 228) LCJ D was convicted of murder, conspiracy to murder police officers, attempted murder, possession of a firearm with intent and robbery. In 2010, he was criminally involved with the offences committed by Raoul Moat (M) in the north-east of England. Upon discovering his former partner, V1, had begun a new relationship, and wrongly believing the relationship was with a police officer, M began a campaign of revenge. D and another assisted M in driving him to various locations, sourcing and holding firearms, and aiding with research to track V1's new partner. D drove M to V1's house. M waited and when V1 and her new partner, V2, exited the house, M shot V2 twice with modified shotgun cartridges. M then reloaded the shotgun and shot V2 in the head, killing him. M then shot V1 in the abdomen, causing serious injury. M and D went their separate ways. D knew that M had killed V2 and seriously injured V1. D, M and another travelled to Rothbury, where they set up camp to watch the events unfold. M made a 999 call in which he said he was "hunting for officers now". The men drove to Newcastle and, upon seeing a parked police car, M jumped out and shot a police officer in the face. Upon realising that the initial shot had not killed him, M fired another shot at the officer's upper body. Both D and the other man knew what M intended to do when he alighted from the car, and that when M returned to the car he had shot the PC. The men thereafter returned to Rothbury, having recovered the first shotgun which was stored by D. M then went to a shop and threatened the owner with a gun. He stole £100. In Rothbury, the police attended and M moved towards them. D and the other man moved away from them and were eventually arrested, having tried to remove all traces of the camp. Held. D was a willing accomplice in M's murder of V2, his mission to hunt out and kill police officers, the attempted murder of the PC, and the armed robbery. They were particularly grave crimes, carefully planned and ruthless in execution. It was not even arguable that we should interfere with a term of **40 years**.

Note: The murder was not of a policeman but the whole campaign was against police officers.

These two cases would only apply to offences committed before 13 April 2015. Ed.

288.56   *Political murders and whole life orders*
Criminal Justice Act 2003 s 269(4) The statutory source of the power of the court to order that the early release provisions should not apply to the offender.
Criminal Justice Act 2003 Sch 21 para 4(1) If:
   a) the court considers that the seriousness of the offence (or combination of the offence and one or more offences associated with it) is exceptionally high, and
   b) the offender was aged 21 or over when he committed the offence,
the appropriate starting point is a whole life order.
para 4(2) Cases that would normally fall within sub-paragraph (1)(a) include:..
   c) a murder done for the purpose of advancing a political, religious, racial[697] or ideological cause.
For more details see **288.90**.
Punish etc., Motive was to see the ***Revenge/Punishment, Motive was to*** para at **288.63**.

288.57   *Racial or religious murders and whole life orders*
Criminal Justice Act 2003 s 269(4) The statutory source of the power of the court to order that the early release provisions should not apply to the offender.
Criminal Justice Act 2003 Sch 21 para 4(1) If:
   a) the court considers that the seriousness of the offence (or combination of the offence and one or more offences associated with it) is exceptionally high, and
   b) the offender was aged 21 or over when he committed the offence,
the appropriate starting point is a whole life order.
4(2) Cases that would normally fall within sub-paragraph (1)(a) include:
   c) a murder done for the purpose of advancing a political, religious, racial[698] or ideological cause.
For more detail see **288.90**.

288.58   *Racial, religious murders   Not whole life*
Criminal Justice Act 2003 Sch 21 para 5(1)-(2) Cases for a defendant aged 21+ that would normally fall within the **30-year** starting point include [unless they fulfil the criteria for a whole life term]: g) a murder that is racially or religiously aggravated or aggravated by sexual orientation, disability or transgender identity.
Old cases: *R v Taylor* 2006 EWCA Crim 1777, 2007 1 Cr App R (S) 59 (p 340) **(24 years)** *R v Blue* 2008 EWCA Crim 769, 2009 1 Cr App R (S) 2 (p 6) **(17 years)**
For a summary of the first case, see the 8th edition of this book and for the second case, see the 9th edition.
See also the ***Gay, lesbian and transgender murders Not whole life*** para at **288.42** and the ***Disability, Aggravated by, Not whole life*** para at **288.34**.

288.59   *Relationship killings   Basic principles*
For using earlier incidents of violence in the sentencing process, see ***Bad character, with/without a conviction/Background of violence*** at **288.77**.
See also the ***Family etc. killings*** para at **288.35**, ***Firearms, With*** para at **288.38** and ***Gain, Defendant's motive was*** para at **288.40**.
For the *Domestic Violence Guideline 2006*, see www.banksr.com Other matters Guidelines tab and the **DOMESTIC VIOLENCE** chapter.

288.60   *Relationship killings   Men killing wives etc. 19 years or less*
R v Davies-Jones 2013 EWCA Crim 2809 D was convicted of the murder of his wife, V. Their relationship was volatile and the police had attended on numerous occasions at the bequest of both parties alleging assaults.[699] V also had a history of self-harming. V and D had both complained to V's family about each other. D attacked V in the living-room

---

[697] The word 'racial' was inserted in the sub-section by Counter-Terrorism Act 2008 s 75(1) and (2)(c). In force 16/2/09, Counter-Terrorism Act 2008 (Commencement No 2) Order 2009 2009/58
[698] The word 'racial' was inserted in the sub-section by Counter-Terrorism Act 2008 s 75(1) and (2)(c). In force 16/2/09, Counter-Terrorism Act 2008 (Commencement No 2) Order 2009 2009/58
[699] This is at para 14. At para 17 there is a contrary suggestion. News reports give his age as 34. Ed.

and there had been a struggle. V retreated to the kitchen and picked up a knife, stabbing D in the neck with it. V then left the house. D, also armed with a knife, pursued her and inflicted the fatal blow in the neck on the driveway. D immediately phoned for an ambulance and said he had stabbed her. D was of good character and had an exemplary army record. He was a former Captain who became a city solicitor. There were extensive testimonials. The Judge ruled out a 25-year starting point and started at 15. He moved this up to 20 years for the sole aggravating factor of the knife. He then considered some provocation, D's positive good character, his job achievements, the lack of premeditation and D's stress as mitigating factors. Held. The use of a knife is and will always be a significant aggravating factor, and the immediate circumstances in which this particular knife was used outside the house to inflict the fatal blow do little to reduce D's culpability. Balancing the aggravating factors against the mitigating factors, a sentence above 15 years was justly deserved. The increase was, however, too high. **18-year minimum term** not 20.

R v Samuel 2014 EWCA Crim 2353 D was convicted of murder. His plea to manslaughter was not accepted. He and V were in a volatile relationship. D had previously assaulted her and witnesses at the trial gave evidence of bruising and injuries to V. A non-molestation order had been made. The prosecution said the violence was escalating. D brutally attacked V. D then stole V's mobile, purse and bicycle. The cause of death was shock and haemorrhage caused by severe blunt trauma to her abdomen which had ruptured her liver. The pathologist's assessment was that the blow was delivered by 'severe force' either by a punch or a shod foot. The injuries to V's face were indicative of a minimum of six punches with a fist. D was aged 35 and was 7½ stone heavier and 6 inches taller than V. The Judge started at 15 years. The Judge found the following aggravating factors: a) V was murdered in her own home where she should have been safe, b) V was vulnerable and to some degree under the control of D, c) the ferocity of the attack, d) D's very substantial record for dishonesty and violence, and e) D stole V's property. The Judge considered the only mitigating factor was that there was no intent to kill. Held. This was a brutal attack on a defenceless woman. Taking into account the factors and that D never denied he had killed V, **18-year minimum term**, not 20.

See also: *R v Birks* 2010 EWCA Crim 1394, 2011 1 Cr App R (S) 48 (p 317) (Very late plea (5% discount) to murder. D and his wife had a troubled relationship. He was violent towards her. He strangled her during an argument and set fire to the house to mask the cause of death. Children in the room below. On bail for assaulting wife. No intent to kill. **19 years** was not manifestly excessive.)

Old cases: *R v Master* 2007 EWCA Crim 142 (**16 years**) *R v McDonald* 2007 EWCA Crim 1081 (**14 years**) *R v Rush* 2007 EWCA Crim 1907, 2008 1 Cr App R (S) 45 (p 244) (**13 years**) *R v Taylor* 2008 EWCA Crim 838, 2009 1 Cr App R (S) 7 (p 31) (**15 years**) *R v Appleyard* 2007 EWCA Crim 3169, 2008 2 Cr App R (S) 42 (p 235) (**17 years**) *R v Thomas* 2009 EWCA Crim 904, 2010 1 Cr App R (S) 14 (p 75) (**17½ years**) *R v Symmons* 2009 EWCA Crim 1304 (**16 years**) *R v Ibe* 2009 EWCA Crim 1489, 2010 1 Cr App R (S) 72 (p 480) (**15 years**)

For a summary of the first, second and third cases, see the 7th edition of this book, for the fifth case, see the 8th edition, for the sixth and eighth cases, see the 9th edition and for the last case, see the 10th edition.

288.61   *Relationship killings*[700]   *Men killing wives etc.*   *20+ years imprisonment*
R v Ahmed 2012 EWCA Crim 251, 2 Cr App R (S) 64 (p 378) D was convicted of murder. He suspected his wife, W, aged 21, of having an affair. Neighbours heard a struggle emanating from D's house. D telephoned his employer to say he could not attend work and subsequently drove to Birmingham, Norwich, and back to Birmingham.

---

[700] This paragraph includes cases where one party wished there to be a relationship with the subsequent victim and also cases where the murder occurred after the relationship had ended.

W's family became concerned and visited D's house. Blood was subsequently found on the walls, carpet and ceiling. D claimed that V had attacked him with a knife and had suffered a wound to the neck as D defended himself. The prosecution claimed that D had used a two-foot-long knife, which weighed three pounds, to inflict blows. A forensic examination of the blood spatter corroborated that assertion. D admitted to disposing of W's body in a bin at the rear of his place of work. W's body was never found. Held. There were numerous aggravating factors: a) the killing was an act of vengeance, b) the murder was brutal and callous, where the knife was used as a blunt instrument, c) it was carried out in the family home, d) D had disposed of W's body. Concealment is one of the aggravating factors of Criminal Justice Act 2003 Sch 21 para 10. We regard it as the most serious of the aggravating factors. **20 years** was not manifestly excessive.

R v Williams 2013 EWCA Crim 933 D was convicted of murder and section 18. He had begun a relationship with V, aged 20, in early 2011. Within a few weeks she was expecting D's baby. D was violent to V and she moved away from D to live with her family. In December 2011, D was charged with threatening behaviour relating to an attack on V in the street. He was released on bail with a condition not to contact her. A few days later V gave birth and there was contact between the two. D sent a text to V saying he would not hit her again so long as she did not do anything that made him angry. V replied saying she did not want to see him that day. D armed himself with a knife and went to V's home. He broke in and went to the bedroom where V and her very young daughter were. She heard D in the house and locked the bedroom door. D kicked the bedroom door open and attacked V. V was holding her child and the force caused her to drop the child, who was less than one month old, onto the floor. He stabbed V with the knife. V's sister tried to protect her. D stabbed her in the arm. V's brother, T, entered the room armed with a dumbbell. He hit D with it causing minor injury. D stabbed him four times in the chest, with one penetrating his lung. He returned to V and repeatedly stabbed her in the chest. V's sister cried out asking why D was acting like this. D replied that her family had been trying to get him sent to prison. He told V that she was coming with him and dragged her down the stairs. She was still alive at this point. D drove for two miles and could be heard shouting, "I just stabbed her" and "She's dead, she ain't breathing". D saw a friend and told him he wanted to hide the body behind some dustbins. V had 29 stab wounds. D, aged 19, had previous convictions for robbery (×2), ABH and common assault. He had a history of violence in his relationships with women. A report revealed D's IQ was within the extremely low range, comparable to a 12- or 13-year-old. Held. Apart from age and intellectual impairment, there are no mitigating features in this case. D showed no remorse. This offence was premeditated and carried out at night. He broke into her house and broke down V's door. He stabbed her nearly 30 times in two persistent attacks. She had a very young child in her arms. He caused injuries to two other people, one of whom, T, was very badly injured. V's body was dumped some miles away in a humiliating way. D disregarded advice to take her to hospital and discarded the murder weapon. This offence was committed against a background of violent offending whilst on bail. There was little difficulty in concluding that the starting point was 30 years. The Judge's decision to move the figure to 32 years before considering the mitigation was reasonable. **28 years** was stern but not manifestly excessive.

R v S 2015 EWCA Crim 1359 D pleaded (full credit) to murder and two counts of GBH with intent. D was known to be a very jealous man. He lived with V and in 2014 there were strains in the relationship. At about 9.30 pm, after both had been drinking and taking amphetamine, D found a text message on V's phone. He falsely accused her of being unfaithful. D lost his temper and there was an argument and D repeatedly thrust a glass into V's face. Next D stabbed V, who was pregnant, 81 times. V's two boys, V2 and V3, aged 11 and 9, heard V's screams. V2 was stabbed numerous times. D pushed V3 to the floor, stamped on his head and stabbed him numerous times. V's six-year-old son starting screaming as V3 was stabbed. D said he would not be stabbing him. V2 escaped and the police attended. All the children were very distressed. D kicked and struggled with the officers. A Taser had to be used. V1 had very extensive injuries, including three deep stab wounds to the chest, 10 deep stab wounds to the back and a deep stab wound to the neck. A piece of glass was removed from her eye. V2 and V3 had multiple wounds to the upper part of their bodies and heads. V died. D was aged 40 with no previous convictions. The Judge found there was no premeditation as the motivation was anger in a possessive rage. He started at 15 years for the murder. This was increased with the aggravating factors to 24 years making 20 years with plea. For the GBH counts he assessed D as dangerous and added 8 years after plea discount making a 28-year global term. The defence said that meant the starting point for the GBH counts would have been 24 years. Held. The murder was aggravated by a) the brutality of attack, b) the use of a broken glass and knife, c) the duration and persistence of the attack and d) the presence of young children. The attack on the children was horrifying. Although their injuries were not life-threatening it was little short of torture. They will have significant psychological damage. Four children have lost their mother. The baby in the womb perished. A minimum term before plea of 24 years was firm but not excessive. There should have been a consecutive element for the GBH counts. For them we start at 18 years which, after the plea discount and the division, would be a minimum term of 6 years. With a discount for totality, that would be 25 years (**20 years** and 5 years). If we had started at the particularly high seriousness starting point, the starting point would have been 30 years and with plea, 25 years. That confirms our conclusion. So **25 years** with a [concurrent] 6-year minimum term for each of the GBH counts.

See also: *R v Ghafelipour* 2011 EWCA Crim 112 (Late plea. Defendant had begun short friendship with victim and then stole from him. 130 stab wounds to head and neck. Removed hair from her head by the roots, removed her right eye. Bite marks. **23 years**.)
R v Bristol 2012 EWCA Crim 1684, 2013 1 Cr App R (S) 81 (p 445) (Convicted. Girlfriend ended relationship and D became jealous of her new partner. Travelled from Trinidad to see her. Turned up at her house and she tried to escape. Stabbed her 'with repeated savage and horrifying ferocity'. 37 wounds to face, neck, torso and legs. Aged 27. Good character. Significant uplift from 15-year starting point merited. **22-year** minimum term upheld.)
Att-Gen's Ref No 19 of 2014 2014 EWCA Crim 1322 (Convicted. Sharing home pending separation. Tried to falsely blacken V's reputation. Talked about killing V. Killed her with commercial rolling pin (taken to the home as a weapon) causing severe brain injury. Motive to obtain sole custody of child. 25-year starting point as weapon taken to scene so **23 years** not 18.)
Old cases: *R v Height and Anderson* 2008 EWCA Crim 2500, 2009 1 Cr App R (S) 117 (p 656) (**22 years** for both) *R v Genestin* 2008 EWCA Crim 3099, 2009 1 Cr App R (S) 97 (p 558) (**20 years**) *Att-Gen's Ref No 116 of 2009* 2010 EWCA Crim 577 (**30 years**) *R v Ahmed* 2010 EWCA Crim 2446 (**18 years**) *R v Entwistle* 2010 EWCA Crim 2828 (**21½ years**)
For a summary of the first case, see the 8th edition of this book and for the last case, see the 10th edition.

288.62   *Relationship killings   Women killing husbands etc.*

R v Khatun 2010 EWCA Crim 138 D was convicted of murder. She carried out a sophisticated plan to kill her husband. She had been married for just over a month and she was bored with him. She stabbed him, returned to the flat with her brother, and rang the emergency services after she said she was unable to enter the flat. In interview she tried to divert suspicion onto someone else and constructed an alibi. At trial she relied on physical abuse by her husband and self-defence. The Judge noted the cultural difficulties and her depressive episodes. Held. **17 years** was not manifestly excessive.
R v Challen 2011 EWCA Crim 2919, 2012 1 Cr App R (S) 20 (p 85) LCJ D, aged 57, was convicted of murder. She had been married to V for 31 years. They had two sons, both in their twenties. D had been suspicious about V's fidelity for a number of years. In

2009, D informed V she was moving out and began divorce proceedings. D moved to a house nearby with her youngest son. She found the separation difficult to deal with as V began to socialise with friends he had met over the Internet. She was convinced that V was having an affair with considerable justification. In 2010, she began to access his voicemails and check his Facebook page. In June 2010, he agreed to her request for reconciliation. A post-nuptial agreement was reached in which D thought V was being unfair in relation to the financial arrangements. The couple, though living apart, decided to let the family home and travel to Australia for six months. D remained suspicious about V's friendships with other women. When V was clearing out the garage in preparation for their trip, D asked him to go out and get some provisions. While he did so, he telephoned a female friend and cancelled an arrangement to meet the following day. D, upon noticing that the phone had been moved, dialled the last dialled number and heard a woman's voice. D asked V whether she could see him the following day, to which V replied, "Don't question me". That was the usual way in which he spoke to her. She made them something to eat and, as V ate, she took a hammer and repeatedly hit him over the head with it. She covered V's body with blankets and left a note which read 'I love you, Sally'. She returned to her home and remained there that evening. Her youngest son noticed nothing out of the ordinary. The following day she telephoned her cousin and told her that she was calling from the car park at Beachy Head and that she had killed her husband. The cousin immediately phoned the police. In her vehicle at Beachy Head, police found a typed note, which stated that she felt V had pressured D into signing the post-nuptial agreement on the basis that they would then reconcile when, in fact, he had no intention of seeing a reconciliation through. V had self-defence type wounds, and there were at least 20 sites of injury on V's head. D, aged 57, was of good character. Held. The Judge proposed to start at 15 years, until it was pointed out that paragraph 5A applied to any weapon, not just knives. The Judge started therefore at 25 years and, considering all the factors, reduced the term to 22 years. That suggests that on its facts the Judge would not have considered this to be a case of particularly high seriousness, justifying a minimum term of above 20 years. We understand why that should be so. Taking all the factors into account, including the degree of premeditation in taking the hammer in her bag, the appropriate sentence is life, with a minimum term of **18 years**.

See also: *R v Singh* 2010 EWCA Crim 2951, 2011 2 Cr App R (S) 19 (p 107) (Convicted of murder and GBH with intent. Struggled to come to terms with ex-partner's new relationship. Poisoned him and his new partner with Indian aconite, bought in India. Partner died, his new partner suffered injuries. **23-year** minimum term.)

R v Hood 2012 EWCA Crim 1260, 2013 1 Cr App R (S) 49 (p 273) (Late plea to murder by H. Victim was girlfriend's ex-partner, V. Motive was that girlfriend didn't want V to see their six-month-old child. Girlfriend lured V to a lake at night. H attacked V with a hammer. 10 blows. Pushed body into a lake. Intention to kill. Gave evidence against his girlfriend. Starting at 25 years. With aggravating including concealment of body, 30 years. Discount for plea 1 year. The discount for the assistance to prosecution should have been 7 years not 5. **22-year** minimum term, not 24.)

Old cases: *R v West* 2007 EWCA Crim 701 (**13 years**) *Att-Gen's Ref No 24 of 2008* 2008 EWCA Crim 2936, 2009 2 Cr App R (S) 41 (p 289) (**10 years**)

For a summary of the first case, see the 7th edition of this book.

See also *Passion, Crime of* at **288.54**.

288.63   *Revenge/Punishment, Motive was*

R v M and Others Re K 2009 EWCA Crim 2544, 2010 2 Cr App R (S) 19 (p 117) at para 20 LCJ K was convicted of murder. A confrontation developed between two groups of youths. B was seen to gesture that he had a knife. He was heard to threaten to use it. A fight broke out, and one of B's friends was struck. Again B was heard to threaten to use his knife. B and his gang ran off. B contacted K and L. The three went back for revenge. One said that someone was going to be 'shanked'. The other group ran away. V, aged 16, was at the back. He was hunted down and knocked down between two parked cars. V received 11 stab wounds. One was so ferocious that one of his ribs was split. K and L disposed of some of their bloodstained clothing. V died. K was just 18. He had six court appearances with a robbery and an affray conviction but had not served custody. K showed no remorse. He had had a difficult upbringing. The Judge found a joint intention to kill. Held. V was a wholly innocent victim. He offered not a shred of provocation. K knew exactly what he was doing. **19 years** cannot remotely be described as excessive.

R v M and Others Re S 2009 EWCA Crim 2544, 2010 2 Cr App R (S) 19 (p 117) at para 33 LCJ S pleaded to murder and wounding with intent on the day that his case was listed for trial. The intent count was added that day as an alternative to attempted murder. S was looking for a fight and wanted others to join him. S, K and X were together. V1 and V2 were in the town centre together, unarmed. There was a confrontation between S and V2. V2 was stabbed with a kitchen knife. V1 was confronted by K and X. S then went to V1 and stabbed him twice. One wound went to the heart. V1 died. In interview S made no comment. S was aged 25 with nine court appearances for 12 offences. One was for GBH with intent (4½ years' detention). He was on licence for that. His defence case statement indicated self-defence. A basis of plea was rejected by the prosecution. The prosecution said that it was revenge. A *Newton* hearing was offered but not taken up. The Judge found that there was a large, dangerous knife used, the victims showed no aggression, there was persistent savagery, the stab wounds were to vulnerable parts of the body, there was recruitment of K, the sentence had to reflect the other very serious stabbing, and that there was no intent to kill but the difference between that and an intent to kill was marginal. Held. Two peaceful men were attacked. The late plea was reflected in the **21 years**.

R v Collier 2014 EWCA Crim 2085 D pleaded at the PCMH to murdering V. V had a history of severe drug and alcohol abuse and lived in a house with individuals with similar problems. J helped both the landlady and tenants. V complained to police that J had been threatening and harassing him over a debt, genuinely fearing for his safety. J, angered by V's actions, arranged for D to give V a beating. A few days later V was in his room, having taken heavy sedatives and cannabis, when D attacked him. V was manually strangled and suffered a severe beating, with 97 injuries. These included extensive bruising and multiple cuts to the head, some of which were almost certainly inflicted by blows from a glass-framed picture. V had severe ribcage fractures, and a detached rib causing a collapsed lung. V weighed just over seven stone when he died and other injuries demonstrated multiple heavy blows to the body. V also had defensive injuries but the attack's ferocity meant he was overcome within a short time. D bragged that he had "battered" a man by jumping all over his chest. He made no comment in interview but confessed to killing V to a nurse. However, he expressed neither regret nor remorse. He proffered a basis of plea, later withdrawn, that either he had acted in self-defence or that he had acted in provocation insufficient to provide a defence. D was aged 20 and had convictions for burglary, robbery and attempted robbery. The Judge found an intent to kill. He started at 15 years. He found a) the victim was vulnerable because of his physical condition, b) the attack was planned and was punishment, c) the attack was at V's home and at night and d) the attack was ferocious. That made just over a 24-year minimum term and the Judge gave D only 5% plea credit because of D's false basis of plea. Held. The discount for D's age and comparative immaturity should be somewhat greater than 5%, so **21-year** minimum term, not 23. Those were the only mitigating factors.

See also: *R v Finlay* 2010 EWCA Crim 503 (LCJ Plea. One murder and one very near murder on his brother-in-law and his 14-year-old nephew after D's divorce. A ferocious attack using a knife repeatedly. No possible ground for interfering with **25 years**.)

Old cases: *Att-Gen's Ref Nos 108-109 of 2005* 2006 EWCA Crim 513 (D **28 years**, P **22 years**) *R v Williamson* 2007 EWCA Crim 44 (**27 years**) *R v Roberts and Mould* 2008 EWCA Crim 59, 2 Cr App R (S) 59 (p 350) (**9 years**) *R v Patterson* 2008 EWCA

Crim 1018, 2009 1 Cr App R (S) 19 (p 103) *R v Martin* 2009 EWCA Crim 1182, 2010 1 Cr App R (S) 38 (p 226) (**13 years**) *R v Khan and Others* 2009 EWCA Crim 966 (**22 years** for M, **20 years** for K)
For a summary of the first case, see the 6th edition of this book, for the second case, see the 7th edition, for the third case, see the 8th edition and for the last but one case see the 9th edition.

288.64   Sadistic murders and whole life orders
Criminal Justice Act 2003 s 269(4) The statutory source of the power of the court to order that the early release provisions should not apply to the offender.
Criminal Justice Act 2003 Sch 21 para 4(1) If a) the court considers that the seriousness of the offence (or combination of the offence and one or more offences associated with it) is exceptionally high, and b) the offender was aged 21 or over when he committed the offence, the appropriate starting point is a whole life order.
(2) Cases that would normally fall within sub-paragraph (1)(a) include:
  a) the murder of two or more persons, where each[701] murder involves any of the following: iii) sadistic conduct,
  b) the murder of a child if involving the abduction of the child or sexual or sadistic motivation.

288.65   Sadistic murders   Judicial guidance
Criminal Justice Act 2003 Sch 21 para 5(1)-(2) Cases for a defendant aged 21+ that would normally fall within the **30-year** starting point include (e) a murder involving sexual or sadistic conduct (unless it fulfils the criteria for a whole life term).
R v Bonellie and Others 2008 EWCA Crim 1417, 2009 1 Cr App R (S) 55 (p 297) LCJ The defendants were sentenced on the basis that it was a sadistic murder. Held. The behaviour of these defendants was appalling. They behaved like a pack of animals for amusement and to make themselves look big. It is often the case that those who attack others derive pleasure from it, including from kicking someone on the ground, baiting an individual or showing off to friends. That is not enough to conclude there was sadistic conduct as envisaged by Criminal Justice Act 2003 Sch 21 para 5(2)(e). That contemplates a greater degree of awareness of pleasure in the infliction of pain, suffering or humiliation.

288.66   Sadistic murders   Cases
Criminal Justice Act 2003 Sch 21 para 10 Aggravating factors (additional to those mentioned in paras 4(2) and 5(2) (see **288.90** and **288.15**) that may be relevant include:..c) mental or physical suffering inflicted on the victim before death.
R v Jones and Smith 2011 EWCA Crim 1553, 2012 1 Cr App R (S) 46 (p 274) LCJ J pleaded to murder (late). S was convicted of murder. R, a co-accused, was also convicted. J, S, R and V all resided at a hostel for former offenders. V was vulnerable. S, R and V were friends. J, R, S and V had been drinking alcohol to celebrate V's birthday. On the way back to the hostel, S, R and J were involved in an altercation. V was not. J was the ringleader. At the hostel, J grabbed V by the throat and punched him. S and R tried to calm him down. J had a knife by his side, and punched V again. V went to his room. S, R and J followed him. Over 50 minutes he was tortured. A knife or knives were used on him, causing wounds 14 and 16 cm deep. V was systematically beaten, and the room was damaged. S recorded part of the incident on a mobile phone. All four men left the hostel at 4.25 am. They went to an ATM armed with two knives with the intention of forcing V to hand over money. V attempted to run away but was prevented from doing so. He was stabbed 20 times and sustained multiple injuries, several of which were fatal. J, R and S returned to the hostel via slightly different routes, attempted to clean the knives and changed their clothes. The Judge found an intention to kill. J, aged 25 at appeal, had convictions for harassment (30 months), ABH and possession of an offensive weapon,

---

[701] There is clearly a drafting error here. It would be absurd if two sadistic murders trigger the whole life provisions but four sadistic murders and one non-sadistic murder do not. Ed.

his previous convictions demonstrating a propensity for serious violence. S, aged 20, had convictions for drugs. R received a 27-year minimum term. Held. Each developed an enthusiasm for inflicting pain and humiliation. J was the ringleader, he initiated the violence and pleaded very late. The photographing of the injuries is a particularly nauseating feature. They acted as a gang and the Judge was fully justified in imposing identical determinate terms. **27 years** was fully justified for J and S.

R v Chalk and Others 2015 EWCA Crim 1053 D, W and C were convicted of murder and N pleaded to murder when he was giving evidence at his trial. All four pleaded to perverting the course of justice. The defendants met V, who was homeless, and invited him to their flat. C stayed in the flat while the three male defendants left. On their return, C a female, alleged falsely that V had sexually assaulted her to cement her relationship with D. She also did this to manipulate N to act violently. As a result, that evening, N beat V up in a supermarket car park. V was found unconscious and taken to hospital. Shortly after, C arrived at the scene and told the police that N was responsible for the attack. V recovered and met the defendants again and went back to their flat. P was present. V's laptop was stolen and the male defendants went out to try to sell it. On their return, C and P told the men that V had made a sexual advance to P. They stole V's bank card. C and P left the flat and the males beat V up with a baseball bat and a knife. V's PIN was obtained and W drew out £20 from V's account. C and P returned and saw that V had been badly beaten. He was put in a wardrobe and made to clean up his blood on the carpet. He was given a kicking every time he failed to do as he was told. Shortly afterwards P left the flat. The following day, V was in an appalling condition. He was left bound and gagged while the defendants went out to try to sell V's laptop. On their return, C looked through V's phone and called him a weirdo. This prompted the males to fatally assault V, which lasted about 30 minutes. Fists, three knives, a baseball bat and a bottle were used. Clothing was removed and the violence interrupted so pictures could be taken. Twenty knife injuries were inflicted. The violence resumed after the pictures were taken. C had one of the photos on her phone. Most of the injuries were inflicted while V was conscious. The four set about disposing of V's body. It was put in a wheelie bin and petrol was purchased by N and W. C was instructed to clean up the flat. The fire service attended a fire and found V's body in the wheelie bin. C's case was based on joint enterprise, by her intentional encouragement. D, N and W had extensive previous convictions but none for serious violence. C was aged 20, had no relevant convictions and was an extremely vulnerable and psychologically dependent person who had had many unfortunate life experiences. The Judge found: a) V was a vulnerable young man, b) the fatal attack was an orgy of violence, c) N was the leader, d) the others played significant roles, e) the mental and physical suffering of V was terrible, f) the violence was sadistic as the only purpose was to gain pleasure from it, g) the photographs had been taken to derive pleasure at what had happened to V, h) C delighted in her sense of power in the fatal attack, i) there was an intent to kill but not for C, j) W had credit for the substantially true account he gave the police, and k) N had given some co-operation to the police and offered to give evidence against the others. Held. The Judge was entitled to find it was a sadistic murder and increase the starting point because of the attempts to dispose of the body. For N, **31 years** not 34. For D, **29 years** not 32. For W, **27 years** not 30. For C, **20 years** not 25.

See also: *R v Nicholls and Others* 2010 EWCA Crim 1548 2011 1 Cr App R (S) 67 (p 413) (Convicted. Systematic, sadistic abuse of man who was very shy and had learning difficulties. A slow and excruciatingly painful death. Burns, cuts, bruises and multiple rib fractures. For sister, aged 28, **32 years**, for brother, aged 28, **25 years**, and for former partner, aged 44, **20 years** was not manifestly excessive.)

R v Watt and Others 2011 EWCA Crim 1325, 2012 1 Cr App R (S) 31 (p 184)[702] (Convicted with perverting count. Homeless vulnerable boy kept as near slave. Severely

---

[702] The Cr App R (S) copy of the judgment misses out key paragraphs. Use the court judgment. Ed.

violently abused for fun for 10 years. Violence recorded on mobiles. Handcuffed to bed to prevent escape. Barely able to walk. Swollen stomach. Dismembered body found in lake with airgun pellets in it. No intent to kill. **36 years** upheld.)

Old cases: *Att-Gen's Ref No 38 of 2008* 2008 EWCA Crim 2122 (**30 years**) *R v Clarke* 2009 EWCA Crim 2484, 2010 2 Cr App R (S) 13 (p 78) (**27 years**)

For a summary of the first case, see the 8th edition of this book and for the second case, see the 10th edition.

288.67   *Secondary parties/Assisting offenders/Aiding and abetting/Accomplices etc.*

Att-Gen's Ref No 24 of 2008 2008 EWCA Crim 2936, 2009 2 Cr App R (S) 41 (p 289) D was convicted of aiding and abetting murder. Held. Schedule 21 starting points do apply to secondary parties. Although the culpability of secondary parties may in many cases be less than that of the principal, the sentence must be viewed proportionately.

See also: *R v Badza* 2009 EWCA Crim 2695 (Aged 18. Co-defendant stabbed youth at bus stop. There should have been a distinction between the two. No previous convictions. Further, for Badza there was no proven intent to kill, so **16 years** not 18.)

R v Ness 2011 EWCA Crim 3105, 2012 2 Cr App R (S) 39 (p 228) (LCJ Against girlfriend's new partner and conspiracy to kill police officers. **40 years** upheld, see **288.55**.)

R v Jogee 2013 EWCA Crim 1433 (Convicted. Encouraged co-defendant to stab victim. **18 years**, see **288.46**.)

288.68   *Sexual murders and whole life orders*

Criminal Justice Act 2003 s 269(4) The statutory source of the power of the court to order that the early release provisions should not apply to the offender.

Criminal Justice Act 2003 Sch 21 para 4(1) If a) the court considers that the seriousness of the offence (or combination of the offence and one or more offences associated with it) is exceptionally high, and b) the offender was aged 21 or over when he committed the offence, the appropriate starting point is a whole life order.

(2) Cases that would normally fall within sub-paragraph (1)(a) include:

   a) the murder of two or more persons, where each[703] murder involves any of the
      following: iii) sexual conduct,

   b) the murder of a child if involving sexual motivation.

288.69   *Sexual murders   Judicial guidance*

Att-Gen's Ref No 149 of 2006 2007 EWCA Crim 965, 2 Cr App R (S) 96 (p 616) In the absence of any material which could properly dissociate the killing from the sexual activity, the only proper inference is that the two were connected.

R v Walker 2007 EWCA Crim 2631, 2008 2 Cr App R (S) 6 (p 38) LCJ The reference to murder 'involving sexual or sadistic conduct' was intended to cover circumstances where the acts which resulted in the death were sexual in nature or accompanied by sexual activity that increased the ordeal of the victim or the depravity of the murder or both. The murder here appears to have occurred shortly after sexual intercourse, not in the course of it. It may or may not have been consensual intercourse. The case does not fall within the paragraph.

For an example of the court's being unable to say that it was sexual, see *R v Davies* 2008 EWCA Crim 1055, 2009 1 Cr App R (S) 15 (p 79) at **288.71**. For an example of the court saying that a murder after a sex act was not sexual, see *R v Morley* 2009 EWCA Crim 1302, 2010 1 Cr App R (S) 44 (p 275) at **288.30**.

288.70   *Sexual murders   Cases*

Att-Gen's Ref No 73 of 2012 2012 EWCA Crim 2924, 2013 2 Cr App R (S) 38 (p 261)[704] D pleaded (late) to murder. V, aged 22, went out with some friends to a nightclub. When she left the nightclub she was extremely drunk and had become separated from her

---

[703] There is clearly a drafting error here. It would be absurd if two sexual murders trigger the whole life provisions but four sexual murders and one non-sexual murder do not. Ed.

[704] This case is called *R v Halliwell* 2012 EWCA Crim 2924 in the judgment in error.

friends. D, a taxi driver, had signed himself off for the evening by turning off his radio. He began looking for a woman with whom to have sexual contact. V got into his taxi and was immediately driven off in the opposite direction to her home. D attacked her. She died from a combination of three injuries: a stab wound to the back of the head which penetrated the brain, a horizontal stab wound to the back of the neck, and pressure to the neck either by way of strangulation or neck restraint, which produced deep bruising and haemorrhages in the linings of the eyes. There were other injuries including blunt trauma to the back of the head, deep bruising to the face, bruising to the chest and damage to the nipple caused by a bite. There were further signs of sexual assault: her bra had been removed and one of its shoulder straps remained within her clothing. Her body was found on the side of a steep bank, having been moved from its original resting place. She was found naked from the waist down with her leggings and underwear around her ankles. Both items had been cut rather than torn. There was no sexual injury to her genitalia, nor any other sign of more severe sexual assault. D had returned to the scene of the murder on a number of occasions and was clearly reconnoitring the countryside to find a safer place to which to move the body. D had attempted to remove evidence which would incriminate him. He cleaned blood from his taxi, burned some seat covers and threw away others. One of the seat covers was recovered and DNA testing showed it was smeared with V's blood. D was aged 48 at appeal. There were previous convictions but these were irrelevant. Held. There was undoubtedly a sexual motivation in the offender's planning, although there was no overt sexual act. V was vulnerable by reason of her drunkenness. This was a feature of D's search for a suitable victim for a sexual encounter. The Judge was entitled to conclude that the limited sexual component of the offence, important though it is in the context of the murder, taken with the other aggravating factors, comprised the particularly high seriousness of the offence, which would properly be reflected in a minimum term of 30 years after a trial, and before a plea of guilty. The Judge found that the factors did not require an uplift. A **25-year** minimum term was not unduly lenient.

Att-Gen's Ref No 68 of 2013 2014 EWCA Crim 125 D pleaded to murder and attempted rape. He had decided to rape a woman and approached three women that day. The first was walking her dog, which deterred him. He approached the second and propositioned her but was deterred by the presence of other people. He returned to his caravan and fetched a knife. The third woman was V. She also had gone for a walk. D approached her and a struggle ensued. He dropped the knife and V threw it a little distance away. D repeatedly punched her in the face and attempted to remove her clothes. He decided he would have to kill her as she 'might be a witness against him'. He sat astride her and strangled her with a piece of her clothing. He dragged her body through vegetation and over a barbed wire fence. He dumped the body in a secluded spot and returned to his caravan. He changed his clothes and fetched items intended to destroy evidence. He used a fork to clean beneath her fingernails and a bleach-based spray and cloth. He took her bracelet to dispose of it. V's body was found the following day, lying with her back against a tree, her head tilted to one side with blood coming from her mouth. She was naked, save for her skirt, which had been pulled around her waist. There was blood around her vagina. Police recovered her underwear, her cardigan and a knife nearby. There were a large number of scratches to the front of V's body, consistent with her being dragged across the ground. There was no evidence of sexual assault. V's DNA was found on the bloodstained clothing. D was aged 30 at appeal. He had convictions for ABH (1999), two attempted rapes (2001) and indecent assault (2003). He was released in 2005 but recalled due to an indecent images charge which was not pursued. He was released in 2013, having been at large for five weeks prior to the murder. Held. The aggravating features were manifest: a) D began the day with an intention to rape, b) he took a knife from his caravan, c) he murdered V to prevent her giving evidence against him, d) he then went to considerable lengths to clean her body to destroy any evidence, e) he left the body virtually naked in the woodland, f) he had only recently been released from prison, and g) had convictions for attempted rape. The only mitigation was that D made full admissions and had pleaded guilty, providing information about his crimes and intentions which would not have otherwise been discovered. This was a case of attempted rape followed by a deliberate killing to avoid prosecution. The violence and sexual assault were inextricably interwoven. There can be no doubt that this was a murder involving sexual conduct. The starting point was therefore 30 years. With the aggravating features, avoiding double-counting, the sentence was 36 years. With the maximum one-sixth credit for plea and taking account of the mitigation, minimum term of **30 years** not 25.

See also: *Att-Gen's Ref No 73 of 2012* 2012 EWCA Crim 2924, 2013 2 Cr App R (S) 38 (p 261) (Plea to murder. Taxi driver killed passenger. A number of aggravating features including offence premeditated, vulnerable victim, severe pain and extreme fear. Sexual motive but no overt sexual act. Starting at 30 years. Judge entitled to end at **30 years** before plea discount. So **25 years**.)

R v Minto 2014 EWCA Crim 297, 2 Cr App R (S) 36 (p 301) (Convicted. Contacted V, aged 16, on Facebook, offered her work at hotel. V's body found nearby with 58 stab wounds. V had been sexually assaulted at point of death, and set on fire. Statutory aggravating factors non-exhaustive. Premeditation of the sexual assault, V's suffering, the abuse of trust and the destruction of the body means aggravating factors listed in Sch 21 para 10 are not exhaustive. **35-year** minimum term was not a day too long.)

Old cases: *R v McGrady* 2007 EWCA Crim 192, 2 Cr App R (S) 56 (p 347) **(whole life)** *R v Archer* 2007 EWCA Crim 536, 2 Cr App R (S) 71 (p 453) **(25 years)** *Att-Gen's Ref No 149 of 2006* 2007 EWCA Crim 965, 2 Cr App R (S) 96 (p 616) **(21 years)** *R v Mullen* 2008 EWCA Crim 592, 2 Cr App R (S) 88 (p 501) **(35 years)** *Att-Gen's Ref Nos 25-26 of 2008* 2008 EWCA Crim 2665, 2009 1 Cr App R (S) 116 (p 648) (For M, **24 years** not 19, for W, **18 years**)

For a summary of the first case, see the 6th edition of this book, for the second case, see the 7th edition, for the fourth case, see the 8th edition and for the last case, see the 9th edition.

Terrorist murders see the TERRORISM *Large-scale terrorism* para at **345.10**.

Torture see the *Sadistic murders* para at **288.66**.

Transitional cases see the 3rd edition of this book.

288.71   Unexplained motive

R v Jones 2005 EWCA Crim 3115, 2006 2 Cr App R (S) 19 (p 121) para 9 A killing for which there is no rational explanation may reflect a mental disorder or disability in the offender. Such murders are sometimes more horrifying than killings that are motivated. It is important to bear in mind that in the case of such a murder it is the task of the Parole Board to ensure that the offender is not released after serving the minimum term unless this presents no danger to the public. Protection of the public is not a relevant factor in fixing the minimum term.

R v Davies 2008 EWCA Crim 1055, 2009 1 Cr App R (S) 15 (p 79) LCJ D was convicted of murder and perverting the course of justice. V was a young woman who was known to exercise and sunbathe on a common. She went missing, and nine days later her mobile phone was traced to D, who was arrested. At his home police found a rucksack containing clothing and a hat stained with V's blood. They also found a holdall containing a knife stained with her blood, two vibrators, tissue paper and an opened packet of liquid Viagra. Her naked, badly decomposed body was found by police three days later on the common in a shallow grave. There was a length of fishing line where her neck would have been. Tissue paper matching that found in D's possession was nearby. Her clothing was never found. The perverting the course of justice count was the concealment of the body. The Judge sentenced D on the basis that the murder involved sexual conduct. D, aged 22, had a number of previous convictions, but none for violence. A psychiatric report said that he had a deprived and disrupted childhood. He abused drugs from an early age. He suffered from emotional instability and had self-harmed. He suffered from a personality disorder. He was likely to harm himself or attempt suicide when feeling depressed. He had a low IQ, although it would not affect his ability to function on a day-to-day basis. Held. The sex aids found in the rucksack bore no trace of the victim's DNA. D said that they were for his personal use and there is no reason to doubt this. His previous convictions showed no suggestion of a propensity to sexual offences or indeed offences of violence. The psychiatric report does not suggest a propensity for sexual offending. The only factor that points to the possibility of sexual conduct was that V's body was naked. That raises the possibility that sexual conduct was involved, but no more than that. D must have removed all her clothing from the scene, and the prosecution accepted it as likely that she would have removed some to sunbathe. So the starting point is 15 years. Concealing the body resulted in additional anxiety and distress for V's family and concealed from the Court the facts of the offence. That was a serious aggravating factor. **18-year** minimum term, not 23.

See also: *R v McFly* 2013 EWCA Crim 729 (Convicted of murder. Drunk. Victim was attacked in the street by the defendant and another, on and off for about 35 minutes. Kicked and stamped upon. Dropped a refrigerator on his head. 24 fractures to the head, neck and ribs. Defendant later shaved off his distinctive hair and burned his clothes. Victim knew the defendant. Significant previous convictions including robbery, violence and possession of an offensive weapon. Gratuitous and senseless violence. Severe personality disorder. Judge fully justified in finding of dangerousness. Intent to kill. 15-year starting point. Minimum term **21 years** not 24.)

Old case: *R v Walker* 2007 EWCA Crim 2631, 2008 2 Cr App R (S) 6 (p 38) (**20 years**) For a summary of this case, see the 8th edition of this book.

288.72   *Vehicles   Using vehicle as a weapon   Disqualification*
Disqualification In motor vehicle manslaughter cases, the driver is liable to 2 years' obligatory disqualification.[705] The power does not exist in murder cases, no doubt because it is so uncertain when the defendant will be released.

288.73   *Vehicle, Using vehicle as weapon   Case*
Example: *R v Beckford* 2014 EWCA Crim 1299, 2 Cr App R (S) 34 (p 285) (D was convicted. V, aged 19, was a member of a rival gang. D drove a stolen car into V, ramming him off his bicycle with tremendous force. D aged 22 but no licence and poor record with three violent offences, including two robberies in 2009. Held. Judge entitled to conclude that D took a weapon to the scene. In setting minimum terms courts should achieve just results, not slavishly follow Criminal Justice Act 2003 Sch 21. 24 year-term upheld.)

288.74   *Victim aged 65+*
Criminal Justice Act 2003 Sch 21 para 10 Aggravating factors (additional to those mentioned in paras 4(2) and 5(2) (see **288.90** and **288.15**) that may be relevant include:...b) the fact that the victim was particularly vulnerable because of age or disability.

R v Zebedee 2012 EWCA Crim 1428, 2013 1 Cr App R (S) 37 (p 207) D was convicted of murder. His elderly father, V, aged 94, suffered from dementia. His illness worsened after the death of his wife, D's mother, in 2009. V went to live with D's sister and her family. They were determined that he would not be forced into a care home. D and D's sister showed their loving devotion to V during his illness. The burden of care was very great, not least because V was doubly incontinent. He could ask the same question 50 times in half an hour and whistle the same tune endlessly. D would stay over at his sister's house to assist with caring for V every other weekend and one full week in five. One evening, D's sister woke her partner, P, because she heard loud noises. He found D at the kitchen sink washing his hands. D had drunk two bottles of wine and smoked a cannabis joint. D had blood on his clothing and he was clearly drunk. P led D back to his

---

[705] Road Traffic Offenders Act 1988 s 9, 34, 97 and Sch 2 Part II

bedroom, which involved going through V's bedroom. P saw V on the bed lying on his back. There were bruises and blood on his face and one eye was completely bloodied. It was clear V was dead. V had woken D as he had soiled himself. D went to V's aid and cleaned him up. 20 minutes later V called him again. D became angry, grabbed V's lip to prevent him from whistling and began to shake V. He put his hands around V's neck. V had died from blunt trauma from punches to the face and head, and had then been strangled by a ligature or with bare hands. In interview, D accepted that he had killed V. He told police that he had not intended to kill him. A doctor assessed D and concluded that he had cracked under the pressure of caring for V. The doctor felt that the burden of caring for V was too great for the whole family. D, aged 55, was of good character. He had a long-standing alcohol problem and had had psychotherapy over the previous 10 years. He was a respected lecturer and author on the topic of housing benefit. D wrote to the trial Judge after his conviction expressing his desire to apologise to his family for the turmoil and heartbreak he had caused. The Judge considered D's vulnerability to be the principal aggravating factor. Held. It was clear D cared for his father very much. While affected by drink, he simply gave in to the enormous frustration of caring for V or gave in to anger triggered by the soiling and disturbance. The Judge gave insufficient weight to those factors. The appropriate minimum term was **10 years** not 15.

Old case: *R v Essilfie* 2008 EWCA Crim 2818, 2009 2 Cr App R (S) 11 (p 65) (Plea. Under stress. Six-month-old baby. Previous violence to child. **13 years** not 15)

For a summary of the case, see the 9th edition of this book.

288.75   *Violent attack, Very*

Att-Gen's Ref No 38 of 2008 2008 EWCA Crim 2122 D was convicted of murder in 1991. He selected a doctor who lived alone and hit him with about 17 blows in what became a vicious and prolonged attack. The motive was a 'preoccupied hatred of authority' and wanting to be brought into direct and physical contact with police. A mass of firearms and weapons were found at his address. A hit list of people in authority, mostly police officers, was also found. He had a persistent disorder or disability of the mind making him behave in a seriously aggressive way. It was untreatable. The Judge, the LCJ and Home Secretary considered whole life appropriate. Held. It was the most appalling sadistic murder. The disorder was some mitigation but it did not diminish his insight or understanding of what he was doing. **30 years** not 18.

R v Griffin 2010 EWCA Crim 149 LCJ D pleaded early to murder. V, aged 44, lived alone in a one-bedroom flat. He was harmless, kind and vulnerable. V regularly used drugs and drank heavily. He allowed drug users to use his flat. D visited V regularly to share drugs. The fire brigade were called, and in the lobby of V's block they had to go on their hands and knees because of smoke infestation. In V's flat they found the fire still burning and V's partly burnt body. There were ten separate fires set in the flat. Also, blood was found at four different sites. A table leg and a wooden rocking chair had V's blood on them. The pathologist found severe injuries on the body far in excess of the majority of cases involving 'blunt-force trauma'. The injuries were of a type found when someone was hit by a car or had fallen from a building. There were at least 80 external injuries and extensive internal injuries, and 18 or 19 cut lacerations caused by broken glass were found. D was aged 33 with a variety of convictions including violence. In 2002 he received 5 years for wounding with intent. He had a serious drug problem. D gave evidence against the co-defendant which was considered truthful. The Judge started at 35 years because of the level of violence. Held. It was a desperately violent attack. The calculated and exceptional brutality, the record of violence, the intent to kill a vulnerable victim, V's suffering and the intent to destroy evidence by fire were dreadful features. These justified a 30-year starting point. With the plea, the co-operation with the police and the giving of evidence reduces it to **22 years**. Had there been a 15-year starting point, the result would have been the same.

See also the *Sadistic murders* para at **288.66**.

Old cases: *Att-Gen's Ref No 12 of 2008* 2008 EWCA Crim 1060, 2009 1 Cr App R (S) 18
(p 97) (**22 years**) *R v Khan and Others* 2009 EWCA Crim 966 (**22** and **20 years**)
For a summary of the first case, see the 8th edition of this book and for the second case,
see the 9th edition.

Matters relating to the defendant

288.76   *Alcohol, Defendant under the influence of*
R v Waters 2006 EWHC 355 (QB) High Court Mere drunkenness leading to extreme
violence cannot be a mitigating factor.
R v Douglas 2014 EWCA Crim 2322, 2015 1 Cr App R (S) 28 (p 214) D was convicted
of murder following the rejection of a diminished responsibility defence. D's mother, V,
was aged 73 and extremely frail with emphysema and a heart condition. She weighed
only five stone and was fairly immobile but was cared for by D's father, who himself
was ill. D assisted her father in caring for V and cared for her father too. One Sunday
afternoon, the father and D's partner went out. Whilst D prepared lunch, she drank a
significant amount of wine. That evening, D was heard crying hysterically from upstairs.
D's partner and father went upstairs and found V inexplicably on the floor next to her
bed. D phoned the ambulance and was distressed. She was cuddling V and shouting at
the paramedics not to resuscitate V. D then wandered outside dangerously into the
middle of the road. She was distressed, saying she had smothered V with a pillow. D was
taken home and later phoned the police, telling them what she had done. A post-mortem
revealed that the smothering provoked rapid cardiac arrest, but V could have died of
heart failure at any time. D was frank in interview, saying she could not bear watching V
being ill but had thought, "What am I doing?" and stopped. She said she called an
ambulance but could not explain why V ended up on the floor. D was aged 49 on appeal
and of good character but regularly drank heavily. The Judge found that V was seriously
under the influence of alcohol ($3\frac{1}{2}$ times driving limit). Had D been sober, she would
not have acted in the way she did. Further D genuinely thought, albeit briefly, it was an
act of mercy. Held. Cases where belief harboured through drunkenness affords mitigation will all be fact-dependent. Life with a **7-year** minimum term, not 12.

288.77   *Bad character with/without a conviction/Background of violence*
Criminal Justice Act 2003 Sch 21 para 12(a) Nothing in this Schedule restricts the
application of section 143(2) [of this Act].
Note: Section 143(2) directs the court to treat previous convictions as an aggravating
factor where they can be so reasonably treated. Ed.
R v Thomas 2009 EWCA Crim 904, 2010 1 Cr App R (S) 14 (p 75) D was convicted of
murder of the woman with whom he was in a relationship. The prosecution was
permitted to put in evidence earlier incidents of domestic violence against V, his ex-wife
and a former partner. The Judge held that the violence to his ex-wife and former partner
was an aggravating feature. Held. It has always been open to a judge, when assessing the
culpability of D, to have regard to D's antecedent behaviour, not all of which is
necessarily evidenced by previous convictions. Pre-sentence reports frequently refer to
attitude and behaviour etc., so the court can determine whether the use of violence
reveals an entrenched disregard for others or is a one-off. The *Domestic Violence
Guideline 2006* list of aggravating factors at paragraph 2.1(v) says, 'a proven history of
violence or threats by the offender in a domestic setting'. Paragraph 3.14 says 'It is
important that an assessment of the seriousness of an offence recognises the cumulative
effect of a series of violent incidents or threats over a prolonged period, where such
conduct has been proved or accepted'. The Judge is not entitled to increase the minimum
term for the violence visited on the ex-wife and former partner, as he was not sentencing
for those offences. Neither could the Judge use Criminal Justice Act 2003 s 143(2) for
the caution over an incident with V. However, the Judge was entitled to assess the
seriousness of the act of violence which led to V's death in the context of the cumulative
effect of a series of violent incidents or threats over a prolonged period. Quite apart from

the common law, that approach is specifically mandated by Criminal Justice Act 2003
s 172(1) (duty to have regard to guidelines) and consistent with Schedule 21 paragraph 10(b) and (c) about vulnerability and suffering of the deceased.

For other paragraphs about bad character, see the **Previous convictions** entry in the back
index.

288.78   *Dangerous defendants, Very*

Att-Gen's Ref No 38 of 2008 2008 EWCA Crim 2122 D was convicted of murder in
1991. He selected a doctor who lived alone and hit him with about 17 blows in what
became a vicious and prolonged attack. The motive was a 'preoccupied hatred of
authority' and wanting to be brought into direct and physical contact with police. Very
many firearms and weapons were found at his address. A hit list of people in authority,
mostly police officers, was also found. He had a persistent disorder or disability of the
mind making him behave in a seriously aggressive way. It was untreatable. The Judge,
the LCJ and Home Secretary considered whole life appropriate. Held. It was the most
appalling sadistic murder. The disorder was some mitigation but it did not diminish his
insight or understanding of what he was doing. **30 years** not 18.

Old case: *R v Henson and Magraw* 2007 EWCA Crim 1308, 2008 1 Cr App R (S) 19
(p 83) (Aged 20, convicted, **35 years**)

For a summary of the case, see the 8th edition of this book.

See also the *Whole life* para at **288.90**.

288.79   *Defendant aged under 18   Starting points and age as a factor*

Criminal Justice Act 2003 Sch 21 para 6 If the offender was aged 18 or over when he
committed the offence and the case does not fall into paras 4(1) or 5(1) (see paras **288.90**
and **288.15**), the appropriate starting point, in determining the minimum term, is
15 years.

Powers of Criminal Courts (Sentencing) Act 2000 s 90 Where a person convicted of
murder appears to the court to have been aged under 18 at the time the offence was
committed, the court shall sentence him to be detained during HM's Pleasure.[706]

Criminal Justice Act 2003 Sch 21 para 11 Mitigating factors that may be relevant
include: g) the age of the offender.

288.80   *Defendant aged under 21   Mandatory sentence*

Powers of Criminal Courts (Sentencing) Act 2000 s 93 Where a person aged under 21 is
convicted of murder the court shall sentence him to custody for life unless he is liable to
be detained under section 90 (detention at HM's Pleasure).

Note: This rule applies however old the defendant is. An example of this is *R v Norris
and Dobson* 2012 The Times News 5/1/12. The defendants were aged 16 and 17 at the
time of the Stephen Lawrence killing and were aged 35 and 36 when sentenced to
detention during HM's Pleasure. Ed.

Criminal Justice Act 2003 Sch 21 para 7 If the offender was aged under 18 when he
committed the offence, the appropriate starting point, in determining the minimum term,
is 12 years.

Note: This means the starting points for offenders aged 18-20 are the same as for those
aged 21+, save that 'whole life' is not available.[707] Those cases have a 30-year starting
point. For offenders aged 10 to 17 the starting point is 12 years. For more details, see
288.12.

Court Martial The provisions are in Armed Forces Act 2006 s 218.

288.81   *Defendant aged under 21   Guideline remarks*

R v Peters 2005 EWCA Crim 605, 2 Cr App R (S) 101 (p 627) It has long been
understood that considerations of age and maturity are usually relevant to the culpability
of an offender and the seriousness of the offence. Schedule 21 underlines this principle.

---

[706] The statute also calls this order 'detention at HM's Pleasure'.
[707] Criminal Justice Act 2003 Sch 21 para 4

Although the passage of an 18th or 21st birthday represents a significant moment in the life of each individual, it does not necessarily tell us very much about the individual's true level of maturity, insight and understanding. These levels are not postponed until, or suddenly accelerated by, an 18th or 21st birthday. Therefore, although the normal starting point is governed by the defendant's age, when assessing his culpability, the sentencing judge should reflect on and make allowances, as appropriate upwards or downwards, for the level of the offender's maturity. Here, where a defendant is 18 years 2 months when the offence was committed, a rigid application of the starting point in Schedule 21 would mean that the three months' difference in age should be reflected by a difference of 3 years in the sentence. Sentencing decisions cannot be prescribed by such accidents of time. We can illustrate this problem a little further by taking the all too familiar case of a group of youths convicted of murder following an attack on a passer-by in the street late at night. They may be 17, 19 and 21 years old. Normally the 21-year-old would be likely to be the most mature. But there are cases where the 17-year-old, although the youngest, is in truth the leader of the group, and the most violent of the three, and the most culpable, who triggered off the attack and indeed inflicted the fatal blow. It may produce an unjust result if, on the basis of his age alone, the minimum term in his case were lower than the sentence on his co-defendants. Therefore, in relation to offenders aged up to 21 or even 22 years, the determination of the minimum term in accordance with the legislative framework in Schedule 21 needs to be approached with an acute sense of how inevitably imprecise the statutory criteria may sometimes be to issues of culpability, and ultimately to 'seriousness' as envisaged in section 269 itself. Schedule 21 does not envisage a movable starting point, upwards or downwards, from the dates fixed by reference to the offender's 18th or 21st birthdays. Nor does it provide a mathematical scale, starting at 12 years for the 18-year-old offender, moving upwards to 13 years for the 19-year-old, through to 14 years for the 20-year-old, culminating in 15 years for the 21-year-old. The principle is simple. Where the offender's age, as it affects his culpability, and the seriousness of the crime justify it, a substantial, or even a very substantial, discount from the starting point may be appropriate. One way in which the judge *may* check that the discount is proportionate would be for him to consider it in the context of the overall statutory framework, as if Schedule 21 envisaged a flexible starting point for offenders between 18 and 21. This would have the advantage of linking the mitigation which would normally arise from the offender's relative youth with the statutory provisions which apply to an offender a year or two older or younger, and would contribute to a desirable level of sentencing consistency. Due allowance should then be made for the relevant aggravating and mitigating features to produce the final determination of the minimum term, and thereafter the judge should explain the reasons for the determination in open court.
Note: This is an old case, but it was a guideline case. If any of the principles in the case had been altered, it would have been made clear in later judgments. Ed.

R v Matthew 2005 EWCA Crim 2399, 2006 1 Cr App R (S) 88 (p 505) D was convicted of murder and wounding with intent. He was aged 18 at the time of the offence. Held. There was no intention to kill. Of greater importance is his age. Although Schedule 21 identifies the age of 18 as a higher starting point, there was no sudden step change and the court has to take into account a certain flexibility as each defendant grows to maturity. D lost the benefit of a significantly lower starting point of 12 years by a few months. The starting point referred to by the Judge of 17 years was too high. An appropriate starting point was 15 years.

Att-Gen's Ref No 126 of 2006 2007 EWCA Crim 53, 2 Cr App R (S) 59 (p 362) D pleaded to murder. He was aged 14 at the time of the offence. Held. It is clear that the appropriate sentence remains fact-specific. It is trite law that irrespective of the 'starting point', the end result may be a minimum term of 'any length', well below or well above the defined starting point. The court must take account of every aggravating and mitigating feature, with specific reference to those in paragraphs 10 to 11 of the

Schedule. These lists are not exhaustive. Schedule 21 underlines the long-established principle that the level of responsibility and ultimate criminality of an offender who is young is likely to be (but may not necessarily be) lower than the culpability and criminality of an older offender. No mathematical table can be produced which calculates the culpability of a young offender with any specific age, and no list, however carefully drawn up, can provide an accurate reflection of the way in which a young offender may or may not have learnt from or been damaged by the experiences to which that young man had been exposed. Detention during HM's Pleasure means that the offender will not be released unless and until it is safe for him to be released. Even after release he will be liable to be recalled for the rest of his life.

Att-Gen's Ref Nos 143-144 of 2006 2007 EWCA Crim 1245, 2008 1 Cr App R (S) 28 (p 136) LCJ The defendants, C and B, were convicted of murder. The victim had come out of an Underground station. He was stabbed in the thigh, in the face and twice in the chest. The prosecution were not able to prove which of them stabbed the murder victim. At the time of the murder, C was aged 18 years 7 months and B 17 years 9 months. The starting point for one was 30 years and for the other, 12 years. Held. Where one defendant is just under and the other just over an age limit, that raises an acute problem. The sentences should not be assessed independently. The sentencer should move from each starting point to a position where any disparity between the two terms is no more than a fair reflection of the age difference. We do not consider that the small disparity in age between C and B could be reflected in more than 1 year's difference in the minimum terms. The minimum terms will be **20** and **21 years**.

R v J 2008 EWCA Crim 2437, 2009 1 Cr App R (S) 108 (p 605) D was convicted of murder. She was aged 15. Age and birthdays are not the only indicators of an individual's true level of maturity and understanding.

R v Martin 2009 EWCA Crim 1182, 2010 1 Cr App R (S) 38 (p 226) D was convicted of murder when aged 18. It is not the case that as soon as a defendant turns 18, the term will automatically be 15 years if there are no mitigating or aggravating factors. A balancing exercise is required taking into account culpability, the seriousness of the crime and the defendant's age.

R v Moore 2010 EWCA Crim 2197, 2011 1 Cr App R (S) 94 (p 561) D pleaded to murder and wounding. Following gang tensions, two innocent youths were stabbed. One died. The minimum term was set at 17 years. It was argued that the minimum term was manifestly excessive, when considering the youth of the defendant (he was aged 16) and the increased starting point for knife murders for defendants over the age of 18, but not under 18. Held. In deference to defence counsel's submissions, we add: a) Even an immature 16-year-old will appreciate that stabbing someone with a knife is utterly wrong. b) We can, insofar as it is a matter for us, readily understand why, in respect of knife murders, Parliament might have left the starting point for under-18s unchanged, whilst raising it in respect of those aged over 18. But the fact that the starting point was left unchanged simply means that the matter is left to the discretion of the judge to deal with as is just on the facts of the particular case. c) So far as concerns the guilty plea, the Judge did have it squarely in mind, and indeed made an allowance greater than that contemplated in the guidelines. d) So far as the authorities go, we think that the facts are altogether too diverse and too different to provide any assistance, still less assistance which points to the minimum term not exceeding 15 years...If (contrary to our view) there was any general level of sentencing to be extracted from the authorities, then the particular facts of this case, for the reasons given by him, justified the Judge fixing a minimum term in excess of 15 years.

Att-Gen's Ref No 25 of 2012 2012 EWCA Crim 2352, 2013 1 Cr App R (S) 124 (p 644) D, a 15-year-old boy, stabbed a student on his way home. The knife was not taken to the scene by him. D had a bad record including robbery with a pointed article. Held. The fact that an offender is of a young age is a very significant matter. However, where

Parliament has reduced the starting point for the minimum term for young offenders, there must be a limit to which further reduction must be made for a 15-year-old with this record who kills in these circumstances.

288.82   *Defendant aged under 16*

R v C 2013 EWCA Crim 2639 C and N were convicted of murder. C was with other youths outside a shop. N lived in the flat above the shop. C became involved in an altercation with V, a man in his 30s. V thought C's younger brother had been seeking to 'wind up' two dogs that he had with him. C's brother shouted up to N that his assistance was needed and N came down. N went over to V and punched him in the face. V stumbled or fell and then began to advance towards N. As he did so, C punched him to the head. V fell to the floor and failed to get up. N kicked him in the head, with witnesses describing the kick as like one would kick a football. V died some hours later. He suffered a subarachnoid haemorrhage resulting from a torn vertebral artery.[708] It could have been the result of a single punch or kick, or a combination of blows. He also suffered a broken right cheekbone and a broken left jaw. N was aged 19 and C was aged 15 at the time of the offence. N had five convictions for common assault and one for ABH. C had a conviction for common assault when aged 13. Held. The Judge found that there were no aggravating features and accepted that the mitigation included the absence of an intention to kill. The death was unexpected and in medical terms highly unusual. C must take responsibility for the fact that he was a party to the joint enterprise but the sentences needed to reflect his role. He directed only one punch and the whole enterprise was over in barely a minute. He also had positive elements to his character and a good prison report. A minimum term of **5 years** would reflect the culpability, action and age of C. N did not appeal his sentence of 11 years. Reducing C's sentence was not in any way based on the premise that N's sentence was too high.

For the manslaughter cases see **MANSLAUGHTER** *Defendant aged 16-17* at **288.12**.

See also: *R v Thomas Re W* 2010 EWCA Crim 148 (Convicted. Planned gang revenge attack. Aged 14 but 15 when sentenced. Three stab wounds to head done by group. Seen carrying bloodstained knife away. Previous for ABH (Referral Order). No intent to kill. **12 years** not 14 to balance with the sentence on one more forceful and older.)

Att-Gen's Ref No 25 of 2012 2012 EWCA Crim 2352, 2013 1 Cr App R (S) 124 (p 644) (Convicted of murder. Argument in a park after victim remonstrated with defendant and his group. Victim aged 21. Defendant aged 15 at the time of the offence. Victim was punched and kicked. He hit the defendant with his skateboard. Defendant stabbed victim once in the chest. Knife obtained at the scene from another. Very bad record including robbery with a pointed article, robbery and dwelling burglary. No intent to kill. **12 years'** not 10½ years.)

R v Rahman and Rashed 2015 EWCA Crim 15 (Convicted. D1 and two others forced their way into elderly victims' house, armed and disguised, at night. All were carrying knives and wearing gloves. V1, aged 69 and with cancer, was subjected to a frenzied attack. He was beaten, kicked and stabbed 11 times. Shouts of "Kill him, kill him." V2, aged 65, tried to protect V1 and was stabbed in the arm. Jewellery of £5-6,000 and £1,000 cash were taken. Aged 15 and of good character. Held. Extremely grave offence planned over several weeks. Detention for life with 19-year minimum term upheld.)

Note: Notwithstanding all those who dealt with the case at the Crown Court and the Court of Appeal, the sentence is now and always has been unlawful. D1 should have been sentenced to Detention during HM's Pleasure, because he was aged under 18 at the time of the offence. Ed.

R v Cornick 2015 EWCA Crim 110, 1 Cr App R (S) 69 (p 483) (LCJ Plea. Aged 15. When aged 12, developed a hatred of Spanish lessons. On Facebook talked of brutally killing and torturing V, a Spanish teacher. Stabbed V, aged 61, seven times in a lesson with large kitchen knife, in front of other pupils. Had responsible, loving and caring

---

[708] This is a rare injury resulting from the hyperextension or rotation of the neck. Ed.

parents. Judge started at 12 years and with aggravating factors moved it up to 25 years. Two years off for plea and three years off for youth and his adjustment disorder made **20 years**. Upheld.)

Old cases: *Att-Gen's Ref No 126 of 2006* 2007 EWCA Crim 53, 2 Cr App R (S) 59 (p 362) (**15-year minimum term**) *R v Taylor and Thomas* 2007 EWCA Crim 803, 2008 1 Cr App R (S) 4 (p 19) (**18 years**) *R v J* 2008 EWCA Crim 2437, 2009 1 Cr App R (S) 108 (p 605) (**12 years**) *R v Yemoh and Others* 2009 EWCA Crim 1775, 2010 1 Cr App R (S) 97 (p 611) (**13 years**)

For a summary of the first and second cases, see the 7th edition of this book, for the third case, see the 9th edition and for the last case, see the 10th edition.

288.83   *Defendant aged 16-17   Cases*

R v M and Others 2009 EWCA Crim 2544, 2010 2 Cr App R (S) 19 (p 117) LCJ M was convicted of murder. He was found not guilty of robbery. V, aged 17, and two others were sitting on a bench listening to music on a phone. D's two co-accused, G and another, approached the three, and one of them snatched the phone. The three remonstrated, and V asked for the phone's return. D, a friend of G, approached the scene with a knife in his hand. G said, "Poke him". D stabbed V with a moderate if not a severe blow in the abdomen. D and G ran off. D disposed of the knife and his clothing. V died. D was aged nearly 18. He had no offences of significant violence but had convictions. He had been the victim of a serious knife crime the year before. The Judge found no proven intent to kill. Held. V died because D went onto the streets armed with a knife. **14 years** gave a heavy discount for his age.

R v Moore 2010 EWCA Crim 2197, 2011 1 Cr App R (S) 94 (p 561) D pleaded late to murder and wounding. He was associated with the Scottie Road Crew in the Everton and Vauxhall areas of Liverpool. There was tension between that gang and the Langley Crew, also local to the area. There was nothing to suggest D was involved in gangland activity. There was a personal animosity between D and W. W was threatened directly and indirectly via telephone. Members of the Scottie Road Crew were attacked, and one member was threatened with knives and a gun and made to say "I love the Langleys" on the phone to his brother, who was also affiliated with the Scottie Road Crew. It was believed that the perpetrators were members of the Langley Crew and associates of W. Two cars containing members of the Scottie Road Crew, including D, agreed they would search for those responsible, and travelled to a youth centre. At the youth centre, three individuals, V1, V2 and V3, who were listening to a friend's band practising, had congregated outside to smoke a cigarette. The youths alighted from their cars and chased V1, V2 and V3 for 200 m. They were cornered and D approached V1 and stabbed him in the chest. He then stabbed V2 in the thigh and abdomen. The youths ran off. V1's heart was punctured and he subsequently died. V2 suffered stab wounds and was discharged from hospital the following day. The Judge noted that this was a group attack, was planned, the victims were young and vulnerable and there was the use of a knife (see *R v AM* 2009 EWCA Crim 2544). In mitigation, D was young and immature. The Judge gave more than the advised 5% for the plea. D, aged 16, had six previous court appearances for 14 offences between November 2007 and July 2009. They included breaches of ASBOs, a Referral Order and a Supervision Order. He had totally disregarded court orders. He had received no positive parenting. Held. D has shown contrition and having regard to all the factors identified by the Judge, specifically the plea, his youth and immaturity, **17 years** was not manifestly excessive.

See also: *R v Mazekelua* 2011 EWCA Crim 2137 (Convicted of murder. Gang tension in East London. Victim suffered stab wounds to the chest and abdomen. Took knife to scene. Aged 16 years 9 months. No convictions. 22-25 years for an adult. **17 years** was not manifestly excessive.)

R v Odegbune and Others 2013 EWCA Crim 711 (D, N and O aged 16, 17 and 16 were convicted of a ferocious and merciless gang attack on a 15-year-old boy, V, at Victoria station. V was stabbed nine times. O had minor convictions and D and N were of good character. Aggravated by planning, mass violence and use of more than one weapon. **18 years** might seem overwhelming but inevitable because of the need to punish and deter. Because D had no intent to kill, for him 16 years.)

R v Rahman and Rashed 2015 EWCA Crim 15 (Convicted. D1 and two others forced their way into elderly victims' house, armed and disguised, at night. All were carrying knives and wearing gloves. V1, aged 69 and with cancer, was subjected to a frenzied attack. He was beaten, kicked and stabbed 11 times. Shouts of "Kill him, kill him." V2, aged 65, tried to protect V1 and was stabbed in the arm. Jewellery of £5-6,000 and £1,000 cash were taken. Aged 15 and of good character. Held. Extremely grave offence planned over several weeks. Detention for life with 19-year minimum term upheld.)

Note: Notwithstanding all those who dealt with the case at the Crown Court and the Court of Appeal, the sentence is now and always has been unlawful. D1 should have been sentenced to Detention during HM's Pleasure, because he was aged under 18 at the time of the offence. Ed.

Old cases: *R v D and JS* 2007 1 Cr App R (S) 67 (p 391) (**10 years**) *R v Taylor and Thomas* 2007 EWCA Crim 803, 2008 1 Cr App R (S) 4 (p 19) (Ta **22 years** and Th **18 years**) *Att-Gen's Ref Nos 143-144 of 2006* 2007 EWCA Crim 1245, 2008 1 Cr App R (S) 28 (p 136) (**20 years**) *R v R* 2007 EWCA Crim 1874, 2008 1 Cr App R (S) 65 (p 379) (**10 years**) *R v Roberts and Mould* 2008 EWCA Crim 59, 2 Cr App R (S) 59 (p 350) (**9 years**) *R v Patterson* 2008 EWCA Crim 1018, 2009 1 Cr App R (S) 19 (p 103) (**12 years**) *R v Malasi* 2008 EWCA Crim 2505, 2009 1 Cr App R (S) 51 (p 276) (Aged 16. **30 years**) *R v Swellings and Sorton* 2008 EWCA Crim 3249, 2009 2 Cr App R (S) 30 (p 220)[709] (**13 years**, see **288.29**)

For a summary of the first, second and third cases, see the 7th edition of this book, for the fourth case, see the 8th edition and for the fifth case, see the 9th edition.

288.84   *Defendant aged 18-20*

R v M and Others Re K 2009 EWCA Crim 2544, 2010 2 Cr App R (S) 19 (p 117) at para 20 LCJ K was convicted of murder. A confrontation developed between two groups of youths. B was seen to gesture that he had a knife. He was heard to threaten to use it. A fight broke out, and one of B's friends was struck. Again B was heard to threaten to use his knife. B and his gang ran off. B contacted K and L. The three went back for revenge. One said that someone was going to be 'shanked'. The other group ran. V, aged 16, was at the back. He was hunted down and knocked down between two parked cars. V received 11 stab wounds. One was so ferocious that one of his ribs was split. K and L disposed of some of their blood-stained clothing. V died. K was aged just 18. He had six court appearances with a robbery and an affray conviction but had not served custody. K showed no remorse. He had had a difficult upbringing. The Judge found a joint intention to kill. Held. V was a wholly innocent victim. He offered not a shred of provocation. K knew exactly what he was doing. **19 years** cannot remotely be described as excessive.

R v Barney and James 2010 EWCA Crim 211, 2 Cr App R (S) 61 (p 407) (Aged 18. **24 years**) See **288.41**.

R v King 2013 EWCA Crim 930 See **288.41**.

R v Williams 2013 EWCA Crim 933 (Aged 19. **28 years**) See **288.61**.

R v Parr 2013 EWCA Crim 2007 (Aged 19. Knife. **23 years**) See **288.45**.

R v De Silva 2014 EWCA Crim 2616, 1 Cr App R (S) 52 (p 359) Convicted. Aged just 19. Stabbed victim in his home 22 times during a burglary. **28 years** not 32. For more details, see **288.41**.

See also: *R v Adeojo and Nyamupfukudza* 2013 EWCA Crim 41 (D was convicted of murder, two attempted murders and possessing a firearm with intent to endanger life. Gang gun killing. Aged nearly 19. **30 years** did reflect the defendant's age and the recent crossing of the age threshold.)

---

[709] The neutral citation in the Cr App R (S) report is wrong.

Old cases: *R v Clarke* 2009 EWCA Crim 2484, 2010 2 Cr App R (S) 13 (p 78) (LCJ **27 years**) See **288.37**. *R v Swellings and Sorton* 2008 EWCA Crim 3249, 2009 2 Cr App R (S) 30 (p 220)[710] (**17 years**) See **288.29**. *R v Martin* 2009 EWCA Crim 1182, 2010 1 Cr App R (S) 38 (p 226) (**13 years**) *Att-Gen's Ref No 30 of 2009* 2009 EWCA Crim 2344, 2010 2 Cr App R (S) 7 (p 37) (**25 years**) *R v Hylton* 2009 EWCA Crim 2604, 2010 2 Cr App R (S) 29 (p 186) (**15 years**) *R v Badza* 2009 EWCA Crim 2695 (**16 years**)

For even older cases, see the 8th edition of this book.

288.85   *Defendant aged over 65 or would be very old on release*
Criminal Justice Act 2003 Sch 21 para 11 Mitigating factors that may be relevant include: g) the age of the offender.
R v Archer 2007 EWCA Crim 536, 2 Cr App R (S) 71 (p 453) D was convicted of murder. He was aged 55. Held. One of the factors which will be taken into account in relation to a sentence as long as 30 years is the possibility of light at the end of the tunnel. This defendant was not given a whole life order, but it may be that the sentence he was given would amount to one in practice. The understood actuarial position is that males will not last much over 80, if at all, in terms of normal life expectancy. If he were considered for parole at the age of 83½ he may well not be immediately released. If released then, or even at a lesser age, he will be nothing like the danger to the public that he might otherwise have been. The Judge should have made allowance for age as a mitigating factor.
R v McDonald 2007 EWCA Crim 1081 D pleaded to a murder committed in 2001. He was aged 55 (49 at the time of the offence). Held. His age is also relevant to physical capacity on release.
R v Troughton 2012 EWCA Crim 1520, 2013 1 Cr App R (S) 75 (p 417) D was convicted of murder. He had two cousins, C and V. V suffered from a mental illness. V broke into C's home under a mistaken impression and started to rearrange the property. C was away but on his return D and a number of others spent six hours cleaning the property up. About two weeks later, C locked V out and ignored him. At about 10.15 am, some family friends summoned D to help and he arrived with a farm vehicle which had a spade in it. D went to confront V with the spade. An argument broke out during which D stuck V with the spade to the left side of the head. V was knocked to the ground, and D struck him again on the top and back of his head as V lay on the ground. D left to carry on working on the farm. D returned about an hour later to recover a broken-down van but did not check on V. At about 1 pm, C called V's mental health team and said V was lying in the garden. An ambulance was called at about 2.40 pm. V was found unconscious with severe head injuries. He died three weeks later. D, aged 75 at his appeal, was of impeccable character. He was in robust health. The Judge found D had lost his temper and started at 15 years. He reduced that to 12 years because of D's character. It was contended that the minimum term did not properly reflect D's age. Held. If the minimum term imposed by the Judge is to stand, D will not be released until he is, at the earliest, 86. D's age justifies a further reduction to **9 years**.
See also: *R v Horseman* 2007 EWCA Crim 2589 (Aged 65. The impact of a life sentence must be greater so we take it into account.)
R v Symmons 2009 EWCA Crim 1304 (Aged 62. That is a factor but it cannot be determinative of the finishing point.)
Diminished responsibility see MANSLAUGHTER *Diminished responsibility* at **284.24**.

288.86   *Good character*
R v Simmons 2006 EWCA Crim 1259, 2007 1 Cr App R (S) 27 (p 140) D was convicted of murder. He believed on the flimsiest of evidence that V had raped his ex-girlfriend. After planning, he lured V to his home, killed him, cut up his body and disposed of it in

---

[710] The neutral citation in the Cr App R (S) report is wrong.

a lake. He was now aged 35 and admitted drug taking with others. The Judge declined to include his good character as a mitigating factor. Held. Parliament did not intend that the lists of aggravating and mitigating factors were exhaustive. Good character could be a factor. Here, however, as his lifestyle could hardly be described as unblemished, it was not a factor.

Note: This is an old case but it is in line with current sentencing practice. Ed.

288.87   *Mental disorder or mental disability, Defendant suffering from   Statute and judicial guidance*

Criminal Justice Act 2003 Sch 21 para 11 Mitigating factors that may be relevant include:

   c) the fact that the offender suffered from any mental disorder or mental disability which (although not falling within Homicide Act 1957 s 2(1)) lowered his degree of culpability.

R v Coonan (formerly Sutcliffe) 2011 EWCA Crim 5 In 1981 D, known as 'the Yorkshire Ripper', was convicted of 13 counts of murder. He had earlier pleaded to seven counts of attempted murder. The defence asserted in respect of the murder counts was diminished responsibility. This was rejected by the jury. The sentencing Judge imposed mandatory life for the murder counts, and discretionary life for the attempt counts. There was a minimum term of 30 years set. In 2010, the Home Secretary made a reference to the High Court for the minimum term to be set under Criminal Justice Act 2003 s 276. D was subject to a whole life minimum term. He appealed. It was argued on behalf of D that, in accordance with Criminal Justice Act 2003 Sch 21 para 11, D's mental disorder should have been taken into account by the High Court and that his minimum term ought to have been reduced to reflect his reduced culpability. Criminal Justice Act 2003 Sch 22 provides that where the seriousness of an offence or offences associated with it is 'exceptionally high', the starting point is a whole life order. Against this background D appealed. Held. The Court of Appeal was bound by the decision of the jury. Notwithstanding that the offender failed to establish that his responsibility was substantially diminished for the purposes of the partial defence, if he in fact suffered from mental disorder or disability which lowered his degree of culpability then this may provide an element of mitigation. We agree that it does not inexorably follow from the verdict of the jury that, for the purposes of assessing the minimum term, the potential mitigation was excluded from further consideration. If the reasoning for the whole life order proceeded on the basis that the decision by the jury that D had failed to establish diminished responsibility meant that the issue whether he suffered from relevant mental disorder or disability capable of providing mitigation was resolved against the appellant, the statute was misread.

The question is whether D was subject to mental disability or disorder which did in fact constitute any, and if so how much, mitigation for his offences. In other words, such disorders do not of themselves automatically lower the degree of the offender's culpability: often they will, but not necessarily. The entire case, whether of substantial impairment of responsibility for the purposes of trial, or indeed mental disorder as potential mitigation for the purposes of paragraph 11(c) of Schedule 21, depended and continued to depend on D's assertion that his actions were the result, as he genuinely believed, of divine inspiration. It is clear to us that this account was rejected by the jury. There is…no reason to conclude that D's claim that he genuinely believed that he was acting under divine instruction to fulfil God's will carries any greater conviction now than it did when it was rejected by the jury. This was criminal conduct at the extreme end of horror. Each of the attempted murders, as well as each of the murder offences, taken on its own was a dreadful crime of utmost brutality: taking all the offences together, we have been considering an accumulation of criminality of exceptional magnitude which went far beyond the legislative criteria for a whole life order. Even accepting that an element of mental disturbance was intrinsic to the commission of these crimes, the interests of justice require nothing less than a whole life order. That is the only available punishment proportionate to these crimes.

R v Langlands 2011 EWCA Crim 1880 D was convicted of murder, having had a plea to manslaughter rejected. He lived with V, his 83-year-old grandmother. She had given him around £30,000 as a result of pressure he had put on her. There was evidence that he verbally abused her. Days before the offence, he was under a delusional belief that he was dying of cancer, and told a number of people so. He had sought medical help and told staff about his alcohol and cocaine consumption. D returned home and in the kitchen repeatedly stabbed V. He then kicked her as she lay on the ground. He then left the house, discarded his blood-stained clothing and spent two days attempting to cover his tracks. He suffered from paranoid psychosis caused by his own ingestion of alcohol and cocaine. D was aged 27 and had no significant offences. Held. This was an appalling case. The aggravating features were much more powerful than the mitigation: a) V's vulnerability, b) the offence occurred in V's home, c) the abuse of trust, d) the verbal abuse, e) the intention to kill, f) the degree of planning, and g) the frenzied, brutal and sustained nature of the attack. **22-year minimum term** had sufficient credit for his diminished responsibility.

See also: *R v Levey* 2012 EWCA Crim 657 (Late plea. Complex and severe personality disorder. Inflicted 25 stab wounds after telling someone the day before he was going to kill someone. History of violent offences and knives. Start at 25 years. Judge made insufficient allowance for his mental state. With aggravating and mitigation features, 26 years. With plea, **22 years** not 24.)

Old cases: Best ignored.

288.88   *Previous conviction for murder or manslaughter*

Criminal Justice Act 2003 Sch 21 para 4(1) If:
    a) the court considers that the seriousness of the offence (or combination of the offence and one or more offences associated with it) is exceptionally high, and
    b) the offender was aged 21 or over when he committed the offence,
the appropriate starting point is a whole life order.
(2) Cases that would normally fall within para 4(1) include:
    d) a murder by an offender previously convicted of murder.

R v Brady and Paton 2006 EWCA Crim 2780, 2007 1 Cr App R 719 P pleaded to murder and section 18 assault. P had a serious record including 15 theft and related offences including two robberies, three offences relating to the police and one drugs offence. His most serious offence was manslaughter. The defence argued that not too much weight should be attached to the manslaughter conviction as that will be considered when there is discussion about his release. Held. We do not agree. The minimum term must be served by way of punishment for these offences against the background of the record and the conviction for manslaughter. The fact he had killed before must weigh very heavily in the Judge's mind.

Note: This is an old case but these principles continue to be applied. Ed.

R v Vinter 2009 EWCA Crim 1399, 2010 1 Cr App R (S) 58 (p 368) LCJ D pleaded to murder. In 1996 he was convicted of the murder of a work colleague. D stabbed him with a knife 13 times. His minimum term was 10 years. On home leave, he met V and they began a relationship. In 2005 he was released on licence and moved in with V and her four children. In 2006 they married. V's friends and family had concerns about domestic violence as they had seen her with injuries. In 2006 D was involved in a fight with several men in a pub, and his licence was revoked. D was charged with affray and received 6 months' imprisonment. In December 2007, because he was a model prisoner, he was released on licence. He returned to his wife, and at the end of January 2008 she told a friend she wanted to leave D, but was too frightened to do so. On 5 February 2008, D emptied all the cupboards in the house, damaged the TV and removed V's passport. He moved out and went to live with his mother. On 10 February 2008 he went drinking with three of his friends. One said that he also took cocaine. V went to four pubs and left each time because D kept appearing. D anticipated that V would return to the pub where her daughter collected the glasses. V asked the door staff to keep an eye on D to ensure that there was no trouble. This, and the fact that V's daughter was sending V text messages about D, irritated D. Trouble flared up, and the door staff intervened. D warned them off, and they backed off. In the car park an argument developed between D and V, and V's daughter tried to persuade V to go home with her. D took extreme exception to this. The daughter called the police, and D ordered V to get in his friend's car. The daughter tried to get in but D removed her and dumped her on the pavement. The argument continued. D was alleging that V had been unfaithful. He took V to his mother's home. The police and a friend contacted V on the phone, and each time she assured them that she was OK. At 1.36 am D phoned the police to say that V was OK. D killed V with a knife. At 2.30 am D called two of his friends and demanded that they pick him up. He then contacted the police to report a murder. D's mother found V's body in her kitchen. V had a broken nose, deep and extensive bruising to the neck consistent with a serious attempt at strangulation, and four stab wounds. In interview D admitted the killing. D was aged 39. Held. This violence had an element of premeditation. D deliberately put the police off track. He intended the death. He kidnapped her. There was no reason to depart from the normal principle that it should be a **whole life** term.

R v Khaleel 2012 EWCA Crim 2035, 2013 1 Cr App R (S) 122 (p 629) LCJ D was convicted of murder. He was aged 39 at his appeal. D met V, a 69-year-old homosexual, on three occasions. D's interest might have been commercial. V enjoyed short-term relationships with Asian or Mediterranean men. V was found at his home lying on his back wearing a pair of boxer shorts. He had a large stab wound on the back of his head and neck with multiple other stab wounds. At the time, D was on licence, having been released from prison following a conviction for manslaughter which was committed in strikingly similar circumstances. The jury in that case accepted that D might have lost his self-control as a result of provocation. The Judge took into account in the second case that there was no evidence of planning, but the attack was ferocious and he considered it a cold-blooded execution. The Judge considered the previous conviction as a highly aggravating factor. The Judge started at 30 years. The defence said he should have started at 15 years and not treated the conviction as an aggravating factor. Held. All we are deciding is whether the previous conviction for manslaughter may lead the Judge to treat a subsequent offence of murder as an offence of particularly high seriousness. Here the Judge was entitled so to do. If the Judge had started at 15 years he would have been entitled to pass a term very close to 30 years. Because the murder was not planned, **28 years** not 33.

See also: *R v Edgington* 2013 EWCA Crim 2185 (In 2006 convicted of manslaughter and given Hospital Order. Stabbed mother in her house. Released in 2009. In 2013, convicted of murder and attempted murder. She left hospital after asking for help, went by bus to an ASDA store. Bought knife and ferociously attacked passer-by in street. Stabbed another passer-by, previous mental health difficulties. **37-year minimum term** upheld.)

For linked paragraphs see the **Previous convictions** entry in the back index.

288.89   *Progress in prison, Exceptional*

Note: This was a factor considered when the court was reviewing sentences passed before Criminal Justice Act 2003 came into force. For details, see this paragraph in the 3rd edition of this book. Ed.

R v J 2008 EWCA Crim 2437, 2009 1 Cr App R (S) 108 (p 605) D was convicted of murder. She was aged 15. Held. We have not taken into account the good progress she has made in the secure training centre. The minimum term has to be set according to the 'seriousness of the offence'. Good progress cannot be relevant to the seriousness of the offence. Following *R v Caines* 2006 EWCA Crim 2915, good progress can only be taken into account in exceptional circumstances. Good behaviour is not enough to constitute exceptional progress.

R v Gill and Others 2011 EWCA Crim 2795, 2012 EWCA Crim 26 (p 136) LCJ The defendants were convicted of murder. They appealed the minimum terms that were specified as part of their mandatory life sentences (under Criminal Justice Act 2003 Sch 22 para 3 or 6 relating to transitional cases) on the basis that they had made exceptional progress after spending a number of years in custody. Held. A reduction in the length of the minimum term could take account of exceptional progress made whilst in custody. However, possible reductions for exceptional progress in prison do not form part of any appeal process for sentences imposed after 18 December 2003. Any reduction in the minimum term to reflect exceptional progress should not realistically be considered until towards the end of the minimum period.

Whole life orders
288.90   *Whole life orders   Basic principles*
Criminal Justice Act 2003 s 269(4) If the offender was 21 or over when he committed the offence and the court is of the opinion that, because of the seriousness of the offence, or of the combination of the offence and one or more offences associated with it, no order should be made under subsection (2) [the early release provisions], the court must order that the early release provisions are not to apply to the offender.
Criminal Justice Act 2003 Sch 21 para 4(1) If:
  a) the court considers that the seriousness of the offence (or combination of the offence and one or more offences associated with it) is exceptionally high, and
  b) the offender was aged 21 or over when he committed the offence, the appropriate starting point is a whole life order.
(2) Cases that would normally fall within sub-paragraph (1)(a) include:
  a) the murder of two or more persons, where each[711] murder involves any of the following: i) a substantial degree of premeditation or planning, ii) the abduction of the victim, or iii) sexual or sadistic conduct,
  b) the murder of a child if involving the abduction of the child or sexual or sadistic motivation.
  ba) the murder of a police officer or prison officer in the course of his or her duty.[712]
  c) a murder done for the purpose of advancing a political, religious, racial[713] or ideological cause, or
  d) a murder by an offender previously convicted of murder.
Criminal Practice Directions 2015 EWCA Crim 1567 para VII M.5 Where the offender was 21 or over at the time of the offence, and the court takes the view that the murder is so grave that the offender ought to spend the rest of his life in prison, the appropriate starting point is a 'whole life order', Criminal Justice Act 2003 Sch 21 para 4(1). The effect of such an order is that the early release provisions in Crime (Sentences) Act 1997 s 28 will not apply. Such an order should only be specified where the court considers that the seriousness of the offence (or the combination of the offence and one or more other offences associated with it) is exceptionally high. Paragraph 4(2) sets out examples of cases where it would normally be appropriate to take the 'whole life order' as the appropriate starting point.
R v Jones 2005 EWCA Crim 3115, 2006 2 Cr App R (S) 19 (p 121) at 131 para 10 A whole life order should be imposed where the seriousness of the offending is so exceptionally high that just punishment requires the offender to be kept in prison for the

---

[711] There is clearly a drafting error here. It would be absurd if two abduction murders trigger the whole life provisions but four abduction murders and one non-abduction murder do not. Ed.
[712] Inserted by Criminal Justice and Courts Act 2015 s 27(1)-(2). In force 13/11/15. The provision only applies to offences committed after the section is in force, Criminal Justice and Courts Act 2015 s 27(4).
[713] The word 'racial' was inserted in the sub-section by Counter-Terrorism Act 2008 s 75(1) and (2)(c). In force 16/2/09, Counter-Terrorism Act 2008 (Commencement No 2) Order 2009 2009/58

rest of his or her life. Often, perhaps usually, where such an order is called for, the case will not be on the borderline. The facts of the case, considered as a whole, will leave the Judge in no doubt that the offender must be kept in prison for the rest of his or her life. To be imprisoned for a finite period of 30 years or more is a very severe penalty. If the case includes one or more of the factors set out in paragraph 4(2) it is likely to be a case that calls for a whole life order, but the Judge must consider all the material facts before concluding that a very lengthy finite term will not be a sufficiently severe penalty. Where a whole life order is called for, the case will not be on the borderline. If the Judge is in doubt, this may well indicate that a finite minimum term which leaves open the possibility that the offender may be released for the final years of his or her life is appropriate.

R v Randall 2007 EWCA Crim 2257, 2008 1 Cr App R (S) 93 (p 556) D pleaded to murder. Held. Vile and grave as the abuse was, it was not at the very top end of the scale. The imposition of a whole life tariff should be reserved for cases where the need for it is clear cut. The sentencer should be left in no doubt that such a course is necessary.

R v Reynolds and Rosser 2014 EWCA Crim 2205, 2015 1 Cr App R (S) 24 (p 174) LCJ D and R pleaded to murder (little or no credit). Each case fell under Criminal Justice Act 2003 Sch 21 para 4(2)(b) in that in each the victims were children and there was a sadistic motivation. For D1 there was also a sexual motivation to his actions. Held. We emphasise four points: a) the guidance given in Schedule 21 is provided to assist the judge to determine the appropriate sentence. The judge must have regard to the guidance but each case will depend critically on its particular facts, b) where a whole life order is called for, often, perhaps usually, the case will not be on the borderline. The facts will leave the judge in no doubt that the defendant must be kept in prison for the rest of his life, c) the court should consider the fact that the defendant has pleaded guilty to murder [on its own] when deciding whether it is appropriate to order a whole life term. The *Reduction in Sentence for a Guilty Plea Guideline* 2007, which states (in its revision) at paragraph 6.6.1, 'Where a court determines that there should be a whole life minimum term, there will be no reduction for a guilty plea', must be read along with the observations in *R v Jones* 2005 EWCA Crim 3115, 2006 2 Cr App R (S) 19 (p 121), d) the whole life order is reserved for the few exceptionally serious offences where, after reflecting on all the features of aggravation and mitigation, the judge is satisfied that the element of just punishment requires the imposition of a whole life order.

When with a mental disorder, see *Mental disorder or mental disability, Defendant suffering from* paras at **288.87**.

For a history of whole life orders, see *Att-Gen's Ref No 69 of 2013* 2014 EWCA Crim 188, 2014 2 Cr App R (S) 40 (p 321) LCJ at para 1.

288.91   *Whole life orders   Defendant aged under 21*
Note: Whole life orders are not available for those aged under 21, see Schedule 21 para 4(b) above. For the starting points for those defendants see **288.12**. Ed.

288.92   *Whole life orders   Article 3*
Vinter and Others v UK 2013 No 66069/09 ECtHR Grand Chamber Three defendants contended their whole life tariffs were incompatible with article 3. Held. para 110 There are a number of reasons why for a life sentence to remain compatible with article 3, there must be both a prospect of release and a prospect of review. para 120 We observe that the comparative and international law materials show clear support for the institution of a dedicated mechanism guaranteeing a review no later than 25 years after the imposition of a life sentence, with further periodic reviews thereafter. para 125 There is a lack of clarity concerning the prospect of release of life prisoners. para 130 The requirements of article 3 have not been met for any of the three defendants.

R v Oakes 2013 EWCA Crim 2982 LCJ para 6 Every civilised country also embraces the principle that just punishment is appropriate for those convicted of criminal offences. The assessment of what should be deemed to constitute just punishment or inhuman or degrading punishment in a particular circumstance can legitimately produce different answers in different countries, and indeed different answers at different times in the same country. Whole life reflects the settled will of Parliament. para 22 It is clear that the European Court has proceeded on the basis that a whole life order imposed as a matter of judicial discretion as to the appropriate level of punishment and deterrence following conviction for a crime of utmost seriousness would not constitute inhuman or degrading punishment. No one doubts that a whole life minimum term is a Draconian penalty, or indeed that it is the order of last resort reserved for cases of exceptionally serious criminality.

Att-Gen's Ref No 69 of 2013 2014 EWCA Crim 188, 2014 2 Cr App R (S) 40 (p 321) LCJ (five-judge court) N pleaded guilty to murder and robbery. Whilst serving a life sentence for murder, he murdered someone when he was on day release. The Judge sentenced him to 40 years believing whole life was unlawful. The prosecution appealed. Held. para 17 No specific passage in *Vinter v UK* 2012 impugns the provisions of Criminal Justice Act 2003 Sch 21 which entitle a judge to make at the time of sentence a whole life order as a sentence reflecting just punishment... para 29 The domestic law of England and Wales is clear as to 'possible exceptional release of whole life prisoners'. As is set out in *R v Bieber* 2008, the Secretary of State is bound to exercise his power under Crime (Sentences) Act 1997 s 30 in a manner compatible with principles of domestic administrative law and with article 3. para 30 [In *Vinter v UK* 2012] it might have been thought that the fact that policy set out in the *Lifer Manual* has not been revised is of real consequence. However, as a matter of law, it is of no consequence. para 31 First, the power of review under the section arises if there are exceptional circumstances. It is not necessary to specify what such circumstances are or specify criteria; the term 'exceptional circumstances' is of itself sufficiently certain. para 32 Second, the Secretary of State must then consider whether such exceptional circumstances justify the release on compassionate grounds. The policy set out in the *Lifer Manual* is highly restrictive and purports to circumscribe the matters which will be considered by the Secretary of State. The Manual cannot restrict the duty of the Secretary of State to consider all circumstances relevant to release on compassionate grounds. para 33 Third, the term 'compassionate grounds' must be read, as the Court made clear in *R v Bieber*, in a manner compatible with article 3. They are not restricted to what is set out in the *Lifer Manual*. It is a term with a wide meaning that can be elucidated, as is the way the common law develops, on a case-by-case basis. para 34 Fourth, the decision of the Secretary of State must be reasoned by reference to the circumstances of each case and is subject to scrutiny by way of judicial review... para 35 The law of England and Wales therefore does provide to an offender 'hope' or the 'possibility' of release in exceptional circumstances which render the just punishment originally imposed no longer justifiable... para 37 Judges should continue to apply the statutory scheme and in exceptional cases, likely to be rare, impose whole life orders in accordance with Schedule 21.

Hutchinson v UK 2015 No 57592/08 ECtHR Fourth Section (6-1 decision) D was convicted of three murders, aggravated burglary and rape in 1984. He was sentenced to life with an 18-year minimum. The Secretary of State imposed whole life in 1994. D had argued that his case was indistinguishable from *Vinter and Others v UK* 2013 No 66069/ 09. All D's appeals failed, including to the Court of Appeal in 2008 and the ECtHR. Since then, *Att-Gen's Ref No 69 of 2013* 2014 EWCA Crim 188, 2014 2 Cr App R (S) 40 (p 321) was decided. Held. In *Vinter and Others v UK* 2013 No 66069/09 the ECtHR held that the law was unclear regarding the existence of an article 3 compliant review mechanism for whole life sentences. However, in *Att-Gen's Ref No 69 of 2013* 2014 EWCA Crim 188, 2014 2 Cr App R (S) 40 (p 321), the Court of Appeal found that the Secretary of State's power to release under Criminal Justice Act 2003 s 30 functioned in precisely the way which the Grand Chamber held was in principle sufficient to render a whole life order reducible and this was compatible with article 3. The Court of Appeal was uniquely well placed to determine this issue and its judgment had put to rest any suggestion that domestic law was in any relevant respect unclear. The national court has specifically addressed those doubts [about the clarity of domestic law] and set out an unequivocal statement of the legal position. [This] Court must accept the national court's interpretation of domestic law. There was no violation of article 3.

Old cases: *R (Wellington) v Secretary of State for the Home Department* 2008 UKHL 720 (Lords Extradition case. The prescribed penalty was death or life without parole. The prosecutor gave an undertaking not to apply for the death penalty. Held. A sentence of whole life would not infringe European Convention on Human Rights art 3.)

R v Bieber 2008 EWCA Crim 1601 (We do not consider that a whole life term should be considered as a sentence that is irreducible. Any article 3 challenge should be made not at the time of the imposition of the sentence but at the stage where the prisoner contends that any further detention will constitute inhuman or degrading treatment. See **288.55** for a fuller report.)

288.93 *Whole life orders   Cases*

R v McGrady 2007 EWCA Crim 192, 2 Cr App R (S) 56 (p 347) D pleaded to murder. He misused alcohol and was sometimes unable to ejaculate during intercourse. He had sex with a woman, and then said that his penis was still hard and he was going to have to go out and look for someone. Shortly afterwards at around 7 pm the victim, V, a 15-year-old girl, phoned her mother but was not heard of after that. Three days later, D's girlfriend called the police. They found D lying on a bed with injuries to his wrists and other parts. The girlfriend said that he had told her that he had killed someone and showed her the body. She took the officers to a pile of bin bags by some external stairs to the flat. V's dismembered body was in the bags. There were also notes confessing to the killing and expressing remorse. A post-mortem showed that the cause of death was strangulation. Injuries showed that V had done her best to defend herself. There was no evidence available to show whether or not there had been any sexual element to the attack. There was a victim impact statement from the girl's mother in which she explained how her life had been devastated. That was exacerbated by not knowing how, why or when D had murdered her daughter. He made no material comment in interview or at any point thereafter, saying that he could not remember what happened. D, aged 48, was sentenced to 6 years in 1988 for rape and indecent assault. In a drunken state he forced two women into a bedroom at knifepoint. He raped one of them, deliberately applying pressure to her windpipe, and said that he would kill her if she didn't do what he said. He attempted to bugger the other one. In 1993 he was sentenced to 5 years for false imprisonment. Again drunk, he grabbed a woman as she got off a bus and dragged her towards a wall. She believed that she was going to be raped but managed to escape from him. A psychiatrist found no evidence of mental illness. He hesitated to accept that he had no memory of the events. The report said that he was a high-risk offender and that there was a high risk of further violent and sexual offences. A pre-sentence report said that the risk of serious harm to the public was high. Held. We do not accept that D has no memory of the offence. We are doubtful of his expression of remorse. If he were truly sorry he would have something to tell the family of the victim as to what happened. This was the murder of a child for his own sexual purposes. He must have known exactly what he was doing when he strangled her. It involves serious force, and he intended that she should die. This was not the first time that he had applied manual pressure to the throat of a young woman. After she was dead he subjected her body to the gross indignity of dismemberment, intending to erase evidence of guilt. This case fell plainly within the rare example for which the statutory starting point was a **whole life order**.

R v Randall 2007 EWCA Crim 2257, 2008 1 Cr App R (S) 93 (p 556) D pleaded to section 18 wounding, murder, and four counts of sexual activity with a child family member. The victim of each count was his daughter, V, aged seven weeks when she died. She was premature and had a heart defect. Her mother suffered from schizophrenia. V was taken to hospital a number of times suffering from various ailments such as sickness and coughing. Doctors noticed bruising and scratching, and social services became involved. Shortly after this the mother called the emergency services to the home, and the baby died shortly afterwards. The cause of death was a fractured skull. The pathologist said that there was evidence of earlier head injury. She had 16 rib fractures aged from one to five weeks. In interview D said that he had abused and in his words 'tortured' V from the time she was two or three weeks old. He had shaken her, tried to suffocate her by squeezing her nose, dropped her from a height on about 12 occasions, and sometimes thrown her against the back of an armchair or sofa when he was angry because she was crying. He had kicked her across the carpet and stamped on her chest, and at least once he had heard something snap. In the evening before she died, he had placed his hand over her mouth and brought her to the point of suffocation. He had shaken her violently, he had put his fingers down her throat to shut her up and he had slapped her. He said that the skull fracture was likely to have been caused by his holding her head against the sofa and pushing it whilst applying pressure. He said that he had not intended to kill her. The section 18 was that, on a number of occasions, he had gripped and shaken her, put his hand over her mouth, flicked her nose and ears, stamped on her and gripped her chest, causing fractures. The sexual offences were that when V was about three weeks old he had inserted his finger into her anus as far as his second knuckle and had touched her inappropriately around her vagina while changing her nappy, and on two or three occasions he had rubbed his penis against her mouth. He said he had thought about killing her and others every day. He had thought about killing his partner. He thought about torturing and imprisoning women, and hurting and killing as many people as he could. He had thought that he would kill someone, but he did not think it would be his daughter. D, aged 34, had no previous convictions. A psychiatric report noted that he denied any intention to kill. He had long-standing sadistic and violent fantasies. There was no evidence of current mental illness, but he might have an underlying depressive disorder. There was no history of aggression towards his partner or others. The report said that he was unable to maintain relationships or develop a meaningful self-identity. He could not cope with being the main carer for his wife and a sickly baby daughter. It was quite likely that he had contradictory feelings towards his daughter including love, anger and resentment. Held. We cannot accept the Judge's analysis that there was a sexual element to the murder. There was no safe evidence that what happened on the day of her death involved sexual activity or motivation. The psychiatric report indicated that the case is a complex one, and there is a degree of ambiguity about what led D to kill his daughter. The fantasising amounted to premeditation, and it is safe to conclude that he had an intention to kill at the time of the murder. Vile and grave as the abuse was, it was not at the very top end of the scale. The imposition of a whole life tariff should be reserved for cases where the need for it is clear cut. The aggravating features are plain: the brutal and cruel acts, the breach of trust, V's vulnerability, her tender age, the course of serious violent and sexual misconduct, the pain and suffering inflicted, the premeditation. There is some mitigation in the plea and lack of previous convictions: **30-year minimum term**, not whole life tariff.

R v Bieber 2008 EWCA Crim 1601 D was convicted of one count of murder, two counts of attempted murder and two counts of possession of a firearm with intent to endanger life. He was in a badly parked stolen car, and two police officers on routine patrol approached because the car's tax disc was not genuine. He was put in their patrol car and, after a check had been made on the car, they told him that he was under arrest. A recovery vehicle arrived to remove the car, and a third officer arrived to take D to the police station. All three officers (B, R and A) went to the car door to handcuff him. He produced a handgun and fired five times. The first shot hit B in the chest. The second hit R, who had turned to run, in the lower back. The third hit both R and A, both now running. B was lying on the ground, and D stood over him and shot him in the head. D ran off with the gun. He approached a car and pointed the gun at the passenger. That car drove off. Holding the gun, D approached a second car and the people in it ran off, leaving him to take the car. The Judge said that the aggravating feature leading him to impose a whole life tariff was the shot to the head of B, which made certain of his death. (D's age and character are not mentioned.) Held. The case fell within the 30-year starting point for two reasons: because the murder was of a police officer, and it involved the use of a firearm. The fact that two criteria were present is a possible reason for raising the term above the 30-year starting point. Added to this is the effect of the associated offences of attempting to murder two other police officers, which justified a substantial increment above the 30-year starting point. It must be remembered that the 30-year point already assumes an intention to kill. The criminal conduct was committed within a space of some eight seconds. Horrifying though this was, a minimum term of **37 years**, not a whole life tariff.

Att-Gen's Ref No 69 of 2013 2014 EWCA Crim 188, 2014 2 Cr App R (S) 40 (p 321) LCJ (five-judge court) N was convicted of murder and theft. Whilst serving a sentence, N and his fellow prisoners considered V, a prisoner who had been convicted of killing a young child, was worthy of particular condemnation. N and S followed V into his cell and engaged the privacy lock. Each had with them, as improvised weapons, a sharpened toothbrush and a pen. They told V they were going to hold him hostage to bargain with the prison authorities. This was merely a pretence to ensure that V did not resist when they tied him up with Sellotape. Once tied up, N used V's tracksuit bottoms as a ligature to strangle him to death. It took significantly in excess of 30 seconds to achieve. When asked why they had done it, N and S replied that they were bored and it was something to do. N was later found wearing V's watch and the Judge considered that N regarded this as a trophy. N was aged 45 at his appeal. In 1989, D had been convicted of murder after gaining entry to a house by deception and after demanding money from the occupier, strangled her to death. He received a 15-year minimum term but was not released. Held. There was no mitigation. This was a second offence of murder and the seriousness was exceptionally high. A **whole life order** was not manifestly excessive.

R v Reynolds and Rosser 2014 EWCA Crim 2205, 2015 1 Cr App R (S) 24 (p 174) LCJ D (very little credit) and R pleaded. D was aged 22 and had also committed three much less serious, but similar incidents before. He was obsessed with sexual violence against women and suffered from recurrent intense sexual urges. He would continue to pose a grave risk to women for the rest of his life. R was aged 33 with several antecedents, including for minor violence. He had an antisocial personality disorder, was dependent on alcohol and was psychopathic. Held. In R's case, a plea of guilty had no relevance to the whole life order. **Whole life** orders in each case upheld.

Note: The Lord Chief Justice asked that the details of the murders should not be distributed, see *R v Reynolds and Rossiter* 2014 EWCA Crim 2317 (post judgment). Ed. See also: *R v Henson and Magraw* 2007 EWCA Crim 1308, 2008 1 Cr App R (S) 19 (p 83) (Aged 20. Not whole life. **35 years.**) See **288.33**.

R v Mullen 2008 EWCA Crim 592, 2 Cr App R (S) 88 (p 501) (The case plainly fell within this category.) See **288.32**.

R v Vinter 2009 EWCA Crim 1399, 2010 1 Cr App R (S) 58 (p 368) (LCJ Previous conviction for murder. Whole life, see **288.88**).

R v Coonan (formerly Sutcliffe) 2011 EWCA Crim 5 (Yorkshire Ripper. 13 murders. This was the extreme end of horror. Whole life upheld.) See **288.87**.

Old cases: *R v Kunowski* 2005 EWCA Crim 2139, 2006 1 Cr App R (S) 81 (p 469) (Sexual with sexual previous. Whole life.) *R v Jones* 2005 EWCA Crim 3115, 2006 2 Cr App R (S) 19 (p 121) at 141 (Four murders. Whole life.) *R v McDowell* 2006 EWCA Crim 1836, 2007 1 Cr App R (S) 56 (p 320) (**20 years**)

For a summary of the last case, see the 8th edition of this book.

See also the **MANSLAUGHTER** *Life sentences Whole life order* paras at **240.3**.

For whole life in cases other than murder and manslaughter, see **75.16**.

The sentence

Global sentences see the CONCURRENT OR CONSECUTIVE SENTENCES *Defendant serving a determinate sentence Life suitable* para at **19.13** in Volume 1.

288.94   *Discount for time on remand/bail*

Criminal Justice Act 2003 s 269(3)[714] The part of his sentence [meaning the minimum term] is to be such as the court considers appropriate taking into account:..b) the effect of Criminal Justice Act 2003 s 240ZA (crediting periods of remand in custody) or of any direction which it would have given under Criminal Justice Act 2003 s 240A (crediting periods of remand on certain types of bail) if it had sentenced him to a term of imprisonment.

Criminal Practice Directions 2015 EWCA Crim 1567 para VII M.13 The third step is that the court should consider the effect of Criminal Justice Act 2003 s 143(2) in relation to previous convictions (see **86.2** in Volume 1), Criminal Justice Act 2003 s 143(3) where the offence was committed whilst the offender was on bail; and Criminal Justice Act 2003 s 144 where the offender has pleaded guilty (Schedule 21 paragraph 12). The court should then take into account what credit the offender would have received for a remand in custody under Criminal Justice Act 2003 s 240 or 240ZA and/or for a remand on bail subject to a qualifying curfew condition under section 240A, but for the fact that the mandatory sentence is one of life imprisonment. Where the offender has been thus remanded in connection with the offence or a related offence, the court should have in mind that no credit will otherwise be given for this time when the prisoner is considered for early release. The appropriate time to take it into account is when setting the minimum term. The court should make any appropriate subtraction from the punitive period it would otherwise impose, in order to reach the minimum term.

288.95   *Funeral expenses of the deceased, Power to make an order for compensation for the*

Powers of Criminal Courts (Sentencing) Act 2000 s 130(1) The court may on application or otherwise make an order requiring him to make payments for funeral expenses or bereavement in respect of a death resulting from an offence other than death due to an accident arising out of the presence of a motor vehicle on a road.

Powers of Criminal Courts (Sentencing) Act 2000 s 130(3) A court shall give reasons if it does not make a compensation order in a case where this section empowers it to do so.

Note: The current specified amount is £12,980.[715] Ed.

R v Williams 1989 Unreported 10/3/89 It is important that sentencers bear in mind the words (which had just been added to the then statute) giving the court power to order compensation for funeral expenses. If the court decides not to order compensation, it must give its reasons.

288.96   *Judge explaining the sentence/Suggested sentencing remarks*

Criminal Practice Directions 2015 EWCA Crim 1567 para VII P.1 Having gone through the three or four steps outlined above, the court is then under a duty, under [Criminal Justice Act 2003 s 270], to state in open court, in ordinary language, its reasons for deciding on the minimum term or for passing a whole life order.

P.2 In order to comply with this duty, the court should state clearly the minimum term it has determined. In doing so, it should state which of the starting points it has chosen and its reasons for doing so. Where the court has departed from that starting point due to mitigating or aggravating features, it must state the reasons for that departure and any aggravating or mitigating features which have led to that departure. At that point, the court should also declare how much, if any, time is being deducted for time spent in custody and/or on bail subject to a qualifying curfew condition. The court must then

---

[714] As amended by Legal Aid, Sentencing and Punishment of Offenders Act 2012 s 110(10)

[715] See Fatal Accidents Act 1976 s 1A(3) and Damages for Bereavement (Variation of Sum) (England and Wales) Order 2013 2013/510 para 2. For deaths before 1/4/13 the figure is £11,800, Damages for Bereavement (Variation of Sum) (England and Wales) Order 2007 2007/3489 para 2.

explain that the minimum term is the minimum amount of time the prisoner will spend in prison, from the date of sentence, before the Parole Board can order early release. If it remains necessary for the protection of the public, the prisoner will continue to be detained after that date. The court should also state that where the prisoner has served the minimum term and the Parole Board has decided to direct release, the prisoner will remain on licence for the rest of his life and may be recalled to prison at any time.

P.3 Where the offender was aged 21 or over when he committed the offence and the court considers that the seriousness of the offence is so exceptionally high that a 'whole life order' is appropriate, the court should state clearly its reasons for reaching this conclusion. It should also explain that the early release provisions will not apply.

Crown Court Bench Book 2013 www.banksr.com Other Matters Other Documents page 9 **Passing the sentence** State that the sentence is one of imprisonment for life/custody for life/detention during Her Majesty's Pleasure.

Either, if D is aged 21 or over and it is the case, state that because of the [extreme] seriousness of the offence/combination of offences, the early release provisions are not to apply and so the sentence is a whole life order, 'life means life'.

Or, in any other case, state the minimum term, giving reasons for having fixed it at the level stated, in particular by reference to the applicable provision(s) of Schedule 21 and the aggravating and mitigating factors, e.g. (having given reasons), "...so having regard to all the aggravating and mitigating features in your case, I fix the minimum term which you will serve in custody, before the Parole Board may consider your possible release, at 18 years."

Credit should (almost invariably) be given, in this order, for: any plea of guilty. Example: "...But for your plea of Guilty I would have fixed the minimum term which you would have to serve in custody before you may apply to the Parole Board for your release at [XX] years. Giving you credit for your plea of Guilty, I reduce that by one sixth and fix the minimum term at [XX] years; and any time spent on remand in custody or half the time spent on remand on qualifying electronic curfew." Example "...From this will be deducted the [XX] days which you have already spent on remand in custody so that the minimum term which you will serve is [XX] years and [XX] days."

Explain the consequences: The minimum term will be served in full before the defendant is eligible to be considered for release by the Parole Board. The decision about whether or when he will be released on licence will be taken by the Parole Board upon consideration of the risk(s) of the defendant causing further harm. If the defendant is released he will be on licence for the rest of his life. The licence will be subject to conditions, which will be set at the time of his release, and if he were to break any condition he would be liable to be returned to prison to continue to serve his sentence and may not be released again.

[Sentencing remarks] example: "It is most important that you and everyone concerned with this case should understand what this in fact means. The minimum term is not a fixed term after which you will automatically be released but the minimum time that you will spend in custody before your case can be considered by the Parole Board and it will be for the Parole Board to say, at that time, whether or not you will be released, and if they do not you will remain in custody. If and when you are released you will still be subject to licence, and this will remain the case for the rest of your life. If for any reason your licence were to be revoked, you would be recalled to prison to continue to serve your life sentence in custody."

Appeals

For prosecution appeals and double jeopardy, see the **ATTORNEY-GENERAL'S REFER-ENCES** *Double jeopardy reduction When not available Murder etc.* para at **8.42** in Volume 1.

289   MURDER, ATTEMPTED, CONSPIRACY TO MURDER, ETC.

289.1

1) Attempted murder
   Criminal Attempts Act 1981 s 1(1)
   Mode of trial Indictable only
   Maximum sentence Life[716]

2) Conspiracy to murder
   Criminal Law Act 1977 s 1(1)
   Mode of trial Indictable only
   Maximum sentence Life[717]

3) Soliciting to murder
   Offences Against the Person Act 1861 s 4
   Mode of trial Indictable only
   Maximum sentence Life[718]

Automatic life Conspiracy to murder, attempted murder, soliciting to murder and incitement to murder are listed in Criminal Justice Act 2003 Sch 15B Part 1. The court must (unless the particular circumstances make it unjust[719]) pass automatic life if: a) the defendant is aged 18+ at the date of the conviction, b) the offence was committed on or after 3 December 2012, c) the court considers a determinate sentence of at least 10 years is appropriate, d) at the time the offender was convicted he had a conviction for a Criminal Justice Act 2003 Sch 15B offence, and e) the defendant at the time of his or her conviction had previously been sentenced to either: i) a life sentence where he or she was not eligible for release during the first five years of the sentence, or ii) a determinate sentence or extended sentence where the custodial part was 10 years or more.[720] For a pre-2012 extended sentence, when determining whether the custodial term was 10+ years, the period deducted for time on remand or on a curfew and tag is included.[721]

Extended sentences This offence is listed in Criminal Justice Act 2003 Sch 15. The court may pass a 2012 extended sentence (EDS) if there is a significant risk of serious harm from future specified offences and either: a) the defendant has a Criminal Justice Act 2003 Sch 15B conviction (applicable only to defendants aged 18+), or b) the offence would justify a determinate sentence of at least 4 years.[722]

Sexual Harm Prevention Orders There is a discretionary power to make this order when it is necessary to protect the public from sexual harm.[723]

Children and vulnerable adults: barred lists Where the defendant is convicted of attempted murder, conspiracy to murder, incitement to murder or aiding, abetting, counselling or procuring murder and is aged 18 or over, he or she is automatically barred from engaging in regulated activity with children and with vulnerable adults.[724] The Judge must tell the defendant that the Disclosure and Barring Service will include him or her in the barred lists.[725] The defendant may ask the Authority to remove him or her from the lists.

289.2   *Crown Court statistics   England and Wales*

Attempted murder Aged 21+

---

[716] Criminal Attempts Act 1981 s 4(1)(a)
[717] Criminal Law Act 1977 s 3(1)(a) and 3(2)(a)
[718] Offences Against the Person Act 1861 s 4
[719] Criminal Justice Act 2003 s 224A(2)
[720] Criminal Justice Act 2003 s 224A as inserted by Legal Aid, Sentencing and Punishment of Offenders Act 2012 s 122. The condition for a) is at section 224A(1)(a), for b) is at section 224A(1)(b), for c) is at section 224A(1)(c), and for d) is at section 224A(4)-(9).
[721] Criminal Justice Act 2003 s 224A(9)-(10)
[722] Criminal Justice Act 2003 s 226A-226B as inserted by Legal Aid, Sentencing and Punishment of Offenders Act 2012 s 124
[723] Sexual Offences Act 2003 s 103A as inserted by Anti-social Behaviour, Crime and Policing Act 2014 Sch 5 para 2 and Sexual Offences Act 2003 Sch 5
[724] Safeguarding Vulnerable Groups Act 2006 s 2 and Sch 3 and Safeguarding Vulnerable Groups Act 2006 (Prescribed Criteria and Miscellaneous Provisions) Regulations 2009 2009/37 Reg 1(2)(a), 4 and 6 and Sch 1 paras 2 and 4
[725] Safeguarding Vulnerable Groups Act 2006 s 2 and Sch 3 para 25

Year	Plea	Total sentenced	Type of sentencing %						Average length of custody in months
			Dis-charge	Fine	Commu-nity sentence	Sus-pended sentence	Custody	Other	
2013	G	43	–	–	–	–	100	–	–
	NG	229	–	–	–	–	100	–	–
2014	G	25	–	–	–	4	44	52	137.3
	NG	39	–	–	–	–	100	–	199.6

Threat or conspiracy to murder[726] Aged 21+

Year	Plea	Total sentenced	Type of sentencing %						Average length of custody in months
			Dis-charge	Fine	Commu-nity sentence	Sus-pended sentence	Custody	Other	
2013	G	253	–	0.4	12.3	24.5	59.7	3.2	24.5
	NG	43	–	–	–	11.6	81.4	7	64.2
2014	G	8	–	–	–	25	75	–	37.8
	NG	15	–	–	–	7	93	–	92.1

For explanations about the statistics see page 1-xii. For more statistics and for statistics about defendants aged 10-20 and statistics for male and female defendants see www. banksr.com Other Matters Statistics tab

289.3   *Guidelines   Attempted murder*
Attempted Murder Guideline 2009, see www.banksr.com Other Matters Guidelines tab page 3 The definitive guideline applies to offenders aged 18+.

Culpability and harm

page 3 para 3 The culpability of the offender is the initial factor in determining the seriousness of an offence. It is an essential element of the offence of attempted murder that the offender had an intention to kill, accordingly an offender convicted of this offence will have demonstrated a high level of culpability. Even so, the precise level of culpability will vary in line with the circumstances of the offence and whether the offence was planned or spontaneous. The use of a weapon may influence this assessment. 4 In common with all offences against the person, this offence has the potential to contain an imbalance between culpability and harm. 5 Where the degree of harm actually caused to the victim of an attempted murder is negligible, it is inevitable that this will impact on the overall assessment of offence seriousness. 6 However, although the degree of (or lack of) physical or psychological harm suffered by a victim may generally influence sentence, the statutory definition of harm encompasses not only the harm actually caused by an offence but also any harm that the offence was intended to cause or might foreseeably have caused. Since the offence can only be committed where there is an intention to kill, an offence of attempted murder will always involve, in principle, the most serious level of harm.

Aggravating and mitigating factors

para 7 The most serious offences of attempted murder will include those which encompass the factors set out in Criminal Justice Act 2003 Sch 21 paras 4-5, that, had the offence been murder, would make the seriousness of the offence 'exceptionally high' or 'particularly high'. 8 In all cases, the aggravating and mitigating factors that will influence the identification of the provisional sentence within the range follow those set out in Schedule 21 with suitable adjustments. These factors are included in the guideline table. 9 Care needs to be taken to ensure that there is no double counting where an

---

[726] It looks as if the statistics include threats to kill, which is a far less serious offence than conspiracy to murder. Ed.

essential element of the offence charged might, in other circumstances, be an aggravating factor. 10 This guideline is not intended to provide for an offence found to be based on a genuine belief that the murder would have been an act of mercy. Whilst the approach to assessing the seriousness of the offence may be similar, there are likely to be other factors present (relating to the offence and the offender) that would have to be taken into account and reflected in the sentence.

Compensation orders

para 11 A court must consider making a compensation order in respect of any personal injury, loss or damage occasioned.

Sentencing ranges and starting points

para 12 The starting points and ranges are based upon an adult 'first-time offender' who has been convicted. A 'first-time offender' is a person who does not have a conviction which, by virtue of Criminal Justice Act 2003 s 143(2), must be treated as an aggravating factor.

page 5 para 16 Where the offender has previous convictions which aggravate the seriousness of the current offence, that may take the provisional sentence beyond the range given, particularly where there are significant other aggravating factors present.

Factors to take into consideration

page 6 para 4 The level of injury or harm sustained by the victim as well as any harm that the offence was intended to cause or might foreseeably have caused, must be taken into account and reflected in the sentence imposed. 5 The degree of harm will vary greatly. Where there is low harm and high culpability, culpability is more significant. Even in cases where a low level of injury (or no injury) has been caused, an offence of attempted murder will be extremely serious.

page 7

Nature of offence	Starting point	Sentencing range
Level 1 The most serious offences including those which (if the charge had been murder) would come within Criminal Justice Act 2003 Sch 21 paras 4 or 5		
A Serious and long-term physical or psychological harm	30 years' custody	27 to 35 years' custody
B Some physical or psychological harm	20 years' custody	17 to 25 years' custody
C Little or no physical or psychological harm	15 years' custody	12 to 20 years' custody
Level 2 Other planned attempt to kill		
A Serious and long-term physical or psychological harm	20 years' custody	17 to 25 years' custody
B Some physical or psychological harm	15 years' custody	12 to 20 years' custody
C Little or no physical or psychological harm	10 years' custody	7 to 15 years' custody
Level 3 Other spontaneous attempt to kill		
A Serious and long-term physical or psychological harm	15 years' custody	12 to 20 years' custody
B Some physical or psychological harm	12 years' custody	9 to 17 years' custody
C Little or no physical or psychological harm	9 years' custody	6 to 14 years' custody

Specific aggravating factors
   a) the victim was particularly vulnerable, for example, because of age or disability,
   b) mental or physical suffering inflicted on the victim,
   c) the abuse of a position of trust,
   d) the use of duress or threats against another person to facilitate the commission of the offence, and
   e) the fact that the victim was providing a public service or performing a public duty.

Specific mitigating factors
   a) the offender suffered from any mental disorder or mental disability which lowered his degree of culpability,
   b) the offender was provoked (for example, by prolonged stress),
   c) the offender acted to any extent in self-defence, and
   d) the age of the offender.

The presence of one or more aggravating features will indicate a more severe sentence within the suggested range and, if any aggravating features are exceptionally serious, the case will move up to the next level.

289.4   Judicial guidance   Attempted murder
R v Powell 1998 1 Cr App R (S) 84 Attempted murder is often more serious than murder, as it involves the intention to kill, which is not necessary in murder cases.

R v Smith 1999 2 Cr App R (S) 212 Factors to have particular regard to are: a) an intent to kill will have been established, b) the failure to implement the intent will not normally be a cause for indulgence or credit to be accorded to the defendant, c) the motive and the premeditation, d) the recognition of some proportional correlation between the sentence and the minimum recommendation the Judge would have made had murder been committed, e) the plea, f) the defendant's age, and g) where there are other sentences, the totality.

R v Barot 2007 EWCA Crim 1119, 2008 1 Cr App R (S) 31 (p 156) LCJ D pleaded to conspiracy to murder. He was a terrorist. Held. In approaching the sentence for an inchoate offence, start by considering the sentence that would have been appropriate had the objective of the offender been achieved.

For a summary of the case, see **345.3**.

Note: It is important to remember that these cases were decided before the new guideline was published. Ed.

289.5   Children as victims
R v Gayzer-Tomlinson 2012 EWCA Crim 1944, 2013 1 Cr App R (S) 98 (p 513) (See **289.13**.)

Old case: *R v Schumann* 2007 EWCA Crim 569, 2 Cr App R (S) 73 (p 465) (Community sentence)

For a summary of the case, see the 8th edition of this book.

Conspiracy not carried out see the CONSPIRACY *Conspiracy not carried out* para at **227.2**.

289.6   Criminal gangs, Attempted killings by/Drug disputes etc.   Contract killings
R v McNee, Russell and Gunn 2007 EWCA Crim 1529, 2008 1 Cr App R (S) 24 (p 108) M, R and G were convicted of conspiracy to murder. They plotted the revenge killing of Mr and Mrs S. They were shot, and the gunmen were never caught. Mrs S's son had previously been convicted of the murder of a man called Bradshaw. G's nephew, JG, was with Bradshaw when he was murdered. Days after Mrs S's son had been convicted of the murder of Bradshaw, JG contracted pneumonia and died. During that trial there was evidence of threats traded between G and Mrs S's son. Mr and Mrs S feared for their safety, and after shots were fired at their home, they left the area and moved to a village in Lincolnshire. On the day JG died, it was decided that revenge should be extracted for his death. As Mrs S's son was serving a sentence of life imprisonment, it was decided to assassinate his mother and her husband. The conspiracy was organised and financed by

G. He traced the victims to their new address by using contacts within British Telecom. He bought phones for use in the conspiracy and recruited the gunmen. Very shortly after JG's death, M and G travelled to the village where the victims lived for a reconnaissance. They stayed in a caravan nearby. Two days later, M and R went to the area. On the day of the murders M and R were on the promenade some 100 yards from the victims' home. They were lookouts. On that day two men wearing boiler suits entered the victims' home and shot them dead. Their burnt-out vehicle was found later. G was regarded as the prime mover of the conspiracy and the dominating leader of the others. The Judge concluded that he initiated and was involved in every aspect of the case, and that the idea came from him. He acted in a calculating and premeditated way, involving others, obtaining firearms and the services of others to pull the trigger, and taking careful measures to cover his tracks. The Judge said that R was a persistent criminal and was a valuable lieutenant, heavily involved in the crime and without scruple, conscience or remorse. G, aged 39, had 28 previous convictions including ABH, wounding and affray. R, aged 30, had 87 previous convictions, although none for violence. M, aged 19 at the time of the offence, had 29 previous convictions, although none for violence. The Judge said that M acted as a pair with R, and was an early recruit, trusted by G. The Judge also said that the parents were wholly innocent, and that the killing was to assert a criminal grip over areas of Nottingham. Further, there was no mitigation. Held. These defendants were convicted of conspiracy to murder and their objective was achieved. The level of their criminality was very high indeed. There was ample material from the trial process from which the Judge could infer that they represented a continuing risk for the indefinite future. The Judge did not need medical evidence suggesting irrationality or instability of the personality to come to this conclusion. The danger could be represented by a wholly rational individual. The features which bear on the sentencing decisions in murder cases apply to this case of conspiracy to murder where the objective of the conspiracy was fulfilled, murder resulted, and the criminal culpability of each appellant was high. The Judge made appropriate distinctions between the defendants. The crime merited punishment of the utmost severity. **Life** was correct with minimum terms of **35 years** for G, **30 years** for R and **25 years** for M upheld.

R v Cameron 2010 EWCA Crim 1282, 2011 1 Cr App R (S) 24 (p 163) D was convicted of the murder of V1 and conspiracy to rob. D was recruited with others to rob V1, who it was thought had large quantities of drugs and money at his address. D, with others, went to V1's home with an imitation firearm and wrench. V1 was tied up and tortured. There were 56 separate injuries. The facial skeleton had been shattered by blows that had also caused underlying brain damage, which it was concluded was the cause of death. A friend of V1, V2, visited V1's address, was dragged inside by two men and assaulted with a blunt object and the imitation handgun, which was also forced into his mouth. V2 lost consciousness and when he came round he saw men dragging V1 out of the house. During the violence, V1 suffered two stab wounds to the chest. V's body was found in the grounds of a disused nursing home, naked save for his underpants. It was argued that D had no intention to kill and had removed himself from the situation. D sought to argue that he had disengaged with the violence. D, aged 29 at appeal, had no relevant convictions. He was ex-Army and very strong. Held. The lack of an intention to kill was but the other side of the coin to the specific intention of keeping V1 alive, if necessary through a period of torture and extreme violence, because only by so doing could he be expected to divulge the assumed presence of the money and the drugs. In those circumstances it is difficult to conceive of a situation in which the lack of an intention to kill counts for as little by way of mitigation. Similarly, with the matter of withdrawal. The Judge concluded, no doubt correctly, that that was not evidence of any remorse or altruism. The most aggravating feature it seems to us was the mental and physical suffering inflicted on V1 before his death. The **33-year** minimum term was not manifestly excessive.

R v Shah 2015 EWCA Crim 1250 D was convicted of attempted murder, section 18 and possession of a firearm with intent. At about 10.30 pm D rang V and asked for a lift. V agreed and they met. V agreed to pick up V2 and later X. With four in the car, V and V2 were sitting in the front seat of a car and D and X were in the back. D or X asked the driver to pull over, which he did. D and X then produced sawn-off shotguns. V and V2 tried to reach for the guns but three shots were fired. Two missed V. The other one took off V's thumb and 50 shotgun pellets lodged in his chest. Thirty-five could not be removed by surgery. V2 was struck in the face with the butt of the gun in the ensuing struggle. V ran away and heard a further shot and D shouting at X to shoot V2 in the head. Both attackers had difficulty in getting out of the car because the child locks were activated. The motive for the shooting was unclear. D was aged about 35 with a domestic violence conviction (10 months' imprisonment). The Judge considered the 30-year minimum term if it had been a successful killing by shooting and said there was no way of knowing what sort of danger D would pose 'years hence'. Considering the *Attempted Murder Guideline 2009*, he selected a 40-year determinate term making a 20-year IPP sentence. Held. IPP was almost inevitable. The protection of the public is [a matter for] the Parole Board. It was not appropriate to go outside the top of the range of the *Attempted Murder Guideline 2009* (35 years) so we substitute a **17-year** minimum term. See also: *R v Barrat* 2009 EWCA Crim 1119 (Conviction. Two of five stab wounds life-threatening. Team of three or four hooded men attack drug dealer over debt. 7½ **years' IPP** upheld.)

Note: It is important to remember that these cases were decided before the guideline was published. Ed.

Old cases: *R v Reynolds and Others Re T* 2007 EWCA Crim 538, 2 Cr App R (S) 87 (p 553) at 576 (**18 years' detention**) *Att-Gen's Ref No 66 of 2007* 2007 EWCA Crim 2630, 2008 1 Cr App R (S) 107 (p 627) (**IPP**) *R v Hills* 2007 EWCA Crim 3152, 2008 2 Cr App R (S) 29 (p 169) (**4½ years**) *R v Hunter* 2007 EWCA Crim 3424, 2008 2 Cr App R (S) 40 (p 226) (**8 years**)

For a summary of the first and second cases, see the 7th edition of this book and for the last two cases, see the 8th edition.

289.7   *Defendant under 21*

Note: The guideline does not apply to offenders aged under 18. Judges normally work out what the offence would be for an adult and make a reduction. Ed.

R v Jolie 2010 EWCA Crim 1816 D pleaded to conspiracy to murder. D and O planned to murder D's 15-year-old pregnant former girlfriend, V. D had disassociated himself with V when he learned of her pregnancy. He did not wish his mother to discover the pregnancy. The scheme was planned over a number of weeks and D and O considered how best to cover their tracks. They were in regular contact, often through the MSN Messenger system. O's computer retained the messages sent between the two and this enabled the conspiracy to be proved against him. D subsequently arranged to meet V, stating that he had changed his mind about her pregnancy. A number of text messages passed between D and O, and D arranged for V to be in a pre-arranged place. D subsequently returned to his halls of residence where he was studying, no doubt to conceal his involvement. O saw V, ran up behind her and struck her with a metal pole. V said, "Please don't, I'm pregnant". O struck V a number of times on the back of the head. V fell to the ground. A member of the public, H, heard her scream and approached O, who punched and kicked V on the floor. He then pushed her into the canal and held her head under water. H confronted O, who ran away, and pulled V from the canal. The Judge placed the offence at Level 2 in the guidelines and took a starting point between 15 and 20 years. There was credit for the plea. The Judge said, "You planned to lure your young victim to her death and you were very willing to plan the murder." D had no previous convictions. Held. The Judge was right in his assessment of the starting point. This was a truly appalling crime. It was a cold and calculated offence motivated by selfishness. Standing back, **14 years' YOI** was not excessive.

R v Gayzer-Tomlinson 2012 EWCA Crim 1944, 2013 1 Cr App R (S) 98 (p 513) see
289.13.

R v CJC 2014 EWCA Crim 525 D pleaded to attempted murder. Not guilty pleas to
committing an offence with the intent to commit a sexual offence and possession of an
offensive weapon were accepted and remained on file. D, aged 16, lived with his parents
and attended the same school as V. V, aged 12, agreed to meet D in a quiet, rural lane not
far from their respective homes. D arrived wearing a hooded jumper with the hood up
and his hands in his pockets. He asked V whether he was scaring her, to which V replied
that he was. D then pounced on her. V saw that D was wearing surgical gloves. He
knocked her to the ground and produced a Swiss Army knife. V shouted "No" and began
to fight back. D said, "I am going to have to kill you now" and threatened her with rape.
He repeatedly stabbed her throat and chest but the knife appeared to be blunt and
fortunately only caused superficial wounds. D then tried to strangle V but was
interrupted by a passer-by who was walking her dog. When D realised that the passer-by
could see him with his hands around V's throat, he got up and left. V had blood on her
hands, was unsteady on her feet and had wet herself. She was treated in hospital. D was
arrested the same day and still had the knife and gloves in his possession. He told
officers he had tried to kill V but declined to comment when formally interviewed. There
was significant background to those events. V had become aware that D was infatuated
with her. He stared at her at school. They occasionally talked on the way home from
school and D had sent her numerous text messages telling V that he was interested in her.
She let him know that she did not share those feelings. Between September 2012 and
March 2013 there was no communication between them and V believed the matter was
over. D had not, however, forgotten about V. He was in regular contact with Childline
via an online chat forum and explained that he really liked an 11- or 12-year-old girl and
wanted to resolve his feelings for her. He said he was depressed because the girl had a
boyfriend and described her as being 'a bit of a bitch'. He said he wanted to do illegal
things to V because her life was too good and he wanted to balance things out. When
asked what he meant he said 'Rape'. Subsequent analysis of his computer revealed that
he had accessed material about rape and murder. Childline contacted the police who in
turn spoke to D. D said he had said those things to attract attention. There was a
psychological report which stated that D had said after V had been 'very cool' to him, he
decided to punish her. Having accessed material about the trauma experienced by rape
victims, he thought that might be a good way to take his revenge on V. The report noted
that D had said he became very depressed and the urge to punish V worsened. He
decided the only way to put an end to his distress was to kill V, not merely traumatise
her. He was worried that he would not go through with the killing and had practised
stabbing a cardboard box in front of a mirror. In the days leading up to the offence, D
had sent V a number of text messages saying that he would kill himself if she did not
meet him. A psychiatric report noted that D had not experienced any appropriate
remorse. He made it clear he regretted the offence because he had been apprehended. D
said his efforts were to no avail as V would suffer no lasting harm. When the psychiatrist
told him it was virtually certain V would suffer lasting harm, D seemed more fulfilled
and said it made him feel better. It was accepted that the dangerousness criteria were
met. D was previously reprimanded for common assault committed against a fellow
student but was highly intelligent and expected to do very well in his GCSEs. The Judge
reduced the minimum term to reflect the days in custody, which appear to be 3 months
21 days. Held. It was argued that an extended sentence would have sufficed. The Judge
could have come to no other conclusion than that a life sentence was appropriate. It was
then argued that a 7-year minimum term was too long. Having given up trying to stab V
to death, D attempted to strangle her. That attempt did not result in significant visible
harm. For an adult, the appropriate starting point would have been 26 years. The
minimum term must reflect D's youth, although there is no requirement that it be
reduced in part at all. D was mature for his age and a very intelligent young man. The

troubling feature of the case is that he was not deterred by the intervention of the police after they were contacted by Childline. The offence was planned and rehearsed and he had shown no remorse. Starting in the region of 26 years, to account for his age that would be reduced to 21 years. Applying the discount for his guilty plea, that is reduced to 14 years. Accordingly, **detention for life** with a minimum of **7 years** was appropriate.
R v Gomes-Monteiro and Others Re NT 2014 EWCA Crim 747, 2 Cr App R (S) 62 (p 483)[727] LCJ D was convicted of attempted murder. D, aged 13, became involved in an altercation with V, aged 14, at McDonald's, where D demanded a battery for a mobile phone from V. At 9.15 pm, the argument continued outside a youth club. D had taken a knife to the club. The disagreement became violent involving a number of people, including V, who hit back at TM and D. V, on roller skates, calmed down and skated a short distance away. D followed, produced a knife and stabbed V twice. V was taken to hospital by air ambulance. The knife entered the chest and penetrated the kidney. He suffered a collapsed lung, a significant gastric injury, a shattered spleen and a very serious renal injury. V will require life-long antibiotic medication. D had a number of convictions, including common assault where he surrounded a 14-year-old girl and held a knife to her throat (a referral order). D denied he had a knife. He received a 9-month rehabilitation order for ABH. He had also used threatening behaviour towards a bus driver. The pre-sentence report indicated a difficult home life and emotional and behavioural difficulties. The report also highlighted D's genuine remorse for his actions. Held. The Judge was entitled to make a finding of dangerousness with the information presented. Further information post-trial highlighted V's vast improvement in behaviour and the positive effect of medication so **10 years' extended** sentence (**7 years'** custody, not 10, 3 years' extended licence).
See also: *R v Khan* 2015 EWCA Crim 1816 (With another, hit 15-year-old boy with hammer a number of times in street. Three skull fractures. Extensive surgical intervention required. Aged 17. No previous convictions. So-called 'honour attack'. **15 years** was appropriate.)
For *Domestic violence* see the *Relationships/Emotional offences* para at **289.16**.

289.8   *Drunken attack*
R v Davison 2010 EWCA Crim 2284 D pleaded to attempted murder. He had been asked to leave a hostel in which he was staying after a dispute. He joined a 60-year-old alcoholic, V, in some gardens and 'drank the afternoon away'. D believed that V had touched him in an inappropriate manner and, afflicted by memories of childhood abuse, he produced a knife and stabbed V nine times. V survived. D made his way to a police station and said, "I killed a man tonight for fucking touching me. I stabbed him so many times he's got to be dead". D was sentenced on the basis that V inappropriately touched D. D, aged 35, had a large number of convictions concerning indecent images of children. A psychiatric report found he was emotionally unstable and suffered from antisocial personality disorder. Held. Giving full credit for the plea, the Judge's starting point must have been 18 years. That is too high. The right starting point here was in the region of **12 years**, so with the plea **8 years**.

289.9   *Firearms, With*
R v Akiniyi 2010 EWCA Crim 345 D was convicted of attempted murder, aggravated burglary and possession of a firearm when committing an offence. D and O forced their way into a family home where a married couple and their son, V, were sleeping. V was woken by banging on his bedroom door. D and O burst into his bedroom. O pointed a double-barrelled shotgun at V. D and O told V not to scream or they would kill his mother. They demanded money and drugs, took a ring from V's finger and took him upstairs. They took £4,000 in cash and a small amount of cannabis and continued to search for more. V was then taken back to his bedroom and told to get on the bed. V was

---

[727] This case is also referred to as *R v Monteiro and Others* 2014 EWCA Crim 747.

convinced they were going to shoot him and was begging them not to. V grabbed the barrel of the gun from O. During the struggle D intervened, produced a knife and began to stab V repeatedly in his leg. V tried to escape but D followed him and stabbed him in total 11 times to the back and front of his body. D and O shot out the glass in the front door and left the premises. V was taken to hospital, where emergency surgery was performed. V sustained life-threatening injuries including a laceration to the liver and a haemothorax. D, aged 20, had two convictions for carrying a bladed instrument and a conviction for violent disorder which was a group fight in which knives were used. The pre-sentence report said D presented a significant risk of committing further violent offences and posed a high risk of harm to the public. Held. This was a Level 1 attempted murder. There was an abundance of material before the Judge which justified the imposition of an IPP. **10 years' IPP** was correct.

Post-guideline case
R v Powell 2014 EWCA Crim 596 D was convicted of attempted murder and possession of a prohibited weapon with intent. D attended a party and E fired shots into the ceiling. This caused panic and everyone rushed outside where E and a friend of D were shot dead by V. D pursued V into an adjacent street, shooting him a number of times at close range. V managed to escape but was shot again from behind. When D finally caught up with V, D stood over him and shot him in the face. There were nine shots in all. D went into hiding. By extraordinary chance V made a full recovery. D had a conviction for possession of a firearm and ammunition (8 years' imprisonment). V was convicted of both murders. Held. D used the gun to inflict serious harm in residential London streets with complete disregard for public safety. **34 years** upheld.

See also: *R v Stevens* 2011 EWCA Crim 827 (Convicted of attempted murder and possessing a firearm with intent. At close range the defendant fired five shots at the victim, three entered body, one entering the jaw and exiting through the neck. Small degree of provocation and self-defence. Treated as good character. Starting at 25, **22 years**.)

See also the *Criminal gangs, Attempted killings by/Drug disputes etc.* para at **289.6**. Old cases: Best ignored.

289.10   Gain   Attempted murder for gain
Att-Gen's Ref No 123 of 2014 2015 EWCA Crim 111, 2015 1 Cr App R (S) 67 (p 470) LCJ D pleaded to aggravated burglary and GBH with intent (×3). Three weeks later he was convicted of three attempted murders and conspiracy to commit aggravated burglary. A family from the United Arab Emirates was staying in a Marble Arch hotel. The group included four sisters, V1, V2, V3 and S, accompanied by V2's three children, aged between 7 and 12. In the early hours, D, who was a 'hotel creeper', entered the room in which V1 and her young nephew were sleeping. The door had been left ajar. D was armed with a hammer which his co-defendant, E, had given him in case D met resistance. Once inside the room, D gathered cash, jewellery and other valuables. He then entered the room next door via an interconnecting door. V2 woke up and D, leaning over her, shouted, "Give me fucking money". D then struck her repeatedly to the head with the hammer. Before V2 became unconscious, her screams woke V3. V3 tried to stop the attack on V2, but was herself hit on the head repeatedly until unconscious. Either before or after these assaults, D also attacked V1, smashing her skull six times with the hammer. V1 was struck even after she was unconscious and a whole side of her skull was destroyed, with part of her brain protruding and brain matter spread over her face.

The injuries to all three victims were life-threatening. V1 was bedridden and will neither walk nor regain proper brain function again. Her speech was severely limited and it was unlikely that she would ever regain enough movement to use a motorised wheelchair. V2 was left with two skull defects and multiple muscular problems on her left hand side. V3 suffered deafness, severe vertigo, significant facial and skull pain and long-term neurological difficulties as well as back and spine problems. The effect on the children was severe as they now lacked any trust of people, were fearful of being alone and did not want to leave home.

Evidence showed that D had deliberately aimed at the victims' heads, using both ends of the hammer, landing at least 15 blows. D had used severe force and had continued to hit both V1 and V2 on the head, even after they were saturated with blood. All the attacks occurred in front of V2's three children, one of whom was deeply distressed and covered in the victims' blood. Some six minutes after D had first entered the hotel, he left the victims for dead and made off with a suitcase full of valuables towards E's home. D also attempted to dispose of the hammer and, an hour or so after the attack, E used the victims' stolen bank cards to withdraw £5,000. Later that day, D handed over the stolen goods to a known handler, boasting that he had stolen £50,000-worth of property. D was arrested a week after the attack but declined to answer police questions and blamed E at trial for the attacks. D was aged 32 and had 37 previous appearances for 62 offences, having begun offending aged 12. He first went to prison in 1997 for section 20 assault and had also been convicted of robbery (2½ years in 1998, his longest sentence), burglary and other assaults. D had also used a hammer during an affray in 2008. He was prone to losing his temper and had a 'mixed type' disorder. D had little insight into his offending, but did express remorse. The Judge found D to be dangerous. Held. D's mental health cannot in any way excuse the appalling criminality. This is a shocking case. We would emphasise, as Lord Judge did in *R v Oakes* 2012 EWCA Crim 2435, 2013 2 Cr App R (S) 22 (p 132), that there may well be cases, exceptional though they may be, where, even if none of the victims has died, a whole life order might nonetheless be appropriate. We can envisage for an exceptional case of attempted murder such a sentence being passed. But this is not that case. However…we are firmly of the view that the minimum term imposed…was unduly lenient. Three concurrent **life** sentences with a **27-year minimum**, not 18-year minimum.

Note: It may be that the gap between an attempted murder with horrific injuries and a murder is closing. It may be that the aggravating features of the horrific injuries, the number of victims and the presence of children made a very large difference. Either way, the courts have no interest in placing ceilings on the sentences they can impose. Ed.

See also: *R v McHugh* 2012 EWCA Crim 123 (Plea to handling and fraud (×2). Convicted of conspiracy to murder. Plotted with mother to kill her father for inheritance. Hit him with bricks. Stole £355. Convictions for assault. 20 years' extended sentence (**15 years**' custody 5 years' licence) not 7½ years' DPP.)

R v Khan 2015 EWCA Crim 1816 (With another, hit 15-year-old boy with hammer a number of times in street. Three skull fractures. Extensive surgical intervention required. Aged 17. No previous. So called 'honour attack'. **15 years** was appropriate.)

See also the **MURDER** *Gain, defendant's motive was* paras at **288.40**.

289.11   *Hammer, Attack with*

R v Terry 2012 EWCA Crim 1411, 2013 1 Cr App R (S) 51 (p 285) (Convicted. Dispute after drinking. 23 years' extended sentence (**18 years**' custody 5 years' licence, see **289.17**.)

R v Hardy 2012 EWCA Crim 2671, 2013 2 Cr App R (S) 24 (p 164) (Plea. Hit wife on head with hammer and then said, "Let's get you to hospital." **10 years**, see **289.16**.)

Att-Gen's Ref No 123 of 2014 2015 EWCA Crim 111, 2015 1 Cr App R (S) 67 (p 470) (LCJ Convicted. Three attempted murders by hotel creeper. 15 blows with severe force. Terrible long-term consequences. Life with **27-year** minimum term, see **289.10**.)

Att-Gen's Ref No 91 of 2014 2014 EWCA Crim 2891 D was convicted of attempted murder. In a discussion at a minorities group D was heard to refer to gays as perverts. Others suggested that was not his own view. V, who was openly gay and often wore women's clothing, was homeless. D's landlord suggested that V move into D's flat, where there was a spare room. D helped V to measure up his room for his bed. On V's first night, D came back to the flat at 5.15 am. Forty minutes later, D sent a series of text messages to various emergency numbers. At 10.30 am, D told a visitor that V was still asleep. At 10.41 am, D dialled 999 and said someone was dead and that he had hit him with a claw hammer when he was asleep. Police arrived and found V on an inflatable bed with a claw hammer embedded in his head. In hospital, the hammer was removed. V had a depressed skull fracture and a penetrating traumatic brain injury. Analysis indicated that V was attacked in his sleep and considerable force was used. V made some recovery but could not pick up objects like cutlery, he suffered from depression and his social life and ability to find work were affected. D had a history of recurring depressive disorders. Four psychiatrists gave evidence. One said D suffered from a depressive illness. One said he suffered from a process psychotic illness, namely schizophrenia. There were periods on the ward where D had applied paranoid misinterpretations to other people's reactions and D had become aroused and agitated. D was now aged 21 and had suffered physical abuse from his father. The Judge started at 20 years and reduced that to 14 years because of D's youth, his mental illness and his lack of previous convictions. He made a Hybrid Order with a Restriction Order. Held. The attack was quite grotesque and had shattering consequences. V was entirely blameless. The Judge was right to find D satisfied the dangerousness criteria. We don't consider 14 years as unduly lenient. It is significant that D's dangerousness was not confined to his mental illness. With his Restriction Order, D will not be released without careful consideration. Despite this, to guard against the possibility of serious harm following D's discharge, 19 years' extended sentence (**14 years'** custody 5 years' extended licence).

Note: Some might think that only a life sentence reflected the seriousness of this terrible attack. Time will tell whether the extended licence provides the public with much protection. Reducing the sentence because of a lack of previous convictions was wrong because the *Attempted Murder Guideline 2009* bases the starting points on first-time offenders, see **289.3** at para 12. Previous convictions aggravate the offence, see para 16 of the guideline and **86.2** in Volume 1. Ed.

289.12   Knife, With   *Judicial guidance*

R v Gayzer-Tomlinson 2012 EWCA Crim 1944, 2013 1 Cr App R (S) 98 (p 513) D pleaded to attempted murder and possession of an offensive weapon. He attacked V with a knife inflicting 20 wounds to the face, neck and head. The Judge considered the introduction of the 25-year minimum term for knife murders meant that an offence between Levels 1 and 2 in the guideline had increased to 17-20 years. Defence counsel did not disagree. Sentence upheld.

289.13   Knives (since new murder starting point)

R v Gayzer-Tomlinson 2012 EWCA Crim 1944, 2013 1 Cr App R (S) 98 (p 513) D pleaded to attempted murder, section 20 on V2, and possession of an offensive weapon. In November 2010, he began a relationship with V1, a 14-year-old schoolgirl. They only met a few times but they corresponded electronically. In early February, V1 told D by text she did not want to see him any more. D took it badly. In February, he sought treatment from his GP, who thought D might have bipolar developing. The GP referred D to the community psychiatric services. On 19 March, D bought a VW Golf, although he could not drive. He also bought some number plates with the numbers of other VW Golfs in the area. He made a to-do list which included buying a knife, petrol, two cans of acetone, spray paint, masking tape and face paint. On 1 April, D disguised himself with hair dye and wore contact lenses instead of his distinctive glasses. He went to V1's school and drove up and down until he saw V1 approach the school. He went up to her and asked why she had not replied to his texts. V1 told him to get lost. D put her head in a headlock and began a frenzied attack on her face, neck and head with a knife with a 4 inch blade. V1 fell to the ground and was kicked by D. V2, a 16-year-old pupil, rugby tackled D, who fought him off with the knife. D cut V2's finger. D returned to his attack on V1. D was finally restrained by pupils and teachers. He asked to see how V1 was and was allowed to do so. He kicked her. V1 received 20 wounds. She was airlifted to hospital. She required 48 stitches. Luckily there was little structural damage to her. There was less scarring than might have been expected. Her personal statement was full of optimism and her positive attitude. Her family was, however, seriously affected by the attack, reducing them to tears on quite a number of occasions. D was aged 17. He wanted to be a vet and it was predicted he would obtain three A-grade A levels. The experts said D was most likely to have a mixed affective state of depressive and manic symptoms. It could be a precursor to a bipolar disorder. Irritability and anger were more common in a mixed state than where depression was alone. His lack of sleep since V1 ended the relationship had almost certainly caused a depersonisation. The Judge considered the introduction of the 25-year minimum term for knife murders meant that an offence between Levels 1 and 2 in the guideline had increased to 17-20 years. He started at 18 years for the attempt and 18 months consecutive for the possession of the knife. With full credit he gave **13 years** in all. Held. We are not persuaded that was too long.

Att-Gen's Ref No 63 of 2013 2014 EWCA Crim 2763 D was convicted of attempted murder, breaching a Restraining Order (×2) and possession of an offensive weapon. He could not come to terms with the break-up of his marriage to V1. In January 2012, D rang V1's doorbell and when V1 opened the door, he stepped inside and put his hands around her throat in a threatening manner. V1 was forced against a wall and V2 stepped in and asked D to leave. D left. In July 2012, a court made a Restraining Order. Three days later, D breached the order. V1 and V2 moved to an address which they assumed D would not know of. In December 2012, the doorbell rang at the new address and V2 opened it. No one was there and suddenly D appeared and sprayed a liquid containing cleaning products and lighter fluid in V2's eyes, causing a stinging sensation. D said "I'll kill you, you bastard". D stabbed him in the chest and V2 fell backwards. V2 grabbed the knife and was able to force it out of D's hand. V2 kept hold of D and shouted for help. Two neighbours restrained D until police arrived, when he was arrested. D had taken parcel tape and cable ties with him. V2 had a penetrating chest wound of at least 5 cm. Had the knife been at a different direction, it would have penetrated V2's heart. An impact statement said that V2 had lived in fear since the attack and his personality had changed as a result of the attack. He had undergone counselling and was taking anti-depressants. D was aged 70 at appeal with no convictions. He expressed remorse but that was wholly absent at trial. Held. The aggravating features were that D took a knife to the scene, there was significant planning and there was a background of harassment and repeated breaches of Restraining Orders. It was correct for the Judge to impose a **discretionary life** sentence, given the risk that D posed to V1 and V2. D's settled intention to kill was undoubted. The offence is in Level 1 for the purposes of the attempted murder guideline bearing in mind the effect of Schedule 21 para 5A. The notional determinate term ought to have been 24 years, not 14. Because of his age, that would be reduced to 20 years. The **minimum term** was therefore **10 years** not 7.

See also: *R v Kela* 2011 EWCA Crim 1277, 2012 1 Cr App R (S) 32 (p 193) (Plea (10%) credit. Behind with rent. Went to landlord and stabbed him continuously. 48 stitches. Good character. Judge entitled to start at 25 years. We agree with **22 years**.)

R v Cooley 2013 EWCA Crim 1988 (Plea to stabbing wife when drunk. **10 years** not 12. For details see **289.16**.)

289.14   *Multiple attempted murders*

R v Onyenaychi 2012 EWCA Crim 1460, 2013 1 Cr App R (S) 59 (p 335) (See **289.15**)
See also: *R v Reeves* 2012 EWCA Crim 2613, 2013 2 Cr App R (S) 21 (p 129) (**3 years 9 months**)
See also the **MURDER** *Multiple murder* paras at **288.50**.

289.15   *Police officers as victims*

R v Onyenaychi 2012 EWCA Crim 1460, 2013 1 Cr App R (S) 59 (p 335) D was convicted of two attempted murders (V3 and V4), section 18 (V1), robbery (V2) and attempted section 18 (V5). D was in a taxi with another. Suddenly, D told the driver that he was going to rob him. As D and X exited the taxi, D dropped his mobile phone in the taxi. The driver, in a panic, sped off, contacted the police, handed the mobile to them and returned to the taxi office. D was waiting for him, threatened him with a knife, dragged him to the office and threatened to kill him unless he got his phone back. D put a balaclava on and the driver managed to get into the taxi office. D followed him into the office, where V1 was visiting his cousin, another driver for the taxi firm. D, who was shouting about his phone, then gratuitously stabbed V1 four times, once each in the chest and abdomen and twice in the arm. V1 was in hospital for four days. Two days later, D met V2 at a tube station. V2 had agreed, via a website, to sell D a laptop. D produced a knife and demanded the laptop. He made off with the laptop and an iPhone. V2 gave chase and D subsequently crashed his car and ran off, taking the property but leaving the knife. Two days later, D was on a bus when a number of ticket inspectors boarded the bus with police support officers, including V3 and V5. D became abusive and he and the inspector alighted onto the pavement. D had one hand in his front pocket and appeared to be holding something. He gave a false name and address. D was recognised by the police support officers as being wanted for the stabbing of V1 and for breach of his prison licence. A police unit was summoned. Two officers including V4 arrived. V4 feared that D might be armed and asked him to remove his hand from his pocket. Without warning, D ripped his hand from his pocket. He was carrying a knife, the blade of which he had extended to its maximum whilst it was still in his pocket. D stabbed V4 on the left side of his face, pulled him towards him and cut him across the throat. The support officers attempted to bring D under control and during the struggle he intentionally stabbed V3 twice in the head. V5 got D in a headlock and D was swinging his arms around wildly, still holding the knife, saying "Let me out, I'll cut them, I'll finish them." V4 suffered two deep lacerations to the scalp and two to the throat. He lost a large amount of blood and his injuries were life-threatening. By chance, a vascular surgeon was passing and intervened. He saved V4's life. D was aged 31 at appeal and had 17 previous court appearances including four assaults, one attempted robbery, three robberies and one section 18 (4 years' detention). There were also convictions for possession of a prohibited weapon, possession of an imitation firearm with intent to cause fear of violence (6 years[728]) and causing death by dangerous driving (2 years). He was on licence for the driving offence at the time of these offences. Held. The knife's blade was extended whilst in D's pocket and therefore it was done plainly to attack V4. The knife had been deliberately carried to the scene, there was significant planning and premeditation and the incidents spanned over five days. Grave harm had been caused to V4 and D's convictions were highly relevant. D did not know that he would be confronted on the bus, but having lost one knife in the previous incident, he went and acquired another and in that sense he came prepared. The sentence of **life imprisonment** on the two attempted murder counts was not challenged. The minimum term of **25 years** (for the offence against V4) did take account of the distinction between murder and attempted murder. (Other sentences were concurrent.) It was a severe sentence, but not one which was manifestly excessive.

289.16   *Relationship/Emotional offences*

R v Walker 2010 EWCA Crim 1108, 2011 1 Cr App R (S) 26 (p 175) D pleaded to attempted murder. He was married to V for 19 years and they had two teenage sons. He was a jealous and controlling man, having lost his temper and damaged property during the marriage, but had not been physically violent towards her. In 2007, during flooding near their house, V allowed a man to use her mobile phone. D became angry and accused V of having an affair. He sent abusive text messages to her and sought to track down the man. V commenced divorce proceedings and D left the matrimonial home. She allowed him to visit her at the address and D punched her and threw her around the room. He

---

[728] Although that is what the report says, it may be that the 6-year sentence was for both firearm offences. Ed.

then took an air rifle and held it to her head. She pleaded with him. He shot her twice in the head and then turned the gun on himself. She was bleeding heavily and sought assistance from neighbours. D was arrested and he smelled of alcohol. A pellet was lodged at the back of her head which was too close to the nerve to remove safely, but there was a possibility it might have to be removed in the future if it became dislodged or the wound became infected. She had cuts and she also had bruising to her upper body, back, arms, shoulders and neck. Four of her upper teeth were badly fractured and that required an extensive course of dental treatment. D, aged 46 at appeal, was of good character with character evidence. The Judge found that D was not dangerous. He said had death resulted, he would have taken the adjusted starting point as 22 years. The current guidelines had not yet come into effect. The Judge, applying the approach indicated in *R v Ford* 2006, then indicated that he would have made a reduction of 40% to reflect the survival of V and then a further reduction of 30% to reflect the plea of guilty, leaving a resulting figure of around 9 years. He then acknowledged that the sentence needed to be increased to reflect potential release at half-time. Held. We can see no fault in the way the Judge, at a time before the guideline had come into effect, approached the matter by reference to Criminal Justice Act 2003 had death in fact resulted. The adjusted starting point of 22 years had death in fact resulted was not wrong. **18 years** was not excessive.

R v Jolie 2010 EWCA Crim 1816 D pleaded to conspiracy to murder. D and O planned to murder D's 15-year-old pregnant former girlfriend, V. D had disassociated himself with V when he learned of her pregnancy. He did not wish his mother to discover the pregnancy. The scheme was planned over a number of weeks and D and O considered how best to cover their tracks. They were in regular contact, often through the MSN Messenger system. O's computer retained the messages sent between the two and this enabled the conspiracy to be proved against him. D subsequently arranged to meet V, stating that he had changed his mind about her pregnancy. A number of text messages passed between D and O, and D arranged for V to be in a pre-arranged place. D subsequently returned to his halls of residence where he was studying, no doubt to conceal his involvement. O saw V, ran up behind her and struck her with a metal pole. V said, "Please don't, I'm pregnant". O struck V a number of times on the back of the head. V fell to the ground. A member of the public, H, heard her scream and approached O, who punched and kicked V on the floor. He then pushed her into the canal and held her head under water. H confronted O, who ran away, and pulled V from the canal. The Judge placed the offence at Level 2 in the guidelines and took a starting point between 15 and 20 years. There was credit for the plea. The Judge said, "You planned to lure your young victim to her death and you were very willing to plan the murder". D had no previous convictions. Held. The Judge was right in his assessment of the starting point. This was a truly appalling crime. It was a cold and calculated offence motivated by selfishness. Standing back, **14 years' YOI** was not excessive.

R v Ntombela 2012 EWCA Crim 2261 D pleaded on the day of trial to attempted murder and section 18. D had been in a relationship with V. D's motivation for this was to marry V to enable him to remain in the UK. She had alleged that D had been violent towards her. V terminated her pregnancy against D's wishes. The relationship was inherently unstable and marked by jealousy on both sides. V considered D to be controlling and aggressive. The relationship eventually broke down. D stayed at her flat. The following day he was drunk and V asked him to leave. He did so, but soon returned, upon which V refused to admit him to the flat. V made it clear that D was no longer welcome and that she would throw D's possessions down to him. D became enraged. D was able to crawl through the lower half of the flat door.[729] V called the police and locked herself in the

---

[729] It is unclear how the defendant made a hole in the door. The Yorkshire Evening Post 25/2/12 said he kicked a hole in the door. Ed.

lavatory. D armed himself with a knife[730] from the kitchen and tried to cut his way through the door. He was shouting that he would kill her for what she had done. V was terrified. There was a short pause in the attack on the door. V and her friend,[731] who was present at the flat, tried to make their escape. D cornered them in the hall. He had two knives. He said to V, "I should have killed you long ago". He then tried to stab her in the chest and repeated that he was going to kill her. V was able to prevent him from doing so only by taking hold of the knife in both hands, receiving in the process very serious cuts. V returned to the lounge. D again tried to stab her and bit her in the back. Her friend tried to intervene and pushed D off her. V ran back to the lavatory and locked herself in again. The police arrived and D could hear them at the door. D stabbed V's friend, despite her telling him she was pregnant. Police heard one of the women shout, "He's got a knife, he is trying to kill me". D shouted, "I've got a knife, you fuckers, and I'm going to kill her if you try to come in". An officer saw that D was holding the knife to the victim's friend's throat. He was asked to put the knife down and responded that he would kill the friend if they entered the flat. D then tried to smash his way through an upstairs window, either in an attempted suicide or self-harm. An officer tasered him and he was arrested. V had multiple stab wounds to both hands and a bite mark on her back. She received hospital treatment for 18 days. V's friend had a wound to the palm of her left hand, and a further wound on her left knee. She was still receiving hospital treatment for loss of mobility at the date of sentence. D denied the offences in interview, suggesting the injuries must have been caused in trying to prevent him from taking his own life. He pleaded but made an application to change his plea, which was refused. D, aged 23, had no previous convictions. He was not mentally ill. The Judge started at 15 years for the attempted murder (Level 3) and 12 years for the section 18 offence. Because of totality he reduced it from 27 to 22 and with plea made it **20 years**. Held. These were terrible offences. The defendant's age is not so young that it in itself constitutes a substantial mitigating factor. The offences occurred in the context of a turbulent interpersonal relationship, exacerbated by alcohol. The Judge was perhaps generous in finding that the defendant was not dangerous. These were terrible offences. The defendant attacked the victims with determination and brutality. Lengthy consecutive sentences were inevitable. **14 years** and 6 years consecutive was not excessive.

R v Gayzer-Tomlinson 2012 EWCA Crim 1944, 2013 1 Cr App R (S) 98 (p 513) D pleaded to attempted murder, section 20 on V2, and possession of an offensive weapon. In November 2010, he began a relationship with V1, a 14-year-old schoolgirl. They only met a few times but they corresponded electronically. In early February, V1 told D by text she did not want to see him any more. D took it badly. In February, he sought treatment from his GP, who thought D might have bipolar developing. The GP referred D to the community psychiatric services. On 19 March, D bought a VW Golf, although he could not drive. He also bought some number plates with the numbers of other VW Golfs in the area. He made a 'to do' list which included buying a knife, petrol, two cans of acetone, spray paint, masking tape and face paint. On 1 April, D disguised himself with hair dye and wore contact lenses instead of his distinctive glasses. He went to V1's school and drove up and down until he saw V1 approach the school. He went up to her and asked why she had not replied to his texts. V1 told him to get lost. D put her head in a headlock and began a frenzied attack on her face, neck and head with a knife with a 4 inch blade. V1 fell to the ground and was kicked by D. V2, a 16-year-old pupil, rugby tackled D, who fought him off with the knife. D cut V2's finger. D returned to his attack on V1. D was finally restrained by pupils and teachers. He asked to see how V1 was and was allowed to do so. He kicked her. V1 received 20 wounds. She was airlifted to hospital. She required 48 stitches. Luckily there was little structural damage to her.

---

[730] The report is not clear. It could be two knives. The Yorkshire Evening Post 25/2/12 said D fetched another knife after the first one broke.

[731] There is no mention of V's friend until this point in the judgment. It is therefore unclear where she was in the flat. Ed.

There was less scarring than might have been expected. Her personal statement was full of optimism and her positive attitude. Her family was, however, seriously affected by the attack, reducing them to tears on quite a number of occasions. D was aged 17. He wanted to be a vet and it was predicted he would obtain three A-grade A levels. The experts said D was most likely to have a mixed affective state of depressive and manic symptoms. It could be a precursor to a bipolar disorder. Irritability and anger were more common in a mixed state than where depression was alone. His lack of sleep once V ended the relationship had almost certainly caused a depersonisation. The Judge considered the introduction of the 25-year minimum term for knife murders meant that an offence between Levels 1 and 2 in the guideline had increased to 17-20 years. He started at 18 years for the attempt and 18 months consecutive for the possession of the knife. With full credit he gave **13 years** in all. Held. We are not persuaded that was too long.

R v Hardy 2012 EWCA Crim 2671, 2013 2 Cr App R (S) 24 (p 164) D pleaded to attempted murder. His wife, V, was accessing bank accounts on the family computer, in a study on the first floor. D took a 2½ pound lump hammer from his garage, went to the study and hit V on the head with it. V looked round and saw D, who raised the hammer again and hit her on the head and the wrist. D then stood back and said, "Let's get you to hospital". V told him to ring the police but he begged her [to change her mind]. V rang the police herself. D immediately said to the police, "I'm really sorry, I've hurt my wife". When arrested he said, "I hit her over the head with a hammer because of money problems". V had a 4 cm laceration on the front top of the scull and a 6 cm laceration to the back of the head. There was no bone injury and no bleeding in the brain tissue. The injuries turned out not to be life-threatening. The medical view was that that was fortuitous. There was also a 4 cm wrist injury. In interview, D said he snapped through stress after a build-up of debts which he had kept secret from his wife. He feared she might leave him if she knew. D was now aged 40 and had no previous convictions. D's basis of plea included that there was no expectation of financial gain. The Judge said V was a vulnerable victim and there was a gross breach of trust. Held. This was a very serious and very nasty attack on a defenceless lady. It was a Level 2 offence. The element of planning might have been brief. The aggravating factors would raise this to something in the order of 15 years. With plea **10 years**.

R v Cooley 2013 EWCA Crim 1988 D pleaded (full credit) to attempted murder. He and V were married for 30 years. In 2010, one of their sons was sent to prison for fighting. In December 2011, another son died in suspicious circumstances. This caused stress to D and V. D had financial difficulties, started drinking heavily and tried to commit suicide. He was prescribed medication by his GP and had regular alcoholic blackouts. In September 2012, he argued with V and struck her on the chin, which she said was out of character. The next day they both drank heavily. V asked D to buy some more wine, which he did. After consuming it, V lay on her bed. V thought they had an argument and she asked him to leave home. D went to the kitchen and stabbed her six or seven times to the chest, abdomen and back. V thought D said, "You're having it". D then dialled 999 and said he had killed his wife. D sounded angry. She could be heard moaning in the background. He then threatened to go back and kill her. D was three times over the drink/drive limit. V was even higher. V was taken to hospital and was initially there for two weeks. She had to be readmitted but made a pretty good physical recovery. D was aged 65 and had no convictions, but did have a caution for pushing his wife in an argument. V was aged 47. A report said D had acute alcohol intoxication, was clinically depressed and had alcohol dependency. V indicated support for D and declined to make a victim impact statement. The Judge considered it was a Level 2 case. Held. The case was on the cusp of Categories 2 and 3. Starting at 15 years, with plea **10 years** not 13.

Att-Gen's Ref No 63 of 2013 2014 EWCA Crim 2763 D was convicted of attempted murder, breaching a Restraining Order (×2) and possession of an offensive weapon. He could not come to terms with the break-up of his marriage to V1. In January 2012, D rang V1's doorbell and when V1 opened the door, he stepped inside and put his hands around her throat in a threatening manner. V1 was forced against a wall and V2 stepped in and asked D to leave. D left. In July 2012, a court made a Restraining Order. Three days later, D breached the order. V1 and V2 moved to an address which they assumed D would not know of. In December 2012, the doorbell rang at the new address and V2 opened it. No one was there and suddenly D appeared and sprayed a liquid containing cleaning products and lighter fluid in V2's eyes, causing a stinging sensation. D said "I'll kill you, you bastard". D stabbed him in the chest and V2 fell backwards. V2 grabbed the knife and was able to force it out of D's hand. V2 kept hold of D and shouted for help. Two neighbours restrained D until police arrived, when he was arrested. D had taken parcel tape and cable ties with him. V2 had a penetrating chest wound of at least 5 cm. Had the knife been at a different direction, it would have penetrated V2's heart. An impact statement said that V2 had lived in fear since the attack and his personality had changed as a result of the attack. He had undergone counselling and was taking anti-depressants. D was aged 70 at appeal with no convictions. He expressed remorse but that was wholly absent at trial. Held. The aggravating features were that D took a knife to the scene, there was significant planning and there was a background of harassment and repeated breaches of Restraining Orders. It was correct for the Judge to impose a **discretionary life** sentence, given the risk that D posed to V1 and V2. D's settled intention to kill was undoubted. The offence is in Level 1 for the purposes of the attempted murder guideline bearing in mind the effect of Schedule 21 para 5A. The notional determinate term ought to have been 24 years, not 14. Because of his age, that would be reduced to 20 years. The **minimum term** was therefore **10 years** not 7.

See also: *R v Wade* 2012 EWCA Crim 2605, 2013 2 Cr App R (S) 12 (p 52) (Plea. Victim was defendant's ex-wife, they having been divorced for three years. She had become seriously ill and he was looking after her. Condition deteriorated. Incontinent. She drank to excess. D couldn't cope. Needed assistance but V wouldn't accept any outside help. He 'snapped' and attempted to smother her. Admitted it to a police officer a week later when they were called to the house by a neighbour. Only evidence was his confession. D had an alcohol problem and a history of depression. Served 8 months. Equivalent to **16 months**, which was appropriate. Immediate release.)

Old cases: *R v Johnson Re J* 2007 1 Cr App R (S) 112 (p 674) at 689 (IPP, **10-year** notional term) *R v Knox-Hooke* 2006 1 Cr App R (S) 87 (p 500) **(9 years)** *R v Ipek* 2006 1 Cr App R (S) 127 (p 740) (After a trial **15 years**) *R v Clark* 2007 EWCA Crim 2195, 2008 1 Cr App R (S) 105 (p 617) **(8 years)** *R v Knight* 2008 EWCA Crim 1444, 2009 1 Cr App R (S) 57 (p 306) **(30 years)** *R v Mayhew* 2008 EWCA Crim 2897, 2009 2 Cr App R (S) 6 (p 30) **(12 years)** *R v Sandhu* 2008 EWCA Crim 2867, 2009 2 Cr App R (S) 10 (p 61) **(15 years)**

For a summary of the third case, see the 6th edition of this book, for the fourth case, see the 7th edition, and for the fifth case, see the 8th edition.

For the *Domestic Violence Guideline 2006*, see the **DOMESTIC VIOLENCE** chapter.

See also the ***Relationship killings*** paras in the **MANSLAUGHTER** chapter at **284.55** and the **MURDER** chapter at **288.59**.

289.17   *Revenge/Vengeance*

R v Davison 2010 EWCA Crim 2284 D pleaded to attempted murder. He had been asked to leave a hostel in which he was staying after a dispute. He joined a 60-year-old alcoholic, V, in some gardens and 'drank the afternoon away'. D believed that V had touched him in an inappropriate manner and, afflicted by memories of childhood abuse, he produced a knife and stabbed V nine times. V survived. D made his way to a police station and said, "I killed a man tonight for fucking touching me. I stabbed him so many times he's got to be dead." D was sentenced on the basis that V inappropriately touched D. D, aged 35, had a large number of convictions concerning indecent images of children. A psychiatric report found emotionally unstable and antisocial personality disorder. Held. Giving full credit for the plea, the Judge's starting point must have been 18 years. That is too high. The right starting point here was in the region of **12 years**, so with the plea **8 years**.

R v Barnaby 2012 EWCA Crim 1327, 2013 1 Cr App R (S) 53 (p 302) D was convicted of attempted murder. D and V were acquaintances and played cards together. An argument had occurred six months before and D had become aggressive. D and V were again playing cards with others and an argument occurred again, regarding an allegation that D had not put money down on the table. V left the bar, closely followed by D and his friend. D said to V, "Watch, watch". D went to the boot of his car and took out a knife, which was in plastic casing. V ran away and armed himself with a clothes line prop. D and his friend returned to the car and searched for V. D drove at him at speed. D and the friend got out and approached V. V warned he would hit them with the piece of wood, and swung it at them but did not connect. V ran away once again. D caught up with V and stabbed him in his left arm and his stomach. V kept running, but was pursued by D. D stabbed him in the back. V asked, "Are you going to kill me?" D replied, "Yes". V continued to run away and D desisted. V sought help from a passer-by. His intestines were visible through his wound. V suffered three stab wounds, to the right scapula, to the back and to the left of the abdomen. The latter had made a 5 cm cut into the liver, severing an artery. His injuries were life-threatening. There was consequential scarring causing a loss of confidence, low self-esteem and a feeling of depression. There were ongoing psychological problems. A few days after the attack, D left the country. He was arrested when he returned from Jamaica six months later. The pre-sentence report assessed D as posing a high risk of serious harm. D, aged 28, had eight convictions for 14 offences, including possession of a bladed article (2003), assaulting a police officer and common assault (2007). Held. The finding of dangerousness was correct. However, considering *R v Kehoe* 2008 EWCA Crim 819, 2009 1 Cr App R (S) 9 (p 41) (LCJ) and *R v Wilkinson and Others* 2009 EWCA Crim 1925 (LCJ) in relation to a discretionary life sentence being reserved for offences of the utmost gravity, IPP (not life) was the appropriate sentence. This was not a spontaneous attempt to kill. The search and chase put this above Level 3 in the guidelines. Had V died, the starting point would have been 25 years (Schedule 21 paragraph 5A). The injuries put this case in the middle band. Leaving the country is an obvious aggravating factor. 30 years is too high for a notional determinate sentence, 22 years was correct. **IPP** with a minimum term of **11 years**, not life with a minimum term of 15 years.

R v Terry 2012 EWCA Crim 1411, 2013 1 Cr App R (S) 51 (p 285) D was convicted of attempted murder. D and V, aged in his 40s, owned flats in the same building. They knew each other 'a little'. One evening, both had been drinking and D invited V up to his flat for a drink and a chat. There was a dispute. D claimed that V hit him with one of his crutches, causing pain to his leg where he had been previously injured. The Judge found that V had done something to cause D to react. D responded by picking up a claw hammer and striking V 16 times in the face. The skull was fractured in many places. Many of the blows were inflicted when V was on the ground and already seriously injured. He bled profusely, one of his eye sockets shattered and his eye was dislodged. D locked the door of the flat and fled the country. He believed V to be dead. V had metal plates inserted into his skull, he lost an eye and required treatment for excruciating headaches. D was aged 33 and had a troubled childhood. He had a long history of offending, including a number of acquisitive offences and some for violence (not serious). He also had a conviction for possession of a firearm with intent. Using the guidelines, the Judge started at 15 years. Held. The Judge's assessment was impeccable. This was a very serious offence by a man with a long record. 23 years' extended sentence (**18 years' custody** 5 years' licence).

See also: *R v Stevens* 2011 EWCA Crim 827 (Convicted of attempted murder and possessing a firearm with intent. At close range the defendant fired five shots at victim,

three entered body, one entering the jaw and exiting through the neck. Small degree of provocation and self-defence. Treated as good character. Starting at 25 years, **22 years**.)
R v Vakas and Others 2011 EWCA Crim 875 (D convicted of conspiracy to murder. Sustained beating and stabbed victim. Attempted to make him drink 91% sulphuric acid. Poured it over his head. Burns on 47% of his head, neck, chest, abdomen and back. Hideously disfigured. 'Unimaginable suffering'. D, aged 25, at the heart of the conspiracy. **30 years** was not manifestly excessive.)
R v McMahon 2012 EWCA Crim 210 (LCJ Convicted. Previous conviction for murder in 2008 (13-year minimum term). Serving prisoner. Victim was an inmate. Previous incident between the two men. Ligature placed around victim's neck. Rendered him unconscious, believing him to be dead. Aged 26. **20-year** minimum term giving D 11½ years extra.)
Old case: *R v Szypusz and Gaynor* 2006 EWCA Crim 1552, 2007 1 Cr App R (S) 49 (p 273) (**25 years' detention**)
For a summary of the case, see the 8th edition of this book.

289.18   *Sexual*

R v Brown 2011 EWCA Crim 2256 D pleaded late (15% credit) to attempted murder. He telephoned an escort agency and asked for V, a prostitute, whom he had used before. He was anxious and telephoned twice to ensure that V would attend. V attended D's address and after D paid V's fee, and the door was locked at V's request, they proceeded to have intercourse. It was V's habit to close her eyes whilst doing so. After five minutes, she felt something sharp in her neck, and saw D holding a knife with an 8-9 inch blade over her throat. There was a struggle and D ended up on the floor. V took the knife from D and ran out of the property naked. The wound was 12 to 15 cm long and caused a permanent scar. D eventually admitted the offence, but pleaded on the basis that it was spontaneous. D suffered from alcohol dependency syndrome and narcissistic personality traits. He also had a history of violence towards women and convictions (all relatively minor) including harassment and breach of a Non-molestation Order. Held. In mitigation, D had telephoned the emergency services immediately and been co-operative. The attack was spontaneous and relatively brief. There was long-term psychological harm. IPP was proportionate but life was not. After a trial, **17-18** years would have been appropriate, with mitigation, 14 years. **7 years' IPP** not life, minimum term 10 years.
See also: *Att-Gen's Ref No 37 of 2011* 2011 EWCA Crim 1919, 2012 1 Cr App R (S) 84 (p 497) LCJ Plea with rape and other offences. Burglary with knife taken from kitchen. Tied victim to her bed. Oral and vaginal rape. Ejaculated wearing no condom. Stabbed and beat victim repeatedly causing punctured lung. Tip of knife embedded in skull. Set fire to the bed. No mitigation. **Life** with **15-year** not 12-year minimum term.)
See also the **MANSLAUGHTER:** *Sexual* para at **284.59**.

290   OBSTRUCTING A POLICE OFFICER
290.1
Police Act 1996 s 89(2)
Mode of trial Summary only
Maximum sentence 1 month and/or a Level 3 fine (£1,000)

290.2   *Magistrates' Court Sentencing Guidelines*
Magistrates' Court Sentencing Guidelines 2008, see www.banksr.com Other Matters Guidelines tab page 80 The guideline applies to the Magistrates' Court and to the Crown Court hearing appeals or sentencing for summary only offences.[732]
Starting points are based on a first-time offender pleading not guilty.

---

[732] See page 15 of the guidelines.

Examples of nature of activity	Starting point	Range
Failure to move when required to do so	Band A fine	Conditional discharge to Band B fine
Attempt to prevent arrest or other lawful police action, or giving false details	Band B fine	Band A fine to Band C fine
Several people attempting to prevent arrest or other lawful police action	Low-level community order	Band C fine to medium-level community order

The following aggravating and mitigating factors may be particularly relevant. Factors indicating higher culpability: 1 Premeditated action, 2 Aggressive words and/or threats, and 3 Aggressive group action. Factors indicating lower culpability: 1 Genuine mistake or misjudgement, and 2 Brief incident.

Consider ancillary orders

A Band A fine is 50% of net weekly income. Bands B and C are 100% and 150%. For more detail, see **60.27** in Volume 1.

Consultation It is expected that the Sentencing Council will issue a consultation document about updating this guideline in May 2016.

For the meaning of a medium-level and a low-level community order, see **16.12** in Volume 1.

For how to apply the guidelines, see the **GUIDELINES** chapter in Volume 1.

291 OBSTRUCTING THE CORONER/BURIAL, PREVENTING

291.1

Both offences are contrary to the common law.

Modes of trial Both offences are indictable only.

Maximum sentences Neither offence has a maximum provided, so the maximum is life. See **PERVERTING THE COURSE OF JUSTICE/CONTEMPT OF COURT/PERJURY ETC.** *Evidence, Interfering with corpses/injured people* at **305.11**.

291.2 *Judicial guidance*

R v Sullivan 2003 EWCA Crim 806 We refer to *R v Godward* 1998 1 Cr App R (S) 385 at 388 where the Lord Chief Justice said, "If it appears that the intention of the accused was to obstruct the course of justice by disposing of or concealing a body, and so making it difficult or impossible for the prosecuting authority to bring home a charge against the defendant or another person, then that is in our judgment an offence which merits a sentence at the top of the appropriate scale. If, on the other hand, the intention of the defendant is not established or is an intention of a more venial kind, then a shorter sentence will be appropriate."

291.3 *Disposing of/Concealing body*

R v Butterworth 2003 EWCA Crim 1995, 2004 1 Cr App R (S) 40 (p 255) D pleaded to obstructing the coroner. He and others were taking drugs at his address. One of them died, and D said that he didn't want to call an ambulance. The deceased's girlfriend protested but she was overruled. After dark the body was taken to a nearby playing field. The clothing was removed and other clothing was put on the body. After D had come back from work the girlfriend tried to change D's mind. He threatened her. The next day the body was found and the girlfriend made a statement to the police about it. D was aged 39. Held. The offence was committed to avoid the detection of drug offences. It was aggravated by the attempt to remove forensic evidence. It was callous and offensive to the friends and family of the deceased. **3 years** not 3 years 10 months.

R v Amin 2014 EWCA Crim 1924 D (**5 years** concurrent to 8 years for perverting the course of justice upheld, see **305.11**.)

Old case: *R v Munday* 2002 EWCA Crim 2529, 2003 1 Cr App R (S) 118 (p 623) (**4½ years** (plus recall))

For a summary of the case, see the 9th edition of this book.

291.4   *Obstructing the coroner*   *Cases*

R v Masefield 2012 EWCA Crim 1873, 2013 1 Cr App R (S) 77 (p 426) LCJ D pleaded to manslaughter. In 1987, then aged 19, he struck a friend, V, over the head with a metal pole after an argument. V died. D then wrapped V's body in bed sheets and pushed it into a sewage pipe under a manhole cover in the garden. About three months later council workers tried to clear the blockage and V's body was found. Unfortunately the council workers had inadvertently used 'robust methods', which masked the fatal injury. About a month later, D was interviewed and denied being involved. He did, however, refer to the bickering between V and his brother, B. B was arrested for different reasons and a number of his family thought B was responsible and turned completely against him. In 2010, in a drunken conversation with H, D said he had killed V. B heard about it and went to the police. D was interviewed and again denied involvement. Meanwhile H died. In 2011, D approached the police and confessed. D aged (presumably) 44 at appeal, had previous convictions including in 1985 an assault with intent to rob when he used a three-foot pole to demand money in a shop. There was also a battery in which D kicked his son and a burglary in 2011. A basis of plea said D had not aimed at V's head and there was a single blow. B said that D had wrecked 25 years of his life. The Judge considered the most serious aggravating factor was the cover-up, which lasted many years. Held. The following were serious aggravating factors: a) V was to an extent vulnerable and killed in his own home, b) a weapon was used (although it was not taken there), and c) D had disposed of the body in the most appalling way with a total lack of respect for V. B and his sister spoke of how [the disposal] had affected them and because of D's lies suspicion fell on B, and D must have known the anguish this had caused. If D had been charged with obstructing the coroner or perverting the course of justice he could have expected a very substantial sentence, see *R v Lang* 2001 EWCA Crim 2690, 2002 2 Cr App R (S) 15 (p 44), where a sentence of 6 years was imposed. The Judge was right to apply *R v H* 2011 EWCA Crim 2753, 2012 2 Cr App R (S) 21 (p 88). With late plea and modest mitigation **11½ years** was well merited.)

Note: In *R v Lang* 2001, the Court reduced an 8-year sentence to 6 years for perverting the course of justice in a drug-related gang case. The victim was killed with a shotgun and the defendant dug a grave and buried the victim. The grave was covered over with a patio. The plea was late and the defendant was aged 33 with a previous conviction for possession of a firearm, for which he received 4½ years. The Judge found D was involved in professional organised crime. Therefore all very different from the facts in *R v Masefield* 2012. For more details about *R v Lang* 2001 see the 7th edition of this book.

292   OFFENCES AGAINST THE PERSON ACT 1861 S 18

292.1

Offences Against the Person Act 1861 s 18 (wounding or causing grievous bodily harm with intent to do some grievous bodily harm or with intent to resist or prevent the lawful apprehension or detainer of any person.)

Mode of trial Indictable only

Maximum sentence Life

There is an offence of committing an offence with intent to commit a sexual offence, see the **Sexual Offences Act 2003 s 62** chapter.

Automatic life This offence is listed in Criminal Justice Act 2003 Sch 15B Part 1. The court must (unless the particular circumstances make it unjust[733]) pass automatic life if: a) the defendant is aged 18+ at the date of the conviction, b) the offence was committed on or after 3 December 2012, c) the court considers a determinate sentence of at least 10 years is appropriate, d) at the time the offender was convicted he had a conviction for a Criminal Justice Act 2003 Sch 15B offence, and e) the defendant at the time of his or her conviction had previously been sentenced to either i) a life sentence where he or she was not eligible for release during the first five years of the sentence or ii) a determinate sentence or extended sentence where the custodial part was 10 years or more.[734] For a pre-2012 extended sentence, when determining whether the custodial term was 10+ years, the period deducted for time on remand or on a curfew and tag is included.[735]

Extended sentences This offence is listed in Criminal Justice Act 2003 Sch 15. The court may pass a 2012 extended sentence (EDS) if there is a significant risk of serious harm from future specified offences and either: a) the defendant has a Criminal Justice Act 2003 Sch 15B conviction (applicable only to defendants aged 18+), or b) the offence would justify a determinate sentence of at least 4 years.[736]

Football Banning Order Where the offence was committed relevant to a football match and where there are reasonable grounds to believe that making a banning order would help to prevent violence or disorder at or in connection with any regulated football match, the court must make a Football Banning Order, under Football Spectators Act 1989 s 14A and Sch 1 para 1.

Licensed premises Where an offence is committed on licensed premises, the court may prohibit defendants from entering those premises or any other specified premises without the express consent of the licensee etc.[737] The minimum period is 3 months and the maximum period is 2 years.[738] Violent Crime Reduction Act 2006 s 65 and Sch 5 repeals these powers and includes powers to make Drinking Banning Orders. Evaluation of the new powers continues. The repeal and the commencement of the new powers is not expected soon.

Sexual Harm Prevention Orders There is a discretionary power to make this order when it is necessary to protect the public from sexual harm.[739]

Children and vulnerable adults: barred lists Section 18 is not a scheduled offence for automatic barring.

The paragraphs The division of the cases into categories does not mean that each category has its own sentencing tariff. The number of categories only indicates the many ways the offence may be committed. Each case depends critically on its own facts. Ed.

Law Commission On 3 November 2015, the Law Commission published its scoping report, 'Reform of Offences against the Person', Law Com No 361. The report proposes abolishing this offence and substituting a new offence of 'intentionally causing serious injury'.

292.2   Crown Court statistics   England and Wales
Wounding or other act endangering life

---

[733] Criminal Justice Act 2003 s 224A(2)
[734] Criminal Justice Act 2003 s 224A as inserted by Legal Aid, Sentencing and Punishment of Offenders Act 2012 s 122 The condition for: a) is at section 224A(1)(a), for b) is at section 224A(1)(b), for c) is at section 224A(1)(c), and for d) is at section 224A(4)-(9).
[735] Criminal Justice Act 2003 s 224A(9)-(10)
[736] Criminal Justice Act 2003 s 226A-226B as inserted by Legal Aid, Sentencing and Punishment of Offenders Act 2012 s 124
[737] Licensed Premises (Exclusion of Certain Persons) Act 1980 s 1(1)
[738] Licensed Premises (Exclusion of Certain Persons) Act 1980 s 1(3)
[739] Sexual Offences Act 2003 s 103A as inserted by Anti-social Behaviour, Crime and Policing Act 2014 Sch 5 para 2 and Sexual Offences Act 2003 Sch 5

Year	Age	Sex	Plea	Total sentenced	Type of sentencing %						Average length of custody in months
					Discharge	Fine	Community sentence	Suspended sentence	Custody	Other	
2013	10-17			Not available							
	18–20	Male	G	166	–	–	1.2	1.2	97	0.6	59.3
			NG	83	–	–	–	–	100	–	82.6
		Female	G	7	–	–	–	–	100	–	58
			NG	2	–	–	–	50	50	–	15
	21+	Male	G	754	–	–	0.7	2.9	93.2	3.2	71.7
			NG	379	–	–	–	1.1	95.8	3.2	93.5
		Female	G	46	–	–	4.3	10.9	78.3	6.5	56.8
			NG	25	–	–	–	4	88	8	79.7
2014	10-17			Not available							
	18–20	Male	G	134	–	–	1	1	93	6	63.4
			NG	50	–	–	–	2	96	2	82.9
		Female	G	10	–	–	–	–	100	–	61.8
			NG	4	–	–	–	–	100	–	Not listed[740]
	21+	Male	G	706	–	–	–	3	89	7	71.3
			NG	376	–	–	–	2	92	5	93.8
		Female	G	40	–	–	–	5	83	13	61.3
			NG	33	–	–	3	15	79	3	69.6

For explanations about the statistics, see page 1-xii. For more statistics about defendants aged 10-20 and statistics for male and female defendants, see www.banksr.com Other Matters Statistics tab

292.3   *Sentencing Council guideline*

Assault Guideline 2011, see www.banksr.com Other Matters Guidelines tab page 3 This guideline applies to all offenders aged 18 and older, regardless of the date of the offence, see page 2 of the guideline. For the usual practice, see **66.21** in Volume 1. In force 13 June 2011.

STEP ONE Determining the offence category

page 4 The court should determine the offence category using the table below.

Category 1	Greater harm (serious injury must normally be present) and higher culpability
Category 2	Greater harm (serious injury must normally be present) and lower culpability or lesser harm and higher culpability
Category 3	Lesser harm and lower culpability

page 4 The court should determine the offender's culpability and the harm caused, or intended, by reference **only** to the factors below (as demonstrated by the presence of one or more). These factors comprise the principal factual elements of the offence and should determine the category.

---

[740] Based on too few cases to be meaningful

Factors indicating greater harm
Injury (which includes disease transmission and/or psychological harm) which is serious in the context of the offence (must normally be present)   Victim is particularly vulnerable because of personal circumstances   Sustained or repeated assault on the same victim

Factors indicating lesser harm
Injury which is less serious in the context of the offence

Factors indicating lower culpability
Subordinate role in group or gang   A greater degree of provocation than normally expected   Lack of premeditation   Mental disorder or learning disability, where linked to commission of the offence   Excessive self-defence

Factors indicating higher culpability
Statutory aggravating factors: Offence racially or religiously aggravated   Offence motivated by, or demonstrating, hostility to the victim based on his or her sexual orientation (or presumed sexual orientation)   Offence motivated by, or demonstrating, hostility to the victim based on the victim's disability (or presumed disability)   *Other aggravating factors:*   A significant degree of premeditation   Use of weapon or weapon equivalent (for example, shod foot, head-butting, use of acid, use of animal)   Intention to commit more serious harm than actually resulted from the offence   Deliberately causes more harm than is necessary for commission of offence   Deliberate targeting of vulnerable victim   Leading role in group or gang   Offender motivated by, or demonstrating, hostility based on the victim's age, sex, gender identity (or presumed gender identity)

292.4

STEP TWO Starting point and category range

page 5 Having determined the category, the court should use the corresponding starting points to reach a sentence within the category range below. The starting point applies to all offenders irrespective of plea or previous convictions. A case of particular gravity, reflected by multiple features of culpability in step one, could merit upward adjustment from the starting point before further adjustment for aggravating or mitigating features, set out below.

Offence category	Starting point (applicable to all offenders)	Category range (applicable to all offenders)
Category 1	12 years' custody	9 to 16 years' custody
Category 2	6 years' custody	5 to 9 years' custody
Category 3	4 years' custody	3 to 5 years' custody

292.5   [Aggravating and mitigating factors]

page 5 The table below contains a non-exhaustive list of additional factual elements providing the context of the offence and factors relating to the offender.

Factors increasing seriousness

Statutory aggravating factors:

Previous convictions, having regard to a) the nature of the offence to which the conviction relates and its relevance to the current offence; and b) the time that has elapsed since the conviction

Offence committed whilst on bail

Other aggravating factors include:

Location of the offence

Timing of the offence

Ongoing effect upon the victim

Offence committed against those working in the public sector or providing a service to the public

Presence of others including relatives, especially children or partner of the victim

Gratuitous degradation of victim

In domestic violence cases, victim forced to leave their home

Failure to comply with current court orders

Offence committed whilst on licence

An attempt to conceal or dispose of evidence

Failure to respond to warnings or concerns expressed by others about the offender's behaviour

Commission of offence whilst under the influence of alcohol or drugs

Abuse of power and/or position of trust

Exploiting contact arrangements with a child to commit an offence

Previous violence or threats to the same victim

Established evidence of community impact

Any steps taken to prevent the victim reporting an incident, or obtaining assistance and/or from assisting or supporting the prosecution

Offences taken into consideration (TICs)

Factors reducing seriousness or reflecting personal mitigation

No previous convictions or no relevant/recent convictions

Single blow

Remorse

Good character and/or exemplary conduct

Determination, and/or demonstration of steps taken to address addiction or offending behaviour

Serious medical conditions requiring urgent, intensive or long-term treatment

Isolated incident

Age and/or lack of maturity where it affects the responsibility of the offender

Lapse of time since the offence where this is not the fault of the offender

Mental disorder or learning disability, where not linked to the commission of the offence

Sole or primary carer for dependent relatives

The court should then consider the following: a) other factors indicating a reduction, such as assistance to the prosecution, b) reduction for a guilty plea, c) dangerousness, d) totality, if sentencing for more than one offence, e) compensation and ancillary orders.

292.6   *Applying the guidelines*

R v Richardson 2012 EWCA Crim 1007, 2 Cr App R (S) 103 (p 606) D pleaded to section 18. Held. The [Sentencing Council] guidelines say that, in order for there to be greater harm, injury which is serious in the context of the offence must normally be present. Without being in any way prescriptive, it may be helpful for the sentencing judge to deal with that point first. If he or she finds serious injury, the reasons for that conclusion should briefly be explained. Then, whatever the view on the seriousness of the injury, the judge would (ordinarily) go on to consider whether either of the other two factors, namely vulnerability or a sustained attack, are present. Again, if they are, brief reasons would be given for this conclusion. There would follow a brief balancing exercise in order for the judge to reach a final conclusion as to whether, on all the facts, greater harm can be said to exist.

R v Fadairo 2012 EWCA Crim 1292 In deciding whether it is appropriate to move outside the identified category range, the judge will take into account both the factors listed in step one and those listed in step two, and any other relevant factors.

R v Anani 2013 EWCA Crim 65, 2 Cr App R (S) 57 (p 370) The [guideline] boxes are not mutually exclusive. There is an inevitable overlap between the scenarios which reflects the fact that real-life offending is found on a sliding scale of gravity with few hard lines.

R v Smith 2015 EWCA Crim 1482, 2016 1 Cr App R (S) 8 (p 49) The Judge categorised the case as Category 1. Held. The differences between Categories 1 and 2 are stark as far as the penalty is concerned. The injuries here were significant but they could be worse. para 4 In the harm category in the guidelines it says, 'serious injury must normally be present'. 'Normally' is an indication that an offence may abnormally be a Category 1 offence even where the harm is less than serious. The only reason the Judge gave for finding 'higher harm' was that the blow required hospital treatment, stitching and had a considerable lasting effect. The question is whether 'the injury was serious in the context of the offence'. That means the violence must go beyond what is inherent or par [for the course] in a standard section 18 case. It must be significantly above the serious level of harm which is normal for section 18. Here, there was one blow amounting to section 18. It was sufficient to break the bat. It was a serious attack. Given the great disparity between Categories 1 and 2, it was nasty but it was not Category 1. However, the previous blow makes it more serious and closer to a Category 1 offence. Because V was dazed when he was hit, he was vulnerable. The two blows, one of which was not a section 18 blow, would not normally amount to a 'sustained or repeated assault'. This case was either at the top end of Category 2 or on the borderline between Categories 1 and 2, so we start at 9 years. For more detail see **292.42.**)

292.7   *Pre-guideline judicial guidance*

Att-Gen's Ref Nos 59-60 and 63 of 1998 1999 2 Cr App R (S) 128 LCJ All offences under section 18 are serious because they involve the deliberate or intentional causing of serious injury. Some instances are more serious than others: the use of a firearm, a razor, a knife, a broken bottle, a club, a baseball bat, or a pick handle, or something of that sort, has usually been held to aggravate the offence. The courts have also, however, been obliged to recognise that injuries of almost equal seriousness can be caused by kicking with a shod foot or biting. It is also, of course, possible to inflict serious injury with the bare fist, although this is usually regarded as less serious, partly because in that instance the offender may lack the premeditation usually shown by a defendant who has armed himself with a dangerous weapon. Perhaps the least inexcusable example of an offence under section 18 is where a defendant entitled to defend himself responds with unreasonable and excessive force directed against an aggressor. Even then a custodial sentence, probably of some length, will usually be appropriate. In any other case a custodial sentence will almost invariably follow.

Att-Gen's Ref Nos 44-45 of 2001 2001 EWCA Crim 1483 In *Att-Gen's Ref No 44 of 1994* 1995 16 Cr App R (S) 865 the Lord Chief Justice said, "It is frequently a misconception that unless some object is held in the hand, no weapon has been used. An attacker who uses shod feet or who bites someone is just as much using a weapon as someone who wields an object in his hand."

Att-Gen's Ref No 29 of 2001 2001 EWCA Crim 1491, 2002 1 Cr App R (S) 60 (p 253) The essence of the offence which marks it out for a substantial custodial sentence is the specific intent to do serious bodily harm which, even in cases of provocation or stress, simply cannot be excused. In section 18 cases the court is less flexible in its approach than in relation to lesser assaults, and is much less inclined to leniency in the face of personal mitigation.

Note: None of these remarks appear inconsistent with the guidelines. Ed.

Types of section 18 offence

292.8   *Attempted section 18   Pre-guideline case*

R v Perks 2011 EWCA Crim 2115 D was convicted of attempted section 18. He had been drinking and taking cocaine with H. They went downstairs to P's flat with the intention of buying more cocaine. The three men left the flat. H attacked P with a claw hammer causing severe skull fractures. H returned to P's flat and was admitted by V. D waited outside. H attacked V with the hammer. V pushed H and managed to run out of the flat. D was invited inside but waited outside with W, who attacked V. The Judge found that D knew that H was going to attack V and realised that serious injury would be caused. Held. While the fact of the relatively minor injury was relevant, the Judge was entitled to view the matter as one involving serious culpability and harm by D. **8 years** was not manifestly excessive.

Biting see the ***Fighting, Biting*** para at **292.13**.

Blackmail, With see BLACKMAIL *Violence occurs, Serious* para at **217.12**.

292.9   *Bullying/Showing off*

R v Mangan 2010 EWCA Crim 1561 D pleaded to GBH with intent and ABH (full credit). V, aged 18, had psychological and learning difficulties. V met O on a bus and travelled with him to meet D and his girlfriend, S. V asked for S's phone number and D punched V in the face several times. V put his hands to his face in an attempt to protect himself. S joined in the punching. D told V to get on his knees and D and S told O to hit V. D stood behind V holding V's hands behind his back whilst holding onto V's head. O punched V hard in the face. V's nose was broken and he fell to the ground. D, S and O laughed at V and insulted him for not fighting back and subjected V to further assaults. The group then went to a nearby car park. D told V to get on his hands and knees and bark like a dog, to lick D's trainers, to call D 'sir' or 'prince', to call S 'madam' and to sniff D's backside. V was punched and kicked. D made V lie on the floor and used a lighter to burn V's hair. D then lit an aerosol can and burned V's hair again. D took V's bank card, demanded the PIN and threatened to shoot V if he said anything to the police. V suffered a bruised and partially closed left eye, a swollen lip, swollen ear, singed patches of hair and a broken nose. V suffered grievous psychological harm and will continue to do so. D, now aged 20, had previous convictions for a number of burglaries, theft, common assault and threatening behaviour and was in breach of a Detention and Training Order. The pre-sentence report said D posed a high risk of reoffending, he had displayed no compassion or remorse and he represented a high risk of serious harm to vulnerable persons as well as a medium risk of serious harm to future partners of his. The medical reports said D met the test of dangerousness. The Judge took a starting point of 9 years. Held. The correct starting point would have been 7 years, so with a third reduction for plea and dividing it in half for IPP, **2 years 4 months' IPP** not 3 years.

See also: *R v H* 2010 EWCA Crim 1547, 2011 1 Cr App R (S) 52 (p 340) (D, aged 15, convicted of GBH with intent and theft. Unprovoked gang attack on youths. Skull fracture and frontal lobe damage. **6 years' detention**, not 7.)

R v Ware 2010 EWCA Crim 1968 (Plea on rearraignment. Unprovoked attack on three females at 3 am. Racist language. D, aged 16, threw brick at victim causing 4-inch cut. **3 years' detention**, not 4.)

Old cases: *R v Hulme and Others* 2008 EWCA Crim 2501 (**DPP** (**5 years 10 months** for one and **4 years 4 months** for the other) *R v Skeggs and Field* 2009 EWCA Crim 439 (**8 years' detention**)

For a summary of the first case, see the 8th edition of this book and for the second case, see the 9th edition.

Post-guideline cases

R v Haynes and Jones 2011 EWCA Crim 2318 D (30% credit) and J (18% credit) pleaded late to section 18. In the early hours of the morning, they had been drinking and were 'chilling out' in a supermarket car park with others. V, aged 34, who had also been drinking and was swaying as a result, walked into the car park. D and J thought it was amusing. V rounded on them and J punched V. V tried to defend himself but was hampered because one of his arms was in plaster. D joined the attack and both punched V and grappled him to the floor. V was kicked numerous times to the head and body. Two others tried to pull D and J away. D and J fled, and discouraged others from calling an ambulance. V was not found until 7 am the following morning. He had suffered an extensive fracture to the front of his skull, extensive brain swelling and was in a coma. A lung injury aggravated the brain injury. There were subsequent complications and, at sentence, V could not speak, walk or stand. J asked a friend to punch him so that he could claim V had generated the attack. D and J sent text messages to the others who were present, encouraging them to join in their fabricated account. D, aged 18 at appeal, had no previous convictions. J, aged 17 at appeal, was treated as of good character. Reports suggested that their remorse was genuine. Held. Following the guidelines, the appalling outcome, the mob-handed thuggery, two on one, merits raising the starting point to 10 years for an adult. Moderated for youth and the eventual pleas, **7 years** not 9 for D and **6½** not 7 for J.

R v King 2014 EWCA Crim 2030 D pleaded to section 18 assault (20% credit). V was walking home with a friend past D, who was in a group of around nine men. V knew some of them, including D. The group were drinking and smoking cannabis. Fighting then broke out. D put V in a headlock and, pulling a ring from V's finger, told him to empty his pockets. D then head-butted V in the face. The group of men then tried to rob V and his friend, but both fled. V ran to a house, asking that they let him in, but the occupants were too scared to do so. As D caught up with V, V shouted in Arabic that he was disabled and had a brain injury. In 2012 V had suffered a compressed skull and a brain injury, a fact which was well known to locals, including D. Two other members of the group caught up with V and one of them punched him and broke his jaw, nearly knocking him over in the process. The other kicked V in the head and foot. All three then repeatedly punched V in the head, jaw and back, notwithstanding that someone had tried to intervene. V's pockets were also rifled through, he suffered facial bruising and his jaw was broken in two places, needing surgery. Upon arrest, D smelt strongly of alcohol and had V's ring and mobile on him. D was aged 26 on appeal and had nine previous convictions. He was on a suspended sentence following a racist ABH in 2013 and had committed five assaults from 2007 to 2012. The pre-sentence report noted that D was impulsive, unpredictable and had no control over his violence. He also posed an imminent risk to the public but did not presently, although he could become dangerous. The Judge accepted this assessment. Held. This was a Category 1 offence but the starting point should have been 12 to 12½ years not 14, so **9 years 10 months**, not 11 years 2 months and the 2 months of the activated suspended sentence consecutive.

Note: What the motive was is far from clear. Ed.

See also the *Torture/Sadistic violence* para at **292.36** and MANSLAUGHTER *Bullying/ Showing off etc.* para at **284.12**.

Burglary, And see *Robbery/Burglary/Aggravated burglary, And* at **292.32**.

Children as victims see the CRUELTY TO CHILDREN **Offences Against the Person Act 1861** section at **231.22**.

Domestic Violence For the general principles, see the DOMESTIC VIOLENCE chapter. See the *Relationship attack* paras at **292.28**.

292.10   *Crime of passion   Post-guideline case*
Example: *R v Smith* 2012 EWCA Crim 2852 (Convicted of section 18 and ABH. Visited ex-partner's home and using a key she retained, wrecked the house. Returned later with a knife, stabbing ex-partner's new partner twice in the back in front of him. When dragged away, she pulled at her hair. Stabs were so forceful the knife broke. No internal organs damaged but there was residual scarring. Wounds 6-8 cm deep. Aged 24. Had 6-month-old child when sentenced. No convictions. Positive references. 8 years not 12.)

292.11 *Domestic violence   Post-guideline case*
R v Halliwell 2015 EWCA Crim 1134, 2 Cr App R (S) 64 (p 454) D pleaded (25%
credit) to section 18 and ABH. D went to a pub to celebrate a windfall with his daughter,
V1 and her boyfriend, V2. D and V2 became drunk. The three returned home and D
carried on drinking. V2 was put to bed. Later, [D went in the room], seized V2 by the
throat and punched V2 repeatedly in the face. This was the ABH. V2 and another tried to
pull D off V2 but couldn't. D threatened to kill both of them. D left the room and
returned with a pair of scissors. D told V1 she should not have tried to help V2. D then
stabbed V1 in the shoulder area and punched her to the face and body. V1 bent forward
and D stabbed her again in the back. V1 fled outside and V2 jumped out of the first floor
window to seek help. V1 had a penetrating wound to her back, a collapsed lung and a
superficial wound to the front of her chest. V2 had facial bruising, particularly to an eye,
and cuts. D was now aged 45 and between 1982 and 2005 he had 13 sentencing hearings
for 29 offences. He had two section 47 offences in 1984 (a fine and 21 days' detention).
In 1987, he had a section 20 wounding (community order). He also had a long history of
alcohol abuse. The pre-sentence report said D posed a high risk of causing serious harm
to those closest to him. The Judge assessed the section 18 as a Category 2 offence with a
starting point of 10 years. Held. The 1984 and 1987 offences were historic and [could
not be used] to assess dangerousness. The Judge was right to consider the underlying
history of domestic violence. The section 18 offence was very close to or within
Category 1, so the penalty was 10-11 years, making 8 years with the plea. The ABH was
a Category 2 not 1 case, so 1 year not 1½. It should be concurrent not consecutive, so **8
years** determinate in all and not 12½ years' extended sentence (9 years' custody 2½
years' extended licence).

292.12   *Drug dealer victims   Post-guideline case*
Att-Gen's Ref No 32 of 2012 2012 EWCA Crim 2588, 2013 2 Cr App R (S) 8 (p 39) D
was convicted of section 18. The victim, V, was with two friends in the living room of
his home. The front door was not locked. D entered and struck V without saying a word.
V already had a fractured cheekbone. He received a series of further blows to his head. D
then left. It was unclear whether he had others with him when he entered, though
evidence suggested he left with two others. V suffered multiple fractures to the mid-face,
which included a broken jaw, fractured cheekbones and fractures to the eye sockets and
nose. There were also extensive bruising and lacerations to his head and upper lip.
Surgery fixed the facial fractures with plates and screws, which necessitated incisions
across the scalp, through the lower eyelids and through the mouth. D was arrested 2
hours after the attack. He had blood spattered on his face and hands, his shirt and his
jeans. The blood staining on the right boot and the distribution of the blood on his jeans
demonstrated beyond doubt that D had stamped on V's face at a time when he was
already significantly injured. D said, "That's what happens to drug dealers" and "I don't
care as I'll get off in the morning. He won't give a statement." Police found at the
address a number of small packs containing cocaine. V declined to give a statement but
there was sufficient evidence to proceed. D, aged 29 at appeal, had convictions for 36
offences including burglary, affray and ABH when aged 20 (3 years' detention). In 2007,
he was convicted of possession of an offensive weapon, threatening words and
behaviour and ABH (extended sentence (30 months' custody 3 years' licence)). The
current offence was committed in breach of licence from the 2007 offence. Held. The
Judge found that this was not a premeditated offence. That is a significant factor which
operates as a limit on the appropriate sentence. There were a number of significant
aggravating factors: a) the offence was committed whilst on licence, b) D's previous
convictions, including violence to the person, and c) committed at night and in V's
home. The fact that V may have been a drug dealer is relevant to a point, in that a drug
dealer who opens his doors to unlawful trade is not in the same position as a householder
who is broken into by an attacker at night. Nevertheless, it was an unprovoked attack in
V's home. The callous remark made by D, to the effect that 'this is what happens to drug

dealers' and that D would be released because V wouldn't make a statement, was highly significant. The courts are no friends of drug dealers, [but] for an offender to think that a particular type of victim, however vile his trade may be, is therefore beyond the protection of the law from serious assault…is totally unacceptable. It was a serious aggravating feature of the offence that D carried out the attack believing himself to be immune. The appropriate sentence was **13 years**, not 7. There was ample material to suggest IPP, but it would not be right to conclude that the Judge was wrong not to impose IPP.

292.13   *Fighting   Biting   Pre-guideline case*
Att-Gen's Ref Nos 44-45 of 2001 2001 EWCA Crim 1483 In *Att-Gen's Ref No 44 of 1994* 1995 16 Cr App R (S) 865, the Lord Chief Justice said, "It is frequently a misconception that unless some object is held in the hand, no weapon has been used. An attacker who uses shod feet or who bites someone is just as much using a weapon as someone who wields an object in his hand."

292.14   *Fighting when the major injuries are caused by the fall, not any blow*
Note: This principle is particularly relevant in manslaughter and Offences Against the Person Act 1861 s 20 cases, see **284.31** and **293.10**. It has less relevance for section 18 cases because there is a specific intent to cause GBH. Ed.
Fire, By see the **ARSON Arson intending life would be endangered** section at **209.20**.

292.15   *Firearms, With*
R v Collins and Others 2009 EWCA Crim 2534, 2010 2 Cr App R (S) 3 (p 15) C, T and B were convicted of GBH with intent. V's brother was assaulted in a pub, and V thought that C was responsible. About a week later, H spoke to C's mother and she was upset. C was told about this. C contacted B, who contacted T, and the three agreed to confront V in a pub. C and T knew that B was bringing a gun. Just after 10 pm the confrontation took place. V argued with C and punched him, knocking him to the floor. B produced a gun and shot V. V initially continued to confront B but retreated. B and C ran after him, and B shot V again. The shootings were at close range. C, T and B then ran. One shot passed close to a kidney and 'shaved' the liver. The second shot went through the colon, perforating it. That bullet could not be removed, and there it remains. V was in hospital for ten days and had a colostomy. There was a reversal which required major surgery. C was aged 21, and B and T were aged 26. T had convictions for attempted robbery and possession of a firearm. C and B were relatively lightly convicted. The pre-sentence report said that T acted out of misplaced loyalty and peer pressure. B was remorseful and had character references. The Judge found that the injuries could have been fatal, and that T was less responsible than the other two. Held. These were particularly grave injuries and potentially lethal. It was in the highest category. There was a gang, two shots not in quick succession were serious aggravating factors. **14 years** for C and B and **10 years** for T upheld.
R v Carty and Others 2010 EWCA Crim 831 C, K and J were convicted of section 18 and a robbery. They responded to an advertisement for a fast car. They met the owner and stole the car using unnecessary gratuitous violence involving kicking V after he had offered them the car keys. Two days later, the three used the car as a getaway vehicle. J stayed in the car while C and K entered a wedding reception wearing balaclavas and carrying at least one gun. C went behind the bridegroom, B, who was at the high table and shot him in the lap. C was trying to shoot B's genitals but missed, hitting an artery causing serious injury. Shots were fired into the ceiling. After using the car it was destroyed. The motive was extreme sexual jealousy. J had a short relationship with the bride, who broke it off and went back to B. J was the organiser. C and K were aged 17. C had convictions but none for violence. He was in the lowest 1% for IQ, had significant learning difficulties, memory problems and a low level of intellectual functioning. The Judge found C was unable to weigh up consequences and was not fully able to resist. K had served 10 months for violent disorder. J was aged nearly 19. He had convictions for

burglary and violent disorder. During their trial the three tried to escape. Only J was successful. Held. It was a meticulous and carefully planned attempt to cause severe injury and horror to all those present and to destroy B's relationship. J's age was no mitigation as he displayed the necessary maturity to execute two such dreadful crimes. C's low IQ and his easy susceptibility did not diminish the fact he was capable of acting in a controlled and planned way to commit extremely dangerous offences. Had they been older, the terms would have been substantially longer. J's pre-sentence report provided chilling reading. He was very dangerous indeed. **7½ years' IPP** for C and K upheld. J was fortunate to have received a low **8-year** term for his **IPP**.

See also: *Att-Gen's Ref No 42 of 2010* 2010 EWCA Crim 2716, 2011 2 Cr App R (S) 3 (p 7) (Plea. Full credit. Section 18, possessing a firearm with intent and possession of prohibited ammunition. After an argument, shot half-brother-in-law in buttocks from close range while he was face down in bed. Premeditated. No relevant convictions. Starting at no less than 16 years, with the plea and because it was a reference, **10 years** not 6.)

Post-guideline case

Example: *R v Rasab* 2012 EWCA Crim 1704 (Plea to attempted section 18 and carrying a firearm with intent. Resentment between gang members and the victim, V, who was an ex-member of the gang. Attempts to blackmail V. Violence between gang and V. Drive-by shooting with double-barrelled shotgun outside V's house. Did not hit V. Committed whilst on licence for section 18. Also found loaded revolver and sub-machine gun with ammunition at his address. Full credit. Starting at 15 years was appropriate. So **5 years' IPP**, not 6.)

Note: These offence are normally charged as firearm offences. Ed.

292.16   Glassing (using a glass as a weapon)   Pre-guideline judicial guidance

Note: It will usually be necessary to consider whether the bottle was: i) picked up broken, ii) broken deliberately just before being used, or iii) whether it broke on impact. Ed.

Att-Gen's Ref No 14 of 2000 2001 1 Cr App R (S) 16 (p 55) Glassing offences are extremely dangerous. Terrible and permanent injuries can be inflicted in a split second.

R v Pritchard 2002 EWCA Crim 1668, 2003 1 Cr App R (S) 55 (p 263) The defendant pleaded to section 18. Held. Using a glass to lacerate the face is a significantly aggravating factor because of the appalling long-term consequences that may occur. Where an offence is committed in cold blood, with premeditation and the motive of revenge, the sentence would be significantly longer.

See also: *R v Anani* 2013 EWCA Crim 65, 2 Cr App R (S) 57 (p 370) (Pleas to two section 18s, affray and possession of an offensive weapon by Algerian asylum-seeker. D saw an attack and went to fetch a bottle. Returned with broken bottle. Attacked man in face with it, hard. Man needed 12 outer and 12 inner stitches. Swung bottle at others. Another was lacerated on the arm. Aged 35. No convictions. Category 1 or upper end of Category 2. 9 years, with the plea **6 years** upheld.)

For using unbroken bottles, see the **Hammers, bars, bottles (unbroken) etc.** para at **292.19**.

292.17   Glassing   Cases

R v Simpson 2011 EWCA Crim 1141, 2012 1 Cr App R (S) 9 (p 38) D was convicted of section 18. V was in a bar and went to the lavatory. D was there attempting to take some cocaine. He accused V of taking the cocaine and preventing him from doing so. V left the lavatory. Some five or ten minutes later, V was standing at the bar waiting to be served. D approached him from behind and struck him between three and five times in the face with a glass. The glass smashed and caused a serious laceration to V's lip. V suffered severe blood loss and multiple lacerations in the mouth. There was permanent scarring and V had substantial psychological problems. V had no feeling in his upper lip and was unable to feel when kissing. He lost his apprenticeship and was only rarely able to socialise. D, aged 47 at appeal, had two cautions in 2006 for violence while drunk, but did have a good character reference. Held. It is not possible to fit every case of assault into one of the brackets used in the guidelines. Moreover, Criminal Justice Act 2003 s 143 requires that regard be had to the intended or foreseeable harm, not just the actual harm. This offence was premeditated. There was an interval of some minutes between the incident in the lavatory and D's actions. D seized the weapon and used it with specific intent. There was a high degree of culpability. **10 years** was severe but not manifestly excessive.

Old cases: *R v Haystead* 2009 EWCA Crim 1177, 2010 1 Cr App R (S) 21 (p 117) (**6 years**) *R v Gayle* 2010 EWCA Crim 2932 (Convicted. Beer poured over girl, punch to face and she walks out. Glass thrown at female victim's face which smashes, causing cuts. Previous good character. **5½ years** was not manifestly excessive.)

For a summary of the first case, see the 9th edition of this book. For numerous other old cases, see the 8th edition.

Post-guideline cases

Att-Gen's Ref No 37 of 2011 2011 EWCA Crim 1720, 2012 1 Cr App R (S) 72 (p 405) D pleaded late to section 18, having earlier admitted section 20. V, who was drunk, asked D about which drink belonged to D. D, who had consumed 16 units of alcohol and 'a couple of lines of coke', picked up a glass and hit V in the face. The glass smashed, causing nine wounds, including an 8 cm cut, and two or three cuts of 3 cm in length. It was likely that V would suffer permanent scarring. D, aged 30 at appeal, was of exemplary good character, was taking anti-depressant medication and had had suicidal thoughts following his ex-fiancée's infidelity. The Judge sentenced him to a Suspended Sentence Order. He had completed 23 of 250 hours of unpaid work and had spent 49 days on a curfew. Held. Too often glasses are used as weapons and lead to serious and permanent consequences. The Judge failed to identify his reason for departing from the guidelines. This case clearly has a starting point of 5 years, when considering the guidelines. Giving credit for the plea (10-16%), his exemplary character, the unpaid work and curfew, and allowing for double jeopardy, **3 years**.

R v Moran 2012 EWCA Crim 263 D was convicted of section 18. She had been involved in a dispute with a waitress in a pub. The manageress, V, had intervened and offered D a refund. D was asked to leave, at which point the waitress began to clear the table. V asked D for the glass which she was holding. D refused and V attempted to take the glass from her, at which point D thrust the glass into V's neck. V suffered an 11.5 cm incised wound causing very noticeable permanent scarring. D, aged 20 at the time of the offence, had four convictions for four offences. When aged 17, she received a 9-month Referral Order for a section 20 offence where she had used a wine glass as a weapon. The pre-sentence report noted that much of D's offending was linked to binge drinking. Held. This came toward the lower end of Category 2. There were six aggravating features: a) the previous conviction for glassing, b) V was providing a public service, c) the offence was witnessed by D's children, d) it was in a public place, e) it was unprovoked, and f) there was permanent scarring. In mitigation: i) D had struck only a single blow, ii) D was now aged only 21, iii) D had demonstrated some remorse, and iv) there were very positive reports from prison. **5 years' YOI** was a fair and reasonable sentence for this offence.

R v Foster 2015 EWCA Crim 916, 2 Cr App R (S) 45 (p 348) D pleaded (full credit) to section 18. He was in a relationship with G for almost one year. Both were at university. D did not accept that the relationship had ended. At 2.30 am, he sent a text to G saying he had seen her with someone. Later, in a night club, he saw G with, V, a friend of hers. V and G hugged and D stabbed V in the back three times with a broken bottle. It was over very quickly. V had three incised wounds to his lower back and buttock area and two superficial wounds. The larger wounds needed six and two sutures. V was a student in his final year. As a result of his injuries he could not train for or attend national and regional ski competitions. V was also fearful of going out. D was aged 24 and of positive good character. The probation officer was impressed by D's appreciation of his offending and accepted that his remorse, regret and shame were genuine. The Judge thought the offence was aggravated by a) the repeated blows, albeit in quick succession, and b) D was under the influence of alcohol. He increased the starting point in Category 2 from 6 to 7 years. Held. This was a cowardly and unprovoked attack. The injuries were far from trivial. The Judge rightly placed this in Category 2. The weapon gave it higher culpability, but there was no greater harm. The mitigation counterbalanced the aggravating factors so we start at 6 years. With plea, **4 years** not 4 years 8 months.

See also: *R v Burtenshaw* 2012 EWCA Crim 3058, 2013 2 Cr App R (S) 41 (p 277) (Convicted. Threw wine glass on the floor in a wine bar. Challenged by door staff. Told to leave and refused. Smashed beer glass he was holding in the doorman's face and then hit him again with the smashed glass. Serious cuts (over 30 stitches). Aged 29. No relevant convictions. Between Categories 1 and 2. Aggravated by the fact that the victim was working at the time of the attack, in a public place and the defendant was drunk. **9 years** was not manifestly excessive.)

R v Anani 2013 EWCA Crim 65, 2 Cr App R (S) 57 (p 370) (Pleas to two section 18s, affray and possession of an offensive weapon by Algerian asylum-seeker. D saw an attack and went to fetch a bottle. Returned with broken bottle. Attacked man in face with it, hard. Man needed 12 outer and 12 inner stitches. Swung bottle at others. Another was lacerated on the arm. Aged 35. No convictions. Category 1 or upper end of Category 2. 9 years, with the plea **6 years** upheld.)

292.18   *Group attacks   Post-guideline cases*

R v Grubb 2011 EWCA Crim 3228, 2 Cr App R (S) 43 (p 248) D was convicted of section 18. Sm and St pleaded guilty. V lived in a bedsit where Sm and St were also residents. Sm was D's ex-partner and father of her son. V kept his room unlocked and was happy for Sm and St to wander in and out. V returned one day and found Sm and St in his room. St and Sm left after a short conversation. St re-entered the room and V was on edge. Sm and D joined shortly after. D accused V of touching her son in a sexual manner. V emphatically denied this. D insisted her son was telling the truth. She went up to V and slapped him twice and punched him. D then stepped back and Sm and St took up the attack. St punched V about the body and head several times, and Sm joined in quickly, also punching V about the head and body. V was pleading with them to stop and protesting that he hadn't done anything to D's child. Sm and St were calling him a paedophile. V felt that the assault carried on for 30 minutes. The assault stopped and D drank some lager and smoked a cigarette. She said, "Tell me the truth and we won't hurt you again." Again, V maintained his emphatic denial. D slapped him in the face and St punched him in the face and pushed him backwards so that his head hit the wall. V passed out and awoke to find his nose bleeding. Sm took photographs of V's injuries on his mobile phone. St turned the sound up on the TV, dragged V into the middle of the floor and stamped on his groin four times. St and Sm punched and kicked V in the face and body. Sm stamped on V's ribs. St then took out his penis, wiped it on V's face and then urinated on V. St then said, "If you grass on us we'll all deny it and we'll kill you. He suggested that V's explanation for his injuries should be that he was beaten up in an alleyway. V had soiled himself twice during the attack. V initially told the police the false story. V suffered a significant amount of bleeding on the brain. There was an extensive fracture of the left eye socket, a fractured rib, a bruised kidney, water on the lungs, a fracture to the skull and bruising to various parts of the body. D, aged 26, was the sole carer of her 4-year-old son. Three of D and Sm's children had been taken into care. Only D's 4-year-old son lived with her. As a result of the offence, the child lived with his paternal grandparents. D had no relevant convictions but did have a caution for cruelty to a child in 2004. Held. The Judge was correct to start at 12 years. This was a joint enterprise and was plainly a Category 1 case. It is right to reflect the respective roles. All the physical injuries were caused by Sm and St. **8 years** not 11.

R v Clifford 2013 EWCA Crim 803 (See **292.19** below.)

R v Law 2014 EWCA Crim 1772 D was convicted of wounding with intent. D and his wife had separated and V was in a relationship with D's wife. D's 18-year-old son, H, was employed by V. D and H pulled up in a car and H got out, crossed the road and spoke to V. After an exchange of words, H returned to the car and was followed by V. The car then drove off and it was accepted that V may have acted in an unpleasant manner towards H during these events. About 20 minutes later, V was on the same stretch of road and D, wielding a 4ft metal pole, ran up behind him and struck V over the head and to the kidney area. V then turned around and was struck on the elbow but managed to disarm D. H then threatened V with a shovel. V suffered a cut to his head requiring stitches, a 3 cm laceration to the elbow and bruising to his back. Blood was also found in his urine but a scan showed nothing abnormal. In interview, D admitted striking in retaliation for V's altercation with H. D was aged 52, of good character and was hard-working and resourceful. The Judge considered Categories 1 and 2 and adopted a starting point of 10 years. Held. These injuries were not more serious than those commonly found in section 18 cases. We do not consider there was 'greater harm' but there was significant premeditation and use of a weapon. This therefore falls into Category 2. The attack was from behind and at night. With good character, **6 years**, not 8.

292.19   *Hammers, bars, bottles (unbroken) etc.*

Att-Gen's Ref No 22 of 2011 2011 EWCA Crim 1473, 2012 1 Cr App R (S) 34 (p 201) D pleaded (late) to section 18. He had a long-standing history of mental ill-health, including grand mal epilepsy and depression. This was worsened by drug and alcohol misuse. There were episodes of self-harm and, upon being made redundant in 2009, his depression worsened. While drinking heavily in a pub, D became convinced that V, another customer, had been responsible for an assault upon him some seven years previously, and that he was muttering derogatory remarks. D was carrying a hammer, as his partner had asked him to purchase one in order to carry out some home repairs. When V went to the lavatory, D followed him and struck him numerous times with the hammer. V's cheekbone and eye socket were shattered and he suffered head wounds causing brain damage which resulted in a stroke. It was necessary to insert plates into his head and V would not make a full recovery. V had permanent eye damage, permanent asymmetry to his face and scarring. He could not continue with his self-employment. Consequently there was considerable loss of income. In the following year, D was admitted to a psychiatric hospital after a realistic suicide threat. The suitability of a hospital order was explored. The doctor confirmed that the treatment required did not justify D's admission and was available as an outpatient. The Judge imposed a 3-year community order with a mental health treatment requirement. It was imposed on the basis that it was the best method by which D could obtain the necessary treatment. D, aged 49, had no convictions, though there were incidents of violence against his partner. Held. There is no doubt that the monitoring, the advice and flexibility of treatment would be greater from D's point of view under the community order than it would be in prison. We understand the route by which the Judge arrived at her conclusion. However, it simply left out one critical factor. There was the very significant degree of culpability which D exhibited, notwithstanding his mental health. The crime was almost certainly largely induced by the fact that he had had too much to drink, which was his own choice. There was enormous harm caused to V, and the irrational delusion that V had assaulted him many years earlier could not have begun to justify the attack, even if it were true. **5 years**.

R v Charlton 2011 EWCA Crim 1651 D pleaded at his PCMH to ABH and section 18. D had argued with his partner and her parents and committed several offences of battery upon them. D, in a drunken state, visited a friend and told him the police were after him. He took a poker, threatened his friend and said he was going to get his father. He visited his father's house, and when he opened the door, head-butted him and struck him about eight times to the head and jaw with the poker. He threatened his father's partner and threatened to kill his father. He remained in the house for around 3 hours. He prevented his father from attending to his wounds. His father suffered deep cuts to his head and suffered scarring on his face. He did not seek medical treatment. D was arrested and released on bail. His father went to stay with a friend, F. D visited F's home, entered and struck F around the head. He had a crowbar and a Bowie-style knife. F was able to defend himself and D fled. D, aged 38, had no previous convictions. Reports showed he had an alcohol dependency and significant disadvantages in childhood. Held. There were aggravating features present. However, with the mitigation, there ought to be a slight reduction from the starting point. Full discount for the plea was warranted, so **5 years** not 6 for the section 20. **2 years** for the ABH could not be complained about, so 7 years in all.

R v Guias 2011 EWCA Crim 2232 D was convicted of section 18. V had a disagreement with D's brother regarding a £50 debt. V then agreed to repair D's laptop computer for £25 and the computer was left with V. V informed D he could collect his laptop and also settle D's brother's debt. D offered only £20 and V declined this suggestion. D visited V's house and barged past V to seize his computer. D produced a metal bar and struck V's head with it a number of times, in front of V's wife and 4-year-old child. V suffered two 3 cm wounds and one 6 cm wound to his forehead. D was sentenced on the basis that he had not brought the bar to V's home. D was of previous good character with good references. Held. D was to be sentenced on the basis that he picked the bar up in self-defence. This was wholly out of character. **4 years** not 7.

Post-guideline cases

R v Welsh and Others 2013 EWCA Crim 409 T, J and K were convicted of section 18. Police officers were called to an address following a report that V had been assaulted. He was on the ground and had clearly been hurt. V had been kicked, punched and struck with an iron bar. K had the iron bar. T and J were brothers. K was T's son. He suffered a broken elbow, a puncture wound to his right leg and numerous cuts and bruises to his arms and legs. V suffered from schizophrenia and took prescribed medication. K, aged 22 at appeal, had convictions as a juvenile for battery, GBH, possession of an offensive weapon and adult convictions for ABH (2010 and 2011). J, aged 49 at appeal, had convictions for ABH in 1982, 1984, 1986, 1995 and 1997, for theft, threatening words and behaviour (1985, 1990, 1991 and 1998) and affray (1992, 2001 and 2009). T was aged 44 at appeal and had convictions for affray (1996) and public order offences (1999 and 2008). Held. There is no doubt that there are factors indicating greater harm. V was vulnerable because of his psychiatric injury and there was a sustained or repeated assault on him. It is recognised that the injury sustained is not serious in the context of the offence. As for culpability, there is no doubt that there was a significant degree of premeditation, the use of a weapon and the targeting of a vulnerable victim. The Judge was right to place this into Category 1. The absence of serious injury is an important factor. That could reduce the sentence within the range for this offence. The proper sentence, with no distinction between them, was **10 years**, not 12.

R v Clifford 2013 EWCA Crim 803 D was convicted of false imprisonment and section 18. D's son, G, was a 28-year-old heroin addict. D suspected that G had stolen a quantity of jewellery belonging to D's wife, G's stepmother. D's wife telephoned the police to report the theft. D sent G a text message offering him some work and offering to pick him up. D picked G up and took him to the workshop at the back of D's house. There, G was tied up by D and G's uncle, P. G was then suspended upside down from the prongs of a fork-lift truck and beaten with a length of rubber hose and a hammer. D contacted JC, who bore great animosity towards G and had assaulted him in the past. When he arrived, JC and P went to search G's house for the jewellery. The search was unsuccessful and they returned. G was lowered from the fork-lift and JC began to beat him with a baseball bat. D was present throughout. He joined in and used a hammer and a hose pipe with a metal end. They stood on his arms and G could hear his bones breaking. The beating lasted for a considerable period of time and D, JC and P took breaks, drinking beer and laughing. G refused to confess to the theft and the men welded him into a metal cage. He claimed he was told that he would be left there for a few weeks. They sprayed him with brake cleaner and threatened to set him alight. The men discussed whether they could delay getting G medical attention. They told him they would inflict worse injuries if he 'grassed them up'. He was placed in a builder's sack and put into the rear of a van. He was given a high-visibility workman's jacket and deposited in a pub car park a few miles away. He called out for help once the van had gone and he was taken to hospital. G's cheekbone was fractured, his chest was bruised, he had an open fracture to his shin bone, his left thigh bone was fractured, both kneecaps had been broken in numerous places and there was a multi-fragmented fracture to his right wrist. He also required a plaster cast for a right arm fracture and an external fixation device to fix the injury to his left leg. Some thought his injuries were life-threatening. D was aged 52 at appeal and also had convictions for 30 offences between 1973 and 1993 including burglary, theft, handling, firearms and violence. He had a 12-year-old autistic son. Held. The finding of greater harm was entirely right. The injuries were extremely severe and the attack was prolonged. Higher culpability was also demonstrable as the attack was planned and premeditated, with the use of weapons. D played a leading role. There was an element of gratuitous degradation, attempts to conceal the evidence and threats made to stop G from reporting the attack. The fact that D was involved in an attack on his own son was an aggravating feature. The Judge gave **5 years concurrent** for the false imprisonment. With that in mind, there can be no complaint that **16 years** was excessive, regardless of the mitigation.

R v Law 2014 EWCA Crim 1772 D was convicted of wounding with intent. D and his wife had separated and V was in a relationship with D's wife. D's 18-year-old son, H, was employed by V. D and H pulled up in a car and H got out, crossed the road and spoke to V. After an exchange of words, H returned to the car and was followed by V. The car then drove off and it was accepted that V may have acted in an unpleasant manner towards H during these events. About 20 minutes later, V was on the same stretch of road and D, wielding a 4 ft metal pole, ran up behind him and struck V over the head and to the kidney area. V then turned around and was struck on the elbow but managed to disarm D. H then threatened V with a shovel. V suffered a cut to his head requiring stitches, a 3 cm laceration to the elbow and bruising to his back. Blood was also found in his urine but a scan showed nothing abnormal. In interview, D admitted striking in retaliation for V's altercation with H. D was aged 52, of good character and was hard-working and resourceful. The Judge considered Categories 1 and 2 and adopted a starting point of 10 years. Held. These injuries were not more serious than those commonly found in section 18 cases. We do not consider there was greater harm but there was significant premeditation and use of a weapon. This therefore falls into Category 2. The attack was from behind and at night. With good character, **6 years**, not 8.

R v Smedley 2016 EWCA Crim 149 D was convicted of section 18. D and V were neighbours and were in a long-running dispute over the ownership of hedges and ditches on their boundary. A civil case about it was continuing. D saw V and believed he was working on the disputed hedges. D left his property and picked up a heavy metal bar. He went to V and struck him on the head once. V fell unconscious into a ditch. D went back to his property. V suffered a 3-inch laceration to his head which required five stitches. V was discharged from hospital the same day. D was aged 76, had no significant convictions and had references. The pre-sentence report said D showed no regret or compassion. The Judge found a) the weapon was taken to V, b) D lacked regret and had intransigent views about the dispute. Held. It was a Category 2 case. D's age requires a greater reduction to be made, so with the provocation as D saw it, **3½ years** not 4½.

See also: *Att-Gen's Ref Nos 39-42 of 2014* 2014 EWCA Crim 1557 (14 years' extended sentence **(10 years'** custody 4 years' extended licence), see **217.12**.)

Old cases: There are plenty of recent cases. If old cases are required, they are listed in the 9th edition of this book.

292.20   Kicking   *Pre-guideline judicial guidance*
Att-Gen's Ref Nos 44-45 of 2001 2001 EWCA Crim 1483 In *Att-Gen's Ref No 44 of 1994* 1995 16 Cr App R (S) 865 the Lord Chief Justice said, "It is frequently a misconception that unless some object is held in the hand, no weapon has been used. An attacker who uses shod feet or who bites someone is just as much using a weapon as someone who wields an object in his hand."
R v Islam 2001 EWCA Crim 2950, 2002 2 Cr App R (S) 33 (p 118) Attacks by kicking with shoes or boots compare with those where weapons are used.

292.21   *Kicking victim on ground after drinking   Pre-guideline cases*
R v Butler and Holifield 2010 EWCA Crim 752[741] B pleaded (full credit) and H was convicted of GBH with intent. There was bad feeling between V's housemates and H over H's girlfriend. In the early hours, V was at a neighbour's house with two female friends when B and H arrived uninvited. H said one of V's housemates had been sleeping with his girlfriend and they seemed intent on taking their anger out on someone. H said to V, "I don't fucking like you" and threw a Hoover at him. V threw a TV at H, and H and B beat him with a mirror off the wall, a steel pan and a pair of scissors. The lights went out. V managed to lock himself in the bathroom. B hammered on the door, so V jumped out of the window. H and B followed him. B kicked and stamped on V and H punched him. V was taken back to the house and the girls were asked to clean him up. When the police arrived H was shouting at V and threatening to kill him. The attack lasted half an hour. V had multiple injuries to the face, head and chest. He was in intensive care for 38 days. His face was badly swollen and initially he was unable to open his eyes. V was on a breathing machine for some days and had to be fed through tubes. V suffered from severe psychological harm with flashbacks. His level of fear affected everything he did. His personality and lifestyle had changed. He had become paranoid about other people. V had to use walking sticks and the pain in his fingers made cooking and cleaning difficult. He also had breathing and swallowing difficulties. B was aged 30 with five convictions and had received a community punishment for common assault. H was aged 34, with 15 appearances for 40 offences including violence. He had received 3 months for ABH. B's pre-sentence report said B was very upset when he heard about the harm caused to V. The Judge said: a) the attack was cowardly, vicious and prolonged, b) B was in H's shadow but he still played a major part, c) B had showed some remorse, and d) the starting point was **11 years**. He gave B 3 years' IPP (based on a 7-year notional sentence and reduction for time on remand) and H **5 years' IPP**. Held. B and H had no dispute with V and the two vented their anger on him as a substitute. B went along to add muscle and willingly joined in. It was a Level 2 offence. The Judge's approach was not wrong and 11 years was at the top end. **7 years** for B not IPP.
Old case: *Att-Gen's Ref Nos 122-123 of 2005* 2006 EWCA Crim 571, 2 Cr App R (S) 91 (p 601) (**3 years 8 months' YOI**)
For a summary of the case, see the 8th edition of this book.

292.22   Knives, With   *Judicial guidance*
Att-Gen's Ref No 49 of 2008 2008 EWCA Crim 2304, 2009 1 Cr App R (S) 109 (p 613) LCJ Those who carry knives in the street and then use them to wound must expect severe punishment – no ifs, no buts, no perhaps.
Note: It is perhaps important to remember that the 'no ifs, no buts' principle relates to those who take knives onto the street. Ed.
Post-guideline case
R v Odegbune and Others 2013 EWCA Crim 711 paras 29-30 From 2 March 2010, the starting point for murders where a knife or other weapon was taken to the scene where

---

[741] There is continual reference to B's problem with alcohol although there is no specific reference to either of the two actually drinking on the night. It seems likely that they did. Ed.

the intention was to commit an offence or have it available as a weapon became 25 years. In order to preserve consistency of approach to sentencing across the range of offences, that change for murder inevitably has an impact on lesser offences of violence committed with a knife or similar weapon.

292.23   Knives, With   8 years or less appropriate

Examples: *R v Lewis* 2011 EWCA Crim 1839 (Plea. After a complaint about a part-full take-away box being thrown from an eighth-floor window, D, aged 16, took a knife to the ground floor and, after a confrontation, stabbed V four times, twice in the chest, and twice as V tried to retreat. V in hospital for nine days and left with permanent scarring. Previous convictions for attempted robbery and ABH. Adult starting point 14 years. **6 years** not 8.)

Att-Gen's Ref No 29 of 2011 2011 EWCA Crim 1668, 2012 1 Cr App R (S) 61 (p 351) (Plea (full credit). After disagreement in a nightclub, some hours later in the street D was struck a number of times by a group of men. Initially did not retaliate. Later kicked to ground, punched and stamped on. D was carrying a 10 cm lock-knife. In rage, caused eight 'nasty' wounds to V. Very considerable provocation. **3 years 8 months** was comfortably within the range.)

Old cases: *R v Baldwin* 2010 EWCA Crim 1359 (**5 years 4 months**) *R v Thompson* 2010 EWCA Crim 1772 (**Extended sentence (7 years 8 months'** custody 5 years' licence)) *R v Graham* 2010 EWCA Crim 2793 (**3 years 8 months**)

Other old cases can be found in the 9th edition of this book.

Post-guideline case

R v Karakas 2012 EWCA Crim 1245, 2013 1 Cr App R (S) 46 (p 261) LCJ D pleaded on rearraignment to section 18. There was an incident of arson at a block of flats. Extensive damage was caused to the landing and to outside three flats, including one where D and his family lived. V, who lived on the same floor, was arrested and bailed. An electrician was carrying out repairs near D's flat when V walked by. They had a brief conversation and V left. D came out of his flat and asked who the electrician had been talking to. Upon hearing that it was V, D re-entered his flat and shortly returned to the hallway and walked to the lift. The electrician heard D and V arguing and heard D shouting that V had been responsible for the fire. He walked towards the lift area and found V lying on the floor with D standing over him. There was a substantial quantity of blood on the floor and walls. Two men emerged from the lift and saw D walking past them carrying an 8-inch knife and saying, "he caused the fire". V told the men he had been stabbed. D left the flats and went to a nearby shop where he was known. He said that he had stabbed the man who had burned down his house and asked to be taken to the police station. He handed himself in to the police three days later. V suffered four stab wounds to his leg and buttocks and one to his chest. The chest wound was superficial but his femoral artery had been severed. There was also an injury to his bladder and bowel. He lost five pints of blood. He was transferred to an intensive care unit and underwent a number of operations. D detailed a number of issues he had had with V including V constantly playing loud music, making noise and smoking cannabis. D stated that V allowed drug addicts into his flat and that he was convinced that V had set the fire in the block in order to kill D and his family. D was aged 48 at appeal and of good character. He had come to the UK from Turkey in 1998 and lived here since then with his wife and family. Held. This was a case of extremely serious injuries caused by the use of a knife. There was an element of premeditation as D returned to his flat to retrieve the knife, but D had obviously been taken by surprise on learning that V was in the block of flats. 10 years failed to sufficiently reflect D's good character and the stresses against the background from which this serious offence arose. Starting at 12 years was appropriate. With credit for the plea, **8 years** not 10.

R v Styler 2012 EWCA Crim 2169, 2013 1 Cr App R (S) 120 (p 620) D pleaded (25% credit) to two section 20s, dangerous driving, perverting the course of justice, excess alcohol and failing to stop. Back calculation showed that he was twice over the limit. He drove at about twice the speed limit in a built-up area for about 1 mile and collided with two women. At impact the speed was estimated to be 56-58 mph. One woman suffered a broken leg, bleeding spleen, skull fracture and a punctured diaphragm. D braked momentarily after the impact then sped away. He burnt out his car, washed his clothes and shaved off his beard. Next day, D handed himself in to police. One victim suffered further complications requiring additional surgery and further scarring. D was aged 36, married with three young children. He had convictions for violence. Racial beating in 2003 (4 months). In 2004, ABH (2 years). Held. **3 years** for the section 20 offences and 18 months concurrent for the dangerous driving was appropriate, not 4 years and 22 months concurrent. **18 months** consecutive for the perverting the course of justice was entirely appropriate. **4½ years** not 6.

Att-Gen's Ref No 101 of 2014 2014 EWCA Crim 2860 D was convicted of wounding with intent and ABH. He developed a stable and loving relationship with the mother of his child and he lived with her. Living at the same house was V, aged 17. D believed V was responsible for a burglary at D's flat. In a park at about midday, D walked up to V, took a hammer from his pocket and hit him on the head and body with it. V put up a fight and agreed to go to D's flat. There, D demanded V return the property from the burglary and V said he didn't know about it. D picked up a kitchen cleaver and slapped V about his head with it. Then holding it to his throat, D said he was going to kill V. D took a smaller kitchen knife and stabbed V twice above the knee. V was told to return the property by Thursday. On arrest, D showed the police where the hammer and knife were. V had four bruises and swellings to the side of his head overlain by a laceration of the scalp. There was no underlying damage to the skull or the brain. He also had two shallow puncture wounds to the leg, some 2½ cm long. D was aged 20 and when he was aged 17, he was remanded for a public disorder offence but he had no convictions. D had arrived from Afghanistan unaccompanied when he was aged 17. Adult Social Services said D was a pleasure to work with and was highly motivated to obtain an education and find work. The risk of reoffending was assessed as low. There were character witnesses. Held. D wanted to terrorise as well as injure. There were the following aggravating factors: a) there were two attacks, b) the attacks were premeditated, c) multiple weapons were used, d) the offence was committed in a public place,[742] e) the victim was detained against his will. and f) threats to kill were made. The mitigation was the youth, the lack of maturity and his good character. The least sentence was **5½ years** not 3½.

R v Guiled 2015 EWCA Crim 57 D pleaded late (10% credit) to wounding with intent and possessing an offensive weapon. D, who was drunk and had taken cannabis, and his cousin, V, got into an argument. There was a scuffle in the High Street. It was possibly due to a conversation that V had had with a woman, who later described D as 'angry and restless'. During the struggle, D produced a kitchen knife, which he swung and thrust at V's head three times. However, only one blow connected and V suffered a 5 cm head wound which required stapling and left a scar. V also had low blood pressure, indicating a significant loss of blood. D then ran and hid the knife and some gloves, which were all later recovered. He denied responsibility for the attack until trial when, viewing the CCTV which captured the whole event, he pleaded. D was remorseful, had made progress in custody and had a favourable pre-sentence report. D was aged 25 on appeal and had a poor record.[743] The Judge placed the offence into Category 2. (Category 2's starting point is 6 years.) The Judge increased the sentence to 10 years to take into account the following: a) D was drunk, b) it was a public place, c) D's convictions, and d) the attempts to conceal the knife. With the plea and the mitigation he reduced it to 8 years. Held. This Court has frequently said that the carrying of a knife is a grave offence and must be met with severe punishment. The use of a knife as against some other less lethal weapon carried to the scene pushed this case up the range from the starting point

---

[742] The report indicates the wounding was in the flat and not in the park. Ed.
[743] The judgment is silent on the nature of D's convictions.

of 6 years in Category 2, as did the repeated use of the knife aimed at V's head. However, the Judge did push the case too far up the range. **7 years.** 12 months concurrent for the offensive weapon upheld.

See also: *R v Collis* 2012 EWCA Crim 1335 (D pleaded to section 18. Full credit. Argument with neighbour regarding drugs. V attacked D's wife. D grabbed a knife and stabbed V in the neck, causing life-threatening injuries. Numerous previous convictions including offensive weapon and violent offences. Borderline of Categories 1 and 2. Starting at 9 years, **6 years**.)

R v Quinn 2013 EWCA Crim 2711 (With affray and assault by beating. Revenge attack on 14-year-old on a crowded bus. Three wounds to thigh. Prevented by others from stabbing another man unknown to defendant. Injuries not particularly grave. D had serious history of mental health difficulties. Defendant significantly injured by passengers when on pavement, including damage to eye by kick. 35 previous convictions including some for violence. **Extended sentence (6 years'** custody not 9 with 3 years' extended licence).)

R v Malin 2014 EWCA Crim 1651 (Plea. Also possessing an offensive weapon (knife) and supply of class A drugs. Category 1. In a shop, V refused to sell vodka to D, because it was out of hours. D left and then immediately returned and repeatedly stabbed V. D stopped when V said, "Take what you want". V had flashbacks and fear of people in his shop. Eight convictions including theft and minor assaults. Held. Carrying and use of knives is one of the most serious factors indicating higher culpability. Because of D's age (22) etc. **6 years 8 months**, not 8 years.)

Att-Gen's Ref No 67 of 2014 2014 EWCA Crim 2263 (Plea, 10% credit. Fight outside nightclub, D racially abused by V. D deeply cut V's face with 7 cm knife. Wound 4-5 cm. V needed surgery and lost two units of blood. D, aged 20, had seven convictions including 2009 for section 20 and 2012 for section 18 (18 months' DTO). **7 years 2 months**, not 4 years.)

292.24   Knives, With   8+ years appropriate

R v Smith 2010 EWCA Crim 364 D pleaded to wounding with intent and possession of a bladed article. D's girlfriend lived in a children's home. D had been involved in an incident there and given a community order for threatening behaviour. The next day the police found him in the vicinity again and searched him. When asked if he had anything he should not have, D produced a lock knife with a 3-inch blade. Two months later V and his girlfriend were sitting on a bus. D and his girlfriend were sitting two rows in front. D was staring at V so V said, "You what?" and D replied, "Wait, I'll bang you when we get off the bus". D then sat in the empty seat in front of V, leant over and said, "I'll bang you now". A scuffle involving V, his girlfriend, and D ensued. D took out a knife, opened it with both hands and stabbed V in the inner thigh. D took the knife, got off the bus and ran away. V's femoral artery and a vein had been severed. He was unable to play any more rugby or taekwondo, which he played at national level. V had been studying for a sports diploma, had hopes of being considered for the Olympics team and of joining the Marines. These were no longer possible as a result of his injury. He could not run more than a few hundred yards without having to stop and was undergoing counselling for post-traumatic stress disorder. D, aged 21, had previous convictions for threatening behaviour and ABH. He was on bail for possession of a knife. The psychiatric report said D had clear difficulties in his upbringing and a history of emotional and physical abuse. It was likely he suffered from a mild learning disability and attention deficit and hyperactive disorder. He had impaired comprehension and expression, and lack of insight. The pre-sentence report said D had long-standing problems with managing emotion and temper, he had never worked and received Disability Living Allowance. There were significant behavioural and thinking issues and D gave no satisfactory explanation for his behaviour on this occasion. Held. Protection of society is the most important factor. It seems IPP would have been appropriate. **9 years** was not excessive in any way.

See also: *R v Seager* 2010 EWCA Crim 841 (Convictions for two section 18 and a violent disorder. An arranged fight between two groups. Six stab wounds to one by another defendant and three stab wounds to another and one wound to a third man. Previous convictions for conspiracy to rob and GBH. **9 years** upheld.)

Post-guideline case

R v McDowell 2012 EWCA Crim 1062 D pleaded (25% credit) to section 18. After he had consumed beer and taken prescription drugs, he became involved in a physical confrontation with the victim, V, at a private address. D obtained a kitchen knife from the kitchen at the address and approached V. V punched out at D, who then stabbed V four to six times. There were four wounds, three to the left of the abdomen and one to the left side of the chest. V needed two operations, the second to remove a segment of his bowel. He would require a third. He remained in hospital for 17 days. Four months after the attack, V was still in a lot of pain and with a colostomy bag. He had been unable to return to work, had trouble sleeping because of flashbacks and nightmares, and was receiving treatment for stress and depression. D, aged 39 at appeal, had numerous convictions between 1988 and 2009, largely for dishonesty and breaches of court orders. There were convictions for ABH (1990), common assault and threatening behaviour (1998), robbery (2000), possession of a bladed article (2003) and possession of an offensive weapon (2004). The pre-sentence report stated there were two options: IPP or an extended sentence. Held. It was beyond question that this was a Category 1 case, and right at the top end of that category. Short of hunting down his victim it is hard to imagine a worse case. This was an extremely aggravated section 18 case. We start at **16 years**, so with plea **15 years' extended sentence (12 years'** custody 3 years' extended licence).

R v Streeter 2014 EWCA Crim 392 D pleaded to section 18. D and V were long-time friends but had recently fallen out over a girl. At about 10.00 pm D visited V's home. Shortly after, D stabbed V twice in the chest and also in the head and hand. A wound required stitches, V lost movement in two fingers and suffered a pneumothorax. D, aged 25, had no previous convictions and the incident was said to be "an isolated incident completely out of character". The Judge was not able to say that the knife was brought to the premises. Held. This was a bad assault aggravated by having taken place in V's own home and involving more than one stabbing. Nevertheless there is significant personal mitigation. Starting point 12 years not 15. With full credit, **8 years** not 10.

See also: *R v O'Callaghan* 2013 EWCA Crim 525 (Plea with 15% credit. With another in a shopping centre attempting to steal mobile phones. In possession of a pair of scissors for that purpose. Verbal altercation with another shopper. Both sides parted company. Victim followed defendant and his friend into another shop. There was an exchange of words and a fight ensued. Victim suffered 10-15 injuries including five puncture wounds to his back. Lacerations on his head, arm, chest and neck. Aged 23. Large number of convictions consistent with acquisitive offending needed to fund drug addiction. Reckless arson conviction aged 14. Starting at 9½ years, **8 years** not 9 years 3 months.)

Att-Gen's Ref Nos 55-56 of 2014 2014 EWCA Crim 1727 (**10 years** for both, see **292.31**.)

Old cases: They add little. Ed.

No reason see the **Unprovoked attack/Drug induced attack** para at **292.37**.

Passion, Crime of/Emotional attack see the **Relationship attacks** paras at **292.28**.

292.25   Police officers on duty as victims   Intent to resist arrest   Post-guideline cases

R v Talbot 2012 EWCA Crim 2322, 2013 2 Cr App R (S) 6 (p 29) D pleaded to section 18 with intent to resist arrest (20% credit) and dangerous driving. D drove with two others towards Tunbridge Wells. En route, they stopped at a chemist's, where his two passengers engaged in shoplifting. They were followed by F, a female member of staff, who thought goods had been stolen. Items were placed in the boot of D's car. An off-duty policeman, V, witnessed this and approached the front of D's vehicle. He was able to confirm he had identified the correct car and approached D. V said to D, "I want to have a word with you", at which point the car shot forward. V was thrown onto the bonnet. He then rolled onto the ground in front of the vehicle, hitting his head. D then drove out of the parking bay and in doing so drove over V's legs. He continued at speed without stopping, ignoring a traffic light which was red against him. Officers travelling in the opposite direction estimated that D was travelling at about 60 mph. The police attempted to use their vehicles to block D's path. He moved into the middle of the road and accelerated towards them. One police car had to retreat to avoid a collision. D continued and later stopped to let the two passengers out of the car. D drove on and was approached by a police officer in another vehicle and was arrested. V had a fractured tibia and fibula and a laceration to the head. The fractures required pins to be inserted. His activities have been severely impaired. He returned to work but was on restricted duties and continued to suffer from aches in his leg. D's basis of plea was: a) that he was aware his two passengers were 'up to no good', b) that a man who was seeking to detain him was in front of the car, c) in his anxiety to get away, he drove forward hoping the man would move, d) he knew he had knocked the man over but continued to try to escape, e) he drove over the man's leg but his thoughts were not concerned with causing really serious harm, and f) notwithstanding that, continuing to drive brought with it almost an inevitability that serious harm would be caused. The pre-sentence report noted that D sought to minimise his culpability. A prison report noted his dedication and hard work in prison and his effort to address his offending behaviour. D had a bad criminal record. There were 20 convictions for sexual offences, fraud, theft and supplying drugs. Held. The assault guideline was not directly applicable. The offence is aggravated by the fact that D was attempting to escape lawful detention with two passengers whom he knew had recently committed a relatively minor offence. He well knew the consequences of driving over V's body. The consequences to V were serious and comparatively long-term. Neither the starting point of 10 years taken by the Judge, nor the resulting sentence of **8 years**, were manifestly excessive.

Note: Although the officer was off duty to start with, he was probably on duty when he approached the car. Perhaps the key matter is that D pleaded to section 18 with 'intent to resist arrest'. Ed.

R v Haywood 2014 EWCA Crim 2006 D pleaded (20% credit) to GBH with intent to resist arrest, aggravated vehicle-taking and going equipped to burgle. During his day release from prison, D borrowed a stolen car. Police later tried to intercept D but he sped away, driving quickly through a red light. In the opposite lane was another marked police car which was waiting for D and the pursuit car. Two officers got out of the waiting car to get the 'stinger' device, used to stop cars, out of the boot. One officer, V, attempted to deploy the stinger in front of D, but it failed to open. D then swerved, trying to drive through a gap between the police car and other vehicles, and hit V, throwing him into the air. D was travelling at 50 mph in a 40 mph zone. He then failed to stop and carried on at 70 mph, eventually crashing and then running away. V suffered a severe head injury with extensive skull fractures and required operations to relieve pressure on his brain. He also had multiple fractures, a partial lung collapse and was in a medically induced coma for several weeks. V's prognosis became uncertain and his condition variable. At sentence, V was significantly disabled and in a state of severely reduced consciousness with an uncertain future. The accident also affected V's family and his police colleague. D expressed remorse and stated that he did not intend to cause GBH, nor did he foresee V's injuries. He had a poor record with 30 offences, some for motoring but no violence. Held. Recklessness of this sort does not fall far short of intent. Remorse can carry little weight when balanced with the dreadful harm which has been caused. Although the section 18 guideline does not cover this offence, it is to be noted that Parliament has imposed the same maximum sentence and so reference to the section 20 guideline was inappropriate. **8 years 9 months** upheld consecutive to 3 months for the burglary charge. This sentence was consecutive to a 6-year sentence D was serving for a conspiracy to burgle count.

Old cases: Best ignored. Ed.

See also the **ASSAULT WITH INTENT TO RESIST ARREST** chapter.

292.26   *Prison officers, Against   Pre-guideline cases*
R v Elmi 2010 EWCA Crim 20 D was convicted of attempting to cause GBH with intent and he pleaded to section 20. D was serving 5 years for section 18, which concerned a fight where he had stabbed the victim in the side and the knife was embedded in the victim's hand, severing tendons. Within a few months of his expected release, a prison officer, V, opened D's cell door intending to push a carton of milk into the cell. D attacked V with a homemade blade which he had fashioned from a metal tray. V raised his arm to defend himself and fended off the blow. V tried to get the keys out of the cell door and D cut him in his arm (the section 20). The cut was small. D left the cell with the weapon and said, "Give me your keys or I'll slash your face", a number of times. Other officers attended and there was a short stand-off. D dropped the weapon and returned to his cell. Another similar weapon was found in D's cell. In interview D said that he had decided to stab another inmate with whom he had had an argument and that he was in a murderous mood. D had been in custody since he was aged 16 and was now aged 21. He was about 19 years old at the time of the offence and was convicted of robbery when he was aged 13 (Referral Order). The pre-sentence report said that there was a medium to high risk of reoffending and a high risk to the public. Also D lacked problem-solving skills. Held. **DPP** was correct and a **4½-year term** was severe but not manifestly excessive.

See also the **PRISONERS: SENTENCING PRINCIPLES** *Offence committed in prison* para at **308.3**.

Old case: *R v Hills and Others Re P* 2008 EWCA Crim 1871, 2009 1 Cr App R (S) 75 (p 441) (**IPP** with a **6-year** minimum term)

Punish the victim see the *Revenge/punishment, Motive was* para at **292.31**.

292.27   *Pubs   Fights in/near pubs and clubs   Post-guideline cases*
R v Cripps 2012 EWCA Crim 806, 2013 1 Cr App R (S) 7 (p 43) D was convicted of GBH with intent. At 11 pm D arrived at a pub and was drunk. He was involved in altercations at the bar and the landlord intervened. D calmed down and went outside. There were another two altercations. V, who had been drinking at the bar, intervened and calmed D down. D then returned and struck V in the face, causing him to fall unconscious to the ground. Then D punched him in the face and kicked him in the head. V sustained extensive fractures to the jaw, cheek bone, eye sockets and nose. Eleven metal plates were used to reconstruct the face. V's left eye socket was reconstructed with the use of mesh. His jaw was wired shut for six weeks. He was using painkillers for months after the incident. It took a year for him to feel much better. V had permanent scarring and had trouble sleeping. He suffered double vision and loss of confidence. V had to give up his job as an HGV driver, had not worked since the attack, was in a dire financial state and could no longer afford to live in his home. When re-interviewed D claimed he acted in self-defence. D was now aged 49 and had seven sentences between 1976 and 2008. There was a section 20 offence, 22 years earlier, and an ABH, 30 years before. D cared for a close relative and had references. The Judge considered the alcohol had made him aggressive. He found the following aggravating factors: D was drunk, he was aggressive to others, he failed to respond to the previous intervention, he ignored the warnings about his conduct and the location. Held. The photographs are a terrible sight. This case lies uneasily on the cusp of Categories 1 and 2. The bottom of one and the top of the other is **9 years** so we start at 9. That was in no way manifestly excessive, so 9 years.

Att-Gen's Ref No 33 of 2012 2012 EWCA Crim 2391 D pleaded to section 18. In 2003, when aged 22, he lived in Ireland and visited his mother in Wales. V attended his local pub to watch the Wales v Ireland Six Nations rugby match. He had consumed over eight pints. At about 11.45 pm, V became involved in a physical confrontation with D. D had been in a different pub and passed V's pub when he was walking back to his mother's home. V's friend described the confrontation as more of a scuffle than a fight, in which V suffered a nose bleed. V's friend dragged V away from D, who walked up the road. V and his friend remained outside the pub. D went to his mother's house, collected a bread knife some 9-10 cm in length and returned to the road outside the pub. He approached V, shouting a challenge as he did so. He slashed V across the face causing a 7 cm wound along the jawline and neck. The wound bled profusely and V ran, pursued by D, who was shouting "Come on you cunt, I'm going to kill you". V fell to the ground and D kicked him repeatedly about the body, continuing to shout threats and obscenities. The wound required 30 sutures. When arrested, D claimed he had been head-butted in the initial confrontation, causing him to suffer a broken nose. He denied using the knife to deliberately wound. He was charged and bailed and subsequently failed to appear and absconded to his native Ireland. In 2012, D arrived in Pembroke Dock on a ferry from Ireland. A passport check revealed he was wanted. He pleaded to section 20, which was rejected by the prosecution. He then pleaded to section 18. V felt deeply embarrassed by the ugly appearance of his scar, which had become more prominent as a result of skin stretching and hardening. He was afraid to go out at night. D was in a stable relationship and had two children aged 7 and 3, the younger of which had been diagnosed with cerebral palsy. D had a previous conviction for threatening words and behaviour in 2001 (fine). He was brought up in a socially deprived area of Dublin and was extremely difficult. He suffered from attention deficit disorder. Held. The attack was sustained and V was chased and repeatedly kicked. We note the impact upon D's family, the delay since the offence and the plea. The principles in *R v H* 2011 EWCA Crim 2753, 2012 2 Cr App R (S) 21 (p 88) about sentencing historical offences applies here. D was at all times a fugitive from justice. Under current guidelines, this is a Category 2 offence. The starting point was 6 years with a range of 5-9 years. With the aggravating features, the provisional starting point was 7 years. The mitigation could bring that down to 5 years. With the plea (full credit) **3 years** not 2.

R v Carey 2013 EWCA Crim 482 D was convicted of section 18. He was at a public house, as was V. They went outside to have a cigarette and D asked V whether the motif on his shirt was Arabic. V took that as an insult and it led to a fight. During the fight, V's eye was 'put out' by D. V said D had gouged out his eye, whereas a doctor for the defence asserted that the injury was most likely caused by a blow to the eye. The doctor for the prosecution felt the most likely cause was gouging. V stated that he was punched in the face several times. D was aged 40 at his appeal. He had no previous convictions. Held. D was of positive good character, the offence was not premeditated and there was no weapon. D had shown some genuine remorse. The offence was, however, at least in part, racially motivated. It was correctly placed into Category 1. **10 years** was appropriate, not 12.

Note: It is a pity the judgment fails to determine the factual dispute, but considering the evidence of the V and the sentences passed, it can be inferred that both courts considered that D had gouged out the eye. Ed.

R v Chamberlain and Others 2013 EWCA Crim 1859 D pleaded to section 18 and common assault. C and R pleaded to section 20. V1 and his girlfriend, V2, were in a nightclub. A disagreement arose between R's sister and V2. C punched V1 and all were asked to leave. The dispute continued outside the club and insults were thrown. C and V1 threw punches at each other, whereupon C asked R and D to assist. V1 was dragged, kicked in the head by D and punched by C. V2 lay across V1 and was kicked in the face by R. V1 attended hospital and was treated for cuts and bruising to the ribs and discharged. The pain worsened and he was later found to have closed fractures to his forearm, face, two ribs and spine. V2 suffered slight swelling and bruising. All three expressed extreme remorse and blamed alcohol for their actions. D, aged 24, had a conditional discharge for criminal damage. The Judge categorised the case as Category 1. Held. It was a joint attack at night. Part of the attack was when V1 was on the ground. It was also not premeditated and of very short duration. The Judge was wrong to categorise V1's injuries as serious with no evidence of residual effect. The case was on the cusp of Category 1. There should be credit for the remorse. We sentence on the basis the offence was out of character. There was no evidence D was wearing boots. Starting at 7 years, with full credit, **4 years 8 months** not 7 years.

For the sentences for C and R see the **OFFENCES AGAINST THE PERSON ACT 1861 S 20** at **293.14**.

R v Thomas 2014 EWCA Crim 917 D pleaded (10% credit) to section 18. D and V were engaged in a game of pool at a pub. D's girlfriend was present and watching. As V was waiting to take his shot, he engaged in a light-hearted conversation with D's girlfriend, and placed his hand on her shoulder. D became jealous and challenged V. He then struck him over the back of the head with a pool cue, holding the cue by the thinner end. The Judge described it as a 'full bloodied swing'. He apologised for his actions and left the pub. V sustained a deep laceration to his scalp which required six sutures. He was prescribed a course of antibiotics and was off work for four weeks. He suffered from headaches in the aftermath. The Judge placed the offence in Category 2. D had previous for section 18 and threatening behaviour. There were also various assaults and batteries 'over the years'. Held. There was no suggestion that D was not rightly considered to be dangerous. The appropriate sentence was **7 years' extended sentence (4 years' custody** (not 5) **3 years' extended licence)**.

R v Czekalinski 2014 EWCA Crim 2124 D pleaded to s 18 (full credit). He had gone out drinking with two friends and they stood next to a door in a lobby area through which V had to pass to exit the bar. D, who had been drinking heavily, pushed V against a door and, when challenged, head-butted him. V suffered a 'fat lip' and had two teeth forced back, requiring dental treatment. He also fell back and D then pulled V's head towards his knee, striking him several times. V went to the ground, hitting his head on a fire extinguisher, and then curled up to try to protect himself. D then kicked him several times on the arms, and continued for some time until D's girlfriend screamed, "Stop it, stop it." The whole incident was captured on CCTV. D caused a fracture initially so swollen that V's arm could not be put in a cast. V also suffered continuous severe back pain for several weeks and his injuries meant he was unable to work for eight weeks, thereby losing almost £4,000. V suffered no lasting damage. D denied involvement, but was picked out by witnesses. D was aged 18 and of good character. He expressed remorse and was described as 'an exemplary prisoner'. Held. This falls between the upper end of Category 2 and the lower end of Category 1. The consumption of alcohol and the offence being in a pub were aggravating factors. The significant mitigation makes it 9 years, so **6 years' detention**, not 7.

Att-Gen's Ref No 24 of 2015 2015 EWCA Crim 927 D pleaded (full credit) to section 18. D was drinking in a pub when he was approached by V, who tried to sell him a watch. D said he had bought one of V's watches before and it had stopped. D ushered V, who was much smaller than him, to outside the pub and the two talked. V turned his back on V and D moved to stop him. D then delivered a considered heavy punch to V which propelled V across the width of the pavement. V hit the side of a low wall next to the kerb. D then kicked V with his steel-capped work boots in the face. D next punched V in the face three times. After the first punch there was a pause. D was left on the ground. He managed to take refuge in a shop. V was found to have suffered injuries under his eye, his nose and his cheek. His jaw had multiple fractures. A metal plate had to be inserted. V's lip was bitten through. Two teeth had to be removed. For months V was frightened, anxious and had trouble sleeping. He also had difficulty eating. D was aged 30 with a conviction in 2009 for common assault on and harassment of his former partner. His family were supportive and he was a hard worker with testimonials. The pre-sentence report assessed he posed a medium risk of causing harm in the future. It was assessed that imprisonment would place a considerable strain on the family's financial stability which included the mortgage on their house. D had performed 19 hours of unpaid work. Held. The three punches were separate, calculated and deliberate blows on an effectively helpless man. It was Category 2 case. The starting point was not less than 5 years. Being generous we reduce that to 4 years for the personal mitigation. With plea discount **2 years 8 months** not 2 years suspended.

See also: *Att-Gen's Ref No 67 of 2014* 2014 EWCA Crim 2263 (Plea, 10% credit. Fight outside nightclub, D racially abused by V. D deeply cut V's face with 7 cm knife. Wound 4-5 cm. V needed surgery and lost two units of blood. D, aged 20, had seven convictions including 2009 for section 20 and 2012 for section 18 (18 months' DTO). **7 years 2 months**, not 4 years.)

Att-Gen's Ref No 6 of 2015 2015 EWCA Crim 625, 2 Cr App R (S) 24 (p 223) (D pleaded on day trial listed. D, after drinking heavily, told glasses could not be taken onto dance floor. D bit V, a member of the door staff. A large piece of his ear severed off. Profound effect on V. Aged 33. Good work record. Because of personal mitigation we start at 5 years making **4½ years** with plea not 2½.)

Old pre-guideline case: *R v Brogan* 2009 EWCA Crim 2683, 2010 2 Cr App R (S) 32 (p 205) (**7 years**)

For a summary of the case, see the 9th edition of this book.

See also the *Glassing (using a glass as a weapon)* paras at **292.16**.

292.28   *Relationship attacks   Guidelines*

The Sentencing Guidelines Council has issued the *Domestic Violence Guideline 2006*, see www.banksr.com Other Matters Guidelines tab. For details see the **DOMESTIC VIOLENCE** chapter.

292.29   *Relationship attacks   Men attacking wives and partners/ex-wives or ex-partners   Post-guideline cases*

R v Barker 2013 EWCA Crim 520 D pleaded to section 18. He had been in a relationship with V for about 2½ years. V was aged 19. D was strong and of a heavy build with a controlling nature and a short temper. Their relationship was beset with bouts of anger and aggression towards V. V and D had a child and V decided that she would try to maintain the relationship. Subsequently, V decided to end the relationship. D took an overdose of drugs. He discharged himself from hospital and attended V's mother's address. After checking that V was alone with the baby, he attacked V. He put his hands around her neck and squeezed until she lost consciousness. V's mother and partner returned some minutes later and when he saw them he locked the door. D was described as being in a frenzy and stabbing V with a pair of kitchen scissors. The scissors did not belong in the house but it was not clear how they had come to be there. V sustained over 20 wounds, eight of which were significant, including wounds to her neck, upper left chest and back. There were also a large number of superficial wounds. D, aged 24, had two convictions for violence: ABH (2007) and affray (2010). Held. The Judge was incorrect to place this offence into Category 1. It is properly placed at the top of Category 2. None of the injuries were very deep and all were capable of being treated without stitches. The correct starting point was 10 years. An extended sentence was appropriate and that was not disputed. With credit, 12 years' extended sentence (**7 years' custody 5 years' licence**), not 10 years' custody 5 years' licence.

R v Foster 2015 EWCA Crim 916, 2 Cr App R (S) 45 (p 348) (Plea, **4 years**, see **292.17.**)

R v Smith 2015 EWCA Crim 1482 (**9 years**, see **292.42**.)

See also: *R v Aubertin* 2011 EWCA Crim 956 (Pre-guideline case Plea to section 18. Over 24-hour period assaulted his girlfriend by kicking, punching, stabbing, burning and banging her head against the wall. Also shaved her head with an electric razor. Serious but not life-threatening. No permanent injuries caused. 10 years' extended sentence (**6 years'** custody 4 years' licence) not 8 years and 4 years.)

R v Lodge 2012 EWCA Crim 1906, 2013 1 Cr App R (S) 87 (p 467) (Plea with full credit to section 18. Relationship with victim since 2005. Years of violence towards her, including convictions for ABH and section 20. Head-butted, punched, strangled and bit her. Threatened to kill her. Extensive bruising and scratches. This was an attempted offence. Committed whilst on licence. Category 2. Vulnerable victim. **6 years** not 8.)

R v Jenkin 2012 EWCA Crim 2557, 2013 2 Cr App R (S) 15 (LCJ Plea. Just released from prison after partner withdrew complaint. D gouged her eyes out with his fingers. *R v Kehoe* 2009 applied. Blocked medical attention for 11-12 hours. Severe force would have been required. The *Kehoe* indications are not cumulative, they are alternative. Serious previous convictions for violence. Life (**6-year** minimum term) and a Hospital Order was correct with Restriction Order.)

R v Smith 2012 EWCA Crim 2852 (Convicted of section 18 and ABH. Visited ex-partner's home and using a key she retained, wrecked the house. Returned later with a knife, stabbing ex-partner's new partner twice in the back in front of him. When dragged away, she pulled at her hair. Stabs were so forceful the knife broke. No internal organs damaged but there was residual scarring. Wounds 6-8 cm deep. Aged 24. Had six-month-old child when sentenced. No convictions. Positive references. **8 years** not 12.)

R v Waruku 2013 EWCA Crim 1440 (Plea (20% credit) and section 47 (25% credit). Relationship of 18 years. Suspected partner of having an affair. Made threats. Boiled 2.5 litres of oil and poured it on her on four occasions. Teenage son could hear mother screaming. Re-boiled the oil whilst making victim clean the floor. Threatened to 'torch' her and watch her slowly die if she informed the police. Sadistic violence. Threats and violence continued the following day including cutting her scalp and kicking the burn injuries. Two teenage children. Aged 40. No convictions. Starting at 12 years was correct. **9½ years** and **8 months** consecutive.)

Att-Gen's Ref No 32 of 2014 2014 EWCA Crim 1320 (Convicted. Section 18 and assault by beating. Locks changed following his violence. Attacked woman who opened door and stabbed partner. Aged 25 with 82 convictions including five offensive weapons/bladed articles and six ABH/battery offences. Held. His default position is to reach for a bladed instrument. **12 years** not 9.)

Att-Gen's Ref No 104 of 2014 2014 EWCA Crim 2920 (After alcohol and an argument, attacked his partner with whom he had had a four-year relationship. Used steak knife with significant force and almost severed her nose from her face. Two-year old child present. Held. It was Category 2 but with an uplift. We start at 12 years so with plea **8 years** not 6.)

Att-Gen's Ref No 17 of 2015 2015 EWCA Crim 868 (Convicted. Section 18 on former boyfriend who was with his girlfriend. Common assault on girlfriend. 3½ years, see **292.31**.)

R v Henning 2015 EWCA Crim 879, 2 Cr App R (S) 37 (p 302) (Plea (10% credit). Lost his temper. Stamped on her head twice. Jaw fractured. Metal plate inserted. Extensive previous including a robbery. On licence. It was Category 1. **10 years** was severe but upheld.)

Old pre-guideline cases: *Att-Gen's Ref No 80 of 2009* 2010 EWCA Crim 470 (**5 years**) *R v Kelly* 2010 EWCA Crim 672 (**4 years**) *Att-Gen's Ref No 1 of 2010* 2010 EWCA Crim 748 (**6 years**) *R v Brown* 2010 EWCA Crim 1103 (**IPP. 9-year** notional term) *R v Sweeney* 2010 EWCA Crim 2355 (**8 years**) *Att-Gen's Ref No 65 of 2010* 2010 EWCA Crim 3051, 2011 2 Cr App R (S) 33 (p 209) (**4 years**)

For a summary of the first, second, fourth and last cases, see the 10th edition of this book.

292.30 *Relationship attacks   Women attacking husbands, partners etc.*
Post-guideline example: *Att-Gen's Ref No 116 of 2014* 2015 EWCA Crim 623 (Convicted. Section 18 plus ABH ×2 and section 20. Under influence of a drug. Ripped up his clothes. Wooden ball hammer causing two fractures to skull and puncture wounds. ABH squeezing testicles causing intense pain and beating him with pole. Section 20 was jagged broken bottle in neck. In all numerous injuries. Category 1. Accepting the defendant's unfortunate history, **12 years** not 8.)

292.31   *Revenge/punishment, Motive was   Post-guideline cases*
R v Evans 2011 EWCA Crim 2662 D was convicted of section 18. At around 3 am in Wigan town centre, D and a friend came across V, who was walking home after celebrating his 21st birthday. D and his friend asked V for some cocaine. V agreed to show them where they could purchase some in exchange for a lift home. D and his friend obliged. At V's home an argument ensued as V did not want to help them buy cocaine. V chased D's car as they began to leave. V struck the car and D reversed at V in order to scare him. D got out to remonstrate with him. V chased the car for a second time and again struck the car. D again reversed, at a speed of around 10 mph, and crushed V between the car and a lamp post. D then drove off. He subsequently posted on Facebook, 'Some lad...kicked off, so I ran him over'. V suffered a fractured right ankle, a fractured left femur, multiple fractures to the pelvis, a ruptured bladder and a tear to his scrotum. He had a catheter inserted for eight weeks and was in hospital for 14 days, during which time he had two operations. His injuries also required 72 stitches. At the time of the appeal, V could not stand for any length of time, his studies had come to an end and he could not obtain a part-time job. He will require a hip replacement, suffers from depression and will never again play competitive sport. D, aged 20 at appeal, had convictions for 15 offences including violence. He was in breach of a 3-year conditional discharge. Held. This was a very deliberate and wicked act with devastating consequences. The Facebook message demonstrated that the act was intentional and in driving off the conduct is aggravated. It is further aggravated by D's convictions, the breach of the conditional discharge, the use of a weapon (the car) and driving whilst under the influence of drink and/or drugs. **8 years' YOI** was fully merited.
R v Harrison 2012 EWCA Crim 433, 2 Cr App R (S) 78 (p 449) D was convicted of section 18. He had attended a party with his girlfriend at the home of V's sister. D consumed a very large amount of alcohol and quarrelled with his girlfriend. V intervened and D and V argued. The argument became heated and the police were called. D was arrested and put in a cell to allow him to sober up. He was released and at around 9 am D took his younger brother and went looking for V. He took with him a tin concealed in a sock. He went to V's flat and V answered the door. D attempted to punch V before striking him with the tin. V lost consciousness for a short time. He suffered a depressed fracture of the skull and a small epidural haematoma. D, aged 22, had 16 appearances for 40 offences. Many were for offences of violence, including GBH in 2006 and battery (×2) in 2007. Held. The aggravating factors were: a) there was a significant degree of premeditation, b) D had used a potentially lethal weapon, c) it was committed in V's home, and d) D had a background of violent offending. The Judge was wrong to categorise this as a Level 1 case. It falls at the top of Level 2. The mitigation was that a) it was a single blow, and b) there was an element of remorse. **9 years** not 10.
R v Opiote 2012 EWCA Crim 438 D was convicted of section 18, having been acquitted of attempted murder. After some 18-24 months V owed D a debt of £580. V had gone on to university and was unable to repay it. There had been an argument and D and V gave each other a wide berth. V was being driven to his mother's house when he saw F, a friend of D's. F approached the car and began to talk with V and the driver. He asked for a lift around the corner and they agreed. They drove around the corner to a house which was D's cousin's address, upon which F pressed a knife against V's neck and removed a chain from around his neck. He called for D while he tried to drag V into the house. D arrived on the scene and, during a scuffle in the street, stabbed V in the chest. There were

three stab wounds and V collapsed. He suffered a collapsed lung and had blood on the diaphragm. D, aged 27, had convictions for possessing an offensive weapon (2002) and possessing a bladed article (2006). There were also convictions for cannabis possession, and destroying and damaging property. Held. V's injuries were life-threatening. The aggravating features were serious and although the attack only lasted a short period of time, the Judge was entitled to find that the offence fell within the guideline that had a starting point of 13 years and a range of 10-16 years. We are unpersuaded that **12 years**, severe as it was, is manifestly excessive.

Att-Gen's Ref No 32 of 2012 2012 EWCA Crim 2588, 2013 2 Cr App R (S) 8 (p 39) D was convicted of section 18. V was with two friends in the living room of his home. The front door was not locked. D entered and struck V without saying a word. V already had a fractured cheek bone. He received a series of further blows to his head. D then left. It was unclear whether he had others with him when he entered, though evidence suggested D left with two others. V suffered multiple fractures to the mid-face, which included a broken jaw, fractured cheekbones and fractures to the eye sockets and nose. There was also extensive bruising and lacerations to his head and upper lip. Surgery fixed the facial fractures with plates and screws, which necessitated incisions across the scalp, through the lower eyelids and through the mouth. D was arrested two hours after the attack and had blood spattered on his face and hands, his shirt and jeans. The blood staining on the right boot and the distribution of the blood on his jeans demonstrated beyond doubt that D had stamped on V's face at a time when he was already significantly injured. D said, "That's what happens to drug dealers" and "I don't care as I'll get off in the morning. He won't give a statement." Police found at the address a number of small packs containing cocaine. V declined to give a statement but there was sufficient evidence to proceed. D, aged 29 at appeal, had convictions for 36 offences including burglary, affray and ABH, when aged 20 (3 years' detention). In 2007, he was convicted of possession of an offensive weapon, threatening words and behaviour and ABH (extended sentence (30 months' custody 3 years' licence)). The current offence was committed in breach of licence from the 2007 offence. Held. The Judge found that this was not a premeditated offence. That is a significant factor which operates as a limit on the appropriate sentence. There were a number of significant aggravating factors: a) the offence was committed whilst on licence, b) D's previous convictions, including violence to the person, and c) the offence was committed at night and in V's home. The fact that V may have been a drug dealer is relevant to a point, in that a drug dealer who opens his doors to unlawful trade is not in the same position as a householder who is broken into by an attacker at night. Nevertheless, it was an unprovoked attack in V's home. The callous remark made by D, to the effect that 'this is what happens to drug dealers' and that D would be released because V wouldn't make a statement, was highly significant. The courts are no friends of drug dealers, [but] for an offender to think that a particular type of victim, however vile his trade may be, is therefore beyond the protection of the law from serious assault...is totally unacceptable. It was a serious aggravating feature of the offence that D carried out the attack believing himself to be immune. The appropriate sentence was **13 years**, not 7. There was ample material to suggest IPP, but it would not be right to conclude that the Judge was wrong not to impose IPP.

Att-Gen's Ref Nos 55-56 of 2014 2014 EWCA Crim 1727 D1 and D2 were convicted of GBH with intent on V1. D1 was also convicted of ABH on V2. They were bouncers of substantial build and D2 was D1's manager. Outside their nightclub, D1 and D2 had an argument with V1 and V2 about entry and there were derogatory remarks and a scuffle. The police were called by a friend of V1 and V2 and searched them looking for a knife but none was found. About 1½ hours later, after their nightclub had closed, four bouncers in a number of cars chased V1, V2 and another, X, in their car. After over 1½ miles, V1 and V2 stopped and X ran off. D1 and D2 smashed the victims' car windows with batons and pulled the victims out through them. D1 used a knife and D2 a baton to injure V1 and V2, including when they were on the ground. The incident lasted at least 2 minutes. They required hospital treatment for multiple serious injuries. V1 required 57 stitches. He had multiple bruises, deep scalp wounds down to the bone, a severe ear laceration, a broken elbow and defensive wounds. V2 (ABH count) had cuts, bruising and a black eye. At sentence D1 was aged 27 and D2 was aged 37. Both were of good character or treated as such, with references. Held. No provocation occurred and one of the victims was vulnerable as he was trapped in a car. Greater harm and higher culpability were present. D2, as manager, could have prevented the attack. Regard was to be had to the short period V1 spent in hospital. This was a premeditated and determined act of revenge aggravated by the weaponry use and that the defendants' job was to keep order. D2 did not carry a knife but had a managerial role. D1, **10 years** not 5 and 8 months concurrent not consecutive. D2, **10 years** not 6.

R v Shearwood 2014 EWCA Crim 2075 D pleaded at trial to section 18. There was a long-standing dispute between D and V which had involved violence. The last incident was in 2011. They reacted instantly and violently when seeing each other. D and T entered a pub where V was drinking intending to attack V. D carried a concealed Stanley knife. V saw D and struck him with a glass. A struggle ensued with T punching V, and then retreating. During the fight, D produced the Stanley knife and wounded V in the neck. Others came to V's aid. V and the others fought D, who went to ground. They kicked and punched him. D suffered an eye injury and a cut eyebrow which was inflicted either by the glassing or afterwards. V had two 6-inch wounds to the neck which had penetrated a deep muscle layer, requiring surgery. D handed himself in to police but made no comment in interview. He was aged 51 on appeal and heavily convicted with 15 years of violent offending, although his last such offence was in 1995 which was common assault. Held. This was at the lower end of Category 1. Starting at 12 years, **11 years**, not 12½.

Att-Gen's Ref No 17 of 2015 2015 EWCA Crim 868 D was convicted of section 18, common assault, criminal damage and possession of an offensive weapon. He pleaded late to two common assaults. D argued with his girlfriend, V1. Then he seized her round the neck and broke her necklace. She had scratches (the first common assault). V1 went to see a female friend and D was able to trace her through a tracking device on her mobile. V1 hid. Sometime later, V1 met up with V2, a male and others. One of them was her ex-boyfriend. D walked to the group and punched V2 hard in the right eye (the section 18). The verdict of the jury on the offensive weapon meant they accepted he had an object in his hand, similar to a knuckleduster. V2 appeared to lose consciousness. V3 went to help him and D punched him on the face and head (the second common assault). V3 had a cut to an eyebrow and some bruising. V3 put V2 in his car. D then kicked V3's car and knocked off the bumper which he used to hit and dent the car (the criminal damage). The repair cost was £1,143. The next day police went to arrest D and D struggled and punched a female PC in her eye (the third common assault). CS spray was used. V2's facial wound was full thickness down to the bone. It needed 40 stitches. There was permanent scarring. V2 felt unable to leave his home for social events. D was aged 19 and had no convictions but had a battery caution for a fight outside a night club. He was well educated, had a strong work ethic and was in his final year of a four-year apprenticeship. D had genuine remorse and had character witnesses. The Judge placed the section 18 in Category 2 with a starting point of 6 years. He considered D was motivated by jealousy, consumed with anger and lost control. He reduced the sentence to two years and suspended it so as to save all that D had worked for. Held. In many ways D was a decent young man. D's personal circumstances reduce the 6-year starting point as does the fact that D now goes into custody. **3½ years** not 2 years suspended.

See also: *R v Vakas and Others* 2011 EWCA Crim 875 (Pre-guideline D and K convicted of conspiracy to cause GBH with intent. Honour killing. Sustained beating and stabbed victim. Attempted to make him drink 91% sulphuric acid. Poured it over his head. Burns on 47% of his head, neck, chest, abdomen and back. Hideously disfigured. 'Unimaginable suffering'. D, aged 19, unaware of acid or knife. K, aged 16, had previous convictions for violence and was on coat tails of conspiracy. **14 years' YOI** and **8 years' detention** under section 91.)

R v Richardson 2012 EWCA Crim 1007, 2 Cr App R (S) 103 (p 606) (Plea to section 18. Revenge attack. Three masked armed men, including defendant, entered a restaurant where victim was eating. Attacked victim. Stabbed him in upper arm and lower leg. Injury to leg 'so large [officer] could fit his hand in it'. Required surgery. Aware his accomplice was to use a knife. Full credit. Good character. Starting at **12 years, 8 years** not 8 years 4 months.)

R v McLeod 2012 EWCA Crim 1794, 2013 1 Cr App R (S) 78 (p 431) (LCJ D was convicted of murder and pleaded to robbery (×2). V was robbed by D. V gathered a group and sought out D. A fight ensued and V had the upper hand. D's friend and sister produced knives. V ran away. D took a knife and followed V. One stab wound to the chest. On bail for section 18 (later pleaded to section 20, 8-month DTO). Aged 15 at the offence. Robbery was a catalyst for the fight. Didn't take knife to scene. **14-year minimum term** entirely appropriate.)

R v Moustafa 2012 EWCA Crim 1865 (Plea to section 18. Breached bail and was arrested. Angry with his girlfriend for 'grassing him up'. Took knife to victim's house. Girlfriend was there. They argued and the victim, V, intervened. Slashed his face. V swung at defendant and defendant lunged at V, stabbing him in the abdomen. 500 ml of blood in V's peritoneal cavity. Aged 27. Previous convictions including use of knife. Extended sentence for section 20 in 2006. Category 1. Starting at 12 years, **4 years' IPP** not 6.)

Att-Gen's Ref No 9 of 2013 2013 EWCA Crim 597, 2014 1 Cr App R (S) 3 (p 7) (Convicted of section 18. Premeditated but unprovoked attack. Armed with a knife. Climbed in a taxi as it was moving to attack victim who was in the passenger seat. Two deep wounds on the face and head. Permanent scarring and damage to the ear. Victim affected psychologically. Significant previous convictions for violence. Had recently served 40 weeks for second dwelling burglary. Aged 21 at appeal. Upper end of Category 2. Sentence for a mature adult could not have been less than 8 years. **5 years** not 3½.)

Old cases: For six 2010 old cases see the 10th edition of this book. For numerous others, see the 8th edition.

Road Rage see the VEHICLES, *After using* paras at **292.38**.

292.32   *Robbery/Burglary/Aggravated burglary, And   Post-guideline cases*

R v Walsh 2012 EWCA Crim 1276 D pleaded (full credit) to section 18 and robbery, and was later convicted of section 20 (as an alternative to section 18). He entered a convenience store run by V, aged 32, and his 29-year-old wife. D wore a balaclava and a hood. In the store were V and his wife, who was 21 weeks pregnant. Their three-year-old daughter was in the flat above the shop. D carried a 30 cm hunting knife and a bag. He demanded money and cigarettes be put in the bag. V walked towards D and took with him an iron bar that he kept for his own protection. D stabbed him twice, and then went for V's eye. Instead he sliced through V's nose. It was almost severed. V's wife had gone to the door to get help. D slashed at her, cutting her arm in two places, one of which exposed tendons. D ran away empty handed, discarding the knife as he did so. V suffered a 7-8 inch laceration to his back, his spinal cord was injured, his right lung penetrated and he suffered incomplete paraplegia. His ribs were fractured, as was his nose, and he required stitches. The injuries were life-threatening. His survival was considered a near miracle. V is now confined to a wheelchair, has lost £46,000 through the forced sale of his business and has lost his job as an IT developer. He is unable to have intercourse with his wife. His wife received two wounds and a cut. The incident caused a great strain on their relationship. He avoids seeing family and friends because of his scarred face and is mentally insecure. D, a 'young man of some promise', had no convictions. Held. The injuries were horrific. The fact that this was a predetermined offence involving such a violent weapon, with violence used, led to the conclusion that IPP was correct, not the gravity of the injuries. There were so many aggravating factors, the injuries, the weapon, the vulnerable victims, it was done for gain, the concealment of evidence and the separate harm caused to V's wife. The Judge was justified in going above the guidelines. Had V died, the starting point would have been 30 years and might have been higher. **18 years** after a trial was not manifestly excessive. With the (generous) discount for plea, **6 years' IPP**.

R v Morgan and Hazelwood 2013 EWCA Crim 2619 H pleaded (10%) to robbery and section 18. He was with M in the early evening. M dragged V from a fish and chip shop. H joined in. Both were under the influence of alcohol. M demanded that V empty his pockets and struck him with a bottle. H said, "I'm not fucking messing" and V handed over £90 in cash. H went behind V and stabbed him twice in the buttocks with a shard of glass. The wounds were not deep. When V realised he had been stabbed, he lost control of his bowels. M struck V again with the bottle and kicked him whilst he was on the floor. V needed sutures and also suffered a broken tooth and cut lip. M was aged 25 and had a poor record including affray and public order offences. H was aged 19 at the offence and had no convictions. Held. M was the ringleader. H was much younger than M and played the minor role in the robbery. There was nothing wrong with **9 years** for M. Looking at the totality of the offending, H was indistinguishable from M. But taking account of the fact that H inflicted the wounds to V's buttocks, the sentence should be **9 years**, not 11.

R v Garcia 2014 EWCA Crim 93 D pleaded to section 18 and burglary. V was the landlady of a pub and lived above the premises. D had formerly been an employee at the pub. In the early hours, D broke in. V was disturbed and she got out of bed, looked down the stairs, got back into bed and called the police. She heard D come upstairs. He entered her room and, whilst she was still on the phone, struck her five or six times on the head, probably with her own phone as blood and clumps of hair were later found on it. Police attended and he was found nearby with blood on his hands and £1,690 that he had stolen from the pub. D was under the influence of alcohol and drugs at the time. V suffered a 3 cm cut to her forehead which had to be stitched. She went to live with her son after the attack and, despite an intention to return to the pub, was unable to do so for several weeks. She was unable to live alone. The Judge described the attack as 'gratuitous and vicious' and noted that V could not understand why D had carried it out. He was treated as being of good character. Held. The theft was an aggravating feature of the wounding and the Judge was entitled to treat it as such. There was minimal premeditation. It was a very serious offence. The correct starting point was at the top of Category 2 or the bottom of Category 1, namely 9 years not 11. With credit for the plea, **6 years**, not 7. The concurrent sentence of 2 years on the burglary would be unaltered.

See also: *R v L* 2014 EWCA Crim 1952 (GBH and burglary. During burglary, V was stabbed, potentially life threateningly, not initially by D. Later on all three burglars stabbed V multiple times. D was aged 16, was involved in gang activity and had grown up in care with little stability where he suffered physical abuse. Just convicted of several serious offences. Refused to engage with probation, no empathy and self-centred. D proud of criminal identity and planned to make a living from crime. Held. For an adult we would start at 15 years. **10 years' detention**, not 12, and 5 years' extended licence upheld.)

Old pre-guideline cases: *R v Azille* 2008 EWCA Crim 43 (**7 years**) *Att-Gen's Ref No 14 of 2009* 2009 EWCA Crim 1143, 2010 1 Cr App R (S) 17 (p 93) (**6 years'** IPP) *Att-Gen's Ref No 114 of 2009* 2010 EWCA Crim 574 (**6½ years** not 4½.) *R v Hall and Woodhead* 2010 EWCA Crim 1136 (For H, **4 years' IPP** not 4½ years' IPP. For W, **6 years 3 months'** detention)

For a summary of the first case, see the 8th edition of this book, for the second case see the 9th edition and for the last two cases, see the 10th edition.

See also the **ROBBERY** *Dwellings* para at **322.9**.
Sadistic pleasure see the *Torture/Sadistic violence* para at **292.36**.

292.33 Self-defence, Excessive
Note: The guidelines state that 'Excessive self-defence' is a 'Factor indicating lower culpability', see **292.3**.

292.34 Sexual
A pre-guideline example: *Att-Gen's Ref No 5 of 2011* 2011 EWCA Crim 1244, 2012 1 Cr App R (S) 20 (p 103) (convicted of section 18 and sexual assault. Met victim in the street. Both had been drinking. Violent attack causing skull fractures and brain damage. Considerable damage to victims' genitalia after a grossly violent attempt at penile or digital penetration. Aged 19. Wholly out of character. 15 years was right so **7½ years' DPP**.)
See also the **OFFENCES AGAINST THE PERSON ACT 1861 S 20** *Sexual* para at **293.19**.

292.35 Slavery   Victim kept and abused as a virtual slave   Pre-guideline case
R v Patel EWCA Crim 1480, 2007 1 Cr App R (S) 33 (p 179) D was convicted of 'a number' of counts of GBH with intent and false imprisonment. V, aged 40, arrived from India in February 2004, stayed with friends and family and then in February 2005 went to stay with D. She worked in D's pickle factory which was at the same address. During her six-week stay she was beaten with a long cooking spoon for not working quickly enough. She was prevented from leaving the home by a mixture of threats and suggestions that the police were looking for her. On at least two occasions D took her knickers off and struck her vagina and anus with the spoon. Her injuries were extremely serious and included a large wound to her scalp, two black eyes, extensive bruising to her body, deep burns to her back shoulder area, broken and bruised fingers on both hands, a large wound separating a finger from her palm, puncture wounds to her thighs, injuries to her genitals and bruising to her shin and feet. She was admitted to hospital where her injuries were considered life-threatening. Gangrene had set in and three fingers had to be amputated. Her ability to move her shoulder had been affected. It was unlikely she would be able to work again. The Judge described her as a virtual slave, and D's actions as sadistic. D was aged 56, had no convictions and showed no remorse. Held. The degree of wickedness is at the upper end of what even this Court sees. The offence was aggravated by the terrible isolation, but **12 years** not 14.
Note: This case is old and should be treated with care. Ed.

292.36 Torture/Sadistic violence   Pre-guideline case
R v BC and JC 2010 EWCA Crim 1140 LCJ JC and BC pleaded to GBH with intent, robbery, child sex and other offences. The first incident involved tricking a young boy aged 11 to follow them to see a 'massive toad'. The boys led him to an isolated area, pushed him to the ground and JC stamped on his face. BC punched him in the face. They sought to extract from the boy his grandmother's address because they said they proposed to kill her.
The second incident involved T and V, brothers aged 11 and 9 respectively, with JC and BC tricking the boys into following them to see a dead fox. It was the day the boys were required to attend the police station to be questioned about the first incident. Once in a concealed area, they were robbed and JC cut T's pocket to ensure nothing was concealed. T and V were told that they would be killed because they had killed JC's and BC's grandmother. T and V were robbed and T was choked by JC so that he could not breathe. T and V were told, "We're going to kill you. We're going to kill the rest of your family if you don't shut up." They were marched to another location. BC kicked V in the head. They targeted T's and V's genitals. Rocks were gathered and thrown at T's and V's heads. Rocks too heavy to throw were carried and dropped onto both victims. V received a deep wound from a tree branch which was sharp at one end. JC then took a cigarette and extinguished it in V's wound. T and V were told to undress and T was told to "bum" V. There was no penetration although V said it hurt. T and V were forced to

"snog" and V was told to urinate in T's mouth. JC was cautious to avoid getting blood on their clothes, saying, "If blood gets onto me, we'll kill you both", subsequently making V lick some blood from his trainers. T and V were forced to lie under a tarpaulin which was set alight, causing burns. Finally, a large piece of ceramic sanitaryware was found and thrown at T's head. It caused a large wound from which blood flowed. BC was laughing.

T was effectively blinded by the swelling and blood streaming from his head wounds. He slipped in and out of consciousness. T had fractures to facial bones, cuts and wounds. He suffered a degree of life-threatening hyperthermia.[744]

BC, aged 10, and JC, aged 11, had grown up in a 'toxic' environment, having been subjected to violence and exposed to their father's pornographic material and cinematic material of a disgusting and grotesque kind. They were involved in the misuse of drugs from the age of 9. Their upbringing was described as grossly negative, neglectful and abusive. JC had four convictions for violence despite being just 11 years 8 months old. Reports noted that BC's actions were calculated to cause maximum injury and that JC intended the ceramic sanitaryware to knock T out so he could not remember their names. Both JC and BC were of low intelligence. Held. The treatment of T and V amounted to torture. JC and BC were both very dangerous. Account was taken of their 'toxic' upbringing. On all the evidence, the risk that they represent is one which means that any sentence other than DPP cannot be justified because no other sentence would provide the necessary element of long-term public protection. There are no possible grounds for criticism in this highly exceptional case. **5 years' DPP** for both.

See also: *R v Mahmood and Others* 2015 EWCA Crim 441, 2 Cr App R (S) 18 (p 182) (Late plea to conspiracy to kidnap, false imprisonment, section 18 and section 20. Claimed man owed them money. With other, seized V from home with violence. V put in shipping container where tortured with hammers etc. Tied up overnight. Stabbed in new location. Total time held 28 hours. Starting at **18 years** cannot conceivably be criticised for principal offender.)

See also the **SLAVERY, SERVITUDE AND FORCED OR COMPULSORY LABOUR** chapter.

292.37   *Unprovoked/Drug induced attack*

R v Smith 2010 EWCA Crim 364 D pleaded to wounding with intent and possession of a bladed article. D's girlfriend lived in a children's home. D had been involved in an incident there and given a community order for threatening behaviour. The next day the police found him in the vicinity again and searched him. When asked if he had anything he should not have, D produced a lock knife with a 3-inch blade. Two months later V and his girlfriend were sitting on a bus. D and his girlfriend were sitting two rows in front. D was staring at V so V said, "You what?" and D replied, "Wait, I'll bang you when we get off the bus". D then sat in the empty seat in front of S, leant over and said, "I'll bang you now". A scuffle involving S, his girlfriend, and D ensued. D took out a knife, opened it with both hands and stabbed V in the inner thigh. D took the knife, got off the bus and ran away. S's femoral artery and a vein had been severed. He was unable to play any more rugby or taekwondo, which he played at national level. V had been studying for a sports diploma, had hopes of being considered for the Olympics team and of joining the Marines. These were no longer possible as a result of his injury. He could not run more than a few hundred yards without having to stop and was undergoing counselling for post-traumatic stress disorder. D, aged 21, had previous convictions for threatening behaviour and ABH. He was on bail for possession of a knife. The psychiatric report said D had clear difficulties in his upbringing and a history of emotional and physical abuse. It was likely he suffered from a mild learning disability and attention deficit hyperactive disorder. He had impaired comprehension and expression, and lack of insight. The pre-sentence report said D had long-standing problems with managing emotion and temper, he had never worked and received Disability Living

---

[744] It may be that this is a typo for hypothermia. Ed.

Allowance. There were significant behavioural and thinking issues and D gave no satisfactory explanation for his behaviour on this occasion. Held. Protection of society is the most important factor. It seems IPP would have been appropriate. **9 years** was not excessive in any way.

R v Fairhurst 2016 EWCA Crim 112 D pleaded to section 18. D's mother, M, had been in a long-term relationship with V, who suffered from epilepsy and asthma and had difficulty walking. He was in his mid-forties and disabled. D had known V for many years, and considered him a father figure. D went to V's flat and told him he had had an argument with his girlfriend. V told him to speak to M and went with him to M's address in a taxi. On the way they stopped and bought alcohol. At M's address, D became extremely argumentative and aggressive towards V. D accused V of spoiling his sons and referred to V as having a lot of money in the bank. V became concerned about D's behaviour and called for a taxi. Before the taxi arrived, D screamed and shouted at V and then repeatedly punched him about the face. D then seized V around the neck and said, "I've waited a long time to do this" and continued to rain blows upon V. D next picked up a pint glass and hit V with it in the face. The glass smashed on impact. Meanwhile M was shouting at the appellant to stop, and called the police. D picked up V's walking stick and hit him a number of times with it. V went to his knees and D continued to attack him with the stick until it broke. V thought he was going to be killed. Eventually D left the scene. In interview D expressed remorse. V continued to suffer from psychological damage. [It is a pity his physical injuries were not listed. Ed.] V said, "I always considered myself a father figure to D. He has shattered my life. I still love him but can't see him again." D was aged 24. The judge found D was intoxicated and on drugs and had no real remorse because of the lateness of his guilty plea. Held. This was a Category 1 case, which means a starting point of 12 years. The greater harm was the vulnerability of the victim due to his personal circumstances and also that it was a sustained and repeated assault. The higher culpability was based on the two weapons, the glass and the walking stick, which were not taken to the scene. We note young children were in the next room. Given D's lack of previous convictions and given that in the pre-sentence report it said D acknowledged his remorse, which the Judge did not recognise, we start at 12 years not 14. With the same 10% discount for the plea, **10½ years** not 12½.

See also: *R v Mayfield and Faulkner* 2010 EWCA Crim 1406 (Plea. Drunken dispute at taxi rank. Victim attempted to calm situation. Single kick to victim's head while on ground. Fractured jaw. Extended sentence (**4½ years'** detention 4½ years' licence).)

R v Graham 2010 EWCA Crim 2793 (Plea to section 18 and having a bladed article. Spontaneous and unprovoked attack. Stabbed victim in chest twice with lock-knife. Shallow wounds caused. Mental health problems. **3 years 8 months**, not 4 years 8 months.)

R v Smythe 2010 EWCA Crim 2404 (Plea to 2 counts (full credit). D, aged 74, drunk, attacked two friends. Repeatedly struck a man with a hockey stick and stamped on his head causing a broken wrist and an aneurysm. Punched a woman, knocking several teeth out. One conviction for ABH. **7 years**, not 8.)

Old cases: Numerous old cases can be found in the 9th edition of this book.

Post-guideline case

R v Arfu 2014 EWCA Crim 2608 D was convicted of section 18. V, who was suffering from depression and epilepsy, was unfit to work. He was walking home and D and another, C, attacked him. D hit V in the face with an iron bar. This forced V into a garden where he [was forced] to the ground. C stamped on his face and D struck him a number of times with the bar. The attack lasted 30-40 seconds. V had multiple bruises, abrasions, swellings to the temple and around the eyes and a wound to the side of his eye. In interview D lied. D was aged 19 with 14 convictions between 2009 and 2011. They included robbery, burglary, a bladed article, affray, and an offensive weapon. He had not received a custodial sentence. Held. The Judge said it was a cowardly, sustained and unprovoked joint attack. Held. The case fell between Categories 1 and 2. **10 years** detention not 13.

292.38   Vehicles, After using (including road rage)   Post-guideline case
R v Wilkins 2014 EWCA Crim 2066, 2015 1 Cr App R (S) 20 (p 152) D pleaded (full credit) to section 18 and possessing an offensive weapon. D's bad driving caused V to flash his lights and V later turned into the road where he lived. D, reversing his car, followed V and there was an altercation. D, who had been drinking, punched V unprovoked and then took hold of a Stanley knife. D and V grappled on the ground with D continuing to punch V. In the course of the fracas the knife caused a 3½ inch slash to V's face and a cut lip. He needed stitches and had a permanent scar. D then drove away. The attack also left V with anxiety and sleeplessness. D was aged 25 on appeal and had several previous convictions for violence, including a section 20 assault on his ex-partner in 2011. There were supportive references. D had received a suspended sentence which expired only four months prior to this attack. He was remorseful and admitted to anger problems. D was also in long-term employment and his partner had given birth whilst he was remanded. The Judge accepted that D had armed himself with the intention of going out to harm others. Held. We agree D is dangerous, but this was not a Category 1 offence. There was in reality no sustained or repeated assault. 8 years' **extended sentence** (**4 years'** custody (not 6) 4 years' extended licence).
Old pre-guideline case: *R v Smith* 2008 EWCA Crim 1212, 2009 1 Cr App R (S) 37 (p 206) (**5 years**)
For a summary of the case, see the 9th edition of this book.
See also the **ROAD RAGE** chapter.

292.39   Vehicles, after using (including road rage)   Disqualification
R v Wilson 2012 EWCA Crim 2792 (Convicted of section 18. Bad example of road rage. Used wheel lock to smash windscreen. Drove at victim causing broken leg. Fled scene. 5 years was not appealed. **4½-year disqualification** not 12 years.)
Victim aged under 10 see the **CRUELTY TO CHILDREN** *Offences Against the Person Act 1861 s 18* para at **231.22**.

292.40   Victim caused permanent disability/Very serious injuries
R v Cross 2010 EWCA Crim 115 D was convicted of GBH with intent. D was with H and another. D and H were in the area to buy heroin. The group were approached by V, a 15-year-old boy who had been drinking. V asked for a cigarette and tried to impress the three by saying that he had a gun. The three laughed and told him to go and get it. V returned with a turntable, which he threw at them. V then ran and was chased by D and H. H punched him, knocking him to the ground. V was now unconscious. D slapped V's head and then gave him a heavy kick to his head. It was described as 'kicking with his body behind it'. V suffered serious injuries to the brain. He was in a coma in intensive care for eight days. He stayed in hospital for eight weeks. V has difficulty formulating words. His memory has been seriously affected. V has difficulty walking and is partially blind. He has evident scarring and is effectively disabled. The injuries have caused behavioural changes and problems at home and at school. D was now aged 30 with 50 court appearances for 84 offences, mostly for dishonesty. There was one robbery conviction (3 years). He was in breach of a suspended sentence imposed for breach of an ASBO (given 60 days concurrent). Held. **9 years** was severe, and rightly so.
See also: *R v Morgan* 2010 EWCA Crim 1529 (Plea on first day of trial. Pushed man who defendant thought was 'trying it on' with his girlfriend from a bridge. Man fell 35 feet onto concrete. Multiple fractures and broken spine. At court in a wheelchair. Not premeditated. Lengthy antecedents. **9 years**, not 11.)
Old cases: *Att-Gen's Ref No 85 of 2007* 2007 EWCA Crim 3218, 2008 2 Cr App R (S) 39 (p 221) (in the range of **15-16 years**) *R v Cross* 2008 EWCA Crim 1194, 2009 1 Cr App R (S) 34 (p 193) (**IPP** with a minimum term of **5 years**)

For a summary of the first case, see the 8th edition of this book and for the second case, see the 9th edition.

Post-guideline cases

R v Walsh 2012 EWCA Crim 1276 (**18 years** after a trial was not manifestly excessive. **6 years' IPP**), see para **292.32**.

R v B and J 2015 EWCA Crim 11, 1 Cr App R (S) 56 (p 396) D1 and D2 were convicted of section 18. They were at a party with B, who was D1's older brother, R and others when there was a disagreement over a missing mobile phone. A fight then broke out between V and B, 'the leader of what happened'. D1 and D2 joined in and were, between them, armed with one or two knives. A knife had been passed to D1 by B. D1, D2 and R pushed V over a wall and pursued him down the street whereupon V collapsed between two parked cars. He had been stabbed three times, principally ascribed to D2. The wounds were all life-threatening. One caused severe blood loss and another led to poisoning. This caused all of V's limbs to be amputated and he now used a colostomy bag, all severely affecting his quality of life. D1 was aged 17 and D2 was aged 16 and both were heavily influenced by their peers. Held. The Judge rightly identified this as a Category 1 case at the very top end but youth cannot be balanced and cancelled out by findings of fact adverse to any defendant. B received 16 years' detention and it was not appealed. Taking ¾ of that due to their youth, **12 years' detention**, not 15 for both D1 (in a YOI) and D2 (under section 91).

292.40a   *Victim particularly vulnerable*

R v Fairhurst 2016 EWCA Crim 112 D pleaded to section 18. D's mother, M, had been in a long-term relationship with V, who suffered from epilepsy and asthma and had difficulty walking. He was in his mid-forties and disabled. D had known V for many years, and considered him a father figure. D went to V's flat and told him he had had an argument with his girlfriend. V told him to speak to M and went with him to M's address in a taxi. On the way they stopped and bought alcohol. At M's address, D became extremely argumentative and aggressive towards V. D accused V of spoiling his sons and referred to V as having a lot of money in the bank. V became concerned about D's behaviour and called for a taxi. Before the taxi arrived, D screamed and shouted at V and then repeatedly punched him about the face. D then seized V around the neck and said, "I've waited a long time to do this" and continued to rain blows upon V. D next picked up a pint glass and hit V with it in the face. The glass smashed on impact. Meanwhile M was shouting at the appellant to stop, and called the police. D picked up V's walking stick and hit him a number of times with it. V went to his knees and D continued to attack him with the stick until it broke. V thought he was going to be killed. Eventually D left the scene. In interview D expressed remorse. V continued to suffer from psychological damage. [It is a pity his physical injuries were not listed. Ed.] V said, "I always considered myself a father figure to D. He has shattered my life. I still love him but can't see him again." D was aged 24. The judge found D was intoxicated and on drugs and had no real remorse because of the lateness of his guilty plea. Held. This was a Category 1 case, which means a starting point of 12 years. The greater harm was the vulnerability of the victim due to his personal circumstances and also that it was a sustained and repeated assault. The higher culpability was based on the two weapons, the glass and the walking stick, which were not taken to the scene. We note young children were in the next room. Given D's lack of previous convictions and given that in the pre-sentence report it said D acknowledged his remorse, which the Judge did not recognise, we start at 12 years not 14. With the same 10% discount for the plea, **10½ years** not 12½.

292.41   *Water, Boiling   Post-guideline cases*

R v B and S 2013 EWCA Crim 1119 B, S and X pleaded (full credit) to section 18. They were friends. V, aged 28, had been to S's house a number of times. He got very drunk and accepted that he could be unpleasant and obnoxious when intoxicated. He was annoying B, S and X. There was an argument about the mess he had made and the fact he had urinated in the flat. He also made fun of S and a failed relationship she had had. B claimed that V tried to have sex with her and had called her a "slut". V was asked to leave but would not. He was thrown out but returned. B, S and X then launched an attack on him. X repeatedly boiled water and poured it on him. S punched him, knocking him to the ground. Both S and B stamped on and kicked V. Witnesses heard V being accused of stealing money and then begging not to be burnt again. A fat fryer was dropped onto his head from a height. B, S and X bragged and giggled about what they had done to V to a friend of theirs who had been at the address earlier. S told him that she had 'shoved a bottle up V's bottom'. It was the Crown's case that X had assisted. B also admitted to hitting V with a plank of wood. X bragged about pouring boiling water over V. One of the group had filmed the attack and B could be heard to ask V whether he had had enough. V was severely scalded and had to remain in hospital for a number of weeks. He suffered scarring which would improve over time. He also suffered from PTSD as a result of the attack. V struggled to sleep, could not trust people and suffered panic attacks. He needed prolonged therapy. S was aged 33 and claimed to have no recollection of the events, stating that she was an alcoholic. She had a number of convictions for drugs and dishonesty offences. There were no previous convictions for violence, save for assault with intent to resist arrest. She had never been to custody. She said she was angry with V prior to the evening as he had exposed himself to her 11-year-old daughter and that S had been repeatedly abused as a child and so her actions were a way of 'getting justice' for her and her daughter, for whom she was the primary carer. B, aged 18, had convictions for shoplifting but also for violence when aged 13, 14 and 17. She claimed that V had made advances towards her in the past, which she had rejected. She claimed on the night he made advances towards her again. She claimed she had been sexually abused as a child and that her actions were punishing V for what had happened to her in the past. She had two young children and had abused alcohol and drugs. Her level of intelligence was just above the level of someone who has learning difficulties. She suffered from PTSD as a result of the sexual abuse she claimed to have suffered. X was aged 15. Held. It was open to the Judge to treat this as: a) a Category 1 case, b) one in which greater harm had been caused (because of V's injuries), and c) a sustained attack. It was also a case of higher culpability as, despite the degree of provocation, the women caused V much more harm than was necessary to get him to leave. V's drunkenness made him vulnerable. In addition they used the equivalent of weapons, boiling water and shod feet. There was also the gratuitous degradation of V not just from the attack but also the insertion of the bottle into his bottom. Some allowance should be made for the fact that the boiling water was not S or B's idea. Full credit, not 25% given by the Judge, was appropriate. For S, **6½ years** not 8 years. For B, **5½ years'** detention, not 7. X received 5 years' detention and did not appeal.

See also: *R v B* 2010 EWCA Crim 1882 (Pre-guideline conviction. Rape of an Eritrean girl whom he had helped. In witness box defendant accepted there was full sex. Afterwards he threw boiling water over her saying, "Nobody can look at you ever again". 36% burns over face and body. No previous convictions. 5 years for the rape unaltered. **7 years** not 10 consecutive for the attack.)

R v Waruku 2013 EWCA Crim 1440 (Plea (20% credit) and section 47 (25% credit). Relationship of 18 years. Suspected partner of having an affair. Made threats. Boiled 2.5 litres of oil and poured it on her on four occasions. Teenage son could hear mother screaming. Re-boiled the oil whilst making victim clean the floor. Threatened to 'torch' her and watch her slowly die if she informed the police. Sadistic violence. Threats and violence continued the following day including cutting her scalp and kicking the burn injuries. Two teenage children. Aged 40. No convictions. Starting at 12 years was correct. **9½ years** and **8 months** consecutive.)

292.42   *Wooden plank, baseball bat etc., With a   Post-guideline cases*

R v Finn 2013 EWCA Crim 1643 D was convicted of section 18. At about 10.30 pm, V was at home watching television. She let her dog out and shortly went outside in her pyjamas. She saw D kicking the dog. D walked away and the dog followed him. V followed D down the road. V's partner caught up with her and D and there ensued a confrontation. D said, "Come on then" and was described as 'spoiling for a fight'. D ran across the road to a fence and removed a fence panel. He returned to V and her partner. The fence panel had large nails in it. D swung the fence panel towards V's partner at head height. It missed and collided with a wall, rebounding towards V, at which moment V stepped forward. The fence panel struck V in the face. D dropped the panel and ran away. V suffered grievous injuries and lost her left eye. The bones behind her eye were fractured, as was her cheekbone. She had multiple visits and stays in hospital. She could no longer drive and described in an impact statement how her life would never again be the same. D was on bail for another offence at the time of the incident. Aged 28 at conviction, he had a lengthy and serious record dating back to the age of 17. There were convictions for section 20, affray, ABH, threats to kill and assaults on police. Held. There was no challenge to the imposition of an extended sentence. This offence fell fairly and squarely in Category 1. There was an abundance of aggravation here, including the serious previous convictions, the fact that D was drunk, the grossly severe attack and the fact that V was vulnerable, in nightclothes outside her house at night. A 17-year **extended sentence** was appropriate (**13 years'** custody 4 years' extended licence), not 14 years 2 months' custody 3 years' licence.

R v Garcia 2014 EWCA Crim 93 D pleaded to section 18 and burglary. V was the landlady of a pub and lived above the premises. D had formerly been an employee at the pub. In the early hours, D broke in. V was disturbed and she got out of bed, looked down the stairs, got back into bed and called the police. She heard D come upstairs. He entered her room and, whilst she was still on the phone, struck her five or six times on the head, probably with her own phone as blood and clumps of hair were later found on it. Police attended and he was found nearby with blood on his hands and £1,690 that he had stolen from the pub. D was under the influence of alcohol and drugs at the time. V suffered a 3 cm cut to her forehead which had to be stitched. She went to live with her son after the attack and, despite an intention to return to the pub, was unable to do so for several weeks. She was unable to live alone. The Judge described the attack as 'gratuitous and vicious' and noted that V could not understand why D had carried it out. He was treated as being of good character. Held. The theft was an aggravating feature of the wounding and the Judge was entitled to treat it as such. There was minimal premeditation. It was a very serious offence. The correct starting point was at the top of Category 2 or the bottom of Category 1, namely 9 years not 11. With credit for the plea, **6 years** not 7. The concurrent sentence of 2 years on the burglary would be unaltered.

R v Smith 2015 EWCA Crim 1482 D was convicted of section 18. He pleaded to two burglaries and section 20 (an alternative to the section 18 count). D was separated from his wife, W, who began a relationship with V. Whilst V and W were away on holiday, D sent texts to W with naked pictures of herself, taken when the two were together. On return V and W went to V's house. At about 3 am, D broke in with a baseball bat. Fearing violence, W threw herself on V. D told her to get out of the way and hit V with the bat causing two fractures to his arm and lacerations to his forehead, requiring nine stitches. W rang the police and the police could hear her screaming. V punched D but V felt disoriented and dazed and lay on the bed. D then swung the bat at V with such force the bat broke in two. This caused V lacerations behind his ear which required two stitches. V carried on resisting and D left. D was of good character. The Judge considered D treated the break-up of the marriage as an affront and he suffered from high self-regard. The Judge found there was some remorse and categorised the case as Category 1. Held. The differences between Category 1 and 2 are stark as far as the penalty is concerned. The injuries were significant but they could be worse. para 4 In the harm category in the guidelines it says, 'serious injury must normally be present'. 'Normally' is an indication that an offence may abnormally be a Category 1 offence even where the harm is less than serious. The only reason the Judge gave for finding 'higher harm' was that the blow required hospital treatment, stitching and had a considerable lasting effect. The question is whether 'the injury was serious in the context of the offence'. That means the violence must go beyond what is inherent or par [for the course] in a standard section 18 case. It must be significantly above the serious level of harm which is normal for section 18. Here there was one blow amounting to section 18. It was sufficient to break the bat. It was a serious attack. Given the great disparity between Categories 1 and 2, it was nasty but it was not Category 1. However, the previous blow makes it more serious and closer to Category 1. Because V was dazed, he was vulnerable. The two blows, one of which was not a section 18 blow, would not normally amount to a 'sustained or repeated assault'. This case was either at the top end of Category 2 or on the borderline between Categories 1 and 2, so we start at 9 years. The aggravating factors were the location, manner of entry, it was at night time, the continuing effects on the victim, W's presence and the [vulnerability] of V prone on the bed. The mitigating factors were the good character, the limited number of blows, the injuries were not that bad, that it was an isolated incident out of character, the lack of premeditation and the part pleas. With all these factors **9 years** not 12.

See also: *R v Doherty* 2011 EWCA Crim 2455 (Plea (20% credit). Unprovoked. Struck V with pool cue twice. Injuries included loss of four teeth and damage to 10 others. 35 stitches needed in mouth, five on his head. Further emergency treatment was necessary. Previous conviction for offensive weapon. **5 years** not 8.)

R v Tomlyn 2013 EWCA Crim 1769 (Plea and ABH. Met V1 in prison. Upon release, with another, burst into V1's house and attacked V1 and his girlfriend, V2, with a baseball bat and a table leg. V1 suffered a fractured arm, and damaged ribs. V2 suffered a cut and bruising. Aged 30. 32 convictions for 82 offences including nine common assaults, battery, two robberies. 10% credit. **8 years** not 10.)

R v Lodi 2014 EWCA Crim 904 (In a YOI. **7 years 4 months**, see **309.4**.)

R v Hunt 2014 EWCA Crim 1010 (D pleaded to possession of an imitation firearm with intent to cause fear. Returned to a party after being told that a friend's brother had been assaulted. Handed a plastic toy gun. Threatened to shoot a neighbour. Struck him with the weapon several times causing heavy bleeding. Punched another neighbour in the face. Threatened other partygoers that he would kill them if they called the police. Boasted about assaulting people with the weapon. One victim left with severe anxiety. Just short of his 19th birthday at the time. Under the influence of alcohol and cocaine. Consecutive sentences appropriate. **4 years** with 18 months consecutive making **5½ years' YOI** not 8.)

Note: The case is listed in the paragraph because the weapon was used like a piece of wood and the firearms paragraph is reserved for cases where a firearm is discharged. Ed.

Old pre-guideline cases: *Att-Gen's Ref No 14 of 2008* 2008 EWCA Crim 1532, 2009 1 Cr App R (S) 62 (p 360) (**5 years**) *R v Brogan* 2009 EWCA Crim 2683, 2010 2 Cr App R (S) 32 (p 205) (**7 years**) *Att-Gen's Ref No 10 of 2006* 2006 EWCA Crim 3335, 2 Cr App R (S) 103 (p 677) (Aged 17. **2½ years**) *Att-Gen's Ref No 124 of 2006* 2007 EWCA Crim 178 (IPP **2 years**) *R v Smythe* 2010 EWCA Crim 2404 (**7 years**) *R v Stenning* 2010 EWCA Crim 2825 (**3½ years' detention**)

For a summary of the first case, see the 8th edition of this book and for the second case, see the 9th edition.

Matters relating to the defendant

292.43   Defendant aged under 21

Note: The *Assault Guideline 2011* does not apply to those aged under 18, see page 2 of the guideline and **292.3**. I would expect most judges would determine the appropriate sentence for an adult and then make a reduction. Offences must be considered with the guideline for children and young offenders in the **CHILDREN AND YOUNG OFFENDERS: GENERAL PRINCIPLES** chapter at **14.29** in Volume 1. Ed.

292.44   *Defendant aged 10-15*

R v BC and JC 2010 EWCA Crim 1140 LCJ JC and BC pleaded to GBH with intent, robbery, child sex and other offences. The first incident involved tricking a young boy aged 11 to follow them to see a 'massive toad'. The boys led him to an isolated area, pushed him to the ground and JC stamped on his face. BC punched him in the face. They sought to extract from the boy his grandmother's address because they said they proposed to kill her.

The second incident involved T and V, brothers aged 11 and 9 respectively, with JC and BC tricking the boys into following them to see a dead fox. It was the day the boys were required to attend the police station to be questioned about the first incident. Once in a concealed area, they were robbed and JC cut T's pocket to ensure nothing was concealed. The victims were told that they would be killed because they had killed JC's and BC's grandmother. T and V were robbed and T was choked by JC so that he could not breathe. T and V were told, "We're going to kill you. We're going to kill the rest of your family if you don't shut up". They were marched to another location. BC kicked V in the head. They targeted T's and V's genitals. Rocks were gathered and thrown at T's and V's heads. Rocks too heavy to throw were carried and dropped onto both victims. V received a deep wound from a tree branch which was sharp at one end. JC then took a cigarette and extinguished it in V's wound. T and V were told to undress and T was told to 'bum' V. There was no penetration although V said it hurt. T and V were forced to 'snog' and V was told to urinate in T's mouth. JC was cautious to avoid getting blood on their clothes, saying, "If blood gets onto me, we'll kill you both", subsequently making V lick some blood from his trainers. T and V were forced to lie under a tarpaulin which was set alight, causing burns. Finally, a large piece of ceramic sanitaryware was found and thrown at T's head. It caused a large wound from which blood flowed. BC was laughing.

T was effectively blinded by the swelling and blood streaming from his head wounds. He slipped in and out of consciousness. T had fractures to facial bones, cuts and wounds. He suffered life-threatening hyperthermia.[745]

BC, aged 10, and JC, 11, had grown up in a 'toxic' environment, having been subjected to violence and exposed to their father's pornographic material and cinematic material of a disgusting and grotesque kind. They were involved in the misuse of drugs from the age of 9. Their upbringing was described as grossly negative, neglectful and abusive. JC had four convictions for violence despite being aged just 11 years 8 months. Reports noted that BC's actions were calculated to cause maximum injury and that JC intended the ceramic sanitaryware to knock T out so he could not remember their names. Both JC and BC were of low intelligence. Held. The treatment of T and V amounted to torture. JC and BC were both very dangerous. Account was taken of their 'toxic' upbringing. On all the evidence, the risk that they represent is one which means that any sentence other than DPP cannot be justified because no other sentence would provide the necessary element of long-term public protection. There are no possible grounds for criticism in this highly exceptional case. **5 years' DPP** for both.

R v M and F 2012 EWCA Crim 399 M and F were convicted of section 18. With another, X, they followed V, aged 34, to a shop. When V left the shop to return home, the men attacked him. X cut V's face with a hunting knife, and V was kicked and punched whilst on the floor. F hit V in the face with a hammer. M stamped on V's face. V lost four teeth and faced losing a fifth. He suffered bruising, grazes and the complete splitting of his upper lip. F, aged 14, had no convictions but had a reprimand and a warning for battery in 2009 and 2010. M was aged 17 at appeal. Held. This was a very serious offence

---

[745] It may be that this is a typo for hypothermia. Ed.

calling for substantial periods of detention, even for defendants as young as these. It was appropriate to differentiate between the three, with X at the top (5 years). M and F would be just below him, each with **4 years'** detention.

See also: *R v M and Others* 2013 EWCA Crim 650 (One plea, three convictions for section 18. One aged 15. Three aged 14. Gang of 12 youths armed with five metal crutches and a baseball bat hunted victim down in an underground station. Assaulted with bat and crutches whilst on the floor. Stabbed in the thigh. Planned revenge attack. All of previous good character. Bottom of Category 1 or top of Category 2. For one, **27 months** not 36. 30 months, with plea, and 36 months for two others who were convicted was not manifestly excessive.)

292.45   *Defendant aged 15*

R v L 2011 EWCA Crim 2497 LCJ D was convicted of section 18. V was standing at a bus stop with his friend. A bus pulled up and D alighted. He said to V, "Come round the corner" and lifted his jacket to reveal a knife. V's friend grabbed D and told V to run. He did, but D pursued him. D swung the knife many times at V. There was a struggle, V's friend pulled D off V, and D ran away. V suffered four stab wounds, including a serious wound to his abdomen which required emergency surgery. D, aged 15 years 8 months, had one conviction for burglary in 2010 (Referral Order). Held. The real mitigation is first D's youth and second the absence of convictions for violence. **6 years' detention**, although stern, was not manifestly excessive.

R v C 2012 EWCA Crim 1397 D was convicted of section 18. Whilst on the phone to a young woman, he overheard an insult said by a group of people. The following day D located the group and confronted one of them. D had a kitchen knife and swung it at V. Numerous swings failed to connect but those that did caused injuries to the forearm, nose and back. The attack came to an end when the knife entered V's back, struck a bone and broke. D left the scene. D, aged 15, had findings of guilt for attempted robbery (2009 ×2) and carrying an offensive weapon (2010 ×3). Held. The finding of dangerousness was entirely right. However, the Court had a pre-appeal report, which the Judge did not. It noted that the promise of improvement had been substantively maintained whilst in custody. Because of D's age, **9 years' extended sentence (4½ years'** custody 4½ years' extended licence), not DPP with a minimum term of 4 years.

R v Latouche 2012 EWCA Crim 2291 D pleaded (full credit) to section 18. D and V, aged 18, were believed to be members of rival gangs. V was shopping in Oxford Street in London with his girlfriend. D lunged at V, knocking him to the floor. A member of the public separated the two men. D then stabbed V six times. There was a 4 cm wound behind the ear, a 1 cm wound below his shoulder blade, a 2 cm wound in the front left chest area, two 1 cm wounds to his abdomen and a half-centimetre wound to his upper right thigh. He suffered a collapsed lung and was treated with a chest drain. At least one witness saw two knives, although D denied having a knife. D suffered bruising, a superficial laceration to the lip and deep lacerations to the left knee and base of the thumb. The knife used to stab V was found at D's address. There was a known history between D and V. D was aged 15 at the time of the offence and had two previous convictions, one for possession of a bladed article and another for cannabis possession. Held. This was clearly a Category 1 case. The appropriate sentence for an adult after a trial would be **14 years**. Taking account of D's age, **10 years 6 months** was appropriate after a trial. With his plea, the appropriate sentence is **7 years** not 8.

R v T 2014 EWCA Crim 1906 D and K were convicted of section 18 assault and K was also convicted of possession of an offensive weapon. D was aged 15 and arranged to meet V in a park as V had been "disrespecting" him over a video. D abruptly changed the venue of the meeting to a take-away shop. On arrival D told V to wait for K. D and V remained separate and then K arrived. K told V to walk along and, as he did so, he stabbed V in the chest. The knife, which was never recovered, penetrated the muscle layer and the wound later required seven stitches. V ran away, bleeding, pursued by D and K. D tried to punch V and the attack stopped only when a friend intervened. When interviewed, D denied arranging K's attendance or any intention that V be stabbed. D had one conviction for robbery, committed a year prior to the instant offence (9-month referral order). He also had been excluded from school for violence. The pre-sentence report noted it was a gang offence and D's impulsivity, poor temper control and aggression. D continued to lie about his involvement. The pre-sentence report recommended an extended sentence for public protection. K was aged 18 and, having received a *Goodyear* indication, pleaded guilty. The Judge held that the section 18 was borderline Category 1 or 2. With a 6-year starting point, he received 4½ years' detention. Held. The discount for D's age and immaturity, borne out at trial and in the pre-sentence report, was insufficient. An appropriate discount from the sentence for an adult results in **4½ years' detention**, not 6.

Old cases: *R v I* 2009 EWCA Crim 2183 (**15 years** would be appropriate for an adult. **10 years'** detention) *Att-Gen's Ref Nos 74-75 of 2009* 2009 EWCA Crim 2934 (For M, **7 years** not 2, for D, **4 years**) *R v Z* 2010 EWCA Crim 741 (**3 years**) *R v H* 2010 EWCA Crim 1547, 2011 1 Cr App R (S) 52 (p 340) (**6 years' detention**)
For a summary of the first case, see the 9th edition of this book and for the second and third cases, see the 10th edition.

292.46   *Defendant aged 16-17*
Att-Gen's Ref No 65 of 2012 2012 EWCA Crim 3168 D pleaded during his trial to section 18. A group of friends were socialising at the home of a friend. Five, including D, knew each other reasonably well. V and G, who were in a relationship, had been recently introduced. Someone took G's phone and cigarettes from her bag. V and G remonstrated with the group and an argument ensued. The five young men, including D, attacked V and he was cut or stabbed four or five times to his flank, elbow and both thighs. The wounds were deep and needed attention under general anaesthetic. The knife was not carried to the scene. V made a full recovery. He had identified D as the one who first wielded the knife. D accepted that he delivered two blows. Others also delivered blows but were not convicted. D was aged 17 and was on bail for violent disorder. He was studying for a BTEC at college. The pre-sentence report assessed him as relatively immature. D had served the equivalent of a 10-month sentence on remand. The Judge imposed an 18-month Youth Rehabilitation Order. Held. D pleaded late so that V and G had to give evidence. The Judge fell into error in attaching too much significance to the possible counter-productive effects of custody on D and too little on what he had done. For an adult, the starting point would have been in the general region of 6 years. For D, the starting point was **about 3 years**. The appropriate sentence was **2½-3 years' detention**. With time on remand and as it was a reference, **18-month DTO**.
R v BB 2013 EWCA Crim 1686 D pleaded to section 18 wounding. She fell out with V, her former friend, who was aged 21 and was 26 weeks pregnant. They had fallen out six months previously and there had been some hostility on social networking sites. D responded threateningly to a message from V, who drove with her partner to D's address to speak with her about it. D went outside to meet them and, in the heated exchanges, D moved her arms towards V between three and six times. V discovered she was bleeding, and told her partner. D replied "Yeah I have, and I'll fucking slash you both up". V had a cut to the forehead and two cuts to the upper arm, one of which was deep. This caused a partial nerve injury. D, aged 16, had no convictions. The pre-sentence report noted D had little understanding of how serious the consequences could have been, suggesting she had an immature manner which would cause her to react aggressively if challenged. Held. This was clearly a serious offence with potentially very serious consequences. However, the Judge failed to give a sufficient discount for the youth and immaturity of D. This was at the lower end of the Category 1 range. With 25% credit, **5 years** not 7.
R v Giles 2014 EWCA Crim 1172 D pleaded (full credit) to section 18. When drunk, he approached V as he walked to evening prayers and asked him, "Are you a white Muslim?" V, aged 79, was dressed in Bangladeshi clothes and had an age-related condition which lightened his skin. D punched V and kicked him to the head after he had

fallen. V suffered life-threatening injuries with a fracture to the skull and the nose, a bruise to the brain which impaired his cognitive functions and damage to the auditory canal. His quality of life had been much reduced. D, aged 17, had spent the day drinking and had no memory of the offence. He had no relevant convictions. The *Assault Guideline 2011* did not apply to D owing to his age, otherwise it would have been a Category 1 offence. Held. Dreadful though the offence was, account should be taken of D's age, his early plea and his otherwise good character. **6 years**, not 8.

R v B and J 2015 EWCA Crim 11, 1 Cr App R (S) 56 (p 396) D1 and D2 were convicted of section 18. They were at a party with B, who was D1's older brother, R and others when there was a disagreement over a missing mobile phone. A fight then broke out between V and B, 'the leader of what happened'. D1 and D2 joined in and were, between them, armed with one or two knives. A knife had been passed to D1 by B. D1, D2 and R pushed V over a wall and pursued him down the street whereupon V collapsed between two parked cars. He had been stabbed three times, principally ascribed to D2. The wounds were all life-threatening. One caused severe blood loss and another led to poisoning. This caused all of V's limbs to be amputated and he now used a colostomy bag, all severely affecting his quality of life. D1 was aged 17 and D2 was aged 16 and both were heavily influenced by their peers. Held. The Judge rightly identified this as a Category 1 case at the very top end but youth cannot be balanced and cancelled out by findings of fact adverse to any defendant. B received 16 years' detention and it was not appealed. Taking ¾ of that due to their youth, **12 years' detention**, not 15 for both D1 (in a YOI) and D2 (under section 91).

R v Gardner 2015 EWCA Crim 1817 D pleaded to section 18. V, aged 15, was walking with his girlfriend and came across a group containing D and T. T called V by his name and 'asked him if he was who he was'. V was confused. T punched V[746] hard twice in the face knocking him to the ground. D and T then repeatedly kicked V in the face five or six times while V was on the ground. V's girlfriend intervened and pushed the two away. D laughed and said, "I don't know who he is". V had two fractures to his jaw which required a plate and screws. He also had a cracked cheekbone. D was interviewed and denied involvement. D had recently had his 16th birthday and only had a burglary previous conviction (Referral Order). The Judge said the attack was sustained and prolonged and put the case in Category 1. She considered the offence was aggravated by there being two against one and the fact that V was only aged 15. The Judge, in error, believed that D's offence was committed on bail. She distinguished between D and T because T started it and had a robbery conviction (12 months). For T, the Judge started at 10 years, gave a third off for his age and with a full plea discount, gave 4 years 5 months. For D, she started at 9 years, gave the same discounts and gave 4 years. On appeal the defence relied on remorse, lower culpability, subordinate role and lack of premeditation. D's prison report showed D was doing extremely well. Held. V must have been terrified. D was in a very different position to T. **30 months**.

See also: *R v He* 2013 EWCA Crim 1500 (Late plea. Aged 17 at the time. On school premises. Stabbed another pupil. Evidence that victim and others had bullied defendant. Armed himself with 3¼ inch blade and sought out the victim. Two blows to arm and shoulder. Committed for revenge. **2½ years** not 4)

R v L 2014 EWCA Crim 1952 (GBH and burglary. During burglary, V was stabbed, potentially life-threateningly, not initially by D. Later on all three burglars stabbed V multiple times. D was aged 16, was involved in gang activity and had grown up in care with little stability where he suffered physical abuse. Just convicted of several serious offences. Refused to engage with probation, no empathy and self-centred. D proud of criminal identity and planned to make a living from crime. Held. For an adult we would start at 15 years. **10 years' detention**, not 12, and 5 years' extended licence upheld.)

Old cases: Best ignored as there are sufficient recent ones. Ed.

---

[746] The report doesn't give any further details.

292.47 *Defendant has relevant convictions*
Att-Gen's Ref No 32 of 2014 2014 EWCA Crim 1320 Convicted. Section 18 and assault by beating. Locks changed following his violence. Attacked woman who opened door and stabbed partner. Aged 25 with 82 convictions including five offensive weapons/ bladed articles and six ABH/battery offences. Held. His default position is to reach for a bladed instrument. **12 years** not 9.

292.48 *Mental disorder, Defendant has*
Assault Guideline 2011, see www.banksr.com Other Matters Guidelines tab page 8
  a) 'Mental disorder or learning disability, where not linked to the commission of the offence' is a 'Factor reducing seriousness or reflecting personal mitigation', and
  b) 'Mental disorder or learning disability, where linked to commission of the offence' is a 'Factor indicating lower culpability'.
For more detail see **292.3**.
Att-Gen's Ref No 22 of 2011 2011 EWCA Crim 1473, 2012 1 Cr App R (S) 34 (p 201) D pleaded (late) to section 18. He had a long-standing history of mental ill-health, including grand mal epilepsy and depression. This was worsened by drug and alcohol misuse. There were episodes of self-harm and, upon being made redundant in 2009, his depression worsened. While drinking heavily in a pub, D became convinced that V, another customer, had been responsible for an assault upon him some seven years previously, and that he was muttering derogatory remarks. He was carrying a hammer, as his partner had asked him to purchase one in order to carry out some home repairs. When V went to the lavatory, D followed him and struck him numerous times with the hammer. V's cheekbone and eye socket were shattered and he suffered head wounds causing brain damage which resulted in a stroke. It was necessary to insert plates into his head and V did not make a full recovery. V had permanent eye damage, permanent asymmetry to his face and scarring. He could not continue with his self-employment. Consequently there was considerable loss of income. In the following year, D was admitted to a psychiatric hospital after a realistic suicide threat. The suitability of a hospital order was explored. The doctor confirmed that the treatment required did not justify D's admission and was available as an outpatient. The Judge imposed a 3-year community order with a mental health treatment requirement. It was imposed on the basis that it was the best method by which D could obtain the necessary treatment. D, aged 49, had no convictions, though there were incidents of violence against his partner. Held. There is no doubt that the monitoring and advice and flexibility of treatment would be greater from D's point of view under the community order than it would be in prison. We understand the route by which the Judge arrived at her conclusion. However, it simply left out one critical factor. There was the very significant degree of culpability which D exhibited, notwithstanding his mental health. The crime was almost certainly largely induced by the fact that he had had too much to drink, which was his own choice. There was enormous harm caused to V, and the irrational delusion that V had assaulted him many years earlier could not have begun to justify the attack, even if it were true. **5 years**.

293 OFFENCES AGAINST THE PERSON ACT 1861 S 20
293.1
Offences Against the Person Act 1861 s 20 (inflicting GBH or wounding)
Mode of trial Triable either way
Maximum sentence On indictment 5 years. Summary 6 months and/or a £5,000 fine for offences committed before 12 March 2015 and an unlimited fine thereafter.[747] There are maximum fines for those aged under 18, see **14.38** in Volume 1.

---

[747] Legal Aid, Sentencing and Punishment of Offenders Act 2012 s 85(1) and (4) and Legal Aid, Sentencing and Punishment of Offenders Act 2012 (Commencement No 11) Order 2015 2015/504

There is an offence of committing an offence with intent to commit a sexual offence, see the SEXUAL OFFENCES ACT 2003 S 62 chapter. A section 20 offence would be an obvious offence to link with this offence.

Extended sentences This offence is listed in Criminal Justice Act 2003 Sch 15. The court may pass a 2012 extended sentence (EDS) if there is a significant risk of serious harm from future specified offences and either: a) the defendant has a Criminal Justice Act 2003 Sch 15B conviction (applicable only to defendants aged 18+), or b) the offence would justify a determinate sentence of at least 4 years.[748]

Criminal Behaviour Orders Where a defendant has engaged in behaviour that caused or was likely to cause harassment, alarm or distress to any persons and a Criminal Behaviour Order will help in preventing the offender from engaging in such behaviour, the court may make this order.[749]

Football Banning Orders Where the offence was committed relevant to a football match and where there are reasonable grounds to believe that making a banning order would help to prevent violence or disorder at or in connection with any regulated football match, the court must make a Football Banning Order, Football Spectators Act 1989 s 14A and Sch 1 para 1.

Sexual Harm Prevention Orders There is a discretionary power to make this order when it is necessary to protect the public from sexual harm.[750]

Children and vulnerable adults: barred lists Section 20 is not a scheduled offence for automatic barring.

Law Commission On 3 November 2015, the Law Commission published its scoping report, 'Reform of Offences against the Person', Law Com No 361. The report proposes abolishing this offence and substituting new offences of 'recklessly causing serious injury', 'recklessly causing injury' and 'aggravated assault'.

293.2   Crown Court statistics   England and Wales
Malicious wounding etc.

Year	Age	Plea	Total sentenced	Type of sentencing %						Average length of custody in months
				Discharge	Fine	Community sentence	Suspended sentence	Custody	Other	
2012	18-20	G	1,568	1	0	21	31	45	1	14.3
		NG	188	1	1	12	34	48	4	24.7
	21+	G	8,051	2	1	15	32	48	1	15.6
		NG	1,291	2	2	11	26	57	2	19.8
2013	18-20	G	1460	0.8	0.7	19.7	26.9	50.8	1.2	13.9
		NG	147	1.4	1.4	12.9	29.3	53.7	1.4	22
	21+	G	10,629	1	0.9	11.6	36.4	47.7	2.4	14.5
		NG	1,070	1.9	1.5	9.4	32.1	51.7	3.4	20.9

For explanations about the statistics, see page 1-xii. For more statistics about defendants aged 10-20 and statistics for male and female defendants, see www.banksr.com Other Matters Statistics tab

293.3   Sentencing Council Guidelines 2011
Assault Guideline 2011, see www.banksr.com Other Matters Guidelines tab page 7 This guideline applies to all offenders aged 18 and older, regardless of the date of the offence, see page 2 of the guideline. For the usual practice, see **293.8**. In force 13 June 2011.

---

[748] Criminal Justice Act 2003 s 226A-226B as inserted by Legal Aid, Sentencing and Punishment of Offenders Act 2012 s 124
[749] Anti-social Behaviour, Crime and Policing Act 2014 s 22(1)-(4)
[750] Sexual Offences Act 2003 s 103A as inserted by Anti-social Behaviour, Crime and Policing Act 2014 Sch 5 para 2 and Sexual Offences Act 2003 Sch 5

STEP ONE Determining the offence category
page 8 The court should determine the offence category using the table below.

Category 1	Greater harm (serious injury must normally be present) and higher culpability
Category 2	Greater harm (serious injury must normally be present) and lower culpability or lesser harm and higher culpability
Category 3	Lesser harm and lower culpability

page 8 The court should determine the offender's culpability and the harm caused, or intended, by reference **only** to the factors identified in the table below (as demonstrated by the presence of one or more). These factors comprise the principal factual elements of the offence and should determine the category.

Factors indicating greater harm
Injury (which includes disease transmission and/or psychological harm) which is serious in the context of the offence (must normally be present)   Victim is particularly vulnerable because of personal circumstances   Sustained or repeated assault on the same victim

Factors indicating lesser harm
Injury which is less serious in the context of the offence

Factors indicating lower culpability
Subordinate role in group or gang   A greater degree of provocation than normally expected   Lack of premeditation   Mental disorder or learning disability, where linked to commission of the offence   Excessive self-defence

Factors indicating higher culpability
Statutory aggravating factors: Offence motivated by, or demonstrating, hostility to the victim based on his or her sexual orientation (or presumed sexual orientation)   Offence motivated by, or demonstrating, hostility to the victim based on the victim's disability (or presumed disability)   *Other aggravating factors:*   A significant degree of premeditation   Use of weapon or weapon equivalent (for example, shod foot, head-butting, use of acid, use of animal)   Intention to commit more serious harm than actually resulted from the offence   Deliberately causes more harm than is necessary for commission of offence   Deliberate targeting of vulnerable victim   Leading role in group or gang   Offender motivated by, or demonstrating, hostility based on the victim's age, sex, gender identity (or presumed gender identity)

293.4

STEP TWO Starting point and category range
page 8 Having determined the category, the court should use the corresponding starting points to reach a sentence within the category range below. The table is applicable to all offenders.

Offence category	Starting point (applicable to all offenders)	Category range (applicable to all offenders)
Category 1	3 years' custody	2 years 6 months' to 4 years' custody

| Category 2 | 1 year 6 months' custody | 1 to 3 years' custody |
| Category 3 | High-level community order | Low-level community order to 51 weeks' custody |

For the meaning of a high-level and a low-level community order, see **16.12** in Volume 1.

293.5   [Aggravating and mitigating factors]

page 9 The table below contains a non-exhaustive list of additional factual elements providing the context of the offence and factors relating to the offender. When sentencing Category 3 offences, the court should consider the custody threshold as follows:

Has the custody threshold been passed?

If so, is it unavoidable that a custodial sentence be imposed?

If so, can that sentence be suspended?

Factors to determine category

Factors increasing seriousness
Statutory aggravating factors: Previous convictions, having regard to a) the nature of the offence to which the conviction relates and its relevance to the current offence, and b) the time that has elapsed since the conviction   Offence committed whilst on bail   ***Other aggravating factors include:***   Location of the offence   Timing of the offence   Ongoing effect upon the victim   Offence committed against those working in the public sector or providing a service to the public   Presence of others including relatives, especially children or partner of the victim   Gratuitous degradation of victim   In domestic violence cases, victim forced to leave their home   Failure to comply with current court orders   Offence committed whilst on licence   An attempt to conceal or dispose of evidence   Failure to respond to warnings or concerns expressed by others about the offender's behaviour   Commission of offence whilst under the influence of alcohol or drugs   Abuse of power and/or position of trust   Exploiting contact arrangements with a child to commit an offence   Established evidence of community impact   Any steps taken to prevent the victim reporting an incident, or obtaining assistance and/or from assisting or supporting the prosecution   Offences taken into consideration (TICs)
Factors reducing seriousness or reflecting personal mitigation
No previous convictions or no relevant/recent convictions   Single blow   Remorse   Good character and/or exemplary conduct   Determination, and/or demonstration of steps taken to address addiction or offending behaviour   Serious medical conditions requiring urgent, intensive or long-term treatment   Isolated incident   Age and/or lack of maturity where it affects the responsibility of the offender   Lapse of time since the offence where this is not the fault of the offender   Mental disorder or learning disability, where not linked to the commission of the offence   Sole or primary carer for dependent relatives

[Racially/religiously aggravated] offences only:
page 9 The court should determine the appropriate sentence for the offence without taking account of the element of aggravation and then make an addition to the sentence, considering the level of aggravation involved. It may be appropriate to move outside the identified category range, taking into account the increased statutory maximum.

The court should then consider the following: a) other factors indicating a reduction, such as assistance to the prosecution, b) reduction for a guilty plea, c) dangerousness, d) totality, if sentencing for more than one offence, [and] e) compensation and ancillary orders.

Magistrates' Court Sentencing Guideline 2011 (as updated), see www.banksr.com Other Matters Guidelines tab page 197 The update repeats the main guideline. In the table indicating ranges and starting points, sentences exceeding the powers of the Magistrates' Court are replaced with 'Crown Court'.

293.6   *Pre-guideline judicial guidance*
R v Clare 2002 2 Cr App R (S) 97 (p 445) Where there has been an attack involving a single blow, the first consideration is the strength of the blow and the second is the consequences for the victim.

Children see the CRUELTY TO CHILDREN ABH and Offences Against the Person **Act 1861 s 20** section at **231.4**.

293.7   *Crime of passion   Post-guideline case*
Example: *R v Van Niekerk* 2012 EWCA Crim 2607 (Plea. Amicable separation from wife. Found wife in bed with his good friend. Pushed friend and punched him once. Confronted him again outside the house. Pulled him out of his van, wrestled him to the ground and punched him more than once. Fractured eye socket, broken nose, fractured ribs, swelling and bruising, some teeth were tender. Full credit. Served 2½ months. **6 months suspended** not 15 months.)

293.8   *Defendant aged 16-17*
Note: The *Assault Guideline 2011* does not apply to those aged under 18, see **293.3**. I suspect most judges would determine the appropriate sentence for an adult and then make a reduction. There are few reported cases since the *Youths Sentencing Guidelines 2009*, no doubt because the courts endeavour to pass non-custodial sentences wherever they can.

R v B 2012 EWCA Crim 2237 D pleaded to section 20. D and V were good friends and were both aged 17. In the early hours they went out and purchased some lager and vodka. They sat on a stairwell and by 6 am they were both very drunk. There was an argument over some cigarettes and then a scuffle. D punched V and V hit his head on a wall. V had a bloody lip and was disorientated. The group they were with returned and D and V said they wanted to be alone again. There was some grappling and then D threw some punches at V. When they were separated, V's face was bloodied and there was serious swelling to one eye. The globe ruptured and V lost the sight in that eye. The basis of plea was that V became aggressive. V was caused significant psychological trauma. In 2010 D received a 12-month Youth Rehabilitation Order for two offences of intimidation. D was in breach of a community order for another section 20, a pre-arranged fight between two groups (no extra penalty). The victim's jaw was broken. Since the offence D had received a Youth Rehabilitation Order for criminal damage. D had spent 179 days on remand. The Judge started at 3½ years for an adult. He then reduced it for D's youth and 15% for the plea. That took him to 24 months, which he reduced to 18 months because of the time on remand. Held. This was a very nasty attack with catastrophic consequences. The maximum sentence was 24 months as section 91 detention was not available. 3½ years was not excessive. Without the restraints it could have been higher. There could be no criticism of the 24 months. However, D was entitled to a plea discount for that figure. The remand time should have been double time, which works out at nearly 12 months. **10 months** not 18 months.

Domestic violence see the *Domestic Violence Guideline 2006*, see www.banksr.com Other Matters Guidelines tab, the DOMESTIC VIOLENCE chapter and the *Relationship attacks* para at **293.17**.

293.9   Glassing (using a glass as a weapon)

R v Goodwin 2011 EWCA Crim 2518 D pleaded to section 20. She was in a pub at a birthday party. An argument broke out during which D's father attempted to head-butt another guest. V attempted to calm the situation. D, who had seen her father knocked to the ground, picked up a glass from the bar and threw it into the crowd of people involved in what had by now become a scuffle. The glass hit V and caused a laceration to his left eye.[751] It bled profusely and had detached the retina. V was permanently blind in his left eye. D, aged 27, had no convictions. Held. This was a spontaneous act. There was no premeditation. D accepted full responsibility for her actions and had expressed remorse. This case was on the cusp of Categories 1 and 2. **2 years** not 2 years 8 months.

See also: *R v Madden-Devaney* 2010 EWCA Crim 182 (Offered to plead to it but convicted of it when jury failed to agree section 18. Hit victim with a bottle twice, causing it to break. Previous record for ABH. 'Very serious attack'. 5 years' extended sentence (**4 years' custody** 1 year's extended licence).)

Old case: *R v McGhee* 2008 EWCA Crim 25, 2 Cr App R (S) 53 (p 330) (**27 months**) *R v Kee* 2009 EWCA Crim 1716, 2010 1 Cr App R (S) 45 (p 281) (**21 months**) For a summary of the first case, see the 8th edition of this book and for the second case, see the 9th edition.

Post-guideline case

R v Gaunt 2012 EWCA Crim 579 D pleaded (full credit) to section 20. V went into Leeds City Centre to celebrate a friend's birthday. Whilst in a bar, he and his group became aware of D and a friend who were taking an interest in three of the girls in their group. D was alleged to have stared at the girls and was described by the group as being "strange", "odd", and "weird". One of the girls felt her bottom being touched and turned to find D behind her. She complained to the rest of her group. The group went to another bar. D was there and was close to the group. N, who was part of a group, thought that D was looking at her daughter, and confronted him. D said, "I wouldn't mind being on the end of that". V asked D to leave the group alone and to stop staring at her. D continued to stare and said, "What's it got to do with you?" V replied that the girl was his friend and she was with her boyfriend. D squared up to V and pushed his head against V's. V turned to hand his bottle of lager to a friend. As he turned back, D struck him to the side of the head with a glass, causing him to fall backwards against the bar. The injuries required 35 deep sutures and 55 superficial sutures. V will be scarred for the rest of his life. One of the girls was splattered with blood on her face, chest and arms. D was detained by the door staff and subsequently arrested. He made a number of comments, including that he was acting in self-defence, "If he's in hospital he deserves it for coming after me," and "I am aware of what I am saying and that it is probably being recorded". V suffered seven lacerations to the side of his face and left ear, with general swelling and bruising. D, aged 24 at appeal, had no previous convictions or cautions. A report noted that D was hypersensitive to public humiliation or reproval and had difficulty fitting in socially. Held. D showed little remorse or victim empathy. This was a serious offence involving the use of a glass as a weapon. The scarring was severe. This offence does not fit naturally into either Category 1 or 2. It was not premeditated. However, there was undoubtedly grave injury. There was excessive self-defence in that it was a reaction to a perceived but not actual threat. Starting at 3 years, **2 years** not 2 years 8 months.

R v Robinson 2013 EWCA Crim 1644 D pleaded to section 20. V's sister, S, picked up D's handbag. It was returned, but D thought that the bag had been stolen, as had some money from the bag. S said nothing had been stolen but £20 was 'returned' to D. Some six months later, on Boxing Day 2012, V and D met each other whilst out, separately, in

---

[751] It is not clear whether the glass broke on impact. Ed.

a pub. The incident with the handbag was raised and a short altercation took place between D and her friends, and V and her friends. There was no violence and V and her friends left to go to a bar across the road. D followed V to the bar, with her partner. They approached the table where V was seated and D poured a drink over V, who reacted by throwing a drink over D. D went to leave at that stage but before doing so threw her now empty glass at V. The glass hit V's head causing a 3 cm cut on the left-hand side of her head. Eight stitches were required and it was necessary to remove glass from her head. The incident was captured on CCTV. D, aged 24, had no convictions, reprimands or warnings. She was the single parent of a five-year-old boy. The pre-sentence report noted that D acted completely out of character when disinhibited through drink. Held. The Judge failed to take account of the mitigation. D, though a single mother, was employed for 16 hours per week, showed remorse and was of good character. The incident was a single blow and she had good references. This was a Category 2 offence with a starting point of 18 months. That should be reduced to 12 months for the mitigation. With the plea, **8 months** not 12. The use of the glass made this a grave offence and therefore a suspended sentence was not appropriate.

293.10   Injuries were caused by the fall not any blow
R v Coleman 1992 13 Cr App R (S) 508 LCJ D was sentenced for manslaughter. Held. We are considering a person who receives a blow, probably one blow only, to the head or face, is knocked over by the blow and unfortunately cracks his head on the floor or the pavement, suffers a fractured skull and dies. It is to be distinguished sharply from the sort of case where a victim on the ground is kicked about the head. It is to be distinguished sharply from the sort of case where a weapon is used in order to inflict injury. It is to be further distinguished from where the actual blow itself causes the death. This is the case of a fall almost accidentally resulting in a fractured skull. The starting point for manslaughter for this type of offence is 12 months on a plea of guilty. Then one looks at the mitigation and aggravating features. No premeditation, a single blow of moderate force, remorse and immediate admissions are all mitigation. Indications that D is susceptible to outbreaks of violence, the assault was gratuitous and unprovoked, and more than one blow all tend to aggravate the offence.
Note: This is an old case so the decision should be treated with care. Ed.
R v Elsley 2010 EWCA Crim 540 D pleaded early to section 20. After drinking there was some turbulence outside a pub, and in it D punched V. V fell backwards and hit his head on the ground. V lost consciousness and required ten staples to the back of his head. V's upper lip was split, and dental work would be needed. D was aged 22 and had a conviction for assaulting a PC. D showed genuine remorse. The Judge said that neither party had gone out looking for a fight, it was a mercy that V did not sustain brain injury, and that it was a particularly grave injury. Held. For assessing which level it was in the guideline, it was not a 'particularly grave injury'. **6 months** not 12.
Post-guideline case
See also: *R v Murphy* 2012 EWCA Crim 394 (**27 months**) See **293.24**.
See also the *Victim seriously injured Unexpected* para at **293.24**.

293.11   Knives   Post-guideline case
R v Hendry 2013 EWCA Crim 504 D pleaded (full credit) to section 20. She was in a relationship with V, and had been so for only a matter of weeks. D claimed that V was a violent bully. They had both drank roughly a bottle of vodka each and had taken heroin and other drugs. D received a text message from another man and V 'flew into a rage'. He smashed her mobile phone and when D said V would have to replace it, he punched her in the face and left the room. D went to the kitchen, picked up a kitchen knife and followed V outside. There she stabbed him in the back, puncturing his lung. He made a full recovery with no long-term consequences. V had convictions for assault, firearm offences, conspiracy to commit robbery (10 years), blackmail and possession of an offensive weapon. D, aged 29, had convictions for being drunk and disorderly and

shoplifting and had been cautioned in 2011 for possession of an offensive weapon. She had a long history of drug and alcohol addiction and suffered from mental disorders which caused her: a) to be emotionally unstable, b) to act impulsively, and c) to have an increased propensity for aggression after drinking. Doctors considered that this was a modest level of psychiatric mitigation. D had suggested in a psychiatric report that she had stabbed previous boyfriends, but she subsequently denied this. Held. It is arguable that this was a Category 1 case, as there was unquestionably greater harm and higher culpability due to the use of the weapon and the degree of premeditation. But it is equally arguable that this was not a case of higher culpability (and therefore a Category 2 case) as it could be said that this was little more than a spur of the moment reaction to V's loss of temper and punch to her face. There were also her mental disorders and the questionable premeditation. The one aggravating factor is that the offence was committed whilst D was under the influence of drink and drugs. The starting point should have been **3½ years**. With full credit, **2 years 4 months**, not 3 years 4 months.

Older cases: I have not listed cases decided before the guideline was published, as sentences for knife crime have been rising. Ed.

293.12   *Life-threatening injuries*
R v Lowe 2012 EWCA Crim 1551 D pleaded (20% credit) to section 20. He was walking along a street when he encountered V, whom he knew. V was building a wall for a neighbour. D began to 'wind V up' and started abusing him. He then offered to fight V. V was shorter than D, but was an amateur boxer. Both men began to swing punches. V was getting the better of the fight and had knocked two of D's teeth out. D then took a screwdriver from his pocket and swung it at V, causing four or five stab wounds. Two wounds were to the chest, one of which punctured the sac around the heart causing it to fill with blood. The injuries were life-threatening. V spent six days in hospital. D was a very large man, well over 6 feet tall. Held. The repeated and violent use of a screwdriver clearly made this offence one of higher culpability. The gravity of the consequences strongly outweighed the countervailing factors of the lack of premeditation and the claimed excessive use of self-defence. This was a Category 1 offence and the severity of the injuries required the starting point to be around the top of the range at the very least. The appropriate starting point was 4 years, so with the plea, **3 years 2 months**.

Motor vehicles as a weapon see the **Vehicle, Caused by a** para at **293.23**.

293.13   *Police officers/Public officials/Persons in authority, Attacking Pre-guideline cases*
R v Jonsyn 2013 EWCA Crim 1655, 2014 1 Cr App R (S) 67 (p 438) D pleaded on rearraignment (full credit) to section 20. He was arrested at his home. On arrest, he was abusive and aggressive and at the police station could not be booked in properly. On removal of the handcuffs, D squared up to V, an officer, and punched him once, hard, in the face. V suffered a fractured eye socket which required surgery. D changed his plea upon learning that full credit would be available. D, aged 19, had convictions for at least 37 offences, including assaulting an officer. A psychiatric report indicated D's remorse for his actions. Held. The Judge was wrong to categorise the case as Category 1 on the basis that the officer was a vulnerable victim. Starting point 2½ years not 3½ so **20 months** not 30.

R v Peet 2014 EWCA Crim 2800, 2015 1 Cr App R (S) 48 (p 34) D pleaded (full credit) to section 20 and two assault charges (presumably common assault). D appeared in court for breach of his Non-Molestation Order. In court when handcuffed, he grabbed the little finger of a custody officer, V1, and said, "I am going to fucking snap it off." He pulled it back and the officer heard his finger crack. D then spat at V1's face hitting his cheek, as he and his colleague, V2, walked D out of the dock. In the custody van D spat at V2 through the grille. Some spit landed on V2. The proximal phalanx of V1's finger was fractured. V1 was unable to work for about six weeks and his right hand was in a cast for four weeks. V1 could not drive or perform normal daily tasks. D had previous convictions for assaulting PCs. The Judge started at 4 years for the section 20 and gave 2 months consecutive for the assault charges and consecutive to each other making with plea 3 years. This was concurrent to the sentences for the breach of the Non-Molestation Order. Held. The culpability was high and the injury significant. We start at 3 years, so with plea **2 years**. We make the spitting offences concurrent but consecutive to the section 20 making 2 years 2 months in all.

See also: *R v McIntosh* 2014 EWCA Crim 1003, 2 Cr App R (S) 64 (p 503) (Convicted. D rode stolen moped into V, a police officer in uniform, who signalled him to stop. V had a non-displaced ankle fracture and left knee ligaments torn. D fled but wrote remorseful letter to V. Injuries not greater harm, Category 2 not 1. **2½ years**, not 3½.) Old cases: Best ignored.

293.14   *Pubs/After drinking*

R v Wagner 2011 EWCA Crim 357 (See **293.18**.)

Post-guideline cases

R v Grogan and MacDonald 2012 EWCA Crim 1757 G and M pleaded to section 20 on the day of their trial, having been initially charged with section 18. They were in a bar with their girlfriends. V was in the same bar, celebrating his 19th birthday with a group of friends. G's and M's girlfriends were receiving 'unwanted attention' from V's group, including G's girlfriend being inappropriately touched. There was a fight and after a complaint V and his group were ejected from the bar. G and M made their way to the car park with their girlfriends. V and his group followed them into the car park and a fight broke out. G and M received minor injuries. V's friends ran off, leaving V on his own. They returned to find him lying on the floor. He had suffered a broken jaw, cuts, bruises and contusions to his face. A metal plate had to be inserted into his jaw. G and M accepted that they had used excessive self-defence. There was evidence that M had been throwing punches but that G had kicked V whilst on the ground. G and M were both aged 27 with previous convictions for violence. G was on bail when he committed the instant offence. M had a conviction for wounding. Both had displayed genuine remorse. Held. This was unquestionably a case of greater harm. The self-defence indicated lesser culpability, although in G's case the kicks indicated higher culpability. Therefore G's case was Category 1, M's case was Category 2. The Judge was correct to give 20% credit for the pleas, as they could have indicated their willingness to plead sooner. Starting at 40 months for G cannot be criticised, so **3 years** with the plea will remain. For M, recognising his lower culpability, starting at 24 months, **18 months** (by rounding down the sentence) not 32.

R v Chamberlain and Others 2013 EWCA Crim 1859 C and R pleaded to section 20. V1 and his girlfriend, V2, were in a nightclub. A disagreement arose between R's sister and V2. C punched V1 and all were asked to leave. The dispute continued outside the club and insults were thrown. C and V1 threw punches at each other, whereupon C asked R and D to assist. V1 was dragged, kicked in the head by D and punched by C. V2 lay across V1 and was kicked in the face by R. V1 attended hospital and was treated for cuts and bruising to the ribs and discharged. The pain worsened and he was later found to have closed fractures to his forearm, face, two ribs and spine. V2 suffered slight swelling and bruising. All three expressed extreme remorse and blamed alcohol for their actions. B, aged 24, had a conditional discharge for criminal damage. C, aged 27, had no relevant convictions. R, aged 24, had two cautions for criminal damage and affray. Held. It was a joint attack at night. Part of the attack was when V1 was on the ground. It was also not premeditated and of very short duration. There was no evidence of the residual effect of the injuries. The case was on the cusp of Category 1. There should be credit for the remorse. We sentence on the basis the offence was out of character. There was no evidence D was wearing boots. Starting at **2 years**, with full credit, for C and R **15 months** not two years.

For more details of B's sentence, see **292.27**.

R v Conner 2013 EWCA Crim 1860 D pleaded (full credit) to section 20 wounding. D was drinking at a pub with two friends, who were regulars and known to the staff. One of them, B, was said by the landlord to be "his usual argumentative self". V was on a pub-crawl with a group of his friends and was very much the worse for drink. B was asked to leave the pub and did so accompanied by V and B's friend. V made an offensive remark to the men as they left. B retaliated and V and his friends followed them outside. D ran towards V and struck him forcefully with a single, swinging punch, putting "everything he had into it". V fell to the floor and D left the scene, reportedly stating that the job was done. He was arrested shortly afterwards. V suffered a significant laceration to his face and damage to his front teeth which persisted for five weeks after the event. The Judge described it as a savage blow causing a lot of damage. D was aged 45 with no convictions. The pre-sentence report proposed a suspended sentence and presented D as a placid and caring man of positively good character. Held. The Judge made insufficient allowance for the mitigating factors (presumably the single blow, the lack of convictions, his remorse and the offence was out of character). Therefore the offence was at the lower end of Category 2. **8 months** not 12.

R v Jones 2015 EWCA Crim 542 D pleaded on the first day of her retrial. D went to a social club and in the ladies lavatory, D said to V, aged 76, "What the fucking hell are looking at, you cow?" V said something like, "What are you on about, you silly woman?" D left first. V left and tried to pass D who was at the top of a small flight of stairs. D said something and pushed V in her chest. V fell backwards and down the stairs. V screamed and lost consciousness. She suffered a comminuted compound fracture (meaning more than two fragments) of two bones in her wrist and a minimally displaced fracture of her humerus. She was in hospital for five days. It was predicted she would have restricted shoulder movement and stiffness. The doctor described the wrist injury as severe. D was aged 47 and had no violent previous convictions, but she had two burglary and other [non-minor] convictions. While in custody her partner had died. The basis of plea said D did not intend to push V down the stairs. The pre-sentence report said D was addressing her alcohol misuse. Held. The victim was particularly vulnerable. There was greater harm. The case was on the cusp of Categories 2 and 3. There was a single push and some remorse. With a slight discount for the plea, **9 months** not 20.

See also: *R v Samuel* 2011 EWCA Crim 522 (Early plea. D and his friends argued with a group. All had been drinking. Punches were thrown, knocking the victim to the floor. D kicked him in the head, causing bruising, swelling, four fractured teeth and a fractured nose. D, aged 23, had two convictions for battery and three cautions, including ABH and common assault. **12 months** not 16.)

R v Morrison 2012 EWCA Crim 796, 2012 2 Cr App R (S) 101 (p 594) (Plea to section 20 and affray. Assault at a pub at which victim was performing as a musician. Further violence broke out as a result of victim's friend approaching the defendant and his friends. Struck with a bottle, which broke. Suffered several skull fractures. 18 stitches. Damage to right eye. Depression and temporary loss of hearing. Starting at 3 years 6 months, with 6 months credit for plea, **3 years** not 4.)

R v Warrender 2013 EWCA Crim 1141 (Late plea. Victim, aged 23, was in a club. Struck by defendant. No glass in his hand but one smashed during the incident. Multiple superficial lacerations and one deeper, 5 cm, laceration to the cheek. Lifelong scarring but no functional deficit. 12 stitches in total. Aged 25 at appeal. Had saved a considerable sum to pay compensation. Regular binge drinker. No previous convictions. Starting at 18 months was appropriate. Unlikely to offend again. **9 months** not 15.)

Old cases: Best ignored.

293.15   *Racially aggravated offences*
Offences Against the Person Act 1861 s 20 and Crime and Disorder Act 1998 s 29 (racially aggravated inflicting GBH or wounding)
Mode of trial Triable either way

Maximum sentence On indictment 7 years. Summary 6 months and/or a £5,000 fine for offences committed before 12 March 2015 and an unlimited fine thereafter.[752] There are maximum fines for those aged under 18, see **14.38** in Volume 1.

The ancillary orders and guidelines are the same as those for the non-aggravated offence, see **293.1**.

For basic principles about racially aggravated offences, see the RACIALLY OR RELI-GIOUSLY AGGRAVATED OFFENCES chapter.

For comparable cases, some assistance can be obtained from the ABH: RACIALLY OR RELIGIOUSLY AGGRAVATED chapter.

293.16   *Racially aggravated offences   Pre-guideline case*
R v Sweet 2011 EWCA Crim 1208, 2012 1 Cr App R (S) 8 (p 35) D pleaded to racially aggravated ABH at his PCMH. On his 18th birthday, and after drinking, D attacked V, a 61-year-old man who had travelled from India to visit his son. D's friends attacked V's son. D grabbed V, punched him in the nose and eye causing two black eyes and a nose bleed. D also pulled V to the floor and fell on him heavily, dislocating his shoulder. D then said, "Paki bastard, why don't you go back to the country where you came from". D, aged 18, had convictions for assault (Referral Order), robbery (Supervision Order and Curfew Order), burglary and theft. He was ashamed of what he had done and professed he did not hold racist views. Held. It was an unprovoked violent attack on an elderly man prompted by racist attitudes. V had suffered significant injuries. The Judge gave an 8-month uplift for the racial element, which cannot be described as excessive or even severe. With the mitigation for his age, the plea and the fact that this is his first custodial sentence, **22 months** for the assault, not 30, with **8 months** for the racial element.

293.17   *Relationship attacks   Post-guideline cases*
For the general principles, see the *Domestic Violence Guideline 2006*, see www.banksr. com Other Matters Guidelines tab and the DOMESTIC VIOLENCE chapter.
R v Thomas 2012 EWCA Crim 89 D pleaded (full credit) to section 20. D's marriage had featured frequent arguments. There had been only one incident of physical violence, around 28 years previously. He had argued with V, his wife of 34 years. Whilst in the kitchen, D pushed or punched V in the back of the head. It caused no injury, but it did cause V to fall and hit her head on the steps to the patio door. There was immediate heavy bleeding. D just stood over V shouting at her. He had a bread knife in his hand, but it was not suggested that D intended, or attempted, to do anything with the knife. D's son manhandled D and took the knife away from him. V's injury required five internal stitches and 19 external stitches. D and V were now in the midst of divorce. D had no relevant convictions. D's aggressive behaviour had worsened since he suffered a series of strokes in 2006. The risk of reoffending was assessed as low. Held. Starting at 18 months, with mitigation, namely the strokes, reducing that to 15 months, and allowing full credit for the plea, **10 months**, not 16. Because he had served virtually 3 months, we suspend the balance.

R v James 2013 EWCA Crim 1009 D pleaded at the PCMH to section 20. V, aged 31, had been in a relationship with D for some 13 years. Their relationship was characterised by violence committed by V against D. In 2008, V received 14 months for an unspecified assault against D. V was made subject to a Restraining Order and breached it repeatedly. D remained emotionally attached to him and on occasions encouraged V to return to stay with her. Police attended the family home at 2 am and found blood and broken crockery on the kitchen floor. V was bare-chested with three wounds to his body, including a puncture wound to the back and one to the shoulder. There were also grazes across V's body. D had barricaded herself into an upstairs room. D was drunk and violent towards the police when they arrived. V said, "I sliced him open, I hope he fucking dies" and "I'll slit his throat, I'll kill him". V claimed to have fallen on a knife

---

[752] Legal Aid, Sentencing and Punishment of Offenders Act 2012 s 85(1) and (4) and Legal Aid, Sentencing and Punishment of Offenders Act 2012 (Commencement No 11) Order 2015 2015/504

and made no complaint. D breached bail by going to visit V. D was in a relationship with a new partner. She was aged 42 at appeal and had convictions for dishonesty, but none since 2008. She had four children, three of whom, aged 19, 15 and 14, lived in the family home. Held. The evidence did not support the conclusion that this was a Category 1 offence. It was probably between Categories 2 and 3. The custody threshold was crossed but the history of domestic violence and the lack of premeditation and possible provocation by V called for a starting point of 12 months. With personal mitigation, 8 months was the correct length. With regard to D's children, it was appropriate to suspend the sentence. **8 months suspended,** not 18 months.

R v Kent 2014 EWCA Crim 244 D pleaded to section 20. He was originally charged with section 18 and offered to plead to section 47. He pleaded to section 20 after the prosecution added that count to the indictment after the medical evidence was served. D, with a friend, F, arrived at the flat of V, his former partner, at about 1 am, worse for drink. They continued drinking at V's flat. D convinced himself that V had been having an affair behind his back. He began to make humiliating comments about V in the presence of F. He then punched V with full force in the face, then rained blows down on her as if she were a punch bag. V begged D to stop. D went to the kitchen and returned with a wrench. He hit V repeatedly with the wrench on the head and legs. F told him to stop. D stopped and V tried to escape. She got to the top of the stairs and D told her to return to the sitting room otherwise he would 'kick her down the stairs'. V, bleeding and dazed, returned to the sitting room whereupon D hit her with the wrench. F had left. D then armed himself with a knife and threatened to disfigure and decapitate her. V thought she would be killed. Not long before 7 am, the attack and the threats came to an end. D got ready for work and left. V called a friend in a distressed state. She had bruises to her face, arms and legs and a laceration to her head which was bleeding. V was in severe pain and was struggling to walk. She had fractured her foot. Four weeks later the swelling had not entirely subsided. D was aged 37 at his appeal and had 27 convictions for 45 offences, mainly for dishonesty. He had convictions for ABH (1997, probation order), affray (2003, short custodial sentence), section 20 and possession of an offensive weapon (2010, 15 months). The pre-sentence report noted that D had also been taking drugs and had become jealous of his partner. He was assessed as posing a high risk of causing serious harm to future partners and those with whom he believed himself to be in conflict. There was a risk of physical violence including from the use of a weapon. Held. This was a sustained and repeated assault on a vulnerable victim with a weapon. D also had a previous section 20 conviction. Starting at 4 years 8 months was at the top of the bracket for this offence but it was not manifestly excessive. It was a savage and prolonged attack. The Judge gave more credit than the 10% D was entitled to for pleading on the day of trial and D was not entitled to significantly more credit for his offer to plead to the lesser offence. 5 years' extended sentence (**4 years' custody** 1 year's licence). No complaint was made about the licence period.

R v Johnson 2014 EWCA Crim 1966 D pleaded (little credit) to section 20 assault. D had been married to V for eight years and they lived together for 21. V had a child, not D's, which was a source of ill-feeling and so V asked her son to live elsewhere. Over time, D became abusive towards V, verbally and physically. He belittled her and complained about her conduct and V then began to drink more. Following drinking by both parties, an argument developed over the amount V was drinking and D pushed V. She fell and hit her head on a door frame, requiring three staples and hospital treatment. She had also broken her wrist, needing an operation to put pins in. She reported the incident to police, having fled the house in her pyjamas. D played the incident down and said that V, drunk, had fallen towards him and he had pushed her away. He also said that this was the first such incident and that he intended no malice or ill-will towards V. D was aged 45 on appeal and had only a caution for possession of an offensive weapon from 2003. He expressed remorse and the pre-sentence report recommended an 18-month community order with supervision. Held. This was Category 2, not 3. We would respectfully doubt whether the fractures to the wrist were serious in the context of this offence…they were not among the more serious injuries within the range of offences to which this offence relates. **9 months** not 12 (immediate), **suspended** with supervision.

See also: *R v Badala* 2011 EWCA Crim 1576 (Pre-guideline case Convicted. Attack on partner after drinking. Punches and kicks causing bruising, fractured eye socket, swelling and a deep brain injury. 3-4 weeks in hospital. Permanent loss of some vision in eye. Not premeditated. Good character. No remorse. **3½ years** not 4½.)

See also: *R v Caceres* 2013 EWCA Crim 924, 2014 1 Cr App R (S) 23 (p 128) (Plea to section 20, ABH, two of common assault and one of criminal damage (victim's clothes which had been destroyed). Domestic violence by a man on male partner. Regular violence. One resulted in broken eye-socket. On another occasion, iron used on head resulting in stitches. Previous conviction for battery. Earlier police caution. Judge bound to take into account as an aggravating factor that each offence not an isolated incident. **4 years 2 months** upheld.)

Old cases: Best ignored.

293.18   *Revenge/punishment, Motive was*

R v Wagner 2011 EWCA Crim 357 D pleaded on rearraignment to section 20. He went out drinking and on several occasions V approached him in a confrontational manner. V suggested that D had been sleeping with his girlfriend. Words were exchanged. Whilst on his way home, drinking cider from a bottle, D was approached by V, who had waited for the opportunity. D shouted "I'm going to smash your face in", and struck V with the bottle. Whilst V was defenceless, D punched V when it was clear V was in no position to fight back. D walked off shouting "Who's the man? Who's the man?" D initially pleaded self-defence but upon seeing the CCTV evidence offered a plea to section 20. V suffered a shattered cheek bone, eye socket, and sinus bones. There was damage to the membrane above the brain. V required emergency surgery during which the front half of his skull was removed. He had a subsequent operation to repair his cheek bone. He also suffered short-term memory loss and depression. D had a reprimand for ABH (2005), and convictions for common assault (2006), threatening words and behaviour (2007 and 2008), and driving offences and affray (2010). He had been released from the last sentence ten days prior to the instant offence. Held. The Judge did not provide a starting point or identify aggravating or mitigating factors. This was an extraordinarily grave offence of its type. 20% discount for the plea was appropriate and perhaps even generous. **4 years' YOI** was deservedly severe.

See also: *R v Marsh and Stokes* 2011 EWCA Crim 3190, 2012 2 Cr App R (S) 31 (p 178) (Convicted. After a pub fight where V, a girl aged 16, was the victim, the defendants and two others set upon V in the street. V was restrained. Bolt cutters brandished to deter her friends. Key used to cut her face. 4 cm laceration. Permanent scarring. Category 1. Both had previous convictions. Aged 25 and 20. **2 years** for one, **20 months** for the other)

Post-guideline case

R v Bathgate 2013 EWCA Crim 243 D was convicted of section 20. He was in a nightclub and came across V, whom he knew, as they were members of the same gym. D and V exchanged 'banter', with D saying that V looked slim, and V saying that D looked fat. V accepted that this had obviously struck a nerve. With that in mind, V called D fat again and made a gesture simulating masturbation. D threw a punch and his elbow connected with V's cheek. Both were asked to leave the nightclub and did so without a fuss. V went to A&E but was sent home. A few days later he returned and an X-ray revealed a fracture to his cheekbone. Two mini-plates were inserted during surgery. Unfortunately an infection developed which required further surgery. V had to undergo painful treatment and was left with a clicking of the jaw and residual pain. D was aged 31 and had three previous summary convictions which did not reveal a violent disposition. D was employed as an aviation engineer at the search and rescue unit. His employers described him as highly trained, skilled and not easy to replace. The Judge

sentenced D on the basis he had lost his temper and the public was sick of this mindless violence. Held. The offence was Category 2 and was a brief and isolated incident. The sentence did not sufficiently reflect the mitigation. **12 months** not 18.
Old cases: Best ignored.

293.19   *Sexual/HIV infection   Post-guideline case*
R v Golding 2014 EWCA Crim 889 D pleaded guilty to reckless section 20. In June 2007 and April 2008, D went to a clinic and was diagnosed with herpes. In July 2009, he met V and their relationship became sexual. V contracted type HSV-2 genital herpes and said D was her only partner at the time. In interview, D admitted he had given V herpes. D was now aged 31 and of good character. He was given 14 months and appealed his conviction and sentence. He was conditionally bailed. Held. There had been a failure to apply CPS guidance about charging sexual assault. Genital herpes was capable of being 'really serious bodily harm'. D's plea had been properly made and was voluntary. No proper criticism could be made of the sentence. However, D had lost his job because of the sentence and that over the three years on bail at the Court of Appeal, he had not found another one, family difficulties caused by that and his period in limbo meant it would be wrong to return him to custody, so **3 months** making immediate release appropriate.
See also: *R v Marangwanda* 2009 EWCA Crim 60 (Pre-guideline case. Pleaded guilty. Knowingly had gonorrhoea and recklessly passed it to his partner's two daughters, aged 4 and 6. **1 year** not 2.)

293.20   *Sporting*
R v Brown 2011 EWCA Crim 786 D was convicted of section 20. Whilst playing rugby, and after the ball had gone, he ran some distance and punched the victim, V, who was playing for the other side, once in the eye. The punch knocked V out. The game was abandoned because of the concern for V. His eye was closed from the swelling and bruising and his cheekbone was sore. The punch caused an extensive defect of the right orbital floor, and his right eye appeared to be sinking. It required surgery and a graft of bone to be taken from his pelvis. V continued to suffer altered sensation in his cheek but was able to use his eye fully, notwithstanding double vision in the downward gaze. D, aged 18 then and 20 at appeal, was of good character and at university. Since the offence he had stopped playing rugby. He had been the victim of a section 18 assault since the instant offence. Held. D delivered one powerful blow resulting in a particularly grave injury. He would lose his university place and be unable to complete his education. Unprovoked assault is not only unacceptable but must be dealt with in a way that such assaults have to be in these courts. **12 months' YOI.**
R v Lawrence 2011 EWCA Crim 3129, 2012 2 Cr App R (S) 42 (p 243) D was convicted of section 20. He was a substitute in a Sunday League football match and was not playing. V, a player on the opposing team, fouled a member of D's team. The player he fouled immediately remonstrated with V and V pushed him to the floor. Members of both teams squared up to one another and the substitutes from D's team, including D, rushed onto the pitch. D aimed a heavy punch at V, causing him a serious injury to the face. D ran towards V and 'took off' as he punched V. V presented no threat to D. The force of the blow broke V's eye socket and cheek in four places. He suffered a depressed fracture which required surgery under general anaesthetic to insert a metal plate to his face. D, aged 25, was of good character and had good references. He had volunteered in youth projects and was pursuing qualifications as a plumber. Held. The ongoing effect on V was an aggravating factor. There was no guilty plea and this was rightly identified as a Category 2 offence. **9 months** could not be faulted.
Old cases: *R v Cotterill* 2007 EWCA Crim 526, 2 Cr App R (S) 64 (p 391) (**4 months**) *R v Garfield* 2008 EWCA Crim 130, 2 Cr App R (S) 364 (**15 months**)
For a summary of the first case, see the 8th edition of this book and for the second case, see the 9th edition.

Post-guideline case

R v Billam-Stevens 2015 EWCA Crim 1636 D pleaded early to section 20. During a seven-a-side football match, V's elbow made contact with D's chin while they were [clashing over the football]. D demanded an apology. V refused to give one. D complained to the referee, who took no action. A few seconds later, D punched V hard on the jaw, knocking him over. V's cheek bone was fractured. V left the pitch but returned to play in the second half. After the game, D said to V if he had apologised it would not have happened. D offered to shake V's hand and advised him to apply ice to his jaw, which was swollen. Both sides went to the police. V's fracture required an internal metal plate and V had to live on a soft food diet over the Christmas period. D was aged 27 and of good character. He was genuinely remorseful and was supported by his employers. Held. There was clearly greater harm. There was an element of premeditation but not significant premeditation, so it was Category 2 not 1. We start at 18 months, so with plea, **12 months** not 20.

293.21   *Torture Pre-guideline case*
R v Khan and Ta 2010 EWCA Crim 1517 K and T were convicted of inflicting GBH. V was taken by K and T to T's flat. A number of young men were summoned into the room and made to line up against a wall with V in the middle. K punched V and told others to search him. V's wallet was taken and the cash distributed amongst those present. K beat V's arms and legs with a stick for one hour whilst the other men present took photos on their mobile phones. K threatened to throw petrol at V's family and to "chop him up" if he reported the incident. V had a fractured forearm and bruising and swelling to his arms. The Judge said there was an intent to torture and T's culpability could not be higher. K, aged 23, and T, aged 26, had previous convictions but none were relevant. Held. This was no ordinary section 20 offence, it was sadistic conduct orchestrated by the defendants. The aggravating features were the duration of the conduct and violence, and the humiliation of V. K **4½ years** and T **2 years 10 months** upheld.

293.22   *Unprovoked/Unwarranted attack*
R v Hopper 2010 EWCA Crim 813 D pleaded to GBH (full credit). Earlier in the evening V had spoken to the girlfriend of one of D's friends. Later on, in the early hours, D was outside a nightclub. V spoke to the girl again outside the club and D's friend warned him off. D came over and punched V to the face. V fell to the ground, hit his head and was unconscious. V had a fractured skull, bleeding to the brain and the bones of his eye socket were broken. V was in a coma for 13 days and had a slow neurological recovery. V said his life had been turned upside down. He could no longer drive, ride a bike or play football, had been left epileptic and had to take medication on a daily basis. He often fell asleep for long periods of time, could no longer work on building sites, his concentration was affected, he had become forgetful and had to claim disability benefit. D, aged 20, claimed he had been acting in defence of his friend. He had appeared in court for five offences, including having a bladed article and breaches of community orders. The pre-sentence report said D accepted he was fully culpable for the offence, that he displayed regret but appeared to minimise his actions. D posed a medium risk of reoffending and a medium risk of harm to the public. D's basis of plea said he thought V had clenched his fist. The punch went beyond lawful self-defence. The Judge said this was a vicious and unprovoked assault. Held. It must have been a very hard blow. **3 years** after trial, so **2 years' detention** not 2 years 8 months.

Old cases: *R v Seit* 2007 EWCA Crim 1108, 2008 1 Cr App R (S) 15 (p 65) (**2 years**) *R v Shannon* 2008 EWCA Crim 2131, 2009 1 Cr App R (S) 95 (p 551) (**8 months**) *R v Abdille* 2009 EWCA Crim 1195, 2010 1 Cr App R (S) 18 (p 99) (**18 months**) *R v King* 2009 EWCA Crim 1990 (**12 months'** detention)

For a summary of the first case, see the 7th edition of this book, for the second case, see the 8th edition and for the last case, see the 9th edition.

Post-guideline case

R v Cleverly 2012 EWCA Crim 749 D pleaded, on the day of his trial, to section 20. D and his father, F, were at a bowling alley. F made a complaint to V, another bowler, that he was being inconsiderate. V made a slightly threatening remark to F. Later, as V was leaving, F was near the exit and lunged for V. V tried to punch F. D's basis of plea was that he did not see the beginning of the assault mounted by F on V, and he intervened in the defence of F. D kicked V twice and punched him to the face. The fighting lasted about a minute and stopped when a cousin of V screamed at them to stop. V's contact lens was knocked out, he sustained a chipped tooth, a fracture to the left orbital floor and other injuries to his eye. His left eye was floating, discoloured and painful. D accepted there came a point at which his actions went beyond the reasonable defence of F. The Judge placed the offence in Category 2. F had died in a motor accident before the trial. Held. This was a difficult sentencing exercise as F was not before the court. It was wrong of the Judge to characterise this as a joint attack. Starting at **18 months**, with a 10% reduction for the plea, **16 months**, not 27.

R v Burgin 2015 EWCA Crim 49 D pleaded (25% credit) to section 20. V and a group of friends went to get a take-away. The group encountered D and his co-accused, Br. Br asked V to fight in a tunnel[753] out of sight of CCTV. Br felled V by punching him in the face. D kicked V's face whilst he was on the floor. V suffered a fractured jaw, requiring the insertion of surgical plates, but suffered no long-term or lasting effects. D denied any involvement in the altercation and was on licence, having been released two months before the offence from 3 years' detention for robberies (×3). He was aged 21 on appeal and had ten court appearances in all between 2009 and 2011, including battery. The pre-sentence report indicated that D had entrenched antisocial attitudes, limited insight and minimum victim awareness and posed a high risk of causing serious harm to the public. Br pleaded to section 47, receiving an 18-month community order, and this caused a nine-month delay to D's sentencing. Held. **30 months' detention** was not manifestly excessive and it had been slightly reduced to take into account the recall.

See also: *R v Knight* 2014 EWCA Crim 293 (Plea. Dispute about a queue at a cash machine. Defendant, worse for drink, punched and then dealt a full-bodied kick to V's head when V was on the ground. V suffered fractures to cheek bone and orbit. He faced continuing disfigurement. Intense remorse, good work record and acceptance of peer group risk factor. Insufficient account given to mitigating factors. We start at 3 years, with 20% credit, **2½ years** not 2 years 9 months.)

Note: It appears the Judge failed to deduct the full 20% as promised. Ed.

293.23   *Vehicle, Caused by a*

R v Collins 2010 EWCA Crim 1342, 2011 1 Cr App R (S) 35 (p 218) D pleaded early to section 20 and dangerous driving. D had an argument with his partner, made threats to her father and took a car and drove off. He did not have a licence or insurance. When spotted by police he drove off at speed. Police officers gave chase but, because of the nature of D's driving, they fell back. D overtook numerous cars in dangerous manoeuvres. He hit a kerb, lost control and collided with a taxi. His car overturned. The driver of the other car suffered broken legs which had to be pinned, severe cuts and bruises, and concussion. He needed the use of a wheelchair and his life was devastated. The chase had lasted 20 minutes over six or seven miles. The car D took had defective tyres and D had known that when he drove the car. The Judge said D's driving was extremely reckless, atrociously dangerous, irresponsible and stupid. He thought it was hard to think of a worse case of dangerous driving. D had 12 appearances for 36 offences, including convictions for driving and violent offences. Held. It was entirely appropriate for the Judge to consider that D was, in effect, using his car as a guided missile. **4 years** for the section 20 was harsh but not excessive. **5 years' disqualification** not 8.

---

[753] Assuming I have amended a typo correctly.

R v Croft 2010 EWCA Crim 1598, 2011 1 Cr App R (S) 66 (p 409) D was convicted of dangerous driving and section 20, having been acquitted of section 18. He was a taxi driver who, while carrying passengers, drove towards the victim, V. V was slow to cross the road and D drove towards him in an attempt to hurry him up. V banged his hands on the bonnet and D nudged V with the car. He then drove forward, throwing V onto the bonnet and off onto the road. D then drove over V with both the front and rear wheels. He then stopped further down the road. V suffered gaping breaks to his right leg, fractures to his right ribs, a punctured lung, a small laceration to his liver and many abrasions to the skin and his body and head. The Judge said that D had used his car 'as a lethal weapon against a defenceless victim'. D had convictions for dishonesty. Held. V could very easily have been killed and suffered very serious injuries. However, any premeditation was very short. The Judge may have misdirected himself by relying on *Att-Gen's Ref No 13 of 2001* 2001 EWCA Crim 721, 2 Cr App Rep (S) 112 page 497, a section 18 case. Bearing in mind the acquittal on the section 18, **3 years** not 4 was appropriate.

See also: *R v Hopkinson* 2010 EWCA Crim 2308 (After argument with girlfriend, V swore at D and said he had slept with D's girlfriend. D drove car at V to frighten him. V thrown in the air and then dragged along by car. Broken jaw and shoulder blade. D reported himself to police. Aged 21. **9 months** not 18.)

Old cases: *R v Honey* 2007 EWCA Crim 2268 (5 years' extended sentence (**4 years'** custody 1 year's extended licence)) *R v Stranney* 2007 EWCA Crim 2847, 2008 1 Cr App R (S) 104 (p 611) (**2½ years**)

For a summary of the first case, see the 7th edition of this book and for the second case, see the 8th edition.

Post-guideline cases

Examples: *R v Kaeppner* 2012 EWCA Crim 158, 2 Cr App R (S) 47 (p 276) (Plea to GBH and aggravated vehicle-taking. D had a provisional licence. Took friend's keys after drinking. 135 mg in the blood. Travelling at speed on wrong side of road. Head-on collision. Victim suffered serious injuries including fractured pelvis and open fractures. Needed extensive use of wheelchair. Possibility of amputation. Victim did not want D sent to prison. Aged 20. Good character. Full credit. It was just chance that victim wasn't killed. **2 years' detention** upheld.)

R v McIntosh 2014 EWCA Crim 1003, 2 Cr App R (S) 64 (p 503) (Convicted. D rode stolen moped into V, a police officer in uniform who signalled him to stop. V had a non-displaced ankle fracture and left knee ligaments torn. D fled but wrote remorseful letter to V. Injuries not greater harm, Category 2 not 1. **2½ years**, not 3½.)

293.24   *Victim seriously injured   Unexpected*

R v Astbury 2011 EWCA Crim 505 D pleaded to section 20 on rearraignment. He and the victim, V, were living in a hostel. V had been drinking cider and fell asleep. He was woken by some noise and lost his temper. D objected and asked V to open his door, which he did. V was aggressive. D punched V no more than twice in pre-emptive but excessive self-defence. V had lost sight in his left eye from an industrial accident and the punches had damaged the eye further. It had to be removed. D, aged 36 at appeal, had 22 convictions for over 50 offences, including assault. He had problems with drugs, alcohol and depression. Held. This was unnecessary violence causing grave injury and had devastating effects on D's vulnerable neighbour. **3 years** not 4.

Old cases: *R v Owen* 2008 EWCA Crim 1724, 2009 1 Cr App R (S) 64 (p 369) (**2 years**) *R v Hopper* 2010 EWCA Crim 813 (**2 years' detention**)

For a summary of the first case, see the 8th edition and for the second case, see the 10th edition.

Post-guideline cases

R v Murphy 2012 EWCA Crim 394 D was convicted of section 20. He was at a bar with his friends. V was at a private party in the basement of the same premises. D sought to enter the basement and was ejected by V and others. At the end of the evening, D was waiting for his wife outside the bar. V approached and sought to shake D's hand. D misinterpreted this as a hostile gesture and punched V twice to the head. The first punch broke V's nose. The second caused V to fall and strike his head on the pavement. This caused serious head injuries and V was unconscious for three weeks. A large proportion of his skull was removed for surgical repair work and to allow access to a blood clot on the brain. He had eight major operations and surgeons feared he would die. D, aged 23 at the time, was of previous good character. He was married a week before the incident and had since become a father. There were positive prison reports. Held. The injuries were very serious indeed. There were two punches, several seconds apart. This is not to be treated as a single act. The fact that the incident took place in the street and at night are aggravating features. The Judge was entitled to go above the Category 2 starting point, towards the upper end of the range. **27 months** may have been severe, but it was not manifestly excessive.

R v Robinson 2014 EWCA Crim 1661 D pleaded (full discount) to s 20 assault. V and a friend walked up some stairs in a pub. D, who had been drinking, walked down the stairs. Words were exchanged and D grabbed V. D then pushed and pulled V to the top of the stairs and punched V once in the face. V was knocked down, fell down the stairs and hit his head on the floor. D left. V was unconscious with a fractured skull and swelling to the brain. V's injuries were life-threatening. V made a good physical recovery but would have serious lifelong problems. In interview D took responsibility, having initially said he acted in self-defence. D was aged 20, had a drink/driving conviction in 2011 and had references. D lived with his parents and was employed. He showed remorse. The Judge found this was Level 1 due to the injuries and the need to deter. Held. The attack was unprovoked. The Judge was unjustified in going above the top of Level 2. **2 years' detention**, not 30 months.

R v Broad 2014 EWCA Crim 2319 D pleaded (full credit) to s 20. D and V, who was with a girl, were dancing in a nightclub. There was bumping between D and the couple just under ten times, most of which was initiated by D. D and V tapped each other in the face and they were smiling. Eventually, V told D to "fuck off". As V walked away, D punched him in the eye from behind. V struggled to see out of his eye and had two tears in the vascular (muscle) layer beneath the retina, resulting in permanent loss of his central vision. It is likely that V may become permanently blind in that eye. D was aged 18 and of good character with impressive references and a promising future. D was remorseful and wrote a letter of apology. The pre-sentence report proposed a suspended sentence with unpaid work and it was agreed this fell into Category 2. Held. There was some deliberation about the assault, it was not completely spontaneous. However, the aggravating and mitigating factors balance out, so starting at 18 months makes **12 months' detention**, not 18.

See also: *R v Topp* 2012 EWCA Crim 1861, 2013 1 Cr App R (S) 82 (p 450) (Plea. Full credit. At almost 5 am, after drinking and taking ecstasy, he became involved in an argument with a group of men. D was not part of the group but was standing close by, behind the victim. Punched him without warning. He fell to the ground. Lost consciousness. Subdural haemorrhage. Needed surgery to reduce pressure on his brain. That saved his life. Cannot play sport or drink alcohol. Reluctant to go out in public. Stayed at the scene but denied hitting V. Previous offences of violence. **30 months** was not manifestly excessive nor too severe.)

R v Robson 2015 EWCA Crim 223 (Plea. D, drunk, pushed V, who pushed D back and started to move away. D punched V unconscious. V's head hit the ground, where D punched V twice more and left. Catastrophic injuries including bleeding on brain. Part of skull missing. D, aged 20, handed himself in the next day. Dishonest account, but remorseful and of positive good character. Category 2. **2 years 4 months' YOI.**)

293.25   *Victim very seriously injured*

R v Hurley 2008 EWCA Crim 2620, 2009 1 Cr App R (S) 100 (p 568) D was convicted of section 20. He was acquitted of section 18. He went to a pub and met up with others, including the victim, V. The group became boisterous and were asked to leave. They went to another pub, and V became involved in a play fight with one of the group and they were asked to leave again. They then went to one of their houses to carry on drinking. There was an argument between V and his wife, which led to their being asked to leave. V left and after a while D followed him. D said that those who attack women and children should be locked up. There was then a confrontation and D punched V four or five times in the face. V fell and hit his head on a piece of wood or a log. D went to find help and was heard to say, "He fucking deserved that". V had a fractured eye socket, a fractured skull and a large 'bleed in the brain'. He remains in a coma, kept alive through tubes. He will be in a vegetative state for the rest of his life. D was aged 23 and effectively of good character. He misused alcohol on a regular basis. Although he had experienced learning difficulties he worked in an animal sanctuary. There were character witnesses. The Judge said that the remorse carried little weight because of D's remark after the attack. Held. There are cases which fall outside the guidelines, although they are similar to one of the guideline categories. The Judge was entitled to sentence outside the guidelines, because the offence was so grave in that D had left the house to confront and punish the victim, the seriousness of the punching and its appalling consequences. **4 years** was not manifestly excessive.

Post-guideline cases

R v Dodds 2013 EWCA Crim 22, 2 Cr App R (S) 54 (p 358) D pleaded (full credit) to section 20. D and V were close friends but they fell out. D then began a relationship with V's partner. She had a 3-year-old child. Animosity grew between D and V. In the early hours, after both had been drinking, there was an altercation between them. V said something to D as D walked away. D kicked V's legs. V turned round and D punched V once in the face with full force. V fell and hit his head hard on a wall and fell unconscious. V had a very badly damaged skull and an acute subdural haematoma in his brain. A craniotomy was performed. V suffered dysphasia (a language disorder), upper limb weakness and significant disability and disfigurement, which was extreme and highly distressing. V's ability to write, eat, dress and communicate was severely affected. Three times the family was told that the doctors might turn off the life support system. V's treatment might last five years. In interview D said he intended to give V 'a fat lip'. D was aged 34 and had 11 previous convictions, including violence, public disorder offences, affray, wounding and assaulting a PC. He had not served a prison sentence. The pre-sentence report said alcohol played a role in the offence and D had a history of alcohol and drug abuse. The Judge said V's life had been effectively ruined and said it was a greater harm case because of the seriousness of the injury and lesser culpability because there was only one punch. The offence was aggravated by the previous convictions, the violence was late at night and the long-term effect on the victim. D was given **3 years**, which D's counsel equated with a 4½-year sentence and was too close to the 5-year maximum and above the top category range. Held. We disagree. The record showed escalating violence. There was no fault in the Judge's approach.

See also: *R v Kaeppner* 2012 EWCA Crim 158, 2 Cr App R (S) 47 (p 276) (Plea to GBH and aggravated vehicle-taking. D had a provisional licence. Took friend's keys after drinking. 135 mg in the blood. Travelling at speed on wrong side of road. Head-on collision. Victim suffered serious injuries, including fractured pelvis and open fractures. Needed extensive use of wheelchair. Possibility of amputation. Victim did not want D sent to prison. Aged 20. Good character. Full credit. It was just chance that victim wasn't killed. **2 years' detention** upheld.)

293.26   Water, Boiling   Pre-guideline case

R v Day 2010 EWCA Crim 126 D pleaded to section 20. He had earlier been tried for section 18 and the jury failed to agree. D was at the home of his former partner, V, and suddenly he demanded money. He shouted at her and picked up a kettle of boiling water. The water went over her right shoulder. She felt excruciating pain. In interview D denied he had poured water over her. D was aged 42 with old convictions including a robbery in 1992. In 1998 he assaulted his former wife. In 1999 he caused criminal damage to her property. In 2001 he was convicted of harassment. In 2003 he assaulted police. He was sentenced on the basis he did not intend to pour the water but during a struggle he was able to foresee that such an injury could be caused. He had offered to plead to section 20 about 2 months before his trial. Held. There was serious damage to V. **3 years determinate** was appropriate, not 6 years' extended sentence (4 years' custody 2 years' licence) (which was unlawful because it was over the 5-year maximum).

294 OFFENCES AGAINST THE PERSON ACT 1861 S 21

294.1

Offences Against the Person Act 1861 s 21 (attempting to choke, suffocate or strangle etc. with intent to commit etc. an indictable offence)

Mode of trial Indictable only

Maximum sentence Life

Extended sentences This offence is listed in Criminal Justice Act 2003 Sch 15. The court may pass a 2012 extended sentence (EDS) if there is a significant risk of serious harm from future specified offences and either: a) the defendant has a Criminal Justice Act 2003 Sch 15B conviction (applicable only to defendants aged 18+), or b) the offence would justify a determinate sentence of at least 4 years.[754]

Law Commission On 3 November 2015, the Law Commission published its scoping report, 'Reform of Offences against the Person', Law Com No 361. The report proposes abolishing this offence and not creating a replacement.

Sexual Harm Prevention Orders There is a discretionary power to make this order when it is necessary to protect the public from sexual harm.[755]

Children and vulnerable adults: barred lists Where the defendant is aged 18 or over, he or she is automatically barred from engaging in regulated activity with children and vulnerable adults.[756] The judge must tell the defendant that the Disclosure and Barring Service will include him or her in the barred lists.[757] The defendant may ask the Service to remove him or her from the lists.

Where the intent is to rape, see the **RAPE AND ASSAULT BY PENETRATION** chapter or the back index.

294.2 *Case*

R v Groombridge 2013 EWCA Crim 274 D pleaded (at the PCMH) to attempting to choke, suffocate or strangle under OAPA 1861 s 21, and two thefts. He had experienced some difficulties at home and he left his mother's house some nine months before the offences, as he did not get on with his mother's new partner, who had moved in very quickly. He stayed with various people, including his aunt. He moved out of his aunt's house because he was not 'paying his way'. He stole £80 from a safe at his friend's house where he was staying. D moved to stay with another friend. He asked the friend to drive him to the home of his great-grandmother, V, so she could give him some money. V had previously lent D money. D promised to give some of the money to his friend for 'board'. V was aged 92 and lived alone. D asked V to lend him some money. V refused on the basis that D had no means by which to repay it. V later told police that she wasn't threatened by D, but that he strangled her. Five minutes later, V's grandchildren arrived and found her gasping and disorientated. V had marks on her neck. She then suffered from anxiety attacks and had a number of falls and was admitted to a care home. When arrested, D said he smothered her with a cushion but stopped because he "couldn't do

---

[754] Criminal Justice Act 2003 s 226A-226B as inserted by Legal Aid, Sentencing and Punishment of Offenders Act 2012 s 124
[755] Sexual Offences Act 2003 s 103A as inserted by Anti-social Behaviour, Crime and Policing Act 2014 Sch 5 para 2 and Sexual Offences Act 2003 Sch 5
[756] Safeguarding Vulnerable Groups Act 2006 s 2 and Sch 3 and Safeguarding Vulnerable Groups Act 2006 (Prescribed Criteria and Miscellaneous Provisions) Regulations 2009 2009/37 Reg 4 and 6 and Sch 1 para 2 and 4
[757] Safeguarding Vulnerable Groups Act 2006 s 2 and Sch 3 para 25

it". As he left, he stole £80 from V's purse. He got back into the car and gave his friend £60. V's false teeth had dropped down in her mouth and she had soiled herself. D, aged 16, had recently left school. He was of good character and his behaviour at school was described as 'impeccable' and he 'displayed a pleasant and polite nature'. He was also described in a report from the YOT as 'very vulnerable'. There were no mental health issues. D had a medical condition which will result in a curvature of the spine. This put an end to a footballing apprenticeship that he had just attained. The Judge described the offence as of the utmost gravity and if D had been an adult he would have been given life. Held. This offence was truly shocking on a number of levels. This was a single, very serious and unexplained outbreak of violence towards an elderly and very vulnerable victim. V could have died. His age warrants a significant deduction from the sentence he would have received as an adult. 10 years would have been appropriate for an adult. That indicates that between 6 and 6½ years was D's starting point. The Judge made insufficient allowance for his youth. An extended sentence was necessary. There was no reason for, or understanding of, how and why D came to act so violently towards his great-grandmother. If he was provoked to act in that way because he was upset or worried by the possibility of not being able to pay for his keep, then there must have been a significant risk of serious harm. We bear in mind D's youth and immaturity. He is at an age where he will still be developing rapidly. A long period of detention will lead to a substantial diminution in any risk which may have existed at the time of sentencing. 7 years' extended sentence (**4 years' custody** (not 5) 3 years' licence (not 5)).

295   OFFENCES AGAINST THE PERSON ACT 1861 S 22/SEXUAL OFFENCES ACT 2003 S 61

295.1

1) Offences Against the Person Act 1861 s 22 (administer etc. to any person chloroform, laudanum or other stupefying drug to commit an indictable offence etc.)
   Mode of trial Indictable only
   Maximum sentence Life
2) Sexual Offences Act 2003 s 61 (administering a substance with intent to stupefy etc.)
   Mode of trial Triable either way
   Maximum sentence On indictment 10 years. Summary 6 months and/or a £5,000 fine for offences committed before 12 March 2015 and an unlimited fine thereafter.[758]
   There are maximum fines for those aged under 18, see **14.38** in Volume 1.

Extended sentences Both offences are listed in Criminal Justice Act 2003 Sch 15. The court may pass a 2012 extended sentence (EDS) if there is a significant risk of serious harm from future specified offences and either: a) the defendant has a Criminal Justice Act 2003 Sch 15B conviction (applicable only to defendants aged 18+), or b) the offence would justify a determinate sentence of at least 4 years.[759]

Sexual Harm Prevention Orders There is a discretionary power to make this order when it is necessary to protect the public from sexual harm.[760]

Notification For a section 61 offence, the defendant must notify the police within three days (or three days from his release from imprisonment, hospital etc.) with his name, home address, national insurance number etc. and any changes, and addresses where he resides for seven days[761] (in one or more periods) or more in any 12-month period.[762]

Children and vulnerable adults: barred lists Where the defendant is convicted of section 61 and is aged 18 or over he or she is automatically barred from engaging in

---

[758] Legal Aid, Sentencing and Punishment of Offenders Act 2012 s 85(1) and (4) and Legal Aid, Sentencing and Punishment of Offenders Act 2012 (Commencement No 11) Order 2015 2015/504
[759] Criminal Justice Act 2003 s 226A-226B as inserted by Legal Aid, Sentencing and Punishment of Offenders Act 2012 s 124
[760] Sexual Offences Act 2003 s 103A as inserted by Anti-social Behaviour, Crime and Policing Act 2014 Sch 5 para 2 and Sexual Offences Act 2003 Sch 3 and 5
[761] Sexual Offences Act 2003 s 84(1)(c) and (6)
[762] Sexual Offences Act 2003 s 83

regulated activity with children and vulnerable adults.[763] The judge must tell the defendant that the Disclosure and Barring Service will include him or her in the barred lists.[764] The defendant may ask the Service to remove him or her from the lists.

Where the intent is to rape, see the RAPE AND ASSAULT BY PENETRATION chapter or back index.

295.2   Sentencing Council guidelines   Sexual Offences Act 2003 s 61
Sexual Offences Guideline 2014 www.banksr.com Other Matters Guidelines tab In force 1 April 2014.

The guideline only applies to offenders aged 18+, see page 7 of the guideline. For the usual practice, see **66.21** in Volume 1.

STEP ONE: Determining the offence category
page 142 The court should determine the offence category using the table below.

Category 1	Raised harm **and** raised culpability
Category 2	Raised harm **or** raised culpability
Category 3	Administering a substance with intent **without** raised harm or culpability factors present

The court should determine culpability and harm caused or intended, by reference only to the factors below, which comprise the principal factual elements of the offence. Where an offence does not fall squarely into a category, individual factors may require a degree of weighting before making an overall assessment and determining the appropriate offence category. Where no substantive sexual offence has been committed the main consideration for the court will be the offender's conduct as a whole including, but not exclusively, the offender's intention.

Factors indicating raised harm
Severe psychological or physical harm
Prolonged detention/sustained incident
Additional degradation/humiliation

Factors indicating raised culpability
Significant degree of planning
Specific targeting of a particularly vulnerable victim
Intended sexual offence carries a statutory maximum of life
Abuse of trust
Recording of offence
Offender acts together with others to commit the offence
Commercial exploitation and/or motivation
Offence racially or religiously aggravated
Offence motivated by, or demonstrating, hostility to the victim based on his or her sexual orientation (or presumed sexual orientation) or transgender identity (or presumed transgender identity)
Offence motivated by, or demonstrating, hostility to the victim based on his or her disability (or presumed disability)

295.3

STEP TWO: Starting point and category range
page 143 Having determined the category, the court should use the corresponding starting points to reach a sentence within the category range below. The starting point

---

[763] Safeguarding Vulnerable Groups Act 2006 s 2 and Sch 3 and Safeguarding Vulnerable Groups Act 2006 (Prescribed Criteria and Miscellaneous Provisions) Regulations 2009 2009/37 Reg 4 and 6 and Sch 1 para 2 and 4
[764] Safeguarding Vulnerable Groups Act 2006 s 2 and Sch 3 para 25

applies to all offenders irrespective of plea or previous convictions. Having determined the starting point, step one allows further adjustment for aggravating or mitigating features, set out below.

A case of particular gravity, reflected by multiple features of culpability or harm in step one, could merit upward adjustment from the starting point before further adjustment for aggravating or mitigating features, set out below.

Offence category	Starting point (applicable to all offenders)	Category range (applicable to all offenders)
Category 1	6 years' custody	4 to 9 years' custody
Category 2	4 years' custody	3 to 7 years' custody
Category 3	2 years' custody	1 to 5 years' custody

295.4 [Aggravating and mitigating factors]
page 143 The table below contains a non-exhaustive list of additional factual elements providing the context of the offence and factors relating to the offender. Identify whether any combination of these, or other relevant factors, should result in an upward or downward adjustment from the starting point. In particular, relevant recent convictions are likely to result in an upward adjustment. In some cases, having considered these factors, it may be appropriate to move outside the identified category range.

Aggravating factors
Statutory aggravating factors Previous convictions, having regard to a) the nature of the offence to which the conviction relates and its relevance to the current offence; and b) the time that has elapsed since the conviction Offence committed whilst on bail **Other aggravating factors** Location of offence Timing of offence Any steps taken to prevent reporting an incident, obtaining assistance and/or from assisting or supporting the prosecution Attempts to dispose of or conceal evidence Failure to comply with current court orders Offence committed whilst on licence
Mitigating factors
No previous convictions or no relevant/recent convictions Remorse Previous good character and/or exemplary conduct* Age and/or lack of maturity where it affects the responsibility of the offender Mental disorder or learning disability, particularly where linked to the commission of the offence Demonstration of steps taken to address offending behaviour * Previous good character/exemplary conduct is different from having no previous convictions. The more serious the offence, the less the weight which should normally be attributed to this factor. Where previous good character/exemplary conduct has been used to facilitate the offence, this mitigation should not normally be allowed and such conduct may constitute an aggravating factor.

295.5 *Pre-guideline cases*
R v Kwiatowski and Marecki 2011 EWCA Crim 1904, 2012 1 Cr App R (S) 77 (p 437) K and M were convicted of robbery and administering a drug with intent. At 7 am, with five other men, K and M visited V's house. They kicked the front door in and entered. V and his girlfriend were asleep. V was held and bound with cable ties. Duct tape was placed over his mouth and M injected V with ketamine on three occasions. V was told

the drug was 'truth serum'. The men demanded to know where the large quantities of cash which they knew he kept in the house were stored. He refused to tell them. V was taken downstairs while his girlfriend was kept upstairs. V was threatened that he would be taken from the house and beaten. M was aged 20 at the time of the offence. Neither had relevant previous convictions. Held. There were serious aggravating features present: the degree of planning and premeditation, the large number of men, the degree of fear and terror inflicted, the threat to inflict more violence and the injection of dangerous drugs. **12 years** for the robbery and **3 years consecutive** for the drug offence, making **15 years,** was severe but justifiably so.

See also: *R v Penfold* 2012 EWCA Crim 1222 (Convicted of sexual assault and administering a noxious substance. Satellite TV installer revisited home of 84-year-old disabled lady. He put BZP and TFMPP ('designer' drugs) in her drink and sexually assaulted her while she was unconscious, causing her pain and distress. No previous convictions for sexual offences. **4½ years'** not 6 years' **IPP.**)

R v W 2013 EWCA Crim 2232 (Convicted. Partner, V, ended eight-year relationship and told D to leave. D unable to accept that. Administered ecstasy in an open can of drink, had intercourse with her. V unable to move. Had seizure, and so ill had to go to hospital. Acquitted of rape but Judge sentenced on basis sex was non-consensual, but she was unable to convey the lack of consent. An allowance should be made for the fact that no non-consensual activity was intended. Treated as of good character. Gross breach of trust. Starting point too high. **4½ years** not 8.)

Old cases: Best ignored.

296   OFFENCES AGAINST THE PERSON ACT 1861 s 23

296.1

Offences Against the Person Act 1861 s 23 (administering etc. poison or noxious thing etc. so as to endanger life or inflict GBH)

Mode of trial Indictable only

Maximum sentence 10 years

Extended sentences This offence is listed in Criminal Justice Act 2003 Sch 15. The court may pass a 2012 extended sentence (EDS) if there is a significant risk of serious harm from future specified offences and either: a) the defendant has a Criminal Justice Act 2003 Sch 15B conviction (applicable only to defendants aged 18+), or b) the offence would justify a determinate sentence of at least 4 years.[765]

Sexual Harm Prevention Orders There is a discretionary power to make this order when it is necessary to protect the public from sexual harm.[766]

296.2   Drugs   Class A

R v MK 2008 2 Cr App R (S) 78 (p 437) D pleaded to administering a noxious substance, methadone, so as to endanger the life of a three-year-old child (OAPA 1861 s 23). He was left in charge of the child by the parents, who were at work. He was part of their extended family. He was about to go to Poland and he needed to present a urine sample positive for methadone but negative for other drugs. This was to get a two-week prescription for methadone. He put methadone in a carton of apple juice and fed it to the child, intending to use the child's urine as his sample. The child became ill, and D called an ambulance. Paramedics found the child unconscious and in respiratory arrest. D claimed he did not know the cause of the illness. He phoned the father but minimised the illness. The father passed the phone to the mother. When she asked him what he had done to the child he hung up. D stayed with the child in the local hospital. When the child was taken to Great Ormond Street because of his serious condition, D left. When challenged by the child's parents, he denied that the child had ingested any drugs. The

---

[765] Criminal Justice Act 2003 s 226A-226B as inserted by Legal Aid, Sentencing and Punishment of Offenders Act 2012 s 124
[766] Sexual Offences Act 2003 s 103A as inserted by Anti-social Behaviour, Crime and Policing Act 2014 Sch 5 para 2 and Sexual Offences Act 2003 Sch 5

child suffered from convulsions, was ventilated and intubated, given a spectrum of medication, and underwent investigative procedures to try to discover what was causing his illness, including scans, swabs and a lumbar puncture, which carried risks with it. He was unconscious for two days and in hospital for ten days. D was arrested and denied that he had given the child any drugs. Blood tests revealed that the child had been given a life-threatening dose of methadone. The opinion of several experts was that he would have died without medical care. There was an impact statement from the child's mother in which she said that a doctor had told her that the child would suffer side effects in his adolescence. The basis of plea included that he did not realise that the methadone would cause anything more serious than sleepiness. He also expressed remorse. D, aged 23, had two previous convictions for theft. Held. The offence was significantly aggravated by D's failure to alert the authorities to the reason for the illness. This was a clear case of recklessness. **4½ years** upheld.

297   OFFENCES AGAINST THE PERSON ACT 1861 S 24
297.1
Offences Against the Person Act 1861 s 24 (administering etc. poison or noxious thing etc. with intent to injure, aggrieve or annoy)
Mode of trial Indictable only
Maximum sentence 5 years

297.2   *General principles*
R v Jones 1990 12 Cr App R (S) 233 The right approach is to equate a section 24 offence with either an Offences Against the Person Act 1861 s 20 offence or a serious ABH.
Note: This is an old case, so treat the decision with care. Ed.

298   OFFENCES AGAINST THE PERSON ACT 1861 S 58 AND 59
298.1
1) Offences Against the Person Act 1861 s 58 (use of poison or instrument to cause miscarriage)
   Mode of trial Indictable only
   Maximum sentence Life
2) Offences Against the Person Act 1861 s 59 (supplying or procuring poison or instrument to cause miscarriage)
   Mode of trial Indictable only
   Maximum sentence 5 years
Medical practitioners are protected from prosecution if they satisfy the provisions in Abortion Act 1967.

298.2   *Cases*
R v Catt 2013 EWCA Crim 1187, 2014 1 Cr App R (S) 35 (p 210) D pleaded to administering poison with intent to procure a miscarriage. D was married with two young children. In 1999, she presented at hospital at 23 weeks' gestation. She did not return until full term and she delivered a child immediately surrendered for adoption. In 2000 she presented at hospital at 23-25 weeks' gestation and had a termination. In 2002, she presented at hospital seeking a termination. Her pregnancy had hitherto been concealed. A scan showed that it was too far advanced. She subsequently gave birth. In 2004, she presented in hospital in labour. Once again the pregnancy had been concealed. In 2009, she again became pregnant. Her last menstrual period had been in mid-August 2009 and D had been contemplating a termination from January 2010. At 23 weeks' gestation, she accessed the Marie Stopes website to search for information about termination. At 26 weeks, she visited the same website. Between January and March 2010, she had intermittent contact with the Marie Stopes clinic. In March, she searched various phrases on the Internet concerning whether her GP could tell Marie Stopes any personal information, what happens if a GP thinks someone has had an illegal abortion

and whether she might be charged with child abduction. In March 2010 she informed the Marie Stopes clinic her last menstrual period was in November 2009. She was booked into the clinic the next day but did not attend. A hospital scan revealed that she was at 29 weeks and 5 days gestation. The same day, she searched for 'Inducing an abortion at 30 weeks', 'Where can I get an illegal abortion?', and 'Where can I buy misoprostol [a drug capable of inducing a miscarriage] without a prescription?' In April 2010, she searched 'What happens if I take Cytotec [another name for misoprostol] at 34 weeks?' D ordered misoprostol and it was delivered in May 2010, by which point she would have been 38 weeks' pregnant. She subsequently searched for 'How soon will misoprostal work?' when she was around 40 weeks' pregnant. The authorities expected D to contact them with a view to antenatal care, as a result of the scans in March. When there was silence, the midwifery department contacted D, who claimed she had had a termination in March at the Marie Stopes clinic. She maintained that lie for a considerable period. D had been having an affair with a man with whom the pregnancy had been discussed. D was aged 35 or 36 at appeal with no previous convictions. There was a supportive letter from her husband which expressed a desire for the family unit to remain together. A doctor's report noted D's remorse and the effect of the sentence on D's two young children. Held. The termination was at full term and the body has not been recovered. There was careful planning and acquisition of the abortifacient. The criminal acts were done despite considerable experience of pregnancy and its range of consequences. The plea and the doctor's report provided mitigation. The sooner that the family unit is back together, the better. Starting at 12 years was manifestly excessive. We start in the region of 5 years, so with the plea, **3½ years** not 8.

R v Fletcher 2014 EWCA Crim 1876 D pleaded (full credit) to procuring poison to be used with intent to procure a miscarriage (section 59). D was in a relationship with V. D told V he was not ready for a family but they had unprotected intercourse and V fell pregnant. D immediately expressed his unhappiness and said there was no alternative to not having the child. In stark contrast V, having had an ectopic pregnancy, was overjoyed. She began taking pregnancy supplements in D's presence. D purchased paint, the same colour as the supplement pills, as well as a drill and drill bits. V opened a package meant for D which contained pills for procuring a miscarriage. A second such package arrived the next day. V at that time had stomach cramps and wrongly thought they were from taking such pills. She then went to A & E. In D's room were two red pills, each with a hole in. The contents had been replaced with a prescription sleeping medicine. Two further pills were found cut open and secured in red putty. A modelling tool, tweezers and grips were also found. D gave a no comment interview. D was aged 35 on appeal and was a corporal with an exemplary record of 18 years' service. He had very positive character and references from two officers. D had been remanded in custody for over 14 months and had received a further discount of 12 months for his good character. Held. A starting point of 4½ years was too high but the prosecution case was overwhelming. From a starting point of 4 years, a 25% discount with the further discount of 12 months gives the same result. However, recognising the time spent on remand and D's service in the Army, a suspended sentence may allow him to continue his career. **2 years' suspended**, not immediate custody.

See also: *R v Magira* 2008 EWCA Crim 1939, 2009 1 Cr App R (S) 68 (p 390) (Plea (worth 25%) to OAPA 1861 s 58. He twice tried to cause his pregnant wife to have a miscarriage by using pills obtained from abroad over the Internet. Once she had acute stomach pains and once she felt ill. Admitted to hospital on both occasions. Healthy son born. **3 years 9 months** upheld.)

299   OFFENSIVE   WEAPON/BLADED   ARTICLE,   POSSESSION OF/THREATENING WITH

299.1

1) Prevention of Crime Act 1953 s 1 (possession of an offensive weapon)

2) Criminal Justice Act 1988 s 139 (possession of a bladed article)

3) Prevention of Crime Act 1953 s 1A[767] (threatening with an offensive weapon in a public place)

4) Criminal Justice Act 1988 s 139AA[768] (threatening with a blade or pointed article or offensive weapon in a public place or school premises)

Modes of trial All four offences are triable either way.

Maximum sentences All four offences: On indictment 4 years. Summary 6 months and/or a £5,000 fine for offences committed before 12 March 2015 and an unlimited fine thereafter.[769] There are maximum fines for those aged under 18, see **14.38** in Volume 1.

Minimum sentences For offences 1) and 2) Criminal Justice and Courts Act 2015 s 28 enacted a new minimum sentence for defendants aged over 16 at the time of the offence who have a 'relevant conviction' and it is not unjust to pass the 'appropriate custodial sentence'. A 'relevant conviction' is a conviction under Prevention of Crime Act 1953 s 1 or 1A, or Criminal Justice Act 1988 s 139, 139A or 139AA, Prevention of Crime Act 1953 s 1ZA. The 'appropriate custodial sentence' is 6 months for those aged 18 when convicted and 4 months for those aged 16-17 when convicted, Prevention of Crime Act 1953 s 1(2C) and Criminal Justice Act 1988 s 139-139A. In force 13 April 2015.[770] The provisions only apply to offences committed after the provisions came into force. For details see **299.9**.

For offences 3) and 4), the court must impose an appropriate sentence (minimum of 6 months for those aged 18+ and 4 months for those aged 16-17) unless the court is of the opinion that there are particular circumstances which would make it unjust.[771] For details see **299.11**.

For both types of minimum sentence, for those aged 16-17[772] the court must have regard to the welfare of the young person, Children and Young Persons Act 1933 s 44(1) (see **14.34** in Volume 1).

Hospital Orders The minimum sentence provisions do not prevent a court from making a Hospital Order, Mental Health Act 1983 s 37(1A)(ba).

Football Banning Orders Possession of an offensive weapon is a relevant offence under Football Spectators Act 1989 s 14A and Sch 1 para 1. Banning orders may also be made for an offence involving the use or threat of violence either: i) by the accused towards another person, or ii) towards property.[773] For both situations where: a) the accused was at or attempting to enter or leave the premises or journeying to and from the football premises or the offence related to a match, the offence was committed during a journey and the court makes a declaration that the offence related to football matches, and b) there are reasonable grounds to believe that making a banning order would help to prevent violence or disorder at or in connection with any regulated football match, the court must make a Football Banning Order (except where the defendant is given an absolute discharge).

---

[767] As inserted by Legal Aid, Sentencing and Punishment of Offenders Act 2012 s 142. In force 3/12/12 by Legal Aid, Sentencing and Punishment of Offenders Act 2012 (Commencement No 3 and Saving Provision) Order 2012 2012/2770 para 2

[768] As inserted by Legal Aid, Sentencing and Punishment of Offenders Act 2012 s 142. In force 3/12/12 by Legal Aid, Sentencing and Punishment of Offenders Act 2012 (Commencement No 3 and Saving Provision) Order 2012 2012/2770 para 2

[769] Legal Aid, Sentencing and Punishment of Offenders Act 2012 s 85(1) and (4) and Legal Aid, Sentencing and Punishment of Offenders Act 2012 (Commencement No 11) Order 2015 2015/504

[770] Criminal Justice and Courts Act 2015 (Commencement No 1, Saving and Transitional Provisions) Order 2015 2015/778 para 3 and Sch 1 para 28

[771] Prevention of Crime Act 1953 s 1A(5)-(7) and Criminal Justice Act 1988 s 139AA(7)-(9)

[772] Children and Young Persons Act 1933 s 107(1) defines a young person as someone who has not attained the age of 17.

[773] Football Spectators Act 1989 s 14(8), 14A and Sch 1 para 1(r)-(s)

Consultation The Sentencing Guidelines Council is expected to publish a consultation paper during the summer of 2016.

299.2   Guideline cases and judicial guidance

R v Celaire 2002 EWCA Crim 2487, 2003 1 Cr App R (S) 116 (p 610) This judgment is guidance, not a straitjacket to sentencers. The carrying of knives is extremely dangerous because the production of a knife to threaten people, in circumstances of potential violence, has the capacity to cause serious escalation of such violence. A balance has to be struck between the fact that the offence does not in itself involve physical injury and the public's legitimate concern that a culture of carrying weapons encourages violence and may lead to more serious criminal behaviour. It is necessary to consider the offender's intention, the circumstances of the offence and the nature of the weapon involved. It may often be helpful for a sentencer to ask the sort of questions posed in relation to firearms in *R v Avis* 1998 2 Cr App R (S) 178, that is to say to consider the nature of the weapon involved, the use to which it may be put, the defendant's intention in carrying it and the defendant's previous record. As to intention, there are three specific factors which may aggravate the offence. First, there may be a specifically planned use of the weapon, to commit violence or threaten violence or intimidate others. Second, the offence may be motivated by hostility towards a minority individual or group, which may give rise to an aggravating feature such as racial motivation within Crime and Disorder Act 1998 s 28. Third, we would regard it as an aggravating aspect if the defendant were acting under the influence of alcohol or drugs while carrying such a weapon.

Aggravating and mitigating factors

As to the circumstances of the offence, these may be aggravated if its commission takes place at particularly vulnerable premises such as a school (which may give rise to the possibility of a separate charge under Criminal Justice Act 1988 s 139A), or a hospital or other place where vulnerable people may be present. Likewise, an offence may be aggravated if committed at a large public gathering, especially one where there may be a risk of disorder, or, if committed on public transport or on licensed premises or on premises where people are carrying out public services, such as in a doctor's surgery or at a social security office. Finally the offence will obviously be aggravated if it is committed while the defendant is on bail. That, of course, is a statutorily aggravating feature under Criminal Justice Act 1991 s 29(2). As to the nature of the weapon, some weapons are inherently more dangerous than others. But the nature of the weapon will not be the primary determinant as to the seriousness of the offence, because a relatively less dangerous weapon, such as a billiard cue or a knuckleduster, may be used to create fear and such an offence may be at least as serious as one in which a more obviously dangerous weapon, such as a knife or an acid spray, is being carried for self-defence or no actual attempt has been made by the offender to use it. On the other hand, light may be shed on an offender's intention if he is carrying a weapon, such as a flick knife or a butterfly knife, which is offensive *per se*, or a weapon designed or adapted to cause serious injury. Mitigation will be found if the weapon was being carried only on a temporary basis. A defendant, with previous convictions for violence or carrying weapons, who is convicted of carrying a particularly dangerous weapon, in circum-stances aggravated by any of the factors which we have identified and doing so with the clear intention of causing injury or fear, can expect to receive a sentence **at or near the statutory maximum**. In relation to an adult offender of previous good character, the custody threshold will almost invariably be passed where there is a combination of dangerous circumstances and actual use of the weapon to threaten or cause fear. The nature of the weapon and other aggravating or mitigating factors will bear on the length of the custodial term. Custody may still be appropriate, depending on the circumstances, where no threatening use was made of the weapon. Alternatively, depending on the circumstances, there will be cases where, absent aggravating features of the kind which we have identified and where no threat has been made and where the weapon is not particularly dangerous, the custody threshold may not be passed and a community sentence towards the top end of the available range may be appropriate. Of course, if the defendant has previous convictions for violence or for other weapon offences, then the sentence imposed on him or her is likely to be longer.

Consecutive to or concurrent with the other offence

Where the weapons offence was committed in conjunction with another offence, the usual considerations in relation to totality will apply. A concurrent sentence will usually be appropriate if the weapons offence is ancillary to another more serious offence. Where the weapons offence is distinct from and independent of another offence, a consecutive sentence will usually be called for.

Other orders

The sentencing court will also wish to bear in mind its powers to order forfeiture, which will almost inevitably follow, and its powers to make a compensation order.

R v Povey 2008 EWCA Crim 1261, 2009 1 Cr App R (S) 42 (p 228) Carrying a knife or an offensive weapon is a crime which is being committed far too often by far too many people. Offences of this kind have recently escalated. Every weapon carried about the streets, even if concealed from sight, even if not likely to be or intended to be used, and even if not used, represents a threat to public safety and public order. That is because even if concealed, even if carried only for bravado, or from some misguided sense that its use in possible self-defence might arise, it takes but a moment of irritation, drunkenness, anger, perceived insult or something utterly trivial such as a look, for the weapon to be produced. Then we have mayhem, and offences of the greatest possible seriousness follow, including murder, manslaughter, GBH, wounding and assault. All those offences have victims. They are reaching epidemic proportions. Every knife or weapon carried in the street represents a public danger, and therefore in the public interest this crime must be confronted and stopped. The courts will do what they can to help reduce and, so far as practicable, eradicate it. It is important for public confidence that those caught in possession of a knife or offensive weapon should normally be brought before the courts and prosecuted. Whatever other considerations may arise in the individual case, courts must have in the forefront of their thinking a focus on the reduction of crime, including its reduction by deterrence, and the protection of the public. Even if the offender does no more than carry the weapon, even when the weapon is not used to threaten or cause fear, when considering the seriousness of the offence courts should bear in mind the harm which the weapon might foreseeably have caused. So the message is stark. This is a serious offence and it should be treated with the seriousness it deserves. Conditions now are much more grave[774] than they were when *R v Celaire* 2002 EWCA Crim 2487, 2003 1 Cr App R (S) 116 (p 610) was decided. *R v Celaire* should be applied with the current grave situation and the sentencing considerations we have just identified clearly in mind. Any relevant guidance from the Sentencing Guidelines Council to magistrates should normally be applied at the most severe end of the appropriate range of sentences.

R v Gomes-Monteiro and Others 2014 EWCA Crim 747, 2 Cr App R (S) 62 (p 483)[775] LCJ It is important that the Youth Court pays the closest attention to the guidance given in *R v Povey* 2008. Given the prevalence of knife crime among young persons, the Youth Court must keep a very sharp focus, if necessary through the use of more severe sentences, on preventing further offending by anyone apprehended for carrying a knife in a public place and to securing a reduction in the carrying of knives. It is important particularly in relation to knife crime that the guidance given in respect of cautions is aligned to the sentencing practice (as it should be in the light of our observation) in the Youth Court, the Magistrates' Court and the Crown Court.

---

[774] Assuming I have correctly amended a typo in the judgment.
[775] This case is also referred to as *R v Monteiro and Others* 2014 EWCA Crim 747.

299.3   *Magistrates' Court Sentencing Guidelines*

Magistrates' Court Sentencing Guidelines 2008, see www.banksr.com Other Matters Guidelines tab page 33 The guideline applies to the Magistrates' Court and to the Crown Court hearing appeals or sentencing for summary only offences.[776]

Starting points are based on a first-time offender pleading not guilty.

page 33 Bladed instrument/offensive weapon

Examples of nature of activity	Starting point	Range
Weapon not used to threaten or cause fear	High-level community order	Band C fine to 12 weeks' custody
Weapon not used to threaten or cause fear but offence committed in dangerous circumstances	6 weeks' custody	High-level community order to Crown Court
Weapon used to threaten or cause fear and offence committed in dangerous circumstances	Crown Court	Crown Court

For the meaning of a high-level community order, see **16.14** in Volume 1.

The following aggravating and mitigating factors may be particularly relevant:

Factors indicating higher culpability: 1 Particularly dangerous weapon, 2 Specifically planned use of weapon to commit violence, threaten violence or intimidate, 3 Offence motivated by hostility towards minority individual or group, 4 Offender under influence of drink or drugs, and 5 Offender operating in group or gang.

Factors indicating lower culpability: 1 Weapon carried only on temporary basis, and 2 Original possession legitimate, e.g. in course of trade or business of individual or group.

Factors indicating greater degree of harm: 1 Offence committed at school, hospital or other place where vulnerable persons may be present, 2 Offence committed on premises where people carrying out public services, 3 Offence committed on licensed premises, 4 Offence committed on public transport, and 5 Offence committed at large public gathering, especially where there may be risk of disorder.

Consider ancillary orders, including compensation, deprivation of property (including weapon).

Notes

   a) Concurrent sentences will be appropriate if the weapons offence is ancillary to a more serious offence. Consecutive sentences will be appropriate if the offences are distinct and independent.
   b) When assessing offence seriousness, consider the offender's intention, the circumstances of the offence and the nature of the weapon involved.
   c) The nature of the weapon is not the primary determinant of offence seriousness. A relatively less dangerous weapon, such as a billiard cue or knuckleduster, may be used to create fear, and such an offence may be at least as serious as one in which a more obviously dangerous weapon, such as a knife or an acid spray, is being carried for self-defence or no actual attempt has been made by the offender to use it.
   d) Nevertheless, the fact that the offender was carrying a weapon which is offensive *per se* may shed light on his or her intentions.

A Band C fine is 150% of net weekly income. For more detail see **60.27** in Volume 1.

For how to apply the guidelines, see the **GUIDELINES** chapter in Volume 1.

The guideline also set out the principles in *R v Povey* 2008 as a note inserted into the guidelines.

---

[776] See page 15 of the guidelines.

299.4   *Article not visible*

R v Povey 2008 EWCA Crim 1261, 2009 1 Cr App R (S) 42 (p 228) D pleaded to having a bladed article, having an offensive weapon and possession of cannabis. At 12.45 am he was seen by police officers in the street wearing army-style clothing. There was an outstanding warrant for his arrest, so officers spoke to him. He had a flick knife and a wooden-handled kitchen knife with a 6-inch blade in his pocket, along with a small amount of cannabis. In interview he made no comment about the knives. D, aged 50, had 97 previous convictions. They included an old offence of manslaughter in which he stabbed his victim. There were other offences of violence. A pre-sentence report said that he tended to minimise his actions and did not take full responsibility for them. He had a lack of consequential thinking, a chaotic lifestyle, had relationship difficulties and was homeless. He accepted that he was angry. He indicated he would use a weapon if he felt he needed to protect himself. He presented a high risk of reoffending with a medium risk of harm to the public. He was not motivated to co-operate with the probation service. Held. D is of unstable temperament with a serious criminal record. It is not arguable that **16 months concurrent** was excessive.

R v Wilson 2011 EWCA Crim 1758 D pleaded to possession of a bladed article and possession of Diazepam. He was bailed after being arrested for a class C drugs offence. A condition of bail was that he lived with his parents. He had been pestering them for money and they no longer wished him to live there. They contacted the police when he refused to leave. D was in the front garden when the officers arrived, and when asked what he was doing there he responded that he was going to hurt someone. He had concealed a knife with a 3- or 4-inch blade up his sleeve. D, aged 27 at appeal, had convictions for low-level offending for which he had been to prison in addition to community disposals. His offending included a conviction for possession of an offensive weapon. He had committed offences whilst on licence. D had an alcohol and drug dependency and limited thinking and problem-solving skills. He had also been detained under mental health legislation. Held. This was the fifth time D had appeared before the court for possession of a knife. It is absolutely clear that D is in need of substantial assistance. It is important the offence is seen within the context of the offender's background, personality and character. The starting point should have been 2 years, so with the plea, **16 months** not 30.

R v Burgess 2012 EWCA Crim 2476, 2013 2 Cr App R (S) 13 (p 57) D was convicted of having a bladed article in a public place. In the immediate aftermath of the London riots in 2011, police in riot gear were on patrol in Lewisham at about 2 am. They spotted a large group of men wearing dark clothing and in some cases with their faces covered. They followed the group and noticed that D walked away from the others once they had spotted the police. An officer shouted at D to stop and he failed to do so, discarding something in a bush as he walked. D had discarded a kitchen knife with a 3-inch blade, wrapped in a bandana. D, aged 30, had no convictions. He had been in the UK for 8 years and was awaiting the outcome of an application for leave to remain. Held. The proximity in time to the riots was an aggravating feature. The Judge was entitled to come to the conclusion that D was carrying the knife in order to use it if necessary to cause injury or threaten or intimidate. However, with regard to D's age and his otherwise good character, **15 months** not 20.

299.5   *Article visible*

R v Bhebe 2010 EWCA Crim 1045 D pleaded at the Magistrates' Court to possessing a bladed article. At about 6.15 pm, D was on the top deck of a bus and he asked a 17-year-old girl to move her bags, which were next to her. After she had moved them, D sat next to her. When she tried to leave, D blocked her path, reached down to his ankle and produced a large kitchen knife. She pushed past him and ran downstairs distressed. The bus driver drove to a police station. D was aged 38, with 29 previous court appearances including in 2003 8 weeks for a bladed article, in 2004 18 months for robbery, in 2006 a conditional discharge for threatening behaviour, in 2007 an unknown sentence for assault with intent to resist arrest, and in 2008 3 months for an affray. D had a long-standing problem with heroin, cocaine and alcohol, suffered from paranoid schizophrenia and was receiving anti-psychotic drugs. The pre-sentence report considered there was a high risk of reoffending and harm to the public being caused. Held. The Judge would have been entitled to reduce the discount because of the incriminating CCTV etc. **30 months** was not manifestly excessive.

R v Gordon 2012 EWCA Crim 970, 2013 1 Cr App R (S) 14 (p 76) D pleaded (full credit) to having a bladed article and using threatening etc. words and behaviour with intent to cause fear (3 months concurrent). At 5 pm he approached two boys and a girl, all aged 15. They were sunbathing on some grass by the roadside. D was a complete stranger to them. They could see D was holding something behind his back. D asked them if they knew Carl and they said they didn't. He then asked, "Are you sure about that? I'm not scared to blaze anyone's throat". D then jogged off and the boys could see he was holding a knife. The police were informed. Quite independently D's sister called the police saying D was angry and had stormed out of the house with a knife. D's father approached the police and told them that he had found D, put him in a car and taken the knife from him. The knife was shown to the police. It was 4½ inches long. D then approached the officers and he appeared drunk and agitated. He was arrested and shouted whether his arrest meant that he would go back to prison. In interview he said he had had an argument with his girlfriend and the only person who would have been harmed was himself. D was aged 19, with convictions for criminal damage (twice and both domestic), harassment (sending over 400 texts in a domestic setting) and threatening behaviour (insults and threats to a social worker responsible for the welfare of his child). Held. The convictions suggest some instability.

See also: *R v Povey Re C* 2008 EWCA Crim 1261, 2009 1 Cr App R (S) 42 (p 228) at para 27 (**9 months** consecutive to 3 years.)

R v Murphy 2012 EWCA Crim 469 (Plea. Seen walking around a Gay Pride festival with 17 cm meat cleaver. Told police, "I was going to get him, he fucking robbed me. I was going to kill him." 97 convictions on 45 occasions including 3½ years for section 18. Terrifying weapon but **2 years** not 3.).

299.6   *Article carried before intended violence*

R v Povey Re M 2008 EWCA Crim 1261, 2009 1 Cr App R (S) 42 (p 228) para 17 M pleaded to possession of an offensive weapon. There was ill-feeling between his brother and a man, S, because his brother was having a relationship with S's estranged wife. M and his brother arranged to meet S in the streets of Jarrow to 'resolve' the matter. They had two others to support them, so they were four against one. Police got to the scene before there was any trouble. S had a knife, M had a kitchen knife and one of D's side had a metal pole. In interview D said that he had had the knife for perhaps five minutes when arrested, and it was for his protection. D, aged 34, had attended a school for children with special educational needs and was not working. A pre-sentence report said that there was nothing to indicate that he was a risk to the public. He had expressed regret. Held. This is a much more serious offence than mere possession of a weapon. This was a scene in the middle of the night when three men were armed. The potential for serious violence was obvious. It is not to the credit of D that the police were able to intervene before there was any violence. Arming yourself and joining with others who have armed themselves for the purpose of confrontation cannot be mitigated by asserting that the weapon was for self-defence. A longer sentence than the **4 months** given would have been appropriate.

299.7   *Article carried/held where public official/shop worker etc. present*

R v Povey Re B 2008 EWCA Crim 1261, 2009 1 Cr App R (S) 42 (p 228) para 41 B was convicted of breach of an ASBO, two counts of possession of a bladed article, and going equipped for theft. He joined a crowd waiting to see the Queen, who was visiting Huddersfield. He pushed his way through them and upset them. A police officer found that he was carrying a felling axe in a carrier bag. In interview he agreed he should not have been walking about the streets with the axe. He was granted police bail. Three weeks later at 1.30 am he was stopped by police and found to be carrying gloves, a torch, a hammer and a Stanley knife. He made no comment in interview. B, aged 34, had a number of previous convictions but no custodial sentences. He was the subject of a community service order. The ASBO had been imposed two years earlier for possession of a bladed article. A pre-sentence report said that there was a medium risk of reoffending and harm being caused to the public. A psychiatric report said that he was slightly odd but did not suffer from any mental illness or learning disability. The Judge was concerned that he intended to approach the Queen as closely as possible and to brandish the axe. He was greatly concerned that firearms might then be discharged. A prison report for the Appeal Court did nothing to dispel the concerns expressed by the trial Judge. Held. The ASBO breach and the bladed article related to the same behaviour. The total sentence (4½ years) for the ASBO and first bladed article was too long. So ASBO breach 6 months not 18. The **3 years** consecutive for the bladed articles was appropriate. 18 months concurrent for the going equipped and **18 months consecutive** for the other bladed article upheld, so **5 years** in total not 6.

R v Moore 2013 EWCA Crim 1590 D pleaded to having a bladed article. He caused a disturbance outside the house of V, his former partner. V called the police. An officer arrived with a police dog and pulled up 3 or 4 metres from D. D was holding a craft knife with a blade of 3-4 cm in length. He first put the blade to his own wrist and then waved it at the officer in a threatening and aggressive manner. He then ran away from the officer. The officer caught up with D, who again waved the knife towards him. D used threatening and abusive language. The officer warned D that he would release the dog, upon which D became compliant and gave up the knife. D was also in possession of some plastic rope with which he claimed he had planned to commit suicide. A *Newton* hearing was held. The Judge rejected D's version about the blade. D was aged 23 at conviction and had 60 previous convictions. They included affray and having a bladed article (2005), assaults on police (×2, 2007), assault, affray (×3) and having a bladed article (×2) (2008), threatening behaviour and sending a letter conveying a threat (2011). Held. D brandished a knife in a threatening and aggressive manner and, in doing so, created a dangerous situation. If the officer had not handled it in the way he did, it could have ended in bloodshed. The offence was aggravated by D's convictions, particularly for those for similar offences. D accepted that the 10% discount for the plea, following the unsuccessful *Newton* hearing, was appropriate. **27 months** was not manifestly excessive.

R v Spencer 2014 EWCA Crim 444, 2014 2 Cr App R (S) 32 (p 262) D pleaded (full credit) to two offensive weapon counts. At about 11.30 pm, D went to a petrol station with a grievance about a pair of sunglasses which he said were scratched. The assistant, V, wanted a receipt and told D to come back the next day. D went away and shortly after returned and stood next to the glass screen with a Samurai sword in his hand pointing upwards. D was laughing. The blade was about 75 cm long. V quickly gave him some sunglasses and D walked away still laughing. D was found nearby and on his person was a lock-knife. D admitted he had been to the petrol station with the sword. D was unable to sign the police notebook as he had inhaled four cans of lighter gas. In interview D said he had consumed two bottles of vodka. He had one previous conviction for battery in 2005. D was diagnosed as having a borderline personality disorder and had had numerous mental health admissions. Held. An employee was put in fear. A display of any sort of blade in public must be dealt with severely. A lock knife, which D also had, was never produced so that sentence should not have been consecutive. There was genuine remorse. **2 years** not 3 for the sword and 4 months concurrent for the lock-knife.

See also: *R v Fryer* 2014 EWCA Crim 1004 (Early plea to possession of a bladed article. Disagreements with staff at the job centre. Decided to make a public protest against what he perceived to be the incorrect stoppage of his benefits. Attended job centre with knife with 6-inch blade. Attached himself to a radiator with plastic handcuffs, put the knife on the floor and declared he wasn't leaving until he received his money. Pre-sentence report noted high risk of harm. Aged 49. Previous conviction for manslaughter by stabbing in 1988. Very serious offence. Not far below the worst category of such offences. Starting at 3½ years, not 4 (the maximum), was appropriate. Full credit. **28 months** not 32.)

Old case: *R v Golebiowski* 2010 EWCA Crim 2964 (**12 months**)

For a summary of the case, see the 10th edition of this book.

299.8   *Previous convictions for knife crime*

R v Lally 2014 EWCA Crim 1090 D pleaded to possession of a bladed article. In the early hours of the morning, he was arrested by the police after a fight. He was not charged, his case being that he was attacked and was defending himself. On arrival at the police station, he informed the police that he had a 'tool' in his sock. A plain knife in a sheath was found. He also had a small amount of cannabis (fined in separate proceedings). D had previous convictions for violence including robbery with a knife and received a 12-year extended sentence for manslaughter committed with a knife. He was subject to a suspended sentence imposed for ABH at the time of the instant offence. A psychiatric assessment revealed no mental illness but a high risk of harming others due to his weapon carrying, use of alcohol and drugs, a propensity for extreme violence when angry and criminal associations. D told the assessor he would stab and torture anyone that crossed him and would have no feelings about it. The Judge imposed 2½ years and activated the 9-month suspended sentence in full. Held. In a case such as the present where D not only had an appalling history of serious knife crime but had also expressed a current intention to use a knife to inflict terrible injuries, a sentence close to the statutory maximum cannot only be expected but is necessary to protect the public. Given D's record and expressed intention of harming people, the Judge was entitled to perceive a sinister intention in his having concealed a knife about his person. With a 20% plea credit, there was nothing excessive about **2½ years**. Suspended sentence activation reduced because of part compliance etc. from 9 months to 3. 2 years 9 months in all.

299.9   *Minimum sentences   Explanation*

Minimum sentences For offences 1) and 2) Criminal Justice and Courts Act 2015 s 28 enacted a new minimum sentence for defendants aged over 16 at the time of the offence who have a 'relevant conviction' and it is not unjust to pass the 'appropriate custodial sentence'. A 'relevant conviction' is a conviction under Prevention of Crime Act 1953 s 1 or 1A, or Criminal Justice Act 1988 s 139, 139A or 139AA, Prevention of Crime Act 1953 s 1ZA. The 'appropriate custodial sentence' is 6 months for those aged 18 when convicted and 4 months for those aged 16-17 when convicted, Prevention of Crime Act 1953 s 1(2C) and Criminal Justice Act 1988 s 139-139A. In force 13 April 2015.[777] The provisions only apply to offences committed after the provisions came into force. For details see **299.9**.

For offences 3) and 4), the court must impose an appropriate sentence (minimum of 6 months for those aged 18+ and 4 months for those aged 16-17) unless the court is of the opinion that there are particular circumstances which would make it unjust.[778] For details see **299.11**.

For both types of minimum sentences, for those aged 16-17,[779] the court must have regard to the welfare of the young person, Children and Young Persons Act 1933 s 44(1) (see **14.34** in Volume 1).

---

[777] Criminal Justice and Courts Act 2015 (Commencement No 1, Saving and Transitional Provisions) Order 2015 2015/778 para 3 and Sch 1 para 28
[778] Prevention of Crime Act 1953 s 1A(5)-(7) and Criminal Justice Act 1988 s 139AA(7)-(9)
[779] Children and Young Persons Act 1933 s 107(1) defines a young person as someone who has not attained the age of 17.

Offence	Minimum sentence Statutory provisions	Definition of relevant conviction
Possession of offensive weapon Prevention of Crime Act 1953 s 1	Prevention of Crime Act 1953 s 1(2A)-(2C), see **299.9**	Prevention of Crime Act 1953 s 1ZA, see **299.10**
Threatening with an offensive weapon Prevention of Crime Act 1953 s 1A	Prevention of Crime Act 1953 s 1A(5)-(9), see **299.12**	Relevant conviction not required
Having a bladed article Criminal Justice Act 1988 s 139	Criminal Justice Act 1988 s 139(6A)-(8), see **299.12**	Criminal Justice Act 1988 s 139AZA The wording is the same as section 1ZA above.
Having bladed article or offensive weapon on school premises Criminal Justice Act 1988 s 139A	Criminal Justice Act 1988 s 139A(6A)-(8) (not listed)	
Threatening with bladed article or offensive weapon Criminal Justice Act 1988 s 139AA	Criminal Justice Act 1988 s 139AA(7)-(11) (not listed)	Relevant conviction not required

Court Martial There is a similar provision for members of the armed forces, Armed Forces Act 2006 s 227A.[780]

299.10   *Minimum sentences   Offensive weapons, Possession of   Statutory provisions*

Prevention of Crime Act 1953 s 1(2A)-(2G)

Prevention of Crime Act 1953 s 1(2A)[781] Subsection (2B) applies where:

a) a person is convicted of an offence under subsection (1) [possession of an offensive weapon] committed after this subsection is commenced, and

b) when the offence was committed, the person was aged 16 or over and had at least one relevant conviction (see section 1ZA).

(2B) Where this subsection applies, the court must impose an appropriate custodial sentence (with or without a fine) unless the court is of the opinion that there are particular circumstances which:

a) relate to the offence, to the previous offence or to the offender, and

b) would make it unjust to do so in all the circumstances.

(2C) In this section 'appropriate custodial sentence' means:

a) in the case of a person who is aged 18 or over when convicted, a sentence of imprisonment for a term of at least 6 months,

b) in the case of a person who is aged at least 16 but under 18 when convicted, a detention and training order of at least 4 months.

(2D) In considering whether it is of the opinion mentioned in subsection (2B) in the case of a person aged 16 or 17, the court must have regard to its duty under the Children and Young Persons Act 1933 s 44 (general considerations).

(2E) Where:

a) an appropriate custodial sentence has been imposed on a person under subsection (2B), and

---

[780] As inserted by Legal Aid, Sentencing and Punishment of Offenders Act 2012 Sch 26 para 23-24. In force 3/12/12 by Legal Aid, Sentencing and Punishment of Offenders Act 2012 (Commencement No 3 and Saving Provision) Order 2012 2012/2770 para 2

[781] As inserted by Criminal Justice and Courts Act 2015 s 28

    b) a relevant conviction without which subsection (2B) would not have applied has
      been subsequently set aside on appeal,
notice of appeal against the sentence may be given at any time within 28 days from the
date on which the conviction was set aside (despite anything in the Criminal Appeal
Act 1968 s 18 (initiating procedure)).

(2F) Where an offence is found to have been committed over a period of two or more
days, or at some time during a period of two or more days, it shall be taken for the
purposes of this section to have been committed on the last of those days.

(2G) In relation to times before the coming into force of Criminal Justice and Court
Services Act 2000 Sch 7 para 180, the reference in subsection (2C)(a) to a sentence of
imprisonment, in relation to an offender aged under 21 at the time of conviction, is to be
read as a reference to a sentence of detention in a Young Offender Institution.

299.11   *'Relevant conviction', Meaning of   Offensive weapons, Possession of*
Prevention of Crime Act 1953 s 1ZA(1) For the purposes of section 1 [possession of an
offensive weapon], 'relevant conviction' means:
    a) a conviction for an offence under:
      i) section 1 [possession of an offensive weapon] or 1A [threatening with offensive
        weapon] of this Act, or
      ii) Criminal Justice Act 1988 s 139, 139A or 139AA, [having a bladed article,
        having a bladed article on school premises and threatening with bladed article]
        (a 'relevant offence'), whenever committed,
    (b) a conviction in Scotland, Northern Ireland or a member State other than the
    United Kingdom for a civilian offence, whenever committed, which would have
    constituted a relevant offence if committed in England and Wales at the time of that
    conviction,
    (c) a conviction for an offence under the Armed Forces Act 2006 s 42, whenever
    committed, in respect of which the corresponding offence under the law of England
    and Wales (within the meaning of that section) is a relevant offence,
    (d) a conviction for an offence under the Army Act 1955 s 70, the Air Force Act 1955
    s 70 or the Naval Discipline Act 1957 s 42, whenever committed, in respect of which
    the corresponding civil offence (within the meaning of the Act in question) is a
    relevant offence, and
    (e) a conviction for a member State service offence, whenever committed, which
    would have constituted a relevant offence if committed in England and Wales at the
    time of conviction.

(2) In this section:
'civilian offence' means an offence other than:
    a) an offence under an enactment mentioned in subsection (1)(c) or (d), or
    b) a member State service offence;
'conviction' includes:
    a) in relation to an offence under the Armed Forces Act 2006 s 42, anything which by
      virtue of section 376(1) and (2) of that Act is to be treated as a conviction, and
    b) in relation to an offence under the Naval Discipline Act 1957 s 42 and a member
      State service offence, a finding of guilt in respect of the person,
'member State service offence' means an offence which was the subject of proceedings
under the law of a member State, other than the United Kingdom, governing all or any of
the naval, military or air forces of that State.

(3) For the purposes of subsection (1)(c) and (d), where the offence was committed by
aiding, abetting, counselling or procuring, it must be assumed that the act aided, abetted,
counselled or procured was done in England and Wales.

299.12   *Minimum sentences   Threatening a member of the public with an offensive weapon*

Prevention of Crime Act 1953 s 1A(5) Where a person aged 16 or over is convicted of an offence under this section [threatening with an offensive weapon in public], the court must impose an appropriate custodial sentence (with or without a fine) unless the court is of the opinion that there are particular circumstances which:

    a) relate to the offence or to the offender, and

    b) would make it unjust to do so in all the circumstances.

(6) In this section 'appropriate custodial sentence' means:

    a) in the case of a person who is aged 18 or over when convicted, a sentence of imprisonment for a term of at least 6 months,

    b) in the case of a person who is aged at least 16 but under 18 when convicted, a detention and training order of at least 4 months.

(7) In considering whether it is of the opinion mentioned in subsection (5) in the case of a person aged under 18, the court must have regard to its duty under the Children and Young Persons Act 1933 s 44.

(8) In relation to an offence committed before the commencement of the Criminal Justice Act 2003 s 154(1), the reference in subsection (4)(a) to 12 months is to be read as a reference to 6 months.

(9) In relation to times before the coming into force of the Criminal Justice and Court Services Act 2000 Sch 7 para 180, the reference in subsection (6)(a) to a sentence of imprisonment, in relation to an offender aged under 21 at the time of conviction, is to be read as a reference to a sentence of detention in a Young Offender Institution.

Note: There is a similar provision for offences of threatening with a bladed article in Criminal Justice Act 1988 s 139AA(7)-(11).

299.13   *Minimum sentences   Bladed articles   Statutory provisions*

Criminal Justice Act 1988 s 139(6A) Subsection (6B) applies where:

    a) a person is convicted of an offence under subsection (1) [having a bladed article] by a court in England and Wales,

    b) the offence was committed after this subsection is commenced, and

    c) when the offence was committed, the person was aged 16 or over and had at least one relevant conviction (see section 139AZA).

(6B) Where this subsection applies, the court must impose an appropriate custodial sentence (with or without a fine) unless the court is of the opinion that there are particular circumstances which:

    a) relate to the offence, to the previous offence or to the offender, and

    b) would make it unjust to do so in all the circumstances.

(6C) In this section 'appropriate custodial sentence' means:

    a) in the case of a person who is aged 18 or over when convicted, a sentence of imprisonment for a term of at least 6 months,

    b) in the case of a person who is aged at least 16 but under 18 when convicted, a Detention and Training Order of at least 4 months.

(6D) In considering whether it is of the opinion mentioned in subsection (6B) in the case of a person aged 16 or 17, the court must have regard to its duty under the Children and Young Persons Act 1933 s 44 (general considerations).

(6E) Where:

    a) an appropriate custodial sentence has been imposed on a person under subsection (6B), and

    b) a relevant conviction without which subsection (6B) would not have applied has been subsequently set aside on appeal, notice of appeal against the sentence may be given at any time within 28 days from the date on which the conviction was set aside (despite anything in the Criminal Appeal Act 1968 s 18 (initiating procedure)).

(6F) Where an offence is found to have been committed over a period of two or more days, or at some time during a period of two or more days, it shall be taken for the purposes of this section to have been committed on the last of those days.

(6G) In relation to times before the coming into force of the Criminal Justice and Court Services Act 2000 Sch 7 para 180, the reference in subsection (6C)(a) to a sentence of imprisonment, in relation to an offender aged under 21 at the time of conviction, is to be read as a reference to a sentence of detention in a Young Offender Institution.

(7) In this section 'public place' includes any place to which at the material time the public have or are permitted access, whether on payment or otherwise.

(8) This section shall not have effect in relation to anything done before it comes into force.

300   OFFICIAL SECRETS ACTS

300.1
Official Secrets Act 1911 s 1 (obtains, collects, records or publishes, or communicates any secret note etc.)

    Mode of trial Indictable only

    Maximum sentence 14 years

300.2   *Judicial guidance*
R v James 2009 EWCA Crim 1261, 2010 1 Cr App R (S) 57 (p 362) The Lord Chief Justice in *R v Prime* 1983 5 Cr App R (S) 127 underlined the importance of deterrence in a case where information of value to a foreign power was or was intended to be disclosed. He said, "It is much better that spying should never start than that spies should subsequently confess". Also in that case, the necessity for deterrence was identified and it was said, "Anyone, particularly those in the Armed Services and Government Service who is tempted, whether by money, threats of blackmail or ideology, to communicate sensitive information to a potential enemy, should have in mind what happened to Mr Prime [who received 35 years consecutive to 3 years for a sex offence]. This is particularly so nowadays when, because of the developments in the gathering and storing of information by electronic means, those in comparatively lowly positions often have access to material which could endanger the security of the state if it got into the wrong hands." In *R v Smith* 1996 1 Cr App R (S) 202 the Lord Chief Justice said, "Anyone who is prepared to betray his country must expect that he will receive a long sentence. It makes no difference that there may be variations in the political situation worldwide, or in the existence or non-existence of the Cold War, or any other possible source of war or threat to the United Kingdom in the future. Anyone who is prepared to betray his country must expect to receive a long sentence. Treachery is treachery. It must be deterred and it must be punished."

Where a member of the Armed Forces, however junior, serving abroad in a theatre of military operations, chooses to disclose information which may be of use to an enemy, the element of intended betrayal of serving colleagues makes it a very serious offence. There must be no doubt that even if the information disclosed is not proven to have caused any actual damage, the deterrent element in the sentence is absolutely fundamental.

300.3   *Foreign power, Giving information to a*
R v James 2009 EWCA Crim 1261, 2010 1 Cr App R (S) 57 (p 362) LCJ D was convicted of communicating information useful to an enemy. In 1987, D joined the Territorial Army and signed the Official Secrets Acts form given to him by the Civil Service. In 2006 he was sent to Afghanistan to serve as an interpreter. D acted for the commanding officer of the International Security Assistance Force. He did not have direct access to the most sensitive of the officer's work, but he was in a unique position to overhear operational and strategic information. He passed information to the Iranian Military Attaché. D believed that it would be useful, but it was imprecise and general.

He appeared to exaggerate his importance with his narcissistic personality. No actual damage to operations was caused. However, relations with other NATO forces and the Government of Afghanistan were damaged. D was aged 46 and born in Iran. In 1986 he became a British citizen and held joint UK and Iranian nationality. His conduct to start with was satisfactory but there was a decline in his discipline. He became dissatisfied with his rank. Held. There was the potential for very serious damage to the safety and operations of the UK and its forces. The gravest part was the fact that it occurred while he was in a war zone. Held. The deterrent element was reflected in the **10-year** sentence. Old case: *R v Smith* 1996 1 Cr App R (S) 202 (**20 years**)

300.4   *Journalists, Handing material to*

R v Shayler 2002 The Times News 6/11/02 D, an ex-Security Service officer, was convicted of three counts under Official Secrets Act 1989 s 1 and 4. He handed documents to *The Mail* and 29 were returned. Most of them related to security and intelligence matters and were classified from 'Classified' up to and including 'Top Secret'. They related to the interception of communications. He left the country, and articles based on the papers were published. Attempts to extradite him from France failed. Sentencing remarks: Your blinkered arrogance has led you to the dock. I accept your motivation was to expose what you thought was wrong, not a desire for money or as a ploy to begin a new career as a journalist. You lack any real insight into what you were doing or any intelligent foresight into its consequences. I was minded to send you to prison for 18 months but I take into account the 3½ months you spent in a French prison.
Note: Treat news reports with care. Where possible the facts were taken from *R v Shayler* 2001 1 WLR 2206, the House of Lords case on a preliminary matter. Ed.

300.5   *Selling defence secrets, Unsuccessful*

R v Bravo 2002 The Times News and The Daily Telegraph News 2/2/00 and Internet sites D pleaded to five counts under the Official Secrets Act (presumably including Official Secrets Act 1911 s 1) and five theft counts. He asked for two secrets counts to be taken into consideration. He was a security guard for a private firm at British Aerospace and obtained documents from unlocked security cabinets while on night patrols. He tried to sell the documents, which contained British and NATO secrets. The documents related to defence systems for Harrier jump jets to stop radar locking onto them, electronic decoy systems for warships and electronic warfare. The documents had a colour-coding system, indicating that the documents could threaten life and cause serious damage to operational effectiveness etc. He telephoned the Russian Embassy but only reached an answerphone. He therefore posted the documents with his pager number. When the documents were found to be missing, he was suspected. His fingerprints were found at the scene. He was followed. Shortly after the theft, an MI5 agent contacted him and arranged a meeting. Bravo said that he had more documents. He was asked what he wanted and he said, "Money, as much as I can get". He was arrested, and 200 pages of defence secrets were found in the carriers of his motorbike. There was no evidence that national or allied secrets were prejudiced. Had he succeeded, those interests would have been substantially prejudiced. He considered that he was in a dead-end job and wanted money to go to Spain. He was aged 30 and a British national of Spanish descent with financial problems. He was described as a loner and a typical opportunist spy. He claimed that he had not appreciated the seriousness of what he had done. Sentencing remarks: Although I accept you were motivated by financial gain, a lengthy jail term was necessary to deter others. Anyone who has put at risk his country's security must receive long sentences. **11 years**.

R v Parr 2003 The Times News and The Daily Telegraph News 30/11/02, The Daily Telegraph News and The Guardian News 5/4/03 and Internet sites CCC The Recorder of London D pleaded to two counts under Official Secrets Act 1911 s 1 and seven counts under Theft Act 1968. He handed over 56 floppy disks and 14 sets of documents relating

to seven sensitive defence projects to someone who he thought was from the Russian Embassy. They included the Stealth cruise-missile system and the Storm Shadow system. In fact, he had been dealing with an MI5 officer from the start. He thought that he would receive £25,000 in the first stage of an espionage operation which would net him £130,000. He was arrested. D had worked at BAE Systems Avionics for 15 years, where he was a test co-ordinator in charge of a department making circuit boards for key weapon systems. It was the same place where Raphael Bravo (see above) worked. He was aged 46 and a former soldier. His sole motive was money. None of the systems was compromised. He was of good character and claimed that he was worried about being made redundant. Sentencing remarks: A substantial sentence was needed to reflect public abhorrence and to deter others. **10 years**.
Note: Treat news reports with care. Ed.

301 OPIUM
See also the **DEFENDANT** *Drug users* paras at **240.21** and the **IMPORTATION OF DRUGS (CLASS A, B AND C), POSSESSION OF DRUGS, PRODUCTION OF DRUGS** and **SUPPLY OF DRUGS** chapters.

301.1 *General characteristics and the proper approach*
R v Mashaollahi 2001 1 Cr App R (S) 96 (p 330) Opium is most often imported from traditional opium-growing countries in small quantities for personal use. It is not commonly traded on the street, and there is no evidence that its use is widespread or that it is likely to increase significantly. The current classification of opium as a class A drug is on the premise that it is to be regarded as being every bit as harmful as other class A drugs. Weight for weight, where street value is concerned, heroin is considered to be approximately eight times more valuable than opium. On this basis, a consignment of 40 kilos of opium at 100% purity would be equivalent in value to 5 kilos of heroin at 100% purity, importation of which, under the current sentencing guidelines, attracts a sentence of 14 years and upwards on a contested case. We understand that the ratio to apply to convert opium to morphine or heroin would be 10:1, i.e. 10 kilos of opium would be needed to produce 1 kilo of morphine or heroin, assuming average levels of purity. In practice, it is virtually impossible to buy heroin or cocaine of 100% purity on the street. They are invariably cut or otherwise adulterated by the admixture of some harmless substance. The extent of criminality depends on the extent of the drug itself and not of the harmless substance. But with opium the position is different. It is a crude mixture of many different chemicals contained in the juice of the seed capsule of the opium poppy, *papaver somniferum.* Incisions are made in the capsule from which the latex oozes out and which, when collected and allowed to dry in the air, forms a dark sticky mass known as raw opium. For non-medical purposes, such as either smoking or eating the substance, the raw opium is boiled in water, strained to remove insoluble materials and then evaporated to form a sticky paste known as prepared opium. The significant feature is that it is still the natural derivative of the plant and, save exceptionally, it is not adulterated by the addition of any further substances. It was pointed out to us that the morphine constituent of opium tended to show a considerable variation. However, since we are dealing with the composite product of the plant, we think that any enquiry as to the percentage of one particular constituent, even though it is by itself a class A drug, would introduce a needless complication to the sentencing process.

302 PASSPORT/ID DOCUMENT OFFENCES
302.1
1) Identity Documents Act 2010
  s 4 (possession of false identity documents etc. with improper intention)
  s 5 (possession etc. of apparatus designed etc. for making false identity documents)
  Modes of trial Sections 4 and 5 are indictable only
  Maximum sentences For both offences 10 years

2) Identity Documents Act 2010 s 6 (possession of false identity documents etc. without reasonable excuse)
Mode of trial Triable either way
Maximum sentence Indictment two years. Summary 6 months and/or a £5,000 fine for offences committed before 12 March 2015 and an unlimited fine thereafter.[782] There are maximum fines for those aged under 18, see **14.38** in Volume 1.
Where the offence is primarily the possession of the documents, whether as simple possession for use in obtaining work or misleading immigration officials etc., the cases are listed in this chapter.
Where the offence is identity fraud, the cases are listed in the FRAUD AND FINANCIAL SERVICES OFFENCES *Identity fraud* paras at **265.37**.
See also the BIGAMY/MARRIAGE OFFENCES *Immigration controls, To evade* para at **216.3** and the IMMIGRATION OFFENCES chapter.

302.2   *Judicial guidance*

R v Takyi 1998 1 Cr App R (S) 372 The integrity of the passport system is of such public importance that, other than in unusual circumstances, custodial sentences will follow convictions for the improper use of a passport. The length of the sentence will vary infinitely with the facts of the case.
Note: This is an old case. However, it is in line with current sentencing policy. Ed.
R v De Oliveira 2005 EWCA Crim 3187, 2006 2 Cr App R (S) 17 (p 115) It is necessary to distinguish between: a) using a passport with the intention of inducing someone to accept it as genuine (Forgery and Counterfeiting Act 1981 s 3), b) having a passport intending to induce someone to accept it (F&CA 1981 s 5(1)), and c) having a passport known to be false (F&CA 1981 s 5(2)). The maximum sentence for a) and b) is 10 years. The maximum for c) is 2 years. *R v Kolawole* 2004 EWCA Crim 3047, 2005 2 Cr App R (S) 14 (p 71) was principally concerned with a) and b).
R v Juma 2007 EWCA Crim 936, 2008 1 Cr App R (S) 5 (p 23) The defendant pleaded guilty to possession of a false identity document with intent. Held. *R v Kolawole* 2004 EWCA Crim 3047, 2005 2 Cr App R (S) 14 (p 71) suggested that penalties apply to cases under Identity Cards Act 2006 s 25. The two offences have the same maximum.
See also the judicial guidance for *False passport/ID document, Using or possessing* at **302.5** and the judicial guidance for *Producing false passports/ID documents, Being involved in* at **302.8**.

302.3   *Disparity with Ministry of Justice return scheme for offenders*[783]

R v Cshako 2011 EWCA Crim 1449, 2012 1 Cr App R (S) 39 (p 231) D pleaded to possession of false identity documents with intent. A French police officer discovered that D had a false passport whilst at St Pancras International station. The issue was whether the existence of a pilot scheme in certain areas, which gave offenders the opportunity to avoid prosecution if they accepted a simple caution and agreed to immediate deportation, should cause the Court to reduce a sentence on the basis of a perceived injustice. Held. It would be totally wrong for this Court to intervene by altering a sentence which was, on the face of it, neither manifestly excessive nor wrong in principle. Such a course would be entirely [outside] the function and duty of this Court. There was no disparity with those who were subject to the scheme.

302.4   *Driving licences, False*

R v Hoxha 2012 EWCA Crim 1765 D was convicted of possessing a false identity document. He was stopped by police while driving his car. He produced a false Albanian driving licence. In fact he had not passed a test, had no insurance but had been driving most days. He had sought work as a driver but was informed that he would need a UK driving licence. He had obtained a UK provisional licence, but still had no right to drive.

---

[782] Legal Aid, Sentencing and Punishment of Offenders Act 2012 s 85(1) and (4) and Legal Aid, Sentencing and Punishment of Offenders Act 2012 (Commencement No 11) Order 2015 2015/504
[783] This scheme is now administered by the Home Office.

D, aged 33, was an Albanian national with indefinite leave to remain. He was not of good character. He had a conviction for a forgery of a different kind. Held. He had a good, respectable job. D had shown some willingness to comply with English rules when he applied for a UK driving licence. There is nothing wrong in principle with a short custodial sentence. **4 months** not 8.

302.5   *False passport/ID document, Using or possessing   Judicial guidance*
R v Singh 1999 1 Cr App R (S) 490 There have been a number of inconsistent cases in offences involving false passports. The use of false passports appears to be on the increase. A passport is an important document that confers rights upon the lawful holder. It is, in our judgment, necessary that the integrity of passports should be maintained. It follows that to use a false passport is a serious offence, whatever the precise nature of the offence. Good character and personal circumstances are of very limited value. Sentences should generally be on a deterrent basis, for the reasons given in *R v Osman* 1999 1 Cr App R (S) 230. Extensive or sophisticated alteration of a passport will always be an aggravating feature. Cases involving the use of false passports will almost always merit a significant period of custody. This will usually be within the range of **12-18 months** (previously 6-9 months), even on a guilty plea by a person of good character.
Note: This extract has been updated by *R v Kolawole* 2004 EWCA Crim 3047, 2005 2 Cr App R (S) 14 (p 71), which increased the penalties. Ed.
R v De Oliveira 2005 EWCA Crim 3187, 2006 2 Cr App R (S) 17 (p 115) It is necessary to distinguish between: a) using a passport with the intention of inducing someone to accept it as genuine (Forgery and Counterfeiting Act 1981 s 3), b) having a passport intending to induce someone to accept it (FCA 1981 s 5(1)), and c) having a passport known to be false (FCA 1981 s 5(2)). The maximum sentence for a) and b) is 10 years. The maximum for c) is 2 years. *R v Kolawole* 2004 EWCA Crim 3047, 2005 2 Cr App R (S) 14 (p 71) was principally concerned with a) and b).
R v Adebayo 2007 EWCA Crim 878, 2008 1 Cr App R (S) 7 (p 30) D pleaded to two counts of possession of an ID document with intent to deceive. One was a passport. It is difficult to see a distinction between using a false passport to enter the country and using one to remain here.
R v Bogoslov 2008 EWCA Crim 676 Possession of a false passport is a serious offence and will almost certainly lead to immediate imprisonment.
R v Ovieriakhi 2009 EWCA Crim 452, 2 Cr App R (S) 91 (p 607) LCJ At one end of the scale is the use or possession for use of false passports for the purpose of evading, or enabling others to evade, the controls on entry into the United Kingdom. Such evasion may at worst be for terrorist or other malign purposes, or at least for the purpose of securing the entry of someone into the United Kingdom which would otherwise be forbidden. The documents may be possessed by those whose business it is to help others to circumvent the rules on entry. At the other end of the scale is the use by someone who is lawfully in the United Kingdom of a document other than a passport for the purpose of obtaining employment or a bank account. Wherever the case is on the spectrum, a custodial sentence is likely, save in exceptional circumstances, for the reasons stated in *R v Carneiro* 2007 EWCA Crim 2170, 2008 1 Cr App R (S) 95 (p 571). In cases in which a false passport is to be used for the purpose of securing entry into the United Kingdom, the guidance contained in *R v Kolawole* 2004 EWCA Crim 3047, 2005 2 Cr App R (S) 14 (p 71) applies. Where, however, a false passport is used to obtain work or a bank account, its use does not enable the offender to obtain entry to the United Kingdom, and for that reason it may properly be treated less severely than the use of a passport which does, or may, have that effect. What the use of a passport to obtain work does, however, do is to facilitate the offender remaining in the United Kingdom in breach of immigration controls. For that reason a custodial sentence is usually required.

But it can justifiably be less, particularly if the offender is of good character and has done no more than use or try to use it to seek employment in order to maintain himself or herself, or his or her family.

See also the general *Judicial guidance* para at **20.2** in Volume 1.

See also the FRAUD AND FINANCIAL SERVICES OFFENCES *Identity frauds Guidelines* paras at **265.37**.

302.6   *False passport/ID documents, Using or possessing*   More serious than using it to obtain employment etc.

R v Farah 2012 EWCA Crim 1597 D pleaded to possession of an identity document with improper intention. He had booked two flights from Heathrow, in his name and the name of his brother. He used a false Portuguese passport he had found in his taxi, affixed a photograph of his brother to it and attempted to board the plane. He had with him his legitimate UK passport. His intention was to travel to Tanzania, using the false passport in order to validate it. He would then allow his brother to travel from Somalia to the UK on the false passport. D would then use his legitimate passport in order to return to the UK. D, aged 31 at appeal, was of good character. Held. The offence demonstrated an element of planning to circumvent the UK immigration laws. There is a need to impose deterrent sentences for this offence. The facts of the case justify a departure from the range indicated in *R v Kolawole* 2004 EWCA Crim 3047, 2005 2 Cr App R (S) 14 (p 71). **20 months** was entirely appropriate.

R v Abokede 2013 EWCA Crim 947 D pleaded to using a false instrument (×3). In 2004, she applied for assistance as a homeless person. She provided supporting documentation in the form of her genuine Nigerian passport, furnished with a false stamp indicating that she had leave to remain in the UK. There was a false birth certificate contending that she had a son and a false child benefit letter confirming she was in receipt of child benefit. Those documents were prerequisites to qualifying for council accommodation, which she subsequently obtained. The offences were discovered in 2012 after an audit. D admitted the wrongdoing in interview. She had come to the UK legitimately in 2000 and said she had fled an abusive family situation in Nigeria. She then overstayed. D had received the false documents from a 'fixer'. D, aged 45, had no convictions and was the sole carer for a five-year-old girl. After having obtained the accommodation, D proceeded to work in numerous jobs and did not claim benefits. Held. The Judge ought to have ordered a pre-sentence report. The young child was to be cared for by relatives and so this was not a case where young children were being deprived of a carer. It was accepted that the custody threshold was passed but anything less than immediate custody could not be justified. **4 months** not 6 would take a fuller account of her personal circumstances.

R v Marques 2014 EWCA Crim 1078 D pleaded (25% credit) to possession of an article designed for the making of false identity documents. Police officers stopped his vehicle during a routine traffic enquiry. On searching the vehicle they found six blank Italian passport covers in mint condition secreted beneath the rubber mat of the driver's footwell. The passport covers were counterfeit and were designed to enable a false Italian passport to be created when the identity and other pages were stitched into the cover. D said he had found them on the street earlier and had retained them. He eventually accepted that he knew the documents were fraudulent but denied any intention to use them personally or on another's behalf. D was aged 46 at appeal and a Portuguese national resident in London. Held. The Judge correctly distinguished this case from that of *R v Ovieriakhi* 2009 EWCA Crim 452, 2 Cr App R (S) 91 (p 607). He did not need the passports to work in the UK as he was an EU citizen. He did not possess one false document but six covers from which a quantity of passports could be produced. Such activity undermines the ability to regulate immigration control. The appropriate starting point was around 18 months, not 2 years (the maximum). With credit for the plea, **12 months** not 18 months.

R v Lasgaa 2014 EWCA Crim 1822 D pleaded (full credit) to having an identification document with improper intention. D was an Algerian who had overstayed on a visitor's visa which expired in 2008. D was stopped at the Channel Tunnel whilst on a coach to Germany. He had on him a Belgian ID document and a bank card, both in the same false name. His explanation for the bank card was that he had used the account of an Algerian to operate as self-employed. He had purchased the ID document off the Internet to visit a German woman he met online and whom he may have been intending to marry to obtain legitimate EU immigration status. D was of good character. The Judge empha-sised the importance of preserving the integrity of the UK's borders. Held. The Judge was right to consider the time D had been an overstayer. D had been unlawfully living and working in the UK for over five years and, although caught leaving the UK, his intention was to return. D had a counterfeit document which would have been used to enable him to continue his long-assumed false identity. The Judge must have started at 27 months. He was entitled to do so. **18 months** was not excessive.

See also: *R v Osagie* 2010 EWCA Crim 2208 (D pleaded to possession of a false identity document with intent and possession of a false identity document. False passports possessed by a Nigerian-born woman attempting to stay in the UK. 6 months on each count consecutive, so **12 months**.)

R v Akinpelu 2010 EWCA Crim 2754 (Pleas to fraud for obtaining employment with false birth certificate and driving licence and possessing a false driving licence with intent. Used to obtain work. **6 months** not 12.)

R v Mtandagai 2013 EWCA Crim 1093 (Plea to possession of an ID document. Zimbabwean national. Came to UK in 2002. Granted leave to remain on a student visa in 2004. Unsuccessfully claimed asylum. In 2007 she obtained a false South African passport, procured by her ex-partner. The purpose was to obtain employment to support her children. Aged 46. Not previously been before the courts. **6 months** not 12.)

Old cases: *R v Wasik* 2010 EWCA Crim 1427 (**12 months**) Rest best ignored. Ed.

302.7   *False passports/ID documents, Using or possessing   To obtain employment/ accommodation etc.*

R v Rajeswaran 2011 EWCA Crim 789 D pleaded to possession of a false identity document with intent. He attended a job centre and applied for an NI number. He produced a Bulgarian passport bearing his photograph but a false name and date of birth. He was also found to be in possession of a Bulgarian driving licence in the same name. D entered the UK in 2008 using his Sri Lankan passport. His application for asylum and subsequent appeal were refused. D, aged 30, had no convictions in the UK. Held. This case bears similarities to *R v Ovieriakhi* 2009, but D had also been through the asylum appeal system and had a false driving licence. Those factors were not present in *R v Ovieriakhi*. **8 months** not 12.

R v Abokede 2013 EWCA Crim 947 D pleaded to using a false instrument (×3). In 2004, she applied for assistance as a homeless person. She provided supporting documentation in the form of her genuine Nigerian passport, furnished with a false stamp indicating that she had leave to remain in the UK. There was a false birth certificate contending that she had a son and a false child benefit letter confirming she was in receipt of child benefit. Those documents were prerequisites to qualifying for council accommodation, which she subsequently obtained. The offences were discovered in 2012 after an audit. D admitted the wrongdoing in interview. She had come to the UK legitimately in 2000 and said she had fled an abusive family situation in Nigeria. She then overstayed. D had received the false documents from a 'fixer'. D, aged 45, had no convictions and was the sole carer for a five-year-old girl. After having obtained the accommodation, D proceeded to work in numerous jobs and did not claim benefits. Held. The Judge ought to have ordered a pre-sentence report. The young child was to be cared for by relatives and so this was not a case where young children were being deprived of a carer. It was accepted that the custody threshold was passed but anything less than immediate custody could not be justified. **4 months** not 6 would take a fuller account of her personal circumstances.

R v Patel 2014 EWCA Crim 647 D pleaded to possession of a false passport (section 4). He bought it for £500 and tried to use it to open a bank account. He needed to use a passport because he did not have 'immigration status'. D was trying to support his late brother's family in India and there was no criminal purpose. He was aged 45 and of good character. D said he was under pressure from his employer who refused to pay him unless he opened an account. **6 months** not 12.

R v Ndjanga 2015 EWCA Crim 2020 D pleaded to possession of a false identity document, (section 4(1)(a)). In 2000, D arrived at Heathrow and sought to board a fight to Canada. His Cameroon passport was found to have a false Canadian entry visa on it. D then claimed asylum, which was refused. D was sentenced on the basis that he was granted bail from a detention centre and then absconded. In 2002, he began work in a gym and used a forged French passport to obtain and retain the employment. In 2015, in an audit, the passport was found to be false. D was now aged 41, was legally entitled to work in the UK and had a British wife who was pregnant. He had no convictions or cautions. Held. This case was entirely on all fours with the case of *R v Ovieriakhi* 2009 EWCA Crim 452, 2 Cr App R (S) 91 (p 607). He was a hard-working family man. **6 months** not 12.

See also: *R v Akudo* 2010 EWCA Crim 44 (Plea. **9 months**.)

R v Kanthasamy 2010 EWCA Crim 425 (Plea. Asylum seeker using forged passport to open bank account. **6 months** not 12.)

R v Abedote 2010 EWCA Crim 3264 (Plea. Defendant's photograph had been put into a genuine passport. Unlawfully entered UK. Good character. In employment. **8 months** not 12.)

Old cases: Best ignored. Ed.

Passports issued wrongly by civil servants see the CORRUPTION/MISFEASANCE IN PUBLIC OFFICE *Public servants* para at **228.10**.

302.8   Producing false passports/ID documents, Being involved in   Judicial guidance

R v Mussa 2012 EWCA Crim 693, 2 Cr App R (S) 99 (p 585) D was near the top in managing two sophisticated passport and ID document factories. Held. The key considerations in sentencing are: a) the role of the offender in the operation, b) its scale and the sophistication of its products, c) the type of false documents produced, d) the damage caused by the distribution of the documents, and e) the income generated.

See also: *R v Velev* 2008 EWCA Crim 2162 (Very sophisticated. Value of illegal goods found £1.5m. Maximum sentence after a trial is **10 years**. Organisers after a trial can expect 10 years. Lieutenants in the order of **6½ years**.)

See also the general *Judicial guidance* para at **20.2** in Volume 1.

302.9   Producing false passports/ID documents, Being involved in   Cases

R v Santos 2010 EWCA Crim 321 D pleaded to two counts of possessing a false identity document with intent, and was convicted of possessing apparatus for making the same and a further count of possessing a false identity document with intent. A search of D's home address revealed Portuguese, Italian and Spanish ID documents, embossing presses, ink stamps, a card printer and a large quantity of passport photographs, passport covers, laminated paper, and material for the creation of false documents. D, aged 24, lied in interview and had no convictions. D was sentenced on the basis he was a custodian. Held. The potential for undermining the immigration and employment laws was enormous. Custodians play a very prominent role and a prominent link in these operations. **5 years** in all was at the top end.

R v Toska 2010 EWCA Crim 2187 D pleaded to possessing apparatus designed for making false identity documents with intent, possessing a false identity document with intent and making articles for sale in breach of copyright. Police officers executed a search warrant at D's address and found a piece of equipment designed to make ID cards with a laminator attached. Computers, ID cards and driving licences were also found. Officers found a driving licence template with photographs awaiting insertion, Home Office immigration nationalisation details, artwork designed for a Belgian identity card, Inland Revenue registration details and a blank birth certificate. Officers also found discs containing material relating to satellite navigation, which D intended to resell. D's basis of plea included the contentions that he did not supply any false identity cards and that he had not received any money for them. The Judge stated that D had done it for money but accepted that D was not involved in a major or significant supply of fake identity cards. An immediate custodial sentence was appropriate. Held. The sentence was unnecessarily high bearing in mind that there was no evidence that the false documents had entered the public domain, whatever D's future intentions were. **3½ years** not 4½.

See also: *R v Mussa* 2012 EWCA Crim 693, 2 Cr App R (S) 99 (p 585) (Plea. Two sophisticated passport and ID document factories. Good-quality forgeries. Documents to avoid driving penalties and enable false bank accounts to be opened. Not far from top of organisation. **6½ years** upheld.)

Old cases: Best ignored. Ed.

302.10   *Solicitor falsely certifying application for passport*

R v Manifold 2011 EWCA Crim 1271 D was convicted of 14 counts concerned with the false countersigning of fraudulent passport applications. He signed between 78 and 150 applications. There was no evidence that he stood to gain financially or otherwise. He was a solicitor who was held in great esteem. D was aged 49 at the appeal. Held. The fact that he was a solicitor is of great significance. It might not have any greater effect on the success or otherwise of the passport application, but for a solicitor to be prepared to be dishonest is a matter of great consequence. With the delay and his good character, **3 years** not 4½.

R v Andrews 2012 EWCA Crim 3001, 2013 2 Cr App R (S) 40 (p 274) D pleaded to making an untrue statement for the purposes of obtaining a passport. On two occasions in 2004, passport applications were made in the names of SH and DH. The photographs supplied with the applications were of LF and CT. LF was awaiting trial (and subsequently failed to attend). CT was given community release from prison whilst serving sentences for attempted robbery and firearm offences. He failed to return to prison. D also countersigned a passport photograph for LF, who failed to answer bail for a Crown Court trial. D's basis of plea was that his role was merely to be a counter-signatory and that he played no part in the planning of the exercise. He claimed he acted under pressure falling short of duress. D was aged 63 at appeal and of previous good character. He had high blood pressure and was taking medication for cardiac problems. Held. It was argued that the Judge, in passing two 16-month sentences, consecutive, sought to circumvent what she perceived to be the low maximum sentence for the offence (2 years). That criticism was not founded. Full account was taken by the Judge of D's good character, his health problems and the basis of plea. There was nothing wrong with the individual length of the sentences on each count, which adequately reflected the seriousness of the offences. However, a shorter overall term than the one imposed by the Judge would suffice. **16 months** on each count, **concurrent**, not consecutive.

302.11   *Victims of trafficking   Judicial guidance*

R v O 2008 EWCA Crim 2835 D pleaded to an offence of possessing a false identity card with intent. She attempted to leave France by using a Spanish identity card and was arrested at Dover. She finally admitted the card was not hers and explained that she had lost her passport and wanted to visit her uncle in France. She gave her date of birth as 10 December 1985. Over the following months, she informed her advisers that her correct date of birth was 10 December 1991, making her aged 16, although she claimed she was 17. She stated that she had fled Nigeria because of threats to her life as a result of her refusal to enter into an arranged marriage to a 63-year-old man. Her travel to the UK was to be repaid through work involving prostitution. She had no family in the UK. The Crown did not oppose the appeal. Held. No steps were taken by the defence to investigate the history. No consideration was given by the defence as to whether she might have a defence of duress. The possibility that she might have been trafficked was ignored. There is nothing in the transcript to suggest that any thought had been given to the state's duty to protect her as a young victim, under the Council of Europe's Convention on Action against Trafficking in Human Beings 197/1975. Nobody considered that if she was aged 17 or less, she should not have been in the Crown Court at all. Counsel for the defence thought it right to refer to 'an inevitable prison sentence'. The Judge passed what she described as an 'inevitable prison sentence' of 8 months and for good measure had no report. If the appellant was aged 17 or less, a sentence of imprisonment as such was unlawful. This appeal against conviction must obviously be allowed.

Note: On 17 December 2008 the Government signed the Council of Europe Treaty 2005. The treaty is designed to prevent trafficking and protect and assist victims of trafficking. In *R v LM and Others* 2010 EWCA Crim 2327 the Court of Appeal explained the obligations under the treaty, the defences of duress, the opportunity to stay proceedings as an abuse and the duties of the prosecution in such cases. In *R v LM* 2010, women who initially were trafficked and then went on to control prostitutes had their convictions quashed. The need for solicitors to refer the trafficked victims to the appropriate agencies was stressed. For the transcript of *R v O* 2008, *R v LM* 2010, the CPS code, the Law Society practice note, *Rantsev v Cyprus and Russia* 2010 No 25965/04 First Section and the 2005 treaty, see www.banksr.com Other Matters Other Documents tab Ed.

For more detail see the **PROSTITUTION OFFENCES** *Trafficking* paras at **311.18** and **311.22**.

303 PATIENTS, ILL-TREATING ETC.

303.1

Mental Health Act 1983 s 127 (ill-treatment or neglect of mental patients)

Mental Capacity Act 2005 s 44 (ill-treatment or neglect of donee of lasting power of attorney etc. in care)

Criminal Justice and Courts Act 2015 s 20 (ill-treatment or wilful neglect: care worker)

Criminal Justice and Courts Act 2015 s 21 (ill-treatment or wilful neglect: care provider)

Sections 20-21 in force 13 April 2015.[784]

Modes of trial All offences are triable either way.

Maximum sentences On indictment section 127, 2 years, and sections 20 and 44, 5 years. Summary 6 months and/or a £5,000 fine for offences committed before 12 March 2015 and an unlimited fine thereafter.[785] There are maximum fines for those aged under 18, see **14.38** in Volume 1. For section 21 offences, the maximum on indictment and summarily is an unlimited fine, Criminal Justice and Courts Act 2015 s 23(1).

Sexual Harm Prevention Orders For section 127 offences, there is a discretionary power to make this order when it is necessary to protect the public from sexual harm.[786]

Children and vulnerable adults: barred lists For section 127 and section 44 offences, where the defendant is aged 18 or over he or she is automatically barred from engaging

---

[784] Criminal Justice and Courts Act 2015 (Commencement No 1, Saving and Transitional Provisions) Order 2015 2015/778 para 3 and Sch 1 para 16-17 and 19

[785] Legal Aid, Sentencing and Punishment of Offenders Act 2012 s 85(1) and (4) and Legal Aid, Sentencing and Punishment of Offenders Act 2012 (Commencement No 11) Order 2015 2015/504

[786] Sexual Offences Act 2003 s 103A as inserted by Anti-social Behaviour, Crime and Policing Act 2014 Sch 5 para 2 and Sexual Offences Act 2003 Sch 5

in regulated activity with children and vulnerable adults.[787] The judge must tell the defendant that the Disclosure and Barring Service will include him or her in the barred lists.[788] The defendant may ask the Authority to remove him or her from the lists.

303.2   Elderly patients   Judicial guidance

R v Strong 2014 EWCA Crim 2744 D pleaded to three section 44 offences. Held. These were mean, cruel and exploitative offences of very vulnerable people. The *Assaults on Children and Cruelty to a Child Guideline 2008* was relevant as there were similarities with this offence. A substantial sentence of detention was required and it is also necessary for an element of deterrence to be achieved by the sentence. Those who entrust their relatives to professional carers are entitled to know that the courts will do their utmost to protect them. For more detail, see **303.3**.

303.3   Elderly patients   Cases

R v Heaney 2011 EWCA Crim 2682 D was convicted of ill-treatment of a person who lacks mental capacity (×2). She was a senior carer in a care home. The residents were elderly and vulnerable people. V1 was in his eighties. He had dementia and could become violent. D was seen putting seven or eight spoonfuls of sugar into V1's tea, and subsequently poured a quantity of vinegar into his tea. V2 was in her nineties and also had dementia. She was sitting in her wheelchair when D came up from behind her and slapped her across the back of the head. When asked why she had done so, D laughed and walked off. D, aged 38, maintained her innocence at the appeal. She had no convictions. Held. The gravamen of these offences was in the thoughtless and heartless unkindness committed in serious breach of trust. The consequences for D were grave. They were very short incidents. She has lost her livelihood and has no realistic prospect of working in her chosen field again, and rightly so. **3 months and 6 months concurrent,** not consecutive.

R v Fitzpatrick 2013 EWCA Crim 730 D was convicted of battery,[789] having been acquitted of ill-treatment of a person lacking capacity. She was employed as a care assistant and was required to visit clients and assist in all aspects of their care. V, an 88-year-old woman, found it very difficult to swallow and was bedridden. She needed visits from two carers four times a day to administer her medication and feed and bathe her. V lacked capacity to run her own affairs and had a very poor short-term memory. She would therefore have been unable to complain about any incident of mistreatment. When D was trying to give V her medication, she shouted at V in an aggressive tone.[790] V spat the medication out and it went down D's front. V shouted, "You're trying to kill me", at which point D swung her arm and struck V with a backhand across the face. D became aware that her co-worker was watching and said, "Oh I've upset you, I'm sorry darling". The co-worker reported the incident. There was no evidence of injury arising out of the assault. D, aged 46 at appeal, had no convictions. She had been a carer for ten years and had obtained qualifications for that occupation. She had a lost a son aged 7 and suffered depression and anxiety. Held. Anyone with these responsibilities, in great trust, and who strikes a patient clearly carries the burden of higher culpability. There was greater harm present. The Judge was correct to conclude that this offence passed the custody threshold because of the level of trust involved. The degree of trust and reliance in circumstances like this and the consequent important breach of trust mean that it will be a rare case where a suspension of sentence, for a real blow, will be justified. **3 months** not 6 (which was the maximum).

R v Strong 2014 EWCA Crim 2744 D pleaded to three section 44 offences. She was a very junior employee in a care home which specialised in dementia. Older and more

---

[787] Safeguarding Vulnerable Groups Act 2006 s 2 and Sch 3 and Safeguarding Vulnerable Groups Act 2006 (Prescribed Criteria and Miscellaneous Provisions) Regulations 2009 2009/37 reg 4 and 6 and Sch para 2 and 4

[788] Safeguarding Vulnerable Groups Act 2006 s 2 and Sch 3 para 25

[789] The report says assault by beating and Criminal Justice Act 1988 s 39 (which is battery), so it is assumed it was battery.

[790] The report states D shouted at Mr Cole but as there is no other mention of Mr Cole in the judgment it is assumed it is a typo for Mrs Cole, V. Ed.

experienced staff conducted a campaign of humiliation, bullying and some violence against elderly patients. D fell under their influence and took photographs of the three incidents of abuse. In the first incident, B pulled down a 96-year-old's underwear and looked up her skirt and at her vagina. D photographed it and sent it to B saying, 'I don't really like…the dirty bitch'. The second incident involved an 84-year old woman, who B poked repeatedly in the face. D made a video clip and sent it with a message saying that was funny. In the third incident, D photographed a third victim on the floor and sent it to B. B[791] said in a text to another care worker about the victim being a stupid bitch etc. D was aged 20 and of good character. She had four references. The pre-sentence report said D wanted to ingratiate herself with B and the other care worker. She expressed remorse. Held. These were mean, cruel and exploitative offences of very vulnerable people. A substantial sentence of detention was required and it is also necessary for an element of deterrence to be achieved by the sentence. The fact that D had left the area because of the hostility the case had generated was a relevant feature of some weight. Because of the limited role of D, we start at 9 months, so with plea **6 months** not 12.

See also: *R v Kenyon* 2013 EWCA Crim 2123, 2014 1 Cr App R (S) 71 (p 455) (Convicted of eight section 44 offences. Care assistant for elderly. Angry not promoted so 'sabotaged her shift'. At end of shift residents not fed. Seven offences related to women wet with urine and some with faeces. Residents distressed. **8 months** not excessive.)

304 PENSION OFFENCES

304.1
Various offences including many under Pensions Act 1995.

304.2 *Failing to pay money into employees' company fund*
R v Dixon 2000 2 Cr App R (S) p 7 D pleaded at the Magistrates' Court to nine offences contrary to Pensions Act 1995 s 49(8) and 115(1). He was company secretary and finance director of a ceramics company and trustee of the occupational pension scheme, which involved payment of part of the 60 employees' pay to the managers of the scheme. Six of the charges related to payments of about £80,000 in total from the company to the scheme, all of which were made but were 10 to 53 days late. The last three charges related to payment of about £40,000 due but not made. This sum will be replaced from public funds with the possibility of lost interest to the fund as a result. A cheque was issued when there appeared to be sufficient overdrawing facilities but the bank did not honour it, and soon afterwards the company went into receivership at the instigation of the bank. During the period of the offences the bank was reducing the overdraft facilities month by month from £1.5m. D was unaware that the delay of payments was a criminal offence. A letter from the pension adviser said that payments should be made to avoid late-payment fees but said nothing about it being a criminal offence. When D discovered that it was an offence, he wrote to the regulatory authority and explained the position. When interviewed he candidly accepted his failure and explained the reasons for it. He delayed payment in an attempt to preserve jobs when the company was beset with debts. He was of good character. A £2,500 penalty had already been paid. Held. The offences have only recently been introduced and were being replaced with one which requires fraudulent evasion of payment. The desire to keep the company going rather than a selfish motive and his frankness with the authority were significant mitigation. 3 years 6 months' custody was wrong and it should have been a financial penalty. £250 fine for the first six charges and £500 for the three others, making **£3,000** fine in total.

Note: This is an old case, so treat the decision with care. Ed.

See also the **FRAUD AND FINANCIAL SERVICES OFFENCES** chapter.

PERSISTENT OFFENDERS see the **Persistent offenders** entry in the back index.

---

[791] It might make more sense if the text was sent by D but the judgment says otherwise.

305   PERVERTING THE COURSE OF JUSTICE/CONTEMPT OF COURT/ PERJURY ETC.

305.1

There are four principal offences of criminal conduct in the justice system.

1) **Perverting the course of justice** A common law offence.
   Mode of trial Indictable only
   Maximum sentence There is no maximum provided, so the maximum is life.
2) **Contempt of court**
   a) The Crown Court has an inherent power to deal with contempts of court.[792]
   b) Other courts, Contempt of Court Act 1981 s 12 and 14
   Section 12 is for the Magistrates' Courts and section 14 is all other courts which have power to commit to prison for contempt.
   Where triable Triable at the court where the offence was committed.
   Procedure Trial on indictment is obsolete.[793] A judge/magistrate has a power to find a contempt of court and sentence for it.
   Maximum sentence At the Crown Court 2 years, and at the Magistrates' Court 1 month and/or £2,500 fine.[794]
   c) The High Court has power to deal with contempts committed in:
      i) the Divisional Court,
      ii) criminal proceedings, and
      iii) proceedings in an 'inferior court', see Civil Procedure Rules 1998 1998/3132 Rule 81.12-81.14 (as inserted by Civil Procedure (Amendment No 2) Rules 2012 2012/2208 para 16).
   d) The Supreme Court and Court of Appeal retain their common law power to commit persons for contempt of court.

For contempt of court under a) to d):
The use of this power in the Crown Court and the Magistrates' Court is set out in Criminal Procedure Rules 2015 2015/1490 Rule 48.
Research, engaging in prohibited conduct and disclosing jury's deliberations etc. offences Criminal Justice and Courts Act 2015 s 71-74 create four offences of 'research by jurors', 'sharing research with other jurors', 'engaging in other prohibited conduct' and 'disclosing jury deliberations' by inserting Juries Act 1974 s 20A-20G. The offences are indictable only and carry a 2-year maximum penalty. Prosecutions require the consent of the Attorney-General. There are similar offences for the Court Martial, Criminal Justice and Courts Act 2015 Sch 14. Prosecutions do not require the consent of the Attorney-General except one of them in certain circumstances. In force 13 April 2015.[795]
Detention Contemnors aged 18-20 may be sentenced to detention.[796] There is no power to sentence a contemnor aged under 18 to custody.[797]
Community Orders A probation order may not be made when someone is found guilty of contempt of court.[798] That principle was also considered to apply to Community Rehabilitation Orders, therefore it could be argued that the same principle would apply to community orders.
Contempt of court sentencing powers The order is committal to prison/[place of] detention. A committal is not a 'custodial sentence' for the purposes of Powers of

---

[792] Senior Courts Act 1981 s 45(4), previously called the Supreme Court Act 1981. Where the Divisional Court has jurisdiction, e.g. a breach of a restraint order, the Crown Court has concurrent jurisdiction, *R v M* 2008 EWCA Crim 1901.
[793] *HM Attorney-General v Dallas* 2012 EWHC 156
[794] Contempt of Court Act 1981 s 14(1). The section says the 2-year maximum is for superior courts and the one-month maximum is for inferior courts.
[795] Criminal Justice and Courts Act 2015 (Commencement No 1, Saving and Transitional Provisions) Order 2015 2015/778 para 3 and Sch 1 para 56-59 and 80
[796] Powers of Criminal Courts (Sentencing) Act 2000 s 108
[797] *R v Byas* 1995 16 Cr App R (S) 869
[798] *R v Palmer* 1992 95 Cr App R 170

Criminal Courts (Sentencing) Act 2000, Powers of Criminal Courts (Sentencing) Act 2000 s 76(2). A Suspended Sentence Order only applies to sentences of imprisonment and detention in a Young Offender Institution (see **113.3** in Volume 1) so that order is not available. However, there is power to suspend the committal by virtue of Civil Procedure Rules 1998 1998/3132 Rule 81.29 (as inserted by Civil Procedure (Amendment No 2) Rules 2012 2012/2208). The power permits suspension 'for such period or on such terms and conditions as [the court] may specify'. The note to the Criminal Procedure Rules 2015 2015/1490 Rule 48.3 says: 'The Court of Appeal and the Crown Court have an inherent power to suspend imprisonment for contempt of court on conditions or for a period or for both, by reason of the Senior Courts Act 1981 s 15 and 45'.

Contempt of court sentencing powers Young offenders There is no power to commit offenders aged 10-17 to custody.[799] Offenders aged 17 can be given an Attendance Order.[800] Offenders aged 18-20 are committed [to a place of] detention.[801] This is detention in a Young Offender Institution.

Adjournments There is no power to remand before sentence. However, there is power to order 'immediate temporary detention', Criminal Procedure Rules 2015 2015/1490 Rule 48.7. The use of adjournments to provide time for apologies and reflection is considered very important and the court is required to explain this, as set out in Rule 48.7.

Appeals for contempt of court orders This is at **305.1**.

Release A committal is not a 'custodial sentence' for the purposes of Powers of Criminal Courts (Sentencing) Act 2000, Powers of Criminal Courts (Sentencing) Act 2000 s 76(2). This means there is no power to grant early release on a curfew and tag.

3) **Perjury**
Perjury Act 1911 s 1 (perjury in judicial proceedings)
Mode of trial Indictable only
Maximum sentence 7 years[802]

4) **Intimidation of witnesses**
Criminal Justice and Public Order Act 1994 s 51 (intimidation of witnesses, jurors etc.)
Mode of trial Triable either way
Maximum sentence On indictment 5 years. Summary 6 months and/or a £5,000 fine for offences committed before 12 March 2015 and an unlimited fine thereafter.[803] There are maximum fines for those aged under 18, see **14.38** in Volume 1.

305.2   *Crown Court statistics   England and Wales*
Perjury Aged 21+

Year	Plea	Total sentenced	Type of sentencing %						Average length of custody in months
			Discharge	Fine	Community sentence	Sus-pended sentence	Cus-tody	Other	
2013	G	44	–	2.3	4.5	63.6	27.3	2.3	11
	NG	6	–	–	–	16.7	83.3	–	20

---

[799] Contempt of Court Act 1981 s 14(2A) This section is repealed by Criminal Justice and Immigration Act 2008 Sch 4 para 25. Commencement is awaited.
[800] Powers of Criminal Courts (Sentencing) Act 2000 s 60 and *R v Byas* 1995 16 Cr App R (S) 869.
[801] Powers of Criminal Courts (Sentencing) Act 2000 s 108 The section is repealed by Criminal Justice and Court Services Act 2000 s 75 and Sch 8 when and if that part of the Act is in force. There also appears a power under Powers of Criminal Courts (Sentencing) Act 2000 s 60 to make an Attendance Centre Order. The power is unlikely ever to be used.
[802] Criminal Justice Act 1948 s 1(1)-(2)
[803] Legal Aid, Sentencing and Punishment of Offenders Act 2012 s 85(1) and (4) and Legal Aid, Sentencing and Punishment of Offenders Act 2012 (Commencement No 11) Order 2015 2015/504

Year	Plea	Total sentenced	Type of sentencing %						Average length of custody in months
			Discharge	Fine	Community sentence	Suspended sentence	Custody	Other	
2014	G	20	–	–	15	35	50	–	7.6
	NG	5	–	–	–	40	60	–	Not listed[804]

Perverting the course of justice

Year	Age	Sex	Plea	Total sentenced	Type of sentencing %						Average length of custody in months
					Discharge	Fine	Community sentence	Suspended sentence	Custody	Other	
2013	18-20	n/a	G	91	–	1.1	9.9	37.4	49.5	2.2	7.5
			NG	16	–	–	–	12.5	81.3	6.3	9.4
	21+	n/a	G	925	0.6	0.3	5.4	38.6	54.9	0.1	9.5
			NG	166	–	0.6	1.8	21.1	73.5	3	21.1
2014	18-20	Male	G	61	2	–	18	46	34	–	10.4
			NG	6	–	–	17	17	67	–	28.5
		Female	G	15	–	7	20	40	33	–	8.2
			NG	3	–	–	–	67	33	–	not listed[805]
	21+	Male	G	523	–	1	6	41	52	–	8.6
			NG	72	3	1	1	21	74	–	17.3
		Female	G	216	2	–	11	61	26	–	9.2
			NG	32	3	–	3	34	59	–	20.3

The statistics also list 'Perverting the course of justice triable either way'. As perverting the course of justice is triable only on indictment, it is assumed this data is for contempt of court which is triable when the offence is committed, and witness intimidation, which is triable either way. As the data is not split into a defined offence, it is not listed but it can be found at www.banksr.com Other matters Statistics.

For explanations about the statistics, see page 1-xii. For more statistics and for statistics for male and female defendants etc., see www.banksr.com Other Matters Statistics tab

305.3   *Contempt of court   Practice direction and judicial guidance*
Criminal Practice Directions 2015 EWCA Crim 1567 para IX 62A.3 The court should allow the person a further opportunity to apologise for his or her contempt, and should follow the procedure at [Criminal Procedure Rules] rule 62.8(4). The court should consider whether it is appropriate to release the person or whether it must exercise its powers to fine the person or to commit the person to custody under Contempt of Court Act 1981 s 12(2). In deciding how to deal with the person, the court should have regard to the period for which he or she has been detained, whether the conduct was admitted and the seriousness of the contempt. Any period of committal to custody should be for the shortest period of time commensurate with the interests of preserving good order in the administration of justice.

R v Robinson 2006 EWCA Crim 613, 2 Cr App R (S) 88 (p 587) D pleaded to contempt of court. He gave evidence for the defence and refused in cross-examination to name a drug dealer. Held. Applying *R v Montgomery* 1995 16 Cr App R (S) 274, an immediate

---
[804] Based on too few cases to be meaningful
[805] Based on too few cases to be meaningful

custodial sentence is the only appropriate sentence for interfering with the administration of justice, unless the circumstances are wholly exceptional. The principal matters affecting sentence are the gravity of the offence, the effect on the trial, the reason for failing to give evidence, whether there was impertinent defiance of the Judge and whether a special deterrent is needed peculiar to the case.

305.4   Contempt of court   Wilfully insulting someone/interrupting the proceedings
Criminal Practice Directions 2015 EWCA Crim 1567 para IX 62A.2 In the majority of cases, an apology and a promise as to future conduct should be sufficient for the court to order a person's release. However, there are likely to be certain cases where the nature and seriousness of the misconduct requires the court to consider using its powers, under Contempt of Court Act 1981 s 12(2), either to fine or to order the person's committal to custody.
See also the **Outbursts in court** para at **305.23**.

305.5   Judicial guidance   Perjury
R v Archer 2002 EWCA Crim 1996, 2003 1 Cr App R (S) 86 (p 446) There are many factors to be considered when determining the appropriate level of sentence for perjury and related offences. There is no distinction to be drawn whether the proceedings contaminated were civil or criminal. Perjury may be comparatively trivial in relation to criminal proceedings or very serious in relation to civil proceedings. No doubt, whether the proceedings were civil or criminal is one of the factors proper to be considered. There are many others. We do not purport to give an exhaustive list. They include the number of offences committed, the timescale over which they are committed, whether they are planned or spontaneous, whether they are persisted in, whether the lies which are told or the fabrications which are embarked upon have any actual impact on the proceedings in question, whether the activities of the defendant draw in others, what the relationship is between others who are drawn in and the defendant.

305.6   Judicial guidance   Perverting the course of justice etc.
R v Williams 1995 16 Cr App R (S) 191 D was convicted of an attempt to intimidate a witness in civil proceedings. Held. People who are tempted to involve themselves in seeking to deter witnesses from giving evidence, or true evidence, must realise that a prison sentence is inevitable, whatever their own personal mitigation and good character might be.
Note: Although this is an old case, this principle is still applied today. Ed.
R v Khan 2001 EWCA Crim 912, 2 Cr App R (S) 129 (p 553) Such offences undermine the whole process of justice and they are to be treated seriously, and will in most cases merit a custodial sentence to run consecutively to any other sentence.
R v Tunney 2006 EWCA Crim 2066, 2007 1 Cr App R (S) 91 (p 565) D pleaded to doing acts intending to pervert the course of justice. The Court should regard: 1 the seriousness of the substantive offence, 2 the degree of persistence in the conduct, and 3 the effect of the attempt to pervert the course of justice.
R v Snow 2008 EWCA Crim 580, 2 Cr App R (S) 87 (p 497) Important factors are the length of time during which the deception continued, the nature of the deception and the success of the deception.
Att-Gen's Ref No 35 of 2009 2009 EWCA Crim 1375, 2010 1 Cr App R (S) 61 (p 410) There is a long-standing principle that perverting the course of justice is so serious that it is almost always necessary to impose immediate custody unless there are exceptional circumstances. The offence undermines the very system of criminal justice.
Att-Gen's Ref No 34 of 2015 2015 EWCA Crim 1152 D was convicted of two counts of perverting the course of justice. She sheltered a murder suspect and a month later gave police a false witness statement. Held. It has long been recognised that perverting the course of justice is so serious that it is almost always necessary to impose a custodial sentence unless there are exceptional circumstances. Here, 18 months not a Suspended Sentence Order.

For more detail see **305.7**.

R v Ratcliffe 2016 EWCA Crim 27 D pleaded (20% credit) to perverting the course of justice. His car was detected by a camera going through a red light. D took a series of steps to pretend he was not driving the car. Held. Cases of perverting the course of justice of this particular kind almost inevitably call for custodial sentences. Such offending strikes at the very heart of the administration of justice. Accordingly, deterrence is called for, although sometimes the necessary deterrence can be found in the making of an immediate custodial sentence and not one necessarily requiring a term of imprisonment of any great length. Matters to be taken into account [include] the seriousness of the underlying offence, the length of time during which the deception was continued, the nature of the deception practised and the success or otherwise of the deception. Because the circumstances of the offending, and indeed the circumstances of the individual offender, can so greatly vary, a wide range of sentencing outcomes can be found. Accordingly, only limited assistance can be found from such authorities for this purpose, even if the underlying relevant principles are clear enough.

305.7   *Assisting defendants/Tipping defendants off etc.*

R v Dawkins 2008 EWCA Crim 2212, 2009 1 Cr App R (S) 103 (p 582) D was convicted of perverting the course of justice. D's two girlfriends, K and V, confronted him in a car about his relationship with each of them. He managed to escape and went to a friend's house. K took V behind some garages and stabbed and killed her. Later D and K went to the cinema together. D was arrested and claimed that V was alive. He also lied about whom he had been with, saying that he had been with an unknown female. Next day he was interviewed again and denied that he knew K's address, maintaining his account of the unknown female. That day K admitted murder. In the next interview he admitted that he had lied. He had 33 convictions including attempted robbery. The lies did not seriously impede the investigation. At trial he claimed that the lies did not pervert the course of justice. Held. Society requires witnesses not to lie. **3 years** was not manifestly excessive.

Note: This is an old case, so treat the decision with care. Ed.

Att-Gen's Ref No 34 of 2015 2015 EWCA Crim 1152 D was convicted of two counts of perverting the course of justice. Early in the morning, a 24-year-old woman, V1, and another woman, V2, were shot by H and C. They had intended to hit members of a rival gang. A submachine gun and a shotgun were used. V1 died and V2's life was only saved by emergency surgery. Gang members were also injured. Within hours of the murder, H contacted D by phone and then H and C travelled to D's home address. D then travelled from where she had been staying back to the home address. H stayed at the home address until the afternoon of that day. In the evening, D contacted H, who then went back to D's address and spent the night there. About six weeks later, after H and C had been arrested, D lied to the police about her contacts with H after the murder. D then made a false witness statement about it. This was the second perverting matter. She continued with the denials in interview and at trial. D was aged 25 and was treated as of good character. She was a single mother who had had a difficult childhood and background. Her two children were aged about five and about nine months. D had a history of substance abuse. H and C were convicted of murder, attempted murder and conspiracy to cause GBH. The prosecution said this was not a case of rushed short-term sheltering. Held. D let H stay at her address during the critical first 24 hours of the police investigation. The underlying substantive offence was extremely serious. The assistance was important. There was no evidence of pressure. The actions of D had the potential to pervert a successful prosecution although in fact they didn't. Ordinarily a custodial sentence of **3 years** or more would be appropriate. The principal mitigating factor was the children. With that and the satisfactory compliance with the 2-year Suspended Sentence Order, **18 months**.

Old cases: *R v Johnson* 2005 EWCA Crim 3602, 2006 2 Cr App R (S) 23 (p 164) **(1 year)** *R v Gonsalves* 2007 EWCA Crim 1408, 2008 1 Cr App R (S) 40 (p 211) **(18 months)**
For a summary of these cases, see the 9th edition of this book.
See also the *Prosecution/conviction, To avoid* paras at **305.28**.

305.8   *Attacking judge, juror or court staff*
R v Russell 2006 EWCA Crim 470 D was convicted of attempted murder, making use of a firearm with intent and other offences. He received 24 years in total for those offences. During the summing-up, he vaulted the dock, ran in front of the jury and attacked the Judge. He shouted, "Do you think you are going to stitch me up? I deserve a fair trial", and other remarks. He tore the Judge's sash off, but the Judge held D and kept him at arm's length for several seconds until he was restrained by police. He was found to be in contempt of court and sentenced to **18 months** consecutive by a different Judge. He appealed against conviction but not sentence. Held. Even in the context of the long sentences, that contempt sentence was merciful. Those who attack a judge, juror or officer of the court in the course of their duties, particularly in the courtroom, can expect very long sentences measured in years. If the attack is an attempt to frustrate the processes of the trial, that is a further aggravating feature.
Note: This is an old case. Since then, the need to protect judges, magistrates and court officials has grown. These principles are very much in line with current sentencing practice. Ed.
See also: *R v Phelps* 2009 EWCA Crim 2308, 2010 2 Cr App R (S) 1 (p 1)[806] (Contempt. Spat at and punched one dock officer and struck another in the face with full force. Held. This behaviour will be dealt with severely. **2-year** maximum starting point not wrong. No appeal over consecutive sentences of 16 months. Reduced to **21 months** because of no cooling-off period.)

305.9 *Evidence, Interfering with   Judicial guidance*
R v Brookes 2014 EWCA Crim 2076 para 10 Where the offence relates to the concealment of evidence, the relevant factors are the seriousness of the substantive offence, the degree of persistence and effects on justice.

305.10   *Evidence, Interfering with   Cases*
R v Talbot 2015 EWCA Crim 1238 D pleaded (25% credit) to perverting the course of justice, possessing indecent photographs and making indecent photographs. D lived with his wife, who was a rector. He was also a Church of England priest. For three years D had been the chaplaincy co-ordinator for the Cambridge Constabulary. It was an unpaid role. For a number of years he had accessed the Internet to view pornography. He became worried that his Internet provider might have become aware of this[807] so he e-mailed the Assistant Chief Constable of Cambridgeshire, C, and offered to resign forthwith. C phoned him and D said he was in a very dark place. D told C about accessing child pornography on the Internet. C said the matter would have to be referred and was worried D might harm himself. Police attended D's home and seized his computer equipment. D explained the computer he used to download material had been destroyed. Police visited the places D had said the parts of the computer had been deposited and it was discovered the bins had been collected that morning. This was the perverting matter. [A news report says the Judge was told D's wife was instantly dismissed from her job as rector and the two were given 24 hours to leave their home.] D was interviewed and said that the missing computer had a small fraction of child pornography on it. The Court accepted that. On D's home computer only 18 images were found and one was Category A. It was oral sex with a 12-14-year-old girl. One was

---

[806] This case is not summarised because the offending would clearly have warranted a higher starting point if a suitable assault charge had been brought to reflect the number of victims, the defendant's very relevant previous convictions and the length of the incident. Also, the case has many factors which would require a lengthy summary. Ed.
[807] A news report says the Judge was told that all that happened was that his Internet went down.

Category B and the rest were Category C. The pictures were of young girls aged 8-16. D was aged 63, of impeccable character and overcome by remorse. There was an array of impressive testimonials. The pre-sentence report was positive, saying he had good motivation to address his behaviour. Held. The perverting was the most serious offence. We start at 12 months not 20. With plea, **9 months**. The image offences remain concurrent.

See also: *R v Brookes* 2014 EWCA Crim 2076 (Plea (25%) and plea to handling. D lent stolen motorbike to drunk friend who crashed it into a tree. D hid bike rather than helping V, who lay dying. Police and V's family, distressed, believed innocent parties involved. Six old antecedents. **18 months**, not 24.)

305.11   *Evidence, Interfering with/false accounts of corpses/injured persons*
R v Matthews 2009 EWCA Crim 1450, 2010 1 Cr App R (S) 59 (p 373) D pleaded to one and was convicted of two 'doing acts' intended to pervert the course of justice. Both he and his company were dealt with for Health and Safety offences (fines imposed). D and his company were acquitted of manslaughter. D ran a scrap metal business which had a machine which cut and compacted scrap metal. It was being operated by D and V, an employee and a close friend of D. Both were operating the machine dangerously. D and V were in it and D was using a remote control device. An old acetylene cylinder was in the machine and it exploded. V suffered extensive burns and later died. D suffered serious injuries and was 'out of commission for three months'. D was in hospital. The directors operated a cover-up. The investigators were lied to. The remote control cable was removed by a co-accused. It was claimed that no one was in the machine. A trial started and the defence claimed that V was not in the machine but was passing it. Near the end of the trial a witness was found who said that the machine was operated by a remote cable and there were two men in it. This witness was not on the list of witnesses that the emergency services compiled. The jury was discharged. After this, D instructed a co-defendant to reinstate the cable and switch so that D could continue to claim that the machine was operated from the cab. This formed one of the perversion counts and D pleaded to it. D continued the false account that was peddled before he returned to work. The other perversion counts related to D's instruction to two employees not to mention that the new witness had been working at the time of the accident. One co-defendant told a nephew of the deceased the true position, and the nephew was given compensation. The Judge found that D lied when interviewed, lied during the reconstruction, lied at the first trial and lied when re-interviewed. Held. There is a very strong public interest that death and particularly work-related deaths are thoroughly investigated. The perverting offence was manslaughter, which is one of the most serious offences. The offence was persistent. It was a serious perversion: **3 years** was not manifestly excessive.
R v Chidgey 2013 EWCA Crim 2816 D pleaded ten days before his trial to an amended perverting count. He was the licensee of a pub and found a customer, V, dead in the women's toilets. V had died of acute alcoholic poisoning. D was worried about the commercial effect of this as it was the start of a busy weekend. He did not tell anybody and told the cleaner, C, that V was coming to paint the pub the next day. Four days later, C was told to tell the police she had found the body that day and she did so. Her statement to the police was misleading. D made a false statement to the police and C went to the police and told the truth. D was interviewed three times and lied on each occasion. D was aged 29, with no relevant convictions. He had an unhappy personal life and was drinking heavily. The pre-sentence report said there was not a shred of real remorse. The Judge said D had disgraced V's dignity. Held. Because V died of natural causes and D was not concealing a crime, **9 months** not 15.
R v Amin 2014 EWCA Crim 1924 D was convicted of perverting the course of justice and preventing a public burial. V was a young female Iraqi Kurd who was found buried in a suitcase, having been murdered by four of her relatives because of their disapproval of a relationship. D was the nephew of two of the murderers. All the participants and D met the night before the murder to discuss the killing and the disposal of V's body.

Cell-site evidence put D at the place of the murder, but several hours after it was committed. D's bank card was used about a mile from the burial site. He told police that he had last seen V six months ago. Four months later, D was arrested and made false and misleading statements about the use of his phone, his whereabouts and that he had not let anyone apart from his cousin use his car. Despite being shown cell-site evidence contradicting him, he maintained his version. D was interviewed a second time and made further false statements about his whereabouts and also the whereabouts of one of the murder suspects. Then, altering his account, D said he had lent his car to one of the murder suspects. D denied his involvement but could not explain the use of his bank card or phone after the murder. D's misleading statements and denials about the use of his phone continued when he was interviewed for a third time. His statements to police contributed to a delay in finding V's body. D later visited the murderers on remand and admitted using the bank card and letting them use his car on the night of the murder. It was also revealed that D's car was outside the relevant address when V was put into a suitcase and suitcase fibres were later found in the car. D was aged 30 at sentencing and of good character but showed no remorse. **8 years** concurrent with **5 years** for burial offence upheld.)

Old cases: *Att-Gen's Ref No 35 of 2009* 2009 EWCA Crim 1375, 2010 1 Cr App R (S) 61 (p 410) (**34 weeks' detention suspended** with 200 hours' unpaid work was unduly lenient.)

For a summary of the case, see the 9th edition of this book.

See also the ***Prosecution/conviction, To avoid*** para at **305.28** and the OBSTRUCTING THE CORONER/BURIAL, PREVENTING chapter.

305.12   *Incriminating innocent people, Trying to   Non-rape claims   Guideline remarks*

R v Reedy 2013 EWCA Crim 338 D pleaded to perverting the course of justice. He made an anonymous phone call to the police reporting a robbery of an elderly lady. There was no robbery. He gave the address of the perpetrators as his ex-partner's address. She was arrested, along with her new partner and two friends, and detained for 14 hours. Held. The fact that the false allegation here was not of rape makes it no less serious than those allegations. Those who commit this type of offence and make bogus allegations as the result of which innocent people are harmed and resources expended must expect immediate custodial sentences, whatever the mitigation. 12 months.

305.13   *Incriminate innocent people, Trying to   Non-rape claims   Cases*

R v Weiner 2011 EWCA Crim 1249, 1 Cr App R (S) 6 (p 24) D was convicted of perverting the course of justice and possession of indecent photographs of children (×2). D contacted police anonymously, and stated that a caretaker at a school was involved in the distribution of child pornography. A month later he sent a CD containing some of the images. Two months later D contacted the police again and named V, a caretaker at a school in London, as the individual, and said that the images on the CD had been downloaded from V's computer. In fact, D had regular access to V's computer, and had helped him with the use of the computer. The computer contained 177 indecent images, including 87 at Level 1 and 33 at Level 4. Many were in hidden files, so that V was unlikely to find them or accidentally delete them. There was no evidence that a normal user of the computer had accessed any kind of pornography. D had altered the dates of the files to show that they were downloaded prior to V's employment at the school. Two women to whom D had spoken stated that he had told them that he did not like a man at work and he and a colleague were going to place child pornography on that man's computer. V and his wife's life had been ruined. D, aged 40 at appeal, was of good character. Held. Any case of perverting the course of justice which wrongly exposes another to the risk of arrest, imprisonment and wrongful conviction is to be viewed as particularly serious. This involved a high degree of careful planning, and a degree of breach of trust. A considerably higher sentence would have followed had the plot led to V being wrongly convicted. **10 to 12 years** was the appropriate range. **10 years** was correct, not 12.

R v Sutcliffe and McGurk 2012 EWCA Crim 2113, 2013 1 Cr App R (S) 103 (p 540) M pleaded to perverting the course of justice. S pleaded on rearraignment to the same. S ran a business and employed E. E left the business after some disputes and attempted to claim £240 in unpaid wages. Those attempts failed and E gave up. S's car was subsequently damaged and S reported to the police that it was occasioned by E. S claimed it was witnessed by M, who was an independent witness, not known to either M or E. In fact, M was known to S and was paid £100 to make a false statement. E was arrested. S had shown M photographs of E, and M duly identified E in an identification parade. E pleaded not guilty and a date for trial was set. M received a summons and subsequently went to the police and requested that he withdraw his witness statement. He gave a full account of his involvement and S was arrested. S, aged 25, had a conviction in relation to a false statement in order to obtain a payment. M, aged 45, had a rape conviction and other offences between 1989 and 2011. Held. This type of offence undermines the whole process of justice and is so serious that, save in exceptional circumstances, an immediate custodial sentence will almost certainly be necessary. For S, starting at 3 years, **2 years 5 months** was not manifestly excessive. M was to be paid for his false witness statement and so his offending was of a high order. However, he was entitled to more than ⅓ credit, as it was his preparedness to give evidence against S that impacted upon S changing his plea. **12 months** not 14.

See also: *R v Johnson* 2011 EWCA Crim 1219, 2012 1 Cr App R (S) 24 (p 147) (Early plea. D made an untrue statement to police about being robbed by J. Described a distinctive tattoo. Motive appeared to be revenge after a criminal enterprise both probably involved in. Claimed victim had duped him. Victim detained for 4 hours. Custody was inevitable. **8 months** not 14.)

R v Reedy 2013 EWCA Crim 338 (Plea. Phoned police reporting a false robbery on an elderly lady. Gave address of his ex-partner. Police attended and arrested the four occupants, including his ex-partner and her new partner. They spent 14 hours in custody. Police resources tied up for 44 hours investigating the offence. Starting at 18 months, **12 months** not 2 years.

R v Laczmanski 2014 EWCA Crim 2026 (Plea. Also pleaded to 'nasty' assault on V. D and V in difficult, controlling and abusive relationship. D worried V unfaithful and an altercation ensued. As V escaped, D stabbed himself and told police it was V. V in custody for 11 hours for attempted murder but D dropped the allegations and voluntarily admitted stabbing himself. Aged 32, no convictions. **2 years**, not 3.)

Old cases: *R v Betteridge* 2008 EWCA Crim 1006 (**3 months**) *R v Clarke* 2010 EWCA Crim 2076 (**12 months suspended**)

For a summary of the last case, see the 10th edition of this book.

305.14   *Incriminate innocent people, Trying to   Rape claims   Judicial guidance*

R v Carrington-Jones 2007 EWCA Crim 2551 Rape is a repulsive crime. No one doubts that the victims of rape should be treated with every possible consideration by the criminal justice system. On the other hand, just because rape is a repulsive crime, a false allegation can have dreadful consequences, obviously and immediately for an innocent man who has not perpetrated the crime, but also because every occasion of a proved false allegation has an insidious effect on public confidence in the truth of genuine complaints, sometimes allowing doubt to creep in where none should in truth exist.

305.15   *Incriminate innocent people, Trying to   Rape claims   Cases*

R v Vine 2011 EWCA Crim 1860, 2012 1 Cr App R (S) 78 (p 442) D pleaded to perverting the course of justice. She met a man and they exchanged phone numbers. They contacted one another and agreed to meet. D travelled from Southampton to London, to the man's flat. They had sexual intercourse. Later, the man's friends went to his flat and D had intercourse with a number of them. A week later she came to the man's flat again. They again had intercourse. The man took D to a friend's house whereupon she had 'sexual relations' with a number of them. She then made a complaint to the police that she had been raped by a number of men. Nine men were arrested, aged from 16 to mid-20s. The 16-year-old was studying for his GCSE examinations and had been wrongly identified by D. The men spent up to 40 hours in custody. An examination of phone messages and CCTV footage showed that D entered the man's address willingly. She admitted she made up the complaints to punish the men for how they had treated her. She also claimed there was money missing from her purse. D, aged 26, was a single mother of three, with all three children living with their respective fathers. She was also pregnant when sentenced and gave birth in prison. She had a low IQ and the pre-sentence report stated that D did not appreciate the seriousness of her actions. Held. The nine men underwent humiliation, fear, anxiety and loss of reputation. D had to be dealt with severely. **4½ years** was justifiably severe.

R v Simpson 2013 EWCA Crim 1250 D pleaded (full credit) to two counts of perverting the course of justice. V was formerly married to D's mother. V had not seen D for about nine years, when she was aged 11. In 2010, D telephoned a police rape team and alleged that V had pulled up in his car and driven her to an address where four other men and a woman had raped her orally, anally and vaginally. Almost three weeks later, she again telephoned the police rape team and alleged that V had called at her grandmother's address and taken her, with her grandmother's partner and another man, to an address where they all raped her. V was arrested and taken into custody. He was detained for 14 hours, physically examined, required to provide intimate samples and was interviewed under caution. The experience was traumatising and upsetting, despite the fact that it was all too apparent that he could have committed neither offence and that the allegations were wholly false. When arrested, D claimed the first allegation was true and that she could not remember making the second allegation. Her basis of plea was that the first allegation was made because she was angry how she had been treated in the abusive relationship between V and her mother. D had been diagnosed with an emotionally unstable personality disorder associated with reactive depression. It was accepted that starting at 3 years could not be criticised, before considering the mitigation. D was aged 22, of good character and had a young baby. Held. Making due allowances for the mental health issues at the relevant time, it is important not to lose sight of the fact that these were very serious offences, the more serious because D made the second allegation quite deliberately to make matters even worse for V. There could be no criticism of **starting at 3½ years**. With the plea and mitigation, **21 months** was necessarily severe and not manifestly excessive.

See also: *R v Ngwata* 2012 EWCA Crim 2015, 2013 1 Cr App R (S) 111 (p 576) (Late plea to perverting the course of justice. Married husband in Congo in 2009. Came to UK in 2010. Subsequently left marital home. False claim that her husband had locked her in the flat every day and subjected her to domestic violence, raped her at knife point and repeated rape. Applied for indefinite leave to remain claiming she had been assaulted. Husband arrested and held in custody for 14 hours. Advised to say what she did by others, claiming that it was in her son's interests. 20% credit. Starting at 3 years was correct. With the plea, **2 years 5 months**.)

Old cases: Best ignored. Judges now consider the trauma of male victims properly.

305.16   *Juror contacting defendants etc.*

Att-Gen v Pardon 2012 EWHC 3402 (Admin) High Court LCJ D admitted he was in contempt of court. He was a juror in a 13-week trial involving a £2m+ conspiracy to steal stainless-steel beer kegs. The defendants were F, G, K and L. D was given the standard documentation and information in relation to the responsibilities of being a juror and the Judge gave unequivocal directions including the instruction not to discuss the case with anyone else. On a Friday, the jury convicted L and G (10-2) and acquitted K. The jury's deliberations in relation to F continued over the weekend. On the Saturday, with a friend, D went to a scrap metal premises where L was known to work. D sat in a van outside the premises and asked an employee whether L was present. The employee confirmed that he was and L then approached the van. D apologised for the guilty verdict and then made a series of disclosures relating to the jury's deliberations, including reasons for the guilty verdict against L, material the jury had considered and an allegation that the jury had looked at certain newspaper websites. The jury were unable to reach a verdict in relation to F and were discharged. L attended court on the Monday and informed his representatives of the conversation and the Judge was informed. The Judge did not raise the issue of contempt with D and sought permission to allow the police to investigate it. Shortly after being discharged, D went to the workplace of G and beckoned him to come over to talk to him. G instructed his employer to tell D to leave, and he did so. G's case was re-listed for the following day and he informed his representatives of D's actions. D was arrested and accepted in interview that he had disclosed the contents the jury's deliberations to L, and he would have done to G, had G come to speak to him. He was fully co-operative. He also acknowledged that he was explicitly told not to do so. D was a man of mature years who was treated as of good character. D had a number of testimonials. It was said that D approached L because he felt sorry for him and was concerned about there being a miscarriage of justice. Held. D deliberately disobeyed the orders of the Judge. Although the trial was not disrupted or aborted, because of the impropriety, the CCRC will have to add to its heavy workload to investigate the issues which may undermine the safety of this conviction. Much of that might have been avoided if D had had the good sense to go to the Judge with his concerns about jury members reading news websites. This contempt involved deliberate disobedience of two distinct orders of the court on two separate occasions. An immediate custodial sentence was virtually inevitable. Allowing for his admission of guilt, **4 months**.

305.17   *Juror using Facebook, Internet etc.   Guideline remark*
Att-Gen v Harkins and Liddle 2013 EWHC 1455 (Admin) High Court H and L admitted contempt. Both placed images of Thomson and Venables on their Facebook page. (For the details see **305.18** below.) Both were given 9 months suspended. Held. If a similar publication occurs after the date of this judgment there will be little prospect of such a person escaping a substantial custodial sentence and little prospect of the sentence being suspended.

305.18   *Juror using Facebook, Internet etc.   Cases*
Att-Gen v Fraill and Sewart 2011 EWHC 1629 (Admin) High Court F admitted contempt of court and S was found to be in contempt. F was a juror in a drugs trial in which S and S's partner, K, were defendants. Repeatedly, the Judge instructed the jury that they were not to access the Internet to research aspects of the case, and that their decision must be based solely on what they heard in court. The jury retired to consider their verdict. S was acquitted but her co-defendants awaited verdicts. The Judge subsequently received information that an unidentified juror had contacted S via Facebook. He questioned the jurors and, upon F's admission, discharged the jury. It was discovered that after S had been acquitted, F contacted her through a false Facebook profile and revealed that she was a juror in the trial. F provided details of jury deliberations and thoughts on the remaining charges. F and S agreed not to reveal that they had been in contact. S said that she would try to get compensation for the 14 months spent on remand, and should F stay in touch, she would get a nice present. S subsequently contacted her solicitor and it was arranged that the Judge would be informed. F also conducted Internet searches into S's co-defendants. F was of good character and claimed that she had contacted S in order to convey her compassionate concern for S. S was arrested when her child was 10 months old, spent 14 months on remand, and on her acquittal had been reunited with her child. Held. Misuse of the Internet by a juror is always a most serious contempt and in the context of the maximum

2-year custodial sentence, custody is virtually inevitable. The sentence is intended to ensure the continuing integrity of trial by jury. F was not involved in an attempt to pervert the course of justice. S's contempt would not have occurred but for F contacting her. However, she did respond knowing that F was a juror. Though her conduct was contumacious, she did not benefit from the information. For F, **8 months**, for S, **2 months suspended** (because of time on remand and the separation from her child).

Att-Gen v Dallas 2012 EWHC 156 (Admin) High Court LCJ D was found guilty of contempt of court. She was a juror in a section 18 case. There was a bad character application in relation to the defendant, M, which was allowed in part. D, a Greek national, was a lecturer at an English university. She lectured in English and was extremely articulate in English. She used the Internet to search for the Greek translation of the word 'grievous'. She subsequently searched for information relating to M. She discovered details of M's ABH conviction (the bad character). However, she also discovered that M's conviction involved an allegation of rape. She subsequently shared this information with her fellow jurors. D was of positive good character with no convictions. Held. The Court was satisfied that D had searched for information relating to M. D knew that the Judge had directed the jury not to seek information from the Internet and that this was an order. D disobeyed that order. Doing so caused prejudice to the administration of justice. Misuse of the Internet by a juror is always a most serious irregularity and an effective custodial sentence is virtually inevitable. **6 months**.

Att-Gen v Harkins and Liddle 2013 EWHC 1455 (Admin) High Court H and L admitted contempt of court. In 1993, Thompson and Venables aged 11 were sentenced to detention at HM's Pleasure for the murder of two-year-old James Bulger. In 2001, prior to their release, a worldwide injunction was granted prohibiting the publication etc. of images or voice recordings, purporting to be of Thompson or Venables, or any description of their physical appearance, voices or accents. H used his Facebook profile to post a photograph of persons said to be Thompson and Venables. He had 141 'friends' on Facebook but his posting of the picture resulted in over 20,000 'sharings'. It was not clear how many people had seen it but it was obviously a very significant number. H also posted two messages rebuking the system for providing Thompson and Venables protection. The Treasury Solicitor wrote to H informing him of the Attorney-General's involvement and asked him to remove the picture. He immediately did so, apologised and de-activated his Facebook account. He stated that he believed the images were not subject to legal constraints as they were freely available on the Internet. H admitted breaching the injunction. L posted images purporting to be Thompson and Venables on his Twitter account under the name 'OpinionatedDad'. That profile was accessible to the general public. L picked up the photograph from elsewhere on the Internet. The images were removed less than an hour later when someone informed him that the images were not of Thompson and Venables. L 'tweeted' 'I heard about it [the injunction] for a while but I posted it as people are talking about being prosecuted for putting it and I don't think it's right.' The same day, he 'tweeted': 'So I get a huge fine. Great. They will get £2 a week off me and the evil men who murdered a child will be known publicly – #worthit.' L had 915 Twitter 'followers'. He later 'tweeted': 'Just been served with court papers…What a joke' and 'Love them to take me to court'. He subsequently telephoned the Treasury Solicitor and was immensely apologetic. He later sent an email acknowledging that he was aware of the injunction but had already seen the image 'hundreds of times'. He also stated that he did not understand what breaking an injunction actually meant. Both were of good character. L had a deaf child and had done charity work. Held. It was a serious contempt of court. The potential consequences, for Venables and Thompson but also for others who might be mistakenly identified as them, aggravate the offences. It is plain both knew of the existence of the injunction, but perhaps not the extent of the consequences of what they did. Both offending pictures were removed and apologies were made. The very serious nature of publication on social media or otherwise on the Internet must be taken into account. Social media can reach very many people. L had significant personal mitigation. **9 months suspended** for 15 months was appropriate.

See also: *Att-Gen v Davey and Beard* 2013 EWHC 2317 (Admin) (D and B found to be in contempt of court when jurors. Both were jurors. D put on Facebook, 'I've always wanted to Fuck up a paedophile & now I'm within the law!' Lied to the court about it. B told jurors what he had discovered about the case on the Internet. B lied to the police. His jury were discharged after sitting for 5½ weeks. He lost his job. An effective and immediate custodial sentence is almost inevitable in cases of this kind. **2 months**.[808])

305.19   *Juror not attending court*

R v Chapman 2012 EWCA Crim 1011, 2013 1 Cr App R (S) 22 (p 117) D was found to be in contempt. She was called for jury service. At the beginning of the trial, D signed a form stating that she knew of no impediment as to why she could not serve for four weeks, which was the predicted length of the trial. At the conclusion of the third week, the Judge began his summing-up. The jury were sent home for the weekend and were told the Judge would complete his summing-up on Monday. D did not attend court on Monday. She rang the court and said she was unfit to attend. The trial did not continue. The following day, D rang the court and left a message saying that she would be unable to attend for two weeks, that she had to return to the doctor's the following week and that she had sciatica. Enquiries were made and it was discovered that on the Monday at 4.45 pm D had attended the doctor's and obtained a 'sick note' stating that she was not fit for work. On the Tuesday, D had left on a flight bound for Malta. The second phone call to the court was made from Malta. D claimed to have suffered severe back pain over the weekend and that the holiday to Malta was booked by her partner as a surprise. The Judge found that the message sent from Malta was 'misleading and a deception' and that D was not unfit to attend court. The trial was delayed for two days and there was, at first, genuine concern for D's welfare. There were significant wasted costs, considerable inconvenience and personal loss to several people. The Judge also said that where a trial is by 11 jurors it may be more difficult for there to be a verdict. Held. This was a serious contempt of court. D cannot have been unaware of the serious consequences of her not attending the trial. The contempt is aggravated by the deviousness of D's conduct. Immediate imprisonment was required and **56 days** was not manifestly excessive.

305.20   *Jury interference*

R v Cameron 2008 EWCA Crim 2493 LCJ D pleaded at the first opportunity to perverting the course of justice. She attended the first day of the trial of a close friend and recognised one of the jurors as someone she knew through a mutual friend, S. She sent a text to S asking her to text the juror, 'Just text her saying not guilty. I will call and explain later but please do this for me.' S duly sent a text to the juror telling her that she had received a text from D saying: 'Please tell friend he is not guilty. He did not do it.' When the Court rose, the Judge gave the usual directions to the jury about what to do if anyone approached them. Then D realised the potential seriousness of what she had done and tried to contact S to prevent the message being sent, but it had already been done. The following morning the juror reported the matter to the Judge. She had not told any of the other jurors. She was discharged, and the trial went ahead. The same day D was arrested and admitted the offence. She said that she had very little knowledge of the court process and did not realise the seriousness of her actions until she heard the Judge's warning. She accepted her actions were wrong. D, aged 20, had no convictions. She was a student at a university and had been offered a prestigious work placement at Disney World in Florida to start shortly. A pre-sentence report recommended a community order or suspended sentence. There was a low risk of reoffending and D was remorseful. There were five character references from responsible people at her

---

[808] The judgment does not deal with the sentence. The 2 months and the comments come from CO/1504/2013.

university and a family friend. Because of the sentence she lost the placement, was currently unable to continue with her degree, and the conviction meant she might never be able to travel to the USA. Held. To deter others, custody, and sometimes substantial periods of custody, is inevitable for those who interfere with jurors. Regard must be had to the individual facts of the case. She is aged 20 with no convictions. She acted out of naïvety. The moment she realised the gravity of what she had done she tried to prevent the juror being contacted. It was an indirect message and was not threatening. She made an immediate and full confession and pleaded at the first opportunity. She has lost her prime job placement and may not be able to travel to the USA in the future. We emphasise that this is a case decided entirely upon its own exceptional facts. It should not be regarded as providing any sort of sentencing guideline. **4 months**' detention not 12.

R v Curtis and Medlan 2012 EWCA Crim 945, 2013 1 Cr App R (S) 28 (p 147) C and M admitted contempt of court on the second and last day of their trial of the issue. T, a friend of M, was a defendant on trial. C's partner had been in the company of T at the time of the alleged offence and C had spent time in T's company shortly after the alleged offence. C and M attended T's trial. The Judge had noticed that M and C had been peering through the tinted glass screen which separated the public area from the courtroom. He was satisfied that this was in order to get a better view of the jury. At the close of one of the day's proceedings, M and C hung around outside court. Two jurors walked past them and M and C followed. The two jurors were joined by a third, and all three boarded a bus. M and C also boarded the bus. M sat next to one juror and C sat directly opposite. The bus was nearly empty. The Judge concluded that M and C had deliberately followed the jurors and were acting in concert. As soon as C sat down, she started speaking unnaturally loudly and clearly into her mobile phone. The content of the conversation was clearly for the benefit of the jurors. She named T and commented on how well his barrister was doing in comparison to the prosecution barrister and said that it was looking good for T. The clear implication, the Judge found, was that if the jury convicted T, it would be the fault of the jury and not T or his barrister. The jurors were perturbed and frightened. They felt intimidated. The jurors got off the bus at the earliest reasonable opportunity. They returned to the court and reported the incident to the court staff. The trial continued and T was convicted. M and C denied that they recognised the jurors when they got onto the bus. M was aged 21 and of effective good character. She was a single parent with a very young child. She was remorseful and ashamed of her actions. C was aged 30 and had no convictions. She was also a single mother with a four-year-old son. Held. Immediate custody was inevitable. Appropriate credit was given for their remorse and personal mitigation. Limited credit was available for their acknowledgement of guilt as it had occurred at a late stage. For C, **5 months** and M, **3 months** was not manifestly excessive and an appropriate distinction between them.
Note: The judgment does not reveal the starting point or what the sentence would have been if the offence had been committed by someone who wasn't a single parent. Ed.

305.21   *Mitigation, Bogus*
R v Bailey 2006 EWCA Crim 136, 2 Cr App R (S) 47 (p 306) D pleaded to perverting the course of justice. He was due to be sentenced for three counts of indecent assault on an 11-year-old girl. He set up an elaborate series of lies. He told his psychiatrist, probation officer, solicitor and counsel that the mother of his child had been murdered and the child was killed by a speeding car within weeks of each other. As a result he received a 3-year community sentence. In fact he had never had a partner and had never had a child. The Judge said that it was utterly repugnant and he could not think of a worse example. Held. The Judge was entitled to his strong view. It was very serious. That and the sentence D avoided merited the **2½ years** given.
Att-Gen's Ref No 123 of 2015 2016 EWCA Crim 28 In 2007, D was convicted of soliciting to murder and racially aggravated public order offences which occurred in 2006. This related to protests outside the Danish Embassy. He received 6 years. In 2012,

D pleaded to three counts under Terrorism Act 2000 s 58. This related to two documents on his laptop. One was of a violent nature but of limited practical assistance to a would-be terrorist. The other referred to the tradition of assassination. It was not said that D had tried to access the documents since 2006. One document was in Arabic, which D could not read. Both documents were freely available on the Internet. The mitigation included reference to the fact that D was now a changed man and was a law-abiding industrious person. The defence produced a reference from a university multi-faith centre which outlined D's 'big role in the success of the centre'. Another reference claimed to be from a satisfied customer admiring the work D had done to his website. D was given 12 months. It turned out the references were inaccurate. D had played no part in the faith centre and the reference was written by D's wife. The signature from the faith centre was genuine. For the other reference the customer had only been helped in a personal capacity and when his employer read the reference, D was sacked. In February 2013, D was arrested for perverting the course of justice. Owing to prosecution failures, the trial did not start until September 2015. D was convicted. The Judge found the references were far from being the heart of the mitigation, but they would have had a limited influence on the sentencing Judge's mind. Taking into account the delay, D was given **4 months**. Held. The [use] of false character references is a very serious matter. Magistrates' and Crown Courts are routinely given references, often on the date of the hearing. The system cannot operate if those references cannot be relied upon. Ordinarily immediate custodial sentences, normally of some significance, can be expected for people putting in false character references. That message must be maintained. However, the Judge was entitled to make a very substantial reduction for the very great delay, as well as other matters. Without these matters, **12 months** would be expected. D now has a young family. His conduct in prison has been exemplary. He is due to be released in just three days' time. We decline to interfere with the sentence.

See also the **GUILTY PLEA, DISCOUNT FOR *False mitigation*** para at **67.30** in Volume 1.

305.22 *Newspaper reporting*

Att-Gen v Times Newspapers 2009 EWHC 1023 (Admin)[809] High Court A defendant was convicted of manslaughter of a child by a 10 to 2 verdict. The foreman of the jury approached *The Times* about his and another juror's concerns about the verdict. The legal editor wrote an article and sent it to the paper's legal department, where it was checked. Some amendments were made. Publication was held up for a few days because of lack of space. The article was then rechecked by another lawyer and then sent to the sub-editors who checked the grammar, style etc. The article was published and revealed that 'a consensus was taken three minutes after the foreman was voted in. It was 10–2 against, all based on the evidence. After that there was no going back, the medical evidence was overwhelming, and ultimately the case was decided by laymen and laywomen using that despicable enemy of correct and logical thinking, that wonderfully persuasive device, common sense.' Both the paper and the juror, S, were found to be in contempt for disclosing jury secrets. S, a former lecturer, apologised to the Court. *The Times* declined to apologise as that would 'ring hollow' as they did not agree with the Court's finding and would seek to appeal. The Court held that there was no harassment of S and he came forward unprompted because of genuine concern. For *The Times*, **£15,000 fine** and £27,426 costs. For S, **£500 fine**.

Note: The fine for S seems needless as: a) he acted with the best intentions, b) he had been through the trauma of arrest and contempt proceedings, and c) he was retired. Ed.

Att-Gen v MGN and News Group Newspapers 2011 EWHC 2383 (Admin) High Court LCJ The defendant companies were found to be in contempt of court relating to headlines and articles published concerning an arrest made in the Joanna Yeates murder inquiry. Chris Jeffries was arrested and later released without charge. Prior to the

---

[809] The report deals with the finding that there was a contempt of court. The sentences were passed nine days later and that hearing is only reported in *The Times* News 23/5/09 and Internet sites.

publication of the articles, the Attorney-General issued a warning of the risks to the administration of justice. Despite that warning, the articles were published. Neither newspaper accepted that the articles constituted a contempt. Held. In every case where an individual has been arrested on suspicion of committing a crime the individual must not be vilified. The two articles in the *Daily Mirror* were more extreme. The risk to justice was therefore greater. *The Sun* subsequently offered an apology. *The Daily Mail* was fined **£50,000,** *The Sun* **£18,000,** both paying the costs equally.

Old case: *Att-Gen v ITV* 2008 EWHC 1984 (Admin) (**£25,000 fine**)
For a summary of the case, see the 9th edition of this book.

305.23   Outbursts in court

Criminal Practice Directions 2015 EWCA Crim 1567 para IX 62A.2 In the majority of cases, an apology and a promise as to future conduct should be sufficient for the court to order a person's release. However, there are likely to be certain cases where the nature and seriousness of the misconduct requires the court to consider using its powers, under Contempt of Court Act 1981 s 12(2), either to fine or to order the person's committal to custody.

R v Baker and Others 2008 EWCA Crim 334 D was judged in contempt of court. The Judge discharged the jury because he thought that the defendants were manipulating the jury by outbursts. In the second trial the Judge warned the defendants that he would use his contempt powers. D gave evidence but refused to return to be cross-examined. During the summing-up D claimed that the papers had been suppressed and the Judge had threatened him with contempt. Held. **1 year** consecutive to 23 years was not excessive.

R v White 2011 EWCA Crim 2804 (Contempt of court. W in public gallery as son was convicted of 'a very serious offence'. Judge warned public gallery not to cause a disturbance. W shouted at the jury. The Judge reprimanded him and he continued. Some members of the jury were shaken. Good character. Reacted in the heat of the moment. He cooled down and apologised. **7 days** not 14.)

Old case: *R v Huggins* 2007 EWCA Crim 732 (**No order**)
For a summary of the case, see the 9th edition of this book.

305.24   Perjury

For the judicial guidance see **305.5**.

R v Archer 2002 EWCA Crim 1996, 2003 1 Cr App R (S) 86 (p 446) The defendant, Lord Archer, was convicted of procuring a false alibi, two counts of perverting the course of public justice, swearing a false affidavit and perjury. In 1986 he was a successful writer, ambitious politician and deputy chairman of the Conservative Party. The *News of the World* published articles saying he had sex with a prostitute and that money was handed to her at Victoria station to silence her. *The Star* newspaper effectively repeated the *News of the World*'s allegation with added details. The co-accused, who was a casual friend, created a false alibi for D. He received £12,000 in cash and was told that D would help him with his film script. At the libel trial against *The Star* newspaper the prostitute gave her account and D gave false evidence. A diary with false entries written by his secretary was relied on. In 1999 the co-accused approached Max Clifford, a public relations man. Held. The secretary was an employee and therefore vulnerable to suggestions made by her employer. The co-accused was corrupted by money. Considering the length of time over which these offences were committed, the perceived involvement of others, and the persistence in dishonest conduct, **4 years** was not manifestly excessive.

Note: This is an old case, but the decision seems in line with current sentencing practice. Ed.

See also: *R v Lefton and Others* 2007 EWCA Crim 1015, 2008 1 Cr App R (S) 14 (p 58) (Mother, father and son. Lied to Magistrates' Court to have convictions *in absentia* set aside. **6 weeks, 6 weeks** and **21 days**, not 3 months each. See **305.30** for more details about the case.)

305.25   *Photographs taken of courtrooms   Judicial guidance*
Note: The CPS invariably charge contempt of court as the offence under Criminal Justice Act 1925 s 41 of taking or attempting to take any photograph, or making or attempting to make any portrait or sketch of a justice or a witness in, or a party to court proceedings has a maximum of a Level 3 fine. Ed.
R v D 2004 EWCA Crim 1271 LCJ D pleaded to a contempt of court. He took photographs in court while a serious case was being heard and where security was an issue. Held. Photographs taken with mobile phones have become a major problem in the Crown Court, the Magistrates' Court and the civil courts. Photographs can easily be passed on electronically. Intimidation of juries and witnesses is a growing problem in criminal cases. Recently there have been physical attacks on prosecution counsel. Illegal photography has the potential gravely to prejudice the administration of justice. Factors to consider are the nature of the trial, the potential disruption of the trial and the potential for misuse. Mitigation factors are plea, youth, a genuine apology and ignorance or naïvety of the person involved. Where security is less of an issue than in this case a sentence of less than the 12 months here may well be appropriate. In some cases 'the clang of prison gates' will be enough. In other cases, e.g. a foreign tourist in ignorance of the law, it may be that imprisonment is inappropriate and a fine would be correct.
Note: This is an old case, but the decision seems in line with current sentencing practice. Ed.
R v Ivanov 2013 EWCA Crim 614 Ordinarily there must be an element of deterrence in situations of this kind. Very often that element of deterrence may be conveyed by the very fact of immediate custody being imposed.

305.26   *Photographs taken of courtrooms   Cases*
R v Ivanov 2013 EWCA Crim 614 D pleaded to contempt of court. He attended Southwark Crown Court to give evidence for the defence in an ongoing trial. He was a friend of the defendant. After giving evidence, he remained in court. After the jury retired, a juror angrily complained to the jury bailiff that D had been filming them. He initially denied it, claiming to have been texting someone. When the Judge asked to see the phone, he admitted taking one picture. In fact he took three. When the phone was seized, he admitted filming for a few seconds, subsequently admitting it was about 30 seconds. It became apparent that D had taken two photographs of the defendant in the witness box through the door of the court and one of the defendant in the dock. He then filmed one minute of the Judge summing up the case. He had in fact not filmed or taken pictures of the jury. The jury was discharged and a fresh trial was ordered. D offered an apology to the Judge, who accepted that D had no intention of frightening the jury. D, aged 22 at appeal, had previously received 33 months for robbery. Held. The comments in *R v D* 2004 EWCA Crim 1271 are relevant and helpful. Such photographs may be easily shared after the event, even if the intention at the time of taking them is not so specific. The potential prejudice remains whatever the intention may have been at the actual time of taking the photographs. Given all the circumstances, D's relative youth and the fact his mother was recently taken very ill, **5 months** not 8.
See also: *Att-Gen v Scarth* 2013 EWHC 194 (Admin) (High Court. LCJ D was found to be guilty of two contempts. Photographed courts on two occasions with disguised equipment. One recording put on YouTube. Been to prison already for an identical offence. Sending this 87-year-old infirm man to prison was the last resort. It was appropriate but suspended. D could apply for permission to record proceedings and courts dealing with such an application urged to grant it.)

305.27   *Police officers as defendants*
R v Evans-Keady 2013 EWCA Crim 1546, 2014 1 Cr App R (S) 66 (p 433) D pleaded
(late) to perverting the course of justice. He had been a police officer for one year. He
was patrolling on his own when he saw what he suspected to be a drug deal taking place
between a woman and two men. He stopped the three of them and searched them. He
found three wraps of what he suspected to be drugs on the woman. Nothing of
significance was found on the men. The woman was arrested and taken to the station.
She began to cry upon being informed that she would need to be strip-searched. It
transpired that she was an Australian solicitor working in London and her immigration
status and her career were therefore something of great concern to her. D felt sorry for
the woman, saying that she "wasn't the normal slag you see". C, a detention officer, aged
23, tested the three wraps at the police station. C reported back to D that the result was
cocaine. D said it was a shame and asked C what they could do. C asked D what he
wanted to do, adding that there was the possibility of 'chucking the test away' and not
providing a statement to say that it was positive. D agreed that that was the best course
of action and C recorded the test as being negative. D interviewed the woman under
caution and told her the test had proved negative and that the police did not therefore
know what the substances were. He repeated that lie to a senior officer who had to
decide what action should be taken. The senior officer decided that no further action
should be taken and the woman was released. Very soon afterwards, C became
concerned about what had happened and before his shift had ended, he confessed what
he had done to a colleague, who reported what C had told her. D put the blame on C
claiming that C had told him that the test was negative. The woman was contacted and
later cautioned for possession. C pleaded guilty at his first appearance at the Crown
Court and provided a witness statement for use at D's trial. D pleaded not guilty but
changed his plea on the day his trial was due to begin. D was aged 25 at the time of the
offence. During D's short time in the police, he had encountered some traumatic events
which had caused him to seek counselling. A surrogacy arrangement had to be put on
hold as a result of the proceedings and he lost his career in the police force. Held. The
mitigation was relevant but the seriousness of the case made immediate custody
absolutely inevitable. C was a civilian employee to whom D should have been setting a
much better example. It was not done for personal gain and was a spontaneous act of
sympathy for someone facing what he thought was a disproportionate consequence with
serious consequences for her immigration status and career. Following a trial, the
sentence should have been somewhere between 12 and 15 months. With 10% credit for
the late plea, the sentence should have been **12 months** not 2 years.

305.28   *Prosecution/conviction, To avoid   Judicial guidance*
Att-Gen's Ref No 109 of 2010 2010 EWCA Crim 2382 Sentences for offences of this
kind are bound to be measured in years, probably 2 to 3.

305.29   *Prosecution/conviction, To avoid   Cases*
Att-Gen's Ref No 109 of 2010 2010 EWCA Crim 2382 D was convicted of conspiracy to
pervert the course of justice. During a murder investigation into a contract killing by
shooting in the street, she gave three wholly false accounts to police in order to protect
her partner, whom she knew to be connected with the offence. He was subsequently
convicted of murder. The murder was committed in October 2004 and the murder trial
concluded in the early months of 2010. The conspiracy lasted for more than a year and
the police inquiry was impeded. Held. The starting point for offences in the particular
circumstances of this kind of case is bound to be measured in years rather than months,
something probably **between 2 and 3 years** and probably at the upper end of that
bracket. Because of the pressure from her partner, a very long delay before she was
sentenced, her good character, her two children and her personal circumstances, **18
months**.

R v Haymer 2012 EWCA Crim 2200, 2013 1 Cr App R (S) 115 (p 594) D and L pleaded to perverting the course of justice. In L's house D assaulted his then girlfriend, V. L was spoken to by police and provided a short statement saying that he did not witness anything and did not wish to be involved. D was arrested. Whilst on remand, D arranged for L to send a series of Facebook messages to V, purporting to be from a woman called SB. Four messages were sent on one day. V notified the police saying that she knew D was behind them and that the messages left her unable to sleep. Phone calls from D to L were logged by prison authorities. They were discussing how to contact V, including a word-for-word dictation of the Facebook messages. V also received three handwritten letters and a card from D. A further five letters were intercepted and handed to the police. The letters were designed to apply emotional blackmail and put V under pressure to withdraw her complaint. At D's behest, L made a statement to police claiming to have changed his mind about becoming involved as he was disgusted at what he had seen V do to D. He gave an account of D being attacked by V and defending himself from her. He claimed it was not the first time that he had seen V be violent towards D. D was convicted of battery (×2) and committed for sentence. He received 12 months for breach of a suspended sentence and 5 months for the batteries. The sentences were all concurrent. D, aged 21, had a large number of convictions, including violence, anti-social behaviour and witness intimidation (Referral Order). Held. There was an absence of any physical threat. What occurred involved a form of witness intimidation causing undoubted distress, but much more serious forms of intimidation are encountered in practice. Causing L to make a false statement adds to the matter. With full credit, **18 months** was appropriate, not 3 years. The sentence remained consecutive to the battery sentence, which was nearly finished.

R v Davies 2013 EWCA Crim 671 D pleaded (20% credit) to perverting the course of justice. At 1 am, a car crashed into the wall of a property. The police were called but the driver could not be found at the scene. The vehicle was registered to C who was, at the time, in a relationship with D. The police attended C's address and she made a statement saying that D had returned to her address minutes before the police arrived and told her to report the vehicle as stolen. D wasn't found at the property but they did see someone, later known to be D, leaving. Telephone records showed that D sent various messages to C over a two-day period encouraging her to contact the police and tell them the vehicle had been stolen and to change her earlier statement about how D had asked her to report the vehicle as stolen. C did not do so, but later became unco-operative with the police. When arrested, D claimed he knew nothing about the vehicle being stolen. D, aged 25 when sentenced, had 29 offences on 18 occasions. Had D been the driver at the time, he would have been in breach of a suspended sentence. Held. This was a serious and persistent offence of perverting the course of justice. The offences that D [delayed in being dealt with] were serious. Starting point at 15 months, with plea **12 months**, was not outside the appropriate range.

Note: The Court said D would have breached his suspended sentence if he had been driving but it would appear the perverting offence would have been a breach of the suspended sentence as well. Ed.

R v Hampton 2014 EWCA Crim 450 D was convicted of perverting the course of justice. He pleaded (25% credit) to causing death by careless driving (simple), two driving whilst disqualified counts and various driving without insurance charges. In June 2012, D was disqualified from driving for 26 months for driving when more than three times the limit. He treated the order with contempt and bought a 4×4. In February 2013, when driving from Kent to Poole for work, he struck a 16-year-old girl, V, on her moped. V was pushed along the road for a considerable distance and then thrown into the middle of the road. D just drove round her and V was hit by another motorist. D did not stop. V received catastrophic injuries and died instantly. D checked into an hotel, inspected the damage to his car and lied to his wife about what had happened. Next he told his employers that he was ill and drove back to Kent but instead of going home he stayed in an hotel. He lied to wife again, saying the car had broken down. He had the car repaired and lied to the garage about the cause. When arrested, D said he had no idea about the accident. In interview he lied about the reasons for his movements. After the interview he drove home and was prosecuted separately for the disqualified offence (8 weeks' imprisonment). D was aged 59. The Judge said the perverting the course of justice offence was a long and persistent act. He took into account D's health and that prison would not be easy for him. Held. Two years was appropriate for the death by driving count. For perverting the course of justice, the seriousness of the substantive offence was considerable. D's approach was lie after lie after lie. **4 years** was towards the top of the range. We might have structured the sentence differently, but 6 years in all was not too long.

R v Walker 2015 EWCA Crim 1526 D pleaded (full credit) to conspiracy to pervert the course of justice. He drove at 37 mph in a 30 mph area and was caught by a speed camera. D was liable to totting up. He agreed with his mother, D2, that she would take the points on her clean licence and she did so. A few days later they agreed to admit it to the police and that was done. D made admissions and was remorseful. Held. Ordinarily a custodial sentence is required. It was appropriate for D2's 4-month sentence to be suspended because she was aged 71. We start at 6 months not 9 and with the plea and the fact that they reported themselves, **3 months**.

R v Ratcliffe 2016 EWCA Crim 27 D pleaded (20% credit) to perverting the course of justice. His car was detected by a camera going through a red light. The next day D said his number plate had been stolen. D was later told he was to be prosecuted and initially gave no response. After a reminder he wrote to the police and said he was not the driver and the plate had been stolen. D sent photos of his car to the police as requested. A comparison of the police camera and these pictures showed the car had been altered. D then told the police that he had purchased new number plates and an employee (no evidence was offered against him) at a discount centre purportedly supported this. However, it was discovered there was no computer record of this. D was aged about 39. He had a number of previous convictions including dishonesty and driving offences. His last custodial sentence was in 2002 (8 months). The Judge described the activity as a persistent course of conduct. Held. The deception was swiftly initiated by D and over a lengthy period of time. He had a clear financial motive to try and maintain that deception as it would stop an increase in his premiums for his car valeting business. That deception was repeated to the police and there was the doctored photograph. Also D purported to purchase a fresh number plate. This was a bad case. A starting point of nearly 19 months was a very severe sentence but not manifestly excessive, so **15 months** upheld.
For the details of the judicial guidance in this case, see **305.6**.
See also: *R v Saunders* 2011 EWCA Crim 12 (Plea. Perverting the course of justice. Informed police he had committed the offence for which his father was arrested. He had 23 previous convictions. **15 months** not 21.)
R v Henderson and Metcalfe 2011 EWCA Crim 1152, 2012 1 Cr App R (S) 18 (p 95) (Pleas. HGV driver caught by speed camera. Work colleague accepted 3 penalty points as driver had 11 already. No financial reward. Both treated as of good character. Starting at 6 months, **4 months** not 6. For the driver, **6-month disqualification** not 12. For the other, disqualification quashed.) See also the *Assisting defendants/tipping defendants off etc.* para at **305.7**.
R v Gray 2012 EWCA Crim 999, 2013 1 Cr App R (S) 29 (p 153) (Plea at second hearing. Caused death by careless driving (12 months' imprisonment). Did not stop. Hid clothes, shoes and car key. Told police his car had been stolen. In interview said it was the travellers who took it. 10 court appearances. **31 months consecutive** not too long.)
R v Macklin 2012 EWCA Crim 1429, 2013 1 Cr App R (S) 62 (p 347) (D was driving and collided with a lorry. Told police he was driving and failed a breath test. Later claimed his passenger, P, was driving and when bailed he telephoned P to tell him what he had said to the police. P did not accept this and telephoned the police. Before retrial

began, text messages between D and P were served and D pleaded. Aged 25. Previous conviction for arson endangering life, TDA and harassment (2 years' YOI). D persisted in his lies and gave false evidence at the first trial. No third party was questioned as a result. **12 months** not 2 years.)

R v Kruger 2012 EWCA Crim 2166, 2013 1 Cr App R (S) 117 (p 608) (Plea (full credit). Caused a minor car crash after drinking. Claimed his girlfriend was driving at the time. Police helicopter searched for her. She was tracked down, arrested at her home and detained for 10 hours. Aged 25. Previous for dangerous driving. **10 months** was severe but not manifestly excessive.)

See also: *R v Stephenson* 2015 EWCA Crim 591 (Pleaded. Two offences. Car had jamming device to avoid speed camera on 4 and 8 August 2014. On first occasion, travelling at 76 mph in 60 mph area. Lied in interview. Aged 65. Good character. Cautioned for similar offence in 2010. Because of caution and the continual use after 4 August, custody inevitable, so **2 months** upheld.)

Old cases: *R v Mercer* 2009 EWCA Crim 2100, 2010 1 Cr App R (S) 104 (p 667) (**3 years**) *Att-Gen's Ref No 16 of 2009* 2009 EWCA Crim 2439, 2010 2 Cr App R (S) 11 (p 64) (**12 years**) *R v Killeen* 2010 EWCA Crim 3341 (**3 months** consecutive)

For a summary of the first two cases, see the 9th edition of this book. If more old cases are needed, see the 8th edition.

305.30   *Prosecution/conviction, To avoid   Frustrating the breath test procedure*

R v Lefton and Others 2007 EWCA Crim 1015, 2008 1 Cr App R (S) 14 (p 58) The three defendants were Mr and Mrs L and their son, J. Mr and Mrs L pleaded to perverting the course of justice. Mrs L and J pleaded to perjury. On two occasions J was caught on speed cameras speeding in his father's car. Notice of intended prosecution was sent to the family home. J was away at university. Mrs L opened the letters and sought advice from a firm of solicitors. In a subsequent statement J made it clear that he was aware that the letters had arrived. Mrs L gave the solicitors an accurate account of what had happened. She sent them copies of the notices of intended prosecution. The solicitors advised her to do nothing. She was told that if she were sent a reminder to write saying that she had not received the first set of notices and that it wasn't possible to say who was driving. A reminder was sent in relation to the second offence. Mr and Mrs L again contacted the solicitors for advice. They were advised to send a letter, which was the basis of the perversion. It was sent on J's behalf and said that no original notice had been sent and asked for further details and/or photographs as the incident was so long ago. That draft by Mr L was sent to the solicitors. A handwritten suggested addition was made by the solicitors and, as a result of that, a further paragraph was added stating that the car was regularly driven by at least four people. J was summoned for speeding and failing to respond to the notice. He sought an adjournment but the Court went ahead and convicted him in his absence. Mr and Mrs L again contacted the solicitors. The solicitors applied to the Court to have the convictions set aside. J for the first time spoke to the solicitors. He told them he had known about the first notice. He was then told about the letter sent on his behalf which said that he had not known about the first notice and advised that he should stick to what was said in that letter. He took that advice. A proof of evidence was prepared for him by the solicitors. It repeated the claim that he didn't know about any notice until he was summoned. A barrister who did not know the true story was instructed. J and his mother went to court for the trial. She had not intended to give evidence, but the barrister asked if she would give evidence about the non-receipt of the notice and she agreed. They both gave untruthful evidence, which was the basis for the perjury. The barrister asked for costs, which led to an examination of the solicitor's file. This revealed the copies of the two original notices which had been sent by Mrs L to the solicitors, and the police were informed. All three defendants immediately confessed what had happened to the police. They co-operated fully and gave frank answers. They agreed to give witness statements for the purposes of consideration of the prosecution of any member of the solicitors' firm. Mrs L was aged 54, Mr L, 50, and J, 21. They were all of good character and had many character references. Mrs L had been a solicitor, although was not in practice at the time. They were genuinely remorseful. Held. These offences were too serious to justify suspended sentences. Their greatest mitigation is in their attitude since the offence, their full admissions and their offers to give evidence if necessary against the solicitors. In our judgment J's culpability is less and there should have been a distinction made between him and his parents. He was not involved at the initial stage. We have no doubt that he was influenced by his parents. If his sentence is unchanged he will be unable to take his university exams and his whole career will be blighted. For J, **21 days'** not 3 months' detention, for Mr and Mrs L **6 weeks'** imprisonment not 3 months.

Note: This is an old case, so the decision should be treated with care. Ed.

Old case: *R v Melender* 2003 EWCA Crim 478, 2 Cr App R (S) 63 (p 370) **(2½ years)** For a summary of this case, see the 9th edition of this book.

305.31   *Prosecution/conviction, To avoid   Giving false name on arrest etc.*

R v Burney 2007 EWCA Crim 1658, 2008 1 Cr App R (S) 57 (p 335) D pleaded to perverting the course of justice. He was out drinking with his son and, against his son's wishes, encouraged his son to drive them both home. As the car approached the junction to the A2 trunk road, the car collided with a lorry. No one was injured. The car was badly damaged but the lorry was not. The son apologised to the lorry driver but D told him not to as the lorry was over the white line. The driver said that if there was a dispute he would call the police. At D's suggestion both men abandoned the car and ran away. The police were called. The lorry driver said that the son was driving. They were arrested later that night. D encouraged the son to say that D was driving. Both men said that D had been driving. Later that day the son admitted that he had been lying and confessed that he had been driving. D stuck to his story that he was the driver. Four days later, when visiting the police station about the car, he admitted that was not true. D, aged 43, was of previous good character. The son was sentenced to a suspended sentence with 120 unpaid hours. Held. We accept that D's motive was to protect his son. Wishing to protect the son is understandable. However, he persisted in his deception for several days. The deception included leaving the scene of an accident, leaving his car in a damaged condition and making it necessary for the police to attend in the early hours. **6 months** not 12.

Note: This case is listed in this paragraph because D was trying to avoid a conviction for his son. Ed.

R v Snow 2008 EWCA Crim 580, 2 Cr App R (S) 87 (p 497) D pleaded to two counts of perverting the course of justice. He was stopped by police and gave his brother's details. A summons was issued. The brother replied that he was not driving the vehicle. D was convicted in his absence. Six months later he was stopped again and he gave a false name. The officer was not fooled and arrested him. In interview D admitted the offence. Held. 9 months for the first offence was entirely reasonable. For the second, 3 months not 9 consecutive, making **12 months** not 18 in all.

Note: Both these case are old, so the decisions in them should be treated with care. Ed.

See also: *R v Rafiq* 2012 EWCA Crim 2646 (Plea. Defendant arrested for a public order offence. Gave his brother's name and was sentenced to a community order. Met all the requirements. Brother didn't know. Six years later, arrested for drink/driving. False name came to light. Aged 32. Strong mitigation. **8 months** not 1 year.)

305.32   *Restraint order, Breach of*

R v Roddy 2010 EWCA Crim 671, 2 Cr App R (S) 107 (p 679) D was convicted for contempt of court. D and his partner owned a property where police found a large quantity of drugs. Prior to trial D was given a Restraining Order which prohibited him from disposing of, dealing with or diminishing the value of his assets, which included a property owned by D. D sold the property for £79,804, went to the Republic of Ireland and stayed with his partner. D returned to England under a false name and received 7 years for the drug offence. **15 months** not 20.

R v Baird 2011 EWCA Crim 459 D pleaded to five breaches of a restraint order. The SFO charged him with fraud and a restraint order prohibited him from disposing etc. of assets (with exceptions for living expenses) and required disclosure of all assets worth over £1,000 transferred to others since 2005. D failed to provide information relating to his assets within 21 days, although this was eventually provided. D did not comply with a provision of the order requiring information of all persons holding his assets. He also transferred property to a former partner for no consideration. This was later sold for £535,000. He also sold an expensive Ferrari, which he failed to mention. He subsequently used a false passport to open a bank account into which he paid €4,000. There were further breaches involving an application for another false passport and payment of sums into a bank account, representing a further disposal of assets. D was sentenced to 6 months for the passport offences. He was otherwise of good character. The Judge regarded the breaches as a serious matter. Held. The Judge was entitled and right to say that enough was enough. The argument that there was engagement with and co-operation with the SFO is fatally undermined by the deceptions which D was perpetrating in false names. **18 months** was not manifestly excessive.

Old case: *R v Adewunmi* 2008 EWCA Crim 71, 2 Cr App R (S) 52 (p 326) (**15 months** was more appropriate but due to part compliance **12 months**)
For a summary of the case, see the 9th edition of this book.

305.33 *Solicitors as defendants*
An example: *R v Ali* 2012 EWCA Crim 2298, 2013 1 Cr App R (S) 126 (p 669) (Plea to two pervertings and solicitor and fraud counts. Offered advice across a number of disciplines, none of which he was qualified to do. Struck off Institute of Legal Executives in 2006 for offering services that he was not qualified to undertake. Took dishonest steps obtaining divorces for husbands without informing their wives that proceedings were ongoing. Forged documents. A severe deterrent sentence was needed. Starting at 7 years. With plea **4 years 8 months** upheld.

305.34 *Statement   Making a false statement/Fabricating material/account for the court/police   Judicial guidance*
R v Josen 2013 EWCA Crim 2103 D pleaded to perverting the course of justice. Held. It is clear from the decisions about giving false information to the police to enable another to escape [justice] that the crucial factors are: a) the nature of the criminal conduct engaged in by the real offender, b) the nature and extent of the false information provided, c) the length of time over which the falsehood [was] maintained, and d) the effect which the falsehood had on the proceedings.

305.35 *Statement   Making a false statement/Fabricating material/account for the court/police*
R v Tibbits 2012 EWCA Crim 1018, 2013 1 Cr App R (S) 25 (p 130) D pleaded to perverting the course of justice. In 2010 he was sentenced to 16 months for making indecent images. A SOPO was also imposed. His daughter, a minor, had discovered some of the images on a memory stick and the matter was referred to the police. The SOPO prohibited him from having access to a computer at his home address unless it was password protected by an adult over the age of 25, approved by the supervising officer. In 2011, D instructed his solicitors to apply to have the SOPO varied on the basis that it was creating difficulties in his daily life. It was emphasised that, in particular, the provision caused difficulties in relation to the seeking of employment. D was advised that his application would be strengthened by some proof of the difficulties he was experiencing. His solicitors subsequently attended court with a letter. The letter purported to be from the transport manager of D's previous employers. It stated that as D was unable to have access to email or the Internet, the company was unable to offer him

any employment. The Crown sought to have the letter verified and it was discovered that it was a forgery. The purported author of the forged letter confirmed that it was not necessary for employees of the company to have access to the Internet and that D had been asked to leave the company in 2010 upon his conviction. Held. It would be wrong to treat D's behaviour as an attempt to revert to his previous offending behaviour. The terms of the order were legitimately subject to an application to vary by reason of subsequent decisions of this Court. D attempted to subvert the due process of the law and sought to vary a court order by use of a forged letter. He subsequently attempted to mitigate that by claims that the letter was never intended for use. Those are aggravating factors, but **2 years** not 3.

R v Livesley 2012 EWCA Crim 1100, 2013 1 Cr App R (S) 27 (p 138) D was convicted of intending to pervert the course of justice. In 2004, he pleaded to a £29,000 benefit fraud. During the sentencing hearing, his counsel placed before the court a bundle of references. Those included one from an Air Commodore who referred to D's distinguished employment at the Imperial War Museum, Duxford, and how he was awarded the Military Medal for bravery in action with the Parachute Regiment in the Falklands War. Another, from a Major, stated that he had served a full career in the Parachute Regiment and had risen to the rank of Colour Sergeant. The makers of these statements relied on what D told them, which was false. In reality, D had joined the Army as a teenager and been discharged as medically unfit after 2½ years. He had served as a cook in the Catering Corps. D, aged 57 at appeal, showed genuine remorse. He was of good character and had difficulties in distinguishing between truth and fantasy. The probation psychiatrist for the Court of Appeal said D was severely impaired by a personality disorder. Held. The Judge would have sentenced D to immediate custody but for the references that were before the Court. The sentence would have been of some length. The deception was sustained and planned in the sense that the references were obtained from two innocent referees and deployed with a view to achieving the purpose of getting a lesser sentence than he otherwise would have done. Those purporting to give these two references were obviously gravely embarrassed, and most importantly of all, the court was very seriously misled. As the Judge rightly said, it is crucially important that judges should be able to rely on character references, so a particular element of deterrent sentencing is appropriate in this context which of its nature (perverting the course of justice) calls for deterrence in any event. Despite the considerable personal mitigation and the fact that some judges might have imposed less, **3 years** could not be described as excessive.

R v Afford 2013 EWCA Crim 633, 2014 1 Cr App R (S) 2 (p 4) D pleaded (full credit) to perverting the course of justice. His brother-in-law contacted the police to report that D had been attacked by four Asian males, one of whom had slashed his face with a knife whilst commenting, "no white person should walk here". The police attended D's address to take a statement. He provided a description of the attackers but gave a different location from that which was originally reported. The officers spent 90 minutes reviewing CCTV footage and investigating the location. No blood was found at the scene and there were inconsistencies with his account. The story was reported in the local press and the police were concerned that community tensions might be engaged and so they gave high priority to their investigation. An article featured a photograph of D and his injuries. There were 16 separate 'slashes' which D had inflicted upon himself. CCTV images showed D walking back after the alleged attack, but showing no sign of injuries. He was interviewed and admitted he had falsely reported the attack. He had had an encounter with someone over a cigarette and had been punched by that person. That person then followed him home and attacked him. The attack had arisen from a dispute between D and his ex-partner over the use of a motor vehicle. D had no convictions since 2002. Held. There were clearly racial elements in the way the offence was reported. Scarce police and health service resources were wasted. There was a clear risk that men fitting the description given by D would be arrested, though in the event no one was arrested. That had to be borne in mind. The self-inflicted injuries were committed to further the complaint. The risk of inflammation of community or race relations could not be ignored but starting at 12 months, **8 months** not 12.

Note: The case is listed here as there was no attempt to incriminate a particular person. Ed.

R v Josen 2013 EWCA Crim 2103 D pleaded to perverting the course of justice. Police searched K's sister's premises and found a Walther pistol, a silencer for the pistol in a box and five bullets in a bag. K's palm print was found on the bag and his fingerprint on the box. It was illegal for K to possess the pistol as he had a relevant conviction. K was charged with possession of the items and pleaded not guilty. His defence case statement said the articles belonged to D. D went to the police with his solicitor saying he had found a silencer and ammunition while walking K's dog and had taken them to K's sister. D was charged with possessing the silencer and the ammunition. Police were highly sceptical about this. K pleaded to the charges and received 5½ years. D was aged 45 and had 37 previous offences including two of perverting the course of justice in 1999 and 2001 (D given unpaid work and community order). Held. There was no material effect upon proceedings against K. The falsehood was over within weeks. The two previous convictions were serious aggravating factors. We start at 3 years not 4, so with the plea, **2 years** not 32 months.

See also: *R v Kincarr* 2012 EWCA Crim 245 (Early plea to perverting the course of justice. Aged 32. Good character. Gave statement that the marriage of two others, one being his long-standing partner, was a sham to bypass immigration controls. Later said the statement (which was true) was untrue before the two pleaded. **6 months** not 12.)

R v Ngwata 2012 EWCA Crim 2015, 2013 1 Cr App R (S) 111 (p 576) (Late plea to perverting the course of justice. Married husband in Congo in 2009. Came to UK in 2010. Subsequently left marital home. False claim that her husband had locked her in the flat every day and subjected her to domestic violence, raped her at knife point and repeated rape. Applied for indefinite leave to remain claiming she had been assaulted. Husband arrested and held in custody for 14 hours. Advised to say what she did by others, claiming that it was in her son's interests. 20% credit. Starting at 3 years was correct. With the plea, **2 years 5 months**.)

R v Coe 2013 EWCA Crim 1253 (Plea to theft (×2) and perverting the course of justice. Stole £1,500 from a safe at veterinary surgery where he worked. Claimed he had been robbed at knife point. Made lengthy police statement to that effect. Previous including multiple thefts, frauds, animal welfare offences. 21 officers including firearms officers searched the local area. 12 months not 18 for the perverting. Consecutive to two 9-month sentences (concurrent with each other) for the theft. **21 months** not 27.)

Old case: *R v Ballard* 2007 EWCA Crim 751, 2 Cr App R (S) 94 (p 608) (**6 months in all**) *R v Khan and Others* 2009 EWCA Crim 966 (**30 months**) *Att-Gen's Ref No 35 of 2009* 2009 EWCA Crim 1375, 2010 1 Cr App R (S) 61 (p 410) (**34 weeks' detention suspended** with 200 hours' unpaid work was unduly lenient.)

For a summary of the cases, see the 9th edition of this book.

305.36 *Tag interference*

R v MacKenzie and Lammie 2012 EWCA Crim 2088, 2013 1 Cr App R (S) 104 (p 546)[810] M and L pleaded (25% credit) to perverting the course of justice. L was M's stepfather. M had been sentenced to a 6-month community order including a 17-week, 8 pm to 8 am electronically monitored curfew requirement. When the tag was fitted, L was present and stated that he was M. He answered a number of questions and showed documentation to prove that he was M. The tag was fitted to L and the monitoring equipment was installed. M was then present. The police received information that M was not abiding by his curfew and that the tag had been fitted to the wrong person. L was spoken to and admitted what he had done. L suggested that M had discussed the possibility of L wearing the tag. M stated that he had been upstairs when the employee of

---

[810] The Criminal Appeal reports list this as '*McKenzie*', which will no doubt affect searching for it.

the security firm attended and the tag had already been fitted by the time he had made his way downstairs. M also claimed that it was L's idea as he felt sorry for him as he was unable to visit his children whilst subject to the curfew. M, aged 27 at his appeal, had a number of convictions for not abiding by court orders such as community orders and Bail Act offences. L, aged 34 at appeal, also had a number of convictions. Held. Immediate custody was correct. Their actions defeated a lawfully imposed sentence, and defeated the ends of justice. A stern sentence was called for, but starting at 3 years was too high. Starting at 2 years was appropriate. So with 25% credit for the plea (as a plea was inevitable), **18 months** not 2 years.

305.37   *Witness intimidation   Magistrates' Court Sentencing Guidelines*
Magistrates' Court Sentencing Guidelines 2008, see www.banksr.com Other Matters Guidelines tab page 116 The guidelines apply to the Magistrates' Court and the Crown Court hearing appeals or sentencing for summary only offences.[811]
page 116 Starting points are based on a first-time offender pleading not guilty.

Examples of nature of activity	Starting point	Range
Sudden outburst in chance encounter	6 weeks' custody	Medium-level community order to 18 weeks' custody
Conduct amounting to a threat, staring at, approaching or following witnesses, talking about the case, trying to alter or stop evidence	18 weeks' custody	12 weeks' custody to Crown Court
Threats of violence to witnesses and/or their families, deliberately seeking out witnesses	Crown Court	Crown Court

The following aggravating and mitigating factors may be particularly relevant: Factors indicating higher culpability: 1 Breach of bail conditions, and 2 Offender involves others. Factors indicating greater degree of harm: 1 Detrimental impact on administration of justice, and 2 Contact made at or in vicinity of victim's home.
Consider ancillary orders, including compensation.
For the meaning of a medium-level community order see **16.13** in Volume 1.

305.38   *Witness intimidation etc. Judicial guidance*
R v Khan 2001 EWCA Crim 912, 2 Cr App R (S) 129 (p 553) Cases where threats are used against potential witnesses are generally more serious than those where the offender merely tries to persuade (with or without a bribe) a witness to retract or change his or her evidence. Where threats are used, the sentence may well be in the range of **12 months to 2 years** depending on the circumstances, including the seriousness of the threats.
R v Chinery 2002 EWCA Crim 32, 2 Cr App R (S) 55 (p 244) D was convicted of two counts of witness intimidation. Held. The offences are very serious. Witnesses are indispensable. They must not be pressurised. Sentences invariably contain an element of deterrence.

305.39   *Witness interference   Cases*
R v Cullen 2010 EWCA Crim 1611 D pleaded to conspiracy to pervert the course of justice. F kidnapped and raped a young woman who was not known to him. F hid a sawn-off shotgun so that he or those close to him could use the weapon to terrify the rape victim into not giving evidence. F said he knew his victim and the sex was consensual. D, aged 36, was a former partner of F and the mother of his daughter. D said she would corroborate F's account that he had met the rape victim before and she knew where the shotgun was hidden. D eventually gave evidence for the prosecution at F's trial. D had no recent significant convictions. The pre-sentence report said she was very remorseful,

---

[811] See page 15 of the guidelines.

she was a single mother and said she needed help. The Judge described her evidence as "very tentative and self-seeking". The prison report commented favourably on D's conduct whilst in prison. Held. It was impossible to say how important her evidence was. The Judge was not impressed, but it did take courage to give it. She did give significant assistance. **10 months** not 2 years.

Att-Gen's Ref No 39 of 2011 2011 EWCA Crim 2617 During his trial, D pleaded to intentionally assisting etc. an offender to commit arson, reckless as to whether life was endangered. When D lost his job, he pursued a course of threats directed toward his employer, V. D was charged under Public Order Act 1986. (There were also pleas to drugs offences.) When V intended to give evidence, D offered £2,000 to an associate (whom he knew to have a history of non-fatal violence) as payment for setting light to the employer's home. D was unconcerned whether the employer or his family would be at home. He instructed his associate that he wanted petrol poured through the main entry of the property. D persisted in his requests and his associate reported the matter to the police. D had 13 convictions for 18 offences, including violence and criminal damage. Held. The offence was motivated by revenge, was premeditated and involved planning. It was also committed on bail. The plea was entered at the last possible moment, which attracts a discount of 10%. The victim's family could have been seriously injured if not killed. Having already had an extended sentence imposed upon him, there is no doubt that the proper sentence is IPP. It is inappropriate to pass a consecutive term for the other offences. Starting at somewhere in the region of 7 years, with plea, 6½ years. We raise that to 8 years for the drugs offences which he pleaded to. With double jeopardy, we arrive at 7 years, so **3½ years' IPP,** not 2 years 2 months determinate.

Note: This case is listed in this paragraph because D's intention was that there should be at the least serious violence to property. Ed.

R v Banbury-Taylor 2014 EWCA Crim 1927 D was convicted of witness intimidation and pleaded to common assault and ABH. D indecently exposed himself outside a school (which he later pleaded to). Six months later, D saw the witness, V1, who had reported him and knocked on her door. V1 and her family answered the door and they then tried persuading D, who was drunk, to go away. D refused and demanded to know why V1 had called the police and for her to apologise for doing so. V1's daughter, V2, filmed the incident but D pushed her phone from her hand. D then punched V2 repeatedly and dragged her to the ground, causing scratches and bruising. In interview, D admitted being drunk, but denied being aggressive. His alleged intention had been to apologise. D was aged 31 at appeal and had four previous convictions, all non-violent and non-custodial. He was remorseful. Held. The assault was a Category 1 offence. **3 years** for the witness intimidation, but the assaults to be concurrent, making 3 years in total, not 5.

R v Nwanokwu 2015 EWCA Crim 813, 2 Cr App R (S) 33 (p 281) D pleaded to perverting the course of justice. D's daughter, R, was arrested for aggravated burglary where one of the victims, V, was stabbed in the leg several times by R. Rings and a handbag were among items stolen. D made phone calls in an attempt to persuade V to withdraw, retract or change his evidence. D visited V at his home and explained that R would lose custody of her baby. There were no threats made. She had a series of 'low-level' shoplifting offences and was in breach of a conditional discharge for theft (one month consecutive). D had been, over 15 years, a foster parent for over 75 children. The Judge said victims suffered stress and pressure and D had added further pressure to them. Held. That was a serious consideration. There were important policy reasons why the Judge passed an immediate 6-month prison sentence, but her conduct was naïve. The fact it was based on parental concern, that no threats were made and her fostering work was outstanding, made this case exceptional. The sentence could have been suspended so we will ensure her immediate release[812].

---

[812] The report says the Court substituted a 172-day sentence because that was the time she had served. As she was serving a 7-month sentence she would have been released much earlier. What the true situation was is unclear.

See also: *R v Smith* 2011 EWCA Crim 972 (Plea on rearraignment to intimidation. In breach of Suspended Sentence Order. In drink, attended home of a witness to an assault. D was not the man who committed the assault, but the victim of the intimidation gave a statement that he was. Made threats to victim's son. No violence. **2 years 8 months**.) *Att-Gen's Ref Nos 14-16 of 2015* 2015 EWCA Crim 822, 2 Cr App R (S) 36 (p 293) (Honey trap to lure witness away on day of trial from giving evidence. Witness not at Court for one day. Plan unsuccessful. No threats made. We would expect, before plea, for the man facing the trial **3 years**, and the others in the plan **2 years**.) Old cases: *R v Bishop* 2009 EWCA Crim 2502, 2010 2 Cr App R (S) 17 (p 100)[813] (**2½ years**) *R v Sharpe* 2009 EWCA Crim 2774, 2010 2 Cr App R (S) 37 (p 240) (**2 years**) *R v Raybone* 2010 EWCA Crim 78, 2 Cr App R (S) 58 (p 390) (**30 months**) For a summary of the first case and other old cases, see the 9th edition of this book.

305.40   *Witness refusing to answer questions/attend court   Judicial guidance*
R v Montgomery 1995 16 Cr App R (S) 274 D refused to take the oath and was dealt with for contempt. Held. The principles are: 1) An immediate custodial sentence is the only appropriate sentence for a person who interferes with the administration of justice, unless the circumstances are wholly exceptional. 2) Whilst interference with, or threats made to, jurors are usually visited with higher sentences than cases of a witness who refuses to give evidence, there is no rule or established practice to that effect, the circumstances of each case being all-important. 3) The 3-month maximum sentence for failing to comply with a witness order should not inhibit the court from imposing a sentence substantially longer than 3 months for a blatant contempt in the face of the court. The principal matters affecting sentence are: a) the gravity of the offence being tried, b) the effect on the trial, c) the contemnor's reason for failing to give evidence, d) whether or not the contempt is aggravated by impertinent defiance of the judge, rather than simple and stubborn refusal to answer...and g) whether or not a special deterrent is needed, e.g. where it is becoming clear at the beginning of a series of trials that witnesses are being systematically threatened or becoming disaffected in numbers. Note: This is an old case, so treat the decisions with care. The cases in this area are old, but can be found in the 9th edition of this book. Ed. For an article about this, see *Archbold News* 12 November 2012.

305.41   *Witness retracting statement   Rape victims   Judicial guidance*
R v A 2011 EWCA Crim 2913 LCJ D pleaded to perverting the course of justice (×2). She admitted falsely retracting rape allegations against her husband. Held. It is worth emphasising that a complaint that an individual has been the victim of a crime is not, and never has been, merely a private matter between the complainant and the alleged perpetrator of the crime. Every crime engages the community at large. The difference between the culpability of the individual who instigates a false complaint against an innocent man and the complainant who retracts a truthful allegation against a guilty man will often be very marked. Experience shows that the withdrawal of a truthful complaint of crime committed in a domestic environment usually stems from pressure, sometimes direct, sometimes indirect, sometimes immensely subtle, which is consequent on the nature of the individual relationship and the characters of the people who are involved in it. The sentence for perverting the course of justice normally is and will normally continue to be a custodial sentence.

305.42   *Witness retracting statement   Rape victims   Case*
R v A 2011 EWCA Crim 2913 LCJ D pleaded to perverting the course of justice (×2). She admitted falsely retracting rape allegations against her husband and the Crown offered no evidence on the count alleging the allegations were false. She had made three allegations of rape against her husband, H, with whom she had lived for nine years. She was in an extremely distressed state and was relocated to a women's refuge. H was

---

[813] Facts in this judgment are in short supply. It is not clear whether threats were made, but the sentence suggests they were.

charged with six counts of rape, remanded in custody and a date was set for trial. He was subsequently granted bail. D informed the police that she wished to retract the allegations, but maintained that they were true. D was informed that the prosecution of H would continue. She then stated that she had had consensual sex with H and she said the allegations were untrue. No evidence was offered against H. D was subsequently interviewed by the CPS. She explained that both H and H's sister had sought to persuade D to retract her statement. Further, she thought that beginning divorce proceedings was sufficient for her own purposes and so she decided to retract the complaint. She claimed she had been the victim of years of domestic abuse at the hands of H. D, aged 28 at appeal, was of effective good character. D and H had four children aged between 2 and 8. Held. The sentence for perverting the course of justice normally is and will normally continue to be a custodial sentence. This is not such a case. **Community order** with supervision for 2 years.

306 PLANNING OFFENCES

306.1

Town and Country Planning Act 1990
  s 179 (failure to comply with an enforcement notice)
  s 187 (contravention of a stop notice)
  s 189 (contravention of orders requiring discontinuance etc.)
  s 194 (false statements etc. in an application for a certificate of lawful use or development)
  s 210 (non-compliance with tree orders)

Modes of trial All the offences are triable either way.

Maximum sentences On indictment fine only (except for section 194 where the maximum is 2 years). Summary maximum £20,000 for sections 179, 187 and 210, and a £5,000 fine for sections 189 and 194 for offences committed before 12 March 2015 and an unlimited fine thereafter.[814]

Need to regard financial benefit In determining the fine for section 179 offences, the court shall have regard to any financial benefit which has accrued, or appears likely to accrue to him in consequence of the offence, Town and Country Planning Act 1990 s 179(9). In *R v Smith* 2014 EWCA Crim 1508, the Court of Appeal dealt with the problem when the benefit was unclear. On the facts they concluded there must have been a considerable benefit.

See also the **ENVIRONMENTAL OFFENCES** *Tree preservation offences, Breaches of* para at **249.9**.

306.2 *Statistics*

Town and Country Planning Act 1990 Aged 21+

Year	2010	2011	2012	2013	2014
Plea	2 pleas	2 pleas		21 pleas	45 pleas
Sentence	1 fine and 1 discharge	2 fines	Not available	1 discharge, 18 fines and 1 other type of sentence	6 discharges, 36 fines and 3 other types of sentence

---

[814] Legal Aid, Sentencing and Punishment of Offenders Act 2012 (Fines on Summary Conviction) Regulations 2015 2015/664 para 4 and Sch 1 para 18 for section 179, 187 and 210 offences. For section 189 and 194 offences Legal Aid, Sentencing and Punishment of Offenders Act 2012 s 85(1) and (4) and Legal Aid, Sentencing and Punishment of Offenders Act 2012 (Commencement No 11) Order 2015 2015/504

306.3   Enforcement notice offences

R v Schonewille 2011 EWCA Crim 811 D was convicted of one count of non-compliance with an enforcement notice contrary to Town and Country Planning Act 1990. He had inherited the land and intended for the caravans to be a temporary residence. D had applied for planning permission for the continuing use of his two caravans for residential use. The application was refused, as was an appeal and a subsequent application. Further visits to the site showed how one caravan was removed, followed by the second. However, subsequently one of the caravans was seen on the site inside a building referred to as a workshop. A wall had been removed and replaced in order to place the caravan inside. There was evidence that D had attempted to sell the remaining caravan. D was of good character. A fine of **£1,051** payable within 6 months was not too high. Costs of £7,500 were unreasonable. £5,000 substituted.

R v Dagim Fish and Deli 2014 EWCA Crim 2927 D was convicted of breaching an enforcement notice. D, a company, owned a ground floor communal unit. In 2002 D was granted planning permission to build a ground floor cold store unit. In 2007, it was discovered that a two-storey building had been built. The company was notified of the breach and, in 2008, an enforcement notice was served. The company appealed and the appeal was dismissed in 2009. A judicial review appeal was made and that was refused. In October 2009, the company was told it would be prosecuted unless there was compliance within 6 months. After that period, the structure was still in place. D's gross profits between 2009 and 2012 were between £173,000 and £212,000. The Judge found a stubborn refusal to comply with a court order and so considered an element of deterrence was required. The Court made a confiscation order of about £10,340 and awarded £13,200 prosecution costs. Held. In *R v Duckworth* 1995 16 Cr App R (S) 529, this court considered there were three relevant factors where a building had been destroyed. First, the degree of damage done to the structure, which did not apply in this case. Second, the financial gain. The financial benefit which was sought to be achieved must be taken into account otherwise the deterrent and punitive effect may be lost. Third, and most important, the culpability of the defendant. There was no permanent destruction, so **£25,000 fine** not £45,000.

See also: *R v Smith* 2014 EWCA Crim 1508 (Wilful defiance of order. Used land for residential purposes. Benefit unclear. **£100,000** fine not £250,000 fine.)

R v Hussain 2014 EWCA Crim 2344 (Convicted. D disregarded planning enforcement notice, preventing premises' use as two flats. Pointed out multiple times. Written to at least four times but ignored authorities over four years. Good character. **£20,000 fine**, the maximum was severe but justifiable. Costs of £38,420 unappealed.)

R v Kohali 2015 EWCA Crim 1757, 2016 1 Cr App R (S) 30 (p 180) (Because of the dates in the count, we reduce the fine from £190,000 to £30,000.)

Note: This case is not summarised in full because of the local authority's failure to prosecute and indict the case properly. Ed.

306.4   Failure to obtain consent

R v Johnson 2012 EWCA Crim 580, 2 Cr App R (S) 87 (p 517) D pleaded to executing works without authorisation. He bought a semi-detached house in a conservation area. The house was considered significant to the history, character and appearance of the street. It was not listed. D was granted permission to partially demolish the property. It was clear the front façade was not to be demolished. D had sought advice on numerous issues about the property from the council. Without warning anyone, D demolished the house. An expert said the damage could never be fully reversed in heritage terms. A rebuild would not remedy the harm. The value of the remaining villas on the estate had been damaged, particularly N's house, which was once attached. N was concerned about structural integrity and the difficulty of selling her house. The benefit of demolition (VAT and other savings) was £109,320. The value of both the original and the rebuilt house was £1.9m. The basis of plea said D was 'grossly negligent' in not obtaining permission. D had agreed to pay the council £42,500. The Judge started at £120,000 and with plea made the fine £80,000. D had to pay prosecution costs of £42,500. Held. The stress to the neighbours was considerable. Because part of the building was to be demolished anyway and it was not done for commercial gain, we start at £50,000 making a fine of **£33,000**.

Note: The sentencing Judge's decisions seem faultless. The Court of Appeal's decision appears to lack sufficient deterrence and puts insufficient weight to the neighbours' distress, particularly the distress of the one whose house was once attached to D's house. Ed.

306.5   *Listed building offence*

Planning (Listed Buildings and Conservation Areas) Act 1990 s 7 and 9 (unauthorised demolition, alteration or extension of a listed building which affects its character)

R v Rance 2012 EWCA Crim 2023, 2013 1 Cr App R (S) 123 (p 636) D, a property developer, was convicted of a planning offence at the Magistrates' Court. D paid over £2m for a Victorian house in Fulham. He made three applications for conversion and it became clear that his intention was to demolish the house because this would save money. D was told that to do so he would need conservation area consent, which was unlikely to be granted. D removed walls and destabilised the spine wall, and the planning officer thought the work amounted to virtual demolition. The front become unstable, it was considered dangerous and D was granted permission to demolish the front elevation. He was then granted permission to build a new house on the site. He was committed for sentence. The prosecution said they considered he had the means to pay. Under Planning (Listed Buildings and Conservation Areas) Act 1990 s 9(5), the Court was required to have regard to any financial benefit which had accrued. The Judge considered that £100,000 represented the benefit. Costs attributed to the trial and appeal were £60,000. Held. The Judge was entitled to take a severe view of this case but **£50,000** not £120,000 fine with £40,000 costs.

Note: Not for the first time, the sentencing Judge's assessment included a deterrent element and an understanding of commercial considerations whereas the Court of Appeal's assessment was based mainly on ancient cases. Ed.

307   POSSESSION OF DRUGS

307.1

Misuse of Drugs Act 1971 s 5(2)

Mode of trial Triable either way

Maximum sentences On indictment: 7 years for class A drugs, 5 years for class B drugs and 2 years for class C drugs[815]

Summary maxima: 6 months and/or a £5,000 fine for class A drugs offences committed before 12 March 2015 and an unlimited fine thereafter.[816] There are maximum fines for those aged under 18, see **14.38** in Volume 1. 3 months and/or £2,500 for class B drugs, and 3 months and/or £1,000 for class C drugs.[817]

Fixed penalties There is a £90 fixed penalty for possession of cannabis, cannabis resin and associated drugs[818] with half the relevant victim surcharge. For more detail see **61.1** in Volume 1.

Psychoactive Substances For possession of a psychoactive substance in a custodial institution, see **309.9**.

See also **DEFENDANT** *Drug users* paras at **240.21** and the **AMPHETAMINE, CANNABIS, LSD,** and **SUPPLY OF DRUGS** chapters.

---

[815] Misuse of Drugs Act 1971 s 25 and Sch 4
[816] Legal Aid, Sentencing and Punishment of Offenders Act 2012 s 85(1) and (4) and Legal Aid, Sentencing and Punishment of Offenders Act 2012 (Commencement No 11) Order 2015 2015/504
[817] Misuse of Drugs Act 1971 s 25 and Sch 4
[818] Penalties for Disorderly Behaviour (Amount of Penalty) Order 2002 2002/1837 as amended.

307.2   *Crown Court statistics   England and Wales*
Possession   Class A[819]

Year	Age	Plea	Total sentenced	Type of sentencing %						Average length of custody in months
				Dis-charge	Fine	Commu-nity sentence	Sus-pended sentence	Cus-tody	Oth-er	
2013	18-20	G	46	2.2	23.9	23.9	17.4	19.6	13	11.1
		NG	4	–	–	50	–	50	–	81
	21+	G	595	5.5	11.8	31.1	18	27.2	6.4	9.2
		NG	10	20	30	10	10	20	10	72.2
2014	18-20	G	71	4	14	25	13	37	7	4.5
		NG	3	–	–	33	67	–	–	–
	21+	G	575	7	15	22	17	33	5	9.0
		NG	19	11	47	11	16	16	–	Not listed[820]

Possession   Class B   Aged 21+

Year	Plea	Total sentenced	Type of sentencing %						Average length of custody in months
			Discharge	Fine	Commu-nity sentence	Sus-pended sentence	Custody	Other	
2013	G	920	12	17.5	25.9	18.2	15.1	11.4	2.6
	NG	14	7.1	50	28.6	–	7.1	7.1	6
2014	G	910	17	20	21	13	16	13	3.3
	NG	14	36	36	14	–	7	7	Not listed[821]

For explanations about the statistics, see page 1-xii. For more statistics including where the class of the drug is unknown and for statistics for male and female defendants etc., see www.banksr.com Other Matters Statistics tab

307.3   *Sentencing Council guideline*
Drug Offences Guideline 2012, see www.banksr.com Other Matters Guidelines tab page 29

STEP ONE Determining the offence category
page 30 The court should identify the offence category based on the class of drug involved.

Category 1	Class A drug
Category 2	Class B drug
Category 3	Class C drug

STEP TWO Starting point and category range
page 30 The court should use the table below to identify the corresponding starting point. The starting point applies to all offenders irrespective of plea or previous convictions. The court should then consider further adjustment within the category range for aggravating or mitigating features, set out [at **307.4**].
Where the defendant is dependent on or has a propensity to misuse drugs and there is sufficient prospect of success, a community order with a drug rehabilitation

---

[819] It is possible that the data for defendants aged 18-20 was included with the 21+ data. It seems unlikely that the figure for not guilty pleas to possession of class A would be 2 people for 2011 and 2012. Ed.
[820] Based on too few cases to be meaningful
[821] Based on too few cases to be meaningful

requirement under Criminal Justice Act 2003 s 209 can be a proper alternative to a short or moderate-length custodial sentence.

Offence category	Starting point (applicable to all offenders)	Category range (applicable to all offenders)
Category 1 (class A)	Band C fine	Band A fine to 51 weeks' custody
Category 2 (class B)	Band B fine	Discharge to 26 weeks' custody
Category 3 (class C)	Band A fine	Discharge to medium-level community order

Note: A Band A fine is 50% of net weekly income. Bands B and C are 100% and 150%. For more detail, see **60.27** in Volume 1. Ed.

For the meaning of a medium-level community order see **16.13** in Volume 1.

307.4   [Aggravating and mitigating factors]

page 31 The table below contains a **non-exhaustive** list of additional factual elements providing the context of the offence and factors relating to the offender. Identify whether any combination of these, or other relevant factors, should result in an upward or downward adjustment from the starting point. **In particular, possession of drugs in prison is likely to result in an upward adjustment.** In some cases, having considered these factors, it may be appropriate to move outside the identified category range.

Where appropriate, consider the custody threshold as follows:

Has the custody threshold been passed?

If so, is it unavoidable that a custodial sentence be imposed?

If so, can that sentence be suspended?

Where appropriate, the court should also consider the community threshold as follows:

Has the community threshold been passed?

Factors increasing seriousness
Statutory aggravating factors:
Previous convictions, having regard to a) nature of the offence to which conviction relates and relevance to current offence; and b) time elapsed since conviction
Offence committed on bail
Other aggravating factors include:
Possession of drug in prison
Presence of others, especially children and/or non-users
Possession of drug in a school or licensed premises
Failure to comply with current court orders
Offence committed on licence
Attempts to conceal or dispose of evidence, where not charged separately
Charged as importation of a very small amount
Established evidence of community impact

Factors reducing seriousness or reflecting personal mitigation
No previous convictions **or** no relevant or recent convictions
Remorse
Good character and/or exemplary conduct
Offender is using cannabis to help with a diagnosed medical condition
Determination and/or demonstration of steps having been taken to address addiction or offending behaviour
Serious medical conditions requiring urgent, intensive or long-term treatment
Isolated incident
Age and/or lack of maturity where it affects the responsibility of the offender
Mental disorder or learning disability
Sole or primary carer for dependent relatives

307.5   *Suggested approach to the guideline*
Att-Gen's Ref Nos 15-17 of 2012 2012 EWCA Crim 1414, 2013 1 Cr App R (S) 52 (p 289) If the Sentencing Council had intended to lower the level of sentencing, that was not reflected in their press release, which said, 'There will be no change in sentencing for possession or drug supply offences'.
R v Russell 2013 EWCA Crim 273 It should…be noted that, in contrast to other drug offences, the simple possession guideline does not identify the quantity of the illicit drug in question as being a feature that should affect sentence. The reason for this appears to be that, as a result of consultation, the Sentencing Council took the view that 'quantity is an arbitrary measure of seriousness which might give rise to perverse outcomes and disproportionality in sentencing'.
Note: I suggest that it is better to simply follow the guideline and ignore the pre-guideline cases. However, it is a pity the guideline provides so little guidance. Ed.

307.6   *Cases   Class A   Post-guideline cases*
R v Russell 2013 EWCA Crim 273 D pleaded (full credit) to possession of cocaine. He drove his car to a petrol station. He entered the shop, purchased a petrol can and filled it with petrol. D then sprinkled the petrol inside the car and set fire to it with a lighter. He shut the car door, which contained the flames. He made no attempt to escape. He was arrested and taken to the police station. During a strip search, he sat down and when he got up he left behind a bag containing 34.1 grams of cocaine with a street value of £5,500. A jury were unable to agree on a count of possession with intent to supply, and D had already pleaded to simple possession and was convicted of arson. D suffered from bipolar disorder and had been a long-term user of drugs including crack and heroin. He described drugs as having ruined his life. A doctor's opinion was that his long-term illicit substance misuse had probably had a detrimental impact upon his mental state and precipitated a relapse some time before the offence at the petrol station. He thought that D was acutely psychotic. D had 13 convictions between 1995 and 2012. There was only one class A offence (supply, 1995) but some others were serious offences. D received 4 years for arson and 12 months consecutive for the drugs. Only the drugs sentence was challenged. Held. If the sheer quantity of cocaine is to be disregarded, as is the approach in the guideline, then it is difficult to identify any basis upon which 12 months could be justified. **9 months** was appropriate after a trial, so taking account of the plea, **6 months**, not 12. The sentence was consecutive to the 4 years for arson.
R v Burns 2013 EWCA Crim 286 D was convicted of possession of class A (×2), namely heroin and crack cocaine. He was arrested for another matter and a search of his address revealed the drugs. Plastic bags were concealed under the mudguard of a bike in the front garden. They contained 84.23 grams of heroin (11-17% purity) and 12.9 grams of crack (26% purity). The drugs had a value of £5,560 and £645 respectively. D was aged 17 (four months off his 18th birthday) at the time of the offence. The pre-sentence report noted that D said he intended to hide the drugs for a short period of time on instructions from someone else. He had been coerced into holding the drugs through threats and he had not been paid. He showed genuine remorse. Held. [The issues surrounding the appropriate starting point when the offender crosses or is close to a relevant age threshold] are not capable of precise mathematical calculation. What is plainly right here is that D's youth at the time he committed the offences should be taken into account, albeit he was not far off his 18th birthday. The appropriate sentence would have been **21 months' detention**, not 30 months.
R v Lawrence 2014 EWCA Crim 2569 D pleaded to possession of MDMA. He was acquitted of supplying the same quantity. D's conduct in a nightclub aroused suspicion. He was searched and 20 packages of MDMA were found in his shoe. The weight was 3.15 grams at 94% purity. He had £30 in cash on him. D was of good character. The Judge gave a 3-month Suspended Sentence Order. Held. There were a number of aggravating factors, a) the location was a nightclub, b) the quantity, and c) the purity. The quantity and the purity were reasons to go significantly beyond the starting point in

the guidelines. The packaging could not be an aggravating factor in a possession case. For a first possession offence the custody threshold is not passed. As he had been on a 3-month curfew, we reduce the unpaid hours in the **community order** to 40 hours.

307.7   *Cases Class B   Post-guideline cases*
R v Wyatt 2014 EWCA Crim 130 D pleaded (full credit) to possession of a class B drug (MCAT). In February 2013, he was sentenced for possession of MCAT with intent to supply (social supply). He received a suspended sentence of detention in a YOI (28 weeks). He failed to attend review hearings on at least two occasions. He was summoned to court in respect of those breaches but before the hearing he was arrested for the simple possession of MCAT. Held. The Judge did not explain why he regarded it necessary to go outside of the guideline for the simple possession offence. The circumstances permitted the Judge to make an upward adjustment from the starting point of a fine to reflect the aggravating features but the facts and circumstances did not justify an upward adjustment outside the category altogether, nor did they justify an upward adjustment to the level of sentence imposed here. It is significant that D was given a real opportunity when he was given the suspended sentence. 28 weeks consecutive was too long. Starting at 9 weeks, with the plea, **6 weeks** consecutive was appropriate. The partial activation of the suspended sentence (24 weeks) was not challenged.

307.8   *Servicemen and women   Service policy considerations*
Guidance on Sentencing in the Court Martial 2013 para 5.7.1 The Armed Forces' policy on drug abuse is published in Joint Service Publication 835. It states that the misuse of drugs is incompatible with the demands of Service life and poses a significant threat to operational effectiveness. The implications of drug misuse are particularly damaging and the illegal possession and use of controlled drugs is an offence under both Service and civil law. Drugs impair judgement and reliability, reduce fitness, damage health, degrade performance, and harm team cohesion and Service ethos, as well as being harmful personally, to family relationships and to society generally. It is Service Personnel Board policy that there is no place in the Armed Forces for those who misuse drugs. Only in exceptional circumstances will any member of the Armed Forces be retained following drug misuse.
For aggravating and mitigating factors, see *Guidance on Sentencing in the Court Martial 2013* para 5.7.3 and 5.7.4.

307.9   *Servicemen and women   Suggested penalties*
Guidance on Sentencing in the Court Martial 2013 para 5.7.5 **Entry points** Simple possession Dismissal + Detention for 90 to 180 days
All other drug-related offences (including supply) – Dismissal + Imprisonment with a Service Community Order as an alternative to imprisonment, particularly where the offender needs treatment for addiction.
For circumstances where the offender may be retained in the Service see *Guidance on Sentencing in the Court Martial 2013* para 5.7.6.

308   PRISONERS: SENTENCING PRINCIPLES

308.1   *Defendant badly treated by other prisoners*
R v Nall-Cain 1998 2 Cr App R (S) 145 The defendant, Lord Brocket, was sentenced to 5 years for a false £4.5m insurance claim. While in prison his diary was stolen by a gang of prisoners for sale to the press. Other prisoners blackmailed him, and threats were made to him and his family. A prisoner went to his aid and was assaulted and wounded. The leader of the gang was arrested and charged with theft, GBH and blackmail, but none of the other prisoners who could give evidence were prepared to give evidence. He was moved from one prison to another on a number of occasions. When prison officers were absent, he was accused of being a grass. He was stabbed in the hand and repeatedly kicked and punched. His shoulder was dislocated and he received a black eye. Since he moved to an open prison 12 months ago there were no further incidents but he said that

he was fearful. Held. The different wording of Criminal Appeal Act 1907 s 4(3) and Criminal Appeal Act 1968 s 11(3) means there is now a wider power to alter sentences. The authorities do not speak with one voice. *R v Kirby* 1979 1 Cr App R (S) 215, *R v Kay* 1980 2 Cr App R (S) 284 and *R v Parker* 1996 2 Cr App R (S) 275 show that a defendant's treatment by other inmates is not generally a factor to which the Court of Appeal can have regard. A maltreated prisoner has a number of avenues of redress open to him. The difficulties of adjudicating upon the disputes preclude us from taking them into account. The appeal is dismissed.

Note: This is an old case. Treat the case with care. Ed.

308.2 Harsh prison conditions

Note: Occasionally, judges do take into account the effect of prison on the defendant. Reductions have been made because the defendant speaks little English, has no family in this country, or is blind or disabled. However, where reductions are made, they are not necessarily particularly large. Ed.

R v Nall-Cain 1998 2 Cr App R (S) 145 The defendant, Lord Brocket, was sentenced to 5 years for a false £4.5m insurance claim. While in prison his diary was stolen by a gang of prisoners for sale to the press. Other prisoners blackmailed him, and threats were made to him and his family. A prisoner went to his aid and was assaulted and wounded. The leader of the gang was arrested and charged with theft, GBH and blackmail, but none of the other prisoners who could give evidence were prepared to do so. He was moved from one prison to another on a number of occasions. When prison officers were absent he was accused of being a grass. He was stabbed in the hand and repeatedly kicked and punched. His shoulder was dislocated and he received a black eye. Since he moved to an open prison 12 months ago there were no further incidents but he said that he was fearful. Held. The different wording of Criminal Appeal Act 1907 s 4(3) and Criminal Appeal Act 1968 s 11(3) means there is now a wider power to alter sentences. The authorities do not speak with one voice. *R v Kirby* 1979 1 Cr App R (S) 215, *R v Kay* 1980 2 Cr App R (S) 284 and *R v Parker* 1996 2 Cr App R (S) 275 show that a defendant's treatment by other inmates is not generally a factor to which the Court of Appeal can have regard. A maltreated prisoner has a number of avenues of redress open to him. The difficulties of adjudicating upon the disputes preclude us from taking them into account. The appeal is dismissed.

R v Soares and Others 2003 EWCA Crim 2488 D was arrested on 12 February 1999 and was made a Category A exceptional risk prisoner. He was detained in the Special Security Unit at Belmarsh prison. The cell was small. There was little natural light. Metal grids and mesh covered the exercise yard and limited the light. There was no proper view of the sky. For most of the time D was alone in his cell with only three prison officers with whom to associate. Contact with the outside world was limited. After he had been in the unit for a year, he was allowed three open visits. His wife and son came from France twice. His mother came from Brazil once. Following conviction there were no open visits. The only free telephone contact was once a month through an interpreter. Otherwise he would have to pay £200 a time. His trial lasted from May 2000 to June 2000 when a new jury was sworn and then to 25 July 2001 (sic). During the trial he was continually strip-searched, sometimes 11 times a day. The High Court sentencing Judge reduced the sentence from 27 to 24 years (11%) because D had no family in this country. A critical report from Amnesty International on the Special Security Unit was relied on by the defence. The defence said that D had suffered serious depressive illnesses as a result of the conditions, which amounted to inhuman and degrading treatment under European Convention on Human Rights art 3. Held. This Court cannot decide whether the conditions amounted to inhuman and degrading treatment because we have heard no argument. The Judge was right not to reduce the sentence because the detention was unlawful. We are inclined to the view that a judge would be entitled to take pre-sentence conditions into account. If he thought they aggravated the effect of the detention he might adjust the sentence. The appeal was dismissed.

Note: These are old cases. Treat them with care. Ed.

308.3   *Offence committed in prison*
TICs and Totality Guideline 2012: Crown Court, see www.banksr.com Other Matters
Guidelines tab page 9 Offender serving a determinate sentence (offence(s) committed
after original sentence imposed)
Generally the sentence will be consecutive as it will have arisen out of an unrelated
incident. The court must have regard to the totality of the offender's criminality when
passing the second sentence, to ensure that the total sentence to be served is just and
proportionate. Where a prisoner commits acts of violence in prison, any reduction for
totality is likely to be minimal.[822]
R v Morley and Others 2012 EWCA Crim 1866 M, C and Y were convicted of
conspiracy to supply class A and class B drugs. Drugs were distributed in Cumbria, West
Yorkshire and the North East. Y ran the operation from inside prison. 875 grams of
cocaine at 1% and 930 grams of amphetamine at 1%, with a combined street value of
just over £50,000, were seized following surveillance. Y was a serving prisoner and ran
the operation. He was assisted by many others. The Judge remarked that the case was not
serious because of the quantity or purity of drugs, but because the operation was
controlled by a serving prisoner. The Judge raised sentences of 8 years to 12 years and 6
years to 8 years to reflect the aggravating feature. Held. The Judge was right to treat the
feature of Y running the operation from inside prison as a gravely aggravating factor.
There is no sensible basis for criticising the increment in the sentences to reflect this
central feature of this serious conspiracy. For M, **8 years** was not manifestly excessive.
For C, **5 years** was not excessive. For Y, **12 years** was not unfair.
Old cases: *R v Ali* 1998 2 Cr App R (S) 123 (The total is very long indeed. The Judge is
to be commended for the stern attitude he took, which the Court supports. We hope the
message will be conveyed to anyone contemplating acts of this sort. It is inevitable the
sentences should be consecutive. The Judge was right not to be persuaded by the
arguments of totality.) *R v Singh* 1999 1 Cr App R (S) 445 (Sentence adjusted to achieve
what the Judge wanted.)
For a fuller summary of these cases, see the 9th edition of this book.

**308.4   *Offence committed in prison   Offence already punished by the prison
authorities***
R v Boyton 2009 EWCA Crim 1773, 2010 1 Cr App R (S) 40 (p 237) D pleaded to
conveying a prohibited article into prison. Held. Because he had served seven days' loss
of privileges for the same matter, one week deducted.
For *Overcrowding, Prison* see **29.20** in Volume 1.
Release see the:
  DEFENDANT *Don't take release/parole into account when sentencing* para at **240.58**,
and the
  LICENCE CONDITIONS, JUDGE RECOMMENDING chapter in Volume 1.
For an example of the principle that release should not be considered when
sentencing, see also the HOME DETENTION CURFEW SCHEME chapter in Volume 1.

309   PRISON OFFENCES
309.1
See also the CORRUPTION/MISFEASANCE IN PUBLIC OFFICE chapter.
For the supply of drugs, see the SUPPLY OF DRUGS *Prisoners* para at **340.35**.

309.2   *Affray in prison*
R v Saliu and De Silva 2010 EWCA Crim 1447 S and D pleaded to affray. S, aged 18,
and D, aged 17, were on remand in a Young Offender Institution. D turned a table upside
down, wrenched off a table leg and smashed several classroom windows, which

---

[822] *R v Ali* 1998 2 Cr App R (S) 123

activated the alarms. D, S and others climbed onto the flat roof, waving pieces of wood and threatening those below. D climbed down at lunchtime, smashed another window, and took a staff member's lunch back onto the roof to eat. D, S and others broke windows, set off alarms and used a fire hose to spray water. After five hours S gave himself up but D and another continued carrying out further vandalism for another eight hours, causing extensive further damage. Most internal doors, windows, furniture and computers were smashed at a total cost of almost £39,000. Members of staff, several of them female, were verbally threatened and put in fear of violence. D had been before the courts on 13 occasions for 19 offences. S was convicted of robbery in 2007 (supervision order). (The maximum sentence for affray was 3 years. The maximum DTO term was 2 years.) Held. For S, the starting point of 18 months should have been identified. **12 months**' detention upheld. For D, there should have been a full ⅓ discount from the 2-year maximum to 16 months. The 4 months he had spent on remand needed to be doubled to 8 months and deducted from the sentence, so an **8-month** Detention and Training Order, not 18 months.

See also the **AFFRAY/VIOLENT DISORDER** chapter.

309.3 *Assaults against staff*

R v Hylton 2011 EWCA Crim 2130 D was convicted of ABH and GBH. He was a serving prisoner in a secure wing. When being escorted to collect his breakfast, he punched a prison officer, V1. D swung at V1, with his prison-issue plastic knife in his hand. D also had on his person his prison-issue plastic fork and electrical cable wrapped round his waist. Two other officers came to V1's aid. A violent struggle ensued. All four ended up on the ground and D applied pressure to V2's eyes. V1 suffered an injury to his head, requiring surgical glue. V2 suffered two abrasions and pain in his shoulder. The jury expressly stated that they were not sure whether D had intended to cause, or had caused, serious harm. D was serving an IPP sentence for robbery, the minimum term of which had expired. He had a bad record for violence. Held. These were two separate attacks in which D deliberately targeted the officers. **5 years** not 6 in total.

See also: *R v Taylor* 2011 EWCA Crim 2236, 2012 1 Cr App R (S) 75 (p 421) (Serving prisoner. Attacked prison officers, causing loss of consciousness and chipped teeth to one, 2.5 cm laceration and swelling to another, and a fracture to the mandible of a third. Three others suffered minor injuries. **3 years** consecutive to 23-year minimum term.)

309.4 *Assaults etc. in prison*

R v Lodi 2014 EWCA Crim 904 D pleaded early to section 18. D was in detention for immigration matters. V, an inmate at a YOI, was playing pool when he was attacked by D with a pool cue. V was hit three or four times around the face and knocked to the floor. There, D kicked V several times until he was restrained by officers. V had lacerations around his eye, a suggested fracture to his eyeball sockets, bleeding in the front of one eye, bruising of the retina and reduced vision in his right eye. D's basis of plea claimed there were several verbal insults and abuse immediately prior to the incident. V, who was by then serving a 14-year sentence for GBH with intent and robbery, refused to co-operate with a *Newton* hearing. Following a witness summons being served on a member of staff, the defence found support for the suggestions of prior abuse. The *Newton* hearing was abandoned. Held. D was entitled to full credit. Starting at 12 years, the aggravating factors (D's convictions (robbery and possession of a knife) and the prison location) warranted an increase. The mitigation (including the provocation) reduced the sentence to 11 years. With the plea, **7 years 4 months**.

See also: *R v Jeter* 2015 EWCA Crim 1804 (In 2008 given a 27-year-term for murder. Convicted of two attempted murders on prison staff. One officer had 10 cm long and 2 cm deep wound to neck with blade that had been created. Three prison adjudications for violence. Worth 26 years so 13-year-minimum term needed to be added to term left to serve. New **34-year minimum term** made. Upheld.)

309.5   *Conveying articles into prison*

Prison Act 1952 s 40B-40C[823] (conveying etc. prohibited articles into or out of prison)

Modes of trial and maximum sentences

For list A offences (drugs, firearms etc.) Indictable only. Maximum sentence 10 years
For list B offences (mobile phone, alcohol etc.) Triable either way. On indictment maximum 2 years. Summary maximum 6 months and/or a £5,000 fine for offences committed before 12 March 2015 and an unlimited fine thereafter.[824] There are maximum fines for those aged under 18, see **14.38** in Volume 1.

For list C offences (tobacco, money etc.) Summary only. Maximum Level 3 fine (£1,000)

R v Simmons 2012 EWCA Crim 2158, 2013 1 Cr App R (S) 109 (p 564) The [drug] guidelines do not cover the offence [of conveying drugs into prison under Prison Act 1952 s 40B].

R v Watson 2013 EWCA Crim 271 D pleaded to conveying a list A article (cannabis) into prison. Held. The drug offences guideline applies by analogy.

Note: These two cases may be trying to say that the guidelines do not strictly apply but judges may use them to assist them. In any event, for supply offences, the guideline gives little assistance as it only refers to those who are prison employees and those who bring drugs into prison for gain. Ed.

R v Melim 2014 EWCA Crim 1915 D pleaded (25% credit) to conveying a listed article into prison contrary to Prison Act 1952 s 40B. D has sent two letters, marked as legal privilege letters, to two prisoners. One contained 33 grams of cannabis resin, the other, 18 grams. D was aged 48 at sentence and had no relevant or recent convictions. The Judge bore in mind the drugs guidelines, but did not follow them. Held. The amount of drugs involved in the instant case would result in Category 4. Three principles in cases such as the present emerge from the case law: a) reflecting culpability in the drugs guidelines, the role is normally said to be at least significant, b) where the quantity would otherwise fall within Category 4 and the supply is by a non-prison employee, then that is the level of harm to be applied, and c) the fact that the offending comprises supply of drugs within or into prison is to be regarded as a highly aggravating feature, normally placing the level of sentence at the top end of the appropriate range as described in the guidelines. 4½ months consecutive, making **9 months** not 3 years concurrent.

309.6   *Conveying articles into prison   Mobiles/SIM cards etc.*

R v Boyton 2009 EWCA Crim 1773, 2010 1 Cr App R (S) 40 (p 237) D pleaded to conveying a prohibited article into prison. He was remanded into custody. At prison reception he was asked to remove his clothing and he attempted to put his trousers into a property box to prevent them being searched. When instructed to give them to an officer he said that there was a phone in them. There was. D was aged 31 with 157 convictions. Held. He knew full well that phones are prohibited articles. A **9-month** starting point was not excessive. With plea **6 months** but, because he had served seven days' loss of privileges, **25 weeks** not 26.

R v McDade and Reynolds 2010 EWCA Crim 249, 2 Cr App R (S) 82 (p 530) M pleaded (full credit) to misconduct in public office and conveying an article into a prison. M worked at a YOI and she was seen on CCTV to enter a cell after lock-down. She was suspended and then she resigned. She then had the child of the inmate, P, whom she was visiting. P was moved to another YOI which housed many dangerous prisoners. A parcel posted to another inmate at this YOI was intercepted. The parcel contained three mobile phones inside a stereo. Her fingerprint was on the phones. She was of good character. Her motivation was love and she was separated from her baby. Held. Deterrence plays a

---

[823] As inserted by Offender Management Act 2007 s 22(1)
[824] Legal Aid, Sentencing and Punishment of Offenders Act 2012 s 85(1) and (4) and Legal Aid, Sentencing and Punishment of Offenders Act 2012 (Commencement No 11) Order 2015 2015/504

prominent part in sentencing in these cases: **12 months** for the misconduct and **18 months** for the phones consecutive was merciful. Had it not been for the young baby the sentence would have been significantly higher.

R v Smak 2012 EWCA Crim 1280, 2013 1 Cr App R (S) 45 (p 258) LCJ D was convicted of conveying a prohibited article into prison. She was visiting her father-in-law, Abu Hamza, in HMP Belmarsh. Hamza was detained following a conviction for inciting murder. When searched, a SIM card for a mobile phone was discovered in her pocket. She was pregnant at the time. At appeal, her child was aged 10 months. The child was being looked after by her grandmother. D was aged 29 with no convictions. Held. Smuggling mobile phones into prison is a serious offence which must be discouraged by passing deterrent sentences. The fact D was visiting Abu Hamza is a seriously aggravating factor due to the risk presented by Hamza unlawfully possessing a SIM card in prison. **12 months** fully reflected D's mitigation.

R v Stirling and Others 2013 EWCA Crim 50, 2 Cr App R (S) 60 (p 386) S, B, C and P were convicted of conveying list A articles (cannabis) and conspiracy to convey list B articles (mobiles and their parts) into prison. A defence solicitor took the contraband [into HMP Pentonville] and S and B traded it in prison. Material was taken in a minimum of five times and a maximum of 15. Payment was made by the recipient prisoner's relatives and put into accounts controlled by S and his partner, P. They had been together since she was aged 16. The Judge put S in a leading role, B in a significant role, and C and P between significant and lesser. S, now aged 29, had 17 previous convictions on seven occasions including four robberies (4 years' YOI), a robbery in 2003 (6 years) and an attempted robbery in 2008 (an indeterminate sentence). B, now aged 28, had 38 previous convictions on 19 occasions. They included robbery in 2009 (30 months). C, now aged 27, had 23 previous convictions on 11 occasions. In 2009 he was convicted of two counts of conveying articles into prison (2 years). P, now aged 24, had no convictions. The Judge made the list B offence 1 year concurrent. Held. This was grave offending. S's **5 years**, B's **4½ years**, C's **3½ years** consecutive to 2 years for an unrelated conspiracy and P's **3 years** were not manifestly excessive.

See also the *Possessing transmitting/receiving devices etc. in prison* para at **309.10**.

309.7   *Conveying articles into prison   Drugs   Cases*

R v Simmons 2012 EWCA Crim 2158, 2013 1 Cr App R (S) 109 (p 564) (Plea to bringing a prohibited article into a prison and supply of cannabis. With another, attended a prison for a social visit to see her boyfriend, S. Embraced S and passed him a package which he placed in his pocket. 21.1g of skunk cannabis. Street value £210. Turned 18 between conviction and sentence. Good character. Subjected to pressure and vulnerable. Substantial mitigation but need for deterrent. Reluctantly, **6 months' YOI** upheld.)

R v Watson 2013 EWCA Crim 271 D pleaded (full credit) to conveying a list A article into prison and possession of cannabis. He was in the visiting room at HMP Preston and picked up a bottle of soft drink. He spat something into it. He then gave the bottle to the prisoner he was visiting. The bottle was seized and found to contain a small piece of cannabis wrapped in cling film. D's home was searched and two small lumps of cannabis were found in his bedroom. D, aged 25 at his appeal, had a chaotic lifestyle and had many previous convictions, mostly for dishonesty. There were convictions for possessing heroin with intent in 2005 and 2007. In 2009, he was convicted for possession of a class B drug. Held. He played a significant role. This was a Category 3 offence. Supply of drugs to a prisoner is a serious matter. A significant sentence was inevitable in light of his class A previous convictions. However, in view of the very small amount of cannabis in the cling film wrap, the appropriate starting point was **2 years**. With the plea, **16 months**, not 2 years. 6 months concurrent for possession remained.

See also **SUPPLY OF DRUGS** *Prisoners, Supply to* para **340.35**.

309.8 *Harbouring an escaped prisoner*
Criminal Justice Act 1961 s 22(2)
Mode of trial Triable either way
Maximum sentence On indictment 10 years. Summary 6 months and/or a £5,000 fine for offences committed before 12 March 2015 and an unlimited fine thereafter.[825] There are maximum fines for those aged under 18, see **14.38** in Volume 1.
R v Forbes 2010 EWCA Crim 1017, 2011 1 Cr App R (S) 23 (p 161) D pleaded to harbouring. P, a prisoner serving life, went missing from an open prison. D booked a hotel room for two using her real name and using a Visa card in her name. She was arrested and it was accepted that she did not know P was an escapee. D continued to associate with P and a month later D booked a hotel in cash using a false name. She was arrested. Held. We must look at the offence committed by the prisoner and the duration over which the offence was committed. D was clearly not in P's company continuously. Taking into account the sentence was for murder, D was emotionally committed to P, P initially duped her, P subjected her to a powerful degree of persuasion, her plea, her good character and the fact that she was a full-time carer for a gravely ill grandmother, **8 months** not 16.
Escape from custody see the ESCAPE FROM CUSTODY ETC. chapter.

309.9 *Possession of a psychoactive substance*
Psychoactive Substances Act 2016 s 9 (Possession of a psychoactive substance in a custodial institution)
Mode of trial Triable either way
Maximum sentence On indictment 2 years. Summary maximum 6 months and/or an unlimited fine
Commencement Commencement is awaited.
Meaning Psychoactive Substances Act 2016 s 2 provides that a psychoactive substance is one that is capable of producing a psychoactive effect subject to the exceptions listed in the Act. A substance produces a psychoactive effect in a person if, by stimulating or depressing the person's central nervous system, it affects the person's mental functioning or emotional state.
Forfeiture The court may make a forfeiture order for the psychoactive substance.[826]

309.10 *Possessing transmitting/receiving devices etc. in prison*
Prison Act 1952 s 40D(3A)[827] (possession transmitting/receiving device etc. in prison)
Modes of trial Triable either way
Maximum sentence On indictment maximum 2 years. Summary maximum 6 months
R v Saliuka 2014 EWCA Crim 1907 D was convicted of possessing class A and B drugs with intent to supply and of possessing a phone and SIM card inside a prison. In D's shared cell, prison officers found a large amount of heroin, several wraps of cannabis and the phone and SIM card. D was aged 24 with an appalling record. He was on recall. The Judge found that D organised the smuggling of the drugs and had done so on several occasions, inferred from the wide range in purity. Held. The unlawful possession of mobile phones is much prized in prison since it gives unlimited and unmonitored access to others outside the prison, by which means harassment, intimidation and interference with the course of justice may be carried out and escapes and other criminal enterprises planned and in cases of modern iPhones also unlimited access to the Internet and communication by unmonitored e-mails giving rise to all manner of dangers. Many decisions of this Court emphasise the need to punish such cases severely. **18 months** on each concurrent, consecutive to 5½ years for the drugs offences upheld.
For the drugs part of the case, see **340.36**.

---

[825] Legal Aid, Sentencing and Punishment of Offenders Act 2012 s 85(1) and (4) and Legal Aid, Sentencing and Punishment of Offenders Act 2012 (Commencement No 11) Order 2015 2015/504
[826] Psychoactive Substances Act 2016 s 54(1)
[827] Inserted by Crime and Security Act 2010 s 45. In force 26/3/12

See also the *Conveying articles into prison* paras at **309.5**.

309.11   *Prison mutiny*
Prison Security Act 1992 s 1
Mode of trial Indictable only
Maximum sentence 10 years
R v Whiteman and Others 2004 2 Cr App R (S) 59 (p 312) The defendants W, B, Bt, S
and D were charged with participating in a prison mutiny at Rochester YOI. W pleaded
guilty, and B and Bt changed their pleas to guilty some six months later. S changed his
plea to guilty three days after B and Bt. D was convicted of this count and a further
count of false imprisonment. The mutiny lasted from 7.30 pm to 4.30 am the following
day. The violence began when D threw a flask towards prison officers. Items were
smashed and B threw a chair towards officers, although it did not hit them. W threw
items at officers, one of whom took refuge in a cell and became trapped there when other
officers were forced out of the wing. D and W demanded his keys, W threatened the
officer with a chair leg and struck him on the hand. The officer could hear threats such as
"torture the screw". At one point a letter opener was held to him as a threat. He was
handcuffed painfully, taped around the chest to a chair, and a pillow case was put over
his head. Another prisoner hit him over the head with a broom handle or pool cue
producing a lot of blood, and possibly he passed out. B and Bt were not involved in any
violence towards this officer and B said that he tried to help him. S, Bt and B helped to
build barricades. Offices were ransacked and beds and sheets were set on fire. When the
control and restraint teams came, they had furniture and hot water thrown at them. Held.
The Judge was right to work from the basis that anyone who joined in was committing a
serious offence, that any involvement required a substantial sentence and that it was not
necessary to take into account the precise degree of involvement. Although W received
credit for an early plea, his conduct was sufficiently serious that it was inevitable that his
starting point would have been higher than others. This was a serious offence of its kind.
W, B, Bt and S were properly sentenced to **4 years**, and D to **6 years**.
R v Lambert and Others 2006 EWCA Crim 827, 2 Cr App R (S) 107 (p 699) LCJ The
three defendants, B, M and L, were convicted of prison mutiny. B and M were also
convicted of section 20 wounding. At 8 pm there was a riot at HMP Lincoln. It was
planned. A prison officer was lured into a cell, attacked with the leg of a bed, and his
keys and radio were stolen. The keys were then used to release other prisoners. The
prison authorities were forced to withdraw to the gatehouse, and the remainder of the
prison was left in the hands of the prisoners. In order to gain control, 168 prison officers
in riot gear were required. Full control was regained after eight hours of mutiny. There
were numerous incidents of violence. There were also fires, barricades, floods and a
wanton orgy of destruction. A well-liked officer was repeatedly coshed, and 35 people
required hospital treatment. The total cost to the Prison Service was over £2.7m, and the
cost to the NHS was £43,300. The sentences were made consecutive to the sentences
they were serving. Held. **9 years** upheld for B and M, who both played a serious role in
the mutiny. **7 years** also upheld for L, who played a lesser role and was not a ringleader.
This sentence was considered severe but not manifestly excessive.
Note: These are old cases, so the decisions should be treated with care. Ed.

309.12   *Prison officers as defendants*
R v Ratcliffe 2009 EWCA Crim 1468, 2010 1 Cr App R (S) 51 (p 326) D pleaded to two
counts of misconduct in public office. One was making calls and sending texts to a
prisoner, P. The other was failing to take any action about P's phone. D was a prison
officer who formed a relationship with P, the extent of which was not clear. Her father,
also a prison officer, informed her and then the prison of his concerns. She was searched
and a mobile was found, which had stored on it pictures of P's face and penis. Over two
weeks her phone contacted P's phone 264 times for 25 hours in total. One call lasted
over 1 hour. She sent him 435 texts. P's phone contacted D's phone 249 times for 29

hours in total. One call was for over an hour. He sent her 229 texts. The Judge said that the activity would put prison officers in danger and make her liable to blackmail. He took into account the difficulties she would have in prison and her remorse. He started at **15 months** and deducted 3 months for personal mitigation. He then deducted 2 months for the late plea, making **10 months**. Held. Neither the starting point nor the sentence can be criticised.

R v McDade and Reynolds 2010 EWCA Crim 249, 2 Cr App R (S) 82 (p 530) M pleaded (full credit) to misconduct in public office and conveying an article into a prison. M worked at a YOI and she was seen on CCTV to enter a cell after lock-down. She was suspended and then she resigned. She then had the child of the inmate, P, whom she was visiting. P was moved to another YOI which housed many dangerous prisoners. A parcel posted to another inmate at this YOI was intercepted. The parcel contained three mobile phones inside a stereo. Her fingerprint was on the phones. She was of good character. Her motivation was love and she was separated from her baby. Held. Deterrence plays a prominent part in sentencing in these cases: **12 months** for the misconduct and **18 months** for the phones consecutive was merciful. Had it not been for the young baby the sentence would have been significantly higher.

R v King 2013 EWCA Crim 1599, 2014 1 Cr App R (S) 73 (p 462) D pleaded (25% credit) to misconduct in public office (×3) and concealing criminal property. When a prison officer, she met a prisoner, DT, who was serving a sentence for sex offences. In 2007, D was promoted to senior prison officer and transferred to a different prison. DT was released at some point. In 2008, after DT's release, he met D apparently by chance. They became friendly and their relationship became a sexual one. The code of conduct discourages relationships between serving prison officers and ex-prisoners. In any event, it requires that they are reported to the authorities. D did not do that. In 2011, DT was arrested for serious drug offences. At the same time, D was arrested and her address and her mother's address were searched. At her mother's address, cash totalling £9,500 was found in various places including a handbag and an envelope. D's fingerprints were on both. Whilst on remand, DT obtained an illicit mobile phone while in prison. There was very frequent phone contact between D and DT, amounting to some 1,667 communications between them. Some may have been malfunctioning or missed calls. The communications continued despite D being on bail. D also obtained 'top-ups' for DT's phone, sending through activation codes via text message. D pleaded to the concealment on the basis that she had no idea it was connected to drugs, but thought it related to motor vehicles and that it was not being reported for tax purposes. D had no convictions and many positive references. She was a single mother with two young daughters, both of whom were in care. Held. By topping up DT's phone, that enabled him to make use of the illicit phone for other purposes. The amount of communication was substantial. This was a pattern of offending requiring an immediate custodial sentence. The correct sentence was **3 years** so with plea, **27 months** not 3 years.

See also: *R v Edman* 2014 EWCA Crim 2654 (Convicted of three misconduct offences. Lowest prison grade groomed and exploited vulnerable 19-year-old prisoner. Led to full sex. Other offences a kiss and sexual letters. Aged 35. No previous convictions. **4 years** was severe but upheld.)

Violence, And see **OFFENCES AGAINST THE PERSON ACT 1861 S 18** *Prison officers, Against* at **292.26** and **ABH** *Prison officers etc., Against* at **201.13**.

310   PRODUCTION OF DRUGS

For production of cannabis, see **CANNABIS** *Cultivation of etc.* at **221.4**.

See also the **IMPORTATION OF DRUGS (CLASS A, B AND C)**, **POSSESSION OF DRUGS** and **SUPPLY OF DRUGS** chapters.

310.1

1 Misuse of Drugs Act 1971 s 4(2)(a)-(b) (producing a controlled drug or being concerned in the production of a controlled drug)

Modes of trial Triable either way, unless the defendant could receive the minimum sentence of 7 years for a third drug trafficking offence, when the offence is triable only on indictment

Maximum sentences On indictment class A life, class B and C[828] 14 years

Summary maxima Class A and B is 6 months and/or a £5,000 fine for offences committed before 12 March 2015 and an unlimited fine thereafter.[829] There are maximum fines for those aged under 18, see **14.38** in Volume 1. Class C is 3 months and/or a £2,500 fine.[830]

Minimum sentences Production carries a minimum 7 years for a third class A drug trafficking offence,[831] see the **SUPPLY OF DRUGS Minimum sentences** section at **340.65**.

Travel Restriction Order Where 4+ years' imprisonment is appropriate, the court is under a duty to consider whether it is appropriate to make a Travel Restriction Order.[832] Where there is a direction in the order, the Secretary of State may retain the defendant's passport.[833]

2 Psychoactive Substances Act 2016 s 4 (producing a psychoactive substance)

Mode of trial Triable either way

Maximum sentence On indictment 7 years. Summary maximum 6 months and/or an unlimited fine

Commencement Commencement is awaited.

Meaning Psychoactive Substances Act 2016 s 2 provides that a psychoactive substance is one that is capable of producing a psychoactive effect subject to the exceptions listed in the Act. A substance produces a psychoactive effect in a person if, by stimulating or depressing the person's central nervous system, it affects the person's mental functioning or emotional state.

Prohibition order Where a person has been convicted of this offence, the court may make a prohibition order if the court considers it necessary and proportionate for the purpose of preventing the person from carrying on any prohibited activity.[834] The proceedings are civil and the standard of proof is the balance of probabilities.[835]

Forfeiture The court may make a forfeiture order for the psychoactive substance.[836]

Confiscation For both offences where a defendant has a criminal lifestyle the court, once the confiscation proceedings are triggered (see **22.11** in Volume 1), <u>must</u> follow the Proceeds of Crime Act 2002 procedure. 'Criminal lifestyle' offences include those under Misuse of Drugs Act 1971 s 4(2)-(3).[837] For what constitutes a criminal lifestyle see **22.48** in Volume 1.

Serious Crime Prevention Orders For all three offences, there is a discretionary power to make this order when it would protect the public etc.[838]

Statistics The statistics are included with the supply statistics, see the **SUPPLY OF DRUGS** chapter at **340.2**.

For production of cannabis, see **CANNABIS** *Cultivation of etc.* at **221.4**.

See also the **IMPORTATION OF DRUGS (CLASS A, B AND C)**, **POSSESSION OF DRUGS** and **SUPPLY OF DRUGS** chapters.

---

[828] Criminal Justice Act 2003 s 284 and Sch 28 para 1
[829] Legal Aid, Sentencing and Punishment of Offenders Act 2012 s 85(1) and (4) and Legal Aid, Sentencing and Punishment of Offenders Act 2012 (Commencement No 11) Order 2015 2015/504
[830] Misuse of Drugs Act 1971 Sch 4 and Magistrates' Courts Act 1980 s 32(5)(b).
[831] Powers of Criminal Courts (Sentencing) Act 2000 s 110
[832] Criminal Justice and Police Act 2001 s 33
[833] Criminal Justice and Police Act 2001 s 33(5)
[834] Psychoactive Substances Act 2016 s 19(1)
[835] Psychoactive Substances Act 2016 s 32(1) and (2)
[836] Psychoactive Substances Act 2016 s 54(1)
[837] Proceeds of Crime Act 2002 s 6 and 75 and Sch 2 para 1(1)(a) and 1A
[838] Serious Crime Act 2007 s 1 and Sch 1 para 1(1) and 1A.

310.2   *Sentencing Council guideline*
Drug Offences Guideline 2012, see www.banksr.com Other Matters Guidelines tab page 17. In force 27 February 2012. The guideline only applies to offenders aged 18+, see page 2 of the guideline. For the usual practice, see **70.20** in Volume 1.

STEP ONE Determining the offence category
page 18 The court should determine the offender's culpability (role) and the harm caused (output or potential output) with reference to the tables below.

In assessing culpability, the sentencer should weigh up all the factors of the case to determine role. Where there are characteristics present which fall under different role categories, the court should balance these characteristics to reach a fair assessment of the offender's culpability.

In assessing harm, output or potential output is determined by the weight of the product or number of plants/scale of operation. For production offences, purity is not taken into account at step one but is dealt with at step two. Where the operation is on the most serious and commercial scale, involving a quantity of drugs significantly higher than Category 1, sentences of 20 years and above may be appropriate, depending on the role of the offender.

Drug Offences Definitive Guideline – Production/Cultivation

Culpability demonstrated by offender's role One or more of these characteristics may demonstrate the offender's role. These lists are not exhaustive.	Category of harm Indicative output or potential output (upon which the starting point is based):
LEADING role: • directing or organising production on a commercial scale • substantial links to, and influence on, others in a chain • expectation of substantial financial gain • uses business as cover • abuses a position of trust or responsibility	**Category** • heroin, cocaine – 5 kilos • ecstasy – 10,000 tablets • LSD – 250,000 squares • amphetamine – 20 kilos • cannabis – operation capable of producing industrial • quantities for commercial use • ketamine – 5 kilos
SIGNIFICANT role: • operational or management function within a chain • involves others in the operation whether by pressure, influence, intimidation or reward • motivated by financial or other advantage, whether or not operating alone • some awareness and understanding of scale of operation	**Category 2** • heroin, cocaine – 1 kilo • ecstasy – 2,000 tablets • LSD – 25,000 squares • amphetamine – 4 kilos • cannabis – operation capable of producing significant quantities for commercial use • ketamine – 1 kilo
LESSER role: • performs a limited function under direction • engaged by pressure, coercion, intimidation • involvement through naivety/exploitation • no influence on those above in a chain very little, if any, awareness or understanding of the scale of operation • if own operation, solely for own use (considering reasonableness of account in all the circumstances)	**Category 3** • heroin, cocaine – 150 grams • ecstasy – 300 tablets • LSD – 2,500 squares • amphetamine – 750 grams • cannabis – 28 plants* • ketamine – 150 grams

Culpability demonstrated by offender's role One or more of these characteristics may demonstrate the offender's role. These lists are not exhaustive.	Category of harm Indicative output or potential output (upon which the starting point is based):
	Category 4 • heroin, cocaine – 5 grams • ecstasy – 20 tablets • LSD – 170 squares • amphetamine – 20 grams • cannabis – 9 plants (domestic operation)* • ketamine – 5 grams * With assumed yield of 40 grams per plant

Note: For assistance in how to determine the indicative output of drugs and into which category that weight should be placed, see the **SUPPLY OF DRUGS** paras in relation to indicative weight at **340.6** and **340.7**. Ed.

310.3

STEP TWO Starting point and category range

page 19 Having determined the category, the court should use the table below to identify the corresponding starting point to reach a sentence within the category range. The starting point applies to all offenders irrespective of plea or previous convictions. The court should then consider further adjustment within the category range for aggravating or mitigating features, set out over the page.

Where the defendant is dependent on or has a propensity to misuse drugs and there is sufficient prospect of success, a community order with a drug rehabilitation requirement under Criminal Justice Act 2003 s 209 can be a proper alternative to a short or moderate-length custodial sentence.

For class A cases, Powers of Criminal Courts (Sentencing) Act 2000 s 110 provides that a court should impose a minimum sentence of at least seven years' imprisonment for a third class A trafficking offence except where the court is of the opinion that there are particular circumstances which: a) relate to any of the offences or to the offender, and b) would make it unjust to do so in the circumstances.

Class A	Leading role	Significant role	Lesser role
Category 1	**Starting point** 14 years' custody	**Starting point** 10 years' custody	**Starting point** 7 years' custody
	Category range 12 to 16 years' custody	**Category range** 9 to 12 years' custody	**Category range** 6 to 9 years' custody
Category 2	**Starting point** 11 years' custody	**Starting point** 8 years' custody	**Starting point** 5 years' custody
	Category range 9 to 13 years' custody	**Category range** 6½ to 10 years' custody	**Category range** 3½ to 7 years' custody
Category 3	**Starting point** 8½ years' custody	**Starting point** 5 years' custody	**Starting point** 3½ years' custody
	Category range 6½ to 10 years' custody	**Category range** 3½ to 7 years' custody	**Category range** 2 to 5 years' custody

Class A	Leading role	Significant role	Lesser role
Category 4	**Starting point** 5½ years' custody	**Starting point** 3½ years' custody	**Starting point** 18 months' custody
	Category range 4½ to 7½ years' custody	**Category range** 2 to 5 years' custody	**Category range** High-level community order to 3 years' custody

Class B	Leading role	Significant role	Lesser role
Category 1	**Starting point** 8 years' custody	**Starting point** 5½ years' custody	**Starting point** 3 years' custody
	Category range 7 to 10 years' custody	**Category range** 5 to 7 years' custody	**Category range** 2½ to 5 years' custody
Category 2	**Starting point** 6 years' custody	**Starting point** 4 years' custody	**Starting point** 1 year's custody
	Category range 4½ to 8 years' custody	**Category range** 2½ to 5 years' custody	**Category range** 26 weeks' to 3 years' custody
Category 3	**Starting point** 4 years' custody	**Starting point** 1 year's custody	**Starting point** High-level community order
	Category range 2½ to 5 years' custody	**Category range** 26 weeks' to 3 years' custody	**Category range** Low-level community order to 26 weeks' custody
Category 4	**Starting point** 1 year's custody	**Starting point** High-level community order	**Starting point** Band C fine
	Category range High-level community order to 3 years' custody	**Category range** Medium-level community order to 26 weeks' custody	**Category range** Discharge to medium-level community order

Class C	Leading role	Significant role	Lesser role
Category 1	**Starting point** 5 years' custody	**Starting point** 3 years' custody	**Starting point** 18 months' custody
	Category range 4 to 8 years' custody	**Category range** 2 to 5 years' custody	**Category range** 1 to 3 years' custody
Category 2	**Starting point** 3½ years' custody	**Starting point** 18 months' custody	**Starting point** 26 weeks' custody
	Category range 2 to 5 years' custody	**Category range** 1 to 3 years' custody	**Category range** High-level community order to 18 months' custody

Class C	Leading role	Significant role	Lesser role
Category 3	**Starting point** 18 months' custody	**Starting point** 26 weeks' custody	**Starting point** High-level community order
	Category range 1-3 years' custody	**Category range** High-level community order to 18 months' custody	**Category range** Low-level community order to 12 weeks' custody
Category 4	**Starting point** 26 weeks' custody	**Starting point** High-level community order	**Starting point** Band C fine
	Category range High-level community order to 18 months' custody	**Category range** Low-level community order to 12 weeks' custody	**Category range** Discharge to medium-level community order

For the meaning of a high-level, a medium-level and a low-level community order, see **16.12** in Volume 1.

310.4   [Aggravating and mitigating factors]

page 21 The table below contains a non-exhaustive list of additional factual elements providing the context of the offence and factors relating to the offender. Identify whether any combination of these, or other relevant factors, should result in an upward or downward adjustment from the starting point. In some cases, having considered these factors, it may be appropriate to move outside the identified category range.

Where appropriate, consider the custody threshold as follows:

Has the custody threshold been passed?

If so, is it unavoidable that a custodial sentence be imposed?

If so, can that sentence be suspended?

Where appropriate, the court should also consider the community threshold as follows:

Has the community threshold been passed?

Factors increasing seriousness
Statutory aggravating factors: Previous convictions, having regard to: a) nature of the offence to which conviction relates and relevance to current offence; and b) time elapsed since conviction Offence committed on bail ***Other aggravating factors include:*** Nature of any likely supply Level of any profit element Use of premises accompanied by unlawful access to electricity/other utility supply of others Ongoing/large-scale operation as evidenced by presence and nature of specialist equipment Exposure of others to more than usual danger, for example drugs cut with harmful substances Attempts to conceal or dispose of evidence, where not charged separately Presence of others, especially children and/or non-users Presence of weapon, where not charged separately High purity or high potential yield Failure to comply with current court orders Offence committed on licence Established evidence of community impact

Factors reducing seriousness or reflecting personal mitigation
Involvement due to pressure, intimidation or coercion falling short of duress, except where already taken into account at step one
Isolated incident
Low purity
No previous convictions **or** no relevant or recent convictions
Offender's vulnerability was exploited
Remorse
Good character and/or exemplary conduct
Determination and/or demonstration of steps having been taken to address addiction or offending behaviour
Serious medical conditions requiring urgent, intensive or long-term treatment
Age and/or lack of maturity where it affects the responsibility of the offender
Mental disorder or learning disability
Sole or primary carer for dependent relatives

310.5   *Suggested approach to the guideline*
Note: I suggest, except for the 'most serious and commercial' cases (see below), it is better to simply follow the guideline and ignore the pre-guideline cases. Ed.
Cannabis For the production of cannabis see the CANNABIS chapter.

310.6   *'Most serious and commercial' offending*
Drug Offences Guideline 2012 page 18, see www.banksr.com Other Matters Guidelines tab Where the operation is on the most serious and commercial scale, involving a quantity of drugs significantly higher than Category 1, sentences of 20 years and above may be appropriate, depending on the role of the offender.
R v Hardison 2006 EWCA Crim 1502, 2007 1 Cr App R (S) 37 (p 200) D was convicted of three counts of producing drugs (2C-B, 2C-I and LSD), possessing drugs with intent (LSD), possessing drugs (5-Methoxy-DMT) and exporting drugs (tablets of ecstasy). A package was randomly tested in the USA and found to contain ecstasy. Documents at the home of the intended recipient led back to D, who lived near Brighton. Police searched his home and found a fully functioning laboratory of some sophistication. The forensic chemist had not been able to analyse all the items found, since that would have taken years to do. £9,450 was found under a mattress. D had purchased chemicals worth £38,386.70 from one company alone. He had equipment and literature and skills to produce ecstasy. An off-shore company was set up in Belize. He used false names and had no bank accounts. The operation lasted almost two years, and there were three laboratories, although not operating at the same time. He bought an ocean-going boat for his father and spoke of purchasing land in Spain, Mexico and the UK. His defence was that he was a victim of society's war on drugs, and it was a human right to explore drugs. He represented himself. He was aged 34 and had come from the USA to exploit the potential market for LSD. He had convictions in the USA which were ignored. The Judge found that his motivation was financial and the operation was on a massive scale. He was sentenced to **20 years** for the production with concurrent sentences for the other counts. The Judge acknowledged that his sentence would be harder than for a local. Held. The case was of the utmost gravity. It was a calculated attempt to introduce new synthetic drugs onto the UK market. The sentence was very tough but not manifestly excessive. (The Court was not able to estimate the minimum production.)
Note: This pre-guideline case needs to be approached with care. This case is only listed so sentencers who wish to factor in the pre-guideline cases for drug amounts significantly more than those listed in Category 1 in step one of the guideline can do so. Ed.

311   PROSTITUTION OFFENCES

311.1

Modern Slavery Act 2015 s 6(2)-(4)

1) Sexual Offences Act 2003

s 47 (paying for sexual services of a child)

s 48 (sexual exploitation of a child)

s 49 (controlling a child in relation to sexual exploitation)

s 50 (arranging or facilitating sexual exploitation of a child)

The three last offences were renamed by Serious Crime Act 2015 s 68(3)-(5). Section 49 and section 50 had a slight alteration made to them by the same section. In force 3 May 2015.

Modes of trial All the offences are triable either way (except for section 47 (paying for sexual services of a child) when the child is aged under 16, then the offence is indictable only).

Maximum sentences For a human trafficking offence the maximum is life. For the other offences, on indictment 14 years. Summary 6 months and/or £5,000 fine for offences committed before 12 March 2015 and an unlimited fine thereafter.[839] There are maximum fines for those aged under 18, see **14.38** in Volume 1.

This maximum sentence is subject to the automatic life provisions, see below.

2) Sexual Offences Act 2003

s 51A[840] (soliciting)

s 53A (paying for sexual services of a prostitute subjected to force etc.)

Modes of trial Both offences are summary only.

Maximum sentences Both maximums are a Level 3 fine (£1,000).

3) Sexual Offences Act 2003 s 52 and 53 (causing or inciting another person to become a prostitute for gain etc. and controlling prostitutes)

Modes of trial Triable either way

Maximum sentences On indictment 7 years. Summary 6 months and/or a £5,000 fine for offences committed before 12 March 2015 and an unlimited fine thereafter.[841] There are maximum fines for those aged under 18, see **14.38** in Volume 1.

4) Modern Slavery Act 2015 s 2 (human trafficking) In force 31 July 2015[842]

Mode of trial Triable either way

Maximum sentences On indictment life imprisonment. Summary 6 months and/or an unlimited fine.[843] There are maximum fines for those aged under 18, see **14.38** in Volume 1.

5) There are also three old offences which were not repealed by Sexual Offences Act 2003:

Sexual Offences Act 1956

s 33 (keeping a brothel)

s 33A (keeping a brothel used for prostitution including premises used for other activities)

s 34 (landlord letting premises for use as a brothel)

Modes of trial All offences are triable either way.

---

[839] Legal Aid, Sentencing and Punishment of Offenders Act 2012 s 85(1) and (4) and Legal Aid, Sentencing and Punishment of Offenders Act 2012 (Commencement No 11) Order 2015 2015/504

[840] Sections 51A and 53A were inserted by Policing and Crime Act 2009 s 14 and 19.

[841] Legal Aid, Sentencing and Punishment of Offenders Act 2012 s 85(1) and (4) and Legal Aid, Sentencing and Punishment of Offenders Act 2012 (Commencement No 11) Order 2015 2015/504

[842] Modern Slavery Act 2015 (Commencement No 1, Savings and Transitional Provisions) Regs 2015 2015/1476 reg 2

[843] Legal Aid, Sentencing and Punishment of Offenders Act 2012 s 85(1) and (4) and Legal Aid, Sentencing and Punishment of Offenders Act 2012 (Commencement No 11) Order 2015 2015/504

Maximum sentences On indictment 7 years. Summary 6 months and/or a £5,000 fine for offences committed before 12 March 2015 and an unlimited fine thereafter.[844] There are maximum fines for those aged under 18, see **14.38** in Volume 1.

Historical offences Prostitution offences committed from 1 January 1957 to 30 April 2004 are prosecuted under Sexual Offences Act 1956. The offences are in sections 22-31. All are indictable only offences, except permitting a girl under 16 to use premises for intercourse (section 26), living on the earnings of prostitution (section 30) and controlling a prostitute (section 31). All have a maximum of 2 years, except sections 30 and 31, where the maximum was 2 years from 1 January 1957 to 15 August 1959 and thereafter 7 years. From 1 January 1957 to 31 December 1967, section 26 only applied to girls aged 13-15. The summary maxima are the same as listed at **330.1**.

Automatic life Sexual Offences Act 2003 s 47-50 is listed in Criminal Justice Act 2003 Sch 15B Part 1. The Lord Chief Justice said in *Att-Gen's Ref No 27 of 2013* 2014 EWCA Crim 334[845] para 8 iii) (*obiter*) that in rare cases the provisions could lead to the imposition of a life sentence where the offence does not carry life imprisonment. Modern Slavery Act 2015 s 2[846] is listed in Criminal Justice Act 2003 Sch 15B Part 1.

The court must (unless the particular circumstances make it unjust[847]) pass automatic life if: a) the defendant is aged 18+ at the date of the conviction, b) the court considers a determinate sentence of at least 10 years is appropriate, c) at the time the offender was convicted he or she had a conviction for a Criminal Justice Act 2003 Sch 15B offence, and e) the defendant at the time of his or her conviction had previously been sentenced to either: i) a life sentence where he or she was not eligible for release during the first five years of the sentence, or ii) a determinate sentence or extended sentence where the custodial part was 10 years or more.[848] For a pre-2012 extended sentence, when determining whether the custodial term was 10+ years, the period deducted for time on remand or on a curfew and tag is included.[849]

Extended sentences Sexual Offences Act 1956 s 33, Sexual Offences Act 2003 s 47-50 and 52-53 and Modern Slavery Act 2015 s 2[850] offences are listed in Criminal Justice Act 2003 Sch 15. The court may pass a 2012 extended sentence (EDS) if there is a significant risk of serious harm from future specified offences and either: a) the defendant has a Criminal Justice Act 2003 Sch 15B conviction (applicable only to defendants aged 18+), or b) the offence would justify a determinate sentence of at least 4 years.[851]

Note: It appears to be a drafting error that section 33A was not listed. Ed.

Confiscation Where a defendant has a criminal lifestyle, the court, once the confiscation proceedings are triggered (see **21.7** in Volume 1), <u>must</u> follow the Proceeds of Crime Act 2002 procedure. 'Criminal lifestyle' offences include those under Sexual Offences Act 1956 s 33-34, Sexual Offences Act 2003 s 14, 48-50 and 52-53[852] and Modern Slavery Act 2015 s 2.[853] For what constitutes a criminal lifestyle see **22.48** in Volume 1.

Forfeiture For Modern Slavery Act 2015 s 2[854] offences there is power to forfeit vehicles, ships and aircraft.

---

[844] Legal Aid, Sentencing and Punishment of Offenders Act 2012 s 85(1) and (4) and Legal Aid, Sentencing and Punishment of Offenders Act 2012 (Commencement No 11) Order 2015 2015/504

[845] This case is also known as *R v Burinskas* 2014 EWCA Crim 334.

[846] As inserted by Modern Slavery Act 2015 s 6(4)

[847] Criminal Justice Act 2003 s 224A(2)

[848] Criminal Justice Act 2003 s 224A as inserted by Legal Aid, Sentencing and Punishment of Offenders Act 2012 s 122. The condition for: a) is at section 224A(1)(a), for b) is at section 224A(1)(b), for c) is at section 224A(1)(c), and for d) is at section 224A(4)-(9).

[849] Criminal Justice Act 2003 s 224A(9)-(10)

[850] As inserted by Modern Slavery Act 2015 s 6(2) and (3)

[851] Criminal Justice Act 2003 s 226A-226B as inserted by Legal Aid, Sentencing and Punishment of Offenders Act 2012 s 124

[852] Proceeds of Crime Act 2002 s 6 and 75 and Sch 2 para 4(2) and 8

[853] As inserted by Modern Slavery Act 2015 s 7

[854] Modern Slavery Act 2015 s 11

Serious Crime Prevention Orders For Sexual Offences Act 1956 s 33A, Sexual Offences Act 2003 s 48-53 and Modern Slavery Act 2015 s 2[855] offences, there is a discretionary power to make this order, when it would protect the public etc.[856]

Sexual Harm Prevention Orders There is a discretionary power to make this order for all the offences when it is necessary to protect the public from sexual harm.[857]

Slavery and Trafficking Prevention Orders For Modern Slavery Act 2015 s 2 offences, the court may make this order when the conditions are met, Modern Slavery Act 2015 s 14 and Sch 1.

Notification For offences of:[858]

a) Sexual Offences Act 2003 s 47 where: i) the victim was aged under 16 and ii) the defendant is aged 18 or over or is sentenced to at least 12 months' imprisonment,

b) Sexual Offences Act 2003 s 48-50 where the defendant is: i) aged 18+ or ii) is sentenced to at least 12 months' imprisonment,

c) Sexual Offences Act 2003 s 51-53 and 57-59A,[859] and

d)   Modern Slavery Act 2015 s 2,[860]

the defendant must notify the police within three days (or three days from his or her release from imprisonment, hospital etc.) with his or her name, home address, national insurance number etc. and any changes, and addresses where he or she resides for seven days[861] (in one or more periods) or more in any 12-month period.[862]

Children and vulnerable adults: barred lists Where the defendant commits a Sexual Offences Act 2003 s 47-50 or 52-53 or a Modern Slavery 2015 s 2 offence and is aged 18 or over he or she is automatically barred from engaging in regulated activity with children and vulnerable adults.[863] The judge must tell the defendant that the Disclosure and Barring Service will include him or her in the barred lists.[864] The defendant can ask the Service to remove him or her from the lists.

Closure Notices Anti-social Behaviour, Crime and Policing Act 2014 s 115 and Sch 6 enables senior police officers to issue child sex closure notices. In force 8 March 2015.[865]

311.2   *Crown Court statistics   England and Wales*
Exploitation of prostitution Aged 21+

Year	Plea	Total sentenced	Type of sentencing %						Average length of custody in months
			Dis-charge	Fine	Commu-nity sentence	Sus-pended sentence	Custody	Other	
2013	G	19	–	–	–	47.4	52.6	–	25.9
	NG	9	–	–	–	–	100	–	23.7
2014	G	30	–	–	17	40	43	–	14.7
	NG	12	–	–	–	8	92	–	36.5

[855] As inserted by Modern Slavery Act 2015 Sch 5 para 7 (1) and (3)

[856] Serious Crime Act 2007 s 1 and Sch 1 para 4

[857] Sexual Offences Act 2003 s 103A as inserted by Anti-social Behaviour, Crime and Policing Act 2014 Sch 5 para 2 and Sexual Offences Act 2003 Sch 3 and 5

[858] The s 47 offence has always been subject to notification. The three other 2003 offences were not included in the Sexual Offences Act 2003 Sch 3 list through what appears to have been a drafting error. This was corrected by Sexual Offences Act 2003 (Amendment of Schedules 3 and 5) Order 2007 2007/296.

[859] Protection of Freedoms Act 2012 s 109 repealed Sexual Offences Act 2003 s 57-59 but the sections would still apply to offences committed before 6/4/13.

[860] Inserted by Modern Slavery Act 2015 Sch 5 para 5(1) and (3)

[861] Sexual Offences Act 2003 s 84(1)(c) and (6)

[862] Sexual Offences Act 2003 s 83 and Sch 3 para 29A-29C and 89A-89C

[863] Safeguarding Vulnerable Groups Act 2006 s 2 and Sch 3 and Safeguarding Vulnerable Groups Act 2006 (Prescribed Criteria and Miscellaneous Provisions) Regulations 2009 2009/37 regs 4 and 6 and Sch para 2 and 4

[864] Safeguarding Vulnerable Groups Act 2006 s 2 and Sch 3 para 25

[865] Anti-social Behaviour, Crime and Policing Act 2014 (Commencement No 8, Saving and Transitional Provisions) Order 2015 2015/373

Trafficking for sexual exploitation Aged 21+

Year	Plea	Total sentenced	Type of sentencing %						Average length of custody in months
			Dis-charge	Fine	Commu-nity sentence	Sus-pended sentence	Custody	Other	
2013	G	7	–	–	–	–	85.7	14.3	27.7
	NG	5	–	–	–	–	100	–	74.4
2014	G	2	–	–	–	–	100	–	Not listed[866]
	NG	2	–	–	–	–	100	–	Not listed

For explanations about the statistics, see page 1-xxii. For statistics for abuse of children through prostitution, see the SEX OFFENCES: IMAGES ETC. *Statistics* para at **331.2**, where the statistics are combined. For more statistics for those aged under 21 and male and female defendants etc., see www.banksr.com Other Matters Statistics tab

The chapter is divided up into five sections:
Brothel offences
Child prostitution
Exploitation of prostitutes
Paying for sexual services
Trafficking of prostitutes

Brothel offences
311.3   *Sentencing Council guideline   Keeping a brothel*
Sexual Offences Act 1956 s 33A (keeping a brothel used for prostitution)
Sexual Offences Guideline 2014 www.banksr.com Other Matters Guidelines tab page 85. In force 1 April 2014.
The guideline only applies to offenders aged 18+, see page 7 of the guideline. For the usual practice, see **66.21** in Volume 1.

STEP ONE: Determining the offence category
page 86 The court should determine which categories of harm and culpability the offence falls into by reference **only** to the tables below. **This guideline also applies to offences committed remotely/online.**

Harm	
Category 1	Under 18-year-olds working in brothel Abduction/detention Violence or threats of violence Sustained and systematic psychological abuse Those working in brothel forced or coerced to participate in unsafe/degrading sexual activity Those working in brothel forced or coerced into seeing many 'customers' Those working in brothel forced/coerced/deceived into prostitution Established evidence of community impact
Category 2	Factor(s) in Category 1 not present

---

[866] Based on too few cases to be meaningful

Culpability A
Keeping brothel on significant commercial basis Involvement in keeping a number of brothels Expectation of significant financial or other gain Abuse of trust Exploitation of those known to be trafficked Significant involvement in limiting freedom of those working in brothel Grooming of a person to work in the brothel including through cultivation of a dependency on drugs or alcohol
Culpability B
Keeping/managing premises Close involvement with those working in brothel, for example control of finances, choice of clients, working conditions, etc. (where offender's involvement is not as a result of coercion)
Culpability C
Performs limited function under direction Close involvement but engaged by coercion/intimidation/exploitation

311.4

STEP TWO: Starting point and category range

page 86 Having determined the category, the court should use the corresponding starting points to reach a sentence within the category range below. The starting point applies to all offenders irrespective of plea or previous convictions. Having determined the starting point, step two allows further adjustment for aggravating or mitigating features, set out below.

A case of particular gravity, reflected by multiple features of culpability or harm in step one, could merit upward adjustment from the starting point before further adjustment for aggravating or mitigating features, set out below.

Where there is a sufficient prospect of rehabilitation, a community order with a sex offender treatment programme requirement under Criminal Justice Act 2003 s 202 can be a proper alternative to a short or moderate-length custodial sentence.

	Culpability A	Culpability B	Culpability C
Category 1	**Starting point** 5 years' custody **Category range** 3 to 6 years' custody	**Starting point** 3 years' custody **Category range** 2 to 5 years' custody	**Starting point** 1 year's custody **Category range** High-level community order to 18 months' custody
Category 2	**Starting point** 3 years' custody **Category range** 2 to 5 years' custody	**Starting point** 12 months' custody **Category range** 26 weeks' to 2 years' custody	**Starting point** Medium-level community order **Category range** Low-level community order to high-level community order

For the meaning of a high-level, a medium-level and a low-level community order, see **16.12** in Volume 1.

311.5   [Aggravating and mitigating factors]

page 87 The table below contains a non-exhaustive list of additional factual elements providing the context of the offence and factors relating to the offender. Identify whether any combination of these, or other relevant factors, should result in an upward or downward adjustment from the starting point. In particular, relevant recent convictions are likely to result in an upward adjustment. In some cases, having considered these factors, it may be appropriate to move outside the identified category range.

When sentencing appropriate Category 1 offences, the court should also consider the custody threshold as follows:

Has the custody threshold been passed?

If so, is it unavoidable that a custodial sentence be imposed?

If so, can that sentence be suspended?

Aggravating factors
Statutory aggravating factors   Previous convictions, having regard to a) the nature of the offence to which the conviction relates and its relevance to the current offence, and b) the time that has elapsed since the conviction   Offence committed whilst on bail   *Other aggravating factors*   Failure to comply with current court orders   Offence committed whilst on licence   Deliberate isolation of those working in brothel   Threats made to expose those working in brothel to the authorities (for example, immigration or police), family/friends or others   Harm threatened against the family/friends of those working in brothel   Passport/identity documents removed   Those working in brothel prevented from seeking medical treatment   Food withheld   Those working in brothel passed around by offender and moved to other brothels   Earnings of those working in brothel withheld/kept by offender or evidence of excessive wage reduction or debt bondage, inflated travel or living expenses or unreasonable interest rates   Any steps taken to prevent those working in brothel reporting an incident, obtaining assistance and/or from assisting or supporting the prosecution   Attempts to dispose of or conceal evidence   Those working in brothel forced or coerced into pornography   Timescale over which operation has been run
Mitigating factors
No previous convictions or no relevant/recent convictions   Remorse   Previous good character and/or exemplary conduct*   Age and/or lack of maturity where it affects the responsibility of the offender   Mental disorder or learning disability, particularly where linked to the commission of the offence   Demonstration of steps taken to address offending behaviour   * Previous good character/exemplary conduct is different from having no previous convictions. The more serious the offence, the less the weight which should normally be attributed to this factor. Where previous good character/exemplary conduct has been used to facilitate the offence, this mitigation should not normally be allowed and such conduct may constitute an aggravating factor.

Note: An exact copy of this guideline has been placed in the *Magistrates' Court Guidelines 2008* at page 291.

311.6   *Suggested approach to the guideline*

Note: It is understood the Sentencing Council intended that the guideline should reflect the Court of Appeal current sentencing tariff. This means the new guideline was intended to bring the previous guideline up to date rather than to increase the penalties for the bulk of the sex offences. Consequently, it is suggested that sentencers should start with the guideline and then consider recent sentencing cases set out by the Court of Appeal to see if they are helpful, and then return to the guideline before deciding the appropriate sentence. Ed.

311.7   Brothel offences

R v Carroll 2010 EWCA Crim 2463 D pleaded (late) to conspiracy to control prostitution and conspiracy to money launder. D's wife, S, pleaded to the same. Their daughter pleaded to conspiracy to money launder. D ran a large-scale highly successful prostitution business in Ireland, operating on both sides of the border. Money would be put into D's daughter's account and transferred to an account to which D had access. In 2007, €1.14 million passed through the account. D controlled 35 brothels. D's basis of plea was that he did not coerce any person into prostitution and did not use violence. Held. Whilst D did not coerce anyone into prostitution, there were clearly those who did and, whilst there was no evidence that he knew specifically about threats or violence used against the women, he took no steps to find out what the position was. This was an extremely serious conspiracy. **5 years** for the prostitution and **2 years** for the money laundering, making 7 years, was in no way manifestly excessive.

R v Heywood and Heywood 2011 EWCA Crim 2223 J and D, husband and wife, pleaded (full credit) to brothel keeping. Police entered premises in Eastbourne which advertised itself as a massage parlour. Officers found a customer with a prostitute, menus with price lists for services, condoms and sex toys. D admitted running the business. She had been employed by the previous proprietor as a maid and working girl, before taking over the business some six years before. J helped D run the business but knew nothing of the financial side. He had other employment. The Judge was referred to *R v Solanki* 2011 EWCA Crim 1038 and placed the offences in the first category. Held. The Judge incorrectly placed the offences in the first category and failed to appreciate the late plea in *Solanki*. For D, **6 months** not 9, and for J, **12 weeks** (immediate release) not 4 months.

See also: *R v Shi and Yang* 2008 EWCA Crim 1930, 2009 1 Cr App R (S) 82 (p 484) (S and Y pleaded to keeping a brothel for about four months. S made at least £5,000. Good character. **16 months** not 21. **10 months** not 15. Deportation recommendations upheld.)

R v Shaxted 2012 EWCA Crim 520 (Pleaded to brothel keeping, controlling a prostitute, making an indecent image and showing an indecent photograph. Aged 60. Served with distinction in RAF for 20 years. Found in her flat with 15-year-old boy who said he was aged 19. With the boy, provided sexual services for clients including domination. Bought the boy clothes but did not make payments to him. Did not exploit the boy financially. Made £5,000+. Very poor health. Full credit. **6 months** not 8.)

Old case: *R v Bao* 2007 EWCA Crim 2781, 2008 2 Cr App R (S) 10 (p 61) (**12 months**) *R v Moir* 2007 EWCA Crim 3317, 2008 2 Cr App R (S) 44 (p 242) (**3 years**) *R v Baker and Griffiths* 2008 EWCA Crim 274, 2 Cr App R (S) 74 (p 416) B **9 months** and G **4 months**)

For a summary of the first case, see the 7th edition of this book and for the other two, see the 9th edition.

Post-2014 guideline case

R v A 2014 EWCA Crim 1882 D pleaded (20% credit) to conspiracy to act or assist in the management of brothels. D was a driver in a 'taxi-flat' brothel operation whereby clients visited Eastern European woman working voluntarily from expensive Mayfair flats. Clients could only visit prostitutes by being driven to the brothels. They would be directed towards drivers by 'arrangers'. The drivers would then give prospective clients a sales pitch and would ring the brothels to let them know they were on their way. They would sometimes return to pick up clients later. Drivers obtained payment directly from brothels, according to how many customers they brought. They would also pay the 'arrangers'. D was one such driver for a year for two brothels. The set-up was high end and included offering clients cocaine and receiving payment, often for thousands of pounds, but D had no part in these activities. D was aged 53 on appeal and had antecedents mostly relating to taxi service offences. He had an entrenched gambling problem and had been made bankrupt and lost his home following a failed business. D was remorseful and the pre-sentence report questioned his ability to deal with custody and recommended a community order. Held. Nothing justified moving from the starting point of 12 months (Category 2 harm and Category B culpability). Therefore, **9 months**, not 14½.

Child prostitution

311.8   *Sentencing Council guideline   Child prostitution*
Sexual Offences Act 2003 s 48-50
Sexual Offences Guideline 2014 www.banksr.com Other Matters Guidelines tab page 89.
In force 1 April 2014.
The guideline only applies to offenders aged 18+, see page 7 of the guideline. For the usual practice, see **66.21** in Volume 1.

STEP ONE: Determining the offence category
page 90 The court should determine which categories of harm and culpability the offence falls into by reference **only** to the tables below.
For offences that involve wide-scale commercial and/or international activity, sentences above the category range may be appropriate.

Harm	
Category 1	Victims involved in penetrative sexual activity Abduction/detention Violence or threats of violence Sustained and systematic psychological abuse Victim(s) participated in unsafe/degrading sexual activity beyond that which is inherent in the offence Victim(s) passed around by the offender to other 'customers' and/or moved to other brothels
Category 2	Factor(s) in Category 1 not present

Culpability A
Directing or organising child prostitution or pornography on significant commercial basis Expectation of significant financial or other gain Abuse of trust Exploitation of victim(s) known to be trafficked Significant involvement in limiting the freedom of the victim(s) Grooming of a victim to enter prostitution or pornography including through cultivation of a dependency on drugs or alcohol
Culpability B
Close involvement with inciting, controlling, arranging or facilitating child prostitution or pornography (where offender's involvement is not as a result of coercion)
Culpability C
Performs limited function under direction Close involvement but engaged by coercion/intimidation/exploitation

311.9

STEP TWO: Starting point and category range
page 91 Having determined the category, the court should use the corresponding starting points to reach a sentence within the category range below. The starting point applies to all offenders irrespective of plea or previous convictions. Having determined the starting point, step two allows further adjustment for aggravating or mitigating features, set out below.

A case of particular gravity, reflected by multiple features of culpability or harm in step one, could merit upward adjustment from the starting point before further adjustment for aggravating or mitigating features, set out below.

Where there is a sufficient prospect of rehabilitation, a community order with a sex offender treatment programme requirement under Criminal Justice Act 2003 s 202 can be a proper alternative to a short or moderate-length custodial sentence.

	Age	Culpability A	Culpability B	Culpability C
Category 1	Under 13	**Starting point** 10 years' custody **Category range** 8 to 13 years' custody	**Starting point** 8 years' custody **Category range** 6 to 11 years' custody	**Starting point** 5 years' custody **Category range** 2 to 6 years' custody
	13 to 15	**Starting point** 8 years' custody **Category range** 6 to 11 years' custody	**Starting point** 5 years' custody **Category range** 4 to 8 years' custody	**Starting point** 2 years 6 months' custody **Category range** 1 to 4 years' custody
	16 to 17	**Starting point** 4 years' custody **Category range** 3 to 7 years' custody	**Starting point** 2 years' custody **Category range** 1 to 4 years' custody	**Starting point** 1 year's custody **Category range** 26 weeks' to 2 years' custody
Category 2	Under 13	**Starting point** 8 years' custody **Category range** 6 to 11 years' custody	**Starting point** 6 years' custody **Category range** 4 to 9 years' custody	**Starting point** 2 years' custody **Category range** 1 to 4 years' custody
	13 to 15	**Starting point** 6 years' custody **Category range** 4 to 9 years' custody	**Starting point** 3 years' custody **Category range** 2 to 5 years' custody	**Starting point** 1 year's custody **Category range** 26 weeks' to 2 years' custody
	16 to 17	**Starting point** 3 years' custody **Category range** 2 to 5 years' custody	**Starting point** 1 year's custody **Category range** 26 weeks' to 2 years' custody	**Starting point** 26 weeks' custody **Category range** High-level community order to 1 year's custody

For the meaning of a high-level, a medium-level and a low-level community order, see **16.12** in Volume 1.

311.10   [Aggravating and mitigating factors]

page 92 The table below contains a non-exhaustive list of additional factual elements providing the context of the offence and factors relating to the offender. Identify whether any combination of these, or other relevant factors, should result in an upward or downward adjustment from the starting point. In particular, relevant recent convictions are likely to result in an upward adjustment. In some cases, having considered these factors, it may be appropriate to move outside the identified category range.

When sentencing appropriate Category 2 offences, the court should also consider the custody threshold as follows:

Has the custody threshold been passed?

If so, is it unavoidable that a custodial sentence be imposed?

If so, can that sentence be suspended?

Aggravating factors
Statutory aggravating factors: Previous convictions, having regard to: a) the nature of the offence to which the conviction relates and its relevance to the current offence, and b) the time that has elapsed since the conviction Offence committed whilst on bail *Other aggravating factors:* Failure to comply with current court orders Offence committed whilst on licence Deliberate isolation of victim(s) Vulnerability of victim(s) Threats made to expose victim(s) to the authorities (for example, immigration or police), family/friends or others Harm threatened against the family/friends of victim(s) Passport/identity documents removed Victim(s) prevented from seeking medical treatment Victim(s) prevented from attending school Food withheld Earnings withheld/kept by offender or evidence of excessive wage reduction or debt bondage, inflated travel or living expenses or unreasonable interest rates Any steps taken to prevent the victim reporting an incident, obtaining assistance and/or from assisting or supporting the prosecution Attempts to dispose of or conceal evidence Timescale over which the operation has been run
Mitigating factors
No previous convictions or no relevant/recent convictions Remorse Previous good character and/or exemplary conduct* Age and/or lack of maturity where it affects the responsibility of the offender Mental disorder or learning disability, particularly where linked to the commission of the offence * Previous good character/exemplary conduct is different from having no previous convictions. The more serious the offence, the less the weight which should normally be attributed to this factor. Where previous good character/exemplary conduct has been used to facilitate the offence, this mitigation should not normally be allowed and such conduct may constitute an aggravating factor. In the context of this offence, previous good character/exemplary conduct should not normally be given any significant weight and will not normally justify a reduction in what would otherwise be the appropriate sentence.

311.11   Child prostitution
R v Abbas and Khan 2010 EWCA Crim 161 D pleaded (full credit) to controlling a child prostitute and to sexual activity with a child. V had been sexually promiscuous from the age of 12. She had numerous encounters with men and boys. She was put into care for her own safety. She escaped aged 14 for the ninth occasion and went with men for alcohol and both penetrative and oral sex. D sold her on the street on five occasions and sold her to a total of 25 men over a week. D also took V down an alleyway and demanded oral sex from her. D did not know about her background. D was aged 30 with disregarded convictions. The basis of plea was that: a) she presented herself and represented herself to be aged at least 16, b) D had no reason to disbelieve this, c) D latterly doubted these assertions, d) there was evidence to suggest that she had been involved in prostitution before, e) V was attracted to D and they had a close relationship, f) their attraction was mutual, g) she remained with D voluntarily with no force or threat of force employed, h) a good part of the money obtained was spent on V and i) on one

occasion he allowed her to perform oral sex on him. Held. The sentencing range was 6 to 8 years for the prostitution offence. The basis of plea made that 7½ years and with plea 5 years not 7. For the sexual activity count, 2 years consecutive was correct, making **7 years** not 9.

Post-2014 guideline case

R v Gribbin 2015 EWCA Crim 736 D was convicted of causing child prostitution and two counts of paying for sexual services. He initiated conversations with V, aged 16, in an Internet chatroom. He posed as a girl of a similar age saying 'she' provided sex for money and asked if V wanted to sell her body. V claimed to be aged 17 and played along with the suggestion. V's mother was ill and V was worried about the family debt. D then posed as 'Dean' and contacted V as a client. He drove to V's home town and took V to a park. D gave V £50 and had sexual intercourse. Although he used a condom, it split and he gave her £20 for a morning-after pill. Four days later he paid her for more sexual intercourse in the park. Another four days later, they met again but V was unwell and there was no sexual intercourse. D paid her anyway. There was no more contact. Police monitoring the chatroom traced R and then D, who admitted the sex but denied paying for it. D was aged 40 and had a caution for sending a letter with an indecent or grossly offensive message. He had texted a sex worker and asked her if she would help him instruct his 13-year-old stepdaughter in the ways of sex with him. In fact he had no stepdaughter. There were character witnesses. He made derogatory remarks about V to the probation officer. He also said that he liked all age groups of women unless they were 'heifers' and that he had no intention of abiding by any restrictions placed on him. He was assessed as having a high risk of re-offending. The Judge said D deceived V who was vulnerable, he made V a prostitute, there was a considerable impact on V who had lost self-esteem and lost some of her friends. Further she was degraded and manipulated. He noted the planning, the grooming and the ejaculation. Held. This was a Category 1 case in Band B. The starting point was **4 years** and that was the right overall sentence not 6.

See also the ***Brothel keeping*** para at **311.7**.

Exploitation of prostitutes

311.12   *Sentencing Council guideline   Exploitation of prostitutes*
Sexual Offences Act 2003 s 52-53

Sexual Offences Guideline 2014 www.banksr.com Other Matters Guidelines tab page 81. In force 1 April 2014.

The guideline only applies to offenders aged 18+, see page 7 of the guideline. For the usual practice, see **66.21** in Volume 1.

STEP ONE: Determining the offence category

page 82 The court should determine which categories of harm and culpability the offence falls into by reference **only** to the tables below.

Harm	
Category 1	Abduction/detention Violence or threats of violence Sustained and systematic psychological abuse Individual(s) forced or coerced to participate in unsafe/degrading sexual activity Individual(s) forced or coerced into seeing many 'customers' Individual(s) forced/coerced/deceived into prostitution
Category 2	Factor(s) in Category 1 not present

Culpability A
Causing, inciting or controlling prostitution on significant commercial basis Expectation of significant financial or other gain Abuse of trust Exploitation of those known to be trafficked Significant involvement in limiting the freedom of prostitute(s) Grooming of individual(s) to enter prostitution including through cultivation of a dependency on drugs or alcohol

Culpability B
Close involvement with prostitute(s), for example control of finances, choice of clients, working conditions, etc. (where offender's involvement is not as a result of coercion)

Culpability C
Performs limited function under direction Close involvement but engaged by coercion/intimidation/exploitation

311.13

STEP TWO: Starting point and category range

page 82 Having determined the category, the court should use the corresponding starting points to reach a sentence within the category range below. The starting point applies to all offenders irrespective of plea or previous convictions. Having determined the starting point, step two allows further adjustment for aggravating or mitigating features, set out below.

A case of particular gravity, reflected by multiple features of culpability or harm in step one, could merit upward adjustment from the starting point before further adjustment for aggravating or mitigating features, set out below.

Where there is a sufficient prospect of rehabilitation, a community order with a sex offender treatment programme requirement under Criminal Justice Act 2003 s 202 can be a proper alternative to a short or moderate-length custodial sentence.

	Culpability A	Culpability B	Culpability C
Category 1	**Starting point** 4 years' custody **Category range** 3 to 6 years' custody	**Starting point** 2 years 6 months' custody **Category range** 2 to 4 years' custody	**Starting point** 1 year's custody **Category range** 26 weeks' to 2 years' custody
Category 2	**Starting point** 2 years 6 months' custody **Category range** 2 to 5 years' custody	**Starting point** 1 year's custody **Category range** High-level community order to 2 years' custody	**Starting point** Medium-level community order **Category range** Low-level community order to High-level community order

For the meaning of a high-level, a medium-level and a low-level community order, see **16.12** in Volume 1.

311.14 [Aggravating and mitigating factors]

page 83 The table below contains a non-exhaustive list of additional factual elements providing the context of the offence and factors relating to the offender. Identify whether any combination of these, or other relevant factors, should result in an upward or downward adjustment from the starting point. In particular, relevant recent convictions are likely to result in an upward adjustment. In some cases, having considered these factors, it may be appropriate to move outside the identified category range.

When sentencing appropriate Category 2 offences, the court should also consider the custody threshold as follows:

Has the custody threshold been passed?

If so, is it unavoidable that a custodial sentence be imposed?

If so, can that sentence be suspended?

Aggravating factors
Statutory aggravating factors: Previous convictions, having regard to a) the nature of the offence to which the conviction relates and its relevance to the current offence; and b) the time that has elapsed since the conviction   Offence committed whilst on bail   ***Other aggravating factors:***   Failure to comply with current court orders   Offence committed whilst on licence   Deliberate isolation of prostitute(s)   Threats made to expose prostitute(s) to the authorities (for example, immigration or police), family/friends or others   Harm threatened against the family/friends of prostitute(s)   Passport/identity documents removed   Prostitute(s) prevented from seeking medical treatment   Food withheld   Earnings withheld/kept by offender or evidence of excessive wage reduction or debt bondage, inflated travel or living expenses or unreasonable interest rates   Any steps taken to prevent the reporting of an incident, obtaining assistance and/or from assisting or supporting the prosecution   Attempts to dispose of or conceal evidence   Prostitute(s) forced or coerced into pornography   Timescale over which operation has been run
Mitigating factors
No previous convictions **or** no relevant/recent convictions   Remorse   Previous good character and/or exemplary conduct*   Age and/or lack of maturity where it affects the responsibility of the offender   Mental disorder or learning disability, particularly where linked to the commission of the offence   Demonstration of steps taken to address offending behaviour   * Previous good character/exemplary conduct is different from having no previous convictions. The more serious the offence, the less the weight which should normally be attributed to this factor. Where previous good character/exemplary conduct has been used to facilitate the offence, this mitigation should not normally be allowed and such conduct may constitute an aggravating factor.

Note: An exact copy of this guideline has been placed in the *Magistrates' Court Guidelines 2008* at page 287.

311.15   *Exploitation of prostitutes   Coercion, violence or threats, With   Pre-2014 guideline case*

R v Owusu-Akyeaw 2012 EWCA Crim 1466 D was convicted of inciting prostitution for gain. Over a nine-week period, D coerced V into working as a prostitute. V was to some extent vulnerable and D dominated her. She was made to have sex with around seven men each day, each paying £50 per time. D had advertised V's availability as a prostitute on the Internet and in shop windows. The accumulated total benefit was £20,000. V had fallen in love with D who, aged 31, was of effective good character. Held. V was young and vulnerable, and had previously been a respectable woman. D planned from the outset to use V as a prostitute and had benefited substantially. The Judge was correct to place this in the highest category of the guidelines. In light of the maximum 7-year sentence, **3 years** not 5.

Paying for sexual services of a child

311.16   *Sentencing Council guideline*

Sexual Offences Act 2003 s 47

Sexual Offences Guideline 2014 www.banksr.com Other Matters Guidelines tab page 95. In force 1 April 2014.

The guideline only applies to offenders aged 18+, see page 7 of the guideline. For the usual practice, see **66.21** in Volume 1.

STEP ONE: Determining the offence category

page 96 The court should determine which categories of harm and culpability the offence falls into by reference **only** to the tables below.

The guideline should only be used where the victim was aged 16 or 17 years.

Harm	
Category 1	Penetration of vagina or anus (using body or object) by, or of, the victim Penile penetration of mouth by, or of, the victim Violence or threats of violence Victim subjected to unsafe/degrading sexual activity (beyond that which is inherent in the offence)
Category 2	Touching of naked genitalia or naked breasts by, or of, the victim
Category 3	Other sexual activity

Culpability A
Abduction/detention Sexual images of victim recorded, retained, solicited or shared Offender acts together with others to commit the offence Use of alcohol/drugs on victim Abuse of trust Previous violence against victim Sexual images of victim recorded, retained, solicited or shared Blackmail or other threats made (including to expose victim to the authorities, family/friends or others) Offender aware that he has a sexually transmitted disease Offender aware victim has been trafficked
Culpability B
Factor(s) in Category A not present

311.17

STEP TWO: Starting point and category range

page 96 Having determined the category, the court should use the corresponding starting points to reach a sentence within the category range below for victims aged 16 or 17. The starting point applies to all offenders irrespective of plea or previous convictions. Having determined the starting point, step two allows further adjustment for aggravating or mitigating features, set out below.

A case of particular gravity, reflected by multiple features of culpability in step one, could merit upward adjustment from the starting point before further adjustment for aggravating or mitigating features, set out below.

Where there is a sufficient prospect of rehabilitation, a community order with a sex offender treatment programme requirement under Criminal Justice Act 2003 s 202 can be a proper alternative to a short or moderate-length custodial sentence.

	Culpability A	Culpability B
Category 1	**Starting point** 4 years' custody **Category range** 2 to 5 years' custody	**Starting point** 2 years' custody **Category range** 1 to 4 years' custody
Category 2	**Starting point** 3 years' custody **Category range** 1 to 4 years' custody	**Starting point** 1 year's custody **Category range** 26 weeks' to 2 years' custody
Category 3	**Starting point** 1 year's custody **Category range** 26 weeks' to 2 years' custody	**Starting point** 26 weeks' custody **Category range** High-level community order to 1 year's custody

For the meaning of a high-level community order see **16.14** in Volume 1.

311.18   [Aggravating and mitigating factors]

page 97 The table below contains a **non-exhaustive** list of additional factual elements providing the context of the offence and factors relating to the offender. Identify whether any combination of these, or other relevant factors, should result in an upward or downward adjustment from the starting point. **In particular, relevant recent convictions are likely to result in an upward adjustment.** In some cases, having considered these factors, it may be appropriate to move outside the identified category range.

When sentencing appropriate **Category 3** offences, the court should also consider the custody threshold as follows:

Has the custody threshold been passed?

If so, is it unavoidable that a custodial sentence be imposed?

If so, can that sentence be suspended?

Aggravating factors
Statutory aggravating factors: Previous convictions, having regard to a) the nature of the offence to which the conviction relates and its relevance to the current offence; and b) the time that has elapsed since the conviction Offence committed whilst on bail ***Other aggravating factors:*** Ejaculation Failure to comply with current court orders Offence committed whilst on licence Any steps taken to prevent the victim reporting an incident, obtaining assistance and/or from assisting or supporting the prosecution Attempts to dispose of or conceal evidence
Mitigating factors
No previous convictions or no relevant/recent convictions Remorse Previous good character and/or exemplary conduct* Age and/or lack of maturity where it affects the responsibility of the offender Mental disorder or learning disability, particularly where linked to the commission of the offence Demonstration of steps taken to address offending behaviour * Previous good character/exemplary conduct is different from having no previous convictions. The more serious the offence, the less the weight which should normally be attributed to this factor. Where previous good character/exemplary conduct has been used to facilitate the offence, this mitigation should not normally be allowed and such conduct may constitute an aggravating factor.

Trafficking of prostitutes

311.19   *Sentencing Council guideline*

Sexual Offences Act 2003 s 59A[867]

Note: On 31 July 2015, this offence was repealed and replaced by Modern Slavery Act 2015 s 2 (human trafficking) Ed.

Sexual Offences Guideline 2014 www.banksr.com Other Matters Guidelines tab page 99. In force 1 April 2014.

The guideline only applies to offenders aged 18+, see page 7 of the guideline. For the usual practice, see **66.21** in Volume 1.

STEP ONE: Determining the offence category

page 100 The court should determine which categories of harm and culpability the offence falls into by reference **only** to the tables below.

Harm	
Category 1	Abduction/detention Violence or threats of violence Sustained and systematic psychological abuse Victim(s) under 18 Victim(s) forced or coerced to participate in unsafe/degrading sexual activity Victim(s) forced/coerced into prostitution Victim(s) tricked/deceived as to purpose of visit
Category 2	Factor(s) in Category 1 not present

Culpability A
Directing or organising trafficking on significant commercial basis Expectation of significant financial or other gain Significant influence over others in trafficking organisation/hierarchy Abuse of trust

Culpability B
Operational or management function within hierarchy Involves others in operation whether by coercion/intimidation/exploitation or reward (and offender's involvement is not as a result of coercion)

Culpability C
Performs limited function under direction Close involvement but engaged by coercion/intimidation/exploitation

311.20

STEP TWO: Starting point and category range

page 100 Having determined the category of harm and culpability, the court should use the corresponding starting points to reach a sentence within the category range below. The starting point applies to all offenders irrespective of plea or previous convictions. Having determined the starting point, step two allows further adjustment for aggravating or mitigating features, set out below.

A case of particular gravity, reflected by multiple features of culpability or harm in step one, could merit upward adjustment from the starting point before further adjustment for aggravating or mitigating features, set out below.

Where there is a sufficient prospect of rehabilitation, a community order with a sex offender treatment programme requirement under Criminal Justice Act 2003 s 202 can be a proper alternative to a short or moderate-length custodial sentence.

---

[867] On 6 April 2013 Sexual Offences Act 2003 s 57-59 were repealed and section 59A was substituted, Protection of Freedoms Act 2012 s 109.

	Culpability A	Culpability B	Culpability C
Category 1	**Starting point** 8 years' custody **Category range** 6 to 12 years' custody	**Starting point** 6 years' custody **Category range** 4 to 8 years' custody	**Starting point** 18 months' custody **Category range** 26 weeks' to 2 years' custody
Category 2	**Starting point** 6 years' custody **Category range** 4 to 8 years' custody	**Starting point** 4 years' custody **Category range** 2 to 6 years' custody	**Starting point** 26 weeks' custody **Category range** High-level community order to 18 months' custody

For the meaning of a high-level community order see **16.14** in Volume 1.

311.21   [Aggravating and mitigating factors]

page 101 The table below contains a **non-exhaustive** list of additional factual elements providing the context of the offence and factors relating to the offender. Identify whether any combination of these, or other relevant factors, should result in an upward or downward adjustment from the starting point. **In particular, relevant recent convictions are likely to result in an upward adjustment.** In some cases, having considered these factors, it may be appropriate to move outside the identified category range.

When sentencing appropriate **Category 2** offences, the court should also consider the custody threshold as follows:

Has the custody threshold been passed?

If so, is it unavoidable that a custodial sentence be imposed?

If so, can that sentence be suspended?

Aggravating factors
***Statutory aggravating factors*:** Previous convictions, having regard to a) the nature of the offence to which the conviction relates and its relevance to the current offence, and b) the time that has elapsed since the conviction Offence committed whilst on bail ***Other aggravating factors*:** Failure to comply with current court orders Offence committed whilst on licence Deliberate isolation of victim(s) Children of victim(s) left in home country due to trafficking Threats made to expose victim(s) to the authorities (for example, immigration or police), family/friends or others Harm threatened against the family/friends of victim Exploitation of victim(s) from particularly vulnerable backgrounds Victim(s) previously trafficked/sold/passed around Passport/identity documents removed Victim(s) prevented from seeking medical treatment Food withheld Use of drugs/alcohol or other substance to secure victim's compliance Earnings of victim(s) withheld/kept by offender or evidence of excessive wage reduction, debt bondage, inflated travel or living expenses, unreasonable interest rates Any steps taken to prevent the victim reporting an incident, obtaining assistance and/or from assisting or supporting the prosecution Attempts to dispose of or conceal evidence Timescale over which operation has been run

Mitigating factors

No previous convictions or no relevant/recent convictions
Remorse
Previous good character and/or exemplary conduct*
Age and/or lack of maturity where it affects the responsibility of the offender
Mental disorder or learning disability, particularly where linked to the commission of the offence
* Previous good character/exemplary conduct is different from having no previous convictions. The more serious the offence, the less the weight which should normally be attributed to this factor. Where previous good character/exemplary conduct has been used to facilitate the offence, this mitigation should not normally be allowed and such conduct may constitute an aggravating factor.
In the context of this offence, previous good character/exemplary conduct should not normally be given any significant weight and will not normally justify a reduction in what would otherwise be the appropriate sentence.

311.22   *Trafficking   Other pre-2014 guideline guidance*
JSB Equal Treatment Bench Book 2013, see www.banksr.com Other Matters Other Documents tab para 1.5 There are also a significant number of trafficked immigrants[868] whose formal status will be unlawful, making them especially vulnerable. In 2010, research commissioned by the Association of Chief Police Officers (ACPO) estimated that of the 17,000 migrant women involved in off-street prostitution in England and Wales 2,600 had been trafficked, whilst a further 9,600 were vulnerable to trafficking. The majority of the women were from China and South-east Asia with around 400 from Eastern Europe.[869]
Note: In *R v LM and Others* 2010 EWCA Crim 2327, the Court laid down principles for prosecuting these offences. The guidance relates entirely to convictions. Ed.

311.23   *Controlling prostitutes for gain*
R v Fowler 2015 EWCA Crim 1745 D pleaded (full credit) to controlling a prostitute for gain and supplying heroin. Police received information and a police officer, P, rang D's number and asked for a girl. D said both his girls were in jail but he might be able to get Emma, who charged £20. P rang again and it was agreed that P would meet Emma. P went to the address he was told to go to and D told him the girl was now Jade. D said he did not know what she charged. D and P went to D's bedsit where Jade was. She was aged 27. D prepared and smoked some crack cocaine. P asked D to get him some heroin and D agreed to do that. D took £20 and purchased two £10 bags. Meanwhile P and Jade agreed on a price of £20 or £30 depending what P wanted. D was expected to receive a cut from that. D returned and Jade gave D £30 to buy some drugs. He left to buy them and no doubt to give the other two some privacy. Jade and D were arrested by other police officers. Jade told police she used D's flat and she would share her crack with him. D was aged 60. The Judge made it a Category 2B case. Held. The mitigation was D's age and he had lived for most of his life as a law-abiding person, until he became involved in drugs. The Judge said the prostitution offence reached the custody threshold because prostitution is illegal. It is not. This was off-street prostitution. That in itself is not a crime. Secondly, the Judge said that prostitution is degrading to the women involved in it. Very frequently that will be true and where it is true, it is a significant aggravating feature. Here, however, there was no evidence of anyone being degraded or that, if they were, that was the result of anything done by D. In that sense it was the least serious kind of offence under section 53 which is capable of being committed. The court is required to focus in assessing seriousness in these prostitution offences on the extent to which the offender is in control of prostitution, identifying any exploitation and harm

---

[868] *Human Trafficking: Practical Guidance 2013* Home Office
[869] *Setting the Record: The trafficking of migrant women in the England and Wales off-street prostitution sector. Project Acumen*, K. Jackson, J. Jeffery and G. Adamson (2010), ACPO.

caused to the prostitutes, and assessing the level of any benefit obtained by the offender. Here there was very little control and no coercion at all. It appears to have been Jade who was in charge of the transactions and the appellant acted as a broker and facilitator. As it was at the lower end of the range of seriousness, the starting point is therefore not the 12 months suggested but (other things being equal) a **high-level community order**. We start at 18 months for the drug offence, reducing it to 15 months for the mitigation and with the plea 10 months. The prostitution offence should be a concurrent 4 months. The sentence could be suspended so because of 2 months served we make the drugs sentence 6 months suspended.

For the supply decision see **340.49**.

311.24   *Trafficking   Cases*

R v Nualpenyai 2010 EWCA Crim 692, 2 Cr App R (S) 102 (p 658) D pleaded late to trafficking, controlling prostitution for gain, and possessing a class A and a class C drug. D ran two brothels, one at her home address. She employed others to service clients and would also on occasion do so herself. D persuaded B by telephone to come from Thailand to the UK and work as a prostitute. B had been told in Thailand that she would have to pay a debt to D from her earnings and believed that it would be £7,000 but when she arrived in the UK D told her it would be about £25,000. S signed a contract in Thailand agreeing to pay a debt of £20,000 out of her earnings as a prostitute in the UK. She was provided with a false Malaysian passport and travelled here. When S arrived D told her that before she could earn her own money she would have to pay off £30,000. D took possession of B's and S's passports as security for the debts they owed her. Both B and S were required to work almost continuously at D's brothels and various others. B had about 30 customers a day, S was required to work even when she was menstruating and both were encouraged to have unprotected sex as there was a greater charge for this. They had to pay rent to all the brothels they worked in, including D's, and handed the rest of their earnings to D as payment toward the debts they believed they owed. B found her passport and ran away. D made telephone threats to B in an unsuccessful attempt to get her to return. In the few months since arriving in the UK B estimated she had paid off £13,000 of the £25,000 debt as well as her rent payments, but had made nothing for herself. D, aged 30, had no convictions. She grew up in Thailand, came to the UK about five years previously to work as a prostitute and had a two-year-old son. **5 years** not 6½.

R v Dunkova 2010 EWCA Crim 1318, 2011 1 Cr App (S) 40 (p 265) D was convicted of trafficking for sexual exploitation (×2), causing child prostitution and controlling child prostitution. In Slovakia LP, aged 15, ran away from the children's home which housed her. She was befriended by a male, R, and raped by him. He compelled her to work as a prostitute for some few days before explaining that he had arranged for her collection by his own family. LP was taken to another house by R, D's brother. He contacted D, who arrived and persuaded LP to come to the United Kingdom for 'a better life'. D and LP travelled to the UK and LP was given a false passport. She was forced to work as a prostitute. She was subjected to violence, but not by D. D, aged 26 at appeal, worked as a prostitute and had no previous convictions. Held. D's role was to fetch, to move and to supervise. On the other hand, it was D's brother and another man, M, who organised the transit. It was M who sent D, and it must be remembered that D was herself a working prostitute, doubtless answering to M. She, unlike R and M, did not fall to be sentenced for allegations of threats and false imprisonment. **14 years** not 16.

R v Brusch and Horvat 2011 EWCA Crim 1554, 2012 1 Cr App R (S) 47 (p 278) LCJ B and H pleaded (late) to trafficking women into the UK for sexual exploitation (×2). Z, aged 19, and G, aged 37, were citizens of the Czech Republic. Both had drug problems and G had at times been a prostitute. B's role was to get the women out of the Czech Republic, and H's role was to enforce their sexual exploitation. Z and G were told they were to travel to Ireland to undergo bogus marriages in order to remain in the EU. They were taken to Ireland by B, where they met H. They were offered to men for sex. The women were then taken to the UK. Text messages made it clear that the intention to make money out of prostitution was clear and did not just involve Z and G. They were told that they owed amounts of money. Z and G were coerced into having sexual intercourse with a number of men. Z subsequently escaped and alerted the police. G described herself as being mentally tortured. B, aged 31, had convictions in the Czech Republic for dishonesty. H, aged 38, had convictions in the Czech Republic, including sexual activity with a child. Held. These were not single offences and B and H were not men of good character, although there were no previous offences of this type. There was a significant degree of coercion. The ordeal was only brought to an end because Z was able to escape. The women were vulnerable and had their liberty removed. B and H were their only means of obtaining drugs. Against a maximum sentence of 14 years, **8 years** not 10.

R v Harrison 2012 EWCA Crim 225 D was convicted of conspiracy to traffic into the UK for sexual exploitation (×2), conspiracy to traffic out of the UK for sexual exploitation (×2) and two false imprisonments. D was a key player in a sophisticated and organised criminal network of West African people traffickers. V and P, aged 14 and 16, were trafficked into the UK in 2009 by D and others. They were brought to the UK on false papers to work as prostitutes. V was kept at D's address in London for six days against her will before she was trafficked to Spain. P was illiterate and spoke no English. She was kept at D's address for two weeks against her will before D attempted to traffic her to Greece. The girls were not prostitutes before they were trafficked. Held. The Judge was entitled to conclude that a deterrent sentence was warranted. **20 years** upheld. See also: *Att-Gen's Ref Nos 9-10 of 2011* 2011 EWCA Crim 1953 (Convicted. D involved in five cases. Aged 48 or 49. Girls tricked into coming here. At least four were aged under 21. Women treated with utter contempt. **9 years** in total, not 6.)

Old case: *R v Pacan and Others* 2009 EWCA Crim 2436 (**11 years** for P, F and D and **14 years**)

If other old cases are needed, see the 9th edition of this book.

Post-guideline case

R v Gabrys 2015 EWCA Crim 93 D pleaded to conspiracy to traffic for sexual exploitation. He and his sister recruited prostitutes in Poland to work in the UK, by placing ads on websites. He ran the operation and was the main point of contact and the main organiser of the travel for the girls. His sister and girlfriend helped. The Judge considered it was a Category 2B case. D also moved them from venue to venue and organised the hotels. Held. It was not suggested there was coercion or violence. He made about £70,000. Held. We start at 4 years, so with full credit, **2 years 8 months** not 4 in all.

Where trafficked victims are raped, see the **Rape and Assault by Penetration** *Prostitutes as victims Trafficked victims* para at **317.50**.

312   Public Decency, Outraging

312.1

1) Common law (outraging public decency)

    Mode of trial Triable either way[870]

    Maximum sentence On indictment, life.[871] Summary 6 months and/or a £5,000 fine for offences committed before 12 March 2015 and an unlimited fine thereafter.[872] There are maximum fines for those aged under 18, see **14.38** in Volume 1.

2) Common law (conspiracy to outrage decency)[873]

    Mode of trial Indictable only

---

[870] Magistrates' Courts Act 1980 Sch 1 para 1A as inserted by Criminal Justice Act 2003 s 320
[871] There is no maximum provided, so under the common law rules the maximum sentence is life.
[872] Legal Aid, Sentencing and Punishment of Offenders Act 2012 s 85(1) and (4) and Legal Aid, Sentencing and Punishment of Offenders Act 2012 (Commencement No 11) Order 2015 2015/504
[873] There is an independent offence of conspiracy to outrage public decency, *Knuller Ltd v DPP* 1972 56 Cr App R 633

Maximum sentence Life[874]

Criminal Behaviour Orders Where a defendant has engaged in behaviour that caused or was likely to cause harassment, alarm or distress to any persons and a Criminal Behaviour Order will help in preventing the offender from engaging in such behaviour, the court may make this order.[875]

Sexual Harm Prevention Orders There is a discretionary power to make this order when it is necessary to protect the public from sexual harm.[876]

Law Commission On 25 June 2015, the Law Commission issued a consultation paper suggesting the offence should be replaced with one which requires the defendant to have greater knowledge of the offence.

See also the SEXUAL ACTIVITY/ASSAULTS/OFFENCES: IMAGES ETC., the SEX OFFENCES: GENERAL PRINCIPLES and the EXPOSURE chapters.

312.2   *Magistrates' Court Sentencing Guidelines*

Magistrates' Court Sentencing Guidelines 2008, see www.banksr.com Other Matters Guidelines tab page 59 The guidelines indicate that the guideline for exposure may be relevant by way of analogy.

312.3   *Cases*

Note: The CPS tend not to charge outraging public decency when they can charge sexual offences so that notification is triggered and the gravity of the sexual offending is marked. Ed.

R v Carton 2012 EWCA Crim 3199 D pleaded (early) to outraging public decency (×5). He had an urge to take photographs of women's legs under their skirts. D and V were on a train. They disembarked at the same station and V indicated that D should climb the steps from the platform ahead of her. D insisted that V go first, and she did. She then felt someone very close behind her and something brush against her leg. She turned around to see D crouching with his mobile phone angled so it could take a picture up her skirt. V asked D what he was doing and he walked away. The police were contacted and D was searched. His mobile phone was found in a bush nearby. It contained 48 images of various women. The fifth offence represented 45 photographs taken between February and July of 2011. The victims had not suspected anything was amiss. D, aged 59, had significant previous convictions but they were from 'some time ago'. There was a conviction from 1997 for possessing child pornography. The Judge sentenced him to 14 months and imposed an ASBO. Held. D's actions caused considerable upset and anxiety and were carried out over a prolonged period. The *Sexual Offences Act 2003 Guideline 2008* is of some assistance as these offences have something in common with the basic offence. There was no evidence that D had showed the films to anyone else. D had already taken steps to reduce his ability to reoffend by obtaining a mobile phone without a camera and ceasing to be connected to the Internet. It was important not to minimise the effect of the offending. Those who were aware became understandably distressed and in some cases it affected their confidence in public. **3-year community order** with a community sex programme, not 14 months. The ASBO made by the Judge, which prohibited, among other things, using a device capable of capturing still or moving images in a railway or bus station, on public transport, in a shop or other public amenity, was appropriate and would remain in place.

R v Vaiculevicius 2013 EWCA Crim 185, 2 Cr App R (S) 55 (p 362) At the Magistrates' Court, D pleaded to outraging public decency. On a Sunday afternoon in a public park where children were playing, he and a woman removed their lower clothing and had consensual sexual intercourse. Both were heavily intoxicated and made no attempt to conceal their actions. D was aged 30 and had 30 previous convictions, mainly involving

---

[874] There is no maximum provided, so under the common law rules the maximum sentence is life.
[875] Anti-social Behaviour, Crime and Policing Act 2014 s 22(1)-(4)
[876] Sexual Offences Act 2003 s 103A as inserted by Anti-social Behaviour, Crime and Policing Act 2014 Sch 5 para 2 and Sexual Offences Act 2003 Sch 5

dishonesty but none for sex. He had a repeated disregard for court orders. The offence must have been committed within a very short time of his release from prison. Held. The aggravating features were the complete disregard for the shock or distress that was likely to be caused and the presence of young children nearby. The custody threshold was passed but with full credit, **3 months** not 6.

See also: *R v Hardy* 2013 EWCA Crim 2125, 2014 1 Cr App R (S) 70 (p 452) (Convicted. Showing his semi-erect penis in a car park. At 4.45 pm, near a takeaway where children were likely to congregate. **4 months** not 12.)

Old cases: *R v Birch* 2007 EWCA Crim 1008, 2008 1 Cr App R (S) 13 (p 55) (**18 months** not 3 years) *R v Anderson* 2008 EWCA Crim 12, 2 Cr App R (S) 343 (**3 years**) *R v Ferguson* 2008 EWCA Crim 2940, 2009 2 Cr App R (S) 8 (p 39) (**21 months**) For a summary of the first and second cases, see the 9th edition of this book.

PUBLIC ORDER ACT 1986 S 2 see the **AFFRAY/VIOLENT DISORDER** chapter.

313   PUBLIC ORDER ACT 1986 S 4 AND 4A

313.1

1) Public Order Act 1986 s 4 (using threatening, abusive or insulting words or behaviour)

Public Order Act 1986 s 4A (intentional harassment, alarm or distress)

Modes of trial Summary only

Maximum sentences 6 months[877] and/or a £5,000 fine for offences committed before 12 March 2015 and an unlimited fine thereafter.[878] There are maximum fines for those aged under 18, see **14.38** in Volume 1.

Football Banning Orders Where:

   i) the offence is under Public Order Act 1986 s 4(1)(a) or 4A,

   ii) the offence was committed relevant to a football match, and

   iii) there are reasonable grounds to believe that making a banning order would help to prevent violence or disorder at or in connection with any regulated football match,

the court must make a Football Banning Order under Football Spectators Act 1989 s 14A and Sch 1 para 1. The Court of Appeal has considered that it did not think there was any reason why the position should be any different for an offence under Public Order Act 1986 s 4(1)(b) but left the point open as the Court had not heard any argument on the point, *R v O'Keefe* 2003 EWCA Crim 2629, 2004 1 Cr App R (S) 67 (p 402).

2) Public Order Act 1986 s 4 and 4A and Crime and Disorder Act 1998 s 31 (racially or religiously aggravated offences)

Modes of trial Triable either way

Maximum sentences On indictment 2 years. Summary 6 months and/or a £5,000 fine for offences committed before 12 March 2015 and an unlimited fine thereafter.[879] There are maximum fines for those aged under 18, see **14.38** in Volume 1.

Criminal Behaviour Orders Where a defendant has engaged in behaviour that caused or was likely to cause harassment, alarm or distress to any persons and a Criminal Behaviour Order will help in preventing the offender from engaging in such behaviour, the court may make this order.[880] Whether the order can be made when the offence

---

[877] Where the jury convict the defendant of an offence under section 4 as an alternative to a racially aggravated offence, the maximum sentence at the Crown Court is the Magistrates' Court's maximum, Public Order Act 1986 s 7(4), *R v Alden* 2002 EWCA Crim 421, 2 Cr App R (S) 74 (p 326)

[878] Legal Aid, Sentencing and Punishment of Offenders Act 2012 s 85(1) and (4) and Legal Aid, Sentencing and Punishment of Offenders Act 2012 (Commencement No 11) Order 2015 2015/504

[879] Legal Aid, Sentencing and Punishment of Offenders Act 2012 s 85(1) and (4) and Legal Aid, Sentencing and Punishment of Offenders Act 2012 (Commencement No 11) Order 2015 2015/504

[880] Anti-social Behaviour, Crime and Policing Act 2014 s 22(1)-(4)

charged is only Public Order Act 1986 s 4 where this aggravating element of 'behaviour that caused or was likely to cause harassment, alarm or distress to any persons' has not been charged, is open to argument.

Licensed premises For all offences: Where an offence is committed on licensed premises, the court may prohibit defendants from entering those premises or any other specified premises without the express consent of the licensee etc.[881] The minimum period is 3 months and the maximum period is 2 years.[882] Violent Crime Reduction Act 2006 s 65 and Sch 5 repeals these powers and includes powers to make Drinking Banning Orders. Evaluation of the new powers continues. The repeal and the commencement of the new powers is not expected soon.

313.2 *Magistrates' Court Sentencing Guidelines   Public Order Act 1986 s 4*
Magistrates' Court Sentencing Guidelines 2008, see www.banksr.com Other Matters Guidelines tab page 86 The guideline applies to the Magistrates' Court and to the Crown Court hearing appeals or sentencing for summary only offences.[883] The guideline also deals with racially or religiously aggravated offences where the sentence should be increased to reflect that element.

page 18 para 1 The starting points and ranges apply to a first-time offender who was convicted after a trial.

page 86

Examples of nature of activity	Starting point	Range
Fear or threat of low-level immediate unlawful violence such as push, shove or spit	Low-level community order	Band B fine to medium-level community order
Fear or threat of medium-level immediate unlawful violence such as punch	High-level community order	Low-level community order to 12 weeks' custody
Fear or threat of high-level immediate unlawful violence such as use of weapon, missile thrown, gang involvement	12 weeks' custody	6 to 26 weeks' custody

The following aggravating and mitigating factors may be particularly relevant: Factors indicating higher culpability: 1 Planning, 2 Offender deliberately isolates victim, 3 Group action, 4 Threat directed at victim because of job, and 5 History of antagonism towards victim. Factors indicating lower culpability: 1 Impulsive action, 2 Short duration, and 3 Provocation. Factors indicating greater degree of harm: 1 Offence committed at school, hospital or other place where vulnerable persons may be present, 2 Offence committed on enclosed premises such as public transport, 3 Vulnerable victim(s), and 4 Victim needs medical help and/or counselling.

Consider ancillary orders, including compensation and a Football Banning Order.

For the meaning of a high-level, a medium-level and a low-level community order, see **16.12** in Volume 1.

313.3 *Magistrates' Court Sentencing Guidelines   Public Order Act 1986 s 4A*
Magistrates' Court Sentencing Guidelines 2008, see www.banksr.com Other Matters Guidelines tab page 18 The guideline applies to the Magistrates' Court and to the Crown Court hearing appeals or sentencing for summary only offences.[884] The guideline also deals with racially or religiously aggravated offences where the sentence should be increased to reflect that element.

---

[881] Licensed Premises (Exclusion of Certain Persons) Act 1980 s 1(1)
[882] Licensed Premises (Exclusion of Certain Persons) Act 1980 s 1(3)
[883] See page 15 of the guidelines.
[884] See page 15 of the guidelines.

page 18 para 1 The starting points and ranges apply to a first-time offender who was convicted after a trial.
page 87

Examples of nature of activity	Starting point	Range
Threats, abuse or insults made more than once but on same occasion against the same person e.g. following down the street	Band C fine	Band B fine to low-level community order
Group action or deliberately planned action against targeted victim	Medium-level community order	Low-level community order to 12 weeks' custody
Weapon brandished or used or threats against vulnerable victim – course of conduct over longer period	12 weeks' custody	High-level community order to 26 weeks' custody

The following aggravating and mitigating factors may be particularly relevant: Factors indicating higher culpability: 1 High degree of planning, and 2 Offender deliberately isolates victim. Factors indicating lower culpability: 1 Very short period, and 2 Provocation. Factors indicating greater degree of harm: 1 Offence committed in vicinity of victim's home, 2 Large number of people in vicinity, 3 Actual or potential escalation into violence, and 4 Particularly serious impact on victim.

Consider ancillary orders, including compensation and Football Banning Order.

A Band B fine is 100% of net weekly income. Band C is 150%. For more detail see **60.27** in Volume 1.

For the meaning of a high-level, a medium-level and a low-level community order, see **16.12** in Volume 1.

313.4   *Public Order Act 1986 s 4   Case*

R v Smith 2013 EWCA Crim 11 D pleaded to section 4 when it was offered as an alternative to affray. D had offered to plead to that in the Magistrates' Court. V, a barrister, represented D at a family court dispute about the custody of D's son. D thought V was half-hearted and uncommitted. After the hearing, V walked up some stairs to a railway platform and D drew alongside her and shouted, "Bitch" in her ear. He turned to her and said, "Yeah, that's right, you fucking bitch". V did not respond and walked to her train. About a minute later, D approached her again and repeated similar aggressive and intimidating abuse. D also threatened to stab her, saying if it was not for his son he would have thrown her onto the tracks. V persuaded others not to intervene. During the incidents she was aware of D's violent past. D appeared to leave and V caught a train only to see D board the train too. She thought he was looking for her. She phoned the police and sought help at a station. In interview, D said he was frustrated at V's shortcomings. V, in her victim impact statement, said she felt spittle on her face and that she was extremely fearful of an attack. The experience affected her professional life. D was assessed as posing a high risk of harm to the public. D, aged 44, had served 12 years for robbery. On his release he breached court orders. He had convictions for assault on a former partner and ABH on a female (21 months). That was after a road traffic incident when he drove his car at the female. He then shouted at her and kicked her. The Judge considered that D was a bully, particularly towards women. Held. We accept there was a loving relationship between D and his son. The offence was at the top of the hierarchy of seriousness for the offence. V was a lone, terrified woman. **4 months** was not manifestly excessive.

313.5 Public Order Act 1986 s 4 and 4A   Racially or religiously aggravated-Case

Old case: *R v Lockey* 2008 EWCA Crim 2149, 2009 1 Cr App R (S) 99 (p 565) (**6 months**)

For a summary of the case, see the 9th edition of this book.

For the **Basic principles** see the RACIALLY OR RELIGIOUSLY AGGRAVATED OFFENCES **Basic principles** para at **315.4**.

314   PUBLIC ORDER ACT 1986 s 5

314.1

Public Order Act 1986 s 5 (using threatening or abusive words or behaviour or disorderly behaviour etc. likely to cause harassment, alarm or distress)[885]

Mode of trial Summary only

Maximum sentence Level 3 fine (£1,000)

Fixed penalty There is a £90 fixed penalty for Public Order Act 1986 s 5 offences[886] with half the relevant victim surcharge. For more detail see **61.1** in Volume 1.

Criminal Behaviour Orders Where a defendant has engaged in behaviour that caused or was likely to cause harassment, alarm or distress to any persons and a Criminal Behaviour Order will help in preventing the offender from engaging in such behaviour, the court may make this order.[887]

Football Banning Orders The offence is a relevant offence under Football Spectators Act 1989 s 14A and Sch 1 para 1. Where: a) the offence was committed during a period relevant to a football match, and b) the accused was at or attempting to enter or leave the premises or journeying to and from the premises or the offence related to a match, the court must make a Football Banning Order, where there are reasonable grounds to believe that making a banning order would help to prevent violence or disorder at or in connection with any regulated football match (except where the defendant is given an absolute discharge).

Licensed premises Where an offence is committed on licensed premises, the court may prohibit defendants from entering those premises or any other specified premises without the express consent of the licensee etc.[888] The minimum period is 3 months and the maximum period is 2 years.[889] Violent Crime Reduction Act 2006 s 65 and Sch 5 repeals these powers and includes powers to make Drinking Banning Orders. Evaluation of the new powers continues. The repeal and the commencement of the new powers is not expected soon.

314.2   Magistrates' Court Sentencing Guidelines

Magistrates' Court Sentencing Guidelines 2008, see www.banksr.com Other Matters Guidelines tab page 88 The guideline applies to the Magistrates' Court and to the Crown Court hearing appeals or sentencing for summary only offences.[890]

page 18 para 1 The starting points and ranges apply to a first-time offender who was convicted after a trial.

page 88

Examples of nature of activity	Starting point	Range
Shouting, causing disturbance for some minutes	Band A fine	Conditional discharge to Band B fine

---

[885] Crime and Courts Act 2013 s 57 removed the words 'abusive or insulting' and replaced them with 'or abusive'. In force 1/2/14

[886] Penalties for Disorderly Behaviour (Amount of Penalty) Order 2002 2002/1837 as amended

[887] Anti-social Behaviour, Crime and Policing Act 2014 s 22(1)-(4)

[888] Licensed Premises (Exclusion of Certain Persons) Act 1980 s 1(1)

[889] Licensed Premises (Exclusion of Certain Persons) Act 1980 s 1(3)

[890] See page 15 of the guidelines.

Examples of nature of activity	Starting point	Range
Substantial disturbance caused	Band B fine	Band A fine to Band C fine

The following aggravating and mitigating factors may be particularly relevant: Factors indicating higher culpability: 1 Group action, and 2 Lengthy incident. Factors indicating lower culpability: 1 Stopped as soon as police arrived, 2 Brief/minor incident, and 3 Provocation. Factors indicating greater degree of harm: 1 Vulnerable person(s) present, 2 Offence committed at school, hospital or other place where vulnerable persons may be present, and 3 Victim providing public service.

Consider ancillary orders, including compensation and Football Banning Orders.

A Band A fine is 50% of net weekly income. Bands B and C are 100% and 150%. For more detail see **60.27** in Volume 1.

314.3   *Racially or religiously aggravated*

Crime and Disorder Act 1998 s 31 and Public Order Act 1986 s 5 (racially or religiously aggravated harassment, alarm or distress)

Modes of trial Summary only

Maximum sentences Level 4 fine (£2,500)

Basic principles see **RACIALLY AGGRAVATED** Offences *Basic principles* at **315.4**.

315   RACIALLY OR RELIGIOUSLY AGGRAVATED OFFENCES

315.1

1) Crime and Disorder Act 1998 s 29-32 deal with racially or religiously aggravated offences of or contrary to:

a) Offences Against the Person Act 1861 s 20, ABH or Protection from Harassment Act 1997 s 4

Modes of trial Triable either way

Maximum sentences Indictment 7 years. Summary 6 months and/or a £5,000 fine for offences committed before 12 March 2015 and an unlimited fine thereafter.[891] There are maximum fines for those aged under 18, see **14.38** in Volume 1.

b) Common assault, Public Order Act 1986 s 4 and 4A and Protection from Harassment Act 1997 s 2

Modes of trial Triable either way

Maximum sentences Indictment 2 years. Summary 6 months and/or a £5,000 fine for offences committed before 12 March 2015 and an unlimited fine thereafter.[892] There are maximum fines for those aged under 18, see **14.38** in Volume 1.

c) Public Order Act 1986 s 5

Mode of trial Summary only

Maximum sentence Level 4 fine (£2,500)

2) Public Order Act 1986 s 29B-29G Using, publishing etc. threatening words etc. with intent to stir up religious hatred

Mode of trial Triable either way

Maximum sentences Indictment 7 years. Summary 6 months and/or a £5,000 fine for offences committed before 12 March 2015 and an unlimited fine thereafter.[893] There are maximum fines for those aged under 18, see **14.38** in Volume 1.

Report On 28 May 2014, the Law Commission published a report, *Hate Crime: Should the Current Offences Be Extended?* LC 348/Cm 8865.

---

[891] Legal Aid, Sentencing and Punishment of Offenders Act 2012 s 85(1) and (4) and Legal Aid, Sentencing and Punishment of Offenders Act 2012 (Commencement No 11) Order 2015 2015/504

[892] Legal Aid, Sentencing and Punishment of Offenders Act 2012 s 85(1) and (4) and Legal Aid, Sentencing and Punishment of Offenders Act 2012 (Commencement No 11) Order 2015 2015/504

[893] Legal Aid, Sentencing and Punishment of Offenders Act 2012 s 85(1) and (4) and Legal Aid, Sentencing and Punishment of Offenders Act 2012 (Commencement No 11) Order 2015 2015/504

For the offences that have racially or religiously aggravated chapters or paragraphs, see the back index.

315.2   Statutory provisions

Criminal Justice Act 2003 s 145(1) This section applies where a court is considering the seriousness of an offence other than one under Crime and Disorder Act 1998 s 29-32 (racially or religiously aggravated assaults, criminal damage, public order offences and harassment etc.).
(2) If the offence was racially or religiously aggravated, the court:
 a) must treat that fact as an aggravating factor, and
 b) must state in open court that the offence was so aggravated.
(3) Crime and Disorder Act 1998 s 28 (meaning of 'racially or religiously aggravated') applies for the purposes of this section as it applies for the purposes of Crime and Disorder Act 1998 s 29-32.

315.3   Court Martial   Statutory provisions

Armed Forces Act 2006 s 240(1) This section applies where a court or officer dealing with an offender for a service offence (other than an offence mentioned in subsection (3)) is considering the seriousness of the offence.
(2) If the offence was racially or religiously aggravated the court or officer:
 a) must treat that fact as an aggravating factor, and
 b) must state in open court that the offence was so aggravated.
(3) This section does not apply in relation to an offence under section 42 as respects which the corresponding offence under the law of England and Wales is an offence under any of Crime and Disorder Act 1998 s 29-32 (racially or religiously aggravated assaults, criminal damage, public order offences and harassment etc.).
(4) Crime and Disorder Act 1998 s 28 (meaning of 'racially or religiously aggravated') applies for the purposes of this section as it applies for the purposes of Crime and Disorder Act 1998 s 29-32.

315.4   Basic principles

Att-Gen's Ref Nos 29-31 of 1994 1995 16 Cr App R (S) 698 LCJ It cannot be too strongly emphasised that where there is a racial element in an offence of violence, that is a gravely aggravating feature.
R v Saunders 2000 2 Cr App R (S) 71 Racism must not be allowed to flourish. The message must be received and understood in every corner of our society. Racism is evil. Those who indulge in racially aggravated violence must expect to be punished severely.
R v Beglin 2002 EWCA Crim 1887, 2003 1 Cr App R (S) 21 (p 88) D pleaded to racially aggravated common assault. Held. Any offence that is racially aggravated is serious because of its impact not only on the victim but on the public, who should rightly be outraged at such behaviour. The Court in *R v Kelly and Donnelly* 2001 EWCA Crim 170, 2 Cr App R (S) 73 (p 341) was astute not to provide any automatic mechanism in respect of the amount which should be added for the racial aggravation since, as is plain, there are so many factors which have to be taken into account which distinguish one racially aggravated assault from another.

315.5   The uplift

R v Saunders 2000 2 Cr App R (S) 71 Generally speaking, following a trial, a period of up to 2 years should be added to the term of imprisonment otherwise appropriate. Consider the sentence in two stages. Relevant factors will include the nature of the hostile demonstration, its length, whether isolated, repeated, or persistent, its location, whether public or private, and the number both of those demonstrating and those demonstrated against.
R v Morrison 2001 1 Cr App R (S) 5 (p 11) The decision in *R v Saunders* 2000 2 Cr App R (S) 71 does not mean that the maximum that can be added is 2 years. The amount will depend on all the circumstances.

R v Kelly and Donnelly 2001 EWCA Crim 170, 2 Cr App R (S) 73 (p 341) First determine what the appropriate sentence was for the offence without the racial element and then determine the appropriate sentence for the racial element. Each part should be publicly identified. The factors seriously aggravating the racial element in relation to the offender's intention are planning, the offence being part of a pattern of racist offending, membership of a group promoting racist activity, and the deliberate setting up of the victim for the purposes of humiliating him or being offensive towards him. The factors seriously aggravating the racial element in relation to the impact on the victim are if the offence took place in the victim's home, or the victim was particularly vulnerable, or providing a service to the public, or if the timing or location of the offence was such as to maximise the harm or distress caused, or the expressions of racial hostility were repeated or prolonged, or if fear and distress throughout a particular community resulted from the offence, or if particular distress was caused to the victim or the victim's family. These factors should be added to the factors in *R v Saunders* 2000 2 Cr App R (S) 71.

R v Beglin 2002 EWCA Crim 1887, 2003 1 Cr App R (S) 21 (p 88) D pleaded to racially aggravated common assault. Held. The Court in *R v Kelly and Donnelly* 2001 EWCA Crim 170, 2 Cr App R (S) 73 (p 341) was astute not to provide any automatic mechanism in respect of the amount that should be added for racial aggravation, since there are so many factors which have to be taken into account which distinguish one racially aggravated assault from another. Counsel are obliged to draw the court's attention to *R v Kelly and Donnelly* 2001 and the judge should announce what the two parts are.

R v O'Brien 2003 EWCA Crim 302, 2 Cr App R (S) 66 (p 390) D pleaded to racially aggravated criminal damage. He was given 2 months with an uplift of 12 months, making a 14-month sentence. The defence said that the uplift was too great. Held. We note the Sentencing Advisory Panel recommended the two-stage approach and an enhancement within the range of 40 to 70% but the sentencer should not be constrained by those figures. There may be cases where the two-stage approach is not appropriate. Take the case of a burning book, with slight monetary value but important racial or religious associations. There could be circumstances in which a mechanical or even the flexible application of the 40 to 70% will not be appropriate. It may fail to regard the overall view. There may be cases where the entire nature of the offence is changed by reason of the racial or religious aggravation.

R v Fitzgerald 2003 EWCA Crim 2875, 2004 1 Cr App R (S) 74 (p 436) The *R v Kelly and Donnelly* 2001 approach is not applicable in all cases. Here, the racial aggravation is so inherent and integral to the offence it is not possible sensibly to assess the overall criminality in such a discrete way. In such cases, the court must assess the seriousness of the conduct and its criminality as a whole.

R v Slater 2005 EWCA Crim 2882, 2006 1 Cr App R (S) 129 (p 751) The defendant was convicted of racially aggravated common assault. Where the assault does not merit custody but the racial element does, make the assault sentence notional and then decide the uplift.

315.6   *Joint enterprise*

R v Davies and Ely 2003 EWCA Crim 3700, 2004 2 Cr App R (S) 29 (p 148) The defendants pleaded guilty to wounding with intent. A group attacked a mixed-race victim. A witness heard a member of the group say, "You black bastard. I am going to cut you." The Judge found that as the group set off there was no element of racial motivation. He sentenced them to 5 years for the wounding with 1 year added to reflect the racial aggravation. Held. The Judge made no finding as to who said the offending words and it would have been impossible for him to do so. It is open to all members of the group to be convicted of the section 18 offence on a joint enterprise basis but that same basis is not apt to make all members of the group liable for the added aggravating feature. **5 years** substituted.

315.7 *No racially aggravated offence charged*

Magistrates' Court Sentencing Guidelines 2008, see www.banksr.com Other Matters Guidelines tab page 178 The court should not normally treat an offence as racially or religiously aggravated if a racially or religiously aggravated form of the offence was available but was not charged.[894] A court should not conclude that offending involved aggravation related to race, religion, disability or sexual orientation without first putting the offender on notice and allowing him or her to challenge the allegation.

R v O'Callaghan 2005 EWCA Crim 317, 2 Cr App R (S) 83 (p 514) D was convicted of ABH. There was no racially aggravated count. The racial angle was not an issue at the trial. The Judge in his sentencing remarks said that there was a racial motive to the offence. He indicated that he had added a 3-month uplift to the sentence because it was a racially enhanced offence. Held. The Judge cannot sentence on the basis that a more serious offence has been committed. Considering *R v Clark* 1996 2 Cr App R (S) 351, this case falls very much on the wrong side of the line. There are also difficulties with using a *Newton* hearing, see *R v Druce* 1993 14 Cr App R (S) 691 and *R v Davies* 1998 1 Cr App R (S) 380. The question of racial aggravation can be dealt with in the sentencing process even if it had not arisen during the trial. But there must be a *Newton* hearing or at the very least plain and adequate notice must be given. Fairness and principle demand that.

R v McGillivray 2005 EWCA Crim 604, 2 Cr App R (S) 60 (p 366) D pleaded to an amended indictment charging him with ABH. He had earlier pleaded not guilty to a count alleging racially aggravated ABH and the prosecution offered no evidence so that a not guilty verdict had been entered for that count. D called the victim "a fucking refugee" and said, "Go back to your own country" and "I cannot wait to see the back of you". He had four previous convictions for assault and had also been fined for using racially threatening abusive or insulting words or behaviour. The Judge sentenced him, saying that the appropriate sentence for the assault was 2 years, but because of the aggravation of circumstances of racism shown by D's comments he would increase that by 50%. Held. It was not open to the Judge to increase the sentence he otherwise would have given on the basis that the assault was racially aggravated when the Crown had offered no evidence on that count and D had been found not guilty of that count. To do that it was necessary for D to plead guilty or be found guilty of a racially aggravated assault.

R v Kentsch 2005 EWCA Crim 2851, 2006 1 Cr App R (S) 126 (p 737) D pleaded to ABH after the particular alleging racial aggravation had been deleted. The Judge sentenced him on the basis that there had been racial taunts. Held. That could not be right. Sentence reduced.

R v O'Leary 2015 EWCA Crim 1306, 1 Cr App R (S) 11 (p 66) D pleaded to assault with intent to rob and two section 20 woundings. He was acquitted of attempted murder and two section 18 woundings arising from the same facts. He tried to rob V1 in a convenience store with a knife and V1 resisted. V1's hand was cut by the knife. On the same day, D went to another convenience store and approached V2 brandishing one of his knives and told V2 he wanted to kill a Muslim. A struggle ensued during which V2 received a deep wound to his hand. D's previous convictions included three for ABH and a 'racially aggravated behaviour' charge. The defence contended the Judge should not have taken into account the racial motivation as there was no count for that. Held. Here, unlike in *R v McGillivray* 2005 and *R v Kentsch* 2005, D had neither been acquitted of a Crime and Disorder Act 1998 s 29 offence, nor had such a count been deleted from the indictment. Moreover, unlike the situation in both *R v Lawrence* 1983 5 Cr App R (S) 220 (a firearm case) and *R v O'Prey* 1999 2 Cr App R (S) 83 (a driving whilst disqualified case), D was dealt with following a trial when he had an opportunity of challenging the evidence and the Judge had an opportunity of making a finding about it.

---

[894] *R v O'Callaghan* 2005 EWCA Crim 317, 2 Cr App R (S) 83 (p 514)

So the case is more akin to *R v Khan* 2009 EWCA Crim 389, 2010 1 Cr App R (S) 1 (p 1) (a perverting the course of justice case). Moreover, unlike the situation in *R v O'Callaghan* 2005 (see above) and *R v Docherty* 2014 EWCA Crim 1404 (an ABH case), here there was clear evidence upon which the trial Judge had been entitled to conclude to the criminal standard that the assault was racially aggravated. Consequently the Judge was entitled to treat this matter as a factor which increased the seriousness of the offence, and we dismiss the appeal. But the prosecution are not relieved of their duty to consider the indictment with care. In the majority of cases where the evidence supports an aggravated form of assault, then it should be placed upon the indictment. However, there was another set of alternative offences so adding further alternatives would have overloaded the indictment.

315.8   *Publishing racially inflammatory material*
Public Order Act 1986 s 19
Mode of trial Triable either way
Maximum sentence On indictment 7 years. Summary 6 months and/or a £5,000 fine for offences committed before 12 March 2015 and an unlimited fine thereafter.[895] There are maximum fines for those aged under 18, see **14.38** in Volume 1.
R v Whittle and Sheppard 2010 EWCA Crim 65 W and S were convicted of five and 13 counts of publishing racially inflammatory material respectively. S was also convicted of three counts of possessing racially inflammatory material. W composed material which he sent by e-mail to S, who edited it and then loaded it onto a Californian remote server. Material could then be accessed. Much of the material questioned the existence of the Holocaust. Other material made derogatory remarks about Jewish and black people. S also distributed two pamphlets, one about the Holocaust. The website had several thousand hits a day. W was the 'brains' behind the construction but his involvement was less than that of S and over a shorter period. W had no convictions, while S had two similar convictions in 2000 (9 months). After the giving of the first convictions W and S fled to the USA (4 months consecutive each for the bail offence and no appeal). The Judge said that he had rarely read or had to consider material so abusive and insulting. Held. This was truly pernicious material. Deterring offenders was an important element. For W **18 months** not 2 years. For S **3½ years** not 4½.

315.9   *Threatening behaviour etc. intending to stir up racial hatred*
Public Order Act 1986 s 18
Mode of trial Triable either way
Maximum sentence On indictment 7 years. Summary 6 months and/or a £5,000 fine for offences committed before 12 March 2015 and an unlimited fine thereafter.[896] There are maximum fines for those aged under 18, see **14.38** in Volume 1.
R v Javed and Others 2007 EWCA Crim 2692, 2008 2 Cr App R (S) 12 (p 70) LCJ J was convicted of soliciting murder and stirring up racial hatred. S was convicted of stirring up racial hatred. M was convicted of two counts of soliciting to murder. They all took part in a demonstration in central London protesting about a cartoon depicting the Prophet Mohammed which had been published in other countries. J spoke to the crowd outside the Danish embassy. He said, "The infidels attack the Muslim nation. They are one group. We will not stand for what Denmark did, for what France did. The whole of the infidels and the Western world are united. You have declared war against Allah and the Muslim nations for which you will pay a heavy price. Take a lesson from Theo Van Gogh and take a lesson from the Jews of Khyber from what you can see, or you will pay with your blood." S had participated in every stage of the demonstration. He drove a car equipped with a public address system which was used to excite the crowd and got out

---

[895] Legal Aid, Sentencing and Punishment of Offenders Act 2012 s 85(1) and (4) and Legal Aid, Sentencing and Punishment of Offenders Act 2012 (Commencement No 11) Order 2015 2015/504
[896] Legal Aid, Sentencing and Punishment of Offenders Act 2012 s 85(1) and (4) and Legal Aid, Sentencing and Punishment of Offenders Act 2012 (Commencement No 11) Order 2015 2015/504

of the car to make a speech. He held a microphone and led chants of "Democracy, hypocrisy! Democracy, go to hell! Freedom go to hell, UK you must pay! Sharia is on its way! Denmark you must pay! Muslims are on their way! Down down UK! Denmark/Europe you will pay! With your blood with your blood! 7/7 is on its way! UK you will pay! Bin Laden is on his way!". After each chant the crowd chanted the words back. M brought placards for the demonstration saying, 'Europe you will pay, 3/11[897] is on its way. Behead the one who insults the prophet! Exterminate those who insult Islam!' He carried a poster saying, 'Annihilate those who insult Islam'. He helped to carry the amplifying equipment for those who led the chants. He had another placard which said, 'Annihilate those who insult Islam'. In front of the Danish embassy he was leading the crowd in chants like 'Denmark you will pay!' and was involved in setting fire to the Danish flag. J, aged 28, had no convictions. He was married with a two-year-old daughter. He had a degree in computer sciences, and character references. S had no convictions. He was married with five children. He had a good employment record. A character reference said that he had worked hard to promote good community relations. He had a favourable pre-sentence report which said that he did not display adverse views or attitudes towards others of different cultures, races or religions and he had said that he did not intend to incite racial hatred. M, aged 24, had one conviction for criminal damage when he pulled down a poster he found offensive. Held. These offences stem from a one-off demonstration mounted at short notice without sophisticated planning. In so far as the crude chanting and the messages on the placards solicited murder, we do not think that this was likely to persuade those who witnessed it live or saw it on TV to resort to killing. We cannot be sure of the effect on those already inclined to terrorist activity. The demeanour of the demonstrators did not appear to be violent or threatening. The demonstration took place only six months after the London bombings, and these, the Madrid bombings and 9/11 were the subject of approbatory chanting. They were a demonstration of and an incitement to racial hatred. This case falls at the lower end of the range of conduct that is capable of amounting to soliciting to murder. For J and M, **4 years** not 6 for soliciting to murder, for J, **2 years** not 3 for stirring up racial hatred, for S, **30 months** not 4 years for stirring up racial hatred.
Note: This is an old case, so the decision should be treated with care. Ed.
See also: *R v El-Faisal* 2004 EWCA Crim 465 (**12 months**)
R v Hamza 2006 EWCA Crim 2918 (**21 months**)

316   RAILWAY OFFENCES

316.1
Various offences and penalties including:
1) Offences Against the Person Act 1861 s 32 (placing wood etc. on railway etc. with intent to endanger passengers)
   Mode of trial Triable either way
   Maximum sentence On indictment life. Summary 6 months and/or a £5,000 fine for offences committed before 12 March 2015 and an unlimited fine thereafter.[898] There are maximum fines for those aged under 18, see **14.38** in Volume 1.
2) Offences Against the Person Act 1861 s 33 (casting stones etc. on railway etc. with intent to endanger passengers)
   Mode of trial Indictable only
   Maximum sentence Life
Extended sentences Offences Against the Person Act 1861 s 33 is listed in Criminal Justice Act 2003 Sch 15. The court may pass a 2012 extended sentence (EDS) if there is a significant risk of serious harm from future specified offences and either: a) the

---

[897] It may be that 3/11 is in fact a typo for 9/11.
[898] Legal Aid, Sentencing and Punishment of Offenders Act 2012 s 85(1) and (4) and Legal Aid, Sentencing and Punishment of Offenders Act 2012 (Commencement No 11) Order 2015 2015/504

defendant has a Criminal Justice Act 2003 Sch 15B conviction (applicable only to defendants aged 18+), or b) the offence would justify a determinate sentence of at least 4 years.[899]

Fixed penalties There is a £60 fixed penalty[900] for: a) trespassing on a railway[901] and b) throwing stones etc. at trains or railways.[902] For more detail see **61.1** in Volume 1.

Sexual Harm Prevention Orders For Offences Against the Person Act 1861 s 32 offences, there is a discretionary power to make this order when it is necessary to protect the public from sexual harm.[903]

316.2   *Crown Court statistics   England and Wales*
Endangering railway passengers Aged 21+

Year	Plea	Total sentenced	Type of sentencing %						Average length of custody in months
			Dis-charge	Fine	Commu-nity sentence	Sus-pended sentence	Custody	Other	
2013	G	7	14.3	–	28.6	14.3	42.9	–	10.3
	NG	0							
2014	G	5	20	–	–	60	–	20	–
	NG	0							

For explanations about the statistics, see page 1-xii. For more statistics, see www.banksr. com Other Matters Statistics tab
Corporate defendants see the HEALTH AND SAFETY OFFENCES *Railway accidents* para at **270.22** and the MANSLAUGHTER *Railway accidents* para at **284.54**.

316.3   *Railway, bus etc. fare evasion*
There are many offences including:
Regulation of Railways Act 1889 s 5(1) and (3) (travelling on a railway without paying and failing to produce a ticket)
Mode of trial Summary only
Maximum sentence Level 2 fine (£500) for section 5(1) offences and 3 months' imprisonment and/or Level 3 fine (£1,000) for section 5(3) offences.

316.4   *Railway, bus etc. fare evasion   Magistrates' Court Sentencing Guidelines*
Magistrates' Court Sentencing Guidelines, see www.banksr.com Other Matters Guide-lines tab
page 89 The guidelines apply to the Magistrates' Court and the Crown Court hearing appeals or sentencing for summary only offences.[904] [The guideline is for a] first-time offender pleading not guilty.

Examples of nature of activity	Starting points	Range
Failing to produce ticket or pay fare on request	Band A fine	Conditional discharge to Band B fine
Travelling on railway without having paid the fare or knowingly and wilfully travelling beyond the distance paid for, with intent to avoid payment	Band B fine	Band A fine to Band C fine

---

[899] Criminal Justice Act 2003 s 226A-226B as inserted by Legal Aid, Sentencing and Punishment of Offenders Act 2012 s 124
[900] Penalties for Disorderly Behaviour (Amount of Penalty) Order 2002 2002/1837 Sch as amended
[901] British Transport Commission Act 1949 s 55
[902] British Transport Commission Act 1949 s 56
[903] Sexual Offences Act 2003 s 103A as inserted by Anti-social Behaviour, Crime and Policing Act 2014 Sch 5 para 2 and Sexual Offences Act 2003 Sch 5
[904] See page 15 of the guidelines.

Factor indicating higher culpability: Offensive or intimidating language or behaviour towards railway staff. Factor indicating greater degree of harm: High level of loss caused or intended to be caused.

Consider ancillary orders, including compensation.

Note: A Band A fine is 50% of net weekly income. Bands B and C are 100% and 150%. For more detail, see **60.27** in Volume 1. Ed.

Consultation It is expected that the Sentencing Council will issue a consultation document about updating this guideline in May 2016.

316.5   *Stealing material which disrupts railway services*

R v Manion 2011 EWCA Crim 234 D and another pleaded on rearraignment to two counts of theft (10% credit). Considerable lengths of cable were stolen from a railway track. D and his companion were captured on CCTV in relation to count 2, and were traced by a receipt from a scrap yard in relation to count 1. The thefts caused disruption to the railway services and the cable was costly to replace. The loss to the railway company caused by the delays was estimated at £25,000 and the cost of replacing the cable was £1,777 and £900. D, aged 30, had 13 convictions for 28 offences including numerous dishonesty offences. Held. The starting point here was too high. **2 years** after a plea was appropriate, not 3.

See also: *R v Mitchell and Kelham* 2011 EWCA Crim 1652, 2012 1 Cr App R (S) 68 (p 387) (Pleas to theft of railway cable and damaging railway cable. £75,000 worth of damage. Considering *Manion* and with full credit for the plea, **2 years**.)

See also the **THEFT** *Metal theft* para at **346.23**.

317   RAPE AND ASSAULT BY PENETRATION

317.1

1) Sexual Offences Act 2003
   s 1 (rape)
   s 2 (sexual assault by penetration)
   s 5 (rape when the victim is a child under 13)
   s 6 (assault of a child under 13 by penetration)
2) Sexual Offences Act 1956 s 1 (rape)

Offences committed on or after 1 May 2004 must be charged under Sexual Offences Act 2003. Offences committed prior to that date must be charged under Sexual Offences Act 1956.

Modes of trial All five offences are indictable only.

Maximum sentences All five offences have a maximum sentence of life.

Automatic life Sexual Offences Act 2003 s 1-2, 5 and 6 are listed in Criminal Justice Act 2003 Sch 15B Part 1. The court must (unless the particular circumstances make it unjust[905]) pass automatic life if: a) the defendant is aged 18+ at the date of the conviction, b) the offence was committed on or after 3 December 2012, c) the court considers a determinate sentence of at least 10 years is appropriate, d) at the time the offender was convicted he had a conviction for a Criminal Justice Act 2003 Sch 15B offence, and e) the defendant at the time of his or her conviction had previously been sentenced to either: i) a life sentence where he or she was not eligible for release during the first five years of the sentence or ii) a determinate sentence or extended sentence where the custodial part was 10 years or more.[906] For a pre-2012 extended sentence, when determining whether the custodial term was 10+ years, the period deducted for time on remand or on a curfew and tag is included.[907]

---

[905] Criminal Justice Act 2003 s 224A(2)
[906] Criminal Justice Act 2003 s 224A as inserted by Legal Aid, Sentencing and Punishment of Offenders Act 2012 s 122. The condition for: a) is at section 224A(1)(a), for b) is at section 224A(1)(b), for c) is at section 224A(1)(c), and for d) is at section 224A(4)-(9).
[907] Criminal Justice Act 2003 s 224A(9)-(10)

Extended sentences Sexual Offences Act 2003 s 1-2, 5 and 6 and Sexual Offences Act 1956 s 1 are listed in Criminal Justice Act 2003 Sch 15. The court may pass a 2012 extended sentence (EDS) if there is a significant risk of serious harm from future specified offences and either: a) the defendant has a Criminal Justice Act 2003 Sch 15B conviction (applicable only to defendants aged 18+), or b) the offence would justify a determinate sentence of at least 4 years.[908]

Sexual Harm Prevention Orders For all five offences under Sexual Offences Act 2003 and rape under Sexual Offences Act 1956 s 1, there is a discretionary power to make this order when it is necessary to protect the public etc.[909]

Notification For all five offences, the defendant must notify the police within three days (or three days from his release from imprisonment, hospital etc.) with his name, home address, national insurance number etc. and any changes, and addresses where he resides for seven days[910] (in one or more periods) or more in any 12-month period.[911]

Children and vulnerable adults: barred lists Where the defendant is convicted of: a) SOA 1956 s 1 against a child, b) SOA 2003 s 1 against a child, c) SOA 2003 s 2, 5 or 6 and is aged 18 or over, he or she is automatically barred from engaging in regulated activity with vulnerable adults and children.[912] The judge must tell the defendant that the Disclosure and Barring Service will include him or her in the barred list.[913] The defendant may ask the Service to remove him or her from the child list except when the offence is SOA 2003 s 5 or 6 or is committed against a child. The defendant may ask the Service to remove him or her from the adult list.

Old cases As the key factor in sentencing is the guideline, few old cases are listed.

317.2   *Crown Court statistics*   *England and Wales*
Rape of a female

Year	Age	Plea	Total sen-tenced	Type of sentencing %						Average length of custody in months
				Dis-charge	Fine	Commu-nity sentence	Sus-pended sentence	Custody	Other	
2013	10-17			Not available						
	18-20	G	42	–	–	9.5	2.4	83.3	4.8	58.5
		NG	33	–	–	–	–	100	–	80.3
	21+	G	294	–	–	0.7	1	96.3	2	106
		NG	598	–	–	0.5	–	98.5	1	121.4
2014	10-17			Not available						
	18-20	G	13	–	–	–	–	100	–	98.2
		NG	21	–	–	–	–	100	–	78.9
	21+	G	142	–	–	–	1	99	1	88.6
		NG	340	–	–	–	–	99	1	113.2

---

[908] Criminal Justice Act 2003 s 226A-226B as inserted by Legal Aid, Sentencing and Punishment of Offenders Act 2012 s 124
[909] Sexual Offences Act 2003 s 103A as inserted by Anti-social Behaviour, Crime and Policing Act 2014 Sch 5 para 2 and Sexual Offences Act 2003 Sch 3
[910] Criminal Justice Act 2003 s 226 and 228
[911] Powers of Criminal Courts (Sentencing) Act 2000 s 161(2)(a)
[912] Safeguarding Vulnerable Groups Act 2006 s 2 and Sch 3 and Safeguarding Vulnerable Groups Act 2006 (Prescribed Criteria and Miscellaneous Provisions) Regulations 2009 2009/37 para 3, 4 and 6 and Sch para 1, 2 and 4
[913] Safeguarding Vulnerable Groups Act 2006 s 2 and Sch 3 para 25

Rape of a male

Year	Age	Plea	Total sen-tenced	Type of sentencing %						Average length of custody in months
				Dis-charge	Fine	Commu-nity sentence	Sus-pended sentence	Custody	Other	
2013	18-20	G	4	–	–	–	25	75	–	75
		NG	2	–	–	–	–	100	–	66
	21+	G	32	–	–	–	–	96.9	3.1	123.2
		NG	38	–	–	–	–	100	–	127.7
2014	18-20	G	2	–	–	–	–	100	–	Not listed[914]
		NG	0							
	21+	G	1	–	–	–	–	100	–	Not listed
		NG	4	–	–	–	–	100	–	Not listed

For explanations about the statistics, see page 1-xii. For more detailed statistics, see www.banksr.com Other Matters Statistics tab

Guidelines: Approach

317.3   *Suggested approach to the guidelines*

Note: The *Sexual Offences Guideline 2014* is very different in structure from the *Sexual Offences Act 2003 Guideline 2008*. I consider the best approach for assessing the appropriate penalty is to simply apply the guideline. In the book, the pre-2014 guideline cases are ignored except in three respects. First, where they assert matters of principle. Second, where the appropriate starting point was 18 years or more. In those cases, I infer the new guideline did not wish to disturb the work of the Court of Appeal in dealing with very serious rapes. Third, for rapes of victims aged under 13. The reason for the third exception is at **317.64**.

The old guideline included the following assistance, 'We would emphasise that guidelines can produce sentences which are inappropriately high or inappropriately low if sentencers merely adopt a mechanistic approach to the guidelines. It is essential that, having taken the guidelines into account, sentencers stand back and look at the circumstances as a whole and impose the sentence which is appropriate having regard to all the circumstances. Double accounting must be avoided and can be a result of guidelines if they are applied indiscriminately.' That seems as true as ever. Ed.

Guidelines: Victim aged 13+

317.4   Sentencing Council guideline   Step One   Both offences

Sexual Offences Act 2003 s 1

Sexual Offences Guideline 2014, see www.banksr.com Other Matters Guidelines tab page 9 (rape) and page 14 (assault by penetration) This section of the guideline is the same. In force 1 April 2014

The guideline only applies to offenders aged 18+, see page 7 of the guideline. For the usual practice, see **66.21** in Volume 1.

STEP ONE: Determining the category offence

page 10 (rape) and page 14 (assault by penetration) The court should determine which categories of harm and culpability the offence falls into by reference only to the tables below.

Offences may be of such severity, for example involving a campaign of rape, that sentences of 20 years and above may be appropriate.

Note: this paragraph only appears in the rape guideline. Ed.

---

[914] 'Not listed' means figure based on too few cases to be meaningful

Harm	
Category 1	The extreme nature of one or more Category 2 factors or the extreme impact caused by a combination of Category 2 factors **may** elevate to Category 1
Category 2	Severe psychological or physical harm Pregnancy or STI as a consequence of offence Additional degradation/humiliation Abduction Prolonged detention/sustained incident Violence or threats of violence (beyond that which is inherent in the offence) Forced/uninvited entry into victim's home Victim is particularly vulnerable due to personal circumstances* * for children under 13 please refer to the guideline [at **317.9**]
Category 3	Factor(s) in Categories 1 and 2 not present

Culpability A
Significant degree of planning Offender acts together with others to commit the offence Use of alcohol/drugs on victim to facilitate the offence Abuse of trust Previous violence against victim Offence committed in course of burglary Recording of the offence Commercial exploitation and/or motivation Offence racially or religiously aggravated Offence motivated by, or demonstrating, hostility to the victim based on his or her sexual orientation (or presumed sexual orientation) or transgender identity (or presumed transgender identity) Offence motivated by, or demonstrating, hostility to the victim based on his or her disability (or presumed disability)

Culpability B
Factor(s) in Category A not present

For **Step Two Assault by penetration** see para **317.7**.

317.5   Step Two   Rape

STEP TWO: Starting point and category range

page 10 Having determined the category, the court should use the corresponding starting points to reach a sentence within the category range [below]. The starting point applies to all offenders irrespective of plea or previous convictions. Having determined the starting point, step two allows further adjustment for aggravating or mitigating features set out [below].

A case of particular gravity, reflected by multiple features of culpability or harm in step one, could merit upward adjustment from the starting point before further adjustment for aggravating or mitigating features, set out [below].

	Culpability A		Culpability B	
	Starting point	**Category range**	**Starting point**	**Category range**
Category 1	15 years' custody	13 to 19 years' custody	12 years' custody	10 to 15 years' custody
Category 2	10 years' custody	9 to 13 years' custody	8 years' custody	7 to 9 years' custody
Category 3	7 years' custody	6 to 9 years' custody	5 years' custody	4 to 7 years' custody

317.6   [Rape: Aggravating and mitigating factors]
page 11 The table below contains a **non-exhaustive** list of additional factual elements providing the context of the offence and factors relating to the offender. Identify whether any combination of these, or other relevant factors, should result in an upward or downward adjustment from the starting point. **In particular, relevant recent convictions are likely to result in an upward adjustment.** In some cases, having considered these factors, it may be appropriate to move outside the identified category range.

Aggravating factors
Statutory aggravating factors:
Previous convictions, having regard to: a) the nature of the offence to which the conviction relates and its relevance to the current offence; and b) the time that has elapsed since the conviction
Offence committed whilst on bail
Other aggravating factors:
Specific targeting of a particularly vulnerable victim
Ejaculation (where not taken into account at step one)
Blackmail or other threats made (where not taken into account at step one)
Location of offence
Timing of offence
Use of weapon or other item to frighten or injure
Victim compelled to leave their home (including victims of domestic violence)
Failure to comply with current court orders
Offence committed whilst on licence
Exploiting contact arrangements with a child to commit an offence
Presence of others, especially children
Any steps taken to prevent the victim reporting an incident, obtaining assistance and/or from assisting or supporting the prosecution
Attempts to dispose of or conceal evidence
Commission of offence whilst under the influence of alcohol or drugs

Mitigating factors
No previous convictions or no relevant/recent convictions
Remorse
Previous good character and/or exemplary conduct*
Age and/or lack of maturity where it affects the responsibility of the offender
Mental disorder or learning disability, particularly where linked to the commission of the offence
*Previous good character/exemplary conduct is different from having no previous convictions. The more serious the offence, the less the weight which should normally be attributed to this factor. Where previous good character/exemplary conduct has been used to facilitate the offence, this mitigation should not normally be allowed and such conduct may constitute an aggravating factor.
In the context of this offence, previous good character/exemplary conduct should not normally be given any significant weight and will not normally justify a reduction in what would otherwise be the appropriate sentence.

317.7   Step Two   Assault by penetration

STEP TWO: Starting point and category range
page 14 Having determined the category, the court should use the corresponding starting points to reach a sentence within the range [below]. The starting point applies to all offenders irrespective of plea or previous convictions.
Having determined the starting point, step two allows further adjustment for aggravating or mitigating features, set out [below].
A case of particular gravity, reflected by multiple features of culpability or harm in step one, could merit upward adjustment from the starting point before further adjustment for aggravating or mitigating features, set out [below].

Where there is a sufficient prospect of rehabilitation, a community order with a sex offender treatment programme requirement under Criminal Justice Act 2003 s 202 can be a proper alternative to a short or moderate-length custodial sentence.

	Culpability A		Culpability B	
	Starting point	**Category range**	**Starting point**	**Category range**
Category 1	15 years' custody	13 to 19 years' custody	12 years' custody	10 to 15 years' custody
Category 2	8 years' custody	5 to 13 years' custody	6 years' custody	4 to 9 years' custody
Category 3	4 years' custody	2 to 6 years' custody	2 years' custody	High-level community order to 4 years' custody

For the meaning of a high-level community order, see **16.14** in Volume 1.

317.8   [Assault by penetration: Aggravating and mitigating factors]
page 15 The table below contains a **non-exhaustive** list of additional factual elements providing the context of the offence and factors relating to the offender. Identify whether any combination of these, or other relevant factors, should result in an upward or downward adjustment from the starting point. **In particular, relevant recent convictions are likely to result in an upward adjustment.** In some cases, having considered these factors, it may be appropriate to move outside the identified category range.

When sentencing appropriate **Category 3** offences, the court should also consider the custody threshold as follows:
   Has the custody threshold been passed?
   If so, is it unavoidable that a custodial sentence be imposed?
   If so, can that sentence be suspended?

Aggravating factors
Statutory aggravating factors:
Previous convictions, having regard to: a) the nature of the offence to which the conviction relates and its relevance to the current offence; and b) the time that has elapsed since the conviction
Offence committed whilst on bail
Other aggravating factors:
Specific targeting of a particularly vulnerable victim
Blackmail or other threats made (where not taken into account at step one)
Location of offence
Timing of offence
Use of weapon or other item to frighten or injure
Victim compelled to leave their home (including victims of domestic violence)
Failure to comply with current court orders
Offence committed whilst on licence
Exploiting contact arrangements with a child to commit an offence
Presence of others, especially children
Any steps taken to prevent the victim reporting an incident, obtaining assistance and/or from assisting or supporting the prosecution
Attempts to dispose of or conceal evidence
Commission of offence whilst under the influence of alcohol or drugs

Mitigating factors
No previous convictions or no relevant/recent convictions Remorse Previous good character and/or exemplary conduct* Age and/or lack of maturity where it affects the responsibility of the offender Mental disorder or learning disability, particularly where linked to the commission of the offence *Previous good character/exemplary conduct is different from having no previous convictions. The more serious the offence, the less the weight which should normally be attributed to this factor. Where previous good character/exemplary conduct has been used to facilitate the offence, this mitigation should not normally be allowed and such conduct may constitute an aggravating factor. In the context of this offence, previous good character/exemplary conduct should not normally be given any significant weight and will not normally justify a reduction in what would otherwise be the appropriate sentence.

Guidelines: Victim aged under 13
317.9   Victim aged under 13   Rape   Sentencing Council guideline
Sexual Offences Act 2003 s 5
Sexual Offences Guideline 2014, www.banksr.com Other Matters Guidelines tab
The guideline only applies to offenders aged 18+, see page 7 of the guideline. For the usual practice, see **66.21** in Volume 1.

STEP ONE: Determining the offence category
page 28 The court should determine which categories of harm and culpability the offence falls into by reference **only** to the tables [below].

Offences may be of such severity, for example involving a campaign of rape, that sentences of 20 years and above may be appropriate.

When dealing with the statutory offence of rape of a child under 13, the court may be faced with a wide range of offending behaviour.

Sentencers should have particular regard to the fact that these offences are not only committed through force or fear of force but may include exploitative behaviour towards a child which should be considered to indicate high culpability.

This guideline is designed to deal with the majority of offending behaviour which deserves a significant custodial sentence. The starting points and ranges reflect the fact that such offending merits such an approach. There may also be exceptional cases, where a lengthy community order with a requirement to participate in a sex offender treatment programme may be the best way of changing the offender's behaviour and of protecting the public by preventing any repetition of the offence. This guideline may not be appropriate where the sentencer is satisfied that on the available evidence, and in the absence of exploitation, a young or particularly immature defendant genuinely believed, on reasonable grounds, that the victim was aged 16 or over and that they were engaging in lawful sexual activity.

Sentencers are reminded that if sentencing outside the guideline they must be satisfied that it would be contrary to the interests of justice to follow the guideline.

Harm	
Category 1	The extreme nature of one or more Category 2 factors or the extreme impact caused by a combination of Category 2 factors **may** elevate to Category 1

Category 2	Severe psychological or physical harm Pregnancy or STI as a consequence of offence Additional degradation/humiliation Abduction Prolonged detention/sustained incident Violence or threats of violence Forced/uninvited entry into victim's home Child is particularly vulnerable due to extreme youth and/or personal circumstances
Category 3	Factor(s) in Categories 1 and 2 not present

Culpability A
Significant degree of planning Offender acts together with others to commit the offence Use of alcohol/drugs on victim to facilitate the offence Grooming behaviour used against victim Abuse of trust Previous violence against victim Offence committed in course of burglary Sexual images of victim recorded, retained, solicited or shared
Deliberate isolation of victim Commercial exploitation and/or motivation Offence racially or religiously aggravated Offence motivated by, or demonstrating, hostility to the victim based on his or her sexual orientation (or presumed sexual orientation) or transgender identity (or presumed transgender identity) Offence motivated by, or demonstrating, hostility to the victim based on his or her disability (or presumed disability)
Culpability B
Factor(s) in Category A not present

317.10   [Victim aged under 13   Rape   Step Two]

STEP TWO: Starting point and category range

page 30 Having determined the category, the court should use the corresponding starting points to reach a sentence within the category range below. The starting point applies to all offenders irrespective of plea or previous convictions. Having determined the starting point, step two allows further adjustment for aggravating or mitigating features, set out [below].

A case of particular gravity, reflected by multiple features of culpability or harm in step one, could merit upward adjustment from the starting point before further adjustment for aggravating or mitigating features, set out [below].

Sentencers should also note the wording set out at step one, which may be applicable in exceptional cases.

	Culpability A		**Culpability B**	
	Starting point	**Category range**	**Starting point**	**Category range**
Category 1	16 years' custody	13 to 19 years' custody	13 years' custody	11 to 17 years' custody
Category 2	13 years' custody	11 to 17 years' custody	10 years' custody	8 to 13 years' custody
Category 3	10 years' custody	8 to 13 years' custody	8 years' custody	6 to 11 years' custody

317.11   [Victim under 13   Rape   Aggravating and mitigating factors]
page 31 The table below contains a **non-exhaustive** list of additional factual elements providing the context of the offence and factors relating to the offender. Identify whether any combination of these, or other relevant factors, should result in an upward or downward adjustment from the starting point. **In particular, relevant recent convictions are likely to result in an upward adjustment.** In some cases, having considered these factors, it may be appropriate to move outside the identified category range.

Aggravating factors
Statutory aggravating factors: Previous convictions, having regard to: a) the nature of the offence to which the conviction relates and its relevance to the current offence; and b) the time that has elapsed since the conviction   Offence committed whilst on bail   *Other aggravating factors:*   Specific targeting of a particularly vulnerable child   Ejaculation (where not taken into account at step one)   Blackmail or other threats made (where not taken into account at step one)   Location of offence   Timing of offence   Use of weapon or other item to frighten or injure   Victim compelled to leave their home, school, etc.   Failure to comply with current court orders   Offence committed whilst on licence   Exploiting contact arrangements with a child to commit an offence   Presence of others, especially other children   Any steps taken to prevent the victim reporting an incident, obtaining assistance and/or from assisting or supporting the prosecution   Attempts to dispose of or conceal evidence   Commission of offence whilst offender under the influence of alcohol or drugs   Victim encouraged to recruit others

Mitigating factors
No previous convictions or no relevant/recent convictions   Remorse   Previous good character and/or exemplary conduct*   Age and/or lack of maturity where it affects the responsibility of the offender   Mental disorder or learning disability, particularly where linked to the commission of the offence   *Previous good character/exemplary conduct is different from having no previous convictions. The more serious the offence, the less the weight which should normally be attributed to this factor. Where previous good character/exemplary conduct has been used to facilitate the offence, this mitigation should not normally be allowed and such conduct may constitute an aggravating factor.   In the context of this offence, previous good character/exemplary conduct should not normally be given any significant weight and will not normally justify a reduction in what would otherwise be the appropriate sentence.

317.12   Victim aged under 13   Assault by penetration   Sentencing Council guideline
Sexual Offences Act 2003 s 6
Sexual Offences Guideline 2014 www.banksr.com Other Matters Guidelines tab page 33
The guideline only applies to offenders aged 18+, see page 7 of the guideline. For the usual practice, see **66.21** in Volume 1.

STEP ONE: Determining the offence category
page 34 The court should determine which categories of harm and culpability the offence falls into by reference **only** to the tables [below].

Harm	
Category 1	The extreme nature of one or more Category 2 factors or the extreme impact caused by a combination of Category 2 factors **may** elevate to Category 1
Category 2	Severe psychological or physical harm Penetration using large or dangerous object(s) Additional degradation/humiliation Abduction Prolonged detention/sustained incident Violence or threats of violence Forced/uninvited entry into victim's home Child is particularly vulnerable due to extreme youth and/or personal circumstances
Category 3	Factor(s) in Categories 1 and 2 not present

Culpability A

Significant degree of planning
Offender acts together with others to commit the offence
Use of alcohol/drugs on victim to facilitate the offence
Grooming behaviour used against victim
Abuse of trust
Previous violence against victim
Offence committed in course of burglary
Sexual images of victim recorded, retained, solicited or shared
Deliberate isolation of victim
Commercial exploitation and/or motivation
Offence racially or religiously aggravated
Offence motivated by, or demonstrating, hostility to the victim based on his or her sexual orientation (or presumed sexual orientation) or transgender identity (or presumed transgender identity)
Offence motivated by, or demonstrating, hostility to the victim based on his or her disability (or presumed disability)

Culpability B

Factor(s) in Category A not present

317.13 [Victim under 13 Assault by penetration]

STEP TWO: Starting point and category range

page 34 Having determined the category, the court should use the corresponding starting points to reach a sentence within the category range [below]. The starting point applies to all offenders irrespective of plea or previous convictions. Having determined the starting point, step two allows further adjustment for aggravating or mitigating features, set out [below].

A case of particular gravity, reflected by multiple features of culpability or harm in step one, could merit upward adjustment from the starting point before further adjustment for aggravating or mitigating features, set out [below].

	Culpability A		Culpability B	
	Starting point	**Category range**	**Starting point**	**Category range**
Category 1	16 years' custody	13 to 19 years' custody	13 years' custody	11 to 17 years' custody
Category 2	11 years' custody	7 to 15 years' custody	8 years' custody	5 to 13 years' custody

	Culpability A		Culpability B	
Category 3	6 years' custody	4 to 9 years' custody	4 years' custody	2 to 6 years' custody

317.14   [Victim under 13   Assault by penetration   Aggravating and mitigating factors]

page 35 The table below contains a **non-exhaustive** list of additional factual elements providing the context of the offence and factors relating to the offender. Identify whether any combination of these, or other relevant factors, should result in an upward or downward adjustment from the starting point. **In particular, relevant recent convictions are likely to result in an upward adjustment.** In some cases, having considered these factors, it may be appropriate to move outside the identified category range.

Aggravating factors

Statutory aggravating factors:
Previous convictions, having regard to: a) the nature of the offence to which the conviction relates and its relevance to the current offence; and b) the time that has elapsed since the conviction
Offence committed whilst on bail
Other aggravating factors:
Specific targeting of a particularly vulnerable child
Blackmail or other threats made (where not taken into account at step one)
Location of offence
Timing of offence
Use of weapon or other item to frighten or injure
Victim compelled to leave their home, school etc.
Failure to comply with current court orders
Offence committed whilst on licence
Exploiting contact arrangements with a child to commit an offence
Presence of others, especially other children
Any steps taken to prevent the victim reporting an incident, obtaining assistance and/or from assisting or supporting the prosecution
Attempts to dispose of or conceal evidence
Commission of offence whilst under the influence of alcohol or drugs
Victim encouraged to recruit others

Mitigating factors

No previous convictions or no relevant/recent convictions
Remorse
Previous good character and/or exemplary conduct*
Age and/or lack of maturity where it affects the responsibility of the offender
Mental disorder or learning disability, particularly where linked to the commission of the offence
*Previous good character/exemplary conduct is different from having no previous convictions. The more serious the offence, the less the weight which should normally be attributed to this factor. Where previous good character/exemplary conduct has been used to facilitate the offence, this mitigation should not normally be allowed and such conduct may constitute an aggravating factor.
In the context of this offence, previous good character/exemplary conduct should not normally be given any significant weight and will not normally justify a reduction in what would otherwise be the appropriate sentence.

General matters and guilty plea
317.15   *Judicial guidance   Pre-2014 guideline case*
Att-Gen's Ref No 6 of 2002 2002 EWCA Crim 1811, 2003 1 Cr App R (S) 71 (p 357)
Where aggravating features have to be taken into account, there is no artificial limit beyond which the Court cannot go in reflecting those aggravating features.

Note: This approach is consistent with the new guideline. Ed.

317.16   *Pre-sentence report, Court must have*
Att-Gen's Ref Nos 73 and 75 of 2010 and 3 of 2011 2011 EWCA Crim 633[915] LCJ When a defendant is convicted of rape or a really serious sexual offence, it is unwise, even after a trial, for the court to pass sentence without seeking at the very least a pre-sentence report. This is no less true for a defendant of good character than it is for one with previous sexual offences recorded against him. Indeed, in some cases it is more important to examine how it has come about that the offence was committed and what underlying problems there may be which have resulted in an individual of good character committing a serious sexual offence. That fact alone may suggest an element of dangerousness which has so far failed to manifest itself. The possibility that a defendant who faces charges like these falls within the provisions designed to provide protection from dangerous offenders should not be overlooked. The pre-sentence report on M is revealing. It underlines why it is appropriate always for a pre-sentence report to be sought in such cases, particularly as the offender was to all intents and purposes a man of good character whose preoccupation with sexual matters did not emerge until after the police investigation had identified him as the criminal.

317.17   *Guilty plea*
R v Millberry 2002 EWCA Crim 2891, 2003 2 Cr App R (S) 31 (p 142) Old guideline case LCJ para 29 The reason why the courts are prepared to and should reduce sentences substantially for a guilty plea is because it is well known that victims of rape can find it an extremely distressing experience to give evidence in open court about what has happened to them, even where their identity is protected. Having to give evidence, and especially being cross-examined, can make a victim relive the offence. We have seen many victim impact statements that make this clear. Obviously the distress which is avoided is greater the earlier the victim is informed, so the discount should be reduced if there is not an early plea. There is also the fact that the plea demonstrates that the offender appreciates how wrong his conduct was and regrets it. While it is desirable to avoid taking up the time of the court and incurring expense unnecessarily, this is less important in mitigation than the other two factors we have just mentioned. We stress that the maximum credit should only be given for a timely guilty plea.

Note: *The Reduction in Sentence for a Guilty Plea Guideline 2007* takes precedence over this case. Ed.

Post-2014 guideline case
Att-Gen's Ref No 115 of 2014 2015 EWCA Crim 200 D pleaded just before trial to rape (×3), assault by penetration and robbery. In interview D denied responsibility and said he had no memory of his actions. The defence said one of the reasons for the late plea was that they had only received the CCTV recently. The victim described the trauma of waiting for the trial. The Judge described the attack as 'evil and wicked' and said D did not need the CCTV to know he was guilty. The Judge started at 11 years and with D's good character and what he described as "the shame and gravity of D's position [that took] a level of courage to plead guilty, albeit on trial day," he reduced the sentence to 8 years. Next he applied the plea discount of 10 months, making 7 years 2 months. Held. This was a horrific incident. For the Judge to give a 3-year discount before the credit for plea discount was wrong. The lowest starting point was 12-13 years, so [with mitigation and plea] **10 years**. For more detail see **317.29**.

See also the **Guilty Plea, Discount for** chapter in Volume 1.

Concurrent or consecutive sentences for two or more sex offences see the *Series of rapes/Campaign of rape Concurrent or consecutive* para at **317.59**.

---

[915] In some reports this case is listed as 73, 75 and 3 of 2010.

False claim of rape, Making see the PERVERTING THE COURSE OF JUSTICE/
CONTEMPT OF COURT/PERJURY ETC. *Incriminate innocent people, Trying to rape
cases* para at **305.14**.

Types of rape and factors

317.18 *Abduction/false imprisonment etc., And   Starting point 18+ years   Pre-
2014 guideline cases*

R v Ayre 2010 EWCA Crim 1063 LCJ D pleaded to two rapes, causing or inciting a child
under 13 to engage in sexual activity and abducting a child. In 1985 D was convicted of
killing a young woman with whom he was in a relationship. The murder involved a
sexual element, namely that she had agreed to have intercourse with him and subsequently asked him to desist. He lost his temper, picked up an iron bar and battered her
with it. In 2005 D was released on licence and less than a year after, he committed these
offences. Two boys, one of whom was ten years old, were playing. D approached them
and persuaded the ten-year-old to go with him. When they arrived at D's flat, the boy
was pulled inside, where he was threatened with a Stanley knife. D forced the boy to
undress, perform oral sex upon him and he raped him orally and anally. D offered to take
the boy home. The pre-sentence report concluded that D posed a very high risk of
reconviction for sexual offences if he were ever free. The psychiatric report said he was
untreatable and extremely dangerous. There were significant aggravating factors: D,
aged 48, was on licence for murder, the abduction of the boy, the use of a knife, the gross
indignity involved, the pain caused to the boy and the use of force on a very young
victim. The Judge ordered whole life. Held. We cannot envisage that he will ever be
released. However, it was inappropriate to order that the early release provisions would
not apply. There are 35 other offenders who have been made subject to such an order, all
of whom were sentenced for murder. Four **life sentences** with a **10-year** minimum
period.

Att-Gen's Ref No 78 of 2012 2013 EWCA Crim 130 D pleaded to two rapes, kidnapping
and false imprisonment at his PCMH. In 1981, when a groundsman at a school and aged
36, he lived in a lodge at the school. V, aged 14, also lived at the school, with her
parents. Her parents had entertained D. V was walking down the drive and D pushed her
into a wooded area and covered her nose and mouth to stop her screaming. He then
wrapped her in a blanket and took her to his cottage. She was screaming so he gagged
her. Once inside he pushed her into a small cupboard. When V kicked out he bound her
hands and feet with rope and put her in his attic. D put her on a mattress and bound her
to the rafters using leather straps. A gas mask was put over her face. She was given water
but no food and she had to urinate in her clothes. D wiped her private parts with a
sponge and digitally penetrated her, causing her pain. He tried to penetrate her with his
penis and eventually succeeded. She continued screaming. D told her he had been
planning this for weeks. After the attack he left her in the dark with the gas mask tied
tightly over her face. Some hours later he returned with some Vaseline, which he applied
to her private parts. He raped her again causing her pain. He left and returned saying the
police were looking for her and he was helping them, which he thought was funny. In
fact, he had tried to appear to help the police. D left her in the attic, he left the school and
went abroad. She eventually rubbed through the rope and ran for help. V had bruising to
her head, legs, nose, neck and stomach. She had burn marks on her ankles and wrists. D
joined the Foreign Legion in a false name. In 2010, he was located in North Africa when
he applied for a Spanish ID card in a false name. D contested his extradition. In her
impact statement V said she expected to die and suffered stress and anxiety. She had a
permanent inability to trust others. D had no convictions before or since the event. Held.
The effect on the victim was serious and continuing. The offence involved two rapes, a
digital attack, kidnapping, false imprisonment, constraint, abuse of trust and violence. It
was planned, degrading, terrifying and over a very substantial time in a dark attic. V was
vulnerable and only 14 years old, and [was] left to her fate when he ran away. The

aggravating factors and any mitigation available (his lack of previous convictions) call for a sentence of close to **20 years**. His character was not unblemished as he was living under a false name and was unlawfully at large. His [good] character is more than outweighed by that and the failure to give V closure. With full credit for the plea, **13 years** not 9½.

Note: For the suggested approach to these pre-guideline cases, see **317.3**.

317.19   *Abuse of trust   Guideline*

'Abuse of trust' is one of the factors in Category 2 when the reader is determining the level of culpability, see *Sexual Offences Guideline 2014* pages 10 (rape) and 14 (assault by penetration), which are the same and are at **317.4**.

317.20   *Abuse of trust   Meaning*

R v Thompson 2012 EWCA Crim 1727 D pleaded to the rape of his stepsister, C. C woke her mother up and told her she had been woken by D on top of her having sex with her. Both had been drinking. Held. We are not convinced that this is an abuse of trust. That phrase, in our experience, contemplates, for example, teacher/student, parent/child relationships. This was two stepsiblings in a familial context, not an abuse of trust. There was, for example, no duty of care on D.

R v Jones 2012 EWCA Crim 2268 D was convicted of causing another to engage in sexual activity. He stayed in a hotel with his 29-year-old daughter's ex-partner, V, when they both worked as shopfitters. D abused V. The Judge treated the offence as a breach of trust. Held. Abuse of trust is not defined in the guidelines. It requires a relationship involving inequality between the parties to some substantive degree. D did not stand *in loco parentis* to V. It was a relationship of equal adults. Sentence reduced.

R v Abdoullahi 2014 EWCA Crim 132 D pleaded to assault by penetration. V was aged 15. At about 2 am and thereafter she attempted to get a taxi from various local firms. At one taxi office, a male answered the door and asked her to come into the office. V described D as working in the taxi office as a controller. They discussed getting her a taxi and the other drivers were not keen to assist. Eventually, it was agreed that D would take V for £12. V was happy to go with D. In fact, D was not a taxi driver and his licence had expired. As D was driving, he inserted a finger or fingers into her vagina. Held. Did this offence involve a position of trust? The *Sexual Offences Act 2003 Guideline 2008* directly refers to *R v Millberry 2002* EWCA Crim 2891, 2003 2 Cr App R (S) 31 (p 142) at para 20 ii: 'the offender is in a position of responsibility towards the victim (e.g. in the relationship of medical practitioner and patient, teacher and pupil); or the offender is a person in whom the victim has placed his or her trust by virtue of his office or employment (e.g. a clergyman, an emergency services patrolman, a taxi driver, or a police officer).' This was an offence involving a position of trust. D was acting as a taxi driver and V would not have entered the taxi had she not believed D was going to take her home. The plan was for her to get £12 from home to pay D. V was worse for alcohol and alone, late at night, many miles from home. She was, to a very high degree, vulnerable.

Note: The guideline does not refer to para 20ii.

See also: *R v R* 2013 EWCA Crim 2056 (Convicted of sexual activity with a child. V, aged 12, was D's partner's friend's child. He was vulnerable with some learning difficulties. V went to stay with D and his partner for a week. Whilst V was in bed, D entered the bedroom and gave V a head massage. He then touched V's penis and put it in his mouth. V gave evidence. Judge was perfectly entitled to find that D had adopted a degree of responsibility for V's welfare and therefore was in breach of trust.)

Post-2014 guideline case

R v O (D) 2014 EWCA Crim 2202, 2015 1 Cr App R (S) 41 (p 299) D pleaded to the rape of his partner and sexual abuse of child relations of his partners. The Judge placed the rape in Category 2 because the victim was particularly vulnerable due to personal circumstances and Category A because of the abuse of trust. Held. Due to the psychological effects on the family which were immeasurable, the Judge was entitled to find the case fell into Category 2, on the basis of severe psychological harm. The gross betrayal was an aggravating factor. The Sentencing Council did not intend that every rape within an established relationship should be treated as a breach of trust. The case fell into Category 2B, but the overall sentence was not manifestly excessive.

R v BK 2015 EWCA Crim 1987 D admitted four rapes committed when he was aged between 12 and 13 and V, his sister, was aged 10-11. The Judge held that this was an abuse of trust. Held. It could not be so described. That phrase contemplates an inequality of power, often involving a duty of care by the abuser, usually an adult, in relationships such as those between teacher and student, or parent and child. This case involved two young siblings in a familial context, see *R v ZBT* 2012 EWCA Crim 1727.

For more details see **317.87**.

317.21   *Abuse of trust   Case   Pre-2014 guideline case*

R v B 2014 EWCA Crim 2124 D pleaded (full discount) to 12 assaults by penetration (ten vaginal and two anal), with ten similar TICs, 11 sexual assaults, with eight similar TICs, and an unknown number of counts of voyeurism, with 47 similar TICs. D also pleaded to sexual activity with a child (×2). D was a GP and knew V's family. V, who was aged 17, stayed with D during half-term when he acted as her legal guardian. She was described as 'willing to please and somewhat gullible'. One evening, whilst watching a film with sexual content and having discussed sexual matters, D gave V alcohol and two tablets, albeit with no medical effect. When she went upstairs, D touched her sexually, including inserting his fingers into her vagina. Although this was consensual, unknown to V, D used a camera hidden in his watch to record the events, thereby vitiating consent. One film lasted 32 minutes and a further film, showing V asleep, lasted 11 minutes. D then filmed V undressing and showering.

V took screenshots of images on D's computer leading to the discovery of a huge number of videos, some lasting over 40 minutes, showing medical examinations of female patients over a three-year period. They were all un-chaperoned, save for one occasion when they moved behind a curtain on D's instruction. The victims, 293 in all, were aged from their early teens to their fifties. Examinations of victims' vaginas or anuses were filmed using D's hidden watch camera. These were then downloaded, but not circulated, by D and were deleted subsequently in large quantities. D also filmed his digital penetration of the vaginas of ten patients, and the anuses of two. It was accepted that this was reasonable for the purposes of legitimate medical examination, but there had been no consent to being filmed for D's sexual gratification. On six of these occasions, D had not worn a glove, and on one D made inappropriate comments. D, again filming, also touched or massaged the naked breasts or bottoms of female patients. This was for legitimate medical examination but, again, the victims did not consent to being filmed. D also fondled the bottoms of two 15-year-old girls attending for contraceptive injections, recording each assault. D was a Malaysian, aged 46 on appeal and of good character. He had co-operated and was remorseful. The Judge considered him dangerous but thought that could be managed by a long prison sentence and a SOPO.

Held. For D there was serious breach of trust and there could have been no medical need for anything that happened. Starting at 3 years, we impose 2 years for the assaults by penetration and 18 months concurrent for the voyeurism. For the patients, no one could have contemplated offending on this scale by a doctor. The gross breach was the most important factor. There can be no doubt that the public places enormous trust in doctors. The maintenance of confidence in that trust is of paramount importance. We view with very considerable seriousness the failure by D and the medical practice at which he worked to inquire whether the patients required a chaperon. It also indicated a very considerable degree of planning. It was particularly serious to abuse the trust that the two children had placed in D when coming for their contraceptive injections. We also place the offences of assault by penetration in the top category. For the penetration, the guideline has a range of 6-11 years.[916] We put the case at the top of that range, because of the breach of trust, although the penetration was minimal and brief. The sentence for the offences involving patients is 12 years. With plea, that is 8 years. The sentence for the offences involving V should be 3 years, with plea 2 years. 8 years and 2 years consecutive makes **10 years** in all, not the 12 ordered by the Judge.

317.22   *Alcohol/drugs, Defendant under the influence of*
'Commission of offence whilst under the influence of alcohol or drugs' is one of the aggravating factors, see *Sexual Offences Guideline 2014* page 11 at **317.5** (rape) and page 15 at **317.8** (assault by penetration).

317.23   *Alcohol/drugs used to facilitate the offence*
'Use of alcohol/drugs on victim to facilitate the offence' is one of the factors in Category 2 when the reader is determining the level of culpability, see *Sexual Offences Guideline 2014* pages 10 (rape) and 14 (assault by penetration), which are the same and are at **317.4**.
AIDS see the **Sexually transmitted disease, Defendant has** para at **317.94**, the **DEFENDANT *AIDS, Defendant has*** para at **240.1** and the VICTIMS *AIDS, Victim fears he or she has contracted AIDS from the sex attack* para at **121.2** in Volume 1.

317.24   *Anal rape (female victim) Pre-2014 guideline cases*
R v Millberry 2002 EWCA Crim 2891, 2003 2 Cr App R (S) 31 (p 142) Guideline case LCJ There is no inherent distinction between anal and vaginal rape. Where a victim is raped both vaginally and anally by the offender, this should be treated (for the purposes of the higher starting point) as repeated rape.
R v Baker 2014 EWCA Crim 242 (**Life 8½ years** minimum term, see **317.26**.)

317.25   *Attempted rape   Pre-2014 guideline cases*
R v Billam 1986 82 Cr App R 347 LCJ The starting point for attempted rape should normally be less than for the completed offence, especially if it is desisted at a comparatively early stage, but attempted rape may be made by aggravating features into an offence even more serious than some examples of the full offence.
Note: The guideline case and the guidelines issued after this case have made no reference to attempted rape. The remarks may assist but the 2014 guideline takes precedence over the old guidance. Ed.
See also: *R v Johnston* 2014 EWCA Crim 2909 (Convicted of two sex assaults by penetration and attempted rape. Ex-partner, after long history of harassment and breaches of court orders. Assaults were digital rapes (3 years). Different day, lay in wait in her garage and pounced on her, ripping her clothes off and digitally raped her. Gagged her and then was disturbed. Suggested there was going to be penile rape. The fact the offence fell short of rape was of real significance. For the attempt, **6½ years** not 8 so in total 16½ years' extended sentence (**9½ years custody** 7 years' extended licence.)

317.26   *Burglar rapists   Pre-2014 guideline case*
'Offence committed in the course of a burglary' is one of the factors in Category 2 when the reader is determining the level of culpability, see *Sexual Offences Guideline 2014* pages 10 (rape) and 14 (assault by penetration), which are the same and are at **317.4**.
R v Baker 2014 EWCA Crim 242 LCJ D was convicted of rape. In 1997, V, then aged 66 and living alone, locked her front door and went to bed. Her friend, G, used to visit her frequently. V was cold and put on a number of layers that night, including thermal underwear. She woke at about 4.20 am and saw a man in her bedroom standing on a chair. She asked him what he was doing and he shouted at her not to look at him. He put blankets over her and began to hit her. He punched her in the face and chest before lifting her clothing and punching her bare stomach. He asked whether there was anyone

---

[916] In part of the judgment, the range is stated to be 6-13 years, which is in error. The guideline has a starting point of 10 years where the victim is aged 13-15 and 8 years where the victim is aged 16+. The range for the first is 8-13 years and for the second, 6-11 years, see page 25 of the guideline. Ed.

else in the house. V replied that there was not. D said he would kill her if there was. D left the room briefly then returned, telling her if she did not give him some money he would kill her. He repeatedly asked for her PIN and said he knew that G gave her money from his business. D placed V on the floor kneeling against the bed. D pulled her trousers down and inserted his penis into her anus causing her considerable pain and distress. Immediately after the rape, she lost bowel and bladder control. D then 'shoved' V into a small cupboard and locked the cupboard from the outside. She remained there for many hours in acute discomfort. She had difficulty breathing and moving and thought she would die there. She was found in the early evening of the following day by G. V's face had been so badly beaten that she was unrecognisable to her son. She had a number of blunt trauma injuries, bruises and abrasions. At the first trial D was acquitted at the direction of the Judge, who ruled that a DNA sample which should have been destroyed, but was not, was inadmissible. That was challenged and the House of Lords ruled that the DNA evidence was admissible. Following the coming into force of CJA 2003 Part 10, a retrial became a possibility. Only after a BBC Panorama documentary and a Daily Mail article criticising the police for losing the relevant papers was a further investigation carried out. D was arrested and was aggressive to the female officer. He said he would "put [his] cock in her mouth and fuck her hard". A DNA sample was taken and compared to the semen taken from V's body. The chance of it originating from someone other than D was one in one billion. V had since died but her son spoke of how V had been frightened to return to her own home and that her life had been ruined. D was aged 56 at conviction and had 28 convictions for 49 offences. They included robbery, residential burglary, ABH and assaults on police. His last conviction was for affray in 2001. Held. The Judge referred to *R v Hodgson* 1968 52 Cr App R 113 and was entitled to come to the view that a **life sentence** was justified. This was an offence which called for a life sentence. There was gratuitous violence before the rape, with threats to kill, and there was gratuitous violence after the rape. The culpability and harm were very high indeed. The correct starting point was 20 years, not 24. With credit of 3 years (as given by the Judge for the delay and double jeopardy and the time spent on remand awaiting the first trial), **8½ years** not 10½ years **minimum** term.

317.27   Burglars/robbers, By   Pre-2014 guideline judicial guidance
Att-Gen's Ref Nos 73 and 75 of 2010 and 3 of 2011 2011 EWCA Crim 633[917] LCJ Sexual offences committed by a burglar should be approached as if they were among the most serious offences of their kind, as the culpability of the criminal is at its highest and the harm done to the victim is at its most grave. Two of the cases represent the ultimate nightmare for any woman asleep alone in her own home at night. Our home should be our safest refuge. There is no room for mercy. All those who live in the house with the victim will suffer. It is wrong in principle for offences like these, where rape has been committed, to be treated as a single offence of rape by a single offender. As these cases show, in many such cases where rape or serious sexual assault is perpetrated in the course of a burglary, several additional aggravating features are usually present. In all such cases the question of dangerousness must be carefully examined.
Note: These remarks appear consistent with the 2014 guideline. Ed.

317.28   Burglars/robbers, By   Starting point 18+ years   Pre-2014 guideline cases
Att-Gen's Ref Nos 73 and 75 of 2010 and 3 of 2011 Re P 2011 EWCA Crim 633[918] LCJ D pleaded at his PCMH to rape, robbery and an unconnected count of possession of a bladed article. V was a young female university student, whose parents lived in China. She had never before had a sexual relationship with a man. V had left the keys to her dormitory room in the outside of the door. At 5 am D, a fellow student, entered V's room, apparently with the intention to steal. He was wearing gloves. V awoke to find him in her room. The room was in darkness. D approached her, put his gloved hand over

---

[917] In some reports this case is listed as 73, 75 and 3 of 2010.
[918] In some reports this case is listed as 73, 75 and 3 of 2010.

her mouth and proceeded to use duct tape to bind her wrists. She begged him to stop. He bound her mouth, covered her eyes and wrapped the tape five times around her head. She knelt down and begged him not to hurt her. D held her by the throat and warned her "If you don't want to die, be quiet". D then removed V's lower clothing, some shorts and underwear. He took photographs of her using his mobile phone. She was aware of what D was doing. He then took further photographs of her using V's own digital camera. Again, V was aware. D removed his gloves and inserted his fingers into her vagina. She struggled and D took V by the neck. She struggled to breathe. She thought that she would die. He climbed on top of her and penetrated her with his penis. He remained there for a minute or so and ejaculated. He wiped semen from around the outside of her vagina. He took the tissue with him in an attempt to avoid detection. D told V that if she reported the attacks he would publish the photographs on the Internet. D picked up V's laptop and her purse containing money and bank cards. He demanded the PINs. He warned her that if she lied about the numbers, he would return. D left with V's room key. V felt 'dirty' as a result of the offences and she had become afraid when alone. She had failed one of her examinations where before the rape there had been hope that she would pass. V found out that D carried hepatitis B and had a traumatic period waiting to hear whether she had contracted it also. Fortunately she had not. After arresting D, the police searched his property and found V's laptop, her bank cards, her bag and purse, her room key and her digital camera with two photographs of V contained within. D initially denied involvement with the offences but when faced with DNA evidence changed his plea to guilty. Reports were prepared and the writers disagreed as to the level of risk that D posed. The Judge sentenced D on the basis that he posed no more than a moderate risk. D, aged 22, was of good character. However, he had started acquisitive crimes at an early age. He had come from South Korea and was very isolated. *Held.* The aggravating features of this case are clear. A young woman, 20 years of age, was alone in a study bedroom. She fell asleep after working hard late into the night. The offender entered her room while she was alone and vulnerable. A threat to kill was made. V was bound and gagged. Photographs were taken and used in attempted blackmail. The Judge gave full credit for the plea. That was not appropriate. With 20% credit, **15 years**, not 8.

Note: For the suggested approach to these pre-guideline cases, see **317.3**.

Campaign of rape see the *Series of rapes/Campaign of rape* para at **317.58**.

317.29 Burglars/robbers Street and other non-dwelling robbery rapes Post-2014 guideline case

Att-Gen's Ref No 115 of 2014 2015 EWCA Crim 200 D pleaded just before trial (10% credit) to rape (×3), assault by penetration and robbery. Very early one morning a student, V, aged 21, was walking home. D, who had also been out, followed her for five to ten minutes. As V approached an alleyway, D punched the back of her head and V fell to the ground, where D punched her again. D asked if V had any money and V offered her purse. D then pulled V to her feet and, with his hands on her shoulders, forced V down the alleyway. D threatened to hurt V if she was unco-operative. He then removed V's tights, pants and bra, feeling her breast. D then forced V to give him oral sex and repeatedly told V not to look at him. He then stood V up and penetrated her with both his finger and then his penis for around two minutes. V was then forced to give D oral sex for around two minutes after which D masturbated, ejaculating onto the ground. Finally, D blindfolded V with her own scarf and made her count to ten until she could remove it, which she did. He then made off with her handbag. The whole episode lasted around 15 minutes. V had sustained two half-centimetre cuts and vaginal bleeding and tenderness. The following day, D told his neighbour that his drink had allegedly been spiked and confessed to attacking or raping V. In interview D denied responsibility and said he had no memory of his actions. V was left feeling unsafe alone and spent nine months prior to the scheduled trial 'on edge and in fear'. D was aged 41 on appeal and of positive good character. The Judge described the attack as 'evil and wicked' but also took into account the 'courage to plead guilty, albeit on the day of trial'. It was agreed the case was a

Category A rape. Held. This was a most horrific incident. For the Judge to give a 3-year discount before the credit for plea discount was wrong. The lowest starting point was 12-13 years, not 11 [so with the mitigation and the plea], **10 years**, not 7 years 2 months. For details of the plea discount, see **317.17**.

317.30   *Children and others present*
'Presence of others, especially children' is one of the aggravating factors, see *Sexual Offences Guideline 2014* page 11 at **317.5** (rape) and page 15 at **317.8** (assault by penetration).

317.31   *Commercial exploitation and/or motivation*
'Commercial exploitation and/or motivation' is one of the factors in Category 2 when the reader is determining the level of culpability, see *Sexual Offences Guideline 2014* pages 10 (rape) and 14 (assault by penetration), which are the same and are at **317.4**.

317.32   *Condom, Failure to use   Pre-2014 guideline case*
R v Cadogan 2010 EWCA Crim 1642, 2011 1 Cr App R (S) 53 (p 343) D pleaded to ABH and was convicted of rape. Held. The absence of a condom was an aggravating feature, as were the threats made to V.
Delay see the *Historical cases* para at **317.40**.

317.33   *Digital penetration   Pre-2014 guideline Judicial guidance*
R v Singh 2012 EWCA Crim 1274, 2013 1 Cr App R (S) 44 (p 254) D was convicted of assault by penetration. He digitally penetrated the victim's vagina. Held. The proposition that non-penile penetration cases should be sentenced less severely not least because there was no risk of impregnation or infection is self-evident. *Att-Gen's Ref No 104 of 2004* 2004 EWCA Crim 2672, 2005 1 Cr App R (S) 117 (p 666) and *R v P* 2008 EWCA Crim 1806, 2009 1 Cr App R (S) 45 (p 247) applied.

317.34   *Digital penetration   Cases*
R v Abdoullahi 2014 EWCA Crim 132 D changed his plea at his PCMH to assault by penetration (25% credit). V was aged 15. One night she was picked up by some friends and they went to Woking. They purchased some alcohol and drank a significant amount. V ran out of money and went back to a flat where they continued to drink. V was not a regular drinker. In the early hours of the morning she needed to get home. She walked to the train station at about 2 am and thereafter attempted to get a taxi from various local firms. At one taxi office, a male answered the door and asked her to come into the office. V described D as working in the taxi office as a controller. They discussed getting her a taxi and the other drivers were not keen to assist. Eventually, it was agreed that D would take V for £12. V was happy to go with D. In fact, D was not a taxi driver and his licence had expired. As D was driving, he reached across to the front passenger seat where V was sat. He placed his hand down her trousers and inserted a finger or fingers into her vagina. She froze with fear. That assault carried on for 5 or 6 minutes. D stopped the car and attempted to kiss her. V did not know what to do and felt that she couldn't get out of the car as it was dark and she was a distance away from her home. D then drove V near her home and she got out, stating that she would go to fetch the £12 fare but D drove away. She went inside and immediately told her father. D was aged 46 and of good character. Held. This was an offence involving a position of trust. D was acting as a taxi driver and V would not have entered the taxi had she not believed D was going to take her home. D had a captive victim and did not care whether she was willing or not. V was worse for alcohol and alone, late at night, many miles from home. She was, to a very high degree, vulnerable. The attack clearly had a very serious effect on her education, her relationships with friends and family as well as leaving her fearful of travelling and being on her own. She had episodes of depression and low self-esteem. **5 years** was entirely justified.
See also: *R v PT* 2014 EWCA Crim 537 (Plea. Committed over 20 years against eight victims, aged 2 to 13. Assault by penetration, indecent assault and sexual assault. Specimen counts. Touching over and under clothing. Breach of trust. Committed further

offences after initially being interviewed. Filmed himself digitally penetrating his niece and her two sisters, aged 2 to 4, 3 and 5 respectively. Indecent images also found including ten at Level 3 and four at Level 4. 25% credit. Life imprisonment was correct. 20-year notional term was severe but within the range. **Life** with **minimum of 7½ years** was not manifestly excessive.)

Post-guideline case[919]

R v S 2015 EWCA Crim 265 D pleaded (full credit) to <u>inciting a child to engage in digital penetration</u>, inciting a child to engage in sexual activity, to numerous counts of possessing, making and distributing indecent child images, sexual assault, blackmail and various computer offences. Between 2007 and 2011, D posed as a teenage boy aged 13 or 14 on Facebook. He groomed children, going on to incite them to provide sexual images of themselves or commit sexual acts in front of a web camera. The acts incited included digital penetration by V1 and V1 asphyxiating himself. D would then distribute the images on the Internet and he also downloaded 46 other child images. D also, whilst watering neighbours' plants whilst they were away, copied photos of their teenage daughter, V2. D blackmailed V3, a 13-year-old girl, into providing more sexually explicit pictures, having incited her to expose her breasts and pose naked. The only physical contact was when D approached V4, a 9-year-old girl, asking to take a photo of her, and sexually touched her neck. V1 suffered from PTSD and was depressed and suicidal and V4 was deeply affected, shaking and crying when she was at the site where it happened. D was aged 65 on appeal and of good character. The Judge said it was all highly devious and planned. He gave: a) for incitement for digital penetration, **5 years**, b) for distributing indecent photographs, 2 years, c) for perverting the course of justice (which was telling a victim to delete incriminating e-mails), 1 year, d) for making indecent photographs, 1 year, e) for sexual assault, 18 months, and f) for blackmail, 18 months. They were all consecutive with the other sentences concurrent, making 12 years in all. That would equate with a starting point of 18 years. Held. By making more of the sentences concurrent, **9 years** in all.

317.35   *Disability, Hostility to/Motivated against*
'Offence motivated by, or demonstrating, hostility to the victim based on his or her disability (or presumed disability)' is one of the factors in Category 2 when the reader is determining the level of culpability, see *Sexual Offences Guideline 2014* pages 10 (rape) and 14 (assault by penetration), which are the same and are at **317.4**.

317.36   *Dispose or conceal evidence, Attempts to*
'Attempts to dispose of or conceal evidence' is one of the aggravating factors, see *Sexual Offences Guideline 2014* page 11 at **317.5** (rape) and page 15 at **317.8** (assault by penetration).
Note: How this factor should be considered is unclear. If a rapist were to dispose of a used condom he would be disposing of vital evidence. However, that would be the normal action for someone to take. If a rapist were to clean a car it might not be disposal of evidence if the defendant regularly cleaned his car. However, if there was extensive cleaning of the inside of a car to remove forensic material that was linked to the victim who had been in the car, that would be 'disposal of evidence'. Expect judges to take a pragmatic view of this difficult-to-apply factor. Ed.
Drugs used to facilitate the offence see the ***Alcohol/drugs used to facilitate the offence*** para at **317.23**.

317.37   *Ejaculated, Defendant*
'Ejaculation (where not taken into account at step one)' is one of the aggravating factors, see *Sexual Offences Guideline 2014* page 11 at **317.5** (rape) and page 15 at **317.8** (assault by penetration).

---

[919] The fact that the case was post-guideline can be found on the Internet.

317.38   *Fathers/Stepfathers etc., By*

'Victim is particularly vulnerable due to personal circumstances*' is one of the factors in Category 2 when the reader is determining harm, see *Sexual Offences Guideline 2014* pages 10 (rape) and 14 (assault by penetration), which are the same and are at **317.4**.
* For children aged under 13 please refer to page 27 [of the guideline] or para **317.9**.
Note: Fathers are not mentioned in the Rape section of the *Sexual Offences Guideline 2014*. This would be a suitable Category 2 factor to raise the suggested penalty for fathers etc. Ed.

Pre-2014 guideline case

Example: *R v DL* 2015 EWCA Crim 74, 1 Cr App R (S) 58 (p 404) (D was convicted of two rapes on his daughter when she was aged 13-14. Two other sex offences against her. She was vulnerable. D was aged 33 with, in 2007, three sex assault previous convictions (Victim just aged 14. 3 years' imprisonment on a plea) and significant non-sex previous convictions. Judge made the offence Category 2A. Held. Particularly gross breach of trust. 20 years' extended sentence (**15 years'** custody 5 years' extended licence) was not manifestly excessive.)

317.39   *Fathers/Stepfathers etc.   Starting point 18+ years*

R v SF 2011 EWCA Crim 2212 D pleaded at the last possible moment to an unspecified number of rapes. In 2005, he picked up a prostitute, V1, in his car. He drove to an alleyway by the side of his house and demanded to "see the merchandise". She refused but D pulled her trousers and underwear down. He grabbed her face and told her not to make him angry. He demanded oral sex and forced his penis into V1's mouth, after she had given him a condom. He pushed her into the back of the car, forced her to take one leg out of her trousers and penetrated her vaginally. V1 said it was painful and asked him to stop. He turned her over and penetrated her anally. That too was painful. V1 shouted and turned around. D removed the condom and penetrated her vaginally again, ejaculating inside her. V1 said she was in fear during the incident. He insisted on driving her back to the street, but V1 was so scared that she jumped out of the car when it was travelling slowly. V1 suffered an abrasion to her perianal area. In 2008, D was driving with his stepdaughter, V2, who was aged 14. They stopped for petrol and V2 asked for a can of Coke. D put some white powder in the can and told V2 not to look. She drank it and felt faint. D drove to a remote location and told V2 to get into the back seat. He penetrated her anally and V2 cried. It lasted about 5 minutes. He later swore on the Bible that he would never do it again. On that basis, V2 agreed to visit D again. Less than one month later, V2 visited D with her two brothers. Whilst her brothers were asleep in V2's room, V2 was anally raped by D again. V2 cried. One month later, D told V2 to have a shower. He watched her, then followed her into the bedroom and removed her towel. He pinned her down and forcibly penetrated her. V2 cried out, "Dad, don't do it". D put his hand over V2's mouth. She asked what would happen if she became pregnant. D got angry and turned V2 over and penetrated her anally. V2 complained that she was bleeding. D allowed V2 to go to the bathroom, but when she came back he penetrated her again vaginally and anally. He ejaculated onto her pubic hair and said that she would not get pregnant. D then told her she must learn to forgive and forget. When she was examined she was found to have significant injury to her vagina. D denied all allegations and refused to co-operate with his probation officer. D, aged 40, was of previous good character. Held. For V1, the starting point of **8 years** was plainly right. D deserved no more than a reduction of one year for his plea. A starting point of **15 years** after a trial for the rapes of his stepdaughter would have been entirely appropriate. These were repeated rapes aggravated by very serious factors, notably the administering of a drug, the use of force and the breach of trust. By giving D the minimal credit for the pleas, the Judge did all that was required of him. **9 years' IPP** was entirely appropriate.

R v G 2013 EWCA Crim 1821 D pleaded (25% credit) to five rapes, four attempted rapes, three assaults by penetration, two engaging in sexual activity counts and two sexual assaults on his daughter, C1. They were all specimen counts. He also pleaded to inciting his other daughter, C2, to engage in sexual activity. C1 was taken from her mother when aged 6. She was totally controlled by D, who made her fall out with C2 so they could not confide in each other. She was allowed no social life. Starting when C1 was aged 10, D graduated from masturbating while watching her to full sexual intercourse with her when she was aged 12 or 13 to 17. Over the years, the abuse was as often as four to five times a week. He incited C2 when she was aged 13 to 'play with his bits'. She told someone at her school and D was arrested. This led to C1 making allegations. D denied being involved. The police cautioned him for some extreme pornography. He denied guilt at a preliminary hearing but pleaded guilty at his PCMH. That was one year after C2's report to her school. C1 suffered from isolation, depression, an eating disorder and emotional trauma. The Judge was satisfied that, but for his arrest, D would have treated C2 as he had treated C1. The Judge gave 19 years in all. Held. That would mean 25 years 4 months before the plea. That was excessive. **17 years**.

R v JM 2015 EWCA Crim 1638, 2016 1 Cr App R (S) 21 (p 145) D was convicted of 12 sex offences including two sample offences of vaginal rape, sexual assaults, assault by penetration, oral rape and sexual activity with a child family member. He systematically abused his daughter, V, when she was aged 9-13. D groomed her by using sexualised language and exposing himself to her when she was aged 9, touched her breasts and genitalia and persuaded her to insert a candle into her vagina. When she was aged 11, D began to rape her vaginally in various rooms in the family home, at least once a week. He did not use a condom and ejaculated, but outside her. On other occasions he raped her orally. He isolated her from her younger siblings and discouraged her from telling anyone by emotional blackmail. The recollection of what D had done to her caused her to be withdrawn and depressed. As D's trial approached, V deliberately took an overdose of paracetamol. There was no remorse. D was aged 37 and of good character. The Judge said the offending fell within Category 2A because of V's attempt on her own life, indicating she had suffered severe psychological harm and because the offending involved planning, grooming and a gross breach of trust. Held. The category was 2A. The suicide attempt did demonstrate severe psychological harm. The Judge was right to depart from the guideline range. The sentence of **22 years** was severe but justifiably so. See also: *R v R* 2010 EWCA Crim 2006 (D, aged 50, pleaded to 18 sexual offences including five rapes over a 10-year period. There were four victims, with the offences occurring when his child and his stepdaughters were aged 6-15. Penetration when aged 14. Significant aggravating factors. **15 years** not 22½.)

R v DP 2012 EWCA Crim 1203 (Convicted. Sample abuse counts against daughter when aged 4-16, abuse against son when aged 2-13, abuse against second daughter when she was aged 12-13 and abuse against friend aged 14. Sample rape counts involving first daughter when it (appears) she was aged 11 onwards. **24 years** in all not excessive.)

R v TR 2012 EWCA Crim 1542 (Convicted of rape, sexual assaults and making indecent photographs. Regularly assaulted his daughter when aged 8-15. Raped her from when she was aged under 13. Digitally penetrated and attempted to rape his niece when aged 7-8. Touched chest and bottom of his daughter's friend. 51 images at Levels 1-4, mostly at lower end. Required the most severe punishment. Because of totality, **20 years** not 24 in all.)

Att-Gen's Ref No 64 of 2012 2013 EWCA Crim 3174 (Convicted of three rapes (two were specimen offences), attempted rape, six indecent assaults and eight counts of indecency with a child. The victims were his child, stepchild and stepgrandchild. The children were aged 3 to 15. Occurred from late 1970s to 2003. Involved coercion. Caused one child to have intercourse with his sister and for one child to play with the penis of another who had learning difficulties. No violence. Dire effect on the victims. Exceptional depravity over a number of years. Aged 56 at appeal. **21 years** not 12.)

For the suggested approach to these pre-guideline cases, see **317.3**.

Post-2014 guideline cases

R v JH 2015 EWCA Crim 54, 1 Cr App R (S) 59 (p 409) D was convicted of five rapes and three indecent assaults. The victim was V, his daughter, who was aged 13-15 at the time of the rapes and 11-15 for the assaults. The offences started in about 1979. D would provide his wife with money to go out and play bingo so he could be left alone with V. D would apply emotional and sometimes physical pressure and there was a degree of degradation and humiliation as D would comment on the level of satisfaction V provided. D told her that she would not be believed and would split up the family. V withdrew her initial complaint in 1984 following pressure from D. The offences had an appalling effect on V, causing very serious and lifelong psychological damage. D denied everything throughout. He had a conviction for indecent assault on another girl, about 13 years prior to the rape offences. Held. There were grave aggravating factors, namely: a) multiple offences over a prolonged period, b) gross breach of trust, c) the offences were planned and money was given to D's wife so she would not be there, d) emotional and sometimes physical pressure was involved, e) there was an element of degradation and humiliation, f) comments were made about the satisfaction provided, and g) V was told if she complained, the family would be split up. One has to focus on the statement in the *Sexual Offences Guideline 2014*, 'Offences may be of such severity, for example involving a campaign of rape that sentences of 20 years and above may be appropriate.' Because of that, it is unnecessary to consider whether the case is a Category 1 case. **22 years** upheld.

See also: *Att-Gen's Ref No 3 of 2015* 2015 EWCA Crim 454 (Plea to two anal rapes, an oral rape and various sex offences. Serving police officer and daughter. Grooming from age 9. Sex offences from age 13 which continued until her early twenties.[920] Subjugated her so they were essentially living like a couple. Regular rapes when she was aged 22-25. Not allowed to go out without offender. Severe psychological harm caused. Took indecent photos of children. We start at 24 years not 15, so with 15% plea discount **20 years**.)

R v G 2015 EWCA Crim 1439 (Two rapes (victim aged 15), three buggeries (representing many occasions) six indecent assaults and six indecencies with a child by D. Some specimen counts. Digital sex and masturbation. Three victims aged from 10 to 16 and his foster children. Consequences for victims significant and one particularly severe. D now aged 74. No convictions. We start at 25 years, so with plea **19 years**.)

317.40   *Historical cases*

Att-Gen's Ref No 78 of 2012 2013 EWCA Crim 130 D pleaded to two rapes, kidnapping and false imprisonment at his PCMH. In 1981, when a groundsman at a school and aged 36, he lived in a lodge at the school. V, aged 14, also lived at the school, with her parents. Her parents had entertained D. V was walking down the drive and D pushed her into a wooded area and covered her nose and mouth to stop her screaming. He then wrapped her in a blanket and took her to his cottage. She was screaming so he gagged her. Once inside, he pushed her into a small cupboard. When V kicked out he bound her hands and feet with rope and put her in his attic. D put her on a mattress and bound her to the rafters using leather straps. A gas mask was put over her face. She was given water but no food and she had to urinate in her clothes. D wiped her private parts with a sponge and digitally penetrated her, causing her pain. He tried to penetrate her with his penis and eventually succeeded. She continued screaming. D told her he had been planning this for weeks. After the attack he left her in the dark with the gas mask tied tightly over her face. Some hours later he returned with some Vaseline, which he applied to her private parts. He raped her again causing her pain. He left and returned saying the police were looking for her and he was helping them, which he thought was funny. In fact, he had tried to appear to help the police. D left her in the attic, he left the school and

---

[920] It may be that the Judge should have said mid-twenties. The report says the original sentence was 14½ years, so there may have been consecutive sentences for the photo offences. The facts are far from clear.

went abroad. She eventually rubbed through the rope and ran for help. V had bruising to her head, legs, nose, neck and stomach. She had burn marks on her ankles and wrists. D joined the Foreign Legion in a false name. In 2010, he was located in North Africa when he applied for a Spanish ID card in a false name. D contested his extradition. In her impact statement V said she expected to die and suffered stress and anxiety. She had a permanent inability to trust others. D had no convictions before or since the event. Held. The effect on the victim was serious and continuing. The offence involved two rapes, a digital attack, kidnapping, false imprisonment, constraint, abuse of trust and violence. It was planned, degrading, terrifying and over a very substantial time in a dark attic. V was vulnerable and only 14 years old and [was] left to her fate when he ran away. The aggravating factors and any mitigation available (his lack of previous convictions) call for a sentence of close to **20 years**. His character was not unblemished as he was living under a false name and was unlawfully at large. His [good] character is more than outweighed by that and the failure to give V closure. With full credit for the plea, **13 years** not 9½.

Att-Gen's Ref No 62 of 2013 2013 EWCA Crim 2297 D was convicted of 14 counts of sexual abuse against his daughter. They were indecent assault for licking her vagina when she was aged between 4 and 7 years, and indecent assault for touching her vagina when she was aged between 4 and 7 years. There were also multiple attempted buggery counts when she was aged between 4 and 7 years, buggery when she was aged between 7 and 11 years and indecency with a child by making her rub his penis when she was aged between 4 and 7 years. Additionally there were multiple indecency with a child counts for masturbating in front of her when she was aged between 7 and 11 years, multiple indecent assaults (described only as 'oral sex') when she was aged between 7 and 11 years, and multiple indecent assaults by digital penetration when she was aged between 10 and 13 years. There were also multiple rapes when she was aged between 10 and 13 and between 12 and 15 years and multiple indecent assaults when she was required to perform oral sex when aged between 12 and 15 years. The abuse was usually committed in the family home and began with licking or touching and progressed to buggery and rape. On occasions, he would give her alcohol and make her watch pornographic films. He wanted her to dress in her mother's underwear. When V was aged 12 or 13 he began to pay her for sex. The activity would often continue until he ejaculated. At no stage did D use a condom. V left home aged 15 or 16 and had a breakdown aged 19. V reported the incidents to the police in 2004 but was not 'strong enough' for an interview. In 2012 she was interviewed. She felt bullied by her father and the abuse had affected her relationships. D was aged 61 when convicted. He was of good character but on the jury's verdict he had not been of good character since he was aged 41. Held. D capitalised upon the absence of maternal love in V's life. At times, he bought sexual favours. He undermined her by claiming that if she spoke out, no one would believe her and that no one would understand, which was arguably a more damaging word to use. **19 years** not 15.

R v Baker 2014 EWCA Crim 242 (**Life with 8½-year** minimum term, see **317.26.**)

Note: For the suggested approach to these pre-guideline cases, see **317.3**.

Post-guideline case

R v JH 2015 EWCA Crim 54, 1 Cr App R (S) 59 (p 409) D was convicted of five rapes and three indecent assaults. The victim was V, his daughter, who was aged 13-15 at the time of the rapes and 11-15 for the assaults. The offences started in about 1979. D would provide his wife with money to go out and play bingo so he could be left alone with V. D would apply emotional and sometimes physical pressure and there was a degree of degradation and humiliation as D would comment on the level of satisfaction V provided. D told her that she would not be believed and would split up the family. V withdrew her initial complaint in 1984 following pressure from D. The offences had an appalling effect on V, causing very serious and lifelong psychological damage. D denied everything throughout. He had a conviction for indecent assault on another girl, about 13 years prior to the rape offences. Held. There were grave aggravating factors namely: a) multiple offences over a prolonged period, b) gross breach of trust, c) the offences were planned and money was given to D's wife so she would not be there, d) emotional and sometimes physical pressure was involved, e) there was an element of degradation and humiliation, f) comments were made about the satisfaction provided, and g) V was told if she complained, the family would be split up. One has to focus on the statement in the *Sexual Offences Guideline 2014*, 'Offences may be of such severity, for example involving a campaign of rape, that sentences of 20 years and above may be appropriate.' Because of that, it is unnecessary to consider whether the case is a Category 1 case. **22 years** upheld.

See also: *R v Carroll* 2014 EWCA Crim 2818, 2015 1 Cr App R (S) 54 (p 381) (Convicted. Strangled a prostitute and then left. She was badly traumatised. Extended sentence with a **12-year** not 15 custodial term, see **317.49**. (The fact the offence was historical was not listed as a factor.))

R v N 2015 EWCA Crim 228 (Convicted of attempted rape (×3), digital rape (×2), indecency with a child (×2) and indecent assault (×2). V1 and V2 were D's sisters-in-law. Allegations made in 2004, not proceeded with but D given 6 months for indecent child images. V1, profoundly deaf, aged 10, and V2, aged 11, when D was aged around 30. Masturbation, inserting fingers into the vaginas of both girls and attempted and actual penetration with penis, also anally. V1 photographed and given money for silence. V2 shown pornography. Victims' relationships affected. D, aged 40, in utter denial. Judge made rapes consecutive. Held. 'Campaign of rape' in guideline does not restrict judges from moving to a higher bracket. 26 years excessive, **22 years** substituted.)

R v P 2015 EWCA Crim 455 (Two rapes on niece only aged 10 or 11. Long-standing abuse on her and another niece. Sentence reduced because for some of the offending defendant was only aged 14 or 15. **17 years** not 20.)

Historical cases Judicial guidance See also the **DEFENDANT** *Historical cases* paras at **240.32**.

Homophobic rape see the ***Sexual orientation, Hostility to/Motivated against*** para at **317.60**.

317.41 Intruder/Uninvited entrant rape
'Forced/uninvited entry into victim's home' is one of the factors in Category 2 when the reader is determining Harm, see *Sexual Offences Guideline 2014* pages 10 (rape) and 14 (assault by penetration), which are the same and are at **317.4**.
See also the ***Burglar rapists*** para at **317.26**.

317.42 Location of the offence
'Location of the offence' is one of the aggravating factors, see *Sexual Offences Guideline 2014* page 11 at **317.5** (rape) and page 15 at **317.8** (assault by penetration).

317.43 Mistake, Acting under   Pre-2014 guideline case
Att-Gen's Ref No 79 of 2006 2006 EWCA Crim 2626, 2007 1 Cr App R (S) 122 (p 752) D pleaded following the Judge's ruling to assault by penetration. D was at a party where he became friendly with a young woman, S. They kissed several times. They were both staying overnight at the address and it was accepted that their relationship would develop further after the party. V was a 51-year-old woman who lived at the house. She returned home having consumed ten shots of vodka and went to bed around 4.30 am, sharing a bed with her sister. D then went into a room where he thought S was sleeping. It was very dark and he assumed the person in the bed was S. He put his fingers into V's vagina. She turned round and said, "Don't. Fuck off." He stopped, apologised and left the room. In interview he gave this account saying that he had understood that he and S were to have sexual intercourse after the party, that when he went into the bedroom he had taken off his glasses and that he began making sexual advances to the person he thought was S. When he realised that it was V he apologised and left. He was sentenced on this account. D, aged 26, was of good character, and had numerous character

references. Held. Although it is true that V was assaulted in her own home after she had consumed a large amount of alcohol, these factors cannot be aggravating features because D did not know the true identity of V and had no reason to think that S had consumed a large amount of alcohol. The 'normal' sentence of 4 years cannot possibly be appropriate in this case as if he had been in bed with S he would not have been committing any offence, so he is to be sentenced on the basis that a reasonable, sober person would have realised that the person in the bed was not S. Taking into account his good character, his immediate apology and withdrawal as well as his sense of shame and guilty plea, a **3-year Supervision Order** was not unduly lenient.

Note: This case is listed for the principles of acting under a mistake. The guidelines should determine the precise sentence. Ed.

317.44   *Objects inserted   Pre-2014 guideline judicial guidance*

R v AT 2013 EWCA Crim 686 D pleaded to assault by penetration and sexual assault. W pleaded to sexual assault. After a New Year's Eve party, V was taken to, or persuaded to go to, W's flat. She was stripped naked, had her breasts bitten and fondled, and made to lie with her legs in the air. W handed D a small truncheon and D inserted it into V's vagina, to a depth of around 6½ inches. This happened at least once. V managed to escape. D had over 100 convictions on 43 occasions. In 1994, he had sexually assaulted a woman with others. The Judge found the motive was domination and humiliation. D was sentenced to consecutive sentences of 5½ years (the assault) and 9 years (the penetration). Held. The use of the truncheon added greatly to the criminality of the incident. The offences called for a very severe sentence. 14½ years was not manifestly excessive.

Note: This case is listed for the judicial guidance. The guidelines should determine the precise sentence. Ed.

317.45   *Others acting with defendant*

'Offender acts together with others to commit the offence' is one of the factors in Category 2 when the reader is determining the level of culpability, see *Sexual Offences Guideline 2014* pages 10 (rape) and 14 (assault by penetration), which are the same and are at **317.4**.

317.46   *Persistent offenders   Pre-2014 guideline case*

R v Phillips 2012 EWCA Crim 2072 D was convicted of assault by penetration and exposure (×2). Twice in three days, he was seen by different women standing in an alcove near the sea-front masturbating. Two to three weeks later, at around 3 am, V was walking back to a nightclub. D approached her, grabbed her and forced her to the ground. He put his hands under her dress and inserted his fingers into her vagina. He then ran off. D, aged 35, had convictions for indecent assault and indecent exposure in 1993 (aged 16, supervision order) and two rapes (2002, 10 years). Following his release from the sentence for rape, he was convicted of indecent exposure (×2) (12 months) and recalled to prison. Held. The offence was premeditated and he had targeted a lone female at night. He caused serious vaginal injury. Although the offence did not go as far as attempted rape, that was clearly in his mind. The offence was the culmination of predatory behaviour spanning two to three weeks. There was also the seriously aggravating factor of his previous convictions. Following conviction, 12 years determinate was appropriate. The offences of exposure, committed in the context of the previous offending and predatory behaviour, each justified the maximum sentence. There could have been no complaint if those sentences were consecutive, [but] with regard to totality, they ought to be consecutive to the **12 years**, but concurrent to one another. Therefore, the notional determinate term would be **14 years**. Therefore **7 years' IPP**, not 8½ years' IPP.

Old cases: *R v Marshall* 2007 EWCA Crim 1193, 2008 1 Cr App R (S) 18 (p 77) (**15 years**) *R v Hogg* 2007 EWCA Crim 1357, 2008 1 Cr App R (S) 22 (p 99) (**Life** with a 10-year term)

For a summary of the cases, see the 7th edition of this book.

317.47 *Planning, Significant degree of*
'Significant degree of planning' is one of the factors in Category 2 when the reader is determining the level of culpability, see *Sexual Offences Guideline 2014* pages 10 (rape) and 14 (assault by penetration), which are the same and are at **317.4**.

317.48 *Prostitutes as victims   Pre-2014 guideline judicial guidance*
R v Cole 1993 14 Cr App R (S) 764 The law will uphold the prostitute's right to say 'No'. But by the very nature of her trade she is prepared to have sex with any man who pays for it, and the hurt she may suffer is to some extent different from another woman, and that is a factor the court can take into account.

R v Masood 1997 2 Cr App R (S) 137 D pleaded to rape and false imprisonment. Held. We do not disagree with *R v Cole* 1993 14 Cr App R (S) 764, but the remarks are not germane here. The very act of intercourse to someone who has never experienced it before, if she is unwilling and is taken by surprise, can be in itself an inexpressibly appalling event. Intercourse by itself with a prostitute might be to some extent less appalling, but the catalogue of other indecencies, of gratuitous violence, of false imprisonment, of gratuitous additional insults and threats is something which is as painful to a prostitute as it would be to anyone else. It was for the courts to give the protection to prostitutes they sadly too often need. We take no account of the fact she was a prostitute.

Att-Gen's Ref No 28 of 1996 1997 2 Cr App R (S) 206 LCJ D was convicted of five rapes over six years. Each was on a different prostitute. He always refused to wear a condom just before sex. Held. Prostitutes were entitled to the protection of the law as much as anyone else. They were in particular need of protection.

Note: These are old cases, but the decisions seem in line with current sentencing practice. Ed.

317.49 *Prostitutes as victims*
R v Buckland 2013 EWCA Crim 91 D was convicted of assault by penetration and robbery. V, an escort, was asked on the phone to do an 'outcall' and declined. The next day D phoned again and asked for an 'overnight' for £900. V agreed. When she arrived at the address it appeared wrong. She phoned D, who said he had given her the wrong address. He directed her to some shops and then approached her. D tried to lure V to some garages. She saw it was unlit and refused to go further. D placed her arm around her shoulders and put his hand on her mouth. He frogmarched her the length of the garages to an area of grass. V was pushed against a wall. D kept one hand on her mouth and he put the other up her skirt and forcibly digitally penetrated her. V fought back. D told her not to scream or he would stab her. She thought she would prefer to be stabbed than raped. She continued struggling and screaming. She managed to move the hand away from her face and screamed even louder. Someone looked out of the window and D wrestled her overnight bag from her and ran away with it. Two people attended and found her crying and upset. The bag contained personal items, keys and her laptop. The bag was recovered. The laptop was not. V suffered bruising to her upper thighs and her breasts. A friend reported the matter to the police. In her impact statement V said she no longer felt safe at night and did not go out unless with a friend. She had stopped being an escort, so was struggling financially. She had had to leave her house and give up her studies. D had 16 previous convictions on six occasions. They included burglary. He had served three custodial sentences. The Judge determined that D was intending to have sex without payment. He said the total offending was worth 6 years and made it 4 years and 2 years consecutive. The defence relied on the range for digital penetration being 1-4 years. Held. Consecutive sentences were appropriate as the offences were separate and discrete. The sex offence was determined with considerable force. There was also the threat to stab. 4 years was appropriate. With his previous convictions, the 2 years consecutive was appropriate.

Old case: *Att-Gen's Ref No 107 of 2007* 2008 EWCA Crim 198, 2 Cr App R (S) 65 (p 373) (Normally it would have been **6 years**)

For a summary of the case, see the 9th edition of this book.

Post-2014 guideline case

R v Carroll 2014 EWCA Crim 2818, 2015 1 Cr App R (S) 54 (p 381) D was convicted of rape and attempting to cause GBH with intent. He was sentenced in August 2014. In 1996, D left a wedding reception near Lowestoft and drove to Norwich, where he stopped his car. V asked him if he was looking for business. The price of £30 in the car was agreed. V gave D directions where to go and she told him she was pregnant. They stopped in a layby and V put a condom on his erect penis. After some minutes of vaginal sex, D put his hands around V's neck and began to strangle her. V struggled, tried to kick him and scratched his face. She lost consciousness. When she came round, she was on the ground and D was gone. V was half naked. She had lacerations, bruising (including her tongue) and two of her teeth were loose. In 2013, D was arrested. He claimed self-defence. D was now aged 56. In 2008, he had a conviction for assaulting his wife. The Judge found that V was in a very dark place and was therefore vulnerable. Furthermore, D had left her severely traumatised and the psychological damage he had caused was extreme. She was still suffering 18 years later. Even now she is wary of men and does not go out at night even to put the dustbin out. The Judge placed the offence at Category 1 and at the top end of Category B. Held. The violence and fear cannot be underestimated. The violence was correctly categorised as extreme. It was Category 1B. However, there was nothing to lift the sentence from the starting point. There were no [extra] aggravating factors. We start at the **12-year** starting point, so 17 years' extended sentence (**12 years' custody** not 15, 5 years' extended licence).

317.50 *Prostitutes as victims   Trafficked victims*

An example: *Att-Gen's Ref Nos 9-10 of 2011* 2011 EWCA Crim 1953 (Convicted. Callous exploitation and brutality of five victims tricked into coming to the UK. Two repeatedly raped. Number of rapes not revealed. Convicted of assaulting all five. Witness intimidation. One had objects inserted into her anus to prepare her for anal intercourse. Tried to trick another girl to come to the UK whilst on remand. **21 years** was in the right bracket but some judges might have made it rather longer. Should have been IPP so **10½ years' IPP**.)

317.51   *Punish, Rape was to/Revenge rape   Pre-2014 guideline case*

R v Cadogan 2010 EWCA Crim 1642, 2011 1 Cr App R (S) 53 (p 343) D pleaded to ABH and was convicted of rape. V worked in a pub and, after staying for drinks afterwards, was followed home by D, one of the customers. D punched V, causing a nosebleed. That was the ABH. He then pulled down V's trousers and anally raped him. D held V down during the rape. The Judge found that there was gratuitous violence above that required to carry out the rape. D told V that he had been paid £1,000 to exact revenge on V for allegedly assaulting his sister, C. There had been an incident where D had 'stood up' to C physically following an argument. V was initially too scared to inform the police. D was aged 27 at appeal. The Judge described the incident as a planned and deliberate attack, which used sexual violence to punish, degrade and humiliate. Held. This was a sustained attack. The absence of a condom was an aggravating feature, as were the threats made to V. This case merited a severe sentence. 12 years' extended sentence (**9 years'** custody 3 years' licence).

317.52   *Racially or religiously aggravated rapes etc.*

'Offence racially or religiously aggravated' is one of the factors in Category 2 when the reader is determining the level of culpability, see *Sexual Offences Guideline 2014* pages 10 (rape) and 14 (assault by penetration), which are the same and are at **317.4**.

317.53   Recording the offence
'Recording of the offence' is one of the factors in Category 2 when the reader is determining the level of culpability, see *Sexual Offences Guideline 2014* pages 10 (rape) and 14 (assault by penetration), which are the same and are at **317.4**.

317.54   Recording the offence   Pre-2014 guideline judicial guidance
Att-Gen's Ref Nos 73 and 75 of 2010 and 3 of 2011 2011 EWCA Crim 633[921] LCJ Two of these cases reveal how modern technology can be grotesquely misused. A pernicious new habit has developed by which criminals take photographs of their victims, often just to show off to their friends, often just to add something to the humiliation which the victim is already suffering, and sometimes, as in two of these cases, either as a form of pressure to discourage any complaint (in that sense a form of blackmail), but also possibly for the purposes of blackmail, as is revealed in one of these three cases. Anyone can understand what a powerful lever may be given to the criminal by his possession of photographs taken of the victim when, as in these cases, she has been subjected to degrading treatment. The problem is acknowledged in the Definitive Guideline on Robbery. That guideline was issued after the guideline in relation to sexual offences. We make it clear that from now onwards the taking of photographs should always be treated as an aggravating feature of any case and, in particular, of any sexual cases. Photography in these circumstances usually constitutes a very serious aggravating feature of the case. For an example of the person filming the attack receiving the same penalty as the perpetrators, see *Att-Gen's Ref Nos 15-17 of 2013* 2013 EWCA Crim 1041 at **317.73**.

317.55   Relationship rape   Pre-2014 guideline judicial guidance
R v Berry 1988 10 Cr App R (S) 13 In some instances the violation of the person and defilement and inevitable features where a stranger rapes a woman are not always present to the same degree when the defendant and victim previously had a long-standing sexual relationship.
R v W 1993 14 Cr App R (S) 256 at 260 LCJ It should not be thought that a different and lower scale of sentencing attaches automatically to rape by a husband as against that set out in *R v Billam* 1986 82 Cr App R 347 (the then guideline case). All will depend on the circumstances of the individual case. Where the parties were cohabiting normally at the time and the husband insisted on intercourse against his wife's will, but without violence or threats, the considerations identified in *R v Berry* 1988 10 Cr App R (S) 13 and approved in *R v Thornton* 1990 12 Cr App R (S) 1 will no doubt be an important factor in reducing the level of sentencing. Where, however, the conduct is gross and does involve threats or violence, the facts of the marriage, of long cohabitation and that the defendant is no stranger will be of little significance. Between these two extremes there will be many intermediate degrees of gravity which judges will have to consider case by case.
R v M 1995 16 Cr App R (S) 770 LCJ Principles considered. There must be a distinction between those who are estranged and return as an intruder and those who share the same house or bed. Here, where the victim consented to sharing the same bed and no violence was used, we do not consider that as grave as when he returns as an intruder.
R v Millberry 2002 EWCA Crim 2891, 2003 2 Cr App R (S) 31 (p 142) LCJ The starting point for sentence is that cases of 'relationship rape' and 'acquaintance rape' are to be treated as being of equal seriousness to cases of 'stranger rape', with the sentence increased or reduced, in each case, by the presence of specific aggravating or mitigating factors. Rape is rape, and cannot be divided in this way into more and less serious offences. It can be just as traumatic to be raped by someone you know and trust who has chosen you as his victim, as by a stranger who sexually assaults the first man or woman who passes by. It is up to the courts to take all particular circumstances of a case into account before determining the appropriate penalty. Where, for example, the offender is

---

[921] In some reports this case is listed as 73, 75 and 3 of 2010.

the husband of the victim there can be, but not necessarily will be, mitigating features that clearly cannot apply to a rape by a stranger. On the other hand, as is confirmed by the research commissioned by the Panel, because of the existence of a relationship, the victim can feel particularly bitter about an offence of rape, regarding it as a breach of trust. This may in a particular case mean that, looking at the offence from the victim's point of view, the offence is as bad as a 'stranger rape'.

Where there is a relationship, the impact on a particular victim can still be particularly serious. In other cases this may not be the situation because of the ongoing nature of the relationship between the offender and the victim. In such a situation the impact on the victim may be less. It may also be the case where, while the offender's conduct cannot be excused, the continuing close nature of the relationship can explain how a particular offender came to commit what is always a serious offence that is out of character. There can be situations where the offender and victim are sharing the same bed on a regular basis and, prior to retiring to bed, both had been out drinking and, because of the drink that the offender consumed, he failed to show the restraint he should have. It would be contrary to common sense to treat such a category of rape as equivalent to stranger rape. In *R v M* 1995 16 Cr App R (S) 770 the Court emphasised that a custodial sentence was inevitable and Lord Taylor CJ said, 'There is a distinction between a husband who is estranged from his wife and has parted from her and returns to the house as an intruder either by forcing his way in or by worming his way in through some device and then rapes her, and a case where as here the husband is still living in the same house and indeed with consent occupying the same bed as his wife. We do not consider this class of case is the same as the former class'.

Note: All these cases were before the guideline was published and are old. Since these cases were reported there has been a greater emphasis on the need to protect women in a relationship from rape. Ed.

For the Domestic Violence Guideline, see the **Domestic Violence** chapter.

317.56   *Relationship rape   Post-2014 guideline cases*

Att-Gen's Ref No 64 of 2014 2014 EWCA Crim 2050 D was convicted of assault by penetration. V was D's partner of 12 years and they had two children. However, the relationship had been on and off and blighted by domestic violence. V had reported the violence on four occasions. D and V went out for the night, having engaged in consensual sex. They consumed drugs and alcohol. On their return to a hotel, V angered D by blowing away some cocaine powder. As V climbed into bed, D pushed her to the floor and then tried to pull down her nightwear. V asked him to stop and D reacted by trying to force two fingers into her vagina. V called D "evil" to which he replied, "Evil. I'll show you fucking evil." D then proceeded to cover V's face and repeatedly forced his hand, in a fist, into her vagina with such force that it moved her entire body. V was in immediate pain and asked D to stop. She was so distressed that people next door heard and raised their concerns. D's violence caused a 10-12 cm tear in V's vagina, which bled considerably. Two hours later, D began to panic and, upset, purportedly threatened to kill himself. D phoned his mother, who later called the emergency services, and he also phoned for an ambulance five times. When the ambulance arrived an hour later, V had breathing problems and had lost two litres of blood. She underwent surgery, receiving the equivalent of ten stitches in one continuous stitch. She had a blood transfusion and was discharged the next day. She made a full recovery. D claimed V's injuries were suffered following "dirty sex" and he had stopped once V said it hurt and he realised she was bleeding. He made no comment in interview. Prior to trial, V changed her statement, saying it must have been accidental due to their intoxication. Her evidence at trial was that she had no recollection of the incident at all. D was aged 31 on appeal and had 14 convictions, including eight assaults. In 2012, he punched V leaving her needing eight stitches (ABH and 12 months' imprisonment). His last assault conviction was in 2013. Nonetheless, V said she did not wish D to go to prison and he was a good father. The Judge did not refer to the domestic violence guidelines but, placing the sexual assault into Category 2, noted that there was some abuse of trust as D had taken advantage of V's state. Held. In addition to the sexual offences guidelines, it is necessary to refer to the domestic violence guidelines. Those guidelines' principles and the victim's views are relevant generally, as was made clear in *Att-Gen's Ref No 38 of 2013* 2013 EWCA Crim 1450, para 86 (see **317.76**). In relation to domestic violence, particularly where there is a history of such conduct, such that the approach of a victim to an offender may well be a consequence of what has happened in the past, that approach is all the more important. In this case, it is beyond argument that this sentence fell well outside the bracket but the Judge effectively ignored not only the guidelines but also the overarching principles on domestic violence. We start at 8 years, so **7 years**, not 3½.

R v A 2015 EWCA Crim 177, 2 Cr App R (S) 12 (p 115)[922] D was convicted of rape and assault by penetration. The counts were multi-allegation counts. D and V were married and they lived with D's parents. In 2010, they had a child. V thought D's family treated her badly because she had been married before. V also thought D had an affair with the consent of his parents. V said D did not show her consideration even when there was consensual sex. When she resisted, D beat and attacked her. In July police were called. Police were able to see a long mark on her arm. The psychological effect on her had been serious. D was now aged 29 and was treated as of good character. The Judge considered that V was very vulnerable and D had treated her appallingly. Held. Because the Judge wrongly applied the multi-allegation provisions, we sentence for just two offences for each count. As the offending was at the bottom of Category 1, **12 years** not 16.

Att-Gen's Ref No 19 of 2015 2015 EWCA Crim 760 (**20 years**, see **351.57**)

R v Hassan 2015 EWCA Crim 2136 D was convicted of three rapes. D had known V for about 3½ years. They were friends but it was not a sexual relationship. D was aged 42 and V was aged 45. To save money V moved into D's flat and they slept in single beds. There was no sexual contact between them. Each worked long hours, so the time they spent in the flat together was limited. On a Sunday, two months after V moved into the flat, they had lunch together at the flat. D drank quite a lot, became aggressive and asked V for sex. When she refused he pushed her down onto the bed and began to remove her clothing. She struggled and ran for the stairs but she fell. The appellant grabbed her by the hair, pulled her back into the flat and he then slapped her. He verbally abused her and then forced his penis into her mouth. D ejaculated on her. After a while D vaginally raped V twice and on each occasion he ejaculated. V felt unable to escape. After the final rape V showered. Afterwards D apologised to her and left the flat. The next day D gave V £800 and his bank card. V said she had lost her trust in people, lost sleep and lost her dignity. She constantly felt fear, and lost an academic year. D had no convictions. Held. It was Category 2A case with a starting point of 10 years. Factors included the rape was repeated, the three acts of ejaculation, the rapes took place in V's home, the bribe to stop her going to the police, and D had been drinking. **10 years** not 15 years' extended sentence (12 years' custody 3 years' extended licence).

See also: *Att-Gen's Ref No 4 of 2015* 2015 EWCA Crim 481 (Plea during trial which D tried to vacate. 4 (it seems) rape counts, two of which were specimen. Rape of three women he was in a relationship with. One when on bail for the other rapes. Violent, abusive, controlling and threatening behaviour. Now aged 28. Relatively few previous convictions. Category 2B. Held. Starting at 14 years, with plea, **12 years** not 9.)

317.57   *Reporting   Trying to prevent victim reporting the offence*

'Any steps taken to prevent the victim reporting an incident, obtaining assistance and/or from assisting or supporting the prosecution' is one of the aggravating factors, see *Sexual Offences Guideline 2014* page 11 at **317.5** (rape) and page 15 at **317.8** (assault by penetration).

---

[922] This case is also known as *R v S* 2015 EWCA Crim 177.

317.58   *Series of rapes/Campaign of rape*
Offences may be of such severity, for example involving a campaign of rape, that sentences of 20 years and above may be appropriate, see *Sexual Offences Guideline 2014* pages 10 (rape) and 14 (assault by penetration), which are the same and are at **317.4**.

R v G 2013 EWCA Crim 1821 D pleaded (25% credit) to five rapes, four attempted rapes, three assaults by penetration, two engaging in sexual activity counts and two sexual assaults on his daughter, C1. They were all specimen counts. He also pleaded to inciting his other daughter, C2, to engage in sexual activity. C1 was taken from her mother when aged 6. She was totally controlled by D, who made her fall out with C2 so they could not confide in each other. She was allowed no social life. Starting when C1 was aged 10, D graduated from masturbating while watching her to full sexual intercourse with her when she was aged 12 or 13 to 17. Over the years, the abuse was as often as four to five times a week. He incited C2 when she was aged 13 to 'play with his bits'. She told someone at her school and D was arrested. This led to C1 making allegations. D denied being involved. The police cautioned him for some extreme pornography. He denied guilt at a preliminary hearing but pleaded guilty at his PCMH. That was one year after C2's report to her school. C1 suffered from isolation, depression, an eating disorder and emotional trauma. The Judge was satisfied that, but for his arrest, D would have treated C2 as he had treated C1. The Judge gave 19 years in all. Held. That would mean 25 years 4 months before the plea. That was excessive. **17 years**.

See also: *Att-Gen's Ref No 64 of 2012* 2013 EWCA Crim 3174 (Convicted of three rapes (two were specimen offences), attempted rape, six indecent assaults and eight counts of indecency with a child. The victims were his child, stepchild and stepgrandchild. The children were aged 3-15. Occurred from late 1970s to 2003. Involved coercion. Caused one child to have intercourse with his sister and for one child to play with the penis of another who had learning difficulties. No violence. Dire effect on the victims. Exceptional depravity over a number of years. Aged 56 at appeal. **21 years** not 12.)

Post-2014 guideline cases
Att-Gen's Ref No 19 of 2015 2015 EWCA Crim 760 D was convicted of six rapes with V1, his wife (all specimen counts), two rapes with V2 and three rapes with V3. D had a relationship with V1 for 28 years. They had six children and he treated her poorly. Her life was miserable. Between 2004 and 2011, D raped her vaginally, anally and orally, usually after he had been drinking. Sometimes their son in a cot was present. The anal rapes often left V bleeding and in pain and fear. If V1 complained D would slap her. Rapes were achieved through violence. In January 2011, the relationship ended. In 1992 and January 2011, V1 reported the rapes but no action was taken. Immediately after the end of the relationship, D began a relationship with V2. There was physical and sexual violence against V2. He raped her vaginally and anally which made her bleed and cry. This annoyed D, who made V2 perform oral sex with her hair grabbed and force used. In one argument, D kicked V2 and shut her head in a wardrobe. The relationship ended in December 2012 and she reported the rapes to the police, who reconsidered the complaints made by V1. In March 2013, D started a relationship with V3. She was raped vaginally and anally after he had been drinking, after which he beat her with a belt and forced his penis into her mouth to the point of ejaculation. He was charged with the rapes of V1 and V2 and said to V3 that as he had been charged he might as well rape V3 again. He had his hand round her neck. She then went to the police. D was now aged 47 with 32 convictions. There were numerous convictions for violence. The pre-sentence report said he posed a serious risk of harm to women if he was in a relationship with them. It was agreed that the rapes on V1 were in Category 1A and those on V2 and V3 were in Category 2A. The Judge found that D had taken steps to prevent the offences being reported. This and the location of the offences he considered to be additional

aggravating factors. Held. The Judge failed to have sufficient regard to the fact there were three victims and the profound consequences the rapes had had. **20 years** in all, not 16.

R v K and Others 2015 EWCA Crim 850 K was convicted of three conspiracies to rape, five rapes, two of arranging child prostitution and trafficking. AD was involved in the same counts save there was one less conspiracy. J and B were convicted of slightly fewer charges. It was a campaign of rape against three vulnerable children aged 11+. [Over what period of time is far from clear. Ed.] The children were ordered to recruit others. The girls were given gifts, supplied with drugs (including cocaine and heroin) and shown apparent affection. They also suffered extreme physical and sexual violence and threats were issued if they tried to escape. V1 was told that her house would be burnt down. In particular there were oral, vaginal and anal rape and gang rape. Knives, meat cleavers and sex toys were used causing physical injuries. A hairbrush was inserted into V1's vagina. Girls were bitten, scratched, urinated on, suffocated, tied up and burnt with cigarettes. Some had to endure men licking their injured vaginas and watch the abusers smell their dirty and stained underwear. The girls were sold to other men to have sex with them. V2 was threatened with a gun. A baseball bat was inserted into V3's vagina. AD was aged 22-26 and had testimonials. He started offending in 2004 and stopped offending in 2008. He was not arrested until 2009. The Judge started at 34 years for D and AD. J was aged 19-21 when he was involved, was of effective good character and was described by the Judge as a follower and not a leader. He was only involved with two victims and stopped offending on his own account. B was involved with two girls and he was not a prime mover. His involvement ended in about 2009. Held. The impact on the girls had been devastating and of the utmost severity. They had been scarred for life. There was a multiplicity of aggravating factors. **Life** was appropriate in all cases. For D and AD a **17-year** minimum term was justified. For J no complaint can be made of a **12-year** minimum term. For B a **15-year** term reflected the behaviour.

Att-Gen's Ref No 35 of 2015 2015 EWCA Crim 1594 D was convicted of five rapes and three ABHs. Between 1997 and 2013, he committed rapes against four females. When aged 25 and 26, he was in a flat where V1, a 15-year-old schoolgirl, sometimes slept. V1 woke up to find D raping her and eventually she managed to push him off. Then and in the morning he treated the rape with callous indifference. D gave her a sexual disease. At the time she was coping with the death of her brother. She later became a police officer dealing with sex cases and endured psychological problems. She only spoke out when she learnt that D had been arrested. In 2001, V2 and D began a sexual relationship, when she was aged 30 and D was 29. D became violent (the ABH counts). In 2001, he strangled her with a scarf. In 2003, there was a) strangulation with D hitting her with a broom and kicking her, and b) 'driving away, she being dragged by her hair'.[923] Intercourse then became non-consensual (where the two counts of rape reflected specimen offences) although on other occasions there was consent. In 2010, D persuaded V3 to get in his car and against her wishes drove her to a club. In the club she had a drink and passed out. She awoke in her home to find him in bed with her and rubbing her clitoris. Her vagina was sore and it was clear he had had sexual intercourse with her. D showed a callous indifference to her. D met V4 in a pub. They drank and D took her back to another woman's flat. V4 woke up to find D having intercourse with her. He treated her with callous indifference. Shortly before she was due to give evidence, V4 tried to hang herself. D had a number of convictions including ABH and possession of an offensive weapon in 2010 (2 years' imprisonment). The pre-sentence report said D posed a very high risk of serious harm to females and he was willing to manipulate the vulnerable. Held. Over 16 years, D had callously sexually degraded four women. One

---

[923] This is what the report says, but what happened is far from clear.

was aged 15, sad, vulnerable and in mourning. We increase one of the concurrent ABH sentences to 4 years. **24 years' extended sentence** (**20 years'** custody not 10, 4 years' extended licence).

317.59   Series of rapes/Campaign of rape   Concurrent or consecutive   Pre-2014 guideline cases
R v Khan 2001 2 Cr App R (S) 59 (p 285) Consecutive sentences for these two rapes was not wrong.
R v Price 2003 2 Cr App R (S) 73 (p 440) D was convicted of rape and indecent assault. V lived with her two children when she met D. A relationship developed and they lived together for four months. She experienced his violent temper and mood swings and as a result the elder daughter, aged 16, moved out. One night, V went to bed and D wanted sex. She refused and he put his hand around her neck, kissed her forcibly and got on top of her. He held her hands above her head, and ignored her protests and crying. There was sex to ejaculation, then he got off and apologised. Within a fortnight, she moved out of her own home (with her remaining daughter). She was persuaded a week later to return but, following further violence, D was persuaded to leave her home. A few days later he phoned her in the early hours and said that he wanted to talk. She firmly told him that the relationship was over, whereupon he became abusive. He arrived uninvited at her home shortly afterwards and let himself in. He was initially calm but threatened to rape her, humiliate her and make her feel as bad as he felt. When she made it clear that she wanted him to leave, he pushed her onto a sofa and removed her trousers as she kicked out. He ripped her knickers and tried to kiss her. He later calmed down but he demanded her knickers to prevent her from showing them to anyone. He remained in the house for a considerable time. Police were eventually called to the house and arrested D. He was interviewed but denied the offences. He was aged 35 with no previous convictions of any significance. A pre-sentence report suggested that he was a 'higher risk of reoffending'. Held. Relationship or acquaintance rape should be treated as equally serious as cases of stranger rape. In cases of this kind, the starting point should be **5 years** in a contested case. Further, in this case, there was nothing wrong in principle or inappropriate with consecutive sentences as these were two quite distinct incidents some time apart. **5 years and 3 years consecutive** upheld.
R v Hinds 2003 2 Cr App R (S) 76 (p 455) D was convicted of 32 serious offences against eight girls aged 11-16 including rape, buggery and indecent assault. Held. For these offences, there was no reason why the Judge should not impose consecutive sentences.
Note: These are old cases. The Court of Appeal now does not consider its task is to worry about whether the sentences should be concurrent or consecutive. It concentrates on whether the total is manifestly excessive or not. Ed.
See also the CONCURRENT OR CONSECUTIVE SENTENCES chapter in Volume 1.

317.60   Sexual orientation, Hostility to/Motivated against
'Offence motivated by, or demonstrating, hostility to the victim based on his or her sexual orientation (or presumed sexual orientation) or transgender identity (or presumed transgender identity)' is one of the factors in Category 2 when the reader is determining the level of culpability, see *Sexual Offences Guideline 2014* pages 10 (rape) and 14 (assault by penetration), which are the same and are at **317.4**.

317.61   Threats made
'Blackmail or other threats made (where not taken into account at step one)' is one of the aggravating factors, see *Sexual Offences Guideline 2014* page 11 at **317.5** (rape) and page 15 at **317.8** (assault by penetration).

317.62   Timing of the offence
'Timing of the offence' is one of the aggravating factors, see *Sexual Offences Guideline 2014* page 11 at **317.5** (rape) and page 15 at **317.8** (assault by penetration).

317.63   Victim compelled to leave their home
'Victim compelled to leave their home (including victims of domestic violence)' is one
of the aggravating factors, see *Sexual Offences Guideline 2014* page 11 at **317.5** (rape)
and page 15 at **317.8** (assault by penetration).

317.64   Victim aged under 13   Guidelines
The guidelines are at **317.9**.

317.65   Victim aged under 13   Judicial guidance
R v Corran and Others 2005 EWCA Crim 192, 2 Cr App R (S) 73 (p 453) para 6 For
rape of a child under 13 the appropriate sentence is likely to lie within a very wide
bracket, depending on all the circumstances. There will be very few cases in which
immediate custody is not called for, even in relation to a young offender, because the
purpose of the legislation is to protect children under 13 from themselves, as well as
from others minded to prey upon them. There will be some offences, for example where
there is no question of consent and where significant aggravating features, as identified
in *R v Millberry* 2002 EWCA Crim 2891, 2003 2 Cr App R (S) 31 (p 142), are present,
where a long determinate sentence, or a life sentence, will be called for. Although
absence of consent is not an ingredient of the offence, presence of consent is material in
relation to sentence, particularly in relation to young defendants. The age of the
defendant, of itself and when compared with the age of the victim, is also an important
factor. If the offender is much older than the victim a substantial term of imprisonment
will usually be called for. Other factors include the nature of the relationship between the
two and their respective characters and maturity, the number of occasions when
penetration occurred, the circumstances of the penetration, including whether contracep-
tion was used, the consequences for the victim, emotionally and physically, the degree of
remorse shown by the defendant and the likelihood of repetition. A reasonable belief that
the victim was 16 will also be a mitigating factor, particularly where the defendant is
young.
Att-Gen's Ref Nos 74 and 83 of 2007 2007 EWCA Crim 2550, 2008 1 Cr App R (S) 110
(p 640) Paras 6-9 in *R v Corran* 2005 remain valuable general guidance. As far as
apparent age is concerned, the [old] SGC guideline only refers to it as being capable of
being a mitigating factor in the case of a young offender (aged under 18), where such an
offender reasonably believes the other person to be aged 16 or over. This reflects two
aspects of the scheme of Sexual Offences Act 2003. The first is that there is a special
sentencing regime for young offenders to which we have already referred but which does
not apply to offences under section 5. Secondly, in relation to offences against those
aged between 13 and 16, it is a defence to establish a reasonable belief that the other
person is aged 16 or over. It seems to us that inherent in this approach is the view that
any adults who embark on sexual activity with a young person do so at their own risk.
Just as anyone in relation to consent has to give due consideration as to whether the
victim was able to or did in fact give consent, failure to give due consideration to age
will in itself be a substantial element in the culpability of the offence. However, that does
not mean that a reasonable belief that the victim is aged 16 or over cannot be a
mitigating factor for an adult, that is a person over the age of 18. But the older the
offender, the less relevant a mistake as to age, even if reasonably held, will be. In
determining the extent to which mitigation relating to consent or age can justify
departing from the sentencing bracket, it may be helpful to consider the guidelines on
penetrative sexual activity with a person under the age of 16 (SOA 2003 s 9), if the
offender does not reasonably believe that the other person is aged 16 or over. We would
not wish, however, to exclude the possibility of a non-custodial sentence in exceptional
circumstances.
Att-Gen's Ref Nos 11-12 of 2012 2012 EWCA Crim 1119, 2013 1 Cr App R (S) 43
(p 237) D and M pleaded to rape of a child under 13, V. Held. While an offence contrary
to section 5 (victim under 13) will always be a serious offence, section 5 embraces a

wide range of seriousness. The [then] Sentencing Guidelines Council recognised the need to do justice by identifying the particular harm caused by and the culpability of the offender. We would summarise the relevant considerations as follows:

1 Careful analysis of the circumstances of a section 5 offence is always required and a *Newton* hearing may be necessary when the claim is made that the victim was consenting in fact and/or that the offender believed the victim to be significantly older than her chronological age. The prosecutor bears a burden of responsibility to ensure that factual concessions to a basis of plea or mitigation of the offence are made only when justified and that, if made, the precise import of the concession is understood by the offender and the court (see further para 3 below).

2 There is a strong element of deterrence in sentencing for sexual offences committed against young children, whether they are sexually experienced and 'willing' or not. They are, by reason of their young age, vulnerable to exploitation and require protection, sometimes from themselves. It can be assumed that, whatever the circumstances, there is likely to be considerable long-term harm caused by such offences.

3 Exploitative sexual behaviour towards a child under 13 without consideration for the vulnerability of that child may be just as serious as submission obtained by the use of force or the threat of force. 'Ostensible consent' and 'willingness' are terms which, in the context of offences against the young in particular, are susceptible to misunderstanding and, even if accurately used, are liable to obscure the true nature of the encounter between the offender and the victim (see *Att-Gen's Ref Nos 74-83 of 2007* 2007 EWCA Crim 2550 at para 11).

4 The culpability of the offender is measured in part by his own understanding of the harm he was causing or was likely to cause. The guideline does not, however, recognise as a mitigating factor a belief by the offender that the victim was aged 13-15 years. There is a good reason for this. Such an offender knew that the victim was not in law consenting. Nevertheless, the younger the victim, the more serious is the harm likely to result and the greater is likely to be the culpability of the offender. We repeat the advice of the court in *R v Corran and Others* 2005 at para 8 that the respective ages of the offender and the victim is an important factor in the assessment of seriousness.

5 The starting point for consideration of the appropriate sentence for a section 5 offence is the table at page 25 of the guideline and not the table at page 53, which applies to offences contrary to section 9. If the judge decides to sentence outside the guideline range, that decision should be justified and explained.

Note: Most of this guidance was issued before the 2014 guideline. It would appear that much of the guidance is still relevant. I have deleted references to consent as the courts have hardened their approach to considering it as mitigation. Lack of trauma would be a better description for defence advocates. Ed.

Post-2014 guideline judicial guidance

Att-Gen's Ref No 105 of 2014 2014 EWCA Crim 2751 D pleaded to rape. *R v Corran* 2005 (see above) where the defendant pleaded to a section 5 rape, has limited value as a sentencing authority. However, the following part holds good today. 'There will be very few cases in which immediate custody is not called for, even in relation to a young offender, because the purpose of the legislation is to protect children under 13 from themselves, as well as from others minded to prey upon them.' para 23 The legislation and the thinking behind the guidelines concentrates on the actions of the offender rather than the attitude of the victim. Girls under 13 are to be regarded as vulnerable and on occasion, if need be, are to be protected from themselves.

317.66   *Victim(s) aged under 10   Defendant aged under 18*

R v DM 2014 EWCA Crim 1905 D was convicted of rape of a child under 13 (×6). The offending occurred when D was aged between 12 and 15 and V was aged between 9 and 11. Whilst their parents were out D would pin down V, his sister. He would then partially undress them both and then penetrate V, ejaculating. Occasionally V would feel pain but D would dig his knees in when she told him it hurt. D would also sometimes cover her mouth to stop her crying out. D would tell V to clean herself up and that if she told anyone, there would be trouble and she could never see him again. This carried on approximately fortnightly over the relevant period until D met his girlfriend when he was aged 15 and then moved out when he was aged 16. D was aged 18 and of good character, with many positive references, but he had denied the allegations throughout. In her victim impact statement, V described being tearful, emotional and having social and school problems. She had also attempted an overdose. Both V and her mother expressed their love of D. D's mother was recently diagnosed with a serious illness and hoped he could become part of the family again. Held. The Judge rightly rejected any suggestion that D posed a high risk of harm to children. It was restricted to when D was a child. These were serious and repeated offences which caused harm to V and substantial custody was inevitable. The offending began as a form of sexual experimentation and D neither used violence above what was necessary to commit the offences nor threatened violence against V. The phrase 'breach of trust' is not apt in the context of siblings in a familial context, particularly when they are children. **5 years' detention** concurrent, not 10 years.

Post-2014 guideline

R v Smith 2015 EWCA Crim 722 D was convicted of rape of a child aged under 13 and pleaded to various sex assault charges on children.[924] When aged 14 he became a volunteer at a deaf club. His job was to look after young children of people who were deaf. When he was aged about 17, he put the penises of boys aged between 5 and 8 in his mouth on various occasions. He put his penis in the mouth of a boy aged 6. It did not go in far and was out in seconds. This was the rape. When his computer was searched it was discovered that D had searched for images of 'oral sex with 7-year-old boy' and 'naked children'. There was a modest number of images of children on his computer. The pre-sentence report said D had major deficits in his thinking and behaviour. He himself had been sexually abused and bullied because of his Tourette's syndrome over a number of years and he suffered from social isolation and low self-esteem. The Judge considered the starting point for an adult was 14 years, because of the grooming and the child's vulnerability. He reduced the sentence by ⅓ because of D's age. Held. This was not a sustained incident and it was very short lived. [All victims for this offence would be vulnerable.] D had significant features over and above his age. He was emotionally damaged and immature. **7 years detention** not 9 years 4 months with the rest of the counts remaining concurrent.

R v W 2015 EWCA Crim 578 D was convicted of rape, assault on a child by penetration, indecent assault, sexual assault and inciting a child to engage in sexual activity. In 2004, D was aged 10 and V1, a friend of his sister, was aged 6. They, with two others, played hide and seek. D found G inside a wardrobe and began to stroke her legs. D picked up a coat hanger and put her feet through it to keep her legs together. Next he took the coat hanger off and began to stroke her side with it and he kissed her. D took off his trainers and trousers and got on top of V and inserted his penis into her vagina. V said it hurt and began to cry. The next day, at D's home, the four children were playing teachers. D told the others it was break time and told G to stay behind as a punishment. The others were sent out of the room. Next he said the punishment was for her to take her clothes off and use a hula hoop. V asked to keep her clothes on and D said 'No'. She took her clothes off and D wrote on the wall 'I love' and then V's name. V was on the bed and D gave her three quick kisses on the lips and told her to lie down. D stroked her hand, legs and vagina. Then he took off his trousers and underwear and said, "Touch me here," meaning his penis. V did not know what to do. D took her hand and put it around his penis. He moved her hand, backwards and forwards. Next he told her to put her finger in a pencil

---

[924] What D pleaded to and was convicted of is not completely clear. Ed.

sharpener which she did. D took the finger out and unscrewed the blade. He gave her the blade and she held it in her hand and cut herself slightly. He told her to take the blade home and every time she thought of him she was to mark her body with the blade.

On Christmas Day 2004,[925] V went to D's house and the two ended up on a bed. D put a pillow over her face and she began to cry. D took off his trousers and began licking and kissing V's vagina. Telling her repeatedly to be quiet, he put his fingers in her vagina and she screamed. D told her she had to touch him and he took her hand and put it on his penis. She still had a pillow over her face so D guided her hand. In 2012, V went to the police. D made denials. V was now aged 17 and said the court proceedings had caused her a lot of pain. D was now aged 22, with a reprimand for ABH and a caution for obstructing a constable. There were positive references. D had an extremely low IQ and probably had deficits in day-to-day functioning. He also had significant speech and language difficulties and struggled socially and academically. His parents had physical and mental health conditions. The family was victimised and they had to move five times in 11 years to try to escape it. The pre-sentence report suggested a community disposal. The Judge accepted that if D had been prosecuted at the time it was likely he would have been given help and not punishment. **12 months** not 18.

317.67   *Victim(s) aged under 10   Defendant aged 18 to 24   Pre-2014 guideline cases*

Examples: *R v Wilson* 2012 EWCA Crim 386, 2 Cr App R (S) 77 (p 440) (LCJ Two rapes. Plea indicated a few days after arrest. In nursery forced two toddlers, both aged 3, to perform oral sex. Acts filmed on mobile. 44 other sex offences against children. 22 victims aged 12-16 on the Internet. Blackmail used. Some Level 5 still and video images. Aged 21 with no previous convictions. Sought to justify actions and to dominate and control the psychiatrist. He must be detained for the rest of his life. Judge started at 30 years, gave nothing for the plea and made it **life** with 15-year term. We give some allowance for plea, giving **27-year** notional term, giving a **13½-year** term.)

R v Saunders and Others 2013 EWCA Crim 1027, 2014 1 Cr App R (S) 45 (p 258) (LCJ Early pleas. Obtained babysitting job with false papers. Very disturbing material on computer. Made five-year-old suck his erect penis on which he had placed chocolate. Entrenched sexual offending towards young girls. Aged 23. **Life**, with notional starting point of 24 years reduced for plea making **8-year** term, upheld.)

317.68 *Victim(s) aged under 10   Defendant aged 25+*

R v TH 2011 EWCA Crim 2434 D pleaded on rearrangement to nine indecent assaults on females and was convicted of an attempted rape and two sexual assaults of a child who was 'about aged 6' under the 2003 Act. D sexually abused Y from the age of 6. D would touch Y's vagina with his hand and penis. The offences would occur when D and Y were together under bedclothes. The abuse continued until Y was aged 12. When D was aged 18 or 19, and Y was aged 12, he attempted to penetrate her. It hurt and Y pushed D away. J, aged 6, was the daughter of D's cousin. When J was staying at her great-aunt's house, D entered her bedroom while J was still asleep. D touched her vaginal area over her underwear. J tried to get up but D pulled her back and repeated his action. When D was aged 24 or 25, he sexually abused M, aged 6, by putting his hand down her trousers and touching her vagina. M's mother was D's aunt. D was aged 31 at the appeal.[926] Held. D's offending against Y had begun when he was aged 14. To some extent that was sexual experimentation, but it was with someone who was eight years younger. It was a serious matter which had affected Y badly. It was noted that D had not offended for five years after his last victim. In relation to the attempted rape, the appropriate sentence would have been 10 years. The other sentences would be concurrent with the attempted rape. Because of the commencement date, an extended sentence under the 2000 Act was appropriate. 15 years' extended sentence (**10 years' custody** 5 years' licence).

---

[925] The report says 2004, but the ages given for D and V would indicate it was 2005.

[926] There is no mention of whether D had previous convictions.

R v MJ 2012 EWCA Crim 132, 2 Cr App R (S) 73 (p 416) LCJ D pleaded (full credit) to rape of a child. He was looking after V, his nearly three-year-old son. When changing V's nappy, D became sexually aroused. He inserted his erect penis into V's anus, and pushed it in and out on at least six occasions, until he ejaculated. V was screaming throughout. D took V to the bathroom and, using the shower attachment, rinsed away the blood and semen. D told V's mother that V had had an accident and suffered an injury to his bottom after falling onto a bedpost. V was taken to hospital and examinations revealed significant injuries to his anus. Some three weeks later there remained some scarring. D subsequently made full and frank admissions. The pre-sentence report showed some guilt and remorse. D had admitted to having sexual fantasies about V before the attack. D demonstrated a high level of motivation to take part in a sex offender treatment programme. D had no convictions and was effectively of good character. [D's age is not given.] Held. The offence fell outside of the guideline. It was not disputed that D was dangerous. IPP was appropriate. Starting at 21 years was severe. However, with the plea, **7 years' IPP** was not manifestly excessive.

R v Flammia 2012 EWCA Crim 554 D pleaded (full credit) to assault by penetration on a child under 13 and on rearraignment to three sexual assaults on a child under 13 and another assault by penetration on a child under 13. V was aged about 9. D knew V's family and had worked for them as a handyman for a number of years. He was treated like a member of the family and on occasions he would be entrusted with the care of V and her two younger siblings. V was downstairs in the house with D, whilst V's parents were upstairs. She bent over to pick something up and D told her to stay there. He lifted her skirt, pulled down her knickers, took out his penis and rubbed it against her bottom for about a minute. He then made her lie down on two chairs and inserted two fingers into her vagina. On another occasion, he told V to lie on the bed and he rubbed his penis against her vagina. On a separate occasion, V returned home from school and was followed to her bedroom by D. He asked her to take off her jeans. She did not want to. He removed her jeans and underwear and inserted two fingers into her vagina. He moved them in and out and V said that it was hurting. D ignored her. V began to get off the bed but D put her back on the bed, took out his penis and rubbed it in the area of her vagina. He ejaculated. D offered V some money but V told him she would tell her mother. D said if she did so he would kill himself. V eventually told her mother, who confronted D. He admitted touching V. He subsequently sent his partner a series of messages informing her of what he had done, went missing for a few days and was later found by police in his car with superficial cuts to his wrists. He said to the officers, "I'm disgusting…I didn't have sex with her, I just touched her". D, aged 58, had previous convictions. In April 2003, for six indecent assaults on a female under 14 he received an extended sentence. The licence expired before the commission of these offences. Held. D had a bad record for sexual offending. That is so even if there was no physical harm. D had resisted any attempt to address his offending behaviour during his extended licence. He had significantly groomed V and her family over a period of time. On one occasion he had hurt the victim. A starting point of 18 years was too long. 15 years was appropriate, so with full credit, **5 years' IPP** not 6.

Att-Gen's Ref No 79 of 2012 2013 EWCA Crim 197 D was convicted of three rapes, three indecent assaults and one indecency with a child. D was aged 36 then and 60 now. He lost his wife and two daughters in a fire on their houseboat and was homeless. D went to live with his sister-in-law and her family including V, who was then aged 6. He slept in the same bedroom as V and her younger brother, B. In incident 1, D invited V into his bed and made her masturbate him. Next he sat astride her and raped her. She was in pain and bleeding. In incident 2, when D was left to look after V and B, he took V down into the cellar, held her legs apart and raped her. In incident 3, D asked V to join him in the lavatory. He exposed his penis and made her masturbate him. He then picked her up, sat her on his lap and raped her. In incident 4, D made V rub his penis through his clothing. In incident 5, D made V perform oral sex on him. She found this disgusting and made her want to vomit. The offending stopped when he moved back to a houseboat. V was severely traumatised. She suffered from depression. When she finally told her mother, her mother refused to support V. When D's brother traced V on Facebook, V was terrified and went to the police. D's first jury could not agree. D's second jury had to be discharged. D's third jury convicted him. V had to give evidence three times. In 1984, D had a conviction for indecent assault on his brother's 8-year-old daughter. There were no further convictions. The Judge considered the evidence overwhelming. He noted V's huge distress, loneliness, inability to mix with people and the breach of trust. The prosecution on appeal said the aggravating factors were: age of victim, disparity of age, number of offences, position of trust, vulnerable victim, impact on the victim and the similar previous conviction. Held. There was absolutely no reason why the Judge should not have started at 15 years as stated by the guidelines. That figure should be increased to reflect the guidelines. The mitigating factors are the reduced risk of reoffending and lack of convictions since. The proper sentence was **15 years** not 10.

R v CH 2013 EWCA Crim 1232 D pleaded (30% credit) to sexual assault on a child aged under 13 and assault by penetration on a child aged under 13. D was the stepgrandfather of four young children. V1, D's two-year-old stepgranddaughter, was left by her mother and D's son in D's charge for two hours or so. D removed her nappy on two occasions. When V1's parents returned, they noticed that she was refusing to sit down and was miserable. When she had her nappy changed, V1 said it was hurting her. Her mother noticed three spots of blood towards the front of the nappy. Two months later, D, who had a good relationship with his five-year-old stepgrandson, V2, agreed that he could come and stay the night with him. D invited him to sleep in the same bed as him, which he did. D was naked and V2 described D as, "pulling that thing back and playing with it", indicating D's penis and foreskin. V2 said D tried to bite his penis whilst he was on the bed and tried to suck it with his mouth whilst he was under the blankets. D tried to dissuade V2 from telling his parents. V2 did so. The parents, aware that D might have been responsible for V1's discomfort, informed the police and V1 was examined. Her hymen had been completely transected. In the doctor's view, that was consistent with penetrative vaginal and sexual abuse. D was aged 59 at appeal and had two convictions, one for burglary and one for indecent assaults on five boys aged 9-16 (1983). Held. The Judge was entitled to place this offending towards the top of the 11 to 17-year range after a trial, especially having regard to the previous, albeit old, conviction for sexual offending. However, the Judge failed to adequately reduce the sentence for totality. The appropriate sentence before discount for the plea was **18 years**. With 30% for the plea (because he had the opportunity to admit the offences in interview) **20½ years'** **extended sentence** (**12½ years'** custody 8 years' licence) not 22 years' extended sentence (14 years' custody 8 years' licence).

See also: *R v H* 2012 EWCA Crim 1585 (Pleas to rape of a child under 13 (×3), assault of a child under 13 by penetration (×3), attempted rape (×2), indecent assault (×2), sexual assault, inciting a child to engage in sexual activity and indecency with a child (×2). One penetration of an eight-year-old. Committed against son, granddaughter, niece and neighbour's daughter. Minimised culpability. Deeply entrenched pattern of sexual offending. Aged 65. Consecutive sentences appropriate for separate victims. **12 years** not 15 for the rapes, **2 years** not 3 for the inciting a child count. Total sentence **19 years** not 23.)

R v Saunders and Others Re G 2013 EWCA Crim 1027, 2014 1 Cr App R (S) 45 (p 258) para 38 (LCJ Early pleas. Father. Oral rape and other abuse on daughters aged 2 and 6, and friend aged about 7. Given money to keep quiet. Aged 35. No previous convictions. Defendant in denial. Offences of the highest culpability. **Life** upheld. 6-year 4-month term not challenged.)

R v Watkins and P 2014 EWCA Crim 1677, 2015 1 Cr App R (S) 6 (p 41) (D pleaded to attempted oral and anal rape, two conspiracies to rape and 19 other sexual assault and image offences. He sexually abused babies anally and orally, with the involvement of their two mothers. The two babies were about a year old. The acts were photographed and there were references to the babies being drugged with crack. [There were the most alarming] messages including that D would like to, "fuck her a little bit every day until she can take all of daddy's dick." The Judge said he passed a **35-year extended sentence** made up of two 15-year (concurrent) and two 14-year (concurrent) sentences but they were consecutive to each other with a 6-year extended licence. The defence said the total was too long. Held. It wasn't. Because of what the Judge said we make one set of the offences determinate.)

Post-2014 guideline case

R v W 2015 EWCA Crim 960 D pleaded (full credit) to four rapes, three indecent assaults and three gross indecencies with a child. The counts were specimen counts covering regular activity. Between 1971 and 1982, starting when he was aged about 25, he abused V (who appears to be his niece) when she was aged 7 to 18. The first act was digital penetration, which was painful. D was told to stop but didn't. D bought her treats and groomed her. Also in 1971, he bought V a large teddy bear and asked her to his flat to see it. He then raped her. V was also obliged to suck D's penis and masturbate him. The second rape was in 1977. During the next five years the rapes became regular. The other sex offences related to when he licked her vagina and put his penis into her mouth. It stopped when V left the country. V said D swore her to secrecy by threats. In interview he did not dispute the account and claimed not to recall specific incidents. He also said he had been running [away] from these allegations for 40 years. D was now aged 68 and had no previous convictions. V now thought a long custodial sentence would not benefit anyone and she did not believe she had sustained long-term harm. The Judge passed consecutive sentences making 19 years 10 months in all. Held. That would mean a starting point of almost 30 years. The case involves the destruction of a childhood. We start at 24 years making **16 years** after the plea.

R v DJ 2015 EWCA Crim 563, 2 Cr App R (S) 16 (p 164) D pleaded to six rapes, 24 child sex offences, 18 child image offences and two extreme image offences. He was convicted of five rapes, 13 child sex offences and two abduction counts. The conviction matters were as follows. When SJ, his daughter, was aged 4½ he started touching her. When she was aged 5, he vaginally and anally raped her. This lasted about 10 years. He said it was punishment for her being bad. He would hit her and verbally abuse her. D also held her nose to force her to open her mouth for oral sex. Threats were made that if she did not comply with his demands he would hurt her and her mother. D met AF, a runaway, when she was aged 15. She was a vulnerable child who functioned like a six to eight-year-old. He had regular sex with her. D also made LS masturbate him when she was aged 8-10. When DC was aged 15 he put his hands on her vaginal area.

The matters he pleaded to were as follows. When his niece, LJ, was aged 8-11, he entered her bedroom at night and touched her. This led to anal and vaginal rape and digital penetration. There was oral abuse as well. Threats were made to keep her quiet. He took photographs of this and on occasions her brother, aged 8, was present. When LJ wanted to end their sex sessions, he threatened to send sex photographs he had taken of them to her father and her school. Sinister texts were also sent to her. D met JD, aged 14, on the Internet and took her to a hotel where he plied her with alcohol and gave her gifts. She declined sex and when she was asleep he raped her. They met again and he was rough with her and made her perform oral sex. He groomed BP, aged 14, to meet him in a hotel. When it happened he received a text from her mother and he took her home. Police were informed and his mobile was searched. BP had to be sectioned when she self-harmed. Between 2007 and 2013, he created or obtained 500 images. Over 200 involved himself. Two videos involved a two-year-old girl masturbating him. Many of the images were of adults pretending to be children and fathers sexually involved with their children.

D was arrested and bailed. He did not co-operate to find the victims in the images and carried on seeking child sex and child sex images. All the abuse was over 12 years. D was now aged 49 and had no convictions. The Judge considered a) in many cases the evidence was overwhelming, b) the defendant was a clever, confident and manipulative sexual predator, c) he manipulated the court processes, and d) there was extreme harm. Held. There was great misery and lasting harm. The paternal breach of trust was serious. All the girls were vulnerable. The Judge's comments were correct. There were multiple aggravating factors namely: a) nine victims, b) breaches of trust, c) recordings made, d) threats made, e) deceit, f) grooming and controlling, g) suborning his daughters to give false evidence, h) his isolation of SJ within the family, and i) the exploitation of the vulnerable. Grave as the offending was, the extended sentence should have an overall custodial term of **30 years** not 33 with a 6-year extended licence.

317.69   Victim(s) aged 10-12   Defendant aged under 18
R v Morrissey 2011 EWCA Crim 3332 D was convicted of attempted rape and five rapes. V worked under the instruction of D's mother at stables. D rode horses and worked at various stables. Between June 2006 and August 2007, he repeatedly raped V, aged 11-12. He pushed her against the stable walls when no-one could see. He pulled her hair and tried to make her suck his penis. He also raped her in a horse box. D was aged 15-16 and much stronger than V. V was powerless to resist. The Judge said had D been an adult, the sentence would have been 15 years. Held. These are very serious offences indeed. **10 years** appropriately represented D's age and immaturity.
See also: *R v S* 2011 EWCA Crim 1238, 2012 1 Cr App R (S) 14 (p 67) (Plea to statutory rape of his girlfriend aged 12-13, who looked 15-16. Aged 16. 20 instances of intercourse, one or two in the week before her 13th birthday. Victim became pregnant (terminated). Victim instigated the sexual activity. **2 years 3 months** not 6.)

Post-guideline case
R v G and M 2015 EWCA Crim 32 G pleaded to rape of a child under 13 (late and on the basis that he believed the victim to be aged 15) and engaging in sexual activity with a girl under 16 (×7) involving four different girls. The sexual activity was unprotected. G and BM became boyfriend and girlfriend, both being aged 14, and had sex. G also had sex with AS, aged 12, who had taken cannabis following pressure. G told her he wanted to take her virginity. AS described being in pain to CH. Later, AS said she did not blame G but wished he had pleaded guilty on an earlier occasion. G later had sex with a girl exactly a year younger, CS, a cousin of AS. G was aged 15 and CS was aged 14 at that time. CS also sent provocative photos of herself to G, who, against her wishes, sent one on to a male friend. A month or so later, G had sex with KG, aged 13, taking her virginity. KG also thought she might be pregnant but was not. BM also had sex with two other youths at a party when G was present. He was then aged 15, and had sex twice with BM. All of the sexual activity with G was consensual.
G was aged 17 on appeal and had been in care since 2009. G was of effectively good character but had a conditional discharge for criminal damage in 2014. There was an element of grooming and an opportunistic use of gatherings where alcohol and cannabis were consumed. He was also influenced by older males and had a lack of real emotional attachments but had a supportive family. However, he had positively engaged in his therapeutic support and work placement. G posed a medium risk of serious harm to the public. Custody was considered unsuitable for or unlikely to address their sexual behaviour. Held. Even a disparity of 12 months [in age between the victims and the defendant] at these ages does not make a difference to the maturity of mind of the individuals involved. For G, we do not consider that the legal label of rape...provided any assistance in the evaluation of its seriousness and accept that G was a sexually precocious young person who put the health and welfare of four separate underage girls at serious risk. However, **18 months' detention** in all, not 3 years.
R v H 2015 EWCA Crim 1579 (Pleaded to four counts of rape of a child under 13. D aged 16 (now 17) and child aged 12. Consent. Good character. Emotionally immature. Because of mitigation **12 months'** DTO not 18.)

317.70   *Victim(s) aged 10-12   Defendant aged 18 to 24*

R v Charles and Others 2011 EWCA Crim 2153, 2012 1 Cr App R (S) 74 (p 414) F and two others pleaded to oral rape of V1. Two further defendants pleaded to vaginal rape of V1. D pleaded to oral rape of V2. The defendants were together and one received a text message from V1 showing her willingness to meet him. The defendants drove in two cars to a party which V1 and V2 were attending. One girl got into each car. The text messages showed that V1, who was 1 month short of her 13th birthday, wanted to have some sexual contact with more than one person. V2 was under 13 years old. One of the defendants asked the girls' ages and was told that they were 16 years old. There was nothing in their physical appearance to suggest they were under 16. Consequently the group believed that any sexual contact would be lawful. The cars drove around and stopped at a park. V1 and V2 went into the park alone to go to the toilet. V1 then collected and invited the defendants, one by one (except D) to accompany her behind a tree. Either oral or vaginal penetration took place. D had sexual contact with V2. Initially at her suggestion, there was oral penetration. V2 then became upset and D comforted her. V1 and V2 were then driven back to where they wanted to be dropped off. There was a suggestion that they were aged under 16 and, when quizzed on this, V1 and V2 refused to acknowledge it. The defendants voluntarily attended the police station. During interviews they admitted the conduct but stated they believed the girls to be aged 16. There was a delay of over 12 months before the defendants were sentenced, despite the early guilty pleas. The matters therefore only came to court as a result of the defendants' responsible confessions. The prosecution were unable to call V1 as she had made a false accusation against another man. The Court therefore had to sentence the defendants on the bases of pleas, namely that there was no absence of consent and the defendants believed the girls to be 16 years old. All defendants were under 21,[927] save F, and all were of good character. The Judge gave them all 2 years' custody. Held. There is no evidence of emotional or physical suffering. V1 had had sexual experiences back to the age of 10. There was ample personal mitigation. The defendants were relatively sexually inexperienced. Custody was merited but immediate detention was not right, taking into account the delay, the confessions and the willingness of the victims. For F, **1 year suspended**. For the rest, **1 year's detention suspended**.

Att-Gen's Ref No 1 of 2015 2015 EWCA Crim 380 D pleaded early to six rapes of a child under 13 (two specimen counts of vaginal, two specimen counts of anal and two specimen counts of oral). D was aged 19. He met V, a 12-year-old virgin, who was a distant relative. D soon progressed to frequent sexual conduct to which V reluctantly acquiesced. V was scared of D. Rapes were several times a week. D did not use a contraceptive but would withdraw and ejaculate. D gave her chlamydia. He persisted in anal rape despite her saying it was painful. Once D raped her in front of a 10 or 11-year-old friend. D sent V pictures of his penis and asked for pictures of herself to 'make it up'. D lied to V's mother about the activity. The mother went to the police. In interview D said there was sexual touching with V's initiation and consent. Further it was V who wanted anal intercourse and it had only happened three or four times. Vaginal and oral penetration was accepted. D had only minor previous convictions. He had a troubled and disruptive upbringing. He was bullied regularly. D had a limited intellectual capacity and in many ways was immature. There had been suicide attempts and regular self-harming. The pre-sentence report assessed a high risk of serious harm to children. It was a Category 2A case. Held. The starting point was 13 years. The conduct was persistent. However, the mitigation was very powerful. **9 years** not 6.

See also: *R v Wilson* 2012 EWCA Crim 386, 2 Cr App R (S) 77 (p 440) (LCJ Two rapes. Plea indicated a few days after arrest. In nursery forced two toddlers, both aged 3, to

---

[927] Unfortunately the judgment does not say how old the defendants were. I assume they were aged over 18 because those aged under 18 cannot have their sentences suspended. Also the sentencing Judge passed Detention in a Young Offender Institution orders. Ed.

perform oral sex. Acts filmed on mobile. 44 other sex offences against children. 22 victims aged 12-16 on the Internet. Blackmail used. Some Level 5 still and video images. Aged 21 with no previous convictions. Sought to justify actions and to dominate and control the psychiatrist. He must be detained for the rest of his life. Judge started at 30 years, gave nothing for the plea and made it **life** with a 15-year term. We give some allowance for plea, giving a **27-year** notional term, giving a **13½-year** term.)

Att-Gen's Ref Nos 11-12 of 2012 2012 EWCA Crim 1119, 2013 1 Cr App R (S) 43 (p 237) (D and M, aged 20, raped V, aged 11. Sentenced on the basis that V consented, and that they could not have believed that V was aged over 14. Others were present and the rape was videoed on a mobile phone. The rape was considered degrading. Held. The willingness of V was of little mitigation. The **starting point was 11 years**. With the pleas, **7 years** not 5.)

R v NA 2014 EWCA Crim 536 (Convicted. Assault by penetration of child under 13 and four sexual assaults of a child under 13. Victim was his foster daughter, aged 11 to 12. He gave her alcohol and then penetrated her vagina with his fingers. Asked for sexual intercourse but she refused. Kissed her on the lips. Touched her breasts inside her clothing. Committed over the course of two years. Dreadful abuse of trust. Aged 52. Effective good character. **14 years** was stiff, but not manifestly excessive.)

Post-2014 guideline case

Att-Gen's Ref No 105 of 2014 2014 EWCA Crim 2751 D pleaded, on the day his case was listed for trial, to rape of a child under 13, sexual assault of a child under 13 and two counts of causing a child under 13 to engage in sexual activity. Soon after D passed his 18th birthday, he met V online and initially D thought she was aged 16. They met and D thought she was aged 14-15. They kissed and V masturbated D. Eight days later they met again. They kissed and D touched V's breast under her clothing. She masturbated him and sucked his penis. The investigating officer thought V looked aged 14-15. D told V to keep their relationship secret. V declined to assist the police. D had no previous convictions. The pre-sentence report said D was disgusted with himself when he discovered V was only aged 12 and he was very immature. The Judge made a community order. Held. The rape falls into Category 3. D did not know V was aged 12. Because of the no previous convictions, the favourable references, his educational qualifications which led him to aspire to university, his respectable and supportive family, his age, his recognition that the activity was wholly wrong, the remorse and the suggestion he was 'very immature', we have regard to the principles in the *Youths Sentencing Guideline 2009*. D had complied well with his community order. We take into account the effect of this reference. Because of the cumulative mitigation, 2½ years' YOI.

317.71 *Victim(s) aged 10-12 Defendant aged 25+*

R v Ayre 2010 EWCA Crim 1063 LCJ D pleaded to two rapes, causing or inciting a child under 13 to engage in sexual activity and abducting a child. In 1985, D was convicted of killing a young woman with whom he was in a relationship. The murder involved a sexual element, namely that she had agreed to have intercourse with him and subsequently asked him to desist. He lost his temper, picked up an iron bar and battered her with it. In 2005, D was released on licence and less than a year later he committed these offences. Two boys, one of whom was 10 years old, were playing. D approached them and persuaded the 10-year-old to go with him. When they arrived at D's flat, the boy was pulled inside where he was threatened with a Stanley knife. D forced the boy to undress, perform oral sex upon him and he raped him orally and anally. D offered to take the boy home. The pre-sentence report concluded that D posed a very high risk of reconviction for sexual offences if he were ever free. The psychiatric report said he was untreatable and extremely dangerous. There were significant aggravating factors: D, aged 48, was on licence for murder, the abduction of the boy, the use of a knife, the gross indignity involved, the pain caused to the boy and the use of force on a very young victim. The Judge ordered whole life. Held. We cannot envisage that he will ever be released.

However, it was inappropriate to order that the early release provisions would not apply. There are 35 other offenders who have been made subject to such an order, all of whom were sentenced for murder. **Four life sentences** with a **10-year** minimum period.

R v Ahmad 2014 EWCA Crim 388 D was convicted of two assaults by penetration of a child under 13 and sexual assault of a child under 13. V was born in 1997 and was D's cousin. She lived near to D and often stayed the night. When she was aged 10 or 11, D entered the bedroom where V lay half asleep. She was lying on her stomach. D pulled off her knickers and pyjama trousers and inserted his finger into her anus. She was frightened and embarrassed. On another occasion, D came into the bedroom and again tried to pull down her knickers and pyjama trousers. V resisted. D touched her breasts over her pyjama top. The next incident occurred when V was aged 12. D sat on the bed beside V and pulled up her pyjama top. He touched and kissed her all over except on her face. He pulled down her knickers and pyjamas again and this time he put his finger into V's vagina, lying on top of her. After D went to the bathroom he tried to do it again. He was unsuccessful. V told D's wife but the offences were not reported for some nine months. D was aged 43 and had no previous convictions. His marriage broke down and he lost contact with his children. V said the offences had had a minimal impact on her life. The Judge treated the case as a bad breach of trust case as V's parents trusted D and allowed V to stay at his house. Held. There was no penile penetration, no threats or any accompanying aggravating circumstances of that kind. However, the offences were committed over some months and in breach of trust. **8 years** was appropriate, not 10.

R v Hall 2014 EWCA Crim 534 D was convicted of assault by penetration of a child under 13 (×4), indecent assault (×9) and sexual assault of a child under 13 (×5). Between 2000 and 2008, when V was aged 5 to 12, D systematically sexually abused her. D was the partner of V's grandmother. V would stay with them at weekends whilst her mother worked. It began with D touching and rubbing V's vagina and progressed to digital penetration. There was one occasion where D licked V's vagina. D denied the allegations but subsequently pleaded guilty. The pre-sentence report noted that he was, in some respects, remorseful but also minimised his culpability. D was aged 73 at appeal. He had no relevant convictions. Held. Given the circumstances and the grave breach of trust, the assault by penetration fell into the top category. The real complaint is as to totality. D had pleaded at an early stage, had no relevant convictions and had not previously been to custody. The Judge had taken an overall starting point of 24 years. That was simply too long. There was a significant impact upon the victim but with the plea and other mitigation, **13 years** not 16.

Note: This gives a starting point of 19½ years. Ed.

R v K and Others 2015 EWCA Crim 850 K was convicted of three conspiracies to rape, 5 rapes, two of arranging child prostitution and trafficking. AD was involved in the same counts save there was one less conspiracy. J and B were convicted of slightly fewer charges. It was a campaign of rape against three vulnerable children aged 11+. [Over what period of time is far from clear. Ed.] The children were ordered to recruit others. The girls were given gifts, supplied with drugs (including cocaine and heroin) and shown apparent affection. They also suffered extreme physical and sexual violence and threats were issued if they tried to escape. V1 was told her house would be burnt down. In particular there was oral, vaginal and anal rape and gang rape. Knives, meat cleavers and sex toys were used causing physical injuries. A hairbrush was inserted into V1's vagina. Girls were bitten, scratched, urinated on, suffocated, tied up and burnt with cigarettes. Some had to endure men licking their injured vaginas and watch the abusers smell their dirty and stained underwear. The girls were sold to other men to have sex with them. V2 was threatened with a gun. A baseball bat was inserted into V3's vagina. AD was aged 22-26 and had testimonials. He started offending in 2004 and stopped offending in 2008. He wasn't arrested until 2009. The Judge started at 34 years for D and AD. J was aged 19-21 when he was involved, was of effective good character and was described by the Judge as a follower and not a leader. He was only involved with two victims and stopped offending on his own account. B was involved with two girls and he was not a prime mover. His involvement ended in about 2009. Held. The impact on the girls had been devastating and of the utmost severity. They had been scarred for life. There was a multiplicity of aggravating factors. **Life** was appropriate in all cases. For D and AD a **17-year** minimum term was justified. For J no complaint can be made of a **12-year** minimum term. For B a **15-year** term reflected the behaviour.

See also: *R v R* 2010 EWCA Crim 2006 (Aged 50, pleaded (full credit) to 18 sexual offences including five rapes over a 10-year period. There were four victims, with the offences occurring when his child and his stepdaughters were aged 6 to 15. Penetration when aged 14. Significant aggravating factors. **15 years** not 22½.)

R v KS 2012 EWCA Crim 126 (Pleas to rape and numerous other sexual offences. Four-year period. Victim aged between 10-12 and 13-14 for the rapes. Related to defendant. Oral rape and digital penetration. Aged 44. Good character. Full credit. **5 years' IPP**, not 7.)

R v H 2012 EWCA Crim 1585 (Pleas to rape of a child under 13 (×3), assault of a child under 13 by penetration (×3), attempted rape (×2), indecent assault (×2), sexual assault, inciting a child to engage in sexual activity and indecency with a child (×2). One penetration of an eight-year-old. Committed against son, granddaughter, niece and neighbour's daughter. Minimised culpability. Deeply entrenched pattern of sexual offending. Aged 65. Consecutive sentences appropriate for separate victims. **12 years** not 15 for the rapes, **2 years** not 3 for the inciting a child count. Total sentence **19 years** not 23.)

For the suggested approach to these pre-guideline cases, see **317.73**.

Post-2014 guideline case

Example: *R v Carroll* 2014 EWCA Crim 2818, 2015 1 Cr App R (S) 54 (p 381) (Convicted. Strangled a prostitute and then left. She was badly traumatised. Extended sentence with a **12-year** not 15-year custodial term. For more detail, see **317.49**.)

317.72   *Victim aged 13-15   Pre-2014 guideline case*

Example: *R v DL* 2015 EWCA Crim 74, 1 Cr App R (S) 58 (p 404) (D was convicted of two rapes on his daughter when she was aged 13-14. Two other sex offences against her. She was vulnerable. D was aged 33 with, in 2007, three sex assault previous convictions (Victim just aged 14. 3 years' imprisonment on a plea) and significant non-sex previous convictions. Judge made the offence Category 2A. Held. Particularly gross breach of trust. 20 years' extended sentence (**15 years'** custody 5 years' extended licence) was not manifestly excessive.)

317.73   *Victim asleep, drunk etc.*

Att-Gen's Ref Nos 15-17 of 2013 2013 EWCA Crim 1041 D, M and W pleaded (on rearraignment) to two assaults by penetration. W also pleaded to sexual assault. A rape count was left to lie on the file. V, an 18-year-old student, left a nightclub. In doing so, she met D, M and W and agreed to go back to W's house. 'Increasing amounts of alcohol' were consumed and the group played drinking games and engaged in 'sexual banter'. V appeared happy to engage in the games and jokes. V went upstairs to the bathroom and thereafter had no memory of what occurred. She awoke on the afternoon of the same day and found herself in bed with D and W lying either side of her. She was naked from the waist down, suspected she had been sexually assaulted and felt sore in the anal region. She ran from the house and reported the matter to her mother, who called the police. She was examined and showed no injuries. She initially decided she did not wish to pursue the matter, but she subsequently became aware of a video recording of the events of that night. The recording shows D saying, "She's gorgeous mate, she's got beautiful breasts, beautiful face, she's just unfortunate enough to have met us tonight". One of the other two could be heard to say, "She'll have a fit when she comes round" and there was some discussion about ensuring their faces could not be seen on the recording. All three could be heard giggling and egging one another on in coarse terms. The footage showed V lying comatose on a bed while W was putting his penis in her face. D and M were encouraging him to put it in her mouth but he did not do so. D could be seen digitally penetrating V's anus, and D or W could be seen penetrating V's anus with a white object. M was filming the incident and did not touch V, but was encouraging the other two. M left the premises after a while and the offending continued. All three claimed V had willingly engaged in sexual activity prior to the filming when arrested. The victim impact statement revealed how V blamed herself for the offences and felt self-hatred. She had to attend a clinic for an HIV test. She was humiliated when she saw the footage and had to take time away from her studies. D displayed a high level of genuine remorse but with a degree of minimisation. D had three excess alcohol convictions. W, aged 34 at appeal, was remorseful. He had no relevant convictions and a good employment history. M, aged 22 at appeal, had qualifications and a good employment history. Held. The offences were carried out whilst V was unconscious and totally helpless. She was highly vulnerable. The offences were recorded, which was a serious matter. It was a sustained sexual assault over a period of 20 minutes. All three were fully involved in the joint enterprise. In mitigation, there was some, limited, prior consensual sexual activity. That was of limited weight as what initially occurred was in a very different league from what happened when she became unconscious. There was also the remorse and the guilty pleas. The Judge gave 20% credit for the pleas, which were entered on the day of trial. That seems appropriate given the earlier indications they would plead. The Judge should have started at 8 years. The aggravation takes the sentence to at least 9 years. The Judge discounted the sentence by 18 months for personal mitigation. That may be generous but we will be faithful to it. Before the plea, the sentence should have been not less than 7½ years. With the pleas, the correct sentence for D, M and W was **5½ years**, not 3½.

R v M 2013 EWCA Crim 1530 D was convicted of three rapes and sexual assault committed against his then partner whilst she was asleep. It was submitted that the offences are less serious for having been committed for the most part whilst his partner was asleep. Held. Whilst it is true that D's partner was not awake to experience much of what was happening, the offending indicates a degree of callousness with regard to her wishes, which cannot be overlooked.

Post-2014 guideline case
See also: *R v W* 2015 EWCA Crim 1021 (Convicted. W and victim, V, both aged 16. W took down her jeans and knickers when V was asleep. V found wet ejaculate between her legs. W apologised. Relationship continued, then broke up. V reported it. Starting point 5 years. With W's age and his good character, **2½ years**, not 3½.)

Att-Gen's Ref No 51 of 2015 2015 EWCA Crim 1699 D pleaded early to rape. V, who was now aged 19 and a virgin, was very drunk. She vomited in a taxi and had to walk home. She was nearly home when D took her to an alleyway where he vaginally raped her causing her pain and a tearing sensation. The impact on V was severe, causing her panic attacks and to break down in tears over little things. D had no convictions. He did have a reprimand for common assault. The pre-sentence report said D posed a high risk of harm to vulnerable women. Held. As the victim was particularly vulnerable, it was in Category 2B not 3B, so we start at 8 years not 6, making **6 years** not 4.

317.74   *Victim changes mind during intercourse*   *Pre-2014 guideline judicial guidance*
Example: *R v J* 2012 EWCA Crim 1008 (J aged 16. Victim aged 22. **4 years** would have been appropriate for an adult. With plea and age, 18 months' DTO.)

317.75   *Victim initially consents to sexual familiarity*   *Pre-2014 guideline judicial guidance*
R v Millberry 2002 EWCA Crim 2891, 2003 2 Cr App R (S) 31 (p 142) LCJ Where, for example, the victim has consented to sexual familiarity with the defendant on the occasion in question, but has said 'No' to sexual intercourse at the last moment, the

offender's culpability for rape is somewhat less than it would have been if he had intended to rape the victim from the outset. This is not to say that any responsibility for the rape attaches to the victim. It is simply to say that the offender's culpability is somewhat less than it otherwise would have been. The degree of the offender's culpability should be reflected in the sentence, but, given the inherent gravity of the offence of rape, the sentence adjustment in such a case should, we think, be relatively small.

R v Benney 2010 EWCA Crim 1288 D pleaded (full credit) to five counts of rape. V was D's wife, who had learning difficulties. V met D when she was aged 16 and they became friendly around the time of her 19th birthday. They moved in together and they were married when V was aged 19 and D was aged 52. They went on to have two children. V reported a number of acts of rape over a five-year period. V stated that after the birth of the first child, she became less inclined to sexual activity, whereas D remained very keen on an active sex life. Despite expressing a lack of interest, she did consent and tolerate such activity for much of the time, perhaps without giving much enthusiasm. D was arrested and bailed. He went to visit V's social worker and described instances where V had told D to get off her during sex and that he had not done so. D admitted rape. D said he had sought medical advice as to how to reduce his sex drive, to no avail. He stated that he had gone to see the social worker as it had been "eating him inside" and that he wanted it all out in the open. The social worker advised him to contact the police. She herself also contacted the police. They were then divorced. There was a letter from D's wife expressing some continuing affection for him and that she was rather lost in practical terms without him whilst caring for their young children. D was of good character and had a significant number of references. He entered pleas on the basis that: a) on five occasions during the marriage, D admitted that he carried on having sexual intercourse with his wife, after she told him to stop, having withdrawn her consent. Sexual intercourse had commenced on a consensual basis, b) on none of these occasions was there any anal intercourse, c) D could not remember any of the dates when these acts occurred, save that none occurred whilst on holiday, d) he has a high sex drive, e) prior to the birth of the children, he and his wife had an active sex life. It was accepted by the Crown specifically that there was consensual sexual intercourse taking place prior to the withdrawal of consent. Held. The appropriate starting point would have been 3 years, so with the plea and early admissions, 2 years on each count, concurrent.

Old case: *Att-Gen's Ref No 96 of 2006* 2006 EWCA Crim 3251, 2007 2 Cr App R (S) 30 (p 170) (Community order)

For a summary of the case, see the 7th edition of this book.

317.76 *Victim does not want the defendant sent to prison/Victim has forgiven him*
Domestic Violence Guideline 2006, see www.banksr.com Other Matters Guidelines tab para 4.1 As a matter of general principle, a sentence imposed for an offence of violence should be determined by the seriousness of the offence, not by the expressed wishes of the victim.

4.2 There are a number of reasons why it may be particularly important that this principle is observed in a case of domestic violence:

    it is undesirable that a victim should feel a responsibility for the sentence imposed;
    there is a risk that a plea for mercy made by a victim will be induced by threats made by, or by a fear of, the offender;
    the risk of such threats will be increased if it is generally believed that the severity of the sentence may be affected by the wishes of the victim.

4.3 Nonetheless, there may be circumstances in which the court can properly mitigate a sentence to give effect to the expressed wish of the victim that the relationship be permitted to continue. The court must, however, be confident that such a wish is genuine, and that giving effect to it will not expose the victim to a real risk of further violence. Critical conditions are likely to be the seriousness of the offence and the history of the relationship.

It is vitally important that the court has up-to-date information in a pre-sentence report and victim personal statement.

4.4 Either the offender or the victim (or both) may ask the court to take into consideration the interests of any children and to impose a less severe sentence. The court will wish to have regard not only to the effect on the children if the relationship is disrupted but also to the likely effect on the children of any further incidents of domestic violence.

R v Perks 2000 Crim LR 606 The opinions of the victim and the victim's close relatives on the appropriate level of sentence should not be taken into account except: a) where the sentence passed on the offender was aggravating the victim's distress, and b) where the victim's forgiveness or unwillingness to press charges provided evidence that his or her psychological or mental suffering must be very much less than would normally be the case.

Att-Gen's Ref No 38 of 2013 2013 EWCA Crim 1450 LCJ para 86 We must of course consider the harm done to victims, but victims do not and cannot decide sentences. We cannot have sentences which depend on whether a victim feels particularly vengeful, moderately vengeful, not vengeful at all, filled with mercy, or even, as some do, believes there should not be a prison sentence.

See also the **VICTIMS** chapter and in particular the *Views of the victims about the sentence* para at **121.13** in Volume 1.

317.77   Victim exposing herself to the risk of rape   Pre-2014 guideline judicial guidance

R v Billam 1986 82 Cr App R 347 LCJ Old guideline case. Victim exposing herself to a risk, e.g. accepting a lift, is not a mitigating factor.

Note: This is an old case, but the guidance seems obviously correct. Ed.

317.78   Victim's previous sexual experience   Pre-2014 guideline judicial guidance

R v Billam 1986 82 Cr App R 347 LCJ Old guideline case. Previous sexual experience is irrelevant.

317.79   Violence or threats of violence, Rapes with

'Violence or threats of violence (beyond that which is inherent in the offence)' is one of the factors in Category 2 when the reader is determining harm, see *Sexual Offences Guideline 2014* pages 10 and 14 at **317.5** (rape) and **317.8** (assault by penetration).

Att-Gen's Ref No 64 of 2014 2014 EWCA Crim 2050 D was convicted of assault by penetration. V was D's partner of 12 years and they had two children. However, the relationship had been on and off and blighted by domestic violence. V had reported the violence on four occasions. D and V went out for the night, having engaged in consensual sex. They consumed drugs and alcohol. On their return to a hotel, V angered D by blowing away some cocaine powder. As V climbed into bed, D pushed her to the floor and then tried to pull down her nightwear. V asked him to stop and D reacted by trying to force two fingers into her vagina. V called D "evil" to which he replied, "Evil. I'll show you fucking evil." D then proceeded to cover V's face and repeatedly forced his hand, in a fist, into her vagina with such force that it moved her entire body. V was in immediate pain and asked D to stop. She was so distressed that people next door heard and raised their concerns. D's violence caused a 10-12 cm tear in V's vagina, which bled considerably. Two hours later, D began to panic and, upset, purportedly threatened to kill himself. D phoned his mother, who later called the emergency services, and he also phoned for an ambulance five times. When the ambulance arrived an hour later, V had breathing problems and had lost two litres of blood. She underwent surgery, receiving the equivalent of ten stitches in one continuous stitch. She had a blood transfusion and was discharged the next day. She made a full recovery. D claimed V's injuries were suffered following "dirty sex" and he had stopped once V said it hurt and he realised she was bleeding. He made no comment in interview. Prior to trial, V changed her statement, saying it must have been accidental due to their intoxication. Her evidence at trial was that she had no recollection of the incident at all. D was aged 31 on appeal and had 14 convictions, including eight assaults. In 2012, he punched V leaving her needing eight stitches (ABH and 12 months' imprisonment). His last assault conviction was in 2013. Nonetheless, V said she did not wish D to go to prison and he was a good father. The Judge did not refer to the domestic violence guidelines but, placing the sexual assault into Category 2, noted that there was some abuse of trust as D had taken advantage of V's state. Held. In addition to the sexual offences guidelines, it is necessary to refer to the domestic violence guidelines. Those guidelines' principles and the victim's views are relevant generally, as was made clear in *Att-Gen's Ref No 38 of 2013* 2013 EWCA Crim 1450, para 86 (see **317.76**). In relation to domestic violence, particularly where there is a history of such conduct, such that the approach of a victim to an offender may well be a consequence of what has happened in the past, that approach is all the more important. In this case, it is beyond argument that this sentence fell well outside the bracket but the Judge effectively ignored not only the guidelines but also the overarching principles on domestic violence. We start at 8 years, so **7 years**, not 3½.

Post-2014 guideline case

R v Carroll 2014 EWCA Crim 2818, 2015 1 Cr App R (S) 54 (p 381) (Convicted. Strangled a prostitute and then left. She was badly traumatised. Extended sentence with a **12-year** not 15-year custodial term. For more detail, see **317.49**.)

317.80   Violence, Previous violence against victim

'Previous violence against victim' is one of the factors in Category 2 when the reader is determining the level of culpability, see *Sexual Offences Guideline 2014* pages 10 (rape) and 14 (assault by penetration), which are the same and are at **317.4**.

317.81   Violence, With   Serious injury caused   Starting point 18+ years   Pre-2014 guideline cases

R v Wilson 2009 EWCA Crim 999, 2010 1 Cr App R (S) 11 (p 56) LCJ D pleaded to attempted rape, wounding with intent and causing a person to engage in sexual activity. At about 10 pm, it appears that D targeted V, aged 71, at a bus stop. D boarded the same bus and then followed her. When V reached her front door, D grabbed her round the neck. He pointed a knife at her face. V was so terrified that she lost her voice. D called her a bitch and punched her repeatedly. He told her that if she screamed or shouted she would be killed. He forced her to handle his penis. He then told her to go on her knees so he could put his penis in her mouth. She was unable to do so and screamed. D punched her in the face. He cut her clothes off from the neck to the mid-body area with the knife. He insisted that she touched his penis, and she started to scream. D cut her face with the knife. She seized the knife and suffered a serious 10 cm laceration to her hand. D was then disturbed by two boys. V had a 5 cm cut to her cheek, bruising, black eyes, two smaller cuts and a fractured cheekbone. Five months later she suffered painful sensations in her fingers with restricted movement. She lived in fear. D was born in 1957 in the UK and emigrated to Australia as a boy. He had 75 convictions on 17 occasions. In 1985 he received 10 years for repeatedly raping an elderly lady in her home. When she was helpless he attacked her violently. Shortly after his release D attacked another elderly lady and beat her to death with his fists. He removed her clothing and left her naked body in a park. In 1992 he was sentenced to life. In 2008 he was released and deported back to the UK. He was monitored, given a home and showed every sign of co-operation. The latest attack occurred about three months after his arrival. The Judge said that D was exceptionally dangerous. Held. We agree. He is not to be re-sentenced for the earlier offences. Giving every allowance for his plea for what was a very strong case, we start at 20 years. So life with a minimum period of **10 years** not a whole life order. He may remain in prison for ever.

R v Baker 2014 EWCA Crim 242 LCJ D was convicted of rape. In 1997, V, then aged 66 and living alone, locked her front door and went to bed. Her friend, G, used to visit her frequently. V was cold and put on a number of layers that night, including thermal underwear. She woke at about 4.20 am and saw a man in her bedroom standing on a chair. She asked him what he was doing and he shouted at her not to look at him. He put blankets over her and began to hit her. He punched her in the face and chest before lifting her clothing and punching her bare stomach. He asked whether there was anyone else in the house. V replied that there was not. D said he would kill her if there was. D left the room briefly then returned, telling her if she did not give him some money he would kill her. He repeatedly asked for her PIN and said he knew that G gave her money from his business. D placed V on the floor kneeling against the bed. D pulled her trousers down and inserted his penis into her anus causing her considerable pain and distress. Immediately after the rape, she lost bowel and bladder control. D then 'shoved' V into a small cupboard and locked the cupboard from the outside. She remained there for many hours in acute discomfort. She had difficulty breathing and moving and thought she would die there. She was found in the early evening of the following day by G. V's face had been so badly beaten that she was unrecognisable to her son. She had a number of blunt trauma injuries, bruises and abrasions. At the first trial D was acquitted at the direction of the Judge, who ruled that a DNA sample which should have been destroyed, but was not, was inadmissible. That was challenged and the House of Lords ruled that the DNA evidence was admissible. Following the coming into force of CJA 2003 Part 10, a retrial became a possibility. Only after a BBC Panorama documentary and a Daily Mail article criticising the police for losing the relevant papers was a further investigation carried out. D was arrested and was aggressive to the female officer. He said he would "put [his] cock in her mouth and fuck her hard". A DNA sample was taken and compared to the semen taken from V's body. The chance of it originating from someone other than D was one in one billion. V had since died but her son spoke of how V had been frightened to return to her own home and that her life had been ruined. D was aged 56 at conviction and had 28 convictions for 49 offences. They included robbery, residential burglary, ABH and assaults on police. His last conviction was for affray in 2001. Held. The Judge referred to *R v Hodgson* 1968 52 Cr App R 113 and was entitled to come to the view that a **life sentence** was justified. This was an offence which called for a life sentence. There was gratuitous violence before the rape, with threats to kill, and there was gratuitous violence after the rape. The culpability and harm were very high indeed. The correct starting point was 20 years, not 24. With credit of 3 years (as given by the Judge for the delay and double jeopardy and the time spent on remand awaiting the first trial), **8½ years** not 10½ years **minimum** term.

317.82   *Vulnerable victim*
'Victim is particularly vulnerable due to personal circumstances' is one of the factors in Category 2 when the reader is determining harm, see *Sexual Offences Guideline 2014* pages 10 (rape) and 14 (assault by penetration), which are the same and are at **317.4**.
'Specific targeting of a particularly vulnerable victim' is one of the aggravating factors, see *Sexual Offences Guideline 2014* page 11 at **317.5** (rape) and page 15 at **317.8** (assault by penetration).

317.83   *Weapon or other item used to frighten or injure*
'Use of weapon to frighten or injure' is one of the aggravating factors, see *Sexual Offences Guideline 2014* page 11 at **317.5** (rape) and page 15 at **317.8** (assault by penetration).

Matters relating to the defendant
317.84   *Child contact arrangements, Exploiting*
'Exploiting contact arrangements with a child to commit an offence' is one of the 'other aggravating factors', see *Sexual Offences Guideline 2014* page 11 at **317.5** (rape) and page 15 at **317.8** (assault by penetration).

317.85   *Court orders, Failure to comply with current*
'Failure to comply with current court orders' is one of the 'other aggravating factors', see *Sexual Offences Guideline 2014* page 11 at **317.5** (rape) and page 15 at **317.8** (assault by penetration).

317.86   *Defendant aged under 18*
'Age and/or lack of maturity where it affects the responsibility of the offender' is one of the mitigating factors, see *Sexual Offences Guideline 2014* page 11 at **317.5** (rape) and page 15 at **317.8** (assault by penetration).
Note: The guideline only applies to offenders aged 18+, see page 7 of the guideline. For the usual practice, see **66.21** in Volume 1. It is understood that the Sentencing Council did not include full guidance about sentencing defendants aged under 18 as this will be dealt when the new Youths definitive guideline is published. Ed.
R v Asi-Akram 2005 EWCA Crim 1543, 2006 1 Cr App R (S) 47 (p 260) D pleaded to two counts of rape. He was aged 17 at the time of the offences. The Judge said that he was a very great danger to women and he looked like a 22-year-old. Held. These were among the very worst examples of this kind of offence. The observation in *R v Millberry* 2002 EWCA Crim 2891, 2003 2 Cr App R (S) 31 (p 142) that in rape cases the sentence for young offenders should be 'significantly shorter' admits of exceptions. This is not a case where the youth of the offender played a part in the offences.

317.87   *Defendant aged 10-14*
Att-Gen's Ref No 96 of 2009 2010 EWCA Crim 350 LCJ D was convicted of rape. D and V were aged 14. He pulled V, a virgin, to the floor, pulled her jeans and knickers down and penetrated her. D was educationally sub-normal with an IQ of 71 and mental problems. D had self-harmed on a number of occasions. The pre-sentence report said a custodial sentence could be extremely damaging to D. Eighteen months after the offence, the Judge made a **Youth Community Order**, with Intensive Supervision and Surveillance, curfew, tag and support. Held. This was a serious offence which had a severe impact on V. The Judge was right to say it is a very rare day when a person responsible for this offence was not sent to custody for a long period of years. The sentence was arguably unduly lenient but we do not alter it because the order was working very well and it was now two years after the offence.
R v B 2010 EWCA Crim 559 LCJ D, aged 11, pleaded to anal rape. V, a 9-year-old vulnerable, autistic boy was well known to D. After school, V knocked on D's door and wanted to play on D's Xbox. D said he would give him a game if he pulled his pants down. V did so and D turned him around, bent him over and ejaculated inside the boy's anus. It lasted about 15 seconds. V had asked him to stop because it hurt. V was very upset and crying. D accepted that his penis was between V's buttocks but denied anal penetration. D was physically well developed but his knowledge of right and wrong was less developed. D's father was murdered in Jamaica. His mother suffered from depression. His stepfather was involved in drug crime. D had problems containing his anger. At school and in a secure home there were serious concerns about D's violence. His period in a secure home had been beneficial but there had been incidents of acute violence by D. Two psychiatrists said he was: a) undoubtedly dangerous, b) there was a high risk of D offending against youngsters and causing serious harm to them, and c) D needed treatment and control. The Judge said that for an adult it would be 12 years. She halved that because of D's age and reduced that to **4½ years** because of the plea. She then **extended** the licence for 3½ years. Held. The Judge was entitled to consider D's other suggested sexual assaults on other youngsters to determine D's culpability. It was an important failure by D not to admit the penetration. The Judge was therefore entitled to give less credit for the plea. The sentence will benefit the public and him.
R v S 2012 EWCA Crim 2927 D pleaded to (presumably) rape (×2). D, aged 13, was in a park with his friend, F, who was of a similar age. V, aged 12, was also in the park with a friend. D and F spoke to V and her friend. A group of older children walked past and D

indicated to V that the group had a tendency to pick on him and that they should hide. D, F and V went into an area of long grass. D pulled V on top of him and tried to pull down her trousers. V pushed D off him and D gave her a 'love bite'. D proceeded to move with F and V further into the long grass and D once again tried to pull V's trousers down. She again resisted. She was on her knees, confused and began to panic. D then took his penis out of his trousers and, holding V's head, put his penis into her mouth. He moved her head backwards and forwards for about 20 seconds until he ejaculated into her mouth (count 1). He was laughing as he did so. He then persuaded F to do likewise. F did so for around 5 seconds and was unable to achieve an erection (count 2). D was aged 13 at the time and 14 when sentenced. Held. This was an extremely grave offence. Although no court likes to impose a sentence of this length on a boy of only 14, a lengthy period of detention was required for the protection of the public, bearing in mind the serious nature of these offences. **2½ years' detention** under section 91 upheld.

R v SC 2015 EWCA Crim 1960 D was convicted of rape, assault by penetration of a child aged under 13 and two sexual assaults on a child aged under 13. D and V were first cousins. When D was aged 14 and V aged 10, he was invited into V's home. He started behaving sexually towards V and rubbed his penis over her clothing and against her bottom, simulating sexual intercourse. V did not like it but did not report it, because she was scared of him. Five months later, when D was aged 15, he was invited to stay the night at V's house and asked V to repeat what he had done earlier. She declined and towards the end of the night the two were alone in the bedroom. He then asked for a cuddle and V agreed. D asked her whether she was a virgin. V said she was and D forced her legs apart and raped her. Immediately after he inserted her fingers into her vagina. The next day, in the kitchen, D asked V to do it again. D then dragged V into the utility room and placed her hand on the top of his penis. She pulled her hand away. V's mother said a taxi then arrived to take D away. The next day the rape was reported. A psychologist considered that D was nearly aged 16, but functioned closer to a nine or ten-year-old in academic and literacy attainments, in emotional matters and in social interactions. Further there were possible characteristics of an autistic spectrum disorder and indications of anxiety and attachment disorder. The report said D required substantial support to achieve his potential. The Judge sentenced the case as a breach of trust case. Held. It was not that. For the rape, 6 years' detention not 7½. Other sentences remained concurrent.

R v BK 2015 EWCA Crim 1987 D admitted four rapes committed when he was aged between 12 and 13 with V, his sister, who was then aged 10-11. V had suffered a brain injury which left her physically weak on her left side. She had difficulty concentrating and expressing herself. S and D lived with their father. D raped her orally and vaginally. It occurred in his bedroom and the activity was taking place over months. There was no coercion, but D did show V a pornographic video clip on his phone and told her not to tell anyone. D made admissions in his interview. He said he did not wear a condom and he ejaculated outside her body. D, now aged 14, had no findings of guilt. V showed no signs of distress or emotional reaction to the rapes. When he was sentenced she missed him. The pre-sentence report said he was extremely remorseful and lacked emotional security. Further D harboured feelings of anger against his absent mother. A psychological report said D had a disrupted upbringing with a lack of appropriate supervision and boundaries within the family. Also, D confused the sexual activity with his need for love and attachment. There was a risk of developing depression which required intervention. D would not function well in custody due to his vulnerabilities. The Judge accepted his vulnerability. She considered that the principal aim of youth sentencing was to prevent offending. For an adult she considered 18 years to be appropriate. With his age the Judge started at 7½ years, making 5 years with plea. Held. This was an unusual case. It did not 'fall within the rape guideline'. The Judge was wrong to consider it was an abuse of trust case. Nor can the showing of a pornographic video clip to S on just one occasion properly be said to amount to grooming behaviour. The offence was clearly serious and persistent. V was particularly vulnerable. The sexual activity was consensual. D was also particularly vulnerable. We apply *Youths Sentencing Guideline 2009* para 11.16: 'an offender aged 14 years or less should be sentenced to long term detention only where that is necessary for the protection of the public, either because of the risk of serious harm from future offending or because of the persistence of offending behaviour; exceptionally, such a sentence may be appropriate where an offender aged 14 years or less has committed a very serious offence but is not a persistent offender and there is no risk of serious harm from future offending'. The Judge made no such finding. These offences cannot be said to be so serious in themselves as to warrant section 91 detention for that reason, so the sentence was wrong in principle. D was a persistent offender so we substitute a **Youth Rehabilitation Order with Intense Supervision and Surveillance** with a curfew and tag.

See also: *R v JW* 2014 EWCA Crim 1407 (Plea. Five rapes of a child under 13. V was D's brother, three years younger than D. D raped V every two to three weeks. Both boys in foster care and autistic. V was an elective mute and D had Asperger's. D was obsessed with violence and death. D told social services about inappropriate touching, admitted rapes and how he was attracted to children. Aged 19, but offending occurred when he was aged 14 to 16. No convictions. D gained gratification from offending and the control he exerted but had had a significantly disturbed childhood. For an adult we would start at 18 years. With age etc. 10-11 years. 11 years' extended sentence (**7 years'** custody 4 years' extended licence) not excessive.)

Old cases: *R v G* 2009 EWCA Crim 265, 2 Cr App R (S) 77 (p 525) (**3 years**) *R v J* 2009 EWCA Crim 2108, 2010 1 Cr App R (S) 89 (p 580) (**6 years**) *Att-Gen's Ref No 67 of 2009* 2009 EWCA Crim 2221, 2010 1 Cr App R (S) 106 (p 676) (**12 months' YOI**) *R v C* 2009 EWCA Crim 2231, 2010 1 Cr App R (S) 98 (p 616) (**Supervision Order**) For a summary of the first three cases and older cases, see the 9th edition of this book.

Post-guideline case

R v E 2014 EWCA Crim 2655 D was convicted of two rapes (oral and vaginal), assault by penetration and an attempt of the same. V, aged 16, was D's brother's girlfriend. The offending occurred at V's family home, which D attended with a stash of drugs that he and a friend had found. D thought the drugs were Valium when in fact they were Phenazepam, a seductive hypnotic drug for anxiety. D and V took the drugs and D also smoked cannabis. That evening D's brother, V and D were upstairs and D was asked to leave. As he left, D asked V into the spare bedroom under the pretence of showing her something. Once there, D pinned V down on the bed and raped her vaginally. He was not wearing a condom and ejaculated. During the rape, D pretended he was his brother but V, despite being under the influence of drugs, knew otherwise. V then returned to her bedroom but was awoken by D putting his fingers in her vagina and attempting to do the same in her anus. V protested and D went to the door, as if to leave, then D returned to V and put his penis in her mouth. The next morning D, his brother and V were found asleep in the same bed. D left and wrote V a letter of apology, claiming his actions were due to Valium. D, aged 13, led a chaotic lifestyle with few boundaries and failed to attend school. He was subject to a referral order for robbery at the time and the pre-sentence report stated that he presented a high re-offending risk. D also wanted to get revenge on V because of her 'false' complaints. The Judge started at 15 years and halved it due to D's age. Held. We see nothing wrong with the Judge reflecting upon what sentence she might have imposed upon an adult to give her some guide...but this would have depended to some extend upon the age of the adult in question. Adopting a hypothetical age of 18-21, 15 years would have been too long. D was immature and undeveloped intellectually. **6 years' detention**, not 7½.

R v K 2014 EWCA Crim 2907 D was convicted of assault by penetration of a child and rape of a child. When he was aged 14, he met V, then aged 12, and he tried to kiss her. He then took her into an alleyway and put his hand in her knickers. Next he put his finger in her vagina and his penis into her anus. D touched her breasts under her clothes and attempted to lick her vagina. After that he inserted the tip of his penis into her vagina (the rape) and after pulling her hair attempted to force his penis into her mouth. At that point she managed to run away. V had a trace of blood in her knickers and some superficial wounds. In interview D lied. D was now aged 16½ years. He had findings of guilt for burglary and theft of a cycle. V had been badly affected by the attack. The Judge said 8 years was suitable for an adult and gave 4 years. Held. The Judge should have given a little more credit for D's [then] age and his lack of maturity. **3 years'** detention. See also: *R v BH* 2015 EWCA Crim 1289 (Convicted. Three rapes and other sex offences. Victim aged 6 to about 12. Defendant then aged 9-15. Now aged 22. At some stage sexual activity turned to rape. Mascara tube inserted. Threats made. **9 years** had a substantial discount.)

317.88   *Defendant aged 15-17   Post-2014 guideline cases*
R v SC 2015 EWCA Crim 1960 D was convicted of rape, assault by penetration of a child aged under 13 and two sexual assaults on a child aged under 13. D and V were first cousins. When D was aged 14 and V aged 10, he was invited into V's home. He started behaving sexually towards V and rubbed his penis over her clothing and against her bottom, simulating sexual intercourse. V did not like it but did not report it, because she was scared of him. Five months later, when D was aged 15, he was invited to stay the night at V's house and asked V to repeat what he had done earlier. She declined and towards the end of the night the two were alone in the bedroom. He then asked for a cuddle and V agreed. D asked her whether she was a virgin. V said she was and D forced her legs apart and raped her. Immediately after he inserted her fingers into her vagina. The next day, in the kitchen, D asked V to do it again. D then dragged V into the utility room and placed her hand on the top of his penis. She pulled her hand away. V's mother said a taxi then arrived to take D away. The next day the rape was reported. A psychologist considered that D was nearly aged 16, but functioned closer to a nine or ten-year-old in academic and literacy attainments, in emotional matters and in social interactions. Further there were possible characteristics of an autistic spectrum disorder and indications of anxiety and attachment disorder. The report said D required substantial support to achieve his potential. The Judge sentenced the case as a breach of trust case. Held. It was not that. For the rape, **6 years'** detention not 7½. Other sentences remained concurrent.
See also: *R v W* 2015 EWCA Crim 1021 (Convicted. W and victim, V, both aged 16. W took down her jeans and knickers when V was asleep. V found wet ejaculate between her legs. W apologised. Relationship continued, then broke up. V reported it. Starting point 5 years. With W's age and his good character, **2½ years**, not 3½.)

317.89   *Good character, Defendant has*
'No previous convictions or no relevant/recent convictions' and 'Previous good character and/or exemplary conduct*' are two of the mitigating factors, see *Sexual Offences Guideline 2014* page 11 at **317.5** (rape) and page 15 at **317.8** (assault by penetration).
*Previous good character/exemplary conduct is different from having no previous convictions. The more serious the offence, the less the weight which should normally be attributed to this factor. Where previous good character/exemplary conduct has been used to facilitate the offence, this mitigation should not normally be allowed and such conduct may constitute an aggravating factor. In the context of this offence, previous good character/exemplary conduct should not normally be given any significant weight and will not normally justify a reduction in what would otherwise be the appropriate sentence.
R v Millberry 2002 EWCA Crim 2891, 2003 2 Cr App R (S) 31 (p 142) para 29 Old guideline case LCJ While the fact that an offender has previous convictions for sexual or violent offences can be a significant aggravating factor, the defendant's good character, although it should not be ignored, does not justify a substantial reduction of what would otherwise be the appropriate sentence.

Note: This is an old guideline case, but the principle seems to apply today. Ed.

317.90 *Licence   Offence committed whilst on licence*
'Offence committed whilst on licence' is one of the aggravating factors, see *Sexual Offences Guideline 2014* page 11 at **317.5** (rape) and page 15 at **317.8** (assault by penetration).

317.91 *Mental disorder or learning disability, Defendant has*
'Mental disorder or learning disability, particularly where linked to the commission of the offence' is one of the mitigating factors, see *Sexual Offences Guideline 2014* page 11 at **317.5** (rape) and page 15 at **317.8** (assault by penetration).
Persistent offenders see the *Previous convictions, Defendant has* para at **317.92** below.

317.92 *Previous convictions, Defendant has*
'Previous convictions, having regard to: a) the nature of the offence to which the conviction relates and its relevance to the current offence, and b) the time that has elapsed since the conviction' is a statutory aggravating factor, see *Sexual Offences Guideline 2014* page 11 at **317.5** (rape) and page 15 at **317.8** (assault by penetration). See also the **PREVIOUS CONVICTIONS** chapter.

317.93 *Remorse*
'Remorse' is one of the mitigating factors, see *Sexual Offences Guideline 2014* page 11 at **317.5** (rape) and page 15 at **317.8** (assault by penetration).

317.94 *Sexually transmitted disease, Defendant has*
Sexual Offences Act 2003 Guideline 2007, see www.banksr.com Other Matters Guidelines tab page 23 para 2A.2 The sentencing starting points established in *R v Millberry* 2002 EWCA Crim 2891, 2003 2 Cr App R (S) 31 (p 142) should apply to all non-consensual offences involving penetration of the anus or vagina or penile penetration of the mouth. The existence of aggravating factors may significantly increase the sentence.
R v Millberry 2002 EWCA Crim 2891, 2003 2 Cr App R (S) 31 (p 142) LCJ Guideline case The **8-year** starting point is appropriate after a contested trial for rape by a man who is knowingly suffering from a life-threatening sexually transmissible disease, whether or not he has told the victim of his condition and whether or not the disease was actually transmitted. The 8-year starting point is recommended either because of the impact of the offence upon the victim or the level of the offender's culpability, or both. The Panel adds that factors reflecting a high level of risk to society, in particular evidence of repeat offending, will indicate a substantially longer sentence. The seven grounds for raising the starting point to 8 years each can vary in gravity. In a really bad case it can mean that a higher figure is appropriate.
Note: This guidance has been replaced by the *Sexual Offences Guideline 2014*. The starting points should be ignored. However, if the defendant is suffering from a life-threatening sexual disease, that would be an obvious aggravating factor. Ed.

318   RETAIL OFFENCES
318.1
1) Copyright, Designs and Patents Act 1988 s 107 and 198. For more detail, see **318.2**.
   Modes of trial and maximum sentences
   For sections 107(1)(a), (b), (d)(iv) and (e) and 198(1)(a), (b) and (d)(iii) Triable either way. On indictment 10 years. Summary 6 months and/or a £5,000 fine
   For sections 107(2A) and 198(1A) offences Triable either way. On indictment 2 years. Summary 6 months and/or a £5,000 fine
   Otherwise summary only. Maximum 3 months[928] and/or a £5,000 fine. For section 107 offences, 6 months for section 198 offences and/or a £5,000 fine

---

[928] Penalty altered for section 107 offences by Copyright, Designs and Patents Act 1988 (Amendment) Regulations 2010 2010/2694 reg 5 from 1/1/11

2) Trade Marks Act 1994 s 92 (unauthorised use of a trademark etc. in the course of business etc.)
Mode of trial Triable either way
Maximum sentence On indictment 10 years. Summary 6 months and/or a £5,000 fine
3) Consumer Protection from Unfair Trading Regulations 2008 2008/1277 reg 8-13 (engaging in an unfair commercial practice, misleading actions under regulation 5, aggressive commercial practice etc.)
Mode of trial Triable either way
Maximum sentence On indictment 2 years. Summary a £5,000 fine[929]

Confiscation Where a defendant has a criminal lifestyle the court, once the confiscation proceedings are triggered (see **22.8** in Volume 1), <u>must</u> follow the Proceeds of Crime Act 2002 procedure. 'Criminal lifestyle' offences include Copyright, Designs and Patents Act 1988 s 107(1)-(2) 198(1) and 297A and Trade Marks Act 1994 s 91(1)-(3) offences.[930] For what constitutes a criminal lifestyle, see **22.43**.

Serious Crime Prevention Orders For Copyright, Designs and Patents Act 1988 s 107(1)(a), (b), (d)(iv) and (e), 198(1)(a), (b), (d)(iii) and 297A and Trade Marks Act 1994 s 92(1)-(3) offences there is a discretionary power to make this order, when it would protect the public etc.[931]

For offences of misusing medicine trademarks etc., see the **MEDICINE OFFENCES** chapter.

318.2   *Copyright offences*

Copyright, Designs and Patents Act 1988 s 107(1) A person commits an offence who, without the licence of the copyright owner:
  a) makes for sale or hire, or
  b) imports into the United Kingdom otherwise than for his private and domestic use, or
  c) possesses in the course of a business with a view to committing any act infringing the copyright, or
  d) in the course of a business:
     i) sells or lets for hire, or
     ii) offers or exposes for sale or hire, or
     iii) exhibits in public, or
     iv) distributes, or
  e) distributes otherwise than in the course of a business to such an extent as to affect prejudicially the owner of the copyright,
an article which is, and which he knows or has reason to believe is, an infringing copy of a copyright work.
(2) A person commits an offence who:
  a) makes an article specifically designed or adapted for making copies of a particular copyright work, or
  b) has such an article in his possession,
knowing or having reason to believe that it is to be used to make infringing copies for sale or hire or for use in the course of a business.
(2A) A person who infringes copyright in a work by communicating the work to the public:
  a) in the course of a business, or
  b) otherwise than in the course of a business to such an extent as to affect prejudicially the owner of the copyright,

---

[929] When Legal Aid, Sentencing and Punishment of Offenders Act 2012 s 85 is in force, the summary fines will be unlimited.
[930] Proceeds of Crime Act 2002 s 6 and 75 and Sch 2 para 7
[931] Serious Crime Act 2007 s 1 and Sch 1 para 12

commits an offence if he knows or has reason to believe that, by doing so, he is infringing copyright in that work.

Copyright, Designs and Patents Act 1988 s 198(1) A person commits an offence who without sufficient consent:

a) makes for sale or hire, or

b) imports into the United Kingdom otherwise than for his private and domestic use, or

c) possesses in the course of a business with a view to committing any act infringing the rights conferred by this chapter, or

d) in the course of a business:
   i) sells or lets for hire, or
   ii) offers or exposes for sale or hire, or
   iii) distributes,

a recording which is, and which he knows or has reason to believe is, an illicit recording.

(1A) A person who infringes a performer's making available right:

a) in the course of a business, or

b) otherwise than in the course of a business to such an extent as to affect prejudicially the owner of the making available right,

commits an offence if he knows or has reason to believe that, by doing so, he is infringing the making available right in the recording.

318.3   *Crown Court statistics   England and Wales*
Trade Descriptions Act and similar offences Aged 21+

Year	Plea	Total sentenced	Type of sentencing %						Average length of custody in months
			Discharge	Fine	Community sentence	Suspended sentence	Custody	Other	
2013	G	184	3.3	3.8	26.1	37.0	29.3	0.5	11.0
	NG	30	6.7	23.3	13.3	40.0	13.3	3.3	20.0
2014	G	168	8	7	17	43	25	–	12.7
	NG	19	–	5	16	58	21	–	20.8

For explanations about the statistics, see page 1-xii. For statistics for male and female defendants and defendants aged under 21, see www.banksr.com Other Matters Statistics tab

318.4   *Trade Marks   Judicial guidance*
R v Ansari 2000 1 Cr App R (S) 94 Trade mark offences undermine reputable companies. The sentencer should consider how professional the enterprise was and the likely or actual profits made.

R v Woolridge 2005 EWCA Crim 1086, 2006 1 Cr App R (S) 13 (p 72) Sentences imposed for trade mark offences have to contain some element of deterrence, especially as trade mark offences are often difficult, time-consuming and expensive to detect. Courts have the duty to protect the owners of trade marks and this means frequently sentencing offenders to prison. A useful starting point is *R v Kemp* 1995 16 Cr App R (S) 941 where it was said offences of counterfeiting normally attract at least a short sentence of imprisonment.

R v Lee 2010 EWCA Crim 268 D pleaded to seven counts of unauthorised use of a trade mark. Held. The offences are difficult to detect, time-consuming to investigate, and expensive to bring to court. The Court had a duty to protect the owners of trade marks and their employees. There had to be an element of deterrence. For more details see **318.10**.

R v Brayford 2010 EWCA Crim 2329 Sentencers should bear in mind the guidance in *R v Yanko* 1996 1 Cr App R (S) 217. The considerations are: a) the fact that the offence undermines reputable companies, b) how professional the enterprise was, and c) the likely or actual profit made from the enterprise.

R v Manders 2012 EWCA Crim 908, 2013 1 Cr App R (S) 13 (p 73) D pleaded to 14 trade mark offences. He set up a small factory producing counterfeit DVDs. Held. A deterrent sentence has to be imposed for this type of offending.

318.5   *Car dealers*

R v Bettridge 2010 EWCA Crim 41 D was convicted of applying a false trade description and supplying a dangerous product. D was a motor trader. D advertised a vehicle as a 'lovely car'. On driving the vehicle away the purchaser, an elderly disabled man, noticed vibration above certain speeds. It was discovered the car had previously been in an accident. D sold another car and told the purchaser that the vehicle had not been involved in an accident when in fact it had. D, aged 56, had no convictions, had traded as a motor trader for approximately 25 years and suffered from long-standing depression. **2 months** not 4.

See also: *R v Dutton-Woolley* 2009 EWCA Crim 811 (Claiming an amphibious vehicle was fit for fare-paying passengers on land and water. Aged 60. No previous offences. 6 months suspended was wrong. **150 hours' unpaid work** would have been suitable.)

Old case: *R v Richards and Evans* 2004 EWCA Crim 192, 2 Cr App R (S) 51 (p 264) (**2-year conditional discharge** with compensation orders.)

318.6   *Clamping, Unlicensed*

Example: *R v Rice* 2013 EWCA Crim 2670 (Late plea to acquiring criminal property. Director of a security firm operating unlicensed wheel clamping organisation using unlicensed operatives. Licensing authority became involved. Resigned and used others' names as they had no convictions. £516,000 made over six years without a licence. Aged 42 at appeal. Previous convictions for handling stolen goods (1990 and 2000). No remorse. The licence offence provided the means of acquiring the proceeds of crime. Professionally planned, significant period, fraudulent from the outset. Otherwise an efficient business. With 10% credit, **27 months** was not in any way manifestly excessive.)

318.7   *Consumer protection offences*

R v Garfoot and Wilsher 2011 EWCA Crim 2043 G pleaded (early) and W pleaded to fraud and Consumer Protection Regulations offences. W ran a business in the building trade. G, a labourer, was his employee. W was a traveller and lived in a caravan park. He did not want customers to discover his true address and so used G's address on flyers bearing the company name. G, who was of large stature, approached V, a woman in her eighties, and stated he could do some work on her drive. A price was agreed and work began immediately. There was no cooling-off period as prescribed by law, nor were there any terms and conditions or an estimate or price breakdown. G then convinced V that further work costing £6,000 was required. W was involved in another incident in similar circumstances. £5,500 was requested following a payment of £2,000. G demonstrated some concern for V. Neither defendant had relevant convictions. Held. There were unscrupulous and high-pressure business techniques applied. G played a lesser role and taking into account his personal mitigation, **3 months** not 6 was appropriate. W was persistent and forceful if not downright bullying. W had had two previous warnings about his trade practices. There were two victims who were vulnerable. However, the Judge did not adhere to the basis of plea that the work was not shoddy, so **8 months** not 10.

R v Hamilton 2015 EWCA Crim 278 D pleaded (full credit) to engaging in a commercial practice contravening the requirement of due diligence contrary to Consumer Protection from Unfair Trading Regulations 2008 2008/1277. V1 and V2, a couple aged 84 and 68 respectively, wanted a dividing wall in their house. D, describing himself as a builder and competent bricklayer, quoted them £800, a figure that was subsequently raised to £2,000. He asked for £500 on account and then a further £800, on top of the £2,000, and all was paid. A surveyor, asked by V2 to inspect D's work, concluded that two lintels were inadequate and badly inserted and that D's bricklaying was poor. The estimated cost of properly done work was £1,200 but it would cost £2,600 to put D's mistakes right. D was aged 28 on appeal with low-level public order convictions but he asserted he had done a good job. Held. Although a custodial sentence was justified, it would have been appropriate to suspend it. **12 weeks suspended for 1 year**, not immediate.

See also: *R v Kayani* 2014 EWCA Crim 2635 (Four offences under Consumer Protection from Unfair Trading Regs 2008 2008/1277 and General Product Safety Regs 2005. Convicted. Used car dealer sold two cars damaged in accidents which were in a defective condition. Described as 'immaculate'. One car illegal and dangerous. Defendant had serious health problems and was carer to parents. Without that the **12 months** was correct. With that we substitute 6 months.)

Credit card fraud Guideline see the *Identity fraud* para at **265.37**.

See also the THEFT *Credit card offences* para at **346.16**.

Dishonesty offences Where the offence is in essence theft, the case is listed in the THEFT ETC. chapter.

318.8 Credit offences

R v Dixon 2012 EWCA Crim 815, 2 Cr App R (S) 100 (p 589) D pleaded to eight counts of engaging in a consumer credit business without a licence. Over a period of 7½ years, D engaged in lending substantial sums of money to individuals whom she knew. She had no licence. She had loaned out about £400,000, in amounts from £50 to £30,000. When police searched D's address, they found £9,000, short loan agreements and loan books containing the personal accounts of the borrowers. It was a well-organised and lucrative illegal money-lending operation. D did not inform the borrowers that the APR rates were between 1,300 and 1,700%. Large charges were levied against borrowers who missed repayments, in addition to threats made by D against those who did so. To ensure that regular payments were made, D took borrowers' bank cards and PINs. Although D pleaded, it was apparent in the pre-sentence report that her pleas were as a result of legal advice to that effect, as opposed to an acceptance of responsibility. D, aged 35 at appeal, was of positive good character. D was a single parent and sole carer for two young children, and D was receiving treatment for depression. Held. Although D's case was serious, it lacked many features of an aggressive loan shark. With the mitigation, 3 years was the starting point. With the plea, **2 years** not 3 years 9 months.

318.9 Trade Marks Magistrates' Court Sentencing Guidelines

Magistrates' Court Sentencing Guidelines 2008, see www.banksr.com Other Matters Guidelines tab page 105 The guidelines apply to the Magistrates' Court and to the Crown Court hearing appeals or sentencing for summary only offences.[932]

Unauthorised use of trademark

Starting points are based on a first-time offender pleading not guilty.

Examples of nature of activity	Starting point	Range
Small number of counterfeit items	Band C fine	Band B fine to low-level community order
Larger number of counterfeit items but no involvement in wider operation	Medium-level community order, plus fine[933]	Low-level community order to 12 weeks' custody, plus fine[934]

---

[932] See page 15 of the guidelines.
[933] This may be an offence for which it is suitable to combine a fine with a community order.
[934] This may be an offence for which it is suitable to combine a fine with a community order.

Examples of nature of activity	Starting point	Range
High number of counterfeit items or involvement in wider operation e.g. manufacture or distribution	12 weeks' custody	6 weeks' custody to Crown Court
Central role in large-scale operation	Crown Court	Crown Court

The following aggravating and mitigating factors may be particularly relevant: Factors indicating higher culpability: 1 High degree of professionalism 2 High level of profit. Factor indicating lower culpability: Mistake or ignorance about provenance of goods. Factor indicating greater degree of harm: Purchasers at risk of harm e.g. from counterfeit drugs.

Consider ordering compensation, forfeiture and destruction of the goods.

A Band A fine is 50% of net weekly income. Band B is 100% and Band C is 150%. For more detail, see **60.27** in Volume 1.

For the meaning of a high-level, a medium-level and a low-level community order see **16.13-16.14** in Volume 1.

For how to apply the guidelines, see the GUIDELINES chapter in Volume 1.

318.10   Trade Marks   Distributing articles in breach of copyright or with false trademarks

R v Lee 2010 EWCA Crim 268 D pleaded (full credit) to seven counts of unauthorised use of a trade mark which were specimen counts. Over two years he purchased counterfeit golfing goods from China and sold them on eBay, and 874 such items were found at his home address. D used a large number of e-mail accounts to conceal his identity. An e-mail was found saying that he normally ordered between $5,000 and $6,000 worth a month. The benefit for confiscation was assessed as £105,000, based on sales. D was aged 55 and of good character. He had been warned by Customs that counterfeit items had been intercepted, and eBay had also warned him. The offending started after he was made redundant. The Judge found that the activity was organised and well researched. Held. There was a persistent and deliberate attempt to hide his identity. The failure to heed the warnings weighs particularly heavily with the Court. **21 months** not 30.

R v Gill 2010 EWCA Crim 324 D pleaded to eight offences of unauthorised application of a trade mark and eight offences of conniving at the possession of a trade mark. He started up a legitimate business and then involved himself in the manufacture of counterfeit designer labels for clothing. Workers made up fake goods, and when his premises were searched 3,000 garments and 6,000 false labels were found. There were also false 'swing' labels and certificates of authenticity. D was aged 54 with one entirely different and exceptionally serious conviction. He was in poor health and was a highly respected member of the local Sikh community. D had carried out a significant amount of charity work and cared for a son with special needs. There was also significant delay. Held. Legitimate businesses are cheated of profits after their investment in design and marketing. After a trial it would be 18 months, so **12 months** not 33.

R v McFarlane 2010 EWCA Crim 1170 D was convicted of conspiracy to sell goods to which a sign identical to or likely to be mistaken for a registered trade mark had been applied. D was involved in a large conspiracy to sell counterfeit clothing on eBay between 2004 and 2007. A search of D's house revealed photographs and descriptions of the counterfeit clothing stored on a computer data stick. D was involved in over 1,700 transactions and over £43,000 was paid into his bank account. D, aged 24, had no convictions. The pre-sentence report said D expressed a high degree of remorse but remained adamant that he was unaware of the criminality of his involvement. The Judge said dealing in such counterfeit goods was effectively stealing from the rightful owners of the brand concerned. Held. This was a substantial, sophisticated conspiracy. **15 months** was not wrong.

318.11   Trade Marks   Making copies in breach of copyright or with false trade marks or descriptions

R v Sheikh and Sheikh 2010 EWCA Crim 921 R and S were convicted of three counts of conspiracy to contravene trade mark and copyright law and money laundering. R and S were brothers and directors of a family-run business by the name of Samrana which was concerned in the production and retail of counterfeit DVDs. Samrana purchased specialised industrial replication machinery which would enable the company to produce hundreds of thousands, if not millions, of DVDs of a significantly higher quality at a cost of over $1m HK. That plant, machinery and raw materials included 1.5 tons of polycarbon resin, the main material from which DVDs are made. A number of counterfeiting factories were found to have links to Samrana, including one of the largest DVD factories yet found in the UK. A search of R's and S's home revealed over £100,000, counterfeit DVDs and other materials. Both R, now aged 27, and S, now aged 29, were of good character. Neither showed any remorse. Held. This was an enduring fraud on a significant scale. The dishonest activity continued over a number of years and it only ceased on detection, R and S were the guiding lights of the operation, the scheme crossed international boundaries, it involved huge gains for the perpetrators but commensurate losses for others, and exploited vulnerable people. **6 years** was justified. 10 years' disqualification for acting as a company director was deservedly severe.

R v Nimley 2010 EWCA Crim 2752 D pleaded to 10 counts relating to fraud and copyright infringement. When viewing films at a cinema, he recorded three films (and was arrested filming the fourth) on his iPhone. He then uploaded the three films to a free-to-view website. He received no remuneration. He initially denied the offences, prior to his computer being examined. The Judge described the offence as deliberately planned and executed. D had a conviction for theft from his employer. A report stated that he committed the offences to gain status with friends and that whilst he realised he was committing an offence, he did not properly consider the consequences. Held. The dissemination of the illegal copy is truly international, being downloaded and posted on other websites. D did not show particular remorse. D had served 2 months in prison. **Community orders** with 120 hours unpaid work, not 6 months.

R v Manders 2012 EWCA Crim 908, 2013 1 Cr App R (S) 13 (p 73) D pleaded (10% credit) to 14 trade mark offences. D lost his job and set up a small factory in his house producing counterfeit DVDs. 32,000 counterfeit films, music and games were found. Computer hard drives to manufacture computer discs, seven DVD writing machines, printers and scanners for packaging discs, blank DVDs and boxes and bags for packaging were found. There was a list of potential customers including those who were going to sell the products at car boot sales. D was aged 39 and a rehabilitated person with a raft of references. Held. The aggravating factors were the professional nature of the operation and the wholesale selling. There were no grounds to interfere with 2 years. Old cases: *R v Hatton* 2007 EWCA Crim 1860, 2008 1 Cr App R (S) 74 (p 429) (**18 months**)

For a summary of the case, see the 8th edition of this book.

318.12   Trade Marks   Retailers/Wholesalers

R v Khan and Others 2013 EWCA Crim 802 YK, AK, YL and IK pleaded (all late) to conspiracy to sell etc. goods with unauthorised trademarks. Dollar Designs, a company, was involved in selling counterfeit clothing and footwear bearing the labels of 22 household names such as Nike and Hugo Boss. IK was the directing mind, setting up and running the day-to-day operation. His basis of plea was that the customers knew the items were fake and the profit margin was 25%. YL was in day-to-day charge of running the shop which sold the goods. He was the manager of one shop for three months and earned £170 per week. AK was the tenant of the flat above the shop and allowed the others to store the counterfeit goods there. YK was a trusted helper and would open up the shop and deal with customers. His basis was that he only helped out on the day he was arrested. Over three premises, 1,700 counterfeit items were recovered, representing an estimated loss of £70,000 (the court expressed some concern over the reliability of the £70,000 figure. Ed.) IK was of good character. YL had eight previous convictions largely for drugs and road traffic offences. AK was of good character. YK had two convictions for burglary and attempted robbery. Held. This was a fairly professional operation and over a period of six months, the profits would not have been insubstantial. There was clearly a need for deterrence and immediate custody was inevitable. For IK, **18 months** not 2 years. For YL, **12 months** not 18. For AK and YK, **8 months** not 15 months and 12 months respectively.

See also: *R v Brayford* 2010 EWCA Crim 2329 (Convicted of trade mark offence. 25,000 kilos bearing the mark 'Persil'. Premises were raided. D was high up in the hierarchy, having dealt with the suppliers in China. **2 years** was not manifestly excessive.)

R v Guest 2013 EWCA Crim 1437 (Pleas to ten trade mark offences. Nine computers sold which had fake or unauthorised Microsoft software on them. The loss to one purchaser was £420. The loss to Microsoft was £200-£385 per copy. Aged 67. Retired. Made bankrupt. Extremely frank about his offending. Had recently moved into sheltered accommodated with his 74-year-old wife. Full credit. **4 months** not 6, which should enable release shortly after the appeal.)

See also the **FRAUD AND FINANCIAL SERVICES OFFENCES** *Confidence frauds Commercial suppliers* para at **265.30**.

318.13   *Trading without a licence*

R v Dixon 2012 EWCA Crim 815, 2 Cr App R (S) 100 (p 589) D pleaded to eight counts of engaging in a consumer credit business without a licence. Over a period of 7½ years, D engaged in lending substantial sums of money to individuals whom she knew. She had no licence. She had loaned out about £400,000, in amounts from £50 to £30,000. When police searched D's address, they found £9,000, short loan agreements and loan books containing the personal accounts of the borrowers. It was a well-organised and lucrative illegal money-lending operation. D did not inform the borrowers that the APR rates were between 1,300 and 1,700%. Large charges were levied against borrowers who missed repayments, in addition to threats made by D against those who did so. To ensure that regular payments were made, D took borrowers' bank cards and PINs. Although D pleaded, it was apparent in the pre-sentence report that her pleas were as a result of legal advice to that effect, as opposed to an acceptance of responsibility. D, aged 35 at appeal, was of positive good character. D was a single parent and sole carer for two young children, and D was receiving treatment for depression. Held. Although D's case was serious, it lacked many features of an aggressive loan shark. With the mitigation, 3 years was the starting point. With the plea, **2 years** not 45 months.

318.14   *Unfair commercial practices*

R v Connolly 2012 EWCA Crim 477 D pleaded on rearraignment to engaging in an unfair commercial practice (×2) and engaging in aggressive commercial practice. He also pleaded to breach of a conditional discharge, imposed in 2010 for engaging in an unfair commercial practice. D was the director of a company in the business of replacement windows and doors. On two occasions, there were disputes with clients over the nature or quality of the work provided. The customers disputed the amount to be paid. D instructed his employees to remove the windows of one, and the door and door frame of another, unless the customers paid the invoice in full. Both duly paid. Complaints were made to Trading Standards. The defence said in the end the work was done satisfactorily. In advertisements, D's company used words which they were not authorised to use. Held. D had a warning when the conditional discharge was imposed and chose to continue with objectionable practices. The Judge did not err in imposing a director's disqualification, nor did he err in imposing immediate custody. The total sentence has to be considered in the light of four offences. **5 months'** custody in total and **5-year director's disqualification** was tough and intentionally so.

See also **FRAUD AND FINANCIAL SERVICES OFFENCES** chapter.

319   RIOT

319.1
Public Order Act 1986 s 1
Mode of trial Indictable only
Maximum sentence 10 years[935]
Extended sentences Public Order Act 1986 s 1 is listed in Criminal Justice Act 2003 Sch 15. The court may pass a 2012 extended sentence (EDS) if there is a significant risk of serious harm from future specified offences and either: a) the defendant has a Criminal Justice Act 2003 Sch 15B conviction (applicable only to defendants aged 18+), or b) the offence would justify a determinate sentence of at least 4 years.[936]
Sexual Harm Prevention Orders There is a discretionary power to make this order when it is necessary to protect the public from sexual harm.[937]

319.2   *Crown Court statistics   England and Wales*

Riot Aged 21+

	2009	2010	2011	2012	2013	2014
Pleas	0	0	1	14	0	0
Convicted	9	0	0	3	0	0
Average custody	72 months		48 months	49 months		

For explanations about the statistics, see page 1-xii. For more statistics, see www.banksr. com Other Matters Statistics tab

319.3   *Judicial guidance*
R v Tyler 1993 96 Cr App R (S) 332 Two defendants were convicted of riot and two offences of violent disorder. After a poll tax demonstration, buildings were damaged and police attacked. Held. It is not the individual act that is the essence of the offence here. It is the use of violence in circumstances where so many people are present as to cause or inspire fear in the general public. One must look at the individual act in the context of that fear. When it occurs in a busy street the dangers are obvious.
Note: This is an old case, but this approach was affirmed by the Lord Chief Justice in *R v Blackshaw and Others* 2011 EWCA Crim 2312. The Court considered the appeals against the sentences imposed for burglary committed during, and as a part of, widespread public disorder. The Court said, "Those who deliberately participate in disturbances of this magnitude, causing injury and damage and fear to even the most stout-hearted of citizens, and who individually commit further crimes during the course of the riots, are committing aggravated crimes...It is a wholly wrong approach to take the acts of any individual participator in isolation", *R v Caird* 1970 54 Cr App R 499. The imposition of severe sentences, intended to provide both punishment and deterrence, must follow. Ed.
R v Chapman 2002 EWCA Crim 2346 There was a full-scale riot which lasted 12 hours. The presiding Judge issued a policy for those being sentenced for the riot. Judges must regard the total picture and the individual's specific acts. The specific acts cannot be regarded in isolation. The court must regard the level and nature of the violence used, the scale of the riot, the extent to which it is premeditated, the number of persons engaged [in the riot] and [all] in the context of the overall picture and the specific acts of the individual defendant. I hope that this message will deter others from engaging in this type of behaviour. Held. We wholeheartedly endorse this and adopt it.

---

[935] Public Order Act 1986 s 1 (6)
[936] Criminal Justice Act 2003 s 226A-226B as inserted by Legal Aid, Sentencing and Punishment of Offenders Act 2012 s 124
[937] Sexual Offences Act 2003 s 103A as inserted by Anti-social Behaviour, Crime and Policing Act 2014 Sch 5 para 2 and Sexual Offences Act 2003 Sch 5

R v Najeeb and Others 2003 EWCA Crim 194, 2 Cr App R (S) 69 (p 408) The defendants pleaded to riot. Held. The authorities stress the importance of the distinction between riots that are premeditated and planned and those that are spontaneous. Deterrent sentences were called for so good character and personal mitigation were of comparatively little weight. If any ringleader had been convicted we would have expected a sentence at or near the statutory maximum of **10 years**. A persistent participant who threw petrol bombs or used a crossbow or drove a car at police if convicted would receive between **8 and 9 years**. Those who participated over a number of hours and threw missiles more dangerous than stones, like gas cylinders, knives, fences or poles or who set fire to cars, would receive after a trial **6-7 years**. Those present for a significant period repeatedly throwing missiles like bricks and stones would expect after a trial **5 years**. Lesser degrees of participation would, we would have expected, attract sentences at a lower level.
Note: For details of this case, see **319.4** below. Ed.

319.4   *Cases*

R v Najeeb and Others 2003 EWCA Crim 194, 2 Cr App R (S) 69 (p 408) The defendants N, Q, M, R, Al, P, L, Az, H, Ha, Qu, K, Kh and Ra pleaded to riot at the first opportunity. There was a disturbance in Oldham. A month and a half later there was another in Burnley, which was held to be a racist attack on Asians. Two weeks later, the leader of the BNP made a speech in Bradford. The City Council cancelled a festival planned for the next day. The Anti-Nazi League assembled in Bradford in response to an assembly by the National Front party which the police had banned. The Asian community was concerned about the need to defend itself. By 2 pm serious disorder broke out between rival Asian and white males. Arrests were made and Asian youths threw missiles, smashing windows. Then the police were targeted. A white man seriously stabbed an Asian male. Asian males were running amok carrying sticks and baseball bats which were used against pubs and shops. Police decided to drive the youths out of the city centre to prevent destruction. As they were pushed back, premises were attacked with stones and petrol bombs etc. Two police horses were stabbed and the police, who were heavily outnumbered, were attacked with metal fencing and a crossbow. Two garages were completely gutted. Stolen cars were set alight and driven at the police. Four hundred police attended from different forces. Three hundred police were injured. Businesses were ruined and £27m worth of damage caused. The prosecution relied on video evidence. Held. The origin of this riot began in fear. This riot was of the utmost gravity. It lasted about 12 hours. As the hours passed there were clear signs of organisation among the rioters. They covered their faces and changed their clothes because of what they intended to do. The rioters defied the senior members of the Asian community who tried to calm matters. All defendants expressed remorse. All except P gave themselves up to police. N was seen at 4 pm and at 6.48 pm when he was in a hostile crowd. He threw one missile. He was aged 28 with references. **3 years** not 4.
Q was in the front line of the riot early in the evening. He threw a missile at the police and armed himself with a broken lamp pole. In a group he struck a police van three times. He threw a gas cylinder towards the police, knocking an officer over. He left for 2½ hours and returned with a change of clothing. His face was covered, and he threw a burning object at a stolen car. He hurled a gas cylinder at police from a short distance and knocked another officer over. He suffered from a mental illness, namely mania, which creates an elation in mood, over-activity, grandiose ideas and over-confidence. A psychiatrist said that at the time his thought processes and reasoning were affected. Held. The Judge gave insufficient reduction for this, so **2 years** not 4.
M was present for five hours and he threw an object at the police lines. He was in the vicinity of two cars which were being damaged, and nearby when a petrol bomb was thrown. He had convictions including a common assault some time ago. His wife spoke no English and they had a child with a congenital heart defect. **4 years** was not excessive.

R was present for between six and seven hours and he covered his face. He threw a missile at police lines four times. His child died in deeply distressing circumstances. He looked after his disabled sister. There was no distinction between him and M, so **4 years** upheld.

Al was seen throwing missiles on several occasions over a 20-minute period. At one stage he was masked. Al was aged 21, of good character, and was described as a highly motivated student with a university place available. Held. Because of the mitigation, **3 years** not 4.

P was first involved at 6.30 pm and he remained in the crowd until the early hours. About 9 pm he threw missiles at police three times and was wearing a mask. P threw two more missiles at about 11 pm and shortly after midnight. On a number of occasions he was at or near the front of those confronting the police. There was nothing wrong with **4 years**.

L was present for a three-hour period and was seen with a metal bar and on a number of occasions throwing stones at police. When arrested he put forward false alibis. He had no relevant convictions. **4 years 9 months** was not manifestly excessive.

Az was seen throwing stones and missiles at the police. He was also seen near a burning barricade and an overturned car. On occasions he was hooded. He was aged 25 and of good character. **4 years 9 months** upheld.

H was repeatedly throwing missiles at the police. He was present for about eight hours. H pulled up the hood on his jacket. He was aged 26 with no relevant convictions. **4½ years** upheld.

Ha participated for over two hours, and on six separate occasions threw stones and other missiles at the police. He also attacked a police van and picked up a metal fence and threw it at a police van. Ha was hooded for most of the time and encouraged others with victory signs. He was aged 21. Obstructing the police was his only relevant conviction. **4 years 9 months** was not manifestly excessive.

Q participated for four hours and threw nine missiles at the police. He brandished a large light tube to encourage others. Q was aged 21, of good character, and with references. **4 years 9 months** was not manifestly excessive.

K was present for about three hours. He threw two missiles at police, carried burning debris and tried to ignite something in his hand. He rolled a beer barrel towards the police and threw a petrol bomb directly at police. He was aged 28 with no relevant convictions except obstructing police. **6½ years** was not manifestly excessive.

Qu participated for five hours and threw nine missiles at the police. He brandished a lighted tube. **4½ years** was not manifestly excessive.

Kh started by behaving peacefully and then he changed his clothes. He then was with a group which damaged a car, helped to erect a barricade and threw missiles at police. When arrested, he lied. He was aged 20 with no relevant convictions and had references. **5 years** was not manifestly excessive.

Ra was present for five hours. He threw missiles several times, instructed others how to damage a car, which was set alight and pushed towards the police. He was repeatedly in the front line. He was aged 20, of good character and had six references. **5 years** was not manifestly excessive.

Note: This is an old case. Even where the evidence is available, the CPS frequently charge other offences so cases at the Court of Appeal are rare. I would imagine similar sentences to these would be passed today. I am confident they would not be any lower. Ed.

Att-Gen's Ref No 5 of 2012 2012 EWCA Crim 964, 2013 1 Cr App R (S) 15 (79) LCJ D pleaded at his PCMH to four robberies, violent disorder, three burglaries and two criminal damage counts. In 2011, D was at the front of rioters advancing towards a police line in the Croydon riots. He was armed with bricks and debris and took someone else's scarf to mask his face. D threw a missile at the officers and another at a shop. Then for several hours the group terrorised shopkeepers and members of the public. The crowd confronted a bus and forced it to stop. The windows of the bus were attacked with weapons and missiles. The driver's windscreen was smashed and the driver, V1, was showered with glass. V1 was so terrified he didn't flee. Property was stolen from his cab. He was attacked with sticks. D also went into a sweetshop armed with a pole. The shop was ransacked. D left with stolen items. A shop assistant was violently attacked. Nearby buildings were set on fire. The owners, V2 and V3, a married couple, feared their shop would be set alight but eventually managed to flee. Their van stopped at a red light and V2 could not see sufficiently to 'jump' the lights. The rioters surrounded the van. V2's window was smashed and the doors opened. V2 was threatened with a knife. Money was taken from his pockets and he was pulled from the van. The group threatened to burn the vehicle and its occupants. D, armed with a metal pole, and another stole items from V3's handbag. V3 was then pulled from the van and forced across the road. D remained with her and stopped her helping V2. D then went to the back of the van and struck it but failed to open it. V2 suffered swelling to his face. V3 had pain to her wrist. They were both traumatised and their clothing was torn. The damage to the shop was £30,000 to £40,000. V2 had to pay large sums of excess insurance to replace stolen stock. Fearful of a repeat attack, V2 left the business and was in great financial difficulty.

V4 was using a cash machine when D attacked him with a hammer. V4 was put in a headlock and forced to enter his PIN. While his throat was squeezed £40 was taken. Next D in a group wearing disguises smashed the windows of a Tesco Express. D climbed the counter, attacked the door to the back of the cash machine but failed to break it down. D and others then climbed over the service counter and took whatever they could. All the windows were broken, the till drawers were missing, the safe was damaged and the refrigeration equipment was extensively damaged. Someone broke an internal wall and damage to the cash machine was estimated to be nearly £30,000. As a result the store closed down. An hour later, D was at the front of a group who forced their way into a William Hill betting office. D kicked and threw a waste bin at the security screen. He and others went to the back office. Gaming machines were pulled from the wall. The damage to the betting shop was just over £18,500. D was now aged 20 and of good character. He told the author of his pre-sentence report that he was in custody for robbing someone of £40. Held. With youth, plea and good character **7 years'** detention not 4.

See also the **Burglary** *Shops Looting during public disturbance* paras at **219.51**.

320   ROAD RAGE

320.1
There are numerous offences which can be road rage offences. The paragraphs are divided up into the various offences. Ed.

320.2   *Judicial guidance*
R v Howells 2002 EWCA Crim 1608, 2003 1 Cr App R (S) 61 (p 292) In dangerous driving road rage cases, where no accident or injury results and there is no consumption of alcohol but there is ample evidence to suggest furious driving in temper with an intent of causing fear and possibly injury, the appropriate sentencing bracket is between **6** and **12 months**.

R v Normanton 2003 EWCA Crim 959 The defendant pleaded to a road rage ABH. Held. Custody is almost inevitable even where the defendant is of good character. Road rage must be firmly dealt with because of its prevalence and unacceptable nature.

R v Khan 2013 EWCA Crim 915 Although for offences of road rage sentences of immediate custody are appropriate, there can be circumstances where another course may be adopted.

320.2a   *ABH/ Offences Against the Person Act 1861 s 20*
For the maximum sentences and ancillary powers, see the **ABH AND OFFENCES AGAINST THE PERSON ACT 1861 S 20** chapters.

R v Simpson 2008 EWCA Crim 485 LCJ D was convicted of unlawful wounding. He parked in a way which blocked in the car of V, a 67-year-old man. There was an exchange of words between V on the one hand and D and his girlfriend on the other. There was an altercation and V ended up with a wound to the back of his head, a wound to his scalp, a fracture of the cheekbone, a displaced fracture to the nose, an injury to his jaw, bruising to his face and a minor injury to his elbow. He was left with a permanent dent to the top of his head. The prosecution case was that D had attacked V with a wooden handle and had head-butted him. D told the police that he had pushed V because V was swinging a pickaxe handle at him. He declined to answer questions in interview. In evidence he said that he had pushed and head-butted V in self-defence. D, aged in his mid-40s, had no convictions and was of positive good character. He called witnesses as to character. He had a good work record, was in responsible employment, and was highly commended by his employers. Held. This was an incident which occurred through loss of temper and significantly in a public place. As an act of mercy to this man of previous good character who will never offend again, **2 years** not 3.

R v Smith 2010 EWCA Crim 23 D pleaded to inflicting GBH. V, while driving, started changing lanes and then changed her mind, causing inconvenience to D, who was in a car behind with her son. D sounded her horn and V raised her hand to apologise. V stopped at a red light and D got out of her vehicle and punched V on the cheek through an open window. D shouted and attempted to throw more punches. V's sister got out of V's car and confronted D. V also left the car and shouted at D. D drove away, accidentally hitting V in the pelvic area. V was pinned between the two vehicles and V's car was dented. V had a bruise to her cheek, a minimal undisplaced fracture to her cheek bone and a step defect in her orbital rim. From the accident V had bruising to her legs. V said that the attack made her very scared and nervous. D was aged 24, of good character and the full-time carer of her 9-year-old son. The pre-sentence report said that D expressed genuine remorse, she would have difficulty with custody, she might lose her accommodation, there was a low risk of reconviction and a low to medium risk of harm. In custody D's parents had stepped in to look after the child. Held. The case had to be marked by a custodial sentence, either immediate or suspended. **4 months** not 9.

See also: *R v Saqib* 2015 EWCA Crim 950 (Plea (10% credit) to ABH. Minor collision. Hard punch. Fractured cheekbone. Aged 27. Many convictions including GBH in 2009 (21 months). In 2013, ABH (2 years) for which on licence. Sentenced on the basis of excessive self-defence. We start at 18 months, so with plea **16 months**.)

See also the **OFFENCES AGAINST THE PERSON ACT 1861 S 20** chapter.

320.3   *Dangerous driving*

For the maximum sentences and ancillary powers, see the **DANGEROUS DRIVING (SIMPLE)** chapter.

R v Watson 2007 EWCA Crim 1595, 2008 1 Cr App R (S) 55 (p 315) D was convicted of dangerous driving. He was the chauffeur of a Mercedes S class, which he parked in a busy London street on a yellow line. The victim, a traffic warden, V, gave him a friendly warning about his parking 15 minutes before the incident, which D ignored. V returned, gave him five more minutes and then issued a ticket. D chased V up the road and threw a stone at him and said that if he saw him again he would run him over. V began to make notes. D got into his car, did a three-point turn and drove at V. Both the nearside wheels mounted the pavement, he speeded up and swerved towards V, who had to jump out of the way. Two minutes later D returned to the scene, speeding towards V and swerving at him as he ran away. The car mounted the pavement again and D again drove at V. Then he drove off. D, aged 53, was of good character apart from relatively minor road traffic offences. A pre-sentence report said that he posed no risk of reoffending. He lost his job because of the conviction. The Judge said that the warden's behaviour was beyond criticism. Held. D used his large and powerful car as a deadly weapon, intending to hurt the warden. That was aggravated by V being a public servant. We have considered *R v Howells* 2003 1 Cr App R (S) 61 (p 292) and *R v Joseph* 2002 1 Cr App R (S) 20 (p 74).

We are constrained by the broad thrust of previous decisions. We do not regard these cases as imposing an absolute ceiling of 12 months' imprisonment but in the circumstances of this case, the appropriate sentence is **12 months** not 20.

R v Bath 2012 EWCA Crim 488, 2 Cr App R (S) 50 (p 286) D was convicted of dangerous driving. In the early hours of the morning, on the M4, when the road was wet, D overtook a car driven by V. He then pulled in front of V's car with only inches to spare. V felt that this was dangerous and so he flashed his lights. D's reaction was to put his fog lights on and to slam his brakes on. V was forced to brake sharply to avoid crashing into D's car. He managed to pull into the middle lane but as he got level with D's car, D stuck his arm out of the window and made gestures to V and V's 11-year-old daughter. He started to move towards the middle lane and V was forced to move to the outside lane. D made out as though he was going to ram V's car. He then moved into the outside lane to stop V from overtaking. D left the motorway at the next junction. V pulled over as his wife was hysterical and his daughter had woken up. He saw that D had stopped his car on the exit slip road and had got out of the car. He was waving his arms, jumping up and down and shouting. He shouted, "I'm going to fucking kill you". V drove off as he was worried what D might do. He thought that was the end of the incident. However, D drove up behind V's car with his full beam headlights on. He pulled in front of V's car and slammed his brakes on. V slowed down, to which D's response was to swerve from one side of the road to the other, to prevent V from overtaking. He left at the next junction. D denied the offence. He was aged 44 and had convictions for excess alcohol, road rage and threatening behaviour (1989 and 1999). He had suffered from depression in the past and claimed he spent each day caring for his elderly father. Held. The maximum was 2 years. We don't think that a sentence of 20 months reflected the absence of factors such as drink or injury. Those factors would have brought D's sentence to near the maximum. **10 months** was appropriate. Given the gravity, it was not appropriate to suspend the sentence.

R v Atkinson 2014 EWCA Crim 1079 D pleaded to dangerous driving. V was in her car waiting for her daughter to collect a package from the post office. V was parked in a turning circle at the back of a post office, which was a restricted area. There was a pedestrian walking area and a barrier to prevent other vehicles from advancing further into a restricted parking zone. D arrived in a minibus. He was a licensed taxi driver. He moved the minibus as far as he could towards the barrier, and then apparently wanted to perform a three-point turn. V's car restricted the space in which D could perform the manoeuvre. D left his vehicle and spoke in abusive terms towards V, telling her that it was not " . . .a fucking parking space, you fucking whore, leave it". She was unable to do so with D's vehicle in front of hers and pedestrians passing in front of her. D returned to his minibus and after a pause reversed his vehicle a few feet and ran into the front of V's car. The collision caused £400 worth of damage. V got out of her car and remonstrated with D. He abused her once again and told her that she should have moved out of the way. D completed his three-point turn and drove away. V was left shaking and very upset. D was aged 37-38 at appeal and had dishonesty convictions in 1997 and 1999. He had no convictions for bad driving or threatening behaviour. Held. This was a road rage incident and the need for deterrent sentences of immediate custody has been made clear since at least *R v Hassan and Schuller* 1989 RTR 129. The aggravating feature was D's aggression directed at a lone woman with the consequences that she described in her impact statement.[938] This was a single act of deliberately reversing into V's car. It was not prolonged and did not involve two moving vehicles. The foul language was all part of the characterisation as a road rage case. Starting at 9 months was appropriate. With full credit, **6 months** not 12.

See also the **DANGEROUS DRIVING (SIMPLE)** chapter.

---

[938] The Court did not set out the details of the impact statement. Ed.

Offences Against the Person Act 1861 s 18 see the OFFENCES AGAINST THE PERSON ACT 1861 S 18 *Vehicles, after using (including road rage)* para at **292.38**.

321   ROAD TRAFFIC
For a list of road traffic offences, see the **Road traffic** entry in the back index.

321.1
Fixed penalties Most of these offences carry fixed penalty points. Many also carry a financial penalty deposit charge. However, whether there is a fixed penalty or a financial penalty deposit and what the penalty is, depends on which statute or regulation is involved. This is not always clear and some offences can be charged in more than one way. Therefore, most of the fixed penalties and the financial penalty deposit charges are not listed. For more detail, see **61.1** in Volume 1. Ed.

321.2   *Magistrates' Court Sentencing Guidelines*
Magistrates' Court Sentencing Guidelines 2008, see www.banksr.com Other Matters Guidelines tab page 135 The guideline applies to the Magistrates' Court and to the Crown Court hearing appeals or sentencing for summary only offences.[939]
Starting points are based on a first-time offender pleading not guilty.
Part 1: Offences concerning the driver

Offence	Maximum penalty	Points	Starting point	Special considerations
Fail to give information of driver's identity as required	Level 3	6	Band C fine	For limited companies endorsement is not available. A fine is the only available penalty
Drive otherwise than in accordance with licence	Level 3	3-6	Band A fine	Aggravating factor if no licence ever held
Failure to produce insurance certificate	Level 4	–	Band A fine	Fine per offence not per document
Failure to produce test certificate	Level 3	–	Band A fine	
Drive otherwise than in accordance with licence (where could be covered)	Level 3	–	Band A fine	

---

[939] See page 15 of the guidelines.

321.3   *Part 2: Offences concerning the vehicle*[940]

Offence	Maximum penalty	Points	Starting point	Special considerations
No excise licence	Level 3 or 5 times annual duty, whichever is greater	–	A (1-3 months unpaid) B (4-6 months unpaid) C (7-12 months unpaid)	Add duty lost
Failing to notify change of ownership to DVLA	Level 3	–	Band A fine	Note 1 below applies
No test certificate[941]	Level 3	–	Band A fine	Note 1 below applies
Brakes defective	Level 4	3	Band B fine	Level 5 if goods vehicle, see Part 5 below
Steering defective	Level 4	3	Band B fine	Level 5 if goods vehicle, see Part 5 below
Tyres defective	Level 4	3	Band B fine	Level 5 if goods vehicle, see Part 5 below Penalty per tyre
Condition of vehicle/ accessories/ equipment/ involving danger of injury (Road Traffic Act 1988 s 40A)	Level 4	3	Band B fine	Level 5 if goods vehicle, see Part 5 below. Note 2 below also applies
Exhaust defective	Level 3	–	Band A fine	Note 1 below applies
Lights defective	Level 3	–	Band A fine	Note 1 below applies

Note 1: For all these Part 2 offences and other offences where specified: Band A fine for driver, Band A fine with at least a 25% uplift for an owner driver, and Band B fine for owner-company.

Note 2: Must disqualify for at least 6 months if offender has one or more previous convictions for same offence within three years.

---

[940] For Road Traffic Act 1988 s 40A offences

[941] There is a £100 fixed penalty with half the relevant victim surcharge, Fixed Penalty Order 2000 2000/2792 Sch 1 as amended. For more detail see **61.1** in Volume 1.

321.4   *Part 3: Offences concerning use of vehicle*

Offence	Maximum penalty	Points	Starting point	Special considerations
Weight, position or distribution of load or manner in which load secured involving danger of injury (Road Traffic Act 1988 s 40A)	Level 4	3	Band B fine	Notes 1 and 2 above apply Level 5 if goods vehicle, see Part 5 below
Position or manner in which load secured (not involving danger) (Road Traffic Act 1988 s 42)	Level 3	–	Band A fine	Level 4 if goods vehicle, see Part 5 below
Overloading/exceeding axle weight	Level 5 (unlimited fine)	–	A	Note 1 above applies Level 5 if goods vehicle, see Part 5 below, see Note 3 below Penalty per axle
Number of passengers or way carried involving danger of injury (Road Traffic Act 1988 s 40A)	Level 4	3	Band B fine	Note 1 above applies Level 5 if goods vehicle, see Part 5 below
Dangerous parking	Level 3	3	Band A fine	
Pelican/Zebra crossing contravention	Level 3	3	Band A fine	

Offence	Maximum penalty	Points	Starting point	Special considerations
Failing to comply with traffic sign (e.g. red traffic light,[942] stop sign, double white lines, and no entry sign)	Level 3	3	Band A fine	
Failing to comply with police constable directing traffic	Level 3	3	Band A fine	
Failing to stop when required by police constable	Level 5 (unlimited fine) (mechanically propelled vehicle)	–	Band B fine	Level 3 if a cycle
Use of mobile telephone	Level 3	3	Band A fine	
Seat belt offences[943]	Level 2 (adult or child in front) Level 2[944] (child in rear)	–	Band A fine	
Failure to use appropriate child car seat	Level 2	–	Band A fine	

Note 3: Starting point caters for cases where the overload is up to and including 10%. Therefore, 10% should be added to the penalty for each additional 1% of overload.

321.5   *Part 4: Motorway offences*

Offence	Maximum penalty	Points	Starting point	Special considerations
Driving in reverse or wrong way on slip road	Level 4	3	Band B fine	
Driving in reverse or wrong way on motorway	Level 4	3	Band C fine	

---

[942] There is power to reduce disqualification for this offence when the defendant attends courses, see the **Disqualification from Driving: Obligatory** *Reduced periods of disqualification for attendance on courses* para at **44.8** in Volume 1.

[943] There is a £100 fixed penalty for seat belt offences under Road Traffic Act 1988 s 14-15(2) and (4) with half the relevant victim surcharge, Fixed Penalty Order 2000 2000/2792 Sch 1 as amended and Road Safety (Financial Penalty Deposit) (Appropriate Amount) Order 2009 2009/492 as amended. For more detail see **61.1** in Volume 1.

[944] As increased by Road Safety Act 2006 s 24 amending Road Traffic Offenders Act 1988 Sch 2. Ed.

Offence	Maximum penalty	Points	Starting point	Special considerations
Drive off carriageway (central reservation or hard shoulder)	Level 4	3	Band B fine	
Making U turn	Level 4	3	Band C fine	
Learner driver or excluded vehicle	Level 4	3	Band B fine	
Stopping on hard shoulder	Level 4	–	Band A fine	
Vehicle in prohibited lane	Level 4	3	Band A fine	
Walk on motorway, slip road or hard shoulder	Level 4	–	Band A fine	

321.6   *Part 5: Offences Re Buses/goods vehicles over 3.5 tonnes (GVW)*
For **Passenger Carrying Vehicles (PCV) and Large Goods Vehicles (LGV) drivers**
see the note at **341.1**.

Offence	Maximum penalty	Points	Starting point	Special considerations
In all cases, take safety, damage to roads and commercial gain into account. Refer to **COMPANIES AND PUBLIC BODIES** *Offence committed for commercial purpose* at **60.10** in Volume 1 for approach to fines for 'commercially motivated' offences.				
No goods vehicle plating certificate	Level 3	–	Note 1 below Part 2 applies	
No goods vehicle test certificate	Level 4	–	Note 4 below applies	
Brakes defective	Level 5 (unlimited fine)	3	Note 4 below applies	
Steering defective	Level 5 (unlimited fine)	3	Note 4 below applies	
Tyres defective	Level 5 (unlimited fine)	3	Note 4 below applies	Penalty per tyre
Exhaust emission	Level 4	–	Note 4 below applies	

Offence	Maximum penalty	Points	Starting point	Special considerations
Condition of vehicle/ accessories/ equipment involving danger of injury (Road Traffic Act 1988 s 40A)	Level 5 (unlimited fine)	3	Note 4 below applies	Note 2 below Part 2 applies
Number of passengers or way carried involving danger of injury (Road Traffic Act 1988 s 40A)	Level 5 (unlimited fine)	3	Note 4 below applies	Note 2 below Part 2 applies
Weight, position or distribution of load or manner in which load secured involving danger of injury (Road Traffic Act 1988 s 42)	Level 5 (unlimited fine)	3	Note 4 below applies	Note 2 below Part 2 applies
Position or manner in which load secured (not involving danger) (Road Traffic Act 1988 s 42)	Level 4	–	Note 4 below applies	
Overloading or exceeding maximum axle weight	Level 5 (unlimited fine)	–	Note 4 below applies	Note 3 below Part 3 applies
No operator's licence	Level 4 (PSV) Level 5 (Goods) Unlimited fine)	–	Note 4 below applies	
Speed limiter not used or incorrectly calibrated	Level 4	–	Note 4 below applies	

Offence	Maximum penalty	Points	Starting point	Special considerations
Tachograph not used/not working	Level 5 (unlimited fine)	–	Note 4 below applies	
Exceed permitted driving time/periods of duty	Level 4	–	Note 4 below applies	
Fail to keep/return written record sheets	Level 4	–	Note 4 below applies	
Falsify or alter written records with intent to deceive	Level 5 (unlimited fine) 2 years	–	Note 4 below applies	Either way offence

Note 2: Must disqualify for at least 6 months if offender has one or more previous convictions for same offence within 3 years.

Note 3: Starting point caters for cases where the overload is up to and including 10%. Therefore, 10% should be added to the penalty for each additional 1% of overload. Penalty per axle.

Note 4: Band B fine for driver, Band B fine with at least 25% uplift for an owner-driver, and Band C fine for owner-company.

A Band A fine is 50% of net weekly income. Band B and C are 100% and 150%. For more detail see **60.27** in Volume 1.

See also the **TACHOGRAPH AND OTHER DRIVERS' HOURS OFFENCES** chapter.

322   ROBBERY

322.1

Theft Act 1968 s 8

Mode of trial Indictable only

Maximum sentence Life

Automatic life In the Criminal Justice Act 2003 Sch 15B Part 1 list is robbery, where, at some time during the commission of the offence, the offender had in his possession a firearm or an imitation firearm within the meaning of Firearms Act 1968. The court, where the offender satisfies this provision, must (unless the particular circumstances make it unjust[945]) pass automatic life if: a) the defendant is aged 18+ at the date of the conviction, b) the offence was committed on or after 3 December 2012, c) the court considers a determinate sentence of at least 10 years is appropriate, d) at the time the offender was convicted he had a conviction for a Criminal Justice Act 2003 Sch 15B offence, and e) the defendant at the time of his or her conviction had previously been sentenced to either: i) a life sentence where he or she was not eligible for release during the first five years of the sentence, or ii) a determinate sentence or extended sentence where the custodial part was 10 years or more.[946] For a pre-2012 extended sentence,

---

[945] Criminal Justice Act 2003 s 224A(2)

[946] Criminal Justice Act 2003 s 224A as inserted by Legal Aid, Sentencing and Punishment of Offenders Act 2012 s 122. The condition for a) is at section 224A(1)(a), for b) is at section 224A(1)(b), for c) is at section 224A(1)(c), and for d) is at section 224A(4)-(9).

when determining whether the custodial term was 10+ years, the period deducted for time on remand or on a curfew and tag is included.[947] For determining the issue where there is no firearm count, see the ***Firearm, With No firearm count*** para at **322.15**.

Extended sentences Theft Act 1968 s 8 is listed in Criminal Justice Act 2003 Sch 15. The court may pass a 2012 extended sentence (EDS) if there is a significant risk of serious harm from future specified offences and either: a) the defendant has a Criminal Justice Act 2003 Sch 15B conviction (applicable only to defendants aged 18+), or b) the offence would justify a determinate sentence of at least 4 years.[948]

Restitution Orders There is power to make a Restitution Order under Powers of Criminal Courts (Sentencing) Act 2000 s 148.

Serious Crime Prevention Orders For Theft Act 1968 s 8(1) and assault with intent to rob offences, where the use or threat of force/the assault involves a firearm, an imitation firearm, an imitation firearm or an offensive weapon there is a discretionary power to make this order, when it would protect the public etc.[949]

Sexual Harm Prevention Orders There is a discretionary power to make this order when it is necessary to protect the public from sexual harm.[950]

322.2   *Crown Court statistics   England and Wales*
Robbery

Year	Age	Sex	Plea	Total sen-tenced	Type of sentencing %						Average length of custody in months
					Dis-charge	Fine	Commu-nity sentence	Sus-pended sentence	Custody	Oth-er	
2013	10-17				Not available						
	18-20	Male	G	992	–	0.2	3.7	11.3	84.5	0.3	31
			NG	173	–	0.6	3.5	10.4	83.8	1.7	36.7
		Fe-male	G	43	–	–	9.3	25.6	62.8	2.3	26.2
			NG	8	–	–	25	37.5	37.5	–	17.3
	21+	Male	G	2,466	–	0.1	2.0	10.1	87	0.7	44
			NG	479	–	0.2	0.8	7.9	89.8	1.3	66.2
		Fe-male	G	197	–	–	5.6	28.9	63.5	2	31.7
			NG	38	–	–	2.6	18.4	78.9	–	38.2
2014	10-17				Not available						
	18-20	Male	G	783	–	–	4	17	78	1	32.8
			NG	125	–	–	4	19	76	1	44.4
		Fe-male	G	54	–	–	11	31	56	2	27.0
			NG	5	–	–	–	20	80	–	Not listed[951]
	21+	Male	G	2,235	–	–	1	9	88	2	42.9
			NG	456	–	–	1	5	92	2	66.3
		Fe-male	G	166	1	–	7	22	69	2	32.5
			NG	42	–	–	–	29	67	5	48.0

For explanations about the statistics, see page 1-xii. For more statistics, see www.banksr. com Other Matters Statistics tab

The chapter is divided into three sections: a) Guidelines, b) Types of robbery and factors, and c) Matters relating to the defendant.

---

[947] Criminal Justice Act 2003 s 224A(9)-(10)
[948] Criminal Justice Act 2003 s 226A-226B as inserted by Legal Aid, Sentencing and Punishment of Offenders Act 2012 s 124
[949] Serious Crime Act 2007 s 1 and Sch 1 para 5
[950] Sexual Offences Act 2003 s 103A as inserted by Anti-social Behaviour, Crime and Policing Act 2014 Sch 5 para 2 and Sexual Offences Act 2003 Sch 5
[951] Based on too few cases to be meaningful

Guidelines

322.3   *How to approach the guideline*

Note: The press release of the Sentencing Council for the new guideline said, 'While the Council has not set out to increase sentence levels, the new guidelines reflect the increases in sentence levels that have occurred over recent years. The increases have come about as case law has made clear that offences involving knives must focus on deterrence. This approach also reflects society's concerns about the problem of robberies involving the use of knives and guns, emphasising the seriousness of these offences and aiming to ensure that robbers who use these weapons, or threaten people with them, get the longest sentences.'

As a result of this, I consider that where a case would fit neatly into one of the three sections of the new guideline, like a street robbery, pre-guideline cases will not assist and I have not listed them. However, where a street robber has previous convictions for robbery I consider that pre-2016 cases may assist and I have listed them. Similarly where sentences of 18 years or more are appropriate for firearm cases I consider that the pre-2016 cases may assist and they are listed. The suggested approach is to start with the guideline, consider the pre-2016 cases to see if they assist and then return to the guideline before passing sentence. Ed.

Att-Gen's Ref No 147 of 2006 2007 EWCA Crim 961, 2008 1 Cr App R (S) 2 (p 9) G was convicted of conspiracy to rob. Held. The definitive guideline is simply a guideline. The immense variety of circumstances in which offences of robbery are committed will necessarily have to be looked at in the context that the guidelines cannot identify each and every category or purport to provide a sentencing grid for each and every category. Between the description of 'less than sophisticated commercial robberies' and 'professionally planned commercial robberies' there will be a wide spectrum of offences.

The guideline that this case relates to is the *Robbery Guideline 2006*. However, similar problems arise with the new guideline with the different categorisation in the new guideline. Ed.

Types of robbery and factors

Armed robbery see the *Firearm, With* paras at **322.13**.

322.4   *Commercial robberies, Less sophisticated   Guideline*

Robbery Guideline 2016, see www.banksr.com Other Matters Guidelines tab page 3, The first guideline applies to street and less sophisticated commercial robberies, and unsophisticated robberies within commercial premises or targeting commercial goods or money. For the guideline see **322.26**.

322.5 *Commercial robberies, Professionally planned commercial   Guideline*

Robbery Guideline 2016, see www.banksr.com Other Matters Guidelines tab page 9 'Professionally planned commercial robbery' refers to a robbery involving a significant degree of planning, sophistication or organisation. For the guideline see **322.26**.

STEP ONE: Determining the offence category

page 10 The court should determine the offence category with reference **only** to the factors listed in the tables below. In order to determine the category the court should assess **culpability** and **harm**.

The court should weigh all the factors set out below in determining the offender's culpability.

Where there are characteristics present which fall under different levels of culpability, the court should balance these characteristics to reach a fair assessment of the offender's culpability.

CULPABILITY demonstrated by one or more of the following	
A – High	• Use of a weapon to inflict violence • Production of a bladed article or firearm or imitation firearm to threaten violence • Use of very significant force in the commission of the offence • A leading role where offending is part of a group activity • Offence motivated by, or demonstrating hostility based on any of the following characteristics or presumed characteristics of the victim: religion, race, disability, sexual orientation or transgender identity • Abuse of position
B – Medium	• Production of a weapon other than a bladed article or firearm or imitation firearm to threaten violence • Threat of violence by any weapon (but which is not produced) • A significant role where offending is part of a group activity • Other cases where characteristics for Categories A or C are not present
C – Lesser	• Performed limited function under direction • Involved through coercion, intimidation or exploitation • Threat or use of minimal force • Mental disability or learning disability where linked to the commission of the offence

322.5a *Harm*

page 10 The level of **harm** is determined by weighing up all the factors of the case to determine the harm that has been caused or was intended to be caused to the victim. The victim relates both to the commercial organisation that has been robbed and any individual(s) who has suffered the use or threat of force during the commission of the offence.

Category 1	• Serious physical and/or psychological harm caused to the victim • Serious detrimental effect on the business • Very high value goods or sums targeted or obtained (whether economic, personal or sentimental)
Category 2	• Other cases where characteristics for Categories 1 or 3 are not present
Category 3	• No/minimal physical or psychological harm caused to the victim • No/minimal detrimental effect on the business • Low-value goods or sums targeted or obtained (whether economic, personal or sentimental)

322.6

STEP TWO: Starting point and category range

page 11 Having determined the category at step one, the court should use the corresponding starting point to reach a sentence within the category range below. The starting point applies to all offenders irrespective of plea or previous convictions. A case of particular gravity, reflected by multiple features of high culpability or harm in step one, could merit upward adjustment from the starting point before further adjustment for aggravating or mitigating features, set out on the next page.

Consecutive sentences for multiple offences may be appropriate particularly where exceptionally high levels of harm have been caused, [*TICs and Totality Guideline 2012: Crown Court*].

Where multiple offences or a single conspiracy to commit multiple offences of particular severity have taken place, sentences in excess of 20 years may be appropriate.

	Culpability		
Harm	**A**	**B**	**C**
Category 1	**Starting point** 16 years' custody **Category range** 12 to 20 years' custody	**Starting point** 9 years' custody **Category range** 7 to 14 years' custody	**Starting point** 5 years' custody **Category range** 4 to 8 years' custody
Category 2	**Starting point** 9 years' custody **Category range** 7 to 14 years' custody	**Starting point** 5 years' custody **Category range** 4 to 8 years' custody	**Starting point** 3 years' custody **Category range** 2 to 5 years' custody
Category 3	**Starting point** 5 years' custody **Category range** 4 to 8 years' custody	**Starting point** 3 years' custody **Category range** 2 to 5 years' custody	**Starting point** 2 years' custody **Category range** 18 months' to 4 years' custody

322.7 [Aggravating and mitigating factors]

page 11 The table [below] contains a **non-exhaustive** list of additional factual elements providing the context of the offence and factors relating to the offender. Identify whether any combination of these, or other relevant factors, should result in an upward or downward adjustment from the sentence arrived at so far. In particular, relevant recent convictions are likely to result in an upward adjustment. In some cases, having considered these factors, it may be appropriate to move outside the identified category range.

Factors increasing seriousness
Statutory aggravating factors: Previous convictions, having regard to: a) the **nature** of the offence to which the conviction relates and its **relevance** to the current offence; and b) the **time** that has elapsed since the conviction Offence committed whilst on bail *Other aggravating factors:* Victim is targeted due to a vulnerability (or a perceived vulnerability) Steps taken to prevent the victim reporting or obtaining assistance and/or from assisting or supporting the prosecution Prolonged nature of attack Restraint, detention or additional degradation of the victim Involvement of others through coercion, intimidation or exploitation Location of the offence (including cases where the location of the offence is the victim's residence) Timing of the offence Attempt to conceal identity (for example, wearing a balaclava or hood) Commission of offence whilst under the influence of alcohol or drugs Attempts to conceal/dispose of evidence Established evidence of community/wider impact Failure to comply with current court orders Offence committed on licence Offences taken into consideration Failure to respond to warnings about behaviour

Factors reducing seriousness or reflecting personal mitigation
No previous convictions **or** no relevant/recent convictions Remorse, particularly where evidenced by voluntary reparation to the victim Good character and/or exemplary conduct Serious medical condition requiring urgent, intensive or long-term treatment Age and/or lack of maturity where it affects the responsibility of the offender Mental disorder or learning disability (where not linked to the commission of the offence) Sole or primary carer for dependent relatives Determination and/or demonstration of steps having been taken to address addiction or offending behaviour

For a suggested approach to the guideline, see **322.3**.

322.8   *Commercial robberies, Professionally planned   Series of robberies*
Robbery Guideline 2016, see www.banksr.com Other Matters Guidelines tab This guideline applies only to offenders aged 18 and over.

STEP TWO: Starting point and category range
page 11 [First paragraph not listed]
Consecutive sentences for multiple offences may be appropriate particularly where exceptionally high levels of harm have been caused, please refer to the [*TICs and Totality Guideline 2012: Crown Court*].
Where multiple offences or a single conspiracy to commit multiple offences of particular severity have taken place, sentences in excess of 20 years may be appropriate.
For the whole section of this guideline, see **322.6**.
For an index of the 'series of robberies' paras see **322.22**.
Death is caused see MANSLAUGHTER *Burglars/Robbers/Thieves, By* at **284.13**.

322.9   *Dwellings   Guideline*
Robbery Guideline 2016, see www.banksr.com Other Matters Guidelines tab page 15 This guideline applies only to offenders aged 18 and over.

STEP ONE: Determining the offence category
page 16 The court should determine the offence category with reference **only** to the factors listed in the tables below. In order to determine the category the court should assess **culpability** and **harm**.
The court should weigh all the factors set out below in determining the offender's culpability.
Where there are characteristics present which fall under different levels of culpability, the court should balance these characteristics to reach a fair assessment of the offender's culpability.

CULPABILITY demonstrated by one or more of the following	
A – High	• Use of a weapon to inflict violence • Production of a bladed article or firearm or imitation firearm to threaten violence • Use of very significant force in the commission of the offence • Sophisticated organised nature of offence • A leading role where offending is part of a group activity • Offence motivated by, or demonstrating hostility based on any of the following characteristics or presumed characteristics of the victim: religion, race, disability, sexual orientation or transgender identity • Abuse of position

B – Medium	• Production of a weapon other than a bladed article or firearm or imitation firearm to threaten violence • Threat of violence by any weapon (but which is not produced) • A significant role where offending is part of a group activity • Other cases where characteristics for Categories A or C are not present
C – Lesser	• Performed limited function under direction • Involved through coercion, intimidation or exploitation • Threat or use of minimal force • Very little or no planning • Mental disability or learning disability where linked to the commission of the offence

322.10 *Harm*

page 16 The court should weigh up all the factors set out below to determine the harm that has been caused or was intended to be caused to the victim.

Category 1	• Serious physical and/or psychological harm caused to the victim • Very high-value goods or sums targeted or obtained (whether economic, sentimental or personal) • Soiling, ransacking or vandalism of property
Category 2	• Other cases where characteristics for Categories 1 or 3 are not present
Category 3	• No/minimal physical or psychological harm caused to the victim • Low-value goods or sums targeted or obtained (whether economic, personal or sentimental) • Limited damage or disturbance to property

322.11

STEP TWO: Starting point and category range

page 17 Having determined the category at step one, the court should use the corresponding starting point to reach a sentence within the category range below. The starting point applies to all offenders irrespective of plea or previous convictions. A case of particular gravity, reflected by multiple features of culpability or harm in step one, could merit upward adjustment from the starting point before further adjustment for aggravating or mitigating features, set out on the next page.

Consecutive sentences for multiple offences may be appropriate particularly where exceptionally high levels of harm have been caused – see the [*TICs and Totality Guideline 2012: Crown Court*].

In a case of particular gravity, reflected by extremely serious violence, a sentence in excess of 13 years may be appropriate.

	Culpability		
Harm	**A**	**B**	**C**
Category 1	**Starting point** 13 years' custody **Category range** 10 to 16 years' custody	**Starting point** 8 years' custody **Category range** 6 to 10 years' custody	**Starting point** 5 years' custody **Category range** 4 to 8 years' custody
Category 2	**Starting point** 8 years' custody **Category range** 6 to 10 years' custody	**Starting point** 5 years' custody **Category range** 4 to 8 years' custody	**Starting point** 3 years' custody **Category range** 2 to 5 years' custody

Category 3	Starting point 5 years' custody Category range 4 to 8 years' custody	Starting point 3 years' custody Category range 2 to 5 years' custody	Starting point 18 months' custody Category range 1 to 3 years' custody

322.12   [Aggravating and mitigating factors]

page 17 The table [below] contains a **non-exhaustive** list of additional factual elements providing the context of the offence and factors relating to the offender. Identify whether any combination of these, or other relevant factors, should result in an upward or downward adjustment from the sentence arrived at so far. In particular, relevant recent convictions are likely to result in an upward adjustment. In some cases, having considered these factors, it may be appropriate to move outside the identified category range.

Factors increasing seriousness

Statutory aggravating factors:
Previous convictions, having regard to: a) the **nature** of the offence to which the conviction relates and its **relevance** to the current offence; and b) the **time** that has elapsed since the conviction
Offence committed whilst on bail
Other aggravating factors:
Victim is targeted due to a vulnerability (or a perceived vulnerability)
Steps taken to prevent the victim reporting or obtaining assistance and/or from assisting or supporting the prosecution
Prolonged nature of event
Restraint, detention or additional degradation of the victim
Involvement of others through coercion, intimidation or exploitation
Timing of the offence
Attempt to conceal identity (for example, wearing a balaclava or hood)
Commission of offence whilst under the influence of alcohol or drugs
Attempts to conceal/dispose of evidence
Child or vulnerable person at home (or returns home) when offence committed
Victim compelled to leave their home
Established evidence of community/wider impact
Failure to comply with current court orders
Offence committed on licence
Offences taken into consideration
Failure to respond to warnings about behaviour

Factors reducing seriousness or reflecting personal mitigation

No previous convictions **or** no relevant/recent convictions
Remorse, particularly where evidenced by voluntary reparation to the victim
Good character and/or exemplary conduct
Serious medical condition requiring urgent, intensive or long-term treatment
Age and/or lack of maturity where it affects the responsibility of the offender
Mental disorder or learning disability (where not linked to the commission of the offence)
Sole or primary carer for dependent relatives
Determination and/or demonstration of steps having been taken to address addiction or offending behaviour

For a suggested approach to the guideline, see **322.3**.

322.13   *Firearm, With   Guideline*

Each of the three sections in the *Robbery Guideline 2016*, see www.banksr.com Other Matters Guidelines tab at pages 4, 10 and 16, have the same factor demonstrating 'High culpability' namely:

| **A High** | • Production of a bladed article or firearm or imitation firearm to threaten violence |

For the full guideline for: a) dwelling robberies, see **322.9**, b) professionally planned commercial robberies, see **322.4**, and c) street and less sophisticated commercial robberies, see **322.26**.

322.14   *Firearm, With   Concurrent or consecutive sentences   Pre-2016 guideline cases*

TICs and Totality Guideline 2012: Crown Court, see www.banksr.com Other Matters Guidelines tab page 6 (*Magistrates' Court Sentencing Guidelines 2008* page 18h)

Where concurrent sentences are to be passed the sentence should reflect the overall criminality involved. The sentence should be appropriately aggravated by the presence of the associated offences. Examples include:...robbery with a weapon where the weapon offence is ancillary to the robbery and is not distinct and independent of it. The principal sentence for the robbery should properly reflect the presence of the weapon. The court must avoid double-counting and may deem it preferable for the possession of the weapon's offence to run concurrently to avoid the appearance of under-sentencing in respect of the robbery.[952]

R v Ajala and Others 2011 EWCA Crim 2507, 2012 1 Cr App R (S) 107 (p 644) The defendants pleaded to robbery and two counts of possession of an imitation firearm with intent. The Judge followed the remarks of the Lord Chief Justice in *R v Greaves and Jaffier* 2003 EWCA Crim 3229, 2004 2 Cr App R (S) 10 (p 41) where it was said, "The policy which should be adopted is to make the firearm sentence consecutive. That gives a clear message to those who commit crimes of this nature that if they carry a weapon when committing a robbery they will receive an additional sentence." Held. We agree that consecutive sentences were appropriate for firearm offences.

322.15   *Firearm, With   No firearm count*

R v Eubank 2001 EWCA Crim 891, 2002 1 Cr App R (S) 4 (p 11) LCJ D pleaded to a single count of robbery. There was an issue whether D had a firearm. The Judge held a *Newton* hearing and concluded that D at least had an imitation weapon. Held. Before D is convicted of such a grave offence he is entitled to have a verdict of the jury. The appropriate course was to include a count in the indictment to make their position clear. As there was no count, it was wrong to sentence him on the basis that he had a firearm.

R v Flamson 2001 EWCA Crim 3030, 2002 2 Cr App R (S) 48 (p 208) The prosecution told the Judge that there was no dispute about the firearm. Automatic life upheld.

R v Murphy 2002 EWCA Crim 1624, 2003 1 Cr App R (S) 39 (p 181) In 1997 D pleaded to robbery. There was no firearm count. The prosecution did not agree the basis of plea, and the Judge held a *Newton* hearing and concluded that D had something with him that looked like a gun. He was sentenced and released. He robbed a petrol station, and his accomplice had a gun. He was convicted of robbery, and again there was no firearm count. The second Judge read the transcript from the *Newton* hearing from the first robbery and passed an automatic life sentence. Held. *R v Eubank* 2001 EWCA Crim 891, 2002 1 Cr App R (S) 4 (p 11) applied. In both cases there should have been separate firearm counts. It was inappropriate to hold a *Newton* hearing. The proceedings were flawed, so the life sentence was quashed.

R v Townsend 2003 EWCA Crim 2210, 2004 1 Cr App R (S) 47 (p 281) D pleaded to robbery, and the prosecution counsel said that leading counsel for the defence had told him the previous robbery conviction involved an imitation firearm. He was sentenced to automatic life. Held. We do not seek to undervalue the authority of *R v Eubank* 2001 EWCA Crim 891, 2002 1 Cr App R (S) 4 (p 11) in the context in which it applies. We are faced with different views in *R v Flamson* 2001 EWCA Crim 3030, 2002 2 Cr App R (S) 48 (p 208) and *R v Murphy* 2002 EWCA Crim 1624, 2003 1 Cr App R (S) 39

---

[952] *Att-Gen's Ref Nos 21-22 of 2003* 2003 EWCA Crim 3089, 2004 2 Cr App R (S) 13 (p 63)

(p 181). It is not proper to gloss the statute to require there be a separate firearms count. We should follow *R v Flamson* 2001 EWCA Crim 3030, 2002 2 Cr App R (S) 48 (p 208). *R v Murphy* 2002 EWCA Crim 1624, 2003 1 Cr App R (S) 39 (p 181) was decided *per incuriam*.

R v Benfield 2003 EWCA Crim 2223, 2004 1 Cr App R (S) 52 (p 307) LCJ D pleaded to robbery. The prosecution case was that he was armed with a firearm. There was no issue about the firearm raised at the hearing. He received automatic life. Held. It appears that his counsel did not direct their minds to the issue of the automatic life provisions. The fact there was no dispute about the possession of the firearm must be established and must be abundantly clear. There should be no doubt about the position for the subsequent and the prior offence. If it isn't dealt with, the matter must be resolved in favour of the defendant. The life sentence is set aside.

R v Hylands 2004 EWCA Crim 2999, 2005 2 Cr App R (S) 25 (p 135) D was convicted of robbery. The defence did not expressly admit that D had a firearm. The Judge held that D was in joint possession of a firearm. Held. We accept that had the jury been asked they would have found D in possession of the firearm. *R v Murphy* 2002 EWCA Crim 1624, 2003 1 Cr App R (S) 39 (p 181) and *R v Eubank* 2002 1 Cr App R (S) 4 (p 11) are binding on us. The provisions only apply where the defendant admits the firearm or the jury return a special verdict. Life sentence quashed.

R v Gore 2010 EWCA Crim 369, 2 Cr App R (S) 93 (p 590) D was given IPP based on a previous offence being with a firearm. Held. CJA 2003 Sch 15A para 10 is wide enough to embrace joint possession in a joint enterprise robbery where the defendant did not actually have possession of the firearm. *R v Flamson* 2002 and *R v Benfield* 2004 applied. The situation must be abundantly clear. This concession by D's leading counsel made it abundantly clear.

See also: *R v Yusuf and Others Re M* 2014 EWCA Crim 1586, 2015 1 Cr App R (S) 4 (p 23) at para 28 (Plea to conspiracy to rob. Judge sentenced on the basis defendant knew the gun had been taken to the scene. That was wrong here because [of the way the case had developed].)

Note: All the cases except the last two were concerned with old automatic life, which has been repealed. Similar issues have developed with Criminal Justice Act 2003 Sch 15A and have developed with the 2012 automatic life sentence for robberies when it is claimed that the defendant had a firearm with him or her. Ed.

322.16   Firearm, With   Series of robberies   Pre-2016 guideline judicial guidance

R v McCartney 2003 EWCA Crim 1372 Those who make a career of crime should receive more severe punishment than those who have been convicted of only one offence. Something must be added to the basic offence for those who commit more than one robbery.

R v Jenkins and Others 2008 EWCA Crim 1372, 2009 1 Cr App R (S) 20 (p 109) The defendants pleaded to armed robberies. Held. The maximum reserved for the most serious offences appears to be in the region of 25 years. *R v Turner* 1975 61 Cr App R 67 is no longer a reliable guide. The maximum sentence for a number of armed robberies where actual violence is used appears to be in the region of 25 years.

R v De Carvalho and Fraser 2013 EWCA Crim 2249 D and F were convicted of robbery (×11). They were also convicted of firearms offences in relation to eight of the robberies. There was a series of robberies of small supermarkets over a period of about two years. Held. It was made clear in *R v Jenkins and Others* 2008 EWCA Crim 1372, 2009 1 Cr App R (S) 20 (p 109) and *R v Knight* 2010 EWCA Crim 237, 2 Cr App R (S) 84 (p 541) that the level of sentence in *R v Turner* 1975 is no longer applicable. The sentence is about 25 years.

Note: The *Robbery Guideline 2016* takes precedence over these cases. Ed.

322.17   Firearm, With   Series of robberies   Pre-2016 guideline cases

R v Cronin 2009 EWCA Crim 3320 H, C and D pleaded to a conspiracy to rob and conspiracy to possess firearms. H also pleaded to other matters (which may not have affected the outcome). H asked for two robberies to be taken into consideration (no details given). H's plea was early, the other pleas were later. H was involved in four robberies and an unsuccessful one. C and D were involved with one each. The robbers were driven to the scene in a stolen car. Security guards were threatened with an imitation gun and ordered to drop their box. The car was driven to a changeover place where the robbers left in another stolen car. £25,000 was the typical gain. H was the prime mover. C's role was at the car changeover. D carried no firearm. H was aged a little under 21 with no convictions. D was aged 19 and of relatively good character. He had made good progress and behaved well in prison. The Judge started at 22 years. For C and D he started at 15 years. Held. Allowance should have been made for the fact that the firearms were imitation and their youth. The starting points were too high. **11 years** not 13 for H. For C and D, **9 years** not 10.

R v De Carvalho and Fraser 2013 EWCA Crim 2249 D and F were convicted of robbery (×11). They were also convicted of firearms offences in relation to eight of the robberies. Additionally, D was convicted of possessing a firearm with intent and possession of ammunition. D and F were involved in a series of robberies of small supermarkets over a period of about two years. They took place early in the morning when the supermarkets were about to open. In eight of the robberies, the robbers were armed with a loaded revolver. In a number of cases, victims were shown the ammunition inside the gun. Staff were made to open safes at gunpoint and in some cases had their wrists bound with cable ties. The robbers wore disguises. The robbers made off with over £100,000 in cash and a quantity of cigarettes. The Judge found that they were planned robberies. When the police arrested D at his home, they found a revolver and ammunition. D was aged 34 at his appeal and F aged 28. D had convictions for much less serious offences but F was of good character. The Judge imposed 16 years for the robberies, consecutive to 8 years for the firearms and an additional 4 years consecutive for D for the additional firearm counts. Held. There can be no doubt that the victims will be affected for a long time. These offences clearly merited long sentences. The offences were outside of the guidelines. They were serious, planned, professional robberies. They may not have been of banks or security vehicles but they involved the use of firearms, were planned, and substantial amounts were taken. D was still in possession of the weapon when he was arrested. To make the sentence for that count consecutive contains an element of double counting. The sentence of 4 years for the gun and ammunition were unlawful sentences as they were subject to the minimum sentence and there was no reason as to why that should not be imposed. They would be increased to 5 years but to be served concurrently. For D, **24 years** not 28. For F, **24 years** upheld.

See also: *R v Wynne and Others* 2013 EWCA Crim 945, 2014 1 Cr App R (S) 14 (p 63) (Pleas (20%) to various offences relating to a conspiracy to commit armed robberies on banks and building societies spanning 12 years. Attacked cash-in-transit security guards at bank premises at night. Wore masks and carried firearms including a Walther PPK pistol and a 0.38 revolver. Restrained guards with cable ties where necessary. Used angle grinder and hydraulic press to gain entry to premises. **19½ years** for H (4 robberies) not 22 and **17½ years** for W (3 robberies) and K (2 robberies, reconnaissance work and work prior to a robbery).

R v Curwen 2014 EWCA Crim 1046 (Convicted of eight robberies. Escaped from prison while serving life for 14 armed robberies. **Life** with a minimum term of **8 years** not 10.) For more detail, see **322.54**.

Old cases: Best ignored.

See also the *Series of robberies* paras at **322.21**.

322.18   *Getaway drivers   Pre-2016 guideline case*
R v McMahon and Others 2010 EWCA Crim 716 The defendants were sentenced for
armed robbery. There were two getaway drivers and two robbers. Held. The Judge was
right to treat the defendants the same.
Highway robbery see the **Vehicles** paras at **322.42**.

322.19   *Looting   Pre-2016 guideline case*
Att-Gen's Ref No 5 of 2012 2012 EWCA Crim 964, 2013 1 Cr App R (S) 15 (79) LCJ D
pleaded at his PCMH to four robberies, violent disorder, three burglaries and two
criminal damage counts. In 2011, D was at the front of rioters advancing towards a
police line in the Croydon riots. He was armed with bricks and debris and took someone
else's scarf to mask his face. D threw a missile at the officers and another at a shop. Then
for several hours the group terrorised shopkeepers and members of the public. The
crowd confronted a bus and forced it to stop. The windows of the bus were attacked with
weapons and missiles. The driver's windscreen was smashed and the driver, V1, was
showered with glass. V1 was so terrified he didn't flee. Property was stolen from his cab.
He was attacked with sticks. D also went into a sweetshop armed with a pole. The shop
was ransacked. D left with stolen items. A shop assistant was violently attacked. Nearby
buildings were set on fire. The owners, V2 and V3, a married couple, feared their shop
would be set alight but eventually managed to flee. Their van stopped at a red light and
V2 could not see sufficiently to 'jump' the lights. The rioters surrounded the van. V2's
window was smashed and the doors opened. V2 was threatened with a knife. Money was
taken from his pockets and he was pulled from the van. The group threatened to burn the
vehicle and its occupants. D, armed with a metal pole, and another stole items from V3's
handbag. V3 was then pulled from the van and forced across the road. D remained with
her and stopped her helping V2. D then went to the back of the van and struck it but
failed to open it. V2 suffered swelling to his face. V3 had pain to her wrist. They were
both traumatised and their clothing was torn. The damage to the shop was £30,000 to
£40,000. V2 had to pay large sums of excess insurance to replace stolen stock. Fearful of
a repeat attack, V2 left the business and was in great financial difficulty.
V4 was using a cash machine when D attacked him with a hammer. V4 was put in a
headlock and forced to enter his PIN. While his throat was squeezed £40 was taken.
Next D in a group wearing disguises smashed the windows of a Tesco Express. D
climbed the counter, attacked the door to the back of the cash machine but failed to break
it down. D and others then climbed over the service counter and took whatever they
could. All the windows were broken, the till drawers were missing, the safe was
damaged and the refrigeration equipment was extensively damaged. Someone broke an
internal wall and damage to the cash machine was estimated to be nearly £30,000. As a
result the store closed down. An hour later, D was at the front of a group who forced
their way into a William Hill betting office. D kicked and threw a waste bin at the
security screen. He and others went to the back office. Gaming machines were pulled
from the wall. The damage to the betting shop was just over £18,500. D was now aged
20 and of good character. He told the author of his pre-sentence report that he was in
custody for robbing someone of £40. Held. With youth, plea and good character **7 years'**
detention not 4.
See also the **Riot** chapter and the **Burglary** *Shops Looting during public disturbance*
paras at **219.51**.

322.20   *Luring victim to secluded spot   Pre-2016 guideline case*
R v Kelly 2012 EWCA Crim 1039 D pleaded (full credit) to robbery. She approached V,
who was sitting in his car. She said that she was lost and V offered her a lift. D used V's
phone under the pretence that she was phoning her father, when in fact she was giving
information to a group of men as to their location. She took V to the agreed destination,
whereupon V was attacked. He was struck with a hammer. V was told one of his
attackers had a gun. He was repeatedly struck in the face with the hammer and punched

by a number of individuals. He was also poked with scissors but protected by his thick clothing. The group demanded money, bank cards and his PIN and took £700, mobile phones, a satellite navigation system and a stereo. V did not suffer serious physical injury, sustaining only cuts and bruises on his head, a lost tooth and cut to his lower lip. The ordeal lasted for three hours. D, aged just 16 at the time of the offence, had convictions for shoplifting and obstructing a police officer (Referral Order in 2009). She also had a warning and a reprimand for low-level offences. D had a troubled background, with considerable vulnerabilities. Her young age, below average cognitive abilities and low self-esteem all increased her vulnerability. A clinical psychologist considered these to be 'significant potential mitigating factors'. The Judge started at 12 years' detention for the co-defendants. Held. This was a robbery of the utmost seriousness with significant aggravating features. The 12 years was correct. It was planned and the victim abducted. He was not severely injured but had to endure the most terrifying ordeal. Taking account of her vulnerability and age, the appropriate starting point was 4½ years not 6. With the plea, **3 years'** detention not 4.

R v Manikum 2012 EWCA Crim 1828 D was convicted of robbery. She was offering sexual services in an area of Bristol. She was talking to two men, who walked away as another man, V, approached her. D and V discussed what V wanted and he asked whether D knew somewhere where the activity could take place. D said she would ask her friends and disappeared. She returned and took V to a disused garage. She began to give V oral sex and two men came in and threatened V. One stood behind him and the other placed his arm around his neck. One of the men said, "If you don't give us your fucking money, I'll kill you". One of the men punched V in the face and the body. V handed over his wallet. On one account, it was handed to D. The men and D left together. V suffered an injury to the eye, bruising and swelling to his body and face. D denied involvement in the robbery, but at trial accepted she was given £30 from V's wallet and told to keep quiet about what she had seen. D, aged 42, had 28 offences between 1992 and 2011. Most of the offences were motoring offences. However, in 2011 she received a community order (with a drug treatment requirement) for two offences of fraud. Held. D's role was to be the bait. It was a serious offence, committed whilst D was subject to a community order. D has no previous violent offending. The appropriate sentence was **3½ years** not 4½.

See also the *Taxi drivers and delivery staff* paras at **322.39**.

322.21   Series of robberies   Pre-2016 guideline judicial guidance
Att-Gen's Ref Nos 24-28 and 41 of 2006 2006 EWCA Crim 1617, 2007 1 Cr App R (S) 50 (p 278) The defendants were involved in robbing 14 small businesses like McDonald's and newsagents in south and south-east London over a three-month period. Three defendants admitted involvement in eight robberies, one in ten and one in five. Held. Deterring others is an important part of sentencing for offences on vulnerable premises. A campaign of robbery like this, committed by adults with knives, crowbars and other weapons carried and sometimes used, would merit **15 years or more** even where there were no previous convictions. It is important to maintain a proper differential between a single robbery or a very few robberies and a campaign of multiple robberies.

Att-Gen's Ref Nos 32-34 of 2007 2007 EWCA Crim 1375, 2008 1 Cr App R (S) 35 (p 187) The three defendants pleaded to two robberies. They carried out two nearly identical robberies within two hours. The Judge passed concurrent sentences. Held. The Judge could not be criticised if he had passed consecutive sentences and he cannot be criticised for passing concurrent ones.

Note: Both these cases are old, but they reflect current sentencing practice. Ed.

322.22   Series of robberies   Pre-2016 guideline case
R v Brennan 2014 EWCA Crim 78 D pleaded on the day of trial to robbery. He was a passenger in a car driven by his cousin. They parked in a country lane so that D could urinate in a field. By chance, a group of four young people were walking up the lane in

order to feed a horse belonging to one of them. There were two boys and two girls, all aged 14. They walked past the car in single file. It was about 7 pm and it was dark. D approached them and blocked their path. He demanded that they hand over their mobile phones and threatened to batter them. He ordered one boy to empty his pockets and the boy handed over £1 and his phone. One girl handed over her phone. D told them to go away or he would hurt them. They ran away and watched from a distance. When the car left, they returned and retrieved one of the phones, which had been dropped on the ground. The first trial was aborted due to there being further evidence available adverse to the defence case. D pleaded on the day of the second trial. D[953] had three previous robberies (5 years' detention, 3 years, and 3 years) on his record in addition to a variety of other offences. The Judge sentenced outside of the guidelines and started at 6 years. Held. This case did not fall squarely within Category 1 (which refers to the threat of minimal force). D threatened more than minimal force. This was not a single robbery but two robberies and two attempted robberies. The fact they were committed on the same occasion makes it less serious than if there had been a spree of separate offences. The Judge was correct in principle to move outside of the guidelines. D had a bad record but also three robbery convictions for similar robberies. The failure to respond to previous sentences is an aggravating feature. He is an habitual robber. **5½ years** was at the top, possibly the very top, of the acceptable range, but it was not manifestly excessive.

See also the *Commercial robberies, Professionally planned Series of robberies* para at **322.8**, *Firearm, With Series of robberies* paras at **322.16**, *Shops, petrol stations etc. More than one offence* para at **322.25**, and the *Street etc. robbery More than one robbery* para at **322.38**.

322.24   *Shops, petrol stations, etc.   Pre-2016 guideline judicial guidance*
Att-Gen's Ref No 7 of 1992 1993 14 Cr App R (S) 122 LCJ It has to be realised that corner shops, sub-post offices etc. are very often staffed by only one person, who may be unable to defend him or herself. It is unlikely there will be any sophisticated security there, and it is a prime target for someone who wants to enrich himself quickly and successfully. It is therefore very important that the courts should indicate by the sentences passed that that type of offence will be punished severely.

Note: This is an old case, but the guidance is as relevant today as it was when given. Ed.

322.25   *Shops, petrol stations, etc.   More than one offence   Pre-2016 guideline case*
R v O'Brien 2015 EWCA Crim 265 D pleaded (full credit) to robberies (×3), attempted robbery (×2), threatening with an article or blade (×3) and unlawful wounding. At 3 am one morning in May 2014 D went to McDonald's. Going behind the counter with a 6-8 inch knife, he shouted at the female manager, V1, "Open your fucking till." He counted down from five to one and threatened to slit her throat. D made off with £100 cash. Two days later, D entered a Co-op store and, in a similar way using the same knife, shouted at a female worker, V2, demanding money. D's face was covered and he made off with £666 of cash and £172 of stamps. Shortly after on the same day, D approached a 66-year-old lady, V3, and demanded her purse, which she had in one hand. Her walking stick was in the other. D took the purse and her handbag, both of which were later recovered. The next incident was an attempted robbery a few days later. D, taking the knife from his waistband, jumped over the counter in a family-run newsagents. He threatened to kill the shop worker, V4, who then tried to grab the knife. A scuffle ensued, causing cuts to V4's hands, needing five stitches. V4 felt that his life was threatened. This incident was seen by two 12-year-old girls, who ran off, scared. D ran off, dropping the knife, before he could take any money. D admitted the offences and had committed them in order to fund his drug habit, which cost £150-250 per day.

---

[953] D's age is not revealed.

D was aged 24 with antecedents mainly for drug possession and burglaries. All the offences had long-lasting effects upon the victims and D had written a letter of apology. Held. There were no aggravating factors for the robbery of V3 beyond the fact that this was one of a series of robberies. Two years, not three for that count, making **12 years** not 13 in all.

R v Baboukhan 2015 EWCA Crim 863 D pleaded to three attempted robberies (full credit). In the early evening, he entered a betting shop and went to the counter. He said to a female cashier, C, "Do me a favour put £500 on the counter. If you don't I'll pull something on these guys," indicating a man on a gambling machine. C asked what he was going to pull and D said, "A knife." C went to a staff area and D followed her. There was a brief struggle between the two and D said, "Do you think I am scared of the police." D then walked off. About a half an hour later he entered another betting shop nearby and D told the manager to go behind the counter and get £500. He appeared to be rambling and the manager, M, didn't take it seriously. D then offered to fight for the money, put his hand in his waistband and said it was a weapon. M thought he was about to be attacked. D left. 20 minutes later, at another betting shop nearby, D again asked for £500. The female staff member thought he was joking even when D said he had a knife. Putting his hands through a gap in the counter, D tried to grab some coins. Then he pushed two machines off the counter, hit the fire alarm and left. D was now aged 24 and had six sentencing appearances. They were mostly when he was a juvenile. In 2008, he received 42 months' detention for attempted robbery and possession of an imitation firearm. D told probation that on the day he had been drinking and taking class A drugs. A psychiatric report said he exhibited traits of an anti-social personality disorder and other disorders, but he was not mentally unwell. Held. The range was up to 3 years after a trial. We start at 6 years not 9, so with plea **4 years** not 6, the sentences to be concurrent not consecutive.

See also: *R v Sykes* 2011 EWCA Crim 2756 (Plea to conspiracy to rob. Implicated in 11 convenience stores robbed with accomplice. Face covered. Claw hammer brandished but not used to inflict violence. Demanded money from tills and, in later robberies, to be taken to the safes. £6,193 stolen. Committed to pay off gambling debts. Aged 25. Previous convictions for supply of cocaine and threatening words and behaviour. Under influence of accomplice. Starting at 12, **8 years** not 9.)

R v Coaker and Asher 2012 EWCA Crim 2771 (Pleas (20% credit) to conspiracy to rob and conspiracy to burgle. Over 10 days, targeted shops and petrol stations late at night. Two shops were ram-raided. Violence on more than one occasion including using a chisel to strike the victim. The wound required 15 stitches. Faces covered. Cigarettes and alcohol taken. Both heavily convicted. One was gratuitously violent and dangerous. The other was violent but not dangerous. **6½ years' IPP** not 8 years' IPP and **11 years** not 6 years' IPP.)

Old cases: Best ignored.

For an index of the 'series of robberies' paras see **322.22**.

322.26   *Street etc. robbery (including premises open to the public) Guideline*
Robbery Guideline 2016, see www.banksr.com Other Matters Guidelines tab
page 3 **Street and less sophisticated commercial robberies**
This guideline applies only to offenders aged 18 and over. [For the usual practice, see **66.21** in Volume 1.]

[This section of the guideline] refers to robberies committed in public places, including those committed in taxis or on public transport. It also refers to unsophisticated robberies within commercial premises or targeting commercial goods or money.

There is relevant guidance for sentencing young offenders within both the Sentencing Guidelines Council's [*Robbery Guideline 2006*], see **322.48**, and the [*Youths Sentencing Guideline 2009*]. These guidelines will continue to be in force until they are replaced by the Sentencing Council's new and updated guidance.

STEP ONE: Determining the offence category

page 4 The court should determine the offence category with reference **only** to the factors listed in the tables below. In order to determine the category the court should assess **culpability** and **harm**.

The court should weigh all the factors set out below in determining the offender's culpability.

Where there are characteristics present which fall under different levels of culpability, the court should balance these characteristics to reach a fair assessment of the offender's culpability.

CULPABILITY demonstrated by one or more of the following	
A – High	• Use of a weapon to inflict violence • Production of a bladed article or firearm or imitation firearm to threaten violence • Use of very significant force in the commission of the offence • Offence motivated by, or demonstrating hostility based on any of the following characteristics or presumed characteristics of the victim: religion, race, disability, sexual orientation or transgender identity
B – Medium	• Production of a weapon other than a bladed article or firearm or imitation firearm to threaten violence • Threat of violence by any weapon (but which is not produced) • Other cases where characteristics for Categories A or C are not present
C – Lesser	• Involved through coercion, intimidation or exploitation • Threat or use of minimal force • Mental disability or learning disability where linked to the commission of the offence

322.27   Harm

page 4 The court should consider the factors set out below to determine the level of harm that has been caused or was intended to be caused to the victim.

Category 1	• Serious physical and/or psychological harm caused to the victim • Serious detrimental effect on the business
Category 2	• Other cases where characteristics for Categories 1 or 3 are not present
Category 3	• No/minimal physical or psychological harm caused to the victim • No/minimal detrimental effect on the business

322.28

STEP TWO: Starting point and category range

page 5 Having determined the category at step one, the court should use the corresponding starting point to reach a sentence within the category range below. The starting point applies to all offenders irrespective of plea or previous convictions. A case of particular gravity, reflected by multiple features of culpability or harm in step one, could merit upward adjustment from the starting point before further adjustment for aggravating or mitigating features, set out on the next page.

Consecutive sentences for multiple offences may be appropriate – see the [*TICs and Totality Guideline 2012: Crown Court*].

Harm	Culpability		
	A	**B**	**C**
Category 1	**Starting point** 8 years' custody **Category range** 7 to 12 years' custody	**Starting point** 5 years' custody **Category range** 4 to 8 years' custody	**Starting point** 4 years' custody **Category range** 3 to 6 years' custody
Category 2	**Starting point** 5 years' custody **Category range** 4 to 8 years' custody	**Starting point** 4 years' custody **Category range** 3 to 6 years' custody	**Starting point** 2 years' custody **Category range** 1 to 4 years' custody
Category 3	**Starting point** 4 years' custody **Category range** 3 to 6 years' custody	**Starting point** 2 years' custody **Category range** 1 to 4 years' custody	**Starting point** 1 years' custody **Category range** High-level community order to 3 years' custody

322.29   [Aggravating and mitigating factors]

page 5 The table [below] contains a **non-exhaustive** list of additional factual elements providing the context of the offence and factors relating to the offender. Identify whether any combination of these, or other relevant factors, should result in an upward or downward adjustment from the sentence arrived at so far. In particular, relevant recent convictions are likely to result in an upward adjustment. In some cases, having considered these factors, it may be appropriate to move outside the identified category range.

Factors increasing seriousness

Statutory aggravating factors:
Previous convictions, having regard to: a) the **nature** of the offence to which the conviction relates and its **relevance** to the current offence; and b) the **time** that has elapsed since the conviction
Offence committed whilst on bail
Other aggravating factors:
High-value goods or sums targeted or obtained (whether economic, personal or sentimental)
Victim is targeted due to a vulnerability (or a perceived vulnerability)
Significant planning
Steps taken to prevent the victim reporting or obtaining assistance and/or from assisting or supporting the prosecution
Prolonged nature of event
Restraint, detention or additional degradation of the victim
A leading role where offending is part of a group activity
Involvement of others through coercion, intimidation or exploitation
Location of the offence (including cases where the location of the offence is the victim's residence)
Timing of the offence
Attempt to conceal identity (for example, wearing a balaclava or hood)
Commission of offence whilst under the influence of alcohol or drugs
Attempts to conceal/dispose of evidence
Established evidence of community/wider impact
Failure to comply with current court orders
Offence committed on licence
Offences taken into consideration
Failure to respond to warnings about behaviour

Factors reducing seriousness or reflecting personal mitigation
No previous convictions **or** no relevant/recent convictions
Remorse, particularly where evidenced by voluntary reparation to the victim
Good character and/or exemplary conduct
Serious medical condition requiring urgent, intensive or long-term treatment
Age and/or lack of maturity where it affects the responsibility of the offender
Mental disorder or learning disability (where not linked to the commission of the offence)
Little or no planning
Sole or primary carer for dependent relatives
Determination and/or demonstration of steps having been taken to address addiction or offending behaviour

Note: Street robbery cases heard before the *Robbery Guideline 2016* applied are not listed unless there is a special feature to the case. Ed.
For a suggested approach to the guideline, see **322.3**.

322.30   *Street etc. robbery   Pre-2016 guideline judicial guidance*
R v Edward and Larter 1987 The Times 3/2/87 LCJ The defendants were convicted of robbery and received 5 years. Held. Judges should impose long sentences on muggers who attack others, particularly women at night in urban areas. The amount of money was beside the point.
Att-Gen's Ref No 6 of 1994 1995 16 Cr App R (S) 343 at 345 LCJ Street robberies make the public afraid to walk out alone. The public require protection. There must be an element of deterrence to protect the public. Even a first offender must expect a period of custody.
Att-Gen's Ref Nos 19-21 of 2001 2001 EWCA Crim 1432, 2002 1 Cr App R (S) 33 (p 136) There can be little doubt that the two forms of criminal conduct which cause the public most concern are domestic burglary and street robberies. The effect of such offences goes way beyond the dreadful trauma suffered by the immediate victim and causes large sections of the public to alter their lifestyle to seek to avoid the danger. People are afraid to go out of their homes.
Att-Gen's Ref Nos 4 and 7 of 2002 2002 EWCA Crim 127, 2 Cr App R (S) 77 (p 345) LCJ We have to adopt a robust sentencing policy. Punishment will be severe. Custodial sentences will be the only option unless there are exceptional circumstances irrespective of age and lack of previous convictions.
Att-Gen's Ref No 22 of 2008 2008 EWCA Crim 1516, 2009 1 Cr App R (S) 54 (p 293) D pleaded to attempted robbery. He and another attacked a man at an ATM. Held. In *Att-Gen's Ref Nos 4 and 7 of 2002* 2002 EWCA Crim 127, 2 Cr App R (S) 77 (p 345) the Lord Chief Justice said, "The information available points to telephones playing a part in the rise in robberies. Those aged under 18 constitute 48% of all victims with a peak at 15 and 16. The courts have no alternative but to adopt a robust sentencing policy. Punishment will be severe. Custodial sentences will be the only option unless there are exceptional circumstances irrespective of age and lack of previous convictions. However, both those factors are very important when considering the length of a sentence." Although that case concerned mobiles, cases about bank cards are no less prevalent.
Note: These cases were heard before the *Robbery Guideline 2016* was issued. They are also old. However, the guidance seems still correct. Ed.

322.31   *Street etc. robbery   Particularly vulnerable victim   Pre-2016 guideline cases*
Note: Clearly all victims of street robbery are vulnerable. This paragraph deals with those particularly vulnerable. Ed.
R v Griffiths 2010 EWCA Crim 1059 D pleaded early to attempted robbery. V, aged 61, was driving along the road in his electric wheelchair. D approached V from behind and asked him for £10. V refused. D snatched V's keys from his pocket. V grabbed D's arm and said "Give them back". For a few seconds they struggled and D continued trying to

pull the keys away. A passer-by shouted at D. D walked away. D, aged 35, had 24 court appearances for 40 offences over a nine-year period, largely for theft, and a conviction for assault with intent to rob (3 years). He had robbed a wheelchair user in his home before tipping him onto the floor. In interview D made admissions. The pre-sentence report said: a) D accepted full responsibility, b) the Probation Service tools indicated that D posed a medium risk of harm and reoffending, c) the probation officer considered that D posed a high risk of reoffending due to his drug addiction, and d) D admitted that he struggled to control his addiction when at liberty. The psychiatric report said D had long-standing personality difficulties. D had an unstable family background, a traumatic childhood, a diagnosis of paranoid schizophrenia and co-morbid diagnosis of opioid dependence. Held. The aggravating features were: targeting a disabled person and a previous conviction for the same offence. **3 years** not 10 years' extended sentence (4 years' custody 6 years' licence).

Att-Gen's Ref No 3 of 2010 2010 EWCA Crim 1256 D pleaded to robbery. X approached V, an 80-year-old woman, from behind and grabbed her bag. V fell to the ground and X ran away with V's bag towards an alleyway where he met D. V had to wait 10 minutes before anyone came to help her. V sustained a fractured shoulder, a broken leg and substantial nerve damage to her arm, which reduced mobility. She had to be helped around in a wheelchair and had very little confidence going out. There was newspaper reporting of the incident with CCTV pictures. D surrendered to police. In interview he made no comment, and in a defence statement he denied the offence but did reveal X's name and address. One month later he pleaded guilty. D, aged 25, had two previous convictions for robbery when aged about 14 years, and also convictions for theft, shoplifting and common assault. D expressed remorse for the offence and towards V and was disgusted at the injuries V had sustained. Held. D did not foresee V's injuries. The starting point was in the region of **6 years**. The cumulative effect of the mitigating factors made it **4 years**. **3½ years** was not unduly lenient.

R v Hume 2011 EWCA Crim 29 D pleaded to robbery and assault by beating. The victim, V, was a 76-year-old pensioner. V had collected her pension, £220, and got back into her car. As she tried to shut the door, D forced it open and took her handbag. There was a struggle in which V suffered a minor injury to her finger. D ran away and was chased by another woman. There was another struggle and D struck the woman. The bag was eventually retrieved by another passer-by. D was subsequently arrested. The Judge said that a more disgusting and low offence of robbery was not imaginable. D, aged 41, had 22 previous convictions including 11 for theft, five for unlawful wounding and four for ABH. Held. This offence falls into the very bottom of the second category. That has a starting point of 4 years' custody. After a trial, the appropriate sentence would have been 4 years' imprisonment. Therefore, with full credit for the plea, **32 months** for the robbery and **4 months** (undisturbed) for the assault consecutive.

R v Weir-Steele 2014 EWCA Crim 682 D pleaded to two separate street robberies. She robbed V1, a 72-year old man, as he sat outside a centre run by the mental health charity MIND. He was pushed hard to the ground, grazing his hand, and his wallet was taken. V2, an 88-year old woman, was robbed as she walked home from the bus stop. D grabbed V2's handbag, causing her to lose her balance and fall, grazing her elbow. Nearly £200 was taken in total. D, aged 28, had convictions in 2001 and 2002 for assault and had a drug dependency. In interview D spoke of how she got an adrenaline rush from stealing, and a psychiatric report concluded she suffered from bipolar disorder. Held. Both robberies targeted very vulnerable elderly people and involved the use of force, resulting in injury. Aggravating and mitigating factors broadly cancel each other out. Concurrent sentences would be wrong. We take a starting point of 42 months for the first, reducing it to 28 months with plea. For the second we start at 54 months making 36 months with the plea. With totality we make that 24 and 30 months, so **4½ years**, which was the Judge's sentence and entirely in accordance with the guideline.

Old cases: Best ignored.

See also the *Victim particularly vulnerable* para at **322.43**.

322.32   Street etc. robbery Victim injured   Guideline
Robbery Guideline 2016, see www.banksr.com Other Matters Guidelines tab Each of the three sections of the guideline have the same entry in the Harm section about the harm caused to the victim, see pages 4, 10 and 16.

STEP ONE: Determining the offence category
[Introductory and Culpability text not listed]
Harm
pages 4, 10 and 16 The court should weigh up all the factors set out below to determine the harm that has been caused or was intended to be caused to the victim.

Category 1	• Serious physical and/or psychological harm caused to the victim • [other factors not listed]

For the full guideline for a) dwelling robberies, see **322.9**, b) professionally planned commercial robberies, see **322.4** and c) street and less sophisticated commercial robberies, see **322.26**.

322.33   Street etc. robbery   Victim injured   Pre-2016 guideline cases
Att-Gen's Ref Nos 77-78 of 2009 2010 EWCA Crim 199 LCJ G and H were convicted of robbery, kidnap, three frauds and ABH. V, aged 22, lived at home and was vulnerable. He had been bullied at school. V was seen at a bowling alley by G and H. He drank three pints of lager, and at about 11 pm he left for home. In an alleyway he was attacked by G and H. V felt a blow to his head from a fist or a foot. His glasses were knocked off. H grabbed him from behind while G pulled out a knife. His wallet was taken. V was marched to an ATM with a knife held to his back. V's family was threatened and V was told, "We're going to make you watch and kill you last". V was very scared. £250 was stolen. He was then taken to a petrol station where £70 of alcohol and cigarettes were paid for with V's debit card at 12.29 am. V was taken to G's home and made to carry the purchases while he was kicked and punched. At the flat, V was pushed down the stairs. He fell and struck his head. He was again assaulted. V managed to escape. He felt unable to tell his father what had happened. V had bruising around both eyes. One eye was almost completely closed. His lip and nose were cut. There were also bruises and scratches. V suffered from blurred vision, panic attacks, insomnia and anxiety. A couple of days later, father and son went to the police station about the card misuse. V was reluctant to name his attackers. H and G were arrested and made denials. Eight months later V was withdrawn, had difficulty sleeping and had spoken of suicide. G, aged 21, had numerous convictions since he was aged 14 for offences of dishonesty, minor violence and public order offences. They included: 2004, dishonesty (6 months' DTO), 2006, attempted theft and battery (4 months' DTO), 2006, attempted arson and aggravated vehicle-taking (51 weeks' suspended) which was breached (6 months), and in 2007 and 2008, four appearances where non-immediate custody was imposed. H, aged 22, had a large number of convictions, including minor violence, public order offences, battery and two threatening behaviours. H was heavily involved with cocaine and heroin misuse. G misused crack and heroin. Held. V was subjected to gratuitous violence. He was terrified. Time and time again G and H were treated with leniency. **5 years** not 3.
R v Tshibangu 2013 EWCA Crim 678 D pleaded (full credit) to robbery. At about 6.30 pm V and his wife returned home to their block of flats. D and another were on the first floor landing inside the communal entrance. V and his wife attempted to walk up the stairs to their flat but their paths were blocked by D. D and another confronted V, who pushed his wife out of harm's way. They grabbed V's arms and tried to pull him to the floor but he resisted. D and another tried to take V's wristwatch. One of them (D denied it was him) bit V on the arm. V was punched about half a dozen times in the chest during the robbery before his watch was forcibly taken from him. D, aged 18, had seven appearances between 2007 and 2011. In 2007, he received a supervision order for

possessing a bladed article. In 2010, he received a Detention and Training Order for two robberies. In 2011, he received a Youth Rehabilitation Order for possession of a bladed article and later a Detention and Training Order for section 20 where he stabbed someone in the back with a kitchen knife arising out of a gang dispute. The pre-sentence report noted that D had a transient and difficult upbringing. He had written a letter of apology to V. References attested to D's positive character. Held. This was a Level 2 offence. There were aggravating features such as the fact that there were two men involved in the robbery, there was plainly an element of planning and the offence occurred in the precincts of V's home. There was also D's record. Mitigation came in the form of his age, his genuine remorse, the letter of apology and the references as to D's character. The appropriate starting point was in the region of **4½-5 years**. With the plea, **3 years 3 months** was appropriate. The issue of dangerousness therefore did not arise and the 8 years' extended sentence (4 years' custody 4 years' licence) was quashed.)

R v May 2013 EWCA Crim 850, 2014 1 Cr App R (S) 13 (p 58) D pleaded to two robberies. After midnight, D's accomplice approached V1 at a bus stop and asked for a cigarette and some change. While V1 was distracted D moved in and punched him. V1 was knocked unconscious and his wallet, mobile and Oyster card were stolen. He received a black eye and a suspected broken nose. D was arrested and lied in his interview. He was bailed. Three days later, at 3 am, V2 was with her male companion, C, in a street. D and H approached V2 in a 'pincer movement'. H asked V2 for a light and may have offered her drugs. V2 said she was not interested. H snatched her handbag, which was over her shoulder, and ran off. The bag had her mobile, keys and Oyster card. D held on to C to prevent him from helping V2. D was arrested by a policeman in a passing car. D was aged 25 when sentenced and had a bad record for dishonesty, some violence and a warning for a robbery. D had a significant drug problem. Held. Because of the force, the first robbery was a Category 2 offence. The starting point was 4 years. The aggravating factors were: a) group action, b) it was at night, and c) V1 was vulnerable because of the alcohol he had consumed. The second robbery was a Category 1 offence but aggravated by: a) the joint enterprise, b) the vulnerability of V2, c) it was at night, d) D was under the influence of drugs and alcohol and e) D was on bail. That moved it to a Category 2 offence. The starting point for both was **8 years**. With 20% credit that would produce a sentence of just over the **6 years 4 months** he received so appeal dismissed.

R v Jalo and Others 2014 EWCA Crim 1910 (**4 years**. For detail, see **322.38**.)

R v Tolbert and Another 2015 EWCA Crim 127 (For T **6½ years** and for R **4 years**, see **322.36**.)

R v Hedley 2015 EWCA Crim 225 D pleaded (full credit) to robbery. With D nearby, V withdrew cash from an ATM in the early hours of the morning. D then followed V, asking for a cigarette, which V gave him. D followed V again and then punched her hard, behind her right ear, and she fell to the ground. D then pulled at V's bag but she resisted and D punched and then kicked her. V relented. As D was walking away, she screamed out for help and D looked back. D realised that V still had her purse and went back to get it but V ran off. V was moderately hurt but unable to carry out normal household duties. She was emotionally affected and severely shaken. D was aged 32 with a poor record, including assaults on females and a wounding ten years or so prior. Held. There were no exceptionally serious aggravating factors. **4 years**, not 5 years 4 months.

See also: *R v Mykoo* 2010 EWCA Crim 989 (Plea. 19 robberies. Victims principally lone females attacked from behind and strangled to the point of unconsciousness. Accomplice would steal high-value items and threats were made to maim or kill. Between March and June in the same year. Knife carried, 65 TIC robberies over 10 years. 50 were strangulation robberies. Aged 29, previous convictions for robbery. Life with **14-year** term.)

R v McAffer 2010 EWCA Crim 2433 (Late plea. Level 2-3 street robbery. Victim was 48-year-old female, who was injured when she fell to the floor. Fracture to upper femur. As a result of injury she lost her job. Previous convictions for violence and dishonesty. Starting at 6 years, **5½ years**, not 7 years 4 months.)

R v Williams 2010 EWCA Crim 2722 (Early plea to attempted street robbery with 15-year-old nephew. One punch to face of victim. Demanded mobile phone. Previous convictions but none for robbery. **20 months**, not 32.)

R v Kulpi 2013 EWCA Crim 371 (With another, followed victim and punched him several times. Stole £4-5 from him. Victim suffered grazes, swollen lip and nose. Aged 18. No previous convictions. Category 2. Element of planning. With his age, good character and 10% for plea, **3½ years** not 4½.)

Att-Gen's Ref Nos 19-21 of 2013 2013 EWCA Crim 1260 (Two convicted of robbery. At least two knives used, one of which was held to the victim's chin. Committed at night. Neither was the ringleader. Three men approached victim talking on his mobile. iPhone stolen. Victim kicked and punched. Aged 19 and nearly 18. Both of positive good character. Cuts to the face, requiring stitches, and a black eye. Young. Good character. Expressed remorse. **5½ years' YOI** not 3½.)

Old cases: Best ignored.

322.34   *Street etc. robbery   Weapon used*
Robbery Guideline 2016, www.banksr.com Other Matters Guidelines tab page 9 Each of the three sections of the guideline have the same entry in the Culpability section about the harm caused to the victim, see pages 4, 10 and 16.

STEP ONE: Determining the offence category
[Introductory text not listed.]

CULPABILITY demonstrated by one or more of the following	
A – High	• Use of a weapon to inflict violence • Production of a bladed article or firearm or imitation firearm to threaten violence • [other factors not listed]
B – Medium	• Production of a weapon other than a bladed article or firearm or imitation firearm to threaten violence • Threat of violence by any weapon (but which is not produced) • [other factors not listed]

For the full guideline for a) dwelling robberies, see **322.9**, b) professionally planned commercial robberies, see **322.4**, and c) street and less sophisticated commercial robberies, see **322.26**.

See also the ***Firearm, With*** paras at **322.13**.

322.35   *Street etc. robbery   Defendant has significant record   Less than 5 years suitable   Pre-2016 guideline cases*
R v Hume 2011 EWCA Crim 29 D pleaded to robbery and assault by beating. The victim, V, was a 76-year-old pensioner. V had collected her pension, £220, and got back into her car. As she tried to shut the door, D forced it open and took her handbag. There was a struggle in which V suffered a minor injury to her finger. D ran away and was chased by another woman. There was another struggle and D struck the woman. The bag was eventually retrieved by another passer-by. D was subsequently arrested. The Judge said that a more disgusting and low offence of robbery was not imaginable. D, aged 41, had 22 previous convictions including 11 for theft, five for unlawful wounding and four for ABH. Held. This offence falls into the very bottom of the second category. That has a starting point of 4 years' custody. After a trial, the appropriate sentence would have been 4 years' imprisonment. Therefore, with full credit for the plea, **32 months** for the robbery and **4 months** (undisturbed) for the assault consecutive.

R v Tshibangu 2013 EWCA Crim 678 D pleaded (full credit) to robbery. At about 6.30 pm, V and his wife returned home to their block of flats. D and another were on the first-floor landing inside the communal entrance. V and his wife attempted to walk up the stairs to their flat but their paths were blocked by D. D and another confronted V, who pushed his wife out of harm's way. They grabbed his arms and tried to pull him to the floor but V resisted. D and another tried to take V's wristwatch. One of them (D denied it was him) bit V on the arm. V was punched about half a dozen times in the chest during the robbery before his watch was forcibly taken from him. D, aged 18, had seven appearances between 2007 and 2011. In 2007, he received a supervision order for possessing a bladed article. In 2010, he received a DTO for two robberies. In 2011, he received a YRO for possession of a bladed article and later a DTO for section 20 where he stabbed someone in the back with a kitchen knife arising out of a gang dispute. The pre-sentence report noted that D had a transient and difficult upbringing. He had written a letter of apology to V. References attested to D's positive character. Held. This was a Level 2 offence. There were aggravating features such as the fact there were two men involved in the robbery, there was plainly an element of planning and the offence occurred in the precincts of V's home. There was also D's record. Mitigation came in the form of his age, his genuine remorse, the letter of apology and the references as to D's character. The appropriate starting point was in the region of **4½-5 years**. With the plea, **3 years 3 months** was appropriate. The issue of dangerousness therefore did not arise and the 8 years' extended sentence (4 years' custody 4 years' licence) was quashed.)

R v Phillips 2013 EWCA Crim 2220 D pleaded to robbery. V, aged 16, was walking home. Whilst drunk and under the influence of drugs, with two others, D jumped over a fence, struck V over the back of the head and said, "Give me your money." D stood in front of V and punched him in the face. The blows caused V pain but left no lasting marks. D demanded V's mobile phone, which V handed over. One of the other two males with D said, "Leave him alone, he's only a kid." D then left the scene. D was aged 20 at appeal and had a bad record. There were convictions for attempted burglary, theft, common assault, both with and without racial aggravation, and public order matters, again both with and without racial aggravation. He had no previous convictions for robbery and had not been to custody for a significant period of time. The offence was committed within the operational period of a conditional discharge imposed for criminal damage. Held. D had showed genuine remorse, which the Judge had failed to refer to when sentencing. The Judge also referred to the robbery as a group attack. There was no evidence to justify that conclusion. The correct starting point was 3 years. With the plea, **2 years' YOI**, not 2 years 8 months.

R v Abraha and Another 2014 EWCA Crim 1889 D and F pleaded (full credit) to robbery. Due to large numbers of robberies of high-value items, undercover police were deployed. Two men approached V, who had been drinking, outside a nightclub in the small hours. V then sat down with D, F and another man. V was concerned that he was about to be robbed and stood up to leave. D then grabbed V tightly around the body, restraining him. F then violently pulled V's wrist, removing V's fake Rolex (although thought to be genuine). Undercover police saw the robbery and stopped D and F. F was seen to throw the watch onto the floor. D was aged 23 on appeal and had convictions for ABH and theft from the person, also committed with F in similar circumstances. F was aged 24 on appeal and had a poor record, including robbery, two further thefts from the person and various other thefts. The only remorse expressed by D or F was that they were caught. Held. The Judge was entitled to sentence outside the range of Level 1. This offence was serious and was prevalent in the area so the Judge was correct to have regard to deterrence. For D1, the appropriate staring point was 3½ years. Therefore **28 months**, not 3 years. For F, a starting point of 4½ years, with plea **3 years**, unaltered. Old cases: Best ignored.

322.36   Street etc. robbery   Defendant has significant record   5+ years suitable
Pre-2016 guideline cases

R v Taylor and Others 2012 EWCA Crim 630 T, H and C were convicted of robbery. V
performed with his band and walked home. He had with him four cans of lager and
kebabs. The ground was covered with snow and ice. He heard X, who had fallen and
broken his leg, call out for help. He rang for an ambulance and agreed to take X's two
dogs to a friend's house for safety. T, H and C arrived and one of them suggested they lift
X. V told him not to. That man shouted, "Don't you shout at me, you knob head". V felt
very intimidated and apologised, saying he had been told by the operator not to move X.
The others asked V for his beer cans. V said they were not his. One of them said, "If you
don't give us a tin we'll fucking kill ya." V feared for his safety, backed away and tried
to run off. Because of the conditions he could not. The defendants chased after V and
caught up with him. They punched V and knocked him to the ground. One produced a
knife and said, "Give me your fucking bag and give us your money or I'll stab you." V
threw his bag to them and asked them not to hurt him. The defendants walked away
laughing. V called the emergency services and returned to X. T was arrested when he
went back to X. T was now aged 26. H was now aged 23. C was aged 20, had never
received immediate custody before and was subject to a suspended sentence.[954] The
Judge described them as a gang of feral animals. Held. Notwithstanding the offence was
unplanned and opportunist in nature, it was a bad case. It was at night, there were three
robbers and V was trying to help X. It was a Level 2 case. T, **6 years** not 7. H and C,
7 years not 8, with C's suspended sentence activated consecutively.

R v Roxburgh 2013 EWCA Crim 230 D pleaded (25% credit) to robbery. He was on a
bus with some friends at about 10.30 pm. He went up to the top deck and saw V with
two friends. D was intimidating and asked V where he was from and said, "What are you
doing in my town?" D told V to get off the bus but when one of V's friends asked to get
off the bus, D prevented him from doing so. D asked what V had for him and how much
money he had. V replied that he had none. D asked about his mobile phone. V held it
out, stating that it was of poor quality. D took it. V saw that D had a Stanley knife. V's
friend also saw the knife and shouted that D had a knife and was mugging V and his
friends. V and his friends pushed past D, who threw a punch. D used the manual release
button to exit the bus after the driver refused to let him off. D was aged 18. He had 33
appearances for 80 offences. On four of those occasions he had faced six charges of
robbery of a similar nature. He was on a curfew at the time of the offence and was still
subject to the training period of a DTO. Held. The Judge should have taken account of
the range recommended both for an adult and an offender aged 17. After a trial, the
appropriate sentence was 80 months. With the plea, **5 years** not 6.

R v May 2013 EWCA Crim 850, 2014 1 Cr App R (S) 13 (p 58) D pleaded to two
robberies. After midnight, D's accomplice approached V1 and asked for a cigarette and
some change. While V1 was distracted, D moved in and punched him. V1 was knocked
unconscious and his wallet, mobile and Oyster card were stolen. He received a black eye
and a suspected broken nose. D was arrested and lied in his interview. He was bailed.
Three days later, at 3 am, V2 was with her male companion, C, in a street. D and H
approached V2 in a 'pincer movement'. H asked V2 for a light and may have offered her
drugs. V2 said she was not interested. H snatched her handbag, which was over her
shoulder, and ran off. The bag had her mobile, keys and Oyster card. D held on to C to
prevent him from helping V2. D was arrested by a policeman in a passing car. D was
aged 25 when sentenced and had a bad record for dishonesty, some violence and a
warning for a robbery. D had a significant drug problem. Held. Because of the force, the
first robbery was a Category 2 offence. The starting point was 4 years. The aggravating
factors were: a) group action, b) it was at night, and c) the victim was vulnerable because
of the alcohol he had consumed. The second robbery was a Category 1 offence but

---

[954] There is no reference to the other defendants' convictions. What was taken is not clear either. Ed.

aggravated by: a) the joint enterprise, b) the vulnerability of V2, c) it was at night, d) D was under the influence of drugs and alcohol, and e) D was on bail. That moved it to a Category 2 offence. The starting point for both was **8 years**. With 20% credit that would produce a sentence of just over the **6 years 4 months** he received so appeal dismissed. *Att-Gen's Ref No 121 of 2014* 2015 EWCA Crim 24 D pleaded (25% credit) to robbery and was convicted of robbery (×3) and attempted robbery (×2). V1 was robbed of his car and iPhone by a group wielding knives. D was involved although he did not have a knife. His DNA was found on a machete/meat cleaver in V1's car and fibres connected D to the car. In a second incident, and whilst D was on bail for the first, a group with five men, aged 16-17, and a young woman were followed by four hooded men, including D. After a mile, each member of the group was targeted by one of the hooded men, who demanded their property. Two out of four victims were assaulted gratuitously and injured, and the other two were robbed. A knife was also used as a threat, which D was not necessarily aware of. Cash and valuables were handed over and later a bus pass and a phone were found where D lived. He was aged 18 at the time and was on licence and on an ASBO from another robbery (40 months' DTO). He had many other antecedents. During that sentencing, 15 group street robberies for cash and/or phones were also TIC'd where a similar *modus operandi* was used. All the instant offences were Category 2. Held. There were many aggravating features and they are, when taken together, an indication of the seriousness of what happened. Here we have a young man who had already been sentenced to custody for a string of robberies, which were nasty robberies sometimes involving violence and the presence of a knife. **7 years' detention** in a YOI, not 4.

R v Tolbert and Another 2015 EWCA Crim 127 T was convicted of and R and L pleaded to robbery. V was out drinking alone in Mansfield town centre when he was befriended by R and L. They were joined shortly after by T. V was drunk and, during the evening, T repeatedly asked to use V's phone and R repeatedly asked V for money. The group then went to purchase alcohol, which V paid for on his credit card, but the other three were taking advantage of him with two of them standing over him as he entered his PIN. V felt uncomfortable and so made excuses to go home to a relative's house. As V was walking, the three men stalked him. V tried to gain access to the house, but his sister-in-law would not let him in as he was drunk. Whilst V was anxiously calling his partner, R and L approached V from behind and punched him to the head. V fell to the floor with a lump on his head and in pain. R and L then searched V's pockets. L made off with V's phone and T, having run over from the other side of the road, took V's phone case containing credit cards, cash, keys and a fishing licence. T and R then withdrew £80 from an ATM using V's card and boarded a taxi, along with L. All three went by taxi to a service station, purchasing cigarettes there, and then to Tesco to buy yet more alcohol. Finally, they returned by taxi to L's sister's house and were arrested the next day. The only property recovered was V's phone, found under T's bed. T and R were both aged 23 on appeal. T had eight previous appearances with one for attempted robbery and two for robbery, the last of which, in 2007, involved a firearm for which he was found to be 'dangerous' and received detention for public protection. His other convictions were for thefts, assaults and weapon offences. T was recalled to prison for a breach of his licence five months before the robbery. R was convicted on nine previous occasions, including for minor violence and for robbery and possession of an offensive weapon in 2008. The Judge viewed the offence as being on the cusp of Categories 1 and 2, but closer to Category 2. L received 4 years (unappealed). Held. There were significant aggravating features…namely, the degree of planning, the fact that there was a group involved, the fact that it was late at night, the fact that the victim was isolated and drunk, and so additionally vulnerable, and there was the unpleasant element of stalking. This took the appropriate starting point towards the 6-year mark. For R, **4 years** upheld and a higher starting point of 7 years was merited for T as his record was significantly more serious. Including the Judge's reduction of 6 months to reflect time in custody being by way of recall on licence, as well as having been remanded in custody, **6½ years** not 7½.

See also: *Att-Gen's Ref Nos 19-21 of 2013* 2013 EWCA Crim 1260 (Two convicted of robbery. At least two knives used, one of which was held to the victim's chin. Committed at night. Neither was the ringleader. Three men approached victim talking on his mobile. iPhone stolen. Victim kicked and punched. Aged 19 and nearly 18. Both positive good character. Cuts to the face, requiring stitches, and a black eye. Young. Good character. Expressed remorse. **5½ years' YOI** not 3½.)

R v Lewis 2015 EWCA Crim 165, 1 Cr App R (S) 66 (p 467) (D pleaded early to robbery. One man attacked a woman from behind, putting her in a stranglehold, while D removed her diamond ring, valued at £40,000. Victim lost consciousness and was injured. Attempts made to steal her Rolex watch. 80 convictions including robbery (33 months) and firearms (5 years). Cat 2 Level 2 with a range of 2-7 years. The aggravating factors meant starting at 9 years making **6 years** on a plea not manifestly excessive.)
Old cases: Best ignored.

322.37   *Street etc. robbery   More than one robber   Pre-2016 guideline case*

R v Taylor and Others 2012 EWCA Crim 630 T, H and C were convicted of robbery. V performed with his band and walked home. He had with him four cans of lager and kebabs. The ground was covered with snow and ice. He heard X, who had fallen and broken his leg, call out for help. He rang for an ambulance and agreed to take X's two dogs to a friend's house for safety. T, H and C arrived and one of them suggested they lift X. V told him not to. That man shouted, "Don't you shout at me, you knob head". V felt very intimidated and apologised, saying he had been told by the operator not to move X. The others asked V for his beer cans. V said they were not his. One of them said, "If you don't give us a tin we'll fucking kill ya". V feared for his safety, backed away and tried to run off. Because of the conditions he could not. The defendants chased after V and caught up with him. They punched V and knocked him to the ground. One produced a knife and said, "Give me your fucking bag and give us your money or I'll stab you". V threw his bag to them and asked them not to hurt him. The defendants walked away laughing. V called the emergency services and returned to X. T was arrested when he went back to X. T was now aged 26. H was now aged 23. C was aged 20, had never received immediate custody before and was subject to a suspended sentence.[955] The Judge described them as a gang of feral animals. Held. Notwithstanding the offence was unplanned and opportunist in nature, it was a bad case. It was at night, there were three robbers and V was trying to help X. It was a Level 2 case. T, **6 years** not 7. H and C, **7 years** not 8, with C's suspended sentence activated consecutively.

R v Tshibangu 2013 EWCA Crim 678 D pleaded (full credit) to robbery. At about 6.30 pm V and his wife returned home to their block of flats. D and another were on the first floor landing inside the communal entrance. V and his wife attempted to walk up the stairs to their flat but their paths were blocked by D. D and another confronted V, who pushed his wife out of harm's way. They grabbed V's arms and tried to pull him to the floor but he resisted. D and another tried to take V's wristwatch. One of them (D denied it was him) bit V on the arm. V was punched about half a dozen times in the chest during the robbery before his watch was forcibly taken from him. D, aged 18, had seven appearances between 2007 and 2011. In 2007, he received a supervision order for possessing a bladed article. In 2010, he received a DTO for two robberies. In 2011, he received a YRO for possession of a bladed article and later a DTO for section 20 where he stabbed someone in the back with a kitchen knife arising out of a gang dispute. The pre-sentence report noted that D had a transient and difficult upbringing. He had written a letter of apology to V. References attested to D's positive character. Held. This was a Level 2 offence. There were aggravating features such as the fact there were two men

---

[955] There is no reference to the other defendant's convictions. What was taken is not clear either. Ed.

involved in the robbery, there was plainly an element of planning and the offence occurred in the precincts of V's home. There was also D's record. Mitigation came in the form of his age, his genuine remorse, the letter of apology and the references as to D's character. The appropriate starting point was in the region of **4½-5 years**. With the plea, **3 years 3 months** was appropriate. The issue of dangerousness therefore did not arise and the 8 years' extended sentence (4 years' custody 4 years' licence) was quashed.)

R v Fagan 2014 EWCA Crim 60 D was convicted of robbery. He and C were sitting in a group on a log in a park. V, who knew them, cycled over to the log on his mountain bike, which was worth £900. V's phone rang and, as he was answering it, C punched him above the right eye. Unknown to D, C was wearing a knuckleduster. He then shouted to D, "Get the fucking bike". C punched V again, this time to the left eye, and restrained him. D rode off on the bike. Meanwhile, C and the rest of the group fled and V gave chase in vain. D was arrested shortly afterwards and V's bike was found in D's back garden. He told lies to the police. D was aged 28 on appeal and had convictions for theft, public disorder and perverting the course of justice. He was of limited intelligence and had attended a special school. The Judge said it was "a cowardly, violent act and wholly unprovoked". However, he found there was no evidence that D knew violence was to be used or C had the knuckleduster and D had a more peripheral role. C received 5½ years. Held. This was a Category 2 offence but had the [Judge] been aware of the limited intelligence of D, he would have had to take that into account. Taking into account the mitigation and D's learning difficulties, **2 years 6 months**, not 3 years 9 months.

R v Abdallah and Others 2015 EWCA Crim 730 D, R and E were convicted of robbery. V, aged 49, was cycling and he was set upon by four or five youths. V tried to keep hold of his bicycle and a holdall containing his laptop. V was hit severely on the back of his head and he continued to struggle. V saw one of them draw a knife which was used to stab him in the back causing injury to his kidney. It was a 4 cm laceration. The group managed to steal the bicycle and the laptop. The Judge found the venue of the robbery was selected because there were no CCTV cameras, unlike the neighbouring streets. D was aged 19 and had a conviction for robbery in 2010 when a knife was used to threaten the victim. He was in breach of a conditional discharge for assaulting a PC. R was aged 19 and had no convictions. He did, however, have a caution for possession of an offensive weapon. D and R had positive references. E was aged just 17 and had a conviction for attempted robbery when he was aged 16. V continues to have long-term problems including bladder control connected with his kidney injury. The Judge found that the defendants knew that a knife was in existence and might be used. Held. The Judge was entitled to conclude it was a Level 3 injury. Bearing in mind the knife was small, the Judge was not able to conclude so he was sure that the defendants knew about the knife. A sentence at the top of Level 2 was appropriate. For D, **6½ years'** YOI not 8. For R, **6 years'** YOI not 7. For E, **5 years 9 months'** YOI not 8.

R v Lewis 2015 EWCA Crim 1088 D was convicted of robbery. V was walking down an alleyway texting. D, another male and a female approached him and he was asked for £5. V tried to walk away saying he had no money. One male pushed him to the ground causing him to drop his phone. That man snatched V's phone and ran. The female threatened V with her dog. The other male picked up a stick and threatened V with it and the two ran off. D was 53 with long-term drug problems. He had 12 previous convictions. Before 2014, there was a 10-year offending gap. Just before the offence there was a shoplifting matter and just after there was a vehicle interference offence. The Judge said the offence was nasty, opportunist and frightening, making it Level 1. Held. More than one robber was an aggravating factor, but **2 years** not 2 years 9 months.

See also: *Att-Gen's Ref Nos 19-21 of 2013* 2013 EWCA Crim 1260 (Two convicted of robbery. At least two knives used, one of which was held to the victim's chin. Committed at night. Neither was the ringleader. Three men approached victim talking on his mobile. iPhone stolen. Victim kicked and punched. Aged 19 and nearly 18. Both positive good character. Cuts to the face, requiring stitches, and a black eye. Young. Good character. Expressed remorse. **5½ years' YOI** not 3½.)

Att-Gen's Ref No 121 of 2014 2015 EWCA Crim 24 (Six robberies and attempted robberies. Aged 18. **7 years' detention** in a YOI, see **322.36**.

R v Tolbert and Another 2015 EWCA Crim 127 (For T **6½ years** and for R **4 years**, see **322.36**.)

Old cases: Best ignored.

322.38   *Street etc. robbery   More than one robbery   Pre-2016 guideline cases*

R v May 2013 EWCA Crim 850, 2014 1 Cr App R (S) 13 (p 58) D pleaded to two robberies. After midnight, D's accomplice approached V1 and asked for a cigarette and some change. While V1 was distracted, D moved in and punched him. V1 was knocked unconscious and his wallet, mobile and Oyster card were stolen. He received a black eye and a suspected broken nose. D was arrested and lied in his interview. He was bailed. Three days later, at 3 am, V2 was with her male companion, C, in a street. D and H approached V2 in a 'pincer movement'. H asked V2 for a light and may have offered her drugs. V2 said she was not interested. H snatched her handbag, which was over her shoulder, and ran off. The bag had her mobile, keys and Oyster card. D held on to C to prevent him from helping V2. D was arrested by a policeman in a passing car. D was aged 25 when sentenced and had a bad record for dishonesty, some violence and a warning for a robbery. D had a significant drug problem. Held. Because of the force, the first robbery was a Category 2 offence. The starting point was 4 years. The aggravating factors were: a) group action, b) it was at night, and c) the victim was vulnerable because of the alcohol he had consumed. The second robbery was a Category 1 offence but aggravated by: a) the joint enterprise, b) the vulnerability of V2, c) it was at night, d) D was under the influence of drugs and alcohol, and e) D was on bail. That moved it to a Category 2 offence. The starting point for both was **8 years**. With 20% credit that would produce a sentence of just over the **6 years 4 months** he received so appeal dismissed.

R v Mangan 2014 EWCA Crim 80 D pleaded to robbery. He was released from custody and went to a Jobcentre to collect a Giro. The Giro was not ready and he became angry. He began talking to V, who was standing outside the building. He asked her for some money, which she refused. D grabbed the bag which V was holding and, in so doing, caused V to fall to the floor, grazing her knee. The bag contained a substantial sum of money which was never recovered. Once it was apparent that the prosecution witnesses were available and present, D pleaded guilty. He had a large number of offences 'of all kinds' including robbery in 2011 (20 months). Held. This case fell between Categories 1 and 2. It is really more serious than a Category 1 street robbery but does not have the features that would put it into Category 2. The aggravating features are that the offence was committed whilst on licence and D's appalling record, including a robbery conviction. Starting at 3 years was appropriate, moving up to 4 years to take account of the aggravating features. With a deduction of 6 months for the plea,[956] **3½ years** not 4½.

R v Willis and W 2014 EWCA Crim 113 Willis and W were convicted of robbery. With others, they were loitering in a stairwell. The police were called. About 20 minutes later, V, aged 47, left his home and walked to a bus stop, which was not far from the stairwell. Willis, W and another youth were in his way. W was on a bicycle and cycled up to V asking if he had a phone. He blocked V's path and said, "Why aren't you talking to me?" He got up close to V's face and V pushed him away. Willis, W and the other youth began to punch V in the head and legs, causing him to fall to the ground. V's mobile phone fell out of his pocket. Willis punched V and demanded his mobile phone. V pointed at where it had fallen. Willis picked it up and ran away. V was taken to hospital and suffered bruises and swelling on his head and face, and extensive swelling on his right shin. He

---

[956] The Court noted that a precise ¹⁄₁₀ reduction would produce 'an untidy figure'. The 6-month figure was a reduction of ⅛. Ed.

had to use a crutch to walk for a period of time. W was aged 14½ at the time of the offence[957] and had no convictions. A few weeks subsequent to the offence, however, he was bailed in respect of a robbery and an attempted robbery of a pizza delivery driver. He later received community sentences in respect of those two offences (he had failed to comply). Willis was aged 17 at the time and had one conviction for possessing an offensive weapon. The pre-sentence reports did not advocate custodial sentences. At appeal, W was aged 15 and Willis was aged 18. W was very immature and there had been problems controlling his behaviour in detention. Held. The Court cannot concentrate solely on the position of the young offender. This was, as the Judge rightly noted, a serious offence of robbery. It involved a group attack on a lone man in the hours of darkness, involving significant violence including punching and kicking. With regard to W, his subsequent offending and failure to comply with his community sentence were highly relevant. Given all the circumstances, the Judge was entitled to impose an **8-month DTO**. Willis was significantly older than W and must bear some responsibility in that regard, given that on one view he may be regarded as the leader of the group by virtue of his age, even if not by virtue of his actual conduct. In any event, he took a full part in the violence and it was he who actually took the phone. **2 years' detention** was not manifestly excessive and there was no unacceptable disparity between the sentences. Appeals dismissed.

R v Jalo and Others 2014 EWCA Crim 1910 D, J and C pleaded to robbery of two women committed at the same time. J and C pleaded to another street robbery. D additionally pleaded to an attempted street robbery. All received full credit. D, with another male, attempted a robbery by pulling at V1's handbag. Her necklace snapped and she screamed. The police chased D and the male and arrested them. D was bailed for this offence. Three days later, a robbery involving D, J and another took place. V2 was asked the time and V2 took out his phone and his phone was seized. V2 was asked what else he had and was threatened. He tried to run but two males approached from behind. One attempted to stab V2 in the eye with a pointed metal bar and V2's eyebrow was cut either with the bar or by the assailant's jewellery. The third male tripped V2 up and pulled him to the ground. V2 was kicked and punched and his pockets were rifled through. The attackers made off with a £1,500 chain and V2 suffered a 2 cm cut to the eye, which needed stitches. Over three months later, there was a robbery involving all three defendants wearing hoods. They ran towards two young women and seized them. They snatched their gold necklaces and ran away. J was aged 18 and C was aged 20 on appeal. Both had previously committed several offences in a sustained pattern, including robbery, attempted robbery and theft or attempted theft. Their convictions were in late 2013, with both receiving custody (either in prison or a YOI). D was aged 19 on appeal and was of effectively good character. The Judge started at 6 years. He gave 6 years' extended sentence (4 years' detention 2 years' extended licence) in each case. Held. There is a need, particularly with young offenders, to consider the offenders as individuals and the application of guidelines to each of their offences. The Judge was wrong to assess the defendants as dangerous. A starting point of 6 years after trial for the attempted robbery is unimpugnable. The rest were Level 1, not Level 2. For C we start at 4½ years, so **3 years' YOI**. D's lack of convictions was balanced out by the extra robbery he faced. So for D and J **4 years' YOI**.

See also: *R v Kulpi* 2013 EWCA Crim 371 (With another, followed victim and punched him several times. Stole £4-5 from him. Victim suffered grazes, swollen lip and nose. Aged 18. No previous convictions. Category 2. Element of planning. With his age, good character and 10% for plea, **3½ years** not 4½.)

R v Donaldson 2013 EWCA Crim 2677 (Plea. 4.40 am in Birmingham city centre. Victim walking alone in a subway. Pursued by D and two other males. Punched to the

---

[957] W had turned 15 years old by the time he was sentenced, enabling the Judge to impose a DTO on him without the requirement that he be considered a 'persistent offender' as this was his first offence. Ed.

ground by co-accused. All three went through his pockets as he lay on the floor dazed. Victim asked for his PIN, punched again by co-accused. Caught on CCTV. Aged 18 at the time. 18 appearances since 2007 including three robberies, ABH and battery. Breach of licence. Entitled to take starting point higher than guideline suggested but starting at 5½ years was correct. With credit for the plea, **3 years 8 months' YOI** not 4 years 2 months' YOI.)

Att-Gen's Ref No 121 of 2014 2015 EWCA Crim 24 (Six robberies and attempted robberies. Aged 18. **7 years' detention** in a YOI, see **322.36**.

Old cases: Best ignored.

For an index of the 'series of robberies' paras see **322.22**.

322.39   Taxi drivers and delivery staff etc.   Guideline

Robbery Guideline 2016, see www.banksr.com Other Matters Guidelines tab page 3 The first guideline applies to robberies committed in taxis. For the guideline see **322.26**.

322.40   Taxi drivers and delivery staff etc.   Pre-2016 guideline judicial guidance

R v Howlett 2010 EWCA Crim 432 D robbed a taxi driver after telling the driver where to go and, when the driver arrived, directing him to a quiet turning. Held. Taxi drivers are particularly vulnerable to being picked on in this manner, and sentences need to reflect that. For more detail see the next paragraph.

Old case: *Att-Gen's Ref No 38 of 1995* 1996 2 Cr App R (S) 103 (LCJ Taxi drivers are particularly vulnerable, they operate alone and they are at the whim of the passenger to be taken where the passenger asks. It is this Court's job to see that they are properly protected, and anyone who is minded to attack a taxi driver must receive a substantial sentence of imprisonment.)

322.41   Trains, buses etc.   Gang activity   Pre-2016 guideline case

Robbery Guideline 2016, see www.banksr.com Other Matters Guidelines tab page 3 The first guideline applies to robberies committed on public transport, see **322.26**.

Note: These offences would fall to be dealt with by the guidelines. The cases would normally have the aggravating factors of gang activity, multiple victims and vulnerable victims present. However, the sheer terror of the event would cause most judges to consider that the sentence would need to be outside the guidelines. The Court of Appeal in *R v Millberry* 2002 EWCA Crim 2891, 2003 2 Cr App R (S) 31 (p 142) said, 'It is essential that having taken the guidelines into account, sentencers stand back and look at the circumstances as a whole and impose the sentence which is appropriate having regard to all the circumstances'. Consequently, I consider that sentences similar to the old law (see below) are likely to be passed for this activity. Ed.

R v RLM and ADW 2011 EWCA Crim 2398, 2012 1 Cr App R (S) 95 (p 574) M pleaded to five robberies and handling stolen goods. W pleaded to five robberies, after failing to attend the PCMH. They were involved with a gang who committed a series of robberies on buses in Birmingham. Not all members of the gang were involved in all of the robberies. The gang, usually 10 to 15 members strong, would board a bus with a view to taking control of it and robbing the passengers at will. They would use intimidation to subdue the passengers, but would use force if necessary. The group would take handbags, mobile phones, iPods and money. Numerous victims were punched and kicked, with one suffering a chipped tooth. M was aged 14 and had one unrelated conviction. W was aged 16 and was of good character. Held. The use of violence and intimidation on passengers who had no means of escape were serious aggravating factors. Theses offences do not easily fit into the categories specified in the guidelines. Perhaps the most appropriate would be a street robbery between Levels 2 and 3. Starting at 8 years for a 17-year-old was not manifestly excessive. **4 years'** detention, though stern, reflected the underlying gravity of the offences.

Old cases: *Att-Gen's Ref Nos 21-22 of 2004* EWCA Crim 3048 (Those in gangs who prey on innocent travellers on the Underground can expect to receive deterrent sentences and, save in the most exceptional cases, e.g. extreme youth, can expect custody. Even

young offenders should expect a significant period of DTO and in some cases long-term detention.) *R v Dallison* 2005 EWCA Crim 422 (**5 years**) *R v Allen* 2005 EWCA Crim 667, 2 Cr App R (S) 95 (p 573) (**4 years'** detention) *Att-Gen's Ref Nos 24-29 of 2006* 2007 EWCA Crim 2217 (For A, **5 years**. For M, **3½ years** For G, **4½ years**. For H, **2½ years**. For O, **3 years**. For B, **2 years**.)
For a summary of the third case, see the 9th edition of this book.

322.42 Vehicles Carjacking Pre-2016 guideline cases
R v Thompson 2002 EWCA Crim 1051, 2003 1 Cr App R (S) 13 (p 54) D pleaded to robbery. Carjacking offences are particularly prevalent at the moment. The offences are committed quickly. The detection rates are not high. Those who commit these offences must expect substantial sentences. For further details, see the 7th edition of this book. Note: This case is old, but the guidance remains valid today. Ed.

322.43 Victim particularly vulnerable Pre-2016 guideline cases
Robbery Guideline 2016, see www.banksr.com Other Matters Guidelines tab page 6 (street and less sophisticated commercial robberies, see **322.29**), page 12 (professionally planned commercial robberies, see **322.7**), and page 18 (dwelling burglaries, see **322.12**) The guideline states what the factors increasing seriousness are:
Other aggravating factors:
Victim is targeted due to a vulnerability (or a perceived vulnerability)
In the dwelling burglary section of the *Robbery Guideline 2016* at page 18 and **322.12**, the following factor is also listed:
Child or vulnerable person at home (or returns home) when offence committed
Att-Gen's Ref No 80 of 2011 2011 EWCA Crim 3211, 2 Cr App R (S) 35 (p 195) D pleaded (on the day of trial) to robbery (×2) and theft. He was employed as a care assistant at a care home. D stole wedding and eternity rings from some of the residents. The values were unknown. V1 was aged 92 and blind. She suffered from dementia and was completely immobile. V2 was aged 88, suffered from slight dementia and had limited mobility. D took the rings from their fingers. He sought to blame an innocent colleague when confronted with the allegations. He subsequently pleaded guilty after a *Goodyear* indication was refused. D had no previous convictions. Held. By his employment he was in a considerable position of trust. The victims were vulnerable and were entitled to feel safe in their own rooms within the care home. D specifically targeted those who he thought were unable to make a credible complaint against him, because of their dementia. He then sought to blame an innocent colleague. Additionally, the items were of sentimental value. In mitigation, D pleaded late, expressed remorse and the force used was minimal. The robberies were worth not less than **4 years** after a trial. With the plea, that would be reduced to something over 3½ years. With double jeopardy, the robbery was worth **3 years** and the theft was worth 2 years, to be served concurrently.
R v Scott and Others 2014 EWCA Crim 201 S, M and P pleaded to robbery (full credit). They attended V's address one evening, banged on his door and demanded to be let in. V was vulnerable and suffered from Asperger's syndrome. This was known to S, M and P. V opened the door and the three demanded that V unplug and hand over all electrical items. He refused and M produced a kitchen knife with a 6-inch blade and threatened V with it. V was then assaulted and threatened and told he would be anally raped and subject to other sexual degradations. He was told that he was a dog and that he must sit on the floor and obey instructions. V's property was removed without any resistance, although at one point, V poked M in the eye. This led to a further violent response. P punched him in the face and M bit his chest. They stole property worth £2,000. Most of it was subsequently recovered. When the three left, they forgot to take the knife and banged on the door demanding its return. V posted it through the letterbox. S's basis of plea was that he was unaware that M had a knife, he was not involved in the use of the knife and did not personally inflict any violence on V. P's basis of plea was that he

inflicted only two punches. At the appeal, M was aged 29 with 35 previous convictions including robbery. He had had custody before. P was aged 19 and had eight previous convictions including two for battery and two for robbery. He was also sentenced to 12 months' detention consecutive, for theft and assault offences arising out of a separate incident. S was aged 20 and had two convictions including attempted robbery (10 months' YOI). The Judge started at 16 years. Held. This was a very serious robbery in the home of a victim who was present. Aggravating features included one of the three carrying a knife to the scene, the knife was produced and used to intimidate V. V was vulnerable and targeted as such, and actual violence was used. P committed this offence whilst on bail for theft and assault. In light of the level of violence actually inflicted and the fact that the knife was used only to threaten, the Judge took too high a starting point. There was a need to reflect their different ages and bases of pleas. For M, **9 years** not 10½. For P, considering totality, **5 years' detention** for the robbery, not 6½. The 12-month consecutive sentence would remain. For S, **4½ years' detention**, not 6. See also the *Street etc. robbery Victim particularly vulnerable* para at **322.31**.

322.44   *Victim seriously injured   Guideline*
Robbery Guideline 2016, see www.banksr.com Other Matters Guidelines tab Each of the three sections of the guideline have the same entry in the Harm section about the harm caused to the victim, see pages 4, 10 and 16.

STEP ONE: Determining the offence category
[Introductory and Culpability text not listed]
Harm
The court should weigh up all the factors set out below to determine the harm that has been caused or was intended to be caused to the victim.

Category 1	• Serious physical and/or psychological harm caused to the victim • [other factors not listed]

For the full guideline for a) dwelling robberies, see **322.9**, b) professionally planned commercial robberies, see **322.4**, and c) street and less sophisticated commercial robberies, see **322.26**.

322.45   *Victim seriously injured   Pre-2016 guideline cases*
R v Danes 2013 EWCA Crim 114 D pleaded to attempted robbery on the day of his trial and to section 20 early. D rang the bell of V's ground-floor flat, which was near to where he lived. V, aged 79, answered the bell and D attacked him demanding money. V fell to the ground and was subjected to a sustained attack which included a bitten ear and most likely kicks and punches. D was caught close by and said he was sorry and needed help. Police found V in a terrible state. He had cuts to his face and head. He had a fractured nose and eye socket. The flat was covered in blood. V had to be rehoused and his whole character changed. D was aged 37. He had convictions but none of this seriousness. He was extremely sorry. The Judge said he started at the top of the range, 12 years, and reduced it by 2 making 10 years. Held. The robbery guidelines do not apply to violent personal robberies. The Judge was entitled to start at **12 years**. The sentence was not manifestly excessive.

322.46   *Violence, Others inflict   Pre-2016 guideline case*
Example: *R v Berger* 2014 EWCA Crim 183 (Plea to robbery, escape, burglary and attempted burglary. Burglary and handling offences TIC'd. Group of men broke into house and violently robbed victim. She was badly injured and seriously distressed. £15,000 of property taken. Another burglary and an attempt. He was not one of the robbers who violently robbed the victim. Bad record including numerous burglaries, robbery and a firearm offence. Sentence must reflect the knowledge that violence might be used, and the other offences. 15 years' **extended sentence** (**10 years' custody** 5 years' licence) upheld.)

322.47   *Weapon used   Guideline and judicial guidance*
Robbery Guideline 2016, see www.banksr.com Other Matters Guidelines tab page 9
Each of the three sections of the guideline have the same entry in the Culpability section
about the harm caused to the victim, see pages 4, 10 and 16.

STEP ONE: Determining the offence category
[Introductory text not listed.]

CULPABILITY demonstrated by one or more of the following	
A High	• Use of a weapon to inflict violence • Production of a bladed article or firearm or imitation firearm to threaten violence • [other factors not listed]
B Medium	• Production of a weapon other than a bladed article or firearm or imitation firearm to threaten violence • Threat of violence by any weapon (but which is not produced) • [other factors not listed]

For the full guideline for a) dwelling robberies, see **322.9**, b) professionally planned
commercial robberies, see **322.4**, and c) street and less sophisticated commercial
robberies, see **322.26**.

Matters relating to the defendant
322.48   *Defendant aged under 18   General*
There is relevant guidance for sentencing young offenders within both the *Robbery
Guideline 2006* and the *Youths Sentencing Guideline 2009*. These guidelines will
continue to be in force until they are replaced by the Sentencing Council's new and
updated guidance.
Robbery Guideline 2006, see www.banksr.com Other Matters Guidelines tab
page 1 Foreword The guideline makes clear that robbery will usually merit a custodial
sentence but that exceptional circumstances may justify a non-custodial penalty for an
adult and, more frequently, for a young offender. In this way it is not intended to make a
significant change to current practice. Over the past 10 years the majority of young
offenders sentenced for robbery have been given a non-custodial sentence.
Young Offenders
page 8 Young offenders may have characteristics relevant to their offending behaviour
which are different from adult offenders. Also, by statute, the youth justice system has
the principal aim of preventing offending by children and young persons. Because of
this, there may be factors which are of greater significance in cases involving young
offenders including:
• age of the offender
• immaturity of the offender
• group pressure.
Sentencers should recognise the varying significance of these factors for different ages.
page 12 para 5 Young offenders may have characteristics relevant to their offending
behaviour which are different from adult offenders. Also, by statute, the youth justice
system has the principal aim of preventing offending by children and young persons.[958]
Because of this, there may be factors which are of greater significance in cases involving
young offenders, including: 1) Age of the offender, 2) Immaturity of the offender, and
3) Group pressure. Sentencers should recognise the varying significance of these factors
for different ages.
Young offenders. Factors to take into consideration
page 12 para 1 A Youth Court cannot impose a custodial sentence on an offender aged 10
or 11. If the offender is aged 12, 13 or 14, a Detention and Training Order can only be

---
[958] Crime and Disorder Act 1998 s 37

imposed by a Youth Court in the case of persistent young offenders. In the Crown Court, however, long-term detention in accordance with Powers of Criminal Courts (Sentencing) Act 2000 can be ordered on any young offender without the requirement of persistence. The Crown Court may also impose an extended sentence, detention for public protection or detention for life where the young offender meets the criteria for being a 'dangerous offender'. The following guidelines apply to offenders who have not been assessed as dangerous.

2 If a Youth Court is considering sending a case to the Crown Court, the Court must be of the view that it is such a serious case that detention above 2 years is required, or that the appropriate sentence is a custodial sentence approaching the 2-year limit which is normally applicable to older offenders.[959]

3 The sentencing ranges and presumptive starting points apply to all three categories of robbery detailed above: Street robbery or 'mugging', Robberies of small businesses, and Less-sophisticated commercial robberies.

4 The 'starting points' are based upon a first-time offender, aged 17 years, who pleaded not guilty. For younger offenders sentencers should consider whether a lower starting point is justified in recognition of the offender's age or immaturity.

5 Young offenders may have characteristics relevant to their offending behaviour which are different from adult offenders. Also, by statute, the youth justice system has the principal aim of preventing offending by children and young persons.[960] Because of this, there may be factors which are of greater significance in cases involving young offenders. Sentencers should recognise the varying significance of such factors for different ages.

6 A reduction to the appropriate sentence, taking account of seriousness, and aggravating and mitigating factors will need to be made if an offender has pleaded guilty. The effect of applying the reduction may be that the sentence imposed for an offence at one level of seriousness may fall within the range suggested for the next lowest level of seriousness.

7 The relative seriousness of each offence will be determined by the following factors:
   1 Degree of force and/or nature and duration of threats, 2 Degree of injury to the victim, 3 Degree of fear experienced by the victim, and 4 Value of property taken.

8 Use of a particular degree of force is more serious than the threat (which is not carried into effect) to use that same degree of force. Depending on the facts, however, a threat to use a high degree of force might properly be regarded as more serious than actual use of a lesser degree of force.

9 If a weapon is involved in the use or threat of force, the offence will be more serious. Possession of a weapon during the course of an offence will be an aggravating factor, even if it is not used, because it indicates planning. If the offence involves a real firearm it will be more serious if that firearm is loaded. Whether the weapon is real or imitation is not a major factor in determining sentence because the amount of fear created in the victim is likely to be the same.

10 The value of the property capable of being taken, as well as the actual amount taken, is important.

11 The presence of one or more aggravating features will indicate a more severe sentence within the suggested range and, if the aggravating feature(s) are exceptionally serious, the case will move up to the next level.

12 In all cases, courts should consider making a Restitution Order and/or a compensation order. Where a non-custodial sentence is imposed, the court may also consider making an Antisocial Behaviour Order.

13 Courts are required by Children and Young Persons Act 1933 s 44(1) to have regard to the welfare of the child, and under section 37 of the Crime and Disorder Act 1998 to have regard to the overall aim of the youth justice system of preventing reoffending.

---

[959] *W v Southampton Youth Court* 2003 1 Cr App R (S) 87 (p 455)
[960] Crime and Disorder Act 1998 s 37

14 Passing the custody threshold does not mean that a custodial sentence should be deemed inevitable.[961]

15 Where there is evidence that the offence has been committed to fund a drug habit and that treatment for this could help tackle the offender's offending behaviour, sentencers should consider a drug treatment requirement as part of a Supervision Order or Action Plan Order.

322.50   Defendant aged 10-15   Pre-2016 guideline case

R v L 2010 EWCA Crim 158 L, aged 15, pleaded early to robbery. L and S, her 18-year-old sister, had been drinking and then set upon V, a 54-year-old man. S hit V on the back of the head as he was walking home. V turned round and S tried to seize his briefcase. V punched her twice. S punched him back twice in the mouth. S seized the bag and the two girls ran off. The bag contained five memory sticks worth £210. V had a cut lip. In interview L admitted the offence. In April 2009, L received a Referral Order for theft and two TICs. In May 2009, the order was extended for another theft and a commercial burglary. In August 2009, the order was revoked for an ABH. A Supervision Order was made. The offence was committed seven weeks later. The probation officer said that she was ashamed and remorseful. When awaiting sentence she was tagged and had attended all her appointments. The Judge started at 12 months and reduced it for the plea and the tag to 6 months' DTO. Held. This was a nasty robbery. The offence was at the upper end of Level 1. The proper course would have been to remit the case to the Youth Court or to impose the **Supervision Order** with intense supervision and surveillance suggested by the pre-sentence report. We impose that order for 18 months.

R v C and T 2014 EWCA Crim 1807 D1 and D2 were convicted of robbery. V was a frail 64-year-old man who lived alone but was known to D2's family. In 2012, D2 was convicted of assaulting V and had also admitted stealing from him. D2 said she would do some cleaning work for V and he reluctantly let D2 into his house giving D2 a second chance. V was unwell and went to bed. D1 then attacked and straddled V, punching his face and body and demanding to know where V's money was. Meanwhile, D2 hit V with a shoe. V said there was no money, but they carried on. They removed V's phone and 'lifeline' connections. V tried to fend them off and they ran away with his watch, keys and two coin jars. V was admitted to hospital with cuts and marks to his upper body with pain and a restriction of movement in his shoulders. D1 was aged 14 and D2 aged 15. D1 had three battery convictions, but made good progress whilst on bail and took steps to turn her life around. D2 lacked empathy, had a propensity for violence and had extremely low cognitive functioning with characteristics of autism and ADHD. Her IQ was 64. However, she had suffered recent bereavements and a miscarriage. Held. The shoe made this a robbery with a weapon. For an adult, before considering the convictions and the aggravating factors, the starting point would have been 3 years. The offence was too serious to resile from imposing custody but insufficient weight was given by the Judge to the defendants' personal factors which should be at the forefront of sentencing offenders of this age. We reduce the sentence because of remand time which is not deductible. **12 months' DTO** for both, not 24.

See also: *R v S* 2011 EWCA Crim 322 (D, aged 10, pleaded to three false imprisonment counts, GBH, two ABHs and two robberies. **3 years**.)

R v L 2012 EWCA Crim 1336, 2013 1 Cr App R (S) 56 (p 317) (Plea to robbery (×3) and an attempted robbery. D and two others approached five boys aged 14 or 15. Demanded their mobile phones. Screwdriver pointed at one victim. Aged 14. Two reprimands, one for theft, one for an imitation firearm. Basis of plea that he aided and abetted the robbery rather than playing an active part, verbally or physically. Genuine remorse. Influenced by others. **12-month YRO** with supervision and a curfew, not a 10-month DTO.)

Att-Gen's Ref Nos 21-22 of 2012 2012 EWCA Crim 1806 (Pleas to three robberies. Aged 14 and 17. Used weapons including metal bar, 8-inch knife and a hammer. Weapons used

---

[961] *Overarching Principles: Seriousness Guideline 2004* para 1.32, see www.banksr.com Guidelines tab

to cause injury, including superficial stab wound. Both dangerous. Substantial convictions for violence, acquisitive offences and possession of bladed articles. Only mitigation was their ages and pleas. For the 14-year-old, 14 years' **extended sentence (10 years' custody** 4 years' licence**),** for the 17-year-old, 13 years' **extended sentence (9 years' custody** 4 years' licence).
Old cases: Best ignored.

322.51   *Defendant aged 13-15   Firearms, With   Pre-2016 guideline case*
R v Kilbride and Others 2012 EWCA Crim 1802 J, C, D, B and K pleaded to 'a number of serious offences of robbery with guns'. B pleaded to possession of a firearm with intent to endanger life. K, and two others unknown, pointed a shotgun at a taxi driver and demanded money. They drove the car away and when the car was recovered, the driver's mobile, GPS system and £100 were stolen. The next day, K and B and another, wearing hoods and scarves, were collected by another cab driver. K pulled the handbrake and one of the others pointed a shotgun at the driver and demanded money. The driver left the car and K drove it away. A mobile, a GPS system and about £140 were stolen. On the same day, B entered a small shop and pointed a gun at the shopkeeper. £500 was taken. Three days later, K walked into a small store and asked for vodka. Another walked in and pointed a long-barrelled gun at the shopkeeper, S, who ran upstairs and locked himself in. S saw four men leave the shop with the till and cigarettes. On an unknown day, C carried out a 'recce' on a shop. Other 'recces' were made. B entered the shop with a gun along with J and C. C stayed at the door but held the gun on one occasion. While B pointed the gun, money was taken from the till by J and C. The incident was very terrifying. The owner, V, who was nearby, came with a friend and saw four leaving. V asked for his money back. The man with the gun looked scared and passed the gun to B. B fired the gun at V, who luckily received only minor injuries. J was aged 13 and had previous convictions. Pictures on his mobile showed him revelling in gang culture. He had considerable physical maturity and his girlfriend was pregnant. He received **4 years' detention**. C was aged 14½ and had previous convictions. He too revelled in gang culture and received **6 years**. D was aged 15 and had no previous convictions. He received **5 years**. K was aged 16 and had received community sentences for a whole series of offences. He received **9 years**. B was aged 18 and had served numerous short custodial sentences. He received **5½ years' DPP**. Held. These crimes show what a serious problem Liverpool has. B was very dangerous. The Judge was right to pass these very severe sentences. J might have received **5 years**.

322.52   *Defendant aged 16-17   Pre-2016 guideline case*
R v Maughan and Others 2012 EWCA Crim 1037 M, Mc and KM were convicted of robbery. KW was convicted of three robberies and one attempted robbery. KW and a co-defendant who pleaded guilty threatened a number of young boys and girls in the street. They threatened or used violence, and demanded iPhones, BlackBerrys and iPods. M, Mc, KW and KM approached an 8-year-old girl in the street. They asked her questions and became aggressive. They forced her along the road where she told them she was not allowed to go. They asked her the time and when she took her BlackBerry out of her pocket, it was snatched from her. M, Mc, KM and KW ran away. The phone was sold for £20, with the proceeds being split between the four defendants. M was aged 17 and had one reprimand for theft. She expressed remorse. Mc was aged 17 and had one caution for common assault. She was attending college. KM was just aged 16. She had one reprimand for theft when aged 10. She was extremely remorseful. KW was aged just 14 at the time of the offence. She had a reprimand for theft, and had learning difficulties and special educational needs. Held. The emphasis ought to have been on preventing reoffending, not punishment. Consequently, immediate custodial sentences were not necessary. For M, Mc and KM, **12-month YRO** with supervision not 4 months'

YOI/DTO. KW committed these offences under pressure from a co-defendant. A **12-month YRO** with programme, supervision and activity requirements was suitable, not a 6-month DTO.

R v V 2012 EWCA Crim 1259[962] D pleaded to robbery. D, aged 16, knew V, aged 20, and had pushed his way into V's flat about ten times. About midday, D again pushed his way into V's flat and demanded money and valuables. When D was told V had neither, D conducted his own search, kicking V's property about. D picked up a fire extinguisher and threw it at V, hitting him on the face. He repeated this and missed. D beat V with a table leg which had a 2-inch screw in it, while referring to some shootings in Bradford and shouting that he was going down for murder. V struck his head on a kitchen unit and passed out. When V came round, D punched him several times, leaving V very dazed and with blurred vision. D left, saying he would batter V if he reported the matter to the police. D stole a computer console, some computer games, a mobile and a door key. V had an 1½-inch laceration to his head, bruising and swelling down the entire left side of his body and cuts to his arms. The property was worth about £455. D had 21 appearances for 31 offences starting with robbery when he was aged 10. He had convictions for affray, battery, attempted robbery, possession of an offensive weapon and a bladed article. About two weeks before the sentence was passed he received a 12-month DTO for ABH. He was also on bail, subject to an ASBO and a YRO at the time of the offence. A psychiatrist said D exhibited signs of an unsocialised conduct disorder. Since the sentence D had had 11 proved governor's reports for assaults and fighting. Held. This would have been a Category 1 aggravated burglary if he had been so charged, with a 10-year starting point. It was worrying so many of the previous offences were for violence or potential violence. The offence was aggravated by the CRO, the threats and D being on bail at the time of the offence. We do not regard the Judge's 12-year starting point as manifestly excessive. The Judge's one-third off for both the plea and D's age could not be criticised. The Judge was entitled to pass the **32-month DPP** sentence.

R v N and Edge 2013 EWCA Crim 81 N pleaded to four robberies and E pleaded to three. N, E and L were responsible for the robberies of Chinese and Indian takeaway delivery staff and a taxi driver. N, aged 16, was living with his mother in a one-bedroom flat. She left him. L argued with his mother and went to stay with N. Neither had enough money to buy food. After about two hours of planning, one of them rang a takeaway restaurant and ordered a meal. The delivery person received no response at the address he was given and N and L approached him. The driver was told to put the food down (or hand it over). Three weeks later, N, E and L were involved in two similar robberies an hour or so apart. In these a small amount of change was handed over as well as the food. In the last robbery the next day, N ordered a taxi, which picked up E and L. They were delivered to their destination. One got out and then returned. They asked to return to where they had been picked up. There E and L produced kitchen knives, pointed them at the driver and demanded money. They were given £50 and about £10 in loose change. Neither defendant had any convictions. N was unusually close to his mother, whom he cared for when she was ill. She did not set appropriate boundaries for him. She was a student and assessed as not being sufficiently aware of his needs. Poverty was at the heart of their problems. N did not get on with her new partner and thought he was using her to be able to stay in the country. N left school with no qualifications. When on bail his co-operation with the youth offending team was described as 'virtually faultless'. E aged [probably] 16 had left home after rows with his parents. He was in an emergency hostel. In 2010, he started to suffer from depression and began to self-harm. He was assessed as lacking in self-confidence and was easily led. Held. The offences were very serious. The aggravating factors were the first three robberies were at night, there was a

---

[962] This case was once 2012 EWCA Crim 3091.

team and they were planned. The starting point for N was **5 years** not 6, so with plea **3 years 4 months** not 4 years. The starting point for E was **4 years** not 5½, so with plea **2 years 8 months** not 3 years 8 months.

R v H 2013 EWCA Crim 353 D pleaded to robbery. At about 5.30 pm V, aged 12, was riding his BMX bicycle. He was approached by D and another. D told V to give him the bike. V refused and D produced a knife with a 7-inch blade. V handed over his bike and D asked if he had anything else on him. V handed over his mobile phone. D's companion told D to leave V alone and D cycled off on the bike. The bike was found nearby. V was frightened and did not want to go outside for a while. He also suffered nightmares. D, aged 16, had no convictions but, whilst on bail for this offence, he received a reprimand for theft of aluminium from a factory. D had ADHD and had been excluded from school aged seven. An e-mail from D's father stated that D had fallen in with the wrong crowd. Held. This was a Level 2 robbery. The starting point was therefore 3 years. D had picked on an extremely vulnerable victim. A report from a secure centre stated that D was progressing educationally but his behaviour wasn't as good. Starting at **3 years** was appropriate. Taking account of D's age and the plea, 2 years' DTO, not 3 years' detention.

Att-Gen's Ref No 52 of 2014 2014 EWCA Crim 1742 D pleaded to robbery at the first opportunity. A charge of possession of a bladed article was dropped. V received a call that someone wanted to buy tobacco from him. V suffered from neuropathy (a nerve disorder) and so had no feeling in his legs. D and two others went to V's house. V came to the door and went to get the tobacco. D and the two others then entered. One pushed V to the floor, held a 6-inch serrated kitchen knife to V's throat and threatened him. He also stood on V's foot, trapping V's big toe. A second man searched the living room and a third stood in the hallway. D was directed upstairs by the man in the hallway and, taking V, mishandled him onto the bed. D then tied V's wrists to the headboard saying, "I don't want to hurt you, but I will." D then demanded the keys to V's safe whilst the knife-wielding male held the blade to V's arm. A male (not D) also held a lamp and threatened V. V, fearing for his life, told the men the keys were held by a neighbour. The robbers left taking a TV and tobacco. V suffered a cut arm and a bruise. His toe had to be amputated and so he now needed a walking stick. V's TV was later found in D's home. In interview D denied the robbery and said the TV was given to him by a friend. D was aged almost 17, of good character and came from a good home, although he had been in trouble at school. Held. The robbery was carefully planned and a vulnerable victim was targeted. A knife and a rope to tie the victim up were taken to the house. Custody was required. It is in the interests of D, other offenders and young people to know that this behaviour attracts a custodial sentence. We would expect a sentence of **3½ years' detention**. Because of his response to the Youth Rehabilitation Order, 3 years.

See also: *Att-Gen's Ref Nos 21-22 of 2012* 2012 EWCA Crim 1806 (Pleas to three robberies. Aged 14 and 17. Used weapons including metal bar, 8-inch knife and a hammer. Weapons used to cause injury, including superficial stab wound. Both dangerous. Substantial convictions for violence, acquisitive offences and possession of bladed articles. Only mitigation was their ages and pleas. For the 14-year-old, 14 years' **extended sentence (10 years' custody** 4 years' licence), for the 17-year-old, 13 years' **extended sentence (9 years' custody** 4 years' licence).)

R v Fadil 2013 EWCA Crim 166 (Pleaded early to robbery. Late plea to imitation firearm. Robbed a taxi driver with imitation firearm. Good character. Aged two days off his 17th birthday. **5 years** was tough but not excessive.)

Old cases: Best ignored.

322.53   *Persistent offenders   Pre-2016 guideline cases*

Att-Gen's Ref No 11 of 2010 2010 EWCA Crim 2095 D pleaded (late) to robbery. D visited V, an 88-year-old widow, who lived alone. He stated that some roofing tiles on her house were loose. V informed D that it was in hand and sent D away. He returned the following day, when V was returning to her home, and pushed her into the house. He put his left arm around her shoulders and said, "I'll have those off you", and proceeded to wrench the rings she wore from the fingers of her left hand. He used his right hand and continued to hold her with his left. He then punched her to the left eye, which knocked her to the ground. The rings were her engagement ring, with obvious sentimental value, and another ring which she had inherited, which was 150 years old. They were valued at in excess of £5,000. V was bleeding from the head, suffered an extensive complex fracture to her left femur which required surgery to insert a metal plate, and other bruising. She spent 12 days in hospital following which she required carers for 24 hours per day. Eventually she regained her independence. D, aged 33, had 51 previous convictions and was a 'career criminal', with offences of dwelling burglaries. Whilst awaiting sentence he admitted 14 other burglaries and attempted burglaries. Held. The aggravating features are obvious, the targeting of an elderly victim in her home, the numerous previous convictions, the pattern of escalating seriousness and the gratuitous violence. There is little mitigation. The starting point, referring to the guidelines, was 8 years on conviction. Had D not admitted the offence, a sentence of **at least 10 years** would have been suitable. With the plea, **8 years,** not 5.

R v Stanford 2014 EWCA Crim 2770 D pleaded to robbery. Just before the 9.30 pm closing time, D entered a bookmakers without a disguise. The sole cashier, V, was told to give D all his money and D said, "I'm serious. Give me all your money or I will stab you." V was terrified and gave D £500 in notes and coins. As D left he said, "Don't call the fucking police." D was aged 29. In 2014, he had committed a strikingly similar robbery on a bookmakers. He was released after 8 months and the offence was committed less than three weeks after that. He had no other convictions. Until he was aged 28 he was in full-time employment but cocaine and drink changed that and made him homeless. Held. This was a Level 2 offence. It was aggravated by the similar previous conviction, D was intoxicated, V was vulnerable on his own and the offence was relatively late at night. The 4-year starting point was unexceptional but the uplift should have been no more than 18 months, making 5½ years. With plea, **3 years 8 months** not 4 years 8 months.

R v Brown 2015 EWCA Crim 707 D pleaded to robbery. He and two others entered a Wandsworth post office. A sliding door was wedged open and all three jumped over the counter. V1, an employee, was knocked backwards in his chair and his shin was cut. V1 struggled and a second robber tried to make V1 release him. This was unsuccessful so the second man seized V2, another employee, around the throat and told V1 not to do anything stupid or V2 would be hurt. V1 released his grip and the robbers began stealing cash. D was in the secure area and stealing cash. As he jumped back over the counter he slipped or was kicked and he fell. He dropped his cash. All three robbers left and £5,000 was stolen. The only injury was V1's shin, which did not need any medical attention. Eight days later, D rang 999 saying he wanted to hand himself in. Later that day he went to the police station and made full admissions. D was aged 37. He had 20 previous offences. In 1994 and 1998, there was a robbery. In 2000, there were five robberies of post offices (8 years). In 2007, there were three conspiracy to rob offences (9 years 8 months). There were also burglaries and other dishonesty offences. The Judge considered it was a Level 2 robbery but disapplied the guidelines. Held. We start at 12 years, so with plea **8 years** not 10.

Att-Gen's Ref No 53 of 2015 2015 Crim EWCA 1580 M and C pleaded to robbery at their PCMH. H was convicted of the same count. After planning, observing the premises for about two hours and stealing a getaway car, M and C approached a security guard, V, who was about to take a cash box from a petrol station to his van. C said, "Cut him" and M produced a large knife and stabbed at V's head and face several times. The knife did not connect. V let go of the cash box and the two men ran with it to the getaway car, where H was waiting. At a safe distance the two changed to another car. £12,000 was stolen. H was aged 34. He had 37 convictions between 1994 and 2009. Six were for robberies. There were: 1997, plea, attempt (business premises with gun, axe and knife),

2 years' detention; 1999, with knife; 2002, convicted (jewellers, £5,000 worth of jewellery taken, two staff attacked), 7 years; and 2009, convicted (jewellers with M and hammers and tools, owner attacked with fists, feet and hammers and slashed about the face), 7 years (M received 56 months). M was aged 30 and had 21 convictions. He had two robberies. The other one was in 2004 (4 years). C was aged 20 and only had minor convictions. The pre-sentence report said H and M had taken advantage of C. Held. The robbery fell outside the guidelines. It was aggravated by planning, the fact it was a group offence, the disguises, the vulnerable victim, the large sum and the stolen car. For H, a 16-year extended sentence (**13 years'** custody not 10, 3 years' extended licence). For M, we start at 11 years, so with plea **7 years 4 months**, not 64 months. For C, because of his age, his lack of criminal experience, manipulation and naivety we start at 5½ years, so with plea **3 years 8 months** not 32 months.

Old cases: Best ignored.

See also the ***Street etc. robbery Defendant has significant record*** paras at **322.35**.

322.54   *Persistent offenders   Firearm, With   Pre-2016 guideline cases*

R v Curwen 2014 EWCA Crim 1046 D was convicted of robbery (×7), attempted robbery and possession of an imitation firearm (×8). Whilst serving a life sentence for armed robbery, he walked out of an open prison. He targeted six banks and two bookmakers' premises. He entered with an imitation handgun and threatened the cashier. On seven occasions, cash was handed over with the total approximately £34,000. The imitation handgun, which was subsequently found at D's address, was in fact a gas-powered gun which appeared to be capable of firing ball bearings.[963] D, aged 51 at appeal, had offended all his life. His first custodial sentence for robbery was in 1981 aged 18 (6 years). There were also custodial sentences in 1994 (armed robbery, 12 years) and 2004 (14 armed robberies, life with minimum of 10 years). Held. The Judge was required by section 224A[964] to pass a life sentence. The appeal was solely in relation to the minimum term. These were not the very worst robberies of their kind. D was a single robber acting alone, threatening people with an imitation firearm. No one was hurt. What made the offences exceptionally serious is that D was a prisoner on the run. He was not just any prisoner but one serving life sentences for similar armed robberies. D's culpability was exceptionally high. If a 20-year determinate term would have been appropriate for these offences without the background of previous armed robberies and escape from prison, then a 10-year uplift to a starting point of 30 years was too long. Starting at 24 years would have been appropriate. With full credit that is reduced to 16 years. Therefore **life** with a **minimum term** of **8 years**, not 10.

R v Fernandez 2014 EWCA Crim 2405, 2015 1 Cr App R (S) 35 (268) D pleaded to two robberies and an attempt and three associated counts of possession of an imitation firearm. In the first two robberies, which were ten weeks apart, he entered a Lloyds Bank wearing a crash helmet and holding a plastic gun. He demanded money and money was handed over. He escaped on a bike. Just under £5,430 and just under £4,040 were taken. Two months later he did exactly the same but before any money was handed over, someone in the bank, R, said, "Look you prick, why don't you just fuck off?" D said he would just start shooting and shoot through the glass and demanded money again. Money was handed over, but R said, "Fuck off you prick. It's a fake gun anyway, it's plastic." D said, "Chris bring the shooter in" as a bluff. D escaped on his bike empty-handed. R chased him and twice threw a fire extinguisher at him knocking him off his bike. D hit R with his helmet. D was chased by R and another and detained. Police found D's van nearby. In interview he denied the first two robberies. One of the cashiers had been subjected to six previous robberies and had suffered severe trauma. D

---

[963] The indictment stated that the firearm was an imitation firearm and the Court treated D as though the weapon was not capable of firing anything. Ed.
[964] The judgment states 'the Judge was required by section 225A'. It is assumed this is a typo for section 224A (automatic life). Ed.

had 35 previous convictions on 12 occasions. In 1986, when aged 19, he was sentenced to 5 years' youth custody for armed robbery. In 1990, when aged 23, he was sentenced to 7 years for robbery. In 1995, when aged 28, he was sentenced to 11 years for robbery and two firearm counts. Held. The offences were planned, D was disguised, vulnerable victims were targeted, the premises were vulnerable and D had caused terror. D was clearly dangerous. **17-18 years**, as given, was an accurate starting point. The Judge was wrong to deduct less than half when fixing the minimum term. With plea, life with a minimum term of **6½ years**.

See also: *R v Brown* 2008 EWCA Crim 736 (Convicted of two counts of conspiracy to rob and two counts of having a firearm with intent. Case based on surveillance and the finding of two pistols. Convictions for similar offences in 1983 and 1989. **Life** (11-year term) is an appropriately severe deterrent sentence at the top end of the appropriate range.)

R v Wheatley 2014 EWCA Crim 2675 (Plea. Imitation firearm. Serving life. Absconded on his first day of day release. Offence 4 days later. Aged 55. Had convictions for 23 robberies, 2 attempted robberies and 18 offences involving firearm. We start at 24 years not 30, so life with a minimum term of **8 years**.)

322.55   *Withdrawing from robbery plan   Pre-2016 guideline case*
Att-Gen's Ref Nos 65-66 of 2001 2001 EWCA Crim 2406 H pleaded to robbery of a guard of a security van. H, then aged 19, sat beside the getaway driver, wearing a balaclava helmet throughout the robbery. H's basis of plea was that when the two assailants who attacked the guard got out of the car, he was unaware that weapons were to be used. When he saw the weapons he decided not to go with the other two and he remained in the car. Held. The basis of plea for H was supported by the fact that he just remained in the car. Courts ought to encourage people who, at the last minute, decide not to go through with a criminal enterprise and who withdraw their own involvement, even if they remain a party to what is going on.
Note: This is an old case, so treat the decision with care. Ed.

323   SCHOOL: FAILURE TO SECURE REGULAR ATTENDANCE
323.1
1) Education Act 1996 s 444(1) (parent with child who fails to attend regularly)
   Mode of trial Summary only
   Maximum sentence Level 3 fine (£1,000)
2) Education Act 1996 s 444(1A) (parent who knows child is failing to attend regularly, and fails to cause him to attend)
   Mode of trial Summary only
   Maximum sentence 3 months and/or Level 4 fine (£2,500)
Fixed penalties Anti-social Behaviour Act 2003 s 23 and Education Act 1996 s 444(1A) introduced the power to authorise local education authorities, school staff and the police to issue Fixed Penalty Notices. The penalty is £60 if paid within 28 days and £120 if paid within 42 days of receipt of the notice.[965]
Parenting Orders For both offences there is power to make a Parenting Order under Crime and Disorder Act 1998 s 8.

323.2   *Magistrates' Court Sentencing Guidelines*
Magistrates' Court Sentencing Guideline 2008 page 90, see www.banksr.com Other Matters Guidelines tab Starting points are based on a first-time offender pleading not guilty.

---

[965] Education (Penalty Notices) (England) Regulations 2007 2007/1867 as amended, reg 3 and 4

Examples of nature of activity	Starting point	Range
Short period following previous good attendance (section 444(1))	Band A fine	Conditional discharge to Band A fine
Erratic attendance for long period (section 444(1))	Band B fine	Band B fine to Band C fine
Colluding in and condoning non-attendance or deliberately instigating non-attendance (section 444(1A))	Medium-level community order	Low-level community order to high-level community order

Factors indicating higher culpability: 1 Parental collusion (section 444(1) only), 2 Lack of parental effort to ensure attendance (section 444(1) only), 3 Threats to teachers and/or officials, 4 Refusal to co-operate with school and/or officials. Factors indicating lower culpability: 1 Parent unaware of child's whereabouts, 2 Parent tried to ensure attendance, and 3 Parent concerned by child's allegations of bullying or unable to get school to address bullying. Factors indicating greater degree of harm: 1 More than one child, and 2 Harmful effect on other children in family.

Consider ancillary orders, including Parenting Order.

Consultation It is expected that the Sentencing Council will issue a consultation document about updating this guideline in May 2016.

A Band A fine is 50% of net weekly income. A Band B fine is 100%. For more detail see **60.27** in Volume 1.

For the meaning of a high-level, a medium-level and a low-level community order, see **16.12** in Volume 1.

324   SCRAP METAL OFFENCES

324.1

Scrap Metal Dealers Act 2013 s 12

Buying scrap metal for cash etc.

Mode of trial Summary only

Maximum sentence Level 5 fine (£5,000 fine for offences committed before 12 March 2015 and an unlimited fine thereafter.[966] There are maximum fines for those aged under 18, see **14.38** in Volume 1).

Commencement Section 12 is in force from 1 October 2013, Scrap Metal Dealers Act 2013 (Commencement and Transitional Provisions) 2013 2013/1966.

See also the RAILWAY *Stealing material which disrupts services* para at **316.5** and the THEFT ETC. *Metal thefts* para at **346.23**.

325   SEX OFFENCES: ANIMALS

325.1

Sexual Offences Act 2003 s 69 (intercourse with an animal)

Mode of trial Triable either way

Maximum sentence On indictment 2 years. Summary 6 months and/or a £5,000 fine for offences committed before 12 March 2015 and an unlimited fine thereafter.[967] There are maximum fines for those aged under 18, see **14.38** in Volume 1.

Extended sentences This offence is listed in Criminal Justice Act 2003 Sch 15. The court may pass a 2012 extended sentence (EDS) if there is a significant risk of serious

---

[966] Legal Aid, Sentencing and Punishment of Offenders Act 2012 s 85(1) and (4) and Legal Aid, Sentencing and Punishment of Offenders Act 2012 (Commencement No 11) Order 2015 2015/504

[967] Legal Aid, Sentencing and Punishment of Offenders Act 2012 s 85(1) and (4) and Legal Aid, Sentencing and Punishment of Offenders Act 2012 (Commencement No 11) Order 2015 2015/504

harm from future specified offences and either: a) the defendant has a Criminal Justice Act 2003 Sch 15B conviction (applicable only to defendants aged 18+), or b) the offence would justify a determinate sentence of at least 4 years.[968]

Sexual Harm Prevention Orders There is a discretionary power to make this order when it is necessary to protect the public from sexual harm.[969]

Notification For offences where the defendant was:

a) aged under 18 and sentenced to imprisonment of at least 12 months, or

b) aged 18 or over and was sentenced to imprisonment or detained in a hospital,

the defendant must notify the police within three days (or three days from his or her release from imprisonment, hospital etc.) with his or her name, home address, National Insurance number etc. and any changes to those, and addresses where he or she resides for seven days[970] (in one or more periods) or more in any 12-month period.[971]

325.2   Sentencing Guidelines Council guideline

Sexual Offences Act 2003 Guideline 2008 page 18 para 1, see www.banksr.com Other Matters Guidelines tab

Note: It is understood that as these offences are not dealt with in the *Sexual Offences Guideline 2014*, the *Sexual Offences Act 2003 Guideline 2008* is still in force. Ed.

The starting points and ranges apply to a first-time offender who was convicted after a trial. page 101 For a basic offence as defined in Sexual Offences Act 2003, assuming no aggravating or mitigating factors, the starting point is a community order and the sentencing range is a fine or a community order.

Additional aggravating factor: Recording activity and/or circulating pictures or videos

Additional mitigating factor: Symptom of isolation rather than depravity.

325.3   Cases

R v H and R 2008 EWCA Crim 1202 The defendants pleaded to causing a person to engage in a sex act, making an indecent photograph of a child and causing unnecessary harm to an animal. H forced the victim, V, to take a dog's erect penis into his mouth and filmed it on his mobile. He then took V and the dog to R's house where he and R forced V to be penetrated in his anus by the dog. This was again filmed. The films were extensively circulated on the Internet, elsewhere and circulated to schoolchildren. V was visibly mentally disabled, had been traumatised by abuse, was vulnerable and had significant learning difficulties. H and R shouted and laughed at V's humiliation. H was aged 17. He was in regular work and had effectively no convictions. H was heavily intoxicated with skunk at the time. R was aged 18. He had two minor convictions for battery in 2003. He had a disruptive childhood and was prone to aggression, violence and bullying. R was unemployed living a pointless life in which cannabis and alcohol figured largely. He was intoxicated with one or the other at the time of the offences. The Judge considered H's good character balanced his involvement in both incidents and sentenced both to 7 years for the anal sex act offence with 3 years for the photograph offence and 3 months for the animal harm offence all concurrent. Held. These acts were deeply unpleasant acts of cruelty and sexual humiliation of a vulnerable, mentally disordered teenage boy. The humiliation and serious psychological harm to the victim was compounded by the event being recorded. This was rape or rape equivalent. The Judge must have considered a starting sentence in the region of 10 years. His approach (in passing the same sentence) was not wrong. Weight was given to the ages of the defendants. **7 years** upheld.

Note: Although this is not an intercourse with an animal case, which has a maximum sentence of 2 years, this case shows the approach of the Court. Ed.

---

[968] Criminal Justice Act 2003 s 226A-226B as inserted by Legal Aid, Sentencing and Punishment of Offenders Act 2012 s 124
[969] Sexual Offences Act 2003 s 103A as inserted by Anti-social Behaviour, Crime and Policing Act 2014 Sch 5 para 2 and Sexual Offences Act 2003 Sch 3
[970] Sexual Offences Act 2003 s 84(1)(c) and (6)
[971] Sexual Offences Act 2003 s 83 and Sch 3 para 35

R v Squires 2010 EWCA Crim 2582 D pleaded late to two counts of buggery and two counts of criminal damage. In 1999 a female donkey was found tied up in a field having been buggered. Its tail had also been cut. In 2004 a pregnant mare was also found with her legs tied together. She had also been subjected to an act of buggery.[972] Her reproductive organs were swollen and bleeding. Traces of semen were found on vaginal swabs. D was arrested on other matters and DNA was taken. D was aged 67 at appeal and had lost his 10-year-old son in a fire. A pre-sentence report noted D's 'low level of intellect' and that he was socially isolated. His deviant sexual interest suggested an increased, medium risk of reconviction. It was also noted that D expressed remorse. The Judge said that the offences were disgusting, distressing and worrying. Slight credit was given for the late plea. Held. These were two very unpleasant offences against animals, aggravated by the fact they were tied up and also that the mare was pregnant. D had served the equivalent of 18 months. Sentences reduced to 6 months for the buggery, concurrent, 2 months for the criminal damage concurrent with the sentences for buggery. **12 months** not 22.

SEX OFFENCES: ABUSE OF TRUST see the SEX OFFENCES: CHILDREN, WITH chapter.

326 SEX OFFENCES: ASSAULT

326.1

Sexual Offences Act 2003 s 3 (sexual touching of another person who does not consent)
Mode of trial Triable either way
Maximum sentence On indictment 10 years. Summary 6 months and/or a £5,000 fine for offences committed before 12 March 2015 and an unlimited fine thereafter.[973] There are maximum fines for those aged under 18, see **14.38** in Volume 1.
Detention The offence is a specified offence enabling defendants aged under 18 to be detained under Powers of Criminal Courts (Sentencing) Act 2000 s 91.[974]
Extended sentences Section 3 is listed in Criminal Justice Act 2003 Sch 15. The court may pass a 2012 extended sentence (EDS) if there is a significant risk of serious harm from future specified offences and either: a) the defendant has a Criminal Justice Act 2003 Sch 15B conviction (applicable only to defendants aged 18+), or b) the offence would justify a determinate sentence of at least 4 years.[975]
Sexual Harm Prevention Orders There is a discretionary power to make this order when it is necessary to protect the public from sexual harm.[976]
Notification For offences where the defendant was:
  a) under 18 and sentenced to imprisonment of at least 12 months, or
  b) aged 18 or over and i) the victim was under 18 or ii) the defendant was sentenced to imprisonment or detained in a hospital or given community service for at least 12 months,
the defendant must notify the police within three days (or three days from his or her release from imprisonment, hospital etc.) with his or her name, home address, National Insurance number etc. and any change of address and any address where he or she resides for seven days[977] (in one or more periods) or more in any 12-month period.[978]
Children and vulnerable adults: barred lists Where the defendant is aged 18 or over, he or she is automatically barred from engaging in regulated activity with children and

---

[972] Under the 1956 Act, vaginal intercourse with an animal appears to have been charged as buggery. Ed.
[973] Legal Aid, Sentencing and Punishment of Offenders Act 2012 s 85(1) and (4) and Legal Aid, Sentencing and Punishment of Offenders Act 2012 (Commencement No 11) Order 2015 2015/504
[974] Powers of Criminal Courts (Sentencing) Act 2000 s 91(1)(b)
[975] Criminal Justice Act 2003 s 226A-226B as inserted by Legal Aid, Sentencing and Punishment of Offenders Act 2012 s 124
[976] Sexual Offences Act 2003 s 103A as inserted by Anti-social Behaviour, Crime and Policing Act 2014 Sch 5 para 2 and Sexual Offences Act 2003 Sch 3
[977] Sexual Offences Act 2003 s 84(1)(c) and (6)
[978] Sexual Offences Act 2003 s 83 and Sch 3 para 18

with vulnerable adults.[979] The Judge must tell the defendant that the Disclosure and Barring Service will include him or her in the barred list.[980] The defendant may ask the Service to remove him or her from the list.

Where the offence is *Sexual assault by penetration*, see the RAPE AND ASSAULT BY PENETRATION chapter.

Where the offence involves children, see the SEX OFFENCES: CHILDREN, WITH chapter.

326.2   Crown Court statistics   England and Wales
Sexual assault on a female

Year	Age	Plea	Total sen-tenced	Type of sentencing %							Average length of custody in months
				Dis-charge	Fine	Commu-nity sentence	Sus-pended sentence	Custody	Other		
2013	18-20	G	42	–	–	9.5	2.4	83.3	4.8		58.5
		NG	33	–	–	–	–	100	–		80.3
	21+	G	805	0.7	0.1	15.7	15.8	66.1	1.6		34.9
		NG	532	0.9	0.4	11.3	10.9	75.2	1.3		46.4
2014	18-20	G	28	–	–	18	25	54	4		18.1
		NG	9	–	–	22	11	56	11		17.4
	21+	G	404	–	–	22	24	50	4		18.8
		NG	223	2	–	15	17	65	1		22.6

Sexual assault on a male   Aged 21+

Year	Plea	Total sen-tenced	Type of sentencing %						Average length of custody in months
			Dis-charge	Fine	Community sentence	Sus-pended sentence	Custody	Other	
2013	G	105	1.9	–	13.3	15.2	69.5	–	34.9
	NG	61	–	–	4.9	16.4	78.7	–	41.3
2014	G	43	5	.	30	21	40	5	20.1
	NG	23	.	.	9	26	57	9	23.2

For explanations about the statistics, see page 1-xii. For more statistics, see www.banksr.com Other Matters Statistics tab

Note: The statistics may not be for Sexual Offences Act 2003 s 3 only. Ed.

326.3   Sentencing Council Guidelines Sexual Offences Act 2003 s 3
Sexual Offences Guideline 2014, see www.banksr.com Other Matters Guidelines tab. In force 1 April 2014. The guideline only applies to offenders aged 18+, see page 7 of the guideline. For the usual practice, see **66.21** in Volume 1.

STEP ONE: Determining the offence category
page 17 The court should determine which categories of harm and culpability the offence falls into by reference only to the tables below. **This guideline also applies to offences committed remotely/online.**

---

[979] Safeguarding Vulnerable Groups Act 2006 s 2 and Sch 3 and Safeguarding Vulnerable Groups Act 2006 (Prescribed Criteria and Miscellaneous Provisions) Regulations 2009 2009/37 reg 4 and 6 and Sch para 2 and 4
[980] Safeguarding Vulnerable Groups Act 2006 s 2 and Sch 3 para 25

Harm	
Category 1	Severe psychological or physical harm Abduction Violence or threats of violence Forced/uninvited entry into victim's home
Category 2	Touching of naked genitalia or naked breasts Prolonged detention/sustained incident Additional degradation/humiliation Victim is particularly vulnerable due to personal circumstances* *For children under 13, please refer to the guideline (at **328.3**)
Category 3	Factor(s) in Categories 1 and 2 not present

Culpability A
Significant degree of planning Offender acts together with others to commit the offence Use of alcohol/drugs on victim to facilitate the offence Abuse of trust Previous violence against victim Offence committed in course of burglary Recording of offence Commercial exploitation and/or motivation Offence racially or religiously aggravated Offence motivated by, or demonstrating, hostility to the victim based on his or her sexual orientation (or presumed sexual orientation) or transgender identity (or presumed transgender identity) Offence motivated by, or demonstrating, hostility to the victim based on his or her disability (or presumed disability)

Culpability B
Factor(s) in Category A not present

326.4

STEP TWO: Starting point and category range

page 18 Having determined the category, the court should use the corresponding starting points to reach a sentence within the category range [below]. The starting point applies to all offenders irrespective of plea or previous convictions. Having determined the starting point, step two allows further adjustment for aggravating or mitigating features, set out below.

A case of particular gravity, reflected by multiple features of culpability or harm in step one, could merit upward adjustment from the starting point before further adjustment for aggravating or mitigating features, set out [below].

Where there is a sufficient prospect of rehabilitation, a community order with a sex offender treatment programme requirement under Criminal Justice Act 2003 s 202 can be a proper alternative to a short or moderate-length custodial sentence.

	A		B	
	Starting point	Category range	Starting point	Category range
Category 1	4 years' custody	3 to 7 years' custody	2 years 6 months' custody	2 to 4 years' custody
Category 2	2 years' custody	1 to 4 years' custody	1 year's custody	High-level community order to 2 years' custody

	A		**B**	
Category 3	26 weeks' custody	High-level community order to 1 year's custody	High-level community order	Medium-level community order to 26 weeks' custody

For the meaning of a high-level and a medium-level community order, see **16.13** in Volume 1.

326.5   [Aggravating and mitigating factors]

page 19 The table below contains a non-exhaustive list of additional factual elements providing the context of the offence and factors relating to the offender. Identify whether any combination of these, or other relevant factors, should result in an upward or downward adjustment from the starting point. In particular, relevant recent convictions are likely to result in an upward adjustment. In some cases, having considered these factors, it may be appropriate to move outside the identified category range.

When sentencing appropriate Category 2 or 3 offences, the court should also consider the custody threshold as follows:

Has the custody threshold been passed?

If so, is it unavoidable that a custodial sentence be imposed?

If so, can that sentence be suspended?

Aggravating factors
Statutory aggravating factors:
Previous convictions, having regard to: a) the nature of the offence to which the conviction relates and its relevance to the current offence, and b) the time that has elapsed since the conviction
Offence committed whilst on bail
Other aggravating factors:
Specific targeting of a particularly vulnerable victim
Blackmail or other threats made (where not taken into account at step one)
Location of offence
Timing of offence
Use of weapon or other item to frighten or injure
Victim compelled to leave their home (including victims of domestic violence)
Failure to comply with current court orders
Offence committed whilst on licence
Exploiting contact arrangements with a child to commit an offence
Presence of others, especially children
Any steps taken to prevent the victim reporting an incident, obtaining assistance and/or from assisting or supporting the prosecution
Attempts to dispose of or conceal evidence
Commission of offence whilst under the influence of alcohol or drugs

Mitigating factors
No previous convictions or no relevant/recent convictions
Remorse
Previous good character and/or exemplary conduct*
Age and/or lack of maturity where it affects the responsibility of the offender
Mental disorder or learning disability, particularly where linked to the commission of the offence
Demonstration of steps taken to address offending behaviour
*Previous good character/exemplary conduct is different from having no previous convictions. The more serious the offence, the less the weight which should normally be attributed to this factor. Where previous good character/exemplary conduct has been used to facilitate the offence, this mitigation should not normally be allowed and such conduct may constitute an aggravating factor.

Note: An exact copy of this guideline has been placed in the Magistrates' Court Guidelines at page 273.

326.6   Suggested approach to the new guideline

Note: It is understood the Sentencing Council intended that the guideline should reflect the Court of Appeal current sentencing tariff. This means the changes were about bringing the guidelines up to date rather than increasing the penalties for the bulk of the sex offences. Consequently, I would suggest that sentencers should start with the guideline and then consider the current level of sentencing set out by the Court of Appeal and then return to the guideline before deciding the appropriate sentence. Ed.

326.7   Abuse of Trust/Abuse of Power   Factor and cases

'Abuse of trust' is one of the factors in Category 2 when the reader is determining harm, see *Sexual Offences Guideline 2014* page 10 and 14 at **326.3**.

R v Finnegan 2013 EWCA Crim 817 D was convicted of sexual assault. The family of V, aged 17, had become very friendly with D. He was a Catholic priest and had been the parish priest at V's church for around four years. V had acted as an altar server throughout the time D was the parish priest. V's grandfather was ill and could not attend the church. D would visit him and give him communion. V would see D then. D was close with the family and it was not uncommon to see V hugging D. After an Easter Sunday service, D drew V into the church and placed one hand on the back of V's head, and the other on her bottom. He then pulled her forcefully towards him. He then kissed her on the lips with an open mouth. She told her mother but no action was taken. Two days later, D visited V's house. V was there with her brother. D told V that he had harboured sexual feelings for her for some time and spoke of buying her an expensive birthday present. V told her mother, who contacted a church welfare agency. The police became involved. D, aged 60, had no previous convictions. In breach of his vows he had married an ex-parishioner. He had been ordained as a priest when aged 24 and had given support to many parishioners for over 30 years. V's A-level studies had been affected and the offence had undermined both V's physical wellbeing and her religious faith. The Judge found that D visited V's home in an attempt to persuade her to keep quiet. He had tried to buy her silence with the promise of an expensive present. Held. The offence was committed in an enormous breach of trust. This represented a considerable fall from grace. There is greater culpability due to the breach of trust placed in D by V and her family. It was aggravated by the fact it was committed in a church and, additionally, the impact of that breach of trust on the harm caused to V was an aggravating factor. D's offence had also caused damage to the wider Catholic Church community at a time when it could ill afford such damage. If committed in other circumstances, a non-custodial sentence might have been appropriate. **6 months** was severe but not manifestly excessive.

R v Dhabeneey 2013 EWCA Crim 2184 D was convicted of sexual assault. At 3.30 am, V and three friends got into a cab driven by D. They had been to a pub and later a restaurant. The cab made two stops, dropping off two of D's friends, both of whom were male. V and her female friend remained in the cab, with V in the front passenger seat. V fell asleep and was awoken by D touching her legs and rubbing her crotch. She also felt D unsuccessfully try to put his hand down her trousers, and then grab her left breast over her clothing. V remonstrated with D and D stopped the cab. V got out and immediately called the police. D was of previous exemplary character. Held. The offence fell on the borderline between Categories 2 and 3. The custody threshold was passed, however, due to the breach of trust. Women must know that they can trust the driver of a taxi they get into late at night. The Judge was right to conclude that D took advantage of the fact that V was intoxicated. In mitigation there was his character and the financial and domestic impact of a custodial sentence upon his wife and young children. Starting at 5 months was appropriate. Taking account of the aggravation and mitigation, 4 months should be added to that, so **9 months** not 15.

R v Ayyoub 2014 EWCA Crim 385 D was convicted of two sexual assaults. He was a doctor whose practice involved preparing reports for claimants seeking compensation in personal injury cases. V was making a claim for whiplash injuries allegedly sustained in a car accident. She attended D's surgery with a male friend. She was taken into the examination room and was alone with D. After an initial examination, D said he thought the problem was muscular, and that he would perform a massage to ease her symptoms. V was asked to lie face down on the examination table. D pulled up her top and undid her bra, exposing her back. He applied massage oil and began to massage her back, working towards her breasts. He touched them on two occasions. At that stage V was unsure whether it was deliberate and thus said nothing. He then left the room to see his next patient and in doing so unlocked the door. V had been unaware that the door was locked. He returned some minutes later and again locked the door. He resumed the massage, focusing more and more on V's breasts. He brought his hands underneath her, onto her breasts, rubbing them and 'moving them down to her stomach'. V said more than once that she needed to go but D did not stop what he was doing. The massage lasted for 10 minutes or more. When V said that she wanted to go, D grabbed her roughly and twice attempted to pull her head towards his groin. She pulled away and went to leave but could not do so because the door was locked. She asked him to unlock it and he did so. She made her exit. As she was waiting to be collected by her friend, D left the building and asked if she would like a lift. She declined. Held. It was a gross breach of trust against a victim who was in a vulnerable situation. The custodial sentence had to be immediate due to the serious breach of the basis on which the doctor/patient relationship is founded. Taking account of the mitigation, good character and the inevitably devastating impact on his family and professional career, **6 months** not 12.

Post-2014 guideline case

See also: *Att-Gen's Ref No 118 of 2014* 2014 EWCA Crim 2898 (Pleas to 11 sexual assaults. Over 19 months V1's breasts and bottom touched, both over clothing. V1 aged in her mid-30s. V2, V3 and V4 worked at D's kennels and aged 16 to early 20s. V2, V3 and V4 assaulted in a similar manner but often under clothing/on bare skin as well. Occurred to V2 over four years, V3 over two, and V4 over one year. Detrimental effects on victims. D denied offences, suggested Vs were making it up. D, aged 77, of good character. Held. Not simple. Abuse of power closely aligned to abuse of trust. **15 months** not suspended.)

See also the SEX OFFENCES: CHILDREN, WITH **Abuse of Trust** section.

326.8   *Alcohol/Drugs, Offence committed when under the influence of   Factor and pre-2014 guideline cases*

'Commission of offence whilst under the influence of alcohol or drugs' is one of the aggravating factors, see *Sexual Offences Guideline 2014* page 19 at **326.3**.

R v Christopher 2010 EWCA Crim 859 D was convicted of sexual assault. D lived in the same block as V, a 57-year-old lady in ill health. D and X had been drinking and visited V's flat. D asked X to go to his flat to get him more drink. X left and D asked V for a kiss but she refused. D kissed V on the cheek, straddled V whilst she was sitting in her armchair, forced his tongue into her mouth and grabbed her breasts. He said he was going to have her 'minge' later on and put his hands inside her jumper. V tried to push D off. D got off and V asked him to leave. D said, "Oh, so I can't have a shag then", and then left. The next morning D apologised to V. V was badly affected by what happened, did not sleep well and was worried that someone would come into her flat. D, aged 57, had nine court appearances for 21 offences, including ABH (12 months). The pre-sentence report said D accepted no responsibility for his criminal behaviour and his risk of reoffending was low. Held. This was a very unpleasant assault involving some degree of force on a disabled woman who was unable to protect herself. **18 months** not 2 years 3 months.

R v Davies 2011 EWCA Crim 2142 D pleaded (full credit) to two sexual assaults and one common assault. D, who was significantly intoxicated, said to two girls, aged 13 and

14, "That's a nice bum, can I touch it?", and similar remarks. The girls ran off. He followed and grabbed outside her clothing one girl's buttocks and breasts. That was the sexual assault. D then attempted to grab the second but only caught her shoulder. That was the common assault. About 30 minutes later, he touched a 17-year-old girl's buttocks and stroked her thigh. That was the second sexual assault. A search of D's address found a box of sanitary towels and computer searches relating to menstruation. D, aged 45, was of good character save for an excess alcohol conviction. He was diagnosed as being schizophrenic and drank daily. D also had gender dysphoria. Held. The drunkenness, the lewd comments and the fact that the offences were committed in public were aggravating features. 2 years 6 months was far outside of the guidelines' range, so **community order**, with 3 years' supervision and a sex offender programme.

R v Borrill 2011 EWCA Crim 2158 D pleaded on rearraignment to sexual assault and breach of a SOPO. D, in an intoxicated state, approached V, who was at an ATM. He rubbed his hand on the inside of her leg, and onto her vaginal area. He said, "Nice arse" and then ran away. He was at the time in breach of a SOPO prohibiting him from speaking to a female in a manner a reasonable person would consider sexual, without express consent. D, aged 48 at appeal, had significant previous convictions: 1990, rape of 69-year-old; 1994, indecent assault of 74-year-old woman. Held. **6 years'** not 8 years' extended sentence (**3 years'** not 5 years' custody and 3 years' extended licence).

R v Janes 2013 EWCA Crim 1504 D pleaded to sexual assault (after the prosecution opening). On the night of the closing ceremony of the London 2012 Olympic Games, special trains ran through the night from London to other parts of the country. At 2.30 am, V boarded a train at Paddington. The train was crowded and V passed D, E and H. D was drunk. D and H tried to pull her onto their laps and all three were grabbing her over her clothes in the area of her groin and buttocks. The train guard entered the carriage and told them that they had to move as the carriage was for passengers with first class tickets only. They moved and V sat in a seat for two people. D and E joined her and squeezed onto the seat, effectively trapping her against the window. They began to touch her breasts and each put his hand inside her brassiere. D said to E, "She has nice nipples, you should touch them as well." Shortly after this, the men moved to a different part of the train. As she tried to leave the train, the three men blocked her path and were making grabbing motions towards her groin. She shouted "Fuck off" at them and they allowed her to leave the train. She pointed the men out to a police officer. D had no previous sexual offences but had served a significant prison term in 2009 for an offence of dishonesty. He was married with six children, the youngest being two years old. Held. The attack was disgraceful, humiliating and frightening. A custodial sentence was appropriate. Given the mitigation (the effect on the family and his parents, whom he supported at his home), **12 months** not 18.

See also: *R v Cannel* 2010 EWCA Crim 485 (Conviction. Been drinking. Victim would not let him in but he pushed his way in. Sucking of neck while masturbating. Victim feared she was to be raped. Aged 25. Ten previous convictions but none for sexual offences. 6 years' extended sentence (**4 years' custody** 2 years' extension.)

R v Coulter 2010 EWCA Crim 2129 (Plea to sexual assault and threatening words/ behaviour. Young women grabbed between the legs. Appeared to be drunk. **12 months** not 18 for sexual assault unaltered.)

326.9   Alcohol/drugs used to facilitate the offence Factor and pre-2014 guideline case

'Use of alcohol/drugs on victim to facilitate the offence' is one of the factors when the reader is determining Category A Culpability, see *Sexual Offences Guideline 2014* page 18 at **326.3**.

An example: *R v Penfold* 2012 EWCA Crim 1222 (Convicted of sexual assault and administering a noxious substance. Satellite TV installer revisited home of 84-year-old disabled lady. He put BZP and TFMPP in her drink and sexually assaulted her while she was unconscious, causing her pain and distress. No previous convictions for sexual offences. **4½ years' IPP** not 6 years' IPP.)

326.10   Intruders, By   Factor and cases

'Forced/uninvited entry into victim's home' is one of the factors when the reader is determining Category 1 harm, see *Sexual Offences Guideline 2014* page 18 at **326.3**.

R v Moulding 2010 EWCA Crim 1690 D pleaded to two offences of sexual assault and trespass with intent to commit a sexual offence. T lived next door to D with her partner and her 14-year-old daughter, V. D entered their property in the early hours. V woke up and D was kneeling by her bed. D put his hand on V's thigh and moved it towards her breast. V swatted D's hand and told him to go away. When V picked up her mobile phone and illuminated it she saw D masturbating. V screamed. D put his hands over her face, pushed her head towards the pillow and walked out of the room. T's partner had heard the screams and chased D out of the house. The screams also woke T. She had a substance in her hair which was identified as D's semen. An attempt was made to call the police but the telephone had been unplugged from the socket. V felt very self-conscious and her relationship with her mother and stepfather was affected. T had a lot of pent-up anger. She said the incident had ruined family relationships and affected her children. D denied the offences were sexually motivated, denied assaulting V and denied unplugging the phone. D, aged 31, had no previous convictions for sexual offences but had five previous court appearances. These included convictions for seven offences of arson, burglary, criminal damage, theft and aggravated vehicle-taking (2 years' detention in 2007). He had developed an extensive drug habit in his twenties. The pre-sentence report said D's denial indicated a high level of risk. The psychiatric report said: a) D had a depressive type of adjustment disorder and schizophrenia, b) D misused psychoactive substances, and c) a personality disorder could not be ruled out. D posed a medium risk of harm but did not represent a significant risk of serious harm to the public. Held. The appropriate total determinate sentence would have been 6 years. 8 years' extended sentence (**4 years' custody** 4 years' licence) not 10 years' extended sentence (6 years' custody 4 years' licence).

R v Rauf 2011 EWCA Crim 2447 D pleaded to sexual assault. He was staying in a hotel as part of a stag party. V, aged 29 and unknown to D, was also staying in the hotel, as part of a hen party. V returned to her room at 2.30 am. She wedged the door open and left the lights on, so that her room-mate could enter without waking her. D entered the room, turned the lights off and closed the door. He grabbed V's hand and placed it on his exposed, erect penis and moved it up and down. He then tried to pull down V's pyjama bottoms. V pushed D off her. He left the room. D, aged 29, was of effective good character with a good work record and a partner and baby son. Held. There were a number of aggravating features. It was committed in a hotel room where V was entitled to feel secure. There must have been some element of premeditation. D then turned off the light and closed the door. In mitigation there is D's character and the fact that he left when asked to do so. With the plea, **20 months** not 3 years 4 months.

See also: *R v Cannel* 2010 EWCA Crim 485 (Conviction. Victim would not let him in but he pushed his way in. Sucking of neck while masturbating. Victim feared she was to be raped. Aged 25. Ten previous convictions but none for sexual offences. 6 years' extended sentence (**4 years' custody** 2 years' extension).

Old cases: Best ignored.

Post-2014 guideline case

Att-Gen's Ref No 37 of 2015 2015 EWCA Crim 1210 D pleaded (full credit) to sexual assault and burglary. D, after drinking, asked a friend to go to a club with him and the friend refused. D left. About four hours later, he smashed a lower floor window with a spade and entered a dwelling. He stole some relatively insignificant articles and then went to V's room. V woke up, saw D and without her glasses was unable to recognise the person and screamed. She was absolutely terrified. D stood over the bed and said,

"You are not going to make any noise are you?" V said she would not. She tried to keep D talking and thought D had a weapon. D pulled the duvet from V's legs, touched her bottom with his hand, and moved it up to her upper thigh area over her clothing. Next he pulled her legs apart and cupped her vagina over her pyjama bottoms. D then moved his hand to the back of her waist band and began to pull at it. At this point another resident came into the bedroom. She directed D out of the house and he left. Shortly afterwards he was seen by a police officer, who considered D was smelling slightly of alcohol. The stolen articles were found in his pockets. D lied then and in interview. D was aged 19 with no convictions. He continued with the lies he told at trial. However, he claimed that he was a victim of sex abuse and that was found to be true. V described her feelings of vulnerability and how she now never felt safe. Held. Forced entry was indicative of greater harm in every case. The offence was committed at night and under the influence of alcohol. The victim exemplifies the feelings of distress, invasion and future fear as to their safety in their own home. We start at **4 years** so with plea and 2 months off as he now goes into custody, **2½ years** not a community order.

326.11   *Previous convictions, Defendant has   Factor and pre-2014 guideline cases*
'Previous convictions, having regard to: a) the nature of the offence to which the conviction relates and its relevance to the current offence, and b) the time that has elapsed since the conviction' is one of the statutory aggravating factors, see *Sexual Offences Guideline 2014* page 19 at **326.3**.
R v Borrill 2011 EWCA Crim 2158 D pleaded on rearraignment to sexual assault and breach of a SOPO. D, in an intoxicated state, approached V, who was at an ATM. He rubbed his hand on the inside of her leg, and onto her vaginal area. He said, "Nice arse" and then ran away. He was at the time in breach of a SOPO prohibiting him from speaking to a female in a manner a reasonable person would consider sexual, without express consent. D, aged 48 at appeal, had significant previous convictions: 1990, rape of 69-year-old, 1994, indecent assault of 74-year-old woman. Held. 6 years' extended sentence (**3 years' custody** 3 years' licence) not 8 years' extended sentence (5 years' custody 3 years' licence).
R v Burkinshaw 2012 EWCA Crim 184 D pleaded to sexual assault. At about 1.15 am, V, aged 17, was walking home. D followed her on a bicycle. She stopped under a streetlight to let him pass. He cycled up to her and said, "Show us your tits". D seized V and held his hand over her mouth. She screamed. He got on top of her and she was unable to move her legs or his hand over her mouth. She screamed as loudly as she could. He told her to stop. She managed to push away and run off. Police found D nearby. V believed she was to be raped. D lied in his first interview and admitted the offence in the second interview. The next day he pleaded guilty. D was aged 47. When aged 17, D was sentenced to 3 years' youth custody for two indecent assaults on women, two ABHs and a wounding. When D was aged 21, he was sentenced to 4 years for an indecent assault. Held. The guidelines do not deal with this type of aggravated offence involving a lone young girl attacked at night in a secluded place with violence and a fear that she is to be raped. The previous convictions were highly significant. However, the offence is not to be equated with the completed offence of rape. Starting at **6 years**, with plea **4 years** not 6.
R v Brown 2012 EWCA Crim 347 D pleaded to sexual assault. V was in London's West End celebrating her friend's birthday. She and her friends had been to several bars and clubs and at about 3 am they left. She became aware that her bag had been lost or stolen. She recalled that a friend of hers had had her phone stolen in the same area and had received the help of a local person who was aware of how to get it back. Trusting that, V spoke to D, who indicated that he would be able to assist her. She was quite drunk. She followed him as he went from place to place making enquiries. She was very cold from the temperature and the effects of the alcohol. D suggested on numerous occasions that they should go to the police. V declined. D went to a phone box, at which point V decided she wished to go home. She informed D of this and D led her to believe that

there was one more place to search, which was a multi-storey car park. They made their way there and got into a lift. D tried to put his arms around her and touched her hips. V rejected his advances and said it felt like she was being assaulted. D said, "Fuck you, I'm not doing so but I will now". After getting out of the lift, he pulled V to the floor, and banged her head repeatedly against the floor or wall. He pulled her underwear down and lowered his trousers, exposing his penis, before trying to pull her legs apart. V screamed for help and a man and the car park attendant made their way towards them. D looked agitated and aggressive, dressed himself and ran off. V was very distressed and vomited a number of times. D denied the offence, claiming that he left V with two people she knew and then heard screaming. D, aged 30, had the following convictions: section 18 (1997, 6 years' YOI), robbery (2002, 12 months), assault with intent to rob (2003, 3 years), possession of an offensive weapon (2005, 4 months) and possession of a bladed article (2006, 2 months), common assault (2007, conditional discharge), violent disorder (2008, 8 months) and possession of an offensive weapon (2008, 3 months). Held. The Judge was entitled to reach the conclusion that an IPP sentence should be imposed. The correct starting point was **9 years.** With full credit for the plea, the nominal determinate term was 6 years. So, **3 years' IPP** not 4 years' IPP.

Note: Although the convictions do not appear to be of a sexual nature, they are important when determining the appropriate sentence. Ed.

R v McCormack 2014 EWCA Crim 681 D pleaded to sexual assault. When V was aged 14, he did some work experience in a shop in Birmingham. D used the shop. Shortly before V's 15th birthday, D spoke to him about doing some work in his garden. V gave D his mobile number. On V's 15th birthday, D sent V a text wishing him a happy birthday. There was then a telephone call about the gardening job. A few days later, V went to D's address. He was asked to remove his coat and shoes. D asked V to remove his trousers because it had been raining. V declined. D offered V a drink of cola, which V later learned had been spiked. D encouraged V to drink the cola in one go, which he did. D said he wanted to 'check V for any wires', which V thought was odd but he complied with the instruction to pull up his jumper and t-shirt. D said, "What's down there?" and pointed to V's legs. With D's encouragement, V pulled down his trousers on one side, exposing his boxer shorts and the top of his leg. D asked what V had on underneath his boxer shorts. V said, "nothing" and D asked to see, saying, "We're only men". V pulled his boxers to one side, exposing the top of his leg but covered his genitals with his hand. D pulled V's wrist, thereby exposing his genitals. D looked at V's genitals and bottom and made complimentary remarks. V pushed D away and was able to re-dress himself. D then hugged V, kissed him on the cheek and tried to kiss him again. V was uncomfortable and shuffled away from D. The spiked drink then began to take effect and V became drowsy. D said V would have 'a lot of money coming [his] way' if he set up a video camera for D. He asked V to close the curtains and left the room. V pretended to be on the phone to his parents and managed to leave the flat. D implored him to come back. V walked to the nearby house of a friend who noticed he had been severely affected by the drink and telephoned V's parents. D was arrested. He had 36 convictions for 91 offences including violence and dishonesty. Amongst others there were two convictions for section 18 and a large number of sexual offences, some of which had similarities to the instant offence. They included two attempted indecent assaults in 1993 (15 months), gross indecency with a child and attempted buggery in 1995, two indecent assaults in 1997 (18 months and 12 months) and indecent assault of a male under 16 in 2002 (8 years' extended sentence). Held. D's previous convictions for very similar offences mean the [old] guidelines are of no direct application. D was a predatory sexual offender. He had previously spiked victims' drinks to commit offences of this kind. V was vulnerable, deliberately targeted, deceived into coming into D's home and drugged. Those factors meant a lengthy prison term was inevitable. The grounds of appeal played down D's behaviour. Having said that, starting at 8 years was too high. The physical contact was less serious than it might have been, but the wider circumstances were of course important. The appropriate starting point was 5½ years. The Judge was entitled to reduce the discount for the plea based on the strength of the evidence. 25% was appropriate. That reduces the custodial term to 4 years, instead of 6. The extended licence should remain at 4 years. It will allow the Probation Service to keep D under proper scrutiny. D clearly poses an obvious danger to the public, particularly children. 8 years' extended sentence (**4 years' custody**, not 6, 4 years' licence).

R v Collins 2014 EWCA Crim 2803 D pleaded to touching two community support officers on duty. Two previous convictions for sexual assault (18 months and 6 months). **18 months**, see **326.13**.

326.12   *Prosecution, Attempts to avoid   Factor and pre-2014 guideline cases*
'Any steps taken to prevent the victim reporting an incident, obtaining assistance and/or from assisting or supporting the prosecution' is one of the aggravating factors, see *Sexual Offences Guideline 2014* page 19 at **326.3**.

R v Moulding 2010 EWCA Crim 1690 D pleaded to two offences of sexual assault and trespass with intent to commit a sexual offence. T lived next door to D with her partner and her 14-year-old daughter, V. D entered their property in the early hours. V woke up and D was kneeling by her bed. D put his hand on V's thigh and moved it towards her breast. V swatted D's hand and told him to go away. When V picked up her mobile phone and illuminated it she saw D masturbating. V screamed. D put his hands over her face, pushed her head towards the pillow and walked out of the room. T's partner had heard the screams and chased D out of the house. The screams also woke T. She had a substance in her hair which was identified as D's semen. An attempt was made to call the police but the telephone had been unplugged from the socket. V felt very self-conscious and her relationship with her mother and stepfather was affected. T had a lot of pent-up anger. She said the incident had ruined family relationships and affected her children. D denied the offences were sexually motivated, denied assaulting V and denied unplugging the phone. D, aged 31, had no previous convictions for sexual offences but had five previous court appearances. These included convictions for seven offences of arson, burglary, criminal damage, theft and aggravated vehicle-taking (2 years' detention in 2007). He had developed an extensive drug habit in his twenties. The pre-sentence report said D's denial indicated a high level of risk. The psychiatric report said: a) D had a depressive type of adjustment disorder and schizophrenia, b) D misused psychoactive substances, and c) a personality disorder could not be ruled out. D posed a medium risk of harm but did not represent a significant risk of serious harm to the public. Held. The appropriate total determinate sentence would have been 6 years. 8 years' extended sentence (**4 years' custody** 4 years' licence) not 10 years' extended sentence (6 years' custody 4 years' licence).

R v Finnegan 2013 EWCA Crim 817 D was convicted of sexual assault. The family of V, aged 17, had become very friendly with D. He was a Catholic priest and had been the parish priest at V's church for around four years. V had acted as an altar server throughout the time D was the parish priest. V's grandfather was ill and could not attend the church. D would visit him and give him communion. V would see D then. D was close with the family and it was not uncommon to see V hugging D. After an Easter Sunday service, D drew V into the church and placed one hand on the back of V's head, and the other on her bottom. He then pulled her forcefully towards him. He then kissed her on the lips with an open mouth. She told her mother but no action was taken. Two days later, D visited V's house. V was there with her brother. D told V that he had harboured sexual feelings for her for some time and spoke of buying her an expensive birthday present. V told her mother, who contacted a church welfare agency. The police became involved. D, aged 60, had no previous convictions. In breach of his vows he had married an ex-parishioner. He had been ordained as a priest when aged 24 and had given support to many parishioners for over 30 years. V's A-level studies had been affected and the offence had undermined both V's physical wellbeing and her religious faith. The

Judge found that D visited V's home in an attempt to persuade her to keep quiet. He had tried to buy her silence with the promise of an expensive present. Held. The offence was committed in an enormous breach of trust. This represented a considerable fall from grace. There is greater culpability due to the breach of trust placed in D by V and her family. It was aggravated by the fact it was committed in a church and, additionally, the impact of that breach of trust on the harm caused to V was an aggravating factor. D's offence had also caused damage to the wider Catholic Church community at a time when it could ill afford such damage. If committed in other circumstances, a non-custodial sentence might have been appropriate. **6 months** was severe but not manifestly excessive.

326.13   *Psychological harm, Severe   Factor and pre-2014 guideline cases*

'Severe psychological or physical harm' is one of the factors when the reader is determining Category 1 harm, see *Sexual Offences Guideline 2014* page 18 at **326.3**.

R v Gomes 2013 EWCA Crim 407 D pleaded to sexual assault and exposure. V was a 67-year-old lady who had difficulty in walking. She lived on an estate where D was employed as a sweeper and she saw him regularly. D must have been aware of V's frailties. V returned from the shops and passed D, who was sweeping up leaves. He asked her if he could have a glass of water as the only water he had access to was dirty. V invited D into her kitchen and passed him a cup of water. He asked to use the bathroom and D said, "of course". She expected D to leave but he sat on the sofa. She said he should sit in a chair and as he moved to do so, V saw that D's trousers were undone and his erect penis was protruding from his trousers. V told D to tidy himself up and to leave. She set off towards her bedroom, expecting D to comply with her request. D helped himself to more water and came up behind V whereupon he groped her breast. He freed his penis from his trousers and said, "Is this big enough?" V was shocked. She asked him to leave and D apologised and left. The effect upon V was severe. Her whole quality of life has been adversely affected and the problems caused by D persisted. D made limited admissions when arrested. D, aged 28 at appeal, had a conviction for exposure in 2008 (community order). Held. There were particular aggravating features. D had a previous conviction for exposure. He targeted a particularly vulnerable woman, knowing of her frailties, and he assaulted her in her own home. After exposing himself and having been asked to leave, he did not do so but persisted in his unpleasant behaviour. The Judge was justified in sentencing outside the guideline to **2 years**.

R v Collins 2014 EWCA Crim 2803 D pleaded (25% credit) to two sexual assaults. Two community support officers, S and P, aged 29 and 49, were patrolling in Greater Manchester. At about 9 pm, D, who was drunk, approached them and asked for a cigarette. S said neither of them smoked. D then stared at S and said, "You have really nice lips." D lunged at her with his arm moving towards her crotch area. S moved backwards and the contact was only for a split second and S did not feel it. S called for assistance. P tried to push D backwards, but D tried to grab her genital area. D only managed to touch the inside of her thighs. P pinned D against a wall and D touched her higher up the thigh. P pinned D harder against the wall. S went to her assistance and D managed to touch P's crotch area. D was restrained and police help arrived. The assisting officers noticed D's buttocks were exposed under a long coat. S was extremely shocked and was now worried about patrolling at night. P had trouble sleeping and was more wary of her safety. D was aged 35 with 42 court appearances for 73 offences. In 2007 and in 2009, he was convicted of sexual assault (18 months and 6 months). In 2010, he was convicted of a sex notification offence (6 months). D had been homeless for most of the last 10 years. When found accommodation he lost it because he caused damage. He used cannabis every day. D was assessed as posing a very high risk of further sex offending. The Judge considered it was a Category 3 case and said D's repetition and lack of insight took the case outside the category range. Held. The offending was grossly offensive and threatening. It was a significant aggravating factor that S and P were performing a public service. The Judge was justified to move the case outside Category 3B, but the highest this case could be elevated to was Category 2A, so we start at 2 years, making with plea **18 months** not 27.

See also: *R v P* 2011 EWCA Crim 1378 (Plea at PCMH (25% credit) to sexual assault. Seized a young woman from behind. Sat on her and simulated intercourse. Undid his trousers and touched her underneath her top. Victim had post-traumatic stress disorder and required counselling. Job and boyfriend lost. Defendant had long-term paranoid schizophrenia. **3 years** not 7½ years' extended sentence (4½ years' custody 3 years' licence).)

See also the *Victim traumatised* paras at **326.22**.

326.14   Public transport, Assault on/street attack   Pre-2014 guideline cases

R v Mohammed 2010 EWCA Crim 21 D pleaded to sexual assault. In the early hours, he came up behind V1, a 19-year-old woman, and her female friend. He put his arm round their shoulders and gave them a cigarette. D said, "Do you want a smoke?" Then he said, "Do you want more than a smoke?" V1 replied, "What?", and D pulled her roughly by the neck and stuck his tongue down her throat. V1 pushed D away, and D touched her over her clothes in the vaginal area. V1 pushed D away again and D ran to a nightclub nearby. V1 followed D in and slapped him in the face. He ran off again. In interview D denied the offence. The pre-sentence report said that he had limited victim empathy and there was a medium risk of his causing serious harm. D was in breach of a community sentence for harassment. The victim of that offence was his former wife, V2, who had to move house. D appeared when V2 was dropping off their children at school. D grabbed V2 by the face and pushed her against a wall so that her head hit it. He shouted abuse at V2, calling her a whore, and threatened to take the children from her. The Judge said that D's attitude to women was appalling, and gave him **6 months** and 4 months consecutive. Held. The case fell into Level 2. 6 months was not manifestly excessive.

Att-Gen's Ref No 121 of 2009 2010 EWCA Crim 452 D pleaded belatedly to three sexual assaults. Over an 8-month period he attacked three women, V1, V2 and V3. The attacks were at night after they had alighted from a bus and were about to enter their home. V1 was grabbed from behind and felt an arm come round her waist and come up between her legs. She felt the pressure of fingers upon her vagina. She screamed, her boyfriend came down the stairs, and D ran off. V1 was extremely shocked and distressed. The incident affected her confidence and quality of life. The second attack was similar. V2 was additionally pulled back and fell on the ground. She had a graze and a bruise. V3 felt an arm come round her side and she was pulled violently to the ground. She felt a hand between her legs, and D poked her vagina aggressively as if trying to penetrate her. She shouted and D continued to touch her vagina over her underwear. D ran off. V3 had a graze and a bruise. Her confidence was severely affected. When seen by the police, D made partial admissions, denials and no comments. The case was listed four times for trial. On one occasion D's counsel withdrew. D, aged 22, was Peruvian with no convictions. The pre-sentence report said that D posed a high risk to lone females. Held. The Judge should have considered the issue of dangerousness. We don't adjourn for the papers for that to be available. The victims were terrified and remain deeply traumatised. We would expect a sentence of **6½ years**. Because this is the third time he has been sentenced, **6 years**.

R v Janes 2013 EWCA Crim 1504 D pleaded to sexual assault (after the prosecution opening). On the night of the closing ceremony of the London 2012 Olympic Games, special trains ran through the night from London to other parts of the country. At 2.30 am, V boarded a train at Paddington. The train was crowded and V passed D, E and H. D was drunk. D and H tried to pull her onto their laps and all three were grabbing her over her clothes in the area of her groin and buttocks. The train guard entered the carriage and told them that they had to move as the carriage was for passengers with first class tickets only. They moved and V sat in a seat for two people. D and E joined her and squeezed onto the seat, effectively trapping her against the window. They began to touch her breasts and each put his hand inside her brassiere. D said to E, "She has nice nipples, you should touch them as well." Shortly after this, the men moved to a different part of the train. As she tried to leave the train, the three men blocked her path and were making grabbing motions towards her groin. She shouted, "Fuck off" at them and they allowed her to leave the train. She pointed the men out to a police officer. D had no previous sexual offences but had served a significant prison term in 2009 for an offence of dishonesty. He was married with six children, the youngest being two years old. Held. The attack was disgraceful, humiliating and frightening. A custodial sentence was appropriate. Given the mitigation (the effect on the family and his parents, whom he supported at his home), **12 months** not 18.

326.15   *Service personnel   Pre-2014 guideline cases*
R v Yard 2013 EWCA Crim 2147 D was convicted of sexual assault. He, then a lance corporal, and V, an able seawoman, were guarding an Afghan detainee in a hospital at Camp Bastion. The work was boring so they chatted. Over two hours, after telling V he liked women with tight leggings, D said he, "like[d] a straight up and down body". He next asked her to stand up and she did so. Then, he twice felt her from the armpits down to 'perhaps the waist'. D pulled her skirt tight and made an appreciative noise and later boasted of his sexual prowess. D then invited V to a private encounter which she took to be sexual. After commenting on the bosom of a nurse, D described her 'set' as 'small'. Next he leant over and touched V's breast and V smacked him. D said, "Sorry, I couldn't help myself." After finishing her duty and chatting with others, she was jokingly told she had had it easy. V said she had been felt or 'touched up'. The matter was reported. V in her victim impact statement said the event had not affected her. D had no convictions or in the 12 years of service any military findings against him. His work was described as exemplary and he was described as an outstanding soldier. Before the trial he was promoted to corporal. The Vice Judge Advocate said had D accepted responsibility he would have taken an exceptionally lenient course. Loss of rank to lance corporal not trooper (one loss not two) and **30 days' detention** not 120.
See also: *R v Rapson* 2012 EWCA Crim 3135 (Convicted of two sexual assaults. Hand inside her pyjama top and on her breast. 16 photos. **3 months** not 12, effecting immediate release.)

326.16   *Significant force used or threatened   Pre-2014 guideline case*
R v Reed 2012 EWCA Crim 2131 D pleaded to sexual assault. V, aged 20, placed a note on Facebook about selling her dog for £60 or nearest offer. D replied from one of his Facebook accounts. D was not permitted to have an account because of the terms of his ISA orders. An appointment was made and about that time V returned to her flat and found D in the corridor. V invited him in and for a short while they talked about the dog. When V bent down to pick something up, D slapped her bottom and said, "You've got a sexy arse". V tried to ignore him and still assumed D had come about the dog. D told V he had just come out of jail for attempted murder and had been "kicked off" the train for not paying his fare. They resumed talking for what she thought was about an hour and D said he would give her £20 for the dog. As she wanted him to leave she said he could have dog for £30. He said he would pay £60 if he could get into her bed. She was really scared. He told her she was sexy and that he was horny. She went into the bathroom to roll a cigarette. D followed her, grabbed her wrist and closed the door. Next he pushed her against a wall holding her arms so she could not move them. D was bigger than V and she could not get away. Next D spun her around and pinned her there by putting his leg between her legs. D started kissing the back of V's neck and pulled V's top off. He told her he knew she wanted it and undid her bra. D then released her and she got away from him only for him to push her onto the bed. D kissed and bit V's neck and tried to pull her trouser zip down. V crossed her legs and curled into a ball. He still tried to pull V's trousers' down. When she bit his hand, D let her go. V jumped off the bed only to find D grabbing her bra and top. Next he took hold of her breasts and said what a nice set

she had. He told her to leave and D then began to apologise. He told her not to tell the police and gave her £30 for the dog. Afterwards V did not like being alone, did not sleep well and wanted to find somewhere else to live. D was aged 31 at appeal and had violence, drug and dishonesty convictions. He had served five custodial sentences. When aged 17, he was cautioned for indecently assaulting a woman in a street. When still 17, he received 1 year's YOI detention for indecently assaulting a 14-year-old girl by pulling her trousers down and touching her with his penis. He received a community sentence for sexually assaulting his partner's 27-year-old cousin by touching her breasts and biting her. Held. She may have been targeted. D knew she was vulnerable and naïve. V was alone in her home. Considerable force was used. The discount should have been 20%. 9 years' extended sentence (**5 years'** custody 4 years' extended licence) was not too long.

R v H 2014 EWCA Crim 168 D pleaded to attempted sexual assault and ABH. V was a housing officer. She was six months pregnant. She attended D's flat to discuss his housing issues. V entered with a colleague and sat down, the further of the two away from D. There was a normal conversation until D got up and moved towards V. He brandished a large kitchen knife and lunged towards her in a downward stabbing motion. V managed to disarm D, screamed and said, "Let us go". D moved to one side and both left the flat. V had sustained a cut to the web on her hand between her thumb and first finger. D was originally charged with section 18 but the prosecution accepted his version of events, namely that D acted as he did in an attempt to subdue V so that he could sexually assault her. The injury sustained by V was caused recklessly. D was aged 30 and he had a caution for a sexual assault on a child. He had sexually assaulted his young nephew on numerous occasions. A report noted that D had suffered physical and emotional abuse as a child. It raised the possibility that he had been sexually abused. The Judge imposed a 10-year extended sentence (4 years' custody 6 years' licence). There was a concurrent sentence for the ABH. Held. D's troubled background did constitute some mitigation. He was not to be treated as a man of good character. The concurrent sentence added nothing and so the sentence for the sexual assault had to take account of the ABH. The circumstances were so severe that the Judge was entitled to move up to twice the upper limit in the guidelines. An appropriate sentence therefore, before credit for the plea, was 4 years. With full credit, **2 years 8 months**.

326.17   *Touching of naked genitalia or naked breasts   Factor and pre-2014 guideline case*

'Touching of naked genitalia or naked breasts' is one of the factors when the reader is determining Category 2 harm, see *Sexual Offences Guideline 2014* page 18 at **326.3**.

An example: *R v Elliott* 2010 EWCA Crim 31, 2 Cr App R (S) 55 (p 377) (Plea to two counts of sexual assault against a 60-year-old female victim. D forced the victim onto the sofa and placed his erect penis inches from her face. He tried to force her legs open. There was also a subsequent assault where D grabbed the victim's breast. **18 months** not 3 years.)

326.18   *Two or more acting together   Pre-2014 guideline cases*

R v Janes 2013 EWCA Crim 1504 D pleaded to sexual assault (after the prosecution opening). On the night of the closing ceremony of the London 2012 Olympic Games, special trains ran through the night from London to other parts of the country. At 2.30 am, V boarded a train at Paddington. The train was crowded and V passed D, E and H. D was drunk. D and H tried to pull her onto their laps and all three were grabbing her over her clothes in the area of her groin and buttocks. The train guard entered the carriage and told them that they had to move as the carriage was for passengers with first class tickets only. They moved and V sat in a seat for two people. D and E joined her and squeezed onto the seat, effectively trapping her against the window. They began to touch her breasts and each put his hand inside her brassiere. D said to E, "She has nice nipples, you should touch them as well." Shortly after this, the men moved to a different part of the train. As she tried to leave the train, the three men blocked her path and were making grabbing motions towards her groin. She shouted, "Fuck off" at them and they allowed her to leave the train. She pointed the men out to a police officer. D had no previous sexual offences but had served a significant prison term in 2009 for an offence of dishonesty. He was married with six children, the youngest being two years old. Held. The attack was disgraceful, humiliating and frightening. A custodial sentence was appropriate. Given the mitigation (the effect on the family and his parents, whom he supported at his home), **12 months** not 18.

See also: *R v Sandes* 2011 EWCA Crim 2400 (Convicted. Followed young woman. Asked for directions. Continued to follow her. Accomplice offered to pay her. Bear-hugged her, grabbed her face and kissed her cheek. Fear she would be raped. Able to escape upon the intervention of passers-by. Aged 26. Good character. **2 years 6 months** was severe but not manifestly excessive.)

326.19   *Victim compelled to leave home   Factor*

'Victim compelled to leave their home (including victims of domestic violence)' is one of the aggravating factors, see *Sexual Offences Guideline 2014* page 19 at **326.3**.

326.20   *Victim harassed   Pre-2014 guideline cases*

R v John 2013 EWCA Crim 2345 D was convicted of sexual assault. V, a young woman in her twenties, worked in an interior design shop. D entered with his son on the pretext of buying some flooring. There came a time when V, who was working alone, needed to go downstairs and D followed her. His son remained upstairs. D grabbed V's arms, pushed her back and attempted to kiss her. The 'sexual contact was limited' but that appeared to be because D was disturbed by another employee entering the shop and walking down the stairs. The Judge said she was in no doubt that if D had not been interrupted, the attack would have been considerably more serious. V was in a state of shock and was disturbed by what happened. She was afraid of D returning to the shop and trying to 'take it further than kissing'. V did not call the police because she did not feel it was serious enough to raise a complaint. Three weeks later, D entered the shop and asked V why she had not called him. V said she had a boyfriend and was not interested. She asked him to leave her alone. Subsequently, D returned to the shop with his son. V told him firmly to leave her alone and D replied that he was leaving and that V should take good care of herself. That comment worried V. She then reported the matter to the police. D, aged 46 at appeal, had convictions in 2003 for two indecent exposure and harassment offences. He had repeatedly exposed himself to a schoolgirl over a period of months. Held. This was a calculated course of conduct against a vulnerable woman working in a shop on her own. The defence accepted that the behaviour after the offence could be described as low-level harassment. D targeted her. The Judge was entitled to conclude that an immediate custodial sentence was necessary. However, **6 months** was appropriate, not 12.

326.21   *Victim particularly vulnerable   Factor and pre-2014 guideline cases*

'Victim is particularly vulnerable due to personal circumstances' is one of the factors when the reader is determining Category 2 harm, see *Sexual Offences Guideline 2014* page 18 at **326.3**.

R v Burkinshaw 2012 EWCA Crim 184 D pleaded to sexual assault. At about 1.15 am, V, aged 17, was walking home. D followed her on a bicycle. She stopped under a streetlight to let him pass. He cycled up to her and said, "Show us your tits". D seized V and held his hand over her mouth. She screamed. He got on top of her and she was unable to move her legs or his hand over her mouth. She screamed as loudly as she could. He told her to stop. She managed to push away and run off. Police found D nearby. V believed she was to be raped. D lied in his first interview and admitted the offence in the second interview. The next day he pleaded guilty. D was aged 47. When aged 17, D was sentenced to 3 years' youth custody for two indecent assaults on women, two ABHs and a wounding. When D was aged 21, he was sentenced to 4 years for an indecent assault.

Held. The guidelines do not deal with this type of aggravated offence involving a lone young girl attacked at night in a secluded place with violence and a fear that she is to be raped. The previous convictions were highly significant. However, the offence is not to be equated with the completed offence of rape. Starting at **6 years**, with plea **4 years** not 6.

R v Fadre 2012 EWCA Crim 336, 2 Cr App R (S) 72 (p 412) D pleaded, on the second day of trial, to sexual assault. V, aged 17, had known D for four or five months. D was Nigerian but visited the UK regularly. D and V had met by prior arrangement four or five times and kept in touch when D was out of the UK. D demonstrated a sexual interest in V, saying that he wanted to marry her. V made it clear that she was not interested in a relationship. V hadn't seen D for a couple of months. She went out to celebrate her birthday and was not expecting to see D. D appeared and he, V and V's friend had a drink. When the bar closed, D asked them to go with him to another bar where D bought V a number of drinks. After being persuaded to get a lift home with D and his friends, V, her friend and D were dropped at an address, on the understanding that D's friend would return and take them home. They waited inside the flat and V fell asleep. She awoke to find that her trousers and underwear had been pulled down. Her friend and D were arguing in another room. The friend called a taxi and D said that V was not leaving. He tricked the friend into thinking the taxi was outside and locked her out of the house. He approached V and tried to kiss her and to remove her clothes. V made it clear that D should desist. D told V he had had sex with her while she was asleep. He held her by the neck, making it difficult for her to breathe. D tried to put his finger into her vagina and said he was going to put his 'dick' in her. V managed to reach her mobile phone and called 999. She pushed D off and said she was going to the kitchen. In fact, she ran into the street, leaving her personal belongings in the flat. D was aged 33. Held. The aggravating features were substantial and manifold. V was in a more vulnerable position because, as D knew, she had drunk a considerable amount of alcohol. He used significant force, causing some injury, despite V making it quite plain that she wished him to desist. The aggravating features took this offence outside of the guideline. Starting at 3 years was perhaps severe and at the top of the permissible range, but was not manifestly excessive. With limited reduction for the plea, **2 years 9 months** was not manifestly excessive.

Note: It would have been fairer if the suggested penetration had either been proved or left out of the facts. Ed.

R v Turner 2013 EWCA Crim 368 D was charged with assault by penetration. On the day of trial, a sexual assault charge was added and D pleaded to that. V travelled to visit her friend, E, at a university, during the 'freshers' period, when students often drink to excess. D was a flatmate of E, who was aged 18. V was aged 20. V and E drank alcohol in preparation for going into the local town for a night out. By 10 pm both E and V were very drunk. Before they went out, someone broke the lock on E's bedroom door. At midnight, they went into the town centre. D and some others joined them. D put his arm around V and tried to kiss her. D had no ID and was refused entry to a nightclub. He returned home, accompanied by E, who was concerned because he was staggering as a result of being so drunk. V went to the nightclub and E joined her shortly after. V and E returned home at about 3 am. E slept in her bed and V slept on the bedroom floor. V had changed into her pyjamas but kept her underwear on. E had been woken by the sound of the door opening and closing. She saw that V's pyjamas and knickers had been pulled down. E was unable to wake V and so pulled the duvet to cover her. Five minutes later, at about 6.30 am, E heard the door open again and the sound of heavy breathing. V woke to find D was lying beside her. He was trying to touch her vagina. V pushed his hand away. Her pyjama bottoms and knickers had been pulled down. D returned to the room saying that he wanted to chat, but E said that she wanted to sleep. V suffered four bruises on the inside of her thigh. In interview, D said he had very little recollection of the night's events as he had been drinking so heavily. Held. This fell into the middle category of the guidelines, which had a starting point of 12 months. This was a serious offence committed in drink at a time when D lost his self-control. D took advantage of V for his own sexual gratification. **12 months' YOI suspended**, not 12 months.

R v Gomes 2013 EWCA Crim 407 D pleaded to sexual assault and exposure. V was a 67-year-old lady who had difficulty in walking. She lived on an estate where D was employed as a sweeper and she saw him regularly. D must have been aware of V's frailties. V returned from the shops and passed D, who was sweeping up leaves. He asked her if he could have a glass of water as the only water he had access to was dirty. V invited D into her kitchen and passed him a cup of water. He asked to use the bathroom and D said, "of course". She expected D to leave but he sat on the sofa. She said he should sit in a chair and as he moved to do so, V saw that D's trousers were undone and his erect penis was protruding from his trousers. V told D to tidy himself up and to leave. She set off towards her bedroom, expecting D to comply with her request. D helped himself to more water and came up behind V whereupon he groped her breast. He freed his penis from his trousers and said, "Is this big enough?" V was shocked. She asked him to leave and D apologised and left. The effect upon V was severe. Her whole quality of life has been adversely affected and the problems caused by D persisted. D made limited admissions when arrested. D, aged 28 at appeal, had a conviction for exposure in 2008 (community order). Held. There were particular aggravating features. D had a previous conviction for exposure. He targeted a particularly vulnerable woman, knowing of her frailties, and he assaulted her in her own home. After exposing himself and having been asked to leave, he did not do so but persisted in his unpleasant behaviour. The Judge was justified in sentencing outside the guideline to **2 years**.

See also: *R v Boles* 2011 EWCA Crim 910 (Plea to sexual assault. Victim was drunk and fell asleep in an alley. Defendant pinned him down, undid his trousers and masturbated him. Alcoholic. Aged 24. Previous convictions but none for sex. Starting at 3 years. **18 months**)

R v Penfold 2012 EWCA Crim 1222 (Convicted of sexual assault and administering a noxious substance. Satellite TV installer revisited home of 84-year-old disabled lady. He put BZP and TFMPP in her drink and sexually assaulted her while she was unconscious, causing her pain and distress. No previous convictions for sexual offences. 4½ years' IPP not 6 years' IPP.)

326.22   *Victim traumatised   Pre-2014 guideline cases*

Att-Gen's Ref No 121 of 2009 2010 EWCA Crim 452 D pleaded belatedly to three sexual assaults. Over an eight-month period he attacked three women, V1, V2 and V3. The attacks were at night after they had alighted from a bus and were about to enter their home. V1 was grabbed from behind and felt an arm come round her waist and come up between her legs. She felt the pressure of fingers upon her vagina. She screamed, her boyfriend came down the stairs, and D ran off. V1 was extremely shocked and distressed. The incident affected her confidence and quality of life. The second attack was similar. V2 was additionally pulled back and fell on the ground. She had a graze and a bruise. V3 felt an arm come round her side and she was pulled violently to the ground. She felt a hand between her legs, and D poked her vagina aggressively as if trying to penetrate her. She shouted and D continued to touch her vagina over her underwear. D ran off. V3 had a graze and a bruise. Her confidence was severely affected. When seen by the police, D made partial admissions, denials and no comments. The case was listed four times for trial. On one occasion D's counsel withdrew. D, aged 22, was Peruvian with no convictions. The pre-sentence report said that D posed a high risk to lone females. Held. The Judge should have considered the issue of dangerousness. We don't adjourn for the papers for that to be available. The victims were terrified and remain deeply traumatised. We would expect a sentence of **6½ years**. Because this is the third time he has been sentenced, **6 years**.

R v Christopher 2010 EWCA Crim 859 D was convicted of sexual assault. D lived in the same block as V, a 57-year-old lady in ill health. D and X had been drinking and visited

V's flat. D asked X to go to his flat to get him more drink. X left and D asked V for a kiss but she refused. D kissed V on the cheek, straddled V whilst she was sitting in her armchair, forced his tongue into her mouth and grabbed her breasts. He said he was going to have her "minge" later on and put his hands inside her jumper. V tried to push D off. D got off and V asked him to leave. D said, "Oh, so I can't have a shag then", and then left. The next morning D apologised to V. V was badly affected by what happened, did not sleep well and was worried that someone would come into her flat. D, aged 57, had nine court appearances for 21 offences, including ABH (12 months). The pre-sentence report said D accepted no responsibility for his criminal behaviour and his risk of reoffending was low. Held. This was a very unpleasant assault involving some degree of force on a disabled woman who was unable to protect herself. **18 months** not 2 years 3 months.

See also the ***Psychological harm, Severe*** para at **326.13**.

326.23   *Violence or threats of violence Factor and pre-2014 guideline cases*

'Violence or threat of violence' is one of the factors when the reader is determining Category 1 harm, see *Sexual Offences Guideline 2014* page 18 at **326.3**.

Att-Gen's Ref No 121 of 2009 2010 EWCA Crim 452 D pleaded belatedly to three sexual assaults. Over an 8-month period he attacked three women, V1, V2 and V3. The attacks were at night after they had alighted from a bus and were about to enter their home. V1 was grabbed from behind and felt an arm come round her waist and come up between her legs. She felt the pressure of fingers upon her vagina. She screamed, her boyfriend came down the stairs, and D ran off. V1 was extremely shocked and distressed. The incident affected her confidence and quality of life. The second attack was similar. V2 was additionally pulled back and fell on the ground. She had a graze and a bruise. V3 felt an arm come round her side and she was pulled violently to the ground. She felt a hand between her legs, and D poked her vagina aggressively as if trying to penetrate her. She shouted and D continued to touch her vagina over her underwear. D ran off. V3 had a graze and a bruise. Her confidence was severely affected. When seen by the police, D made partial admissions, denials and no comments. The case was listed four times for trial. On one occasion D's counsel withdrew. D, aged 22, was Peruvian with no convictions. The pre-sentence report said that D posed a high risk to lone females. Held. The Judge should have considered the issue of dangerousness. We don't adjourn for the papers for that to be available. The victims were terrified and remain deeply traumatised. We would expect a sentence of **6½ years**. Because this is the third time he has been sentenced, **6 years**.

R v Fadre 2012 EWCA Crim 336, 2 Cr App R (S) 72 (p 412) D pleaded, on the second day of trial, to sexual assault. V, aged 17, had known D for four or five months. D was Nigerian but visited the UK regularly. D and V had met by prior arrangement four or five times and kept in touch when D was out of the UK. D demonstrated a sexual interest in V, saying that he wanted to marry her. V made it clear that she was not interested in a relationship. V hadn't seen D for a couple of months. She went out to celebrate her birthday and was not expecting to see D. D appeared and he, V and V's friend had a drink. When the bar closed, D asked them to go with him to another bar where D bought V a number of drinks. After being persuaded to get a lift home with D and his friends, V, her friend and D were dropped at an address, on the understanding that D's friend would return and take them home. They waited inside the flat and V fell asleep. She awoke to find that her trousers and underwear had been pulled down. Her friend and D were arguing in another room. The friend called a taxi and D said that V was not leaving. He tricked the friend into thinking the taxi was outside and locked her out of the house. He approached V and tried to kiss her and to remove her clothes. V made it clear D should desist. D told V he had had sex with her while she was asleep. He held her by the neck, making it difficult for her to breathe. D tried to put his finger into her vagina and said he was going to put his 'dick' in her. V managed to reach her mobile phone and called 999. She pushed D off and said she was going to the kitchen. In fact, she ran into the street, leaving her personal belongings in the flat. D was aged 33. Held. The aggravating features were substantial and manifold. V was in a more vulnerable position because, as D knew, she had drunk a considerable amount of alcohol. He used significant force, causing some injury, despite V making it quite plain that she wished him to desist. The aggravating features took this offence outside of the guideline. Starting at 3 years was perhaps severe and at the top of the permissible range, but was not manifestly excessive. With limited reduction for the plea, **2 years 9 months** was not manifestly excessive.

Note: It would have been fairer if the suggested penetration had either been proved or left out of the facts. Ed.

R v Brown 2012 EWCA Crim 347 D pleaded to sexual assault. V was in London's West End celebrating her friend's birthday. She and her friends had been to several bars and clubs and at about 3 am they left. She became aware that her bag had been lost or stolen. She recalled that a friend of hers had had her phone stolen in the same area and had received the help of a local person who was aware of how to get it back. Trusting that, V spoke to D, who indicated that he would be able to assist her. She was quite drunk. She followed him as he went from place to place making enquiries. She was very cold from the temperature and the effects of the alcohol. D suggested on numerous occasions that they should go to the police. V declined. D went to a phone box, at which point V decided she wished to go home. She informed D of this and D led her to believe that there was one more place to search, which was a multi-storey car park. They made their way there and got into a lift. D tried to put his arms around her and touched her hips. V rejected his advances and said it felt like she was being assaulted. D said, "Fuck you, I'm not doing so but I will now". After getting out of the lift, he pulled V to the floor, and banged her head repeatedly against the floor or wall. He pulled her underwear down and lowered his trousers, exposing his penis, before trying to pull her legs apart. V screamed for help and a man and the car park attendant made their way towards them. D looked agitated and aggressive, dressed himself and ran off. V was very distressed and vomited a number of times. D denied the offence, claiming that he left V with two people she knew and then heard screaming. D, aged 30, had the following convictions: section 18 (1997, 6 years' YOI), robbery (2002, 12 months), assault with intent to rob (2003, 3 years), possession of an offensive weapon (2005, 4 months) and possession of a bladed article (2006, 2 months), common assault (2007, conditional discharge), violent disorder (2008, 8 months) and possession of an offensive weapon (2008, 3 months). Held. The Judge was entitled to reach the conclusion that an IPP sentence should be imposed. The correct starting point was **9 years.** With full credit for the plea, the nominal determinate term was 6 years. So, **3 years' IPP** not 4 years' IPP.

See also: *R v Law* 2011 EWCA Crim 204 (Plea. Defendant grabbed victim from behind. Threatened to stab her. Took her to a wooded area for 20 minutes. Forcibly removed her clothes but was disturbed and ran away. Aged 29. Previous convictions, but none for sex. **4 years** not 4½.)

R v Aman 2013 EWCA Crim 580 (Convicted. Pestered young woman on a bus at 4 am. She got off and he followed. He spoke of 'doing more than talking' then pinned her against a shop front and pulled at her top and trousers. They were on the ground for 5-10 seconds. He made his escape after she screamed. Aged 21. No convictions. Aggravating factor of targeting vulnerable victim. The gravamen of the offence was the obvious sexual purpose of the attack. 3 years.)

Old case: *Att-Gen's Ref No 26 of 2009* 2009 EWCA Crim 1393, 2010 1 Cr App R (S) 41 (p 240) (**4 years**)

For a summary of the case, see the 9th edition of this book.

327 SEX OFFENCES: CAUSING A PERSON TO ENGAGE IN SEXUAL ACTIVITY

327.1

Sexual Offences Act 2003 s 4 (causing a person to engage in sexual activity without consent)

Modes of trial and maximum sentences

1) Where the activity caused involves:
   a) penetration of the victim's anus or vagina,
   b) penetration of the victim's mouth with a person's penis,
   c) penetration of a person's anus or vagina with a part of the victim's body or by the victim with anything else, or
   d) penetration of a person's mouth with the victim's penis,

the offence is indictable only and the maximum sentence is life.

2) Otherwise, the offences are triable either way. On indictment 10 years. Summary maximum 6 months and/or a £5,000 fine for offences committed before 12 March 2015 and an unlimited fine thereafter.[981] There are maximum fines for those aged under 18, see **14.38** in Volume 1.

Automatic life Section 4 is listed in Criminal Justice Act 2003 Sch 15B Part 1. The Lord Chief Justice said in *Att-Gen's Ref No 27 of 2013* 2014 EWCA Crim 334[982] para 8 iii) *(obiter)* that in rare cases the provisions could lead to the imposition of a life sentence where the offence does not carry life imprisonment.

The court must (unless the particular circumstances make it unjust[983]) pass automatic life if: a) the defendant is aged 18+ at the date of the conviction, b) the offence was committed on or after 3 December 2012, c) the court considers a determinate sentence of at least 10 years is appropriate, d) at the time the offender was convicted he had a conviction for a Criminal Justice Act 2003 Sch 15B offence, and e) the defendant at the time of his or her conviction had previously been sentenced to: i) a life sentence where he or she was not eligible for release during the first five years of the sentence or ii) a determinate sentence or extended sentence where the custodial part was 10 years or more.[984] For a pre-2012 extended sentence, when determining whether the custodial term was 10+ years the period deducted for time on remand or on a curfew and tag is included.[985]

Extended sentences This offence is listed in Criminal Justice Act 2003 Sch 15. The court may pass a 2012 extended sentence (EDS) if there is a significant risk of serious harm from future specified offences and either: a) the defendant has a Criminal Justice Act 2003 Sch 15B conviction (applicable only to defendants aged 18+), or b) the offence would justify a determinate sentence of at least 4 years.[986]

Sexual Harm Prevention Orders There is a discretionary power to make this order when it is necessary to protect the public from sexual harm.[987]

Notification The defendant must notify the police within three days (or three days from his release from imprisonment, hospital etc.) with his name, home address, National Insurance number etc. and any change of address and any address where he resides for seven days[988] (in one or more periods) or more in any 12-month period.[989]

---

[981] Legal Aid, Sentencing and Punishment of Offenders Act 2012 s 85(1) and (4) and Legal Aid, Sentencing and Punishment of Offenders Act 2012 (Commencement No 11) Order 2015 2015/504

[982] This case is also known as *R v Burinskas* 2014 EWCA Crim 334.

[983] Criminal Justice Act 2003 s 224A(2)

[984] Criminal Justice Act 2003 s 224A as inserted by Legal Aid, Sentencing and Punishment of Offenders Act 2012 s 122. The condition for a) is at section 224A(1)(a), for b) is at section 224A(1)(b), for c) is at section 224A(1)(c), and for d) is at section 224A(4)-(9).

[985] Criminal Justice Act 2003 s 224A(9)-(10)

[986] Criminal Justice Act 2003 s 226A-226B as inserted by Legal Aid, Sentencing and Punishment of Offenders Act 2012 s 124

[987] Sexual Offences Act 2003 s 103A as inserted by Anti-social Behaviour, Crime and Policing Act 2014 Sch 5 para 2 and Sexual Offences Act 2003 Sch 3

[988] Sexual Offences Act 2003 s 84(1)(c) and (6)

Children and vulnerable adults: barred lists Where the defendant is aged 18 or over he or she is automatically barred from engaging in regulated activity with vulnerable adults with children.[990] The judge must tell the defendant that the Disclosure and Barring Service will include him or her in the barred list.[991] The defendant may ask the Service to remove him or her from the list.

327.2   *Sentencing Council guideline   Sexual Offences Act 2003 s 4*
Sexual Offences Guideline 2014, see www.banksr.com Other Matters Guidelines tab. In force 1 April 2014. The guideline only applies to offenders aged 18+, see page 7 of the guideline. For the usual practice, see **66.21** in Volume 1.

STEP ONE: Determining the offence category
page 21 The court should determine which categories of harm and culpability the offence falls into by reference **only** to the tables below.

Harm	
Category 1	The extreme nature of one or more Category 2 factors or the extreme impact caused by a combination of Category 2 factors **may** elevate to Category 1
Category 2	Severe psychological or physical harm Penetration using large or dangerous object(s) Pregnancy or STI as a consequence of offence Additional degradation/humiliation Abduction Prolonged detention/sustained incident Violence or threats of violence Forced/uninvited entry into victim's home Victim is particularly vulnerable due to personal circumstances* *For children under 13 please refer to the guideline on page 41
Category 3	Factor(s) in Categories 1 and 2 not present

Culpability A
Significant degree of planning Offender acts together with others to commit the offence Use of alcohol/drugs on victim to facilitate the offence Abuse of trust Previous violence against victim Offence committed in course of burglary Recording of the offence Commercial exploitation and/or motivation Offence racially or religiously aggravated Offence motivated by, or demonstrating, hostility to the victim based on his or her sexual orientation (or presumed sexual orientation) or transgender identity (or presumed transgender identity) Offence motivated by, or demonstrating, hostility to the victim based on his or her disability (or presumed disability)

Culpability B
Factor(s) in Category A not present

---

[989] Sexual Offences Act 2003 s 83 and Sch 3 para 19
[990] Safeguarding Vulnerable Groups Act 2006 s 2 and Sch 3 and Safeguarding Vulnerable Groups Act 2006 (Prescribed Criteria and Miscellaneous Provisions) Regulations 2009 2009/37 reg 4 and 6 and Sch para 2 and 4
[991] Safeguarding Vulnerable Groups Act 2006 s 2 and Sch 3 para 25

327.3

STEP TWO: Starting point and category range

page 22 Having determined the category, the court should use the corresponding starting points to reach a sentence within the category range [below]. The starting point applies to all offenders irrespective of plea or previous convictions. Having determined the starting point, step two allows further adjustment for aggravating or mitigating features, set out [below].

A case of particular gravity, reflected by multiple features of culpability or harm in step one, could merit upward adjustment from the starting point before further adjustment for aggravating or mitigating features, set out [below].

Where there is a sufficient prospect of rehabilitation, a community order with a sex offender treatment programme requirement under Criminal Justice Act 2003 s 202 can be a proper alternative to a short or moderate-length custodial sentence.

Where offence involved penetration

	A		B	
	Starting point	Category range	Starting point	Category range
Category 1	15 years' custody	13 to 19 years' custody	12 years' custody	10 to 15 years' custody
Category 2	8 years' custody	5 to 13 years' custody	6 years' custody	4 to 9 years' custody
Category 3	4 years' custody	2 to 6 years' custody	2 years' custody	High-level community order to 4 years' custody

Where offence did not involve penetration

	A		B	
	Starting point	Category range	Starting point	Category range
Category 1	4 years' custody	3 to 7 years' custody	2 years 6 months' custody	2 to 4 years' custody
Category 2	2 years' custody	1 to 4 years' custody	1 year's custody	High-level community order to 2 years' custody
Category 3	26 weeks' custody	High-level community order to 1 year's custody	High-level community order	Medium-level community order to 26 weeks' custody

For the meaning of a high-level and a medium-level community order, see **16.13** in Volume 1.

327.4 [Aggravating and mitigating factors]

page 24 The table below contains a **non-exhaustive** list of additional factual elements providing the context of the offence and factors relating to the offender. Identify whether any combination of these, or other relevant factors, should result in an upward or downward adjustment from the starting point. **In particular, relevant recent convictions are likely to result in an upward adjustment**. In some cases, having considered these factors, it may be appropriate to move outside the identified category range.

When sentencing appropriate **Category 2 or 3 offences**, the court should also consider the custody threshold as follows:

Has the custody threshold been passed?
If so, is it unavoidable that a custodial sentence be imposed?
If so, can that sentence be suspended?

Aggravating factors

Statutory aggravating factors:
Previous convictions, having regard to: a) the nature of the offence to which the conviction relates and its relevance to the current offence, and b) the time that has elapsed since the conviction
Offence committed whilst on bail
Other aggravating factors:
Specific targeting of a particularly vulnerable victim
Ejaculation (where not taken into account at step one)
Blackmail or other threats made (where not taken into account at step one)
Location of offence
Timing of offence
Use of weapon or other item to frighten or injure
Victim compelled to leave their home (including victims of domestic violence)
Failure to comply with current court orders
Offence committed whilst on licence
Exploiting contact arrangements with a child to commit an offence
Presence of others, especially children
Any steps taken to prevent the victim reporting an incident, obtaining assistance and/or from assisting or supporting the prosecution
Attempts to dispose of or conceal evidence
Commission of offence whilst under the influence of alcohol or drugs

Mitigating factors

No previous convictions or no relevant/recent convictions
Remorse
Previous good character and/or exemplary conduct*
Age and/or lack of maturity where it affects the responsibility of the offender
Mental disorder or learning disability, particularly where linked to the commission of the offence
*Previous good character/exemplary conduct is different from having no previous convictions. The more serious the offence, the less the weight which should normally be attributed to this factor. Where previous good character/exemplary conduct has been used to facilitate the offence, this mitigation should not normally be allowed and such conduct may constitute an aggravating factor.

327.5   Cases
Note: There are old cases but sentencing in this area has changed. For relevant cases, it is suggested the reader looks at comparable sentencing cases on the other SEX OFFENCES chapters. Ed.

328   SEX OFFENCES: CHILDREN, WITH
328.1
Sexual Offences Act 2003
   s 3 (sexual assault)
   s 7 (sexual assault of a child)
   s 8 and 10 (causing etc. a child to engage in sexual activity)
   s 9 (sexual activity with a child)
   s 11 (engaging in sexual activity in the presence of a child)
   s 12 (causing a child to watch a sex act)
   s 13 (section 9-12 offences committed by persons under 18)
   s 14 (arranging or facilitating a child sex offence)
   s 15 (grooming)

s 15A (sexual communication with a child) Inserted by Serious Crime Act 2015 s 67. Commencement is awaited.

s 16 (abuse of trust: sexual activity with a child)

s 17 (abuse of trust: causing or inciting a child to engage in sexual activity)

s 18 (abuse of trust: sexual activity in the presence of a child)

s 19 (abuse of trust: causing a child to watch a sex act)

s 25 (sexual activity with a child family member)

s 26 (inciting a child family member to engage in sexual activity)

Modes of trial Sections 8, 9 and 10 are indictable only where there is penetration. For sections 25 and 26 where the defendant is aged 18+ and where there is penetration,[992] the offences are indictable only. Otherwise, those offences are triable either way. Sections 3, 7, and 12-19 are therefore triable either way. Sections 3, 7, and 12-19 are triable either way.

Maximum sentences They are:

Section 8 (where there is penetration), life

Sections 7, 8 (no penetration), 9, 10 and 14, 14 years

Sections 3, 11-12 and 15, 10 years

Sections 13, 16-19, 5 years

Section 15A 2 years

Sections 25 and 26, 14 years, and 5 years if the defendant is aged under 18

Some of these maximum sentences are subject to the automatic life provisions.

Summary maximum 6 months and/or a £5,000 fine for offences committed before 12 March 2015 and an unlimited fine thereafter.[993] There are maximum fines for those aged under 18, see **14.38** in Volume 1.

Changes to the grooming offence Criminal Justice and Courts Act 2015 s 36 widened the Sexual Offences Act 2003 s 15 'Grooming etc.' offence to reduce the number of meetings required from 'at least two' to 'on one or more occasions'. In force 13 April 2015.[994]

Automatic life Sexual Offences Act 2003 s 7-12, 14-15 and 25-26 are listed in Criminal Justice Act 2003 Sch 15B Part 1. The Lord Chief Justice said in *Att-Gen's Ref No 27 of 2013* 2014 EWCA Crim 334[995] para 8 iii) (*obiter*) that in rare cases the provisions could lead to the imposition of a life sentence where the offence does not carry life imprisonment.

The court must (unless the particular circumstances make it unjust[996]) pass automatic life if: a) the defendant is aged 18+ at the date of the conviction, b) the offence was committed on or after 3 December 2012, c) the court considers a determinate sentence of at least 10 years is appropriate, d) at the time the offender was convicted he had a conviction for a Criminal Justice Act 2003 Sch 15B offence, and e) the defendant at the time of his or her conviction had previously been sentenced to either: i) a life sentence where he or she was not eligible for release during the first five years of the sentence or ii) a determinate sentence or extended sentence where the custodial part was 10 years or more.[997] For a pre-2012 extended sentence, when determining whether the custodial term was 10+ years the period deducted for time on remand or on a curfew and tag is included.[998]

---

[992] 'Penetration' means 'penetration of a vagina or anus or a mouth with a penis', Sexual Offences Act 2003 s 25(6) and 26(6).

[993] Legal Aid, Sentencing and Punishment of Offenders Act 2012 s 85(1) and (4) and Legal Aid, Sentencing and Punishment of Offenders Act 2012 (Commencement No 11) Order 2015 2015/504

[994] Criminal Justice and Courts Act 2015 (Commencement No 1, Saving and Transitional Provisions) Order 2015 2015/778 para 3 and Sch 1 para 30

[995] This case is also known as *R v Burinskas* 2014 EWCA Crim 334.

[996] Criminal Justice Act 2003 s 224A(2)

[997] Criminal Justice Act 2003 s 224A as inserted by Legal Aid, Sentencing and Punishment of Offenders Act 2012 s 122. The condition for a) is at section 224A(1)(a), for b) is at section 224A(1)(b), for c) is at section 224A(1)(c), and for d) is at section 224A(4)-(9).

[998] Criminal Justice Act 2003 s 224A(9)-(10)

Detention Defendants aged under 18 who are convicted of section 3, 13, 25 or 26 offences can be detained under Powers of Criminal Courts (Sentencing) Act 2000 s 91.[999]

Extended sentences All these offences are listed in Criminal Justice Act 2003 Sch 15. The court may pass a 2012 extended sentence (EDS) if there is a significant risk of serious harm from future specified offences and either: a) the defendant has a Criminal Justice Act 2003 Sch 15B conviction (applicable only to defendants aged 18+), or b) the offence would justify a determinate sentence of at least 4 years.[1000]

Sexual Harm Prevention Orders There is a discretionary power to make this order when it is necessary to protect the public from sexual harm.[1001]

Notification For offences under:

a) section 3, where:
   i) where the offender was aged under 18, he or she is sentenced to imprisonment for a term of at least 12 months,
   ii) in any other case: 1) the victim was aged under 18, or 2) the defendant is sentenced to a term of imprisonment, detained in a hospital, or made the subject of a community sentence of at least 12 months,
b) sections 7, 14, 25 and 26 where the defendant
   i) was aged 18 or over or
   ii) was sentenced to at least 12 months' imprisonment,
c) sections 8-12, 15 and 15A(when in force), and
d) section 13 where the defendant has been sentenced to at least 12 months' imprisonment,
e) sections 16-19 where the defendant was sentenced to imprisonment or detained in a hospital or given community service for at least 12 months,

the defendant must notify the police within three days (or three days from his release from imprisonment, hospital etc.) of his name, home address, National Insurance number etc. and any change of address and any address where he resides for seven days[1002] (in one or more periods) or more in any 12-month period.[1003]

Children and vulnerable adults: barred lists Where the defendant is aged 18 or over he or she is automatically barred from engaging in regulated activity with children and vulnerable adults.[1004] The judge must tell the defendant that the Disclosure and Barring Service will include him or her in the barred lists.[1005] Except for section 7-8 offences, the defendant may ask the Service to remove him or her from the child list. The defendant may also ask the Service to remove him or her from the adult list.

Young offenders The *Sexual Offences Guideline 2014* only applies to offenders aged 18+, see page 7 of the guideline. For the usual practice, see **66.21** in Volume 1. For detail about youth offending, see **328.57**.

Old cases: Old cases which contain no judicial guidance are not listed and are best ignored.

For Sexual Offences Act 2003 s 5 (rape of a child under 13) and s 6 (assault of a child under 13 by penetration) see the RAPE and ASSAULT BY PENETRATION chapter.

328.2   *Crown Court statistics   England and Wales*
Abuse of trust   Sexual offences   Aged 21+

---

[999] Powers of Criminal Courts (Sentencing) Act 2000 s 91(1)(b)
[1000] Criminal Justice Act 2003 s 226A-226B as inserted by Legal Aid, Sentencing and Punishment of Offenders Act 2012 s 124
[1001] Sexual Offences Act 2003 s 103A as inserted by Anti-social Behaviour, Crime and Policing Act 2014 Sch 5 para 2 and Sexual Offences Act 2003 Sch 5
[1002] Sexual Offences Act 2003 s 84(1)(c) and (6)
[1003] Sexual Offences Act 2003 s 83
[1004] Safeguarding Vulnerable Groups Act 2006 s 2 and Sch 3 and Safeguarding Vulnerable Groups Act 2006 (Prescribed Criteria and Miscellaneous Provisions) Regulations 2009 2009/37 regs 3, 4 and 6 and Sch paras 1, 2 and 4
[1005] Safeguarding Vulnerable Groups Act 2006 s 2 and Sch 3 para 25

Year	Plea	Total sentenced	Type of sentencing %						Average length of custody in months
			Discharge	Fine	Commu- nity sentence	Sus- pended sentence	Custody	Other	
2013	G	19	–	–	10.5	10.5	73.7	5.3	15
	NG	1	–	–	100	–	–	–	–
2014	G	26	–	–	8	35	58	–	13.7
	NG	5	–	–	–	20	80	–	not listed[1006]

Sexual activity with child under 13   Aged 21+

Year	Plea	Total sentenced	Type of sentencing %						Average length of custody in months
			Discharge	Fine	Commu- nity sentence	Sus- pended sentence	Custody	Other	
2013	G	106	–	–	18.9	13.2	67	0.9	37.8
	NG	37	–	–	10.8	5.4	83.8	–	55.3
2014	G	120	–	–	18	12	68	2	40.9
	NG	55	–	–	3	2	95	–	65.4

Sexual activity with child under 16   Aged 21+

Year	Age	Plea	Total sen- tenced	Type of sentencing %						Average length of custody in months
				Dis- charge	Fine	Commu- nity sentence	Sus- pended sentence	Custody	Other	
2013	n/a	G	509	–	0.2	16.9	15.1	66.6	1.2	36
	n/a	NG	117	–	–	6.8	4.3	88.9	–	48
2014	Aged under 18	G	3	–	33	–	–	67	–	not listed[1007]
		NG	2	–	–	–	50	50	–	not listed
	Aged 18+	G	195	1	–	33	19	47	1	31.0
		NG	49	–	–	4	22	71	2	34.3

For explanations about the statistics, see page 1-xii. For more statistics and for statistics for male and female defendants etc., see www.banksr.com Other Matters Statistics tab

Guidelines

328.3 *Sentencing Council guideline   Sexual Offences Act 2003 s 7*
Sexual assault of a child (section 7)
Sexual Offences Guideline 2014, see www.banksr.com Other Matters Guidelines tab. In force 1 April 2014. The guideline only applies to offenders aged 18+, see page 7 of the guideline. For the usual practice, see **66.21** in Volume 1.
Section 3 offences: Where the offence is sexual assault (section 3) and the victim is a child, it would be sensible to use this section 7 guideline. Ed.
Note: An exact copy of the section 7 guidelines has been placed in the *Magistrates' Court Guidelines 2008* at pages 277-280. Ed.

STEP ONE: Determining the offence category
page 37 The court should determine which categories of harm and culpability the offence falls into by reference **only** to the tables below.

[1006] Based on too few cases to be meaningful
[1007] Based on too few cases to be meaningful

Harm	
Category 1	Severe psychological or physical harm Abduction Violence or threats of violence Forced/uninvited entry into victim's home
Category 2	Touching of naked genitalia or naked breast area Prolonged detention/sustained incident Additional degradation/humiliation Child is particularly vulnerable due to extreme youth and/or personal circumstances
Category 3	Factor(s) in Categories 1 and 2 not present

Culpability A
Significant degree of planning Offender acts together with others to commit the offence Use of alcohol/drugs on victim to facilitate the offence Grooming behaviour used against victim Abuse of trust Previous violence against victim Offence committed in course of burglary Sexual images of victim recorded, retained, solicited or shared Deliberate isolation of victim Commercial exploitation and/or motivation Offence racially or religiously aggravated Offence motivated by, or demonstrating, hostility to the victim based on his or her sexual orientation (or presumed sexual orientation) or transgender identity (or presumed transgender identity) Offence motivated by, or demonstrating, hostility to the victim based on his or her disability (or presumed disability)

Culpability B
Factor(s) in Category A not present

328.4

STEP TWO: Starting point and category range

page 38 Having determined the category, the court should use the corresponding starting points to reach a sentence within the category range [below]. The starting point applies to all offenders irrespective of plea or previous convictions. Having determined the starting point, step two allows further adjustment for aggravating or mitigating features, set out [below].

A case of particular gravity, reflected by multiple features of culpability or harm in step one, could merit upward adjustment from the starting point before further adjustment for aggravating or mitigating features, set out [below].

Where there is a sufficient prospect of rehabilitation, a community order with a sex offender treatment programme requirement under Criminal Justice Act 2003 s 202 can be a proper alternative to a short or moderate-length custodial sentence.

	A		B	
	Starting point	**Category range**	**Starting point**	**Category range**
Category 1	6 years' custody	4 to 9 years' custody	4 years' custody	3 to 7 years' custody
Category 2	4 years' custody	3 to 7 years' custody	2 years' custody	1 to 4 years' custody

	A		B	
Category 3	1 year's custody	26 weeks' to 2 years' custody	26 weeks' custody	High-level community order to 1 year's custody

For the meaning of a high-level community order, see **16.14** in Volume 1.

328.5   [Aggravating and mitigating factors]
page 39 The table below contains a **non-exhaustive** list of additional factual elements providing the context of the offence and factors relating to the offender. Identify whether any combination of these, or other relevant factors, should result in an upward or downward adjustment from the starting point. **In particular, relevant recent convictions are likely to result in an upward adjustment**. In some cases, having considered these factors, it may be appropriate to move outside the identified category range.

Aggravating factors
Statutory aggravating factors: Previous convictions, having regard to: a) the nature of the offence to which the conviction relates and its relevance to the current offence, and b) the time that has elapsed since the conviction   Offence committed whilst on bail   ***Other aggravating factors:***   Specific targeting of a particularly vulnerable child   Blackmail or other threats made (where not taken into account at step one)   Location of offence   Timing of offence   Use of weapon or other item to frighten or injure   Victim compelled to leave their home, school, etc.   Failure to comply with current court orders   Offence committed whilst on licence   Exploiting contact arrangements with a child to commit an offence   Presence of others, especially other children   Any steps taken to prevent the victim reporting an incident, obtaining assistance and/or from assisting or supporting the prosecution   Attempts to dispose of or conceal evidence   Commission of offence whilst under the influence of alcohol or drugs   Victim encouraged to recruit others
Mitigating factors
No previous convictions or no relevant/recent convictions   Remorse   Previous good character and/or exemplary conduct*   Age and/or lack of maturity where it affects the responsibility of the offender   Mental disorder or learning disability, particularly where linked to the commission of the offence   *Previous good character/exemplary conduct is different from having no previous convictions. The more serious the offence, the less the weight which should normally be attributed to this factor. Where previous good character/exemplary conduct has been used to facilitate the offence, this mitigation should not normally be allowed and such conduct may constitute an aggravating factor.   In the context of this offence, previous good character/exemplary conduct should not normally be given any significant weight and will not normally justify a reduction in what would otherwise be the appropriate sentence.

Note: An exact copy of the section 7 and section 3 guidelines have been placed in theMagistrates' Court Guidelines 2008 at pages 277-280 and 273-276 respectively. Ed.

328.6   *Sentencing Council guideline   Sexual Offences Act 2003 s 8*
Causing or inciting a child under 13 to engage in sexual activity (section 8).
Sexual Offences Guideline 2014, see www.banksr.com Other Matters Guidelines tab. In force 1 April 2014. The guideline only applies to offenders aged 18+, see page 7 of the guideline. For the usual practice, see **66.21** in Volume 1.

STEP ONE: Determining the offence category
page 41 The court should determine which categories of harm and culpability the offence falls into by reference **only** to the tables below.

Harm	
Category 1	The extreme nature of one or more Category 2 factors or the extreme impact caused by a combination of Category 2 factors **may** elevate to Category 1
Category 2	Severe psychological or physical harm Penetration of vagina or anus (using body or object) by, or of, the victim Penile penetration of mouth by, or of, the victim Additional degradation/humiliation Abduction Prolonged detention/sustained incident Violence or threats of violence Forced/uninvited entry into victim's home Child is particularly vulnerable due to extreme youth and/or personal circumstances
Category 3	Factor(s) in Categories 1 and 2 not present

Culpability A
Significant degree of planning Offender acts together with others to commit the offence Use of alcohol/drugs on victim to facilitate the offence Grooming behaviour used against victim Abuse of trust Previous violence against victim Offence committed in course of burglary Sexual images of victim recorded, retained, solicited or shared Deliberate isolation of victim Commercial exploitation and/or motivation Offence racially or religiously aggravated Offence motivated by, or demonstrating hostility to the victim based on his or her sexual orientation (or presumed sexual orientation) or transgender identity (or presumed transgender identity) Offence motivated by, or demonstrating, hostility to the victim based on his or her disability (or presumed disability)

Culpability B
Factor(s) in Category A not present

328.7

STEP TWO: Starting point and category range
page 42 Having determined the category, the court should use the corresponding starting points to reach a sentence within the category range [below]. The starting point applies

to all offenders irrespective of plea or previous convictions. Having determined the
starting point, step two allows further adjustment for aggravating or mitigating features,
set out [below].

A case of particular gravity, reflected by multiple features of culpability or harm in step
one, could merit upward adjustment from the starting point before further adjustment for
aggravating or mitigating features, set out [below].

	A		B	
	Starting point	**Category range**	**Starting point**	**Category range**
Category 1	13 years' custody	11 to 17 years' custody	11 years' custody	10 to 15 years' custody
Category 2	8 years' custody	5 to 10 years' custody	6 years' custody	3 to 9 years' custody
Category 3	5 years' custody	3 to 8 years' custody	2 years' custody	1 to 4 years' custody

328.8   [Aggravating and mitigating factors]
page 43 The table below contains a **non-exhaustive** list of additional factual elements
providing the context of the offence and factors relating to the offender. Identify whether
any combination of these, or other relevant factors, should result in an upward or
downward adjustment from the starting point. **In particular, relevant recent convictions are likely to result in an upward adjustment**. In some cases, having considered
these factors, it may be appropriate to move outside the identified category range.

Aggravating factors
Statutory aggravating factors:
Previous convictions, having regard to: a) the nature of the offence to which the conviction relates and its relevance to the current offence, and b) the time that has elapsed since the conviction
Offence committed whilst on bail
Other aggravating factors:
Specific targeting of a particularly vulnerable child
Ejaculation (where not taken into account at step one)
Blackmail or other threats made (where not taken into account at step one)
Pregnancy or STI as a consequence of offence
Location of offence
Timing of offence
Use of weapon or other item to frighten or injure
Victim compelled to leave their home, school, etc.
Failure to comply with current court orders
Offence committed whilst on licence
Exploiting contact arrangements with a child to commit an offence
Presence of others, especially other children
Any steps taken to prevent the victim reporting an incident, obtaining assistance and/or from assisting or supporting the prosecution
Attempts to dispose of or conceal evidence
Commission of offence whilst offender under the influence of alcohol or drugs
Victim encouraged to recruit others

Mitigating factors
No previous convictions or no relevant/recent convictions Remorse Previous good character and/or exemplary conduct* Age and/or lack of maturity where it affects the responsibility of the offender Mental disorder or learning disability, particularly where linked to the commission of the offence Sexual activity was incited but no activity took place because the offender voluntarily desisted or intervened to prevent it *Previous good character/exemplary conduct is different from having no previous convictions. The more serious the offence, the less the weight which should normally be attributed to this factor. Where previous good character/exemplary conduct has been used to facilitate the offence, this mitigation should not normally be allowed and such conduct may constitute an aggravating factor. In the context of this offence, previous good character/exemplary conduct should not normally be given any significant weight and will not normally justify a reduction in what would otherwise be the appropriate sentence.

328.9   *Sentencing Council guideline   Sexual Offences Act 2003 s 9-10*

Sexual Offences Guideline 2014, see www.banksr.com Other Matters Guidelines tab. In force 1 April 2014. The guideline only applies to offenders aged 18+, see page 7 of the guideline. For the usual practice, see **66.21** in Volume 1.

page 45 **[Explanatory note:] Arranging or facilitating the commission of a child offence** (Sexual Offences Act 2003 s 14) page 61 or **328.15**

The starting points and ranges in this guideline are also applicable to offences of arranging or facilitating the commission of a child offence. In such cases, the level of harm should be determined by reference to the type of activity arranged or facilitated. Sentences commensurate with the applicable starting point and range will ordinarily be appropriate. For offences involving significant commercial exploitation and/or an international element, it may, in the interests of justice, be appropriate to increase a sentence to a point above the category range. In exceptional cases, such as where a vulnerable offender performed a limited role, having been coerced or exploited by others, sentences below the starting point and range may be appropriate.

STEP ONE: Determining the offence category

page 46 The court should determine which categories of harm and culpability the offence falls into by reference **only** to the tables below.

This guideline also applies to offences committed remotely/online.

Harm	
Category 1	Penetration of vagina or anus (using body or object) Penile penetration of mouth In either case by, or of, the victim
Category 2	Touching, or exposure, of naked genitalia or naked breasts by, or of, the victim
Category 3	Other sexual activity

Culpability A
Significant degree of planning
Offender acts together with others to commit the offence
Use of alcohol/drugs on victim to facilitate the offence
Grooming behaviour used against victim
Abuse of trust
Previous violence against victim
Offence committed in course of burglary
Sexual images of victim recorded, retained, solicited or shared
Deliberate isolation of victim
Commercial exploitation and/or motivation
Offence racially or religiously aggravated
Offence motivated by, or demonstrating hostility to the victim based on his or her sexual orientation (or presumed sexual orientation) or transgender identity (or presumed transgender identity)
Offence motivated by, or demonstrating, hostility to the victim based on his or her disability (or presumed disability)

Culpability B
Factor(s) in Category A not present

328.10

STEP TWO: Starting point and category range

page 47 Having determined the category, the court should use the corresponding starting points to reach a sentence within the category range below. The starting point applies to all offenders irrespective of plea or previous convictions. Having determined the starting point, step two allows further adjustment for aggravating or mitigating features, set out [below].

A case of particular gravity, reflected by multiple features of culpability or harm in step one, could merit upward adjustment from the starting point before further adjustment for aggravating or mitigating features, set out [below].

Where there is a sufficient prospect of rehabilitation, a community order with a sex offender treatment programme requirement under Criminal Justice Act 2003 s 202 can be a proper alternative to a short or moderate-length custodial sentence.

	A		B	
	Starting point	**Category range**	**Starting point**	**Category range**
Category 1	5 years' custody	4 to 10 years' custody	1 year's custody	High-level community order to 2 years' custody
Category 2	3 years' custody	2 to 6 years' custody	26 weeks' custody	High-level community order to 1 year's custody
Category 3	26 weeks' custody	High-level community order to 3 years' custody	Medium-level community order	Low-level community order to high-level community order

For the meaning of a high-level, a medium-level and a low-level community order, see **16.12** in Volume 1.

328.11 [Aggravating and mitigating factors]

page 48 The table below contains a non-exhaustive list of additional factual elements providing the context of the offence and factors relating to the offender. Identify whether any combination of these, or other relevant factors, should result in an upward or downward adjustment from the starting point. In particular, relevant recent convictions are likely to result in an upward adjustment. In some cases, having considered these factors, it may be appropriate to move outside the identified category range.

When sentencing appropriate Category 2 or 3 offences, the court should also consider the custody threshold as follows:

Has the custody threshold been passed?

If so, is it unavoidable that a custodial sentence be imposed?

If so, can that sentence be suspended?

Aggravating factors
Statutory aggravating factors:
Previous convictions, having regard to: a) the nature of the offence to which the conviction relates and its relevance to the current offence, and b) the time that has elapsed since the conviction
Offence committed whilst on bail
Other aggravating factors:
Severe psychological or physical harm
Ejaculation
Pregnancy or STI as a consequence of offence
Location of offence
Timing of offence
Victim compelled to leave their home, school, etc.
Failure to comply with current court orders
Offence committed whilst on licence
Exploiting contact arrangements with a child to commit an offence
Presence of others, especially other children
Any steps taken to prevent the victim reporting an incident, obtaining assistance and/or from assisting or supporting the prosecution
Attempts to dispose of or conceal evidence
Failure of offender to respond to previous warnings
Commission of offence whilst under the influence of alcohol or drugs
Victim encouraged to recruit others
Period over which offence committed

Mitigating factors
No previous convictions or no relevant/recent convictions
Remorse
Previous good character and/or exemplary conduct*
Age and/or lack of maturity where it affects the responsibility of the offender
Mental disorder or learning disability, particularly where linked to the commission of the offence
Sexual activity was incited but no activity took place because the offender voluntarily desisted or intervened to prevent it
*Previous good character/exemplary conduct is different from having no previous convictions. The more serious the offence, the less the weight which should normally be attributed to this factor. Where previous good character/exemplary conduct has been used to facilitate the offence, this mitigation should not normally be allowed and such conduct may constitute an aggravating factor.
In the context of this offence, previous good character/exemplary conduct should not normally be given any significant weight and will not normally justify a reduction in what would otherwise be the appropriate sentence.

328.12   Sentencing Council guideline   Sexual Offences Act 2003 s 11-12
Engaging in sexual activity in the presence of a child (section 11) and Causing a child to watch a sex act (section 12)

Sexual Offences Guideline 2014, see www.banksr.com Other Matters Guidelines tab. In force 1 April 2014. The guideline only applies to offenders aged 18+, see page 7 of the guideline. For the usual practice, see **66.21** in Volume 1.

page 57 **[Explanatory note:] Arranging or facilitating the commission of a child offence** (Sexual Offences Act 2003 s 14) page 61 or **328.15**

The starting points and ranges in this guideline are also applicable to offences of arranging or facilitating the commission of a child offence. In such cases, the level of harm should be determined by reference to the type of activity arranged or facilitated. Sentences commensurate with the applicable starting point and range will ordinarily be appropriate. For offences involving significant commercial exploitation and/or an international element, it may, in the interests of justice, be appropriate to increase a sentence to a point above the category range. In exceptional cases, such as where a vulnerable offender performed a limited role, having been coerced or exploited by others, sentences below the starting point and range may be appropriate.

STEP ONE: Determining the offence category

page 58 The court should determine which categories of harm and culpability the offence falls into by reference **only** to the tables below.

Harm	
Category 1	Causing victim to view extreme pornography Causing victim to view indecent/prohibited images of children Engaging in, or causing a victim to view live, sexual activity involving sadism/violence/sexual activity with an animal/a child
Category 2	Engaging in, or causing a victim to view images of or view live, sexual activity involving: penetration of vagina or anus (using body or object) penile penetration of the mouth masturbation
Category 3	Factor(s) in Categories 1 and 2 not present

Culpability A
Significant degree of planning Offender acts together with others in order to commit the offence Use of alcohol/drugs on victim to facilitate the offence Grooming behaviour used against victim Abuse of trust Use of threats (including blackmail) Specific targeting of a particularly vulnerable child Significant disparity in age Commercial exploitation and/or motivation Offence racially or religiously aggravated Offence motivated by, or demonstrating, hostility to the victim based on his or her sexual orientation (or presumed sexual orientation) or transgender identity (or presumed transgender identity) Offence motivated by, or demonstrating, hostility to the victim based on his or her disability (or presumed disability)

Culpability B
Factor(s) in Category A not present

328.13

STEP TWO: Starting point and category range

page 58 Having determined the category, the court should use the corresponding starting points to reach a sentence within the category range [below]. The starting point applies to all offenders irrespective of plea or previous convictions. Having determined the starting point, step two allows further adjustment for aggravating or mitigating features, set out [below].

A case of particular gravity, reflected by multiple features of culpability or harm in step one, could merit upward adjustment from the starting point before further adjustment for aggravating or mitigating features, set out [below].

Where there is a sufficient prospect of rehabilitation, a community order with a sex offender treatment programme requirement under Criminal Justice Act 2003 s 202 can be a proper alternative to a short or moderate-length custodial sentence.

	A		B	
	Starting point	**Category range**	**Starting point**	**Category range**
Category 1	4 years' custody	3 to 6 years' custody	2 years' custody	1 to 3 years' custody
Category 2	2 years' custody	1 to 3 years' custody	1 year's custody	High-level community order to 18 months' custody
Category 3	26 weeks' custody	High-level community order to 1 year's custody	Medium-level community order	Low-level community order to medium-level community order

For the meaning of a high-level, a medium-level and a low-level community order, see **16.12** in Volume 1.

328.14   [Aggravating and mitigating factors]
page 59 The table below contains a **non-exhaustive** list of additional factual elements providing the context of the offence and factors relating to the offender. Identify whether any combination of these, or other relevant factors, should result in an upward or downward adjustment from the starting point. **In particular, relevant recent convictions are likely to result in an upward adjustment.** In some cases, having considered these factors, it may be appropriate to move outside the identified category range.

When sentencing appropriate **Category 2 or 3 offences**, the court should also consider the custody threshold as follows:

Has the custody threshold been passed?
If so, is it unavoidable that a custodial sentence be imposed?
If so, can that sentence be suspended?

Aggravating factors
Statutory aggravating factors: Previous convictions, having regard to: a) the nature of the offence to which the conviction relates and its relevance to the current offence, and b) the time that has elapsed since the conviction   Offence committed whilst on bail

> **Other aggravating factors:**
> Location of offence
> Timing of offence
> Victim compelled to leave their home, school, etc.
> Failure to comply with current court orders
> Offence committed whilst on licence
> Exploiting contact arrangements with a child to commit an offence
> Presence of others, especially other children
> Any steps taken to prevent the victim reporting an incident, obtaining assistance and/or from
> assisting or supporting the prosecution
> Attempts to dispose of or conceal evidence
> Failure of offender to respond to previous warnings
> Commission of offence whilst offender under the influence of alcohol or drugs
> Victim encouraged to recruit others
>
> **Mitigating factors**
>
> No previous convictions or no relevant/recent convictions
> Remorse
> Previous good character and/or exemplary conduct*
> Age and/or lack of maturity where it affects the responsibility of the offender
> Mental disorder or learning disability, particularly where linked to the commission of the
> offence
> Demonstration of steps taken to address offending behaviour
> *Previous good character/exemplary conduct is different from having no previous
> convictions. The more serious the offence, the less the weight which should normally be
> attributed to this factor. Where previous good character/exemplary conduct has been used to
> facilitate the offence, this mitigation should not normally be allowed and such conduct may
> constitute an aggravating factor.

328.15   *Sentencing Council guideline   Sexual Offences Act 2003 s 14*

Arranging or facilitating the commission of a child sex offence (section 14)

Sexual Offences Guideline 2014, see www.banksr.com Other Matters Guidelines tab. In force 1 April 2014. The guideline only applies to offenders aged 18+, see page 7 of the guideline. For the usual practice, see **66.21** in Volume 1.

page 61 Sentencers should refer to the guideline for the applicable, substantive offence of arranging or facilitating under sections 9 to 12, or pages 45 to 49, see **328.9** and 57 to 60, see **328.12**. The level of harm should be determined by reference to the type of activity arranged or facilitated. Sentences commensurate with the applicable starting point and range will ordinarily be appropriate. For offences involving significant commercial exploitation and/or an international element, it may, in the interests of justice, be appropriate to increase a sentence to a point above the category range. In exceptional cases, such as where a vulnerable offender performed a limited role, having been coerced or exploited by others, sentences below the starting point and range may be appropriate.

Sexual Offences Act 2003 s 15 Sentencing Council guideline see para **328.38**.

Sexual Offences Act 2003 s 25 and 26 Sentencing Council guideline see para **328.28**.

328.16   *Suggested approach to the new guideline*

Note: It is understood the Sentencing Council intended that the guideline should reflect the Court of Appeal current sentencing tariff for sentencing. This means the new guideline was intended to bring the previous guideline up to date rather than intending to increase the penalties for the bulk of the sex offences. Consequently, I would suggest that sentencers should start with the guideline and then consider recent sentencing cases set out by the Court of Appeal to see if they are helpful and then return to the guideline before deciding the appropriate sentence. Ed.

328.17   *Victims   Assessing victims who may encourage offence*
Att-Gen's Ref No 53 of 2013 2013 EWCA Crim 2544, 2014 2 Cr App R (S) 1 (p 1) LCJ
D pleaded (full credit) to sexual activity with a child, making indecent photographs of a child and possession of extreme pornographic images (×2). V, aged 13, was an unwilling complainant. The prosecution evidence was substantially on the basis of D's account. V played truant from school. She approached D in a town centre and asked him for cigarettes. D said he had none but agreed to buy some for her. V said she was aged 16 and asked if she could use his home phone to call a family member. He agreed and took her back to his flat. D and V chatted and watched television. D hugged V to comfort her. V kissed his neck and placed her hands over his trousers on his penis. D rejected her advances. He did not ask her to leave but gave her his mobile phone number in case she wanted someone to talk to. In the following days, D and V exchanged a number of text messages. V indicated that she was younger than 16. D sent V messages of a sexual nature. He claimed that this was an attempt to 'scare her with sex'. D told V he felt guilty and that they should not contact one another. A few days later, V posted a note through D's door and sent him a text message. Contact resumed. About a week later, V again went to D's flat. When D let V in, she was in her school uniform and asked to change. She re-appeared wearing nothing but a t-shirt. D told V to put her clothes back on but V began to kiss and touch him. She then undid his trousers and masturbated him. D became angry and told her to stop. V turned around and attempted to lower herself onto his penis. There was contact between D's penis and V's vagina. D pushed her away and V left. V told her friend about the incident. D was arrested and his computer was examined. There were eight indecent images found; two Level 1, two Level 2 and four Level 3. The Level 3 images included two very young female children holding the erect penis of an adult male. There were also 11 extreme pornographic images including a naked female adult being penetrated by a dog's penis and a woman performing oral sex on a horse's penis. D was bailed and moved address. Another search of his computer uncovered further extreme pornographic images displaying sexual activity between humans and dogs and horses. D was aged 40 at appeal. The Judge imposed 8 months suspended for the child sex offence and 4 months suspended, consecutive, for the images. Held. Far from it being any mitigation that, on D's account, the victim had initiated what happened, that was an aggravating not a mitigating factor. The purpose of the legislation prohibiting sexual relations with those aged under 16 is to protect those aged under 16. The reduction of punishment on the basis that the person who needed protection encouraged the commission of the offence is therefore simply wrong. Such a person needs more protection, not less. D took advantage of V and that aggravated the offence. V's vulnerability therefore aggravated the offence. A further feature of the offending was D's actions in inviting V back to his flat, giving her his mobile number and sending sexually explicit messages. The age gap between the two also provided for some aggravation. The only mitigating feature was his plea. Immediate imprisonment should have been imposed. **2 years** not 8 months suspended, for the sexual activity. 4 months concurrent, not 4 months suspended, consecutive, for the images.

Types of offending
Note: The statutory child sex offences have considerable overlap between them. When considering the offences it is always important to remember: a) that the majority of the cases were heard before the guideline was in force, and b) the specific offence that was charged. It is also important to start and end with a consideration of the guideline. Ed.

Abuse of trust
328.18   *Sentencing Council guideline   Sexual Offences Act 2003 s 16-17*
Sexual Offences Guideline 2014, see www.banksr.com Other Matters Guidelines tab. In force 1 April 2014. The guideline only applies to offenders aged 18+, see page 7 of the guideline. For the usual practice, see **66.21** in Volume 1.
Sexual Offences Act 2003 s 16 and 17

STEP ONE: Determining the offence category

page 68 The court should determine which categories of harm and culpability the offence falls into by reference only to the tables below. **This guideline also applies to offences committed remotely/online.**

Harm	
Category 1	Penetration of vagina or anus (using body or object) Penile penetration of mouth In either case by, or of, the victim
Category 2	Touching, or exposure, of naked genitalia or naked breasts by, or of, the victim
Category 3	Factor(s) in Categories 1 and 2 not present

Culpability A
Significant degree of planning Offender acts together with others to commit the offence Use of alcohol/drugs on victim to facilitate the offence Grooming behaviour used against victim Use of threats (including blackmail) Sexual images of victim recorded, retained, solicited or shared Specific targeting of a particularly vulnerable child Commercial exploitation and/or motivation Offence racially or religiously aggravated Offence motivated by, or demonstrating, hostility to the victim based on his or her sexual orientation (or presumed sexual orientation) or transgender identity (or presumed transgender identity) Offence motivated by, or demonstrating, hostility to the victim based on his or her disability (or presumed disability)

Culpability B
Factor(s) in Category A not present

328.19

STEP TWO: Starting point and category range

page 68 Having determined the category, the court should use the corresponding starting points to reach a sentence within the category range [below]. The starting point applies to all offenders irrespective of plea or previous convictions. Having determined the starting point, step two allows further adjustment for aggravating or mitigating features, set out [below].

A case of particular gravity, reflected by multiple features of culpability or harm in step one, could merit upward adjustment from the starting point before further adjustment for aggravating or mitigating features, set out [below].

Where there is a sufficient prospect of rehabilitation, a community order with a sex offender treatment programme requirement under Criminal Justice Act 2003 s 202 can be a proper alternative to a short or moderate-length custodial sentence.

	A		B	
	Starting point	**Category range**	**Starting point**	**Category range**
Category 1	18 months' custody	1 to 2 years' custody	1 year's custody	26 weeks' to 18 months' custody

	A		B	
Category 2	1 year's custody	26 weeks' to 18 months' custody	26 weeks' custody	High-level community order to 1 year's custody
Category 3	26 weeks' custody	High-level community order to 1 year's custody	Medium-level community order	Low-level community order to high-level community order

For the meaning of a high-level, a medium-level and a low-level community order, see **16.12** in Volume 1.

328.20   [Aggravating and mitigating factors]
page 69 The table below contains a non-exhaustive list of additional factual elements providing the context of the offence and factors relating to the offender. Identify whether any combination of these, or other relevant factors, should result in an upward or downward adjustment from the starting point. In particular, relevant recent convictions are likely to result in an upward adjustment. In some cases, having considered these factors, it may be appropriate to move outside the identified category range.

When sentencing appropriate Category 2 or 3 offences, the court should also consider the custody threshold as follows:

Has the custody threshold been passed?

If so, is it unavoidable that a custodial sentence be imposed?

If so, can that sentence be suspended?

Aggravating factors
Statutory aggravating factors:
Previous convictions, having regard to: a) the nature of the offence to which the conviction relates and its relevance to the current offence, and b) the time that has elapsed since the conviction
Offence committed whilst on bail
Other aggravating factors:
Ejaculation
Pregnancy or STI as a consequence of offence
Location of offence
Timing of offence
Victim compelled to leave their home, school, etc.
Failure to comply with current court orders
Offence committed whilst on licence
Presence of others, especially other children
Any steps taken to prevent the victim reporting an incident, obtaining assistance and/or from assisting or supporting the prosecution
Attempts to dispose of or conceal evidence
Failure of offender to respond to previous warnings
Commission of offence whilst under the influence of alcohol or drugs
Victim encouraged to recruit others

Mitigating factors
No previous convictions or no relevant/recent convictions
Remorse
Previous good character and/or exemplary conduct*
Age and/or lack of maturity where it affects the responsibility of the offender
Mental disorder or learning disability, particularly where linked to the commission of the offence
Sexual activity was incited but no activity took place because the offender voluntarily desisted or intervened to prevent it
Demonstration of steps taken to address offending behaviour
*Previous good character/exemplary conduct is different from having no previous convictions. The more serious the offence, the less the weight which should normally be attributed to this factor. Where previous good character/exemplary conduct has been used to facilitate the offence, this mitigation should not normally be allowed and such conduct may constitute an aggravating factor.

328.21   Sentencing Council guideline   Sexual Offences Act 2003 s 18-19
Sexual Offences Guideline 2014, see www.banksr.com Other matters Guidelines tab. In force 1 April 2014. The guideline only applies to offenders aged 18+, see page 7 of the guideline. For the usual practice, see **66.21** in Volume 1.

page 71 The court should determine which categories of harm and culpability the offence falls into by reference only to the tables below.

STEP ONE: Determining the offence category

Harm	
Category 1	Causing victim to view extreme pornography Causing victim to view indecent/prohibited images of children Engaging in, or causing a victim to view live, sexual activity involving sadism/violence/sexual activity with an animal/a child
Category 2	Engaging in, or causing a victim to view images of or view live, sexual activity involving: penetration of vagina or anus (using body or object) penile penetration of mouth masturbation
Category 3	Factor(s) in Categories 1 and 2 not present

Culpability A
Significant degree of planning
Offender acts together with others to commit the offence
Use of alcohol/drugs on victim to facilitate the offence
Grooming behaviour used against victim
Use of threats (including blackmail)
Specific targeting of a particularly vulnerable child
Commercial exploitation and/or motivation
Offence racially or religiously aggravated
Offence motivated by, or demonstrating, hostility to the victim based on his or her sexual orientation (or presumed sexual orientation) or transgender identity (or presumed transgender identity)
Offence motivated by, or demonstrating, hostility to the victim based on his or her disability (or presumed disability)

Culpability B
Factor(s) in Category A not present

328.22

STEP TWO: Starting point and category range

page 72 Having determined the category, the court should use the corresponding starting points to reach a sentence within the category range [below]. The starting point applies to all offenders irrespective of plea or previous convictions. Having determined the starting point, step two allows further adjustment for aggravating or mitigating features, set out [below].

A case of particular gravity, reflected by multiple features of culpability or harm in step one, could merit upward adjustment from the starting point before further adjustment for aggravating or mitigating features, set out [below].

Where there is a sufficient prospect of rehabilitation, a community order with a sex offender treatment programme requirement under Criminal Justice Act 2003 s 202 can be a proper alternative to a short or moderate-length custodial sentence.

	A		B	
	Starting point	**Category range**	**Starting point**	**Category range**
Category 1	18 months' custody	1 to 2 years' custody	1 year's custody	26 weeks' to 18 months' custody
Category 2	1 year's custody	26 weeks' to 18 months' custody	26 weeks' custody	High-level community order to 1 year's custody
Category 3	26 weeks' custody	High-level community order to 1 year's custody	Medium-level community order	Low-level community order to high-level community order

For the meaning of a high-level, a medium-level and a low-level community order, see **16.12** in Volume 1.

328.23   [Aggravating and mitigating factors]

page 73 The table below contains a non-exhaustive list of additional factual elements providing the context of the offence and factors relating to the offender. Identify whether any combination of these, or other relevant factors, should result in an upward or downward adjustment from the starting point. In particular, relevant recent convictions are likely to result in an upward adjustment. In some cases, having considered these factors, it may be appropriate to move outside the identified category range.

When sentencing appropriate Category 2 or 3 offences, the court should also consider the custody threshold as follows:

Has the custody threshold been passed?

If so, is it unavoidable that a custodial sentence be imposed?

If so, can that sentence be suspended?

Aggravating factors
Statutory aggravating factors: Previous convictions, having regard to: a) the nature of the offence to which the conviction relates and its relevance to the current offence, and b) the time that has elapsed since the conviction   Offence committed whilst on bail

> **Other aggravating factors:**
> Location of offence
> Timing of offence
> Victim compelled to leave their home, school, etc.
> Failure to comply with current court orders
> Offence committed whilst on licence
> Presence of others, especially other children
> Any steps taken to prevent the victim reporting an incident, obtaining assistance and/or from assisting or supporting the prosecution
> Attempts to dispose of or conceal evidence
> Failure of offender to respond to previous warnings
> Commission of offence whilst under the influence of alcohol or drugs
> Victim encouraged to recruit others

> **Mitigating factors**
>
> No previous convictions or no relevant/recent convictions
> Remorse
> Previous good character and/or exemplary conduct*
> Age and/or lack of maturity where it affects the responsibility of the offender
> Mental disorder or learning disability, particularly where linked to the commission of the offence
> Demonstration of steps taken to address offending behaviour
> *Previous good character/exemplary conduct is different from having no previous convictions. The more serious the offence, the less the weight which should normally be attributed to this factor. Where previous good character/exemplary conduct has been used to facilitate the offence, this mitigation should not normally be allowed and such conduct may constitute an aggravating factor.

328.24   Suggested approach to the guideline
Note: It is understood the Sentencing Council intended that the guideline should reflect the Court of Appeal's current sentencing tariff for sentencing. This means the new guideline intends to bring the previous guideline up to date rather than intending to increase the penalties for the bulk of the sex offences. Consequently, it is suggested that sentencers should start with the guideline and then consider recent sentencing cases set out by the Court of Appeal to see if they are helpful, and then return to the guideline before deciding the appropriate sentence. Ed.

328.25   Causing sexual activity   Judicial guidance   Post-2014 guideline case
Att-Gen's Ref No 94 of 2014 2014 EWCA Crim 2752 The harm is the impact on the victim of behaving as he or she has done, whether in the presence of the offender or remotely or online. To that extent, the offence of causing sexual activity is potentially more serious than inciting such activity because the actual activity is a necessary part of the offence. Where incitement does not lead the child to behave in the manner incited, although the culpability is likely to be identical, the harm is necessarily less: the same is so in relation to attempts.

328.26   Abuse of trust
R v Sheppard 2011 EWCA Crim 1882 D pleaded (early) to two counts of causing or inciting a child to engage in sexual activity by a person in a position of trust. He was a teaching assistant at a school where V1, aged 14, and V2, aged 15, were students. The girls initiated contact with D via Facebook. D then engaged in sexually explicit conversations with the girls. D asked V2 to send pictures of herself in various states of undress. D commented on the photographs. D repeatedly asked V1 for a video of her masturbating. There was no video. D offered V1 help with schoolwork and drove her home on one occasion. He repeated his requests for a video of her masturbating. The communication took place over a period of five days and it was D who ceased the inappropriate contact. There was no direct physical contact. D, aged 30 or 31 at appeal, had no convictions. Held. There was an element of grooming, but no intimidation. There is really no guideline which

can be appropriately looked at to reach a starting point for sentencing purposes, and comparison with guidelines for offences which do not correspond are apt to be misleading. This was a case of sexual exploitation and a serious breach of trust. **Starting at 2½ years** and with mitigation, **21 months**, not 2½ years.

R v Cornwall 2012 EWCA Crim 1227, 2013 1 Cr App R (S) 30 (p 158) D pleaded (full credit) to three counts of inciting a child to engage in sexual activity by a person in a position of trust. He was a PE teacher. D contacted V via Facebook when she was aged 14-15. They also spoke via text message. During the conversations, D described sexual activity which he wanted to conduct with her, including sucking her clitoris. He expressed a desire to meet up, although no meeting took place. V was aware that D had also been in contact with H, aged 17. H had contacted D via Facebook. They also spoke via text message. He sent her sexual messages including 'my cock is hard' and describing sexual activity he wished to have with her. This included references to 'blow jobs' and H sitting on D's face. H subsequently moved to another school but D remained in contact with her. H sent D pictures of her in a low-cut top, a bikini and without a top on. D denied sending V or H sexual messages when interviewed. D, aged 26-27, was of good character with character references. He was deeply remorseful and had contacted a psychotherapist as he recognised that he had a problem. Held. This was a case of inciting activity, but no activity occurred. The Judge misjudged the activity. H had initiated the contact with D. The Judge had wrongly rejected the loss of D's career as a mitigating factor. After a trial, the appropriate sentence was one of no more than 6 months. With the plea, **4 months** not 16.

Post-2014 guideline cases

R v TW 2015 EWCA Crim 63 D pleaded (full credit) to sexual assault on a child under 13 (×5), inciting a child to engage in sexual activity, taking (×4) and making (×4) indecent photos of a child. V, D's stepgranddaughter, was aged 4-6 at the time and she regularly stayed with D and his wife. When V and D were alone, D sexually assaulted V, photographing and videoing the activity on his mobile phone. This occurred around 20 times. V later described this as D touching her 'fiffy' with his 'willy'. On D's phone were: seven images, two of which were from the Internet and not of V, and three videos (Level 1), one video (Level 2) and two images and nine videos (Level 3). D denied any wrongdoing until his phone was analysed, whereupon he admitted the offences. V now faced acute difficulties with the 'scars persisting for the rest of her life' and the events placed great strain on her family as a whole. D was aged 49-51 during the offending and of effective good character. He had a settled and stable life and struggled to explain his behaviour, appearing quite distressed at it, and expressing remorse. D was described as 'honest, caring and hardworking' with a low reoffending risk, and a suspended sentence with unpaid work and a sex offender treatment programme was proposed. The Court of Appeal received further character references emphasising the adverse effect on D's family. The Judge placed the sexual assaults into Category 2. Held. The Judge was right to stress that D's offending involved a gross breach of trust. The sentence plainly…had to go beyond the bracket for a single offence as the gross breach occurred repeatedly over a prolonged period which called for a severe sentence. A non-custodial sentence would have been quite inappropriate. Starting at 10 years, **6½ years** was severe but not manifestly excessive.

R v Bradbury 2015 EWCA Crim 1176, 2 Cr App R (S) 72 (p 485) D pleaded (full credit) 'to various counts of sexual activity with children', sex assault counts, making indecent photographs of children and voyeurism. 18 boys aged 10-16 were abused over a 4½-year period. Many of the boys were very seriously ill. The counts were largely specimen. He was a consultant paediatric haematologist in a hospital in Cambridge. His patients had illnesses and treatments which could lead to concerns about pubertal development which was monitored. Up to a certain age, young patients would be seen with another person, usually a parent. D encouraged a number of young boys to see him alone, when he would fondle their genitals. When there was a parent present he would see the boys behind a curtain. For some boys he would pretend their problems were more serious than they were and they were given more appointments than necessary. Three boys were required to masturbate themselves. D then measured the length and width of their penises. On 12 of the counts, boys had unnecessary examination of their genitals. The boys were told to strip and D fondled their penises and testicles. The victims on seven counts were aged under 13 and their penises and genitals were touched. D attempted to use a camera pen to take images of partially clothed boys. The pen had 170,000 images but none were indecent. D had purchased DVDs. 98% of them involved boys aged 10-16. Some were at the most serious levels. Contacting 800 of the most affected families was a significant undertaking and extremely emotionally demanding. The work distracted the hospital's team from their primary role of caring for their most vulnerable patients. The impact on the children and parents had been devastating. Many parents saw significant changes in their child's personality. Boys suffered from clinical depression, panic attacks, nightmares, lack of sleep, loss of confidence etc. and needed counselling. More than one suffered severe psychological harm. Hospital colleagues felt guilt, anger and shame. The hospital's reputation suffered. D was now aged 41. The pre-sentence report assessed a high risk of serious harm to children. The Judge found that D was dangerous but believed 22 years was sufficient protection for the public. The defence said that was the equivalent of a 33-year sentence after a trial. Held. This was a very difficult sentencing exercise. D appears to have targeted the particularly vulnerable. The behaviour was escalating. It was a Category 2A case. We substitute 22 years' **extended sentence (16 years' custody** 6 years' extended licence). The licence was attached to the total term.

Note: For a 22-year determinate sentence, D would be released after 11 years. For the extended sentence, he would be released sometime between 10 years 8 months and 16 years with an extended licence to follow. D appears to be significantly worse off after his so-called successful appeal. The judgment does not refer to whether consideration was given to whether the new sentence was more severe than the original sentence or whether counsel were given any warning of the extended sentence. A more fundamental problem is that the Court attached the 6-year extended licence to the total term, which is unlawful, see **58.79**. Prosecution counsel drew the court's attention to the error. The court documents show changes have been made to sentence, but the circumstances of that are not known. The judgment remains unaltered. The changes appear unlawful as they were not made in open court, nor was D present. Ed.

For the Sexual Offences Act 2003 s 16-17 and 18-19 (Abuse of trust) offences guidelines, see **328.18** and **328.21**.

328.27   Breach of trust, Grave   Pre-2014 guideline case

Att-Gen's Ref No 13 of 2013 2013 EWCA Crim 681 D was convicted of sexual activity with a child (×5) and indecent assault on males (×5). D was an osteopath. Over a period of 12 years, between 1998 and 2010, D abused his position in relation to his patients. The offences included touching MW's groin and testicles through his clothing during treatment. MW was aged 31. D asked another patient, LJ, aged 28, to pull down his underwear. D proceeded to massage his pelvis, picking up the patient's penis and moving it to one side. He did not wear gloves. D massaged the buttocks of another patient, MG, aged 18. He then purported to show MG how to check for testicular cancer. He then touched MG's testicles and perineum, saying that he required MG to achieve an erection in order for D to "work on this bit properly". Another patient, JB, aged 13, was asked to strip naked and D massaged his thighs, telling JB it did not matter if he became erect. He then asked JB to turn over so that his erect penis was exposed. D applied some cream to JB's penis and masturbated him, asking inappropriate questions about puberty and whether he had a girlfriend. He also said he needed to ascertain how tight JB's prostate muscles were and put his thumb on JB's perineum. AR, aged 15, was usually accompanied to treatment by his mother. On one occasion when he was not, D took the opportunity to lock the door. He asked AR to strip naked and pulled back AR's foreskin. D said, "oops" and that AR should not worry if he became erect whilst D massaged his buttocks. There was a significant period spent on bail (about 2 years) during which he was barred from living in his own home by social services and he was unable to work. D, aged 40, was married with two daughters and of previous good character. Held. All the offences occurred within the context of D's therapeutic relationship with the victims and therefore they were committed in breach of trust. The offences were committed over an extended period and were repeated in relation to most of the victims. There was an escalation of offending, from touching over clothing to masturbating a young boy to the point of ejaculation. In mitigation, there was his good character, references and the fact he had lost his good standing in the community as well as his profession as an osteopath. There were ten offences against five victims. The sentences would remain as they were but would run consecutively rather than concurrently: for the offences against JB, 18 months, for the offences against AR, 12 months (consecutive), for the offence against MG, 9 months (consecutive), for the offences against LJ, 9 months (consecutive) and the offences against MW, 6 months (concurrent). In total, **4 years** not 18 months.

Note: Almost all child sex offences involve a breach of trust. This case is listed here as there was not only a breach of trust when the children were left in D's care but there was the additional breach of trust when D abused the medical examination procedure. Ed.

Child family member

328.28   Child family member   Sentencing Council guideline   Sexual Offences Act 2003 s 25-26

Sexual activity with a child family member (section 25) and Inciting a child family member to engage in sexual activity (section 26)

Sexual Offences Guideline 2014 page 51, see www.banksr.com Other Matters Guidelines tab. In force 1 April 2014. The guideline only applies to offenders aged 18+, see page 7 of the guideline. For the usual practice, see **66.21** in Volume 1.

STEP ONE: Determining the offence category

page 51 The court should determine which categories of harm and culpability the offence falls into by reference **only** to the tables below. This offence involves those who have a family relationship with the victim and it should be assumed that the greater the abuse of trust within this relationship the more grave the offence.

Harm	
Category 1	Penetration of vagina or anus (using body or object) Penile penetration of mouth In either case by, or of, the victim
Category 2	Touching of naked genitalia or naked breasts by, or of, the victim
Category 3	Other sexual activity

Culpability A
Significant degree of planning
Offender acts together with others to commit the offence
Use of alcohol/drugs on victim to facilitate the offence
Grooming behaviour used against victim
Use of threats (including blackmail)
Sexual images of victim recorded, retained, solicited or shared
Specific targeting of a particularly vulnerable child
Significant disparity in age
Commercial exploitation and/or motivation
Offence racially or religiously aggravated
Offence motivated by, or demonstrating, hostility to the victim based on his or her sexual orientation (or presumed sexual orientation) or transgender identity (or presumed transgender identity)
Offence motivated by, or demonstrating, hostility to the victim based on his or her disability (or presumed disability)

Culpability B
Factor(s) in Category A not present

328.29

STEP TWO: Starting point and category range

page 53 Having determined the category, the court should use the corresponding starting points to reach a sentence within the category range [below]. The starting point applies to all offenders irrespective of plea or previous convictions. Having determined the starting point, step two allows further adjustment for aggravating or mitigating features, set out [below].

A case of particular gravity, reflected by multiple features of culpability or harm in step one, could merit upward adjustment from the starting point before further adjustment for aggravating or mitigating features, set out [below].

Where there is a sufficient prospect of rehabilitation, a community order with a sex offender treatment programme requirement under Criminal Justice Act 2003 s 202 can be a proper alternative to a short or moderate-length custodial sentence.

	A		B	
	Starting point	**Category range**	**Starting point**	**Category range**
Category 1	6 years' custody	4 to 10 years' custody	3 years 6 months' custody	2 years 6 months' to 5 years' custody
Category 2	4 years' custody	2 to 6 years' custody	18 months' custody	26 weeks' to 2 years 6 months' custody
Category 3	1 year's custody	High-level community order to 3 years' custody	Medium-level community order	Low-level community order to high-level community order

For the meaning of a high-level, a medium-level and a low-level community order, see **16.12** in Volume 1.

328.30   [Aggravating and mitigating factors]

page 54 The table below contains a **non-exhaustive** list of additional factual elements providing the context of the offence and factors relating to the offender. Identify whether any combination of these, or other relevant factors, should result in an upward or downward adjustment from the starting point. **In particular, relevant recent convictions are likely to result in an upward adjustment**. In some cases, having considered these factors, it may be appropriate to move outside the identified category range.

When sentencing appropriate **Category 3 offences**, the court should also consider the custody threshold as follows:

Has the custody threshold been passed?

If so, is it unavoidable that a custodial sentence be imposed?

If so, can that sentence be suspended?

Aggravating factors
Statutory aggravating factors: Previous convictions, having regard to: a) the nature of the offence to which the conviction relates and its relevance to the current offence, and b) the time that has elapsed since the conviction   Offence committed whilst on bail

Other aggravating factors:
Severe psychological or physical harm
Ejaculation
Pregnancy or STI as a consequence of offence
Location of offence
Timing of offence
Victim compelled to leave their home, school, etc.
Failure to comply with current court orders
Offence committed whilst on licence
Exploiting contact arrangements with a child to commit an offence
Presence of others, especially other children
Any steps taken to prevent the victim reporting an incident, obtaining assistance and/or from assisting or supporting the prosecution
Attempts to dispose of or conceal evidence
Failure of offender to respond to previous warnings
Commission of offence whilst under the influence of alcohol or drugs
Victim encouraged to recruit others
Period over which offence committed
Mitigating factors
No previous convictions or no relevant/recent convictions
Remorse
Previous good character and/or exemplary conduct*
Age and/or lack of maturity where it affects the responsibility of the offender
Mental disorder or learning disability, particularly where linked to the commission of the offence
Sexual activity was incited but no activity took place because the offender voluntarily desisted or intervened to prevent it
*Previous good character/exemplary conduct is different from having no previous convictions. The more serious the offence, the less the weight which should normally be attributed to this factor. Where previous good character/exemplary conduct has been used to facilitate the offence, this mitigation should not normally be allowed and such conduct may constitute an aggravating factor.
In the context of this offence, previous good character/exemplary conduct should not normally be given any significant weight and will not normally justify a reduction in what would otherwise be the appropriate sentence.

328.31   *Child family member   Pre-2014 guideline Judicial guidance*
R v Thomas 2006 1 Cr App R (S) 101 (p 602) D pleaded to sexual activity with a child family member (section 25(1) and (6)). Held. The gravamen of this offence lies in the abuse of the relationship with a child. There are three particular factors pertinent to sentence: the age of the parties, the nature of the sexual activity engaged in and the number of occasions when sexual activity occurs. The younger the child and the greater the age gap the more serious the offence is likely to be. The nature and length of the penetration are relevant: penile penetration will usually, though not always, be more serious than non-penile penetration. Full sexual intercourse is likely to be near the top of the range of seriousness.
Note: This seems to be in line with the guidelines and current sentencing practice. Ed.

328.32   *Child family member   Child aged 16+   Sexual intercourse   Pre-2014 guideline cases*
R v Alderson 2012 EWCA Crim 1824 D pleaded, at his PCMH, to a specimen count of sexual activity with a child family member. D married M and they had a child. In 1992, D and M's relationship ended. In 1993, after M had begun another relationship, V was born. D and M were then reconciled for the next five to six years. V knew D as 'Dad' and they had a normal father/daughter relationship. In 1999, when V was aged 6, all the

children were removed by social services. Between then and 2010, D had no involvement or contact with V. V then contacted D and she moved in with him in a one-bedroom flat. There began the sexual relationship. In 2011 V, now aged 16, gave birth to his child. V initially told people the child was fathered by a boy she had met. When she revealed the truth, the police were contacted and she initially stated that D had raped her. After he was interviewed, in which D was very frank, the allegation was withdrawn. Proceedings then continued on much of the evidence provided by D. D, aged 55, was treated as being of good character. Held. A custodial sentence was inevitable to mark the breach of trust and that D undoubtedly took advantage of V's immaturity. With credit for plea and for frank admissions, **2 years** not 3.

See also: *R v B* 2012 EWCA Crim 349 (Plea to sexual activity with a child family member (×3). Stepfather with close family relationship to 16-year-old stepdaughter, V. Intercourse on three occasions in three months. Wore a condom and ejaculated. Significant intimidation/coercion. Offered V money. Made threats to prevent her from reporting his offences. He was later violent to V following the allegations. V was very distressed. Outside guidelines. 25% credit. Starting at **5 years**, 3 years 9 months.)

328.33   *Child family member   Child aged 16+   Non-penetrative sex   Post-2014 guideline case*

R v B 2013 EWCA Crim 438 D was convicted of sexual activity with a child family member (×3). V, aged 17, had left home after a dispute with her mother regarding the degree of freedom she was permitted. D, who lived with his wife and daughter, had known V and her mother for ten years or more and was said to be a father figure to V. D and V were in the sitting room. D's wife was in Ghana. D put some pornography on the television and drank alcohol to disinhibit himself. He asked V to check that his daughter was asleep. When V returned, he began stroking her arm. He made her sit on the sofa and pulled her across so she was lying alongside him. He placed her hand on his penis and said that she could masturbate him. He removed some of her clothes and licked her vagina. He left the room, put a condom on, took a Viagra-type tablet and then had sexual intercourse with V. V waited until D was in another room and left the house by getting out of a window. She told a number of people what had happened and was in a state of distress. D said that V consented and had initiated the activity. V said the incident was scary. She had become withdrawn and spent a great deal of time crying in her bedroom. She did not wish to be intimate with anyone. D, aged 47, was of good character. He lost his job, marriage and home. He displayed some remorse. The Judge noted that there was no affectionate relationship between D and V. He said there was an element of planning, gross breach of trust and that V was vulnerable. Held. The offending had a substantial impact upon V. The Judge was incorrect in his approach to the guidelines. V was not a blood relative nor the equivalent of one. The relationship between D and V and the breach of trust is implicit in the offences themselves. There was a degree of preparation and planning. The licking of V's vagina and getting her to masturbate him were additional elements to the abuse. The aggravating features justified a sentence above the starting point. **3 years** not 5.

R v Davies 2013 EWCA Crim 3166 D pleaded to sexual activity with a child family member. In 2003 and 2004, D and his then partner, L, fostered children. V was a foster child living in their home between October 2003 and June 2004. V's 16th birthday was in March 2004. Shortly before V left the foster home, there were arguments between D, L and V, but no allegations of sexual impropriety were made against D. In 2011, V contacted L. L and D had separated. V told L that D had raped her twice. L then confronted D, who admitted that sexual intercourse had taken place between D and V on two or three occasions but only because he was being blackmailed by V. D pleaded on the basis that V had instigated the events and that intercourse occurred in the family home on two occasions. V was aged 16 and D was aged 43 when the sexual intercourse occurred. D had no convictions and had testimonials. Held. After a trial, the appropriate sentence would have been 2 years. With full credit, **16 months** not 2 years.

Att-Gen's Ref No 95 of 2014 2014 EWCA Crim 2514 D was convicted of activity with a child family member, V. V, D's daughter, was aged 16 and had had a difficult upbringing as her depressed mother drank heavily. V had also been estranged from D for most of her life and they got in contact via social media around six months before the offence and whilst V was in foster care. They began seeing each other daily and V would visit D at her grandmother's house, where D also lived. D and V were lying clothed on a bed when they began watching lesbian pornography on D's phone. D then massaged V's back but also massaged her buttocks and touched V's breasts, both under her clothing. V moved away and D apologised. However, several days later, D texted V wanting intercourse, even though he knew it was wrong. There was then an exchange of messages which D told V to delete, which she did, save for the ones used to incriminate D. The exchange ended in an argument and an apology from D. The messages lacked sexual motivation and D also apologised for the purportedly accidental touching of V's breast. Later, V informed D that her mother knew and D told her to 'forget about it' but V could not, messaging, 'You fucked me up.' D then pointed out that V had replied to his messages and V said that she did so because she was scared. D then alleged that he was scared too for the same reason.[1008] They continued to see each other for a month or so until D ended the contact due to 'insufficient funds and his depression following the incident'. D, aged 44, was of good character and was a valued and trusted worker. He admitted to the massaging of V's back but not her buttocks and maintained that the touching of V's breasts was accidental. Meanwhile V had begun drinking heavily and staying out all night. She also suffered mental health problems and was medicated for depression. The pre-sentence report concluded that D's denials meant he posed a high risk of sexual and emotional harm to female children. Held. These facts position the matter squarely within Category 2A. **2 years** not 9 months.

Digital/oral penetration

328.34   *Digital/oral penetration   Child   aged   under   10   Defendant   aged 25+   Pre-2014 guideline case*

Att-Gen's Ref No 74 of 2011 2011 EWCA Crim 2855 D pleaded (after two trial witnesses had given evidence) to sexual assault of a child, after a *Goodyear* indication was sought. The Judge stated a sentence of not more than 4 years would be passed. D was babysitting V, a five-year-old girl, and inserted his finger into her anus, while kissing and blowing on the back of her neck. V's mother returned and saw D lying on the bed with V. V's mother made D leave. When D subsequently returned to the house, V was frightened and distressed. The Judge imposed a community order on the basis that it would provide the most appropriate treatment for D. D, aged 51, had no relevant or recent convictions. Held. Because of the way in which the categories have had to be drafted, there is sometimes a temptation to rely too strictly on the precise physical nature of the act and to pay insufficient attention to all the circumstances. Those circumstances include V's age, her distress, which lasted for some considerable time, the gross breach of trust and the delayed plea of guilty. A significant departure from the range provided by the guideline could not be justified. 4 years was appropriate after a trial. Allowing for D's compliance with the community order, **3 years** not a community order.

328.35   *Digital/oral penetration   Child aged 13-15   Defendant aged 18-24*

R v T 2013 EWCA Crim 1998 D pleaded at his PCMH to sexual activity with a child and causing or inciting a child to engage in sexual activity. V1 and V2 were cousins. V1 was aged 14 when she came to know D through V2. Contact was made through Facebook and D asked V1 to meet up with him. V1 told D she was aged 15, when actually she was aged 14, during their Facebook conversations. D picked V2 up in his car and drove her to a car park. D asked V1 if she wanted to have sex. She agreed and they both removed their trousers. Another car drove past causing them to move to a more secluded spot.

[1008] It is not entirely clear from the judgment what this reason was.

They removed their trousers again. D digitally penetrated V1 and ejaculated as a result of her masturbating him. D dropped V1 off in town. The next day she told a teacher, who informed her mother, who in turn called the police. After the incident came to light, V2's parents began to question her about her contact with D. V2 was aged 13 when she began frequent contact with D. Despite knowing her age, D had repeatedly tried to convince V2 to meet him and engage in sexual activity. He sent messages to her such as 'Do I get a hand job or a blowy?' and 'Do you want sex when I come back?' D was aged 20 at the time of the offences and of good character. The pre-sentence report stated that D described himself as selfish, immature and stupid. He had a history of depression. Held. There was a significant age gap between D and the victims. His actions were predatory and penetrative activity took place in relation to V1. However, in imposing a sentence of 4 years 8 months, the Judge failed to have regard to totality. 2 years 8 months for the offence against V1 would remain unchanged but 12 months, not 2 years, consecutive, for the offence against V2, making **3 years 8 months**.

Post-2014 guideline case

R v BA 2015 EWCA Crim 1295, 2 Cr App R (S) 78 (p 520) D pleaded on the third day of his trial to five counts of sexual activity with a child. D, now aged 24, in 2013 created a false Facebook page claiming to be an 18-year-old. He made contact with V, a 15-year-old, who soon claimed to be in love with D. Four days after the first contact the two arranged to meet at a station. They did so and they went to a park. D brought alcohol with him and encouraged V to drink it, knowing that she did not normally drink. D took V into some bushes and removed her clothes. He [encouraged] her to give him oral sex. His penis went in so far she 'gagged'. D videoed this on his phone. D also digitally penetrated her, which was rough, making her bleed. During the activity D pulled her hair, spat at her and spanked her. V dressed and still believed they were in a relationship. A short time later there was more oral sex and D ejaculated over her face. D then left. A week later 'he dumped her'. These events were three of the counts. Three months later, D contacted V again. He asked for a meeting and she refused. D said if she did not meet him he would put the video of the sex on the Internet. They agreed to meet. D told V to shave her pubic hairs and send him a photograph of her naked vagina or he would publish the video. They met at a hotel and D demanded oral sex or he would publish the video. V complied and D ejaculated in her mouth. A short time later this was repeated. D left and she reported the events. D had in 2006 sex convictions against five separate victims, one the same age as V (12 months' DTO). The Judge found that D was a dangerous offender. She found that V was particularly vulnerable. The Judge told D that he would be released after serving ⅔ of his sentence, which was in error. Held. There were many aggravating features. We substitute consecutive extended sentences totalling 19 years 9 months (custodial term of **9 years 9 months**, not 11 years, 10 years' extended licence) so he will be released at ⅔ of his sentence as the Judge intended (because the prison term was now less than 10 years, so would not be referred to the Parole Board). Note: It is impossible to reconcile the differing accounts about what sentences were substituted. However, the sentence listed is the Court's summary of what was substituted. The 10-year extended licence is unlawful as the maximum (whether on its own or as a consecutive term) is 8 years. It was wrong to take into account what the Judge thought was the release date, see **87.49** in Volume 1. Ed.

328.36   *Digital/oral penetration   Child aged 13–15 Defendant 25+*

R v J 2013 EWCA Crim 584 D was convicted of sexual activity with a child family member. V, aged 13, was his stepdaughter. D and V's mother had been in a relationship for about ten years. V had regarded D as her father from about the age of 2. D treated V as his daughter. D went into V's room when V's mother was downstairs. He thought V was asleep and he penetrated her vagina with his finger. V reported the incident at school the next day. D denied the offence and continued to do so. V's mother accepted D's innocence. D was aged 56 and of good character. He had served in the Army and since discharge had been a hard-working man. He had favourable references and there were pleas of clemency from his family. Held. This offence did not justify a sentence more severe than the recommended starting point of 5 years. There was no blood relationship between D and V. **4 years** not 6½.

Post-2014 guideline case

R v Pearce 2015 EWCA Crim 543 D was convicted of sexual activity with a child and meeting a child following sexual grooming. B's mother answered his phone and she saw numerous sexual text messages. She spoke to B, who was aged 14. He said he was experimenting with his sexuality and had visited gay web sites. He had had an online conversation with D and they met. D took the boy home and they kissed and undressed each other. They also gave each other oral sex and D licked B's anus. D drove B back to the meeting place and they did not meet again. The mother contacted the police. D was a teacher at a grammar school, aged 38. He taught boys aged 12-16. The Judge found that B consented at all times and there was no coercion. Held. D was of impeccable good character. It was a Category 1A offence. There were no aggravating factors. There were [many] of the listed mitigating factors present. There was a lengthy delay. A sentence at the bottom of the range was appropriate so **4 years** not 5.

328.37   *Digital/oral penetration, Conduct falling short of   Child aged 13-15   Defendant 25+   Pre-2014 guideline case*
Att-Gen's Ref No 53 of 2013 2013 EWCA Crim 2544, 2014 2 Cr App R (S) 1 (p 1) LCJ See **328.17**.

Grooming

328.38   *Grooming   Sexual Offences Act 2003 s 15   Sentencing Council guideline*
Grooming
Sexual Offences Guideline 2014, see www.banksr.com Other Matters Guidelines tab. In force 1 April 2014. The guideline only applies to offenders aged 18+, see page 7 of the guideline. For the usual practice, see **66.21** in Volume 1.

STEP ONE: Determining the offence category

page 64 The court should determine the offence category using the table below.

Category 1	Raised harm **and** raised culpability
Category 2	Raised harm **or** raised culpability
Category 3	Grooming **without** raised harm or culpability factors present

The court should determine culpability and harm caused or intended by reference only to the factors below, which comprise the principal factual elements of the offence. Where an offence does not fall squarely into a category, individual factors may require a degree of weighting before making an overall assessment and determining the appropriate offence category.

Factors indicating raised harm
Continued contact despite victim's attempts to terminate contact Sexual images exchanged Victim exposed to extreme sexual content (for example, extreme pornography) Child is particularly vulnerable due to personal circumstances

Factors indicating raised culpability
Offender acts together with others to commit the offence
Communication indicates penetrative sexual activity is intended
Offender lied about age/persona
Use of threats (including blackmail), gifts or bribes
Abuse of trust
Specific targeting of a particularly vulnerable child
Abduction/detention
Commercial exploitation and/or motivation
Offence racially or religiously aggravated
Offence motivated by, or demonstrating, hostility to the victim based on his or her sexual orientation (or presumed sexual orientation) or transgender identity (or presumed transgender identity)
Offence motivated by, or demonstrating, hostility to the victim based on his or her disability (or presumed disability)

328.39

STEP TWO: Starting point and category range

page 65 Having determined the category, the court should use the corresponding starting points to reach a sentence within the category range below. The starting point applies to all offenders irrespective of plea or previous convictions. Having determined the starting point, step two allows further adjustment for aggravating or mitigating features, set out below.

A case of particular gravity, reflected by multiple features of culpability or harm in step one, could merit upward adjustment from the starting point before further adjustment for aggravating or mitigating features, set out below.

	Starting point	Category range
Category 1	4 years' custody	3 to 7 years' custody
Category 2	2 years' custody	1 to 4 years' custody
Category 3	18 months' custody	1 year to 2 years 6 months' custody

328.40   [Aggravating and mitigating factors]

page 65 The table below contains a non-exhaustive list of additional factual elements providing the context of the offence and factors relating to the offender. Identify whether any combination of these, or other relevant factors, should result in an upward or downward adjustment from the starting point. In particular, relevant recent convictions are likely to result in an upward adjustment. In some cases, having considered these factors, it may be appropriate to move outside the identified category range.

Aggravating factors
Statutory aggravating factors:
Previous convictions, having regard to: a) the nature of the offence to which the conviction relates and its relevance to the current offence, and b) the time that has elapsed since the conviction
Offence committed whilst on bail
Other aggravating factors:
Failure to comply with current court orders
Offence committed whilst on licence
Any steps taken to prevent the victim reporting an incident, obtaining assistance and/or from assisting or supporting the prosecution
Attempts to dispose of or conceal evidence
Victim encouraged to recruit others

Mitigating factors
No previous convictions or no relevant/recent convictions Remorse Previous good character and/or exemplary conduct* Age and/or lack of maturity where it affects the responsibility of the offender Mental disorder or learning disability, particularly where linked to the commission of the offence Demonstration of steps taken to address offending behaviour *Previous good character/exemplary conduct is different from having no previous convictions. The more serious the offence, the less the weight which should normally be attributed to this factor. Where previous good character/exemplary conduct has been used to facilitate the offence, this mitigation should not normally be allowed and such conduct may constitute an aggravating factor.

328.41   *Grooming   Pre-2014 guideline cases*

R v M 2012 EWCA Crim 2148 D pleaded (full credit) to three counts of causing a child to watch a sex act. He was a bus driver and travelling on the bus were V1, aged 13, with her brother, B and a friend, F. D sent a message to V1's mobile with a picture of his erect penis and the words 'If you want it, call me'. V1 was really upset and close to tears. B took the phone and sent a message back, asking why he had sent the message. D was told V1 was only 13 years old and D responded he would have F and then later he would have them both. V1, B and F were scared. That was count 1. D was told by V1's mother that she was going to tell the police. On the next day, V2, aged 12, received a similar message. Her friend sent a message back, asking why he had sent the message. D responded by suggesting a sexual threesome. V2's mother spoke to D and D was abusive. In the next month, V3, who was aged 13, was travelling on a bus. She was not confident. She received a photo of D's penis with the message, 'Suck it dry'. V3 felt sick and scared. Later the picture was sent again, with a message saying, 'Use me now. If you are under 16, I will pay you'. Her mother also rang D, who pretended he didn't know anything about the message. V3 felt unable to travel on a bus and became depressed. In interview, D blamed someone else. In 2001, D received a community penalty for six thefts, which was ignored. He had no sex offences. He had a stress disorder caused by his experiences in the first Gulf War. The pre-sentence report said there was a high risk of reoffending. It recommended a 3-year community order with supervision and a Sex Offender Group programme. Held. The offences were in the bottom category of the guideline. As D had served the equivalent of **6 months**, the recommendation was appropriate.

Note: Although this activity was not charged as grooming, the seriousness appears not to be what the defendant did but what he was seeking to arrange. Ed.

Seeking/asking for sexual activity with children

(incl. requests by e-mail, Facebook etc. to meet up)

For sexual activity taking place on the Internet etc. see the **Internet/Mobile phone/E-mail offences** section at **328.43**.

328.42 *Seeking/asking for sexual activity with children   Child aged under 13*

R v Holmes 2013 EWCA Crim 577 D pleaded to inciting a child to engage in sexual activity. When aged 34, he was 'house-sitting' for his sister, V. V was aged 10 and a friend of D's niece. V would come to the house to walk the dog and on one such occasion and came upon D lying on a bed exposing the lower half of his body. He had an erection and when he saw her, he put a condom on his penis and asked her to get on top of him and to have sex with him. V thought she was going to be raped, refused and left. He told her not to tell anyone about it. The offence only came to light some four years later when D went to the police and volunteered an account of the offence. His account involved more serious offending than the reality, in that it involved physical contact, but he sought to attribute some of the responsibility for the offence on to V. D, aged 39 at appeal, was single and lived alone. He suffered from complex and systematised delusional beliefs. A second report diagnosed paranoid schizophrenia. He had previously attempted to take his own life. D was of previous good character. Held. Given the offence was not attributable to D's mental condition, there was no error in imposing immediate custody. This was an invitation to a sexual activity which was rebuffed and not pursued. There was no contact. The nature of the offence, the manner in which it came to the attention of the authorities and D's mental condition justify the view that starting at 4 years was too long. We agree with the Judge that the plea and the mental illness justify the starting point being halved. **15 months** not 2 years.

Note: With there being no physical contact between D and V, D's good character and D volunteering the account, I suspect that many Judges would consider a community order a far more constructive way of dealing with D's problems than immediate imprisonment. Ed.

R v Wilson 2013 EWCA Crim 1251 D pleaded to inciting a child to engage in sexual activity (×2). Over a two-month period, D, aged 24, contacted V1, aged 12, and V2, aged 13, via Facebook. He also contacted both by text message and spoke to V1 by phone. The later Facebook and text message exchanges were sexual in nature and D had sent V1 a picture of his erect penis. D made a number of requests to both V1 and V2 for 'naughty pics'. D viewed images of them in their school uniforms on Facebook. D tried to persuade both girls to meet him and flattered them both. Before matters developed further, a teacher at their school discovered that they were in contact with an older man and, upon learning the content of the messages, alerted the police. Held. A community-based sentence would have been wholly inappropriate. The [then] grooming guideline provided some assistance. This offence fell short of the completed offence, but it was aggravated by the fact that D sent a picture of his erect penis to V1 and V2, D persisted in contacting the girls and the content of the messages was sexually explicit. He also attempted to persuade both to meet him. Both V1 and V2 had experienced anxiety as a result of the offences and continued to suffer nightmares. D's belief that V1 was aged 13 (not 12) provides little mitigation. The starting point should have been 18 months. There was no need to pass a more severe sentence for V1 than V2. With limited credit for the plea, **15 months**, not 18, would have had regard to the mitigating features.

R v Willett 2014 EWCA Crim 194 D, a female aged 20, pleaded to causing a child under 13 to engage in sexual activity (×2). In 2012, V, a girl, was aged under 13.[1009] V registered with an adult social networking site. In her profile, she stated that she was aged 15. P, a male aged 26, was D's partner. P targeted V via the website to become sexually involved in his relationship with D. Over a two-week period, P asked V if she would like to meet D and P and said that they thought she was cute. He engaged in an explicit discussion with her as to what they would do together, and asked her for her address, details of her sexual experience, for telephone sex and for explicit pictures. P sent V photographs of himself and D having sex. An email account was set up to make communication easier, with V referring to D and P as 'mummy' and 'daddy' and them referring to V as 'their little girl' or 'baby girl'. V's mother discovered what had been going on and contacted the police. D's role was limited to two sexually explicit exchanges on the Internet where D described what was going to happen when they met. In interview, D said: a) that P had told her that he had found a 15-year-old for a threesome, b) D said she did not want to do anything until the girl was aged 16, but P asked her to communicate with V and she had done so, and c) P made sexual demands against her including degradation and mother and child scenarios. D had a troubled background and had had a number of failed relationships acquired via the Internet. D had also suffered abuse and violence at P's hands and she feared that the relationship would end if she refused P's requests. D was aged 21 with no convictions. The pre-sentence

---

[1009] In the judgment, V is said to be 15, which cannot be right.

report recommended a community order as a custodial sentence would have a detrimental effect on her emotional well-being. P pleaded to 13 child sex counts. He was aged 26 and was sentenced to 2 years' imprisonment. Held. D is not far from being a victim in her own right who had been under the influence of a much older man. That caused her to commit these offences out of character. The gap between V and D was not as large as between V and P. A suspended sentence was inappropriate. The supervision requirement imposed as part of that had been in force for five months at the appeal. An **18-month community order with 18 months' supervision**, not 2 years suspended with a 2-year supervision requirement.

See also: *R v Bayliss* 2012 EWCA Crim 269, 2 Cr App R (S) 61 (p 360) (Pleas (25% credit). Attempting to arrange child sex offence and possessing and making indecent images. Police officer posed as a woman with a ten-year-old son in an Internet chat room. They discussed sexual activity with children. Agreed to meet. Defendant intended to have oral sex with the fictional son. Images at Levels 1, 3 and 4. Aged 29. No convictions. Starting at 3 years not 4, **2 years 3 months** not 3 years.)

R v Nadli 2013 EWCA Crim 1620 (Inciting a girl to engage in sexual activity. Late plea. D followed a girl, aged 12, from a shop and asked her to go to a flat. Girl went and was taken to a shabbily furnished room. Two sets of doors locked. Girl asked whether she wanted sex. Girl declined. Offered £2. Girl let out. D, aged 35, of good character. Because of what in fact happened, **2½ years** not 3½.)

Post-2014 guideline case

Example: *R v Collins* 2015 EWCA Crim 915, 2 Cr App R (S) 50 (p 38) (Convicted of arranging a child sex offence (section 14) and arranging a child sexual image offence (section 50). Many e-mails with police officer pretending to be the stepmother of an eight-year-old girl. Plans for anal sex and photography. Aged 51. 12 years' **extended sentence (10 years'** custody 2 years' extended licence) not manifestly excessive.)

328.42a *Seeking/asking for sexual activity with children*   *Child aged 13-15*

R v Evans 2012 EWCA Crim 2183 D was convicted of two counts of causing[1010] a child to engage in sexual activity. He was a coach at a swimming club and he used his BlackBerry to send a message along the lines of, "Would you fuck me? Where would you fuck me? Fast or slow? Skin to skin?" He sent it to everyone in his contacts, including members of his own family and two girls aged 13 and 14. The text was sent on more than one occasion. D was now aged 24 and had no previous convictions. The Judge found a significant breach of trust and that the girls were not specifically targeted because everybody received the message. Held. This falls below Category 3. The correct starting point is **9 months** not 18. Given the unusual circumstances, it can be suspended.

See also: *R v W* 2013 EWCA Crim 237 (Pleas to 17 various sex offences with seven TICs involving 19 girls aged 13 or 14. No penetrative sex. Explicit text messages, sent images of his penis and invited girls to have intercourse or perform oral sex on him. He met up with some of the girls. Committed over 2½ years. Aged 22-24. No previous convictions. Dangerousness test met. The volume of offending was the dominant feature. 10 years' **extended sentence (5 years'** custody 5 years' licence).)

Post-2014 guideline case

R v Simms 2014 EWCA Crim 1888 D pleaded (25% credit[1011]) to attempting to meet a child after sexual grooming, thereby breaching a SOPO. D also pleaded to possessing indecent photographs of a child (×4), with one Level 4 and the others at Level 1. The offences were committed shortly after D had been released on licence. Police discovered these offences following a check of D's laptop, pursuant to the SOPO. D had accessed a chatroom called 'Teen chat' and contacted a 14-year-old girl whom he had arranged to meet. There was an intent to have sexual relations conveyed by the conversation. D was

---

[1010] The judgment refers to 'causing'. The relevant section refers to 'or inciting' as well, which is more likely to have been the offence. Ed.

[1011] This is what the Judge gave for one offence and it is assumed that is what he gave for all the offences.

emotionally immature and displayed some remorse but he had almost ten similar convictions. Two involved meeting or communicating with girls under 16. The Judge said he arrived at 7 years by giving the meeting offence 4 years, the SOPO offence 2 years and 2 years for the photos. Held. The critical feature is that D committed precisely the same sorts of offending very recently, committed whilst on licence and breaching a SOPO. 10 years' **extended sentence (7 years'** custody 3 years' extended licence) was severe, but not excessive.

Att-Gen's Ref No 94 of 2014 2014 EWCA Crim 2752 D pleaded (full credit) to inciting a child under 16 to engage in sexual activity. V, aged 13, was a friend of D's neighbour and also used to play with D's own children. One Sunday, D invited his neighbour around for a barbecue to celebrate V's daughter's Holy Communion and V came along. D permitted both his children and V to have alcohol. D asked V for her phone number but V said she didn't know it. However, she later accepted D on Facebook and WhatsApp but it was at D's instigation. During a ten-hour exchange of messages which D made gradually more flirtatious and sexual in nature, V said that she wanted an iPhone, which D offered to buy if she was 'nice' to him. When V asked what D meant, he messaged her 'suck' and 'dick'. The conversation moved onto V's sexual experience and ended with D saying not to worry about the iPhone, which was 'a silly idea'. D said the messages were 'only a joke' and made full admissions in interview. V said the messages made her feel 'cringey'. D was aged 34 on appeal with no previous convictions but he did breach bail conditions. He lived with his partner and three children aged 4-8. He showed insight into the harm caused and expressed shame, embarrassment and remorse but refuted suggestions that he had a sexual preoccupation with female children, feelings he suppressed. D posed a low risk of harm to the public and a medium risk to children. Held. The *Sexual Offences Guideline 2014* covers very different offending and the language used within it must be construed by particular reference to the offence under consideration. Where incitement does not lead the child to behave in the manner incited, although the culpability is likely to be identical, the harm is necessarily less: the same is so in relation to attempts. What happened here was Category 3, not 1, and with high culpability. **180 days' imprisonment** was entirely appropriate.

R v Buchanan 2015 EWCA Crim 172, 2 Cr App R (S) 13 (p 129) D pleaded to inciting a child to engage in sexual activity. He lived in south-east England. He exchanged explicit messages with G, a 14-year-old living on Merseyside. Messages from D included, 'and I would prefer to have unprotected sex with you,' and 'the thought of you playing with yourself in class is a turn on xx" G's messages referred to cum, boobs, big dick and fucking me. There was no suggestion he had attempted to meet G. D was aged 46 and was then unemployed. At the sentence hearing he was in employment. He was married with a young child and had no convictions. Held. There was a significant disparity in age. D had very significant mitigation [in the efforts he had made to address his offending] and the personal difficulties he was suffering at the time. On the face of it, it was a Category 1A case but these categories do not provide very much assistance. With full discount, **8 months** not 12.

R v S 2015 EWCA Crim 265 D pleaded (full credit) to inciting a child to engage in digital penetration, inciting a child to engage in sexual activity, to numerous counts of possessing, making and distributing indecent child images, sexual assault, blackmail and various computer offences. Between 2007 and 2011, D posed as a teenage boy aged 13 or 14 on Facebook. He groomed children, going on to incite them to provide sexual images of themselves or commit sexual acts in front of a web camera. The acts incited included digital penetration by V1 and V1 asphyxiating himself. D would then distribute the images on the Internet and he also downloaded 46 other child images. D also, whilst watering neighbours' plants whilst they were away, copied photos of their teenage daughter, V2. D blackmailed V3, a 13-year-old girl, into providing more sexually explicit pictures, having incited her to expose her breasts and pose naked. The only physical contact was when D approached V4, a nine-year-old girl, asking to take a photo of her, and sexually touched her neck. V1 suffered from PTSD and was depressed and suicidal and V4 was deeply affected, shaking and crying when she was at the site where it happened. D was aged 65 on appeal and of good character. The Judge said it was all highly devious and planned. He gave: a) for incitement for digital penetration, 5 years, b) for distributing indecent photographs, 2 years, c) for perverting the course of justice (which was telling a victim to delete incriminating e-mails), 1 year, d) for making indecent photographs, 1 year, e) for sexual assault, 18 months, and f) for blackmail, 18 months. They were all consecutive with the other sentences concurrent, making 12 years in all. That would equate with a starting point of 18 years. Held. By making more of the sentences concurrent, **9 years** in all.

Internet/Mobile phone/E-mail offences

328.43   *Internet/Mobile phone offences   Pre-2014 guideline judicial guidance*
Att-Gen's Ref No 39 of 2003 2003 EWCA Crim 3068, 2004 1 Cr App R (S) 79 (p 468) Where a man considerably older than a teenager makes contact with young girls using the Internet and this leads to sexual offences against the girls, it needs to be clearly understood that sentences will be towards the top of the range.
Note: This is an old case but the guidance still appears to be valid. This is partly because these offences are so hard to detect and deterrent sentences are required. Ed.
R v Westerman 2013 EWCA Crim 1133 The starting point [in the old guidelines] assumes that the defendant is actually present when the activity he has incited is taking place.
See also the **Grooming** section at **328.38** and the seeking/asking for sexual activity with children section at **328.42**.

328.44   *Internet/Mobile phone/E-mail offences   Directing children to penetrate themselves Pre-2014 guideline cases*
R v Phillips 2013 EWCA Crim 48 D pleaded to: a) two counts of inciting a child to engage in sexual conduct, b) 20 counts of making indecent images of a child, c) possessing indecent images of a child, and d) distributing indecent images of a child. D found V, aged 15, on Facebook and he gave a false name, an age of 15 when he was actually aged 56, falsely stated he lived with his parents and falsely stated he went to a school for the performing arts. D and V spoke online and on their mobiles. After a time, the conversation moved to sex and V said she was horny. D asked her to masturbate, which was conduct a) above. She did this. Unbeknown to V, D recorded this, which was conduct b) above. Had she known this, she would not have done it. D asked his wife to pose as his mother, and she did. V was close to her grandmother. When V was at her grandmother's house, D asked V to prove her love for him by performing sex acts with her grandmother's German shepherd dog. D asked V to simulate intercourse with the dog, take the dog's penis in her mouth and masturbate the dog, which was conduct a) above. She did this except she only simulated taking the dog's penis in her mouth. D recorded this. There it might have remained had not D's wife as 'an act of spite, jealousy and revenge' uploaded the recording on Facebook. Further she changed the password so the recordings could not be removed. V felt physically sick when she knew she had been deceived. When she went to school she was called a 'dog-shagger'. She did not return to school. She self-harmed and felt unable to leave home without someone with her because when she had, insults had been thrown at her. A firework had also been thrown. She was prescribed valium. D's wife received 2 years' imprisonment for the recording. D was arrested and 160 images of children were found on his computer, of which 102 were of V made by D. This was conduct c) above. D admitted sharing these images, which was conduct d) above. D had two recent convictions for indecent assault on a woman almost 40 years ago. The Judge said these were unspeakable offences committed by an unspeakable person. He started at 10 years and gave 3 years 4 months' IPP. Held. We are doubtful whether D posed a significant risk of serious harm to girls. The fact there was

no physical conduct between D and V was of little significance since he had incited her to act in the way she did. Equating this with other offending does not help. We start at 8 years, so **5½ years** not IPP.

R v Westerman 2013 EWCA Crim 1133 D pleaded (25% credit) to causing a 13-year-old girl to engage in penetrative sexual activity, causing the same girl to engage in non-penetrative sexual activity and attempting to incite a 15-year-old girl to engage in non-penetrative sexual activity. When aged 17, D engaged with a 13-year-old, V1, through an Internet chatroom. V1 knew D as 'Westie'. D subsequently pretended to be a bisexual woman called Laura. D asked V1 to put her webcam on and demonstrate how she took off her bra. V1 refused and D threatened her, saying that she ('Laura') and her boyfriend, Brian, would come to 'get' V1. During this conversation, V1 was in contact with D in his real persona. He told her that Laura and Brian were people to be feared. He told her to remove her top and shorts and to turn around and show him her bottom. Then, he told her to remove her bra and show him her breasts. He then told her to pull her knickers to one side, to rub her 'pussy' and place her other hand on her 'boob'. He asked if she was wet and V1 half answered, 'yes'. She kept asking to be left alone. V1 described feeling sick whilst that activity was going on. D had also contacted V2, who informed him she was aged 15. He pretended to be from a modelling agency and asked her to remove her top and show him her body via her webcam. V2 was also told to take photographs of herself in her underwear. D later contacted V2 pretending to be 'Danny', and asked her to send a picture of what she had done to 'Greg' (presumably himself). D was aged 20 at appeal and had no relevant convictions. He was living with his parents. Two and a half years elapsed between arrest and sentence. Held. The Judge made a number of factual errors in his remarks. He started at 28 months. There was a degree of deception. D's basis of plea contended that if there was any penetration, it was minimal. The starting point assumes that the defendant is actually present when the activity he has incited is taking place. A starting point of 20 months would have been adequate. With the same 25% credit as given by the Judge, **15 months** not 21.

328.45   *Internet/Mobile phone/E-mail offences   Directing children to abuse themselves   Pre-2014 guideline cases*
Example: *Att-Gen's Ref No 35 of 2013* 2013 EWCA Crim 1757 (Plea. The defendant encouraged children aged 9 and over to engage in sex acts, like masturbation for him. Arrested and carried on offending. Aged 32. Starting at 6 years, with the plea, **4 years** not 6 months.)

328.46   *Internet/Mobile phone/E-mail offences   Directing children to watch defendant abusing himself   Pre-2014 guideline cases*
R v Jenkins 2012 EWCA Crim 1393 D pleaded (27% credit) to attempting to engage in sexual activity in the presence of a child (×2), making indecent photographs (×16) and possessing indecent photographs of a child. He began a relationship with V, an 11-year-old friend of his daughter, via the Internet. They would chat and, latterly, use the webcam on D's computer. V's mother discovered the relationship and alerted the police. An officer assumed V's identity, unbeknown to D. D showed 'V' a picture of a naked female bottom, and then allowed his dressing gown to fall open, exposing his erect penis. He flopped it from side to side and zoomed in on it using the webcam. He was arrested and his computer seized. There were 51,562 indecent images, with some 45,000 at Level 1, and 176 at Level 5. There were also snuff movies and images depicting bestiality. D, aged 34, had one conviction for ABH when aged 18. Held. There were no aggravating features justifying sentencing outside of the guideline ranges, save for the fact that the real criminality consisted of not only the actual activity but also of the abuse of a relationship. After a trial, 2½ years for the photographs, consecutive to 3 years for the sexual activity, making 5½ years. With the plea, the notional determinate term is reduced to 4 years. D was assessed as dangerous and therefore the sentence is **IPP 2-year minimum term**.

R v Ellis 2014 EWCA Crim 586 D pleaded early to attempting to engage in sexual activity in the presence of a child (×2), attempting to cause a child to look at an image[1012] and making an indecent image of a child. D engaged with a policewoman, P, posing as a 12-year-old child on a social media site for children. D said he was aged 54 and from Watford. D sent P a picture of his erect penis and invited P to watch him masturbating on a webcam. About three weeks later, that activity was repeated. Ten days later, during an online chat, he sent a girl a video clip of a man masturbating, saying untruthfully that that was him. When D was arrested at his home, which wasn't in Watford, police found a film of a girl aged 14 or 15, in school uniform, doing a striptease although stopping short of being naked. D was of good character. The Judge said he did not feel bound by the guideline as there was more than one offence. Held. There is no reason to depart from the guideline. With the mitigation (which must have included that there was no 12-year old girl. Ed.) and full credit for the plea, 18 months was appropriate for the first two offences. For the next offence, 9 months concurrent, and for the making an indecent image offence, no penalty, making **18 months** in all not 3 years.

R v Alderton 2014 EWCA Crim 2204 D pleaded (full credit) to breaching a SOPO (×5), engaging in sexual activity in the presence of a child, attempting to engage in sexual activity in the presence of a child and exposure (×6). The offences involved D using Facebook and FaceTime to contact victims, sometimes persistently, and asking them to watch him. He would then masturbate on camera. D knew several of the victims already. They included girls aged under 18, which D was aware of. One of them was aged only 8. He used different e-mail addresses and identities, sometimes posing as a child. D was aged 43 and posed a very high risk of sexual re-offending. No child was met face-to-face. The offending was committed whilst D was subject to a community order for similar offences when an indefinite SOPO was also imposed. Held. A substantial sentence of imprisonment was merited but **6 years** in all, not 7.

Physical non-penetrative contact

328.47   *Physical contact under clothing   Child aged under 10*

R v L 2014 EWCA Crim 164 D was convicted of sexual assault on V, his daughter. The first set of offences was when she was aged 9 or 10. In 2012, he received 21 months for four counts of sexual assault on V. D had given her 'adult kisses' and touched her private parts. Some months later V was further interviewed by the police. She said she had been too scared to go into full detail about what D had done to her when she was initially interviewed. She said D had done more than she had previously said. He would pick her up from school with her friends on a Friday. He would leave the others playing downstairs and would take V upstairs. He would take off his trousers, make her lie on top of him on the bed and rub his penis against her vagina. She said some things which suggested the rubbing had led to penile penetration. D denied the allegations. He was acquitted of rape and convicted of a single sexual assault. He was sentenced as though it was an isolated incident. D was aged 43 at appeal. He also had a number of convictions for dishonesty. Held. The gross breach of trust involved aggravated the offence. In mitigation, there was the delay in prosecution, the guilty pleas to the earlier activity and good progress made in prison. These were extremely serious offences against his daughter. When associated with the earlier offences, a lengthy prison sentence was fully justified. The Judge's approach was logical and appropriate. Considering totality, starting at **5 years**, not 6, was appropriate. 21 months for the earlier offences should be deducted. The result is **3 years 3 months**, not 4 years 4 months.

Post-2014 guideline cases

Att-Gen's Ref Nos 86-87 of 2014 2014 EWCA Crim 2467 D1 pleaded to sexually touching a child under 13 and making indecent images of children. D2 pleaded to the same sexual touching of a child under 13, and three further counts of the same offence.

[1012] Presumably this is Sexual Offences Act 2003 s 12 (causing a child to watch a sexual act). Ed.

D2 also pleaded to making indecent images. Both received full credit. D1 and D2 discussed and organised mutual masturbation sessions in the presence of children at D2's home. D1 then asked D2 to bring V1, D2's daughter, who was aged 2, to him. V1 was sexually touched by D1, who put his mouth on her vagina, whilst D2 aided and abetted him. More perverted internet chat followed. During the last of the mutual masturbation sessions, D2 instructed his older children, one of whom was V2, aged 7 or 8, not to enter the kitchen. The children heard 'lots of crying and banging about'. D1 left red-faced and D2 told the children not to mention the visit or what they had seen and heard. In addition, D2, over a six-month period, sexually touched V2's vagina under her clothing. V2 only reported the behaviour upon seeing a Childline advert making her realise the behaviour was wrong. D2 was bailed for the various offences, but persisted in making indecent photos, including of sex with children to ejaculation. He pleaded guilty once more. Both D1 and D2 had an interest in sexually abusive images of children which was 'consuming' and they had accessed child pornography at all levels of seriousness which depicted all types of penetrative activity with young children. D1 was aged 47 on appeal and of good character with steady continuous employment and references. His father had died after a long illness and he had also accepted his wife's 13-year-old daughter as his own. However, due to the offending, the family home would have to be sold. D1 had deleted the illicit images well before his arrest and expressed considerable remorse. Probation opined that the next step would be a contact offence and that D1 presented a clear risk of serious harm to children. However, D1 had sought and was receiving counselling. D2 was aged 42 on appeal and also of good character. He was married with three daughters and saw viewing the images as a 'thrill'. D2 allowed the abuse of his own daughter as it was 'fantasy become reality'. He too expressed remorse and presented a high risk of sexual harm to children. He had handed over his family home to his wife and children. Held. The two offenders acted together. Both knew of the betrayal of trust by D2. One had encouraged the other to make his own two-year-old child available for sexual abuse. The child was specifically targeted...there was a significant disparity in age. Other children were in the near vicinity. The oldest child was instructed to say nothing. There was undoubted remorse. The offenders were, on reflection, shocked by their own depravity. For D1, **4 years 8 months**, not 2 years 8 months in all. For D2, **8 years**, not 6 in all.

R v TW 2015 EWCA Crim 63 D pleaded (full credit) to sexual assault on a child under 13 (×5), inciting a child to engage in sexual activity, taking (×4) and making (×4) indecent photos of a child. V, D's stepgranddaughter, was aged 4-6 at the time and she regularly stayed with D and his wife. When V and D were alone, D sexually assaulted V, photographing and videoing the activity on his mobile phone. This occurred around 20 times. V later described this as D touching her 'fiffy' with his 'willy'. On D's phone were: seven images, two of which were from the Internet and not of V, and three videos (Level 1), one video (Level 2) and two images and nine videos (Level 3). D denied any wrongdoing until his phone was analysed whereupon he admitted the offences. V now faced acute difficulties with the 'scars persisting for the rest of her life' and the events placed great strain on her family as a whole. D was aged 49-51 during the offending and of effective good character. He had a settled and stable life and struggled to explain his behaviour, appearing quite distressed at it, and expressing remorse. D was described as 'honest, caring and hardworking' with a low reoffending risk, and a suspended sentence with unpaid work and a sex offender treatment programme was proposed. The Court of Appeal received further character references emphasising the adverse effect on D's family. The Judge placed the sexual assaults into Category 2. Held. The Judge was right to stress that D's offending involved a gross breach of trust. The sentence plainly...had to go beyond the bracket for a single offence as the gross breach occurred repeatedly over a prolonged period which called for a severe sentence. A non-custodial sentence would have been quite inappropriate. Starting at 10 years, **6½ years** was severe but not manifestly excessive.

328.48   ***Physical contact under clothing   Child aged 10-12   Defendant aged 25+***
Att-Gen's Ref No 33 of 2011 2011 EWCA Crim 2028 D pleaded on the day of trial, after
a *Goodyear* indication, to specimen counts of sexual assault on a child under 13 (×4),
sexual assault on a child (×2), causing a child to watch a sexual act (×3) and causing a
child under 13 to engage in a sexual act. Over a three-year period D, V's father, touched
his daughter V's breasts and vagina, made V touch his erect penis and made V watch
sexually explicit adult films. V was then aged between 11 and 14. The offences occurred
both when V was in the bath with D and in the sitting room of the family home. D told
V it was 'their secret'. When V confided in her mother, D tried to make V say that she
had lied. V was angry, insecure and had thoughts of self-harming. D, aged 48, had no
previous convictions. The Judge gave 50% credit for the late plea as he had spared V the
trauma of giving evidence. Held. This was a gross abuse of trust in which a father
gravely abused his daughter. V was in a vulnerable position and the offence is further
aggravated by the fact that the abuse occurred weekly over a long period of some three
years. In mitigation, there is the plea, and his character. Credit for the plea should not
have exceeded 15%. Starting in the range of 5 years, with plea and it was a reference,
3½ years not 15 months.
R v FR 2013 EWCA Crim 168 D pleaded on rearraignment to: a) two counts of sexual
activity with a child (section 9(1)) and b) causing a child to engage in sexual activity
(section 10(1)). The counts were specimen counts. D would stay at V's parents' house on
a sofa when he was in London. D kissed V, who was then aged about 12, on the lips and
bit his lips if V did not open his mouth. D put his hand down V's trousers and touched
his penis. D also invited V to touch his penis, which was the section 10(1) offence. D
was aged 32 and of good character. Held. The Judge was not wrong to place the touching
of the penis in Category 2. The majority of the offending was in Category 3. The
touching was of the lower order. There was a breach of trust. 20% discount was
reasonable. We start at 30 months so with plea, **2 years**.
See also: *Att-Gen's Ref No 65 of 2011* 2011 EWCA Crim 2277 (Early plea. Sexually
touched two stepgranddaughters (one once and one three times) in 2004 and 2005.
Kissing with tongues. Touched their breasts and pubic areas. Victims aged 10-11. Aged
82 at appeal. Not in good health. **6 months** not 12 months suspended.)
Post-2014 guideline case
Att-Gen's Ref No 7 of 2015 2015 EWCA Crim 963 D was convicted of eight sex offences
including four of causing a child to engage in sexual activity and three of sexual assault.
In a residential street, he befriended V, aged 12, whose parents lived close to him. They
would play badminton together in the street. During one game, D hit a shuttlecock into
an enclosed garden and while the two looked for the shuttlecock D took out his penis
and asked V to touch it. Reluctantly V did so. Other activity took place on different days.
Three further times D asked V to masturbate him. V was told not to tell anyone. V was
also asked to suck D's penis and V refused to do so. In the garden, D 'required' V to
remove his trousers and pants and to bend over. D put his penis between the boy's
buttocks. A similar incident took place in a park. Finally D touched V's bottom and said
it was like his wife and said, "I could fuck you". D reached for V's penis but V resisted.
When told, V's family was outraged. V felt misery and anger. D accused V of lying. He
was married with children. The pre-sentence report said D was manipulative and
predatory. The writer said D presented a high risk of causing serious harm to young
boys. The Judge put the sexual assaults in Category 2A. He put the causing sexual
activity in Category 3A. Held. The aggravating factors included that there were multiple
offences against the same boy over 5 months. D's good character was a mitigating factor.
5½ years was the least sentence, not 3½ years.
328.49   ***Physical contact under clothing   Child aged 13-15   Defendant aged 21+***
Post-2014 guideline cases
R v DE 2014 EWCA Crim 1960 D was convicted of sexual activity with a child family
member, V, who was his granddaughter. V was aged 13 and visited D's home to be

congratulated on her school report. When V's mother and D's wife were out of the way, D showed V some holiday pictures on a computer, also intended for V's mother. D, sitting on the computer chair, put his arm around V and moved it under her skirt. He squeezed V's bottom, which was bare, her knickers having ridden up. D denied the offence throughout. He was aged 71 on appeal and of positive good character with flattering references. The episode caused huge family upset. D became suicidal but showed no empathy and was arrogant. He was assessed as suitable for a sexual offenders treatment programme and a 3-year community order was also recommended. The Judge concluded the offending straddled Categories 2 and 3. Held. It is hard to see how this offence is other than a straightforward Category 3 offence. It is to be distinguished from touching naked genitalia or naked breasts. The single culpability factor of age disparity certainly does not take the matter into Category 3A, but the Judge was required to bear in mind there was only the single factor operating to do so. **8 months**, not 12.

See also: *Att-Gen's Ref No 81 of 2014* 2014 EWCA Crim 2083 (Early plea. D lived with but was not related to V, then aged 13. When drunk, D touched V's vagina and apologised. Later he fondled her vagina four times over a short period but D desisted when told by V. 150 lurid texts sent. D, now aged 52, good character and with his drinking now addressed. V withdrawn and isolated. Focus should be on effects on V. Starting at 3 years, **2 years** in all not a suspended sentence.)

R v Jones 2015 EWCA Crim 31 (Plea (25% credit) to sexual activity with a child (×6), causing or inciting a child to engage in sexual activity (×3) and attempting to engage in sexual activity with a child. V1 and V2, aged 13, twin sisters. D knew this. Flirted, kissed and touched both girls over a month-long period. D rubbed V1's thigh, breast and vaginal area in a sexual manner over clothing and placed her hand on his erect penis. Also massaged and touched V2's vagina over clothing twice. Category 3A case. D revealed his clothed erect penis. Aged 29 with no relevant convictions. **2 years' 8 months** overall, not 5 years.)

328.50   Masturbating in front of children   Defendant aged 25+   Post-2014 guideline case

R v A 2014 EWCA Crim 2020 D was convicted of engaging in sexual activity in the presence of a child and inciting a child to engage in sexual activity. V was aged 14 and her father was D's best friend. The two families were close. When V was alone in her house, D asked if he could 'finger her' but V refused. D then removed his penis and began to masturbate in front of V but she filmed the event on her phone as evidence. D was aged 41 on appeal and of positively good character. He continued to maintain his innocence. The Judge found a grave breach of trust. He placed the sexual activity offence into Category 2 and the incitement offence into Category 1A. Held. The incitement offence did not go beyond masturbation but was a serious aggravation overall of the criminality. 2 years and **3 years** (for the incitement), not 4, concurrent.

328.51   Seeking/asking for sexual activity with children   Child aged 13-15

See also: *R v Haldane* 2015 EWCA Crim 1991 (Aged 48. Answered social media profile put out by adult members of the public. Reply indicated defendant was seeking anal and oral sex with a 13-year-old. Had a previous conviction for sex with a 15-year-old in 1991 (4 years). Arrested after agreeing to meet a boy (who did not exist). Police found unconnected downloaded photos. Held. We start at 5 years. With the previous convictions and photos we move to about 7 years. With plea, 10 years 3 months' extended sentence (**5 years 3 months'** custody 5 years' extended licence)).

Sexual intercourse

Sexual intercourse Child aged 10-12 see the RAPE AND ASSAULT BY PENETRATION chapter.

328.52   Sexual intercourse   Child aged 13-15   Defendant aged 18-24

R v Wood 2012 EWCA Crim 1409 D pleaded (full credit) to meeting a child following grooming (×3) and sexual activity with a child (×7). He met S aged 13 and K aged 14 in an Internet chat room designed for teenage girls. After the mutual exchange of sexually suggestive text messages, D travelled to meet S in her home town. They met at a hotel. There was kissing and D fondled S's breasts. On a separate occasion, D travelled to meet S again. Again they met in a hotel room. They had intercourse and D ejaculated on S's body. He did not wear a condom. Initially, D was cautioned for these offences. This was withdrawn four months later. In the interim, he was required to visit an offender manager with whom he was candid about the offences. He volunteered that he had met K and that they had also had intercourse and K had performed oral sex on him. K had denied that such activity had occurred, but D persisted in his candour. It follows that a prosecution for the offences relating to K arose solely out of D's admissions. D, aged 21, was of good character. Held. Starting at 6 years not 7½, **4 years** not 5 was appropriate.

R v McGowan 2013 EWCA Crim 867 D pleaded to sexual activity with a child (×2). J, aged 14, had been pretending to be aged 18 on the Internet. She had created false Facebook profiles. J's mother was aware that J had been contacting older men and was concerned. A police officer spoke to J about her behaviour. J told her mother she was staying with her grandmother but travelled to meet D. J never revealed her true age to D but it was common ground that D could not have reasonably believed she was over the age of 16 once he had met her. D and J spent the evening and all of the following day together. They had consensual sex on two occasions in secluded areas of Manchester known to J. D had a small number of convictions (community order imposed). D was aged 18 at the time of the offence and the Judge accepted that he was immature. Held. Had D been aged under 18, the maximum sentence would have been 5 years, not 14. The age gap between D and J was only 4 years. The starting point should have been 9 months. With full credit, **6 months** not 18.

Post-2014 guideline cases

Att-Gen's Ref No 124 of 2015 2015 EWCA Crim 103 D pleaded (25% credit) to four counts of sexual activity with a child. He was a dance instructor and from October 2012 he had an emotional relationship with a pupil when she was aged 15. It became sexual. D was aware of her age and promised her parents that he would not risk what he had by sleeping with her. It lasted until the end of March or the beginning of April 2013. The girl told her friend, also aged 15, about it. D admitted he had been emotionally and sexually involved with both at the same time. D was now aged 23 and had no convictions. The psychologist's report said D probably sought sexual intimacy with significantly younger females at a time when he was struggling to trust others after bad experiences with women of his own age. Held. This case came well within Category 1A. There were two women, abuse of trust, an element of grooming, sexual images retained, an element of planning, some disparity in age, although not significant and the period of time the offences lasted. We start at 6 years, so with plea, the community order that was part completed and that it was a reference, **4 years** in all not a community order.

R v K 2015 EWCA Crim 1141 D pleaded to sexual activity with a child (section 9) and failing to answer his bail (4 months concurrent, no appeal). D, aged 19, took V, then aged 13, to his home. She was in care but had absconded. After watching TV, they had consensual sexual intercourse. V stayed the night. Next evening, the police attended and took V to the station where she denied there had been sex. She later admitted there had been sex but refused to co-operate with the police. D on the other hand co-operated fully with the police, made full admissions and gave details of his electronic contact with V. Later D was given custody for ABH and breached his bail for this matter. He had 13 sentencing hearings for 18 offences but none for sex. D was assessed as immature for his age, with a poor educational record and a medium risk of causing harm to children. The Judge said there was no force, no threats and no intimidation. She considered D knew V was aged 14 or less and made the offence Category 1A. On appeal, the defence said it was 1B. Held. His unusual immaturity rendered the age difference less stark than the guideline is aimed at. The offence straddled the two categories, so **2 years** YOI not 3 years 4 months.

See also: *R v Richardson* 2015 EWCA Crim 1682, 2016 1 Cr App R (S) 20 (p 141) (Convicted. Defendant aged 20. Other party was a vulnerable 15-year-old girl. Eight occasions of penetrative sex. Held. The age disparity was not significant. Case clearly fell into Category 1B. We start at 18 months. With strong mitigation, **12 months** not 3 years.)

328.53   *Sexual intercourse Child aged 13-15 Defendant aged 25+ Up to 3 years*

R v Wicks 2012 EWCA Crim 330 D pleaded to sexual activity with a child (×6) and abducting a child. D was a chef in a pub. V, aged 15 from a troubled background, began to work in the kitchen. V was under the supervision of social services, at least partly because she was known to be sexually active with older men. D and V became friendly. V made it clear to D that she was attracted to him and their relationship became sexual. In January/February 2011 they started to have sexual intercourse and did so frequently over the following months. D told the police it was about 20 times. D knew from the start that: a) V was aged under 16, b) that she turned 16 in August 2011, and c) that it was an offence for him to have sexual relations with her. The police became involved at an early stage and D was given an informal warning by a police officer to 'stay away from V'. D ignored the warning and took care that their sexual encounters should be conducted thereafter surreptitiously. The police concern continued and in May 2011 D had a formal meeting with an officer from the protection of vulnerable children unit. D was then served with a notice under Child Abduction Act 1984 s 2, prohibiting D from allowing V to enter his flat, travel in his car, meet or contact V in any way. D signed to say he understood the notice and that it had been explained to him by an officer. D ignored the notice and the relationship continued. It was a somewhat volatile relationship and when V suggested she might bring the relationship to an end, D suggested that he would kill himself. In June 2011, D and V drove in D's father's car to nearby woodland. They pitched a tent and consumed a 'fair amount' of alcohol. They had vaginal and anal intercourse. V left the tent wearing only pants and a T-shirt. She felt ill because of the heat and what she had drunk the previous night. She was found by a neighbour, clearly unwell and in a distressed state. D had left the tent and did not go to find her. D, aged 32 at appeal, was of good character. It was said that, having regard to D's personality and the nature of his offence, he was finding life particularly difficult in prison. The Judge imposed 3 years 8 months on each count concurrently. Held. Aggravating features were the number of offences committed over a lengthy period of time during which D was given two warnings. The warnings should have left D in no doubt that V was a vulnerable person. It is also relevant that D put pressure on V to continue the relationship. Starting at 4½ years, with the plea, **3 years**.

Post-2014 guideline case

R v Hopkins 2015 EWCA Crim 1409 D pleaded to two sexual activity with a child counts. He and his cousin, F, invited C, aged 15 years 4 months, to join them for a sleepover. The three slept in a tent in the back garden. At about 4 am, F was woken by the sound of D and C kissing. F left the tent. The activity went beyond kissing but C did not wish to make a complaint so D was sentenced on his account. That was that C and he had been attracted to each other before that day and on the day C had approached him, undone his trousers and he knew she was only aged 15. He had licked one of her breasts and she had sucked his penis three times. He had ejaculated over himself. D was now aged 25 and had no convictions. He had learning disabilities and some history of mental health problems. D could not read or write very well. He lived with his aunt as he spent all his money on drugs and alcohol. The Judge started at 5 years, went down to three years and with the plea gave two years. Held. The case was exceptional because he had provided the evidence against himself. The disparity in the ages was mitigated by D's learning difficulties. The mitigating factors in the guideline were all present except for one. We start at 16 months, so with plea **16 months**.

Note: C was in a joint enterprise. The fact C was a few months below the age of consent is not a factor in the guideline and was not mentioned in the judgment. This is a classic example of how the guidelines encourage sentencers to pass unnecessary sentences when there is no victim. The Puritans' relentless search for victims continues.

328.54   *Sexual intercourse Child aged 13-15 Defendant aged 25+ 3 to 4 years Pre-2014 guideline cases*

R v Razaq and Razaq 2011 EWCA Crim 2677 R was convicted of sexual activity with a child (×2) and breach of a SOPO (3 years concurrent). U was convicted of sexual activity with a child. R and U met two 13-year-old girls. R had sex with both girls in his car. U tried to have sex with one girl but she resisted. He then threatened her. The girls thought the men were aged 17 or 18. R and U knew the girls were aged 13. R, aged 30, had a conviction for sexual activity with a child and was subject to a SOPO. U, aged 25, had convictions but none for sexual offences. Held. There were elements of grooming and vulnerability. Substantial custodial sentences were warranted. For R, 5½ years ×2 consecutive, making 11 years, was severe but not manifestly excessive. Manifestly U's case fell outside the guidelines. Reflecting the fact he had not been charged with facilitating further sexual offences by others, **3½ years** not 4½.

R v Pearce 2012 EWCA Crim 1337, 2013 1 Cr App R (S) 54 (p 309) D was convicted of sexual activity with a child (×3). He employed V, aged 15, as a stable hand at weekends. He was aware of her age. Over a period of approximately three or four weeks, they had sexual intercourse, twice at D's address and once in his car. Matters came to light when V's mother found text messages on V's phone suggesting there had been a sexual relationship. The intercourse was consensual. V lost her self-confidence, lost her friends as a result of rumour and gossip and struggled to concentrate at school. D, aged 54 at the appeal, had no convictions and eight impressive character references. His wife had decided to stand by him. The Judge noted that D had first denied any sexual contact, and then contended there was one incident falling short of intercourse, despite there being clear evidence. Held. These offences were committed in breach of trust and there was a significant age gap. However, this was not a case that involved a significant element of grooming or manipulation. The offences occurred over a comparatively short period of time and with V's consent. **4 years** not 7.

R v Rutland 2012 EWCA Crim 2048 D pleaded (full credit) to sexual activity with a child (×2) with two of the same offences TIC'd. D met V, aged 14, through a relative. It was arranged that V would tutor D's ten-year-old daughter. The first session was at V's house, thereafter it occurred at D's house. V's mother became suspicious of the relationship between the two and accessed V's Facebook account, which suggested a relationship. She confronted D, who 'stared like a rabbit caught in headlights'. He said he would drop his children off and go to the police, which he did. He admitted they had sex the previous weekend and had used protection once, and that three times they had unprotected sex and oral sex which included ejaculation. A report suggested D had a mild to moderate depressive disorder, low self-esteem and an immature self-concept. D, aged 31 at appeal, was of previous good character. He was separated from his wife, who was the mother of his children. He was the sole carer for the four children who were aged from 3 to 10 years. They were now in care. Held. There was the plainest breach of trust, ejaculation on three or four occasions, the grooming of V and changing her from a friend to a sexual object. After a trial, a sentence in the region of 5 years could have been expected. With the plea, **3½ years** not 5.

R v Garrett 2013 EWCA Crim 1166 D pleaded (full credit) to grooming and sexual activity with a child. V was aged 14 and was uncertain about his sexuality. He had contacted gay men on the BlackBerry messaging service (BBM) to talk about the issue. One of V's contacts had broadcast a number of contact PINs, including D's. V contacted D and asked if he was gay. D said that he was and asked V if he was gay. V said that he wasn't sure. They exchanged around 3,000 messages between 28 June and 6 July. At first, V told D that he was aged 16. Within a couple of days he said he was 15 and then

14. D told V he was aged 26, a millionaire, having won the lottery, and had finished a relationship. None of that was true. They had explicit sexual discussions. D did not use any intimidation or coercion but continued to encourage and reassure V. He said he was rich and held out promises of treats and luxuries. They arranged to spend a weekend together and D promised to take V to London. V felt excited but also indebted to D. V told three friends and they were concerned. One of them sent D a message on BBM asking if he thought his relationship with V was 'right' as he was aged 26 and V aged 14. D replied that he did not know V was 14 at the start. D later sent V a message telling him someone he knew had contacted him and tried to 'put him off' V. D said, "I don't see age, I see you, the guy who likes me and [the] guy I really like." They met at a public house a few weeks prior to going away for the weekend. They spoke about having sex and V said he was nervous. D reassured him and said they would, "take it slow and see what happens". V said he was being bullied at school for being gay. V told his mother he was spending a weekend with his friends. He exchanged messages with D who said it was exciting and romantic. The conversation then became sexual in nature. D picked V up and they went to a restaurant. They drank wine although there was no suggestion that V was drunk. They went to their hotel room and D put on a film about two boys who were struggling with their sexuality. It was not pornographic. D encouraged V to remove his shirt. V said he was not sure that he wanted matters to continue but he felt he didn't want to upset D, who had spent money on him. D did not pressurise V and said they could stop at any point. D had brought with him baby oil but no condoms. V performed oral sex on D and D reciprocated. D then had anal sex with V, culminating in ejaculation. One of V's friends told V's mother where he was and she tried to contact him. V replied the following morning and D was arrested at the hotel. In V's victim impact statement he said his life would never be the same again and that D had filled his head with lies in order to take advantage of him. V's mother said it was psychologically destroying. D was aged 37 at the time of the offences. He was of good character and had expressed genuine remorse. Held. D had made V believe that he was in a loving relationship. The offences fell into the highest category of the guideline for sexual activity with a child. The activity had culminated in ejaculation, there was a significant age gap, D had lied about his age from the outset and D knew that V was uncertain about his sexuality and began to groom V as a prelude to committing these serious offences. The grooming was committed over an extensive period. D did not take the opportunity to desist when it presented itself. The effect on V and his family was severe. However, the three activities took place on a single occasion. We start at 6 years, not 9. With the plea, **4 years** not 6.

328.55   *Sexual intercourse Child aged 13-15 Defendant aged 25+ 4+ years*

R v Razaq and Razaq 2011 EWCA Crim 2677 R was convicted of sexual activity with a child (×2) and breach of a SOPO (3 years concurrent). U was convicted of sexual activity with a child. R and U met two 13-year-old girls. R had sex with both girls in his car. U tried to have sex with one girl but she resisted. He then threatened her. The girls thought the men were aged 17 or 18. R and U knew the girls were aged 13. R, aged 30, had a conviction for sexual activity with a child and was subject to a SOPO. U, aged 25, had convictions but none for sexual offences. Held. There were elements of grooming and vulnerability. Substantial custodial sentences were warranted. For R, 5½ years ×2 consecutive, making 11 years, was severe but not manifestly excessive. Manifestly U's case fell outside the guidelines. Reflecting the fact he had not been charged with facilitating further sexual offences by others, **3½ years** not 4½.

Att-Gen's Ref No 74 of 2012 2013 EWCA Crim 149 D was convicted of seven sexual offences against his niece, V, and pleaded to two such offences. These included sexual assault, sexual activity with a child family member and assault of a child aged under 13 by penetration. A number were specimen counts. The age difference between the two was about 15 years. The offending began in 2003 and temporarily ceased in 2004. In December 2009 the offending resumed and finally stopped in January 2011. When V was aged 8, she would stay at her grandmother's home, where D was living. He was aged about 22. At night, he would take his mother's cat into V's room as a cover for his activity. He would fondle her and penetrate her vagina with his finger. The offences took place for around a 12-month period. In 2009, D's girlfriend was pregnant and contact between D and V resumed. He was then aged 28 and V aged 14. He would take her shopping, pay attention to her and buy her gifts. He touched her inappropriately, kissed her and told her that he loved her. He would drive her to a secluded spot and penetrate her vagina with his fingers. D showed V how to masturbate him and encouraged her to do so. When V's mother was in hospital giving birth, D was asked to stay at the family home to help with V and her sister. He did so and asked the sister to run an errand. He removed V's pyjama bottoms and licked V's vagina. The offending progressed to sexual intercourse on more than one occasion. D became possessive and jealous of V's friendships with boys her own age. V expressed discomfort at the situation and D said that it must mean that V didn't love him and that D would do something stupid and it would be V's fault. V described being entirely under his influence during that period. V eventually told her mother and D was arrested. He alleged that they were 'close' but that a sexual relationship was a fabrication. D had convictions but none for sexual offences. Held. There were a large number of offences committed over a considerable number of years. D abused his position of trust and there was an element of premeditation. The large age gap is also an aggravating factor. There would be some credit for his pleas. The Judge appears to have made an error when identifying the starting point. The starting point was 13 years not 8. With credit for his late pleas (2 years), the appropriate sentence was **11 years**.

R v Pipe 2014 EWCA Crim 2570, 2015 1 Cr App R (S) 42 (p 306) LCJ D was convicted of three specimen counts of sexual activity with a 15-year-old girl, V. V's sister worked with D and V moved in with D and his wife. V was unhappy, naïve, immature, quiet and lonely. D groomed her by text, plied her with alcohol and filled her head with 'spiritual mumbo-jumbo'. This led to digital penetration and full sex. V could not extricate herself. D was now aged 31. Held. It was an extensive campaign of sexual abuse. The case was Category 1A, because of the planning, use of alcohol, grooming and gross breach of trust. It was at the top of the range because a) D ejaculated, b) it was in his home, c) threats were made if V reported the activity, and d) the period of time over which the offending occurred (September to December 2009). The mitigation was the absence of previous convictions. **9 years** in total was appropriate.

Post-2014 guideline case

See also: *Att-Gen's Ref No 106 of 2014* 2015 EWCA Crim 379 (Five pleas of sexual activity by D, a 33-year-old, with a child, C, aged 15 in hotels. Unprotected and ejaculation outside vagina. Wife and her parents lied to. C said to police she loved D. Held. D had groomed C. We start at around 7 years, so with plea and mitigation **4½ years** not 30 months.)

For *Sexual intercourse with a child family member*, see **328.32**.

Particular defendants

328.57 *Defendant under 18 Sentencing Council guideline*

Youths Sentencing Guideline 2009, see www.banksr.com Other Matters Guidelines tab para 3.3 When sentencing a young offender whose offence involves sexual activity but there is no evidence of a coercive or abusive relationship or of anything other than consensual activity, a court will need to be aware that a desire to explore gender identity or sexual orientation may result in offending behaviour. Depending on the seriousness of the offending behaviour, offender mitigation may arise where that behaviour stems from sexual immaturity or confusion.

Sexual Offences Guideline 2014, see www.banksr.com Other Matters Guidelines tab. In force 1 April 2014. The guideline only applies to offenders aged 18+, see page 7 of the guideline. For the usual practice, see **66.21** in Volume 1.

page 151, Definitive guidelines for the sentencing of offenders under 18 years old are not included.

When sentencing offenders aged under 18, a court must in particular follow the *Youths Sentencing Guideline* 2009, see www.banksr.com Other Matters Guidelines tab, and have regard to the principal aim of the youth justice system (to prevent offending by children and young people) and the welfare of the young offender.

Note: I understand that the Sentencing Council decided not to issue a guideline for those aged under 18 because those matters are due to dealt with by a new guideline for youths. A consultation paper for that is expected soon.

328.58   *Defendant aged under 16*

R v F 2013 EWCA Crim 52 D pleaded to three assaults by digital penetration, nine counts of sexual assault and four counts of causing a child under 13 to engage in sexual activity. The counts were specimen counts. The victim was V, D's first cousin, who [it appears] was aged 7. The two families were close and D and V were often alone together. The conduct was licking her vagina (three times), touching it with his fingers (three times), inciting her to masturbate him (three times), inciting her to penetrate her own vagina (once) and putting his penis between her buttocks (three times). D made partial admissions and said he was abused when he was younger. D was [it appears] aged 15 and of good character and from a loving family giving him a good upbringing. The pre-sentence report assessed a low risk of sexual re-offending. The author thought D was motivated by sexual curiosity underpinned by poor judgement and impulsivity and latterly an inability to control his sexual urges. The Judge rejected this and said D was very blameworthy. He thought the conduct was close to rape. He also thought the activity was increasing in gravity and only stopped when V was brave enough to inform. He assessed the risk of further offences as high. He also found a significant risk of serious harm. Held. Experience teaches us that 16-year-olds of good character who lose their liberty for a very long time are vulnerable to influences decent families would not wish on them, which is itself a risk for the future. We are not convinced he was right to reject the risk assessment. **Youth Rehabilitation Order** with an NSPCC 'Change for good' programme, not 12 years' extended sentence (6 years' detention (an unlawful sentence) with 6 years' extension in all).

See also: *R v K and Others* 2013 EWCA Crim 649, 2014 1 Cr App R (S) 5 (p 16) (Pleas to sexual activity with a child and making indecent photographs by four boys aged 14, 15, 15 and 16. Initially indicted with rape. The victim, V, was a girl aged 14. She was very drunk. One boy called V over to a wooded area. He pulled down her trousers and penetrated her vagina with his penis. Another penetrated her mouth with his penis. A third penetrated her vagina with his penis whilst the first gripped her. A fourth boy, aged 16, filmed what happened on his phone. The boys boasted after the event. None had convictions. Significant impact upon V. With allowances for youth and the pleas, a **12-month DTO** was not in any way excessive.)

Post-2014 guideline case

R v G 2014 EWCA Crim 1939 D pleaded to two and was convicted of three assaults on a child under 13 and of three offences of causing or inciting a child under 13 to engage in sexual activity. The offences began in 2008 when D was 11 and went on for four years. V1 was almost three years younger and V2 two and a half years younger than D and they were D's female and male cousins respectively. The offending was minor to begin with, but grew more serious once D realised that, as instructed, V1 would not tell anyone. D touched V1's vaginal area and, around six times a year, would digitally penetrate her. V1 was made to masturbate D to ejaculation. This continued even when V1 wept. V2 witnessed many such assaults, which were committed in D's room during family gatherings. V2 also fell victim to one such assault himself as D made V2 masturbate him. D would also masturbate in front of both V1 and V2 and showed them pornography. Both V1 and V2 said, "no", but D threatened them and told them not to tell anyone as they wouldn't be believed and any allegations would lead to their father being ill and give their grandmother a heart attack. V1 reported the offences six months after D had ceased them. D was deceitful and sought to minimise his actions and blamed both V1 and V2 for initiating activities. D was aged 17 and only had a warning for robbery in 2011. He posed a moderate risk of future sexual offending. He was bullied and exposed to emotional abuse, neglect and violence in his adolescence, leaving him with a sense of no control over his life. He was a 'tremendous academic success', but suffered from setbacks since sentencing, being excluded after his arrest. D was noted to have helped students with revision and was universally admired as a mentor for the young at school. D also showed no remorse and the family was split but his mother unswervingly supported him, despite her own grave health difficulties. There was also a stark difference in his life during the offending and now. D would have no access to treatment in custody and an expert was worried that it would expose him to a highly delinquent population. V1's behaviour at home was affected and she avoided male attention, drastically changing her appearance to do so. She also self-harmed. The Judge identified the adult starting point as 6 years. Held. There is no abuse of trust here. This case is odd as D is highly intelligent, is more than capable of devoting himself to his studies, and came extremely close to a scholarship at a prestigious school. This case is singular and very difficult, even for this Court, to categorise. Reflecting the traumas endured by V1 and V2 and to acknowledge the circumstances of the offending but also ensuring that D, at the earliest possible opportunity, comes back into a community capable of welcoming him and picks up his life again, we impose a **12-month DTO**, not 3½ years' detention.

328.59   *Defendant aged 16-17*
R v B 2013 EWCA Crim 2774 (Plea to sexual assault and sexual activity with a child (×4). Aged 15. Three victims. Ejaculated onto knickers of previous girlfriend aged 16 whilst she was asleep. Simulated intercourse with another aged 15 and pressed erect penis against her. Whilst on bail, he pulled down clothing of a third girl aged 13 and inserted his finger into her vagina. Third victim suffered ongoing psychological effects. Caution for theft. Aged 17 at appeal. Persistent offender over ten-month period. 18-month DTO was severe but reflected the totality of the offending. SOPO quashed as due to his age the test was not met and the terms were unworkably wide.)

Post-2014 guideline case
R v G and M 2015 EWCA Crim 32 M was convicted of one section 13 count and three sexual activity counts against two girls. Aged 15, M and CH were boyfriend and girlfriend and had sex, leading to CH falling pregnant. Months later, when M had turned 16, he and BM, aged 14, had sex at a party at which alcohol and cannabis were consumed. BM also had sex with two other youths that night. G was also present at the party. He was then aged 15, and had sex twice with BM. All of the sexual activity in both G and M's offending was consensual. M, aged 18 on appeal, had previous convictions for criminal damage, disorder, assault, burglary and cannabis possession. He continued to deny sexual involvement in one of the offences. A probation officer said M had a tendency to treat women as objects and had failed at school due to his challenging behaviour. Notwithstanding M's emotional immaturity, there were planning and grooming elements. For both G and M, custody was considered unsuitable for or unlikely to address their sexual behaviour. Held. Even a disparity of 12 months [in age between the victims and the defendant] at these ages does not make a difference to the maturity of mind of the individuals involved. For G, we do not consider that the legal label of rape…provided any assistance in the evaluation of its seriousness and accept that G was a sexually precocious young person who put the health and welfare of four separate underage girls at serious risk. However, **18 months' detention** in all, not 3 years. For M, the significant disparity in ages between him and BM is why we agree with the Judge in imposing custody. The appropriate total sentence for M, after trial, is **18 months' detention**, not 3 years.

328.60   *Female defendants   Judicial guidance   Post-2014 guideline case*
(Guidance that applies to all sex offending)
Att-Gen's Ref No 85 of 2014 2014 EWCA Crim 2088, 2015 1 Cr App R (S) 14 (p 111) D,
a woman, pleaded to sexual activity with a child under 16. When aged 43, she had
penetrative sex with a 14-year-old boy. Held. At least since 2008, this Court has
proceeded on the basis that sex guidelines are gender neutral.

328.61   *Female defendants*
R v Smith 2012 EWCA Crim 2408 D pleaded (full credit) to sexual assault on a child
under 13 by penetration. When aged 17, D became pregnant. She had had a difficult
upbringing and was sexually abused by her mother's new partner. She gave birth to V
and V's father took no part in the child's upbringing. D was plainly overwhelmed by
motherhood. She presented symptoms of post-natal depression. D moved in with her
partner, B, who was not V's father. B heard V screaming and when he went to change
her nappy he discovered that V was bleeding extensively. D and B took V to the hospital
where it was discovered that the bleeding was coming from the vagina. D could offer no
explanation. There was a laceration to the vaginal orifice. Self-evidently the injury was
non-accidental and some instrument must have been used. D offered no explanation, was
unable to remember what had happened and showed no emotion. The community did not
react well to reports of the incident and eggs were thrown at her house. At appeal, D
accepted she had caused the injury but did not remember doing so. D, aged 20, had no
convictions. She had suffered from post-natal depression and resultant chronic stress so
much so that it was identifiable as post-traumatic stress. Held. The motivation was not
perverted sexual gratification, it arose entirely from D's troubled state of mind. She was
entirely unable to deal with the stresses and strains of motherhood and was at the time of
the offence in a pathetic and wretched condition. She really was more to be pitied than
punished. Custody was wrong in principle. **3-year community order** with 3 years'
supervision, not 3 years' detention.
See also: *R v Willett* 2014 EWCA Crim 194 (Internet. **Community order** not a
suspended sentence.)

Post-2014 guideline cases
Att-Gen's Ref No 85 of 2014 2014 EWCA Crim 2088, 2015 1 Cr App R (S) 14 (p 111) D
pleaded on the day of trial to sexual activity with a child under 16 (×3). D was a close
friend of V's mother. D was asked to join V, aged 14, and his mother at an awards
ceremony, during which D became drunk. They all returned to D's house and continued
to drink, including V, and D and V kissed. The party then moved onto V's house
whereupon D asked V to "get his cock out" so she could suck it, which D did. They were
interrupted but it was decided that D should stay over and the drinking continued. D was
warned to keep away from V. The next morning, V entered the room where D was
sleeping and she sucked and masturbated his penis to ejaculation, then leading to full
sex. Noises were heard, including D's disbelief at being in bed with a 15-year-old (even
though V was aged 14), and they were discovered. D said she was sorry and, expressing
self-disgust, left immediately. D admitted only to kissing V to his mother, but word got
out at V's school. D was aged 43, of positive good character, and a conscientious mother
with references. However, after conviction she continued to maintain her innocence and
that V had initiated the offences. V was not sexually naïve, having engaged in sexual
activity with children around his age and both he and his mother did not wish D to be
punished. Held. The proper approach is to treat V's lack of sexual naïvety as an absence
of aggravation which otherwise might have existed. The risk of harm is always present.
The least possible sentence is **2 years** concurrent, not 9 months suspended.
See also: *Att-Gen's Ref No 32 of 2015* 2015 EWCA Crim 1110 (Court Martial Appeal.
Plea to four sexual activity with a child offences. Breach of trust. 13-14 year old boy
groomed by wife of soldier. Full sex. Two warnings by military police ignored. Full

unprotected sex with ejaculation. Claimed boy raped her. Now aged 28 and of good character. With aggravating features, starting point should have been more than 5 years. **3 years** at the very least, sentence not suspended.)

Att-Gen's Ref No 28 of 2015 2015 EWCA Crim 1267 (D, aged 33, pleaded during trial to sexual activity with a child, a vulnerable boy aged 15½. Full sex unknown number of times. No previous convictions. Category 1A. A great deal of powerful mitigation. **30 months** not 2 years suspended.)

328.62   *Persistent offenders   Pre-2014 guideline cases*
R v Glancey 2011 EWCA Crim 118 D pleaded to arranging or facilitating the commission of a child sex offence and distributing indecent photographs of children. He lived in a multi-occupancy house run by a Christian family. He had access to the family computer and Internet through a router, allowing him access via his laptop. He downloaded 100 images at Level 1, 12 at Level 2, 33 at Level 3, 37 at Level 4 and seven at Level 5. He was arrested and bailed. Police ran a covert investigation and an undercover officer began to chat online with D. They discussed webcams and moving images of girls aged 10 to 12. D also revealed a sophisticated understanding of computers and how to avoid detection by the police. D and the officer agreed to meet in a public house. D identified himself by a pre-arranged sign. D stated that he wanted to masturbate whilst watching a 10- to 12-year-old girl dancing for him and ejaculate on the child. D again explained his knowledge of computers and how to avoid detection. D subsequently downloaded 68 images at Level 1, 11 at Level 3, ten at Level 4 and one at Level 5. D had previous convictions for child sex offences: in 2001, exposure (×3), in 2002 possession of child abuse images and conspiracy to commit an act of gross indecency. D, then aged 19, had sexual relations with his 13-year-old girlfriend and asked her 13-year-old friend to masturbate over her. The pre-sentence report noted that the offending was escalating in seriousness. It also considered that D did not have the necessary skills to manage the risks that he posed. Held. We conclude that this case is right at the margin between Imprisonment for Public Protection and an extended sentence and we fully understand why the Judge thought that only Imprisonment for Public Protection would contain the significant risk posed by D. However, taking account of the factors that we have mentioned, 9 years 2 months' **extended sentence (4 years 2 months' custody** 5 years' extended licence).

R v J 2012 EWCA Crim 1888 D pleaded to sexual assault and breaching his SOPO. The SOPO forbade him from approaching or communicating directly or indirectly with any child under 18. V, a 13-year-old boy, was fishing on the banks of a river. D, who was very drunk, engaged V in conversation for 15 minutes, then grabbed V's wrists and tried to kiss him. V struggled free and ran away. He was badly affected by the incident and had trouble sleeping. D, aged 36, had a terrible record, including possessing indecent photographs (×4), gross indecency with a child (×2), indecent assault on a male (×1) and breaches of his SOPO (×10). Held. D was an alcoholic with strong sexual urges towards young boys. Starting at 6 years (3 for the sexual assault and 3 for the breach) was too much. Consequently, because of the minimum term requirement, IPP was wrong. The appropriate sentence was 2 years for the assault and 1 year consecutive for the breach. **3 years** in all not IPP.

Post-2014 guideline case
R v Alderton 2014 EWCA Crim 2204 D pleaded (full credit) to breaching a SOPO (×5), engaging in sexual activity in the presence of a child, attempting to engage in sexual activity in the presence of a child and exposure (×6). The offences involved D using Facebook and FaceTime to contact victims, sometimes persistently, and asking them to watch him. He would then masturbate on camera. D knew several of the victims already. They included girls aged under 18, which D was aware of. One of them was aged only 8. He used different e-mail addresses and identities, sometimes posing as a child. D was aged 43 and posed a very high risk of sexual re-offending. No child was met

face-to-face. The offending was committed whilst D was subject to a community order for similar offences when an indefinite SOPO was also imposed. Held. A substantial sentence of imprisonment was merited but **6 years** in all, not 7.

329   SEX OFFENCES: CORPSES
329.1
Sexual Offences Act 2003 s 70 (sexual penetration of a corpse)
Mode of trial Triable either way
Maximum sentences On indictment 2 years. Summary 6 months and/or a £5,000 fine for offences committed before 12 March 2015 and an unlimited fine thereafter.[1013] There are maximum fines for those aged under 18, see **14.38** in Volume 1.
Extended sentences Sexual Offences Act 2003 s 70 is listed in Criminal Justice Act 2003 Sch 15. The court may pass a 2012 extended sentence (EDS) if there is a significant risk of serious harm from future specified offences and either: a) the defendant has a Criminal Justice Act 2003 Sch 15B conviction (applicable only to defendants aged 18+), or b) the offence would justify a determinate sentence of at least 4 years.[1014]
Sexual Harm Prevention Orders There is a discretionary power to make this order, when the notification criteria are present (see below) or when it is necessary to protect the public from sexual harm.[1015]
Notification For offences where the defendant was:
   a) aged under 18 and sentenced to imprisonment of at least 12 months, or
   b) aged 18 or over and was sentenced to imprisonment or detained in a hospital,
the defendant must notify the police within three days (or three days from his or her release from imprisonment, hospital etc.) with his or her name, home address, National Insurance number etc. and any changes to those, and addresses where he or she resides for seven days[1016] (in one or more periods) or more in any 12-month period.[1017]

329.2   *Sentencing Guidelines Council guideline*
Sexual Offences Act 2003 Guideline 2007 page 103, see www.banksr.com Other Matters Guidelines tab
page 18 para 1 The starting points and ranges apply to a first-time offender who was convicted after a trial.
page 103

Type/nature of activity	Starting points	Sentencing ranges
Repeat offending and/or aggravating factors	26 weeks' custody	4 weeks' to 18 months' custody
Basic offence as defined in SOA 2003, assuming no aggravating or mitigating factors	Community order	Community order or a fine

Additional aggravating factors: 1 Distress caused to relatives or friends of the deceased, 2 Physical damage caused to body of the deceased, 3 The corpse was that of a child, and 4 The offence was committed in a funeral home or mortuary.
Note: The *Sexual Offences Guideline 2014* does not have a guideline for this offence. I understand it is intended that the guidance in the 2007 guideline continue in force. Ed.

[1013] Legal Aid, Sentencing and Punishment of Offenders Act 2012 s 85(1) and (4) and Legal Aid, Sentencing and Punishment of Offenders Act 2012 (Commencement No 11) Order 2015 2015/504
[1014] Criminal Justice Act 2003 s 226A-226B as inserted by Legal Aid, Sentencing and Punishment of Offenders Act 2012 s 124
[1015] Sexual Offences Act 2003 s 103A as inserted by Anti-social Behaviour, Crime and Policing Act 2014 Sch 5 para 2 and Sexual Offences Act 2003 Sch 5
[1016] Sexual Offences Act 2003 s 84(1)(c) and (6)
[1017] Sexual Offences Act 2003 s 83 and Sch 3 para 18

330   Sex Offences: Historical
330.1
Sexual Offences Act 1956
> s 5 (unlawful sexual intercourse with a girl aged under 13)
> s 10 (incest by a man)
> s 12 (buggery)
> s 13 (Indecency between men)
> s 14 (indecent assault on a woman)
> s 15 (indecent assault on a man)

Indecency with Children Act 1960 s 1(1) (gross indecency with a child under 14 or 16 depending on the date of the offence)

Sexual Offences (Amendment) Act 2000 s 3 (Abuse of position of trust)

Modes of trial Buggery is triable only on indictment. The other seven offences listed above are triable either way.

Maximum sentences On indictment for offences committed during the following periods:

Sexual Offences Act 1956 s 5 Life (for the full offence).[1018] For an attempt, 2 years from 1 January 1957 to 1 June 1960[1019] and 7 years from 2 June 1960 to 30 April 2004.[1020]

Sexual Offences Act 1956 s 10 From 1 January 1957 to 30 April 2004, life if with a girl aged under 13, otherwise 7 years.

Sexual Offences Act 1956 s 12 From 1 January 1957 to 30 April 2004, life. Sexual Offences Act 1967 and Criminal Justice and Public Order Act 1994 s 143 made changes for adult partners (initially aged over 21 and then over 18) which are not listed.

Sexual Offences Act 1956 s 12 (attempt) From 1 January 1957 to 2 November 1994, 10 years. From 3 November 1994 to 30 April 2004, life.

Sexual Offences Act 1956 s 13 From 1 January 1957 to 30 April 2004, male defendant aged over 21 with another male under the age of consent, 5 years. Otherwise 2 years. The differing ages of consent are now not material as the CPS does not prosecute offences of consensual sex when both parties were aged over 16.

Sexual Offences Act 1956 s 14 From 1 January 1957 to 15 September 1985, 5 years when the victim was under 13 and 2 years otherwise.[1021] From 16 September 1985 to 30 April 2004, the penalty was 10 years irrespective of the victim's age.[1022]

Sexual Offences Act 1956 s 15 From 1 January 1957 to 30 April 2004, 10 years.[1023]

Indecency with Children Act 1960 s 1(1) From 2 July 1960 to 30 September 1997, 2 years (the victim had to be under 14 years old for it to be an offence).[1024] From 1 October 1997 to 10 January 2001, the penalty was 10 years.[1025] From 11 January 2001 to 30 April 2004, the victim had to be under 16 and the penalty remained at 10 years.[1026]

Sexual Offences (Amendment) Act 2000 s 3 (Abuse of position of trust) From 8 January 2001 to 30 April 2004, 5 years.

[1018] Sexual Offences Act 1956 Sch 2 para 1(2)(a)
[1019] Sexual Offences Act 1956 Sch 2 para 1(2)(b)
[1020] Indecency with Children Act 1960 s 2(3)(a)
[1021] Sexual Offences Act 1956 Sch 2 para 1(17)
[1022] Sexual Offences Act 1985 s 3(3)
[1023] Sexual Offences Act 1956 Sch 2 para 1(18)
[1024] Indecency with Children Act 1960 s 1(1)
[1025] Crime (Sentences) Act 1997 s 52
[1026] Criminal Justice and Court Services Act 2000 s 39

Summary maxima: For the triable either way offences the summary maxima were 6 months and/or a fine (from 17 September 1977, £1,000,[1027] from 1 May 1984, £2,000,[1028] from 1 October 1992, £5,000.[1029])

Buggery From 3 November 1994, non-consensual acts of buggery were defined as rape.[1030]

Consent Prosecutions for Sexual Offences Act 1956 s 10 (incest by a man) require the consent of the DPP, Sexual Offences Act 1956 Sch 2 Part 2 para 14, as amended by Criminal Law Act 1977 Sch 12.

Extended sentences Sexual Offences Act 1956 s 5 and 14-15, and Indecency with Children Act 1960 s 1(1) are listed in Criminal Justice Act 2003 Sch 15. The court may pass a 2012 extended sentence (EDS) if there is a significant risk of serious harm from future specified offences and either: a) the defendant has a Criminal Justice Act 2003 Sch 15B conviction (applicable only to defendants aged 18+), or b) the offence would justify a determinate sentence of at least 4 years.[1031]

Sexual Harm Prevention Orders For all the offences there is a discretionary power to make this order, when the notification criteria are present (see below) or when it is necessary to protect the public from sexual harm.[1032]

Notification For all offences, when the conditions are satisfied, the defendant must notify[1033] the police within three days (or three days from his or her release from imprisonment, hospital etc.) with his or her name, home address, National Insurance number etc. and any changes to those, and addresses where he or she resides for seven days[1034] (in one or more periods) or more in any 12-month period.[1035] The conditions are that a) in Sexual Offences Act 1956 s 12-15 cases, the victim/other party must have been under 18, b) in Sexual Offences Act 1956 s 10 and 12-13 and Sexual Offences (Amendment) Act 2000 s 3 cases the offender must be aged 20 or over and c) in Sexual Offences Act 1956 s 14-15 cases the offender must be sentenced to 30 months or more or admitted to a hospital subject to restrictions.

Children and vulnerable adults: barred lists For a) i) buggery and ii) indecency between men, b) when the other party is aged under 16 or did not consent and c) the defendant is aged 18 or over, the defendant is automatically barred from engaging in regulated activity with vulnerable adults and with children.[1036] For Sexual Offences Act 1956 s 10 offences, if a) the offence is committed against a child and b) the defendant is aged 18 or over he or she is automatically barred from engaging in regulated activity with vulnerable adults.[1037] For Sexual Offences Act 1956 s 10 offences, if a) the offence is committed against a child or the other party did not consent and b) the defendant is aged 18 or over he or she is automatically barred from engaging in regulated activity with children.[1038] For Sexual Offences (Amendment) Act 2000 s 3 offences, if the defendant is aged 18 or over he or she is automatically barred from engaging in regulated activity with children.[1039] For the other four offences, where the

---

[1027] Criminal Law Act 1977 s 28(7)
[1028] Criminal Justice Act 1982 s 37 as amended by Criminal Penalties etc. (Increase) Order 1984 1984/447 art 2(4) and Sch 4
[1029] Criminal Justice Act 1982 s 37
[1030] Criminal Justice and Public Order Act 1994 s 142
[1031] Criminal Justice Act 2003 s 226A-226B as inserted by Legal Aid, Sentencing and Punishment of Offenders Act 2012 s 124
[1032] Sexual Offences Act 2003 s 103A as inserted by Anti-social Behaviour, Crime and Policing Act 2014 Sch 5 para 2 and Sexual Offences Act 2003 Sch 5
[1033] Sexual Offences Act 2003 s 80(1)(a) and Sch 3 para 7, 8 and 11
[1034] Sexual Offences Act 2003 s 84(1)(c) and (6)
[1035] Sexual Offences Act 2003 s 83
[1036] Safeguarding Vulnerable Groups Act 2006 s 2 and Sch 3 and Safeguarding Vulnerable Groups Act 2006 (Prescribed Criteria and Miscellaneous Provisions) Regulations 2009 2009/37 regs 4 and 6 and Sch para 2 and 4
[1037] Safeguarding Vulnerable Groups Act 2006 s 2 and Sch 3 and Safeguarding Vulnerable Groups Act 2006 (Prescribed Criteria and Miscellaneous Provisions) Regulations 2009 2009/37 reg 6 and Sch para 4
[1038] Safeguarding Vulnerable Groups Act 2006 s 2 and Sch 3 and Safeguarding Vulnerable Groups Act 2006 (Prescribed Criteria and Miscellaneous Provisions) Regulations 2009 2009/37 reg 4 and Sch para 2
[1039] Safeguarding Vulnerable Groups Act 2006 s 2 and Sch 3 and Safeguarding Vulnerable Groups Act 2006 (Prescribed Criteria and Miscellaneous Provisions) Regulations 2009 2009/37 para 4 and Sch para 2

defendant is aged 18 or over he or she is automatically barred from engaging in regulated activity with vulnerable adults and with children.[1040] The judge must tell the defendant that the Disclosure and Barring Service will include him or her in the barred list(s).[1041] For all the offences, except the Sexual Offences Act 1956 s 5 child list, the defendant may ask the Service to remove him or her from the lists.

Guidelines Although the *Sexual Offences Guideline 2014* does not specifically apply to these historical and repealed offences, the Court of Appeal has decided that a 'measured reference to any definitive sentencing guideline' should be made, *R v H* 2011 EWCA Crim 2753, 2012 2 Cr App R (S) 21 (p 88), see **330.3**. Consequently the cases are divided into those decided before and those decided after the guideline.

Old cases: Sentencing has changed recently. No old cases are listed and old cases are best ignored.

Where the defendant is aged under 18 at the date of the offence, see also the **CHILDREN AND YOUNG OFFENDERS The age of the offender** section at **14.3** in Volume 1.

For the principles about offences which have been repealed, see the **DEFENDANT** *Historical cases Offences which have been repealed* para at **240.35**.

For cases where the maximum penalty has changed, see the **DEFENDANT** *Historical cases/Old cases Penalties change* para at **240.36**.

For cases where the release provisions change, see the **DEFENDANT** *Historical cases Release provisions change* para at **240.37**.

Note: There is a danger in using comparable cases in historical sex offence matters because: a) where the offending straddles statutory amendments to the maximum penalties, it is not always clear what the maximum sentence was for each offence, b) frequently, the abuse occurs against multiple victims, both under and over the age of 13, and c) frequently the abuse spans a period of time during which the maximum sentence may have been increased. Ed.

330.2   Sentencing Council guideline
Sexual Offences Guideline 2014 Annex B page 155, www.banksr.com Other Matters Guidelines tab. In force 1 April 2014. The guideline only applies to offenders aged 18+, see page 7 of the guideline. For the usual practice, see **66.21** in Volume 1.

Approach to sentencing historical sexual offences
When sentencing sexual offences under Sexual Offences Act 1956, or other legislation pre-dating Sexual Offences Act 2003, the court should apply the following principles:

1 The offender must be sentenced in accordance with the sentencing regime applicable at the date of sentence. Under Criminal Justice Act 2003[1042] the court must have regard to the statutory purposes of sentencing and must base the sentencing exercise on its assessment of the seriousness of the offence.

2 The sentence is limited to the maximum sentence available at the date of the commission of the offence. If the maximum sentence has been reduced, the lower maximum will be applicable.

3 The court should have regard to any applicable sentencing guidelines for equivalent offences under Sexual Offences Act 2003.

4 The seriousness of the offence, assessed by the culpability of the offender and the harm caused or intended, is the main consideration for the court. The court should not seek to establish the likely sentence had the offender been convicted shortly after the date of the offence.

5 When assessing the culpability of the offender, the court should have regard to relevant culpability factors set out in any applicable guideline.

[1040] Safeguarding Vulnerable Groups Act 2006 s 2 and Sch 3 and Safeguarding Vulnerable Groups Act 2006 (Prescribed Criteria and Miscellaneous Provisions) Regulations 2009 2009/37 regs 1, 4 and 6 and Sch para 2 and 4
[1041] Safeguarding Vulnerable Groups Act 2006 s 2 and Sch 3 para 25
[1042] *R v H and Others* 2011 EWCA Crim 2753, 2012 2 Cr App R(S) 21 (p 88)

6 The court must assess carefully the harm done to the victim based on the facts available to it, having regard to relevant harm factors set out in any applicable guideline. Consideration of the circumstances which brought the offence to light will be of importance.

7 The court must consider the relevance of the passage of time carefully as it has the potential to aggravate or mitigate the seriousness of the offence. It will be an aggravating factor where the offender has continued to commit sexual offences against the victim or others or has continued to prevent the victim reporting the offence.

8 Where there is an absence of further offending over a long period of time, especially combined with evidence of good character, this may be treated by the court as a mitigating factor. However, as with offences dealt with under Sexual Offences Act 2003, previous good character/exemplary conduct is different from having no previous convictions. The more serious the offence, the less the weight which should normally be attributed to this factor. Where previous good character/exemplary conduct has been used to facilitate the offence, this mitigation should not normally be allowed and such conduct may constitute an aggravating factor.

9 If the offender was very young and immature at the time of the offence, depending on the circumstances of the offence, this may be regarded as personal mitigation.

10 If the offender made admissions at the time of the offence that were not investigated this is likely to be regarded as personal mitigation. Even greater mitigation is available to the offender who reported himself to the police and/or made early admissions.

11 A reduction for an early guilty plea should be made in the usual manner.

330.3   *Historical abuse   Judicial guidance*

Att-Gen's Ref Nos 91, 119-120 of 2002 2003 EWCA Crim 5, 2 Cr App R (S) 55 (p 338) We accept the approach in *R v Millberry* 2002 EWCA Crim 2891, 2003 2 Cr App R (S) 31 (p 142). The fact that the offences are of some age is not necessarily a sufficient reason for imposing a lesser sentence than might otherwise have been the case. In *R v Millberry* the Court said at para 17: 'In "historic" cases where the offence is reported many years after it occurred and where the offender can be in his eighties at the time of the sentence, the same starting point should apply [as for recent activity]. The fact that the offences are stale can be taken into account but only to a limited extent. It is, after all, always open to an offender to admit the offences and the fact that they are not reported earlier is often explained because of the relationship between the offender and the victim, which is an aggravating factor of the offence. A different factor that could cause the court to take a more lenient view than it would otherwise is the consequences which result from the age of the offender. In these cases the experience is that the offender may be only a danger to members of the family with whom he has a relationship. So this is a dimension which can be taken into account if there is a reduced risk of reoffending'. The same approach is equally applicable to all categories of sexual offending. Where the victims have kept secret what had happened, sometimes following threats made or inducements offered and sometimes out of a sense of shame about what has been done to them, this of itself can aggravate the harm caused by the offence. Before passing a lighter sentence because the offences are stale, the court should weigh the impact on the victim of the matter having remained secret for so long.

R v H 2011 EWCA Crim 2753, 2012 2 Cr App R (S) 21 (p 88) LCJ para 28 When passing sentence, the court should reflect on all the facts, including events since the offence was committed, with, according to *R v Bird* 1987 9 Cr App R (S) 77, account to be taken of the defendant's subsequent positive good character. para 46 [Only] *R v Millberry* 2003, the definitive sentencing guideline, used in the measured way we suggest, and this guidance [should be used]. Reference to earlier decisions is unlikely to be helpful, and, dealing with it generally, to be discouraged. Subsequent decisions of this court which do not expressly state that they are intended to amend or amplify this guidance should be treated as fact-specific decisions, and therefore unlikely to be of assistance to courts.

The following considerations should be treated as guidance.

para 47 a) Sentence will be imposed at the date of the sentencing hearing, on the basis of the legislative provisions then current, and by measured reference to any definitive sentencing guidelines relevant to the situation revealed by the established facts.

b) Although sentence must be limited to the maximum sentence at the date when the offence was committed, it is wholly unrealistic to attempt an assessment of sentence by seeking to identify [at the date of sentence] what the sentence for the individual offence was likely to have been if the offence had come to light at or shortly after the date when it was committed. Similarly, if maximum sentences have been reduced, as in some instances, e.g. theft, they have, the more severe attitude to the offence in earlier years, even if it could be established, should not apply.

c) As always, the particular circumstances in which the offence was committed and its seriousness must be the main focus. Due allowance for the passage of time may be appropriate. The date may have a considerable bearing on the offender's culpability. If, for example, the offender was very young and immature at the time when the case was committed, that remains a continuing feature of the sentencing decision. Similarly if the allegations had come to light many years earlier, and when confronted with them, the defendant had admitted them, but for whatever reason, the complaint had not been drawn to the attention of, or investigated by, the police, or had been investigated and not then pursued to trial, these too would be relevant features.

d) In some cases it may be safe to assume that the fact that, notwithstanding the passage of years, the victim has chosen spontaneously to report what happened to him or her in his or her childhood or younger years would be an indication of continuing inner turmoil. However, the circumstances in which the facts come to light vary, and careful judgement of the harm done to the victim is always a critical feature of the sentencing decision. Simultaneously, equal care needs to be taken to assess the true extent of the defendant's criminality by reference to what he actually did and the circumstances in which he did it.

e) The passing of the years may demonstrate aggravating features if, for example, the defendant has continued to commit sexual crime or he represents a continuing risk to the public. On the other hand, mitigation may be found in an unblemished life over the years since the offences were committed, particularly if accompanied by evidence of positive good character.

f)[1043] Early admissions and a guilty plea are of particular importance in historical cases. Just because they relate to facts which are long past, the defendant will inevitably be tempted to lie his way out of the allegations. It is greatly to his credit if he makes early admissions. Even more powerful mitigation is available to the offender who, out of a sense of guilt and remorse, reports himself to the authorities. Considerations like these provide the victim with vindication, often a feature of great importance to them.

Note: Because of what was said at para 46, no earlier cases are listed, other than *R v Millberry* 2003. Ed.

R v Clifford 2014 EWCA Crim 2245, 2015 1 Cr App R (S) 32 (p 242) D was convicted of eight indecent assaults. Four young vulnerable victims, one of whom was under 16, were assaulted over a number of years. Some, under pretence of entry into show business, were made to remove clothing. The victims were groped and some were forced to masturbate D to ejaculation. D's actions had long-term adverse consequences. One also threatened to kill herself. D was aged 71 and of good character with some health difficulties, but he caused additional trauma to the victims by intentionally issuing press statements maintaining his innocence. The Judge observed that some of the offending would nowadays be charged as rape or assault by penetration. Held. What is required is that sentencing should reflect modern attitudes...in the course of which the court may take account of modern guidelines. The Judge was entitled to draw attention to the

---

[1043] This paragraph is listed as g) in the judgment, which is assumed to have been a typo. Ed.

gravity of this offending by modern standards, which are to be reflected if old offences such as these are sentenced in the present day. The Judge was entitled to structure his sentence by imposing consecutive sentences which would reflect overall criminality involved according to modern standards and attitudes. Moreover, the use of consecutive sentences was consistent with the Sentencing Council's guideline on totality. Great care needs to be taken by sentencing courts not to elevate denials, albeit vehement, into something deserving of further punishment in the absence of some more explicit traducing of the victim. The court, of course, is perfectly entitled to reflect these matters in withholding available mitigation since the offender has shown no sign of remorse-...but they should not have been used by way of positive aggravation.
For the basic position, see the **DEFENDANT** *Historical cases Basic approach* para at **240.33**.

Abuse of trust
330.4   *Abuse of trust*
Att-Gen's Ref No 28 of 2013 2013 EWCA Crim 1190 D pleaded (at different times) to seven indecent assaults and sexual activity with a child. The indecent assaults were committed between 1973 and 2004 and involved touching the leg and bottom and rubbing the vaginal area of various children aged between five and 12 years. Between 1996 and 2004 whilst he was the coach of a gymnastics and dance display team he touched the bottom and crotch of one of the girls who trained with his team. He was arrested in relation to these matters and subsequently a victim of his earlier offending reported other offences. Between 1970 and 1982, he was a gymnastics coach at a school and indecently assaulted girls on the gymnastics team. One of the earlier offences occurred at D's home. All victims were assaulted once, save for one who was assaulted twice. Victim impact statements revealed that some victims felt that their personal relationships had been affected and some still endure difficulties in trusting men. D, aged 66 at appeal, had health problems including a heart condition, depression and anxiety. Held. A permissible amount of credit would have been 30%. Each victim was spared the trauma of giving evidence. These offences were at the low end of offending and starting at 12 months, we are not inclined to disturb the 15 months on which the Judge settled, despite it being a lenient sentence. The question was whether the Judge properly suspended the sentence. With D's age, health, positive good character, the age of the offences and nature of the offences, **15 months suspended** was lenient, but not unduly so.
R v Folks 2013 EWCA Crim 1240 D pleaded (on the day of trial) to indecent assault on a male and attempted indecent assault on a male. D was a vicar in Ambleside, where V grew up. D gave V guitar lessons at D's home when V was aged about 13. Between 2003 and 2004, when V was aged around 15-16, the guitar lessons began to change in their nature, at D's instigation. They became more about physical exercise and D began to take an interest in V's physical appearance. D engaged in what he termed 'boy talk', commenting on V's physique and touching his pectoral and abdominal muscles in an inappropriate way. In interview he admitted that he had become sexually attracted to V. That was count 1. Count 2 occurred when, after a lesson, D asked V if he could see his penis. V reluctantly obliged but would not let D touch it when he asked to do so. V's parents stopped the lessons after D had written V a letter which implied that he wished V to come to live with him. V's parents noticed that around this time V had become aggressive and moody. V complained that D had been waiting for him at the bus stop. The incidents led V to leave home at the age of 16 and become estranged from his family for around ten years. D, aged 70 at appeal, had no previous convictions and many positive character references from the community which he had served. He was no longer a vicar. Held. The Judge was right that a custodial sentence was called for. There was a very serious breach of trust; he was trusted because of his position. He was trusted by V and V's parents. The *Sexual Offences Act 2003 Guideline 2008* Assault section

does not provide much assistance. The appropriate sentence could be calculated in two ways. First, starting at 12 months for count 2, a one-quarter reduction was appropriate to reflect that it was an attempt. There should be full credit for the plea. Alternatively, focusing on count 1, reduce the sentence by one third for the plea, then recognise the candour shown by D which led him to be charged. **6 months**, not 8, was appropriate.

Att-Gen's Ref No 38 of 2013 2013 EWCA Crim 1450 LCJ D pleaded to 14 counts of indecent assault. He was a well-known, popular and successful public figure through his TV and radio career. The offences occurred over a period of about 20 years, between 1967 and 1986, during which he indecently assaulted 13 female victims aged 9 to 17 years. D was aged between 38 and his mid-fifties when the offences were committed and was a figure of power and influence. The offences included touching under and over clothing, kissing and stroking but also the digital penetration of a 13-year-old and placing his hand on the thigh of a 9-year-old whilst she was in bed, then moving up towards her naked genitalia. The offences were committed in serious breaches of trust, often where the victims' parents had entrusted D to care for their children unsupervised. D provided alcohol to some victims and there was an element of planning in one of the offences, namely that he had prepared a bath on one occasion when three girls attended his house under the guise of receiving elocution lessons. D, aged 83 at appeal, had no convictions and had positive references. Held. D had got away with his offences for decades. The impact on the victims has been life-long. All of the offences were real assaults. There was no question of any of the victims consenting to anything. D's successful career provided no mitigation. On the contrary, it was the career that put him in a position of trust which he was then able to exploit. The last incident occurred in 1986 and no further offence has been recorded. D no longer presented a risk to children or young women and his age and level of infirmity were relevant to the sentencing decision, but must be approached with a degree of caution. Making every allowance that can be made for the mitigation, the sentence [of 15 months] was inadequate. Double jeopardy does not apply. **30 months** not 15.

Att-Gen's Ref No 36 of 2013 2013 EWCA Crim 2574 LCJ Artist and photographer. He kept asking young girls to wash his penis in the bath. **2 years 3 months**, see 330.15.

Att-Gen's Ref No 2 of 2014 2014 EWCA Crim 553 D was convicted of three specimen counts of buggery, one attempted buggery and two gross indecencies with a child. D was a kickboxing instructor who between 1987 and 1990 abused two sisters, V1 and V2. The girls hero-worshipped him. Kissing started on the pretext of passing sweets, when V1 was aged around 11 or 12. This progressed to vaginal sex and oral sex. Sometimes D tied her up when she was using a weight bench to build up her arms. Next, when V1 was aged 13, he made promises to take her round the world. He then penetrated her anally. V2, who was two years older than V1, was taught kickboxing by D starting when she was 9 or 10. He also kissed her using the sweet trick. After she was aged 14, D digitally penetrated V2 and she performed oral sex on D. When she was aged 15, there was vaginal sex when V2 was tied to a bed and on one occasion D tried to anally penetrate her. It hurt V2 and she asked him to stop. The conduct stopped when she was aged 17. D was aged 55 at appeal with no convictions. The prosecution accepted there was no force used and (putting aside their ages) they agreed to the activity. The factors the prosecution relied on were the grave breach of trust, the grooming, the period over which the offending occurred and the considerable long-lasting harm done. Held. This was very serious and sustained offending. We apply the *Sexual Offences Act 2003 Guideline 2008* section 9 guideline (sexual activity with a child) because of the obscure circumstances. The girls were in no position to consent. The sentences relating to each girl are to be consecutive. **10 years** not 4½ in total. It could have been longer without complaint.

See also: *R v Moss* 2012 EWCA Crim 528 (Pleas to multiple specimen sexual offences. Between 1979 and 1993, when aged between 14 and 28, he sexually abused five of his nieces and nephews. Victims aged 5-10. Masturbation, simulated intercourse and sexual assault. Breach of trust (babysitting). Committed for sexual gratification. He bribed or threatened the victims. Had long-standing partner and two children. Risk of similar offences was relatively low. **4½ years** not 7.)

R v Islam 2013 EWCA Crim 2355 (Convicted of numerous indecent assaults committed between the 1970s and 1990s. He was a doctor and the victims were six female patients aged 13 to mid-20s and one practice nurse. Put penis in patient's mouth and ejaculated. Previous good character. **11 years** was severe but not manifestly excessive. For more details see **18.30** in Volume 1.)

Post-2012 guideline case

R v Kerr 2015 EWCA Crim 1234 D, a teacher, was convicted of three indecent assaults committed between 1999 and 2002 or 2003. Two were against his pupils. D was highly regarded and popular. He was an enthusiastic supporter of extracurricular activity. In 1999, following an allegation of sexual misconduct which was not sustained, D was warned not to invite pupils unaccompanied to his home. He developed a particularly close relationship with V1, who had personal difficulties at home. They would share a shower together naked. V1 found this uncomfortable. When V1 was aged 15 or 16 he complained of some muscle pain. D took V1 to his home and put V1 on a bed and massaged his back. Next he pulled down his lower clothing and massaged his naked buttocks and touched his anus for about five seconds without penetrating it. V1 said he did not want to be touched there and D stopped. On the pretext of helping him with a bad exam mark, D invited V2, aged 17, to his home. They played squash and showered naked afterwards. Next, D took him to a pub and bought him two pints and drove V2 to his home. V2 complained of pain from the squash game, and D said he would give V2 a massage. D rubbed V2's back with oil for five minutes and then pulled D's trunks down exposing his bottom. D told V2 to close his eyes and turned him over and massaged his penis for 30 seconds. V2 then left. V2 complained and D resigned as a teacher. Other pupils disapproved because they had lost a popular teacher. V3, aged 17, was openly gay and was not a pupil of D. He declined to shower with D. D called him to his office to ask why. Later he asked V3 to have a coffee in his house. There he tried to kiss V3. V3 said he was not going to kiss D. D said it was acceptable and tried to hug and kiss him. V3 resisted. D was aged 53, with no convictions. V1 and V2's victim impact statements focused on the stress of the trial. Held. There was obviously a clear breach of trust. For the offences involving V2, there had been planning and the supply of alcohol. There was high culpability. The offences involving V1 and V2 were Category 2A, so 2½ years (V1) and 2 years (V2). The offence involving V3 was Category 3 (6 months). The Judge was entitled to make the sentences consecutive, making **5 years** in all not 7.

Buggery/anal rape

330.5   *Crown Court statistics   England and Wales*

Buggery 21+

Year	Plea	Total sentenced	Type of sentencing %						Average length of custody in months
			Dis-charge	Fine	Commu-nity sentence	Sus-pended sentence	Custody	Other	
2013	G	21	–	–	–	–	100	–	110
	NG	30	–	–	–	–	100	–	110.5
2014	G	19	–	–	5	–	95	–	97.2
	NG	30	–	–	–	–	100	–	133.9

Warning: There is a danger in using comparable cases in historical sex offence matters because: a) since the end of 2013 the sentences have increased markedly, b) the maximum penalties increased for indecent assault in 1985 and 2004, c) it is not always clear how the sentences were structured, and d) the frequency of the abuse is sometimes hard to determine from the judgments. Ed.

330.6   *Buggery/anal rape   Cases*
Pre-2014 guideline cases
R v S 2014 EWCA Crim 272 D pleaded (in the same month as his retrial was due to start) to buggery (×2). In 1977, D was aged 17 and V, D's cousin, was aged 8. D began an apprenticeship and would frequently visit his aunt's house while his aunt and uncle were out at work. While he was there, D would take V upstairs and penetrate him until ejaculation. He then used V's underwear to wipe both of them. Thereafter relationships remained on an outwardly friendly basis. There was frequent contact over the ensuing years and there were 'happy' photographs of the two together. In 2010, V suffered flashbacks and mood swings. After seeing a social worker, V confronted D whilst wearing a recording device. A confession followed, including an indication that D had suffered far worse at the hands of others before he himself was brought to the UK from India. D offered an apology and agreed to see a social worker. There was some discussion as to whether sums of money should be paid to a reputable charity in addition to a full letter of apology in order for the matter to be finally dealt with. D was unable to pay the sum of money and things developed such that the police were involved and D was arrested. There was a trial but the prosecution decided the tape should be analysed and the trial was stopped. The Judge ordered a retrial. In the pre-sentence report, D accepted that V was vulnerable and unable to forget the experiences. He only then realised the full impact of his actions. D suffered from depression and was taking medication. There were over 100 character references of a universally high character. Held. The sentencing exercise was extraordinarily difficult. The Judge noted this was not a case of experimentation and, at the time, D was twice V's age. The Judge correctly identified the starting point was around 15 years. D had spent the intervening 35/36 years in an exemplary way, was a happy family man, and had contributed hugely to the community. These were objectively atrocious acts. There were sufficient exceptional circumstances to take the sentence well below the guidelines. The appropriate starting point was 6½ years on each count, concurrent so with the plea, **6 years** not 9½.
Att-Gen's Ref No 2 of 2014 2014 EWCA Crim 553 D was convicted of three specimen counts of buggery, one attempted buggery and two gross indecencies with a child. D was a kickboxing instructor who between 1987 and 1990 abused two sisters, V1 and V2. The girls hero-worshipped him. Kissing started on the pretext of passing sweets, when V1 was aged around 11 or 12. This progressed to vaginal sex and oral sex. Sometimes D tied her up when she was using a weight bench to build up her arms. Next, when V1 was aged 13, he made promises to take her round the world. He then penetrated her anally. V2, who was two years older than V1, was taught kickboxing by D starting when she was 9 or 10. He also kissed her using the sweet trick. After she was aged 14, D digitally penetrated V2 and she performed oral sex on D. When she was aged 15, there was vaginal sex when V2 was tied to a bed and on one occasion D tried to anally penetrate her. It hurt V2 and she asked him to stop. The conduct stopped when she was aged 17. D was aged 55 at appeal with no convictions. The prosecution accepted there was no force used and (putting aside their ages) they agreed to the activity. The factors the prosecution relied on were the grave breach of trust, the grooming, the period over which the offending occurred and the considerable long-lasting harm done. Held. This was very serious and sustained offending. We apply the *Sexual Offences Act 2003 Guideline 2008* section 9 guideline (sexual activity with a child) because of the obscure circumstances. The girls were in no position to consent. The sentences relating to each girl are to be consecutive. **10 years** not 4½ in total. It could have been longer without complaint.
See also: *R v G* 2014 EWCA Crim 1221 (LCJ D Convicted of rape and other sex offences. Main victims were a boy aged 15-17 and wife. Boy repeatedly raped over two years. Wife raped on number of occasions which hurt her and made her cry. Former Chief Superintendent. Aged 64. Good character. **20 years** not life with a 12-year minimum term.)
Note: Buggery is not an offence that is specifically dealt with in the new *Sexual Offences Guideline 2014*. However, the offence is very similar to rape and from 1994

non-consensual buggery is prosecuted as rape. Judges will inevitably consider the rape guideline when considering this offence as *R v H* 2011 EWCA Crim 2753, 2012 2 Cr App R (S) 21 (p 88) says that judges should consider the modern penalty. The guidelines are at **317.4**.

Post-2014 guideline case

Att-Gen's Ref No 44 of 2015 2015 EWCA Crim 1330 D was convicted of four specimen counts of buggery, four rapes, seven indecent assaults/indecency counts/sexual assaults and ABH. D had a relationship with W since she was aged 15. He married her and W said he had a violent temper and was excessively controlling. She was afraid of him. Between 1982 and 1985, when he was aged 15-18, he encouraged his nephew, N, to masturbate him. This led to touching of N's penis, oral sex and after gifts, anal rape of N. N was then aged between 9 and 12. N treated D like an uncle. D made threats that if N told anyone, D would kill him. N didn't report the abuse because he thought D was a violent man. In about 2004, when D's daughter, M, was aged about 9, D demanded she took an ashtray to his bedroom. When she did, he got out of bed naked and seized her. He forced her to suck his penis and then undressed her. Next he forced her onto his bed and raped her. M was told not to tell anyone. When M was between 10 and 13, D would touch her breasts, which was dealt with by one specimen count. When S, another daughter, was aged between 13 and 15, he touched her breasts and genitals. It happened about once a month. On an unknown date, he raped W. She cried during the rape and it lasted 25 minutes. In 2014, he anally raped W. Also in 2014, S intervened in an argument and D hit her with his fist or hand. It caused bruising over a large area of S's cheek. That led her school to report the matter to the police. In interview, D made denials of all matters. He was now aged 48 with one trifling conviction. He had had a heart attack and there were indications he had been abused as a child. The pre-sentence report said D had a complete lack of insight into what he had done and was preoccupied with his sexual gratification. The risk of serious harm to family members and others was high. N had experienced significant psychological harm. He had attempted suicide and had become an alcoholic and drug user. The police considered the victims as part of a travelling community who found it difficult to talk to the authorities. The Judge was misled into believing the maximum for the historic buggery counts was only one year. Held. Bearing in mind his age when N was abused, the least sentence that can be imposed is **20 years** not 16.

Sexual intercourse

For rape see the **RAPE AND ASSAULT BY PENETRATION** chapter.

330.7   Unlawful sexual intercourse   Defendant then aged 21+   Pre-2014 guideline case

R v BM 2010 EWCA Crim 1454, 2011 1 Cr App R (S) 34 (p 214) D pleaded to unlawful sexual intercourse under Sexual Offences Act 1956. Six rapes and another offence were allowed to lie on the file. The offence occurred between 1984 and 1985. The victim, V, was 12 years old at the time. D, who would have been about 40 years of age at the material time, was a teacher of music at V's school. D gave V attention at school. He took her on a shopping trip to Nottingham. Because of the trust which had built up between her and D and with V's parents, permission was given. After the shopping D took V back to his house, and in the bedroom they had full sexual intercourse. No words were spoken. She could not recall whether he ejaculated. She did not resist, and she never told him to stop. In 2007 D had pleaded to an offence of sexual assault upon another child, and a number of counts of making and possessing indecent photographs of children.[1044] A report of this was published in a local newspaper. V then made her complaint. By this time D was aged 65 years and had generalised osteoarthritis of his joints and the spine with limited mobility. He had suffered three strokes, was wheelchair-bound and was incontinent of urine. The Judge felt a starting point after a trial would

---

[1044] The sentence is not revealed in the report.

have been 8 years. He considered D's health, and that the offence would have today been charged as rape of a child under 13. Held. That was an incorrect approach. We observe that the offence of unlawful sexual intercourse in SOA 1956 was a different offence from the offence of rape of a child under 13 within the current Act. Considering the relevant case law, **3 years** not 6.

Incest

330.8   *Incest*

R v GB 2015 EWCA Crim 1501, 2016 1 Cr App R (S) 17 (p 127) D pleaded (full credit) to incest and two indecent assaults. D was now aged 68. When he was a child he lived with his parents, his sister, V and two younger siblings. All six slept in the same bedroom. V was 15 months younger than D. When D was aged 14 and V aged 13, D would touch V between her legs under her bedsheets. He would also digitally penetrate her. This lasted for six months and ended when the family moved house and V was given her own bedroom. Subsequently when D was aged 15 and V aged 14, he came home from work and went to V's bedroom. He told her to lie on her side and told her not to make a sound. He had vaginal sex with her but did not ejaculate. When he had finished he gave her a £1 note. V had a troubled adult life. She suffered from depression and self-harmed and made two attempts to kill herself. She blamed D for the breakdown of all three of her marriages. In 2008, V confronted D about the incidents and recorded admissions and an apology by him. D was of positive good character and had nine letters of support from his family including V's daughter, whom he had looked after at V's request when V was aged 18. D has supported the whole family financially including V. He paid for one of her weddings and took her on family holidays. Held. The maximum sentence for incest at the time was 7 years and the maximum for the assaults was 2 years. The modern equivalent offences would be Sexual Offences Act 2003 s 25 (sexual activity with a child family member). The current guideline provides a starting point of 18 months' DTO when there is penetration. In cases where there are no aggravating factors the starting point is a community order. The guideline also states that for younger offenders, that is those aged under 17, a court should consider a lower starting point because of the offender's age and lack of maturity. There were no aggravating factors here and the disparity in age was small.

D is not being sentenced as a 15-year old youth. It is necessarily artificial for a court to put itself directly into the position of [sentencing him as if he was]. The court must do its best. Today a 15-year-old offender might receive a non-custodial sentence. D had not contributed to the delay [by threats etc.]. He had lived an honest and industrious life for 50 years. He had been of considerable assistance to his family. He is remorseful. We do not overlook the harm suffered by V, but an immediate custodial sentence was wrong in principle. Because D had served 11 weeks, we substitute a community order with a one-week residential condition.

Note: The Court did not say it had factored in the early acceptance of guilt and the full plea discount, which would be a significant factor. Ed.

Digital/oral penetration

330.9   *Digital/oral penetration   Victim(s) aged under 10   Fathers/Stepfathers etc.*
Example: *Att-Gen's Ref No 104 of 2011* 2012 EWCA Crim 366 (Convicted of sexual and cruelty offences against his daughters in 1967-1980. Indecent assault on a girl under 13 and indecency with a child. Aged 7-12. He digitally penetrated them, and forced them to masturbate him to ejaculation. He forced one daughter to perform oral sex. No remorse. Aged 70. No relevant convictions. **11 years** in total not 5½.)

Post-2014 guideline cases
Att-Gen's Ref No 53 of 2014 2014 EWCA Crim 1929[1045] D was convicted of two indecent assaults and indecency with a child. The offences occurred in 1991 against a backdrop of

---

[1045] There are two Att-Gen's Refs No 53 of 2014. They are different cases. The other is 2014 EWCA Crim 2262.

persistent regular violence towards both children of D's then partner. V was aged 7 and her brother aged 10. They both saw D as a stepfather figure. D confronted V when she was on the toilet. D slapped V's head and told her to kneel and close her eyes. He then placed his penis in her mouth, instructing her to suck it. When she did not, he hit her again. A few minutes later, D told V to bend over. He then touched V's stomach, waist and vagina, going on to insert his fingers. He also struck her bottom and threatened to kill V if she told anyone. Sometime later in 1991, in similar circumstances to the first assault, D told V to kneel and kiss his penis. She refused and was hit. The assault ended when V's mother called from downstairs. V complained to police in 1999, but withdrew her evidence when D resumed the relationship with V's mother. The offences considerably affected V and she had left school and suffered panic attacks continuing into adulthood. D's denial persisted throughout. D was now aged 48 and had several convictions. He pleaded in 1991 to ABH against V and assault against her brother but had only had a caution since. D had a back problem, bipolar disorder, depression and anxiety. D's references were positive, especially of his behaviour since 1991. The Judge, although aware of *R v H* 2011 EWCA Crim 2753, 2012 2 Cr App R (S) 21 (p 88), was reluctant to transpose these offences into their modern-day equivalents. Held. V was cowed by a background of bullying and violence and today [the penetration] would be rape. Offences under Sexual Offences Act 2003 s 7 and 9 contain factors in the guideline capable of encompassing the sort of conduct in this case. But the court should also have regard to factors which are in play when more serious offences of rape and assault by penetration on a child under 13 are considered. The approach should be to look at relevant guidelines in the round and make adjustments for the change in sentencing levels. **7 years** in all, not 4.

R v JW and KW 2015 EWCA Crim 572 D was convicted of three indecent assaults, four gross indecency offences, two watching sex act offences, one engaging in sexual activity, two sexual assaults, two cruelty offences and an ABH. The offences took place between 1988 and 2013 against his children and grandchildren. When V1 was aged about 6, D and another pinned him to a bed, took down his trousers, squirted washing up liquid over his anus and inserted the tip of the bottle into the anus. V1 felt that he had been cut. When N was aged between 5 and 13, D showed him pornographic films, while D masturbated in the presence of V1 and other children. When V1 was aged 10-11, D told his wife, K, to remove her lower clothing and told V1 to lick K's vagina. V1, when aged between 11 and 13, watched D and K engaging in sexual conduct. D tickled and kissed V2, who was aged 8 to 9. D also rubbed her knicker area. D slapped, punched and pushed V2 when she was aged 10. When V2 was aged 17, D punched and kicked her when she was on the ground, causing bleeding. D threw hot coffee over V3 when he was aged between 6 and 12. D went into V3's bedroom and touched his visible erect penis in front of V3. This action was repeated when V3 was a little older. The other offences were similar. V1 went on to commit the most appalling series of sexual offences, for which he was given life. The Judge said: a) D was without moral purpose, b) he never cared or loved or disciplined V1, and c) the impact on the children and grandchildren was catastrophic with extreme psychological harm. **15 years** in all, not 19.

330.10   *Digital/oral penetration   Victim(s) aged under 10   Defendant then under 16   Post-2014 guideline cases*

R v GM 2014 EWCA Crim 2403 D pleaded to four counts under Indecency with Children Act 1960. D, when aged 13 or 14, made his two younger sisters, V1 and V2, either touch his penis or put it in their mouth. V1 was then aged 3 or 4 and V2 was then aged 5 or 6. At the time, D was a victim of serious sexual abuse by an adult male. The girls at the time told their mother, who contacted social services. D made admissions. When aged 15, D was taken into care. Police on the [then state of the law for prosecuting sex abuse] decided to take no action. Also at that time D was ready to give evidence against his abuser, who then pleaded. D, now aged 28 and a heroin addict, had an appalling record but no sex offences. Held. Offences of this nature attract immediate and substantial custody in almost every circumstance. These facts were extraordinary. **18 months suspended**, not immediate.)

Note: It can be inferred that one reason why D, a sexually abused 13-year-old, was not charged was his welfare. The decision then to charge him 13 years later is open to question. Ed.

R v MW 2014 EWCA Crim 2668 D was convicted of indecent assault. When he was aged between 15 and 17 he put his penis in V's mouth. She was his half-sister and was aged between 8 and 10. It was a single incident. V said the incident had blighted and ruined her life. She had fled the family home. The Judge treated D as aged 15. D was now aged 51 and in the 35 years since the offence he had committed no offence and had consistently been in employment. He had glowing references. D's upbringing had been very austere and the household had verbal and physical violence. **15 months** not 2 years.

R v CG 2015 EWCA Crim 316 D was convicted of three indecent assaults dating from when V was aged between 7 and 9 and D was aged between 11 and 13. The counts involved two occasions when V sucked D's penis and one occasion when D put his penis between V's legs. He started with a dare, which required V to kiss D or his friend. The dares escalated to digital penetration and other forms of sexual touching. V reported these matters when D was aged 19. He was now aged 29 and was serving a 14-year extended sentence for a section 18 wounding. He had no sex convictions. The Judge decided the case was in Category 1A and made the sentence consecutive to that sentence. Held. There is something slightly repugnant about sentencing an adult for offences committed when he was a child or young teenager. The maximum D could have received at the Youth Court if prosecuted [at the time] was 2 years. That is not conclusive but we take it into account. **2 years** not 4.

330.11   *Digital/oral penetration   Victim(s) aged under 10   Defendant then aged 16-20*

Example: *R v C* 2013 EWCA Crim 445 (Convicted of 12 indecent assaults and two indecencies with a child. Systematically abused younger sister aged 9-13 between 1980 and 1983. He was aged 19-23. Masturbated in front of her. Digitally penetrated her vagina. Put his penis in her mouth. **7 years** not 9.)

Post-2014 guideline case

Att-Gen's Ref No 57 of 2015 2015 EWCA Crim 1762 D was convicted of two indecent assaults and two indecencies with a child. When aged 20 or 21 he lived opposite V, aged 7 or 8. When babysitting V, D played what he called a game which ended with both of them fully naked. They touched each other's penises. Later, with V's mother's permission, D took V to an isolated wooded area. D produced his erect penis and made V masturbate him. At the same time D touched V's penis and told V to kiss it and to open his mouth. He held V's head back and put his penis in V's mouth and thrust it back and forth. The impact on V was lasting and severe. He suffered with depression and suicidal thoughts. Recently V visited D and assaulted him. D was now aged 48 and had previous convictions including arson, which was the only one for which he was given custody. There were none after 1991 and no sexual convictions. D was injured in a motorcycle accident and was on disability benefits. Held. We consider the modern appropriate guideline would be the *Sexual Offences Guideline 2014* (sexual assault of a child under 13 section). With the severe psychological harm the case would be in Category 1A. The last count was aggravated by the breach of trust, the victim's age was significantly below 13, the isolated location and that D ejaculated. The lack of later sex offending and D's personal difficulties were mitigation. **5 years** was indeed lenient but not unduly lenient.

330.12   *Digital/oral penetration   Victim(s) aged under 10   Defendant then aged 21+*

Att-Gen's Ref No 38 of 2013 2013 EWCA Crim 1450 LCJ D pleaded to 14 counts of indecent assault. He was a well-known, popular and successful public figure through his

TV and radio career. The offences occurred over a period of about 20 years, between 1967 and 1986, during which he indecently assaulted 13 female victims aged 9 to 17. D was aged between 38 and his mid-fifties when the offences were committed and was a figure of power and influence. The offences included touching under and over clothing, kissing and stroking but also the digital penetration of a 13-year-old and placing his hand on the thigh of a 9-year-old whilst she was in bed, then moving up towards her naked genitalia. The offences were committed in serious breaches of trust, often where the victims' parents had entrusted D to care for their children unsupervised. D provided alcohol to some victims and there was an element of planning in one of the offences, namely that he had prepared a bath on one occasion when three girls attended his house under the guise of receiving elocution lessons. D, aged 83 at appeal, had no convictions and had positive references. Held. D had got away with his offences for decades. The impact on the victims has been life-long. All of the offences were real assaults. There was no question of any of the victims consenting to anything. D's successful career provided no mitigation. On the contrary, it was the career that put him in a position of trust which he was then able to exploit. The last incident occurred in 1986 and no further offence has been recorded. D no longer presented a risk to children or young women and his age and level of infirmity were relevant to the sentencing decision, but must be approached with a degree of caution. Making every allowance that can be made for the mitigation, the sentence [of 15 months] was inadequate. Double jeopardy does not apply. **30 months** not 15.

Att-Gen's Ref No 26 of 2013 2013 EWCA Crim 1137 D pleaded (full discount) to five counts of indecent assault (at least one was a specimen count). D, who was aged 50 at appeal, had ten years previously abused his 7-year-old niece, V. D lived with his mother. V visited them. Over a period of one to two months D: a) placed his hands in V's underwear leading to digital penetration on five occasions, b) rubbed his penis over her clothing, and c) kissed V. The abuse ended when V refused to go into a bedroom with D and she was overheard by a friend. D made full admissions. He had convictions for theft, burglary and driving with excess alcohol. The pre-sentence report said a custodial sentence would not address the issues and suggested a community order. This was imposed because the Judge considered that sentence provided better protection for children. Held. That approach was commendable but it failed to take account of the very serious impact this offending had on V. The very least sentence that could be imposed is **3 years**.

R v G 2014 EWCA Crim 393 D was convicted of four indecent assaults. V1 and V2 were sisters. V3 was their cousin. All three were nieces of D's wife. Between 1987 and 1994, when the victims were aged 8 and 11 and D was aged around 30, the victims used to visit D. Over that period, D gave each victim rides on a fork-lift truck and on a lawn mower, sitting on his lap. He would touch their vaginas and, in many instances, penetrate them with his finger. There were similar episodes in the garden shed in respect of V1, and in the house in respect of V3. There were also incidents of sexual assault where D touched V3 over clothing. D was aged 55 on appeal. In February 1991, he had been cautioned for an assault on V1. He had put his hand inside her knickers and touched her vagina. D still protested his innocence to the writer of the pre-sentence report. Held. There were a large number of glowing testimonials attesting to D's positive good character and he had not offended since 1993. A just and proportionate sentence was **8 years**, not 10.

Post-2014 guideline case

R v P 2015 EWCA Crim 1320 D was convicted of six specimen indecent assaults. Between 1983 and 1986, D was a close friend of V's father and was a regular visitor. V was aged between 8 and 10. Once a week, while V's mother was preparing the evening meal, D and V would play fight and then D would push V against a sofa and touch and digitally penetrate her vagina under her clothes. This stopped when V went to secondary school. V was never threatened. She was, however, adversely affected and later had difficulties in forming relationships. D was now aged 70 and of good character. There were five character witnesses. The pre-sentence report said he presented a low risk of offending and recommended a non-custodial penalty. The Judge described him as an unofficial uncle. Held. There was devastating long-term impact for V. The Judge should have given more weight to D's good character and that there was no offending for 30 years. **8 years** in all not 10.

Att-Gen's Ref No 75 of 2015 2015 EWCA Crim 2116 D was convicted of three counts of indecent assault. The first two were for specific offences. The last was representative of a substantial course of conduct. D lived with V's mother. Between early 2000 and late 2003, when V was aged between 5 and 9 and D was aged between 29 and 33, he made V perform oral sex on him and on every occasion made V swallow the ejaculate. The offending was 'continuous' and took place when V's mother was out and either in D's bed or in his living room. V was told if she did not comply with the demands, she would never see her mother again and V would go to prison. On occasions D bribed her. V believed the threats and was frightened of D. It happened so regularly V thought it was normal. In 2013, when V was at university, she went to the police. V suffered from persistent nightmares as a child. When aged 16 she was diagnosed with depression and has taken anti-depressant medication ever since. She has very low self-esteem and has self-harmed. In 2014, she suffered severe anxiety attacks. V felt that the abuse she had suffered had affected her education, her employment, her ability to sustain personal relationships and her ability to trust people. Her anxiety etc. about D's trial caused her to resign her employment. D was now aged 45 with a good work record and had no previous convictions. He cared for his disabled elderly parents. Held. V was particularly vulnerable and has suffered significant psychological harm. The offending was an abuse of trust and was compounded by threats. D showed no remorse. The ongoing psychological consequences for this victim are severe. [Because of the change in the law], the relevant section of the *Sexual Offences Act 2003 Guideline 2008* is not the rape of a child under 13 section but the causing a child under 13 to engage in sexual activity with a child section. The offending would be in Category 2A with a starting point of 8 years. The lowest suitable sentence is **14 years**. The Judge should not have felt restricted by the 10-year maximum for the offence. We keep the specimen count at 9 years but make the other two offences 5 years consecutive.

See also: *R v C* 2014 EWCA Crim 2607 (Pleas (full credit) 12 specimen counts with five different granddaughters or stepgranddaughters. Over 10 years when girls aged 5 to 11. Two fingers in vagina. Penis against body in swimming pool. Now aged 68. Good character and good work record. We start in the region of 18 years not 22, making with age and plea **11 years**.)

330.13   *Digital/oral penetration   Victim(s) aged 10-12   Defendant then aged 21+*
R v AD 2013 EWCA Crim 1017 D pleaded (25%) to three indecent assault counts and two other sex offences, each with a maximum of 2 years. The counts were specimen counts against his niece, V. He admitted: a) five digital penetrations when V was aged 12 and 13, b) penal oral penetration on seven occasions when V was aged 12 or 13, and c) placing his erect penis against V's naked vagina when she was aged 13. V said she had changed from a studious, happy-go-lucky girl to someone who started to 'disregard and hate [people]'. She found relationships very difficult. She self-abused and had physical fights. She tried to numb the pain with cannabis. She told her mother when she was aged 25 and then, after the strain on the two families, had a breakdown. D was aged 68 at appeal, with no convictions or cautions and with references. The Judge found a gross abuse of trust and planning, and further that he could not use consecutive sentences to subvert the statutory maximums. For two indecent assaults he received 18 months. He received 9 months for two other counts and 6 months for the third indecent assault. The sentences were made consecutive making **5 years** in all. Held. It was open to the Judge to impose consecutive sentences. He provided an appropriate balance between the competing factors. The sentence was not manifestly excessive.

Post-2014 guideline
Att-Gen's Ref No 72 of 2014 2014 EWCA Crim 2003 D was convicted of five specimen indecent assault counts. D was V's stepgrandfather and V was between the ages of 11

and 16. D had always been physically affectionate towards V but on one occasion, when V was aged 11, D put her on his knee and, placing his hand inside her knickers, D digitally penetrated V, hurting her. Afterwards, D asked V whether she had been "enjoying it". On another occasion, D stroked V's genitalia and penetrated her, pretending to be affectionate. There were nine or ten incidents of abuse, with some occurring when V's family was present but D would disguise his actions, for example, by using a cushion. On the final occasion, D was babysitting V and stroked her under her bedclothes and at some point, either then or on a separate occasion, exposed his penis to her. D was aged 67 on appeal and was of good character, but expressed no remorse. V felt that her childhood had ended when D began the abuse and she had become shy and wary of contact with males. Held. **6 years**, not 3½ concurrent.

Att-Gen's Ref No 52 of 2015 2015 EWCA Crim 1581 D pleaded on the day his trial was listed to seven indecent assaults and four indecency counts. When D was aged between 25 and 30, he abused his sister, V1, who was then aged between 11 and 15. On five occasions, once in each year, D digitally abused V1. On two occasions, when she was aged 13 and 15, he rubbed his erect penis on her vagina. He also asked his brother, V2, who was V1's twin, aged 11, to perform oral sex on him. V2 refused in vehement terms and ran off. D was then married with children. D was now aged 68. After the offending ceased he did not offend again. D had some health problems. The trial process was delayed and this was very stressful to the victims. Held. There were no threats of violence or force. V2 was not touched. The victims were vulnerable. In some cases D was brought to ejaculation. The starting point should have been at least 6 years. 10% credit makes 5 years 4 months. Because D had complied with his supervision we make it 5 years.

See also: *R v W* 2015 EWCA Crim 569 (Plea. Plea discounts, full and 25%. Three indecent assaults. Two sexual activity with a child counts. Sexually abused four boys aged between 11 and 15 over 15 years. Oral sex. No complaints. Evidence in photos. 13 indecent photograph counts. Four other child sex offences. A perverting the course of justice count for destroying a hard drive with photos on it. D now aged 49. **8 years** not 11 years 8 months.)

330.14   *Digital/oral penetration   Victim(s) aged 13-15   Defendant then aged 21+* Pre-2014 guideline case

Example: *R v Islam* 2013 EWCA Crim 2355 (Convicted of numerous indecent assaults committed between the 1970s and 1990s. He was a doctor and the victims were six female patients aged 13 to mid-twenties and one practice nurse. Put penis in patient's mouth and ejaculated. Previous good character. **11 years** was severe but not manifestly excessive. For more details see **18.30** in Volume 1.)

Physical non-penetrative contact

330.15   *Physical non-penetrative contact   Victim(s) aged under 10   Defendant then aged 16-20   Pre-2014 guideline cases*

R v Fenton 2013 EWCA Crim 1619 D was convicted of four indecent assaults. When aged between 15 and 18, D masturbated V1, who was aged between 7 and 9. D also simulated sexual intercourse with V1 and rubbed their penises together. Later V1 tried to commit suicide. When aged between 17 and 19, D abused V2, aged 8-10. D put his hand on V2's penis and also forced V2 to put his penis in his mouth for 20-30 seconds. D was aged 28 at appeal and was affected by physical and mental difficulties. They were hydrocephalus from birth, mild cerebral palsy, a cranial fossa arachnoid cyst and some signs of cerebral atrophy. He had no convictions. A probation officer considered when he committed the offences he was functioning at an age of between 10 and 14 years. At the time of the offences he was experiencing increased sexual feelings after frequent periods in hospital. D had, however, worked at Morrisons for 10 years and had been promoted. Held. **2 years** not 4 was appropriate.

R v MS 2013 EWCA Crim 1960 D pleaded (20% credit) to eight specimen counts of indecent assault (maximum 10 years). At the time of the offending the victims were aged about 12, 4, and 9 or 10. D was aged 13 or 14 to 16 or 17 at the time of the offences and was aged 28 at appeal. Held. These were nasty and shocking offences. The activity was touching the victims' breasts and vaginas under their clothing, and using their hands to masturbate him. D's basis of plea stated that there was no licking. There was undisputed evidence that on occasions he masturbated himself to ejaculation in front of them. The victim impact statements gave vivid descriptions of the damage caused. D had no convictions and showed remorse. He was bullied at school and suffered violence at home. Held. The passage of time between the offence and the sentence cannot have the result of increasing the penalty he now faces. The maximum then was a 2-year DTO. Starting at 2 years with plea, **18 months** not 3 years.

330.16 *Physical non-penetrative contact   Victim(s) aged under 10   Defendant then aged 21+*

Att-Gen's Ref No 28 of 2013 2013 EWCA Crim 1190 D pleaded (at different times) to seven indecent assaults and sexual activity with a child. The indecent assaults were committed between 1973 and 2004 and involved touching the leg and bottom and rubbing the vaginal area of various children aged between five and 12 years. Between 1996 and 2004 whilst he was the coach of a gymnastics and dance display team he touched the bottom and crotch of one of the girls who trained with his team. He was arrested in relation to these matters and subsequently a victim of his earlier offending reported the offences. Between 1970 and 1982, he was a gymnastics coach at a school and indecently assaulted girls on the gymnastics team. One of the earlier offences occurred at D's home. All victims were assaulted once, save for one who was assaulted twice. Victim impact statements revealed that some victims felt their personal relationships had been affected and some still endure difficulties in trusting men. D, aged 66 at appeal, had health problems including a heart condition, depression and anxiety. Held. A permissible amount of credit would have been 30%. Each victim was spared the trauma of giving evidence. These offences were at the low end of offending and starting at 12 months, we are not inclined to disturb the 15 months on which the Judge settled, despite it being a lenient sentence. The question was whether the Judge properly suspended the sentence. With D's age, health, positive good character, the age of the offences and nature of the offences, **15 months suspended** was lenient, but not unduly so.

Att-Gen's Ref No 36 of 2013 2013 EWCA Crim 2574 LCJ D was convicted of indecency with children (×6) and indecent assault. D was an artist and photographer. In 2006, police executed a search warrant and his computer was seized. A number of pseudo-images were discovered. This led to victims telling of abuse. That conduct occurred between 1972 and 1987. D took photographs of V1 when she was aged about 10. She was naked. On one occasion, V1 was naked and D placed Sellotape over her eyes. V1 could hear D breathing heavily. He photographed her. On another occasion, he photographed her as she posed, naked, on some rocks. V2 was the child of D's wife's friend. They would visit D's address when V2 was a child. She gave evidence that when she was aged about 6, she was having a bath with D's daughter (aged about 5). D entered the bathroom, naked, and got into the bath. His penis was erect. He kept asking them to wash his penis. His daughter did so. D left the bathroom and returned, and photographed V2. Those were two gross indecency counts. When V2 was aged about 10, D cupped her breasts in his hands and V2 kicked him in the shins. That was the indecent assault. V3 was photographed when aged 9-14 having been dressed up in Victorian clothes. D would ask her to move or would move her so that her genitals were exposed. There were a substantial number of pseudo-photographs found on D's computer. 138 images had been created by use of a computer software program which enabled photographs to be manipulated or brought together to create images. D claimed they were for a forthcoming publication and that they were for his artistic purposes. V1 said that giving evidence was the worst experience of her life. V2 echoed that. V3 felt that the handing round of nude photographs of her 'robbed her of her dignity'. There was strong evidence of D's good character. He was aged over 70 when sentenced. Held. There was no doubt that D had a sexual interest in children. The offences were committed between 25 and 40 years ago. The only mitigation was D's good character and his age. There were a large number of aggravating factors including the number of victims, the serious abuse of position of trust (in that his reputation as an artist enabled him to get close to the children) and the serious impact the offences had on the victims, magnified by the way in which he had grossly manipulated and degraded them by the photography in which he had engaged. D's lack of contrition seriously aggravated the offending. He claimed to be a victim of a global witch hunt. D suffered from age-related illnesses which would be taken into account. The incident in the bath was a very serious offence. 18 months was appropriate for that. The photograph offences should be marked with a consecutive sentence. Regard needed to be had to totality. The sentence should not have been suspended. **2 years 3 months,** not 12 months suspended.

Att-Gen's Ref No 61 of 2014 2014 EWCA Crim 1933, 2015 1 Cr App R (S) 25 (p 187) D was convicted of seven indecent assaults. One count was a specimen count against V2. In the late 1980s D was aged 15 or 16 and he would lie naked on top of V1, his stepbrother, make him remove his clothing in bed and rub up and down until D ejaculated. He told V1 not to tell anyone and this occurred over a 12-month period. This was similarly perpetrated against V2, D's stepsister, but over an 18-month period. In addition, D had touched V2's vagina and had rubbed his groin against V2's under the pretence of playing a game. The offences took place when their parents were out of the house and D was left in charge. V1 was aged 5 and V2 6 or 7 at the time. The abuse ended when V1 told his mother, coinciding with D leaving for the Army at age 16. D admitted the offences to his parents, who then sought advice from a vicar. V1 and V2 received counselling and the Judge found the offences to have had a profound effect. D was now aged 42 and had a conviction for other sexual offences from 2010 (taking a child, who was aged 15, without authority and meeting her following grooming when he was a teacher). D was made subject to a SOPO, which he breached three years later by still being in contact with that victim. It was then varied when she became an adult, to permit contact between the two. He was currently engaged in a Sexual Offender Treatment Programme (SOTP), and had continued on the community order imposed then, but now breached. The pre-sentence report noted that custody would be of insufficient length to enable work to occur with D to reduce his risk of harm. Research showed that non- or partial completion can increase the risk of reoffending. There was some acceptance of guilt. Held. D's conviction shows that, many years after the [instant] offending, he was prepared to indulge his proclivities at the expense of his responsibilities. To bring the SOTP to an end by imposing immediate custody would not only frustrate such work, but might exacerbate the situation. This is a difficult and unusual case. We conclude that the interruption of the SOTP, with concomitant exacerbation of the situation, is an exceptional circumstance justifying the suspension of the sentence. **18 months, suspended for 2 years** unaltered.

See also: *R v Moss* 2012 EWCA Crim 528 (Pleas to multiple specimen sexual offences. Between 1979 and 1993, when aged between 14 and 28, he sexually abused five of his nieces and nephews. Victims aged 5-10. Masturbation, simulated intercourse and sexual assault. Breach of trust (babysitting). Committed for sexual gratification. He bribed or threatened the victims. Had long-standing partner and two children. Risk of similar offences was relatively low. **4½ years** not 7.)

Post-2014 guideline case

R v G 2015 EWCA Crim 261 D pleaded (full credit) to indecent assault (×4) and indecency with a child committed in the early 1980s when D was aged 29 or 30. V, aged 5 or 6, was D's then partner's daughter and they all lived together. D sat V astride him in her bedroom and he played with his penis. V reciprocated, thinking it was a game. Another time, D invited V to touch and kiss his penis (the indecency with a child). D also made V masturbate him several times, including in the bath and to ejaculation. The conduct lasted under a month and D stopped of his own accord. In 2013, V confronted D about the conduct, which he admitted, immediately apologising. D was aged 63 on appeal and expressed deep shame, remorse and a high level of victim empathy. He was of good character but lost his long-standing employment as a result, causing him to lose his accommodation and family. He had also behaved well in prison. Held. The appropriate starting point for each of the offences, except for the indecency with a child, would be 45 months. **30 months concurrent**, not 40 months.

330.17   *Physical non-penetrative contact   Victim(s) aged 10-12   Defendant then aged 16-20*
Pre-2014 guideline cases
R v Kane 2013 EWCA Crim 1254 D was convicted of indecent assault. V, aged 10, visited D's house with her parents. D was aged 17-18. D grabbed her and put her on his knee. He put his hand inside her knickers and touched her vaginal area. When V moved away, D grabbed her again and repeated the action. D laughed. D, aged 36 when sentenced, had convictions in 1997 and 2002 for minor dishonesty offences which were not relevant. He was married with a child and in full-time employment. The Judge made a 6-month reduction from the starting point stated in the guidelines to reflect that the guidelines applied to sexual assault (maximum sentence 14 years) whereas the instant offence was indecent assault (maximum sentence 10 years). Held. That reduction was insufficient. The sentence must reflect that this was one offence committed by a 17- or 18-year-old offender. The offence was fortunately short-lived and not repeated. The appropriate starting point was one of 12 months. **12 months** not 18.
R v B 2015 EWCA Crim 2046 D was convicted of four indecent assaults and three gross indecencies. D was heavily involved with his local church and when he was aged 18, in his gap year, he went to the Philippines to work with disadvantaged children. There he met a woman, W, whom he brought back to the UK and then married. When aged 18 or 19, D helped a mother with two daughters who was in financial difficulties. He allowed them to move from a shelter and into his flat. One daughter, V1, was aged 13 and slept on a sofa-bed. On one occasion, V1 felt the bed covers move off her body and D touching her nipples. She saw D kneeling on the floor next to her masturbating. He asked her to masturbate him and she refused. She was frightened. On a different occasion, D put his hand up V1's skirt and touched the top of her inner thigh. D put her hand on his erect penis through his trousers. V1 pulled away and screamed. V1 moved back to the shelter and while D was giving V1 assistance he groped her buttocks. When V1 complained, her mother was unsupportive and their relationship was devastated for many years. The church minister gave no support, saying the matters were all in the past. A year or so later V2, aged 9 or 10, was staying in D's flat and she shared a bed with W. D got in the bed with V2 and touched her naked vagina. Next morning V2 saw D in the bath with an erection. D invited her to join him in the bath (not subject to a count). Both V1 and V2 were adversely affected by the experience, particularly V1. There was no offending since then although there was an incident in the Philippines which could not be charged (which the Court should have ignored). D was now aged 50 and after the gap year he went to an ecclesiastical college and then was ordained. He had devoted himself to charitable work in the Philippines over 30 years, for which he was awarded an MBE. Held. The Judge was entitled to pass consecutive sentences (2 years, 1 year and 2 years applying to each of three occasions). **5 years** was severe but not manifestly excessive. For details about D's foreign travel prohibition, see **107.11** in Volume 1.

330.18   *Physical non-penetrative contact   Victim(s) aged 13-15   Pre-2014 guideline cases*
R v O 2010 EWCA Crim 1509 D pleaded (full credit) to six counts of indecent assault, occurring between 1990 and 1996 when D was aged between 58 and 63, and one count of sexual activity with a child, occurring between 2003 and 2007 when D was aged between 70 and 74. The indecent assault related to D's stepdaughter, P, when she was aged 14-19. He would touch her breasts both above and beneath her clothing, he would kiss her on the

mouth, inserting or attempting to insert his tongue on one occasion, and he touched her vaginal area over her nightdress. The incidents happened on many occasions. P planned to become pregnant as a way of moving out of the house in order to end the abuse. P did become pregnant in 1996 and the abuse did indeed cease. P's daughter, V, was born in 1997. P would take V to stay with her parents regularly, believing that because P's mother was there, D would not abuse V. This was not so. D pulled down his trousers and underpants and sat on the bed so that V could see his penis. V said she wanted to go to the park but D said, "This will be better". He touched V's shoulder and pulled her towards him. She was reluctant and he let V leave the room. Other incidents occurred when D bounced V up and down on his lap. V said that she could feel his penis each time. V would also dress up in her grandmother's clothes and D would slap her bottom and say that she looked sexy. D was of good character. A pre-sentence report stated that: a) D felt self-revulsion at what he had put his victims through, b) he recognised that he had been in a position of trust and had betrayed that trust, and c) D was assessed as posing a low risk of reoffending and a small risk to children. D attempted suicide and wrote several suicide notes. The Judge stated that the offences "could be said to come towards the lower end of the scale of seriousness" but that the sentence to be passed was to be judged by the second bracket for sexual assault in the guidelines "because of the persistence of the conduct, because of the gross breach of trust" and that what D had done was to effectively rob P of many of the joys of schooling, of adolescence and of normal home life. The offence relating to V was more serious and fell within the same bracket as the counts relating to P. Held. The Judge's comments were amply justified. Both sets of offences represented gross breaches of trust. One year's imprisonment on counts 1-6 concurrent and one year's imprisonment on count 7 consecutive, making **2 years**, did reflect his age, remorse and unfortunate personal background.

R v Folks 2013 EWCA Crim 1240 D pleaded (on the day of trial) to indecent assault on a male and attempted indecent assault on a male. D was a vicar in Ambleside where V grew up. D gave V guitar lessons at D's home when V was aged about 13. Between 2003 and 2004, when V was aged around 15-16, the guitar lessons began to change in their nature, at D's instigation. They became more about physical exercise and D began to take an interest in V's physical appearance. D engaged in what he termed 'boy talk', commenting on V's physique and touching his pectoral and abdominal muscles in an inappropriate way. In interview he admitted that he had become sexually attracted to V. That was count 1. Count 2 occurred when, after a lesson, D asked V if he could see his penis. V reluctantly obliged but would not let D touch it when he asked to do so. V's parents stopped the lessons after D had written V a letter which implied that he wished V to come to live with him. V's parents noticed that around this time V had become aggressive and moody. V complained that D had been waiting for him at the bus stop. The incidents led V to leave home at the age of 16 and become estranged from his family for around ten years. D, aged 70 at appeal, had no previous convictions and many positive character references from the community which he had served. He was no longer a vicar. Held. The Judge was right that a custodial sentence was called for. There was a very serious breach of trust; he was trusted because of his position. He was trusted by V and V's parents. The *Sexual Offences Act 2003 Guideline 2008* Assault section does not provide much assistance. The appropriate sentence could be calculated in two ways. First, starting at 12 months for count 2, a one-quarter reduction was appropriate to reflect that it was an attempt. There should be full credit for the plea. Alternatively, focusing on count 1, reduce the sentence by one third for the plea, then recognise the candour shown by D which led him to be charged. **6 months**, not 8, was appropriate.

330.14b   Victim(s) aged 16-17   Breach of trust   Post-2014 guideline case
R v Kerr 2015 EWCA Crim 1234 D, a teacher, was convicted of three indecent assaults committed between 1999 and 2002 or 2003. Two were against his pupils. D was highly regarded and popular. He was an enthusiastic supporter of extracurricular activity. In 1999, following an allegation of sexual misconduct which was not sustained, D was

warned not to invite pupils unaccompanied to his home. He developed a particularly close relationship with V1, who had personal difficulties at home. They would share a shower together naked. V1 found this uncomfortable. When V1 was aged 15 or 16 he complained of some muscle pain. D took V1 to his home and put V1 on a bed and massaged his back. Next he pulled down his lower clothing and massaged his naked buttocks and touched his anus for about five seconds without penetrating it. V1 said he did not want to be touched there and D stopped. On the pretext of helping him with a bad exam mark, D invited V2, aged 17, to his home. They played squash and showered naked afterwards. Next, D took him to a pub and bought him two pints and drove V2 to his home. V2 complained of pain from the squash game, and D said he would give V2 a massage. D rubbed V2's back with oil for five minutes and then pulled D's trunks down exposing his bottom. D told V2 to close his eyes and turned him over and massaged his penis for 30 seconds. V2 then left. V2 complained and D resigned as a teacher. Other pupils disapproved because they had lost a popular teacher. V3, aged 17, was openly gay and was not a pupil of D. He declined to shower with D. D called him to his office to ask why. Later he asked V3 to have a coffee in his house. There he tried to kiss V3. V3 said he was not going to kiss D. D said it was acceptable and tried to hug and kiss him. V3 resisted. D was aged 53, with no convictions. V1 and V2's victim impact statements focused on the stress of the trial. Held. There was obviously a clear breach of trust. For the offence involving V2, there had been planning and the supply of alcohol. There was high culpability. The offences involving V1 and V2 were Category 2A, so 2½ years (V1) and 2 years (V2). The offence involving V3 was Category 3, so 6 months. The Judge was entitled to make the sentences consecutive, making **5 years** in all not 7.

331   SEX OFFENCES: IMAGES ETC.

331.1
1) Obscene Publications Act 1959 s 2 (publishing an obscene article or having an obscene article for publication for gain)
   Mode of trial Triable either way
   Maximum sentence On indictment 5 years. Summary 6 months and/or a £5,000 fine for offences committed before 12 March 2015 and an unlimited fine thereafter.[1046] There are maximum fines for those aged under 18, see **14.38** in Volume 1.
Note: Prosecutors tend to avoid this Act, perhaps because it does not trigger notification, automatic barring and other orders. Ed.
2) Protection of Children Act 1978 s 1 (taking, distributing, publishing etc. indecent photographs etc.)
   Mode of trial Triable either way
   Maximum sentence On indictment 10 years. Summary 6 months and/or a £5,000 fine for offences committed before 12 March 2015 and an unlimited fine thereafter.[1047] There are maximum fines for those aged under 18, see **14.38** in Volume 1.
3) Criminal Justice Act 1988 s 160 (possession of indecent photographs etc.)
   Mode of trial Triable either way
   Maximum sentence On indictment 5 years. Summary 6 months and/or a £5,000 fine for offences committed before 12 March 2015 and an unlimited fine thereafter.[1048] There are maximum fines for those aged under 18, see **14.38** in Volume 1.
4) Sexual Offences Act 2003 s 48-50 (causing etc. a person to be involved in pornography, controlling a child involved in pornography or arranging child pornography)
   Modes of trial Triable either way

[1046] Legal Aid, Sentencing and Punishment of Offenders Act 2012 s 85(1) and (4) and Legal Aid, Sentencing and Punishment of Offenders Act 2012 (Commencement No 11) Order 2015 2015/504
[1047] Legal Aid, Sentencing and Punishment of Offenders Act 2012 s 85(1) and (4) and Legal Aid, Sentencing and Punishment of Offenders Act 2012 (Commencement No 11) Order 2015 2015/504
[1048] Legal Aid, Sentencing and Punishment of Offenders Act 2012 s 85(1) and (4) and Legal Aid, Sentencing and Punishment of Offenders Act 2012 (Commencement No 11) Order 2015 2015/504

Maximum sentences On indictment 14 years. Summary 6 months and/or a £5,000 fine for offences committed before 12 March 2015 and an unlimited fine thereafter.[1049] There are maximum fines for those aged under 18, see **14.38** in Volume 1.

5) Criminal Justice and Immigration Act 2008 s 63 (possession of extreme pornographic images e.g. animals and violence)

Mode of trial Triable either way

Maximum sentence On indictment 3 years (or 2 years where it is not a section 63(7)(a) or (b) image). Summary 6 months and/or a £5,000 fine for offences committed before 12 March 2015 and an unlimited fine thereafter.[1050] There are maximum fines for those aged under 18, see **14.38** in Volume 1.

Criminal Justice and Courts Act 2015 s 37 extends the definition of 'extreme image' in section 63 to include 'possession of pornographic images of rape and assault by penetration'. In force 13 April 2015.[1051]

6) Coroners and Justice Act 2009 s 62 (possession of prohibited images of children)[1052]

Mode of trial Triable either way

Maximum sentence On indictment 3 years. Summary 6 months and/or a £5,000 fine for offences committed before 12 March 2015 and an unlimited fine thereafter.[1053] There are maximum fines for those aged under 18, see **14.38** in Volume 1.

7) Serious Crime Act 2015 s 69 (possession of paedophile material) In force 3 May 2015.[1054]

Mode of trial Triable either way

Maximum sentence On indictment 3 years. The summary penalty is 6 months and/or an unlimited fine.[1055] There are maximum fines for those aged under 18, see **14.38** in Volume 1.

8) Criminal Justice and Courts Act 2015 s 33 (disclosing private sexual photographs and films with intent to cause distress)

Mode of trial Triable either way

Maximum sentence On indictment 2 years. Summary 6 months and/or an unlimited fine[1056] for those aged 18+. For those under 18, see **14.37** in Volume 1. In force 13 April 2015.[1057]

Automatic life Protection of Children Act 1978 s 1, Sexual Offences Act 2003 s 48-50 are listed in Criminal Justice Act 2003 Sch 15B Part 1. The Lord Chief Justice said in *Att-Gen's Ref No 27 of 2013* 2014 EWCA Crim 334[1058] para 8 iii) (*obiter*) that in rare cases the provisions could lead to the imposition of a life sentence where the offence does not carry life imprisonment.

The court must (unless the particular circumstances make it unjust[1059]) pass automatic life if: a) the defendant is aged 18+ at the date of the conviction, b) the offence was committed on or after 3 December 2012, c) the court considers a determinate sentence of at least 10 years is appropriate, d) at the time the offender was convicted he had a conviction for a Criminal Justice Act 2003 Sch 15B offence, and e) the defendant at the

---

[1049] Legal Aid, Sentencing and Punishment of Offenders Act 2012 s 85(1) and (4) and Legal Aid, Sentencing and Punishment of Offenders Act 2012 (Commencement No 11) Order 2015 2015/504

[1050] Legal Aid, Sentencing and Punishment of Offenders Act 2012 s 85(1) and (4) and Legal Aid, Sentencing and Punishment of Offenders Act 2012 (Commencement No 11) Order 2015 2015/504

[1051] Criminal Justice and Courts Act 2015 (Commencement No 1, Saving and Transitional Provisions) Order 2015 2015/778 para 3 and Sch 1 para 27 and 31

[1052] In force 6/4/10, Coroners and Justice Act 2009 (Commencement No 4, Transitional and Saving Provisions) Order 2010 2010/816

[1053] Legal Aid, Sentencing and Punishment of Offenders Act 2012 s 85(1) and (4) and Legal Aid, Sentencing and Punishment of Offenders Act 2012 (Commencement No 11) Order 2015 2015/504

[1054] Serious Crime Act 2015 (Commencement No 1) Regulations 2015 2015/820 para 2

[1055] Legal Aid, Sentencing and Punishment of Offenders Act 2012 s 85(1) and (4)

[1056] Legal Aid, Sentencing and Punishment of Offenders Act 2012 s 85(1) and (4)

[1057] Criminal Justice and Courts Act 2015 (Commencement No 1, Saving and Transitional Provisions) Order 2015 2015/778 para 3 and Sch 1 para 27 and 31

[1058] This case is also known as *R v Burinskas* 2014 EWCA Crim 334.

[1059] Criminal Justice Act 2003 s 224A(2)

time of his or her conviction had previously been sentenced to either: i) a life sentence where he or she was not eligible for release during the first 5 years of the sentence, or ii) a determinate sentence or extended sentence where the custodial part was 10 years or more.[1060] For a pre-2012 extended sentence, when determining whether the custodial term was 10+ years the period deducted for time on remand or on a curfew and tag is included.[1061]

Historical offences The maximum sentence for Protection of Children Act 1978 s 1 was, from 20 August 1978 to 10 January 2001, 3 years, and thereafter 10 years. Criminal Justice Act 1988 s 160 was a summary only offence from 29 September 1988 to 10 January 2001. Thereafter it was a triable either way offence with a maximum of 5 years. The summary maxima are the same as listed at **330.1**.

Extended sentences Protection of Children Act 1978 s 1, Criminal Justice Act 1988 s 160, Sexual Offences Act 2003 s 48-50 and Serious Crime Act 2015 s 69 are listed in Criminal Justice Act 2003 Sch 15. The court may pass a 2012 extended sentence (EDS) if there is a significant risk of serious harm from future specified offences and either: a) the defendant has a Criminal Justice Act 2003 Sch 15B conviction (applicable only to defendants aged 18+), or b) the offence would justify a determinate sentence of at least 4 years.[1062]

Sexual Harm Prevention Orders There is a discretionary power (except for the 1959 offence) to make this order, when the notification criteria are present (see below) or when it is necessary to protect the public from sexual harm.[1063]

Notification For the following offences:[1064]

   a) Protection of Children Act 1978 s 1 and Criminal Justice Act 1988 s 160, where the photograph etc. showed a person aged under 16, and i) the defendant is aged 18 or over or ii) the defendant is sentenced to at least 12 months' imprisonment,

   b) Sexual Offences Act 2003 s 48-50, where: i) the defendant is aged 18 or over, or ii) the defendant is sentenced to at least 12 months' imprisonment,

   c) Criminal Justice and Immigration Act 2008 s 63 and Coroners and Justice Act 2009 s 62(1) where i) the defendant is aged 18 or over, or ii) the defendant is sentenced to at least 2 years' imprisonment,

   d) Serious Crime Act 2015 s 69,

the defendant must notify the police within three days (or three days from his or her release from imprisonment, hospital etc.) with his or her name, home address, National Insurance number etc. and any changes, and addresses where he or she resides for seven days[1065] (in one or more periods) or more in any 12-month period.[1066] See the NOTIFICATION chapter.

Children and vulnerable adults: barred lists Where the defendant is convicted of Protection of Children Act 1978 s 1, Criminal Justice Act 1988 s 160 and Sexual Offences Act 2003 s 48-50 and is aged 18 or over, he or she is automatically barred from engaging in regulated activity with children and vulnerable adults.[1067] The Judge must

---

[1060] Criminal Justice Act 2003 s 224A as inserted by Legal Aid, Sentencing and Punishment of Offenders Act 2012 s 122. The condition for a) is at section 224A(1)(a), for b) is at section 224A(1)(b), for c) is at section 224A(1)(c), and for d) is at section 224A(4)-(9).

[1061] Criminal Justice Act 2003 s 224A(9)-(10)

[1062] Criminal Justice Act 2003 s 226A-226B as inserted by Legal Aid, Sentencing and Punishment of Offenders Act 2012 s 124

[1063] Sexual Offences Act 2003 s 103A as inserted by Anti-social Behaviour, Crime and Policing Act 2014 Sch 5 para 2 and Sexual Offences Act 2003 Sch 5

[1064] The two older offences have always been subject to notification. The three 2003 offences were not included in the Sexual Offences Act 2003 Sch 3 list through what appears to have been a drafting error. This was corrected by Sexual Offences Act 2003 (Amendment of Schedules 3 and 5) Order 2007 2007/296. The new extreme pornographic image offence was added by Criminal Justice and Immigration Act 2008 s 148 and Sch 26 para 58. The section 62 offence was added by Coroners and Justice Act 2009 Sch 21(3) para 62(2).

[1065] Sexual Offences Act 2003 s 84(1)(c) and (6)

[1066] Sexual Offences Act 2003 s 83 and Sch 3 para 13 and 15

[1067] Safeguarding Vulnerable Groups Act 2006 s 2 and Sch 3 and Safeguarding Vulnerable Groups Act 2006 (Prescribed Criteria and Miscellaneous Provisions) Regulations 2009 2009/37 regs 4 and 6 and Sch para 2 and 4

tell the defendant that the Disclosure and Barring Service will include him or her in the barred lists.[1068] The defendant may ask the Authority to remove him or her from the lists. Old cases. Old cases which do not deal with procedure or sentencing orders are not listed and are best ignored.

See also the **VOYEURISM** chapter and **IMPORTATION OF PROHIBITED/RESTRICTED GOODS** *Sexual images, Unlawful* para at **274.7**.

331.2   *Crown Court statistics   England and Wales*
Possession of obscene material etc. Aged 21+

Year	Age	Plea	Total sentenced	Type of sentencing %						Average length of custody in months
				Dis-charge	Fine	Commu-nity sentence	Sus-pended sentence	Cus-tody	Other	
Taking, permitting to be taken or making, distributing or publishing indecent photographs or pseudo photographs of children										
2014	18-20	G	50	–	–	54	30	16	–	22.9
		NG	0	–	–	–	–	–	–	–
	21+	G	1,255	–	–	39	29	31	–	19.1
		NG	34	6	–	21	15	53	6	24.8
Possession of indecent photograph of a child										
2014	18-20	G	17			65	29	6	–	not listed[1069]
		NG	0							
	21+	G	297	1	–	42	30	27	–	13.2
		NG	8	–	–	25	13	50	13	not listed
Possessing prohibited images of children										
2014	18-20	G	1	–	–	–	100	–	–	–
		NG	0							
	21+	G	7	–	–	29	57	14	–	not listed
		NG	1	–	–	–	–	100	–	not listed
Other Possession of Obscene Material etc.										
2014	18-20	G	3	–	–	33	33	33	–	not listed
		NG								
	21+	G	73	8	3	34	34	21	–	11.1
		NG	2	–	50	–	50	–	–	–

For explanations about the statistics, see page 1-xii. For more statistics and for statistics for male and female defendants etc., see www.banksr.com Other Matters Statistics tab

Note: It is a pity these two very different offences were put in the same category. Ed.

Guidelines and Judicial guidance
331.3   *Sentencing Council guideline   Sexual Offences Act 2003 s 160 and Protection of Children Act 1978 s 1*
Sexual Offences Guideline 2014, see www.banksr.com Other Matters Guidelines tab. In force 1 April 2014. The guideline only applies to offenders aged 18+, see page 7 of the guideline. For the usual practice, see **66.21** in Volume 1.

STEP ONE: Determining the offence category
page 75 The court should determine the offence category using the table below.

[1068] Safeguarding Vulnerable Groups Act 2006 s 2 and Sch 3 para 25
[1069] 'Not listed' means the statistic is based on too few cases to be meaningful

	Possession	Distribution*	Production**
Category A	Possession of images involving penetrative sexual activity Possession of images involving sexual activity with an animal or sadism	Sharing images involving penetrative sexual activity Sharing images involving sexual activity with an animal or sadism	Creating images involving penetrative sexual activity Creating images involving sexual activity with an animal or sadism
Category B	Possession of images involving non-penetrative sexual activity	Possession of images involving non-penetrative sexual activity	Possession of images involving non-penetrative sexual activity
Category C	Possession of other indecent images not falling within Categories A or B	Possession of other indecent images not falling within Categories A or B	Possession of other indecent images not falling within Categories A or B

*Distribution includes possession with a view to distributing or sharing images.
**Production includes the taking or making of any image at source, for instance the original image.
Making an image by simple downloading should be treated as possession for the purposes of sentencing.
In most cases the intrinsic character of the most serious of the offending images will initially determine the appropriate category. If, however, the most serious images are unrepresentative of the offender's conduct, a lower category may be appropriate. A lower category will not, however, be appropriate if the offender has produced or taken (for example photographed) images of a higher category.

331.4

STEP TWO: Starting point and category range

page 77 Having determined the category, the court should use the corresponding starting points to reach a sentence within the category range below. The starting point applies to all offenders irrespective of plea or previous convictions. Having determined the starting point, step two allows further adjustment for aggravating or mitigating features, set out [below].
Where there is a sufficient prospect of rehabilitation, a community order with a sex offender treatment programme requirement under Criminal Justice Act 2003 s 202 can be a proper alternative to a short or moderate-length custodial sentence.

	Possession	Distribution	Production
Category A	**Starting point** 1 year's custody **Category range** 26 weeks' to 3 years' custody	**Starting point** 3 years' custody **Category range** 2 to 5 years' custody	**Starting point** 6 years' custody **Category range** 4 to 9 years' custody
Category B	**Starting point** 26 weeks' custody **Category range** High-level community order to 18 months' custody	**Starting point** 1 year's custody **Category range** 26 weeks' to 2 years' custody	**Starting point** 2 years' custody **Category range** 1 to 4 years' custody

	Starting point High-level community order **Category range** Medium-level community order to 26 weeks' custody	Starting point 13 weeks' custody **Category range** High-level community order to 26 weeks' custody	Starting point 18 months' custody **Category range** 1 to 3 years' custody
Category C			

For the meaning of a high-level and a medium-level community order, see **16.13** in Volume 1.

331.5   [Aggravating and mitigating factors]

page 78 The table below contains a non-exhaustive list of additional factual elements providing the context of the offence and factors relating to the offender. Identify whether any combination of these, or other relevant factors, should result in an upward or downward adjustment from the starting point. In particular, relevant recent convictions are likely to result in an upward adjustment. In some cases, having considered these factors, it may be appropriate to move outside the identified category range.

When sentencing appropriate Category B or C[1070] offences, the court should also consider the custody threshold as follows:

Has the custody threshold been passed?

If so, is it unavoidable that a custodial sentence be imposed?

If so, can that sentence be suspended?

Aggravating factors
Statutory aggravating factors:
Previous convictions, having regard to: a) the nature of the offence to which the conviction relates and its relevance to the current offence, and b) the time that has elapsed since the conviction
Offence committed whilst on bail
Other aggravating factors:
Failure to comply with current court orders
Offence committed whilst on licence
Age and/or vulnerability of the child depicted
Discernable pain or distress suffered by child depicted*
Period over which images were possessed, distributed or produced
High volume of images possessed, distributed or produced
Placing images where there is the potential for a high volume of viewers
Collection includes moving images
Attempts to dispose of or conceal evidence
Abuse of trust
Child depicted known to the offender
Active involvement in a network or process that facilitates or commissions the creation or sharing of indecent images of children
Commercial exploitation and/or motivation
Deliberate or systematic searching for images portraying young children, Category A images or the portrayal of familial sexual abuse
Large number of different victims
Child depicted intoxicated or drugged
*Age and/or vulnerability of the child should be given significant weight. In cases where the actual age of the victim is difficult to determine sentencers should consider the development of the child (infant, pre-pubescent, post-pubescent).

[1070] The guideline originally stated 'Category 2 or 3'. This was amended to 'Category B or C'.

Mitigating factors
No previous convictions or no relevant/recent convictions Remorse Previous good character and/or exemplary conduct* Age and/or lack of maturity where it affects the responsibility of the offender Mental disorder or learning disability, particularly where linked to the commission of the offence Demonstration of steps taken to address offending behaviour *Previous good character/exemplary conduct is different from having no previous convictions. The more serious the offence, the less the weight which should normally be attributed to this factor. Where previous good character/exemplary conduct has been used to facilitate the offence, this mitigation should not normally be allowed and such conduct may constitute an aggravating factor.

Note: An exact copy of this guideline has been placed in the *Magistrates' Court Guidelines 2008* at page 282.

331.6   *Sentencing Guidelines Council guideline   Sexual Offences Act 2003 s 48-50*
Sexual Offences Guideline 2014, see www.banksr.com Other Matters Guidelines tab. In force 1 April 2014. The guideline only applies to offenders aged 18+, see page 7 of the guideline. For the usual practice, see **66.21** in Volume 1.

STEP ONE: Determining the offence category
page 89 The court should determine which categories of harm and culpability the offence falls into by reference **only** to the tables below.
For offences that involve wide-scale commercial and/or international activity sentences above the category range may be appropriate.

Harm	
Category 1	Victims involved in penetrative sexual activity Abduction/detention Violence or threats of violence Sustained and systematic psychological abuse Victim(s) participated in unsafe/degrading sexual activity beyond that which is inherent in the offence Victim(s) passed around by the offender to other 'customers' and/or moved to other brothels
Category 2	Factor(s) in Category 1 not present

Culpability A
Directing or organising child prostitution or pornography on significant commercial basis Expectation of significant financial or other gain Abuse of trust Exploitation of victim(s) known to be trafficked Significant involvement in limiting the freedom of the victim(s) Grooming of a victim to enter prostitution or pornography including through cultivation of a dependency on drugs or alcohol

Culpability B
Close involvement with inciting, controlling, arranging or facilitating child prostitution or pornography (where offender's involvement is not as a result of coercion)

Culpability C
Performs limited function under direction Close involvement but engaged by coercion/intimidation/exploitation

331.7

STEP TWO: Starting point and category range

page 91 Having determined the category, the court should use the corresponding starting points to reach a sentence within the category range [below]. The starting point applies to all offenders irrespective of plea or previous convictions. Having determined the starting point, step two allows further adjustment for aggravating or mitigating features, set out [below].

A case of particular gravity, reflected by multiple features of culpability or harm in step one, could merit upward adjustment from the starting point before further adjustment for aggravating or mitigating features, set out [below].

Where there is a sufficient prospect of rehabilitation, a community order with a sex offender treatment programme requirement under Criminal Justice Act 2003 s 202 can be a proper alternative to a short or moderate-length custodial sentence.

	Age	A	B	C
Category 1	Under 13	**Starting point** 10 years' custody **Category range** 8 to 13 years' custody	**Starting point** 8 years' custody **Category range** 6 to 11 years' custody	**Starting point** 5 years' custody **Category range** 2 to 6 years' custody
	13 to 15	**Starting point** 8 years' custody **Category range** 6 to 11 years' custody	**Starting point** 5 years' custody **Category range** 4 to 8 years' custody	**Starting point** 2 years 6 months' custody **Category range** 1 to 4 years' custody
	16 to 17	**Starting point** 4 years' custody **Category range** 3 to 7 years' custody	**Starting point** 2 years' custody **Category range** 1 to 4 years' custody	**Starting point** 1 year's custody **Category range** 26 weeks' to 2 years' custody
Category 2	Under 13	**Starting point** 8 years' custody **Category range** 6 to 11 years' custody	**Starting point** 6 years' custody **Category range** 4 to 9 years' custody	**Starting point** 2 years' custody **Category range** 1 to 4 years' custody
	13 to 15	**Starting point** 6 years' custody **Category range** 4 to 9 years' custody	**Starting point** 3 years' custody **Category range** 2 to 5 years' custody	**Starting point** 1 year's custody **Category range** 26 weeks' to 2 years' custody
	16 to 17	**Starting point** 3 years' custody **Category range** 2 to 5 years' custody	**Starting point** 1 year's custody **Category range** 26 weeks' to 2 years' custody	**Starting point** 26 weeks' custody **Category range** High-level community order to 1 year's custody

For the meaning of a high-level community order, see **16.14** in Volume 1.

331.8   [Aggravating and mitigating factors]

page 92 The table below contains a **non-exhaustive** list of additional factual elements providing the context of the offence and factors relating to the offender. Identify whether any combination of these, or other relevant factors, should result in an upward or downward adjustment from the starting point. **In particular, relevant recent convictions are likely to result in an upward adjustment**. In some cases, having considered these factors, it may be appropriate to move outside the identified category range.

When sentencing appropriate Category 2 offences, the court should also consider the custody threshold as follows:

Has the custody threshold been passed?

If so, is it unavoidable that a custodial sentence be imposed?

If so, can that sentence be suspended?

Aggravating factors
Statutory aggravating factors:
Previous convictions, having regard to: a) the nature of the offence to which the conviction relates and its relevance to the current offence, and b) the time that has elapsed since the conviction
Offence committed whilst on bail
Other aggravating factors:
Failure to comply with current court orders
Offence committed whilst on licence
Deliberate isolation of victim(s)
Vulnerability of victim(s)
Threats made to expose victim(s) to the authorities (for example, immigration or police), family/friends or others
Harm threatened against the family/friends of victim(s)
Passport/identity documents removed
Victim(s) prevented from seeking medical treatment
Victim(s) prevented from attending school
Food withheld
Earnings withheld/kept by offender or evidence of excessive wage reduction or debt bondage, inflated travel or living expenses or unreasonable interest rates
Any steps taken to prevent the victim reporting an incident, obtaining assistance and/or from assisting or supporting the prosecution
Attempts to dispose of or conceal evidence
Timescale over which the operation has been run

Mitigating factors
No previous convictions or no relevant/recent convictions
Remorse
Previous good character and/or exemplary conduct*
Age and/or lack of maturity where it affects the responsibility of the offender
Mental disorder or learning disability, particularly where linked to the commission of the offence
*Previous good character/exemplary conduct is different from having no previous convictions. The more serious the offence, the less the weight which should normally be attributed to this factor. Where previous good character/exemplary conduct has been used to facilitate the offence, this mitigation should not normally be allowed and such conduct may constitute an aggravating factor.
In the context of this offence, previous good character/exemplary conduct should not normally be given any significant weight and will not normally justify a reduction in what would otherwise be the appropriate sentence.

331.9   *Suggested approach to the guideline*

Note: It is particularly important to remember that: a) there are two guidelines and each has very different penalties, and b) three of the offences in para **331.1** have no guideline.

It is understood the Sentencing Council intended that the guideline should reflect the Court of Appeal's current sentencing tariff. Further, the new guideline was intended to bring the previous guideline up to date rather than intending to increase the penalties for the bulk of the sex offences. Consequently, I would suggest that sentencers should start with the guideline and then consider recent sentencing cases set out by the Court of Appeal to see if they are helpful, and then return to the guideline before deciding the appropriate sentence. Because there are new guidelines and the emphasis is on recent Court of Appeal authority, I have removed most old cases. Ed.

331.10   *Judicial guidance*

R v Oliver 2002 EWCA Crim 127, 2003 2 Cr App R (S) 15 (p 64) The increased access to the Internet has greatly exacerbated the problem in this area by making pornographic images more easily accessible, and increasing the likelihood of such material being found accidentally by others who may subsequently become corrupted by it. This additional risk adds to the culpability of offenders who distribute material of this kind, especially if they post it on publicly accessible areas of the Internet. Merely locating an image on the Internet will generally be less serious than downloading it. Downloading will generally be less serious than taking an original film or photograph of indecent posing or activity.

R v Terrell 2007 EWCA Crim 3079, 2008 2 Cr App R (S) 49 (p 292) LCJ D pleaded to four counts of making indecent photographs. Held. Downloading indecent images perpetuated the [problem of] 'market or distribution networks' and so encouraged the making of further images. Children of whom such images had been made might be harmed by knowledge of the perverted gratification which adults gained from looking at those images of them, even if they only came to realise that as they grew older.

Note: Although these cases were decided before the 2014 guideline was issued, the approach may be helpful. Ed.

Procedure, deprivation orders and extended sentences

331.11   *Procedure for indecent images*

R v Thompson 2004 EWCA Crim 669, 2005 1 Cr App R (S) 1 (p 1) The following practices should be adopted in the drafting of indictments. The same practices might also be adopted in the selection of images for presentation in summary proceedings.

i) In cases where there are significant numbers of photographs, in addition to the specific counts, the inclusion of a comprehensive count covering the remainder is a practice that should be followed.

ii) The photographs used in the specific counts should, if it is practicable, be selected so as to be broadly representative of the images in the comprehensive count. If agreement can then be reached between the parties that (say) five images at Level 2, ten at Level 3, and two at Level 4 represent 500 Level 2, 100 Level 3 and 200 Level 4 images in the comprehensive count of 800 images, the need for the judge to view the entirety of the offending material may be avoided.

Note: Now this categorisation has been replaced, prosecutors divide images of children into Categories A, B and C, see **331.3**. Ed.

iii) Where it is impractical to present the court with specific counts that are agreed to be representative of the comprehensive count, there must be available to the court an approximate breakdown of the number of images at each of the levels. This may best be achieved by the prosecution providing the defence with a schedule setting out the information and ensuring that the defence have an opportunity, well in advance of the sentencing hearing, of viewing the images and checking the accuracy of the schedule.

iv) Each of the specific counts should, in accordance with what was stated by this court in *R v Oliver* 2002 EWCA Crim 127, 2003 2 Cr App R (S) 15 (p 64), make it clear whether the image in question is a real image or a pseudo-image. The same count should not charge both. As this court pointed out in *R v Oliver* 2002, there may be a significant difference between the two and where there is a dispute, then there should be alternative counts. In the majority of cases there will be no doubt as to whether the image in question should be dealt with either as a real image or a pseudo-image.

v) Each image charged in a specific count should be identified by reference to its 'jpg' or other reference so that it is clear with which image the specific count is dealing.

vi) The estimated age range of the child shown in each of the images should, where possible, be provided to the court.

331.12   *Need for sentencer to address the behaviour as well as punish*

This paragraph applies to other sex offending as well as image offences.

'Where there is a sufficient prospect of rehabilitation, a community order with a sex offender treatment programme requirement under Criminal Justice Act 2003 s 202 can be a proper alternative to a short or moderate-length custodial sentence', see *Sexual Offences Guideline 2014* page 78 at **331.4**.

R v McGreen 2010 EWCA Crim 2776 D pleaded to possession of extreme pornographic images and other similar counts. The Judge sentenced D to imprisonment. Held. These are very difficult sentencing exercises. There is a public interest in punishing people who view and download this kind of material, but there is also a public interest to try to ensure that people who do commit such offending are dealt with in a way which is likely to reduce, rather than leave untreated, their need for this kind of imagery. Immediate release.

R v V 2013 EWCA Crim 488 D pleaded at the PCMH to breach of a SOPO and making indecent images. In 2010 he was sentenced to a 3-year community order and an indefinite SOPO for 31 offences of making indecent images. He made frank admissions to breaching a term of the SOPO and making indecent images. There were 46,000 indecent images: 3,220 at Level 1, 559 at Level 2, 313 at Level 3, 341 at Level 4 and 53 at Level 5. The first pre-sentence report discussed D's Community Sex Offender Group Work Programme and how, at the time of the offences, D had only just begun the programme, whereas when he was to be sentenced, he had nearly completed it. The report recommended a suspended sentence as it would assist in addressing D's behaviour. Held. We agree with the comments in *R v McGreen* 2010 (see above). There is a public interest in trying, by appropriate measures, to reduce future offending as well as punishing past offending. The Judge on this occasion failed to address that particular element of the undoubtedly difficult sentencing exercise which this particular case presented. Had he done so, he would have followed the recommendation of the pre-sentence report. We now do so. **16 months suspended** with a Sex Offender Treatment Programme, not 18 months.

Att-Gen's Ref No 61 of 2014 2014 EWCA Crim 1933, 2015 1 Cr App R (S) 25 (p 187) D was convicted of seven indecent assaults. One count was a specimen count against V2. In the late 1980s D was aged 15 or 16 and he would lie naked on top of V1, his stepbrother, make him remove his clothing in bed and rub up and down until D ejaculated. He told V1 not to tell anyone and this occurred over a 12-month period. This was similarly perpetrated against V2, D's stepsister, but over an 18-month period. In addition, D had touched V2's vagina and had rubbed his groin against V2's under the pretence of playing a game. The offences took place when their parents were out of the house and D was left in charge. V1 was aged 5 and V2 6 or 7 at the time. The abuse ended when V1 told his mother, coinciding with D leaving for the Army at age 16. D admitted the offences to his parents, who then sought advice from a vicar. V1 and V2 received counselling and the Judge found the offences to have had a profound effect. D was now aged 42 and had a conviction for other sexual offences from 2010 (taking a child, who was aged 15, without authority and meeting her following grooming when he was a teacher). D was made subject to a SOPO, which he breached three years later by still being in contact with that victim. It was then varied when she became an adult, to permit contact between the two. He was currently engaged in a Sexual Offender Treatment Programme (SOTP), and had continued on the community order imposed then, but now breached. The pre-sentence report noted that custody would be of insufficient length to enable work to occur with D to reduce his risk of harm. Research showed that non- or partial completion can increase the risk of reoffending. There was some acceptance of guilt. Held. D's conviction shows that, many years after the [instant] offending, he was prepared to indulge his proclivities at the expense of his responsibilities. To bring the SOTP to an end by imposing immediate custody would not only frustrate such work, but might exacerbate the situation. This is a difficult and unusual case. We conclude that the interruption of the SOTP, with concomitant exacerbation of the situation, is an exceptional circumstance justifying the suspension of the sentence. **18 months, suspended for 2 years** unaltered.

331.13   *Basis of plea   No proper basis of plea*
R v Thompson 2004 EWCA Crim 669, 2005 1 Cr App R (S) 1 (p 1) D pleaded to 12 counts of possessing indecent photographs or pseudo-photographs of children. D's computer was seized and was found to contain over 3,700 indecent images of children downloaded from commercial sites on the Internet which had subsequently been deleted. He was aged 52, married with three children and of good character. Two of the photographs in two of the counts contained 5- or 6-year-old girls engaged in intercourse with adults. The other nine counts were representative of the other photographs seized. Held. Because the photographs were not categorised into the quantities at the different levels, it was impossible to say how many of the remaining photographs fell into Category 4. It would not be right to make an assumption against D as to the number of images at the different levels which were encompassed within the remaining images. On the information before him, the Judge could not properly conclude that D was in possession of that large quantity of material at Level 4. 9 months not 2 years.

331.14   *Concurrent or consecutive offending*
R v Smith 2014 EWCA Crim 2383 D pleaded to specimen counts of making indecent photos of a child (×9). The first three counts totalled 374 Category C images and depicted erotic posing with no sexual activity. Counts 4-7 totalled 60 images at Category B and counts 8-9 were 28 images at Category A. The prosecution said the offending should be classified as Category A. The Judge passed a series of consecutive sentences. Held. para 14 This was correct. However, there should not have been consecutive sentences for the other categories. Where there are multiple images spanning different levels of seriousness, [the judge] should impose a sentence on the most serious category which took into account the overall offending and other factors. We pass 18 months on the Category A offences with lesser concurrent sentences on the other counts.

331.15   *Deprivation orders*
R v Connelly 2012 EWCA Crim 2049 D pleaded to six counts of taking indecent photos of a child, V. His computer was examined and there were six photos of the same seven-year-old child clearly taken on two different days. Her poses for the camera were clearly sexualised. In one V had pulled down her underclothes and exposed her genitalia. D was a keen amateur photographer. He had many thousands of innocent pictures of his family, family occasions, his grandchildren and his military career. The photos of V had been deleted. The Judge made a SOPO which restricted D's possession and use of photographic equipment with a police inspection requirement. The Judge also made a deprivation order after hearing that V's family wanted complete confidence that the images would not resurface. Held. We take judicial notice of the fact that an expert with sophisticated software can always retrieve deleted files. But that is not a risk that we consider is sufficiently real to deprive him of the computer and its legitimate contents. The SOPO provided sufficient checks on D and his computer.

331.16   *Extended sentences*

Note: The case below was decided before IPP was abolished and before the Criminal Justice and Immigration Act 2008 changes. The case is only listed to show the approach to assessing 'significant risk of serious harm'. Ed.

R v Lang 2005 EWCA Crim 2864, 2006 2 Cr App R (S) 3 (p 13) para 11 Downloading indecent images of children may cause serious psychological injury to a child arising not only from what the child has been forced to do but also from the knowledge that others will see what they were doing (see *R v Collard* 2004 EWCA Crim 1664, 2005 1 Cr App R (S) 34 (p 155)).

R v Terrell 2007 EWCA Crim 3079, 2008 2 Cr App R (S) 49 (p 292) LCJ D pleaded to four counts (Levels 1, 2, 3 and 5) of making indecent photographs. There were 36 TICs (Levels 1, 2 and 3, mostly at Level 1). He was a student. His computer was seized by police at his parents' home. He said that he searched the Internet for boys aged 7-13. He viewed some more than once. In 2003, when he was aged 16, he had been convicted of 26 offences of making indecent photographs of children. There were over 1,200 images recovered, largely at Levels 3 and 4. He received a 4-month Detention and Training Order. The pre-sentence report said that he was isolated and wanted to talk to counsellors. It said that there was a medium risk of reoffending. There was a high risk of sexual harm to male children aged 7-12. The RM 2000/S assessment put him into the very-high-risk category. However, it recommended a suspended sentence and treatment. This was not available locally. The Judge found no coercion or boys in distress. Held. Downloading indecent images perpetuated the market [and the] distribution networks and so encouraged the making of further images. Children of whom such images had been made might be harmed by the knowledge of the perverted gratification which adults gained from looking at those images of them, even if they came to realise that as they grew older. As was said in *R v Lang* 2005 EWCA Crim 2864, 2006 2 Cr App R (S) 3 (p 13), 'repetitive violent or sexual offending at a relatively low level without serious harm does not itself give rise to a significant risk of serious harm in the future'. The Judge did not find that the offences which might be committed in the future were different from or graver than those that D had already committed. It was not suggested that D risked progressing to physical contact. The harm relied on is the harm to children of being forced to participate in the activities. It cannot reasonably be said that there is a significant risk of this defendant's reoffending, occasioning harm to a child or children, whether through perpetuating the market or through further indecent images being taken, or through a child becoming aware of the indecent purposes to which the photographs might be put. The link between the act of downloading and the possible harm which might be done to children is too remote. The IPP provisions do not apply here.

R v Cheshire 2014 EWCA Crim 627, 2 Cr App R (S) 53 (p 430) D pleaded early to 'child pornography offences'. Police visited his home and he tried to conceal a stylus pen. It was seen and he claimed it was for a sat nav device. He showed the officers such a device and they left. They later discovered that the stylus pen could be used on devices such as Internet smartphones and iPads. They returned to D's home and D denied having any device that could access the Internet. Police found a hidden pouch on D containing a mobile phone capable of accessing the Internet. The mobile had about 1,700 child images in it which were Level 1-5. On a memory card and the memory within the phone there were 55 Level 4 images and at least three Level 5 images including a nine- or ten-year old girl having oral sex with a dog. D was now aged 63. In 1978, he received 9 months for indecent assault on a man aged over 16. In 1995, he received 3 months for distributing indecent images of children. In 1998, he was convicted of inciting a child to commit gross indecency by leaving notes and money in a park. In 1999, a Sex Offender Order was made following his approach to two children under the age of 10. By 2000, there were eight breaches of a Sex Offender Order. Also in 2000, there were three offences involving him being in prohibited areas, four other breaches and five sexual image offences. D received 7 years. In 2006, D pleaded to further child pornography offences and was sentenced to IPP (subsequently quashed by the Court of Appeal, which substituted a sentence of two years). In 2011, D was sentenced for further indecent images offences. The Judge felt unable to pass an extended sentence and sentenced D to 3 years and a SOPO. D breached that order by committing the instant offences. In 2013, for the instant offences the Judge gave him a 7-year extended sentence (4 years' custody 3 years' extended licence). The pre-sentence report had requested such a sentence saying, 'should the opportunity arise, D would commit contact sexual offences against children'. D was aged 63 at appeal. Held. A finding of dangerousness may be appropriate if the significant risk of serious harm can properly be inferred from, for example, a greater frequency of offending, a risk of contact offending or an escalation in the gravity of the relevant images. Since 2009, there had been a significant escalation in the risk posed by D, in particular the sheer persistence and scale of offending since 2009, the extreme lengths to which D was prepared to go to conceal his offending (including the concealed pouch) and D's failure to engage with processes designed to help him. There was an escalation in offending and there was a clear risk that D could revert to contact offences of the type he committed previously. The Judge was therefore entitled to find that D was dangerous and impose a 7-year extended sentence (4 years' custody 3 years' extended licence). Appeal dismissed.

Note: The problem is that the decision was formulated by the author of the pre-sentence report, who does not give any convincing reasons why there would be an escalation to contact offences involving serious harm and was not available for cross-examination. The reason given by the sentencing Judge and the Court of Appeal appears to be the frequency of the offending and that the image seriousness is escalating. Why that would establish an escalation is not revealed. Normally one looks to someone's past behaviour to determine future behaviour. That past from when he was aged 18, over 45 years ago, indicated that D did not progress to child contact offences. Now D was aged 63, it would be hoped his interest would wane, not escalate. Although the result might be attractive, the reasons don't point to the substantial risk of serious harm. Ed.

R v D 2015 EWCA Crim 1456 D pleaded (full credit) to five counts of making indecent photographs and six counts of possession of indecent photographs. Police on a SOPO check visited D at home. He tried to put them off saying he was expecting guests. In his bedroom they found various USB sticks in a vase and one in his hand. About 44,000 indecent images were found. They were categorised as follows:

		Category A	Category B	Category C
Possession offences	**Still**	2	64	21,858
	Moving images	22	2	6
Making images	**Still**	0	64	22,619
	Moving images	29	2	14

The age range of the children was from 4 to 13. In interview, D explained he downloaded the images straight onto a USB stick. In 2010, D pleaded to 18 offences of making or possessing indecent photographs. He was given 28 months and a SOPO. He had breached one of the computer conditions but no indecent images were found. The pre-sentence report said D had a history of mental health difficulties and there was a high risk of serious harm to children. There was, however, a clear motivation to address his behaviour. A psychiatrist said D had an adjustment disorder. The Judge put the case in Category A and passed an extended sentence (4 years' custody 2 years' extended licence). Held. For an extended sentence there must be a close link between the type of offending and the serious harm that would be occasioned. Here there was no escalation in the seriousness of the offences committed. The level of image was essentially the same as the previous time. There was no suggestion D actually took or distributed the photographs. There was no evidence there was a potential for contact offences. We quash the extended sentence. **18 months**.

R v Richardson 2016 EWCA Crim 146 D pleaded guilty to more than one count of [presumably] possession of unlawful images. Police searched his home and found two mobiles and a tablet. That possession breached his SOPO because the devices were capable of accessing the Internet. The devices had images of gross sexual abuse of children, some of whom were very young, including babies. There were 51 Category A images (including 14 moving images), 35 Category B (including eight moving images) and 90 Category C (including three moving images). Whilst D was on bail, police visited his home again and found a Samsung Notepad, which a neighbour of his had said he always carried around with him. This device had more illegal images on it. 84 were Category A (including 38 moving images), 52 were Category B (including 23 moving images) and 837 were Category C (including 10 moving images). D was aged 26. In 2009, he received a community order for possession of indecent images and in 2010 he was given a SOPO. In the same year, he breached the community order and a more stringent SOPO was made. The Judge found a very high risk of D committing further offences and considered the awful nature of the images. He found that D satisfied the dangerousness criteria. The Judge passed an 8-year extended sentence (4 years' custody 4 years' extended licence). D appealed his extended sentence and his custodial term. Held. The images were extremely serious. Those who download these images obviously contribute to the market in them and to the harm done thereby to children. For dangerousness, usually but not always, there is a link or nexus between the instant offence and that issue. The awful nature of some of the images does not have a sufficient nexus for the finding of dangerousness, so we quash the extended sentence.

For details of the appeal against the 4-year custodial term, see **331.20**.

See also: *R v Joy* 2007 EWCA Crim 3281 (It was not reasonable to draw such an inference. IPP was not appropriate.)

R v Cheshire 2009 EWCA Crim 447 (IPP was not appropriate.)

R v Hicks 2009 EWCA Crim 733 (*R v Terrell* 2007 applied, so no to IPP.)

R v Sackman 2010 EWCA Crim 19, 2 Cr App R (S) 56 (p 380) (*R v Terrell* 2007 applied, so no to IPP.)

R v Stubbings 2010 EWCA Crim 710 (IPP was appropriate. See **331.17** below.)

R v Waller 2010 EWCA Crim 728, 2 Cr App R (S) 101 (p 652) (*R v Terrell* 2007 applied.)

Note: Criminal Justice and Immigration Act 2008 changes ensured that IPP and extended sentences could only be passed where the offence warranted a determinate sentence of 4 or more years or where the defendant had been convicted of a Schedule 15B offence. These provisions were extended by the 2012 Criminal Justice Act 2003 s 226A(3) and 226B(1)(d) extended sentences which were inserted by Legal Aid, Sentencing and Punishment of Offenders Act 2012, so consequently, the rule in *R v Terrell* 2007 above would be less applicable now. Ed.

Child offences

Note: For many of the pre-2014 guideline cases it can be difficult to determine which category of the 2014 guidelines the case fits into. 'Making' is often not distribution but downloading material from the Internet. It is particularly important to remember that: a) there are two guidelines and each has very different penalties, and b) three of the offences listed in para **331.1** have no guideline. Ed.

331.17   *Category A   Part of large network   Pre-2014 guideline case*
'Active involvement in a network or process that facilitates or commissions the creation or sharing of indecent images of children' and 'Commercial exploitation and/or motivation' are aggravating factors, see *Sexual Offences Guideline 2014* page 78 at **331.5**.

R v Stubbings 2010 EWCA Crim 710 D pleaded at the earliest opportunity to two counts of procurement of a pornographic video, two counts of arranging or facilitating a child sex offence, three counts of making etc. indecent images and an indecent assault. D founded a closely knit group of 50-60 international paedophiles. D was second in command and played a leading role in the maintenance of the system. He was interested in the commercial exploitation of the material so that funds could be obtained for the production of more child pornography. The group used highly sophisticated encryption methods to stop people infiltrating the group. D adopted several pseudonyms. He encouraged the production of extreme pornography. The material included masturbation, vaginal and oral sex, ejaculation over children, the use of dogs for oral sex, bestiality and sadism through tying up with chains or ropes, sometimes with objects inserted into children's vaginas. There was caning, birching, whipping and the binding of children to expose their genitalia and anuses. This was sometimes in close contact with or being penetrated by adult male genitalia or other objects such as knives, wires, needles or rods. Some children were as young as one or two years old. The majority were 11+. The pain of the children was evident from their expressions or welts on their bodies. Captions emphasised the degradation to which the victims were subjected. Screams could be heard on the videos when the children were beaten on their buttocks or had objects inserted into their vaginas or anuses. Bleeding could be seen on the videos. E-mails disclosed that girls should masturbate to orgasm, that they should use toys, they should moan with pleasure and they should have sexual activity together. When D was arrested, police found the following numbers of images, still and (moving): Level 1, 17,000 (31), Level 2, 152 (7), Level 3, 1,219 (3), Level 4, 1,514 (8), and Level 5, 640 (85). The indecent assault was D rubbing the vagina of a seven- or eight-year-old daughter of a friend under her trousers. This continued over a five-year period. D said he preferred girls aged 8 to 10 and claimed they were able to decide whether they were enjoying themselves. D was aged 55 when sentenced and had been a management consultant living a comfortable life. He had lived an unblemished life with no convictions. The Judge started at **12 years** for the two arrangement offences: 9 years for the making offences (concurrent to each other) and 3 years for the possession offences. She gave 1 year for the assault and made the 12, 12, and 9 consecutive making **33 years**. The deduction for the plea was 25% because D was caught red-handed making it **25 years**. The result was **12½ years' IPP**. Held. The group involved the grooming, degradation and corruption of children worldwide over a four-year period. To reflect the extreme pornography the terms should be consecutive. Those who engage in child pornography must expect severe punishment. It was right to take the starting points close to the maximum. The Judge's approach could not be faulted in any way.

331.18   Category A   Penetration   Distribution   Pre-2014 guideline cases
R v Wolverson 2010 EWCA Crim 2132 D pleaded to three counts of distributing indecent photographs of a child. He met B, whom he worked with. D set up a website for B, who wanted to advertise his escort agency. B was also involved in child prostitution. There was no suggestion that D was aware of this before B's arrest. B provided D with some material which D put onto a DVD and made a number of copies. The material contained Level 4 images of a girl of 16 years of age being penetrated by objects and performing oral sex on B. Held. The offences were strict liability offences. As the distribution offences in this case were limited in number and were not committed for gain, the starting point should have been significantly less than 3 years, which was provided for in the guideline. However, the sentence must reflect the fact that D made a number of copies and, despite thinking that they were for B's personal use, must have at least contemplated the risk of wider distribution from the number of copies he made for B. **1 year** in all not 2.

R v Glancey 2011 EWCA Crim 118 D pleaded to arranging or facilitating the commission of a child sex offence and distributing indecent photographs of children. He lived in a multi-occupancy house run by a Christian family. He had access to the family computer and Internet through a router, allowing him access via his laptop. He downloaded 100 images at Level 1, 12 at Level 2, 33 at Level 3, 37 at Level 4 and seven at Level 5. He was arrested and bailed. Police ran a covert investigation and an undercover officer began to chat online with D. They discussed webcams and moving images of girls aged 10-12. D also revealed a sophisticated understanding of computers and how to avoid detection by the police. D and the officer agreed to meet in a public house. D identified himself by a pre-arranged sign. D stated that he wanted to masturbate whilst watching a ten- to twelve-year-old girl dancing for him and ejaculate on the child. D again explained his knowledge of computers and how to avoid detection. D subsequently downloaded 68 images at Level 1, 11 at Level 3, 10 at Level 4 and one at Level 5. D had previous convictions for child sex offences. In 2001, exposure (×3), in 2002 possession of child abuse images and conspiracy to commit an act of gross indecency. D, then aged 19, had sexual relations with his 13-year-old girlfriend and asked her 13-year-old friend to masturbate over her. The pre-sentence report noted that the offending was escalating in seriousness. It also considered that D did not have the necessary skills to manage the risks that he posed. Held. 9 years 2 months' extended sentence (**4 years 2 months'** custody 5 years' extended licence) would be sufficient.

R v Heathcote-Smith and Melton 2011 EWCA Crim 2846, 2012 2 Cr App R (S) 2 (p 133) H pleaded to conspiracy to distribute indecent images of children, inciting etc. a child to engage in sexual activity, making indecent photographs (×10) and possession of an indecent image. M pleaded to conspiracy to distribute indecent images of children, making indecent photographs (×10) and possession of an indecent image. H and M were part of an electronic ring of more than 200 paedophiles who shared amongst them tens of thousands of indecent images. When D's computers were examined, over 75,000 indecent images were found. 71,973 were at Level 1, 676 at Level 4 and 208 at Level 5. They also found that D had contacted a girl under the age of 14 and had encouraged her to send him numerous indecent photographs of her touching herself. When interviewed, he made a full and frank confession. He named M as someone who he regularly exchanged images with. M was arrested and his computers were searched. There were 10,385 images, of which 1,865 were at Level 4 and 562 were at Level 5. A lot of the images on M's computers showed children under the age of 5 being abused. M admitted looking at the images and said it had "gotten out of control". The Judge sentenced outside of the guidelines, suggesting that when they were written, they did not contemplate the scale of such offending. H and M were of good character. Held. The Judge erred in sentencing outside of the guidelines. There were a vast number of photographs at Levels 4 and 5, shared among a large number of people. H went on a course at his own expense, with a positive outcome. M was depressed at the time of the offences and attempted suicide after his arrest. Both were co-operative. There is no reason to draw a distinction between H and M. For M, **2½ years**, not 4 years. For H, **2½ years** not 4 years, and **12 months consecutive** for the incitement.

See also: *R v Packwood* 2011 EWCA Crim 621 (Pleas. Distributing (×5) and possessing (×10) an indecent image of a child. Possessing an extreme pornographic image (×5). Largely Level 1-2 with one image Level 4. For the Level 4 image, **20 months** not 3 years.)

331.19   Category A   Penetration   Distribution   No sexual motive   Pre-2014 guideline case

R v M 2011 EWCA Crim 2064 D and W pleaded to taking and distributing indecent photographs of a child. F and V, who were friends of D and W, were in a casual sexual relationship. V was around the age of 16. With D and W, F arranged for V to meet him in a caravan on D's property. There, F and V had sexual intercourse whilst D and W were hiding in the lavatory. Their presence became known and V was deeply embarrassed. They filmed the incident and the video was shown to a small group of friends. V was further distressed. Almost 12 months later, V discovered that the video clip had been posted to YouTube. V was emotionally distressed and had a history of self-harm. D was aged 16 and had no previous convictions. W was aged 18 and had no convictions but one caution for alcohol-related violence. The Judge asked for reports addressing the suitability of unpaid work. Held. There was no sexual motivation. The offences were committed as a prank. For D, **community order** with **120 hours**' unpaid work, not 16 months. For W, community order with **60 hours**' unpaid work, not 8 months.

331.20   *Category A   Penetration   Possessing   Fewer than 1,000 images*
'High volume of images possessed, distributed or produced' is an aggravating factor, see *Sexual Offences Guideline 2014* page 78 at **331.5**.
Note: It is unknown what a high volume is. Many collectors of unlawful images have thousands of images. Over 1,000 images is likely to be considered a 'high volume'. Fewer than that is more problematic. Ed.
R v Davidson 2012 EWCA Crim 703 D pleaded (full credit) to 11 counts of possessing indecent photographs of children. Police executed a search warrant at D's address after information that he had downloaded and shared images of children. His computer and two 'thumb drives' were found to contain images of children. There were 7,106 images, with 6,490 at Level 1, 282 at Level 2, 156 at Level 3, 170 at Level 4, and eight at Level 5. Within those numbers, there were the following moving images: 130 at Level 1, 110 at Level 2, two at Level 3, 56 at Level 4, and nine at Level 5. Examination of chat logs showed a clear intention to share the images with others via a 'peer2peer' site. D, aged 35, was married with two daughters. Held. The criminality was the intention that others would share this material with a view to reciprocity. The Judge described the material as vile and cannot be criticised for doing so. The correct range was 2-5 years. There were still a substantial number of images at Level 4 and a small number at Level 5. There were also a huge number at Level 1. There was a full ⅓ discount for the plea and a small reduction for personal mitigation. The starting point was therefore a little higher than 3 years. **2 years** properly reflects the criminality in this case.
R v Clarke 2012 EWCA Crim 1559 D pleaded (early) to 17 counts of making and possessing indecent photographs of a child. D's computer was seized and 4,538 static and 578 moving images were found. The images were at Levels 1-5, with most being at Level 1. This conduct occurred over a sustained period of time. In addition D was able to observe young males masturbating themselves over the webcam. D, aged 30, was in many respects of positive good character. He had acknowledged the need to address his offending and voluntarily made contact with an organisation with expertise in this field. Held. It seems beyond argument that an immediate sentence of imprisonment was inevitable. Although there were aspects of the offence enabling the Judge to aggravate the offence, he did not give the necessary weight to the mitigation. **2 years** not 3 was appropriate.
R v King 2013 EWCA Crim 320 D pleaded to possession of indecent photographs (×1) and making indecent photographs (×27). D's home was searched after his partner telephoned the police upon finding an album with images of young girls. The album included four photographs at Level 1 of D's partner's late daughter in a state of undress. He had never met the girl in question and had misappropriated the pictures after being shown them by his partner. Held. The images of his partner's daughter were misappropriated in a gross breach of trust. Four computers and three memory cards were examined and 4,267 still and moving images were found. About 60% of the images were in the 'active' area of the computer. The images were of girls aged between 2 and 15. The overwhelming majority were at Level 1 (4,151 images). There were 27 images at Level 2, 30 images at Level 3, 56 images at Level 4 and three images at Level 5. The police also found website details written in notebooks. In interview, D admitted that the images would be found but denied that any would involve penetration. He admitted that he had been accessing child pornography two or three times a week over a four-year period. He was aged 42 and had no similar convictions. An unrelated matter was dealt with by a community order in 2006. The pre-sentence report noted a low risk of reoffending but a high risk of harm. It recommended a community disposal. The Judge

justified his departure from the guidelines by the 'grotesque nature' of the four photographs from his partner. Held. The photographs from her partner were completely innocent when taken by a parent in a domestic setting but not so in D's possession. There was large-scale downloading of images of children, focusing on girls aged under 13. The material was held for personal use and there was no question of distribution or commercial gain. Immediate custody was entirely justified. That in itself is likely to result in an increase in starting point. We may have left in place a custodial sentence, [but] we consider that the community will be best protected by an order that allows some constructive work to be done. It is the course most likely to prevent repetition in contrast to being released from custody where no course has been undertaken. Because D had been in custody for several months, **3-year community order** with an Internet sex offender treatment programme (which would not have been available with the Judge's 2-year sentence).

R v Horn 2014 EWCA Crim 653 D pleaded early to nine child sex image offences. D said he was interested in children aged between 10 and 14 and had collected 'a large number' of images. About half of the 90 videos were Level 4 or 5. Some involved the rape of children as young as 6. He admitted to using file-sharing software to search for images. He was a deputy headmaster of a primary school with specific responsibilities for child protection. The pre-sentence report said he was extremely remorseful and distressed. He suffered from a genetic disorder which affected his skin. He was bullied as a child and had low self-confidence. D was socially isolated and suffered from stress at work. He was assessed as having a low risk of further offending. Held. There was no suggestion he had assaulted any children in his care. The low risk assessment related to image offences and not contact offences. Starting at 12 months, which would be increased to 18 to reflect the young age of some of the victims. That would be reduced to 15 months because of the strong personal mitigation. With the plea, **10 months** not 18.

Post-2014 guideline case

R v Jones 2014 EWCA Crim 1859, 2015 1 Cr App R (S) 9 (p 68) D pleaded (full credit) to making indecent photos of a child (×10) and possession of indecent photos of a child. On D's laptop there were around 30 videos at Levels 1-4 and six cartoons and images at Level 5. One Level 4 video was of a female child aged around 11 being penetrated anally by a man to ejaculation. In interview D provided the laptop password, although commented no further. D was aged 64 at sentence. He had two previous convictions for similar offences, the last being in 2006 for which he received custody. However, as the sentence was too short, he was unable to complete the Sex Offender Treatment Programme. D was diagnosed with a 'disorder of sexual preference' but not paedophilia. The pre-sentence report noted that D was remorseful, accepted responsibility for his behaviour and also demonstrated awareness of his offending's impact. He understood that viewing indecent images and videos creates a market perpetuating victims' abuse and that they are likely to suffer psychological trauma. D's behaviour was part of an emerging pattern and not an escalation of behaviour and D posed a low risk of carrying out contact sexual offences. He also voluntarily removed his access to the Internet. The pre-sentence report expressed concern about D's emotional wellbeing and ability to cope with custody. It recommended a suspended sentence with a requirement to engage with the SOTP. Held. The Judge rightly placed this in Category A but the public will be better protected by preventing further offending than by a short sentence. Adopting the pre-sentence report proposal, 36-month **community order** with an SOTP requirement and 36 months' supervision (concurrently), not 2 years concurrent. No unpaid work due to custody already served on remand.

R v Smith 2014 EWCA Crim 2383 D pleaded, and then attempted to renounce his pleas, to specimen counts of making indecent photos of a child (×9). The first three counts totalled 374 Category C images and depicted erotic posing with no sexual activity. Counts 4-7 totalled 60 images at Category B and counts 8-9 were 28 images at Category A. The images were discovered on a large amount of sophisticated computer equipment following a large-scale planned police operation but the computers could be accessed by anyone in the house. The images were all in deleted file space and could only be retrieved using specialist software, which D had. D had accessed sites known for illegal child content. D was aged 51 on appeal and of effective good character with a wife and five children. He said the images were pop-ups and thought he might come across pictures of himself, following his experiences in care. Held. A discount of 20%, not one-third. Considering totality, starting at 2 years, **18 months**, not 34.

R v Richardson 2016 EWCA Crim 146 D pleaded to more than one count of [presumably] possession of unlawful images. Police searched his home and found two mobiles and a tablet. That possession breached his SOPO because the devices were capable of accessing the Internet. The devices had images of gross sexual abuse of children, some of whom were very young, including babies. There were 51 Category A images (including 14 moving images), 35 Category B (including eight moving images), 90 Category C (including three moving images). Whilst D was on bail, police visited his home again and found a Samsung tablet, which a neighbour of his had said he always carried around with him. This device had more illegal images on it. 84 were Category A (including 38 moving images), 52 were Category B (including 23 moving images) and 837 were Category C (including 10 moving images). D was aged 26. In 2009, he received a community order for possession of indecent images and in 2010 he was given a SOPO. In the same year, he breached the community order and a more stringent SOPO was made. The Judge found a very high risk of D committing further offences and considered the awful nature of the images. The Judge passed an 8-year extended sentence (4 years' custody 4 years' extended licence). Held. The images were extremely serious. The guideline indicates that for Category A images the starting point is 1 year with a range up to 3 years. Here there were aggravating features: a) there were a significant number of Category A images (some of which were moving), b) his previous convictions, and c) the offences in the second indictment were committed whilst on bail. Considering the reports, this relatively young man is not irredeemable. On the first indictment we start at 3 years, so with plea discount 2 years. For the second indictment, considering totality we start at 2 years, so with plea discount 16 months. Because those offences were committed on bail the sentences are consecutive. That makes **3 years 4 months** which we impose on both indictments concurrent.

For details about quashing the extended sentence, see **331.16**.

331.21   *Category A   Penetration   Possessing   1,000+ images*
R v Rollason 2010 EWCA Crim 2146 D pleaded to five counts of making indecent photographs of a child. D's adoptive father was arrested for having a large number of indecent images on his computer. D was a significant witness and, when interviewed, admitted that he too had viewed such images. He informed police where they could find his hard drive. There were 58 images which had been deleted spanning Levels 1 to 4 with the majority at Level 1. He made full and frank admissions and showed remorse. A pre-sentence report disclosed a medium risk of reoffending. He admitted having an interest in post-pubescent children. The report recommended a community order and a supervision requirement. D was of previous good character. The Judge passed 6 months. Held. The guidelines did not compel a custodial sentence in this case. Even if we are wrong about that then given his good character, his remorse, the plea and the limited number of images, it should not have been 6 months. D has served a short sentence, the appropriate sentence now is to impose a **community order** which will run for 2 years with a requirement to attend an Internet Sex Offender Treatment Programme and a supervision requirement.

R v McGreen 2010 EWCA Crim 2776 D was convicted of possession of extreme pornographic images and making indecent photographs of children. D's flatmate noticed some images on his computer which caused concern. The police were notified. The images[1071] were at Level 5 portraying acts of intercourse and oral sex with a dog and horses. There were indecent videos at Levels 1 and 4, including girls under the age of 12 showing their underwear. D denied all knowledge of the images, claiming his former wife was responsible. D, aged 58, was of previous good character. A pre-sentence report noted that D eventually accepted responsibility for the offences and that he posed a low risk of reoffending. The Judge accepted that D's remorse was genuine. Held. These are difficult sentencing exercises. There is a need to punish offenders who commit these offences, but also a need to deal with them in a way which is likely to reduce, not leave untreated, their need for this kind of imagery. For the indecent images of children, **7 months** not 9.

Post-2014 guideline case

R v M 2014 EWCA Crim 2384 D pleaded (full credit) to making (×3, which was downloading) and distributing indecent photos of children. A total of 1,500 separate images and over 80 videos were involved. 954 were at Level 1/Category C, 124 were at Level 2 and 370 at Level 3, of which 12 were videos. 377 were at Level 4, of which 48 were videos, and 15 were at Level 5, of which four were videos. Levels 2 and 3 were Category B. Levels 4 and 5 were Category A. The children depicted were babies to 13-year-olds. Over four months D had used Skype to distribute 92 images to 13 other people. 17 were at Level 4. The Judge accepted that this exchange was to enable the electronic chatting to continue. D was aged 59 on appeal and of effective good character. He was frank with police, accepting he had been looking at such images for ten years and indicated the website he used. D, whilst on bail, and over an eight-month period, voluntarily attended several weekly psychological assessments to address his behaviour. D was highly committed and motivated to do so, developing considerable insight into his offending. D had lost his job and a quarter of his pension. His wife was a prison officer at the prison where D spent his first night of custody. The pre-sentence report also noted that D was remorseful and presented no risk to children. The defence said the sentence did not reflect the mitigation. Held. The significant and exceptional mitigation was that D had voluntarily embarked upon rehabilitation to address his offending behaviour-…with a reported degree of success. So **16 months** concurrent, not 21. £5,000 fine quashed.

R v Nestoros 2015 EWCA Crim 1424, 2016 1 Cr App R (S) 5 (p 19) D pleaded (full credit) to ten counts of making and possessing indecent images and two counts of possession of prohibited images. Police visited D at home and he was candid and helpful. Over two years he had downloaded 4.2 million images. 10,000 were graded. 5,000 were Grade A. 643 were Grade B. 2,009 were Grade C. There were 60 prohibited images. There were 463 Category B moving images and 1,000 Category C moving images. D was aged 64 and in 1989 he was fined £75 for possession of one indecent photograph. He had chronic health issues which required three-monthly visits to a hospital. The defence said it was difficult to see how he could have used so many images. Held. The guidelines give a starting point of 12 months. The Judge must have started at more than 7½ years. We start at 4 years, so with the plea, **2 years 8 months** not 5 years.

R v E 2015 EWCA Crim 1599 D pleaded to 32 offences of indecent photographs of a child and an extreme pornographic image count. Police searched D's home and found on various devices about 2,600 indecent images. There were 394 Category A images (39 moving), 535 Category B images (17 moving), and 1,674 Category C images (36 moving). There was oral sex, vaginal sex, a child performing oral sex on a dog, and a dog's penis in a child's vagina. For the Category A offences, the children were aged 4-5 years to 10-11 years. For the Category B offences, the children were aged 3-4 years to about 12 years. The Category C offences included children as young as 12 months. D was aged 41 and in good and stable employment. There were testimonials. In 2008, D

[1071] It is not clear what material related to what count. However, it appears the possession charge concerned animals. Ed.

was sentenced to a community order for making an indecent photograph of a child. He received a police caution for a breach of his notification requirements. The Judge noted the following aggravating factors: a) the children's ages, b) the children's distress, c) the number of images, d) the moving images, e) the large number of different victims, f) the convictions, g) D's notification period ended shortly before these offences were committed, and h) D had been involved in a paedophile Internet chat room. Held. We start at 4½ years not 6, making **3 years** not 4.

See also: *R v Wakeling* 2010 EWCA Crim 2210 (Plea to 11 counts of making indecent photographs of a child, four of having indecent photographs of a child and one of possessing extreme pornographic images. 453 in total. 11 at Level 5. Guidelines are not rigid. **10 months**.)

331.21a   *Category A   No penetration*

R v Moxham 2016 EWCA Crim 182 D pleaded guilty to indecent image offences. Police searched D's home and found 25 DVDs containing indecent images of children. The images, some of which were moving, showed boys aged between 9 and 15. The boys were naked or semi-naked, but there was no overt sexual activity involved. They were Category C images. The police also found a memory stick and a computer containing around 3,600 images, which included some duplication. The images were similar to those on the DVDs. There was a limited number of Category A images which showed boys with their hands tied and/or gags in their mouths. The images did not involve overt sexual activity. Neckties were used to tie the boys. It was considered that the binding of the children amounted to sadism. D was aged 62. He was of good character and had been in work for the whole of his working life. The Judge started at 1 year. He increased that to 2 years because of the Category C images and then reduced it to 12 months because of D's age, character and plea.

Held. The guideline identifies a starting point of 1 year and also says that for many sexual offences of lesser seriousness, where there is a sufficient prospect of rehabilitation, a community order with a Sex Offender Treatment Programme requirement can be a proper alternative to a short or moderate-length custodial sentence. There was no basis for a starting point of 2 years. First, the images themselves were not sadistic in the way that such images so often are in this kind of case. No suffering was intended to be portrayed, and none was apparent. This offending fell at the lower end of the relevant category range. The large number of Category C images did not aggravate the possession of the Category A images. The proper starting point was **less than 12 months**. With the mitigation and the credit for the guilty plea, the sentence for the count involving Category A images, were it to be a custodial sentence, should not have exceeded 6 months' imprisonment. The Category C images sentences should not have exceeded 2 months' imprisonment, if immediate custody was to be the sentence. As he has almost served his sentence and to enable D to attend a treatment programme, we substitute a community order.

Note: Whether it was open to the Court to pass a community order when D had virtually served the appropriate sentence is open to question. For the principles, see **113.20** in Volume 1.

331.22   *Category B   Post-2014 guideline case*

R v Bingham 2015 EWCA Crim 1342, 2016 1 Cr App R (S) 3 (p 10) D pleaded (10% credit) to distributing an indecent photograph. Using a fake name, D made contact with V, a 17-year-old who functioned as a 12-year-old because of his autism. D showed V a video of an adult male with a female child. V asked how old the child was and D said seven. D asked V to show his penis to the child. V seemed disgusted. D had experienced shame, his relationship broke up, he lost contact with friends and family and he was in employment.[1072] Held. It was a Category B offence with a range of 26 weeks to 2 years.

[1072] D's age and whether he was of good character are not revealed.

The image was distributed to engage V in sexual activity. D's failure to spare V the misery of worrying about giving evidence reduced the mitigation. **16 months** was severe but not inappropriate.

R v D 2015 EWCA Crim 1456 D pleaded (full credit) to five counts of making indecent photographs and six counts of possession of indecent photographs. Police on a SOPO check visited D at home. He tried to put them off saying he was expecting guests. In his bedroom they found various USB sticks in a vase and one in his hand. About 44,000 indecent images were found. They were categorised as follows:

	Category A	Category B	Category C
Possession offences	24	66	21,864
Moving images	22	2	6
Making images	29	66	22,633
Moving images	29	2	14

The age range of the children was from 4 to 13. In interview, D explained he downloaded the images straight onto a USB stick. In 2010, D pleaded to 18 offences of making or possessing indecent photographs. He was given 28 months and a SOPO. He had breached one of the computer conditions but no indecent images were found. The pre-sentence report said D had a history of mental health difficulties and there was a high risk of serious harm to children. There was, however, a clear motivation to address his behaviour. A psychiatrist said D had an adjustment disorder. The Judge put the case in Category A. Held. [As there were so many Category C images] it was a Category B case which reflected an overall assessment, so adjusting for his previous convictions, **18 months** not 6 years' extended sentence (4 years' custody 2 years' extended licence.

331.23   *Victim unaware of filming/Images of associates misused/Breach of trust*
R v Clark 2012 EWCA Crim 1707 D pleaded (full credit) to possession of indecent images of children (×3), possession of an extreme pornographic image and making indecent images of children (×17). A search of D's home and computer equipment uncovered a number of bestial images depicting women and girls with horses and dogs. There were also 937 indecent images and movies of children, 613 at Level 1. There were 227 at Level 4. The images were predominantly of children aged 8-14. There were 18 images of a girl's face superimposed on adult bodies engaged in intercourse and bestiality. That girl was D's girlfriend's niece, aged 13 or 14. D said that he found it sexually arousing to look at what the women and girls were doing with animals. D was aged 37 and had shown remorse. Held. There was a lack of distribution, co-operation and the generous full credit for the plea. The Judge was entitled to be concerned about the potential danger D posed. The maximum 2-year sentence for one offence of extreme pornography is not wrong. With regard to the mitigation and totality, and despite the aggravating features, the sentences would be concurrent, making **2 years** overall, not 2½ years.

R v King 2013 EWCA Crim 320 D pleaded to possession of indecent photographs (×1) and making indecent photographs (×27). D's home was searched after his partner telephoned the police upon finding an album with images of young girls. The album included four photographs at Level 1 of D's partner's late daughter in a state of undress. He had never met the girl in question and had misappropriated the pictures after being shown them by his partner. Held. The images of his partner's daughter were misappropriated in a gross breach of trust. Four computers and three memory cards were examined and 4,267 still and moving images were found. About 60% of the images were in the 'active' area of the computer. The images were of girls aged between 2 and 15. The overwhelming majority were at Level 1 (4,151 images). There were 27 images at Level 2, 30 images at Level 3, 56 images at Level 4 and three images at Level 5. The police also found website details written in notebooks. In interview, D admitted that the images would be found but denied that any would involve penetration. He admitted that he had been accessing child pornography two or three times a week over a four-year period. He was aged 42 and had no similar convictions. An unrelated matter was dealt with by a community order in 2006. The pre-sentence report noted a low risk of reoffending but a high risk of harm. It recommended a community disposal. The Judge justified his departure from the guidelines by the 'grotesque nature' of the four photographs from his partner. Held. The photographs from her partner were completely innocent when taken by a parent in a domestic setting but not so in D's possession. There was large-scale downloading of images of children, focusing on girls aged under 13. The material was held for personal use and there was no question of distribution or commercial gain. Immediate custody was entirely justified. That in itself is likely to result in an increase in starting point. We may have left in place a custodial sentence, however, we consider that the community will be best protected by an order that allows some constructive work to be done. It is the course most likely to prevent repetition in contrast to being released from custody where no course has been undertaken. Because D had been in custody for several months, **3-year community order** with an Internet sex offender treatment programme (which would not have been available with the Judge's 2-year sentence).

R v GC 2013 EWCA Crim 999 D pleaded to making indecent images of a child (×8) and taking indecent images (×5). D's partner looked at his mobile phone and computer hard drive. The hard drive contained adult pornography and some images of herself, which she deleted. On closer inspection she saw that the mobile phone contained a folder in the cache memory in which there were six images of her four-year-old daughter lying naked on her back with her genitalia exposed. D was effectively her stepfather. There was a further image of D's partner's daughter which was on a USB stick found in the house. Another image of a seven-year-old child was recovered from the same source. Those images were categorised as Level 1. Following his arrest, a further 174 images of pre-pubescent girls at Level 1 were found on D's computer. D accepted that he had taken the images of his partner's daughter, after putting their son to bed and waiting for his partner to go out. D's partner said that as a result of the offences she had had to leave a university course halfway through, which put her in financial difficulty. D, aged 24 at appeal, had no convictions. Held. The offences concerning the stepdaughter were on any view extremely serious. They were deeply unattractive principally because of the gross breach of trust. The images were not shared and there were no aggravating features identified by the guidelines, save that they were of a very young child. Allowing for the breach of trust element, after a trial, 21 months for the offences relating to his stepdaughter was appropriate. With the plea, **14 months** not 18 months. 8 weeks concurrent for the other offences would remain.

R v B 2014 EWCA Crim 2124 D pleaded (full discount) to 12 assaults by penetration (10 vaginal and two anal), with ten similar TICs, 11 sexual assaults, with eight similar TICs, an unknown number of counts of voyeurism, with 47 similar TICs. D also pleaded to sexual activity with a child (×2). D was a GP and knew V's family. V, who was aged 17, stayed with D during half-term when he acted as her legal guardian. She was described as 'willing to please and somewhat gullible'. One evening, whilst watching a film with sexual content and having discussed sexual matters, D gave V alcohol and two tablets, albeit with no medical effect. When she went upstairs, D touched her sexually, including inserting his fingers into her vagina. Although this was consensual, unknown to V, D used a camera hidden in his watch to record the events, thereby vitiating consent. One film lasted 32 minutes and a further film, showing V asleep, lasted 11 minutes. D then filmed V undressing and showering.

V took screenshots of images on D's computer leading to the discovery of a huge number of videos, some lasting over 40 minutes, showing medical examinations of female patients over a three-year period. They were all un-chaperoned, save for one occasion when they moved behind a curtain on D's instruction. The victims, 293 in all, were aged from their early teens to their fifties. Examinations of victims' vaginas or anuses were filmed using D's hidden watch camera. This was then downloaded, but not circulated, by D and was deleted subsequently in large quantities. D also filmed his digital penetration of the vagina of ten patients, and the anus of two. It was accepted that this was reasonable for the purposes of legitimate medical examination, but there had been no consent to being filmed for D's sexual gratification. On six of these occasions, D had not worn a glove, and on one D made inappropriate comments. D, again filming, also touched or massaged the naked breasts or bottoms of female patients. This was for legitimate medical examination but, again, the victims did not consent to being filmed. D also fondled the bottoms of two 15-year-old girls attending for contraceptive injections, recording each assault. D was a Malaysian, aged 46 on appeal and of good character. He had co-operated and was remorseful. The Judge considered him dangerous but thought that could be managed by a long prison sentence and a SOPO.

Held. For D there was serious breach of trust and there could have been no medical need for anything that happened. Starting at 3 years, we impose 2 years for the assaults by penetration and 18 months concurrent for the voyeurism. For the patients, no one could have contemplated offending on this scale by a doctor. The gross breach was the most important factor. There can be no doubt that the public places enormous trust in doctors. The maintenance of confidence in that trust is of paramount importance. We view with very considerable seriousness the failure by D and the medical practice at which he worked to inquire whether the patients required a chaperon. It also indicated a very considerable degree of planning. It was particularly serious to abuse the trust that the two children had placed in D when coming for their contraceptive injections. We also place the offences of assault by penetration in the top category. For the penetration, the guideline has a range of 6-11 years.[1073] We put case at the top of that range, because of the breach of trust, although the penetration was minimal and brief. The sentence for the offences involving patients is 12 years. With plea, that is 8 years. The V sentence should be 3 years, with plea 2 years. 8 years and 2 years consecutive makes **10 years** in all, not the 12 ordered by the Judge.

Post-2014 guideline case
R v Norval 2015 EWCA Crim 1694 D pleaded to various sex offences including outraging public decency. Using his mobile phone, D attempted to take a photograph up the skirt of a 14-year-old girl while both were waiting at a till in a supermarket. D was aged 53 and of good character. Held. The offence would not normally attract a custodial sentence. On its own it should have resulted in a high-level community order. Sentence reduced for all offending and suspended.

See also: *R v GW* 2014 EWCA Crim 2471 (Pleas to 29 counts of voyeurism and making indecent photographs of children, aged 9-17. Deputy head at school photographing pupils and other children elsewhere. Internet programme to defeat police detectors. Nearly 16,500 images, almost all at Level 1. 26 moving images. Exemplary good character. We start at 6 years, so with plea **4 years** not 5.

331.24   *Pseudo-photographs, cartoons, drawings etc.*
Sexual Offences Act 2003 Guideline 2008 para 6A.3, see www.banksr.com Other Matters Guidelines tab Pseudo-photographs should generally be treated as less serious than real images. However, they can be just as serious as photographs of a real child, for example where the imagery is particularly grotesque and beyond the scope of normal photography.

Note: I understand this guideline has not been replaced. The new guideline only repeals parts which are covered in the new guideline. Ed.

[1073] In part of the judgment, the range is stated to be 6-13, which is in error. The guideline has a starting point of 10 years where the victim is aged 13-15, and 8 years where the victim is aged 16+. The range for the first is 8-13 years and for the second, 6-11 years, see page 25 of the guideline. Ed.

R v Gregory 2012 EWCA Crim 2099 D pleaded to possession of prohibited images of children (sections 62(1) and 66(2)). Prison officers found 107 hand-drawn indecent images of children and a large amount of indecent writing relating to sexual abuse of children. Another prisoner was found to have indecent drawings which had been obtained from D. D's drawings were cartoonish but were technically proficient and very graphic. They depicted young children involved in sexual acts with adults, group activity and images involving a dog. Some showed a child distressed. The writings involved fantasy stories of abuse. In 2006 D was convicted of 10 offences of making indecent photographs (251 days suspended). In 2007 he pleaded to three offences of sexual assault on a female aged under 13 (extended sentence with 21 months' custody). In 2009 for taking indecent photographs he received 15 months' imprisonment. He was released and recalled. D had taken part in sex offending courses with no effect. The Judge started with the maximum (3 years) and gave a full discount for the plea. Held. The images were absolutely sickening. There is an important difference between this type of offending and where there is a photograph of an actual victim. But one must avoid pressing the point too far. There is an aggravating feature that D had made these images and passed them within a prison where their presence could adversely affect the keeping of good order and the effectiveness of sex offender work. We start at **27 months** not the maximum, so with plea **18 months**.

Post-2014 guideline case

R v Norval 2015 EWCA Crim 1694 D pleaded to various sex offences including making indecent photographs of children involving pseudo-images. D had created them by superimposing photographs of a child's head on photographs of naked adult females in indecent poses. The superimposition looked realistic. Held. This should not be treated as production even if it was that technically. It should be treated as possession. Sentence reduced for all offending and suspended.

Extreme pornographic offences (incl. animal and violent images)

331.25 **Animals, Sexual activity with   Distribution   Selling   Pre-2014 guideline case**

'Commercial exploitation and/or motivation' is an aggravating factor, see *Sexual Offences Guideline 2014* page 78 at **331.5**.

Note: Although the offence is not dealt with in the guidelines, this principle is of universal application to sex offences. Ed.

R v Snowden 2009 EWCA Crim 1200, 2010 1 Cr App R (S) 39 (p 233) D pleaded early to seven specimen counts of publishing an obscene article. A letter for D was put through the wrong letter box. The householder opened it and took it to the police. They searched D's house and found DVD copying equipment and 55 obscene DVDs, mostly dealing with animals. A woman was shown having oral and/or vaginal sex with a dog, a horse and a pig. Men were having sex with a cow and a chicken. A woman was masturbating a horse and a dog. A mouse in a tube was inserted into a woman's vagina. An eel was inserted into a woman's vagina and anus. Fists were inserted into women's vaginas and they were evidently unwilling and showing distress. Other activity involved defecation, vomiting and urination. There was a list of films that D had sent to 69 customers. D made full admissions. He said that some of the material was sold and some exchanged. D was aged 53 and of good character. He was unemployed and drawing benefits. The Judge said that he was caught red-handed and said that the supply was only to those who requested DVDs. Held. It was proper to sentence for the previous trading. Being caught red-handed made the discount for plea 20%. It was commercial, and the number and extreme obscenity made **2½ years** not excessive.

331.26 **Animals, Sexual activity with   Possession**

R v Oliver 2011 EWCA Crim 3114, 2012 2 Cr App (R) 45 (p 269) D pleaded to possession of extreme pornographic images (×2). He visited an Internet chat room and his computer equipment was seized from his home and searched. There were eight movies and three still images which depicted sexual intercourse or oral sex between human beings and animals. D claimed to have no recollection of the images and was unsure how they came to be on his computer. After their discovery, there was publicity about it and D retired from a position as Governor of HMP Doncaster, taking redundancy. The pre-sentence report noted the additional hardship of a custodial sentence for a man with D's background. The Judge noted that when D downloaded the images, it was not an offence to possess them. D was sentenced on the basis that: a) he downloaded the images when they were legal and did not later re-access them, and b) after the criminalisation of possession of extreme pornography, D downloaded a program called Team Viewer, which enabled persons other than D to remotely take control of D's computer. The Judge noted that D had thereby exposed himself as a governor to blackmail, and also made the images accessible to others. For that reason, the Judge concluded the offences crossed the custody threshold. D, aged 54 at appeal, was of previous good character. Held. D was of exemplary character and had paid a high price for his exposure to shame and ridicule. **3 months** following a trial was sufficient punishment. With plea, **2 months** not 6.

R v Burns 2012 EWCA Crim 192, 2 Cr App R (S) 66 (p 384) D pleaded to possession of extreme pornographic images. V, aged 16, was in contact with D via Facebook. V's father became concerned because the chat log between V and D was sexual. Officers attended D's home and he was arrested. His house was searched and he admitted that there were pornographic movies involving sexual activity between women and animals stored on his laptop. There were eight movies which had been sent to D by a person with whom he was in contact in America. D, aged 42 at appeal, had a number of previous convictions, including offences of sexual activity with a child (2008). The child was aged 14 at the time. Held. These matters clearly crossed the custody threshold. Even allowing for D's previous convictions, 12 months after a trial was excessive. With full credit for the plea, **4 months** not 8.

R v Clark 2012 EWCA Crim 1707 D pleaded (full credit) to possession of indecent images of children (×3), possession of an extreme pornographic image and making indecent images of children (×17). A search of D's home and computer equipment uncovered a number of bestial images depicting women and girls with horses and dogs. There were also 937 indecent images and movies of children, of which 613 were at Level 1. There were 227 at Level 4. The images were predominantly of children aged 8-14. There were 18 images of a girl's face superimposed on adult bodies engaged in intercourse and bestiality. That girl was D's girlfriend's niece, aged 13 or 14. D said that he found it sexually arousing to look at what the women and girls were doing with animals. D was aged 37 and had shown remorse. Held. There was a lack of distribution, co-operation and the generous full credit for the plea. The Judge was entitled to be concerned about the potential danger D posed. The maximum 2-year sentence for one offence of extreme pornography is not wrong. With regard to the mitigation and totality, and despite the aggravating features, the sentences would be concurrent, making **2 years** overall, not 2½ years.

R v Lewis 2012 EWCA Crim 1978 D pleaded to making indecent photographs of children (×16) and possession of extreme pornographic images. The police received information regarding D and searched his home address. His computers were seized and D made full admissions before his equipment was examined. There were 121 images of children including moving images: five at Level 5, 42 at Level 4, 17 at Level 3, 34 at Level 2, and 23 at Level 1. Nearly all the children were aged under 13, but some of the higher-level images involved children as young as 8. There was one image of a child aged 3 or 4. The extreme images mainly involved adults with animals. D, aged 45 at appeal, had no convictions. The pre-sentence report assessed him as posing a medium risk to the public, but with a low risk of reoffending. He had a history of emotional vulnerability and the report writer said he would struggle to cope with a custodial sentence. The report recommended a suspended sentence. D sought to minimise his

responsibility including offering explanations of the offences such as his redundancy, his night job leading to drinking in the day and the serious illness of his partner. Held. Given the very early plea and strong personal mitigation, 12 months is too long. The gravity of the offending is sufficiently recognised by a sentence of **6 months**.
See also: *R v Livesay* 2013 EWCA Crim 1600 (Plea. 329 still images and five moving images. Horses or dogs penetrating women. No previous. Full credit. Strong personal mitigation. **4 months** not 14. Suspension was a very serious possibility.)
Post-2014 guideline conviction
R v R 2014 EWCA Crim 1976 D pleaded (20% credit) to making indecent photos of a child (×16), possessing indecent photos of a child, possessing extreme pornographic images (×5). D's wife found a memory stick with voyeuristic images of her adult daughter (D received 6 months) and police then examined D's computer which contained three and a half years' worth of material. 392 child images were found. Three were Category B, but the remainder were Category C. The children depicted were aged between 7 and 12. 19 extreme pornographic images were found, depicting adult bestiality. D was aged 57 on appeal and was convicted in 2000 of making indecent photos of children (×11). He showed little remorse and minimised his conduct. Held. The Judge had erroneously equated the possession of extreme pornography with a Category A offence under the indecent photos of children guidelines. **8 months**, not 16.

331.27   *Possession   Pre-2014 guideline case*
Example: *R v Blyth* 2011 EWCA Crim 2399 (Plea to making an indecent photograph of a child (×3), 126 images and 21 movies and possessing an extreme pornographic image (bestiality). Levels 1 and 2 only. Children aged between 6 and 13. Aged 56. Good character. **Community order** not suspended sentence with unpaid work.)

Matters relating to the defendant
331.28   *Defendant on licence   Pre-2014 guideline case*
'Offence committed whilst on licence' is an aggravating factor, see *Sexual Offences Guideline 2014* page 78 at **331.5**.
R v Hatchett 2010 EWCA Crim 13 D pleaded early to 16 counts of making indecent photos. While on licence after his release from prison, concerns were raised and police searched his home. They found 502 indecent images of children or films of children aged between 1 and 13 years. 397 were at Level 1, 39 at Level 2, 28 at Level 3, 32 at Level 4 and four at Level 5. The images had been downloaded over a 10-month period for personal use. He made full and frank admissions in interview and was recalled to prison. D expressed remorse. The pre-sentence report gave a low risk of reoffending but a high risk of serious harm to children if he did so. In 2002, D was sentenced to an extended sentence of 10½ years (5½ years' custody 5 years' licence) for ten indecent assaults on children (the youngest child was aged 3), six offences of taking indecent photos of children and having indecent photos of children. Held. The starting point was 9 months. The extreme aggravating factors lifted that to 3 years, and with the plea discount **2 years** not 2 years' IPP. This to be consecutive to 1 year for the breach of licence.
See also: *R v Britton* 2010 EWCA Crim 2079 (Plea. 685 images with 24 at Level 5. Aged 58. Own use. Previous convictions for taking indecent photographs (5½ years' extended sentence (2½ years' custody 3 years' licence)). Some of the offences were committed when he was on licence. After trial 2 years, so **15 months** not 27.)

331.29   *Persistent offenders/Previous image conviction(s)*
'Previous convictions, having regard to: a) the nature of the offence to which the conviction relates and its relevance to the current offence, and b) the time that has elapsed since the conviction' is a statutory aggravating factor, see *Sexual Offences Guideline 2014* page 78 at **331.5**.
R v Sperl 2011 EWCA Crim 208 D pleaded to making indecent photographs of a child. There were five counts to represent the five different levels of photograph. Some of the

images at Level 3 and 4 involved babies from 6-12 months old. There were 2,731 live images: that is 1,569 at Level 1, 345 at Level 2, 394 at Level 3, 343 at Level 4 and 81 at Level 5. D, aged 33, had a previous conviction in 2001 for five offences of making indecent photographs of children. He told probation that the offences were "like a drug, you have to keep doing it more and more". Held. The offence was aggravated by D's previous convictions for the same offences. In D's favour there was a timely plea and there is no evidence that he distributed the images. We appreciate that that sentence itself is significantly outside the appropriate guidelines, but that can be justified by reference to the nature of the material, and to the fact of the previous conviction, which inevitably has aggravated this matter. Because of the plea and the range in the guidelines, **2 years**, not 3½.

R v Burns 2012 EWCA Crim 192, 2 Cr App R (S) 66 (p 384) D pleaded (full credit) to possession of extreme pornographic images. He had been contacting a 16-year-old girl on Facebook. The content of the messages was sexual and her father became concerned. Police searched D's address and seized his laptop. It contained eight video images of sexual activity between women and animals involved in sexual activity. He volunteered that information in interview. D, aged 42 at appeal, had a number of convictions, most notably for a number of offences of sexual activity with a 14-year-old child in 2008 (3 years). Held. The offence passed the custody threshold. The previous convictions were a factor to be taken into account. With the plea and his co-operation, **4 months** not 8 was appropriate.

Note: It seems likely that at least one of the films showed penetrative activity. Ed.

R v Lewis 2012 EWCA Crim 1071, 2013 1 Cr App R (S) 23 (p 121) D pleaded to possessing an extreme pornographic image (×2). He was subject to a SOPO as a result of a 2007 conviction for causing or inciting a female child to engage in sexual activity (×2), one grooming, making indecent photographs (×2) and one possessing indecent photographs. As a part of the monitoring of his activities, his computers were examined. There were 44 static images of an adult female engaged in sexual activities with horses and dogs, and 19 moving images of similar acts. Twelve of the static images were duplicates. The pre-sentence report noted that whilst D accepted possession of the images, he sought to minimise the offence by denying he used them for sexual gratification. It recommended a community order with a Community Sex Offender Group Programme. D was aged 43 at appeal. He was university educated and suffered from worsening colitis. He had to give up work due to poor health. The Judge had regard to the guidelines for possession of child pornography. Held. This was not a victimless crime because quite often the women were trafficked or forced into involvement in making the images. The women had to be protected from sexual exploitation. The downloading of material of this sort contributed to the demand for such images and further exploitation of such women. The Judge had regard to the 2007 convictions and noted that the instant offences were not identical to possession of child pornography. **12 months** was not manifestly excessive.

See also: *R v Officer* 2012 EWCA Crim 1685 (Pleas to offences of making indecent photographs of children (two at Level 4, three at Level 2) and possessing extreme pornography. Conviction for sexual assault on a girl aged under 13 in 2007 (54 months). Images of children aged between 4 and 10, including three movies at Level 4. He stated he downloaded the images so he would be sent back to prison. Report identified he posed a very serious danger to children. Every reason to think that he might progress to contact offences again. **3 years** was untouched, without hesitation.)

Post-2014 guideline cases

R v R 2014 EWCA Crim 1976 D pleaded (20% credit) to making indecent photos of a child (×16), possessing indecent photos of a child, and possessing extreme pornographic images (×5). D's wife found a memory stick with voyeuristic images of her adult daughter (D received 6 months) and police then examined D's computer, which contained 3½ years' worth of material. 392 child images were found. Three were

Category B, but the remainder were Category C. The children depicted were aged between 7 and 12. 19 extreme pornographic images were found, depicting adult bestiality. D was aged 57 on appeal and was convicted in 2000 of making indecent photos of children (×11). He showed little remorse and minimised his conduct. Held. The Judge had erroneously equated the possession of extreme pornography with a Category A offence under the indecent photos of children guidelines. **8 months**, not 16.

R v Kerry 2015 EWCA Crim 827 D pleaded guilty to three counts of making indecent photographs of a child and three counts of distribution of such photographs. He sold his phone and the new owner found it had five indecent images of children on it. One photo was Category B and four were Category C. D told the police he liked young boys and had requested images of young boys from other men. In recent years he had taken M-CAT which had increased his sexual arousal. D was aged 52, and between 1982 and 2005 he had nine court appearances for 51 offences, including four buggeries, two gross indecencies, 14 indecent assaults on boys aged under 16 with 63 TICs, five indecent assaults on girls aged under 13 and a conspiracy to commit gross indecency (given 8 years). He breached his licence and was not released until March 2013. The pre-sentence report said there was a very high risk of him committing 'further offences of this nature'. The psychiatrist said his risk of sexual offending had reduced in recent years. The Judge departed from the guideline and gave D 10 years' **extended sentence (4 years' custody** 6 years' extended licence). Held. D is a prolific sex offender and throughout his life has failed to abide by his licence conditions. The court should always have a note of the guidelines. The Judge was entitled to conclude that D satisfied the dangerousness criteria, but applying the guideline, **2½ years**, with little discount for the plea because of the weight [of evidence] against him.

331.30   *Persistent offenders/Previous image conviction   More than one child/sex sentence   Pre-2014 guideline cases*

'Previous convictions, having regard to: a) the nature of the offence to which the conviction relates and its relevance to the current offence, and b) the time that has elapsed since the conviction' is a statutory aggravating factor, see *Sexual Offences Guideline 2014* page 78 at **331.5**.

R v Hicks 2009 EWCA Crim 733 D pleaded to 14 offences of making indecent photographs. In January 2006, police searched his home and found two computers with 1,139 indecent images of children on them: 1,133 were at Level 1, one at Level 2, one at Level 3, and four at Level 4. He was in breach of various computer and/or web orders. D was aged 54. In July 2003 he was sentenced to 9 months with a 24-month extended licence for making indecent photographs (relating to the period from September 1998 to November 2002). Shortly after his release he, using the web, invited girls to be photographed. A 13-year-old girl arrived with her mother, and the mother indicated there were to be no inappropriate underwear shots. There was a doctored photo but it had not been circulated. In February 2005, for more indecent photographs (relating from his release in November 2003 to June 2004), he was sentenced to 39 months' extended sentence (**15 months'** custody 24 months' licence). This time the Judge imposed IPP. Held. There were no contact offences. **12 months** with a stringent Sexual Offences Prevention Order substituted.

R v Bain and Best 2009 EWCA Crim 2970 D and B pleaded (full credit) to possessing indecent photographs of a child (×20). B also pleaded on rearraignment to breach of a SOPO. D and B had been in a relationship for 12 years. B was released from custody and took out a lease on a property. A search warrant was executed and a computer seized. DVDs were also seized and both were found to contain indecent images. The DVDs were primarily made at a time when B was in prison. There were also DVDs that were dated 2001. The images found were as follows: Still and (Moving) Level 1, 106 (0), Level 2, 47 (84), Level 3, 0 (3) and Level 4, 45 (90). B, aged 44, had convictions for burglary and theft, but also buggery (1987, 11 years), making and distributing indecent photographs (2000, extended sentence) and possessing indecent images (2006, 2 years).

D, aged 59, had convictions for possessing (×15) and making (×2) indecent images (1999, 2 years' probation) and making and distributing indecent photographs (2003, extended sentence). B's offending had reduced in seriousness from contact to non-contact offences, but this was his fourth conviction in eight years. This was D's third offence for child pornography. Held. The offences fell outside the guidelines. The appropriate starting point was near the 5-year maximum. Starting at 4 years 9 months, the appropriate sentence for both is **3 years 2 months**.

R v Gregory 2012 EWCA Crim 2099 D pleaded to possession of prohibited images of children (sections 62(1) and 66(2)). Prison officers found 107 hand-drawn indecent images of children and a large amount of indecent writing relating to sexual abuse of children. Another prisoner was found to have indecent drawings which had been obtained from D. D's drawings were cartoonish but were technically proficient and very graphic. They depicted young children involved in sexual acts with adults, group activity and images involving a dog. Some showed a child distressed. The writings involved fantasy stories of abuse. In 2006 D was convicted of 10 offences of making indecent photographs (251 days suspended). In 2007 he pleaded to three offences of sexual assault on a female aged under 13 (extended sentence with 21 months' custody). In 2009 for taking indecent photographs he received 15 months' imprisonment. He was released and recalled. D had taken part in sex offending courses with no effect. The Judge started with the maximum (3 years) and gave a full discount for the plea. Held. The images were absolutely sickening. There is an important difference between this type of offending and where there is a photograph of an actual victim. But one must avoid pressing the point too far. There is an aggravating feature that D had made these images and passed them within a prison where their presence could adversely affect the keeping of good order and the effectiveness of sex offender work. We start at 27 months, not the maximum, so with plea **18 months**.

331.31   *Rehabilitation*
'Where there is a sufficient prospect of rehabilitation, a community order with a sex offender treatment programme requirement under Criminal Justice Act 2003 s 202 can be a proper alternative to a short or moderate-length custodial sentence', see *Sexual Offences Guideline 2014* page 78 at **331.5**.

331.32   *Servicemen and women*
Guidance on Sentencing in the Court Martial 2013 para 10.2. The incidence of child pornography cases has risen significantly in the Service jurisdiction over the past few years. This sort of offending and the management of sexual offenders of this kind (involving e.g. restrictions on working with young persons) is often incompatible with their continued service in the Armed Forces. Trust is undermined and in a close-knit community an offender of this kind may be ostracised by his peers; that can lead to a breakdown of unit cohesion and operational effectiveness. In addition to the sentences in the SC guidelines, which depend partly on the quantity and level of seriousness of the images, offenders should therefore be dismissed (with or without disgrace) unless there are exceptional reasons for retention in the Service.

332   SEX OFFENCES: MENTALLY DISORDERED PERSONS, WITH
332.1
Sexual Offences Act 2003
   s 30 (sexual activity with a person with a mental disorder impeding choice)
   s 31 (causing or inciting a person with a mental disorder impeding choice to engage in sexual activity)
   s 32 (engaging in sexual activity in the presence of a person with a mental disorder impeding choice)
   s 33 (causing a person with a mental disorder impeding choice to watch a sexual act)

s 34 (inducement/threat/deception to procure sexual activity with a person with a mental disorder)

s 35 (causing a person with a mental disorder to engage etc. in sexual activity by inducement/threat/deception)

s 36 (sexual activity in the presence of a person with a mental disorder, by inducement/threat/deception)

s 37 (causing a person with a mental disorder to watch a sexual act by inducement/threat/deception)

s 38 (care workers: sexual activity with a person with a mental disorder)

s 39 (care workers: causing or inciting sexual activity)

s 40 (care workers: sexual activity in the presence of a person with a mental disorder)

s 41 (care workers: causing a person with a mental disorder to watch a sexual act)

Modes of trial and maximum sentences Sections 30, 31, 34, 35, 38 and 39 where there is penetration, the offences are triable only on indictment. Maximum sentence is life. Otherwise the offences are triable either way. On indictment the maximum for sections 30, 31, 34 and 35 is 14 years, and for sections 38 and 39, the maximum is 10 years. Sections 32, 33, 36, 37, 40 and 41 are triable either way. On indictment the maximum for sections 32, 33, 36 and 37 is 10 years and for sections 40 and 41, the maximum is 7 years.

Summary maximum for all offences, 6 months and/or a £5,000 fine for offences committed before 12 March 2015 and an unlimited fine thereafter.[1074] There are maximum fines for those aged under 18, see **14.38** in Volume 1.

Some of these maximum sentences are subject to the automatic life provisions.

Automatic life Sexual Offences Act 2003 s 30-31 and 34-35 are listed in Criminal Justice Act 2003 Sch 15B Part 1. The Lord Chief Justice said in *Att-Gen's Ref No 27 of 2013* 2014 EWCA Crim 334[1075] para 8 iii) (*obiter*) that in rare cases the provisions could lead to the imposition of a life sentence where the offence does not carry life imprisonment.

The court must (unless the particular circumstances make it unjust[1076]) pass automatic life if: a) the defendant is aged 18+ at the date of the conviction, b) the offence was committed on or after 3 December 2012, c) the court considers a determinate sentence of at least 10 years is appropriate, d) at the time the offender was convicted he had a conviction for a Criminal Justice Act 2003 Sch 15B offence, and e) the defendant at the time of his or her conviction had previously been sentenced to either: i) a life sentence where he or she was not eligible for release during the first 5 years of the sentence, or ii) a determinate sentence or extended sentence where the custodial part was 10 years or more.[1077] For a pre-2012 extended sentence, when determining whether the custodial term was 10+ years the period deducted for time on remand or on a curfew and tag is included.[1078]

Extended sentences Offences Against the Person Act 1861 s 33 is listed in Criminal Justice Act 2003 Sch 15. The court may pass a 2012 extended sentence (EDS) if there is a significant risk of serious harm from future specified offences and either: a) the defendant has a Criminal Justice Act 2003 Sch 15B conviction (applicable only to defendants aged 18+), or b) the offence would justify a determinate sentence of at least 4 years.[1079]

[1074] Legal Aid, Sentencing and Punishment of Offenders Act 2012 s 85(1) and (4) and Legal Aid, Sentencing and Punishment of Offenders Act 2012 (Commencement No 11) Order 2015 2015/504

[1075] This case is also known as *R v Burinskas* 2014 EWCA Crim 334.

[1076] Criminal Justice Act 2003 s 224A(2)

[1077] Criminal Justice Act 2003 s 224A as inserted by Legal Aid, Sentencing and Punishment of Offenders Act 2012 s 122. The condition for a) is at section 224A(1)(a), for b) is at section 224A(1)(b), for c) is at section 224A(1)(c), and for d) is at section 224A(4)-(9).

[1078] Criminal Justice Act 2003 s 224A(9)-(10)

[1079] Criminal Justice Act 2003 s 226A-226B as inserted by Legal Aid, Sentencing and Punishment of Offenders Act 2012 s 124

Sexual Harm Prevention Orders There is a discretionary power to make this order when it is necessary to protect the public from sexual harm.[1080]
Notification For: a) section 30-37 offences and b) section 38-41 offences where:
  i) the defendant was aged under 18, he or she is sentenced to imprisonment for a term of 12+ months, or
  ii) in any other case: 1) the victim was aged under 18, or 2) the defendant is sentenced to: a) a term of imprisonment, b) detained in a hospital, or…d) made the subject of a community sentence of at least 12 months,
the defendant must notify the police within three days (or three days from his or her release from imprisonment, hospital etc.) with his or her name, home address, National Insurance number etc. and any change of address and any address where he or she resides for seven days[1081] (in one or more periods) or more in any 12-month period.[1082]
Children and vulnerable adults: barred lists Where the defendant is convicted of any of these offences and is aged 18 or over he or she is automatically barred from engaging in regulated activity with vulnerable adults and with children.[1083] The judge must tell the defendant that the Disclosure and Barring Service will include him or her in the barred list.[1084] The defendant cannot ask the Service to remove him or her from the child list for offences under SOA 2003 s 30-41 where the offence involved a child. Where the offence involved an adult he or she can ask for removal. The defendant cannot ask the Service to remove him or her from the vulnerable adults list when convicted for any of the offences listed above.
Old cases. Only one is listed. Sentencing policy has changed. All but that one are best ignored.

332.2   *Crown Court statistics   England and Wales*
Sexual activity etc. with a person with a mental disorder   Aged 21+

Year	Plea	Total sentenced	Type of sentencing %						Average length of custody in months
			Discharge	Fine	Commu-nity sentence	Sus-pended sentence	Custody	Other	
2013	G	13	–	–	–	15.4	84.6	–	44.8
	NG	9	–	–	–	11.1	88.9	–	77.3
2014	G	19	–	–	5.3	10.5	84.2	–	57.0
	NG	16	–	–	6.3	–	93.7	–	58.7

For explanations about the statistics, see page 1-xii. For more statistics and for statistics for male and female defendants etc., see www.banksr.com Other Matters Statistics tab

Guidelines
332.3   *Sentencing Council guideline Sexual Offences Act 2003 s 30-31*
Sexual Offences Guideline 2014, see www.banksr.com Other Matters Guidelines tab. In force 1 April 2014. The guideline only applies to offenders aged 18+, see page 7 of the guideline. For the usual practice, see **66.21** in Volume 1.

STEP ONE: Determining the offence category
page 103 The court should determine which categories of harm and culpability the offence falls into by reference only to the tables below.

[1080] Sexual Offences Act 2003 s 103A as inserted by Anti-social Behaviour, Crime and Policing Act 2014 Sch 5 para 2 and Sexual Offences Act 2003 Sch 3
[1081] Sexual Offences Act 2003 s 84(1)(c) and (6)
[1082] Sexual Offences Act 2003 s 83 and Sch 3
[1083] Safeguarding Vulnerable Groups Act 2006 s 2 and Sch 3 and Safeguarding Vulnerable Groups Act 2006 (Prescribed Criteria and Miscellaneous Provisions) Regulations 2009 2009/37 For offences without a right to make representation, see regs 3 and 5 and Sch paras 1 and 3. For offences with a right to make representation, see regs 4 and 6 and Sch para 2 and 4.
[1084] Safeguarding Vulnerable Groups Act 2006 s 2 and Sch 3 para 25

Harm	
Category 1	The extreme nature of one or more Category 2 factors or the extreme impact caused by a combination of Category 2 factors **may** elevate to Category 1
Category 2	Severe psychological or physical harm Pregnancy or STI as a consequence of offence Additional degradation/humiliation Abduction Prolonged detention/sustained incident Violence or threats of violence Forced/uninvited entry into victim's home or residence
Category 3	Factor(s) in Categories 1 and 2 not present

Culpability A
Significant degree of planning Offender acts together with others to commit the offence Use of alcohol/drugs on victim to facilitate the offence Grooming behaviour used against victim Abuse of trust Previous violence against victim Offence committed in course of burglary Sexual images of victim recorded, retained, solicited or shared Deliberate isolation of victim Commercial exploitation and/or motivation Offence racially or religiously aggravated Offence motivated by, or demonstrating, hostility to the victim based on his or her sexual orientation (or presumed sexual orientation) or transgender identity (or presumed transgender identity) Offence motivated by, or demonstrating, hostility to the victim based on the victim's disability (or presumed disability)
Culpability B
Factor(s) in Category A not present

332.4

STEP TWO: Starting point and category range

page 105 Having determined the category of harm and culpability, the court should use the corresponding starting points to reach a sentence within the category range below. The starting point applies to all offenders irrespective of plea or previous convictions. Having determined the starting point, step two allows further adjustment for aggravating or mitigating features, set out [below].

A case of particular gravity, reflected by multiple features of culpability or harm in step one, could merit upward adjustment from the starting point before further adjustment for aggravating or mitigating features, set out [below].

Where there is a sufficient prospect of rehabilitation, a community order with a sex offender treatment programme requirement under Criminal Justice Act 2003 s 202 can be a proper alternative to a short or moderate-length custodial sentence.

Where offence involved penetration

	A		B	
	Starting point	**Category range**	**Starting point**	**Category range**
Category 1	16 years' custody	13 to 19 years' custody	13 years' custody	11 to 17 years' custody

	A		B	
Category 2	13 years' custody	11 to 17 years' custody	10 years' custody	8 to 13 years' custody
Category 3	10 years' custody	8 to 13 years' custody	8 years' custody	6 to 11 years' custody

Where offence did not involve penetration

	A		B	
	Starting point	**Category range**	**Starting point**	**Category range**
Category 1	6 years' custody	4 to 9 years' custody	4 years' custody	3 to 7 years' custody
Category 2	4 years' custody	3 to 7 years' custody	2 years' custody	1 to 4 years' custody
Category 3	1 year's custody	26 weeks' to 2 years' custody	26 weeks' custody	High-level community order to 1 year's custody

For the meaning of a high-level community order, see **16.14** in Volume 1.

332.5   [Aggravating and mitigating factors]
page 106 The table below contains a **non-exhaustive** list of additional factual elements providing the context of the offence and factors relating to the offender. Identify whether any combination of these, or other relevant factors, should result in an upward or downward adjustment from the starting point. **In particular, relevant recent convictions are likely to result in an upward adjustment**. In some cases, having considered these factors, it may be appropriate to move outside the identified category range.

When appropriate, the court should also consider the custody threshold as follows:

Has the custody threshold been passed?

If so, is it unavoidable that a custodial sentence be imposed?

If so, can that sentence be suspended?

Aggravating factors
Statutory aggravating factors:
Previous convictions, having regard to: a) the nature of the offence to which the conviction relates and its relevance to the current offence, and b) the time that has elapsed since the conviction
Offence committed whilst on bail
Other aggravating factors:
Ejaculation (where not taken into account at step one)
Blackmail or other threats made (where not taken into account at step one)
Location of offence
Timing of offence
Use of weapon or other item to frighten or injure
Victim compelled to leave their home or institution (including victims of domestic violence)
Failure to comply with current court orders
Offence committed whilst on licence
Presence of others, especially children
Any steps taken to prevent the victim reporting an incident, obtaining assistance and/or from assisting or supporting the prosecution
Attempts to dispose of or conceal evidence
Commission of offence whilst under the influence of alcohol or drugs

Mitigating factors
No previous convictions **or** no relevant/recent convictions Remorse Previous good character and/or exemplary conduct* Age and/or lack of maturity where it affects the responsibility of the offender Mental disorder or learning disability, particularly where linked to the commission of the offence Sexual activity was incited but no activity took place because the offender voluntarily desisted or intervened to prevent it *Previous good character/exemplary conduct is different from having no previous convictions. The more serious the offence, the less the weight which should normally be attributed to this factor. Where previous good character/exemplary conduct has been used to facilitate the offence, this mitigation should not normally be allowed and such conduct may constitute an aggravating factor. In the context of this offence, previous good character/exemplary conduct should not normally be given any significant weight and will not normally justify a reduction in what would otherwise be the appropriate sentence.

332.6 Sentencing Council Guideline Sexual Offences Act 2003 s 32-33
Sexual Offences Guideline 2014, see www.banksr.com Other Matters Guidelines tab. In force 1 April 2014. The guideline only applies to offenders aged 18+, see page 7 of the guideline. For the usual practice, see **66.21** in Volume 1.

STEP ONE: Determining the offence category
page 110 The court should determine which categories of harm and culpability the offence falls into by reference **only** to the tables below.

Harm	
Category 1	Causing victim to view extreme pornography Causing victim to view indecent/prohibited images of children Engaging in, or causing a victim to view live, sexual activity involving sadism/violence/sexual activity with an animal/a child
Category 2	Engaging in, or causing a victim to view images of or view live, sexual activity involving: penetration of vagina or anus (using body or object) penile penetration of mouth masturbation
Category 3	Factor(s) in Categories 1 and 2 not present

Culpability A
Significant degree of planning Offender acts together with others in order to commit the offence Use of alcohol/drugs on victim to facilitate the offence Grooming behaviour used against victim Abuse of trust Use of threats (including blackmail) Commercial exploitation and/or motivation Offence racially or religiously aggravated Offence motivated by, or demonstrating, hostility to the victim based on his or her sexual orientation (or presumed sexual orientation) or transgender identity (or presumed transgender identity) Offence motivated by, or demonstrating, hostility to the victim based on his or her disability (or presumed disability)

Culpability B
Factor(s) in Category A not present

332.7

STEP TWO: Starting point and category range

page 110 Having determined the category of harm and culpability, the court should use the corresponding starting points to reach a sentence within the category range [below]. The starting point applies to all offenders irrespective of plea or previous convictions. Having determined the starting point, step two allows further adjustment for aggravating or mitigating features, set out [below].

A case of particular gravity, reflected by multiple features of culpability or harm in step one, could merit upward adjustment from the starting point before further adjustment for aggravating or mitigating features, set out [below].

Where there is a sufficient prospect of rehabilitation, a community order with a sex offender treatment programme requirement under Criminal Justice Act 2003 s 202 can be a proper alternative to a short or moderate-length custodial sentence.

	A		B	
	Starting point	**Category range**	**Starting point**	**Category range**
Category 1	4 years' custody	3 to 6 years' custody	2 years' custody	1 to 3 years' custody
Category 2	2 years' custody	1 to 3 years' custody	1 year's custody	High-level community order to 18 months' custody
Category 3	26 weeks' custody	High-level community order to 1 year's custody	Medium-level community order	Low-level community order to medium-level community order

For the meaning of a high-level, a medium-level and a low-level community order, see **16.12** in Volume 1.

332.8   [Aggravating and mitigating factors]

page 111 The table below contains a **non-exhaustive** list of additional factual elements providing the context of the offence and factors relating to the offender. Identify whether any combination of these, or other relevant factors, should result in an upward or downward adjustment from the starting point. **In particular, relevant recent convictions are likely to result in an upward adjustment**. In some cases, having considered these factors, it may be appropriate to move outside the identified category range.

When appropriate, the court should also consider the custody threshold as follows:

Has the custody threshold been passed?

If so, is it unavoidable that a custodial sentence be imposed?

If so, can that sentence be suspended?

Aggravating factors
Statutory aggravating factors: Previous convictions, having regard to: a) the nature of the offence to which the conviction relates and its relevance to the current offence, and b) the time that has elapsed since the conviction Offence committed whilst on bail

Other aggravating factors:	

Other aggravating factors:
Location of offence
Timing of offence
Failure to comply with current court orders
Offence committed whilst on licence
Any steps taken to prevent the victim reporting an incident, obtaining assistance and/or from assisting or supporting the prosecution
Attempts to dispose of or conceal evidence
Commission of offence whilst under the influence of alcohol or drugs

Mitigating factors

No previous convictions or no relevant/recent convictions
Remorse
Previous good character and/or exemplary conduct*
Age and/or lack of maturity where it affects the responsibility of the offender
Mental disorder or learning disability, particularly where linked to the commission of the offence
Demonstration of steps taken to address offending behaviour
*Previous good character/exemplary conduct is different from having no previous convictions. The more serious the offence, the less the weight which should normally be attributed to this factor. Where previous good character/exemplary conduct has been used to facilitate the offence, this mitigation should not normally be allowed and such conduct may constitute an aggravating factor.

332.9   Sentencing Council Guideline   Sexual Offences Act 2003 s 34-35
Sexual Offences Guideline 2014, see www.banksr.com Other Matters Guidelines tab. In force 1 April 2014. The guideline only applies to offenders aged 18+, see page 7 of the guideline. For the usual practice, see **66.21** in Volume 1.

STEP ONE: Determining the offence category
page 114 The court should determine which categories of harm and culpability the offence falls into by reference **only** to the tables below.

Harm	
Category 1	Penetration of vagina or anus (using body or object) Penile penetration of mouth In either case by, or of, the victim
Category 2	Touching, or exposure, of naked genitalia or naked breasts by, or of, the victim
Category 3	Other sexual activity

Culpability A

Significant degree of planning
Offender acts together with others to commit the offence
Use of alcohol/drugs on victim to facilitate the offence
Abuse of trust
Sexual images of victim recorded, retained, solicited or shared
Commercial exploitation and/or motivation
Offence racially or religiously aggravated
Offence motivated by, or demonstrating, hostility to the victim based on his or her sexual orientation (or presumed sexual orientation) or transgender identity (or presumed transgender identity)
Offence motivated by, or demonstrating, hostility to the victim based on his or her disability (or presumed disability)

Culpability B
Factor(s) in Category A not present

332.10

STEP TWO: Starting point and category range

page 114 Having determined the category of harm and culpability, the court should use the corresponding starting points to reach a sentence within the category range [below]. The starting point applies to all offenders irrespective of plea or previous convictions. Having determined the starting point, step two allows further adjustment for aggravating or mitigating features, set out [below].

A case of particular gravity, reflected by multiple features of culpability or harm in step one, could merit upward adjustment from the starting point before further adjustment for aggravating or mitigating features, set out [below].

Where there is a sufficient prospect of rehabilitation, a community order with a sex offender treatment programme requirement under Criminal Justice Act 2003 s 202 can be a proper alternative to a short or moderate-length custodial sentence.

	A		B	
	Starting point	**Category range**	**Starting point**	**Category range**
Category 1	5 years' custody	4 to 10 years' custody	1 year's custody	High-level community order to 2 years' custody
Category 2	3 years' custody	2 to 6 years' custody	26 weeks' custody	High-level community order to 1 year's custody
Category 3	26 weeks' custody	High-level community order to 3 years' custody	Medium-level community order	Low-level community order to high-level community order

For the meaning of a high-level, a medium-level and a low-level community order, see **16.12** in Volume 1.

332.11   [Aggravating and mitigating factors]

page 115 The table below contains a non-exhaustive list of additional factual elements providing the context of the offence and factors relating to the offender. Identify whether any combination of these, or other relevant factors, should result in an upward or downward adjustment from the starting point. In particular, relevant recent convictions are likely to result in an upward adjustment. In some cases, having considered these factors, it may be appropriate to move outside the identified category range.

When sentencing appropriate **Category 2 or 3 offences**, the court should also consider the custody threshold as follows:

Has the custody threshold been passed?

If so, is it unavoidable that a custodial sentence be imposed?

If so, can that sentence be suspended?

Aggravating factors
Statutory aggravating factors: Previous convictions, having regard to: a) the nature of the offence to which the conviction relates and its relevance to the current offence, and b) the time that has elapsed since the conviction   Offence committed whilst on bail   ***Other aggravating factors:***   Severe psychological or physical harm   Ejaculation   Pregnancy or STI as a consequence of offence   Location of offence   Timing of offence   Victim compelled to leave their home or institution (including victims of domestic violence)   Failure to comply with current court orders   Offence committed whilst on licence   Any steps taken to prevent the victim reporting an incident, obtaining assistance and/or from assisting or supporting the prosecution   Attempts to dispose of or conceal evidence   Commission of offence whilst under the influence of alcohol or drugs

Mitigating factors
No previous convictions or no relevant/recent convictions   Remorse   Previous good character and/or exemplary conduct*   Age and/or lack of maturity where it affects the responsibility of the offender   Mental disorder or learning disability, particularly where linked to the commission of the offence   *Previous good character/exemplary conduct is different from having no previous convictions. The more serious the offence, the less the weight which should normally be attributed to this factor. Where previous good character/exemplary conduct has been used to facilitate the offence, this mitigation should not normally be allowed and such conduct may constitute an aggravating factor.   In the context of this offence, previous good character/exemplary conduct should not normally be given any significant weight and will not normally justify a reduction in what would otherwise be the appropriate sentence.

For the general principles and starting points etc., see **SEX OFFENCES: CAUSING A PERSON TO ENGAGE IN SEXUAL ACTIVITY** *Guidelines* at **327.2**. (The guidelines are the same. Ed.)

332.12   *Sentencing Council guideline   Sexual Offences Act 2003 s 36-37*
Sexual Offences Guideline 2014, see www.banksr.com Other Matters Guidelines tab. In force 1 April 2014. The guideline only applies to offenders aged 18+, see page 7 of the guideline. For the usual practice, see **66.21** in Volume 1.

STEP ONE: Determining the offence category
page 118 The court should determine which categories of harm and culpability the offence falls into by reference **only** to the tables below.

Harm	
Category 1	Causing victim to view extreme pornography Causing victim to view indecent/prohibited images of children Engaging in, or causing a victim to view live, sexual activity involving sadism/violence/sexual activity with an animal/a child

Category 2	Engaging in, or causing a victim to view images of or view live, sexual activity involving: penetration of vagina or anus (using body or object) penile penetration of mouth masturbation
Category 3	Factor(s) in Categories 1 and 2 not present

Culpability A
Significant degree of planning Offender acts together with others in order to commit the offence Use of alcohol/drugs on victim to facilitate the offence Abuse of trust Commercial exploitation and/or motivation Offence racially or religiously aggravated Offence motivated by, or demonstrating, hostility to the victim based on his or her sexual orientation (or presumed sexual orientation) or transgender identity (or presumed transgender identity) Offence motivated by, or demonstrating, hostility to the victim based on his or her disability (or presumed disability)

Culpability B
Factor(s) in Category A not present

332.13

STEP TWO: Starting point and category range

page 118 Having determined the category of harm and culpability, the court should use the corresponding starting points to reach a sentence within the category range [below]. The starting point applies to all offenders irrespective of plea or previous convictions. Having determined the starting point, step two allows further adjustment for aggravating or mitigating features, set out [below].

A case of particular gravity, reflected by multiple features of culpability or harm in step one, could merit upward adjustment from the starting point before further adjustment for aggravating or mitigating features, set out [below].

Where there is a sufficient prospect of rehabilitation, a community order with a sex offender treatment programme requirement under Criminal Justice Act 2003 s 202 can be a proper alternative to a short or moderate-length custodial sentence.

	A		B	
	Starting point	**Category range**	**Starting point**	**Category range**
Category 1	4 years' custody	3 to 6 years' custody	2 years' custody	1 to 3 years' custody
Category 2	2 years' custody	1 to 3 years' custody	1 year's custody	High-level community order to 18 months' custody
Category 3	26 weeks' custody	High-level community order to 1 year's custody	Medium-level community order	Low-level community order to medium-level community order

For the meaning of a high-level, a medium-level and a low-level community order, see **16.12** in Volume 1.

332.14   [Aggravating and mitigating factors]
page 119 The table below contains a non-exhaustive list of additional factual elements providing the context of the offence and factors relating to the offender. Identify whether any combination of these, or other relevant factors, should result in an upward or downward adjustment from the starting point. In particular, relevant recent convictions are likely to result in an upward adjustment. In some cases, having considered these factors, it may be appropriate to move outside the identified category range.
When sentencing appropriate Category 2 or 3 offences, the court should also consider the custody threshold as follows:
  Has the custody threshold been passed?
  If so, is it unavoidable that a custodial sentence be imposed?
  If so, can that sentence be suspended?

Aggravating factors
Statutory aggravating factors: Previous convictions, having regard to: a) the nature of the offence to which the conviction relates and its relevance to the current offence, and b) the time that has elapsed since the conviction Offence committed whilst on bail *Other aggravating factors:* Location of offence Timing of offence Failure to comply with current court orders Offence committed whilst on licence Any steps taken to prevent the victim reporting an incident, obtaining assistance and/or from assisting or supporting the prosecution Attempts to dispose of or conceal evidence Commission of offence whilst under the influence of alcohol or drugs
Mitigating factors
No previous convictions or no relevant/recent convictions Remorse Previous good character and/or exemplary conduct* Age and/or lack of maturity where it affects the responsibility of the offender Mental disorder or learning disability, particularly where linked to the commission of the offence Demonstration of steps taken to address offending behaviour *Previous good character/exemplary conduct is different from having no previous convictions. The more serious the offence, the less the weight which should normally be attributed to this factor. Where previous good character/exemplary conduct has been used to facilitate the offence, this mitigation should not normally be allowed and such conduct may constitute an aggravating factor.

For the general principles and starting points etc. see **SEX OFFENCES: CHILDREN, WITH** *Guidelines* at **328.3**. (The guidelines are the same. Ed.)

332.15   *Sentencing Council guideline   Sexual Offences Act 2003 s 38-39*
Sexual Offences Guideline 2014, see www.banksr.com Other Matters Guidelines tab. In force 1 April 2014. The guideline only applies to offenders aged 18+, see page 7 of the guideline. For the usual practice, see **66.21** in Volume 1.

STEP ONE: Determining the offence category
page 122 The court should determine which categories of harm and culpability the offence falls into by reference **only** to the tables below.
This guideline also applies to offences committed remotely/online.

Harm	
Category 1	Penetration of vagina or anus (using body or object) Penile penetration of mouth In either case by, or of, the victim
Category 2	Touching, or exposure, of naked genitalia or naked breasts by, or of, the victim
Category 3	Factor(s) in Categories 1 and 2 not present

Culpability A
Significant degree of planning Offender acts together with others to commit the offence Use of alcohol/drugs on victim to facilitate the offence Grooming behaviour used against victim Use of threats (including blackmail) Sexual images of victim recorded, retained, solicited or shared Commercial exploitation and/or motivation Offence racially or religiously aggravated Offence motivated by, or demonstrating, hostility to the victim based on his or her sexual orientation (or presumed sexual orientation) or transgender identity (or presumed transgender identity) Offence motivated by, or demonstrating, hostility to the victim based on his or her disability (or presumed disability)

Culpability B
Factor(s) in Category A not present

332.16

STEP TWO: Starting point and category range

page 122 Having determined the category of harm and culpability, the court should use the corresponding starting points to reach a sentence within the category range [below]. The starting point applies to all offenders irrespective of plea or previous convictions. Having determined the starting point, step two allows further adjustment for aggravating or mitigating features, set out [below].

A case of particular gravity, reflected by multiple features of culpability or harm in step one, could merit upward adjustment from the starting point before further adjustment for aggravating or mitigating features, set out [below].

Where there is a sufficient prospect of rehabilitation, a community order with a sex offender treatment programme requirement under Criminal Justice Act 2003 s 202 can be a proper alternative to a short or moderate-length custodial sentence.

	A		B	
	Starting point	**Category range**	**Starting point**	**Category range**
Category 1	5 years' custody	4 to 10 years' custody	18 months' custody	1 to 2 years' custody
Category 2	3 years' custody	2 to 6 years' custody	26 weeks' custody	Medium-level community order to 1 year's custody
Category 3	26 weeks' custody	High-level community order to 3 years' custody	Medium-level community order	Low-level community order to high-level community order

For the meaning of a high-level, a medium-level and a low-level community order, see **16.12** in Volume 1.

332.17 [Aggravating and mitigating factors]
page 123 The table below contains a **non-exhaustive** list of additional factual elements providing the context of the offence and factors relating to the offender. Identify whether any combination of these, or other relevant factors, should result in an upward or downward adjustment from the starting point. **In particular, relevant recent convictions are likely to result in an upward adjustment**. In some cases, having considered these factors, it may be appropriate to move outside the identified category range.
When sentencing appropriate **Category 2 or 3 offences**, the court should also consider the custody threshold as follows:

Has the custody threshold been passed?
If so, is it unavoidable that a custodial sentence be imposed?
If so, can that sentence be suspended?

Aggravating factors
Statutory aggravating factors: Previous convictions, having regard to: a) the nature of the offence to which the conviction relates and its relevance to the current offence, and b) the time that has elapsed since the conviction Offence committed whilst on bail *Other aggravating factors:* Ejaculation Pregnancy or STI as a consequence of offence Location of offence Timing of offence Victim compelled to leave their home or institution (including victims of domestic violence) Failure to comply with current court orders Offence committed whilst on licence Any steps taken to prevent the victim reporting an incident, obtaining assistance and/or from assisting or supporting the prosecution Attempts to dispose of or conceal evidence Failure of offender to respond to previous warnings Commission of offence whilst under the influence of alcohol or drugs
Mitigating factors
No previous convictions or no relevant/recent convictions Remorse Previous good character and/or exemplary conduct* Age and/or lack of maturity where it affects the responsibility of the offender Mental disorder or learning disability, particularly where linked to the commission of the offence Sexual activity was incited but no activity took place because the offender voluntarily desisted or intervened to prevent it *Previous good character/exemplary conduct is different from having no previous convictions. The more serious the offence, the less the weight which should normally be attributed to this factor. Where previous good character/exemplary conduct has been used to facilitate the offence, this mitigation should not normally be allowed and such conduct may constitute an aggravating factor. In the context of this offence, previous good character/exemplary conduct should not normally be given any significant weight and will not normally justify a reduction in what would otherwise be the appropriate sentence.

332.18 *Sentencing Council guideline   Sexual Offences Act 2003 s 40-41*
Sexual Offences Guideline 2014, see www.banksr.com Other Matters Guidelines tab The guideline only applies to offenders aged 18+, see page 7 of the guideline. For the usual practice, see **66.21** in Volume 1.

STEP ONE: Determining the offence category

page 126 The court should determine which categories of harm and culpability the offence falls into by reference **only** to the tables below.

Harm	
Category 1	Causing victim to view extreme pornography Causing victim to view indecent/prohibited images of children Engaging in, or causing a victim to view live, sexual activity involving sadism/violence/sexual activity with an animal/a child
Category 2	Engaging in, or causing a victim to view images of or view live, sexual activity involving: penetration of vagina or anus (using body or object) penile penetration of mouth masturbation
Category 3	Factor(s) in Categories 1 and 2 not present

Culpability A
Significant degree of planning Offender acts together with others to commit the offence Use of alcohol/drugs on victim to facilitate the offence Grooming behaviour used against victim Use of threats (including blackmail) Commercial exploitation and/or motivation Offence racially or religiously aggravated Offence motivated by, or demonstrating, hostility to the victim based on his or her sexual orientation (or presumed sexual orientation) or transgender identity (or presumed transgender identity) Offence motivated by, or demonstrating, hostility to the victim based on his or her disability (or presumed disability)
Culpability B
Factor(s) in Category A not present

332.19

STEP TWO: Starting point and category range

page 126 Having determined the category of harm and culpability, the court should use the corresponding starting points to reach a sentence within the category range [below]. The starting point applies to all offenders irrespective of plea or previous convictions. Having determined the starting point, step two allows further adjustment for aggravating or mitigating features, set out [below].

A case of particular gravity, reflected by multiple features of culpability or harm in step one, could merit upward adjustment from the starting point before further adjustment for aggravating or mitigating features, set out [below].

Where there is a sufficient prospect of rehabilitation, a community order with a sex offender treatment programme requirement under Criminal Justice Act 2003 s 202 can be a proper alternative to a short or moderate-length custodial sentence.

	A		B	
	Starting point	**Category range**	**Starting point**	**Category range**
Category 1	18 years' custody	1-2 years' custody	1 year's custody	26 weeks' to 18 months' custody
Category 2	1 year's custody	26 weeks' to 18 months' custody	26 weeks' custody	High-level community order to 1 year's custody

	A		B	
Category 3	26 weeks' custody	High-level community order to 1 years' custody	Medium-level community order	Low-level community order to high-level community order

For the meaning of a high-level, a medium-level and a low-level community order, see **16.12** in Volume 1.

332.20   [Aggravating and mitigating factors]
page 127 The table below contains a **non-exhaustive** list of additional factual elements providing the context of the offence and factors relating to the offender. Identify whether any combination of these, or other relevant factors, should result in an upward or downward adjustment from the starting point. **In particular, relevant recent convictions are likely to result in an upward adjustment**. In some cases, having considered these factors, it may be appropriate to move outside the identified category range.

When sentencing appropriate Category 2 or 3 offences, the court should also consider the custody threshold as follows:

Has the custody threshold been passed?

If so, is it unavoidable that a custodial sentence be imposed?

If so, can that sentence be suspended?

Aggravating factors
Statutory aggravating factors:
Previous convictions, having regard to: a) the nature of the offence to which the conviction relates and its relevance to the current offence, and b) the time that has elapsed since the conviction
Offence committed whilst on bail
Other aggravating factors:
Location of offence
Timing of offence
Failure to comply with current court orders
Offence committed whilst on licence
Any steps taken to prevent the victim reporting an incident, obtaining assistance and/or from assisting or supporting the prosecution
Attempts to dispose of or conceal evidence
Failure of offender to respond to previous warnings
Commission of offence whilst under the influence of alcohol or drugs

Mitigating factors
No previous convictions or no relevant/recent convictions
Remorse
Previous good character and/or exemplary conduct*
Age and/or lack of maturity where it affects the responsibility of the offender
Mental disorder or learning disability, particularly where linked to the commission of the offence
Demonstration of steps taken to address offending behaviour
*Previous good character/exemplary conduct is different from having no previous convictions. The more serious the offence, the less the weight which should normally be attributed to this factor. Where previous good character/exemplary conduct has been used to facilitate the offence, this mitigation should not normally be allowed and such conduct may constitute an aggravating factor.
In the context of this offence, previous good character/exemplary conduct should not normally be given any significant weight and will not normally justify a reduction in what would otherwise be the appropriate sentence.

332.21   Suggested approach to the guideline
Note: It is understood the Sentencing Council intended that the guideline should reflect the Court of Appeal current sentencing tariff for sentencing. Further, the new guideline was intended to bring the previous guideline up to date rather than intending to increase the penalties for the bulk of the sex offences. Consequently, I would suggest that sentencers should start with the guideline and then consider recent sentencing cases set out by the Court of Appeal to see if they are helpful, and then return to the guideline before deciding the appropriate sentence. Ed.

Cases   All offences
332.22   Judicial guidance   Pre-2014 guideline
R v Jones 2005 EWCA Crim 3414, 2006 2 Cr App R (S) 18 (p 117) D was convicted of causing or inciting a person with a mental disorder to engage in sexual activity (SOA 2003 s 31). Held. These offences, depending on the facts, can be compared in terms of seriousness to sexual offences against children.
Note: The guidelines take precedence over this case. Ed.

332.23   No sexual intercourse   Pre-2014 guideline cases
R v Holland 2011 EWCA Crim 1890 D pleaded at the last moment to sexual activity with a person with a mental disorder. D had been friends with V and her late husband for 50 years. V was an 84-year-old widow and suffered from Alzheimer's. D would visit V, care for her, do jobs for her and demonstrated affection for her. It was an intimate friendship in which D had applied cream to the lips of V's vagina and had washed her clothes. On one occasion, D said to V, "You had better suck me then". Oral sex, without force or coercion, lasted a matter of seconds. D admitted another incident of oral sex. V's illness meant that she was unaware of the act and there was no effect upon her. D was impotent and could not have gained any sexual gratification from the act. D, aged 75, was of good character and was a force for good in the community. Held. D only marginally crossed over the line of criminality. It is not necessary to impose immediate imprisonment. The Judge gave insufficient weight to the circumstances of this highly unusual case and D's remorse. **51 weeks suspended** with supervision, not 3 years.
See also: *R v Van Rijn* 2011 EWCA Crim 2828 (Convicted of sexual activity with a person with a mental disorder and causing or inciting sexual activity with a person with a mental disorder. Victim was a man aged 40 suffering from Down's syndrome and schizophrenia. Victim performed oral sex on a male care worker. Witnessed by manager carrying out spot checks. Victim 'liked' care worker and denied events took place. Late fifties with no relevant convictions. No aggravating features and very powerful testimonials. **2 years 9 months** well within the legitimate range.)

332.24   Sexual intercourse/Penetration, With
Att-Gen's Ref No 35 of 2010 2010 EWCA Crim 2555, 2011 1 Cr App R (S) 123 (p 711) LCJ D pleaded to nine sample counts of sexual activity with a person with a mental disorder, after the jury had been sworn. He was in a relationship with M, the mother of V. V suffered from severe learning difficulties arising from her epilepsy. As the sexual relationship between D and M deteriorated, D sought to establish a sexual relationship with V. D was trusted by V's family to care for her, and often cooked and read books to her. V would sometimes visit D and stay overnight. D and V had sexual intercourse. On the first occasion, V told D to stop and she was concerned that D was doing these things with her and not her mother. The intercourse hurt V. D instructed V not to tell anyone. On subsequent occasions he would give her alcohol to relax her. D knew that V ought not to drink alcohol as it conflicted with her medication. The abuse continued for about a year. There was vaginal and anal intercourse and digital penetration. He never used a condom and would ejaculate inside V's vagina or over her body. D told V that he loved her. V, aged 30, was extremely vulnerable and her cognitive function was below the bottom 1% of people of her age. She wanted to commit suicide.

D, aged 67, was of positive good character. Held. These were sexual offences of considerable seriousness, featuring a very serious breach of trust. V was treated like a sex toy by D. 6 years on each count was unduly lenient, so **9 years**.

Post-2014 guideline case

R v S 2014 EWCA Crim 2980 D pleaded (almost full credit) to sexual activity with a person with a mental disorder procured by an inducement (section 34(1)). V was aged 22 and did not have the capacity to make decisions for herself. She had an IQ of 71-72. V had previously been in an abusive relationship and had a son for whom she wanted parental access and custody. When V talked about this she would get upset. She was a very vulnerable lady. In 2010, D met V's parents and befriended them. He saw them regularly and encouraged V to visit him to meet his daughter who was the same age as V. D said he would help V and listen to her problems. It was agreed that V could stay with D and did so. V and D had sex. When returning V home, D asked V's mother, "How she would feel if V and I were in a relationship?" She said she would not mind as long as V was not hurt. V's aunt, R, said it was up to V and then began to become increasingly concerned. The next day she asked why V was with someone old enough to be her father. D told R that X had contacted him and said he had a DVD of V[1085] having sex with X. Further X had threatened to show the DVD to the father of V's son and V's family and this would make it more difficult for V to win her court case. V agreed to have sex with D because of the DVD. Next D said he had bought the DVD with copies from X and that V was told she would never see her son if the court got a copy of the video. V told the police that D had threatened her with the DVD if she did not have a relationship with him. The prosecution were unable to say whether the DVD existed. D was then aged 48 and now aged 51. He was then of good character but since then had a conviction for harassment and wasting police time. He was of limited intellectual capacity (with an IQ of 61) and fragile mental health. The Judge found D had used V's vulnerability to manipulate, threaten and blackmail her. Held. There was an unpleasant side of the deception. We are cautious about ascribing the whole responsibility for any serious psychological harm suffered by V to D. It was a Category A offence. The effect on the victim moved it to Category 1 giving a 5-year starting point. There was no need to move the case higher, so **3½ years** not 5.

R v Taylor 2015 EWCA Crim 322 D was convicted of five counts of sexual activity with a person with a mental disorder. He was a care manager at a hospital for those with learning difficulties complicated by mental health difficulties. One count was a specimen count covering three incidents of vaginal intercourse with V1, who was aged 24-25 at the time. She suffered from mental retardation, post-traumatic [stress] disorder and an emotionally unstable personality disorder. Another count dealt with D touching V1's vagina under her underwear. These offences took place when D took V1 back to his house within the hospital grounds. The Judge said V1 craved attention and friendship which is why D targeted her. D also unlocked the door of V2's room and had sex with her. The observation window was covered. She was aged 25-26 with an emotionally unstable personality. He also took V2 cycling and had sex with her in a secluded place. In 1999, D was warned about inappropriate behaviour to staff. D was aged 51 with no convictions. He had lost his accommodation. D was suspended from his job in May 2007. He was charged in January 2013 but was not convicted until April 2014. The Judge put the offending in the top category. He considered the aggravating factors were the high degree of planning, the repetitive nature of the offending, there were two victims, steps were taken to conceal the evidence and the warning given. Held. These offences were extremely grave and were an appalling breach of trust. The victims were extremely vulnerable and fragile individuals. Their recent deterioration was attributable to the offences. We pay some regard to the fact that under the guideline that was

---

[1085] The judgment appears to suggest the DVD was about S and X having sex but in the context of the case that would not make sense.

enforced at the time, the penalties were less. The delay was a mitigating factor. The sentencing for each victim (V1 6 years and V2 6½ years) was at the very top of the bracket. Because of totality we reduce the sentences to 4 years 9 months and 5 years 3 months making **10 years** not 12½ years in all.

See also: *R v P* 2014 EWCA Crim 2646, 2015 2 Cr App R (S) 28 (p 257) (Convicted. Sex with 30-year-old stepdaughter. Event filmed. **13 years** upheld.)

Att-Gen's Ref No 54 of 2014 2014 EWCA Crim 2999 (Convicted. Regular buggery and oral sex on V who had significant impairment of intelligence and social functioning. This is to be contrasted with only four specific counts. V distressed with deteriorating behaviour. **12 years** not 9.)

333   SEX OFFENCES: TRESPASS WITH INTENT

333.1

Sexual Offences Act 2003 s 63 (trespass with intent to commit a sexual offence)

Mode of trial Triable either way

Maximum sentence On indictment 10 years. Summary 6 months and/or a £5,000 fine for offences committed before 12 March 2015 and an unlimited fine thereafter.[1086] There are maximum fines for those aged under 18, see **14.38** in Volume 1.

Extended sentences Sexual Offences Act 2003 s 63 is listed in Criminal Justice Act 2003 Sch 15. The court may pass a 2012 extended sentence (EDS) if there is a significant risk of serious harm from future specified offences and either: a) the defendant has a Criminal Justice Act 2003 Sch 15B conviction (applicable only to defendants aged 18+), or b) the offence would justify a determinate sentence of at least 4 years.[1087]

Sexual Harm Prevention Orders There is a discretionary power to make this order when it is necessary to protect the public from sexual harm.[1088]

Notification For offences where the defendant was:
  a) aged under 18 and sentenced to imprisonment of at least 12 months, or
  b) aged 18 or over, and: i) the victim was under 18, or ii) the defendant was sentenced to imprisonment or detained in a hospital or given community service for at least 12 months,

the defendant must notify the police within three days (or three days from his or her release from imprisonment, hospital etc.) with his or her name, home address, National Insurance number etc. and any change of address and any address where he or she resides for seven days[1089] (in one or more periods) or more in any 12-month period.[1090]

Children and vulnerable adults: barred lists Where the defendant is aged 18 or over and the relevant sexual offence is one specified for (barring), he or she is automatically barred from engaging in regulated activity with children and vulnerable adults.[1091] The Judge must tell the defendant that the Disclosure and Barring Service will include him or her in the barred list.[1092] The defendant may ask the Service to remove him or her from the list.

333.2   *Sentencing Council guideline   Sexual Offences Act 2003 s 63*

Sexual Offences Guideline 2014, see www.banksr.com Other Matters Guidelines tab. In force 1 April 2014. The guideline only applies to offenders aged 18+, see page 7 of the guideline. For the usual practice, see **66.21** in Volume 1.

[1086] Legal Aid, Sentencing and Punishment of Offenders Act 2012 s 85(1) and (4) and Legal Aid, Sentencing and Punishment of Offenders Act 2012 (Commencement No 11) Order 2015 2015/504

[1087] Criminal Justice Act 2003 s 226A-226B as inserted by Legal Aid, Sentencing and Punishment of Offenders Act 2012 s 124

[1088] Sexual Offences Act 2003 s 103A as inserted by Anti-social Behaviour, Crime and Policing Act 2014 Sch 5 para 2 and Sexual Offences Act 2003 Sch 3

[1089] Sexual Offences Act 2003 s 84(1)(c) and (6)

[1090] Sexual Offences Act 2003 s 83 and Sch 3 para 18

[1091] Safeguarding Vulnerable Groups Act 2006 s 2 and Sch 3 and Safeguarding Vulnerable Groups Act 2006 (Prescribed Criteria and Miscellaneous Provisions) Regulations 2009 2009/37 regs 4 and 6 and Sch paras 2 and 4

[1092] Safeguarding Vulnerable Groups Act 2006 s 2 and Sch 3 para 25

STEP ONE: Determining the offence category

page 148 The court should determine the offence category using the table below.

Category 1	Raised harm and raised culpability
Category 2	Raised harm or raised culpability
Category 3	Trespass with intent to commit a sexual offence without raised harm or culpability factors present

The court should determine culpability and harm caused or intended by reference only to the factors below, which comprise the principal factual elements of the offence. Where an offence does not fall squarely into a category, individual factors may require a degree of weighting before making an overall assessment and determining the appropriate offence category. Where no substantive sexual offence has been committed the main consideration for the court will be the offender's conduct as a whole including, but not exclusively, the offender's intention.

Factors indicating raised harm
Prolonged detention/sustained incident
Additional degradation/humiliation
Offence committed in victim's home

Factors indicating raised culpability
Significant degree of planning
Specific targeting of a particularly vulnerable victim
Intended sexual offence attracts a statutory maximum of life imprisonment
Possession of weapon or other item to frighten or injure
Abuse of trust
Offender acts together with others to commit the offence
Commercial exploitation and/or motivation
Offence racially or religiously aggravated
Offence motivated by, or demonstrating, hostility to the victim based on his or her sexual orientation (or presumed sexual orientation) or transgender identity (or presumed transgender identity)
Offence motivated by, or demonstrating, hostility to the victim based on his or her disability (or presumed disability)

333.3

STEP TWO: Starting point and category range

page 149 Having determined the category, the court should use the corresponding starting points to reach a sentence within the category range below. The starting point applies to all offenders irrespective of plea or previous convictions. Having determined the starting point, step two allows further adjustment for aggravating or mitigating features, set out below.

A case of particular gravity, reflected by multiple features of culpability or harm in step one, could merit upward adjustment from the starting point before further adjustment for aggravating or mitigating features, set out below.

	Starting point	**Category range**
Category 1	6 years' custody	4 to 9 years' custody
Category 2	4 years' custody	3 to 7 years' custody
Category 3	2 years' custody	1 to 5 years' custody

333.4   [Aggravating and mitigating factors]
page 149 The table below contains a non-exhaustive list of additional factual elements
providing the context of the offence and factors relating to the offender. Identify whether
any combination of these, or other relevant factors, should result in an upward or
downward adjustment from the starting point. In particular, relevant recent convictions
are likely to result in an upward adjustment. In some cases, having considered these
factors, it may be appropriate to move outside the identified category range.

Aggravating factors
Statutory aggravating factors: Previous convictions, having regard to: a) the nature of the offence to which the conviction relates and its relevance to the current offence, and b) the time that has elapsed since the conviction Offence committed whilst on bail *Other aggravating factors:* Location of offence Timing of offence Any steps taken to prevent reporting an incident, obtaining assistance and/or from assisting or supporting the prosecution Attempts to dispose of or conceal evidence Failure to comply with current court orders Offence committed whilst on licence

Mitigating factors
No previous convictions or no relevant/recent convictions Remorse Previous good character and/or exemplary conduct* Age and/or lack of maturity where it affects the responsibility of the offender Mental disorder or learning disability, particularly where linked to the commission of the offence Demonstration of steps taken to address offending behaviour *Previous good character/exemplary conduct is different from having no previous convictions. The more serious the offence, the less the weight which should normally be attributed to this factor. Where previous good character/exemplary conduct has been used to facilitate the offence, this mitigation should not normally be allowed and such conduct may constitute an aggravating factor.

333.5   *Cases   Post-2014 guideline case*
R v M 2015 EWCA Crim 1628, 2016 1 Cr App R (S) 27 (p 168) D pleaded guilty to
trespass with intent and having a bladed article. V returned to her home address which
was being renovated and D was at her front gate on the pavement. He was smoking. She
asked him for a cigarette, which he gave her. V continued to put various items of rubbish
in a bin. For about 10 minutes she was near the front door of her house, going in and out.
As V stepped into her house, D followed her. He produced a knife and put his hands
around her. D held the knife up to her cheek. V felt it digging in and she tried to distract
him by saying that her boyfriend was due back at any time and then she began to wrestle
with him. She thought D would either ask for money or rape her. She was terrified. She
fought harder and bit his finger and scratched at his face. D moved the knife to her throat
area. D pushed her away and ran from the property. He left behind a bank card so he was
traced. V had a cut finger and had scratches to her cheek and chin. She was extremely
distressed. D also had scratches. The impact on V was devastating. Since the attack her
life had fallen apart. D was aged 33 and of good character. There were references stating
his support for projects in the community. The pre-sentence report assessed him as
having a high risk of re-offending. The Judge said there was a dark side to this
respectable married man because of his abuse of alcohol and drugs. Held. This was a
very serious offence with a number of aggravating features, namely the violation of V's

home, D was carrying a knife and he used the knife, holding it to the victim's face and neck. It was a terrifying attack and it had caused the victim grave psychological harm. There was also D's good character and his immediate admission. The use of the knife justified increasing the starting point. We start at 7½ years, so **5 years** not 6.

Old cases: There is only one old usable case that I know of, *R v Moulding* 2010 EWCA Crim 1690 (**8 years' extended sentence** (**4 years'** custody 4 years' extended licence)). There is a summary of the case at **326.10** but it is an old case. Readers should consider looking at the cases that relate to the sexual activity that was intended to be committed. Ed.

334   SEXUAL OFFENCES ACT 2003 S 62

334.1

Sexual Offences Act 2003 s 62 (committing any offence with the intention of committing a relevant sexual offence)

Mode of trial Triable either way

Maximum sentence On indictment, life where 'the offence is committed by kidnap or false imprisonment' and 10 years otherwise. Summary 6 months and/or £5,000 fine for offences committed before 12 March 2015 and an unlimited fine thereafter.[1093] There are maximum fines for those aged under 18, see **14.38** in Volume 1. This maximum sentence is subject to the automatic life provisions.

Automatic life This section is listed in Criminal Justice Act 2003 Sch 15B Part 1. The Lord Chief Justice said in *Att-Gen's Ref No 27 of 2013* 2014 EWCA Crim 334[1094] para 8 iii) (*obiter*) that in rare cases the provisions could lead to the imposition of a life sentence where the offence does not carry life imprisonment.

The court must (unless the particular circumstances make it unjust[1095]) pass automatic life if: a) the defendant is aged 18+ at the date of the conviction, b) the offence was committed on or after 3 December 2012, c) the court considers a determinate sentence of at least 10 years is appropriate, d) at the time the offender was convicted he had a conviction for a Criminal Justice Act 2003 Sch 15B offence, and e) the defendant at the time of his or her conviction had previously been sentenced to either: i) a life sentence where he or she was not eligible for release during the first 5 years of the sentence or ii) a determinate sentence or extended sentence where the custodial part was 10 years or more.[1096] For a pre-2012 extended sentence, when determining whether the custodial term was 10+ years, the period deducted for time on remand or on a curfew and tag is included.[1097]

Extended sentences Sexual Offences Act 2003 s 62 is listed in Criminal Justice Act 2003 Sch 15. The court may pass a 2012 extended sentence (EDS) if there is a significant risk of serious harm from future specified offences and either: a) the defendant has a Criminal Justice Act 2003 Sch 15B conviction (applicable only to defendants aged 18+), or b) the offence would justify a determinate sentence of at least 4 years.[1098]

Sexual Harm Prevention Orders There is a discretionary power to make this order when it is necessary to protect the public from sexual harm.[1099]

Notification For offences where the defendant was:

[1093] Legal Aid, Sentencing and Punishment of Offenders Act 2012 s 85(1) and (4) and Legal Aid, Sentencing and Punishment of Offenders Act 2012 (Commencement No 11) Order 2015 2015/504

[1094] This case is also known as *R v Burinskas* 2014 EWCA Crim 334.

[1095] Criminal Justice Act 2003 s 224A(2)

[1096] Criminal Justice Act 2003 s 224A as inserted by Legal Aid, Sentencing and Punishment of Offenders Act 2012 s 122 The condition for a) is at section 224A(1)(a), for b) is at section 224A(1)(b), for c) is at section 224A(1)(c) and for d) is at section 224A(4)-(9).

[1097] Criminal Justice Act 2003 s 224A(9)-(10)

[1098] Criminal Justice Act 2003 s 226A-226B as inserted by Legal Aid, Sentencing and Punishment of Offenders Act 2012 s 124

[1099] Sexual Offences Act 2003 s 103A as inserted by Anti-social Behaviour, Crime and Policing Act 2014 Sch 5 para 2 and Sexual Offences Act 2003 Sch 3

a) aged under 18 and sentenced to imprisonment of at least 12 months, or

b) aged 18 or over, and: i) the victim was under 18, or ii) the defendant was sentenced to imprisonment or detained in a hospital or given community service for at least 12 months,

the defendant must notify the police within three days (or three days from his or her release from imprisonment, hospital etc.) with his or her name, home address, National Insurance number etc. and any change of address and any address where he or she resides for seven days[1100] (in one or more periods) or more in any 12-month period.[1101]

Children and vulnerable adults: barred lists Where the relevant sexual offence is one specified for barring and the defendant is aged 18 or over, he or she is automatically barred from engaging in regulated activity with vulnerable adults and children.[1102] The judge must tell the defendant that the Disclosure and Barring Service will include him or her in the barred list.[1103] The defendant may ask the Service to remove him or her from the list.

334.2   Sentencing Council guideline   Sexual Offences Act 2003 s 62

Sexual Offences Guideline 2014 page 145, see www.banksr.com Other Matters Guidelines tab. In force 1 April 2014.

The starting point and range should be commensurate with that for the preliminary offence actually committed, but with an enhancement to reflect the intention to commit a sexual offence.

The enhancement will vary depending on the nature and seriousness of the intended sexual offence, but 2 years is suggested as a suitable enhancement where the intent was to commit rape or assault by penetration.

334.3   *Judicial guidance   Pre-2014 guideline*

R v Wisniewski 2004 EWCA Crim 3361, 2005 2 Cr App R (S) 39 (p 236) D pleaded to two counts of battery with intent to commit a sexual offence (section 62). Held. The offence is new but the conduct is not new. In relation to battery with intent, the factors of particular relevance include the method and degree of force used, the nature and extent of the indecency perpetrated and intended, the degree of vulnerability of and harm to the victim, the duration and general circumstances of the attack, including the time, day and place where it occurred, and the level of risk posed by the offender to the public. The good character of the offender will afford only limited mitigation. In consequence of the maximum sentence of 10 years compared with life for rape, save where a great deal of violence is used, the level of sentence for battery with intent will generally be lower than the appropriate sentence for rape.

Note: It is important to apply the guidelines but none of these remarks conflict with them. Ed.

334.4   *Pre-2014 guideline cases*

R v Baker 2011 EWCA Crim 1507 D was convicted of assault by beating and committing an offence with intent to commit a sexual offence. D and V had been friends and then were in a relationship for around a year. D arrived at V's home, having drunk seven or eight beers. They chatted. V suggested D sleep on the sofa, causing D to become aggressive. He said that he would rape her. He ripped her top and bra. V fell on the floor and D slapped her. A neighbour intervened and D left. D returned and was arrested by police. He denied the allegation. D, aged 31, had one excess alcohol conviction and a caution. There were good references. The Judge found that the attack was in breach of trust, and that it was a serious attempt to rape. The Judge sentenced D

[1100] Sexual Offences Act 2003 s 84(1)(c) and (6)
[1101] Sexual Offences Act 2003 s 83 and Sch 3 para 18
[1102] Safeguarding Vulnerable Groups Act 2006 s 2 and Sch 3 and Safeguarding Vulnerable Groups Act 2006 (Prescribed Criteria and Miscellaneous Provisions) Regulations 2009 2009/37 regs 4 and 6 and Sch para 2 and 4
[1103] Safeguarding Vulnerable Groups Act 2006 s 2 and Sch 3

to 30 months for the sex offence saying it was 6 months for the assault (the maximum) and a 2-year enhancement. Held. It was a nasty attack and a very frightening experience. **2 years 6 months** was tough but not manifestly excessive.

R v N 2012 EWCA Crim 2563 D was convicted of committing an offence with intent to commit a sexual offence. V, a cannabis user, approached D. She had some cannabis but no papers with which to roll a spliff. D was a cannabis user and agreed to help V. They walked for 20 or 30 minutes, exchanging names and telephone numbers, to D's uncle's home. D's uncle had visitors, so D took V to another address which was commonly used for smoking cannabis. They shared a spliff and subsequently V wanted to leave. D demanded oral sex. V refused and D held the door, grabbed V's mobile phone and forced her head towards his erect penis. She put her hand on his penis to stop him forcing it into her mouth, and managed to struggle free. V asked D to return her phone, but D said she had to give him oral sex before he would do so. She refused and tried to get out of the room. D stopped her again. She eventually said she would perform oral sex and got D to sit on the sofa, at which point she made a break for the door. D tried to stop her and in doing so pulled some of her hair out. She managed to get out of the address and called the police. D had convictions but none for sex offences. He looked after his sick mother and she was at a real disadvantage by his absence. Held. The Judge was not wrong to sentence outside of the guideline. The guideline appears to indicate a maximum of 2 years. The guideline does not properly cater for a situation such as this. A sentence above 2 years was appropriate, however 4½ years was excessive. **3 years** was appropriate.

R v F 2014 EWCA Crim 539 LCJ D was convicted of common assault and committing an offence with intent to commit a sexual offence. His neighbour, V, asked D if she could borrow his lawn mower as hers was broken. D said he would mow the lawn for her. V said she would pay him or give him a bottle of wine. D said a blow job would do. V thought he was joking. The next day, D mowed the lawn and afterwards V offered him £10. D said that that was not what they had agreed, that V knew what he wanted and that he had "…been thinking about it all night". D then grabbed V's arms and pulled her into the living room onto a couch. D said, "It won't take long" and, "it's not that big". V managed to free herself and noticed D's flies were unzipped. There was a bruise on one of V's arms. D was aged 69 with no convictions. Since the offence he had received three conditional discharges for benefit fraud. V felt she had no option but to move house because of her apprehension if she stayed. Held. The sex offence for the section 62 count must have been rape (oral sex). However, he didn't get very far and stopped when he realised she would not agree. The incident was over very quickly. D was now prepared to move. With that and the other factors, **1 year** not 2.

Note: The reader may find help by looking at the appropriate sentence for the offence that was intended to have been committed. Ed.

335 SMOKING
335.1
Health Act 2006
  s 6(5) (failure to display a no-smoking sign)
  s 7(2) (smoking in a smoke-free place)
  s 8(4) (failing to prevent smoking in a smoke-free place)
Modes of trial Summary only
Maximum sentences Level 3 fine (£1,000), Level 1 fine (£200) and Level 4 fine (£2,500) respectively[1104]

[1104] Smoke-free (Penalties and Discounted Amounts) Regulations 2007 2007/764 para 1

Fixed penalties The amounts are £200 (£150 if paid in 15 days) for section 6(5), and £50 (£30 if paid within 15 days) for section 7(2).[1105] There is no power for a section 8(4) offence.

336   SOLICITORS

336.1
There is no tariff for solicitor defendants. The fact that a defendant is a solicitor may or may not be relevant to the sentence. Where the offence is committed as part of the defendant's work as a solicitor, it is likely to be a relevant factor. Each case will depend critically on its own facts. Ed.

336.2   *Approach, Proper*
R v McQuoid 2009 EWCA Crim 1301 LCJ The defendant was convicted of insider dealing. As a solicitor working in a company he knew about a proposed takeover and made nearly £49,000 profit. Held. In assessing sentence full weight must be given to the destruction of his professional reputation. For more details see the FRAUD AND FINANCIAL SERVICES OFFENCES chapter.
See also the DEFENDANT *Professional defendants* para at **240.56**.

336.3   *Theft etc.   Pre-guideline cases*
R v Hunt 2012 EWCA Crim 2313, 2013 2 Cr App R (S) 2 (p 6) D pleaded (full credit) to fraud by abuse of position. D and G were partners in a firm of solicitors. Between 1 October 2008 and 21 October 2009, D and G used the client account to support the firm through a period of significant economic and banking crisis. By October 2009, there was a shortfall in the client account in the region of £1m. The firm had suffered a 50% reduction in its income within a six-month period. Both D and G had put capital into the firm, and the firm had attempted to cut costs and attract different types of work. D wrote a cheque for £35,000 from a personal account to the client account, in order that the firm's wages could be paid. The personal account had a balance of £2,000 and no overdraft facility. That cheque was dishonoured leaving a shortfall in the client account as the client account had reached its overdraft limit. D sanctioned the practice cashier to transfer £35,000 from the client account to the office account to pay the wages. G knew of the activity and engaged in using the client account to keep the firm afloat. D was responsible for 80% of the subsequent transfers. D had told G that he would replenish the client account with funds from his own personal assets, when he was able to access them. The Crown accepted that this was a genuine belief. D was aged 66 at appeal and was of positive good character. Held. It was agreed that the case would be sentenced as theft in breach of trust. D acted with an honest (yet unrealistic) belief that he would replace the funds in order to try to save his firm. It was not done to fund an extravagant lifestyle. D suffered a large, personal, financial loss of over £1m due to the creditors and the SRA looking to him for recompense. It was appropriate to start at somewhere around 4½ to 5 years. With full credit, **3 years** not 4.
R v Iyer 2013 EWCA Crim 754 D pleaded (full credit) to false accounting and forgery (×2). He was a solicitor and later became a partner. Over a 12-year period D submitted fictitious invoices from external suppliers to the accounts department in his firm totalling about £2.8m. D was in possession of a blank invoice document in the name of a company which had gone into administration in the 1990s. The firm had done some work on that administration under D's direction. Most invoices had been expensed to, and paid by, clients of the firm with about £200,000 paid for by the firm itself. The money had been spent on an extravagant lifestyle including a yacht, expensive cars and properties. D admitted the offences when challenged by the firm. He paid back about £2.15m as a result of a civil action by the firm. The forgery offences were unconnected and related to false documents created by D in support of an application that he be

---

[1105] Smoke-free (Penalties and Discounted Amounts) Regulations 2007 2007/764 para 2

honoured with an OBE. The application claimed he had written a book and donated the proceeds to Cancer Research. D was aged 46. He had no convictions and showed remorse. He had written letters of apology to the affected clients. Held. The offending occurred over a lengthy period and the amount stolen was very considerable. There was a significant amount recovered but there remained a considerable loss outstanding. The offending was well planned, determined and was used to fund high living. There was an obvious profound breach of trust of the firm at which he was a partner, but also in relation to a number of the firm's clients. However, D made immediate admissions, followed by early guilty pleas, and he co-operated in the recovery of a very substantial amount of the money. D had been struck off as a solicitor and had become bankrupt, which led to the breakdown of his marriage. 6 years after a trial would adequately reflect aggravation and mitigation. With the plea, **4 years 8 months** was correct.

See also: *R v Crickmore* 2014 EWCA Crim 1499 (D pleaded (full credit) to seven counts of theft and eight of fraud. From 1998 to 2010, D took £1.8 million from his clients, including £900,000 from an estate. The widow lost almost all of it. D concealed this by submitting inflated costs and making false and fraudulent letters of authority. Part was used to keep D's ailing practice afloat. Part was used to support a lifestyle he could not afford. D was of good character and had done charitable work. He was depressed and felt shame. Held. Stiff sentences are required for such offences. **8 years** was not excessive.)

Note: Since these cases were heard the new guideline has come into force. Ed.

337 SPEEDING

337.1
Road Traffic Regulation Act 1984 s 89(1) (driving a motor vehicle on a road at a speed exceeding the limit)
Mode of trial Summary only
Maximum sentences Level 3 fine (£1,000). Level 4 fine (£2,500) if on a motorway
Disqualification Discretionary[1106]
Endorsement Obligatory,[1107] unless there are special reasons
Penalty points 3-6 points.[1108] When certain conditions are met, the court may order reduced penalty points for attendance on courses.[1109]
Fixed penalty There is a fixed penalty of £60[1110] and 3 penalty points[1111] for this offence with half the relevant victim surcharge. For more detail see **61.1** in Volume 1.
Courses For defendants convicted of Road Traffic Regulation Act 1988 s 89(1), there is power to order reduced disqualification for attendance on courses.[1112] On 24 June 2013, the Road Safety Act 2006 changes came into force. For details see the **DISQUALIFICATION FROM DRIVING: OBLIGATORY** *Reduced periods of disqualification for attendance on courses* para at **44.8** in Volume 1.
For **Passenger Carrying Vehicles (PCV) and Large Goods Vehicles (LGV) drivers** see the note at **341.1**.

337.2 *Magistrates' Court Sentencing Guidelines*
Magistrates' Court Sentencing Guidelines 2008 page 131, see www.banksr.com Other Matters Guidelines tab

---

[1106] Road Traffic Offenders Act 1988 Sch 2 Part 1
[1107] Road Traffic Offenders Act 1988 Sch 2 Part 1
[1108] When the Road Safety Act 2006 s 17(b) changes are implemented the points will be 2-6. Currently there are no plans to implement the section.
[1109] Road Traffic Act 1988 s 30A substituted by Road Safety Act 2006 s 34
[1110] Fixed Penalty Order 2000 2000/2792 Sch 1 as amended
[1111] Road Traffic Offenders Act 1988 Sch 2 Part 1
[1112] Road Traffic Offenders Act 1988 s 34A(2)(d) as inserted by Road Safety Act 2006 s 34(3)

Speed limit (mph)	Recorded speed (mph)		
20	21-30	31-40	41-50
30	31-40	41-50	51-60
40	41-55	56-65	66-75
50	51-65	66-75	76-85
60	61-80	81-90	91-100
70	71-90	91-100	101-110
Starting point	Band A fine	Band B fine	Band B fine
Range	Band A fine	Band B fine	Band B fine
Points/disqualification	3 points	4-6 points or disqualify for 7-28 days	Disqualify 7-56 days or 6 points

The following aggravating and mitigating factors may be particularly relevant. Factors indicating higher culpability: 1 Poor road or weather conditions, 2 LGV, HGV, PSV etc., 3 Towing caravan or trailer, 4 Carrying passengers or heavy load, and 5 Driving for hire or reward. Factor indicating lower culpability: Genuine emergency established. Factors indicating greater degree of harm: 1 Location, e.g. near school, and 2 High level of traffic or pedestrians in the vicinity.

Consider ancillary orders.

Starting point fine Band A (50% of weekly take-home pay/weekly benefit payment) Starting point fine Band B (100% of weekly take-home pay/weekly benefit payment). For more detail see **60.27** in Volume 1.

Consultation It is expected that the Sentencing Council will issue a consultation document about updating this guideline in May 2016.

For details about applying the guidelines, see the **GUIDELINES** chapter in Volume 1.

337.3 *Charging threshold*
Road Traffic Offences: Guidance on Fixed Penalty Notices
http://www.cps.gov.uk/legal/p_to_r/road_traffic_offences_guidance_on_fixed_penalty_notices/#speed

The Association of Chief Police Officers (ACPO) has issued speed enforcement policy guidance, which suggests that enforcement will normally occur when a driver exceeds the speed limit by a particular margin. This is normally 10 per cent over the speed limit plus 2 mph. It also sets guidelines for when it would not be appropriate to issue a fixed penalty notice but to issue a summons instead (see below). Note that these are guidelines and that a police officer has discretion to act outside of them providing he acts fairly, consistently and proportionately.

Speed limit (mph)	20	30	40	50	60	70
ACPO charging threshold (mph)	24	35	46	57	68	79
Summons (mph)	35	50	66	76	86	96

337.4 *Court Martial*
Guidance on Sentencing in the Court Martial 2013 para 5.11.1 There is no power to impose penalty points.

para 5.11.4 The suggested penalty (when the speeding is not dangerous) is a fine of five days' pay with a recommendation that the military driving permit be withdrawn.

338 STALKING

338.1

1) Protection from Harassment Act 1997 s 2A ([simple] stalking)[1113]

Mode of trial Summary only

Maximum sentence 6 months and/or a £5,000 fine for offences committed before 12 March 2015 and an unlimited fine thereafter.[1114] There are maximum fines for those aged under 18, see **14.38** in Volume 1.

2) Protection from Harassment Act 1997 s 4A (stalking involving fear of violence or serious alarm or distress)

Mode of trial Triable either way

Maximum sentence On indictment 5 years. Summary maximum 6 months and/or a £5,000 fine for offences committed before 12 March 2015 and an unlimited fine thereafter.[1115] There are maximum fines for those aged under 18, see **14.38** in Volume 1.

3) Offences Against the Person Act 1861 s 18, 20 and 47

For penalties and ancillary orders, see the **ABH ASSAULT OCCASIONING ACTUAL BODILY HARM, OFFENCES AGAINST THE PERSON ACT 1861 S 18** and **OFFENCES AGAINST THE PERSON ACT 1861 S 20** chapters.

Extended sentences All the above offences are listed in Criminal Justice Act 2003 Sch 15. The court may pass a 2012 extended sentence (EDS) if there is a significant risk of serious harm from future specified offences and either: a) the defendant has a Criminal Justice Act 2003 Sch 15B conviction (applicable only to defendants aged 18+), or b) the offence would justify a determinate sentence of at least 4 years.[1116]

Criminal Behaviour Orders Where a defendant has engaged in behaviour that caused or was likely to cause harassment, alarm or distress to any person and a Criminal Behaviour Order will help in preventing the offender from engaging in such behaviour, the court may make this order.[1117]

Restraining Orders There is power to make this order to protect a victim etc. from further conduct.[1118] These powers were amended by Domestic Violence, Crime and Victims Act 2004 s 12 etc., which also inserted a power to impose an order after an acquittal.[1119]

Sexual Harm Prevention Orders For all the above offences, there is a discretionary power to make this order when it is necessary to protect the public from sexual harm.[1120]

Research Research by Lorraine Sheridan, a lecturer in psychology at Leicester University who has written extensively about stalking, has identified four types of stalker.

1 Angry or bitter former partners account for half of the incidents. They often threaten violence against their ex-partners and his or her property. The threats should be taken seriously.

2 Infatuated harassers account for 20% and see their target as a fantasy 'beloved'. They generally seek out their victims by non-malicious means. These include leaving notes, quizzing their friends or loitering near their address or place of work, hoping for an accidental meeting. The threat is not considered high risk, and such behaviour can often be discouraged through discussion.

[1113] Sections 2A and 4A were inserted by Protection of Freedoms Act 2012 s 111. In force 25/11/12

[1114] Legal Aid, Sentencing and Punishment of Offenders Act 2012 s 85(1) and (4) and Legal Aid, Sentencing and Punishment of Offenders Act 2012 (Commencement No 11) Order 2015 2015/504

[1115] Legal Aid, Sentencing and Punishment of Offenders Act 2012 s 85(1) and (4) and Legal Aid, Sentencing and Punishment of Offenders Act 2012 (Commencement No 11) Order 2015 2015/504

[1116] Criminal Justice Act 2003 s 226A-226B as inserted by Legal Aid, Sentencing and Punishment of Offenders Act 2012 s 124

[1117] Anti-social Behaviour, Crime and Policing Act 2014 s 22(1)-(4)

[1118] Protection from Harassment Act 1997 s 5

[1119] Domestic Violence, Crime and Victims Act 2004 (Commencement No 11) Order 2009 2009/2501

[1120] Sexual Offences Act 2003 s 103A as inserted by Anti-social Behaviour, Crime and Policing Act 2014 Sch 5 para 2 and Sexual Offences Act 2003 Sch 5

3 Delusional fixation stalkers are more sinister. They genuinely believe that they are having a relationship with their victim. Making up 15% of stalkers, they talk about their sexual intentions, rather than romantic love, and often suffer from mental illness or borderline personality disorders. They might bombard their victims, who are often professionals of elevated status, with telephone calls, letters or visits. Victims are advised to take legal advice.

4 The most dangerous type is sadistic stalkers, who make up 13% of cases. They consider their target to be their prey and want to make their target feel powerless. They target those who seem stable and content, leaving subtle, nasty clues to show they have been in their victims' homes. They should be taken very seriously. Victims should consider moving to a secret address.

338.2   *Cases*

R v Marchese 2008 EWCA Crim 389 LCJ D was convicted of two counts of harassment (section 4), threats to kill and perverting the course of justice. In about 1997 she had a relationship with G, who had a psychiatric illness and was treated by Dr V, who saw G every two to three months. D occasionally accompanied G at the consultations. In 2001, Dr V became engaged to Miss V. In 2002 the victims received threatening calls on their mobiles. Dr V received anonymous texts including, 'You will never know how much I feel for you in the last 4 years'. The police were contacted, and the victims received very many calls which revealed close knowledge of their personal lives. They contained considerable hostility to Miss V and the planned wedding. Dr V kept a boat in Limehouse Basin, and the victims found lights turned on when they had been switched off and two days later a gas stove that had been turned on. The lock-keeper said that a woman attempted to enter, claiming to have a dinner invitation from Dr V. A month later Dr V received a text suggesting that Miss V could end up in Limehouse Pool. The calls and text messages intensified as the wedding approached. D visited the hotel where it was to take place. There were clear death threats, e.g., '2 weeks left before gunman visit u, 6.9 the date'. The stress on the victims was very severe and their relationship was destroyed. The police asked them to pretend that the marriage was to go ahead. Miss V received a text telling her to get Dr V to call off the wedding or many would be dead. On the day the wedding would have taken place there was a flurry of calls. D was arrested by the phone box where calls had just been made. Dr V started a new relationship, and 15 months after the wedding day the CPS dropped the charges. Shortly afterwards Dr V received a threatening phone call from D. About three weeks later in December 2003, Miss V's flat was entered. Lights were left on, windows left open and objects moved. Three weeks later D was arrested, and when interviewed alleged that Dr V had raped her. She produced a pair of her pants which had Dr V's sperm on them. Dr V was arrested for rape and the pants were found to contain a partial match with Dr V's new partner's DNA. Dr V was suspended at work. However, he had noticed that his rubbish, where he had placed his condoms, had been disturbed. In August 2005 Dr V's charge was dropped. D was re-arrested. D was born in Argentina in 1961. The pre-sentence report said D was fixated with Dr V and she was exceptionally devious. D did not suffer from a mental illness. The Judge sentenced her to 3½ and 4½ years for the harassment, 3 years concurrent for the threats to kill and 4½ years consecutive for the perversion, making **9 years** in all. Held. Dr V might never fully recover his practice. The prolonged campaign had a devastating effect on Miss V and a serious psychiatric effect on Dr V. It was a living nightmare. D went to extraordinarily devious lengths to procure a rape conviction. There is no ground to suggest that the overall sentence was inappropriate.

R v Newton 2015 EWCA Crim 1088 D was convicted of stalking. D and V were in a relationship for 15 years and she split from him after D became controlling. V went abroad and after seven or eight years she bumped into D. V thought D had changed and they started seeing each other. Two months later V stopped seeing him when D became jealous and abusive. D then started sending her very abusive texts and voicemails. D said he would not contact her once she had paid a small sum. V received 40 calls and 26 voicemails. D was aged 43 and had 18 previous convictions between 1994 and 2009. They included assaults and one for harassment. The Judge said D was an entirely self-centred man who thought of no one but himself. Held. It was very unpleasant but **6 months** not 12.

339   SUICIDE, ASSISTING

339.1
Suicide Act 1961 s 2 (aiding, abetting, counselling or procuring the suicide of another etc.)
Mode of trial Indictable only
Maximum sentence 14 years
Extended sentences Suicide Act 1961 s 2 is not a specified offence, so the sentence is not available.

339.2   *Crown Court statistics   England and Wales*
In 2010, one person was convicted of this offence. It appears from the data that in 2011-14, no one was convicted.

339.3   *Judicial guidance*
R v Howe 2014 EWCA Crim 114, 2014 2 Cr App R (S) 38 (p 311) LCJ D was convicted of encouraging or assisting suicide. As far as intention is concerned, we note that [the intention is to cause] the death of the other person [not to cause] serious harm. That is clearly a highly important factor inherent in the nature of the offence. In *R v Hough* 1984 6 Cr App R (S) 406 Lord Lane CJ said, "In terms of gravity it can vary from the borders of cold-blooded murder down to the shadowy area of mercy killing or common humanity." Clearly the resolution of cases coming before the court will involve a particularly fact-specific examination. There is understandably little authority and it is clear from the DPP's guidelines to prosecutors that some cases at the compassionate end of the spectrum will not result in prosecution, even if the ingredients of the offence are satisfied. *R v England* 1991 12 Cr App R (S) 1998 suggests that a term of about **3 years** will generally be appropriate in a suicide pact case. The guidance we give relates to what can be described as face-to-face encouragement or assistance as opposed to cases involving remote encouragement over the Internet, which may take the form of encouragement given to multiple individuals unknown to the encourager.

Harm
As to harm, the most serious cases will be those where death resulted. Next in the scale will be attempted suicides where serious harm resulted. The court will need in addition to take account of adverse consequences for people other than the primary victim. In addition, if serious harm has occurred, the court should assess whether the harm has been resolved, or whether it will continue into the foreseeable future. Harm in this context will include psychological as well as physical harm. Risk of harm to others, as occurred in this case, will be a less serious but relevant factor. At the bottom end of the harm range will be those cases where, despite encouragement with the necessary intent, the victim does not go on to attempt suicide. A little higher up the scale than that will be the case where a substance is provided with intent, but which in fact turns out to be harmless. There will clearly be cases which fall between the levels of harm just described and the upper end of the range.

Culpability
[With regard] to culpability, the court will need to consider a number of factors in deciding the level of the offender's blameworthiness. They would include the presence of premeditation, persistence, and the extent of encouragement provided or assistance given, and the means by which the suicide is to take place. The offender's motivation may be important, with compassion at one end of the range, and malice or the prospect of gain at the other. In this context the existence of a duty of care or trust may play a part in determining the extent of culpability. A court should consider whether the victim had

a settled, voluntary and informed intention to commit suicide, or whether his or her state of mind was less certain. Whether the victim solicited assistance or encouragement is relevant, as is the victim's capacity to make a decision as to suicide. In this context, knowledge by the offender of the extent of any vulnerability of the victim will be important. Again, evidence of threats, pressure or persuasion applied to the victim will have a bearing on culpability.

Suggested range

In those cases where the custodial threshold is crossed, we would envisage the range running from 3 years to 12 years or more where an attempt at suicide or actual suicide has taken place. Where the victim has not attempted suicide, but the offence has nonetheless been committed, there may be cases which do not cross the custody threshold, but that will very much depend on the circumstances of the case. Naturally, in any case once an assessment of seriousness has been made, the court will need to consider aggravating and mitigating features of a more generic nature.

339.4   *Cases*

R v McGranagham 1987 9 Cr App R (S) 447 D, a prisoner, made an early plea to aiding an attempted suicide. V contracted polio and as a result suffered from physical disabilities. He was blind in one eye, had no use of his right arm or right foot and he suffered from epilepsy. D and V were in the segregation unit and the events took place over 36 hours. D was aggressive to him and taunted him over his disabilities and the offences V had committed. D had no confidence. D repeatedly told V he would be better off if he committed suicide. D induced V to write a suicide note. D made a noose from a dirty sheet and assisted V to climb onto a cupboard. D then put the noose, which was tied to a pipe on the ceiling, around V's neck. V thought D was trying to kill him and wanted to make it look like suicide. V fell off the cupboard and the noose started to strangle him. D waited half a minute. When D saw blood was coming out of V's mouth he thought V had died. He seized V and rang an alarm bell. Prison officers cut V down. V recovered and made a statement. D made no admissions. A note sent by D was found which said, 'There was no way he could do it by himself. I thought the cripple was brown bread when I raised the alarm (what a pity) the scum stabbed a little kid.' At the committal proceedings D told police V's account was true. He said he did not get on with V and felt anger and hatred towards him. He knew V's father had committed suicide and he thought it was the right idea. The pressure had become too much for V and he had agreed to do what D told him to do. D was aged 25 with a long criminal career. He had progressed from dishonesty and motoring to burglary and aggravated burglary. He was serving 4 years for indecent assault. He broke into a nursing home, beat up an 80-year-old woman and sexually assaulted her. D was institutionalised. Held. V was obviously a pathetic person. His wickedness was quite startling. **8 years** concurrent to the sentence D was serving could not be criticised.

R v Howe 2014 EWCA Crim 114, 2014 2 Cr App R (S) 38 (p 311) LCJ D was convicted of encouraging or assisting suicide. D and V were friends and described as 'inseparable'. V was aged 30 and 'a vulnerable character'. He suffered from mental health problems and had threatened to take his own life on a number of occasions. D knew that they were not idle threats. The two met and spent the day drinking. D was aware that drinking vodka was bad for V. In the evening, D left V's home taking with him a petrol can. He made a 1½ mile round trip to a petrol station, buying nearly 3 litres of petrol and a cigarette lighter. As he was setting off, a neighbour told D not to buy petrol for V, but D ignored him. Whilst D was making that journey, V spoke to his neighbour in terms that showed that he was contemplating suicide. D gave the petrol to V and then left. He said to the neighbour that V had the petrol and D was going to 'get out of the way'. The neighbour then saw that V had poured petrol on himself and was 'singeing' his arm with the lighter. The neighbour put the flames out around the petrol can and went to fetch help. The neighbour's cousin attempted to wrestle the petrol can from V but was unsuccessful. V poured more petrol on his head and the neighbour and his cousin left the house through fear. The petrol ignited and the house burst into flames. The windows all shattered and the flames extended one foot above V's head. V sustained 95% burns, most of which were third degree or full thickness burns. Miraculously he survived. The house suffered extensive damage. When interviewed, D said "I will never speak to him again for what he has put me through". D was aged 19 at the time of the offence and of previous good character. Held. D showed no remorse. The harm falls short of death resulting, the injuries caused will have permanent effect and are of the gravest nature. D was aware of V's vulnerability and knew the previous threats were not idle. There was a degree of premeditation and D provided immediate assistance to V by handing him the newly acquired petrol container. There were no compassionate circumstances. This was a case of very high seriousness. There was no apparent ulterior motive and D did not force V to act as he did. More weight should have been given to D's age, immaturity and lack of convictions. **10 years' YOI** not 12.

See also: *R v Gilderdale* 2010 Times News 26/1/10 and Internet sites (Crown Court High Court judge. G pleaded to assisting the suicide of her daughter with ME, who begged help to die. Daughter's existence described as wretched. In a bed for 16 years. Acquitted of attempted murder. Former nurse aged 54. 1-year **conditional discharge**.)

Note: Treat news reports with care. Ed.

R v Howe 2014 EWCA Crim 114, 2014 2 Cr App R (S) 38 (p 311) LCJ We do not disagree with the level of sentence in *R v McGranagham* 1987 9 Cr App R (S) 447.

Old case: *Att-Gen's Ref No 85 of 2006* 2006 EWCA Crim 2623, 2007 1 Cr App R (S) 104 (p 637) (The starting point should have been **3 to 4 years**)

For a summary of the case see the 9th edition of this book.

340   SUPPLY OF DRUGS (CLASS A, B AND C)

340.1

1 Misuse of Drugs Act 1971

   s 4(3)(a) (supply)

   s 4(3)(c) (offer to supply)

   s 5(3) (possession with intent to supply)

Modes of trial Triable either way unless the defendant could be sentenced to a 7-year minimum sentence under Powers of Criminal Courts (Sentencing) Act 2000 s 110(2), when the offence is triable only on indictment.

Maximum sentences On indictment: life for class A drugs, and 14 years for class B and C[1121] drugs. Summary maximum 6 months and/or a £5,000 fine for class A and B drugs offences committed before 12 March 2015 and an unlimited fine thereafter.[1122] There are maximum fines for those aged under 18, see **14.38** in Volume 1. 3 months and/or £2,500 fine for class C drugs.[1123] Supply of drugs carries a minimum 7 years for a third class A drug trafficking offence.[1124]

Temporary class drugs Police Reform and Social Responsibility Act 2011 s 151 and Sch 17 para 2 amends Misuse of Drugs Act 1971 s 2(1) and widens the definition of 'controlled drugs' to include 'temporary class drugs'. The relevant penalties for supplying this category of drugs are the class B penalties, Misuse of Drugs Act 1971 s 25(2B).

Travel Restriction Orders For offences under Misuse of Drugs Act 1971 s 4(2) and (3) where 4 or more years' imprisonment is appropriate, the court is under a duty to consider whether it is appropriate to make a Travel Restriction Order.[1125] There is no

---

[1121] Criminal Justice Act 2003 s 284 and Sch 28 para 1
[1122] Legal Aid, Sentencing and Punishment of Offenders Act 2012 s 85(1) and (4) and Legal Aid, Sentencing and Punishment of Offenders Act 2012 (Commencement No 11) Order 2015 2015/504
[1123] Misuse of Drugs Act 1971 Sch 4 and Magistrates' Courts Act 1980 s 32(5)(b)
[1124] Powers of Criminal Courts (Sentencing) Act 2000 s 110
[1125] Criminal Justice and Police Act 2001 s 33

power to make an order for possession with intent to supply (section 5(3)).[1126] Where there is a direction in the order, the Secretary of State may retain the defendant's passport.[1127]

Children: barred list For section 4(3) offences where the defendant is aged 18 or over and the person to whom controlled drugs were offered or supplied was a child, he or she is automatically barred from engaging in regulated activity with children.[1128] The judge must tell the defendant that the Disclosure and Barring Service will include him or her in the barred list.[1129] The defendant may ask the Service to remove him or her from the list.

2 Psychoactive Substances Act 2016

s 5 (supplying, or offering to supply, a psychoactive substance)

s 7 (Possession of a psychoactive substance with intent to supply)

Modes of trial Both offences are triable either way.

Maximum sentence On indictment 7 years. Summary maximum 6 months and/or an unlimited fine.

Commencement Commencement is awaited.

Meaning Psychoactive Substances Act 2016 s 2 provides that a psychoactive substance is one that is capable of producing a psychoactive effect subject to the exceptions listed in the Act. A substance produces a psychoactive effect in a person if, by stimulating or depressing the person's central nervous system, it affects the person's mental functioning or emotional state.

Aggravating factors For Psychoactive Substances Act 2016 s 5 offences, the offence is aggravated if committed in the vicinity of a school premises, see **340.12**.

Prohibition order Where a person has been convicted of this offence, the court may make a prohibition order if the court considers it necessary and proportionate for the purpose of preventing the person from carrying on any prohibited activity.[1130] The proceedings are civil and the standard of proof is the balance of probabilities.[1131]

Extended sentences None of the offences are specified offences, so the sentence is not available.

Confiscation For all offences, where a defendant has a criminal lifestyle the court, once the confiscation proceedings are triggered (see **22.11** in Volume 1), must follow the Proceeds of Crime Act 2002 procedure. 'Criminal lifestyle' offences include those under Misuse of Drugs Act 1971 s 4(2)-(3), 5(3).[1132] For what constitutes a criminal lifestyle see **22.48** in Volume 1.

Serious Crime Prevention Orders For Misuse of Drugs Act 1971 s 4(3) and 5(3) and Psychoactive Substances Act 2016 s 5 offences, there is a discretionary power to make this order when it would protect the public etc.[1133]

Forfeiture The court may make a forfeiture order for the drugs and the psychoactive substances.[1134]

[1126] *R v Whittle* 2007 2 Cr App R (S) 578
[1127] Criminal Justice and Police Act 2001 s 33(5)
[1128] Safeguarding Vulnerable Groups Act 2006 s 2 and Sch 3 and Safeguarding Vulnerable Groups Act 2006 (Prescribed Criteria and Miscellaneous Provisions) Regulations 2009 2009/37 reg 4 and Sch para 2
[1129] Safeguarding Vulnerable Groups Act 2006 s 2 and Sch 3 para 25
[1130] Psychoactive Substances Act 2016 s 19(1)
[1131] Psychoactive Substances Act 2016 s 32(1) and (2)
[1132] Proceeds of Crime Act 2002 s 6 and 75 and Sch 2 para 1(1) and 1A.
[1133] Serious Crime Act 2007 s 1 and Sch 1 para 1(1) and 1A
[1134] Misuse of Drugs Act 1971 s 27 and Psychoactive Substances Act 2016 s 54(1)

General
340.2   *Crown Court statistics   England and Wales*
Production and supply   Class A

Year and age	Sex	Plea	Total Sentenced	Type of sentencing %							Average length of custody in months
				Discharge	Fine	Commu-nity sentence	Sus-pended sentence	Custody	Other		
2013 18-20	Both	G	653	–	–	3.4	14.9	80.9	0.9		29.4
		NG	38	–	–	2.6	7.9	81.6	7.9		33.5
2013 21+	Male	G	3,914	0.1	0.1	3.2	16.1	80.1	0.4		42.1
		NG	425	–	–	0.9	5.6	91.8	1.6		69.8
	Fe-male	G	305	0.3	0.3	12.8	37.4	48.5	0.7		31.3
		NG	28	–	–	3.6	17.9	78.6	–		41.7
2014 18-20	Both	G	755	–	–	3	29	68	–		30.5
		NG	46	–	–	2	13	85	–		46.5
2014 21+	Male	G	4,027	–	–	2	17	81	–		43.3
		NG	454	–	–	1	5	94	–		74.8
	Fe-male	G	366	–	–	9	43	47	–		32.7
		NG	35	–	–	–	23	77	–		51.5

Production and supply   Both sexes   Class B

Year	Age	Plea	Total sen-tenced	Type of sentencing %							Average length of custody in months
				Discharge	Fine	Commu-nity sentence	Sus-pended sentence	Custody	Other		
2013	18-20	G	456	0.4	0.2	28.3	40.1	30.3	0.7		12.9
		NG	13	–	–	15.4	23.1	61.5	–		28.9
	21+	G	6,005	0.8	0.9	15.8	44.8	37.3	0.4		17.6
		NG	274	0.7	0.4	4.7	25.5	68.2	0.4		30
2014	18-20	G	698	1	–	23	50	25	–		11.5
		NG	18	–	–	–	56	39	6		11.1
	21+	G	5,788	1	1	15	49	34	–		17.7
		NG	251	1	2	5	30	62	–		33.1

For explanations about the statistics, see page 1-xii. For more statistics, see www.banksr. com Other Matters Statistics tab

Guidelines and the proper approach
340.3   *Sentencing Council Guideline*
Drug Offences Guideline 2012, see www.banksr.com Other Matters Guidelines tab In force 27 February 2012. Page 10. The guideline only applies to offenders aged 18+, see page 2 of the guideline. For the usual practice, see **66.21** in Volume 1.

STEP ONE: Determining the offence category
page 10 The court should determine the offender's culpability (role) and the harm caused (quantity/type of offender) with reference to the tables below.

In assessing culpability, the sentencer should weigh up all the factors of the case to determine role. Where there are characteristics present which fall under different role categories, the court should balance these characteristics to reach a fair assessment of the offender's culpability.

In assessing harm, quantity is determined by the weight of the product. Purity is not taken into account at step one but is dealt with at step two. Where the offence is street dealing or supply of drugs in prison by a prison employee, the quantity of the product is less indicative of the harm caused and therefore the starting point is not based on quantity.

Where the operation is on the most serious and commercial scale, involving a quantity of drugs significantly higher than Category 1, sentences of 20 years and above may be appropriate, depending on the role of the offender.

Culpability demonstrated by offender's role One or more of these characteristics may demonstrate the offender's role. These lists are not exhaustive.	Category of harm Indicative quantity of drug concerned (upon which the starting point is based):
LEADING role: • directing or organising buying and selling on a commercial scale • substantial links to, and influence on, others in a chain • close links to original source • expectation of substantial financial gain; uses business as cover • abuses a position of trust or responsibility, for example prison employee, medical professional	**Category 1** • heroin, cocaine – 5 kilos • ecstasy – 10,000 tablets • LSD – 250,000 squares • amphetamine – 20 kilos • cannabis – 200 kilos • ketamine – 5 kilos
SIGNIFICANT role: • operational or management function within a chain • involves others in the operation whether by pressure, influence, intimidation or reward • motivated by financial or other advantage, whether or not operating alone • some awareness and understanding of scale of operation • supply, other than by a person in a position of responsibility, to a prisoner for gain without coercion	**Category 2** • heroin, cocaine – 1 kilo • ecstasy – 2,000 tablets • LSD – 25,000 squares • amphetamine – 4 kilos • cannabis – 40 kilos • ketamine – 1 kilo
LESSER role: • performs a limited function under direction • engaged by pressure, coercion, intimidation • involvement through naivety/exploitation • no influence on those above in a chain • very little, if any, awareness or understanding of the scale of operation • if own operation, solely for own use (considering reasonableness of account in all the circumstances) • if own operation, absence of any financial gain, for example joint purchase for no profit, or sharing minimal quantity between peers on non-commercial basis	**Category 3** • Where the offence is selling directly to users* ('street dealing'), the starting point is not based on a quantity, OR • where the offence is supply of drugs in prison by a prison employee, the starting point is not based on a quantity[1135] OR • heroin, cocaine – 150 grams • ecstasy – 300 tablets • LSD – 2,500 squares • amphetamine – 750 grams • cannabis – 6 kilos • ketamine – 150 grams *Including test purchase officers

---

[1135] Some words which complicate matters and add nothing have been removed. Ed.

Culpability demonstrated by offender's role One or more of these characteristics may demonstrate the offender's role. These lists are not exhaustive.	Category of harm Indicative quantity of drug concerned (upon which the starting point is based):
	Category 4 • heroin, cocaine – 5 grams • ecstasy – 20 tablets • LSD – 170 squares • amphetamine – 20 grams • cannabis – 100 grams • ketamine – 5 grams OR • where the offence is selling directly to users* ('street dealing') the starting point is not based on quantity – go to Category 3 *Including test purchase officers

Note: For how to determine the indicative quantity of drugs and into which category that weight should be placed, see **340.6** and **340.7**. Ed.

340.4

STEP TWO: Starting point and category range

page 12 Having determined the category, the court should use the corresponding starting point to reach a sentence within the category range below. The starting point applies to all offenders irrespective of plea or previous convictions. The court should then consider further adjustment within the category range for aggravating or mitigating features, set out on page 14. In cases where the offender is regarded as being at the very top of the 'leading' role it may be justifiable for the court to depart from the guideline.

Where the defendant is dependent on or has a propensity to misuse drugs and there is sufficient prospect of success, a community order with a drug rehabilitation requirement under Criminal Justice Act 2003 s 209 can be a proper alternative to a short or moderate-length custodial sentence.

Class A	Leading role	Significant role	Lesser role
Category 1	**Starting point** 14 years' custody	**Starting point** 10 years' custody	**Starting point** 7 years' custody
	Category range 12 to 16 years' custody	**Category range** 9 to 12 years' custody	**Category range** 6 to 9 years' custody
Category 2	**Starting point** 11 years' custody	**Starting point** 8 years' custody	**Starting point** 5 years' custody
	Category range 9 to 13 years' custody	**Category range** 6½ to 10 years' custody	**Category range** 3½ to 7 years' custody
Category 3	**Starting point** 8½ years' custody	**Starting point** 4½ years' custody	**Starting point** 3 years' custody
	Category range 6½ to 10 years' custody	**Category range** 3½ to 7 years' custody	**Category range** 2 to 4½ years' custody

Class A	Leading role	Significant role	Lesser role
Category 4	**Starting point** 5½ years' custody	**Starting point** 3½ years' custody	**Starting point** 18 months' custody
	Category range 4½ to 7½ years' custody	**Category range** 2 to 5 years' custody	**Category range** High-level community order to 3 years' custody

Class B	Leading role	Significant role	Lesser role
Category 1	**Starting point** 8 years' custody	**Starting point** 5½ years' custody	**Starting point** 3 years' custody
	Category range 7-10 years' custody	**Category range** 5-7 years' custody	**Category range** 2½-5 years' custody
Category 2	**Starting point** 6 years' custody	**Starting point** 4 years' custody	**Starting point** 1 year's custody
	Category range 4½-8 years' custody	**Category range** 2½-5 years' custody	**Category range** 26 weeks' to 3 years' custody
Category 3	**Starting point** 4 years' custody	**Starting point** 1 year's custody	**Starting point** High-level community order
	Category range 2½-5 years' custody	**Category range** 26 weeks' to 3 years' custody	**Category range** Low-level community order to 26 weeks' custody
Category 4	**Starting point** 18 months' custody	**Starting point** High-level community order	**Starting point** Low-level community order
	Category range 26 weeks' to 3 years' custody	**Category range** Medium-level community order to 26 weeks' custody	**Category range** Band B fine to medium-level community order

Class C	Leading role	Significant role	Lesser role
Category 1	**Starting point** 5 years' custody	**Starting point** 3 years' custody	**Starting point** 18 months' custody
	Category range 4-8 years' custody	**Category range** 2-5 years' custody	**Category range** 1-3 years' custody
Category 2	**Starting point** 3½ years' custody	**Starting point** 18 months' custody	**Starting point** 26 weeks' custody
	Category range 2-5 years' custody	**Category range** 1-3 years' custody	**Category range** 12 weeks' to 18 months' custody
Category 3	**Starting point** 18 months' custody	**Starting point** 26 weeks' custody	**Starting point** High-level community order
	Category range 1-3 years' custody	**Category range** 12 weeks' to 18 months' custody	**Category range** Low-level community order to 12 weeks' custody

Class C	Leading role	Significant role	Lesser role
Category 4	**Starting point** 26 weeks' custody	**Starting point** High-level community order	**Starting point** Low-level community order
	Category range High-level community order to 18 months' custody	**Category range** Low-level community order to 12 weeks' custody	**Category range** Band A fine to medium-level community order

For the meaning of a high-level, a medium-level and a low-level community order, see **16.12** in Volume 1.

340.5   [Aggravating and mitigating factors]

page 14 The table below contains a non-exhaustive list of additional factual elements providing the context of the offence and factors relating to the offender. Identify whether any combination of these, or other relevant factors, should result in an upward or downward adjustment from the starting point. In some cases, having considered these factors, it may be appropriate to move outside the identified category range.

For appropriate class B and C ranges, consider the custody threshold as follows:

Has the custody threshold been passed?

If so, is it unavoidable that a custodial sentence be imposed?

If so, can that sentence be suspended?

Factors increasing seriousness
Statutory aggravating factors:
Previous convictions, having regard to:
a) nature of the offence to which conviction relates and relevance to current offence, and
b) time elapsed since conviction
Offender used or permitted a person aged under 18 to deliver a controlled drug to a third person
Offender aged 18 or over supplies or offers to supply a drug on, or in the vicinity of, school premises either when school in use as such or at a time between one hour before and one hour after they are to be used
Offence committed on bail
Other aggravating factors:
Targeting of any premises intended to locate vulnerable individuals or supply to such individuals and/or supply to those aged under 18
Exposure of others to more than usual danger, for example drugs cut with harmful substances
Attempts to conceal or dispose of evidence, where not charged separately
Presence of others, especially children and/or non-users
Presence of weapon, where not charged separately
Charged as importation of a very small amount
High purity
Failure to comply with current court orders
Offence committed on licence
Established evidence of community impact

Factors reducing seriousness or reflecting personal mitigation
Involvement due to pressure, intimidation or coercion falling short of duress, except where already taken into account at step one Supply only of drug to which offender addicted Mistaken belief of the offender regarding the type of drug, taking into account the reasonableness of such belief in all the circumstances Isolated incident Low purity No previous convictions or no relevant or recent convictions Offender's vulnerability was exploited Remorse Good character and/or exemplary conduct Determination and/or demonstration of steps having been taken to address addiction or offending behaviour Serious medical conditions requiring urgent, intensive or long-term treatment Age and/or lack of maturity where it affects the responsibility of the offender Mental disorder or learning disability Sole or primary carer for dependent relatives

340.6 Guideline   Determining the 'indicative quantity of the drug concerned'
Drug Offences Guideline 2012 page 10, see www.banksr.com Other Matters Guidelines tab
Step one In assessing harm, quantity is determined by the weight of the product. Purity is not taken into account at step one but is dealt with at step two. Where the offence is street dealing or supply of drugs in prison by a prison employee, the quantity of the product is less indicative of the harm caused and therefore the starting point is not based on quantity.
page 11 The title above the list of various weights says (see **340.3**):

Category of harm
Indicative quantity of drug concerned (upon which the starting point is based):

R v Singh 1988 10 Cr App R (S) 402 at 406 LCJ It should be noted…that the assistance which can be derived from the amount of the drug actually found in the possession of D is limited. It is the scale and nature of the dealing which are the material factors.
R v Djahit 1999 2 Cr App R (S) 142 D pleaded to possession of heroin with intent to supply and possession of cannabis. The police arrived to execute a search warrant at his shop and adjoining flat. Two bags of heroin were found in a door panel near his kitchen. Two further bags were found in a kitchen cupboard. A small amount of heroin was found in one of his socks. The total weight was 21.5 grams with a street value of £2,150. The purity was not ascertained. £6,005, a list of names and addresses, a set of scales and bags were found. D accepted that the paraphernalia belonged to him but the list did not. Held. One count of possession with intent to supply does not prevent the Judge from taking into account the admitted level of dealing as reflected by the sums of money and drugs paraphernalia found. If, however, there is a dispute about the level of dealing and no conviction on a count which reflects dealing over a period of time, then the sentencing judge must exercise care, see for example *R v Canavan* 1998 1 Cr App R (S) 243, *R v Thompson and Smith* 1997 1 Cr App R (S) 289 and *R v Johnson* 1984 6 Cr App R (S) 227.
R v Brown 2000 1 Cr App R (S) p 300 D was convicted of being concerned in the supply of controlled drugs and possession with intent to supply. The counts were based on one occasion. D's car was stopped and he was searched. Police found five small bags of cannabis and nearly £700. At his home in his sister's room there were scales, 100 self-sealing bags, £7,520 in cash and two building society account books in her name. £43,000 was in the accounts. There was no scientific link between any of the money and

D. The Judge sentenced him on the basis of 'the wider picture'. He was sentenced on the basis of a period of 33 months with profits of £33,000. Held. The Judge was bound to sentence for the single offence. The prosecution could have avoided the difficulties if they had drafted six substantive counts against him which the sister faced (assisting another to retain the proceeds of drug trafficking). Sentence reduced.

R v Morris 2001 1 Cr App R (S) 87 (p 297) at para 18 The amount of class A or B drug with which a defendant is involved is very important but not solely the determinative factor in sentencing. Evidence as to the scale of dealing can come from many sources other than the amount with which a defendant is directly connected.

R v Lee 2005 EWCA Crim 443 D pleaded to two supply counts. She claimed she was holding the drugs for another as a custodian. A *Newton* hearing was held. After hearing D the Judge asked the prosecution counsel if there was any PII material. Counsel elected not to adduce any. The Judge then saw him in chambers. Afterwards counsel gave defence counsel information that D had been dealing in drugs on a different day. The Judge sentenced her on the basis that she had been dealing on other days. Held. The Judge erred. There was no evidence to support the claim about the other day.

R v Ahmadzay and Ahmad 2009 EWCA Crim 1115 D and A were convicted of conspiracy to supply 4.93 kilos of heroin. An undercover officer met D, A and another in a hotel. D showed the officer 4.93 kilos of heroin (51 to 59% pure). The prosecution and the Judge said that there was the prospect of regular supplies. Held. As the count in the indictment referred to just 4.93 kilos it could not be widened.

R v Nnamani 2015 EWCA Crim 596, 2 Cr App R (S) 23 (p 219) D was convicted of possession of heroin and cocaine with intent to supply. Police searched a car connected to him and found about 695 grams of cocaine, 27 grams of heroin and 595 grams of a cutting agent used with class A drugs. The Judge said this case was Category 2. Held. It was because guidelines have to be applied with a degree of realism. The quantity of drugs could not be considered in isolation. Taking the purity of the drugs, if the police had not intercepted the drugs there would have been a considerably larger amount of drugs ready for distribution. The total weight came to more than 1 kilo.

Note: The test under the guidelines in the Category of harm table is the 'Indicative quantity of drug concerned'. The principles in these cases appears consistent with the new approach. Ed.

340.7   *Guideline   Relating the indicative quantity to the category weights*

R v Boakye and Others 2012 EWCA Crim 838, 2013 1 Cr App R (S) 2 (p 6) para 39 In step one, the quantities of drug which are listed under the categories of harm in the new guideline are deliberately described as 'indicative quantity of drug upon which the starting point is based'. They are not thresholds at which the sentencing range changes. They are indications of the general region of weight which goes into the relevant category. They could not be [thresholds] because by definition [the starting point] is in the middle of the range.[1136]

Note: I read this to mean that: a) in fixing the starting point, sentencers take the given weight and the given starting point and adjust them either up or down to reflect the actual weight in the case, and b) the starting point given is flexible. Ed.

R v Healey and Others 2012 EWCA Crim 1005, 2013 1 Cr App R (S) 33 (p 176) The quantities that appear in the pictorial boxes as broad indicators of harm are neither fixed points nor are they thresholds. They are 'indicative', designed to enable the judge to put the case into the right context on the sliding scale.

Att-Gen's Ref Nos 15-17 of 2012 2012 EWCA Crim 1414, 2013 1 Cr App R (S) 52 (p 289) The categories do not provide some kind of straightjacket into which every case must be squeezed.

[1136] The judgment at this point says, 'They could not be if the starting point, which by definition is a mid-range of sentence, is to be based upon it.' It is hoped what I have substituted is what the Judge meant to say.

R v Faruqe and Anwar 2015 EWCA Crim 179 D1 and D2 pleaded to conspiracy to possess class A drugs (heroin) with intent to supply. They were stopped by police, who found a kilo of high-purity heroin in their car. A further 8 kilos of heroin and a large number of mobile phones were recovered from D1's home. The Judge took starting points of 13½ years (for a significant role) and 18 years (for a leading role) respectively. Held. We would deprecate the submission that a formulaic approach should be adopted when quantities of drugs significantly in excess of the guideline amount of 5 kilos are seized in the circumstances which we have described. The Judge was entitled to sentence above the ranges in the guidelines.

340.8   Guideline   Drugs not listed in the guideline
R v Pitts and Others 2014 EWCA Crim 1615 The majority of the sentence appeals involved M-CAT. The Judge used the amphetamine guideline for sentence. Held. para 8 *Att-Gen's Ref Nos 15-17 of 2012* 2012 EWCA Crim 1414, 2013 1 Cr App R (S) 52 (p 289) supports the approach that where a drug is not referred to in the guideline, the defence are entitled to the most favourable comparison [with the drugs that are in the guideline].

340.9   Guideline   Determining the role
(Guidance for importation cases as well.)
Att-Gen's Ref Nos 15-17 of 2012 2012 EWCA Crim 1414, 2013 1 Cr App R (S) 52 (p 289) If the Sentencing Council had intended to lower the level of sentencing, that was not reflected in its press release: 'There will be no change in sentencing for possession or drug supply offences.' The essential nature of a drugs hierarchy remains the same even if the terminology has changed. There was a time when some judges divided offenders according to military ranks: generals, lieutenants and foot soldiers. The Council has chosen the categories of 'leading', 'significant' and 'lesser' roles. This is not a change in substance.
R v Descombre and Thomas 2013 EWCA Crim 72, 2 Cr App R (S) 51 (p 345) D pleaded to cultivating cannabis. Held. The proposition that a leading role should be reserved for cases where there is an operational hierarchy, and a chain of employees and a significant role should apply to where there is no chain, is an incorrect analysis of the guideline.
R v Khatib 2013 EWCA Crim 566 D pleaded to supplying class A drugs (×7). On seven occasions, an undercover officer arranged to buy drugs from D, and met him to carry out the transaction. Each 'deal' cost £15. On six of the occasions, the drug was heroin and on the seventh it was crack cocaine. D had become involved with drug dealing when he built up a debt for cannabis which he could not pay. D was aged 18 when the offences were committed and 19 at sentence. He had no previous convictions. He explained to the probation officer that he supplied drugs to around 10-15 people a day, for which he received a £10 or £15 reduction in his debt. He started dealing at the end of February and finished in March, when the debt was repaid. He explained that his dealer had given him a patch of a few roads to cover and he was instructed where to attend in order to supply drugs. The Judge described him as a runner and made the role 'significant', because of the two types of drugs on seven occasions over two weeks. The range was 3½ to 7 years and he started at 4½. With plea he gave 3 years. Held. The Judge's reasons for role went to the level of harm and not to role. D was clearly motivated by financial advantage and must have had some awareness and understanding of the scale of what was clearly a large operation. In contrast, D performed a limited function under direction. It was a lesser role. There was an element of pressure from the dealer. Placing D into Category 3, at the higher end, was reasonable. Taking account of D's age and good character, **2½ years' YOI**.
R v Samuel 2013 EWCA Crim 931 D pleaded to possession of cocaine with intent. His basis of plea was rejected by the Judge. The submission was that had it been accepted, the Judge would have been obliged to sentence him as playing a lesser, not significant, role. The Judge described him as 'the local controlling hand'. Held. para 7 It was wrong

to consider that one or more factors in the 'lesser role' list will automatically place a defendant in that category. The task of the sentencing judge is to analyse carefully all the various factors listed in the various categories and then place the offender in the category which best reflects the offender's role.

R v Dyer and Others 2013 EWCA Crim 2114, 2014 2 Cr App R (S) 11 (p 61) The Court considered sentences imposed for offences of class A drug supply to test purchasers in Soho. The Court addressed the terms 'some awareness and understanding of the scale of the operation' in relation to significant role and 'very little, if any, awareness or understanding of the scale of the operation' in the lesser role used in the guideline. Held. This is intended to encompass not only street dealers but also those who are being sentenced based on the quantity of drug concerned: it is not difficult to visualise a courier or low-level participant in a very substantial drug dealing operation who had no idea of the scale of that operation but who, unless these descriptors were provided, could find the starting point for the sentence at a level far in excess of that which would be justified for the criminality of which the offender was aware. Given that street dealing is always likely to be at low level and the category is fixed, this descriptor has far less relevance.

R v Nunez-Lopez 2015 EWCA Crim 1451 D pleaded to importation of cocaine. He was stopped in his Spanish-registered lorry at Dover. Under a false floor in his cab, customs found about 50 kilos of cocaine. In interview he said he had bought the vehicle himself. The Judge considered that D's role was between a leading and a significant role. He also held that D was using his business as cover and there was an expectation of substantial financial reward. The defence contended that D was a courier who had no involvement higher up the chain. Held. There was no evidence that D was acting in a leading role. The use of a legitimate business cover was limited to the concealment of the drugs amongst a legitimate cargo. There was no evidence of an expectation of substantial gain. In order for there to be a significant role there had to be evidence of an operational or management function within a chain, or that he involved others, or was motivated by financial or other advantage, or had some awareness of the scale of the operation. Whether or not he had an operational function or had involved others, clearly this appellant was motivated by financial reward and in our view he had some awareness of the scale of this operation. His role was therefore a significant one. However, there was no evidence that he personally had helped to load the cocaine into this lorry or knew precisely how extensive the operation was. With plea, 10 years not 14.

See also: *R v Wilson* 2014 EWCA Crim 2998 (Plea to importing a kilo of cocaine. Defendant said ticket, cash and passport put though letter box. Category 2 and lesser role makes starting point 6 years. 3 years extra because of previous conviction for importing. With plea, 6 years not 8.)

340.10   *Guideline   Making an overall assessment*

Att-Gen's Ref Nos 15-17 of 2012 2012 EWCA Crim 1414, 2013 1 Cr App R (S) 52 (p 289) The categories do not provide some kind of straightjacket into which every case must be squeezed. The judge must do his or her best to reach a fair assessment of the overall offending, namely culpability and harm, before proceeding to the next stage (step two). Judges should declare their conclusions on step one in their sentencing remarks, for the benefit of the offender, those advising the offender, and this Court.

R v Hood 2012 EWCA Crim 2666 D pleaded to supply. His advocate used mathematics to arrive at 2 years for the sentence. Held. Despite the guideline, sentencing is still not that precisely mathematical or scientific. Any sentence must take into account all of the relevant circumstances, not only the type and weight of drugs. That is why, for example, there is an overlap between the sentencing ranges for Category 3 and Category 2 where an offender has a 'significant' role in respect of the supply of class B drugs.

Guideline introduced after the date of the offence see **66.18** in Volume 1.

340.11   *Suggested approach to the guidelines*
Note: The *Drug Offences Guideline 2012* increased some penalties for supply and decreased others. Consequently, I consider that the bulk of the tariff cases for the individual drugs are no longer relevant. However, it appears that some of the non-tariff cases remain valid and they are listed. As the guidelines do not suggest suitable penalties for exceptionally large conspiracies, I list those cases as well. Judges continue to apply them. There are some drugs which are not listed in the 'Category of harm' section, see para **340.8**.
Since the guidelines have been in force, the vast majority of reported cases provide little or no assistance. Judges approach supply cases by deciding the category, deciding the role and then deciding where in the range the case fits. This is a very fact-specific series of decisions. A small number of new cases are listed that do not concern large quantities of drugs or drugs which are not listed in the guideline. They are listed as illustrations for practitioners and others. I do not expect the Court of Appeal will consider they are helpful. Ed.

340.12   *Psychoactive Substances Act 2016 s 5 offences in vicinity of school premises*
Aggravation of offence under section 5
Psychoactive Substances Act 2016 s 5(1) This section applies if:
    a) a court is considering the seriousness of an offence under section 5, and
    b) at the time the offence was committed the offender was aged 18 or over.
(2) If condition A, B or C is met the court:
    a) must treat the fact that the condition is met as an aggravating factor (that is to say, a factor that increases the seriousness of the offence), and
    b) must state in open court that the offence is so aggravated.
(3) Condition A is that the offence was committed on or in the vicinity of school premises at a relevant time.
(4) For the purposes of subsection (3) a "relevant time" is:
    a) any time when the school premises are in use by persons under the age of 18;
    b) one hour before the start and one hour after the end of any such time.
(5) In this section:
"school premises" means land used for the purposes of a school, other than any land occupied solely as a dwelling by a person employed at the school;
"school" has the same meaning:
    a) in England and Wales, as in section 4 of the Education Act 1996;
    b) and c) [Relate to Scotland and Northern Ireland]
(6) Condition B is that in connection with the commission of the offence the offender used a courier who, at the time the offence was committed, was under the age of 18.
(7) For the purposes of subsection (6) a person ("P") uses a courier in connection with an offence under section 5 if P causes or permits another person (the courier):
    a) to deliver a substance to a third person, or
    b) to deliver a drug-related consideration to P or a third person.
(8) A drug-related consideration is a consideration of any description which—
    a) is obtained in connection with the supply of a psychoactive substance, or
    b) is intended to be used in connection with obtaining a psychoactive substance.
(9) Condition C is that the offence was committed in a custodial institution.
(10) In this section:
"custodial institution" means any of the following:
    a) a prison,
    b) a Young Offender Institution, secure training centre, secure college, Young Offenders Institution, young offenders centre, juvenile justice centre or remand centre,
    c) a removal centre, a short-term holding facility or pre-departure accommodation;
    d) service custody premises;

"removal centre", "short-term holding facility" and "pre-departure accommodation" have the meaning given by section 147 of the Immigration and Asylum Act 1999, "service custody premises" has the meaning given by section 300(7) of the Armed Forces Act 2006.

340.13   *Judicial guidance*

Att-Gen's Ref Nos 82-96 and 104-109 of 2011 2012 EWCA Crim 155, 2 Cr App R (S) 56 (p 320) All dealers are not of course the same. Each must be considered on the facts of his individual case. On the whole the greater the quantity, the more serious the offence is likely to be. Similarly, the longer the period over which supplies were made, the graver the case is likely to be. The greater the profit, the more serious the case is likely to be. On the whole, wholesale supplies, that is to say supplies to those who then supply onward to individual consumers, are likely to be more serious than retail supply because of the quantity involved.

340.14   *Indictment/Charge, Must restrict yourself to what is alleged in the*

R v Twisse 2001 2 Cr App R (S) 9 (p 37) We recognise the importance of only sentencing for the criminality proved or admitted. This established principle of law is now reinforced by European Convention on Human Rights art 6. If the prosecution can prove that D has been acting as a supplier over a substantial time, it can put the court in a position to sentence properly by one of three ways: 1) charging a number of offences of supply or possession and supply at different dates, 2) charging a conspiracy over a prescribed period, and 3) charging him with being concerned in the supply over a specified period contrary to Misuse of Drugs Act 1971 s 4(3)(b). If the indictment is not drawn as we have suggested and D does not ask for offences to be taken into consideration, judges should refrain from drawing inferences to the extent of D's criminal activities, even if those inferences are inescapable having regard to admissions made or equipment found. In other words, a defendant charged with one offence of supply cannot receive a more substantial sentence because it is clear that he has been dealing for 9 months, but the court is not required to blind itself to the obvious. If he claims that the occasion in question was an isolated transaction, that submission can be rejected. He can be given the appropriate sentence for that one offence without the credit he would receive if he really were an isolated offender.

R v Ahmadzay and Ahmad 2009 EWCA Crim 1115 D and A were convicted of conspiracy to supply 4.93 kilos of heroin. An undercover officer met D, A and another in a hotel. D showed the officer 4.93 kilos of heroin (51 to 59% pure). The prosecution and the Judge said that there was the prospect of regular supplies. Held. As the count in the indictment referred to just 4.93 kilos it could not be widened.

See also the **Guidelines Determining the 'indicative quantity of the drug concerned'** para at **340.6**.

340.15   *Distinction between drugs in the same class, Don't draw a*

R v Thompson 1997 2 Cr App R (S) 223 The defendant pleaded to two counts of supplying ecstasy. The Judge sentenced him on the basis that ecstasy was more serious than other class A drugs, so passed a higher sentence than the guidelines. Held. The court has said on a number of occasions that there should be no distinction between the various drugs in a class. The sentence was reduced.

340.16   *Purity   Proper approach   Post-guideline*

Drug Offences Guideline 2012 page 10, see www.banksr.com Other Matters Guidelines tab Purity is not taken into account at step one but is dealt with at step two. For details see **340.3**.

Note: In step two 'High purity' is listed as an 'Other aggravating factor'.

R v Kelly and McGirr 2014 EWCA Crim 1141, 2 Cr App R (S) 70 (p 549) M pleaded to conspiracy to supply class A and class B drugs and K was convicted of a conspiracy to supply class A drugs. M had been dealing with other co-defendants in supplying drugs to Scotland. In December 2011, 1.5 kilos of high-purity heroin was dealt, and 167 grams in

May 2012. That did not represent the totality of the offending. The offending was at either end of an extended period of active dealing. Held. The guidelines make absolutely clear that the purity of the drugs is of high importance, for very obvious reasons. No authorities precluded what the Judge did in this case. He took account of the weight and purity, with the purity first confirming the ascription of senior roles for both K and M. It is an obvious inference that offenders who deal with high-purity drugs are closer to the centre of operations than those who deal with drugs which have been diluted for street use. Second, the Judge relied on purity as meaning that a quantity of nearly 2 kilos at very high purity falls to be regarded as offending in the higher category. That was entirely appropriate. para 16 It would, however, be unjust if someone high up the drugs hierarchy was sentenced for a quantity of drugs by just their weight whereas someone lower down the chain dealt with the same amount of drugs after they had been cut making their quantity of drugs many times larger than the person higher up the chain. That approach would also be a misuse of the guideline.

340.17   *Purity   What is required?*
R v Morris 2001 1 Cr App R (S) 87 (p 297) Purity analysis is essential for sentencing purposes for cases of importation, or in other circumstances where 500 grams or more of cocaine, heroin or amphetamine are seized. It may be desirable in cases where quantities less than 500 grams of those substances are seized. But, bearing in mind the cost of purity analysis and that analysis may cause delay, purity analysis will not generally be required where a defendant is in possession of only a small amount consistent with either personal use or only limited supply to others. As purity can indicate proximity to the primary source of supply, if there is reason for the prosecution to believe that a defendant in possession of a small quantity of drugs is close to the source of supply and is wholesaling rather than retailing, it will be necessary for purity analysis to be undertaken before a court can be invited to sentence on this more serious basis. In the absence of purity analysis or expert evidence, it is not open to a court to find or assume levels of purity, except in the case of ecstasy and LSD [because sentencing for them is based on tablets and squares] and currently with an assumed average purity of 100 mg of ecstasy (*R v Warren and Beeley* 1996 1 Cr App R (S) 233) and 50 µg of LSD (*R v Hurley* 1998 1 Cr App R (S) 299) unless prosecution or defence, by expert evidence, show the contrary (*R v Warren and Beeley* 1996 1 Cr App R (S) 233 and *R v McPhail* 1997 1 Cr App R (S) 321).

R v Boakye and Others 2012 EWCA Crim 838, 2013 1 Cr App R (S) 2 (p 6) Whereas the previous case law proceeded upon the basis of quantity of drugs measured at 100% purity, the new guideline does not. The reason is that the Council was advised that in many cases, especially at the lower end of offending, scientific analysis of purity may not be available. For this reason, amongst others, the indicative quantities of weight, which the new guideline adopts as a broad measure of harm, are not the same as those spoken of in *R v Aramah* 1982 76 Cr App R 190, as subsequently modified. They are gross, not 100% purity weights. Of course, in dealing with a large consignment where there has been analysis and the weight at 100% purity is known, a court may well pay attention to the additional information which it has been given. It may determine to adjust up or down, either for very high or very low purity. However, the initial indicator of the category of offence is the weight as seized.

Note: The explanation for the change given in lines two to six does not deal with the problem of those who import or supply at cocaine at 1%. Consider two individuals who both have 1 kilo of cocaine at 88% and intend to cut it to make 5 kilos. If police arrest the first before he cuts it and the second just after he cuts it, why should they have different starting points? The ability to adjust the sentence for purity is of little help as different judges would no doubt give different adjustments for similar cases. Ed.

340.18   *Purity, Low*
Drug Offences Guideline 2012 page 10, see www.banksr.com Other Matters Guidelines tab

| **Factors reducing seriousness or reflecting personal mitigation** |
| Low purity |

R v Parker 2014 EWCA Crim 51 D pleaded to conspiracy to supply a class B drug, namely MDPV. The conspiracy lasted about six months. 9.5 kilos of MDPV was seized in an attempt to trace the supply. The purity was between 2% and 5%. D played a leading role. Held. The Court applied *R v Brown* 2013 EWCA Crim 1726, 2014 1 Cr App R (S) 84 (p 518). The low purity should be factored into the sentence. **3 years 4 months**, not 3 years 8 months to reflect the purity.

Factors

340.19   *Assisting the authorities*
R v Aramah 1982 76 Cr App R 190 at 192 It is particularly important that offenders should be encouraged to give information to the police. A confession of guilt coupled with considerable assistance to the police can properly be marked by a substantial reduction.
Note: The discounts that have been given show that Crown Court judges and Court of Appeal judges believe that very considerable ones are appropriate, no doubt because of the importance that is attached to arresting and prosecuting drug traffickers. Ed.
See also the **INFORMANTS/GIVING EVIDENCE FOR THE PROSECUTION** chapter in Volume 1.

340.20   *Believing the drugs to be a different drug*
R v Bilinski 1987 9 Cr App R (S) 360 The amount of mitigation for this will obviously depend upon all the circumstances, amongst them the degree of care exercised by the defendant.
R v Ngiam 2001 EWCA Crim 1332, 2002 1 Cr App R (S) 35 (p 150) The defendant pleaded to possessing 50 kilos of heroin (at 47%) with intent to supply. She was sentenced on the basis that she thought it was cannabis and she was a courier. Held. The fact that she believed it was cannabis was a mitigating factor but it did not mean that the Judge was obliged to sentence her as if it were cannabis.
Att-Gen's Ref No 146 of 2002 2003 EWCA Crim 1010, 2 Cr App R (S) 107 (p 640) D pleaded to possessing 982 grams of heroin (363 grams at 100%) at the first opportunity. Police boarded a train, believing that a gun was on board, and inspected a holdall. D denied that it was his. Police found a plastic gun, and D then admitted that it was his holdall. He took the heroin from his carrier bag and tried to conceal it on his body. When challenged he said it was cannabis. The basis of plea was that he was a courier who believed that it was cannabis, and acted because he had a drug debt. There were differences about the debt in his account to the police and the pre-sentence report writer. He was aged 35 with a conviction for supplying cannabis for which he received 6 months. Held. We consider the opportunity the offender might have had to satisfy himself of the true nature of the drugs. The drugs were wrapped. The false account was to water down the degree of his admission in that regard. The degree of discount need not be particularly high. **7-7½ years** as a starting point was not excessive. Because he believed that it was cannabis, **5 years** was proper. Because it was a reference, **4 years**.
R v Bird 2013 EWCA Crim 1765, 2014 1 Cr App R (S) 77 (p 478) D pleaded (10% credit) to two counts of possession with intent to supply class A drugs and other less serious drug counts. The two counts related to a drug commonly known as M-CAT which were found on him and at his home address. The prosecution case was that D would have assumed the drugs were amphetamine (class B). D was aged 33 with a very poor record. The defence said D should be sentenced on the basis of a class B drug.

Held. We reject that. The guideline starting point was 4½ years. That would be increased because of the other drug counts and his appalling record. **42 months**, which would give a starting point of just short of 4 years, not 54 months.

See also the **IMPORTATION OF DRUGS** *Believing the goods to be a different drug* para at **273.39**.

340.21   *Children etc.   Supplying to/using as couriers*

Misuse of Drugs Act 1971 s 4A[1137] Where the offender has reached the age of 18 and the offence under section 4(3) was committed on or in the vicinity of school premises at a relevant time or the offender uses a courier aged under 18 the court must treat that factor as an aggravating factor.

340.22   *Conspiracies*

R v Khan and Others 2013 EWCA Crim 800, 2014 1 Cr App R (S) 10 (p 42) The defendants pleaded to conspiracy to supply cocaine. Held. The court is entitled to reflect the fact that the offender has been part of a wider course of criminal activity. The fact of involvement in a conspiracy is an aggravating feature since each conspirator playing his part gives comfort and assistance to others knowing that he is doing so, and the greater his or her awareness of the scale of the enterprise in which he is assisting, the greater his culpability. A particular individual within a conspiracy may be shown only to have been involved for a particular period during the conspiracy, or to have been involved only in certain transactions within the conspiracy, or otherwise to have had an identifiably smaller part in the whole conspiracy. In such circumstances, the judge should have regard to those factors which limit an individual's part relative to the whole conspiracy. It will be appropriate for the judge to reflect that in sentence, perhaps by adjusting the category to one better reflecting the reality.

R v Pitts and Others 2014 EWCA Crim 1615 The defendants were convicted of conspiracy to supply. Held. We bear in mind the parameters of the *Drug Offences Guideline 2012* which do not explicitly encompass the offences of conspiracy to import, supply or produce drugs. We see no error in the Judge seeking to derive some assistance from relevant entry points into sentencing categories by virtue of the relevant weights of drugs recovered, subject to the recognition that the criminality of the conspiracy is not necessarily thereby confined. That which must also be considered is the degree of participation in the illegal agreement and its scope. We accept that the broad brush of defining leading, significant and lesser roles may be a helpful indicator as to participation but these categories are themselves likely to be subject to further refining on the facts. In summary, in sentencing for the conspiracies indicted, caution should be exercised against a slavish following of the guidelines on the basis of weights of drugs discovered at the conclusion of a surveillance operation.

340.23   *Conspiracies and the guideline*

R v Khan and Others 2013 EWCA Crim 800, 2014 1 Cr App R (S) 10 (p 42) The defendants pleaded to conspiracy to supply cocaine. Held. para 21 The guideline should be applied to an offence of conspiracy to supply a controlled drug because: a) there is no positive exclusion in the guideline, b) the guideline does not explicitly comprehend inchoate offences such as attempts, which are clearly covered by the guideline, c) substantive offences under Misuse of Drugs Act 1971 s 4(3)(b)-(c) are not specifically referred to but it could not sensibly be said they are not covered by the guideline, and d) this court has already applied the guideline to conspiracies in the past, see for example *R v McCalla* 2012 EWCA Crim 2252.

340.24   *Couriers*

Att-Gen's Ref Nos 82-96 and 104-109 of 2011 2012 EWCA Crim 155, 2 Cr App R (S) 56 (p 320) Just as dealers vary, so do transporters or, as they are often conveniently labelled, couriers. Some people fulfilling the role of transporting drugs may in fact be very close

---

[1137] Inserted by Drugs Act 2005 s 1.

to the central organisers of the trade, the entrepreneurs. Judges will be alert to the efforts that such people are likely to make to assert that they are mere functionaries when they are not and judges are not only entitled but bound to draw proper inferences from the evidence before them as to the true state of affairs. Other couriers, however, are little more than hired hands. They operate under the direction of the entrepreneurs and are likely to be paid in one way or another per task.

R v Bowman 2014 EWCA Crim 2542 D pleaded to supply. Police stopped a taxi and found D with 956 grams of heroin (64% and 67% purity) and 255 grams of a cutting agent. The street value was about £100,000. D was aged 17 and now 18 and this was her first offence. The prosecution accepted she was a courier. Held. It will not always follow that a courier will have a lesser role. It will depend on their knowledge of the wider operation, the trust placed in them by those up the chain and matters of detail of that sort. But it will usually be the case that a courier acting on instructions will have a lesser role. In our view, the appellant here plainly played a lesser role. She was young, gullible and there was indeed some evidence of intimidation. The fact that she was being paid £100 (or 0.1 per cent of the value of the drugs) did not in our view give her a financial stake in the operation. She was obeying the instructions she was given. She was plainly in the lesser role category. We start at 4 years not 6. The high value and high purity stop the case being at the bottom of the range. The youth reduction will depend on age, maturity and all the circumstances. A third off not a quarter off was required for her age. With full credit that makes 22 months' detention, not 3 years.

For when the courier is involved with wraps of drugs for street dealing, see **340.39**.

340.25   *Custodians/Warehousing*

R v Hartley and Dale 2013 EWCA Crim 542 H and D were convicted of conspiracy to supply cocaine, heroin and amphetamine. Between 2005 and 2008, D headed a criminal organisation that imported and supplied nearly 36 tonnes of chemicals. The chemicals were sold to drug dealers on a nationwide basis and used as cutting agents. Evidence suggested that the chemicals were to be used to cut cocaine at a ratio of 1:1. The resulting powders would therefore have had a street value of no less than £3.5bn. Held. A drugs supplier at the top of an operation of this scale could contemplate a sentence after a trial in the region of **30 years**.

R v Langley 2013 EWCA Crim 1034 D pleaded (25% credit) possession of cocaine. Police officers observed D's co-accused, X, enter the porch of an address. He left a minute later carrying a plastic bag. Officers approached X but he ran off, discarding the bag as he did so. He was arrested and recovered the bag, which contained 246 grams of cocaine at 76% purity. It had a street value of around £76,000. Officers returned to the property and spoke to D's grandfather. He said that he lived there with D and that D had gone out and told him that someone would come to collect something from the porch. Officers searched D's bedroom and found a small quantity of cocaine. His basis of plea stated that D was asked to store some cocaine by X. D agreed that he would, on the basis that he would receive some cocaine for his own use. D agreed to leave the bag of cocaine in the porch so that someone could pick it up. This was on X's instruction. There was no financial reward. D had previous convictions but not for drugs and had not been to custody before. Held. D was unaware of the scale of the operation, despite warehousing a large quantity of cocaine. The Judge did not have sufficient regard to the basis of plea. **2 years 3 months** not 3 years 3 months. 3 weeks consecutive for breach of the community order remained.

R v Bush 2013 EWCA Crim 1164, 2014 1 Cr App R (S) 40 (p 232) D pleaded to possessing ecstasy with intent. He attended a music festival where staff thought they overheard a conversation about ecstasy. D was arrested. He was searched and 55 individual bags of the drug were found on him. Each bag contained just less than 1 gram of ecstasy in powder form. In total there was 37.8 grams, with a street level value of about £1,900. It was accepted that: a) D was looking after the drugs for another, b) D was not involved in the sale of drugs, and c) D was acting as a custodian. The police thought that D appeared rather naïve. He was aged 21 and of good character. Held. D's culpability was at a low level. He had extensive personal mitigation: his difficult domestic circumstances, his youth, his remorse, his good character and positive references. Starting at 21 months, with the plea, 14 months not 2 years. There were very good reasons not to suspend that.

340.26   *Death occurs   Post-guideline cases*

R v Hood 2012 EWCA Crim 2666 D pleaded to being concerned in the supply of cannabis. B was observed by undercover police officers pulling into a pub car park. B approached another car and took a holdall from his car's boot. D got out of the other car and B placed the holdall in the boot of D's car. Both cars were driven away. D was arrested with drugs, £240, two mobile phones and a book on hydro-gardening. The bag was recovered and contained 9.9 kilos of cannabis resin. D admitted to being paid £200 to deliver the package to someone in the car park. The man to whom he gave the bag, B, had convictions for drugs offences, including supply. D had known B for some years and had been offered £200 to deliver some items. D suspected the bag to contain drugs. D, aged 33, had left school without qualifications, but had studied for a BTEC, obtained a BSc with first class honours and was studying for an MSc, with just his dissertation to submit. Through the university, he had begun to mentor challenging schoolchildren and had lectured. He had three convictions for simple possession of cannabis, having been a user aged 13-22. Held. This conviction was a personal disaster for someone who worked so hard for his academic and community achievements. D was a courier and no more. His awareness or understanding was limited. He had much that was positive in his good character. Despite some understanding of the scale of the operation (a marker of 'significant' role), his role as a simple courier had most hallmarks of a 'lesser' role. This was at the top of the Category 3 band, and at worst, this was towards the bottom of Category 2. With the full discount for the plea, **2 years** not 3.

R v Harrod 2013 EWCA Crim 1750, 2014 1 Cr App R (S) 76 (p 474) D pleaded to supply (full credit). He and V were very close friends and had been for many years. Once a month they would spend a weekend together watching sport and taking drugs. They took it in turns to buy the drugs. One weekend D bought the drugs believing them to be MDMA, which they had taken many times before. In fact, it was PMA, which was similar but more toxic. They both reacted adversely but V stopped breathing. D called an ambulance but he and the paramedics could not resuscitate him. V died. D admitted his part to the police. D was aged 39, in employment and of positive good character. V's father said he did not "hold D responsible in any way". He said that D had "suffered greatly since the death and will continue to suffer for the rest of his life". The father asked the court to be merciful. Held. There is no doubt D was very affected by the death. The offence was probably categorised as Category 4, lesser role. It was sharing minimal quantities on a non-commercial basis. There was remorse and the sentence could be at the bottom of the range if one leaves out the death. That would be a high-level community order. The death was a substantial aggravating factor. Starting at **9 months**, with plea **6 months** not 9. The decision whether to suspend was a matter for the Judge. We can't say he erred.

Note: There is a clear implication that if the Judge had suspended the sentence that would not have been wrong. Ed.

R v Priest 2013 EWCA Crim 2018 D pleaded (full credit) to permitting premises to be used for supplying class A drugs, namely morphine. D was a tenant in a flat. AM brought round 200 prescription tablets of morphine contained in 10 boxes of blister packs, and left them in a drawer in D's kitchen. D was present and aware that AM had left the drugs in the flat. Some days later, AM and three other friends were in D's flat. AM produced three or four tablets and crushed them into a powder. Most of those present snorted the powder. D and EE consumed 10-20 tablets, combining them with alcohol. D and EE went into the town centre and continued to drink. They returned early in the morning and were both sick. The next afternoon, D and the others woke up. EE was breathing heavily and then stopped breathing. They called an ambulance. He died of a morphine overdose. The police were called and a search of the flat recovered 118 of the tablets. D was aged 19 and had no previous convictions. She had originally been assigned the flat by social services as she had been a vulnerable child. There had been a history of self-harm. AR pleaded to supply and received 52 months. Held. The starting point of 20 months taken by the Judge was too high. Because of the loss of life, an immediate custodial sentence was required. Starting at 9 months was appropriate. With the plea, **6 months** not 14.

See also: *R v Walker* 2010 EWCA Crim 2977 (Pre-guideline case Plea to supply of methadone. Defendant was a heroin addict. He allowed an acquaintance, V, to consume residue of his partner's methadone prescription. V died. It did not cause the death but did not help. Third conviction for supply of class A. **4 years** was not excessive.)

Note: These cases are listed to show the approach in cases where death occurs and not to indicate the tariff, which is set by the new tables in the guidelines. Ed.

See also the **MANSLAUGHTER** *Drug abuse* paras at **284.28**.

340.27 *Helping others to obtain drugs*

R v Leeworthy 2010 EWCA Crim 464 D pleaded at the first opportunity to supplying heroin and cocaine. Police were targeting drug dealing, and D was a known user but not thought to be a supplier. Undercover officers approached D and asked for his help in obtaining drugs. The officers provided D with the phone number of the 'general' but a call was unsuccessful. D and the officers then went to an address, and D went inside with the officers' money and came out with the drugs. (The amount of money and weight are not revealed.) It was not suggested that D made any money out of the supply, or that he had any drug stock. D had a dreadful record with ten drug possession convictions and a 'general criminal lifestyle'. He had no supply convictions. D was on bail and in breach of a suspended sentence (30 days consecutive.) Held. D was a drug user who helped out a perceived user. He was a facilitator. **3 years** not 4.

340.28 *Informing on the defendant, Defendant's family*

R v Catterall 1993 14 Cr App R (S) 724 The defendant's father called the police because he and his wife were concerned that the defendant was under the influence of drink or drugs. They did it entirely in the interests of their son. Held. His father and mother care so much about his future that they were prepared to disclose the offences to the police. They are likely to support his efforts to give up his habit. The Court should take those facts into account and give him a further discount. The sentence will be reduced from 4 years to **2 years**, a reduction entirely due to his father's action.

R v Ferrett 1998 2 Cr App R (S) 384 D pleaded to four counts of supplying ecstasy, a count of supplying amphetamine and two counts of supplying cannabis. A teenage girl died after taking ecstasy and amphetamine. D's mother and others told the police that he might have been the supplier of the drugs. D was interviewed and denied supplying the deceased but admitted supplying another. He was aged 18 when sentenced and of good character. Held. A total of **5 years** would have been appropriate. However, applying *R v Catterall* 1993 14 Cr App R (S) 724, he is entitled to a further discount because of the credit due to his family for taking the course they did. So **4½ years'** YOI not 7.

Note: These are old cases, so they may help with deciding whether such information is a factor, but not what the suitable penalties are. Ed.

340.29 *Joint purchase of drugs*

Drug Offences Guideline 2012 page 11, see www.banksr.com Other Matters Guidelines tab [When determining the offence category] one or more of these characteristics may demonstrate the offender's [lesser] role:..if own operation, absence of any financial gain, e.g. joint purchase for no profit, or sharing minimal quantity between peers on non-commercial basis.

Note: As the examples for what may demonstrate a 'lesser role' are generally more serious than this, it can be inferred that joint purchase cases should be sentenced at the lower end of the range for that group. Ed.

R v Denslow 1998 EWCA Crim 432 D pleaded to supplying heroin after a ruling of law. He had offered to plead to possession. D and another each put £150 together to purchase heroin. D paid the money to the dealer and received two bags of heroin. He handed one to his co-purchaser. The Judge gave him an absolute discharge. D appealed his conviction. Held. We wonder why it was necessary to charge supply. It was inevitable that D would be dealt with at worst as though he were in possession of the drugs. His plea to possession should have been accepted.

Att-Gen's Ref Nos 82-96 and 104-109 of 2011 2012 EWCA Crim 155, 2 Cr App R (S) 56 (p 320) [Supplying to friends] is to be contrasted with a genuine case of a supply which is wholly technical. That can happen, for example, if two friends together purchase an evening's supply and one alone concludes the transaction before passing over a share to the friend. That is not supply in the ordinary sense and is absent any financial or benefit component at all. That kind of transaction is rightly treated differently, see *R v Denslow* 1998 EWCA Crim 432.

Note: There is a clear distinction between joint purchase and social supply. *R v Wolfe* 2011 EWCA Crim 2301 doubted the correctness of the *R v Denslow* 1998 decision but the 2012 case (above) affirms it. Ed.

R v Harrod 2013 EWCA Crim 1750, 2014 1 Cr App R (S) 76 (p 474) D pleaded to supply (full credit). He and V were very close friends and had been for many years. Once a month they would spend a weekend together watching sport and taking drugs. They took it in turns to buy the drugs. One weekend D bought the drugs believing them to be MDMA, which they had taken many times before. In fact it was PMA, which was similar but more toxic. V died. Held. We agree with the Court in *R v Wolfe* 2011 EWCA Crim 2301 that the comments in *R v Denslow* 1998 EWCA Crim 432 should not be promoted into a statement of law. *R v Denslow* 1998 predates the guidelines and deals with offences of joint purchase of minimal quantities and it is that guidance that judges should refer to.

For more detail see **340.26**.

340.30 *Legal substances, Material turns out to be*
R v Szmyt 2009 EWCA Crim 1507, 2010 1 Cr App R (S) 69 (p 468) D was convicted of attempting to import ecstasy. He was stopped in France driving a car in which there were 2 kilos of cannabis (a guilty plea), and hidden in a television were 1,998 harmless tablets which had the appearance of ecstasy. D said that he was on his way to the UK to visit his brother-in-law. D, aged 30, was Polish and had received a caution in 2008 for possession of an offensive weapon. He was treated as a courier. There was a favourable prison report before the Court. Held. *R v Warren and Beeley* 1996 1 Crim App R (S) 233 proposes that the sentence should reflect the strength of the drugs. We must presume that D believed that he was importing tablets of usual strength, but the sentence should reflect the fact that the tablets contained no ecstasy. If they had, the correct sentence would have been 6½ to 7 years. As it was an attempt and there was no ecstasy, **4½ years** not 6.

See also: *R v Chambers* 2009 EWCA Crim 2742 D was convicted of conspiracy to supply ecstasy. **16 years** was proper.

340.31 *Music festivals, Selling at*
R v Bush 2013 EWCA Crim 1164, 2014 1 Cr App R (S) 40 (p 232) Teenagers go to summer music festivals in groups and are particularly vulnerable to those trying to sell drugs. Anyone who is involved in such an enterprise, even on a relatively low-level basis, must expect an immediate custodial sentence.

340.32 *Peripheral role*
R v Evans 2012 EWCA Crim 1758 D pleaded to conspiring to supply class B drugs. He worked at a garage and as he was closing up for the evening, a van drove onto the forecourt of the premises opposite. The van was followed by another van. A man, whom D knew as a regular customer, got out and asked him to help move some boxes from one van to another.

He began to help and as he did so noticed that some of the boxes were damaged, resulting in the contents spilling out. He saw that they were bars of cannabis resin. He panicked and was worried about what would happen to him if he refused to carry on. He re-stuck the Sellotape and continued to load the boxes. The vans left and the man said he would "sort" D out with a "drink". D was never paid for his assistance. D was arrested as his fingerprints were on the boxes. He volunteered information about his involvement and the name of the man whom he knew. The consignment of cannabis resin weighed 226 kilos and had a street value in excess of £1.1m. D was aged 33 at appeal and was treated as having no previous convictions. He lived with his parents and his daughter, for whom he was the primary carer. He showed genuine remorse. Held. The Judge must have started at 2 years, placing the offence at a low level for Category 1, with D playing a lesser role. The factors reducing the seriousness of the offence were significant. This was an isolated incident which started out entirely innocently, and it was only fear which caused him to continue. There was also a delay of eight months before being sentenced. A short prison sentence may have been unavoidable, but as D had served the equivalent of a 6-month sentence, **50 weeks suspended** with unpaid work, not 16 months.

340.33 *Pretending goods were prohibited drugs*
R v Reid 2008 EWCA Crim 202, 2 Cr App R (S) 68 (p 383) D pleaded to one count of offering to supply crack cocaine and heroin and one count of theft. He approached an undercover police officer and offered a wrap. The officer agreed to buy for £20 and handed the money over. D came back some time later but refused to hand over any drugs. He pleaded on the basis that he did not have a wrap on him when he made the offer, and his intention was to steal money and not to supply drugs. D, aged 41, was a long-term drug addict. He had almost 100 previous convictions going back to when he was a teenager. He had served several custodial sentences, the longest being 3½ years. He had seven convictions for offering to supply drugs, five for actual supply and three for possession. These mostly related to class A drugs. He had three previous offences falling within the terms of Powers of Criminal Courts (Sentencing) Act 2000 s 110, triggering a minimum prison term of 7 years (less maximum 20% for plea) unless this would be unjust. Held. The criminality of D was more akin to obtaining money by deception than drug dealing. **12 months** not 5 years.
Old cases: *R v Tugwell* 2001 2 Cr App R (S) 113 (p 501) (It involves a lesser degree of criminality than supplying real drugs.) *R v McNab* 2001 EWCA Crim 1605, 2002 1 Cr App R (S) 72 (p 304) (It was a fraud on a massive scale. There can be no criticism of M's **11 years** and L and B's **9 years**.) *Att-Gen's Ref No 90 of 2001* 2002 EWCA Crim 3173, 2003 2 Cr App R (S) 33 (p 164) (Enough powder to manufacture another 850,000 tablets. The appropriate starting point was in the order of **10 years**.)
For a summary of the second and third cases, see the 9th edition of this book.
See also the *Lawful substance, Material turns out to be* para at **340.30**.

340.34 *Previous conviction for drug trafficking/Persistent offenders*
R v Miller 2012 EWCA Crim 2614 D was convicted of possession of crack cocaine with intent to supply. Upon searching D's address, police officers found hidden in the kitchen 86.5 grams of crack cocaine at 22% purity. The street value was nearly £8,000. D had convictions for possession of cocaine and cannabis (1997 and 1998) and supplying half a kilo of heroin and 420 grams of crack cocaine in 2009, worth £57,500. The instant offence was committed whilst on licence from that sentence. Held. This was a Category 3, significant role case. The amount found was little over half of the indicative figure for Category 3. An upward adjustment was warranted to reflect D's previous convictions and the fact he was on licence. **6 years** not 7.
R v Kotun 2013 EWCA Crim 1039 D pleaded to supplying class A drugs (×4). D supplied undercover police officers with heroin (143 mg, 100 mg and 148 mg) and crack cocaine (132 mg) over the course of two months. D was a street dealer and was able to source drugs to sell to people, whether they asked for them or not. D had a very bad

record. In 2000, 2003 (×2), 2004 and 2007 he was convicted of possession of cannabis with intent (imprisonment on all but one occasion). In 2009 he was convicted of heroin supply and subsequently heroin and crack cocaine supply (6 years). It was argued that, had the minimum sentence provisions applied, the sentence would have been 7 years less 20% for the plea. D was in fact sentenced to 7 years. Held. This was a Category 3 case and D's role was significant. The offences were committed on licence. We have no doubt the Judge was fully justified in sentencing at the top of the range and indeed somewhat above it. The starting point taken by the Judge took this case into a category appropriate for either a greater role or quantity of drugs than applied in this case. The appropriate starting point was **7½ years**. With the plea, **5 years** not 7.

R v Hornby 2014 EWCA Crim 136 D pleaded to possession of class B with intent to supply (×2). Police executed a search warrant and discovered 95 grams of cannabis and 14 grams of amphetamine (41-59% purity). There were digital scales, snap bags, tick lists and £915 in cash. D was aged 28 at appeal and had 17 convictions for 65 offences including possession of class A and B with intent to supply, possession of class A and C and possession of an offensive weapon (32 months). Held. This was an established pattern of drug offending as a street dealer. The current offences were committed on licence after release from a sentence of 39 months. He had been recalled to prison. The Judge was wrong to treat the previous convictions as a reason to move up a category. D had accepted full culpability and explained to the probation officer that he 'thrived' off supplying drugs to others. The offences warranted a sentence starting at in excess of 3 years. D's role, on his own admission to the probation officer, could be categorised as leading, as he was running his own drugs operation. The high purity indicated that D was close to the source. The appropriate starting point was 4 years. With full credit for his pleas, **32 months** not 40.

See also: *R v McLeary* 2009 EWCA Crim 925 (D pleaded to possessing cocaine with intent to supply. D had a conviction in 1996 for importing cocaine (10 years). Held. 7 years would be appropriate after a trial. No more than 2 years should be added for the previous conviction. So **9 years** with full discount for the plea makes **6 years** not 8.)

R v Arif 2013 EWCA Crim 1545 (Plea to possession of cannabis with intent. Police searched his flat. He threw a shoe box containing 34 self-sealable bags each containing a quantity of cannabis out of the window. £1,400 in cash, eight mobile phones, a piece of paper with more than 50 phone numbers on it, 59 self-sealable bags, a razor and digital scales were also found. 44.3 grams of skunk cannabis. Significant role. String of previous convictions for drug dealing, including heroin and crack. Committed on licence. Aged 24 when arrested. The sentence could not be less than his 2010 sentence for cannabis dealing (30 months). Starting at 4½ years was on the high side but not too long. With plea, **3 years**.)

340.35   *Prisoners, Supplying to   Guideline/ Judicial guidance*

Drug Offences Guideline 2012 page 10, see www.banksr.com Other Matters Guidelines tab Where the offence is street dealing or supply of drugs in prison by a prison employee, the quantity of the product is less indicative of the harm caused and therefore the starting point is not based on quantity.

page 11 [When determining the offence category] one or more of these characteristics may demonstrate the offender's [significant] role: supply, other than by a person in a position of responsibility, to a prisoner for gain without coercion.

R v Bower 2001 EWCA Crim 2040, 2002 1 Cr App R (S) 111 (p 483) The message has to go out to those who succumb to threat or persuasion to take drugs into prison that if they do so they will lose their liberty for a very long time indeed, good character and absence of previous convictions notwithstanding.

R v Rogers 2007 EWCA Crim 2438 D pleaded to supplying cannabis. Deterrent sentences are imposed on those who take drugs into prison because drugs inside a prison have a much greater value than they have on the streets. Drugs are a form of currency in prison. They can be responsible for injury to persons, particularly prison staff. Such offences are too prevalent and require the imposition of deterrent sentences. These are not offences for which a nominal period of imprisonment is appropriate, despite the mitigation which may exist for the individual offender.

R v Akhtar 2008 EWCA Crim 791 Those who attempt to supply drugs to prisoners require exemplary sentences. Drugs within a prison, even where the drugs are not heroin, cocaine or crack cocaine, are entirely inimical to the rule of law within a prison. They are used to extort or bully and the evil that they do is even worse than the evil done within our open society. Those who try to smuggle drugs into prison are dealt with by extremely harsh sentences because of the problems in detection. People have to be deterred.

Note: The three cases above are consistent with the severe penalties in the new guidelines. Ed.

R v Wilkinson 2011 EWCA Crim 2415 D pleaded to smuggling drugs into prison. Held. We are told, and we accept, that the drugs were three times more valuable within prison than they would be on the street.

Post-2014 guideline cases

R v Sanchez-Canadas 2012 EWCA Crim 2204, 2013 1 Cr App R (S) 114 (p 588) The Judge moved the category from 4 to 3 because the supply was into prison. Held. That was wrong. The supply of drugs into prison is in itself inherently more serious than is the supply of drugs generally. That is because drugs in prison are a currency, an instrument of power, extortion and oppression and they fundamentally undermine the discipline and good order which is essential to running a prison properly. The supply of drugs into prison ought usually [to] be described as [better] fitting into the significant role category than the lesser role category. It will ordinarily demand a prison sentence, even where there is no commercial motive and indeed where the supplier has come under some moral pressure. The Judge's starting point of **5 years** (which was the top of the range. Ed.) could be justified.

For more detail of the case, see **340.36**.

R v Saliuka 2014 EWCA Crim 1907 In D's cell were found 40 wraps of heroin and wraps containing 7 grams of skunk cannabis and 8½ grams of cannabis resin. D organised the smuggling of the drugs and had done so on several occasions. Held. The supply of drugs within the prison system is a serious social evil. Because of the high price that drugs fetch within prison, it enriches and gives power to ruthless prisoners who may exploit others to create debts which are difficult to service without resorting to bullying and intimidation or the commission of further crime inside or outside the prison. The trade has an inherently corrosive and corrupting influence. Furthermore, it is capable of feeding the addiction of other prisoners who should be able to make use of their time in prison to become drug free.

See also the **PRISON OFFENCES** *Conveying articles into prison* paras at **309.5**.

340.36   *Prisoners, Supplying to   Cocaine or heroin   Cases*

R v Wilkinson 2011 EWCA Crim 2415 D pleaded (full credit) to smuggling 6.62 grams of heroin, 1.75 grams of cocaine and 27 subutex tablets (a heroin substitute) into prison. In 2004, D was in a relationship with M. The relationship broke down but D remained loyal to M. They had a son. M was sent to prison in 2010 and D visited him, taking their son with her. M repeatedly asked her to bring him drugs. He stated that he was in danger and that there were people who would harm and kill him. She initially refused but eventually acquiesced. She was not paid anything. She received instructions that the drugs would be left in a suitcase in her back garden. She took the drugs to the prison in two packages. Subutex has a particularly high value in prison. She went to the lavatory to move the drugs from her bra, the purpose of which was to avoid detection by the sniffer dogs. She then passed the drugs to M. In prison, the drugs were worth over £2,000. D was of good character and the carer for her five children. Held. D was manipulated by M, and she was precisely the type of woman who is targeted by those in prison. She made good progress in prison. The separation from her children is undoubtedly difficult. However, **4 years** cannot be said to be manifestly excessive.

Note: Although the case was decided before the guidelines were issued, it is listed to show the principle that in these cases deterrence takes precedence over personal mitigation. Ed.

Post-guideline cases

R v Sanchez-Canadas 2012 EWCA Crim 2204, 2013 1 Cr App R (S) 114 (p 588) D pleaded to supplying class A and class B drugs into prison. He sent a prisoner in Winchester prison a box containing a pair of trainers with hidden in them 10.75 grams of heroin and around 23 grams of cannabis resin in 11 different wraps. The package was intercepted. D was traced by a fingerprint left on the package. The drugs were destined for a friend, LC, a drug addict, who had pleaded with D to send the drugs to him. D said that LC had arranged for a third party, whom D did not know, to bring the trainers and the heroin to him. D hollowed out the trainers and made up the package, including adding the cannabis resin. The package was addressed to another prisoner who would be able to deny any connection and the return address on the package was not D's. D told police that he was managing LC's money, allowing him to transact business in prison. After his first appearance, he absconded to Spain, where he remained for 10 years. He was eventually arrested and brought back to the UK. D was aged 42 when he committed the offences and in his fifties when he was sentenced. He had a conviction in 1992 for drug supply. Held. This was a significant role, Category 4 case. The fact that this was an attempt somewhat mitigates the sentence. This was a carefully thought out and well-concealed supply. The Judge's starting point of 5 years could be justified by the combination of factors. D pleaded, but only after the public had been put to the trouble and expense of hunting him in Spain. The time and effort which D saved by his extremely belated plea of guilty on the first day of trial, after endeavouring to evade justice for 10 years, is certainly not greater than the time saved by a man who pleads guilty on the first day of trial. We would give no more than 10% credit. With that in mind, there is nothing wrong with **3 years 9 months**.

R v Tongo 2014 EWCA Crim 331 D pleaded (on the day of trial) to possession with intent to supply heroin (22 grams, cocaine (12.5 grams at 14-20%), cannabis (319 grams) and anabolic steroids (60 tablets). D was seen on CCTV outside the perimeter fence of a prison. He was carrying a sports bag and holding a mobile phone to his ear. He threw the bag into the bushes. After a time he retrieved the bag and appeared to hide in the bushes himself until he was seen by police entering the rear of a car parked in a nearby lay-by. He still had the bag with him. The drugs found in the bag had a value of £10,000. D said he had acquired a drug habit, particularly for cannabis and cocaine. He then lost his job and had no way of repaying the £3,000 debt that he had accumulated. As a result, his dealer had threatened D and his mother. His mother made some repayments but continued to receive threats. He was then told he could pay the balance off and make himself £200 by throwing a bag over a prison wall. He was collected and taken to the prison. He claimed he decided not to go through with it and returned to the car. He knew or suspected that the bag contained drugs but did not know which drugs or in what quantities. D had one conviction for possession of cannabis (fine) and three for attempted robbery, having a bladed article and causing damage to property. Held. The weight of class A drugs does not come near 150 grams but Category 3 applies to those such as prison employees supplying drugs in prisons. Category 3 was the correct starting point. The supply of drugs for money signifies a significant role although on the contrary, an offence committed in consequence of intimidation etc. may signify a lesser role. D played a lesser role but had to an extent brought his misfortune on himself. However, he did not go through with the supply. The correct starting point was in the order of 4 to 4½ years.[1138] He was due some credit for his late plea. The appropriate sentence was **4 years** not 5.

[1138] Though stating that D played a lesser role, the Court then appeared to select a starting point close to or at the level for a Category 3 significant role offence. Ed.

R v Saliuka 2014 EWCA Crim 1907 D was convicted of possessing class A and B drugs with intent to supply and of possessing a phone and SIM card inside a prison. In D's shared cell, prison officers found 40 wraps of heroin and wraps containing 7 grams of skunk cannabis and 8½ grams of cannabis resin. The phone and SIM card were also discovered. D blamed his cell mate but recordings on a prison-issue mobile phone showed both men discussing drugs and getting them into the prison. D was aged 24 with an appalling record. He was on recall. The Judge found that D organised the smuggling of the drugs and had done so on several occasions, inferred from the wide range in purity. Held. **7 years** (5½ years for the drugs and 18 months consecutive for the phone and SIM possession) was perfectly proper.

See also: *R v Bayliss and Others* 2013 EWCA Crim 1067 (Pleas to supply of class B (cannabis) and class C (buprenorphine). Supply into prison by family members via post. Numerous occasions. 1.5 grams of buprenorphine. Over a two-month period. Numerous phone calls to arrange the supply. Cards sent to other inmates to avoid detection. 20% credit. It was Category 4. Leading role. **2½ years** for the prisoner who instigated the offences not manifestly excessive. **10 months** for the two family members with young children.)

340.37   *Prisoners, Supplying to   Prison staff   Guideline/Judicial guidance*
Drug Offences Guideline 2012 page 11, see www.banksr.com Other Matters Guidelines tab [When determining the offence category] one or more of these characteristics may demonstrate the offender's [leading] role: abuses a position of trust or responsibility, e.g. prison employee.
Pre guideline case
R v Jibona 2010 EWCA Crim 1390 A health visitor tried to smuggle cannabis into prison. Held. Every member of the staff of a prison knows that the majority of prisoners come into prison with a history of substance abuse and that great efforts are made to wean them from such habits, both for their own sake and for the sake of society. Every member of the prison staff knows that drugs, however, do find their way into prisons and that they are a source of evil, they form a kind of currency, they give rise to a hierarchy of drug barons and the like, and their presence in prison is contrary to the work which the Prison Service tries to perform. Every member of prison staff knows the steps which are taken to try to stop drugs being brought into prison, but there is a limit to that which can be done and is practicable and respectful of the human dignity of prison visitors. Those who work in prisons are in a position of special trust because they are not subjected to the same degree of scrutiny as other visitors. The appellant knew all these things, but he broke the trust imposed on him and let down his fellow prison staff. For all those reasons, the Judge was right to regard this offence as more serious than an attempt to smuggle drugs into a prison by a friend or family member of an inmate.

340.38   *Social supply   Pre guideline case*
Att-Gen's Ref Nos 82-96 and 104-109 of 2011 2012 EWCA Crim 155, 2 Cr App R (S) 56 (p 320) These defendants, caught dealing, asserted that it was significant mitigation that they supplied to their friends. It is not. If a man is an habitual supplier of dangerous drugs it is scarcely surprising that he should choose to supply, if he can, those whom he trusts rather than strangers whom he cannot trust. Nor is it more than scant mitigation that he does. A man who makes himself an outlet for drugs to a circle of acquaintances or friends is engaged in trading and in a commercial exercise. That kind of situation is to be contrasted with a genuine case of a supply which is wholly technical. That can happen, for example, if two friends together purchase an evening's supply and one alone concludes the transaction before passing over a share to the friend. That is not supply in the ordinary sense and is absent any financial or benefit component at all. That kind of transaction is rightly treated differently. Otherwise the assertion that only friends were supplied, like the much over-used expression 'social supply', is all too often advanced when there is no merit in the underlying contention.

Note: Advocates rely on 'social supply' to indicate that the supply was less organised, provided additional income to their defendant's main income and of a smaller scale than those who run an established supply service to all. Clearly it is the extent of the dealing and the type of organisation involved that are the key factors. Ed.

340.39   *Street dealing   General principles*
R v Leigh 2015 EWCA Crim 1045, 2 Cr App R (S) 42 (p 332) D pleaded to possession of cocaine and possession of cocaine with intent to supply. D was stopped on his bike and found to have a wrap of cocaine in his mouth. He was bailed. A month later, D was stopped again and strip-searched. Police found 142 wraps of heroin and cocaine in his anus. The Judge held it was Category 4. Held. It was Category 3 as the wraps were in due course to be dealt with in the street. He was part of the group street dealing. His role was a lesser role. The starting point was 3 years. Because D was on bail and had previous convictions for class A supply, that would increase the sentence beyond the Judge's starting point of 3 years 3 months, so appeal dismissed.

R v Reid and Higgins 2015 EWCA Crim 1165 R and H pleaded to two conspiracies to supply (heroin and cocaine). Police in an undercover operation made test purchases to catch street dealers. R was involved in 12 transactions and H was involved in ten. On one occasion they told the buyer there would be a slight delay as they were "still cutting up the gear". R was aged 24 years and had 11 court appearances for 17 offences. In 2010, he was given 9 weeks' YOI for possession of cannabis with intent to supply. In 2014 he was given 18 days' imprisonment for possession of heroin. H was aged 25 with convictions for dishonesty and disorder. He had no drug convictions. The Judge ascribed them with a leading role. The defence said there was no evidence of substantial gain and the role should be significant. Held. It was agreed it was Category 3. Both R and H had substantial links and some influence on the chain. They were motivated by financial gain and had involved others for reward. They were trusted with cutting the drugs. The roles were clearly appreciably above that of a sole street dealer. Their role was significant. The range was 3½ to 7 years. For R **7 years** and for H **6 years**.

R v Mellor 2015 EWCA Crim 1243 D pleaded to supplying heroin. Police saw him meet a female, have a short conversation and walk off. The female was stopped and found to have three wraps of heroin. The weight was 0.9 grams. D was searched and found to have £25 in notes. D was aged 43 and had a significant criminal record but no convictions for supply. For 10 years he had a serious crack and heroin problem. In a *Newton* hearing the Judge determined that D was caught in a single supply for gain to feed his own addiction. He placed D at the bottom of Category 3 at a significant role, making 3½ years and with plea, 28 months. Held. We need not decide whether this was a significant or lesser role. The only aggravating factor was the previous convictions. As it was an isolated incident we start at 2½ years making, with plea, **20 months**.

340.40   *Test purchases/Entrapment (and similar situations)*
R v Springer 1999 1 Cr App R (S) 217 D pleaded at the Magistrates' Court to three charges of supplying heroin and was committed to the Crown Court. D was a suspected drug dealer. The police tested their suspicions by making three telephone calls. He was asked, "Have you got anything?" He replied, "Yeah", and arrangements were made to meet him. In response to each call a meeting was arranged, and about 1.5 grams of heroin was supplied. The calls were recorded and the meetings were videoed. The defence argued that he was entitled to a discount because of entrapment. Held. There was a need for the police to adopt this method of detection. There was a need for there to be more than one supply to provide evidence he was a dealer. This was not a case of entrapping a suspect into supplying drugs who would otherwise never have engaged in that activity. *R v Underhill* 1979 1 Cr App R (S) 270 at 272 applied. Here there was legitimate police activity and not activity that could provide mitigation or a reduction at all.

R v Mayeri 1999 1 Cr App R (S) 304 D pleaded at the earliest opportunity to four counts of supplying ecstasy. One tablet was involved in each case. Four undercover police officers approached him in a nightclub, and he agreed to sell them a tablet for £10. He claimed there was an element of entrapment. D relied on *R v Tonnessen* 1998 2 Cr App R (S) 328 Held. The entrapment argument is not a good one. Where undercover officers discover that a man is prepared to sell drugs by approaching him, it is not a matter the courts need normally take into account as amounting to entrapment. It might be said, 'Seller beware'. These premises are frequently used to sell drugs.

R v Davidson 2002 EWCA Crim 879, 2003 1 Cr App R (S) 4 (p 12) Although the police behaved impeccably, the escalating progress of the supply was to a degree fuelled by their suggestions [which contributed to the reduced sentence].

Note: The above cases are old. However, they are in line with current sentencing practice. Ed.

Att-Gen's Ref Nos 82-96 and 104-109 of 2011 2012 EWCA Crim 155, 2 Cr App R (S) 56 (p 320) Supplying a police officer [who is making a test purchase] does less damage than other supplying. However, ordinarily making supplies of that kind will be an indication that the defendant has a practice of general supplying and that is likely to remove any mitigation which derives solely from the identity of the particular recipient in question. (Note: Although the case was heard before the guidelines were produced, the principles appear to be of general application. Ed.)

R v Dyer and Others 2013 EWCA Crim 2114, 2014 2 Cr App R (S) 11 (p 61) The Court considered sentences for class A drug supply to police officers who were making test purchases in Soho. Held. The guideline states that where the supply is 'direct to users' the appropriate category is Category 3. There is a footnote which states that selling direct to users includes test purchase officers. The fact that supply is to a test purchase or undercover police officer is…not a reason to reduce the category. In reality, there is no question of a street dealer deliberately approaching an undercover officer (intending less harm) and the identity of the person with whom the defendant engages when supplying or offering to supply drugs is entirely a matter of chance. For that reason, 'supply to an undercover officer'…[was not] included in the definitive guideline [as a mitigating factor].

For more information about entrapment, see the **ENTRAPMENT/AGENTS PROVOCATEURS, SIMILAR SITUATIONS** chapter.

Types of drugs

340.41

Note: Since the guidelines have been in force, the vast majority of Court of Appeal cases provide little or no assistance to court users. Judges approach supply cases by deciding the category, deciding the role and then deciding where in the range the case fits. This is a very fact-specific series of decisions. A small number of new cases are listed and they are listed as illustrations for practitioners and others. I do not expect the Court of Appeal will consider they are helpful when they check a sentencer's approach.

The two main exceptions to this approach are that first, very large drug conspiracy cases are listed in line with *R v Walker and Gosling* 2013 EWCA Crim 1940, which said that cases decided before the guideline which have extremely long sentences are a relevant consideration for sentencers. The second exception is drugs that are not listed in the Category of harm section in the guidelines, see **340.3**. Ed.

Amphetamine class B

340.42   *Amphetamine   Class B   Sentencing Council guideline*

Drug Offences Guideline 2012 page 11, see www.banksr.com Other Matters Guidelines tab and **340.3**.

Note: Amphetamine is a listed drug in the Category of harm section in the guidelines. Category 1 is 20 kilos,[1139] Category 2 is 4 kilos, Category 3 is 750 grams and Category 4 is 20 grams. Ed.

[1139] For determining the weight of drugs to apply to the guideline, see **340.6** and **340.7**.

Cannabis class B

340.43   *Cannabis   Class B   Sentencing Council guideline*
Drug Offences Guideline 2012 page 11, see www.banksr.com Other Matters Guidelines tab and **340.3**.
Note: Cannabis is a listed drug in the Category of harm section in the guidelines. Category 1 is 200 kilos,[1140] Category 2 is 40 kilos, Category 3 is 6 kilos and Category 4 is 100 grams. Ed.

340.44   *Cannabis   Class B   How cannabis is supplied*
R v Auton 2011 EWCA Crim 76 Cannabis for individual use commonly changes hands in quantities of one-eighth, one-quarter or one-half of an ounce (3.5, 7 or 14 grams), although of course supplies may be in larger quantities. The cases before us, which do not appear in any way unusual, involve operations. A defendant who embarks upon such cultivation likely to produce not less than 1 kilo (35 ounces) and sometimes quite a lot more, even exclusively for his own use, is avoiding the risk of being caught buying on the open market and making available to himself large quantities of strong cannabis. The total drug available in the community is appreciably increased by these operations.

340.45   *Cannabis   Class B   Local dealer   Post-guideline case*
R v Hornby 2014 EWCA Crim 136 D pleaded to possession of class B with intent to supply (×2). Police executed a search warrant and discovered 95 grams of cannabis and 14 grams of amphetamine (41-59% purity). There were digital scales, snap bags, tick lists and £915 in cash. D was aged 28 at appeal and had 17 convictions for 65 offences including possession of class A and B with intent to supply, possession of class A and C and possession of an offensive weapon (32 months). Held. This was an established pattern of drug offending as a street dealer. The current offences were committed on licence after release from a sentence of 39 months. He had been recalled to prison. The Judge was wrong to treat the previous convictions as a reason to move up a category. D had accepted full culpability and explained to the probation officer that he 'thrived' off supplying drugs to others. The offences warranted a sentence starting at in excess of 3 years. D's role, on his own admission to the probation officer, could be categorised as leading, as he was running his own drugs operation. The high purity indicated that D was close to the source. The appropriate starting point was 4 years. With full credit for his pleas, **32 months** not 40.
R v Lindo 2015 EWCA Crim 735 D pleaded to possession of cannabis with intent to supply, driving without a licence and driving without insurance. His car was stopped by police and 17.33 grams of skunk (street value £173-£346) were found in a bag with five small packets of herbal cannabis (street value £50-£100). Scales, a grinder and self-sealing bags were found at his home. Supply messages were found on his mobile. D was aged 25 and had ten previous convictions including four possession of cannabis and one possession of cocaine convictions. The Judge considered the case as Category 3 with a significant role. He increased the sentence because of the driving matters. Held. That was wrong because those convictions did not carry imprisonment. 12 months was appropriate so with plea **8 months** not 18. 3-month disqualification to remain.

340.46   *Cannabis   Class B   Significantly more than 200 kilos   Pre-guideline* cases
Note: The listed amount for cannabis in the guideline for Category 1 is 200 kilos,[1141] see **340.3**. Ed.
R v Dines 2010 EWCA Crim 1811 D pleaded to conspiracy to supply cannabis resin. D arrived at a storage unit which was under surveillance by police. W arrived shortly afterwards. Police moved in after about an hour and found both D and W inside. W, kneeling, was passing D a number of wrapped blocks of cannabis resin while D was

---

[1140] For determining the weight of drugs to apply to the guideline, see **340.6** and **340.7**.
[1141] For determining the weight of drugs to apply to the guideline, see **340.6** and **340.7**.

weighing the blocks. The blocks were **593 kilos** of cannabis resin with a street value of more than £1.7m. D tried to minimise his involvement. However, his basis of plea was as follows: he was asked by W to help in the movement of some cannabis. He agreed for the payment of £100 to ensure the cannabis would be moved as the container had previously been used to store his own equipment. He was not aware of the amounts or quality of the cannabis involved. A pre-sentence report noted that he was of effective good character and that this was his first venture into crime. Held. Given the basis of plea, **3 years'** imprisonment, not 4.

R v Chalkley and Others 2011 EWCA Crim 611 C pleaded to conspiracy to supply cannabis, E was convicted of possession of cannabis with intent to supply, and F was convicted of attempting to possess cannabis with intent to supply. **1.64 tonnes** had been imported in mid-June 2009 and was planned to be distributed from an industrial yard belonging to C. C provided a lorry from which the drugs were being unloaded at his yard. Others divided the cannabis up and couriers or customers contacted persons at the yard by mobile phone. Customers or couriers were instructed to stop at a pub nearby, where they would be collected, driven in their own cars to the yard and the cannabis would be loaded into their vehicle. E and another were stopped with 196 kilos of cannabis, worth around £564,000. F arrived at the yard, but before any boxes could be loaded into another customer's car, arrests were made. A further **547 kilos** of cannabis was found. It was estimated to be worth £1.5m. There was a second consignment of drugs which the defendants were not involved with. Held. Considering the authorities, for C, **6 years 3 months** was not manifestly excessive. It is clear E was only involved on the day of the offence and was not allowed to see the drugs or to enter the yard. However, E must have been a trusted courier. **5 years** was appropriate. F should have been sentenced on the basis of one box only (23.5 kilos). He was also a trusted courier and had previous relevant convictions. **4½ years** was appropriate.

See also: *R v Alexander and Others Re B* 2011 EWCA Crim 89 (Late plea. Conspiracy to supply cannabis and conspiracy to conceal the proceeds. **18,000 kilos** worth £61m. B was right at the top of the conspiracy. So serious were these importations, for which B was to a great extent responsible, that the maximum sentence of 14 years was fully justified. 9 years, and 7 for money laundering, making **16 years**, was not manifestly excessive.)

340.47   Cannabis   Class B   Street dealing   Post-guideline cases
R v Wetheridge 2012 EWCA Crim 2365 D was convicted of possession of cannabis with intent to supply, having the previous day pleaded to simple possession. A search of D's house found a sandwich box containing numerous packages of skunk cannabis, weighing 46.4 grams, and two further packages containing 0.6 and 0.7 grams of skunk cannabis. There was also a wallet containing £560, a cannabis grinder, empty self-seal bags, electronic scales, two mobile phones and a SIM card. One of the phones received a text message saying, "Its jay sam you got any green?" D, aged 24, was employed and this was his first drug trafficking offence, although he had cautions for simple possession in 2006 and 2011 (cannabis) and 2008 (cocaine). Held. This was a Category 3 case. The Judge was entitled to find that this was not an isolated offence, but was obliged to pass a sentence which reflected the specific offending. Considering D's age, record and the amount of cannabis involved, a 12-month increase from the starting point was not warranted. **15 months** not 2 years.

R v Tahid 2013 EWCA Crim 613 D pleaded (full credit) to possession of cannabis with intent to supply. Police saw D riding his bicycle and talking on his mobile phone. Later he was seen standing next to a stationary car, astride his bicycle, apparently talking to the driver through the window. As one of the officers approached him, he dropped a package on the floor which contained 6.31 grams of skunk cannabis. When his home was searched, a further 70 grams were found, along with a quantity of self-seal bags. In interview, D claimed the drugs were for his own use. D, aged 23, had a conviction for possession of cannabis (2008) and a caution for possession of cocaine and cannabis (2007). D was unemployed and lived at home. D's basis of plea claimed social supply.

That was rejected and the Judge found that D was a street dealer. He treated D as playing a significant role and placed him into Category 3 in the guidelines. A letter from D's GP stated that he suffered myofascial pain and had told the doctor that he used cannabis as relief. Held. Starting at **12 months, 8 months**, not 10 months.

R v Trotter 2015 EWCA Crim 1298 D pleaded to five counts of supplying small quantities of cannabis and amphetamine. Police had made test purchases. D was aged 37 and was treated as being of good character. The Judge started at 2 years and because the case was overwhelming gave 25% credit. Held. **12 months** in all not 18.

Cocaine/Heroin class A

340.48   *Cocaine/Heroin   Class A   Couriers   Post-guideline case*
R v Adekunle 2013 EWCA Crim 415 D was convicted of possession of heroin with intent to supply. He was stopped whilst driving from Liverpool to London. When asked whether there was anything in the car that should not be there, he indicated a bag behind the passenger seat. It contained three compressed vacuum-packed blocks of heroin. The total weight was 2.99 kilos at 13% purity, equating to 388 grams at 100%. The street value was over £298,000. When asked what was in the bag, D said, "I don't know. They just told me to go and collect something." D, aged 49 at appeal, was a Nigerian national of good character. Held. The Judge placed D's role between the lesser and significant role categories. That is a fair summary considering that he was a courier dealing with a very substantial quantity of drugs. However, the Judge failed to take account of his previous good character, the fact that D was a family man and had been in employment and that this offence appeared to be a one-off journey. **6 years** not 8.

340.49   *Cocaine/Heroin   Less than 50 grams*
R v Fowler 2015 EWCA Crim 1745 D pleaded (full credit) to controlling a prostitute for gain and supplying heroin. Police received information and a police officer, P, rang D's number and asked for a girl. P went to the address he was told to go to and D and P went to D's bedsit where Jade was. D prepared and smoked some crack cocaine. P asked D to get him some heroin and D agreed to do that. D took £20 and purchased two £10 bags. Meanwhile P and Jade agreed on a price of £20 or £30. D returned and Jade gave D £30 to buy some drugs. He left to buy them. Jade and D were arrested by other policemen. Jade told police she used D's flat and she would share her crack with him. D was aged 60. The Judge found it was a Category 3 case with a lesser role. She passed 1 year for the prostitution offence and 30 months for the drug offence concurrent. Held. The mitigation was D's age and he had lived for most of his life as a law-abiding person, until he became involved in drugs. Category 3 applies to street dealing but that is what actually happened here. D was a user of drugs who agreed to go and buy some drugs from his dealer in order to supply them to the police officer. He did not profit on that single transaction at all, he merely operated as a broker. He agreed to buy drugs for Jade on a similar basis, although he expected that she would share them with him. [We regard] this as a Category 4 offence and a lesser role which would mean we start at 18 months, reducing it to 15 months for the mitigation and with the plea 10 months. The prostitution offence should be a concurrent 4 months. The sentence could be suspended so because of 2 months served we make for the drugs 6 months suspended.
For the prostitution decision see **311.23**.

340.50   *Cocaine/Heroin   Class A   Significantly more than 5 kilos   Judicial guidance*
Att-Gen's Ref 99-102 of 2005 2005 EWCA Crim 294, 2 Cr App R (S) 82 (p 505) We compare the present case with *R v Soares and Others* 2003 EWCA Crim 2488, where sentences in excess of **30 years** would have been regarded as properly representing the starting point, following a trial, for the prime mover in importing 2,000 to 3,000 kilos of class A drugs.

Note: This decision was before the guidelines were issued. However, judges continue to use pre-guideline material in cases where there are amounts significantly over 5 kilos because there is little else to help them. Ed.

340.51   Cocaine/Heroin   Class A   Significantly more than 5 kilos
Note: The listed amount in the guideline for Category 1 is 5 kilos,[1142] see **340.3**.
These cases are listed here in line with *R v Walker and Gosling* 2013 EWCA Crim 1940. See the note at **340.41**. Ed.

R v Daly 2010 EWCA Crim 2518 D pleaded (20% credit) to conspiracy to supply cocaine. He had previously pleaded to conspiracy to supply cocaine and amphetamine. D was involved in a plan to import **1,554 kilos** of cocaine (average purity of 75%) from the Caribbean to Ireland, using a boat called the *Lucky Day* purchased in Florida. The cocaine had a street value of £235m. The plan was to use a second boat to rendezvous with the *Lucky Day* to ferry the drugs ashore. The second boat got into difficulty and the drugs and the men aboard ended up in the sea. The alarm was raised and the men were arrested. False passports, Land Rovers registered in false names and satellite phones were found. D's basis of plea was that he was employed by the others to transport the drugs and had received a fee for that alone. D, aged 50, was of effective good character. He had been a police officer in the drugs squad. Held. It was a sophisticated conspiracy. D played a crucial role in the conspiracy. A starting point of **30 years** was not manifestly excessive. This was D's third attempt at importation. The 20% discount was entirely appropriate. **22 years** consecutive to 8 years, making for the supply counts **30 years**, properly reflects the gravity of the offending and does not offend the principle of totality.
R v Hurtado 2011 EWCA Crim 147 D and E were convicted of conspiracy to supply cocaine. There were co-accused who pleaded guilty. D met two undercover officers. There were discussions between one of the officers and D as to how much would be paid for **299 kilos** of cocaine. The sellers wanted £521,000 and the purchasers wanted to pay only £300,000. There was evidence of telephone traffic between D, E and another conspirator, P. D telephoned one of the officers and informed him that 'his people' had agreed that the money would be handed over the day after delivery. Another conspirator telephoned an undercover officer to inform him that £300,000 was available to make the purchase. The same man was seen taking hessian shopping bags into his house which were later found to contain £322,000. The money was driven to a retail park where it was placed in the boot of the undercover officer's car. The undercover officer was given money to purchase a mobile phone. A number of telephone calls resulted in an arrangement to pick up a set of keys to a van from a service station on the M6. The van was then collected from another location. The van was stopped en route to the M1 and the drugs retrieved. The 299 kilos were between 60 and 70% purity and after dilution would yield a street value of around £80m. The Judge described D and E as being at the heart of the operation. Neither defendant had serious drug convictions. Held. Despite the misery that is caused to the individuals who get hooked on this type of drug, we think 28 years as a starting point was too high. This was not a case of importation and the tendency is to sentence a little lower for supply. We also bear in mind that *R v Soares and Others* 2003 EWCA Crim 2488 pointed out that an appropriate starting point for the prime mover importing 2,000 to 3,000 kilos of class A drugs was 30 years. We also see some force in the disparity argument. A co-defendant, S, received 12 years discounted to 9 on plea. However, D should not be sentenced in an equivalent way to S. **23 years** not 28.
R v Gonal 2011 EWCA Crim 587 D was convicted of conspiracy to supply cocaine. D was released from prison having served a previous sentence of imprisonment for supplying cocaine. He was stopped at Dover heading for the continent with nearly £25,000 in cash on him or in the vehicle. The Crown viewed that money as showing that D was dealing in cocaine. A number of people were changing cash on his behalf in the Exeter area, up to a value of approximately £35,000. This was further evidence of

---

[1142] For determining the weight of drugs to apply to the guideline, see **340.6** and **340.7**.

cocaine dealing by D. Those changing money were arrested and D left the country, not to return until his extradition two years later. It was alleged that on his departure D handed over his existing cocaine dealing network to his first lieutenant. From then on, while living abroad D continued to receive a share of the proceeds of the cocaine network that was being run in Devon. The Judge regarded D as the prime mover in a **wide-ranging conspiracy** lasting almost four years. The Judge also noted that the offences were aggravated by the fact that the offences began immediately upon D's release from prison from his previous sentence for a drugs offence. When D's lieutenant was sentenced, the Judge accepted a profit figure of £1.3m for the conspiracy. D, aged 49 at appeal, had a large number of previous convictions for drug offences. Held. This was plainly a very serious conspiracy of a substantial scale, continuing over a lengthy period, with D as the prime mover, having set it up and retaining a connection with it after he had fled this country. There was no mitigation of any substance available to D. **22 years** not 26.

See also: *R v Litwinski and Others* 2011 EWCA Crim 727 (*Re S* Plea. Large-scale conspiracy to supply cocaine and/or MDMA. 70 journeys totalling **35 kilos** at 100%. Began as a mule. Progressed to a minder and supervisor of the other mules. Involved for four months, travelling between UK and Amsterdam. Aged 19. **10 years** not 12. *Re N* Convicted. Involved in importation from Amsterdam by car. 5-7 journeys. **15 years**. *Re B* Plea. 35 kilos of cocaine. 5-7 journeys by car. Foot soldier. 50% credit for plea. Starting at 11 years, **5½ years** was appropriate.)

R v Khan and Ahmed 2011 EWCA Crim 2049 (Convicted. Well organised and sophisticated conspiracy. D was a first-line wholesale dealer. In total, **154.5 kilos** at 100% worth, when diluted, £50m. **20 years** was severe for supply but not unwarranted.)

R v Kotecha and Others 2011 EWCA Crim 2229 (Conspiracy to supply cocaine, heroin and amphetamine. **14-21 kilos** of cocaine, less than 100 kilos cannabis. Consecutive sentences could not be justified as the sentences reflected the overall criminality. Appropriate starting point for ringleader after trial, **20 years**. So, **17 years** (right-hand man, convicted, consecutive to 3 years for supply of cannabis**), 17 and 12 years** (both fully involved and convicted) and **15 years** (ringleader, on plea).)

R v Evans 2013 EWCA Crim 889 (Convicted of conspiracy to supply class A, acquiring and converting criminal property. Kidnapped by criminal associates and reported missing. A police search found he had modified a van to create storage for drugs. **£3m worth** of drugs were seized. 23 kilos of benzocaine, bulking agent for cocaine, found at his work premises. Organised movement of drugs on commercial scale. Leading role. Aged 76. Numerous previous convictions but not for drugs. Treated as good character. Starting at 23 years was appropriate. **18 years** was entirely correct.)

Old cases: There are enough new cases so old cases are not listed. If needed they can be found in the 9th edition of this book. Ed.

Post-guideline cases

R v Reed and Others 2015 EWCA Crim 171 R, J and G were convicted of and C and S pleaded to conspiracy to supply class A drugs. The police seized 10.9 kilos of cocaine at 92% purity, having carried out surveillance on the operation for at least nine months. The drugs had been brought in from the Netherlands by W. The conspiracy had lasted a minimum of 18 months and concerned so much cocaine that, "it [was] truly off [the] scale", regarding the guidelines. Each consignment weighed 4-11 kilos and not less than 46.9 kilos was imported. C was aged 49 on appeal and had a leading role of crucial importance, organising transport and controlling the organisation. He had threatened W with violence when he tried to leave the conspiracy. An unknown quantity of cash was also found at C's house. He pleaded shortly before trial, gaining 20% credit. G was aged 64 on appeal and was ascribed an essential albeit lesser role. He had been 'a pawn' and had not appreciated the full scale of the operation. He was convicted. Also convicted was R, aged 67 on appeal. He was the mastermind and £24,155 cash was found in his house. The Judge was conscious of R's age but also that he had been convicted of armed robbery and firearms offences, receiving 17 years in 1987. J was aged 53 and he had an important but lesser role, acting as a link between C and R. However, at the time of the offending, J was in an open prison serving a sentence for another serious drugs conspiracy. S was aged 42 on appeal and had played a significant role. He received full credit. Held. R's **28-year** sentence, even if undoubtedly severe, was not manifestly excessive. Regarding C, we must query how…C had been accorded a starting point of some 31 years, when R, who had been the mastermind and had a role somewhat above C's, and who had the significant previous conviction, was sentenced after a trial to 28 years. C's starting point should have been in the order of 25 years' imprisonment, so **20 years**, not 25. For S, the starting point taken by the Judge of 24 years was too high. In our view, the appropriate starting point…should have been in the order of 21 years, so **14 years** not 16. For J, to maintain a degree of parity with regard to the adjusted starting points, we will reduce that sentence which had started at 18 years, reduced for unknown reasons to 15, further by one year, so **14 years**, not 15. For G, whose position…is significantly different from others in the conspiracy, we think that a sentence of 12 years' imprisonment, albeit after a trial, was too long. We substitute **9 years**.

See also: *R v Clark* 2015 EWCA Crim 1771 (Plea to class A and B drugs including 25 kilos of cocaine, 10 kilos of heroin, 19½ kilos of heroin and 50 kilos of amphetamine (18 years). Consecutive to 7 years for about £1.5m drugs money laundering. Because of totality **23 years**, not 25 years (which had a starting point of 34½ years.)

340.52   *Cocaine/Heroin   Class A   Street dealing   Post-guideline cases*

R v Gaffney 2013 EWCA Crim 535 D pleaded at the PCMH to possession of cocaine with intent. Police officers were on the lookout for a vehicle believed to be involved with drug supply. D was stopped whilst driving his car. The vehicle was searched and nothing found. D was sitting in the rear of the police car and was 'fidgeting'. He was told to get out of the car and a bag containing 30.21 grams of cocaine (estimated street value £1,558) was found where he had been sitting. D claimed it was not his. His home address was searched and a set of scales, sandwich bags and disposable gloves were found. D, aged 37 at appeal, had 26 offences between 1993 and 2007. They included possession of class A and C with intent to supply (12 years). He was released on licence in August 2012 but recalled after being charged with this offence. The Judge placed D in Category 3, significant role. Held. It was noteworthy that he was on licence for previous relevant offences whilst he committed this offence. With a range of 3½ to 7 years, starting at **6 years** was appropriate. With full credit, **4 years** not 5.

R v Khatib 2013 EWCA Crim 566 D pleaded to supplying class A drugs (×7). On seven occasions, an undercover officer arranged to buy drugs from D, and met him to carry out the transaction. Each 'deal' cost £15. On six of the occasions, the drug was heroin and on the seventh it was crack cocaine. D had become involved with drug dealing when he built up a debt for cannabis which he could not pay. D was aged 18 when the offences were committed and 19 at sentence. He had no previous convictions. He explained to the probation officer that he supplied drugs to around 10-15 people a day, for which he received a £10 or £15 reduction in his debt. He started dealing at the end of February and finished in March when the debt was repaid. He explained that his dealer had given him a patch of a few roads to cover and he was instructed where to attend in order to supply drugs. The Judge described him as a 'runner' and made the role 'significant', because of the two types of drugs on seven occasions over two weeks. The range was 3½ to 7 years and he started at 4½. With plea he gave 3 years. Held. The Judge's reasons for role went to the level of harm and not to role. D was clearly motivated by financial advantage and must have had some awareness and understanding of the scale of what was clearly a large operation. In contrast, D performed a limited function under direction. It was a lesser role. There was an element of pressure from the dealer. Placing D into Category 3, at the higher end was reasonable. Taking account of D's age and good character, **2½ years'** YOI.

R v Reid and Higgins 2015 EWCA Crim 1165 12 transactions for R and ten for H. R had previous drug convictions. **7 years** for R and **6 years** for H, see **340.39**.

See also: *R v Dyer and Others* 2013 EWCA Crim 2114, 2014 2 Cr App R (S) 11 (p 61) (The Court considered sentences imposed for offences of class A drug supply to test purchasers in Soho. Held. **5½ years**, **4 years** (×2), **40 months** and **3 years** (×4) substituted.)
R v Mellor 2015 EWCA Crim 1243 (Plea. 1 wrap. No previous supply convictions. **20 months**, see **340.39**.)

Cutting agents
340.53   *Cutting agents   Class A drugs, For   Pre-guideline cases*
R v Hartley and Dale 2013 EWCA Crim 542 H and D were convicted of conspiracy to supply cocaine, heroin and amphetamine. Between 2005 and 2008, D headed a criminal organisation that imported and supplied nearly 36 tonnes of chemicals. The chemicals were sold to drug dealers on a nationwide basis and used as cutting agents. All of the chemicals were legal at the time. The scale of the enterprise was enormous. For example, in a two-month period, D imported over 5 tonnes of benzocaine. Evidence suggested that the chemicals were to be used to cut cocaine at a ratio of 1:1. The resulting powders would therefore have had a street value of no less than £3.5bn. D initially used a false name and false identities to obtain the chemicals and rent storage facilities. Eventually, he used his own company as a vehicle for larger importations from Asia. In less than a year, he imported more than 10 tonnes of benzocaine, 3 tonnes of lidocaine and 625 kilos of paracetamol. D was in regular contact with H, an advisor. H was an expert in chemicals and their use in the drugs trade. H was also in contact with others associated with drug dealing, both by phone and through actual meetings, and acted as a go-between linking D with drug dealers. H was in his mid-sixties at appeal. He had convictions in 1995 for possession with intent to supply a class A drug, supplying a class A drug and conspiracy to supply amphetamine (10 years). He also had a conviction in 2008 for possession of ecstasy with intent to supply (5 years), which was a part of the conspiracy. D was aged 34 at appeal and of previous good character. Held. D was the organiser of the conspiracy, which ran for about three years. He imported massive quantities of cutting agents, which had a significant effect on the drug market. A drugs supplier at the top of an operation of this scale could contemplate a sentence after a trial in the region of 30 years. A starting point for D of **21 years** is in no way arguably excessive. With a discount for the plea, **18 years**. H was a vital adviser in relation to technical matters relating to the chemical supply. He was also an essential link in the onward supply of D's chemicals to drug wholesalers. He was fully aware of the scale of the conspiracy. He played a very substantial role, but somewhat lower than D. The Judge started at **20 years** and deducted the 5 years served for the ecstasy offence. **11 years** was not manifestly excessive.
R v Woodford 2013 EWCA Crim 1098, 2014 1 Cr App R (S) 32 (p 194) D was convicted of encouraging or assisting an offence of supply of class A drugs. At 11.30 pm, D's co-accused, L, was stopped by officials at Dover Docks. He was driving a hired van which contained 18 sacks, each containing a light brown powder. The total weight was just under 150 kilos. Analysis showed that it was a mixture of paracetamol and caffeine which had been baked in order to turn it brown. The powder is a cutting agent known as 'bash'. Calculations made on the basis that the powder was to be cut with heroin in equal proportions would have produced £5.7m worth of heroin at 50% purity. D and L had hired the van the day before, using L's name but D's mother's email address. D provided L with a satnav for the trip. During L's absence on the continent, there was close telephone contact between D and L. Two months after L's arrest, D contacted the police, stating that the powder belonged to him and that it was amino acid powder for his mother's lawn. D had two convictions for simple cannabis possession and aggravated vehicle-taking. He had never served a custodial sentence. He also had caring responsibilities for his family, far beyond that expected of a man in his mid-twenties. Held. The Judge was fully entitled to hold that D had a significant organisational role. Had D been convicted of supply of heroin, the guideline starting point was 10 years. The Judge

clearly had regard to this. The offence came very close to the full offence, for which D would have been likely to receive 10 years or more. Looking at the case as a whole, **6 years** not 8 was appropriate.

Note: The decision in *R v Whittam and Others* 2012 Canterbury Crown Court deals with 143 kilos of 'bash' (a cutting agent) which would generate 286 kilos of cut heroin. Starting at 6½ years, with plea, 4 years 4 months was imposed. This case does not create a precedent. It just illustrates what has happened in the past and in Canterbury Crown Court, where so many importation cases are heard. See www.banksr.com Other Matters Other Documents tab for a copy of the decision. Ed.

R v Nnamani 2015 EWCA Crim 596, 2 Cr App R (S) 23 (p 219) D was convicted of possession of heroin and cocaine with intent to supply. Police searched a car connected to him and found about 695 grams of cocaine, 27 grams of heroin and 595 grams of a cutting agent used with class A drugs. The Judge said this case was Category 2. Held. It was because guidelines have to be applied with a degree of realism. The quantity of drugs could not be considered in isolation. Taking the purity of the drugs, if the police had not intercepted the drugs there would have been a considerably larger amount of drugs ready for distribution. The total weight came to more than 1 kilo.

Ecstasy class A

340.54 *Ecstasy Class A Sentencing Council guideline Post-guideline cases*
Drug Offences Guideline 2012 page 11, see www.banksr.com Other Matters Guidelines tab and **340.3**.

Note: Ecstasy is a listed drug in the Category of harm section in the guidelines. Category 1 is 10,000 tablets,[1143] Category 2 is 2,000 tablets, Category 3 is 300 tablets and Category 4 is 20 tablets. Ed.

R v Bush 2013 EWCA Crim 1164, 2014 1 Cr App R (S) 40 (p 232) D pleaded to possession of ecstasy with intent to supply. He went to a music festival and staff overheard a conversation in which reference was made to ecstasy. As a result, D was searched and found to be in possession of 55 individual bags containing just less than 1 gram of ecstasy in powdered form in each. There was a total of 37.8 grams with a street value of around £1,900. D's basis of plea, that his intention to supply arose out of his acting as a custodian for the drugs but that he was not involved in the sale of the drugs, was accepted. D was aged 21 and of good character. Held. It appears the Judge adopted the recommended starting point of 3 years and gave full credit for the plea. The correct starting point was **21 months**, which is below the range stated in the guidelines. That reflects the basis of plea, the mitigation and the quantity of drugs. Teenagers go to summer music festivals in groups and are particularly vulnerable to those trying to sell drugs. Anyone who is involved in such an enterprise, even on a relatively low-level basis, must expect an immediate custodial sentence. With the plea, **14 months** not 2 years was appropriate reflecting the quantity, the basis of plea and the mitigation.

R v Walker and Gosling 2013 EWCA Crim 1940 G pleaded to [conspiracy to] supply 32 kilos of amphetamine and nearly 30,000 ecstasy tablets. He was convicted of possession with intent to supply 14 kilos of amphetamine and 9 kilos of skunk cannabis. G and another were the principal conspirators. The 32 kilos were seized from their couriers. Another 12 kilos of amphetamine were also seized. Police visited an industrial estate and found the ecstasy with digital scales, a machine for sealing plastic bags, large plastic containers and an industrial paddle mixer. The 14 kilos of amphetamine and the skunk cannabis were also found with a large amount of cutting agents. G was aged 45. In 1995 he had a conviction for cultivating cannabis. In 1998, he had a conviction for possessing class C drugs. Held. G was involved in an extensive and commercial operation designed to make very large profits. A total sentence of **20 years** rather than 24 was appropriate before the plea discount. With the plea (full credit), **13 years**.

[1143] For determining the weight of drugs to apply to the guideline, see **340.6** and **340.7**.

340.55 *Ecstasy   Joint purchase   Post-guideline case*
R v Clare 2013 EWCA Crim 369 D pleaded to possession of cocaine, MDMA (class A) and M-CAT (class B) with intent. A police officer on duty at the V Festival saw what he thought was a drug deal. He followed the supplier to his tent and found D, who had on his person two pots, one containing white powder and one containing 71 MDMA tablets. His basis of plea was that he and six friends had pooled their money in order to buy drugs to use amongst themselves whilst at the festival. He was in possession of them when the officer attended the tent. D, aged 24, was self-employed as a roof joiner and had no relevant convictions. Held. The Judge was correct to treat this as a Category 4 case (notwithstanding that the 71 MDMA tablets would have placed that offence into Category 3). He also identified, correctly, the aggravating factor of drug supply at music festivals. The appropriate sentence was **4 months** concurrent on the class A counts and **2 months** concurrent on the class B count, not 12 months (×2) and 4 months concurrent.

Ketamine class B
340.56 *Ketamine   Class B   Sentencing Council guideline*
Drug Offences Guideline 2012 page 11, see www.banksr.com Other Matters Guidelines tab and **340.3**.
Reclassification: Ketamine is a class B drug for offences committed on or after 10 June 2014, Misuse of Drugs Act 1971 (Ketamine etc.) (Amendment) Order 2014 2014/1106 para 4.
Note: Ketamine is a listed drug in the Category of harm section in the guidelines. Category 1 is 5 kilos,[1144] Category 2 is 1 kilo, Category 3 is 150 grams and Category 4 is 5 grams. For offences committed before 10 June 2014, the class C tables must be used. Ed.

LSD class A
340.57 *LSD   Class A   Sentencing Council guideline*
Drug Offences Guideline 2012 page 11, see www.banksr.com Other Matters Guidelines tab and **340.3**.
Note: LSD is a listed drug in the Category of harm section in the guidelines. Category 1 is 250,000 squares,[1145] Category 2 is 25,000 squares, Category 3 is 2,500 squares and Category 4 is 170 squares.

M-CAT/Mephedrone
340.58 *M-CAT/M-KAT/Mephedrone/Pentedrone/Meow meow   Class B*
Drug Offences Guideline 2012 page 11, see www.banksr.com Other Matters Guidelines tab and **340.3**.
Note: The drug is to be equated with amphetamine, see below. Amphetamine is a listed drug in the Category of harm section in the guidelines. Category 1 is 20 kilos,[1146] Category 2 is 4 kilos, Category 3 is 750 grams and Category 4 is 20 grams. Ed.
Post-guideline cases
R v Howland 2013 EWCA Crim 1448 D pleaded to possession of class B with intent to supply. D's girlfriend was stopped by the police. Her home was later searched and police found 667 grams of white powder. D went to the police station the following day to accept responsibility for the drug and make clear that it was not his girlfriend's. He said he believed it to be M-CAT but in fact it was pentedrone, which has a similar chemical composition. It had a street value of over £8,000 if sold in single deals but a value of around £4,000 if sold by the ounce. D's basis asserted that he only sold to friends without making a profit. A *Newton* hearing was ordered but a couple of days before the hearing, D conceded that he sold the drug making a 'modest profit'. D, aged 24, had convictions for cannabis cultivation and possession of cannabis with intent (2010,

---

[1144] For determining the weight of drugs to apply to the guideline, see **340.6** and **340.7**.
[1145] For determining the weight of drugs to apply to the guideline, see **340.6** and **340.7**.
[1146] For determining the weight of drugs to apply to the guideline, see **340.6** and **340.7**.

suspended sentence) and supplying class B drugs (2011, 9 months). Held. This was a Category 3 offence. The Judge found that D had played a significant role. This gave a starting point of 1 year. It was correct to raise that due to D's convictions. Around 20 months was appropriate. D was entitled to 25% credit because of his abandoned basis of plea. **15 months** not 2 years.

Note: I imagine the courts equated both drugs with amphetamine. Ed.

See also: *R v Pitts and Others* 2014 EWCA Crim 1615 (The majority of the sentence appeals involved M-CAT. The Judge used the amphetamine guideline for sentence. Held. That was correct.)

MDPV   class B

340.59   MDPV Class B
Drug Offences Guideline 2012 page 11, see www.banksr.com Other Matters Guidelines tab and **340.3**.

Note: Amphetamine is a listed drug in the Category of harm section in the guidelines. Category 1 is 20 kilos,[1147] Category 2 is 4 kilos, Category 3 is 750 grams and Category 4 is 20 grams. Ed.

Post-guideline case
R v Brown 2013 EWCA Crim 1726, 2014 1 Cr App R (S) 84 (p 518) D pleaded to conspiracy to supply MDPV (full credit). He travelled from Kent to Skegness to collect 4 kilos of the drug. Later he collected another kilo of the drug from the same source. He also collected two other consignments. D was aged 35 with two children. He had no drug convictions but had received 2 years for tobacco smuggling. The Judge considered he played a leading role, although not at the highest level. He equated the drug with amphetamine. He was not told about the purity. For the appeal a pharmacological report was obtained. The purity was estimated to be 2-5%. Held. MDPV comes in a powder form and is a derivative of cathinone, which is a stimulant occurring naturally in a plant found in the Horn of Africa and the Arabian Peninsula. The effect of the report is that cathinones are structurally very similar to amphetamines. Also, the effect of the drug and the capacity for dependency is similar to amphetamine. The potential for causing harm was equivalent to amphetamine. Had the Judge known about the low purity, he was likely to have started at **4½ years** not 5. So with the plea, **3 years** not 3 years 4 months.

Medicines
Medicines Where the drugs are not class A, B or C, see the **MEDICINE OFFENCES** chapter.

Opium class A

340.60   Opium   Class A   Judicial guidance
R v Mashaollahi 2001 1 Cr App R (S) 96 (p 330) The current classification of opium as a class A drug is on the premise that it was to be regarded as being every bit as harmful as other class A drugs. Weight for weight, where street value is concerned, heroin is considered to be approximately eight times more valuable than opium. On this basis, a consignment of 40 kilos of opium at 100% purity would be equivalent in value to 5 kilos of heroin at 100% purity. There is at least the remote possibility that opium might be imported to convert it into morphine or heroin. In those cases, base the sentence on the amount of heroin or morphine that could be produced from the opium seized. We understand that the ratio to apply in these circumstances would be 10:1, i.e. 10 kilos of opium would be needed to produce 1 kilo of morphine or heroin, assuming average levels of purity. Because opium is the natural extract from the poppy and not a drug adulterated with other material, the court should assume that it is unadulterated and of 100% purity. Should the defence wish, by way of mitigation, to persuade a judge that the active ingredient was of a lesser percentage, it is open to them to call the appropriate evidence. If the judge is presented with evidence which persuades him that a calculation

---

[1147] For determining the weight of drugs to apply to the guideline, see **340.6** and **340.7**.

based on the equivalent street value of heroin or cocaine would produce an unacceptably high sentence for opium offences, he would be entitled to disregard any cross-check based on the street value of heroin or cocaine.
See also the **OPIUM** chapter.

Steroids (those which are class C drugs)
Note: Steroids are not listed in the *Drug Offences Guideline 2012*. Ed.

340.61   Steroids   Class C
Example: *R v Nagle* 2014 EWCA Crim 2559 (D pleaded to conspiracy to supply. He sold anabolic androgenic steroids (AAS) on his website for a total of £137,000. The Judge was right to make it a Category 1 offence. The Judge was right to start at **4 years**.)

340.62   Steroids   Class C   Street dealing   Post-guideline cases
R v Pearce 2015 EWCA Crim 1291, 2 Cr App R (S) 70 LCJ D pleaded to possession with intent to supply and importing steroids. He was interested in bodybuilding. He imported steroids from China and sold them. The amount was agreed to be in Category 3. The steroids had a street value of about £58,000 and D made about £20,000 profit. D was aged 35. He had some serious offences on his record but had no serious convictions in the last 15 years. Held. It is important to remember that possession of steroids is lawful. However, it is a serious criminal offence to import them and sell them on. The evil of steroids is well known. D's role was somewhere between leading and significant. **20 months** concurrent not 30 months in all.

Defendants aged under 18
The guideline only applies to offenders aged 18+, see page 2 of the guideline. For the usual practice, see **66.21** in Volume 1.

340.63   *Defendant aged under 18*
R v Yusuf 2012 EWCA Crim 2210 D pleaded on rearraignment to conspiracy to supply class A (×2). The drugs were crack cocaine and diamorphine. Police officers searched a man outside a block of flats. He was in possession of a small wrap of crack cocaine, some money, a telephone and some keys to one of the flats. The officers searched a flat. Inside were D and another man. D was lying on a bed next to a coffee table on which there were 76 wraps of crack cocaine and diamorphine, and some mobile phones which were ringing frequently. The drugs were worth £780, weighing 13 grams. Analysis of the telephones showed that D had received text messages instructing him where to go to deliver drugs. The basis of plea accepted he was a courier for a period of around three weeks as it was the only way to feed and house himself. D, aged 18, was of previous good character. The Judge characterised D as playing a significant role as his motivation was financial, and described the offending as street dealing. He started at 4½ years. Held. There could be no criticism of the Judge's assessment of the dealing. Because of his age and plea, **2 years 3 months' detention** not 3 years.
R v Bowman 2014 EWCA Crim 2542 D pleaded to supply. Police stopped a taxi and found D with 956 grams of heroin (64% and 67% purity) and 255 grams of a cutting agent. The street value was about £100,000. D was aged 17 and now 18 and this was her first offence. The prosecution accepted she was a courier. Held. She was plainly in the lesser role category. We start at 4 years not 6. The high value and high purity stop the case being at the bottom of the range. The youth reduction will depend on age, maturity and all the circumstances. A third off, not a quarter, was required for her age. With full credit that makes 22 months' detention not 3 years. For more detail, see **340.24**.
See also: *R v Taj* 2015 EWCA Crim 1081 (Here the Judge should have given greater weight to the fact that the defendant was only just 18.)

340.64   *Drug addicts*
Drug Offences Guideline 2012 page 12, see www.banksr.com Other Matters Guidelines tab Where the defendant is dependent on or has a propensity to misuse drugs and there is

sufficient prospect of success, a community order with a drug rehabilitation requirement under Criminal Justice Act 2003 s 209 can be a proper alternative to a short or moderate-length custodial sentence.

Theft Offences Guideline 2016, www.banksr.com Other matters Guidelines tab In the General theft section, see page 6 and **346.5**, and the Theft from a shop or stall section, see page 12 and **346.37** of the guideline, there is the same instruction as in the Drug Offences Guideline 2012.

Note: This replaces the *R v Afonso* 2004 EWCA Crim 2342, 2005 1 Cr App R (S) 99 (p 560) principle with another, perhaps more generous, approach. Ed.

Att-Gen's Ref Nos 82-96 and 104-109 of 2011 2012 EWCA Crim 155, 2 Cr App R (S) 56 (p 320) Absent addiction, however, the fact that a defendant is himself a user of the drug which he supplies is likely to be of little and usually will be no mitigation. But the fact that a defendant chooses to spend the money which he makes from drug dealing on drug use for himself usually has little more relevance to sentence than if he spends it on gambling, exotic travel or expensive automobiles. The same will apply if his benefit from drug dealing is the free or cheap supply of drugs for himself.

Post-guideline case

R v Priest 2013 EWCA Crim 2018 D pleaded (full credit) to permitting premises to be used for supplying class A drugs, namely morphine. D was a tenant in a flat. AM brought round 200 prescription tablets of morphine contained in 10 boxes of blister packs, and left them in a drawer in D's kitchen. D was present and aware that AM had left the drugs in the flat. Some days later, AM and three other friends were in D's flat. AM produced three or four tablets and crushed them into a powder. Most of those present snorted the powder. D and EE consumed 10-20 tablets, combining them with alcohol. D and EE went into the town centre and continued to drink. They returned early in the morning and were both sick. The next afternoon, D and the others woke up. EE was breathing heavily and then stopped breathing. They called an ambulance. He died of a morphine overdose. The police were called and a search of the flat recovered 118 of the tablets. D was aged 19 and had no previous convictions. She had originally been assigned the flat by social services as she had been a vulnerable child. There had been a history of self-harm. AR pleaded to supply and received 52 months. Held. The starting point of 20 months taken by the Judge was too high. Because of the loss of life, an immediate custodial sentence was required. Starting at 9 months was appropriate. With the plea, **6 months** not 14.

Minimum sentences

340.65   *Minimum 7 years sentence for class A suppliers   Statute*

Powers of Criminal Courts (Sentencing) Act 2000 s 110(1) This section applies where:
   a) a person is convicted of a class A drug trafficking offence committed after 30 September 1997,
   b) at the time when that offence was committed, he was aged 18 or over and had two relevant drug convictions,[1148] and
   c) one of those other offences was committed after he had been convicted of the other.

(2) The court shall impose an appropriate custodial sentence for a term of at least 7 years except where the court is of the opinion that there are particular circumstances which:
   a) relate to any of the offences or to the offender, and
   b) would make it unjust to do so in all the circumstances.

Powers of Criminal Courts (Sentencing) Act 2000 s 110(6) In this section 'an appropriate custodial sentence' means:..
   b) in relation to a person who is under 21 at that time, a sentence of detention in a Young Offender Institution.

[1148] Powers of Criminal Courts (Sentencing) Act 2000 s 110(2A). For the purposes of subsection (1)(a) a 'relevant drug conviction' means: i) a conviction in any part of the United Kingdom of a class A drug trafficking offence, or ii) a conviction in another member State of the EU of an offence which was committed after the relevant date and would, if done in the United Kingdom at the time of the conviction, have constituted a class A drug trafficking offence.

Powers of Criminal Courts (Sentencing) Act 2000 s 115 Where an offence is found to have been committed over a period of two or more days, or at some time during a period of two or more days, it shall be taken for the purposes of section 110 (third drug offence) to have been committed on the last of those days.

Mental Health Act 1983 s 37(1A)(b) Nothing in section 110(2) shall prevent the court from making a (Hospital Order or a Guardianship Order).

Serious Organised Crime and Police Act 2005 s 73(5) Nothing in any requirement which requires that a minimum sentence is passed affects the power of the court to act under section 73(2) (power to take into account assistance given by the defendant where there is a written agreement). (Section summarised.)

Note: Coroners and Justice Act 2009 s 144 and Sch 17 para 10(2) widened the convictions that can be taken into account to include EU drug-trafficking offences committed after the commencement date, which is awaited. Ed.

340.66   *Minimum 7 years for class A suppliers   Servicemen/women*
Powers of Criminal Courts (Sentencing) Act 2000 s 114(1) Where:
   a) a person has at any time been convicted of an offence under (criminal conduct), and
   b) the corresponding offence under the law of England and Wales (within the meaning given by that section) was a class A drug trafficking offence,
the relevant section of this chapter shall have effect as if he had at that time been convicted in England and Wales of that corresponding offence.

(1A) Where a) a person has at any time been found guilty of a member State service offence committed after the relevant date, and b) the corresponding UK offence was a class A drug trafficking offence, the relevant section of this chapter and subsection (1) above shall have effect as if the person had at that time been convicted in England and Wales of that corresponding UK offence.

340.67   *Minimum 7 years sentence for class A Statistics   England and Wales*
Note: Statistics are produced but in the past there was serious under-reporting. Nowadays, the statisticians just total up the numbers of those who received 7 years or more. This leaves out those whose sentence started at 7 years and who received up to 20% off for their plea. I think the statistics are best ignored. Ed.

340.68   *Minimum 7 years for class A suppliers   How to determine whether Act applies*
R v Hoare 2004 EWCA Crim 191, 2 Cr App R (S) 50 (p 261) D pleaded to three burglaries and other counts. In 2000 he was sentenced for a dwelling house burglary and three TICs. In 2003 he committed the instant offence. The total number of dwelling house burglaries on his record was seven. In the Crown Court the Judge was wrongly informed by both counsel that D qualified for a 3-year sentence. Held. In fact D had only been convicted of one dwelling burglary at the commission of the third burglary. Powers of Criminal Courts (Sentencing) Act 2000 s 111 requires that in order for the automatic sentence to be triggered, the sequence required is: a) commission of first offence, b) conviction for first offence, c) commission of second burglary, d) conviction for second burglary, e) commission of third burglary, f) conviction for third burglary. This was not so in D's case. The sentence is therefore unlawful.
Note: Although the drug section for minimum sentences is slightly different from the burglary section for minimum sentences, the structure is the same, so the two sections should be applied in the same way. Ed.

340.69   *Minimum 7 years for class A suppliers   Plea of guilty*
Powers of Criminal Courts (Sentencing) Act 2000 s 152(3) Where a sentence is to be imposed under Powers of Criminal Courts (Sentencing) Act 2000 s 110 after a plea of guilty, nothing in that section shall prevent the court from imposing a sentence of 80% or more of the minimum period.
Note: This section is summarised. The section means that if he or she pleads guilty, the court can impose a sentence which is 80% or more of the minimum term. Ed.

R v Brown 2000 2 Cr App R (S) p 435 D pleaded at the first opportunity to supplying crack cocaine, supplying heroin and possession of cocaine. Police were conducting a drugs operation in the Kings Cross area of London, and D gave an officer a piece of paper with a telephone number on it and told them to call it if they wanted drugs. An officer rang the number, and D told them where they should meet. Two officers went to a flat as directed, and one purchased 164 mg of crack for £20. Another officer asked for heroin and crack but was told there was no crack left, and he was given 105 mg of heroin for £20. When D was arrested nearly three months later he had 1.6 mg of crack on him. He was aged 45 and had three convictions for supplying drugs, two of which were for class A drugs. He also had two convictions for possession of an offensive weapon and one for possession of a bladed article. He was sentenced to 6½ years for the supply counts with 6 months consecutive for a breach of a CSO. There was a concurrent sentence for the possession offence. The defence said that either the Judge started too high or failed to give the full 20% discount for the guilty plea. Held. We agree, and as he didn't indicate which, we adjust the supply sentence to **5 years 8 months,** and because of totality the 6 months should run concurrently.

R v Gray 2007 EWCA Crim 979, 2 Cr App R (S) 78 (p 494) D pleaded to a burglary and an attempted burglary. The Judge considered 5 years was the starting figure with a 30% discount for the plea. He then gave a 20% discount to the first 3 years (because of the Act) and 30% to the other 2 years. Held. The Judge should have applied 30% to the whole figure as all the Act does is to say the judge may not impose less than a certain figure.
Note: The principles for minimum sentences for both burglary and supply offences are similar. Ed.

R v Darling 2009 EWCA Crim 1610, 2010 1 Cr App R (S) 63 (p 420) The Judge found that it would be unjust to impose the minimum but considered that he was restricted to a 20% discount for the plea. Held. He was not restricted. One-third discount given.

R v Kemp 2014 EWCA Crim 200 D pleaded to possession with intent to supply class A drugs at his adjourned PCMH. He qualified for a 7-year minimum sentence and the Judge gave him 6 years 3 months, which was just over 10% plea credit. Held. D had pleaded reasonably early and before the trial date was fixed. Had there been no minimum sentence he would have been entitled to 25%. He was entitled to just under the statutory maximum 20%, which makes 5 years 9 months.

340.70   *Minimum 7 years class A suppliers   Pre-sentence report*
R v Densham 2014 EWCA Crim 2552, 2015 1 Cr App R (S) 37 (p 279) D was convicted of possession with intent to supply. He had already been served a 7-year minimum term. The defence argued that a pre-sentence report should have been ordered. A report was obtained. Held. para 8 Unless a defendant can show that it would be unjust to impose a minimum term, the judge should adjourn for a pre-sentence report. That course should usually be taken where the burden is on the defendant to show that a minimum term should not be imposed. On the facts, appeal dismissed.
Note: The Lord Chief Justice is very keen to reduce the obtaining of unnecessary reports. I suspect he would wish each decision to be carefully made on the facts of that particular case. Ed.

340.71   *Minimum 7 years class A suppliers   Unjust, Meaning of*
R v Hickson 2002 1 Cr App R (S) 71 (p 298) One is not looking for exceptional circumstances. One is looking at the particular circumstances of the offence and the offender.

340.72   *Minimum 7 years class A suppliers   Cases*
R v Stenhouse 2000 2 Cr App R (S) p 386 D pleaded to supplying heroin on four separate occasions. A police officer called a number and was told to ring back in 15 minutes. He did so and spoke to D. They agreed to meet. D was given £10, and the undercover officer was given a wrap which contained 52 mg of heroin. The other offences were similar. D had convictions for possession of drugs, including two for supplying class A drugs. The

last conviction was in 1997 for supplying one methadone tablet, for which he was given probation at the Magistrates' Court. He had been in custody from December 1998 to July 1999, when he was released because of the custody time limit provisions. He was sentenced in December 1999 to the 7-year minimum term. Since his arrest he had made valiant attempts to conquer his drug addiction. Held. His efforts to break his drug habit were rare, and he should be encouraged to continue with his efforts. Because of the combination of circumstances the sentence was unjust, so **3 years** substituted.

R v Willoughby 2003 EWCA Crim 208, 2 Cr App R (S) 60 (p 357) D pleaded to five counts of supplying heroin. Over three weeks he sold wraps of heroin to undercover officers five times. The amounts were five wraps for £40 (212 mg), a wrap for £10 (26 mg), five wraps for £50 (389 mg), a number of wraps for £40 (253 mg) and four wraps (199 grams). The amounts were at 100% purity. He was aged 46 with numerous convictions, primarily for theft and related matters. In 1986 he received 30 months for supply and in 1992, again for supply, he received 42 months. He qualified for a minimum 7-year sentence. He was in breach of a conditional discharge for possession of heroin. The Judge said that he started at 9 years and gave him 6½ years. Held. The Judge did not have to start at 7 years here. No complaint could have been made if the Judge had started at 8 years. **6½ years** meets the justice of the case.

R v Turner 2005 EWCA Crim 2363, 2006 1 Cr App R (S) 95 (p 565) D pleaded to supplying heroin on three occasions. The police mounted a drugs operation, and D was one of the first to be seen. He engaged a number of drug users, acted as an intermediary and, as a result, a large amount of drugs was supplied. He collected about £40 to £100 from seven people. Test purchases were made. The plea was on the basis of a continuous course of conduct over two days. D's home was searched, and cannabis and heroin paraphernalia was found. He said that he was an addict. In interview he made denials. He was aged 23. His convictions included: November 1998, possession of heroin and cannabis (3-month Curfew Order), January 1999, supplying heroin (50-hour community service order), October 2000, possessing heroin with intent (2 years), and May 2003, possessing cannabis (18-month Community Rehabilitation Order). The Judge said that it was the bottom end of street dealing but for a third time. Held. It was unjust to impose the minimum sentence. The first conviction was for heroin bought on behalf of friends. The second was similar, and in the third he acted as an intermediary between existing drug users known to him and the street dealers. **4½ years** not 5½, which would be the same as for the co-defendant higher up the chain.

R v McDonagh 2005 EWCA Crim 2742, 2006 1 Cr App R (S) 111 (p 647) D pleaded to three counts of supplying heroin and two counts of supplying crack cocaine. Undercover police officers mounted a drugs operation in Liverpool city centre. On 22 October 2003 he supplied an officer with 209 mg of heroin. On 6 November he supplied an officer with 139 mg of heroin and 135 mg of crack. On 10 December he supplied an officer with 104 mg of heroin and 83 mg of crack. On 25 November he committed a burglary and was sentenced on 12 October 2004 to a DTTO. He had a number of other convictions, including in 1990 3 years' detention for supplying and in 1993 2½ years for supplying. A report said that he had made good progress and asked for the matter to be held over for 6 months. The Judge held there were no exceptional circumstances. On appeal it was argued that he was in the *R v Afonso* 2004 EWCA Crim 2342, 2005 1 Cr App R (S) 99 (p 560) group, which made the minimum sentence unjust. Held. There is a difference between particular and exceptional circumstances. The Court will decline to specify what will and what will not amount to particular circumstances. The fact that a defendant may come within the *R v Afonso* 2004 group does not mean that he can escape the section. The Judge was right not to accede to the DTTO suggestion. The relevant factors are: the previous convictions occurred some time ago, the second occurred 10 years before, and in the middle of the offending he committed burglary. The antiquity of the offences, the circumstances surrounding the burglary sentence and the delay constitute particular circumstances such as to make it unjust. **4½ years** not 5 years 7 months.

R v Reid 2008 EWCA Crim 202, 2 Cr App R (S) 68 (p 383) D pleaded to one count of offering to supply crack cocaine and heroin and one count of theft. He approached an undercover police officer and offered a wrap. The officer agreed to buy for £20 and handed the money over. D came back some time later but refused to hand over any drugs. He pleaded on the basis that he did not have a wrap on him when he made the offer, and his intention was to steal money and not to supply drugs. D, aged 41, was a long-term drug addict. He had almost 100 previous convictions going back to when he was a teenager. He had served several custodial sentences, the longest being 3½ years. He had seven convictions for offering to supply drugs, five for actual supply and three for possession. These mostly related to class A drugs. He had three previous offences falling within the terms of Powers of Criminal Courts (Sentencing) Act 2000 s 110, triggering a minimum prison term of 7 years (less maximum 20% for plea) unless this would be unjust. Held. We regard the present case on all fours with *R v Prince* 1999 2 Cr App R (S) 419. In that case, the Court accepted that the criminality of D was more akin to obtaining money by deception than drug dealing. **12 months** not 5 years.

R v Timperley 2012 EWCA Crim 1782 D pleaded (full credit) to supply of class A (×3). Police mounted an undercover operation to tackle class A drug supply. Officers attempted to make contact and subsequently test purchases from dealers. An officer approached D and asked where he could 'score a couple of bags'. D contacted a dealer and took the officer to a park. The officers gave D £20 and he took it to a dealer and came back with two wraps of heroin weighing 0.17 (12%) and 0.22 grams (19%), which he gave the officers. There were two other incidents of D obtaining drugs on behalf of undercover officers at similar weights. The third transaction concerned heroin of a purity around 44%. D was aged 39 at appeal and had convictions for supply of class A (×2) and possession of class A with intent (×2). He had been released from prison 10 days before the first offence. Held. D's role was less than an actual dealer but could not be described as extremely low. The deals were for modest amounts with little financial reward. This was a third strike case but the Judge appropriately disapplied the minimum sentence, because of the relative antiquity of the qualifying convictions (the last one was eight years ago), the circumstances of the three offences in which he was a go-between, the absence of his own stocks, the modest amount supplied, the limited rewards and the fact that he was 'effectively seduced' to act. Starting at 4½ years, with full credit, **3 years** was appropriate, not 4.

See also: *R v Gallone* 2014 EWCA Crim 1140, 2 Cr App R (S) 57 (p 469) (The fact that one of the previous convictions was in 1997 and the previous convictions involved community-based sentences did not amount to exceptional circumstances. This street dealing was as serious a case as there was, so the sentence was fully justified.)

The sentence

340.73   *Disqualification from driving*
R v Sofekun 2008 EWCA Crim 2035, 2009 1 Cr App R (S) 78 (p 460) D pleaded to possession of cannabis with intent to supply and two driving offences. He was stopped in his car, and hidden under the bonnet were found cannabis and 30 self-seal bags. For the supply matter he was sentenced to **8 months** and disqualified from driving for **15 months**. He was aged 19 and at university with three years to complete. Held. The car was being used to commit etc. the supply offence. The disqualification was neither wrong in principle nor too long.

Permitting premises to be used for the supply etc. of drugs

340.74
Misuse of Drugs Act 1971 s 8
An occupier or a person concerned in the management of premises, knowingly permitting etc. the: a) production etc. of a controlled drug, b) supply etc. of controlled drugs, c) preparation of opium for smoking and d) smoking of cannabis, cannabis resin or prepared opium.

Modes of trial Triable either way unless the offence could qualify for a minimum 7-year sentence when the offence is triable only on indictment.

Maximum sentences On indictment: 14 years for class A and B drugs and 5 years for class C drugs. Summary maxima: 6 months and/or a £5,000 fine for class A and B drugs offences committed before 12 March 2015 and an unlimited fine thereafter.[1149] There are maximum fines for those aged under 18, see **14.38** in Volume 1. 3 months and/or £2,500 fine for class C drugs.

Confiscation Where a defendant has a criminal lifestyle the court, once the confiscation proceedings are triggered (see **22.11** in Volume 1), must follow the Proceeds of Crime Act 2002 procedure. 'Criminal lifestyle' offences include those under Misuse of Drugs Act 1971 s 8.[1150] For what constitutes a criminal lifestyle see **22.48** in Volume 1.

Minimum sentences For supply offences the minimum sentence provision of 7 years for the third class A drug trafficking offence[1151] applies, see **340.65**.

Serious Crime Prevention Orders There is a discretionary power to make this order, when it would protect the public etc.[1152]

Guidelines and the proper approach
340.75 *Sentencing Council Guideline*
Drug Offences Guideline 2012, see www.banksr.com Other Matters Guidelines tab In force 27 February 2012. The guideline only applies to offenders aged 18+, see page 2 of the guideline. For the usual practice, see **66.21** in Volume 1.

STEP ONE: Determining the offence category
page 24 The court should determine the offender's culpability and the harm caused (extent of the activity and/or the quantity of drugs) with reference to the table below.

In assessing harm, quantity is determined by the weight of the product. Purity is not taken into account at step one but is dealt with at step two.

Category 1	Higher culpability **and** greater harm
Category 2	Lower culpability **and** greater harm, **or** higher culpability **and** lesser harm
Category 3	Lower culpability **and** lesser harm

Factors indicating culpability (non-exhaustive)
Higher culpability: Permits premises to be used primarily for drug activity, for example crack house Permits use in expectation of substantial financial gain Uses legitimate business premises to aid and/or conceal illegal activity, for example public house or club *Lower culpability:* Permits use for limited or no financial gain No active role in any supply taking place Involvement through naivety

---

[1149] Legal Aid, Sentencing and Punishment of Offenders Act 2012 s 85(1) and (4) and Legal Aid, Sentencing and Punishment of Offenders Act 2012 (Commencement No 11) Order 2015 2015/504
[1150] Proceeds of Crime Act 2002 s 6 and 75 and Sch 2 para 1(1)(c)
[1151] Applying Drug Trafficking Act 1994 s 1(1)(a), which defines a drug trafficking offence as doing or being concerned in...supplying a controlled drug where the...supply contravenes Misuse of Drugs Act 1971 s 4(1). (Section 4(1) does not create an offence.)
[1152] Serious Crime Act 2007 s 1 and Sch 1 para 1(c)

Factors indicating harm (non-exhaustive)
Greater harm: Regular drug-related activity Higher quantity of drugs, for example: heroin, cocaine – more than 5 grams, cannabis – more than 50 grams **Lesser harm:** Infrequent drug-related activity Lower quantity of drugs, for example: heroin, cocaine – up to 5 grams, cannabis – up to 50 grams

340.76

STEP TWO: Starting point and category range

page 25 Having determined the category, the court should use the table below to identify the corresponding starting point to reach a sentence within the category range. The starting point applies to all offenders irrespective of plea or previous convictions. The court should then consider further adjustment within the category range for aggravating or mitigating features, set out over the page.

Where the defendant is dependent on or has a propensity to misuse drugs and there is sufficient prospect of success, a community order with a drug rehabilitation requirement under Criminal Justice Act 2003 s 209 can be a proper alternative to a short or moderate-length custodial sentence.

Class A		
Offence category	Starting point (applicable to all offenders)	Category range (applicable to all offenders)
Category 1	2½ years' custody	18 months' to 4 years' custody
Category 2	36 weeks' custody	High-level community order to 18 months' custody
Category 3	Medium-level community order	Low-level community order to high-level community order
Class B		
Offence category	Starting point (applicable to all offenders)	Category range (applicable to all offenders)
Category 1	1 year's custody	26 weeks' to 18 months' custody
Category 2	High-level community order	Low-level community order to 26 weeks' custody
Category 3	Band C fine	Band A fine to low-level community order
Class C		
Offence category	Starting point (applicable to all offenders)	Category range (applicable to all offenders)
Category 1	12 weeks' custody	High-level community order to 26 weeks' custody*
Category 2	Low-level community order	Band C fine to high-level community order
Category 3	Band A fine	Discharge to Band C fine
*When tried summarily, the maximum penalty is 12 weeks' custody		

For the meaning of a high-level, a medium-level and a low-level community order, see **16.12** in Volume 1.

340.77   [Aggravating and mitigating factors]
page 26 The table below contains a non-exhaustive list of additional factual elements providing the context of the offence and factors relating to the offender. Identify whether any combination of these, or other relevant factors, should result in an upward or downward adjustment from the starting point. In some cases, having considered these factors, it may be appropriate to move outside the identified category range.
Where appropriate, consider the custody threshold as follows:
   Has the custody threshold been passed?
   If so, is it unavoidable that a custodial sentence be imposed?
   If so, can that sentence be suspended?
Non-exhaustive list of additional factual elements

Factors increasing seriousness
Statutory aggravating factors: Previous convictions, having regard to: a) nature of the offence to which conviction relates and relevance to current offence, and b) time elapsed since conviction Offence committed on bail *Other aggravating factors:* Length of time over which premises used for drug activity Volume of drug activity permitted Premises adapted to facilitate drug activity Location of premises, for example proximity to school Attempts to conceal or dispose of evidence, where not charged separately Presence of others, especially children and/or non-users High purity Presence of weapons, where not charged separately Failure to comply with current court orders Offence committed on licence Established evidence of community impact
Factors reducing seriousness or reflecting personal mitigation
Involvement due to pressure, intimidation or coercion falling short of duress Isolated incident Low purity No previous convictions **or** no relevant or recent convictions Offender's vulnerability was exploited Remorse Good character and/or exemplary conduct Determination and/or demonstration of steps having been taken to address addiction or offending behaviour Serious medical conditions requiring urgent, intensive or long-term treatment Age and/or lack of maturity where it affects the responsibility of the offender Mental disorder or learning disability Sole or primary carer for dependent relatives

340.78   *Suggested approach to the guidelines*
Note: I consider that the pre-guideline cases add nothing. It is better just to follow the guideline. Ed.

341   TACHOGRAPH AND OTHER DRIVERS' HOURS OFFENCES
341.1
Transport Act 1968
   s 96(11) (contravention of the requirements of the domestic drivers' hours code)
   s 97(1) (use of etc. an applicable vehicle without compliant vehicle recording equipment)

s 97AA (forgery etc. of seals on recording equipment)
s 98 (contravention of the written records requirements)
s 99(5) (making a false entry for the purposes of records under section 98)

Modes of trial and maximum sentences Sections 97AA and 99(5) are triable either way. On indictment maximum 2 years. Summary maximum a £5,000 fine for offences committed before 12 March 2015 and an unlimited fine thereafter.[1153] There are maximum fines for those aged under 18, see **14.38** in Volume 1.

Sections 96(11), 97(1) and 98 are summary only. The maximum fines are: a) Level 4 (£2,500), b) a £5,000 fine for offences committed before 12 March 2015 and an unlimited fine thereafter.[1154] There are maximum fines for those aged under 18, see **14.38** in Volume 1, and c) Level 4, respectively.

Fixed penalties There is a fixed penalty (and financial penalty deposit) of £100, £200 or £300[1155] for the various offences. Many of them are graduated penalties. There are graduated fixed penalties of £60, £120 and £200 depending on the number of hours. The table can be found in Fixed Penalty Order 2000 2000/2792 Sch 2, as amended by Fixed Penalty (Amendment) Order 2009 2009/488. All the penalties have half the relevant victim surcharge added. For more detail see **61.1** in Volume 1.

Passenger carrying vehicle (PCV) and Large goods vehicle (LGV) drivers Drivers of PCVs and LGVs who: a) accumulate penalty points (9 points in 3 years for those aged 21+ and 6 points in 2 years for those aged under 21) or b) receive 56 days' or more disqualification or 3) are referred by the DVLA because of endorsements including speed limiter or tachograph offences will be dealt with by the Traffic Commissioners. They will consider whether to warn the driver or suspend or revoke his or her licence. They consider that their role is not to punish but to determine whether the person is fit to have a PCV or LGV licence. Their decisions follow their Statutory Document No 6 *Vocational Driver Conduct* of December 2011, see https://www.gov.uk/government/ uploads/system/uploads/attachment_data/file/251199/6-driver-conduct.pdf or www- .banksr.com Other Matters Other Documents tab

341.2   *Crown Court statistics   England and Wales*
Fraud, forgery etc. associated with vehicle or driver records Aged 21+

Year	Plea	Total sentenced	Type of sentencing %						Average length of custody in months
			Discharge	Fine	Commu- nity sentence	Sus- pended sentence	Custody	Other	
2013	G	26	3.8	15.4	7.7	42.3	30.8	–	5.6
	NG	7	–	14.3	14.3	28.6	42.9	–	3.7
2014	G	24	–	4	25	42	25	4	4.7
	NG	1	–	–	–	100	–	–	–

For explanations about the statistics see page 1-xii. For more statistics see www.banksr. com Other Matters Statistics tab

341.3   *Magistrates' Court Sentencing Guidelines*
Magistrates' Court Sentencing Guidelines 2008 page 138, see www.banksr.com Other Matters Guidelines tab The guidelines apply to the Magistrates' Courts and the Crown Court hearing appeals or sentencing for summary only offences.[1156] page 138

[1153] Education (Penalty Notices) (England) Regulations 2007 2007/1867 as amended, reg 3 and 4
[1154] Legal Aid, Sentencing and Punishment of Offenders Act 2012 s 85(1) and (4) and Legal Aid, Sentencing and Punishment of Offenders Act 2012 (Commencement No 11) Order 2015 2015/504
[1155] Legal Aid, Sentencing and Punishment of Offenders Act 2012 s 85(1) and (4) and Legal Aid, Sentencing and Punishment of Offenders Act 2012 (Commencement No 11) Order 2015 2015/504
[1156] Criminal Justice Act 2003 s 226A-226B as inserted by Legal Aid, Sentencing and Punishment of Offenders Act 2012 s 124

Offence	Starting point
Speed limiter not used or incorrectly calibrated Tachograph not used/not working Exceeding permitted driving time/periods of duty Failure to keep/return written record sheets Falsifying or altering records with intent to deceive	Band B fine for driver, Band B fine with at least a 25% uplift for an owner driver and Band C fine for owner company

Starting point fine Band B is 100% of weekly take-home pay/weekly benefit payment and starting point fine Band C is 150% of that payment. For more detail see **60.27** in Volume 1.

For details about how to apply the guidelines see the GUIDELINES chapter in Volume 1.

341.4   *Judicial guidance*

R v McCabe 1989 11 Cr App R (S) 154 These offences were serious and caused danger to the public. The very fact that employees or drivers may regard them as bureaucratic interference with their livelihood was a reason for imposing a significant sentence.

R v Livingstone 2008 EWCA Crim 789, 2 Cr App R (S) 96 (p 539) The defendant pleaded to falsifying records (×7). A broken fuse was found to have been inserted in the vehicle which stopped the tachograph from recording. Held. This offence was so serious that there could be few circumstances that would not justify immediate custody. Immediate custody is necessary because it is very easy to interfere with tachographs and other devices on lorries. In view of the potential fatal consequences of doing so, an immediate custodial sentence is one that will be passed.

Note: These are old cases, but they are in line with current sentencing practice. Ed.

341.5   *Judicial guidance   Persons in authority*

R v Raven 1988 10 Cr App R (S) 354 D was concerned in the management of a haulage company. He pleaded to six charges of making false entries on a driver's sheet. The Judge said, 'The deliberate alteration of tachographs with a view to profit is a shocking state of affairs. One only needs to have regard to the news on an almost daily basis to realise how important it is that safety regulations with regard to the use of heavy vehicles on the road are complied with and it must be obvious that those who come before the courts charged with effectively fraud but which give rise to matters of public danger, as these offences have done, must understand there will be serious consequences when and if they come to light. Where it is done for profit it is dangerous and unfair competition for other traders'. Held. We agree with those comments.

R v McCabe 1989 11 Cr App R (S) 154 Where someone in authority was corrupting employees the offence was more serious than when committed by the employees, and demanded a severe sentence to discourage others.

R v Saunders 2001 2 Cr App R (S) 63 (p 301) We agree with the comments in *R v Raven* 1988 10 Cr App R (S) 354.

Note: These are old cases, but they are in line with current sentencing practice. Ed.

341.6   *Disqualification*

R v Livingstone 2008 EWCA Crim 789, 2 Cr App R (S) 96 (p 539) The defendant pleaded to seven offences of falsifying records. Held. He will lose his HGV licence. Because of the Traffic Commissioners' Practice Direction 2005[1157] and to enable him to work rather than live off the state, **1-year** disqualification not 3. (The Practice Direction reference may be to the 6-12 month disqualification guideline for those who commit this offence.)

[1157] Sexual Offences Act 2003 s 103A as inserted by Anti-social Behaviour, Crime and Policing Act 2014 Sch 5 para 2 and Sexual Offences Act 2003 Sch 3

341.7   *Interfering with equipment to hide true recordings*
R v Livingstone 2008 EWCA Crim 789, 2 Cr App R (S) 96 (p 539) D pleaded to seven offences of falsifying records. He drove an articulated lorry carrying stone on the M5. He was stopped by police, who found his tachograph sheet blank. There were documents which suggested that he had completed a journey which, because of its length, could not be lawfully completed in a day. A broken fuse was found to have been inserted in the vehicle which stopped the tachograph from recording. The Judge imposed 6 months' suspended with community work because of prison overcrowding. He appealed the disqualification. Held. He should have received **immediate imprisonment**.
See also the **ROAD TRAFFIC** chapter.

342   TAKING MOTOR VEHICLES
See also the **AGGRAVATED VEHICLE-TAKING** chapter.

342.1
Theft Act 1968 s 12 (taking a motor vehicle or other conveyance without authority)
Mode of trial Summary only. Triable on indictment as an alternative to theft[1158]
Maximum sentence 6 months and/or a £5,000 fine for offences committed before 12 March 2015 and an unlimited fine thereafter.[1159] There are maximum fines for those aged under 18, see **14.38** in Volume 1.
Disqualification Discretionary disqualification[1160]
Endorsement The offence does not enable the recording of an endorsement.[1161]
Penalty points There are no penalty points.[1162]
Criminal Behaviour Orders Where a defendant has engaged in behaviour that caused or was likely to cause harassment, alarm or distress to any persons and a Criminal Behaviour Order will help in preventing the offender from engaging in such behaviour, the court may make this order.[1163]

342.2   *Crown Court statistics   England and Wales*
Theft or unauthorised taking of motor vehicle

Year	Age	Plea	Total sen-tenced	Type of sentencing %						Average length of custody in months
				Dis-charge	Fine	Commu-nity sentence	Sus-pended sentence	Custody	Oth-er	
2013	18-20	G	21	–	–	23.8	14.3	57.1	4.8	8.2
		NG	1	–	–	100	–	–	–	–
	21+	G	194	–	1.5	7.7	22.2	67.5	1	13.8
		NG	15	–	–	20	20	60	–	28.6
2014	18-20	G	16	–	–	13	25	63	–	13.4
		NG	1	–	–	–	–	100	–	not listed[1164]
	21+	G	225	–	–	7	24	69	–	18.4
		NG	16	–	–	19	44	38	–	31.3

For explanations about the statistics see page 1-xii. For more statistics and for statistics for male and female defendants etc. see www.banksr.com Other Matters Statistics tab

---

[1158] Theft Act 1968 s 12(4)
[1159] Legal Aid, Sentencing and Punishment of Offenders Act 2012 s 85(1) and (4) and Legal Aid, Sentencing and Punishment of Offenders Act 2012 (Commencement No 11) Order 2015 2015/504
[1160] Road Traffic Offenders Act 1988 s 9, 34, 97 and Sch 2 Part II
[1161] Road Traffic Offenders Act 1988 s 9, 34, 97 and Sch 2 Part II
[1162] Road Traffic Offenders Act 1988 s 9, 34, 97 and Sch 2 Part II
[1163] Anti-social Behaviour, Crime and Policing Act 2014 s 22(1)-(4)
[1164] Based on too few cases to be meaningful

For details about applying the guidelines see the GUIDELINES chapter in Volume 1.

342.3   *Magistrates' Court Sentencing Guidelines*

Magistrates' Court Sentencing Guideline, see www.banksr.com Other Matters Guidelines tab page 110 The guidelines apply to the Magistrates' Courts and the Crown Court hearing appeals or sentencing for summary only offences.[1165]

page 110 Starting points are based on a first-time offender pleading not guilty.

Examples of nature of activity	Starting point	Range
Exceeding authorised use of e.g. employer's or relative's vehicle, retention of hire car beyond return date	Low-level community order	Band B fine to medium-level community order
As above with damage caused to lock/ignition, or stranger's vehicle involved but no damage caused	Medium-level community order	Low-level community order to high-level community order
Taking vehicle from private premises, Causing damage to e.g. lock/ignition of stranger's vehicle	High-level community order	Medium-level community order to 26 weeks' custody

The following aggravating and mitigating factors may be particularly relevant: Factors indicating greater degree of harm: 1 Vehicle later burnt, 2 Vehicle belonging to elderly/disabled person, 3 Emergency services vehicle, 4 Medium to large goods vehicle, and 5 Passengers carried. Factor indicating lower culpability: Misunderstanding with owner. Factor indicating lesser degree of harm: Offender voluntarily returned vehicle to owner.

Consider compensation and disqualification from driving.

Consultation It is expected that the Sentencing Council will issue a consultation document about updating this guideline in May 2016.

Band B has a £200 fine starting point with a £100-£500 range. For more details see **60.27** in Volume 1.

For the meaning of a high-level, a medium-level and a low-level community order, see **16.12** in Volume 1.

342.4   *Cases*

R v Sivyer and Others 2012 EWCA Crim 66 D, C and H pleaded to TDA and criminal damage. With others, the three men broke into a shed on a golf course. Using some chain cutters, which were legitimately in D's car, they freed six golf buggies. Their bases of plea were that they cut six chains, and drove the buggies but caused no damage. In the event, the greens and fairways were damaged, and the six buggies went over a cliff, whereupon they smashed. The total damage was £30,000. D, aged 19, had a conviction for criminal damage (conditional discharge) and two dwelling house burglaries (suspended sentence). H, aged 17, had a conviction for a bladed article. He received a Referral Order which he subsequently breached. C, aged 19, had two criminal damage convictions (£100 fine) and a fare evasion offence (£130 fine). Held. This level of criminal behaviour by men with relatively light convictions does not warrant a custodial sentence. It was not the defendants' fault that their pleas were not acceptable earlier. Consequently they were entitled to significant credit. The Judge erred in this regard. **Community order** with **150 hours' unpaid work**, not a 6-month suspended sentence. Note: The serious element seems to be the damage to the buggies and the golf course. However, the report does not explain what the damage was the defendants pleaded to. It may have been the chains. Ed.

[1165] See page 15 of the guidelines.

343   TAX FRAUD AND DUTY EVASION

343.1

There are many different offences and penalties but in particular there are:

1) Cheating the public revenue

Contrary to common law

Mode of trial Indictable only

Maximum sentence Life

2) Value Added Tax Act 1994 s 72 (knowingly concerned in or taking steps with a view to the fraudulent evasion of VAT)

Mode of trial Triable either way

Maximum sentence On indictment 7 years. Summary maximum 6 months and/or a £5,000 fine for offences committed before 12 March 2015 and £20,000 fine thereafter.[1166]

Why the maximum fine is £20,000 and not unlimited is far from clear. It may be because the appropriate forum for large-scale tax frauds is considered to be the Crown Court.

3) **Duty evasion**

Customs and Excise Management Act 1979

s 50(2) (improper importation of goods chargeable with a duty that has not been paid)

s 50(3) (importing goods contrary to any prohibition or restriction with intent to evade the prohibition etc.)

s 170(2) (fraudulent evasion of duty)

s 170B (knowingly concerned in or taking steps with a view to the fraudulent evasion of duty)

Modes of trial Triable either way

Maximum sentences On indictment maximum sentence 7 years. Summary maximum is 6 months and/or a £5,000 fine for offences committed before 12 March 2015 and a £20,000[1167] fine thereafter, or three times the value of the goods, whichever is greater.

Confiscation Where a defendant has a criminal lifestyle the court, once the confiscation proceedings are triggered (see **22.11** in Volume 1), <u>must</u> follow the Proceeds of Crime Act 2002 procedure. 'Criminal lifestyle' offences include those under Customs and Excise Management Act 1979 s 50(2)-(3), 68(2) and 170 (though not 170B) but only when connected with the prohibition by virtue of Misuse of Drugs Act 1971 s 3.[1168] For what constitutes a criminal lifestyle, see **22.48** in Volume 1. The categories of persons liable to pay tobacco duty are set out in HMRC *Excise Notice 476: Tobacco Products Duty*. As a result it is more difficult to make confiscation orders for those defendants who were not holding the tobacco products at an excise duty point or caused the tobacco products to reach such a point, *R v Khan and Others* 2009 EWCA Crim 588. The expression 'cigarettes of that description' includes both genuine goods and counterfeit goods of substantially the same type made up to resemble them. Therefore the prosecution can calculate from the duty on genuine cigarettes, *R v Varsani* 2010 EWCA Crim 1938. For more detail see the **CONFISCATION** *Determining the benefit Duty evasion (tobacco smuggling etc.)* para at **22.96** in Volume 1.

Forfeiture There are powers to forfeit the goods and cars, ships etc. used in duty evasion.[1169]

[1166] Legal Aid, Sentencing and Punishment of Offenders Act 2012 (Fines on Summary Conviction) Regulations 2015 2015/664 para 2 and Sch 1 para 60-64 and Sch 2 para 8
[1167] Legal Aid, Sentencing and Punishment of Offenders Act 2012 (Fines on Summary Conviction) Regulations 2015 2015/664 para 2 and Sch 1 para 2, 3, 23 and 24 Sch 2 para 1(3), 1(21) and 1(22)
[1168] Proceeds of Crime Act 2002 s 6 and 75 and Sch 2 para 1(2)
[1169] Customs and Excise Management Act 1979 s 49, 53, 66, 74, 88, 141 and 159

Disqualification from driving This order may be appropriate for a defendant whether or not he or she is the actual driver.[1170]

Serious Crime Prevention Orders For Customs and Excise Management Act 1979 s 170, Value Added Tax Act 1994 s 72, Taxes Management Act 1970 s 106A, Tax Credits Act 2002 s 35 and cheating the public revenue offences there is a discretionary power to make this order, when it would protect the public etc.[1171]

Deferred Prosecution Agreements A designated prosecutor may apply to the court under Crime and Courts Act 2013 Sch 17 para 7 for this procedure to be applied for the following offences: a) cheating the public revenue, b) Customs and Excise Management Act 1979 s 167 and 170, d) Value Added Tax Act 1994 s 72, and e) certain other offences (see Crime and Courts Act 2013 Sch 17 para 15-30). The procedure is laid down in Crime and Courts Act 2013 Sch 17. Commencement was on 24 February 2014.

Old cases All old tariff cases are best ignored. None are listed.

See also the BENEFIT FRAUD and FRAUD AND FINANCIAL SERVICES OFFENCES chapters.

For **corporate offenders** see the *Fraud, Bribery and Money Laundering: Corporate Offenders Guideline 2014* at **225.9**.

343.2   Crown Court statistics   England and Wales
Revenue law offences 21+

Year	Plea	Total sentenced	Type of sentencing %						Average length of custody in months
			Discharge	Fine	Community sentence	Suspended sentence	Custody	Other	
2013	G	56	0.0	1.8	3.6	58.9	35.7	0.0	14.4
	NG	4	0.0	0.0	0.0	50.0	50.0	0.0	13.5
2014	G	71	3	–	8	49	38	1	15.6
	NG	6	–	–	17	50	33	–	not listed[1172]

Note: I suspect that some of the offences used to prosecute tax fraudsters are not listed in 'Revenue offences'. Perhaps they are listed in the 'Other fraud' category. Figures are only available up to 2011 but have been requested for subsequent years. Ed.

For more statistics see www.banksr.com Other Matters Statistics tab

For **corporate offenders** see the *Fraud, Bribery and Money Laundering: Corporate Offenders Guideline 2014* at **225.9**.

343.3   Sentencing Council guideline
Fraud, Bribery and Money Laundering Offences Guideline 2014, see www.banksr.com Other matters Guideline tab This guideline applies to Fraud Act 2006 s 1, Theft Act 1968 s 17 (false accounting), Value Added Tax Act 1994 s 72, Taxes Management Act 1970 s 106A, Customs and Excise Management Act 1979 s 50, 170 and 170B, and cheating the public revenue. In force 1 October 2014. The guideline only applies to offenders aged 18+, see page 4 of the guideline. For the usual practice, see **66.21** in Volume 1.

STEP ONE: Determining the offence category
page 20 The court should determine the offence category with reference to the tables below. In order to determine the category the court should assess culpability and harm.
Culpability

[1170] *R v Skitt* 2004 EWCA Crim 3141, 2005 2 Cr App R (S) 23 (p 122) The defendants were sentenced for importing large quantities of cigarettes where excise duty had not been paid. Held. Disqualification is designed to deal with just these sorts of offence.
[1171] Serious Crime Act 2007 s 1 and Sch 1 para 8
[1172] Based on too few cases to be meaningful

The level of culpability is determined by weighing up all the factors of the case to determine the offender's role and the extent to which the offending was planned and the sophistication with which it was carried out.

Where there are characteristics present which fall under different levels of culpability, the court should balance these characteristics to reach a fair assessment of the offender's culpability.

Culpability
Culpability A – High culpability
A leading role where offending is part of a group activity Involvement of others through pressure/influence Abuse of position of power or trust or responsibility Sophisticated nature of offence/significant planning Fraudulent activity conducted over sustained period of time
Culpability B – Medium culpability
Other cases where characteristics for Categories A or C are not present A significant role where offending is part of a group activity
Culpability C – Lesser culpability
Performed limited function under direction Involved through coercion, intimidation or exploitation Not motivated by personal gain Opportunistic 'one-off' offence; very little or no planning Limited awareness or understanding of the extent of fraudulent activity

Harm – gain/intended gain to offender or loss/intended loss to HMRC

Category 1	£50 million or more Starting point based on £80 million
Category 2	£10 million–£50 million Starting point based on £30 million
Category 3	£2 million–£10 million Starting point based on £5 million
Category 4	£500,000–£2 million Starting point based on £1 million
Category 5	£100,000–£500,000 Starting point based on £300,000
Category 6	£20,000–£100,000 Starting point based on £50,000
Category 7	Less than £20,000 Starting point based on £12,500

343.4

STEP TWO: Starting point and category range

page 21 Having determined the category at step one, the court should use the appropriate starting point to reach a sentence within the category range in the table below. The starting point applies to all offenders irrespective of plea or previous convictions.

Where the value is larger or smaller than the amount on which the starting point is based, this should lead to upward or downward adjustment as appropriate.

Where the value greatly exceeds the amount of the starting point in Category 1, it may be appropriate to move outside the identified range.

Table 1 Fraud Act 2006 s 1 and conspiracy to defraud

Culpability			
Harm	**A**	**B**	**C**
Category 4 £500,000– £2 million	**Starting point** 7 years' custody	**Starting point** 5 years' custody	**Starting point** 3 years' custody
Starting point based on £1 million	**Category range** 5 to 8 years' custody	**Category range** 3 to 6 years' custody	**Category range** 18 months' to 4 years' custody
Category 5 £100,000– £500,000	**Starting point** 5 years' custody	**Starting point** 3 years' custody	**Starting point** 18 months' custody
Starting point based on £300,000	**Category range** 3 to 6 years' custody	**Category range** 18 months' to 4 years' custody	**Category range** 26 weeks' to 3 years' custody
Category 6 £20,000– £100,000	**Starting point** 3 years' custody	**Starting point** 18 months' custody	**Starting point** 26 weeks' custody
Starting point based on £50,000	**Category range** 18 months' to 4 years' custody	**Category range** 26 weeks' to 3 years' custody	**Category range** Medium-level community order to 1 year's custody
Category 7 £5,000– £20,000	**Starting point** 18 months' custody	**Starting point** 36 weeks' custody	**Starting point** Medium-level community order
Starting point based on £12,500	**Category range** 36 weeks' to 3 years' custody	**Category range** Medium-level community order to 18 months' custody	**Category range** Low-level community order to high-level community order

For the meaning of a high-level, a medium-level and a low-level community order, see
16.12 in Volume 1.

Table 2

Theft Act 1968 s 17, Value Added Tax Act 1994 s 72, Taxes Management Act 1970
s 106A, Customs and Excise Management Act 1979 s 50, 170 and 170B

Culpability			
Harm	**A**	**B**	**C**
Category 4 £500,000– £2 million	**Starting point** 5 years 6 months' custody	**Starting point** 4 years' custody	**Starting point** 2 years 6 months' custody
Starting point based on £1 million	**Category range** 4 years' to 6 years 6 months' custody	**Category range** 2 years 6 months' to 5 years' custody	**Category range** 15 months' to 3 years 6 months' custody
Category 5 £100,000– £500,000	**Starting point** 4 years' custody	**Starting point** 2 years 6 months' custody	**Starting point** 15 months' custody

Culpability			
Harm	**A**	**B**	**C**
Starting point based on £300,000	**Category range** 2 years 6 months' to 5 years' custody	**Category range** 15 months' to 3 years 6 months' custody	**Category range** 26 weeks' to 2 years 6 months' custody
Category 6 £20,000–£100,000	**Starting point** 2 years 6 months' custody	**Starting point** 15 months' custody	**Starting point** High-level community order
Starting point based on £50,000	**Category range** 15 months' to 3 years 6 months' custody	**Category range** High-level community order to 2 years 6 months' custody	**Category range** Low-level community order to 36 weeks' custody
Category 7 £5,000–£20,000	**Starting point** 15 months' custody	**Starting point** 26 weeks' custody	**Starting point** Medium-level community order
Starting point based on £12,500	**Category range** 26 weeks' to 2 years 6 months' custody	**Category range** Medium-level community order to 15 months' custody	**Category range** Band C fine to high-level community order

For the meaning of a high-level, a medium-level and a low-level community order, see **16.12** in Volume 1.

343.5   Table 3 Cheating the public revenue

Culpability			
Harm	**A**	**B**	**C**
Category 1 £50 million or more	**Starting point** 12 years' custody	**Starting point** 8 years' custody	**Starting point** 6 years' custody
Starting point based on £80 million	**Category range** 10 to 17 years' custody	**Category range** 7 to 12 years' custody	**Category range** 4 to 8 years' custody
Category 2 £10 million–£50 million	**Starting point** 10 years' custody	**Starting point** 7 years' custody	**Starting point** 5 years' custody
Starting point based on £30 million	**Category range** 8 to 13 years' custody	**Category range** 5 to 9 years' custody	**Category range** 3 to 6 years' custody
Category 3 £2 million–£10 million	**Starting point** 8 years' custody	**Starting point** 6 years' custody	**Starting point** 4 years' custody
Starting point based on £5 million	**Category range** 6 to 10 years' custody	**Category range** 4 to 7 years' custody	**Category range** 3 to 5 years' custody

343.6   [Aggravating and mitigating factors]
page 24 The table below contains a non-exhaustive list of additional factual elements providing the context of the offence and factors relating to the offender.
Identify whether any combination of these or other relevant factors should result in an upward or downward adjustment from the sentence arrived at so far.
Consecutive sentences for multiple offences may be appropriate where large sums are involved.

Factors increasing seriousness
Statutory aggravating factors: Previous convictions, having regard to: a) the nature of the offence to which the conviction relates and its relevance to the current offence; and b) the time that has elapsed since the conviction   Offence committed whilst on bail   *Other aggravating factors:*   Involves multiple frauds   Number of false declarations   Attempts to conceal/dispose of evidence   Failure to comply with current court orders   Offence committed on licence   Offences taken into consideration   Failure to respond to warnings about behaviour   Blame wrongly placed on others   Damage to third party (for example as a result of identity theft)   Dealing with goods with an additional health risk   Disposing of goods to under-age purchasers
Factors reducing seriousness or reflecting personal mitigation
No previous convictions or no relevant/recent convictions   Remorse   Good character and/or exemplary conduct   Little or no prospect of success   Serious medical condition requiring urgent, intensive or long-term treatment   Age and/or lack of maturity where it affects the responsibility of the offender   Lapse of time since apprehension where this does not arise from the conduct of the offender   Mental disorder or learning disability   Sole or primary carer for dependent relatives   Offender co-operated with investigation, made early admissions and/or voluntarily reported offending   Determination and/or demonstration of steps having been taken to address addiction or offending behaviour   Activity originally legitimate

343.7   *Suggested approach to the new guideline*
Note: There is nothing in the guideline to suggest it is intended that there should be a radical departure from the existing sentencing principles. I would suggest sentencers: a) start with the guideline, b) consider the recent cases from the Court of Appeal to see if they are helpful, and then c) return to the guideline before deciding the appropriate sentence. Ed.

343.8   *Magistrates' Court Sentencing Guideline*
Magistrates' Court Sentencing Guideline 2008 (as amended), see www.banksr.com p 341 The section on revenue fraud of the *Fraud, Bribery and Money Laundering Offences Guideline 2014* has been inserted, see www.banksr.com Other matters Guideline tab

343.9   *Pre-guideline judicial guidance*

R v Ward 2005 EWCA Crim 1926, 2006 1 Cr App R (S) 66 (p 356) The defendant pleaded to cheating the public revenue. It was a 'missing trader' VAT case involving a loss of £9m. The defence argued that the sentence should be restrained by the statutory maximum for VAT evasion (7 years) and relied on *R v Czyzewski* 2003 EWCA Crim 2139, 2004 1 Cr App R (S) 49 (p 289). Held. Where the allegation is that many millions have been lost to the country's revenue it is entirely appropriate for the court to approach the matter on the basis that the appropriate charge is conspiracy to cheat so that a sentence in excess of the maximum for the single substantive offence is available.

Att-Gen's Ref Nos 88-91 of 2006 2006 EWCA Crim 3254, 2007 2 Cr App R (S) 28 (p 155) The defendants were involved in a missing trader tax fraud. The total tax loss for the first and second defendant was just under £24m. The company controlled by the third defendant caused a £28m loss. Held. Those who organise such fraudulent activity should now expect sentences well into double figures.

R v Randhawa and Others 2012 EWCA Crim 1, 2 Cr App R (S) 53 (p 298) The defendants were convicted of an MTIC carousel fraud. Identifiable falsely reclaimed VAT was just under £19m. Held. The total value of identifiable VAT reclaims made or intended to be made, and the total amount actually paid out by way of VAT reclaim, will in most cases provide the most reliable starting point for sentencing. It will also provide the most reliable basis for a comparison with sentencing decisions in other cases, though we would emphasise that sentencing decisions are inevitably fact-specific and that a 'like for like' comparison between cases will often be particularly difficult in frauds of this nature. However, it should not be thought that the total value of the transactions is irrelevant: on the contrary, it will assist the court to gauge the overall size, complexity and sophistication of the conspiracy. Nor should it be thought that the total value of reclaims and repayments will always be a reliable indication of the true gain to the fraudsters or the true loss to HM Revenue: for the reasons which we have mentioned above, a sophisticated carousel fraud may involve successful VAT reclaims which HM Revenue are unable to identify as linked to the conspirators. There is, plainly, a risk that a focus on the total amount of identifiable VAT reclaims and repayments might understate the true seriousness of a particularly sophisticated conspiracy. As a matter of principle, therefore, it does not seem to us to be possible to say that the courts must invariably focus upon the amount of VAT reclaimed and repaid: there may be circumstances in which that approach will not assist the court in its assessment of the seriousness of the crime. But in general, we are persuaded that such a focus will best assist the court both to assess the seriousness of a particular case and to set it into the context of sentencing decisions in other cases.

Old case: *Att-Gen's Ref Nos 86-87 of 1999* 2001 1 Cr App R (S) 141 (p 505) (The length of sentence will depend on a number of factors: the amount of tax evaded, the period of time the evasion took place, the efforts made to conceal the fraud, whether others were drawn in and corrupted, the character of the defendant, his personal gain, his plea and the amount recovered.)

343.10   *Deprivation orders/Disqualification from driving*

R v Czyzewski 2003 EWCA Crim 2139, 2004 1 Cr App R (S) 49 (p 289) Sentencers should also bear in mind their powers to order: confiscation of assets under Proceeds of Crime Act 2002 (Crown Court only), compensation in a clear case under Powers of Criminal Courts (Sentencing) Act 2000 s 130 (Crown Court and, subject to a limit of £5,000, Magistrates' Court also), deprivation, particularly of vehicles, under Powers of Criminal Courts (Sentencing) Act 2000 s 143 (both Crown Court and Magistrates' Court), and disqualification from driving, where a motor vehicle has been used (Crown Court only). The court should warn the defence before making the order.

343.11   Confiscation orders   Tax frauds
Proceeds of Crime Act 2002 s 13(4) The court shall leave the confiscation order out of account in determining the appropriate sentence (except for fines, drug forfeiture orders and Deprivation Orders etc.[1173]).
R v Andrews 1997 1 Cr App R (S) 279 The defendant who was sentenced for a £300,000 tax fraud was ordered to pay a **£250,000** confiscation order. The Court of Appeal reduced the sentence because of the large order.
R v Rogers 2001 EWCA Crim 1680, 2002 1 Cr App R (S) 81 (p 338) The decision in *R v Andrews* 1997 1 Cr App R (S) 279 was without reference to section 72(5) (the repealed but similar Criminal Justice Act 1988 section. Ed.) and the court cannot reduce a sentence because of the confiscation order.

343.12   Loss less than £5m   Cheating the Revenue   Pre-guideline cases
R v Robinson 2010 EWCA Crim 1040 D was convicted of three counts of making a false statement to the Revenue and cheating the public revenue. In 2001, his used car company's tax return showed a profit of £3,453 when the actual profit was £125,966. £37,408 tax was evaded. In 2002, the declared profit was £6,093 when the actual profit was £189,641. £56,626 tax was evaded. In 2003 the stated profit was £9,137 when the actual profit was £359,853. £112,130 tax was evaded. The total tax loss over the three years was £206,165. D also failed to register for VAT although the trading was over the compulsory figure and over the same period the VAT loss was £140,672. D had a conviction in 1996 for applying false descriptions to his cars and received 3 months. He suffered from anxiety, depression and diabetes and his mother had had a stroke and needed assistance. The tax had been paid. Held. It could not be said that **3 years** was outside the appropriate bracket.
See also: *R v Wood* 2010 EWCA Crim 1742 (Plea to conspiracy to cheat the public revenue of £1.7m in a VAT fraud. Other defendant, 4 years upheld. Former tax officer. Starting point 7 years. With his previous good character, the delay and his level of involvement in the conspiracy, **3 years 8 months**.)
R v Panchak 2011 EWCA Crim 3119, 2012 2 Cr App R (S) 40 (p 235) (Conviction for conspiracy to cheat public revenue etc. HMRC self-assessments used to obtain false repayments of income tax. £4.5m was paid into accounts controlled by the defendant and his group. 1,200 false identities. 600 false bank accounts. Ringleader of the conspiracy. Aged 29. **5 years 8 months** upheld.)
R v James and Courtney 2013 EWCA Crim 559, 2 Cr App R (S) 84 (536) (Pleas. Two car import VAT conspiracy frauds using buffer companies. Revenue loss in two conspiracies about £1m. For J, starting at 6 years, with his plea, age, poor health, good character and delay, **3 years 4 months**. C's loss to the Revenue was about £600,000. C had previous convictions including carrying on a business with intent to defraud. On bail for first conspiracy when he was involved in second conspiracy. **3 years** upheld.)
R v Hackney 2013 EWCA Crim 1156, 2014 1 Cr App R (S) 41 (p 235) (Prime mover in a missing trader fraud. About £2.3 claimed. All but about £800,000 received. Starting at 9 years was too high. With 40% discount (plea and assistance) **5 years 3 months**[1174] not 6.)

343.13   Loss over £15m   Cheating the Revenue   Pre-guideline cases
R v Foster and Sophocleous 2011 EWCA Crim 755 S and F pleaded (25% credit) on rearraignment to cheating the public revenue (×4). With another, they were engaged in a substantial VAT fraud spanning 10 years. The losses were around £16m, most of which was never recovered. It involved the submission of false claims for the repayment of VAT from building supplies and reclaiming tax from those supplies. The Judge remarked that, "from first registration to last claim, the only business of the trading entities was VAT fraud". F was estimated to have benefited by £3.5m. F, in his early fifties, was

---

[1173] For details of the limited exceptions see Proceeds of Crime Act 2002 s 13(2)-(3).
[1174] It seems the Court of Appeal got their maths wrong. Ed.

treated as being of good character. He showed symptoms of alcohol dependency syndrome. Held. F had used some of the money to improve his quality of life. Both S and F played major roles. S was head of this vast and elaborate fraud and benefited most. For S, starting at 11 years, **8 years 3 months**. F was at a lower level and his gains were less than S. Starting at 7 years, **5 years 3 months**.

R v Dosanjh and Others 2013 EWCA Crim 2366, 2014 2 Cr App R (S) 25 (p 191) D, G and C were convicted of conspiracy to cheat the Revenue. They manipulated the EU Emissions Trading Scheme. Two artificial trading chains were set up and missing traders were used to cheat the VAT system. Offshore banking platforms were used. The loss was £39m. D's profit was £6.6m. G's profit was £309,000 and C's profit was £40,000, half of which he paid the Revenue. D was near the top of the hierarchy. He ordered G, C and others. G and C played organisational roles. All defendants were of good character. D was aged 31, G was aged 33 and C was aged 36. Held. This was an extremely sophisticated conspiracy. There were huge gains. Our analysis of the previous decisions sets the bar for D at about 13 years, so D **13 years** not 15, G **10 years** not 11, C **8 years** not 9.

See also: *R v Castillo* 2010 EWCA Crim 658 LCJ (£250m missing trader fraud. 540 trading chains. £300m went through D's account. D was one of the principal organisers. **10 years** upheld. Note: The arguments were mostly about role. Ed.)

R v Randhawa and Others 2012 EWCA Crim 1, 2 Cr App R (S) 53 (p 298) (Multiple defendants convicted of conspiracy to cheat the public revenue in relation to an MTIC fraud concerning VAT due on mobile phones. Numerous false transactions relating to mobile phones. Combined sum of fraudulent outputs of the companies controlled by the defendants was in excess of £300m. Identifiable falsely reclaimed VAT was just under £19m. Some companies established for a wholly fraudulent purpose. Sentences of **14, 10, 10 and 6½ years** were not manifestly excessive. For one defendant, 15 years was reduced to **14**.)

343.14   *Duty evasion   Not tobacco   Pre-guideline cases*

R v McCreesh and Lennon 2010 EWCA Crim 314 M and L pleaded (full credit) to a conspiracy to contravene Customs and Excise Management Act 1979 s 170(2). The conspiracy involved rebated diesel fuel, which carries a significantly lower duty than diesel used in road vehicles. Their bases of plea asserted that they were merely drivers and not concerned in the organisation of the conspiracy in any way. M and L were, however, aware of the contents of the lorries that they were driving. The Judge declined to hold a *Newton* hearing and stated that he was satisfied that both M and L were involved in the organisation and were more than merely drivers. However, he did not identify the evidence on which he based those conclusions. M, aged 29, was of previous good character and L, aged 48, was effectively of good character. Held. Referring to *R v West* 2007 EWCA Crim 701, the defendants ought to have been sentenced on their bases of plea. There was a significant delay, through no fault of M or L. This was a large-scale scam and the Judge concluded that the duty evaded was in the region of £1m. After a trial, 2 years would have been appropriate, so with the pleas, **16 months**.

R v Pitt 2012 EWCA Crim 583 D pleaded (full credit) to evasion of duty, supplying etc. an article for use in fraud and control of computer equipment etc. in connection with fraud. There were seven co-accused who were convicted or pleaded. Members of the group travelled to various UK airports and entered the security-controlled zones using boarding passes for domestic flights. They then purchased cigarettes using boarding passes for flights to destinations outside of the EU. There is no limit to the amount of cigarettes which can be purchased in such transactions. The cigarettes were then concealed in empty suitcases. Flexible tickets, through which flights may be booked, cancelled and rebooked, were used in order to obtain boarding passes to allow the transactions to be carried out on multiple occasions. D produced counterfeit boarding passes on his home computer and at Internet cafés. He used some of the passes himself, others he distributed to the group. D and another went to Stansted airport having booked a flight to Belfast. His colleague was stopped at security and found to be in possession of a number of boarding passes. D had accessed 'airside' and went to the duty free outlet. He purchased 2,000 cigarettes which were recorded against a boarding pass for a flight to Norway. D was arrested the following day and released on bail. He continued to be involved in the operation from January to May of 2010. He was subsequently arrested at Manchester airport with 2,600 cigarettes and £2,000 in cash. The Crown stated that the operation concerned the evasion of £546,000 worth of duty on the purchase of 2.5m cigarettes between February 2009 and May 2010, but D claimed that the figure was much lower. The Judge treated D as falling within the £100,000-£500,000 category in the guidelines, with a starting point of £300,000. D, aged 47, had 23 convictions for 39 offences, the majority of which were for burglary, handling stolen goods and theft. There were duty evasion offences in 2004 (small fine), 2006 (3 months) and 2007 (18 months). Held. This was a well-organised and professional fraud. D's convictions and the fact that he continued his offending whilst on bail were seriously aggravating features. A substantial term of imprisonment was necessary. The Judge was correct in placing D into the £100,000-£500,000 guideline category, which has a range of 3-5 years. With full credit for the plea, the Judge must have started at the statutory maximum 7 years. That was too high. It was appropriate to go beyond the top of the category range to reflect D's previous convictions. Starting at 6 years for count 1, with full credit, **4 years** not 4 years 8 months. The consecutive sentence of 4 months should have been concurrent.

343.15   *Duty evasion   Cigarettes and tobacco   Pre-guideline cases*
R v Bevan 2012 EWCA Crim 2258 D pleaded to being knowingly concerned in the fraudulent keeping of restricted goods (×5). His co-accused pleaded to two counts of the same (suspended sentence). Three properties connected to D were searched. In the first property (owned by D's father), half a kilo of hand-rolling tobacco and 12,400 cigarettes on which duty had not been paid were found. The total amount of duty evaded was £2,246. In the second property (D's home), 3,600 cigarettes (some of which were counterfeit) were found. The total amount of duty evaded was £660. In the third property (owned by D's co-accused) 43.4 kilos of hand-rolling tobacco and 117,264 cigarettes (some of which were counterfeit) were found. The duty evaded was £25,563. The total duty evaded was £28,469. D, aged 62, had convictions for being knowingly concerned in the fraudulent keeping of restricted goods (21 months and a £121,428 confiscation order). Held. The *Fraud Guideline 2009* indicated a starting point of 6 months and a range of 6 weeks to 12 months, for a single transaction, fraudulent from the outset with the amount between £20,000 and £100,000. The most serious aggravating factor was his previous conviction for the same offence. Starting at 23 months was too high. **15 months** was correct, so with credit, **10 months** not 16.
R v Lamb and Thompson 2013 EWCA Crim 1365 L was convicted of fraudulently evading duty. T pleaded to the same. Between July 2007 and October 2009, 21 shipping containers were sent to the UK. 13 were seized by HMRC, six of which contained paving slabs, and seven of which contained 60 million cigarettes on which a little under £11m worth of duty and VAT should have been paid. The estimated street value of the cigarettes was £10.4m. The remaining eight containers were not accounted for and their contents remained unknown. L, T and a third man, X, were parties to a conspiracy to avoid duty due on cigarettes. The group rented ten residential or commercial addresses in England using false names. They used another false name to install landline telephones, the calls to which were diverted to an unregistered mobile. They used those addresses and phone numbers to make use of the names of ten genuine companies. In some cases they created false company stationery. They used the identities of the companies to make the necessary arrangements for the containers. They also used names and addresses of private individuals which they used to obtain identification documents and to register for utilities. They set up false VAT registrations and opened bank accounts. There was a significant amount of telephone and e-mail traffic to link T to those activities. T was the prime mover, using bank accounts to launder the proceeds of

the enterprise, estimated to be over £2m. L was seen with T on a number of occasions. X was a haulier, collecting the containers from the docks. Both T and L were former police officers. T was aged 44 and of previous good character. He had served in the Army. He ran into financial difficulties and had turned to crime. L was aged 51 and had served in the RAF. He was of previous good character. He suffered from ischaemic heart disease and depression. Held. This was a very serious offence. The Judge was correct to place it in the highest category of offences. T may not have been the prime mover in the sense that he was making the arrangements for the cigarettes to reach the UK, but he played a crucial role in enabling them to enter without paying VAT or duty. That was a key element of the enterprise and its sole purpose. This was one of the more serious examples of its kind. The Judge was therefore right to take a starting point close to the maximum. For T, the Judge must have started at about 6½ years and with about 10% credit for the plea, **6 years** was not manifestly excessive. For L, **5 years** was not manifestly excessive.

R v Lowe and Sheekey 2013 EWCA Crim 2218 D was convicted of duty evasion (×3). L pleaded on rearraignment to duty evasion (×7). From July 2008 to May 2009 in seven importations, 3.5 million cigarettes and 1.5 tonnes of loose tobacco were brought into the UK from the Far East. L had a long-established family furniture company in London. In 2000 he began to import furniture from the Far East. He set up a business with W, a co-accused, in 2002 and they set up a factory in Indonesia. Initially this was an entirely legitimate business. In 2006, W and a shipping agent began to ship cigarettes and tobacco hidden inside the furniture being sent to the UK. D was a long-standing friend of L and had a furniture business in London. In 2009, W, L, D and the other co-accused were arrested in the UK. In total, there were 22 importations, with the final importation not making it to the UK. The total duty in L's case amounted to over £500,000 in six importations and the attempted importation. D was involved in the professional planning of the four importations in which he was involved. The Judge described L as the instigator and the leader. L was aged 52 and D was aged 51 at the appeal, and both were of previous good character. Held. The Judge was entirely right to place L into Category 1 of the guidelines. Once he entered the [agreement] he was a full and active participant in the importations. He played a significant role in the UK in what was clearly a sophisticated and professionally planned operation involving multiple fraudulent evasions of duty. There was insufficient evidence for the Judge to sentence L as the architect and the leader of the entire enterprise. The appropriate range for these offences over a 12-month period was 2 to 6 years. With a small discount for the plea, **3½ years**, not 4 years 9 months. D was properly placed in Category 2. D understood the risk he was taking in committing these offences entirely for profit. **4 years** was not manifestly excessive.

R v Worboys 2014 EWCA Crim 1429 D changed his plea to guilty to conspiracy to evade duty on tobacco. There were 22 defendants and there was a £5m duty loss. Large consignments of tobacco were imported from the continent. D was a driver and delivered 16-17 consignments of smaller loads into this country. His consignments were goods involving £4+m worth of duty.[1175] D was paid £250 a trip with travel costs. The Judge started at 6 years for the top end and started at 4 years for the bottom end. Held. D was not a planner or an organiser. We start at 2½ years, not 5½. Giving 6 months for the personal mitigation and 25% credit, so **18 months**.

See also: *R v Allin* 2010 EWCA Crim 262 (Plea. Bad record. 7.7m cigarettes. The defendant had some role in setting the trip up. **5 years**.)

R v Wroblewski 2011 EWCA Crim 2093 (Plea. Lorry driver. Over 1 million cigarettes. £200,000 evaded. Stopped at Dover docks. Aged 48. No convictions. **7 months** not 12.)

R v Hareem and Salih 2013 EWCA Crim 1470, 2014 1 Cr App R (S) 580 (p 299) (Late pleas. Conspiracy involving 12 trips over 21 months. Cigarettes worth £1.3m seized,

---

[1175] In para 5 the judgment says D only delivered a fraction of the imported goods. What the situation was is unclear. Ed.

forming small part of smuggled goods. H involved in transporting goods which caused just over £330,000 duty loss. **2 years 4 months upheld**. S had senior role in duty loss of just over £980,000. **5 years 4 months** upheld.)

344 TAXI TOUTING

344.1
Criminal Justice and Public Order Act 1994 s 167 (touting for hire care services)
Mode of trial Summary only
Maximum sentence Level 4 fine (£2,500)

344.2 *Magistrates' Court Sentencing Guidelines*
Magistrates' Court Sentencing Guidelines 2008, see www.banksr.com Other Matters Guidelines tab page 98 The guidelines apply to the Magistrates' Court and the Crown Court hearing appeals or sentencing for summary only offences.[1176]
page 98 Starting points are based on a first-time offender pleading not guilty.

Examples of nature of activity	Starting point	Range
Licensed taxi-driver touting for trade (i.e. making approach rather than waiting for a person to initiate hiring)	Band A fine	Conditional discharge to Band A fine and consider disqualification 1-3 months
PHV licence held but touting for trade rather than being booked through an operator, an accomplice to touting	Band B fine	Band A fine to Band C fine and consider disqualification 3-6 months
No PHV licence held	Band C fine	Band B fine to Band C fine and disqualification 6-12 months

The following aggravating and mitigating factors may be particularly relevant: Factors indicating higher culpability: 1 Commercial business/large-scale operation, 2 No insurance/invalid insurance, 3 No driving licence and/or no MOT, and 4 Vehicle not roadworthy. Factor indicating lower culpability: Providing a service when no licensed taxi available. Factors indicating greater degree of harm: 1 Deliberately diverting trade from taxi rank, and 2 PHV licence had been refused/offender ineligible for licence. Consider disqualification from driving and deprivation of property.
Consultation It is expected that the Sentencing Council will issue a consultation document about updating this guideline in May 2016.
A Band A fine is 50% of net weekly income. Bands B and C are 100% and 150%. For more detail see **60.27** in Volume 1.

345 TERRORISM

345.1
Terrorism Act 2000 and Terrorism Act 2006 contain many offences, including:
Terrorism Act 2000
    s 11 (belonging to proscribed organisations)
        Mode of trial Triable either way
        Maximum sentence On indictment 10 years. Summary maximum 6 months and/or a £5,000 fine for offences committed before 12 March 2015 and an unlimited fine thereafter.[1177] There are maximum fines for those aged under 18, see **14.38** in Volume 1.

[1176] Guidelines page 15.
[1177] Legal Aid, Sentencing and Punishment of Offenders Act 2012 s 85(1) and (4) and Legal Aid, Sentencing and Punishment of Offenders Act 2012 (Commencement No 11) Order 2015 2015/504

s 57(1) (possessing an article when there is a reasonable suspicion for a purpose connected with the commission etc. of an act of terrorism)

Mode of trial Triable either way

Maximum sentence On indictment 15 years[1178] Summary 6 months and/or a £5,000 fine for offences committed before 12 March 2015 and an unlimited fine thereafter.[1179] There are maximum fines for those aged under 18, see **14.38** in Volume 1.

s 58(1) (collecting or making a record of information likely to be useful to a person committing or preparing an act of terrorism)

Mode of trial Triable either way

Maximum sentence On indictment 10 years. Summary 6 months and/or a £5,000 fine for offences committed before 12 March 2015 and an unlimited fine thereafter.[1180] There are maximum fines for those aged under 18, see **14.38** in Volume 1.

s 59 (inciting another to commit an act of terrorism[1181] wholly or partly outside of the UK)

Mode of trial Indictable only

Maximum sentence A person guilty of an offence under this section shall be liable to any penalty to which he would be liable on conviction of the offence listed in subsection (2) which corresponds to the act which he incites.[1182] Where the offence incited is murder, the maximum sentence is discretionary life, not mandatory life, *Att-Gen's Ref Nos 85-87 of 2007* 2007 EWCA Crim 3300, 2008 2 Cr App R (S) 45 (p 247) para 35.

Terrorism Act 2006

s 2(1) (dissemination of terrorist publications)

Mode of trial Triable either way

Maximum sentence On indictment 7 years. Summary 6 months and/or a £5,000 fine for offences committed before 12 March 2015 and an unlimited fine thereafter.[1183] There are maximum fines for those aged under 18, see **14.38** in Volume 1.

Automatic life Anti-terrorism, Crime and Security Act 2001 s 47, 50 and 113, Terrorism Act 2000 s 56-57 and 59, and Terrorism Act 2006 s 5 and 9-11 are listed in Criminal Justice Act 2003 Sch 15B Part 1. The Lord Chief Justice said in *Att-Gen's Ref No 27 of 2013* 2014 EWCA Crim 334[1184] para 8 iii) (*obiter*) that in rare cases the provisions could lead to the imposition of a life sentence where the offence does not carry life imprisonment.

The court must (unless the particular circumstances make it unjust)[1185] pass automatic life if: a) the defendant is aged 18+ at the date of the conviction, b) the offence was committed on or after 3 December 2012, c) the court considers a determinate sentence of at least 10 years is appropriate, d) at the time the offender was convicted he had a conviction for a Criminal Justice Act 2003 Sch 15B offence, and e) the defendant at the time of his or her conviction had previously been sentenced to either: i) a life sentence where he or she was not eligible for release during the first five years of the sentence or ii) a determinate sentence or extended sentence where the custodial part was 10 years or

---

[1178] Words substituted by Terrorism Act 2006 s 13(1)

[1179] Legal Aid, Sentencing and Punishment of Offenders Act 2012 s 85(1) and (4) and Legal Aid, Sentencing and Punishment of Offenders Act 2012 (Commencement No 11) Order 2015 2015/504

[1180] Legal Aid, Sentencing and Punishment of Offenders Act 2012 s 85(1) and (4) and Legal Aid, Sentencing and Punishment of Offenders Act 2012 (Commencement No 11) Order 2015 2015/504

[1181] Those offences are murder, Offences Against the Person Act 1861 s 18, 23 or 24, 28 or 29, and Criminal Damage Act 1971 s 1(2).

[1182] Terrorism Act 2000 s 59(3)

[1183] Legal Aid, Sentencing and Punishment of Offenders Act 2012 s 85(1) and (4) and Legal Aid, Sentencing and Punishment of Offenders Act 2012 (Commencement No 11) Order 2015 2015/504

[1184] This case is also known as *R v Burinskas* 2014 EWCA Crim 334.

[1185] Criminal Justice Act 2003 s 224A(2)

more.[1186] For a pre-2012 extended sentence, when determining whether the custodial term was 10+ years, the period deducted for time on remand or on a curfew and tag is included.[1187]

Extended sentences Anti-terrorism, Crime and Security Act 2001 s 47, 50 and 113, Aviation and Maritime Security Act 1990 s 1, 9-13, Aviation Security Act 1982 s 1-4, Terrorism Act 2000 s 54-57 and 59 and Terrorism Act 2006 s 5, 6 and 9-11 are listed in Criminal Justice Act 2003 Sch 15, Terrorism Act 2000 s 56-57, and 59, Anti-terrorism, Crime and Security Act 2001 s 47, 50 and 113 and Terrorism Act 2006 s 5 and 9-11 are listed in Criminal Justice Act 2003 Sch 15B. The court may pass a 2012 extended sentence (EDS) if there is a significant risk of serious harm from future specified offences and either: a) the defendant has a Criminal Justice Act 2003 Sch 15B conviction (applicable only to defendants aged 18+), or b) the offence would justify a determinate sentence of at least 4 years.[1188] Criminal Justice and Courts Act 2015 s 3(1) and (3)-(5) adds Terrorism Act 2000 s 54 and Terrorism Act 2006 s 6 to the Schedule 15B list of offences. In force 13 April 2015[1189]

Confiscation Where a defendant has a criminal lifestyle the court, once the confiscation proceedings are triggered (see **22.11** in Volume 1), <u>must</u> follow the Proceeds of Crime Act 2002 procedure. Only Terrorism Act 2000 s 56 is a 'criminal lifestyle' offence.[1190] For what constitutes a criminal lifestyle and conducting confiscation procedures under another route, see **22.48** in Volume 1.

Forfeiture There are extra powers to forfeit in terrorist cases.

Notification For specified terrorist offences notification requirements are triggered. These are similar to those for sex offenders, see the **NOTIFICATION: TERRORISM** chapter in Volume 1.

Temporary Exclusion Orders The Secretary of State has power to make such an order when the conditions are met, Counter-Terrorism and Security Act 2015 s 2.

345.2 *Statutory need to determine whether there is a terrorist connection*

Counter-Terrorism Act 2008 s 30(2) If it appears to the court that the offence (among a list contained in Sch 2 to the Act) has or may have a terrorist connection, the court must determine whether this is the case.

Counter-Terrorism Act 2008 s 30(4) If the court determines that the offence has a terrorist connection, the court:

a) must treat that fact as an aggravating factor, and

b) must state in open court that the offence was so aggravated.

345.3 *Guideline cases and judicial guidance*

R v Martin 1999 1 Cr App R (S) 477 LCJ The defendants were convicted of conspiracy to cause explosions likely to endanger life or cause serious injury to property. They planned to attack electricity sub-stations with 37 bombs. Held. This crime was clearly abnormal within Lawton LJ's description in *R v Turner* 1975 61 Cr App R 67 at 90. We fully agree with the extract from *R v Byrne* 1976 62 Cr App R (S) 159 at 163. The reported cases show that the most severe sentences have been passed in cases involving a deliberate threat to human life. For example: *R v Al-Banna* 1984 6 Cr App R (S) 426 (**30, 35 years**), *R v Hindawi* 1988 10 Cr App R (S) 104 (**45 years**), *R v Basra* 1989 11 Cr App R (S) 527 (**35 years**), *R v Mullen* 1991 12 Cr App R (S) 754 (**30 years**), *R v Kinsella* 1995 16 Cr App R (S) 1035 (**35, 25, 16 years**), *R v Taylor and Hayes* 1995 16 Cr App R (S) 873 (**30 years**), and *R v McGonagle and Heffernan* 1996 1 Cr App R

[1186] Criminal Justice Act 2003 s 224A as inserted by Legal Aid, Sentencing and Punishment of Offenders Act 2012 s 122. The condition for a) is at section 224A(1)(a), for b) is at section 224A(1)(b), for c) is at section 224A(1)(c) and for d) is at section 224A(4)-(9).

[1187] Criminal Justice Act 2003 s 224A(9)-(10)

[1188] Criminal Justice Act 2003 s 226A-226B as inserted by Legal Aid, Sentencing and Punishment of Offenders Act 2012 s 124

[1189] Criminal Justice and Courts Act 2015 (Commencement No 1, Saving and Transitional Provisions) Order 2015 2015/778 para 3 and Sch 1 para 3

[1190] Proceeds of Crime Act 2002 s 6 and 75 and Sch 2 para 3

(S) 90 (25, 23 years). The current level of sentencing in cases concerning terrorist explosions appears to be in the range of **20 to 35 years**. But there are some cases which fall outside the bracket, either above or below. The appropriate sentence will plainly depend on a large number of factors, including the likely result of any explosion, the target, the role, the nature, size and likely effect of any explosive device, the motivation and, where death, injury or damage has been caused, the nature and extent of the death, injury or damage. When imposing sentences for conspiracies of this sort, the courts should remind themselves of the term actually served for murder, particularly murder in its more aggravated forms. But there can be no precise equivalence, and conduct threatening the democratic Government and the security of the State and the daily life and livelihood of millions of people has a seriousness all of its own. For conspiracies directed purely to the destruction of property the starting point should be somewhat wider than 'below 20 years'. In some cases below 15 will be appropriate. In a case such as this it would be unrealistic to ignore the threat to life and limb, since had the conspirators' plan been implemented it seems probable that some injury and loss of life would have resulted, whether intended or not. It is not appropriate to recast English sentencing practice to bring it into line with that in Northern Ireland, even assuming the level of sentences there are lower.

R v Barot 2007 EWCA Crim 1119, 2008 1 Cr App R (S) 31 (p 156) LCJ D pleaded to conspiracy to murder. Held. The *R v Martin* 1999 guidelines require review. A terrorist who is in the grip of idealistic extremism to the extent that, over a prolonged period, he has been plotting to commit murder of innocent citizens is likely to pose a serious risk for an indefinite period if he is not confined. If he commits an offence that permits the court to impose an indeterminate sentence, this is likely to be the appropriate course. The fanaticism that is demonstrated by the current terrorists is undoubtedly different in degree [from] that shown by sectarian terrorists with which the UK had become familiar. It is this fanaticism that makes it appropriate to impose indeterminate sentences on today's terrorists, because it is impossible to say when, if ever, such terrorists will cease to pose a danger. The element of public protection is achieved where an indeterminate sentence is imposed. This factor should not influence the minimum term. Although some extremists may not be deterred by the length of sentences it is important that those who might be tempted to accept the role of camp follower should know they are at risk of very severe punishment. The other important element in sentencing is punishment. The increase in the level of sentencing for the most serious murders is a factor that supports an increase in the level of sentences for terrorist conspiracies and attempts to commit mass murder. A life sentence with a minimum of 40 years should, save in quite exceptional circumstances, be the maximum sentence for a terrorist who sets out to achieve mass murder but is not successful in causing any harm. This sentence should be reserved for a terrorist who has been convicted after a trial of a serious attempt to commit mass murder by a viable method. Where the court is unable to be sure that the conspiracy would have been put into practice, or would have led to a successful attempt to murder, the sentence should be significantly lower than for an attempt.

R v Dart and Others 2014 EWCA Crim 2158 The Court heard two preparation (section 5) cases together. The main thrust of the terrorist acts was aimed abroad. Held. That was not a relevant factor in determining the sentence.

345.4 *Guilty plea*

R v Girma and Others 2009 EWCA Crim 912, 2010 1 Cr App R (S) 28 (p 172) After presumably a long wait for his multi-handed terrorist trial, K pleaded to assisting an offender (who committed conspiracy to murder) and failing to disclose information about terrorism. Held. In a multi-handed trial which is likely to last many months, which will be conducted at immense public expense, particular credit must be given to those who break ranks and plead guilty, particularly in the context of allegations like this. Even where a plea is entered only 10 days before the trial, very considerable savings are made. K should have received not 10% but something in the region of **20%**.

Specific terrorist offences

345.5   *Collecting or possessing etc. terrorist information or articles   Statute and judicial guidance*

For the offences, mode of trial and maximum sentences, see **345.1**.

R v Rahman and Mohammed 2008 EWCA Crim 1465, 2009 1 Cr App R (S) 70 (p 402) LCJ R pleaded to Terrorism Act 2000 s 57. Held. Whether the defendant intended dissemination or was reckless as to the consequences is likely to be significant when assessing culpability. The volume and content of the material disseminated will be relevant to the harm caused, intended or foreseeable. Terrorist acts are usually extremely serious and the sentence must reflect the need to deter others. Care must, however, be taken to ensure the sentence is not disproportionate to the facts of the particular offence. If higher sentences are imposed than the case warrants, this will be likely to inflame rather than deter extremism.

345.6   *Collecting or possessing etc. terrorist information or articles   Cases*

R v Worrell 2009 EWCA Crim 1431, 2010 1 Cr App R (S) 27 (p 168) D was convicted of possessing articles for terrorist purposes (TA 2000 s 57) and racially aggravated harassment. D called himself a 'White Nationalist' and espoused the compulsory repatriation of the UK's non-white population. His one-bedroom council flat was searched by police, and a significant quantity of books, stickers, DVDs, videos and Nazi memorabilia were found. The books included manuals about weapons, bombs and how to manufacture them. The books were entitled 'White Urban Survival Guide', 'The black book on Improvised Ammunition' and 'The black book of Arson' etc. Within the books were step-by-step diagrams of how to construct electric circuit detonators and contact boards. Police found sodium chlorate, weedkiller, matches, lighter fuel and fireworks. A large number of match heads were found, of which the expert said that there was no innocent reason for their preparation, and that they were used for pipe bombs. There was also a candle with a fuse wire, indicating that it was an experimental timing device. 'Niggers will die in Grimsby' and other offensive remarks were written on pieces of paper. There was no evidence that he was part of a terrorist cell. The harassment count related to a married couple on the same estate as D. The husband was a Bangladeshi immigrant, and she was a white native of Grimsby. They were subject to racial abuse and harassment month after month. Stickers were placed on a lamp post near their back gate. One read, 'Don't be a mixed-race slut'. The couple felt intimidated and vulnerable, and their relationship suffered as a result. D was aged 34, and in 1995 he received 4 years for various robberies and attempted robberies. In 1999 there was an offensive weapon count. In 2000 there was a bladed article charge and later a threatening material count (12 months). The Judge bore in mind that D had not actually assembled or started to assemble an explosive device. Held. **6 years** was at the top of the range but was not manifestly excessive. 15 months consecutive for the harassment was not wrong and the total was appropriate.

See also:

R v Muhammed 2010 EWCA Crim 227 (Convicted of three counts of possessing an article for a purpose connected with terrorism. No appeal. Convicted of making a record of information likely to be useful in terrorism (section 58(1)). Found in possession of the largest collection of data, stored on hard drives and CDs, including terrorist propaganda and bomb-making instructions. On one count, **2 years** not 4.)

R v Lusha 2010 EWCA Crim 1761 (Convicted. Section 57(1). 71 litres of petrol, computer with instructions about weapons, hard drive with instructions about explosives, bombs etc. Good character. Failed asylum seeker. The top end is 15 years, not the 6 mentioned in *R v Worrell* 2009. **7 years** was impeccably correct.)

R v Khan and Others Re R 2013 EWCA Crim 468 (Plea (20% credit). Section 57(1) Possession of two magazines which contained a bomb-making recipe with hints about how Muslims should kill people in UK. Trusted member of a group. **4½ years** not 5.)

Old cases: *R v Mansha* 2007 1 Cr App R (S) 70 (p 410) (Section 58. **6 years**) *R v Yahya* 2007 The Times News 6/11/07 and Internet sites (**6 years 9 months**) *R v Rahman* 2008 EWCA Crim 1465, 2009 1 Cr App R (S) 70 (p 402) (**5½ years**) *R v Mohammed* 2008 EWCA Crim 1465, 2009 1 Cr App R (S) 70 (p 402) (**2 years**) *R v Muhammed and Khan* 2009 EWCA Crim 2653, 2010 1 Cr App R (S) 103 (p 662) (For K, **12 years**. For M, **10 years**.)

For a summary of the first case, see the 7th edition of this book and for the third and fourth cases, see the 9th edition.

345.7 *Encouraging or inciting others to commit terrorism/Soliciting to murder*

For the offence, mode of trial and maximum sentences, see **345.1**.

Att-Gen's Ref Nos 85-87 of 2007 2007 EWCA Crim 3300, 2008 2 Cr App R (S) 45 (p 247) D pleaded one day after the day fixed for the start of trial to a count of conspiracy to defraud. Some days later, T and M pleaded to a different charge of conspiracy to defraud. A jury was sworn. Nine weeks into the trial T, M and D pleaded to the overarching count of incitement to commit an offence of terrorism, namely murder. D also pleaded to the further charge of conspiracy to defraud to which T and M had previously pleaded. All had received *Goodyear* indications before entering these pleas. The terrorism charge related to material posted on websites between June and October 2005. T set up the websites using stolen credit cards. Originally the stolen credit card details came to T from M, although the originator of the card details was always D. At one point T and M used a different supplier of cards, but there were difficulties with these cards so they went back to D. M and D knew that the websites would be used to publish jihadi material. D was also defrauding credit card companies for his own benefit, separate from the terrorist purpose. In all T had set up or attempted to set up 32 websites. Others posted the material on the websites. Much of the posted material came from the media section of Al Qaeda in Iraq. The theme of the material is that Islam is under threat from a global conspiracy and that the prime movers of this conspiracy are the USA and its western allies, including Britain, but also many other states. Democratic states are all enemies of Islam. The only answer to the conspiracy is jihad or holy war. It is argued that jihad means only fighting by armed conflict with the express purpose of visiting death, destruction and humiliation on all enemies of Islam. Posted on the websites were examples of living wills, where those about to kill themselves parade with bombs and weapons, with a commentary which glorified them and their actions and sanctified their memory, clips of attacks by the mujahedeen on US and UK forces and clips of the terrorist attacks on New York, Washington, Madrid and London and in many other places, with death and destruction glorified. There were also many clips of beheadings mainly in Iraq, showing deliberate public humiliation of the victim, the cutting off of the head, and the severed head produced as a trophy. T was also an administrator of the al-Ansar forum. This was a closed forum on which jihadi issues were discussed, and T posted links on it to videos of beheadings. He permitted discussion in which young men asked for help in going to Iraq and helping in the insurgency.

The Judge found that T was subordinate in the scheme of things but the most prominent of these defendants. It was accepted that M had not been engaged in administering the sites or selecting the material to be posted, but he knew precisely what T had in mind with these sites. He had nothing to do with the al-Ansar site. There was some evidence that he had been engaged in translating and editing for publication books and articles encouraging violence including one which incited believers to fight and kill disbelievers. D accepted the furnishing of nine sets of information about stolen credit cards to set up websites. He knew that there would be extreme jihadi material on the websites, and intended that it would amount to an incitement to murder. He did not visit the sites and did not know T. All the defendants possessed large amounts of jihadi material. All had clips showing beheadings and films showing mujahedeen or Al Qaeda attacks. The Judge found that of the material posted on the websites, much of it amounted to an incitement to murder. D was also involved in a separate credit card conspiracy lasting over a year. This was a sophisticated fraud involving obtaining the identities of genuine credit card holders, changing their addresses to receive the cards when sent out in the post, and the collection of the cards by an accomplice. The overall loss was at least £1.8m, and D's part would have led to a loss of between £250,000 and £300,000, although the extent of his personal gain would have been rather less than that. T and M were aged 22, D 21. None had previous convictions. T came to the UK in 2001 with his parents. He had been granted a residence permit with indefinite leave to remain. For two years he attended an IT and computing course. M was born in Britain. He had a first-class degree in biochemistry. He was highly competent in computer usage. D came originally from the UAE and was granted British citizenship in 2004. He had applied to read law at university. *Held.* They were involved in the planning of a sophisticated and intricate misuse of computers. The offence was funded by the proceeds of fraud. Their purpose was to facilitate publication of material exhorting in strong terms others to participate in acts of extreme violence on a very large scale. But for their arrest their conduct would have covered a much longer period. They intended that others should be moved to commit atrocities on a large scale. The sentences on the terrorism count were unduly lenient. For T after a trial the sentence should have been in the region of 16 to 20 years. Taking into account his plea and the fact that this was a reference, **16 years** not 10. **3½ years concurrent** for the fraud count unchanged. For M, **12 years** not 7½, **3½ years concurrent** on the fraud count unchanged. For D, **10 years** not 6½, **3½ years concurrent** on the joint fraud count unchanged. As this was a reference, **2½ years consecutive** on the separate fraud count not 3½ years concurrent.

R v Saleem and Others 2009 EWCA Crim 920 H and M were convicted of count 1, fundraising for terrorism purposes (Terrorism Act 2000 s 15(1)), S was convicted of count 2, inciting terrorism overseas (Terrorism Act 2000 s 59(1) and (2)(a)), and B and K of both counts. On 9 and 10 November 2004 they had made speeches at a mosque in Central London. Count 1 related to attempts to raise money to send to Fallujah in Iraq and count 2 to attempts to incite members of the audience to join the mujahideen particularly in Fallujah to take part in the jihad and murder members of the coalition forces. The defendants were all members of or associated with the group Al-Muhajiroun, which was not then proscribed. They sought to persuade the audience that that was their obligation and applauded others who had become martyrs to their cause including those responsible for the 9/11 attacks. 9 November was the holiest day of Ramadan and coincided with significant events in Iraq. Coalition forces were attempting to establish control over insurgent forces there and had been engaged in battle over the city of Fallujah, which was being used as a base for Al Qaeda activities. Someone made a DVD of the speeches and this was recovered by police in February 2006. The defendants did not dispute that they made the speeches, only that what they had said amounted to the offences. There was no evidence that any funds had been collected or that any act of terrorism had been committed abroad as a result of the speeches. S played the leading role. At the time of the offences, H and M were aged 22. S and Brooks were aged 29. K was aged 33. The defendants either had no convictions or their convictions did not aggravate their offences. The Judge said the defendants may have felt sincere and deep emotions about the part played by coalition forces. *Held.* While sentences for these kind of offences are likely now to be much higher we take the view that their sentences should reflect the decision in *R v Saleem, Muhid and Javed* 2007 EWCA Crim 2692, 2008 2 Cr App R (S) 12 (p 70) (the Danish cartoon case). This case is probably less serious. The speeches were delivered in private in the context of religious observance and when emotions were running high. We doubt whether any of the defendants thought they were committing or were at risk of committing serious criminal offences. For S, taking into account that this sentence is consecutive to one of 2½ years for inciting racial hatred, **2 years** not 3 years 9 months. For M, taking into account that the sentence is consecutive to one of 4 years' imprisonment for soliciting to murder, **9 months** not 2 years. For B and K, **18 months** not 2½ years on count 1 and **3½ years concurrent** not 4½ years on count 2. For H, **18 months** not 2 years.

Note: These cases are old, so should be treated with care. Ed.

See also: *R v Da Costa and Others* 2009 EWCA Crim 482, 2 Cr App R (S) 98 (p 647) (H was convicted of three counts and D pleaded to three similar counts. H organised a number of training trips. Both spoke at meetings.)

R v Ahmad 2012 EWCA Crim 959, 2013 1 Cr App R (S) 17 (p 89) (LCJ Plea to soliciting to murder and other counts involving separate terrorist activity. Advising people how to kill Members of Parliament who voted for the war in Iraq at their surgeries. **17 years' extended sentence (12 years'** custody and 5 years' licence) was appropriate.)

345.8   *Failure to disclose information/assisting offenders   Judicial guidance*
R v Sherif and Others 2008 EWCA Crim 2653, 2009 2 Cr App R (S) 33 (p 235) The defendants were convicted of offences of failing to disclose information and assisting bombers. Held. There is nothing wrong in principle with imposing consecutive sentences where both limbs of Terrorism Act 2000 s 38B have been charged – failure to provide information both before and after the event. They are entirely separate offences. Where, as here, the offence of assisting an offender is also charged care must be taken to ensure there is criminality over and above the failure to inform if consecutive sentences are to be justified. There may be cases where the court may be able to show some understanding and mercy when someone, if vulnerable either because of age or a particular relationship with an offender, for a time mistakenly and misguidedly puts loyalty to a family member or a friend before the duty to disclose.

345.9   *Failure to disclose information/Assisting offenders   Cases*
R v Sherif and Others 2008 EWCA Crim 2653, 2009 2 Cr App R (S) 33 (p 235) S, Al, Mu, Mo and Ab were convicted after a lengthy trial of offences of failing to disclose information and assisting bombers (four in all, noted here as B1 to B4: see *R v Osman* 2008 EWCA Crim 880) in the failed 21 July 2005 London bombings.

S, B1's brother, was convicted of one count of assisting B1 and one count of failing to disclose information about B1. Both counts were based on his providing his passport to Ab so that B1 could use it to flee the country. S agreed that he provided the passport but said that he did not think about whether his brother was involved in the bombings. He was fearful for his brother's life because of the De Menezes shooting,[1191] as he thought that the police were operating a shoot-to-kill policy.

Al was convicted of two offences of failure to disclose information prior to the bombings and two offences of failing to disclose information after the bombings. All related to the activities of B1 and B2, and one offence of assisting B2. Al and B3 had been in the care of the same foster parents as children. They lived in the same block of flats, and B2 stayed at Al's flat sometimes. The bombs were assembled in B3's flat. In Al's flat there was a notepad with B2's fingerprints on it, with calculations relating to detonators and charges, a handwritten note containing steps to martyrdom, a list of bomb-making equipment and cards from two suppliers of hydrogen peroxide, an essential ingredient in the bombs. The prosecution case was that the documents showed that the bombers had used Al's flat when making their plans, and that the bombers lived in his flat while using B3's flat to boil hydrogen peroxide, which gave off fumes. In the communal bins for the block police found a large number of empty peroxide bottles, a plastic tub identical to that used by the bomber to hold the main explosive charge, a pipette with traces of sulphuric acid, some light bulbs and holders of the type used by the bombers, receipts for the hydrogen peroxide and various bomb-making electrical components and documents, including a rota for concentrating the peroxide by boiling.

[1191] De Menezes was shot by police in a tube train at Stockwell station. The police accepted that he was completely unconnected with terrorism. Ed.

Al was arrested before any of the bombers. In interview he first denied that he had seen B2 or B3 for some time. Later he said that B2 had a key to his flat but denied responsibility for any of the incriminating items in the flat or for disposing of anything in the bins.

M was convicted of one count of assisting an offender, B1, and one count of failure to give information after the event. He was a close friend of B1. Before the bombings he received B4's suicide note, together with a mass of Islamic tapes. He retained the suicide note, and it was in his possession when he was arrested. In the hours and days after the bombings he was involved in a number of phone calls with B4 and B1's wife. He offered B1 the opportunity to stay in his flat. That was the assisting an offender count.

Mo was convicted of four counts of offences concerning prior knowledge relating to each of the four bombers, two counts of assisting an offender, B1 and B4, and four counts relating to post-event knowledge. He was B4's brother. He was present at the address from which the bombers set off on the morning of 21 July. He encouraged them to carry out their attacks by showing them films. He took away the video camera used by them to make their suicide videos. He handed the camera to F to give to B1 after the bombings. After the bombings he provided his brother with a mobile phone, a SIM card, a charger and food while B4 was in hiding with B2. There was considerable telephone contact between this defendant and both B1 and B4 before the bombings. Within a short time of the bombings, M, B1 and his brother all tried to contact him.

Ab was convicted of one count of assisting B1 and four counts of failing to disclose information after the event. He had met B1 at a station on 25 July and B1 stayed with him until the morning of 26 July. He collected S's passport from him and gave it to B1. He also collected a video camera which had been used to film suicide messages by the bombers and gave it to B1. On 26 July he went with B1 to a bus stop where B1 caught a bus for Waterloo. B1 then used S's passport to go to Paris and on to Italy. B1 made two calls to Ab on 26 July and tried unsuccessfully to call him twice from Italy. He was first seen by police as a witness and gave an account that the meeting at the station was by chance, and that although B1 said that he was the would-be bomber on the CCTV, Ab did not believe him. He was subsequently arrested and gave essentially the same account. Ab pleaded late to one count of assisting an offender, B1.

F pleaded to assisting an offender. She stayed in a hotel with her fiancé B3 on the night of 21 July. She helped him to escape to Birmingham disguised as a woman in a full-length burka. She accompanied him to near to the coach station in London from where he took a coach to Birmingham. She provided him with a mobile phone. She was aged 17 and had been engaged to him for a year. She was put under pressure by him and it was accepted that he had a powerful personality. She suffered from post-traumatic stress disorder because of childhood events. She had a child while in custody.

None of these defendants had shown any remorse.

Held. There is nothing wrong in principle with imposing consecutive sentences where both limbs of Terrorism Act 2000 s 38B have been charged – failure to provide information both before and after the event. They are entirely separate offences. Where, as here, the offence of assisting an offender is also charged care must be taken to ensure there is criminality over and above the failure to inform if consecutive sentences are to be justified.

For S, he played a critical part in enabling his brother to escape to Italy. We acknowledge divided loyalties where a brother is involved in such activity. Failing to give information adds little to the seriousness of the matter. Taking into account 467 days under house arrest, **6 years 9 months** for the assisting count, not 10 years in all.

For Al, we can see nothing wrong in imposing the maximum for the failures to inform the authorities before the event. Assisting an offender by cleaning up the flat adds little to the failure to give information after the bombings. For the two counts of failure to inform before the event, **5 years concurrent** upheld. For the two counts of failure to give information after the event, **4 years** consecutive so **9 years** not 12.

For M, he was prepared to give assistance by way of accommodation to B1 when he was on the run. A proper sentence would have been in the region of **5 years**. Taking into account the period of 479 days of house arrest, for the assisting an offender **4 years 9 months** not 7 years with consecutive sentences.

For Mo, he knew the bombings were about to take place and failed to give information. He was present when final preparations were being made. He gave particularly important assistance to B4. The present sentence shows too great a disparity between him and Al, who also had knowledge before the event. Taking into account 304 days of house arrest, **5 years** on the four counts of failure to give information before the event, all concurrent upheld, **4 years and 4 years** concurrent for assisting B1 and B4, consecutive to the 5 years making **13 years** not 17 in all.

For Ab, the assistance he gave B1 was of the utmost significance. We can and should reflect the fact that albeit only after he had been seen by the police, he at least gave some help and information. The failure to give information in relation to B1 adds little to the criminality involved in the assisting. For assisting an offender, **4 years** not 5, and for failure to give information about B1 post event, 4 years concurrent, not 5 consecutive, for failure to give information post event about the four bombers, a consecutive sentence is justified, so **4 years** not 5 concurrent with but consecutive to the other sentences, making a total of **8 years** not 10.

For F, this case could have justified a sentence of up to 7 years, but there was powerful personal mitigation. 5 years was a generous starting point, and the Judge adequately reflected the mitigation in the sentence of **3 years**.

For a linked case see: *R v Girma and Others* 2009 EWCA Crim 912, 2010 1 Cr App R (S) 28 (p 172) (Information non-disclosure (TA 2000 s 38B(1)(a)) sentences were made concurrent to assisting offender counts. For Y, **11 years 9 months** not 15 in all (**5 years** maximum for failing to disclose, consecutive to 7 years maximum for assisting an offender less bail tag discount concurrent to **5 years** for failing to disclose), for E and M, 5 years not 10 in all, for K, 4 years not 9 in all.)

Note: This is an old case, so it should be treated with care. Ed.

345.10   *Group terrorism*

R v Osman and Mohamed 2008 EWCA Crim 880 Os and M were convicted with two others of conspiracy to murder. On 21 July 2005 all four had taken bombs onto the London transport system and detonated them. The bombs did not explode because the main charges failed. The bombs had been made using ingredients including hydrogen peroxide, which had been boiled in an attempt to concentrate it to the required strength, and chapatti flour, and packed with screws, tacks, washers and nuts to act as shrapnel. The bombs were in rucksacks carried by the defendants with wires fed through a slit in their clothing so that they could detonate the bombs by means of battery contact. In 2004 Os and M with others had attended a training camp in the Lake District to train for jihad. Os attended sermons of the extremist cleric Abu Hamza. There was extremist material showing beheadings and other atrocities at Os's flat. There was also a lengthy video film showing how to make a ball-bearing suicide vest. There was telephone evidence of association between him and the other defendants throughout April 2005 showing planning meetings near his home and culminating in the first purchase of hydrogen peroxide at the end of April. His fingerprints were found among the 228 empty bottles of hydrogen peroxide and associated boxes found at the flat of Omar, a co-defendant who carried a bomb to a tube station. M left a farewell letter for his family using the same pad which was used to construct part of the detonators. M was arrested in West London on 29 July. In interview he initially denied knowing anything about the attempted bombings. Later in interview he remained silent. In his defence case statement he accepted he carried a bomb onto the Underground. He said that he helped move some of the peroxide used to manufacture the devices, and on 21 July he mixed the peroxide with the flour and placed it in a container and attached metal washers and screws to it. He said that it was intended to make a noise and not to injure. Os fled to Rome and was arrested there on 30 July. In interview he said that the devices were a hoax to frighten people. He did not give evidence. Os was said to have behavioural and psychiatric problems, to be a follower not a leader, and a vulnerable character. Held. They resolved to commit mass murder and die in the process. By the time each operated the detonator, distinctions of any possible significance which might have been drawn between them at an earlier stage in the conspiracy evaporated. These were merciless and extreme crimes. Sentences for all of **life imprisonment** with a minimum term of **40 years** were severe, extreme and utterly justified.

R v Amin and Others 2008 EWCA Crim 1612 Am, Ak, G and M were convicted after a long trial of conspiracy to cause explosions likely to endanger life or cause serious injury to property. The main conspirator was K (no appeal). K and G were also convicted of possessing fertiliser containing ammonium nitrate for the purposes of terrorism. The defendants held extremist jihadist views. K was at the centre of the conspiracy and involved the others but each of them was only given sufficient information to fulfil his own particular function. The conspiracy had participants in the US and in Pakistan. Its objective was to further their cause by using violence wherever possible with proposed terrorist attacks on the London Underground, nightclubs, public houses and synagogues. They considered bombing the Ministry of Sound and Bluewater shopping centre. K attended a training camp in Pakistan where he was given training in the use of explosives. On his return to the UK he arranged to obtain ingredients for an ammonium nitrate fertiliser-based explosive device. He brought aluminium powder back from Pakistan, and just over half a ton of ammonium nitrate was found at storage premises rented by him. G was K's personal assistant and close confidant. He received explosives training in Pakistan and helped organise a camp attended by some of the conspirators. He was director of finances and played a full part in the purchase and storage of the ammonium nitrate. Ak was a committed terrorist who said he was willing and able to bomb the Ministry of Sound nightclub. Intercepted conversations showed his enthusiasm for terrorist activity and his frustration that it was not happening as quickly as he would have liked. He arranged for a lease in the name of his wife to provide a safe place for the conspirators to meet. He provided disks to plot terrorist activities in the UK. M was the oldest of the conspirators, who commanded respect and had authority over others. His presence in Pakistan where he arranged for others to be trained in the use of explosives was important. He suggested terrorist operations in the UK, and was prepared to bomb Bluewater. M had said that he and others had connections to one of Al-Qaeda's operatives. Am was deeply involved in the jihadist cause in Pakistan. He was K's and the other conspirators' contact in Pakistan, and K's main agent there. He knew the ingredients required by K to make bombs and their intended purpose. He supplied the formula, knowing that it was for use in the UK. The conspirators were under surveillance. All these defendants save Am were arrested in the UK. Two months later Am surrendered to the authorities in Pakistan, and some 10 months later was returned by the Pakistani authorities to the UK when he was arrested and charged. Held. Each of these defendants was a highly dangerous man, willing to participate in wholesale death and destruction. But for the intervention of the security services, their common objectives would have been achieved. They represent a continuing danger and will continue to do so for the indefinite future. For all, **life** imprisonment was inevitable and rightly imposed. For M, given the fact that he was the oldest conspirator and had considerable standing in his own community so that he provided leadership as well as spurious respectability for the conspirators, a minimum term of **20 years**, the same as for K, was correct. For Am and Ak, active and enthusiastic participants although with a relatively reduced involvement, minimum terms of **17½ years** were justified. For G, his sentence should be aligned with Am and Ak, so **17½ years'** minimum term not 20 years. For Am, the Judge was wrong to decline to make any allowance for the period he was held in

Pakistan by the ISI. His detention arose directly from his suspected involvement in this conspiracy. His minimum term will be reduced from 17½ years to **16 years 9 months** to reflect the period of detention in Pakistan.

R v Asiedu 2008 EWCA Crim 1725, 2009 1 Cr App R (S) 72 (p 420) D pleaded to conspiracy to cause an explosion or explosions likely to endanger life or property. He had been tried with the four 21 July 2005 bombers (see *R v Osman and Mohamed* 2008 EWCA Crim 880 above) on a count of conspiracy to murder but the jury had failed to agree on a verdict in his case. Before his retrial the Crown accepted his plea on 'entirely pragmatic grounds'. The other four men, including Om, took their bombs onto the London transport system and detonated them but the main charges failed to explode. He lived at the house where the bombs were made. His role had been to buy and help process the hydrogen peroxide needed to make the bombs. He was in frequent telephone contact with the other conspirators from mid-March onwards. He was the central figure in researching what was the maximum concentration hydrogen peroxide available for commercial purchase. He ordered and bought 450 litres of hydrogen peroxide at the maximum available concentration over the course of weeks and from several different suppliers. He was well placed to do this as he was a painter and decorator, so could talk knowledgeably with the suppliers about the legitimate uses of hydrogen peroxide in decorating. He later said that he knew only the night before 21 July that the bombings were to take place, and that in the morning he took part in the making up of the bombs including mixing the hydrogen peroxide and flour and packing the devices with 80 screws etc. On 21 July he was also carrying a lethal bomb, but he abandoned it in a shrubbery in scrubland and did not detonate it. He separated the battery from the main charge before abandoning it. After realising that the plot had failed he disposed of the remaining hydrogen peroxide down the sink and disposed of other incriminating items. D enabled members of Om's family to collect clothing for him from the flat they lived in. The following day, he remained at the flat and continued to try to dispose of evidence. He dismantled a booby trap bomb at the flat. He met Om's brother and said that he knew nothing about the plot. He did eventually go to the police but only when Om's brother said he was going to. Thereafter he lied 'on an epic scale'. His basis of plea was that pressure was put on him by other defendants who had provided him with a home, that he did not know initially that the hydrogen peroxide was to make bombs, that he refused to take part in the boiling process to concentrate the hydrogen peroxide to the required strength but that he did continue to buy it when asked. He said that he refused to take part in the actual bombings. The prosecution said that he must have been involved in the manufacture process before 21 July and that he was a trusted conspirator, although not one of the inner circle. His fingerprints were on many of the containers of the explosives. The Judge accepted the prosecution's view, and said that he did not accept that D refused to take part in the intended bombings of 21 July. He gave no warning of the plan to commit murder although he knew of it. When he went to the police he told lies. At trial he said that he had bought the hydrogen peroxide for legitimate purposes. It was said if he had not agreed to participate he would have lost his home. Held. The Judge was entitled to conclude, and we do, that he was an important member of the conspiracy which had developed to the point where the level and danger and the extent of risk came at the extreme end of criminality for a conspiracy of this kind. **33 years** was amply justified.

R v Jalil and Others 2008 EWCA Crim 2910, 2009 2 Cr App R (S) 40 (p 276) J, B and H pleaded to conspiracy to cause explosions likely to endanger life (Explosive Substances Act 1883 s 2). That count had recently been added to the indictment. B then pleaded. J and H pleaded seven days later. The principal in the plot was Dhiren Barot, see *R v Barot* 2007 EWCA Crim 1119. He had been plotting terrorist attacks on major cities in the US and the UK since at least 2000. He was drawing up plans for Al Qaeda to approve. After the US attacks in 2001 he turned his attention to the UK. The most detailed plans discovered were for the 'gas limo' project in which it was proposed a number of stretch limos should be packed with propane gas cylinders and explosives and detonated in underground car parks. There were other proposals for a radioactive bomb, sabotage of a major rail artery perhaps in a tunnel under the Thames, and the hijacking of a petrol tanker to ram into a building. Some of the attacks were to be on the same day. J, B and Barot were arrested on 3 August 2004, having been under surveillance for about six weeks. J was Barot's most trusted associate, even if he did not know the specifics of what Barot had in mind. He was seen almost continuously in Barot's company. He had on his laptop and memory stick vital research and planning files including the critical 'Final Presentation'. J rented a safe house for himself and Barot to use, and had made use of the store of material in Barot's garage. He had worked on the plans when Barot was out of the country. B had a garage in which was a mass of detailed working plans. His own computer had been used to work on the plans, including when Barot was out of the country. He was frequently in Barot's company. He had documents relating to two false identities used by Barot and had retained an advertisement for a job as a driver of an LGV petrol tanker. H had experience in the construction and surveying of buildings which was useful in the plot. He was a long-standing associate of Barot and used his training to help him plan attacks. He was peripherally involved in the US stage and he had helped Barot research UK plans. He gave himself up to police when he learned they wanted him. A prison report for B said he had distanced himself from extremist prisoners. His mental health was fragile and he had developed obsessive compulsive order and depression in prison, and normal treatment was not available in that location. Held. The conspiracy did not involve an intention to kill but it had a vast potential for mass injury and loss of life. Even if the gas limo explosions did not work as envisaged, mismanaged explosions are unlikely to be other than extremely hazardous to life, to say the least. J was Barot's most trusted associate. B correctly received the largest reduction for his plea, which must have taken some courage without the security (as the others had to a limited extent) of an indication on sentence. It is possible his plea encouraged others to plead guilty. However, a deduction of 15-20% was about right. For J, **26 years**, for B, **20 years**, and for H, **18 years** all upheld.

R v Khan 2009 EWCA Crim 1085, 2010 1 Cr App R (S) 35 (p 215) D pleaded to two counts of engaging in conduct (TA 2006 s 5) and two counts of possessing records (TA 2000 s 58(1)(b)). D was the leader and recruiter of a group of terrorists. He planned the kidnapping of a Muslim soldier in the British Army who would be filmed being beheaded. The film was then to be distributed. The act was to undermine army morale especially among Muslims. D had not identified a soldier. D approached others about the plan and decided how to kidnap the soldier and where to hold him. On four occasions D also shipped range finders, fire accelerants for detonators, computer peripherals, flash-lights etc. to Pakistan for use by Al Qaeda. The last two shipments weighed nearly 1½ tonnes. The records included 'The Encyclopaedia of the Jihad'. D was aged 37, with no convictions. The Judge considered after a plea 18 years, 8 years and 2½ years (for the records) was appropriate. He then considered that the overall term should be **28 years** and gave **life** with a minimum term of **14 years**. Held. The Judge's starting points would equate with about 27 years, 12 years and 3½ to 4 years after a trial. 14 years was not too long.

All these cases are old, so should be treated with care. Ed.

See also: *R v Karim* 2011 EWCA Crim 2577, 2012 1 Cr App R (S) 85 (p 503) (Plea to five and convicted of four terrorism offences including sending funds, possessing documents, preparatory acts and producing a video. Joined British Airways and indicated his willingness to plan terrorist acts. Acted as a 'sleeper'. Documents and messages sent in sophisticated code. **35 years' extended sentence** (**30 years'** custody 5 years' licence.)

R v Khan and Others 2013 EWCA Crim 468 (Pleas (20% credit). Meetings and planning for training and explosions. Venue not determined. Three groups with different roles. For the leader, S, 22 years 8 months' extended sentence (**17 years 8 months'** custody 5 years' extended licence). For two marginally below him, K and H, 21 years' extended sentence (**16 years'** custody 5 years' extended licence). For L, who attended two meetings and was in the group providing money, 15 years 4 months' extended sentence (**10 years 4 months'** custody[1192] 5 years' extended licence.)

R v Khan and Others 2014 EWCA Crim 1766 (Pleas by six. Attack nearly executed on English Defence League's march with explosive device, two sawn-off shot guns, swords and knives. Motive was that they had [insulted] Mohammed and Islam. Device had 359 nails and 93 ball-bearings. Serious injuries planned and deaths envisaged with an intent to trigger escalating spiral of violence. Police and shoppers endangered. Some remorse. All aged in their twenties. Judge started at 26 and 25 years. For three defendants, with plea, 24½ years' extended sentence (**19½ years'** custody 5 years' licence) and for the other three 23 years 9 months' extended sentence (**18 years 9 months'** custody 5 years' extended licence). Appeals dismissed.)

Old cases: *R v Bourgass* 2006 EWCA Crim 3397, 2007 2 Cr App R (S) 40 (p 253) (**17 years**) *R v Ibrahim and Others* 2007 The Times News 10/7/07 and 12//7/07 Crown Court (**Life** with 40-year term for all four defendants) *R v Rowe* 2007 EWCA Crim 635, 2 Cr App R (S) 92 (p 598) (**7½ years** and **2½ years** consecutive) *R v Barot* 2007 EWCA Crim 1119, 2008 1 Cr App R (S) 31 (p 156) (**30 years**) *R v Khyam* 2008 EWCA Crim 1612, 2009 1 Cr App R (S) 77 (p 455) (**Life** with 20-year minimum term for two, and **life** with 17½ years for the other three) *R v Ali and Others* 2009 The Times News 15/9/09 and Internet sites (Crown Court Leader of plot to murder thousands by placing bombs on seven transatlantic airlines. Convicted. **Life** with minimum term of 40 years) For a summary of the fourth case, see the 8th edition of this book.

345.11 *Preparing terrorist acts/Fighting foreign wars   Judicial guidance*
R v Dart and Others 2014 EWCA Crim 2158 The Court heard two preparation cases together. Held. para 72 This was a serious case, in which (in accordance with established principles) the starting point was the notional sentence which would have been imposed if that intention had been achieved. We also reject the suggestion that the Judge was bound by the maximum sentence for a section 6 (training offence) case as that is what the defence claimed it was about.

345.12   *Preparing terrorist acts/Fighting foreign wars*
R v Dart and Others 2014 EWCA Crim 2158 The Court heard two preparation cases together. D pleaded (25% credit) to engaging in conduct in preparation for acts of terrorism. Two others also pleaded (no appeal). D, a fundamentalist, went to Pakistan for terrorist training and to secure terrorist documents. He discussed contact with the Taliban and targeting soldiers in Afghanistan, so civilians could have been at risk. However, no targets were identified. D made concerted efforts to avoid detection. Phones, SIM cards, a will, £4,800 cash for contacts and a video of a proscribed group were found. D was aged 31 and of good character. Held. It was necessary to examine the factual nexus between each applicant's conduct in preparation for giving effect to his intention and the future commission of the intended act(s) of terrorism. For D, 11 years' extended sentence (**6 years'** custody 5 years' licence) upheld. The [provisional sentence] could have been significantly longer.

R v Dart and Others Re UA and SH 2014 EWCA Crim 2158 The Court heard two preparation cases together. UA, SH and others pleaded (25% credit) to engaging in conduct in preparation for acts of terrorism. UA and SH accompanied a co-defendant on several physical training trips and SH discussed obtaining firearms with the same co-defendant. SH was also encouraged by others to travel abroad in the cause of jihad but this never got beyond an aspirational stage. UA meanwhile was sending money to Pakistan for terrorist purposes. When their respective properties were raided by police, it was clear that all defendants accessed and had access to documents espousing violent

---

[1192] The report says 10 years but unless it was 10 years 4 months the constituent parts of the sentence would not add up to the total. Ed.

jihad. The men were not, however, arrested until eight months later when their homes were searched for a second time, but nothing was found. Upon arrest, they made no or no relevant comment in interview and pleaded at the PCMH. All were of good character. UA was aged 26 on appeal and expressed remorse, with a letter from his brother. SH was aged 23 on appeal, remorseful, and had continuing support from his family, including a letter. The Judge concluded that neither was dangerous. Held. It was necessary to examine the factual nexus between each applicant's conduct in preparation for giving effect to his intention and the future commission of the intended act(s) of terrorism. For UA, **5 years 3 months**, not 6 years 9 months. For SH, **3 years 5 months**, not 5 years 3 months. Two co-defendants who intended acts 'at the upper end of the spectrum of operational acts of terrorism' had their extended sentences of 16 years 3 months (11 years 3 months' custody' 5 years' licence) upheld.

R v Sarwar and Another 2015 EWCA Crim 1886 S and D pleaded (20% credit) to preparation of terrorist acts (section 5). In May 2013, S and D travelled from the UK to Turkey and then on to Syria, where with Islamist forces they fought against the regime of President Assad. Before they went to Syria each of them had misled their families as to the purpose of the trip. When S's family discovered that he was travelling to Syria intent on jihad, that he did not intend to return and that he wished to be martyred on the battlefield in Syria, they went to the police. S and D returned to the UK in January 2014 and were arrested. There had been a similarly well-planned but aborted trip in March 2013. S referred to joining KAM, said to be part of Al-Nusra, which was proscribed in June 2013. S and D's homes were searched and computers when examined provided a wealth of material showing a very high level of commitment to violent Islamist extremism. Both had large quantities of jihadist literature and other material which showed D describing Al-Qaeda as 'the best' and America and NATO as the clear enemy, combat activity in Syria and sectarian anti-Shia material. On their return two memory cards containing over 1,600 deleted images were found. They showed places very close to combat and depicted the preparation of weapons and ordnance in Syria. Traces of high explosive were found on items attributable to each of them. When interviewed S and D lied. Their basis of plea downplaying their involvement was not accepted by the prosecution. Both were of previous good character with references. When they travelled abroad they were aged nearly 21. The Judge held that both were fundamentalists who had become deeply committed to violent extremism. He said that they intended to commit terrorist acts against President Assad's forces in Syria, but he could not be sure that either appellant had formed any specific intent to commit acts of terrorism in the UK although the retention of the memory card with detailed instructions as to how to make an improvised explosive device was deeply disturbing. Held. The significant planning over several months prior to departure showed the arrangements were not a spontaneous response to a developing humanitarian crisis in Syria, but instead a well-planned operation for sinister reasons. We take judicial notice of the general nature of the conflict in Syria and the fact that there have been appalling consequences for the civilians of that country arising from the fighting. para 43 Noble cause terrorism is not mitigation. Although there was no prospect of S and D fighting Western forces [which was not mitigation], that aggravating feature was not present. para 46 The fact that preparations were for acts abroad was not mitigation. The preparations were over a long period of time and significant. The Judge was wrong to reject the basis of plea without a *Newton* hearing. With that and other reasons, we start at 13 years not 16 so the custodial term for the **extended sentence** is **10 years 3 months** not 12 years 8 months for both. The 5-year licence extension was not altered.

See also: *R v Khan* 2013 EWCA Crim 1364 (Plea (25% credit). Components for a bomb and extremist CDs and DVDs found. Laptop had extremist literature about violence. Appearance for two ABHs, aggravated burglary and dangerous driving (4 years).

Previous for GBH with intent (8 years). Dominant force in partnership with wife. Preparations detailed and extensive. Judge started at 20 years and with plea, **7½ years'** **IPP**. Appeal dismissed.)

345.13 *Selling or distributing terrorist material*

R Khan 2015 EWCA Crim 1341, 2 Cr App R (S) 76 (p 510) D pleaded to four charges of disseminating terrorist publications. D, who held extreme Islamist views, communicated with T, who was going to Syria to fight. T sent D his route and D expressed a wish to join the conflict. D was contacted by an undercover officer, U, who posed as a jihadi fighter. U was able to view D's texts and posted images. There was an article claiming to be a blueprint for raising mujahid children. D's phone revealed pictures of her youngest son (then aged 2) holding a toy assault rifle, her nine-year-old and teenaged sons with a sword each and pictures of T holding a handgun. There were pictures of D with a sword. Another picture showed a small child with an ammunition belt and a caption saying, "His grandfather became a jihadi so now he wants to be a mujahid." Other pictures showed young children with what appeared to be real firearms and one child with a grenade. D was aged 35 with six children under 18. She was in poor health. The Judge started at 7 years (the maximum) and with plea gave 5 years 3 months. He also said that the promotion of terrorism using the Internet was of national concern. On appeal, the defence said the material was restricted to 241 Facebook friends and the pictures came from the Internet. Further, no one had actively been encouraged to be involved with terrorist activity. Held. We accept the mitigation and the positive elements in her character. However, five of her children live with D's mother and D had talked about leaving to fight in Syria. These offences are serious because of her intentions to be involved in a particular conflict and her deep commitment to the radicalisation of children, including very young children, into becoming violent jihadist activists. Giving the maximum sentence must be seen in the light of the four offences which could have been made consecutive. Appeal dismissed.

See also: *R v Brown* 2011 EWCA Crim 2751, 2012 2 Cr App R (S) 10 (p 39) (LCJ D was convicted of nine offences of collecting or making a record useful to a terrorist (2 years concurrent), two counts of selling or distributing terrorist material (3 years concurrent). He produced and sold material via his website containing information relating to the preparation of explosives, bombs and poisons running to tens of thousands of pages. Very large scale. Committed over a number of years for financial reward. Sold 2,000 disks to 32 countries. Aged 48 at appeal. One conviction for eight copyright offences. Not motivated by ideological beliefs. **3 years** was not arguably manifestly excessive.)

346 THEFT ETC.

346.1

The cases listed in this chapter include forgery, false accounting, making or using a false instrument and public nuisance where the essence of those offences is theft.

1) Theft Act 1968 s 1 (theft)
   Mode of trial Triable either way.
   Maximum sentence Indictment 7 years. Summary 6 months and/or a £5,000 fine for offences committed before 12 March 2015 and an unlimited fine thereafter.[1193] There are maximum fines for those aged under 18, see **14.38** in Volume 1.
2) Fraud Act 2006 s 11 (obtaining services dishonestly)
   Mode of trial Triable either way.

[1193] Legal Aid, Sentencing and Punishment of Offenders Act 2012 s 85(1) and (4) and Legal Aid, Sentencing and Punishment of Offenders Act 2012 (Commencement No 11) Order 2015 2015/504

Maximum sentence Indictment 5 years. Summary 6 months and or a £5,000 fine for offences committed before 12 March 2015 and an unlimited fine thereafter.[1194] There are maximum fines for those aged under 18, see **14.38** in Volume 1.

There are also other offences under Fraud Act 2006.

Anti-social Behaviour, Crime and Policing Act 2014 s 176 created a low-value shoplifting offence which initially is a summary only offence. For details see **346.34**. The section came into force on 13 May 2014.[1195]

Confiscation Where a defendant has a criminal lifestyle the court, once the confiscation proceedings are triggered (see **22.11** in Volume 1), <u>must</u> follow the Proceeds of Crime Act 2002 procedure. The list of 'Criminal lifestyle' offences only includes blackmail (section 21) in the Theft Act 1968 offences.[1196] For what constitutes a criminal lifestyle see **22.48** in Volume 1.

Criminal Behaviour Orders For an example of what conditions can be appropriate and inappropriate see *R v McGrath* 2005 EWCA Crim 353, 2 Cr App R (S) 85 (p 525). For an example of another ASBO being upheld see *R v Vittles* 2004 EWCA Crim 1089, 2005 1 Cr App R (S) 8 (p 31). For conditions see the PREVENTIVE ORDERS *Shoplifting* para at **85.82** in Volume 1.

Disqualification from driving If the offence is theft or attempted theft of a motor vehicle, the offence carries discretionary disqualification.[1197] The Crown Court may disqualify where a motor vehicle was used (by the defendant or another) to commit etc. the offence.[1198]

Endorsement The relevant entries were removed from Road Traffic Offenders Act 1988, so endorsement is no longer applicable for stealing a motor vehicle.[1199]

Fixed penalty There is a £90 fixed penalty for theft[1200] with half the relevant victim surcharge. For more detail see **61.1** in Volume 1.

Restitution Orders There is power to make an order that the stolen goods etc. in the possession of the defendant or a third party be restored to the owner etc.[1201]

Sexual Harm Prevention Orders There is a discretionary power to make this order when it is necessary to protect the public from sexual harm.[1202]

Deferred Prosecution Agreements A designated prosecutor may apply to the court under Crime and Courts Act 2013 Sch 17 para 7, for this procedure to be applied to Theft Act 1968 s 1, 17, 20 and 24A and certain other offences (see Crime and Courts Act 2013 Sch 17 para 15-30). The procedure is laid down in Crime and Courts Act 2013 Sch 17. In force from 24 February 2014.

For *Making off without payment* see the MAKING OFF WITHOUT PAYMENT chapter.

For **corporate offenders** see the *Fraud, Bribery and Money Laundering: Corporate Offenders 2014* guideline at **225.9**.

[1194] Legal Aid, Sentencing and Punishment of Offenders Act 2012 s 85(1) and (4) and Legal Aid, Sentencing and Punishment of Offenders Act 2012 (Commencement No 11) Order 2015 2015/504
[1195] Anti-social Behaviour, Crime and Policing Act 2014 (Commencement No 2, Transitional and Transitory Provisions) Order 2014 2014/949 Sch 1 para 17
[1196] Proceeds of Crime Act 2002 s 6 and 75 and Sch 2 para
[1197] Road Traffic Offenders Act 1988 s 9, 34, 97 and Sch 2 Part II
[1198] Powers of Criminal Courts (Sentencing) Act 2000 s 147(1)(a) and (3)
[1199] Road Traffic Act 1991 s 26 and Sch 2, para 32
[1200] Penalties for Disorderly Behaviour (Amount of Penalty) Order 2002 2002/1837 as amended.
[1201] Powers of Criminal Courts (Sentencing) Act 2000 s 148(2)
[1202] Sexual Offences Act 2003 s 103A as inserted by Anti-social Behaviour, Crime and Policing Act 2014 Sch 5 para 2 and Sexual Offences Act 2003 Sch 5

346.2 *Crown Court statistics   England and Wales*
Theft by employee aged 21+

Year	Plea	Total sentenced	Type of sentencing %							Average length of custody in months
			Discharge	Fine	Community sentence	Suspended sentence	Custody	Other	
2013	G	523	0.6	0.6	11.1	50.3	37.1	0.4	17.4
	NG	37	2.7	2.7	32.4	27	35.1	–	18
2014	G	485	1	1	12	54	33	–	17.7
	NG	33	–	3	18	24	55	–	25.4

Theft from the person of another[1203]

Year	Age	Plea	Total sentenced	Type of sentencing %							Average length of custody in months
				Discharge	Fine	Community sentence	Suspended sentence	Custody	Other	
2013	18-20	G	176	2.8	1.1	35.8	17.6	41.5	1.1	7.1
		NG	15	–	–	26.7	20	53.3	–	7.9
	21+	G	1,143	1.7	2.2	14.3	21.4	59.5	0.8	11.9
		NG	98	5.1	8.2	18.4	21.4	45.9	1	20.8
2014	18-20	G	125	3	2	24	26	44	–	5.9
		NG	5	20	–	40	–	40	–	not listed[1204]
	21+	G	1,197	3	2	14	24	57	1	11.4
		NG	100	2	11	12	32	42	1	22.5

For explanations about the statistics see page 1-xii. For more statistics for male and female defendants, theft from a dwelling, theft of mail, theft of pedal cycles, theft from vehicles and theft from automatic machines see www.banksr.com Other Matters Statistics tab

For *Abstracting electricity or stealing gas statistics* see **346.17**.
For theft by *Postmen/Postwomen* see **346.29**.
For shop theft *Statistics* see **346.33**.

Guidelines
346.3 *Sentencing Guidelines Council guideline*
Theft Offences Guideline 2016, see www.banksr.com Other matters Guidelines tab In force 1 February 2016. The guideline only applies to offenders aged 18+, see page 2 of the guideline. For the usual practice, see **66.21** in Volume 1.

page 3 [The types of offending] included in this guideline are: theft from the person, theft in a dwelling, theft in breach of trust, theft from a motor vehicle, theft of a motor vehicle, theft of a pedal bicycle and all other Theft Act 1968 s 1 offences, except theft from a shop or stall.

STEP ONE: Determining the offence category
page 4 The court should determine the offence category with reference only to the factors identified in the following tables. In order to determine the category the court should assess culpability and harm.

[1203] This is the table's title. I am unaware of what it means. One explanation is 'theft from a person'. Ed.
[1204] Based on too few cases to be meaningful

The level of culpability is determined by weighing up all the factors of the case to determine the offender's role and the extent to which the offending was planned and the sophistication with which it was carried out.

CULPABILITY demonstrated by one or more of the following:
A – High Culpability
A leading role where offending is part of a group activity Involvement of others through coercion, intimidation or exploitation Breach of a high degree of trust or responsibility Sophisticated nature of offence/significant planning Theft involving intimidation or the use or threat of force Deliberately targeting victim on basis of vulnerability
B – Medium Culpability
A significant role where offending is part of a group activity Some degree of planning involved Breach of some degree of trust or responsibility All other cases where characteristics for categories A or C are not present
C – Lesser Culpability
Performed limited function under direction Involved through coercion, intimidation or exploitation Little or no planning Limited awareness or understanding of offence

Where there are characteristics present which fall under different levels of culpability, the court should balance these characteristics to reach a fair assessment of the offender's culpability.

346.4   General theft   Harm

page 5 Harm is assessed by reference to the financial loss that results from the theft and any significant additional harm suffered by the victim or others – examples of significant additional harm may include but are not limited to:

Items stolen were of substantial value to the loser – regardless of monetary worth
High level of inconvenience caused to the victim or others
Consequential financial harm to victim or others
Emotional distress
Fear/loss of confidence caused by the crime
Risk of or actual injury to persons or damage to property
Impact of theft on a business
Damage to heritage assets
Disruption caused to infrastructure

Intended loss should be used where actual loss has been prevented.

Category 1	Very high value goods stolen (above £100,000) **or** High value [goods stolen (£10,000 to £100,000)] with significant additional harm to the victim or others
Category 2	High value goods stolen (£10,000 to £100,000) **and** no significant additional harm **or** Medium value [goods stolen (£500 to £10,000)] with significant additional harm to the victim or others
Category 3	Medium value goods stolen (£500 to £10,000) **and** no significant additional harm **or** Low value [goods stolen (up to £500)] with significant additional harm to the victim or others

Category 4	Low value goods stolen (up to £500) **and** Little or no significant additional harm to the victim or others

346.5   General theft

STEP TWO: Starting point and category range

page 6 Having determined the category at step one, the court should use the starting point to reach a sentence within the appropriate category range in the table below. The starting point applies to all offenders irrespective of plea or previous convictions.

Culpability			
Harm	**A**	**B**	**C**
Category 1 Adjustment should be made for any significant additional harm factors where very high value goods are stolen.	**Starting point** 3 years 6 months' custody	**Starting point** 2 years' custody	**Starting point** 1 year's custody
	Category range 2 years 6 months to 6 years' custody	**Category range** 1 to 3 years 6 months' custody	**Category range** 26 weeks' to 2 years' custody
Category 2	**Starting point** 2 years' custody	**Starting point** 1 year's custody	**Starting point** High-level community order
	Category range 1 to 3 years 6 months' custody	**Category range** 26 weeks' to 2 years' custody	**Category range** Low-level community order to 36 weeks' custody
Category 3	**Starting point** 1 year's custody	**Starting point** High-level community order	**Starting point** Band C fine
	Category range 26 weeks' to 2 years' custody	**Category range** Low-level community order to 36 weeks' custody	**Category range** Band B fine to low-level community order
Category 4	**Starting point** High-level community order	**Starting point** Low-level community order	**Starting point** Band B fine
	Category range Medium-level community order to 36 weeks' custody	**Category range** Band C fine to Medium-level community order	**Category range** Discharge to Band C fine

The table above refers to single offences. Where there are multiple offences, consecutive sentences may be appropriate, [see the *TICs and Totality Guideline 2012: Crown Court*]. Where multiple offences are committed in circumstances which justify consecutive sentences, and the total amount stolen is in excess of £1 million, then an aggregate sentence in excess of 7 years may be appropriate.

Where the offender is dependent on or has a propensity to misuse drugs or alcohol and there is sufficient prospect of success, a community order with a drug rehabilitation requirement under [Criminal Justice Act 2003 s 209], or an alcohol treatment requirement under [Criminal Justice Act 2003 s 212], may be a proper alternative to a short or moderate[-length] custodial sentence.

Where the offender suffers from a medical condition that is susceptible to treatment but does not warrant detention under a hospital order, a community order with a mental health treatment requirement under [Criminal Justice Act 2003 s 207] may be a proper alternative to a short or moderate[-length] custodial sentence.

346.6   General theft   [Aggravating and mitigating factors]
Seriousness
page 7 The court should then consider further adjustment for any aggravating or mitigating factors. The following is a non-exhaustive list of additional factual elements providing the context of the offence and factors relating to the offender. Identify whether any combination of these, or other relevant factors, should result in an upward or downward adjustment from the sentence arrived at so far.

Factors increasing seriousness
Statutory aggravating factors: Previous convictions, having regard to: a) the nature of the offence to which the conviction relates and its relevance to the current offence; and b) the time that has elapsed since the conviction Offence committed whilst on bail Offence motivated by, or demonstrating hostility based on any of the following characteristics or presumed characteristics of the victim: religion, race, disability, sexual orientation or transgender identity *Other aggravating factors:* Stealing goods to order Steps taken to prevent the victim reporting or obtaining assistance and/or from assisting or supporting the prosecution Offender motivated by intention to cause harm or out of revenge Offence committed over sustained period of time Attempts to conceal/dispose of evidence Failure to comply with current court orders Offence committed on licence Offences taken into consideration Blame wrongly placed on others Established evidence of community/wider impact (for issues other than prevalence) Prevalence – see below

Factors reducing seriousness or reflecting personal mitigation
No previous convictions or no relevant/recent convictions Remorse, particularly where evidenced by voluntary reparation to the victim Good character and/or exemplary conduct Serious medical condition requiring urgent, intensive or long-term treatment Age and/or lack of maturity where it affects the responsibility of the offender Mental disorder or learning disability Sole or primary carer for dependent relatives Determination and/or demonstration of steps having been taken to address addiction or offending behaviour Inappropriate degree of trust or responsibility

Prevalence
There may be exceptional local circumstances that arise which may lead a court to decide that prevalence should influence sentencing levels. The pivotal issue in such cases will be the harm caused to the community.

It is essential that the court before taking account of prevalence:

has supporting evidence from an external source, for example, Community Impact Statements, to justify claims that a particular crime is prevalent in their area, **and** is causing particular harm in that community, **and**

is satisfied that there is a compelling need to treat the offence more seriously than elsewhere.

346.7   *General theft   Suggested approach to the guideline*
Note: The new guideline has a different method of determining the sentence from the previous guideline and recent cases. On the other hand, the Sentencing Council, in its press release introducing the new guideline said, 'the Sentencing Council has not set out to change overall sentencing levels, but rather to provide comprehensive guidance and introduce a standard approach.' In balancing these factors I have included most of the old cases. If the old cases are used, it would be wise to begin and end with a consideration of the guideline. Where the main factor in an old case is the financial value I have not included it because the reader would be wise to simply apply the guideline, which is based on value. Ed.

Types of theft
Advance fee fraud see the FRAUD AND FINANCIAL SERVICES OFFENCES *Confidence fraud* paras at **265.28.**
For bank thefts see the ***Cash machines*** paras at **346.12**, the ***Cheque theft etc.*** para at **346.14** and the FRAUD *Banking, insurance frauds and obtaining credit through fraud* paras at **265.22.**

346.8   *Airport thieves   Pre-2016-guideline case*
R v Bond 2013 EWCA Crim 2713 D was convicted of two thefts. He stole expensive items of luggage from Heathrow airport. One item had contents worth £1,400. D was aged 53 and was a professional thief who specialised in high-value items from travellers. He often carefully targeted his victims, including in this instance. His record was appalling with 34 offences over many years, mainly for dishonesty. They included offences committed abroad in airports and elsewhere. In 2002 he was convicted of conspiracy to steal in similar circumstances. Held. The *Theft and Burglary in a Building other than a Dwelling Guideline 2008* does not provide for the current case and to follow it "would produce a wholly unjust result". **4 years** was wholly justified.

346.9   *Bicycle theft   Pre-2016 guideline cases*
Note: Theft of a pedal cycle is specifically included in the **General theft** section of the *Theft Offences Guideline 2016*, www.banksr.com Other matters Guidelines tab, see page 3 and **346.3**. Ed.
R v Jeffries and Jeffries 2013 EWCA Crim 1239 A week before his trial date, J pleaded to 11 counts of theft and T pleaded the next day to seven counts of theft. In 2011, over a four-month period, J and T, who were brothers, stole 13 bicycles between them, worth in total £6,620. The bikes ranged in value from £260 to £1,100. They stole them from 11 railway stations. In doing so they caused nearly £300 worth of damage to padlocks and chains. One witness saw T and J loading a bike into a van which contained other bikes and bike parts. T pleaded to the theft of seven bikes valued at just over £2,000 with nearly £80 damage to locks and chains. J pleaded to the theft of 11 bikes worth a total of £4,500 and £217 worth of damage to locks and chains. There were five counts in common. Bolt cutters and pliers were found at their addresses and the van used in the thefts was found outside T's address. J was aged 23 and T aged 25 at their appeal. J had 23 previous offences on ten occasions mostly for dishonesty but included drugs and public order offences. T had two recent drug offences but had not been to custody. Both expressed a desire to compensate their victims. J had a cocaine and cannabis habit and had been unemployed for 18 months. He had since obtained work as a locksmith's apprentice. Held. J and T had indicated their intentions to plead guilty before they did so, but to unidentified counts, contingent on the Crown providing further evidence. In those circumstances a full ⅓ discount was not appropriate. 25% credit was the correct amount. The Judge rightly described the offences as the well-organised, systematic theft of bicycles. The timescale and extent of travel indicated a large degree of planning. They obviously had a 'fence' organised to dispose of the bikes. There was no genuine remorse.

There would be no difference between J and T despite their disparate previous and differing numbers of convictions. The previous [convictions were] of no real significance. Starting at 30 months, **22 months** not 30 months.
R v Scott 2015 EWCA Crim 411 D was convicted of six thefts and one count of misfeasance in a public office. She was a police community support officer. When on duty, in uniform and working at Gatwick airport, D would approach passengers very shortly before their plane was due to leave. She would take them to an area where they could not be overheard and ask them if they were taking any cash out of the country. She told them they were only able to take out £1,000, which was a lie. She told them any surplus had to be left with her and collected when they returned. She appeared to be writing down details in her notebook. In all she had obtained £13,500 with this trick. If a receipt was asked for she refused to give one and in panic they handed over the money. Impact statements revealed the profound effects the thefts had had. Some victims were not treated seriously and one or two were thought of as being involved in a scam. D had two children aged 16 years and 4 months. The Judge emphasised the loss of morale of officers when they discovered they had disbelieved victims and in some cases treated them quite severely. Held. We bear in mind the vulnerability of the victims, the persistence of the behaviour and that the offence will erode confidence in the police. The money, whilst objectively small, was of great value to victims. There must be a deterrent sentence. In light of her good character, positive references and other factors, **5 years** not 6½ years in all.
See also: *R v Whitehead and Others* 2013 EWCA Crim 2401 (Pleas to conspiracy to steal. One also pleaded to burglary, 15 months consecutive not challenged. Targeted high-value mountain bikes at car parks in Cumbria. Travelled from Liverpool in a van. Cutting tools used. Stole £13,850 worth of bikes. Items totalling £2,750 taken. Aged 27-41. Each had a poor record. Planning and targeting of high-value items. Short-lived conspiracy. All 25% credit. For three, **3 years** not 3 years 9 months. For one, **27 months** not 3 years. 10-year ASBOs for all reduced to 5 years.)

346.10   Breach of trust
Note: Theft in breach of trust is specifically included in the **General theft** section of the *Theft Offences Guideline 2016*, www.banksr.com Other matters Guidelines tab, see page 3 and **346.3**. In that section one of the Level A High culpability factors in the guideline is 'Breach of a high degree of trust or responsibility', see page 4 and **346.3**. I do not think the pre-2016 cases can assist, except where there is an uplift because the victim was vulnerable. These are listed. Ed.
See also the *Postmen/Postwomen, Theft by* paras at **346.29**.

346.11   Breach of trust   Victim vulnerable
Examples: *R v Yates* 2013 EWCA Crim 2252 (Four counts. D called on V, in her seventies, offering to do work. The work was done to a poor standard and D took V to ATMs to get paid. D obtained V's bank details and PIN etc. then made **£7,295** of unauthorised transactions. V had lost her life savings. D aged 29. Multiple convictions including fraud, dwelling burglaries and robbery. Had targeted the vulnerable before. D had a long-standing gambling problem but repaid around £550. Held. Starting at **4 years,** with late plea, making 43 months, "not a day too long".)
Old cases: *R v Kinuthia* 2010 EWCA Crim 299 (**15 months**) *R v Daniell* 2010 EWCA Crim 2206 (Plea. Jailor at Lewisham Police Station. Stole **£921.16** from a detained person. Held. This was a despicable offence and **9 months** was fully justified.)
For a summary of the cases, see the 10th edition of this book.

346.12   Cash machines: Lebanese loops etc.   Pre-2016 guideline cases
Note: A Lebanese loop is a device for committing fraud which is inserted into the card slot of an ATM. It retains customers' cards within the ATM, which are later collected by the fraudster. This is sometimes coupled with the installation of a hidden camera so that the fraudster has both customers' cards and their PINs. Ed.

R v Graduiaru 2012 EWCA Crim 1312, 2013 1 Cr App R (S) 50 (p 282) D was convicted of possession of articles for use in fraud. He was arrested operating with a gang who had inserted a Lebanese loop device into an ATM. It was unclear whether D was a 'shoulder surfer' who would obtain PINs, or whether he had inserted the device. The device was basic in that it was designed to retain the cards as opposed to reading or photographing the PIN. The prosecution conceded that this case fell into the lower bracket of the guidelines. Held. There was no evidence that the gang was involved in more extensive fraud, but this was a well-planned and executed operation. **8 months** not 12.

R v Strachinaru 2012 EWCA Crim 1612 D pleaded to fraud (×2) and possessing an article for use in fraud (6 months consecutive). Over a 4-4½-hour period, D and another carried out frauds at various ATMs. They made 11 attempts to withdraw money, with nine of those being successful. They obtained £2,750. They used 'transactional reversal fraud' where the machine is tampered with in order to obtain the money requested in the transaction, but the machine does not register the withdrawal and therefore the account is not debited. D had an MP3 player which contained a video demonstrating how to perform a transactional reversal fraud. The MP3 player had been partially modified in a manner associated with skimming frauds, although there was no evidence that it had been used on the night of these frauds. The MP3 player was seized from D's address, along with £9,000 in cash. The Judge described the outfit as a professional, skilful, criminal enterprise. D, aged 29, had been present in the UK since 2007 and had no convictions or cautions. Held. The nature and seriousness of the offences justify treating these offences as falling into a higher category than the amount stolen would indicate. The correct starting point was 12 months. With the plea, **8 months** making 14 months in all not 22.

R v Munteanu 2012 EWCA Crim 2221, 2013 1 Cr App R (S) 107 (p 555) D pleaded to possession of an article for use in fraud. V tried to use an ATM in High Holborn. She was unable to withdraw any cash and her card was retained by the machine. The machine displayed an 'Out of service' message. Two men had been intending to use the ATM after her. They observed two people approach the machine, remove items from it and then drive away. The police were called and the car was stopped nearby. A 'Lebanese loop' was found. D entered the UK from his native Romania in 2011. He had no regular employment since then and had previous convictions for theft and possession of an article for use in fraud (2011, arising out of the same incident). This was the same offence as the instant offence. D was aged 25. Held. The only aggravation was D's previous convictions. Our starting point is the guidance applicable to possession of 'articles intended for use in an extensive and skilfully planned fraud', which is indeed the appropriate guideline for cases of this character. Cases of this kind inherently fall to be sentenced at the top end of the recommended range, particularly where the item is used. Of its nature it is sophisticated and requires deliberate planning. The Judge was justified in starting far above the recommended range. This was deliberate reoffending with the same co-defendants as his previous convictions. **2 years** was severe but not manifestly excessive.

R v Chandrarajah 2015 EWCA Crim 55 D pleaded (full credit) to conspiracy to defraud bank account holders. ATMs were tampered with by using skimming devices and miniature cameras. Customers' cards would be retained and then shortly afterwards, using the cards and the customers' information, unauthorised withdrawals would be made. The fraud was planned, well-organised and covered a large geographical area. The evidence against D was of him being with the ringleaders when they made fraudulent ATM withdrawals and D's car being filled with fuel paid for with the same stolen card as was used for the withdrawals. The Judge identified D's role as somewhere between the principals and the drivers. D was aged 32 on appeal and had one conviction, for drink/driving. Held. Notwithstanding D's lies, he should have been sentenced on the basis of the evidence, which demonstrated involvement on one day only and at the very outset and as a driver. **16 months**, not 2 years.

See also: *R v Ciomaga* 2012 EWCA Crim 2679, 2013 1 Cr App R (S) 106 (p 553) (Plea to possession of an article for use in fraud. Lebanese loop device. Romanian. Placed device on a cash machine. A number of users had their cards retained. Also in possession of a mobile phone which had been used to record customers inputting their PINs. No convictions in UK. Full credit. **12 months** was not too long.)

See also the **FRAUD** *Articles, Possessing, making or supplying articles for use in fraud Cases* para at **265.15**.

346.13   *Cash machines, Stealing from: Ram-raiding   Pre-2016 guideline cases*

R v Skuce 2010 EWCA Crim 626 D pleaded on rearraignment to conspiracy to steal ATMs. Over 12 months, D and others attacked 24 ATMs in the early hours with car jacks, angle grinders and crowbars. £400,000 was stolen. Bin liners were put over cameras, or they were painted. Faces were concealed by clothing. D was involved in 14 such attacks in which £53,810 was stolen. D had convictions, including six for theft. Held. What stands out was the degree of professionalism. It is unavoidable to take a rough-and-ready approach to role. D played a full and active part. We have not overlooked his family commitments. **5 years** was tough but not manifestly excessive.

R v Burciu 2010 EWCA Crim 875 D pleaded early to theft (full credit). D and X placed a device on an ATM which retained three bank cards. D retrieved the cards and X used two of them to withdraw £530 in cash. £520 was recovered. D, aged 24, had no convictions. The pre-sentence report said D was unemployed, had expressed remorse and posed a low risk of reoffending. The basis of plea was that it was someone else's device and he would have given some of the money to the other man. X wasn't caught. The prison report said D was a good worker and a quiet and compliant prisoner. **4 months** not 8.

R v Igbinovia 2013 EWCA Crim 2562 D was convicted of attempted theft. In the early hours of the morning, a 4×4 was stolen from outside a house. Later, D and another drove it to a petrol station. They were wearing dark clothing and had their hoods pulled up. They took a ratchet rope out of the boot, attached one end to the car and the other to the cash machine, which was in a stand-alone pod on the forecourt. The car was moved forwards but the rope detached. They reattached it and took tools from the car and began hitting the cash machine. The car was moved forward again and this time the cash machine came away. Neighbours were alerted by the noise and called the police. The police arrived and one of the men threw something at the police car. They ran off and climbed over a high wall into a cemetery. A helicopter was deployed and the area was contained. D and his accomplice were arrested. The door of the safe had been torn off, but no cash stolen. Tools, including an angle-grinder, were lying on the floor. The car remained on the forecourt and its ignition was damaged. The maximum amount of cash the machine could hold was £60,000. D's record began in his mid-teens and was characterised by offences of dishonesty, driving offences and occasional violence. In 2007 he was sentenced to 6½ years for a ram-raid on a bank where money being loaded into a cash machine was stolen. The instant offence was committed whilst D was on licence from the 2007 offence. Held. The Judge was right to call D a 'career criminal'. **6 years** was severe but not manifestly excessive.

Old case: *R v Welford* 2009 EWCA Crim 1019 (**4½ years** for W. **2½ years** for B) For a summary of the case, see the 9th edition of this book.

Charging for work that is not necessary or not done see **265.24**.

346.14   *Cheque thefts etc.   Pre-2016 guideline case*

Example: *R v Martin* 2011 EWCA Crim 2418 (Plea (10% credit) to converting criminal property (×4). Paid fraudulently written business cheques totalling £45,000 into her account. Kept £8,800. 'Suspected' the cheques were criminal property. Previous good character. Co-accused had stolen more than £70,000. Starting at **7 months** not 12, **26 weeks** not 46 weeks was appropriate.)

See also the **FRAUD AND FINANCIAL SERVICES OFFENCES** *Identity frauds* paras at **265.37**.

Company frauds see the **FRAUD AND FINANCIAL SERVICES OFFENCES** chapter.

346.15   *Confidence tricks*

Fraud Guideline 2009, see www.banksr.com Other Matters Guidelines tab This lays down the sentencing principles for confidence frauds, see the **FRAUD AND FINANCIAL SERVICES OFFENCES** *Confidence frauds* para at **265.28**.

346.16   *Credit card offences (including credit card fraud)   Pre-2016 guideline cases*

R v Gharib 2011 EWCA Crim 1257 D was convicted of 11 counts of handling stolen goods. Police searched a shop in which seven iPhones and four laptops were found, totalling just in excess of £8,000. The items had been purchased within the previous month via the unauthorised use of credit cards. D claimed he had paid £5,000 for the laptops and denied dealing in stolen goods. D, aged 41 at appeal, had no previous convictions. Held. Far more important than the location of the outlet is the speed at which the goods can be moved on. In D's case that demonstrated a degree of sophistication. The custody threshold was crossed and there is a need for a deterrent element to the sentence. **12 months** was not manifestly excessive.

R v McGrath 2012 EWCA Crim 2018, 2013 1 Cr App R (S) 108 (p 560) D pleaded (full credit) to 14 counts of fraud by false representation. D met H and let him know that he needed somewhere to live. H allowed D to become his lodger. Within a month, D began to make credit card applications to various institutions pretending to be H. Cards were issued and he proceeded to use them to purchase goods and services and to pay off his gambling debts. One purchase was a car worth £3,908. He paid for the insurance with one of the fraudulent cards and named H as the driver of the vehicle. In order to conceal the fraud, he diverted correspondence intended for H, including those relating to genuine bills. H eventually found a bill from a credit card account in his name of which he was completely unaware. H contacted D, who told him that 'people were after him'. He claimed he had acquired debts of £40,000 which he owed to a drug dealer. D also purchased luxury goods and funded stays in hotels. H unknowingly fell into debt of around £1,000. Two finance houses failed to reinstate H's credit rating so he could not obtain credit. He was required to take a loan from members of his family. The total sum expended in D's fraud was almost £22,000. D committed the offences in breach of a suspended sentence imposed for fraud in 2010. He had cashed bogus cheques in a 'sophisticated fraud' involving producing complex documents. He was dealt with for the breach of the suspended sentence at the Magistrates' Court (6 weeks). Held. The aggravating features were the use of H's identity, his previous fraud offences, the breach of the suspended sentence and the loss caused to H. These were mean and utterly selfish offences. The Judge's starting point of 3 years 8 months was not manifestly excessive. **30 months** upheld.

R v Ibraheem 2013 EWCA Crim 527 D pleaded on rearraignment to two frauds. PBC was a company responsible for leasing property throughout the country. They leased a property to BLM, of which D was listed as the sole director. D was due to pay £4,262 to PBC for the rental of the property. He attempted to pay using a credit card but the transactions were unsuccessful. He attended PBC in person and asked that the payment be taken from two credit cards, one of which belonged to his business partner. The transactions were successful but later identified as fraudulent. The cards belonged to two individuals who knew nothing about it. The total sum obtained, but later refunded by the credit card companies, was £4,262.40. D was aged 25 at sentence. He had convictions for credit card fraud (community order, 2008), possessing criminal property and conspiracy to defraud involving credit cards (2 years, 2010), and credit card fraud (4 months consecutive, 2010). Held. The motive was financial gain. D obtained the use of commercial office space to which he was not entitled. The previous convictions were highly relevant. 15% credit for the pleas was appropriate. **15 months** not 2 years.

R v Li 2013 EWCA Crim 2733 D pleaded to three fraud offences and three possessing an article for use in fraud offences. D visited a shop in Oxford Street and purchased three watches using a cloned credit card. He then went on to another shop, where he attempted to purchase £200 worth of vouchers using another cloned card. A loss prevention officer noticed irregularities with the card and detained D. D, aged 35 and originally from Singapore, had been in the UK illegally for ten years and had no proof of identity. He had recent convictions for using cloned credit cards. The pre-sentence report highlighted a drug addiction. Held. This was a serious and well-planned offence with the specific purpose of defrauding retailers. D's situation was aggravated by the number of cards in his possession and his convictions. It was not, however, appropriate to sentence outside the guideline. Starting at 2 years, with full credit, **16 months** not 3 years.

Old case: *R v Militaru and Bujor* 2007 EWCA Crim 2531, 2008 1 Cr App R (S) 108 (p 631) (The appropriate starting point was in the order of **4-5 years**.)

For a summary of the case see the 7th edition of this book.

For large-scale frauds on banks and credit card companies etc. see the FRAUD AND FINANCIAL SERVICES OFFENCES *Identity fraud* para at **265.37**.

Credit facilities, Obtaining see the FRAUD AND FINANCIAL SERVICES OFFENCES *Banking frauds* para at **265.22**.

346.17 *Electricity or gas (including abstracting electricity)* *Statute and statistics*
Theft Act 1968 s 13
Mode of trial Triable either way
Maximum sentence On indictment 5 years. Summary 6 months and/or a £5,000 fine for offences committed before 12 March 2015 and an unlimited fine thereafter.[1205] There are maximum fines for those aged under 18, see **14.38** in Volume 1.
Abstracting of electricity Aged 21+

Year	Plea	Total sentenced	Type of sentencing %						Average length of custody in months
			Discharge	Fine	Community sentence	Suspended sentence	Custody	Other	
2013	G	1	–	–	–	100	–	–	–
	NG	0							
2014	G	38	8	–	16	55	13	8	8.2
	NG	6	–	17	83	–	–	–	–

For explanations about the statistics see page 1-xii. For more statistics see www.banksr.com Other Matters Statistics tab

346.18 *Electricity or Gas* *Sentencing Council Guideline*
The *Theft Offences Guideline 2016* only deals with abstracting electricity. However, where there is no guideline for a particular offence, such as stealing gas, guidelines for similar offences should be considered, see **66.27** in Volume 1.
Theft Offences Guideline 2016, see www.banksr.com Other matters Guidelines tab In force 1 February 2016. The guideline only applies to offenders aged 18+, see page 2 of the guideline. For the usual practice, see **66.21** in Volume 1.

[1205] Legal Aid, Sentencing and Punishment of Offenders Act 2012 s 85(1) and (4) and Legal Aid, Sentencing and Punishment of Offenders Act 2012 (Commencement No 11) Order 2015 2015/504

STEP ONE: Determining the offence category

page 26 The court should determine the offence category with reference only to the factors identified in the following tables. In order to determine the category the court should assess culpability and harm.

The level of culpability is determined by weighing up all the factors of the case to determine the offender's role and the extent to which the offending was planned and the sophistication with which it was carried out.

CULPABILITY demonstrated by one or more of the following:
A – High Culpability
A leading role where offending is part of a group activity Involvement of others through coercion, intimidation or exploitation Sophisticated nature of offence/significant planning Abuse of position of power or trust or responsibility Commission of offence in association with or to further other criminal activity
B – Medium Culpability
A significant role where offending is part of a group activity All other cases where characteristics for categories A or C are not present
C – Lesser Culpability
Performed limited function under direction Involved through coercion, intimidation or exploitation Limited awareness or understanding of offence

Where there are characteristics present which fall under different levels of culpability, the court should balance these characteristics to reach a fair assessment of the offender's culpability.

346.19   *Electricity or Gas   Harm*

page 26 The level of harm is assessed by weighing up all the factors of the case to determine the level of harm caused.

HARM
Greater harm
A significant risk of, or actual injury to persons or damage to property Significant volume of electricity extracted as evidenced by length of time of offending and/or advanced type of illegal process used
Lesser harm
All other cases

346.20   *Electricity or Gas*

STEP TWO: Starting point and category range

page 27 Having determined the category at step one, the court should use the starting point to reach a sentence within the appropriate category range in the table below. The starting point applies to all offenders irrespective of plea or previous convictions.

Culpability			
Harm	**A**	**B**	**C**
Greater	**Starting point** 12 weeks' custody	**Starting point** Medium-level community order	**Starting point** Band C fine
	Category range High-level community order to 1 year's custody	**Category range** Low-level community order to 12 weeks' custody	**Category range** Band B fine to low-level community order
Lesser	**Starting point** High-level community order	**Starting point** Low-level community order	**Starting point** Band A fine
	Category range Medium-level community order to 12 weeks' custody	**Category range** Band C fine to medium-level community order	**Category range** Discharge to Band C fine

346.21   *Electricity or Gas*   [Aggravating and mitigating factors] [Seriousness]

The court should then consider further adjustment for any aggravating or mitigating factors. The table below contains a non-exhaustive list of additional factual elements providing the context of the offence and factors relating to the offender.

Identify whether any combination of these, or other relevant factors, should result in an upward or downward adjustment from the starting point.

Factors increasing seriousness
Statutory aggravating factors: Previous convictions, having regard to: a) the nature of the offence to which the conviction relates and its relevance to the current offence; and b) the time that has elapsed since the conviction Offence committed whilst on bail *Other aggravating factors:* Electricity abstracted from another person's property Attempts to conceal/dispose of evidence Failure to comply with current court orders Offence committed on licence Offences taken into consideration Blame wrongly placed on others Established evidence of community/wider impact
Factors reducing seriousness or reflecting personal mitigation
No previous convictions or no relevant/recent convictions Good character and/or exemplary conduct Serious medical condition requiring urgent, intensive or long-term treatment Age and/or lack of maturity where it affects the responsibility of the offender Mental disorder or learning disability Sole or primary carer for dependent relatives Determination and/or demonstration of steps having been taken to address addiction or offending behaviour

346.22   *Historic or rare articles   Pre-2016 guideline cases*

Theft Offences Guideline 2016, see www.banksr.com Other matters Guidelines tab One of the harm factors in the guideline is 'Damage to heritage assets', see page 5 and **346.4**. *R v Hakimzadeh* 2009 EWCA Crim 959, 2010 1 Cr App R (S) 10 (p 49) D pleaded (full credit) to 14 specimen counts of theft. He asked for 20 TICs to be considered. D stole books and cut maps and illustrations out of books when using the Bodleian and British libraries. He used a scalpel or sharp instrument. The books dealt with cultural contacts between Europe and Persia from the 15th century. It was not known over what period he took the material but it appeared that the thefts came to an end in 2004. He lied when interviewed. One book was sold at auction for £2,000. All the books and pages had been recovered. D was Iranian and had lived in the UK for over 30 years. He had no convictions. D had an international reputation as a scholar and an expert. He was a distinguished collector, and he said that his library was the fourth most significant in the world. A report indicated that he might have some form of acquisitive personality disorder. Held. Cultural property cannot be valued in the same way as cash. The gravamen is the damage to the rare items. A significant element of deterrence is always necessary. There was an element of breach of trust, so those guidelines come into play. We consider that the books were worth well over £20,000 but probably under £145,000. The replacement value was in the region of £100,000-£145,000. Restoration costs would be well over £20,000, but it is the destruction of cultural property that is the gravamen of the offence. The motive was to improve D's library. There was extremely powerful mitigation relating to his family circumstances and his philanthropic and charitable works, which were exceedingly generous. D had offered his library to a university, so that he was not preventing scholars from accessing them in the future. He had suffered a very considerable loss of reputation and humiliation. **2 years** was the starting point, so with the plea and mitigation **12 months** not 2 years.

Note: It would be unwise to assume anyone else is going to be as fortunate as Mr Hakimzadeh was. Ed.

R v Maughan 2012 EWCA Crim 692 D pleaded early to theft. V, a world-famous violinist, was in a Euston station café with her boyfriend. She placed a case containing her Stradivarius violin and two bows at her side. The violin was worth about £1.2m and was insured for £750,000. The bows were worth about £65,000. X distracted the café staff while D and Y sat next to V. D took the case and all three left. Next day all three researched 'Stradivarius' and '1698' at an Internet café. They tried to sell the violin for £100 but the offer was refused. The items were not found. The violin was V's life savings. D had 59 convictions including a great number for theft and kindred offences. He had just been released from prison. D used about 40 aliases. He had never worked and was a drink and drug abuser. The Judge noted that the CCTV evidence was compelling and considered D the promoter and corrupter of the other two younger accomplices. Held. The offence had had a devastating effect on V. **3½ years** not 4½.

Note: A news report says a bus conductor refused the £100 offer as his daughter already had a recorder. The violin was recovered in March 2013 and sold at auction for £1.38m. Ed.

See also: *R v Jacques* 2010 EWCA Crim 3233, 2011 2 Cr App R (S) 39 (p 237) (Convicted of theft and going equipped. Stole 13 books from Royal Horticultural Society library. He returned to the library, and was found with a list of books with their respective values. Conviction for similar theft (4 years). Guidelines provide inadequate basis to sentence. **3½ years** was the minimum appropriate.)

Making off without payment see the **MAKING OFF WITHOUT PAYMENT** chapter.

346.23   Metal thefts   Pre-2016 guideline cases

Note: *Theft Offences Guideline 2016*, see www.banksr.com Other matters Guidelines tab page 5 Two of the harm factors in the guideline are 'High inconvenience caused by victim or others' and 'Consequential financial harm to victim or others', see **346.4**. Ed.

R v Johnson and Pearce 2011 EWCA Crim 2354 J and P pleaded (25% credit) to theft. They were seen wearing high-visibility jackets and loading a metal manhole cover into a trailer, and subsequently driving away. A member of the public informed the police and the men were arrested. The manhole cover, worth £200, was duly returned. The Judge noted the prevalence of the theft of manhole covers in the local area, with 128 covers being stolen in January 2011, at a cost of £25,600. J, aged 39 at appeal, had four convictions for six offences, including one for theft. P, aged 24 at appeal, had nine convictions for 23 offences including theft, criminal damage and assault. The Judge noted that the offences were easy to commit and hard to detect. Held. The Judge was entitled to have regard to the prevalence of the offending in the local area, but J and P would not be sentenced for the theft of any other manhole covers. The offence was premeditated, given the high-visibility clothing. Referring to *R v Mitchell and Kelham* 2011 EWCA Crim 1652, starting at 4 months, not 12, **3 months** was appropriate.

R v Stokes and Stokes 2012 EWCA Crim 612, 2 Cr App R (S) 92 (p 55) para 31 The acquisitive theft of metals from a whole range of sources has reached in some cases epidemic proportions. Those who are tempted to engage in this sort of criminal activity, for what they might consider easy money, can expect significant sentences. For more details of the case see **346.42**.

R v Sargent 2013 EWCA Crim 1382 D pleaded (full credit) to theft of electricity cables. Manhole covers were removed to enable the removal of 100 m or so of thick copper cabling from ducting within the manholes. It was then attached to a 4×4 vehicle and driven away, with the cable being towed behind the vehicle. The police were called and gave chase. D crashed the vehicle and was arrested nearby. The value was £7,500 but the cost of the damage and repairs was more than £20,000. As a result of the theft, more than 400 customers lost their telephone lines and it took engineers three days to rectify the problem. D, aged 25 at appeal, had convictions for robbery, burglary and theft, amongst others. He had been given an 18-month sentence for burglary in 2007. Held. The proper starting point was 3 years 9 months. With full credit, **2½ years** not 3 years 4 months.

R v Paxon 2013 EWCA Crim 2260 D pleaded (early) to theft and destroying property. In the early hours of the morning, D gained access to the secure compound at a Tesco store and removed copper piping. During the theft he cut himself and left blood on one of the units, which led the police to arrest him. D had 27 convictions for 64 offences spanning 2000 to 2013. There were 41 offences of theft from shops, buildings and from the person. There were 20 for failure to comply with court orders. Held. D can properly be described as a prolific offender. The copper piping cost the store a substantial sum of money, including, but not limited to, £7,500 worth of stock. The Judge generously accepted D's mitigation that he did not realise it would cause significant financial loss to Tesco. D sold the piping to fund his class A drug habit. He had a long history of acquisitive crime and the pre-sentence report noted a high risk of reoffending (95% within 24 months). The correct starting point was 18 months. There would be full credit for the plea. For the destroying property count, **12 months** not 16 months. 4 months consecutive for theft would be untouched. **20 months** not 24.

Note: The case is listed here as the enterprise was about stealing the metal. Ed.

R v Predusca and Others 2013 EWCA Crim 2433, 2014 2 Cr App R (S) 17 (p 121) P, B, T and M pleaded (late) to conspiracy to steal. Ma had pleaded earlier. Over a period of three months, there were 14 recorded thefts of copper cable and similar materials. The value of the cable taken was £28,000 and the cost of restoring the cabling was £90,000. On one occasion, a neighbour noted the registration number of a van parked near to where there had been a previous metal theft. He alerted the police. Those carrying out the thefts had shown obvious technical knowledge and ability which included, among other things, the ability to isolate a section of wire before removing it. On one evening, cable was stolen and power cuts resulted. Traffic police were alerted and chased two vehicles on the M6. One was the same vehicle as had been reported by the neighbour on a previous occasion. The other was a car which was stopped. Ma was driving, M was in the front passenger seat and P and B were in the back. The van was chased and was eventually stopped. T got out and ran across the motorway. All told lies about what they were doing. In the car there was a piece of paper containing addresses which corresponded to electric power lines. There was equipment in the car which was used to scale up posts. In the van there was a quantity of copper cable which was identified as being stolen from a particular site. The satnav in the car had postcodes corresponding to past locations of cable thefts programmed into it. After the five were arrested and remanded, some cable thefts continued. This indicated that there were probably more people involved in the conspiracy. P was only involved on one occasion. He was a paid foot soldier. He was Romanian, aged 24 at appeal and of good character. B, T and M were much more heavily involved in the conspiracy. There was extensive telephone contact between M and B. M also made some calls to T. M was of good character. T was aged 20 when arrested. There were 43 calls between him and B. B had previous convictions for theft, albeit not cable theft. Held. For P, starting at or in excess of 4 years was manifestly excessive. Allowing for his plea and good character, **2 years 6 months** not 3 years 4 months. For the others, the direct financial gain was modest and very much less than the cost of repairing and replacing what was stolen. For M, the Judge started in the region of 5 years 2 months. With the plea and a discount for his good character, **4 years 2 months** was an appropriate reflection of his involvement. T was considered mature and reliable enough to be trusted with the entire proceeds of one of the thefts. There was no reason to differentiate between T and M, so **4 years 2 months** upheld. B was the driving force of the conspiracy. There were fingerprints on the documents evidencing the conspiracy, considerable telephone contact and the van was insured by him. The Judge must have started at or even above the statutory maximum 7 years. Even allowing for his previous convictions and his important position in the conspiracy, the appropriate starting point could not be in excess of 6 years. After the plea, **5 years** not 6.

R v Antonala 2014 EWCA Crim 256 D pleaded (a week before trial) to conspiracy to steal and driving whilst disqualified. Over a period of three months there were 14 thefts of copper cable and similar materials. The value of the cable taken was £28,000 and the cost of restoring the cabling was £90,000. After an observant neighbour telephoned the police, D and his co-defendants were chased in a van and a car, driven by D, by police along the M6. D was stopped and arrested. There were others involved besides the four men arrested with D, indicating the size of the conspiracy. D's basis of plea stated that he was only involved in the activities immediately prior to his arrest. He had been contacted the day before and asked if he wanted to earn some money. He drove the vehicle but was not involved in the planning or the sale of the material. He had 17 convictions including two for disqualified driving, two of stealing cabling in 2009 (36 weeks) and theft from a scrapyard in 2010 (16 weeks). D's co-defendants appealed their sentences in *R v Predusca* 2013 EWCA Crim 2433. Held. D's level of involvement was of equal seriousness to that of P in *R v Predusca*. P received 40 months, reduced to 30 months on appeal. The strongly distinguishing feature between D and P was D's bad record. D was a recent recruit to the conspiracy. The Judge must have started at 5 years which, even taking account of his convictions, was too high. The starting point should not have been more than 4 years. The appropriate discount for his late plea was a little less than 20%. **3 years 4 months** for the conspiracy. The 4-month sentence for the driving was unimpeachable and rightly imposed consecutively.

R v Harding and Others 2014 EWCA Crim 538 LCJ H was convicted of conspiracy to steal BT cabling. W, R, M and D pleaded (full credit) to the same count. Nine people were convicted. With an inside man, BT uniforms, BT equipment and a security key, they stole redundant cables from BT. As the cabling was redundant it was not alarmed. However, the team did cut a live wire which disrupted services to London City airport, the Excel Centre and the University of London. This caused chaos. The cost of replacing the cables was estimated at £230,000 although there was no plan to replace it. The Judge described the plan as 'extremely professional' and 'meticulously executed'. Held. **6 years** was the right starting point for those who played a strategic role. For H, who allowed his yard to be used, **4 years** not 5. For R, M and D who were involved with the stealing, with plea, **3 years** not 3 years 8 months or 3½ years. For W, with plea, few previous convictions and having trouble with his work, **2½ years** not 3 years 8 months.

See also: *R v Birch and Others* 2012 EWCA Crim 1000 (Pleas to theft of cabling. Stopped by police and found with equipment for theft, including heavy-duty cable-cutting tools. Operating as a gang. Cable valued at £9,588 found in another van. £3,500 labour costs to replace the cables. Their previous convictions were not treated as an aggravating factor. Starting point of 3¼ years was excessive. **2½ years** for all three upheld.)

R v Parkin 2012 EWCA Crim 2167, 2013 1 Cr App R (S) 118 (p 614) (Convicted. At 4 am victim looked out of bedroom window to find a man kneeling down and removing lead from the flat roof outside. Arrested with another, aged 16. Rucksacks found containing lead. Aged 26. Convictions for 30 offences including handling, robbery and theft. Four previous custodial sentences. Recently gained employment. **12 months** not 18 was appropriate.)

R v Coffey 2012 EWCA Crim 2550, 2013 2 Cr App R (S) 14 (p 60) (LCJ Plea to conspiracy to steal and handling. Metal thefts from [Network Rail]. Principal offender. Teams of between two and six men committed 16 thefts over 12 months. Defendant involved in 12. Made £25,000 from sale of scrap metal. Extensive planning. Breach of trust as several co-conspirators had been employed by [Network Rail]. Burglary committed on bail TIC'd. Deterrent sentences required. Full credit. 3 years 8 months (conspiracy) and 16 months consecutive (handling) making **5 years** was not manifestly excessive.)

R v Boyd-Hiscock 2013 EWCA Crim 833, 2 Cr App R (S) 78 (p 511) (LCJ Plea to theft. Removed 123 brass plaques with a screwdriver from a memorial garden in a crematorium. With an angle grinder, removed the details of the deceased. Sold the plaques for £94.30. Purchasers had paid nearly £70,000 for them. Cost of replacing the plaques was around £3,500.[1206] High sentimental value. Planned. One conviction for criminal damage. Aged 21. Remorseful. Cruel and heartless crime with high degree of harm and distress, and high culpability. **2 years** was severe but not manifestly excessive.)

Old case: *R v Moss and Biddle* 2010 EWCA Crim 1097, 2011 1 Cr App R (S) 31 (p 199) For M, **2 years**. For B, **30 months**.)

For a summary of the case, see the 10th edition of this book.

See also the SCRAP METAL OFFENCES chapter and the RAILWAY *Stealing material which disrupts services* para at **316.5**.

346.24   *Persistent offenders   Pre-2016 guideline cases*

R v Mathews 2014 EWCA Crim 1839 D pleaded (full credit) to theft (×9). He had earlier been committed for theft and attempted theft and also asked for four further thefts to be TIC'd. Eight of nine counts were thefts of charity collection boxes over a period of three years from all across the country. He would distract staff by talking to them and then take the boxes, which were each estimated to contain between £50 and £100, although one Royal British Legion box was stolen around Remembrance Sunday. On one occasion he went prepared by taking and using a knife to cut string attaching a box. The other theft was of a bottle of wine, stolen using the same distraction technique. D was aged 55 at appeal. He was co-operative and made full admissions in interview. The offences he was committed for and the TICs all occurred whilst he was on licence during a 12-month sentence for theft and driving matters. He had an appalling record with 111 offences, mostly for dishonesty, and the Judge considered the guidelines had no direct application due to his criminal past. Held. This was the calculated, cynical and shameless targeting of sums given to good causes and a lengthy prison sentence was called for. However, a starting point of 7½ years was too long. We start at **5 years**, so 24 months, not 32 for the nine thefts, and 16 months consecutive for the two offences committed from the Magistrates' Court, not 18 months, making **3 years 4 months**.

R v Jamal 2015 EWCA Crim 914, 2 Cr App R (S) 46 (p 351) D pleaded to six counts of theft. He took a schoolboy's mobile and made threats to him afterwards. The phone was

---

[1206] These are the figures in the report. Ed.

worth £300. D was arrested and released on bail. Two days later, he went to Hatton
Garden and was given three rings and a chain. He then left the store with them. Just over
a week later, he took another schoolboy's mobile and again made threats. That phone
was worth £300 too. The next day, D approached two people in the street and made one
empty his pockets. D took his iPhone, which was worth between £400 and £500. Two
days later, he committed a very similar theft on the pretext that someone had been
robbed. Both individuals had their phones stolen. The iPhones were worth £300 and
£400. D was aged 33. In 2006, he received 27 months for robbery. In 2012, he received
27 months for robbery and two thefts from persons. He was on licence from that offence.
The pre-sentence report said he only thought of himself and his need to fund his drug
addiction. The Judge noted that there was intimidation and that the victims were
vulnerable. Held. The starting point would have been about 8 years. 5½ years was not
manifestly excessive.
See also: *R v Arthey* 2015 EWCA Crim 965 (D pleaded to theft of a bike and breach of
an ASBO imposed for bike theft. He used bolt cutters to steal a bike placed there by
police so they could see who stole it. In breach of a suspended sentence for burglary. 23
appearances for 56 offences between 2012 and 2014. Many of them for dishonesty. Drug
addict. **18 months** not 3 years, consecutive to the suspended sentence of 10 months.)
See also the ***Persons in public places, Theft from Persistent offenders Cases*** para at
346.28.

346.25   *Person, Theft from the   Guidelines*
For the guideline, see **346.3**.

346.26   *Person, Theft from   Pre-2016 guideline judicial guidance*
R v Gwillim-Jones 2002 1 Cr App R (S) 6 (p 19) A handbag may contain within it credit
cards, diaries, telephone numbers and personal items. The theft of a handbag may cause
both inconvenience and distress to the victim, quite out of proportion to the intrinsic
value of the handbag itself or any cash within it.

346.27   *Persons in public places, Theft from   Pre-2016 guideline cases*
R v Varga 2014 EWCA Crim 703 D pleaded early (although not at the first opportunity)
to theft. D went to a Primark store with his cousin, C, who was eight years older than
him. On an escalator, C removed his baseball cap and placed it over his other hand. He
placed his hand into V's coat pocket, removed a camera and passed it to D. V was
unaware of the theft but the incident was caught on CCTV. Both D and C had previous
convictions for dishonesty but C's were worse. D was in breach of a conditional
discharge. The Judge said the offence was planned, more serious because there were two
of them and cameras often had photographs important to the victims. He started at 12
months and with the plea gave **9 months**. Held. The guideline is not to be read like a
statute. V was not vulnerable as defined by the guideline. The first aggravating factor is
the offence was planned by two people. The second aggravating factor is, if the victim
had resisted, there could have been a very unpleasant confrontation. Appeal dismissed.
R v Gonaciu 2014 EWCA Crim 2051, 2015 1 Cr App R (S) 19 (p 148) D pleaded (full
credit) to two thefts. In October 2012, D and three others followed V1, aged 79, from a
bank onto a bus. D stole her bag which had £700 in it. In December 2013, V2, a nun,
withdrew £500 of convent money from a bank. D and another followed her to a bus stop.
D and V2 got on a bus, and D sat next to her and stole the money. In February 2014, D
was arrested in a betting shop with £200 on him. He said he had just arrived from Milan,
Paris and Amsterdam. D was a Romanian and had served a prison sentence of 26 weeks.
The Judge said D was a member of a professional gang of thieves travelling around
Europe, because he could not speak English and was not in the UK for work or study. He
considered the offences as nastily planned and threateningly executed on vulnerable
victims. Held. These were very serious thefts. They were by a group, planned, and
vulnerable old ladies were targeted. Their distress was obvious. The Judge was wrong to
assume the defendant and other gang members had gone round Europe stealing from

vulnerable members of the public [when there were no foreign convictions admitted or proved]. For each we start at the top of the bracket, so 3 years not 5. With plea 2 years and consecutive, making **4 years** not 6.

R v Racman 2014 EWCA Crim 2133, 2015 1 Cr App R S 18 (p 143) D pleaded to theft, assault and impersonating a police officer. D and two others approached V1, a tourist who was very frail, and engaged him in conversation. A fake police warrant card was produced and the men said they needed to check V1's money. They removed £2,500 in V1's bag and replaced it, unseen by V1, with a £50 note enclosed in high-denomination counterfeit euros. V1 gave chase as the men made off, but they shouted that he should stay put. A near-identical *modus operandi* was used again on two Japanese tourists. This time it was D himself who produced the fake warrant card. The tourists resisted the taking of the money and a scuffle ensued. The male tourist, V2, was pushed to the ground and D ran off. He was pursued by V2 and his wife and was detained by members of the public. D's two accomplices escaped, however. Senior police outlined a worrying trend of such offences in Westminster, which were rife. D was aged 40 on appeal and had a conviction for dishonesty in his native Romania. He used drugs and was in debt and although he offered to pay compensation, he declined to name his accomplices out of fear. D was also unprepared to accept that he had engaged in organised crime. The Judge concluded that there was an important public dimension to the offences. Held. A starting point of 5 years was neither excessive nor disproportionate and the Judge was entitled to pass a deterrent sentence. **3 years and 4 months** upheld.

Old cases: Best ignored.

346.28   *Persons in public places, Theft from   Persistent offenders   Pre-2016 guideline cases*

R v Edgar 2011 EWCA Crim 2438 D pleaded early to theft. He entered a coffee shop, saw a woman's handbag and slid it towards him. He took the bag and left. Police officers witnessed the theft and arrested him. He had on his person the proceeds from two similar thefts committed two days earlier. The offence was committed six days after being released from a custodial sentence. D, aged 44 at appeal, had 43 appearances, mostly for theft from the person. Held. He was a habitual drug user and every effort had been made by the courts to help him tackle his drug problem. D had an appalling record and it is right to depart from the normal range for offences of this kind. However, the sentence must bear a proportionate relationship to the kind of sentence passed for offences of this type. We start at about 4 years so **2 years 8 months** not 4 years.

R v Ali 2013 EWCA Crim 17 D pleaded to theft at the Magistrates' Court. V, who was in his eighties, withdrew £50 from a cash machine and D snatched the cash and ran. V and then police followed and D was caught. He said, "Sorry. I was desperate." D was aged 38 and had 19 previous convictions, many for dishonesty. He showed genuine remorse and had a long-standing drug addiction. Held. There must have been an element of targeting of V, but **12 months** not 18.

R v Wilson 2013 EWCA Crim 33 D pleaded late to theft. D and his mother, M, were on a train. Another passenger, W, saw D lean over and remove a black bag from the handbag of V, aged 72. It contained cash, a railcard, a Metro card, a bus pass, a debit card, car keys and the key to the suitcase she was travelling with. G was shaken by this. She moved and D and M followed her. W reported the theft and D denied following her. The black bag was not found but the keys were found on M. D was aggressive and abusive to the train staff. D had 261 previous convictions on 64 occasions. They were mainly for theft and dishonesty. Some of the offences had a similar *modus operandi* to the train theft. The Judge considered D was a cynical criminal who manipulated the system. He considered the intimidation to staff a serious aggravating factor. Starting at 2 years he gave **21 months**. Held. The Judge was right to consider the offence was aggravated by D's appalling record. We cannot fault the Judge's analysis and conclusions.

R v Nourine 2013 EWCA Crim 73 D pleaded to theft. In August 2012, V was shopping in Primark and D took her iPhone while she was listening to music on it. He moved briskly away and she confronted him, demanding the phone back. When security staff came to assist, D gave the phone back. D was arrested. D was aged 31 with 28 convictions on 18 occasions between 1998 and 2011. They were mostly for theft or attempted theft with generally non-custodial disposals. In May 2011, he received 20 months for theft and in June 2011 he received 12 months for theft. The offending was six thefts from persons. D was on licence having recently been released. Held. This was a Category 3 case. The aggravating factors were the numerous convictions for like offending, his failure to respond to earlier sentences and the commission of the offence when he was on licence. So we move the case to the top of Category 2. With 20% discount for the plea to an overwhelming case, **3 years 6 months**.

R v Allen 2013 EWCA Crim 93 D pleaded at the Magistrates' Court to theft, obstructing a constable and breach of an ASBO. An off-duty police officer, P, saw D very close to V on an escalator at Waterloo station. P saw D had a purse in his hand and approached V, who found her purse was missing. He called D to stop and he ran off. P caught up with D and both lost their balance and cut themselves. P also suffered some mild concussion. D had an ASBO prohibiting him from using main-line stations. When interviewed, D lied. D had 39 previous convictions on 18 occasions. They were mostly for dishonesty but included burglary and ABH. He had served 11 custodial sentences. Eleven months before the offence, D had received 30 months for theft and assault, a like offence. He was on licence for that offence. Held. The offending was worth 18 months (**12 months for the theft**, and 3 months each for the other offences). As he was caught red-handed, a 20% discount giving **15 months** for the theft and the rest concurrent, not 3 years 1 month in total.

Note: This sentence was unlawful because the maximum for obstruction is one month. Ed.

R v Thomas 2013 EWCA Crim 1084, 2 Cr App R (S) 86 (p 546) D pleaded (full credit) to theft. V was in a Mothercare shop with her baby in a pram. She had her purse in a basket under the pram. She then went to a nearby supermarket. When she went to pay for some goods, she discovered that her purse was missing. She returned to Mothercare and reported the incident. CCTV footage was checked and it showed D stealing the purse. A description of D was circulated and an officer spotted her standing at a bus stop. D admitted that she had taken the purse, removed the contents, including £80 cash, gift cards, a National Insurance card and a driving licence. At the police station she was found to be in possession of £104, which she said she had stolen in order to pay for a removal van. D had convictions for 66 theft and related offences. Her first conviction was in 1984. By 1986 she had attracted a custodial sentence. In 1994 she received 12 months for theft (×3). In 2000 there were convictions for theft and going equipped (3 years) and in 2002 for attempted theft (×3) (2 years). In 2004 she received 4 years for wounding and attempted wounding. There were regular appearances in the Magistrates' Court resulting in various non-custodial penalties. The pattern continued. The pre-sentence report noted a 100% negative attitude towards offending and that she failed to acknowledge her criminality. The Judge started at 3 years and reduced that to 2 years for the plea. Held. The question must be asked: what was the Judge to do with a determined thief who is unable or unwilling to take advantage of the previous community penalties, drug treatment orders, suspended sentences and the like imposed, and furthermore, seemingly undeterred by sentences of varying degrees of gravity of imprisonment? The overall criminality cannot simply be assessed by reference to the circumstances of the offence committed. The overall criminality involved necessarily requires consideration of the appalling record of precisely this kind on D's part. It is of some significance that courts have in the past imposed sentences of some years of imprisonment for offences of theft. **2 years** was a severe sentence, but it was deliberately designed to be so. There was no reason to interfere.

R v Mangan 2014 EWCA Crim 2807 D pleaded to two thefts. As V1 left a supermarket, D pointed out a bicycle to her and said someone had left it there. While V1 looked away, D stole her purse, which contained £100. Two days later, at the same supermarket, V2 put her handbag on her trolley. D approached her and asked where the cheap meat was. While V2 was distracted, D stole her purse. It contained £80 and her pension card. Neither victim wanted to make an impact statement as they did not want to go over it all again. D had 84 convictions, 37 of which were theft or 'kindred' offences. Many were distraction offences. In 2012, for five fraud offences and theft from a person, he received 45 months. He was on licence for that offence. He used 37 aliases. D had a problem with crack and heroin. The Judge said D was a cunning, skilful thief who deliberately targeted elderly and vulnerable victims. Held. He continued to commit offences on vulnerable elderly persons. The victims were trusting and public-spirited elderly ladies. We do not underestimate the impact these offences had on elderly persons. D was prepared to use violence when it suited him. We start at 18 months and 12 months. With the victim impact, the record [and] the commission of the offences on licence we move to 5 years. With totality we arrive at 4 years 4 months. With a 25% plea discount, **3 years 3 months**.

Note: It appears the Court (a High Court Judge and the Crown Court Judge) paid too much attention to the guideline (which is only a launchpad for sentencing) and failed to give an adequate uplift for the exceptionally important cumulative aggravating factors. Ed.

See also: *R v Noel* 2013 EWCA Crim 1107 (Pleas to two thefts. Theft and breach of an ASBO TIC'd. Thefts committed on the London Underground. Acted with another. Multiple breaches of ASBOs in 2004, 2005, 2008 and 2009. Serial pickpocket. Aged 46. 44 convictions for 91 offences, the vast majority of which were for pickpocketing. Previous sentences had not deterred him. **3 years**, which meant a starting point of 4½ years, was not arguably manifestly excessive for the thefts and TICs.)

Old case: *R v Lewis* 2010 EWCA Crim 1909 (**16 weeks suspended**)

For a summary of the case, see the 10th edition of this book.

See also the ***Persistent offenders*** para at **346.24**.

346.29   *Postmen/Postwomen, Thefts by*   Statistics   Crown Court
Theft or unauthorised taking from mail Aged 21+

Year	Plea	Total sentenced	Type of sentencing %						Average length of custody in months
			Discharge	Fine	Community sentence	Suspended sentence	Custody	Other	
2013	G	41	2.4	–	9.8	31.7	56.1	–	15.1
	NG	11	–	–	45.5	9.1	45.5	–	30.1
2014	G	46	2	4	4	37	50	2	11.9
	NG	0							

For explanations about the statistics see page 1-xii. For more statistics and for statistics for male and female defendants etc. see www.banksr.com Other Matters Statistics tab

346.30   *Postmen/Postwomen, Thefts by*   Pre-2016 guideline   Judicial guidance
R v Murray 2008 EWCA Crim 2771, 2009 2 Cr App R (S) 14 (p 81) D pleaded to a conspiracy to steal parcels. Held. There is a distinction between theft by a postman and a theft by an employee. The latter only damage their employer. Thefts by postmen cause alarm, disappointment and perhaps distress among members of the public who expect to receive registered letters and parcels. The gravity of the offending goes beyond those simple factors set out in [the then guidance case].

346.31   *Postmen/Postwomen, Thefts by   Pre-2016 guideline cases*
R v Kerling 2011 EWCA Crim 182 D pleaded to theft (×2) and intentionally delaying a postal packet. He began working as a postman in 2006 and after a month or so started to steal mail, the driving force for which was a gambling addiction. Royal Mail investigators became suspicious and put test packages into his post. He stole four out of five. When his house was visited, the following were found: 8,000 pieces of door-to-door mail, six rental DVDs (rightly pointed out to be nothing to do with raising money for a gambling debt), and 587 postal packages. It was estimated that this represented about half of D's theft. He admitted the thefts in interview. D, aged 35, had one previous conviction for theft (shoplifting) committed 12 months prior to his employment as a postman. Held. The Judge rightly stated that the gambling addiction provided little mitigation. D had been stealing postal packages for nearly four years. This case is not simply a case of theft with a gross breach of trust. D received a concurrent sentence for the 8,000 pieces of door-to-door mail. However, this could have represented a separate offence. It should not therefore be thought that the guidelines for simple theft can be applied to this type of case. **16 months** not 2 years.
R v Wogui 2013 EWCA Crim 1483 D, a postman, pleaded to theft. Over a two-week period, he was involved in the theft of around 30 mobile phones which had been ordered under false names and delivered to incorrect addresses on his delivery round. His role was to intercept the packages and pass them to a third party. After the offending came to light, D was kept under surveillance. Phones4U sent two special delivery items. The tracking system showed that on receipt one of the items had been signed for but not at the address to which it should have been delivered. The other package had had the tracking system switched off so it was impossible to tell where it had been signed for. Enquiries at the address to which it was sent showed that it had not been delivered to, or ordered by, anyone at that address. He was seen to go to some bins and then, when back at the delivery office, D appeared to place something in his locker. Police found a mobile phone in his locker and £1,200 in cash on his person. Two mobile phones and a mobile phone box were found at his address. D stated in interview that he was paid £50 per mobile phone. Held. There was a high degree of breach of trust. Starting at 2 years was correct. The sentence of **16 months** may be arguably at the top of the range, but was certainly not manifestly excessive.
Old cases: Best ignored.
Railway, bus etc. fare evasion see the Railway Offences *Fare evasion* paras at **316.3**.
Railway track thefts see the Railway Offences *Stealing material which disrupts services* para at **316.5**.

346.32   *Servicemen and women*
Guidance on Sentencing in the Court Martial 2013 para 5.4. A higher sentence is justified where the offence is potentially corrosive of Service discipline, for example theft from fellow Service personnel…
Guidance on Sentencing in the Court Martial 2013 para 5.8.1 Dishonesty is not consistent with service in the Armed Forces because it is corrosive to unit cohesiveness and morale.
para 5.8.2 deals with theft from employer or theft in breach of trust.
para 5.8.3 deals with Barrack Room theft or Messdeck theft.
Guidance on Sentencing in the Court Martial 2013 para 5.9.1 to 5.9.4 sets out the service policy, the aggravating and mitigating factors, and the suggested penalties.
Note: The details are omitted to save space. Ed.

346.33   *Shop and stall thefts   Crown Court statistics   England and Wales*
Shop and stall thefts

Year	Age	Sex	Plea	Total sentenced	Type of sentencing %						Average length of custody in months
					Discharge	Fine	Community sentence	Suspended sentence	Custody	Other	
2013	18-20	Male	G	99	7.1	3	23.2	15.2	43.4	8.1	4.3
			NG	4	–	–	25	–	75	–	6.5
		Female	G	15	13.3	–	40	6.7	40	–	2.9
			NG	0							
	21+	Male	G	1,156	2.7	3.3	18.8	13.8	58.4	3.1	5.1
			NG	23	8.7	30.4	21.7	13	26.1	–	4.8
		Female	G	326	4.6	4	28.5	17.2	42.3	3.4	4.4
			NG	16	12.5	25	31.3	18.8	12.5	–	3
2014	18-20	Male	G	58	5	2	24	14	55	–	2.6
			NG	0							
		Female	G	13	8	–	23	15	38	15	5.2
			NG	0							
	21+	Male	G	687	4	2	18	15	58	3	5.4
			NG	38	13	26	18	11	32	–	24.2
		Female	G	202	9	1	28	18	42	1	4.5
			NG	15	–	33	33	20	13	–	not listed

For explanations about the statistics see page 1-xii. For more statistics for male and female defendants, theft from a dwelling, theft of mail, theft of pedal cycles, theft from vehicles and theft from automatic machines, see www.banksr.com Other Matters Statistics tab

346.34   *Shop and stall thefts   Statutes*
Anti-social Behaviour, Crime and Policing Act 2014 s 176 makes low-value shoplifting initially a summary only offence. In force from 13 May 2014.[1207]
Theft Act 1968 s 1 (low-value shoplifting when goods value £200 or less)
  Mode of trial Summary only with the ability of those over 18 to elect for trial[1208]
  Maximum sentence Indictment 7 years.[1209] Summary 6 months and/or a £5,000 fine for offences committed before 12 March 2015 and an unlimited fine thereafter.[1210]
  There are maximum fines for those aged under 18, see **14.38** in Volume 1.
Note: Criminal Justice and Courts Act 2015 s 52 amends the method of sending cases to the Crown Court by requiring them to be sent by Crime and Disorder Act 1998 s 51(1). In force 12 April 2015, Criminal Justice and Courts Act 2015 95(2). Ed.

346.35   *Shop and stall theft   Sentencing Council Guideline*
Theft Offences Guideline 2016, see www.banksr.com Other matters Guidelines tab In force 1 February 2016. The guideline only applies to offenders aged 18+, see page 2 of the guideline. For the usual practice, see **66.21** in Volume 1.

[1207] Anti-social Behaviour, Crime and Policing Act 2014 (Commencement No 2, Transitional and Transitory Provisions) Order 2014 2014/949 Sch 1 para 17
[1208] Theft Act 1968 s 22A(2)
[1209] The new section 22 does not refer to the penalty for trial at the Crown Court. As the offence remains a section 1 offence, it can be assumed the maximum sentence is the section 1 maximum.
[1210] Legal Aid, Sentencing and Punishment of Offenders Act 2012 s 85(1) and (4) and Legal Aid, Sentencing and Punishment of Offenders Act 2012 (Commencement No 11) Order 2015 2015/504

STEP ONE: Determining the offence category

page 10 The court should determine the offence category with reference only to the factors identified in the following tables. In order to determine the category the court should assess culpability and harm.

The level of culpability is determined by weighing up all the factors of the case to determine the offender's role and the extent to which the offending was planned and the sophistication with which it was carried out.

CULPABILITY demonstrated by one or more of the following:
A – High Culpability
A leading role where offending is part of a group activity Involvement of others through coercion, intimidation or exploitation Sophisticated nature of offence/significant planning Significant use or threat of force Offender subject to a banning order from the relevant store Child accompanying offender is actively used to facilitate the offence (not merely present when offence is committed)
B – Medium Culpability
A significant role where offending is part of a group activity Some degree of planning involved Limited use or threat of force All other cases where characteristics for categories A or C are not present
C – Lesser Culpability
Performed limited function under direction Involved through coercion, intimidation or exploitation Little or no planning Mental disorder/learning disability where linked to commission of the offence

Where there are characteristics present which fall under different levels of culpability, the court should balance these characteristics to reach a fair assessment of the offender's culpability.

346.36   Shop and stall theft   Harm

page 11 Harm is assessed by reference to the financial loss that results from the theft and any significant additional harm suffered by the victim – examples of significant additional harm may include, but are not limited to:

Emotional distress
Damage to property
Effect on business
A greater impact on the victim due to the size or type of their business
A particularly vulnerable victim

Intended loss should be used where actual loss has been prevented.

Category 1	High-value goods stolen (above £1,000) **or** Medium-value [goods stolen (£200 to £1,000)] with significant additional harm to the victim
Category 2	Medium-value goods stolen (£200 to £1,000) **and** no significant additional harm **or** Low-value [goods stolen (up to £200)] with significant additional harm to the victim
Category 3	Low-value goods stolen (up to £200) **and** Little or no significant additional harm to the victim

346.37   Shop and stall theft

STEP TWO: Starting point and category range
page 12 Having determined the category at step one, the court should use the starting point to reach a sentence within the appropriate category range in the table below.
The starting point applies to all offenders irrespective of plea or previous convictions.

Culpability			
Harm	**A**	**B**	**C**
Category 1 Where the value greatly exceeds £1,000 it may be appropriate to move outside the identified range. Adjustment should be made for any significant additional harm where high-value goods are stolen.	Starting point 26 weeks' custody	Starting point Medium-level community order	Starting point Band C fine
	Category range 12 weeks' to 3 years' custody	Category range Low-level community order to 26 weeks' custody	Category range Band B fine to low-level community order
Category 2	Starting point 12 weeks' custody	Starting point Low-level community order	Starting point Band B fine
	Category range High-level community order to 26 weeks' custody	Category range Band C fine to medium-level community order	Category range Band A fine to Band C fine
Category 3	Starting point High-level community order	Starting point Band C fine	Starting point Band A fine
	Category range Low-level community order to 12 weeks' custody	Category range Band B fine to low-level community order	Category range Discharge to Band B fine

Consecutive sentences for multiple offences may be appropriate, [see the *TICs and Totality Guideline 2012: Crown Court*].
Previous diversionary work with an offender does not preclude the court from considering this type of sentencing option again if appropriate.
Where the offender is dependent on or has a propensity to misuse drugs or alcohol and there is sufficient prospect of success, a community order with a drug rehabilitation requirement under [Criminal Justice Act 2003 s 209], or an alcohol treatment requirement under [Criminal Justice Act 2003 s 212] may be a proper alternative to a short or moderate[-length] custodial sentence.
Where the offender suffers from a medical condition that is susceptible to treatment but does not warrant detention under a hospital order, a community order with a mental health treatment requirement under [Criminal Justice Act 2003 s 207] may be a proper alternative to a short or moderate[-length] custodial sentence.

**346.38   Shop and stall theft   [Aggravating and mitigating factors]
[Seriousness]**
page 13 The court should then consider further adjustment for any aggravating or mitigating factors. The following is a non-exhaustive list of additional factual elements

providing the context of the offence and factors relating to the offender. Identify whether any combination of these, or other relevant factors, should result in an upward or downward adjustment from the sentence arrived at so far.

Factors increasing seriousness
Statutory aggravating factors: Previous convictions, having regard to: a) the **nature** of the offence to which the conviction relates and its **relevance** to the current offence; and b) the **time** that has elapsed since the conviction Relevant recent convictions **may** justify an upward adjustment, including outside the category range. In cases involving significant persistent offending, the community and custodial thresholds may be crossed even though the offence otherwise warrants a lesser sentence. Any custodial sentence must be kept to the necessary minimum Offence committed whilst on bail Offence motivated by, or demonstrating hostility based on any of the following characteristics or presumed characteristics of the victim: religion, race, disability, sexual orientation or transgender identity ***Other aggravating factors:*** Stealing goods to order Steps taken to prevent the victim reporting or obtaining assistance and/or from assisting or supporting the prosecution Attempts to conceal/dispose of evidence Offender motivated by intention to cause harm or out of revenge Failure to comply with current court orders Offence committed on licence Offences taken into consideration Established evidence of community/wider impact (for issues other than prevalence) Prevalence – see below

Factors reducing seriousness or reflecting personal mitigation
No previous convictions or no relevant/recent convictions Remorse, particularly where evidenced by voluntary reparation to the victim Good character and/or exemplary conduct Serious medical condition requiring urgent, intensive or long-term treatment Age and/or lack of maturity where it affects the responsibility of the offender Mental disorder or learning disability (where not linked to the commission of the offence) Sole or primary carer for dependent relatives Determination and/or demonstration of steps having been taken to address addiction or offending behaviour Offender experiencing exceptional financial hardship

Prevalence

There may be exceptional local circumstances that arise which may lead a court to decide that prevalence should influence sentencing levels. The pivotal issue in such cases will be the harm caused to the community.

It is essential that the court before taking account of prevalence:

has supporting evidence from an external source, for example, Community Impact Statements, to justify claims that a particular crime is prevalent in their area, **and** is causing particular harm in that community, **and**

is satisfied that there is a compelling need to treat the offence more seriously than elsewhere.

346.39   *Shop theft   Organised groups*

Note: *Theft Offences Guideline 2016*, see www.banksr.com Other matters Guidelines tab page 4 As step one culpability determines the category by the type of 'group activity', see **346.3**, I do not think the pre-2016 cases can assist. Ed.

346.40   *Shop theft   Single thief   Pre-2016 guideline cases*

R v Jackson 2010 EWCA Crim 1396 D pleaded at the first opportunity to theft. D went into a jewellery shop and asked to see a bracelet with a retail value of £10,000 and some rings. When shown the bracelet, D offered £8,000 and his own watch in payment, which was accepted. D said he would come back with some cash and pay the balance with a Visa card. D returned later and offered two sealed envelopes which appeared to be full of money. D grabbed the bracelet and escaped from the shop. The bracelet was 18 carat gold with 5.6 carats of diamonds with a replacement value of £7,500 and was never recovered. The envelope contained pieces of paper. In interview D made admissions. D had been released on licence one month before this offence following convictions for robbery and theft from jewellery shops (2 years), and had 59 convictions for 146 offences including three robberies, attempted robbery, theft from the person, threatening behaviour, affray and possessing an offensive weapon. **2 years** not 3½.

R v Webb 2013 EWCA Crim 2213 D pleaded (late) to theft. He bought a second-hand BlackBerry phone from a shop for £100. There were problems with the phone and D returned it asking for a refund. The shop manager said the problems were with the software not the hardware and refused to refund the purchase. D was annoyed and picked up a laptop (worth £350) that was sitting on top of a cabinet in the shop and ran out. He was chased by the shop manager and stopped by two police officers shortly after. The Judge treated the offence as more akin to theft from the person. D had no convictions. Held. This was not a case which deserved a custodial sentence, even one that was suspended. **Community order with 150 hours' unpaid work**, not 12 weeks suspended with 100 hours' unpaid work.

Solicitors see the **Solicitors** *Theft etc.* para at **336.3**.

346.41   *Shop and stall theft   Persistent offenders   Pre-2016 guideline cases*

R v Argyelan 2013 EWCA Crim 1266 D pleaded to breach of a community order and failure to surrender (no penalty). In November 2012, he was given a 6-month community order for theft (total value £4). In December 2012, he stole cosmetics valued at £198 from Boots and seven packets of cheese from Tesco valued at £15.75. He was sentenced for theft and the court gave D the opportunity to comply with his community order. Probation tried to contact D but he had lost his temporary housing. In March 2013, D failed to maintain contact with probation and failed to surrender. He was brought to court and sentenced for his breach, failing to surrender and re-sentenced for the December and November thefts. D had 22 convictions for 37 offences, the majority of which were for theft and kindred offences. D had a history of substance abuse from the age of 14. D was homeless and without welfare support. The Judge revoked the community order. Held. The previous convictions and the failure to respond to previous sentences meant that the custody threshold was passed. His previous convictions took him outside of the guideline. The Court was impressed with the three-month period after the December matter during which D did not reoffend. 30 weeks concurrent on the thefts, with 4 weeks consecutive for the breach of the community order. **34 weeks** not 12 months (10 months for theft with 2 months consecutive).

R v Raisis 2014 EWCA Crim 1887, 2015 1 Cr App R (S) 26 (p 194) D pleaded (full credit) to two thefts from jewellers' shops. D also breached a suspended sentence, which was activated concurrently. D asked to look closely at a ring worth £11,500 and then ran off with it. He then, with an accomplice, stole five rings and a chain, though he later handed the chain back. D had a very poor record, including violence offences and five dishonesty offences, but this was an escalation in offending. He was a drug user and assessed at high risk of reconviction, albeit that he had managed to break his habit. Held. The fact that D's offences were motivated by drug addiction is not a reason for reducing a sentence. **3 years** concurrent, not 3 years and 18 months consecutive.

R v Futcher 2015 EWCA Crim 243 D pleaded (full credit) to theft (×3), attempted theft and fraud (×8) with 13 more frauds TIC'd. D took a body warmer from a shop and then, appearing upset and crying, pretended to staff that she had bought the item as a gift for her father, who had since died. Consequently, she could not produce a receipt so they gave her £40 worth of store vouchers. In interview, D admitted theft, saying that she needed money for rent arrears. A week later, and on bail, D took items worth £47 and, having cut the tags off, simply walked out of the shop. Four days later, she returned but was arrested. A corkscrew and secateurs were found in D's bag and clothes with their tags removed were found in the shop's changing rooms. Seven weeks later, also on bail, D stole a £70 baby monitor. During D's theft spree, she also knocked on the doors of at least eight houses and told false heart-rending stories to get people to give her cash but there were only one or two victims and they parted with very little cash. D, aged 34 on appeal, was a persistent, prolific offender and was well known in the area. She had 145 dishonesty convictions since 1998 and breached a recent community order. Her offending was linked to an entrenched drug addiction and there were concerns about her mental health as she had emotionally unstable personality disorder and self-harmed. Held. A significant sentence of imprisonment was appropriate but regard had to be had to totality. **18 months**, not 28.

R v Megia-Grande 2015 EWCA Crim 1205 D pleaded to two thefts. He went into John Lewis and put fragrances worth £460 into an empty John Lewis bag and tried to leave the shop. He held the bag above his head to try to avoid the detectors. He was stopped and he lied. He was bailed and five months later went to Waitrose and took items of clothing into a fitting room. He concealed the clothing about his person and equipped himself with an empty Waitrose bag. He then stole some food. The total value of the Waitrose goods was £250. When he was arrested he lied. He was bailed. About three weeks later D pleaded to both matters and was bailed. Two days later he shoplifted some clothing and footwear (worth over £100) and he had with him a de-tagging device. He was given a community sentence the next day. D was aged 22 and had no previous convictions. Held. There was a significant element of deliberation and planning. The third matter could not aggravate the earlier conduct, but the Judge could have it in mind. We start at 3 months, so with plea **2 months** not 6.

Street crime see the *Persons, Theft from* paras at **346.25**.

346.42 *Vehicles, Stealing (including parts and handling) etc.* *Pre-2016 guideline cases*

Note: Theft from a motor vehicle and theft of a motor vehicle are specifically included in the **General theft** section of the *Theft Offences Guideline 2016*, www.banksr.com Other matters Guidelines tab, see page 3 and **346.3**. Ed.

R v Evans 1996 1 Cr App R (S) 104 The Judge said, "Car crime is rampant and police resources are so limited they can only deal with a small proportion of the car crimes reported. The public are sick to death of having to subsidise the activities of people like you by ever-increasing insurance premiums and having to suffer the heartache of the loss of an expensive piece of property and large sums of money which they hardly ever get back." Held. We agree. For a ringleader after a trial **4 to 5 years** would not be excessive, even when the defendant is of good character. For a lieutenant after a trial, **3 years** notwithstanding good character.

Note: This is an old case. I'm sure the anger against car thieves is as high as ever. The more recent cases in this section indicate that the penalties now are similar to those in 1996. Ed.

R v Stokes and Stokes 2012 EWCA Crim 612, 2 Cr App R (S) 92 (p 55) P and W pleaded (25% credit) to conspiracy to steal. They engaged in a protracted spree of stealing catalytic converters from parked cars. They were stopped and searched by police after approximately 1 month, but continued their efforts thereafter after not being charged. They would drive around in a car with cloned registration plates, searching for suitable targets. Their targets were usually cars unattended in car parks. They would use hydraulic cutters to cut the exhaust pipe either side of the converters. The converters contained precious metals. In 4½ months, P and W stole 348 converters. They sold them to a company dealing in the recycling of catalytic converters. Their invoices showed that the company had paid P and W £55,000, at an average price of £150 each. There was £4,000 outstanding. The effect of having the converter stolen is that the car cannot be driven for very long and the exhaust needs repair. 27 victims were traced and the damage to their vehicles was assessed at £26,000. W, aged 27 at appeal, had two convictions involving vehicles. P, aged 34 at appeal, had learning difficulties. Both were treated as being of good character. Held. Starting at **3 years** was justified. This was a systematic campaign lasting 4½ months, targeting cars at a rate of 17-18 per week. It involved planning, equipment and false plates. It was also indiscriminate, for example they targeted a car parked at a hospital and other people's vehicles involved in public duties. It was striking that P and W continued in their efforts despite being stopped by police. P and W yielded significant sums (over £50,000) but if one takes into account the cost of the repairs, the increased insurance premium and the cost to their insurance companies, the figure runs into several hundred thousand pounds. 25% credit was generous. W was fortunate to be treated as of good character but there was no disparity to be found between W and P. The sentences of **3 years** cannot be faulted.

R v Fiddimore 2013 EWCA Crim 762 D pleaded (20% credit) to conspiracy to convert criminal property and converting criminal property. The conspiracy concerned high-value cars stolen where, largely, the keys were obtained in burglaries. Within a short period of time, the vehicles were dismantled and attempts were made to conceal their origin. The parts were then sold for profit. The conspiracy embraced a 16-17 month period and involved 37 vehicles with a value of over £700,000. The parts were mainly sold through an eBay account with the money received (in excess of £120,000) ending up in a Lloyds TSB bank account. D's basis of plea accepted that his part in the conspiracy amounted to disposing of the car parts and that resulted in him being involved in about £60,000 of the overall figure. D, aged 33 at appeal, had five convictions for 18 offences including 11 for handling, two for TDA and two for theft of a vehicle. In 2001 he had been sentenced for offences of a similar nature (3 years). Three years earlier, he had received 2 years' detention for similar offences. Held. D played an important role. A six-month reduction was appropriate, so 3½ years not 4. 6 months for the converting criminal property would remain, but it was an integral part of the conspiracy so concurrent sentences were appropriate. **3½ years** not 4½ years.

R v Khan and Others 2013 EWCA Crim 1003 K was convicted of conspiracy to handle stolen goods. MM and TM pleaded to conspiracy to handle and conspiracy to defraud. Burglaries to steal keys to high-value cars were committed. K arranged for the cars to be passed on to TM and MM whereupon they fitted new number plates and created false documents to support the identities of the vehicles. Some vehicles were exported to Japan and sold. This occurred over about 12 months. TM and MM were also responsible for altering the odometers on legitimately obtained cars. That occurred over about 16 months. The police identified 18 stolen vehicles with a combined value of £419,380, 16 of which were stolen during dwelling burglaries, committed at night and invariably while the properties were occupied. Eight of the vehicles were dispatched to Japan. In relation to the odometer offences, 21 vehicles were identified as being advertised with lower mileage than was the case. They were sold on eBay or other websites. Sixteen of the vehicles were sold for a total of £90,741. The profit was about £27,000. TM had brought MM, his younger brother, into the criminal enterprise. TM offered to give evidence for the prosecution. That wasn't accepted. MM was aged 23 at the time of the offence and 27 at appeal. All three defendants were well educated and showed promise. Held. All three knew how to set up companies and had knowledge of company law. This conspiracy involved a large number of cars, many of high value, stolen at night during dwelling-house burglaries. The system used was a highly developed one. They used their contacts in the transportation business and in Japan. All the equipment for forging the documents and creating false number plates was there. This was a sophisticated conspiracy. For K, **9 years** was at the top of the range but was not manifestly excessive. For TM, **6½ years** (for the handling) and a consecutive sentence of 14 months (the fraud) would not be reduced. For MM, the same considerations apply. The starting point was appropriate, as was the differentiation between MM and TM. For MM, **4 years** with 9 months consecutive would not be reduced.

See also: *R v Whittingham and Others* 2010 EWCA Crim 2890 (Pleas to conspiracy to steal (×2). Group of no fewer than 12 men stealing lorries and their loads. 28 attacks over 9 months. In excess of £1m stolen. Violence used on occasion. Starting point was **7 years**, so organiser with full plea discount 4 years 8 months. For lieutenant starting at **6 years 3 months** (one-third discount), 4 years 2 months. For quartermaster starting at **6 years** (10% discount), 5 years 5 months. Rest start at **5 years 3 months** (one-third discount), 3 years 6 months.)

R v Disbrey 2011 EWCA Crim 628 (Pleas to four counts of handling. Found with the keys to two stolen cars and stolen number plates. Shocking record for dishonesty including three burglaries and four handlings. **2 years**, not 3 consecutive to 1 year for aggravated vehicle-taking.)

R v Gordon 2013 EWCA Crim 1594 (Plea to conspiracy to handle stolen goods. Seven high-value vehicles found at a garage, stolen during burglaries. Value approaching if not over six figures. D had worked there in the evenings for two weeks and knew the vehicles were stolen but did not know how. He received a little extra cash for his work but was not involved in the organisation. Sentenced two years after arrest and one year after plea. Delays not his fault. In breach of a suspended sentence for theft of a vehicle. **20 months** in total was correct, not 24, with the 4-month activated suspended sentence concurrent not consecutive.)

Old cases: Best ignored.

346.43   *Vehicles   Stealing from them   Pre-2016 guideline cases*

R v Foulger and Others 2012 EWCA Crim 1516 Ba and Bu were convicted of conspiracy to steal. A container load of cigarettes worth between £750,000 and £900,000 on the black market was stolen. Over £1m in duty would have been payable on the cigarettes. F was employed by a firm sub-contracted to collect the cigarettes from a warehouse. F passed on the details to Bu and Ba, including codes needed to secure the release of the container. Arrangements had been made for a bogus lorry to collect the cigarettes, and for the legitimate lorry to attend afterwards. Neither the lorry nor the cigarettes were recovered. Ba was the organiser, F was the inside man and Bu was the right-hand man, responsible for recruiting another to drive the lorry. Ba, aged 31, had 11 convictions for 33 offences between 1998 and 2009. These included theft of a lorry containing goods worth £30,000 (2001) and of a lorry with a load worth £84,000 (2004). He also had an offence of handling 8 million cigarettes (2009). Bu, aged 52, had an appearance for stealing a fully loaded lorry with Ba in 2002 (15 months). F did not appeal his sentence. Held. The offence was planned, deliberately targeted the warehouse, featured a high level of gain and high-value property and featured a breach of trust in relation to F. Ba was a professional criminal who has taken little or no notice of previous sentences for similar offences. **7 years** would not be altered. For Bu, as he had an important but limited role, a comparative lack of convictions and had partial responsibility for his daughter, **4½ years** not 5.

R v McDonagh and Lawrence 2014 EWCA Crim 478 M and L pleaded to theft. One night, they went out in a car looking for parked lorries from which to steal diesel. For that purpose they had in their car 13 25-litre containers, gloves and two screwdrivers. They went to a lorry park and were seen acting suspiciously. They then went to a layby where four lorries were parked. They forced open the fuel cap on one of the lorries whose driver was asleep and stole diesel worth £150-180. At about 11.50 pm, a police car saw their car and stopped them. M and L ran off and the police gave chase. A police helicopter was summoned and M and L were arrested about a mile away. M claimed they had been having a picnic. M had no convictions. He assisted his mother with the care of his brothers and sisters. L had a caution for making off without payment and theft from a vehicle. He also had a conviction for fraud (2013). The pre-sentence report noted that he did not accept responsibility for the offence. The Judge imposed deterrent sentences on the basis that the offence was prevalent in that area. Held. The Judge was entitled to consider that the case against M and L was overwhelming and reduced their plea credit accordingly, presumably to 20%. There were a number of aggravating features including that the offence was planned, it was committed at night and there were two offenders. The lorry driver was vulnerable because he was asleep and was deliberately targeted. On the other hand, the value of the diesel stolen was relatively modest and both defendants were young and neither had previously been to custody. Whilst there was an element of being on the cusp in this case, the Judge was entitled to impose a custodial sentence. For M, **2 months' YOI** not 8 and for L, **3 months' YOI** not 10.

R v Buttler 2015 EWCA Crim 1028 D pleaded (full credit) to 23 thefts and an attempted theft. He asked for 14 TICs to be considered. Nine of the counts were committed when D was on bail for the others and in breach of a bail term. D was a persistent thief of property in cars parked in secluded spots. He would smash the rear window and steal what he could. They included mobiles, computers, shoes and some items of sentimental value like jewellery. D was aged 40 with eight children and said he wanted to pay off his debts. He had 48 previous convictions for theft or dishonesty offences. The defence said the starting point the Judge must have had was nearly 7 years. Held. Keeping the sentences in proportion, 21 months for each set of counts consecutive making **42 months** in all.

See also: *R v Rodriguez and Mitchell* 2015 EWCA Crim 1284 (R and M pleaded to vehicle conspiracy. M also pleaded to theft (£550). R admitted 11 occasions, H nine. R had 42 previous convictions, which included many for theft from vehicles (including a 3-year sentence). For R, the Judge started at 6½ years, making with plea 4½ years. For M, 3 years and 1 year consecutive. Sentences near the top end of the range but not manifestly excessive.)

Victim believes plan is dishonest but is tricked as to who the victim is see the FRAUD AND FINANCIAL SERVICES OFFENCES *Confidence frauds* para at **265.28**.

346.44   *Victim over 65   Pre-2016 guideline cases*
R v O'Farrell 2014 EWCA Crim 170 D pleaded to two thefts. The offences were committed over a three-year period beginning in 2007 but did not come to light until D had been sentenced for fraud offences committed between 2008 and 2010 (6 years 8 months). His methodology for the 2008-2010 offences was to befriend vulnerable adults who were elderly, disabled or lonely and by various dishonest means obtain or attempt to obtain money and possessions from them. For the instant offences, D befriended V, aged 70, and repeatedly lied to him to steal money and possessions. Count 1 was theft of about £377,000 and count 2 was theft of a large quantity of personal belongings, including a number of items of sentimental value. None were recovered. D had used a false name, pretended to be gay and fooled V into thinking they would get married. He also lied about his purported ill-health and financial affairs. V was left with nothing and the impact statement stated that his life had been destroyed. D was aged 43 at appeal and had convictions for obtaining property by deception in 1990 (community order) and 1992 (18 months). There was then a long gap before he began to reoffend (presumably in 2007). The Judge considered the 2008-2010 offences and concluded that had the first Judge been sentencing for all offences, the sentence would have been 8½ years. With 10% credit, he imposed two concurrent sentences of 7½ years. Held. Taking account of the 18 months D had spent in custody for the 2008-2010 offences, D had served the equivalent of a 3-year sentence when the Judge sentenced him to 7½ years. Therefore, the total was 10½ years. The correct approach was to ask whether 10½ years after deductions for the pleas was manifestly excessive. The aggravating features were D's previous convictions, the length of time over which the offences were committed, the number of victims, the large amounts stolen and the fact there were some committed whilst on bail. [Although the police did not know about the offences], when sentenced for the 2008-2010 offences, D had the opportunity to ask for the 2007 offences to be

taken into consideration. He did not. It was entirely appropriate for a lengthy sentence to be imposed. 10½ years was too long. The sentences for the two counts of theft would be **6½ years** not 7½ years, concurrent.

Old cases: Best ignored.

347 THREATS TO KILL

347.1

Offences Against the Person Act 1861 s 16 (making a threat to kill)

Mode of trial Triable either way

Maximum sentence On indictment 10 years. Summary 6 months and/or a £5,000 fine for offences committed before 12 March 2015 and an unlimited fine thereafter.[1211] There are maximum fines for those aged under 18, see **14.38** in Volume 1.

Extended sentences This offence is listed in Criminal Justice Act 2003 Sch 15. The court may pass a 2012 extended sentence (EDS) if there is a significant risk of serious harm from future specified offences and either: a) the defendant has a Criminal Justice Act 2003 Sch 15B conviction (applicable only to defendants aged 18+), or b) the offence would justify a determinate sentence of at least 4 years.[1212]

Criminal Behaviour Orders Where a defendant has engaged in behaviour that caused or was likely to cause harassment, alarm or distress to any persons and a Criminal Behaviour Order will help in preventing the offender from engaging in such behaviour, the court may make this order.[1213]

Sexual Harm Prevention Orders There is a discretionary power to make this order when it is necessary to protect the public from sexual harm.[1214]

347.2 *Magistrates' Court Sentencing Guidelines*

Magistrates' Court Sentencing Guidelines 2008, see www.banksr.com Other Matters Guidelines tab

page 104 Starting points are based on a first-time offender pleading not guilty.

Examples of nature of activity	Starting point	Range
One threat uttered in the heat of the moment, No more than fleeting impact on victim	Medium-level community order	Low-level community order to high-level community order
Single calculated threat or victim fears that threat will be carried out	12 weeks' custody	6 to 26 weeks' custody
Repeated threats or visible weapon	Crown Court	Crown Court

Identify dangerous offenders for the purposes of the public protection provisions in Criminal Justice Act 2003. The following aggravating and mitigating factors may be particularly relevant: Factors indicating higher culpability: 1 Planning, 2 Offender deliberately isolates victim, 3 Group action, 4 Threat directed at victim because of job, and 5 History of antagonism towards victim. Factor indicating lower culpability: Provocation. Factors indicating greater degree of harm: 1 Vulnerable victim, and 2 Victim needs medical help/counselling.

Consider ancillary orders, including compensation and Football Banning Order.

For the meaning of a medium-level and a low-level community order, see **16.12** in Volume 1.

[1211] Legal Aid, Sentencing and Punishment of Offenders Act 2012 s 85(1) and (4) and Legal Aid, Sentencing and Punishment of Offenders Act 2012 (Commencement No 11) Order 2015 2015/504

[1212] Criminal Justice Act 2003 s 226A-226B as inserted by Legal Aid, Sentencing and Punishment of Offenders Act 2012 s 124

[1213] Anti-social Behaviour, Crime and Policing Act 2014 s 22(1)-(4)

[1214] Sexual Offences Act 2003 s 103A as inserted by Anti-social Behaviour, Crime and Policing Act 2014 Sch 5 para 2 and Sexual Offences Act 2003 Sch 5

347.3   Judicial guidance

Att-Gen's Ref No 84 of 1999 2000 2 Cr App R (S) 213 LCJ It is relevant to regard the vulnerability of the party threatened and, most importantly, the reality of the threat – the likelihood, in the view of the party threatened, that the threat will be carried out and the extent the party is put in genuine fear. It is very relevant to consider whether the party making the threat is known to be violent, and whether the party making the threat is known to have some grudge or animus or grievance which may cause him to act.

Note: This is an old case. The guidance appears to reflect current sentencing practice. Ed.

347.4   Cases (non-relationship)

R v Davidson 2010 EWCA Crim 273 D pleaded to threats to kill, harassment and threatening to take revenge. V, a probation officer, supervised D in prison. D was released twice and recalled twice and D blamed V for that. D wrote to V from prison blaming V for her recall and her separation from her children. V also told a psychiatric nurse that she was going to slit V's throat. D was released again and she phoned V's office and spoke to a receptionist and said V would have her throat slit. A message was left saying D was on her way. Another call was made to a senior manager, saying V had betrayed her etc. Next day there was an apology for a letter that had been sent and saying she was in drink. The letter arrived containing threats to kill V. D was arrested and told a liaison officer in prison that a) someone was going to kneecap V, V's legs were going to be blown off and she wanted to murder V. D was aged 38 with two convictions for arson. She had set fire to her home while her children were there. She also had convictions for ABH and harassment. A report said she had mental health and alcohol problems. Another report said that a) D had a long history of instability, b) D was a vulnerable lady in emotional turmoil and c) D continued to experience intense anger towards V. Held. She has a sad history but her lack of control caused great anguish and fear. There was a sustained campaign with an appalling level of threats. The starting point should have been **9 years** so with plea 6 years making **3 years' IPP** not 4 years' IPP. We hope she receives the help she requires.

R v Tyas 2013 EWCA Crim 2291 D pleaded (full credit) to making a threat to kill and assault by beating. D lived with his partner, V. There were four children in the flat, two of whom were D and V's children, two of whom were V's from a previous relationship. D and V had a furious argument between 8.30 pm and midnight during which D accused her of infidelity. V went to bed in a bedroom in which one of the children, aged 10 months, slept. D stormed in and demanded V's mobile phone. He pushed her into the bed, took it from her and went downstairs. He returned with a 6-inch kitchen knife. D shouted and swore at V and held the knife to his throat saying that he would kill himself. He then put the knife to her throat (without touching it) and threatened to kill her. Still holding the knife, he then went to stand over the baby's cot. V tried to prevent him but he pushed her against a wardrobe, causing bruising. He said he would kill himself over the baby. He went downstairs and returned with a pair of scissors which he used to cut up her SIM card. D went to get the baby and pushed V aside when she sought to prevent him. D said he proposed to take the baby. D dressed him, put him in his pushchair and took him roughly downstairs and outside. Neighbours tried to stop D but he threatened to kill them. The police were called and D was arrested. He made an immediate and full confession. He appeared genuinely remorseful. He had convictions for violence without weapons in 2004 (×3) and 2008 (×2) for which he received non-custodial sentences. He also had a conviction for harassment by text and telephone against a former partner (2009). Held. An immediate custodial sentence was necessary. The offence was seriously aggravated by the production of the knife and the previous convictions for violence and harassment. The 45-month starting point adopted by the Judge was above that for a completed section 20 offence in Category 1 (serious injury and higher culpability). To sentence a man for an incident in which he inflicted no injury and was rapidly remorseful to a sentence at least as great as for a man who actually caused serious injury was more than was justified by the offence. 30 months was manifestly excessive. Starting at 30 months, **20 months** was appropriate.

R v Humphries 2014 EWCA Crim 2033 D was convicted of threats to kill at the Magistrates' Court. He later pleaded to another threats to kill count. D suffered from depression and was visited by mental health services. For the first offence, D told them he had thoughts about killing two people. One of them, V1, had abused him during childhood and, since the CPS had decided not to prosecute, he was going to kill him. D had already researched and obtained photos of V1. D said he would kill the other man 'as a trial run'. He was visited again, the next day, and spoke again of killing another two people, one of whom was his neighbour, V2, and the other his drug dealer. On both visits, D appeared calm and rational and in interview D denied intending to harm V2. Following his first conviction, D was unrepresented and said that upon leaving court he would kill his former abuser and did not care for the consequences. D was arrested and told police that it was not a threat to kill, but a promise to do so and pleaded guilty the next day. D was aged 52 on appeal with no relevant convictions and with references. A psychiatrist reported that D's depression was a major factor in causing him to act as he did and that he did not pose a high risk of violence to others. However, increasing alcohol and drug abuse as well as a preoccupation with his abuse would increase D's risk. D's mental state had improved and a mental health disposal was unneeded. The pre-sentence report said D's threat to kill V2 was a cry for help but he still intended to kill V1 and was not remorseful. The Judge concluded that D was dangerous. Held. This is an anxious case and the Judge faced a difficult task but his conclusions were justified. **10 years'** extended sentence (**5 years' custody** 5 years' extended licence) upheld.

See also: *R v Fuller* 2011 EWCA Crim 85 (Late plea to making a threat to kill. Threat to shoot a man with whom D had animosity over him giving evidence for the prosecution against D's cousin. Related to the drugs scene. Five previous convictions including threatening behaviour. 25% credit for plea. **2 years** not 40 months.)

R v Bond 2011 EWCA Crim 1197, 2012 1 Cr App R (S) 29 (p 173) (Convicted. Told nurse at A&E of his thoughts of killing people and in particular a female cousin of his. 30 previous convictions including burglary, but nothing 'serious'. Not mentally ill. Clearly 'dangerous'. As he was seeking help, **2 years'** not 30 months' IPP.)

R v Gomersall 2014 EWCA Crim 2481 (Plea. Full credit. Repeated threats to staff and others supervising his release from prison that he would kill the complainant in the blackmail case he was serving a sentence for and who was the same complainant in another previous offence of blackmail. Made the threats so he would not be released as he was not ready for that. Mental problems. **3 years**, not an extended sentence with a 4-year custodial element.)

Old case: *R v C* 2007 EWCA Crim 1358 (6 years' extended sentence (**2½ years'** custody 3½ years' licence)

347.5   Knife, With

Att-Gen's Ref No 52 of 2013 2013 EWCA Crim 1733 D pleaded at the Magistrates' Court to threats to kill and possession of an offensive weapon (no penalty). He lived in a flat for elderly, disabled and vulnerable people. D had a dispute with V, whom he accused of cadging tobacco. At 9 pm, D, while talking to another resident, referred to V as "that black bastard upstairs…a cadger". D had been drinking and he jumped from a balcony to a grassed area and challenged V to fight man-to-man. D shouted to V (who was presumably in his flat), "I'll come up there and cut your throat". Next D said he would get a knife and obtained an 11 cm kitchen knife from his flat. D confronted V, who obtained a golf club from his flat. D lunged towards V with the knife, saying, "Black bastard, Nigger. And I'll kill you, you Nigger." V defended himself and ran. Officers attended and D said, "This isn't finished. I'll sort the black bastard out." In 1977, when aged 13, D pleaded to arson (supervision). Since then, he had 121 offences on 31 occasions. Between 1982 and 1998, he had 16 assault convictions. In 1995 he was convicted of manslaughter (probation) which was a fight between homeless people. He also had convictions for a public order offence and an offensive weapon offence. He had breached many court orders but had no convictions since 2005. He walked out of a video conference with the probation officer, claiming she had accused him of having a murder conviction. He suffered from alcohol dependency syndrome. If he missed an injection he was prone to psychotic episodes. He suffered from arthritis and was given a mobility scooter. D was given a 3-month suspended sentence but interfered with the tag. The sentence was activated in full. Held. Were it not for D's fragile mental condition and the lack of offending since 2005, **4 years** before plea would be appropriate. The proper sentence was in the region of **2 years**. Here **18 months** was appropriate (presumably the double jeopardy). It would have been **15 months** without the racial element. Because of the served activated sentence, **15 months**.

R v Pilat 2014 EWCA Crim 668 **18 months** see **347.6**.

347.6   *Relationship/ex-partners etc. offences*

R v Patel 2012 EWCA Crim 2172, 2013 1 Cr App R (S) 119 (p 617) D pleaded to making a threat to kill. He had been in a relationship with V for some three years. They had a son. When he was aged 16 months, D and V separated. V was renting a home from D's parents. V lived there with her son and from time to time D would stay with them. V encouraged contact throughout the separation. There had been a number of arguments between V and D and on one occasion, D showed V a weapon which was said to be an air gun. He had been extremely aggressive and said that if V formed a relationship with another man, he would kill V, the child and the man. The following morning, V went to work, leaving the child with D. D phoned her at about 6.20 am and said she must come home immediately. D shouted at V and told her that he was going to kill the child. V phoned the police and D's mother. As V was on her way home, D sent her a text message saying 'the job is done, you are too slow'. V believed for a period of about an hour that her son had been killed. Police met up with V en route home. D phoned V more than once and police were able to hear the vile sexual insults and bullying comments D made to V. Officers entered the house and D was entirely compliant. He stated, "I didn't hurt him, I wouldn't hurt him". D, aged 31, was of good character. D regularly used cannabis and had a history of depression. Held. V suffered extreme distress. Starting at 6 years was too high. Full credit was also unwarranted as the plea was not tendered at the earliest opportunity. The period over which the threats to kill were made was relatively short. D demonstrated his remorse. Starting at 2 years, with a 4-month reduction for the late plea, **20 months,** not 4 years.

R v Pilat 2014 EWCA Crim 668 D pleaded to making a threat to kill. He was married to V for about 30 years. He lost his job and developed a drink problem. He started to abuse V and tried to make her feel worthless. The police were called on numerous occasions. One evening, V woke to find D sitting on the bed, holding a large knife above her with the blade pointing towards her. V said it was the sharpest knife in their knife block. D told her he would kill her and then himself. V tried to phone the police but D stopped her. V locked herself in the lavatory and called the police. D, aged 53, had a drink/drive conviction for which he was then on bail. The pre-sentence report was 'distinctly unfavourable' to D, saying that D did not recognise the harm he had caused and minimised his responsibility. Held. This domestic violence was the culmination of months of worsening behaviour from D towards his wife. We start at 27 months not 5 years 3 months, so with the early plea, **18 months** not 3½ years.

R v J 2014 EWCA Crim 849, 2 Cr App R (S) 47 (p 378) D pleaded to making threats to kill (×2). He had been in a relationship with V for four years. It was tempestuous and characterised by frequent arguments and subsequent reconciliations. He became aware that V was carrying his child. At that time they were not speaking due to an unrelated argument. D attempted to contact V but she did not respond. He was upset because V said she was considering terminating the pregnancy. When V was not answering her phone or responding to text messages, D asked his mother to intervene. He told his mother that he intended to kill V if she aborted the child. However, the basis of plea stated that he did not intend to carry out the threat. His mother reported the threat to the police and while she was at the police station D phoned her, again threatening to kill V if she aborted the child. Officers overheard the conversation and described D as being very angry. They heard him say he had taken legal advice as to the likely sentence he would receive for murder in these circumstances. D had a poor record, involving 30 previous offences including criminal damage, arson, perverting the course of justice and dishonesty offences. A number of his convictions involved him assaulting or harassing previous girlfriends. In 2010 he received a Restraining Order for harassment and was subsequently given a custodial sentence for breaching that order. He was in breach of a Community Order imposed in 2012 for assault and battery on a young woman when he committed the instant offences. D had been physically and sexually abused and was taken into care at an early age. He had had over 500 foster carers. Held. The threats persisted over a very short period of time (less than two days) and were not communicated to V. D was unstable and vulnerable and was acting under some real emotional pressure. Allowing for his previous convictions, 24 months was appropriate. The late plea would attract no more than ⅙ discount. **20 months** not 30.

See also: *R v Jones* 2011 EWCA Crim 2430 (Pleas to making a threat to kill and common assault on former wife. Committed ten days after release from prison. After drinking a bottle of brandy and some lager, he assaulted her, then held a long kitchen knife to her throat for some minutes. Aged 44. Numerous convictions including threatening behaviour. 6 years' **extended sentence (4 years'** custody, 2 years' licence.))

Old case: *R v Russell* 2010 EWCA Crim 778 (**IPP with 2½-year** minimum term)

For a summary of the case, see the 10th edition of this book.

For the Domestic Violence Guideline, see the **DOMESTIC VIOLENCE** chapter.

348 TRAFFICKING/SLAVERY, SERVITUDE AND FORCED OR COMPULSORY LABOUR

348.1

Modern Slavery Act 2015 s 1 (Slavery, servitude and forced or compulsory labour)
Modern Slavery Act 2015 s 2 (Human trafficking)
Modern Slavery Act 2015 s 4 (Committing any offence with the intension of committing a section 2 offence)

Modes of trial All three offences are triable either way.[1215]

Maximum sentences[1216] On indictment sections 1 and 2 offences life, and section 4 offences 10 years, unless the offence in section 4 is kidnapping or false imprisonment, when the penalty is life. Summary conviction, 6 months and/or an unlimited fine.

Automatic life Modern Slavery Act 2015 s 1-2 will be listed in Criminal Justice Act 2003 Sch 15B Part 1, when commencement has taken place. When that happens, the court must (unless the particular circumstances make it unjust[1217]) pass automatic life if: a) the defendant is aged 18+ at the date of the conviction, b) the court considers a determinate sentence of at least 10 years is appropriate, c) at the time the offender was convicted, he had a conviction for a Criminal Justice Act 2003 Sch 15B offence, and d) the defendant, at the time of his or her conviction, had previously been sentenced to either: i) a life sentence where he or she was not eligible for release during the first five years of the sentence, or ii) a determinate sentence or extended sentence where the

---

[1215] Modern Slavery Act 2015 s 5(1)-(2)
[1216] Modern Slavery Act 2015 s 5(1)-(3)
[1217] Criminal Justice Act 2003 s 224A(2)

custodial part was 10 years or more.[1218] For a pre-2012 extended sentence, when determining whether the custodial term was 10+ years, the period deducted for time on remand or on a curfew and tag is included.[1219]

Confiscation Where a defendant has a criminal lifestyle the court, once the confiscation proceedings are triggered (see **22.11** in Volume 1), <u>must</u> follow the Proceeds of Crime Act 2002 procedure. 'Criminal lifestyle' offences will include those under Modern Slavery Act 2015 s 1-2.[1220] For what constitutes a criminal lifestyle, see **22.48** in Volume 1.

Extended sentences Sections 1 and 2 are listed in Criminal Justice Act 2003 Sch 15. The court may pass a 2012 extended sentence (EDS) if there is a significant risk of serious harm from future specified offences and either: a) the defendant has a Criminal Justice Act 2003 Sch 15B conviction (applicable only to defendants aged 18+), or b) the offence would justify a determinate sentence of at least 4 years.[1221]

Sexual Harm Prevention Orders There is a discretionary power to make this order when it is necessary to protect the public from sexual harm.[1222]

Serious Crime Prevention Orders For Modern Slavery Act 2015 s 1 and 2 offences, there is a discretionary power to make this order, when it would protect the public etc.[1223]

Forfeiture There is power to forfeit land vehicles, ships and aircraft, Modern Slavery Act 2015 s 11.

Children and vulnerable adults: barred lists For Modern Slavery Act 2015 s 2 offences, where the defendant is aged 18 or over, he or she is automatically barred from engaging in regulated activity with vulnerable adults and with children.[1224] The judge must tell the defendant that the Disclosure and Barring Service will include him or her in the barred lists.[1225] The defendant may ask the Service to remove him or her from the lists. The relevant entries were added by Modern Slavery Act 2015 (Consequential Amendments) Regs 2015 2015/1472 paras 4-6.

Slavery and Trafficking Prevention Orders There is power to make a Slavery and Trafficking Prevention Order for these three offences after a conviction, a finding of not guilty by reason of insanity and a finding of disability with a finding the offender did the act when the Modern Slavery Act 2015 s 14-16 conditions are met, Modern Slavery Act 2015 s 14.

Slavery and Trafficking Reparation Orders These orders can be made when the Modern Slavery Act 2015 s 8 complex conditions are met.

Slavery and Trafficking Risk Orders There is power to make a Slavery and Trafficking Risk Order, Modern Slavery Act 2015 s 23. This is a stand-alone civil order. The court may make an interim risk order, Modern Slavery Act 2015 s 28. Commencement is awaited for the risk order.

Commencement The offences and the preventive orders above came into force on 31 July 2015, Modern Slavery Act 2015 (Commencement No 1, Savings and Transitional Provisions) Regs 2015 2015/1476 para 2. The offences can apply to offending committed wholly or partly before 31 July 2015, see paras 3-8. The provisions are complex.

See also:

IMMIGRATION *Exploiting immigrants though employment* at **272.13**, and

---

[1218] Criminal Justice Act 2003 s 224A as inserted by Legal Aid, Sentencing and Punishment of Offenders Act 2012 s 122. The condition for a) is at section 224A(1)(a), for b) is at section 224A(1)(b), for c) is at section 224A(1)(c), and for d) is at section 224A(4)-(9).

[1219] Criminal Justice Act 2003 s 224A(9)-(10)

[1220] Proceeds of Crime Act 2002 s 6 and 75 and Sch 2 para 3A, as inserted by Modern Slavery Act 2015 s 7(1)-(2)

[1221] Criminal Justice Act 2003 s 226A-226B as inserted by Legal Aid, Sentencing and Punishment of Offenders Act 2012 s 124

[1222] Sexual Offences Act 2003 s 103A as inserted by Anti-social Behaviour, Crime and Policing Act 2014 Sch 5 para 2 and Sexual Offences Act 2003 Sch 5 para 63B as inserted by Modern Slavery Act 2015 Sch 5 para 5(3)

[1223] Serious Crime Act 2007 s 1 and Sch 1 para 1A and 2(4)

[1224] Safeguarding Vulnerable Groups Act 2006 s 2 and Sch 3, and Safeguarding Vulnerable Groups Act 2006 (Prescribed Criteria and Miscellaneous Provisions) Regulations 2009 2009/37 para 3 and Sch 1 para 2 and 4

[1225] Safeguarding Vulnerable Groups Act 2006 s 2 and Sch 3 para 25

OFFENCES AGAINST THE PERSON ACT 1861 S 18 *Slavery Victim kept and abused as a virtual slave* at **292.35**.

348.2 *Judicial guidance*

Att-Gen's Ref Nos 2-5 of 2013 2013 EWCA Crim 324, 2 Cr App R (S) 71 (p 451)[1226] LCJ The Court considered Coroners and Justice Act 2009 s 71 (now repealed). An offence of slavery is likely to be more severely punished than one of servitude, and one of servitude more severely than one of forced labour. It is, however, important to emphasise that distinctions of this kind only apply where the manifestations of criminal behaviour, in the context of[1227] culpability and magnitude and complexity and profit, are indeed similar.

The relevant considerations include:

  a) the nature and degree of the deception or coercion involved in persuading the worker to join the organisation,
  b) the nature and degree of subsequent exploitation after arrival at the workplace,
  c) conditions at the workplace,
  d) the level and methods of control to ensure that the individual remained trapped within the organisation,
  e) the level and extent of his vulnerability, and
  f) the degree of harm, including physical, psychological and financial harm, suffered by him.

Plainly the nature and extent of the organisation and the financial objectives and profits actually achieved, and the number of those exploited within the organisation and the individual offender's role within the organisation all contribute to the assessment of the seriousness of the offence. Sentences must make clear, not merely that the statutory minimum wage should not be undermined, but much more important, that every vulnerable victim of exploitation will be protected by the criminal law. They must also emphasise that there is no victim so vulnerable to exploitation that he or she somehow becomes invisible or unknown to or somehow beyond the protection of the law. Exploitation of fellow human beings in any of the ways represents deliberate degrading of a fellow human being or human beings. It is far from straightforward for them even to complain about the way they are being treated, let alone to report their plight to the authorities so that the offenders might be brought to justice. Therefore when they are, substantial sentences are required, reflective, of course, of the distinctions between enslavement, serfdom, and forced labour, but realistically addressing the criminality of the defendants.

348.3 *Cases*

Att-Gen's Ref Nos 2-5 of 2013 2013 EWCA Crim 324, 2 Cr App R (S) 71 (p 451) LCJ Five members of the same family were convicted of conspiracy to require a person to perform forced or compulsory labour. The prosecution appealed four of the sentences. W, the head of the family and criminal organisation, ran a business involving roofing, paving, tarmacking and general property maintenance. The male members of the family joined the family business. JC and JoC were sons of W. MC was a son-in-law. All helped to cajole, persuade and bully vulnerable men to join their small workforce on the basis of false promises that they would be provided with accommodation and food, paid reasonably well and consistently for the work they were to do. Often the men were homeless, addicted to alcohol, friendless and isolated. The men were usually paid something like £10 per day, for a day's work, and sometimes £5 or occasionally £20 per day, but on other days they were not paid at all. They worked very long hours, sometimes seven days a week. They would be expected to work in very poor conditions without proper equipment or clothing. The accommodation provided for them was of a very poor standard indeed, sometimes without heating or even running water. On

---

[1226] The judgment refers to this case as *R v Connors and Others* 2013 EWCA Crim 324 in error.
[1227] The judgment says 'for example' here. It has been removed to enable the sentence to make sense.

occasion they were subjected to violence or the threat of violence as well as verbal abuse. Some were told they would never leave. The offences were committed over a period of about one year. A number of the employees effectively worked for different members of the family, and although W, JC, JoC and MC were members of the conspiracy, and their employees were mistreated in accordance with the conspiracy, the level of mistreatment by each was not identical. When arrested, W, aged 52, had £370,000 in his bank account. Other members of the family had £66,000, £50,000, £13,000 and £4,500. JaC, aged 17 at the start of the offences, was heavily influenced by W, his father. He was involved for a relatively short period of time. JoC was aged 20. MC, aged 24, had intervened in an assault upon the workers by JoC on one occasion. (The characters of the defendants are not revealed.) The Judge noted that their freedom was 'significantly curtailed' but not to a degree amounting to servitude. Further, the Inland Revenue (now HMRC) was defrauded. Some of the workers' state benefit documentation was taken from them and kept by the family. Nevertheless benefits were collected on their behalf but seldom passed to them. This provided substantial funding for the conspirators, to be added to the profits made from work, performed by a cheap, degraded, vulnerable, intimidated and sometimes physically assaulted workforce. The Judge discounted the offences because of the delay which the defendants were not to blame for. Held. The **6½ years** for W and **4 years** for JoC were lenient but could not be said to be unduly so. Sentences of **3 years** for MC and **3 years' detention** for JoC were within the appropriate range, if at the lower end of the bracket.

R v Connors and Others 2013 EWCA Crim 1165 LCJ T and his son, P, were convicted of conspiracy to hold a person in servitude and conspiracy to require forced labour. T's daughter, JC, and her husband were convicted of holding a person in servitude and requiring a person to perform forced labour. T, P and C were convicted of three different ABHs. They recruited vulnerable adults on the pretence that they would be paid, fed and housed. The victims, once caught, had no means of escape. They were forced to perform forced labour for extensive hours without payment. They suffered actual violence and threats of violence. The victims were held against their will at travellers' sites. V1 was homeless in London, begging in a doorway. He was offered a place to live and work by J and JC. He never received any pay and his possessions (phone, birth certificate etc.) were taken from him. He was told if he tried to leave he would be killed. V1 was made to work from 6 am to 10 pm. There were no breaks. He was assaulted. Once he was hit in the eye and imprisoned in the boot of a car. There was no access to hot water or a lavatory. V1 and V2 had to use a field. He was taken to a post office to receive his benefits and they were taken from him. The benefits stopped because he was prevented from obtaining a sick note. If given tips at work they were taken. V1 and V2 lived in a caravan. There was a TV but there was no time to watch it. There was a rusty microwave to heat up eggs. Some days there was nothing to eat. JC's kittens used the caravan floor as their lavatory. V1 was too frightened to leave but eventually he escaped into someone's garden and police were called. This led to V2, who was a registered alcoholic and suffered from depression. He was thin, frail, unkempt and dirty. To start with he was too frightened to tell the police the truth and said he loved his work. Gradually he outlined his deprivation and the violence against him. V2 was punched, kicked and hit with a broom handle. He too was too frightened to leave. He was forced to accept the blame for the theft of some bricks. V2 fell through a garage roof and was not permitted to see a doctor. When he could not walk he was taken to hospital and was forced to discharge himself early. Even with a foot in plaster he was forced to continue to work. V2 was mentally abused and treated as a slave. P severely kicked him in the head and beat him while JC watched. V3 was homeless and an alcoholic. He too was promised work, a home and food. He was found with a severe infection to his foot because he did not take his shoes or socks off enough. He said this was in case he was called upon to do something. He lived with ten others in a horsebox. Heaters were taken away by T, who broke them and threw them away. The food was inadequate. V3's possessions were taken from him. His work started at 4-5 am. V3 feared showing pain as he would be picked on like a wounded animal. He felt compelled to report on other workers. He saw boiling water poured on others. T told P to inflict violence. V4 was underweight, stooped, extremely gaunt, smelling, dirty, bewildered and frightened. Police found £16,000 in cash and £130,000 in bank deposits. T had convictions for dishonesty and public order offences over many years. In 1999, he had a false imprisonment conviction when he locked a worker in a barn (12 months). He also had an assault conviction. J had no previous convictions for violence. P had no convictions and was aged 18-19 when the offences against V3 occurred. JC had no convictions and was the mother of three children. The Judge took into account offending 'over very many years involving hundreds of workers'. He treated the pre-2010 offending (i.e. before the Act was in place) as aggravating the offences. He considered T had a very heavy responsibility for bringing his children into this way of life. Held. The offending had an appalling impact. The victims were exploited, brutalised and reduced to servitude and penury. In effect they were brutalised and reduced to abject, medieval serfdom. T's **8 years** was not a day too long. J's **11 years** was at the top end of the appropriate scale but was not manifestly excessive. JC actively contributed to the victim's servitude and was integral in the control and management of the victims. There was no reason to interfere with her **4 years**. P was aged only 14 when the offending started but he was not overborne by a more powerful adult. He enthusiastically mistreated the victims. **5 years** was not manifestly excessive.

349   TV LICENCE EVASION
349.1
Communications Act 2003 s 363 (television receiver installed not authorised by a licence)
Mode of trial Summary only
Maximum sentence Level 3 fine (£1,000)
Draft legislation Deregulation Act 2015 s 77 enables the Secretary of State to introduce regulations to replace the statutory s 363 offence with a civil penalty. The repeal of the offence is said to have cross-party support. No regulations have yet been issued.
349.2   *Magistrates' Court Sentencing Guidelines*
Magistrates' Court Sentencing Guidelines 2008, see www.banksr.com Other Matters Guidelines tab
page 106 Starting points are based on a first-time offender pleading not guilty.

Examples of nature of activity	Starting point	Range
Up to 6 months' unlicensed use	Band A fine	Band A fine
Over 6 months' unlicensed use	Band B Fine	Band A fine to Band B fine

The following aggravating and mitigating factors may be particularly relevant: Factors indicating lower culpability: 1 Accidental oversight or belief licence held, 2 Confusion of responsibility, and 3 Licence immediately obtained.
Consider ancillary orders.
Consultation It is expected that the Sentencing Council will issue a consultation document about updating this guideline in May 2016.
Band A and B are 50% and 100% of net weekly income. For more detail see **60.27** in Volume 1.

350   VEHICLE INTERFERENCE/IMMOBILISATION
350.1
1) Criminal Attempts Act 1981 s 9 (interference with vehicles)
   Mode of trial Summary only

Maximum sentence 3 months and/or level 4 fine (£2,500)

2) Protection of Freedoms Act 2012 s 54 (vehicle immobilisation/unlawful clamping)

Mode of trial Triable either way

Maximum sentence On indictment a fine. Summary only a £5,000 fine for offences committed before 12 March 2015 and an unlimited fine thereafter.[1228] There are maximum fines for those aged under 18, see **14.38** in Volume 1.

350.2   *Magistrates' Court Sentencing Guidelines   Vehicle interference*

Magistrates' Court Sentencing Guideline 2008, see www.banksr.com Other Matters Guidelines tab

page 108 Starting points are based on a first-time offender pleading not guilty.

Examples of nature of activity	Starting point	Range
Trying door handles, no entry gained to vehicle, no damage caused	Band C fine	Band A fine to low-level community order
Entering vehicle, little or no damage caused	Medium-level community order	Band C fine to high-level community order
Entering vehicle, with damage caused	High-level community order	Medium-level community order to 12 weeks' custody

Factor indicating higher culpability: Targeting vehicle in dark/isolated location. Factors indicating greater degree of harm: 1 Emergency services vehicle 2 Disabled driver's vehicle 3 Part of series.

Consider ancillary orders, including compensation and disqualification from driving.

Consultation It is expected that the Sentencing Council will issue a consultation document about updating this guideline in May 2016.

A Band A fine is 50% of net weekly income. Band C is 150%. For more detail see **60.27** in Volume 1.

For the meaning of a high-level, a medium-level and a low-level community order, see **16.12** in Volume 1.

For details about applying the guidelines see the **GUIDELINES** chapter in Volume 1.

VIOLENT DISORDER see **AFFRAY/VIOLENT DISORDER**

351   VOYEURISM

351.1

Sexual Offences Act 2003

s 67(1) (observing, for sexual gratification, without consent, a person doing a private act)

s 67(2) (operating equipment, for sexual gratification etc., without consent, with the intention of enabling another person to observe a third person doing a private act)

s 67(3) (recording another person doing a private act, for sexual gratification etc., without consent)

s 67(4) (installing equipment, or constructing or adapting a structure or part of a structure, with the intention of enabling himself or another person to commit an offence under the subsection)

Modes of trial All four offences are triable either way.

[1228] Legal Aid, Sentencing and Punishment of Offenders Act 2012 s 85(1) and (4) and Legal Aid, Sentencing and Punishment of Offenders Act 2012 (Commencement No 11) Order 2015 2015/504

Maximum sentences For all four offences, on indictment 2 years. Summary is 6 months and/or a £5,000 fine for offences committed before 12 March 2015 and an unlimited fine thereafter.[1229] There are maximum fines for those aged under 18, see **14.38** in Volume 1.

Extended sentences Section 67 is listed in Criminal Justice Act 2003 Sch 15. The court may pass an extended sentence if there is a significant risk of serious harm from future specified offences and the defendant has a Criminal Justice Act 2003 Sch 15A conviction (applicable only to defendants aged 18+).[1230]

Sexual Harm Prevention Orders There is a discretionary power, when the notification (see below) criteria are present or when it is necessary to protect the public etc. to make this order.[1231]

Notification Where:

a) the defendant is aged less than 18 and is sentenced to imprisonment of 12 months or more, or

b) the defendant is aged 18 or over and: i) the victim was under 18, or ii) the defendant was sentenced to imprisonment or detained in a hospital or given community service for at least 12 months,

the defendant must notify[1232] the police within three days (or three days from his/her release from imprisonment, hospital etc.) with his/her name, home address, National Insurance number etc. and any changes to those, and addresses where he or she resides for seven days[1233] in one or more periods or more in any 12-month period.[1234]

Children and vulnerable adults: barred lists Where the defendant is aged 18 or over and the offence was committed against a child he or she is automatically barred[1235] from engaging in regulated activity with children and with vulnerable adults.[1236] The judge must tell the defendant that the Disclosure and Barring Service will include him or her in the barred lists.[1237] The defendant may ask the Service to remove him or her from the list.

351.2   Sentencing Council guideline   Sexual Offences Act 2003 s 67
Sexual Offences Guideline 2014 www.banksr.com Other Matters Guidelines tab
The guideline only applies to offenders aged 18+, see page 7 of the guideline. For the usual practice, see **66.21** in Volume 1.

STEP ONE: Determining the offence category
page 134 The court should determine the offence category using the table below.

Category 1	Raised harm **and** raised culpability
Category 2	Raised harm **or** raised culpability
Category 3	Voyeurism **without** raised harm or culpability factors present

The court should determine culpability and harm caused or intended, by reference only to the factors below, which comprise the principal factual elements of the offence.

[1229] Legal Aid, Sentencing and Punishment of Offenders Act 2012 s 85(1) and (4) and Legal Aid, Sentencing and Punishment of Offenders Act 2012 (Commencement No 11) Order 2015 2015/504

[1230] Criminal Justice Act 2003 s 225-229 as amended by Criminal Justice and Immigration Act 2008 s 13-20 and commenced by Criminal Justice and Immigration Act 2008 (Commencement No 2 and Transitional and Saving Provisions) Order 2008 2008/1586 para 2

[1231] Sexual Offences Act 2003 s 103A as inserted by Anti-social Behaviour, Crime and Policing Act 2014 Sch 5 para 2 and Sexual Offences Act 2003 Sch 5

[1232] Sexual Offences Act 2003 s 80(1)(a) and Sch 3 para 34

[1233] Sexual Offences Act 2003 s 84(1)(c) and (6)

[1234] Sexual Offences Act 2003 s 83

[1235] As amended by Safeguarding Vulnerable Groups Act 2006 (Controlled Activity and Miscellaneous Provisions) Regulations 2010 2010/1146 para 9(4)

[1236] Safeguarding Vulnerable Groups Act 2006 s 2 and Sch 3 and Safeguarding Vulnerable Groups Act 2006 (Prescribed Criteria and Miscellaneous Provisions) Regulations 2009 2009/37 regs 4 and 6 and Sch para 2 and 4

[1237] Safeguarding Vulnerable Groups Act 2006 s 2 and Sch 3 para 25

Where an offence does not fall squarely into a category, individual factors may require a degree of weighting before making an overall assessment and determining the appropriate offence category.

Factors indicating raised harm	Factors indicating raised culpability
Image(s) available to be viewed by others Victim observed or recorded in their own home or residence	Significant degree of planning Image(s) recorded Abuse of trust Specific or previous targeting of a particularly vulnerable victim Commercial exploitation and/or motivation Offence racially or religiously aggravated Offence motivated by, or demonstrating, hostility to the victim based on his or her sexual orientation (or presumed sexual orientation) or transgender identity (or presumed transgender identity) Offence motivated by, or demonstrating, hostility to the victim based on his or her disability (or presumed disability)

351.3

STEP TWO: Starting point and category range

page 134 Having determined the category, the court should use the corresponding starting points to reach a sentence within the category range on the next page. The starting point applies to all offenders irrespective of plea or previous convictions. Having determined the starting point, step two allows further adjustment for aggravating or mitigating features, set out on the next page.

A case of particular gravity, reflected by multiple features of culpability or harm in step one, could merit upward adjustment from the starting point before further adjustment for aggravating or mitigating features, set out on the next page.

Where there is a sufficient prospect of rehabilitation, a community order with a sex offender treatment programme requirement under Criminal Justice Act 2003 s 202 can be a proper alternative to a short or moderate-length custodial sentence.

Category	Starting point	Category range
1	26 weeks' custody	12 weeks' to 18 months' custody
2	High-level community order	Medium-level community order to 26 weeks' custody
3	Medium-level community order	Band A fine to high-level community order

For the meaning of a high-level and a medium-level community order, see **16.13** in Volume 1.

351.4   [Aggravating and mitigating factors]

page 135 The table below contains a non-exhaustive list of additional factual elements providing the context of the offence and factors relating to the offender. Identify whether any combination of these, or other relevant factors, should result in an upward or downward adjustment from the starting point. In particular, relevant recent convictions are likely to result in an upward adjustment. In some cases, having considered these factors, it may be appropriate to move outside the identified category range.

When sentencing Category 2 offences, the court should also consider the custody threshold as follows:

Has the custody threshold been passed?
If so, is it unavoidable that a custodial sentence be imposed?
If so, can that sentence be suspended?
When sentencing Category 3 offences, the court should also consider the community order threshold as follows:
has the community order threshold been passed?

Aggravating factors
Statutory aggravating factors: Previous convictions, having regard to: a) the nature of the offence to which the conviction relates and its relevance to the current offence, and b) the time that has elapsed since the conviction Offence committed whilst on bail ***Other aggravating factors:*** Location of offence Timing of offence Failure to comply with current court orders Offence committed whilst on licence Distribution of images, whether or not for gain Placing images where there is the potential for a high volume of viewers Period over which victim observed Period over which images were made or distributed Any steps taken to prevent victim reporting an incident, obtaining assistance and/or from assisting or supporting the prosecution Attempts to dispose of or conceal evidence
Mitigating factors
No previous convictions or no relevant/recent convictions Remorse Previous good character and/or exemplary conduct* Age and/or lack of maturity where it affects the responsibility of the offender Mental disorder or learning disability, particularly where linked to the commission of the offence Demonstration of steps taken to address offending behaviour *Previous good character/exemplary conduct is different from having no previous convictions. The more serious the offence, the less the weight which should normally be attributed to this factor. Where previous good character/exemplary conduct has been used to facilitate the offence, this mitigation should not normally be allowed and such conduct may constitute an aggravating factor.

Note: An exact copy of this guideline has been placed in the *Magistrates' Court Sentencing Guidelines 2008* at page 299.

351.5   *Suggested approach to the guideline*
Note: It is understood that the Sentencing Council intended that the guideline should reflect the Court of Appeal current sentencing tariff. Further, the new guideline was intended to bring the previous guideline up to date rather than intending to increase the penalties for the bulk of the sex offences. Consequently, I suggest that sentencers should start with the guideline and then consider recent sentencing cases set out by the Court of Appeal to see if they are helpful, and then return to the guideline before deciding the appropriate sentence. Ed.

351.6   *Pre-2014 guideline cases*
R v Proch 2010 EWCA Crim 714 D pleaded to voyeurism. He was a marketing manager from the US staying at an hotel. D was in the woman's toilet. A girl, V (age unspecified), who was in the adjacent toilet, saw D's hand holding a mirror. V could see his eyes in the mirror and D, realising he had been seen, left the cubicle. V was too afraid to leave the cubicle and tried to contact friends on her mobile, which was unsuccessful. She was

caused extreme distress. In interview, D said he had walked into the wrong toilet by mistake and told other lies. D was of good character (age unspecified). A report said he had a long-standing voyeurism problem and was taking steps to address it. As he lived in the USA the Judge could not make an effective community sentence. Held. A suspended sentence was not in accordance with the guidelines so **£500** fine instead.

R v Carton 2012 EWCA Crim 3199 D pleaded (early) to outraging public decency (×5). He had an urge to take photographs of women's legs under their skirts. D and V were on a train. They disembarked at the same station and V indicated that D should climb the steps from the platform ahead of her. D insisted that V go first, and she did. She then felt someone very close behind her and something brush against her leg. She turned around to see D crouching with his mobile phone angled so it could take a picture up her skirt. V asked D what he was doing and he walked away. The police were contacted and D was searched. His mobile phone was found in a bush nearby. It contained 48 images of various women. The fifth offence represented 45 photographs taken between February and July 2011. The victims had not suspected anything was amiss. D, aged 59, had significant previous convictions but they were from 'some time ago'. There was a conviction from 1997 for possessing child pornography. The Judge sentenced him to 14 months and imposed an ASBO. Held. D's actions caused considerable upset and anxiety and were carried out over a prolonged period. The voyeurism section of the *Sexual Offences Act 2003 Guideline 2008* is of some assistance as these offences have something in common with the basic offence. There was no evidence D had showed the films to anyone else. D had already taken steps to reduce his ability to reoffend by obtaining a mobile phone without a camera and ceasing to be connected to the Internet. It was important not to minimise the effect of the offending. Those who were aware became understandably distressed and in some cases it affected their confidence in public. **3-year community order** with a community sex programme, not 14 months. The ASBO made by the Judge, prohibiting among other things, using a device capable of capturing still or moving images in a railway or bus station, on public transport, in a shop or other public amenity, was appropriate and would remain in place.

See also *R v Moss* 2010 EWCA Crim 294 (Pleaded. Prowler outside bedroom window when resident was naked. She suffered fear and anxiety. Activity had been repeated. Defendant had served many custodial sentences. 105 convictions. **3 months** not 12 consecutive to 6 months for breach of a suspended sentence.)

R v Sturgess 2010 EWCA Crim 2550, 2011 1 Cr App R (S) 117 (p 686) (Plea. Voyeurism (×12) and taking indecent photographs of a child (×3). He installed video cameras in a property which was rented out to holidaymakers. Cameras in bedrooms, bathroom and living room, disguised as burglar alarms. Victims included two 17-year-old girls and one 14-year-old girl. Committed over a period of 12 months. **2½ years** in all was not manifestly excessive.)

Old cases: Best ignored.

351.7 *Post-2014 guideline cases*

R v Adams 2014 EWCA Crim 1898 D pleaded (at the earliest opportunity) to voyeurism (×6) and making indecent photos of a child (×3). D sold an MP3 player to a shop and staff found footage of people using a lavatory in a local hospital. D had placed a disguised camera under the sink, pointing at the lavatory. About 50 people, male and female, were filmed and their genitals were seen. D had been filming once or twice a week for three years, but had stopped of his own accord in about 2012. Upon a search of D's home, the camera was found and data storage devices with deleted films of a dozen or so people using the same toilet were found. This included girls of 10-14. That particular film had been copied three times. D denied involvement initially but later handed himself in and made frank admissions. D was aged 54 on appeal and effectively of good character. He had Parkinson's and also mild depression following his wife's death. The positive pre-sentence report recommended a community order with SOTP. Held. The facts here are unusual. There were aggravating factors. This was in effect a campaign of voyeurism with a significant degree of planning. The toilet was used by hospital outpatients who may have been vulnerable or unwell and where they were entitled to feel entirely safe. The images of girls were isolated and copied. These factors justify this as a serious Category 1 case. However, due to D's Parkinson's, custody would be harder for him to cope with than others. For the voyeurism, we adopt an overall starting point of 27 months and for the indecent images, 18 months on each count. The sentences ought to be concurrent, not consecutive, as they related to a single course of conduct. Taking into account D's plea, **18 months** for voyeurism with the indecent image counts concurrent.

See also: *R v M(A)* 2015 EWCA Crim 792 (Convicted. Duty manager of Paddington station told cleaner to come to office. Made her watch him masturbate. She was extremely distressed and lost her job. Very serious breach of trust. Should have been sentenced for one incident so **6 months** not 9.)

352   WANTON OR FURIOUS DRIVING

352.1

Offences Against the Person Act 1861 s 35 (wanton or furious driving etc. causing bodily harm to any person)

Mode of trial Indictable only

Maximum sentence 2 years

Disqualification The offence carries discretionary disqualification.[1238]

Endorsement The obligation to order endorsement applies only 'if committed in respect of a mechanically propelled vehicle'. A bicycle is not such a vehicle.[1239]

Penalty points 3-9 points[1240]

Extended sentences The offence is a specified offence under Criminal Justice Act 2003 Sch 15. As the maximum sentence is only 2 years, the opportunity to pass an extended sentence is exceptionally limited.

Depriving defendant of vehicle used There is power to deprive the defendant of the vehicle used[1241] for the purposes of committing the offence.

Problems This offence is in urgent need of radical reform. The maximum penalty is too low. Where they can, prosecutors charge a summary only offence or ABH and Offences Against the Person Act 1861 s 20, where the maximum penalty is 5 years. The first two cases below are old and restrained by the maximum sentence. I consider they are a poor guide to the appropriate sentence. The causing injury by dangerous driving offence does not cover driving on private roads and it should have done. The pain of victims and the need to protect road users is the same whether the injury took place on a public road or a private road.

352.2   Guidelines

The guidelines in the **DANGEROUS DRIVING (SIMPLE)** and **DEATH BY DRIVING: GENERAL PRINCIPLES** chapters may provide assistance. Ed.

352.3   Cases

R v Lambert 2008 EWCA Crim 2109, 2009 1 Cr App R (S) 92 (p 542) D pleaded at the first opportunity to causing bodily harm by wanton driving. He rode his mountain bike near a bus stop. A bus overtook him and three people at the bus stop moved towards the road. The bus slowed and he mounted the pavement at 12-13 mph and hit an 82-year-old woman. She went into the air, struck her head on the ground and died. His rear brake was wholly ineffective and the front brake could only be applied with great effort. The victim's death was a tragedy for her family. D was aged 17½ with no convictions. Held.

[1238] Road Traffic Offenders Act 1988 s 28, 34 and 44 and Sch 2
[1239] *R v Hall* 2009 EWCA Crim 2236, 2010 1 Cr App R (S) 95 (p 603)
[1240] Road Traffic Offenders Act 1988 s 28, 34 and 44 and Sch 2 Part II
[1241] It appears that the power is available generally under Powers of Criminal Courts (Sentencing) Act 2000 s 143(2), and Powers of Criminal Courts (Sentencing) Act 2000 s 143(6)-(7) extended the power to where a motor vehicle is used to commit manslaughter. Ed.

This was a bad case of wilful misconduct with the gravest consequences. He deliberately mounted the pavement. A collision with a person was at least highly likely and injury was likely to result. Death was not wholly unforeseeable, even to a 17-year-old. A sentence at or near the statutory maximum would have been appropriate after a trial. **12 months'** detention was not in the least excessive.

R v Hall 2009 EWCA Crim 2236, 2010 1 Cr App R (S) 95 (p 603) D pleaded to causing bodily harm by wanton or furious driving. In the early evening, D was cycling home from work. Going downhill towards a T-junction he was intending to turn right. D claimed he was forced to mount the pavement in order to avoid a vehicle which had pulled in front of him. He remained on the narrow pavement, turned a blind corner and hit V, an 84-year-old man. V was knocked to the ground and into the road. D remained at the scene in a state of shock and expressed severe regret. V's head was injured and 12 days later he unexpectedly died of a pulmonary embolism. D accepted he should have returned to the road. D said he was coasting and a witness said he was cycling 'like a bat out of hell'. D was aged 19, living with his parents, his fiancée and 4-month-old daughter. He worked in a bakery. When aged 18 he was cautioned for common assault and had impressive character witnesses. **7 months'** YOI and 12 months' disqualification was not manifestly excessive.

See also: *R v Gittoes* 2015 EWCA Crim 1608, 2016 1 Cr App R (S) 23 (p 150) (Plea (full credit). D cycled in a pedestrian area where bikes were prohibited. The bike had no brakes and no bell. D struck a 73-year-old who fell, received devastating head injuries and later died. **12 months** upheld.)

353   WASTEFUL EMPLOYMENT OF THE POLICE

353.1
(This offence is commonly called 'wasting police time'.)
Criminal Law Act 1967 s 5(2) (wasteful employment of police)
Mode of trial Summary only
Maximum sentence 6 months and/ or Level 4 fine (£2,500)
Where the offence warrants a greater penalty, expect the CPS to charge attempting to pervert the course of justice. For details of that offence see that chapter. Ed.
Fixed penalty There is a fixed penalty of £90 for wasting police time or giving a false report.[1242] All the penalties have half the relevant victim surcharge added. For more detail see **61.1** in Volume 1.

353.2   *Case*
R v Afford 2013 EWCA Crim 633, 2014 1 Cr App R (S) 2 (p 4) D pleaded (full credit) to perverting the course of justice. His brother-in-law contacted the police to report that D had been attacked by four Asian males, one of whom had slashed his face with a knife whilst commenting, "no white person should walk here". The police attended D's address to take a statement. He provided a description of the attackers but gave a different location from that which was originally reported. The officers spent 90 minutes reviewing CCTV footage and investigating the location. No blood was found at the scene and there were inconsistencies in his account. The story was reported in the local press and the police were concerned that community tensions might be engaged and so they gave high priority to their investigation. An article featured a photograph of D and his injuries. There were 16 separate 'slashes' which D had inflicted upon himself. CCTV images showed D walking back after the alleged attack, but showing no sign of injuries. He was interviewed and admitted he had falsely reported the attack. He had had an encounter with someone over a cigarette and had been punched by that person. That person then followed him home and attacked him. The attack had arisen from a dispute between D and his ex-partner over the use of a motor vehicle. D had no convictions since 2002. Held. There were clearly racial elements in the way the offence was

---

[1242] Penalties for Disorderly Behaviour (Amount of Penalty) Order 2002 2002/1837 as amended.

reported. Scarce police and health service resources were wasted. There was a clear risk that men fitting the description given by D would be arrested, though in the event no one was arrested. That had to be borne in mind. The self-inflicted injuries were committed to further the complaint. The risk of inflammation of community or race relations could not be ignored but starting at 12 months was appropriate, so **8 months** not 12.

Note: Although this was a perverting case, it may be of assistance. Ed.

Contents Index

References are to paragraph numbers.
Paragraphs 1.1 to 127.32 are in Volume 1.
Paragraphs 200.1 to 353.2 are in Volume 2.

Contents Index

Contents Index

Contents Index

Contents Index

Contents Index

Contents Index

Contents Index

Contents Index

Contents Index